Problems and Materials on Commercial Law

ASPEN CASEBOOK SERIES

Problems and Materials on Commercial Law

Twelfth Edition

Douglas J. Whaley
Professor Emeritus
Moritz College of Law
The Ohio State University

Stephen M. McJohn
Professor of Law
Suffolk University Law School

ASPEN
PUBLISHING

To contact Customer Service, e-mail customer.service@aspenpublishing.com, call 1-800-950-5259, or mail correspondence to:

Aspen Publishing
Attn: Order Department
PO Box 990
Frederick, MD 21705

Printed in the United States of America.

3 4 5 6 7 8 9 0

ISBN 978-1-5438-2590-9

Library of Congress Cataloging-in-Publication Data

Names: Whaley, Douglas J., author. | McJohn, Stephen M., 1959- author.
Title: Problems and materials on commercial law / Douglas J. Whaley, Professor emeritus, Moritz College of Law, The Ohio State University; Stephen M. McJohn, Professor of Law, Suffolk University Law School.
Description: Twelfth edition. | Frederick, MD: Aspen Publishing, [2021] | Series: Aspen casebook series | Includes bibliographical references and index. | Summary: "This is a problem-based commercial law casebook"—Provided by publisher.
Identifiers: LCCN 2020053082 (print) | LCCN 2020053083 (ebook) | ISBN 9781543825909 (hardcover) | ISBN 9781543825916 (ebook)
Subjects: LCSH: Commercial law—United States—Cases. | LCGFT: Casebooks (Law)
Classification: LCC KF889 .W47 2021 (print) | LCC KF889 (ebook) | DDC 346.7307—c23
LC record available at https://lccn.loc.gov/2020053082
LC ebook record available at https://lccn.loc.gov/2020053083

About Aspen Publishing

Aspen Publishing is a leading provider of educational content and digital learning solutions to law schools in the U.S. and around the world. Aspen provides best-in-class solutions for legal education through authoritative textbooks, written by renowned authors, and breakthrough products such as Connected eBooks, Connected Quizzing, and PracticePerfect.

The Aspen Casebook Series (famously known among law faculty and students as the "red and black" casebooks) encompasses hundreds of highly regarded textbooks in more than eighty disciplines, from large enrollment courses, such as Torts and Contracts to emerging electives such as Sustainability and the Law of Policing. Study aids such as the *Examples & Explanations* and the *Emanuel Law Outlines* series, both highly popular collections, help law students master complex subject matter.

Major products, programs, and initiatives include:

- **Connected eBooks** are enhanced digital textbooks and study aids that come with a suite of online content and learning tools designed to maximize student success. Designed in collaboration with hundreds of faculty and students, the Connected eBook is a significant leap forward in the legal education learning tools available to students.
- **Connected Quizzing** is an easy-to-use formative assessment tool that tests law students' understanding and provides timely feedback to improve learning outcomes. Delivered through CasebookConnect.com, the learning platform already used by students to access their Aspen casebooks, Connected Quizzing is simple to implement and integrates seamlessly with law school course curricula.
- **PracticePerfect** is a visually engaging, interactive study aid to explain commonly encountered legal doctrines through easy-to-understand animated videos, illustrative examples, and numerous practice questions. Developed by a team of experts, PracticePerfect is the ideal study companion for today's law students.
- The **Aspen Learning Library** enables law schools to provide their students with access to the most popular study aids on the market across all of their courses. Available through an annual subscription, the online library consists of study aids in e-book, audio, and video formats with full text search, note-taking, and highlighting capabilities.
- Aspen's **Digital Bookshelf** is an institutional-level online education bookshelf, consolidating everything students and professors need to ensure success. This program ensures that every student has access to affordable course materials from day one.
- **Leading Edge** is a community centered on thinking differently about legal education and putting those thoughts into actionable strategies. At the core of the program is the Leading Edge Conference, an annual gathering of legal education thought leaders looking to pool ideas and identify promising directions of exploration.

To my husband, David Vargo

DW

To Lorie, Ian, and all the McJohns

SM

Summary of Contents

Contents

PREFACE

This book explores commercial law by focusing on a series of Problems designed to encourage the student to concentrate on the exact statutory language in the Uniform Commercial Code and related statutes.

Representative cases and textual notes are also included. Unfortunately, students reared on the case method sometimes have trouble concentrating on Problem after Problem. Such an attitude here can be academically fatal. As a guide to the degree of concentration required, we have used a hierarchy of signals. When the Problem states "Read §3-302," we mean "Put down this book, pick up the Uniform Commercial Code, and study §3-302 carefully." When the instruction is "See §3-302," the reader need look at the cited section only if unsure of the answer. "Cf. §3-302," or simply "§3-302," is a lesser reference, included as a guide for the curious.

We have edited the footnotes out of most cases; the ones that remain have been stripped of their original numbering and have been consecutively numbered with our other textual footnotes. Unless clearly indicated otherwise, all footnotes in the cases are the court's own.

We would like to thank Gregory Krabacher, Whaley's 2004 research assistant, for creating the very helpful chart in Chapter 18 illustrating a typical letter of credit transaction. As always, Whaley is indebted to the fine people at Aspen Publishers, who have taken good care of him through seven casebooks. McJohn adds his thanks to our friends at Aspen and his colleagues at Suffolk. Finally, our grateful thanks go to our many students, who through the years have taught us as much about the law as we taught them.

The authors would also like to thank the following:

Photograph of Karl Llewellyn, Courtesy of Yale Law School.

Douglas J. Whaley
Columbus, Ohio

Stephen M. McJohn
Boston, Massachusetts

February 2021

Problems and Materials on Commercial Law

CHAPTER 1

INTRODUCTION TO THE UNIFORM COMMERCIAL CODE

I. A BIT OF HISTORY

During medieval times, commercial law varied widely from place to place throughout the trading world, and the statutes of the various countries either didn't address the relevant issues that traders cared about or reached results that were at odds with what those traders thought either realistic or fair. During much of English history, for example, the common law courts were lumbered by such arcane rules of procedure that justice was either unavailable or so slow as to come far too late.

To solve this dilemma the traders developed their own legal system, the so-called law merchant (or *lex mercatoria* in Latin). By agreement they created their own courts, chose their own judges, and developed mercantile understandings that made trade efficient and fair (in their own eyes). At some point the real courts became aware that they were being bypassed and began to incorporate the law merchant into their own rules. During the time of the American Revolution, the English court system had as its Chief Justice the great jurist Lord Mansfield. He believed in pragmatism in his courtroom, and during his tenure the law merchant was given much influence in English decisions. Lord Mansfield would call merchants into court to testify as to what mercantile understandings were in the matter before

Lord Mansfield

the court, and was not above putting merchants on the jury and then asking them questions as cases proceeded.

II. THE CREATION OF THE UNIFORM COMMERCIAL CODE

Starting in the 1940s, two private bodies, the American Law Institute (ALI) and the National Conference of Commissioners on Uniform State Law (NCCUSL), decided it was time to modernize the state laws on commercial matters. Over the coming years, they gathered together the greatest commercial experts in the country to draft a new giant statute that would supersede existing ones for the areas that were covered. Chief draftsman was Professor Karl N. Llewellyn, the leading voice for the "legal realism" school of jurisprudence (very much in Lord Mansfield's tradition), and he led a drafting team that by 1952 produced the first version of what was called the "Uniform Commercial Code."

Karl Llewellyn

The Uniform Commercial Code went through various versions from that day to this (though Article 2 on "Sales" has remained largely unchanged). The UCC (or, in this course, simply "the Code") is divided into "Articles" covering different aspects of commercial law.

It is important to appreciate that the UCC is not federal law. Instead, the two drafting bodies submitted it for adoption to the states, and it had to be individually enacted into law state by state. The idea was that if commercial law were uniform throughout the country, commerce would be more certain and efficient (the same goals animating the law merchant centuries before). Most states did adopt the Code with few changes (though some have sneaked in through the years, and you, budding lawyer, should always check your own state's enactment to make sure some evil alteration hasn't muddled what you've learned in this course). By the end of the last quarter of the twentieth century, all states, most U.S. territories, and a number of Native American tribes had adopted the UCC, though most importantly for this course, Louisiana, with its French law, Napoleonic Code, tradition did not enact Article 2 on the Sale of Goods, but has its own civil law version thereof.

III. FEDERAL LAW

The federal government, of course, has a great interest in commercial matters, and thus has enacted a wide number of statutes that exist alongside the states' UCC mandates. Federal law supersedes inconsistent state laws, and in this book we will explore these collisions as they occur.

IV. ARTICLE 1 OF THE CODE

The first Article of the UCC covers "General Provisions," and it applies to all UCC matters unless a more specific section elsewhere in the Code says otherwise. Article 1's most recent rewrite occurred in 2001, and that version, now adopted by most of the states, is the one referred to in this book.

Look at §1-103 and let's highlight some of what it says. Subsection 1-103(a)(1) tells us that the UCC shall be "liberally construed." This is not a political statement, but instead is meant to combat the old presumption that the common law (meaning the law as created by precedent with no statutory guidance) was thought so wise that a rule of statutory construction arose stating that "statutes in derogation of the common law are to be *strictly* construed" so as to change the common law result as little as possible. Karl Llewellyn was having none of that: the UCC is to be read broadly, the common law be damned.

Subsection 1-103(a)(3) commands the courts of the various states to work to make the law "uniform" throughout the country. This gives the attorney finding a favorable ruling in one state a strong argument that it's a good precedent in another—a valuable thing to remember.

Finally §1-103(b) preserves all of the common law rules (including the rules of equity and even the law merchant) to the extent that they do not contradict the statutory rules contained in the UCC. If the UCC doesn't speak to an issue, then attorneys must look to other laws to find the desired result.

One of the most important sections in the Code is §1-201, which is a huge definition section containing definitions for 43 different words and phrases. You will consult it often when exploring the matters we'll discuss in later chapters. Section 1-202 has complicated definitions of *notice* and *knowledge* that answer important questions such as what the two terms mean and at what moment a notice is effective (when sent? when received?). Section 1-204 defines *value* and §1-205 explores the issues of *reasonable time* and *seasonable.*

There's a choice of law provision in §1-301 that generally applies the law of the enacting state if "appropriate," but allows the parties by agreement to choose the law of any state having a "reasonable relation" to the transaction.

Another important section, often referred to in this book and the case law, is §1-303, which explains what are sometimes called "construction" terms: the items that make up the understanding of the parties as to what the contract means. Section 1-303(c) explains that a *usage of trade* is a *custom* within the industry (sort of a throwback to the law merchant) and this custom binds all of those who should know about it, sometimes including even consumers. Ask yourself this: is it the "usage of trade" that car dealers can lie about the attributes of the vehicle being sold and therefore get away with that? (Of course not—a usage of trade can't violate the law, and such lies would be fraud.) *Course of dealing* in §1-303(b) refers to what the parties did in their *past* contacts with one another. If the parties have dealt with each other in prior dealings, that history creates an expectation of what will happen in this contract, and the Code thusly recognizes it. Finally *course of performance* in §1-303(a) means what the parties do in performing this one particular contract, especially important where the contract goes on over a period of time and creates its own history and expectations. The common law called *course of performance* by the term *practical construction* and found that it gave great guidance to the true boundaries of the contract. Then, in §1-303(e), there is a hierarchy of importance of these construction terms, with the more relevant ones beating out the less relevant. Under this idea, express terms control course of performance, but course of performance is more important than both course of dealing or usage of trade, and course of dealing beats out an inconsistent usage of trade. One caveat to this little list: §1-303(f) explains that an express term in a contract ("deliveries must be made on time or the contract is breached") can be *waived* by course of performance (accepting late deliveries without protest means one cannot suddenly call a breach for this reason—a result codified by §2-209 for the sale of goods).

Section 1-304 provides that "[e]very contract or duty within the Uniform Commercial Code imposes an obligation of good faith in its performance and enforcement." The definition of *good faith* is "honesty in fact and the observance of reasonable commercial standards of fair dealing." §1-201(b)(20). Note that good faith has both a subjective component (honesty in fact) and an objective component (observance of reasonable commercial standards of fair dealing). This standard has changed over time. Some states have kept to the old definition of good faith, which required only "honesty in fact." Failure to act in good faith, by itself, "does not support an independent cause of action." Official Comment to §1-304; see, e.g., Brooklyn Bagel Boys, Inc. v. Earthgrains Refrigerated Dough Products, Inc, 212 F.3d 373 (7th Cir. 2000). Courts have held that failure to act in good faith, by itself, does not make a party liable, but a party that has performed in bad faith may be unable to assert rights under the Code. In one case, for example, a creditor who behaved in a blatantly evil manner had the usual Article 9 priorities reversed and ended up losing its collateral; see Ninth Dist. Prod. Credit Assn. v. Ed Duggan, Inc., 821 P.2d 788 (Colo. 1991).

V. *THE OFFICIAL COMMENTS*

All of the sections of the Code are followed by the Official Comments (such as the one quoted in the previous paragraph), which explain how the drafters wanted the sections to be interpreted. These Comments, the courts have said clearly, are not the law, but they are important to in understanding the meaning of the relevant section and are to be studied in that light. If in a future case you have an Official Comment in your favor, you will of course call it to the court's attention and remind the court that this Comment was written by the very experts who wrote the statute and therefore it should be given great weight. If the relevant Comment hurts your case and has, annoyingly, been raised by the other side, remind the court that the Comment are not the law, and that sometimes these Comments have the look of "Oops, we meant to say this, but knew we couldn't get it through the legislature so we're trying to amend the law through a more devious channel."

CHAPTER 1 REVIEW QUESTIONS

Who developed the law merchant and why?

How did the law merchant affect the development of commercial law in the courts?

Who drafted the Uniform Commercial Code and why?

How does the UCC become law?

How does the UCC define "good faith"?

PART 1

Sale and Lease of Goods

CHAPTER 2

BASIC CONCEPTS

I. *INTRODUCTION*

Disputes about sales have always been with us. In what has been called the earliest documented customer service complaint, a Babylonian clay tablet from 1750 B.C. bears a letter from an aggrieved buyer, Nanni, to the seller, Ea-nasir. Nanni complains that the wrong grade of copper ore was delivered, that goods were misdirected after a gulf voyage, and that the seller was guilty of further delays and failures to respect the buyer as a merchant.[1] Nanni further protests that the buyer wrongfully retained money bags and forced Nanni's messengers to return home empty-handed through enemy territory. We will see the same concerns arise today in sales of goods as diverse as smart home systems, thoroughbred racehorses, diving boards, uranium stockpiles, diamond rings, paintings, stock cars, grass seed, truckloads of seafood, communications satellites, and more. Nanni's concerns echo in the cases in this book: A seller

1. See description of clay tablet, Museum number 131236, at the site of the British Museum, http://www.britishmuseum.org/research/collection_online/.

promises to create web application software but delivers it late and full of bugs. A corn seller complains that a buyer has refused to honor their custom of meeting each month to confirm sales. A seller of merchandise ships boxes filled with garbage and uses the shipping receipt to draw on a letter of credit (today's equivalent of money bags carried by messengers). A clothing shopper tries on a pair of slacks and is bitten by a poisonous spider. Enemy territory problems for seller's servants do not come up much in the 21st century.

From the beginning of civilization buyers and sellers have traded things across great distances, even in very primitive times. Over 14,000 years ago, Native American peoples living in the middle of the continent possessed items such as beads and weapons that could only have originated on the East Coast, demonstrating that tribal merchants were at work moving goods around even then. The need to trade and the desire to acquire goods both for necessities and more luxurious purposes has fueled much of the development of our world. During times of major international wars, trade still flourished (and sometimes thrived, as in the sale of weapons), and in countries where private bargains have been severely regulated or even forbidden (as in some communist regimes), black markets arise to slide deals past the eyes of the authorities.

In all transactions there is a commonality of expectations: the parties must agree on the terms of the bargain, those terms must be honored, the product being sold must meet some standard of quality or suitability, and if the transaction hits snags, the parties must have recourse to a viable remedy. In the materials that follow, we will explore how the Uniform Commercial Code provides a legal framework to resolve these matters.

II. SCOPE OF ARTICLE 2

A. "Transactions in Goods"

Article 2 of the Uniform Commercial Code applies to *transactions in goods*. Read §2-102. The word *transactions* is not defined in the Code. Look at §2-106(1); does that help? Much is encompassed within these parameters. Both the delivery of a multibillion-dollar space craft to the U.S. government and the purchase of a package of chewing gum at a local store trigger the application of Article 2 of the Code. *Goods* is defined in §2-105. Read it, and work through the following materials.

PROBLEM 1

Whether Article 2 applies may determine the outcome of a case. If Article 2 applies, its rules may favor one party (such as the implied warranty of merchantability that automatically 3is given to many buyers by §2-314). Does Article 2 of the Code apply to the following matters?

(a) The sale of an insurance policy? See Call v. Czaplicki, 2010 WL 3724275 (D.N.J. 2010).

(b) The sale of real property? What about the sale of a house apart from the realty? See §2-107.

(c) The sale of building materials as part of a construction project? See the case following this Problem.

(d) The sale of standing timber? Crops? See §2-107.

(e) A defective spinal plate given a patient in a hospital operating room? See Brandt v. Boston Scientific Corp., 204 Ill. 2d 640, 792 N.E.2d 296 (2003). The preparation of false teeth by a dentist? See Carroll v. Grabavoy, 77 Ill. App. 3d 895, 396 N.E.2d 836 (1977). The injection of a drug (for which the patient was separately billed) into a patient's eye as part of an operation? See Providence Hospital v. Truly, 611 S.W.2d 127 (Tex. Civ. App. 1980).

(f) The sale of membership in a health spa?

(g) The sale of electricity? See GFI Wisconsin, Inc. v. Reedsbury Utility Commn., 440 B.R. 791 (W.D. Wis. 2010).

(h) Devices signed a distribution agreement giving Detail Retail the exclusive right to sell Gooseberry phones in the Midwest. Is this an Article 2 transaction? Same result if Detail Retail also agreed to buy 1 million Gooseberry phones directly from Devices? See MidAmerican Distribution, Inc. v. Clarification Technology, Inc., 807 F. Supp. 2d 646 (E.D. Ky. 2011); Franklin Publications, Inc. v. General Nutrition Corp., 2007 WL 2071914 (S.D. Ohio 2007).

(i) Specially manufacturing and supplying a yacht? See §2-105(1); Fed. Ins. Co. v. Mathews Bros., LLC, 2015 WL 4879194 (D. Md. 2015).

(j) When a customer paid for groceries at the counter she was given a plastic bag to put them in. The bag proved defective such that the groceries spilled and she suffered serious injuries from broken glass in the bag. Is there a sale of goods as to the plastic grocery bag by the grocery store? See Fuller v. Winn-Dixie Montgomery, LLC, 2017 WL 3098104 (S.D. Ala. 2017).

PROBLEM 2

Heather Oberdorf purchased a dog collar on Amazon.com from a third-party vendor identified as "The Furry Gang." The Furry Gang shipped the dog collar from its place of business, and Amazon never had possession of the dog collar. About a month later, Ms. Oberdorf attached a retractable leash to this collar to take her dog for a walk. During the walk, the D-ring on the collar broke. The leash recoiled, hitting Oberdorf's face and eyeglasses. As a result, she is permanently blind in one eye. Neither Amazon nor Oberdorf has been able to locate The Furry Gang or the manufacturer of the dog collar. Is Amazon a "seller of goods" and therefore liable for this injury? Look carefully at the definitions of "seller" and "sale" in §§2-103(d) and 2-106(1). Did Amazon have "title" to the goods at any point?

The actual case is Oberdorf v. Amazon.com Inc., 2020 WL 3023064 (3d Cir. 2020), in which the court discusses the issue only in terms of strict product liability law (an issue we will get to later in this book), and reviews cases that mostly have held that Amazon is not a "seller" of the goods that pass through its system, at least for third party goods it never even possesses, but then the court decided to send this issue to the Pennsylvania Supreme Court for resolution (and at this book's creation there had not yet been a response from that court).

Amazon's liability for defective products is a hot issue all over the United States, and Amazon frequently—but not always—escapes, particularly in pure UCC cases, because it has no "title" to third party goods sold through its website. Compare Erie Insurance Company v. Amazon.com, Inc., 925 F.3d 135 (4th Cir. 2019) (Amazon not "seller" of defective headlamp that burned down a house causing $300.000 in damages since it never had title to the headlamp), with Legal Aid of Nebraska, Inc. v. Chaina Wholesale, Inc., 2020 WL 42471 (D. Neb. 2020) (Amazon liable for breach of warranty on space heater that caught fire and caused $783,000.00 in damages—no discussion of title); and note that suing the actual manufacturer of the defective goods can fail for another reason, lack of *privity* ("legal connection"), an issue we will explore later in this book; see Loomis v. Slendertone Distribution, Inc., 420 F. Supp. 3d 1046 (S.D. Ca. 2019).

But, say the commentators, "not so fast." Amazon has much control over these third parties, frequently commingling their identical goods so it is not clear whose goods Amazon actually shipped, and for other reasons so dominates the transaction that it is far from the usual sort of independent market (like an antique store in which the true owners of the items display them on consignment to the store). For a detailed discussion of Amazon's practices see Edward J. Janger & Aaron D. Twerski, The Heavy Hand of Amazon: a Seller not a Neutral Platform, 14 Brook. J. Corp. Fin. & Com. L. 259 (2020). The issue is very important because frequently the third party seller either can't be found, or is defunct, or is beyond legal service, and in the meantime a defective product sold through Amazon has caused a woman to be blind for life in one eye or a house to burn to the ground.

Audio Visual Artistry v. Tanzer

Court of Appeals of Tennessee, 2012
403 S.W.3d 789

J. STEVEN STAFFORD, J.

This is a breach of contract case. Appellant/Homeowner contracted with Appellee for the installation of a "smart home" system. After myriad problems arose, Appellant fired Appellee, who filed the instant lawsuit to collect the unpaid balance for equipment and installation. The trial court determined that the primary purpose of the parties' agreement was the sale of goods and applied Article 2 of the Uniform Commercial Code. The court granted judgment in favor of Appellee, but allowed certain offsets for items rejected by Appellant. Appellant appeals, arguing that the trial court erred in applying the UCC, and in its calculation of damages. Appellant also appeals the trial court's determination that the Tennessee Consumer Protection Act does not apply. Discerning no error, we affirm.

On or about March 26, 2004, Appellant Stephen Tanzer and Appellee Audio Video Artistry ("AVA") entered into discussions for the sale and installation of electronic and entertainment equipment in Mr. Tanzer's home. AVA is a residential entertainment and communications firm specializing in custom design projects. AVA is a general partnership; its partners, Chris Rogers and Brad Parsley, founded the firm in 1999 to offer state-of-the-art home theater, multi-room music and television, lighting control and phone/intercom systems. The sale, installation, and integration of these systems for the creation of a "smart home" (also known as "domotics") is AVA's specialty.

In March 2004, Chris Rogers met with Mr. Tanzer to discuss Mr. Tanzer's desires for the home he was building. Based upon their discussion, AVA submitted a proposal to Mr. Tanzer for components, parts, and installation, totaling $78,567.13. The written proposal specifically provided for the following work:

- 6 "independent" zones of music consisting of 13 rooms and related equipment to switch, power, and control the music system;
- phone system throughout the house with door communications;
- lighting control system throughout the house to include 64 standard wattage (600w) loads;
- network wiring for television, phone, music, and computers throughout the home.

The systems pricing for this work (i.e., the total price of $78,567.13) was broken out in the original proposal as follows:

- Equipment: $56,375.00
- Labor/Programming: $9,880.00

- Cable: Misc. Parts: $5,660.00
- Total: $71,915.00
- Tax: $6,652.13

On September 22, 2004, AVA and Mr. Tanzer entered into a written contract, which incorporates the original proposal, adding an additional "seventh zone" for music, and also adding seven automated shades. These shades were included as a "purchase incentive" at no cost to Mr. Tanzer. The contract provides that, in the event the shades do not work in an acceptable fashion, Mr. Tanzer would receive an additional $8,400 credit. The contract further contemplates that Mr. Tanzer's needs and desires for the "smart system" would likely evolve during the course of the project; therefore, the contract specifically provides that "[v]erbal agreements throughout the life of the project may also be honored as part of this contract and will be documented by AVA."

As originally contemplated, the contract called for a Concierge whole-house audio system. The audio/visual items were to be integrated via the Crestron system, which would allow Mr. Tanzer to play music in the seven, independently controlled music "zones." Remote control "touch-panels" would control and integrate DVD, television, music, and other smart home functions. The contract further included a Lutron automated lighting system, which would be integrated into the Crestron system, along with an intercom/phone/whole house networking system.

At the time the parties entered their contract, construction had just commenced on Mr. Tanzer's home. The home is not a usual residence; rather, it is an approximately 15,000 square foot, $3.5 million dollar build. Because of the size and scope of the project, AVA was to install certain wiring and equipment during the construction process. Pre-wiring began on the house as the framing went in, but equipment installation and programming of the smart system did not begin in earnest until March, 2006. Mr. Tanzer and his family moved into the home in April, 2006.

During the project, and as contemplated in the contract, the original scope of work was changed and AVA performed additional work. One significant change was the decision to use an Escient music system in lieu of the Concierge music system. Mr. Rogers allegedly represented to Mr. Tanzer, after the job had begun, that the Escient system was better able to do what Mr. Tanzer wanted, i.e., stream music from his PC, which was not a function that the Concierge system offered. AVA agreed to sell and install the Escient system for the same price as the Concierge system. Later, an art frame and shade were also added to conceal the television in the sitting room. The "art shade" is a custom-painted, frame-mounted piece of artwork on canvas, which can be rolled down to conceal a television at the push of a button. Other changes related to the Crestron touch panels, which were changed from radio-frequency panels to Wi-Fi panels (Crestron came out with a Wi-Fi product before installation commenced). The Wi-Fi panels were changed at the same cost as that previously quoted for the radio-frequency panels. Another change was the switch in the music distribution equipment, which would allow for future expansion of the system. Further changes included equipment for the media room and five additional pairs of speakers. AVA also integrated the pool system, the alarm system, and the HVAC system with the Crestron control system.

Mr. Tanzer eventually became unsatisfied with AVA's work. Mr. Tanzer contends that, based upon Mr. Parsley's statements, he thought that the installation, programming, and debugging of the "smart home" system would take less than three months. However, Mr. Tanzer claims that, after fifteen months, he was still having significant problems with the functionality of the system. Specifically, Mr. Tanzer states, in his brief, that: (1) the punch list ebbed and flowed; (2) [t]he programming was unstable; (3) "[i]t seemed every time AVA would come out to resolve one problem, two or three new problems would crop up in its place"; (4) [t]hings that AVA fixed didn't stay fixed. As a result, Mr. Tanzer became "extremely frustrated and inconven[ienced]." To compound these alleged issues, in July, 2006, the basement of the house flooded, damaging the media room. A year later, in July of 2007, while AVA was allegedly still trying to "debug" the system, the home was struck by lightning. The power surge from the lightning caused damage to the Crestron processor and Ethernet card. Although the damaged components had no warranty against "Acts of God," it is not disputed that AVA replaced them without additional charge. In August 2007, Mr. Tanzer fired AVA and requested a final billing.

Both the original equipment and work and the additional work, equipment, and changes were set out in Invoice #3036, which was presented by AVA to Mr. Tanzer. This Invoice shows a total project cost of $119,402.15, and reflects an outstanding balance of $43,824.55. Mr. Tanzer disputed this balance and the instant lawsuit ensued.

On November 19, 2007, AVA filed suit against Mr. Tanzer for breach of contract. On December 31, 2007, Mr. Tanzer filed his answer, in which he denies any liability. Concurrent with the answer, Mr. Tanzer filed a counter-complaint against AVA, alleging that AVA breached the contract and seeking damages for the breach. AVA answered the counter-complaint, denying any liability.

After the lawsuit had commenced, in February or March of 2008, a second lightning strike to the house shut down the entire "smart home" system. Mr. Tanzer then hired Marquis Home Solutions ("Marquis") to make repairs. Tom Brown, an employee of Marquis, testified that there were numerous problems with AVA's installation of the systems, including:

(1) improper power source to the Lutron processor; (2) improper surge protection; (3) failure to install the Lutron processor in a proper recessed and covered enclosure; (4) failure to label wiring and improper wiring; (5) instability of the Wi-Fi handles for the Crestron system. Marquis charged Mr. Tanzer $67,587 for the repairs. Mr. Tanzer avers that the amount Marquis charged includes only the cost of repairs to the systems that AVA installed, and does not include the price of any upgrades.

The parties filed various trial briefs, which are incorrectly included in this record. Tenn. R. App. P. 24(b) ("The following papers filed in the trial court are excluded from the record . . . (4) trial briefs. . . ."). Regardless, on May 19, 2011, the trial court entered its preliminary findings of fact and conclusions of law, which were based upon the parties' briefs. Therein, the court states, in relevant part, that:

> [T]he Court finds that the parties' agreement in this matter involved the sale of consumer goods governed by the Uniform Commercial Code found at T.C.A. §47-2-101 et seq. Although the parties' agreement involved some provision of labor and services, an examination of the entire transaction and application of the "predominant factor" test, leads the Court to the conclusion that this was simply an agreement for the sale and installation of electronic equipment. The labor and services provided under the terms of the parties' agreement was insignificant in comparison to the cost of equipment provided. As such, the Uniform Commercial Code is applicable to this transaction and the Court is required to consider its provisions in determining the rights and remedies afforded the parties under the agreement in this case.

The trial court then allowed additional time for the parties to prepare and present supplemental evidence on the issue of remedies under the Uniform Commercial Code ("UCC"). In addition, the preliminary findings of fact include a specific finding that the Tennessee Consumer Protection Act ("TCPA") is not applicable to the case. Specifically, the court found that there was insufficient proof to show that AVA had "engaged in any unfair or deceptive acts or practices," and that there was "insufficient proof that Chris Rogers held himself out to [Mr. Tanzer] as an electrical engineer."

In response to the trial court's preliminary findings, Mr. Tanzer filed a motion for reconsideration on June 14, 2011. AVA opposed the motion, which was ultimately denied by the trial court's July 22, 2011 order. By order of October 17, 2011, the trial court granted judgment in favor of AVA. The order includes the following, relevant, findings:

> 1. That within a reasonable time after delivery and installation of the equipment involved in the parties' contract, AVA had actual knowledge and

notice that the Escient music system and phone system did not perform properly even after repeated attempts by AVA to fix the problems complained of by Tanzer. As such, the Court finds from the proof that these items were never accepted by Tanzer and were rejected in accordance with the requirements of the UCC.

2. That, under the facts in this case, Tanzer is entitled to an offset for these items in the amounts indicated below:

a. Escient Music System	$14,098.00
b. Phone System	$3,825.00

3. That in addition to these offsets against the balance owed AVA, Tanzer is entitled to the following credits for items that were improperly charged:

a. 5 Sonance volume controls	$400.00
b. 4 Lutron switches	$1,200.00
c. Overcharge on wire run	$330.00

4. That the charges paid to Marquis Solutions by Tanzer are not appropriate for a consequential damage claim under the facts here. Marquis made extensive upgrades and changes to Tanzer's whole house system and there was insufficient detail in Mr. Brown's testimony regarding the specific work performed and the amount charged for each specific item for the Court to make an award for consequential damages. Additionally, the Court has offset the amount owed by Tanzer for the items that were rejected. Tanzer is not entitled to an offset for the rejected items and to receive an award for repairs to these items. It is also noted that Marquis' repair bill is unreasonably high and grossly exceeds the amount charged by AVA for these items in its contract with Tanzer.

5. That HVAC integration was not included in AVA's original proposal to Tanzer. I further find from the proof that AVA completed this additional work at Tanzer's request and is entitled to the amount charged for this work. Tanzer also failed to prove that the HVAC integration was not functioning properly when AVA completed its work.

6. That Tanzer failed to establish through his proof that AVA had any responsibility for the lightning strike which damaged some of the components installed by AVA and which was later repaired by Marquis. As such, Tanzer is not entitled to recover for the amount charged by Marquis for such repairs.

7. That AVA is entitled to the equipment rejected by Tanzer which is in his possession. Tanzer is hereby ordered to make these items available to AVA if requested by AVA.

Based upon the foregoing findings, the court awarded offsets and credits to Mr. Tanzer in the total amount of $19,842.00. Accordingly, AVA was awarded judgment in the amount of $23,982.55. On October 31, 2011,

AVA filed a motion to alter or amend the judgment under Tennessee Rule of Civil Procedure 59. The motion was granted and, on December 12, 2011, the trial court amended its previous order. . . . AVA's total judgment was increased from $23,982.55 to $35,580.55. Upon Mr. Tanzer's motion, the judgment was stayed pending appeal. By separate order, entered on February 23, 2012, the trial court also denied both parties' requests for attorney's fees and costs.

Mr. Tanzer appeals. He raises four issues for review as stated in his brief:

> I. The trial court erred in finding that the UCC applied to the services rendered by AVA.
>
> II. The Court erred in not declaring the failure to complete its work a material breach on the part of AVA and denying damages to [Tanzer].
>
> III. The trial court erred in not awarding Tanzer the cost incurred to make the system work properly and get the benefit of his bargain.
>
> IV. The trial court erred in finding that AVA did not violate the Tennessee Consumer Protection Act. . . .

I. Applicability of UCC Article 2

In his first issue, Mr. Tanzer asserts that the trial court erred in applying UCC Article 2 to his contract with AVA. Specifically, Mr. Tanzer argues that thrust of the contract is for services and not for the sale of goods such that common law breach of contract principles apply. We begin our analysis with 67 Am. Jur. 2d Sales §37, which provides:

> Article 2 [of the UCC] applies to transactions in goods but does not apply to construction contracts or contracts for the rendition of services. However, the existence of a sale in and of itself does not automatically implicate the Uniform Commercial Code. In many cases, a contract or transaction may involve both the transaction of a sale and the rendition of services, presenting a "mixed" or hybrid transaction or contract. To determine whether such "mixed" or "hybrid" contracts are governed by Article 2, a court must examine the whole transaction and look to the essence or main objective of the parties' agreement or the primary or overall purpose of the transaction.
>
> Ordinarily, a court determines whether a mixed contract for goods and services is subject to Article 2 by considering whether the contract, reasonably stated, is for goods with labor incidentally involved or for services with goods incidentally involved. The question is generally one of fact, involving a consideration of the contract in its entirety. Depending upon whether the contract or transaction is predominantly for the sale of goods or the rendition of services, Article 2 applies to the entire contract or not at all.

Id. (footnotes omitted). As further discussed in 1 Stephen W. Ramp & Katherine Simpson Allen, Tennessee Practice: Uniform Commercial Code Forms §2-106 (2d ed. 2002):

> A sale is the passing of title from the seller to the buyer for a price. Courts will consider the substance of the transaction rather than how the parties chose to label the transaction. Where the service component of a contract for sale overrides the goods aspect of the transaction it will not fall within Article 2 once the transaction is determined to be a service and not a sale.

The question of whether UCC Article 2 or common law contract principles apply is important in terms of available warranties and the measure of damages. As discussed in R. Alan Pritchard, The Predominant Factor Test Under the Uniform Commercial Code, Tenn. B. J., July, 2001, at 23:

> Article 2 of the Uniform Commercial Code (UCC) sets forth the provisions that govern certain sales transactions involving goods. The provisions establish the terms that will govern such a transaction including, among other items, warranty provisions, remedies provisions for both the buyer and the seller, and damages provisions. Section 2-313 establishes the express warranty that governs the sales transaction, and §§2-314 and 2-315 establish the implied warranties of merchantability and fitness for a particular purpose. All of these warranties are subject to exclusion under the sales contract between the parties; however, such exclusions must be in accordance with the specific provisions of the Uniform Commercial Code. In the event there is a breach of these warranties, the Uniform Commercial Code sets forth the remedies that are available for such breach. A claim for breach must be brought within four years from the date the cause of action accrues. See UCC 2-725. The cause of action accrues at the time the breach occurs, which is at the time the tender of delivery is made. See 2-725.

As noted above in 67 Am. Jur. 2d Sales §37, many transactions are neither pure sale of goods nor pure service transactions, but a combination of the two, i.e., a hybrid contract. As discussed in Barkley Clark and Christopher Smith, The Law of Product Warranties §2:19 (2012):

> When faced with these hybrids, the courts have generally employed a predominant element test: If the service aspect predominates, tort theories must control (even as to defective goods), but if the goods aspect predominates, Article 2 warranties come into play (sometimes even with respect to the service component). This is a rather mechanical approach, but the courts favor it. Sometimes they are swayed by the wording of the contract, as when the plaintiff is denominated as an "owner" rather than a "buyer," and the defendant is denominated as the "contractor" rather than the "seller." Sometimes the courts look at the price factor, attempting to analyze the billing, and

> sometimes the decision is based on nothing more than a judicial hunch as to which element predominates. In the usual case, the plaintiff will push to persuade the court that the goods element predominates, so the more lenient standard of the Article 2 implied warranties can be used to measure liability, and the defendant will shove in the opposite direction in a real tug-of-war.

Id. (footnotes omitted). One of the earliest cases to adopt the predominant purpose test was Bonebrake v. Cox, 499 F.2d 951 (8th Cir. 1974), which involved a contract for the sale and installation of pre-fabricated bowling equipment. The *Bonebrake* Court noted that such hybrid contracts are legion and then proposed its test:

> The test for inclusion or exclusion is not whether they are mixed, but granting that they are mixed, whether their predominant factor, their thrust, their purpose, reasonably stated, is the rendition of service, with goods incidentally involved (e.g., contract with artist for painting), or is a transaction of sale, with labor incidentally involved (e.g., installation of a water heater in a bathroom).

Id. at 960. In *Bonebrake,* the court concluded that the goods element predominated, thus invoking the rules of Article 2, including the warranty provisions. Id.

In the case of Pass v. Shelby Aviation, No. W1999-00018-COA-R9-CV, 2000 WL 388775 (Tenn. Ct. App. April 13, 2000), Tennessee adopted and applied the *Bonebrake* predominant purpose test. Applying the test, the *Pass* Court determined that a mixed transaction of goods and services was "predominantly the provision of a service, not subject to the warranty provisions of the UCC." Id. at *6. In that case, Max E. Pass, Jr., and his wife, Martha N. Pass, were both killed when their aircraft, piloted by Mr. Pass, crashed outside of Opelika, Alabama. Approximately four-and-one-half months prior to the fatal flight, Mr. Pass had taken the aircraft to defendant, Shelby Aviation, Inc., for inspection and service. During the servicing, Shelby Aviation replaced both rear wing attach point brackets on the plane.

After the crash, the administrators of the Pass's estates filed a lawsuit against Shelby Aviation. The suit alleged that the rear wing brackets, which were sold and installed by Shelby Aviation, were defective and asserted claims for breach of common law warranties, and for breach of express and implied warranties under Article 2 of the UCC. Shelby Aviation filed a motion to dismiss for failure to state a claim, contending that, because the contract was primarily for services, Article 2 did not apply. The motion was denied, and Shelby Aviation requested, and was granted, permission to file an interlocutory appeal to this Court. The main issue on appeal was whether the transaction between Mr. Pass and Shelby Aviation was governed by Article 2.

This Court determined that the predominant purpose test was the appropriate test to apply because it looks at the transaction as a whole. In applying the test, the Court stated:

> In order to determine whether the predominant purpose of a mixed transaction is the sale of goods or the provision of a service, we examine the language of the parties' contract, the nature of the business of the supplier of the goods and services, the reason the parties entered into the contract (i.e., what each bargained to receive), and the respective amounts charged under the contract for goods and for services. [Citations omitted.]. None of these factors alone is dispositive. BMC Industries, Inc. v. Barth Industries, Inc., 160 F.3d 1322, 1330 (11th Cir. 1998). The party seeking application of the UCC bears the burden of proof to show that the predominant purpose of the contract was the sale of goods. *Insul-Mark,* 612 N.E.2d at 555; Northwestern Equipment, Inc. v. Cudmore, 312 N.W.2d 347, 351 (N.D. 1981).

Pass, 2000 WL 388775, at *4. In concluding that the foregoing relevant factors should be considered in determining the choice of law for mixed contracts for sales of goods and service, the *Pass* Court relied upon an Indiana Supreme Court Case, Insul-Mark Midwest, Inc. v. Modern Materials, Inc., 612 N.E.2d 550 (Ind. 1993), wherein the Indiana Court stated:

> To determine whether the predominant thrust of a mixed contract is to provide services or goods, one looks first to the language of the contract, in light of the situation of the parties and the surrounding circumstances. Specifically one looks to the terms describing the performance of the parties, and the words used to describe the relationship between the parties.
>
> Beyond the contractual terms themselves, one looks to the circumstances of the parties, and the primary reason they entered into the contract. One also considers the final product the purchaser bargained to receive, and whether it may be described as a good or a service.
>
> Finally, one examines the costs involved for the goods and services, and whether the purchaser was charged only for a good, or a price based on both goods and services. If the cost of the goods is but a small portion of the overall contract price, such fact would increase the likelihood that the services portion predominates.

Pass, 2000 WL 388775, at *4 (citing *Insul-Mark,* 612 N.E.2d at 555 (citations omitted)).

Applying the foregoing principles, the *Pass* Court determined that "the invoice clearly emphasizes the repair and inspection aspects of the transaction, indicating that the predominant purpose was the sale of service, with the sale of goods incidental to that service." *Pass,* 2000 WL 388775, at *4. Further, the overall nature of Shelby Aviation's business was service rather than the sale of parts, and "Mr. Pass took the plane to Shelby Aviation primarily to have a service performed, i.e., the annual inspection." Id. at *5. Finally, the court looked to allocation of costs between goods and services. Id. The court indicated that it did not favor adding the labor charges for installing the parts to the cost of the parts as was proposed by the plaintiffs, and then the court stated that:

> Regardless of how the percentage of the cost of goods is calculated, viewing the transaction as a whole, we must conclude that the predominant purpose of the transaction was the provision of a service rather than the sale of goods. . . . As such, it is not subject to the warranty provisions of Article 2 of the UCC. Shelby Aviation is entitled to judgment as a matter of law on the [p]laintiffs' UCC breach of warranty claims.

Id. at *6. The decision denying Shelby Aviation's motion for summary judgment on the UCC breach of warranty claims was reversed, and the case was remanded for further proceedings. *Id.*

From *Pass,* we understand that, in applying the predominant purpose test, the court looks to four factors:

(1) the language of the contract;
(2) the nature of the business of the supplier of goods and services;
(3) the reason the parties entered into the contract, and
(4) the amounts paid for the rendition of the services and goods, respectively.

We now turn to address each of these factors based on the evidence contained in the record to determine whether the trial court correctly found that the contract at issue in this case predominantly involves the sale of goods such that UCC Article 2 is applicable.

A. LANGUAGE OF THE CONTRACT

The first factor set out by the *Pass* Court requires us to look "to the language of the contract, in light of the situation of the parties and the surrounding circumstances. Specifically, [the court] looks to the terms describing the performance of the parties, and the words used to describe the relationship between the parties." *Pass,* 2000 WL 388775, at *4 (quoting *Insul-Mark,* 612 N.E.2d at 555). Contractual language that refers to the transaction as a "purchase," for example, or identifies the parties as the "buyer" and "seller," indicates that the transaction is for goods rather than services. See *Bonebrake,* 499 F.2d at 958 (stating that language referring to "equipment" is peculiar to goods rather than services); Bailey v. Montgomery Ward & Co., 690 P.2d 1280, 1282 (Colo. Ct. App. 1984) (holding that a contract that identifies the transaction as a "purchase" and one of the parties as the "customer" signals a transaction in goods); Meeker v. Hamilton Grain Elevator Co., 110 Ill. App. 3d 668, 66 Ill. Dec. 360, 442 N.E.2d 921, 923 (1982) (stating that a contract that calls the parties "seller" and "purchaser" indicates a contract for goods).

Turning to the contract between Mr. Tanzer and AVA, we first note that it is titled "Systems Sale and Installation Contract." From the plain language, it is clear that this is a hybrid contract, contemplating both the sale of goods and the installation of the goods. The question, then, is whether the language, when viewed in context, indicates the predominant purpose of the contract.

Throughout the contract, Mr. Tanzer is referred to as the "purchaser," a term that connotes a sale of goods contract. *Bonebrake,* 499 F.2d at 958. In various sections, the contract states that: (1) "[p]er this contract, AVA agrees to deliver and install **equipment** included in the proposal"; (2) "AVA retains ownership of the equipment until contract is paid in full"; (3) "Delays . . . by parties other than AVA that prohibit proper installation of **delivered equipment** shall not delay payment . . .;" (4) "Prices are subject to change on items . . . between the time of execution of this contract and the **delivery of goods**"; (5) "All **pre-paid goods** shall be delivered at the price agreed"; (6) "Model numbers may change . . . therefore Product delivered may not . . . be the same model number agreed to in the Proposal"; and (7) "Final installation of most **electronic hardware** corresponds with purchaser['s] actual move-in date. . . ." (Emphases added). As noted in *Bonebrake,* "equipment" is a term of art, which is "peculiar [to the sale of goods.]" *Bonebrake,* 499 F.2d at 958. Furthermore, the contract incorporates, by reference, the earlier proposal, which sets out the specific equipment that AVA would install in the Tanzer home.

In his brief, Mr. Tanzer urges this Court to read the disputed contract as a construction or building contract based, *inter alia,* upon the fact that the equipment and installation occurred during the building process and the items installed allegedly became part of the completed home. In support of his argument, Mr. Tanzer relies upon the case of Aluminum Vinyl Sales Company v. Woerz, No. 03A01-9304-CV-00172, 1993 WL 367125 (Tenn. Ct. App. Sept. 20, 1993). *Woerz* involved a contract for the installation of vinyl siding on a home. In pertinent part, the *Woerz* Court stated:

> "The Uniform Commercial Code does not apply to a contract for the rendition of services or to construction contracts." The subject matter of the contract before us is to furnish "all the materials and labor necessary for" the installation of vinyl siding to the entire exterior of Defendant's house.
>
> A contract to furnish a movable thing and affix it to the freehold is not a contract for the sale of goods, but one to furnish materials and affix them to the freehold by work and labor, and, until the materials are affixed, title to the materials does not pass.

1993 WL 367125, at *3 (citing 67 Am. Jur. 2d, Sales, §39 (1985); 77 C.J.S., Sales, §2, p. 585). Despite Mr. Tanzer's reading of *Woerz*, we cannot extend its holding so far as to conclude that it stands for the proposition that any and all contracts that contemplate the sale of goods, which are installed in a home or affixed to realty, are to be construed as predominantly service contracts. Rather, as noted in 1 Barkley Clark and Christopher Smith, The Law of Product Warranties §2:22 (2012):

> Contracts for the installation of products that were identifiable goods before installation and that, when installed, constitute only a small portion of a total building, are covered by Article 2. . . . As long as the transaction involves defective products that were moveable before installation and thus once qualified as "goods" under §2-105(1), the courts assume that the service elements are also covered.

Id. Accordingly, cases have held that the installation of the following are all sale of goods: (1) carpet, Snyder v. Herbert Greenbaum & Associates, Inc., 38 Md. App. 144, 380 A.2d 618 (1977), Colorado Carpet Installation, Inc. v. Palermo, 668 P.2d 1384 (Colo. 1983); (2) electrical equipment, E.C. Ernst, Inc. v. Manhattan Const. Co. of Texas, 551 F.2d 1026 (5th Cir. 1977); (3) trees, shrubs and sod, Burton v. Artery Co., Inc., 279 Md. 94, 367 A.2d 935 (1977); (4) steel lockers, Anderson Const. Co., Inc. v. Lyon Metal Products, Inc., 370 So. 2d 935 (Miss. 1979); (5) overhead doors, Meyers v. Henderson Const. Co., 147 N.J. Super. 77, 370 A.2d 547 (1977); (6) water heaters, Shapiro v. Long Island Lighting Co., 71 A.D.2d 671, 418 N.Y.S.2d 948 (1979); (7) a furnace, O'Laughlin v. Minnesota Natural Gas Co., 253 N.W.2d 826 (Minn. 1977); (8) an air-conditioning system, B & B Refrigeration & Air Conditioning Service, Inc. v. Haifley, 1978 WL 23510 (D.C. Super. Ct. Nov. 6, 1978); and (9) interior window panels, The Plantation Shutter Co. v. Ezell, 328 S.C. 475, 492 S.E.2d 404 (1997).

In Glazer, et ux v. Tri-State Tile and Marble Co., Inc., 1985 Tenn. App. LEXIS 2767 (Tenn. Ct. App. March 22, 1985), a suit for breach of express warranty in connection with the resurfacing of plaintiffs' patio with "prairie film," which is "a mixture of epoxy and very fine gravel," Id. at *1, this Court noted that, in cases "involving building useful improvements out of raw materials," courts have held that these contracts are "outside the scope of the U.C.C." Id. at *3. Such cases involved: (1) the sale and installation of blacktop, Rose Acre Farms v. L.P. Cavett Co., 151 Ind. App. 268, 279 N.E.2d 280 (1972); (2) construction of a house with a builder furnishing all materials and labor, Vernali v. Centrella, 28 Conn. Supp. 476, 266 A.2d 200 (1970); and (3) construction of electrical equipment, Mainland v. Alfred Brown Co., 85 Nev. 654, 461 P.2d 862 (Nev. Sup. Ct. 1969). On the other hand, in cases where the courts have found the contract to be one for the sale of goods, and thus governed by the UCC, "the items therein involved have been tangible things, movable at the time they are identified to the contract and where installation has not been a major or predominant factor in the contract." *Glazer,* 1985 Tenn. App. LEXIS 2767, at *3. Such cases involved: (1) installation of water tank, Pittsburgh-Des Moines Steel Co. v. Brookhaven Manor Water Co., 532 F.2d 572 (7th Cir. 1976); (2) installation of a bowling alley and equipment, *Bonebrake,* 499 F.2d at 951; and (3) installation of a liner for the bottom of a swimming pool, Riffe v. Black, 548 S.W.2d 175 (Ky. Ct. App. 1977). The *Glazer* Court applied the foregoing principles in reaching its conclusion that the installation of "prairie film" is not a sale of goods. In reaching its holding, the Court noted:

> [T]his is clearly not a sale of "goods," but is closely akin to some of the cases cited above, such as, the sale and installation of a blacktop driveway, or building or painting a house. We see no difference between installing a Prairie Film system over a patio and overlaying the patio with concrete or quarry tile. Plaintiffs were contracting to obtain a service from the defendant, not to purchase a quantity of gravel.
>
> By the same token, materials, such as the Prairie Film, when attached to realty, such as a patio cover, lose their character as goods. See T.C.A. §47-9-313. Once the patio was resurfaced by defendant the resurfacing lost any characteristics of personalty and became part of an improvement of the real estate, not severable therefrom.

Glazer, 1985 Tenn. App. LEXIS 2767, at *3.

Tennessee Code Annotated Section 47-2-105 sets out the current definition of "goods" under the UCC. The statute provides, in relevant part, that: "'Goods' means all things (including specially manufactured goods) which are movable at the time of identification to the contract for sale. . . ." The comments to the code section clarify that: "The definition of goods is based on the concept of movability. . . . It is not intended to deal with things which are not fairly identifiable as movables before the contract is performed." The comment goes on to explain that:

> The use of the word "fixtures" is avoided in view of the diversity of definitions of that term. This Article in including within its scope "things attached to realty" adds the further test that they must be capable of severance without material harm thereto. As between the parties any identified things which fall within that definition becomes "goods" upon the making of the contract for sale.

In light of the foregoing statutory provisions, the holding in *Glazer* is still applicable. Because the "prairie film" became "attached to the realty," such that it could not be removed "without material harm" to the structure, the

Court correctly held that the contract was one for service, thus excluding application of the UCC. By contrast, in Highland Rim Contractors v. Atlantic Software Corp., No. 01-A-01-9104CV00147, 1992 WL 184872 (Tenn. Ct. App. Aug. 5, 1992), this Court held that a contract involving the sale of a computer system to a construction company was a sale of goods contract. The Court noted that the contract was a hybrid contract, involving both sale of goods and service. The Court then applied the predominant purpose test to determine that the UCC applied to the transaction; in so holding, the Court stated:

> Other courts, using the predominant [purpose] test, have found that contracts for the sale of computer systems or related components, including hardware, software, training, and support services, are contracts for the sale of goods governed by Article 2. RRX Indus., Inc. v. Lab-Con, Inc., 772 F.2d 543, 546 (9th Cir. 1985) (software, training, systems repairs, and upgrades); Triangle Underwriters, Inc. v. Honeywell, Inc., 604 F.2d 737, 742-43 (2d Cir. 1979) (hardware and software); Neilson Business Equip. Ctr., Inc. v. Monteleone, 524 A.2d 1172, 1174 (Del. 1987) (computer system); USM Corp. v. Arthur D. Little Sys., Inc., 28 Mass. App. Ct. 108, 546 N.E.2d 888, 894 (1989) (computer system); Communications Group, Inc. v. Warner Communications, Inc., 138 Misc. 2d 80, 527 N.Y.S.2d 341, 344 (N.Y. Civ. Ct. 1988) (software); Camara v. Hill, 157 Vt. 156, 596 A.2d 349, 351 (1991) (computer system).
>
> We agree with the reasoning of these precedents. Atlantic's agreement with Highland Rim was predominately for the sale of an integrated computer system. Its obligation to provide training in the use of the system was incidental to the purchase of the system itself. Accordingly, the transaction is one involving goods, and the parties' rights are governed by Article 2.

Highland Rim Constructors, 1992 WL 184872, at *6. We find the reasoning and cited cases in *Highland Rim* persuasive in the instant appeal. As set out in the contract, and in the incorporated proposal, it is clear that the contract contemplates the sale of various, moveable components, which were to be integrated via a control system. Unlike the *Glazer* case, the fact that the components were installed in the home did not result in an attachment that would change the movability of the goods sold. Accordingly, we are not persuaded by Mr. Tanzer's argument that the integration of the components constitutes a "construction" contract. The plain language of the contract simply does not support such a finding.

B. Nature of AVA's Business

In addition to the plain language of the contract, the court may also consider the nature of the seller's business. *Pass,* 2000 WL 388775, at *4. It is not disputed in the record that AVA is in the business of design and sale of custom, state-of-the-art, home theater, multi-room music/television/

lighting control, and phone/intercom systems. AVA does not manufacture or promote one brand of product; rather, it sells and installs products from various manufacturers. From our review of the record, it appears that AVA's "design" role really constitutes a determination of what goods the customer needs and what integration system(s) will work to link the various components. In this sense, the "integration" of the whole system is done by the controlling system, i.e., Escient, Concierge, Crestron, Lutron. The sale of these respective systems is, in the opinion of this Court, similar to the sale of an integrated computer system. *See Highland Rim Constructors,* 1992 WL 184872, at *6-7. The installation and service that AVA performs is incidental to the overarching purpose of its business, which is to sell "smart home" components.

C. Reason for the Contract

The third factor instructs the court to "consider the final product the purchaser bargained to receive, and whether it may be described as a good or a service." *Pass,* 2000 WL 388775, at *12 (quoting *Insul-Mark,* 612 N.E.2d at 555). Whether the purchaser sought to procure a good or a service by entering into the subject contract is "a strong indication of the predominant purpose of the contract." Id. at *15 (citing Stafford v. Int'l Harvester Co., 668 F.2d 142, 147 (2d Cir. 1981) ("underlying nature of a hybrid transaction is determined by reference to the purpose with which the customer contracted with the defendant")); NW Equip. Inc. v. Cudmore, 312 N.W.2d 347, 349 (N.D. 1981) ("*Bonebrake* test looks to the predominant purpose or thrust of the contract as it would exist in the minds of reasonable parties."). In analyzing this factor, the *Pass* Court found guidance from the Michigan Supreme Court, in Neibarger v. Universal Cooperatives, Inc., 439 Mich. 512, 486 N.W.2d 612 (1992), wherein the Michigan court described its analysis of the purpose of the parties' dealings as follows:

> If the purchaser's ultimate goal is to acquire a product, the contract should be considered a transaction in goods, even though service is incidentally required. Conversely, if the purchaser's ultimate goal is to procure a service, the contract is not governed by the UCC, even though goods are incidentally required in the provision of this service.

Id. at 622.

As discussed above, even in cases where labor and services were contemplated by the parties to be an integral part of the contract, courts have still held that Article 2 applies. See, e.g., *Highland Rim Constructors,* 1992 WL 184872, at *7 (noting that the seller's "obligation to provide training in the use of the system was incidental to the purchase of the system itself."); see also IBP, Inc. v. HK Sys., No. 98cv00480, 2000 WL 35725320 (D. Neb. Sept. 21,

2000) (holding that contract for purchase of a computer system was a sale of goods, with rendition of services such as design, construction, manufacturing and installation incidental); *Bonebrake,* 499 F.2d at 958 (holding that installation of pre-fabricated bowling lanes incidental to the contract because the lanes remained "movable"); Meyers v. Henderson Constr. Co., 147 N.J. Super. 77, 370 A.2d 547, 549 (1977) (holding that installation of pre-fabricated disassembled doors was incidental to the contract for sale of the tangible goods).

Turning to the record in the instant case, in his answer, Mr. Tanzer admits that he contracted for electronic equipment. It is not disputed that AVA orders all of the equipment it sells from the manufacturer or from the distributor. In other words, none of the equipment was "constructed" at Tanzer's home; it was merely installed there. The record further indicates that the equipment maintained its characteristics as personalty and was never rendered immovable from the residence. In support of this conclusion, Mr. Tanzer presented a spreadsheet at trial, which indicated all of the equipment he was willing to return to AVA. The fact that Mr. Tanzer could return this equipment supports a finding that it had not become a permanent improvement to his realty. The fact that the original proposal, which was incorporated into the contract, breaks apart the costs of the "equipment," i.e., tangible goods, from the cost of "cable/misc. parts," i.e., materials also supports a finding that Mr. Tanzer bargained for the purchase of equipment, and that the services rendered by AVA in connection with that sale, including delivery and installation, were necessary but incidental to the ultimate purpose of the contract, i.e., to obtain the various components and the integration system that would link them.

D. Amounts Paid for Services and Goods, Respectively

The final factor to be considered is the respective amounts charged under the contract for the goods and services. *Pass,* 2000 WL 388775, at *4. "If the cost of the goods is but a small portion of the overall contract price, such fact would increase the likelihood that the services portion predominates." Id. at *12 (quoting *Insul-Mark,* 612 N.E.2d at 555). Conversely, where "the charge for goods exceeds that for services, the contract is more likely to be for goods." *BMC Indus.,* 160 F.3d at 1330 (citations omitted).

In this case, the trial court found that the costs of labor and services were "insignificant" compared to the cost of the equipment. As set out above, under the original contract, equipment sales constituted $56,375 of the total price of $71,915 (before taxes); on the other hand, labor accounted for only $9,880. In the final invoice, equipment totaled $89,640.03 of the total contract price of $109,830.03 (before taxes), with labor constituting only $13,260.00. Viewed as a percentage, equipment constitutes roughly 82% of the final contract price. Accordingly, this factor weighs heavily in favor of a finding that the contract was predominantly for the sale of goods.

Based upon the foregoing, we conclude that all four of the *Pass* factors favor the trial court's conclusion that the instant contract was predominantly for the sale of goods. Accordingly, we conclude that the trial court did not err in applying UCC Article 2 to this transaction.

[The court then concluded that Mr. Tanzer had accepted the system and could only offset the amount of damages he could prove AVA's breaches of warranty caused him, but that, with some exceptions, his proof was inadequate due to complication caused by the lightning strike, extra work done by the new contractor, and the excessive size of that contractor's bill.]

For the foregoing reasons, we affirm the judgment of the trial court. The case is remanded for all further proceedings as may be necessary and are consistent with this opinion. Costs of this appeal are assessed against the Appellant, Stephen Tanzer, and his surety.

One thorny area that is much litigated concerns the extent to which contracts for the sale of software are governed by Article 2 of the Uniform Commercial Code. This was briefly discussed in the last case, and the next one considers the issue in more depth.

Simulados Software, Ltd. v. Photon Infotech Private, Ltd.

United States District Court, Northern District of California, 2014
40 F. Supp. 3d 1191

EDWARD J. DAVILA, United States District Judge

Presently before the Court is Defendant Photon Infotech Private, Ltd.'s ("Photon" or "Defendant") Motion to Dismiss Plaintiff Simulados Software, Ltd.'s ("Simulados" or "Plaintiff") Amended Complaint ("AC"). See Docket Item No. 46. Federal jurisdiction arises under 28 U.S.C. §1332(a). This case is proceeding in this Court because of the parties' venue selection clause in their contract. See Docket Item No. 15. Having fully reviewed the parties' papers, the Court will GRANT Defendant's motion for the reasons stated below.

I. BACKGROUND

Simulados is a Texas software development company based in Houston, Texas. Photon is a technology consulting corporation incorporated in New Jersey with its principal place of business in Chennai, India, and a virtual office in San Jose, California. See AC, Docket Item No. 44 ¶¶1-2. Simulados developed a program called Certify Teacher, which is a test simulation program used by educators to prepare for the Texas Examinations of Educator

Standards ("TExES") certification exam. Simulados decided to produce a version of its product compatible with Apple Macintosh ("Mac") computers as well as an internet web application. *Id.* ¶¶3-4.

In early 2009, Photon called Simulados, representing Photon's ability to create a Mac-compatible product and develop a web application. *Id.* ¶¶6-7. Simulados and Photon entered into a contract ("Contract") on March 31, 2009, which consisted of a Statement of Work ("SOW") and a Master Professional Services Agreement ("MPSA"). See Docket Item No. 1-1 (the SOW incorporates all the terms and conditions of the MPSA). In the Contract, Photon represented that the project would start on May 20, 2009, and finish on September 17, 2009. The Contract provided that Photon would complete: CD mastering, migrating the existing source code to Real Basic, convert VB project, add Mac specific BASIC code, add support for New DB format, address performance bottlenecks in product, customize for Mac operating systems, add platform specific paths, tweak for Mac Human Interface Guidelines, provide license key generation and key validation, create a web application, create website authentication certification for downloads, upgrade to database content creator, provide support for reading the content, provide support for modifying content, migrate up to three sample products, and code review. Simulados agreed to pay $23,560 in four installments, the final of which was to be made upon delivery of a complete workable product. Id. at 10-12. The Contract contained the following choice-of-law and forum selection provision: "[t]his Agreement shall be governed by and construed and enforce [sic] in accordance with the laws of the State of California." Id. at 23.

Simulados contends that Photon never fulfilled its obligations under the Contract. On June 9, 2009, Photon communicated to Simulados that it was initiating the project, and represented that there would not be any outstanding serious or critical defects at the time of the site launch, with fewer than five medium defects and fewer than ten low defects. On August 14, 2009, Photon requested that Simulados approve completion of the project's development phase. A teleconference demonstration was held on August 19, 2009 and on September 24, 2009 Simulados received an access link for user testing and approval. During the review, Simulados found 38 low level and 8 critical issues. Simulados requested a status update on the web application and expressed dissatisfaction that the product was not complete. On May 3, 2010, Simulados gave Photon a deadline of June 3, 2012, to correct an additional 17 errors. On May 17, 2010, Photon responded to Simulados' notice, providing a link to incomplete software. To date, Photon has not provided Simulados with fully functioning web application. Dkt. No. 44 ¶¶12-16.

Simulados filed a complaint on May 11, 2012 in the District Court for the Southern District of Texas. See Docket Item No. 1. The case was transferred to this Court on August 20, 2012, based on the choice-of-law provision in the

Contract. See Docket Item No. 16. Simulados filed an Amended Complaint ("AC") on December 11, 2012. Dkt. No. 44. On December 24, 2012, Photon filed a Motion to Dismiss, which is presently before the Court. Dkt. No. 46. Plaintiffs have filed written opposition to this motion. See Docket Item No. 51. The parties engaged in mediation, but failed to reach an agreement regarding arbitration. See Docket Item No. 63. Photon re-noticed its Motion on July 23, 2013. See Docket Item No. 67. Pursuant to Civil Local Rule 7-1(b), the Court took the motion under submission without oral argument. . . .

C. Claims Arising Under the Uniform Commercial Code

Photon contends that Simulados' claim that it is entitled to remedies outside the contract by virtue of the UCC is implausible and must be dismissed because Article 2 of the UCC applies only to contracts for the sale of goods, not services, and the Contract between the parties is for services. Simulados argues that the Contract is for sale of software, which is considered a good, and thus the UCC applies. For the reasons outlined below, the Court will dismiss any claims arising from the UCC.

The UCC applies to the transaction of goods. Cal. Com. Code §2102. The UCC defines goods as "all things (including specially manufactured goods) which are movable at the time of identification to the contract for sale . . ." Cal. Com. Code § 2105. Applying the UCC to software poses a complex issue because transactions for software often combine elements of both goods and services. As such, courts have arrived at different decisions concerning whether software transactions are covered by the UCC.

The primary test used by courts to determine whether software is a good under the UCC is the predominant factor test, where courts look to the "essence of the agreement" on a case-by-case basis to decide how to characterize the transaction. Gross v. Symantec Corp., No. C-12-00154-CRB, 2012 WL 3116158, at *8 (N.D. Cal. July 31, 2012) (citing RRX Indus., Inc. v. Lab-Con, Inc., 772 F.2d 543, 546 (9th Cir. 1985)). Courts determine whether the predominant factor or purpose of the contract is rendition of services, with goods incidentally involved, or is rendition of goods, with labor incidentally involved.

Generally, courts have found that mass-produced, standardized, or generally available software, even with modifications and ancillary services included in the agreement, is a good that is covered by the UCC. In RRX Industries, Inc. v. Lab-Con, Inc., the Ninth Circuit found that a license for mass-produced software for use in medical laboratories was covered by the UCC, even when the software contract also provided for ancillary services such as training, repair, and system upgrading. *RRX Indus.*, 772 F.2d 543 (9th Cir. 1985). The court noted, "[h]ere, the sales aspect of the transaction predominates. The [services] were incidental to sale of the software package and did not defeat characterization of the system as a good." Id.

at 546. See also *Gross*, 2012 WL 3116158, at *8-9 (where a user purchased and downloaded Symantec's pre-existing software from the internet, this court determined that the "essence of the agreement" was the sale of a good); Olcott Intern v. Micro Data, 793 N.E.2d 1063 (Ind. Ct. App. 2003) ("generally-available standardized software" was found to be a good under the UCC); Rottner v. AVG Tech. USA, Inc., 943 F. Supp. 2d 222, 230 (D. Mass. 2013) (noting that the sale of a downloadable computer software is like a sale of tangible goods and that courts nationally have consistently classified the sale of a software package as the sale of a good for UCC purposes); Advent Sys. Ltd. v. Unisys Corp., 925 F.2d 670, 675-76 (3d Cir. 1991) (noting that the majority of academic commentary supports the view that software fits with the definition of a good under the UCC).

Software may still be considered a good even when accompanied by ancillary services, which "are not substantially different from those generally accompanying package sales of computer systems consisting of hardware and software." *Advent Sys.*, 925 F.2d at 676. Such ancillary services include installation, training, and technical support. See Dahlmann v. Sulcus Hosp. Tech. Corp., 63 F. Supp. 2d 772, 775 (E.D. Mich. 1999) (a contract for property management systems incorporating hardware, software, installation, training, and technical support services for plaintiffs' hotels was a contract for goods because the provisions for services were incidental to the agreements for the system); ePresence v. Evolve, 190 F. Supp. 2d 159 (D. Mass. 2002) (a contract for software licensing which also included services was determined to be a transaction for goods, as the software programs themselves were the essence of the parties' agreement); Wachter Mgmt. Co. v. Dexter & Chaney, Inc., 282 Kan. 365, 369, 144 P.3d 747 (2006) (even when incidental services such as modifications, corrections, maintenance, training, and consulting were provided with software, the services would have been unnecessary if the software had not been purchased, so the transaction is predominantly for a good).

Even software adapted for specific needs has been considered a good. In Micro Data Base Systems, Inc. v. Dharma Systems, Inc., 148 F.3d 649 (7th Cir. 1998), the Seventh Circuit determined that the UCC governed a contract for software where one party agreed to adapt its software program for use in the other party's system. The court noted that "labor is a service" that is part of the manufacture of every good and opined, "we can think of no reason why the UCC is not suitable to govern disputes arising from the sale of custom software." Id. 654-55. Similarly, the Third Circuit found that the software contracted for was a good where one party planned to modify its existing software and hardware interfaces for the other party's use. *Advent Sys.*, 925 F.2d 670. The court noted, "[t]he fact that some programs may be tailored for specific purposes need not alter their status as 'goods' because the Code definition includes 'specially manufactured goods.'" Id. at 675. The Third Circuit found that the advantages of applying the UCC to software transactions (namely uniformity on a range of questions) and the importance of software to the commercial world were strong policy arguments favoring the application of the UCC and that the majority of academic commentary espoused the view that software falls under the UCC. Id. at 675-76. See also Commc'ns Groups, Inc. v. Warner Commc'ns, 138 Misc. 2d 80, 83, 527 N.Y.S.2d 341 (N.Y. Civ. Ct. 1988) (determining that a contract which provided for the installation of specially designed software equipment for one party's telephone and computer systems, including recording, accounting and traffic analysis and optimizations, modules, buffer, directories and an operational user guide was a transaction of software equipment involving movable, tangible and identifiable products or goods); Waterfront Properties v. Xerox Connect, 58 U.C.C. Rep. Serv. 2d 809, 2006 WL 266581 (W.D.N.C. 2006) (agreements for the provision of custom adapted pre-existing computer software and attendant hardware were contracts predominately for goods, which are governed by the UCC).

On the other end of the spectrum, courts in this district and beyond have determined that certain software transactions are better defined as services and therefore are not covered by the UCC. Where software is designed from scratch, or the transaction is mainly for one party's knowledge and skills in creating software, the software is often found to be a service rather than a good.

In Systems America, Inc. v. Rockwell Software, Inc., No. C-03-2232, 2007 WL 218242 (N.D. Cal. Jan. 26, 2007), the agreement entered into between the parties called for development of a final software product for reproduction and distribution to one party's customers. The developing party developed new software to supplement existing software, provided the source code to an escrow agent, and retained all ownership rights to the software. The court determined that the contract was for services, not goods, because the essence of the contract was the development of software from scratch and the granting of a license for use of the software. Id. at *4. Where a contract required a party to design, develop, and implement a tailored, highly complex automated software system, that contract was deemed to be for services, not goods. State v. Lockheed Martin, No. C-036815, 2002 WL 99554, at *18 (Cal. Ct. App., Jan. 25, 2002). This district found that even in a situation where an agreement was made for production of physical prototypes, since most of the price paid was for the other party's "knowledge, skill, and ability" to develop software code and test prototypes, the agreement was for services rather than goods. TK Power v. Textron, 433 F. Supp. 2d 1058, 1062 (N.D. Cal. 2006). See also Data Processing Serv. v. L.H. Smith Oil Corp., 492 N.E.2d 314, 318-19 (Ind. Ct. App. 1986) (custom-designed accounting software is not a good because no hardware was involved and the contract bargained for the programmer's "knowledge, skill, and ability" rather than standardized software); Pearl Inv. v. Standard I/O, 257 F. Supp. 2d 326 (D. Me. 2003) (custom-made software is distinguishable from pre-existing software—even with custom modifications and upgrades—and is a service); Multi-Tech Sys. v. Floreat, No. Civ-01-1320, 2002 WL 432016, at *3 (D. Minn. March 18, 2002) ("work" toward "jointly developing" a new product is a service . . . the UCC does not apply to an agreement to design and develop a product, even if compensation under that agreement is based in part on later sales of that product"); Wharton Mgmt. Grp. v. Sigma Consultants, Inc., 50 U.C.C. Rep. Serv. 2d 678, 1990 WL 18360 (Del. Super. Ct. 1990) (software contract is for services where a party was hired for its skills to "design, develop, and install computer software which would meet . . . specific needs and objectives . . .").

In this instance, Photon was meant to produce a Mac-compliant version of Simulados' existing Windows-based software and an internet web application. Based on an analysis of the cases concerning the application of the UCC to software transactions, this Court determines that in this particular case, Simulados contracted for a service and the UCC does not apply to this software transaction. Following other courts, this Court uses the predominance test on a case-by-case basis to analyze a transaction that involves elements of both a good and a service. The Contract between the parties calls for Photon to provide services, skills, and knowledge to customize Simulados' existing product for sale to Simulados' customers. Although customized software may still be considered a good, here Simulados was not purchasing any software from Photon. Rather, Photon was only providing services to modify Simulados' already-existing software. As such, Simulados was contracting only for the modifications, a service, and not for software as a separate good. Thus, the UCC does not apply to this transaction and any claims arising from it are dismissed. . . .

IT IS SO ORDERED.

QUESTION

The court makes much of the fact that the computer program to be sold was a modification of an existing program. No mention is made of the clear inclusion of "specially manufactured goods" in the definition of "Goods" in §2-105(1). Had this been pointed out to the court might it have made a difference in the result?

The "predominate purpose" test doesn't entirely carry the day in all situations. It's wildly unpredictable, and that instability has caused some courts to look for a test that will lead to more predictable outcomes. Maryland's highest court led the way in the following case.

Anthony Pools v. Sheehan

Maryland Court of Appeals, 1983
295 Md. 285, 455 A.2d 434

Rodowsky, J.

This products liability case presents questions of implied warranty and of defense to strict liability in tort involving an in-ground, gunite swimming pool and its diving board. Analysis of whether there is any implied warranty and, if so, whether it can be excluded takes us into the problem of hybrid transactions and into Md. Code (1975), §2-316.1(1) and (2) of the Commercial Law Article (C.L.).[1]

Plaintiffs, John B. Sheehan (Sheehan) and his wife, Pilar E. Sheehan, of Potomac Woods, Maryland, sued Anthony Pools, a division of Anthony Industries, Inc. (Anthony) in the Circuit Court for Montgomery County. Sheehan sustained bodily injuries when he fell from the side of the diving board of the plaintiffs' new, backyard swimming pool. The swimming pool had been designed and built by Anthony. Anthony also designed and manufactured the diving board which it installed as part of the swimming pool transaction.

The swimming pool is 16 feet by 40 feet, with a depth from 3 feet to 8 feet. Its style is "Grecian," which means that there is a curved alcove in the center of each of the 16 foot sides. The 6-foot-long diving board in question was installed over an imaginary centerline bisecting the alcove at the deep end of the pool. Anthony had completed its work by mid-June of 1976. On August 21, 1976, the plaintiffs entertained at a pool party. Sheehan testified that he had not previously used the diving board. He said that on that evening he emerged from swimming in the pool, stepped up onto the diving board, and, while walking toward the pool end of the diving board, slipped and fell from the right side of the diving board and struck the coping of the pool.

Plaintiffs advanced two theories of liability. First, skid resistant material built into the surface of the top of the diving board did not extend to the very edge of the board on each side. It stopped approximately one inch short of each edge. This condition, it was claimed, breached an implied warranty of merchantability. Plaintiffs also presented testimony directed toward

1. C.L. §2-316.1 in relevant part provides:

"(1) The provisions of §2-316 do not apply to sales of consumer goods, as defined by §9-109, services, or both.

"(2) Any oral or written language used by a seller of consumer goods and services, which attempts to exclude or modify any implied warranties of merchantability and fitness for a particular purpose or to exclude or modify the consumer's remedies for breach of those warranties, is unenforceable. However, the seller may recover from the manufacturer any damages resulting from breach of the implied warranty of merchantability or fitness for a particular purpose." [This is a nonuniform addition to the UCC, and is not the law in most other states.—Ed.]

proving that use of the "defective" diving board, particularly as positioned in the alcove, was unreasonably dangerous.

At the end of the plaintiffs' case, the trial court directed a verdict for Anthony as to liability founded on warranty, because the written contract between the parties conspicuously provided that the express warranties which it contained were in lieu of any other warranties, express or implied. The case went to the jury on a strict liability in tort theory. Verdict was in favor of the defendant, and judgment was so entered.

Plaintiffs appealed to the Court of Special Appeals which reversed and remanded for a new trial. That court said that "the swimming pool package purchased by the Sheehans constitute[d] 'consumer goods'" so that C.L. §2-316.1 rendered ineffective Anthony's attempt to limit the implied warranty of merchantability. Sheehan v. Anthony Pools, 50 Md. App. 614, 619, 440 A.2d 1085, 1088 (1982). The granting of the directed verdict based on the contractual limitation was held to be error. Judgment based on the jury verdict was reversed because of error in the instructions. As to that issue, Judge Moore, writing for the court, concluded:

> In the instant case, it is our view that while the trial court was eminently correct in rejecting the defendant's request for a contributory negligence instruction, the matter should not have ended there. On the basis of the facts involved and of the Sheehans' specific request, an instruction should have been granted that Mr. Sheehan's inadvertent or careless use of the diving board and the pool would not bar his recovery. On the other hand, giving such an instruction would also have required an appropriate instruction on assumption of risk, i.e., that the defendant was entitled to prevail if Mr. Sheehan had discovered the defect, was aware of the danger, and then proceeded unreasonably to use the diving board and pool. [Id. at 625-626, 440 A.2d at 1092.]

We granted Anthony's petition for certiorari which raised three questions. In essence, the petition asks us to review (1) the implied warranty issue; (2) the inadvertent use instruction issue; and (3) whether the Court of Special Appeals erred "in holding, as dictum that contributory negligence is not a defense in a strict liability case."

1

The warranty issue, as presented here, involves only the implied warranty of merchantability under C.L. §2-314. Plaintiffs do not argue that their warranty claim is based upon any express warranty or that the diving board was to be used for other than its ordinary purpose. Anthony contends that the Sheehans' swimming pool is not "goods," that exclusion of implied warranties is allowed, and that a directed verdict on the plaintiffs' warranty count was proper. We agree with the Court of Special Appeals that the directed verdict was improper in this case, but we reach that conclusion by a somewhat different route.

Title 2 of the Commercial Law Article is the Maryland Uniform Commercial Code Sales. C.L. §2-101. Unless the context otherwise requires, that title "applies to transactions in goods. . . ." C.L. §2-102. For purposes of title 2, and with certain exclusions not here relevant, "goods" means "all things (including specially manufactured goods) which are movable at the time of identification to the contract for sale. . . ." C.L. §2-105(1). C.L. §2-314(1) in part provides that "[u]nless excluded or modified (§2-316), a warranty that the goods shall be merchantable is implied in a contract for their sale if the seller is a merchant with respect to goods of that kind." C.L. §2-316(2) permits the exclusion or modification of the implied warranty of merchantability by language which mentions merchantability and which, in the case of a writing, is conspicuous. The Maryland UCC, in §2-316.1, then states that the "provisions of §2-316 do not apply to sales of consumer goods, as defined by §9-109, services, or both," and that any "language used by a seller of consumer goods and services, which attempts to exclude or modify any implied warranties . . . is unenforceable." C.L. §9-109(1) provides that goods are "'[c]onsumer goods' if they are used or bought for use primarily for personal, family or household purposes."

The May 25, 1976 contract between Anthony and the plaintiffs is a printed form designed for use in Anthony's Washington, D.C., region. It is a single sheet of paper, approximately 15" by 20," with printing on both sides. The face of the document is three columns wide. The lefthand column on the face is headed "Retail Installment Contract." Under that column are set forth Anthony's contractor license numbers in Virginia, Maryland and the District of Columbia, a statement of the buyer's right to cancel a home solicitation contract, federal truth-in-lending disclosures and a detachable notice of cancellation. The next two columns on the face are entitled "Swimming Pool Construction Agreement." Anthony "agrees to construct for and sell to" the plaintiffs, called "'Buyer,'" the "swimming pool and related equipment described below (herein collectively called the 'work') to be installed at" the plaintiffs' home for a fixed cash price. Below this covenant, under the heading "Plans and Specifications," are two columns listing 47 items, some of which are automatically included and some of which are optional. These items appear under the headings, "General Construction Specifications," "Hydraulic and Filtering Specifications," "Color-Coordinated Exclusive Deck Equip.," "Automatic Pool Equipment" and "Other Anthony Features." In the subject contract Anthony's obligations included pool layout, structural engineering, obtaining construction permits, excavation, use of engineered steel reinforcing throughout the pool structure, guniting the pool structure, finishing the pool interior with hand troweled, waterproof plaster, installation both of a six-inch band of water-line tile and of coping and installation of a filter, a pump, a skimmer and a specified model of six foot diving board. The reverse side of the contract contains two columns of terms and conditions, including the implied warranty exclusion. The subject contract presents a mixed or hybrid transaction. It is in part a contract for the rendering of services and in part a contract for the sale of goods.

Burton v. Artery Company, 279 Md. 94, 367 A.2d 935 (1977) addressed the applicability vel non of the Maryland UCC Sales to hybrid contracts. The issue presented was whether the four-year statute of limitations under §2-725(1), or the general three-year statute, applied to a contract to landscape around a construction project of 13 buildings. The contract called for the furnishing and planting of hundreds of trees, of hundreds of shrubs, and of sod. We there adopted the test enunciated in Bonebrake v. Cox, 499 F.2d 951 (8th Cir. 1974), a case holding that the sale and installation of bowling lanes, with associated equipment, is a contract of sale and not of services. That test is whether "the predominant factor . . ., the thrust, the purpose, reasonably stated, is a transaction of sale with labor incidentally involved," or vice versa. 279 Md. at 114-115, 367 A.2d at 946. Applying that test, the court held the contract in *Burton* to be predominantly a transaction in goods. See also Snyder v. Herbert Greenbaum & Associates, 38 Md. App. 144, 380 A.2d 618 (1977) (contract to furnish and install over 17,000 yards of carpet in 228 apartments was predominantly a sale of goods).

G. Wallach, The Law of Sales Under the Uniform Commercial Code (1981), §11.05[3] at 11-28 describes the current state of the law concerning implied warranties in hybrid transactions to be as follows:

> The general pre-Code approach to this issue was to examine the transaction to see whether the goods aspect or the service aspect of the transaction predominated. If the service aspect predominated, no warranties of quality were imposed in the transaction, not even if the defect or complaint related to the goods that were involved rather than to the services. This mechanical approach remains the most popular method of resolving the issue.[2]

The few reported holdings concerning whether Article 2 of the UCC applies to swimming pool installations have involved a variety of types of

2. Among recent decisions applying the predominant purpose test are: White v. Peabody Construction Co., Inc., 386 Mass. 121, 434 N.E.2d 1015 (1982) (contract for the construction of a housing project was one for services so that there was no warranty implied under the UCC on the windows or frames, which leaked); Milau Associates v. North Avenue Development Corp., 42 N.Y.2d 482, 368 N.E.2d 1247, 398 N.Y.S.2d 882 (1977) (there is no warranty of merchantability on a section of pipe which ruptured and which had been installed as part of a sprinkler system in the course of construction of a new building); Northwestern Equipment, Inc. v. Cudmore, 312 N.W.2d 347 (N.D. 1981) (contract for the repair of the transmission in a used bulldozer is a contract for services and carries no implied warranty of fitness for a particular purpose, even though the charges for parts exceeded the charges for labor).

pools and are not uniform. A Connecticut trial court decision dealt with the alleged breach of the implied warranty of merchantability in the installation of an aboveground swimming pool. Its sides were plywood panels, braced by a 29×4' support. A vinyl liner was laid within the sides. That court applied the predominant purpose test. It held that the owners did not offer any adequate evidence on the apportionment between labor and material and equipment, and so they failed to meet the burden of establishing the existence of a warranty under the UCC. Gulash v. Stylarama, Inc., 33 Conn. Supp. 108, 364 A.2d 1221 (1975). A vinyl liner pool was also involved in Riffe v. Black, 548 S.W.2d 175 (Ky. App. 1977). The walls of that pool consisted of prefabricated steel which was set into an excavated site. Sand was troweled for the bottom of the pool. Leaking had resulted from the contractor's failure both to reseal the liner after a wrinkle had developed during installation and to repair the hole which developed later. The Kentucky court applied a predominant purpose test and necessarily classified the contract as one for the sale of goods. It was held that the warranty provisions of that state's UCC "apply to services when the sale is primarily one of goods and the services are necessary to insure that those goods are merchantable and fit for the ordinary purpose." Id. at 177. Judgment for the pool owners was affirmed. Ben Construction Corp. v. Ventre, 23 A.D.2d 44, 257 N.Y.S.2d 988 (1965) is not a UCC case, but it is analogous. It presented the claim of the pool owners for return of moneys paid, based on a section of the New York Personal Property Law. The pool is described in the opinion only as "installed." Judgment for the defendant contractor was affirmed, 3-2. In the majority's view, the contract was for work, labor and services and was not a sale, while the dissent viewed the transaction as primarily a sale of a swimming pool with an incidental agreement to install.

The Court of Special Appeals has recently held that C.L. §2-601's "perfect tender" provisions do not apply to a contract for the installation of an in-ground, concrete swimming pool. There was no transaction in goods because the pool was not movable. Chlan v. KDI Sylvan Pools, Inc., 53 Md. App. 123, 452 A.2d 1279 (1982) [No. 192, September Term, 1982, decided December 7, 1982].

Here, Anthony undertook the construction of an in-ground, steel reinforced, gunite swimming pool with hand finished plaster surfacing, tile trim, and coping. The Sheehans were not buying steel rods, or gunite, or plaster or tiles. The predominant factor, the thrust, the purpose of the contract was the furnishing of labor and service by Anthony, while the sale of the diving board was incidental to the construction of the pool itself. The question thus resolves itself into whether the predominant purpose test, which we applied in *Burton* for the purpose of determining whether the UCC statute of limitations governed that transaction, should be applied to determine whether the sale of the diving board, included in the Anthony-Sheehans transaction, carries an implied warranty of merchantability under §2-314.

Were the predominant purpose test mechanically to be applied to the facts of this case, there would be no quality warranty implied as to the diving board. But here the contract expressly states that Anthony agrees not only to construct the swimming pool, but also to sell the related equipment selected by the Sheehans. The Sheehans are described as "'Buyer.'" The diving board itself is not structurally integrated into the swimming pool. Anthony offered the board as an optional accessory, just as Anthony offered the options of purchasing a pool ladder or a sliding board. When identified to the contract, the diving board was movable. See C.L. §2-105. The board itself remains detachable from its support, as reflected by a photograph in evidence. The diving board, considered alone, is goods. Had it been purchased by the Sheehans in a transaction distinct from the pool construction agreement with Anthony, there would have been an implied warranty of merchantability.

A number of commentators have advocated a more policy-oriented approach to determining whether warranties of quality and fitness are implied with respect to goods sold as part of a hybrid transaction in which service predominates. See Farnsworth, Implied Warranties of Quality in Non-Sales Cases, 57 Colum. L. Rev. 653 (1957); Comment, Sale of Goods in Service-Predominated Transactions, 37 Fordham L. Rev. 115 (1968); Note, Products and the Professional: Strict Liability in the Sale-Service Hybrid Transaction, 24 Hastings L.J. 111 (1972); Note, Contracts for Goods and Services and Article 2 of the Uniform Commercial Code, 9 Rut.-Cam. L.J. 303 (1978); Comment, Sales-Service Hybrid Transactions: A Policy Approach, 28 Sw. L.J. 575 (1974). To support their position, these commentators in general emphasize loss shifting, risk distribution, consumer reliance and difficulties in the proof of negligence. These concepts underlie strict liability in tort. See Phipps v. General Motors Corp., 278 Md. 337, 363 A.2d 955 (1976).

A leading case applying a policy approach in this problem area is Newmark v. Gimbel's Incorporated, 54 N.J. 585, 258 A.2d 697 (1969). There the patron of a beauty parlor sued for injury to her hair and scalp allegedly resulting from a lotion used in giving her a permanent wave. Because the transaction was viewed as the rendering of a service, the trial court had ruled that there could be no warranty liability. The intermediate appellate court's reversal was affirmed by the Supreme Court of New Jersey which reasoned in part as follows (id., at 593, 258 A.2d at 701):

> The transaction, in our judgment, is a hybrid partaking of incidents of a sale and a service. It is really partly the rendering of service, and partly the supplying of goods for a consideration. Accordingly, we agree with the Appellate Division that an implied warranty of fitness of the products used in giving the permanent wave exists with no less force than it would have in the case of a simple sale. Obviously in permanent wave operations the product is taken into consideration in fixing the price of the service. The no-separate-charge

> argument puts excessive emphasis on form and downgrades the overall substance of the transaction. If the beauty parlor operator bought and applied the permanent wave solution to her own hair and suffered injury thereby, her action in warranty or strict liability in tort against the manufacturer-seller of the product clearly would be maintainable because the basic transaction would have arisen from a conventional type of sale. It does not accord with logic to deny a similar right to a patron against the beauty parlor operator or the manufacturer when the purchase and sale were made in anticipation of and for the purpose of use of the product on the patron who would be charged for its use. Common sense demands that such patron be deemed a customer as to both manufacturer and beauty parlor operator. [Citations omitted.]

The court was careful to limit its holding to commercial transactions, as opposed to those predominantly involving professional services. Id. at 596-597, 258 A.2d at 702-703.

1 R. Anderson, Uniform Commercial Code (1970), §2-102:5 at 209 refers to *Newmark* as illustrative of a possible trend in the law and states:

> It is probable that a goods-services transaction will come to be subjected to Article 2 of the Code insofar as the contractor's obligations with respect to the goods themselves are involved, at least where the goods involved could have been purchased in the general market and used by the plaintiff-customer.

A warranty of fitness for particular purpose under §2-315 of the UCC was implied in Worrell v. Barnes, 87 Nev. 204, 484 P.2d 573 (1971). In that case a contractor was engaged to do some carpentry work and to connect various appliances in the plaintiff's home to an existing liquefied petroleum gas system. The appliances were not supplied by the contractor. Suit was for damage to the plaintiff's home resulting from a fire. The plaintiff produced evidence that the fire was caused by a defective fitting installed by the contractor which had allowed propane to escape. Dismissal of the plaintiff's claims, based on the Nevada version of strict liability in tort and based on implied warranty, was reversed. The court reasoned that, because it had held that the contractor had sold a product so as to bring into operation the doctrine of strict liability, "so also must we deem this case to involve 'goods' within the purview of the Uniform Commercial Code." Id. at 208, 484 P.2d at 576.

1 W. Hawkland, Uniform Commercial Code Series (1982), §2-102:04, at Art. 2, p. 12 has suggested what might be called a "gravamen" test in light of the decision in *Worrell*. He writes:

> Unless uniformity would be impaired thereby, it might be more sensible and facilitate administration, at least in this grey area, to abandon the "predominant factor" test and focus instead on whether the gravamen of the action involves goods or services. For example, in Worrell v. Barnes, if the gas escaped because of a defective fitting or connector, the case might be

characterized as one involving the sale of goods. On the other hand, if the gas escaped because of poor work by Barnes the case might be characterized as one involving services, outside the scope of the UCC.

In this state, the provisions of C.L. §2-316.1(1) and (2) reflect an implicit policy judgment by the General Assembly which prevents the mechanical application of the predominant purpose test to cases like the one under consideration. Subsection (1) states that §2-316, dealing in part with the manner in which an implied warranty of merchantability may be excluded or modified, does not apply to "consumer goods . . . services, or both." Under subsection (2) language "used by a seller of consumer goods and services" to exclude or modify implied warranties is unenforceable. The hybrid transaction is covered by, or at least embraced within, those terms.

Under the predominant purpose test, as applied by a majority of the courts, a hybrid transaction must first be classified as a sale of goods in order for there to be UCC-based, implied warranties on the goods included in the transaction. If goods predominate and they are consumer goods, §2-316.1 would render contractual disclaimers of implied warranties ineffective because that section applies to a seller of consumer goods. In such cases the result of applying the predominant purpose test is consistent with §2-316.1. If, however, the predominant purpose test results in classifying the transaction as a contract for services there would, under the majority approach, be no UCC-based, implied warranties on goods included in the transaction. But, §2-316.1 declares that a seller of consumer services may not contractually disclaim implied warranties. In the hybrid transaction, at least one effect of §2-316.1 is to render ineffective contractual disclaimers of implied warranties on consumer goods included in a consumer service transaction. Section 2-316.1 is at least partially predicated on a legislative understanding that warranties under the UCC are implied as to the goods included in such transactions. An all or nothing classification of the instant transaction under the predominant purpose test would mean there could be no UCC-based, implied warranties on the diving board and would be contrary to the legislative policy implicit in §2-316.1. Consequently, we cannot use that test in order to determine whether UCC-based warranties are implied as to consumer goods in a transaction that is predominantly for the rendering of consumer services.

The gravamen test of Dean Hawkland suggests the vehicle for satisfying the legislative policy. Accordingly, we hold that where, as part of a commercial transaction, consumer goods are sold which retain their character as consumer goods after completion of the performance promised to the consumer, and where monetary loss or personal injury is claimed to have resulted from a defect in the consumer goods, the provisions of the Maryland UCC dealing with implied warranties apply to the consumer goods, even if the transaction is predominantly one for the rendering of consumer services.

The facts of the instant case, however, make it unnecessary for us presently to decide whether §2-316.1 would require that UCC-based, implied warranties also extend to consumer goods which are used up in the course of rendering the consumer service to the consumer.

Thus the diving board which Anthony sold to the Sheehans as part of the swimming pool construction contract carried an implied warranty of merchantability under C.L. §2-314. Anthony's contractual disclaimer of that warranty was ineffective under C.L. §2-316.1. As a result, the trial court erred in relying on the disclaimer as a basis for directing a verdict in favor of Anthony on the warranty count. . . .

Judgment of the court of special appeals affirmed. Costs to be paid by Anthony Industries, Inc.

PROBLEM 3

Boswell Consultants purchased a Hawking 2020 printer from Ganges Devices. For the contract price, Ganges Devices agreed to deliver the internet-enabled printer along with its software, to store printed files in Ganges's cloud, to provide remote diagnostic and maintenance, and to provide software updates tailored to Boswell Consultants' pattern of use. Is the transaction covered by Article 2? See §2-105(1); Stacy-Ann Elvy, Hybrid Transactions and the Internet of Things: Goods, Services or Software?, 34 Wash. & Lee L. Rev. 77, 134 (2017) (citing Douglas J. Whaley & Stephen M. McJohn, Problems and Materials on Commercial Law 32 (11th ed. 2016)).

B. *Merchants*

PROBLEM 4

Portia Moot, a third-year law student, sold her car to a fellow student. Does Article 2 of the UCC apply to this transaction? Would §2-314 apply to the sale?

Frix v. Integrity Medical Systems, Inc.

United States District Court, Western District of Tennessee, Eastern Division, 2017
2017 WL 4171987

S. Thomas Anderson, Chief United States District Judge

. . .

Plaintiff, as the owner and operator of several medical clinics throughout west Tennessee, wanted to expand the services at his clinics to include mammography. In order to do so, Plaintiff specifically sought to place a 64-slice CT scanner, then located at his Henderson clinic, inside a mobile trailer with the new mammography equipment. Plaintiff owned the mobile trailer, but it was currently occupied by a 4-slice CT scanner. Plaintiff sought to solve all of these issues at once and solicited bids from three medical equipment companies (1) to uninstall and remove the four-slice CT scanner from his trailer, (2) to transport and install the 64-slice CT scanner inside that same trailer, and (3) for new mammography equipment that would also be installed in the trailer. Defendant ultimately submitted the lowest bid to Plaintiff. Though the parties disagree on the legal results of what occurred next, they do not dispute that informal discussions took place. Nor do they dispute that the discussions eventually resulted in a contract between the parties (the "Contract"). Plaintiff alleges he simply accepted Defendant's bid and e-mailed David Denholtz, owner of Defendant, to confirm the terms of the deal. . . .

For section 2-207 to have the effect that Defendant desires upon the Contract—the addition of the terms of the Purchase Agreement to the Contract despite the lack of evidence of Plaintiff ever having seen or agreed to them—the Contract must be "between merchants." Tenn. Code Ann. §47-2-207(2)(c). "Between merchants," in the UCC, "means in any transaction with respect to which both parties are chargeable with the knowledge or skill of merchants." Id. §47-2-104(3). Defendant relies on the statutory definition of merchant and Official Comment 1 to this provision in its assertion that Plaintiff is a merchant under the UCC. Def.'s Resp., at 12 n.2 (citing Fla. Stat. Ann. §672.104, cmt. 1) ("This Article assumes that transactions between professionals in a given field require special and clear rules which may not apply to a casual or inexperienced seller or buyer."). Plaintiff argues that Defendant has offered no evidence that Plaintiff is a merchant within the meaning of the statute. Indeed, Plaintiff points out that he does not deal in medical equipment and lacks particular knowledge or skill with respect to such equipment. Reply, at 2 n.3. Plaintiff relies on two Florida cases in support of his position. Id. at 2-3 n.3. Neither the Tennessee Supreme Court nor the Sixth Circuit has spoken to the issue of whether a physician that purchases equipment for his practice constitutes a merchant under the UCC. As there is no binding authority upon the Court as to this issue, it begins its analysis with the statutory language of the definition.

The UCC defines "[m]erchant" as "a person who deals in goods of the kind or otherwise by his occupation holds himself out as having knowledge or skill peculiar to the practices or goods involved in the transaction. . . ." Tenn. Code Ann. §47-2-104(1). No evidence before the Court suggests that Plaintiff is a seller of CT scanners or mammography equipment, so it will restrict its analysis to the latter portion of the definition. To discern whether Plaintiff is a merchant under the UCC, the Court must decide whether

Plaintiff is "a person who . . . by his occupation holds himself out as having knowledge or skill peculiar to the practices or goods involved in the transaction." Id. Plaintiff insists that he does not hold himself out as having such knowledge or skill. Pl.'s Reply, at 2 n.3. But that is not the relevant inquiry. The definition does not require a person who holds himself out as having a particular knowledge or skill but who does so "*by his occupation*." Tenn. Code Ann. §47-2-104(1) (emphasis added); see also Loeb & Co. v. Schreiner, 321 So. 2d 199, 202 (Ala. 1975) ("[A] person cannot be considered a 'merchant' [under section 2-104] simply because he is a braggart or has a high opinion of his knowledge in a particular area.").

To Plaintiff's credit, the Tennessee Court of Appeals has adopted an individualized approach for farmers. Brooks Cotton Co. v. Williams, 381 S.W.3d 414 (Tenn. Ct. App. 2012). The test adopted by the court provides a nonexhaustive list of four factors for use in determining whether a *particular* farmer is a merchant based upon his own personal business sophistication. Id. at 425. While the decisions of the Tennessee Court of Appeals are not binding upon this Court, and this particular analysis seems applicable only to farmers, the departure in reasoning between the Court of Appeals and this Court is worth highlighting nonetheless. An individualized approach stands in stark contrast to the occupation-based approach that the language of the statute plainly calls for. The court seems to ultimately distinguish between a regular farmer and an "experienced commercial farmer[]." Id. at 427-28. The Tennessee Court of Appeals was faced with persuasive authority that ranged from "It is inconceivable that the drafters of the [UCC] intended to place the average farmer, who merely grows his yearly crop and sells it to the local elevator, etc., on equal footing with the professional commodities dealer whose sole business is the buying and selling of farm commodities," Pierson v. Arnst, 534 F. Supp. 360, 362 (D. Mont. 1982), to "This court does not believe that anyone in this day and age looks upon any person or corporation who conducts a farming operation as a simple tiller of the soil," Rush Johnson Farms, Inc. v. Mo. Farmers Ass'n, 555 S.W.2d 64 (Mo. Ct. App. 1977). *Brooks Cotton Co.*, 381 S.W.3d at 423-26. The court ultimately adopted its test from the Colorado Court of Appeals, which noted an evolution in the general sophistication of the farmer. Id. at 425 (quoting Colo.-Kan. Grain Co. v. Reifschneider, 817 P.2d 637 (Colo. Ct. App. 1991)). Unless experience and sophistication are capable of dividing farmers into distinguishable occupations, however, this Court cannot reconcile an individualized test with the clear dictates of the statute. According to section 47-2-104(1), the person must hold himself out with the peculiar knowledge by his occupation rather than by his individual experience or level of sophistication. A person's occupation is his or her "usual or principal work or business, esp[ecially] as a means of earning a living." Occupation, *The Random House Dictionary of the English Language* (2d unabridged ed. 1987). The novice that manages to make his living from the smallest patch of earth may call himself a farmer as much as any agricultural corporate giant. Any distinction is therefore immaterial to this Court's analysis of section 47-2-104(1). What changes from case to case are the goods or practices involved in transactions. Thus, the issue then becomes whether a physician inherently holds himself out as having knowledge or skills peculiar to medical equipment or the installation thereof.

This is of course a much narrower reading of "merchant" than Defendant argues for. But Defendant's apparent assertion that the UCC envisions merchants as encompassing all professionals is inconsistent with the statutory language, which significantly restricts the knowledge or skill that would trigger the merchant provisions to such "knowledge or skill *peculiar to the practices or goods involved in the transaction.*" Tenn. Code Ann. §47-2-104(1) (emphasis added). The Tennessee General Assembly did not include the Official Comments in the provisions of 47-2-104. United Foods, Inc. v. Hadley-Peoples Mfg. Co., 1994 Tenn. App. LEXIS 277, at *13, 1994 WL 228773 (Tenn. Ct. App. May 20, 1994) (citing Tenn. Code Ann. §47-2-207(2) & cmt. 3) (rejecting the argument that the use by Official Comment 3 to section 47-2-207 of "additional or different terms" was applicable when section 47-2-207(2) only called for "additional terms" because "the drafters could easily have included 'or different' in [section] 47-2-207(2) if they had so intended"). Defendant would perhaps be correct in relying on the legislature's use of "practices" in hopes that "practice" is meant in the sense of "the business of a professional person." Practice, *The Random House Dictionary of the English Language* (2d unabridged ed. 1987). Defendant could then argue that Plaintiff, by virtue of being a doctor, is charged with the requisite knowledge and skill peculiar to the practice of medicine, and this is sufficient to constitute a merchant under the UCC. It is true that one such rule, known as the last-reasonable-referent canon, provides that subsequent modifying language usually only modifies the closest reasonable word. Carroll v. Sanders (In re Sanders), 551 F.3d 397, 399 (6th Cir. 2008) (quoting Bryan A. Garner, *Garner's Modern American Usage* 523-24 (2003)) ("[W]hen a word . . . points back to a [] . . . referent, the true referent should generally be the closest appropriate word."); see also Lockhart v. United States, 136 S. Ct. 958, 962 (2016) (citing Barnhart v. Thomas, 540 U.S. 20, 26 (2003); Rule of the last antecedent, *Black's Law Dictionary* 1532-33 (10th ed. 2014); Scalia & Garner, supra note 8, at 144) ("The rule provides that 'a limiting clause or phrase . . . should ordinarily be read as modifying only the noun or phrase that it immediately follows.'"). Under that rule, it would not be unreasonable to suggest that the modifier "involved in the transaction" modifies the word "goods" but not "practices." But the rule of the last reasonable referent "can assuredly be overcome by other indicia of meaning." *Barnhart,* 540 U.S. at 26. For example, "the . . . rule does not generally apply . . . when '[t]he modifying clause appear[s] . . . at the end of a single, integrated list.'" *Lockhart*, 136 S. Ct. at 970 (Kagan, J., dissenting) (quoting Jama v. Immigration and Customs Enforcement, 543 U.S. 335, 344 n.4 (2005)). "'When there is a straightforward, parallel construction that involves all nouns or verbs in a series,' a modifier at the end of the list 'normally applies to the entire series.'" Id. (quoting Scalia & Garner, supra note 8, at 147). Here, the phrase "the practices or goods" is written in a parallel construction. Both words are plural, and the definite article "the" is carried over to both words. See Scalia & Garner, supra note 8, at 147 (citations omitted) ("The typical way in which syntax would suggest no carryover modification is that a determiner (*a, the, some,* etc.) will be repeated before the second element."). Thus, "involved in the transaction" modifies both "practices" and "goods," restricting the meaning of practices in the instant case to the "business of a professional person" involved in the sale or installation of medical equipment. The Court now turns to resolving whether a physician inherently holds himself out as having knowledge or skills peculiar to medical equipment or the installation thereof.

In response to Defendant's assertion that Plaintiff is a merchant under the UCC, Plaintiff cites two cases: first, Czarnecki v. Roller, 726 F. Supp. 832, 843 (S.D. Fla. 1989), for the proposition that a "a party who engages in only a handful of transactions with respect to a particular good is not a 'merchant'"; and, second, Porter v. Rosenberg, 650 So. 2d 79, 81-82 (Fla. Dist. Ct. App. 1995), for the proposition that physicians are "more akin to the consumer or user of the product, especially where the product is not transferred to the patient but utilized incidental [sic] to the provision of medical services." Pl.'s Reply, at 2-3. The Court finds the first case irrelevant to its analysis. How often a person engages in the sales for a particular good goes to whether he is a "deal[er] in goods of the kind," a portion of the definition that clearly does not apply to Plaintiff. See Tenn. Code Ann. §47-2-104(1). A person's occupation can present that person to the world as having certain knowledge regardless of how many times they actually enter into a transaction so long as the knowledge is distinctive to the practices or goods involved in the disputed transaction. See id. The proposition Plaintiff draws from the second case certainly makes a lot of sense, but it speaks more to a common understanding of merchant rather than the UCC's definition. Common sense and understanding, however, are what must finally decide this dispute lest the Court and the parties remain forever more entangled in the UCC's provisions. A physician, put simply, is "a person qualified to practice medicine." Physician, *New Oxford American Dictionary* (3d ed. 2010). And medicine is "the science or practice of the diagnosis, treatment, or prevention of disease." Medicine, supra. This practice necessarily includes the ability to use various types of medical equipment, but the ability to use a machine is not a skill peculiar to one's practice.

> Physicians, like hospitals, are providers of medical services. The physician's expertise lies in the diagnosis, treatment and cure of illness, not in the research or development of prosthetics or devices used to aid medical diagnosis or treatment. . . . Products . . . case are supplied and utilized only as needed to deliver the professional medical service. They are incidental, or integral, to a physician's service, but they are not the focus of the physician's delivery of health care.

Porter v. Rosenberg, 650 So. 2d 79, 81-82 (Pa. Super. Ct. 1995) (discussing health care providers in a strict liability context). Yes, the physician is more like the consumer in these transactions. But the reason that physicians are not merchants under the UCC is that physicians are not experts in the equipment itself. There is nothing peculiar about being able to use a machine for its intended purpose. And there is no indication that physicians generally know how to take apart, put back together, install, or repair complicated pieces of machinery. Nor is there an indication that physicians can converse easily about the market for medical equipment. Cf. Brooks Cotton Co. v. Williams, 381 S.W.3d 414, 424-25 (Tenn. Ct. App. 2012) (holding that farmers could constitute merchants under the UCC because of their "extensive knowledge and sophistication regarding the purchase and sale of crops on the various agricultural markets"). The Court finds that a physician, by mere virtue of being a physician, does not hold himself out as having skills or knowledge peculiar to the sale or installation of medical equipment. Accordingly, the Court must conclude that Plaintiff is not a merchant under the UCC, and, therefore, the Purchase Agreement cannot be part of the Contract under section 2-207.

Plaintiff's Motion for Partial Summary Judgment is hereby GRANTED.

Notice that the definition of *merchant* in §2-104(1) refers not only to those who deal in the goods involved, but also those merchants who deal in the *practices* of the kind involved in the transaction. Official Comment 2 explains:

> The special provisions as to merchants appear only in this Article and they are of three kinds. Sections 2-201(2), 2-205, 2-207 and 2-209 dealing with the statute of frauds, firm offers, confirmatory memoranda and modification rest on normal business practices which are or ought to be typical of and familiar to any person in business. For purposes of these sections almost every person in business would, therefore, be deemed to be a "merchant" under the language "who . . . by his occupation holds himself out as having knowledge or

skill peculiar to the practices . . . involved in the transaction . . ." since the practices involved in the transaction are non-specialized business practices such as answering mail. In this type of provision, banks or even universities, for example, well may be "merchants." But even these sections only apply to a merchant in his mercantile capacity; a lawyer or bank president buying fishing tackle for his own use is not a merchant.

On the other hand, in Section 2-314 on the warranty of merchantability, such warranty is implied only "if the seller is a merchant with respect to goods of that kind." Obviously this qualification restricts the implied warranty to a much smaller group than everyone who is engaged in business and requires a professional status as to particular kinds of goods. The exception in Section 2-402(2) for retention of possession by a merchant-seller falls in the same class; as does Section 2-403(2) on entrusting of possession to a merchant "who deals in goods of that kind."

A third group of sections includes 2-103(1)(b), which provides that in the case of a merchant "good faith" includes observance of reasonable commercial standards of fair dealing in trade; 2-327(1)(c), 2-603, and 2-605 dealing with responsibilities of merchant buyers to follow seller's instructions, etc.; 2-509 on risk of loss; and 2-609 on adequate assurance of performance. This group of sections applies to persons who are merchants under either the "practices" or the "goods" aspect of the definition of merchant.

PROBLEM 5

Are the following persons merchants?

(a) Amanda, who quit her teaching job on Friday and on Monday opened a clothing store?

(b) Tom Tiller, a farmer selling his produce to a wholesaler? Compare Loeb & Co. v. Schreiner, 294 Ala. 722, 321 So. 2d 199 (1975) ("Although a farmer might sell his cotton every year, we do not think that this should take him out of the category of a 'casual seller' and place him in the category with 'professionals.'") with Continental Grain Co. v. Brown (W.D. Wis. 1976) ("A sale of 75,000 bushels of corn for a total price in excess of $212,000 is not a 'casual' sale."). See also Vince v. Broome, 443 So. 2d 23 (Miss. 1983) ("Some farming operations are worth millions of dollars. . . . It would stretch the imagination to conclude that all these operations were exempt from coverage under the Commercial Code."); Ohio Grain Co. v. Swisshelm, 40 Ohio App. 2d 203, 318 N.E.2d 428 (1973) (the modern farmer is more than "a simple tiller of the soil, unaccustomed to the affairs of business and the marketplace. . . . Only an agribusinessman may hope to survive."); Harvest States Cooperatives v. Anderson, 217 Wis. 2d 154, 577 N.W.2d 381 (1998) (man who had some cows and made occasional sales of corn not a merchant).

III. SCOPE OF ARTICLE 2A

In recent years, equipment leasing has become big business, topping $1 trillion in 2019. Leasing goods (as opposed to purchasing them with cash or on credit) has certain advantages. It may be desirable for accounting reasons because the lease obligation is not reflected as an asset/liability, thus improving the balance sheet ratios. At various times there have been tax advantages to leasing goods, though the tax laws have fluctuated on this through the years.[3]

A major problem with all this is that the law of personal property leasing has not been clearly defined. It originally developed from the law of bailments and, by analogy, from the law governing the lease of real property, though it fit comfortably into neither. Where the law was unfavorable or nonexistent, model equipment leases were promulgated by various bodies. See, e.g., Antin, An Equipment Lease Form, 8 A.L.I.-A.B.A. Course Materials J. 117 (1983). Since the adoption of the Uniform Commercial Code, many courts have applied Article 2 to leases, either stating that this was the intention of the drafters—see §2-102, stating that Article 2 applies to "transactions" in goods—or using Article 2 by analogy. Since many of Article 2's sections apply only if a "sale" occurs—defined in §2-106(1) to require the passing of title from the seller to the buyer—the Code's rules have to be stretched a great deal to encompass a true lease of goods.

In 1987, the last of the various bodies involved approved for adoption a new version of the Uniform Commercial Code containing Article 2A, entitled "Leases." It is modeled in large part (some say too much)[4] on Article 2. Throughout the rest of this book, reference will be made to sections of Article 2A, particularly where those sections deviate from the similar rules in Article 2.

It is important to appreciate the kind of leases to which Article 2A applies. Sometimes a transaction is called a "lease" when it is in reality a sale of goods. This is done for various reasons: the bookkeeping and tax

3. It has always been malpractice for the authors to say the word tax out loud, and this book therefore expresses no opinion on the current position of the Internal Revenue Code on this or any other subject.

4. "The Article 2A draftsmen's desire to follow the Article 2 model on occasion resulted in virtual unintelligibility to all but the most experienced and knowledgeable." Report of the Uniform Commercial Code Committee of the Business Law Section of the State Bar of California on Proposed California Commercial Code Division 10 (Article 2A) (1987), reprinted in 39 Ala. L. Rev. at 979, 984 (1988). California has adopted Article 2A with major overhauls to some of its sections. See also Kripke, Some Dissonant Notes About Article 2A, 39 Ala. L. Rev. 791 (1988).

considerations mentioned above, plus the desire to escape from the necessity of complying with either Article 2 or the secured transaction rules of Article 9. If a so-called lease does not pass the tests described therein, Article 2A is not triggered. Instead, the "lease" will be governed by those Articles and treated as a disguised sale on credit, with the "lessor's" interest in reality being nothing more than the "reservation of a security interest."[5] If the so-called lease is really a sale disguised as a lease, then it qualifies as what Article 9 of the UCC calls a "secured transaction," meaning, in this case, a sale on credit, with the seller having the right to repossess the goods if payment is not made by using its "security interest" (i.e., a lien on the goods) to reclaim them (and being also required to follow the formidable rules of Article 9). If the "lease" is really a "sale," and the seller did not follow the Article 9 rules, it runs the substantial risk of losing the ability to repossess the goods and/or having junior priority in them to other creditors (or to the buyer's bankruptcy trustee). It is therefore very important for the so-called lessor to prevail in this argument, or (the smart thing) to take the precautionary step of complying with the rules of Article 9 in case it has to battle other Article 9 claimants to the goods; see §9-505 (allowing a filing without it necessarily being an admission of a disguised sale). Read the very complicated definition of *security interest* in §1-203, concentrating on the major part of it that attempts to distinguish between a true lease and a security interest (that is, a sale on credit disguised as a lease). What are we to make of this definition? The happiest thing about it (despite its formidable size) is that it does draw some bright lines to help attorneys tell leases from secured transactions:

(1) As under the original definition, if at the end of the lease period the lessee becomes the owner of the property for little or no consideration, a secured transaction and not a lease has been created.
(2) If the contract contains a clause that permits the lessee to terminate the lease at any time and return the leased goods (the so-called walk away test), a true lease has resulted. Such a right of termination is not an attribute of a sale of goods.
(3) If the lease is for the entire economic life of the leased goods, with or without renewal, a disguised sale has occurred.

Other than that, each lease must be evaluated on its own. It does not necessarily answer the central question if the lessee pays consideration equal

5. Professors James White and Robert Summers deal with Article 2A in their splendid treatise on the Uniform Commercial Code: see Chapters 15 and 16 in Volume 2 (6th ed. Practitioner Treatise Series 2014). This work is published in two editions: a multi-volume work for practitioners and a one-volume student edition. All further citations, unless noted, are to the student edition: J. White & R. Summers, Uniform Commercial Code (6th ed. 2010) [hereinafter White & Summers].

to or even greater than the fair market value of the leased goods as long as the lease does not cover the total economic life of the goods. Nor does the lessee's assumption of major duties (taxes, risk of loss, etc.) necessarily indicate a lease or a sale of goods.

Use the definition and the above tests to answer the following Problem.

PROBLEM 6

BIG Machines, Inc., leased a computer to Helen's Flower Shoppe for a five-year period. The machine was new and had cost BIG Machines $10,000. Helen's Flower Shoppe promised to pay $225 a month as rent. Is this a lease or a disguised sale? Is your answer affected by the following considerations?

(a) The lease provided that the lessee could terminate the lease at any time and return the computer to the lessor.

(b) Assume there was no such option as described in (a), but the goods had no value at the end of the five-year period.

(c) Assume instead that the rental amount is only $150 a month and the computer will be worth $3,500 at the end of the five-year period. The lease has a clause giving Helen's Flower Shoppe the option to purchase the computer for that amount at that time. Is this a true lease? What if the lease *requires* the lessee to renew this lease at the end of the five-year period for another five years?

IV. INTERNATIONAL SALES

Effective January 1, 1988, the United States became bound by a treaty: the United Nations Convention on Contracts for the International Sale of Goods (hereinafter CISG). The Convention covers only issues of contract formation and the rights and duties of the parties thereto. It excludes coverage of products liability issues; it does not address matters touching on contract validity, such as fraud, illegality, etc. As of this writing, 89 countries, including most of the important trading states, are parties.[6] The leading text on the CISG is J. Honnold, Uniform Law for International Sales Under the 1980 United Nations Convention (4th ed. 2009).

6. As of 2018, the largest trading states not parties to the CISG were India, South Africa, Taiwan, and the United Kingdom. See http://www.uncitral.org/uncitral/en/uncitral_texts/sale_goods/1980CISG_status.html.

PROBLEM 7

Hegemony Enterprises, headquartered in New York, is about to sign a contract for the sale of men's clothing to Cosas Americana, a retailer in Mexico City. You are the lawyer for Hegemony Enterprises, and a company official calls you with the following questions:

(a) Will the CISG apply to this transaction? See CISG Articles 1 and 2.

(b) If Hegemony Enterprises wants the law of New York to apply, can the parties so stipulate in the contract and avoid the CISG? See Article 6.

(c) If Hegemony Enterprises were selling toys to Cosas Americana, would the CISG apply? See Article 2(a).

CHAPTER 2 REVIEW QUESTIONS

What difference does it make if a transaction is a transaction in goods?
What law governs transactions in services?
How do courts differentiate between transactions in goods versus services?
What difference does it make if someone is a merchant, for purposes of Article 2 of the UCC?
How do courts distinguish between a sale of goods and a lease? Why?
When does the CISG apply to a transaction?

ASSESSMENT: MULTIPLE CHOICE QUESTIONS

1. Which of the following cases would most likely be governed by Article 2?
   a. Gately Construction provided detailed specifications for inventory control software. Van Dyne Apps agreed to design, develop, and test software to meet those specifications.
   b. Van Dyne Apps agreed to provide inventory control software, update the software periodically, make any adaptations necessary to run it on Gately Construction's system, and train Gately Construction's employees to use the software.
   c. Van Dyne Apps sold Gately Construction a standard software package, identical to the package Van Dyne Apps sold to many small businesses.
   d. All of the above.

2. Incandenza liked a Marconi sedan offered at Pemulis Auto for $14,000, but wished to keep options open. Incandenza and Pemulis Auto signed a "Sales Contract," under which Incandenza would pay $400 per month to Pemulis Auto to use the car. Incandenza could at any time return the car and be obliged to make no more payments. Incandenza may also keep

the car forever, as long as he makes the monthly payment. Does Article 2 apply to the transaction?

a. Yes. The contract clearly states that it is a sales contract.
b. No. The transaction is governed by UCC Article 2A, Leases.
c. Article 2 will apply until Incandenza returns the car.
d. Yes. The subject of the contract is a car, which falls into the category of goods, not services.

3. Avril agreed to design and build a custom wheelchair for Mario. The contract specified capabilities and dimensions of the chair and provided for Avril to determine the design and build the chair. Upon completion and delivery, Avril would be entitled to a lump-sum payment based on her time and other specified costs. Does Article 2 apply to the transaction?
   a. Yes, because Article 2 applies to specially made goods.
   b. No, because the predominant purpose of the contract is services in designing and building the chair.
   c. No, because Avril is not a merchant.
   d. Yes, because Avril is a merchant.

4. Steeply runs an art gallery in Baldwinsville, New York. She signs a contract to purchase a security system from Marathe Prevention of Montreal, Quebec. The contract provides that it is governed by Article 2 of the UCC. Is the contract governed by Article 2 of the UCC or by the Convention on Contracts for the International Sale of Goods (CISG)?
   a. CISG, because the parties live in two countries that are party to the CISG.
   b. UCC Article 2, because the CISG allows the parties to choose the law to govern their transaction.
   c. Conduct in Quebec is governed by the CISG and conduct in the United States by UCC Article 2.
   d. The parties must comply with all provisions of both the UCC and the CISG. Citizens do not choose the law.

5. Van Dyne Apps sold Gately Construction some software that would run its inventory control systems. What difference would it make if the transaction is governed by Article 2 of the UCC, rather than the common law of contracts?
   a. Article 2 provides an implied warranty of merchantability, even if Van Dyne Apps did not make any specific promises about the software.
   b. Article 2's rules on contract formation are more flexible, finding an enforceable contract even where there is no matching offer and acceptance.
   c. Article 2's perfect tender rule may require the seller to deliver exactly the software agreed upon to be entitled to the price. Common law contract may only require substantial performance.

d. Article 2 will readily fill in gaps that the parties did not address, such as price or time for performance.
e. All of the above.

6. Wilson had the highest bid on eBay, the online auction site, for a painting, which the seller described as an original Jackson Pollock. After some email exchanges with the seller, Wilson sent a cashier's check, and a few days later received a suspiciously fresh painting, although Pollock died in 1956. Unable to locate the seller, Wilson sued eBay for breach of express warranty under Article 2 of the UCC. Which is likely to be the best argument for eBay?
   a. Fraud is legal, in order to encourage buyers to be careful.
   b. Article 2 of the UCC does not apply to paintings.
   c. Article 2 does not apply, because the transaction was not a sale of goods, rather was a service transaction (shipping a painting).
   d. eBay is not liable, because it did not sell the painting.

ANSWERS

1. *C* is the best answer. Courts routinely hold that the sale of standard software is a transaction in goods, subject to Article 2. *B* is at the other end of the goods/services spectrum. The contract not only requires the design and coding of software, but continued services to update and adapt the software, not to mention training employees. This would be predominantly services, not subject to Article 2. Answer *A* is a little more in the middle. As the cases in the chapter indicate, courts are somewhat split on whether a contract to design, develop, and implement software is a contract for services or for goods. So the case most likely to be governed by Article 2 is *C*.
2. *B* is the best answer. The parties called it a sale, but this is a lease: Incandenza may keep the car only as long as he pays for it, may terminate at any time, and never becomes the owner. The fact that the parties call it a sale has little weight, contrary to *A*. Both leases and sales may apply to goods, so *D* is misguided. *C* would give strange results.
3. *A* is the best answer. The contract calls for some services, but all geared toward providing the wheelchair, a specially made item of goods. All goods require services to be made, so any transaction in goods necessarily will require performance of services. This contract ultimately requires Avril to deliver goods, not to perform associated services such as training or maintenance. *C* and *D* are red herrings. They should remind us that Article 2 applies to transactions in goods, whether the parties are merchants or not. Some of the rules within Article 2 apply only to merchants.
4. *B* is the best answer. The CISG would apply to the contract, because the parties are residents of different CISG states. But Article 6 of the CISG allows parties to choose governing law. They chose Article 2, so Article 2

will provide the rules that govern their duties and rights under the contract. So parties can choose the law, sometimes, contrary to *D*. *C* is not the law, and would be strange to enforce.

5. *E* is the best answer. This question (instructive if not really fair, because it previews material ahead in the book) collects some of the biggest differences between UCC Article 2 and the common law of contracts. In the cases on the scope of Article 2, one party may be arguing that Article 2 applies so that the party gets an implied warranty of merchantability (answer *A*), or so that there will be an enforceable contract where the parties' forms or conduct show an agreement, even though there is no offer and acceptance (answer *B*), or so that the buyer can reject goods that did not match the contract, even if the seller substantially performed (answer *D*) or to use some other gap-filler in Article 2, such as finding a price where the parties did not specifically agree on price (answer *D*). That's really a lot of preview of what later chapters will cover. But that look ahead is helpful to show why it matters whether Article 2 applies to a transaction.
6. *D* is the best answer. This question raises the issue raised in Problem 2, which Amazon has litigated: When does an online marketplace qualify as a seller of goods? As noted above, most courts have held that Amazon is not a seller, although some incisive commentary has argued for a different result. The case to hold eBay liable as a seller would seem to be weaker. eBay operates a site where buyers and sellers deal more directly, set the prices for transactions, and handle the shipping details. The other possible answers are deliberately way off. We have not gone through Article 2 yet, but fraud is never encouraged. Article 2 applies to goods, and we saw no exemption for paintings. *C* is off the mark, because the transaction was to buy a specific item of goods, a painting, not just to ship a painting.

CHAPTER 3

CONTRACT FORMATION

The bargain of the parties to a sales contract must conform to most of the usual rules you learned in the course on Contracts, though Article 2 of the Uniform Commercial Code does change some of them. Thus the basics of contract formation should be reassuringly familiar to you already. Perhaps the UCC's approach to the Statute of Frauds, the parol evidence rule, and offer and acceptance were covered in the Contracts course. If not, as you learn these rules, rather than review them, contrast the UCC approach with the common law result and ask yourself why the drafters of the Code would have made these changes.

I. THE STATUTE OF FRAUDS

Read §2-201, which is quite a change from the original English Statute of Frauds from which it is descended. Passed in 1677 by Parliament, it was a statute that attempted to prevent fraud by requiring certain kinds of contracts to be in writing in order to be enforceable in a court of law (those involving real property, surety promises, etc.). The statute required certain sales contracts to be in writing, and §2-201 is its latest iteration.

At common law, when a contract fell within the Statute, *all* its terms and conditions had to be in writing or the contract was not enforceable. Under §2-201, a contract can be enforced even if a main term is omitted or misstated. The only term necessary for a sufficient memorandum under §2-201(1) is *quantity*.[1] Not only are the standards lessened by the Code, but also four exceptions are provided: merchant confirmation letters, special manufacture, part performance, and admission in legal proceedings.

Ellig v. Molina

United States District Court, Southern District of New York, 2014
996 F. Supp. 2d 236

Katherine B. Forrest, District Judge:

Diamonds are not always a girl's best friend. Here, the particular diamond ring at issue—a 10-carat center stone in a platinum setting that included dozens of baguettes—drove friends apart.

The story starts with a cruise around the world, and ends in a courtroom in Manhattan. The cast of characters includes a jet-setting jeweler from Arizona; a financially conservative husband who is intent on investing wisely and who wants to (and does) buy his wife a special ring for a significant birthday, trusting in the ring's value; and a wife appreciative of the gesture, but concerned about the ring's cost and actual value. Buyer's and receiver's remorse set in; that might have been the end of the story, if it were not for the fact that the jeweler had promised that plaintiffs could return the ring within one year and that he would buy it back. In fact, plaintiffs claim that said jeweler, Alfred Molina himself, had also agreed to pay them 10% in addition to the purchase price—in effect, guaranteeing the price of the ring and a 10% return on the investment if returned within a year.

Unfortunately, this promise was not in writing. The parties generally agree that there was a promise of some sort; but, rather unsurprisingly, disagree as to important details. This lawsuit followed; a bench trial was held on January 10, 2014. At that trial, the now former friends testified as to their version of events. This Opinion & Order constitutes the Court's findings of fact and conclusions of law.

In summary, the Court finds that, in exchange for plaintiffs' purchase of the ring, defendants agreed to buy it back at full price plus 10% if tendered within one year. By failing to hold up their end of the bargain, defendants have breached the contract.

1. White and Summers note that one could (contrary to the weight of authority) interpret §2-201(1) *not* to require a quantity, but rather to say only that *if* a quantity is specified, the agreement cannot be enforced beyond that quantity. White & Summers §3-4, at 97 n.12.

I. Findings of Fact

At trial, the Elligs and Mr. Molina provided direct testimony by written declaration and were subject to live cross-examination and re-direct. The Court found both of the Elligs very credible. Mrs. Ellig is an articulate and sophisticated businesswoman; her answers were consistent and direct. She was never evasive. The Court credits her testimony *in toto.* Mr. Ellig is also a sophisticated businessperson who is clearly very detail-oriented and careful. He was clear, consistent and articulate in Court. He was never evasive. The Court similarly credits his testimony *in toto.* In contrast, the Court found Mr. Molina lacking in credibility; he was evasive, argumentative and inconsistent. The Court does not believe his version of the agreement between the parties.

Plaintiffs and defendant Molina met on an around-the-world trip in 2007. (Decl. of Janice Ellig ("JE Decl.") ¶4, ECF No. 74.) He introduced himself as a world-renowned jeweler. (Decl. of Bruce R. Ellig ("BE Decl.") ¶5, ECF No. 75.) Mr. Molina is the sole shareholder in Molina, Inc., which operates two jewelry stores under the name Molina Fine Jewelers ("MFJ"). (Trial Decl. of Alfred Molina ("Molina Decl.") ¶3, ECF No. 77.) The Elligs and Mr. Molina became close friends and socialized together with Mr. Molina's then wife. (JE Decl. ¶¶5-6.) Mr. Molina was a regular guest in the Elligs' home when he came to New York for business. (Id. ¶8.) Mr. Molina would use the word "brother" when he contacted Mr. Ellig regarding a prospective visit—stating, for instance, "Hey, brother, I am coming to visit you and will arrive on __________." (BE Decl. ¶7.) The Elligs and Molinas also travelled together to Eastern Europe, Sicily and the Caribbean. (JE Decl. ¶9.)

During the time the Elligs and Molinas spent together, Mr. Molina spoke about diamonds as an investment. (BE Decl. ¶9.) Mr. Ellig considers himself fiscally conservative. (Id.) He has invested primarily in municipal bonds. (Id.) He conveyed this to Mr. Molina on a number of occasions. (Id.)

Mrs. Ellig's 65th birthday was in 2011. In December 2010, Mr. Ellig told Mr. Molina that Mrs. Ellig's 65th birthday was approaching, as was their 17th wedding anniversary, and that he wanted to do something special to mark those occasions. (BE Decl. ¶10.) Mr. Molina suggested that Mr. Ellig buy her a large diamond ring. (Id.) Mr. Molina stated that diamonds appreciate and therefore were a safe investment. (Id.) Mr. Ellig was initially skeptical; he was contemplating a gift in the range of a couple of hundred thousand dollars, and Mr. Molina told him that a large diamond befitting his wife would cost three times that amount. (BE Decl. ¶11.) Mr. Ellig told Mr. Molina that if he were even to consider spending that kind of money, the purchase would have to be not only a gift but also an investment. (Id.)

Mr. Ellig stated that, as much as he wanted to do something special for his wife, the appropriateness of the investment depended on his ability to get his money back. (BE Decl. ¶12.) In that very first conversation in December 2010, Mr. Molina stated that, if the Elligs purchased the ring and were unhappy with it for any reason at all, he would buy it back within a year for the full purchase price plus a guaranteed 10%. (Id. ¶13.) The agreement was not reduced to writing. Mr. Ellig and Mr. Molina had a number of conversations about the ring following this first one, and in each, Mr. Molina repeated the benefits of investing in diamonds and the guarantee he was providing. (Id. ¶¶15-16.) In each of these conversations, the terms of the guarantee remained the same. (Id. ¶16.)

At no time prior to the Elligs' purchase of the ring—and indeed not until July 2012—did Mr. Molina mention a consignment arrangement or a waiting period before their money would be returned. (See BE Decl. ¶¶16-17.)

As her birthday approached, the Elligs discussed the possibility of Mr. Ellig buying his wife a diamond ring. (JE Decl. ¶15; BE Decl. ¶19.) The Elligs never discussed purchasing a loose diamond (that is, a diamond not yet set into a ring or other piece of jewelry); their discussions always related to a wearable diamond ring. (JE Decl. ¶21.)

Mrs. Ellig then spoke with Mr. Molina about acquiring a ring with a diamond in the 8-to-10 carat range. (JE Decl. ¶16.) Mrs. Ellig informed Mr. Molina that their budget was $300,000 to $350,000. (Id.) During April to June, the conversations became more serious. (Id. ¶17.)

Prior to receipt of the ring, Mrs. Ellig had a conversation with Mr. Molina in her kitchen in which she expressed to Mr. Molina her concern that, given the price of the ring, she had to be certain it was a good investment. (Trial Tr. 40, Jan. 10, 2014.) Molina told her in substance not to worry, that diamonds were an investment that did not lose value, and that he would repurchase the ring and guarantee another 10% if the Elligs were not happy with it. (Tr. 40-41.) Mrs. Ellig testified credibly at trial that Mr. Molina repeated his promise to buy the ring back (plus 10%) on multiple occasions. (JE Decl. ¶19.) The Elligs subsequently agreed to buy a ring for over $700,000. (Id. ¶¶25-26.) They both testified credibly that they did so in reliance on the specific and repeated representations by Mr. Molina regarding the buy-back promise. (Id. ¶¶21, 23.)

On June 21, 2011, Mr. Molina came to Manhattan with a ring with a more than 10-carat diamond center stone; he showed it to Mrs. Ellig. (JE Decl. ¶24; BE Decl. ¶¶21, 23.) The diamond was in a setting when Mr. Molina first showed it to her. (Tr. 64-65; JE Decl. ¶24.) Mrs. Ellig had some concerns about clarity and expressed them to Mr. Molina. (BE Decl. ¶20.) Mr. Molina stated that the ring was a good deal, and that what she was noticing was its blue fluorescence, which made it even more valuable. (Id.) At trial, Mr. Molina maintained that the blue fluorescence was an advantage and added value. (Molina Decl. ¶11.)

To address Mrs. Ellig's clarity concerns, Mr. Molina suggested boiling the ring; when Mrs. Ellig was still dissatisfied with the color of the ring, Mr. Molina suggested the addition of baguettes in the setting. (BE Decl. ¶¶21-22.)

Mr. Ellig paid for the diamond stone and the setting in two separate payments: he wired Mr. Molina $580,000 on June 21, 2011, and $71,188 on June 30, 2011. (BE Decl. ¶¶23-24.)

The Elligs' negotiations regarding purchase of the ring and the terms of return were solely with Mr. Molina; he made statements to them as an individual and not purporting to act through or on behalf of a corporate entity. However, the invoices for the ring were in the name of Molina Fine Jewelers, and the payments sent for the ring were to Molina Inc. (See PX1, PX2, PX12, DX1-DX4.) The Court finds that Mr. Molina made a personal promise that he and/or his wholly owned company—acting with regard to the ring indistinguishably—would buy back the ring within one year.

Mr. Molina did not leave the ring behind, but returned with it to Arizona, where a new setting was designed. (JE Decl. ¶29; BE Decl. ¶22.) The ring in the form in which it currently exists was finished and presented to Mrs. Ellig in late July or early August 2011; this was approximately two to three weeks after he showed the original ring to Mrs. Ellig. (Tr. 51-52; JE Decl. ¶¶28-29.) Mr. Molina provided the Elligs with a valuation by Mr. Molina himself, which they could use for insurance purposes, which valued the ring for $925,000. (BE Decl. ¶¶25-26.)

Shortly after receiving the ring, Mrs. Ellig began to have misgivings. She continued to be bothered by the center stone's strong blue fluorescence. (JE Decl. ¶30.) She expressed her concerns to Mr. Molina soon after she received it; he told her that the blue fluorescence made the ring whiter. (Id.)

Over the course of the next 10 months, Mrs. Ellig's concerns about the color of the ring continued. (Id. ¶33.) She had several people she believed were knowledgeable in the area provide her with their views as to the value of the ring; their valuations came in at a number far lower than the Elligs had paid. (JE Decl. ¶¶34, 37.) During the holiday season of 2011, Mrs. Ellig informed Mr. Molina of the third-party opinions regarding the ring's value; their relationship began to sour. (Id. ¶¶36-37.) In May 2012, Mrs. Ellig and Mr. Molina were both in attendance at a shareholders' conference in Omaha, Nebraska. (Id. ¶39.) Mrs. Ellig and Mr. Molina visited a jewelry store in town, and Mrs. Ellig was struck by how her ring compared to others at lower prices; she believed hers lacked the same sparkle. (Id.) Later that same month, the Elligs decided to return the ring. (Id. ¶41.) She called Mr. Molina at the end of May or beginning of June 2012 and informed him of that decision. (Tr. 61; JE Decl. ¶41; BE Decl. ¶¶29-30.)

On July 11, 2012, Mr. Molina sent the Elligs a letter, which was referred to throughout the trial as the "Dear Brother letter," (JE Decl. ¶42.) That letter confirms that the parties had an agreement with respect to the return of the ring. (See id.) The letter provided a chronology of the Elligs' purchase of the ring. It states that Mr. Molina presented the "diamond" to Mrs. Ellig in June and that she subsequently wanted changes to the setting. (Tr. 46-48; JE Decl. ¶42.) At trial, Mr. Molina testified that he had never presented Mrs. Ellig with a loose stone. (Tr. 116-17.) The letter reads in relevant part as follows:

> When we discussed the risk of you purchasing the diamond, I made several statements to both of you.
>
> 1. If you decide that you do not want the diamond a year from now, I would get your money back and a 10% return on your money. I understand that is your understanding that I committed to buy the stone and you are correct. The only gray area is that for me to do so I have to sell the stone. (I am prepared to provide you with a financial note that guarantees the funds and a return.)

(JE Decl. ¶42; BE Decl. ¶31; PX4.)

The "gray area" referred to in the letter (selling the diamond prior to giving the Elligs their money back) was not part of the original agreement between the parties. (BE Decl. ¶32.) Mr. Ellig testified credibly that a consignment arrangement emerged for the first time after the Elligs told Mr. Molina that they wanted to return the ring. Mr. Molina initially explained the need to sequence the events in this manner as due to a lack of immediate funds on his part. (Tr. 75.) The Court agrees that any consignment arrangement was an *ex post facto* attempt to avoid the terms of the guarantee that Mr. Molina had made to the Elligs.

Mr. Ellig declined to provide the ring—even with the financial guarantee offered—prior to receiving full payment. (Tr. 84-86.) At trial, he explained that he is a conservative investor, and that he did not want and had not bargained for the uncertainty that came with such an arrangement. (Tr. 86; BE Decl. ¶9.) In addition, Mrs. Ellig stated that she knew that Molina had debts and was concerned that if he sold the ring, the proceeds could be used to satisfy some other creditor. (JE Decl. ¶47.)

On July 12, 2012, Mr. Molina sent the Elligs a consignment agreement along with a guarantee of payment over time upon return of the ring. (JE Decl. ¶44; BE Decl. ¶33.) The Elligs did not enter into this agreement.

At trial, Mr. Molina testified that in his 45 years in the jewelry business, he has never promised or agreed to buy back any jewelry. (Molina Decl. ¶39.)

II. Conclusions of Law

This is a straightforward breach of contract case: is there an enforceable buy-back guarantee between the parties and, if so, what are its terms?

Plainly, resolution of this dispute would have been far easier had the agreement between the parties been in writing at the outset. A clear writing would have provided certainty as to terms and therefore clarity as to breach. Neither party disputes that there was an oral agreement—but, as is clear from the above, they disagree as to certain provisions. Defendants argue that the lack of a writing at the outset dooms plaintiffs' claim: the statute of frauds requires, *inter alia,* contracts over a certain value or which cannot be completed within one year to be in writing. See N.Y. U.C.C. §2-201(1) (explaining that "a contract for the sale of goods for the price of $500 or more is not enforceable . . . unless there is some writing sufficient to indicate that a contract for sale has been made between the parties and signed by the party against whom enforcement is sought"); Dallas Aerospace, Inc. v. CIS Air Corp., 352 F.3d 775, 782 (2d Cir. 2003). The Elligs find themselves in the rather lucky position of having a confirming writing, with Mr. Molina's signature, that satisfies the statute of frauds: the "Dear Brother" letter is all that they need in this regard. Defendants also argue that the letter is not admissible under Federal Rule of Evidence 408 or that it cannot satisfy the statute of frauds, since the parties disagree as to whether the terms of the buy-back are accurately set forth in the letter. These arguments are both unavailing. . . .

Defendants' primary legal argument is that the statute of frauds requires a written contract, and that the lack of a written contract between the parties here therefore renders any promises unenforceable. Plaintiffs bear the burden of overcoming any statute of frauds requirement. See Trebor Sportswear Co., Inc. v. The Limited Stores, Inc., 865 F.2d 506, 509 (2d Cir. 1989). To carry this burden, plaintiffs must present sufficient admissible evidence of an agreement. Id. at 510. All that is required is that there is a writing that affords a basis for believing that the offered oral evidence of a contract and its terms refer to a real transaction. See Apex Oil Co. v. Vanguard Oil & Serv. Co., 760 F.2d 417, 423 (2d Cir. 1985). A sufficient writing in this regard (1) indicates that an agreement with obligations exists between the parties, (2) is signed, and (3) specifies a quantity of goods. See N.Y. U.C.C. §2-201(1). Several writings may be considered together. See Hawley Fuel Coalmart, Inc. v. Steag Handel GmbH, 796 F.2d 29, 30 (2d Cir. 1986).

THE CLASSIC PHRASE "HOISTED WITH HIS OWN PETARD" APPLIES HERE

Defendant Molina himself drafted and sent to plaintiffs the written instrument that lays out the chronology leading up to the agreement for the purchase and sale of one ring, concedes that a guarantee exists, and further concedes that Mrs. Ellig's version of events is "correct." (JE Decl. ¶42; BE Decl. ¶31; PX4.) This writing is sufficient to meet the requirements of the statute of frauds. See Great Destinations, Inc. v. Transportes Aereos Portugueses S.A.R.L., 460 F. Supp. 1160, 1163-64 (S.D.N.Y. 1978) (finding several letters setting forth the essential terms of contracts to satisfy the statute of frauds); Crabtree v. Elizabeth Arden Sales Corp., 305 N.Y. 48, 53-54, 110 N.E.2d 551 (1953) (finding payroll cards to constitute sufficient writings under the statute although they came into existence subsequent to the contract's execution, because they contained essential elements such as the parties to the contract, the compensation to be received, and the duration of the contract); Nausch v. AON Corp., 2 A.D.3d 101, 769 N.Y.S.2d 481, 483 (App. Div. 1st Dep't 2003) (finding that documents such as a letter agreement, internal memorandum, and handwritten notes satisfied the statute of frauds).

To the extent that the price paid itself is contained in separate writings (the invoices tendered by Mr. Molina and the wire transfers tendered by the Elligs), the fact that they are not signed in the classic sense of bearing a personal signature is not fatal. Under the circumstances here, neither party has contested the amount paid; the wires bear indicia of reliability, as do the invoices, though the date upon which the invoices were sent or whether they were sent was disputed. Under these circumstances, that the purchase price is contained in separate, not-classically signed documents is nonetheless sufficient. See Babdo Sales, Inc. v. Miller-Wohl Co., 440 F.2d 962, 966 (2d Cir. 1971) (explaining that only one writing "must bear the signature of the party to be charged," while the unsigned document must "refer to the same transaction"); *Crabtree,* 305 N.Y. at 54, 110 N.E.2d 551 (explaining that "separate writings, connected with one another either expressly or by the internal evidence of subject-matter and occasion," satisfy the statute of frauds). . . .

Defendants argue that the Dear Brother letter is inadmissible as an offer of settlement. They raised this before trial in a motion *in limine.* The Court denied that motion at that time, but specifically invited defendants to bring out any facts they desired at trial which would support their position that the letter was an offer of settlement. (Tr. 3-6.) Defendants failed to do so.

Defendants also argue that, even if admissible, the Dear Brother letter is insufficient to satisfy the statute of frauds because it lacks certain terms, including that the return needed to be exercised within a year, as well as the date from which that year would run. In addition, defendants assert that the Dear Brother letter does not specify that there was any agreement with regard to the "setting" for the ring, as opposed to only the center diamond stone. According to defendants, the absence of clarity (no pun intended) as to whether the guarantee is with respect to the stone or the entire ring, as well as the amount of time within which the return needed to be exercised, are material terms that must be in a writing. Put another way, while plaintiffs argue that the Dear Brother letter is a sufficient writing to constitute confirmation of a contract, they then disagree with the terms of the letter.

Under these circumstances, the issue becomes: if the letter satisfies the statute of frauds, must this Court take as true the additional terms of the contract as reflected in the letter? No. See, e.g., *Nausch,* 769 N.Y.S.2d at 483.

While the Dear Brother letter is sufficient to confirm the contract between the parties—because it contains the essential terms related to Mr. Molina's commitment to buy the stone within a year—the terms expressed in the letter relating to a "gray area" do not, and need not for purposes of the statute of frauds, form part of the contract. Rather, the oral contract, whose existence the letter confirms, obligated defendants to buy back the ring within one year for the purchase price plus 10%. . . .

III. Conclusion

For the reasons set forth above, the Court finds that defendants Alfred Molina and Molina, Inc. d/b/a Molina Fine Jewelers have breached their contract with plaintiffs Janice and Bruce Ellig. Plaintiffs shall submit a proposed judgment within seven days, or by Monday, February 17, 2014.

SO ORDERED.

PROBLEM 8

On December 10, James Ross, president of Ross Ice Cream Shoppes, Inc., phoned Robert Scott, president of Amundsen Ice Company, and negotiated the purchase of two tons of ice from Amundsen at $256/ton. As they talked on the phone, Scott picked up a memo pad inscribed "Amundsen Ice Company From the Desk of the President," wrote on it "2 tons Ross Co.," and then scribbled his initials on it. When the parties hung up the phones, Scott placed the memo on a spindle marked "Orders." Ross wrote Scott a letter beginning "Dear Bob: This is to confirm our ice purchase deal . . . ," which described their transaction completely. Scott received the letter on December 14. On January 17, Scott phoned Ross and denied the existence of the contract detailed in the Ross letter. Answer these questions:

(a) Does the memo pad note satisfy §2-201(1)? See §1-201(b)(37) and Official Comment 37.

(b) What legal effect did the December 14 letter have? Same result if Ross's letter failed to mention the quantity? Even if the letter satisfies the Statute of Frauds, is it conclusive as to the existence and terms of the contract? See Hinson-Barr, Inc. v. Pinckard, 292 S.C. 267, 356 S.E.2d 115 (1987).

(c) Did Scott's denial of the terms contained in Ross's letter avoid the operation of §2-201(2)? Suppose Scott had immediately written Ross a letter stating, "You haven't stated the terms correctly. We only agreed to sell you 1 ton." Would that letter be a sufficient notice of objection? See Simmons Oil Corp. v. Bulk Sales Corp., 498 F. Supp. 457 (D.N.J. 1980); Annot., 82 A.L.R.4th 709.

(d) Would an unsigned receipt for artworks satisfy §2-201? Beard v. Chase, 2017 WL 2674494 (N.Y. Sup. Ct. 2017).

St. Ansgar Mills, Inc. v. Streit

Supreme Court of Iowa, 2000
613 N.W.2d 289

Cady, Justice.

A grain dealer appeals from an order by the district court granting summary judgment in an action to enforce an oral contract for the sale of corn based on a written confirmation. The district court held the oral contract was unenforceable because the written confirmation was not delivered within a reasonable time after the oral contract as a matter of law. We reverse the decision of the district court and remand for further proceedings.

I. Background Facts and Proceedings

St. Ansgar Mills, Inc. is a family-owned agricultural business located in Mitchell County. As a part of its business, St. Ansgar Mills buys corn from local grain farmers and sells corn to livestock farmers for feed. The price of the corn sold to farmers is established by trades made on the Chicago Board of Trade for delivery with reference to five contract months. The sale of corn for future delivery is hedged by St. Ansgar Mills through an offsetting futures position on the Chicago Board of Trade.

A sale is typically made when a farmer calls St. Ansgar Mills and requests a quote for a cash price of grain for future delivery based on the Chicago Board of Trade price for the delivery. The farmer then accepts or rejects the price. If the price is accepted, St. Ansgar Mills protects the price through a licensed brokerage house by acquiring a hedge position on the Chicago Board of Trade. This hedge position, however, obligates St. Ansgar Mills to purchase the corn at the stated price at the time of delivery. Thus, St. Ansgar Mills relies on the farmer who purchased the grain to accept delivery at the agreed price.

Duane Streit formerly resided in Mitchell County and currently practices veterinarian medicine in Carroll County. He also raises hogs. He owns a large hog farrowing operation in Carroll County and a hog finishing operation in Mitchell County near Osage. Streit purchased the Osage farm from his father in 1993. Duane's father, John Streit, resides in Mitchell County and helps Duane operate the Osage finishing facility.

Duane and his father have been long-time customers of St. Ansgar Mills. Since 1989, Duane entered into numerous contracts with St. Ansgar Mills for the purchase of large quantities of corn and other grain products. Duane would generally initiate the purchase agreement by calling St. Ansgar Mills on the telephone to obtain a price quote. If an oral contract was made, an employee of St. Ansgar Mills would prepare a written confirmation of the sale and either mail it to Duane to sign and return, or wait for Duane or John to sign the confirmation when they would stop in to the business.

John would regularly stop by St. Ansgar Mills sometime during the first ten days of each month and pay the amount of the open account Duane maintained at St. Ansgar Mills for the purchase of supplies and other materials. On those occasions when St. Ansgar Mills sent the written confirmation to Duane, it was not unusual for Duane to fail to sign the confirmation for a long period of time. He also failed to return contracts sent to him. Nevertheless, Duane had never refused delivery of grain he purchased by telephone prior to the incident which gave rise to this case.

On July 1, 1996, John telephoned St. Ansgar Mills to place two orders for the purchase of 60,000 bushels of corn for delivery in December 1996 and May 1997. This order followed an earlier conversation between Duane and St. Ansgar Mills. After the order was placed, St. Ansgar Mills completed the written confirmation but set it aside for John to sign when he was expected to stop by the business to pay the open account. The agreed price of the December corn was $3.53 per bushel. The price of the May corn was $3.73 per bushel.

John failed to follow his monthly routine of stopping by the business during the month of July. St. Ansgar Mills then asked a local banker who was expected to see John to have John stop in to the business.

John did not stop by St. Ansgar Mills until August 10, 1996. On that date, St. Ansgar Mills delivered the written confirmation to him.

Duane later refused delivery of the corn orally purchased on July 1, 1996. The price of corn had started to decline shortly after July 1, and eventually plummeted well below the quoted price on July 1. After Duane refused delivery of the corn, he purchased corn for his hog operations on the open market at prices well below the contract prices of July 1. St. Ansgar Mills later told Duane it should have followed up earlier with the written confirmation and had no excuse for not doing so.

St. Ansgar Mills then brought this action for breach of contract. It sought damages of $152,100, which was the difference between the contract price of the corn and the market price at the time Duane refused delivery.

Duane filed a motion for summary judgment. He claimed the oral contract alleged by St. Ansgar Mills was governed by the provisions of the Uniform Commercial Code, and was unenforceable as a matter of law under the statute of frauds. He claimed the written confirmation delivered to John on August 10, 1996 did not satisfy the statute of frauds for two reasons. First, he was not a merchant. Second, the confirmation was not received within a reasonable time after the alleged oral agreement.

The district court determined a jury question was presented on whether Duane was a merchant under the Uniform Commercial Code. However, the district court found the written confirmation did not satisfy the writing requirements of the statute of frauds because the delivery of the confirmation to John, as Duane's agent, did not occur within a reasonable time after the oral contract as a matter of law. The district court found the size of the order, the volatility of the grain market, and the lack of an explanation by St. Ansgar Mills for failing to send the confirmation to Duane after John failed to stop by the business as expected made the delay between July 1 and August 10 unreasonable as a matter of law.

St. Ansgar Mills appeals. It claims a jury question was presented on the issue of whether a written confirmation was received within a reasonable time. . . .

III. Statute of Frauds

The statute of frauds is one of the most well-known and venerable rules applicable to contract law. Generally, it establishes an exception to the proposition that oral contracts are enforceable in a lawsuit if sufficiently proven by requiring certain types of contracts to be in writing and signed by the party against whom enforcement is sought. See Iowa Code §554.2201(1).

The statute of frauds originated in 17th century England to combat the use of fraud and perjury by litigants in court proceedings to establish oral contracts. See 2 E. Allan Farnsworth, Contracts §6.1, at 82-83 (2d ed. 1990). At the time, court rules prohibited parties to a lawsuit from testifying as witnesses in their case, and, consequently, an oral contract could only be established with testimony of third parties. See Azevedo v. Minister, 86 Nev. 576, 471 P.2d 661, 663 (1970). This prohibition allowed witnesses to be persuaded to give false testimony on behalf of a party in an effort to establish an oral contract, leaving the other party at a distinct disadvantage. See James J. O'Connell, Jr., Boats Against a Current: The Courts and the Statute of Frauds, 47 Emory L.J. 253, 257 (1998) [hereinafter O'Connell].

In 1677, in response to this unsavory practice of using perjury to establish oral contracts, Parliament enacted the statute of frauds to require certain contracts to be supported by written evidence to be enforceable. 29 Car. 2, ch. 3 (1677) (Eng.); see Hugh E. Willis, Statute of Frauds—A Legal Anachronism, 3 Ind. L.J. 427, 427 (1928). The statute included contracts which were not only particularly susceptible to fraud, but those which posed serious consequences of fraud, including contracts for the sale of goods or property. See O'Connell, 47 Emory L.J. at 258.

Despite a difference in the court rules which gave rise to this statute of frauds, our American legal culture quickly adopted the principle. James J. White & Robert S. Summers, Uniform Commercial Code §2-1, at 50 (2d ed. 1980) [hereinafter White & Summers]. Iowa adopted the statute of frauds in 1851. See Iowa Code §§2409-2410 (1851). The statute of frauds also became a part of the Uniform Sales Act in 1906, which Iowa subsequently adopted in 1924. See 1919 Iowa Acts ch. 396 (initially codified at Iowa Code §§9930-10007 (1924)). This statute required all contracts for the sale of goods to be in writing. Over time, the Uniform Sales Act was replaced by the Uniform

Commercial Code.[2] The Uniform Commercial Code continued to adhere to the statute of frauds, but was limited in its provisions to the sale of goods in excess of $500. Iowa enacted its version of the Uniform Commercial Code in 1966 including the statute of frauds. See 1965 Iowa Acts ch. 413. Iowa's statute of frauds for the sale of goods now provides:

> Except as otherwise provided in this section, a contract for the sale of goods for the price of $500 or more is not enforced by way of action or defense unless there is some writing sufficient to indicate that a contract for sale has been made between the parties and signed by the party against whom enforcement is sought or by that party's authorized agent or broker.

Iowa Code §554.2201(1) (1995).

Although the statute of frauds has been deeply engrained into our law, many of the forces which originally gave rise to the rule are no longer prevalent. White & Summers §2-1, at 51. This, in turn, has caused some of the rigid requirements of the rule to be modified.

One statutory exception or modification to the statute of frauds which has surfaced applies to merchants. Id. §554.2201(2). Under section 554.2201(2), the writing requirements of section 554.2201(1) are considered to be satisfied if, within a reasonable time, a writing in confirmation of the contract which is sufficient against the sender is received and the merchant receiving it has reason to know of its contents, unless written notice of objection of its contents is given within ten days after receipt. Id. Thus, a writing is still required, but it does not need to be signed by the party against whom the contract is sought to be enforced. The purpose of this exception was to put professional buyers and sellers on equal footing by changing the former law under which a party who received a written confirmation of an oral agreement of sale, but who had not signed anything, could hold the other party to a contract without being bound. See White & Summers §2-3, at 55; Kimball County Grain Coop. v. Yung, 200 Neb. 233, 263 N.W.2d 818, 820 (1978). It also encourages the common, prudent business practice of sending memoranda to confirm oral agreements. White & Summers §2-3, at 55.

2. After six years of deliberating, the National Conference of Commissioners on Uniform State Laws produced the 1952 Official Text of the Uniform Commercial Code. See William A. Schnader, A Short History of the Preparation and Enactment of the Uniform Commercial Code, 22 U. Miami L. Rev. 1, 1-2 (1967). In 1954, Pennsylvania was the first state to formally adopt the text. See 13 Pa. Const. Stat. §§1101 to 9507 (1953). By 1968, the Uniform Commercial Code was effective in 49 states, the District of Columbia, and the Virgin Islands. See Uniform Commercial Code Table, 1 U.L.A. 1-2 (Master ed. 1989). There have been three official revisions, the 1972, the 1978, and the 1987 Official Texts, offered by the Permanent Editorial Board, a board established in 1961 to keep the Code up to date. See William A. Schnader, The Permanent Editorial Board for the Uniform Commercial Code: Can it Accomplish its Object?, 3 Am. Bus. L.J. 137, 138 (1965).

While the written confirmation exception imposes a specific ten-day requirement for a merchant to object to a written confirmation, it employs a flexible standard of reasonableness to establish the time in which the confirmation must be received. Iowa Code §554.2201(2). The Uniform Commercial Code specifically defines a reasonable time for taking action in relationship to "the nature, purpose and circumstances" of the action. Id. §554.1204(2) [UCC §1-204[3]]. Additionally, the declared purpose of the Uniform Commercial Code is to permit the expansion of commercial practices through the custom and practice of the parties. See Iowa Code Ann. §554.1102 cmt. 2 (course of dealings, usage of trade or course of performance are material in determining a reasonable time). Furthermore, the Uniform Commercial Code relies upon course of dealings between the parties to help interpret their conduct. Iowa Code §554.1205(1). Thus, all relevant circumstances, including custom and practice of the parties, must be considered in determining what constitutes a reasonable time under section 554.2201(2).

Generally, the determination of the reasonableness of particular conduct is a jury question. See Pirelli-Armstrong Tire Co. v. Reynolds, 562 N.W.2d 433, 436 (Iowa 1997); see also Harvey v. Great Atl. & Pac. Tea Co., 388 F.2d 123, 125 (5th Cir. 1968) (passing judgment on the reasonableness of conduct of the parties must be accomplished in light of all the circumstances of the case and should rarely be disposed of by summary judgment). Thus, the reasonableness of time between an oral contract and a subsequent written confirmation is ordinarily a question of fact for the jury. Mortgageamerica Corp. v. American Nat'l Bank, 651 S.W.2d 851, 856 (Tex. Ct. App. 1983); Schiavi Mobile Homes, Inc. v. Gagne, 510 A.2d 236, 238 (Me. 1986) (reasonableness of parties' time for action is a question of fact). It is only in rare cases that a determination of the reasonableness of conduct should be decided by summary adjudication. Harvey, 388 F.2d at 125. Summary judgment is appropriate only when the evidence is so one-sided that a party must prevail at trial as a matter of law. Ridgeway v. Union County Comm'rs, 775 F. Supp. 1105, 1109 (S.D. Ohio 1991).

There are a host of cases from other jurisdictions which have considered the question of what constitutes a reasonable time under the written confirmation exception of the Uniform Commercial Code. See Gestetner Corp. v. Case Equip. Co., 815 F.2d 806, 810 (1st Cir. 1987) (roughly five-month delay reasonable in light of merchants 'relationship and parties' immediate action under contract following oral agreement); Serna, Inc. v. Harman, 742 F.2d 186, 189 (5th Cir. 1984) (three and one-half month delay reasonable in light of the parties' interaction in the interim, and

3. Now §1-302(b).—Ed.

non-fluctuating prices, thus no prejudice); Cargill, Inc. v. Stafford, 553 F.2d 1222, 1224 (10th Cir. 1977) (less than one-month delay unreasonable despite misdirection of confirmation due to mistaken addressing); Starry Constr. Co. v. Murphy Oil USA, Inc., 785 F. Supp. 1356, 1362-63 (D. Minn. 1992) (six-month delay for confirmation of modification order for additional oil unreasonable as a matter of law in light of Persian Gulf War, thus increased prices and demand); Rockland Indus., Inc. v. Frank Kasmir Assoc., 470 F. Supp. 1176, 1179 (N.D. Tex. 1979) (letter sent eight months after alleged oral agreement for two-year continuity agreement unreasonable in light of lack of evidence supporting reasonableness of delay); Yung, 263 N.W.2d at 820 (six-month delay in confirming oral agreement delivered one day prior to last possible day of delivery unreasonable); Azevedo, 471 P.2d at 666 (ten-week delay reasonable in light of immediate performance by both parties following oral agreement); Lish v. Compton, 547 P.2d 223, 226-27 (Utah 1976) (twelve-day delay "outside the ambit which fair-minded persons could conclude to be reasonable" in light of volatile price market and lack of excuse for delay other than casual delay). Most of these cases, however, were decided after a trial on the merits and cannot be used to establish a standard or time period as a matter of law. Only a few courts have decided the question as a matter of law under the facts of the case. Compare *Starry,* 785 F. Supp. At 1362-63 (granting summary judgment), and *Lish,* 547 P.2d at 226-27 (removing claim from jury's consideration), with Barron v. Edwards, 45 Mich. App. 210, 206 N.W.2d 508, 511 (1973) (remanding for further development of facts, summary judgment improper). However, these cases do not establish a strict principle to apply in this case. The resolution of each case depends upon the particular facts and circumstances.

In this case, the district court relied upon the large amount of the sale, volatile market conditions, and lack of an explanation by St. Ansgar Mills for failing to send the written confirmation to Duane in determining St. Ansgar Mills acted unreasonably as a matter of law in delaying delivery of the written confirmation until August 10, 1996. Volatile market conditions, combined with a large sale price, would normally narrow the window of reasonable time under section 554.2201(2). However, they are not the only factors to consider. Other relevant factors which must also be considered in this case reveal the parties had developed a custom or practice to delay delivery of the confirmation. The parties also maintained a long-time amicable business relationship and had engaged in many other similar business transactions without incident. There is also evidence to infer St. Ansgar Mills did not suspect John's failure to follow his customary practice in July of stopping by the business was a concern at the time. These factors reveal a genuine dispute over the reasonableness of the delay in delivering the written confirmation, and make the resolution of the issue appropriate for the jury. Moreover, conduct is not rendered unreasonable solely because the acting party had no particular explanation for not pursuing different conduct, or regretted not pursuing different conduct in retrospect. The reasonableness of conduct is determined by the facts and circumstances existing at the time.

Considering our principles governing summary adjudication and the need to resolve the legal issue by considering the particular facts and circumstances of each case, we conclude the trial court erred by granting summary judgment. We reverse and remand the case for further proceedings.

Article 2A (Leases) has a Statute of Frauds similar to §2-201, though the amount of the lease must be at least $1,000 before a writing is required, and the writing must describe the leased goods and the lease term in order to satisfy the Statute. See §2A-201. There is no "merchant's confirmation" subsection in this section because (according to the Official Comment) that situation does not often arise in lease transactions.

There is no Statute of Frauds for international sales under the CISG unless the country adopting the Convention stipulates that its own Statute of Frauds will apply. See Articles 11 and 96.

PROBLEM 9

The city manager of Thebes, Utah, which is world-famous for its beautiful desert golf course, orally ordered a huge water tank to be made in the shape of a golf ball on a tee from Tanks of America, Inc. The price was agreed to be $30,000, and the city sent Tanks a down payment check for $3,000, signed by the city comptroller and marked "Tank" on the memo line. Tanks of America built the tank and was in the process of painting "City of Thebes" on the side when a representative of a newly elected city administration called and said that the new administration considered the contract unenforceable. Answer these questions:

(a) Does the check satisfy §2-201(1)? Where is the *quantity?* See Beautiful Jewellers Private, Ltd. v. Tiffany & Co., 2007 WL 867202 (S.D.N.Y. 2007).

(b) What legal argument can Tanks of America make based on §§2-201(3)(a) and 2-201(3)(c)? Does the City of Thebes have a good response to the §2-201(3)(c) argument? See W.I. Snyder Corp. v. Caracciolo, 373 Pa. Super. 486, 541 A.2d 775 (1988).

(c) If the city had promised to sign a written contract but had never gotten around to doing so, can promissory estoppel or equitable estoppel be used to circumvent §2-201? Reread §1-103(b), and see Allen M. Campbell Co.

v. Virginia Metal Indus., Inc., 708 F.2d 930 (4th Cir. 1983); Amber Chemical, Inc. v. Reilly Industries, Inc., 2007 WL 512410 (E.D. Cal. 2007).

(d) Would it make a difference if the city had a Vender Buying Agreement posted on its website, which disclaimed the effectiveness of any oral agreements with the city? See Grandoe Corp. v. Gander Mt. Co., 761 F.3d 876 (8th Cir. 2014).

PROBLEM 10

Tomorrow, Inc. (a computer software company), and Systems Unlimited (a company specializing in advising other companies how to maximize their computer operations) entered into a written joint venture contract by which Tomorrow, Inc., promised to design and sell to Systems Unlimited software that would enable the latter's customers to receive engineering drawings by phone. The parties agreed that their arrangement was "non-exclusive" (meaning either was allowed to deal with other buyers and sellers of the same product). The contract described the obligations of the parties in some detail and stated that the contract would terminate after two years unless renewed. In fact, after working with Tomorrow, Inc., for only six months, Systems Unlimited decided it could develop its own software more cheaply than buying it from Tomorrow, Inc., so it faxed a letter to the latter stating that their contract was at an end. Systems Unlimited declined to purchase any further software. Tomorrow, Inc., which had incurred substantial startup costs in developing the software for this contract, was astounded and promptly filed suit. Systems Unlimited sought refuge in the Statute of Frauds, arguing that the contract signed by the parties stated no quantity. Does §2-201(1) always require a specific quantity? Look at the statutory language very carefully. Compare §2-306. See also Advent Sys. Ltd. v. Unisys Corp., 925 F.2d 670 (3d Cir. 1991); White & Summers §3-4, at 97 n.12.

PROBLEM 11

Sued by a trusting seller after refusing delivery, Renege Retail's president calmly testifies that he had agreed to buy the goods, but the parties never put anything in writing. Without a signed contract, memorandum, confirmation or any other writing, is Renege Retail off the hook? See §2-201(3)(b).

At both the federal and state level, statutes have been enacted to facilitate electronic commerce as civilization moves from the world of paper into cyberspace. The states acted first, with many of them adopting the Uniform Electronic Transactions Act (UETA), and the federal government followed with the similar Electronic Signatures in Global and National Commerce Act, 15 U.S.C. §7001, commonly known as "E-Sign." The latter statute applies only in jurisdictions not adopting UETA. As of 2015, Illinois, New York, and Washington were the only states not to have enacted UETA. Both statutes should be in your statute book. White and Summers have a clear discussion of the statutes. See White & Summers §§1-3, 3-9.

The basic thrust of these statutes is to allow electronic records in most commercial transactions even if other statutes, such as the Statute of Frauds, require a writing or a written signature. With certain exceptions (utility cut-off notices, notices of default, repossession, foreclosure and eviction, insurance cancellations, etc.), almost all legal communications by the parties to a transaction can now be accomplished electronically. The statutes provide only that electronic communications may meet the requirements for a writing or signature. They do not provide substantive rules, such as how contracts are formed or what terms will be included in the contract. See Alliance Laundry Systems, LLC v. Thyssenkrupp Materials, NA, 570 F. Supp. 2d 1061 (E.D. Wis. 2008).

J.B.B. Investment Partners, Ltd. v. Fair

Court of Appeals of California, 2015
232 Cal. App. 4th 974, 182 Cal. Rptr. 3d 154

Kline, P.J.

R. Thomas Fair (Fair), Bronco RE Corporation (Bronco), BRE Boulevard LLC (Boulevard) and BRE Cameron Creek LLC (Cameron; collectively, defendants) appeal from a judgment following the trial court's grant of a motion pursuant to Code of Civil Procedure section 664.6 by J.B.B. Investment Partners, Ltd. (JBB) and Silvester Rabic (collectively, plaintiffs) to enforce a settlement between plaintiffs and defendants. The trial court found that Fair's printed name at the end of his e-mail where he had agreed to settlement terms set forth in an e-mail from plaintiffs' counsel was an "electronic signature" within the meaning of California's Uniform Electronic Transactions Act (Civ. Code, §1633.1 et seq.) (UETA) and what the trial court referred to as the "common law of contract" or "contract case law."

Subsequently, plaintiffs requested attorney fees pursuant to a provision in an arbitration agreement between the parties. The trial court found plaintiffs to be the prevailing parties but denied the request for attorney fees because the matter never proceeded to arbitration and plaintiffs had failed to show that any contract authorized fees in the present litigation. Plaintiffs appeal from the order denying them attorney fees. . . .

Background

Fair, an attorney and inactive member of the California State Bar, is the founder of Bronco, and Bronco is the managing member of Boulevard and Cameron. Boulevard and Cameron are Arizona limited liability companies formed in 2007, and they each own apartment units in Arizona.

Rabic is a non-attorney individual investor. JBB is a limited partnership based in Atherton, California, and Jonathan B. Buckheit is the general partner of JBB. In late 2007 and early 2008, JBB invested $150,000 and Rabic invested $100,000 in Boulevard and Cameron, and both became members of the limited liability companies.

Subsequently, plaintiffs asserted that they had discovered defendants had made various fraudulent representations and omissions; the parties attempted to negotiate a settlement of those disputes. One of plaintiffs' attorneys, Giacomo A. Russo, sent a settlement offer by e-mail on July 4, 2013 (the July 4 offer). The July 4 offer addressed to Fair stated, among other things, that Fair "must represent and warrant (and provide full disclosure that) no monies moved illegally from one entity to another[,]" that he must enter a stipulated judgment for $350,000, and that "[a]ll litigation would be stayed pending the payments" made by Fair.

The last section in the July 4 offer provided, in relevant part: "The Settlement paperwork would be drafted in parallel with your full disclosure of all documents and all information as required by the first paragraph hereof; it is a material inducement to this settlement that you demonstrate that there is, IN FACT, not a Ponzi or Ponzi-like scheme at work here and the misrepresentations and non-disclosures of which [plaintiffs] have complained are, in fact, simply at most a negligent mistake on your part—as was the failure to get signatures on the ACTUAL FULL-LENGTH LLC Operating Agreements AND at that time, you disclosed that 'priority' really has NO MEANING in the context of the 'priority payments' which they were promised." This section concluded with the following final paragraph: "WE require a YES or NO on this proposal; you need to say 'I accept.' . . . Anything less shifts all focus to the litigation and to the Court Orders we will seek now as well as in the future as well as the subpoenas we will serve. . . . It is now up to you to decide whether you would rather resolve this amicably or not. Let me know your decision." The July 4 offer and e-mail did not have a signature line or signature block, and the e-mail sent to Fair did not include any signature by Rabic and Buckheit.

Rabic and Buckheit both declared that they authorized Russo to make a final settlement offer to defendants and that they signed the July 4 offer on July 5, 2013. Fair declared that he did not receive the July 4 offer with the signatures of Rabic and Buckheit until August 6, 2013.

At 10:17 A.M., on July 5, Fair sent the following e-mail to Russo from his cell phone: "[Russo], the facts will not in any way support the theory in your e-mail. I believe in Cameron. So I agree. Tom [F]air[.]" Russo and another attorney for plaintiffs, Ansel J. Halliburton, responded that they did not understand Fair's e-mail and could not determine whether he was accepting or rejecting the settlement offer. Halliburton stated, "Please be unambiguous, because I am about to file the complaint and *ex parte* papers unless we hear an unambiguous acceptance."

Plaintiffs filed their lawsuit against defendants just before noon on July 5, 2013. Counsel for plaintiffs sent an e-mail at 12:25 P.M. to Fair, which attached the filed complaint and copies of an *ex parte* application for, among other things, expedited discovery.

At 1:02 P.M., on July 5, Fair sent Halliburton the following message from his cell phone: "I said I agree. Took wording right from [Russo's] e-mail. I agree[.]" At 1:04 P.M., Fair left the following voicemail message for Halliburton: "Hey Ansel, I just got your e-mail and your—and your voice-mail. I was playing golf on a course that doesn't allow cell phones. So anyway, I thought I was quite clear on my first response, I made another response by e-mail, I said I agree with [plaintiffs' counsel's] terms. You know? So, that's it."

Shortly thereafter, at 1:07 P.M., Fair sent a message from his cell phone to Halliburton and stated: "I do not believe you gave proper notice. Also I agreed with your terms. You should mot [*sic*] have filed. We clearly have an agreement. [T]om [F]air[.]" At 1:36 P.M., Fair sent by his cell phone the following message to Russo: "Filing does not obviate agreement/acceptance. Pls acknowledge[.]"

Russo responded to Fair at 1:53 P.M. with the following e-mail: "This confirms full agreement; I will work on the formal settlement paperwork which will conform to the settlement agreement made today based on the 10 numbered paragraphs below with no admission of liability or wrongdoing by anyone. I will seek to get that settlement paperwork to you for review by Monday with the goal of getting it all finalized and signed next week. The settlement is otherwise binding under [Code of Civil Procedure section] 664.6. . . ."

Two minutes later, at 1:55 P.M., Fair sent the following text message to Halliburton: "I have accepted by phone and [e-mail]. Stop proceeding. I said accept which is same as 'agreed.' You must stop and you must tell the court we have an agreement." Fair also left a voice message for Russo at some unknown time on July 5, 2013.

On July 11, 2103, Halliburton sent to Fair a draft of the final settlement (July 11 writing). This writing specified the names of plaintiffs and defendants and stated that the agreement was between them. It advised that the agreement could be "signed and delivered by facsimile" and that it could be "electronically signed" by each party. It also included signature blocks for each party.

On July 16, Halliburton sent an e-mail to Fair stating that he had not heard from Fair. In a separate e-mail, he indicated that he would get [Rabic's] signature once he received Fair's signature and a check for the initial payment. A few days later, on July 18, Fair responded that he expected to have comments for Halliburton by the following day and that his attorney had been out of town but was returning that day.

Fair sent an e-mail to Halliburton on July 19, and stated that he had spoken to his accounting firm and the firm suggested a call or a meeting to discuss "the unfounded suspicions and allegations of your clients." Halliburton, responding by e-mail on that same day, said, in relevant part: "It's a good thing we have a settlement, then; let's put pen to paper and close it." "We are not going to stay anything until we have a signed deal."

Fair did not sign the July 11 writing.

On August 6, 2013, plaintiffs filed a motion pursuant to Code of Civil Procedure section 664.6 to enforce the settlement. In support of the motion, plaintiffs submitted the various e-mail, voicemail, and text communications between Fair and their attorneys on July 5, 2013. They also submitted the videotaped deposition of Fair. At his deposition, Fair acknowledged that he deliberately typed his name when his name appeared at the end of an e-mail message and that his phone or software did not automatically place his name there. When asked whether he thought he had an agreement when he sent his e-mail on July 5, 2013, Fair replied: "I thought I had agreed to terms that were suggested in an e-mail during the morning, which had become moot, but I didn't know it until I reviewed all of this stuff later. I didn't read that long e-mail of the morning until maybe a couple of days later." When asked why he believed the agreement had become moot, he answered: "Because they did file, and I changed my mind."

In opposition to the motion, Fair filed, among other things, his declaration. He maintained that Russo's statements that he would contact other investors or go to newspapers to disclose "frivolous allegations" against defendants had made him fearful in July 2013. Additionally, he had not slept during the first week of July 2013 because he had to check repeatedly on his ailing mother. He noted that he was not represented by counsel when he sent the messages to plaintiffs and their counsel and his messages "were sent under severe duress, in particular because [p]laintiffs' counsel was barraging me with phone calls and e-mails, and demanding the names of the other investors in the [limited liability companies]—threatening to contact the other members of the [limited liability companies]." He insisted that his e-mail messages on July 5, 2013, simply signified his good faith and desire to work out a settlement. He asserted that there was no meeting of the minds and that he had not read more than the first paragraph of the

July 5 offer. He declared that he did not consider his name on the e-mail to be a signature to a settlement agreement. He maintained that he did not sign important legal documents, such as settlement agreements, without the assistance of counsel.

The superior court held a hearing on plaintiffs' motion to enforce the settlement under Code of Civil Procedure section 664.6 on October 18, 2013. At its commencement the court advised counsel that it "had some real problems with Mr. Fair's declaration as far as credibility, I'll tell you that at the start," and the court felt entitled to take "the comparative credibility of the witnesses" into account. Indicating credibility was not the question, counsel for Fair answered that the central issue was whether there was an electronic signature that satisfied the requirements of UETA. Fair's printed name did not satisfy UETA, counsel insisted, because the July 7 offer did not authorize an electronic signature, nor did any other communication between the parties prior to the draft final settlement Halliburton sent Fair on July 11, which did state that it could be "electronically signed." Counsel for the plaintiffs agreed that whether Fair's printed name complied with UETA was the chief issue but maintained that it clearly complied, resting on the provision of UETA which states that "[i]f a law requires a signature, an electronic record satisfies the law." (§1633.7, subd. (d).)

As will be seen, although the court wondered how plaintiff's counsel can "be here asking me under [Code of Civil Procedure section] 664.6 to enforce a settlement that you didn't yourself think was binding" when counsel sent Fair a draft final settlement on July 11, the court adopted plaintiffs' contention.

It is clear from the court's explanation of its granting of plaintiffs' motion to enforce the settlement that it conceived the chief issue to be whether there was a meeting of the minds as to the terms of the settlement, which is a factual question. As the court stated, "I think that the preponderance of the evidence that's in front of me here is that there was an agreement struck on July 5th. It may not have been reduced to the more formal writing signed by both sides, but I think that there was more likely than not Mr. Fair's agreement that the matter had been settled according to what the e-mails and the voice mails said. The reason why I'm not stating that in more detail is that would have to go into things that are under seal, under the sealing order, but I think that is the case. And so that makes a commercial sense in my view because we have sophisticated parties on both sides."

The trial court continued: "You have at that point in time the equivalent of a situation of yesteryear that would have been not electronic where a lot of deals were done on backs of envelopes and maybe at that point down the road the parties would get lawyers to draft a more formal agreement. But there is older case law that recognizes that a preliminary scribbling like that, if it entailed out all of the materials [*sic*], it was good enough for a contract to warrant to be in place [*sic*]."

The trial court concluded that there was a settlement and that Fair was not under duress but "knew exactly what he was doing." The court emphasized that "[t]here is no coercion or duress here." The court said it was following the federal case law and finding that the e-mail coupled with the corroborating voicemail qualified as an "electronic signature" under UETA. The court added that, even if it should not follow the guidance of the federal case law, it found "that the communications that went back and forth electronically are tantamount to today's modern version of telegrams that used to go back and forth in the commercial world and follow the old cases." The court certified its ruling for interlocutory appeal under Code of Civil Procedure section 166.1.

On November 1, 2013, the trial court filed its judgment granting plaintiffs' motion to enforce the settlement. The court found that plaintiffs proved by a preponderance of the evidence that Fair, on behalf of all defendants, "did more likely than not agree to a settlement with counsel for [p]laintiffs by e-mail on July 5, 2013, confirmed by later e-mails and voicemails." The court found that the e-mails "include electronic signatures within the meaning of" UETA and "[p]laintiffs provided sufficient evidence that Mr. Fair deliberately typed his name at the end of those e-mails. Those e-mails were further corroborated with later e-mails and voicemails, as reflected in the record." The court added, "even without resort to the UETA and instead under contract common law, Mr. Fair's July 5 communications constitute acceptances of [p]laintiffs' offer to settle. The court follows the reasoning set out in Lamle v. Mattel [(Fed. Cir. 2005) 394 F.3d 1355 (*Lamle*)], as well as prior California cases finding typed names on telegrams sufficient to form a contract. . . ." The court concluded: "As stated on the record, the court is of the opinion that there are 'substantial grounds for difference of opinion' regarding the court's resolution of this motion" and "there is no California case law to guide the court's opinion, and the appellate court should look into this matter." The court retained jurisdiction to enforce the judgment.

On November 7, 2013, the trial court entered final judgment in favor of plaintiffs and ordered defendants to pay plaintiffs $362,810.96. Defendants filed a timely notice of appeal. . . .

C. *Fair's Printed Signature Was Not an "Electronic Signature" Within the Meaning of UETA*

At the hearing on the motion pursuant to Code of Civil Procedure section 664.6, counsel for the parties both stated that, in their view, the dispositive issue was whether Fair's printed signature on the e-mail responding to Russo's July 4 e-mail constituted an "electronic signature" within the meaning of UETA. According to counsel for Fair, Civil Code section 1633.7 is "really the meat of all of the issues that we are going to get to today, whether there was a signature or not, and I think that that is driving everything."

Section 1633.7 provides that "(a) A record or signature may not be denied legal effect of enforceability solely because it is in electronic form. (b) A contract may not be denied legal effect or enforceability solely because an electronic record was used in its formation. (c) If a law requires a record to be in writing, an electronic record satisfies the law. (d) *If a law requires a signature, an electronic signature satisfies the law.*" (Italics added.)

Counsel's argument that Fair's printed name was not an "electronic signature" within the meaning of the statute consisted of three points: First, that in subsequent e-mails to Fair, Russo, and Halliburton repeatedly indicated that there can be no genuine settlement until a formal agreement had been drafted "signed and delivered by facsimile" and thereafter "electronically signed." As Halliburton stated in one of his subsequent e-mails, " 'Once we have your signature [on a final agreement] we will have the other plaintiff come in for his signature and we can be done.' " Counsel maintained, in other words, that there was no meeting of the minds as to a final agreement at the time Fair printed his name on the e-mail offer. Second, counsel argued the July 4 settlement offer indicated that, if the parties agreed, "there will be no litigation; everything would be stayed," so that, even if there was a settlement agreement, by filing the complaint on July 5 the plaintiffs either withdrew or breached it. Finally, counsel pointed out that, at the time Fair printed his name on the July 4 e-mail, none of the correspondence between the parties authorized the use of an electronic signature, such as that later included in the July 11 writing.

Counsel for plaintiffs agreed that section 1633.7 was controlling, but maintained that it definitively established that Fair's printed name was an "electronic signature" within the meaning of the UETA. Given the simplicity of the pertinent provision—"If the law requires a signature, an electronic signature satisfies the law" (§1633.7, subd. (d).)—counsel for plaintiffs felt there was no need to consult the case law or any other legal authority.

After the court pointed out that by proffering the July 11 draft settlement his clients did not act as if they had an executed final settlement after Fair printed his name on the July 4 offer, the court asked plaintiffs' counsel "how can you be here asking me under [Code of Civil Procedure] 664.6 to enforce the settlement that you didn't yourself think was binding." Counsel answered that plaintiffs "are not seeking to enforce that July 11th document; we are seeking to enforce the July 5th agreement which has ten clear, precise numbered paragraphs; that's what we are seeking to enforce. We are seeking to enforce against all of the defendants because doing anything else wouldn't make any sense," and "Mr. Fair controls all of those defendants. So when he says, 'I agree; I accept' he is speaking for all of them, clearly by context."

The trial court adopted plaintiffs' view. Finding that, a preponderance of the evidence showed that an agreement was struck on July 5th, the court reasoned that it was "more likely than not Mr. Fair's agreement that the matter had been settled according to what the e-mails and the voicemails said." Referring to section 1633.7, the court also found that "the e-mails in this case coupled with the corroborating voice mail can qualify as an electronic signature under the statute."

The views of counsel to the contrary notwithstanding, section 1633.7 is not the provision of UETA most applicable to the motion before the court, and the court's determination that Fair's printed name was an enforceable "electronic signature" was manifestly erroneous.

Under UETA (§1633.1 et seq.), which became effective January 1, 2000, an electronic record satisfies the requirement that a record be in writing (§1633.7, subd. (c)), and an electronic signature satisfies the requirement that the writing be signed (§1633.7, subd. (d)). "An electronic record or electronic signature is attributable to a person if it was the act of the person. The act of the person may be shown in any manner. . . ." (§1633.9, subd. (a); see also Ni v. Slocum (2011) 196 Cal. App. 4th 1636, 1647, 127 Cal. Rptr. 3d 620 ["the Legislature has, through these provisions, expressed general approval of the use of electronic signatures in commercial and governmental transactions"].)

Section 1633.2, subdivision (h) defines an "'[e]lectronic signature'" as "an electronic sound, symbol, or process attached to or logically associated with an electronic record and executed or adopted by a person with the intent to sign the electronic record." UETA applies, however, only when the parties consent to conduct the transaction by electronic means. (§1633.5, subd. (b).) "Whether the parties agree to conduct a transaction by electronic means is determined from the context and surrounding circumstances, including the parties' conduct. . . ." (Ibid.) "A party that agrees to conduct a transaction by electronic means may refuse to conduct other transactions by electronic means. . . ." (§1633.5, subd. (c).)

Nothing in the record indicates counsel or the court were aware of any of the provisions of UETA just cited, other than section 1633.7, or appreciated the complexity of the statutory scheme. Focusing only on section 1633.7, the court appears to have simplistically assumed, as did counsel for plaintiffs, that because Fair admitted at deposition that the signature was his, and the signature was indisputably electronic, the printed signature on the July 4 offer was therefore an "electronic signature" within the meaning of UETA.

We agree that a printed name or some other symbol might, under specific circumstances, be a signature under UETA and might satisfy the even more rigorous requirements under Code of Civil Procedure section 664.6. Courts in other jurisdictions that have adopted a version of UETA have concluded that names typed at the end of e-mails *can* be electronic signatures. (See, e.g., Preston Law Firm, L.L.C. v. Mariner Health Care Mgmt. Co. (5th

Cir. 2010) 622 F.3d 384, 391 [affirming that "[e]mails can qualify as the signed writings needed to form contracts" under Louisiana's UETA]; Cloud Corp. v. Hasbro, Inc. (7th Cir. 2002) 314 F.3d 289, 295-296 [holding that "the sender's name on an e-mail satisfies the signature requirement of the [Illinois] statute of frauds" and noting that it would be a valid signature under the federal Electronic Signatures in Global and National Commerce Act as well]; see also *Lamle,* supra, 394 F.3d at p. 1362 [e-mail was written prior to the enactment of California's UETA, but court opined that inclusion of individual's name on e-mail would be valid signature under California's UETA]; Gillis v. Wells Fargo Bank (E.D. Mich. 2012) 875 F. Supp. 2d 728, 734-735 [signed letter and e-mail messages that included the sender's salutation were sufficient to satisfy statute of frauds].)

The trial court's analysis was incomplete. Attributing the name on an e-mail to a particular person and determining that the printed name is "[t]he act of [this] person" is a necessary prerequisite but is insufficient, by itself, to establish that it is an "electronic signature." (§1633.9, subd. (a).) As counsel and the court seemed unaware, UETA defines the term "electronic signature." Subdivision (h) of section 1633.2 states that "'[e]lectronic signature' means an electronic sound, symbol, or process attached to or logically associated with an electronic record and *executed or adopted by a person with the intent to sign the electronic record.*" (Italics added. See also Cal. Civ. Jury Inst. No. 380 [party suing to enforce an agreement formalized by electronic means must prove "based on the context and surrounding circumstances, including the conduct of the parties, that the parties agreed to use (e.g., e-mail) to formalize their agreement"].)

We have independently reviewed the record and conclude, as a matter of law, that it does not show that Fair printed his name at the end of his e-mail with any intent to formalize an electronic transaction. Indeed, substantial evidence in the record refutes such a finding.

"Whether the parties agree to conduct a transaction by electronic means is determined from the context and surrounding circumstances, including the parties' conduct. . . ." (§1633.5, subd. (b).) The absence of an explicit agreement to conduct the transaction by electronic means is not determinative; however, it is a relevant factor to consider.

Plaintiffs argue that the July 4 offer expressly contemplated acceptance by electronic means as it specified that Fair needed to say, "I accept." They also cite Fair's testimony that he personally typed his name and that he refused to sign the July 11 writing because he had simply changed his mind. Plaintiffs' evidence is legally insufficient.

The exchange of e-mail messages shows that the parties clearly agreed to negotiate the terms of the settlement by e-mail, but plaintiffs did not demonstrate, as they must (§1633.5, subd. (b)), that the parties ever agreed to conduct transactions by electronic means or that Fair intended with his printed name at the end of his e-mail to sign electronically the July 4 offer. The July 4 offer did not contain any statement indicating that the parties agreed to enter into a final settlement by electronic means. The plain language of the July 4 offer made it clear that no signature was being requested as the offer included no signature line or signature block, contained no signature by any of the plaintiffs, and advised that future paperwork was forthcoming. The last section in the July 4 offer provided that "[t]he Settlement paperwork would be drafted. . . ." Additionally, this section advised that plaintiffs require "a YES or NO on this proposal; you need to say 'I accept[.]' " The last sentence in this section stated: "Let me know your decision." None of these sentences in the July 4 offer supports a conclusion that the parties agreed that Fair's agreement to the proposal was an agreement to sign a legally binding settlement. (See *Sully-Miller,* supra, 103 Cal. App. 4th at p. 37, 126 Cal. Rptr. 2d 400 [a party's signature added "to a document that does not call for it" is not a signed writing under Code of Civil Procedure section 664.6 because "[a] party's signature fails to convey" knowledge and express consent "unless it is contained in a document that was clearly intended by that party to be a binding settlement agreement"]; Powell v. City of Newton (2010) 364 N.C. 562, 703 S.E.2d 723, 727-728 [applying North Carolina's UETA and concluding that the parties did not agree to the use of electronic signatures "[i]n light of the express indication by [one party] that [the other party] should sign and forward the [agreements]"].) Moreover, Fair's subsequent voicemail and text messages from his cell phone did not indicate that he intended for his e-mail to be a signature to the electronic record as he simply stated that he "agree[d] with" or accepted Russo's terms.

Subsequently, the statements of plaintiffs' counsel provided further evidence that no party considered the July 4 offer attached to the July 5 e-mail as a final document requiring a signature. Russo stated that Fair's response "confirms full agreement" and he promised to work "on the formal settlement paperwork" and "get the settlement paperwork" for Fair's review "with the goal of getting it all finalized and signed next week." He added that the "settlement is otherwise binding under" Code of Civil Procedure section 664.6, but the settlement could not be binding without all of the parties' signatures. Halliburton sent Fair an e-mail on July 19, 2013, stating in relevant part: "It's a good thing we have a settlement, then; let's put pen to paper and close it." "We are not going to stay anything until we have a signed deal."

In contrast to the July 4 offer, the July 11 writing included a signature line at the end of the settlement agreement. Additionally, it specified that an electronic signature could be used. The July 11 writing provided: "This Settlement Agreement may be signed and delivered by facsimile and in counter-parts. It may also be electronically signed by each of the Parties through the use of EchoSign, DocuSign, or such other commercially available electronic signature software which results in confirmed signatures delivered electronically to each of the Parties, which shall be treated as an original as though in-signed by officers or other duly authorized representatives of each Party." No similar language was in the July 4 offer and, as already stressed, the July 4 offer did not indicate that a printed name at the bottom of an e-mail would be an electronic signature.

Accordingly, we conclude that the evidence in the record is as a matter of law insufficient to establish that Fair signed electronically a settlement agreement. Since Fair's printed name was not a signature under UETA, the trial court erred when it concluded that Fair's printed name at the bottom of the e-mail satisfied the strict signature requirements under Code of Civil Procedure section 664.6. . . .

DISPOSITION

The order enforcing the settlement pursuant to Code of Civil Procedure section 664.6 is reversed and the judgment is vacated. We affirm the order denying plaintiffs' attorney fees. Defendants are awarded costs in both appeals.

QUESTIONS

Is this case right in your opinion? Fair? What does the result suggest that you, as an attorney practicing in a jurisdiction adopting this result, should tell your clients to do when contracting through e-mails?

There are a number of unsettled issues as to electronic signatures. Both of the statutes mentioned before the case require that if a consumer is involved, he or she must have *agreed* to electronic disclosures, but it is unclear exactly what this means. The federal statute is broader, requiring that there be *electronic agreement or confirmation of agreement,* and this agreement must be "affirmative"; 15 U.S.C. §7001(c)(1)(C)(ii). This means that the consumer must have agreed electronically to receive electronic records or have confirmed this consent electronically. UETA is less clear about this, though Comment 4 to §5 indicates that the consumer's agreement to receive electronic communications must be actual and not imposed unconscionably as part of the fine print in a written contract.

There is also no consensus on what electronic communication means. Is it sufficient for the required information to be posted on a website (the so-called "Come and Get It" notice) that the consumer must periodically access (which, of course, most won't do) to keep informed? In the 1990s,

AOL posted rate changes only on its website, making customers agree that this was sufficient notice of any hike in the rate, only to back down when 19 attorneys general objected that the practice was unfair and deceptive. What about e-mail notification? Must it be highlighted in such a way that the consumer will recognize its importance and not delete it as "spam"? If the consumer has switched e-mail addresses, then what? Must the sender do something with bounced-back messages? These matters and others will have to await judicial determination. For a summary of the consumer issues and suggested resolutions, see Jean Braucher, Rent-Seeking and Risk-Fixing in the New Statutory Law of Electronic Commerce: Difficulties in Moving Consumer Protection Online, 2001 Wis. L. Rev. 527.

II. THE PAROL EVIDENCE RULE

Read §2-202 and its Official Comment.

PROBLEM 12

Lawyers for Swinging Singles Magazine negotiated for an entire year with Space Age Aircraft Co. to obtain a contract for the construction of a special Swinging Singles airplane. (The plane was to be black and silver, with the Swinging Singles emblem painted on the tail; it was to contain a living room, bed chamber, swimming pool, hot tub, and a dance floor.) The resulting 30-page contract also contained a *merger* clause, stating that all prior negotiations were merged into the written contract that contained all the terms of the agreement. The contract was signed by both parties. Does §2-202 bar the introduction of evidence of the following?

(a) An alleged precontract agreement that Space Age would provide free flying lessons to Hi Handsome, president of Swinging Singles, Inc.? The contract says nothing about this. See the test found in Official Comment 3 to §2-202.

(b) An alleged precontract agreement that Swinging Singles could use the plane for two months, and if they did not like it, they could return it for a full refund?

To aid in the construction of agreements, the Code looks to the customs within the industry (called *usage of trade*), the parties' past contacts with one another (called *course of dealing*), and the parties' behavior during the existence of the contract in question (called *course of performance*) and presumes that these matters are relevant in fleshing out the express terms of the contract. See Nanakuli Paving & Rock Co. v. Shell Oil Co., 664 F.2d 772 (9th Cir. 1981) (good discussion of these terms). Read §1-303 carefully. Their relationship to §2-202 is explored in the case below.

Columbia Nitrogen Corp. v. Royster Co.

United States Court of Appeals, Fourth Circuit, 1971
451 F.2d 3

Butzner, J. . . .

I

Royster manufactures and markets mixed fertilizers, the principal components of which are nitrogen, phosphate and potash. Columbia is primarily a producer of nitrogen, although it manufactures some mixed fertilizer. For several years Royster had been a major purchaser of Columbia's products, but Columbia had never been a significant customer of Royster. In the fall of 1966, Royster constructed a facility which enabled it to produce more phosphate than it needed in its own operations. After extensive negotiations, the companies executed a contract for Royster's sale of a minimum of 31,000 tons of phosphate each year for three years to Columbia, with an option to extend the term. The contract stated the price per ton, subject to an escalation clause dependent on production costs.

Phosphate prices soon plunged precipitously. Unable to resell the phosphate at a competitive price, Columbia ordered only part of the scheduled tonnage. At Columbia's request, Royster lowered its price for diammonium phosphate on shipments for three months in 1967, but specified that subsequent shipments would be at the original contract price. Even with this concession, Royster's price was still substantially above the market. As a result, Columbia ordered less than a tenth of the phosphate Royster was to ship in the first contract year. When pressed by Royster, Columbia offered to take the phosphate at the current market price and resell it without brokerage fee. Royster, however, insisted on the contract price. When Columbia refused delivery, Royster sold the unaccepted phosphate for Columbia's account at a price substantially below the contract price.

II

Columbia assigns error to the pretrial ruling of the district court excluding all evidence on usage of the trade and course of dealing between the parties. It offered the testimony of witnesses with long experience in the trade that because of uncertain crop and weather conditions, farming practices, and government agricultural programs, express price and quantity terms in contracts for materials in the mixed fertilizer industry are mere projections to be adjusted according to market forces.[4]

Columbia also offered proof of its business dealings with Royster over the six-year period preceding the phosphate contract. Since Columbia had not been a significant purchaser of Royster's products, these dealings were almost exclusively nitrogen sales to Royster or exchanges of stock carried in inventory. The pattern which emerges, Columbia claimed, is one of repeated and substantial deviation from the stated amount or price, including four instances where Royster took none of the goods for which it had contracted. Columbia offered proof that the total variance amounted to more than $500,000 in reduced sales. This experience, a Columbia officer offered to testify, formed the basis of an understanding on which he depended in conducting negotiations with Royster.

The district court held that the evidence should be excluded. It ruled that "custom and usage or course of dealing are not admissible to contradict the express, plain, unambiguous language of a valid written contract, which by virtue of its detail negates the proposition that the contract is open to variances in its terms. . . ."

A number of Virginia cases have held that extrinsic evidence may not be received to explain or supplement a written contract unless the court finds the writing is ambiguous. E.g., Mathieson Alkali Works v. Virginia Banner Coal Corp., 147 Va. 125, 136 S.E. 673 (1927). This rule, however, has been

4. Typical of the proffered testimony are the following excerpts: "The contracts generally entered into between buyer and seller of materials has always been, in my opinion, construed to be the buyer's best estimate of his anticipated requirements for a given period of time. It is well known in our industry that weather conditions, farming practices, government farm control programs, change requirements from time to time. And therefore allowances were always made to meet these circumstances as they arose." "Tonnage requirements fluctuate greatly, and that is one reason that the contracts are not considered as binding as most contracts are, because the buyer normally would buy on historical basis, but his normal average use would be per annum of any given material. Now that can be affected very decidedly by adverse weather conditions such as a drought, or a flood, or maybe governmental programs which we have been faced with for many, many years, seed grain programs. They pay the farmer not to plant. If he doesn't plant, he doesn't use the fertilizer. When the contracts are made, we do not know of all these contingencies and what they are going to be. So the contract is made for what is considered a fair estimate of his requirements. And, the contract is considered binding to the extent, on him morally, that if he uses the tonnage that he will execute the contract in good faith as the buyer. . . ." "I have never heard of a contract of this type being enforced legally. . . ." Well, it undoubtedly sounds ridiculous to people from other industries, but there is a very definite, several very definite reasons why the fertilizer business is always operated under what we call gentlemen's agreements. . . . "The custom in the fertilizer industry is that the seller either meets the competitive situation or releases the buyer from it upon proof that he can buy it at that price. . . . [T]hey will either have the option of meeting it or releasing him from taking additional tonnage or holding him to that price. . . ." And this custom exists "regardless of the contractual provisions." "[T]he custom was that [these contracts] were not worth the cost of the paper they were printed on."

changed by the Uniform Commercial Code which Virginia has adopted. The Code expressly states that it "shall be liberally construed and applied to promote its underlying purposes and policies," which include "the expansion of commercial practices through custom, usage and agreement of the parties. . . ." §1-102.[5] The importance of usage of trade and course of dealing between the parties is shown by §2-202, which authorizes their use to explain or supplement a contract. The official comment states this section rejects the old rule that evidence of course of dealing or usage of trade can be introduced only when the contract is ambiguous. And the Virginia commentators, noting that "[t]his section reflects a more liberal approach to the introduction of parol evidence . . . than has been followed in Virginia," express the opinion that *Mathieson,* supra, and similar Virginia cases no longer should be followed. §2-202, Va. Comment. See also Portsmouth Gas Co. v. Shebar, 209 Va. 250, 253 n.1, 163 S.E.2d 205, 208 n.1 (1968) (dictum). We hold, therefore, that a finding of ambiguity is not necessary for the admission of extrinsic evidence about the usage of the trade and the parties' course of dealing.

We turn next to Royster's claim that Columbia's evidence was properly excluded because it was inconsistent with the express terms of their agreement. There can be no doubt that the Uniform Commercial Code restates the well-established rule that evidence of usage of trade and course of dealing should be excluded whenever it cannot be reasonably construed as consistent with the terms of the contract. Division of Triple T Service, Inc. v. Mobil Oil Corp., 60 Misc. 2d 720, 304 N.Y.S.2d 191, 203 (1969), *aff'd mem.*, 311 N.Y.S.2d 961 (1970). Royster argues that the evidence should be excluded as inconsistent because the contract contains detailed provisions regarding the base price, escalation, minimum tonnage, and delivery schedules. The argument is based on the premise that because a contract appears on its face to be complete, evidence of course of dealing and usage of trade should be excluded. We believe, however, that neither the language nor the policy of the Code supports such a broad exclusionary rule. Section 2-202 expressly allows evidence of course of dealing or usage of trade to explain or supplement terms intended by the parties as a final expression of their agreement. When this section is read in light of §1-205(4),[6] it is clear that the test of admissibility is not whether the contract appears on its face to be complete in every detail, but whether the proffered evidence of course of dealing and trade usage reasonably can be construed as consistent with the express terms of the agreement.

The proffered testimony sought to establish that because of changing weather conditions, farming practices, and government agricultural

5. Now §1-103(a)(2).—Ed.
6. Now §1-303(e).—Ed.

programs, dealers adjusted prices, quantities, and delivery schedules to reflect declining market conditions. For the following reasons it is reasonable to construe this evidence as consistent with the express terms of the contract:

The contract does not expressly state that course of dealing and usage of trade cannot be used to explain or supplement the written contract.

The contract is silent about adjusting prices and quantities to reflect a declining market. It neither permits nor prohibits adjustment, and this neutrality provides a fitting occasion for recourse to usage of trade and prior dealing to supplement the contract and explain its terms.

Minimum tonnages and additional quantities are expressed in terms of "Products Supplied Under Contract." Significantly, they are not expressed as just "Products" or as "Products Purchased Under Contract." The description used by the parties is consistent with the proffered testimony.

Finally, the default clause of the contract refers only to the failure of the buyer to pay for delivered phosphate. During the contract negotiations, Columbia rejected a Royster proposal for liquidated damages of $10 for each ton Columbia declined to accept. On the other hand, Royster rejected a Columbia proposal for a clause that tied the price to the market by obligating Royster to conform its price to offers Columbia received from other phosphate producers. The parties, having rejected both proposals, failed to state any consequences of Columbia's refusal to take delivery—the kind of default Royster alleges in this case. Royster insists that we span this hiatus by applying the general law of contracts permitting recovery of damages upon the buyer's refusal to take delivery according to the written provisions of the contract. This solution is not what the Uniform Commercial Code prescribes. Before allowing damages, a court must first determine whether the buyer has in fact defaulted. It must do this by supplementing and explaining the agreement with evidence of trade usage and course of dealing that is consistent with the contract's express terms; §§1-205(4),[7] 2-202. Faithful adherence to this mandate reflects the reality of the marketplace and avoids the overly legalistic interpretations which the Code seeks to abolish.

Royster also contends that Columbia's proffered testimony was properly rejected because it dealt with mutual willingness of buyer and seller to adjust contract terms to the market. Columbia, Royster protests, seeks unilateral adjustment. This argument misses the point. What Columbia seeks to show is a practice of mutual adjustments so prevalent in the industry and in prior dealings between the parties that it formed a part of the agreement governing this transaction. It is not insisting on a unilateral right to modify the contract.

7. Now §1-303(e).—Ed.

Nor can we accept Royster's contention that the testimony should be excluded under the contract clause:

> No verbal understanding will be recognized by either party hereto; this contract expresses all the terms and conditions of the agreement, shall be signed in duplicate, and shall not become operative until approved in writing by the Seller.

Course of dealing and trade usage are not synonymous with verbal understandings, terms and conditions. Section 2-202 draws a distinction between supplementing a written contract by consistent additional terms and supplementing it by course of dealing or usage of trade. Evidence of additional terms must be excluded when "the court finds the writing to have been intended also as a complete and exclusive statement of the terms of the agreement." Significantly, no similar limitation is placed on the introduction of evidence of course of dealing or usage of trade. Indeed the official comment notes that course of dealing and usage of trade, unless carefully negated, are admissible to supplement the terms of any writing, and that contracts are to be read on the assumption that these elements were taken for granted when the document was phrased. Since the Code assigns course of dealing and trade usage unique and important roles, they should not be conclusively rejected by reading them into stereotyped language that makes no specific reference to them. Cf. Provident Tradesmen's Bank & Trust Co. v. Pemberton, 196 Pa. Super. 180, 173 A.2d 780 (1961). Indeed, the Code's official commentators urge that overly simplistic and overly legalistic interpretation of a contract should be shunned.[8]

We conclude therefore that Columbia's evidence about course of dealing and usage of trade should have been admitted. Its exclusion requires that the judgment against Columbia must be set aside and the case retried. . . .

QUESTION

Sometimes the contract will specify that no usage of trade shall be relevant to modify the agreement, but courts are suspicious of such clauses. See Wells Fargo Bank v. Cherryland Mall Ltd. P'ship, 812 N.W.2d 799, 810

8. Referring to the general provisions about course of dealing and trade usage, §1-205, Comment 1 states:

> This Act rejects both the "lay dictionary" and the "conveyancer's" reading of a commercial agreement. Instead the meaning of the agreement of the parties is to be determined by the language used by them and by their action, read and interpreted in the light of commercial practices and other surrounding circumstances. The measure and background for interpretation are set by the commercial context, which may explain and supplement even the language of a formal or final writing.

(Mich. Ct. App. 2011) (admitting usage of trade to explain an undefined technical term despite a clause in the parties' agreement stating in capital letters that "no trade practice . . . shall be used to contradict, vary, supplement or modify any term of this guaranty agreement"); U.C.C. §2-202 cmt. 2 (indicating that usage of trade and course of dealing become an element of the meaning of the words used in the parties' agreement "[u]nless *carefully* negated") (emphasis added).

III. OFFER AND ACCEPTANCE

A. General Rules

Common law rules of contract formation had too many technicalities and formalities to suit the drafters of the UCC. If, as often happens, people in business create contracts on a very informal basis, the Code does all it can to give legal meaning to the resulting deal.[9] Read §§2-204, 2-205, and 2-206 before doing the next Problems.

PROBLEM 13

Mastervoice TV ordered 20,000 fuses from the Generous Electric Company, the order stating "Reply by return mail." Instead of a formal reply, Generous immediately shipped the fuses. When the fuses arrived, they were found to be defective. Mastervoice, which had to procure substitute goods elsewhere to meet its production schedule, sued Generous Electric for breach of warranty. Answer these questions:

(a) At what moment was the contract formed?

(b) Can Generous make this defense: "There was never any contract since our alleged act of acceptance (the shipment of *defective* goods) did not comply with requirements of Mastervoice's offer (which contemplated only shipment of *good* fuses)"?

(c) Instead of the above, assume that when Generous received the order it discovered that it no longer manufactured the type of fuses Mastervoice wanted, but that it did carry a very similar type of fuse that it believed would

9. Article 2 specifically addresses the issue of when a binding contract to sell is formed at an *auction.* See §2-328; Callimanopulos v. Christie's Inc., 621 F. Supp. 2d 127 (S.D.N.Y. 2009) (holding that §2-328 authorized auctioneer to reopen bidding, after gavel had fallen on $3 million bid for painting, because auctioneer had not seen another bidder raise her paddle).

suit Mastervoice's needs. The shipping manager for Generous was unable to get through to the relevant people at Mastervoice, so in the end Generous shipped the slightly different fuses along with a cover note saying, "These are similar to the fuses you ordered, but may not be right for you. If they are not suitable, we will gladly take them back without charge." Is Generous now in breach because it shipped nonconforming goods? See §2-206(1)(b).

PROBLEM 14

For years P. Dreamer had wanted a Rolls Royce Silver Shadow with burgundy-colored trim (he had seen one in an ad and salivated). He saw one on the lot of Posh Motors. After Dreamer had dickered loud and long over the terms with Paula Posh, president of Posh Motors, they finally agreed on a price. Dreamer said he wanted to clear the deal with his wife before signing anything, so Posh promised she would hold the car for the Dreamers until the next day at noon. When Mr. and Mrs. Dreamer arrived at the dealership the next morning, the car was gone. Posh had made a better deal with another buyer. Do the Dreamers have a good cause of action? See §2-205.

B. The Battle of the Forms

> As long as there are merchant buyers and sellers of goods, there will be forms with self-serving boilerplate. And as long as the transactions proceed without incident—which may be after a long while and many sales—their forms will pass like ships on a foggy sea. But when at last one of their transactions sinks, each retreats to the shelter of its favorable terms to claim victory.

Dependable Component Supply, Inc. v. Pace Electronics Inc., 772 So. 2d 582 (Fla. App. 2000).

The "battle of the forms" is a much litigated problem that arises from two sources: (1) the business practices of either negotiating deals orally and then exchanging printed forms that no one reads until a dispute arises, or dealing at arm's length with non-matching purchase orders and acknowledgments, and (2) the complexities of §2-207 and its Official Comment.

Subsection (1) to §2-207 is meant to reverse the common law rule that an *acceptance* that was not the *mirror image* of the offer was (impliedly) both a rejection and a counteroffer. Under §2-207(1), an acceptance adding new terms creates a contract based on the original offer, unless the *acceptance* very clearly states otherwise. As to what happens to the additional terms, see §2-207(2).

If, in spite of all logic and business judgment, the parties exchange documents that cannot be reconciled so as to produce a contract, no contract results, and either party may, on discovering this mishap, back out of the deal *if* that party acts prior to the beginning of performance. If performance has begun (with the parties wrongly believing a contract exists), subsection (3) of §2-207 regulates the ensuing mess.

Judges recognize that §2-207 is not a model of clarity: "Referred to as 'a murky bit of prose,' and 'like the amphibious tank that was originally designed to fight in the swamps, but was ultimately sent to fight in the desert,' §2-207 is a defiant, lurking demon patiently waiting to condemn its interpreters to the depths of despair. Nevertheless, §2-207 must and can be conquered." Reaction Molding Technologies, Inc. v. General Electric Co., 585 F. Supp. 1097, 1104 (E.D. Pa. 1984).

PROBLEM 15

The Magic Carpet Co. had a long and profitable business relationship with Alibaba Carpet Manufacturers of Bagdad, Illinois. Fifty-five times Alibaba had sold carpets to Magic Carpet. Each sale was carried out in the following manner. A partner of Magic Carpet telephoned Alibaba's order department and ordered a certain quantity of carpet at the price listed in Alibaba's catalog. After each oral order was placed, the credit department was consulted to determine if Magic Carpet was paid up. Then, if the credit was okay, the order department of Alibaba typed the information from the order on one of its printed acknowledgment forms, each of which had the following paragraph printed conspicuously on its face:

> The acceptance of your order is subject to all of the terms and conditions on the face and reverse side hereof, all of which are accepted by buyer; it supersedes buyer's order form, if any. It shall become a contract either (a) when signed and delivered by buyer to seller and accepted in writing by seller, or (b) at seller's option, when buyer shall have given to seller specification of assortments, delivery dates, shipping instructions, or instructions to bill and hold as to all or any part of the merchandise herein described, or when buyer has received delivery of the whole or any part thereof, or when buyer has otherwise assented to the terms and conditions hereof.

The provisions on the reverse side of the form provided, among other things, that the seller disclaimed all warranties, express or implied. Each acknowledgment form was signed by an employee in Alibaba's order department and mailed to the Magic Carpet Co. Shortly thereafter, the carpet was shipped. Magic Carpet always received the acknowledgment form before the carpet. They placed each form in a file, accepted delivery of the carpet, and paid for it promptly. On the 56th sale, the accepted and paid-for carpet proved to be nonconforming. Magic Carpet sued Alibaba for breach of warranty. Alibaba replied that its form disclaimed all warranties.

Answer these questions:

(a) Was a contract formed between Magic Carpet and Alibaba? See §2-207(1).

(b) Was the disclaimer of warranties part of that contract? See §2-207(2).

Problem 15 is based on Dorton v. Collins & Aikman Corp., 453 F.2d 1161 (6th Cir. 1972), where the court clearly and competently sorted through the complexities of §2-207. White and Summers discuss §2-207 exhaustively. See White & Summers §2-3.

Diamond Fruit Growers, Inc. v. Krack Corp.

United States Court of Appeals, Ninth Circuit, 1986
794 F.2d 1440

WIGGINS, J.

Metal-Matic, Inc. (Metal-Matic) appeals from judgment entered after a jury verdict in favor of Krack Corporation (Krack) on Krack's third-party complaint against Metal-Matic. Metal-Matic also appeals from the district court's denial of its motion for judgment n.o.v. We have jurisdiction under 28 U.S.C. §1291 (1982) and affirm.

Facts and Proceedings Below

Krack is a manufacturer of cooling units that contain steel tubing it purchases from outside suppliers. Metal-Matic is one of Krack's tubing suppliers. At the time this dispute arose, Metal-Matic had been supplying tubing to Krack for about ten years. The parties followed the same course of dealing during the entire ten years. At the beginning of each year, Krack sent a blanket purchase order to Metal-Matic stating how much tubing Krack would need for the year. Then, throughout the year as Krack needed tubing, it sent release purchase orders to Metal-Matic requesting that tubing be shipped. Metal-Matic responded to Krack's release purchase orders by sending Krack an acknowledgment form and then shipping the tubing.

Metal-Matic's acknowledgment form disclaimed all liability for consequential damages and limited Metal-Matic's liability for defects in the tubing to refund of the purchase price or replacement or repair of the tubing. As one would expect, these terms were not contained in Krack's purchase order. The following statement was printed on Metal-Matic's form: "Metal-Matic, Inc.'s acceptance of purchaser's offer or its offer to purchaser is hereby expressly made conditional to purchaser's acceptance of the terms and provisions of the acknowledgment form." This statement and the disclaimer of liability were on the back of the acknowledgment form. However, printed at the bottom of the front of the form in boldface capitals was the following statement: "SEE REVERSE SIDE FOR TERMS AND CONDITIONS OF SALE."

On at least one occasion during the ten-year relationship between Metal-Matic and Krack, Allen Zver, Krack's purchasing manager, discussed the limitations of warranty and disclaimer of liability terms contained in Metal-Matic's acknowledgment form with Robert Van Krevelen, Executive Vice President of Metal-Matic. Zver told Van Krevelen that Krack objected to the terms and tried to convince him to change them, but Van Krevelen refused to do so. After the discussions, Krack continued to accept and pay for tubing from Metal-Matic.

In February 1981, Krack sold one of its cooling units to Diamond Fruit Growers, Inc. (Diamond) in Oregon, and in September 1981, Diamond installed the unit in a controlled-atmosphere warehouse. In January 1982, the unit began leaking ammonia from a cooling coil made of steel tubing.

After Diamond discovered that ammonia was leaking into the warehouse, Joseph Smith, the engineer who had been responsible for building Diamond's controlled-atmosphere warehouses, was called in to find the source of the leak. Smith testified that he found a pinhole leak in the cooling coil of the Krack cooling unit. Smith inspected the coil while it was still inside the unit. He last inspected the coil on April 23, 1982. The coil then sat in a hall at Diamond's warehouse until May 1984, when John Myers inspected the coil for Metal-Matic.

Myers cut the defective tubing out of the unit and took it to his office. At his office, he did more cutting on the tubing. After Myers inspected the tubing, it was also inspected by Bruce Wong for Diamond and Paul Irish for Krack.

Diamond sued Krack to recover the loss in value of fruit that it was forced to remove from the storage room as a result of the leak. Krack in turn brought a third-party complaint against Metal-Matic and Van Huffel Tube Corporation (Van Huffel), another of its tubing suppliers, seeking contribution or indemnity in the event it was held liable to Diamond. At the close of the evidence, both Metal-Matic and Van Huffel moved for a directed verdict on the third-party complaint. The court granted Van Huffel's motion based on evidence that the failed tubing was not manufactured by Van Huffel. The court denied Metal-Matic's motion.

The jury returned a verdict in favor of Diamond against Krack. It then found that Krack was entitled to contribution from Metal-Matic for thirty percent of Diamond's damages. Metal-Matic moved for judgment n.o.v. The court denied that motion and entered judgment on the jury verdict.

Metal-Matic raises two grounds for reversal. First, Metal-Matic contends that as part of its contract with Krack, it disclaimed all liability for consequential damages and specifically limited its liability for defects in the tubing to refund of the purchase price or replacement or repair of the tubing. Second, Metal-Matic asserts that the evidence does not support a finding that it manufactured the tubing in which the leak developed or that it caused the leak. We address each of these contentions in turn. . . .

DISCUSSION

A. METAL-MATIC'S DISCLAIMER OF LIABILITY FOR CONSEQUENTIAL DAMAGES

If the contract between Metal-Matic and Krack contains Metal-Matic's disclaimer of liability, Metal-Matic is not liable to indemnify Krack for part of Diamond's damages. Therefore, the principal issue before us on this appeal is whether Metal-Matic's disclaimer of liability became part of the contract between these parties.

Relying on Uniform Commercial Code (U.C.C.) §2-207, Or. Rev. Stat. §72.2070 (1985), Krack argues that Metal-Matic's disclaimer did not become part of the contract. Metal-Matic, on the other hand, argues that §2-207 is inapplicable to this case because the parties discussed the disclaimer, and Krack assented to it.

Krack is correct in its assertion that §2-207 applies to this case. One intended application of §2-207 is to commercial transactions in which the parties exchange printed purchase order and acknowledgment forms. See U.C.C. §2-207 comment 1. The drafters of the UCC recognized that "[b]ecause the [purchase order and acknowledgment] forms are oriented to the thinking of the respective drafting parties, the terms contained in them often do not correspond." Id. Section 2-207 is an attempt to provide rules of contract formation in such cases. In this case, Krack and Metal-Matic exchanged purchase order and acknowledgment forms that contained different or additional terms. This, then, is a typical §2-207 situation. The fact that the parties discussed the terms of their contract after they exchanged their forms does not put this case outside §2-207. See 3 R. Duesenburg & L. King, Sales and Bulk Transfers under the Uniform Commercial Code (Bender's U.C.C. Service) §3.05[2] (1986). Section 2-207 provides rules of contract formation in cases such as this one in which the parties exchange forms but do not agree on all the terms of their contract.

A brief summary of §2-207 is necessary to an understanding of its application to this case. Section 2-207 changes the common law's mirror-image rule for transactions that fall within article 2 of the U.C.C. At common law, an acceptance that varies the terms of the offer is a counteroffer and operates as a rejection of the original offer. See Idaho Power Co. v. Westinghouse Electric Corp., 596 F.2d 924, 926 (9th Cir. 1979). If the offeror goes ahead with the contract after receiving the counteroffer, his performance is an acceptance of the terms of the counteroffer. See C. Itoh & Co. v. Jordan International Co., 552 F.2d 1228, 1236 (7th Cir. 1977); J. White & R. Summers, Handbook of the Law Under the Uniform Commercial Code §1-2 at 34 (2d ed. 1980).

Generally §2-207(1) "converts a common law counteroffer into an acceptance even though it states additional or different terms." Idaho Power, 596 F.2d at 926; see U.C.C. §2-207(1). The only requirement under §2-207(1) is that the responding form contain a definite and seasonable expression of acceptance. The terms of the responding form that correspond to the offer constitute the contract. Under §2-207(2), the additional terms of the responding form become proposals for additions to the contract. Between merchants the additional terms become part of the contract unless the offer is specifically limited to its terms, the offeror objects to the additional terms, or the additional terms materially alter the terms of the offer. U.C.C. §2-207(2); see J. White & R. Summers, §1-2 at 32.

However, §2-207(1) is subject to a proviso. If a definite and seasonable expression of acceptance expressly conditions acceptance on the offeror's assent to additional or different terms contained therein, the parties' differing forms do not result in a contract unless the offeror assents to the additional terms. See J. White & R. Summers, §1-2 at 32-33. If the offeror assents, the parties have a contract and the additional terms are a part of that contract. If, however, the offeror does not assent, but the parties proceed with the transaction as if they have a contract, their performance results in formation of a contract. UCC §2-207(3). In that case, the terms of the contract are those on which the parties' forms agree plus any terms supplied by the UCC. Id.; see Boise Cascade Corp. v. Etsco, Ltd., 39 U.C.C. Rep. Serv. (Callaghan) 410, 414 (D. Or. 1984); J. White & R. Summers, §1-2 at 34.

In this case, Metal-Matic expressly conditioned its acceptance on Krack's assent to the additional terms contained in Metal-Matic's acknowledgment form. That form tracks the language of the §2-207(1) proviso, stating that "Metal-Matic, Inc.'s acceptance . . . is hereby *expressly made conditional* to purchaser's acceptance of the terms and provisions of the acknowledgment form" (emphasis added). See *C. Itoh & Co.*, 552 F.2d at 1235. Therefore, we must determine whether Krack assented to Metal-Matic's limitation of liability term.

Metal-Matic argues that Krack did assent to the limitation of liability term. This argument is based on the discussions between Zver for Krack and Van Krevelen for Metal-Matic. Some time during the ten-year relationship between the companies, these two men discussed Krack's objections to the warranty and liability limitation terms in Metal-Matic's acknowledgment form. Krack attempted to persuade Metal-Matic to change its forms, but Metal-Matic refused to do so. After the discussions, the companies continued to do business as in the past. Metal-Matic contends that Krack assented to the limitation of liability term when it continued to accept and pay for tubing after Metal-Matic insisted that the contract contain its terms.

To address Metal-Matic's argument, we must determine what constitutes assent to additional or different terms for purposes of §2-207(1). The parties have not directed us to any cases that analyze this question and our research has revealed none. We therefore look to the language and structure of §2-207 and to the purposes behind that section to determine the correct standard.

One of the principles underlying §2-207 is neutrality. If possible, the section should be interpreted so as to give neither party to a contract an advantage simply because it happened to send the first or in some cases the last form. See J. White & R. Summers, §1-2 at 26-27. Section 2-207 accomplishes this result in part by doing away with the common law's "last shot" rule. See 3 R. Duesenberg & L. King, §3.05[1][a][iii] at 3-73. At common law, the offeree/counterofferor gets all of its terms simply because it fired the last shot in the exchange of forms. Section 2-207(3) does away with this result by giving neither party the terms it attempted to impose unilaterally on the other. See id. at 3-71. Instead, all of the terms on which the parties' forms do not agree drop out, and the UCC supplies the missing terms.

Generally, this result is fair because both parties are responsible for the ambiguity in their contract. The parties could have negotiated a contract and agreed on its terms, but for whatever reason failed to do so. Therefore, neither party should get its terms. See 3 R. Duesenberg & L. King §3.05[2] at 3-88. However, as White and Summers point out, resort to §2-207(3) will often work to the disadvantage of the seller because he will "wish to undertake less responsibility for the quality of his goods than the Code imposes or else wish to limit his damages liability more narrowly than would the Code." J. White & R. Summers §1-2 at 34. Nevertheless, White and Summers recommend that §2-207(3) be applied in such cases. Id. We agree. Application of §2-207(3) is more equitable than giving one party its terms simply because it sent the last form. Further, the terms imposed by the code are presumably equitable and consistent with public policy because they are statutorily imposed. See 3 R. Duesenberg & L. King, §3.05 [2] at 3-88.

With these principles in mind, we turn now to Metal-Matic's argument that Krack assented to the disclaimer when it continued to accept and pay for tubing once Metal-Matic indicated that it was willing to sell tubing only if its warranty and liability terms were part of the contract. Metal-Matic's argument is appealing. Sound policy supports permitting a seller to control the terms on which it will sell its products, especially in a case in which the seller has indicated both in writing and orally that those terms are the only terms on which it is willing to sell the product. Nevertheless, we reject Metal-Matic's argument because we find that these considerations are outweighed by the public policy reflected by Oregon's enactment of the UCC.

If we were to accept Metal-Matic's argument, we would reinstate to some extent the common law's last shot rule. To illustrate, assume that the parties in this case had sent the same forms but in the reverse order and that Krack's form contained terms stating that Metal-Matic is liable for all consequential damages and conditioning acceptance on Metal-Matic's assent to Krack's terms. Assume also that Metal-Matic objected to Krack's terms but Krack refused to change them and that the parties continued with their transaction anyway. If we applied Metal-Matic's argument in that case, we would find that Krack's term was part of the contract because Metal-Matic continued to ship tubing to Krack after Krack reaffirmed that it would purchase tubing only if Metal-Matic were liable for consequential damages. Thus, the result would turn on which party sent the last form, and would therefore be inconsistent with §2-207's purpose of doing away with the last shot rule.

That result is avoided by requiring a specific and unequivocal expression of assent on the part of the offeror when the offeree conditions its acceptance on assent to additional or different terms. If the offeror does not give specific and unequivocal assent but the parties act as if they have a contract, the provisions of §2-207(3) apply to fill in the terms of the contract. Application of §2-207(3) is appropriate in that situation because by going ahead with the transaction without resolving their dispute, both parties are responsible for introducing ambiguity into the contract. Further, in a case such as this one, requiring the seller to assume more liability than it intends is not altogether inappropriate. The seller is most responsible for the ambiguity because it inserts a term in its form that requires assent to additional terms and then does not enforce that requirement. If the seller truly does not want to be bound unless the buyer assents to its terms, it can protect itself by not shipping until it obtains that assent. See *C. Itoh & Co.*, 552 F.2d at 1238.

We hold that because Krack's conduct did not indicate unequivocally that Krack intended to assent to Metal-Matic's terms, that conduct did not amount to the assent contemplated by §2-207(1). See 3 R. Duesenberg & L. King, §3.05[1][a][iii] at 3-74. . . .

The jury verdict is supported by the evidence and consistent with the UCC. Therefore, the district court did not err in denying Metal-Matic's motion for a judgment n.o.v.

PROBLEM 16

Would the following clause in the seller's acknowledgment to the buyer's order form be a material alteration under §2-207(2)(b): "Any disputes concerning this contract shall be subject to binding arbitration"? See ICC Chemical Corp. v. Vitol, Inc., 425 Fed. Appx. 57 (2d Cir. 2011) (arbitration clause not a material alteration where sometimes used in chemical industry sales); In re Cotton Yarn Antitrust Litigation, 505 F.3d 274 (4th Cir. 2007) (not a material alteration where arbitration was the usage of trade in the textile industry). How about a forum-selection clause providing that all disputes must be litigated in the seller's state? See Ridgelawn Cemetery Assn. v. Grantie Resources Corp., 2017 WL 3783401 (N.D. Ind. 2017).

If these clauses were in an acknowledgment of an international sale of goods to which CISG applies, would it be valid? See Article 19; Filanto, S.p.A. v. Chilewich Intl. Corp., 789 F. Supp. 1229 (S.D.N.Y. 1992), *appeal dismissed,* 984 F.2d 58 (2d Cir. 1993); Comment, The U.N. Convention on the International Sale of Goods and the "Battle of the Forms," 13 Fordham Intl. L.J. 649 (1990).

Bayway Refining Co. v. Oxygenated Marketing and Trading A.G.

United States Court of Appeals, Second Circuit, 2000
215 F.3d 219

Jacobs, Circuit Judge.

Plaintiff-appellee Bayway Refining Company ("Bayway") paid federal excise tax on a petroleum transaction, as the Internal Revenue Code requires a petroleum dealer to do in a sale to a buyer who has not procured an exemption under the applicable tax provision. In this diversity suit against the buyer, Oxygenated Marketing and Trading A.G. ("OMT"), Bayway seeks to recover the amount of the tax it paid. One question in this "battle of the forms" contract case is whether, under N.Y. U.C.C. §2-207(2)(b) (McKinney 1993), a contract term allocating liability to the buyer for an excise tax is an additional term presumed to have been accepted (as the seller contends) or (as the buyer contends) a material alteration presumed to have been rejected. The United States District Court for the Southern District of New York (McKenna, J.) granted summary judgment in favor of the seller, Bayway.

We conclude that, in the circumstances presented: (i) the party opposing the inclusion of an additional term under §2-207(2)(b) bears the burden of proving that the term amounts to a material alteration; (ii) the district court properly granted summary judgment in favor of the seller, because the additional term here did not materially alter the contract; and (iii) the district court properly admitted evidence of custom and practice in the industry despite the fact that it was first proffered in the moving party's reply papers. Accordingly, we affirm.

Background

Bayway and OMT are in the business of buying and selling petroleum products. Bayway contracted to sell to OMT 60,000 barrels of a gasoline blendstock called Methyl Tertiary Butyl Ether ("MTBE"). On February 12,

1998, OMT faxed Bayway a confirmation letter, which operated as the offer, and which stated in pertinent part:

> We are pleased to confirm the details of our purchase from you of MTBE as agreed between Mr. Ben Basil and Roger Ertle on [February 12, 1998.] . . .
>
> This confirmation constitutes the entire contract and represents our understanding of the terms and conditions of our agreement. . . . Any apparent discrepancies or omissions should be brought to our notice within the next two working days.

Bayway faxed its confirmation to OMT the next day. That document, which operated as the acceptance, stated in pertinent part: "We are pleased to confirm the following verbal agreement concluded on February 12, 1998 with your company. This document cancels and supersedes any correspondence in relation to this transaction." Bayway's acceptance then set forth the parties, price, amount and delivery terms, and undertook to incorporate the company's standard terms:

> Notwithstanding any other provision of this agreement, where not in conflict with the foregoing, the terms and conditions as set forth in Bayway Refining Company's General Terms and Conditions dated March 01, 1994 along with Bayway's Marine Provisions are hereby incorporated in full by reference in this contract.

The Bayway General Terms and Conditions were not transmitted with Bayway's fax, but Paragraph 10 of its General Terms and Conditions states:

> Buyer shall pay seller the amount of any federal, state and local excise, gross receipts, import, motor fuel, superfund and spill taxes and all other federal, state and local taxes however designated, other than taxes on income, paid or incurred by seller directly or indirectly with respect to the oil or product sold hereunder and/or on the value thereof.

This term is referenced as the "Tax Clause."

OMT did not object to Bayway's acceptance or to the incorporation of its General Terms and Conditions (which included the Tax Clause). OMT accepted delivery of the MTBE barrels on March 22, 1998.

The Internal Revenue Code imposes an excise tax, payable by the seller, on the sale of gasoline blendstocks such as MTBE "to any person who is not registered under [26 U.S.C. §4101]" for a tax exemption. 26 U.S.C.A. §4081(a)(1)(A)(iv) (West Supp. 1999). After delivery, Bayway learned that OMT was not registered with the Internal Revenue Service for the tax exemption. The transaction therefore created a tax liability of $464,035.12, which Bayway paid.

Invoking the Tax Clause, Bayway demanded payment of the $464,035.12 in taxes in addition to the purchase price of the MTBE. OMT denied that it had agreed to assume the tax liability and refused to pay that invoice item. In response, Bayway filed this diversity suit alleging breach of contract by OMT.

Upon Bayway's motion for summary judgment, the district court held that the Tax Clause was properly incorporated into the contract. See Tosco Corp. v. Oxygenated Mktg. & Trading A.G., No. 98 Civ. 4695, 1999 WL 328342, at *3-*6 (S.D.N.Y. May 24, 1999). The fact that Bayway had failed to attach a copy of the General Terms and Conditions was irrelevant because OMT could have obtained a copy if it had asked for one. See id. at *3. The court then analyzed the contract-forming documents, applied the "battle of the forms" framework set forth in N.Y. U.C.C. §2-207(2), and concluded that OMT failed to carry its burden of proving that the Tax Clause materially altered the contract. See id. at *3-*6. The court therefore granted summary judgment in favor of Bayway.

Discussion

On appeal, OMT argues (i) that it succeeded in raising genuine issues of fact as to whether the Tax Clause materially altered the Bayway/OMT contract and (ii) that the evidence of custom and practice in the industry, upon which the grant of summary judgment turns, was improperly admitted. . . .

We affirm for substantially the reasons stated by the district court. We hold—on an issue of first impression in this Court—that in a "battle of the forms" case governed by N.Y. U.C.C. §2-207(2)(b), the party opposing the inclusion of an additional term bears the burden of proving that the term works a material alteration. Viewing the evidence in the light most favorable to OMT, we conclude that OMT failed to shoulder that burden. Finally, we hold that the district court properly admitted the evidence concerning industry custom and practice.

A. Battle of the Forms

Bayway argued its motion for summary judgment on the basis of New York law, presumably because one of the additional terms incorporated by its acceptance is a New York choice-of-law provision. OMT has accepted New York law as controlling for purposes of Bayway's summary judgment motion. [The court quoted §2-207(1) and (2).]

It was undisputed in the district court that Bayway's confirmation fax is effective to form a contract as an acceptance—even though it stated or referenced additional terms (including the Tax Clause)—because it was not made expressly conditional on OMT's assent to the additional terms. See id. §2-207(1). Therefore, under §2-207(2), the Tax Clause is a proposal for an addition to the contract. See id. §2-207(2). The parties are both merchants within the meaning of the U.C.C. See id. §2-104(1), (3). The Tax Clause therefore is presumed to become part of the contract unless one of the three enumerated exceptions applies. See id. §2-207(2). In its defense, OMT invokes the "material alteration" exception of §2-207(2)(b).

1. *Burden of Proof*

The allocation of the burden of proof under this exception to §2-207(2) is a question of New York law, see United States v. McCombs, 30 F.3d 310, 323-24 (2d Cir. 1994) (holding that, under the Erie doctrine, federal courts sitting in diversity apply the forum state's law concerning burdens of proof), and is answered in the text of New York's U.C.C. §2-207(2). Section 2-207(2)(b) is an exception to the general rule of §2-207(2) that additional terms become part of a contract between merchants. That general rule is in the nature of a presumption concerning the intent of the contracting parties. Thus if neither party introduced any evidence, the Tax Clause would, by the plain language of §2-207(2), become part of the contract. To implement that presumption, the burden of proving the materiality of the alteration must fall on the party that opposes inclusion. Accordingly, we hold that under §2-207(2)(b) the party opposing the inclusion of additional terms shoulders the burden of proof. In so doing, we join almost every court to have considered this issue. [Citations omitted.]

2. *Materiality and Per Se Materiality*

A material alteration is one that would "result in surprise or *hardship* if incorporated without express awareness by the other party." N.Y. U.C.C. §2-207 cmt. 4 (emphasis added).

Certain additional terms are deemed material as a matter of law. For example, an arbitration clause is per se a material alteration in New York because New York law requires an express agreement to commit disputes to arbitration. See Marlene Indus. v. Carnac Textiles, Inc., 45 N.Y.2d 327, 408 N.Y.S.2d 410, 413, 380 N.E.2d 239 (1978); see also N.Y. U.C.C. §2-207 cmt. 4 (listing as examples of per se material alterations, inter alia, waivers of warranties of merchantability or fitness for a particular purpose and clauses granting the seller the power to cancel upon the buyer's failure to meet any invoice). OMT characterizes the Tax Clause as a broad-ranging indemnity clause, and analogizes it to these per se material alterations. We reject the analogy. The Tax Clause allocates responsibility for the tax payable on a specific sale of goods. See Union Carbide Corp. v. Oscar Mayer Foods Corp., 947 F.2d 1333, 1335, 1337 (7th Cir. 1991) (distinguishing between "open-ended" tax liability, which is a material alteration, from "responsibility for taxes shown on an individual invoice," which is not). And unlike an arbitration clause, which waives a range of rights that are solicitously protected, the Tax Clause is limited, discrete and the subject of no special protection. Unable to show that the Tax Clause is a material alteration per se, OMT must prove that in this case the Tax Clause resulted in surprise or hardship.[10]

3. Surprise

Surprise, within the meaning of the material alteration exception of §2-207(2)(b), has both the subjective element of what a party actually knew and the objective element of what a party should have known. See American Ins. Co. v. El Paso Pipe & Supply Co., 978 F.2d 1185, 1191 (10th Cir. 1992); In re Chateaugay, 162 B.R. at 956-57. A profession of surprise and raised eyebrows are not enough: "[C]onclusory statements, conjecture, or speculation by the party resisting the motion will not defeat summary judgment." Kulak v. City of New York, 88 F.3d 63, 71 (2d Cir. 1996). To carry the burden of showing surprise, a party must establish that, under the circumstances, it cannot be presumed that a reasonable merchant would have consented to the additional term. See Union Carbide, 947 F.2d at 1336.

OMT has adduced evidence that the Tax Clause came as an amazement to OMT's executives, who described the term's incorporation as "contract by ambush" and a "sl[e]ight-of-hand proposal." Thus OMT has sufficiently exhibited its subjective surprise. As to objective surprise, however, OMT has alleged no facts and introduced no evidence to show that a reasonable petroleum merchant would be surprised by the Tax Clause. See In re Chateaugay, 162 B.R. at 957 (including as types of evidence proving objective surprise "the parties' prior course of dealing and the number of written confirmations that they exchanged, industry custom and the conspicuousness of the term"). OMT had no prior contrary course of dealing with Bayway, and offered nothing concerning trade custom or practice.

Ordinarily, our inquiry into surprise would end here. However, in response to OMT's claim of surprise, Bayway introduced evidence that the Tax Clause reflects custom and practice in the petroleum industry, and on appeal OMT argues that Bayway's own evidence raises a genuine issue of material fact as to whether such a trade practice exists. Although the evidence was introduced by Bayway, we are "obligated to search the record and independently determine whether or not a genuine issue of fact exists." Jiminez v. Dreis & Krump Mfg. Co., 736 F.2d 51, 53 (2d Cir. 1984) (quoting

10. Even if an additional term that places the tax liability on the opposing party was a material alteration per se, New York law allows a party to rebut this conclusion in some limited circumstances with a sufficient showing that the additional term reflects the custom and practice in the particular industry. See Avedon Eng'g, 126 F.3d at 1285 & n.15 (discussing New York law); Schubtex, Inc. v. Allen Snyder, Inc., 49 N.Y.2d 1, 424 N.Y.S.2d 133, 135, 399 N.E.2d 1154 (1979). As discussed below, Bayway's evidence that the Tax Clause reflects the custom and practice in the petroleum industry is compelling and unrebutted.

Higgins v. Baker, 309 F. Supp. 635, 639 (S.D.N.Y. 1970)) (internal quotation marks omitted).

Upon our review of the evidence, we conclude that Bayway has adduced compelling proof that shifting tax liability to a buyer is the custom and practice in the petroleum industry. Two industry experts offered unchallenged testimony that it is customary for the buyer to pay all the taxes resulting from a petroleum transaction. One expert stated that "[t]his practice is so universally understood among traders in the industry, that I cannot recall an instance, in all my years of trading and overseeing trades, when the buyer refused to pay the seller for excise or sales taxes."

OMT cites the standard contracts of five major petroleum companies that Bayway introduced to illustrate contract terms similar to the Tax Clause. OMT argues that only three of the five place the tax liability on the buyer, and that there is therefore an issue of fact as to whether the Tax Clause would objectively surprise a merchant in this industry.

OMT misconstrues the evidence. Three of the contracts—those of CITGO Petroleum, Conoco, and Enron—mirror the Tax Clause. A fourth, Chevron's, differs from the others only in that the cost of the taxes is added into the contract price rather than separately itemized. Thus Chevron's standard contract affords OMT no support.

The fifth example, the Texaco contract, is silent as to the tax allocation issue in this case. But on this unrebutted record of universal trade custom and practice, silence supports no contrary inference.

Moreover, common sense supports Bayway's evidence of custom and practice. The federal excise tax is imposed when taxable fuels are sold "to any person who is not registered under [26 U.S.C. §4101]." 26 U.S.C. §4081(a)(1)(A)(iv). The buyer thereby controls whether any tax liability is incurred in a transaction. A trade practice that reflects a rational allocation of incentives (as trade practices usually do) would place the burden of the tax on the party that is in the position to obviate it—here, on OMT as the buyer.

Viewing Bayway's evidence in the light most favorable to OMT, we conclude that allocating the tax liability to the buyer is the custom and practice in the petroleum industry. OMT could not be objectively surprised by the incorporation of an additional term in the contract that reflects such a practice.

4. Hardship

To recapitulate: A material alteration is one that would "result in surprise *or* hardship if incorporated without express awareness by the other party." N.Y. U.C.C. §2-207 cmt. 4 (emphasis added). Although this Official Comment to the U.C.C. seemingly treats hardship as an independent ground for finding that an alteration is material, courts have expressed doubt: "You cannot walk away from a contract that you can fairly be deemed to have agreed to, merely because performance turns out to be a hardship for you, unless you can squeeze yourself into the impossibility defense or some related doctrine of excuse." *Union Carbide,* 947 F.2d at 1336 ("Hardship is a consequence [of material alteration], not a criterion. (Surprise can be either.)"); see also, e.g., Suzy Phillips Originals, Inc. v. Coville, Inc., 939 F. Supp. 1012, 1017-18 (E.D.N.Y. 1996) (citing *Union Carbide* with approval and limiting the test for material alteration to surprise); In re Chateaugay, 162 B.R. at 957 (same).

We need not decide whether hardship is an independent ground of material alteration, because even if it were, OMT failed to raise a genuine issue of material fact as to hardship. OMT's only evidence of hardship is (generally) that it is a small business dependent on precarious profit margins, and it would suffer a loss it cannot afford. That does not amount to hardship in the present circumstances.

Typically, courts that have relied on hardship to find that an additional term materially alters a contract have done so when the term is one that creates or allocates an open-ended and prolonged liability. See, e.g., St. Charles Cable TV, Inc. v. Eagle Comtronics, Inc., 687 F. Supp. 820, 827 (S.D.N.Y. 1988) (finding a hardship in "shift[ing] all risks for any dispute to the buyers"), *aff'd,* 895 F.2d 1410 (2d Cir. 1989) (unpublished table disposition); Charles J. King, Inc. v. Barge LM-10, 518 F. Supp. 1117, 1120 (S.D.N.Y. 1981).

The Tax Clause places on a buyer a contractual responsibility that bears on a specific sale of goods, that is (at least) not uncommon in the industry, and that the buyer could avoid by registration. The cry of hardship rings hollow, because any loss that the Tax Clause imposed on OMT is limited, routine and self-inflicted.

OMT failed to raise a factual issue as to hardship or surprise. Summary judgment was therefore appropriately granted in favor of Bayway. . . .

For the foregoing reasons, we affirm the judgment of the district court.

PROBLEM 17

The purchase order of the buyer ordered a tugboat, and the fine print demanded that the tugboat be warranted for a two-year period. The tugboat seller's acknowledgment form contained a statement that disclaimed all warranties. Neither party read the other's form, so the tugboat was shipped, accepted, and then had major problems remaining afloat. You are the attorney for the buyer. Advise your client whether the contract includes a warranty.

The last Problem raised the issue of how §2-207 resolves an exchange of forms containing *different* terms. While subsection (1) of the statute talks about both "additional" and "different" terms, subsection (2) mentions only "additional" ones. Official Comment 6, at first glance, appears to resolve the matter, but a careful reading of it shows that it is addressed only to written confirmations of an oral contract containing different terms, which the Official Comment says cancel each other out. The courts facing the different terms scenario of Problem 17 have divided into two major camps, as discussed in the following case.

Ultraflex Systems of Florida, Inc. v. Veritev Operating Co.

United States District Court, District of New Jersey, 2019
2019 WL 7207483

MICHAEL A. HAMMER, United States Magistrate Judge.

. . .

II. BACKGROUND

This action arises out of allegedly unpaid invoices for the sale of commercial substrate materials for digital printing. Plaintiff/counter-defendant Ultraflex Systems of Florida, Inc. ("Plaintiff") is a "worldwide distribution company of substrate fabrics and accessories used for digital printing" that is incorporated and headquartered in Florida. Compl. ¶2, June 3, 2019, D.E. 1. Plaintiff maintains a distribution warehouse and offices in Randolph, New Jersey. *Id.* ¶3. Defendant is a "business-to-business distributor of packaging, facility solutions, print and publishing products and services." *Id.* ¶5. Defendant is a Delaware corporation with a principal place of business in Atlanta, Georgia, and conducts business in New Jersey from two offices located in this state. *Id.* ¶4."

The parties have regularly done business together for the past decade. *Id.* ¶9. "At all times, the parties exchanged routine documents such as purchase orders, sales order confirmations, and invoices." Decl. of John E. Schleicher, Jr. in Opp'n to Def.'s Mot. to Transfer ("Schleicher Decl.") ¶7, Aug. 5, 2019, D.E. 13-1. Defendant would initiate the parties' transactions by electronically sending purchase orders that contained Defendant's Terms and Conditions of Purchase ("Veritiv Terms and Conditions"). Decl. of Scott Dickerson in Supp. of Def.'s Mot. to Transfer ("Dickerson Decl.") ¶¶4-5, Aug. 20, 2019, D.E. 19. Paragraph One of the Terms and Conditions prescribes:

> **Acceptance; Entire Agreement**—Unless otherwise agreed to in writing, these Terms and Conditions of Purchase ("Terms") apply to all purchases by Veritiv Operating Company ("Buyer") from the supplier of any goods and/or services ("Seller") hereunder. These Terms constitute Buyer's offer and may be accepted by Seller only in accordance with the terms hereof. Seller's acceptance of these Terms and any order hereunder shall occur either through commencement of performance or acknowledgment of the order.

> By accepting an order hereunder, Seller waives all terms and conditions contained in its quotation, acknowledgment, invoice or other documents which are different from or additional to those contained herein and all such different or additional terms and conditions shall be null and void. No addition to, waiver or modification of, any provisions herein contained shall be of any force or effect unless made in writing and executed by Buyer's authorized representative.

Dickerson Decl., Ex. A, D.E. 19-1. Paragraph Seventeen, titled "Miscellaneous," contains both a choice-of-law provision and a forum-selection clause:

> These terms, any order hereunder, and the rights and obligations of the parties thereto, shall be governed by the laws of the State of Delaware, without giving effect to its principles of conflicts of law. Seller agrees to subject itself to the courts of Delaware and such venue shall be exclusive regarding disputes arising out of these Terms.

Id.; *see also* Def.'s Answer & Countercls. ¶16, June 27, 2019, D.E. 4."

Upon receipt of a purchase order, Plaintiff would promptly transmit to Defendant a sales order confirmation that included a copy of its own terms and conditions of sale ("Ultraflex Terms and Conditions"). *See* Schleicher Decl. ¶8; Dickerson Decl. ¶¶7-8. The final provision of the Ultraflex Terms and Conditions prescribes:

> **MISCELLANEOUS:** This agreement is effective upon shipment of the Product by Ultraflex. This agreement is governed by New Jersey law and Purchaser agrees that in the event of any dispute arising under or relating to this purchase and sale agreement that Purchaser shall submit to the exclusive personal jurisdiction of the state and federal courts situated in the State of New Jersey.

Schleicher Decl., Ex. 1, D.E. 13-2."

Defendant submitted multiple purchase orders for substrate materials to Plaintiff between September 2018 and March 2019. *See* Compl. ¶10; Schleicher Decl. ¶2. Following delivery, Plaintiff issued invoices to Defendant from its New Jersey office. Compl. ¶¶11-13. However, Defendant refused to pay those invoices on the basis that an October 2017 order was deemed defective by one of Defendant's customers, Circle Graphics, Inc. *See id.* ¶14-15; Schleicher Decl. ¶¶3-4. Plaintiff avers that it provided an appropriate credit for the allegedly defective shipment towards Defendant's unpaid balance from the 2018-19 purchases. Compl. ¶¶16-17. As a result, Plaintiff filed this breach-of-contract action seeking the unpaid balance plus interest, attorneys' fees, and late charges pursuant to the Ultraflex Terms and Conditions. *Id.* ¶¶18-26."

Defendant filed three counterclaims arising from the October 2017 order of allegedly defective goods. Answer & Countercls., ¶¶28-43. Defendant alleges that it ordered 239 rolls of graphic printing product from Plaintiff for the purpose of resale to one of its own customers. *Id.* ¶17. Defendant's customer "experienced immediate printing failures" with respect to thirty of the first sixty printing rolls shipped. *Id.* ¶18. "As a result, [Defendant's] customer returned the remaining 30 rolls from [Defendant's] 60-roll delivery and refused to receive any further deliveries from that same batch of rolls provided by [[Plaintiff]." *Id.* ¶19. Despite continued efforts by Defendant to obtain a full refund, Plaintiff only issued Defendant a credit for twelve of the 239 printing rolls. *Id.* ¶¶20-22. Defendant seeks money damages, lost profits, and other relief in conjunction with the defective sale from Plaintiff. *Id.* ¶¶23-27. Defendant submits that the Veritiv Terms and Conditions supplies many of its remedies it seeks by way of its counterclaims. *See id.* ¶¶2-4, 11-15, 24-26, 33, 39."

Defendant now moves to have this case transferred to the United States District Court for the District of Delaware pursuant to the forum-selection clause in the Veritiv Terms and Conditions or, in the alternative, dismissed on the grounds of *forum non conveniens. See generally* Mot. to Transfer or Dismiss, June 27, 2019, D.E. 6."

III. Discussion

A. Battle of the Forms

Relying on their respective term sheets, the parties dispute whether New Jersey or Delaware law applies to this action and whether Plaintiff properly filed suit in this forum. To ultimately determine whether this case must be transferred to the District of Delaware, this Court must first resolve a "battle of the forms" under Section 2-207 of the Uniform Commercial Code ("U.C.C.").

Section 2-207 addresses the situation when parties consummate a sale of goods notwithstanding their exchange of non-identical term sheets. *See* U.C.C. §2-207 cmt. 1; *Olefins Trading, Inc. v. Han Yang Chem Corp.*, 9 F.3d 282, 287-88 (3d Cir. 1993). To simplify business transactions, the drafters of the U.C.C. recognized that "a proposed deal which in commercial understanding has in fact been closed is recognized as a contract." U.C.C. §2-207 cmt. 2. Proof of a contract can be established by either "[a] definite and seasonable expression of acceptance or a written confirmation which is sent within a reasonable time" after the offer. *Id.* §2-207(1). If the confirmation makes acceptance expressly conditional on the offeror's assent to the new terms, the parties' writings do not give rise to a valid contract. *See id.* In that context, "[c]onduct by both parties which recognizes the existence of a contract is sufficient to establish a contract for sale although the writings of the parties do not otherwise establish a contract." *Id.* §2-207(3)."

The dispute here is not over the existence of a contract arising from the purchase orders, but the terms thereof. Plaintiff's mailing of the sales confirmation constituted its acceptance of the purchase order (the offer) because Plaintiff did not condition its acceptance on Defendant's assent to the Ultraflex Terms and Conditions. *See Corestar Int'l Pte. Ltd v. LPB Commc'ns, Inc.*, 513 F. Supp. 2d 107, 116-17 (D.N.J. 2007) (holding that confirmatory purchase order in response to price quotation constituted acceptance "because it was not 'expressly made conditional on asset to the additional or different terms'" (quoting U.C.C. §2-207(1))."

With respect to the additional or different terms, UCC §2-207 establishes a legal rule that proceeding with a contract after receiving a writing that purports to define the terms of the parties' contract is not sufficient to establish the party's consent to the terms of the writing to the extent that the terms of the writing either add to, or differ from, the terms detailed in the parties['] earlier writings or discussions. *Step-Saver Data Sys, Inc.*, 939 F.2d at 99. In a dealing between merchants, however, the *additional* terms become part of the contract unless any one of three enumerated exceptions apply:

> (a) the offer expressly limits acceptance to the terms of the offer;"
> (b) they materially alter it; or"
> (c) notification of objection to them has already been given or is given within a reasonable time after notice of them is received.

U.C.C. §2-207(2). The fate of *conflicting* terms is less clear. The drafters of the U.C.C. provided two comments regarding that issue. Comment Three provides:

> Whether or not *additional or different* terms will become part of the agreement depends upon the provisions of subsection (2). If they are such as materially to alter the original bargain, they will not be included unless expressly agreed to by the other party. If, however, they are terms which would not so change the bargain they will be incorporated unless notice of objection to them has already been given or is given within a reasonable time.

Id. §2-207 cmt. 3 (emphasis added). On the other hand, Comment Six states:

> Where clauses on confirming forms sent by both parties *conflict* each party must be assumed to object to a clause of the other conflicting with one on the confirmation sent by himself. As a result the requirement that there be notice of objection which is found in subsection (2) is satisfied and the conflicting terms do not become a part of the contract. The contract then consists of the terms originally expressly agreed to, terms on which the confirmations agree, and terms supplied by this Act, including subsection (2).

Id. §2-207 cmt. 6 (emphasis added)."

As a result, jurisdictions have developed divergent approaches for dealing with conflicting terms sent in a confirmatory writing. The majority rule is that conflicting terms are "knocked out" and not included in the resulting contract. *See Flender Corp. v. Tippins Int'l, Inc.* 830 A.2d 1279, 1285-87 (Pa. Sup. Ct. 2003) (noting that the knockout rule "has now been adopted by a strong majority of U.S. jurisdictions that have considered the issue, and the federal courts have predicted its adoption in others"); *Richardson v. Union Carbide Indus. Gases, Inc.*, 790 A.2d 962, 967-68 (N.J. Sup. Ct. App. Div. 2002) (surveying the different approaches to the issue of conflicting terms and holding that "the majority approach, the 'knock-out' rule, is preferable and should be adopted in New Jersey"). There are two minority approaches: (1) the offeror's terms control because conflicting terms constitute material alterations under U.C.C. §2-207(2)(b) and Comment Three; and (2) the offeror's terms control because conflicting terms are outside the scope of U.C.C. §2-207(2) and thus are never considered. *See Daitom, Inc. v. Pennwalt Corp.*, 741 F.2d 1569, 1579 (10th Cir. 1984) (outlining the three approaches and predicting that the Pennsylvania Supreme Court would adopt the knockout rule)."

"Advocates of the knockout rule interpret Comment 6 to require the cancellation of terms in *both* parties' documents that conflict with one another, whether the terms are in confirmation notices or in the offer and acceptance themselves." *Reilly Foam Corp. v. Rubbermaid Corp.*, 206 F. Supp. 2d 643, 654 (E.D. Pa. 2002) (emphasis added). An additional rationale for the knockout rule flows from the U.C.C.'s rejection of the anachronistic mirror-image rule that existed at common law. Under the mirror-image rule, any difference in the terms between the parties' writings converted the putative acceptance into a counteroffer. *See Step-Saver Data Sys, Inc.*, 939 F.2d at 99.

If the offeror proceeded with the contract despite the differing terms of the supposed acceptance, he would, by his performance, constructively accept the terms of the "counteroffer", and be bound by its terms. As a result of these rules, the terms of the party who sent the last form, typically the seller, would become the terms of the parties'[] contract. *Id.* The impetus for U.C.C. §2-207 was the belief that "it would be unfair to bind the buyer of goods to the standard terms of the seller, when neither party cared sufficiently to establish expressly the terms of their agreement, simply because the seller sent the last form." *Id.*

Courts that have adopted the knockout rule have expressed similar sentiments about not binding the offeree to the boilerplate terms of the offer when those terms were not deemed sufficiently important to be negotiated by the parties:

> One should not be able to dictate the terms of the contract merely because one sent the offer. Indeed, the knockout rule recognizes that merchants are

> frequently willing to proceed with a transaction even though all terms have not been assented to. It would be inequitable to lend greater force to one party's preferred terms than the other's. As one court recently explained, "An approach other than the knock-out rule for conflicting terms would result in . . . [] any offeror . . . [] always prevailing on its terms solely because it sent the first form. That is not a desirable result, particularly when the parties have not negotiated for the challenged clause.

Reilly Foam Corp., 206 F. Supp. 2d at 653-54 (alterations in original) (quoting *Richardson*, 790 A.2d at 968).

The parties dispute whether the knockout rule should apply in this case. Defendant relies on two of the three exceptions set forth in U.C.C. §2-207(2). Defendant submits that Paragraph One of the Veritiv Terms and Conditions expressly limited acceptance to the terms contained therein. Def.'s Br. at 7-8, D.E. 8; Def.'s Reply Br. at 8, 10-11, D.E. 17. Defendant thus contends that, pursuant to U.C.C. §2-207(2)(a), Plaintiff "could not unilaterally impose *any* additional terms via its acknowledgement forms without [[Defendant's] written acceptance, and *any* attempt to impose new terms without [[Defendant's] written assent would be null and void." Def.'s Reply Br. at 8. Defendant further asserts that Plaintiff's "choice of law and forum selection clause terms constitute 'material alter[ations]' that are not incorporated into and are excluded from the agreement between the parties." *Id.* at 9 (quoting N.J. Stat. Ann. §12A:2-207(2)(b) <<UCC §2-207>>; Del. Code Ann. tit. 6, § 2-207(2)(b)). Defendant cites Comment Three for the proposition that conflicting terms are encompassed by U.C.C. §2-207(2)(b), and as a result, the terms of the offer control. *Id.* For its part, Plaintiff submits that the knockout rule cancels out the parties' conflicting choice of law and forum selection provisions. Pl.'s Br. at 6-7, D.E. 13. Plaintiff predominately relies on *Richardson* and Comment Six to U.C.C. §2-207. *See id.* at 9-11."

Given the parties' conflict regarding which state law applies, this Court must engage in a choice-of-law analysis. Because the knockout rule is a principle of contract interpretation, its application is a matter of state substantive law. *See Collins v. Mary Kay, Inc.*, 874 F.3d 176, 182 (3d Cir. 2017). As a federal court sitting in diversity, this Court applies New Jersey choice-of-law rules. *See id.* at 183. The first inquiry, which is dispositive in this case, "is whether the laws of the states with interests in the litigation are in conflict." *In re Accutane Litig.*, 194 A.3d 503, 517 (N.J. 2018) (quoting *McCarrell v. Hoffman-La Roche, Inc.*, 153 A.3d 207, 216 (N.J. 2017)). The Court must "examin[e] the substance of the potentially applicable laws to determine whether 'there is a distinction' between them." *P.V. ex rel. T.V. v. Camp Jaycee*, 962 A.2d 453, 460 (N.J. 2008) (quoting *Lebegern v. Forman*, 471 F.3d 424, 430 (3d Cir. 2006)). If there is no distinction, there is no choice-of-law issue and the forum state applies its own law. *See In re Accutane Litig.*, 194 A.3d at 517."

Although neither the Delaware Supreme Court nor the New Jersey Supreme Court has considered the knockout rule, this Court holds that there is no conflict. Both states have adopted U.C.C. §2-207 without modification and this Court predicts that both states would align themselves with the majority of jurisdictions that have adopted the knockout rule. Indeed, one of the primary policies of the U.C.C. is to "[t]o make uniform the law among the various jurisdictions." N.J. Stat. Ann. §12A:1-103(a)(3) <<UCC §1-103>>; Del. Code. Ann. tit. 6, §1-103(a)(3)."

This Court treats *Richardson* as persuasive authority that the New Jersey Supreme Court would adopt the knockout rule. *See Travelers Indem. Co. v. Dammann & Co., Inc.*, 594 F.3d 238, 244 (3d Cir. 2010) ("Furthermore, in the absence of direct authority from the New Jersey Supreme Court, we may treat as persuasive authority decisions of the Appellate Division of the Superior Court of New Jersey."). With respect to Delaware, a review of Delaware case law provides this Court with no reason to believe that the Delaware Supreme Court would depart from the majority approach in this case. *See, e.g., Acienro v. Worthy Bros. Pipeline Corp.*, 656 A.2d 1085, 1089 (Del. 1995) (adopting majority rule that the adoption of the U.C.C. did not displace the common law doctrine of accord and satisfaction); *Johnson v. Hockessin Tractor, Inc.*, 420 A.2d 154, 158 (Del. 1980) (adopting majority rule that the U.C.C.'s statute of limitations applies to a breach of implied warranty action where personal injury is also alleged). Accordingly, the Court holds that the knockout rule governs this case."

Applied here, the knockout rule operates to cancel out the conflicting litigation provisions. The Court reaches this conclusion notwithstanding the putative restrictions on acceptance contained in the Veritiv Terms and Conditions for several reasons. *See* Dickerson Decl., Ex. A (stating that "[t]hese Terms constitute Buyer's offer and may be accepted by Seller only in accordance with the terms hereof[]" and that "all such different or additional terms and conditions shall be null and void"). First, U.C.C. §2-207(2)(a) and N.J. Stat. Ann. §12A:2-207(2)(a) <<UCC §2-207>>, by their plain language, apply only to additional terms-not conflicting terms. Pursuant to Comment Six to U.C.C. §2-207, neither parties' proffered term becomes part of the contract. *See id.* (prescribing that "the conflicting terms do not become a part of the contract"). Second, the Superior Court of New Jersey, Appellate Division applied the knockout rule in light of similar restrictive language contained in the offer in that case. *See Richardson*, 790 A.2d at 963-64 (noting that the offer stated that "[t]his sale . . . limited to and expressly made conditional on Purchaser's asset to these Terms and Conditions"). Finally, this Court is persuaded by the rationale underlying the knockout rule and concludes that it is the most equitable approach. Defendant, as the offeror, had the opportunity to include the litigation provisions among the dickered terms if it deemed those provisions to be of sufficient importance. The inclusion of disagreeable terms should not depend on which party initiated the transaction. *See Daitom, Inc.*, 741 F.2d at 1580 ("To refuse to adopt the 'knock-out' rule . . . would serve to re-enshrine the undue advantages derived solely from the fortuitous positions of when a party sent a form.")."

B. MOTION TO TRANSFER

Having concluded that neither party's forum selection clause was incorporated into the contract for the sale of the commercial substrate materials, Defendant's motion to transfer is subject to a straightforward analysis under 28 U.S.C. §1404. "[A] district court may transfer a civil action to another district where the case might have been brought, or to which the parties have consented, for the convenience of the parties and witnesses and in the interest of justice." *In re McGraw-Hill Glob. Educ. Holdings LLC*, 909 F.3d 48, 57 (3d Cir. 2018) (citing *Jumara v. State Farm Ins. Co.*, 55 F.3d 873, 879-80 (3d Cir. 1995)). "Factors the court must consider include the three enumerated under the statute-convenience of the parties, convenience of the witnesses, and the interests of justice-along with all other relevant private and public factors, including the plaintiff's choice of forum and the local interest in deciding local controversies close to home." *Id.* at 57 (citing *Atlantic Marine Constr. Co. v. U.S. District Court*, 571 U.S. 49, 62 n.6 (2013)); *see also* 28 U.S.C. § 1404."

More specifically, the private interests to be balanced include:

> The plaintiff's forum preference as manifested in the original choice; the defendant's preference; whether the claim arose elsewhere; the convenience of the parties as indicated by their relative physical and financial condition; the convenience of the witnesses; and the location of books and records, well as all other practical problems that make trial of a case easy, expeditious and inexpensive.

In re: Howmedica Osteonics Corp, 867 F.3d 390, 402 (3d Cir. 2017) (internal quotation marks and citations omitted). The public interests to be considered include: "the enforceability of the judgment; the relative administrative difficulty in the two fora resulting from court congestion; the local interest in deciding local controversies at home; the public policies of the fora; and the familiarity of the trial judge with the applicable state law in diversity cases." *Id.* (internal quotation marks and citations omitted). The movant bears the burden of establishing that transfer is warranted and must "show the proposed alternative forum is not only adequate, but also more appropriate than the present forum." *Hoffer v. InfoSpace.com, Inc.*, 102 F. Supp. 2d 556, 575 (D.N.J. 2000)."

Aside from Defendant's preference to sue and be sued in Delaware, this Court finds that many of the private factors weighs against transfer. Plaintiff filed this breach-of-contract action in New Jersey and the parties issued the purchase orders and invoices in this state. *See* Compl. ¶7, 10, 13; Schleicher Decl. ¶6. Both parties operate on a national scale and do business in New Jersey. *See* Compl. ¶¶2, 5; Schleicher Decl. ¶6. At least some of Plaintiff's witnesses and its books and records are associated with its Randolph, New Jersey facility. With respect to Defendant's counterclaim, the client who allegedly received the defective good is based in Colorado and has no clear ties to either desired forum. Accordingly, it would not inconvenience the parties and witnesses to litigate this matter in New Jersey where they engaged in many of the commercial dealings at issue as opposed to Delaware, which has little to no connection to the disputed transactions. *See Yocham v. Novartis Pharm. Corp.*, 565 F. Supp. 2d 554, 558 (D.N.J. 2008) ("[I]n light of the paramount consideration accorded to a plaintiff's choice of venue, courts in this district have recognized that unless the balance of inconvenience of the parties is strongly in favor of Defendant, [Plaintiff's] choice of forum should prevail." (internal quotation marks and citations omitted))."

Nor is the Court convinced that the balancing of the public interest factors weighs in favor of transfer. Although this Court's docket is busy, there are no other administrative burdens in resolving this relatively straightforward breach of contract and warranty action that is governed by the Uniform Commercial Code. Accordingly, venue is proper in New Jersey and this Court will deny Defendant's motion to transfer this action to the District of Delaware."

IV. Conclusion

For the foregoing reasons, the Court denies Defendant's Motion to Transfer."

Courts call the clause that ends subsection (1) of §2-207 ("unless acceptance is expressly made conditional on assent to the additional or different terms") the *proviso* clause. The proviso clause acts just like a railroad switch. If it is *not* used as part of the accepting form, then the purported acceptance does create a contract, and the parties are directed to subsection (2) to determine its terms. If the proviso is put into the accepting document, the exchange of forms does not create a contract, and the parties are directed to subsection (3) to see what results from their dealings. Our point is this: the presence or absence of the proviso shunts the parties into either subsection (2) or subsection (3), *but never both.*

PROBLEM 18

On April 25, Plastic Furniture Mart sent a purchase order for 100 tables to the Ersatz Manufacturing Company. In addition to the usual boilerplate language, the purchase order also stated: "BUYER OBJECTS IN ADVANCE TO ANY TERMS PROPOSED BY SELLER THAT DIFFER IN ANY WAY FROM THE TERMS OF THIS PURCHASE ORDER." Ersatz received the order, and on May 3 it sent back its own acknowledgment form, which disclaimed all warranties and contained this clause: "THIS IS NOT AN ACCEPTANCE UNLESS BUYER ASSENTS TO ALL CHANGES MADE BY THIS ACKNOWLEDGMENT FORM." Neither party read the details of the other's form. On May 6, Ersatz shipped the tables. Is there a contract? See §§2-207(3), 2-206(1)(b); see Building Materials Corporation of America v. Henkel Corporation, 2016 WL 7666151 (M.D. Fla. 2016). Did Ersatz make a warranty as to the condition of the tables? See §2-314. On May 3 was there a contract?

QUESTION

Assume that you are an associate at a law firm that represents a seller who frequently receives purchase orders triggering §2-207's rules. Your client wants to disclaim warranties, and the senior partner asks you to come up with a way of doing this. What do you advise? How comfortable will be you be sleeping that night?

PROBLEM 19

Through a series of phone calls, the parties reached a complete oral agreement on the terms of a sales contract. Seller then sent buyer an e-mail saying "I'm delighted we've made this deal. The contract is attached." The attachment was seller's usual Acknowledgement Form, and it first disclaimed warranties (which had not been discussed in the oral communications), and then clearly tracked the language of §2-207(1)'s proviso, by stating that this was not an acceptance unless buyer expressly agreed to seller's new terms. Buyer responded by sending payment, and seller promptly shipped the goods. When the goods proved to be unmerchantable, buyer sued, and seller pointed to the disclaimer of warranties in its Acknowledgement Form. Can seller use the proviso in this situation? See Air Prods. & Chem., Inc. v. Fairbanks Morse, Inc., 58 Wis. 2d 193, 206 N.W.2d 414, 422-423 (1973).

Klocek v. Gateway, Inc.

United States District Court, Kansas, 2000
104 F. Supp. 2d 1332

Vratil, District Judge.

William S. Klocek brings suit against Gateway, Inc. and Hewlett-Packard, Inc. on claims arising from purchases of a Gateway computer and a Hewlett-Packard scanner. . . . For reasons stated below, the Court overrules Gateway's motion to dismiss, sustains Hewlett-Packard's motion to dismiss, and overrules the motions filed by plaintiff.

I. Gateway's Motion to Dismiss

Plaintiff brings individual and class action claims against Gateway, alleging that it induced him and other consumers to purchase computers and special support packages by making false promises of technical support. *Complaint,* ¶¶3 and 4. Individually, plaintiff also claims breach of contract and breach of warranty, in that Gateway breached certain warranties that its computer would be compatible with standard peripherals and standard internet services. *Complaint,* ¶¶2, 5, and 6.

Gateway asserts that plaintiff must arbitrate his claims under Gateway's Standard Terms and Conditions Agreement ("Standard Terms"). Whenever it sells a computer, Gateway includes a copy of the Standard Terms in the box which contains the computer battery power cables and instruction manuals. At the top of the first page, the Standard Terms include the following notice:

> Note to the Customer:
>
> This document contains Gateway 2000's Standard Terms and Conditions. By keeping your Gateway 2000 computer system beyond five (5) days after the date of delivery, you accept these Terms and Conditions.

The notice is in emphasized type and is located inside a printed box which sets it apart from other provisions of the document. The Standard Terms are four pages long and contain 16 numbered paragraphs. Paragraph 10 provides the following arbitration clause:

> DISPUTE RESOLUTION. Any dispute or controversy arising out of or relating to this Agreement or its interpretation shall be settled exclusively and finally by arbitration. The arbitration shall be conducted in accordance with the Rules of Conciliation and Arbitration of the International Chamber of Commerce. The arbitration shall be conducted in Chicago, Illinois, U.S.A. before a sole arbitrator. Any award rendered in any such arbitration

> proceeding shall be final and binding on each of the parties, and judgment may be entered thereon in a court of competent jurisdiction.[11]

Gateway urges the Court to dismiss plaintiff's claims under the Federal Arbitration Act ("FAA"), 9 U.S.C. §1 et seq. The FAA ensures that written arbitration agreements in maritime transactions and transactions involving interstate commerce are "valid, irrevocable, and enforceable." 9 U.S.C. §2. Federal policy favors arbitration agreements and requires that we "rigorously enforce" them. Shearson/American Exp., Inc. v. McMahon, 482 U.S. 220, 226, 107 S. Ct. 2332, 96 L. Ed. 2d 185 (1987) (quoting Dean Witter Reynolds, Inc. v. Byrd, 470 U.S. 213, 105 S. Ct. 1238, 84 L. Ed. 2d 158 (1985)); *Moses,* 460 U.S. at 24, 103 S. Ct. 927. "[A]ny doubts concerning the scope of arbitrable issues should be resolved in favor of arbitration." *Moses,* 460 U.S. at 24-25, 103 S. Ct. 927.

FAA Section 3 states:

> If any suit or proceeding be brought in any of the courts of the United States upon any issue referable to arbitration under an agreement in writing for such arbitration, the court in which such suit is pending, upon being satisfied that the issue involved in such suit or proceeding is referable to arbitration under such agreement, shall on application of one of the parties stay the trial of the action until such arbitration has been had in accordance with the terms of the agreement, providing the applicant for the stay is not in default in proceeding with such arbitration.

9 U.S.C. §3. . . . [T]he Court concludes that dismissal is appropriate if plaintiff's claims are arbitrable.

Gateway bears an initial summary-judgment-like burden of establishing that it is entitled to arbitration. [Citations omitted.] Thus, Gateway must present evidence sufficient to demonstrate the existence of an enforceable agreement to arbitrate. See, e.g., Oppenheimer & Co. v. Neidhardt, 56 F.3d 352, 358 (2d Cir. 1995). If Gateway makes such a showing, the burden shifts to plaintiff to submit evidence demonstrating a genuine issue for trial. Id.; see also Naddy v. Piper Jaffray, Inc., 88 Wash. App. 1033, 1997 WL 749261, *2, Case Nos. 15431-9-III, 15681-8-III (Wash. App. Dec. 4, 1997). In this case,

11. Gateway states that after it sold plaintiff's computer, it mailed all existing customers in the United States a copy of its quarterly magazine, which contained notice of a change in the arbitration policy set forth in the Standard Terms. The new arbitration policy afforded customers the option of arbitrating before the International Chamber of Commerce ("ICC"), the American Arbitration Association ("AAA"), or the National Arbitration Forum ("NAF") in Chicago, Illinois, or any other location agreed upon by the parties. Plaintiff denies receiving notice of the amended arbitration policy. Neither party explains why—if the arbitration agreement was an enforceable contract—Gateway was entitled to unilaterally amend it by sending a magazine to computer customers.

Gateway fails to present evidence establishing the most basic facts regarding the transaction. The gaping holes in the evidentiary record preclude the Court from determining what state law controls the formation of the contract in this case and, consequently, prevent the Court from agreeing that Gateway's motion is well taken.

Before granting a stay or dismissing a case pending arbitration, the Court must determine that the parties have a written agreement to arbitrate. See 9 U.S.C. §§3 and 4; Avedon Engineering, Inc. v. Seatex, 126 F.3d 1279, 1283 (10th Cir. 1997). When deciding whether the parties have agreed to arbitrate, the Court applies ordinary state law principles that govern the formation of contracts. First Options of Chicago, Inc. v. Kaplan, 514 U.S. 938, 944, 115 S. Ct. 1920, 131 L. Ed. 2d 985 (1995). The existence of an arbitration agreement "is simply a matter of contract between the parties; [arbitration] is a way to resolve those disputes—but only those disputes—that the parties have agreed to submit to arbitration." *Avedon,* 126 F.3d at 1283 (quoting *Kaplan,* 514 U.S. at 943-945, 115 S. Ct. 1920). If the parties dispute making an arbitration agreement, a jury trial on the existence of an agreement is warranted if the record reveals genuine issues of material fact regarding the parties' agreement. See *Avedon,* 126 F.3d at 1283. . . .

The Uniform Commercial Code ("UCC") governs the parties' transaction under both Kansas and Missouri law. See K.S.A. §84-2-102; V.A.M.S. §400.2-102 (UCC applies to "transactions in goods."); Kansas Comment 1 (main thrust of Article 2 is limited to sales); K.S.A. §84-2-105(1) V.A.M.S. §400.2-105(1) ("'Goods' means all things . . . which are movable at the time of identification to the contract for sale. . . ."). Regardless whether plaintiff purchased the computer in person or placed an order and received shipment of the computer, the parties agree that plaintiff paid for and received a computer from Gateway. This conduct clearly demonstrates a contract for the sale of a computer. See, e.g., Step-Saver Data Sys., Inc. v. Wyse Techn., 939 F.2d 91, 98 (3d Cir. 1991). Thus the issue is whether the contract of sale includes the Standard Terms as part of the agreement.

State courts in Kansas and Missouri apparently have not decided whether terms received with a product become part of the parties' agreement. Authority from other courts is split. Compare *Step-Saver,* 939 F.2d 91 (printed terms on computer software package not part of agreement); Arizona Retail Sys., Inc. v. Software Link, Inc., 831 F. Supp. 759 (D. Ariz. 1993) (license agreement shipped with computer software not part of agreement); and U.S. Surgical Corp. v. Orris, Inc., 5 F. Supp. 2d 1201 (D. Kan. 1998) (single use restriction on product package not binding agreement); with Hill v. Gateway 2000, Inc., 105 F.3d 1147 (7th Cir.), *cert. denied,* 522 U.S. 808, 118 S. Ct. 47, 139 L. Ed. 2d 13 (1997) (arbitration provision shipped with computer binding on buyer); ProCD, Inc. v. Zeidenberg, 86 F.3d 1447 (7th

Cir. 1996) (shrinkwrap license binding on buyer)[12] and M.A. Mortenson Co., Inc. v. Timberline Software Corp., 140 Wash. 2d 568, 998 P.2d 305 (2000) (following *Hill* and *ProCD* on license agreement supplied with software).[13] It appears that at least in part, the cases turn on whether the court finds that the parties formed their contract *before* or *after* the vendor communicated its terms to the purchaser. Compare *Step-Saver,* 939 F.2d at 98 (parties' conduct in shipping, receiving and paying for product demonstrates existence of contract; box-top license constitutes proposal for additional terms under §2-207 which requires express agreement by purchaser); *Arizona Retail,* 831 F. Supp. at 765 (vendor entered into contract by agreeing to ship goods, or at latest by shipping goods to buyer; license agreement constitutes proposal to modify agreement under §2-209 which requires express assent by buyer); and *Orris,* 5 F. Supp. 2d at 1206 (sales contract concluded when vendor received consumer orders; single-use language on product's label was proposed modification under §2-209 which requires express assent by purchaser); with *ProCD,* 86 F.3d at 1452 (under §2-204 vendor, as master of offer, may propose limitations on kind of conduct that constitutes acceptance; §2-207 does not apply in case with only one form); *Hill,* 105 F.3d at 1148-49 (same); and *Mortenson,* 998 P.2d at 311-314 (where vendor and purchaser utilized license agreement in prior course of dealing, shrinkwrap license agreement constituted issue of contract formation under §2-204, not contract alteration under §2-207).

Gateway urges the Court to follow the Seventh Circuit decision in *Hill.* That case involved the shipment of a Gateway computer with terms similar to the Standard Terms in this case, except that Gateway gave the customer 30 days—instead of 5 days—to return the computer. In enforcing the arbitration clause, the Seventh Circuit relied on its decision in *ProCD,* where it enforced a software license which was contained inside a product box. See *Hill,* 105 F.3d at 1148-50. In *ProCD,* the Seventh Circuit noted that

12. The term "shrinkwrap license" gets its name from retail software packages that are covered in plastic or cellophane "shrinkwrap" and contain licenses that purport to become effective as soon as the customer tears the wrapping from the package. See *ProCD,* 86 F.3d at 1449.

13. The *Mortenson* court also found support for its holding in the proposed Uniform Computer Information Transactions Act ("UCITA") (formerly known as proposed UCC Article 2B) (text located at www.law.upenn.edu/library/ulc/ucita/UCITA_99.htm), which the National Conference of Commissioners on Uniform State Laws approved and recommended for enactment by the states in July 1999. See *Mortenson,* 998 P.2d at 310 n.6, 313 n.10. The proposed UCITA, however, would not apply to the Court's analysis in this case. The UCITA applies to computer information transactions, which are defined as agreements "to create, modify, transfer, or license computer information or informational rights in computer information." UCITA, §§102(11), 103. In transactions involving the sale of computers, such as our case, the UCITA applies only to the computer programs and copies, not to the sale of the computer itself. See UCITA §103(c)(2).

the exchange of money frequently precedes the communication of detailed terms in a commercial transaction. See *ProCD,* 86 F.3d at 1451. Citing UCC §2-204, the court reasoned that by including the license with the software, the vendor proposed a contract that the buyer could accept by using the software after having an opportunity to read the license.[14] *ProCD,* 86 F.3d at 1452. Specifically, the court stated:

> A vendor, as master of the offer, may invite acceptance by conduct, and may propose limitations on the kind of conduct that constitutes acceptance. A buyer may accept by performing the acts the vendor proposes to treat as acceptance.

ProCD, 86 F.3d at 1452. The *Hill* court followed the *ProCD* analysis, noting that "[p]ractical considerations support allowing vendors to enclose the full legal terms with their products." *Hill,* 105 F.3d at 1149.[15]

The Court is not persuaded that Kansas or Missouri courts would follow the Seventh Circuit reasoning in *Hill* and *ProCD.* In each case the Seventh Circuit concluded without support that UCC §2-207 was irrelevant because the cases involved only one written form. See *ProCD,* 86 F.3d at 1452 (citing no authority); *Hill,* 105 F.3d at 1150 (citing *ProCD).* This conclusion is not supported by the statute or by Kansas or Missouri law. Disputes under §2- 207 often arise in the context of a "battle of forms," see, e.g., Diatom, Inc.

14. Section 2-204 provides: "A contract for sale of goods may be made in any manner sufficient to show agreement, including conduct by both parties which recognizes the existence of such contract." K.S.A. §84-2-204; V.A.M.S. §400.2-204.

15. Legal commentators have criticized the reasoning of the Seventh Circuit in this regard. See, e.g., Jean R. Sternlight, *Gateway* Widens Doorway to Imposing Unfair Binding Arbitration on Consumers, Fla. Bar J., Nov. 1997, at 8, 10-12 (outcome in *Gateway* is questionable on federal statutory, common law and constitutional grounds and as a matter of contract law and is unwise as a matter of policy because it unreasonably shifts to consumers search cost of ascertaining existence of arbitration clause and return cost to avoid such clause); Thomas J. McCarthy et al., Survey: Uniform Commercial Code, 53 Bus. Law. 1461, 1465-66 (Seventh Circuit finding that UCC §2-207 did not apply is inconsistent with official comment); Batya Goodman, Honey, I Shrink-Wrapped the Consumer: the Shrinkwrap Agreement as an Adhesion Contract, 21 Cardozo L. Rev. 319, 344-352 (Seventh Circuit failed to consider principles of adhesion contracts); Jeremy Senderowicz, Consumer Arbitration and Freedom of Contract: A Proposal to Facilitate Consumers' Informed Consent to Arbitration Clauses in Form Contracts, 32 Colum. J.L. & Soc. Probs. 275, 296-299 (judiciary (in multiple decisions, including *Hill*) has ignored issue of consumer consent to an arbitration clause). Nonetheless, several courts have followed the Seventh Circuit decisions in *Hill* and *ProCD.* See, e.g., M.A. Mortenson Co., Inc. v. Timberline Software Corp., 140 Wash. 2d 568, 998 P.2d 305 (license agreement supplied with software); Rinaldi v. Iomega Corp., 1999 WL 1442014, Case No. 98C-09-064-RRC (Del. Super. Sept. 3, 1999) (warranty disclaimer included inside computer Zip drive packaging); Westendorf v. Gateway 2000, Inc., 2000 WL 307369, Case No. 16913 (Del. Ch. March 16, 2000) (arbitration provision shipped with computer); Brower v. Gateway 2000, Inc., 246 A.D.2d 246, 676 N.Y.S.2d 569 (N.Y. App. Div. 1998) (same); Levy v. Gateway 2000, Inc., 1997 WL 823611, 1060 (N.Y. Sup. Oct. 31, 1997) (same).

v. Pennwalt Corp., 741 F.2d 1569, 1574 (10th Cir. 1984), but nothing in its language precludes application in a case which involves only one form. The statute provides:

> Additional terms in acceptance or confirmation.
>
> (1) A definite and seasonable expression of acceptance or a written confirmation which is sent within a reasonable time operates as an acceptance even though it states terms additional to or different from those offered or agreed upon, unless acceptance is expressly made conditional on assent to the additional or different terms.
>
> (2) The additional terms are to be construed as proposals for addition to the contract [if the contract is not between merchants]. . . .

K.S.A. §84-2-207; V.A.M.S. §400.2-207. By its terms, §2-207 applies to an acceptance or written confirmation. It states nothing which requires another form before the provision becomes effective. In fact, the official comment to the section specifically provides that §2-207(1) and (2) apply "where an agreement has been reached orally . . . and is followed by one or both of the parties sending formal memoranda embodying the terms so far agreed and adding terms not discussed." Official Comment 1 of UCC §2-207. Kansas and Missouri courts have followed this analysis. See Southwest Engineering Co. v. Martin Tractor Co., 205 Kan. 684, 695, 473 P.2d 18, 26 (1970) (stating in dicta that §2-207 applies where open offer is accepted by expression of acceptance in writing or where oral agreement is later confirmed in writing); Central Bag Co. v. W. Scott and Co., 647 S.W.2d 828, 830 (Mo. App. 1983) (§2-207(1) and (2) govern cases where one or both parties send written confirmation after oral contract). Thus, the Court concludes that Kansas and Missouri courts would apply §2-207 to the facts in this case. Accord *Avedon,* 126 F.3d at 1283 (parties agree that §2-207 controls whether arbitration clause in sales confirmation is part of contract).

In addition, the Seventh Circuit provided no explanation for its conclusion that "the vendor is the master of the offer." See *ProCD,* 86 F.3d at 1452 (citing nothing in support of proposition); *Hill,* 105 F.3d at 1149 (citing *ProCD).* In typical consumer transactions, the purchaser is the offeror, and the vendor is the offeree. See Brown Mach., Div. of John Brown, Inc. v. Hercules, Inc., 770 S.W.2d 416, 419 (Mo. App. 1989) (as general rule orders are considered offers to purchase); Rich Prods. Corp. v. Kemutec Inc., 66 F. Supp. 2d 937, 956 (E.D. Wis. 1999) (generally price quotation is invitation to make offer and purchase order is offer). While it is possible for the vendor to be the offeror, see *Brown Machine,* 770 S.W.2d at 419 (price quote can amount to offer if it reasonably appears from quote that assent to quote is all that is needed to ripen offer into contract), Gateway provides no factual evidence which would support such a finding in this case. The Court therefore assumes for purposes of the motion to dismiss that plaintiff offered to purchase the computer (either in person or through catalog order) and that Gateway accepted plaintiff's offer (either by completing the sales transaction in person or by agreeing to ship and/or shipping the computer to plaintiff).[16] Accord *Arizona Retail,* 831 F. Supp. At 765 (vendor entered into contract by agreeing to ship goods, or at latest, by shipping goods).

Under §2-207, the Standard Terms constitute either an expression of acceptance or written confirmation. As an expression of acceptance, the Standard Terms would constitute a counter-offer only if Gateway expressly made its acceptance conditional on plaintiff's assent to the additional or different terms. K.S.A. §84-2-207(1); V.A.M.S. §400.2-207(1). "[T]he conditional nature of the acceptance must be clearly expressed in a manner sufficient to notify the offeror that the offeree is unwilling to proceed with the transaction unless the additional or different terms are included in the contract." *Brown Machine,* 770 S.W.2d at 420. Gateway provides no evidence that at the time of the sales transaction, it informed plaintiff that the transaction was conditioned on plaintiff's acceptance of the Standard Terms. Moreover, the mere fact that Gateway shipped the goods with the terms attached did not communicate to plaintiff any unwillingness to proceed without plaintiff's agreement to the Standard Terms. See, e.g., *Arizona Retail,* 831 F. Supp. At 765 (conditional acceptance analysis rarely appropriate where contract formed by performance but goods arrive with conditions attached); Leighton Indus., Inc. v. Callier Steel Pipe & Tube, Inc., 1991 WL 18413, *6, Case No. 89-C-8235 (N.D. Ill. Feb. 6, 1991) (applying Missouri law) (preprinted forms insufficient to notify offeror of conditional nature of acceptance, particularly where form arrives after delivery of goods).

Because plaintiff is not a merchant, additional or different terms contained in the Standard Terms did not become part of the parties' agreement unless plaintiff expressly agreed to them. See K.S.A. §84-2-207, Kansas Comment 2 (if either party is not a merchant, additional terms are proposals for addition to the contract that do not become part of the contract unless the original offeror expressly agrees). Gateway argues that plaintiff demonstrated acceptance of the arbitration provision by keeping the computer more than five days after the date of delivery. Although the Standard Terms purport to work that result, Gateway has not presented evidence that plaintiff expressly agreed to those Standard Terms. Gateway states only that it enclosed the Standard Terms inside the computer box for plaintiff to

16. UCC §2-206(b) provides that "an order or other offer to buy goods for prompt or current shipment shall be construed as inviting acceptance either by a prompt promise to ship or by the prompt or current shipment. . . ." The official comment states that "[e]ither shipment or a prompt promise to ship is made a proper means of acceptance of an offer looking to current shipment." UCC §2-206, Official Comment 2.

read afterwards. It provides no evidence that it informed plaintiff of the five-day review-and-return period as a condition of the sales transaction, or that the parties contemplated additional terms to the agreement.[17] See *Step-Saver*, 939 F.2d at 99 (during negotiations leading to purchase, vendor never mentioned box-top license or obtained buyer's express assent thereto). The Court finds that the act of keeping the computer past five days was not sufficient to demonstrate that plaintiff expressly agreed to the Standard Terms. Accord *Brown Machine,* 770 S.W.2d at 421 (express assent cannot be presumed by silence or mere failure to object). Thus, because Gateway has not provided evidence sufficient to support a finding under Kansas or Missouri law that plaintiff agreed to the arbitration provision contained in Gateway's Standard Terms, the Court overrules Gateway's motion to dismiss. . . .

There are many cases disagreeing with the court's analysis and requiring arbitration or allowing warranty disclaimers in spite of §2-207's provisions. These courts typically find that an "approve or return" clause in the paperwork arriving with the goods prevents formation of the contract until the buyer assents to the new terms (usually by doing nothing more than retaining the goods); see Fiser v. Dell Computer Corp., 142 N.M. 331, 165 P.3d 328 (2007). These decisions are all of a piece with the *ProCD* and *Hill* opinions discussed in the last case, which create so-called rolling or layered contracts through the negotiations plus the shipment with new terms, followed by the buyer's failure to object to the changes first mentioned in documents that come with the shipment, while ignoring §2-207 as irrelevant. By contrast, the Ninth Circuit squarely rejected *Hill,* reasoning that "silence alone does not constitute assent" and so "Samsung's inclusion of a brochure in the Galaxy S4 box, and Norcia's failure to opt out, does not make the arbitration provision enforceable against Norcia." Norcia v. Samsung Telecommunications America, LLC, 845 F.3d 1279, 1289 (9th Cir. 2017).

Looking to the future, consumers may sometimes have little opportunity to review contract terms, in the coming era of the Internet of Things. Web-enabled devices from printers to washing machines to thermostats may order supplies and components without direct supervision of consumers. Such machine-to-machine transactions may raise many issues of contract formation and content. See Stacy-Ann Elvy, Contracting in the Age of the

17. The Court is mindful of the practical considerations which are involved in commercial transactions, but it is not unreasonable for a vendor to clearly communicate to a buyer—at the time of sale—either the complete terms of the sale or the fact that the vendor will propose additional terms as a condition of sale, if that be the case.

Internet of Things: Article 2 of the UCC and Beyond, 44 Hofstra L. Rev. 839 (2016). What contract formation and content issues do you see arising?

CHAPTER 3 REVIEW QUESTIONS

What are the exceptions to the UCC Article 2 Statute of Frauds?
What sorts of parol evidence are admissible and subject to what conditions?
What are the requirements for an effective electronic signature?
What different ways may an offer be accepted under UCC Article 2?
What is the structure of the Battle of the Forms rule?

ASSESSMENT: MULTIPLE CHOICE QUESTIONS

1. Avril and Mario had a long conversation, ending with them agreeing that Avril would build Mario a custom wheelchair for an agreed price. When the wheelchair was almost finished, Avril contacted Mario to arrange delivery and payment. Mario denied that they had an enforceable contract, because he had not signed a contract and she had not sent him a confirmation. Is there an enforceable contract?
   a. No, for lack of a signed writing.
   b. Yes, because an oral agreement for specially manufactured goods is enforceable where the seller has made a substantial beginning.
   c. Yes, because no writing is required where the parties are not both merchants.
   d. No, because a writing is required to enforce a contract against a nonmerchant.

2. Steeply agreed over the phone with Orin to purchase a painting by Joelle for $7,000. Not long after, Joelle disappeared in a volcanic explosion, which drove the price of her artwork up. Orin refused to deliver the painting. In court, Orin testified, "We had an agreement, but sorry to say that it cannot be enforced without a writing." Can Steeply enforce the contract?
   a. No, for lack of a signed writing.
   b. Yes, because the goods are unique.
   c. Yes, because Orin admitted they had a contract.
   d. No, because Steeply could have sent a confirmation.

3. Pemulis Auto signs a contract with Lyle for the sale of a 2007 Pluto automobile. Which of the following could be introduced as evidence of terms that were not included in the writing?
   a. A common practice in the used car business that sellers would replace any parts that failed for the first year.
   b. A practice between Pemulis Auto and Lyle, in their previous transactions, that Lyle could return the car within 30 days and get his money back.

c. An oral agreement between the two that Pemulis Auto would provide free service for the first two years.
d. All of the above.

4. Gately Construction faxes an order to Van Dyne Apps for 50 tablet computers. Van Dyne faxes back an acceptance, with the following provision: "THERE ARE NO WARRANTIES EXPRESS OR IMPLIED, INCLUDING NO WARRANTY OF MERCHANTABILITY FOR THE TABLET COMPUTERS." The tablet computers are duly shipped, accepted, and paid for. Not long after, Gately Construction finds the performance of the computers to be sub-par. Did Van Dyne's provision excluding warranties become part of the parties' contract?
   a. Yes, because Gately Construction did not object to the provision.
   b. Yes, because Gately Construction's offer did not expressly limit acceptance to the terms of the offer.
   c. No, because the provision would materially alter the contract.
   d. No, because an acceptance that is different from the offer is not effective to form a contract.

5. Enfield Academy sent Microcenter an order for 25 Yushituyo Media Players. The order provided that "[a]n acceptance of this offer is not effective if the acceptance changes any of the terms of the offer." Microcenter quickly sent back an acceptance letter, which contained an arbitration provision. Enfield Academy paid for the media players on delivery, but was dissatisfied to learn they lack the capacity to show tennis videos shot with a special slow-motion feature. Will Enfield Academy be subject to the arbitration clause, if there is a dispute?
   a. No, because the parties never formed a contract.
   b. No, because the arbitration clause would not be part of the contract.
   c. Yes. The arbitration clause would be part of the contract because it was not a material alteration.
   d. Yes, the arbitration clause would be part of the contract because Enfield Academy did not object to the clause.

ANSWERS

1. *B* is the best answer. Section 2-201 provides that a signed contract is generally required, but, contrary to *A*, then provides several generous exceptions. One applies here. No writing is required if the goods are specially manufactured for the buyer, not suitable for sale to others, and seller has made a "substantial beginning of their manufacture." §2-201(3)(a). Merchant status is not a factor in the rule, contrary to *C* and *D*.
2. *C* is the best answer. One of the biggest exceptions to the writing requirement is that no writing is necessary if the defendant admits in court that

there was a contract. This means that a defendant cannot rely on the mere formality of a writing requirement, unless the defendant can avoid admitting the truth in court. Answer *B*'s reference to unique goods is misdirected. There is an exception for specially manufactured goods, but not unique goods. No confirmation is required to be sent, contrary to *D*.

3. *D* is the best answer. This question reminds us that the written contract may be explained or supplemented by usage of trade (as in *A*), course of dealing (as in *B*), and consistent additional terms (as in *C*), where writing is not shown to be the complete and exclusive statement of the parties' terms.
4. *C* is the best answer. The acceptance is effective, under the Battle of the Forms provision, §2-207(1). Unlike a stricter view under some common law cases, the UCC allows an acceptance to be effective even if it does not match the offer, contrary to *D*. But the additional terms become part of the contract only if they are not excluded by §2-207(2). The exclusion of all warranties would be excluded by §2-207(2)(b), because it is a material alteration. This would be the case even though Gately Construction did not object (contrary to *A*) or limit its original offer to its terms (contrary to *B*).
5. *B* is the best answer. Microcenter's acceptance is not effective to form a contract. Under §2-207(1), if the offer limits acceptance to the terms of the offer, an acceptance on different terms is not effective. So even if the arbitration clause is not a material alteration, the parties' writings do not form a contract. But, contrary to *A*, their conduct may form a contract, under §2-207(3). The terms of that contract would be the agreed terms, which would not include the arbitration clause.

Chapter 4
Warranties

There is sometimes confusion in the minds of the parties to a sales transaction as to what a warranty is and how it relates to other terms of the contract, such as "if not satisfied, return within 30 days for a full refund." If a customer receives such a promise and does not return the item within the specified period but then the product malfunctions, the expired 30-day period has nothing to do with the subsequent assertion that the seller is in breach of warranty. A warranty is a contractual obligation by the seller to remedy certain possible defects in the goods. It may be useful to think of it as a sort of insurance policy issued by the seller to the buyer at the time of sale that promises a remedy if the product does not work or meet some claimed level of performance. If the warranty is breached it's no defense that the seller was free of negligence or that the fault lies with some other party, such as the manufacturer. Just like an insurance policy, it is a promise to pay if something goes wrong, regardless of fault.

The UCC divides warranties into two basic types: warranties of *title* and warranties of *quality,* and we start with the former. Read §2-312.

I. THE WARRANTY OF TITLE

PROBLEM 20

Fast Eddie stole Mabel Stanley's car from a shopping center in Phoenix. He drove it to Las Vegas, where he sold it for $500 to Sealed Lips Used Cars. This firm somehow obtained a Nevada certificate of title for the car, which showed clean title in Sealed Lips. The car was then sold for $2,000 to a bona fide purchaser, Frederick Duty. Duty drove it for a month until a bad run at the roulette wheel forced him to sell it in order to finance further recreational activity. Another bona fide purchaser, Samuel Pirate, bought the car from Duty for $1,900. He drove it for only one week before the Nevada State Police impounded it and returned it to Mabel in Phoenix. Pirate sued Duty for breach of the warranty of good title.

(a) Duty argues that he *thought* he had good title, and since he was not negligent or in any way at fault in so believing, the warranty was not breached. Does this defense succeed? See Brokke v. Williams, 766 P.2d 1311 (Mont. 1989).

(b) Duty argues that he *did* have good title, and hence the warranty was not breached. Did he? See §2-403(1); Inmi-Etti v. Aluisi, 63 Md. App. 293, 492 A.2d 917(1985) (*Nemo dat qui non habet*—"He who hath not cannot give."); Executive Cars, LLC v. Western Funding II, Inc., 2019 349 Ga. App. 517, 826 S.E.2d 370 (2019) (stolen car still belongs to owner even when transferred through good faith purchasers).

(c) Would your answer to (b) change if Fast Eddie had bought the car from Mabel with a bad check? See §2-403; Allan Nott Enters., Inc. v. Nicholas Starr Auto, L.L.C. 110 Ohio St. 3d 112, 851 N.E.2d 479 (2006).

(d) Does the law give any relief to Duty? See §2-607(5)(a) (describing a procedure known as *vouching in*).

PROBLEM 21

Before the Nevada State Police found Mabel's car, discussed in the last Problem, they accidentally impounded a very similar car owned by P.T. Boss. Boss had recently purchased the car from Croupier Motors. In order to convince the police that they had made a mistake and should release the car to him, Boss had to hire an attorney, Arnold Sunglasses. The latter did retrieve the car and then sent Boss a bill for $4,100. Boss forwarded the bill to Croupier Motors, along with a cover letter to the effect that title problems were the seller's headache per §2-312. Should the car dealership pay Sunglasses's bill? See Official Comment 1 to §2-312; White & Summers §10-15(b), at 501-502; Saber v. Dan Angelone Chevrolet, Inc., 811 A.2d 644 (R.I. 2002). See also §2-607(5).

PROBLEM 22

Sellers can sometimes evade or disclaim the warranty of title. Determine if the warranty is present in the following situations:

(a) The sales contract has this clause: "The product is sold 'As Is' and seller makes no warranties, express or implied, as part of this sale." See Official Comment 6 to §2-312.

(b) Repossession Motors sold a car on credit to a customer who returned it after failing to make the first payment. It then conducted an Article 9-type resale. (See §9-610(d).) Does the resale buyer get the benefit of a §2-312 warranty? See Official Comment 5.

(c) Ted Traveler walked into the men's room of the bus depot and, to his surprise, was offered an expensive watch at a bargain rate from a stranger. He bought the watch. Is there a warranty of title in this transaction? See §1-303(c).

Moore v. Pro Team Corvette Sales, Inc.

Court of Appeals of Ohio, 2002
152 Ohio App. 3d 71, 786 N.E.2d 903

WALTERS, J.

Plaintiff-Appellant, Bryon Moore, brings this appeal from a Henry County Common Pleas Court decision which dismissed his action against Defendant-Appellee, Pro Team Corvette Sales, Inc., regarding a contract for the sale of a 1974 Chevrolet Corvette, which was subsequently discovered to be stolen. On appeal, Moore argues that terms within the agreement did not effectively disclaim the implied warranty of title under U.C.C. 2-312. Because U.C.C. 2-312 provides for a buyer's basic needs with respect to the type of title he in good faith expects to acquire by his purchase, namely, a good, clean title transferred to him in a rightful manner, we find that the provision lacks sufficient specificity to disclaim the implied warranty of title. Accordingly, we reverse the judgment of the trial court.

Facts and procedural history relevant to issues raised on appeal are as follows: In October 1994, Moore drove from his Gross Isle, Michigan, residence to Pro Team Corvette Sales, Inc. ("Pro Team"), located in Napoleon, Ohio, in order to purchase a Chevrolet Corvette. On October 17, 1994, he signed an agreement to purchase a 1974 Corvette, as well as a separate agreement to trade in his 1975 Corvette. When Moore attempted to register the car with the Michigan Bureau of Motor Vehicles, he learned that the car had been reported stolen in Texas, and therefore could not be registered. The Michigan State Police subsequently confiscated the car and returned it to Texas.

On October 15, 1996, Moore filed suit against Pro Team, arguing that its failure to provide good title to the vehicle was negligent. He also claimed unjust enrichment, breach of statutory warranties, and violations of Ohio's Consumer Sales Practices Act. Pro Team denied all liability, claiming that it had excluded all warranties, including the warranty of title, in the purchase agreement. Pro Team also filed a third-party complaint against the dealership that sold the car to Pro Team, as well as the person who sold the car to that dealer, the Michigan State Police, and the sheriff of San Patricio County, Texas.

In defending the suit, Pro Team relied upon language in its contract indicating that the Corvette was being sold "as is" and that the all warranties, including the warranty of title, were excluded from the agreement. Moore sought summary judgment, arguing that the language contained in the agreement was not sufficient to constitute a valid disclaimer of statutorily implied warranties of title. This motion was denied. Moore subsequently dismissed all counts unrelated to the warranty provisions. In February 2002, the trial court dismissed his remaining claims, concluding that the language contained in the agreement was sufficiently specific to permit exclusion of the warranty of title under U.C.C. 2-312.

Moore appeals the trial court's judgment, presenting the following single assignment of error for our review: "The Trial Court erred when it concluded that the dealer's contract properly excluded the warranty of title."

In Ohio, "a seller warrants that he will convey good title free from any security interest or other lien or encumbrance of which the buyer is without knowledge when the contract is made." This implied warranty of title is codified in U.C.C. 2-312 [which the court then quoted].

Accordingly, "[u]nless excluded or modified, U.C.C. 2-312(1) adds to a sales contract a warranty by the seller that the title conveyed shall be good and its transfer rightful." As provided by U.C.C. 2-312(2), a warranty of title may be excluded or modified by specific language giving the purchaser reasons to know that the vendor is only selling what title he possesses.

> [T]his code section provides for a buyer's basic needs in respect to the type of title he in good faith expects to acquire by his purchase, namely, a good, clean title transferred to him in a rightful manner so that he will not be exposed to a lawsuit in order to protect it. . . . In the usual case, the buyer expects to get a good title, and regards disclaimers as affecting only risks with regard to quality.[1]

1. 1 Hawkland UCC Series (2001) §2-312:5, Disclaimer of Warranty of Title-Contractual Terms.

The Michigan Court of Appeals, in Jones v. Linebaugh, held that "very precise and unambiguous language must be used to exclude a warranty so basic to the sale of goods as is title." Specific language is necessary to relieve the buyer of the idea that any disclaimer of warranty relates only to quality.[2] In Sunseri v. RKO-Stanley Warner Theaters, Inc.,[3] the court found language stating that the seller "shall in nowise be . . . liable . . . upon or under guaranties [*sic*] or warranties . . . including, but not limited to, the implied warrant[y] of title" lacked sufficient specificity to disclaim the warranty of title. The court reasoned that the language used was ineffective because it was "couched in negative terminology," expressing what the seller will not be liable for rather than what the buyer is or is not receiving. The inadequacy of such a caveat is best illustrated by juxtaposing it with title disclaimer provisions suggested by authorities in the subject area. For example, 18 Am. Jur. Legal Forms 2d §253:825 (1974), provides:

> Seller makes no warranty as to the title to the goods, and buyer assumes all risks of nonownership of the goods by seller. . . . [W]here the language in a purported disclaimer expresses how the seller's liability will be limited rather than what title (or lack thereof) the seller purports to transfer, the purported disclaimer is ineffective.[4]

The relevant portion of the sale contract states: "All warranties pursuant to U.C.C. 2-312 are hereby excluded from this transaction." In light of the foregoing discussion, we find this language to be akin to that which expresses how the seller's liability will be limited, rather than what title the seller purports to transfer, and conclude that the provision lacks sufficient specificity to disclaim the implied warranty of title. Accordingly, Moore's assignment of error is sustained.

Having found error prejudicial to the appellant herein, in the particulars assigned and argued, the judgment of the trial court is hereby reversed and the matter is remanded for further proceedings in accordance with this opinion.

Judgment reversed and cause remanded.

QUESTION

Why is the court being so picky here? What policy is at work? Could this case have been better decided on the grounds that a disclaimer of "UCC 2-312" is always insufficient because no one will know what that strange

2. 1 Hawkland UCC Series (2001) §2-312:5, Disclaimer of Warranty of Title-Contractual Terms.

3. Sunseri v. RKO-Stanley Warner Theaters, Inc. (1977), 248 Pa. Super. 111, 374 A.2d 1342, 1344.

4. *Kel-Keef,* 738 N.E.2d at 536.

citation means? If you, future attorney, are going to draft a clause disclaiming liability for breach of the warranty of title, how should you phrase it?

The next Problem is called "The Treasure in the Attic":

PROBLEM 23

When his aged uncle was very ill Ralph Rackstraw moved into the uncle's house to care for him. The old man, who had a colorful history that included several run-ins with the law and a couple of minor prison terms, was very grateful, and Ralph dutifully cared for him for four years until the uncle died. Ralph was very surprised to learn that his uncle had left him the house and all its contents; the house was quite large, though old and in need of repair.

In the attic Ralph found a locked chest and when he opened it he was amazed to find a small figurine of a woman that was made entirely of jewels, almost a hundred of them. Ralph took it to a jeweler, who told him he'd never seen anything like it—that is was a major find. The jeweler offered to buy it from Ralph for $50,000.

Ralph calls you, his attorney-cousin, and asks you to draw up a bill of sale for this transaction that makes it clear that Ralph doesn't know the origin of this figurine and won't give back the money if it turns out that there is some prior claimant to the object. "Who the hell knows how my uncle got it," he mutters.

Draft the sales clause that will protect Ralph if it turns out this is a stolen piece that rightly belongs to someone else. Be prepared to read the clause out loud when you are called upon.

Note that the warranty of title in §2-312 also includes:

(1) a warranty that there are no security interests (or other liens) on the goods other than those of which the buyer knows (§2-312(1)(b)), and
(2) a warranty given by merchant sellers against claims based on patent infringement or the like (§2-312(3)).

See Big Lots Stores, Inc. v. Luv N' Care, 2007 WL 1026448 (S.D. Ohio 2007) (breach of warranty of title to supply inventory bearing infringing trademark); Phoenix Solutions, Inc. v. Sony Electronics, Inc., 637 F. Supp. 2d 683 (N.D. Cal. 2009) (breach of warranty of title where buyer subject to patent infringement claim).

If the buyer furnishes specifications to the seller (which happens where the goods are to be specially manufactured to the buyer's order), the *buyer* automatically makes a warranty to the seller that protects the latter from infringement claims. Section 2-312(3). This is the *only* situation under the UCC where the buyer is the warrantor.

Entrustment of Goods. Closely related to the warranty of title is the doctrine of entrustment, under which a merchant may pass good title to goods someone has entrusted to the merchant, even though the merchant neither owns the goods nor has actual authority to sell them.

PROBLEM 24

Yankees fan Billy Slider bought a baseball at an auction that was supposedly signed by both Babe Ruth and Lou Gehrig. He was worried it wasn't authentic, so he took it to Sports Confidence, a company that specialized in examining the bona fides of sports memorabilia. He asked them to look into its history and authenticity. The owner of the company immediately recognized it as a major find and decided to steal it. He sold it a man named Alex Stewart and told Billy Slider that the baseball was a fake. On learning the truth, can Slider recover the baseball from Stewart? Do you need to know anything more about Stewart? See §2-403(2) and (3); Zaretsky v. William Goldberg Diamond Corp., 820 F.3d 513, 525 (2d Cir. 2016) (sale of diamond).

Lindholm v. Brant

Supreme Court of Connecticut, 2007
283 Conn. 65, 925 A.2d 1048

SULLIVAN, J.

[Lindholm entrusted her painting, *Red Elvis* by Andy Warhol, to Malmberg, a respected art dealer, who arranged for it to be displayed at several leading museums in the United States and Europe—and then sold it for $2.9 million to Brant. Brant had ordered a lien search and a search of the Art Loss Register, neither of which disclosed any problems with title. Brant's presale efforts to get documents showing that the art dealer indeed owned the painting he was selling were unsuccessful.]

Section 42a-2-403 (2) provides that "[a]ny entrusting of possession of goods to a merchant who deals in goods of that kind gives him power to transfer all rights of the entruster to a buyer in ordinary course of business." "'Entrusting'" is defined as "any delivery and any acquiescence in retention of possession regardless of any condition expressed between the parties to the delivery or acquiescence and regardless of whether the procurement of the entrusting or the possessor's disposition of the goods have been such as to be larcenous under the criminal law." General Statutes §42a-2-403 (3).

There is no dispute in the present case that the plaintiff's March 20, 2000, letter authorizing the Guggenheim to release *Red Elvis* to Malmberg constituted an entrustment under §42a-2-403 (3), or that Malmberg, an art dealer, is a merchant dealing in "goods of that kind"—works of art—under §42a-2-403 (2). Under the plain language of §42a-2-403 (2) and (3), therefore, Malmberg, as a merchant dealing in art entrusted with the painting, had the power to transfer all the rights of the entruster to a buyer in the ordinary course of business.

A "'[b]uyer in [the] ordinary course of business'" is defined as "a person that buys goods in good faith, without knowledge that the sale violates the rights of another person in the goods, and in the ordinary course from a person . . . in the business of selling goods of that kind. A person buys goods in the ordinary course if the sale to the person comports with the usual or customary practices in the kind of business in which the seller is engaged or with the seller's own usual or customary practices. . . ." General Statutes §42a-1-201 (9). A person buys goods in good faith if there is "honesty in fact and the observance of reasonable commercial standards of fair dealing" in the conduct or transaction concerned. General Statutes §42a-1-201 (20).

We are required, therefore, to determine whether the defendant followed the usual or customary practices and observed reasonable commercial standards of fair dealing in the art industry in his dealings with Malmberg. As we have indicated, the defendant presented expert testimony that the vast majority of art transactions, in which the buyer has no reason for concern about the seller's ability to convey good title, are "completed on a handshake and an exchange of an invoice." It is not customary for sophisticated buyers and sellers to obtain a signed invoice from the original seller to the dealer prior to a transaction, nor is it an ordinary or customary practice to request the underlying invoice or corroborating information as to a dealer's authority to convey title. Moreover, it is not customary to approach the owner of an artwork if the owner regularly worked with a particular art dealer because any inquiries about an art transaction customarily are presented to the art dealer rather than directly to the principal. It is customary to rely upon representations made by respected dealers regarding their authority to sell works of art. A dealer customarily is not required to present an invoice establishing when and from whom he bought the artwork or the conditions of the purchase.

We are compelled to conclude, however, that the sale from Malmberg to the defendant was unlike the vast majority of art transactions. The defendant had good reason to be concerned that Lindholm might have claims to the painting. Several courts have held that, under such circumstances, a handshake and an exchange of invoice is not sufficient to confer status as a buyer in the ordinary course. In Porter v. Wertz, 416 N.Y.S.2d 254, 68 A.D.2d 141 (1979), *aff'd,* 53 N.Y.2d 696, 421 N.E.2d 500, 439 N.Y.S.2d 105 (1981), for example, the owner of a painting entrusted it to an individual with whom he previously had conducted art transactions for display in the individual's home. This individual then used the services of a delicatessen employee, posing as an art dealer, to sell the painting to a merchant art buyer. Id., 145-46. In discussing the good faith obligation of a merchant, the court stated that although the definition of good faith "by its terms embraces the reasonable commercial standards of fair dealing in the trade, it should not—and cannot—be interpreted to permit, countenance or condone commercial standards of sharp trade practice or indifference as to the provenance, i.e., history of ownership or the right to possess or sell an object d'art. . . ." (Internal quotation marks omitted.) Id., 146. The buyer made no inquiry as to whether the purported art dealer, who was in fact a delicatessen employee, was the owner of the painting or had been authorized by the owner to sell the painting. Id. Because a simple telephone call would have revealed the fact that the defendant was not an art merchant, thereby leading to doubt that would have required further verification, the court concluded that the buyer could not claim buyer in the ordinary course of business status. Id., 146-47.

In Howley v. Sotheby's, Inc., New York Law Journal, Vol. 195 (February 20, 1986) p. 6, col. 3B, the owner of a painting sought its recovery from the defendant art dealer. The defendant had purchased the painting from the caretaker of the owner's home, who had posed as the owner's nephew, even though the defendant was unsure whether the "owner's nephew" had authority to sell the painting. Id. The court concluded that, because the defendant was a professional art dealer, he should have been "scrupulously concerned with taking proper title in anything he purchases." Id. Because the defendant had not taken any steps to verify title, even after the "owner's nephew" informed him that the sale first needed the owner's approval, the defendant did not fulfill his obligation and was liable for conversion. Id.

In Cantor v. Anderson, 639 F. Supp. 364, 367-68 (S.D.N.Y.), *aff'd*, 833 F.2d 1002 (2d Cir. 1986), the court, citing *Howley*, imposed a duty upon a sophisticated buyer to inquire into a painting's ownership when circumstances dictate. In *Cantor*, the buyer and the seller had engaged in numerous previous art transactions. Id., 366. When the buyer sought the return of several of his artworks that were on consignment with the seller, the seller gave the buyer a painting, to which he claimed ownership, as security for the artworks on consignment. Id., 367. The buyer, who had been aware of the seller's financial difficulties and was familiar with the seller's practice of selling works on consignment, had reason to doubt the seller's ownership of the painting. Id., 368. This doubt led to a duty to obtain some verification that the seller had good title. Because the buyer had made no efforts to verify title to the painting, choosing to rely solely on the seller's assurances, the court concluded that the buyer had not fulfilled his duty and was liable for conversion. Id., 368-69.

Finally, in Morgold, Inc. v. Keeler, 891 F. Supp. 1361, 1369 (N.D. Cal. 1995), the court held that an art dealer buyer had obtained good title to a painting by satisfying "the reasonable commercial standards in the art industry. . . ." In that case, the buyer and the seller had engaged in previous art transactions for several years. Id., 1364. When the buyer purchased the painting from the seller, he was unaware that the seller had only a one-half interest in the painting. Id., 1363-65. The court imposed a duty on "dealers in art [to] take reasonable steps to inquire into the title to a painting, particularly if there are warnings that something is wrong with a transaction." Id., 1368. In *Morgold, Inc.*, the buyer had engaged in previous art transactions with the seller and had contacted an expert on the artist, who gave no indication of problems with the painting's title. Id., 1365. Because there were no other warning signs indicating problems with title, the court concluded that the buyer had fulfilled his duty to make a reasonable inquiry and had acquired good title and a right to possession of the painting. Id., 1369.

We agree with these courts that a merchant buyer has a heightened duty of inquiry when a reasonable merchant would have doubts or questions regarding the seller's authority to sell. We further conclude that the steps that a merchant must take to conform to reasonable commercial standards before consummating a deal depend on all of the facts and circumstances surrounding the sale. In the present case, the defendant had concerns about Malmberg's ability to convey good title to *Red Elvis* because he believed that Lindholm might have had a claim to the painting. The defendant also was concerned that Malmberg had not yet acquired title to the painting or that the transaction might be a "flip."

Because of his concern that Lindholm might make a claim to *Red Elvis*, the defendant took the extraordinary step of hiring counsel to conduct an investigation and to negotiate a formal contract of sale on his behalf. He also insisted on and obtained a formal contract containing representations and warranties that Malmberg had title to the painting. In addition, during the course of the investigation, the defendant's counsel conducted both a lien search and an Art Loss Register search that revealed no competing claims to *Red Elvis.* Although the defendant was cautioned that the searches provided only minimal assurance that Malmberg had good title to the painting, such searches typically are not conducted during the course of a normal art transaction and, therefore, provided the defendant with at least some assurance that Lindholm had no claims to the painting.

Moreover, the evidence was sufficient for the trial court reasonably to conclude that at all times during the transaction, both Malmberg and Holm had reputations as honest, reliable, and trustworthy art dealers. This is not like the situation in Porter v. Wertz, supra, 68 A.D.2d 146, in which the court concluded that the buyer was not a buyer in the ordinary course of business because he did not know the dealer or his reputation. The defendant had little reason to doubt Malmberg's claim that he was the owner of *Red Elvis,* and any doubts that he did have reasonably were allayed by relying on Holm's assurances that Malmberg had bought the painting from the plaintiff because she needed money due to her divorce. The defendant established at trial that it is customary to rely on the assurances of respected art dealers when conducting a transaction, and the defendant had no reason to depart from this practice.

The defendant's concerns were further allayed when Malmberg delivered *Red Elvis* to a bonded warehouse in Denmark, the delivery location the parties had agreed to in the contract of sale. At the time of the sale, the painting was on loan to the Guggenheim, whose policy it was to release a painting on loan only to the true owner, or to someone the true owner had authorized to take possession. The defendant was not informed that the plaintiff had authorized release to Malmberg for the sole purpose of lending the painting to a museum in Denmark. Knowing that the Guggenheim would release the painting to an authorized party only, it was reasonable for the defendant to believe that Malmberg was the true owner of the painting. We conclude that these steps were sufficient to conform to reasonable commercial standards for the sale of artwork under the circumstances and, therefore, that the defendant had status as a buyer in the ordinary course of business.

We recognize that the customary practice in the art industry of not requiring a merchant buyer to obtain documentary proof that the seller owns the work of art whenever there are reasonable doubts or questions regarding the seller's authority to sell imposes risks on persons who entrust art to an art dealer. Section 42a-1-201(9) evinces a legislative desire, however, for courts to respect "the usual or customary practices in the kind of business in which the seller is engaged. . . ." We are not entitled to impose the type of business practices that we would prefer.

Moreover, the evidence presented at trial established that the reason that documentary proof of ownership customarily is not required is to protect the confidentiality of the owner and the buyer. Requiring a merchant buyer to obtain an invoice or other supporting documentation proving the seller's ownership would in every transaction destroy the privacy and confidentiality that buyers and sellers have come to desire and expect. Accordingly, only when circumstances surrounding the sale cast severe doubt on the ownership of the artwork are merchant buyers required to obtain documentary assurance that the seller has good title. In this instance, the Swedish-English letter was produced at Holm's suggestion to give the defendant assurance that the *plaintiff* had good title when she sold the painting to Malmberg. In light of the customary practices in the industry, the defendant reasonably could have concluded that Malmberg was unwilling to produce a signed copy of the letter because of his desire to protect the owner's expectation of confidentiality in their transaction. The purpose of the letter was not to give the defendant assurance that *Malmberg* had good title to the painting, and any concerns about Malmberg's title that could be inferred from the refusal to show the defendant a signed copy of the letter were quickly allayed by Malmberg's subsequent delivery of the painting to Denmark. Accordingly, we conclude, on the basis of all the circumstances surrounding this sale, that the defendant's failure to obtain an invoice from the plaintiff to Malmberg or a signed copy of the Swedish-English letter does not strip him of his status as a buyer in the ordinary course of business. For the same reasons, we conclude that the defendant was not required to contact directly the plaintiff or other parties who might have had knowledge concerning *Red Elvis*' title.

We conclude that the trial court properly determined that the defendant was a buyer in the ordinary course of business and, therefore, took all rights the plaintiff had to the painting pursuant to §42a-2-403(2).

The judgment is affirmed.

PROBLEM 25

Going on a family vacation, Kahr stowed sterling silver and credit cards in a bag in the attic. Not long after returning, Kahr took several bags of clothing to donate to Goodwill—and unknowingly brought along the bag of valuables. Kahr handed the bags over to Goodwill, and signed a form describing the donation as "used clothing." After sorting through the bags, a Goodwill employee set the credit cards aside, but put the silver out for sale. A bargain hunter soon snapped it up. Can Kahr recover the silver? See §2-403(2) and (3); Kahr v. Markland, 543 N.E.2d 579 (Ill. App. 1989).

II. WARRANTIES OF QUALITY

A. Express Warranties

An express warranty arises when the seller does something affirmative to create buyer expectations about the characteristics or performance of the goods. Typically this means that the seller will make oral or written representations about the product in advertisements, the verbal sales pitch, or the written contract. These representations must have some substance to them (more than mere "puffing") to rise to the dignity of an express warranty. In the Code's words, they must "relate to the goods" (an obvious requirement) and become part of the *basis of the bargain* (a not-so-obvious or explainable requirement). Under the now-replaced Uniform Sales Act (§12), the buyer had to prove *reliance* on the statement alleged to be an express warranty. Does *basis of bargain* mean this? Read Official Comment 3 to §2-313. Most courts (but not all) have not required a buyer to prove any specific reliance, but instead hold that a statement goes to the basis of the bargain if its natural tendency is to induce the buyer to purchase (even though that is not the sole reason). See In re General Motors Corp. Dex-Cool Products Liability Litigation, 241 F.R.D. 305 (S.D. Ill. 2007); White & Summers §10-5. This means that if the statement, however made, has any substance to it so that it *might* have played some part in the buyer's decision to buy, the burden is on the *seller* to prove that the buyer did *not* rely on the statement. If the seller cannot meet this burden, the buyer has the benefit of an express warranty. See Official Comment 8 to §2-313.

PROBLEM 26

(a) The salesman at the lot of Smiles Pre-Owned Vehicles told the woman buying the car that it was in "A-1 shape." She bought the car, but it broke down the next day, stranding her in the country. Was this oral statement mere puffing? See Wat Henry Pontiac Co. v. Bradley, 202 Okla. 82, 210 P.2d 348 (1949); White & Summers §10-4. Is it an easier case if the seller tells the buyer that the used car is in "mint condition"? See Taylor v. Alfama, 481 A.2d 1059 (Vt. 1984); Nigro v. Lee, 882 N.Y.S.2d 346 (App. Div. 2009) (no express warranty where eBay seller described Mercedes Benz automobile as "gorgeous" with "minor blemishes," but sold "as is").

(b) When the farmer looked over the young chickens he was contemplating purchasing from the poultry company, he complained that they looked pretty scruffy. The salesman explained that that was because they were on half-feed and that when they were placed on full-feed, they would "bloom out, straighten up, and fly right," and they would "do a good job in your chicken house." The farmer purchased the chickens, and two months later they started dying in droves. The farmer sued, claiming breach of an express warranty. Is he right? Is this a question of law or of fact for the jury? See Woodruff v. Clark County Farm Bureau Coop, 153 Ind. App. 31, 286 N.E.2d 188 (1972).

(c) Portia Moot, a third-year law student, had taken the course in Sales, so when she went to buy a used car, she listened very carefully to the sales pitch. The smarmy salesman was quite friendly, but he only made two statements about the car she bought: "This is a great car!" and "You're going to love it!" In fact, the car broke down a great deal, and Portia quickly grew to hate it. Does she have a cause of action here?

(d) Assume that the car salesman told Portia that the used car she was contemplating purchasing had been thoroughly inspected by the car dealership's crack repair department and was "mechanically in perfect condition." Is that an express warranty? See Bobholz v. Banaszak, 655 N.W.2d 547 (Wis. App. 2002). Portia was suspicious about the reliability of the car and before she bought it, she took it to her own favorite mechanic for an inspection. She didn't buy the car until her mechanic cleared it as fine. When the car broke down a few days later, she decided to bring suit on the express warranty. What defense will the car dealership raise?

(e) David Vargo purchased only very healthy foods. A vegetable oil he bought stated on the label that it was "All Natural" but then was found to contain genetically modified organisms. Has an express warranty been breached? See Ault v. J.M. Smucker Co., 2014 WL 1998235 (S.D.N.Y. 2014).

(f) Should a court accept the argument that a "Manufacturer's Suggested Retail Price" is an express warranty of product quality, because "status-conscious consumers tend to use a price cue also as a surrogate indicator of prestige"? Marino v. Coach, Inc., 2017 WL 3731954 (S.D.N.Y. 2017).

In re Toshiba America HD DVD Marketing and Sales Practices Litigation

United States District Court, District of New Jersey, 2009
WL 2940081

DEBEVOISE, Senior District Judge.

[Plaintiffs bought an HD DVD Player from Toshiba after the company had decided to discontinue future production of the product because it had lost the technological battle for its format's supremacy, but while Toshiba was still advertising the player as "'For Today, Tomorrow and Beyond.'" When Plaintiffs discovered this deception, they sued for, among other things, breach of an express warranty.]

High Definition Digital Versatile Disc ("HD DVD") is an optical disc storage format for encoding audio-visual entertainment such as movies, and is available for playback on compatible HD DVD players, including Toshiba's HD DVD Player. (Id. ¶13.) Toshiba developed the HD DVD format to be a "next generation" format to succeed the standard DVD. (Id.) The HD DVD Player allows consumers to view movies in higher definition and fidelity than allowed by previous technologies. (Id.)

Toshiba introduced the HD DVD Player for sale to consumers in the United States in April 2006. (Id. ¶14.) At that time the list prices ranged from \$499 to \$799. (Id.) Plaintiffs allege that these prices were 200% to 500% of the cost of standard DVD players without high definition capabilities. (Id.)

The HD DVD Player faced competition from Blu-ray Disc, an optical disc format largely developed and supported by the Sony Corporation ("Sony"). (Id. ¶18.) Blu-ray Disc was also marketed as a "next generation" format for the encoding and playback of audio-visual entertainment. (Id.)

Several major movie studios, which regularly release movies in the DVD format, chose to release movies in Blu-ray format rather than HD DVD. (Id. ¶25.) Disney (including Touchstone and Miramax), Sony Pictures (including MGM/Columbia Tristar) and 20th Century Fox all supported Blu-ray technology rather than HD DVD. (Id.) Plaintiffs allege that Toshiba "consistently failed to disclose to its customers" this information regarding the support of certain movie studios for Blu-ray rather than HD DVD technology. (Id.) In what the Plaintiffs characterize as "a desperate attempt by Toshiba to increase its market share and garner HD DVD movie studio support," on August 21, 2007, *The New York Times* reported that Paramount and Dream Works Animation would receive approximately $150 million in financial incentives for their commitment to HD DVD. (Id.)

The competition between Blu-ray and HD DVD was well reported in the media and was likened to the competition 30 years ago between the VHS and Betamax formats for home video recording. (Certification of David E. Sellinger, February 17, 2009 ("Sellinger Cert.") Ex. C at 2 and Ex. E at 1.) As *Business Week* reported in its December 6, 2007 edition,

> For two years now, rival camps have been battling over which new DVD format will prevail: Blu-ray, which is backed by Sony (SNE) and a consortium of 170 other companies, or HD DVD, which is being championed by Toshiba (TOSBF), Microsoft (MSFT), and others. Both technologies promise crisper video that looks better on the new generation of flat-panel, high definition TVs. And the winner stands to control a lucrative new market worth billions. Each side has been competing to win the backing of the major movie studios. Only Warner Bros. (TWX), which currently uses both formats, is still playing hard to get.

(Sellinger Cert. Ex. D at 1.) That same article reported that there were rumors that "Warner [was] coming aboard-[Sony] soon," meaning that Warner Brothers was planning to discontinue production of movies in the HD DVD format and instead use the Blu-ray format. (Id.; CCAC ¶35.) *Business Week* also reported that the head of Toshiba's HD DVD business in Japan had made three trips since the summer to meet with Warner Brothers regarding its HD DVD business. (Sellinger Cert. Ex. D at 1; CCAC ¶35.) On December 10, 2007, *The New York Times* reported that Warner Brothers had signaled that it would choose one format—HD DVD or Blu-ray—after the 2007 holiday shopping season and that its choice would be determined by which format sold more DVDs during that season. (CCAC ¶35.)

Toshiba continued to market its HD DVD Players, with the slogan "For Today, Tomorrow and Beyond," throughout the 2007 holiday shopping seasons and thereafter. (Id. ¶27.) During that season, Plaintiffs allege that Toshiba lowered prices on its Players in order to induce additional sales. (Id.)

On January 4, 2008, Warner Brothers announced that it would no longer release movies in the HD DVD format. (Id. ¶26.) This announcement led to "a chain reaction in the industry," which included decisions by Best Buy, Wal-Mart and Circuit City to drop HD DVD from their stores. (Id.) Once Warner Brothers decided in favor of Blu-ray, that system's market share increased from 49% to 70%. (Id. ¶35.)

Toshiba continued marketing its HD DVD Players in January and the first weeks of February 2008. On January 14, 2008, Toshiba issued a press release stating "that it [was] stepping up its successful marketing campaign for HD DVD as it experienced record-breaking unit sales in the fourth quarter of 2007" (Id. ¶28.) That press release also stated that "HD DVD is proven to be the format of choice for consumers" and that Toshiba planned to execute an extended advertising campaign to further enhance consumer awareness of the benefits of HD DVD and drive sales. (Id.) On February 3, 2008, Toshiba ran an ad during the Super Bowl, "highlighting its HD-A3, HD-A30 and HD-A35 Players," which the Plaintiffs allege "thereby [characterized] the long-term viability of the Players." (Id. ¶29.)

Plaintiffs allege that "[m]arket insiders" predicted that Blu-ray would win the battle with the HD DVD format if for no other reason than the fact that Blu-ray was backed by Disney. (Id. ¶35.) Plaintiffs also allege that "Toshiba was aware of market trends and knew, despite its misleading marketing campaign, that it was only a matter of time before the company withdrew from the marketplace abandoning its customer base." (Id. ¶35.) Plaintiffs claim that, as a "direct result of Toshiba's abrupt exit from the HD DVD market," their investments in the HD DVD Players "lost significant value." (Id. ¶31.) . . . An express warranty by a seller is created by: "[a]ny affirmation of fact or promise made by the seller to the buyer which relates to the goods and becomes part of the basis of the bargain," or "[a]ny description of the goods which is made part of the basis of the bargain." N.J.S.A. § 12A:2-313(1)(a) & (b); Cal. Comm. Code §2313(1)(a) & (b); Fla. Stat. Ann. 672.313(1)(a) & (b); Idaho Code §28-2-313(1)(a) & (b); 810 Ill. Comp. Stat. 5/2-313(1)(a) & (b); Mich. Comp. Laws §440.2313(1)(a) & (b). The use of "formal words of promise or that the seller have a specific intention to warrant the good" is not necessary to create an express warranty. Liberty Lincoln-Mercury, Inc. v. Ford Motor Co., 171 F.3d 818, 824 (3d Cir. 1999) (citing N.J. Stat. Ann. §12A:2-313(2)). But "an affirmation merely of the value of the goods or a statement purporting to be merely the seller's opinion or commendation of the goods does not create a warranty." N.J. Stat. Ann §12A:2-313(2); Cal. Comm. Code §2313(2); Fla. Stat. Ann. 672.313(2); Idaho Code §28-2-313(2); 810 Ill. Comp. Stat. 5/2-313(2); Mich. Comp. Laws §440.2313(2).

Plaintiffs allege that Toshiba's "affirmations of fact and/or promises relating to the [HD DVD] Players created express warranties that Toshiba would continue to support the HD DVD format and continue to manufacture such players." (CCAC ¶117.) They allege that Toshiba breached these warranties when it announced in February 2008 that it would exit the HD DVD market. (Id. ¶118.) Specifically, Plaintiffs argue that "Toshiba warranted that its [HD DVD] Players could play HD DVDs 'Today, Tomorrow, and Beyond.'" (Plts.' Opp'n Br. 17.) Yet there is no allegation that the HD DVD Players cannot still play HD DVDs. Rather, the problem is that the availability of new HD DVDs has severely decreased. Plaintiffs further argue that the long-term viability of the HD DVD market "was a large part of the basis of the bargain between Toshiba and the putative Class, because consumers were concerned with choosing a high definition DVD player which would have long term viability." (Id. 17 & 18.) Toshiba's exit from the HD DVD market has, according to Plaintiffs, "substantially limited that viability." (Id. 18.)

Plaintiffs do not allege that their HD DVD Players no longer can play HD DVDs. Rather, they argue that Toshiba's tag line that its HD DVD Players were for "Today, Tomorrow, and Beyond" created an express warranty that, essentially, Toshiba would remain in the HD DVD market forever. As discussed with respect to the Plaintiffs' consumer fraud claims, the statement that HD DVD Players were for "Today, Tomorrow, and Beyond" is puffery and not specific enough to create an express warranty. Plaintiffs cite to L.S. Heath & Son, Inc. v. AT & T Information Systems, Inc., 9 F.3d 561, 570 (7th Cir. 1993), where the Court of Appeals for the Seventh Circuit, applying New Jersey law, noted that, "A statement can amount to a warranty, even if unintended to be such by the seller, 'if it could fairly be understood . . . to constitute an affirmation or representation that the [product] possesse[s] a certain quality or capacity relating to future performance.'" Id. (quoting Gladden v. Cadillac Motor Car Div., Gen. Motors Corp., 83 N.J. 320, 416 A.2d 394, 396 (N.J. 1980)). While it is certainly true that a statement relating to future performance *may* create an express warranty, even if not intended by the seller, Toshiba's statement regarding its HD DVD Players does not rise to that level. In *L.S. Heath & Son,* the court found that AT & T's statement that its "complete intregated [sic] data processing and voice/data communications network [will] satisf[y] all of your aforementioned objectives," may have constituted an express warranty. Id. AT & T's statement was far more specific than Toshiba's statement that its HD DVD Players were for "Today, Tomorrow, and Beyond." Additionally, even if Toshiba created an express warranty of future *performance,* there is no allegation that the HD DVD Players do not perform as they are intended—i.e., to play HD DVDs.

The CCAC fails to state a claim for breach of express warranty. Count Five of the CCAC is therefore dismissed.

PROBLEM 27

Upon graduation from law school, Andrew Loner hung out his shingle and waited. Mr. and Mrs. Consumer were his first clients, and they told him the following story. Two weeks earlier they had visited a wallpaper store, Paper & Paste, Inc., and inquired about vinyl wallpaper for their dining room. The salesman told them that the "finest" wallpaper in the store was Expenso-Paper, a vinyl wallpaper selling at $75 a roll. When he learned that the Consumers had never before put up wallpaper, the salesman assured them that Expenso-Paper "goes up easily, can be put on with any paste, and dries immediately." He said that it "would look wonderful" and, moreover, that Expenso-Paper "was used by Mary Magic," the famous movie star, in her dining room. He showed them a sample book, and they picked out a pattern they liked and ordered ten rolls. When the paper arrived the next week, it proved to be very stiff and hard to work with. It tore easily and refused to stay flat on the wall (it either bubbled or, due to its heavy weight, fell down on drying). In addition, it was dyed a darker color than the version of the pattern in the sample book. The final result was that the Consumers' dining room looked terrible. To top it all off, the Consumers discovered that Mary Magic did not own a home (she lived exclusively in hotels).

Upon complaining to Paper & Paste, the Consumers were told by the manager that Expenso-Paper needs a special brand of paste, to wit, Expenso-Paste. They were also told that Expenso-Paper was an inferior brand and that next time they should buy Super Wall, a better product that the store carried.

The Consumers told Loner that they signed the contract without reading it and that the statement about Mary Magic's dining room was made *after* they signed the agreement. Loner (and you) have to answer these questions:

(a) Which of the salesman's representations amount to express warranties?

(1) finest?
(2) goes up easily?
(3) can be put on with any paste?
(4) dries immediately?
(5) would look wonderful?
(6) was used by Mary Magic?

Do you see any other express warranties?

(b) Is the Mary Magic statement part of the *basis of the bargain,* arising as it did after the contract was signed? See §2-209(1); Official Comment 7 to §2-313.

PROBLEM 28

Balding Paul bought a wig from Hair, Inc. He became annoyed when the wig changed colors slightly from season to season. He did not do anything about it until one day, while thumbing through a newspaper, he noticed an ad for Hair, Inc., that claimed that their wigs did not shrink or change color. On checking back, he discovered that Hair, Inc., had run an identical ad during the week prior to his purchase of the wig. He sues. On the witness stand Paul confesses that he never saw the ad until a year after his purchase of the wig. Is this admission fatal to his recovery on a theory of express warranty? See Winston Indus., Inc. v. Stuyvesant Ins. Co., 55 Ala. App. 525, 317 So. 2d 493 (1975) (buyer held protected by manufacturer's warranty on mobile home even though he never received a copy).

B. *Implied Warranties*

In many ways implied warranties are the legal opposites of express warranties. An express warranty is created only where sellers do something *affirmative* (open their mouth and say something, take out a newspaper ad, display a sample). Implied warranties, on the other hand, are *automatically* part of the contract unless the seller (or the circumstance) does something affirmative to get rid of them. Implied warranties are implied as a matter of law; they are sometimes referred to as "children of the law." Like express warranties, the seller's intention to create any implied warranty is completely irrelevant.

1. Merchantability

The implied warranty of merchantability (which is easier to spell and pronounce if you think of it as two words—*merchant* and *ability*—tacked together) is not given a precise definition in the Code. The basic idea is that the item must be saleable and conform to the normal expectations of the parties. Notice that §2-314(2), which you should now read, sets minimum standards for its meaning. Clever lawyers can make much of the laundry list found in that subsection.

Shaffer v. Victoria Station, Inc.

Supreme Court of Washington, 1978
91 Wash. 2d 295, 588 P.2d 233

DOLLIVER, J.

On March 26, 1974, plaintiff Shaffer ordered a glass of wine at the Victoria Station, a restaurant operated by defendant. In the course of taking his first or second sip, the wine glass broke in Mr. Shaffer's hand, resulting in alleged permanent injury.

Plaintiff brought this action based upon three theories: negligence, breach of implied warranty under the Uniform Commercial Code, and strict liability under the theory of Restatement (Second) of Torts §402A (1965). The manufacturer of the glass was named as a defendant, but was never served. Prior to trial, as counsel and the trial judge were discussing proposed instructions, plaintiff's attorney indicated that he could not prove negligence, and wished to submit the case to the jury on the grounds of breach of warranty and strict liability. Plaintiff then took a voluntary nonsuit on the negligence issue. At the same time, the court ruled the case sounded in negligence alone, and granted the defendant's motion for dismissal. The Court of Appeals affirmed. Shaffer v. Victoria Station, Inc., 18 Wash. App. 816, 572 P.2d 737 (1977). We reverse the Court of Appeals.

I

Defendant argues the Uniform Commercial Code does not apply since the restaurant was not a merchant with respect to wine glasses as defined in §2-104 and, since the glass itself was not sold, there was no passing of title as required under §2-106. Plaintiff, however, points to §2-314 as being decisive. We agree. Section 2-314 reads, inter alia:

> (1) Unless excluded or modified (§2-316), a warranty that the goods shall be merchantable is implied in a contract for their sale if the seller is a merchant with respect to goods of that kind. Under this section the serving for value of food or drink to be consumed either on the premises or elsewhere is a sale.
>
> (2) Goods to be merchantable must be at least such as . . .
>
> (c) are fit for the ordinary purposes for which such goods are used; and . . .
>
> (e) are adequately contained, packaged, and labeled as the agreement may require;. . . .

It is our opinion that, when the Uniform Commercial Code states "the serving for value of food or drink to be consumed either on the premises or elsewhere is a sale" and that such food and drink must be "adequately contained, packaged, and labeled as the agreement may require," it covers entirely the situation before us. Plaintiff ordered a drink (a glass of wine) from defendant. Defendant sold and served the glass of wine to plaintiff to be consumed by plaintiff on the premises. The wine could not be served as a drink nor could it be consumed without an adequate container. The drink sold includes the wine and the container both of which must be fit for the ordinary purpose for which used. Plaintiff alleges the drink sold—wine in a glass—was unfit and has, therefore, stated a cause of action.

In addition to the language of §2-314, we believe the language of §1-103 is applicable. It states:

> Unless displaced by the particular provisions of this Title, the principles of law and equity, including the law merchant and the law relative to capacity to contract, principal and agent, estoppel, fraud, misrepresentation, duress,

> coercion, mistake, bankruptcy, or other validating or invalidating cause shall supplement its provisions.

Plaintiff urges that cases which apply the Uniform Commercial Code where the goods are leased rather than sold (see, e.g., Baker v. Seattle, 79 Wash. 2d 198, 484 P.2d 405 (1971)), or are under a bailment for mutual benefit (see, e.g., Fulbright v. Klamath Gas Co., 271 Ore. 449, 533 P.2d 316 (1975)), be extended to the facts before us. We believe this is unnecessary. A more straightforward and less tortuous approach is that adopted in Hadley v. Hillcrest Dairy, Inc., 341 Mass. 624, 171 N.E.2d 293 (1961). In that case, a bottle of milk delivered to the plaintiff's home shattered and cut the plaintiff's hand. The Massachusetts Supreme Judicial Court, relying on the Massachusetts sales act (which was not, as argued by defendant, significantly different in its applicable part from the Uniform Commercial Code), held at 627, "In our view it is immaterial whether or not the property in the jug passed to the plaintiff." The court goes on to cite Geddling v. Marsh, (1920) 1 K.B. 668. In that case, a retailer received bottled mineral water from the manufacturer and was injured by an exploding bottle. The court found the bottles were not sold to the retailer but held the retailer could recover under a breach of an implied warranty of fitness. The court said at 671-672:

> In this case there was only one contract—namely, a contract between the plaintiff and the defendant that the plaintiff should be supplied with mineral waters. Mineral waters could not be supplied except in bottles, and therefore the plaintiff was asking to be supplied with mineral waters in bottles. That undoubtedly is a contract of sale, and I will assume that in that contract there might be a condition that the bottles should not be bought by the plaintiff but should be hired; but the question the county court judge had to consider was whether the bottles were not "supplied under a contract of sale." This was a contract of sale none the less because there was a special provision with regard to the bottles. The section, in my opinion, extends not only to the goods actually bought under the contract but to goods "supplied under the contract of sale." This particular bottle was thus "supplied under a contract of sale," and it follows that it should be reasonably fit for the purpose for which it was supplied. In fact it was not reasonably fit and in consequence of that unfitness the plaintiff was injured.

See also Sartin v. Blackwell, 200 Miss. 579, 28 So. 2d 222 (1946). Plaintiff has a cause of action both on the face of the statute and under the principles of case law elucidated above.

II

We also hold an action lies under the strict liability theory of Restatement (Second) of Torts §402A (1965). The policy questions of strict liability and their application to retailers have been previously determined.

See Seattle-First Natl. Bank v. Tabert, 86 Wash. 2d 145, 542 P.2d 774 (1975); Ulmer v. Ford Motor Co., 75 Wash. 2d 522, 452 P.2d 729 (1969). The only question remaining is whether §402A applies to the transaction here. In addressing this issue, the Court of Appeals expressed concern over an uncontrollable broadening of the doctrine of strict liability:

> Were the wine glass in question held to be a mere facet of the sale of the "glass of wine" and thus a "product" for the purposes of section 402A, the theory of strict liability would be greatly and unnecessarily expanded. The reasonably clear standard of engagement "in the business of selling . . . a product" would be abandoned in deference to a less predictable question—whether the injury-producing aspect of the sale was necessary to the sale. If a wine glass renders a restaurateur strictly liable because he could not sell wine without it, what of other tablewear, the waiters and the bus boys, the furnishings to effect an attractive atmosphere, or the building housing the establishment? The argument could be made that numerous aspects of a restaurant's operation, or that of any other retailer, are integral to each sale. To ignore the fact that this allegedly defective glass was never sold would create great uncertainty as to the limits of strict liability.

Shaffer, at 820-821.

We do not agree with the gloomy view of the Court of Appeals of the consequences of allowing the plaintiff to proceed with this action. We hold the sale of a glass of wine is subject to the strict liability provisions of §402A. If their predictions as to future lawsuits come to pass, we will deal with the litigation at that time. Confirmation of the applicability of §402A to this case is given in comment h, which says:

> The defective condition may arise not only from harmful ingredients, not characteristic of the product itself either as to presence or quantity, but also from foreign objects contained in the product, from decay or deterioration before sale, or from the way in which the product is prepared or packed. No reason is apparent for distinguishing between the product itself and the container in which it is supplied; and the two are purchased by the user or consumer as an integrated whole. Where the container is itself dangerous, the product is sold in a defective condition. Thus a carbonated beverage in a bottle which is so weak, or cracked, or jagged at the edges, or bottled under such excessive pressure that it may explode or otherwise cause harm to the person who handles it, is in a defective and dangerous condition. The container cannot logically be separated from the contents when the two are sold as a unit, and the liability stated in this Section arises not only when the consumer drinks the beverage and is poisoned by it, but also when he is injured by the bottle while he is handling it preparatory to consumption.

Restatement (Second) of Torts §402A, comment h at 351-352 (1965).

Plaintiff has stated a cause of action under theories of implied warranty of fitness and strict liability. The Court of Appeals is reversed.

QUESTIONS

1. Would it be a defense to the restaurant that it was not negligent in any way in connection with its handling of the wine glass? See La Fountain v. Sears, Roebuck & Co., 680 F. Supp. 251 (E.D. Mich. 1988).

2. If a casino serves its patrons free drinks at the gaming tables and one of the drinks proves to contain chips of glass, would the Washington Supreme Court reach the same result it did in the last case? Phrased another way: is there a "sale" going on? See Levondosky v. Marina Assocs., 731 F. Supp. 1210 (D.N.J. 1990).

By far the most important segment of §2-314(2) is found in subsection (2)(c): to be merchantable the goods must be "fit for the ordinary purposes for which such goods are used." (Or, as the South Carolina courts have put it since 1793, "a sound price warrants a sound commodity.") When you think about it, a warranty that the goods are fit for their *ordinary purpose* is a big warranty. It is the warranty that the goods will work, and it is typically the only warranty that the buyer needs. When sellers disclaim the implied warranty of merchantability (and they often do), why do buyers not routinely complain?

PROBLEM 29

Consider the following:

(a) Are cigarettes that cause lung cancer merchantable if used over a period of years? See Haglund v. Philip Morris, Inc., 446 Mass. 741, 847 N.E.2d 315 (2006); Franklin E. Crawford, Fit for Its Ordinary Purpose? Tobacco, Fast Food, and the Implied Warranty of Merchantability, 63 Ohio St. L.J. 1165 (2002); White & Summers §10-12; Annot. 80 A.L.R.2d 681. See also Hoyte v. Yum! Brands, Inc., 489 F. Supp. 2d 24 (D.D.C. 2007) (KFC did not breach implied warranty of merchantability, although its products contained trans fats); Bodie v. Purdue Pharma Co., 489 F. Supp. 2d 24 (D.D.C. 2007) (addictive nature of painkiller OxyContin did not breach warranty of merchantability). If the seller's advertisements stated that the cigarettes were "mild," would that create an express warranty?

(b) To treat menopausal symptoms, plaintiff took medicines manufactured by the defendant that combined the drug progestin and estrogen. As a consequence she developed breast cancer. Contending that the warranty of merchantability was breached when the defendant failed to warn her of this possibility, she sued. Does that warranty contain a "failure to warn" component? See Hines v. Wyeth, 2011 WL 1990496 (S.D. W.Va. 2011).

(c) Following a recipe in the Exotic Cookbook, Martha prepared pufferfish fillet for Thanksgiving. The book, however, neglected to advise chefs to remove the pufferfish's poisonous organs. After a lengthy recuperation,

Martha sued the book store and publisher for breach of the implied warranty of merchantability. What result? See Cardozo v. True, 342 So. 2d 1053 (Fla. Dist. Ct. App. 1977). *Cardozo* emphasized one major consideration: "It is unthinkable that standards imposed on the quality of goods sold by a merchant would require that merchant, who is a book seller, to evaluate the thought processes of the many authors and publishers of the hundreds and often thousands of books which the merchant offers for sale. One can readily imagine the extent of potential litigation. Is the newsdealer, or for that matter the neighborhood news carrier, liable if the local paper's recipes call for inedible ingredients? We think not." Do you agree?

(d) Officer Krupke, a New York policeman by profession, sold his family car to his next-door neighbor, Maria, telling her it was a "good car." In fact, it was falling apart and blew up the first time she drove it. Has Krupke breached the implied warranty of merchantability? See §2-104(1); Official Comment 3 to §2-314; §1-304. Should §2-314 be extended so that the warranty is made by all sellers? See Ingrid Hillinger, The Merchant of §2-314: Who Needs Him?, 34 Hastings L.J. 747 (1983).

(e) If the dashboard touchscreen, which controlled the radio, climate control, and navigation systems, was defective, would that make a new automobile unmerchantable? See Rasnic v. FCA US LLC, 2017 WL 6406880 (D. Kan. 2017).

Webster v. Blue Ship Tea Room, Inc.

Massachusetts Supreme Judicial Court, 1964
347 Mass. 421, 198 N.E.2d 309

Reardon, J.

This is a case which by its nature evokes earnest study not only of the law but also of the culinary traditions of the Commonwealth which bear so heavily upon its outcome. It is an action to recover damages for personal injuries sustained by reason of a breach of implied warranty of food served by the defendant in its restaurant. An auditor, whose findings of fact were not to be final, found for the plaintiff. On a retrial in the Superior Court before a judge and jury, in which the plaintiff testified, the jury returned a verdict for her. The defendant is here on exceptions to the refusal of the judge (1) to strike certain portions of the auditor's report, (2) to direct a verdict for the defendant, and (3) to allow the defendant's motion for the entry of a verdict in its favor under leave reserved.

The jury could have found the following facts: On Saturday, April 25, 1959, about 1 p.m., the plaintiff, accompanied by her sister and her aunt, entered the Blue Ship Tea Room operated by the defendant. The group was seated at a table and supplied with menus.

This restaurant, which the plaintiff characterized as "quaint," was located in Boston "on the third floor of an old building in T Wharf which overlooks the ocean."

The plaintiff, who had been born and brought up in New England (a fact of some consequence), ordered clam chowder and crabmeat salad. Within a few minutes she received tidings to the effect that "there was no more clam chowder," whereupon she ordered a cup of fish chowder. Presently, there was set before her "a small bowl of fish chowder." She had previously enjoyed a breakfast about 9 a.m. which had given her no difficulty. "The fish chowder contained haddock, potatoes, milk, water and seasoning. The chowder was milky in color and not clear. The haddock and potatoes were in chunks" (also a fact of consequence). "She agitated it a little with the spoon and observed that it was a fairly full bowl. . . . It was hot when she got it, but she did not tip it with her spoon because it was hot . . . but stirred it in an up and under motion. She denied that she did this because she was looking for something, but it was rather because she wanted an even distribution of fish and potatoes." "She started to eat it, alternating between the chowder and crackers which were on the table with . . . [some] rolls. She ate about 3 or 4 spoonfuls then stopped. She looked at the spoonfuls as she was eating. She saw equal parts of liquid, potato and fish as she spooned it into her mouth. She did not see anything unusual about it. After 3 or 4 spoonfuls she was aware that something had lodged in her throat because she couldn't swallow and couldn't clear her throat by gulping and she could feel it." This misadventure led to two esophagoscopies at the Massachusetts General Hospital, in the second of which, on April 27, 1959, a fish bone was found and removed. The sequence of events produced injury to the plaintiff which was not insubstantial.

We must decide whether a fish bone lurking in a fish chowder, about the ingredients of which there is no other complaint, constitutes a breach of implied warranty under applicable provisions of the Uniform Commercial Code, the annotations to which are not helpful on this point. As the judge put it in his charge, "Was the fish chowder fit to be eaten and wholesome? . . . [N]obody is claiming that the fish itself wasn't wholesome. . . . But the bone of contention here—I don't mean that for a pun—but was this fish bone a foreign substance that made the fish chowder unwholesome or not fit to be eaten?"

The plaintiff has vigorously reminded us of the high standards imposed by this court where the sale of food is involved (see Flynn v. First Natl. Stores Inc., 296 Mass. 521, 523) and has made reference to cases involving stones in beans (Friend v. Childs Dining Hall Co., 231 Mass. 65), trichinae in pork (Holt v. Mann, 294 Mass. 21, 22), and to certain other cases, here and elsewhere, serving to bolster her contention of breach of warranty.

The defendant asserts that here was a native New Englander eating fish chowder in a "quaint" Boston dining place where she had been before; that "[f]ish chowder, as it is served and enjoyed by New Englanders, is a hearty dish, originally designed to satisfy the appetites of our seamen and fishermen"; that "[t]his court knows well that we are not talking of some insipid broth as is customarily served to convalescents." We are asked to rule in such fashion that no chef is forced "to reduce the pieces of fish in the chowder to minuscule size in an effort to ascertain if they contained any pieces of bone." "In so ruling," we are told (in the defendant's brief), "the court will not only uphold its reputation for legal knowledge and acumen, but will, as loyal sons of Massachusetts, save our world-renowned fish chowder from degenerating into an insipid broth containing the mere essence of its former stature as a culinary masterpiece." Notwithstanding these passionate entreaties we are bound to examine with detachment the nature of fish chowder and what might happen to it under varying interpretations of the Uniform Commercial Code.

Chowder is an ancient dish preexisting even "the appetites of our seamen and fishermen." It was perhaps the common ancestor of the "more refined cream soups, purees, and bisques." Berolzheimer, The American Woman's Cook Book (Publisher's Guild Inc., New York, 1941) p. 176. The word "chowder" comes from the French "chaudiere," meaning a "cauldron" or "pot." "In the fishing villages of Brittany . . . 'faire la chaudiere' means to supply a cauldron in which is cooked a mess of fish and biscuit with some savoury condiments, a hodgepodge contributed by the fishermen themselves, each of whom in return receives his share of the prepared dish. The Breton fishermen probably carried the custom to Newfoundland, long famous for its chowder, whence it has spread to Nova Scotia, New Brunswick, and New England." A New England Dictionary (MacMillan and Co., 1893) p. 386. Our literature over the years abounds in references not only to the delights of chowder but also to its manufacture. A namesake of the plaintiff, Daniel Webster, had a recipe for fish chowder which has survived into a number of modern cookbooks[5] and in which the removal of fish bones is not mentioned at all. One old-time recipe recited in the

5. "Take a cod of ten pounds, well cleaned, leaving on the skin. Cut into pieces one and a half pounds thick, preserving the head whole. Take one and a half pounds of clear, fat salt pork, cut in thin slices. Do the same with twelve potatoes. Take the largest pot you have. Try out the pork first, then take out the pieces of pork, leaving in the drippings. Add to that three parts of water, a layer of fish, so as to cover the bottom of the pot; next a layer of potatoes, then two tablespoons of salt, 1 teaspoon of pepper, then the pork, another layer of fish, and the remainder of the potatoes. Fill the pot with water to cover the ingredients. Put over a good fire. Let the chowder boil twenty-five minutes. When this is done have a quart of boiling milk ready, and ten hard crackers split and dipped in cold water. Add milk and crackers. Let the whole boil five minutes. The chowder is then ready to be first-rate if you have followed the directions. An onion may be added if you like the flavor." "This chowder," he adds, "is suitable for a large fishing party." Wolcott, The Yankee Cook Book (Coward-McCann, Inc., New York City, 1939) p. 9.

New English Dictionary study defines chowder as "A dish made of fresh fish (esp. cod) or clams, stewed with slices of pork or bacon, onions, and biscuit. Cider and champagne are sometimes added." Hawthorne, in The House of the Seven Gables (Allyn and Bacon, Boston, 1957) p. 8, speaks of "[a] codfish of sixty pounds, caught in the bay [which] had been dissolved into the rich liquid of a chowder." A chowder variant, cod "Muddle," was made in Plymouth in the 1890s by taking "a three or four pound codfish, head added. Season with salt and pepper and boil in just enough water to keep from burning. When cooked, add milk and a piece of butter." The recitation of these ancient formulae suffices to indicate that in the construction of chowders in these parts in other years, worries about fish bones played no role whatsoever. This broad outlook on chowders has persisted in more modern cookbooks. "The chowder of today is much the same as the old chowder. . . ." The American Women's Cook Book, supra, p. 176. The all embracing Fannie Farmer states in a portion of her recipe, fish chowder is made with a "fish skinned, but head and tail left on. Cut fish in 2-inch pieces and set aside. Put head, tail, and backbone broken in pieces, in stew-pan; add 2 cups cold water and bring slowly to boiling point. . . ." The liquor thus produced from the bones is added to the balance of the chowder. Farmer, The Boston Cooking School Cook Book (Little Brown Co., 1937) p. 166.

Thus, we consider a dish which for many long years, if well made, has been made generally as outlined above. It is not too much to say that a person sitting down in New England to consume a good New England fish chowder embarks on gustatory adventure which may entail the removal of some fish bones from his bowl as he proceeds. We are not inclined to tamper with age-old recipes by any amendment reflecting the plaintiff's view of the effect of the Uniform Commercial Code upon them. We are aware of the heavy body of case law involving foreign substances in food, but we sense a strong distinction between them and those relative to unwholesomeness of the food itself, e.g., tainted mackerel (Smith v. Gerrish, 256 Mass. 183), and a fish bone in a fish chowder. Certain Massachusetts cooks might cavil at the ingredients contained in the chowder in this case in that it lacked the heartening lift of salt pork. In any event, we consider that the joys of life in New England include the ready availability of fresh fish chowder. We should be prepared to cope with the hazards of fish bones, the occasional presence of which in chowders is, it seems to us, to be anticipated, and which, in the light of a hallowed tradition, do not impair their fitness or merchantability. While we are buoyed up in this conclusion by Shapiro v. Hotel Statler Corp., 132 F. Supp. 891 (S.D. Cal.), in which the bone which afflicted the plaintiff appeared in "Hot Barquette of Seafood Mornay," we know that the United States District Court of Southern California, situated as are we upon a coast, might be expected to share our views. We are most impressed, however, by Allen v. Grafton, 170 Ohio St. 249, where in Ohio, the Midwest, in a case where the plaintiff was injured by a piece of oyster shell in an order of fried oysters, Mr. Justice Taft (now Chief Justice) in a majority opinion held that "the possible presence of a piece of oyster shell in or attached to an oyster is so well known to anyone who eats oysters that we can say as a matter of law that one who eats oysters can reasonably anticipate and guard against eating such a piece of shell. . . ." (p. 259)

Thus, while we sympathize with the plaintiff who has suffered a peculiarly New England injury, the order must be

Exceptions sustained.

Judgment for the defendant.

QUESTIONS

1. Is the court saying that a natural substance does not breach the warranty or that the plaintiff's reasonable expectation should have included the bone? See Phillips v. Town of West Springfield, 405 Mass. 411, 540 N.E.2d 1331 (1989).

2. Would the plaintiff have recovered if she had been born and reared in South Dakota and was on her first visit to New England?

3. Would the result be the same if the plaintiff had purchased a *can* of fish chowder and encountered the bone?

PROBLEM 30

Natty Bumpo was driving through upstate New York when a deer ran in front of his car. He swerved to avoid it and ran into a tree. His major injuries came from his sudden contact with the steering wheel and the inside of the driver's door, where he smashed up against sharp points on the dashboard's GPS system. Natty sued the car manufacturer, the Mohican Motor Company, for breach of the warranty of merchantability. His theory was that the manufacturer should have designed a much safer dashboard. The manufacturer's defense was that the car was fit for its ordinary purpose and that Natty had misused it. How should this come out? See Larsen v. General Motors Corp., 391 F.2d 495 (8th Cir. 1968); Comment, Intended Use and the Unsafe Automobile: Manufacturers' Liability for Negligent Design, 28 Md. L. Rev. 386 (1968); Annot., 76 A.L.R.2d 91.

PROBLEM 31

Carry Nation, on the advice of her beautician, Parker Pillsbury, bought a hair dye named "Intoxicating Fragrance" and proceeded to use it in accordance with the instructions on the package. Unfortunately the product contained alcohol, to which Ms. Nation was allergic, and she suffered considerable burn damage to her scalp and ears. When she sued the manufacturer, Harper's Hair Products, Inc., the basic defense was that only 0.5 percent of the population had this allergic reaction. Is this a good defense?

In re Carrier IQ, Inc.

United States District Court, Northern District of California, 2015
2015 WL 274054

Edward M. Chen, United States District Judge

I. Introduction

Plaintiffs in this multidistrict litigation—eighteen (18) individuals from thirteen different states—have filed a second consolidated amended complaint ("SCAC" or "Complaint") against Defendant Carrier IQ, Inc. and a number of manufacturers of mobile devices. The Complaint alleges that Defendants have violated the Federal Wiretap Act as well as a number of state's privacy and consumer protection statutes through the creation and use of Carrier IQ's software on Plaintiffs' mobile devices. Plaintiffs allege that Carrier IQ designed, and the Device Manufacturers Defendants embedded, the Carrier IQ Software on their mobile devices and, once embedded, this software surreptitiously intercepted personal data and communications and transmitted this data to Carrier IQ and its customers. Pending before the Court is Defendants' joint motion to dismiss the SCAC in its entirety. For the reasons that follow, the Court **GRANTS** in part and **DENIES** in part Defendants' joint motion, and will afford Plaintiffs leave to file a third consolidated amended complaint.

II. Factual and Procedural Background

A. *Plaintiffs*

There are 18 plaintiffs in this action, from 13 different states. . . . In describing each Plaintiff, the SCAC provides that "[u]pon information and belief, [the Plaintiff's] mobile device came with the Carrier IQ Software and implementing or porting software pre-installed. In addition to using his devices to make phone calls, [the Plaintiff] has used it for web browsing and text messaging, including accessing, inputting, and transmitting personal, private, confidential, and sensitive information. [The Plaintiff] would not have purchased his mobile device had he known that the Carrier IQ Software and related implementing or porting software was installed and operating on his device, and taxing his device's battery, processor, and memory, as alleged herein." See SCAC ¶¶8-25.

B. *Defendants*

The remaining defendants in this action are a number of mobile device manufacturers. Plaintiffs allege that Carrier IQ is the "designer, author, programmer, and vendor" of the IQ Agent software and provided the mobile device manufacturers the "guide or template" needed for the "related implementing or porting software known as the CIQ Interface." Id. ¶26. The IQ Agent and CIQ Interface software forms the basis of Plaintiffs' claims, as described *infra.*

The remaining Defendants are: (1) HTC America, Inc. and HTC Corporation (collectively "HTC"); (2) Huawei Device USA, Inc. ("Huawei"), (3) LG Electronics MobileComm U.S.A., Inc. and LG Electronics, Inc. (collectively "LG"); (4) Motorola Mobility LLC ("Motorola"); (5) Pantech Wireless, Inc. ("Pantech"); (6) Samsung Telecommunications America, Inc. and Samsung Electronics Co., Ltd. (collectively "Samsung"). Each Defendant is alleged to have installed the Carrier IQ Software and CIQ Interface software on at least some of their mobile device models.

C. *Asserted Causes of Action*

The SCAC alleges five causes of action:

- **Count 1: Violation of the Federal Wiretap Act (18 U.S.C. §2551)**
- **Count 2: Violation of State Privacy Laws:** Plaintiffs assert their claims on behalf of all residents of the United States under Cal. Penal Code §502 and on behalf of citizens of the following 35 states under those states' respective privacy laws: Arizona, California, Connecticut, Delaware, Florida, Hawaii, Idaho, Illinois, Indiana, Iowa, Louisiana, Maine, Maryland, Massachusetts, Michigan, Minnesota, Nebraska, Nevada, New Hampshire, New Jersey, New Mexico, North Carolina, Ohio, Oregon, Pennsylvania, Rhode Island, South Carolina, Tennessee, Texas, Utah, Virginia, Washington, West Virginia, Wisconsin, and Wyoming.
- **Count 3: Violation of State Consumer Protection Acts:** Asserted on behalf of residents of the following 21 states under those states' respective consumer protection statutes: Arkansas, California, Connecticut, Delaware, Florida, Hawaii, Kansas, Maryland, Michigan, Missouri, Nevada, New Hampshire, New Jersey, Oklahoma, Rhode Island, South Carolina, South Dakota, Texas, Vermont, Washington, and West Virginia.
- **Count 4: Violation of the Magnuson-Moss Warranty Act (15 U.S.C. §2301-2312):** Asserted on behalf of the residents of the following 34 states (and the District of Columbia): Alaska, Arkansas, California, Colorado, Delaware, District of Columbia, Hawaii, Indiana, Kansas,

Louisiana, Maine, Maryland, Massachusetts, Michigan, Minnesota, Mississippi, Missouri, Montana, Nebraska, Nevada, New Hampshire, New Jersey, New Mexico, North Dakota, Oklahoma, Pennsylvania, Rhode Island, South Carolina, South Dakota, Texas, Utah, Virginia, Washington, West Virginia, and Wyoming.

- **Count 5: Violation of the Implied Warranty of Merchantability:** asserted on behalf of residents of the states enumerated under Count 4.

D. *Carrier IQ Software Background*

Carrier IQ "designed, authored, programmed, and caused the installation and activation of the Carrier IQ Software, including the so-called IQ Agent, on the devices at issue in this case." Id. ¶62. It also "designed, authored, and provided guides to the Device Manufacturers for designing, authoring, programming, installing, and activating the CIQ Interface in deployments" through the "embedded" method of installation. Id.

Carrier IQ represents that its software is a "network diagnostics tool" for cell phone service providers. Id. ¶40. It is alleged that in reality, the software collects, and transfers, sensitive personal data off of a user's mobile device. See id. ¶¶1-2. Specifically, the CIQ Interface software is alleged to be a "wrapping or porting layer of code designed to see, recognize, and intercept a host of data and content, including SMS text message content and URLs containing search terms, user names, and passwords . . . and to send that material down to the IQ Agent for further processing and possible transmittals." Id. ¶63. The SCAC alleges that the Device Manufacturers "design and program" the CIQ Interface (with Carrier IQ's aid) and then install the CIQ Interface and IQ Agent software on their mobile devices. Id. Once installed, the software "operates in the background," such that the typical user has no idea that it is running and cannot turn it off. Id. ¶64. Users are never given the choice of opting into or out of the Carrier IQ Software's functionality. Id. Because it is always running, the Plaintiffs allege that it "taxes the device's battery power, processor functions, and system memory." Id.

Plaintiffs allege that the data intercepted by the Carrier IQ Software includes the following: (1) URLs (including those which contain query strings with embedded information such as search terms, user names, passwords, and GPS-based geo-location information); (2) GPS-location information; (3) SMS text messages; (4) telephone numbers dialed and received; (5) the user's keypad presses/keystrokes; and (6) application purchases and uses. Id. ¶65. This information is intercepted as part of the Carrier IQ Software's "calls" on the device operating system for "metrics." Id. It then stores the information in the mobile device's RAM memory on a rolling basis. Id.

The Carrier IQ Software also has a feature referred to as "Profiles." Via Profiles, Carrier IQ customers (who are typically wireless carriers, but can also include device manufacturers) will specify which data they want from the above described "metrics." Id. ¶68. At designated times (or as requested), the Profile-specified data would then be transmitted from the mobile device to the requesting customer (the wireless carriers or device manufacturers). Id.

The SCAC quotes from a number of letters which the various Device Manufacturers sent to Senator Al Franken in response to his inquiries regarding the Carrier IQ Software. These letters provide a glimpse into the potential scope of the Carrier IQ Software deployment. AT & T stated that Carrier IQ's Software was installed on approximately "900,000 devices, with about 575,000 of those collecting and reporting wireless and service performance information to AT & T." Id. ¶53. Sprint indicated that there were "26 million active Sprint devices that have Carrier IQ Software Installed" and stated that Sprint queried information from a fraction of those (c. 1.3 million) at any given time for diagnostic needs and that a 30,000 device subset of this 1.3 million were used for "research specific problems." Id. ¶54. T-Mobile stated that there were "approximately 450,000 T-Mobile customers [that] use devices that contain Carrier IQ's diagnostic software." Id. ¶56.

The SCAC recounts two ways where deployment of the Carrier IQ Software has resulted in "grave breaches of privacy." Id. ¶69. First, due to a "programming error," the SCAC alleges that AT & T has admitted that the "Carrier IQ Software transmitted text message content to it." Id. Plaintiffs use this as evidence that the Carrier IQ Software does, in fact, intercept and capture text message content. Id. Second, Plaintiffs state that "with some deployments, including those on HTC mobile devices and possibly on certain other devices," the data and content intercepted by the Carrier IQ Software was sent in unencrypted, human-readable form into the system logs of the affected devices. Id. ¶71. Accordingly, this information was vulnerable to anyone with access to the system logs, including to individuals with malicious intent. Id. ¶72. Further, because this information was contained in system logs, the private information improperly intercepted and stored was transmitted to Google (who is the author of the Android Operating System) as part of crash reports. Id. ¶73. Similarly, HTC has acknowledged that they have also received this private information through its "Tell HTC" tool which "draws on content stored in the device logs." Id. Accordingly, Plaintiffs contend that this information "may have gone to application developers who draw on device logs as a means of diagnosing application crashes (or for other purposes), including via widely available software tools." Id.

Plaintiffs allege that the Carrier IQ Software continues to operate even if the consumer is using the device solely on a Wi-Fi network (as opposed to a cellular network). Id. ¶74.

E. *FTC Investigation of and Action Against HTC Re: Carrier IQ Software*

Since the filing of the First Consolidated Amended Complaint in this action, the FTC commenced an investigation into HTC regarding the Carrier IQ Software and a "related privacy and security flaw" in HTC mobile devices. Id. ¶75. This investigation culminated in a Consent Order agreement in February 2013. Id. ¶76.

The FTC found that HTC had "failed to take reasonable steps to secure the software it developed for its smartphones and tablet computers, introducing security flaws that placed sensitive information about millions of consumers at risk." Id. One of the failures cited, was HTC's failure to use "documented secure communications mechanisms in implementing logging applications," thus placing sensitive information at risk. Id. ¶77. Because of HTC's failure to implement security measures, "any third-party application that could connect to the internet could communicate with the logging applications on HTC devices and access a variety of sensitive information." Id. One of the "logging" applications noted by the FTC was the Carrier IQ Software. Relevant to this case, the Consent Order noted: The information collected by the Carrier IQ software was supposed to have been accessible only by network operators, but because HTC used an insecure communications mechanism, any third-party application on the user's device that could connect to the internet could exploit the vulnerability to communicate with the CIQ Interface." Id. This permitted interception of "the sensitive information being collected by the Carrier IQ software" and potentially allowed individuals to perform "malicious actions" such as "sending text messages without permission." Id.

The FTC Consent Order explained how this security flaw occurred. During the development of its CIQ Interface, HTC activated "debug code" in the operating system to test whether the CIQ Interface was operating properly. "The debug code accomplished this by writing the information to a particular device log known as the Android system log, which could then be reviewed. However, HTC failed to deactivate the debug code before its devices shipped for sale to consumers." Id. Thus, "all information that the CIQ Interface sent to the Carrier IQ software . . . was also written to the Android system log on the device." Id. Once in the system log, the sensitive information was then "[a]ccessible to any third-party application with permission to read the system log" and was sent to HTC through its "Tell HTC" error reporting tool." Id. The FTC noted the consumers had "little, if any, reason to know their information was at risk because of the vulnerabilities introduced by HTC." Id. ¶78. Ultimately, the FTC found that HTC had engaged in unfair or deceptive acts or practices in violation of the Federal Trade Commission Act given deceptive statements in its user manuals and user interface. Id. ¶79. . . .

F. *Plaintiffs' Implied Warranty of Merchantability Claims*

Plaintiffs' fifth cause of action alleges a breach of the implied warranty of merchantability under the laws of over thirty states and the District of Columbia against the Device Manufacturers. The Device Manufacturers have moved to dismiss these claims on a variety of grounds. First, Defendants argue that the implied warranty claims under California, Maryland, Michigan, New Hampshire, Texas, and Washington law should be dismissed as Plaintiffs failed to afford them pre-suit notice of any alleged breach. Second, Defendants argue that Plaintiffs California-based implied warranty claims fail because Plaintiffs were not in privity with the Device Manufacturer and have failed to allege that they purchased their mobile devices in California. Finally, Defendants contend that Plaintiffs have failed to allege that their mobile devices were not "merchantable."

4. *Plaintiffs Have Sufficiently Alleged That Their Mobile Devices Were Unmerchantable for Purposes of Their Implied Warranty Claims*

Defendants substantively attack Plaintiffs' implied warranty of merchantability claims alleging that Plaintiffs have not—and cannot—allege that the presence and operation of the Carrier IQ Software rendered their mobile devices unmerchantable. Docket No. 304, at 72. Defendants accordingly seek dismissal of Plaintiffs' implied warranty claims arising under the laws of California, Maryland, Michigan, Mississippi, New Hampshire, Texas, and Washington.

Under the laws of each of these states, the implied warranty of merchantability warrants that a purchased good is "fit for the ordinary purposes for which such goods are used." See, e.g., Cal. Comm. Code §2314(2)(c); Md. Code, Comm. Law §2-314(2)(c); Miss. Code Ann. §75-2-314(2)(c); N.H. Rev. Stat. §382-A:2-314(2)(c); Tex. Bus. & Com. Code §2.314(b)(3); Wash. Rev. Code §62A.2-314(2)(c). Courts across various jurisdictions have recognized that the concept of whether a product is "fit for ordinary purposes" necessarily "incorporates . . . the consumer's reasonable expectations into the concept of merchantability." Robinson v. American Honda Motor Co., Inc., 551 F.3d 218 (4th Cir. 2009); see also Venezia v. Miller Brewing Co., 626 F.2d 188, 190 (1st Cir. 1980) ("Under Massachusetts law the question of fitness for ordinary purposes is largely one centering around reasonable consumer expectations."); Denny v. Ford Motor Co., 87 N.Y.2d 248, 639 N.Y.S.2d 250, 662 N.E.2d 730, 736 (1995) (noting that the "fit for the ordinary purposes for which such goods are used" inquiry "focuses on the expectations for the performance of the product when used in the customary, usual and reasonably foreseeable manners").

At the same time, the implied warranty of merchantability merely guarantees that the product will perform at a "minimum level of quality." Birdsong

v. Apple, Inc., 590 F.3d 955, 958 (9th Cir. 2009). As such, the implied warranty "does not impose a general requirement that goods precisely fulfill the expectation of the buyer," Am. Suzuki Motor Corp. v. Superior Court, 37 Cal. App. 4th 1291, 1296, 44 Cal. Rptr. 2d 526 (1995). Therefore, a product which "performs its ordinary function adequately does not breach the implied warranty of merchantability merely because it does not function as well as the buyer would like, or even as well as it could." Gen. Motors Corp. v. Brewer, 966 S.W.2d 56, 57 (Tex. 1998). Rather, the alleged defect in the product must be so fundamental as to render the product unfit for its ordinary purpose. See Tietsworth v. Sears, Roebuck & Co., 720 F. Supp. 2d 1123, 1142 (N.D. Cal. 2010) ("The mere manifestation of a defect by itself does not constitute a breach of the implied warranty of merchantability. Instead, there must be a fundamental defect that renders the product unfit for its ordinary purpose.").

Defendants contend that the "ordinary purpose" of mobile devices is communication—making and receiving phone calls, text messages, facilitating internet usage, and allowing usage of apps. Because of this, Defendants argue, Plaintiffs cannot establish that the Carrier IQ Software renders their mobile devices unfit for this ordinary purpose because there are no allegations that the software rendered the devices unable to make and receive phone calls, text messages, and the like. See Docket No. 304, at 73.

Defendants' definition of mobile devices' "ordinary purpose" finds some support in case law from courts in this District. Specifically, in In re iPhone 4S Consumer Litig., No. C12-1227 CW, 2013 WL 3829653 (N.D. Cal. July 23, 2013), the court stated that the "iPhone 4S's intended and ordinary use is as a smartphone, 'which the court safely presumes includes functions like making and receiving calls, sending and receiving text messages, or allowing for use of mobile applications.'" Id. at *16 (quoting Williamson v. Apple, Inc., No. 5:11-cv-0377 EJD, 2012 WL 3835104, at *8-9 (N.D. Cal. Sept. 4, 2012)). Notably, as this quote demonstrates, the court merely found that a mobile device's ordinary and intended use "includes" making and receiving calls, text messages, and the like, suggesting that the courts were not intending to provide an exhaustive definition of a mobile device's ordinary and intended use. Cf. Dairy v. Bonham, No. C-13-1519 EMC, 2013 WL 3829268, at *3 (N.D. Cal. July 23, 2013) ("[U]se of the word 'including' indicates the enumerated ways . . . is not exhaustive.").

Nonetheless, these courts have found that alleged defects which did not affect this core functionality did not render the mobile devices unfit for their ordinary purposes. For example, in *In re iPhone,* plaintiffs alleged that the iPhone was rendered unfit because Apple's "Siri" feature did not perform as advertised. 2013 WL 3829653, at *16. The court, however, found that this allegation failed to state a claim for breach of the implied warranty because plaintiffs had "not alleged that the iPhone 4S is deficient" in "making and receiving calls, sending and receiving text messages, or allowing the use of mobile applications." Rather, plaintiffs had alleged that the iPhone was deficient "in providing the Siri feature to access these functions." Id. Similarly, in *Williamson,* plaintiffs alleged that the glass on their iPhone was defective as it was easily scarred and broken, despite Apple's representations to the contrary. See *Williamson,* 2012 WL 3835104, at *1. The court rejected plaintiff's implied warranty claim, finding that the glass defect did not render deficient the iPhone's ability to make calls, send or receive text messages, or use mobile applications. Id. at *8. Finally, in In re Google Phone Litig., No. 10-CV-0117-EJD, 2012 WL 3155571 (N.D. Cal. Aug. 2, 2012), plaintiffs did allege defects which touched on the core functionality of the Google phone—specifically, they alleged, *inter alia,* that the phone's 3G data connectivity was inconsistent and the phone occasionally dropped or missed phone calls. The court found, however, that plaintiffs had failed to "demonstrate that this alleged defect is more than inconvenience" such that the phone was unfit for its ordinary purpose. Id. at *5.

This Court finds that Defendants' argument that the Carrier IQ Software does not render Plaintiffs' mobile devices unfit for the devices' ordinary purpose simply because the devices could make and receive phone calls, text messages, use mobile apps, and access the internet is overly simplistic and underinclusive. While a defect must be "fundamental" to implicate the implied warranty, "this does not mean the alleged defect must preclude any use of the product at all." Stearns v. Select Comfort Retail Corp., No. 08-2746 JF, 2009 WL 1635931, at *8 (N.D. Cal. June 5, 2009). There are a number of examples of courts which have held that a defect can render a product unfit notwithstanding the fact the product at issue could, in a technical sense, perform its base function. These courts have found that the implied warranty can be breached when, although capable of performing its ordinary function, the product nonetheless fails in a significant way to perform as a reasonable consumer would expect.

Thus, in *Stearns,* plaintiffs alleged an implied warranty claim against a bed manufacturer on the basis of mold growing on its beds. The court determined that the plaintiffs had adequately alleged that the beds at issue "did not conform to expectations regarding ordinary use," and simply because "a person still may sleep on a moldy bed does not bar as a matter of law a claim for breach of the implied warranty of merchantability." Id. at *8. Similarly, in Long v. Graco Children's Products Inc., No. 13-cv-01257-WHO, 2013 WL 4655763 (N.D. Cal. Aug. 26, 2013), plaintiff alleged that defendants' car seats contained a defective buckle that was "unreasonably difficult or impossible to unlatch." Id. at *1. Even though it was not disputed that the car seat provided "adequate protective restraint" for the child, the court found plaintiffs adequately alleged the car seat was unfit. Id. at *12. It held that "[c]onsumers do not merely expect a car seat to serve its bare-minimum purpose" but rather would expect that they "would be able to quickly unlatch the harness or buckle in case of an emergency." Id. Finally, in Isip v. Mercedes-Benz USA, 155 Cal. App. 4th 19, 65 Cal. Rptr. 3d 695 (2007), a car manufacturer argued that so long as a vehicle provided transportation from point A to point B, it necessarily was fit for its ordinary purpose. The court rejected this argument, finding it to be an "unjustified dilution" of the implied warranty. Rather, it held that a vehicle that "smells, lurches, clanks, and emits smoke over an extended period of time is not fit for its intended purpose. Id. at 27, 65 Cal. Rptr. 3d 695; see also Fleisher v. Fiber Composites, LLC, No. 12-1326, 2012 WL 5381381 (E.D. Pa. Nov. 2, 2012) (plaintiffs adequately alleged outdoor deck that became discolored by mold as a result of a defect was unfit for ordinary purpose as consumers expect outdoor decks to not only provide structural support, but to also to meet "a certain aesthetic expectation").

The Court concludes that in determining if a defect rises to the level of rendering a product unfit for its ordinary purpose, the Court must ask two questions. First, the defect in question must be "fundamental" in that it affects the core functionality of the product. See, e.g., *Stearns,* 2009 WL 1635931, at *7 (requiring a "fundamental defect'). Thus defects which only affect functionality that is peripheral or tangential to the core function of the product—for example the strength of glass used in a mobile device or the effectiveness of Apple's Siri function, see, e.g., *In re iPhone,* 2013 WL 3829653, at *16—would be insufficient. In defining a product's core functionality, a court should not seek to reduce a product to its most basic, bare minimum purpose, but rather should take a common sense view informed by reasonable consumers' expectations about the function of the type of product in a general sense. See *Long,* 2013 WL 4655763, at *12 (rejecting "bare-minimum" view of a car seat's purpose in light of consumer expectations); see also *Robinson,* 551 F.3d at 224 ("This definition of merchantability incorporates trade quality standards and the consumer's reasonable expectations into the concept of merchantability."). Thus, the core function of a vehicle is not to provide transportation, it is to provide safe and reliable transportation, see *Isip,* 155 Cal. App. 4th at 27, 65 Cal. Rptr. 3d 695, and the core function of a bed is not simply to provide a place on which an individual can sleep, but rather to provide a place where an individual can sleep that is free from mold, see *Stearns,* 2009 WL 1635931, at *7. Second, just because a defect affects the core functionality of a product does not automatically mean that the product is unfit for its ordinary purposes. Rather, as discussed, the implied warranty only ensures that a product will meet a "minimum level of quality." *Birdsong,* 590 F.3d at 958. The impairment of the core functionality must be significant enough to prevent the product from reaching a reasonably expected minimum level of quality.

On this basis, the Court finds, for purposes of the motion to dismiss, that Plaintiffs have adequately alleged that the Carrier IQ Software rendered their mobile devices unmerchantable. While there is no dispute that the Carrier IQ Software did not make it impossible for Plaintiffs to make and receive phone calls, text messages, and the like on their devices, that alone is not dispositive. Consumers have a reasonable expectation that mobile devices, in general, will allow them to communicate with others without having a third party surreptitiously intercept and transmit those communications to third parties. Stated another way, it is beyond controversy that individuals have a reasonable expectation of privacy as to the contents of communications made with their mobile devices. Cf. Riley v. California, __ U.S. __, 134 S. Ct. 2473, 2489-91, 189 L. Ed. 2d 430 (2014) (discussing the privacy interests at stake in searches of cell phones by law enforcement and recognizing the user's expectation of privacy). Just as a consumer would likely choose not to sleep on a bed contaminated with mold, a consumer would likely choose to not use a mobile device that actively intercepted his or her private communication data and potentially share that data with third parties.

Plaintiffs have, in the SCAC, provided sufficient factual allegations for the Court to conclude, at this stage, that the Carrier IQ Software intercepts and/or transmits personal communication data to third parties. See, e.g., SCAC ¶65, 68 (alleging that the Carrier IQ Software intercepts and transmits to Carrier IQ and its customers data that can include URLS which contain internet search terms, user names and passwords; text messages; app purchases and uses; a user's keystrokes; numbers dialed and received; etc.). Taking all inferences in favor of the Plaintiffs, these allegations are sufficient for the Court to conclude that the Carrier IQ Software undermines consumers' reasonable expectations in privacy to such a degree so as to render their mobile devices unfit to perform their core functions. During discovery, the parties will have the opportunity to flesh out the precise way the Carrier IQ Software operates, including the degree to which Plaintiffs' personal data or communications were in fact compromised by the Carrier IQ Software. Based on development of a factual record, Carrier IQ Software may renew their argument via motion for summary judgment.

Accordingly, for the foregoing reasons, Plaintiffs have adequately alleged that their mobile devices were unmerchantable and Defendants motion to dismiss the implied warranty claims on this ground is **DENIED**. . . .

2. Fitness for a Particular Purpose

Where the buyer wants to use the goods for something beyond their *ordinary* purpose, a warranty of merchantability is not enough. But the buyer may be able to sue for breach of the implied warranty of fitness for a particular purpose if the buyer can satisfy all of the elements of §2-315. Read the section and its Official Comment.

PROBLEM 32

When Christopher Wren finished building a recreation room in his basement, he wanted a heater for it. He saw an ad for the A-1 Hotblast Heater, which seemed to be what he needed. A good friend of Wren's named Inigo Jones ran a nearby appliance store. Wren went there and told Jones that he wanted the A-1 Hotblast Heater for the new room. Jones knew the room well; he had helped build it. When the heater arrived, it worked perfectly, but it simply did not have the capacity to heat the room. May Wren sue Jones for breach of either §2-314 or §2-315? See Comment 5 to §2-315; Englebreacht v. W.D. Brannan & Sons, Inc., 501 S.W.2d 707 (Tex. Civ. App. 1973).

PROBLEM 33

Lee Matheson went to the Easy Paint Store and bought a can of green paint, which the store mixed on the premises from various pigments. Lee used the paint on his dining room walls, but due to a miscalculation on his part, he ran out when he was half finished. He took the empty paint can back to the store. He told the clerk that he was only half done with the job and needed another can, which the clerk promptly mixed and sold him. Lee finished the painting and then noticed two things: (1) the dried paint gave off an offensive odor, and (2) the paint from the second can did not match the first. What cause(s) of action does he have?

PROBLEM 34

Donald Souse ordered a martini at the Tired Executives Club. When he bit into the olive, he cracked his new $2,000 dentures on a pit. Is there a cause of action under either §2-314 or §2-315? See Hochberg v. O'Donnell's Restaurant, Inc., 272 A.2d 846 (D.C. 1971).

Courts faced with this last Problem (harmful substances in food) have split into two camps: those that deny liability if the object is a *natural substance,* as opposed to a *foreign object,* and those that permit recovery even where the consumer is injured by a natural substance as long as the biter's "reasonable expectation" is that it would have been removed. The problem reoccurs in the cases as gourmands encounter stones in cherry pies, pits in olives, or, as in the *Webster* case above, bones in fish. See Annot., 7 A.L.R.2d 1027.

C. *Warranty Disclaimers and Limitations*

1. Disclaiming Express Warranties

The drafters of the Uniform Commercial Code thought that it was basically unfair for a seller to create an express warranty and then try to disclaim it, so they drafted §2-316(1) in such a way as to make disclaimer of an express warranty virtually impossible. Read it. The proper way to avoid liability for an express warranty is *to not make it in the first place.* Note that express warranties are created by *affirmative* seller conduct. The seller must take out an ad, publish a booklet, say something orally about the product, or point to a sample or model, or the warranty will never arise. Having done one of these things and created buyer expectations that the product will comply with the representations made, the seller must live with the liability assumed. See Official Comment 4 to §2-313; Travis v. Washington Horse Breeders Assn., 111 Wash. 2d 396, 759 P.2d 418 (1988).

Bell Sports, Inc. v. Yarusso

Supreme Court of Delaware, 2000
759 A.2d 582

WALSH, Justice:

This is an appeal from a Superior Court denial of judgment as a matter of law, or alternatively, for a new trial following an award of damages in a product liability action. The defendant-appellant claims error on the part of the trial judge in ruling on the qualifications of plaintiff's expert witnesses and in permitting the substance of that testimony to establish a jury question on claims for breach of warranty. The appellant further asserts that the jury verdict was internally inconsistent and that the Superior Court should have declared a mistrial after discharging a juror for cause during trial. Upon careful review of the record, we conclude that the Superior Court did not abuse its discretion in permitting the testimony of plaintiff's experts nor in submitting the issues of breach of warranty to the jury. We further conclude that the jury's verdict did not lack consistency and that the refusal to grant a mistrial was not error.

I

On October 20, 1991, Brian J. Yarusso ("Yarusso"), then 22 years of age, was riding his off-road motorcycle[6] at a dirt motocross track located off

6. "Off-road" motorcycles are equipped with motors, tires, seats and suspension components specifically designed to function effectively under adverse riding conditions typical of motocross tracks, woods and fields. They are generally much lighter in weight than motorcycles designed for street use, have a higher degree of suspension clearance/compliance and are usually not equipped with horns, lights and other features required for legal street operation.

Church Road in Newark, Delaware. Yarusso was wearing a full complement of safety equipment in addition to the helmet that is the subject of this dispute. While traveling over a series of dirt moguls, or bumps, Yarusso hit one of the moguls in such a way that he was catapulted over the handlebars of the motorcycle. He landed on his head, flipped over and came to rest face down in the dirt. As a result of his fall, Yarusso sustained a burst fracture of the C5 vertebral body and was rendered a quadriplegic.[7]

Yarusso filed suit in the Superior Court against Bell Sports, Inc. ("Bell"), the manufacturer of the Bell Moto-5 helmet he was wearing at the time of the accident. Yarusso's suit against Bell was predicated on a claim that the enhanced injuries he suffered were the proximate result of a defect in the helmet's design. The Bell Moto-5 is a full-face motocross helmet that was designed for off-road use. It complies with federal Department of Transportation ("DOT") standards and is also certified by the Snell Foundation, a leading worldwide helmet research and testing laboratory. The helmet is constructed of a fiberglass outer shell, an inner crushable liner, and a retention system consisting of a chinstrap and D-ring pull-tab. While all three of these components are designed to interact, the inner liner is considered the most important safety feature of the helmet. The expanded polystyrene material of which this liner is primarily constructed is designed to compress upon contact with a solid object.

Yarusso's complaint contained alternative grounds for recovery. He alleged negligence in the design and construction of the helmet, breach of express warranties and breach of an implied warranty of merchantability. Yarusso's express warranty claim arose from specific textual representations in the helmet's accompanying owner's manual (the "manual"), the relevant portions of which are as follows (emphasis printed in manual also reproduced below):

> Five Year Limited Warranty: Any Bell helmet found by the factory to be defective in materials or workmanship within five years from the date of purchase will be repaired or replaced at the option of the manufacturer, free of charge, when received at the factory, freight pre-paid. . . . This warranty is expressly in lieu of all other warranties, and any implied warranties of merchantability or fitness for a particular purpose created hereby, are limited in duration to the same duration as the express warranty herein. Bell shall not be liable for any incidental or consequential damages. . . .
>
> Introduction: Your new Moto-5 helmet is another in the long line of innovative off-road helmets from Bell. . . . (T)he primary function of a helmet is to reduce the harmful effects of a blow to the head. However, it is

7. Dr. Joseph Cusick, a neurosurgeon, described Yarusso's specific injuries. He testified that Yarusso's C5 vertebral body sustained major damage due to a "severe axiocompression load, usually . . . without much extension or flexion." The magnitude of the load was sufficient to crack the bone, push the spinal disk into the soft bone, and "explode" the disc into the spinal cord and some of the other disks.

> important to recognize that the wearing of a helmet is not an assurance of absolute protection. NO HELMET CAN PROTECT THE WEARER AGAINST ALL FORESEEABLE IMPACTS.
>
> Helmet Performance: The Moto-5 is designed to absorb the force of a blow first by spreading it over as wide an area of the outer shell as possible, and second by the crushing of the non-resilient inner liner. Damage to the helmet after an impact is not a sign of any defect in the helmet design or construction. It is exactly what the helmet is designed to do.
>
> NOTICE: No helmet can protect the user from all foreseeable impacts. To obtain the maximum protection offered by any helmet, it must fit firmly on the head and the chinstrap must be securely fastened.

Yarusso testified at trial that he purchased this particular helmet based on the specific assertions, quoted above, that "(t)he primary function of a helmet is to reduce the harmful effects of a blow to the head."

Yarusso's implied warranty of merchantability claim arose out of his contention that the helmet was not merchantable because it was sold as an off-road helmet but was designed to function for "on-road" use. Because the helmet met DOT street helmet standards, Yarusso claimed that it was actually designed with a very stiff liner that would effectively function for on-road use but would not protect a rider against foreseeable off-road falls, where the impact surface could conceivably be softer.

A pivotal factual issue at trial was whether the helmet liner properly crushed, as designed, at the time Yarusso's head impacted the ground after his fall. Yarusso claimed that the injuries to his neck were caused by the stiffness or density of the liner material at the helmet crown. At trial, he offered expert testimony by Maurice Fox ("Fox"), a safety consultant who had been employed by a helmet manufacturer during the 1970s. Fox opined that Yarusso's helmet sustained the majority of the fall's impact at its crown where the liner was too dense to crush sufficiently, thereby transmitting excessive force to Yarusso's neck, resulting in his paralysis. Fox's testimony however, was directed primarily at Yarusso's negligence claim against Bell, which the jury subsequently rejected.

Joseph Cusick, M.D. ("Cusick"), a neurological expert, similarly testified that the neck injuries sustained by Yarusso were consistent with impact at the top, or crown, of the helmet. Cusick further testified that a 20-30% reduction of force to Yarusso's body would have been sufficient to avoid injury because his body would have been able to withstand this lower level of force.

Richard Stalnaker, Ph.D. ("Stalnaker"), a biomechanical engineer, also testified on behalf of Yarusso and largely affirmed Fox's opinion. His testimony was crucial in the jury's determination that Bell had breached express and implied warranties. Stalnaker determined that the force of Yarusso's impact with the ground was equivalent to 60 foot pounds, and that adequate crush of the helmet liner would have reduced it significantly to avert injury. Although Stalnaker modified the analytical process used to reconstruct the accident to coincide with that presented by Bell's expert reconstruction witness at trial, Bell's counsel rejected an opportunity to delay the trial and requested only a mistrial. Because the trial judge determined that the factual foundation for Stalnaker's testimony was unchanged despite his use of an alternative analytical, she denied the motion for mistrial leaving the matter for attack through cross-examination.

Bell offered its own expert testimony at trial disputing the helmet's point of impact from the accident and asserting the inability of any helmet to protect its user from severe neck injuries. The principal designer of the helmet, James Sundahl ("Sundahl"), testified that any helmet must be designed to protect its user from a multitude of accident types. He further opined that in circumstances involving a helmet's impact with a soft surface, the surface itself, rather than the helmet, absorbs a greater portion of the energy. When questioned about the representation in the helmet's manual, Sundahl testified that it was "wrong."

James McElhaney, Ph.D. ("McElhaney"), a professor of biomechanics at Duke University, testified for Bell and disputed Yarusso's contention that the helmet was impacted at its crown. McElhaney testified that the front of Yarusso's helmet liner was crushed in a fashion indicating a substantial blow to that area. Both Sundahl and McElhaney presented evidence of industry-wide research to the effect that no helmet can offer "any significant protection of the neck because the mass of the torso is so much more than the energy levels that a helmet can manage." Bell's experts claimed that this helmet and helmets in general are designed to protect users from head and brain injuries and the helmet in this case did precisely that.

Upon the conclusion of Yarusso's case, he abandoned his failure to warn claim. At the close of all the evidence, Bell moved for judgment as a matter of law as to liability. The trial court granted judgment as a matter of law on Yarusso's breach of implied warranty for a particular purpose claim, but denied Bell's motion on the remaining counts. The jury was then charged on the remaining claims of negligence, breach of implied warranty of merchantability and breach of express warranty.

On the second day of jury deliberations, one juror notified the trial court that he had reviewed outside information regarding motorcycle helmets in connection with securing a motorcycle licensing examiner's certificate. The jury also notified the court that they were deadlocked. The trial judge subsequently interrogated the juror who had disclosed his outside knowledge out of the presence of the remaining jurors. The trial judge determined that while the juror had not yet shared this extraneous information with other jurors, he had violated the direct instruction to decide the case solely from the evidence presented. The trial judge dismissed the juror prompting a motion from Bell for a mistrial, which was denied. Because both parties had agreed at the outset of the trial to accept a jury of eleven members, the remaining jurors were permitted to deliberate.

Through specific answers to interrogatories, the jury ultimately found that Bell was not negligent, but had breached an express or implied warranty, which proximately caused Yarusso's enhanced injury. Yarusso was awarded $1,812,000 in damages. Bell objected that the verdict was inconsistent and renewed its motions for judgment as a matter of law or alternatively for a new trial on liability only, all of which were denied by the Superior Court. This appeal followed. . . .

II

By its verdict, the jury specifically determined that Bell had not negligently designed the Moto-5 helmet but that Bell had breached "an express or implied warranty" when it sold the helmet and that "conduct proximately caused Brian Yarusso to suffer enhanced injuries." Bell argues on appeal that Yarusso failed, as a matter of law, to establish an evidentiary basis for recovery under either express or implied warranty and the trial court should have granted judgment in its favor as to those claims.

Preliminarily, we note that the jury was permitted to find liability under alternative forms of breach of warranty, express or implied, without differentiating between the two. Bell did not object to the warranty claims being submitted in that format and, thus, the verdict may be sustained if there is record and legal support for recovery under either theory.

A.

The statutory basis for a claim for damages based on breach of an express warranty arising out of a sale of goods under Delaware law is found in this State's counterpart of the Uniform Commercial Code. Title 6, section 2-313 [which the court quotes— Eds.].

The official commentary to that section under the U.C.C. indicates that the drafters intended its warranty provisions to be construed and applied liberally in favor of a buyer of goods. See U.C.C. §2-313 cmt. 1 (1977) ("Express warranties rest on 'dickered' aspects of the individual bargain, and go so clearly to the essence of that bargain that words of a disclaimer in a form are repugnant to the basic dickered terms."); U.C.C. §2-313 cmt. 3 ("In actual practice affirmations of fact made by a seller about the goods during a bargain are regarded as part of the description of those goods; hence no particular reliance on such statements need be shown in order to weave them into the fabric of the agreement."); U.C.C. §2-313 cmt. 4 ("[A] contract is normally a contract for a sale of something describable and described. A clause generally disclaiming 'all warranties, express or implied' cannot reduce the seller's obligation with respect to such description. . . ."). The language of the U.C.C.'s official commentary may be applied by analogy to the sale of goods governed by 6 Del. C. §2-313 in the reconciliation of any ensuing express warranty disputes. Thus, Bell's argument in this case that the express warranty terms in the manual are strictly limited to the "Five Year Limited Warranty" section, which also contained a purportedly effective disclaimer of those terms, is unfounded.

Formal wording is not necessary to create a warranty and a seller does not have to express any specific intention to create one. See Pack & Process, Inc. v. Celotex Corp., Del. Super., 503 A.2d 646, 658-59 (1985). Here the additional terms found in the manual's "Introduction" and "Helmet Performance" sections (stating that "the primary function of a helmet is to reduce the harmful effects of a blow to the head . . ." and ". . . the [helmet] is designed to absorb the force of a blow by spreading it over as wide an area of the outer shell as possible . . .") are textual representations constituting affirmations of fact upon which a buyer is entitled to rely. While this Court does not appear to have specifically addressed the issue, other courts have held that express warranties can arise from similar textual representations found in owners' manuals even where not specifically labeled as such. See e.g., Kinlaw v. Long Mfg. N.C., Inc., 298 N.C. 494, 259 S.E.2d 552, 557 (1979); Hawkins Constr. Co. v. Matthews Co., 190 Neb. 546, 209 N.W.2d 643, 654-55 (1973).

The restrictive provision of 6 Del. C. §2-316(1), renders Bell's effort to disclaim any express warranties in the manual's "Five Year Limited Warranty" ineffective as a matter of law. See U.C.C. §2-316(1) cmt. 1 (stating that "this section . . . seeks to protect a buyer from unexpected and unbargained language of disclaimer by denying effect to such language when inconsistent with language of express warranty. . . ."). While the manual contains disclaimers warning potential users that the helmet cannot prevent all injuries, other representations were made to assure a potential buyer that the helmet's liner was designed to reduce the harmful effects of a blow to the head. Those representations constituted essential elements of a valid express warranty that may not be effectively disclaimed as a matter of law. See Jensen v. Seigel Mobile Homes Group, 105 Idaho 189, 668 P.2d 65, 71-72 (1983) (holding that one principle of the law of warranty is to hold a seller responsible for its representations and assuring that a buyer receives that which he bargained for).

Bell argues that even if an express warranty was created and not effectively disclaimed here, the manual's textual representations promise only to prevent injuries to the head, not to a user's neck. Furthermore, Bell argues, the helmet's liner did crush as designed, thereby precluding a finding that the warranty was breached. Yarusso counters this argument by pointing out that injuries to the neck may logically follow a blow to the head, the helmet's liner did not sufficiently crush to prevent his injury and, as a result, he did not get what he bargained for. Upon review of the evidence, much of which was admittedly supplied by testimony of Yarusso's experts, the jury came to a logical conclusion that an express warranty was made in the helmet's manual. Upon consideration of this representation in relation to the specific facts of this case, they also concluded that the warranty was breached. In view of the evidence presented by the experts for both parties on the relationship between the helmet's design and the risk of neck injury, a factual predicate existed for the jury to determine whether there was a basis for recovery under the express warranty claim. The Superior Court did not err in submitting that issue to the jury.

B.

Our holding sustaining the jury's verdict on the claim of breach of express warranty renders an in-depth consideration of Bell's implied warranty arguments unnecessary, since the jury was permitted to find a breach of warranty on alternative grounds. The Superior Court in rejecting Bell's post-trial motions also declined to rule on the merits of Bell's attack on the implied warranty finding in view of the jury's finding of liability on the express warranty claim. We also are not required to address Bell's contention that Yarusso was obligated, as a matter of law, to present evidence of a safer alternative design. See Mazda Motor Corp. v. Lindahl, Del. Supr., 706 A.2d 526, 530 (1998). We note, however, that Yarusso's experts never claimed that a helmet can reduce the probability of a user's neck injury in all circumstances, and they were not required to present evidence that a helmet could be designed to achieve this. Expert evidence was presented, however, that a helmet could be designed with a softer liner that would, in theory, limit the amount of force placed on the user's neck, thereby reducing the probability of partial-load direct downward neck injuries, particularly upon impact with harder surfaces. There was, thus, a sufficient factual predicate for submission of the implied warranty claim to the jury.

III

In a related vein, Bell next argues that the jury's finding for Yarusso on breach of express and implied warranties is inconsistent with its finding that Bell was not negligent. Because the jury found no product defect leading to negligent conduct on Bell's part, it could not have properly found, the argument runs, that a defect existed in the helmet upon which any warranty claims relied. See Ruffin v. Shaw Indus., Inc., 4th Cir., 149 F.3d 294, 301 (1998) (holding that the requirements of both actions are nearly alike and that a finding on one claim often "applies equally" to the other); Prentis v. Yale Mfg. Co., 421 Mich. 670, 365 N.W.2d 176, 186 (1984) (both actions "involve identical evidence and require proof of exactly the same elements"). In essence, Bell contends that because its product was not defective, a verdict in favor of Yarusso on warranty and negligence claims was precluded.

A claim for breach of warranty, express or implied, is conceptually distinct from a negligence claim because the latter focuses on the manufacturer's conduct, whereas a breach of warranty claim evaluates the product itself. See Cline v. Prowler Indus. of Md., Inc., Del. Supr., 418 A.2d 968, 978, n.19 (1980) (the focus of a negligence claim is the manufacturer's conduct and the breach of an accepted standard of conduct); Borel v. Fibreboard Paper Prod. Corp., 5th Cir., 493 F.2d 1076, 1094 (1973) (in a products liability case with inconsistent verdicts, it is within the jury's prerogative so long as evidence supports the finding); Community Television Serv. v. Dresser Indus., Inc., D.S.D., 435 F. Supp. 214, 216 (1977) (jury could find defendant neither negligent nor strictly liable while finding as a matter of law that representations in a brochure created an express warranty that defendant breached). Based on the foregoing authorities, we find no fatal inconsistency between the jury's verdict negating negligence but finding breach of warranty. . . .

The judgment of the Superior Court is AFFIRMED.

PROBLEM 35

When Portia Moot went to buy a new car, she asked the salesman how many miles to the gallon it would get. He replied that it would get "between 30 and 35 MPG in the city and 40 to 45 on the highway." Delighted, she bought the car. The very best the car ever did, even in highway driving, was 27 MPG, and Portia was upset. When she threatened a lawsuit, the dealership pointed out the following three clauses in the contract she had signed that it relied on to avoid liability. This contract said nothing about miles per gallon of gas. In your opinion is there any way around these clauses?

(1) "This is the entire contract, and there are no other matters agreed to by the parties that are not contained herein." Would this clause be more effective in a business contract to exclude oral statements made during negotiations on the theory that the written disclaimer keeps such oral matters from being part of the "basis of the bargain"? See Lincoln Sav. Bank v. Open Solutions, Inc., 2013 WL 997894 (N.D. Iowa 2013).

(2) "There are no other express or implied warranties except those contained herein."

(3) "No salesperson has the authority to give express warranties other than those contained herein." (As to this last clause, see White & Summers §13-4, and the brief reference to the matter in Official Comment 2 to §2-316.)

2. Disclaiming Implied Warranties

In contrast to express warranties, implied warranties are much more easily disclaimed. Since they are created by the legislature of the enacting state and not by seller conduct, there is less unfairness in their destruction as long as the seller or the circumstances alert the buyer to the disclaimer. Read §2-316(2) and (3) carefully.

Cate v. Dover Corp.

Supreme Court of Texas, 1990
790 S.W.2d 559

DOGGETT, J.

We consider the enforceability of a disclaimer of implied warranties. The trial court upheld the disclaimer and granted summary judgment in favor of Dover Corporation. The court of appeals affirmed. 776 S.W.2d 680. We reverse the judgment of the court of appeals and remand this cause to the trial court for further proceedings consistent with this opinion.

In September 1984, Edward Cate, doing business as Cate's Transmission Service, purchased from Beech Tire Mart three lifts manufactured and designed by Dover Corporation to elevate vehicles for maintenance. Despite repairs made by Beech and Dover, the lifts never functioned properly. Dover contends that Cate's subsequent claim against it for breach of the implied warranty of merchantability is barred by a disclaimer contained within a written, express warranty.

This warranty is set forth on a separate page headed in blue half inch block print, with the heading: "YOU CAN TAKE ROTARY'S NEW 5-YEAR WARRANTY AND TEAR IT APART." The statement is followed by bold black type stating, "And, when you are through, it'll be just as solid as the No. 1 lift company in America, Rotary." The text of the warranty itself is in black type, contained within double blue lines, and appears under the blue three-eighths inch block print heading "WARRANTY." The disclaimer of implied warranties, although contained in a separate paragraph within the warranty text, is in the same typeface, size, and color as the remainder of the text.

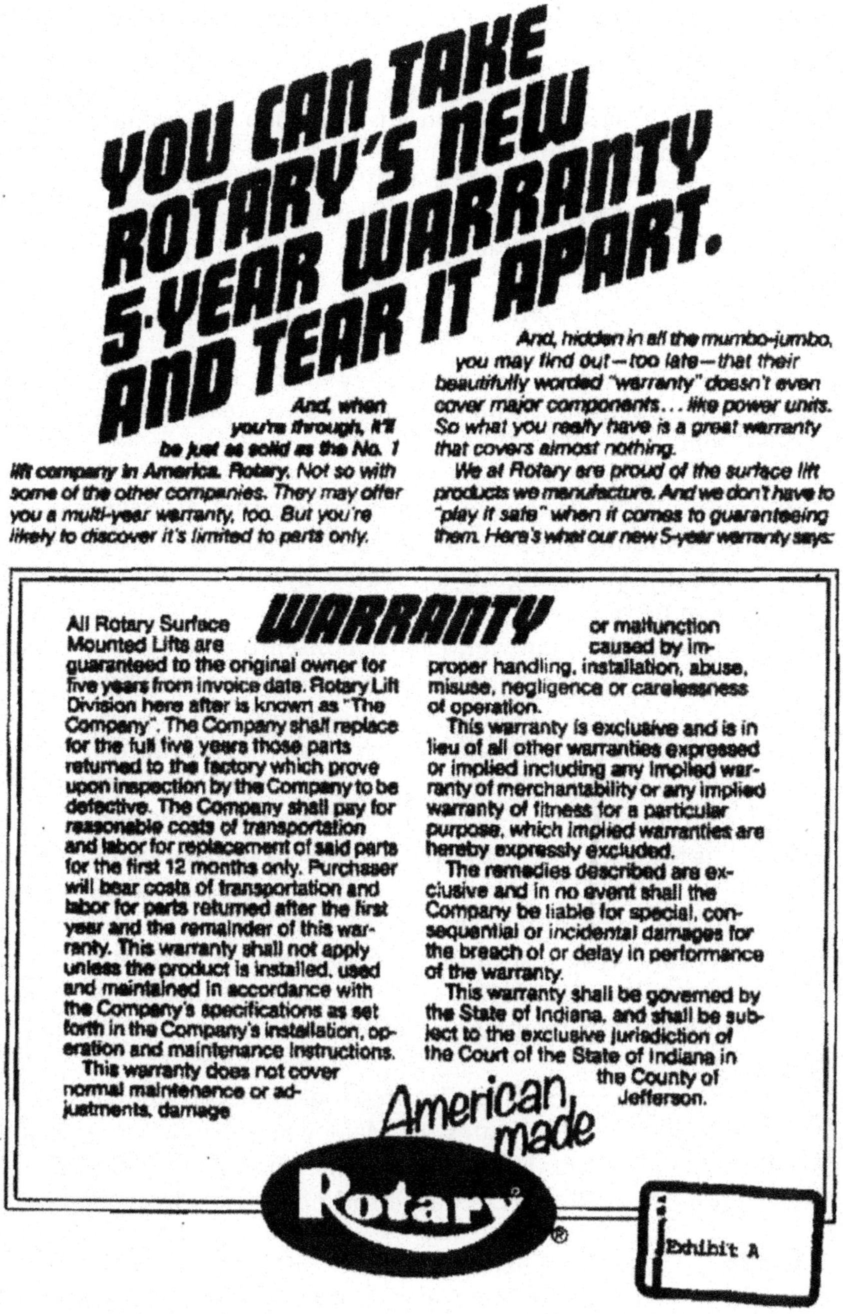

An implied warranty of merchantability arises in a contract for the sale of goods unless expressly excluded or modified by conspicuous language. Tex. Bus. & Com. Code Ann. §§2.314(a), 2.316(b) (Vernon 1968). Whether a particular disclaimer is conspicuous is a question of law to be determined by the following definition:

> A term or clause is conspicuous when it is so written that a reasonable person against whom it is to operate ought to have noticed it. A printed heading in capitals (as: NON-NEGOTIABLE BILL OF LADING) is conspicuous. Language in a body of a form is conspicuous if it is larger or of other contrasting type or color. But in a telegram, any stated term is conspicuous.

Id. §1.201(10). Further explanation is provided by comment 10 thereto:

> This [section] is intended to indicate some of the methods of making a term attention-calling. But the test is whether attention can reasonably be expected to be called to it.

In interpreting this language, Dover argues that a lesser standard of conspicuousness should apply to a disclaimer made to a merchant, such as Cate. Admittedly, an ambiguity is created by the requirement that disclaimer language be conspicuous to "a reasonable person *against whom it is to operate.*" Comment 10, however, clearly contemplated an objective standard, stating the test as "whether attention can reasonably be expected to be called to it."

We then turn to an application of an objective standard of conspicuousness to Dover's warranty. The top forty percent of the written warranty is devoted to extolling its virtues. The warranty itself, contained within double blue lines, is then set out in five paragraphs in normal black type under the heading "WARRANTY." Nothing distinguishes the third paragraph, which contains the exclusionary language. It is printed in the same typeface, size and color as the rest of the warranty text. Although the warranty in its entirety may be considered conspicuous, the disclaimer is hidden among attention-getting language purporting to grant the best warranty available. . . .

Although this is a case of first impression in Texas, the facts here parallel those reviewed in other states. In Massey-Ferguson, Inc. v. Utley, 439 S.W.2d 57, 59 (Ky. Ct. App. 1969), a disclaimer hidden under the heading "WARRANTY and AGREEMENT" was found not to be conspicuous:

> It is true that the *heading was* in large, bold-face type, but there was nothing to suggest that an exclusion was being made; on the contrary, the words of the headings indicated a *making* of warranties rather than a *disclaimer.*

(Emphasis in original.) Similarly, in Hartman v. Jensen's, Inc., 289 S.E.2d 648 (S.C. 1982), the court found that placing a disclaimer under the bold heading "Terms of Warranty" failed to alert the consumer to the fact that an exclusion was intended. Dover's disclaimer similarly fails to attract the attention of a reasonable person and is not conspicuous. . . .

Dover argues that even an inconspicuous disclaimer should be given effect because Cate had actual knowledge of it at the time of the purchase. Because the object of the conspicuousness requirement is to protect the buyer from surprise and an unknowing waiver of his or her rights, inconspicuous language is immaterial when the buyer has actual knowledge of the disclaimer. This knowledge can result from the buyer's prior dealings with the seller, or by the seller specifically bringing the inconspicuous waiver to the buyer's attention. The Code appears to recognize that actual knowledge of the disclaimer overrides the question of conspicuousness. For example, §2.316(b) does not mandate a written disclaimer of the implied warranty of merchantability but clearly provides that an oral disclaimer may be effective.[8] Similarly, §2.316(c)(3) allows an implied warranty to be excluded or modified by methods other than a conspicuous writing: course of dealing, course of performance, or usage of trade. When the buyer is not surprised by the disclaimer, insisting on compliance with the conspicuousness requirement serves no purpose. See R. Anderson, Uniform Commercial Code §2-316:49-50 (1983). The extent of a buyer's knowledge of a disclaimer of the implied warranty of merchantability is thus clearly relevant to a determination of its enforceability. See Singleton v. LaCoure, 712 S.W.2d 757, 759 (Tex. App. Houston [14th Dist.] 1986, writ ref'd n.r.e.) (relying in part on buyer's acknowledgement to enforce disclaimer). The seller has the burden of proving the buyer's actual knowledge of the disclaimer.

As this is a summary judgment case, the issue on appeal is whether Dover met its burden by establishing that there exists no genuine issue of material fact thereby entitling it to judgment as a matter of law. City of Houston v. Clear Creek Basin Authority, 589 S.W.2d 671, 678 (Tex. 1979). All doubts as to the existence of a genuine issue of material fact are resolved against the movant, and we must view the evidence in the light most favorable to the Petitioner. Great American Reserve Ins. Co. v. San Antonio Plumbing Supply Co., 391 S.W.2d 41, 47 (Tex. 1965). In support of its claim that Cate had actual knowledge of the disclaimer, Dover relies on Cate's deposition testimony, as follows:

8. Tex. Bus. & Com. Code §2.136, comment 1 (section seeks to protect buyer from unexpected and unbargained language of disclaimer by permitting exclusion of implied warranties only by conspicuous language or other circumstances which protect buyer from surprise); see also Weintraub, Disclaimer of Warranties and Limitation of Damages for Breach of Warranty Under the UCC, 53 Tex. L. Rev. 60, 66 (1974); J. White & R. Summers, Uniform Commercial Code §12-5, n.76 (2d ed. 1980) (seller may effectively disclaim by orally explaining inconspicuous written disclaimer, provided word "merchantability" used).

Q: Do you know, or do you remember what kinds of warranties you received when you bought the lifts?
A: I may be wrong, but I think it was a five-year warranty.
Q: What was your understanding of that warranty?
A: Any problems would be taken care of within the five year period.
Q: Do you know if that warranty was from Beech Equipment, or from Dover?
A: I believe it was from Dover.
Q: Did you receive any written documentation in regard to that warranty?
A: Yes, ma'am.

Although it is clear that Cate understood the warranty to extend for only five years, it is not clear that he understood any other limitations or exclusions. Merely providing a buyer a copy of documents containing an inconspicuous disclaimer does not establish actual knowledge. Dover has failed to establish that as a matter of law Cate had actual knowledge of the disclaimer.

We hold that, to be enforceable, a written disclaimer of the implied warranty of merchantability made in connection with a sale of goods must be conspicuous to a reasonable person. We further hold that such a disclaimer contained in text undistinguished in typeface, size or color within a form purporting to grant a warranty is not conspicuous, and is unenforceable unless the buyer has actual knowledge of the disclaimer. For the reasons stated herein, we reverse the judgment of the court of appeals and remand to the trial court for further proceedings consistent with this opinion.

SPEARS, J. concurs and files a separate opinion (in which Mauzy, J. joins).

RAY, J. files a concurring and dissenting opinion.

SPEARS, J. Although I concur in the court's opinion, I write separately to declare that the time has come for the legislature to consider the realities of the marketplace and prohibit all disclaimers of the implied warranties of merchantability and fitness.

These implied warranties, created by common-law courts long before the adoption of the UCC, developed to protect purchasers from losses suffered because of "the frustration of their expectations about the worth, efficacy, or desirability" of a product. W. Keeton, Prosser and Keeton on the Law of Torts §95A (5th ed. 1984). Implication of these warranties into every goods contract, without regard to the parties' actual assent to their terms, served "to police, to prevent, and to remedy" unfair consumer transactions. Llewellyn, On Warranty of Quality, and Society, 39 Colum. L. Rev. 699, 699 (1936); Humber v. Morton, 426 S.W.2d 554, 557-558 (Tex. 1968).

These implied warranties also serve other important purposes: they create incentives to produce and market higher quality products; they discourage shoddy workmanship and unethical trade practices; and they place responsibility on those who profit from the sale of goods, have the greatest control over the products, and are better able to bear the risk of loss. See *Humber,* 426 S.W.2d at 562; Decker & Sons v. Capp, 139 Tex. 609, 610, 164 S.W.2d 828, 829 (1942). Section 2-316 of the U.C.C., however, subverts all of these purposes by giving sellers almost unlimited license to disclaim implied warranties.

We live in an age when sellers of goods "saturate the marketplace and all of our senses" with the most extraordinary claims about the worth of their products. Anderson, The Supreme Court of Texas and the Duty to Read the Contracts You Sign, 15 Tex. Tech L. Rev. 517, 544 (1984); Henningsen v. BloomField Motors, Inc., 161 A.2d 69, 84 (N.J. 1960). Yet, the same sellers under the carte blanche granted them by §2-316 of the U.C.C. refuse to guarantee and indeed expressly disclaim that their products are merchantable or even fit for their intended purposes. Under §2-316, not much is actually required for an effective disclaimer. To disclaim the implied warranty of merchantability the seller need only include the word "merchantability" in a conspicuous fashion. Tex. Bus. & Com. Code Ann. §2-316(b) (Vernon 1968). To disclaim the implied warranty of fitness the seller must use a writing and must make the disclaimer conspicuous. Id. at §2-316(2). No particular form of words is needed to disclaim an implied warranty of fitness, nor does §2-316 require the buyer to be actually aware of the disclaimer before it will be enforced. All implied warranties can be disclaimed by the mere inclusion of expressions like "as is" or "with all faults." Id. at §2-316, comment 1. Finally, as today's majority makes clear, §2-316 does not even require the disclaimer to be conspicuous if the buyer's actual knowledge of the disclaimer can be shown.

By establishing specific "requirements" for disclaimers §2-316 ostensibly "seeks to protect a buyer from unexpected and unbargained language of disclaimer." Tex. Bus. & Com. Code §2-316, comment 1 (Vernon 1968). In reality, however, §2-316 completely undermines implied warranties. Implicitly, §2-316 adopts the position that disclaimers should be enforced because society benefits when parties to a contract are allowed to set *all* the terms of their agreement. The problem with this position, and with §2-316 generally, is two-fold: it ignores the fact that governmental implication of protective terms into private contracts is commonplace (e.g., the *implied* warranties of merchantability and fitness); and, more importantly, it rests on the faulty premise that contractual disclaimers are generally freely bargained for elements of a contract.

Freedom of contract arguments generally, and §2-316 specifically, presuppose and are based on "the image of individuals meeting in the marketplace" on equal ground to negotiate the terms of a contract. Rakoff, Contracts of Adhesion: An Essay in Reconstruction, 96 Harv. L. Rev. 1174, 1216 (1983). At one time, this image may have accurately reflected marketplace realities. However, the last half of the twentieth century has witnessed "the rise of the corporation" and, increasingly, the displacement of physical persons as sellers in consumer and commercial contracts. Phillips, Unconscionability and Article 2 Implied Warranty Disclaimers, 62 Chi.-Kent L. Rev. 199, 239 (1985). This development has led to innumerable situations in which consumers deal from an unequal bargaining position, the most prominent example being the ubiquitous standard form contract which is now used by most sellers of goods and which invariably contains an implied warranty disclaimer. See Melody Home Mfg. Co. v. Barnes, 741 S.W.2d 349, 355 (Tex. 1987); *Henningsen,* 161 A.2d at 86-89; Slawson, Standard Form Contracts and Democratic Control of Lawmaking Power, 84 Harv. L. Rev. 529, 529 (1971) ("standard form contracts probably account for more than ninety-nine percent of all the contracts now made"); L. Vold, Handbook of the Law of Sales 447 (2d ed. 1959) (dramatic rise in corporate power has yielded the standard form contract whose terms are drafted by the seller and usually contain implied warranty disclaimers).

The great majority of buyers never read an implied warranty disclaimer found in a standard form contract.[9] Even when implied warranty disclaimers are read, their legal significance is not generally understood. Such disclaimers include unfamiliar terminology (e.g., "implied warranty of merchantability"), and comprehending their legal effect requires one not only to understand what substantive rights are involved, but also to grasp that these rights have been lost via the disclaimer. Phillips, Unconscionability and Article 2 Implied Warranty Disclaimers, 62 Chi.-Kent L. Rev. 199, 243 (1985); see also Federal Trade Commission, Facts for Consumers (Mar. 23, 1979) (more than 35% of those surveyed mistakenly believed that an "as is" disclaimer meant the dealer would have to pay some, if not all, costs if a car broke down within 25 days of

9. See Restatement (Second) of Contracts §211, Comment b (1981):

> A party who makes regular use of a standardized form of agreement does not ordinarily expect his customers to understand or even to read the standard terms. One purpose of standardization is to eliminate bargaining over details of individual transactions, and that purpose would not be served if a substantial number of customers retained counsel and reviewed the standard terms. . . . Customers do not in fact ordinarily understand or even read the standard terms.

Id.; see also Rakoff, Contracts of Adhesion: An Essay in Reconstruction, 96 Harv. L. Rev. 1174, 1179 n.21 (1983) (citing numerous commentators who declare that standard terms not read or understood, and some empirical studies asserting same proposition); Phillips, Unconscionability and Article 2 Implied Warranty Disclaimers, 62 Chi.-Kent L. Rev. 199, 243 (1985) (many sales do not involve a written sales contract that is presented before the goods change hands; usually, the disclaimer is inside the package and is not seen until after the sale is completed).

a sale). Finally, even if a buyer reads and understands an implied warranty disclaimer, chances are he will be without power to either strike these terms or "shop around" for better ones. If the buyer attempts the former, he will likely run into an employee who is unauthorized to alter the form contract; if he attempts the latter, he will likely confront a competitor who offers substantially the same form terms. *Henningsen,* 161 A.2d at 87. In short, the "marketplace reality" suggests that freedom of contract in the sale of goods is actually nonexistent; a buyer today can either take the contract with the disclaimer attached or leave it and go without the good. . . .

The realities of the modern marketplace demand that the legislature prohibit implied warranty disclaimers by repealing §2-316 of the U.C.C. Without such action, Texas courts will be forced to rely on "covert tools," such as the unconscionability provision in §2-302 or the "conspicuous" requirement in §2-316, to reach a just and fair result in disclaimer suits. When these tools are used, guidance, predictability and consistency in the law is sacrificed, while limited judicial resources are spent policing unjust bargains that could have been avoided. Were it up to the judicial branch, the courts could declare such disclaimers void as against public policy. If the legislature has the interests of Texas citizens at heart, it will repeal §2-316 because, no matter how conspicuous, such disclaimers are abusive of consumers.

Mauzy, J. joins in this concurring opinion.

Ray, J. I concur in that portion of the court's opinion requiring that a written disclaimer of the implied warranty of merchantability must be conspicuous to a reasonable person. I write separately, however, to take issue with the court's immediate erosion of that standard by permitting a showing of actual knowledge of the disclaimer to override a lack of conspicuousness.

The statute, on its face, provides for no actual knowledge exception. There is no room for judicial crafting of those omitted by the legislature. I would hold that the extent of a buyer's knowledge of a disclaimer is irrelevant to a determination of its enforceability under §2-316(b) of the U.C.C.

The effect of actual knowledge is subject to debate among leading commentators on commercial law. The purpose of the objective standard of conspicuousness adopted by the court today reflects the view that "the drafters intended a rigid adherence to the conspicuousness requirement in order to avoid arguments concerning what the parties said about the warranties at the time of the sale." J. White and R. Summers, Uniform Commercial Code §12-5 (2d ed. 1980). An absolute rule that an inconspicuous disclaimer is invalid, despite the buyer's actual knowledge, encourages sellers to make their disclaimers conspicuous, thereby reducing the need for courts to evaluate swearing matches as to actual awareness in particular cases. See

W. Powers, Texas Products Liability Law §2.0723 (1989). Today's decision condemns our court to a parade of such cases.

PROBLEM 36

(a) A statement buried in the fine print of a used car purchase agreement states that "There are no express or implied warranties that are part of this sale." See §§2-316(2), 1-201(b)(10).

(1) Are the implied warranties effectively disclaimed?

(2) If the car dealership asks you to redraft this clause so as to comply with the Code, what changes would you make in the language? See the extended discussion, particularly in the dissent, in Hicks v. Superior Court, 8 Cal. Rptr. 3d 703 (Cal. App. 2004).

(3) What changes would you make in the physical appearance of the clause in the contract? Is it all right to put the disclaimer in a clause labeled *WARRANTY*? See Benedict v. Hankook Tire Co. Ltd., 295 F. Supp. 3d 632 (E.D. Va. 2018); Agropur, Inc. v. Scoular Company, 2017 WL 3411944 (D. Minn. 2017) (disclaimer in contract section titled "CONTAMINATION & GUARANTEE").

(4) Can the car dealer win the legal dispute by arguing that usage of trade (§1-303(c)) permits the burial of warranty disclaimers in the fine print? (For an annotation collecting the automobile warranty disclaimer cases, see Annot., 54 A.L.R.3d 1217.)

(b) The words *AS IS* are written with soap in large letters across the front windshield of the used car. See §2-316(3)(a). Is this effective to disclaim implied warranties? Express warranties? See Woodard v. Labrada, 2017 WL 3309765 (C.D. Cal. 2017); Annot., 24 A.L.R.3d 465. Must the "as is" language be conspicuous? See §2-316(3)(a); Lumber Mut. Ins. Co. v. Clarklift of Detroit, Inc., 224 Mich. App. 737, 569 N.W.2d 681 (1997); R.J. Robertson, Jr., A Modest Proposal Regarding the Enforceability of "As Is" Disclaimers of Implied Warranties: What the Buyer Doesn't Know Shouldn't Hurt Him, 99 Com. L.J. 1 (1994). Would a conspicuous statement of AS IS on a *new* recreational vehicle exclude the implied warranty of merchantability? See Chaudoin v. Thor Motor Coach, Inc., 2017 WL 3485803 (E.D. Mich. 2017). Certainly it is clear that "As Is" will not protect a seller from tort theories such as fraud. Sorchaga v. Ride Auto, LLC, 893 N.W.2d 360 (Wis. App. 2017).

(c) The car salesman asks the buyer, "Would you like to examine the car?" and the buyer, who is in a hurry, says, "No." Effective disclaimer? See §2-316(3)(b); see also Official Comment 8.

(d) Remember Ted Traveler (Problem 22), who walked into the men's room of the bus depot and bought an expensive watch? We decided there was no warranty of title in that transaction. However, a warranty of quality is a separate question. Are there implied warranties in this sale? See §2-316(3)(c).

PROBLEM 37

If your client is the manufacturer of products and asks you to draft up contracts for the sale of the company's products, should you recommend disclaiming warranties? You could do this by making no express warranties except vague puffs—"This product is outstanding!"—and carefully disclaim all implied warranties, mentioning "merchantability" conspicuously. Is this a good idea either from a business or legal standpoint? Be prepared to discuss this in class.

Carrigg v. General R.V. Center, Inc.

United States District Court, Eastern District of Michigan, 2019
421 F. Supp. 3d 480

TERRENCE G. BERG, United States District Judge.

Plaintiffs Everette L. Carrigg and Patsy O. Carrigg purchased a used recreational vehicle ("RV") from Defendant General R.V. Center, Inc. ("General RV"). According to the Carriggs, shortly after they purchased the RV, it became clear the vehicle was defective and not safe for its intended use. Plaintiffs are now asserting claims for violation of the Magnuson-Moss Warranty Act, 15 U.S.C. §2301 *et seq.*, breach of express and implied warranties, fraudulent misrepresentation, and breach of contract. The case is before the Court on motions for summary judgment filed by General RV and by Defendant Cornerstone United, Inc., a party to the service contract Plaintiffs purchased through General RV. ECF Nos. 22, 23. For reasons explained below, the Court will grant Cornerstone's and General RV's motions for summary judgment.

BACKGROUND

In late 2016, Plaintiffs Everett Carrigg and Patsy Carrigg, a retired couple in their mid-to-late 70's, purchased a used 2013 Thor Challenger recreational vehicle ("RV") from Defendant General R.V. Center, Inc. ("General RV"). ECF No. 16, PageID.494 (Am. Compl.). As part of the sale, Plaintiffs traded in their old RV and agreed to pay an additional $62,228.33. *Id.* at PageID.496; ECF No. 22-1, PageID.562 ("Purchase Agreement"). Along with the Thor Challenger RV, they also purchased a three-year service warranty serviced by Cornerstone United, Inc. ECF No. 16, PageID.494. Plaintiffs contend that throughout the process of purchasing the RV a General RV salesman, Julius "Juice" Tatum, as well as other agents of General RV-including a sales manager, financing manager, general manager, and service manager-made misrepresentations about the condition and quality of the RV, as well as the applicable warranties. ECF No. 16, PageID.496; ECF No. 29-2, PageID.722-23 (Patsy Carrigg Aff.). These alleged misrepresentations, which Plaintiffs say they relied on to their detriment, form the basis of this lawsuit.

According to Plaintiffs, representatives of General RV on multiple occasions averred that the RV they ultimately purchased was in excellent condition and "came with the remainder of a 10-year manufacturer's bumper-to-bumper factory warranty that specifically covered any structural defects." ECF No. 16, PageID.496; ECF No. 29-2, PageID.722-23. Contrary to General RV's alleged representations that the vehicle was "like new" at the time of purchase, Plaintiffs contend the RV had "major structural damage" and, as they later claim to have discovered, had previously been totaled and its chassis replaced with a salvage chassis. ECF No. 16, PageID.497; ECF No. 29-2, PageID.730. The advertised "bumper-to-bumper" manufacturer's warranty had in fact expired in 2014, two years before Plaintiffs purchased the vehicle. ECF No. 35, PageID.1005 (Celina Tyler Aff.). Plaintiffs further urge that representatives of General RV misrepresented the scope of the three-year Cornerstone warranty they purchased at the dealership, reassuring them that the warranty would cover any needed repairs to fix structural or mechanical problems with the vehicle. ECF No. 29-2, PageID.724. Essentially, Plaintiffs maintain that General RV's salesman and managers made express oral representations to them about the condition of the vehicle and the manufacturer's warranty, that those representations were false, and that Plaintiffs relied on them to their detriment."

The purchase agreement governing the RV's sale is a two-sided document with an "all-caps" integration clause above the purchasers' signature line explaining that the written agreement contains the entire agreement between Plaintiffs and General RV. ECF No. 22-1, PageID.562. That provision also alerts signatories to other terms and conditions contained in the agreement-including an "as is" and exclusion of warranties provision located on the reverse side of the agreement. *Id.* The integration clause reads:

> THIS PURCHASE AGREEMENT CONTAINS THE ENTIRE UNDERSTANDING BETWEEN GENERAL RV AND PURCHASER. NO ONE HAS AUTHORITY TO MAKE ANY REPRESENTATION BEYOND THIS AGREEMENT. NO OTHER REPRESENTATIONS OR INDUCEMENTS, VERBAL OR WRITTEN HAVE BEEN MADE, WHICH ARE NOT CONTAINED ON THIS DOCUMENT. PURCHASER HAS NOT RELIED ON ANYTHING NOT WRITTEN INTO THIS PURCHASE AGREEMENT

> SUCH THAT NOTHING ELSE IS THE BASIS OF THE BARGAIN OR IS ENFORCEABLE AGAINST GENERAL RV, EVEN IF ALLEGED TO BE A MISREPRESENTATION. BY SIGNING BELOW, PURCHASER ACKNOWLEDGES THAT PURCHASER HAS RECEIVED A COPY OF THIS AGREEMENT AND THAT PURCHASER HAS READ AND UNDERSTANDS THE TERMS OF THIS AGREEMENT, INCLUDING THOSE PRINTED ON THE REVERSE SIDE, WHICH INCLUDE AN "AS IS" CLAUSE, A NON-REFUNDABLE DEPOSIT STATEMENT, AND A CHOICE OF LAW AND FORUM SELECTION CLAUSES INDICATING THAT MICHIGAN LAW APPLIES TO ALL POTENTIAL DISPUTES AND THAT ALL CLAIMS MUST BE FILED IN MICHIGAN.

ECF No. 22-1, PageID.562.

The "as is" purchase warning and express exclusion of warranties on the reverse side of the agreement states:

> **EXCLUSION OF WARRANTIES, "AS IS" PURCHASE** PURCHASER UNDERSTANDS THAT THERE MAY BE WRITTEN WARRANTIES COVERING THIS RV, BUT THAT THESE WARRANTIES ARE OFFERED BY THE MANUFACTURER OF THE RV.... PURCHASER UNDERSTANDS THAT DEALER OFFERS NO WARRANTIES, EXPRESS OR IMPLIED, ON THIS RV. **THIS RV IS SOLD "AS IS" BY DEALER, AND DEALER DISCLAIMS ALL WARRANTIES EXPRESS OR IMPLIED, INCLUDING, BUT NOT LIMITED TO ANY IMPLIED WARRANTY OF MERCHANTABILITY OR FITNESS FOR A PARTICULAR PURPOSE.** This document is not a warranty and nothing that Dealer says or does creates a warranty.... This is true even if Purchaser purchases a service contract.... Also, since Dealer provides no warranties from Dealer, any written warranty from a manufacturer of the vehicle or its components is Purchaser's sole and exclusive remedy for any problem that Purchaser may have with the vehicle or any appliance or component.

ECF No. 22-1, PageID.563. This "as is" provision is the eleventh of sixteen different terms and conditions described on the reverse side of the purchase agreement:"

The font, which is small and somewhat difficult to read, appears to be no larger than that used for other provisions on this same page of the purchase agreement, though portions of the "as is" disclaimer are capitalized, and some parts both capitalized and bolded. ECF No. 22-1, PageID.563. No other provision in the purchase agreement is both capitalized and bolded. *See id.*

Plaintiffs also signed a separate General RV "as is" and warranty disclaimer form, thereby again acknowledging that the RV was purchased "as is" and that the two-sided purchase agreement is "the only document that contains the terms and conditions of [the] agreement with General RV."

ECF No. 22-1, PageID.565. The form uses the phrase "as is" in its title and capitalizes, bolds, and underlines that term[.]

The same warranty disclaimer former also includes an additional exclusion of warranties provision which Plaintiffs signed, affirming:

> I understand that **GENERAL RV OFFERS NO WARRANTIES, EXPRESS OR IMPLIED, ON THIS RV AND THAT I AM PURCHASING THE RV "AS IS" FROM GENERAL RV. GENERAL RV DISCLAIMS ALL WARRANTIES, EXPRESS OR IMPLIED, INCLUDING, BUT NOT LIMITED TO ANY IMPLIED WARRANTY OF MERCHANTABILITY OR FITNESS FOR A PARTICULAR PURPOSE.**

ECF No. 22-1, PageID.565; *see also* ECF No. 22-1, PageID.569-70 (General RV Service Call Agreement) ("General RV Center has sold the unit to you "AS IS" and does not issue any warranties whatsoever either express or implied. All warranties received by you are solely issued by the manufacturer of your recreational vehicle/unit.").

According to the amended complaint, Everette Carrigg is "not functionally literate" and therefore "could not understand the terms of the documents he signed and initialed at General RV." ECF No. 29-2, PageID.722. Patsy Carrigg apparently also has poor eyesight-she has had two surgeries on her eyes and continues to be treated for vision issues. ECF No. 29-2, PageID.721. Despite these limitations Plaintiffs signed several forms, including the purchase agreement, in the process of purchasing their RV. ECF 22-1, PageID.4-5. Everette Carrigg, the primary buyer, also signed an additional acknowledgment averring that he had received the purchase agreement, "was allowed the necessary and requested amount of time to review its contents" and "fully underst[ood] the terms and conditions." ECF No. 22-1, PageID.571. Yet Plaintiffs allege that General RV rushed them through the sales process, without any meaningful opportunity to review the paperwork or to examine the "fine print," which Patsy Carrigg found difficult to read (and Everett Carrigg apparently could not read at all). ECF No. 16, PageID.499; ECF No. 29-2, PageID.722, 724.

After purchasing the RV, Plaintiffs claim they immediately discovered it was "mechanically unsound, unsafe to drive, and did not conform to the representations that [General RV] had made." ECF No. 16, PageID.503; ECF No. 29-2, PageID.726-27. Repairs were needed at the outset, according to Plaintiffs, to address the following problems: broken driver's seat; defective step control modules; seeping jack seals; malfunctioning R/R thermistor, camera, radio and monitors; and an unsealed or leaking toilet. ECF No. 16, PageID.503; ECF No. 29-2, PageID.726-27. Plaintiffs also brought their recently purchased RV back to the General RV service department to address a litany of more serious structural and mechanical problems, including a windshield that popped out of the vehicle, a defective leveling device, a malfunctioning awning system, and unstable interior walls. ECF No. 16, PageID.504; ECF No. 29-2, PageID.727. But General RV then explained that there was in fact no manufacturer's warranty on the vehicle and apparently declined to make the repairs Plaintiffs requested, or at least to do so free of charge. ECF No. 16, PageID.505-06. Likewise, General RV refused to let Plaintiffs trade in the apparently defective RV for a different, similarly priced one. ECF No. 16, PageID.506.

Plaintiffs assert they have been left with a worthless RV along with an equally ineffective manufacturer's warranty and service contract. ECF No. 29-02, PageID.26. Seeking relief from this court, they now claim that: (1) General RV breached implied warranties inherent in the sale of any good; (2) General RV breached express warranties it made to Plaintiffs about the condition of the Thor RV, the existence of a manufacturer's warranty, and General RV's commitment to fulfilling the Cornerstone service contract; (3) General RV breached warranties and employed deceptive practices in violation of the Magnuson-Moss Warranty Act, 15 U.S.C. § 2301 *et seq.*; (4) General RV made fraudulent misrepresentations to them regarding the condition of the Thor RV; and (5) Cornerstone breached its service contract by failing to repair the RV. ECF No. 16, PageID.19-27.

Discussion

. . .

I. Cornerstone's Motion for Summary Judgment

Plaintiffs' only claim against Cornerstone is for breach of contract in connection with Cornerstone's alleged failure to repair their RV. They assert that Cornerstone was required to make these repairs under the service contract they purchased through General RV. But the plain language of the contract provides that Cornerstone was only obligated to *pay* authorized service centers to make covered repairs to the RV-not to make those repairs itself. *See* ECF No. 30-3, PageID.830 (Cornerstone Contract). Even if the Court construes Plaintiffs' "failure to repair" claim as one for failure or refusal by Cornerstone to pay for needed repairs (rather than to make repairs itself), as Plaintiffs request, the record shows Cornerstone in fact paid each claim it received related to Plaintiffs' RV. Because the undisputed material facts demonstrate that Cornerstone performed its obligations under the service contract, the Court must grant summary judgment in favor of Cornerstone on Plaintiffs' claim for breach of contract.

The elements of a claim for breach of contract under Michigan law are: "(1) that there was a contract, (2) that the other party breached the contract and, (3) that the party asserting breach of contract suffered damages as a result of the breach." *Lossia v. Flagstar Bancorp, Inc.*, No. 15-12540, 2016 WL 520867, *2 (E.D. Mich. Feb. 10, 2016) (quoting *AFT Mich. v. Michigan*, 846 N.W.2d 583, 590 (Mich. Ct. App. 2014)). Plaintiffs purchased their Cornerstone service contract from General RV the same day they purchased their vehicle. ECF No. 23-1, PageID.630. Although the contract was purchased through General RV, it makes clear that it is an agreement between Plaintiffs and Cornerstone only. *See* ECF No. 23-1, PageID.630 ("This Contract is between You and the Obligor (hereinafter referred to as We, Us, and Our)-Cornerstone United Administrative Services, Inc."). General RV is not a party to the contract and the contract did not establish any warranty by or service contract with General RV. *See* ECF No. 30-3; *Chaudoin v. Thor Motor Coach, Inc.*, No. 15-13871, 2017 WL 3485803, at *14 (E.D. Mich. Aug. 15, 2017) (examining an apparently identical Cornerstone service contract in a similar case and determining that it established no obligation on the part of General RV). Under the service contract Plaintiffs signed, Cornerstone was required only to reimburse Plaintiffs for covered repairs to the RV completed by authorized service centers. *See* ECF No. 30-3, PageID.830-35. Plaintiffs were not required to have their RV serviced at General RV and in fact could have gone to any authorized service dealer for repairs. *See* ECF No. 35, PageID.1002. The record is unclear as to why Plaintiffs did not seek to have repairs performed by other service centers under the Cornerstone warranty, if General RV refused to help them.

Four different claims were submitted to Cornerstone for repairs to Plaintiffs' vehicle, all of which were completed at General RV. ECF No. 23-1, PageID.632-39. Claim detail summaries produced by Cornerstone establish that it in fact paid each of these four claims. *See* ECF No. 23-1, PageID.632-39; ECF No. 35, PageID.1001 (Frank Caballero Aff.) ("CornerStone had performed under the service contract on each occasion where a claim for benefits was made to CornerStone on behalf of Mr. and Mrs. Carrigg."). Cornerstone paid each of Plaintiffs' claims in full, minus a $150 deductible. ECF No. 23-1, PageID.632-39. Though Plaintiffs contend that "Cornerstone failed or refused to pay for the needed repairs to the RV," they have produced no evidence to support this assertion. ECF No. 30, PageID.800. The evidentiary record therefore does not suggest that Cornerstone in any way breached its obligations to Plaintiffs under the service contract.

Another argument Plaintiffs raise in opposition to Cornerstone's summary judgment motion is that the service contract "appears to be void *ab initio*" because it states that coverage will not be available "[i]f the original warranty has ever been voided by the manufacturer." ECF No. 30, PageID.799-800 (Plaintiffs' Resp. Br.); ECF No. 30-3, PageID.831 (Cornerstone Contract). Plaintiffs assert that the original manufacturer's warranty on Plaintiffs' RV had in fact been voided. ECF No. 30,

PageID.799-800 (Plaintiffs' Resp. Br.). But Plaintiffs have not produced evidence in support of their argument that the manufacturer's warranty or Cornerstone service contract was ever voided. According to the text of the service contract, the agreement with Cornerstone remains in force and will not expire until November 20, 2019. ECF No. 30-3, PageID.830 (Cornerstone Contract); ECF No. 35, PageID.1002 (Frank Caballero Aff.). Further, General RV has provided an affidavit by a consumer affairs manager at Thor Motor Coach, Inc., manufacturer of the RV at issue, averring that the manufacturer's warranty was provided only to the RV's initial purchaser and was valid just "for 12 months or 15,000 miles on the covered portions of the house portion of the motorhome, and for 24 months or 24,000 miles on the steel or aluminum frame structure, only." ECF No. 35, PageID.1004-05 (Celina Tyler Aff.). The manufacturer's warranty thus had expired before Plaintiffs purchased the RV. *Id.* It was not voided. *Id.* Besides, if the Cornerstone service contract *was* void *ab initio*, as Plaintiffs argue, their claim for breach of contract against Cornerstone would necessarily fail. The existence of a contract is a required element for breach of contract. *AFT Mich.*, 846 N.W.2d at 590.

Because the undisputed material facts demonstrate that Cornerstone paid in full each of the claims it received for covered repairs to Plaintiffs' RV and thereby fulfilled its obligations under the service contract, Plaintiffs have failed to establish a genuine issue of material fact as to whether Cornerstone breached the terms of the contract. ECF No. 23-1, PageID.632-39. On this basis, summary judgment will be granted in favor of Cornerstone on Plaintiffs' breach of contract claim.

II. General RV's Motion for Summary Judgment

Plaintiffs assert several claims against Defendant General RV for breach of implied and express warranties, related violations of the Magnuson-Moss Warranty Act, 15 U.S.C. §2301 *et seq.*, and for fraudulent misrepresentation. General RV asserts that it is entitled to summary judgment on these claims because Plaintiffs purchased the RV "as is," with all warranties disclaimed by the purchase agreement. The Court agrees and will accordingly grant General RV's motion for summary judgment.

A. Violation of implied warranties

Every contract for the sale of goods includes implied warranties of merchantability and fitness for a particular purpose, unless the warranty is excluded or modified. *Lumber Mut. Ins. Co. v. Clarklift of Detroit, Inc.*, 569 N.W.2d 681, 682 (Mich. Ct. App. 1997) (per curiam) (citing Mich. Comp. Laws §§ 440.2314, 440.2315); *Davis v. LaFontaine Motors, Inc.*, 719 N.W.2d 890, 895 (Mich. Ct. App. 2006). Implied warranties may "be negated by contrary contractual terms meeting the requirements of [Mich. Comp.

Laws § 440.2316(2), (3)]." *Rokicsak v. Colony Marine Sales and Serv., Inc.*, 219 F. Supp. 2d 810, 815 (E.D. Mich. 2002) (quoting *McGhee v. GMC Truck & Coach Div.*, 296 N.W.2d 286, 289 (Mich. Ct. App. 1980)). Under Mich. Comp. Laws § 440.2316, "unless the circumstances indicate otherwise, all implied warranties are excluded by expressions like 'as is', 'with all fault' or other language which in common understanding calls the buyer's attention to the exclusion of warranties and makes plain that there is no implied warranty." Additionally, "[t]o exclude or modify the implied warranty of merchantability . . . the [[disclaimer] language must mention merchantability and in case of a writing must be conspicuous." Mich. Comp. Laws §440.2316(2). Likewise, "to exclude or modify any implied warranty of fitness the exclusion must be by a writing and conspicuous." *Id.* "[A] printed heading in capitals is conspicuous and language in the body of a form is conspicuous if it is larger or in contrasting type or color." *HRL Land or Sea Yachts v. Travel Supreme, Inc.*, No. 1:07-cv-945, 2009 WL 427375, *3 (W.D. Mich. Feb. 20, 2009) (citing Mich. Comp. Laws § 440.1201(j)). The statute goes on to expressly state that language is sufficient to exclude all implied warranties of fitness "if it states, for example, that 'There are no warranties which extend beyond the description on the face hereof.'" *Id.*

Here, the purchase agreement at issue plainly includes language-in bolded, capital letters-expressly warning that "this RV is sold 'as is' by dealer, and dealer disclaims all warranties express or implied, including, but not limited to any implied warranty of merchantability or fitness for a particular purpose." ECF No. 22-1, PageID.563 (Purchase Agreement). This disclaimer specifies the "as is" nature of the sale and, consistent with Michigan law's requirements for disclaimer of the implied warranty of merchantability, specifically mentions merchantability. *See* Mich. Comp. Laws § 440.2316(2). Further, as required by state law to negate the implied warranties of merchantability and fitness, the disclaimer is conspicuous and in writing. *Id.* The language appears on the reverse side of the relatively concise two-page purchase agreement, in bolded, capitalized, albeit small font. ECF No. 22-1, PageID.563. Further, the same "as is" sale language and exclusion of warranties appears not only in the purchase agreement, but also in the following documents signed by Plaintiffs: (1) "General RV 'As Is' and Warranty Disclaimer Form," ECF No. 22-1, PageID.565; (2) "Delivery Receipt, Storage, Agreement and Risk of Loss Notice and Acknowledgment," ECF No. 22-1, PageID.567; and (3) "Service Call Agreement," ECF No. 22-1, PageID.569. Courts interpreting almost identical warranty disclaimers in cases applying Michigan law have found them sufficient. *See, e.g., Dolores v. General R.V. Center, Inc.*, No. 19-10413, 2019 WL 2601311, at *3 (E.D. Mich. June 25, 2019); *Rokicsak*, 219 F. Supp. 2d at 815; *Pidcock v. Ewing*, 371 F. Supp. 2d 870, 880 (E.D. Mich. 2005); *HRL Land or Sea Yachts*, 2009 WL 427375 at **1-3. Michigan law allows for the disclaimer of implied warranties and the Courts finds that the multiple disclaimers included in the purchase documents at issue (and most critically, in the purchase agreement) are effective.[10]

Plaintiffs' contention that they were unable to read the text of the purchase agreement and related documents, and were therefore unaware of the warranty disclaimers, will not prevent summary judgment in favor of General RV. "It is well established that failure to read an agreement is not a valid defense to enforcement of a contract. A contracting party has a duty to examine a contract and know what the party has signed, and the other contracting party cannot be made to suffer for neglect of that duty." *Montgomery v. Fid. & Guar. Life Ins. Co.*, 713 N.W.2d 801, 804 (Mich. Ct. App. 2005) (citations omitted). "[I]n Michigan, a party who signs a document is deemed to know the contents of those documents and may not claim ignorance to avoid enforcement of the instrument." *HRL Land or Sea Yachts*, 2009 WL 427375 at *4 (citing *Scholz v. Montgomery Ward & Co., Inc.*, 468 N.W.2d 845, 848 (Mich. 1991)). Plaintiffs' alleged inability to read the purchase agreement is not a defense to enforcement of the contract against them.

The contents of the purchase agreement and related sale documents are not in dispute. The Court finds that the implied warranty disclaimers contained therein meet the requirements for disclaimers established by Michigan law. General RV's disclaimer of any implied warranties was effective and, as a result, Plaintiffs' claim for violation of implied warranties fails as a matter of law. Summary judgment in favor of General RV is warranted on this claim."

B. VIOLATION OF EXPRESS WARRANTIES

Under Michigan law, a seller who makes "[a]n affirmation of fact or promise . . . to the buyer which relates to the goods and becomes part of the basis of the bargain" creates an express warranty that "the goods shall conform to the affirmation or promise." Mich. Comp. Laws §440.2313(1)(a). Likewise, a seller who gives the buyer "[a] description of the goods which is made part of the basis of the bargain creates an express warranty that the goods shall conform to the description." Mich. Comp. Laws §440.2313(1)(b). As explained by the Michigan Court of Appeals, however, "any alleged oral statements made by [a seller's] representatives about the reliability of the

10. To the extent Plaintiffs are arguing that the Magnuson-Moss Warranty Act, 15 U.S.C. §2308(a), does not permit disclaimer of implied warranties where a written warranty is provided, it is clear from the record that no written warranty was provided by General RV. The purchase agreement plainly states that General RV disclaimed all express and implied warranties, and that any written warranties "are offered by the manufacturer of the RV." ECF No. 22-1, PageID.563. Moreover, "an MMWA claim for breach of warranty depends on the plaintiff having a valid state law implied warranty claim," which Plaintiffs have not presented. *HRL Land or Sea Yachts*, 2009 WL 427375 at *5 (citing *Harnden v. Ford Motor Co.*, 408 F. Supp. 2d 300, 308 (E.D. Mich. 2004).

[[product] . . . are subject to the UCC statute of frauds and are therefore excluded to the extent they are inconsistent with the parties' written expressions." *Rodger v. Ford Motor Co.*, No. 275578, 2008 WL 4646140, *5 (Mich. Ct. App. Oct. 21, 2008) (citing Mich. Comp. Laws §440.2202) ("Terms . . . to which . . . the parties agree or which are otherwise set forth in a writing intended by the parties as a final expression of their agreement with respect to those terms . . . may not be contradicted by evidence of any prior agreement or of a contemporaneous oral agreement."). Accordingly, where a written agreement exists between the parties and that agreement is clear and unambiguous, "parol evidence of prior negotiations and representations cannot be adduced to create an express warranty and thereby vary the terms of the contract." *Heritage Res., Inc. v. Caterpillar Fin. Serv. Corp.*, 774 N.W.2d 332, 342 (Mich. Ct. App. 2009) (quoting *Salzman v. Maldaver*, 24 N.W.2d 161, 165 (Mich. 1946))."

It is undisputed that the parties' agreement was put into writing in the form of the fully executed purchase agreement. *See* ECF No. 22-1, PageID.562-63. That agreement also contains an integration clause explicitly acknowledging that the purchase agreement "contains the entire understanding between General RV and Purchaser" and that no other representations, verbal or written, had been made by General RV or relied on by Plaintiffs in entering into the agreement. *Id.* at PageID.562; *Wonderland Shopping Ctr. Venture Ltd. P'ship v. CDC Mortg. Capital, Inc.*, 274 F.3d 1085, 1095 (6th Cir. 2001) ("[A]n integration clause in a written contract conclusively establishes that the parties intended the written contract to be the complete expression of the agreement.") (applying Michigan law). Plaintiffs are therefore precluded from suing General RV under a theory of violation of express warranties not contained in the purchase agreement. *See Irwin Seating Co. v. Int'l Bus. Mach. Corp.*, No. 1:04CV568, 2005 WL 1475390, at *9 (W.D. Mich. June 22, 2005) (explaining that plaintiff was precluded from suing on a theory of violation of express warranties because the agreement contained a conspicuous disclaimer of any prior statements to the contrary and an integration clause). Summary judgment on Plaintiffs' claim for breach of express warranties must be entered in General RV's favor."

QUESTION

Is this case right? Think about it carefully. In any dispute (legal or otherwise) a good starting point is to ask yourself "what is really going on here?" This was the sale of a RV that was never functional as promised but the consumers gave away all their legal rights in the contract and were punished by having to live with the bad deal they made and the expenses of a losing lawsuit.

On the one hand a federal court applying state law must abide by that law; on the other hand when this case was over the consumers, old and having major problems reading a contract full of legalese, believed the outrageous lies told to them by the sales personnel (such as there was an existing manufacturer's warranty on the RV), only to be slapped down by a mysterious thing called the parol evidence rule which kept evidence of those conversations from being considered at all. Thus the Carriggs traded in their old vehicle for a RV that was worthless on the day they purchased it and, due to a lot of Uniform Commercial Code provisions lined up like an army, they had no legal recourse at all. They should have read the fine print on the contract and not believed a word told to them by the salespeople as they put those contracts in front of the trusting buyers. Those employees were free to say anything they liked since, apparently, none of it had any legal meaning. Is that our law?

Were there arguments that the plaintiffs could have made under the Uniform Commercial Code or other laws that they did not make? See §1-304 (mentioned in the first chapter of this book as a powerful tool for lawyers to wield) and §2-302 (unconscionability). Tort law will tell you that the making of a promise without any intent to fulfill it is "promissory fraud," and that the common law maxim is that "fraud vitiates all transactions"—nothing can hide fraud. In fraud suits the injured party can frequently recover punitive damages and attorney fees. Plus all states have consumer laws for the sale of goods that typically would make a major difference in the result here (including the recovery of attorney fees). Why were these possibilities never mentioned? Think about that carefully too.

3. Timing of the Disclaimer

PROBLEM 38

Joe College bought a new car from Flash Motors, relying on the seller's extravagant claims about the car's superior qualities. He signed a purchase order on August 1, and the car was delivered two weeks later. In the glove compartment he found the warranty booklet and on reading it was dismayed to learn that the actual written warranty was very limited in coverage. Is he bound by the written warranty's terms? What argument can he make? See Comment 7 to §2-313; §2-209; White & Summers §13-5, at 582-583.

Bowdoin v. Showell Growers, Inc.

United States Court of Appeals, Eleventh Circuit, 1987
817 F.2d 1543

WISDOM, J.

This appeal raises a single question: whether the defendants effectively disclaimed the implied warranties of fitness and merchantability with respect to a high pressure spray rig that caused injuries to the plaintiffs. The district court concluded that a disclaimer found in the instruction manual that accompanied the spray rig when it was delivered to the purchaser was conspicuous and therefore effective. We disagree. Even assuming that the disclaimer was otherwise conspicuous, it was delivered to the purchaser *after* the sale. Such a post-sale disclaimer is not effective because it did not form a part of the basis of the bargain between the parties to the sale. The decision of the district court is therefore reversed.

Facts

At the time this controversy arose, the plaintiffs in this action, Rachel and Billy Bowdoin, raised chickens in Sampson, Alabama, for Showell Growers, Inc., a Maryland corporation. Under their contract with Showell Growers, the Bowdoins were required once a year to give a thorough cleaning to their chicken house and the chicken coop pallets. To aid them in this annual task, Showell Growers lent the Bowdoins a high pressure spray rig. In December 1980, Mrs. Bowdoin was using the spray rig to clean the pallets when an article of her clothing caught in the safety shield covering the spray rig's power take-off shaft. Mrs. Bowdoin was pulled into the shaft and suffered severe injuries.

The spray rig in question was manufactured by FMC Corporation, an Illinois corporation. The safety shield and drive shaft component was manufactured for FMC by NEAPCO, Inc., a Pennsylvania corporation. Showell purchased the spray rig from FMC through an FMC dealer, Brushy Mountain Co-op of Moravian Falls, North Carolina. Two weeks after the sale, the spray rig was shipped to Brushy Mountain and then delivered to Showell Growers. An instruction manual was included with the spray rig when it was delivered to Showell Growers. The last page of the instruction manual included a purported warranty disclaimer, which stated: *"The foregoing warranty is expressly in lieu of any and all other warranties, express, implied, statutory or otherwise (including, but without limitation, the implied warranties of merchantability and fitness for a particular purpose). . . ."*

Usually, FMC required its dealer and the purchaser to complete an "agriculture delivery report" before a sale. The report contains a disclaimer of the implied warranties of fitness and merchantability. The purchaser is required to read the report and sign it acknowledging that he has read the warranty information. The report is then returned to FMC. The record shows that no agriculture delivery report was completed in connection with the purchase by Showell Growers.

In 1982, the Bowdoins filed a diversity action against Showell Growers and FMC in the United States District Court for the Northern District of Florida. The Bowdoins later added NEAPCO as a defendant. The Bowdoins sought to recover on a number of counts including one count alleging breach by

FMC and NEAPCO of the implied warranties of fitness and merchantability. FMC and NEAPCO moved for summary judgment on this count. The district court concluded that the law of Alabama applied to the warranty claims and that under Alabama law, FMC and NEAPCO had effectively disclaimed the implied warranties with the disclaimer in the instruction manual. The district court therefore granted summary judgment in favor of FMC and NEAPCO, and dismissed with prejudice the Bowdoins' implied warranties claims.

The Bowdoins now appeal that ruling. The sole issue on appeal is whether the district court correctly determined that FMC and NEAPCO had effectively disclaimed the implied warranties. The Bowdoins contend that the district court's ruling in favor of FMC and NEAPCO is erroneous for several reasons: the disclaimer was not part of the bargain and is therefore ineffective; the disclaimer is not conspicuous as required under Alabama law; the spray rig comes within the classification of "consumer goods" and therefore a manufacturer cannot disclaim implied warranties; the disclaimer is unconscionable; and finally, even if the disclaimer is effective as to FMC, it is ineffective as to NEAPCO, which manufactured the drive shaft and safety shield component. We conclude that the disclaimer is ineffective as to both FMC and NEAPCO because it did not form a part of the basis of the bargain. We therefore do not reach the Bowdoins' other arguments.

DISCUSSION

Under the Uniform Commercial Code as adopted by Alabama and virtually every other state, a manufacturer may disclaim the implied warranties of merchantability and fitness provided that the disclaimer is in writing and conspicuous, and provided that the disclaimer is part of the parties' bargain. If a disclaimer was conspicuous to the purchaser *before the sale,* a court will generally hold the disclaimer effective based on the assumption that the disclaimer formed a part of the basis of the bargain. If, however, the disclaimer was not presented to the purchaser before the sale, the court will hold such a disclaimer ineffective because it did not form a part of the basis of the bargain. This "basis of the bargain" rule protects purchasers from unexpected and coercive disclaimers.

We turn now to determine whether the FMC disclaimer was a part of the basis of the bargain. The parties agree that for purposes of this analysis, the Bowdoins stand in the shoes of Showell Growers. The question therefore is whether the disclaimer is effective as to Showell Growers. We conclude that it is not.

Showell Growers purchased the spray rig at least two weeks before it was delivered. When the rig was delivered, an instruction manual was enclosed, and in that instruction manual is the disclaimer upon which FMC and NEAPCO rely. The disclaimer was never brought to Showell's attention.

Such a post-sale disclaimer is ineffective. "By definition, a disclaimer that appears for the first time after the sale in something supplied by the seller is not a part of the basis of the bargain and therefore is not binding on the buyer. Thus, the buyer is not bound by the disclaimer to which he had never agreed at the time of the sale and which first appears in the manufacturer's manual delivered to the buyer with the goods [or] the manufacturer's printed material brochure, or warranty booklet that accompanies the goods. . . ."[11]

The leading Alabama decision on disclaimers of implied warranties is in harmony with this position. In Tiger Motor Co. v. McMurtry, the Alabama Supreme Court addressed the validity of a disclaimer of implied warranties with respect to an automobile. The evidence showed that the day after the sale took place, the automobile was delivered to the purchaser along with the disclaimer. The evidence also showed that the disclaimer was never called to the purchaser's attention before the sale. The court concluded that the disclaimer was ineffective. Decisions of other courts construing the same provisions of the Uniform Commercial Code have also concluded that a post-sale disclaimer is not effective. [Citations omitted.]

FMC attempts to distinguish these cases on three grounds. First, FMC argues that unlike the purchasers involved in most of the cases, who were, for the most part, individual consumers, Showell Growers is a sophisticated commercial enterprise. But FMC has not offered and we have not found a post-sale disclaimer case in which such a distinction was material. Indeed, several of the cases in other states did involve commercial transactions between sophisticated commercial enterprises or businessmen, and the results reached were not affected: Courts consistently held that post-sale disclaimers were ineffective.

FMC next argues that here the post-sale disclaimer was effective because it was conspicuous. Specifically, FMC asserts that the cases which have held post-sale disclaimers ineffective involved "egregious facts involving the combination of the failure of a disclaimer to be conspicuous and its appearance subsequent to the parties' transaction."

FMC's argument is, however, wrong on both the facts and the law. Several of the cases holding post-sale disclaimers ineffective did not even mention whether the disclaimer was otherwise conspicuous. And the cases to which FMC is apparently referring typically involved not one disclaimer but two: one in the sales contract and the other in a document delivered after the sale, such as an instruction manual or a warranty. In those cases, the courts held both disclaimers ineffective: the disclaimer in the sales contract because it was in small print and therefore not conspicuous, and the

11. R. Anderson, 3 Uniform Commercial Code §2-316:32, p. 345 (footnotes omitted).

post-sale disclaimer because it was not a part of the basis of the bargain. In these cases, as in the cases involving only a post-sale disclaimer, the courts generally did not discuss whether the disclaimer was otherwise conspicuous. The absence of such a discussion is not surprising, because as a general rule the conspicuousness of a post-sale disclaimer is immaterial. By definition, a post-sale disclaimer is not conspicuous in the full sense of that term because the reasonable person against whom it is intended to operate could not have noticed it before the consummation of the transaction. A post-sale disclaimer is therefore not effective merely because it was otherwise conspicuous.

Finally, FMC argues that its post-sale disclaimer is effective because of prior dealings with Showell Growers that put Showell on notice that FMC's practice was to disclaim implied warranties with respect to high pressure spray rigs. Showell Growers had previously purchased an FMC spray rig similar to the one that caused Mrs. Bowdoin's injuries. The instruction manual accompanying the first spray rig contained a disclaimer of implied warranties, and according to one Showell employee, that instruction manual appeared to be identical to the one accompanying the spray rig in question. From this, FMC argues that Showell was on notice that FMC was disclaiming the implied warranties with respect to the second spray rig.

This argument misses the point. Even assuming that the mere similar appearance of two instruction manuals could put a purchaser on notice that a disclaimer in the first would also be found in the second, FMC's argument fails for the same reason its argument that a post-sale disclaimer can be effective if it was otherwise conspicuous failed. A disclaimer must be conspicuous before the sale, for only then will the law presume that the disclaimer was part of the bargain. In this case, Showell Growers did not receive the second instruction manual until after the second sale was consummated. The disclaimer in that instruction manual was therefore without significance. This is not less true merely because earlier Showell had received a similar instruction manual. Until it received the second instruction manual, it could not know what it would look like or what it would contain.

Conclusion

We conclude that the post-sale disclaimer of implied warranties found in the instruction manual that accompanied the FMC spray rig is ineffective because it did not form a part of the basis of the bargain. The decision of the district court is therefore reversed, and the district court is instructed to reinstate the Bowdoins' breach of implied warranties of fitness and merchantability claims against FMC and NEAPCO.

Rinaldi v. Iomega Corp.

Delaware Superior Court, 1999
WL 1442014

COOCH, J.

I. INTRODUCTION: FACTUAL AND PROCEDURAL HISTORY

This proposed class action was commenced in September 1998 on behalf of all persons who have purchased purportedly defective "Zip drives" from January 1, 1995, to the present. The Zip drives are manufactured by defendant Iomega Corporation, a computer storage device maker incorporated in Delaware and based in Utah. A Zip drive is a large capacity personal computer data storage drive. The complaint alleges inter alia that the alleged defect, said by Plaintiffs to be commonly known as the "Click of Death," causes irreparable damage to the removable magnetic media storage disks on which the drives store data. Plaintiffs also allege that the defect renders the data on the disks unreadable and that when another drive attempts to read the data from a disk that has been infected, the defect transfers to the second drive, causing further damage.

Plaintiffs' complaint has four counts. Count I alleges that Defendant breached the implied warranty of merchantability by manufacturing a product that was not fit for the ordinary purpose for which such products are used and that Defendant's disclaimer of the implied warranty of merchantability contained in the packaging of the product was ineffective because it was not sufficiently "conspicuous" as required by 6 Del. C. §2-316(2). Count II alleges that Defendant was negligent in manufacturing and designing the Zip drive without using the reasonable care, skill, and diligence required when placing such a product into the stream of commerce. Count III alleges that Defendant committed consumer fraud in violation of the Delaware Consumer Fraud Act by falsely misrepresenting through advertising to the consuming public that the Zip drives were suitable for their intended purpose. Count IV alleges that Defendant was negligent in failing to warn the consuming public about the risks of its product when it knew or should have known that the product could cause damage when used for its intended purpose. . . .

Defendant's Motion to Dismiss Count I on the grounds that Plaintiffs have failed to state a claim for breach of the implied warranty of merchantability is GRANTED since the Court finds that the disclaimer is "conspicuous." . . .

Defendant contends that Plaintiffs' claim for breach of the implied warranty of merchantability has failed to state a claim because Defendant's disclaimer of the implied warranty of merchantability, contained within the packaging of the Zip drive, effectively disclaimed all liability. The sole issue to be resolved here is whether Count I of the complaint should be dismissed because Defendant's disclaimer of the implied warranty of merchantability was not "conspicuous," as required by 6 Del. C. §2-316, because the disclaimer was contained within the packaging of the Zip drive product itself and therefore not "discovered" by the purchaser prior to the purchaser's purchase of the product.

Defendant's disclaimer inside the Zip drive package provides:

> EXCEPT AS STATED ABOVE IN THIS PARAGRAPH, THE FOREGOING WARRANTIES ARE IN LIEU OF ALL OTHER CONDITIONS OR WARRANTIES, EXPRESS, IMPLIED, OR STATUTORY, INCLUDING, WITHOUT LIMITATION, ANY IMPLIED CONDITION OR WARRANTY OF MERCHANTABILITY OR FITNESS FOR A PARTICULAR PURPOSE AND OF ANY OTHER WARRANTY OBLIGATION ON THE PART OF IOMEGA (capitals in original).

The above disclaimer appears near the bottom of a document labeled "IOMEGA LIMITED WARRANTY' located inside the packaging.

6 Del. C. §2-316(2) provides, in pertinent part, ". . . to exclude or modify the implied warranty of merchantability or any part of it the language must mention merchantability and in the case of a writing must be conspicuous. . . ." 6 Del. C. §2-316(2) is identical to §2-316(2) of the Uniform Commercial Code.

The usual arguments concerning the conspicuousness requirement of U.C.C. §2-316(2) have been based on issues such as the size of the type set and the location of the disclaimer in the warranty itself. Defendant contends that the conspicuousness requirement has been met regardless of the location of the disclaimer inside the Zip drive package so long as the disclaimer is "noticeable and easily readable." Defendant asserts that "modern commercial realities of how contracts are formed with consumers of prepackaged products necessitates that the terms of [its] warranty disclaimer be given effect."

Plaintiffs do not claim that the disclaimer was improperly worded, that the text of the disclaimer was improperly placed in the rest of the warranty or that the typeface of the disclaimer was too small, but instead argue that the disclaimer, located in the packaging of the product, could not realistically be called to the attention of the consumer until after the sale had been consummated, thus rendering the disclaimer not "conspicuous" as a matter or law and therefore ineffective. Although similar issues of additional terms to a contract such as a shrinkwrap license,[12] an arbitration clause[13] and a license agreement,[14] each physically located within the

12. ProCd, Inc. v. Zeidenberg, 7th Cir., 86 F.3d 1447 (1996).

13. Hill v. Gateway 2000, Inc., 7th Cir., 105 F.3d 1147 (1997), *cert. denied,* 118 S. Ct. 47 (1997).

14. M.A. Mortenson Co. v. Timberline Software Corp., Wash. App., 970 P.2d 803 (1999).

packaging of the product, has been litigated in other jurisdictions, the parties have cited no case directly addressing the effectiveness, under U.C.C. §2-316(2), of a disclaimer of the implied warranty of merchantability by virtue of its location within the packaging of a product itself, nor has the Court found any such case.

The issue of conspicuousness, generally, under §2-316 has been the topic of various law review articles, periodicals and texts,[15] and has been the subject of much litigation. As stated, however, no authorities have been located that squarely addressed the issue in this case. The traditional focus has been on the "mention"[16] of merchantability and the visible characteristics of the disclaimer, such as type set and location within the warranty document itself. In determining if a disclaimer of the implied warranty of merchantability is effective as being "conspicuous," the secondary authorities and courts have often looked to the purpose of §2-316.[17] The purpose of that section is to "protect a buyer from unexpected and unbargained for language of disclaimer."[18] That purpose is the real backbone in determining if a disclaimer is conspicuous when looking at factors beyond the mentioning of merchantability and type set.

Analogous support for this Court's conclusion that the physical location of the disclaimer of the implied warranty of merchantability inside the Zip drive packaging does not make the disclaimer inconspicuous can be found in some cases from other jurisdictions. In ProCD, Inc. v. Zeidenberg,[19] the Seventh Circuit held that a shrinkwrap license located inside the packaging of the computer program was enforceable as an additional term of the contract, and stated that the commercial practicalities of modern retail purchasing dictate where terms such as a shrinkwrap license should be located. The *ProCD* court held that it would be otherwise impractical for these additional terms to be located on the outside of the box in "microscopic" type. The *ProCD* court stated, "[t]ransactions in which the exchange of money precedes the communication of detailed terms are common." The *ProCD* court then looked to other sections of the U.C.C. that dealt with the issue in terms of acceptance and rejection of goods: "A buyer accepts goods under

15. See, e.g., Bernard F. Kistler, Jr., U.C.C. Article Two Warranty Disclaimers and the "Conspicuousness" Requirement of Section 2-316, 43 Mercer L. Rev. 943, 945-953 (1992); Jeffrey C. Selman and Christopher S. Chen, Steering the Titanic Clear of the Iceberg: Saving the Sale of Software from the Perils of Warranties, 31 U.S.F. L. Rev. 531, 533-536 (1997); William H. Danne, Jr., Construction and Effect of UCC §2-316(2) Providing That Implied Warranty Disclaimer Must Be "Conspicuous," 73 A.L.R.3d 248, Vol. 73 (1976).

16. 6 Del. C. §2-316(2).

17. Ronald A. Anderson, Anderson on the Uniform Commercial Code, §2-316:144-153 (3d ed. 1983); Debra L. Goetz, Special Project: Article Two Warranties in Commercial Transactions, An Update, 72 Cornell L. Rev. 1159, 1264-1275 (1978).

18. U.C.C. §2-316 cmt. 1 (1962).

19. 7th Cir., 86 F.3d at 1447.

§2-606(1)(b) when, after an opportunity to inspect, [the buyer] fails to make an effective rejection under §2-602(1). [The seller] extended an opportunity to reject if a buyer should find the license unsatisfactory." The *ProCD* court continued its analysis and observed that

> [c]onsumer goods work the same way. Someone who wants to buy a radio set visits a store, pays and walks out with a box. Inside the box is a leaflet containing some terms, the most important of which usually is the warranty, read for the first time in the comfort of home. By [the buyer's] lights, the warranty in the box is irrelevant; every consumer gets the standard warranty implied by the UCC in the event the contract is silent; yet so far as we are aware no state disregards warranties furnished with consumer products.[20]

Plaintiffs argue that *ProCD* is inapposite because it specifically concerned the validity of a shrinkwrap license which is not governed by U.C.C. §2-316(2). Although that is correct, *ProCD* stressed that "the U.C.C. . . . permits parties to structure their relations so that the buyer has a chance to make a final decision after a detailed review" of the contract terms.[21] All of the additional terms, which included the shrinkwrap license, became part of the contract in *ProCD*.

In Hill v. Gateway 2000, Inc.,[22] the Seventh Circuit relied on *ProCD* in holding that an arbitration clause located inside the packaging of a computer was enforceable as an additional term to the contract, and stated, "[p]ractical considerations support allowing vendors to enclose the full legal terms with their products. . . . [C]ustomers as a group are better off when vendors skip costly and ineffectual steps such as telephonic recitation, and use instead a simple approve-or-return device."[23] In holding that the arbitration clause was effective, the Hill court concluded that an additional term physically located outside of the contract was nevertheless an enforceable term of the contract.

In M.A. Mortenson Co. v. Timberline Software Corp.,[24] the Washington Court of Appeals relied on *ProCD* and *Hill* and held that a licensing agreement located inside the packaging of a software program was enforceable as an additional term to the contract. In *Mortenson* the court stated, ". . . the terms of the present license agreement are part of the contract as formed between parties. We find that [the purchaser's] installation and use of the software manifested its assent to the terms of the license. . . ."[25] As in *ProCD*

20. Id. at 152.
21. Id. at 1453.
22. 7th Cir., 105 F.3d at 1147.
23. Id. at 1149.
24. 970 P.2d at 803.
25. Id. at 831.

and *Hill,* the *Mortenson* court held that a licensing agreement located within the packaging of the product, not in the contract itself, was an enforceable additional term of the contract.

Other courts have also addressed the issue of the physical location of the disclaimer of the implied warranty of merchantability from different perspectives. Thus in Step-Saver Data Systems, Inc. v. Wyse Technology,[26] the United States District Court for the Eastern District of Pennsylvania discussed the location of a disclaimer of the implied warranty of merchantability inside computer software packaging and held the location of an additional term (in *Step-Saver,* a disclaimer) is to be considered independently of conspicuousness. The *Step-Saver* court held that "[t]here is no question that pursuant to the U.C.C., limitation of warranty and remedies are valid when packaged with the product so long as the limitation is clear, conspicuous and one that a reasonable person would have noticed and understood."[27] The holding in *Step-Saver* that conspicuousness and location are to be considered independently is not directly on point with the issue at bar. However, the *Step-Saver* court relied on the purpose behind §2-316 in finding that so long as a disclaimer of the implied warranty of merchantability is one that could be noticed and understood, the disclaimer is conspicuous.

This Court has addressed the issue of conspicuousness under §2-316(2) in Lecates v. Hertrick Pontiac Buick Co.[28] In *Lecates,* a case on which Plaintiffs rely, the issue was whether the implied warranties were effectively disclaimed by an automobile dealer when the car that was sold malfunctioned, causing physical injuries. The court held that the seller's disclaimer of the implied warranty of merchantability located in a sales invoice satisfied the conspicuous requirement of §2-316(2). In *Lecates,* the specific question was whether or not the disclaimer had been delivered by the seller to the buyer only after the sale had already been consummated. The *Lecates* court addressed this narrow issue in light of the specific facts in that case and observed that disclaimer clauses have been held ineffective "if it appeared that the documents in which such clauses appeared were given to the buyer after the sale had been consummated."[29] *Lecates* addressed the issue of what terms and conditions were a part of the contract at the point of contract consummation, but here, Defendant's disclaimer of the implied warranty of merchantability was an additional term of each contract between each plaintiff and Defendant to purchase the Zip drives. Defendant's sales of the Zip drives to the six plaintiffs were each not "consummated" until after each plaintiff had had an opportunity to inspect and then to reject or to accept the product

26. E.D. Pa., C.A. No. 89-7203, 1990 WL 87334, Broderick, J. (June 21, 1990).
27. Id. at *7.
28. Del. Super., 515 A.2d 163 (1986).
29. Id. at 170.

with the additional terms that were enclosed within the packaging of the Zip drive.

The commercial practicalities of modern retail purchasing make it eminently reasonable for a seller of a product such as a Zip drive to place a disclaimer of the implied warranty of merchantability within the plastic packaging. The buyer can read the disclaimer after payment for the Zip drive and then later have the opportunity to reject the contract terms (i.e., the disclaimer) if the buyer so chooses. This Court concludes that Defendant's disclaimer of the implied warranty of merchantability was effective despite its physical placement inside the packaging of the Zip drive and has satisfied the conspicuousness requirement of 6 Del. C. §2-316(2).

Defendant's Motion to Dismiss Count I on the grounds that Plaintiffs have failed to state a claim for breach of the implied warranty of merchantability is granted. . . .

QUESTION

Do these last two cases conflict? If so, which is right and which wrong? The second case, of course, is part of the "rolling contracts" theory of offer and acceptance advanced in cases such as the Seventh Circuit's famous *ProCD* opinion, discussed both in this case and in another case earlier in this book at page 119.

We will return to the issue of whether the buyer can return a defective item directly to the manufacturer later in the book. Note that even if a seller disclaimed all express and implied warranties, there might still be liability in some states for breach of the obligation of good faith, such as where the goods sold were virtually unusable. See Accessdata Corporation v. Alste Technologies Gmbh, 2009 WL 2338172 (D. Utah 2009).

4. Limitations on the Warranty

Sometimes a seller is willing to give a warranty to the buyer, but wants in some way to limit the scope of the liability that a breach creates. The Code permits such a limitation, but puts various restrictions on its use. Read §§2-316(4) and 2-719.

Wilson Trading Corp. v. David Ferguson, Ltd.

Court of Appeals of New York, 1968
23 N.Y.2d 398, 244 N.E.2d 685, 297 N.Y.S.2d 108

JASEN, J.

The plaintiff, the Wilson Trading Corporation, entered into a contract of sale with the defendant, David Ferguson, Ltd., for the sale of a specified quantity of yarn. After the yarn was delivered, cut and knitted into sweaters, the finished product was washed. It was during this washing that it was discovered that the color of the yarn had "shaded"—that is, "there was a variation of color from piece to piece and within the pieces." This defect, the defendant claims, rendered the sweaters "unmarketable."

This action for the contract price of the yarn was commenced after the defendant refused payment. As a defense to the action and as a counterclaim for damages, the defendant alleges that "[p]laintiff has failed to perform all of the conditions of the contract on its part required to be performed, and has delivered . . . defective and unworkmanlike goods."

The sales contract provides in pertinent part:

> 2. No claims relating to excessive moisture content, short weight, count variations, twist, quality or shade shall be allowed *if made after weaving, knitting, or processing,* or more than 10 days after receipt of shipment. . . . The buyer shall within 10 days of the receipt of the merchandise by himself or agent examine the merchandise for any and all defects. [Emphasis supplied.]
>
> 4. This instrument constitutes the entire agreement between the parties, superseding all previous communications, oral or written, and no changes, amendments or additions hereto will be recognized unless in writing signed by both seller and buyer or buyer's agent. It is expressly agreed that no representations or warranties, express or implied, have been or are made by the seller except as stated herein, and the seller makes no warranty, express or implied, as to the fitness for buyer's purposes of yarn purchased hereunder, seller's obligations, except as expressly stated herein, being limited to the *delivery of good merchantable yarn of the description stated herein.* [Emphasis supplied.]

Special Term granted plaintiff summary judgment for the contract price of the yarn sold on the ground that "notice of the alleged breach of warranty for defect in shading was not given within the time expressly limited and is not now available by way of defense or counterclaim." The Appellate Division affirmed, without opinion.

The defendant on this appeal urges that the time limitation provision on claims in the contract was unreasonable since the defect in the color of the yarn was latent and could not be discovered until after the yarn was processed and the finished product washed.

Defendant's affidavits allege that its sweaters were rendered unsaleable because of latent defects in the yarn which caused "variation in color from piece to piece and within the pieces." This allegation is sufficient to create a question of fact concerning the merchantability of the yarn (Uniform Commercial Code, §2-314, subd. [2]). Indeed, the plaintiff does not seriously dispute the fact that its yarn was unmerchantable, but instead, like Special

Term, relies upon the failure of defendant to give notice of the breach of warranty within the time limits prescribed by paragraph two of the contract.

Subdivision (3) (par. [a]) of section 2-607 of the Uniform Commercial Code expressly provides that a buyer who accepts goods has a reasonable time after he discovers or should have discovered a breach to notify the seller of such breach. (Cf. 5 Williston, Contracts [3d ed.] §173.) Defendant's affidavits allege that a claim was made immediately upon discovery of the breach of warranty after the yarn was knitted and washed, and that this was the earliest possible moment that the defects could reasonably be discovered in the normal manufacturing process. Defendant's affidavits are, therefore, sufficient to create a question of fact concerning whether notice of the latent defects alleged was given within a reasonable time. (Cf. Ann., 17 A.L.R.3d 1010, 1112-1115 [1968]).

However, the Uniform Commercial Code allows the parties, within limits established by the code, to modify or exclude warranties and to limit remedies for breach of warranty. The courts below have found that the sales contract bars all claims not made before knitting and processing. Concededly, defendant discovered and gave notice of the alleged breach of warranty after knitting and washing.

We are, therefore, confronted with the effect to be given the time limitation provision in paragraph two of the contract. Analytically, paragraph two presents separate and distinct issues concerning its effect as a valid limitation on remedies for breach of warranty (Uniform Commercial Code, §§2-316, subd. [4]; 2-719) and its effect as a modification of the express warranty of merchantability (Uniform Commercial Code, §2-316, subd. [1]) established by paragraph four of the contract.

Parties to a contract are given broad latitude within which to fashion their own remedies for breach of contract (Uniform Commercial Code, §2-316, subd. [4]; §§2-718; 2-719). Nevertheless, it is clear from the official section 2-719 of the Uniform Commercial Code that it is the very essence of a sale contract that at least minimum adequate remedies be available for its breach. "If the parties intend to conclude a contract for sale within this Article they must accept the legal consequence that there be at least a fair quantum of remedy for breach of the obligations or duties outlined in the contract. Thus any clause purporting to modify or limit the remedial provisions of this Article in an *unconscionable manner* is subject to deletion and in that event the remedies made available by this Article are applicable as if the stricken clause had never existed." (Uniform Commercial Code, §2-719, official comment 1; emphasis supplied.)

It follows that contractual limitations upon remedies are generally to be enforced unless unconscionable. This analysis is buttressed by the fact that the official comments to section 2-302 of the Uniform Commercial Code, the code provision pertaining to unconscionable contracts or clauses, cites

Kansas City Wholesale Grocery Co. v. Weber Packing Corp. (93 Utah 414 [1937]), a case invalidating a time limitation provision as applied to latent defects, as illustrating the underlying basis for section 2-302. . . .

However, it is unnecessary to decide the issue of whether the time limitation is unconscionable on this appeal for section 2-719, subd. (2) of the Uniform Commercial Code provides that the general remedy provisions of the code apply when "circumstances cause an exclusive or limited remedy to fail of its essential purpose." As explained by the official comments to this section: "where an apparently fair and reasonable clause because of circumstances fails in its purpose or operates to deprive either party of the substantial value of the bargain, it must give way to the general remedy provisions of this Article." (Uniform Commercial Code, §2-719, official comment 1.) Here, paragraph 2 of the contract bars all claims for shade and other specified defects made after knitting and processing. Its effect is to eliminate any remedy for shade defects not reasonably discoverable within the time limitation period. It is true that parties may set by agreement any time not manifestly unreasonable whenever the code "requires any action to be taken within a reasonable time" (Uniform Commercial Code, §1-204, subd. [1][30]), but here the time provision eliminates all remedy for defects not discoverable before knitting and processing and section 2-719, subd. (2) of the Uniform Commercial Code therefore applies.

Defendant's affidavits allege that sweaters manufactured from the yarn were rendered unmarketable because of latent shading defects not reasonably discoverable before knitting and processing of the yarn into sweaters. If these factual allegations are established at trial, the limited remedy established by paragraph two has failed its "essential purpose" and the buyer is, in effect, without remedy. The time limitation clause of the contract must give way to the general code rule that a buyer has a reasonable time to notify the seller of breach of contract after he discovers or should have discovered the defect. (Uniform Commercial Code, §2-207, subd. [3], par. [a].) As indicated above, defendant's affidavits are sufficient to create a question of fact concerning whether notice was given within a reasonable time after the shading defect should have been discovered.

It can be argued that paragraph two of the contract, insofar as it bars all claims for enumerated defects not reasonably discoverable within the time period established, purports to exclude these defects from the coverage of the express warranty of merchantability. By this analysis, the contract not only limits its remedies for its breach, but also purports to modify the warranty of merchantability. An attempt to both warrant and refuse to warrant goods creates an ambiguity which can only be resolved by making one term yield to the other (cf. Hawkland, Limitation of Warranty under the Uniform

30. Now §1-302(b) — Ed.

Commercial Code, 11 How. L.J. 28 [1965]). Section 2-316 (subd. [1]) of the Uniform Commercial Code provides that warranty language prevails over the disclaimer if the two cannot be reasonably reconciled.

Here, the contract expressly creates an unlimited express warranty of merchantability while in a separate clause purports to indirectly modify the warranty without expressly mentioning the word merchantability. Under these circumstances, the language creating the unlimited express warranty must prevail over the time limitation insofar as the latter modifies the warranty. It follows that the express warranty of merchantability includes latent shading defects and defendant may claim for such defects not reasonably discoverable within the time limits established by the contract if plaintiff was notified of these defects within a reasonable time after they should have been discovered. . . .

In sum, there are factual issues for trial concerning whether the shading defects alleged were discoverable before knitting and processing, and if not, whether notice of the defects was given within a reasonable time after the defects were or should have been discovered. If the shading defects were not reasonably discoverable before knitting and processing and notice was given within a reasonable time after the defects were or should have been discovered, a further factual issue of whether the sweaters were rendered unsaleable because of the defect is presented for trial.

The order of the Appellate Division should be reversed, with costs, and plaintiff's motion for summary judgment should be denied.

Chief Judge Fuld (concurring). I agree that there should be a reversal but on the sole ground that a substantial question of fact has been raised as to whether the clause limiting the time in which to make a claim is "manifestly unreasonable" (Uniform Commercial Code, §1-204[31]) as applied to the type of defect here complained of. In this view, it is not necessary to consider the relevancy, if any, of other provisions of the Uniform Commercial Code (e.g., §§2-302, 2-316, 2-719), dealing with "unconscionable" contracts or clauses, exclusion of implied warranties or limitations on damages.

PROBLEM 39

On November 1, Jack Frost of Portland, Maine, bought a snowmobile from King Cold Recreationland. Jack used the snowmobile to get to work during the week in the winter and for fun on the weekends. The contract that he signed stated that the seller warranted that the vehicle was merchantable, but that, in the event of breach, "the buyer's remedy was limited solely to repair or

31. Now §1-302(b).—Ed.

replacement of defective parts." Moreover, the contract conspicuously stated that the seller was not responsible for "any consequential damages."

One week after he received the snowmobile, Jack noticed a strange rumble in the engine. He took the machine back to the King Cold service department. The machine was returned to him in three days allegedly repaired. These events repeated themselves three times over the next three weeks. Four weeks after he bought the snowmobile, Frost was seriously injured when it blew up while he was riding it. The machine, which cost $1,200, was destroyed. Frost temporarily lost the use of his left arm, incurred hospital expenses of $2,500, and lost pay of $1,600. Moreover, when he did return to work, he had to rent a snowmobile for $40 a week until spring (16 weeks—spring is very late in Maine). In addition, a $350 camera he was carrying was also destroyed. Frost brought suit against King Cold. King Cold defended on the ground that its liability was limited to the cost of repair or replacement. Frost argued that the remedy limitation was "unconscionable" and failed of its "essential purpose." All the parties pointed to §§2-316(4), 2-302, 2-719, and 2-715. How should this suit come out? See Beal v. General Motors Corp., 354 F. Supp. 423 (D. Del. 1973); Earl M. Jorgensen Co. v. Mark Constr., Inc., 56 Haw. 466, 540 P.2d 978 (1975).

The New Jersey Supreme Court has produced two leading opinions on the validity of a disclaimer of liability for consequential damages in automobile tire blowout cases. In Collins v. Uniroyal, Inc., 64 N.J. 260, 315 A.2d 16 (1974), a consumer was killed in an automobile accident when his right rear tire failed. The tire manufacturer tried to avoid §2-719(3) by saying that its disclaimer of liability for personal injury damages overcame the prima facie presumption of unconscionability because its warranty made a conspicuous statement limiting the remedy for blowout to repair or replacement. The court held that this argument was not "consonant with the commercial and human realities," and added:

> A tire manufacturer warrants against blowouts in order to increase tire sales. Public advertising by defendant relative to these tires stated: "If it only saves your life once, it's a bargain." The seller should be held to realize that the purchaser of a tire buying it because so warranted is far more likely to have made the purchase decision in order to protect himself and the passengers in his car from death or personal injury in a blowout accident than to assure himself of a refund of the price of the tire in such an event. That being the natural reliance and the reasonable expectation of the purchaser flowing from the warranty, it appears to us patently unconscionable for the manufacturer to be permitted to limit his damages for a breach of warranty proximately resulting in the purchaser's death to a price refund or replacement of the tire.

In a later case, no personal injury occurred, but the car was destroyed when the tire blew. The tire manufacturer argued that since §2-719(3)'s "prima facie unconscionable" language applies only to "injury to the person," the consumer was limited in her recovery to a replacement of the defective tire. The New Jersey Supreme Court, however, still applied §2-719(3) because it found the warranty limitation to be "seriously lacking in clarity." The court stated:

> [T]he booklet presents the owner with a linguistic maze. Throughout the document there is an admixture of terms relating to quality, capacity, and performance, together with disclaimers and exclusions of coverage, as well as limitations and restrictions upon liability and remedies. There are fulsome and repeated references to the term "guarantee," seemingly relating to quality and performance followed by the rather sudden, isolated use of the term "promise," purportedly limiting the entire contractual undertaking to tire replacement. What is thus given to a purchaser is not a simple and straightforward document defining on the one hand that which constitutes an affirmation of quality or performance and, on the other, the liability which flows from a breach thereof. Rather what is presented is a melange of overlapping, variant, misleading, and contradictory provisions.

Gladden v. Cadillac Motor Car Div., 83 N.J. 320, 333, 416 A.2d 394, 401 (1980). For a similar result in a commercial setting, see Andover Air Ltd. Partnership v. Piper Aircraft Corp., 7 U.C.C. Rep. Serv. 2d 1494 (D. Mass. 1989) (remedy limitation to repair or replacement held unconscionable where defective and inexpensive bracket caused $100,000 in damages in an airplane crash). Not all courts are this sympathetic to buyers. In NEC Technologies, Inc. v. Nelson, 267 Ga. 390, 478 S.E.2d 769 (1996), the Georgia Supreme Court held that a disclaimer of liability for consequential damages was not unconscionable where a TV malfunctioned, and the resulting fire caused extensive damage to the consumer's home but no personal injuries.

PROBLEM 40

Since you are in charge of drafting the warranty provisions for your manufacturing client's sales contracts, you have decided to make some express warranties and disclaim all implied ones. For the express warranties you are thinking about limiting the buyer's remedies to just repair and replacement so that (as in the Georgia case just cited) your client at most will have to return the purchase price but never pay consequential damages, which could be huge, particularly if there is personal injury involved. Is this a good idea? Are there moral questions here? Who should bear these types of damages?

See Hennings v. Camping Time RV Centers, LLC, 2017 WL 4552896 (N.D. Ga. 2017).

One other point: although §2-719 does not say so, most courts have required that any remedy limitation be *conspicuous* in order to be effective. See, e.g., Stauffer Chem. Co. v. Curry, 778 P.2d 1083 (Wyo. 1989) (any other result "absurd"); but see Apex Supply Co. v. Benbow Indus., 189 Ga. App. 598, 376 S.E.2d 694 (1988) (conspicuousness not required because a limitation of remedy is not as serious a matter as a disclaimer of warranty).

Pierce v. Catalina Yachts, Inc.

Supreme Court of Alaska, 1999
2 P.3d 618

BRYNER, Justice.

I. INTRODUCTION

After finding that Catalina Yachts, a sailboat manufacturer, breached its limited warranty to repair a defect in a boat that it sold to Jim and Karen Pierce, a jury awarded the Pierces monetary damages for the reasonable cost of repair. Before submitting the case to the jury, the trial court dismissed the Pierces' claim for consequential damages, finding it barred by an express provision in the warranty. On appeal, the Pierces contend that they were entitled to consequential damages despite this provision. We agree, holding that because Catalina acted in bad faith when it breached the warranty, the company cannot conscionably enforce the warranty's provision barring consequential damages. Accordingly, we remand for a trial to determine consequential damages.

II. FACTS AND PROCEEDINGS

In June 1992 Jim and Karen Pierce purchased a forty-two-foot sailboat newly built by Catalina Yachts. Catalina gave the Pierces a limited warranty, promising to repair or pay for repair of any below-waterline blisters that might appear in the gel coat—a smooth outer layer of resin on the boat's hull.[32] The warranty expressly disclaimed Catalina's responsibility for consequential damages.

In June 1994 the Pierces hauled the boat out of the water to perform maintenance and discovered gel-coat blisters on its hull and rudder.

32. This limited warranty provided, in relevant part: "Catalina will repair or, at its option, pay for 100% of the labor and material costs necessary to repair any below-the-waterline gel coat blisters that occur within the first year after the boat is placed in the water."

They promptly notified Catalina of the problem and submitted a repair estimate of $10,645, which included the cost of removing and replacing the gel coat below the waterline. Catalina refused to accept this estimate, insisting that the hull only needed minor patching. Six months later, after their repeated efforts failed to convince Catalina that the gel coat needed to be replaced, the Pierces sued the company, claiming tort and contract damages. They later amended their complaint to allege a separate claim for unfair trade practices. Before trial, the superior court ruled that the limited warranty's provision barring consequential damages was not unconscionable. Based on this ruling, the court later precluded the Pierces from submitting their consequential damages claim to the jury, restricting the Pierces' recovery on their claim of breach of contract to their cost of repair, as specified in the limited warranty. The jury awarded the Pierces $12,445 as the reasonable cost of repair, specifically finding that the Pierces had given Catalina timely notice of the blister problem, that Catalina breached its gel-coat warranty, that it acted in bad faith in failing to honor its warranty obligations, and that the Pierces could not have avoided any of their losses.

The Pierces appeal, contending that the trial court erred in striking their claim for consequential damages, in excluding evidence supporting their unfair trade practices claim, and in calculating the attorney's fee award. Catalina cross-appeals, also contesting the attorney's fee order.

III. Discussion

A. The Pierces Are Entitled to Consequential Damages

The Pierces' consequential damages argument requires us to consider a question of first impression concerning how a warranty provision that creates a limited remedy interacts with another provision that excludes consequential damages: if the limited remedy fails, should the exclusion of consequential damages survive?

Alaska's commercial code addresses these issues in AS 45.02.719. The first paragraph of this provision, subsection .719(a), authorizes limited warranties, allowing parties entering into commercial transactions to "limit or alter the measure of damages recoverable under [chapter 7 of the U.C.C.], as by limiting the buyer's remedies to . . . repair and replacement of nonconforming goods or parts" and to agree that the limited remedy is "exclusive, in which case it is the sole remedy." But when a limited remedy fails, the second paragraph of AS 45.02.719, subsection .719(b), nullifies the warranty's limitation, restoring the buyer's right to rely on any authorized remedy: "If circumstances cause an exclusive or limited remedy to fail of its essential purpose, remedy may be had as provided in the code."

Courts construing U.C.C. subsection 719(b) agree that a limited warranty to repair "fails of its essential purpose," "when the seller is either unwilling or unable to conform the goods to the contract."[33]

The policy behind the failure of essential purpose rule is to insure that the buyer has "at least minimum adequate remedies." Typically, a limited repair/replacement remedy fails of its essential purpose where (1) the "[s]eller is unsuccessful in repairing or replacing the defective part, regardless of good or bad faith; or (2) [t]here is unreasonable delay in repairing or replacing defective components.[34]

Here, by specifically finding that the Pierces' boat experienced gel-coat blisters, that the Pierces gave Catalina timely notice of the problem, that Catalina thereafter breached its obligations under the limited gel-coat warranty, and that the Pierces could not have avoided their damages, the jury effectively determined that the gel-coat warranty had failed of its essential purpose. Under subsection .719(b), then, the Pierces seemingly can pursue any remedy available under the commercial code, including consequential damages.

But the Pierces' right to consequential damages under subsection .719(b) is not as certain as it seems. The last paragraph of AS 45.02.719, subsection .719(c), separately provides that consequential damages may be limited or excluded "unless the limitation or exclusion is unconscionable." By validating consequential damages exclusions subject only to unconscionability, subsection .719(c) casts doubt upon subsection .719(b)'s implied promise that, when a limited remedy fails, the buyer may claim consequential damages because they are a "remedy . . . provided in the code."

The commercial code does not directly resolve this tension between subsections .719(b) and .719(c).[35] When, as here, a limited repair remedy fails, and a separate provision of the warranty bars consequential damages, the code fails to say whether a court should apply subsection .719(b) by restoring the buyer's right to seek consequential damages, or whether it should instead apply subsection .719(c) by enforcing the bar against consequential damages "unless . . . unconscionable."

33. Chatlos Sys., Inc. v. National Cash Register Corp., 635 F.2d 1081, 1085 (3d Cir. 1980).

34. McDermott, Inc. v. Clyde Iron, 979 F.2d 1068, 1073 (5th Cir. 1993) (internal citations omitted), *rev'd on other grounds*, McDermott, Inc. v. AmClyde, 511 U.S. 202, 114 S. Ct. 1461, 128 L. Ed. 2d 148 (1994). See also S.M. Wilson & Co. v. Smith Int'l, Inc., 587 F.2d 1363, 1375 (9th Cir. 1978); Liberty Truck Sales, Inc. v. Kimbrel, 548 So. 2d 1379, 1384 (Ala. 1989). See generally Daniel C. Hagen, Sections 2-719(2) & 2-719(3) of the Uniform Commercial Code: The Limited Warranty Package & Consequential Damages, 31 Val. U. L. Rev. 111, 115 (1996).

35. See *S.M. Wilson & Co.*, 587 F.2d at 1375 ("The failure of the limited repair warranty to achieve its essential purpose makes available . . . the remedies 'as may be had as provided in this code.' This does not mean, however, that the bar to recovery of consequential damages should be eliminated.").

Courts addressing this dilemma in other jurisdictions have come to differing conclusions. Some have found the two subsections to be dependent, ruling that when a warranty fails, subsection .719(b)'s command to restore all available remedies trumps subsection .719(c)'s approval of a specific clause that bars consequential damages, regardless of whether that clause might itself be unconscionable. [Citations omitted.] Other courts have applied a case-by-case analysis. [Citations omitted.] But the majority of jurisdictions view these subsections to be independent, ruling that when a warranty fails, a separate provision barring consequential damages will survive under subsection .719(c) as long as the bar itself is not unconscionable. [Citations omitted.]

We believe that the majority approach best serves the Uniform Commercial Code's underlying purposes "to simplify, clarify and modernize the law governing commercial transactions; to permit the continued expansion of commercial practices through custom, usage and agreement of the parties; [and] to make uniform the law among the various jurisdictions."[36] Moreover, this approach balances the purposes of subsections .719(b) and (c) by allowing parties latitude to contract around consequential damages, while protecting buyers from unconscionable results.[37] We therefore adopt the independent approach as the most sensible rule in light of precedent, reason, and policy.

Courts applying this approach recognize that contractual provisions limiting remedies and excluding consequential damages shift the risk of a limited remedy's failure from the seller to the buyer; they examine the totality of the circumstances at issue—including those surrounding the limited remedy's failure—to determine whether there is anything "in the formation of the contract or the circumstances resulting in failure of performance that makes it unconscionable to enforce the parties' allocation of risk."[38]

In determining whether an exclusion is unconscionable, courts examine the circumstances existing when the contract was signed, asking whether "there was . . . reason to conclude that the parties could not competently agree upon the allocation of risk."[39] Courts are more likely to find unconscionability when a consumer is involved, when there is a disparity in bargaining

36. U.C.C. §1-102(2) (1996).

37. See McKernan v. United Tech. Corp., 717 F. Supp. 60, 71 (D. Conn. 1989). The comments to U.C.C. §2-719 provide that, while "minimum adequate remedies must be available" to the buyer when a contract fails, "parties are left free to shape their remedies to their particular requirements and reasonable agreements limiting or modifying remedies are to be given effect." U.C.C. §2-719 cmt. 1. In discussing subsection 2-719(3), the U.C.C. comments also recognize that clauses limiting consequential damages are "merely an allocation of unknown or undeterminable risks." U.C.C. §2-719 cmt. 3.

38. *Chatlos*, 635 F.2d at 1087.

39. Id. at 1087.

power, and when the consequential damages clause is on a pre-printed form; conversely, they are unlikely to find unconscionability when "such a limitation is freely negotiated between sophisticated parties, which will most likely occur in a commercial setting. . . ."[40]

In addition to inquiring into the circumstances at the time of the sale, courts examine the case "[f]rom the perspective of later events," inquiring whether "it appears that the type of damage claimed . . . came within the realm of expectable losses."[41] The reason for the limited warranty's failure affects this analysis:

> Whether the preclusion of consequential damages should be effective in this case depends upon the circumstances involved. The repair remedy's failure of essential purpose, while a discrete question, is not completely irrelevant to the issue of the conscionability of enforcing the consequential damages exclusion. The latter term is "merely an allocation of unknown or undeterminable risks." Recognizing this, *the question . . . narrows to the unconscionability of the buyer retaining the risk of consequential damages upon the failure of the essential purpose of the exclusive repair remedy.*[42]

And in examining why a limited remedy failed of its essential purpose, courts consider it significant if the seller acted unreasonably or in bad faith.

In the present case, the nature of the Pierces' warranty and the circumstances surrounding Catalina's breach weigh heavily against enforcing the consequential damages bar. The contract at issue was a consumer sale, not a commercial transaction between sophisticated businesses with equivalent bargaining power. Catalina unilaterally drafted the damages bar and evidently included it in a preprinted standard limited warranty. Moreover, the jury's sizable award for the reasonable cost of repairing the boat's gel coat establishes that Catalina's breach deprived the Pierces of a substantial benefit of their bargain. Though some gel-coat blistering might have been foreseeable, a defect of this magnitude does not fit neatly "within the realm of expectable losses."

But the decisive factor in this case is the nature of Catalina's breach, which caused the limited remedy to fail of its essential purpose. The jury specifically found that Catalina acted in bad faith in failing to honor its warranty. This finding virtually establishes a "circumstance[] resulting in failure of performance that makes it unconscionable to enforce the parties' allocation of risk." Because the jury found that Catalina consciously deprived the

40. *Schurtz,* 814 P.2d at 1114; see also Associated Press v. Southern Ark. Radio Co., 34 Ark. App. 211, 809 S.W.2d 695, 697 (1991); Construction Assocs. v. Fargo Water Equip. Co., 446 N.W.2d 237, 242 (N.D. 1989).

41. *Chatlos,* 635 F.2d at 1087.

42. Id. at 1086-87 (internal citation omitted; emphasis added).

Pierces of their rights under the warranty, the company cannot conscionably demand to enforce its own warranty rights against the Pierces:

> This Court would be in an untenable position if it allowed the defendant to shelter itself behind one segment of the warranty when it has allegedly repudiated and ignored its very limited obligations under another segment of the same warranty, which alleged repudiation has caused the very need for relief which the defendant is attempting to avoid.[43]

Moreover, in light of Catalina's bad faith, allowing the company to enforce the consequential damages bar would conflict with the commercial code's imperative that "[e]very contract or duty in the code imposes an obligation of good faith in its performance or enforcement."[44] Finally, because it is self-evident that the Pierces did not bargain to assume the risk of a bad faith breach by Catalina, enforcing the bar against consequential damages would thwart AS 45.02.719's basic goal of implementing the parties' agreement.

For these reasons, we hold the superior court erred in ruling that it would be conscionable to enforce the warranty's bar against consequential damages and in declining to allow the Pierces to present their consequential damages claim to the jury. We further hold that this error requires us to remand the case for a trial to determine the extent of these damages. . . .

IV. Conclusion

For these reasons, we VACATE the judgment and REMAND for a trial to determine the amount of the Pierces' consequential damages.

NOTE

As this decision notes, there was once sharp judicial disagreement on the issue presented in this last case, but the trend in recent years is to read §2-719(2) and (3) as *independent* of one another, so that an essential failure of the remedy limitation's purpose does not automatically create a claim for

43. Jones and McKnight Corp. v. Birdsboro Corp., 320 F. Supp. 39, 43-44 (N.D. Ill. 1970).
44. See AS 47.01.203; U.C.C. §1-304.

1. In "Changing Times, the Kiplinger Magazine," issue of April, 1969, Page 45, there is an interesting article with reference to this spider, entitled "Beware the Brown Recluse." The views of several Arkansas physicians are set out, this state being one with a large infestation of this particular species of spider.
2. The evidence reflected that Mrs. Flippo had, at some previous time, been in the business of raising chickens, and owned a chicken house. She said that she had seen spiders in this chicken house, though not at the time chickens were being raised. It is suggested by appellees that she could have brought the spider into the store with her.

disclaimed consequential damages; see Razor v. Hyundai Motor America, 222 Ill. 2d 75, 854 N.E.2d 607 (2006). Predictably, as the court notes, consumers have had an easier time recovering disclaimed consequential damages than have commercial buyers.

Helena Chemical Co. v. Williamson

United States District Court, Western District of Louisiana, 2015
2015 WL 1298435

Robert G. James, District Judge.

This action was brought by Plaintiff Helena Chemical Co. ("Helena") against Defendant Lavelle Williamson ("Williamson") to recover amounts due for goods and services provided to Williamson under a Credit Sales and Services Agreement. Williamson filed a counterclaim asserting that Helena was negligent for selling him wet corn seed, which resulted in his decreased production, loss of higher contract price, and increased farming expenses.

Pending before the Court is Helena's Motion for Summary Judgment on Consequential Damages. . . . For the following reasons, Helena's motion is DENIED.

I. Facts and Background

Williamson began farming in 2010. Prior to that time, he had worked in the oilfield industry, marked timber, and as a painter. He has a tenth-grade education.

Until 2010, Williamson had never purchased seeds or chemicals for farming purposes. During his first year of farming, he sought to purchase goods and services from Helena on credit. Helena presented him with a Credit Sales and Services Agreement ("the Agreement"), which he signed. [Doc. No. 1-2, Exh. A]. The terms were not discussed or explained to him.

Between 2010 and 2013, Williamson purchased seed, fertilizer, and chemicals from Helena under the Agreement. The Agreement was not superseded or cancelled at any time.

For the 2013 crop year, Helena provided certain goods and services to Williamson, including corn seed and soybeans and related products, for a total price of $79,188.50. After Helena's delivery, Williamson had difficulty getting the corn seed out of Helena's tender. He contacted Helena's sales representative, Paul McKinley, to complain about this issue, but proceeded with planting the corn seed.

Williamson's corn seed failed to germinate, and a sufficient stand of corn was not realized for the 2013 crop year. He avers that "it was determined" that Helena's corn seed was wet when it was delivered in Helena's tender. [Doc. No. 16, Williamson Aff., ¶4]. According to Williamson, the wet corn seed absorbed more chemicals than it would normally, resulting in a loss of "at least eighty (80) bushels of corn per acre." [Doc. No. 16, Williamson Aff., ¶3]. Helena contends, however, that Williamson's corn crop failure was a result of his own improper application of fertilizer.

Williamson made one payment to Helena, but has not made any further payments on his account, arguing that Helena is liable to him in negligence. Helena has filed the instant motion seeking a ruling by the Court that Williamson cannot recover consequential damages based on the exclusion/limitations of remedies provision of the Agreement. Williamson opposes the motion.

The Court is now prepared to rule.

II. Law and Analysis

* * *

B. Consequential Damages

In his counterclaim, Williamson seeks to recover damages from Helena based on its alleged negligence, claiming that he suffered damages in the amount of $148,964.15 for decreased corn production, $64,439.16 for loss of a higher contract price, and $13,491.50 for increased farming expenses for the 2013 crop year.

Helena moves the Court for judgment as a matter of law that Williamson cannot recover on his counterclaim, arguing that the clear and unambiguous language of the Agreement prevents him from recovering consequential damages.

Williamson opposes Helena's motion and argues that the exclusion/limitations of remedy provision in the Agreement is unenforceable under Tennessee law.

The Agreement contains the following pertinent provisions:

> THE EXCLUSIVE REMEDY FOR ANY CAUSE OF ACTION BY OR ON BEHALF OF PURCHASER UNDER THIS STATEMENT AND RELATED TRANSACTION(S) IS A CLAIM FOR DAMAGES AND IN NO EVENT SHALL DAMAGES OR ANY OTHER RECOVERY OF ANY KIND AGAINST HELENA . . . EXCEED THE PRICE OF THE SPECIFIC GOODS OR SERVICES WHICH CAUSE THE ALLEGED LOSS, DAMAGE, INJURY OR OTHER CLAIM. NEITHER HELENA . . . SHALL BE LIABLE AND ANY AND ALL CLAIMS AGAINST HELENA . . . ARE WAIVED FOR SPECIAL, DIRECT OR CONSEQUENTIAL DAMAGES, OR EXPENSES, OF ANY NATURE INCLUDING, BUT NOT LIMITED TO, LOSS OF PROFITS OR INCOME, CROP OR PROPERTY LOSS OR DAMAGE, LABOR CHARGES AND FREIGHT CHARGES, WHETHER OR NOT BASED ON HELENA'S, ITS OFFICERS', DIRECTORS', EMPLOYEES' AND/OR AFFILIATES' NEGLIGENCE, BREACH OF WARRANTY, STRICT LIABILITY IN TORT OR ANY OTHER CAUSE OF ACTION. . . .

The Agreement's choice of law clause provides that Tennessee law governs, which the parties do not dispute. Under Tennessee law, "[t]he interpretation of a contract is a matter of law." Guiliano v. Cleo, Inc., 995 S.W.2d 88, 95 (Tenn. 1999). Consequently, "[q]uestions of contract interpretation . . . are especially well-suited for resolution by summary judgment." Ross Prods. Div. Abbott Labs. v. Tennessee, No. M2006-01113-COA-R3-CV, 2007 Tenn. App. LEXIS 752, at *7 (Tenn. Ct. App. Dec. 5, 2007). "If the language [of a contract] is clear and unambiguous, the literal meaning controls the outcome of the dispute." Allstate Ins. Co. v. Watson, 195 S.W.3d 609, 611 (Tenn. 2006). . . . [The court then quoted §2-719 of the UCC.]

The comments following the statute explain:

> 1. Under this section parties are left free to shape their remedies to their particular requirements and reasonable agreements limiting or modifying remedies are to be given effect.
>
> However, it is of the very essence of a sales contract that at least minimum adequate remedies be available. If the parties intend to conclude a contract for sale within this Article they must accept the legal consequence that there be at least a fair quantum of remedy for breach of the obligations or duties outlined in the contract. Thus any clause purporting to modify or limit the remedial provisions of this Article in an unconscionable manner is subject to deletion and in that event the remedies made available by this Article are applicable as if the stricken clause had never existed. Similarly, under subsection (2), where an apparently fair and reasonable clause because of circumstances fails in its purpose or operates to deprive either party of the substantial value of the bargain, it must give way to the general remedy provisions of this Article.
>
> . . .
>
> 3. Subsection (3) recognizes the validity of clauses limiting or excluding consequential damages but makes it clear that they may not operate in an unconscionable manner. Actually such terms are merely an allocation of unknown or undeterminable risks. The seller in all cases is free to disclaim warranties in the manner provided in Section 2-316.

Tenn. Code Ann. 47-2-719 cmts. 1, 3. Thus, Tennessee permits the limitation of remedies unless circumstances causes the remedy to fail of its essential purpose. Specifically, commercial parties may limit or exclude consequential damages unless the limitation or exclusion is unconscionable.

The Court considers, first, whether the Agreement's clause excluding consequential damages is unconscionable. Whether a contract term is unconscionable is a question of law, and a presumption of permissible dealings exists between commercial parties. [Citations omitted.] "In contrast with failure of essential purpose, the determination of unconscionability focuses on the circumstances as they existed when the parties entered into the contract." Baptist Memorial Hosp. v. Argo Const. Corp., 308 S.W.3d 337, 346 (Tenn. Ct. App. 2009).

The Tennessee Court of Appeals has discussed unconscionability in the commercial context:

> Is the limitation on consequential damages unconscionable? This is a question of law for the court in light of the commercial setting, purpose and effect of the provision. (Citation omitted.) Unconscionability may arise from a lack of meaningful choice on the part of one party (procedural unconscionability) or from contract terms that are unreasonably harsh (substantive unconscionability). (Citation omitted.) In Tennessee we have tended to lump the two together and speak of unconscionability resulting when the inequality of the bargain is so manifest as to shock the judgment of a person of common sense, and where the terms are so oppressive that no reasonable person would make them on one hand, and no honest and fair person would accept them on the other. (Citation omitted.) Where the parties possess equal bargaining power the courts are unlikely to find that their negotiations resulted in an unconscionable bargain, and terms that are common in the industry are generally not unconscionable. (Citation omitted.)

Trinity Industries, Inc. v. McKinnon Bridge Company, Inc., 77 S.W.3d 159 (Tenn. Ct. App. 2001).

Although there are no Tennessee cases directly on point, Williamson has cited to the Court nine cases in other state and federal jurisdictions which have addressed this issue and found that the exclusion or limitations of remedies provision was unconscionable. In many of those cases, the seller or manufacturer held such a strong bargaining position that it could impose a provision on the farmer which deprived him of "virtually all protection." Martin v. Joseph Harris Co., 767 F.2d 296, 301 (6th Cir. 1985) (internal quotation marks omitted) (quoting J. White & R. Summers, the Handbook of the Law Under the Uniform Commercial Code, §12-11, at 477 (2d ed. 1980)). In Hanson v. Funk Seeds, Int'l, 373 N.W.2d 30 (S.D. Sup. Ct. 1985), the Supreme Court of South Dakota reviewed and upheld a trial court's determination that a corn seed supplier could not enforce a remedy provision limiting the farmer/buyer to a refund of the corn seed price because the provision was unconscionable. The *Hanson* Court explained:

> Appellee Hanson, like most farmers, was not in a position to bargain for more favorable contract terms, nor was he able to test the seed before the purchase. A crop failure is inevitable if the corn seed is ineffective and to enforce the provisions here in question, which would only allow the return of the purchase price, would leave appellee without any substantial recourse for his loss. In essence, appellee would be left without a remedy for another's breach. Cf. Rozeboom v. Northwestern Bell Telephone Co., 358 N.W.2d 241, 242 (S.D. 1984). The trial court's determination that these provisions were unconscionable is therefore not in error and we uphold its decision in this regard.

Id. at 35; cf. Jones v. Asgrow Seed Co., 749 F. Supp. 836 (N.D. Ohio 1990) (limitation of liability not unconscionable where limitation was conspicuous, buyer was experienced commercial tomato seed buyer, and seed contained undiscoverable latent defect); Nunes Turfgrass v. Vaughan-Jacklin Seed Co., 200 Cal. App. 3d 1518, 246 Cal. Rptr. 823 (1988) (seller's limitation of consequential damages clause in sales confirmation for sale of commercial sod seed mix was not unconscionable where buyer and seller were large commercial entities familiar with sod seed business and had done business together for 20 years).

In this case, at the time the Agreement was entered, Williamson was a first-time farmer with a tenth-grade education and no apparent experience in the agricultural industry. He needed the goods and services Helena provided to begin his farming career. Helena then presented him with an agreement which had to be signed if he wished to purchase from Helena. Although the Agreement was not *prima facie* unconscionable under Tennessee law and commercial parties are presumed to have engaged in permissible dealings, this simply was not a commercial transaction between two parties on equal footing. See *Aquascene,* 831 F. Supp. at 604 (The state legislature "intended to allow merchants to allocate risks when making business contracts," but a provision may be invalidated "where one party is overwhelmed."). Williamson was in no position to bargain and thus signed an Agreement which left him without recourse, even if Helena's action resulted in substantial damages to him. Under these circumstances and finding the decisions of every other court to consider this issue persuasive, the Court finds that the exclusion/limitations of remedies provision is unconscionable and unenforceable. . . .

III. Conclusion

For the foregoing reasons, Helena's Motion for Summary Judgment on Consequential Damages [Doc. No. 10] is DENIED. If Williamson prevails on his counterclaim, he may seek to recover consequential damages from Helena.

D. Defenses in Warranty Actions

1. Notice

In all warranty actions a buyer loses all UCC rights if there is a failure to give the seller *notice* of the breach within a reasonable period of time after the breach should have been discovered. Read §2-607(3)(a) and Official Comment 4 to that section. The reason for this technical requirement is to preserve for the seller the right to inspect the goods (§2-515) and the right to *cure* (§2-508) and, of course, to facilitate an early settlement of the dispute.

PROBLEM 41

Pearl, a farmer, exhibited to Dave samples of her apples, but said that the bulk of the apples had less color and were one-fifth smaller in size than the samples. Dave said, "Bring your apples to my warehouse; such size apples are worth $3 a bushel, and I will pay you that for them." Pearl agreed to do so.

The next day Pearl delivered 150 bushels of apples to Dave's warehouse. These apples were not as good, on an average, as the samples and were one-third smaller in size than the samples were. Dave, without inspecting the apples, delivered them ten days later to his commission merchant, who the same day sold them on the market, bringing only $1.50 per bushel.

The commission merchant, immediately upon making the sale, called Dave and informed him of the price brought by the apples. Dave was disgusted and decided to wait until Pearl billed him for the apples, at which time he would give her a piece of his mind. Sixty days later Pearl billed Dave in the amount of $450 for the 150 bushels of apples. Dave refused to pay, telling Pearl that the apples had not measured up to the contract. Pearl sued Dave. Dave contended that Pearl breached an express warranty under the Uniform Commercial Code since a contract of sale by sample was involved. What result? Review §2-313.

Fitl v. Strek

Supreme Court of Nebraska, 2005
269 Neb. 51, 690 N.W.2d 605

WRIGHT, J.

NATURE OF CASE

James G. Fitl purchased a baseball card from Mark Strek, doing business as Star Cards of San Francisco. When Fitl discovered that the baseball card had been altered and was of no value, he sued Strek for what he argued was the current fair market value of an unaltered version of the same card. Following a bench trial, judgment was entered against Strek in the amount of $17,750 plus costs. Strek appeals. . . .

FACTS

In September 1995, Fitl attended a sports card show in San Francisco, California, where Strek was an exhibitor. Fitl subsequently purchased from Strek a 1952 Mickey Mantle Topps baseball card for $17,750. According to Fitl, Strek represented that the card was in near mint condition. After Strek delivered the card to Fitl in Omaha, Nebraska, Fitl placed it in a safe-deposit box.

In May 1997, Fitl sent the baseball card to Professional Sports Authenticators (PSA), a grading service for sports cards that is located in Newport Beach, California. PSA reported to Fitl that the baseball card was ungradable because it had been discolored and doctored.

On May 29, 1997, Fitl wrote to Strek and indicated that he planned to pursue "legal methods" to resolve the matter. Strek replied that Fitl should have initiated a return of the baseball card in a timely fashion so that Strek could have confronted his source and remedied the situation. Strek asserted that a typical grace period for the unconditional return of a card was from 7 days to 1 month.

In August 1997, Fitl sent the baseball card to ASA Accugrade, Inc. (ASA), in Longwood, Florida, for a second opinion. ASA also concluded that the baseball card had been refinished and trimmed.

On September 8, 1997, Fitl sued Strek, alleging that Strek knew the baseball card had been recolored or otherwise altered and had concealed this fact from him. Fitl claimed he had reasonably relied upon Strek's status as a reputable sports card dealer. Strek's answer generally denied Fitl's allegations.

In a trial to the court, Fitl appeared with counsel and offered evidence. Strek was represented by counsel but did not appear or offer any evidence. Fitl testified that he was in San Francisco over the Labor Day weekend of 1995, where he met Strek at a sports card show. Fitl subsequently purchased from Strek a 1952 Mickey Mantle Topps baseball card and placed it in a safe-deposit box. In 1997, Fitl retrieved the baseball card and sent it to PSA, a sports card grading service.

Steve Orand testified that he had been a sports card collector for 27 years and that he bought, sold, and traded cards. He testified that PSA originated in 1996 or 1997 and was a leader in the sports card grading industry. He stated that PSA would not grade an altered card because alteration would totally devalue the card. He opined that any touchup or trimming of a card would render the card valueless and that an altered card is worth no more than the paper on which it is printed.

Orand examined the baseball card in question the week before trial and said that the edges of the card had been trimmed and reglued. One spot on the front of the baseball card and a larger spot on the back had been repainted, which left the card with no value. He testified that the standard for sports memorabilia was a lifetime guarantee and that a reputable collector would stand behind what he sold and refund the money if an item were fake or had been altered.

The district court entered judgment for Fitl in the amount of $17,750 and costs. The court found that Fitl had notified Strek as soon as he realized the baseball card was altered and worthless and that Fitl had notified Strek of the defect within a reasonable time after its discovery. The court rejected

Strek's theory that Fitl should have determined the authenticity of the baseball card immediately after it had been purchased.

Assignment of Error

Strek claims that the district court erred in determining that notification of the defective condition of the baseball card 2 years after the date of purchase was timely pursuant to Neb. U.C.C. §2-607(3)(a) (Reissue 2001).

Analysis

In a bench trial of a law action, a trial court's factual findings have the effect of a jury verdict and will not be set aside on appeal unless clearly erroneous. Webb v. American Employers Group, 268 Neb. 473, 684 N.W.2d 33 (2004). The district court found that Fitl had notified Strek within a reasonable time after discovery of the breach. Therefore, our review is whether the district court's finding as to the reasonableness of the notice was clearly erroneous.

Section 2-607(3)(a) states: "Where a tender has been accepted . . . the buyer must within a reasonable time after he discovers or should have discovered any breach notify the seller of breach or be barred from any remedy[.]" "What is a reasonable time for taking any action depends on the nature, purpose and circumstances of such action." Neb. U.C.C. §1-204(2) (Reissue 2001).

The notice requirement set forth in §2-607(3)(a) serves three purposes. It provides the seller with an opportunity to correct any defect, to prepare for negotiation and litigation, and to protect itself against stale claims asserted after it is too late for the seller to investigate them. See Cheyenne Mountain Bank v. Whetstone Corp., 787 P.2d 210 (Colo. App. 1990). "Whether the notice given is satisfactory and whether it is given within a reasonable time are generally questions of fact to be measured by all the circumstances of the case." Id. at 213.

In Maybank v. Kresge Co., 302 N.C. 129, 273 S.E.2d 681 (1981), the court reviewed the policies behind the notice requirement. The most important one is to enable the seller "to make efforts to cure the breach by making adjustments or replacements in order to minimize the buyer's damages and the seller's liability." Id. at 134, 273 S.E.2d at 684. A second policy is to provide the seller "a reasonable opportunity to learn the facts so that he may adequately prepare for negotiation and defend himself in a suit." Id. A third policy, designated the "least compelling" by the court, is the same as the policy behind statutes of limitation: "to provide a seller with a terminal point in time for liability." Id. at 135, 273 S.E.2d at 684.

Fitl purchased the baseball card in 1995 and immediately placed it in a safe-deposit box. Two years later, he retrieved the baseball card, had it appraised, and learned that it was of no value. Fitl testified that he had relied on Strek's position as a dealer of sports cards and on his representations that the baseball card was authentic. In Cao v. Nguyen, 258 Neb. 1027, 607 N.W.2d 528 (2000), we stated that a party is justified in relying upon a representation made to the party as a positive statement of fact when an investigation would be required to ascertain its falsity. In order for Fitl to have determined that the baseball card had been altered, he would have been required to conduct an investigation. We find that he was not required to do so. Once Fitl learned that the baseball card had been altered, he gave notice to Strek.

As the court noted in Maybank v. Kresge Co., supra, one of the most important policies behind the notice requirement of North Carolina's equivalent to §2-607(3)(a) is to allow the seller to cure the breach by making adjustments or replacements to minimize the buyer's damages and the seller's liability. However, even if Fitl had learned immediately upon taking possession of the baseball card that it was not authentic and had notified Strek at that time, there is no evidence that Strek could have made any adjustment or taken any action that would have minimized his liability. In its altered condition, the baseball card was worthless.

Strek claimed via his correspondence to Fitl that if Strek had received notice earlier, he could have contacted the person who sold him the baseball card to determine the source of the alteration, but there is no evidence to support this allegation. In fact, Strek offered no evidence at trial. His letter is merely an assertion that is unsupported. Earlier notification would not have helped Strek prepare for negotiation or defend himself in a suit because the damage to Fitl could not be repaired. Thus, the policies behind the notice requirement, to allow the seller to correct a defect, to prepare for negotiation and litigation, and to protect against stale claims at a time beyond which an investigation can be completed, were not unfairly prejudiced by the lack of an earlier notice to Strek. Any problem Strek may have had with the party from whom he obtained the baseball card was a separate matter from his transaction with Fitl, and an investigation into the source of the altered card would not have minimized Fitl's damages.

Strek represented himself as a sports card dealer at a card show in San Francisco. After Fitl expressed interest in a specific baseball card, Strek contacted Fitl to sell him just such a card. Orand stated that a reputable dealer will stand behind what he sells and refund the money if an item is fake or has been altered. In the context of whether a rejection of goods was made in a reasonable amount of time, we have stated that "when there is no precise rule of law which governs, the question of what, under the circumstances of a particular case, is a reasonable amount of time is usually a question for the jury." See Smith v. Paoli Popcorn Co., 255 Neb. 910, 917, 587 N.W.2d 660, 664 (1999).

The district court found that it was reasonable to give Strek notice of a defect 2 years after the purchase. This finding was not clearly erroneous. Pursuant to §2-607(4), the burden is on the buyer to show a breach with respect to the goods accepted. Fitl presented evidence that the baseball card was not authentic, as he had been led to believe by Strek's representations. Strek did not refute Fitl's evidence.

CONCLUSION

The judgment of the district court is affirmed.

PROBLEM 42

Icarus Airlines ordered 40 new airplanes from the Daedalus Aircraft Company. Twenty were to be delivered on May 8 and the rest on November 10. The first shipment actually came on September 11, but Icarus did not complain. The second came on January 12 of the next year. On January 30 the president of Icarus wrote Daedalus that "[w]e are very disappointed by your late shipment, which has caused us much expense and inconvenience." Three months later Icarus sued, claiming some $24 million in damages caused by the delayed deliveries. In its answer Daedalus responded by stating that it had received no notice of the breach as to the first shipment and that the notice concerning the second shipment was defective because it did not announce Icarus's intention to claim a breach as a result of the late delivery. At trial, Icarus countered by stating that no notice is required where, as here, the breach is obvious to the seller. As to the lack of formal notice of breach in the January letter, Icarus pointed to Official Comment 4 to §2-607.

As the trial court judge, how would you rule on the notice issues? See Aqualon Co. v. MAC Equipment, Inc., 149 F.3d 262 (4th Cir. 1998); Peavey Electronics Corp. v. Baan U.S.A., Inc., 10 So. 3d 945 (Miss. App. 2009) (noting split among courts and holding that merchant did not give notice by merely giving notice of problems, because notice requirement "exists to prevent commercial bad faith, promote mitigation and cure, enable the seller to collect evidence while still fresh, and promote settlement"); Wheeler v. Subaru of America, Inc., 2020 WL 1550744 (D. Minn. 2020) (consumer inquiry whether warranty on car would cover chipped paint not sufficient as notice of defect). What if on January 30 Icarus had filed suit against Daedalus rather than waiting three months? Would the notice requirement have been satisfied by the filing itself? See Armco Steel Co. v. Isaacson Structure Steel Co., 611 P.2d 507 (Alaska 1980). In *Armco,* the court held that filing suit was not sufficient notice. However, the dissenting judge said: "[F]iling suit without prior notice may be impolite but it is not deceptive or dishonest and it certainly is no hindrance to 'normal settlement through negotiation.' Often, in fact, serious settlement negotiations do not take place until a lawsuit is filed." See also In re Bridgestone/Firestone, Inc. Tires Products Liability Litigation, 155 F. Supp. 2d 1069 (S.D. Ind. 2001). Some courts have held that consumers can give adequate notice by filing suit, particularly in personal injury actions (see Buzadzhi v. Bexco Enter., Inc., 2011 WL 43086 (N.D. Wis. 2011)), but others have not relaxed the law for consumers with complaints alleging only financial losses (see In re Carrier IQ, Inc., 2015 WL 274054 (N.D. Cal. 2015)). Is notice required if the seller is already aware of the nonconformity on the delivery date? See Muir v. Nature's Bounty, Inc., 2017 WL 4310650 (N.D. Ill. 2017).

PROBLEM 43

Alonso Quijano invited his good friend Sancho to dinner and served him a pheasant for the meal. The wine specially uncorked for the meal had been bottled by La Mancha Vineyards. It proved to be laced with a poisonous chemical, but only Sancho drank enough to have a serious reaction: it put him in the hospital for eight months. When he was discharged, he hired an attorney and filed suit against La Mancha Vineyards, which defended on the lack of notice required by §2-607(3)(a). How should this come out? Read §2-318 and Official Comment 5 to §2-607. If the person who had been injured had been Alonso Quijano and if he had given notice of breach to the retail seller, Carrasco Liquors, would that preserve his rights against the manufacturer, La Mancha Vineyards? See Danielkiewicz v. Whirlpool Corporation, 426 F.Supp.3d 426 (E.D. Mich. 2019).

2. Privity

Because suits on warranties are contract actions, the buyer must establish that there was in fact and in law a contract between the two parties. This "legal connection" is called *privity*. Where a buyer has purchased the goods directly from the retailer who gave the warranty, there is obviously privity between the two parties. Suppose, however, the warranty was made by the manufacturer, who sold to a wholesaler, who sold to a retailer, who sold to the buyer. If the buyer wishes to sue the manufacturer, the issue of lack of privity arises. At common law the manufacturer could successfully maintain a defense based on lack of privity, because the manufacturer did not deal directly with the buyer. The problem of how far back up the distribution chain the buyer can go is said to be an issue of *vertical privity*. To complicate matters, there is a second type of privity called *horizontal privity*. Horizontal privity deals with identifying to whom the retail seller is liable other than the immediate purchaser. The next Problem illustrates the difference.

PROBLEM 44

The Girard Instruments Corporation manufactured a pocket calculator called the Descartes 1000. It bought the paint used on the machine from the Hamilton Paint Company. Girard sold the calculators to the retailer, Leibnitz Department Store, which sold a calculator to Sylvester Cayley. He in turn gave it to his wife as a birthday gift. The Descartes 1000 was a popular gift. Joan Cayley used it all the time, as did the Cayley children (for homework) and even Mr. Gauss, the mailman, who borrowed it one day to compute the distance he walked on his route. After this last use, Mr. Gauss went home, where his dog, Diophantus, eagerly licked his hand and promptly dropped dead of lead poisoning. It turned out that the paint used on the Descartes 1000 had an extraordinarily high lead content. All the Cayleys and Mr. Gauss became very ill and, on recovery, brought suit for their pain and suffering, lost wages, medical expenses, and, in Mr. Gauss's case, the value of his dog. Whom should they sue?

The privity problem looks like the following diagram.

Hamilton Paint Co.

↕

Girard Inst. Corp.

↕

Leibnitz Dept. Store

↕

Sylvester Cayley ↔ Joan Cayley ↔ Children ↔ Mr. Gauss

The question "Can Mr. Gauss sue the Leibnitz Department Store?" is a question of horizontal privity. The question "Can Mr. Cayley sue the

Hamilton Paint Company?" is a question of vertical privity. The question "Can Mr. Gauss sue the Hamilton Paint Company?" is a question involving both horizontal and vertical privity.

If the Hamilton Paint Company had made express warranties (either in ads or in writings contained in the calculator box), most courts would have had no problem finding a cause of action in contract on the warranty in favor of anyone relying thereon. And if negligence could be proved (the doctrine of *res ipsa loquitur* helps here), a tort action was possible. Another theory Mr. Cayley (the retail buyer) could have tried, where no express warranty was involved, was that he was a third-party beneficiary of the implied warranties made in the sales between Hamilton and Girard and between Girard and Leibnitz. The other potential plaintiffs might also try the third-party beneficiary argument.

However, all these theories have technical, practical, or historical problems. Even with the doctrine of *res ipsa loquitur*, negligence can be hard to prove. Contract/warranty actions are bound by centuries of "no privity–no lawsuit" decisions. And, as we have seen, warranty suits have upheld requirements like that in §2-607(3)(a), *notice* within a reasonable amount of time (a requirement the mailman is not likely to meet even if his attorney remembers it).

The original 1962 version of the UCC had §2-318, which spoke in a limited fashion to the question of how much horizontal privity was excused under the Code. That version (now called Alternative A) protected the retail buyer's family and house guests from personal injury. Official Comment 3 to §2-318 invited the courts to extend warranty protection. But this version did not help the buyer's employees or casual bystanders, nor did it protect property losses (for example, the loss of the dog by Mr. Gauss). In 1966, the UCC's Permanent Editorial Board proposed two more versions of §2-318: Alternative B, which spoke to privity in terms of a foreseeable personal injury test, and Alternative C, which protected even property damage and nonnatural persons (for example, corporations). Read these versions and the Official Comments (especially Official Comment 3).

Does §2-318 restrict the limits of *vertical* privity so as to answer the question "Can Sylvester Cayley sue the Hamilton Paint Company?" See Official Comment 3 to §2-318, second sentence, and consider the following Problem.

PROBLEM 45

When Alan Turing needed a new computer he went to Big Sale Department Store and bought the Enigma 1000, the best selling computer on the market, made by Code Manufacturing Company. The computer worked well for a few months, but then had a spectacular electrical event that turned it into a useless piece of machinery and caused a fire, burning up much of Turing's office. Turing sued both Big Sale and Code Manufacturing, but the latter filed a motion for dismissal for lack of privity since it had no direct dealings with Alan Turing and had made no express warranty that the computer would be defect free to anyone. eCode Manufacturing also argued that any implied warranty of merchantability was only made to the retailer, Big Sale, with which it had direct dealings, and not to Turing, with whom it did not. The trial court bought these arguments and dismissed Code Manufacturing from the lawsuit. Is this right? Compare Hyundai Motor America, Inc. v. Goodin, 822 N.E.2d 947 (Ind. 2005) (no privity needed to sue manufacturer) with Curl v. Volkswagen of America, Inc., 114 Ohio St. 3d 266, 871 N.E.2d 1141 (2007) (manufacturer's implied warranty to retailer did not create necessary privity with buyer). Suppose you are the attorney for Big Sale. You are annoyed that your client really did nothing wrong except pass on a defective product from the manufacturer, but is nonetheless liable (due to a technicality—lack of privity—that this state stupidly adopts) to the consumer. Is there anything you can do to make Code Manufacturing interested in defending this lawsuit even if privity would otherwise protect it? See §2-607(5)(a).

Reed v. City of Chicago

United States District Court, Northern District of Illinois, 2003
263 F. Supp. 2d 1123

MORAN, Senior District Judge.

Plaintiff Ruby Reed brought this action against defendants City of Chicago (City), police officers Timothy Gould, Bruce Young, Brian Pemberton, and Susan Madison (officers), and Edwards Medical Supply, Inc. (Edwards), Cypress Medical Products, Ltd. and Cypress Medical Products, Inc. (together, Cypress), and Medline Industries (Medline) arising from her son's death in a Chicago jail cell. Defendant Cypress filed a motion to dismiss count VI of the complaint—breach of warranty—pursuant to Federal Rule of Civil Procedure 12 (b)(6). For the following reasons, Cypress' motion is denied.

BACKGROUND

Plaintiff Ruby Reed filed this suit as the special administrator of her son J.C. Reed's estate. On November 12, 2000, J.C. Reed (Reed) was allegedly arrested and brought to the City's Fifth District Police Station, where he was placed in a detention cell controlled and managed by the officers. The officers allegedly knew that Reed was mentally unstable, had witnessed him attempting suicide by slitting his wrists, and failed to adequately monitor the cell. The officers removed his clothing and provided him with a paper isolation gown. Plaintiff claims that Reed used this gown to hang himself, and that officers found him in the cell and failed to give him proper medical care, resulting in his death.

Plaintiff further alleges that the gown was manufactured and designed by defendants Edwards, Cypress and Medline, and that these defendants breached implied and express warranties when the gown failed to tear away when used by Reed in an attempt to hang himself.

Discussion

The single issue we must decide is whether plaintiff, as a non-purchaser, can recover from the manufacturer and designer of the gown for breach of warranty. Historically, Illinois law has required plaintiffs suing for breach of warranty to establish both horizontal and vertical privity.[45] [The court quotes Alternative A to §2-318, the version adopted in Illinois.— Eds.]

The Illinois Supreme Court has determined that the privity is no longer an absolute requirement for breach of warranty actions. Berry v. G.D. Searle & Co., 56 Ill. 2d 548, 309 N.E.2d 550 (Ill. 1974) (stating "privity is of no consequence when a buyer who purportedly has sustained personal injuries predicates recovery against a remote manufacturer for breach of an implied warranty under the code"); see also Suvada v. White Motor Co., 32 Ill. 2d 612, 210 N.E.2d 182 (Ill. 1965), *overruled on other grounds* (holding, prior to the enactment of the UCC in Illinois, that the privity requirement should be abolished in food and drug cases). While section 2-318 lists specific exceptions to the privity requirement, Illinois courts have noted that this list is not necessarily exhaustive. See Wheeler v. Sunbelt Tool Co., Inc., 181 Ill. App. 3d 1088, 1099, 537 N.E.2d 1332, 1340, 130 Ill. Dec. 863, 871 (1989); see also UCC §2-318, comment 3 (stating that "the section in this form is neutral and is not intended to enlarge or restrict the developing case law on whether the seller's warranties, given to his buyer who resells, extend to other persons in the distributive chain").

The vast majority of cases examining the limits of section 2-318 in Illinois have dealt with the employment context, expanding the class of potential breach of warranty plaintiffs to employees of the ultimate purchaser. [Citing cases.] In these cases courts have allowed employees to sue for breach of warranty despite a lack of horizontal privity.

In [Whitaker v. Lian Feng Mach. Co., 156 Ill. App. 3d 316, 509 N.E.2d 591 (1987)] plaintiff was injured while using a band-saw that had been purchased by his employer. . . . The court determined that section 2-318 does

45. Lack of vertical privity occurs when a consumer seeks to sue a remote manufacturer who was not involved in the sale to the consumer. Lack of horizontal privity occurs when a user of the product, beside the consumer, is injured. See Thomas v. Bombardier-Rotax Motorenfabrik, 869 F. Supp. 551, 557 n.7 (N.D. Ill. 1994).

not state any limitation on the rights of persons to recover for breach of warranty, nor does it differentiate between horizontal and vertical privity (id. at 593-94). It reasoned that the purpose of warranties is to determine what the seller has agreed to sell . . ., quoting UCC §2-313, comment 4. The employee was essentially a third-party beneficiary to the sale in that the employee's safety while using the bandsaw was "either explicitly or implicitly part of the basis of the bargain when the employer purchased the goods" (id. at 595). . . .

While no Illinois courts have expanded the plaintiff class for breach of warranty actions beyond employees, we believe that the law requires us to do so here. The beneficiary of any warranty made by the manufacturer and designer of the gown is necessarily a potentially suicidal detainee like Reed. If protection is not provided to plaintiffs like Reed, any warranty as to the safety of the gown would have little, if any, effect. In designing and manufacturing the gown, defendants contemplated that the users of the gown would be detainees. Moreover, the safety of these detainees was necessarily a part of the bargain, whether explicitly or implicitly, between the seller and buyer. For these reasons, a detainee of the City like Reed must be able to enforce the protections of any warranties made by the manufacturer and designer of the gown.

CONCLUSION

For the foregoing reasons, defendants' motion to dismiss count VI of the complaint is denied.

4. A Note on Strict Products Liability

About the same time that the UCC drafters were wrestling with §2-318, another legal revolution was occurring: the development of *strict products liability*. See W. Prosser, Torts 692 (5th ed. 1984). This concept has been described by Professor William Prosser as "a freak hybrid born of the illicit intercourse of tort and contract." Prosser, The Fall of the Citadel (Strict Liability to the Consumer), 50 Minn. L. Rev. 791, 800 (1966). Basically, strict products liability permits recovery by an injured consumer in a suit against the manufacturer as long as the consumer can prove that the manufacturer distributed into commerce a product that contained a dangerous defect. There is no necessity of proving either negligence or privity.

The primary source of the doctrine is §402A of the Restatement (Second) of Torts:

> *§402A Special Liability of Seller of Product for Physical Harm to User or Consumer*
>
> (1) One who sells any product in a defective condition unreasonably dangerous to the user or consumer or to his property is subject to liability

for physical harm thereby caused to the ultimate user or consumer, or to his property, if

(a) the seller is engaged in the business of selling such a product, and

(b) it is expected to and does reach the user or consumer without substantial change in the condition in which it is sold.

(2) The rule stated in Subsection (1) applies although

(a) the seller has exercised all possible care in the preparation and sale of his product, and

(b) the user or consumer has not bought the product from or entered into any contractual relation with the seller.

Strict products liability as a separate cause of action has been adopted by most (but not all) courts. Starting with Henningsen v. Bloomfield Motors, Inc., 32 N.J. 358, 161 A.2d 69 (1960), and proceeding through landmark opinions such as Greenman v. Yuba Power Prods., Inc., 59 Cal. 2d 57, 377 P.2d 897, 27 Cal. Rptr. 697 (1962); Seely v. White Motor Co., 63 Cal. 2d 9, 403 P.2d 145, 45 Cal. Rptr. 17 (1965); State ex rel. Western Seed Prod. Corp. v. Campbell, 250 Or. 262, 442 P.2d 215 (1968); and Kassab v. Central Soya, 432 Pa. 217, 246 A.2d 848 (1968), the courts have worked one by one what Prosser has called "the most rapid and altogether spectacular overturn of an established rule in the entire history of the law of torts." W. Prosser, Torts 690 (5th ed. 1984). A cause of action based on strict products liability is very similar to the UCC implied warranty of merchantability ("fitness for ordinary purpose" is only slight degrees away from freedom from "unreasonably dangerous" defects, the §402A test), and some courts have held the two doctrines are to be measured by the same rules as to privity and defenses. See, e.g., Gregory v. White Truck & Equip. Co., 163 Ind. App. 240, 323 N.E.2d 280 (1975) (held contributory negligence is not a defense in a §2-315 suit nor in a §402A suit unless it amounts to an assumption of the risk so that plaintiff proceeded to encounter a known danger); see also Annot., 4 A.L.R.3d 501, and Annot., 46 A.L.R.3d 240, on the defense of contributory negligence in warranty/products liability suits.

In 1997, the American Law Institute published a new Restatement, the Restatement (Third) of Torts: Products Liability, designed to update the law in this field. The new promulgation answers a host of questions that had been raised under old Restatement §402A, and is a lot more complicated than its predecessor. The primary change made by Restatement Third is that while it retains strict liability for manufacturing defects, it shifts to a negligence standard for design defects and injuries caused by failure to give a proper warning. See Restatement (Third) of Torts: Products Liability §2. For a summary of the new Restatement, see David G. Owen & Mary J. Davis, 1 Madden & Owen on Products Liability chs. 5-8 (2014). Courts have been split on whether to adopt the new Restatement. See, e.g., Bifolck v. Philip

Morris, Inc., 324 Conn. 402, 152 A.3d 1183 (2016) (declining to adopt the Restatement Third and noting broad disagreement among jurisdictions on whether to follow the Restatement Third).

Lincoln Company v. Detroit Diesel Corporation General Insurance

Supreme Court of Tennessee, 2009
293 S.W.3d 487

JANICE M. HOLDER, C.J.

* * *

FACTS AND PROCEDURAL HISTORY

Senators Rental, Inc. ("Senators Rental"), an insured of Lincoln General Insurance Company ("Lincoln General"), purchased a bus manufactured by Prevost Car (US) Inc. ("Prevost"). The engine in the bus was produced by Detroit Diesel Corporation ("Detroit Diesel"). On May 8, 2006, the bus was traveling south on Interstate 65 near Goodlettsville, Tennessee, when it caught fire due to an alleged engine defect. The fire did not cause personal injury or damage to any property other than the bus itself. Lincoln General paid Senators Rental $405,250 for the fire damage pursuant to its insurance policy.

Lincoln General filed a complaint against Prevost and Detroit Diesel. The complaint included counts of breach of express and implied warranties, negligence, and strict products liability. Prevost and Detroit Diesel removed the case to the United States District Court for the Middle District of Tennessee. Prevost filed a motion to dismiss for failure to state a claim pursuant to Federal Rule of Civil Procedure 12(b)(6), arguing that Lincoln General's tort claims are barred by the economic loss doctrine.

On July 1, 2008, the United States District Court certified one question of law to this Court, which we accepted pursuant to Tennessee Supreme Court Rule 23. . . .

ANALYSIS

The United States District Court certified the following question of law: Does Tennessee law recognize an exception to the economic loss doctrine under which recovery in tort is possible for damage to the defective product itself when the defect renders the product unreasonably dangerous and causes the damage by means of a sudden, calamitous event?

This certified question presupposes that Tennessee recognizes the economic loss doctrine, a judicially created principle that reflects an attempt to maintain separation between contract law and tort law by barring recovery in tort for purely economic loss. See generally, Vincent R. Johnson, The Boundary-Line Function of the Economic Loss Rule, 66 Wash. & Lee L. Rev. 523 (2009). Although this Court has never expressly adopted the economic loss doctrine, we expressed agreement with the policies underlying the doctrine in Ritter v. Custom Chemicides, Inc., 912 S.W.2d 128 (Tenn. 1995). In Ritter, this Court stated that "Tennessee has joined those jurisdictions which hold that product liability claims resulting in pure economic loss can be better resolved on theories other than negligence. . . . In Tennessee, the consumer does not have an action in tort for economic damages under strict liability." Id. at 133 (footnote omitted); see also First Nat'l Bank of Louisville v. Brooks Farms, 821 S.W.2d 925, 930-31 (Tenn. 1991) (finding that actions under the Tennessee Products Liability Act are limited to those brought on account of personal injury, death, or property damage and do not include actions brought for pecuniary loss).

The economic loss doctrine is implicated in products liability cases when a defective product damages itself without causing personal injury or damage to other property. In this context, "economic loss" is defined generally as "the diminution in the value of the product because it is inferior in quality and does not work for the general purposes for which it was manufactured and sold." Comment, Manufacturers' Liability to Remote Purchasers for "Economic Loss" Damages—Tort or Contract?, 114 U. Pa. L. Rev. 539, 541 (1966). Two types of economic loss, direct and consequential, occur when a defective product is damaged. See, e.g., Restatement (Third) of Torts: Products Liability §21, cmt. d (1998). Direct economic loss may be measured by the defective product's cost of repair or replacement. Id. Consequential economic losses, such as lost profits, result from the product owner's inability to use the product. Id.

The question certified presents us with our first opportunity to examine the proper application of the economic loss doctrine when only the defective product is damaged. In the seminal case of East River Steamship Corp. v. Transamerica Delaval, Inc., 476 U.S. 858, 868-71, 106 S. Ct. 2295, 90 L. Ed. 2d 865 (1986), the United States Supreme Court examined three approaches to the economic loss doctrine used by various state and federal courts, which it described as the "majority," "minority," and "intermediate" positions, and adopted the majority approach. In *East River*, a shipbuilder contracted with a manufacturer for the production of turbines to propel four oil-transporting super tankers. While at sea, the turbines malfunctioned due to design and manufacturing defects. Only the turbines themselves were damaged. In a unanimous decision, the Supreme Court held that the economic loss doctrine barred the shipbuilder's products liability suit in admiralty against the manufacturer.

In adopting the "majority approach" to the economic loss doctrine, the Supreme Court chose a bright-line rule that precludes recovery in tort when a product damages itself without causing personal injury or damage to other property. In reaching this conclusion, the Supreme Court observed that "[w]hen a product injures only itself the reasons for imposing a tort duty are weak and those for leaving the party to its contractual remedies are strong." Id. at 871, 106 S. Ct. 2295. Specifically, the Supreme Court reasoned that damage to a defective product is merely a failure of the product to meet the purchaser's expectations, a risk that the parties had the opportunity to allocate by negotiating contract terms and acquiring insurance. Id. at 871-72, 106 S. Ct. 2295. In contrast, the "'cost of an injury and the loss of time or health may be an overwhelming misfortune,' and one the person is not prepared to meet." Id. at 871, 106 S. Ct. 2295 (quoting Escola v. Coca Cola Bottling Co., 24 Cal. 2d 453, 150 P.2d 436, 441 (1944)). Finally, the Supreme Court expressed concern that permitting recovery in tort for purely economic loss could subject the manufacturer to an indefinite amount of damages. Id. at 874, 106 S. Ct. 2295. A warranty action, on the other hand, has a "built-in limitation on liability." Id.

In contrast, the "minority approach" to the economic loss doctrine permits tort recovery for purely economic loss. The Supreme Court explained that jurisdictions following the minority approach do not distinguish between economic loss and personal injury or property damage because in either circumstance, the damage was caused by the defendant's conduct. Id. at 869, 106 S. Ct. 2295; see *Farm Bureau Ins. Co.*, 878 S.W.2d at 743. In the minority view, the manufacturer's duty to produce non-defective products and tort law's corresponding concern with safety apply equally when the harm is purely economic. *E. River S.S. Corp.*, 476 U.S. at 868-69, 106 S. Ct. 2295; see *Thompson*, 647 P.2d. at 337. Ultimately, the Supreme Court rejected the minority approach because it "fails to account for the need to keep products liability and contract law in separate spheres and to maintain a realistic limitation on damages." *E. River S.S. Corp.*, 476 U.S. at 870-71, 106 S. Ct. 2295.

Lincoln General urges us to recognize a variation of the third approach to the economic loss doctrine, the "intermediate approach." States that follow the intermediate approach permit tort recovery for damage to the defective product alone under limited exceptions that "turn on the nature of the defect, the type of risk, and the manner in which the injury arose." Id. at 870, 106 S. Ct. 2295. The exception advanced by Lincoln General would permit recovery for unreasonably dangerous products that cause damage to themselves during sudden, calamitous events. This exception would require courts to distinguish between those products that expose a product owner to an unreasonable risk of injury during an abrupt and disastrous occurrence and those products that merely disappoint a product owner's expectations. See id. at 869-70, 106 S. Ct. 2295.

The *East River* Court rejected the dichotomy between disappointed and endangered product owners as "too indeterminate to enable manufacturers easily to structure their business behavior." Id. at 870, 106 S. Ct. 2295. The Court also found unpersuasive an exception that focuses on the manner in which the harm occurred:

> We realize that the damage may be qualitative, occurring through gradual deterioration or internal breakage. Or it may be calamitous. But either way, since by definition no person or other property is damaged, the resulting loss is purely economic. Even when the harm to the product itself occurs through an abrupt, accident—like event, the resulting loss due to repair costs, decreased value, and lost profits is essentially the failure of the purchaser to receive the benefit of its bargain—traditionally the core concern of contract law.

Id. (citations omitted).

We agree with the United States Supreme Court that the owner of a defective product that creates a risk of injury and was damaged during a fire, a crash, or other similar occurrence is in the same position as the owner of a defective product that malfunctions and simply does not work. It follows that the remedies available to these similarly situated product owners should derive from the parties' agreements, not from the law of torts, lest we disrupt the parties' allocation of risk. See Prosser & Keeton on the Law of Torts §101(3), at 709 (5th ed. 1984) ("[R]isk of harm to the product itself due to the condition of the product would seem to be a type of risk that the parties to a purchase and sale contract should be allowed to allocate pursuant to the terms of the contract."). To hold otherwise would make it more difficult for parties to predict the consequences of their business transactions, the cost of which ultimately falls on consumers in the form of increased prices. See *E. River S.S. Corp.*, 476 U.S. at 872, 106 S. Ct. 2295 ("The increased cost to the public that would result from holding a manufacturer liable in tort for injury to the product itself is not justified."); Bocre Leasing Corp. v. Gen. Motors Corp. (Allison Gas Turbine Div.), 84 N.Y.2d 685, 692, 621 N.Y.S.2d 497, 645 N.E.2d 1195 (1995) ("In essence, all consumers would subsidize or 'pay premiums' for purchasers of assertedly 'unduly dangerous' products.").

It is difficult, moreover, for parties and courts to apply a rule that focuses on the degree of risk and the manner in which the product was damaged as opposed to a rule that hinges on harm the plaintiff actually sustains. Lincoln General suggests, nonetheless, that adopting the bright-line rule espoused in *East River* would come at too great a price—the decreased safety of Tennessee citizens. We believe, however, that deterrence is adequately promoted by existing law that permits tort recovery for personal injury and damage to property other than the product itself. As explained by the Illinois Supreme Court, "[b]ecause no manufacturer can predict with any certainty that the damage his unsafe product causes will be confined to the product itself, tort liability will continue to loom as a possibility." Trans States Airlines v. Pratt & Whitney Can., Inc., 177 Ill. 2d 21, 224 Ill. Dec. 484, 682 N.E.2d 45, 53 (1997).

Finally, Lincoln General argues that adopting the *East River* approach is inconsistent with the General Assembly's intentions under the Tennessee Products Liability Act of 1978, Tenn. Code Ann. §§29-28-101 to 108 (2000). We disagree. Application of the Tennessee Products Liability Act is limited to "actions brought for or on account of personal injury, death or property damage." Tenn. Code Ann. §29-28-102(6) (emphasis added). We interpret "property damage" to mean damage to property other than the defective product. See Progressive Ins. Co. v. Gen. Motors Corp., 749 N.E.2d 484, 487-89 (Ind. 2001). A product's self-destruction is naturally understood as "economic loss" because it "is indistinguishable in consequence from the product's simple failure to function." *Progressive Ins. Co.*, 749 N.E.2d at 488. This Court previously held in *Ritter* that the Tennessee Products Liability Act does not afford the right to recover purely economic losses. 912 S.W.2d at 132-33; see also *First Nat'l Bank*, 821 S.W.2d at 931 ("[T]he rights and liabilities of parties to actions based on diminished economic expectations can be better adjudicated on other legal theories."); Olin Corp. v. Lambda Elecs., Inc., 39 F. Supp. 2d 912, 914 (E.D. Tenn. 1998). In the almost fourteen years since our decision in *Ritter*, the General Assembly has not amended the Tennessee Products Liability Act to permit claims for purely economic loss.

In our view, the *East River* approach fairly balances the competing policy interests and clearly delineates between the law of contract and the law of tort. We therefore hold that Tennessee law does not recognize an exception to the economic loss doctrine under which recovery in tort is possible for damage to the defective product itself when the defect renders the product unreasonably dangerous and causes damage by means of a sudden, calamitous event.

In so holding, we join the majority of state appellate courts that have considered the adoption of an exception to the economic loss doctrine based on unreasonably dangerous products; sudden, calamitous events; or both. [Citations omitted.]

Finally, our holding is consistent with the Restatement (Third) of Torts: Products Liability (1998). Section 21 specifically excludes harm to "the defective product itself" from the definition of "harm to persons or property" for which economic loss is recoverable. Comment (d) to section 21 further explains:

> A plausible argument can be made that products that are dangerous, rather than merely ineffectual, should be governed by the rules governing products

liability law. However, a majority of courts have concluded that the remedies provided under the Uniform Commercial Code—repair and replacement costs and, in appropriate circumstances, consequential economic loss—are sufficient. Thus, the rules of this Restatement do not apply in such situations.

Conclusion

In addressing the United States District Court's certified question, we are persuaded that the rationale proffered by the United States Supreme Court in *East River* is sound. We therefore hold that Tennessee does not recognize an exception to the economic loss doctrine under which recovery in tort is possible for damage to the defective product itself when the defect renders the product unreasonably dangerous and causes the damage by means of a sudden, calamitous event. The costs of this appeal are taxed to the respondent, Lincoln General Insurance Company, for which execution may issue if necessary.

Strict products liability suits are largely similar to implied warranty suits, though some courts struggle mightily to draw distinctions between the two causes of action; see Denny v. Ford Motor Co., 87 N.Y.2d 248, 662 N.E.2d 730 (N.Y. 1995). Typically, either a suit under §402A or a suit for breach of the implied warranty of merchantability can be a viable legal alternative under the same facts. There are some differences that are immediately visible:

(1) A §402A cause of action does not require notice; a UCC cause of action does. See §2-607(3)(a).
(2) In a §402A cause of action, damages are limited to those for physical injury; the damages in a UCC cause of action are not. See §2-715.
(3) A §402A cause of action has the statute of limitations imposed by state law for tort actions; the UCC action is governed by §2-725. The time periods may differ significantly.
(4) A §402A cause of action is not affected by disclaimers or remedy limitations; a UCC action may be so limited. See §§2-316, 2-719.
(5) Privity is not an issue in §402A suits; privity may be an issue in UCC suits.
(6) Section 402A requires that the product contain a "defect," but a UCC warranty may be breached even if the product is not defective. For example, a perfectly good product may neither fulfill the express warranty nor be fit for the particular purpose for which the buyer needs the goods. See Malawy v. Richards Mfg. Co., 150 Ill. App. 3d 549, 501 N.E.2d 376 (1986).

PROBLEM 46

The axle on Monty Python's new car snapped in two while he was driving at a high rate of speed on the interstate. Python's car skidded across the median and ran into a hitchhiker, Thumbs Bystander, killing him instantly. As Bystander's attorney, decide which is the best cause of action: negligence, §402A, or §2-314. Whom should you sue? See Martin v. Ryder Truck Rental, Inc., 353 A.2d 581 (Del. 1976).

E. UCC Warranties and the Magnuson-Moss Act

In 1975, Congress passed the Magnuson-Moss Warranty Act,[46] which applies to all consumer products manufactured after July 4, 1975, that are covered by a written warranty. Magnuson-Moss was enacted in response to many years of consumer complaints about warranties—in particular about manufacturers' statements that were labeled warranties, but that upon testing in the courts took away more rights than they gave. The stated purposes of the statute are to improve the adequacy of information available to consumers, to prevent deception, and to improve competition in the marketing of consumer products.[47] For a comprehensive study, see C. Reitz, Consumer Protection Under the Magnuson-Moss Warranty Act (1978).

To apply Magnuson-Moss, the warranty given must fall within its scope. Read Mag.-Moss §101,[48] and answer the following Problems.

PROBLEM 47

Attorney Sam Ambulance formed a professional corporation, Ambulance, LPC, under which he practices law. When the corporation buys a company car, is it entitled to the protection of the Magnuson-Moss Warranty Act? See §101(1) and (3).

46. The full name of the statute is the Magnuson-Moss Warranty—Federal Trade Commission Improvement Act, 15 U.S.C. §§2301-2312 (1975). Title I deals with consumer product warranties. Title II deals with Federal Trade Commission powers. Only Title I will be discussed in this text.

47. Title I, 15 U.S.C. §2302(a).

48. Citations styled Mag.-Moss § _____ refer to 15 U.S.C. §2301 et seq., Magnuson-Moss Warranty—Federal Trade Commission Improvement Act (1975). Note: section enumeration in textbooks is not always consistent with the enumeration in the U.S.C. In some texts, §2301 of the U.S.C. is labeled as §101, §2302 is labeled as §102, etc.

PROBLEM 48

(a) When Tom Jeffire bought his car from Sharp Sam's Used Car lot, Sam said, "I refuse to warrant my cars in any way." Is there a possible Magnuson-Moss action? See Mag.-Moss §102(b)(2). Is there a UCC warranty?

(b) When Michele Bean bought her car from Sharp Sam, she demanded that he warrant the car. Sam said, "I promise that this car has a sound engine that will last five years." Is there a possible Magnuson-Moss action? See Mag.-Moss §102(a). Is there a UCC warranty?

(c) When Norman Anderson bought his car from Sharp Sam, he demanded that Sam write down his warranty. Sam wrote the following: "I guarantee that the only person to ever own this car was a little old lady who only drove it to church every Sunday." If it turns out that in fact the car was owned by Hotdog Harry, a speedway racer, is there a possible Magnuson-Moss action? See Mag.-Moss §101(6). Is there a UCC warranty? See Skelton v. General Motors Corp., 500 F. Supp. 1181 (N.D. Ill. 1981).

(d) When Ann Leonard bought her car from Sharp Sam, she, too, demanded a written warranty. Before the sale Sam took her into his salesroom and pointed out two loose-leaf binders. Inside one of the binders under the model name of the car that Ann desired, Super Z, there was written the following statement:

The Super Z Has a Full Life-Time Guarantee.

Has Sam subjected himself to Magnuson-Moss? See Mag.-Moss §104. Is there a UCC warranty?

(e) Mammoth Motors phones you, its corporate counsel, and says that it has heard that two types of written warranties are possible under Magnuson-Moss: a *Full* (statement of duration, e.g., 1 year or 90 days) *Warranty* and a *Limited Warranty.* It is very proud of the performance of its vehicles and is considering giving the full warranty. What differences are there between the two types? See Mag.-Moss §§103, 104, 105, 108. What do you advise?

The most important intersection between the UCC and the Magnuson-Moss Act lies in the area of implied warranties. Read Mag.-Moss §108.

PROBLEM 49

Fenton Hardy bought a new car from Dixon Motors. The car carried a full three-month warranty, which guaranteed all the parts except the tires as defect-free. The warranty conspicuously stated that "this warranty is in lieu of all other warranties, express or implied, particularly the warranty of merchantability." One day after the three-month period expired, every part in the car (except the tires) malfunctioned. Hardy sued in state court using UCC §2-314 as his theory. Was the warranty disclaimer effective? See Mag.-Moss §108. Would it have been effective had Dixon offered only a "limited warranty"? See Mag.-Moss §108 again. In an action based on §2-314, may Hardy recover his attorney fees? See Mag.-Moss §110(d); Champion Ford Sales, Inc. v. Levine, 49 Md. App. 547, 433 A.2d 1218 (1981).

Pursuant to the Act's command, the Federal Trade Commission has promulgated rules to supplement the statute; see 16 C.F.R. §701 et seq. These regulations have delineated the precise information required for the §102 warranties, provided for presale availability of the warranty through signs or warranty binders to be kept at the place of sale, and specified the makeup and procedure to be followed by entities (called *mechanisms*) engaging in §110's informal settlement of disputes. The rules also call for mandatory language about protection of implied warranties, quoted in the second footnote of the next case, which must be included in warranty disclosures.

Ventura v. Ford Motor Corp.

New Jersey Superior Court, Appellate Division, 1981
180 N.J. Super. 45, 433 A.2d 801

BOTTER, J.

Ford Motor Company (Ford) appeals from the final judgment in this action in which plaintiff, the purchaser of a new 1978 Mercury Marquis Brougham, sued Ford's authorized dealer, Marino Auto Sales, Inc. (Marino Auto), and Ford, as manufacturer, for damages due to defects in the vehicle. Marino Auto cross-claimed against Ford for indemnification. The final judgment (a) granted plaintiff rescission of the purchase and damages of $6,745.59 against Marino Auto Sales (representing the purchase price of $7,847.49 less an allowance for plaintiff's use of the car and the sales tax), (b) awarded damages in favor of Marino Auto against Ford on the cross-claim in the sum of $2,910.59 (representing $6,745.59 less the resale value of the car), and (c) awarded counsel fees to plaintiff against Ford in the sum of $5,165. Plaintiff's demands for interest, punitive damages in excess of $2,000,000 and treble damages were denied. The trial court's published opinion was limited to the issue of counsel fees awarded under the

Magnuson-Moss Warranty—Federal Trade Commission Improvement Act, 15 U.S.C. §2301 et seq., 173 N.J. Super. 501 (Ch. Div. 1980).

Plaintiff took delivery of the automobile on April 12, 1978. According to the testimony of plaintiff and his wife they experienced engine hesitation and stalling problems early in their use of the car which continued without interruption despite repeated attempts by Marino Auto to cure the problem. Stanley Bednarz, Ford's zone service manager and mechanical specialist who assists dealers in satisfying customers, inspected the vehicle on July 13, 1978 and recommended replacing the exhaust regulator valve. Plaintiff testified that he was told by Bednarz that there was nothing wrong with the car and he would "have to live with this one." Plaintiff also testified that later in July 1978 he returned to Marino Auto intending to ask Mr. Marino to take the car back if it could not be fixed but that he was prevented from doing so and was forcibly removed from the premises. . . .

At the conclusion of plaintiff's case against Ford the trial judge announced his findings and conclusions that Ford had breached its warranty, that the car was substantially impaired because of persistent and continual stalling and hesitation, but that plaintiff had not proven damages against Ford. He held that the only remedy to which plaintiff was entitled was rescission or revocation of acceptance against Marino Auto, see §2-608; Herbstman v. Eastman Kodak Co., 68 N.J. 1, 9-10 (1975), except that plaintiff would also have a claim for attorney's fees against Ford under the Magnuson-Moss Warranty Act, supra, 15 U.S.C. §2310(d)(2). Various reasons were given for affording plaintiff the right to rescind the purchase and receive a refund of the purchase price from Marino Auto. At one point in his oral decision the trial judge alternatively relied upon the theory of strict liability in tort and breach of an implied warranty of merchantability and fitness. In his written opinion he stated that this result "pierced through the dealership system, granting rescission against the selling dealer Marino, based upon defects in breach of the manufacturer Ford's express warranty." 173 N.J. Super. At 504. He also said: "The only remedy under the Magnuson-Moss Warranty Act for Ford's violation of the act was rescission against the selling dealer Marino"; and he viewed Marino Auto as Ford's "authorized agent to remedy defects. . . ." Id. Punitive damages against Ford were denied because of the absence of "deliberate, willful, malicious fraud or wanton and gross negligence or unconscionable commercial practice. . . ." Thus, the case was continued to permit plaintiff to claim a refund of the purchase price, less an allowance for the use of the car, on a rescission basis against Marino Auto, and to permit Marino Auto to claim indemnification against Ford. Ford was to be afforded the opportunity to defend by establishing Marino Auto's fault in failing properly to repair the auto.

On the next trial date Marino Auto stipulated the sale of the car to plaintiff and seemingly conceded at one point that plaintiff would be entitled to a judgment against Marino Auto based on the finding of Ford's breach of warranty on the proofs offered by plaintiff against Ford. The issues to be tried, then, were declared to be damages on rescission or revocation of acceptance, §2-608, i.e., the purchase price less the value of the car to be returned to the dealer, minus an allowance for the limited use of the car. (There was evidence that plaintiff was financially compelled to continue to use the vehicle in its imperfect state. Upon the seller's breach the buyer has the right to "cover" by acquiring substituted goods but is not barred from any other remedy if he fails to effect "cover." Sections 2-711 and 712. See also §2-711(3) which gives the buyer a security interest in and the right to retain or resell goods after revocation of acceptance.) The case proceeded on the cross-claim although Ford contended that no claim ever could arise until plaintiff recovered a judgment against Marino Auto. On the assumption that proof of Ford's breach of an express warranty established plaintiff's right to recover against Marino Auto, 173 N.J. Super. at 503-504, the trial judge ordered the trial to proceed on Marino Auto's indemnification claim. Proof of plaintiff's damage claim was also anticipated before a final judgment was to be entered on the complaint and cross-claim.

Proofs were presented by Ford to show that the car was not defective and that there could be other causes for engine hesitation or stalling, such as contaminated fuel. Although Ford contends that Marino Auto was negligent in not checking the fuel system, there was no proof that contaminated fuel was the actual cause of the problem. Thus, there was no proof that the defect in the vehicle would have been discovered but for Marino Auto's lack of reasonable care in attempting to repair the car. Marino Auto cannot be denied indemnification because it failed to successfully diagnose the cause of the problem. Ford's expert could find nothing wrong with the car, and, on the facts of this case the trial judge could properly have rejected Ford's contention that Marino Auto was at fault for not correcting it, regardless of where the burden of proving Marino Auto's negligence was placed.

At the conclusion of this testimony Marino Auto contended that there was no proof of any wrongdoing by Marino Auto and no basis for rescission. However, Marino Auto also claimed indemnification from Ford for any damage award granted to plaintiff against Marino Auto. Ford contended that no judgment should be entered against Marino Auto, that there was no basis for rescission and therefore no need for indemnification. Ford also protested the lack of sufficient notice of plaintiff's complaints about the car's performance.

We have considered the merits of this appeal on the assumption that, although Marino Auto has not appealed the judgment against it, Ford can contend that no judgment should have been entered against Marino Auto. Ford has an interest in the judgment against Marino Auto since it was the basis for Ford's indemnification obligation. In fact, the trial judge did consider Ford's arguments against Marino Auto's liability to plaintiff.

Our reasoning through the body of law applicable to this commonplace contractual skein, which binds consumers, car dealers and manufacturers together, differs from that of the trial judge. But we affirm plaintiff's recovery. We conclude that, despite Marino Auto's attempted disclaimer of all warranties, plaintiff can recover from Marino Auto for the breach of implied warranty of merchantability. We also uphold the award of counsel fees against Ford pursuant to the Magnuson-Moss Warranty Act.

The contract of sale between Marino Auto and plaintiff conspicuously contained the following legend on its face:

> The seller, MARINO AUTO SALES, Inc., hereby expressly disclaims all warranties, either expressed or implied, including any implied warranty of merchantability or fitness for a particular purpose, and MARINO AUTO SALES, Inc., neither assumes nor authorizes another person to assume for it any liability in connection with the sale of the vehicle.

On the back of this sales order-contract were the following terms which were made part of the contract:

> 7. It is expressly agreed that there are no warranties, express or implied, made by either the selling dealer or the manufacturer on the motor vehicle, chassis or parts furnished hereunder except, in the case of a new motor vehicle the warranty expressly given to the purchaser upon the delivery of such motor vehicle or chassis.
>
> The selling dealer also agrees to promptly perform and fulfill all terms and conditions of the owner service policy.

For the purpose of this opinion we will assume that the disclaimer of implied warranties of merchantability and fitness was effective under the Uniform Commercial Code §2-316. Since the dealer passed on to the purchaser a warranty from the manufacturer, we will not consider whether the attempted disclaimer by Marino Auto should be voided as unconscionable and contrary to public policy under §2-302 even though such disclaimer could foreclose rescission or other remedies against the dealer and, without privity between buyer and manufacturer, rescission has been held ordinarily unavailable under the Code against the manufacturer. Edelstein v. Toyota Motors Distributors, 176 N.J. Super. 57, 64 (App. Div. 1980); see Henningsen v. Bloomfield Motors, Inc., 32 N.J. 358, 372-373, 406-408 (1960); Gladden v. Cadillac Motor Car Div., 83 N.J. 320, 330-331 (1980); Herbstman v. Eastman Kodak Co., supra, 68 N.J. at 9-10; cf. Santor v. A. & M. Karagheusian, Inc., 44 N.J. 52 (1965). Section 2-316(1) provides that "words or conduct tending to negate or limit warranty shall be construed wherever reasonable as consistent with each other; but subject to the provisions of this Chapter on parol or extrinsic evidence (§2-202) negation or limitation is inoperative to the extent that such construction is unreasonable." It may be argued that the dealer's conduct in transmitting Ford's warranty to plaintiff, the reference to such warranty in paragraph 7 on the back of the purchase order-contract, and the undertaking "to promptly perform and fulfill all terms and conditions of the owner service policy," are inconsistent with a disclaimer of all warranties and that such a disclaimer is an unreasonable construction. See Gladden v. Cadillac Motor Car Div., supra, 83 N.J. at 330; Henningsen v. Bloomfield Motors, Inc., supra, 32 N.J. at 407-408; cf. Murray v. Holiday Rambler, Inc., 83 Wis. 2d 406, ___, 265 N.W.2d 513, 519 (Sup. Ct. 1978). The contract in the *Henningsen* case contained the identical obligation to perform all terms and conditions of the owner service policy. Id. The combination of the dealer's undertaking and the automobile manufacturer's warranty was interpreted in *Henningsen* to rebut the disclaimer of implied warranty of merchantability by the dealer. The court held that the attempt to limit liability to the replacement of defective parts was contrary to public policy and void with respect to a claim for personal injuries resulting from an accident caused by defects in an automobile. However, we need not explore these issues further because the Magnuson-Moss Warranty Act has solved many of the problems posed by the intricacies confronting consumers under the pre-existing law of sales.

The Magnuson-Moss Warranty—Federal Trade Commission Improvement Act, supra, was adopted on January 4, 1975, 88 Stat. 2183. Its purpose was to make "warranties on consumer products more readily understandable and enforceable." Note, 7 Rutgers-Camden L.J. 379 (1976). The act enhances the consumer's position by allowing recovery under a warranty without regard to privity of contract between the consumer and warrantor, by prohibiting the disclaimer of implied warranties in a written warranty, and by enlarging the remedies available to a consumer for breach of warranty, including the award of attorneys' fees. Id. The requirement of privity of contract between the consumer and the warrantor has been removed by assuring consumers a remedy against all warrantors of the product.[49] A consumer is defined in 15 U.S.C. §2301(3) as follows:

> (3) The term "consumer" means a buyer (other than for purposes of resale) of any consumer product, any person to whom such product is transferred

49. In Miller and Kanter, "Litigation Under Magnuson-Moss: New Opportunities in Private Actions," 13 U.C.C. L.J. 10, 21-22 (1980), the authors discuss the broad definition of a *consumer* and state that "an assumption is now created that no privity restriction exists."

during the duration of an implied or written warranty (or service contract) applicable to the product, and any other person who is entitled by the terms of such warranty (or service contract) or under applicable State law to enforce against the warrantor (or service contractor) the obligations of the warranty (or service contract).

A "supplier" is defined as any person engaged in the business of making a consumer product directly or indirectly available to consumers, §2301(4), and a "warrantor" includes any supplier or other person who gives or offers to give a written warranty or who is obligated under an implied warranty. §2301(5). The term "written warranty" is defined in §2301(6) to include:

(A) any written affirmation of fact or written promise made in connection with the sale of a consumer product by a supplier to a buyer which relates to the nature of the material or workmanship and affirms or promises that such material or workmanship is defect free or will meet a specified level of performance over a specified period of time, or

(B) any undertaking in writing in connection with the sale by a supplier of a consumer product to refund, repair, replace or take other remedial action with respect to such product in the event that such product fails to meet the specifications set forth in the undertaking.

The Magnuson-Moss Warranty Act provides for two types of written warranties on consumer products, those described as "full" warranties and those described as "limited" warranties. 15 U.S.C. §2303. The nature of the "full" warranty is prescribed by §2304. It expressly provides in subsection (a)(4) that a consumer must be given the election to receive a refund or replacement without charge of a product or part which is defective or malfunctions after a reasonable number of attempts by the warrantor to correct such condition. For the breach of any warranty, express or implied, or of a service contract (defined in 15 U.S.C. §2301(8)), consumers are given the right to sue for damages and "other legal and equitable relief afforded under state or federal law, 15 U.S.C.A. §2310(d); 15 U.S.C. §2311(b)(1).

Appellant Ford contends that the trial judge improperly invoked section 2304 of the act as a basis for allowing "rescission" in the case since the warranty given by Ford was a limited warranty and not a full warranty. 15 U.S.C. §2303(a)(2) provides that all warranties that do not meet federal minimum standards for warranty contained in §2304 shall be conspicuously designated a "limited warranty." "Limited warranties" protect consumers by prohibiting disclaimers of implied warranties, §2308, but are otherwise not described in the act. Note, supra 7, Rutgers-Camden L.J. at 381. Clearly, Ford's warranty, which is quoted later in this opinion, was a limited warranty.

15 U.S.C. §2308 provides as follows:

> (a) No supplier may disclaim or modify (except as provided in subsection (b) of this section) any implied warranty to a consumer with respect to such consumer product if (1) such supplier makes any written warranty to the consumer with respect to such consumer product, or (2) at the time of sale, or within 90 days thereafter, such supplier enters into a service contract with the consumer which applies to such consumer product.
>
> (b) For purposes of this chapter (other than section 2304(a)(2) of this title), implied warranties may be limited in duration to the duration of a written warranty of reasonable duration, if such limitation is conscionable and is set forth in clear and unmistakable language and prominently displayed on the face of the warranty.
>
> (c) A disclaimer, modification, or limitation made in violation of this section shall be ineffective for purposes of this chapter and State law.

We will first consider the application of this act to the dealer, Marino Auto. As quoted above, paragraph 7 of the purchase order-contract provides that there are no warranties, express or implied, made by the selling dealer or manufacturer except, in the case of a new motor vehicle, "the warranty expressly given to the purchaser upon delivery of such motor vehicle. . . ." This section also provides: "The selling dealer also agrees to promptly perform and fulfill all terms and conditions of the owner service policy." Ford contended in the trial court that Marino Auto had "a duty" to properly diagnose and make repairs, that such duty was "fixed both by the express warranty . . . which they passed on . . . and by the terms of [paragraph 7 of the contract with plaintiff]" by which Marino Auto expressly undertook "to perform its obligations under the owner service policy." See 15 U.S.C. §2310(f); 16 C.F.R. §700.4 (1980). The provision in paragraph 7 in these circumstances is a "written warranty" within the meaning of §2301(6)(B) since it constitutes an undertaking in connection with the sale to take "remedial action with respect to such product in the event that such product fails to meet the specifications set forth in the undertaking. . . ." In our view the specifications of the undertaking include, at the least, the provisions of the limited warranty furnished by Ford, namely:

> LIMITED WARRANTY (12 MONTHS OR 12,000 MILES/19,312 KILOMETRES) 1978 NEW CAR AND LIGHT TRUCK
>
> Ford warrants for its 1978 model cars and light trucks that the Selling Dealer will repair or replace free any parts, except tires, found under normal use in the U.S. or Canada to be defective in factory materials or workmanship within the earlier of 12 months or 12,000 miles/19,312 km from either first use or retail delivery.
>
> All we require is that you properly operate and maintain your vehicle and that you return for warranty service to your Selling Dealer or any Ford or

Lincoln-Mercury Dealer if you are traveling, have moved a long distance or need emergency repairs. Warranty repairs will be made with Ford Authorized Service or Remanufactured Parts.

THERE IS NO OTHER EXPRESS WARRANTY ON THIS VEHICLE.[50]

The record does not contain a written description of the "owner service policy" which the dealer agreed to perform. Nevertheless, since Ford is the appellant here, we take its contentions at trial and documents in the record to establish the dealer's obligation to Ford and to plaintiff to make the warranty repairs on behalf of Ford (subject to the right of reimbursement or other terms that may be contained in their agreement). For the purpose of this appeal we are satisfied that the dealer's undertaking in paragraph 7 constitutes a written warranty within the meaning of 15 U.S.C. §2301(6)(B). Accordingly, having furnished a written warranty to the consumer, the dealer as a supplier may not "disclaim or modify [except to limit in duration] any implied warranty to a consumer. . . ." The result of this analysis is to invalidate the attempted disclaimer by the dealer of the implied warranties of merchantability and fitness. Being bound by those implied warranties arising under state law, §§2-314 and 315, Marino Auto was liable to plaintiff for the breach thereof as found by the trial judge, and plaintiff could timely revoke his acceptance of the automobile and claim a refund of his purchase price. §§2-608, 2-711. Zabriskie Chevrolet, Inc. v. Smith, 99 N.J. Super. 441 (L. Div. 1968). In this connection we note that the trial judge found that plaintiff's attempted revocation of acceptance was made in timely fashion, and that finding has adequate support in the evidence.

As the trial judge noted, 15 U.S.C. §2310(d)(1) provides that a consumer who is damaged by the failure of a warrantor to comply with any obligation under the act, or under a written warranty or implied warranty or service contract, may bring suit "for damages and other legal and equitable relief. . . ." Although the remedy of refund of the purchase price is expressly

50. The warranty also provided:

TO THE EXTENT ALLOWED BY LAW:

1. ANY IMPLIED WARRANTY OF MERCHANTABILITY OR FITNESS IS LIMITED TO THE 12 MONTH OR 12,000-MILE/19,312-KM DURATION OF THIS WRITTEN WARRANTY.

2. NEITHER FORD NOR THE SELLING DEALER SHALL HAVE ANY RESPONSIBILITY FOR LOSS OF USE OF THE VEHICLE, LOSS OF TIME, INCONVENIENCE, COMMERCIAL LOSS OR CONSEQUENTIAL DAMAGES.

Some states do not allow limitations on how long an implied warranty lasts or the exclusion or limitation of incidental or consequential damages, so the above limitations may not apply to you.

This warranty gives you specific legal rights, and you also may have other rights which vary from state to state.

provided by the Magnuson-Moss Warranty Act for breach of a full warranty, granting this remedy under state law for breach of a limited warranty is not barred by or inconsistent with the act. 15 U.S.C. §2311(b)(1) provides that nothing in the act restricts "any right or remedy of any consumer under State law or other Federal law." See also 15 U.S.C. §2311(c)(2). Thus, for breach of the implied warranty of merchantability, plaintiff was entitled to revoke acceptance against Marino Auto, and a judgment for the purchase price less an allowance for the use of the vehicle was properly entered against Marino Auto. Sections 2-608 and 711. Cf. 15 U.S.C. §2301(12) which defines "refund" as the return of the purchase price "less reasonable depreciation based on actual use where permitted" by regulations.

Plaintiff also could have recovered damages against Ford for Ford's breach of its written limited warranty. Marino Auto was Ford's representative for the purpose of making repairs to plaintiff's vehicle under the warranty. See Henningsen v. Bloomfield Motors, Inc., supra, 32 N.J. at 374; cf. Conte v. Dwan Lincoln-Mercury, Inc., 172 Conn. 112, ___, 374 A.2d 144, 149-150 (Sup. Ct. 1976). The limited warranty expressly required the purchaser to return the vehicle "for warranty service" to the dealer or to any Ford or Lincoln-Mercury dealer if the purchaser is traveling or has moved a long distance or needs emergency repairs. Ford contends that it put purchasers on notice that they should advise Ford's district office if they have problems with their cars that a dealer is unable to fix. The record contains a document listing "frequently asked warranty questions" which states:

> The Dealership where you purchased your vehicle has the responsibility for performing warranty repairs; therefore, take your vehicle to that Dealership. . . .
>
> If you encounter a service problem, refer to the service assistance section of your Owner's Guide for suggested action.

We do not read these provisions as requiring notice to Ford as a condition of relief against Ford when Ford's dealer has failed after numerous attempts to correct defects under warranty. . . .

One question posed by this case is whether recovery of the purchase price from the manufacturer was available to plaintiff for breach of the manufacturer's warranty. If the warranty were a full warranty plaintiff would have been entitled to a refund of the purchase price under the Magnuson-Moss Warranty Act. Since Ford's warranty was a limited warranty we must look to state law to determine plaintiff's right to damages or other legal and equitable relief. 15 U.S.C. §2310(d)(1). Once privity is removed as an obstacle to relief we see no reason why a purchaser cannot also elect the equitable remedy of returning the goods to the manufacturer who is a warrantor and claiming a refund of the purchase price less an allowance for use of the product. See Seely v. White Motor Co., 45 Cal. Rptr. 17, ___, 403 P.2d 145, 148 (Sup. Ct. 1965); Durfee v. Rod Baxter Imports, Inc., supra, 262 N.W.2d at 357-358, where the Minnesota Supreme Court held as a matter of state law that lack of privity does not bar a purchaser of a foreign car from revoking acceptance and recovering the purchase price from the distributor of such cars as distinguished from the local dealer. The decision was made without regard to the Magnuson-Moss Warranty Act.

We are dealing with the breach of an express contractual obligation. Nothing prevents us from granting an adequate remedy under state law for that breach of contract, including rescission when appropriate. Under state law the right to revoke acceptance for defects substantially impairing the value of the product (§2-608) and to receive a refund of the purchase price (§2-711) are rights available to a buyer against a seller in privity. Where the manufacturer gives a warranty to induce the sale it is consistent to allow the same type of remedy as against that manufacturer. See Durfee v. Rod Baxter Imports, Inc., supra; cf. Seely v. White Motor Co., supra. Only the privity concept, which is frequently viewed as a relic these days, Koperski v. Husker Dodge, Inc., 208 Neb. 29, ___, 302 N.W.2d 655, 664 (Sup. Ct. 1981); see Kinlaw v. Long Mfg. N.C., Inc., 298 N.C. 494, 259 S.E.2d 552 (Sup. Ct. 1979), has interfered with a rescission-type remedy against the manufacturer of goods not purchased directly from the manufacturer. If we focus on the fact that the warranty creates a direct contractual obligation to the buyer, the reason for allowing the same remedy that is available against a direct seller becomes clear. Although the manufacturer intended to limit the remedy to the repair and replacement of defective parts, the failure of that remedy, see §2-719(2); Goddard v. General Motors Corp., 60 Ohio St. 2d 41, 396 N.E.2d 761 (Sup. Ct. 1979); Seely v. White Motor Co., supra, and the consequent breach of the implied warranty of merchantability which accompanied the limited warranty by virtue of the Magnuson-Moss Warranty Act, make a rescission-type remedy appropriate when revocation of acceptance is justified. Durfee v. Rod Baxter Imports, Inc., supra, 262 N.W.2d at 357.

Lastly, we consider Ford's contention that a counsel fee was improperly granted to plaintiff since no judgment was entered in favor of plaintiff against Ford and Ford contends it was not given adequate notice of the defects in the car. 15 U.S.C. §2310(d)(2) provides that a consumer who "prevails in any action brought [in any court] under paragraph (1) of this subsection . . . may be allowed by the court to recover as part of the judgment . . . expenses (including attorneys' fees based on the actual time expended). . . ." This section is subject to the provisions contained in §2310(e). Subsection (e) provides that, with certain exceptions, no action based upon breach of a written or implied warranty or service contract may be prosecuted unless a person obligated under the warranty or service contract "is afforded a reasonable opportunity to cure such failure to comply." Here that opportunity was given to Ford's designated representative to whom the purchaser was required to bring the car. A direct employee of Ford, Bednarz, also met with plaintiff or his wife and was made aware of some difficulty with the car. We are not certain of the extent of Ford's knowledge of those difficulties. However, in our view the opportunities given to Marino Auto to repair the vehicle satisfied the requirements of 15 U.S.C. §2310(e) in this case.

As noted, Ford also contends that a counsel fee could not be awarded against Ford because plaintiff did not recover a judgment against Ford. The Magnuson-Moss Warranty Act permits a prevailing consumer to recover attorney's fees "as part of the judgment." The trial judge found that Ford had breached its warranty and that the car's value was substantially impaired. He entered no damage judgment against Ford. However, in the absence of proof of actual damages, plaintiff was entitled to a judgment against Ford for nominal damages. Ruane Dev. Corp. v. Cullere, 134 N.J. Super. 245, 252 (App. Div. 1975); Ench v. Bluestein, 52 N.J. Super. 169, 173-174 (App. Div. 1958); Winkler v. Hartford Accident and Indem. Co., 66 N.J. Super. 22, 29 (App. Div.), *cert. den.*, 34 N.J. 581 (1961); Packard Englewood Motors, Inc. v. Packard Motor Car Co., 215 F.2d 503, 510 (3d Cir. 1954). Ford was not prejudiced by the failure of the trial judge to enter a judgment for nominal damages to which the award of attorney's fees could be attached. See Nobility Homes, Inc. v. Ballentine, 386 So. 2d 727, 730-731 (Sup. Ct. Ala. 1980). The award of counsel fees fulfills the intent of the Magnuson-Moss Warranty Act. Without such an award consumers frequently would be unable to vindicate warranty rights accorded by law.

As to the amount of counsel fees allowed by the trial judge, we find no abuse of discretion. The allowance was for actual time spent at an hourly rate of $75.00. Consideration could properly be given to the fact that plaintiff's attorney undertook this claim on a contingency basis with a relatively small retainer. D.R. 2-106(A)(8). The normal breach of warranty case ought not require four separate appearances before the trial court. To some extent this was not in the control of plaintiff's attorney; and plaintiff might have obtained all the relief required against Ford on the first day of trial. But it did not work out that way. In other cases it may be possible to stipulate damages and simplify the issues, thus limiting the cost of this type of litigation for consumers and suppliers alike. But the issues raised in this case were novel in this state, and no one can be faulted for the difficulty and time consumed in this litigation. . . .

Affirmed.

At one point in its opinion the court says that the Magnuson-Moss Act does away with the requirement of privity. That was certainly the intention of the drafters, who wanted a broad statute that would give consumers an effective remedy against any entity warranting a product sold to them that breached the warranties provided either by the law or the contract.

PROBLEM 50

When consumer Alan Turing learned of a new computer called "The Quantum" manufactured by Bletchley Corporation, he bought one from Morcom Electronics, a local store in his city. The Quantum worked well for a while but then exploded one day when Turing was sitting at it, putting him in the hospital and burning down a portion of his house. Bletchley Corporation had issued a written Limited Warranty for the Quantum promising that it would be defect free for one year, and limiting the implied warranty of merchantability to the same period. When Turing comes to your office for legal advice he has done some research and has a number of questions.

(a) May he use the Magnuson-Moss Act to sue Morcom Electronics? The retail contract conspicuously disclaimed all warranties, mentioning merchantability especially. Morcom made no express warranties when it sold him the product, but merely passed on the one given by Bletchley. Study the language of §110(d)(1) carefully. He wants to use the federal statute because it provides him with attorney fees. See McNamara v. Nomero, 26 F. Supp. 2d 1168 (D. Minn. 1998) (no, since that section applies only to the entity that gave an express warranty).

(b) In the jurisdiction that Turing lives in, the state courts have always said that privity is required before a consumer can sue the manufacturer, though Magnuson-Moss had not been enacted when those decisions were decided. Does the statute now mandate that the state courts must allow the direct suit against Enigma Corporation?

It was clear that Congress thought it was abolishing privity when it passed the Magnuson-Moss Act, but the courts have divided on that question. A splendid law review article written by Professor Janet Stevenson, The Unfulfilled Promise of the Magnuson-Moss Warranty Act, 18 Lewis & Clark L. Rev. 155 (2014), lists the decisions going each way and explains that those finding that lack of privity can still block suits against the manufacturer are wrong. However, until the United States Supreme Court takes up the question (which it has never done) and holds that the states can't circumvent the clear intention of Congress by this route, those decisions cause many consumers with defective products to have no remedy at all if the retailer either made no warranties or is judgment-proof. In some states the manufacturer is liable for express warranties made on the product on the theory that this creates sufficient privity with the eventual purchaser, but even in those jurisdictions some courts will not extend this same logic to create privity for breach of implied warranties. Does this make sense? Is it good policy for these jurisdictions to protect manufacturers but not retailers from implied warranties? In warranties suits who should bear the ultimate responsibility for a product that won't work?

F. Warranties and Article 2A

The warranty rules for the lease of goods found in Article 2A are, with minor variations, mere carbon copies of the Article 2 rules. There is one major difference, however, which arises in what Article 2A calls a "finance lease."

PROBLEM 51

Chemicals of Tomorrow Corp. decided that the safest way to work with hazardous materials was through the use of an advanced robot. It persuaded Aurora Robotics, Inc., to design a robot that would meet its needs. To finance the purchase of the robot, Chemicals of Tomorrow went to Octopus National Bank, which bought the robot from Aurora Robotics and then leased it to Chemicals of Tomorrow. The robot was subject to both express and implied warranties, which became important when the robot ran amok in one of Chemicals of Tomorrow's laboratories and caused extensive damage. Answer these questions:

(a) Is this a "finance lease"? What factors do and do not influence this decision? See §2A-103(1)(g) and its Official Comment (g); Information Leasing Corp. v. King, 155 Ohio App. 3d 201, 800 N.E.2d 73 (2003). As the leasing officer for the bank, what steps would you have recommended to make sure that a court would hold that this lease so qualified? See Construction Resources Group, LLC v. Element Fin. Corp., 2017 WL 2266894 (W.D. Okla. 2017).

(b) What name does Article 2A give to Aurora Robotics in this situation? See §2A-103(1)(x).

(c) Does Chemicals of Tomorrow Corp. have the benefit of whatever warranties Aurora gave to Octopus National? See §2A-209 and its Official Comment.

(d) Is Octopus National Bank responsible for breach of the implied warranty of merchantability? See §2A-212.

(e) If Octopus National's leasing officer had told Chemicals of Tomorrow's president, "We have investigated this robot, and I guarantee you it will cause you no trouble," must the lessor then respond in a warranty lawsuit to a claim for damages? See §2A-210 and Official Comment (g), third paragraph, to §2A-103.

(f) The lease between Octopus National Bank and Chemicals of Tomorrow contained a clause stating that the lessee had to pay the lessor even if the goods did not work, a "hell or high water" clause, so called because the lessee binds itself to pay the lessor no matter what happens in connection with the performance of the leased goods. After the robot ruins the laboratory, must Chemicals of Tomorrow nonetheless pay Octopus National Bank? See §2A-407 and its Official Comment. Would we reach the same result if the lessee were a consumer?

Information Leasing Corporation v. GDR Investments, Inc., d/b/a/ Pinnacle Exxon

Court of Appeals of Ohio, 2003
152 Ohio App. 3d 260, 787 N.E.2d 652

GORMAN, Judge.

[¶1] The plaintiff-appellant, Information Leasing Corporation ("ILC"), appeals from the order of the trial court rendering judgment in favor of the defendants-appellees, GDR Investments, d.b.a. Pinnacle Exxon, and Avtar S. Arora, in an action to recover $15,877.37 on a five-year commercial lease of an Automated Teller Machine ("ATM"). In its sole assignment of error, ILC argues that the trial court's judgment constituted "an abuse of discretion" because it failed to address the effect of [§2A-103(A)(7)] on the issue of GDR's liability under the lease. For the following reasons, we reverse and remand this cause to the trial court.

[¶2] This is one of many cases involving ILC that have been recently before this court. ILC is an Ohio corporation wholly owned by the Provident Bank. ILC is in the business of leasing ATMs through a third party, or vendor. In all of these cases, the vendor has been a third-party corporation, JRA 222, Inc., d.b.a. Credit Card Center ("CCC"). CCC was in the business of finding lessees for the machines and then providing the services necessary to operate them, offering the lessees attractive commissions. Essentially, CCC would find a customer, usually a small business interested in having an ATM available on its premises, arrange for its customer to sign a lease with ILC, and then agree to service the machine, keeping it stocked with cash and paying the customer a certain monthly commission. Usually, as in the case of GDR, the owner of the business was required to sign as a personal guarantor of the lease. The twist in this story is that CCC soon went bankrupt, leaving its customers stuck with ATMs under the terms of leases with ILC but with no service provider. Rather than seeking to find another company to service the ATMs, many of CCC's former customers, like GDR, simply decided that they no longer wanted the ATMs and were no longer going to make lease payments to ILC.

[¶3] The terms of each lease, however, prohibited cancellation. The pertinent section read, "LEASE NON-CANCELABLE AND NO WARRANTY. THIS LEASE CANNOT BE CANCELED BY YOU FOR ANY REASON, INCLUDING EQUIPMENT FAILURE, LOSS OR DAMAGE. YOU MAY NOT REVOKE ACCEPTANCE OF THE EQUIPMENT. YOU, NOT WE, SELECTED THE EQUIPMENT AND THE VENDOR. WE ARE NOT RESPONSIBLE FOR EQUIPMENT FAILURE OR THE VENDOR'S ACTS. YOU ARE LEASING THE EQUIPMENT 'AS IS', [sic] AND WE DISCLAIM ALL WARRANTIES, EXPRESS OR IMPLIED. WE ARE NOT RESPONSIBLE FOR SERVICE OR REPAIRS."

[¶4] Either out of a sense of fair play or a further desire to make enforcement of the lease ironclad, ILC put a notice on the top of the lease that stated, "NOTICE: THIS IS A NON-CANCELABLE, BINDING CONTRACT. THIS CONTRACT WAS WRITTEN IN PLAIN LANGUAGE FOR YOUR BENEFIT. IT CONTAINS IMPORTANT TERMS AND CONDITIONS AND HAS LEGAL AND FINANCIAL CONSEQUENCES TO YOU. PLEASE READ IT CAREFULLY; FEEL FREE TO ASK QUESTIONS BEFORE SIGNING BY CALLING THE LEASING COMPANY AT 1-513-421-9191."

[¶5] Arora, the owner of GDR, was a resident alien with degrees in commerce and economics from the University of Delhi, India. Arora wished to have an ATM on the premises of his Exxon station in the hope of increasing business. He made the mistake of arranging acquisition of the ATM through CCC. According to his testimony, a representative of CCC showed up at the station one day and gave him "formality papers" to sign before the ATM could be delivered. Arora stated that he was busy with other customers when the CCC representative asked him to sign the papers. He testified that when he informed the CCC representative that he needed time to read the documents before signing them, he was told not to worry and, in effect, given the CCC representative's word that the papers did not need his attention and that his signature was a mere formality. Arora signed the ILC lease, having never read it.

[¶6] Within days, CCC went into bankruptcy. Arora found himself with an ATM that he no longer wanted. Although the testimony was spotty, it appears that he never attempted to look for another service provider. According to his testimony, he tried unsuccessfully to contact ILC to take back the ATM. Soon Arora suffered a mild heart attack, the gas station went out of business, and the ATM, which had been in place for approximately eighteen days, was left sitting in the garage, no longer in use until ILC came and removed it several months later.

[¶7] Unfortunately for Arora, the lease also had an acceleration clause that read, "DEFAULT. If you fail to pay us or perform as agreed, we will have the right to (i) terminate this lease, (ii) sue you for all past due payment AND ALL FUTURE PAYMENTS UNDER THIS LEASE, plus the Residual Value we have placed on the equipment and other charges you owe us, (iii) repossess the equipment at your expense and (iv) exercise any other right or remedy which may be available under applicable law or proceed by court act."

[¶8] The trial court listened to the evidence in this case, which was awkwardly presented due in large part to Arora's decision to act as his own trial counsel. Obviously impressed with Arora's honesty and sympathetic to his situation, the trial court found that Arora owed ILC nothing. In so ruling, the court stated that ILC "ha[d] not complied with any of its contractual obligations and that [Arora] appropriately canceled any obligations by him, if there really were any." The court also found that ILC, "if they did have a contract, failed to mitigate any damages by timely picking up the machine after [Arora] gave them notice to pick up the machine."

[¶9] In its assignment of error, ILC asserts that the trial court "abused its discretion" by not applying [§2A-103(1)(g)]. Initially we note that the assignment is miscast, as it actually challenges the judgment as being contrary to law, not an abuse of discretion. The decision whether to apply the correct law to the case is, thankfully, not a matter of judicial discretion. This aside, we turn our attention to the Uniform Commercial Code and the world of lease financing.

[¶10] ILC contends, and we do not disagree, that the lease in question satisfied the definition of a "finance lease" under the UCC. See [§2A-103(1)(g)]. A finance lease is considerably different from an ordinary lease in that it adds a third party, the equipment supplier or manufacturer (in this case, the now defunct CCC). As noted by White and Summers, "In effect, the finance lessee * * * is relying upon the manufacturer * * * to provide the promised goods and stand by its promises and warranties; the [lessee] does not look to the [lessor] for these. The [lessor] is only a finance lessor and deals largely in paper, rather than goods." 1 White & Summers, Uniform Commercial Code (3d Ed. 1988) 20.

[¶11] One notorious feature of a finance lease is its typically noncancelable nature, which is specifically authorized by statute. [§2A-407(A)] provides in the case of a finance lease that is not a consumer lease, "[T]he lessee's promises under the lease contract become irrevocable and independent upon the lessee's acceptance of the goods." The same statutory section also makes clear that the finance lease is "not subject to cancellation, termination, modification, repudiation, excuse, or substitution without the consent of the party to whom it runs." [§2A-407(2)(b)].

[¶12] Because of their noncancelable nature, finance leases enjoy somewhat of a reputation. The titles of law review articles written about them reveal more than a little cynicism regarding their fairness: Strauss,

Equipment Leases Under U.C.C. Article 2A—Analysis and Practice Suggestions. U.C.C. Revisions: Promises and Pitfalls (1992), 43 Mercer L. Rev. 853; King, Major Problems with Article 2A: Unfairness, Cutting Off Consumer Defenses, Unfiled Interest and Uneven Adoption (1992), 43 Mercer L. Rev. 869; Breslauer, Finance Lease, Hell or High Water Clause and Third Party Beneficiary Theory in Article 2A of the Uniform Commercial Code (1992), 77 Cornell L. Rev. 318; Heckman, Article 2A of the Uniform Commercial Code: Government of the Lessor, by the Lessor, and for the Lessor (1992), 36 S. & L.U.L.J. 303.

[¶13] The "hell or high water clause" referred to in one of these titles makes the lessee's obligations to the lessor survive no matter what—come hell or high water. As described by Professors White and Summers, "The parties can draft a lease agreement that carefully excludes warranty and promissory liability of the finance lessor to the lessee, and that sets out what is known in the trade as a 'hell or high water clause,' namely, a clause that requires the lessee to continue to make rent payments to the finance lessor even though the [equipment] is unsuitable, defective, or destroyed." 1 White & Summers, supra, at 20. To offset this one-sidedness, the lessee is generally considered a third-party beneficiary of any warranties between the manufacturer and the lessor. Id. In short, the lessor is merely a disinterested provider of financing. As White and Summers describe the relationship, "The lessor's responsibility is merely to provide the money, not to instruct the lessee like a wayward child concerning a suitable purchase * * *. Absent contrary agreement, even if[, for example, a finance-leased] Boeing 747 explodes into small pieces in flight and is completely uninsured, lessee's obligation to pay continues." Id. at 25.

[¶14] Although fortunately not finding himself in the same situation as the hypothetical, Arora did find himself with an ATM that he did not want, and for which he felt he had no use after CCC dropped out of the picture. Some people complain about being stuck with the bill; Arora's complaint was that he was stuck with the ATM.

[¶15] Initially, we reject the trial court's analysis, which was that ILC did not satisfy its contractual obligations. This was an obvious error. ILC's only contractual obligation was to provide the ATM, which it did. Clearly ILC had an expectancy interest of $15,877.73 that it would lose if the lease were not enforced. We must reject also the trial court's doubts about whether Arora had any obligations under the lease—clearly he did—as well as the court's assertion that he "appropriately cancelled any obligations by him"—a statement that seems to willingly ignore the noncancelable nature of the lease.

[¶16] To begin the proper legal analysis, we note first that this was not a "consumer lease" expressly excepted from [§2A-407(A)]. A "consumer lease" is defined in [§2A-103(1)(e)] as one in which the lessee is "an individual and who takes under the lease primarily for a personal, family, or household purpose." This would definitely not apply here, where the ATM was placed on the business premises of the Exxon station, and where the lessee was GDR Investments and not Arora individually. (Arora was liable individually as the personal guarantor of GDR's obligations under the lease.)

[¶17] Even commercial finance leases, however, are subject to certain defenses, including lack of acceptance and unconscionability. It is noteworthy that ILC argues that Arora irrevocably accepted the ATM by merely signing a certificate of acceptance. (ILC also indicates in its brief that five payments were made on the lease, but it is unclear from the record who made these payments and when.) According to the UCC, however, in the case of finance leases, acceptance occurs only after the lessee has been given a reasonable time to inspect the goods and either (1) signifies acceptance, (2) fails to make an effective rejection, or (3) does any act that signifies acceptance. [§2A-515(A)]. The requirement that the lessee be given a reasonable time cannot be circumvented. "Taking possession of the goods is not determinative of acceptance, nor is the signing of a form of acceptance before receipt of the goods, nor the making of a lease payment." Colonial Pacific Leasing Corp. v. J.W.C.J.R. Corp. (Utah App. 1999), 977 P.2d 541, 545. "A 'reasonable time to inspect' under the UCC must allow an opportunity to put the product to its intended use, or for testing to verify its capability to perform as intended." Capitol Dodge Sales v. Northern Concrete Pipe (1983), 131 Mich. App. 149, 158, 346 N.W.2d 535. See also, Tri-Continental Leasing Corp. v. Law Office of Richard W. Burns (Tex. App. 1985), 710 S.W.2d 604, and Horrocks v. Westfalia Systemat (Utah App. 1995), 892 P.2d 14.

[¶18] Although it was available as a defense, it does not appear that Arora was entitled to claim a valid rejection of the goods in this case. [§2A-509(1)] applies the UCC's "perfect tender" rule to finance leases, allowing the lessee to reject any goods that "fail in any respect to conform to the lease contract." Nothing in the record, however, indicates that Arora rejected the ATM because of its nonconformity, i.e., its failure to work mechanically as intended. Rather, the record demonstrates quite clearly that he rejected it only because he no longer wanted an ATM after CCC went bankrupt. Although the UCC adopts the "perfect tender" rule, it does not adopt the "perfectly happy tenderee" rule.

[¶19] Certain defenses do remain, however. First, the UCC expressly allows for the application of the doctrine of unconscionability to finance leases, both consumer and commercial. [UCC §2A-108authorizes the trial court to find "any clause of a lease contract to have been unconscionable at the time it was made * * *." If it so finds, the court is given the power to "refuse to enforce the lease contract, * * * enforce the remainder of the lease contract without the unconscionable clause, or * * * limit the application of the unconscionable clause as to avoid any unconscionable result." Id.

[¶20] In this case, the trial court made no findings as to whether the finance lease was unconscionable. The primary purpose of the doctrine of unconscionability is to prevent oppression and unfair surprise. Calamari & Perillo, Contracts (3d Ed. 1982), Section 9-40. "Oppression" refers to substantive unconscionability and arises from overly burdensome or punitive terms of a contract, whereas "unfair surprise" refers to procedural unconscionability and is implicated in the formation of a contract, when one of the parties is either overborne by a lack of equal bargaining power or otherwise unfairly or unjustly drawn into a contract. Id. at Sections 9-37 and 9-38.

[¶21] It should be pointed that, although harsh, many characteristics of a finance lease are not inherently unconscionable and, as we have discussed, are specifically authorized by statute. Simply because a finance lease has a "hell or high water clause" does not make it unconscionable. As noted, a finance lease is a separate animal—it is supposed to secure minimal risk to the lessor. At least one court has rejected the argument that an acceleration clause in a commercial finance lease is punitive and unconscionable in the context of parties of relatively equal bargaining power. See Emlee Equip. Leasing Corp. v. Waterbury Transmission, Inc. (1993), 31 Conn. App. 455, 468, 626 A.2d 307.

[¶22] At the heart of Arora's defense in this case was his claim that he was misled into signing the finance lease by the CCC representative and was unfairly surprised to find himself the unwitting signatory of an oppressive lease. This is clearly an argument that implicated procedural unconscionability. His claim of being an unwitting signatory, however, must be carefully balanced against the law in Ohio that places upon a person a duty to read any contract before signing it, a duty that is not excused simply because a person willingly gives into the encouragement to "just go ahead and sign." See Whelan v. E.F. Hutton Credit Corp. (1983), 8th Dist. No. 46724, 1983 WL 2923.

[¶23] Moreover, we note that courts have also recognized that the lessor may give, through word or conduct, the lessee consent to cancel an otherwise noncancelable lease. [§2A-407(2)(b)] makes a finance lease "not subject to cancellation, termination, modification, repudiation, excuse, or substitution *without the consent of the party to whom it runs.*" (Emphasis supplied.) As noted by the court in *Colonial Pacific Leasing,* supra, the UCC does not say anything with respect to the form or content of the consent. 977 P.2d at 548. The *Colonial Pacific* court concluded, therefore, "that the consent may be oral and may be established by conduct that reasonably manifests an intent. * * * Any manifestations that the obligation of the lessee will not be enforced independently of the obligation that runs to the consenting party is sufficient." Id. The question whether consent has been given to a cancellation is a question of fact for the trier of fact. Id.

[¶24] We raise this point because the evidence indicates that there was some communication between Arora and ILC before ILC retrieved the ATM. It is unclear whether ILC removed the ATM at Arora's request, or whether the company was forcibly repossessing the equipment pursuant to the default provision of the lease. In view of the murkiness of the testimony, it is unclear when the ATM was taken back and when the final lease payment was made. One interesting question that arises from ILC's retrieval of the ATM, not addressed in the record, is what ILC did with the equipment afterward. Did ILC warehouse the equipment for the next four and one-half years (conduct that would appear unprofitable and therefore unlikely) or did the company then turn around and lease the ATM to someone else? If there was another lease, was ILC actually seeking a double recovery on the ATM's rental value? In this regard, we note that the trial court ruled that ILC had failed to mitigate its damages, a finding that is not supported by the current record, but may well prove to be true upon further trial of the matter.

[¶25] In sum, this is a case that requires a much more elaborate presentation of evidence by the parties, and much more detailed findings of fact and conclusions of law than those actually made by the trial court. We sustain ILC's assignment of error upon the basis that the trial court did not apply the correct legal analysis, and that the evidence of record did not mandate a judgment in Arora's favor. Because of the number of outstanding issues and unresolved factual questions, we reverse the trial court's judgment and remand this case for a new trial consistent with the law set forth in this opinion.

Judgment reversed and cause remanded.

G. Warranties in International Sales

The warranty provisions of the CISG for the international sale of goods are very similar to the UCC rules. The major difference is not one of substance, but one of terminology: the treaty drafters, wanting to write on a clean slate, eschewed use of the term *warranty* and all the historical baggage that comes with it. Read Articles 35 to 44 of the Convention, and see whether you can nevertheless find within them counterparts to the following:

(a) a warranty of title;

(b) express warranty liability; and

(c) implied warranties of merchantability and/or fitness for a particular purpose.

How are warranties disclaimed under the treaty? See Articles 6 and 35.

CHAPTER 4 REVIEW QUESTIONS

How does a seller's status as merchant affect warranties?
When are express and implied warranties created?
How can a seller disclaim implied warranties? Express warranties?
What is the difference between basis of the bargain and reliance?
What is the consequence of failing to give notice of breach of warranty?
How does the Magnuson-Moss Act affect warranty law?

ASSESSMENT: MULTIPLE CHOICE QUESTIONS

1. Barnet burglarized Alban's home and stole a painting, *Blue Memphis.* Finchley Gallery innocently bought the painting from Barnet and sold it to Totteridge. Alban managed to track the painting down and demanded it back. Is Alban entitled to the painting?
   a. No, because Totteridge bought the painting in good faith with no notice that it was stolen.
   b. No, because Alban and Totteridge had no contract with each other to rescind.
   c. Yes. The entrustment doctrine does not protect Totteridge, because Alban did not entrust the painting to Finchley Gallery.
   d. Yes. "Buyer Beware" governs sales law.

2. Is Totteridge entitled to recover from Finchley Gallery?
   a. No. Totteridge has not been harmed, because Totteridge is entitled to keep the painting.
   b. No. "Buyer Beware" governs sales law.
   c. Yes. Finchley Gallery breached the warranty of title.
   d. Yes. Finchley Gallery defrauded Totteridge.

3. Euston visited Pemulis Auto looking for a sports car. The sales person showed Euston a 2001 Hal Roadster, telling Euston that the Roadster had a top speed of 120 m.p.h. The manager, however, advised Euston that the car was not that speedy and that the sales person was misguided. Euston purchased the car, signing a contract with a merger clause and clause conspicuously stating that the car was sold "AS IS, with no warranties whatsoever." The car disappointed Euston, who found it was capable of 120 m.p.h. only when going steeply downhill. Was there a breach of warranty?
   a. No, due to the exclusion of warranties.
   b. No, because the top speed of the car was not an express warranty.
   c. No, because warranties must be in writing.
   d. Yes, because express warranties are not excluded by language to the contrary.

4. When Pemulis Auto decided to close one of its sales locations, it got a visit from the manager of a competitor, Stice Auto. The manager purchased Pemulis Auto's computer system. Within a week, the system burned up due to a faulty microchip. Did Pemulis Auto breach any warranty?
   a. Pemulis Auto breached the implied warranty of merchantability, because Pemulis Auto is a merchant and the computer system was defective.
   b. Pemulis Auto breached an express warranty, because the system had a latent defect.
   c. Pemulis Auto breached the warranty of fitness for a particular purpose, because Pemulis Auto knew that Stice Auto desired a functional computer system.
   d. Pemulis Auto did not breach any warranty.

5. Joelle's stay at the Ennet Hotel is marred by bedbugs. When the hotel refused to refund her payment, she sued for breach of the implied warranty of merchantability under §2-314. Will she succeed?
   a. Yes, because a hotel room with bed bugs is not merchantable.
   b. No. As long as someone could stay overnight in the room, it was merchantable.
   c. No, because there was no express warranty about bed bugs.
   d. No, because the Ennet Hotel did not make a warranty under §2-314.

ANSWERS

1. *C* is the best answer. The entrustment doctrine does not apply, because Alban did not entrust the painting to a merchant. Rather, Barnet stole the painting from Alban. So Barnet did not have title to the painting or the power to give title to Finchley Gallery. Likewise, when Finchley Gallery sold the painting, Totteridge received only Finchley Gallery's interest in the painting, which was nothing. *A* is wrong, because a good faith buyer does not take priority over the interest of the owner, unless something like the entrustment doctrine applies. *B* is wrong, because Alban is not trying to rescind a contract, Alban is simply seeking return of Alban's property.
2. *C* is the best answer. Although Totteridge must return the painting to Alban, Totteridge is entitled to recover from Finchley Gallery for breach of the warranty of title. Under §2-312, a seller warrants that the seller that rightful title will be conveyed. Finchley Gallery breached the warranty, because it did not have title to the goods or power to transfer title. Contrary to *B*, "Buyer Beware" no longer governs sales law. Rather, sellers make the warranties created by Article 2, unless excluded. Finchley Gallery did not intend to deceive, so it did not defraud Totteridge. But warranty is breached even if the seller does not know of the defect.

3. *B* is the best answer. The question illustrates the basic practical rule for express warranties: the only way to exclude an express warranty is not to make it. An exclusion of warranty will not exclude express warranties, because any inconsistent language is inoperative to exclude the express warranty. Nor need warranties be in writing, contrary to *C.* But here Pemulis Auto took steps to avoid any representation about the top speed of the car becoming an express warranty. An express warranty is an affirmation of fact that is part of the basis of the bargain of the parties. Pemulis Auto advised Euston that the car was not capable of 120 m.p.h. The contract also included a merger clause, indicating the oral statements were not part of the agreement.
4. *D* is the best answer. Pemulis Auto did not make an implied warranty of merchantability, because Pemulis Auto was not a merchant with respect to computer systems. Pemulis Auto did not make any express warranties, because it made no representations about the computer system. Pemulis Auto did not make a warranty of fitness for a particular purpose, because Stice Auto was not relying on Pemulis Auto's skill or judgment to select suitable goods.
5. *D* is the best answer. The question reminds us that UCC Article 2 applies only to sales of goods. This was a contract for services, lodging at a hotel. Article 2 does not apply, so §2-314 does not apply.

CHAPTER 5

TERMS OF THE CONTRACT

Most law students do not come to the study of law with experience in dealing with commercial matters. This chapter will in part rectify that by exposing you to legal terminology used in trade and to practices that the Uniform Commercial Code deals with by specific rules. We begin with how the law fills in missing terms in contracts, then move on to the regulation of unfair bargaining practices, and finally to how the law determines which goods are meant for the contract at issue and how it distributes unexpected losses (such as destruction of the goods).

I. FILLING IN THE GAPS

In the nineteenth and early twentieth centuries, if the parties left a major term out of the contract, the courts typically found no legally enforceable agreement. Judges declared themselves powerless to "make a contract for the parties." As the twentieth century progressed, the courts became more willing to save the contract by implying reasonable terms where possible.

The drafters of the Code fueled this practice by giving the courts statutory guidance in their gap-filling role. Glance through §§2-305 to 2-311.

PROBLEM 52

Edwin Drake wrote to the Watsons Flat Motor Oil Company and said that he wanted to buy 100 cases of its motor oil, some cases to be Type A (the expensive oil) and some to be Type B (a cheaper kind). He said he would let the company know later how much he wanted of each type. The company told him that Type B was selling for $30 a case, but that since the price of Type A was fluctuating, the sale price would have to be set by the company at the time of delivery. Drake agreed. The parties signed a written contract for the delivery of 100 cases, types to be specified by Drake one week prior to the delivery date, which was set for April 8. On April 1, the agent of the oil company called Drake to ask how much he would take of each type. Drake said, "April Fool! I'm not taking any," and hung up the phone. The company calls you, its attorney, for advice. In the past dealings that it has had with Drake, he always has ordered 100 cases and has taken 50 to 65 percent in Type A and the rest in Type B. The usual price for Type A has been $50 a case, but due to a Middle East oil situation, the price has now jumped to $125 a case. What should the company do? See §§2-305, 2-311, 1-205; Citgo Petroleum Corporation v. US Lubes, LLC, 2014 WL 3887773 (E.D. Pa. 2014). If this were an international sale of goods under the CISG, what result? See Article 65. What if Drake had simply said, "April Fool!" and hung up? Is this a definite repudiation? See §§2-610, 2-611. What action can the oil company take to clear up Drake's ambiguous statement? Read §2-609 and its Official Comment; see Pittsburgh-Des Moines Steel Co. v. Brookhaven Manor Water Co., 532 F.2d 572 (7th Cir. 1976). Would a seller have the right to adequate assurance of performance, if shortly before making the goods seller learned that buyer had a poor history of paying sellers? Starchem Laboratories, LLC v. Kabco Pharmaceuticals, Inc., 988 N.Y.S.2d 525 (2014).

Section 1-304 provides that every contract or duty within the Uniform Commercial Code "imposes an obligation of good faith in its performance and enforcement." Many of the UCC provisions specifically require good faith. Good faith is defined in §1-201(b)(20) to include a subjective component ("honesty in fact") and an objective component ("observance of reasonable commercial standards of fair dealing."). Courts often struggle to determine whether good faith limits a party's ability to enforce the literal terms of the contract and the relevant provisions of the UCC.

Casserlie v. Shell Oil Company

Supreme Court of Ohio, 2009
121 Ohio St. 3d 25, 902 N.E.2d 1

Moyer, C.J.

I

Appellants' proposition of law proposes that "[t]he definition of Good Faith under the [Uniform Commercial Code] incorporating an 'honesty in fact' component requires a subjective inquiry." We disagree and affirm the judgment of the court of appeals.

II

Appellants, Donald Casserlie and others, are a group of independent Shell lessee-dealers in the greater Cleveland area (collectively, "the dealers"). The appellees in this case are Shell Oil Company, its partners, and its successors (collectively, "Shell"), who at various times between 1995 and the time the complaint was filed sold Shell-branded gasoline to the dealers in the greater Cleveland area. The dealers leased gas stations, including equipment and land, from Shell and operated them as franchisees. The parties' contracts obligated the dealers to buy gasoline only from Shell at a wholesale price set by Shell at the time of delivery. This type of term in a contract is known as an open-price term.

The price paid by the dealers is referred to as the dealer-tank-wagon ("DTW") price because it includes the cost of delivery to the stations. Shell charged the dealers a DTW price that was based on market factors including the prices offered by its major competitor, British Petroleum ("BP"), and the street price within areas of Cleveland. In each area of the city, called a price administration district ("PAD"), Shell charged all dealers the same DTW price.

In 1998, Shell, Texaco, and Saudi Aramco formed Equilon Enterprises L.L.C.; Shell's agreements with service stations in Cleveland were assigned to Equilon. In November 1999, Equilon and appellee Lyden Company entered into a joint venture called True North Energy, L.L.C. True North became the distributor of Shell-branded gasoline in the Cleveland area, including to the stations operated by the dealers. True North set the DTW price as the wholesale price it had paid Equilon for gasoline plus six or seven cents per gallon.

Shell also sold gasoline to "jobbers," which were independent companies operating non-Shell-owned gas stations. Jobbers purchased gasoline directly at the oil company's terminal and paid the "rack" price, which was the cost of purchasing gasoline at the oil company's terminal and thus did not include delivery costs.

In 1999, the dealers filed suit against Shell, alleging, among other claims, that Shell had engaged in bad faith when it set the DTW price. The dealers alleged that the rack price was often substantially lower than the DTW price. This allowed jobbers, including Lyden Company, to offer wholesale DTW prices that were substantially lower than the DTW price charged to the dealers. The dealers contend that this pricing is unreasonable and is part of a marketing plan proposed by Shell that was designed to drive them out of business. The dealers assert that Shell's goal was to eliminate them so that Shell could take over operation of the gas stations, thus profiting from all of the sales, including nonfuel sales, at the stations, and not just from wholesale gasoline sales to and rental income from the dealers.

The parties agreed to bifurcate the proceedings and move forward only on the bad-faith claim. On April 13, 2005, the trial court granted summary judgment for Shell. The court found that Shell did not violate R.C. 1302.18, which codifies Uniform Commercial Code ("UCC") section 2-305 and requires a price to be fixed in good faith, when it set the DTW price and that the dealers had not proven that the price had been set in a commercially unreasonable manner.

The dealers appealed, arguing that bad faith may be shown either by evidence of a party's intent, a subjective standard, or by evidence of its commercial unreasonableness, which is an objective standard. The court of appeals affirmed the trial court's ruling and adopted an objective standard based on Tom-Lin Ents. v. Sunoco, Inc. (R&M) (C.A.6, 2003), 349 F.3d 277. The court determined that the dealers failed to show that Shell's prices were not commercially reasonable. The cause is before this court upon our acceptance of a discretionary appeal.

III

As a preliminary matter, we review de novo the granting of summary judgment. Comer v. Risko, 106 Ohio St. 3d 185, 2005 Ohio 4559, 833 N.E.2d 712, ¶8.

The parties agree that Shell has authority pursuant to the dealer agreements to set the price of gasoline at the time of delivery. They agree that the price must be set subject to R.C. 1302.18, which requires the price to be "reasonable." R.C. 1302.18(A). Pursuant to R.C. 1302.18(B) (UCC section 2-305(2)), the price must be set "in good faith." "Good faith" is defined generally as "honesty in fact in the conduct or transaction concerned," R.C. 1301.01(S), but in the case of a merchant, "'good faith' . . . means honesty in fact and the observance of reasonable commercial standards of fair dealing in the trade." R.C. 1302.01(A)(2). It is undisputed that Shell is a "merchant," as defined in R.C. 1302.01(A)(5).

Shell argues that good faith requires an objective inquiry and is demonstrated when a seller's price is within the range of its competitors and the seller has not discriminated between similarly situated buyers. Shell also contends that "an inquiry into the seller's subjective intent is neither permitted nor required." The dealers argue that good faith requires a subjective inquiry and ask, "[H]ow can an open price, specifically calculated to drive a contractual partner out of business, be a 'good faith' price."

The trial court and court of appeals agreed with Shell, relying on *Tom-Lin Enters.*, 349 F.3d 277. In *Tom-Lin*, the court confronted an agreement nearly identical to the one between the dealers and Shell and concluded, applying Ohio law, that an inquiry into good faith required "an objective analysis of the merchant-seller's conduct." (Emphasis sic and footnote omitted.) Id. at 281-282. Thus, neither the trial court nor the court of appeals considered whether an examination into "good faith" required a subjective inquiry, and neither court engaged in a subjective inquiry.

It is not disputed that the latter half of the definition of good faith, "the observance of reasonable commercial standards of fair dealing in the trade," requires only an objective analysis. The issue before us is whether there is room for a subjective inquiry within the honesty-in-fact analysis in these circumstances. . . .

Official Comment 3 to UCC section 2-305 does provide some guidance. That comment provides, in full:

"[UCC section 2-305(2)], dealing with the situation where the price is to be fixed by one party rejects the uncommercial idea that an agreement that the seller may fix the price means that he may fix any price he may wish by the express qualification that the price so fixed must be fixed in good faith. Good faith includes observance of reasonable commercial standards of fair dealing in the trade if the party is a merchant. (Section 2-103 [R.C. 1302.01]). But in the normal case a 'posted price' or a future seller's or buyer's 'given price,' 'price in effect,' 'market price,' or the like satisfies the good faith requirement."

Comment 3 explains that the purpose of R.C. 1302.18(B) is to restrict the price a seller or buyer may set when the contract price has been left open, by requiring the price to be fixed in good faith. The second sentence of the comment does not remove honesty in fact from the definition of good faith in this context, because it uses the nonexclusive term "includes." The last sentence, however, is not limited to part of the good-faith definition but rather provides a safe harbor where a "posted price" satisfies good faith in its entirety.

A number of cases from other jurisdictions considering open price terms have relied on the posted-price comment. This court has noted in the past that "it is desirable to conform our interpretations of the Uniform Commercial Code to those of our sister states." Edward A. Kemmler Mem. Found. v. 691/733 E. Dublin-Granville Rd. Co. (1992), 62 Ohio St. 3d 494, 499, 584 N.E.2d 695. Relying on the Official Comments to the UCC helps to achieve this uniformity, as does reviewing case law that has previously interpreted particular provisions.

The Supreme Court of Texas addressed the very issue before us here in an essentially identical fact pattern in Shell Oil Co. v. HRN, Inc. (Tex. 2004), 144 S.W.3d 429. Independent gasoline dealers brought suit against Shell, alleging that the prices were not set in good faith under UCC section 2-305(2) because Shell had set the prices intending to put them out of business. 144 S.W.3d 429, 431-432. The court held that Shell did not violate its duty of good faith, because the posted price was both commercially reasonable and nondiscriminatory. Id. at 435-436. It noted that "'[i]t is abundantly clear . . . that the chief concern of the UCC Drafting Committee in adopting § 2-305(2) was to prevent discriminatory pricing.'" Id. at 434, quoting *Wayman*, 923 F. Supp. at 1346-1347. A subjective good-faith inquiry "injects uncertainty into the law of contracts and undermines one of the UCC's primary goals—to 'promot[e] certainty and predictability in commercial transactions.'" Id. at 435, quoting Am. Airlines Emps. Fed. Credit Union v. Martin (Tex. 2000), 29 S.W.3d 86, 92, quoting Putnam Rolling Ladder Co., Inc. v. Mfrs. Hanover Trust Co. (1989), 74 N.Y.2d 340, 349, 547 N.Y.S.2d 611, 546 N.E.2d 904. The drafters of the UCC, therefore, incorporated the posted-price safe harbor to prevent extensive litigation involving any open-price term, "while seeking 'to avoid discriminatory prices.'" Id., quoting Malcolm, The Proposed Commercial Code: A Report on Developments from May 1950 Through February 1951 (1951), 6 Bus. Law. 113, 186. The court concluded that subjective intent was not intended to stand alone as a basis for liability: "[A]llegations of dishonesty under this section must also have some basis in objective fact which at a minimum requires some connection to the commercial realities of the case." Id. at 435-436.

A few cases note the posted-price comment but conclude that it does not provide a safe harbor where there is subjective bad faith. See Marcoux v. Shell Oil Prods. Co. L.L.C. (C.A.1, 2008), 524 F.3d 33, 50; *Mathis*, 302 F.3d at 455-456; Bob's Shell, Inc. v. O'Connell Oil Assoc., Inc. (Aug. 31, 2005), D. Mass. No. 03-30169, 2005 U.S. Dist. LEXIS 21318, 2005 WL 2365324; see also Allapattah Servs., Inc. v. Exxon Corp. (S.D. Fla. 1999), 61 F. Supp. 2d 1308, 1322 (finding that when the seller double charged for credit-card processing, the action was not a "normal case," because the dispute was not over the actual price charged but over the manner in which the price was calculated; thus, the safe-harbor provision did not apply). Those cases contend that the comment is limited to the "normal case," which does not include a situation where the seller is purposefully trying to drive the buyer out of business.

This interpretation would eviscerate the safe harbor in any action in which the plaintiff alleges circumstantial evidence of an improper motive, leading to drawn-out litigation "even if the prices ultimately charged were undisputedly within the range of those charged throughout the industry." *HRN*, 144 S.W.3d at 435. See Berry, Byers, & Oates, Open Price Agreements: Good Faith Pricing in the Franchise Relationship (2007), 27 Franchise L.J. 45, 49. If a subjective inquiry could determine bad faith, a seller charging a fair price, even exactly the same price as another, good-faith seller, could be deemed to be acting in bad faith. . . .

All of this is not to say that intent is necessarily irrelevant to an analysis of good faith under UCC section 2-305(2), but only that a subjective inquiry is not permitted when the posted-price safe harbor applies. By its language, the safe harbor does not apply when it is not the "normal case" or when the price setter is not imposing a "posted price," "given price," "price in effect," "market price," or the like. As long as a price is commercially reasonable, it qualifies as the "normal case." The touchstone of prices set through open-price term contracts under UCC section 2-305 is reasonableness. A price that is nondiscriminatory among similarly situated buyers correspondingly qualifies as a "posted price" or the like. A discriminatory price could not be considered a "posted" or "market" price, because, in effect, the seller is not being "honest in fact" about the price that it is charging as a posted price, since it is charging a different price to other buyers.

Therefore, a price that is both commercially reasonable and nondiscriminatory fits within the limits of the safe harbor and complies with the statute's good-faith requirement. Given our conclusion below that the safe harbor applies to the facts of this case, we are not required to precisely define good faith as it is used in section 2-305(2). We offer no opinion, in particular, on the role of subjective intent within the good-faith analysis beyond the safe harbor.

IV

The facts of this case demonstrate that the prices set by Shell were both commercially reasonable and nondiscriminatory. Aside from claiming that Shell's goal in setting prices was to drive the dealers out of business, the only evidence of bad faith was that the prices set were too high for dealers to remain profitable and compete with jobbers in the Cleveland area. However, Shell is not required to sell gasoline at a price that is profitable for buyers. "A good-faith price under section [2-305] is not synonymous with a fair market price or the lowest price available." HRN, 144 S.W.3d at 437. As noted by the court of appeals: "The trial court . . . found that Shell submitted expert testimony which established that the DTW prices set by the company were within the range set by its competitors." Casserlie v. Shell Oil Co., 2007 Ohio 2633, at P 31. The dealers failed to rebut this evidence. Id.

The dealers also point out that Shell's prices varied throughout the area because of PAD pricing. But the fact that Shell's DTW prices varied by

PADs does not itself demonstrate unreasonable or discriminatory pricing. It is reasonable for Shell to adjust according to competition, and there is no evidence that Shell discriminated among similarly situated buyers, such as dealers within a given PAD or dealers in similar PADs.

Finally, the only other argument of discrimination put forth by the dealers is that jobbers were charged significantly less, specifically, the rack price rather than the DTW price. Jobbers and dealers are not, however, similarly situated buyers. The price difference is partially explained by the fact that the DTW price includes a delivery charge, while the rack price does not. We further find the Sixth Circuit Court of Appeals analysis comparing jobbers and dealers in *Tom-Lin* instructive, just as the lower courts did. See *Tom-Lin Ents.*, 349 F.3d at 285-286. *Tom-Lin* noted that jobbers perform additional functions compared to dealers, such as maintaining the properties they own and bearing the risk of environmental liability. Id. at 285. Because jobbers relieve Shell of these obligations, they are charged a lower price. The dealers have not challenged these differences. The disparate pricing between jobbers and dealers is not evidence of discrimination.

V

When a price that has been left open in a contract is fixed at a price posted by a seller or buyer, and the posted price is both commercially reasonable and nondiscriminatory, the price setter has acted in good faith as required by R.C. 1302.18(B), and a subjective inquiry into the motives of the price setter is not permitted. In this case, the dealers have not provided any evidence that the prices set by Shell were commercially unreasonable or discriminatory. The posted-price safe harbor therefore applies, and we affirm the judgment of the court of appeals.

Judgment affirmed.

[A dissenting judge argued that good faith for open-price terms should, as in other contexts, have both subjective and objective components. The Official Comment, in the dissent's view, should not be given such authority, because it was not enacted as law by the Ohio legislature.]

II. UNCONSCIONABILITY

The opposite of the incomplete contract is the one that contains too much. In the name of *freedom of contract, caveat emptor,* and the *duty to read,* courts have permitted some rapacious merchants to insulate themselves in legally formidable contracts that have bordered on fraud and were filled with "I win—you lose" provisions. Early attacks on these *adhesion contracts* (so called because the lesser party had to adhere to the will of the stronger) were made in well-known articles like Friedrich Kessler's famous article: Contracts of Adhesion—Some Thoughts About Freedom of Contract, 43 Colum. L. Rev. 629 (1943). Later, the chief reporter for the UCC, Karl Llewellyn, proposed this famous "true answer" to the problem:

> The answer, I suggest, is this: Instead of thinking about "assent" to boilerplate clauses, we can recognize that so far as concerns the specific, there is no assent at all. What has in fact been assented to, specifically, are the few dickered terms, and the broad type of the transaction, and but one thing more. That one thing more is a blanket assent (not a specific assent) to any not unreasonable or indecent terms the seller may have on his form, which do not alter or eviscerate the reasonable meaning of the dickered terms. The fine print which has not been read has no business to cut under the reasonable meaning of those dickered terms which constitute the dominant and only real expression of agreement, but much of it commonly belongs in.

K. Llewellyn, The Common Law Tradition: Deciding Appeals 370 (1960).

The UCC tackled the problem in §2-302. This provision caused whole forests to be stripped to supply the paper for scholarly analysis on a grand scale. The redoubtable Professor Arthur Leff set the tone in a celebrated article attacking §2-302 and its unconscionability principle as "an emotionally satisfying incantation" having "no reality referent"; see Leff, Unconscionability and the Code—The Emperor's New Clause, 115 U. Pa. L. Rev. 485 (1967). Professor Leff's chief contribution to the analysis of §2-302 was his division of "unconscionability" into two types: unfair conduct in the formation of the contract (called *procedural unconscionability*), and unfairness in the terms of the resulting bargain (called *substantive unconscionability*). It was Leff's idea that both are required before a court can make a finding of §2-302 unconscionability.

In a major book entitled Boilerplate: The Fine Print, Vanishing Rights, and the Rule of Law (2012), Professor Margaret Jane Radin discusses boilerplate from many angles. She begins by comparing two worlds: "World A," where parties actually negotiate the terms of their contract, and "World B," where one party dictates all the terms and refuses to negotiate at all. In World B she states that the so-called contracts are in reality "contracts *not* to contract." Rather, the contracts are dictated by the superior party and filled with what she calls "boilerplate rights deletion schemes." Professor Radin has a raft of solutions: legislative action to forbid such clauses, private rating systems of contracts according to how odious they are, etc., but when it comes to judicial treatment of offending boilerplate she urges the courts to look beyond existing doctrines like unconscionability and treat the use of harmful boilerplate as an intentional tort resulting in both punitive damages and attorney fees.

Read §2-302 and its Official Comment, and then answer the following questions.

QUESTIONS

1. Is *unconscionability* defined in the Code? If asked, how would you define the meaning to a judge? Are the example cases in the Official Comment helpful?

2. Is the unconscionability issue one for the judge or the jury? What is the policy reason for the Code drafters' decision on this matter?

3. Is the §2-302(2) hearing mandatory as a technical step prior to a finding of unconscionability? See Haugen v. Ford Motor Co., 219 N.W.2d 462 (N.D. 1974), holding that the hearing *is* mandatory and that summary judgment is inappropriate without such a hearing.

4. Would the answers to these questions change if this were a lease of goods to a consumer? See §2A-108.

Sacramento E.D.M., Inc. v. Hynes Aviation Industries

United States District Court, Eastern District of California, 2017
WL 1383289

KENDALL J. NEWMAN, United States Magistrate Judge.

Order

. . . In addition to concluding that Hynes both breached his fiduciary duty of loyalty and committed constructive fraud with regard to his misrepresentations concerning the interest and duration terms of the equipment leases, the court also concludes that those terms are unconscionable as a matter of law at the time they were made. See Langemeier v. Nat'l Oats Co., 775 F.2d 975, 977 (8th Cir. 1985) (holding that U.C.C. §2-302, which Missouri has adopted verbatim via Missouri Revised Statute §400.2-302, permits a court to raise the issue of unconscionability of a contract *sua sponte*).

Under applicable Missouri law, a contract's term may be deemed invalid when there is both procedural and substantive unconscionability. Funding Sys. Leasing Corp. v. King Louie Int'l, Inc., 597 S.W.2d 624, 634-35 (Mo. App. 1979). Procedural unconscionability arises during the contracting process when there is fine print in the contract, there has been some misrepresentation, or there is unequal bargaining power. World

Enterprises, Inc. v. Midcoast Aviation Servs., Inc., 713 S.W.2d 606 (Mo. App. 1986). Substantive unconscionability, on the other hand, occurs when the contractual terms are unduly harsh. Id.; Lyster v. Ryan's Family Steak Houses, Inc., 239 F.3d 943 (8th Cir. 2001). Provisions that an objective reasonable person would find unexpected and unconscionably unfair are unenforceable. Hartland Computer Leasing Corp., Inc. v. Insurance Man, Inc., 770 S.W.2d 525, 527-28 (Mo. App. 1989). Procedural and substantive unconscionability are considered on a sliding scale, so that when more substantive unconscionability is present less procedural unconscionability is necessary to invalidate a contract and vice versa. *Funding Sys. Leasing Corp.*, 597 S.W.2d at 634-45.

Here, procedural unconscionability arose when Hynes misrepresented the lease contracts' terms regarding the rate of interest being charged and the lease period. Furthermore, the leases' terms with regard to interest and duration are also substantively unconscionable as they are unduly harsh. As discussed above, the 30 percent interest added on to each month's payment is usurious under the applicable Missouri law, which allows for only 10 percent interest under the circumstances. Similarly, the actual duration of each lease is nearly twice as long as Hynes represented they would be, and would result in Sac EDM paying more than double what defendants paid for each piece of equipment, including the equipment that Sac EDM had owned outright prior to the sale, before it could finally buyout that equipment and conclude the lease term if it were to follow the payment schedule contemplated in the terms of each lease agreement. Such a lease term was both contrary to the parties' intentions and goals set forth in their business plan, which was to obtain more favorable lease terms for Sac EDM, and was structured in such a fashion as to clearly benefit defendants to the long-term detriment of Sac EDM. Finally, Sac EDM could apply only 50 percent of its lease payments towards its purchase of the equipment, a substantial portion of which was equipment that it had previously owned outright. This fact not only substantially increased the overall duration of each lease, but also ensured that Sac EDM would have paid more than double defendants' purchase cost for that equipment by the time it could exercise its purchase option. Such a term is entirely contrary to the provisions of the parties' agreement and business plan regarding the operation of the OK EDM joint venture that stated that defendants were to obtain more favorable purchase options with regard to any equipment Sac EDM leased. Accordingly, the court concludes that the interest, duration, and purchase terms of the leases are unconscionable.

[The court ordered that Sac EDM recover interest payments made beyond the rate of 10 percent interest.]

Green Tree Servicing, LLC v. Duncan

Navajo Nation Supreme Court, 2008
7 Am. Tribal Law 633, 2008 WL 5435566

Judges: Before YAZZIE, Chief Justice, and FERGUSON and BLACK, Associate Justices.

. . . The final issue is whether the arbitration clause in the contract bars Duncan's claims. The lengthy arbitration clause in the contract states "[a]ll claims and controversies arising from or relating to this [c]ontract . . . shall be resolved by binding arbitration by one arbitrator selected by Assignee [Green Tree] with consent of the Buyer(s) [Duncan]." It further states that "[t]he parties agree and understand that they choose arbitration instead of litigation to resolve disputes." In all capital letters, it further states that "THE PARTIES VOLUNTARILY AND KNOWINGLY WAIVE ANY RIGHT THEY HAVE TO A JURY TRIAL EITHER PURSUANT TO ARBITRATION UNDER THIS CLAUSE OR PURSUANT TO A COURT ACTION BY ASSIGNEE (AS PROVIDED HEREIN)." The court action referenced at the end of the last sentence is authorized later in the clause, stating that "Assignee [Green Tree] retains an option to use judicial or non-judicial relief to enforce a security agreement relating to the [mobile home] secured by a transaction underlying this arbitration agreement, to enforce the monetary obligation to be secured by the [mobile home] or to foreclose on the [mobile home]." In other words, Duncan agreed to waive her right to file any court action and to instead arbitrate any dispute with Green Tree, and waived her right to a jury completely, but agreed to allow Green Tree to file a court action to repossess the mobile home.

The question is whether such an agreement is enforceable under Navajo law. Green Tree submits that under Navajo law words are sacred. This Court has upheld contracts if the language is clear and the parties voluntarily entered into the agreement. See, e.g., Smith v. Navajo Nation Dept. of Headstart, No. SC-CV-50-04, slip op. at 4-6, 2005 Navajo Sup. LEXIS 8 (Nav. Sup. Ct. September 21, 2005). However, despite the clarity of language, the Court has also stricken agreements if they violate Navajo public policy expressed in our statutory law or in *Diné bi beenahaz'áanii.* See Allstate Indemnity Co. v. Blackgoat, No. SC-CV-15-01, slip op. at 8, 2005 Navajo Sup. LEXIS 5 (Nav. Sup. Ct. May 20, 2005) (striking liability cap in insurance contract for purposes of prejudgment interest as violative of Navajo principle of *nályééh*); see also *Smith,* No. SC-CV-50-04, 2005 Navajo Sup. LEXIS 8, slip op. at 5 (stating test).

To discern Navajo public policy, the Court turns first to several provisions of the Navajo Nation Code. One important principle is that contracts are not enforceable if they are "unconscionable." The clearest articulation of this principle is in Section 2-302(A) of the Navajo Uniform

Commercial Code. That provision states that if a court determines whether a contract, or any part of it, is "unconscionable," it is empowered (1) to refuse enforcement of the entire contract, (2) to enforce the remainder of the contract without the unconscionable clause or clauses, or (3) limit the application of any clause to avoid an unjust result. Id. The basic test is whether, "in the light of the general commercial background and the commercial needs of the particular trade or case, the clauses involved are so one-sided as to be unconscionable under the circumstances existing at the time of the making of the contract." Official Comment, 5A N.N.C. §2-302 (2005). The concept of unconscionability "recognizes that in some cases the lack of bargaining power of one party compared to that of the other party will result in an oppressive contract." Special Plain Language Comment, 5A N.N.C. §2-302 (2005). Similarly, the Navajo Nation Unfair Consumer Practices Act discusses the concept of "unconscionable trade practice," which also considers the difference in understanding and bargaining power, and prohibits acts that result in unfair transactions. See 5 N.N.C. §1103(E) (2005).

The Navajo Nation Code also includes provisions encouraging arbitration. The recently enacted Navajo Nation Arbitration Act authorizes the use of arbitration clauses, but lacks a definition of "arbitration." See 7 N.N.C. §§1001, et seq. Black's Law Dictionary defines "Arbitration" as, "a method of dispute resolution involving one or more neutral third parties and whose decision is binding." Black's Law Dictionary, Seventh Edition, at 100 (1999). The Arbitration Act's provisions are consistent with this general concept, and through the Act the Council appears to encourage the use of non-judicial dispute resolution as a matter of contract.[1] However, the Act does not recognize all arbitration agreements, as it states that "[a] written agreement to submit any existing or future controversy to arbitration is valid, enforceable and irrevocable, save upon such grounds as exist at law or in equity for the revocation of the contract." 7 N.N.C. §1103 (2005) (emphasis added). The Act then balances the value of arbitration agreements with the value of fairness, and states that not all agreements to arbitrate are enforceable in the Navajo Nation.

There are also Fundamental Law principles that inform Navajo public policy on arbitration agreements in mobile home contracts. The Navajo maxim of * házhó'ógó* mandates "more than the mere provision of an English form stating certain rights . . . and requires a patient, respectful discussion . . . before a waiver is effective." Eriacho v. Ramah District Court, No. SC-CV-61-04, slip op. at 7, 2005 Navajo Sup. LEXIS 1 (Nav. Sup. Ct. January

1. Of course, Peacemaking is another type of non-judicial dispute resolution. However, Peacemaking, unlike arbitration, is based on Navajo principles of non-adversarial decision making that emphasize bringing the parties back into harmony.

5, 2005). *Házhó'ógó* requires a meaningful notice and explanation of a right before a waiver of that right is effective. Id. *Házhó'ógó* is not man-made law, but rather a fundamental tenet informing us how we must approach each other as individuals. Navajo Nation v. Rodriguez, No. SC-CR-03-04, slip op. at 10, 2004 Navajo Sup. LEXIS 13 (Nav. Sup. Ct. December 16, 2004). It is "an underlying principle in everyday dealings with relatives and other individuals." Id. Though primarily discussed previously in the criminal context, *házhó'ógó* equally applies in civil situations. See Kesoli v. Anderson Security Agency, No. SC-CV-01-05, slip op. at 6, 2005 Navajo Sup. LEXIS 4 (Nav. Sup. Ct. October 12, 2005).

Several other principles are relevant. In a recent case, the Court discussed the Navajo concept of *nábináheezlágo be t'áá lahj↑ algha' deet'*, which is, finality is established when all participants agree that all of the concerns or issues have been comprehensively resolved in the agreement. Casaus v. Dine College, No. SC-CV-48-05, slip op. at 7, 2007 Navajo Sup. LEXIS 18 (Nav. Sup. Ct. March 8, 2007). It is also said that in the process of "talking things out," or meeting the Navajo common law procedural requirement that everything must be talked over, see Navajo Nation v. Crockett, 7 Nav. R. 237, 241, 1996 Navajo Sup. LEXIS 14 (Nav. Sup. Ct. 1996), there is a requirement of *íishjání ádooniíl*, that is, making something clear or obvious. See Phillips v. Navajo Housing Authority, No. SC-CV-13-05, slip op. at 7, 2005 Navajo Sup. LEXIS 15 (Nav. Sup. Ct. December 8, 2005) (applying Navajo concept of iishjani & Iowa to require clear intent to retroactively grant sovereign immunity to Navajo Housing Authority); Yazzie v. Thompson, No. SC-CV-69-04, slip op. at 4, 2005 Navajo Sup. LEXIS 7 (Nav. Sup. Ct. July 21, 2005) (same for Court rules on fees in domestic violence cases); Rough Rock Community School v. Navajo Nation, 7 Nav. R. 168, 174, 1995 Navajo Sup. LEXIS 4 (Nav. Sup. Ct. 1995) (same for qualifications of school board candidates). Navajo decision-making is practical and pragmatic, and the result of "talking things out" is a clear plan. Rough Rock Community School v. Navajo Nation, 7 Nav. R. 168, 174, 1995 Navajo Sup. LEXIS 4 (Nav. Sup. Ct. 1995). When faced with important matters, it is inappropriate to rush to conclusion or to push a decision without explanation and consideration to those involved. *Áádóó na'nile'dii éi dooda*, that is, delicate matters and things of importance must not be approached recklessly, carelessly, or with indifference to consequences. *Rodriguez*, No. SC-CR-03-04, 2004 Navajo Sup. LEXIS 13, slip op. at 10. This is *házhó'ógó*. Id. If things are not done *házhó'ógó*, it is said that it is done *t'aa bizaka*.

An arbitration clause must be set in the manner of *házhó'ogó* (standard of care), so as to make a clause *íishjání ádooniíl* (clear and obvious), therefore it will not be made *t 'aa na 'nile'dii* (not recklessly, carelessly or with indifference to consequences) resulting in making the arbitration clause *nábináheezlágo be t'áá lahjí algha' deet'* (comprehensive agreement). This was shown in *Eriacho,* wherein the Navajo Nation argued that the explanation of right to a jury trial was not necessary due to Ms. Eriacho's apparent education level. See No. SC-CV-61-04, 2005 Navajo Sup. LEXIS 1, slip op. at 7 n. 2. In response, this Court rejected "any rule that conditions the respectful explanation of rights under Navajo due process on subjective assumption concerning the defendant. This right exists for all defendants in our system." Id.

Finally, these principles must be applied in the context of the importance of a home in Navajo thought. This Court has noted that a home is not just a dwelling, but a place at the center of Navajo life. Fort Defiance Housing Corp. v. Lowe, No. SC-CV-32-03, slip op. at 4, 2004 Navajo Sup. LEXIS 11 (Nav. Sup. Ct. April 12, 2004). Based on this principle, the Court scrutinizes procedures to make sure they protect a home owner's ability to maintain a healthy home and family. See id.; *Phillips,* No. SC-CV-13-05, 2005 Navajo Sup. LEXIS 15, slip op. at 7.

Considering all of these principles together, the Court holds that the specific arbitration clause in the financing contract is unenforceable. Though arbitration generally is encouraged, clauses that mandate arbitration are not immune from scrutiny for unconscionability or consistency with Fundamental Law. This case ultimately concerns the repossession of a mobile home, and the ability to keep the home may depend on the availability of a home owner's counterclaims against a finance company seeking to take the home. The requirement that Duncan engage in arbitration instead of filing counterclaims in an action brought by Green Tree in a Navajo district court greatly burdens her ability to defend herself. She must figure out the arbitration process, spend potentially significant amounts of money and travel off the Nation to participate. Importantly, Green Tree is under no similar obligation; under the agreement it may file a Navajo court action to assert its rights, and is protected from defending counterclaims. The burden is then only one way. The effect of this grossly unequal position is not clearly explained in the clause. An arbitration clause in a mobile home finance contract cannot be enforced if the contract does not contain clear and specific language explaining that the Navajo consumer understands that he or she is surrendering his or her rights to bring claims in a Navajo court, but nonetheless is allowing claims against him or her to compel surrender of the home.

Let the parties be clear on the effect of this holding. The Court does not say that all arbitration clauses are unenforceable. Arbitration serves important purposes, and is one of the possible methods of dispute resolution approved by the Navajo Nation Council. The holding of this case only applies to the specific clause under the circumstances of this case.

VIII

Based on the above, the Court VACATES the District Court's dismissal of Duncan's counterclaims. The case is REMANDED for further proceedings consistent with this opinion.

III. IDENTIFICATION OF THE GOODS

The Code's provisions on risk of loss, casualty to goods, damages, and other matters frequently draw distinctions based on whether the goods have been *identified* as the specific goods to which the contract refers. Read §2-501, and note the general policy favoring early identification found in Official Comment 2.

PROBLEM 53

Decide if *identification* per §2-501 has occurred in the following situations.

(a) Seller, a fisherman, contracts to sell his entire catch for the coming season. Does identification occur on the making of the contract, on the catching of the fish, or on their packaging with a label indicating they belong to this particular buyer? See Official Comment 6.

(b) Three Ring Circus contracted to sell the unborn calf of the circus's elephant Nancy as soon as the calf was born; the contract was made when Nancy was two months pregnant. Does the identification occur on the date of contracting, on the calf's birth, or when the calf is marked for shipment?

(c) Farmer Carl agreed to sell to Breakfast Cereals, Inc. one-half of the grain he had stored in Rural Silo, where Farmer Carl's grain was mixed with that of other farmers. Does identification occur on contracting or on segregation of the grain? Read Official Comment 5. See §§2-105(3), 2-105(4).

(d) Wonder Widgets contracted to sell 5,000 widgets to a buyer. Its warehouse contained 2 million widgets, all alike. Does identification occur on contracting or when the goods are picked out and marked as pertaining to this contract?

(e) Laputa agreed to sell its wrecked helicopter to Sheeta, and agreed to repair it extensively before delivery. After Sheeta paid the contract price but before Laputa did any repairs, Laputa filed bankruptcy. When would the helicopter be identified to the contract: at the time of contracting (meaning title would pass to Sheeta) or not until the helicopter was repaired (meaning that it would stay in the bankruptcy estate)? See In re Phoenix Heliparts Inc., 2018 WL 2107796 (B.A.P. 9th Cir. 2018).

IV. RISK OF LOSS: NO BREACH

A. General Rules

Under the old Uniform Sales Act, risk of loss stayed with the person having technical title to the goods and passed to the buyer only when *title* to the goods switched to the buyer. The UCC expressly states that its rules as to who bears the risk of loss have nothing to do with who has technical title (§2-401(1)). This astounded Samuel Williston, the original drafter of the Uniform Sales Act, who called this abandonment of title the "most iconoclastic" idea in the Code; in a famous and rather sad article, he vainly argued against the adoption of the UCC. See Williston, The Law of Sales in the Proposed Uniform Commercial Code, 63 Harv. L. Rev. 561 (1950). Compare Corbin, The Uniform Commercial Code—Sales; Should It Be Enacted?, 59 Yale L.J. 821 (1950), in which Professor Arthur Corbin announced his enthusiastic indorsement of the Code. The general Code rule on the transfer of the risk of loss is that, absent contrary agreement, (1) where the seller is a *merchant,* the risk of loss passes to the buyer on the buyer's actual *receipt* of the goods; and (2) where the seller is not a merchant, risk of loss passes to the buyer when the seller tenders delivery. See §2-509(3).

PROBLEM 54

William College bought a car from Honest John, the friendly car dealer. He paid the price in full, and Honest John promised delivery on the next Monday. On Monday the car was ready, and Honest John phoned College and said, "Take it away." College said he was busy and that he would pick it up the next day, to which Honest John agreed. That night the car was stolen from the lot due to no fault of Honest John, who had taken reasonable precautions against such a thing. Who had the risk of loss? See §2-509(3) and Official Comment 3. Ramos v. Wheel Sports Center, 96 Misc. 2d 646, 409 N.Y.S.2d 505 (Civ. Ct. 1978). Might Honest John claim he was a *bailee* so that §2-509(2) applies? See White & Summers §6-3; Galbraith v. American Motor Home Corp., 14 Wash. App. 754, 545 P.2d 561 (1976).

PROBLEM 55

Janice Junk decided to hold a garage sale to clean up her home and get some extra cash. In the course of the sale, which was a huge success, her neighbor, Barbara Bargain, offered Junk $200 for her piano, and the two women shook hands. Junk said to Bargain, "Take it away. It's yours." Bargain replied that she would come to get it the next day with four strong friends and a truck. That night Junk's home burned to the ground, and the piano was destroyed. Did the risk of loss pass from Junk to Bargain? See §2-503. If Bargain never picked up the piano and if it was destroyed in a fire *six months* after the sale, what result? See §2-709(1)(a).

Section 2-509(3) applies only when §2-509(1) or §2-509(2) does not.

In many contracts where the goods are in an independent warehouse, the seller must arrange for the warehouse company (bailee) to change its records to show the buyer as the new owner. Subsection (2) of §2-509 sets out the rules as to when the risk of loss passes to the buyer in such a situation. In essence, the risk of loss rests on whoever has control over the bailee. Read §2-509(2).

Since understanding Subsection (2) of §2-509 depends in large part on understanding the nature of warehouse receipts and delivery orders, both negotiable and nonnegotiable, risk of loss under §2-509(2) will be covered in greater depth later in the book, in the Article 7 chapter.

In some contracts, the seller is required to ship the goods by independent carrier to the buyer. Such transportation contracts are governed by §2-509(1). Read that section. Note that in transportation contracts the test as to when the risk passes depends on whether the contract requires the seller to "deliver [the goods] at a particular destination." How do you know whether the contract requires the seller to deliver the goods to the buyer or merely to see that they are delivered to the carrier? The next section deals with that issue.

B. *Delivery Terms*

In sales contracts, the parties often agree that the seller need only get the goods to the carrier and then the buyer will take the risk of loss. This type of contract is called a *shipment contract.* On the other hand, the parties may agree that the goods must be delivered by the carrier before the risk passes from seller to buyer. Such a contract is called a *destination contract.* According to Official Comment 5 to §2-503, the presumption made by Article 2 is in favor of a shipment contract. Read that Comment. Where the contract is silent on risk of loss, the courts have enforced this presumption that a shipment contract was intended; Deiter v. Coons, 162 Idaho 44, 394 P.3d 87 (2017). Through the years, merchants have developed a set of *delivery terms* like F.O.B. (free on board), F.A.S. (free along-side), C.I.F. (cost, insurance, freight), C. & F. (cost and freight), and ex-ship (off the ship), which are shorthand methods of stating whether the sale calls for a shipment or a destination contract. These terms (and similar ones) are defined and their legal implications stated clearly in §§2-319 through 2-324. Not only are these terms *delivery* terms, defining the passage of the risk of loss, but also they are *price* terms that inform the buyer that the price quoted includes freight paid to the point indicated. Thus, if the seller is in New York and the buyer is in Chicago, a *$2,000 F.O.B. New York* term means that the risk of loss passes on delivery to the carrier and that the price quoted includes only delivery to the carrier (the buyer must pay the freight charges to get the goods to Chicago). Remember:

(1) C.I.F. and C. & F. always indicate a *shipment* contract. C.I.F. means that the price stated includes the *cost* of the item, the *insurance* premium, and the *freight* charge. The law merchant concluded the C.I.F. was obviously a shipment contract (where the buyer takes the risk of loss during shipment) because the buyer agreed to pay insurance as part of the price. If the buyer did not have the risk of loss, why would insurance be needed? C. & F. is the same as C.I.F. without the buyer's agreeing to pay the insurance. One might think therefore that C. & F. would indicate a destination contract. It does not for two reasons. First, the buyer frequently asks for a C. & F. price because a blanket insurance policy already covers goods the buyer owns. Second, the law merchant regarded C. & F. as a shipment term, and businesses have arranged their affairs accordingly ever since. Read §2-320.

(2) F.A.S. and ex-ship are delivery terms used in connection with ships. Read §§2-319(2) and 2-322, and use them in answering Problem 56.

(3) F.O.B. can indicate *either* a shipment or a destination contract. In a contract it is always followed by a named place (like F.O.B. Pittsburgh). The risk of loss passes *at the named place.* Thus, if the named place is the seller's warehouse, the F.O.B. term calls for a shipment contract; if it is the buyer's store, a destination contract results. Read §2-319.

PROBLEM 56

Seller in New York City contracted to sell 80 boxes of clothing to buyer in Savannah, Georgia. The delivery term was "$1,800 F.A.S. S.S. Seaworthy, N.Y.C." Seller delivered the 80 boxes to the dock alongside the *S.S. Seaworthy* and received a bill of lading from the ship as a receipt. Before the boxes could be loaded, the dock collapsed, and everything thereon disappeared into the water. Under §2-319(2) must buyer pay the $1,800 anyway? What if the delivery term had been "Ex-ship S.S. Seaworthy, Savannah," and the boxes had been properly unloaded just before the dock collapsed? Would §2-322 make the buyer pay?

PROBLEM 57

Seller in Detroit, Michigan, contracted to sell and ship 50 automobiles to buyer in Birmingham, Alabama. Assume lightning strikes, destroying the vehicles *after* the carrier has received them but before they are loaded on board the railroad car that was to take them to Birmingham. Who had the risk of loss if (a) the contract said, "F.O.B. Detroit"? (see §2-319(1)(a)); (b) the contract said, "F.O.B. railroad cars Detroit"? (see §2-319(1)(c) and Pagano v. Occidental Chem. Corp., 629 N.E.2d 569 (Ill. App. 1994)); or (c) the contract said, "C.I.F. Birmingham"? (see §2-320). If the buyer had inspected the automobiles and accepted them at the factory, would the risk shift to buyer or remain on seller until the automobiles reached the railroad cars? See Southern Recycling, LLC v. Gibbs International, Inc., 2016 WL 1258402 (D.S.C. 2016).

PROBLEM 58

The dispatcher for Perfect Pineapples, Inc., had just finished loading five boxcars of the company's product on board the cars of an independent railroad carrier when he received a notice from PPI's sales department that the company had agreed to sell one boxcar load to Grocery King Food Stores "F.O.B. seller's processing plant." The dispatcher agreed to divert one of the boxcars to Grocery King, but before he could do so, a hurricane destroyed all five boxcars and their contents. Who bears the risk of loss? See Official Comment 2 to §2-509 and §2-501.

Cook Specialty Co. v. Schrlock

United States District Court, Eastern District of Pennsylvania, 1991
772 F. Supp. 1532

WALDMAN, J.

Defendant Machinery Systems, Inc. ("MSI") contracted to sell plaintiff a machine known as a Dries & Krump Hydraulic Press Brake. When the machine was lost in transit, plaintiff sued defendants to recover for the loss. Presently before the court is plaintiff's motion for summary judgment and defendant MSI's cross-motion for summary judgment. . . .

II. Facts

The pertinent facts are not contested and are as follow.

Plaintiff entered into a sales contract with defendant MSI for the purchase of a Dries & Krump Press Brake in August of 1989 for $28,000. The terms of the contract were F.O.B. MSI's warehouse in Schaumburg, Illinois. Defendant R.T.L., also known as Randy's Truck Lines, ("the carrier") was used to deliver the press brake from the defendant's warehouse to the plaintiff in Pennsylvania. MSI obtained a certificate of insurance from the carrier with a face amount of $100,000 and showing a $2,500 deductible. (See dfdt. ex. D.)

On October 20, 1989, the carrier took possession of the press brake at MSI's warehouse. While still in transit, the press brake fell from the carrier's truck. The carrier was cited by the Illinois State Police for not properly securing the load. Plaintiff has recovered damages of $5,000 from the carrier's insurer, the applicable policy limit for this particular incident. The machine was worth $28,000.[2]

III. Discussion

This dispute is governed by the Uniform Commercial Code ("U.C.C.") provisions regarding risk of loss. The parties agree that there is no meaningful distinction between the pertinent law of Pennsylvania and Illinois, both of which have adopted the UCC.

The term "F.O.B., place of shipment," means that "the seller must at that place ship the goods in the manner provided in this Article (§2-504) and bear the expense and risk of putting them into the possession of the carrier." 13 Pa. C.S.A. §2319. Thus, MSI bore the expense and risk of putting the machine into the carrier's possession for delivery. At the time the carrier takes possession, the risk of loss shifts to the buyer. The UCC provides:

> Where the contract requires or authorizes the seller to ship the goods by carrier
>
> a) if it does not require him to deliver them at a particular destination, the risk of loss passes to the buyer when the goods are duly delivered to the carrier. . . .

13 Pa. C.S.A. §2509.

Goods are not "duly delivered" under §2-509, however, unless a contract is entered which satisfies the provisions of §2-504. See 13 Pa. C.S.A.

2. Plaintiff, who also sued for certain consequential damages, asserts a claim for a total of $81,000.

§2509, Official Comment 2. Section 2-504, entitled "Shipment by Seller" provides that:

> Where the seller is required or authorized to send the goods to the buyer and the contract does not require him to deliver them at a particular destination, then unless otherwise agreed he must a) put the goods in the possession of such a carrier and make such a contract for their transportation *as may be reasonable having regard to the nature of the goods* and other circumstances of the case.

13 Pa. C.S.A. §2504 (emphasis added).

Plaintiff argues that the contract MSI made for the delivery of the press brake was not reasonable because defendant failed to ensure that the carrier had sufficient insurance coverage to compensate plaintiff for a loss in transit. Plaintiff thus argues that the press brake was never duly delivered to a carrier within the meaning of §2-509 and accordingly the risk of loss never passed to plaintiff.

Plaintiff relies on two cases. In the first, La Casse v. Blaustein, 93 Misc. 2d 572, 403 N.Y.S.2d 440 (Civ. Ct. 1978), the defendant seller shipped calculators to the plaintiff buyer, a college student, in two cartons by fourth class mail. The buyer authorized the seller to spend up to $50 for shipping and insurance. The seller spent only $9.98 and insured each carton, valued at $1,663, for $200. The seller wrongly addressed one of the cartons, and inscribed a theft-tempting notation on it. The New York County Civil Court held that the defendant had improperly arranged for transportation of the calculators.

La Casse is the only reported case which suggests that a seller's failure to obtain adequate insurance may breach his duty to make a reasonable contract for shipment under §2-504. The dearth of support for plaintiff's position is instructive. A leading UCC authority has remarked: "Under this subsection [§2-504], what constitutes an 'unreasonable' contract of transportation? *Egregious* cases do arise." See J. White and R. Summers, Uniform Commercial Code §5-2 (1988). The only such "egregious case" identified by White and Summers is *La Casse,* where "the package was underinsured, misaddressed, shipped by fourth class mail, and bore a 'theft-tempting' inscription." White and Summers, supra, at §5-2.

The actions taken by the defendant in *La Casse* were utterly reckless. Moreover, unlike the defendant in that case, MSI did not undertake the responsibility to insure the shipment, and did not ship the press brake at a lower cost than the plaintiff expressly authorized it to pay.

Plaintiff also relies on Miller v. Harvey, 221 N.Y. 57, 116 N.E. 781 (1917). This pre-Code case is inapplicable. In *Miller,* by failing to declare the actual value of goods shipped on a form provided for that purpose, the seller effectively contracted away the buyer's rights against the carrier. Official Comment 3 to §2-504 states:

> [i]t is an improper contract under paragraph (a) for the seller to agree with the carrier to a limited valuation below the true value and thus cut off the buyer's opportunity to recover from the carrier in the event of loss, when the risk of shipment is placed on the buyer.

Thus, a contract is improper if the seller agrees to an inadequate valuation of the shipment and thereby extinguishes the buyer's opportunity to recover from the carrier. That is quite different from a seller's failure to ensure that a carrier has sufficient insurance to cover a particular potential loss, in which case the carrier is still liable to the buyer.

Plaintiff's focus on a single sentence of Official Comment 3 ignores the explicit language of the statute which defines reasonable in the context of "having regard to the nature of the goods," 3 Pa. C.S.A. §2504, and the portion of the Comment which states:

> Whether or not the shipment is at the buyer's expense the seller must see to any arrangements, *reasonable in the circumstances,* such as refrigeration, watering of live stock, protection against cold . . . and the like. . . .

Id., Official Comment 3.

The clear implication is that the reasonableness of a shipper's conduct under §2-504 is determined with regard to the mode of transport selected. It would be unreasonable, for example, to send perishables without refrigeration. See Larsen v. A.C. Carpenter, Inc., 620 F. Supp. 1084, 1119 (E.D.N.Y. 1985). No inference fairly can be drawn from the section that a seller has an obligation to investigate the amount and terms of insurance held by the carrier.

The court finds as a matter of law that MSI's conduct was not unreasonable under §2-504. MSI obtained from the carrier a certificate of insurance and did nothing to impair plaintiff's right to recover for any loss from the carrier.[3] Accidents occur in transit. For this reason, the UCC has specifically established mercantile symbols which delineate the risk of loss in a transaction so that the appropriate party might obtain insurance on the shipment.

3. Plaintiff's argument that because the carrier used an allegedly unprofessional sounding name, Randy's Truck Line, and inelegant stationery, MSI was on notice that the carrier was unreliable is untenable. The Philadelphia telephone directory alone lists dozens of moving companies bearing the name, often just the first name, of an individual. Moreover, plaintiff has made no showing that the carrier, which is a party defendant, does not in fact have the means to satisfy a judgment in the amount sought.

The contract in this case was "F.O.B." seller's warehouse. Plaintiff clearly bears the risk of loss in transit.

There are no material facts in dispute and MSI is entitled to judgment as a matter of law.

Rheinberg-Kellerei GmbH v. Vineyard Wine Co.

Court of Appeals of North Carolina, 1981
53 N.C. App. 560, 281 S.E.2d 425

Plaintiff, a West German wine producer and exporter, instituted this action to recover the purchase price of a shipment of wine sold to defendant and lost at sea en route between Germany and the United States. Subsequent to a hearing, the court, sitting without a jury, made the following findings of fact.

Plaintiff is a West German corporation engaged in the business of producing, selling, and exporting wine. Defendant, a North Carolina corporation, is a distributor of wine, buying and selling foreign and domestic wines at wholesale. Frank Sutton, d/b/a Frank Sutton & Company and d/b/a The Empress Importing Company, and other names, of Miami Beach, Florida, is a licensed importer and seller of wines. During 1978-1979 Sutton served as an agent for plaintiff and was authorized to sell and solicit orders for plaintiff's wine in the United States. During 1978 and early 1979, Randall F. Switzer, then of Raleigh, North Carolina, was a broker soliciting orders of wine on behalf of several producers and brokers, including Sutton, on a commission basis.

During the summer of 1978, Switzer, on behalf of Frank Sutton, began to solicit orders from prospective customers in North Carolina for wines produced by plaintiff. He contacted Bennett Distributing Company in Salisbury, North Carolina and the defendant in Charlotte, North Carolina, soliciting orders for sale through Sutton of wine produced by plaintiff to be shipped from West Germany consolidated in one container. Switzer, in late August 1978, called the office of Sutton in Miami Beach, Florida, reporting that he had secured orders from Bennett Distributing Company and defendant for 625 cases and 620 cases, respectively, of plaintiff's wines. Switzer then mailed to Sutton a copy of the proposed orders. Switzer also left a copy of the proposed order by defendant with the defendant's sales manager.

On 25 August 1978, the office of Sutton prepared a written confirmation of the orders and mailed them to defendant. Defendant received the written confirmation of orders, but never gave written notice of objection to the contents thereof to plaintiff or plaintiff's agent, Sutton. Written confirmation of the orders together with "Special Instructions" which reflected the instructions to plaintiff regarding the proposed consolidated shipment, were mailed to the plaintiff in West Germany on or about 25 August 1978.

According to the stated prices for the wine, the purchase price of the 620 cases of wine ordered by the defendant was 15.125,00 German marks. On 15 September 1980, the rate of exchange of German marks to United States dollars was such that one German mark equals $.57. Therefore, the purchase price of the 620 cases of wine, 15.125,00 German marks, equals $8,621.25.

Between August and December 1978, defendant's president, Cremilde D. Blank, and Switzer made telephone inquiries to Sutton concerning the status of the wine orders, but were not furnished any information concerning when and how the wine would be shipped or when and where it would arrive. On or about 8 November 1978, Mrs. Blank telephoned Sutton's office and obtained certain details concerning the consolidated order and then wrote to Bennett Distributing Company. Thereafter, in November 1978, Bennett Distributing Company informed Mrs. Blank that it had cancelled its order with the plaintiff, and Switzer thereafter attempted to resell Bennett's share of the order.

On or about 27 November 1978, plaintiff issued notice to Sutton giving the date of the shipment, port of origin, vessel, estimated date of arrival and port of arrival. Sutton did not give any of such information to defendant or to Switzer and did not notify defendant of anything. There was never any communication of any kind between plaintiff and defendant, and defendant was not aware of the details of the shipment.

Plaintiff delivered the wine ordered by defendant, consolidated in a container with the other wine, to a shipping line on 29 November 1978, for shipment from Rotterdam to Wilmington, North Carolina, on board the *M.S. Munchen.* Defendant did not request the plaintiff to deliver the wine ordered to any particular destination, and plaintiff and its agent, Sutton, selected the port of Wilmington for the port of entry into the United States. The entire container of wine was consigned by plaintiff to defendant, with freight payable at destination by defendant.

After delivering the wine to the ocean vessel for shipment, plaintiff forwarded the invoice for the entire container, certificate of origin and bill of lading, to its bank in West Germany, which forwarded the documents to Wachovia Bank and Trust Company, N.A., in Charlotte, North Carolina. The documents were received by Wachovia on 27 December 1978. The method of payment for the sale was for plaintiff's bank in West Germany to send the invoice, certificate of origin and bill of lading, to Wachovia whereupon defendant was to pay the purchase price to Wachovia and obtain the shipping documents. Wachovia then would forward payment to plaintiff's bank, and defendant could present the shipping documents to the carrier to obtain possession.

Wachovia mailed to defendant on 29 December 1978, a notice requesting payment for the entire consolidated shipment, by sight draft in exchange for documents. The notice was not returned by the Post Office to the sender.

On or about 24 January 1979, defendant first learned that the container of wine had left Germany in early December 1978 aboard the *M.S. Munchen*, which was lost in the North Atlantic with all hands and cargo aboard between 12 December and 22 December 1978.

Defendant did not receive any wine from plaintiff and did not pay Wachovia for the lost shipment. Plaintiff released the sight draft documents to Frank Sutton. Defendant was not furnished with any copy of said documents until receiving some in March and April 1979 and the others through discovery after this action was filed.

The order and "Special Instructions," mailed by Sutton to plaintiff, but not to defendant, provided inter alia: (1) "Insurance to be covered by purchaser"; (2) "Send a 'Notice of Arrival' to both the customer and to Frank Sutton & Company"; and (3) "Payment may be deferred until the merchandise has arrived at the port of entry."

Based upon the foregoing findings of fact, the trial court made the following pertinent conclusions of law:

> 2. The defendant agreed to purchase 620 cases of wine from the plaintiff through its agent or broker, Frank Sutton, in late August 1978.
>
> 3. Plaintiff failed to comply with §2-504, which provides:
>
> Where the seller is required or authorized to send the goods to the buyer and the contract does not require him to deliver them at a particular destination, then unless otherwise agreed he must . . .
>
> "(c) promptly notify the buyer of the shipment.
>
> 4. The purpose of such notification requirement is so the buyer (as defendant in this instance would have been) may make necessary arrangements for cargo insurance and otherwise to protect itself against any ensuing loss.
>
> 5. The plaintiff failed to deliver any such notice to defendant herein prior to the sailing of the ship and the ensuing loss. While plaintiff gave such notice to its agent, Frank Sutton did not pass such information on to defendant, so defendant was unaware of details vital to securing cargo insurance or otherwise protecting itself against loss in transit. The mailing of documents after shipment to Wachovia Bank & Trust Company, N.A. to collect the invoice amount plus freight and charges from defendant by sight draft, of which defendant was unaware until some weeks after the loss of the ship was not prompt notice to the defendant as required by the above statute.
>
> 6. Risk of loss of the wine therefore did not pass from the plaintiff to defendant upon delivery of the container of wine to the carrier, as provided in §2-509(1)(a).
>
> 7. Plaintiff is not entitled to recover any amount from the defendant due to such lack of notice.
>
> From judgment in favor of the defendant, dismissing plaintiff's action, both plaintiff and defendant have appealed. . . .
>
> WELLS, J.

The first question presented by plaintiff's appeal is whether the trial court was correct in its conclusion that the risk of loss for the wine never passed from plaintiff to defendant due to the failure of plaintiff to give prompt notice of the shipment to defendant. Plaintiff made no exceptions to the findings of fact contained in the judgment and does not contend that the facts found were unsupported by the evidence. Our review on appeal is limited to a determination of whether the facts found support the court's conclusions and the judgment entered. Rule 10(a), N.C. Rules of Appellate Procedure; Swygert v. Swygert, 46 N.C. App. 173, 180-81, 264 S.E.2d 902, 907 (1980).

All parties agree that the contract in question was a "shipment" contract, i.e., one not requiring delivery of the wine at any particular destination. See J. White & R. Summers, Uniform Commercial Code §5-2, at 140-42 (1972). The Uniform Commercial Code, as adopted in North Carolina, dictates when the transfer of risk of loss occurs in this situation. Section 2-509(1)(a) provides, in pertinent part:

> Risk of loss in the absence of breach.—(1) Where the contract requires or authorizes the seller to ship the goods by carrier (a) if it does not require him to deliver them at a particular destination, the risk of loss passes to the buyer when the goods are duly delivered to the carrier even though the shipment is under reservation (§2-505). . . .

Before a seller will be deemed to have "duly delivered" the goods to the carrier, however, he must fulfill certain duties owed to the buyer. In the absence of any agreement to the contrary, these responsibilities, set out in §2-504, are as follows: [the court quotes §2-504—Eds.].

The trial court concluded that the plaintiff's failure to notify the defendant of the shipment until after the sailing of the ship and the ensuing loss, was not "prompt notice" within the meaning of §2-504, and therefore, the risk of loss did not pass to defendant upon the delivery of the wine to the carrier pursuant to the provisions of §2-509(1)(a). We hold that the conclusions of the trial court were correct. The seller is burdened with special responsibilities under a shipment contract because of the nature of the risk of loss being transferred. See W. Hawkland, 1 A Transactional Guide to the UCC §1.2104, at 102-107 (1964). Where the buyer, upon shipment by seller, assumes the perils involved in carriage, he must have a reasonable opportunity to guard against these risks by independent arrangements with the carrier. The requirement of prompt notification by the seller, as used in §2-504(c), must be construed as taking into consideration the need of a buyer to be informed of the shipment in sufficient time for him to take action to protect himself from the risk of damage to or loss of the goods while in transit. But see J. White & R. Summers, Uniform Commercial Code §5-2, fn.12 (1972). It would not be practical or desirable, however, for the courts to attempt to engraft onto §2-504 of the U.C.C. a rigid definition of prompt notice. Given the myriad factual situations which arise in business dealings, and keeping in mind the commercial realities, whether notification has been "prompt" within the meaning of UCC will have to be determined on a case-by-case basis, under all the circumstances. See W. Hawkland, 1 A Transactional Guide to the U.C.C. §1.2104, at 106 (1964).

In the case at hand, the shipment of wine was lost at sea sometime between 12 December and 22 December 1978. Although plaintiff did notify its agent, Frank Sutton, regarding pertinent details of the shipment on or about 27 November 1978, this information was not passed along to defendant. The shipping documents were not received by defendant's bank for forwarding to defendant until 27 December 1978, days after the loss had already been incurred. Since the defendant was never notified directly or by the forwarding of shipping documents within the time in which its interest could have been protected by insurance or otherwise, defendant was entitled to reject the shipment pursuant to the term of §2-504(c). . . .

In the plaintiff's appeal, the judgment is affirmed.

In the defendant's appeal, the appeal is dismissed.

PROBLEM 59

The University of Beijing in China ordered video equipment to be shipped from Applied Technology, Inc., in San Jose, California. If nothing is said about the subject, as a matter of international law, will this create a shipment or a destination contract? See CISG Articles 67 and 69. If the parties had been negotiating for the purchase of this equipment but had not gotten around to signing the contract until the goods were already on board an airplane crossing the Pacific Ocean, does the buyer have the risk of loss only from the moment of the signing of the contract or from the delivery of the equipment to the air carrier? See Article 68.

PROBLEM 60

Dime-A-Minute Rent-A-Car rented a new sports car to Joseph Armstrong. Due to a snafu at the rental office, Armstrong did not sign a rental agreement. As he was leaving the rental car lot, the car was struck by a city bus due to no fault of Armstrong (who was unhurt). The sports car was totaled. Dime-A-Minute demanded that Armstrong look to his insurance to replace the car. Did he have the risk of loss here? See §2A-219. If he had signed a rental agreement making him responsible for the car, would that agreement be valid? See §§1-302, 2A-108.

The above discussion of risk of loss, both under the UCC and under the CISG, presupposes that neither of the parties is in breach of their agreement at the moment when the risk would normally pass. If this is not true (for instance, when the seller is in breach because the goods do not conform to the warranties made in the contract), §2-509 does not apply (and neither does Article 67 of the CISG); the relevant risk of loss section is §2-510 (§2A-220 for leases and Articles 66 and 70 in the CISG). Before considering §2-510, we need to explore the UCC's definition of *breach,* and that brings us to the standards of performance set by the Code.

CHAPTER 5 REVIEW QUESTIONS

When does a party have a right to adequate assurance of performance?

Are unfair contract terms necessarily unconscionable?

What is the effect of this provision in Amazon's Terms of Use: "All purchases of physical items from Amazon are made pursuant to a shipment contract. This means that the risk of loss and title for such items pass to you upon our delivery to the carrier"?

What are the meanings of F.O.B., C.I.F., C. & F., F.A.S., and ex-ship?

Does risk of loss depend on ownership of the goods or whether they have been accepted by buyer?

ASSESSMENT: MULTIPLE CHOICE QUESTIONS

1. Curious Liquids signed a contract to sell Pemulis Auto its requirements of motor oil for the year, in monthly shipments at a price of $5 per quart. Pemulis Auto usually needed about 3,000 quarts per month. After fracking-related earthquakes shut down production of many wells, motor oil prices spiked. Pemulis Auto signed another contract to sell Josephson Jobber 100,000 quarts at $10 per quart. Pemulis Auto then informed Curious Liquids that the requirement for the next month would be 103,000 quarts. Is Curious Liquids obliged to deliver 103,000 quarts next month, which would be ruinous for it?
   a. Yes. Curious Liquids made a bad deal, but is bound by the contract.
   b. No. The parties have no sales contract, because they did not agree about the most basic term, the quantity of goods.
   c. No. Pemulis Auto is entitled only to its good faith, actual requirement. Its demand is not good faith or its actual requirement.
   d. Yes. Pemulis Auto has an actual requirement for 103,000 gallons, because it is obliged to deliver 100,000 quarts to Josephson Jobber and needs 3,000 quarts for its own operations.

2. On June 1, Pemulis Auto signed a contract to sell Redford a "2016 Model Excalibur Hardtop" automobile. A week later, Pemulis Auto received three 2016 Model Excalibur Hardtops from the manufacturer. Two days after that, Pemulis Auto placed a sticker on one of the three cars, designating it for delivery to Redford. On July 1, Redford tendered payment, Pemulis Auto signed the certificate of title and handed over the keys, and Redford drove away. When were goods identified to the contract?
   a. On June 1, when the parties signed a contract specifically identifying the car to be sold.
   b. When Pemulis Auto received three cars, meaning it could now deliver one to Redford.
   c. When Pemulis Auto put a sticker on one of the cars.
   d. When the car was paid for and driven away.

3. Word got around that Pemulis Auto had some 2016 Model Excalibur Hardtops in stock. Pompeia soon made a contract with Pemulis Auto to buy one as her retirement present to herself. Pompeia wired the full payment, and Pemulis Auto parked one of the cars to deliver to her the next day. It was stolen overnight. Is Pompeia entitled to either get her payment back or a different car delivered?
   a. No. She had bought and paid for the car, so it was her car that was stolen.
   b. No. She would be reasonably required to obtain insurance for the car.
   c. Yes. The risk of loss would not pass to her until delivery, which did not occur.
   d. Yes. A merchant is required to insure the goods.

4. Blackhorse Goods signed a contract to sell 100 washing machines to Otto Automats. The washing machines were stored in a warehouse. Blackhorse Goods negotiated the warehouse receipt to Otto Automats, who promised to pay the contract price in 30 days. Before that time, the warehouse was destroyed by a fire, through no fault of the warehouse operator. Is Otto Automats obliged to pay for washing machines that are now scrap?
   a. No. Blackhorse Goods has not delivered the goods.
   b. No. The machines still belonged to Blackhorse Goods.
   c. Yes. The risk of loss of the goods passed to Otto Automats with the warehouse receipt.
   d. Yes. The risk of loss passed to Otto Automats upon signing the contract.

5. Obergefell Furniture, in Boston, MA, entered into a contract with Unterwasser Healthcare, in Charleston, S.C., for the sale of medical devices, to be delivered by a trucking company. In which case would the

risk of loss pass from the seller to the buyer when the goods were tendered to the carrier?

a. If the parties did not specifically address the issue in the contract.
b. If they used the shipping term "C.I.F. Charleston."
c. If the used the shipping term "F.O.B. Boston."
d. All of the above.

ANSWERS

1. *C* is the best answer. Article 2 does allow the parties flexibility in forming a contract, without specifying all terms. Section 2-306 permits quantity to be measured by the seller's output or buyer's requirements, contrary to *B*. But it means the "actual output or requirements as may occur in good faith." §2-306(1). Here, Pemulis Auto asked for more than its actual requirements, as contemplated at the time of the agreement. Nor did Pemulis Auto act in good faith, where it misrepresented its actual requirements to take advantage of changing market conditions.
2. *C* is the best answer. Identification of goods to the contract is not the same as specifying what the seller is obliged to deliver, so *A* is not correct. Nor does it require the goods to be paid for and delivered, contrary to *D*. Rather, §2-501 states how the seller, in effect, marks specific goods as the ones to be delivered to the buyer. If the contract is for goods already existing and identified, identification occurs when the contract was made. §2-501(1)(a). When the contract was made, Pemulis Auto was obliged to deliver *a* 2016 Model Excalibur Hardtop, but no particular car had been designated to deliver to Redford. Even when three Hardtops were delivered, no particular one was designated for Redford. Rather, when Pemulis Auto put a sticker on one, that identified that particular car to the contract.
3. *C* is the best answer. The general rule, for nonmerchant buyers, is that risk of loss passes when the goods are delivered. §2-509(3). There are other rules where the goods are being transported, §2-509(1), or held by a bailee, §2-509(2), but neither is the case here. The parties can agree that one should provide insurance, but did not do so, so *B* and *D* are incorrect. Likewise, the parties can agree about when the risk of loss will pass, but did not do so here, so the general rule will apply. The risk of loss does not depend on whether payment has been made, contrary to *A*.
4. *C* is the best answer. When goods are held by a bailee, the risk of loss passes when a negotiable document covering the goods is delivered to the buyer. §2-509(2)(a). The provision also addresses the issue when there is no document covering the goods or when the document is not negotiable.

5. *D* is the best answer. This question illustrates the role of shipping terms. In a transportation contract, if the parties do not address the issue, the contract is a "shipment" contract, meaning risk of loss shifts upon shipment. The parties may decide when the risk of loss shifts. The term *C.I.F.* designates a shipment contract, so the risk of loss would also shift upon shipment in *B. F.O.B.* means the risk of loss shifts at the place designated. *F.O.B. Boston* means risk of loss shifts in Boston, where the seller is, so this is also a shipment contract. So "all of the above" is correct.

Chapter 6

Performance of the Contract

Most contracts are performed without incident, but life, with all its complexities, snares many a deal, and the parties can end up in litigation arguing about who did what to whom. Sometimes the difficulty is with the product, sometimes with the delivery schedule, sometimes with an unwillingness to perform, and sometimes completion of the contract is outright impossible. In this chapter, we explore what levels of performance are required for compliance with contractual duties, the choices available for nonperformance by the other side, and the duties of each party when things go south.

Section 2-301 states that the seller's basic obligation is "to transfer and deliver" and the buyer's is "to pay in accordance with the contract." Thus, the seller must tender (offer to deliver) conforming goods, and the buyer must pay for them. Read and compare §2-507(1) with §2-511(1). They appear to be conflicting, don't they? The conflict disappears when the sections are considered in light of the technical/procedural snarl that they are designed to unravel. It is this: in any contract action, the plaintiff loses unless it can be shown that the other party is in breach. Where a sale of goods is involved, it is frequently true that the parties contemplated a contemporaneous swap of money for the goods. If at the appointed time neither party shows up, the buyer is not in breach because the seller did not tender, and vice versa. If the parties did not intend a contemporaneous swap, but instead contracted so that one or the other's performance was to come first, then either §2-507(1) or §2-511(1) will not apply, since the parties will have "otherwise agreed." When, for example, the parties agree that buyer is to be given six months after delivery in which to pay, failure of the seller to deliver on time is a breach, and the seller may be sued without the buyer's having to allege a §2-511(1) tender of payment. Knowing that the seller's basic duty is to tender conforming goods, and that the buyer's duty is to pay for them, leaves unanswered a host of legal questions. What does the seller's *tender* entail? (Answer: §§2-503, 2-504.) What does *conforming* mean? (Answer: §2-106(2).) What means of payment can the buyer use? (Answer: §2-511(2), (3).) These and other questions are the subject of this portion of the book.

I. INSTALLMENT SALES

At common law, successful plaintiffs in contract actions were generally required to prove *substantial performance* (as opposed to a technically perfect performance) of the terms of the contract. From your Contracts course you may remember Judge Cardozo's opinion in Jacob & Youngs Inc. v. Kent, 230 N.Y. 239, 129 N.E. 889 (1921), the so-called *Reading Pipe* case. The court held that the construction contract was substantially performed even though the contractor installed a different but similar brand of pipe instead of the Reading brand called for under the explicit terms of the contract.

In installment contracts, defined in §2-612(1), substantial performance is still the law. The seller is entitled to payment even where the tender of the goods fails to conform exactly to the contract as long as it "substantially" conforms. Read §2-612. For a good discussion of this section (and many others), see Ellen A. Peters, Remedies for Breach of Contracts Relating to the Sale of Goods Under the Uniform Commercial Code: A Roadmap for Article Two, 73 Yale L.J. 199, 223-229 (1963).

PROBLEM 61

Travis Galleries developed a market in copies of famous statues. It ordered monthly shipments of the statues from Ersatz Imports, agreeing to take 12 shipments of 20 statues each over the coming year. The first month all of the statues arrived upside down in their cartons. The manager of Travis Galleries was amazed that most had survived the trip in this condition. Only one was broken, and a phone call to Ersatz Imports resulted in a promise to ship a replacement at once. The next month the statues were again packaged upside down, and half of them were broken. Does §2-612 permit rejection for this reason? Assume that Ersatz replaced the broken statues within a week, but that the next month the shipment contained no statues at all. Instead, Ersatz had mistakenly shipped Travis poor copies of 20 French Impressionist paintings. Travis Galleries called you, its attorney. May it reject this shipment? Under what theory? May it now cancel the remainder of the Ersatz contract? In any rejection situation, is it wise for attorneys to ask their clients what really underlies their own actions?

Cherwell-Ralli, Inc. v. Rytman Grain Co.

Supreme Court of Connecticut, 1980
433 A.2d 984

PETERS, J.

This case involves a dispute about which of the parties to an oral installment contract was the first to be in breach. The plaintiff, Cherwell-Ralli, Inc., sued the defendant, Rytman Grain Co., Inc., for the nonpayment of moneys due and owing for accepted deliveries of products known as Cherco Meal and C-R-T Meal. The defendant, conceding its indebtedness, counterclaimed for damages arising out of the plaintiff's refusal to deliver remaining installments under the contract. The trial court, Bordon, J., trial referee, having found all issues for the plaintiff, rendered judgment accordingly, and the defendant appealed.

The trial court's unchallenged finding of fact establishes the following: The parties, on July 26, 1974, entered into an installment contract for the sale of Cherco Meal and C-R-T Meal on the basis of a memorandum executed by the Getkin Brokerage House. As modified, the contract called for shipments according to weekly instructions from the buyer, with payments to be made within ten days after delivery. Almost immediately the buyer was behind in its payments, and these arrearages were often quite substantial. The seller repeatedly called these arrearages to the buyer's attention but continued to make all shipments as requested by the buyer from July 29, 1974 to April 23, 1975.

By April 15, 1975, the buyer had become concerned that the seller might not complete performance of the contract, because the seller's plant might close and because the market price of the goods had come significantly to exceed the contract price. In a telephonic conversation between the buyer's president and the seller's president on that day, the buyer was assured by the seller that deliveries would continue if the buyer would make the payments for which it was obligated. Thereupon, the buyer sent the seller a check in the amount of $9,825.60 to cover shipments through March 31, 1975.

Several days later, on April 23, 1975, the buyer stopped payment on this check because he was told by a truck driver, not employed by the seller, that this shipment would be his last load. The trial court found that this was not a valid reason for stoppage of payment. Upon inquiry by the seller, the buyer restated his earlier concerns about future deliveries. Two letters, both dated April 28, 1975, describe the impasse between the parties: the seller again demanded payment, and the buyer, for the first time in writing, demanded adequate assurance of further deliveries. The buyer's demand for assurance was reiterated in its direct reply to the seller's demand for payment. The buyer, however, made no further payments, either to replace the stopped check or otherwise to pay for the nineteen accepted shipments for which balances were outstanding. The seller made no further deliveries after April 23, 1975, when it heard about the stopped check; the buyer never made specific requests for shipments after that date. Inability to deliver the goods forced the seller to close its plant, on May 2, 1975, because of stockpiling of excess material.

The trial court concluded, on the basis of these facts, that the party in breach was the buyer and not the seller. The court concluded that the seller was entitled to recover the final balance of $21,013.60, which both parties agreed to be due and owing. It concluded that the buyer could not prevail on its counterclaim because it had no reasonable grounds to doubt performance from the seller and had in fact received reasonable assurances. Further, the buyer had presented no reasonably accurate evidence to establish the damages it might have sustained because of the seller's failure to deliver.

The buyer on this appeal challenges first the conclusion that the buyer's failure to pay "substantially impaired the value of the whole contract" so as to constitute "a breach of the whole contract," as is required by the applicable law governing installment contracts. U.C.C. §2-612(3). What constitutes impairment of the value of the whole contract is a question of fact; Graulich Caterer, Inc. v. Holterbosch, Inc., 101 N.J. Super. 61, 75, 243 A.2d 253 (1968); Holiday Mfg. Co. v. B.A.S.F. Systems, Inc., 380 F. Supp. 1096, 1102 (D. Neb. 1974). The record below amply sustains the trial court's conclusion in this regard, particularly in light of the undenied and uncured stoppage of a check given to comply with the buyer's promise to reduce significantly the amount of its outstanding arrearages. See Frigiking, Inc. v. Century Tire & Sales Co., 452 F. Supp. 935, 938 (N.D. Tex. 1978).

The buyer argues that the seller in an installment contract may never terminate a contract, despite repeated default in payment by the buyer, without first invoking the insecurity methodology of §2-609. That is not the law. If there is reasonable doubt about whether the buyer's default is substantial, the seller may be well advised to temporize by suspending further performance until it can ascertain whether the buyer is able to offer adequate assurance of future payments. Kunian v. Development Corporation of America, 165 Conn. 300, 312, 334 A.2d 427 (1973); Dangerfield v. Markel, 252 N.W.2d 184, 192-93 (N.D. 1977). But if the buyer's conduct is sufficiently egregious, such conduct will, in and of itself, constitute substantial impairment of the value of the whole contract and a present breach of the contract as a whole. An aggrieved seller is expressly permitted, by §2-703(f), upon breach of a contract as a whole, to cancel the remainder of the contract "with respect to the whole undelivered balance." See Frigiking, Inc. v. Century Tire & Sales Co., supra. Nor is the seller's remedy to cancel waived, as the buyer argues, by a lawsuit seeking recovery for payments due. While §2-612(3) states that a contract is reinstated if the seller "brings an action with respect *only* to past installments" (emphasis added), it is clear in this case that the seller intended, as the buyer well knew, to bring this contract to an end because of the buyer's breach.

The buyer's attack on the court's conclusions with respect to its counterclaim is equally unavailing. The buyer's principal argument is that the seller was obligated, on pain of default, to provide assurance of its further performance. The right to such assurance is premised on reasonable grounds for insecurity. Whether a buyer has reasonable grounds to be insecure is a question of fact. AMF, Inc. v. McDonald's Corp., 536 F.2d 1167, 1170 (7th Cir. 1976). The trial court concluded that in this case the buyer's insecurity was not reasonable and we agree. A party to a sales contract may not suspend performance of its own for which it has "already received the agreed return." At all times, the buyer had received all the goods which it had ordered. The buyer could not rely on its own nonpayments as a basis for its own insecurity. The presidents of the parties had exchanged adequate verbal assurances only eight days before the buyer itself again delayed its own performance on the basis of information that was facially unreliable. Contrary to the buyer's argument, subsequent events proved the buyer's fears to be incorrect, since the seller's plant closed due to a surplus rather than due to a shortage of materials. Finally, it is fatal to the buyer's appeal that neither its oral argument nor its brief addressed its failure to substantiate, with probative evidence, the damages it alleged to be attributable to the seller's nondeliveries.

There is no error.

In this opinion the other judges concurred.

II. THE PERFECT TENDER RULE

The substantial performance rule has never (at least in theory) applied to single-delivery contracts between merchants. Learned Hand once stated that "[t]here is no room in commercial contracts for the doctrine of substantial performance." Mitsubishi Goshi Kaisha v. J. Aron & Co., 16 F.2d 185, 186 (2d Cir. 1926). To prevail in a single-delivery sale, the seller must make a *perfect tender*, one that complied with all of the terms of the contract, and then show that the buyer refused to take the goods. The reason for this higher standard in single-delivery sales is that in such cases the buyer does not have the same bargaining position a buyer would have in installment sales (where the seller needs to keep dealing with the buyer on repeated occasions and therefore must, as a business matter, keep the buyer happy).

The Code's perfect tender rule is found in §2-601. Read it. (*Commercial unit* is defined in §2-105(6).)

PROBLEM 62

Stella Speculator, a wealthy investor, signed a contract with Swank Motors to buy five new cars. All five were to be delivered on October 1. When the cars arrived, she test drove each of them and then returned two of them, saying she would keep the other three. She rejected the two cars because the audio system did not work in one of them (she was a great music lover) and the carpeting in the trunk of the other was ripping. Swank Motors offered to repair both defects. When Speculator refused to permit repair, Swank sued. Answer these questions:

(a) Does the common law doctrine *de minimis non curat lex* ("the law does not notice small defects") survive §2-601? If so, in spite of the tiny defects, the cars would be conforming. See Official Comment 2 to §2-106; see D.P. Technology Corp. v. Sherwood Tool, Inc., 751 F. Supp. 1038 (D. Conn. 1990) (where goods specially manufactured, buyer not in good faith in rejecting because of insubstantial delay in delivery).

(b) A seller has a right to *cure* in some circumstances; see §2-508. Is this section of use to Swank Motors? See Wilson v. Scampoli, 228 A.2d 848 (D.C. 1967), reprinted below.

(c) Suppose Swank can demonstrate that it is common for car sellers to correct small defects. Will Swank succeed if it argues that such correction is a *usage of trade* (§1-303(c)) and thus either that the goods are *conforming* or that because of this usage of trade, the parties have impliedly agreed that a §2-601 perfect tender is not required? See §§1-302, 1-201(b)(3).

Larson v. Burton Construction, Inc.

Supreme Court of Wyoming, 2018
421 P.3d 538

Fox, Justice.

After a bench trial, the circuit court cancelled the mobile home sale between Respondent, Burton Construction, Inc., and Petitioner, Justin

James Larson, finding that the parties made a mutual mistake in drafting their contract. On appeal, the district court reversed the circuit court's decision and found that Mr. Larson breached the contract. We granted Mr. Larson's petition for a writ of review. We affirm in part, reverse in part, and remand for further proceedings.

Issues

We reframe the parties' issues as follows:

1. Did the district court erroneously overturn the circuit court's application of the doctrine of mutual mistake?

2. Did the district court err when it found that Mr. Larson breached the contract before Burton Construction, Inc.'s performance was due by making a clearly erroneous finding of fact, and as a matter of law?

Facts

In December 2015, Ken Burton, on behalf of Burton Construction, Inc., and Mr. Larson entered into a written contract (the Contract) in which Mr. Larson agreed to purchase from Burton a 2015 Skyline mobile home for $43,000. The Contract was a "form" contract, consisting of boilerplate provisions and blank lines on which parties could enter information. Mr. Larson's agent completed the form by hand, obtained Mr. Larson's signature, and delivered the document to Burton with $500 in earnest money. Burton went through the Contract carefully, made a few minor changes, and countersigned it.

Although the Skyline mobile home was new and the parties intended to convey a new mobile home, the form was designed for the sale of a used mobile home. Thus, the Contract required Burton, as the "Owner" of the mobile home, to execute and deliver a Wyoming title at closing (handwritten portions in italics):

> 6. At closing, Owner shall execute and deliver a Wyoming title and Bill of Sale free and clear of all liens and encumbrances except: *all will be free and clear.*
>
> 7. Title shall be conveyed to the following named purchaser(s): *Justin James Larson* as *Sole Owner.* Title and the Bill of Sale shall be executed but escrowed if sold under contract.
>
> 8. Title shall be merchantable in the Seller, except as stated in this paragraph. Subject to payment or tender as above provided and compliance with other terms and conditions hereunder by Purchaser, the Seller shall execute and deliver a good and sufficient title in favor of those persons named in Paragraph 7 above, and a good and sufficient Bill of Sale, and deliver the same to said Purchaser at closing, which shall occur on or before *January*

15, 2016, conveying said personal properties free and clear of all liens and encumbrances, except:

(a) Personal property taxes for *2016*, which shall be prorated to date of closing;

(b) Purchaser shall be responsible for sales tax, if any.

Despite the Contract's clear language, Burton testified that it was not his custom to deliver a Wyoming title to purchasers of new mobile homes at closing. As a reseller, Burton did not take title himself. Burton would purchase the mobile home from the manufacturer with borrowed funds, and the manufacturer would deliver the mobile home with a Manufacturer's Certificate of Origin (MCO). The lender held the MCO as collateral until the mobile home was sold. At closing, Burton would use the purchaser's funds to repay the lender, and the lender would return the MCO. Burton would collect sales tax from the purchaser, submit it to the state, and record the taxes as paid on the Bill of Sale. Under his reseller's tax exemption, Burton would pay no sales tax on his initial purchase from the manufacturer so long as he resold the mobile home directly to the consumer. After closing, Burton or the purchaser would bring the MCO and the Bill of Sale to the County Treasurer to issue a Wyoming title in the purchaser's name as the first assignee of the mobile home.

Accordingly, Burton never intended to deliver a Wyoming title to Mr. Larson at closing because "[t]hat's not how you do it." Burton testified that he "couldn't" deliver the Wyoming title at closing for three reasons. First, he would have to repay his lender in full to obtain the MCO necessary to issue title, which he presumably could not do before receiving Mr. Larson's purchase money. Second, if Burton obtained a Wyoming title before closing, he would become the first "owner" of the mobile home, which would require him to pay sales tax on his initial purchase of the mobile home from the manufacturer, and, because the State of Wyoming taxes only the first sale of a mobile home, Mr. Larson would pay no sales tax on his purchase from Burton. Third, Burton testified that the manufacturer's warranty extended only to the first titleholder. Mr. Larson, as the second titleholder, would be deprived of the warranty.

Burton's realtor, however, did not know the difference between an MCO and a Wyoming title. Thus, each time the escrow officer inquired, the realtor confirmed that Burton would deliver a Wyoming title for the closing. Based on the language of the Contract, confirmed by the realtor's assurances, the escrow officer expected Burton to deliver a Wyoming title at closing and therefore prepared settlement statements indicating that no sales tax was due from Mr. Larson.

When the parties agreed to move the closing date forward by two days, the escrow officer and the parties' agents rushed to assemble the paperwork. Shortly before closing, for the first time, Burton instructed his realtor to pick up the MCO from his lender and bring it to the escrow officer. When Mr. Larson's agent arrived at closing, she discovered that Burton had provided an MCO instead of a Wyoming title, which added $1,806 in sales tax to Mr. Larson's purchase obligation. She called Mr. Larson, who was outside the building:

> *A.* [Mr. Larson] . . . She actually called me and told me what the deal was; that I was required to pay $1,800 more for sales tax that was never agreed upon anywhere, or had ever showed up on anywhere, even in our closing paper that we had.
>
> And, I said, "Well, that's not what we agreed to. We agreed to the 43,000-something.
>
> *Q.* [Burton's counsel] Well, did you ever look at the Contract and ask her about Page 2, Line 61, that said you promised to pay the sales tax at that point?
>
> *A.* No, because I saw up here on the—What line is it?—like, 49 and 50, it says all will be free and clear. She'll deliver a Wyoming Bill of Sale and a, and a Title, and it will all be free and clear, meaning, to me, that there was nothing above and beyond after what we had agreed upon the price of the house.
>
> I had to pay the closing cost and whatever. The only thing I would have to pay after that would be the ten or $15 at the Courthouse to transfer the Title from Mr. Burton's name to my name.

Mr. Larson never entered the building. He cancelled the closing before Burton arrived, refusing to complete the sale upon the delivery of an MCO instead of a title. That same day, Mr. Larson sent a letter to Burton requesting the return of his earnest money and declaring the Contract null and void due to, among other things, Burton's failure to deliver a Wyoming title. Burton's attempts to reschedule the closing before the January 15 deadline failed. Mr. Larson would not close the sale without Burton providing a Wyoming title, which Burton would not do.

Burton brought suit in circuit court for breach of contract, seeking either specific performance or damages, as well as attorney fees and costs. After a bench trial, the circuit court found that the parties made a mutual mistake, cancelled the Contract, and ordered Burton to return Mr. Larson's earnest money. On appeal, the district court reversed, ruling that the circuit court erroneously applied the doctrine of mutual mistake, that it was "factually unknown" whether Burton delivered a Wyoming title at closing, and that Mr. Larson breached the Contract when he refused to attend closing and to pay sales tax. Pursuant to W.R.A.P. 13, we granted Mr. Larson's petition for writ of review.

DISCUSSION

I. DID THE DISTRICT COURT ERRONEOUSLY OVERTURN THE CIRCUIT COURT'S APPLICATION OF THE DOCTRINE OF MUTUAL MISTAKE?

[The court concluded there was no mutual mistake in the transaction.]

II. DID THE DISTRICT COURT ERR WHEN IT FOUND THAT MR. LARSON BREACHED THE CONTRACT BEFORE BURTON CONSTRUCTION, INC.'S PERFORMANCE WAS DUE BY MAKING A CLEARLY ERRONEOUS FINDING OF FACT, AND AS A MATTER OF LAW?

Mr. Larson argued that Burton breached the Contract by failing to deliver a Wyoming title at closing. The district court disagreed, concluding that it is "factually unknown" whether Burton delivered a Wyoming title at closing because Mr. Larson abandoned the closing before Burton arrived. The district court instead held Mr. Larson in breach, finding that he refused to attend closing and tender sales tax as required by the Contract.

To prove a breach of contract, the proponent must show "a lawfully enforceable contract, an unjustified failure to timely perform all or any part of what is promised therein, and entitlement of injured party to damages." *Schlinger v. McGhee*, 2012 WY 7, ¶12, 268 P.3d 264, 268 (Wyo. 2012), *as amended on reh'g* (Feb. 7, 2012) (quoting *Reynolds v. Tice*, 595 P.2d 1318, 1323 (Wyo. 1979)). Here, the Contract is lawfully enforceable. Mr. Larson delivered the Contract to Burton with his signature and $500 earnest money as an offer to purchase the mobile home. Burton countersigned and accepted the earnest money, thus perfecting the Contract. Next, the Contract entitles a nonbreaching party to damages. Thus, to find a breach, we must interpret the Contract to identify each party's obligations and determine whether either party unjustifiably failed to perform as promised. . . .

The fundamental goal of contract interpretation is to determine the intent of the parties. *Whitney Holding Corp. v. Terry*, 2012 WY 21, ¶36, 270 P.3d 662, 673 (Wyo. 2012). The "language of the parties expressed in their contract must be given effect in accordance with the meaning which that language would convey to reasonable persons at the time and place of its use." *Ultra Res., Inc. v. Hartman*, 2010 WY 36, ¶22, 226 P.3d 889, 905 (Wyo. 2010) (quoting *Moncrief v. Louisiana Land Exploration Co.*, 861 P.2d 516, 524 (Wyo. 1993)). This Court employs "common sense in interpreting contracts and ascribe[s] the words with a rational and reasonable intent." *Id.*, ¶22, 226 P.3d at 905. "When the provisions in the contract are clear and unambiguous, the court looks only to the 'four corners' of the document in arriving at the intent of the parties." *Claman v. Popp*, 2012 WY 92, ¶26, 279 P.3d 1003,

1013 (Wyo. 2012) (citations omitted). "In the absence of any ambiguity, the contract will be enforced according to its terms because no construction is appropriate." *Id.* (citation omitted). *Id.* at ¶20, 361 P.3d at 830 (quoting *Wallop Canyon Ranch, LLC v. Goodwyn,* 2015 WY 81, ¶35, 351 P.3d 943, 953 (Wyo. 2015)).

There is no reason to venture beyond the four corners of the Contract to determine that Burton was required to deliver a Wyoming title at closing. The parties argued, and both lower courts found, that the Contract's language is unambiguous, and we agree. The Contract states that closing must occur by January 15, 2016, at which time Burton must deliver a Wyoming title: "At closing, Owner shall execute and deliver a Wyoming title and Bill of Sale free and clear of all liens and encumbrances."

On the other hand, the Contract also stated that Mr. Larson "shall be responsible for sales tax, if any." The words "if any" indicate that Mr. Larson's responsibility to pay sales tax is conditioned on sales tax being generated by the transaction. "Our rules of interpretation require that we interpret a contract as a whole, reading each provision in light of all the others to find their plain meaning." *Pope,* 2015 WY 142, ¶20, 361 P.3d at 830 (citations omitted). Here, the Contract plainly requires Burton's delivery of a Wyoming title. In this light, the Contract requires Mr. Larson to pay the sales tax associated with Burton's delivery of a Wyoming title. Accordingly, we conclude that Mr. Larson was not obligated to pay sales tax on the transaction, as none would be generated. To obtain a Wyoming title before closing, Burton would become the first owner of the mobile home and would have to pay sales tax on his initial purchase of the mobile home from the manufacturer. The State of Wyoming taxes only the first sale of a mobile home. Wyo. Stat. Ann. §39-15-101(a)(xiii)(B) (LexisNexis 2017); Wyo. Stat. Ann. §39-15-103(b)(iv) (LexisNexis 2017). As the second titleholder, Mr. Larson would not be subject to "any" sales tax.

Burton urges us to give the Contract's language its "full effect together in the context of a normal closing of the parties' contract for the sale of a new mobile home" (emphasis in original). Burton explains that the

> contextual fair meaning of the parties' contract, evident from the contract itself, always was that the parties agreed formally to effectuate a sale and transfer of title and possession of a new mobile home with a manufacturer's warranty. Larson agreed to pay the sales tax on that sale. Burton agreed to collect the sales tax at closing from Larson and to then promptly effectuate the issuance of one certificate of title by the County Clerk to Larson with Larson's Bank's lien shown on it as a first lien. . . .

"[C]ourts apply an objective theory of intent whereby one party's intention is deemed to be that meaning a reasonable person in the position of the other contracting party would ascribe to the first party's manifestations of assent." 17A Am. Jur. 2d *Contracts* § 29 (May 2018 update). A reasonable layperson, such as Mr. Larson, would not be privy to a dealer's process of transferring title. Further, although parties to a contract are presumed to know the law, we do not attribute to them a complete understanding of the statutes governing sales of mobile homes. "According to our established standards for interpretation of contracts, the words used in the contract are afforded the plain meaning that a reasonable person would give to them." *Caballo Coal Co. v. Fid. Expl. & Prod. Co.*, 2004 WY 6, ¶11, 84 P.3d 311, 314 (Wyo. 2004) (citation omitted).

While Mr. Larson testified that he knew he had contracted to purchase a new mobile home, we are unable to discern from the record that "new" meant anything more to Mr. Larson than that the mobile home had not been previously occupied. Although Burton testified that by obtaining a Wyoming title, the mobile home would no longer be "new," thus voiding the warranty to Mr. Larson; he also testified that he never discussed this concept with Mr. Larson. In fact, there is no evidence of any agreement regarding a warranty at the time the Contract was made: the listing agent could not say for sure that the online listing advertised the mobile home as having a warranty, and the Contract did not refer to a warranty. The only evidence that the parties discussed a warranty was testimony of a conversation that occurred during a walk-through of the mobile home after the Contract was signed, just before closing. "Our primary purpose is to determine the true intent and understanding of the parties ***at the time and place the agreement was made.***" *Pennaco Energy, Inc. v. KD Co. LLC*, 2015 WY 152, ¶25, 363 P.3d 18, 25 (Wyo. 2015) (citations omitted) (emphasis added).

Likewise, the record shows that Mr. Larson did not share Burton's unilateral intent to deliver an MCO, collect the sales tax at closing, and "promptly effectuate the issuance" of a title. Although Burton apparently had it in his mind that he would follow his customary process of transferring ownership, he signed an enforceable contract that promised otherwise. "Because we use an objective approach to interpret contracts, evidence of a party's subjective intent is not admissible, regardless of whether the court determines a contract is ambiguous or clear." *Ultra Res., Inc. v. Hartman*, 2010 WY 36, ¶23, 226 P.3d 889, 905 (Wyo. 2010). We decline to rewrite the Contract to conform to Burton's subjective intentions.

A. Clearly Erroneous Finding of Fact

We review a district court acting in its appellate capacity under the authority of Wyo. Stat. Ann. §5-2-119 (LexisNexis 2017), which directs this Court to set the standards and extent of our review. Neither the rules of appellate procedure nor our caselaw addresses whether we should review factual findings of the district court under these circumstances and, if so, our level of deference. "Ordinarily, the review in the higher appellate court of the actions of the intermediate appellate court is limited to errors of law only." 5 C.J.S. *Appeal and Error* §985 (June 2018 update). Nonetheless, we recognize that some issues involve mixed questions of law and fact; and, following a bench trial, we generally do not accept factual findings from the lower court that are clearly erroneous. *E.g.*, *Gould v. Ochsner*, 2015 WY 101, ¶16, 354 P.3d 965, 971 (Wyo. 2015). In civil cases, the United States Supreme Court follows the "two court rule," by which "the Court will not review findings of fact concurred in by two courts below in the absence of a very obvious and exceptional showing of error." 20 Charles A. Wright and Mary Kay Kane, *Federal Practice and Procedure Deskbook* §115 (April 2018 update); *see also Graver Tank & Mfg. Co., v. Linde Air Products Co.*, 336 U.S. 271, 275, 69 S. Ct. 535, 538, 93 L. Ed. 672 (1949). Likewise, we will not accept, without scrutiny, the findings of a district court that contradict the trial court and, if clearly erroneous in light of the record, we will disregard the findings.

Here, the two courts below did not concur, and the record does not support the district court's conclusion that the circuit court erred. Specifically, the circuit court found that "[Burton's] agent did not appear with a title" at closing, and "[Burton] could not provide a title at closing as required by the contract." Nevertheless, the district court found that "whether or not Burton tendered a . . . title, remains factually unknown." Burton's testimony refutes the district court's findings:

> *Q.* [Mr. Larson's counsel] Okay. So, at any of these closings that you testified under Direct, under questioning from your attorney, at any of these closings did you bring a Wyoming Title?
>
> *A.* [Mr. Larson] No.
>
> . . .
>
> *Q.* So, essentially we can agree that in none of these proposed closings did you bring a Wyoming Title.
>
> *A.* On a new home, no.
>
> . . .
>
> *Q.* Okay. And, I guess at the risk of repeating myself, you never offered Mr. Larson any written or verbal communication to provide him with a Wyoming Title.
>
> *A.* No.

Although Burton rescheduled the closing for January 15, he remained unwilling to deliver a Wyoming title. In preparation for the rescheduled closing, he directed the escrow officer to create a new settlement sheet showing an additional $1,806 in sales tax due from Mr. Larson, based on his planned delivery of an MCO. The record establishes that Burton neither delivered nor intended to deliver a Wyoming title before January 15. Thus, we set aside the district court's incompatible finding.

B. Breach as a Matter of Law

Throughout the proceedings and on appeal, Burton argued that his obligation to deliver a Wyoming title at closing could be performed by delivering an MCO and a bill of sale, which could be presented to the County Treasurer for a title after closing. Burton rests his argument on the doctrine of substantial performance, which "allows a party that has substantially complied with a contract to recover for its performance despite the fact that it has breached the contract by failing to comply fully with its terms." *Bear Peak Res., LLC v. Peak Powder River Res., LLC*, 2017 WY 124, ¶40, 403 P.3d 1033, 1047 (Wyo. 2017), *reh'g denied* (Nov. 7, 2017) (quoting 15 *Williston on Contracts* §44:58 (4th ed. 2017)). "The doctrine is rooted in fairness and 'is intended to protect a party's right to be compensated when it has performed in all material and substantive respects and to avoid the possibility of a forfeiture due to technical, minor, inadvertent, or unimportant deficiencies.'" *Id.* (quoting *Williston, supra*, §44:52).

We could find that Burton did not "substantially perform" his obligation to deliver a Wyoming title, as the added tax burden rendered the delivery of an MCO to be more than a "technical, minor, inadvertent, or unimportant" performance defect. *Bear Peak Res., LLC*, 2017 WY 124, ¶40, 403 P.3d at 1047. However, the doctrine of substantial performance is inapplicable here. Even though neither party argued for its application—and, even though it leads to the same result—we cannot ignore that Article 2 of the Uniform Commercial Code (UCC)[5] and the "perfect tender" rule govern the Contract. In *Meuse-Rhine-Ijssel Cattle Breeders of Canada Ltd. v. Y-Tex Corp.*, 590 P.2d 1306, 1309 (Wyo. 1979), the Court considered applicable provisions of the UCC in a breach of contract case where the parties had not called them to the attention of the district court. We determined that the UCC "became a part of the contract as though written into its terms." *Id.* (citing *Tri-Cty. Elec. Ass'n, Inc. v. City of Gillette*, 584 P.2d 995, 1007 (Wyo. 1978).) "There is no reason to keep secret the proper law applicable to a case just because overlooked." *Id.* Likewise, we decline to ignore the UCC where we are bound by statute to apply it.

The mobile home that Mr. Larson contracted to purchase is personal property and a "good" governed by the UCC. Wyo. Stat. Ann. §34.1-2-105 (LexisNexis 2017) ("'Goods' means all things (including specially manufactured goods) which are movable at the time of identification to the contract for sale. . . ."); *Milnes v. Milnes*, 2008 WY 11, ¶9, 175 P.3d 1164, 1168 (Wyo. 2008) (mobile homes are ordinarily taxed as personal property unless converted to real property, i.e. installed on a permanent foundation, under Wyo. Stat. Ann. §31-2-502(b)); *Reposa v. Buhler*, 770 P.2d 235, 238 (Wyo. 1989) (applying personal property measure of damages to a mobile home); *see also Singletary, III v. P & A Invs., Inc.*, 212 N.C. App. 469, 712 S.E.2d 681, 685-86 (2011); *Hensley v. Ray's Motor Co. of Forest City, Inc.*, 158 N.C. App. 261, 580 S.E.2d 721, 723 (2003); *Cooper v. Bluff City Mobile Home Sales, Inc.*, 78 S.W.3d 157, 163 (Mo. Ct. App. 2002); *Waggoner v. Town & Country Mobile Homes, Inc.*, 808 P.2d 649, 653 (Okla. 1990). The UCC "does not rely on concepts of substantial performance, but instead requires that the seller make a perfect tender, meaning that the seller must tender goods that conform in all respects to those specified in the parties' agreement." 77A C.J.S. *Sales* §273 (March 2018 update) (citing *Pomerantz Paper Corp. v. New Cmty. Corp.*, 207 N.J. 344, 25 A.3d 221, 231-32 (2011)). In Wyoming, the perfect tender rule is found at Wyo. Stat. Ann. §34.1-2-601 (LexisNexis 2017), stating in pertinent part: "if the goods or the tender of delivery ***fail in any respect to conform to the contract***, the buyer may: (i) Reject the whole. . . ." (Emphasis added.) Generally, under the rule, "the buyer may reject a seller's tender for any trivial defect, whether it be in the quality of the goods, the timing of performance, or the manner of delivery." *Midwest Mobile Diagnostic Imaging, L.L.C. v. Dynamics Corp. of Am.*, 965 F. Supp. 1003, 1011 (W.D. Mich. 1997), *aff'd*, 165 F.3d 27 (6th Cir. 1998) (unpublished opinion).

Here, the Contract plainly states: "At closing, Owner shall execute and deliver a Wyoming title and Bill of Sale free and clear of all liens and encumbrances." Delivering an MCO that can be submitted to the County Treasurer for a Wyoming title after closing is not a perfect tender. The Contract unambiguously stated that the title was due "at closing"—not "promptly effectuated" afterward. Burton failed to perfectly perform his obligation to deliver a Wyoming title at closing under the plain terms of the Contract.[7]

We note that the obligation of good faith limits a buyer's seemingly unhindered right to reject under the perfect tender rule. William H. Lawrence, *Appropriate Standards for a Buyer's Refusal to Keep Goods Tendered by a Seller*, 35 Wm. & Mary L. Rev. 1635, 1651 (1994) ("The perfect tender rule does not give buyers the power to seize upon the slightest contract deviation, even though it is not important to the buyer, as a pretext for discontinuing the contract. . . . The good faith requirement of the Code effectively prevents such improper strategic behavior, and thus assures that application of the perfect tender rule will occur only in those instances when it is invoked honestly." (citations omitted)); *see also generally Printing Ctr. of Texas, Inc. v. Supermind Pub. Co.*, 669 S.W.2d 779, 784 (Tex. App. 1984); *Y & N Furniture, Inc. v. Nwabuoku*, 190 Misc.2d 402, 734 N.Y.S.2d 382, 385 (N.Y. Civ. Ct. 2001); *Hubbard v. UTZ Quality Foods, Inc.*, 903 F.Supp. 444, 451 (W.D.N.Y. 1995); *Clark v. Zaid, Inc.*, 263 Md. 127, 282 A.2d 483, 484 n.1 (1971). Under the UCC, "[e]very contract or duty within this act imposes an obligation of good faith in its performance and enforcement." Wyo. Stat. Ann. §34.1-1-304 (LexisNexis 2017). Good faith includes "both the subjective element of honesty in fact and the objective element of the observance of reasonable commercial standards of fair dealing." 67 Am. Jur. 2d *Sales* §433 (May 2018 update); Wyo. Stat. Ann. §34.1-1-201 (LexisNexis 2017). Here, the law did not oblige Mr. Larson to pay sales tax upon Burton's delivery of a Wyoming title. *See supra* ¶18. As Mr. Larson testified, by accepting an MCO, "I was required to pay $1,800 more for sales tax that was never agreed upon anywhere." It was neither pretextual nor commercially unreasonable for Mr. Larson to reject the MCO as an imperfect tender, as Burton's delivery of an MCO added $1,806 to Mr. Larson's contractual obligation.

Finally, we disagree with the district court that Mr. Larson's failure to attempt to close the sale constituted an unjustified failure to perform under the Contract. The parties' agents were present at closing, and Mr. Larson was outside. Mr. Larson's funds had been issued. Mr. Larson's agent left the closing, and Mr. Larson declined to enter, only because Burton and his agent failed to deliver or undertake delivery of a Wyoming title. Burton's further attempts to close the sale before January 15 consisted of insisting that Mr. Larson accept an MCO in the place of a Wyoming title.

Mr. Larson argues that "Burton breached the contract, which breach excuses Mr. Larson's performance." We agree. The UCC, however, compels us to frame his refusal to close the sale in terms of anticipatory repudiation, which allows a party to suspend his own performance "[w]hen either party repudiates the contract with respect to a performance not yet due the loss of which will substantially impair the value of the contract to the other." Wyo. Stat. Ann. § 34.1-2-610(a) (LexisNexis 2017). "[A]nticipatory repudiation centers upon an overt communication of intention or an action which renders performance impossible or demonstrates a clear determination not to continue with performance." *Id.*, cmt. 1. Mr. Larson was justified to treat Burton's clear determination to deliver an MCO as a repudiation of Burton's contractual obligation to deliver a Wyoming title. In the face of Burton's ongoing repudiation, Mr. Larson justifiably abandoned the initial closing and refused to join Burton's subsequent attempts to close the sale before January 15.

Conclusion

We affirm the district court's reversal of the circuit court's finding of a mutual mistake of the parties. We reverse the district court's decision to hold Mr. Larson in breach of the Contract and conversely find that Burton breached the Contract. We remand for further proceedings consistent with this opinion.

KAUTZ, J., dissenting, in which DAVIS, C.J., joins.

I concur with the majority's determination that the circuit court erred in concluding the parties' written contract mistakenly deviated from their actual prior agreement. The record does not show that prior to the written contract the parties had any specific agreement about the documents to be used in transferring title to Mr. Larson.

I also concur that the parties made an enforceable contract, and that the evidence clearly establishes their intent. I do not agree, however, that the contract's language about the documents to be used in transferring title was unambiguous in the context of this case. . . .

The written contract in this case suffers from a latent ambiguity. The parties' contract stated that Burton would "execute and deliver a Wyoming title" in order to transfer the mobile home to Mr. Larson. Those words, read independently, appear to be definite and not subject to double meaning.[8] However, the evidence is unequivocal that the parties intended and required Burton to transfer a new mobile home with a new mobile home warranty. The evidence is equally unequivocal that it was impossible for Burton to give Mr. Larson an official Wyoming title and also transfer the mobile home as a new mobile home with a new warranty. Wyo. Stat. Ann. §31-2-502(a)(i) and (iii) (LexisNexis 2017) states that **"no certificate of title shall be issued . . . for mobile homes . . . held for sale by a Wyoming mobile home dealer."** Our statutes state that Burton could not get a title, and the evidence established that in the trade dealers do not provide certificates of title for new mobile homes. Instead, Burton used the appropriate document for a dealer to transfer a new mobile home—a manufacturer's certificate of origin. . . .

UNIFORM COMMERCIAL CODE

The majority opinion correctly points out the Uniform Commercial Code as adopted in Wyoming applies to this transaction, even though the parties did not present arguments based on the UCC. The majority concludes that the "perfect tender" statement of Wyo. Stat. Ann. §34.1-2-601 (LexisNexis 2017) required Burton to provide a Wyoming certificate of title. Because he did not (and could not) the majority then concludes Mr. Larson was permitted to reject the transaction and terminate the contract.

Other portions of the UCC, however, show that in this circumstance Mr. Larson was required to accept the manufacturer's certificate of origin as the document used to transfer title. Assuming the parties' contract actually required Burton to provide an official certificate of title, when the buyer (Mr. Larson) objected to the certificate of origin, the UCC then required the seller (Burton) be given the opportunity to cure the defect (§34.1-2-508) or to substitute (§34.1-2-504 and 614). The official UCC comment to

§34.1-2-504 addresses the exact situation present here, stating "when a prescribed document cannot be procured, a question of fact arises under the provision of the Article on substituted performance as to whether the agreed manner of delivery is actually commercially impracticable and whether the substitute is commercially reasonable." In this case, the evidence showed it was not just impracticable, but impossible, for a dealer to provide a title on a new mobile home. The evidence also showed that a manufacturer's certificate of origin was not only reasonable, but was the statutorily recognized method of transferring title on a new mobile home. Wyo. Stat. Ann. §34.1-2-614(a) (LexisNexis 2017) goes on to state that the buyer (Burton) was required to accept the certificate of origin because it was the commercially reasonable method of transferring title. "Where without fault of either party the . . . agreed manner of delivery . . . becomes commercially impracticable but a commercially reasonable substitute is available, such substitute performance **must be tendered and accepted**." (Emphasis added.) *Id.* . . .

The dissent gets into other issues that we will explore next, one by one. We start with "Cure."

III. CURE

If the seller has not made a *perfect* tender, and as a result the buyer has rejected the goods, the seller has the right in some circumstances to *cure* the defective performance. The key section is §2-508. Read it and its Official Comments. For an annotation on the subject, see Annot., 36 A.L.R.4th 544.

PROBLEM 63

On August 8, Francis and Sophie Ferdinand ordered a new car from Princip Motors for $22,000. The car was scheduled for delivery "no later than September 1" (it had special accessories that had to be installed at the factory). On August 15, Princip Motors told the Ferdinands that the car was ready, so they picked it up. Halfway home (three miles from the car dealer), the engine blew up without warning. The Ferdinands were not hurt, but the engine was destroyed. On being informed that the Ferdinands wanted their money back, Princip made the following responses:

(a) Princip offered to take an engine out of a car of the same model and install it in the original automobile (which was otherwise undamaged).

(b) Princip refused to refund the money; instead, it claimed a right to give the Ferdinands a new car to be delivered fresh from the factory on August 20.

Does §2-508 require the Ferdinands to accept either of these cure offers?

In resolving this Problem it may help you to know about the *Shaken Faith Doctrine,* developed in a similar situation by the court in a leading case (worth reading):

> For a majority of people the purchase of a new car is a major investment, rationalized by the peace of mind that flows from its dependability and safety. Once their faith is shaken, the vehicle loses not only its real value in their eyes, but becomes an instrument whose integrity is substantially impaired and whose operation is fraught with apprehension. The attempted cure in the present case was ineffective.

Zabriskie Chevrolet, Inc. v. Smith, 99 N.J. Super. 441, 458, 240 A.2d 195, 205 (1968).

And, in the words of one pedant, "The court should be willing to take judicial notice of what all modern day consumers 'know': things that do not work well at the start are not likely to work well in the future unless the original defect is minor in nature." Douglas Whaley, Tender, Acceptance, Rejection and Revocation—The UCC's "TARR-Baby," 24 Drake L. Rev. 52, 58 (1974).

Wilson v. Scampoli

Court of Appeals of the District of Columbia, 1967
228 A.2d 848

MYERS, J.

This is an appeal from an order of the trial court granting rescission of a sales contract for a color television set and directing the return of the purchase price plus interest and costs.

Appellee purchased the set in question on November 4, 1965, paying the total purchase price in cash. The transaction was evidenced by a sales ticket showing the price paid and guaranteeing ninety days' free service and replacement of any defective tube and parts for a period of one year. Two days after purchase the set was delivered and uncrated, the antennae adjusted and the set plugged into an electrical outlet to "cook out."[1] When the set was turned on, however, it did not function properly, the picture having a reddish tinge. Appellant's delivery man advised the buyer's daughter, Mrs. Kolley, that it was not his duty to tune in or adjust the color but that a service representative would shortly call at her house for that purpose. After

1. Such a "cook out," usually over several days, allows the set to magnetize itself and to heat up the circuit in order to indicate faulty wiring.

the departure of the delivery men, Mrs. Kolley unplugged the set and did not use it.[2]

On November 8, 1965, a service representative arrived, and after spending an hour in an effort to eliminate the red cast from the picture advised Mrs. Kolley that he would have to remove the chassis from the cabinet and take it to the shop as he could not determine the cause of the difficulty from his examination at the house. He also made a written memorandum of his service call, noting that the television "Needs Shop Work (Red Screen)." Mrs. Kolley refused to allow the chassis to be removed, asserting she did not want a "repaired" set but another "brand new" set. Later she demanded the return of the purchase price, although retaining the set. Appellant refused to refund the purchase price, but renewed his offer to adjust, repair, or, if the set could not be made to function properly, to replace it. Ultimately, appellee instituted this suit against appellant seeking a refund of the purchase price. After a trial, the court ruled that "under the facts and circumstances the complaint is justified. Under the equity powers of the court I will order the parties put back in their original status, let the $675 be returned, and the set returned to the defendant."

Appellant does not contest the jurisdiction of the trial court to order rescission in a proper case, but contends the trial judge erred in holding that rescission here was appropriate. He argues that he was always willing to comply with the terms of the sale either by correcting the malfunction by minor repairs or, in the event the set could not be made thereby properly operative, by replacement; that as he was denied the opportunity to try to correct the difficulty, he did not breach the contract of sale or any warranty thereunder, expressed or implied. [The court quotes §2-508.—Eds.] A retail dealer would certainly expect and have reasonable grounds to believe that merchandise like color television sets, new and delivered as crated at the factory, would be acceptable as delivered and that, if defective in some way, he would have the right to substitute a conforming tender. The question then resolves itself to whether the dealer may conform his tender by adjustment or minor repair or whether he must conform by substituting brand new merchandise. The problem seems to be one of first impression in other jurisdictions adopting the Uniform Commercial Code as well as in the District of Columbia.

Although the Official Code Comments do not reach this precise issue, there are cases and comments under other provisions of the Code which indicate that under certain circumstances repairs and adjustments are contemplated as remedies under implied warranties. In L & N Sales Co. v. Little Brown Jug, Inc., 12 Pa. D. & C. 2d 469 (Phila. County Ct. 1957), where the language of a disclaimer was found insufficient to defeat warranties under §§2-314 and 2-315, the court noted that the buyer had notified the seller of

2. Appellee, who made his home with Mrs. Kolley, had been hospitalized shortly before delivery of the set. The remaining negotiations were carried on by Mrs. Kolley, acting on behalf of her father.

defects in the merchandise, and as the seller was unable to remedy them and later refused to accept return of the articles, it was held to be a breach of warranty. In Hall v. Everett Motors, Inc., 340 Mass. 430, 165 N.E.2d 107 (1960), decided shortly before the effective date of the Code in Massachusetts, the court reluctantly found that a disclaimer of warranties was sufficient to insulate the seller. Several references were made in the ruling to the seller's unsuccessful attempts at repairs, the court indicating the result would have been different under the Code.

While these cases provide no mandate to require the buyer to accept patchwork goods or substantially repaired articles in lieu of flawless merchandise, they do indicate that minor repairs or reasonable adjustments are frequently the means by which an imperfect tender may be cured. In discussing the analogous question of defective title, it has been stated that:

> The seller, then, should be able to cure [the defect] under subsection 2-508(2) in those cases in which he can do so without subjecting the buyer to any great inconvenience, risk or loss. [Hawkland, Curing an Improper Tender of Title to Chattels: Past, Present and Commercial Code, 46 Minn. L. Rev. 697, 724 (1962).]

See also Willer & Hart, Forms and Procedures under the U.C.C., §24.07[4]; D.C. Code §28:2-608(1)(a) (Supp. V, 1966).

Removal of a television chassis for a short period of time in order to determine the cause of color malfunction and ascertain the extent of adjustment or correction needed to effect full operational efficiency presents no great inconvenience to the buyer. In the instant case, appellant's expert witness testified that this was not infrequently necessary with new televisions. Should the set be defective in workmanship or parts, the loss would be upon the manufacturer who warranted it free from mechanical defect. Here the adamant refusal of Mrs. Kolley, acting on behalf of appellee, to allow inspection essential to the determination of the cause of the excessive red tinge to the picture defeated any effort by the seller to provide timely repair or even replacement of the set if the difficulty could not be corrected. The cause of the defect might have been minor and easily adjusted or it may have been substantial and required replacement by another new set but the seller was never given an adequate opportunity to make a determination.

We do not hold that appellant has no liability to appellee,[3] but as he was denied access and a reasonable opportunity to repair, appellee has not shown a breach of warranty entitling him either to a brand new set or to

3. Appellant on appeal has renewed his willingness to remedy any defect in the tender, and thus there is no problem of expiration of his warranties. He should be afforded the right to inspect and correct any malfunction. If appellee refuses to allow appellant an opportunity to do so, then no cause of action can lie for breach of warranty, express or implied, and the loss must be borne by appellee.

rescission. We therefore reverse the judgment of the trial court granting rescission and directing the return of the purchase price of the set.

Reversed.

QUESTIONS

1. Is the court following the perfect tender rule here? See §2-601.

2. What portion of §2-508 is relevant to this case?

3. The court says that a "retail dealer would certainly expect . . . that merchandise like color television sets, new and delivered as crated at the factory, would be acceptable as delivered and that, if defective in some way, he would have the right to substitute a conforming tender." How does the court know this? Is this a matter of judicial notice (which means that judges can assume something everyone knows—for example, that we are living on the planet Earth)? Color televisions were very new in 1967 and frequently did need adjustments to work properly. Would the same thing be presumed in the twenty-first century?

4. In this case, the buyer rejected the goods but refused to return them to the seller. Is this permissible? See §2-711(3).

IV. REJECTION AND ACCEPTANCE

When the seller makes a tender of the goods, the buyer must choose between two possible legal responses: rejection (§2-602) and acceptance (§§2-606, 2-607). A buyer cannot do both since rejection and acceptance are mutually exclusive actions. Failure to act results in a technical *acceptance,* since rejection must come within a reasonable period of time after delivery of the goods. Read §2-602. The definition of *acceptance* is found in §2-606, and its legal consequences are spelled out in §2-607. Note two important things about these sections as you read them: (1) a buyer is entitled to a reasonable *trial-use* period to see if the goods conform (this is phrased in the Code as a "reasonable opportunity to inspect"; see §2-513), and (2) on acceptance, the burden of proof as to defects shifts to the buyer (§2-607(4)). Prior to acceptance, the seller must prove that a perfect tender was made under §2-601.

Koviack Irrigation and Farm Services, Inc. v. Maple Row Farms, LLC

Court of Appeals of Michigan, 2017
2017 WL 4182409

PER CURIAM.

Plaintiff appeals by right the trial court's judgment in favor of defendant, following a bench trial. The court determined that defendant was not liable to plaintiff for the cost of equipment that plaintiff supplied for defendant's irrigation system because defendant properly rejected the equipment under the Uniform Commercial Code (UCC), MCL 440.1101 *et seq.* The court ordered defendant to return the equipment to plaintiff at defendant's own expense. Plaintiff also appeals the trial court's award of case evaluation sanctions of $11,362.50. We affirm in both appeals.

Plaintiff sold defendant component parts for an irrigation system for defendant's farm, which included a pump for distributing water from a retention pond. Plaintiff also helped design and install the system. Because the pump was delivered late in the harvest season, defendant waited until the following spring to install it. At that time, plaintiff was unwilling to assist in installing the pump because defendant had not paid for it or its operating panel. Defendant was unwilling to pay for the pump and panel until they were installed, and defendant could confirm that they would work as intended with the irrigation system. Defendant therefore hired another irrigation specialist to install the pump; he was then advised that the pump would not work with defendant's retention pond. Defendant then purchased another type of pump that was compatible with its retention pond and irrigation system. Plaintiff sued defendant for breach of contract, account stated, and unjust enrichment. Defendant filed a counterclaim, alleging that plaintiff had not provided a proper pump for the irrigation system, and that plaintiff refused to correct the problem. Following a two-day bench trial, the trial court found that defendant properly rejected the pump and its panel; consequently, plaintiff was not entitled to recover the costs of those items under the parties' agreement. The court ordered defendant to return the goods at its own expense.

I. Rejection of Goods

The trial court ruled that defendant properly rejected the pump and its operating panel in the spring of 2014 and, therefore, was not liable for the cost of that equipment under the parties' contract. [UCC §2-602(1)] provides, in relevant part:

> (1) Rejection of goods must be within a reasonable time after their delivery or tender. It is ineffective unless the buyer seasonably notifies the seller.
>
> (2) Subject to the provisions of the two following sections on rejected goods (sections 2-603 and 2-604),
>
> (a) after rejection any exercise of ownership by the buyer with respect to any commercial unit is wrongful as against the seller; and
>
> (b) if the buyer has before rejection taken physical possession of goods in which he does not have a security interest under the provisions of this article (subsection (3) of section 2-711), he is under a duty after rejection to hold them with reasonable care at the seller's disposition for a time sufficient to permit the seller to remove them; but
>
> (c) the buyer has no further obligations with regard to goods rightfully rejected.

Plaintiff first argues that defendant did not timely reject the pump. Where goods are rejected, what constitutes a reasonable time to act depends on the nature, purpose, and circumstances of the case. See [UCC §1-205]; Kelynack v. Yamaha Motor Corp., USA, 152 Mich. App. 105, 113; 394 N.W.2d 17 (1986). Where the product at issue involves goods of a complex nature and the buyer depends on the seller's expertise that the goods will perform properly for the intended use, a buyer has an opportunity to put those goods to use or to test the goods before determining whether the goods conform to the contract. See Capitol Dodge Sales, Inc. v. Northern Concrete Pipe, Inc., 131 Mich. App. 149, 157-158; 346 N.W.2d 535 (1983).

In this case, the pump was delivered late in the harvest season, so it could not be put to use right away. Also, some installation work still needed to be performed, such as hooking it up to the electrical system to see if it would work. Under the circumstances, it was reasonable for defendant to wait until the pump was actually installed to see if it would work before deciding whether to reject it, particularly considering that defendant relied on plaintiff's expertise in selecting a pump appropriate for its intended use. The trial court did not clearly err in finding that defendant rejected the goods within a reasonable time when it determined the following spring that the pump was not appropriate for defendant's irrigation system. During the interim period, the pump sat in its original packaging until it could be installed to determine if it would work as intended for defendant's purposes.

Plaintiff also argues that defendant did not actually reject the pump because it did not formally give notice that it was rejecting the pump. We disagree. Again, the reasonableness of defendant's action depends on the nature, purpose, and circumstances of the case. See UCC [§1-205(a).]

Plaintiff's salesman, Anthony Belcher, met with defendant's owner, Dean McClenathen, in April 2014 to inquire about defendant's intention to pay for the pump. Belcher agreed that McClenathen told him that he did not intend to pay for anything more until he saw that the irrigation system would work as planned. Belcher admitted that the pump and panel were still in their original packaging at that time; however, plaintiff's owner, Terry Koviack, refused to do any more work on the project until defendant paid for the equipment. At that point, plaintiff was on notice that defendant intended to reject the pump if it would not work as planned. When Koviack refused to do any further work to assist in installing the pump, defendant reasonably took steps to follow through with the parties' agreement by hiring another irrigation specialist, Mark Ackerman, to install the pump. Ackerman informed defendant that because the pump was not appropriate for defendant's retention pond and irrigation system, it would not work as intended. At that time, defendant had grounds to reject the pump and panel. According to the evidence, however, plaintiff had ceased communications with defendant. While defendant could have more effectively conveyed to plaintiff its reasons for rejecting the pump, such as send a letter or email, given that plaintiff had refused to further communicate with defendant or perform any more work on the project, defendant's failure to take more formal steps to communicate its rejection was not unreasonable. See, e.g., Fargo Machine & Tool Co. v. Kearney & Trecker Corp., 428 F. Supp. 364, 375 (E.D. Mich. 1977). It is apparent that plaintiff had notice that defendant would not accept the pump until it was determined that it would work as intended, and defendant had agreed to pay for it when it was installed and properly working. This evidence supports that plaintiff had notice of defendant's intent to reject the pump if it were to not work as intended, and Ackerman's testimony supports that the pump was not suitable for defendant's intended purposes.

Accordingly, the trial court did not err in finding that under these circumstances defendant properly rejected the pump and panel in a reasonably timely manner. . . .

We affirm. As the prevailing party, defendant may tax costs pursuant to MCR 7.219.

PROBLEM 64

Midwestern Seafoods, headquartered in Iowa, ordered 50 live lobsters from Maine Exports, "F.O.B. Portland." On September 1, Maine Exports loaded the lobsters on board an airplane in Portland, from where they were flown to Boston and then to Des Moines. Maine Exports failed to notify Midwestern Seafoods of the date of the flight until two days later, when Midwestern's purchasing agent called to inquire. He then made a few calls and located the lobsters in Des Moines, where they had been sitting for a day. Midwestern signed a receipt and picked the lobsters up. Twenty of them were clearly dying (15 due to bad handling by Maine Exports before they were handed over to the airline and 5 due to damage in transit); the other 30 were fine. Midwestern decided, for reasons that are unclear, that it wanted none of the lobsters.

(a) Is the seller's failure to notify Midwestern of the shipment a ground for rejection? See §2-504.

(b) May Midwestern reject because of the 20 defective lobsters? See §§2-601, 2-503, 2-509(1), 2-510(1).

(c) How quickly must Midwestern act if it wishes to reject? What technical steps is it required to take? See §§2-602, 1-205.

(d) Must Midwestern reship the goods to Maine Exports if the latter offers to pay the freight? See §2-602(2) with its Official Comment 2; §§2-603, 2-604.

(e) If Midwestern decides to keep 30 of the lobsters for resale, is this allowed? See §§2-602(2)(a), 2-606; cf. §§2-601, 2-105(6); Annot., 67 A.L.R.3d 363.

(f) If Midwestern rejects the goods, must it give its reasons in the notice of rejection? What penalty is there for not doing so? See §2-605 and its Official Comment 2.

(g) If Midwestern gives a valid notice of rejection within a reasonable period of time after the lobsters are delivered, what should it then do with the lobsters? See §2-602(2).

Ramirez v. Autosport

Supreme Court of New Jersey, 1982
88 N.J. 277, 440 A.2d 1345

POLLOCK, J.

This case raises several issues under the Uniform Commercial Code ("the Code" and "UCC") concerning whether a buyer may reject a tender of goods with minor defects and whether a seller may cure the defects. We consider also the remedies available to the buyer, including cancellation of the contract. The main issue is whether plaintiffs, Mr. and Mrs. Ramirez, could reject the tender by defendant, Autosport, of a camper van with minor defects and cancel the contract for the purchase of the van.

The trial court ruled that Mr. and Mrs. Ramirez rightfully rejected the van and awarded them the fair market value of their trade-in van. The Appellate Division affirmed in a brief per curiam decision which, like the trial court opinion, was unreported. We affirm the judgment of the Appellate Division.

I

Following a mobile home show at the Meadowlands Sports Complex, Mr. and Mrs. Ramirez visited Autosport's showroom in Somerville. On July 20, 1978, the Ramirezes and Donald Graff, a salesman for Autosport, agreed on the sale of a new camper and the trade-in of the van owned by Mr. and Mrs. Ramirez. Autosport and the Ramirezes signed a simple contract reflecting a $14,100 purchase price for the new van with a $4,700 trade-in allowance for the Ramirez van, which Mr. and Mrs. Ramirez left with Autosport. After further allowance for taxes, title and documentary fees, the net price was $9,902. Because Autosport needed two weeks to prepare the new van, the contract provided for delivery on or about August 3, 1978.

On that date, Mr. and Mrs. Ramirez returned with their checks to Autosport to pick up the new van. Graff was not there so Mr. White, another salesman, met them. Inspection disclosed several defects in the van. The paint was scratched, both the electric and sewer hookups were missing, and the hubcaps were not installed. White advised the Ramirezes not to accept the camper because it was not ready.

Mr. and Mrs. Ramirez wanted the van for a summer vacation and called Graff several times. Each time Graff told them it was not ready for delivery. Finally, Graff called to notify them that the camper was ready. On August 14, Mr. and Mrs. Ramirez went to Autosport to accept delivery, but workers were still touching up the outside paint. Also, the camper windows were open, and the dining area cushions were soaking wet. Mr. and Mrs. Ramirez could not use the camper in that condition, but Mr. Leis, Autosport's manager, suggested that they take the van and that Autosport would replace the cushions later. Mrs. Ramirez counteroffered to accept the van if they could withhold $2,000, but Leis agreed to no more than $250, which she refused. Leis then agreed to replace the cushions and to call them when the van was ready.

On August 15, 1978, Autosport transferred title to the van to Mr. and Mrs. Ramirez, a fact unknown to them until the summer of 1979. Between August 15 and September 1, 1978, Mrs. Ramirez called Graff several times urging him to complete the preparation of the van, but Graff constantly advised her that the van was not ready. He finally informed her that they could pick it up on September 1.

When Mr. and Mrs. Ramirez went to the showroom on September 1, Graff asked them to wait. And wait they did—for one and a half hours. No one from Autosport came forward to talk with them, and the Ramirezes left in disgust.

On October 5, 1978, Mr. and Mrs. Ramirez went to Autosport with an attorney friend. Although the parties disagreed on what occurred, the general topic was whether they should proceed with the deal or Autosport should return to the Ramirezes their trade-in van. Mrs. Ramirez claimed they rejected the new van and requested the return of their trade-in. Mr. Lustig, the owner of Autosport, thought, however, that the deal could be salvaged if the parties could agree on the dollar amount of a credit for the Ramirezes. Mr. and Mrs. Ramirez never took possession of the new van and repeated their request for the return of their trade-in. Later in October, however, Autosport sold the trade-in to an innocent third party for $4,995. Autosport claimed that the Ramirezes' van had a book value of $3,200 and claimed further that it spent $1,159.62 to repair their van. By subtracting the total of those two figures, $4,159.62, from the $4,995.00 sale price, Autosport claimed a $600-700 profit on the sale.

On November 20, 1978, the Ramirezes sued Autosport seeking, among other things, rescission of the contract. Autosport counterclaimed for breach of contract.

II

Our initial inquiry is whether a consumer may reject defective goods that do not conform to the contract of sale. The basic issue is whether under the UCC, adopted in New Jersey as N.J.S.A. 12A:1-101 et seq., a seller has the duty to deliver goods that conform precisely to the contract. We conclude that the seller is under such a duty to make a "perfect tender" and that a buyer has the right to reject goods that do not conform to the contract. That conclusion, however, does not resolve the entire dispute between buyer and seller. A more complete answer requires a brief statement of the history of the mutual obligations of buyers and sellers of commercial goods.

In the nineteenth century, sellers were required to deliver goods that complied exactly with the sales agreement. See Filley v. Polk, 115 U.S. 213, 29 L. Ed. 372, 373 (1885) (buyer not obliged to accept otherwise conforming scrap iron shipped to New Orleans from Leith, rather than Glasgow, Scotland, as required by contract); Columbian Iron Works & Dry-Dock Co. v. Douglas, 84 Md. 44, 34 A. 1118, 1120-1121 (1896) (buyer who agreed to purchase steel scrap from United States cruisers not obliged to take any other kind of scrap). That rule, known as the "perfect tender" rule, remained part of the law of sales well into the twentieth century. By the 1920's the doctrine was so entrenched in the law that Judge Learned Hand declared "[t]here is no room in commercial contracts for the doctrine of substantial performance." Mitsubishi Goshi Kaisha v. J. Aron & Co., Inc., 16 F.2d 185, 186 (2d Cir. 1926).

The harshness of the rule led courts to seek to ameliorate its effect and to bring the law of sales in closer harmony with the law of contracts, which allows rescission only for material breaches. LeRoy Dyal Co. v. Allen, 161 F.2d 152, 155 (4th Cir. 1947). See 5 Corbin, Contracts §1104 at 464 (1951); 12 Williston, Contracts §1455 at 14 (3d ed. 1970). Nevertheless, a variation of the perfect tender rule appeared in the Uniform Sales Act. N.J.S.A. 46:30-75 (purchasers permitted to reject goods or rescind contracts for any breach of warranty); N.J.S.A. 46:30-18 to -21 (warranties extended to include all the seller's obligations to the goods). See Honnold, "Buyer's Right of Rejection, A Study in the Impact of Codification Upon a Commercial Problem," 97 U. Pa. L. Rev. 457, 460 (1949). The chief objection to the continuation of the perfect tender rule was that buyers in a declining market would reject goods for minor nonconformities and force the loss on surprised sellers. See Hawkland, Sales and Bulk Sales Under the Uniform Commercial Code, 120-122 (1958), cited in N.J.S.A. 12A:2-508, New Jersey Study Comment 3.

To the extent that a buyer can reject goods for any nonconformity, the UCC retains the perfect tender rule. Section 2-106 states that goods conform to a contract "when they are in accordance with the obligations under the contract." Section 2-601 authorizes a buyer to reject goods if they "or the tender of delivery fail in any respect to conform to the contract." The Code, however, mitigates the harshness of the perfect tender rule and balances the interests of buyer and seller. See Restatement (Second), Contracts, §241 comment (b) (1981). The Code achieves that result through its provisions for revocation of acceptance and cure. N.J.S.A. 2-608, 2-508.

Initially, the rights of the parties vary depending on whether the rejection occurs before or after acceptance of the goods. Before acceptance, the buyer may reject goods for any nonconformity. N.J.S.A. 2-601. Because of the seller's right to cure, however, the buyer's rejection does not necessarily discharge the contract. N.J.S.A. 2-508. Within the time set for performance in the contract, the seller's right to cure is unconditional. Id., subsec. (1); see id., Official Comment 1. Some authorities recommend granting a breaching party a right to cure in all contracts, not merely those for the sale of goods. Restatement (Second), Contracts, ch. 10, especially §§237 and 241. Underlying the right to cure in both kinds of contracts is the recognition that parties should be encouraged to communicate with each other and to resolve their own problems. Id., Introduction p. 193.

The rights of the parties also vary if rejection occurs after the time set for performance. After expiration of that time, the seller has a further reasonable time to cure if he believed reasonably that the goods would be acceptable with or without a money allowance. N.J.S.A. 2-508(2). The determination of what constitutes a further reasonable time depends on the surrounding circumstances, which include the change of position by and the amount of inconvenience to the buyer. N.J.S.A. 2-508, Official Comment 3. Those circumstances also include the length of time needed by the seller to correct the nonconformity and his ability to salvage the goods by resale to others. See Restatement (Second), Contracts, §241 comment (d). Thus, the Code balances the buyer's right to reject nonconforming goods with a "second chance" for the seller to conform the goods to the contract under certain limited circumstances. N.J.S.A. 2-508, New Jersey Study Comment 1.

After acceptance, the Code strikes a different balance: the buyer may revoke acceptance only if the nonconformity substantially impairs the value of the goods to him. N.J.S.A. 2-608. See Herbstman v. Eastman Kodak Co., 68 N.J. 1, 9 (1975). See generally, Priest, "Breach and Remedy for the Tender of Non-Conforming Goods Under the Uniform Commercial Code: An Economic Approach," 92 Harv. L. Rev. 960, 971-973 (1978). This provision protects the seller from revocation for trivial defects. *Herbstman*, supra, 68 N.J. at 9. It also prevents the buyer from taking undue advantage of the seller by allowing goods to depreciate and then returning them because of asserted minor defects. See White & Summers, Uniform Commercial Code, §8-3 at 391 (2d ed. 1980). Because this case involves rejection of goods, we need not decide whether a seller has a right to cure substantial defects that justify revocation of acceptance. See Pavesi v. Ford Motor Co., 155 N.J. Super. 373, 378 (App. Div. 1978) (right to cure after acceptance limited to trivial defects) and White & Summers, supra, §8-4 at 319 n.76 (open question as to the relationship between §§2-608 and 2-508).

Other courts agree that the buyer has a right of rejection for any nonconformity, but that the seller has a countervailing right to cure within a reasonable time. Marine Mart Inc. v. Pearce, 480 S.W.2d 133, 137 (Ark. 1972). See Intermeat, Inc. v. American Poultry, Inc., 575 F.2d 1017, 1024 (2d Cir. 1978); Moulton Cavity & Mold, Inc. v. Lyn-Flex Industries, 396 A.2d 1024, 1027 n.6 (Me. 1979); Uchitel v. F.R. Tripler & Co., 434 N.Y.S.2d 77, 81, 107 Misc. 2d 310 (App. Term 1980); Rutland Music Services, Inc. v. Ford Motor Co., 422 A.2d 248, 249 (Vt. 1980). But see McKenzie v. Alla-Ohio Coals, Inc., 29 U.C.C. Rep. 852, 856-857 (D. D.C. 1979).

One New Jersey case, Gindy Mfg. Corp. v. Cardinale Trucking Corp., suggests that, because some defects can be cured, they do not justify rejection. 111 N.J. Super. 383, 387 n.1 (Law Div. 1970). Accord, Adams v. Tremontin, 42 N.J. Super. 313, 325 (App. Div. 1956) (Uniform Sales Act). But see Sudol v. Rudy Papa Motors, 175 N.J. Super. 238, 240-241 (D. Ct. 1980) (§2-601 contains perfect tender rule). Nonetheless we conclude that the perfect tender rule is preserved to the extent of permitting a buyer to reject goods for any defects. Because of the seller's right to cure, rejection does not terminate the contract. Accordingly, we disapprove the suggestion in *Gindy* that curable defects do not justify rejection.

A further problem, however, is identifying the remedy available to a buyer who rejects goods with insubstantial defects that the seller fails to cure within a reasonable time. The Code provides expressly that when "the buyer rightfully rejects, then with respect to the goods involved, the buyer may cancel." N.J.S.A. 2-711. "Cancellation" occurs when either party puts an end to the contract for breach by the other. N.J.S.A. 2-106(4). Nonetheless, some confusion exists whether the equitable remedy of rescission survives under the Code. Compare Ventura v. Ford Motor Corp., 173 N.J. Super. 501, 503 (Ch. Div. 1980) (rescission under UCC) and Pavesi v. Ford Motor Corp., supra, 155 N.J. Super. at 377 (equitable remedies still available since not specifically superseded, §1-103) with Edelstein v. Toyota Motors Dist., 176 N.J. Super. 57, 63-64 (App. Div. 1980) (under UCC rescission is revocation of acceptance) and Sudol v. Rudy Papa Motors, supra, 175 N.J. Super. at 241-242 (under UCC, rescission no longer exists as such).

The Code eschews the word "rescission" and substitutes the terms "cancellation," "revocation of acceptance," and "rightful rejection." N.J.S.A. 2-106(4); 2-608; and 2-711 & Official Comment 1. Although neither "rejection" nor "revocation of acceptance" is defined in the Code, rejection includes both the buyer's refusal to accept or keep delivered goods and his notification to the seller that he will not keep them. White & Summers, supra, §8-1 at 293. Revocation of acceptance is like rejection, but occurs after the buyer has accepted the goods. Nonetheless, revocation of acceptance is intended to provide the same relief as rescission of a contract of sale of goods. N.J.S.A. 2-608 Official Comment 1; N.J. Study Comment 2. In brief, revocation is tantamount to rescission. See Herbstman v. Eastman Kodak Co., supra, 68 N.J. at 9; accord, Peckham v. Larsen Chevrolet-Buick-Oldsmobile, Inc.,

99 Idaho 675, ___, 587 P.2d 816, 818 (1978) (rescission and revocation of acceptance amount to the same thing). Similarly, subject to the seller's right to cure, a buyer who rightfully rejects goods, like one who revokes his acceptance, may cancel the contract. N.J.S.A. 2-711 & Official Comment 1. We need not resolve the extent to which rescission for reasons other than rejection or revocation of acceptance, e.g., fraud and mistake, survives as a remedy outside the Code. Compare N.J.S.A. 1-103 and White & Summers, supra, §8-1, p. 295, with N.J.S.A. 2-721. Accordingly, we approve *Edelstein* and *Sudol,* which recognize that explicit Code remedies replace rescission, and disapprove *Ventura* and *Pavesi* to the extent they suggest the UCC expressly recognizes rescission as a remedy.

Although the complaint requested rescission of the contract, plaintiffs actually sought not only the end of their contractual obligations, but also restoration to their pre-contractual position. That request incorporated the equitable doctrine of restitution, the purpose of which is to restore plaintiff to as good a position as he occupied before the contract. Corbin, supra, §1102 at 455. In UCC parlance, plaintiffs' request was for the cancellation of the contract and recovery of the price paid. N.J.S.A. 2-106(4), 2-711.

General contract law permits rescission only for material breaches, and the Code restates "materiality" in terms of "substantial impairment." See Herbstman v. Eastman Kodak Co., supra, 68 N.J. at 9; id. at 15 (Conford, J., concurring). The Code permits a buyer who rightfully rejects goods to cancel a contract of sale. N.J.S.A. 2-711. Because a buyer may reject goods with insubstantial defects, he also may cancel the contract if those defects remain uncured. Otherwise, a seller's failure to cure minor defects would compel a buyer to accept imperfect goods and collect for any loss caused by the nonconformity. N.J.S.A. 2-714.

Although the Code permits cancellation by rejection for minor defects, it permits revocation of acceptance only for substantial impairments. That distinction is consistent with other Code provisions that depend on whether the buyer has accepted the goods. Acceptance creates liability in the buyer for the price, N.J.S.A. 2-709 (1), and precludes rejection. N.J.S.A. 2-607(2); N.J.S.A. 2-606, New Jersey Study Comment 1. Also, once a buyer accepts goods, he has the burden to prove any defect. N.J.S.A. 2-607(4); White & Summers, supra, §8-2 at 297. By contrast, where goods are rejected for not conforming to the contract, the burden is on the seller to prove that the nonconformity was corrected. Miron v. Yonkers Raceway, Inc., 400 F.2d 112, 119 (2d Cir. 1968).

Underlying the Code provisions is the recognition of the revolutionary change in business practices in this century. The purchase of goods is no longer a simple transaction in which a buyer purchases individually made goods from a seller in a face-to-face transaction. Our economy depends on a complex system for the manufacture, distribution, and sale of goods, a system in which manufacturers and consumers rarely meet. Faceless manufacturers mass-produce goods for unknown consumers who purchase those goods from merchants exercising little or no control over the quality of their production. In an age of assembly lines, we are accustomed to cars with scratches, television sets without knobs and other goods with all kinds of defects. Buyers no longer expect a "perfect tender." If a merchant sells defective goods, the reasonable expectation of the parties is that the buyer will return those goods and that the seller will repair or replace them.

Recognizing this commercial reality, the Code permits a seller to cure imperfect tenders. Should the seller fail to cure the defects, whether substantial or not, the balance shifts again in favor of the buyer, who has the right to cancel or seek damages. N.J.S.A. 2-711. In general, economic considerations would induce sellers to cure minor defects. See generally Priest, supra, 92 Harv. L. Rev. 973-974. Assuming the seller does not cure, however, the buyer should be permitted to exercise his remedies under N.J.S.A. 2-711. The Code remedies for consumers are to be liberally construed, and the buyer should have the option of cancelling if the seller does not provide conforming goods. See N.J.S.A. 1-106.

To summarize, the UCC preserves the perfect tender rule to the extent of permitting a buyer to reject goods for any nonconformity. Nonetheless, that rejection does not automatically terminate the contract. A seller may still effect a cure and preclude unfair rejection and cancellation by the buyer. N.J.S.A. 2-508, Official Comment 2; N.J.S.A. 2-711, Official Comment 1.

III

The trial court found that Mr. and Mrs. Ramirez had rejected the van within a reasonable time under N.J.S.A. 12A:2-602. The court found that on August 3, 1978, Autosport's salesman advised the Ramirezes not to accept the van and that on August 14, they rejected delivery and Autosport agreed to replace the cushions. Those findings are supported by substantial credible evidence, and we sustain them. See Rova Farms Resort v. Investors Ins. Co., 65 N.J. 474, 483-484 (1974). Although the trial court did not find whether Autosport cured the defects within a reasonable time, we find that Autosport did not effect a cure. Clearly the van was not ready for delivery during August, 1978, when Mr. and Mrs. Ramirez rejected it, and Autosport had the burden of proving that it had corrected the defects. Although the Ramirezes gave Autosport ample time to correct the defects, Autosport did not demonstrate that the van conformed to the contract on September 1. In fact, on that date, when Mr. and Mrs. Ramirez returned at Autosport's invitation, all they received was discourtesy.

On the assumption that substantial impairment is necessary only when a purchaser seeks to revoke acceptance under N.J.S.A. 2-608, the trial court correctly refrained from deciding whether the defects substantially impaired the van. The court properly concluded that plaintiffs were entitled to "rescind"—i.e., to "cancel"—the contract.

Because Autosport had sold the trade-in to an innocent third party, the trial court determined that the Ramirezes were entitled not to the return of the trade-in, but to its fair market value, which the court set at the contract price of $4,700. A buyer who rightfully rejects goods and cancels the contract may, among other possible remedies, recover so much of the purchase price as has been paid. N.J.S.A. 2-711. The Code, however, does not define "pay" and does not require payment to be made in cash. . . .

For the preceding reasons, we affirm the judgment of the Appellate Division.

QUESTIONS

1. Did the defendant's grounds for cure fit within §2-508?
2. Is the court creating a right to cure outside of §2-508?

PROBLEM 65

Ulysses Sinon ran a dude ranch in Troy, Colorado. He decided to erect a statue of a giant horse near the entrance to the ranch as a tourist attraction. The horse was specially manufactured by Epeius of Paris and arrived in six boxes to be assembled by Sinon. When the horse was put together, Sinon was displeased with the appearance of the tail. The horse had been designed by Epeius, and the scale model Sinon had seen when he decided to buy the horse had had a different tail. Sinon removed the tail and substituted one of his own design. He returned the original to Epeius along with a letter of rejection. In the meantime, Sinon painted the rest of the horse black (in the delivered state it was white) and used it extensively in advertising for the ranch. The horse failed to attract new business to the ranch. After three months of display, Sinon took it down and shipped it back to Epeius with a letter of rejection that stated that the problem with the tail made the horse unattractive and unusable. Epeius sues. Did Sinon make a rejection or an acceptance? See Technology and Supply Management, LLC v. Johnson Controls Building Automation Systems, LLC, 2017 WL 3219281 (E.D. Va. 2017). If the tail did not conform to the model, is that a ground for rejection? See §2-601. If Sinon had made a technical acceptance, does that fact preclude a suit for breach of warranty? See §2-607(2). What steps should Sinon take to preserve his legal rights? See §2-607(3)(a). What reasons lie behind the notice requirement? See §§2-508, 2-515.

Plateq Corp. of North Haven v. Machlett Laboratories, Inc.

Supreme Court of Connecticut, 1983
189 Conn. 433, 456 A.2d 786

PETERS, J.

In this action by a seller of specially manufactured goods to recover their purchase price from a commercial buyer, the principal issue is whether the buyer accepted the goods before it attempted to cancel the contract of sale. The plaintiff, Plateq Corporation of North Haven, sued the defendant, The Machlett Laboratories, Inc., to recover damages, measured by the contract price and incidental damages, arising out of the defendant's allegedly wrongful cancellation of a written contract for the manufacture and sale of two lead-covered steel tanks and appurtenant stands. The defendant denied liability and counterclaimed for damages. After a full hearing, the trial court found for the plaintiff both on its complaint and on the defendant's counterclaim. The defendant has appealed.

The trial court, in its memorandum of decision, found the following facts. On July 9, 1976, the defendant ordered from the plaintiff two lead-covered steel tanks to be constructed by the plaintiff according to specifications supplied by the defendant. The parties understood that the tanks were designed for the special purpose of testing x-ray tubes and were required to be radiation-proof within certain federal standards. Accordingly, the contract provided that the tanks would be tested for radiation leaks after their installation on the defendant's premises. The plaintiff undertook to correct, at its own cost, any deficiencies that this post-installation test might uncover. The plaintiff had not previously constructed such tanks, nor had the defendant previously designed tanks for this purpose. The contract was amended on August 9, 1976, to add construction of two metal stands to hold the tanks. All the goods were to be delivered to the defendant at the plaintiff's place of business.

Although the plaintiff encountered difficulties both in performing according to the contract specifications and in completing performance within the time required, the defendant did no more than call these deficiencies to the plaintiff's attention during various inspections in September and early October, 1976. By October 11, 1976, performance was belatedly but substantially completed. On that date, Albert Yannello, the defendant's engineer, noted some remaining deficiencies which the plaintiff promised to remedy by the next day, so that the goods would then be ready for delivery. Yannello gave no indication to the plaintiff that this arrangement was in any way unsatisfactory to the defendant. Not only did Yannello communicate general acquiescence in the plaintiff's proposed tender but he specifically led the plaintiff to believe that the defendant's truck would pick up the tanks and the stands within a day or two. Instead of sending its truck, the defendant sent a notice of total cancellation which the plaintiff received on October 14, 1976. That notice failed to particularize the grounds upon which cancellation was based.

On this factual basis, the trial court, having concluded that the transaction was a contract for the sale of goods falling within the Uniform Commercial Code, General Statutes §§2-101 et seq., considered whether the defendant had accepted the goods. The court determined that the defendant had accepted the tanks, primarily by signifying its willingness to take them despite their nonconformities, in accordance with General Statutes §2-606(1)(a), and secondarily by failing to make an effective rejection, in accordance with General Statutes §2-606(1)(b). Once the tanks had been accepted, the defendant could rightfully revoke its acceptance under General Statutes §2-608 only by showing substantial impairment of their value to the defendant. In part because the defendant's conduct had foreclosed any post-installation inspection, the court concluded that such impairment had not been proved. Since the tanks were not readily resalable on the open market, the plaintiff was entitled, upon the defendant's wrongful revocation of acceptance, to recover their contract price, minus salvage value, plus interest. General Statutes §§2-703; 2-709(1)(b). Accordingly, the trial court awarded the plaintiff damages in the amount of $14,837.92.

In its appeal, the defendant raises four principal claims of error. It maintains that the trial court erred: (1) in invoking the "cure" section, General Statutes §2-508, when there had been no tender by the plaintiff seller; (2) in concluding, in accordance with the acceptance section, General Statutes §2-606(1), that the defendant had "signified" to the plaintiff its willingness to take the contract goods; (3) in misconstruing the defendant's statutory and contractual rights of inspection; and (4) in refusing to find that the defendant's letter of cancellation was occasioned by the plaintiff's breach. We find no error.

Upon analysis, all of the defendant's claims of error are variations upon one central theme. The defendant claims that on October 11, when its engineer Yannello conducted the last examination on the plaintiff's premises, the tanks were so incomplete and unsatisfactory that the defendant was rightfully entitled to conclude that the plaintiff would never make a conforming tender. From this scenario, the defendant argues that it was justified in cancelling the contract of sale. It denies that the seller's conduct was sufficient to warrant a finding of tender, or its own conduct sufficient to warrant a finding of acceptance. The difficulty with this argument is that it is inconsistent with the underlying facts found by the trial court. Although the testimony was in dispute, there was evidence of record to support the trial court's findings to the contrary. The defendant cannot sustain its burden of establishing that a trial court's findings of fact are clearly erroneous; Practice Book §3060D; Pandolphe's Auto Parts, Inc. v. Manchester,

181 Conn. 217, 221-22, 435 A.2d 24 (1980); by the mere recitation in its brief of conflicting testimony entirely unsupported by reference to pages of the transcript. Practice Book §3060F(b). There is simply no fit between the defendant's claims and the trial court's finding that, by October 11, 1976, performance was in substantial compliance with the terms of the contract. The trial court further found that on that day the defendant was notified that the goods would be ready for tender the following day and that the defendant responded to this notification by promising to send its truck to pick up the tanks in accordance with the contract.

On the trial court's finding of facts, it was warranted in concluding, on two independent grounds, that the defendant had accepted the goods it had ordered from the plaintiff. Under the provisions of the Uniform Commercial Code, General Statutes §32a-2-606(l) "[a]cceptance of goods occurs when the buyer (a) after a reasonable opportunity to inspect the goods signifies to the seller . . . that he will take . . . them in spite of their nonconformity; or (b) fails to make an effective rejection."

In concluding that the defendant had "signified" to the plaintiff its willingness to "take" the tanks despite possible remaining minor defects, the trial court necessarily found that the defendant had had a reasonable opportunity to inspect the goods. The defendant does not maintain that its engineer, or the other inspectors on previous visits, had inadequate access to the tanks, or inadequate experience to conduct a reasonable examination. It recognizes that inspection of goods when the buyer undertakes to pick up the goods is ordinarily at the seller's place of tender. See General Statutes §§42a-2-503, 42a-2-507, 42a-2-513; see also White & Summers, Uniform Commercial Code §3-5 (2d ed. 1980). The defendant argues, however, that its contract, in providing for inspection for radiation leaks after installation of the tanks at its premises, necessarily postponed its inspection rights to that time. The trial court considered this argument and rejected it, and so do we. It was reasonable, in the context of this contract for the special manufacture of goods with which neither party had had prior experience, to limit this clause to adjustments to take place after tender and acceptance. After acceptance, a buyer may still, in appropriate cases, revoke its acceptance, General Statutes §42a-2-608, or recover damages for breach of warranty, General Statutes §42a-2-714. The trial court reasonably concluded that a post-installation test was intended to safeguard these rights of the defendant as well as to afford the plaintiff a final opportunity to make needed adjustments. The court was therefore justified in concluding that there had been an acceptance within §42a-2-606(1)(a). A buyer may be found to have accepted goods despite their known nonconformity; [citations omitted].

The trial court's alternate ground for concluding that the tanks had been accepted was the defendant's failure to make an effective rejection. Pursuant to General Statutes §42a-2-606(1)(b), an acceptance occurs when, after a reasonable opportunity to inspect, a buyer has failed to make "an effective rejection as provided by subsection (1) of section 42a-2-602." The latter subsection, in turn, makes a rejection "ineffective unless the buyer reasonably notifies the seller." General Statutes §42a-2-605(1)(a) goes on to provide that a buyer is precluded from relying, as a basis for rejection, upon unparticularized defects in his notice of rejection, if the defects were such that, with reasonable notice, the seller could have cured by making a substituted, conforming tender. The defendant does not question the trial court's determination that its telegram of cancellation failed to comply with the requirement of particularization contained in §2-605(1). Instead, the defendant argues that the plaintiff was not entitled to an opportunity to cure, under General Statutes §2-508, because the plaintiff had never made a tender of the tanks. That argument founders, however, on the trial court's finding that the seller was ready to make a tender on the day following the last inspection by the defendant's engineer and would have done so but for its receipt of the defendant's telegram of cancellation. The trial court furthermore found that the defendant's unparticularized telegram of cancellation wrongfully interfered with the plaintiff's contractual right to cure any remaining post-installation defects. In these circumstances, the telegram of cancellation constituted both a wrongful and an ineffective rejection on the part of the defendant. See Uchitel v. F.R. Tripler & Co., 107 Misc. 2d 310, 434 N.Y.S.2d 77, 81-82 (Supreme Court 1980); White & Summers, supra, §8-3, p. 315.

Once the conclusion is reached that the defendant accepted the tanks, its further rights of cancellation under the contract are limited by the governing provisions of the Uniform Commercial Code. "The buyer's acceptance of goods, despite their alleged non-conformity, is a watershed. After acceptance, the buyer must pay for the goods at the contract rate; General Statutes §2-607(1); and bears the burden of establishing their non-conformity. General Statutes §2-607(4)." Stelco Industries, Inc. v. Cohen, 182 Conn. 561, 563-64, 438 A.2d 759 (1980). After acceptance, the buyer may only avoid liability for the contract price by invoking the provision which permits revocation of acceptance. That provision, General Statutes §2-608(1), requires proof that the "nonconformity [of the goods] substantially impairs [their] value to him." See Superior Wire & Paper Products, Ltd. v. Talcott Tool & Machine, Inc., 184 Conn. 10 (42 C.L.J. 44, pp. 4, 6), 441 A.2d 43 (1981); Conte v. Dwan Lincoln-Mercury, Inc., 172 Conn. 112, 120-21, 374 A.2d 144 (1976). On this question, which is an issue of fact; Superior Wire & Paper Products, Ltd. v. Talcott Tool & Machine, Inc., supra, 6-7; Conte v. Dwan Lincoln-Mercury, Inc., supra, 121; the trial court again found against the defendant. Since the defendant has provided no basis for any argument that the trial court was clearly erroneous in finding that the defendant had not met its burden of proof to show that the goods were substantially nonconforming, we can find no error in the conclusion that the defendant's cancellation constituted an unauthorized and hence wrongful revocation of acceptance.

Finally, the defendant in its brief, although not in its statement of the issues presented, challenges the trial court's conclusion about the remedial consequences of its earlier determinations. Although the trial court might have found the plaintiff entitled to recover the contract price because of the defendant's acceptance of the goods; General Statutes §§2-703(e) and 2-709(1)(a); the court chose instead to rely on General Statutes §2-709(1)(b), which permits a price action for contract goods that cannot, after reasonable effort, be resold at a reasonable price. Since the contract goods in this case were concededly specially manufactured for the defendant, the defendant cannot and does not contest the trial court's finding that any effort to resell them on the open market would have been unavailing. In the light of this finding, the defendant can only reiterate its argument, which we have already rejected, that the primary default was that of the plaintiff rather than that of the defendant. The trial court's conclusion to the contrary supports both its award to the plaintiff and its denial of the defendant's counterclaim.

There is no error.

NOTE

If the parties specifically provide that the buyer will have the right to inspect and test the goods, that will extend the reasonable time to accept or reject the goods. See Virginia Elec. and Power Co. v. Bransen Energy, Inc., 2015 WL 2061983 (E.D. Va. 2015) (time for rejection extended where contract provided for buyer to send coal samples for independent laboratory analysis).

V. REVOCATION OF ACCEPTANCE

Having made a technical acceptance, a buyer may still bring a breach of warranty action provided that a proper §2-607(3)(a) notice has been given. If the buyer wins, damages based on §§2-714 and 2-715 will be awarded, and the buyer will still have the goods. If the buyer does not want the goods, but wants the return of the price, the proper UCC method is called *revocation of acceptance.* Read §2-608. At common law this action was called *rescission.* However, revocation of acceptance differs from common law rescission because the buyer not only recovers the price, but may recover consequential damages as well. See Official Comment 1 to §2-608; cf. §§2-711(1), 2-715 (also note Official Comment 1 to §2-715).

In both rejection and revocation of acceptance, the buyer in essence disclaims the goods. The standards under which a buyer can revoke acceptance are more difficult to meet than are the standards for rejection. In rejection, a buyer can in theory reject if the goods "fail in any respect"; however, to revoke an acceptance, the buyer must show that the defect "substantially impairs the value" of the goods. See Annot., 98 A.L.R.3d 1183.

Waddell v. L.V.R.V. Inc.

Supreme Court of Nevada, 2006
122 Nev. 15, 125 P.3d 1160

GIBBONS, J.

This is an appeal and cross-appeal from a district court judgment allowing revocation of acceptance of a contract and an order awarding attorney fees and costs.

Respondent/cross-appellant L.V.R.V. Inc., D/B/A Wheeler's Las Vegas RV (Wheeler's) sold a 1996 Coachmen Santara motor home (the RV) to appellants/cross-respondents Arthur R. Waddell and Roswitha M. Waddell (the Waddells). The Waddells noticed numerous problems with the RV and "continually" had to return it to Wheeler's service department for repairs. Eventually, the Waddells stopped attempting to have Wheeler's make repairs and filed a complaint seeking to revoke their acceptance of the RV or, in the alternative, money damages. Wheeler's answered the complaint and filed a third-party complaint seeking indemnification from respondent Coachmen Recreational Vehicle Company, Inc. (Coachmen). After a bench trial, the district court granted judgment in favor of the Waddells and Coachmen.

On appeal, Wheeler's argues that (1) the district court erred in allowing the Waddells to revoke their acceptance, (2) the district court abused its discretion by admitting two documents into evidence, (3) the district court erred in denying Wheeler's motion for attorney fees, and (4) the district court erred in denying indemnification from Coachmen. The Waddells argue on cross-appeal that the district court erred in denying them (1) computerized research costs and (2) post-judgment interest on their attorney fees award.

FACTS

In 1996, the Waddells served jointly as president of the Las Vegas area Coachmen Association Camping Club. During the course of that group's meetings, the Waddells spoke with Tom Pender, Wheeler's sales manager, about upgrading from the motor home they then owned to a "diesel pusher" motor coach. As a result of that conversation, Pender took the Waddells to the Wheeler's lot and showed them a 1996 Coachmen Santara model diesel pusher coach.

The Waddells test-drove and eventually agreed to purchase the RV and an extended warranty. Before they took possession of the RV, the Waddells requested that Wheeler's perform various repairs. The Waddells' request included a service on the RV's engine cooling system, new batteries, and alignment of the door frames. Wheeler's told Arthur Waddell that the repairs had been performed as requested. The Waddells took delivery of the RV on September 1, 1997.

The Waddells first noticed a problem with the RV's engine shortly after they took possession of it. They drove the RV from Las Vegas to Hemet, California. On the return trip, the entry door popped open and the RV's engine overheated while ascending a moderate grade to such a degree that Mr. Waddell had to pull over to the side of the road and wait for the engine to cool down.

When the Waddells returned from California, they took the RV back to Wheeler's for repairs. Despite Wheeler's attempts to repair the RV, the Waddells continually experienced more problems with the RV, including further episodes of engine overheating. Between September 1997 and March 1999, Wheeler's service department spent a total of seven months during different periods of time attempting to repair the RV.

On June 9, 2000, the Waddells filed a complaint in district court seeking both equitable relief and money damages. Wheeler's answered the complaint and ultimately filed a third-party complaint against Coachmen seeking equitable indemnification and contribution.

Following a three-day bench trial, the district court issued its findings of fact, conclusions of law, and judgment. The district court concluded that the RV's nonconformities substantially impaired its value to the Waddells. The district court allowed the Waddells to revoke their acceptance of the RV and ordered Wheeler's to return all of the Waddells' out-of-pocket expenses, but further concluded that Wheeler's was not entitled to indemnification from Coachmen. Following entry of judgment, the district court awarded the Waddells $15,000 in attorney fees, entered supplemental findings of fact and conclusions of law, issued an amended judgment, entered a separate order denying post-judgment interest on the attorney fee award, and denied the Waddells' motion to retax their costs to include computerized research fees. This timely appeal and cross-appeal followed.

Discussion

Wheeler's argues that the district court erred in allowing the Waddells to revoke their acceptance of the RV because the Waddells failed to prove that the RV suffered nonconformities that substantially impaired its value. We disagree.

The district court found that despite Wheeler's good-faith attempts to repair the RV, the nonconformities persisted and rendered the RV unfit for its intended use. Some of those nonconformities identified by the district court included: the bedroom air conditioning does not cool, the front air conditioning does not cool, the dash heater does not blow hot air, RV batteries do not stay charged, and chronic engine overheating. The district court concluded that these nonconformities and others substantially impaired the RV's value to the Waddells and that the Waddells had revoked their acceptance of the RV within a reasonable time.

SUBSTANTIAL IMPAIRMENT

NRS 104.2608(1) provides that a buyer may revoke his acceptance if the item suffers from a "nonconformity [that] substantially impairs its value *to him*" and (a) the buyer accepted the goods on the understanding that the seller would cure the nonconformity or (b) the buyer was unaware of the nonconformity and the nonconformity was concealed by the difficulty of discovery or by the seller's assurances that the good was conforming. (Emphasis added.)

We have never before determined when a nonconformity substantially impairs the value of a good to the buyer. Other jurisdictions treat this determination as an issue of fact,[4] which "is made in light of the 'totality of the circumstances' of each particular case, including the number of deficiencies and type of nonconformity and the time and inconvenience spent in downtime and attempts at repair."[5]

The Supreme Court of Oregon has established a two-part test to determine whether a nonconformity, under the totality of the circumstances, substantially impairs the value of the goods to the buyer. The test has both an objective and a subjective prong:

> Since [the statute] provides that the buyer may revoke acceptance of goods "whose nonconformity substantially impairs its value to him," the value of conforming goods to the plaintiff must first be determined. This is a subjective question in the sense that it calls for a consideration of the needs and circumstances of the plaintiff who seeks to revoke; not the needs and circumstances of an average buyer. The second inquiry is whether the nonconformity in fact substantially impairs the value of the goods to the buyer, having in mind his particular needs. This is an objective question in the sense that it calls for evidence of something more than plaintiff's assertion that the nonconformity

4. See, e.g., Frontier Mobile Home Sales, Inc. v. Trigleth, 256 Ark. 101, 505 S.W.2d 516, 517 (1974); Rester v. Morrow, 491 So. 2d 204, 209 (Miss. 1986); McCullough v. Bill Swad Chrysler-Plymouth, 5 Ohio St. 3d 181, 449 N.E.2d 1289, 1294 (1983).

5. Fortin v. Ox-Bow Marina, Inc., 408 Mass. 310, 557 N.E.2d 1157, 1162 (1990) (quoting *Rester*, 491 So. 2d at 210).

> impaired the value to him; it requires evidence from which it can be inferred that plaintiff's needs were not met because of the nonconformity.[6]

Since Nevada, like Oregon, adopted Uniform Commercial Code §2-608 verbatim, we conclude that this test applies to NRS 104.2608. Accordingly, we adopt the Supreme Court of Oregon's two-part test for determining whether a nonconformity substantially affects the good's value to the buyer under NRS 104.2608(1).

SUBJECTIVE VALUE TO THE WADDELLS

Arthur Waddell testified that he purchased the RV to enjoy the RV lifestyle. Before purchasing the RV, the Waddells owned similar vehicles that they used both as a residence and for camping trips. In fact, Mr. Waddell testified that he and his wife intended to sell their house and spend two to three years traveling around the country.

Mr. Waddell further testified that he shopped at Wheeler's based on Wheeler's advertisements. Marlene Wheeler, president and chief operating officer, testified that Wheeler's advertising encouraged the purchase of an RV to find unlimited freedom. When Mr. Waddell spoke with Tom Pender, sales manager at Wheeler's, about upgrading to an RV for those purposes, Pender told him that he had an RV on the lot that would meet his needs.

Mr. Waddell's testimony demonstrates that the RV's subjective value to the Waddells was based on their ability to spend two or three years driving the RV around the country. Thus, we must consider whether the RV's nonconformities substantially impaired the value of the RV based on the Waddells' particular needs.

OBJECTIVE IMPAIRMENT

Mr. Waddell testified that as a result of the RV's defects, he and his wife were unable to enjoy the RV as they had intended. Mr. Waddell further testified that the RV's engine would overheat within ten miles of embarking if the travel included any climbing. As a result of the overheating, the Waddells were forced to park on the side of the road and wait for the engine to cool down before continuing. Consequently, the RV spent a total of 213 days, or seven months and one day, at Wheeler's service department during the

6. Jorgensen v. Pressnall, 274 Or. 285, 545 P.2d 1382, 1384-85 (1976) (footnote omitted), quoted with approval in McGilbray v. Scholfield Winnebago, Inc., 221 Kan. 605, 561 P.2d 832, 836 (1977); see also Milicevic v. Mercedes-Benz USA, LLC, 256 F. Supp. 2d 1168, 1176 (D. Nev. 2003) (applying a two-part test that addressed both objective and subjective considerations); Haight v. Dales Used Cars, Inc., 139 Idaho 853, 87 P.3d 962, 966 (App. 2003) (applying a similar two-part test).

eighteen months immediately following the purchase. This testimony is sufficient to demonstrate an objective, substantial impairment of value.

The Supreme Court of Ohio has stated that a nonconformity effects a substantial impairment of value if it "shakes the buyer's faith or undermines his confidence in the reliability and integrity of the purchased item."[7] The Supreme Judicial Court of Massachusetts has recognized that "even cosmetic or minor defects that go unrepaired . . . or defects which do not totally prevent the buyer from using the goods, but circumscribe that use . . . can substantially impair the goods' value to the buyer."[8] The United States District Court for the District of Nevada recently reiterated that " 'the [seller's] inability to correct defects in [motor] vehicles creates a major hardship and an unacceptable economic burden on the consumer.' "[9]

In this case, the chronic engine overheating shook the Waddells' faith in the RV and undermined their confidence in the RV's reliability and integrity. Not only did this problem make travel in the RV unreliable and stressful to the Waddells, the overheating made travel in the vehicle objectively unsafe.

Accordingly, we conclude that substantial evidence exists to support revocation of acceptance under NRS 104.2608(1).

Reasonable Time for Revoking Acceptance

Wheeler's argues that the Waddells should not have been allowed to revoke their acceptance because they did not attempt to revoke within a reasonable time after purchasing the RV. We disagree.

Under NRS 104.2608(2), "[r]evocation of acceptance must occur within a reasonable time after the buyer discovers or should have discovered the ground for it and before any substantial change in condition of the goods which is not caused by their own defects." The statute further provides that revocation "is not effective until the buyer notifies the seller of it." We have never before determined a reasonable timeline for revocation of acceptance. However, other jurisdictions have held that the reasonable time determination "depends upon the nature, purpose and circumstances of the transaction."[10] The reasonable time determination is generally considered to be an issue of fact for the trial court.

7. *McCullough,* 449 N.E.2d at 1294; see also *Rester,* 491 So. 2d at 210-211.

8. *Fortin,* 557 N.E.2d at 1162.

9. *Milicevic,* 256 F. Supp. 2d at 1176 (quoting Berrie v. Toyota Motor Sales, USA, Inc., 267 N.J. Super. 152, 630 A.2d 1180, 1181 (1993)).

10. DeVoe Chevrolet-Cadillac v. Cartwright, 526 N.E.2d 1237, 1240 (Ind. Ct. App. 1988); see also Golembieski v. O'Rielly R.V. Center, Inc., 147 Ariz. 134, 708 P.2d 1325, 1328 (Ariz. Ct. App. 1985) (noting that "[r]easonableness of the time for revocation is a question of fact unique to the circumstances of each case").

Here, the district court found that the Waddells were entitled to revoke their acceptance since they notified Wheeler's of their intent to revoke within a reasonable time. Mr. Waddell testified that he first noticed the RV's defects immediately after his purchase. Mr. Waddell took the RV to Wheeler's service department whenever he noticed a defect and Wheeler's always attempted, often unsuccessfully, to repair the RV. In September 1998, Mr. Waddell took the RV to Wheeler's after continued engine overheating. As a result of these defects, Wheeler's service department kept the RV for approximately seven months of the eighteen months that the Waddells owned the RV. Roger Beauchemin, a former employee of Wheeler's service department, testified that Wheeler's was unable to repair some of the defects, including the engine's chronic overheating problems. In January 1999, the Waddells again brought the RV to Wheeler's complaining of persistent engine overheating. The Waddells demanded a full refund of the purchase price in March 1999 and sought legal counsel. Through counsel, the Waddells wrote to Wheeler's during the summer of 1999 to resolve the matter. Wheeler's did not respond to these inquiries until early 2000. Unable to resolve the dispute with Wheeler's, the Waddells revoked their acceptance of the RV in June 2000.

The seller of nonconforming goods must generally receive an opportunity to cure the nonconformity before the buyer may revoke his acceptance. However, as the Supreme Court of Mississippi has recognized, the seller may not "postpone revocation in perpetuity by fixing everything that goes wrong."[11] Rather, "[t]here comes a time when . . . [the buyer] is entitled to say, 'That's all,' and revoke, notwithstanding the seller's repeated good faith efforts to [cure]."

Furthermore, the seller's attempts to cure do not count against the buyer regarding timely revocation. The United States District Court for the District of Nevada has held that the "time for revocation of acceptance will be tolled while the seller attempts repairs."[12] Tolling the reasonable time for revocation of acceptance is appropriate given "the buyer's obligation to act in good faith, and to afford the seller a reasonable opportunity to cure any defect in the goods."

The Waddells gave Wheeler's several opportunities to repair the defects before revoking their acceptance. Because Wheeler's was unable to repair the defects after a total of seven months, the Waddells were entitled to say "that's all" and revoke their acceptance, notwithstanding Wheeler's good-faith attempts to repair the RV. Also, the reasonable time for revocation was tolled during the seven months that Wheeler's kept the RV and attempted

11. See *Rester,* 491 So. 2d at 210.

12. Sierra Diesel Injection Service v. Burroughs Corp., 651 F. Supp. 1371, 1378 (D. Nev. 1987).

to repair the defects. Accordingly, the district court's determination is supported by substantial evidence and is not clearly erroneous. . . .

Conclusion

The district court did not err in allowing the Waddells to revoke their acceptance of the RV within a reasonable time because chronic engine overheating problems substantially impaired the RV's value to the Waddells. . . .

QUESTIONS

1. Sometimes the buyer will return the car to the seller when giving a notice of revocation. Need the buyer do this? Read carefully §§2-711(3); cf. §2-706. See Mobile Home Sales Management, Inc. v. Brown, 562 P.2d 1378 (Ariz. App. 1977) ("when the buyer has a security interest in the goods and the seller makes no request for their return, the buyer should not be penalized by making tender back a prerequisite to revocation of acceptance"). See also Deaton, Inc. v. Aeroglide Corp., 99 N.M. 253, 657 P.2d 109 (1982). What if the buyer did not have a security interest in the car? See §§2-608(3), 2-602.

2. Should the court, when allowing revocation, make an allowance for the use the buyer got from the car? Is the seller entitled to a setoff for the amount of benefits the purchaser received? See §1-103; compare Barco Auto Leasing Corp. v. House, 202 Conn. 106, 520 A.2d 162 (1987) with Moore v. Howard Pontiac-American, Inc., 492 S.W.2d 227 (Tenn. App. 1973).

3. If the buyer keeps the car after revoking acceptance, may the buyer keep driving it without negating the effectiveness of the revocation of acceptance? See §§2-606(1)(c), 2-602(2)(a), (b). Compare Computerized Radiological Serv. v. Syntex Corp., 786 F.2d 72 (2d Cir. 1986) (use of CAT scanner for 22 months after sending letter of revocation constituted acceptance), Wadsworth Plumbing & Heating Co., Inc. v. Tallycraft Corp., 277 Or. 433, 560 P.2d 1080 (1977) ("such use would appear to be an 'act inconsistent with the seller's ownership' "), and Fecik v. Capindale, 54 Pa. D. & C.2d 701 (1971) (post-revocation use destroys buyer's §2-608 suit), with Deere & Co. v. Johnson, 271 F.3d 613 (5th Cir. 2001) (farmer's continued use of combine excused where replacement cost high); Pittman v. Henry Moncure Motors, Inc., 243 N.C. App. 207 (2015) (reasonable for buyers to continue to reside in manufactured home for 11 years, pending resolution of dispute); Star of the West Milling Company v. Hartwick Sales and Service Limited, 2016 WL 3753530 (E.D. Mich. 2016) ("Following Hartwick's refusal to honor Star's revocation, it appears from the evidence that continued use of the System is the only reasonable way for Star to mitigate damages while it awaits a new system"), and Keller v. Inland Metals All Weather Conditioning, Inc., 76 P.3d 977 (Idaho 2003) (use of rejected dehumidifier excused where unavoidable). In a leading case involving vehicles, the

Kansas Supreme Court permitted post-revocation use (with a setoff to seller for the benefit buyer received thereby); Johnson v. General Motors Corp., 233 Kan. 1044, 668 P.2d 139 (1983) ("Here buyers were placed in a position where if they stored the truck . . . they would not have had a vehicle for transportation. . . . With little or no low-cost public transportation available to the public, private transportation has changed from a luxury to a necessity."). The Massachusetts Supreme Judicial Court has agreed with this, stating that a jury should be instructed to consider a number of circumstances in deciding the reasonableness of the buyer's actions: the seller's instructions to the buyer after revocation of acceptance; the degree of economic and other hardship that the buyer would suffer if he or she discontinued using the defective goods; the reasonableness of the buyer's use after revocation as a method of mitigating damages; the degree of prejudice to the seller; and whether the seller acted in bad faith; Liarikos v. Mello, 418 Mass. 669, 639 N.E.2d 716 (1994).

Given this, if your client tells you, the attorney, that it is necessary to continue to use the goods following rejection/revocation, what do you advise? Cf. §2-714.

Accettura v. Vacationland, Inc.

Supreme Court of Illinois, 2019
2019 WL 4509017

Justice Garman delivered the judgment of the court, with opinion.

¶1 Plaintiffs Kimberly Accettura and Adam Wozniak purchased a recreational vehicle (RV) from defendant Vacationland, Inc. When it leaked during a rainstorm, they brought it in for repair. When it leaked again, they brought it back. A little more than two weeks after they dropped it off the second time and without a timetable for when the vehicle would be repaired, they told the seller that they no longer wanted the RV and asked for their money back. At issue is whether plaintiffs properly revoked their acceptance without permitting defendant a reasonable opportunity to cure the defect.

¶2 Background

¶3 On April 19, 2014, plaintiffs purchased a new 2014 Palomino trailer from defendant for $26,000.25. They took possession of the RV on April 25. That June, they discovered water leaking into the RV from the emergency exit window. They brought the RV back to defendant for repair, which defendant performed without charge.

¶4 In July 2014, plaintiffs took the RV to Michigan. During a rainstorm, the RV leaked extensively into the dinette area, damaging the walls and causing electrical failure. Plaintiffs towed the RV back to defendant for repair on July 14. Defendant was unable to repair the defect itself, so one of its employees told plaintiffs that it would have to send the RV to the manufacturer for repair. Defendant's employees could not estimate how long the manufacturer would take to repair the RV. Plaintiffs state that they called the manufacturer, which also would not give them a time estimate and referred them to defendant. On August 2, before the manufacturer picked up the RV, plaintiffs called defendant and verbally revoked acceptance of the RV. The manufacturer picked the RV up on or around August 4 and returned it on or around September 23. Defendant called plaintiffs on September 23 to inform them that the RV was repaired and that they could pick it up. Plaintiffs' attorney sent defendant a letter on September 28 confirming the earlier revocation of acceptance of the RV.

¶5 On October 29, 2014, plaintiffs filed a complaint in the circuit court of Kane County, seeking return of their purchase price and other damages under four theories of recovery: revocation of acceptance under the Magnuson-Moss Warranty-Federal Trade Commission Improvement Act (Magnuson-Moss Act) (15 U.S.C. § 2310(d) (2012)); breach of implied warranty of merchantability under the Magnuson-Moss Act (*id.*); revocation of acceptance and cancellation of contract under Illinois's adoption of the Uniform Commercial Code (UCC) (810 ILCS 5/2-608(1)(b), 2-711(1) (West 2014)); and return of purchase price under section 2-711(1) of the UCC (*id.*). Defendant moved for summary judgment pursuant to section 2-1005 of the Code of Civil Procedure (735 ILCS 5/2-1005 (West 2016)), arguing that plaintiffs' failure to give it a reasonable opportunity to cure was fatal to their claims. The circuit court granted summary judgment to defendant on all four counts, finding that the record clearly showed that plaintiffs revoked acceptance on or before August 2, 2014, and did not give defendant a reasonable time to cure. The appellate court affirmed. On appeal to this court, plaintiffs only seek review of the revocation of acceptance claim under the UCC (810 ILCS 5/2-608(1)(b) (West 2014)). We allowed the National Association of Consumer Advocates and Consumers for Auto Reliability and Safety to jointly file an *amicus* brief. Ill. S. Ct. R. 345 (eff. Sept. 20, 2010).

¶6 Analysis

¶7 Although plaintiffs alleged several counts against defendant, the only issue on appeal to this court is whether plaintiffs could revoke acceptance of the RV under Illinois's adoption of the UCC (810 ILCS 5/1-101 *et seq.* (West 2014)). The statute at issue, adopted verbatim from the UCC, states:

> "(1) The buyer may revoke his acceptance of a lot or commercial unit whose non-conformity substantially impairs its value to him if he has accepted it
>
> (a) on the reasonable assumption that its non-conformity would be cured and it has not been seasonably cured; or
>
> (b) without discovery of such non-conformity if his acceptance was reasonably induced either by the difficulty of discovery before acceptance or the seller's assurances." 810 ILCS 5/2-608(1) (West 2014).

See U.C.C. §2-608(1) (Am. Law Inst. & Unif. Law Comm'n 1952)."

¶8 On appeal to this court, defendant does not dispute that the defect, without repair, substantially impaired the RV's value to plaintiffs. Plaintiffs' expert opined that the defective unit was worth a mere 10% of its purchase price. The record does not show that defendant rebutted this opinion. Rather, defendant relied on its argument that plaintiffs must have given it an opportunity to seasonably cure, which would have remedied any impairment of value.

¶9 Defendant likewise does not dispute that plaintiffs were unaware of the defect in the RV at the time they accepted it. Thus, subsection (1)(a) cannot apply, for that subsection, by its plain language, contemplates a buyer who accepted a good she knew to be nonconforming "on the reasonable assumption that its non-conformity would be cured." *Id.* §2-608(1)(a). Thus, if plaintiffs can revoke their acceptance, they can do so because they accepted the RV "without discovery of such nonconformity" and their "acceptance was reasonably induced either by the difficulty of discovery before acceptance or the seller's assurances." *Id.* §2-608(1)(b).

¶10 Plaintiffs brought the RV to defendant for repair on July 14. Before defendant sent the RV to the manufacturer, one of its employees gave plaintiffs what plaintiffs described as a "very vague and extended" timeline. Plaintiffs state that they then called the manufacturer, who referred them back to defendant. Upset with defendant's and the manufacturer's inability to give them a timeline for repair, plaintiffs thereafter called defendant to revoke their acceptance of the RV. Defendant argues that plaintiffs were required to give it a reasonable time to cure before they could revoke acceptance.

¶11 Interpretation of subsection (1)(b) is an issue of first impression in Illinois. The standard of review for questions of statutory interpretation is *de novo*. *Taylor v. Pekin Insurance Co.*, 231 Ill. 2d 390, 395, 326 Ill. Dec. 34, 899 N.E.2d 251 (2008). The primary objective of our analysis is to ascertain and give effect to the legislative intent. *Illinois Graphics Co. v. Nickum*, 159 Ill. 2d 469, 479, 203 Ill. Dec. 463, 639 N.E.2d 1282 (1994). The most reliable indicator of the legislature's intent is the statutory language itself, given its plain and ordinary meaning. *Id.* "It is a basic rule of statutory construction that the words of a statute should be given their plain, ordinary[,] and accepted meaning, unless to do so would defeat the legislative intent." *Peoria Savings & Loan Ass'n v. Jefferson Trust & Savings Bank of Peoria,* 81 Ill. 2d 461, 468, 43 Ill. Dec. 712, 410 N.E.2d 845 (1980). We do not depart from the plain language of the statute by reading into it exceptions, limitations, or conditions that conflict with the expressed intent. *Blum v. Koster,* 235 Ill. 2d 21, 29, 335 Ill. Dec. 614, 919 N.E.2d 333 (2009).

¶12 Plaintiffs argue that the statutory language is plain: subsection (1)(a) contemplates and expressly mentions a cure; subsection (1)(b) does not. Under subsection (1)(a), they argue, the cure is part of the contract while under subsection (1)(b) it is not. They illustrate their argument with an analogy: subsection (1)(a) would apply to a buyer who purchased an RV that she knew leaked and included in the sales contract an agreement that the seller would seasonably cure the leak. Subsection (1)(b), they assert, contemplates a buyer who purchases an RV that she reasonably believes does not leak but, she later finds out, does leak. Under plaintiffs' theory, the buyer who knows of the leak and has an agreement with the seller to cure must give the seller a reasonable time to do so, but the buyer who is not aware of the leak can just return the RV to the seller and revoke acceptance, as long as the leak substantially impairs the RV's value. Plaintiffs argue that a majority of other jurisdictions have reached this conclusion.

¶13 We agree with this interpretation. The plain language of the statute evinces the General Assembly's intention to allow a buyer to revoke acceptance of a substantially impaired commercial unit under two separate and distinct circumstances. The first circumstance is when the buyer knows of the nonconformity, the buyer accepts the nonconforming unit with a reasonable assumption that the nonconformity will be cured, and the seller fails to seasonably cure it. 810 ILCS 5/2-608(1)(a) (West 2014). The second is when the buyer accepts the nonconforming unit without knowledge of the nonconformity and either the nonconformity was difficult to discover or the seller assured her that the unit conformed to the specifications. *Id.* § 2-608(1)(b).

¶14 Both situations contemplate a nonconformity that substantially impairs the unit's value to the buyer. Where they diverge is in the buyer's expectation. The first contemplates a buyer who accepts a nonconforming unit and expects the seller to cure the nonconformity. When she does not get that cure seasonably, she can revoke her acceptance. The second contemplates a buyer who accepts what she believes to be a conforming unit. When she does not get that conforming unit, she can revoke her acceptance. Because we find this language plain and because subsection (1)(b) does not require that a buyer give the seller an opportunity to cure, we need not consider the requirements of other statutes that defendant argues are analogous.

¶15 Defendant first argues that Illinois "courts will resort to revocation of acceptance only after attempts at adjustment have failed." *Belfour v. Schaumburg Auto,* 306 Ill. App. 3d 234, 242, 239 Ill.Dec. 383, 713 N.E.2d 1233 (1999). The appellate court below relied on *Belfour* in finding that subsection (1)(b) requires that the buyer give the seller an opportunity to cure. 2018 IL App (2d) 170972, ¶ 40, 425 Ill. Dec. 389, 112 N.E.3d 1054.

¶16 In *Belfour,* the plaintiffs bought a car that later caught on fire as one of the plaintiffs drove it. 306 Ill. App. 3d at 236, 239 Ill. Dec. 383, 713 N.E.2d 1233. The defendants did not dispute that this was due to a defect in the car. See *id.* at 236-39, 239 Ill. Dec. 383, 713 N.E.2d 1233. The opinion does not discuss whether the plaintiffs purchased the vehicle with knowledge of a nonconformity that they reasonably assumed the defendants would fix. The opinion cites only subsection (1)(a) and analyzes only that subsection. *Id.* at 241-42, 239 Ill. Dec. 383, 713 N.E.2d 1233. Subsection (1)(b) was not at issue. As we are considering a revocation of acceptance under subsection (1)(b), we find *Belfour* distinguishable.

¶17 Defendant argues that this case involves more than statutory interpretation of subsection (1)(b). Defendant claims that it offered and plaintiffs accepted repair as their remedy for the defect before plaintiffs revoked acceptance. Because they elected that remedy, defendant asserts, they were obligated to allow defendant a reasonable time to complete the repair.

¶18 Although a situation could arise in which a buyer acts unreasonably in revoking acceptance of a good after requesting that the seller cure a nonconformity, this is not such a situation. Nothing in the record indicates that plaintiffs agreed to an open-ended repair timeline. The fact that they considered allowing defendant to cure does not obligate them to accept an unreasonable cure. Further, it does not obviate their right to revoke under subsection 2-608(1)(b) (810 ILCS 5/2-608(1)(b) (West 2014)).

¶19 Defendant further argues that the cases plaintiffs cite do not comprise a majority of foreign jurisdictions. Rather, it contends, a split of authority exists. It argues that many jurisdictions, and "probably a majority of the commentators," find that the seller has a right to cure when a buyer attempts to revoke acceptance under subsection (1)(b).

¶20 Because we find the language plain, we need not look to our sister states' interpretations of this provision. Even if we review those decisions, however, our research indicates that, although a split of authority exists, a majority of other jurisdictions have interpreted their state's adoption of the statutory provision consistent with our decision today. See, *e.g., Head v. Phillips Camper Sales & Rental, Inc.,* 234 Mich. App. 94, 593 N.W.2d 595, 600 (1999) ("A majority of courts considering this question have concluded that a seller has no right to cure after a buyer revokes his acceptance under § 2-608(1)(b) of the UCC."); *Bowen v. Foust,* 925 S.W.2d 211, 215 n.6 (Mo. Ct. App. 1996) ("[T]he rule that a seller has no right to cure when a buyer justifiably revokes his acceptance remains the majority view." (citing Unif. Commercial Code §4 U.L.A. 63 (1995))); *Gappelberg v. Landrum*, 666 S.W.2d 88, 90 (Tex. 1984) ("The only reference to cure in [section 2-608] is in situations when the buyer knew of the defects at the time of acceptance of the goods."); *Johannsen v. Minnesota Valley Ford Tractor Co.*, 304 N.W.2d 654, 657 (Minn. 1981) ("[T]he seller has no right to cure defects which substantially impair the good's value."); *Werner v. Montana*, 117 N.H. 721, 378 A.2d 1130, 1136-37 (1977) ("In the context of revocation, [section 2-608(1)(a)] speaks to the seller's opportunity to seasonably cure a defect," as distinguished from subsection (1)(b).).

¶21 Notably, although it appears that the courts in some of our sister states would rule to the contrary, we did not find a case in which a court expressly interpreted the statutory language and found that subsection (1)(b) required that the buyer give the seller an opportunity to cure. Rather, the decisions that run contra to ours seem to base their decision on policy grounds (see, *e.g.*, *Conte v. Dwan Lincoln-Mercury, Inc.*, 172 Conn. 112, 374 A.2d 144, 149 (1976) ("'One policy of the Code is to encourage the parties to work out their differences and so to minimize losses resulting from defective performance.'" (quoting White & Summers, Uniform Commercial Code §8-2 n.15))) or gloss over interpretation (see, *e.g.*, *Cuesta v. Classic Wheels, Inc.*, 358 N.J. Super. 512, 818 A.2d 448, 451 (N.J. Super. Ct. App. Div. 2003) (citing section 12A:2-508 of the New Jersey Statutes Annotated (N.J. Stat. Ann. § 12A:2-508 (West 2002)) but not further elaborating); *Rester v. Morrow*, 491 So. 2d 204, 210 (Miss. 1986) ("[T]he seller has a right to attempt cure." (citing section 75-2-508 of the Mississippi Code Annotated (Miss. Code Ann. §75-2-508 (1972)) but not further elaborating)); *Waddell v. L.V.R.V. Inc.*, 122 Nev. 15, 125 P.3d 1160, 1165 n.12 (2006) (citing *Rester*, 491 So. 2d at 210, without explanation or elaboration)).

¶22 Defendant next argues that when the language of the UCC is ambiguous, which it argues the statute here is, we may consider the committee comments. As we find the language unambiguous, we need not consider them. Even if we did, however, they do not support defendant's position. Defendant cites comment 4 of section 2-608, which states that revocation "will be generally resorted to only after attempts at adjustments have failed," and comment 5, which discusses "considerations of good faith, prevention of surprise, and reasonable adjustment." 810 ILCS Ann. 5/2-608, Uniform Commercial Code Comment, at 482 (Smith-Hurd 1993). These comments both discuss the notice that a revoking buyer must give the seller. As the comment states, a court should consider that most buyers will usually seek a cure before revoking in determining whether the notice of revocation was timely. In determining whether the notice of revocation sufficiently notifies the seller of the nonconformity, the court should consider what information the seller has as a result of the buyer previously seeking a cure. Such consideration, however, is irrelevant to whether the buyer *must* seek a cure before revoking.

¶23 Finally, defendant argues that section 2-608(3), which states that "[a] buyer who so revokes has the same rights and duties with regard to the goods involved as if he had rejected them" (810 ILCS 5/2-608(3) (West 2014)), invokes section 2-508 (*id.* §2-508). Some of our sister jurisdictions agree. See, *e.g.*, *Cuesta*, 818 A.2d at 451 (citing N.J. Stat. Ann. §12A:2-508 (West 2002)); *Rester*, 491 So. 2d at 210 (citing Miss. Code Ann. §75-2-508 (West 1972)); *Conte*, 374 A.2d at 149 (citing Conn. Gen. Stat. Ann. §42a-2-508 (West 1975)). Section 2-508 allows a seller to cure a rejected nonconforming delivery if "the time for performance has not yet expired" or if "the seller had reasonable grounds to believe [the nonconforming tender] would be acceptable." 810 ILCS 5/2-508 (West 2014).

¶24 We disagree. Rather, we agree with the Michigan appellate court's analysis of this argument. See *Head*, 593 N.W.2d at 600-01 (interpreting UCC section 2-608, discussing the differences between rejection and revocation of acceptance, and finding that subsection (3) does not incorporate UCC section 2-508). Defendant's argument ignores the distinction between rejection and revocation of acceptance. A buyer may reject goods if they "fail in any respect to conform to the contract." 810 ILCS 5/2-601 (West 2014). Once the buyer accepts the goods, however, he may only revoke that acceptance if the "non-conformity substantially impairs its value to him." *Id.* §2-608(1). When a buyer rejects nonconforming goods, the seller may have a right to cure. *Id.* §2-508. In the case of a revocation, however, as aptly stated by the *Head* court, "[t]he seller, in turn, loses the right to cure, but gains the benefit of the higher substantial impairment standard for revocation." 593 N.W.2d at 601. We further agree that the "rights and duties" referred to in section 2-608(3) (810 ILCS 5/2-608(3) (West 2014)) are found in sections 2-602, 2-603, and 2-604 (*id.* §§2-602, 2-603, 2-604), not section 2-508 (*id.* §2-508). See *Head*, 593 N.W.2d at 600.

¶25 CONCLUSION

¶26 We hold that the plain language of subsection 2-608(1)(b) of the Illinois Commercial Code does not require that the buyer give the seller an opportunity to cure a substantial nonconformity before revoking acceptance. We reverse and remand for further proceedings consistent with this opinion.

¶27 Reversed and remanded.

NOTE: LEMON LAWS

A number of states have enacted so-called Lemon Laws that resolve some of the disputes we have been exploring when they arise in connection with a consumer's purchase of an automobile. For example, the issue addressed in the last question is specifically covered by many of these statutes. New York General Business Law §198a says that a refund from the defendant may be reduced by "a reasonable allowance for the consumer's use of the vehicle in excess of the first 12,000 miles of operation and a reasonable allowance for any damage not attributable to normal wear or improvements." For an exploration of what the various states have done, see Annot., 51 A.L.R.4th 872.

PROBLEM 66

The day after Alice Bluegown bought her new car, the right rear fender fell off. May she use §2-608 or must she give the car dealer a right to cure? Pretend she is sitting in your office expecting an immediate answer; glance at §2-608 and decide. The next day she took the car back to have the fender repaired; this made her late for work. The dealer fixed it, and the fender gave her no more trouble. However, the first time it rained all the paint washed off the car. May she revoke now? She took the car back to the dealer when the rain stopped and rode the bus to work (late again). The car dealer did a nice job repainting the car. Two weeks later the engine quit on her when she was in the middle lane of a superhighway at rush hour. The car had to be towed to the car dealer, and Alice missed an important sales meeting. The car dealer fixed the engine. Now Alice is back in your office. The car's trunk will not open. Must she permit them to fix it, or can she revoke? See Foss, The Seller's Right to Cure When the Buyer Revokes Acceptance: Erase the Line in the Sand, 16 S. Ill. U. L.J. 1 (1991). She has missed enough work to worry about hurting her career. She's also concerned that the car is going to keep breaking down right through and past the warranty period. What do you advise? Is §2-609 of use to her? If she decides to revoke acceptance and if the court agrees that this is allowed, would it also permit her to recover for the cost of a rental car used as substitute transportation while she was attempting to purchase a new car? See McGinnis v. Wentworth Chevrolet Co., 295 Or. 494, 668 P.2d 365 (1983). If she goes out and buys a *new* car, can she make the first car dealer pay for it? See §2-712.

PROBLEM 67

Suppose in the last Problem the contract between the dealer and Bluegown explicitly limits the remedy for breach to repair or replacement of defective parts. The dealer argues that all defects have been promptly and successfully repaired and that the remedy of revocation of acceptance is therefore unavailable to Bluegown. See §2-719(2); Durfee v. Rod Baxter Imports,

Inc., 262 N.W.2d 349 (Minn. 1977); see also Andover Air Ltd. Partnership v. Piper Aircraft Corp., 1989 WL 110453 (D. Mass. 1989).

PROBLEM 68

Arthur Author ordered an expensive computer (the ION #740) from ION Business Machines. ION sent him model #745, a newer and better version of the machine he had ordered, at the same price. When he saw the computer, he liked it and wrote them a letter of acceptance, enclosing a check in payment. However, when he began to use it, he was horrified to learn that the computer was turned on by a hidden switch under the front panel. Arthur Author's father had lost a finger when he reached under a machine to activate it. Arthur had witnessed the accident as a child. Arthur sent a notice of revocation of acceptance to ION, stating that the #740 had a visible switch and explaining that the hidden switch on the #745 brought back childhood memories that kept him from wanting the computer. Does §2-608 permit him to revoke for this reason? See Official Comment 2. Is §2-508(2) relevant? How would you advise ION to respond to Arthur Author's letter? See Annot., 98 A.L.R.3d 1183.

PROBLEM 69

After his car had broken down with the same defect six times, Zack Taylor decided to revoke acceptance and return the car to Fillmore Motors, the dealership that had sold him the vehicle but that had been unable to repair it. To Zack's dismay, he discovered that Fillmore Motors had gone bankrupt and was out of business. Zack is now in your office with this issue: may he revoke acceptance against the *manufacturer* of the car (which had covered its product with a limited warranty)? Compare Newmar Corp. v. McCrary, 309 P.3d 1021 (Nev. 2013), with Gasque v. Mooers Motor Car Co., Inc., 227 Va. 154, 313 S.E.2d 384 (1984); Gregory J. Krabacher, Revocation of Tripartite Rolling Contracts: Finding a Remedy in the Twenty-First Century Usage of Trade, 66 Ohio St. L.J. 397 (2005).

Note that the Magnuson-Moss Warranty Act might help consumers win this battle. Section 110(d) of the Act allows a civil action against the warrantor that includes both legal and *equitable* relief (and, revocation of acceptance, being a form of rescission, qualifies as an equitable remedy). Revocation of acceptance, being a form of rescission, arguably qualifies as an equitable remedy, but the courts have split on whether it can be used in Magnuson-Moss actions against a manufacturer not in privity with the consumer; see Mydlach

v. DaimlerChysler Corp., 226 Ill. 2d 307, 314 Ill. Dec. 760, 875 N.E.2d 1047, 1062-1065 (2007) (discussing split among courts on the issue).

Just as the United Nations CISG treaty does not use the value-loaded word *warranty*, it substitutes the word *avoidance* for concepts such as rescission, rejection, and revocation of acceptance, while keeping much of the substance. The concept of avoidance under the treaty is the subject of the next Problem.

PROBLEM 70

Jeans of the World, a retail clothing outlet in Helsinki, Finland, ordered 20 boxes of jeans from Grey Goods of Manhattan in New York, to be delivered September 1. Use the CISG to answer these questions:

(a) If the goods arrive on July 20, must Jeans of the World take them? See Article 52(1).

(b) If the goods arrive on the appointed date, but there are only 18 boxes, must Jeans of the World accept them? See Articles 35, 49, 51, and 25. Can the buyer get the other two boxes? See Article 46. If the buyer avoids the contract, can the seller reinstate it by delivering the missing two boxes? See Articles 48 and 49.

(c) If a flood causes water damage to the boxes before Jeans of the World tries to avoid the contract, does this affect its ability to do so? See Article 82.

PROBLEM 71

Ambiance Hotel decided to acquire ten horse-carriages to be specially designed to carry its guests around the tourist areas of the scenic city in which it is located. It had the plans for the carriages transmitted to Buggies, Inc., a carriage manufacturer, which assured Ambiance that there would be no problem with the creation of the carriages. Ambiance financed this transaction by having Octopus National Bank purchase the carriages from Buggies, Inc., and then lease them to Ambiance for a ten-year period. Assume that this transaction qualifies as a finance lease; see §2A-103(1)(g).

(a) If the carriages are delivered to the hotel and Ambiance rejects them because they are the wrong color, must Ambiance pay the lease amounts to Octopus National Bank? (You may assume that the finance lease contained a "hell or high water" clause.) See §§2A-407(1), 2A-515.

(b) If the hotel accepts the carriages, but becomes upset when they constantly break down, can it revoke its acceptance and refuse to pay the lessor? See §§2A-407, 2A-516 and its Official Comment, 2A. See GreatAmerica Fin. Serv. Corp. v. Meisels, 2016 WL 5480718 (Iowa App. 2016).

VI. RISK OF LOSS: BREACH

The Code's general rules on risk of loss are found in §2-509, but that section applies only where neither party has breached the sales contract. If a breach has occurred, §2-510 is the relevant section. Read it.

Jakowski v. Carole Chevrolet, Inc.

New Jersey Superior Court, 1981
180 N.J. Super. 122, 433 A.2d 841

NEWMAN, J.

Plaintiff seeks summary judgment on Count I alleging breach of a new car sales contract by the defendant, Carole Chevrolet.

The essential facts are not in dispute. On March 8, 1980, plaintiff, Jakowski, (hereinafter referred to as buyer), entered into a contract of sale with defendant, Carole Chevrolet, (hereinafter referred to as seller), calling for the purchase by plaintiff of one brand new 1980 Chevrolet Camaro. The parties also agreed that the car would be both undercoated and that its finish would have a polymer coating. While there is some disagreement as to exactly when the buyer ordered the coatings, it is undisputed that prior to delivery the seller agreed to deliver the car with the coatings applied. Likewise, it is undisputed that the car in question was delivered to the buyer without the required coatings on May 19, 1980.

The next day, May 20, 1980, the seller contacted the buyer and informed him that the car delivered to him lacked the coatings in question and seller instructed buyer to return the car to seller so that the coatings could be applied. On May 22, 1980, the buyer returned the auto to the seller for application of the coatings. Sometime during the evening of the 22nd or the morning of the 23rd the car was stolen from seller's premises and it was never recovered. Seller has refused to either provide a replacement auto to buyer or to refund the purchase price. Buyer remains accountable on the loan, provided through GMAC, for the purchase of the car.

The narrow question thus presented is upon whom, as between buyer and seller, this loss should fall. In UCC terminology, on May 22, 1980, which party bore the risk of the car's loss.

Seller argues that the risk of loss passed to the buyer upon his receipt of the auto. This is consistent with U.C.C. §2-509(3) pursuant to which the risk of loss passes to the buyer upon his receipt of the goods. Section 2-509(4), however, expressly provides that the general rules of §2-509 are subject to the more specific provisions of §2-510 which deals with the effect of breach upon risk of loss.

Buyer relies upon §2-510(1) which provides:

> Where a tender or delivery of goods so fails to conform to the contract as to give a right of rejection the risk of their loss remains on the seller until cure or acceptance.

Application of this section to the instant facts requires that three questions be answered. First, did the car "so fail to conform" as to give this buyer a right to reject it? If so, did the buyer "accept" the car despite the non-conformity? Finally, did the seller cure the defect prior to the theft of the auto?

The first question must be answered in the affirmative. The contract provided that the car would be delivered with undercoating and a polymer finish and it is undisputed that it was delivered without these coatings. The goods were thus clearly non-conforming and despite seller's assertion to the contrary, the degree of their non-conformity is irrelevant in assessing the buyer's concomitant right to reject them. Section 2-106 is clear in its intent to preserve the rule of strict compliance; that is, the "perfect tender" rule:

> Goods . . . are "conforming" or conform to the contract *when they are in accordance with* the obligations under the contract. [Section 2-106(2). (Emphasis supplied.) See also Comment 2 to §2-106.]

The language of §2-510(1), "so fails to conform," is misleading in this respect: no particular quantum of non-conformity is required where a single delivery is contemplated. The allusion is to §2-612 which substitutes a rule of substantial compliance where, *and only where,* an installment deal is contemplated. White & Summers, Uniform Commercial Code (2d ed. 1980), §5.5 at 187-188.

Secondly, did buyer "accept" the auto by taking possession of it? This question was presented in Zabriskie Chevrolet, Inc. v. Smith, 99 N.J. Super. 441 (Law Div. 1968). In *Zabriskie* it was held that the mere taking of possession by the purchaser is not equivalent to acceptance. Before he can be held to have accepted, a buyer must be afforded a "reasonable opportunity to inspect" the goods. *Zabriskie,* supra, at 452-453; §2-606.

Seller's actions in this matter preclude analysis in conventional "acceptance" terms. Buyer had no opportunity, indeed, no reason, to reject given seller's own communication to buyer shortly after delivery, to the effect that the goods did not conform and that the seller was exercising its right to cure said non-conformity. See §2-508 (seller's right to cure). This communication, in effect an acknowledgment of non-conformity, obviated the need for a formal rejection on buyer's part, if, indeed, §2-510(1) imposes such an obligation. Put another way, it precluded the buyer from rejecting the car. Consistent with this analysis, I find as a matter of law that there was no acceptance by buyer of this non-conforming auto.

As to the final question of whether the seller effected a cure, there is no evidence, in fact defendant does not even contend, that cure was ever effected.

Given the undisputed facts the operation of §2-510(1) is inescapable. The goods failed to conform, the buyer never accepted them and the defect was never cured. Accordingly, the risk of loss remained on the seller and judgment is granted for plaintiff.

A further note on the law is in order. It is possible to conjure up a host of hypotheticals leading to seemingly perverse results under §2-510. The section has been the subject of some scholarly criticism. See, e.g., White & Summers, supra, §5.5 at 187. Williston, "The Law of Sales in the Proposed Uniform Commercial Code," 63 Harv. L. Rev. 561, 583 (1950).

The fact is, however, that those courts considering it have had little difficulty in applying it as written. See, e.g., United Airlines, Inc. v. Conductron Corp., 69 Ill. App. 3d 847, 26 Ill. Dec. 344, 387 N.E.2d 1272 (Ill. App. 1979) (Flight trainer destroyed in fire after delivery to buyer); Southland Mobile Home v. Chyrchol, 255 Ark. 366, 500 S.W.2d 778 (Ark. Sup. 1973) (Mobile home destroyed in fire after delivery to buyer); Graybar Elec. Co. v. Shook, 283 N.C. 213, 195 S.E.2d 514 (N.C. Sup. 1973) (Non-conforming cable stolen while in buyer's possession); Wilkie v. Cummins Diesel Eng. Inc., 252 Md. 611, 250 A.2d 886 (Md. Ct. App. 1969) (Engine block frozen while in buyer's possession).

The rule is simple enough: under §2-510(1) where goods fail to conform to the contract of sale, the risk of loss remains on the seller until the buyer accepts the goods or until the seller cures the defect. In the aforecited cases, such was the result even though in all of them the goods were still in the *buyer's* possession at the time of their destruction.

For present purposes it is adequate to hold simply that where a seller obtains possession of the goods in an effort to cure defects in them so as to comply with his end of the bargain, he is under a contractual duty to redeliver them to the buyer. In failing to do so, he has breached the contract.

Pursuant to §2-711 buyer is entitled to a refund of so much of the purchase price as has been paid to seller. Included in the cost of the automobile are the finance charges incurred by the buyer who secured financing from GMAC pursuant to a retail installment sales contract entered into with the seller. There is no dispute about including these charges in the purchase cost and the buyer, as of March 30, 1981, indicated the total amount due on any judgment to be $9,398.75. However, since this case was first heard some additional time has passed and a current pay off figure should be obtained for inclusion in this judgment. Plaintiff is directed to submit an appropriate order.

PROBLEM 72

The Lamia Museum's director, Mandrake Griffin, ordered three new pieces for the museum: an Egyptian sphinx, an Old World gargoyle, and an Etruscan statue of a centaur. These objets d'art were purchased under separate contracts from Empusa Exports of London, England. All were to be shipped "F.A.S. S.S. Titanic" on or about April 9, on their way to the museum, which was located in New Jersey. The parties agreed that New Jersey law would apply. Prior to April 9, Empusa Exports received a call from Griffin cancelling the purchase of the centaur statue. Empusa protested the cancellation, but agreed to ship the other two pieces. Empusa's manager discovered that the sphinx was a phony, but kept her mouth shut and shipped it anyway. She also discovered that the gargoyle's condition was such that it could not survive the exposure to sea air, so she decided to send it by air in spite of the contract's F.A.S. *Titanic* term. This decision proved wise since the *Titanic* encountered an obstacle on its sea voyage and foundered, taking the sphinx with it. The gargoyle arrived in good condition, and Griffin wrote a letter to Empusa accepting the gargoyle and enclosing the museum's check. A week later Griffin learned that the gargoyle was not from the "Old World," but instead had been cast in Hoboken many years ago, had somehow found its way to Europe, and now was home again. He sent Empusa a letter demanding that the museum's money be returned and stating that he canceled the sale. Before Empusa could respond, two things happened: the museum burned to the ground, and the centaur statue was stolen from Empusa's warehouse (through no fault of Empusa, which was not negligent in guarding it). Both the museum and Empusa were fully insured. Answer these questions:

(a) By shipping the other two objects after the museum refused to take the centaur statue, did Empusa waive its right to sue for the repudiation? See §§2-209(1), 2-106(3), 2-106(4). Would §1-308 have helped Empusa? What should it have done to use this section?

(b) Which party took the risk of loss on

(1) the centaur?

(2) the sphinx?

(3) the gargoyle?

(c) When Empusa shipped the gargoyle by air instead of by sea, could Lamia have treated this as an imperfect tender and rejected the gargoyle for that reason? See §§2-503(1), 2-503(2), 2-504, 2-614.

(d) The Lamia Museum's insurance policy with the Pegasus Insurance Company contains two clauses relevant to §2-510. One provided that on payment of a claim the insurance company was subrogated to any claim its insured had against any other person. The other stated that the policy should not be deemed to provide protection for any claim where the risk of loss rested with another person. What is the effect of these provisions? See Official Comment 3 to §2-510; White & Summers §6-7.

VII. IMPOSSIBILITY OF PERFORMANCE

The Code has four provisions designed to straighten out the legal tangles created by those unexpected events of life that make the performance of a contract impossible or (the UCC equivalent) *commercially impracticable.* By creating a new standard of commercial impracticability, the Code drafters intended to broaden the common law concept of *impossibility.* Many commentators believe that the courts have essentially ignored the drafters' intentions and treated commercial impracticability as synonymous with common law impossibility. See Annot., 93 A.L.R.3d 584.

Read §§2-613 to 2-616, and work through the following Problems.

PROBLEM 73

Virgil Escapement had always wanted a sundial for his garden, and he ordered one for $250 from Horology Timepieces, Inc. The latter had 12 sundials of the type Escapement ordered in its storage room when an earthquake shook the building. All 12 fell over, and all but 3 were smashed. The remaining three were slightly damaged. Escapement, on being informed of the problem, insisted on the right to look over the three remaining sundials and to select one for his purchase, possibly at a reduced price due to the damage. Horology comes to you. Is §2-613 or §2-615 relevant? Must it let Escapement pick out a sundial, and must it offer to let him purchase at a reduced price, or can it simply cancel without fear of legal liability? For the test for impossibility of performance in international sales, see CISG Article 79; cf. Articles 71 and 72.

If the agreed-upon delivery or payment means become unavailable, §2-614 may require use of a substitute. See Macromex v. Globex International, 330 Fed. Appx. 241 (2d Cir. 2009) (under §2-614 Romanian importation ban triggered obligation to change delivery location where original facilities unavailable).

PROBLEM 74

Suppose the following, using the basic facts of the last Problem. When Horology received Virgil's order, one of their salespersons immediately put a red tag on one of the sundials. It said, "Hold for Virgil Escapement." Then the earthquake occurred, and miraculously only Virgil's sundial was destroyed. The other 11 sundials, all exactly like Virgil's, were undamaged. When Virgil demanded his sundial, Horology pleaded §2-613. Will that section excuse them? See Valley Forge Flag Co. v. New York Dowel & Molding Import Co., 90 Misc. 2d 414, 395 N.Y.S.2d 138 (Civ. Ct. 1977).

Arabian Score v. Lasma Arabian Ltd.

United States Court of Appeals, Eighth Circuit, 1987
814 F.2d 529

WOLLMAN, J.

Beating dead horses is the sport of appellate judges, a generally harmless pastime painful only to the readers of appellate opinions. Paying for the promotion of dead horses can be an expensive proposition, however, as the facts of this case make abundantly clear.

Arabian Score (Arabian), a Minnesota limited partnership, appeals from the district court's orders granting summary judgment in favor of Lasma Arabian Ltd. (Limited), a Florida limited partnership, and Lasma Corporation (Lasma), an Arizona corporation. We affirm.

On October 27, 1983, Arabian entered into an agreement to purchase from Limited an Arabian colt named Score. The agreement, which the parties agreed would be governed by and construed in accordance with the laws of Arizona, provided that Arabian would pay Limited $1 million "for the purchase of Score and the performance by Lasma of various services in the promotion of Score." The contract required Lasma to spend $250,000 for the performance of those services which consisted of advertising and promoting Score as a 2 Star Stallion under a license agreement with Lasma Star Stallion, Inc., a separate corporation that is not a party to this lawsuit.

Paragraph 4 of the agreement provided that for a period of five years after the date of his purchase, Score would be a 2 Star Stallion, as defined by the Star Stallion license agreement, with the result that Score's foals would be eligible for nomination to all Lasma-sponsored sales open to the get of Lasma stallions.[13] If Lasma Star Stallion, Inc., in its sole discretion, determined that Score was not eligible to participate in the Star Stallion Program, Lasma would, at Arabian's option, replace Score with an eligible stallion or refund to Arabian the unused portion of the money Lasma would otherwise

13. As near as we can tell from the materials presented to the trial court, the Star Stallion program is to the ranking of Arabian horses what the Mobil Guide is to the ranking of restaurants. This may not be a totally accurate description, but it will do for the purposes of this case.

be required to spend promoting Score pursuant to the terms of the paragraph 5 of the agreement.

Paragraph 5 of the agreement provided that for five consecutive calendar years commencing with 1984, Lasma would implement a complete annual program for the promotion of Score as a 2 Star Stallion. Lasma was to pay $70,000 for the 1984 program and $45,000 for each of the remaining four annual programs. The annual programs were to "include advertising in various trade publications, direct mail programs and the training, boarding, conditioning and showing of SCORE by Lasma."

Pursuant to paragraph 6 of the agreement, Lasma guaranteed that Score was not infertile.

Paragraph 9 of the agreement provided: "Except as provided by paragraphs 4 and 6 above, the Partnership accepts SCORE *AS IS,* all implied warranties being excluded. Risk of loss passes upon closing. All incidental and consequential damages are excluded."

On February 8, 1984, Arabian obtained a mortality insurance policy from Transit Casualty Company insuring Score for his actual cash value. Alas—memento mori—Score went to his reward within the year, dying on September 11, 1984, having sired two foals during his brief life. Misfortune compounding, Transit Casualty Company (its name bespeaks its character?) went broke. Lasma having expended only $52,891.14 for the promotion of Score, Arabian brought suit against Lasma and Limited, seeking recovery of the $197,108.86 not expended from the $250,000 that the purchase agreement allocated for the promotion of Score.

Count I of Arabian's complaint (later dismissed by stipulation) alleged that Lasma and Limited had breached the contract by not promoting Score. Count II sought recovery of the unspent portion of the $250,000 on the ground of impossibility of performance. Count III sought recovery under paragraph 4 of the purchase agreement.

The district court ruled that because Score's death was a foreseeable risk that was assumed by Arabian by the terms of the purchase agreement, neither the doctrine of impossibility nor of commercial frustration was applicable. Likewise, because the unrebutted evidence established that it is not unusual for Lasma Star Stallions, Inc. and Lasma to promote deceased horses, it was not an arbitrary, capricious, or irrational exercise of discretion by Lasma to determine that Score was still eligible postmortem to participate in the Star Stallion Program.

As provided by the agreement, we look to Arizona law to resolve the issues presented by Arabian's complaint.

In Garner v. Ellingson, 18 Ariz. App. 181, 501 P.2d 22 (1972), the Arizona Court of Appeals defined commercial frustration as circumstances beyond the control of the parties which render performance of the contract impossible and exonerate the party failing to perform. The court did not limit the doctrine to strict impossibility but included impracticability caused by extreme or unreasonable difficulty or expense. Id. at 23. The court did require, however, proof that the supervening frustrating event was not reasonably foreseeable. Id. at 24.

In Mohave County v. Mohave-Kingman Estates, 120 Ariz. 417, 586 P.2d 978, 983 (1978), the Arizona Supreme Court stated that "while Arizona recognizes the doctrine of commercial frustration . . . we do not see fit to interpret it as general absolution whenever performance under the contract becomes difficult or expensive. Proper application of this doctrine requires us to examine whether the allegedly frustrating event was reasonably foreseeable." In that case, the court refused to apply the doctrine where a zoning change had affected the economic feasibility of a contract to buy and develop land. The court reasoned that "the doctrine of commercial frustration does not apply to the instant case because the risk of change in the zoning ordinances was an event properly foreseeable by the defendants, and one which they would have contracted against." Id. at 984.

Arizona rejects the application of the commercial frustration doctrine when a party assumes the risk of the frustrating event. Kintner v. Wolfe, 102 Ariz. 164, 426 P.2d 798 (1967). In *Kintner,* the Arizona Supreme Court rejected a commercial frustration claim by a guarantor who had agreed to remain liable for the rent due on a liquor license lease "without respect to future changes in conditions." A change in law made renting liquor licenses illegal, but the court required the guarantor to pay, stating: "If the parties to a contract have agreed in express or implied terms that the risk of loss shall fall upon one or the other of the parties, full effect is given to such provision." Id. at 803.

We conclude that the trial court was correct in holding that the commercial frustration doctrine is inapplicable in this case, both because Score's death was foreseeable, as evidenced by Arabian's purchase of insurance, and because Arabian assumed the risk that Score might die prematurely. Moreover, the doctrine of impossibility/commercial frustration is not applicable because the party obligated to perform—Lasma—does not contend that it is unable or unwilling to complete its duty to promote Score.

Arabian further contends that by virtue of his death Score is no longer eligible to participate in the Star Stallion Program; consequently, paragraph 4 of the agreement obligates Lasma to return any unspent portion of the funds earmarked for promotional purposes.

As indicated earlier, Lasma Star Stallion, Inc. is not a party to this lawsuit, and there are no findings by the district court that Lasma or Limited controls Lasma Star Stallion, Inc. in the exercise of its discretion. Because Lasma Star Stallion, Inc. has not declared Score to be ineligible for the Star Stallion Program, the condition precedent to Lasma's obligation under paragraph 4 of the agreement has not been satisfied.

Even if it were within Lasma's discretion to declare Score ineligible to participate in the Star Stallion Program, we could not say that the decision that Score is still eligible for the program was an arbitrary or capricious abuse of discretion.

Arabian argues that the decision to promote a dead horse is per se arbitrary.[14] As indicated above, however, Lasma's unrebutted evidence shows that Lasma Star Stallion, Inc. and Lasma regularly promote deceased horses. This is done to enhance the owning entity's reputation and to increase the value of the stallion's progeny. Further, the language of paragraph 4 was not intended to cover the risk of death but of ineligibility for other reasons, such as infertility or substandard offspring.

It is with some reluctance that we affirm the district court's grant of summary judgment. That reluctance stems from the thought that spending $197,108.86 to promote a dead horse borders on the bizarre. The parties to this agreement were sophisticated and, we assume, well-heeled business-persons, however, and that which we find to be somewhat unusual may be commonplace to those who inhabit the wealthy world of the horsey set.

The judgment dismissing Arabian's complaint is affirmed.

PROBLEM 75

In the mid-1960s, in an effort to boost sales of its nuclear reactors, Westinghouse Corporation agreed to sell 27 utility companies 80 million pounds of uranium over the next 20 years. The average sale price per pound was $10. When Westinghouse made the sale, it actually owned only 15 million pounds of uranium. By the mid-1970s, the price of uranium had risen to $40 a pound. In late 1975, Westinghouse announced that it would not honor its contract. The utilities sued. Westinghouse argued that the best evidence in the late 1960s and early 1970s indicated uranium prices would be stable over the long term. The Corporation claimed that the price rise was unforeseeable and that the contracts were excused under §2-615 as "commercially impracticable." In particular, Westinghouse blamed the 1973 oil embargo and worldwide price fixing for the "unpredictable" price rises. See Official Comments 4 and 5 to §2-615. How should the dispute be resolved? See Publicker Indus. v. Union Carbide Corp., 1975 WL 22890 (E.D. Pa. 1975); Ecology Services, Inc. v. Granturk Equipment, Inc., 443 F. Supp. 2d 756 (D. Md. 2006); Eagan, The Westinghouse Uranium Contracts: Commercial

14. At oral argument, counsel for Arabian asked, rhetorically we assume, "How are you going to show a dead horse?" Considerations of judicial decorum and a due regard for the financial loss suffered by Arabian dissuaded us from suggesting the construction of a mausoleum—an equestrian Lenin's Tomb, if you will.

Impracticability and Related Matters, 18 Am. Bus. L.J. 281 (1980); Rochester Gas and Electric Corporation v. Delta Star, Inc., 2009 WL 368508 (W.D.N.Y. 2009) (seller of goods at a fixed price was not relieved of obligation where price of component increased due to Hurricane Katrina). If you could advise Westinghouse on how to avoid this problem in the future, what would you suggest? See §2-305.

Louisiana Power & Light Co. v. Allegheny Ludlum Industries, Inc.

United States District Court, Eastern District of Louisiana, 1981
517 F. Supp. 1319

GORDON, J.

This breach of contract case is before the court on plaintiff's motion for summary judgment. The material facts which are not in dispute are as follows:

Plaintiff, Louisiana Power & Light Company (hereinafter referred to as "LP & L"), entered into a contract with defendants, Allegheny Ludlum Industries, Inc. and Allegheny Ludlum Steel Corporation (hereinafter referred to collectively as "Allegheny,") in which Allegheny agreed to supply condenser tubing to LP & L for use at LP & L's Waterford 3 nuclear power plant. The contract was awarded to Allegheny Ludlum Steel Corporation, then a division of Allegheny Ludlum Industries, Inc., after the solicitation of bids by LP & L's agent, Ebasco Services, Incorporated. The contract, dated February 8, 1974, was accepted by Allegheny in mid-March of 1974.

Pursuant to the terms of the contract Allegheny undertook to furnish, fabricate and deliver to LP & L stainless steel condenser tubing in accordance with the specifications of LP & L's agent, Ebasco. Equal shipments of the tubing were to be made on June 1, 1976, June 15, 1976, and July 1, 1976, for a total price of $1,127,387.82. The contract also provided that if LP & L delayed shipment beyond August 31, 1976, but not later than January 31, 1977, the contract price would be increased by three percent (3%). A further adjustment at the rate of ten percent (10%) would take place if LP & L delayed shipment beyond January 31, 1977, but not later than January 31, 1978. No other escalation clauses were included in the contract.

On May 19, 1975, Allegheny sent a letter to LP & L seeking "additional compensation" for performance under the contract. Allegheny informed LP & L that subsequent to the formulation of the contract its "costs [had] risen at such a high rate that escalators built into our contracts have in no way adequately compensated for them. For example, since March of 1974 the price of electrolytic nickel has increased 24%, low carbon ferrochrome 185% and labor 21%." Allegheny sought the opportunity to meet with representatives of LP & L in order to discuss Allegheny's price increases and possible solutions to Allegheny's problem. Allegheny suggested a renegotiation of the contract price, but LP & L chose not to meet with Allegheny to discuss the matter.

In October of 1975, LP & L, through Ebasco, advised Allegheny that it considered Allegheny's price increases to be business risks which must be absorbed by Allegheny. On November 4, 1975, Allegheny informed LP & L, by letter from C.R. Hastings, General Manager of Allegheny's Wallingford Tubular Products Division, that a "[c]urrent review of this matter suggests that Allegheny Ludlum might be well advised not to perform under the contract." On November 19, 1975, Ebasco wrote to Allegheny's Wallingford Tubular Products Division, and demanded written assurances within thirty days, pursuant to §2-609 of the New York Commercial Code,[15] that Allegheny would fully and properly perform under the contract.

As of January 19, 1976, LP & L had not received any such written assurance of performance from Allegheny and on January 30, 1976, LP & L notified Allegheny by letter that it considered the contract repudiated by Allegheny. Thereafter, on February 17, 1976, C.R. Hastings at Allegheny wrote to LP & L informing it that Allegheny was willing to "make delivery under the subject purchase order at $1.80 per lb . . . [Allegheny's] full cost of producing the material. . . ."

LP & L rejected Allegheny's offer to supply the tubing at Allegheny's cost and through its agent, Ebasco, LP & L solicited bids from other vendors for supply of the requisite condenser tubing. LP & L steadfastly rejected the offer of Allegheny to supply the tubing at Allegheny's cost, a price higher than that specified in the LP & L/Allegheny contract. On June 16, 1976, LP & L, through Ebasco, entered into a contract with Trent Tube Division of Crucible, Inc. for the purchase of condenser tubing at a price of $1,729,278.

Allegheny intended that the condenser tubing which was the subject of its contract with LP & L would be supplied by its Wallingford Tubular Products Division at Wallingford, Connecticut. C. R. Hastings, General Manager of the Wallingford Tubular Division, stated in his deposition that performance under the terms of the LP & L/Allegheny contract would have caused Allegheny to sustain a projected loss of $428,500 on the contract. Hastings indicated that such a loss would have reduced the planned profit for 1976 at the Wallingford plant from $1,018,000 to $589,500.

Plaintiff seeks by way of its lawsuit to recover from Allegheny the costs of its "cover," the monetary difference between the LP & L/Allegheny contract and the LP & L/Trent Tube contract, plus the expenses which it incurred

15. The contract between LP & L and Allegheny stated that the contract was to be governed by the laws of the State of New York, hence the invocation of §2-609 of the New York Commercial Code.

in the re-solicitation of bids for the tubing. Allegheny has defended this action on four principal bases: commercial impracticability, mutual mistake, unconscionability and alleged bad faith conduct by LP & L. Plaintiff's claim and Allegheny's defenses will be considered in accord with the appropriate standards for summary judgment motions.

LP & L claims that Allegheny breached its contract to supply condenser tubing to LP & L. The first evidence which LP & L received that indicated that Allegheny would not perform under the contract as written was Allegheny's letter of May 19, 1975, to LP & L in which Allegheny sought "additional compensation" for supplying the condenser tubing. In response to that submission, LP & L sent a letter to Allegheny, invoking the provisions of §2-609 of the New York Uniform Commercial Code and requesting assurance from Allegheny that it would perform under the contract.

The pertinent provisions of §2-609 of the UCC, invoked by LP & L, provide:

> *§2-609 Right to Adequate Assurance of Performance*
>
> (1) A contract for sale imposes an obligation on each party that the other's expectation of receiving due performance will not be impaired. When reasonable grounds for insecurity arise with respect to the performance of either party the other may in writing demand adequate assurance of due performance. . . .
>
> (4) After receipt of a justified demand failure to provide within a reasonable time not exceeding thirty days such assurance of due performance as is adequate under the circumstances of the particular case is a repudiation of the contract.

The letter which LP & L received from Allegheny requesting "additional compensation" provided LP & L with a reasonable basis for insecurity as to Allegheny's performance under the contract. LP & L's letter of November 19, 1975, to Allegheny constituted an adequate demand on Allegheny for an assurance of performance. When LP & L failed to receive such an assurance by January 19, 1976, it was justified in characterizing the contract as repudiated. LP & L notified Allegheny of that fact on January 30, 1976. Subsequently, Allegheny indicated to plaintiff that it would perform under the contract for added compensation. Such a belated and qualified offer of performance cannot, however, be viewed as an assurance of performance under §2-609 of the U.C.C. Allegheny's failure to supply an assurance of performance within the allotted time period operated as a repudiation of the contract.

The UCC provides that:

> When either party repudiates the contract with respect to a performance not yet due the loss of which will substantially impair the value of the contract to

> the other, the aggrieved party may . . . (b) resort to any remedy for breach (Section 2-703 or Section 2-711). . . . [Uniform Commercial Code §2-610.]

One available remedy in the event of a breach is for the buyer to obtain a "cover" by purchasing goods in substitution for the goods due from the seller. A buyer and non-breaching party may then seek to recover from the seller and breaching party the price of such substituted goods plus incidental and consequential damages. See U.C.C. §2-711 and §2-712. It is just such a claim that plaintiff is making in the instant case. Based on the undisputed facts in this case, plaintiff is entitled to recover on that claim, unless Allegheny prevails on one of its defenses.

COMMERCIAL IMPRACTICABILITY

The first of Allegheny's defenses to be considered is that of commercial impracticability. The Uniform Commercial Code provides that performance under a contract may be excused if performance under the contract is commercially impracticable. Section 2-615 of the UCC, upon which Allegheny relies in its defense of commercial impracticability, states in pertinent part:

> *§2-615 Excuse by Failure of Presupposed Conditions*
>
> Except so far as a seller may have assumed a greater obligation and subject to the preceding section on substituted performance:
>
> (a) Delay in delivery or non-delivery in whole or in parts by a seller who complies with paragraphs (b) and (c) is not a breach of his duty under a contract for sale if performance as agreed has been made impracticable by the occurrence of a contingency the non-occurrence of which was a basic assumption on which the contract was made. . . .

In reliance upon that rule of law Allegheny argues that its performance under the contract with LP & L was rendered commercially impracticable because of a "severe shortage of critical raw materials and an increase in the cost of labor, an unexpected contingency which caused a dramatic increase in the price of those raw materials and the condenser tubing. The non-occurrence of such was a basic assumption on which the contract was founded and altered the essential nature of performance."

There are three conditions which must be met pursuant to §2-615 before performance under a contract can be excused because of commercial impracticability: "(1) a contingency must occur, (2) performance must thereby be made 'impracticable' and (3) the non-occurrence of the contingency must have been a basic assumption on which the contract was made." Neal-Cooper Grain Co. v. Texas Gulf Sulphur Co., 508 F.2d 283, 293 (7th Cir. 1974).

The rule has also been stated as "excus[ing] delay or nondelivery when the agreed upon performance has been rendered 'commercially impracticable' by an unforeseen supervening event not within the contemplation of the parties at the time the contract was entered into." Eastern Air Lines, Inc. v. McDonnell Douglas Corp., 532 F.2d 957, 988 (5th Cir. 1976). The rationale behind the doctrine of commercial impracticability is that when an event occurs which renders performance so "vitally different" from that which is anticipated, the contract cannot be reasonably considered to govern and performance under that contract is excused. Eastern Air Lines, Inc., supra, at 991.

The burden of proof on a claim of commercial impracticability rests with the party making the claim, in this case the defendants. Allegheny must meet its burden as to each of the requisite three elements in order to be successful in this defense. See Eastern Air Lines, Inc. v. Gulf Oil Corp., 415 F. Supp. 429, 438 (S.D. Fla. 1975), citing Ocean Air Tradeways, Inc. v. Arkay Realty Corp., 480 F.2d 1112, 1117 (9th Cir. 1973).

The undisputed facts in this case show that Allegheny has not and cannot meet its burden of proof as to this defense because it is unable to show that performance under the contract was commercially impracticable. Allegheny contacted LP & L in May of 1975 and informed LP & L that between March of 1974 and May of 1975, its costs for electrolytic nickel had risen by 24%, for low carbon ferrochrome had risen by 185%, and that its labor costs had risen by 21%. C.R. Hastings, General Manager of Allegheny's Wallingford Tubular Division stated in his deposition that had Allegheny performed under the contract as written, it would have sustained a loss of $428,500 on the contract and that the planned profitability of the Wallingford plant would have been reduced to an overall profit of $589,500 for the year of performance.

There are no facts which indicate that Allegheny's costs increased by more than the amount indicated to LP & L in the Allegheny letter of May 19, 1975. Moreover, there are no facts which indicate that Allegheny would have sustained a greater loss than that attested to by C.R. Hastings had it performed under the contract. There are also no facts which indicate that Allegheny would have been unprofitable during 1976 in either its overall corporate structure or in its Wallingford Tubular Division had it performed under the contract as written. Hastings testified in his deposition that a profit was anticipated for the Wallingford plant even had Allegheny been required to perform under the contract's terms. The material facts in this regard are clear, simple and undisputed. When viewed in the context of a claim of commercial impracticability, as that term has been interpreted in the case law, it must be said that performance under the contract was not commercially impracticable.

The mere fact that performance under the contract would have deprived Allegheny of its anticipated profit and resulted in a loss on the contract is not sufficient to show commercial impracticability. Rather, ". . . [t]he party seeking to excuse his performance must not only show that he can perform only at a loss but also that the loss will be especially severe and unreasonable." Gulf Oil Corp. v. Federal Power Commission, 563 F.2d 588, 600 (3d Cir. 1977), *cert. denied,* 434 U.S. 1062 (1978), *petition for cert. dismissed,* 435 U.S. 911 (1978).

Allegheny's loss by performance would not have been especially severe and unreasonable in this case. On the contrary, by Allegheny's own estimate its costs of performance under the contract increased only 38% over the original contract price of $1,127,387.82. While no seller desires to be called upon to perform under a contract when performance will result in a financial loss, such are the realities of commercial life. Whereas the law quite properly provides relief for situations in which performance can only be had at an excessive and unreasonable cost, see Transatlantic Financing Corp. v. United States, 363 F.2d 312 (D.C. Cir. 1960), Allegheny's cost of performance did not increase to the extent necessary to excuse its performance under the doctrine of commercial impracticability.[16]

Eastern Air Lines, Inc. v. Gulf Oil Corp., 415 F. Supp. 429, 438 (S.D. Fla. 1975) is instructive:

> The modern U.C.C. §2-615 doctrine of commercial impracticability has its roots in the common law doctrine of frustration or impossibility and finds its most recognized illustrations in the so-called "Suez Cases," arising out of the various closings of the Suez Canal and the consequent increases in shipping costs around the Cape of Good Hope. Those cases offered little encouragement to those who would wield the sword of commercial impracticability. As a leading British case arising out of the 1957 Suez closure declared, the unforeseen cost increase that would excuse performance "must be more than merely onerous or expensive. It must be positively unjust to hold the parties bound." Ocean Tramp Tankers v. V/O Sovfracht (The Eugenia), 2 Q.B. 226, 239 (1964). To the same effect are Tsakiroglou and Co. Ltd. v. Noblee Thorl G.m.b.H., 2 Q.B. 348, (1960), *aff'd,* A.C. 93 (1962), and Caparanoyoti & Co., Ltd. v. E.T. Green, Ltd., 1 Q.B. 131, 148 (1959). These British precedents were followed by the District of Columbia Circuit, which gave specific consideration to UCC §2-615, Comment 4, in Transatlantic Financing Corp. v. United States, 124 U.S. App. D.C. 183, 363 F.2d 312, 319 (1966).

In *Transatlantic Financing Corp.*, supra, Judge J. Skelly Wright considered a claim of commercial impracticability and impossibility in connection with

16. When consideration is given to Allegheny's anticipated profitability in 1976, it becomes more apparent that this was not a situation wherein performance under the contract would have been especially severe and unreasonable.

a suit seeking additional compensation for transport of a cargo of wheat around the Cape of Good Hope. The plaintiff was forced to abandon its customary route through the Suez Canal when Egypt obstructed the canal and closed it to traffic. Plaintiff argued that it was subjected to an additional expense of $43,972.00 above the contract price of $305,842.92 because of the longer journey necessitated by the closing of the canal. The court stated:

> . . . While it may be an overstatement to say that increased cost and difficulty of performance never constitute impracticability, to justify relief there must be more of a variation between expected cost and the cost of performing by an available alternative than is present in this case, where the promisor can legitimately be presumed to have accepted some degree of abnormal risk, and where impracticability is urged on the basis of added expense alone. [363 F.2d at 319.] The court affirmed the dismissal of the plaintiff's action because performance under the contract had not been rendered legally impossible.

In a similar case resulting from the closure of the Suez Canal, it was held that extra expense of 31.6% of the contract price, incurred in bringing the vessel around the Cape of Good Hope, was not sufficient to constitute commercial impracticability. American Trading and Production Corp. v. Shell International Marine, Ltd., 453 F.2d 939 (2d Cir. 1972). In discussing the degree of increase in costs that would constitute impossibility or commercial impracticability, it was stated that:

> Mere increase in cost alone is not a sufficient excuse for non-performance (Restatement of Contracts §467 (1932)). It must be an "extreme and unreasonable" expense (Restatement of Contracts §454 (1932)). While in the *Transatlantic* case supra, the increased cost amounted to an increase of about 14% over the contract price, the court did cite with approval the two leading English cases Ocean Tramp Tankers Corp. v. V/O Sovfracht (The Eugenia), [1964] 2 Q.B. 226, 233 (C.A. 1963) (which expressly overruled Societe Franco Tunisienne D'Armement v. Sidemar S.P.A. (The Messalia), [1961] 2 Q.B. 278 (1960), where the court had found frustration because the Cape route was highly circuitous and involved an increase in cost of approximately 50%), and Tsakiroglou & Co. Ltd. v. Noblee Thorl G.m.b.H., [1960] 2 Q.B. 318, 348, *aff'd,* [1962] A.C., 93 (1961) where the House of Lords found no frustration though the freight costs were exactly doubled due to the Canal closure. [453 F.2d at 942.]

In Iowa Electric Light and Power Company v. Atlas Corp., 467 F. Supp. 129 (N.D. Iowa, 1978) the court held that an increase in seller's costs by 52.2%, resulting in the seller's loss of approximately $2,673,125.00, failed to constitute commercial impracticability thereby precluding judicial adjustment or discharge of the contract for supply of uranium concentrate. In making such a determination, the court noted that cost increases of

50-58 percent had generally not been considered of sufficient magnitude to excuse performance under a contractual agreement.

As the jurisprudence indicates, Allegheny's performance under the contract was not commercially impracticable. Even if Allegheny were to show that its increased costs constituted a contingency, the non-occurrence of which was a basic assumption on which the contract was made, it still could not show that performance had been rendered commercially impracticable as a result. Allegheny bears the burden of proof as to each of the requisite three elements on its claim of commercial impracticability. Being unable to prove all three elements, its defense must fall.

Allegheny has suggested that claims of commercial impracticability are inherently insusceptible of resolution by summary judgment. That position is incorrect. While great care should be exercised in granting summary judgment motions in cases of this sort, the mere invocation of the term "commercial impracticability" is not a talisman behind which a defaulting seller may hide and be guaranteed a trial in the absence of a dispute as to the material facts in the matter. Were that the case, every seller or buyer caught in a burdensome position under a contract would find it hard to resist the natural temptation to compel renegotiation of unprofitable contracts by threatening to invoke a claim of commercial impracticability, knowing that it would be assured of a trial on the merits and knowing that even if it lost at trial, it would be required to do no more than fulfill its obligation under the contract. Such a rule of law would constitute a misuse of the protections afforded by the doctrine of commercial impracticability, particularly in cases of this sort where the facts are clear and undisputed and in which the seller in breach has been unable to cite a case wherein a claim of commercial impracticability has been upheld under similar factual circumstances.[17]

The clear undisputed facts require resolution of the commercial impracticability defense in plaintiff's favor. Allegheny is unable to meet its burden of proof. . . .

UNCONSCIONABILITY

Section 4 of the Supplementary Terms and Conditions of the LP & L/Allegheny contract provides that:

> *4. Provision for Cancellation*
>
> At any time after the acceptance of this Order the Purchaser shall have the absolute right to cancel the entire Order upon the payment to the Seller for all disbursements and expenses which the Seller has incurred or become obligated

17. In Aluminum Company of America v. Essex Group, Inc., 499 F. Supp. 53 (W.D. Pa. 1980), a claim of commercial impracticability was upheld. The facts surrounding the claim of commercial impracticability in *Alcoa* are, however, distinguishable from those in the instant

> for prior to date of notice of cancellation, less the reasonable resale value of equipment which shall have been obtained or ordered to become an integral part of the Equipment plus a sum as profit bearing the same ratio to the profit that the Seller would have received upon completing the Work as that portion of Work done bears to the entire amount of Work to be done by the Seller under this Order.

Allegheny argues that the aforementioned cancellation provision is unconscionable, that it taints the contract in its entirety and that as a result the contract is unenforceable. Accordingly, Allegheny urges that LP & L be barred from any recovery for damages.

The unconscionability which Allegheny suggests is rooted in the alleged one-sidedness of the provision which provides a right of cancellation to LP & L with no concomitant right given to Allegheny. The defendants submit that until production commenced, LP & L could cancel its order with impunity and would only be required to pay a penalty for cancellation "if Allegheny would be making a profit on the order, which LP & L now knew it would not. . . ."

Section 2-302 of the U.C.C., which is the basis for Allegheny's claim of unconscionability states: [the court quotes §2-302—EDS.].

Comment 1 to U.C.C. §2-302 sets forth the standards to be used in making a determination on an unconscionability claim. "The basic test is whether in the light of the general commercial background and the commercial needs of the particular trade or case, the clauses involved are so one-sided as to be unconscionable under the circumstances existing at the time of the making of the contract. . . . The principle is one of prevention of oppression and unfair surprise . . . and not of disturbance of allocation of risks because of superior bargaining power."

Allegheny's allegation of unconscionability presents a question of law to be decided by the court. It is not a jury issue. U.C.C. §2-302. W.L. May Co., Inc. v. Philco-Ford Corp., 543 P.2d 283 (Or. 1975). However, plaintiff's claim that the cancellation clause and the contract were unconscionable entitles the parties to "a reasonable opportunity to present evidence as to . . . commercial setting, purpose and effect to aid the court in making . . . [its] determination." U.C.C. §2-302(2). The unconscionability claim is not susceptible of resolution by summary judgment. The court's determination of the issue cannot be made without a hearing. Zicari v. Joseph Harris Co., 304 N.Y.S.2d

---

case. Plaintiff stood to lose $60,000,000.00 in *Alcoa* if its performance under the contract was compelled while the defendant stood to gain a concomitant "windfall profit." There are no comparable facts in the instant case. Allegheny stood to lose $428,500 on a $ 1,127,387.82 contract. It cannot be said that LP & L would be the beneficiary of a "windfall profit" like that in *Alcoa*.

918 (N.Y. 1969). Accordingly, plaintiff's motion for summary judgment must be denied in this regard.

Bad Faith

Allegheny also asserts that bad faith conduct by LP & L serves as a defense to LP & L's claim for breach of contract. The basis of Allegheny's allegation of bad faith is that LP & L refused to meet with it in a timely fashion to discuss renegotiation of the contract. Allegheny argues that its bad faith allegation must be resolved at trial by the finder of fact.

The Uniform Commercial Code imposes an obligation of good faith on the performance or enforcement of contracts under the Code. U.C.C. §1-203.[18] "Good faith" is defined as "honesty in fact and the observance of reasonable commercial standards of fair dealing in the trade." U.C.C. §2-103(1)(b).

Allegheny's defense of bad faith based on LP & L's failure to engage in timely renegotiation of the contract is without merit. There is no obligation imposed under law which would have required LP & L to engage in renegotiation or even discuss renegotiation of its contract with Allegheny. See Missouri Public Service Company v. Peabody Coal Co., 583 S.W.2d 721, 725 (Mo. App. 1979), *cert. denied,* 444 U.S. 865. Allegheny has not attempted to show any requirement for renegotiation. Allegheny's claim that LP & L was in bad faith for failure to do what it had no obligation to do cannot withstand scrutiny. It cannot survive the test of plaintiff's summary judgment motion.

Insofar, however, as Allegheny makes a claim of bad faith conduct in connection with LP & L's purchase of goods in substitution for those due from Allegheny, the "cover" under U.C.C. §2-712(1), that defense relates to the damages portion of LP & L's lawsuit. The issue awaits resolution with LP & L's claim for damages.

In that regard, this court cannot now say that there are no genuine issues of material fact surrounding LP & L's claim for damages. The facts surrounding the obtaining of a "cover," timeliness, mitigation of damages, good faith and costs cannot be decided at this time. Unlike the liability portion of plaintiff's claim and consideration of certain of Allegheny's defenses, the issue of LP & L's damages awaits resolution at trial.

Conclusion

Based on the foregoing authorities and analysis, the court hereby grants the motion of Louisiana Power & Light Co. for summary judgment on the

18. Now §1-304.—Ed.

issue of liability and Allegheny's defenses of commercial impracticability, mistakes of fact and bad faith. The motion for summary judgment must be denied insofar as Allegheny's defense of unconscionability and the issue of LP & L's damages are concerned.

CHAPTER 6 REVIEW QUESTIONS

Is a buyer obliged to accept the goods if the seller has substantially performed?
What are the exceptions to the perfect tender rule?
How can a buyer avoid accepting the goods?
What is an ineffective rejection?
Can a buyer make an effective rejection that breaches the contract?
Is a buyer bound by an acceptance of the goods if seller has breached?
What is the difference between rejection and revocation of acceptance?
What is the effect of breach, by seller or buyer, on risk of loss?
When will a party be excused from performance by failure of presupposed conditions?

ASSESSMENT: MULTIPLE CHOICE QUESTIONS

1. Wambach Retail ordered 10,000 folding chairs from Lloyd Furniture, to be delivered in 5 shipments of 2,000 chairs, on the first days of July, August, and September. The first shipment arrived on July 1, missing a chair. On July 2, may Wambach Retail rightfully reject the shipment?
   a. Yes. In sales law, buyer may reject a seller's tender unless it is a perfect tender.
   b. Yes. The missing chair can never be delivered on time, because July 1 is in the past, so the defect cannot be cured.
   c. No. The non-conformity is not substantial enough to reject.
   d. No. Buyers must always accept a good faith attempt by sellers to meet the contract requirements.

2. A question with a slight but important difference: *can* Wambach Retail reject the shipment?
   a. No. The non-conformity is not substantial enough to reject.
   b. Yes. A buyer can reject a shipment, even if the rejection is wrongful, although buyer would then be in breach.
   c. No. If seller makes a tender that may not be rejected, then buyer cannot reject the tender.
   d. Yes. Buyer always has complete discretion about whether to accept a tender.

3. Lloyd Furniture carefully counted the chairs for a different contract, a single delivery of 1,000 chairs to Rapinoe Raptures, made on the agreed delivery date. Finding the shipment 1 chair short, Lloyd made the delivery as scheduled, arranging for another chair to be delivered the following day. But Rapinoe Raptures rejected the tender of 999 chairs and refused to allow Lloyd Furniture to cure the defect, because the delivery date was now past. Does Lloyd Furniture have a right to cure the defect?
   a. No. The delivery date is past and so the defect cannot be cured.
   b. No. The shaken faith doctrine would apply to prevent cure.
   c. Yes. Lloyd Furniture may cure the defect, where it reasonably believed the tender was conforming.
   d. Yes. A seller always has a right to cure.

4. Pemulis Auto signed yet another contract, to sell a 2016 Model Excalibur Hardtop to Hamlet. As agreed, Hamlet showed up Monday morning at Pemulis Auto to pick up the car. But after Hamlet paid and the papers were signed, Hamlet abruptly decided to wait a couple of days before driving away. That delay breached the contract, which required Hamlet to take delivery upon payment. The next day, the car was struck by lightning and destroyed. Pemulis Auto did not have insurance covering the car. Is Hamlet entitled to return of the price paid?
   a. No. Once the car was paid for and the papers signed, the car belonged to Hamlet.
   b. No. Hamlet was in breach, so the risk of loss was on Hamlet.
   c. Yes. Hamlet had not taken delivery, so the risk of loss was still on the seller.
   d. Yes. Pemulis Auto was at fault for failure to obtain insurance.

5. Pemulis Auto sold a used Hekla sedan to Rapinoe, assuring her that the engine had been thoroughly tested for reliability and safety. Rapinoe agreed to take the car, signed the papers to get title transferred, and set off for home in the car. The engine burst into flames after a mile. Pemulis Auto offers to set off the price of a new engine, but refuses to take the car back. Is Rapinoe obliged to pay for the car, minus the cost of a new engine?
   a. Yes. Rapinoe accepted the car, so is obliged to pay for it, minus damages for the breach.
   b. Yes. Rapinoe should have tested the car herself.
   c. No. Rapinoe may revoke her acceptance.
   d. No. A buyer is never obliged to pay for defective goods.
   e. Yes. Rapinoe cannot revoke acceptance, because the car is damaged and cannot be returned intact.

ANSWERS

1. *C* is the best answer. In sales contract generally, a buyer may reject a tender "if the goods or the tender of delivery fail in any respect to conform to the contract." §2-601. This requirement of perfect tender protects buyers from being required to accept and pay unless the seller delivers exactly as promised. But a lower standard exists for installment contracts, where the parties have repeated dealings and so the buyer is at less of a bargaining disadvantage. In installment contracts, a buyer may reject only "an installment which is non-conforming if the non-conformity substantially impairs the value of that installment and cannot be cured or if non-conformity is a defect in the required documents." One missing chair of 2,000 is not substantial (unless there were special circumstances, not present here). Even if it were, it could be quickly cured. We are not told of any problems with the documents. Grounds for rejecting an installment delivery are lacking.
2. *B* is the best answer. Wambach Retail does not have grounds to reject the shipment. But Wambach Retail can still reject the shipment. That would be an effective, but wrongful rejection. As the next chapter discusses, Wambach Retail would not be liable for the price, because it did not accept the goods, but would be liable for any damages, such as Lloyd Furniture reselling the chairs at a loss.
3. *C* is the best answer. A seller does not always have a right to cure. Under §2-508, a seller has a right to cure if the time for performance has not expired (not applicable here) or the seller had reasonable grounds to believe the tender would be accepted. Here, the seller could reasonably believe that one missing chair of one thousand would not result in rejection of the delivery.
4. *B* is the best answer. Normally, when the buyer is not a merchant, the risk of loss does not pass until the goods have been delivered. §2-509(3). But when one party breaches, a different set of rules may apply under §2-510. Where the buyer is in breach, the seller may treat the risk of loss as resting on the buyer for a commercially reasonable time. §2-510(3). The parties may agree on different rules for risk of loss or for one party to obtain insurance, but they did not do so here. So, contrary to *D*, Pemulis Auto was not required to obtain insurance.
5. *C* is the best answer. Rapinoe accepted the car. She agreed to take the car, and had ownership transferred, either of which would be acceptance. §2-606. Normally a buyer that accepts the goods must pay the price, with a counterclaim for any breach by seller. §2-607. But sometimes a buyer may revoke acceptance. §2-608. Rapinoe meets the requirements

for revocation of acceptance. She accepted the goods with assurances from the seller that the engine was not defective. §2-608(1)(b). The non-conformity substantially impairs the value of the car to Rapinoe. §2-608. There has been a substantial change in the condition of the goods, but that does not prevent revocation where that change was caused by the defect in the goods. §2-608(2).

Chapter 7
Remedies

When the deal has collapsed and the parties have turned to their lawyers with questions such as what steps can be taken to minimize damages and then what should be done to recover those that cannot be avoided, of particular interest are any mandatory actions imposed by the law and what choices the law gives to the aggrieved party. Sometimes the attorney will be asked by the client, "What is the smart thing to do"? At this point the lawyer should be careful to draw a distinction between what the law mandates while being careful not to make business decisions that the lawyer is typically unqualified to assess. The Uniform Commercial Code tends to reward conduct that is "reasonable" and taken "in good faith" and with "ordinary care." Those terms call for a business judgment the lawyer doesn't usually have. Instead, go for the practical: ask the client what steps would be taken if there were no possible legal relief, and that will often give surprising guidance by which to frame the legal battle that follows. Often this leads to a settlement, which is almost always a better result than a lawsuit.

I. SPECIAL REMEDIES

The 2-700s of the UCC are the basic remedy provisions (though some remedies, such as rejection and revocation of acceptance, which we covered earlier, found in other parts of Article 2). The 2-700s may be further divided into two parts: the seller's remedies when the buyer is in breach (§§2-703 to 2-710) and the buyer's remedies when the seller is in breach (§§2-711 to 2-717). These two areas will be discussed below; but before getting to them, pedagogical tidiness calls for a quick look at some special situations.

A. *Remedies on Insolvency*

When one contracting party becomes insolvent while in possession of goods that have been identified to the contract, the other may, in some circumstances, elect to forgo damages and try to get the goods themselves. This action is called *reclamation.* The key Code sections are §§2-502 and 2-702; read them. Both refer to the *insolvency* of the seller as a triggering event, but what does that term mean? In the Bankruptcy Code, it is defined as having more liabilities than assets, a bookkeeping test that is hard to determine without much investigation. The equitable definition of *insolvency,* however, defined the term as being unable to pay one's debts as they matured, a much easier thing to prove. Which of these does the UCC adopt? See §1-201(b)(23).

PROBLEM 76

Ratchett Tools delivered a truckload of inventory to Madoff Hardware. The next day, Ratchett Tools read that Madoff Hardware had shut its doors, failed to pay its many creditors, and has few assets to go after. Can Ratchett get the inventory back? See §2-702(2). Would it help sellers to include a clause in their sales contract forms making buyers promise they had the wherewithal to pay for goods ordered? See §2-702(2). What if Ratchett learned of the financial distress before delivery? §2-702(1). What if Madoff Hardware files for bankruptcy? See 11 U.S.C. §546(c).

Quite often a battle develops between a party (buyer or seller) seeking to reclaim goods and either a trustee in bankruptcy or a secured creditor of the party with the goods. If the battle is between the reclaiming seller and the trustee in bankruptcy, a section of the Bankruptcy Reform Act protects a seller's reclamation right from the trustee's avoiding powers even more broadly than §2-702; see 11 U.S.C.A. §546(c) (allowing seller to reclaim goods that were delivered to insolvent buyer within 45 days before buyer's bankruptcy). The battle between the secured creditor and the reclaiming party is governed by meshing Article 2 with Article 9, not always an easy task. The leading case is In re Samuels & Co., 510 F.2d 139 (5th Cir. 1975), *rev'd on other grounds,* 526 F.2d 1238 (5th Cir. 1976), *cert. denied,* 429 U.S. 834

(1976), where the secured creditor won over an unpaid cash seller. See also White & Summers §24-7 (suggesting that courts are likely to continue to favor secured creditors, under Bankruptcy Code §546(c)).

B. Liquidated Damages

At common law, if the parties put a liquidated damages clause in their contract, it was upheld by the courts only if the parties truly intended the figure named to be compensatory and had made in good faith an attempt to pre-estimate the damages. The courts struck the clause and made the aggrieved party prove actual damages if the courts decided that the parties had intended the liquidated figure to be a penalty amount to be forfeited in the event of breach. See Equitable Lumber Co. v. IPA Land Dev. Corp., 38 N.Y.2d 516, 344 N.E.2d 391, 381 N.Y.S.2d 459 (1976); J. Perillo, Contracts §§14-31, 14-32 (7th ed. 2014).

The Code's liquidated damages provision is §2-718(1). It makes little change from the common law rules except that it provides that the validity of the liquidated damages clause is to be tested, in part, against the *actual* harm caused by the breach (a criterion of no importance at common law). See Note, A New Standard for Liquidated Damage Provisions Under the Uniform Commercial Code?, 38 Ohio St. L.J. 437 (1977). For a case exploring the relationship between the liquidated damages clause and the actual damages incurred in the particular breach at issue, see Garden Ridge, L.P. v. Advance Intl., Inc., 2013 WL 1410145 (Tex. App. 2013).

Interestingly enough, the liquidated damages provision in Article 2A for the leasing of goods no longer refers to actual damages, specifically allows a *formula* to be used to compute damages, and drops all reference to the effect of an unreasonably large liquidated damages clause. Read §2A-504 and its Official Comment. Would this section permit the parties to contract for an outrageous amount (obviously a penalty) in the event of lessee default? See Benfield, Lessor's Damages Under Article 2A After Default by the Lessee as to Accepted Goods, 39 Ala. L. Rev. 915, 953 (1988); In re Republic Airways Holdings Inc., 598 B.R. 118 (S.D.N.Y. 2019) (liquidated damages clause for leases must be reasonable).

C. The Breaching Buyer's Restitution

PROBLEM 77

The zoo officials for the Minerun (West Virginia) Zoo contracted to buy an elephant from the zoo in White Cliffs, Delaware. The terms of the deal were that the West Virginia zoo would deliver a black bear worth $300 as a down payment and pay $100 a month for 20 months, at the end of which time the Delaware zoo would deliver the elephant. The bear was tendered and accepted. The West Virginia zoo duly made its $100 payments for 15 months before it ran out of money and could pay no more. The West Virginia zoo comes to you. Can it recover the $1,500 it has paid? The bear? Look at §§2-718(2), 2-718(3), and 2-718(4). Assuming the bear was and is still worth $300, calculate the amount that the West Virginia zoo is likely to recover in a restitution action.

II. SELLER'S REMEDIES

The plan of the 2-700s is to describe briefly the seller's remedies in §2-703 and the buyer's in §2-711 and then to flesh out these brief descriptions in the sections immediately following. All of these remedies sections are to be read in light of the Code's guiding remedial principle, §1-305(a):

> The remedies provided by this Act shall be liberally administered to the end that the aggrieved party may be put in as good a position as if the other party had fully performed but neither consequential or special nor penal damages may be had except as specifically provided in this Act or by other rule of law.[1]

Now read §2-703 and its Official Comment.

A. Accepted Goods

The seller's recovery of damages is measured by §2-709 (Action for the Price) if the buyer has made a technical *acceptance* of the goods or if the goods are destroyed within a commercially reasonable period of time after the risk of loss shifts to the buyer. In effect, §2-709 is the equivalent of a specific performance remedy for the seller. As discussed below, if the seller still has possession of the goods (or had the risk of loss at the time of their destruction), damages are measured by other sections in the 2-700s. For now, read §2-709. This section is annotated in 90 A.L.R.3d 1141.

1. The Wyoming Supreme Court has read this section as prohibiting punitive damages awards in suits alleging fraud; Waters v. Trenckmann, 503 P.2d 1187 (Wyo. 1972). Other courts have disagreed; see the discussion in Seaton v. Lawson Chevrolet-Mazda, Inc., 821 S.W.2d 137 (Tenn. 1991).

PROBLEM 78

Backslappers Auto Sales sold a new blue sports car to Dwane Diletante on credit. He accepted the car and drove it for a month. He then sent Backslappers a notice of revocation of acceptance and gave as his reason the recent repainting of his garage in a color that clashed with the blue car. The notice stated that Diletante had parked the car down the block from his home (away from the clashing garage) and that Backslappers should come and get it. Dwane also refused to make any more car payments. Three days after Backslappers received the notice, the car disappeared and has never been found. May the seller recover the price under §2-709? Who had the risk of loss? See §§2-608(1) and (3), 2-606(1), 2-510; note Official Comment 5 to §2-709. There is a good discussion of this problem in White & Summers §8-3. Would it make a difference if Diletante had *rejected* the goods for the same reason? Would a seller be entitled to recover the price if the market price for the goods had declined considerably after the delivery date? See Brewer v. J-Six Farms, 350 P.3d 420 (Okla. App. 2015).

B. Unaccepted Goods

When the buyer repudiates before delivery or rejects the goods, the relevant Code section is §2-706 if the seller resells the goods to someone else. If no resale occurs, damages are measured under §2-708. Other relevant sections are cited in the following Problems.

PROBLEM 79

Lannie Light was the sole proprietor of Light's Bulbs, a lighting fixtures business in Austin, Texas. She contracted to sell 80 neon light fixtures to Signs, Inc., a firm in San Antonio. The price was $1,500 "F.O.B. Austin," and the shipment date was to be March 15. On March 5, Signs, Inc., phoned Light and told her that the deal was off, but Lannie refused to agree to a cancellation. She went to her warehouse and picked 80 of the fixtures from her large stock. Then she posted a notice on the bulletin board near the cash register in her store, stating that 80 of the fixtures would be sold to the person making the best offer. Carl Customer (who was always buying these types of items) saw the sign and offered Light $1,000 for the fixtures. Light sold Customer the goods and took payment. Now Light comes to you. She tells you that on March 5 the fixtures were selling on the open market at $800 for 80 and that on March 15 the price for 80 such fixtures was $900 in Austin and $800 in San Antonio. Answer these questions:

(a) Does the UCC permit Light to select goods from the warehouse *after* the buyer repudiates? See §2-704.

(b) Was the resale proper? See §2-706 and Official Comment 2.

(c) Suppose Signs, Inc. had no cash for the purchase price, but offered to take the light fixtures on credit, even offering to provide a motorcycle as collateral. Could Light sell the light fixtures to someone else at a lower price and recover damages? Star Funding, Inc. v. Vault Minerals, LLC, 2018 WL 1581685 (S.D.N.Y. 2018).

(d) If Light's damages are measured under §2-708(1), what amount may she collect? What amount under §2-706?

(e) Does Light have the choice between the §2-706 (Resale) computation and the §2-708 (Repudiation) computation? See Official Comment 1 to §2-703; White & Summers §8-7. The next case deals with this issue in some detail.

Peace River Seed Co-Operative, Ltd. v. Proseeds Marketing, Inc.

Supreme Court of Oregon, 2014
355 Or. 44, 322 P.3d 531

BALMER, C.J.

In this breach of contract case, we examine the availability of different remedies under the Uniform Commercial Code (UCC) for an aggrieved seller of goods after a buyer breaches a contract to purchase those goods. Specifically, we consider the relationship between ORS 72.7080(1), which measures a seller's damages as the difference between the unpaid contract price and the *market* price at the time and place for tender, and ORS 72.7060, which measures a seller's damages as the difference between the contract price and the *resale* price. We examine those provisions to determine whether an aggrieved seller who has resold goods can recover a greater amount of damages using the market price measure of damages than the seller would recover using the resale price measure of damages.

Plaintiff, a seller seeking damages from a buyer that breached contracts to purchase goods, argued at trial that it was entitled to recover its market price damages. The trial court determined that plaintiff was entitled to the lesser of its market price damages or its resale price damages, and the court ultimately awarded plaintiff its resale price damages. The Court of Appeals reversed and remanded, because the court determined that plaintiff could recover its market price damages, even though it had resold some of the goods at issue. Peace River Seed Co-Op. v. Proseeds Marketing, 253 Or. App. 704, 717, 293 P.3d 1058 (2012). The Court of Appeals also reversed the trial court's decision not to award plaintiff its attorney fees under the parties' contracts, and remanded for the trial court to determine whether the parties intended the ambiguous contract term "charges for collection" to include attorney fees. Id. at 724-25, 293 P.3d 1058. For the reasons that follow, we agree that plaintiff was entitled to recover its market price damages, even if those damages exceeded plaintiff's resale price damages. We conclude, however, that plaintiff is not entitled to recover its attorney fees under the parties' contracts.

FACTS AND PROCEEDINGS BELOW

The facts material to our discussion are mostly undisputed. Peace River Seed Co-Operative ("plaintiff") is a Canadian company that buys grass seed from and sells grass seed for grass seed producers. Proseeds Marketing ("defendant") is an Oregon corporation that purchases grass seed from various sources to resell to end users. A broker prepared and the parties agreed to multiple contracts for defendant to purchase from plaintiff the total production of grass seed from a certain number of acres for a fixed price over a period of two years. The contracts incorporated the NORAMSEED Rules for the Trade of Seeds for Planting, which have been adopted by the American and Canadian Seed Trade Associations to govern the trade of seed. The NORAMSEED Rules provide that the UCC applies to transactions within the United States, and both parties have litigated this case under the UCC.

Under the contracts, defendant was to provide shipping and delivery instructions to plaintiff. During the contract period, however, the price of grass seed fell dramatically. Although defendant initially provided shipping instructions and plaintiff shipped conforming seed, defendant eventually refused to provide shipping instructions for delivery of additional seed under the contracts. After multiple requests for shipping instructions, and defendant's continued refusal to provide them, plaintiff cancelled the contracts. Over the next three years, plaintiff was able to sell at least some of the seed that defendant had agreed to purchase to other buyers.

The parties submitted their contract dispute to arbitration. Following an arbitrator's award in plaintiff's favor, plaintiff sought to enforce the award in court, and the trial court entered judgment over defendant's objection. Defendant appealed, and the Court of Appeals remanded for trial after concluding that the arbitration was not binding. Peace River Seed Co-Op v. Proseeds Marketing, 204 Or. App. 523, 526, 534, 132 P.3d 31, *rev. den.*, 341 Or. 216, 140 P.3d 1133 (2006). In the subsequent bench trial, the court concluded that defendant had breached the contracts and that plaintiff had been entitled to cancel the contracts and seek damages. When the trial court awarded plaintiff its damages, the court noted that the parties had entered into fixed price contracts, "regardless of the market price at the time of harvest and shipment," and the court explained that "[e]ach party takes certain risks and hopes for certain benefits in this type of a contract." Nonetheless, the court concluded that plaintiff had an "obligation to mitigate damages" and was "not entitled to recover damages in an amount greater than actually incurred." Accordingly, the trial court awarded plaintiff the lesser of two measures of damages: the difference between the unpaid contract price and the market price (the measure under ORS 72.7080(1)) or the difference between the contract price and the resale price (the measure under ORS 72.7060). The trial court directed plaintiff to submit calculations of each measure of damages.

Both parties sought reconsideration. At a hearing on those motions, the trial court stated that it would not be "absolutely one-hundred percent convinced" about the appropriate measure of damages until it could see how each party calculated market price damages and resale price damages. The trial court acknowledged that plaintiff previously had submitted its calculation of market price damages and had proven those damages, but the court also directed the parties to calculate damages to account for any seed that had been resold. Subsequently, defendant submitted its analysis of damages based on the prices that plaintiff had received when it resold. Plaintiff criticized defendant's analysis and stuck by its calculation of market price damages, without submitting an analysis of damages based on resale prices.

Each party's calculation of damages for one of the breached contracts, contract 1874, illustrates the implications of using the market price or the resale price to calculate damages. The evidence at trial showed that the contract price for contract 1874 was $0.72 per pound. Plaintiff sought damages of $3,736.00 for that contract, apparently based on a market price of $0.64 per pound, resulting in a contract price minus market price differential of $0.08 per pound for 46,700 pounds of seed not accepted by defendant. Defendant argued, however, that plaintiff had resold at least some of that seed for $0.75 per pound, $0.03 per pound above the contract price and $0.11 per pound above plaintiff's market price calculation. Thus, according to defendant, plaintiff did not have any damages for that resold seed because plaintiff had resold for more than the contract price. If plaintiff recovered $0.08 per pound in market price damages, in addition to the $0.75 per pound that plaintiff allegedly had received on the resale, plaintiff ultimately would recover $0.83 per pound, which was $0.11 more than the contract price.

For that same contract, however, where the contract price was $0.72 per pound, defendant noted that some of the seed had been resold for $0.60 per pound. That meant that the resale price damages would be $0.12 per pound. That is, for at least some of the resold seed from contract 1874, plaintiff's resale price damages of $0.12 per pound would exceed plaintiff's claimed market price damages of $0.08 per pound. In sum, the parties' calculations of damages for contract 1874 showed that, with regard to some seed, the market price damage calculation would lead to a larger award, but that, with regard to other seed, the resale price damage calculation would lead to a larger award. On the whole, however, defendant calculated that plaintiff would receive a smaller amount of damages using the resale price measure of damages than plaintiff calculated that it would receive using the market price measure of damages.

The trial court awarded plaintiff damages using the resale price measure of damages as calculated by defendant. The trial court reasoned that plaintiff had not calculated damages as ordered by the court. The court stated that "even if Plaintiff [was] correct that Defendant's calculations [were] somehow flawed or incorrect, no alternative calculation ha[d] been offered." Thus, the trial court concluded that it was "left with no option but to accept Defendant's calculation." . . .

The Court of Appeals reversed and remanded. On the first issue, the court noted that, at least on its face, the UCC allows a seller to recover damages as calculated under either ORS 72.7060 (contract price less resale price) or ORS 72.7080(1) (contract price less market price). Id. at 713, 293 P.3d 1058. After reviewing the relevant statutory provisions, the court went on to conclude that, "[i]n the absence of a restriction within the UCC that precludes an aggrieved seller from seeking its remedy pursuant to ORS 72.7080 if the seller has resold, we would decline to impose such a restriction." Id. at 715, 293 P.3d 1058. In support of that conclusion, the court explained that, once the buyer breaches, the buyer loses any right to control the goods or to "insist upon a different measure of damages." Id. at 716-17, 293 P.3d 1058. Moreover, the court noted, market price damages require the buyer to fulfill only the bargain to which it agreed. Id. at 717, 293 P.3d 1058. Although the court acknowledged that the UCC policy is that remedies should put an aggrieved party "in as good a position as if the other party had fully performed," ORS 71.3050(1), the court concluded that the intent of the UCC is to allow an aggrieved seller to recover market price damages, even if the seller has resold the goods. Id. at 715-16 n.7, 293 P.3d 1058. The court remanded the case for a proper calculation of plaintiff's market price damages. Id. at 717, 293 P.3d 1058. . . .

An Aggrieved Seller's Remedies Under the UCC

The UCC provides a variety of remedies to an aggrieved seller. See ORS 72.7030 (providing an index of a seller's remedies). As noted, the issue in this case is whether an aggrieved seller who has resold goods can recover the difference between the unpaid contract price and the market price under ORS 72.7080(1), even when market price damages would exceed resale price damages under ORS 72.7060.

Commentators and courts have taken two different approaches to this issue. Relying on the text and context of the sellers' remedies provisions, some commentators have argued that the drafters of the UCC intended for sellers to be able to recover either market price damages or resale price damages, even if the seller resold the goods for more than the market price. See, e.g., Henry Gabriel, The Seller's Election of Remedies Under the Uniform Commercial Code: An Expectation Theory, 23 Wake Forest L. Rev. 429, 429 (1988) (arguing that an aggrieved seller "should be allowed to elect between the two remedies regardless of the seller's good faith post-breach activities concerning the non-accepted goods"); Ellen A. Peters, Remedies for Breach of Contracts Relating to the Sale of Goods Under the Uniform Commercial Code: A Roadmap for Article Two, 73 Yale L.J. 199, 260 (1963) (arguing for a "non-restrictive reading of the various remedies sections to preserve full options to use or to ignore substitute transactions as a measure of damages"). On the other hand, Professors White and Summers, whose view has been adopted by a number of courts, have argued that the UCC's general policy is that damages should put a seller only in "as good a position as if the other party had fully performed," ORS 71.3050(1), meaning a seller who has resold should not be allowed to recover more in market price damages than it could recover in resale price damages. James J. White, Robert S. Summers and Robert A. Hillman, 1 Uniform Commercial Code §8:13, 689 (6th ed. 2012) (so stating). We agree with those commentators who have observed that the drafters did not clearly resolve this issue. See, e.g., id. at 691 (noting that the UCC and the comments are "equivocal" about whether a seller can recover more under section 2-708(1) than it could recover under section 2-706); Gabriel, 23 Wake Forest L. Rev. at 430 (noting "the failure of the drafters to clearly resolve the problem of election between sections 2-706 and 2-708(1)"). Nonetheless, we conclude that the text, context, and legislative history of the sellers' remedies provisions support a seller's right to recover either market price damages or resale price damages, even if market price damages lead to a larger recovery.

We analyze the relevant statutory provisions using the framework described in State v. Gaines, 346 Or. 160, 171-72, 206 P.3d 1042 (2009). We begin by examining the statute's text and context to determine the legislature's intent regarding a seller's remedies under the UCC. Because the relevant statutes are part of the UCC, we also consider the official UCC comments as an indication of the legislature's intent. Security Bank v. Chiapuzio, 304 Or. 438, 445 n.6, 747 P.2d 335 (1987) (noting that the Oregon legislature took note of the official comments of the UCC, which are "statements of the purpose of each section"). In addition, "the legislative intent to make the UCC a uniform code makes relevant the decisions of other courts that have examined these questions and the discussions of the questions by scholars in the field, especially those scholars who participated in drafting the UCC." Id. We also examine legislative history. The Oregon legislature enacted the UCC in 1961 "with little debate or discussion of the legislative intent," but the UCC was proposed so that Oregon could "obtain the same advantages that other states had gained from the adoption of a uniform and comprehensive set of commercial statutes." Id. Given "the legislative intent to make the UCC a uniform code," id., we consider prior drafts of the UCC, as drafted by the National Conference of Commissioners on Uniform State Laws (NCCUSL), as part of the legislative history. Cf. Datt v. Hill, 347 Or. 672, 680, 227 P.3d 714 (2010) (examining history of uniform act in interpreting Oregon statute taken from that act).

Before examining the statutory scheme, however, we briefly review the law as it existed prior to the enactment of the UCC in Oregon. At common law, an aggrieved seller

> ha[d] the election of three remedies: (1) To hold the property for the purchaser, and to recover of him the entire purchase money; (2) to sell it, after notice to the purchaser, as his agent for that purpose, and recover the difference between the contract price and that realized on the sale; (3) to retain it as his own, and recover the difference between the contract and market prices at the time and place of delivery[.]"

Krebs Hop Co. v. Livesley, 59 Or. 574, 588, 118 P. 165 (1911). *Krebs Hop Co.* suggests that, before Oregon adopted the UCC, an aggrieved seller had to elect between remedies, and if the seller resold the goods, it had elected its remedy and could recover only resale price damages, but not market price damages. See Gabriel, 23 Wake Forest L. Rev. at 446 (explaining that, under pre-UCC law, an aggrieved seller who resold the goods was assumed to have elected the resale remedy and was barred from using an inconsistent remedy, such as market price damages). Although the UCC retained some aspect of each of the remedies available at common law, as explained below, it specifically rejected the doctrine of election of remedies. See Legislative Comment 1 to ORS 72.7030, reprinted in Legislative Counsel Committee, Oregon's Uniform Commercial Code with Comments and Index and Tables 101 (1962) (noting that the UCC chapter on sales "reject[s] any doctrine of election of remedy as a fundamental policy"); Peters, 73 Yale L.J. at 204 n.16 (noting that many sections of the UCC were "designed to mitigate the effect of prior law insofar as it forced a choice of remedy on the party aggrieved without regard to the adequacy of compensation").

[The court quoted §2-703 on Seller's Remedies.] That section lists the seller's remedies, which, as relevant here, include resale price damages, ORS 72.7060, and market price damages, ORS 72.7080. Moreover, it lists those remedies without any limiting conjunction, such as "or," that might suggest that the remedies are mutually exclusive. In contrast, a similar index of a buyer's remedies after a seller's breach provides that the buyer may "(a) 'Cover' and have damages . . . *or* (b) Recover damages for nondelivery." ORS 72.7110(1) (emphasis added.) Thus, although the buyer's index of remedies suggests that a buyer who covers may be precluded from seeking market price damages, the seller's index of remedies does not contain a similar limitation if the seller chooses to resell. It follows that the text of ORS 72.7030 supports plaintiff's argument that a seller who has resold is not necessarily limited to its resale price damages under ORS 72.7060, but has the option of seeking to recover market price damages under ORS 72.7080.

The UCC comments to the statute describing a seller's remedies confirm that interpretation. Although the comments acknowledge that, in a particular case, the pursuit of one remedy may prevent a seller from obtaining certain damages, the comments also state that the UCC chapter on sales "reject[s] any doctrine of election of remedy as a fundamental policy and thus the remedies are essentially cumulative in nature and include all of the available remedies for breach." Legislative Comment 1 to ORS 72.7030 at 101; id. ("Whether the pursuit of one remedy bars another depends entirely on the facts of the individual case."). In contrast, the comments to the statute describing a buyer's market price remedy explain that that remedy "is completely alternative to 'cover' under ORS 72.7120 and applies *only when and to the extent that the buyer has not covered.*" Legislative Comment 5 to ORS 72.7130 at 110 (emphasis added). Thus, while the comments to the statute describing a seller's remedies expressly reject the doctrine of election of remedies, the comments to the statute describing a buyer's market price remedy appear to adopt that doctrine. Those comments further indicate that a seller who resells goods after a buyer's breach would not be considered to have "elected" the resale remedy and thus would not be precluded from seeking a larger damage recovery using the market price measure of damages.

The text of ORS 72.7060, which sets forth the seller's resale remedy, similarly suggests that a seller who resells goods is not necessarily precluded from using the market price measure of damages, even if it leads to a larger recovery. ORS 72.7060(1) states that "the seller *may* resell the goods concerned or the undelivered balance thereof," which suggests that an aggrieved seller is not required to resell. (Emphasis added.) See White, Summers and Hillman, 1 Uniform Commercial Code §8:6 at 671 ("Resale is not mandatory."). Similarly, the text of ORS 72.7060 indicates that a seller who resells is not required to seek damages using the resale remedy. See ORS 72.7060(1) ("Where the resale is made in good faith and in a commercially reasonable manner the seller *may* recover the difference between the resale price and the contract price. . . ." (Emphasis added.)). In fact, the unqualified text of ORS 72.7080(1) seems to suggest that market price is in fact the default measure of damages. See ORS 72.7080(1) ("Subject to . . . the provisions of ORS 72.7230 with respect to proof of market price, *the* measure of damages for nonacceptance or repudiation by the buyer is the difference between the market price at the time and place for tender and the unpaid contract price. . . ." (Emphasis added.)). Thus, the text of the remedy provisions does not limit a seller who resells to its resale price damages.

As defendant notes, however, one of the comments to ORS 72.7060 does indicate that the drafters intended ORS 72.7060 to be a seller's primary remedy, and did not intend to allow a seller to recover more under the market price remedy. Comment 2 to ORS 72.7060 explains that "[f]ailure to act properly under ORS 72.7060 *deprives* the seller of the measure of damages there provided and *relegates* him to that provided in ORS 72.7080 [market price damages]." Legislative Comment 2 to ORS 72.7060 at 104 (emphasis added). That language suggests that the comment drafters viewed market price damages as less favorable, but it does not indicate *why* they viewed them that way. The pejorative language used in the comments does not necessarily lead to the conclusion that a seller who resells cannot use the market price remedy or must use the resale price remedy if it would yield the same or a smaller amount of damages than the market price remedy. That language instead could indicate that market price damages are considered less favorable because market price is often hard to prove, as many commentators have noted. See, e.g., Henry J. Bailey III, 1 The Oregon Uniform Commercial Code §2.140, 279 (2d ed. 1990) (noting that the remedy under ORS 72.7080(1) "is often a less advantageous remedy for the seller because of difficulty of proof of market price"). As a result, that comment language is not dispositive, particularly in light of the text of the remedy provisions.

Turning to legislative history, prior drafts of the UCC provide additional insight into the drafters' intent to allow a seller to recover its market price damages, even if the seller has resold. In particular, in an earlier draft of the section describing the resale price remedy, section 2-706, one of the comments stated that that section provided

> "the *exclusive* measure of the seller's damages where the resale has been made in accordance with the requirements of this section. Evidence of market or current prices at any particular time or place is relevant *only* on the question of whether the seller acted with commercially reasonable care and judgment in making the resale."

See Gabriel, 23 Wake Forest L. Rev. at 436 (quoting UCC §2-706 cmt. 3 (May 1949 Draft) (emphasis added)). Under that version of the UCC, a seller who had met the resale requirements would be required to use the resale price measure of damages. That comment later was revised, however, and when Oregon adopted the UCC, the comment included language that also had been in the 1949 draft comment, but the mandatory language had been removed, leaving only the permissive wording: "If the seller complies with the prescribed standard of duty in making the resale, he *may* recover from the buyer the damages provided for in subsection (1)." Legislative Comment 3 to ORS 72.7060 at 104 (emphasis added). That shift, from resale as the exclusive remedy to resale as a permissible remedy, indicates that the drafters intended for a seller to be able to choose to recover market price damages, even after reselling under ORS 72.7060.

Defendant argues, however, that even if a seller who resells can recover market price damages under ORS 72.7080(1), those damages cannot exceed the seller's resale price damages. Defendant primarily relies on the general policy statement set forth in ORS 71.3050 to support its argument. ORS 71.3050(1) provides,

> The remedies provided by the Uniform Commercial Code must be liberally administered to the end that the aggrieved party may be put *in as good a*

> *position as if the other party had fully performed* but consequential damages, special damages or penal damages may not be had except as specifically provided in the Uniform Commercial Code or by other rule of law.

(Emphasis added.) Defendant reasons that the reference in ORS 71.3050(1) to putting an aggrieved party "in as good a position as if the other party had fully performed" acts as a limit on the damages that a party can receive. Commentators and courts likewise have relied on that provision in concluding that a seller's market price damages should be limited to the actual loss suffered, by taking into account any goods that have been resold. See, e.g., White, Summers and Hillman, 1 Uniform Commercial Code §8:13 at 689 ("We conclude that a seller should not be permitted to recover more under 2-708(1) [market price damages] than under 2-706 [resale price damages]. . . . Section 1-305 indicates that a seller who has resold may not invoke 2-708(1)."); Coast Trading Co. v. Cudahy Co., 592 F.2d 1074, 1081-83 (9th Cir. 1979) (adopting approach of White and Summers and reducing section 2-708(1) market price damages of seller who conducted commercially unreasonable resale to what seller could have recovered under section 2-706 if resale had been commercially reasonable); Tesoro Petroleum Corp. v. Holborn Oil Co., 145 Misc. 2d 715, 547 N.Y.S.2d 1012, 1016-17 (N.Y. Sup. Ct. 1989) (adopting approach of White and Summers and limiting seller to resale price damages because higher market price damages would create a "windfall" inconsistent with the general policy of the UCC).

The text of ORS 71.3050(1) indicates that the drafters of the UCC intended a seller's remedies to be compensatory. See Legislative Comment 1 to *former* ORS 71.1060 at 6 (1963), amended and renumbered as ORS 71.3050 (2009) (noting that statute is intended to "make it clear that compensatory damages are limited to compensation"). The text of that section, however, also provides that the remedies in the UCC are to be "liberally administered." ORS 71.3050(1); see also Legislative Comment 4 to ORS 72.7030 at 101 ("It should also be noted that the Uniform Commercial Code requires its remedies to be liberally administered. . . ."). Nonetheless, we agree with defendant that the general policy of compensation provided in ORS 71.3050(1) must be taken into account.

We do not agree, however, that that policy necessarily limits an aggrieved seller who has resold to its resale price damages. Defendant argues that if it had fully performed, plaintiff could expect to recover only the contract price, and that limiting plaintiff to the difference between the contract price and the resale price therefore gives it the benefit of its bargain. As Professor Gabriel notes, however, limiting a seller to its resale price damages does not account fully for either party's expectations upon entering into the contract. He explains that a seller expects to be able to recover the difference between the contract price and the market price because it is the "logical and expected measure of damages," and because the ability to recover market price damages "is the natural assumption the seller makes in return for the risk inherent in the contract that the sale may not turn out to be economically beneficial to the seller. That the seller then resells the goods in no way diminishes this expectancy regarding the first contract." Gabriel, 23 Wake Forest L. Rev. at 449, 453. From the buyer's perspective, he argues that "the [buyer] has specific obligations and will suffer the consequences of the failure to perform these obligations because this is the [buyer's] expectation." Id. at 450. In other words, contrary to defendant's argument, an aggrieved seller expects to be able to recover market price damages under the contract, and a breaching buyer expects to have to fulfill its obligation to the seller—even if a seller resells and recovers market price damages, "the buyer's obligation is no more than the right the buyer originally conferred upon the seller." Id. at 449.

Moreover, limiting an aggrieved seller to its resale price damages ignores the risk for which the parties bargained. When parties bargain for fixed price contracts, each party assumes the risk of market price fluctuations. The parties are willing to take that risk because of the benefits that they might receive: if the market price decreases, the seller benefits, and if the market price increases, the buyer benefits. In a fixed price contract, therefore, market price damages represent the risk for which both parties bargained. Cf. id. ("The logical and expected measure of damages is the contract price-market price differential. *This measure of damages is the risk the buyer assumed by entering into the contract;* it is the right conferred upon the seller by the buyer." (Emphasis added.)).[2] For those reasons, we conclude that a seller can recover market price damages, even if the seller resells some of the goods at above the market price at the time and place for tender.

Defendant argues, however, that that conclusion does not account for an aggrieved party's duty to mitigate, which is consistent with the UCC's policy of minimizing damages. See Legislative Comment 1 to *former* ORS 71.1060 at

2. Professor Gabriel's explanation also responds to the argument that to permit a seller to recover market price damages when it has resold some or all of the goods confers an improper "windfall" on the seller. If a seller is limited to its resale price damages, it is just as accurate to say that the breaching buyer has received a "windfall," because the seller's success in reselling reduces the damages that the buyer must pay—and not because of anything the buyer did, but only because of the seller's successful efforts. As discussed in the text, the UCC imposes no obligation on the seller to resell, and the buyer's expectation, at the time the buyer entered into the contract, was that it might have to pay market price damages if it breached the contract. The point is not that one party or the other gets an undeserved "windfall," but rather that the provisions of the UCC, as we have interpreted them here, determine the rights and obligations of each party and therefore what is expected of each party and what each may expect of the other, as well as the consequences of either party's breach. The result we reach here is consistent with those expectations. *See generally* Gabriel, 23 Wake Forest L. Rev. at 453.

6 (1963) ("[T]he Code elsewhere makes it clear that damages must be minimized."); Roy Ryden Anderson, 1 Damages Under the Uniform Commercial Code §1:6, 11-12 (2012) (noting that the duty to mitigate is "implicit in every damage remedy" and typically is justified under section 1-305). We do not understand the duty to mitigate to be a limit on a seller's market price damages because, as noted, the text demonstrates and commentators agree that a seller is not required to resell goods after a buyer's breach. If the duty to mitigate does not require the aggrieved seller to resell its goods, we do not think that the duty to mitigate can require the seller to use the resale price measure of damages. See Gabriel, 23 Wake Forest L. Rev. at 445 ("The seller has no obligation to resell, and the failure to resell the goods does not affect the right to proceed under section 2-708(1). If non-action by the seller does not impact on the statutory right under section 2-708(1), common sense dictates that an affirmative act by the seller to resell should not have any impact on that right." (Footnote omitted.)). The comments to the resale remedy provision also acknowledge that the seller who resells does so for its own benefit, and not for the benefit of the breaching party as mitigation. See Legislative Comment 2 to ORS 72.7060 at 104 (noting that the seller resells "in his own behalf, for his own benefit and for the purpose of fixing his damages"); *cf.* ORS 72.7060(6) ("The seller is not accountable to the buyer for any profit made on any resale."). Therefore, the principle of mitigation does not appear to limit an aggrieved seller's recovery to resale price damages under ORS 72.7060; the seller may instead seek market price damages under ORS 72.7080(1).

In sum, when viewed in light of the bargained-for market risks and the UCC's rejection of the doctrine of election of remedies, the text, context, and legislative history of the sellers' remedy provisions demonstrate that an aggrieved seller can seek damages under either ORS 72.7080(1) or ORS 72.7060. That means that an aggrieved seller can seek damages under ORS 72.7080(1) even if the seller has resold the goods and market price damages exceed resale price damages. . . .

Conclusion

For the reasons explained above, we conclude that plaintiff can recover its market price damages under ORS 72.7080(1). Because the trial court determined that plaintiff had proven its market price damages at trial, but later declined to award those damages for reasons that we have concluded were legally erroneous, plaintiff is entitled to recover market price damages in the amount calculated in plaintiff's Exhibit 409, together with prejudgment interest on that amount. However, we agree with the trial court, although for different reasons, that plaintiff is not entitled to recover its attorney fees under the NORAMSEED Rule that allows a seller to recover "charges for collection."

The decision of the Court of Appeals is affirmed in part and reversed in part. The judgment of the circuit court is affirmed in part and reversed in part, and the case is remanded to the circuit court.

PROBLEM 80

Fun in the Sun, Inc., sells swimming pools. Its president comes to your law office with this problem. A customer named Esther Swimmer ordered one of the standard above-ground pools, retailing for $2,000. The pool's components are purchased by Fun in the Sun at a wholesale price of $800 and are assembled into the finished product. The assembly process costs the seller $400. Swimmer has now repudiated the contract, and Fun in the Sun wants to sue. The current market price is $2,000 for such a pool. Fun in the Sun is sure it can find another buyer at that price if it resells the pool. Does it have damages? How are they measured? See §2-708(2), along with Official Comment 2. See also White & Summers §§8-8 to 8-13.

The problem with sellers in Fun in the Sun's position (sellers having an unlimited supply of goods) is that if the law forces them to measure damages under §2-706 or §2-708(1), they lose the profit they would have made from the sale to the second customer. A seller in such a position is called a *lost volume seller.* The drafters meant for §2-708(2) to rescue such a seller from this dilemma, but the actual mechanics of the operation of the section are not clear. The problem arises in part from the undefined phrase "profit (including reasonable overhead)," which contains accounting terms having no fixed legal meaning. For an analysis of their import, see Speidel & Clay, Seller's Recovery of Overhead Under U.C.C. Section 2-708(2): Economic Cost Theory and Contract Remedial Policy, 57 Cornell L. Rev. 681 (1972). See also Scott, The Case for Market Damages: Revisiting the Lost Profits Puzzle, 57 U. Chi. L. Rev. 1155 (1990).

Teradyne, Inc. v. Teledyne Industries, Inc.

United States Court of Appeals, First Circuit, 1982
676 F.2d 865

WYZANSKI, J.

In this diversity action, Teradyne, Inc. sued Teledyne Industries, Inc. and its subsidiary for damages pursuant to §2-708(2) of the U.C.C. Teledyne does not dispute the facts that it is bound as a buyer under a sales contract with Teradyne, that it broke the contract, and that Teradyne's right to damages is governed by §2-708(2). The principal dispute concerns the calculation of damages.

The district court referred the case to a master whose report the district court approved and made the basis of the judgment here on appeal.

The following facts, derived from the master's report, are undisputed.

> On July 30, 1976 Teradyne, Inc. ["the seller"], a Massachusetts corporation, entered into a Quantity Purchase Contract ["the contract"] which, though made with a subsidiary, binds Teledyne Industries, Inc., a California corporation ["the buyer"]. That contract governed an earlier contract resulting from the seller's acceptance of the buyer's July 23, 1976 purchase order to buy at the list price of $98,400 (which was also its fair market value) a T-347A transistor test system ["the T-347A"]. One consequence of such governance was that the buyer was entitled to a $984 discount from the $98,400 price.
>
> The buyer canceled its order for the T-347A when it was packed ready for shipment scheduled to occur two days later. The seller refused to accept the cancellation.
>
> The buyer offered to purchase instead of the T-347A a $65,000 Field Effects Transistor System ["the FET"] which would also have been governed by "the contract." The seller refused the offer.
>
> After dismantling, testing, and reassembling at an estimated cost of $614 the T-347A, the seller, pursuant to an order that was on hand prior to the cancellation, sold it for $98,400 to another purchaser [hereafter "resale purchaser"].
>
> Teradyne would have made the sale to the resale purchaser even if Teledyne had not broken its contract. Thus if there had been no breach, Teradyne would have made two sales and earned two profits rather than one.
>
> The seller was a volume seller of the equipment covered by the July 23, 1976, purchase order. The equipment represented standard products of the seller and the seller had the means and capacity to duplicate the equipment for a second sale had the buyer honored its purchase order.

Teradyne being of the view that the measure of damages under §2-708(2) was the contract price less ascertainable costs saved as a result of the breach—see Jericho Sash and Door Company, Inc. v. Building Erectors, Inc., 362 Mass. 871, 872, 286 N.E.2d 343 (1972) [hereafter *"Jericho"*]—offered as evidence of its cost prices its Inventory Standards Catalog ["the Catalog"]—a document which was prepared for tax purposes not claimed to have been illegitimate, but which admittedly disclosed "low inventory valuations." Relying on that Catalog, Teradyne's Controller, McCabe, testified that the *only* costs which the seller saved as a result of the breach were:

direct labor costs associated with production	$3,301
material charges	17,045
sales commission on one T-347A	492
expense	1,800
Total	$22,638

McCabe admitted that he had not included as costs saved the labor costs of employees associated with testing, shipping, installing, servicing, or fulfilling 10-year warranties on the T-347A (although he acknowledged that in forms of accounting for purposes other than damage suits the costs of those employees would not be regarded as "overhead"). His reason was that those costs would not have been affected by the production of one machine more or less. McCabe also admitted that he had not included fringe benefits which amounted to 12% in the case of both included and excluded labor costs.

During McCabe's direct examination, he referred to the 10-K report which Teradyne had filed with the SEC. On cross-examination McCabe admitted that the 10-K form showed that on average the seller's revenues were distributed as follows:

profit	9%
"selling and administrative" expense	26%
interest	1%
"costs of sales and engineering" (including substantial research and development costs incidental to a high technology business)	64%

He also admitted that the average figures applied to the T-347a.

Teledyne contended that the 10-K report was a better index of lost profits than was the Catalog. The master disagreed and concluded that the more appropriate formula for calculating Teradyne's damages under §2-708(2) was the one approved in *Jericho,* supra—" 'gross' profit including fixed costs but not costs saved as a result of the breach." He then stated:

> In accordance with the statutory mandate that the remedy "be liberally administered to the end that the aggrieved party may be put in as good a position as if the other party had fully performed," MGL c106 §1-106(1),[3] I find that the Plaintiff has met its burden of proof of damages, and has established the accuracy of its direct costs and the ascertainability of its variable costs with reasonable certainty and "whatever definiteness and accuracy the facts permit." Comment 1 to §1-106(1) of the U.C.C.

In effect, this was a finding that Teradyne had saved only $22,638 as a result of the breach. Subtracting that amount and also the $984 quantity discount from the original contract price of $98,400, the master found that the lost "profit (including reasonable overhead)" was $74,778. To that amount the master added $614 for "incidental damages" which Teradyne incurred in

3. Now §1-305(a).—EDS.

preparing the T-347A for its new customer. Thus he found that Teradyne's total §2-708(2) damages amounted to $75,392.

The master declined to make a deduction from the $75,392 on account of the refusal of the seller to accept the buyer's offer to purchase an FET tester in partial substitution for the repudiated T-347A.

At the time of the reference to the master, the court, without securing the agreement of the parties, had ordered that the master's costs should be paid by them in equal parts.

Teradyne filed a motion praying that the district court (1) should adopt the master's report allowing it to recover $75,392, and (2) should require Teledyne to pay all the master's costs. The district court, without opinion, entered a judgment which grants the first prayer and denies the second. Teledyne appealed from the first part of the judgment; Teradyne appealed from the second part.

1. The parties are agreed that §2-708(2) applies to the case at bar. Inasmuch as this conclusion is not plain from the text, we explain the reasons why we concur in that agreement.

Section 2-708(2) applies only if the damages provided by §2-708(1) are inadequate to put the seller in as good a position as performance would have done. Under §2-708(1) the measure of damages is the difference between unpaid contract price and market price. Here the unpaid contract price was $97,416 and the market price was $98,400. Hence no damages would be recoverable under §2-708(1). On the other hand, if the buyer had performed, the seller (1) would have had the proceeds of two contracts, one with the buyer Teledyne and the other with the "resale purchaser" and (2) *it seems* would have had in 1976-7 one more T-347A sale.

A literal reading of the last sentence of §2-708(2)—providing for "due credit for payments or proceeds of resale"—would indicate that Teradyne recovers nothing because the proceeds of the resale exceeded the price set in the Teledyne-Teradyne contract. However, in light of the statutory history of the subsection, it is universally agreed that in a case where after the buyer's default a seller resells the goods, the proceeds of the resale are not to be credited to the buyer if the seller is a lost volume seller[4]—that is, one who had there

4. The term "lost volume seller" was apparently coined by Professor Robert J. Harris in his article A Radical Restatement of the Law of Seller's Damages: Sales Act and Commercial Code Results Compared, 18 Stan. L. Rev. 66 (1965). The terminology has been widely adopted. See Famous Knitwear Corp. v. Drug Fair Inc., 493 F.2d 251, 254 n.5 (4th Cir. 1974); Snyder v. Herbert Greenbaum & Assoc. Inc., 38 Md. App. 144, 157, 380 A.2d 618, 624 (1977); Publicker Industries, Inc. v. Roman Ceramics Corp., 652 F.2d 340, 346 (3d Cir. 1981). See Restatement (Second) Contracts §347 Comment f; J. White and R. Summers, Uniform Commercial Code, 2d ed. (1980) [hereinafter "White and Summers"] §7-9, particularly p. 276 first full paragraph.

been no breach by the buyer, could and would have had the benefit of both the original contract and the resale contract.[5]

Thus, despite the resale of the T-347A, Teradyne is entitled to recover from Teledyne what §2-708(2) calls its expected "profit (including reasonable overhead)" on the broken Teledyne contract.[6]

2. Teledyne not only "does not dispute that damages are to be calculated pursuant to §2-708(2)" but concedes that the formula used in Jericho Sash & Door Co. v. Building Erectors Inc., 362 Mass. 871 (1972), for determining lost profit including overhead—that is, the formula under which direct costs of producing and selling manufactured goods are deducted from the contract price in order to arrive at "profit (including reasonable overhead)" as that term is used in §2-708(2)—"is permissible provided all variable expenses are identified."

What Teledyne contends is that all variable costs were not identified because the cost figures came from a catalog, prepared for tax purposes, which did not fully reflect all direct costs. The master found that the statement of costs based on the catalog was reliable and that Teledyne's method of calculating costs based on the 10-K statements was not more accurate. Those findings are not clearly erroneous and therefore we may not reverse the judgment on the ground that allegedly the items of cost which were deducted are unreliable. Fed. R. Civ. P. 52(a); Merrill Trust Co. v. Bradford, 507 F.2d 467, 468 (1st Cir. 1974); Van Alen v. Dominick & Dominick, Inc., 560 F.2d 547, 551 (2d Cir. 1977).

Teledyne's more significant objection to Teradyne's and the master's application of the *Jericho* formula in the case at bar is that neither of them made deductions on account of the wages paid to testers, shippers, installers, and other Teradyne employees who directly handled the T-347A, or on account of the fringe benefits amounting in the case of those and other employees to 12 per cent of wages. Teradyne gave as the reason for the omission of the wages of the testers, etc. that those wages would not have been affected if each of the testers, etc. handled one product more or less. However, the work of those employees entered as directly into producing and supplying the T-347A as did the work of a fabricator of a T-347A. Surely

5. Famous Knitwear Corp. v. Drug Fair Inc., supra, 493 F.2d 254 n.7; Snyder v. Herbert Greenbaum & Assoc. Inc., supra, 380 A.2d 625-626; Neri v. Retail Marine Corp., 30 N.Y.2d 393, 399, 285 N.E.2d 311, 314 (1972). See White and Summers, §7-13, particularly 284-285.

6. Ibid. White and Summers at pp. 284-285 give the following suppositious case which parallels the instant case. Boeing is able to make and sell in one year 100 airplanes. TWA contracts to buy the third plane off the assembly line, but it breaks the contract and Boeing resells the plane to Pan Am which had already agreed to buy the fourth plane. Because of the breach Boeing sells only 99 aircraft during the year. White and Summers say that the right result, despite the words of §2-708(2), is that Boeing recovers from TWA both the net profit and the overhead components of the TWA contract price, no credit being given for any part of the proceeds Boeing received from its sale to Pan Am.

no one would regard as "reasonable overhead" within §2-708(2) the wages of a fabricator of a T-347A even if his wages were the same whether he made one product more or less. We conclude that the wages of the testers, etc., likewise are not part of overhead and as a "direct cost" should have been deducted from the contract price. A fortiori fringe benefits amounting to 12 per cent of wages should also have been deducted as direct costs. Taken together we cannot view these omitted items as what *Jericho* called "relatively insignificant items." We, therefore, must vacate the district court's judgment. In accordance with the procedure followed in Publicker Industries, Inc. v. Roman Ceramics Corp., 603 F.2d 1065, 1072-3 (3d Cir. 1979) and Famous Knitwear Corp. v. Drug Fair, Inc., 493 F.2d 251, 255-256 (4th Cir. 1974), we remand this case so that with respect to the omitted direct labor costs specified above the parties may offer further evidence and the court may make findings "with whatever definiteness and accuracy the facts permit, but no more." *Jericho,* p. 872.

There are two other matters which may properly be dealt with before the case is remanded to the district court.

3. Teledyne contends that Teradyne was required to mitigate damages by acceptance of Teledyne's offer to purchase instead of the T-347A the FET system.

That point is without merit.

The meaning of Teledyne's offer was that if Teradyne would forego its profit-loss claim arising out of Teledyne's breach of the T-347A contract, Teledyne would purchase another type of machine which it was under no obligation to buy. The seller's failure to accept such an offer does not preclude it from recovering the full damages to which it would otherwise be entitled. As Restatement (Second) Contracts, §350 Comment c indicates, there is no right to so-called mitigation of damages where the offer of a substitute contract "is conditioned on surrender by the injured party of his claim for breach." "One is not required to mitigate his losses by accepting an arrangement with the repudiator if that is made conditional on his surrender of his rights under the repudiated contract." 5 Corbin, Contracts 2d (1964) §1043 at 274. Acc. Campfield v. Sauer, 189 F. 576 (6th Cir. 1911); Stanspec Corp. v. Jelco, Inc., 464 F.2d 1184, 1187 (10th Cir. 1972). Teradyne acted in a commercially reasonable manner in refusing to accept Teledyne's offer. . . .

The district court's judgment is vacated and the case is remanded to the district court to proceed in accordance with this opinion.

QUESTIONS

1. Exactly who qualifies as a "lost volume seller"? If a college student advertises his guitar for sale in the campus newspaper, he contracts to sell it to a caller, the caller then backs out, and the student sells the guitar to someone else, can the student qualify as a lost volume seller?

2. Why does the court draw a distinction between overhead costs and variable expenses (which the court calls "direct costs")? Which was which here?

3. Section 2-708(2) specifically requires a subtraction of the "proceeds of resale." Doesn't this language always defeat the lost volume seller, who will typically have resold the unaccepted goods? See R.E. Davis Chem. Corp. v. Diasonics, Inc., 826 F.2d 678 (7th Cir. 1987).

4. For a case requiring the seller to measure damages at no more than the lost profit amount where the market price/contract price differential under §2-708(1) would overcompensate the seller, see Purina Mills, L.L.C. v. Less, 295 F. Supp. 2d 1017 (N.D. Iowa 2003).

5. The lost volume concept also applies to lessors of goods. See §2A-529's Official Comment 2 and C.I.C. Corp. v. Ragtime, Inc., 319 N.J. Super. 662, 726 A.2d 316 (N.J. App. 1999).

PROBLEM 81

Milo Veep, sales agent for the Complex Computer Corporation (CCC), negotiated a contract whereby his company was to design and manufacture a special computer that would regulate the timing of subway trains for the City of Plantation, Mississippi. The price was $20,000 F.O.B. CCC's plant in Atlanta, Georgia. When the computer was half completed, the City of Plantation underwent a change of administration, and the new city leaders decided to dump the subway renovations. They phoned CCC and canceled the computer order. Now Veep phones your law office for advice. To help in your decision, Veep states that as scrap the computer and its components are now worth $5,000. Veep has heard that three other cities have subway systems similar to Plantation's, and if the computer is finished, they might be enticed to buy it at a price between $15,000 and $20,000. On the other hand, it will cost CCC $9,000 to complete the computer.

(a) Should CCC stop the manufacture of the computer and sell it for scrap or complete manufacture and then try to resell it? See §2-704(2) and its Official Comment 2.

(b) If CCC completes manufacture and then, after a good faith effort, is unable to find a new buyer for the computer, can it make Plantation pay for the finished product? See §2-709(1)(b); Official Comment 1 to §2-704.

PROBLEM 82

Stern Oil entered into a ten-year Motor Fuel Supply Agreement with James Brown, which required Brown each year to purchase a certain amount of ExxonMobil branded fuel from Stern Oil for Brown's two convenience stores. Brown breached the agreement and stopped purchasing fuel from Stern. As a result, Stern Oil did not receive profits from a 1.5 cent markup per gallon or a 1.25 percent discount from ExxonMobil. Brown conceded the 1.5 cent markup per gallon was duly awarded as lost profits, but argued that the lost discount was not recoverable as damages. Should it be? See §§1-305(a), 2-715(2), 1-103, 2-708(2); Stern Oil Co. v. Brown, 2018 S.D. 15, 908 N.W.2d 144 (2018).

Courts routinely hold that sellers are not entitled to consequential damages (but see §2-710, allowing sellers to recover *incidental* damages). For example, a seller was denied a recovery where lost sales due to buyer's breach caused seller not to qualify for quantity discounts on other contracts with its own seller. Nobs Chemical, U.S.A., Inc. v. Koppers Co., Inc., 616 F.2d 212 (5th Cir. 1980). Section 1-305(a) provides that consequential damages may only be had "as specifically provided in [the Uniform Commercial Code] or by other rule of law." In Article 2, §2-715(2) provides that *buyers* may receive consequential damages, but does not say so for sellers. White & Summers question cases like *Nobs*, arguing that consequential damages could be permitted on the theory that §1-103 incorporates general rules of contract law, which could qualify as a permissible "other rule of law" under §1-305(a).

The *Stern Oil* court did not reach the question. Rather, it distinguished cases like *Nobs*, holding the lost discount in the case before it (on which the Problem above is based) was recoverable because it was not consequential damages but direct damages, allowed by §2-710:

> Thus, while it is true that lost profits may fall within the larger category of consequential damages, lost profits that flow directly from the contract itself are properly characterized as direct damages. They are damages that reflect a party's loss of the benefit of the bargain from the agreement between the parties, not other economic harm caused by agreements collateral to the contract.

Stern Oil Co. v. Brown, 2018 S.D. 15, 908 N.W.2d 144, 153 (2018).
The remedies provided for the parties in a lease of goods by Article 2A have been slavishly copied from the corresponding provisions in Article 2. For the most part this does no harm, but the Article 2A equivalent to §2-709's "Action for the Price" has generated a lot of discord. Read §2A-529, "Lessor's Action for the Rent."

PROBLEM 83

Lawyer Portia Moot decided to rent a computer from Machines Unlimited and use it in her office. The computer arrived, and Portia found it most satisfactory, but her struggling practice made it difficult for her to make the lease payments on time. After she had missed two payments in a row, Machines

Unlimited sent a goon to her office to repossess the computer. Portia was not there at the time, but her loyal administrative assistant protested mightily when the goon grabbed the machine, at one point blocking the door with her body, but she was shoved aside and the computer was taken. The lease still had a year to run, with payments of $100 due each month. Machines Unlimited sued Portia for $1,200.

(a) Was Machines Unlimited's repossession valid? See §2A-525. What remedy does Portia have if it was not?

(b) Assuming there was no problem with the repossession, is the lessor required to try to mitigate damages by re-leasing the machine? See §2A-529 and its Official Comment.

(c) Could the lessor avoid any possible duty to mitigate by so stipulating in the lease agreement? See §§1-302, 2A-503; Homer Kripke, Some Dissonant Notes About Article 2A, 39 Ala. L. Rev. 792, 795-796 (1988).

III. BUYER'S REMEDIES

The general list of the buyer's remedies is found in §2-711. This section also gives the buyer a right to cancel and recover the price if the buyer has already paid. In most circumstances, the buyer has further recoverable damages, as identified in other sections. All the sections are designed to follow §1-305's admonition that the Code's goal is to put the aggrieved party in as good a position as performance would have. As for which sections are appropriate in a given case as far as monetary damages are concerned, the answer depends on whether the buyer has *accepted* the goods or not.

A. *Accepted Goods*

If a technical §2-606 acceptance of the goods has been made and is not later revoked, the buyer may still sue for breach of warranty (or other breach of contract) if a notice of the defect has been given to the seller within a reasonable time after the defect should have been discovered; §2-607(3)(a). Damages are then measured by §§2-714 and 2-715. Read those sections. See Annot., 96 A.L.R.3d 299.

PROBLEM 84

The world-famous pianist Bart Cristofori made $50,000 a year giving concerts. Recently he decided to experiment with some new sounds. He purchased an electric piano for $3,000 from the Silbermann Electronic Music Company. The purchase was negotiated orally; there was no written contract. Cristofori practiced day and night to master the new instrument. After three months of arduous practice, he noticed a strange ringing in his ears. Subsequent medical examination revealed that Cristofori was going deaf. The cause was a high-pitched whine (above the level of human perception) emanating from the electric piano. On learning that the piano had done this to him, Cristofori took an axe and chopped the piano into unrecognizable bits. (This action ended his ability to revoke his acceptance; §§2-608(3), 2-602(2)(b).) When he calmed down, he brought suit against the piano company for breach of warranty. His damages were claimed as $1,755,505, based on the following elements: $3,000 was the cost of the piano, $2,000 was doctor's fees, $500 was paid to experts to examine the piano and determine if it was the cause of the ear problem, $750,000 was lost income for the next 15 years, $1,000,000 was the value of Cristofori's hearing, and $5 was for the axe. Silbermann Electronic Music defended by (1) denying that it had warranted the piano in any way, and (2) proving that the whine was harmless to everybody in the world except Cristofori. (The company proved that the accident occurred to him only because of the bone structure of his skull coupled with the fact that he had a metal plate installed in his head as a result of an auto accident in his youth.) Answer these questions:

(a) What warranty, if any, did the Silbermann Company breach? Does the company's care in manufacturing the piano or the freakishness of the injury keep the warranty from being breached?

(b) Which, if any, of Cristofori's damages are recoverable under §2-714?

(c) Which, if any, of the items claimed are *incidental damages* under §2-715(1)?

(d) The §2-715(2)(a) test of consequential damages with its "reason to know" language is a restatement of our old friend Hadley v. Baxendale. Is it relevant here?

(e) If you were the judge of both the facts and the law, what amount would you award Cristofori, and why?

PROBLEM 85

Sheila Spin made it to the finals of the USA Yo-Yo Championship, where she was widely thought to be a cinch to win the $10,000 first prize. The day of the competition she went into the Smalltime Drug Store owned by her Uncle Mort and told him that she wanted to buy a four-foot nylon yo-yo cord to use in the competition. Mort sold her one for $1.50 (he put it on her bill) and wished her luck. That she did not have. The cord was defective and broke during her first trick, thus eliminating her from the competition. When the bill came from the drug store, Sheila refused to pay it. In fact, she filed suit against Mort, asking for $50,000 consequential damages. Every expert witness who testified stated that Sheila's ability with the yo-yo was the greatest in the world. Mort defended on two grounds: (1) merely knowing about the intended use of the yo-yo in the competition was not enough to impose liability on him unless the parties had agreed to put this risk on him, and (2) her damages were too speculative. Answer these questions:

(a) Does the UCC permit Sheila to refuse to pay the bill? See §2-717. If a buyer feels obligated to pay only part of the bill, what procedure should be followed? See §3-311 (dealing with payment-in-full checks).

(b) Are the consequential damages for which Sheila asked too speculative? See Official Comment 4 to §2-715; White & Summers §11-4. Cf. Wachtel v. National Alfalfa Journal, 190 Iowa 1293, 176 N.W. 801 (1920) (leading contender in canceled contest entitled to value of the chance of winning).

(c) Is knowledge of the possible consequential damages alone sufficient to impose liability on a seller? Or is Mort right in saying that the liability for consequential damages attaches only if the seller has agreed (expressly or impliedly) to assume the risk? See Official Comment 2 to §2-715; White & Summers §11-4; Beal v. General Motors Corp., 354 F. Supp. 423 (D. Del. 1973).

(d) May Sheila recover her attorney fees as consequential damages? See Equitable Lumber Corp. v. IPA Land Dev. Corp., 38 N.Y.2d 516, 344 N.E.2d 391, 381 N.Y.S.2d 459 (1976) (may be recovered if the contract so provides, but any specified amount must be valid as a liquidated damages provision); Too Marker Products, Inc. v. Creation Supply, Inc., 2014 WL 3818675 (D. Or. 2014) (no fees awarded under Illinois law without statutory or contractual provision). Cady v. Dick Loehr's, Inc., 100 Mich. App. 543, 299 N.W.2d 69 (1980) (trial court has discretion to award attorney fees as consequential damages); Modine Mfg. Co. v. North East Indep. Sch. Dist., 503 S.W.2d 833 (Tex. Civ. App. 1974) (no, because such fees are penal in nature and the Code does not authorize punitive damages).

PROBLEM 86

Rambo Trucks, Inc., sold Hercules Moving Company a large moving van. The contract of sale limited the buyer's remedy for breach of warranty to replacement or repair only and clearly disclaimed liability for consequential damages. The first day on the job, the truck proved incapable of climbing even small hills, so Hercules Moving Company revoked its acceptance of the truck. It claimed a security interest in the truck pursuant to §2-711(3) and pending sale stored it at a truck depot, which charged it $50 a day for storage.

Must Rambo Trucks pay the storage charges, or is the company protected by the disclaimer of consequential damages? See §§2-719(3),

2-715(1); Commonwealth Edison Co. v. Allied Chem. Nuclear Prods., Inc., 684 F. Supp. 1429 (N.D. Ill. 1988) (storage charges of $293 million!); Dietec Co., Ltd. v. Osirius Group, LLC, 2017 WL 6039557 (E.D. Mich. 2017) (seller's costs caused by buyer's breach, in securing additional raw materials and financing, held to be incidental damages).

Suppose Rambo Trucks had delivered the van without a bill of sale or proper title, but delivered the title months later. What would be the damages for breach of the warranty of title? See McCoolidge v. Oyvetsky, 2016 WL 852059 (Neb. 2016).

B. *Unaccepted Goods*

Where the seller never delivers the goods or where the buyer rejects or revokes acceptance, §2-711 states that the buyer may recover the price and other damages. These generally include incidental and consequential damages under §2-715. See Official Comment 1 to that section. In addition, the buyer may seek specific performance or replevin under §2-716. Read §2-716 and its Official Comment.

As Comment 1 indicates, the drafters intended to "liberalize" the application of the doctrine of specific performance. Thus, §2-716 provides for the use of specific performance not only when goods are unique, but also "in other proper circumstances." What are "proper circumstances"? See Laclede Gas Co. v. Amoco Oil Co., 522 F.2d 33 (8th Cir. 1975), *rev'd on other grounds*, 531 F.2d 942 (8th Cir. 1975) (the court gave the buyer, a distributor of propane gas, a mandatory injunction against the seller, who had promised to supply gas over a long term); Eastern Airlines Inc. v. Gulf Oil Corp., 415 F. Supp. 429 (S.D. Fla. 1975) (Gulf Oil was enjoined from breaching its contract with Eastern for jet fuel); Sedmak v. Charlie's Chevrolet, Inc., 622 S.W.2d 694 (Mo. App. 1981) (holding buyers entitled to specific performance of contract to buy one of a limited edition of Corvette automobiles); Almetals, Inc. v. Wickeder Westfalenstahl, GmbH, 2008 WL 4791377 (E.D. Mich. 2008) (specific performance awarded where the varieties of clad metal supplied by the seller were unique, with no known alternative source); Annot., 26 A.L.R.4th 294.

Mirion Technologies (Canberra), Inc. v. Sunpower, Inc.

United States District Court, Southern District of Ohio, 2017
2017 WL 5090436

James L. Graham, United States District Judge

This contract dispute is before the court on the motion of plaintiff Mirion Technologies (Canberra), Inc. for a preliminary injunction. Mirion alleges that it entered into a supply agreement with defendant Sunpower, Inc., whereby Sunpower would produce and supply cryocoolers, a device used in nuclear radiation detectors. Mirion asserts that it placed a valid purchase order for 250 cryocoolers but Sunpower breached the agreement by refusing to fill the purchase order.

Mirion seeks a preliminary injunction requiring specific performance of the supply agreement, such that Sunpower would be ordered to manufacture 250 cryocoolers and supply them to Mirion. The court conducted an evidentiary hearing on September 25, 2017. For the reasons that follow, the motion for a preliminary injunction is denied.

I. Background

A. The Parties and Their Products

Mirion is a Delaware corporation based in Connecticut which offers products and support services for the nuclear energy industry. Among other things, Mirion manufactures radiation detection instruments and offers radiation monitoring systems. The president of Mirion's Spectroscopy Division is Sheila Webb, who formerly served as vice president of engineering at Canberra Industries, Inc.

Mirion acquired Canberra in July 2016. Canberra manufactures high-purity germanium detectors, an instrument described by Webb as the most sensitive type of sensor available for detecting radioisotopes. Canberra also manufactures cryostats, which is a device that can be used on radiation detectors in order to maintain extremely low temperatures.

Webb testified that a germanium crystal inside a high-purity germanium detector needs to be kept at a temperature of about negative 296 degrees Fahrenheit. This is accomplished in one of three ways: (1) a dewar, or open-mouth container, filled with liquid nitrogen and having a lead shield at the mouth; (2) an electrically-cooled system; or (3) a hybrid cooler having a closed system with a container of liquid nitrogen, which, as it evaporates, is condensed by a cryocooler. The drawback of the dewar method is that the liquid nitrogen supply needs to be replenished. The drawback of the electrically-cooled method is the need for a constant power supply. Webb testified that the hybrid method is viewed as the best solution because it recirculates liquid nitrogen and can operate without a power supply for a period of several days.

Mirion and Canberra produce and sell a hybrid cooler called the Canberra Cryo-Cycle II. The Cryo-Cycle II is a cryostat and is comprised three basic parts: a cryocooler, a container holding about 22 liters of liquid nitrogen and electrical components which connect the cryostat to a germanium detector. The Cryo-Cycle II keeps the detector at the temperature required for it to operate. According to Webb, there are several other manufactures of hybrid coolers, but Sunpower is not one of them.

Sunpower is an Ohio corporation based in Athens, Ohio. It manufactures CryoTel GT cryocoolers. A cryocooler is a small electrical device that performs a cooling function in certain kinds of radiation detectors, including in high-purity germanium detectors. Sunpower is owned by AMETEK, Inc., which is a global manufacturer of electronic instruments and electromechanical devices.

Webb testified that there are only a handful of manufacturers in the world who produce high-purity germanium detectors. One of those entities is ORTEC, Inc., which is owned by AMETEK. Germanium detectors are sold to various interests associated with the nuclear energy industry, including nuclear power plants and laboratories, research facilities and other entities in the governmental, military, energy and educational sectors. Webb testified that Mirion/Canberra and AMETEK/ORTEC each have nearly a 50% share of the market for high-purity germanium detectors that use hybrid coolers. . . .

F. THE SUPPLY AGREEMENT AND ENSUING PURCHASE ORDER

On June 16, 2017, Mirion and Sunpower entered into a Supply Agreement, under which Sunpower agreed to supply CryoTel GT cryocoolers to Mirion for a three-year period whenever Mirion submitted a purchase order. The parties agreed that the per-unit cost of the cryocoolers would be $9,835. For orders of 1 to 10 cryocoolers, Sunpower agreed to make delivery in 6 weeks. For quantities greater than 10 cryocoolers, the parties would determine a mutually agreeable delivery schedule. The cryocoolers came with a two-year warranty.

Alec Bounds, Mirion's chief procurement officer, negotiated the Supply Agreement on behalf of Mirion. Bounds testified that he and Jim Wade, his point of contact at Sunpower, discussed and agreed to a "ramp-up schedule" on June 7, 2017, prior to the signing of the Supply Agreement. The ramp-up schedule provided a forecast of the number of cryocoolers that Mirion would want supplied each month. The schedule accommodated Mirion's transition away from Lihan and provided Sunpower with time to increase production in order to meet Mirion's supply demand. Under this schedule, Sunpower would supply a smaller number of units in the first few months of the Agreement and then increase production, such that Sunpower would supply 110 units in the first six months of the Agreement and 20 units per month for several additional months.

On or about June 23, 2017, Wade called Bounds and communicated that Mirion should place a "large" purchase order soon. On that same day, individuals at AMETEK/Sunpower emailed the ramp-up schedule amongst themselves. (Hearing Ex. 18).

On June 29, 2017, Mirion submitted a purchase order for 250 CryoTel GT units. (Hearing Ex. 7). When combined with miscellaneous costs, the total purchase order was for $2.65 million. The purchase order was based upon Canberra's forecast that it would need 250 units over the next 18 months.

On June 29, the President of Sunpower, who was not involved in negotiating or signing the Supply Agreement, emailed a letter to Mirion in which he purported to "elect[] not to enter into the proposed Supply Agreement." (Hearing Ex. 6). On June 30, a Sunpower representative sent Mirion an email purporting to reject the Agreement and the June 29 purchase order. (Hearing Ex. 8).

After legal counsel for Mirion objected to the purported rejection, legal counsel for Sunpower responded with a July 7, 2017 letter in which it withdrew the purported notice of rejection. (Hearing Ex. 32). In the same letter, Sunpower exercised its contractual right to terminate the Supply Agreement with six months' notice. Under the Agreement, Sunpower was obligated to fill purchase orders placed prior to the effective date of termination, January 7, 2018.

On July 10, 2017, Mirion delivered a revised purchase order for 250 cryocoolers. Sunpower refused to fill the order and this litigation followed.

G. MIRION'S ABILITY TO OBTAIN AN ALTERNATIVE SUPPLY OF CRYOCOOLERS

Following Sunpower's refusal to fill the purchase order, Mirion continues to obtain cryocoolers from Lihan. James Colaresi, Mirion's director of detector engineering and manufacturing, testified that Mirion is able to obtain an adequate supply of cryocoolers from Lihan to produce the Cryo-Cycle II and to replace defective cryocoolers returned under warranty. According to Webb and Colaresi, Lihan's cryocoolers still suffer from a reliability problem, and Mirion and Lihan continue to work together to address that problem. Bounds testified that Mirion has increased its efforts with Lihan and meets with Lihan on a weekly basis and has implemented a quality improvement plan.

Mirion also has continued to have discussions with Thales. However, it will take at least 18 months to have a product ready from Thales because of the research and development that must be done. Bounds testified that cost and the per-unit price point continues to be an obstacle with Thales.

. . .

C. ENTITLEMENT TO SPECIFIC PERFORMANCE

Specific performance is a remedy that is available only when "there is no adequate remedy at law, i.e., damages." Sashti, Inc. v. Glunt Industries, Inc., 140 F. Supp. 2d 813, 817 (N.D. Ohio 2001) (citing Gleason v. Gleason, 64 Ohio App. 3d 667, 672, 582 N.E.2d 657, 661 (Ohio Ct. App. 1991)). This principle is reflected in the Uniform Commercial Code with the concept of the "commercial feasibility of replacement." U.C.C. §2-716, Off. Cmt.

2. Ohio Revised Code §1302.90(A) states, "Specific performance may be decreed where the goods are unique or in other proper circumstances." The Official Comment to the statute provides that the "inability to cover is strong evidence of 'other proper circumstances.' " O.R.C. §1302.90, Off. Cmt. 2. See also Triple-A Baseball Club Assocs. v. Northeastern Baseball, Inc., 832 F.2d 214, 224 (1st Cir. 1987) (noting in the case law an "emphasis on ability to 'cover' as a major criterion in deciding the appropriateness of specific performance").

"[O]utput and requirements contracts involving a particular or peculiarly available source or market present today the typical commercial specific performance situation." O.R.C. §1302.90, Off. Cmt. 2. Although the statute does not exclude non-requirements contracts from its scope, practically speaking, a buyer to a non-requirements sales contract may well face difficulties of proof in seeking specific performance. As one court put it, "[o]utput and requirements contracts, explicitly cited as examples of situations in which specific performance may be appropriate, by their nature call for a series of continuing acts and an ongoing relationship." Copylease Corp. of Am. v. Memorex Corp., 408 F. Supp. 758, 760 (S.D.N.Y. 1976). And it is "where a contract calls for continuing sale of unique or 'noncoverable' goods" that the Official Comment "contemplate[s] that at least in some circumstances specific performance will issue contrary to the historical reluctance to grant such relief in these situations." Id.

Sunpower argues that because the Supply Agreement is not a requirements contract, Mirion can prevail only if the goods are unique. That is, Sunpower would remove the "other proper circumstances" prong of the statute as a way in which Mirion could show it is entitled to specific performance. If Mirion did not obligate itself to refrain from obtaining cryocoolers from another supplier, so the argument goes, then Mirion has the contractual ability to obtain cover. The court, however, has not found any authority to support Sunpower's categorical proposition that a buyer to a non-requirements contract cannot avail itself of the "other proper circumstances" prong of the statute. A buyer might have the contractual freedom to obtain cover, but the statute and case law look to the commercial feasibility of finding cover and whether the buyer has the ability to go to the marketplace and actually obtain a replacement.

The focus of the court's inquiry, therefore, is twofold: whether Sunpower's cryocoolers are unique and, even if they are not unique, whether Mirion is able to obtain cover.

Courts have said that a good is unique if it is rare, "one of a kind," or nearly impossible to replace. See, e.g., King Aircraft Sales, Inc. v. Lane, 68 Wash. App. 706, 711, 717, 846 P.2d 550, 553, 556-57 (Wash. Ct. App. 1993). Other courts look to the "uncertainty of valuing" the good, in keeping with the precept that specific performance is available only when there is no adequate remedy at law. Van Wagner Advert. Corp. v. S & M Enterprises, 67 N.Y.2d 186, 193, 492 N.E.2d 756, 760 (N.Y. 1986). The U.C.C. provides that "test of uniqueness . . . must be made in terms of the total situation which characterizes the contract." O.R.C. §1302.90, Off. Cmt. 2.

The court finds no support for Mirion's claim that Sunpower's CryoTel GT cryocooler is unique. It may be that high-purity germanium detectors are one of a kind, in comparison to other radiation detectors, in their sensitivity to radioactivity. It may be that hybrid cryostats are the best option available for cooling germanium crystals. And it may be that cryocoolers, which make the detectors and cryostats operational, are devices which reflect sophisticated design and technology. But within the nuclear energy industry in which the parties operate, cryocoolers are not unique or rare goods, nor are they incapable of being valued. Mirion's own witness, James Colaresi, testified that when Sunpower terminated the prior supply agreement with Canberra in 2013, Canberra "came up with a fairly long list of potential companies" with whom it could approach about supplying a cryocooler for Canberra's Cryo-Cycle II. Canberra "pared down that list to about five and then ultimately selected two [Twinbird and Thales] out of the five." He further testified that cost was the consideration that drove Canberra's selection of Twinbird. During the hearing, the court heard of no material changes in the marketplace from 2013 to present day. Sunpower remains one of many potential suppliers of cryocoolers. (Hearing Exs. 12, 13) (charts listing at least six more manufacturers beyond those named in this Opinion and Order). The value of these goods—as expressed by their cost—is ascertainable to Mirion. Indeed, the reason Mirion pursued Sunpower over Thales in early 2017 was not the uniqueness of Sunpower's product but the higher costs associated with Thales.

Mirion argues that cryocoolers have a number of important features and that reliability is one of them. The court agrees that in evaluating uniqueness, it should view the totality of the situation and consider the characteristics or attributes of a good which are important to the parties and to others in the relevant marketplace or industry. See *King Aircraft Sales*, 68 Wash. App. at 711, 846 P.2d at 553 (examining the claim that two aircraft were "rare in terms of their exceptional condition"); Sedmak v. Charlie's Chevrolet, Inc., 622 S.W.2d 694, 699-700 (Mo. Ct. App. 1981) (examining the "mileage, condition, ownership and appearance" of a collectible automobile). Sunpower does not dispute, and common sense dictates, that reliability is an important feature of a machine or a scientific instrument.

According to Mirion, Sunpower is uniquely able to produce a cryocooler that drops into the Cryo-Cycle II and performs reliably. This claim has slim factual support. Though Webb and Colaresi testified that Lihan's product is generally less reliable than Sunpower's, Mirion failed to produce documents or data regarding the respective reliability of Lihan's and

Sunpower's cryocoolers. This leaves the court without specific information from which it could determine, for instance, the comparative failure rates of the two makes of cryocoolers, the average lifespan of a Lihan cryocooler before it fails and whether the failure rate or lifespan of Lihan devices has improved over time.

The court finds that Mirion has shown only that the Sunpower cryocooler perhaps is better than Lihan's on the reliability front, not that the Sunpower device is unique. Lihan's device is not so unreliable that Mirion is unable to sell its Cryo-Cycle II, as was the case when Canberra attempted to work with Twinbird. Mirion/Canberra has sold its product with the Lihan cryocooler since December 2014 and has addressed the reliability issues with Lihan's product through a warranty return program. As Webb and Colaresi testified, Mirion has a "fairly large" service team that is equipped to "immediately" replace defective cryocoolers with new ones.

For the same reasons that Mirion has not shown that Sunpower's product is unique, Mirion has not established that it is unable to obtain cover. See Kaiser Trading Co. v. Associated Metals & Minerals Corp., 321 F. Supp. 923, 932 (N.D. Cal. 1970) (noting that cover can refer to the "scarcity of goods" or to "when the goods contracted for cannot be purchased on the open market"). Mirion's experience with Lihan proves that it is commercially feasible for Mirion to obtain an alternative supply of cryocoolers. Mirion has access to enough of a supply from Lihan to produce the Cryo-Cycle II and fill warranty returns.

Again, numerous potential suppliers exist for Mirion. Bounds testified that while Mirion negotiated with Sunpower in May 2017, Mirion looked at "multiple options," including staying with Lihan, switching to Thales, proceeding with Sunpower and various combinations thereof. Bounds emphasized that Mirion "wanted those options" and wanted the opt-out provision in the Supply Agreement—"knowing the history with Sunpower, I wanted to make sure that we would have the agility or the option to find another source if this agreement failed and . . . I would then be able to adjust and go find another supplier."

Webb similarly testified that Mirion "knew that there was some risk associated with the agreement with Sunpower" and that they were considering their options with Lihan and Thales because they wanted to avoid relying on a single source for cryocoolers. According to Webb, Mirion viewed Sunpower as "the best solution without a lot of engineering effort and design work." The court finds that Sunpower is simply Mirion's preferred supplier among many options and that any extra engineering and design costs associated with choosing another supplier are quantifiable and redressable by monetary damages.

Now that the relationship with Sunpower has indeed failed, Mirion remains able to obtain cryocoolers from Lihan, including during any interim period in which Mirion would seek to work with Thales or another potential supplier on research and development.

Accordingly, the court finds that Mirion has not established a strong likelihood of success on its claim for specific performance. . . .

VI. CONCLUSION

For the reasons stated above, Mirion's motion for a preliminary injunction (doc. 2) is denied.

An important buyer remedy is found in §2-712, where the buyer is authorized to *cover*—that is, purchase substitute goods. If a buyer covers properly, the damages are measured by a comparison of the original contract price and the cost of the cover. Read §2-712.

PROBLEM 87

Mr. and Mrs. Transient ordered a 2025 Blocklong model mobile home for $8,000 from the Home on Wheels Sales Corporation, delivery to be made on May 20. The Transients planned on spending an additional $500 to build a foundation that the Blocklong trailer had to have for maximum utility. Due to widespread industry strikes, the price of trailers rose dramatically in the early spring, and on May 10 Home on Wheels informed the Transients that the deal was off. The Transients shopped around and on September 25 bought a 2025 Behemoth model mobile home for $15,000 from another dealer. The Behemoth was larger than the Blocklong model (it had a basement and a laundry room), but it did not require a foundation. The Transients then brought suit. Home on Wheels defended by offering to show that (a) the Behemoth was selling for $10,000 up to September 5 when the price rose to $15,000, and (b) the Behemoth always sells for $2,000 more than the Blocklong since the former is a snazzier trailer. What damages can the Transients get under §2-712? See Official Comment 2 of that section; White & Summers §7-3; Annot., 79 A.L.R.4th 844.

Hughes Communications Galaxy, Inc. v. United States

United States Court of Appeals, Federal Circuit, 2001
271 F.3d 1060

RADER, Circuit Judge.

Following a trial on damages for breach of contract, the United States Court of Federal Claims awarded Hughes Communications Galaxy, Inc.

$102,680,625. Hughes Communications Galaxy, Inc. v. United States, 47 Fed. Cl. 236 (2000) *(Hughes V)*. Because the Court of Federal Claims did not abuse its discretion in calculating damages, this court affirms.

I.

This case has received extensive factual analysis in prior opinions. . . . This appeal addresses only the Court of Federal Claims' breach of contract damage determination in *Hughes IV* and *Hughes V.*

In December 1985, NASA and Hughes entered into a Launch Services Agreement (LSA), which required NASA to use its "best efforts" to launch ten of Hughes' HS-393 satellites on space shuttles. The LSA required NASA to continue using its best efforts to launch Hughes' HS-393s until it launched all ten HS-393s or until September 30, 1994, whichever was earlier. NASA compiled "manifests" of all shuttle payloads scheduled for launch on shuttles. NASA reissued these manifests periodically to account for changed circumstances. The manifests listed commercial payloads in order of their planned or firm launch dates and scheduled a shuttle for each launch. After NASA and Hughes entered the LSA, NASA assigned Hughes' satellites specific slots on a manifest.

In January 1986, the space shuttle Challenger exploded. Following the Challenger explosion, NASA suspended operation of the shuttles until September 1988. Further, in August 1986, President Reagan announced that NASA would no longer launch commercial satellites on shuttles. On July 10, 1986, NASA completed the last manifest before President Reagan's announcement. It projected that NASA would launch eight Hughes satellites on shuttles by September 1994. Thereafter, NASA compiled a new manifest that only included "shuttle unique" and "national security and foreign policy" payloads. That manifest did not list any Hughes satellites. Later NASA informed Hughes that it would almost certainly not launch any Hughes satellites on shuttles.

After 1986, Hughes launched three of its HS-393s on expendable launch vehicles (ELVs), one of which was the JCSAT-1. Hughes also launched several similar satellites on ELVs, including six HS-601 satellites. The HS-601s are similar to the HS-393s, except they are more powerful and better suited for ELV launches. While the ELV launches provided an alternative to shuttle launch services under the LSA, Hughes incurred more costs by launching satellites on ELVs rather than on shuttles.

Hughes sued the United States Government for breach of contract and for taking its property without providing just compensation. The Court of Federal Claims granted summary judgment to the Government on both claims based on the sovereign act defense. *Hughes I,* 26 Cl. Ct. at 144-46. This court reversed that summary judgment and remanded. *Hughes II,* 998

F.2d at 959. On remand, the Court of Federal Claims granted summary judgment for Hughes for breach of contract. *Hughes III,* 34 Fed. Cl. at 634. Before holding a trial on damages, the Court of Federal Claims ruled that the Government could not produce evidence to reduce its damages by the amount Hughes had passed on to its customers in increased prices. *Hughes IV,* 38 Fed. Cl. at 582.

At the damages trial, Hughes sought to prove damages by showing its increased costs in launching satellites on ELVs, rather than on shuttles. Hughes presented two main methods for calculating the increased costs. The first method, the Ten HS-393 Satellites Method, compared the costs of launching ten HS-393s on shuttles under the LSA with the costs of launching ten HS-393s on ELVs. Because Hughes had actually launched only three HS-393s on ELVs, the method based the ELV launch costs on the actual costs of launching the three HS-393s. The second method, the Primary Method, compared Hughes' actual costs of launching ten satellites on ELVs with the costs that Hughes would have incurred by launching ten satellites on shuttles under the LSA. The ten satellites included the three HS-393s, the six HS-601s, and one HS-376.

The Court of Federal Claims used the Ten HS-393 Satellites Method to calculate Hughes' increased costs of "cover." *Hughes V,* 47 Fed. Cl. at 244. However, the court modified the method in several important respects. First, the court found that even using its best efforts, NASA would have only launched five HS-393s under the LSA. Accordingly, the court only awarded Hughes increased costs for five satellites, rather than ten. Id. Second, the court averaged the costs of launching on shuttles the three HS-393s that were actually launched on ELVs and used that average for the fourth and fifth satellites, rather than individually calculating the cost of launching each satellite on a shuttle, as Hughes' expert had done. Id. at 244 n.12. Third, in calculating the ELV launch costs for the fourth and fifth satellites, the court escalated the costs using the midpoint between March 1989 and September 1994, rather than the midpoint between March 1989 and December 1995, as Hughes' expert had done. Id. at 244. Fourth, the court refused to award Hughes prejudgment interest on its damages. Id. at 244-45. Fifth, the court refused to award Hughes reflight insurance costs and increased launch insurance costs for the five satellites. Id. at 245-46.

Based on its modified HS-393 method, the court awarded Hughes $102,680,625 in damages for its increased launch costs. Id. at 247. Hughes and the Government both appeal. This court has jurisdiction under 28 U.S.C. §1295(a)(3) (1994).

II. . . .

"The general rule in common law breach of contract cases is to award damages sufficient to place the injured party in as good a position as he or she would have been had the breaching party fully performed." San Carlos Irrigation & Drainage Dist. v. United States, 111 F.3d 1557, 1562-63 (Fed. Cir. 1997). Thus, "[a] plaintiff must show that but for the breach, the damages alleged would not have been suffered." Id. Moreover, the damages must have been foreseeable at the time the parties entered the contract, which requires that they "be the natural and proximate result of the breach." Locke v. United States, 151 Ct. Cl. 262, 283 F.2d 521, 526 (Ct. Cl. 1960). The LSA itself further limits damages to "direct damages only" and excludes consequential damages from any recovery.

The Court of Federal Claims awarded Hughes its increased costs of "cover." If a seller breaches a contract for goods, the buyer may "cover" or, in other words, obtain substitute goods from another seller. U.C.C. §2-712 (1997); E. Allan Farnsworth, Farnsworth on Contracts, §12.11 (2d ed. 1998). Additionally, courts often award an analogous remedy for breach of service contracts such as the LSA. Farnsworth, supra, §12.11. While the cover remedy of the Uniform Commercial Code does not govern this analogous remedy under the LSA, the Uniform Commercial Code provides useful guidance in applying general contract principles. Because both parties and the Court of Federal Claims have referred to this remedy as a "cover" remedy, this court will also use this term to refer to the remedy for Hughes' increased costs of obtaining substitute launch services.

The substitute goods or services involved in cover need not be identical to those involved in the contract, but they must be "commercially usable as reasonable substitutes under the circumstances." U.C.C. §2-712 cmt. 2. Whether cover provides a reasonable substitute under the circumstances is a question of fact. Bigelow-Sanford, Inc. v. Gunny Corp., 649 F.2d 1060, 1065 (5th Cir. 1981) (stating that whether cover is reasonable is a "classic jury issue" (quoting Transammonia Export Corp. v. Conserv, Inc., 554 F.2d 719, 724 (5th Cir. 1977))).

When a buyer of goods covers, the buyer's remedy for the seller's breach as to those goods equals the difference between the cost of the replacement goods and the contract price plus other losses. U.C.C. §2-712; Farnsworth, supra, §12.11. Similarly, if the seller breaches a contract for services, the buyer's remedy for cover equals the difference between the cost of the substitute services and the contract price plus other losses. Farnsworth, supra, §12.11 (where a building contractor breaches a first contract and the owner obtains substitute performance under a second contract, the owner can recover "any additional amount required by the second contract beyond what the owner would have had to pay under the first").

The Government cross appeals, arguing that Hughes should only be able to recover damages for the three HS-393s that it actually launched. While Hughes did not actually launch the fourth and fifth HS-393s that the Court of Federal Claims used to calculate damages, Hughes did incur costs in launching the HS-601s. The Court of Federal Claims found that Hughes developed the HS-601s to replace the HS-393s because the HS-601s were better suited for ELV launches, and that Hughes would have launched ten HS-393s on shuttles, given the opportunity. *Hughes V,* 47 Fed. Cl. at 240-41. The Government disputes these findings, asserting that Hughes developed the HS-601s for independent business reasons, specifically, the more powerful HS-601s were more marketable. On this point, however, the Court of Federal Claims specifically credited testimony of Hughes' witnesses that Hughes would not have developed the HS-601 if the Government had not breached the LSA and that Hughes could have designed the HS-393 to accommodate the additional power of the HS-601. Id. at 240. This testimony directly supports the Court of Federal Claims' finding that "the HS-393 could have been used in place of the HS-601" for HS-601 launches during the contract period. *Hughes V,* 47 Fed. Cl. at 240. Thus, the trial court found that the HS-601 launches were reasonable substitutes under the circumstances of this breach.

Additionally, the Court of Federal Claims specifically found that no credible evidence supported the Government's attack on the HS-601 as a reasonable substitute. Specifically, the Government argues that at the time of contracting, the Government could not have foreseen "the demise of the HS-393" as a result of its breach. However, the Court of Federal Claims' damages method does not compensate Hughes for the "demise of the HS-393." Rather it compensates Hughes for increased launch costs. Had Hughes kept using the HS-393s, it would likely have incurred the same damages that the Court of Federal Claims awarded.

In sum, the Court of Federal Claims hinged its determination of this issue on credibility. Such determinations are virtually never clear error. First Interstate Bank v. United States, 61 F.3d 876, 882 (Fed. Cir. 1995). Furthermore, while the damages calculation might have been easier if Hughes had kept launching HS-393s on ELVs, ease of proof in potential future litigation is not sufficient justification to require Hughes to continue launching satellites that were ill-suited for ELV launches. As the victim of the breach, Hughes was within its rights to obtain commercially reasonable substitute launch services even if the substitute services were not identical to those covered by the LSA. The Court of Federal Claims thus did not clearly err in holding that Hughes successfully covered by launching HS-601s on ELVs. Accordingly, this court rejects the Government's cross appeal.

The Court of Federal Claims' use of increased HS-393 launch costs provided reasonable certainty in calculating damages. The trial court compared the costs of launching HS-393s on ELVs with the costs of launching the same HS-393s on shuttles. That comparison provided a basis for assessing Hughes' increased costs in launching the HS-601s. Under this method, the Court of Federal Claims accounted for any measurable difference in value to Hughes between the HS-393 launches and the HS-601 launches. See Farnsworth, supra, §12.11 ("[A]ny measurable difference in quality [of a substitute] can be compensated for by a money allowance."). Accordingly, the Court of Federal Claims used the increased costs for HS-393s as a reasonable approximation of the increased costs incurred by Hughes in launching the substitute HS-601s. Under this method, the trial court did not abuse its discretion. See S.W. Elecs. & Mfg. Corp. v. United States, 228 Ct. Cl. 333, 655 F.2d 1078, 1088 (Ct. Cl. 1981) (the trial court need only "make a fair and reasonable approximation").

The LSA states that damages "shall be limited to direct damages only and shall not include any loss of revenue, profits or other indirect or consequential damages." As discussed above, the increased costs represent direct damages incurred by Hughes in obtaining substitute launch services. Additionally, the damages do not include any lost revenues or profits, only increased costs. Finally, the damages are not consequential. The Uniform Commercial Code is instructive on this point. It allows recovery of the difference between the cost of cover and the contract price "together with any incidental and consequential damages," U.C.C. §2-712 (emphasis added), thereby distinguishing between consequential damages and the direct cost of cover. In sum, the Court of Federal Claims did not abuse its discretion by awarding Hughes damages for its increased costs incurred by obtaining substitute launch services for two HS-601s in addition to the three HS-393s.

Hughes decided to launch the JCSAT-1 satellite, a particular HS-393, on an ELV several months before President Reagan's announcement in 1986 that NASA would no longer launch commercial satellites on shuttles. NASA only breached its best efforts obligation after President Reagan's announcement. *Hughes III,* 34 Fed. Cl. at 630-34; *Hughes V,* 47 Fed. Cl. at 243. However, the LSA is not limited to launching particular satellites, such as the JCSAT-1. Rather, the LSA specifies a particular type of satellite (HS-393) in its preamble, and refers to the ten satellites as "HC-9 through HC-18." Thus, Hughes could have substituted another HS-393 for JCSAT-1, and Hughes still would have launched ten HS-393s on shuttles if NASA had provided those services under the LSA. Accordingly, the Court of Federal Claims did not abuse its discretion by awarding Hughes damages for the increased costs of launching the JCSAT-1.

III.

The Court of Federal Claims found that NASA could have launched five HS-393s during the LSA contract period using its best efforts. The Court of Federal Claims based this finding on the July 1986 manifest, but credited a report by Barrington Consulting Group that unexpected delays beyond NASA's control reduced the number of shuttle launches below the projections in the July 1986 manifest. *Hughes V*, 47 Fed. Cl. at 243. Under the priorities in the July 1986 manifest, the Barrington report concluded that NASA would have launched five HS-393 satellites.

If NASA had given commercial satellites priority over NASA satellites, Hughes asserts, NASA would have launched ten HS-393s. However, before President Reagan's statement, NASA did not elevate commercial launches above its other priorities. NASA did not breach its best efforts obligation before President Reagan's statement. The priorities before President Reagan's statement gave approximately equal priority to commercial and NASA payloads. As the Court of Federal Claims correctly reasoned, Hughes could not have reasonably expected NASA priorities to elevate commercial satellites above other goals for the remainder of the contract period.

Similarly, the LSA's best efforts requirement did not obligate NASA to use the 1984 policy announced in a House sub-committee hearing. In the event of shuttle scheduling conflicts, the 1984 policy gave commercial satellites priority over NASA research and development missions. Under this policy, Hughes asserts, NASA would have launched all ten HS-393s. The LSA itself specifically included a 1982 listing of priorities, but said nothing about the 1984 policy. Without the 1984 policy in the contract, the LSA did not incorporate those priorities into NASA's best efforts obligation.

The Court of Federal Claims also correctly found that circumstances prevented NASA from increasing its launch rates to include all ten HS-393s. In testimony to Congress in 1992, NASA asserted its ability to launch more shuttles than its budget allowed. According to Hughes, the Government chose to limit the number of launches by limiting NASA's budget. The record amply supports the trial court's finding that the post-Challenger investigation and technical problems prevented NASA from launching more shuttles. *Hughes V*, 47 Fed. Cl. at 242-43. The record shows that, in all years except 1994, the Government budgeted for more shuttle launches than NASA was able to launch. In 1994, the Government budgeted for eight launches and NASA actually launched eight. Thus, the Court of Federal Claims did not clearly err in finding that technical obstacles, rather than budget choices, prevented NASA from launching more shuttles during the LSA contract period.

Additionally, Mr. Kiraly, the Government's expert, estimated the number of HS-393s that NASA's best efforts could have launched at between one and six. The variance in this estimate does not undercut the Court of Federal Claims' finding. The Court of Federal Claims relied on the Barrington report, which specifically concluded that NASA's best efforts would have launched five HS-393s. Id. at 243. Thus, the Court of Federal Claims did not clearly err in finding that NASA's best efforts would have produced five HS-393 launches.

IV.

Because Hughes actually launched only three HS-393s, the Court of Federal Claims calculated the average costs of launching those three satellites on shuttles. Then, using the report of Hughes' expert, Mr. Hammer, the trial court applied that average to project the shuttle launch costs of the fourth and fifth satellites. Id. at 244. Hughes asserts that the Court of Federal Claims should have used the shuttle launch costs for each individual satellite shown in Mr. Hammer's report. However, the trial court's method is symmetrical with its calculation of the costs of ELV launches. For ELV launch costs, the trial court averaged the actual ELV launch costs for the three HS-393s and applied that average to project the ELV launch costs of the fourth and fifth satellites. Id. at 244. Hughes does not disagree with the method of calculating ELV launch costs; the Court of Federal Claims merely did the same thing with the shuttle launch costs. The trial court reasonably exercised its discretion in using this symmetrical approach in calculating damages. . . .

IX.

The Government sought to reduce Hughes' damages by the amount Hughes recouped by increasing prices to customers, in other words, by the amount Hughes "passed through" to its customers. The Court of Federal Claims did not allow the Government to assert this defense at the damages trial. *Hughes IV,* 38 Fed. Cl. at 582. According to the Court of Federal Claims, this type of mitigation is too remote to consider. Id.

Although not in the breach of contract context, the Supreme Court has addressed this issue. In Southern Pacific Co. v. Darnell-Taenzer Lumber Co., 245 U.S. 531, 38 S. Ct. 186, 62 L. Ed. 451 (1918), a railroad overcharge case, the Court addressed the reduction of damages because the damaged party allegedly passed the unreasonable charge on to its customers. The Court stated: "The answer is not difficult. The general tendency of the law, in regard to damages at least, is not to go beyond the first step. As it does not attribute remote consequences to a defendant so it holds him liable if proximately the plaintiff has suffered a loss." Id. at 533-34, 38 S. Ct. 186. In an antitrust case, the Court noted that calculating pass-through damages reductions would present "the nearly insuperable difficulty of demonstrating that the particular plaintiff could not or would not have raised his prices absent the overcharge or maintained the higher price had the overcharge been discontinued." Hanover Shoe, Inc. v. United Shoe Mach. Corp., 392 U.S. 481, 493, 88 S. Ct. 2224, 20 L. Ed. 2d 1231 (1968). Similarly, allowing a pass-through damages reduction in a breach of contract action would destroy symmetry between reduction and escalation of damages. Moreover a standard for pass-through reductions would entail extremely difficult burdens for the trial court. Thus, the Supreme Court's reasoning also applies to this breach of contract action. The Court of Federal Claims did not abuse its discretion by disallowing pass-through damages reductions.

CONCLUSION

Because the Court of Federal Claims did not abuse its discretion in determining Hughes' damages for the Government's breach of the LSA, this court affirms.

Technically, a buyer does not have to cover. See, e.g., Turner v. NJN Cotton Company, 485 S.W.3d 513 (Tex. App. 2015) (buyer may choose between cover damages under §2-712 and market differential damages under §2-713). If a buyer fails to cover in an appropriate situation, however, consequential damages that could have been avoided are denied. See §2-715(2)(a). If a buyer decides to cover, the legal effect of the steps taken, as well as when cover should be effectuated, is measured against a standard of reasonableness in the given factual situation. Financial inability is an excuse for non-cover. See REB, Inc. v. Ralston Purina Co., 525 F.2d 749, (10th Cir. 1975). One practical test by which to gauge the reasonableness of the buyer's covering actions is to ask if the buyer would have made the same arrangements if there was no prospect of a successful suit against the breaching seller. See White & Summers §7-3, at 287-288.

If the buyer does not cover, damages may be measured under the next section, §2-713, a much criticized provision. See Childres, Buyer's Remedies: The Danger of Section 2-713, 72 Nw. U. L. Rev. 837 (1978). Read §2-713.

PROBLEM 88

The Student Bar Association (SBA) of the Gilberts Law School decided to hold a mammoth wine-and-cheese-tasting party for the students, faculty, staff, and alumni. The SBA ordered the wine from Classy Caterers. They agreed to pay $1,000 for it; the wine to be delivered on March 30, the day of the party. Classy Caterers ordered the wine from Grapes Vineyards in California, "F.O.B. San Francisco" for $750, but Grapes Vineyards went bankrupt on March 25. Classy Caterers was able to find identical wine in its own city for $750, and it bought the wine on March 25 for that amount. On March 25, the price of similar wine in San Francisco was $900. The cost of transporting the wine from San Francisco to the site of the party would have been $100. The SBA paid Classy Caterers $1,000 for the wine. Classy Caterers filed claims for damages in the bankruptcy proceeding of its defaulting supplier.

(a) Compute the damages due Classy for the failure to deliver the wine under §2-712. Now do it under §2-713. See Official Comment 5 to §2-713; White & Summers §7-4.

(b) What role does the $100 transportation cost play in computing damages? Note the definition of "market place" in §2-723.

Tongish v. Thomas

Supreme Court of Kansas, 1992
251 Kan. 728, 840 P.2d 471

McFarland, Justice:

This case presents the narrow issue of whether damages arising from the nondelivery of contracted-for sunflower seeds should be computed on the basis of K.S.A. 84-1-106 or K.S.A. 84-2-713. That is, whether the buyer is entitled to its actual loss of profit or the difference between the market price and the contract price. The trial court awarded damages on the basis of the buyer's actual loss of profit. The Court of Appeals reversed the judgment, holding that the difference between the market price and the contract price was the proper measure of damages (Tongish v. Thomas, 16 Kan. App. 2d 809, 829 P.2d 916 [1992]). The matter is before us on petition for review.

The pertinent facts are as follows. Denis Tongish entered into a contract on April 28, 1988, with the Decatur Coop Association (Coop) where Tongish agreed to grow 160 acres of sunflower seeds, said crop to be purchased by Coop at $13 per hundredweight for large seeds and $8 per hundredweight for small seeds. By agreement, the acreage was subsequently reduced to 116.8 acres. The crop was to be delivered in increments of one-third by December 31, 1988, March 31, 1989, and May 31, 1989.

Coop had a contract to deliver the seeds purchased to Bambino Bean & Seed, Inc. Coop was to be paid the same price it paid the farmers less a 55 cent per hundredweight handling fee. Coop's only anticipated profit was the handling fee.

In October and November 1988, Tongish delivered sunflower seeds to Coop. In January, a dispute arose over the amount of dockage charged against Tongish's seeds. Tongish's seeds were of higher quality than those of many other farmers selling to Coop, and Coop's practice of commingling seeds prior to sampling was disadvantageous to Tongish. This was resolved by Coop issuing an additional check to Tongish reflecting a lower dockage charge.

Due to a short crop, bad weather, and other factors, the market price of sunflower seeds in January 1989 was double that set forth in the Tongish/Coop contract. On January 13, Tongish notified Coop he would not deliver any more sunflower seeds.

In May 1989, Tongish sold and delivered 82,820 pounds of sunflower seeds to Danny Thomas for approximately $20 per hundredweight. Tongish was to receive $14,714.89, which was $5,153.13 more than the Coop contract price. Thomas paid for approximately one-half of the seeds. Tongish brought this action to collect the balance due. Thomas paid the balance of $7,359.61 into court and was ultimately dismissed from the action.

Meanwhile, Coop intervened in the action, seeking damages for Tongish's breach of their contract. Following a bench trial, the district court held that Tongish had breached the contract with no basis therefor. Damages were allowed in the amount of $455.51, which was the computed loss of handling charges. Coop appealed from said damage award. The Court of Appeals reversed the district court and remanded the case to the district court to determine and award damages pursuant to K.S.A. 84-2-713 (the difference between the market price and the contract price).

The analyses and rationale of the Court of Appeals utilized in resolving the issue are sound and we adopt the following portion thereof:

"The trial court decided the damages to Coop should be the loss of expected profits. Coop argues that K.S.A. 84-2-713 entitles it to collect as damages the difference between the market price and the contract price. Tongish argues that the trial court was correct and cites K.S.A. 84-1-106 as support for the contention that a party should be placed in as good a position as it would be in had the other party performed. Therefore, the only disagreement is how the damages should be calculated.

"The measure of damages in this action involves two sections of the Uniform Commercial Code: K.S.A. 84-1-106 and K.S.A. 84-2-713. The issue to be determined is which statute governs the measure of damages. Stated in another way, if the statutes are in conflict, which statute should prevail? The answer involves an ongoing academic discussion of two contending positions. The issues in this case disclose the problem.

"If Tongish had not breached the contract, he may have received under the contract terms with Coop about $5,153.13 less than he received from Danny Thomas. Coop in turn had an oral contract with Bambino to sell whatever seeds it received from Tongish to Bambino for the same price Coop paid for them. Therefore, if the contract had been performed, Coop would not have actually received the extra $5,153.13.

"We first turn our attention to the conflicting statutes and the applicable rules of statutory construction. K.S.A. 84-1-106(1) [Now §1-305—Eds.] states:

> 'The remedies provided by this act shall be liberally administered to the end that the aggrieved party may be put in as good a position as if the other party had fully performed but neither consequential or special nor penal damages may be had except as specifically provided in this act or by other rule of law.'

"If a seller breaches a contract and the buyer does not 'cover,' the buyer is free to pursue other available remedies. K.S.A. 84-2-711 and 84-2-712. One remedy, which is a complete alternative to 'cover' (K.S.A. 84-2-713, Official comment, ¶5), is K.S.A. 84-2-713(1), which provides:

> 'Subject to the provisions of this article with respect to proof of market price (section 84-2-723), the measure of damages for nondelivery or repudiation by the seller is the difference between the market price at the time when the buyer learned of the breach and the contract price together with any incidental and consequential damages provided in this article (section 84-2-715), but less expenses saved in consequence of the seller's breach.'

"Neither party argues that the Uniform Commercial Code is inapplicable. Both agree that the issue to be determined is which provision of the UCC should be applied. As stated by the appellee: 'This is really the essence of this appeal, *i.e.,* whether this general rule of damages [K.S.A. 84-1-106] controls the measure of damages set forth in K.S.A. 84-2-713.' However, Tongish then offers no support that K.S.A. 84-1-106 controls over K.S.A. 84-2-713. The authority he does cite (M & W Development, Inc. v. El Paso Water Co., 6 Kan. App. 2d 735, 634 P.2d 166 [1981]) is not a UCC case and K.S.A. 84-2-713 was not applicable.

"The statutes do contain conflicting provisions. On the one hand, K.S.A. 84-1-106 offers a general guide of how remedies of the UCC should be applied, whereas K.S.A. 84-2-713 specifically describes a damage remedy that gives the buyer certain damages when the seller breaches a contract for the sale of goods.

"The cardinal rule of statutory construction, to which all others are subordinate, is that the purpose and intent of the legislature govern. State ex rel. Stephan v. Kansas Racing Comm'n, 246 Kan. 708, 719, 792 P.2d 971 (1990); Cedar Creek Properties, Inc. v. Board of Johnson County Comm'rs, 246 Kan. 412, 417, 789 P.2d 1170 (1990); and Stauffer Communications, Inc. v. Mitchell, 246 Kan. 492, Syl. ¶1, 789 P.2d 1153 (1990). When there is a conflict between a statute dealing generally with a subject and another statute dealing specifically with a certain phase of it, the specific statute controls unless it appears that the legislature intended to make the general act controlling. State v. Wilcox, 245 Kan. 76, Syl. ¶1, 775 P.2d 177 (1989). The Kansas Supreme Court stated in Kansas Racing Management, Inc. v. Kansas Racing Comm'n, 244 Kan. 343, 353, 770 P.2d 423 (1989): 'General and special statutes should be read together and harmonized whenever possible, but to the extent a conflict between them exists, the special statute will prevail unless it appears the legislature intended to make the general statute controlling.'

"K.S.A. 84-2-713 allows the buyer to collect the difference in market price and contract price for damages in a breached contract. For that reason, it seems impossible to reconcile the decision of the district court that limits damages to lost profits with this statute.

"Therefore, because it appears impractical to make K.S.A. 84-1-106 and K.S.A. 84-2-713 harmonize in this factual situation, K.S.A. 84-2-713 should prevail as the more specific statute according to statutory rules of construction.

"As stated, however, Coop protected itself against market price fluctuations through its contract with Bambino. Other than the minimal handling charge, Coop suffered no lost profits from the breach. Should the protection require an exception to the general rule under K.S.A. 84-2-713?

"In Panhandle Agri-Service, Inc. v. Becker, 231 Kan. 291, 292, 644 P.2d 413 (1982), a farmer agreed to sell 10,000 tons of alfalfa to the buyer for $45 per ton. At the time the seller breached the contract, the market price was $62 per ton. 231 Kan. at 293 [644 P.2d 413]. The court found, pursuant to K.S.A. 84-2-713, that the damages amounted to $17 per ton or the difference between the market price and the contract price. The court stated: 'We find nothing which would justify the trial court in arriving at damages using loss of business profits which are consequential damages.' 231 Kan. at 298 [644 P.2d 413].

"In Baker v. Ratzlaff, 1 Kan. App. 2d 285, 564 P.2d 153 (1977), the seller contracted to sell all the popcorn planted on 380 acres for $4.75 per hundredweight. The seller breached, and the trial court found that the market price for popcorn was $8 per hundredweight when the buyer learned of the breach. The court held that the proper measure of damages would be the difference between the market price and the contract price as provided in K.S.A. 84-2-713. 1 Kan. App. 2d at 290 [564 P.2d 153].

"Neither Panhandle nor Baker involved a conflict between the two UCC provisions. The difference between the market price and the contract price placed the nonbreaching party in as good a position as that party would have been if the contract had been performed. The decisions can be distinguished from this case, however, in that Coop protected itself against market price fluctuations with the Bambino contract.

"There is authority for appellee's position that K.S.A. 84-2-713 should not be applied in certain circumstances. In Allied Canners & Packers, Inc. v. Victor Packing Co., 162 Cal. App. 3d 905, 209 Cal. Rptr. 60 (1984), Allied contracted to purchase 375,000 pounds of raisins from Victor for 29.75 cents per pound with a 4% discount. Allied then contracted to sell the raisins for 29.75 cents per pound expecting a profit of $4,462.50 from the 4% discount it received from Victor. 162 Cal. App. 3d at 907-08 [209 Cal. Rptr. 60].

"Heavy rains damaged the raisin crop and Victor breached its contract, being unable to fulfill the requirement. The market price of raisins had risen to about 80 cents per pound. Allied's buyers agreed to rescind their contracts so Allied was not bound to supply them with raisins at a severe loss. Therefore, the actual loss to Allied was the $4,462.50 profit it expected, while the difference between the market price and the contract price was about $150,000. 162 Cal. App. 3d at 908-09 [209 Cal. Rptr. 60].

"The California appellate court, in writing an exception, stated: 'It has been recognized that the use of the market-price contract-price formula under section 2-713 does not, absent pure accident, result in a damage award reflecting the buyer's actual loss. [Citations omitted.]' 162 Cal. App. 3d at 912 [209 Cal. Rptr. 60]. The court indicated that section 2-713 may be more of a statutory liquidated damages clause and, therefore, conflicts with the goal of section 1-106. The court discussed that in situations where the buyer has made a resale contract for the goods, which the seller knows about, it may be appropriate to limit 2-713 damages to actual loss. However, the court cited a concern that a seller not be rewarded for a bad faith breach of contract. 162 Cal. App. 3d at 912-14 [209 Cal. Rptr. 60].

"In Allied, the court determined that if the seller knew the buyer had a resale contract for the goods, and the seller did not breach the contract in bad faith, the buyer was limited to actual loss of damages under section 1-106. 162 Cal. App. 3d at 915 [209 Cal. Rptr. 60].

"The similarities between the present case and Allied are that the buyer made a resale contract which the seller knew about. (Tongish knew the seeds eventually went to Bambino, although he may not have known the details of the deal.) However, in examining the breach itself, Victor could not deliver the raisins because its crop had been destroyed. Tongish testified that he breached the contract because he was dissatisfied with dockage tests of Coop and/or Bambino. Victor had no raisins to sell to any buyer, while Tongish took advantage of the doubling price of sunflower seeds and sold to Danny Thomas. Although the trial court had no need to find whether Tongish breached the contract in bad faith, it did find there was no valid reason for the breach. Therefore, the nature of Tongish's breach was much different than Victor's in *Allied.*

"Section 2-713 and the theories behind it have a lengthy and somewhat controversial history. In 1963, it was suggested that 2-713 was a statutory liquidated damages clause and not really an effort to try and accurately predict what actual damages would be. Peters, *Remedies for Breach of Contracts Relating to the Sale of Goods Under the Uniform Commercial Code: A Roadmap for Article Two,* 73 Yale L.J. 199, 259 (1963).

"In 1978, Robert Childres called for the repeal of section 2-713. Childres, *Buyer's Remedies: The Danger of Section 2-713,* 72 Nw. U. L. Rev. 837 (1978). Childres reflected that because the market price/contract price remedy 'has been the cornerstone of Anglo-American damages' that it has been so hard to see that this remedy 'makes no sense whatever when applied to real life situations.' 72 Nw. U. L. Rev. at 841-42.

"In 1979, David Simon and Gerald A. Novack wrote a fairly objective analysis of the two arguments about section 2-713 and stated:

'For over sixty years our courts have divided on the question of which measure of damages is appropriate for the supplier's breach of his delivery obligations. The majority view, reinforced by applicable codes, would award market damages even though in excess of plaintiff's loss. A persistent minority would reduce market damages to the plaintiff's loss, without regard to whether this creates a windfall for the defendant. Strangely enough, each view has generally tended to disregard the arguments, and even the existence, of the opposing view.' Simon and Novack, *Limiting the Buyer's Market Damages to Lost Profits: A Challenge to the Enforceability of Market Contracts,* 92 Harv. L. Rev. 1395, 1397 (1979).

"Although the article discussed both sides of the issue, the authors came down on the side of market price/contract price as the preferred damages theory. The authors admit that market damages fly in the face 'of the familiar maxim that the purpose of contract damages is to make the injured party whole, not penalize the breaching party.' 92 Harv. L. Rev. at 1437. However, they argue that the market damages rule discourages the breach of contracts and encourages a more efficient market. 92 Harv. L. Rev. at 1437.

"The *Allied* decision in 1984, which relied on the articles cited above for its analysis to reject market price/contract price damages, has been sharply criticized. In Schneider, *UCC Section 2-713: A Defense of Buyers' Expectancy Damages,* 22 Cal. W. L. Rev. 233, 266 (1986), the author stated that *Allied* 'adopted the most restrictive [position] on buyer's damages. This Article is intended to reverse that trend.' Schneider argued that by following section 1-106, 'the court ignored the clear language of section 2-713's compensation scheme to award expectation damages in accordance with the parties' allocation of risk as measured by the difference between contract price and market price on the date set for performance.' 22 Cal. W. L. Rev. at 264.

"Recently in Scott, *The Case for Market Damages: Revisiting the Lost Profits Puzzle,* 57 U. Chi. L. Rev. 1155, 1200 (1990), the *Allied* result was called 'unfortunate.' Scott argues that section 1-106 is 'entirely consistent' with the market damages remedy of 2-713. 57 U. Chi. L. Rev. at 1201. According to Scott, it is possible to harmonize sections 1-106 and 2-713. Scott states, 'Market damages measure the expectancy ex ante, and thus reflect the value of the option; lost profits, on the other hand, measure losses ex post, and thus only reflect the value of the completed exchange.' 57 U. Chi. L. Rev. at 1174. The author argues that if the nonbreaching party has laid off part of the market risk (like Coop did) the lost profits rule creates instability because the other party is now encouraged to breach the contract if the market fluctuates to its advantage. 57 U. Chi. L. Rev. at 1178.

"We are not persuaded that the lost profits view under *Allied* should be embraced. It is a minority rule that has received only nominal support. We believe the majority rule or the market damages remedy as contained in K.S.A. 84-2-713 is more reasoned and should be followed as the preferred measure of damages. While application of the rule may not reflect the actual loss to a buyer, it encourages a more efficient market and discourages the breach of contracts." Tongish v. Thomas, 16 Kan. App. 2d at 811-17 [829 P.2d 916].

At first blush, the result reached herein appears unfair. However, closer scrutiny dissipates this impression. By the terms of the contract Coop was obligated to buy Tongish's large sunflower seeds at $13 per hundredweight whether or not it had a market for them. Had the price of sunflower seeds plummeted by delivery time, Coop's obligation to purchase at the agreed price was fixed. If loss of actual profit pursuant to K.S.A. 84-1-106(1) would be the measure of damages to be applied herein, it would enable Tongish to consider the Coop contract price of $13 per hundredweight plus 55 cents per hundredweight handling fee as the "floor" price for his seeds, take advantage of rapidly escalating prices, ignore his contractual obligation, and profitably sell to the highest bidder. Damages computed under K.S.A. 84-2-713 encourage the honoring of contracts and market stability. . . .

The judgment of the Court of Appeals reversing the district court and remanding the case for the determination and award of damages pursuant to the provisions of K.S.A. 84-2-713 is affirmed. The judgment of the district court is reversed.

Remedies Under the CISG Treaty. The damages provisions in the CISG for the international sale of goods are modeled after the similar provisions of the UCC and should look reassuringly familiar to you. Read Articles 74 to 78. There are some new words that the treaty must teach American ears. One is the concept of "fundamental breach," an idea that comes from the civil law. Read Articles 46(2) and 25. Fundamental breach is roughly equivalent to "material breach" (the opposite of "substantial performance"). The Restatement (Second) of Contracts §241 states:

> *Section 241. Circumstances Significant in Determining Whether a Failure Is Material*
>
> In determining whether a failure to render or to offer performance is material, the following circumstances are significant:
>
> (a) the extent to which the injured party will be deprived of the benefit which he reasonably expected;
>
> (b) the extent to which the injured party can be adequately compensated for the part of that benefit of which he will be deprived;
>
> (c) the extent to which the party failing to perform or to offer to perform will suffer forfeiture;
>
> (d) the likelihood that the party failing to perform or to offer to perform will cure his failure, taking account of all the circumstances including any reasonable assurances;
>
> (e) the extent to which the behavior of the party failing to perform or to offer to perform comports with standards of good faith and fair dealing.

Another new concept is *Nachfrist* (German for "extension"). It is illustrated in the following Problem.

PROBLEM 89

Experimental Transportation, Inc., of Los Angeles designed an all-terrain vehicle for rugged hill country travel (called the "Clod Jumper") and agreed to sell one for $30,000 to Dingo Ranch of Australia. Neither party was willing to be bound by the laws of the other's country, so they agreed to adopt the law of the CISG. Experimental Transportation was supposed to deliver the Clod Jumper by December 1, but it had problems with Customs and that date came and went with no activity. Dingo Ranch sent a letter to Experimental Transportation proposing that the date of delivery be moved to February 1. Having sent such a letter, is Dingo Ranch now bound to wait until that date before suing? See Article 47. Is Dingo Ranch bound to wait even if Experimental Transportation's reply is "Go to hell!"? What if instead of the buyer proposing the *Nachfrist,* the seller, Experimental Transportation, is the one to propose a grace period? Can this be done? Compare Articles 48 and 63. If the machine is delivered and then fails to work, can Dingo Ranch force Experimental Transportation to fix it? See Article 46(3). Is this remedy available in American law? See Uniform Commercial Code §2-716.

The treaty has a strong presumption in favor of specific performance. See Articles 46 and 62. However, Article 28 does not require specific performance if the court that would be asked to grant it would not do so if its own law applied. For example, in the United States there are major limits on equitable remedies (there must be no adequate remedy at law—i.e., damages; the court must not become involved in undue supervision of the resulting performance; etc.), and an American court might use these rules to duck an order for specific performance.

IV. ANTICIPATORY REPUDIATION

Ever since the classic case of Hochster v. De La Tour, 2 El. & Bl. 678, 118 Eng. Rep. 922 (Q.B. 1853), it has been settled that if one party to a contract makes a definite repudiation of the contract before the date set for performance, the other party could treat the repudiation as a breach and sue immediately. But the common law also permitted the innocent party to ignore the repudiation and await the performance date to see if the repudiator would retract the repudiation. As long as the innocent party had not changed position in reliance on the repudiation (say, by covering), the repudiator was free to retract the repudiation, reinstate the contract, and perform as originally agreed.

To what extent has the Code changed these common law rules? Read §§2-610 and 2-611. These sections do not define *repudiation,* which is, of course, their triggering event. A repudiation must be a definite refusal to perform; mere equivocation is not enough. See Official Comment 1 to §2-610; White & Summers §7-2; Copylease Corp. of Am. v. Memorex Corp., 403 F. Supp. 625 (S.D.N.Y. 1975). The equivocating party can be forced into performance or repudiation by use of the procedure outlined in §2-609 (Right to Adequate Assurance of Performance).

Unfortunately, in the process of drafting the Code's damages sections, the drafters became careless when dealing with the time for measuring damages in an anticipatory repudiation situation, and the UCC sections simply do not fit together. The following Problem should help you see the difficulty.

PROBLEM 90

The United States Army contracted with the Hawaiian Cattle Company for the purchase of 1,000 pounds of beef. Delivery was set six months later, on October 8, the agreed price to be $5,000. Shortly thereafter, the price of beef rose sharply, and Hawaiian Cattle repudiated the contract on July 10, when the price was $6,000. The Army's procurement officer scrambled around and on July 15 discovered it was possible to cover by buying similar cattle from Texas at a cost of $7,000. Instead, the Army sent Hawaiian Cattle a telegram stating that it did not accept or recognize the repudiation and expected performance on October 8. By October 8 the price had risen to $8,000. The Army decided not to cover at all and instead served the troops beans. As general counsel for the Army, advise the Army of the amount it can recover from Hawaiian Cattle. Read §§2-610, 2-713, and 2-723(1). Does it help reconcile these sections to know that the drafters of §2-713 were thinking of a buyer who learns of the repudiation *after* the date set for the original performance, not (as in this Problem) *before* the due date?

V. THE STATUTE OF LIMITATIONS

The Code drafters decided that it was important to have a uniform statute of limitations for transactions in goods, and they chose four years "as the most appropriate to modern business practice. This is within the normal commercial record keeping period." Official Comment to §2-725. Read §2-725, and note that the four-year period begins to run at the *accrual* of the cause of action (the moment a suit could be brought). The parties may reduce the period by agreement down to one year, but they may not extend it beyond four.

One court has decided that an agreement so reducing the limitation period need not be conspicuous to be enforced. Jandreau v. Sheesley Plumbing & Heating Co., 324 N.W.2d 266 (S.D. 1982). In most jurisdictions the statute of limitations is an affirmative defense and is waived if not pleaded and proved. See, e.g., Mysel v. Gross, 70 Cal. App. 3d 10, 138 Cal. Rptr. 873 (1977).

PROBLEM 91

Four years and two days after delivery of his new car, Joe Suburb came out of his house to discover he had a flat tire. He changed it and, for the first time, put on the spare tire. That afternoon as he was driving on the interstate, the tire burst due to a manufacturing flaw. Joe was killed. Has the statute of limitations run under these situations?

(a) The tire warranty read: "These tires are merchantable." If this were a lease of goods, would Article 2A reach a different result? See §2A-506.

(b) The tire warranty read: "These tires have a lifetime guarantee." See Kelleher v. Lumber, 152 N.H. 813, 891 A.2d 477 (2005); Rawls v. Associated Materials, LLC, 2011 WL 3297622 (S.D. W. Va. 2011); Annot., 93 A.L.R.3d 690.

(c) The sales material said with regard to the tires: "Many tires are still on the road after five years." See Jones & Laughlin Steel Corp. v. Johns-Manville Sales Corp. v. Brown & Kerr, Inc., 626 F.2d 280 (3d Cir. 1980) (a statement of future performance is "explicit" if it does not arise by implication, but is instead "distinctly stated; plain in language; clear; not ambiguous; express; unequivocal").

(d) The tire warranty read: "These tires are warranted for seven years from date of purchase." If a tire first malfunctioned at the beginning of the third year, when would the statute of limitations expire? See Joswick v. Chesapeake Mobile Homes, Inc., 765 A.2d 90 (Md. 2001).

(e) There were no express warranties given with regard to the tires; there were also no warranty disclaimers. See Note, When Does the Statute of Limitations Begin to Run on Breaches of Implied Warranties?, 30 Baylor L. Rev. 386 (1978).

Mydlach v. DaimlerChrysler Corporation

Supreme Court of Illinois, 2007
226 Ill. 2d 307, 314 Ill. Dec. 760, 875 N.E.2d 1047

Justice FITZGERALD delivered the judgment of the court, with opinion:

BACKGROUND

On June 20, 1998, plaintiff purchased a used 1996 Dodge Neon, manufactured by defendant, from McGrath Buick-Nissan (McGrath) in Elgin, Illinois. The vehicle was originally put into service on June 24, 1996, with a three-year/36,000-mile limited warranty. The warranty provided, in relevant part, as follows:

> The "Basic Warranty" begins on your vehicle's Warranty Start Date which is the earlier of (1) the date you take delivery of your new vehicle, OR (2) the date the vehicle was first put into service. . . .
>
> The "Basic Warranty" covers the cost of all parts and labor needed to repair any item on your vehicle (except as noted below) that's defective in material, workmanship, or factory preparation. You pay nothing for these repairs.
>
> The "Basic Warranty" covers every Chrysler-supplied part of your vehicle, EXCEPT its tires and cellular telephone.
>
> . . .
>
> These warranty repairs or adjustments (parts and labor) will be made by your dealer at no charge using new or remanufactured parts.
>
> . . .
>
> The "Basic Warranty" lasts for 36 months from the vehicle's Warranty Start Date OR for 36,000 miles on the odometer, whichever occurs first. (Emphasis in original.)

At the time of plaintiff's purchase in 1998, the car's mileage was 26,296. Thus, the warranty had approximately one year or 10,000 miles remaining.

Beginning July 7, 1998, plaintiff brought the car to McGrath and another authorized dealership several times for a variety of problems, including a recurring fluid leak. Plaintiff claimed that the dealerships' repair attempts were unsuccessful and, as a result, she could not use the vehicle as intended. Plaintiff ultimately filed suit against defendant on May 16, 2001, seeking legal and equitable relief, as well as attorney fees and costs, under the Magnuson-Moss Act. . . .

III

Although the Magnuson-Moss Act provides a private right of action for breach of a written warranty, the Act does not contain a limitations provision for such an action. Where a federal statute fails to specify a limitations period for suits under it, "courts apply the most closely analogous statute of limitations under state law." Del Costello v. International Brotherhood of Teamsters, 462 U.S. 151, 158, 103 S. Ct. 2281, 2287, 76 L. Ed. 2d 476, 485 (1983); accord Wilson v. Garcia, 471 U.S. 261, 268, 105 S. Ct. 1938, 1942, 85 L. Ed. 2d 254, 261 (1985); Teamsters & Employers Welfare Trust v. Gorman Brothers Ready Mix, 283 F.3d 877, 880 (7th Cir. 2002). In suits brought under the Magnuson-Moss Act, our appellate court, as well as courts in other jurisdictions, generally consider the UCC to be the most closely analogous statute and have borrowed the limitations provision contained therein. See, e.g., *Nowalski*, 335 Ill. App. 3d at 628, 269 Ill. Dec. 781, 781 N.E.2d 578 (collecting Illinois cases); Hillery v. Georgie Boy Manufacturing, Inc., 341 F. Supp. 2d 1112, 1114 (D. Ariz. 2004); Poli v. DaimlerChrysler Corp., 349 N.J. Super. 169, 181, 793 A.2d 104, 111 (2002); Murungi v. Mercedes Benz Credit Corp., 192 F. Supp. 2d 71, 79 (W.D.N.Y. 2001); Keller v. Volkswagen, 1999 PA Super. 153, ¶5, 733 A.2d 642. We agree with the foregoing authorities and will look to the limitations provision contained in the UCC to determine the timeliness of plaintiff's complaint. Specifically, we will look to article 2 of the UCC, which applies to "transactions in goods." 810 ILCS 5/2-102 (West 2006).

Section 2-725 of the UCC, titled "Statute of limitations in contracts for sale," generally provides a four-year limitations period:

> (1) An action for breach of any contract for sale must be commenced within 4 years after the cause of action has accrued. By the original agreement the parties may reduce the period of limitation to not less than one year but may not extend it.
>
> (2) A cause of action accrues when the breach occurs, regardless of the aggrieved party's lack of knowledge of the breach. A breach of warranty occurs when tender of delivery is made, except that where a warranty explicitly extends to future performance of the goods and discovery of the breach must await the time of such performance the cause of action accrues when the breach is or should have been discovered.

810 ILCS 5/2-725 (West 2006).

Preliminarily, we note that the future-performance exception to the four-year limitations period, set forth in subsection (2) above, is not at issue in this case. As will be discussed in greater detail below, a repair or replacement warranty like the one issued by defendant here "has nothing to do with the inherent quality of the goods or their future performance." *Cosman*, 285 Ill. App. 3d at 261, 220 Ill. Dec. 790, 674 N.E.2d 61. See also C. Reitz, Manufacturers' Warranties of Consumer Goods, 75 Wash. U. L.Q. 357, 364 n.24 (1997) ("Promises to repair or replace refer to future performance of sellers, not to future performance of goods"); L. Lawrence, Lawrence's Anderson on the Uniform Commercial Code §2-625:129, at 332 (3d ed. 2001) (discussing difference between a warranty of future performance and a covenant to repair or replace). Accordingly, we turn our attention to the balance of the statute and the parties' arguments relative thereto.

Defendant argues that section 2-725 should be applied as written. Thus, because the statute provides that a "breach of warranty occurs when tender of delivery is made," and tender of delivery of the Dodge Neon was first made in June 1996, plaintiff's suit, filed in May 2001, was untimely. See *Nowalski*, 335 Ill. App. 3d at 632, 269 Ill. Dec. 781, 781 N.E.2d 578 (holding that cause of action for breach of three-year/36,000-mile limited warranty accrued when the vehicle was delivered and not when defendant failed to successfully repair the vehicle). Plaintiff argues that a repair warranty cannot be breached until the manufacturer fails to repair the vehicle after a reasonable opportunity to do so, and that the appellate court did not err in finding her complaint was timely filed. See *Cosman,* 285 Ill. App. 3d at 260, 220 Ill. Dec. 790, 674 N.E.2d 61 (holding that breach of six-year/60,000-mile limited power-train warranty "cannot occur until Ford refuses or fails to repair the powertrain if and when it breaks"); Belfour v. Schaumburg Auto, 306 Ill. App. 3d 234, 241, 239 Ill. Dec. 383, 713 N.E.2d 1233 (1999) (following *Cosman* and holding that breach of three-year/50,000-mile repair warranty "cannot occur until Audi refuses or fails to repair the defect"); *Cogley,* 368 Ill. App. 3d at 96-97, 306 Ill. Dec. 243, 857 N.E.2d 336 (following *Cosman* and holding that suit for breach of three-year/36,000-mile repair warranty filed within four years of repair attempt was timely).[7]

We begin our analysis by turning to the language of article 2 of the UCC. Section 2-725(2) plainly states that "[a] breach of warranty occurs when tender of delivery is made." 810 ILCS 5/2-725(2) (West 2006). The *Nowalski* opinion, on which defendant relies, concluded that once article 2 of the UCC is chosen as the analogous state statute from which to borrow the statute of limitations, the analysis begins and ends with the "tender of delivery" language quoted above. *Nowalski,* 335 Ill. App. 3d at 632, 269 Ill. Dec. 781, 781 N.E.2d 578. We disagree.

Although courts generally consider article 2 of the UCC to be the statute most closely analogous to the Magnuson-Moss Act, the two enactments are not identical. For example, article 2 addresses warranties that are created by the "seller." See 810 ILCS 5/2-312, 2-313, 2-314, 2-315 (West 2006). The Magnuson-Moss Act, however, addresses warranties from a "supplier" or "warrantor" who may or may not be the immediate seller. See 15 U.S.C. §§2301(4), (5), (6) (1994). In addition, the term "warranty," as used in the two enactments, is not the same. As discussed above, the Act speaks of implied warranties and written warranties, the latter of which may be either full or limited. 15 U.S.C. §§2301(6), (7), 2303 (1994). In contrast, the UCC speaks of express warranties (which may be oral or written), implied warranties, and warranty of title. 810 ILCS 5/2-312, 2-313, 2-314, 2-315 (West 2006).

Although the parties agree that defendant's warranty is a "written warranty" under the Magnuson-Moss Act, they disagree as to whether the warranty is an "express warranty" under the UCC. Defendant argues that the repair warranty qualifies as an express warranty and that plaintiff's claim

7. The same divergence of opinion on the limitations issue that is exemplified by *Nowalski* and *Cosman* exists among our sister states. See generally L. Garvin, Uncertainty and Error in the Law of Sales: The Article Two Statute of Limitations, 83 B.U. L. Rev. 345, 377-81 (2003) (discussing the split among state courts in their approach to repair or replacement promises).

is therefore governed by the tender-of-delivery rule in section 2-725(2). Plaintiff argues that it does not qualify as an express warranty and that her claim is not subject to the tender-of-delivery rule.

Section 2-313 of the UCC explains how express warranties are created.

> Express warranties by the seller are created as follows:
>
> (a) Any affirmation of fact or promise made by the seller to the buyer which relates to the goods and becomes part of the basis of the bargain creates an express warranty that the goods shall conform to the affirmation or promise.
>
> (b) Any description of the goods which is made part of the basis of the bargain creates an express warrant
>
> (c) Any sample or model which is made part of the basis of the bargain creates an express warranty that the whole of the goods shall conform to the sample or model." 810 ILCS 5/2-313(1) (West 2006).

The UCC makes plain that an express warranty is related to the quality or description of the goods. See Moorman Manufacturing Co. v. National Tank Co., 91 Ill. 2d 69, 78, 61 Ill. Dec. 746, 435 N.E.2d 443 (1982) (observing that UCC warranty rules "determine the quality of the product the manufacturer promises and thereby determine the quality he must deliver"); Alloway v. General Marine Industries, L.P., 149 N.J. 620, 630, 695 A.2d 264, 269 (1997) (stating that "the U.C.C. provides for express warranties regarding the quality of goods"); Allis-Chalmers Credit Corp. v. Herbolt, 17 Ohio App. 3d 230, 233, 17 OBR 496, 479 N.E.2d 293, 297 (1984) (identifying UCC express warranties as one of the "warranties of quality"); 1 W. Hawkland, Uniform Commercial Code Series §2-313.4, at 546 (2002) ("express warranties relate exclusively to quality, description and title of the goods and have nothing to do with the other terms of the contract").

In other words, an express warranty, for purposes of the UCC, obligates the seller to deliver goods that conform to the affirmation, promise, description, sample or model. If a seller delivers conforming goods, the warranty is satisfied. If the seller delivers nonconforming goods, the warranty is breached at that time. Even if the buyer is unaware that the goods, as delivered, do not conform to the seller's affirmation, promise, description, sample or model, the warranty has been breached. Under this scenario, the statutory pronouncement that "[a] breach of warranty occurs when tender of delivery is made" (810 ILCS 5/2-725(2) (West 2006)) makes perfect sense, and the four-year limitations period commences at that time. See M. Klinger, The Concept of Warranty Duration: A Tangled Web, 89 Dick. L. Rev. 935, 939 (1985) ("Section 2-725(2) presumes that all warranties, expressed or implied, relate only to the condition of the goods at the time of sale" and "[a]s a result, the period of limitations begins to run at that time"); L. Garvin, Uncertainty and Error in the Law of Sales: The Article Two Statute of Limitations, 83 B.U. L. Rev. 345, 379 (2003) ("Article Two defines a range of express and implied warranties" which "[a]ll go to the quality of the goods at tender").

The warranty in the present case, however, is not related to the quality or description of the goods at tender. It does not warrant that the vehicle will conform to some affirmation, promise, description, sample or model. Rather, the warranty promises only that the manufacturer will repair or replace defective parts during the warranty period. As defendant made clear in its brief before this court:

> DaimlerChrysler's limited warranty was not a promise that the vehicle would be defect free and in the event of a breach of warranty, Plaintiff would be limited to repair or replacement of the vehicle. Rather, DaimlerChrysler's limited warranty promised to cover the cost to repair or replace defective parts in the automobile for the time period covering 36 months or 36 thousand miles.

Although defendant's warranty qualifies as a "written warranty" under the Act, it is not an "express warranty" under the UCC, and is thus not the type of warranty that can be breached on "tender of delivery" (810 ILCS 5/2-725(2) (West 2006)). See *Cogley*, 368 Ill. App. 3d at 96, 306 Ill. Dec. 243, 857 N.E.2d 336; *Cosman*, 285 Ill. App. 3d at 258-60, 220 Ill. Dec. 790, 674 N.E.2d 61; C. Dewitt, Note, Action Accrual Date for Written Warranties to Repair: Date of Delivery or Date of Failure to Repair, 17 U. Mich. J.L. Reform 713, 722 n.35 (1984) (promise to repair "relates not to the goods and their quality, but to the manufacturer and its obligation to the purchaser," and thus "a repair 'warranty' falls beyond the scope of . . . the on-delivery rule"); C. Reitz, Manufacturers' Warranties of Consumer Goods, 75 Wash. U. L.Q. 357, 364 n.24 (1997) (tender-of-delivery date for commencement of four-year UCC limitations provision is "completely inappropriate to promises to repair or replace goods that are later determined to be defective"). Accordingly, we reject defendant's argument that the four-year limitations period for breach of the repair warranty commenced upon delivery of the Dodge Neon in 1996, and we overrule the *Nowalski* opinion on which defendant relies.

Our conclusion that the repair warranty is not a UCC express warranty, and thus not subject to the tender-of-delivery rule set forth in the second sentence of section 2-725(2), does not render section 2-725(2) irrelevant for purposes of determining when the limitations period began on plaintiff's claim under the Magnuson-Moss Act. The first sentence of section 2-725(2) remains applicable. The first sentence states: "[a] cause of action accrues when the breach occurs, regardless of the aggrieved party's lack of knowledge of the breach." (Emphasis added.) 810 ILCS 5/2-725(2) (West 2006).

Although the UCC does not expressly state when the breach of a repair promise occurs, we may refer to the law that exists outside of the UCC. See 810 ILCS 5/1-103 (West 2006) ("Unless displaced by the particular provisions of this Act, the principles of law and equity . . . shall supplement its provisions"); L. Lawrence, Lawrence's Anderson on the Uniform Commercial Code §2-725:99, at 301 (3d ed. 2001) (because the UCC provides no assistance as to when a nonwarranty breach of contract "occurs" for purposes of computing the limitations period, "it is necessary to resort to the general non-Code law of contracts," which "has not been displaced by the Code and therefore continues in force").

Generally, "[w]hen performance of a duty under a contract is due any non-performance is a breach." Restatement (Second) of Contracts §235, at 211 (1979). Performance under a vehicle manufacturer's promise to repair or replace defective parts is due not at tender of delivery, but only when, and if, a covered defect arises and repairs are required. In that event, if the promised repairs are refused or unsuccessful, the repair warranty is breached and the cause of action accrues, triggering the four-year limitations period. See *Cosman*, 285 Ill. App. 3d at 260, 220 Ill. Dec. 790, 674 N.E.2d 61 (holding that breach of six-year/60,000-mile limited power-train warranty "cannot occur until Ford refuses or fails to repair the power train if and when it breaks"); *Belfour*, 306 Ill. App. 3d at 241, 239 Ill. Dec. 383, 713 N.E.2d 1233 (holding that breach of three-year/50,000-mile repair warranty "cannot occur until Audi refuses or fails to repair the defect"); *Cogley*, 368 Ill. App. 3d at 96-97, 306 Ill. Dec. 243, 857 N.E.2d 336 (holding that suit for breach of three-year/36,000-mile repair warranty filed within four years of repair attempt was timely). See also Monticello v. Winnebago Industries, Inc., 369 F. Supp. 2d 1350, 1356-57 (N.D. Ga. 2005) (under Georgia law, a written warranty that provides for repair or replacement of parts is breached when the purchaser returns the product to the dealer for repair and repair is refused or unsuccessful); *Poli*, 349 N.J. Super. at 180, 793 A.2d at 110-11 (under New Jersey law, cause of action for breach of seven-year/70,000-mile power-train warranty would not have accrued when the car was delivered, but rather when persistent problems appeared or when DaimlerChrysler was unable to repair the defect); Long Island Lighting Co. v. Imo Industries Inc., 6 F.3d 876, 889-90 (2d Cir. 1993) (under New York law, cause of action for breach of a repair promise accrued when the generator malfunctioned and the seller refused to make the necessary repairs).

This is the approach advocated by some commentators. For example, in his discussion of the appropriate treatment of a manufacturer's express warranty to repair or replace defective parts, Professor Lawrence states:

> The sounder approach is to recognize that the failure to repair or replace is merely a breach of contract and not a breach of warranty, and therefore

> no cause of action arises until the seller has refused to repair or replace the goods. This is because until the seller has failed or refused to make the repairs or provide a replacement, the buyer, not being entitled to such a remedy, has no right to commence an action for damages. As a result, the action is timely if brought within four years of the seller's failure or refusal.

L. Lawrence, Lawrence's Anderson on the Uniform Commercial Code §2-725:101, at 303 (3d ed. 2001). Accord L. Garvin, Uncertainty and Error in the Law of Sales: The Article Two Statute of Limitations, 83 B.U. L. Rev. 345, 381 (2003).

The correctness of this approach is manifest when we consider consumer claims for breach of repair warranties that run for periods longer than the three years/36,000 miles at issue here. For example, consider the case of a consumer who purchases a vehicle carrying a five-year/50,000-mile repair warranty. If the four-year limitations period commences at "tender of delivery," the limitations period for a breach of the repair promise occurring in year five will expire before the breach even occurs, thus rendering the repair warranty unenforceable during its final year. Statutes of limitations, however, are intended "to prevent stale claims, not to preclude claims before they are ripe for adjudication." Guzman v. C.R. Epperson Construction, Inc., 196 Ill. 2d 391, 400, 256 Ill. Dec. 827, 752 N.E.2d 1069 (2001). Even a four-year warranty could be rendered unenforceable if breach of the repair promise occurred near the end of the warranty period. In that case, the buyer would have only the briefest of periods in which to file suit. See Nationwide Insurance Co., 533 Pa. at 434, 625 A.2d at 1178.

Defendant argues that concerns about the enforceability of longer-term repair warranties are inapplicable to the facts of this case and without merit. We disagree. Although the repair warranty at issue here ran for three years, our holding in this case will apply equally to longer-term warranties. Such warranties are common in the automobile industry. Adoption of defendant's position would be an invitation to manufacturers and sellers of automobiles, as well as other goods, to engage in misleading marketing. That is, a manufacturer or seller could use the marketing advantage of a longer repair warranty, yet escape the accompanying obligations of that warranty by pleading the statute of limitations in defense. C. Williams, The Statute of Limitations, Prospective Warranties, and Problems of Interpretation in Article Two of the UCC, 52 Geo. Wash. L. Rev. 67, 105 (1983). Such a result is contrary to the very purpose of the Magnuson-Moss Act: "to improve the adequacy of information available to consumers" and "prevent deception." 15 U.S.C. §2302(a) (1994).

Defendant also argues that unless the tender-of-delivery rule in section 2-725 is given effect, the limitations period for breach of limited warranty actions will be "limitless" and "uncertain." This argument is without merit. Because the promise to repair or replace defective parts is only good during the warranty period, the latest a breach of warranty can occur is at the very end of that period. Accordingly, the statute of limitations will expire, at the latest, four years after the warranty period has run. If breach of a repair warranty occurs earlier in the warranty period, the limitations period for that breach will expire sooner, but in no event will the warrantor's exposure extend beyond the warranty period, plus four years. Thus, contrary to defendant's argument, commencing the four-year limitations period from the date the warrantor fails or refuses to repair the vehicle does not result in a limitless limitations period.

We recognize, of course, that a fact question may arise as to the date on which a repair warranty was breached which, in turn, would create some uncertainty as to when the four-year limitations period should commence. Fact questions of this nature, however, frequently arise in cases where the statute of limitations has been pled in defense. Resolution of this type of uncertainty is a classic function of the trier of fact. See, e.g., County of Du Page v. Graham, Anderson, Probst & White, Inc., 109 Ill. 2d 143, 153-54, 92 Ill. Dec. 833, 485 N.E.2d 1076 (1985) (remanding the matter to the circuit court for a factual determination as to when the statute of limitations began to run against the county on its claims for defective design and construction of the county's administration building); Knox College v. Celotex Corp., 88 Ill. 2d 407, 417, 58 Ill. Dec. 725, 430 N.E.2d 976 (1981) (holding that trier of fact must determine when the plaintiff had sufficient information as to the roof defect to start the running of the limitations period); Witherell v. Weimer, 85 Ill. 2d 146, 156, 52 Ill. Dec. 6, 421 N.E.2d 869 (1981) ("In many, if not most, cases the time at which an injured party knows or reasonably should have known both of his injury and that it was wrongfully caused will be a disputed question to be resolved by the finder of fact"). We therefore reject defendant's argument that commencing the limitations period when the warrantor fails or refuses to repair the defect—rather than at tender of delivery—will create unacceptable uncertainty in the limitations period.

Turning to the facts of this case, the record indicates that plaintiff brought her vehicle to McGrath and another authorized dealer on several occasions beginning in July 1998. At that point, assuming the alleged defects were covered defects, defendant was obligated (through its authorized dealer) to make good on its repair promise. Plaintiff's lawsuit, filed in May 2001, is therefore timely. Accordingly, we affirm that portion of the judgment of the appellate court which reversed the grant of summary judgment in favor of defendant as to count I of the complaint.

Affirmed in part and reversed in part; cause remanded.

PROBLEM 92

If the manufacturer of a vehicle sold it to the dealership, and the dealership then resold the vehicle to a consumer, would the four-year period on the manufacturer's *implied* warranty start running on the date of delivery to the dealership or on the date of the sale to the ultimate consumer? See Wilson v. Class, 605 A.2d 907 (Del. Super. 1992). Would we reach the same result on an *express* warranty given by the manufacturer?

PROBLEM 93

Painter Sally Smock had no luck selling her own works, but made good money by creating phony works supposedly by Salvador Dali, signing Dali's name to them, and selling them to DaDa Gallery. In 2025, DaDa Gallery unwittingly sold two of Smock's forgeries to Mr. and Mrs. America, tourists who paid $150,000. The Americas proudly exhibited the supposed Dalis in their Cincinnati living room, until 2030 when Smock made the national news as she went to jail for art forgery. The Americas then sued DaDa Gallery for breach of express warranty, only to be met with the argument that the statute of limitations under §2-725 had run out. How should this come out? See Balog v. Center Art Gallery, 745 F. Supp. 1556 (D. Haw. 1990); Doss, Inc. v. Christie's, Inc., 2009 WL 3053713 (S.D.N.Y. 2009) (holding that a cause of action for selling a painting, which had been stolen by the Nazis from a Paris art dealer, accrued in 1991 when the painting was sold by Christie's, not in 2006 when there was a challenge to the buyer's ownership); Equinox Gallery Ltd. v. Dorfman, 306 F. Supp. 3d 560 (S.D.N.Y. 2018).

PROBLEM 94

In 2027, Notheby's Auction Company sold Max Collector a painting expressly warranted to be by Degas for $1 million. Experts hired by Notheby's had all agreed it was created by Degas in 1886. In 2044, Max Collector sold the painting to Grandiose Museum for $5 million, making an express warranty that it was by Degas. Two years later, the museum learned conclusively that the painting was in fact a forgery created in 1923. It sued Max Collector for return of the purchase price. Does Max Collector have an indemnification action against Notheby's, or has the statute of limitations expired on that claim? See §2-725 and the following case.[8]

8. Some states regulate art authenticity problems by special statute; see L. Garvin, Uncertainty and Error in the Law of Sales: The Article Two Statute of Limitations, 83 B.U. L. Rev. 345, 371 n.116 (2003), citing Fla. Stat. Ann. §686.504; Mich. Comp. Laws Ann. §442.322; N.Y. Arts & Cult. Aff. Law §13.01; R.I. Gen. Laws §5-62-9(1).

Central Washington Refrigeration, Inc. v. Barbee

Supreme Court of Washington, 1997
133 Wash. 2d 509, 946 P.2d 760

SANDERS, Justice.

We are asked whether a buyer of goods may bring an indemnity action against the seller for liability incurred to a third party for a defect in the goods, and, if so, when the statute of limitations begins to run. We hold a buyer may maintain such indemnity action and that the statute of limitations begins to run when the buyer pays damages to the third party or the third party obtains judgment against the buyer, whichever is first in time.

In 1987 petitioner Central Washington Refrigeration, Inc. (Central) contracted with a Yakima orchard to install a set of cold storage rooms to store apples and other fruit. Central in turn contracted with respondent McCormack Engineering (McCormack) to purchase the refrigeration coils which Central was to install. Pursuant to the sales agreement McCormack specially manufactured the coils according to Central's specifications and timely delivered them in August 1987 at which time Central installed the coils in the cold storage rooms.

From the start, however, the orchard experienced problems with the cold storage rooms. After several repair attempts and an intervening bankruptcy by the orchard, the orchard defaulted on payments for the cold storage rooms and Central subsequently sued for payment. In March 1989 the orchard counterclaimed for damages asserting Central misdesigned the cold storage system, used poor workmanship in building it, installed improper components, and failed to repair the system.

On May 22, 1992—over four-and-a-half years after McCormack delivered the coils—Central filed a third-party complaint against McCormack alleging the coils were defective and caused all the problems, seeking contribution and/or indemnity from McCormack for any damages due the orchard from Central. [The court below held that] to the extent Central's claim was either contractual or for indemnity, it was barred by the four-year U.C.C. statute of limitations governing contracts. Central Washington Refrigeration, Inc. v. Barbee, 81 Wash. App. 212, 220, 223-24, 913 P.2d 836 (1996). We granted review to determine whether a buyer may maintain an indemnity action against the seller based on breach of warranty, and, if so, when the applicable statute of limitations commences to run. . . .

Indemnity in its most basic sense means reimbursement (Black's Law Dictionary 769 (6th ed. 1990)) and may lie when one party discharges a liability which another should rightfully have assumed. Stevens v. Security Pac. Mortgage Corp., 53 Wash. App. 507, 517, 768 P.2d 1007, *review denied*, 112 Wash. 2d 1023 (1989) ("Indemnity requires full reimbursement and transfers liability from the one who has been compelled to pay damages to another who should bear the entire loss.").[9]

While indemnity sounds in contract and tort it is a separate equitable cause of action. The variety of indemnity relevant to this case is implied contractual indemnity, also referenced to as "implied in fact" indemnity. Such arises when one party incurs a liability the other party should discharge by virtue of the nature of the relationship between the two parties. . . . The nature of the relationship between the parties gives rise to the right of implied indemnity. . . .[10] The question here is whether the contractual relationship between buyer and seller under the U.C.C. is sufficient to give rise to an implied right of indemnity when a defect in the good causes damage to a third party user and such defect constitutes breach of seller's warranties.

A minority of courts addressing the issue under comparable facts has found the contractual relationship between buyer and seller under the U.C.C. insufficient to give rise to an indemnity action. See, e.g., Perry v. Pioneer Wholesale Supply Co., 681 P.2d 214, 219 (Utah 1984). Jurisdictions following this minority rule are Utah, Idaho, and South Dakota. The minority rule would view Central's claim as nothing more than a claim for damages under a sales contract between merchants for breach of implied warranties resulting in consequential damages owed to a third party.[11] Use of the label "indemnity" would not alter the perception that the action still sounds in contract. The claim would be governed in whole by the U.C.C. Under the U.C.C. actions for breach of contract must be commenced within four years of date of delivery of goods regardless of when the buyer discovers the

9. See also McDermott v. City of New York, 50 N.Y.2d 211, 406 N.E.2d 460, 462, 428 N.Y.S.2d 643 (1980) ("Conceptually, implied indemnification finds its roots in the principles of equity. It is nothing short of simple fairness to recognize that '[a] person who, in whole or in part, has discharged a duty which is owed by him but which as between himself and another should have been discharged by the other, is entitled to indemnity' (Restatement, Restitution, §76). To prevent unjust enrichment, courts have assumed the duty of placing the obligation where in equity it belongs.").

10. See 42 C.J.S. Indemnity §31, at 121 (1991) ("A right to indemnity, while not implied in every contract or contractual relationship, may be claimed on the basis of an implied contract, which can arise either from the conduct of the parties or be implied from the nature of their relationship, whether it be a contractual or other legal relationship, and from given warranties and covenants, or be otherwise implied from unique special factors indicating the parties' intent that the party from whom indemnity is sought should be ultimately liable.") (citations omitted).

11. Two legal commentaries argue the minority rule has it right. See Paul J. Wilkinson, An Ind. Run Around the U.C.C.: The Use (or Abuse?) of Indemnity, 20 Pepp. L. Rev. 1407, 1438 (1993) (such "indemnity" actions are nothing more than actions for consequential damages resulting from breach of contract and there is no reason to treat consequential damages paid to a third party any differently from any other damages incurred as a result of a breach of contract); Thomas A. Leggette, When Can an Implied Indemnity Cause of Action Be Used to End-Run a Limitations Bar?, 42 Fed'n Ins. & Corp. Couns. Q. 33, 33 (1991) (a party should not be able to end-run the strict four-year U.C.C. statute of limitations period for suing on contracts by simply denominating the action one for "indemnity").

defect. Because Central failed to bring its claim against McCormack within four years of delivery, its suit would be time-barred under the minority rule. The Court of Appeals chose to follow the minority rule.

Central, however, argues the minority rule errs in failing to recognize an indemnity claim here. We agree. Central points to the majority of courts addressing the issue which have ruled the contractual relationship between buyer and seller under the U.C.C. is a sufficient relationship to give rise to an implied right of indemnity. Jurisdictions following the majority rule include California, Maine, Michigan, Minnesota, Missouri, Nebraska, New Hampshire, New York, North Carolina, Pennsylvania, and Virginia.

A clear statement of the majority rule appears in Bellevue South Assocs. v. HRH Constr. Corp., 78 N.Y.2d 282, 579 N.E.2d 195, 574 N.Y.S.2d 165 (1991). In Bellevue a subcontractor installed defective floor tiles in an apartment complex and was sued by the apartment complex owner. The subcontractor eventually sued the tile manufacturer for indemnity, seeking to shift the entire liability, alleging the manufacturer breached the implied warranties. The manufacturer argued the suit was nothing more than one on the contract and thus the U.C.C. four-year statute of limitations must govern to bar the suit. The New York high court rejected the manufacturer's argument, concluding the contractual relationship and the U.C.C.'s implied warranties provided "the requisite basis for an indemnification claim." Id., 574 N.Y.S.2d at 171, 579 N.E.2d at 201.

We adopt the majority rule and hold a contractual relationship under the U.C.C., with its implied warranties, provides sufficient basis for an implied indemnity claim when the buyer incurs liability to a third party as a result of a defect in the goods which would constitute a breach of the seller's implied or express warranties. In so holding we acknowledge "[t]here is a substantial difference between an instance where a product simply fails as opposed to a situation where the product fails and causes damage to a third party." Carrier Corp. v. Detrex Corp., 4 Cal. App. 4th 1522, 6 Cal. Rptr. 2d 565, 569 (1992). We also understand our decision to join the majority camp comports with the equitable principles underlying indemnity.[12]

12. See, e.g., City of Willmar v. Short-Elliott-Hendrickson, Inc., 512 N.W.2d 872, 874 (1994) (indemnity is an equitable action and "is not based on contract or tort, although either may secondarily be involved, but on one party paying more than its fair share."); City of Clayton v. Grumman Emergency Prods., Inc., 576 F. Supp. 1122, 1127 (E.D. Mo. 1983) ("A party who buys and then resells a product is not in a position to discover the latent defect within the warranty's limitation period because the product is in the hands of the consumer during that time. Only when the consumer sues the retailer does the retailer gain notice of the latent defect."). We note indemnity may not be available when equity does not so require. See Sheehan v. Morris Irr., Inc., 460 N.W.2d 413, 417 (S.D. 1990); Farmers Nat'l Bank v. Wickham Pipeline Constr., 114 Idaho 565, 759 P.2d 71, 75 (1988) (equity does not require an indemnity action to be recognized where parties could have sued at law but slept on their rights). As the parties have not so requested, we refrain from assessing the particular equities in this case.

The remaining question is when the statute of limitations commences to run on the indemnity claim. Indemnity actions are distinct, separate causes of action from the underlying wrong and are governed by separate statutes of limitations. It is settled law that indemnity actions accrue when the party seeking indemnity pays or is legally adjudged obligated to pay damages to a third party. The statute of limitations on the indemnity action therefore begins to run at that point. . . .

Thus, the statute of limitations on Central's alleged indemnity claim began to run when Central paid the orchard to settle the orchard's claims. Because Central brought suit at the same time it settled, we hold its indemnity action is not time barred. Central's indemnification suit must be determined on its merits. The Court of Appeals is reversed, the case is remanded for trial and Central shall recover its costs on appeal.

Guy, Justice (dissenting).

Article 2 of the Uniform Commercial Code (U.C.C.) establishes one general law governing all commercial sales for the purpose of providing predictability and consistency for all commercial sales transactions. In my view the majority opinion is inconsistent with this purpose. By holding contract-based indemnity claims are outside the U.C.C.'s four-year statute of repose, RCW 62A.2-725, the majority leaves commercial retailers susceptible to indemnity claims indefinitely.[13] Therefore, I dissent.

The transaction between Central and McCormack was a sale of goods. I would hold that any claim stemming from this commercial sales transaction, including one for indemnity, is governed by article 2 of the U.C.C. and its four-year statute of repose. Further, I would hold that Central's claim for indemnity was time barred since it was raised after the four-year time period had expired.

The majority is compelled by the belief that this court must follow the lead of other jurisdictions and find that when commercial buyers have paid damages to a third party due to defective products purchased from a commercial retailer, the buyer has two avenues for compensation. The jurisdictions on which the majority relies found that such commercial buyers not only have a breach of warranty claim against the commercial retailer under article 2 but also have an implied right of indemnity against the retailer founded in common law and governed by general statutes of limitations.

13. Although a third party's claim against a commercial buyer for breach of warranty continues to be bound by the four-year time period, under the majority opinion there is no predictability as to how long a commercial retailer will be held liable for indemnity. Because accrual of an indemnity claim against a commercial retailer does not occur until a judgment is entered against a commercial buyer or when a commercial buyer pays damages to a third party, a commercial retailer cannot predict on what date an action for indemnity will accrue against it.

The majority does not thoroughly discuss why this policy decision is correct but instead places great importance on the fact that a "majority" of other jurisdictions follow it. Contrary to the majority's conclusion, there is no majority/minority view on whether indemnity claims are independent of the U.C.C. Rather, there exists a split of authority. Four states, South Dakota, Idaho, Utah and Georgia, find that such claims fall exclusively under the U.C.C. Courts in six states, Minnesota, California, New York, Nebraska, New Hampshire and Maine, hold indemnity claims may be raised independent of the U.C.C. Therefore, there exists authority from other jurisdictions to support both sides of this policy debate as to whether all contract-based claims, including those of indemnity, are bound by the U.C.C. I would hold that a decision finding contract-based indemnity claims are governed by the U.C.C. is correct because it creates a policy consistent with the purpose of the U.C.C. — one of predictability and uniformity.

Although the jurisdictions cited by the majority claim fairness requires that a commercial buyer who pays out-of-pocket damages to a third party has a remedy unrestricted by a statute of repose, I believe at some point the law must recognize commercial practices and concepts, including the concept of bargained-for risk. Commercial buyers do not purchase items with the notion they are receiving an implied lifetime guarantee. They know products may not last forever. However, there does exist an implied warrantability that lasts for four years after delivery, in order to create a balance between fairness and bargained-for risk. The U.C.C. has identified this four-year period, commencing at the time of delivery, as a fair period of time for a commercial buyer to expect guaranteed warrantability and a commercial retailer to expect to be held liable.

Section 2-725 was adopted to "[take] sales contracts out of the general laws limiting the time for commencing contractual actions and selects a four-year period as the most appropriate to modern business practice. This is within the normal commercial record keeping period." RCWA 62A.2-725 U.C.C. cmt. at 415 (Purposes). Section 2-725 provides "a time when [a merchant] ought to be secure in his reasonable expectation that the slate has been wiped clean of ancient obligations, and he ought not to be called on to resist a claim when 'evidence has been lost, memories have faded, and witnesses have disappeared.' " Paul J. Wilkinson, Comment, An Ind. Run Around the U.C.C.: The Use (or Abuse?) of Indemnity, 20 Pepp. L. Rev. 1407, 1412 (1993) (quoting Developments in the Law, Statutes of Limitations, 63 Harv. L. Rev. 1177, 1185 (1950)). These comments illustrate the U.C.C.'s goal to establish an across-the-board governing law for all commercial sales transactions that adequately addresses fairness and bargained-for risk. By allowing a common law remedy in a commercial sale relationship, the majority contradicts this goal. In order to remain consistent with the purpose of the U.C.C.,

I would hold that Central's action against McCormack is governed by article 2 and that section 2-725 applies.

I would also hold that Central's action, under article 2, is barred under section 2-725. In my view, section 2-725 is a statute of repose, not a statute of limitation. A statute of limitation bars plaintiffs from bringing an already accrued claim after a specified period of time; a statute of repose terminates a right of action after a specified time, even if the injury has not yet occurred. . . .

The language of U.C.C. §2-725 unambiguously creates a statute of repose. Because it is unambiguous, the meaning of the statute is derived from the words of the statute. State v. McDougal, 120 Wash. 2d 334, 350, 841 P.2d 1232 (1992); State v. Olson, 47 Wash. App. 514, 516, 735 P.2d 1362 (1987). The statute states a claim must be made within "four years after the cause of action has accrued." RCW 62A.2-725(1). According to the statute "[a] cause of action accrues when the breach occurs," and "[a] breach of warranty occurs when tender of delivery is made. . . ." RCW 62A.2-725(2). Therefore, all claims must be made no more than four years after delivery, whether or not the buyer is aware of the product's defect. Based on this clear language, I would hold that Central's contractual indemnity claim, based on the breach of an implied warranty, was barred when the action was filed in May 1992, since the coils were delivered more than four and a half years earlier—in August 1987.

Section 2-725 actually "poses few problems: it simply bars a buyer from bringing an action for breach of warranty more than four years after tender of delivery. This straight-forward rule forces buyers to sue when evidence is most readily available and allows sellers to continue with their businesses without fear of suit after a reasonable definite period." Debra L. Goetz et al., Project, Article Two Warranties in Commercial Transactions: An Update, 72 Cornell L. Rev. 1159, 1324-29 (1987).

I would find that Central's claim is governed by U.C.C. §2-725, a statute of repose, and was properly dismissed by the trial court. I would affirm the decision of the Court of Appeals.

Tolling. Finally note that (4) of §2-725 preserves "the law on tolling of the statute of limitation." What does this mean? All states have special statutes or court-made rules that stop the running of the usual statute of limitations if something has happened to make it inappropriate to allow it to expire: the defendant cannot be served with legal process, for example, or the defendant concealed the defect that would have led to the lawsuit if known; see Laurel Grocery Company, LLC v. Freshway, Inc., 2019 WL 7290469 (.E. D. Ky. 2019) (seller cooked the accounting books so that buyer could not discover the fraud); Canfield v. FCA US LLC, 2019 WL 1089798 (D. Del. 2019) (seller sold product that was known to always fail shortly after sale and fraudulently concealed this information).

CHAPTER 7 REVIEW QUESTIONS

When is a seller entitled to reclaim the goods?
Is a penalty clause for nonperformance enforceable?
When is a breaching buyer entitled to restitution?
Why is the measure of remedies different depending on whether the goods were accepted?
Can buyer be liable for the price if seller breached?
Can seller be liable if buyer has effectively rejected the goods?
Can *buyer* be liable if buyer has effectively rejected the goods?
What is the difference, in seller's remedies, between market price damages, resale damages, and lost profits damages?
When is a party liable for consequential damages?
How might buyer's damages differ for breach of warranty and for failure to deliver?

ASSESSMENT: MULTIPLE CHOICE QUESTIONS

1. Cold Feet Labs entered into a contract to purchase a popular genetic sequencing machine from Precision Devices. The machine was delivered on time and met all the contract specifications. The manager of Cold Feet Labs inspected the machine and found no problems, but refused to take delivery. The manager cited budgetary concerns. The market price for the machine had become lower than the contract price, so it would be cheaper to buy the machine elsewhere. How much is the liability of Cold Feet Labs to Precision Devices?
   a. Cold Feet Labs is liable for the contract price, because the seller tendered conforming goods in timely fashion.
   b. Cold Feet Labs is liable for the market price of the machine.
   c. Cold Feet Labs is not liable for anything, because Precision Devices still has the machine.
   d. Cold Feet Labs could be liable for the difference between the contract price and the market price.

2. Pursuant to contract, Gdansk Boats delivered a wooden sailing ship to Historic Cruises. The purchasing agent for Historic Cruises inspected the ship, and quickly noted that many of the fixtures were mahogany rather than the promised teak, that various repairs and adjustments would be required in some of the cabins, and that several sails were missing. Historic Cruises indicated they would take the ship but sue for breach of contract, listing the defects. Is Gdansk Boats liable to Historic Cruises?
   a. No. Historic Cruises accepted the goods and must pay the contract price.

b. Yes. Historic Cruises is liable for the price, but has a counterclaim for damages for breach of warranty, which could be the difference between the value of the boat promised and the boat delivered, and possible consequential damages.
c. Yes. Gdansk Boats did not deliver the boat promised, so Historic Cruises is not liable for the price unless all the shortcomings are cured.
d. No. Gdansk Boats is not liable for defects of which Historic Cruises was aware.

3. Gdansk Boats delivered a defective boat to another customer, Tolerant Harbor. The buyer noted quite a list of defects in the boat, but took it and paid without complaint. After a year, however, Tolerant Harbor realized the defects substantially impaired the value of the boat and resulted in higher repair and service costs. Can Tolerant Harbor recover for breach of contract?
   a. No, because it accepted the boat with defects.
   b. No, because the statute of limitations has run.
   c. Yes, because the statute of limitations has not yet run.
   d. No, because it did not give timely notice of breach.

4. Pemulis Auto had a contract to sell a 2016 Fireworks Rambler to Suzie Sousa for $35,000. On the agreed day of delivery, Pemulis Auto notified Suzie Sousa that they would not be able to perform their obligations. Suzie Sousa shopped around, and found the market price for the car had risen to $40,000. After some thought, she decided to stick with her current automobile. Is Pemulis Auto liable to Suzie Sousa?
   a. Yes, for the $35,000 contract price.
   b. Yes, for the $5,000 difference between the contract and market price.
   c. No, because she did not purchase a substitute.
   d. No, because they gave timely notice of nondelivery.

5. Gdansk Boats sold a fishing boat to Olivier Robeson, an actor. Not long afterwards, the boat's defective engine left Robeson floating for several hours. As a result, he missed a call offering a juicy part, which was quickly offered to a rival. Is Gdansk Boats liable for damages for Robeson's lost role?
   a. Yes, the damages were caused by their breach and Gdansk Boats knew that the boat needed an engine to travel.
   b. No, a breach of sales contract results in damages only for a lost bargain or diminished value.
   c. No, because the damages were not caused by a requirement known to the seller.
   d. Yes, because the breach was a but-for cause of the lost role.

ANSWERS

1. *D* is the best answer. Cold Feet Labs has breached the contract. But Cold Feet Labs is not liable for the price of the machine. The buyer becomes liable for the price under §2-709 if the buyer accepts the goods, but Cold Feet Labs did not accept the goods. The buyer can be liable for the price if the goods cannot reasonably be resold, §2-709(1)(b), but the machine is popular, not a unique product for the buyer. The buyer is also liable for the price of goods destroyed while the risk of loss is on the buyer, §2-709(1)(a), but that likewise does not apply here. Rather, Cold Feet is liable for nonacceptance under §2-708, which could be market differential damages under §2-708(1) or lost profits under §2-708(2). Contrary to *C*, Precision Devices is entitled to damages even though it still has the machine, because it lost the benefit of the bargain.
2. *B* is the best answer. If the buyer accepts the goods, the buyer is liable for the price under §2-709, even if the goods do not conform to the contract. But such a buyer may have a claim for breach of warranty under §2-714, provided the buyer gives notice under §2-607(3)(a), which the buyer did here.
3. *D* is the best answer. A buyer who accepts the goods may still recover for breach of warranty, but only if the buyer gives notice of breach to the seller within a reasonable time. §2-607(3)(a). Tolerant Harbor knew of the breaches for a year before giving notice, which would not be a reasonable time (absent unusual circumstances). So, contrary to *C*, the statute of limitations is not the key limit on time in such sales cases. Rather, buyers may lose their right to sue much more quickly if they fail to give timely notice of breach.
4. *B* is the best answer. Where a seller fails to deliver, a buyer may recover for the loss of the benefit of the bargain. If the buyer purchases the goods elsewhere, the buyer may seek damages calculated by the cover price under §2-712. But the buyer is not required to cover, and may also seek damages for loss of the bargain under §2-713, measured by the difference between the contract price and the market price. Notice of nondelivery is not required, as opposed to where the buyer has accepted the goods and must give notice of any breach. The seller is the one who did not deliver so seller would not need notice.
5. *C* is the best answer. A buyer may recover consequential damages (contrary to *B*), including "any loss resulting from general or particular requirements and needs of which the seller at the time of contracting had reason to know and which could not reasonably be prevented by cover or otherwise." §2-715. The damages here do not fall within that description.

Where seller delivers a machine that seller knows buyer needs to operate a factory, seller could be liable if the defective machine shuts down the factory. But the seller of a boat would not reasonably expect that failure of an engine could result in missing a telephone call that in turn would result in loss of an acting role. Mere but-for causation is insufficient, contrary to *A* and *D*.

PART 2

PAYMENT

Chapter 8
Negotiability

I. INTRODUCTION

We begin our exploration of payment law with Article 3 of the Uniform Commercial Code, titled "Negotiable Instruments." It should be noted that Article 3 was rewritten in 2002 and that is the version that is likely to be in your statute book. But that version is only the law in the following jurisdictions: Arkansas, District of Columbia, Indiana, Kentucky, Michigan, Minnesota, Mississippi, New Mexico, Nevada, Oklahoma, South Carolina, and Texas. The 2002 revision only made slight changes from the version in effect in the other states, and the important ones will be noted as they arise.

Let's start with the question of why our ancestors created negotiable instruments in the first place. There is not, of course, enough money to go around, and what money is available is frequently too physically awkward to be moved easily. Human civilization has been able to create additional sources of money in the form of transferable contractual debt. Thus one can borrow money and give the lender a written promise to repay it (a promissory note) and in this way realize early expected future prosperity. We solved the problem of the awkwardness of the physical transfer of money, and the concomitant possibility of its theft while in transit, by putting the money in the hands of a guarded depository (typically a bank) and then issuing written orders (drafts) for the money's transfer to various people.

In time, complicated things began to happen to these pieces of paper. For one thing, they were transferred (negotiated) through many hands before being presented for payment. If payment was then refused for some reason (the goods proved defective, the maker was financially embarrassed, the bank failed to open its doors one morning), rules had to be invented to straighten out who owed what to whom and to establish which defenses would be good against the person demanding payment and which would not. Similarly, if the instrument was stolen or forged, rules had to be established to put the risk of loss on somebody. Article 3 (Negotiable Instruments) and Article 4 (Bank Deposits and Collections) of the Uniform Commercial Code are designed to supply these rules.

II. TYPES OF NEGOTIABLE INSTRUMENTS

There are many types of negotiable instruments in the world. *Money* itself is technically an instrument. A dollar *bill* is a *bill of exchange*—that is, a *draft* (defined below) drawn on the United States Treasury. The Code deals with investment securities (stocks and bonds) in Article 8, and with wire transfers in Article 4A, these matters being specifically excluded from the coverage of Article 3 by §3-102(a).

The types of negotiable instruments that Article 3 does cover can be divided into two basic categories: *notes* and *drafts.*

A *note* is a written promise to pay money. If the note is created by a *bank,* it is called a *certificate of deposit* (or CD for short). Read §3-104(j). Investors buy CDs because they pay higher rates of interest than a normal savings account, but CDs have the disadvantage that the investor is not able to reclaim the money until the CD *matures* (comes due).[1] The typical note is not made by a bank but is the promissory note signed by those who borrow money or make credit purchases, most commonly when buying a home via a bank loan.

1. If a certificate of deposit states that it is non-negotiable, then Article 3 would not apply (though Article 8 on Investment Securities might). In re Isaacson, 508 So. 2d 1131 (Miss. 1987).

A *draft* is a written order by one person (the *drawer*—see §3-103(a)(5)) to another (the *drawee*, §3-103(a)(4)), directing the latter to pay money to a third person (the *payee*). The most common situation involving drafts arises when someone deposits money in a checking account and then writes checks ("drafts") addressed to the bank, ordering it to pay out the account money to those nominated. In this situation, the bank's customer is the *drawer*, the bank is the *drawee*, and the nominee (the electric company, the book club, the IRS, etc.) is the *payee*. A draft written on a bank and payable on demand is called a *check*; read §3-104(f). If the check is drawn by the bank on itself (the bank is both the drawer and the drawee), the instrument is called a *cashier's check*; see §3-104(g). If one bank draws a draft on another or makes the draft "payable through" another bank, the instrument is called a *teller's check*; see §3-104(h).[2]

PROBLEM 95

When law student Portia Moot went to buy a used car from a man who sold it through the newspaper, the seller told her he refused to take her personal check, demanding instead a cashier's check payable to his order. Portia went to Octopus National Bank and paid the bank the amount required, and the bank then issued the cashier's check, with Portia's car seller being named as payee. The bank gave the check to Portia, and she in turn handed it over to the payee. What is the name that the Code gives to Portia in this situation? See §3-103(a)(15).

If the drawee on a draft is *not* a bank, Article 3 still applies, but the instrument no longer meets the technical definition of a check (which requires that the drawee be a bank). The most common situation in which non-bank drafts are written occurs in the sale of goods. Seller in Boston contracts to sell 100 boxes of goods to buyer in San Francisco, buyer agreeing to pay $5,000 one month after receipt of the goods. Seller ships the goods, but decides that it would be nice to get the money now, before, for instance, going bankrupt. Seller sits down and draws up a $5,000 draft with *buyer as drawee*, leaving the payee line blank. Seller then goes down to a bank and asks the bank if it would be willing to buy the draft at a discount—say, $4,750. The bank investigates buyer's credit rating and,

2. Section 3-104 also contains a definition of a *traveler's check* in §3-104(i) and a *money order* in §3-104(f), and their legal significance is described in Official Comment 4 to that section.

finding it good, buys the draft from seller for $4,750, having seller fill in the payee line with the bank's name. At the end of one month, the bank presents the draft to buyer for payment and receives $5,000, thus making a $250 profit on the deal. Buyer doesn't care who gets the payment as long as the debt to seller is discharged; seller, getting the money early, doesn't mind losing $250. Everybody is happy (unless buyer discovers the goods are defective and refuses to pay the draft when the bank represents it; more on that later).[3]

Thus a negotiable instrument containing a *promise* to pay money is a note and one containing an *order* to pay money is a draft. Read §3-104(e).

III. THE NEGOTIABILITY CONCEPT

Whenever the word *negotiable* is applied to any type of paper, the concept always means this: if the paper is technically *negotiable* (which refers to

3. Drafts, then called *bills of exchange*, originated in Europe in the Middle Ages and were used to transfer money during travels. Merchants wishing to journey from City *A* to City *B* in the year 1220 faced the very real possibility of robbery en route. They solved this problem by going to a banking company in City *A* and there exchanging their money for a letter addressed to a corresponding banking company in City *B*, telling it to give a like amount of money to the merchants on arrival. In an era of rampant illiteracy, this bill of exchange was a lot easier to slip past the brigands than were coins of the realm. Here is a bill of exchange from the nineteenth century:

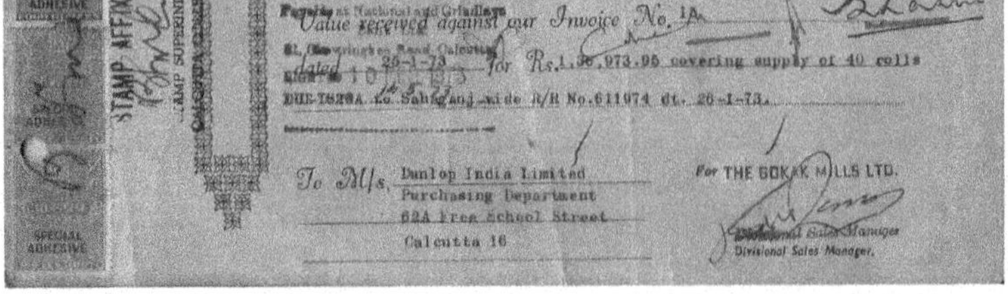

This Bill of Exchange has been drawn under National & Grindlays Bank Ltd., Calcutta, irrevocable letter of authority No.G.110/283 dt. 22-12-72 for supply of tyre cord.

No. CA/6 D/A CALCUTTA 7-2-73 19

Exchange for Rs.1,36,973.95 L. B. P. I/G/111/6

90 days after sight of this Sola of Exchange Pay to the Order of

M/s. NATIONAL & GRINDLAYS BANK LTD., CALCUTTA

the sum of Rupees One lac Thirtysix thousand Ninehundred Seventy Three and Paise Ninetyfive only

ACCEPTED

Value received against our Invoice No. 1A dated 25-1-73 for Rs.1,36,973.95 covering supply of 40 rolls

To M/s. Dunlop India Limited
Purchasing Department
62A Free School Street
Calcutta 16

For THE GOKAK MILLS LTD.
Divisional Sales Manager.

its form), it is technically *negotiated* (which refers to the transfer process) and reaches the hands of a purchaser for value who has no knowledge of problems with the transactions giving rise to the paper's creation (such a person is called a *holder in due course*); then the later purchaser becomes *super-plaintiff* [4] and can sue the parties to the instrument who are not (with certain exceptions) permitted to defend the lawsuit; the defendants simply lose and pay up.

Before the rules of Article 3 apply to an instrument, regardless of whether it is a note or a draft, the instrument must be technically *negotiable* within the rigid definitional requirements of §3-104(a). Every element specified therein must be met or the instrument is non-negotiable, and Article 3 does not apply, except by analogy; see §3-104(b). Read §3-104(a) carefully; it is almost (but not quite) worth memorizing, since the first issue an attorney should explore when dealing with a problem involving commercial paper is this: "Is the instrument technically *negotiable*?"

The question is also important because negotiable instruments pass more freely in commerce than do non-negotiable ones. The transferee of negotiable paper, if qualifying as a holder in due course, has the protection of the rule mentioned above, and the original maker and all other parties to the paper will have to pay it at maturity even if they have defenses arising from the transactions in which they signed the paper. This rule promotes the desirability of buying *negotiable* instruments. If the paper is non-negotiable, its transfer is nothing more than the assignment of a contract right, and, as is the basic rule of contracts law, later holders (assignees) of a contract take subject to *all* defenses arising from the underlying transaction. As Lord Mansfield, when developing the concept of holding in due course, said in Peacock v. Rhodes, 2 Douglas 633, 99 Eng. Rep. 402 (K.B. 1781):

> The holder of a bill of exchange, or promissory note, is not to be considered in the light of an assignee of the payee. An assignee must take the thing assigned, subject to all the equity to which the original party was subject. If this rule applied to bills and promissory notes, it would stop their currency. The law is settled, that a holder, coming fairly by a bill or note, has nothing to do with the transaction between the original parties; unless, perhaps, in

4. The designation "super-plaintiff" to describe a holder in due course is taken from J. White & R. Summers, Uniform Commercial Code 15-1 (6th ed. 2010); for a more specialized treatise, see J. White, R. Summers, D. Barnhizer, W. Barnes & F. Snyder, Principles of Payment Law (2d ed. 2019), or B. Clark, The Law of Bank Deposits, Collections, and Credit Cards (revised edition, updated quarterly).

the single case, (which is a hard one, but has been determined) of a note for money won at play.[5]

It follows then that it is important for everyone to know without question whether or not any given instrument is negotiable as soon as it is examined. In situations in which the deviation from the Code's requirements for negotiability is small, pleas are sometimes made to extend Article 3 by analogy to permit the non-complying instruments to be deemed negotiable. The courts are usually deaf to such entreaties:

> Because the prerequisites to negotiability are formal, it is both simple and necessary to comply with them. To hold that [the notes in question] are negotiable would certainly preserve the integrity of these notes and in that limited sense serve the interests of commerce; however, it would reward shoddy drafting and introduce unnecessary doubt into the formalities of negotiability. The reason for employing formalities in legal rules is to preclude the kinds of arguments that the banks offer to circumvent them here. It will not do to argue that the goal of promoting the expansion of commerce with predictably negotiable paper is served by artful reconstruction of the formalities set up initially to serve that same goal.

In re Boardwalk Marketplace Sec. Litig., 668 F. Supp. 115, 122 (D. Conn. 1987).

Each element of the negotiability requirements listed in §3-104(a) and related sections is discussed below.

A. *"Writing"*

A negotiable instrument cannot be oral (how could it be transferred around?), and the definitions of both *promise* and *order* in §3-103(a) require a "written" instruction or undertaking. However, there is no requirement that the writing be on a piece of paper. See Sir Alan Herbert's article, The Negotiable Cow, reprinted in A.P. Herbert, More Misleading Cases 117 (1930). Banks must sometimes cope with instruments written on odd surfaces (and frequently balk at doing so). The IRS is sometimes the payee of a negotiable shirt.

No one could be the holder of an oral promise to pay. But the law now provides that someone may be the holder of an *electronic* promissory note, as the next case discusses.

5. This last statement refers to instruments that arise from gambling. More on that issue later when we discuss holders in due course in Chapter 10.

Good v. Wells Fargo Bank, N.A.

Court of Appeals of Indiana, 2014
18 N.E.3d 618

BARNES, Judge.

. . .

FACTS

On March 14, 2008, Good purchased real estate in Elkhart. Good executed an electronic promissory note ("the Note") in favor of Synergy Mortgage Group, Inc. ("Synergy"). The Note included the following term:

> 11. Issuance of Transferable Record; Identification of Note Holder; Conversion from Electronic Note to Paper-Based Note
>
> * * *
>
> (B) Except as indicated in Sections 11(D) and (E) below, the identity of the Note Holder and any person to whom this Electronic Note is later transferred will be recorded in a registry maintained by *MERS CORP, Inc., a Delaware corporation* or in another registry to which the records are later transferred (the "Note Holder Registry"). The authoritative copy of this Electronic Note will be the copy identified by the Note Holder after loan closing but prior to registration in the Note Holder Registry. If this Electronic Note has been registered in the Note Holder Registry, then the authoritative copy will be the copy identified by the Note Holder of record in the Note Holder Registry or the Loan Servicer (as defined in the Security Instrument) acting at the direction of the Note Holder, as the authoritative copy. The current identity of the Note Holder and the location of the authoritative copy, as reflected in the Note Holder Registry, will be available from the Note Holder or Loan Servicer, as applicable. *The only copy of this Electric Note that is the authoritative copy is the copy that is within the control of the person identified as the Note Holder in the Note Holder Registry (or that person's designee). No other copy of this Electronic Note may be the authoritative copy.* . . .

Appellee's App. p. 29 (emphasis added). The loan was secured by a mortgage. The mortgage identified Synergy as the lender and Mortgage Electronic Registration Systems, Inc. ("MERS") as a nominee for the lender.

In 2011, Good stopped making payments on the loan. On November 9, 2011, MERS, as nominee for Synergy, assigned the mortgage to Wells Fargo. This assignment was recorded on November 14, 2011.

On November 7, 2012, Wells Fargo filed a complaint to foreclose the mortgage. Good, acting pro-se, filed an answer alleging that Wells Fargo was not a holder in due course of the Note and that it lacked standing.

On April 5, 2013, Wells Fargo moved for summary judgment. In support of its motion, Wells Fargo designated an Affidavit in Support of Judgment ("the Affidavit") in which Shemeka Moye, Wells Fargo's Vice President of Loan Documentation, stated Wells Fargo "directly or through an agent, has possession of the Promissory Note at issue in the plaintiff's cause of action. Wells Fargo Bank, N.A., is either the original payee of the Promissory Note or the Promissory Note has been duly indorsed [sic]." *Id.* at 95. Good responded, arguing that Wells Fargo held only a photocopy of the Note without any endorsements and, without more, did not establish that it was entitled to enforce the Note.

Wells Fargo replied claiming Good failed to designate evidence that creates a genuine issue[] of material fact for trial. Wells Fargo also asserted that it controlled the electronic note and was entitled to enforce it as the holder pursuant to 15 U.S.C.A. §7021(d). In support of this argument, Wells Fargo relied on a Certificate of Authentication ("the Certificate") in which Assistant Vice President of Wells Fargo, Theresa Russell, stated:

> 1. . . . The Bank acts as a servicer for the Federal National Mortgage Association ("Fannie Mae") with respect to the residential mortgage loan executed on the [sic] 3/14/2008 by BRYAN GOOD ("Borrowers"). . . . The promissory note evidencing the Borrowers' obligation to repay the Loan is an electronic record, as authorized by the federal ESIGN Act, 15 USC §7001 et seq., and in particular 15 USC §7021.
>
> 2. As part of its function as servicer, the Bank maintains a copy of the Borrowers' electronic promissory note on behalf of Fannie Mae. I am responsibilities [sic] for overseeing the process by which the Bank maintains the electronic promissory notes evidencing residential mortgage loans. ("Electronic Records").
>
> 3. Each Electronic Record is received in accordance with established procedures and processes for reliable receipt, storage and management of Electronic Records (the "Electronic Record Procedures"). The Electronic Record Procedures provide controls to assure that each Electronic Record is accurately received as originally executed and transmitted, and indexed appropriately for later identification and retrieval. Each Electronic Record is protected against undetected alteration by industry-standard encryption techniques and system controls. The Electronic Record is an official record of the Bank and is readily accessible for later reference.
>
> 4. Each Electronic Record is maintained and stored by the Bank in the ordinary course of business. The Electronic Records are maintained and stored by the Bank continuously from the time of receipt.
>
> 5. The paper copy of the Electronic Record attached . . . is a true and correct copy of the Borrowers' promissory note described above, as maintained and stored by the Bank in accordance with the procedures in Paragraphs 3 and 4 of this Certificate.

Id. at 130.

After a hearing, the trial court concluded that Wells Fargo had standing to enforce the Note and mortgage and partially granted Wells Fargo's motion for summary judgment as to that issue. The trial court also concluded that there were genuine issues of material fact regarding the validity of Good's electronic signature on the Note and the amount due and owing on the Note. Both parties filed motions to reconsider, which were discussed at the September 16, 2013 bench trial on the unresolved issues. After the trial, the trial court reaffirmed its initial ruling on the motion for summary judgment and concluded in part:

> 11. Plaintiff Wells Fargo Bank presented attached to the copy of the Promissory Note in its control a Certificate of Authentication which affirms that the Promissory Note was accurately received as it was originally executed and transmitted electronically. Plaintiff also affirmed that the record was protected against undetected alteration by industry standard encryption techniques and system controls. In this respect, the court concludes that Plaintiff maintained control of the subject Promissory Note which was originally signed by the Defendant, Bryan Good. Further endorsement of an electronic promissory note is not required and the promissory note is self-authenticating pursuant to Ind. Rule of Evidence 902. Accordingly, Defendant is liable on the Promissory Note and related Mortgage.

Appellant's App. P. 134. The trial court determined the payoff amount and entered judgment for Wells Fargo in that amount. The trial court then issued a judgment of foreclosure. Good now appeals.

Analysis

Among other things, Good appeals the trial court's entry of partial summary judgment on the issue of whether Wells Fargo was entitled to enforce the Note. "We review an appeal of a trial court's ruling on a motion for summary judgment using the same standard applicable to the trial court." Perdue v. Gargano, 964 N.E.2d 825, 831 (Ind. 2012). "Therefore, summary judgment is appropriate only if the designated evidence reveals 'no genuine issue as to any material fact and that the moving party is entitled to a judgment as a matter of law.' " *Id.* (quoting Ind. Trial Rule 56(C)). Our review of summary judgment is limited to evidence designated to the trial court. *Id.* (citing T.R. 56(H)). All facts and reasonable inferences drawn from the evidence designated by the parties is construed in a light most favorable to the non-moving party, and we do not defer to the trial court's legal determinations. *Id.*

There is no dispute that the mortgage was assigned from Synergy to Wells Fargo in 2011. The issue is whether Wells Fargo was entitled to enforce the Note. Regarding traditional paper notes, "Indiana has adopted Article 3 of the Uniform Commercial Code (UCC), which governs negotiable instruments, and it is well-established that a promissory note secured by a mortgage is a negotiable instrument." Lunsford v. Deutsche Bank Trust Co. Americas as Tr., 996 N.E.2d 815, 821 (Ind. Ct. App. 2013). According to the UCC, a negotiable instrument may be enforced by "the holder of the instrument." Ind. Code §26-1-3.1-301(1). The term "holder" means "the person in possession of a negotiable instrument that is payable either to bearer or to an identified person if the identified person is in possession of the instrument[.]" I.C. §26-1-1-201(20). In this context, "bearer" means the person in possession of a negotiable instrument "payable to bearer or endorsed in blank." I.C. §26-1-1-201(5).

Wells Fargo initially asserted that it had possession of the Note and was either the original payee or the Note had been duly endorsed. Good responded, challenging Wells Fargo's status as holder because the Note designated by Wells Fargo was not endorsed. In its reply, Wells Fargo asserted that, because the Note was an electronic note, "delivery, possession, and endorsement of an electronic promissory note are not required pursuant to federal statute." Appellee's App. p. 91. Wells Fargo claimed it controlled the Note and was entitled to enforce it pursuant to 15 U.S.C. §7021, which provides:

> *(a) Definitions*
> *For purposes of this section:*
> *(1) Transferable record*
> *The term "transferable record" means an electronic record that—*
> *(A) would be a note under Article 3 of the Uniform Commercial Code if the electronic record were in writing;*
> *(B) the issuer of the electronic record expressly has agreed is a transferable record; and*
> *(C) relates to a loan secured by real property.*
> *A transferable record may be executed using an electronic signature.*
> *(2) Other definitions*
> *The terms "electronic record," "electronic signature," and "person" have the same meanings provided in section 7006 of this title.*
> *(b) Control*
> *A person has control of a transferable record if a system employed for evidencing the transfer of interests in the transferable record reliably establishes that person as the person to which the transferable record was issued or transferred.*
> *(c) Conditions*
> *A system satisfies subsection (b) of this section, and a person is deemed to have control of a transferable record, if the transferable record is created, stored, and assigned in such a manner that—*
> *(1) a single authoritative copy of the transferable record exists which is unique, identifiable, and, except as otherwise provided in paragraphs (4), (5), and (6), unalterable;*

(2) the authoritative copy identifies the person asserting control as—

(A) the person to which the transferable record was issued; or

(B) if the authoritative copy indicates that the transferable record has been transferred, the person to which the transferable record was most recently transferred;

(3) the authoritative copy is communicated to and maintained by the person asserting control or its designated custodian;

(4) copies or revisions that add or change an identified assignee of the authoritative copy can be made only with the consent of the person asserting control;

(5) each copy of the authoritative copy and any copy of a copy is readily identifiable as a copy that is not the authoritative copy; and

(6) any revision of the authoritative copy is readily identifiable as authorized or unauthorized.

(d) Status as holder

Except as otherwise agreed, a person having control of a transferable record is the holder, as defined in section 1-201(20) of the Uniform Commercial Code, of the transferable record and has the same rights and defenses as a holder of an equivalent record or writing under the Uniform Commercial Code, including, if the applicable statutory requirements under section 3-302(a), 9-308, or revised section 9-330 of the Uniform Commercial Code are satisfied, the rights and defenses of a holder in due course or a purchaser, respectively. *Delivery, possession, and endorsement are not required to obtain or exercise any of the rights under this subsection.*

(e) Obligor rights

Except as otherwise agreed, an obligor under a transferable record has the same rights and defenses as an equivalent obligor under equivalent records or writings under the Uniform Commercial Code.

(f) Proof of control

If requested by a person against which enforcement is sought, the person seeking to enforce the transferable record shall provide reasonable proof that the person is in control of the transferable record. Proof may include access to the authoritative copy of the transferable record and related business records sufficient to review the terms of the transferable record and to establish the identity of the person having control of the transferable record.

(g) UCC references

For purposes of this subsection, all references to the Uniform Commercial Code are to the Uniform Commercial Code as in effect in the jurisdiction the law of which governs the transferable record.

15 U.S.C. §7021 (emphases added).

Wells Fargo is correct that, pursuant to §7021(d), a person having control of a transferable record, which includes the Note, is the holder for purposes of the UCC and that delivery, possession, and endorsement are not required. According to §7021(b), to show it controlled the note, Wells Fargo was required to designate evidence that a system employed for evidencing the transfer of interests in the Note reliably established Wells Fargo as the person to whom the Note was transferred. A system that satisfies the control requirement is described in §7021(c). Wells Fargo contends that its "possession of the Note and the recitation of its electronic record keeping procedures in the Certificate evidences Well Fargo's control of the Note. . . ." Appellee's Br. p. 15. We disagree.

Regarding possession, the Affidavit, which does not mention an electronic note, provides only that Wells Fargo, directly or through an agent, "has possession of the Promissory Note at issue in the plaintiff's cause of action." Appellee's App. p. 95. When considering Wells Fargo's assertion that the note in its possession was endorsed and its argument that the endorsement of an electronic note is not required pursuant to §7021(d), it is not clear from the Affidavit whether Wells Fargo was claiming to have possession of an endorsed paper copy or the electronic note.

Even if the Affidavit established that Wells Fargo possessed the electronic note, control, not possession, is the relevant consideration under §7021, and the Certificate does not establish that Wells Fargo controlled the Note. The Certificate does establish that Wells Fargo, as servicer of Good's mortgage loan for Fannie Mae, "maintains a copy of [Good's] promissory note on behalf of Fannie Mae." *Id.* at 26. The Certificate also establishes that Wells Fargo's electronic records are received, stored, and managed in a secure manner with controls to assure they are accurately received as originally executed and protected against alteration. However, the Certificate does not suggest that Wells Fargo maintains the single authoritative copy of the Note as described in §7021(c)(1). Even if we were to assume that the copy of the Note maintained by Wells Fargo is the authoritative copy, it does not indicate that the Note has been transferred or identify either Wells Fargo or Fannie Mae as the person to whom the Note was most recently transferred. *See* 15 U.S.C. §7021(c)(2)(B).

Such a record of transfer is described in the Note, which calls for the recording of any transfer of the Note in a note holder registry. The Note also specifies, "The only copy of this Electric Note that is the authoritative copy is the copy that is within the control of the person identified as the Note Holder in the Note Holder Registry (or that person's designee). No other copy of this Electronic Note may be the authoritative copy." *Id.* at 29. Wells Fargo has not designated any evidence of a note holder registry, let alone evidence showing that Wells Fargo, or even Fannie Mae, is identified as the note holder in the note holder registry.

Pursuant to statute, upon Good's request, Wells Fargo was required to provide "reasonable proof" that it was in control of the Note. 15 U.S.C. §7021(f). "Proof may include access to the authoritative copy of the transferable record and related business records sufficient to review the terms of the transferable record and to establish the identity of the person having control of the transferable record." *Id.* Although Good repeatedly requested such proof, Wells Fargo did not provide any evidence documenting the transfer or assignment of the Note from Synergy to either Wells Fargo or Fannie Mae. Thus, Wells Fargo did not demonstrate it controlled the Note by showing that a system employed for evidencing the transfer of interests in the Note reliably established that the Note had been transferred to Wells Fargo. *See* 15 U.S.C. §7021(b).

Because Wells Fargo did not establish that it controlled the Note as described in §7021, it did not establish that it was the person entitled to enforce the Note as the holder for purposes of the UCC. *See* 15 U.S.C. §7021(d); I.C. §26-1-3.1-301(1). Thus, partial summary judgment for Wells Fargo on this issue was improper.

Wells Fargo goes on to argue that, irrespective of the trial court's summary judgment ruling, it presented uncontroverted evidence at the bench trial that it controlled the Note. Procedurally, however, the issue of Wells Fargo's right to enforce the Note was not before the trial court during the bench trial because it had been resolved, albeit improperly, in the summary judgment proceedings. It would be inappropriate for us to use evidence from the subsequent trial to justify the judgment when Good did not have notice that this issue would be relitigated. Regardless, we are not convinced that the trial testimony establishes that Wells Fargo controlled the Note for purposes of §7021.

Wells Fargo relies on the testimony of Donna Mouzon, a loan verification analyst for Wells Fargo, who testified at trial that Wells Fargo "acquired" the loan on August 1, 2008. Tr. pp. 17-18. Mouzon was also questioned as follows:

> *Q.* Thank you. Is [Wells Fargo] presently in control of the electronic note?
> *A.* Yes.
> *Q.* Does [Wells Fargo] currently maintain the electronic note?
> *A.* Yes.
> *Q.* Does [Wells Fargo] also service the loan?
> *A.* Yes.
>
> * * *
>
> *Q.* Who's the owner of the note?
> *A.* Fanny Mae.
> *Q.* Who's the holder of the note?
> *A.* Wells Fargo.

Id. at 18.

Given the lack of evidence regarding a transfer or assignment from Synergy to Wells Fargo or Fannie Mae, Mouzon's conclusory testimony was not sufficient to establish that it controlled the Note as defined in §7021. Thus, Mouzon's trial testimony did not establish that Wells Fargo is entitled to enforce the note as the holder, and is not a basis for affirming the judgment of foreclosure.

Conclusion

Wells Fargo has not shown that it controls the Note for purposes of §7021(b) and, accordingly, has not established its status as holder for purposes of the UCC. Because Wells Fargo has not established that it was entitled to enforce the Note as its holder, the trial court's grant of summary judgment was improper and the resulting judgment must be set aside. We reverse and remand.

Reversed and remanded.

B. *"Signed"*

Section 3-103(a)'s definitions of both "promise" and "order" require that the instrument be "signed." This is an obvious requirement, but it has interesting wrinkles.

PROBLEM 96

Texas millionaire Howard Chaps signs all of his checks with a small branding iron that prints a fancy "X" on the signature line. Are his checks negotiable? See §1-201(b)(37); cf. Official Comment 37.

PROBLEM 97

Walter Capitalist is the sole proprietor of the Capitalist Company. He signs all of the store's checks by writing "Capitalist Company" on the drawer's line, but the checks are drawn on his personal checking account at the Octopus National Bank. Can the bank treat the check as if Walter had signed his own name? See §3-401(b).

C. *"Unconditional Promise or Order"*

A promissory note must contain an unconditional *promise* to pay; a draft must contain an unconditional *order* to the drawee requiring payment. See §3-104(a). The rule that the promise or order be *unconditional* is obviously a necessity if negotiable paper is to circulate without question. If conditional paper were negotiable, prospective holders of the paper would not feel safe in taking it until they had checked to see if the condition had occurred. See First State Bank v. Clark, 91 N.M. 117, 570 P.2d 1144 (1977); Annot., What Constitutes an Unconditional Promise, 88 A.L.R.3d 1100. To prevent this kind of worry, the Code requires that the promise or order be unconditional, or the paper will be technically non-negotiable. Nonetheless, certain conditions are permitted in the instrument without destroying negotiability. Read §3-106 carefully. (The plan of the §§3-100s, which deal generally with negotiability, is to set out all of the requirements in §3-104(a), and then, section by section, to elaborate on them. Section 3-106 is the first elaboration.)

1. Implied Conditions

The fact that it is possible to think up things that *might* happen to destroy the maker's liability on the instrument does not destroy negotiability unless the instrument makes itself *expressly* conditional as to these matters. For example, if Joanie Singer leases a theater from Music Hall, Inc., and gives the lessor the following signed note, "(Date), I have this day rented a theater from Music Hall, Inc., and I promise to pay $800 to the order of Music Hall, Inc.," the possibility that the theater may burn down prior to Joanie's use of it does not make the note conditional (and therefore non-negotiable); this condition is only implied. On the other hand, if the note had said, "I promise to pay $800 to the order of Music Hall, Inc., *only if* the theater does not burn down before I use it," the note would have been non-negotiable, since it would then be subject to an *express* condition. See §3-106(a)(i).

Triffin v. Dillabough

Supreme Court of Pennsylvania, 1998
552 Pa. 550, 716 A.2d 605

Newman, Justice.

Appellant American Express Travel Related Services Company, Inc. (American Express) asks this Court to decide whether certain of its money orders are negotiable instruments pursuant to the Pennsylvania version of the Uniform Commercial Code, 13 Pa. C.S. §1101, et seq. (Commercial Code), and if they are, whether appellee Robert J. Triffin (Triffin) has the rights of a holder in due course who may recover the face value of those money orders from American Express. We hold that the money orders in question are negotiable instruments and Triffin has the rights of a holder in due course, entitling him to recover the value of the money orders from American Express.

FACTS AND PROCEDURAL HISTORY

American Express, among other endeavors, sells money orders through its authorized agents. In a typical transaction, an agent collects an amount of cash from the purchaser, also known as the sender, equal to the face value of the money order plus a small fee. The sender receives a partially completed money order embossed with the amount of the money order and blank spaces for the sender to fill in his or her own name and address, the name of the payee and the date.

On an unknown date, three American Express money orders were stolen from the premises of one of its agents, Chase Savings Bank. In an apparently unrelated incident, one hundred American Express money orders were stolen while being shipped to another agent, I.W. Levin & Company. When they were stolen, all of the money orders contained the pre-printed signature of Louis Gerstner, then Chairman of American Express, but they were blank as to amount, sender, payee and date.

On December 11, 1990, Stacey Anne Dillabough (Dillabough) presented two American Express money orders for payment at Chuckie Enterprises, Inc. (Chuckie's), a check cashing operation in Philadelphia. The money orders were in the amounts of $550.00 and $650.00, respectively, and listed Dillabough as the payee and David W. (last name indecipherable) of 436 E. Allegheny Avenue as the sender. On February 25, 1991, Robert Lynn (Lynn) presented one American Express money order at Chuckie's in the amount of $200.00, which listed himself as payee and Michael C. Pepe as the sender. In each instance, Charles Giunta (Giunta), the owner of Chuckie's, recognized Dillabough and Lynn from their previous visits to Chuckie's. Dillabough and Lynn provided photographic identification to Giunta and properly endorsed their money orders. Giunta paid the face amounts of the money orders to Dillabough and Lynn, less his standard 2 percent fee.

Giunta was unaware the American Express money orders that he cashed had been stolen. The two Dillabough money orders were stolen from the premises of Chase Savings Bank and the Lynn money order was stolen from the shipment to I.W. Levin and Company. After being cashed at Chuckie's, the money orders traveled the regular bank collection routes and were presented for payment at the United Bank of Grand Junction, Colorado. Because American Express had noted on its "fraud log" that the money orders were stolen, they were returned to Chuckie's bearing the stamp "reported lost or stolen. do not redeposit." American Express refused to pay Chuckie's the face amounts of the money orders. Chuckie's then sold the Dillabough and Lynn money orders to Triffin, a commercial discounter.[6]

6. Triffin testified that he regularly purchases various types of choses in action from members of the check cashing industry. Although a law school graduate, Triffin is not a member of the Pennsylvania Bar and he is proceeding *pro se* in this appeal.

Pursuant to written agreements, Chuckie's assigned all of its right, title and interest in the money orders to Triffin.

Triffin filed separate complaints in the Court of Common Pleas of Philadelphia County (trial court) against Dillabough and American Express in July 16, 1992, and against Lynn and American Express on August 20, 1992, seeking payment of the money orders. The trial court consolidated the two actions. Triffin obtained default judgments against Dillabough and Lynn and proceeded to a non-jury trial with American Express. The trial court found that the money orders were not negotiable instruments and entered a verdict in favor of American Express. On appeal, the Superior Court reversed and trial court and held that the money orders were negotiable instruments and Triffin had the status of a holder in due course, entitling him to recover the face amount of the money orders from American Express. We granted American Express' Petition for Allowance of Appeal from the Order of the Superior Court, and we now affirm. . . .

1. NEGOTIABILITY

The Superior Court has described the purpose of negotiable instruments and the Commercial Code as follows:

> A negotiable instrument is an instrument capable of transfer by endorsement or delivery. Negotiability provides a means of passing on to the transferee the rights of the holder, including the right to sue in his or her own name, and the right to take free of equities as against the assignor/payee. [Citations omitted.] The purpose of the Commercial Code is to enhance the marketability of negotiable instruments and to allow bankers, brokers, and the general public to trade in confidence. [Citations omitted.] As a matter of sound economic policy, the Commercial Code encourages the free transfer and negotiability of commercial paper to stimulate financial interdependence.

Manor Bldg. Corp. v. Manor Complex Assocs., 435 Pa. Super. 246, 252-53, 645 A.2d 843, 846 (1994) (en banc). With these principles in mind, we turn to a discussion of the American Express money orders at issue here.

The threshold question is whether the money orders qualify as negotiable instruments under Division Three of the Commercial Code, 13 Pa. C.S. §3101, et seq., which governs negotiability. Both parties agree that if the money orders are not negotiable instruments then Triffin's claims against American Express must fail. Initially, we note that the Commercial Code does not specifically define the term "money order," nor does it provide a descriptive list of financial documents that automatically qualify as negotiable instruments. Instead, 13 Pa. C.S. 3104(a) sets forth the following four part test to determine if a particular document qualifies as a negotiable instrument:

> (A) Requisites to negotiability—Any writing to be a negotiable instrument within this division must: (1) be signed by the maker or drawer; (2) contain an

> unconditional promise or order to pay a sum certain in money and no other promise, order, obligation or power given by the maker or drawer except as authorized by this division; (3) be payable on demand or at a definite time; and (4) be payable to order or to bearer.

13 Pa. C.S. §3104(a).

The Superior Court described the face of the money orders in question as follows:

> Prior to being stolen[,] the American Express money orders read: "AMERICAN EXPRESS MONEY ORDER . . . CHASE SAVINGS BANK . . . DATE (blank). PAY THE SUM OF (blank), NOT GOOD OVER $1,000, TO THE ORDER OF (blank). Louis V. Gerstner, Chairman. SENDER'S NAME AND ADDRESS (blank). Issued by American Express Travel Related Services Company, Inc., Englewood, Colorado. Payable at United Bank of Grand Junction, Downtown, Grand Junction, Colorado." The two Dillabough instruments were in this form. The third Lynn instrument was identical, except it did not bear an authorized agent's name, e.g., Chase Savings Bank, and was not good for over $200.

Triffin v. Dillabough, 448 Pa. Super. 72, 82, 670 A.2d 684, 689 (1996). When presented at Chuckie's, the sections for date, amount, payee and sender had been completed.

The first requisite of negotiability, a signature by the drawer or maker, "includes any symbol executed or adopted by a party with present intention to authenticate a writing." 13 Pa. C.S. §1201. "Authentication may be printed, stamped or written; it may be by initials or by thumbprint. . . . The question always is whether the symbol was executed or adopted by the party with present intention to authenticate the writing." 13 Pa. C.S. §1201, Comment 39. Additionally, section 3307(a)(2) states that when the effectiveness of a signature is challenged, it is presumed to be genuine or authorized unless the signer has died or become incompetent. 13 Pa. C.S. §3307(a)(2). Here, the drawer, American Express, affixed the pre-printed signature of Louis Gerstner, its then Chairman, to the money orders in question before forwarding them to its agents. American Express does not argue that Gerstner's signature was affixed to the money orders for any reason other than to authenticate them. Accordingly, the money orders satisfy the first requisite for negotiability.

The second requisite, American Express argues, is lacking because the money orders do not contain an unconditional promise or order to pay. Specifically, American Express claims that a legend it placed on the back of the money orders qualifies an otherwise unconditional order on the front directing the drawee to "PAY THE SUM OF" a specified amount "TO THE ORDER OF" the payee. The legend provides as follows:

IMPORTANT
DO NOT CASH FOR STRANGERS

THIS MONEY ORDER WILL NOT BE PAID IF IT HAS BEEN ALTERED OR STOLEN OR IF AN ENDORSEMENT IS MISSING OR FORGED. BE SURE YOU HAVE EFFECTIVE RECOURSE AGAINST YOUR CUSTOMER.

____
PAYEE'S ENDORSEMENT

According to American Express, this legend renders the order to pay conditional on the money order not being altered, stolen, unendorsed or forged and destroys the negotiability of the instrument.

We disagree. In a factually similar case, the Louisiana Court of Appeal construed a legend on the bank of an American Express money order similar to the one at issue here. Hong Kong Importers, Inc. v. American Express Co., 301 So. 2d 707 (La. App. 1974). The legend there stated "cash only if recourse from endorser IS AVAILABLE. IF THIS MONEY ORDER HAS NOT BEEN VALIDLY ISSUED OR HAS BEEN FRADULENTLY NEGOTIATED, IT WILL BE RETURNED." Id. at 708. The money order also had the following language printed on its face: "know your endorser cash only if recourse is available." Id. The Louisiana Court held that the legend on the back and the language on the front did not convert the money order into a conditional promise to pay, but merely operated as a warning to the party cashing the money order to protect himself against fraud. Although *Hong Kong* was decided before Louisiana adopted the Uniform Commercial Code, we find its rationale to be persuasive and applicable to 13 Pa. C.S. §3104.

American Express attempts to distinguish *Hong Kong* by asserting that the legend in this case is more specific because it explicitly conditions payment on the money orders not being altered, stolen, unendorsed or forged. This argument misses the point. "Any writing which meets the requirements of subsection [(a)] and is not excluded under Section [3103] is a negotiable instrument, and all sections of this [Division] apply to it, *even though it may contain additional language beyond that contemplated by this section.*" 13 Pa. C.S. §3104, Comment 4 (emphasis added). An otherwise unconditional order to pay that meets the section 3104 requirements is not made conditional by including implied or constructive conditions in the instrument. 13 Pa. C.S. §3105(a)(1). Moreover, purported conditions on an otherwise negotiable instrument, that merely reflect other provisions of the law, do not vitiate negotiability. State v. Phelps, 125 Ariz. 114, 608 P.2d 51 (App. 1979); see also Falk's Food Basket, Inc. v. Selected Risks Ins. Co., 214 Pa. Super. 522, 257 A.2d 359 (1969); 4 William D. Hawkland & Larry Lawrence, Uniform Commercial Code Series §3-105:03 (Clark Boardman Callaghan) (1994). Here, the alleged conditions on the back of the money orders are nothing more than a restatement of American Express's statutory defenses against payment because of alteration, 13 Pa. C.S. §3407, theft, 13 Pa. C.S. §3306(4), absence of signature, 13 Pa. C.S. §3401, and forgery, 13 Pa. C.S. §3404. Contrary to American Express's claims, expressing those statutory defenses in a legend with the conditional phrase "this money order will not be paid if . . ." does not elevate the legend to a condition for the purposes of 13 Pa. C.S. §3104(a) because it is merely a restatement of the defenses present in the Commercial Code. See 13 Pa. C.S. §3104, Comment 4; Phelps. The legend is simply a warning that American Express has reserved its statutory defenses. Whether these defenses are effective against Triffin is a separate question to be answered after resolving the issue of negotiability. See 13 Pa. C.S. §3104, Comment 4. We hold, therefore, that the money orders contain an unconditional order to pay, and satisfy the second requisite of negotiability.

The third requisite, that the writing be payable on demand or at a definite time, and the fourth requisite, that the writing be payable to order or bearer, are clear from the face of the money orders and are not disputed by the parties. Thus, the American Express money orders qualify as negotiable instruments pursuant to 13 Pa. C.S. §3104. . . .

[The court then found that Triffin had the rights of a holder in due course, so as to be free of American Express's defense of non-issue. As to this, see §3-105 of the Revision, and its Official Comment 2.]

As previously discussed, the legend on the back of the money orders is merely a warning that restates American Express's defenses against persons other than holders in due course in the event of alteration, theft, lack of endorsement or forgery. These defenses are ineffective against a holder in due course. 13 Pa. C.S. §3305; 13 Pa. C.S. §3407(c). Because Triffin has attained holder in due course status through the assignment of the money orders from Chuckie's, American Express cannot enforce the defenses against him. Accordingly, American Express is liable to Triffin for the face value of the money orders.

The Order of the Superior Court is affirmed and this matter is remanded to the trial court for the entry of an order consistent with this Opinion.

Castille, Justice, dissents.

The majority concludes that appellee Robert J. Triffin ("appellee") is entitled to recover the value of the money orders at issue because the money orders were negotiable instruments and because appellee was a holder in due course of those negotiable instruments. However, since the money orders at issue contained express conditional language which precluded negotiability under the relevant statute, I must respectfully dissent from the majority's conclusion. . . .

At issue here is the second of the four statutory prerequisites to negotiability, the requirement of an "unconditional" promise or order. Regarding this prerequisite, section §3105 provides:

> (A) Unconditional promise or order.—A promise or order otherwise unconditional is not made conditional by the fact that the instrument: (1) is subject to implied or constructive conditions; . . .

The comment to section 3105 states:

> 1. . . . Nothing in [paragraph (a) subsection (1)] is intended to imply that language may not be fairly construed to mean what it says, but implications, whether the law or fact, are not to be considered in determining negotiability.

Thus, the statute clearly distinguishes between language which creates an implied condition and language which creates an express condition. The latter renders a promise or order non-negotiable while the former does not. This conclusion derives further support from the revised §3106(a), which provides that ". . . a promise or order is unconditional unless it states (1) an express condition to payment. . . ."

Here, the operative language in the money orders at issue clearly created an "express" condition and thereby rendered the money orders non-negotiable. [Reprints language on the money order.]

This language explicitly conditions payments on the money orders' not being altered or stolen and the endorsements' not being missing or forged. The use of the word "if" renders the condition an express one, since "if" by definition means "on *condition* that; in case that; supposing that." Webster's New World Dict., 2d College ed. (Emphasis added.)

Furthermore, the official comment to revised section 3106 explains what the code intends by drawing the distinction between implied and express conditions: If the promise or order states an express condition to payment, the promise or order is not an instrument. For example, a promise states, "I promise to pay $100,000 to the order of John Doe if he conveys title to Blackacre to me." The promise is not an instrument because there is an express condition to payment. However, suppose a promise states, "In consideration of John Doe's promise to convey title of Blackacre I promise to pay $100,000 to the order of John Doe." That promise can be an instrument *if* [section 3104] is otherwise satisfied. 13 Pa. C.S. §3106 (1992 amended version) (emphasis added). Accordingly, the use of the word "if" creates an express condition which otherwise might be lacking, and thereby precludes a money order from being a negotiable instrument under the statute. The language at issue in this case created the same type of express condition which is embodied in the Comment; consequently, the language precludes the money orders from being negotiable instruments.[7]

The reasons proffered by the majority to justify its departure from this seemingly inescapable statutory logic are strained. First, the majority cites a case, decided by the Louisiana Court of Appeal in 1974, in which a condition incorporating the word "if was construed not to bar negotiability. In that case, the Louisiana Court did not evaluate the significance of the word "if" or the significance of the condition which that word introduced. Moreover, in 1974, Louisiana had not yet adopted Article III of the Uniform Commercial Code ("UCC"). Hence, it appears that the Louisiana decision was decided against the backdrop of the Code of Napoleon. See 9 to 5 Fashions, Inc. v. Petr L. Spurney, 538 So. 2d 228, 233 (La. 1989) (discussing roots of Louisiana's civil code in the Napoleonic code). Pennsylvania, on the other hand, has adopted Article III of the UCC, which speaks directly to the issue presented in this case, as explained supra. A decision by an intermediate Louisiana appellate court interpreting French legal principles should not override the explicit statutory guidance furnished by the Pennsylvania legislature on an issue of Pennsylvania law.

The majority also seizes on Comment 4 to 13 Pa. C.S. §3104, which states that "any writing which meets the requirements of subsection [(a)] and is not excluded under Section [3103] is a negotiable instrument, and all sections of this [Division] apply to it, *even though it may contain additional language beyond that contemplated by this section*" (emphasis added by majority). Since, as explained supra, the money orders contained language which precluded them from satisfying subsection (a), the quoted language from Comment 4 does not further the majority's argument.

Finally, the majority attempts to support its conclusion by referring to the principle that "purported conditions on an otherwise negotiable instrument, that merely reflect other provisions of the law, do not vitiate negotiability." Op. at 609 (citations omitted). The majority contends that the language at issue amounts merely to a restatement of appellant's statutory defenses against payment where there has been alteration (13 Pa. C.S. §3407), theft (3306(4)), absence of signature (3401) and forgery (3404). The majority overlooks the fact that all of these statutory defenses are, by their own terms, ineffective against holders in due course. On the other hand, the language at issue here—which categorically states that the money order will not be paid if it was stolen—is operative even against holders who have taken in due course. As noted in the Comment to section 3105(a)(1), conditional

7. Additionally, I note that if there was any doubt about this conclusion, the doubt would be resolved against negotiability. See United States v. Gonzalez, 797 F.2d 1109, 1113 (1st Cir. 1986) ("when a writing is ambiguous with respect to negotiability, the conclusion to be reached is that it is *not negotiable*") (emphasis added) (other citations omitted).

language may be fairly construed to mean what it says. By its plain terms, the language at issue here sweeps beyond the scope of appellant's statutory defenses, and therefore does more than simply "reflect other provisions of the law." In sum, the statute at issue in this case is devoid of ambiguity, and the application of that statute to these facts compels a conclusion contrary to that reached by the majority. Consequently, I respectfully dissent.

CAPPY, J., joins this dissenting opinion.

This case has been cited with approval by the Montana Supreme Court in Smith v. Farmers Union Mut. Ins. Co., 361 Mont. 516, 260 P.3d 163 (2011).

It is generally accepted that federally guaranteed student loan notes are not negotiable instruments, because they are discharged upon death or disability, thus creating a condition on time of payment; Trent v. North Carolina, 2014 WL 2773579 (W.D.N.C. 2014).

2. Consideration Stated

In the example before the last reprinted case, the note mentioned that it was given in return for the leasing of the theater—that is, it stated exactly what the consideration was that caused the note to be written. Section 3-106 permits the instrument to mention the details of the underlying contract without destroying negotiability as long as payment of the note is not made "subject to" the performance of that contract. Section 3-106(a)'s last sentence clearly permits a *reference* to the underlying contract, though an incorporation of the terms of that contract (without restating them in the note itself) would be fatal to negotiability. The reason is that the prospective holder should never be required to investigate whether all is well with the original agreement; if the instrument requires the current holder to check on this, it is non-negotiable. Gem Global Yield Fund, Ltd. v. Surgilight, Inc., 2006 WL 2389345 (S.D.N.Y. 2006). Another reason is that the separate agreement might contain terms placing a condition on payment; the requisites of *negotiability* will not even entertain such a possibility. The holder must be able to determine the negotiability of an instrument from within its own four corners alone. Bibler v. Arcata Investments 2, LLC, 2005 WL 3304127 (Mich. App. 2005).

PROBLEM 98

Are the following notes negotiable?

(a) "(Date), I promise to pay bearer $500, subject to the contract I signed with Honest John today, (Signature)." See Official Comment 1, second paragraph, to §3-106; Jackson v. Luellen Farms, Inc., 877 N.E.2d 848 (Ind. App. 2007).

(b) "(Date), I promise to pay bearer $500 as per contract I signed today with Honest John, (Signature)." Cf. §3-117, which says that a separate agreement affects only the parties thereto and not a subsequent holder in due course.

(c) "(Date), I promise to pay bearer $500 on January 1, 2022. For rights as to prepayment and acceleration, see the contract signed September 25, 2021, between the maker and the payee. (Signature)." See §3-106(b)(i).

PROBLEM 99

Whenever it mails out a check, the Adhesion Insurance Company marks it "Void After 90 Days." Is such an instrument technically negotiable?

PROBLEM 100

The promissory note contained this clause: "The collateral for this note is a security interest in the maker's art collection; for rights and duties on default, see the security agreement signed this day creating the security interest." Does this clause destroy negotiability? See §3-106(b)(i) and its Official Comment 1, third paragraph.

D. "Fixed Amount of Money"

It is elementary that an instrument will be non-negotiable if one cannot look at it and readily calculate the amount that the maker or drawer has promised to pay.

PROBLEM 101

The promissory note stated that the rate of interest was "2% above the prime rate as of the date of maturity." The prime rate is the interest charged by banks to their best customer and can be ascertained by reference to financial publications. Does the fact that the holder of the note has to consult sources outside of the instrument in order to calculate the interest due destroy negotiability? See §3-112.

A note provides for "negative amortization," meaning that unpaid interest will be added to the original principal amount of the note. Is this note negotiable? Hanna v. PennyMac Holdings, LLC, 2019 WL 1371928 (Fla. App. 2019).

Money. "I promise to pay 100 bales of cotton to bearer" is a non-negotiable promise; a negotiable instrument must promise or order payment in *money.* This requirement then raises this amusing question: Exactly what is money? If in Borneo a note is made payable with "50 boar's teeth," is the note negotiable? Section 1-201(b)(24) defines *money* as the "medium of exchange authorized or adopted by a domestic or foreign government as a part of its currency." The Official Comment to that section states that the "test adopted is that of the sanction of government . . . which recognizes the circulating medium as a part of the official currency of that government."

Note that *money* does not mean only U.S. currency. According to §3-107 an instrument payable in foreign currency is presumed to be payable in either that currency or the U.S. dollar equivalent on the date due *unless the instrument limits payment to the foreign currency.* As a test in statutory reading, read §3-107 and answer this question: If an instrument states that it is payable only with French francs, is it or is it not negotiable? See §3-107's Official Comment.

Heritage Bank v. Bruha

Supreme Court of Nebraska, 2012
283 Neb. 263, 812 N.W.2d 260

CONNOLLY, J.

Heritage Bank (Heritage) sued Jerome J. Bruha on promissory notes that it had purchased from the Federal Deposit Insurance Corporation (FDIC). The FDIC had obtained the notes after it became a receiver for the failed bank that had initially lent the money to Bruha. The notes secured lines of credit for Bruha's benefit. The district court granted summary judgment to Heritage and awarded it $61,384.67 on one of the notes. Bruha appeals. The primary issues are whether either the holder-in-due-course rule of Nebraska's Uniform Commercial Code or federal banking law bars Bruha's defenses to the enforcement of the note. We conclude that federal law bars Bruha's defenses, and thus, we affirm in part. But because of a minor error in the court's calculation of interest, we reverse in part, and remand for correction.

I. BACKGROUND

1. PROMISSORY NOTES

On four different occasions in 2008, Bruha signed promissory notes with Sherman County Bank. Although the district court ultimately granted summary judgment to Heritage on all four notes, Bruha's arguments relate only to the fourth and final note. So we will limit our discussion to the facts regarding this note. We will, however, provide some background to put the note in context.

The notes secured lines of credit under which Bruha could borrow money from Sherman County Bank. Bruha then apparently invested the money in accounts with a trading company, which allegedly shared management with Sherman County Bank. In brief, Bruha claims that Sherman County Bank misled him into borrowing money that, in turn, he invested with a trading company that generated trade commissions through risky and speculative commodity trading.

In an affidavit, Bruha claimed that representatives of Sherman County Bank repeatedly advised him against taking money out of his trading account, stating that he would lose more money if he did so than he would by leaving it in. Bruha claimed that the representatives often understated the potential losses he would suffer by staying in the account. Also, Bruha claims he was told that the existing collateral would cover the credit he later took. Further, although he admittedly knew he was increasing his debt burden, he thought it was under one note as opposed to four. The record, however, contains no internal records or documents of Sherman County Bank evidencing any of the representations regarding his account that Bruha claims Sherman County Bank made.

Bruha signed the fourth note, No. 1723, on December 16, 2008. The note evidenced a promise to pay "the principal amount of Seventy-five Thousand & 00/100 ($75,000.00) or so much as may be outstanding, together with interest on the unpaid outstanding principal balance of each advance." The note stated that it "evidence[d] a revolving line of credit."

The note contained a variable interest rate. The rate was subject to change every month and calculated on an index maintained by Sherman County Bank. The interest rate on Bruha's note was 1 percentage point under the percentage on the index at any given time. The initial rate was 7.25 percent, and was later adjusted to 6.75 percent. On default, this interest rate would increase by 5 percentage points. . . .

On note No. 1723, Bruha received the following advancements: He received $10,000 on December 16, 2008; $40,000 on December 17; and $1,000 on January 30, 2009. This totaled $51,000. There is no dispute that Bruha received all of this money.

An affidavit also established the interest rate on the notes. It shows that the initial rate was 7.25 percent. This rate was adjusted to 6.75 percent on February 1, 2009. Then, on August 2, after Bruha defaulted, the rate increased to 11.75 percent.

Sherman County Bank eventually failed, and the FDIC was appointed as receiver. The FDIC then sold and assigned some of Sherman County Bank's assets to Heritage. These assets included the notes signed by Bruha.

Heritage sued Bruha to enforce the notes. The complaint alleged that Bruha owed Heritage on the four notes and that Heritage had received the notes from the FDIC after Sherman County Bank had been placed into receivership. But as mentioned, only note No. 1723 is the subject of this appeal. As to note No. 1723, Heritage claimed that the principal was $75,000 and that the initial interest rate was 8.25 percent. Heritage also alleged that the interest rate was to jump 5 percentage points upon default. Heritage alleged that it was a holder in due course and entitled to enforce the note.

In his amended answer, Bruha admitted that he signed note No. 1723 but claims that he did not do it voluntarily. He claimed that Sherman County Bank had procured his signature "by fraud and/or misrepresentation." Bruha admitted that he had not paid the note but denied that he was obligated to do so.

[The District Court found that the bank was a holder in due course and took free of Bruha's defense of fraud.]

IV. Analysis

1. Because Note No. 1723 Was Not Negotiable, Heritage Is Not a Holder in Due Course

Bruha argues that Heritage is not a holder in due course. Similarly, he argues that the FDIC was not a holder in due course when it held the note. A holder in due course is, with some exceptions, "immune to defenses, claims in recoupment, and claims of title that prior parties to commercial paper might assert. The holder in due course always enjoys certain pleading and proof advantages."[8] So if Heritage were a holder in due course, it would enjoy an advantageous position in litigation with Bruha.

We conclude, however, that Heritage is not a holder in due course because the note was not "negotiable" and article 3 of the Uniform Commercial Code does not apply to this case.

Neb. U.C.C. §3-104(a) (Cum. Supp. 2010) provides: "Except as provided in subsections (c) and (d), 'negotiable instrument' means an unconditional promise or order to pay *a fixed amount of money,* with or without interest or other charges described in the promise or order. . . ." (Emphasis supplied.) Here, the note fails to meet the definition of a "negotiable instrument" because it was not a promise "to pay a fixed amount of money."

8. 2 James J. White & Robert S. Summers, Uniform Commercial Code §17-1 at 168-69 (5th ed. 2008).

Although the Uniform Commercial Code allows notes to have a variable interest rate,[9] under §3-104(a), the principal amount must be fixed.[10] "A fixed amount is an absolute requisite to negotiability."[11] This is because unless a purchaser can determine how much it will be paid under the instrument, it will be unable to determine a fair price to pay for it, which defeats the basic purpose for negotiable instruments.[12]

We applied this principle in Rodehorst v. Gartner,[13] in which we stated that "[a] guaranty is not an agreement to pay a fixed amount and is therefore not a negotiable instrument subject to article 3 of the Nebraska Uniform Commercial Code." To meet the fixed amount requirement, the fixed amount generally must be determinable by reference to the instrument itself without any reference to any outside source.[14] If reference to a separate instrument or extrinsic facts is needed to ascertain the principal due, the sum is not " 'certain' " or fixed.[15]

Here, the text of the note states that Bruha "promises to pay . . . the principal amount of Seventy-five Thousand & 00/100 Dollars ($75,000.00) *or so much as may be outstanding*. . . ." (Emphasis supplied.) Further, the note states that it "evidences a revolving line of credit" and that Bruha could request advances under the obligation up to $75,000. This fails the "fixed amount of money" requirement of §3-104(a); one looking at the instrument itself cannot tell how much Bruha has been advanced at any given time. So, the note is not negotiable. Stated simply, "[a] note given to secure a line of credit under which the amount of the obligation varies, depending on the extent to which the line of credit is used, is not negotiable. . . ."[16]

For a person to be a holder in due course, the instrument must be negotiable.[17] Because the note was not a negotiable instrument, neither the FDIC nor Heritage could ever become a holder in due course of it under Nebraska law. And further, because this note is not a negotiable instrument, article 3 does not apply.[18]

9. See Neb. U.C.C. §3-112 (Reissue 2001).

10. See id., comment 1. See, also, 6 William D. Hawkland & Lary Lawrence, Uniform Commercial Code Series §3-104:7 (rev. 1999).

11. 6 Hawkland & Lawrence, *supra* note [10] at 3-45.

12. *Id.*

13. Rodehorst v. Gartner, 266 Neb. 842, 848, 669 N.W.2d 679, 684 (2003).

14. 4 William D. Hawkland & Lary Lawrence, Uniform Commercial Code Series §3-106:2 (rev. 1999).

15. See *id.* at 3-100. See, also, Resolution Trust v. Oaks Apts. Joint Venture, 966 F.2d 995 (5th Cir. 1992); Branch Banking and Trust Co. v. Creasy, 301 N.C. 44, 269 S.E.2d 117 (1980).

16. 11 Am. Jur. 2d *Bills and Notes* §84 at 463-64 (2009). See, also, Yin v. Society National Bank Indiana, 665 N.E.2d 58 (Ind. App. 1996); Farmers Production Credit Assoc. v. Arena, 145 Vt. 20, 481 A.2d 1064 (1984).

17. See Neb. U.C.C. §3-302 (Reissue 2001).

18. See Neb. U.C.C. §3-102 (Reissue 2001).

[The court, however, still ruled in favor of the bank as an assignee from the FDIC, and that portion of the case will be studied in Chapter 10, when we get to the issue of holding in due course.]

E. "Courier Without Luggage" Requirement

Pennsylvania's Chief Justice John Gibson once said that a negotiable instrument must be a "courier without luggage." Overton v. Tyler, 3 Pa. 346, 347 (1846). This oft-repeated description means that the instrument must not be burdened with anything other than the simple and clean unconditional promise or order; it cannot be made to truck around other legal obligations. If the maker of a note adds any *additional* promises to it, the note becomes non-negotiable because the prospective holder is then given notice that the note is or may be conditioned on the performance of the other promise. Section 3-104(a)(3) specifies the few additional items that may be mentioned in an instrument without destroying its negotiable character; read it and then do Problem 102.

PROBLEM 102

Do the following clauses in an otherwise negotiable promissory note destroy negotiability?

(a) "Maker agrees that signing this note also indicates acceptance of the contract of sale for which it is given."

(b) "Maker agrees and promises that if the holder of this note deems himself insecure at any time, he may so inform the maker, who will then supply additional collateral in an amount and kind to be specified by the holder."

(c) "Maker agrees to let the holder select an attorney for the maker; at any time the holder directs, said attorney is hereby given the authority to confess judgment against the maker in any appropriate court."

(d) The promissory note contained the following clause:

> I have the right to make payments of Principal at any time before they are due. A payment of Principal only is known as a "Prepayment." When I make a Prepayment, I will tell the Note Holder in writing that I am doing so. I may not designate a payment as a Prepayment if I have not made all the monthly payments due under this Note.

Does it destroy negotiability? See HSBC Bank USA, Natl. Assn. v. Gouda, 2010 WL 5128666 (N.J. Super. 2010).

(e) "Maker hereby grants the payee a security interest in the collateral described below."

DZ Bank AG Deutsche Zentral-Genossenschaftsbank v. McCranie

United States Court of Appeals, Eleventh Circuit, 2018
720 F. App'x 576

MELLOY, Circuit Judge:

In this breach-of-contract action, the district court conducted a bench trial and concluded a written contract ("the Note") was a negotiable instrument, Plaintiff-Creditor DZ Bank AG Deutsche Zentral-Genossenschaftsbank ("DZ Bank") was a holder in due course, and this status alone defeated Defendant-Debtor Michael McCranie's defenses to enforcement of the Note. The district court held in the alternative that, even if McCranie could assert his defenses, he failed to prove them. The district court then determined McCranie defaulted on the Note and was liable for damages. McCranie appeals. We conclude the Note is not a negotiable instrument but was properly transferred to DZ Bank. Moreover, we conclude McCranie's defenses fail and the Note is enforceable. Accordingly, we affirm the judgment of the district court. . . .

A. NEGOTIABLE INSTRUMENT

Pursuant to the U.C.C., as adopted in Kansas, " 'negotiable instrument' means an unconditional promise . . . to pay a fixed amount of money, with or without interest . . . to bearer or to order . . . [that] does not state any other undertaking or instruction by the person promising . . . payment." Kan. Stat. Ann. §84-3-104(a). Although this definition appears rigid, certain conditions and additional promises or undertakings are permitted without defeating negotiability: those that relate to security interests, prepayment rights, or duties surrounding the preservation of collateral. See id. §84-3-104(a)(3) ("[T]he promise . . . may contain (i) an undertaking or power to give, maintain, or protect collateral to secure payment, [or] (ii) an authorization or power to the holder to confess judgment or realize on or dispose of collateral. . . .").

A hallmark of negotiability, however, is the self-contained nature of the instrument and the ability to determine the entirety of the parties' rights and duties without consulting additional writings. See 6 William D. Hawkland & Larry Lawrence, Uniform Commercial Code Series §3-106:2 (rev. supp. 2016) ("An instrument does not freely circulate in commerce if a purchaser must examine a separate agreement to determine whether payment of the instrument is conditioned upon the performance of some act or event. . . . The mere existence of the requirement that another writing be consulted is sufficient to destroy negotiability; it is irrelevant that examination of the other writing does not reveal a condition precedent to payment."). In general, a *mere reference* to a separate document does not preclude a note from being deemed a negotiable instrument. See A.I. Trade Fin., Inc. v. Laminaciones de Lesaca, S.A., 41 F.3d 830, 836 (2d Cir. 1994) ("[A] note containing an otherwise unconditional promise is not made conditional merely because it refers to, or states that it arises from, a separate agreement or transaction."); see also Williams v. Regency Fin. Corp., 309 F.3d 1045, 1049 (8th Cir. 2002) ("[W]here there is a paucity of [controlling] case law interpreting a provision of the U.C.C., . . . courts . . . look for guidance to decisions of other jurisdictions. . . ."); Black v. Don Schmid Motor, Inc., 232 Kan. 458, 657 P.2d 517, 523-24 (1983) (looking to other jurisdictions). Mere references provide context for the commercial transactions giving rise to the instrument and do not, on their face, suggest the promise to pay is subject to additional terms, conditions, or promises.

In contrast, a "disqualifying" reference is one that indicates a need to examine a separate document to determine the parties' rights and duties, *i.e.*, one that indicates the promise to pay is "subject to" or "governed by" the other writing. Kan. Stat. Ann. §84-3-106(a) ("[A] promise or order is unconditional unless it states . . . (2) that the promise or order is subject to or governed by another writing."). Even a reference indicating a need to consult a separate writing, however, will not defeat negotiability if the reference makes clear that the terms in the separate writing relate to a grant or preservation of collateral or to prepayment or acceleration. These exceptions are express on the face of §84-3-106(b)(1), and they relate simply to the permissible undertakings and promises pursuant to §84-3-104(a)(3).

The distinction between when a note's reference to another writing does or does not defeat negotiability, therefore, rests on two factors: the completeness and clarity of the note itself in setting forth the parties' obligations and the clarity and completeness of the reference. This is true regardless of whether the separate writing actually amends the material terms of the parties' agreement. It is the need to consult the other writing that makes the note incomplete on its face and defeats negotiability. The applicable official U.C.C. comment makes this clear:

> [A] promissory note is not [a negotiable] instrument . . . if it contains any of the following statements: 1. "This note is subject to a contract of sale dated . . . between the payee and maker of this note." 2. "This note is subject to a loan and security agreement dated . . . between the payee and maker of this note." 3. "Rights and obligations of the parties with respect to this note are stated in an agreement dated . . . between the payee and maker of this note." *It is not relevant whether any condition to payment is or is not stated in the writing to which reference is made. The rationale is that the holder of a negotiable instrument should not be required to examine another document to determine rights with respect to payment.* But subsection (b)(i) permits reference to a separate writing for information with respect to collateral, prepayment, or acceleration.
>
> For example, a note would not be made conditional by the following statement: "This note is secured by a security interest in collateral described

> in a security agreement dated . . . between the payee and maker of this note. Rights and obligations with respect to the collateral are [stated in] [governed by] the security agreement." The bracketed words are alternatives, either of which complies.

U.C.C. §3-106, cmt. (emphasis added).

Here, McCranie argues the Note's reference to the Advancement Agreement which states, "ADDITIONAL TERMS: See Agreement for Advancement of Loan dated October 30, 2000," defeats negotiability because this reference indicates not merely the existence of a separate agreement, but the existence of unidentified "additional terms." According to McCranie the phrase "additional terms" necessarily describes contractual terms that govern the parties' relationship under the Note, unambiguously informing a reader of the Note that the Note is not wholly self-contained. DZ Bank counters that the Advancement Agreement creates no additional rights for DZ Bank and imposes no additional duties on McCranie other than rights and duties that are permissible under Kansas Statutes §§84-3-104 and 106, namely, rights and duties concerning the grant of security interests, the preservation of collateral, and the right of the lender to declare default and demand accelerated payment in the event of default. In the alternative, DZ Bank asserts the quoted reference is a mere reference indicating the existence of a separate agreement.

Given the Advancement Agreement's myriad protections for Brooke Credit and obligations for McCranie, we have serious doubts as to DZ Bank's assertion that the Advancement Agreement contains only permissible undertakings. Regardless, the actual contents of the Advancement Agreement do not matter for our analysis of this issue. The reference in the Note, in and of itself, defeats negotiability. The Note does not merely recite the existence of the Advancement Agreement, but instead, indicates that the Advancement Agreement contains "additional terms." This reference is akin to a disqualifying statement that the Note is "subject to" or "governed" by the separate writing. Kan. Stat. Ann. §84-3-106(a)(2). Further, nothing about the reference to the Advancement Agreement, as expressed in the Note, suggests that these additional terms relate solely to the permissible subjects of granting or preserving collateral or spelling out acceleration or prepayment rights. Simply put, no party examining the Note can know with any reasonable assurance what the subject matter of the "additional terms" might be without obtaining and consulting the Advancement Agreement.

Further, and importantly, the reference to the Advancement Agreement is additional to and wholly apart from the Note's separate reference to the Security Agreement. The Note, several lines below the reference to the Advancement Agreement, employs a box to set off text from the balance of the document and draw attention to the statement, "SECURITY: This note is separately secured by (describe separate document by type and date): Security Agreement dated October 30, 2000." This identification of a second separate writing as governing the parties' security arrangement—a different writing separate and apart from the referenced Advancement Agreement—most naturally suggests that the additional terms in the Advancement Agreement relate to something *other than* a security interest. At a minimum, the inclusion of this separate reference does nothing to clarify that the Advancement Agreement might contain only permissible undertakings pursuant to §84-3-106(b)(1).

DZ Bank's arguments concerning the actual contents of the Advance Agreement, therefore, are misplaced. Given the inability to determine from the face of the Note that the "additional terms" might relate solely to permissible topics under §84-3-106(b)(1), the Note is not negotiable. Because we conclude the Note is not a negotiable instrument, we need not address whether DZ Bank is a "holder in due course" as that term is a term of art under the UCC.

[The court then found that none of the defenses offered were valid, so that DZ Bank was entitled to payment of the note even if it was not a holder in due course of a negotiable instrument. It prevailed under basic breach of contract principles.]

Because the note was properly transferred and McCranie's defenses fail, we affirm the judgment of the district court.

AFFIRMED.

The following case was decided before the effective date of the 1990 version of Articles 3 and 4 of the Uniform Commercial Code, but the rule of law it states has not changed. The court cites the original numbering of Article 3; you need look only at the current version of §3-104(a).

Woodworth v. The Richmond Indiana Venture

Ohio Court of Common Pleas, 1990
1990 WL 293436

JOHNSON, J.

This matter is before the court on plaintiff's motion for partial summary judgment and defendant Signet Bank's motion for summary judgment. On December 18, 1987, plaintiff executed a promissory note in which he promised to pay to the order of The Richmond Indiana Venture, A Limited Partnership or holder the sum of $655,625.00. The promissory note was given to pay part of the deferred portion of plaintiff's investment in the partnership. The promissory note was subsequently assigned or negotiated to defendant, Signet Bank. Plaintiff is in default on the promissory note having failed to make payments that fell due on July 1, 1989 and July 1, 1990. Plaintiff filed this action on November 2, 1989.

The standard for granting summary judgment is clear. On a motion for summary judgment, the moving party bears the burden of demonstrating that no genuine issue of material fact exists and that it is entitled to judgment as a matter of law. Adickes v. S.H. Kress and Co. (1970), 398 U.S. 144; Harless v. Willis Day Warehousing Co. (1978), 54 Ohio St. 2d 64, 66. The court will construe the evidence most strongly in favor of the party against whom the motion for summary judgment is made. *Harless*, 54 Ohio St. 2d at 66.

In order to be negotiable, a promissory note must be a signed, unconditional promise to pay a sum certain in money which is payable on demand or at a definite, stated time. The note must be payable to order or bearer and contain no other promise, order, obligation, or power given by the maker except as authorized by §§3-101 to 3-805, inclusive, of the Revised Code. UCC §3-104.

The policy under pre-Code law was that instruments should be as concise as possible and free from collateral engagements. Akron Auto Finance Co. v. Stonebraker (1941), 66 Ohio App. 507. As noted above, the Code continues this policy by mandating that the unconditional promise to pay not be cluttered by other promises, orders, obligations, or powers unless otherwise authorized.

The promissory note at issue contains the following term:

> The undersigned agrees that, in the event any payment due pursuant to the terms of this note be not timely made, at the option of the Partnership, the undersigned shall retroactively lose any interest in the Partnership from the date hereof and the Partnership shall have no obligation to account for any payments theretofore made by the undersigned, and that this remedy is in addition to other remedies afforded by the Partnership Agreement.

This term is clearly a promise by the maker resulting in a forfeiture of his partnership interest and payments in the event of default. The term is more than a mere reference to the partnership agreement, a recitation of security, or an agreement to protect collateral; it is a forfeiture provision in addition to other remedies under the referenced partnership agreement.

In Pacific Finance Loans v. Goodwin (1974), 41 Ohio App. 2d 141, the court held that the requirement of an unconditional promise to pay is contravened by a term providing for the repossession of collateral by a seller without judicial process. The case sub judice is analogous since the term at issue is a forfeiture without resort to judicial process.

Nothing in R.C. §3-104 or §3-112 authorizes the forfeiture term at issue. Based on the above analysis, the court finds that the negotiability of this promissory note is doubtful. Where there is doubt, the decision should be against negotiability. Official Code Comment 5 to UCC §3-104. Since the promissory note is not negotiable, defendant Signet Bank cannot claim the status of a holder in due course and is subject to ordinary contract defenses that plaintiff may assert.

Having considered the pleadings and memoranda filed herein, the court finds that plaintiff has fulfilled his burden. Accordingly, plaintiff's motion is sustained. Defendant's motion is denied. Counsel for plaintiff shall prepare an appropriate entry. . . .

Motion for Reconsideration

This matter is before the court on defendant's motion for reconsideration. Upon consideration of the memoranda filed herein, the court affirms its decision of September 19, 1990.

The court finds persuasive the fact that the forfeiture provision may be exercised at the option of the *partnership*, not the holder of the instrument. The provision does not require that the holder must declare a default before the partnership may exercise its option. Instead, the partnership may declare a forfeiture if payments are not timely made. A situation could develop, by mistake or otherwise, wherein the partnership exercises its option before the holder declares a default. In such case, the maker might well decline to cure an overdue payment or to make future payments because of the forfeiture. This exemplifies the reason why negotiable instruments may contain no other promise, order, obligation, or power except as authorized by statute.

The forfeiture provision at issue is not, as defendant suggests, analogous to collateral. It is a basic maxim of law that collateral follows the debt; here the option to declare a forfeiture remains with the partnership and the benefit of its exercise flows to the partnership, not the holder of the instrument.

This case is distinguishable from Standard Premium Plan Corp. v. Hirschorn (N.Y. Sup. Ct., 1968), 5 U.C.C. Rep. Serv. 163. In *Hirschorn*, the payee or assignee, in the event of default, could cancel an underlying insurance policy and apply returned premiums against the unpaid balance. Here the forfeiture flows to the partnership, not the holder and the forfeited interest is not applied to the unpaid balance on the instrument.

Any deleterious effects upon the flow of commercial instruments can be avoided by confining forfeiture provisions such as this one to the partnership agreement. Including such provision in the instrument clutters the unconditional promise to pay and thereby makes the commercial viability of this instrument less certain. . . .

. . . Counsel for plaintiff shall prepare an appropriate entry.

F. "Payable on Demand or at a Definite Time"

A holder of an instrument must be able to tell when it comes due, or the instrument is non-negotiable; however, there is no requirement that the instrument be dated. An undated instrument that specifies no time of payment is treated as an instrument payable on demand by the holder. Read §§3-108 and 3-113.

PROBLEM 103

Do the following clauses in a promissory note destroy negotiability?

(a) "Payable 30 days after sight."

(b) "Payable in eleven successive monthly installments of $2,414.92 each and in a final payment of $2,415.03 thereafter. The first installment being payable on the _____ day of _____ 20___, and the remaining installments on the same date of each month thereafter until paid." The blanks were not filled in. See Barclays Bank PLC v. Johnson, 129 N.C. App. 370, 499 S.E.2d 768 (1998).

(c) "Payable on November 8, 2022, but the holder may demand payment at any time prior thereto if he deems himself insecure." Cf. §1-309 (Option to Accelerate at Will).

(d) "Payable when the sun comes up tomorrow."

(e) "Payable on November 8, 2022, but if my potato crop fails that year, payment shall be extended until November 8 of the following year."

(f) "Payable on November 8, 2022, but the maker hereby reserves the option to extend the time of payment until he can pay without serious financial hardship." See Smith v. Vaughn, 174 Ohio App. 3d 473, 882 N.E.2d 941 (2007).

(g) "Payable 120 days after my rich uncle Al dies." Such notes are called *post-obituary* notes.

(h) "Payable 100 years from the date of this note, but if my rich uncle Al dies before this note is due, it shall become payable 10 days after his death." See Smith v. Gentilotti, 371 Mass. 839, 359 N.E.2d 953(1977).

(i) "Payable on my next birthday."

PROBLEM 104

A paragraph in a promissory note required the maker to give written notice to the holder of the note in the event that the maker wanted to make a prepayment of the principal amount before the scheduled date of maturity of the loan. Is this note payable at a definite time, in your opinion? Consider whether such an obligation makes the payment of the note less certain, and note §3-108(b). See In re Steinberg, 498 B.R. 391 (B.A.P. 10th Cir. 2013).

G. *"Payable to Bearer or to Order"*

The early English common law courts would not permit a subsequent holder of a contract to sue one of the original parties to it; the courts said that there was no *privity* (connection) between the plaintiff and the defendant. These cases were frustrating to the merchants of the day because they recognized the desirability of permitting a direct suit by a remote transferee against the original promisor. These merchants and their attorneys devised two clever ways of establishing privity between the original creator of the paper and the later holder.

The first way was to make the original promise or order payable to *bearer*—that is, payable to the holder of the paper and not to any specific person. In this way, privity passed with the physical delivery of the instrument. The only problem with bearer paper, which is still with us, is that it is too negotiable; it is a little bit too much like money for safety. In Miller v. Race, 1 Burr. 452, 97 Eng. Rep. 398 (K.B. 1758), Lord Mansfield was faced with the problem of a bearer note that had been stolen from the mails and negotiated to plaintiff by one "who had the appearance of a gentleman." Lord Mansfield held that title to bearer paper passes with the instrument since negotiable paper is to be "treated as money, as cash." Plaintiff, a holder in due course, took free of the defense of theft, and defendant had to pay the note.

The second means of establishing privity was to have the creator of the instrument make it payable to a specified person or to whomever that person further ordered the paper paid; thus, notes were made payable to "John Smith or Order" or "John Smith or his assigns." This means the person to whom Doe ordered payment acquired privity, since the original promise ran directly to the assignee. This order paper today simply says "Pay to the order of John Smith," meaning that the instrument will be paid to John Smith or to whomever he orders as his nominee. Until John Smith makes some sort of *order*, the instrument cannot be validly transferred. He usually does this by writing his order on the back of the instrument and then signing his own name.

Section 3-104(a)(1) of the Code continues this ancient requirement that the maker or drawer use either bearer or order language (*words of negotiability*) on an instrument before it is technically negotiable. These special words have become so associated with negotiable instruments that they now serve as one means of easily identifying contracts that are meant to be negotiable, and thus warn people that they may be creating paper having the legal consequences of negotiable transfer (loss of defenses on the underlying contract). Read §3-109.

PROBLEM 105

Do the following clauses in a promissory note create bearer paper?

(a) "Pay to John Smith." See Sunrizon Homes, Inc. v. American Guar. Inv. Corp., 782 P.2d 103 (Okla. 1988).

(b) "Pay to the order of John Smith or bearer." See Official Comment 2 to §3-109.

(c) "Pay to bearer."

(d) "Pay to the order of Cash."

(e) "Pay to a Merry Christmas."

PROBLEM 106

Do the following clauses create order or bearer paper, or do they make the instrument non-negotiable for failure to create either?

(a) "Pay to the order of (blank)." See §3-115 and Official Comment 2.

(b) A promissory note with this language: "Pay to John Doe's estate." See §3-110(c)(2)(i); Sirius LC v. Erickson, 144 Idaho 38, 156 P.3d 539 (2007).

(c) "Pay to the order of the President of the United States." See §3-110(c)(2)(iv).

(d) The drawer of a check drew a line through the words "the order of" that were printed on the check prior to the space for the payee's name. Is the check, as altered, negotiable? See §3-104(c). If the drawer of a check or the maker of a promissory note wants to destroy negotiability, what should be done? See §3-104(d). Why would this ever be desirable?

H. Consumer Notes

Because the creation of a negotiable instrument deprives a maker of the usual contract defenses, most commentators have argued that it is unwise to permit consumers to sign promissory notes. Many state consumer statutes forbid a seller or a lessor to take a negotiable instrument (other than a check) as part of a consumer sale or lease. These statutes do not typically destroy the negotiability of such an instrument, however, and if a consumer note were to get into the hands of a holder in due course, the consumer would still be unable to assert contract defenses when the holder in due course demanded payment. See Circle v. Jim Walter Homes, Inc., 535 F.2d

583 (10th Cir. 1976); see also Jefferson v. Mitchell Select Furniture Co., 56 Ala. App. 259, 321 So. 2d 216 (1975) ("Of course, it is difficult to conceive how one could be a holder of a negotiable instrument which showed that it was taken in the credit sale of consumer merchandise with retention of title and a purchase money security interest, without knowledge that it arose from [a violation of the statute]."). Some states have special statutes allowing some defenses to be raised even against a holder in due course. The Uniform Consumer Credit Code (adopted in a number of jurisdictions) §3.404(1) (1974 text) preserves all consumer's defenses even if the instrument is owned by a holder in due course.

The Federal Trade Commission has promulgated a regulation, 16 C.F.R. part 433, requiring that all promissory notes and contracts taken in consumer sales or *purchase money loans* (defined as loans made to purchase goods or services from a seller who refers the consumer to the lender or who is affiliated with the lender by common control, contract, or business arrangement) contain the following language:

NOTICE

ANY HOLDER OF THIS CONSUMER CREDIT CONTRACT IS SUBJECT TO ALL CLAIMS AND DEFENSES WHICH THE DEBTOR COULD ASSERT AGAINST THE SELLER OF GOODS OR SERVICES OBTAINED PURSUANT HERETO OR WITH THE PROCEEDS HEREOF. RECOVERY HEREUNDER BY THE DEBTOR SHALL NOT EXCEED AMOUNTS PAID BY THE DEBTOR HEREUNDER.

The regulation applies to all such notes or contracts signed after May 14, 1976; see J. White & R. Summers, Uniform Commercial Code (6th ed. 2010) §15-9. Failure to include the required statement violates §5 of the Federal Trade Commission Act (forbidding Unfair and Deceptive Practices), and §3-305(e) in the 2002 Revision of Article 3 of the Uniform Commercial Code automatically adds the missing statement to all consumer transactions that should carry it.

QUESTION

Does the required FTC language destroy negotiability? See §3-106(d).

PROBLEM 107

Sonata, about to take music lessons, purchased a violin on credit from Barenboim Music, which negotiated the note to Titolare Finance Co. The note bore the above FTC legend. When the note came due, Sonata refused to pay Titolare Finance because the violin fell apart after three lessons. Can Titolare Finance claim it is a holder in due course and thus entitled to enforce the note in spite of her defense? See §3-305(e); Timmons v. SunTrust Bank, 834 S.E.2d 298 (Ga. App. 2019). Is this true even if the note had failed to contain the FTC notice? See also §§9-403(d) and 9-404(d). Would we reach the same result if Sonata were a professional musician?

CHAPTER 8 ASSESSMENT: MULTIPLE CHOICE QUESTIONS

1. Djuna purchased a 3D printer from Joyce for $19,390. As part of the transaction, Djuna signed a piece of paper promising to pay $19,390. What difference does it make if that piece of paper is a negotiable instrument?
   a. If it is a negotiable instrument, Djuna would have to pay $19,390 to a holder in due course of the paper, even if Joyce delivered a defective printer or no printer at all.
   b. If it is not a negotiable instrument, Djuna would have to pay only if she was obliged to pay under contract law. If Joyce does not deliver as promised, that would reduce or excuse Djuna's obligation to pay.
   c. If it is a negotiable instrument, UCC Article 3 would govern most issues that would arise: how to transfer rights in the paper to someone else, who is liable if the paper is stolen, how to present the paper for payment, what effect it would have if there were a mistake in the numbers on the paper, etc.
   d. All of the above.

2. The paper that Djuna signed contains this provision: "Djuna is obliged to pay if Joyce delivers the 3D printer as promised." Can the paper be a negotiable instrument?
   a. Yes. She has made an unconditional promise to pay once the printer is delivered.
   b. Yes, but she only has to pay if Joyce delivers the 3D printer as promised.
   c. No. It is conditional and so not a negotiable instrument.
   d. No. Negotiable instruments are used only in loan transactions, not sales.

3. Shaun got a loan from Isobel for $50,000. He signed a mortgage, putting up his house as collateral for the loan. The parties then realized they had forgotten to prepare a promissory note. Shaun copied the text of a negotiable promissory note into an email message, edited it to be payable to the order of Isobel for the amount of $50,000, typed his name at the bottom, and sent it to Isobel. Could someone be a holder in due course of that electronic promissory note?
   a. Yes, if the text meets all the requirements of Article 3.

b. No. It is neither a writing nor made effective by UETA, because there is no "single authoritative copy of the transferable record."
c. Yes. Shaun will be bound by his promise to pay, without regard to formalities.
d. No. Only paper documents can be negotiable instruments.

4. Shem Bank loaned $45,000 to Issy. Issy signed a promissory note payable to the order of Shem Bank, which contains this clause: "Issy hereby promises Shem Bank to have right of first refusal, should she need to borrow money in the future." Can the promissory note be negotiable?
   a. No, because it has an undertaking in addition to the promise to pay the money.
   b. No, because the clause did not read "Issy hereby promises *to the order of* Shem Bank."
   c. Yes. Issy has promised to pay the money without any conditions. The extra promise does not detract from that.
   d. Yes. Otherwise Issy would not have to repay the loan, which would defeat the purpose of the transaction.

5. Which of the following could be on a negotiable check?
   a. Pay to the order of Freddie.
   b. Pay to bearer.
   c. Pay to Freddie.
   d. Pay to Freddie or bearer.
   e. All of the above.

ANSWERS

1. *D* is the best answer. This fact pattern illustrates the role of negotiability. UCC Article 3 applies to negotiable instruments. If the piece of paper is a negotiable instrument, then it will be governed by Article 3, so *C* is correct. One of the rules in Article 3 is the holder in due course doctrine. Later chapters cover that doctrine in detail, but basically a holder in due course can recover from anyone who signed the instrument, even if that person has a defense to payment. A holder in due course could recover from Djuna if Joyce delivered a defective printer. So *A* is also correct. The holder in due course doctrine only applies to negotiable instruments. So if the piece of paper is not a negotiable instrument, that promise would be governed by contract law. As you learned in contracts, if Joyce breached, then Djuna's promise to pay would be reduced or excused—even if the contract had been assigned. *B* is correct as well, so the best answer is *D*. All of the above.

   Note that, as the last section in this chapter explains, the holder in due course doctrine does not apply to notes in consumer credit sales, but such notes may still be negotiable, and so governed by the other rules in Article 3.

2. *C* is the best answer. The provision states an express condition to payment, so the promise to pay is conditional, making the promissory note non-negotiable. The fact pattern shows the reason for the rule. The promissory note says, right on its face, that Djuna is obliged only if Joyce performs as promised. It would not make sense to apply Article 3's holder in due course doctrine, under which Djuna would have to pay a holder in due course even if Joyce did not perform as promised (i.e., Djuna could not raise any defense to payment against a holder in due course).

   The condition (like all conditions) may be fulfilled. The question is whether there is an express condition to payment. So *B* and *C* are both wrong. *D* is incorrect. Negotiable instruments may be used in loans, sales, or any other type of transactions—or even as gifts.
3. *B* is the best answer. As discussed in Good v. Wells Fargo Bank, the UETA provides that an electronic promissory note for a mortgage loan may be treated as a negotiable instrument, so *D* is wrong. But, to be effective as a negotiable instrument, the record must meet all the conditions in the UETA. The key requirement is that there be a "single authoritative copy of the transferable record." Negotiable instrument law assumes that there is only one copy of the instrument, and so only one holder of the instrument entitled to payment. If there were multiple copies, then there could be multiple holders entitled to payment. The UETA accommodates this policy, by providing that for electronic promissory notes, there must be the equivalent, just one authoritative copy. An email can be freely copied and forwarded, so the email would not qualify. *A* is incorrect, because negotiability does not depend only on the text. *C* has it backward. Article 3 and the UETA use formalities to ensure that Article 3 only applies to the sort of promises it was intended to apply to. Contract law has flexibility to deal with other promises.
4. *A* is the best answer. The clause is an additional undertaking, making the promissory note non-negotiable, under §3-104(a)(3). *B* simply misleads, referring to a different and irrelevant rule. To be negotiable, an instrument must be unconditional *and* must not have extra undertakings, so *C* is incorrect.

   If a promissory note is non-negotiable, that does not mean that the promise is not enforceable. Rather, it simply means that the promise is not governed by UCC Article 3, but is governed by some other body of law, usually contract law. *A* promise to pay money may be enforced under contract law. *D* is incorrect.

5. *E* is the best answer. Someone who signs a negotiable promissory note is really promising to pay. Even if the person does not get what was promised, or the person has some other defense to payment, the person will nevertheless have to pay, if the note ends up in the hands of a holder in due course. To limit the rule to notes that the signer should expect to be presented by such strangers, a negotiable note must be payable to order ("I'll pay whomever payee orders me to pay") or bearer ("I'll pay whomever shows up with this note"). A promise to pay Freddie (as opposed to "pay to the order of Freddie"), by contrast, is a personal obligation to pay Freddie, and if Freddie is not entitled to payment, should not be enforceable. If this were a promissory note, only *A*, *B*, and *D* could be negotiable. But that rule does not apply here, because the facts involve a check, not a promissory note.

   Some promissory notes are negotiable, some are not. But everyone expect checks to be passed on. So the rule requiring order or bearer language is not required on checks. Any of the possibilities is permitted on a negotiable check, so the best answer is *E*. All of the above.

CHAPTER 9
NEGOTIATION

The movement of negotiable instruments from one person to another can be as involuntary as a theft or as deliberate as a sale. It is the lawyer's job to make sure that clients observe the formalities so that transfers are valid and clients won't be thinking ugly thoughts about malpractice.

I. SOME TECHNICAL TERMS

A. Parties

Those whose names appear on a negotiable instrument are given definite labels with specific legal consequences varying according to the label affixed.

A promissory note in its most pristine state is a two-party instrument. The person who issues the instrument and promises to pay is called the *maker.* According to §3-412, the legal duty of the issuer of a promissory note is to "pay the instrument (i) according to its terms at the time it was issued . . . (ii) if the issuer signed an incomplete instrument, according to its terms when completed."[1] The person to whom the note is made payable is the *payee*. If the note is made payable to *bearer*, there is no specific payee, and whoever has possession of the paper is presumptively entitled to payment by the maker.

A draft (or check) is always a three-party instrument. The person who creates the draft and orders the drawee to pay is called the *drawer*. Though the courts, and others who should know better, frequently do so, be careful that you do not confuse a *drawer* with a *maker*; there are important differences between their legal responsibilities. A *drawer* creates a *draft*, a *maker* creates a *note*. According to §3-414(b), by drawing a draft, the drawer engages that upon dishonor of the draft by the drawee the drawer will pay the amount of the draft. The *drawee* is the person to whom the drawer addresses the order of payment. On a check, the drawee is the bank at which the drawer has an account.[2] The *payee* of a draft is the person specified by the drawer as entitled to receive payment. As with notes, if the draft is payable to bearer, there is no specific payee, and any holder is entitled to payment from the drawee. If a check is drawn payable to the order of a specific person, that person is the *payee* and may further transfer (*negotiate*) the check in the manner described below.

B. *Negotiability vs. Negotiation*

Be careful not to confuse these two very similar terms. The question "Is an instrument negotiable?" asks if the instrument is in the proper form to meet the technical requirements of negotiability found in §3-104(a). The question "Has the instrument been negotiated?" asks about the legal validity of the attempted transfer of the instrument. Thus, negotiability refers to *form*, negotiation to *transfer*.

II. TRANSFER AND NEGOTIATION

A negotiable instrument goes through three stages in its life. The first stage is called *issuance*. Read §3-105. Skipping for a moment the middle stage, the final stage in the existence of a negotiable instrument is its *presentment* for payment. Read §3-501(a). We will consider the legal ramifications

1. The issuer of a cashier's check assumes the same liability according to §3-412.

2. As we shall see when we get to bank collection, in Article 4 of the Code the drawee is referred to there as the *payor bank*. See §4-105(3).

of both issuance and presentment elsewhere. For now, we focus on the middle stage: the *transfer* of the instrument, meaning every legally significant movement of the paper between issuance and presentment.

It was a basic rule at common law and is now a statutory rule, §3-203(b), that the physical transfer of an instrument, if intended to give the recipient rights to the instrument (whether or not a technical *negotiation*), vests in the transferee whatever rights the transferor had in the instrument. This is the called the "shelter rule" because the transferee takes shelter in the rights of the transferor. We will consider the shelter rule in detail in Chapter 10 when it is used to even pass holder in due course rights to parties who themselves do not qualify as HIDCs. For now just write the words "shelter rule" next to §3-203(b).

Under the Code, if the physical transfer is done in such a manner as to make the transferee a technical *holder* of the instrument, then the transfer is called a *negotiation.*[3] This is important because no one can become a *holder in due course* unless that person is first a holder, and becoming a holder is tied up with proper negotiation. Carefully read §1-201(b)(21)(A), defining *holder,* and §3-201, discussing *negotiation.* Think of it this way: a proper negotiation confers holder status on the transferee, with all the benefits holder status carries (including the possibility of becoming a holder in due course). Without a valid negotiation, the transferee is not a holder and has much more limited rights.

The negotiation of order paper is accomplished by (a) the indorsement by the proper person (who thereby becomes an *indorser*) and (b) the delivery of the instrument to the transferee (who thereupon qualifies as a *holder*). An *indorsement* is a signature placed on an instrument by the payee or any later transferees. The negotiation of bearer paper needs no indorsement; delivery to the transferee is all that is required for the transferee to qualify as a holder. Read all of §3-201.

III. SPECIAL AND BLANK INDORSEMENT

If the instrument is made payable to the order of a specific payee, that payee will be required to indorse the instrument to transfer it to another. A drawee bank, as a matter of course, will require the payee's indorsement

3. The issuance of the instrument to the first taker also creates *holder* status in that person without a negotiation having occurred. A named payee becomes a holder on getting possession of the instrument, and if the instrument is payable to bearer, anyone in possession of it is automatically a holder.

before it makes payment ("Please sign the back of the check here" the teller will say if you present the check across the counter); see §3-501(b)(2)(iii). As we shall see in Chapter 13 when we get to check collection, the bank in which checks are deposited into the payee's own account need not get its customer's signature as payee, but can pass the checks on to other banks unindorsed, while at the same time making a warranty that the check went into the payee's account at the depositary bank. The idea here was to speed up check collection by eliminating unneeded indorsements for items deposited in the correct accounts.

There are two different ways the payee can indorse any instrument. The payee can simply sign the back of the instrument. Such a signature is called a *blank indorsement* and has the legal effect of converting the instrument into bearer paper. If the payee wishes to preserve the *order* character of the instrument, the original payee may specify a new payee by writing "Pay (name of new payee)" above the indorsement. Such an indorsement is called a *special indorsement* and has the legal effect of making the instrument the sole property of the new payee, who becomes a *holder* as soon as the instrument is delivered. Further, the common law always provided that, until that moment, the original payee can strike out the special indorsement and do anything with the instrument—after all, until delivered to someone else it still belongs to the original payee.

No further "order" language is necessary as part of the special indorsement; the negotiability of an instrument is not affected by language written on the instrument during the course of negotiation. An indorsement that reads "Pay to Jane Doe" is legally the same as one that says "Pay to the order of Jane Doe." Read §3-205.

PROBLEM 108

David Hansen banked with the Mechanical National Bank. Hansen owed $50 to William Egger and decided to pay him by writing out a check for $50, using one of the checks Mechanical furnished him when he opened his account. He gave the check to Egger, who wrote his name on the back of the check. Egger gave the check to his wife, Cynthia, who took it down to the No Questions Check Cashing Store and asked the manager to cash it. The manager paid Cynthia $50 and then took the check and wrote "Pay to No Questions Check Cashing Store" just above William Egger's signature. When Billy Speed, the No Questions Check Cashing Store's messenger, came by, the manager gave the check to him for delivery to the Octopus National Bank, where the store had an account. Speed delivered the check to Octopus National Bank, where the bank's check processing machine merely stamped the words "Octopus National Bank" on the back of the check. Octopus National Bank then forwarded the check to the Mechanical National Bank. Answer the following questions:

(a) To which parties should these labels be attached: drawer, drawee, payee, or depositary bank (defined in §4-105(2))?

(b) Did the following people qualify as *holders*: David Hansen, William Egger, Cynthia Egger, the manager of No Questions Check Cashing Store, No Questions Check Cashing Store, Billy Speed, Octopus National Bank, and Mechanical National Bank?

(c) If William Egger had failed to indorse the check, but simply deposited it in his account with Octopus National Bank, would the bank have been a *holder*? See §4-205.

(d) What was the legal effect of the language written on the check by the check cashing store manager?

(e) Which of the parties are properly called *indorsers*? See §3-204.

PROBLEM 109

Mary and Donald Colpitts worked out a great deal for a new car with Façade Motors and promised the dealership to bring by a check for the agreed-upon amount the next day when they would pick up the vehicle. The couple then went to their bank, which had agreed to lend them the money for the car, and had the bank issue a check to them for the relevant amount. If the check is made payable to "Mary and Donald Colpitts," must both payees indorse it in order to negotiate it? What if the check were payable to "Mary or Donald Colpitts"? Must both payees indorse now? Finally, what if it simply is payable to "Mary Colpitts, Donald Colpitts" with no connecting word? Are two indorsements needed here? To answer all these questions, see §3-110(d) and its Official Comment 4.

Frequently in situations like the one in this Problem the bank will include the dealership's name and have all the payees' names "stacked" like this:

Mary Colpitts
Donald Colpitts
Pay to the order of Facade Motor Company

In that case do all three have to sign the check to properly negotiate it? See Pelican National Bank v. Provident National Bank of Maryland, 381 Md. 327, 849 A.2d 475 (2004). If a check payable to multiple payees is indorsed by only one of them, is that a proper negotiation? See McAllen Hospitals, L.P. v. State Farm County Mut. Ins. Co. of Texas, 57 Tex. Sup. Ct. J. 579 (Tex. 2014).

PROBLEM 110

When Portia Moot received her first paycheck from the law firm that recently hired her, she was annoyed to discover that it was made out to "Portia Mort." When she took the check to her bank to cash it, she mentioned the problem to the bank clerk, who promptly called you, the bank's attorney. What steps would you suggest the bank follow in this situation? See §3-204(d) and its Official Comment 3.

In the original version of Article 3, only a *holder* has the right to sue on an instrument to enforce payment, but §3-301 in the revised version would allow owners who are non-holders to sue in some circumstances, replacing the original word *holder* with the more inclusive *person entitled to enforce the instrument* (sometimes called the "PETE"). This term generally means a holder, but it also includes certain parties to whom other sections of the Code give similar rights (matters we will explore later). Read §3-301. To qualify as a holder under §1-201(b)(21), a person must meet two requirements: (a) possession of the instrument and, for non-bearer instruments, (b) be the *person identified* in the instrument (either as payee or special indorsee). Failure to establish *holder* status because of defects in negotiation can be legally fatal.

There is no requirement that the PETE also be the owner of the note. If the instrument is in the hands of a PETE, that's enough to allow enforcement; see Los Alamos National Bank v. Velasquez, 446 P.3d 1220 (N.M. App. 2019) (mortgage servicer to whom mortgage payments were made could enforce the note even though not the technical owner of the note).

Sometimes the indorsement is not made on the promissory note, but on a separate piece of paper, called an "allonge," which is formally defined as a piece of paper attached to the original note for purposes of indorsement.[4] An allonge has an interesting history, traceable to the days in which instruments circulated for long periods before being presented for payment. Consider, for example, the early period in United States history before it was even a country. People living in the Americas frequently had their banks back in Great Britain. If they drew up drafts ("checks") on these banks and gave them to another American, that person was unlikely to immediately send it across the Atlantic to the mother country. Instead, the payee would simply indorse it over to one of the payee's creditors, who would do the same. In those days drafts would circulate, more or less like

4. See Official Comment 1 (last paragraph) to §3-204.

money, for extended periods of time. But the drafts quickly ran out of room on which to place indorsements, so a separate piece of paper, called an "allonge," was glued to the original draft and the new indorsements were placed on the allonge. There are cases from Great Britain where the allonge had over a hundred indorsements before finally being presented to the drawee for payment.

The Uniform Commercial Code still allows the use of an allonge, and given the large number of transfers that some mortgage promissory notes have had in the last few years, there are many new cases dealing with the allonge. These cases frequently reveal problems with negotiation that give the current holder of the instrument difficulties in trying to establish "holder" status.

PROBLEM 111

Desert Paradise, Inc., initiated a scam in which hundreds of middle-class people signed promissory notes in order to invest in the supposed development of a retirement community to be built in the Southwest. Desert Paradise, the payee on all these notes, sold them in bulk to Octopus National Bank (ONB). Rather than indorsing its name hundreds of times on each of the notes, Desert Paradise had its indorsement printed on a separate sheet of paper, which it then folded into each promissory note, not connecting it in any way other than the fold. Desert Paradise's officials then absconded with the money and left the desert land untouched. Octopus National Bank demanded payment from the makers of the notes, and when they tried to raise defenses of breach of contract and fraud, ONB claimed to be a holder in due course, so as to take free of these defenses. Is ONB even a holder? See §3-204(a) and the last paragraph in its Official Comment 1. For a case with somewhat similar facts, see Adams v. Madison Realty & Dev., Inc., 853 F.2d 163 (3d Cir. 1988) ($19.5 million involved). The last sentence of §3-204(a) says that an allonge must be *affixed* to the instrument. What does "affixed" mean? Would a staple do the trick? See Lamson v. Commercial Credit Corp., 187 Colo. 382, 531 P.2d 966 (1975) ("Stapling is the modern equivalent of gluing or pasting. Certainly as a physical matter it is just as easy to cut by scissors a document pasted or glued to another use as it is to detach the two by unstapling."). One court has blessed the used of an Acco fastener; Federal Home Loan Mortg. Corp. v. Madison, 2011 WL 2690617 (D. Ariz. 2011). Do you think a paper clip "affixes" the allonge to the instrument? See Olive Portfolio Alpha, LLC v. 116 West Hubbard Street, LLC, 75 N.E.3d 381 (Ill. App. 2017).

IV. FORGERY OF THE PAYEE'S NAME

Understanding the following rule is crucial to an appreciation of many of the issues we will study in this course.

If an instrument is payable to the *order* of a named payee, only that payee can become a *holder*, and even this status is not conferred until the payee gets possession of the instrument. Thereafter no one can qualify as a *holder* until the payee indorses the instrument; without the payee's valid indorsement, no later transferees will have taken by a valid *negotiation* of the instrument, which remains the payee's property. An unauthorized signature (i.e., a forgery or a signature by a non-agent) is *not* effective to negotiate the instrument, so following a forgery of the payee's name, no later transferee (no matter how innocent, no matter how good the forgery, no matter how far down the line the taker is, etc.) can qualify as a holder.

PROBLEM 112

When Laura Lawyer's briefcase was stolen, it contained her monthly paycheck from the law firm for which she worked, made payable to her order. She had not indorsed it. The thief who stole the briefcase forged her name to the back of the paycheck and transferred it to an innocent party, Quickie Check Cashing. When the latter tried to cash the check at the drawee bank, the bank alerted Laura, and she arrived at the bank immediately. Can she retrieve the check from Quickie Check Cashing? See §3-306.

PROBLEM 113

Assume that on receiving her paycheck, Laura Lawyer (from the last Problem) had signed her name to the back of the instrument, which then was blown out a window and landed at the feet of a criminal, Harry Thief. Harry took the check down to Quickie Check Cashing and told the manager that he (Harry) was Lance Lawyer, Laura's father, and asked the manager to cash it for him. The manager made Harry indorse the instrument (reason: to make Harry contractually liable thereon (§3-415(a)), so Harry wrote "Lance Lawyer" under Laura's indorsement. Is Quickie Check Cashing a holder?

PROBLEM 114

Assume that Laura (from the above Problems) wanted to indorse the instrument over to her mother, so on the back she wrote "Pay to Lilly Lawyer" and then signed her own name. Thus indorsed, the instrument was blown out a window, and Harry Thief found it. He indorsed "Lilly Lawyer" under Laura's name and transferred the check to Quickie Check Cashing. Is Quickie Check Cashing now a holder? See §3-205(a).

The important rule to understand here is that any unauthorized indorsement of the payee's name or any special indorsee's name is *not* a valid negotiation and gives subsequent transferees no legal rights in the instrument, no matter how innocent they are or how far removed from the forgery. The same rule applies to missing indorsements of the payee or special indorsee; later possessors of the instrument do not qualify as holders. BUT once an instrument becomes bearer paper, anyone in possession of it is a holder. Subsequent unauthorized signatures have no effect on the holder status of later takers of bearer paper, or, phrased another way, valid indorsements are not required to negotiate bearer paper (§3-201(b)), mere transfer of possession is enough.

PROBLEM 115

Laura (again from the above Problems) never had a course in commercial paper, so when she received her paycheck, she simply wrote her name on the back and mailed the check to her mother. Her mother (who had had a commercial paper course) needed for some reason to hold onto the check for a week before cashing it, so she wrote "Pay to Lilly Lawyer" *above* Laura's indorsement. Has the check now become order paper requiring the mother's indorsement for further negotiation? See §3-205(c).

CHAPTER 9 ASSESSMENT: MULTIPLE CHOICE QUESTIONS

1. Micawaber borrowed money from Wickfield, signed a negotiable promissory note payable to the order of Wickfield, and handed it to Wickfield. What term applies to that transfer of possession?
   a. Transfer.
   b. Issuance.
   c. Negotiation.
   d. All of the above.

2. Wickfield sold the note and delivered it to Trotwood. Wickfield neglected to indorse the note. What term applies to that transfer of possession?
   a. Transfer.
   b. Issuance.
   c. Negotiation.
   d. None of the above, because the note was not properly indorsed.

3. Spenlow issued a check to his employee, Copperfield. Murdstone stole the check. After much practice, Murdstone wrote a perfect copy of Copperfield's signature on a piece of paper, wrote "Pay to Gummidge" over the forged signature, stapled the paper to the check, and sold it to Gummidge. Is Gummidge a holder?
   a. Yes, if she took the check for value, in good faith, and with no notice of the theft and forgery.
   b. No, because the check was not indorsed by Copperfield.
   c. Yes, because an indorsement on an allonge is effective and the indorsement looked perfectly genuine.
   d. No, because Murdstone did not write "Pay to the order of Gummidge."

4. Traddles stopped by his bank one evening to deposit his paycheck. Just after Traddles signed his name on the back of the check, Little Em'ly appeared with a revolver and relieved him of the instrument. Was Little Em'ly a holder?
   a. Yes. She is in possession of bearer paper.
   b. No. She stole the check, which still belongs to Traddles.
   c. No. Traddles indorsed the check in blank, not specifically to Little Em'ly.
   d. No. Traddles is still the holder.

ANSWERS

1. *B* is the best answer. The first time the instrument is delivered is the issuance. An issuance is not a transfer or a negotiation (even if it makes the payee a holder). That means (as we will see in later chapters) that the issuer has different rights and liabilities than a transferor. For example, a transferor makes a transfer warranty, that there are not legal problems with the instrument.
2. *A* is the best answer. Any time an instrument is physically transferred with intent to give the recipient the right to enforce the instrument, that is a transfer. A transfer that makes the recipient a holder is a negotiation. But Wickfield did not indorse the note, so Trotwood is not a holder. The transfer was not a negotiation, so *C* is incorrect. A transfer that does not make the recipient a holder is still a transfer, so *D* is incorrect. That will be important for several reasons. For example, a transfer conveys all the rights of the transferor to the transferee. Only the first delivery is an issuance, so *B* is not correct.
3. *B* is the best answer. As stated earlier in this chapter: "To qualify as a holder under §1-201(b)(21), a person must meet two requirements: (a) possession of the instrument and, for non-bearer instruments, (b) be the person identified in the instrument (either as payee or special indorsee)." Gummidge is in possession. But the instrument was payable

to Copperfield and he has not made it payable to anyone else. It is not payable to Gummidge, so she is not a holder. *B* is correct. The forged indorsement does not count as Copperfield's indorsement, no matter how skillfully done, so *C* is incorrect. *D* gives the wrong reason. Order language is not required on an indorsement, but the indorsement fails here because it is not authorized. Answer *A* likewise looks to irrelevant matters. We mention them here, because good faith, notice, and value do become relevant in later chapters, when we ask if a holder is a holder in due course—or a mere holder.

4. *A* is the best answer. Traddles indorsed the check in blank, making it bearer paper. Little Em'ly is in possession of bearer paper, so she is a holder. The check still belongs to Traddles, but that is a different question, so *B* is incorrect. Little Em'ly would be a holder either if in possession of an instrument made specifically payable to her or (as here) in possession of bearer paper, which is payable to whoever is in possession. *C* misstates the rule. Traddles is not in possession, so he is not a holder, contrary to *D*.

   Traddles need not give up hope! As we will see, just because Little Em'ly is a holder does not mean she is entitled to payment or even has the right to keep the check. Rather, *holder* is a key term we will meet in later chapters, just like *issuer, indorser, transfer, negotiation,* and the other terms we learned in this chapter.

Chapter 10
Holders in Due Course

I. ACQUIRING HOLDER IN DUE COURSE STATUS

A. Some History of the Doctrine

Let it be clear at the outset that most contracts are assignable but they travel with their defenses into the hands of the assignee; Restatement of Contracts (Second) §336. For example, if the owner of land hires a contractor to build a building on it and promises to pay the contractor a set amount of money, the contractor could sell the contractual right to this money to someone else. The terminology of the law would call the contractor the assignor, the entity buying the contract would be the assignee, and the owner of the land would be the obligor (the one who owes the money). The assignee gets the right to collect the money from the owner of the land (the obligor), but if the original contractor failed to construct the building according to the contract, the obligor could subtract whatever damages this caused from the amount being paid to the assignee. It is against this background that we study the contrary rule that has developed through the centuries for negotiable instruments.

Lord Mansfield was responsible for popularizing the idea that a holder in due course takes free of most of the defenses the parties to the original transaction have against one another, a doctrine that makes it easy to see why it is important to determine if the person currently possessing the instrument qualifies as a holder in due course. The basic definition is found in §3-302(a), which you should read carefully. The doctrine was thought necessary in a historical era where notes and drafts would often circulate from one person to another, or one business to another, for months, sometimes even years before being presented for payment. This was particularly true in an age when people were living far from their homes (in foreign countries, for example) and great distances from the cities where the banks on which drafts were drawn were located or the makers of promissory notes were living, and rapid communications between these locales was impossible. Many innocent holders of these instruments took them as sort of a private form of money, exchanging them back and forth by indorsements, and if defenses from the original transactions were good against these people financial chaos would reign. Thus there arose the rule that if these innocents qualified as a "holders in due course" they could force payment from the creators of the instruments even if those creators could have avoided paying their original transferee (who knew of the defense and was still subject to it) were it still in that person's hands. The creator, having paid, could then press the original transferee for reimbursement, using breach of contract as the cause of action. Once everyone understood this system, it didn't seem unfair to protect holders in due course and let them take free of defenses. As you read the cases that follow, ask if this doctrine still makes sense in the twenty-first century, when most people have never heard of it, but still sign mortgage notes when buying a house, wrongly thinking that if the seller gyps them they surely won't have to pay the note no matter who owns it now.

B. The Payee as Holder in Due Course

Official Comment 4 to §3-302 makes it clear that the *payee* can qualify as a holder in due course in some rare situations. Normally, the payee is so involved in the underlying transaction that he or she has notice of problems affecting payment obligations, and thus cannot be a holder in due course. But the examples given in Official Comment 4 describe fact patterns where the payee is innocent of such knowledge and can therefore qualify for the protection given to holders in due course. See also Eldon's Super Fresh Stores, Inc. v. Merrill Lynch, Pierce, Fenner & Smith, Inc., 296 Minn. 130, 207 N.W.2d 282 (1973), for an example of the payee as a holder in due course.

Subsection (c) gives a list of extraordinary transactions—creditors seizing instruments by judicial process, the sale of an inventoried business (a "bulk transaction"), or the appointment of the administrator of an estate containing negotiable instruments—in which the transferee is statutorily denied holder in due course status.

In spite of §3-302(c), which would seem to reach the opposite result, the federal courts have held that federal agencies such as the Federal Deposit Insurance Corporation, when taking over failed financial institutions, acquire holder in due course status as a matter of federal law. The following case is a continuation of a case that we first looked at in Chapter 8, when the court explored whether a promissory note was negotiable when no fixed amount of money was to be lent. The court decided no. The part of the opinion below continues with the issue of holding in due course under federal law.

Heritage Bank v. Bruha

Supreme Court of Nebraska, 2012
283 Neb. 263, 812 N.W.2d 260

[Part I of the opinion can be found in Chapter 8 at page 475.

In this case, Mr. Bruha alleged that the Sherman County Bank, which was the payee on the note he signed, committed fraud by exposing him to investment risks about which the bank lied in recommending. The note was taken over by the Federal Deposit Insurance Company when Sherman County Bank failed, and the FDIC then sold the note to Heritage Bank. In Part I of the opinion, the Nebraska Supreme Court held that the note was not negotiable due to lack of a fixed amount to be paid, and thus under the Uniform Commercial Code, the defense of holding in due course was not available to anyone possessing a non-negotiable note. The court then turned to other arguments in the case.]

2. DEFENSES . . .

(b) Allegations of Fraud

Bruha's brief also makes glancing, undeveloped references to fraud. Bruha's fraud allegations are sketchy at best.

We begin by noting that there are potentially two different types of fraud at issue: fraud in the execution and fraud in the inducement.

> Fraud in the execution goes to the very existence of the contract, such as where a [contract] is misread to the [party] or where one paper is surreptitiously substituted for another, or where a party is tricked into signing an instrument he or she did not mean to execute. . . . Fraud in the inducement,

> by contrast, goes to the means used to induce a party to enter into a contract. In such cases, the party knows the character of the instrument and intends to execute it, but the contract may be voidable if the party's consent was obtained by false representations. . . .[1]

In liberally construing his complaint, it appears that Bruha has alleged fraud in the inducement. Bruha submitted his own affidavit. The gist of the affidavit is that officials at Sherman County Bank repeatedly told Bruha he would be better off if he maintained his trading account rather than closing it. They allegedly induced Bruha into taking additional loans by misrepresenting the profitability of the trading accounts. But nowhere does Bruha claim that he was unaware that he was incurring additional debt in his negotiations with the bank, although he might have thought it was under one note instead of four notes. In sum, Bruha knew the character of the transactions he was entering, although he might have been led there by false pretenses. This sounds in fraud in the inducement, not fraud in the execution.

3. §1823(e) BARS BRUHA'S FRAUD IN THE INDUCEMENT DEFENSE

Having concluded that if Bruha has stated any defense, he has stated a defense of fraud in the inducement, we move on to Bruha's next argument. For this purpose, we assume, but do not decide, that Bruha could prove the elements of his fraud-in-the-inducement defense.

Bruha argues that the district court erred in applying the *D'Oench* doctrine and its codification at 12 U.S.C. §1823(e). We begin our discussion of this issue with the U.S. Supreme Court case that gave rise to these rules.

In D'Oench, Duhme & Co. v. F.D.I.C.,[2] the U.S. Supreme Court recognized a common-law rule that barred the invocation of secret agreements to defeat a claim of the FDIC. The case involved the FDIC's efforts to enforce notes it had acquired from a failed bank. The signer of the notes and the bank, however, had secretly agreed that the bank would never seek to enforce the notes; the bank had taken the notes to make it appear in better financial shape than it actually was. The FDIC did not learn of this secret agreement until after it had demanded payment on the notes. When the FDIC sought to enforce one of the notes, the defendant pointed to the secret agreement, arguing that the parties had never intended the notes to be enforced and that the notes lacked consideration. Citing "a federal policy to protect [the FDIC], and the public funds which it administers, against misrepresentations as to the securities or other assets in the portfolios of

1. Gonzalez v. Union Pacific R.R. Co., 282 Neb. 47, 66, 803 N.W.2d 424, 442 (2011).
2. [315 U.S. 447 (1942).]

the banks [that the FDIC] insures or to which it makes loans," the Court ruled that the defendant could not rely on the secret agreements in its defense.

The *D'Oench* doctrine generally applies to bar defenses or claims against federal regulators in those instances where a financial institution enters into an oral or secret agreement that alters the terms of an existing unqualified obligation. The doctrine provides well-reasoned, unchallengeable finality to the lender's books and records when used by regulatory agencies to assess the lending institution's solvency. We stress that this doctrine is separate from the doctrine of holder in due course, so whether the document is negotiable is irrelevant.[3]

The *D'Oench* doctrine is codified at 12 U.S.C. §1823(e), which provides in relevant part:

> No agreement which tends to diminish or defeat the interest of the Corporation in any asset acquired by it under this section or section 1821 of this title, either as security for a loan or by purchase or as receiver of any insured depository institution, shall be valid against the Corporation unless such agreement—
>
> (A) is in writing,
>
> (B) was executed by the depository institution and any person claiming an adverse interest thereunder, including the obligor, contemporaneously with the acquisition of the asset by the depository institution,
>
> (C) was approved by the board of directors of the depository institution or its loan committee, which approval shall be reflected in the minutes of said board or committee, and
>
> (D) has been, continuously, from the time of its execution, an official record of the depository institution.

Section 1823(e)'s most obvious purpose "is to allow federal and state bank examiners to rely on a bank's records in evaluating the worth of the bank's assets."[4] These evaluations, which sometimes "must be made 'with great speed,'"[5] would be virtually impossible if "bank records contained seemingly unqualified notes that [were] in fact subject to undisclosed conditions."[6]

3. See, e.g., Resolution Trust Corp. v. Kennelly, 57 F.3d 819 (9th Cir. 1995); Randolph v. Resolution Trust Corp., 995 F.2d 611 (5th Cir. 1993); Adams v. Madison Realty & Development, Inc., 937 F.2d 845 (3d Cir. 1991); Federal Deposit Ins. Corp. v. P.L.M. Intern., Inc., 834 F.2d 248 (1st Cir. 1987).

4. Langley v. F.D.I.C., 484 U.S. 86, 91, 108 S. Ct. 396, 98 L. Ed. 2d 340 (1987).

5. *Id.*, quoting Gunter v. Hutcheson, 674 F.2d 862 (11th Cir. 1982).

6. *Id.*, 484 U.S. at 92, 108 S. Ct. 396.

All courts agree that §1823(e) is a codification of the *D'Oench* doctrine.[7] Further, courts agree this doctrine also protects assignees of the FDIC.[8] We note that there is an "open question whether the judicially created doctrine and its statutory counterpart are coterminous."[9] There is also a dispute whether subsequent U.S. Supreme Court case law[10] has effectively disapproved of the common-law rule.[11] But we need not decide these issues because §1823(e) bars Bruha's defense; so deciding whether a common-law rule would provide greater protection for Heritage is unnecessary.

As mentioned, the only defense that Bruha has alleged is a defense of fraud in the inducement. We now consider whether under §1823(e), Bruha may assert this defense against Heritage. Our starting point in this analysis is Langley v. F.D.I.C.,[12] the seminal case interpreting §1823(e).

In *Langley*, a bank (later received by the FDIC) sued the defendants to collect on promissory notes that the defendants had signed in order to receive money to purchase land. The defendants argued that the bank had procured their signatures by misrepresentation. They claimed that the bank had misrepresented the size of the tract of land, the amount of mineral deposits on the land, and the lack of existing mineral leases on the land. The bank records, the minutes of the board of directors, and the minutes of the bank's loan committee, however, contained no evidence of such misrepresentations.

The Court held that §1823(e) barred the misrepresentation defense, which the Court characterized as fraud in the inducement. The Court reasoned that generally, the truthfulness of a warranty was a condition of a contract, and that the word "agreement" in §1823(e) encompassed such warranties, even if such warranties were made fraudulently. So the terms of the agreement were subject to §1823(e). And fraud in the inducement would not be a defense unless such fraud met the requirements of §1823(e).

Thus, *Langley* holds that §1823(e) bars the defense of fraud in the inducement unless the defense meets the requirements of the statute. In this case, Bruha has failed to show that his defense does so.

7. See, e.g., Young v. F.D.I.C., 103 F.3d 1180 (4th Cir. 1997); DiVall Insured Income v. Boatmen's First Nat. Bank, 69 F.3d 1398 (8th Cir. 1995); Vasapolli v. Rostoff, 39 F.3d 27 (1st Cir. 1994); *Adams, supra* note [3].

8. See, e.g., Beal Bank, SSB v. Pittorino, 177 F.3d 65 (1st Cir. 1999); Caires v. JP Morgan Chase Bank, 745 F. Supp. 2d 40 (D. Conn. 2010) (collecting cases); AAI Recoveries, Inc. v. Pijuan, 13 F. Supp. 2d 448 (S.D.N.Y. 1998); Santopadre v. Pelican Homestead and Sav. Ass'n, 782 F. Supp. 1138 (E.D. La. 1992); OCI Mortg. Corp. v. Marchese, 255 Conn. 448, 774 A.2d 940 (2001); AGI v. Pacific Southwest Bank, F.S.B., 972 S.W.2d 866 (Tex. App. 1998).

9. *Vasapolli, supra* note [7], 39 F.3d at 33 n.3.

10. See, Atherton v. F.D.I.C., 519 U.S. 213, 117 S. Ct. 666, 136 L. Ed. 2d 656 (1997); O'Melveny & Myers v. F.D.I.C., 512 U.S. 79, 114 S. Ct. 2048, 129 L. Ed. 2d 67 (1994).

11. Compare, e.g., *DiVall Insured Income, supra* note [7], with Motorcity of Jacksonville v. Southeast Bank N.A., 120 F.3d 1140 (11th Cir. 1997).

12. *Langley, supra* note [6].

To assert his defense of fraud in the inducement, Bruha must show that the agreement, including the allegedly fraudulent assertions made by Sherman County Bank regarding the profitability of the accounts, has met §1823(e)'s requirements as follows: The agreement is in writing; was executed by the depository institution and any person claiming an adverse interest thereunder, including the obligor, contemporaneously with the acquisition of the asset by the depository institution; was approved by the board of directors of the depository institution or its loan committee, with such approval reflected in the minutes of said board or committee; and has been, continuously, from the time of its execution, an official record of the depository institution.

Bruha does not point to anything regarding the fraud in any writing. Nor does he explain how the alleged fraudulent misrepresentations satisfy any of the other requirements of §1823(e). Summed up, his defense does not meet the requirements §1823(e). . . .

V. CONCLUSION

We agree with the district court that §1823(e) bars Bruha's defense. Because the court erred in applying an initial interest rate of 7.75 percent instead of 7.25 percent, we reverse in part, and remand to the district court to recalculate the interest on the judgment.

Affirmed in part, and in part reversed and remanded.

We now turn to the elements of holding in due course under the Uniform Commercial Code.

C. *"Holder"*

Note, first of all, that in order to be a holder in due course, the possessor of the instrument must qualify as a *holder*. This means that the instrument must be technically *negotiable* and must have been technically *negotiated* into the hands of its current possessor (however, the named payee becomes a holder on issuance of the instrument without the necessity of a negotiation, as does anyone to whom a bearer instrument is issued). No one can be a holder in due course of a non-negotiable instrument, nor even of a negotiable instrument if there is some defect in the transfer (negotiation) process.

Further, the holder must have *possession* of the instrument; §§1-201(b)(21), 3-301. Obviously, you can't be "holder" unless you hold. The Code nowhere defines the word "possession," leaving attorneys who must do so looking at property cases, some of which were decided many centuries ago.

One technical point: the drawee bank on which a check is drawn, taking the check for payment, does not qualify as a "holder." The reason is that an instrument must be *negotiated* to a holder, and the process by which the drawee bank acquires the instrument is not a "negotiation," it is a mere surrender for payment (a "presentment"). Thus the drawee bank is not a holder, and consequently cannot be a holder in due course.

D. "Value"

It is important to emphasize that whether or not someone qualifies as a holder in due course is measured at the moment he or she gave value for the instrument (assuming there has been a valid negotiation so as to create holder status). Things that happen after value is given (such as receiving notice of problems with the instrument) do not destroy holder in due course status once achieved.

What is "value"?

First of all, the *gift* of an instrument will never create holder in due course status in the donee (though the donee may get similar rights under the *shelter* rule, discussed below). The confusing part of the value requirement is that giving value is not the same thing as giving *consideration.* Read §3-303's Official Comment 1, first paragraph. The drafters of the Code decided that one gives value only to the extent that the holder has performed the consideration or made some irrevocable commitment in connection with it. If all that has been exchanged for the instrument is an unexecuted promise and then a problem arises, the holder has the self-help remedy of refusing to perform and does not need the extraordinary status of holding in due course; thus the holder has not given *value* under the Code. This is true even though the promise would be sufficient consideration at common law. Read §3-303 and its Official Comment and then resolve the Problems that follow.

PROBLEM 116

Joe Lunchpail arrived home one day to find a note from his wife stating that she was divorcing him and that he should get a lawyer. Since he had just been paid that day, he took his paycheck down to the law office of Nathan Novice and indorsed it over to Nathan in return for the latter's promise to represent Joe in his divorce. Later that evening, Joe's wife sent the sheriff to seize his paycheck. Joe laughingly referred the sheriff to his attorney. Can the sheriff succeed in wresting the check from Nathan's hands? See §§3-306, 3-303; Carter & Grimsley v. Omni Trading, Inc., 306 Ill. App. 3d 1127, 716 N.E.2d 320 (1999).

PROBLEM 117

Zach Taylor bought a car for his business from Fillmore Motors, signing a promissory note for $23,000 payable to Fillmore. Fillmore sold the note to the Pierce Finance Company for $22,800, a $200 discount. The car fell apart, and Zach refused to pay. Is the finance company (assuming good faith and lack of notice) a holder in due course for $23,000 or $22,800? See Bankers Guar. Title & Trust Co. v. Fisher, 2 Ohio Misc. 18, 204 N.E.2d 103 (C.P. 1964). If Millard Fillmore, the owner of Fillmore Motors, owed his mother $21,000 and gave her the note with the understanding that the extra $2,000 was a Mother's Day gift, would the mother be a holder in due course for the full amount? See §3-303.

PROBLEM 118

Tom Winker tricked old Mrs. Nodding into writing a check payable to Tom (she thought he was the agent for a local charity). The check for $1,000 was drawn on her bank, the First County Bank. Tom took the check to his bank, the Last National Bank, and, after indorsing it, put it in his checking account. Last National Bank sent the check to the First County Bank for payment, but by the time it got there Mrs. Nodding had stopped payment so that the check was dishonored and returned to Last National. Is Last National Bank a holder in due course? This question will be important if Tom has skipped town and Last National decides to sue Mrs. Nodding under §3-414.

The bank's major problem in situations like Problem 118 is in proving that it *paid* value for the check. Is the bank out of pocket anything? If so, the Code will permit the bank to recover. Thus, if the bank had permitted Tom to get the money *before* the check cleared through the drawee bank, the Last National Bank would be a holder in due course. Article 4 of the UCC (which deals with bank collection) sets out special rules for this kind of value. Section 4-211 provides that for purposes of determining its holder in due course status, a bank gives *value* whenever it has a security interest in the instrument. The situations in which this occurs are spelled out in §4-210(a). Read these sections, and consider the following case.

Falls Church Bank v. Wesley Heights Realty, Inc.

District of Columbia Court of Appeals, 1969
256 A.2d 915

Hood, J.

The sole issue on this appeal is whether and under what circumstances, may a depositary bank achieve the status of holder in due course of negotiable paper deposited with it by a customer. The facts are undisputed.

The appellees drew a check for $1,400.00, payable to the order of a customer of appellant bank. The customer deposited this check in his account with the bank and was given a provisional credit of this amount. The customer was permitted to withdraw $140.00 from this account prior to the bank's discovering that appellees had stopped payment on the $1,400.00 check. When the check was returned to the bank dishonored, the bank's customer had "skipped," leaving no credits in his account on which to charge the $140.00. The bank, thereupon, made demand on appellees for that amount and when appellees refused, this action was brought.

At trial appellees moved for, and were granted, judgment on grounds that the bank "was an agent for collection only and did not have a security interest and was not a holder in due course for value."

We reverse. The Uniform Commercial Code, which controls in this case, expressly provides that a bank acquires a security interest in items deposited with it to the extent that the provisional credit given the customer on the item is withdrawn. UCC §4-208 [§4-210 in the revised version of Article 4—Eds.]. It further provides that, for purposes of achieving the status of holder in due course, the depositary bank gives value to the extent that it acquires a security interest in the item in question. UCC §4-209 [§4-211 in the Revision—Eds.].

We agree that appellant bank is deemed by the Uniform Commercial Code to be an agent of its customers (§4-201) but under the scheme of the Code, a "bank may be a holder in due course while acting as a collecting agent for its customer." Citizens Bank of Booneville v. National Bank of Commerce, 334 F.2d 257, 261 (10th Cir. 1964). See also cases collected at 18 A.L.R.3d 1388-1391.

As a holder in due course as to $140.00, appellant's claim cannot be defeated except by those defenses set out in UCC §3-305(2), none of which are herein alleged. The judgment below is accordingly reversed with instructions to enter judgment for appellant.

A depositary bank that has permitted a customer to withdraw a deposited check has only given value up to the amount withdrawn, and therefore can only be a holder in due course for that amount of the check; see Wells Fargo Bank NA v. Ferruggio Insurance Services of LA, Inc., 358 F. Supp. 3d 887 (D. Ariz. 2019).

PROBLEM 119

Same situation as the last Problem except that when Tom deposits the $1,000 check in his account, the account contains $500. Later that afternoon he withdraws $500. Is the bank a holder in due course for any amount? See §4-210(b) (the FIFO rule: First In, First Out). What result if he withdraws $750?

E. "Good Faith" and "Notice"

To become a holder in due course the owner of the instrument must be, in effect, a bona fide purchaser—that is, the owner must have given value for the instrument in *good faith,* defined in §1-201(b)(20)[13] as "honesty in fact and the observance of reasonable commercial standards of fair dealing," thus making the test one that is both subjective and objective. The holder must also be without *notice* that there are problems with the instrument. These two concepts—good faith and notice—are inevitably intertwined: if, at the time value is given for the instrument, a holder has *notice* of a defense the maker of a note has against the payee, the holder cannot be said to take the note with the good faith expectation that it should be paid in spite of the defense. See Annot., 36 A.L.R.4th 212. In the cases that follow, you should note how often the court fails to separate these two issues.

In re Dixon-Ford

United States Bankruptcy Court, District of New Jersey, 2011
2011 WL 6749083

DONALD H. STECKROTH, Bankruptcy Judge.

On June 17, 2010, the Debtor filed a single-count adversary complaint alleging claims for fraud at common law and under New Jersey's Consumer Fraud Act, N.J.S.A. 56:8-1 *et seq.* ("CFA"), against each of the defendants in this adversary proceeding. Before the Court is a pair of summary judgment motions filed against the Plaintiff-Debtor, Mary L. Dixon-Ford ("Debtor"), by the Movant-Defendant U.S. Bank National Association, as Trustee for CMLTI 2007-10 ("US Bank") and Movants-Defendants Weichert Co., d/b/a Weichert Realtors ("Weichert Realtors") and Mortgage Access Corp. d/b/a Weichert Financial Services ("WFS") (together, "Weichert") (collectively, the "Defendants"). . . .

13. As discussed in Chapter 1, some states still have a version of §1-201(b)(20) that requires only "honesty in fact." The present version of Article 3 recommends that such states adopt, for the purposes of Article 3, the definition of good faith requiring both "honesty in fact and the observance of reasonable commercial standards of fair dealing." Legislative Note to §3-103. This is a reminder that, as always, in an actual UCC case, you should go by the UCC as in effect in your jurisdiction.

Facts and Procedural History

I. MOVANTS' FACTS

A. Property Taxes

In 2006, the Debtor engaged Weichert as her real estate representative for the purpose of locating a multi-family home. (Weichert's 56.1 Stmt. of Material Facts, ¶1) ("Weichert's Stmt. of Facts") On February 19, 2007, the Debtor executed a sale contract in which she offered to purchase a residence located in Hillside, New Jersey. (*Id.* at ¶10) The Debtor was represented by attorney John B. D'Alessandro in the transaction. (*Id.* at ¶15) Mr. D'Alessandro has testified that he discussed post-closing property taxes with the Debtor and further instructed that "she and the realtor . . . should really go to town hall to check it out." (Decl. of Michael Millar, Ex. H at 20:10-21:10) ("Millar Decl.") One of the Debtor's real estate agents, Lillian PeloteHodges, testified that they did not have information regarding property taxes. (Weichert's Reply Br. in Further Supp., p. 6) Lastly, Weichert alleges that prior to closing, the Debtor had no communication with her real estate agents. (Weichert's Stmt. of Facts, ¶19)

B. The Mortgage

The Debtor sought to finance the purchase of real property with a mortgage loan from WFS. At all times relevant to this transaction, the Debtor was employed by the Social Security Administration ("SSA") as a "telephone service representative" earning approximately $45,000 annually. (Weichert's Stmt. of Facts, ¶¶20-1; Millar Decl., Ex. B at 10:7-16, 21:16-20) The Debtor contracted with WFS to obtain a "stated income" mortgage loan. (*Id.* at ¶29) In a stated income loan program, the borrower applies for financing based on her income as stated in her loan application. (*Id.* at ¶30) The lender then performs a Verification of Employment ("VOE") directly with the borrower's employer to confirm the borrower's stated income. (*Id.* at ¶31) On February 24, 2007, the Debtor executed a loan application indicating she was employed as the "Vice President" of the SSA earning $11,900 monthly ($142,800 annually). (Weichert's Stmt. of Facts, ¶22)

On April 9, 2007, the Debtor accepted a mortgage loan commitment with WFS. (*Id.* at ¶28) Also on April 9, and again on April 10, WFS submitted a VOE form to the SSA. (Weichert's Br. in Supp. of Mot. for Summ. J., pp. 5-6) ("Weichert's Br.") Weichert alleges that on or about April 10, 2007, someone at the SSA provided a VOE form to the Debtor together with a handwritten note to the Debtor's attention, arguably, before it was returned to WFS. (*Id.* at ¶35; Millar Decl., Ex. P) On April 18, 2007, the Debtor closed on the property and executed a second loan application which also misstated her employment and income information. (Weichert's Stmt. of Facts, ¶¶36-7)

Post-closing review revealed the existence of two VOEs. One correctly stated the Debtor's employment as a "Telephone Service Rep[resentative]" while the other incorrectly stated she was the "Vice President" of the SSA. (Weichert's Stmt. of Facts, ¶¶46-7) The incorrect VOE was supplied to the WFS underwriter. (Weichert's Stmt. of Facts, ¶48)

The Debtor occupied the property with several family members, some of whom contributed to household expenses, including the mortgage. (*Id.* at ¶¶42-3) The Debtor defaulted on her mortgage when one of the contributing family members relocated. (*Id.* at ¶45)

C. Assignment of the Debtor's Mortgage

On October 31 2007, Citigroup Mortgage Loan Trust Inc. ("Buyer") and Citigroup Markets Realty Corp. ("Seller") executed a Mortgage Loan Purchase Agreement ("MLPA") as part of a mortgage-backed securities transaction. (U.S. Bank's 56.1 Statement of Facts, ¶21-23) ("US Bank's Stmt. of Facts") The details of the transaction are set forth in a Pooling and Servicing Agreement ("PSA") that provides for the "selling, purchase, [and] deposit . . . of a series of residential mortgage loans . . . in trust CMLTI 2007-10," with U.S. Bank as trustee. (*Id.* at ¶23) The mortgage loan schedule attached to the MLPA and the PSA indicate that the Debtor's mortgage was included in the transaction and deposited in the trust. (*Id.* at ¶24) U.S. Bank did not conduct an independent review of the individual mortgages because the Seller warranted that the mortgages were enforceable and underwritten in accordance with its guidelines at the time of their originations. (*Id.* at ¶28)

Pursuant to the PSA, U.S. Bank received the Debtor's mortgage note and the original recorded mortgage. (*Id.* at ¶32) There are no indicia of fraud, alteration, or invalidity on the face of the Debtor's mortgage or note. (*Id.* at ¶35-36) Further, neither Weichert nor the Debtor alerted U.S. Bank to any alleged misrepresentations or other flaw in the origination of the mortgage. (*Id.* at ¶18-20)

II. PLAINTIFF'S ADDITIONAL AND DISPUTED FACTS

The Debtor asserts that pursuant to WFS's loan officer's request, she provided documentation that accurately described her employment and overall financial position. (*Id.* at p. 6; Ex. B at 15:20-25, 16:1-9, 17:24-25, 18:1-6) The Debtor provided the following documentation: (1) pay stubs; (2) tax returns; (3) a bank statement for the period between February 14, 2007 and March 16, 2007, which includes an entry for the direct deposit of the Debtor's wages in the amount of $782.60; and (4) a credit report, indicating the Debtor's employment as "Teller Service." (*Id.* at p. 6-7) Nevertheless, the WFS loan officer prepared the loan application containing the incorrect employment information. (Pl.'s Br. in Opp'n, p. 6)

In addition, during post-closing review, the WFS Vice President of Processing, Laura Williamson, spoke with the Debtor's supervisor at the SSA, John Elder, regarding the VOE. (*Id.* at p. 7; Williamson Dep. 25:12-13) Mr. Elder confirmed that he completed a VOE accurately stating the Debtor's employment as a telephone service representative. (*Id.* at 7-8; Williamson Dep. 30:1-10) Importantly, Ms. Williamson testified that the VOE containing incorrect information appeared to have been altered. (*Id.* at p. 8; Williamson Dep. 35:13-18) Lastly, Ms. Williamson stated that the altered VOE was faxed to Weichert from a number with a 908 area code. (*Id.* at p. 7; Williamson Dep. 25:1-3) The office where the loan application was allegedly completed is located in Union, New Jersey and has an area code of 908. (*Id.* at p. 8) Accordingly, the Debtor opines that the WFS loan officer altered the VOE in order to qualify the Debtor for a larger loan.

Discussion

* * *

III. US BANK'S MOTION FOR SUMMARY JUDGMENT: HOLDER IN DUE COURSE

The Debtor brings claims for fraud against U.S. Bank, arguing that U.S. Bank knew or should have known of the alleged misrepresentations made in connection with the origination of the Debtor's mortgage. In its defense, U.S. Bank asserts holder in due course status. Where a defense exists against the payee, the party "claiming the rights of a holder in due course has the burden of establishing that he is . . . such a holder." Gen. Inv. Corp. v. Angelini, 58 N.J. 396, 403-404, 278 A.2d 193 (1971). The Uniform Commercial Code, as adopted in New Jersey, provides that a holder of an instrument becomes a holder in due course when he takes the instrument "for value, in good faith, and without notice of any defense or claim against it." Carnegie Bank v. Shalleck, 256 N.J. Super. 23, 33, 606 A.2d 389 (App. Div. 1992); N.J. Stat. Ann. §12A:3-302(a)(2). Additionally, it is required that "the instrument when . . . negotiated to the holder does not bear such apparent evidence of forgery or alteration or is not otherwise so irregular or incomplete as to call into question its authenticity." N.J. Stat. Ann. §12A:3-302(a)(1). A holder in due course takes an instrument free of any personal defenses the maker may assert against the payee. Bancredit Inc. v. Bethea, 65 N.J. Super. 538, 544, 168 A.2d 250 (App. Div. 1961).

That U.S. Bank took the mortgage instrument for value is undisputed. Instead, the Debtor alleges that U.S. Bank "knew or should have known of the misrepresentations made by [WFS] and [Weichert Realtors]. . . ." (Pl.'s Compl., ¶32) Such allegations implicate the holder's good faith. Good faith is defined by statute in N.J.S.A. 12A:3-103(a)(4) as "honesty in fact and the observance of reasonable commercial standards of fair dealing." Good faith then, concerns both the subjective actions of the holder and the objective elements of the transaction. Wawel Savings Bank v. Jersey Tractor Trailer Training Inc. (In re Jersey Tractor Trailer Training Inc.), 580 F.3d 147, 157 (3d Cir. 2009) (citing Trifin v. Pomerantz Staffing Services, L.L.C., 370 N.J. Super. 301, 308, 851 A.2d 100 (App. Div. 2004)). Often, the critical issue is whether "[a] party [] fails to make an inquiry[] reasonably required by the circumstances. . . ." Trifin v. Pomerantz Staffing, 370 N.J. Super. at 309, 851 A.2d 100. As the court in *Carnegie Bank* observed,

> [o]rdinarily where the note appears to be negotiable in form and regular on its face, the holder is under no duty to inquire as to possible defenses . . . unless the circumstances of which he has knowledge rise to the level that the failure to inquire reveals a deliberate desire on his part to evade knowledge because of a belief or fear that investigation would disclose a defense from the transaction.

Carnegie Bank, 256 N.J. Super. at 35, 606 A.2d 389 (quoting *Gen. Inv. Corp.,* 58 N.J. at 403-404, 278 A.2d 193).

The above derives from the oft quoted rule laid down in Rice v. Barrington, 71 N.J.L. 806 (E. & A. 1968): "[b]ad faith, i.e. fraud, not merely suspicious circumstances, must be brought home to a holder . . . in order to defeat his recovery on a[] note upon the ground of fraud in its inception or between the parties to it." *Rice,* 71 N.J.L. at 807, 60 A. 1134; *see* HSBC Bank USA, N.A. v. Gouda, 2010 N.J. Super. Unpub. Lexis 3029 at *11, 2010 WL 5128666 (App. Div. Dec. 17, 2010). In the present matter, the note has been supplied to the Court for evaluation. (Standing Certif., [ECF Doc. 48], Oct. 19, 2011) The note is facially free from any irregularity that could have alerted U.S. Bank to the existence of a potential fraud. While U.S. Bank does possess the mortgage file containing the allegedly altered VOE, it was under "no duty to inquire" under the circumstances. *Carnegie Bank,* 256 N.J. Super. at 35, 606 A.2d 389; *see* Triffin v. Somerset Valley Bank, 343 N.J. Super. 73, 85, 777 A.2d 993 (App. Div. 2001) ("to preclude liability from a holder in due course under [N.J.S.A. 12A:3-302], it must be apparent on the face of the instrument that it is fraudulent"). Failure to investigate inconsistencies in the mortgage file regarding the Debtor's income, without more, does not evidence bad faith sufficient to prevent U.S. Bank from a holder in due course status. *See* HSBC Bank USA, N.A. v. Gouda, 2010 N.J. Super. Unpub. Lexis 3029, 2010 WL 5128666 (that loan documents indicated the material terms of a loan changed shortly before closing did not implicate the holder's good faith); *see also* Ocwen Loan Servicing, LLC v. Branaman, 554 F. Supp. 2d 645, 649 (N.D. Miss. 2008) ("while the [d]efendants have alleged a potential forgery in the loan documents, no specific evidence has been presented which casts doubt on the authenticity of the promissory note"). Certainly, fraud is one explanation in the array of possibilities, however, constructive notice requires "circumstances [] so strong that if ignored they will be deemed to establish bad faith on the part of the transferee." Provident Sav. Bank v. Pinnacle Mortg. Inv. Corp. (In re Pinnacle Mortg. Inv. Corp.), 1998 U.S. Dist. Lexis 23289 at *32 (D.N.J. Dec. 9, 1998) (simultaneously construing holder in due course status under Pennsylvania and New Jersey law as the law of the two states "[was] largely consistent on the issues," raised therein).

Moreover, the undisputed facts show that U.S. Bank did not participate in the origination of the mortgage, nor is there evidence of collusion or communication between Weichert and U.S. Bank regarding the Debtor's mortgage. *See* Davis v. Clark, 85 N.J.L. 696, 699, 90 A. 303 (E. & A. 1914) (there was no showing that the holder in due course had any knowledge of fraud perpetrated upon a debtor in the original transaction); *see also* Driscoll v. Burlington-Bristol Bridge Co., 8 N.J. 433, 480, 86 A.2d 201 (1952) (the subsequent holder "must have had actual knowledge of such facts that his action in taking the instrument amounted to bad faith"); *accord* Westfield Inv. Co. v. Fellers, 74 N.J. Super. 575, 583, 181 A.2d 809 (Law Div. 1962). On the record, there are simply no facts which tend to apprise U.S. Bank of potential defenses at the time of taking and impair good faith. Thus, U.S. Bank holds the Debtor's mortgage in due course and is entitled to the benefits of its status.

The instant case involves alleged fraudulent inducement in connection with the origination of the Debtor's mortgage, that is, "the [Debtor] was led by deception to execute what [s]he knew to be a negotiable instrument. . . ." New Jersey Mortg. & Inv. Co. v. Dorsey, 60 N.J. Super. 299, 302, 158 A.2d 712 (App. Div. 1960). Under New Jersey law, fraud in the inducement is a personal defense against "transferees who have been parties to any fraud or illegality affecting the instrument or transferees who were prior holders with notice of the defenses or claims and not against holders in due course." *Carnegie Bank,* 256 N.J. Super. at 43, 606 A.2d 389; *see Bancredit,* 65 N.J. Super. at 544, 168 A.2d 250 ("a holder in due course plaintiff is, of course, immune to all personal defenses of the maker against the payee, including that of fraud in the inducement"); *see also New Jersey Mortg.,* 60 N.J. Super. at 302, 158 A.2d 712 (fraudulent inducement is a personal defense not available against a holder in due course). Thus, U.S. Bank is immune to the Debtor's claims and the Court will grant U.S. Bank's motion for summary judgment against the Debtor.

Conclusion

Summary judgment is granted in favor of U.S. Bank and Weichert Realtors against Plaintiff. The Plaintiff's common law and statutory fraud claims survive as to WFS because material questions of fact remain in connection with the Debtor's mortgage application.

As we saw at the end of Chapter 8, the Federal Trade Commission has promulgated a regulation abolishing the holder in due course doctrine, where a consumer gives a promissory note to a seller or lender when purchasing goods or services. But that rule does not apply to checks or to promissory notes in real property purchases, perhaps where consumers like Mary Dixon-Ford in this case need it most. Is the application of the doctrine here fair? Why would the FTC have created such a gap, do you suppose?

PROBLEM 120

Dubious Mortgage Lender convinced a 91-year-old widower to refinance his home by granting him an adjustable rate mortgage, along with bountiful fees, after making fraudulent promises galore to him about the benefits of the new mortgage. Dubious kept the promissory note in a safe deposit box down at its own bank, where it remains to this day. Shortly after the mortgage was given and the mortgage deed recorded in the mortgage records, Dubious sold the note and the mortgage contract to Investment National Bank, which paid good value but did not bother to take possession of the note. When the widower learned he had been defrauded, he stopped making payments on the note and Investment National Bank filed a foreclosure action against him. Is the bank a holder in due course?

PROBLEM 121

The corporate treasurer of the Business Corporation was having major troubles paying his personal bills, so finally he decided to embark on a life of crime. He used a corporate check to pay his American Express bill, making the check out to "Amerex Corp., 770 Broadway, N.Y., N.Y. 10003" (the actual address of American Express). On the corporate check requisition form he wrote a phony explanation that this check represented shipping expenses. This caused no suspicions at Business Corporation and, thus encouraged, he did it every month for two years. When Business Corporation finally figured out what had happened, it sued American Express in quasi-contract for all the money it had received in this fashion. American Express replied that it was a holder in due course of these checks and, as such, was not amenable to this suit. Business Corporation pointed to the suspicious circumstances and to UCC §§3-302(a) and 3-307 (arguing that the corporate treasurer was a fiduciary). How should this be resolved? See Hartford Accident & Indem. Co. v. American Express Co., 74 N.Y.2d 153, 542 N.E.2d 1090, 544 N.Y.S.2d 573 (1989); Grand Rapids Auto Sales, Inc. v. MBNA American Bank, 227 F. Supp. 2d 721 (W.D. Mich. 2002).

Any Kind Checks Cashed, Inc. v. Talcott

District Court of Appeal of Florida, 2002
830 So. 2d 160

GROSS, J.

The issue in this case is whether a check cashing store qualifies as a holder in due course so that it can collect on a $10,000 check written by an elderly man who was fraudulently induced to issue the check by the person who cashed it.

We hold that the check cashing store was not a holder in due course, because the procedures it followed with the $10,000 check did not comport with reasonable commercial standards of fair dealing.

The case is the story of John G. Talcott, Jr., a ninety-three-year-old Massachusetts resident, D.J. Rivera, a "financial advisor" to Talcott, and Salvatore Guarino, a cohort of Rivera. In the mid-1990's, Rivera sold Talcott an investment for "somewhere in the amount of $75,000." The investment produced no returns.

On December 7, 1999, Guarino established check cashing privileges at Any Kind Checks Cashed, Inc. ("Any Kind") by filling out a customer card. The card included his social security number and identification by driver's license. On the card, Guarino listed himself as a broker. That day, he cashed a $450 check without incident.

On January 10, 2000, Rivera telephoned Talcott and talked him into sending him a check for $10,000 made out to Guarino, which was to be used for travel expenses to obtain a return on the original $75,000 investment. Talcott understood that Guarino was Rivera's partner. Rivera received the check on January 11.

Talcott spoke to Rivera on the morning of January 11. Rivera indicated that $10,000 was more than what was needed for travel. He said that $5,700 would meet the travel costs. Talcott called his bank and stopped payment on the $10,000 check.

In spite of what Rivera told Talcott, Guarino appeared at Any Kind's Stuart, Florida office on January 11 and presented the $10,000 check to Nancy Michael. She was a supervisor with the company with the authority to approve checks over $2,000. Guarino showed Michael his driver's license and the Federal Express envelope from Talcott in which he received the check. She asked him the purpose of the check. Consistent with the information on the customer card, he told her that he was a broker and that the maker of the check had sent it as an investment. She was unable to contact the maker of the check by telephone. Based on her experience, Michael believed the check was good; the Federal Express envelope was "very crucial" to her decision, because it indicated that the maker of the check had sent it to the payee trying to cash the check. After deducting the 5 percent check cashing fee, Michael cashed the check and gave Guarino $9,500. The next day she deposited the check in the company's bank.

On January 15, 2000, Rivera called Talcott and asked about the $5,700, again promising to send him a return on his investment. The same day, Talcott sent a check for $5,700. He assumed that Rivera knew that he had stopped payment on the $10,000 check.

On January 17, 2000, Guarino went into the Stuart Any Kind store and presented the $5,700 check to the teller, Joanne Kochakian. He showed her the Federal Express envelope in which the check had come. Company policy required a supervisor to approve a check over $2,000. Kochakian noticed that Michael had previously approved the $10,000 check. She called Michael, who was working at another location, and told her about Guarino's check.

Any Kind had no written procedures that a supervisor was required to follow in deciding which checks over $2,000 to cash. Michael had the discretionary "decision-making power as a supervisor to decide whether or not the check [was] any good." She relied on "instinct and judgment" in deciding what inquiry to make before cashing a check. In the brief non-jury trial, there was no evidence concerning the general practice of the check cashing industry.

Michael instructed the cashier not to cash the check until she contacted the maker, Talcott, to obtain approval. On her first attempt, Kochakian received no answer, using the number on the back of Guarino's check cashing card. When she told Guarino that she would not cash his check, he gave her another number to call, which was the same as the first number except that two numbers were reversed. On the second call, a woman answered the phone. Kochakian identified herself and asked for Talcott. Talcott approved cashing the $5,700 check. There was no discussion of the $10,000 check. Any Kind cashed the second check for Guarino, from which it deducted a 3 percent fee.

On January 19, Rivera called Talcott to warn him that Guarino was a cheat and a thief. Talcott immediately called his bank and stopped payment on the $5,700 check. Talcott's daughter called Any Kind and told it of the stop payment on the $5,700 check. There was no dispute at trial that Guarino and Rivera had pulled a scam on Talcott to get him to issue the checks. Any Kind filed a two-count complaint against Guarino and Talcott, claiming that it was a holder in due course. Talcott's defense was that Any Kind was not a holder in due course and that his obligation on the checks was nullified because of Guarino's illegal acts.

The trial court entered final judgment in favor of Any Kind for only the $5,700 check. On the $10,000 check, the judge found for Talcott. The court found that the circumstances surrounding the cashing of the $10,000 check

> were sufficient to put [Any Kind] on notice of potential defenses and/or infirmities. The best evidence of this is that the plaintiff attempted to contact the maker but was unable to do so on the first check, and did so on the second. The circumstances of a person describing himself as a broker, receiving funds in the amount of $10,000 and negotiating the check for those funds at a $500 discount are sufficient to put [Any Kind] on inquiry notice that some confirmation or explanation should be obtained.

Using the terminology of the Uniform Commercial Code, Talcott was the maker or "drawer" of the check, the person who signed the draft "as a person ordering payment." §3-103(a)(3). By Federal Expressing the check to Guarino, Talcott issued the check to him. See §3-105(a) (defining "issue" as "the first delivery of an instrument by the maker or drawer. . . for the purpose of giving rights on the instrument to any person"). Guarino indorsed the check and cashed it with Any Kind. See §3-204(a) (defining "indorsement"). Any Kind immediately made the funds available to Guarino, less its fee. Talcott stopped payment on the check with his bank, so the check was returned to Any Kind. See §4-403 (regarding a customer's right to stop payment).

When Guarino negotiated the check with Any Kind, it became a holder of the check, making it a "person entitled to enforce" the instrument. See §§1-201(20), 3-301. As the drawer of the check dishonored by his bank, Talcott's obligation was to pay the draft to a person entitled to enforce the draft "[a]ccording to its terms at the time it was issued. . . ." §3-414(b).

Unless Any Kind is a holder in due course, its right to enforce Talcott's obligation to pay the draft is subject to (1) all defenses Talcott could raise "if the person entitled to enforce the instrument were enforcing a right to payment under a simple contract," and (2) a claim of "ecoupment" Talcott could raise against Guarino. §3-305(a)(2) and (3). Because Talcott was fraudulently induced to issue the checks, this case turns on Any Kind's entitlement to holder in due course status.

A "holder in due course" is a holder who takes an instrument without "apparent evidence of forgery or alteration" for value, in good faith, and without notice of certain claims and defenses. See §3-302(a). As the party claiming that it was a holder in due course, Any Kind had the burden to prove that status by a preponderance of the evidence. See §3-308(b); Seinfeld v. Commercial Bank & Trust Co., 405 So. 2d 1039, 1041 (Fla. 3d DCA 1981).

The question for this court is whether the trial court erred in finding that Any Kind was not a holder in due course of the $10,000 check based on the findings of fact made at trial, keeping in mind that Any Kind bore the burden of proof. That question turns on whether Any Kind acted "[i]n good faith" within the meaning of §3-302(a).

The good faith requirement of the holder in due course doctrine "has been the source of an ancient and continuing dispute." White & Summers, Uniform Commercial Code §17-6 (4th ed. 1995). On the one hand,

> [s]hould the courts apply a so-called objective test, and ask whether a reasonably prudent person, behaving the way the alleged holder in due course behaved, would have been acting in good faith? Or should the courts instead apply a subjective test and examine the person's actual behavior, however stupid and irrespective of the reaction a reasonably prudent person would have had in the same circumstance? The legal establishment has steered a crooked course through this debate.

Id.; see Patricia L. Heatherman, Comment, Good Faith in Revised Article 3 of the Uniform Commercial Code: Any Change? Should There Be?, 29 Willamette L. Rev. 567 (1993).

Prior to 1992, section §1-201(19) defined "good faith" as "honesty in fact in the conduct of the transaction concerned." Florida courts interpreted this definition as creating a subjective test. See Cash-A-Check of S. Fla., Inc. v. Sunshine Elec. Contractors, Inc., 26 Fla. Supp. 2d 17, 19 (Fla. Palm Beach County Ct. 1987). For example, we wrote in Barnett Bank of Palm Beach County v. Regency Highland Condo. Ass'n, 452 So. 2d 587, 590 (Fla. 4th DCA 1984), that "good faith" under the holder in due course doctrine did "not include due care; rather lack of good faith must be the result of actual, not constructive, knowledge of the wrongdoing tantamount to dishonesty or bad faith." In another case, Judge Schwartz wrote that the "Florida version of the holder in due course provision of the U.C.C. does seem to protect the objectively stupid so long as he is subjectively pure of heart." *Seinfeld*, 405 So. 2d at 1042.

Application of *Barnett Bank*'s "honesty in fact" standard to Any Kind's conduct in this case would clothe it with holder in due course status. It is undisputed that Any Kind's employees were pure of heart, that they acted without knowledge of Guarino's wrongdoing.

However, in 1992, the legislature adopted a new definition of "good faith" that applies to the §3-302's definition of a holder in due course: "'[g]ood faith' means honesty in fact and the observance of reasonable commercial standards of fair dealing." Ch. 92-82, §2, at 759, Laws of Fla.—U.C.C. §3-103(a)(4). To the old, subjective good faith, "honesty in fact" standard, the legislature added an objective component—the "pure heart of the holder must now be accompanied by reasoning that assures conduct comporting with reasonable commercial standards of fair dealing." Maine Family Fed. Credit Union v. Sun Life Assurance Co. of Canada, 727 A.2d 335, 342 (Me. 1999). No longer may a holder of an instrument act with "a pure heart and an empty head and still obtain holder in due course status." Id.

Comment 4 to §3-103 attempts to shed light on how to interpret the new standard:

> Although fair dealing is a broad term that must be defined in context, it is clear that it is concerned with the fairness of conduct rather than the care with which an act is performed. Failure to exercise ordinary care in conducting a transaction is an entirely different concept than failure to deal fairly in conducting the transaction.

The Code does not define the term "fair dealing." As the Maine Supreme Court has observed, the "most obvious question arising from the use of the term fair is: fairness to whom?" *Maine Family*, 727 A.2d at 343.

Application of holder in due course status is the law's value judgment that certain holders are worthy of protection from certain types of claims. For example, it has been argued that application of the old subjective standard facilitated the transfer of checks in the stream of commerce; arguably one would be "more willing to accept the checks if . . . she knows . . . she can be a holder in due course of that instrument and take it free of defenses that might have existed between the buyer and the seller in the underlying transaction." White & Summers, §17-1. In applying the new standard, "fairness" should be measured by taking a global view of the underlying transaction and all of its participants. A holder "must act in a way that is fair according to commercial standards that are themselves reasonable." *Maine Family*, 727 A.2d at 343.

To apply the law requiring "good faith" under §3-302(a), we adopt the analysis set forth by the Supreme Court of Maine:

> The factfinder must . . . determine, first, whether the conduct of the holder comported with industry or "commercial" standards applicable to the transaction and, second, whether those standards were reasonable standards intended to result in fair dealing. Each of those determinations must be made in the context of the specific transaction at hand. If the factfinder's conclusion on each point is "yes," the holder will be determined to have acted in good faith even if, in the individual transaction at issue, the result appears unreasonable. Thus a holder may be accorded holder in due course status where it acts pursuant to those reasonable commercial standards of fair dealing—even if it is negligent—but may lose that status, even where it complies with commercial standards, if those standards are not reasonably related to achieving fair dealing.

Id.

There was no evidence at trial concerning the check cashing industry's commercial standards. Even assuming that Any Kind's procedures for checks over $2,000 met the industry's gold standard, we hold that in this case the procedures followed were not reasonably related to achieve fair dealing with respect to the $10,000 check, taking into consideration all of the participants in the transaction, Talcott, Guarino, and Any Kind.

Check cashing businesses are regulated by Chapter 560, Florida Statutes (2001), the Money Transmitters' Code. See §560.101, Fla. Stat. (2001). Among the purposes of Chapter 560 are to provide for and promote:

> (b) The maintenance of public confidence in the money transmitter industry.
>
> (c) The protection of the interests of the public in the money transmitter system. . . .
>
> (e) The opportunity for money transmitters to be and remain competitive with each other and with other business organizations. . . .
>
> (f) The opportunity for money transmitters to effectively serve the convenience and needs of their customers and the public. . . .
>
> (g) The opportunity for the management of money transmitter businesses to exercise its business judgment within the framework of the code.

§560.102(2). Nothing in Chapter 560 purports to alter or amend any of the provisions of Chapter 673, leading to a conclusion that the legislature did not intend to bend the holder in due course provision of the Uniform Commercial Code—Negotiable Instruments to specially accommodate check cashing businesses.

Check cashing businesses occupy a special niche in the financial industry. They are part of the "alternative financial services"[14] or "fringe banking"[15] sector, a part of the market that "has become a major source of traditional banking services for low-income and working poor consumers, residents of minority neighborhoods, and people with blemished credit histories." Lynn Drysdale & Kathleen E. Keest, The Two-Tiered Consumer Financial Services Marketplace: The Fringe Banking System and its Challenge to Current Thinking About the Role of Usury Laws in Today's Society, 51 S.C. L. Rev. 589, 591 (2000). Check cashing involves "charging a service fee for providing instant cash to unbanked customers." Joseph R. Falasco, Who's Getting Used in Arkansas: An Analysis of Usury, Check Cashing, and the Arkansas Check-Cashers Act, 55 Ark. L. Rev. 149, 156 (2002); see Drysdale & Keest, at

14. See, e.g., John Burton et al., The Alternative Financial Sector: Policy Implications for Poor Households, 42 Consumer Interests Ann. 279, 279 (1996).

15. See John P. Caskey, Fringe Banking: Check Cashing Outlets, Pawnshops, and the Poor (1994).

626. Check cashing customers "generally have limited resources available to access immediate cash." Falasco, at 155.

Check cashing stores are often in locations where traditional banks fear to tread. Drysdale and Keest report the research that demonstrates that check cashing outlets are usually located in lower income neighborhoods:

> For example, the Federal Reserve Bank of Boston looked at multi-census tract areas in cities in New England where check cashers were most densely clustered—Boston, Hartford, and Providence. The Boston study found that the cities with high [check cashing outlet] clusters tended "to have high percentages of low- and moderate-income census tracts and households," high percentages of households below the poverty level, and higher shares of households on fixed incomes (either public assistance or social security). More dramatic is the Woodstock Institute's study of the relative distribution of banks and [check cashing outlets and currency exchanges] in Chicago, which examines specific census tracts. This study found that the currency exchanges are predominately located in lower income, minority communities. The currency exchange to bank ratio in five predominately minority communities with median household incomes below $22,000 exceeded ten to one. The lowest income communities, with median incomes of $7908 and $12,570, each had twelve check cashers for every one or two banks.[16]

Drysdale & Keest, at 629 (footnotes omitted). In such areas, the typical check presented for cashing is not a large one—a paycheck, child support, social security, or public assistance check. Section 560.309(4)(b) contemplates that such checks will be presented at check cashing outlets; it limits the fee charged for the payment of "any kind of state public assistance or federal social security benefits payable to the bearer."

Attractions of check cashing outlets are convenience and speed. As the amicus points out, many check cashing businesses are open twenty-four hours a day, seven days a week. Unlike banks, check cashing stores cannot place a hold on a check before releasing funds. The Florida Administrative Code requires payment to be made "immediately in currency for every payment instrument received by a person engaging in the activities of a check casher." Fla. Admin. Code R. 3C-560.804(1). The statute and administrative rules also contemplate that a check cashing business will engage in various types of "verification" of a check. §560.309. Rule 3C 560.801

16. The two studies referred to in this paragraph are Lesly Jean Paul & Luxman Nathan, Check Cashers: Moving from the Fringe to the Financial Mainstream, Communities & Banking (Federal Reserve Bank of Boston) 5, 8 (1999), and Woodstock Inst., Reinvestment Alert: Currency Exchanges Add to Poverty Surcharge for Low Income Residents (1997).

of the Florida Administrative Code permits a check casher to collect the "direct costs associated with verifying a payment instrument holder's identity, residence, employment, credit history, account status, or other necessary information." (Italics supplied). "Other necessary information" could include long distance or telephone charges incurred to contact the drawer of a check.

Against this backdrop, we cannot say that the trial court erred in finding that the $10,000 check was a red flag. The $10,000 personal check was not the typical check cashed at a check cashing outlet. The size of the check, in the context of the check cashing business, was a proper factor to consider under the objective standard of good faith in deciding whether Any Kind was a holder in due course. See *Maine Family*, 727 A.2d at 344.

Guarino was not the typical customer of a check cashing outlet. As the trial judge observed, because of the 5 percent fee charged, it is unusual for a small businessman such as a broker to conduct business through a check cashing store instead of through a traditional bank. Guarino did not have a history with Any Kind of cashing checks of similar size without incident. The need for speed in a business transaction is usually less acute than for someone cashing a paycheck or welfare check to pay for life's necessities. The need for speed in cashing a large business check is consistent with a drawer who, for whatever reason, might stop payment. Fair dealing in this case required that the $10,000 check be approached with a degree of caution.

If a drawer has a right to stop payment of a check, and a traditional bank usually places a hold on uncollected funds after a payee deposits a check into an account, then the legal dispute after a stop payment will usually be between the drawer of the check and the payee, the two parties that had the dealings leading to the payment. Thus, where a check is cashed at a bank or savings and loan, the law will often place the loss on the wrongdoer in the underlying transaction. This is a desirable goal.

Where a check cashing store releases funds immediately, the holder in due course doctrine steps in, frequently putting the loss on a wronged maker, in furtherance of the policy that facilitating the transfer of checks benefits the economy. In this case, the policy reasons behind easy negotiability do not outweigh the reasons for caution. Very loose application of the objective component of "good faith" would make check cashing outlets the easy refuge of scam artists who want to take the money and run. The concept of "fair dealing" includes not being an easy, safe harbor for the dishonest.

To affirm the trial court is not to wreak havoc with the check cashing industry. Verification with the maker of a check will not be necessary to preserve holder in due course status in the vast majority of cases arising from check cashing outlets. This was neither the typical customer, nor the typical transaction of a check cashing outlet.

We disagree with the amicus, who worries that requirement of verification by the maker in this case "would inhibit the long standing policy of the free negotiation of instruments." Again, this is not the usual case. Also, as White and Summers have written, "there has been debate about the importance of the holder in due course doctrine in facilitating" check transactions. The Federal Trade Commission's abolition of the holder in due course doctrine in most consumer credit transactions has "not had the catastrophic impact upon the consumer market that some predicted. Indeed, twenty years from now we may conclude that it caused barely a ripple on the consumer credit pond." White & Summers, §17-1.

The legislature's addition of an objective standard of conduct may well have the effect of "slowing the 'wheels of commerce' " in some transactions. *Maine Family*, 727 A.2d at 344. However, by adopting changes to the "good faith" standard in the holder in due course doctrine, the legislature "necessarily must have concluded that the addition of the objective requirement to the definition of 'good faith' serves an important goal. The paramount necessity of unquestioned negotiability has given way, at least in part to the desire for reasonable commercial fairness in negotiable transactions." Id. In this case, reasonable commercial fairness required Any Kind to approach the $10,000 check with some caution and to verify it with the maker if it wanted to preserve its holder in due course status.

Affirmed.

QUESTION

Would a check cashing business be in good faith if it acquired a postdated check before the date of the check? Compare RR Maloan Investments, Inc. v. New HE, Inc., 428 S.W.3d 355 (Tex. App. 2014) (yes), with Buckeye Check Cashing, Inc. v. Camp, 159 Ohio App. 3d 784, 825 N.E.2d 644 (2005) (no). In State Sec. Check Cashing, Inc. v. American General Financial, 409 Md. 81, 972 A.2d 882 (2009), the court found a check-cashing company that took a $10,000 check from a stranger to be a holder in due course; the decision quoted White and Summer's leading UCC treatise, §17-6, as saying:

> [C]ourts . . . are quick to deny holder in due course status to check cashing facilities. We wonder how these courts would have handled these cases had the plaintiffs been banks and not check cashing facilities. In effect the courts are asking check cashers to adhere to a higher standard than might be required of a bank. Given the clientele of check cashing facilities, the courts' skepticism might be justified, but we would like to see a little more evidence that check-cashing facilities are a home for persons engaged in fraudulent behavior before we would subject them to higher standards than might be applied to a bank.

Winter & Hirsch, Inc. v. Passarelli

Illinois Appellate Court, 1970
122 Ill. App. 2d 372, 259 N.E.2d 312

McCormick, J.

This appeal is taken from an order denying a motion to vacate a judgment by confession. The judgment was entered against the defendants, Dominic and Antoinette Passarelli, on behalf of the plaintiff, Winter & Hirsch, Inc. Defendants made a motion before the trial court to vacate the judgment; the motion was denied, and from that order of the trial court this appeal is taken. The questions before this court are: 1) whether the loan entered into between the parties provided for a usurious rate of interest, and 2) whether the plaintiff was a holder in due course of the note evidencing the loan in question.

The defendants first contacted the Equitable Mortgage & Investment Corporation (hereinafter referred to as Equitable), attempting to secure a loan. Equitable is a brokerage firm which makes its profit by selling loan contracts to finance companies at a discount. In this case Equitable was to lend the defendants $10,000. Of the several provisions in the note, we will consider the following: 1) a provision whereby the defendants agreed "for value received" to repay a total of $16,260 over a period of 60 monthly payments of $271 each; and 2) a confession of judgment clause. The promissory note signed by the defendants provided for payment to the bearer and was secured by a trust deed.

The maximum legal rate of interest which could have been charged the defendants was exceeded by Equitable, and it is uncontested that Equitable charged a usurious rate of interest. The question to be resolved by this court, however, is whether the defense of usury is available for use against the plaintiff, who claims to be holder in due course of the promissory note and therefore claims to have taken it free from the defense of usury. In the trial court the defense of usury was rejected and judgment was entered against the defendants based on the court's conclusion that the plaintiff was a holder in due course of the promissory note.

In this appeal the defendants pray that the trial court's order be reversed and that the loan be held to be usurious. Defendants further ask that the trial court be directed to enter an order allowing them twice the rate of interest, plus attorney's fees and court costs. They seek this relief based on Ill. Rev. Stat. 1965, c.74, 6. At the time of the original transaction that section allowed one aggrieved by the imposition of a usurious rate of interest to be freed of the obligation to pay any interest at all, but an amendment to the statute, in effect at the time of trial, granted one the right to a penalty in the amount of double the usurious interest charged, plus attorney's fees and court costs.

Defendants defaulted on the note and the plaintiff obtained a judgment by confession. At the trial the defendants attempted to show that before the plaintiff purchased the note it knew of the usurious interest being charged, and consequently could not have become a holder in due course. Defendants point out that the loan application which the defendants filled out on January 7, 1963, has on it the name of the plaintiff. They also call attention to the testimony of Dominic Passarelli that he had been told by an agent of Equitable that Winter & Hirsch might give them $10,000. By the terms of the promissory note the monthly payments were to be made at the office of Ralph E. Brown, an attorney for plaintiff.

The most compelling fact presented to the court is that plaintiff issued a check to Equitable for $11,000 on February 18, 1963, with the notation on the stub that the funds were for "the Passarelli deal," but the defendants did not receive the $10,000 until February 28, 1963, ten days later. In other words, the plaintiff had extended the money to Equitable for the Passarelli loan prior to the time the defendants executed the note which plaintiff claims to have bought from Equitable. This fact renders inapposite an entire series of cases upon which plaintiff relies. Those cases hold that a loan may be discounted at more than the usury rate if the purchaser is without knowledge that the note was originally tainted with usury. Stevenson v. Unkefer, 14 Ill. 103; Sherman v. Blackman, 24 Ill. 345; Colehour v. State Sav. Institution, 90 Ill. 152. The critical factual distinction between those cases and the one before us is that the plaintiff in the instant case provided the money for the usurious loan before the loan was actually made, whereas in the cited cases the party claiming to be the innocent holder of the usurious note had purchased it subsequent to its execution.

On oral argument counsel for plaintiff argued that there must have been a clerical error in the dates, and that no loan company would have given out money without the loan contract in its possession. The insurmountable difficulty with counsel's argument is that the date of the check issued to Equitable (February 18) and the date of the note executed by the defendants (February 28) are clearly established through the admission into evidence, without objection, of the check issued to Equitable and the note signed by the defendants. This court must accept those dates as accurate.

From these dates it appears that the plaintiff was a co-originator of the note since it advanced the funds for the usurious loan before the loan was formalized. As a co-originator it is charged with the knowledge of the terms of the loan, and that knowledge includes information regarding anticipated return on its investment. Such information should have made it clear that a usurious rate of interest was being charged the defendants; nevertheless, the plaintiff still elected to consummate the transaction, and it must now accept the consequences.

We note, however, that the plaintiff has argued that it did not give the $11,000 to Equitable until after it saw the loan contract; in other words, that it was a purchaser of the note after it had already been executed. Although the facts do not sustain this contention because of the respective dates on which the check to Equitable was issued and the note signed by the defendants, even if that version were correct, we would hold for the defendants.

If the note was seen, as alleged by plaintiff, prior to its giving Equitable $11,000, then the plaintiff also saw that the defendants had signed a note promising to repay $16,260. From the face of the note one cannot ascertain the principal amount the defendants had received; it can only be known that "for value received" the defendants agreed to repay $16,260. We feel, however, that as reasonable businessmen, assuming arguendo that plaintiff did not know the truth, it should have raised the question of why Equitable was willing to sell a $16,260 note for $11,000. The difference between what the plaintiff was paying Equitable and the amount of the note was a charge beyond that permitted under the usury statute, and plaintiff should, therefore, have inquired how much money the defendants were receiving. We cannot permit parties to intentionally keep themselves in ignorance of facts which, if known, would defeat their unlawful purpose. The Uniform Commercial Code (Ill. Rev. Stat. 1965, c.26, §3-304(1)) provides that when an instrument is so incomplete as to call its validity into question, a purchaser of that instrument is on notice of the possibility of a claim against it [in the Revision, see §3-302(a)(1)—Eds.]. In this case we feel that the instrument, without the information as to the principal sum of the loan extended to the defendants, was "so incomplete" as to call its validity into question after plaintiff learned that it was able to buy it for only $11,000.

In Springer v. Mack, 222 Ill. App. 72, the court said at p. 75:

> The question of usury was discussed exhaustively and the authorities reviewed in the case of Clemens v. Crane, 234 Ill. 215, where it was held in substance, that in determining whether the essential elements of usury are present in a particular case, the intention of the parties, as the same appears from the facts and circumstances of the case, may be considered in connection with other evidence.

The court also said, p. 230:

> The form of the contract is not conclusive of the question. The desire of lenders to exact more than the law permits and the willingness of borrowers to concede whatever may be demanded to obtain temporary relief from financial embarrassment have resulted in a variety of shifts and cunning devices designed to evade the law. The character of a transaction is not to be judged by the mere verbal raiment in which the parties have clothed it, but by its true character as disclosed by the whole evidence. If, when so judged, it appears to be a loan or forbearance of money for a greater rate of interest than that allowed by law, the statute is violated and its penalties incurred, no matter what device the parties may have employed to conceal the real character of their dealings.

By failing to include the principal amount loaned to the borrower on the face of the loan contract or note, a subsequent purchaser of that contract is able to say "I had no idea that usury was involved. I simply bought the paper because it was a good buy." If the principal amount were shown, however, all subsequent purchasers would be put on notice if usury were involved, and they could not avoid their own involvement in the charging of a usurious rate by the purchase of such paper.

We feel we are justified in saying that where it appears from the facts and circumstances of the particular transaction under review that a reasonably prudent businessman would have found the purchase suspicious, he should inquire as to the truth. One should become suspicious when, as here, he is himself able to purchase paper at a price which is in itself so far below the amount to be repaid from the borrower that because of that differential the contract would have been usurious had it been the original transaction. The suspicion should be all the more compelling when the paper is bought from a broker or other company that is in the business of selling such paper. Since brokers are in the business of selling loan contracts for a profit, they are likely to have loaned out less than the amount for which they are willing to sell the contract to another. Thus, if one is able to buy a loan contract from a broker for $11,000, it is more than likely that the broker had loaned some figure less than the $11,000, and the broker's profit then becomes the difference between the amount he actually loaned and that for which he sold the contract. It would then appear likely that when this difference is itself usurious, the original transaction was also. Stevenson v. Unkefer, 14 Ill. 103, and similar cases do not dictate a contrary result. . . .

Under the circumstances, if the plaintiff was a purchaser, as it claims to be, it was on notice of a defense, since section 3-304 [in the Revision, §3-302(a)(1)—Eds.], chapter 26 of Ill. Rev. Stat. 1965 provides:

> (1) The purchaser has notice of a claim or defense if
>
> (a) the instrument is so incomplete, bears such visible evidence of forgery or alteration, or is otherwise so irregular as to call into question its validity, terms or ownership or to create an ambiguity as to the party to pay. . . .

This code provision is consistent with the earlier definition of "notice" found in section 1-201(25), chapter 26, providing:

> A person has "notice" of a fact when . . .
>
> (c) from all the facts and circumstances known to him at the time in question he has reason to know that it exists.

The intendment of these provisions would seem to be an attempt to prevent those dealing in the commercial world from obtaining various rights when, from a reasonable inquiry into the true facts that person would have discovered that a fact existed which prevented him from obtaining the rights which he was seeking. Under the circumstances in the present case, it is fair to say that the plaintiff had "reason to know" there was a good defense against the note in question. Even the earlier cases point out that notice of usury destroyed one's rights in the note. . . .

The judgment of the Circuit Court is reversed, and the cause is remanded with directions to enter a judgment for defendants and for further proceedings in conformity with this opinion.

Reversed and remanded with directions.

LYONS, J. concurs.

[The dissenting opinion of BURKE, J., is omitted.]

QUESTION

Would the Federal Trade Commission holder in due course rule (see page 489) apply to the promissory note signed in this case if the transaction had taken place after May 14, 1976 (the effective date of that rule)?

PROBLEM 122

Fred wrote a check on January 5, 2023, but mistakenly put down "2022" as the year. He saw his error, crossed out the last digit, and wrote "3" above it. Can anyone become a holder in due course of this instrument?

PROBLEM 123

Ace Finance Company was the payee on a promissory note signed by John Maker. On its face, the note calls for John to make 12 monthly interest payments before the note matures. Ace sold the note at a discount to Big Town Bank (BTB). If the note has written on it, in big letters, a penciled notation, "Missed Paying First Installment," can BTB ever qualify as a holder in due course? See §3-304(b) and (c) and its Official Comment 2.

PROBLEM 124

Dan Drawer wrote a check dated April 30 to Dr. Paine, his dentist, for $80, in payment for services rendered. Dr. Paine was not aware that the check fell to the floor behind his desk, where it lay until the end of August, when the janitor found it. Dr. Paine then deposited the check in his bank on August 31, and it bounced on September 3, when the drawee bank informed the depositary bank that Dan had stopped payment because the dental work had been done badly. Is the depositary bank a holder in due course? See §3-304(a)(2).

Dawda, Mann, Mulcahy & Sadler, P.L.C. v. Bank of America, N.A.

United States District Court, Eastern District of Michigan, 2014
2014 WL 6669277

TERRENCE G. BERG, District Judge.

This matter is before the Court on Defendant Bank of America, N.A.'s ("Defendant's") motion to dismiss under Federal Rule of Civil Procedure 12(b)(6). (Dkt. 10.) This motion was fully briefed and the parties presented oral argument on June 9, 2014. For the reasons set out below, Defendant's motion to dismiss is DENIED.

I. INTRODUCTION

This is a negligence case. Plaintiff, the law firm of Dawda, Mann, Mulcahy & Sadler, P.L.C. ("Plaintiff"), alleges that it suffered significant monetary losses because of Defendant Bank of America, N.A.'s negligence in accepting over $500,000 in diverted trust account checks. As part of a fraudulent scheme, a former partner of Plaintiff caused Plaintiff to write a number of checks made payable to Defendant from Plaintiff's IOLTA account.[17] The partner, an account holder and customer of Defendant, presented these checks to Defendant, and Defendant deposited the funds into the partner's personal account maintained by Defendant. Though Plaintiff did not owe Defendant any money and did not have a business relationship with Defendant, it is alleged that Defendant made no inquiry regarding the checks before depositing them. As a result, Plaintiff alleges that Defendant violated the common law "duty of inquiry." Defendant counters that it did not owe Plaintiff any duty and that it held the checks as a holder in due course under the Uniform Commercial Code ("UCC"), free from any claims on the checks. For the reasons that follow, Defendant's motion to dismiss is DENIED.

II. FACTUAL AND PROCEDURAL BACKGROUND

Plaintiff is a law firm located in Bloomfield Hills, Michigan. (Second Amended Complaint, Dkt. 9, at ¶1.) Beginning on or about November 15,

17. An IOLTA ("Interest on Lawyer's Trust Account") account is an interest-bearing account maintained by an attorney or law firm to pool funds being held in trust for a client or clients, as required under Michigan Rule of Professional Responsibility 1.15(d).

2010, Plaintiff's former partner Kenneth Flaska ("Flaska") defrauded Plaintiff by laundering funds through Defendant.[18] (*Id.* at ¶6.) Flaska's fraud consisted of presenting and depositing checks drawn on Plaintiff's IOLTA account into Flaska's personal bank account maintained by Defendant. (*Id.*) From November 2010 until March 2013, Defendant received and credited nine of these checks into Flaska's account, totaling $529,676.50. (*Id.* at ¶7.) All of the checks were drawn from Plaintiff's IOLTA account and were payable on their face to "Bank of America," the Defendant. (*Id.* at ¶¶6-7, Exs. A-I.) Despite the fact that Plaintiff was not one of Defendant's customers and was not indebted to Defendant, Defendant allegedly never inquired into these checks before crediting them to Flaska's account. (Second Amended Complaint, Dkt. 9 at ¶¶9, 13.)

On November 15, 2013, Plaintiff sued Defendant in Oakland County Circuit Court. (Dkt. 1, Ex. 1.) Plaintiff amended its state court complaint on February 5, 2014, alleging four counts against Defendant, including: (1) breach of the common law duty of inquiry; (2) common law conversion; (3) statutory conversion; and (4) negligence. (*Id.*) Defendant removed the case to this Court on February 11, 2014. (Dkt. 1.) Plaintiff subsequently amended its complaint, eliminating Counts 2 and 3 and proceeding solely on Counts 1 and 4. (*Id.*)

III. Analysis

* * *

1. THE COMMON LAW DUTY OF INQUIRY

Plaintiff alleges that Defendant was negligent because it breached its common law "duty of inquiry." In diversity jurisdiction actions, federal courts must "appl[y] the substantive law of the forum state—in this case, Michigan." Conlin v. Mortg. Elec. Registration Sys., Inc., 714 F.3d 355, 358 (6th Cir. 2013). The Michigan Court of Appeals first recognized a common law duty of inquiry in Allis Chalmers Leasing Servs. Corp. v. Byron Ctr. State Bank, 129 Mich. App. 602, 341 N.W.2d 837 (1983). In *Allis Chalmers,* the plaintiff wrote a check payable to the defendant, Byron Center State Bank, as part of a purchase and leaseback agreement that the plaintiff had entered into with Gary Deneen, a customer of the defendant. *Id.* at 839. Deneen presented the check to the defendant as part of a fraudulent scheme Deneen devised to defraud the plaintiff. *Id.* The defendant's employee distributed the proceeds according to Deneen's instructions without making any inquiry into how the funds should be used. *Id.*

18. Flaska pled guilty to bank fraud and money laundering for this scheme, and was sentenced to 64 months in prison. *See* E.D. Mich. Case No. 14-20131.

Seeking to recover its losses, the plaintiff brought a negligence action against the defendant bank for the amount of the check. The plaintiff alleged that the defendant bank was negligent in disbursing the check to Deneen without first inquiring into how the funds should be disbursed. *Id.* On appeal, the Michigan Court of Appeals affirmed the trial court's grant of summary judgment in favor of the plaintiff, citing the general rule that "[w]here a check is drawn to the order of a bank to which the drawer is not indebted, the bank is authorized to pay the proceeds only to persons specified by the drawer; it takes the risk in treating such a check as payable to bearer and is placed on inquiry as to the authority of the drawer's agent to receive payment." *Id.* (internal citation omitted).

In addition, the Michigan Court of Appeals, adopting a California Supreme Court decision, held that plaintiff's negligence action was not abrogated by the UCC's "holder in due course" doctrine. The defendant in *Allis Chalmers* argued that it was a holder in due course under the UCC and not liable under the common law duty of inquiry. A holder in due course then, and now, takes an instrument free of any claims on the instrument. *See* Mich. Comp. Laws §440.3306. The Michigan Court of Appeals rejected the defendant's argument and instead adopted the California Supreme Court's holding in Sun 'n Sand, Inc. v. United Cal. Bank, 21 Cal. 3d 671, 148 Cal. Rptr. 329, 582 P.2d 920 (1978). *Id.* at 840.

In *Sun 'n Sand*, the California Supreme Court recognized that banks have a duty of inquiry that is "activated only when checks, not insignificant in amount, are drawn payable to the order of a bank and are presented to the payee bank by a third party seeking to negotiate the checks for his own benefit." 148 Cal. Rptr. 329, 582 P.2d at 937. *Sun 'n Sand* explained that the duty of inquiry is narrow in scope, stating

"[T]he bank's obligation is minimal. We hold simply that the bank may not ignore the danger signals inherent in such an attempted negotiation. There must be objective indicia from which the bank could reasonably conclude that the party presenting the check is authorized to transact in the manner proposed. In the absence of such indicia the bank pays at its peril." *Id.* Since the bank was under the duty of inquiry, *Sun 'n Sand* held that the UCC's holder in due course doctrine was not a defense to the common law duty of inquiry because banks were on notice "so as to preclude UCB from holder in due course status[.]" *Id.*, 148 Cal. Rptr. 329, 582 P.2d at 933.

2. THE 1993 REVISION TO THE UCC

In response, Defendant argues that *Allis Chalmers* is old law, and that Michigan's 1993 revision to the UCC abrogated the common law duty of inquiry. Defendant cites no case law in support of its position that the duty of inquiry was preempted or overturned in Michigan as a result of the 1993 UCC revisions, and the Court finds little precedential support for this assertion.

Indeed, contrary to Defendant's position, there is case law holding that the duty of inquiry recognized in *Allis Chalmers* remains in force in Michigan and may preclude a party from taking as a holder in due course under the UCC. In Grand Rapids Auto Sales, Inc. v. MBNA Am. Bank, 227 F. Supp. 2d 721, 725-726 (W.D. Mich. 2002), citing *Allis Chalmers*, the court held that there is a duty of inquiry that "arises only in circumstances where the check is physically presented to the bank for negotiation by the dishonest employee and the bank, through its agent, has the opportunity to inspect the check for irregularities that should alert the bank that fraud is amiss." *Grand Rapids* involved an employee of a Michigan company who defrauded the company by taking company checks made payable to defendant MBNA bank and having MBNA apply the checks to her husband's credit card. *Id.* at 723. The bank accepted the checks through automatic electronic processing. *Id.* The company, who did not have a relationship with MBNA, sued MBNA alleging that MBNA violated its common law duty of inquiry. *Id.* at 722.

Although the court rejected the company's argument and held that MBNA was a holder in due course, it did so because it ruled that the duty of inquiry did not *extend* to automatic credit card payments, not because the duty of inquiry did not *exist. Id.* at 726. And the court explicitly distinguished its holding from *Allis Chalmers* based on the factual circumstances of the case, "[t]he key distinction between this case and *Sun 'n Sand* and *Allis Chalmers* is that the banks in those cases actually inspected the checks and should have been alerted by the circumstances—a check drawn payable to the order of the bank by a drawer not indebted to the bank and presented by a third party seeking to negotiate the check for his own benefit—that the employee's conduct may have been improper." *Id.* at 726-727 (internal citations omitted). The factual scenario offered by the court as an example of the situation where the duty of inquiry should still apply is exactly what Plaintiff alleges happened in the case at bar. . . .

3. *SUN 'N SAND*'S HOLDING THAT A PARTY UNDER A DUTY OF INQUIRY TAKES WITH NOTICE AND IS NOT A HOLDER IN DUE COURSE REMAINS GOOD LAW

Defendant next attempts a collateral attack on *Allis Chalmers* by arguing that *Sun 'n Sand*, the basis for *Allis Chalmers*, is no longer good law. This argument is not well taken. . . .

Defendant's second point fares no better. Defendant argues that the 1993 revision of the UCC abrogated *Sun 'n Sand*'s holding that defendant had notice and as such was not a holder in due course. . . .

Additionally, Mich. Comp. Laws §440.3302(1)(a), the current section that defines a holder in due course, retains the language concerning irregularity on the instrument that the *Sun 'n Sand* court interpreted. Mich. Comp. Laws §440.3302(1)(a) states that a party is a "holder in due course" if both of the following apply:

(a) The instrument when issued or negotiated to the holder does not bear such apparent evidence of forgery or alteration *or is not otherwise so irregular or incomplete as to call into question its authenticity.*

(b) The holder took the instrument (*i*) for value, (*ii*) in good faith, (*iii*) without notice that the instrument is overdue or has been dishonored or that there is an incurred default with respect to payment of another instrument issued as part of the same series, (*iv*) without notice that the instrument contains an unauthorized signature or has been altered, (*v*) without notice of any claim to the instrument described in section 3306, and (*vi*) without notice that any party has a defense or claim in recoupment described in section 3305(1).

(emphasis added). A check written to a bank as a payee by a non-customer who does not owe it any money is likely an irregularity under Mich. Comp. Laws §440.3302. This is consistent with the position of the court in *Grand Rapids* where the court held that banks that physically inspect a suspect check are in a position to be placed on notice. 227 F. Supp. 2d at 726 ("the banks in those cases actually inspected the checks and should have been alerted by the circumstances . . .").

Defendant counters that under Mich. Comp. Laws §440.3302, the irregularity must be on the face of an instrument and not merely based on the circumstances of a transaction. In support of this argument, Defendant points to Comment One of Mich. Comp. Laws §440.3302(a)(1), which states in relevant part:

Subsection (a)(1) is a return to the N.I.L. rule that the taker of an irregular or incomplete instrument is not a person the law should protect against defenses of the obligor or claims of prior owners. This reflects a policy choice against extending the holder in due course doctrine to an instrument that is so incomplete or irregular "as to call into question its authenticity." The term "authenticity" is used to make it clear that the irregularity or incompleteness must indicate that the instrument may not be what it purports to be. Persons who purchase or pay such instruments should do so at their own risk. Under subsection (1) of former Section 3-304, irregularity or incompleteness gave a purchaser notice of a claim or defense. But it was not clear from that provision whether the claim or defense had to be related to the irregularity or incomplete aspect of the instrument. This ambiguity is not present in subsection (a)(1).

Defendant's reading of Comment One to say that any irregularity must be on the face of an instrument is not supported by the language of the Comment itself. A more accurate reading of this Comment is that where the irregularity *is* present on the face of the instrument, so that a doubt is created that the instrument is what it purports to be, the taker of an instrument with such an irregularity is not protected as a holder in due course.

The Comment does not preclude a finding that the actual language of Mich. Comp. Laws §440.3302(a)(1) contemplated the possibility of irregularities arising both on the face of the instrument and in the circumstances of its negotiation. That language speaks not only of the face of the instrument but also of its negotiation when it states: "[t]he instrument when issued *or negotiated* to the holder does not bear such apparent evidence of forgery or alteration *or is not otherwise so irregular or incomplete as to call into question its authenticity*." (*Id.*) (emphasis added). An instrument that has no marks of forgery or alteration on its face may nevertheless have its authenticity called into question by the surrounding circumstances of its negotiation. Further, had the drafters of the UCC intended to change the holder in due course section to require that an irregularity must be on the face of an instrument, they would have so stated. Indeed, the drafters were clear in their express rejection of *Sun 'n Sand*'s warranty holding. This Court does not find support in the statutory text to hold that an irregularity must be on the face of the check. . . .

5. MICH. COMP. LAWS §440.3307

Defendant also seeks refuge in another section of the UCC, claiming that Mich. Comp. Laws §440.3307 [U.C.C. §3-307] effectively abrogates the common law duty of inquiry. Mich. Comp. Laws §440.3307 defines when a taker of a negotiable instrument has notice of a breach of fiduciary duty and thus does not take as a holder in due course. Mich. Comp. Laws §440.3307(2) provides:

> If (*i*) an instrument is taken from a fiduciary for payment or collection or for value, (*ii*) the taker has knowledge of the fiduciary status of the fiduciary, and (*iii*) the represented person makes a claim to the instrument or its proceeds on the basis that the transaction of the fiduciary is a breach of fiduciary duty, the following rules apply:
>
> (a) Notice of breach of fiduciary duty by the fiduciary is notice of the claim of the represented person.
>
> * * *
>
> (d) If an instrument is issued by the represented person or the fiduciary as such, to the taker as payee, the taker has notice of the breach of fiduciary duty if the instrument is (*i*) taken in payment of or as security for a debt known by the taker to be the personal debt of the fiduciary, (*ii*) taken in a transaction known by the taker to be for the personal benefit of the fiduciary, or (*iii*) deposited to an account other than an account of the fiduciary, as such, or an account of the represented person. . . .

The Court begins with a plain reading of Mich. Comp. Laws §440.3307. Comment Two of Mich. Comp. Laws §440.3307 states that the section applies where a "fiduciary in effect embezzles money of the represented person by applying the proceeds of an instrument that belongs to the represented person to the personal use of the fiduciary." Mich. Comp. Laws §440.3307(1)(a) defines "fiduciary" narrowly, as an "an agent, trustee, partner, corporate officer or director, or other representative *owing a fiduciary duty with respect to an instrument.*" (emphasis added). So, even if a party is a fiduciary of an organization, Mich. Comp. Laws §440.3307 is inapplicable if the party is not a fiduciary with respect to the check itself. This is what the Seventh Circuit held in *Elizabeth State Bank.* There, the Seventh Circuit found that a controller for a company who managed the company's books and accounts was not a fiduciary under Illinois' version of Mich. Comp. Laws §440.3307 because he had "no authority to direct the proceeds" of checks on the company's account at issue. 265 F.3d at 622. As such, the Seventh Circuit held that the controller "may have been a fiduciary for some purposes, but he did not qualify as a fiduciary with respect to checks drawn on the operating account and made payable to the bank's order." *Id.* Because this section applies only where a fiduciary (as to a particular check) is involved, it is narrowly drawn and does not cover every situation where a third-party attempts to divert the proceeds of a check by presenting a check made payable to a taker. It follows that the scope of Mich. Comp. Laws §440.3307, like its Illinois counterpart, does not encompass every situation where the common law duty of inquiry applies.

The Court must also consider that the UCC by its own terms provides for supplementation by other sources of law, such as the common law duty of inquiry. Mich. Comp. Laws §440.1103 provides that "[u]nless displaced by the particular provisions of this act, the principles of law and equity . . . shall supplement its provisions." As discussed above, Mich. Comp. Laws §440.3307 only applies where a fiduciary with respect to a certain instrument presents that instrument to a taker as payee. Because the duty of inquiry applies more broadly to situations that do not involve a fiduciary, the common law duty of inquiry is not displaced by a particular provision of the UCC.

Similarly, the holder in due course section specifically provides for supplementation by other sources of law. Mich. Comp. Laws §440.3302(7) provides that "[t]his section is subject to any law limiting status as a holder in due course in particular classes of transactions." As evidenced by the considerable body of case law discussed above, numerous jurisdictions deny banks holder in due course status when they are "presented with a check made out to it by someone who owes it no money, for deposit in the presenter's account." *Travelers,* 374 F.3d at 527-528. Consequently, the duty of inquiry limits the holder in due course section.

Finally, the UCC's underlying purpose of promoting uniformity among jurisdictions weighs against a finding that Mich. Comp. Laws §440.3307 has abrogated the common law duty of inquiry. Mich. Comp. Laws §440.1103 provides:

> (1) This act must be liberally construed and applied to promote the following underlying purposes and policies:
>
> (a) To simplify, clarify, and modernize the law governing commercial transactions.
>
> * * *
>
> (c) To make uniform the law among the various jurisdictions.

Various jurisdictions have upheld the common law duty of inquiry both before and after the enactment of the UCC. This Court has found no case abrogating the common law duty of inquiry in any jurisdiction. Hence, the interest of uniformity militates against abrogating the common law duty of inquiry.

For the foregoing reasons, this Court holds that the Mich. Comp. Laws §440.3307 does not abrogate the common law duty of inquiry.

6. PLAINTIFF HAS RAISED A PLAUSIBLE CLAIM THAT DEFENDANT HAD A DUTY OF INQUIRY

Having found that the common law duty of inquiry remains viable as a legal claim, we must now analyze whether Plaintiff's facts present a plausible claim that Defendant had a duty of inquiry in this case. *Sun 'n Sand* held that the duty is "activated only when checks, not insignificant in amount, are drawn payable to the order of a bank and are presented to the payee bank by a third party seeking to negotiate the checks for his own benefit." 148 Cal. Rptr. 329, 582 P.2d at 937. Here, Plaintiff's checks were payable to Defendant. These checks were for a significant amount; together the nine checks totaled $529,676.50. And Flaska, a third-party, presented the checks to Defendant for his own benefit. Under these circumstances, a "bank may not ignore the danger signals inherent in such an attempted negotiation." *Id.* Based on these allegations, Plaintiff has raised a plausible claim that Defendant had a duty of inquiry. . . .

IV. CONCLUSION

For the foregoing reasons, Plaintiff has stated a plausible claim for relief and Defendant's motion to dismiss is DENIED.

SO ORDERED.

PROBLEM 125

When Ellen Brown found out that the computer she had purchased didn't work, she was furious and decided not to pay the promissory note she had signed. The note stated that it was "payable at Busy State Bank" (which in this case means that the bank would pay the note when presented and then expect reimbursement from the maker; cf. §4-106(b)). Harold Slow, the head cashier at the bank, took Ellen's phone call and promised not to pay the note when it was presented. Four months went by, and, on one hectic afternoon, the bank paid the note by accident. Slow said he had forgotten the request not to pay. The bank now demands payment, claiming to be a holder in due course. Is it?

The last Problem involves the *forgotten notice doctrine,* which under the NIL permitted a holder to *forget* notice and thus become a holder in due course if sufficient time passed between the notice and the acquisition of the instrument. See First Natl. Bank of Odessa v. Fazzari, 10 N.Y.2d 394, 179 N.E.2d 493, 233 N.Y.S.2d 483 (1961) ("[W]e think that the doctrine should be applied with great caution in the case where a simple promissory note is involved. A lapse of memory is too easily pleaded and too difficult to controvert to permit the doctrine to be applied automatically irrespective of the circumstances surrounding each transaction and the relationship of the parties."). The UCC has no position on the *forgotten notice doctrine;* see §1-202's Official Comment; McCook County Natl. Bank v. Compton, 558 F.2d 871 (8th Cir. 1977).

PROBLEM 126

Giant Earthmovers bought some machinery from Tractors, Inc., and in payment executed a promissory note payable to the order of Tractors for $2,000. Tractors sold the note without indorsement to the Friendly Finance Company for $1,500. The maker of the note refused to pay the note when it matured, stating that the machinery did not operate properly. Friendly decided to sue Giant Earthmovers, and the day before the lawsuit was filed, Friendly's lawyer noticed that the note had never been indorsed by Tractors, Inc. He had Tractors' president specially indorse the note over to Friendly right away, and then the suit was filed. Is Friendly a holder in due course? See §3-203(c) and its Official Comment 3, and Case #4 in Official Comment 4; Ballengee v. New Mexico Fed. Sav. & Loan Assn., 109 N.M. 423, 786 P.2d 37 (N.M. 1990).

Jones v. Approved Bancredit Corp.

Delaware Supreme Court, 1969
256 A.2d 739

HERRMANN, J.

The dispositive question in this appeal is whether the plaintiff finance company is a holder in due course of the defendant's note. We hold that the finance company was not a holder in due course under the party-to-the-transaction rule.

I

The relevant facts are undisputed for present purposes.

The defendant, Myrtle V. Jones, owned a lot of land in Delaware and wished to have a house built on it. She responded to a newspaper advertisement by Albee Dell Homes, Inc. (hereinafter "Dell"), a sales agency for precut homes in Elkton, Maryland. After selecting a type of house from various plans presented, Mrs. Jones signed a purchase order contract and credit application and made a deposit. Several weeks later, Dell's representative presented to Mrs. Jones for signature a series of documents evidencing an obligation of $3,250,[19] to be paid by Mrs. Jones in monthly installments over a period of years for the house. The documents evidencing the obligation included the following papers: a mortgage; a judgment bond and warrant; a promissory note; a construction contract; a request for insurance; an affidavit that the masonry work and foundation were completed and paid for (when in fact none of the work had been commenced); and an affidavit that no materials were delivered or work started as of the date of the mortgage.

Mrs. Jones demurred to the signing of the mass of documents thus placed before her and stated that she would like to consult her attorney before signing because she did not understand the documents. Dell's representative objected, stating that it was not necessary for Mrs. Jones to have an attorney; that it would be a waste of money to do so; that he would advise her. Although Mrs. Jones reiterated her wish for an attorney several times, Dell's representative insisted upon her signing the papers then and there, stating that it was necessary to do so if the work was to start seasonably. He assured her that Dell would take care of the entire situation to her satisfaction. Mrs. Jones finally acquiesced and signed all the documents. Immediately thereafter, the paper was endorsed and assigned by Dell to the plaintiff Approved Bancredit Corp. (hereinafter "Bancredit") which paid Dell $2,250.00 for the $3,250.00 note.

During the construction, an employee of the builder drove a bulldozer into the side of the partially completed house and knocked it off its foundations. Thereafter, the builder refused to go forward with the work. Dell disclaimed responsibility on the ground that the damage to the structure was a result of a "cave-in" and was "a work of God." The structure was left in a dangerous condition with the water-filled basement constituting an attractive nuisance to children. The County authorities demanded that this unsafe

19. The principal amount of the obligation was $2,500. The balance consisted of "charges."

condition be rectified. Mrs. Jones consulted an attorney who notified Dell and Bancredit that Mrs. Jones would be obliged to remove the remnants of the building and fill the basement, in order to make the area safe, unless another satisfactory course of action was suggested. There was no reply and the demolition was accomplished at Mrs. Jones' expense. Later, Dell closed its office and terminated its business except for the servicing of certain contracts through a representative in Delaware.

Thereafter, Bancredit brought this action against Mrs. Jones, seeking foreclosure on the mortgage and collection of an unpaid balance of $2,560.23, with interest. Mrs. Jones interposed several defenses, mainly that of fraud by Dell. During pretrial proceedings, the action developed into a suit upon the promissory note, which Bancredit contended was secured by the mortgage and was negotiable in its hands as a holder in due course by assignment of Dell. Thereupon, Bancredit moved for summary judgment on the ground that the defenses claimed against Dell were not available against it as a holder in due course. The Superior Court denied summary judgment, stating that Mrs. Jones should have the opportunity to "demonstrate the precise relationship" between Dell and Bancredit. Thereafter, depositions were taken and the following facts, inter alia, appeared regarding that relationship:

Dell and Bancredit were both wholly owned subsidiaries of Albee Homes, Inc. (hereinafter "Homes"). The business of the parent corporation was to process pre-cut lumber and sell pre-cut homes. It had between 50 and 70 sales agencies in 19 states. Dell was its Maryland sales agency. Ninety-nine percent of Bancredit's business came from Dell and the other wholly owned sales agency subsidiaries of Homes; it was organized for this purpose. Bancredit examined into the laws of the various states in which the sales agencies operated and prescribed the forms of contracts and financing documents to be used by each agency, including Dell, in concluding a transaction. Homes and Bancredit had the same officers and directors; Homes named the directors and officers of Dell. Checks of Bancredit, issued to consummate a financing transaction like that entered into by Mrs. Jones and Dell, were countersigned by Homes. During the construction of a house, Bancredit routinely requested and received progress reports. Specifically, the manager of Bancredit testified on deposition that Bancredit was a "finance department" of Homes; that each transaction of Dell, like the transactions of each of the other sales agencies, was approved in advance by Bancredit; that the first paper received was the application of the purchaser for extension of credit which was reviewed and passed upon in advance by Bancredit, with directions back to Dell as to any special condition to be imposed upon the purchaser in connection with the loan under consideration. Bancredit had the exclusive power of approval, condition, or rejection of a transaction tendered by the sales agency.

As the result of a pretrial conference, the trial judge stated that with a full understanding of the evidence to be adduced by each side at trial, he had concluded that a directed verdict in favor of Bancredit must necessarily result because, in his opinion, Bancredit was a holder in due course and the defenses sought to be interposed by Mrs. Jones were not available to it. Each of the parties then made a detailed offer of proof on the record and, thereupon, the Superior Court entered judgment for Bancredit on the ground that it was a holder in due course. Mrs. Jones appeals.

II

The question before us has not been heretofore answered by this court. It is a difficult question, as to which the authorities are in sharp conflict.

In dealing with the holder in due course status, a basic problem has been recognized by the courts in cases involving the financing of installment sales, especially of consumer goods and household improvements. The problem arises from the increasingly apparent need for a balancing of the interest of the commercial community in the unrestricted negotiability of commercial papers, on the one hand, against the interest of the installment buyers of the community, on the other hand, in the preservation of their normal remedy of withholding payment whenever there has been misrepresentation, failure of consideration, or other valid reason for refusal to pay. This problem and this need have given rise to this concept: The more the holder knows about the underlying transaction which is the source of the paper, the more he controls or participates in it, the less he fits the role of good faith purchaser for value, and the less justification there is for according to him the protected status of holder in due course considered necessary for the free flow of paper in the commercial world.

The rule, balancing the needs of the installment-buying community and the commercial community, has evolved in various ways. Many courts have solved the problem by denying holder in due course status to the finance company where it maintains a close business relationship with the dealer whose paper it buys; where the financier is closely connected with the particular credit transaction under scrutiny; or where the financier prescribes to the dealer the forms of the papers, the buyer signs the purchase agreement and the note concurrently, and the dealer endorses the note and assigns the contract immediately thereafter. In such situations, many courts look upon the transaction as a species of tri-partite transaction; and the tenor of the cases is that the finance company, in such situation, should not be permitted to hide behind "the fictional fence" of the UNIL or the UCC and thereby achieve an unfair advantage over the purchaser. See Unico v. Owen, 50 N.J. 101, 232 A.2d 405 (1967); Buffalo Industrial Bank v. DeMarzio, 162 Misc. 742, 296 N.Y.S. 738 (1937).

The rule of balance thus evolved is exemplified by Mutual Finance Co. v. Martin, 63 So. 2d 649 (Fla. 1953). There a finance company was held not to be a holder in due course where it appeared that the finance company furnished to the payee electrical appliance dealer the form of conditional sales contract and promissory note with its name imprinted thereon; that before the sales transaction occurred the finance company had investigated the purchaser's credit standing, had approved the proposed terms and agreed to purchase the contract and note in the event the transaction was consummated; that over a period of years immediately prior to the transaction, the finance company had provided much financing for the dealer in other transactions. In holding that, under those circumstances, the finance company was sufficiently a party to the transaction to deprive it of holder in due course status, the Supreme Court of Florida stated:

> . . . It may be that our holding here will require some changes in business methods and will impose a greater burden on the finance companies. We think the buyer—Mr. & Mrs. General Public—should have some protection somewhere along the line. We believe the finance company is better able to bear the risk of the dealer's insolvency than the buyer and in a far better position to protect his interests against unscrupulous and insolvent dealers. . . .
>
> If this opinion imposes great burdens on finance companies it is a potent argument in favor of a rule which will afford protection to the general buying public against unscrupulous dealers in personal property. . . .

Another leading case supporting the rule of balance is Commercial Credit Co. v. Childs, 199 Ark. 1073, 137 S.W.2d 260 (1940), wherein the automobile sales contract, note, and assignment forms were attached together, were furnished by the finance company, and were all executed on the same day. The Supreme Court of Arkansas there stated:

> We think appellant was so closely connected with the entire transaction or with the deal that it can not be heard to say that it, in good faith, was an innocent purchaser of the instrument for value before maturity. . . . Rather than being a purchaser of the instrument after its execution it was to all intents and purposes a party to the agreement and instrument from the beginning. . . .

See also Commercial Credit Corporation v. Orange County Machine Works, 34 Cal. 2d 766, 214 P.2d 819 (1950), where the Supreme Court of California held:

> When a finance company actively participates in a transaction . . . from its inception, counseling and aiding the future vendor-payee, it cannot be regarded as a holder in due course. . . .

And in Unico v. Owen, 50 N.J. 101, 232 A.2d 405 (1967), wherein the finance company was formed expressly to handle the financing of sales by the dealer exclusively, the Supreme Court of New Jersey summarized its position on the question before us as follows:

> For purposes of consumer goods transactions, we hold that where the seller's performance is executory in character and when it appears from the totality of the arrangements between dealer and financier that the financier has had a substantial voice in setting standards for the underlying transaction, or has approved the standards established by the dealer, and has agreed to take all or a predetermined or substantial quantity of the negotiable paper which is backed by such standards, the financier should be considered a participant in the original transaction and therefore not entitled to holder in due course status. . . .

The factual situation in the *Unico* case is especially analogous to the instant case.

The divergent line of cases, reflecting an underlying conflict in policy considerations, accords determinative importance to the maintenance of a free flow of credit. These cases protect the finance company from purchaser defenses on the ground that this is an overriding consideration in order to assure easy negotiability of commercial paper and the resultant availability of the rapid financing methods required by our present-day economy. The cases of both lines of authority are collected at Annots., 128 A.L.R. 729 (1940), 44 A.L.R.2d 8, 134-157 (1955), 4 A.L.R.2d Later Case Serv. 929 (1965). See also Swanson v. Commercial Acceptance Corporation (9th Cir.), 381 F.2d 296 (1967); 39 S. Cal. L. Rev. 48, 68-74 (1966); 10 Vill. L. Rev. 309 (1965); 65 Colum. L. Rev. 733 (1965); 53 Harv. L. Rev. 1200 (1940); 1958 Wash. U. L.Q. 177; 35 U. Chi. L. Rev. 739 (1968); 939 Minn. L. Rev. 775 (1954).

Under the totality of facts and circumstances of this case, we hold that the rule of balance should be adopted and applied; that it should operate in favor of the installment buyer for the reason that, in our opinion, Bancredit was so involved in the transaction that it may not be treated as a subsequent purchaser for value. By reason of its sister corporation relationship to Dell and the established course of dealing between them, Bancredit was more nearly an original party to the transaction than a subsequent purchaser of the paper; and, for the reasons of fairness and balance stated in the foregoing authorities, Bancredit should be denied the protected status of holder in due course which would prevent Mrs. Jones from having her day in court on the defenses she would have otherwise had against Dell.

The rule we here adopt must be applied carefully because of the delicate balance of the interests of the installment buying community and the commercial community. But the need for special care in application should not foreclose the adoption of the rule and its application in a proper case. In this day of demonstrated need for emphasis upon consumer protection and truth in lending, special consideration must be given to preventing the misuse of negotiable instruments to deprive installment purchasers of legitimate defenses. In a proper case, such as the one before us, this becomes the controlling consideration.

For the reasons stated, we conclude that the Superior Court erred in holding that Bancredit was a holder in due course. Accordingly, the judgment below is reversed and the cause remanded for further proceedings consistent herewith.

This decision is typical of a large number of cases in which the courts have held that the buyer-transferee of the paper is too "closely connected" with the seller-transferor to be permitted to obtain holder in due course status. The doctrine has been chiefly of benefit to consumers, but it has been applied in purely commercial settings. See, e.g., St. James v. Diversified Commercial Fin. Corp., 102 Nev. 23, 714 P.2d 179 (1986). Following are some of the tests the courts use to assess the connection.

(1) Is the buyer-transferee the alter ego of the seller-transferor? Do they have the same officers, same personnel, same location?
(2) Who drafted the original promissory note?
(3) Is the buyer-transferee mentioned in the note?
(4) Does the seller-transferor sell paper to other buyers, or is the buyer-transferee the only market?
(5) Did the buyer-transferee get involved in the transaction by which the note was created? Did it, for instance, conduct a credit investigation of the maker?
(6) Did the buyer-transferee have some knowledge of the seller-transferor's poor past performance of similar contracts?

If the court concludes that the buyer-transferee is too *closely connected* to the seller-transferor, the court has a variety of ways to deny holder in due course status to the plaintiff. It can say that the plaintiff was not acting in *good faith*, that the plaintiff had notice of underlying defenses, or that the plaintiff is the same entity as the seller-transferor and can stand in no better situation.

In light of this problem, what would you advise Bancredit to do in the future to become a holder in due course of notes that pass through the hands of payees like Dell?

Lest you get the idea that in promissory note lawsuits the finance company always loses (which is not even vaguely true), read the following case. It makes the important point that knowledge of the underlying transaction is not the same thing as notice of a claim or a defense arising out of that transaction.

Sullivan v. United Dealers Corp.

Kentucky Court of Appeals, 1972
486 S.W.2d 699

REED, J.

The sole issue presented is whether appellee, United Dealers Corporation, a finance company, was a holder in due course of a promissory note executed and delivered by appellants, James Earl Sullivan and Norma Jean Sullivan, his wife, in payment for building materials and labor furnished by Memory Swift Homes, Inc., the payee of the note.

Memory Swift Homes, Inc., contracted with the Sullivans to construct a prefabricated dwelling house for them. The contract was dated March 26, 1963, and on April 9, 1963, the Sullivans executed and delivered to Memory Swift, the contractor, their promissory negotiable note in the sum of $18,224.64 secured by a mortgage on the real property and the improvement to be located thereon. On the same day, the contractor negotiated the note and assigned the mortgage to the finance company.

On June 25, 1963, the finance company negotiated the note to a bank which took the instrument with right of recourse. After the negotiation of the note to the finance company but prior to its negotiation by the finance company to the bank, the Sullivans delivered written statements to the finance company that the foundation of the house had been properly installed and also certified that all framing members in the house were properly and sufficiently nailed to make it a sound and sturdy structure and that all work had been performed in a workmanlike manner.

Beginning in August 1963, the Sullivans made several monthly payments according to the terms of the note but then defaulted. The last monthly payment was made in April 1966, but this covered the monthly installment due in August 1965. On April 25, 1966, the bank transferred the note back to the finance company, for value, without recourse. The finance company then instituted action against the Sullivans for collection of the note and foreclosure of the mortgage. The Sullivans pleaded that the finance company was not a holder in due course of the note and that the contractor had constructed the house in an unworkmanlike manner by reason of which they had been damaged; they sought to assert their claim against the contractor as a defense against the finance company. The parties to the action failed to demand a jury trial and, with their consent, the factual issues were tried by the court without a jury.

The trial court found from the evidence that the finance company was a holder in due course of the note; therefore, the defenses arising from the alleged breaches of contract by the contractor and payee of the note were held nonassertable against the finance company. Judgment was entered for the unpaid balance of the note and foreclosure of the mortgage was ordered. The Sullivans appeal and argue the single proposition that the finance company did not become a holder in due course at the time the note was transferred and negotiated to it by the payee. We affirm the judgment of the circuit court.

The entire case for the Sullivans may be summarized by the following quotation from the brief filed on their behalf:

> The testimony shows that the appellee [the finance company] was cognizant and knew about this contract. The appellee [the finance company] had done around $500,000 with Memory Swift Homes, Inc., over a period of a number of years beginning in 1951. The appellee also knew at the time they purchased this note and mortgage that no work had been performed on the construction of the house. The appellee [the finance company] knowing about this contract, they were put on notice that there *might be* a defense on the note because of the faulty construction of the dwelling house and is, therefore, not a holder in due course and did not take the instrument in good faith—that is the note and mortgage. [Parenthetical expressions and emphasis supplied.]

Notice, in order to prevent one from being a bona fide holder under the law merchant, or a holder in due course under the NIL or the Commercial Code, means notice at the time of the taking or at the time the instrument is negotiated, and not notice arising subsequently. The time when value is given for the instrument is decisive. The moment value is given without notice the status as a holder in due course generally is definitely and irrevocably fixed. The Commercial Code, which has been adopted in Kentucky, provides that to be effective notice to a purchaser must be received at such time and in such manner as to give a reasonable opportunity to act on it. K.R.S. §3-304(6) [in the Revision, see §3-302(f)—Eds.]. See 11 Am. Jur. 2d, Bills and Notes, §428, pp. 458, 459.

Where a close business association between the payee and one who purchases an instrument from him implies the knowledge of such facts as to show bad faith or renders himself a participant in the transaction between the payee and the maker, a finding that such purchaser is not a holder in due course has been regarded as supportable. See 44 A.L.R.2d 154. In Massey-Ferguson v. Utley, Ky., 439 S.W.2d 57 (1969), we discussed several aspects of the basic problem. Therein we expressed the thought that the policy of the

Commercial Code was to encourage the supplying of credit for the buying of goods by insulating the lender from lawsuits over the quality of the goods. The insulation provided, however, appears intended primarily for finance institutions acting independently to supply credit, rather than to protect a manufacturer who finances his own sales either in his own name or by a dominated and controlled agency.

In the case before us, there is no allegation of fraud involving the payee of the note and the finance company. There is no claim any fact existed that the finance company could have discovered at the time of the transfer of the instrument and that would have indicated any deficiency or defect. The maker of the note represented that the state of facts at that time was one of compliance by the contractor with the duties imposed by the contract. The evidence failed to demonstrate any direct connection between the contractor and the finance company except a frequent course of dealing between them. In short, the evidence failed to demonstrate any bad faith on the part of the finance company at the time of the negotiation and transfer of the note to it. All of the evidence demonstrated a complete lack of notice to the finance company that would justify a finding that it failed to acquire the status of a holder in due course.

The judgment is affirmed.

All concur.

F. The Shelter Rule

It has always been a basic rule of the common law that the unqualified transfer of a chose in action places the transferee in the transferor's shoes and gives the transferee all the rights of the transferor. This rule is codified in §3-203(b), where it is made clear that even holder in due course rights can pass to a person not otherwise entitled to them. Because the transferee of a holder in due course takes "shelter" in the status of the transferor, §3-203(b) is called the *shelter rule*. Read §3-203(b) and its Official Comments, paying particular attention to Comment 4 and the examples therein. (Similar shelter rules abound throughout the UCC: for sales of goods, see §2-403(1); for documents of title, see §7-504(a); and for investment securities, see §8-302(a).)

PROBLEM 127

Happy Jack, the used car salesman, sold Manny a lemon car for his business, taking in payment a promissory note for $2,000 made payable to the order of Happy Jack. Jack discounted the note with Alfred, a local licensed money broker, who paid him $1,700 and took the note without knowledge of the underlying transaction. Alfred's daughter Jessica had a birthday shortly thereafter, so Alfred indorsed the note in blank and gave it to her as a present. When the note matured, Manny refused to pay it to Jessica—the car had fallen apart, and he felt that he shouldn't have to pay for a pile of junk. Is Jessica a holder in due course?

PROBLEM 128

If in the above Problem Jessica had thereafter made a gift of the note to her husband, Lorenzo, would Lorenzo have holder in due course rights? Does it matter if Lorenzo, prior to the gift, knows of Manny's problems with the car? If Manny won't pay, is Alfred liable to Lorenzo? See §§3-305(a)(2) and 3-303.

PROBLEM 129

After Lorenzo (from the last Problem) acquired the note, he sold it for $1,800 to Portia, a local attorney. She had no notice of problems with the instrument. When she presented it to Manny for payment, he refused to pay and instead filed for bankruptcy. May she recover from Alfred? See §3-305(b). If she does and prevails, Alfred will reacquire the instrument. Does the shelter rule give him Portia's holder in due course rights? Does Alfred reacquire his *original* holder in due course status when he gets the instrument back? Could he sue Jessica or Lorenzo? See the following discussion.

Reacquisition of an Instrument. If Alfred is forced to pay Portia, he will get the instrument back into his possession. In such a case, §121 of the now-repealed NIL provided that on reacquisition a holder "is remitted to his former rights as regards all prior parties." See Chafee, The Reacquisition of a Negotiable Instrument by a Prior Party, 21 Colum. L. Rev. 538 (1921).[20] Thus, if Alfred used to be a holder in due course, on reacquiring the instrument he would get that status back vis-à-vis parties prior to his first holding. Although the UCC never expressly states the same rule, the idea is implicit throughout the Code, and the NIL rule is therefore still the law. As to the issue of whether Alfred can sue Jessica and Lorenzo, we will explore the liability of an indorser in the next chapter.

20. Section 3-207 discusses reacquisition, but the rules therein are not relevant to the issues raised by the preceding Problems.

Section 3-207 provides that when a previous holder reacquires the instrument, he or she has the power to strike the intervening indorsements. As one court explained:

> Intervening indorsements simply vanish from the chain of title when called by a reacquirer. That concept is the obvious product of the principle that permits the current holder of a negotiable instrument to sue its predecessor in the indorsement chain, in which event that party can in turn look to its own predecessor. If those lawsuits up the chain would ultimately lead back to the current holder, that pointless circular process is best avoided by the cancellation of the intervening indorsements and the discharge of those intermediate parties from liability.

Resolution Trust Corp. v. Juergens, 965 F.2d 149, 154 (7th Cir. 1992).

Triffin v. Somerset Valley Bank

New Jersey Superior Court, Appellate Division, 2001
343 N.J. Super. 73, 777 A.2d 993

CUFF, J.A.D.

This case concerns the enforceability of dishonored checks against the issuer of the checks under Article 3 of the Uniform Commercial Code (UCC), as implemented in New Jersey in N.J.S.A. 12A:3-101 to 3-605.

Plaintiff purchased, through assignment agreements with check cashing companies, eighteen dishonored checks, issued by defendant Hauser Contracting Company (Hauser Co.). Plaintiff then filed suit in the Special Civil Part to enforce Hauser Co.'s liability on the checks. The trial court granted plaintiff's motion for summary judgment. Hauser Co. appeals the grant of summary judgment. It also argues, for the first time, that plaintiff lacked standing to file suit against Hauser Co. We affirm.

In October 1998, Alfred M. Hauser, president of Hauser Co., was notified by Edwards Food Store in Raritan and the Somerset Valley Bank (the Bank), that several individuals were cashing what appeared to be Hauser Co. payroll checks. Mr. Hauser reviewed the checks, ascertained that the checks were counterfeits and contacted the Raritan Borough and Hillsborough Police Departments. Mr. Hauser concluded that the checks were counterfeits because none of the payees were employees of Hauser Co., and because he did not write the checks or authorize anyone to sign those checks on his behalf. At that time, Hauser Co. employed Automatic Data Processing, Inc. (ADP) to provide payroll services and a facsimile signature was utilized on all Hauser Co. payroll checks.

Mr. Hauser executed affidavits of stolen and forged checks at the Bank, stopping payment on the checks at issue. Subsequently, the Bank received more than eighty similar checks valued at $25,000 all drawn on Hauser Co.'s account.

Plaintiff is in the business of purchasing dishonored negotiable instruments. In February and March 1999, plaintiff purchased eighteen dishonored checks from four different check cashing agencies, specifying Hauser Co. as the drawer. The checks totaled $8,826.42. Pursuant to assignment agreements executed by plaintiff, each agency stated that it cashed the checks for value, in good faith, without notice of any claims or defenses to the checks, without knowledge that any of the signatures were unauthorized or forged, and with the expectation that the checks would be paid upon presentment to the bank upon which the checks were drawn. All eighteen checks bore a red and green facsimile drawer's signature stamp in the name of Alfred M. Hauser. All eighteen checks were marked by the Bank as "stolen check" and stamped with the warning, "do not present again." Each of the nine payees on the eighteen checks are named defendants in this case.

Plaintiff then filed this action against the Bank, Hauser Co., and each of the nine individual payees. Plaintiff contended that Hauser Co. was negligent in failing to safeguard both its payroll checks and its authorized drawer's facsimile stamp, and was liable for payment of the checks.

The trial court granted plaintiff's summary judgment motion, concluding that no genuine issue of fact existed as to the authenticity of the eighteen checks at issue. Judge Hoens concluded that because the check cashing companies took the checks in good faith, plaintiff was a holder in due course as assignee. Judge Hoens also found that because the checks appeared to be genuine, Hauser Co. was required, but had failed, to show that plaintiff's assignor had any notice that the checks were not validly drawn. . . .

As to the merits of the appeal, Hauser Co. argues that summary judgment was improperly granted because the court failed to properly address Hauser Co.'s defense that the checks at issue were invalid negotiable instruments and therefore erred in finding plaintiff was a holder in due course. . . .

As a threshold matter, it is evident that the eighteen checks meet the definition of a negotiable instrument. N.J.S.A. 12A:3-104. Each check is payable to a bearer for a fixed amount, on demand, and does not state any other undertaking by the person promising payment, aside from the payment of money. In addition, each check appears to have been signed by Mr. Hauser, through the use of a facsimile stamp, permitted by the UCC to take the place of a manual signature. N.J.S.A. 12A:3-401(b) provides that a "signature may be made manually or by means of a device or machine . . . with present intention to authenticate a writing." It is uncontroverted by Hauser Co. that the facsimile signature stamp on the checks is identical to Hauser Co.'s authorized stamp.

Hauser Co., however, contends that the checks are not negotiable instruments because Mr. Hauser did not sign the checks, did not authorize their signing, and its payroll service, ADP, did not produce the checks. Lack of authorization, however, is a separate issue from whether the checks are negotiable instruments. Consequently, given that the checks are negotiable instruments, the next issue is whether the checks are unenforceable by a holder in due course, because the signature on the checks was forged or unauthorized.

N.J.S.A. 12A:3-203 and N.J.S.A. 12A:3-302 discuss the rights of a holder in due course and the rights of a transferee of a holder in due course. Section 3-302 establishes that a person is a holder in due course if:

> (1) the instrument when issued or negotiated to the holder does not bear such apparent evidence of forgery or alteration or is not otherwise so irregular or incomplete as to call into question its authenticity; and
>
> (2) the holder took the instrument for value, in good faith, without notice that the instrument is overdue or has been dishonored or that there is an uncured default with respect to payment of another instrument issued as part of the same series, without notice that the instrument contains an unauthorized signature or has been altered, without notice of any claim to the instrument described in 12A:3-306, and without notice that any party has a defense or claim in recoupment described in subsection a. of 12A:3-305.

Section 3-203 deals with transfer of instruments and provides:

> a. An instrument is transferred when it is delivered by a person other than its issuer for the purpose of giving to the person receiving delivery the right to enforce the instrument.
>
> b. Transfer of an instrument, whether or not the transfer is a negotiation, vests in the transferee any right of the transferor to enforce the instrument, including any right as a holder in due course, but the transferee cannot acquire rights of a holder in due course by a transfer, directly or indirectly, from a holder in due course if the transferee engaged in fraud or illegality affecting the instrument.

The official comment to N.J.S.A. 12A:3-203 adds that in situations where a transferee does not take the instrument by indorsement (as in this case), the transferee still assumes the rights of the transferor, so long as the transferee can show that the transferor had valid rights to the instrument, and that the transferee acquired the instrument in accordance with section 3-203's requirements. Specifically, Comment 2 reads:

> Subsection (b) states that transfer vests in the transferee any right of the transferor to enforce the instrument "including any right as a holder in due course." *If the transferee is not a holder because the transferor did not indorse, the transferee is nevertheless a person entitled to enforce the instrument under Section 3-301 if the transferor was a holder at the time of transfer. Although the transferee is not a*

> *holder, under subsection (b) the transferee obtained the rights of the transferor as holder. Because the transferee's rights are derivative of the transferor's rights, those rights must be proved.* Because the transferee is not a holder, there is no presumption under Section 3-308 that the transferee, by producing the instrument, is entitled to payment. The instrument, by its terms, is not payable to the transferee and the transferee must account for possession of the unindorsed instrument by proving the transaction through which the transferee acquired it. Proof of a transfer to the transferee by a holder is proof that the transferee has acquired the rights of a holder. At that point the transferee is entitled to the presumption under Section 3-308.
>
> Under subsection (b) a holder in due course that transfers an instrument transfers those rights as a holder in due course to the purchaser. The policy is to assure the holder in due course a free market for the instrument.

[N.J.S.A. 12A:3-203, Comment 2 (emphasis added).]

The record indicates that plaintiff has complied with the requirements of both sections 3-302 and 3-203. Each of the check cashing companies from whom plaintiff purchased the dishonored checks were holders in due course. In support of his summary judgment motion, plaintiff submitted an affidavit from each company; each company swore that it cashed the checks for value, in good faith, without notice of any claims or defenses by any party, without knowledge that any of the signatures on the checks were unauthorized or fraudulent, and with the expectation that the checks would be paid upon their presentment to the bank upon which the checks were drawn. Hauser Co. does not dispute any of the facts sworn to by the check cashing companies.

The checks were then transferred to plaintiff in accordance with section 3-203, vesting plaintiff with holder in due course status. Each company swore that it assigned the checks to plaintiff in exchange for consideration received from plaintiff. Plaintiff thus acquired the check cashing companies' holder in due course status when the checks were assigned to plaintiff. See N.J.S.A. 12A:3-203, Comment 2. Moreover, pursuant to section 3-203(a)'s requirement that the transfer must have been made for the purpose of giving the transferee the right to enforce the instrument, the assignment agreements expressly provided plaintiff with that right, stating that "all payments [assignor] may receive from any of the referenced Debtors . . . shall be the exclusive property of [assignee]." Again, Hauser Co. does not dispute any facts relating to the assignment of the checks to plaintiff.

Hauser Co. contends, instead, that the checks are per se invalid because they were fraudulent and unauthorized. Presumably, this argument is predicated on section 3-302. This section states a person is not a holder in due course if the instrument bears "apparent evidence of forgery or alteration" or is otherwise "so irregular or incomplete as to call into question its authenticity." N.J.S.A. 12A:3-302(a)(1).

In order to preclude liability from a holder in due course under section 3-302, it must be apparent on the face of the instrument that it is fraudulent. The trial court specifically found that Hauser Co. had provided no such evidence, stating that Hauser Co. had failed to show that there was anything about the appearance of the checks to place the check cashing company on notice that any check was not valid. Specifically, with respect to Hauser Co.'s facsimile signature on the checks, the court stated that the signature was identical to Hauser Co.'s authorized facsimile signature. Moreover, each of the check cashing companies certified that they had no knowledge that the signatures on the checks were fraudulent or that there were any claims or defenses to enforcement of the checks. Hence, the trial court's conclusion that there was no apparent evidence of invalidity was not an abuse of discretion and was based on a reasonable reading of the record.

To be sure, section 3-308 (a) does shift the burden of establishing the validity of the signature to the plaintiff, but only if the defendant specifically denies the signature's validity in the pleadings. The section states:

> In an action with respect to an instrument, *the authenticity of, and authority to make, each signature on the instrument is admitted unless specifically denied in the pleadings.* If the validity of a signature is denied in the pleadings, the burden of establishing validity is on the person claiming validity, but the signature is presumed to be authentic and authorized unless the action is to enforce the liability of the purported signer and the signer is dead or incompetent at the time of trial of the issue of validity of the signature.

[N.J.S.A. 12A:3-308(a) (emphasis added).]

Comment 1 explains that a specific denial is required

> to give the plaintiff notice of the defendant's claim of forgery or lack of authority as to the particular signature, and to afford the plaintiff an opportunity to investigate and obtain evidence. . . . In the absence of such specific denial the signature stands admitted, and is not in issue. Nothing in this section is intended, however, to prevent amendment of the pleading in a proper case.

[N.J.S.A. 12A:3-308, Comment 1.]

Examination of the pleadings reveals that Hauser Co. did not specifically deny the factual assertions in plaintiff's complaint.

Even if Hauser Co.'s general denial was sufficient, the presumption that the signature is valid still remains, unless Hauser Co. satisfies the evidentiary requirements of N.J.S.A. 12A:3-308. Comment 1 to that section explains that even when the defendant has specifically denied the authenticity of a signature, the signature is still presumed to be authentic, absent evidence of forgery or lack of authorization. Comment 1 states:

> The burden is on the party claiming under the signature, *but the signature is presumed to be authentic and authorized* except as stated in the second sentence of subsection (a). *"Presumed" is defined in Section 1-201 and means that until some evidence is introduced which would support a finding that the signature is forged or unauthorized, the plaintiff is not required to prove that it is valid.* The presumption rests upon the fact that in ordinary experience forged or unauthorized signatures are very uncommon, and normally any evidence is within the control of, or more accessible to, the defendant. *The defendant is therefore required to make some sufficient showing of the grounds for the denial before the plaintiff is required to introduce evidence.* The defendant's evidence need not be sufficient to require a directed verdict, but it must be enough to support the denial by permitting a finding in the defendant's favor. Until introduction of such evidence the presumption requires a finding for the plaintiff.

[N.J.S.A. 12A:3-308, Comment 1 (emphasis added).]

Here, Hauser Co. has not provided any evidence of the invalidity of the signature. Hauser Co.'s reliance on conclusory statements does not constitute such a "sufficient showing." See Coupounas v. Madden, 401 Mass. 125, 514 N.E.2d 1316, 1320 (1987) (defendant disputing validity of notes "had to do more than 'call into question' the 'integrity' of the notes").

In addition, as a matter of summary judgment, Hauser Co.'s reliance on its answer, amended answer and Mr. Hauser's affidavit as material, disputed facts is inadequate. In order to defeat a motion for summary judgment, a party must show that there are genuine issues of material fact. *Brill*, supra, 142 N.J. at 540, 666 A.2d 146. "Bare conclusions in the pleadings, without factual support in tendered affidavits, will not defeat a meritorious application for summary judgment." United States Pipe and Foundry Co. v. American Arbitration Ass'n, 67 N.J. Super. 384, 399-400, 170 A.2d 505 (App. Div. 1961); see also Brae Asset Fund v. Newman, 327 N.J. Super. 129, 134, 742 A.2d 986 (App. Div. 1999). Hauser Co. provided no factual evidence tending to disprove the authenticity of the signature, relying instead on self-interested and conclusory statements. Consequently, the trial court did not err in finding that Hauser Co. had failed to provide any evidence of the invalidity of the checks.

In conclusion, we hold that Judge Hoens properly granted summary judgment. There was no issue of material fact as to: (1) the status of the checks as negotiable instruments; (2) the status of the check cashing companies as holders in due course; (3) the status of plaintiff as a holder in due course; and (4) the lack of apparent evidence on the face of the checks that they were forged, altered or otherwise irregular. Moreover, Hauser Co.'s failure to submit some factual evidence indicating that the facsimile signature was forged or otherwise unauthorized left unchallenged the UCC's rebuttable presumption that a signature on an instrument is valid. Consequently, the trial court properly held, as a matter of law, that plaintiff was a holder in due course and entitled to enforce the checks.

Affirmed.

Robert Triffin is sometimes called a professional holder in due course for acquiring dishonored checks at a discount and then enforcing them in legal actions he brings against those who should have paid them, making a profitable use of the shelter rule to assume the holder in due course status of the checks' payees. See, e.g., Triffin v. TWC Administration LLC, 2017 WL 6757231 (N.J. App. 2017).

It may seem unfair to use the shelter rule to give holder in due course status to non-purchasers and those who take with notice of defenses, but on reflection the unfairness disappears. If the rule were otherwise, the current holder would simply pass the instrument back up the chain until it reached a former holder in due course, who would then reacquire that status, sue the instrument's creator, and prevail. The shelter rule accomplishes the same result without all these maneuvers and has the further benefit of promoting commercial confidence in the soundness of the instrument once it has floated through the hands of multiple purchasers.

II. REAL AND PERSONAL DEFENSES/CLAIMS

A. Defenses Against a Holder in Due Course

Holder in due course status has as its primary attribute the ability to enforce the instrument free from the usual legal excuses that could be raised in an ordinary contracts action. The key Uniform Commercial Code section reaching this extraordinary result is §3-305, to which we now turn.

Section 3-305 is difficult to read, primarily because a number of the concepts therein are complicated to sort out. Let's take it a point at a time.

First of all, the *obligor* mentioned throughout §3-305 is the party to the instrument who is being sued by the holder of the instrument. Thus the obligor could be the drawer of a draft, the maker of a note, or someone who indorsed the instrument. In the next chapter, we shall discuss the nature of the obligations these parties incur by virtue of having signed the instrument in one of the above capacities.

A "defense," of course, is the legal excuse the obligor may have to avoid paying the obligation. Subsection (b) tells us that a holder in due course takes subject to the defenses listed in subsection (a)(1), meaning that these defenses, if true, defeat the right of the holder in due course to enforce the instrument. Defenses that are good against a holder in due course are commonly called *real defenses,* a label you might wish to write next to §3-305(a)(1). Subsection (b) tells us that a holder in due course is not subject to the defenses raised in subsection (a)(2), the so-called *personal defenses.*

Subsection (b) also states that a holder in due course holds free of "claims in recoupment" per §3-305(a)(3), but what does that mean? Recoupment is the legal ability to *subtract* from any payment due the amount the person trying to collect the debt (or that person's predecessor) happens to owe the debtor. For example, if I owe you $500 pursuant to our contract, and, as a result of your breach of that same contract, you have caused me $200 worth of damages, my claim in recoupment permits me to subtract those damages and only pay you $300. A claim in recoupment is so similar to a defense that the original version of Article 3 seemed to lump it in with the other personal defenses, but the revised version of Article 3 gives it its own special treatment (leading to awkward references throughout to a "defense or claim in recoupment"). Read Official Comment 3 to §3-305.

PROBLEM 130

Stephen Maturin bought a sailboat from Jack Aubrey, paying $500 down and signing a $1,000 promissory note for the balance due. Maturin loved everything about the boat except its color, and he promptly repainted it his favorite color, black. Prior to the sale Aubrey had told Maturin that the boat was constructed so that it wouldn't sink even in the roughest weather. This proved to be untrue when the sailboat went down in the first storm that came along, and it cost Maturin $300 to have it dredged from the bottom and restored. In the meantime, Aubrey had given the promissory note to his father as a birthday gift, and the father presented it to Maturin for payment at maturity. May Maturin assert his damages against the father's demand for payment? Same result if the boat never sank, but Aubrey's dog bit Maturin on the leg one week after the delivery of the sailboat, and Maturin incurred $100 in medical bills as a consequence? See Zener v. Velde, 135 Idaho 352, 17 P.3d 296 (Idaho App. 2000).

Federal Deposit Insurance Corp. v. Culver

United States District Court, District of Kansas, 1986
640 F. Supp. 725

O'CONNOR, J.

This matter comes before the court on defendant's motion to dismiss for lack of personal jurisdiction, on plaintiff's motion for summary judgment, and on defendant's motion for leave to file a demand for jury trial out of time. After reciting the material facts (construed most favorably to defendant), we will address these pending motions.

In 1984, defendant entered into a business arrangement with a Mr. Nasib Ed Kalliel. Kalliel was to assume control over the financial aspects of defendant's farm, while defendant was to manage the farming operation—receiving both a salary and a share of the profits. In July or August of that year, defendant informed Kalliel that he urgently needed money in order to stave off foreclosure. One week later, $30,000.00 was wire-transferred from the Rexford State Bank in Rexford, Kansas, to defendant's bank in King City, Missouri. Although defendant knew that the money had come from the Rexford State Bank, he thought that Kalliel would be responsible for its repayment.

About one week later, defendant was approached by a Mr. Jerry Gilbert, whom defendant believed was working for Kalliel. Gilbert told defendant that "Rexford State Bank wanted to know where the $30,000.00 went, . . . for their records." Gilbert presented defendant with a document and asked defendant to sign it. Apparently, Gilbert either told defendant, or at least led him to believe, that the document was merely a receipt for the $30,000.00 he had received. In any event, defendant signed the document without thereby intending to commit himself to the repayment of any money.

The document defendant signed was a preprinted promissory note form. As might be expected, the form contained a number of blanks into which the parties were expected to insert terms specific to their own transaction. At the time defendant signed the document, none of those blanks had been completed. Thus, the note contained no execution date, no maturity date, no principal amount, and no interest rate. The name of the payee, "THE REXFORD STATE BANK, Rexford, Kansas," *was* printed on the note at that time. Moreover, the note did provide that the principal and accrued interest were to be paid to the payee "at its offices."

Although defendant assumed that the figure $30,000.00 would eventually be written on the document, some unknown individual completed the note as follows:

(1) The principal amount was shown as $50,000.00;
(2) the execution date was shown as August 2, 1984;
(3) the maturity date was shown as February 2, 1985; and
(4) the interest rate was shown as 14 percent per annum until maturity, and 18½ percent per annum thereafter.

Although defendant received only $30,000.00, the Rexford State Bank did deposit the full $50,000.00 in an account controlled by Kalliel. The $30,000.00 apparently came from that account.

Eventually, the note was returned to the Rexford State Bank. When that bank became insolvent, the Federal Deposit Insurance Corporation ["FDIC"] was appointed as its receiver. In its *corporate* capacity, the FDIC then purchased a number of the bank's assets from the receiver—including the note at issue here. At that time, the FDIC had no actual knowledge of the events that had transpired prior to its purchase of the note. As of yet, defendant has made no payment of either principal or interest.

Other than receiving the $30,000.00 wire-transfer from the Rexford State Bank, and then signing the note naming the bank as payee, defendant has had no other relevant contact with the state of Kansas. . . .

II. Plaintiff's Motion for Summary Judgment

. . . Recognizing that "[t]here is no doubt that state and federal law provide the Federal Deposit Insurance Corporation with holder in due course status in the instant litigation" (Defendant's Brief of May 2, 1986, at 11), defendant concedes that the "personal" defenses of fraud in the inducement, estoppel, and failure of consideration would be ineffective against plaintiff's claim. See F.D.I.C. v. Vestering, 620 F. Supp. 1271 (D. Kan. 1985). Accordingly, defendant seeks to assert the "real" defense of fraud in the factum. See K.S.A. 84-3-305(2)(c) [in the Revision, see §3-305(a)(l)(iii)—Eds.]. Plaintiff denies that the facts as alleged by defendant constitute fraud in the factum. Alternatively, even assuming that defendant can establish the elements of fraud in the factum, plaintiff contends that such a defense is ineffective against the FDIC because of the doctrine enunciated in D'Oench, Duhme & Co. v. F.D.I.C., 315 U.S. 447 (1942), and codified at 12 U.S.C. §1823(e). Because we conclude that defendant cannot demonstrate fraud in the factum, we do not reach plaintiff's arguments regarding *D'Oench, Duhme* and section 1823(e).

The "fraud in the factum" defense is codified at K.S.A. 84-3-305(2)(c) [in the Revision, see 3-305(a)(1)(iii)—Eds.], which provides as follows:

> Rights of a holder in due course. To the extent that a holder is a holder in due course he takes the instrument free from . . .
>
> (2) all defenses of any party to the instrument with whom the holder has not dealt *except* . . .
>
> (c) such misrepresentation as has induced the party to sign the instrument with neither knowledge nor reasonable opportunity to obtain knowledge of its *character* or its *essential terms.*

(Emphasis added.) As suggested by our factual summary, defendant contends that he signed the note under the misapprehension that it was merely a receipt. He thus denies having knowledge of the document's "character" at the time he signed it. Moreover, because the note's execution date, maturity date, principal amount and interest rate were all blank at the time he signed it, defendant contends that he had neither knowledge nor reasonable opportunity to obtain knowledge as to the note's "essential terms."

To determine whether these facts fit the definition of fraud in the factum, we look elsewhere in the Kansas Uniform Commercial Code. For instance, Official UCC Comment 7 to §3-305 provides this advice:

> Paragraph (c) of subsection (2) is new. It follows the great majority of the decisions under the original Act in recognizing the defense of "real" or "essential" fraud, sometimes called fraud in the essence or fraud in the factum, as effective against a holder in due course. The common illustration is that of the maker who is tricked into signing a note in the belief that it is merely a receipt or some other document. The theory of the defense is that his signature on the instrument is ineffective because he did not intend to sign such an instrument at all. Under this provision the defense extends to an instrument signed with knowledge that it is a negotiable instrument, but without knowledge of its essential terms.
>
> *The test of the defense here stated is that of excusable ignorance of the contents of the writing signed.* The party must not only have been in ignorance, but must also have had no reasonable opportunity to obtain knowledge.

(Emphasis added.) A portion of the 1983 Kansas Comment to this same section offers guidance as to the proper construction of the term "excusable ignorance." The Comment provides as follows:

> Kansas decisional law would seem to be in accord on the possibility of fraud in the factum as a real defense, the decision in Ort v. Fowler, 31 Kan. 478, 2 P. 580 (1884), being a good example of facts not satisfying the defense because of the failure of the maker to satisfy a standard of conduct comparable to that required by this subsection.

Given this Kansas Comment's reference to *Ort*, an examination of the facts and the holding in that case should be useful in determining whether defendant showed "excusable ignorance" in mistaking the note at issue here for a receipt.

In *Ort*, a farmer was working alone in his field. A stranger came up to him and represented himself to be the state agent for a manufacturer of iron posts and wire fence. After some conversation, the stranger persuaded the farmer to accept a township-wide agency for the same manufacturer. The stranger then completed two documents which he represented to be identical versions of an agency contract. Because the farmer did not have his glasses with him and, in any event, "could not read without spelling out every word," 31 Kan. at 480, the stranger purported to read the document to the farmer. No mention was made of any note. Both men signed each document, with the farmer not intending to sign anything but a contract of agency. Ultimately, it was established that at least one of those documents was a promissory note. A bona fide purchaser of that note brought suit against the farmer, and the farmer attempted to defend the action on the basis of fraud in the factum. After the trial court rejected that defense, the farmer appealed.

The Kansas Supreme Court, in an opinion by Justice David Brewer (later a United States Supreme Court Associate Justice), phrased the issue on appeal as follows: "A party is betrayed into signing a bill or note by the assurance that it is an instrument of a different kind. Under what circumstances ought he to be liable thereon?" 31 Kan. at 482. Three alternative answers were then suggested:

> One view entertained is, that as he never intended to execute a bill or note, it cannot be considered his act, and he should not be held liable thereon any more than if his name had been forged to such an instrument. A second view is, that it is always a question of fact for the jury whether under the circumstances the party was guilty of negligence. A third is the view adopted by the trial court, that as [a] matter of law, one must be adjudged guilty of such negligence as to render him liable who, possessed of all his faculties and able to read, signs a bill or note, relying upon the assurance or the reading of a stranger that it is a different instrument.

Id. Defendant herein would obviously prefer either the first or second alternative. The court, however, made its preference clear:

> *We approve of the latter doctrine.* It presents a case, of course, of which one of two innocent parties must suffer; but the bona fide holder is not only innocent, but free from all negligence. He has done only that which a prudent, careful man might properly do, while on the other hand the maker of the note has omitted ordinary care and prudence. A party cannot guard against forgery; but if in possession of his faculties and able to read, he can know the character of every instrument to which he puts his signature; and it is a duty which he owes to any party who may be subsequently affected by his act, to know what it is which he signs. By his signature he invites the credence of the world to every statement and promise which is in the instrument he has subscribed; and he is guilty of negligence if he omits to use the ordinary means of ascertaining what those provisions and statements are. If he has eyes and can see, he ought to examine; if he can read, he ought to read; and he has no right to send his signature out into the world affixed to an instrument of whose contents he is ignorant. If he relies upon the word of a stranger, he makes that stranger his agent. He adopts his reading as his own knowledge. What his agent knows, he knows; and he cannot disaffirm the acts of that agent done within the scope of the authority he has intrusted to him.

Id., 31 Kan. at 482-483 (emphasis added). Although *Ort is* of rather ancient vintage, this aspect of the decision has been cited with approval as recently as 1966. See Mid Kansas Federal Savings & Loan Assn. v. Binter, 197 Kan. 106, 110, 415 P.2d 278, 282 (1966).

It is obvious from reading defendant's deposition that he is able to read and understand the English language. Thus, under the rule announced in *Ort,* defendant was negligent in relying on Gilbert's assurance that the note was only a receipt. Given the 1983 Kansas Comment referring to the *Ort* absence-of-negligence standard as "comparable to that required by [K.S.A. 84-3-305(2)(c)]," we must also conclude that defendant has failed to show the "excusable ignorance" necessary to establish fraud in the factum. In the words of the statute, we conclude as a matter of law that defendant had a "reasonable opportunity to obtain knowledge of [the document's] character" before he signed it.

Defendant's second argument, assuming that we reject his contention that he neither knew nor had reasonable opportunity to know the "character" of the document he signed, is that he had no such opportunity to learn of the note's "essential terms." Because the note's execution date, maturity date, principal amount and interest rate were all blank when defendant signed the note, he asserts that he had no (let alone a reasonable) opportunity to learn of those terms. On its face, this argument has great appeal; but defendant's reliance thereon is foreclosed by other Code provisions.

Questions arising from incomplete instruments and material alterations are governed by K.S.A. 84-3-115 and -407, respectively. The former provides as follows:

> (1) When a paper whose contents at the time of signing show that it is intended to become an instrument is signed while still incomplete in any necessary respect it cannot be enforced until completed, but when it is completed in accordance with authority given it is effective as completed.
>
> (2) *If the completion is unauthorized the rules as to material alteration apply (section 84-3-407).*

K.S.A. 84-3-115 (emphasis added). Because defendant claims not to have authorized anyone to complete the note as it now reads, we are referred by part (2) of this section to K.S.A. 84-3-407. The latter statute provides, in part, as follows:

> (3) A subsequent holder in due course may in all cases enforce the instrument according to its original tenor, *and when an incomplete instrument has been completed, he may enforce it as completed.*

K.S.A. 84-3-407(3) (emphasis added). As a holder in due course, plaintiff is thus entitled to enforce this note as it was eventually completed—and not merely as defendant would have authorized it to be completed.

The fraud allegedly committed by Gilbert does not affect this conclusion. We learn from Official UCC Comment 4 to K.S.A. 84-3-407 that "this result is intended even though the instrument was stolen from the maker or drawer and completed after the theft." In other words, one who signs an instrument before all essential terms have been completed creates a "blank Check" that may be enforced by a subsequent holder in due course according to any terms that are completed by an intervening holder. See K.S.A. 84-3-305, Kansas Comment 1983. That was precisely what happened here. Defendant executed the note in blank; an intervening holder completed the note as it reads today; and plaintiff, as a holder in due course, is entitled to enforce the note according to its present terms. Defendant's only legal recourse is against the intervening holder who actually completed the note without defendant's authorization. As between the parties now before the court, we must grant plaintiff's motion for summary judgment. . . .

PROBLEM 131

(a) When Ronald Rube, newly rich, moved to New York City, he was impressed by the Brooklyn Bridge when first he saw it. Simon Mustache, a con man, told Rube that he was the owner of the bridge (a lie, of course), and offered to sell it to Rube for $2,000,000 (described as "a bargain"). Rube paid $20,000 cash as a down-payment and signed a promissory note, payable to the order of Mustache, for the rest. Mustache negotiated the note to a finance company, which claimed to be a holder in due course. When Rube discovered that Mustache lacked title to the bridge, he refused to pay the note. Does he have a real defense of fraud here? See Brown v. Carlson, 26 Mass. L. Rptr. 61, 2009 WL 2914191 (Mass. Super. 2009).

(b) William asked his wife Anne to sign a document that he described as some paperwork necessary to keep their mortgage up to date. In reality, it was a negotiable promissory note for a new loan William was taking out for his struggling theater company. Anne, trusting her spouse, signed the document without reading it. If the note winds up in the hands of a holder in due course, can Anne raise fraud as a defense? See Deutsche Bank National Trust Company v. Johnson, 2017 WL 1210144 (Minn. App. 2017).

PROBLEM 132

A child prodigy, Thomas Minor, had been playing the piano since he was three and making professional tours of the world since he was 12. He looked much older than his 17 years. He signed a promissory note for $800 payable to the order of Merry Music Company as payment for a piano, planning to tour with it. The company was unaware of Minor's age. The payee indorsed the note over to the Big National Bank for $725. When the first payment came due, Minor refused to pay. He told the bank to come pick up the piano—he was disaffirming the sale. Who wins?

PROBLEM 133

Childe Harold, also age 17, received a check for $1,000 from his employer and decided to use it to buy a car from Byron Auto Sales, a used car dealership. He picked out the car he wanted, indorsed the check in blank, and handed it over to the salesman. Byron Auto Sales indorsed the check on the back and cashed it at its own bank, the Crusaders National Bank. Before this bank could present the check to the drawee bank, Childe Harold decided to buy a horse instead of an automobile, so he returned the car to the dealer and asked for the check back. Informed that the bank had it, Childe Harold called up the bank and informed it of his rescission of the contract. When the bank refused to return the check to Childe Harold, he filed suit, asking the court to restrain the bank from presenting the check to the drawee and to order replevin of the check. How should the court rule? It is clear that a holder in due course takes subject to the defense of infancy, but does he take subject to a claim to the instrument based on infancy? See §§3-202, 3-305(a) and (b), and 3-306.

Mental Incapacity. Notes signed by those who are mentally incompetent are *void* or *voidable* depending on the equities of the situation (i.e., the knowledge of the person dealing with the incompetent, the benefit received by the incompetent, the degree of incompetency, etc.). If someone has been judicially declared incompetent, his or her instruments are more likely to be declared void (hence a nullity) than if no adjudication has taken place. See Annot., Insanity as Defense Against Holder in Due Course, 24 A.L.R.2d 1380.

Sea Air Support, Inc. v. Herrmann

Nevada Supreme Court, 1980
613 P.2d 413

PER CURIAM.

Ralph Herrmann wrote a check for $10,000 payable to the Ormsby House, a hotel-casino located in Carson City, Nevada, and exchanged it for three counter checks he had written earlier that evening to acquire gaming chips. The Ormsby House was unable to collect the proceeds from the check because Herrmann had insufficient funds in his account. The debt evidenced by the check was assigned to Sea Air Support, Inc., dba Automated Accounts Associates, for collection. Sea Air also was unsuccessful in its attempts to collect and, therefore, filed this action against Herrmann to recover $10,567.

The district judge dismissed the action on the ground that Sea Air's claim is barred by the Statute of Anne. Sea Air appeals the dismissal. We are asked to reconsider the long line of Nevada cases refusing to enforce gambling debts. We refuse to do so, and affirm the dismissal.

Nevada law incorporates the common law of gambling as altered by the Statute of 9 Anne, c.14, 1, absent conflicting statutory or constitutional provisions. N.R.S. 1.030; West Indies v. First National Bank, 67 Nev. 13, 214 P.2d 144 (1950); Burke v. Buck, 31 Nev. 74, 99 P. 1078 (1909). The Statute provides that all notes drawn for the purpose of reimbursing or repaying any money knowingly lent or advanced for gaming are "utterly void, frustrate, and of none effect." Despite the fact that gambling, where licensed, is legal in Nevada, this court has long held that debts incurred, and checks drawn, for gambling purposes are void and unenforceable. Corbin v. O'Keefe, 87 Nev. 189, 484 P.2d 565 (1971); Wolpert v. Knight, 74 Nev. 322, 330 P.2d 1023 (1958); Weisbrod v. Fremont Hotel, 74 Nev. 227, 326 P.2d 1104 (1958); *West Indies*, 67 Nev. at 31; *Burke*, 31 Nev. at 80; Evans v. Cooke, 11 Nev. 69 (1876); Scott v. Courtney, 7 Nev. 419 (1872).

In this case, Herrmann's $10,000 check clearly was drawn for the purpose of repaying money knowingly advanced for gaming. See Craig v. Harrah, 66 Nev. 1, 201 P.2d 1081 (1949). The check is void and unenforceable in this state. If the law is to change, it must be done by legislative action.

Sea Air seeks to avoid the defense that the check is void and unenforceable because of gaming purpose by claiming to be a holder in due course, immune to most defenses. N.R.S. 3-305. "A holder in due course is a holder who takes the [negotiable] instrument (a) For value; and (b) In good faith; and (c) Without notice that it is overdue or has been dishonored or of any defense against or claim to it on the part of any person." N.R.S. 3-302(1). Sea Air promised to take "such legal action as may be necessary to enforce collection" of the $10,000. The promise to perform services in the future does not constitute taking for value under N.R.S. 3-303. Anderson, 2 Uniform Commercial Code (2d ed.) §3303:3. In addition, Sea Air had at least constructive notice of a defense against collection because the check was payable to a casino, and Sea Air knew the check had been dishonored. Consequently, Sea Air is not a holder in due course. The action was properly dismissed.

Affirmed.

QUESTION

If Sea Air had been a holder in due course, would it have been able to enforce the check? See §3-305(a); Casanova Club v. Bisharat, 189 Conn. 591, 458 A.2d 1 (1983). It should be noted that following the decision in *Sea Air Support,* the Nevada legislature amended its gaming laws to permit casinos to sue on credit instruments received in payment of gambling debts. Nev. Rev. Stat. §463.368. Many states have now permitted casinos to flourish within their borders and enacted similar special statutes to avoid the common law rule that all gambling debts are legally unenforceable even against a holder in due course.

Kedzie & 103rd Currency Exchange, Inc. v. Hodge

Illinois Supreme Court, 1993
156 Ill. 2d 112, 619 N.E.2d 732

FREEMAN, J.

We consider here whether a holder in due course of a check is precluded from payment as against the drawer where the check was given in exchange for contract services for which the provider was required to be, but was not, a licensed plumber. We conclude such a claim is not precluded.

BACKGROUND

Pursuant to a written "work order," Fred Fentress agreed to install a "flood control system" at the home of Eric and Beulah Hodge of Chicago for $900. In partial payment for the work, Beulah Hodge drafted a personal check payable to "Fred Fentress—A-OK Plumbing" for $500 from the Hodges' joint account at Citicorp Savings.

The system's components were not delivered to the Hodges' home as scheduled. And, when Fentress failed to appear on the date set for installation, Eric Hodge telephoned him to announce the contract "cancelled." Hodge also told Fentress that he would order Citicorp Savings not to pay the check Fentress had been given.

Records of Citicorp Savings confirm acknowledgment of a stop-payment order entered the same day.

Nevertheless, Fentress presented the check at the Kedzie & 103rd Street Currency Exchange (Currency Exchange), endorsing it as "sole owner" of A-OK Plumbing, and obtained payment. However, when the Currency Exchange later presented the check for payment at Citicorp Savings, payment was refused in accordance with the stop-payment order.

The Currency Exchange, alleging it was a holder in due course (see Ill. Rev. Stat. 1989, ch. 26, par. 3-302), then sued Beulah Hodge, as drawer of the check, and Fentress for the amount stated. Hodge, in turn, filed a counterclaim against Fentress. Hodge also moved to dismiss the Currency Exchange's action against her (see Ill. Rev. Stat. 1989, ch. 110, par. 2-619). The disposition of Hodge's motion gives rise to this appeal.

Hodge asserted a defense provided by 3-305 of the Uniform Commercial Code (UCC) (Ill. Rev. Stat. 1989, ch. 26, par. 3-305). Under that section, the claim of a holder in due course of a negotiable instrument may be barred based on "illegality of the transaction." (Ill. Rev. Stat. 1989, ch. 26, par. 3-305(2)(b).)[21] Hodge contended Fentress was not a licensed plumber as was required under the Illinois Plumbing License Law (see Ill. Rev. Stat. 1989, ch. 111, pars. 1101 through 1140). The director of licensing and registration of the Chicago department of buildings and the keeper of plumbing licensing records of the Illinois Department of Public Health provided affidavits supporting that contention. Hodge asserted that, because Fentress was in violation of the Illinois Plumbing License Law, his promised performance under the contract gave rise to the requisite "illegality" to bar the Currency Exchange's claim for payment.

The circuit court granted the motion and dismissed the Currency Exchange's action against Hodge. The appellate court, with one justice dissenting, affirmed. (234 Ill. App. 3d 1017.) Pursuant to Supreme Court Rule 315(a) (134 Ill. 2d R. 315(a)), we allowed the Currency Exchange's petition for leave to appeal.

DISCUSSION

. . . The Illinois Plumbing License Law requires that all plumbing, including "installation. . . or extension" of "drains," be performed by plumbers licensed under the Act. (Ill. Rev. Stat. 1989, ch. 111, pars. 1102(5), (8), 1103.) The affidavits establish that Fentress was not licensed either by the City of Chicago or the State of Illinois. That failure is a violation of the Illinois Plumbing License Law and is punishable as a misdemeanor. Ill. Rev. Stat. 1989, ch. 111, pars. 1103, 1128. . . .

. . . The concern is whether noncompliance by Fentress with the Illinois Plumbing License Law gives rise to "illegality of the transaction" with respect to the contract for plumbing services so as to bar the claim of the Currency Exchange, a holder in due course of the check initially given Fentress.

The issue of "illegality" arises "under a variety of statutes." (Ill. Ann. Stat., ch. 26, par. 3-305, Uniform Commercial Code Comment, at 66 (Smith-Hurd Supp. 1992).) In view of the diverse constructions to which statutory enactments are given, "illegality" is, accordingly, a matter "left to the local law." (Ill. Ann. Stat., ch. 26, par. 3-305, Uniform Commercial Code Comment, at

21. [Now §3-305(a)(1)(ii)—EDS.]

66 (Smith-Hurd Supp. 1992).) Even so, it is only when an obligation is made "entirely null and void" under "local law" that "illegality" exists as one of the "real defenses" under 3-305 to defeat a claim of a holder in due course. (Ill. Ann. Stat., ch. 26, par. 3-305, Uniform Commercial Code Comment, at 66 (Smith-Hurd Supp. 1992).) In effect, the obligation must be no obligation at all. If it is "merely voidable" at the election of the obligor, the defense is unavailable. Ill. Ann. Stat., ch. 26, par. 3-305, Uniform Commercial Code Comment, at 66 (Smith-Hurd Supp. 1992).

Historically, this court has recognized "illegality" to arise only in view of legislative declaration affecting both the underlying contract or transaction and the instrument exchanged upon it. (Pope v. Hanke (1894), 155 Ill. 617, 628-630; Town of Eagle v. Kohn (1876), 84 Ill. 292, 295-296.) A contract or transaction which is void must certainly negate the obligation to pay arising from it as between the contracting parties. (*Pope*, 155 Ill. at 626; *Kohn*, 84 Ill. at 296.) But, unless an instrument memorializing the obligation is also made void, an innocent third party who has no knowledge of the circumstances of the initial contract or transaction may yet claim payment of it against the drawer or maker. *Pope*, 155 Ill. at 626; *Kohn*, 84 Ill. at 296.

Thus, "illegality" has been held to defeat the claims of holders in due course in cases involving contracts of a gaming nature or for retirement of gambling debts. [Citations omitted.] Owing to a deep-seated hostility toward nongovernmental-sanctioned gambling, our legislature has declared that any instrument associated with such activity is void, independent of the status of who may possess it. [Citations omitted.] The absence of similar legislative declaration as for an instrument given upon a usurious contract must account, in part, for the conclusion that usury has not been held to give rise to "illegality" as a defense against a holder in due course. [Citations omitted.]

That the existence or absence of legislative declaration controls the issue was recognized by our appellate court in McGregor v. Lamont (1922), 225 Ill. App. 451, a case involving circumstances similar to those here. John T. Lamont was the maker of a note used to pay for shares of stock issued by the Corn Belt Farmers' Cooperative Association (Association). Lamont's note subsequently came into the possession of Robert Roy McGregor, a holder in due course. When Lamont failed to pay on the note, McGregor filed suit and obtained a judgment against him.

Lamont moved to vacate the judgment. Lamont asserted that the purchase of the shares of stock was void under the Illinois Securities Law because the Association had not complied with its requirements. Because the transaction was void, Lamont concluded, the note given in payment must also be void despite McGregor's status as a holder in due course.

The appellate court noted that the Illinois Securities Law did, indeed, make transactions for the sale of shares of stock void based on noncompliance with the Law's requirements. (*McGregor*, 225 Ill. App. at 453-454, 455.) But the court noted that only the "sale and contract of sale" of shares of stock were expressly made void, not instruments exchanged upon such contracts. (*McGregor*, 225 Ill. App. at 455.) Absent legislative declaration making such instruments void, the court declined to recognize a defense to McGregor's action for payment on the note. *McGregor*, 225 Ill. App. at 455.

The same rule obtains in New Jersey. In New Jersey Mortgage & Investment Corp. v. Berenyi (App. Div. 1976), 140 N.J. Super. 406, 356 A.2d 421, a holder in due course of a note was permitted to maintain a claim for its payment even though the note had been initially obtained by a corporation in a transaction which violated an injunctive order. No statute rendered the note void, and the holder in due course had no knowledge or notice of the injunction. (*Berenyi*, 140 N.J. Super. at 408, 356 A.2d at 423.) But in Westervelt v. Gateway Financial Service (Ch. Div. 1983), 190 N.J. Super. 615, 464 A.2d 1203, the "illegality" defense was held to bar the claim of a holder in due course of a secondary mortgage and note because New Jersey's Secondary Mortgage and Loan Act specifically made void "[a]ny obligation on the part of the borrower arising out of a secondary mortgage loan." (*Westervelt*, 190 N.J. Super. at 620, 464 A.2d at 1205.) *Westervelt* involved what *Berenyi* did not: applicability of a direct statutory expression that an instrument, itself, arising from a particular contract or transaction was void. *Westervelt*, 190 N.J. Super. at 623, 464 A.2d at 1207.

Several other jurisdictions also find reason to draw a distinction between the voidness of a negotiable instrument and the underlying contract or transaction upon which it is exchanged. (See Annot., 80 A.L.R.2d 465, 472-476 (1961) (summarizing several state decisions in which holders in due course were permitted to claim payment of instruments executed in favor of foreign corporations doing business in states without complying with local licensing requirements).) Although recognition of that distinction is not universal (see Columbus Checkcashiers v. Stiles (1990), 56 Ohio App. 3d 159, 565 N.E.2d 883; Wilson v. Steele (1989), 211 Cal. App. 3d 1053, 259 Cal. Rptr. 851 (holding that "illegality" need only be present in the underlying contract between an unlicensed contractor and the drafter of a negotiable instrument to bar the claim of a holder in due course)), we are convinced it remains the better rule.

A plaintiff is precluded from recovering on a suit involving an illegal contract because the plaintiff is a wrongdoer. (See Bankers Trust Co. v. Litton Systems, Inc. (2d Cir. 1979), 599 F.2d 488, 492 (citing the Restatement of Contracts and Restatement (Second) of Contracts).) Enforcement of the illegal contract makes the court an indirect participant in the wrongful conduct. See *Litton*, 599 F.2d at 493.

But a holder in due course is an innocent third party. (*Litton*, 599 F.2d at 492-493.) Such a holder is without knowledge of the circumstances of the contract upon which the instrument was initially exchanged. (Ill. Rev. Stat.

1989, ch. 26, par. 3-302(1)(c) (defining a holder in due course, in part, as a holder who is "without notice. . . of any defense against or claim to [the instrument] on the part of any person").) The same rationale that precludes recovery by a wrongdoing plaintiff is inapplicable in determining such a holder's right to claim payment. (*Litton*, 599 F.2d at 492-493.) Enforcement of that claim does not sully the court. *Litton*, 599 F.2d at 492-493.

The holder in due course concept is intended to facilitate commercial transactions by eliminating the need for "elaborate investigation" of the nature of the circumstances for which an instrument is initially exchanged or of its drafting. (*Litton*, 599 F.2d at 494.) If "illegality" means simply negation of the initial obligation to pay, a holder in due course enjoys no more protection than a party to the original contract or transaction. The "real" defense of "illegality" is reduced to a "personal" one. See Vedder v. Spellman (1971), 78 Wash. 2d 834, 839-840, 480 P.2d 207, 210 (Neill, J., concurring).

It is, therefore, not enough simply to conclude that the initial obligation to pay arising from a void contract or transaction is void. Negation of that obligation as between the contracting parties has little bearing on whether a holder in due course of an instrument arising from the contract or transaction should nevertheless be permitted to make a claim for payment.

The "local law" (Ill. Ann. Stat., ch. 26, par. 3-305, Uniform Commercial Code Comment, at 66 (Smith-Hurd Supp. 1992)) of this state has been formulated upon this court's recognition, in cases predating the UCC, of legislative prerogative regarding negotiable instruments. In adopting the UCC and, in particular, 3-305, our legislature chose to confer upon a holder in due course of a negotiable instrument considerable protection against claims by persons to it. Our legislature also continues to declare certain obligations void because of the circumstances of the agreements from which they arise and without regard to the status of who may claim ownership. (Ill. Rev. Stat. 1989, ch. 38, par. 28-7(b) (subjecting "[a]ny obligation" made void by reason of gambling to be "set aside and vacated" by any court).) The selective negation of obligations reflects a legislative aim to declare what will and will not give rise to "illegality" in cases now governed by the UCC. As legislative direction indicates which obligations are always void, legislative silence indicates when the protection afforded a holder in due course must be honored.

We therefore reaffirm, today, the view this court has consistently recognized in cases predating the UCC. Unless the instrument arising from a contract or transaction is, itself, made void by statute, the "illegality" defense under §3-305 is not available to bar the claim of a holder in due course.

CONCLUSION

To determine whether Hodge is entitled to a judgment of dismissal, we need not engage in an analysis aimed at characterizing the contract between Fentress and the Hodges. Whether the underlying contract should be considered void because Fentress was not licensed as required by the Illinois Plumbing License Law is not dispositive of the Currency Exchange's right, as a holder in due course, to claim payment of the check. It is relevant only to determine whether the Illinois Plumbing License Law provides that any obligation arising from a contract for plumbing services made in violation of its requirements is void. It does not.

For the reasons stated, the judgments of the appellate and circuit courts are reversed, and the cause is remanded to the circuit court for further proceeding. Judgments reversed; cause remanded.

BILANDIC, J., dissenting. . . .

The plain language of §3-305 and the comments to §3-305 make it clear that where the illegality of a transaction renders the obligation of the maker of an instrument a nullity, the illegality of the transaction can be raised as a defense by the maker of the instrument, even against a holder in due course. Section 3-305 does not state that illegality is a defense only where the instrument arising from a contract or transaction has been expressly declared void by the legislature due to the illegality of the transaction. Had the legislature intended for illegality to be a defense only where it had expressly declared an instrument void due to the illegality of the underlying transaction, it could easily have said so in §3-305. It did not say so, however.

The only inquiry necessary to resolve the issue presented in this case, then, is whether the contract between Hodge and Fentress is void on the grounds of illegality. The comments to the UCC instruct that one must look to Illinois statutory and case law to determine whether the underlying contract was illegal and, as a result of that illegality, void. (Ill. Ann. Stat., ch. 26, par. 3-305. Uniform Commercial Code Comment, at 66 (Smith-Hurd Supp. 1992).) An examination of the statute providing for the licensing of plumbers, the public policy behind that statute, and Illinois case law concerning the illegality of contracts made in contravention of professional licensing laws establishes that the contract between Hodge and Fentress is illegal and void.

The Illinois Plumbing License Law (Ill. Rev. Stat. 1989, ch. 111, par. 1101 et seq.) specifically prohibits the performance of plumbing work by nonlicensed plumbers. Pursuant to the Act, "all plumbing shall be performed only by plumbers licensed under the provisions of this Act." (Ill. Rev. Stat. 1989, ch. 111, par. 1103(1).) The Act imposes criminal penalties on anyone performing plumbing services without a license. (Ill. Rev. Stat. 1989, ch. 111, par. 1128.) The rationale behind the prohibition of plumbing work by nonlicensed plumbers is set forth in the Plumbing License Law. The portion of the Law setting forth its purpose and underlying policy states:

> It has been established by scientific evidence that improper plumbing can adversely affect the health of the public. . . . Faulty plumbing is

> potentially lethal and can cause widespread disease and an epidemic of disastrous consequences.
>
> To protect the health of the public it is essential that plumbing be installed by persons who have proven their knowledge of the sciences of pneumatics and hydraulics and their skill in installing plumbing.
>
> Consistent with its duty to safeguard the health of the people of this State, the General Assembly therefore declares that individuals who plan, inspect, install, alter, extend, repair and maintain plumbing systems shall be individuals of proven skill. . . . [T]his Act is therefore declared to be essential to the public interest. (Ill. Rev. Stat. 1989, ch. 111, par. 1101.)

Here, the contract between Hodge and Fentress presents the kinds of dangers the Illinois Plumbing License Law was intended to guard against. Affidavits attached to Hodge's 2-619 motion to dismiss, which were not contradicted by the plaintiff, establish that Fentress was not a licensed plumber. The affidavits also establish that Hodge and her husband, Eric, believed that Fentress was a licensed plumber at the time they contracted with him for plumbing services. Had Fentress performed the work required of him pursuant to the contract with Hodge, it is likely that his work would not have conformed to acceptable plumbing standards and would have posed the kinds of dangers which the Plumbing License Law was intended to prevent. . . .

The majority asserts that to bar recovery by the Currency Exchange in this case would be unfair because the Currency Exchange is an innocent third party which had no knowledge of the circumstances of the contract between Hodge and Fentress. However, section 3-305 clearly provides that the general policy favoring free negotiability is not absolute. There is a competing policy disfavoring certain transactions, such as those involving infancy, duress, illegality or misrepresentation as to the true nature of an instrument (i.e., fraud in the factum). (Ill. Rev. Stat. 1989, ch. 26, par. 3-305.) Pursuant to §3-305, the Currency Exchange takes a check subject to these and certain other real defenses. The Illinois legislature has provided that, by definition, a holder in due course is one who does not have notice of any of the real defenses listed in §3-305. (See Ill. Rev. Stat. 1989, ch. 26, par. 3-302(1)(c).) By statute, the innocence of the holder in due course cannot defeat *any* of the real defenses listed in §3-305, including illegality. Accordingly, the argument that the Currency Exchange could not have known that the underlying transaction was illegal is simply misplaced. Such reasoning would lead to the conclusion that all of the defenses listed in §3-305 should be unavailable to defeat the claim of a holder in due course, a conclusion obviously contrary to the provisions of §3-305.

For the above reasons, I dissent. I would affirm the judgment of the appellate court which affirmed the circuit court's dismissal of the Currency Exchange's action against Hodge.

PROBLEM 134

When she heard her creditors fighting over priorities on her doorstep, Elsie Maynard knew that she had no choice but bankruptcy. Among the debts that she reported to the bankruptcy court was the loan she had taken from Point National Bank, which was evidenced by a promissory note she had signed. In due course the bankruptcy proceeding culminated in the judge's ordering that Elsie be discharged from all her scheduled debts. Two years later, the promissory note surfaced in the possession of Shadbolt State Bank, which claimed quite convincingly to be a holder in due course. Must Elsie pay? See §3-305(a)(1) and (b).

A Little Lecture on Discharge as a Real Defense

Subsection (b) to §3-302 tells us that:

> Notice of discharge of a party, other than discharge in an insolvency proceeding, is not notice of a defense under subsection (a), but discharge is effective against a person who becomes a holder in due course with notice of the discharge. . . .

What does this mean? Well, first of all, as the above Problem illustrates, discharge in bankruptcy *is always a real defense,* regardless of what the subsequent holder knows or doesn't know at the time of acquisition of the instrument. Any other discharge that the Code or common law creates is not effective against a holder in due course *unless* that holder, at the time of acquisition, knew of the discharge, in which case the discharge is, in effect, a real defense and assertable against the holder in due course. For example, suppose that there are four sureties who have signed their names as indorsers on a promissory note. The current holder of the note decides to excuse one of them from future liability, and so draws a line through that surety's name, thus discharging that person from all liability (see §3-601 and its Official Comment). Even a later holder in due course of the note, seeing the line drawn through the former surety's name, would know that that surety is no longer liable on the note, and therefore could only enforce it against the other obligors.

PROBLEM 135

Malvolio, a traveling salesman, bought a new car from Valentine Auto Sales, signing a note for $25,000. The payee discounted the note for $16,800 to the Orsino Finance Company, which notified Malvolio that he should make all future payments to them. Malvolio immediately sent them a check for the outstanding balance (he had come into some money when his aunt died). He asked for the note back, but Orsino was evasive. A week later Malvolio received a note from the Olivia Finance Company saying that his note had been assigned to them and that he should direct his payments to their office. When Malvolio protested, they made holder in due course noises and became quite nasty. Malvolio, worried, comes to you for advice. What should he do? See §3-501(b)(2); read §§3-601 and 3-602. For the result in the 2002 version of Article 3, see §3-602(b). Does Malvolio have remedies outside the Code? Think back to your course in Contracts.

B. A Special Note on Forgery

Forgery creates very complicated problems under the Code, and these will be dealt with later. The important issue for now is whether forgery is a real defense under the Code, so that it can be raised against a holder in due course, or a personal defense, so that it cannot. The answer to this question lies in §3-401(a): "A person is not liable on an instrument unless (i) the person signed the instrument . . ." and in §3-403(a):

> Unless otherwise provided in this Article or Article 4, an unauthorized signature is ineffective except as the signature of the unauthorized signer in favor of a person who in good faith pays the instrument or takes it for value. . . .

Consider the following Problem.

PROBLEM 136

Jimmy Slick, an expert con man, went into John's Jewelers and told John, the owner, that he was Milton Money, the richest man in town. John was too awed to ask for identification. Slick then picked out several very expensive pieces of jewelry and signed Money's name to a promissory note to pay for them. Slick skipped town with the jewelry. When the note matured, the Tenth National Bank (a holder in due course to whom John has negotiated the paper) presented it to Milton Money for payment. May Money refuse to pay a holder in due course?

The answer to this Problem is obviously that Money is not liable, but as an attorney how do you get away from the all-encompassing language of §3-305(a) and (b)? Read §3-305(a) and (b) again and see if you can determine how Money's forgery defense fits into the statute; see State Bank v. Smith, 2014 WL 6088513 (Mich. Ct. App. 2014).

Additionally, if the forgery is of a name necessary to a valid negotiation, there can be no holder in due course following the forgery because no later transferee will qualify as a *holder*. See the discussion supra at pages 502-503.

C. *Procedural Issues*

One does not have to be a holder in due course in order to sue on the instrument; a "person entitled to enforce the instrument," a phrase defined in §3-301, may do so. Generally a "person entitled to enforce the instrument" means the *holder* of the instrument (someone in possession pursuant to a valid negotiation), though the phrase does include some non-holders—namely, someone who gets holder rights under the shelter rule (or a depositary bank per §4-205), the rightful owner of a lost instrument (§3-309), or the defendant in a successful restitution action (§3-418(d), yet to be discussed). Only if a defense or claim to the instrument arises will the holder's due course status become relevant, at which time the holder has the burden of establishing the position as a holder in due course. Read §3-308(b).

As mentioned above, and elaborated on later in the forgery discussion, a holder must take through a chain of indorsements that is free of forgeries affecting the title. When the genuineness of signatures becomes an issue, §3-308(a) allocates the procedural burdens. Read it.

Virginia National Bank v. Holt

Virginia Supreme Court, 1975
216 Va. 500, 219 S.E.2d 881

COMPTON, J.

. . . In May 1974, the plaintiff, Virginia National Bank, filed a motion for judgment against the defendants, Edgar M. Holt and Gustava H. Holt, his wife, jointly and severally, seeking recovery of the face amount of a "Homestead Waiving Promissory Note," plus interest and attorney's fees. The instrument, payable to the order of the Bank and allegedly made by the Holts to evidence an indebtedness, was dated December 12, 1973, was due 90 days after date, and was in the amount of $6,000.

Edgar M. Holt was duly served with process, but failed to appear on file pleadings in response. A default judgment in the amount sued for was entered against him in August 1974.

In her pleadings, Gustava H. Holt generally denied liability and specifically denied that the instrument was signed by her. On November 20, 1974, judgment was entered on a jury verdict in her favor and we granted the Bank a writ of error.

The dispositive issue is whether the evidence relating to the genuineness of Mrs. Holt's signature on the instrument presented a question of fact to be decided by the jury. We hold that it did not and reverse.

We will summarize only the evidence pertinent to the issue we decide. Testifying for the Bank was one of its commercial loan officers, who did not handle the Holt transaction but through whom the instrument in question was introduced into evidence, and two other witnesses, one of whom was an expert in handwriting analysis, whose statements supported the Bank's position that the signature on the note was in fact the defendant's.

Mrs. Holt did not appear at the trial, but her attorney endeavored to show that his client did not execute the instrument. During cross-examination, the loan officer, over the Bank's objection based on the hearsay rule, was required to answer whether he was present during the taking of Mrs. Holt's discovery deposition in July 1974 when she "denied that she signed the note." The record shows that the witness responded, "Yes, I was. Somewhat surprised." No other statement was elicited by defendant's counsel from any of the Bank's witnesses which would support the defendant's claim that she did not sign the writing.

The only evidence offered in the defendant's behalf was a set of answers previously filed by the Bank to six interrogatories propounded by her attorney. Those responses indicated that the Bank did not know of any witness who saw the defendant sign the note or who heard her admit that she signed it. They further indicated that the Bank had no information that she ever authorized her husband to sign her name to any promissory note or that she ever ratified any act of his in signing her name to such a writing.

By a motion to strike at the conclusion of the evidence, and again by a motion to set aside after the verdict, the Bank moved for judgment in its favor contending, as it does on appeal, that the foregoing hearsay testimony on cross-examination was erroneously admitted and, in the alternative, that even if such evidence was properly received, the defendant had failed, as a matter of law, to overcome the presumption established by §3-307 [§3-308 in the Revision—Eds.] that her signature was genuine and authorized. The trial court, in refusing to sustain the motion to strike and in overruling the motion to set aside, ruled that the question of whether the signature was genuine was for the jury. This was error.

Section 3-307, inter alia, sets out the burden of proof in an action which seeks recovery upon an "instrument" and deals with issues arising, in such a suit, from a challenge of the genuineness or authorization of signatures. 2 R. Anderson, Uniform Commercial Code §3-307:3 (2d ed. 1971). Under that section, each signature on an instrument is admitted unless, as in this case, the "effectiveness" of the signature is put in issue by a specific denial. The burden of establishing the genuineness of the signature is then upon the party claiming under the signature and relying on its "effectiveness," but such party is aided by a presumption that it is genuine or authorized. In this context, "presumption" means that "the trier of fact must find the existence of the fact presumed unless and until evidence is introduced which would support a finding of its nonexistence." Code §1-201(31).

The effect of the presumption is to eliminate any requirement that the plaintiff prove the signature is authentic until some evidence is introduced which would support a finding that the signature is forged or unauthorized. §3-307, Official Comment 1. It is based upon the fact that in the normal course of events forged or unauthorized signatures are very uncommon, and that evidence of such is usually within the defendant's control or more accessible to him. Id. Therefore, under §3-307, the party denying a signature must make some sufficient showing of the grounds for the denial before the plaintiff is put to his proof. The evidence need not be sufficient to require entry of summary judgment in the defendant's favor, "but it must be enough to support his denial by permitting a finding in his favor." Id. "Until the party denying the signature introduces such sufficient evidence, the presumption requires a finding for the party relying on the effectiveness of the signature." §3-307, Virginia Comment. See 2 F. Hart & W. Willier, Commercial Paper Under the Uniform Commercial Code §2.07(2) (1975).

An application of the foregoing analysis of the statute to the facts of this case demonstrates that the Bank was entitled to entry of summary judgment in its favor at the conclusion of all the evidence, since no material issue of fact requiring resolution by a jury was presented. Rule 3:18.

The defendant's specific denial put the genuineness of the defendant's signature in issue. Because of the foregoing presumption, the signature, which appeared to be that of Gustava H. Holt, was presumed to be genuine and the defendant was thus required to present "sufficient evidence" in support of the denial of genuineness. This she failed to do. We will assume, but not decide, that the disputed answer during cross-examination was properly admitted in evidence. Nonetheless, we conclude that this bit of testimony is insufficient to sustain a finding that the signature was forged or unauthorized. Furthermore, the answers to interrogatories furnish no support to the defendant's claimed defense. A forgery or an unauthorized signature may not be shown by merely demonstrating the plaintiff's apparent lack of evidence on that issue.

We hold, therefore, that the defendant has failed, as a matter of law, to make a sufficient showing to support a finding that she, or her authorized representative, did not in fact write her name on the instrument. The presumption then requires a finding that the signature on the instrument is genuine and effective. Accordingly, production of the instrument entitled the Bank to recover, because the defendant established no defense, 3-307(2), and it was error to submit the case to the jury. For these reasons, the judgment in favor of Gustava H. Holt will be reversed and final judgment will be entered here in favor of the Bank.

Reversed and final judgment.

QUESTION

Would it have been sufficient to overcome the presumption if Mrs. Holt had taken the stand and denied the signature? See Metropolitan Mortgage Fund v. Basiliko, 407 A.2d 773 (Md. App. 1979); Freeman Check Cashing, Inc. v. State, 97 Misc. 2d 819, 412 N.Y.S.2d 963 (Ct. Cl. 1979); Bates & Springer, Inc. v. Stallworth, 56 Ohio App. 2d 223, 382 N.E.2d 1179 (1978). If you were her attorney, what sort of evidence would you present to the court?

D. Defenses Against a Non-Holder in Due Course

Read §§3-305(a) and (b) and 3-306 carefully. Note the legal result: all *claims* and both real and personal *defenses* may be asserted against anyone who does not qualify as a holder in due course.[22] The most common personal defenses are *want of consideration* (no consideration) and *failure of consideration* (breach of contract, called a *claim in recoupment* in the Revision).

Herzog Contracting Corp. v. McGowen Corp.

United States Court of Appeals, Seventh Circuit, 1992
976 F.2d 1062

POSNER, Circuit Judge.

The district judge granted summary judgment in favor of Herzog Contracting Corporation in its diversity suit to enforce two promissory notes, aggregating $400,000, against the issuer, McGowen Corporation. The appeal raises a tangle of jurisdictional and substantive questions, the latter governed, the parties agree, by Indiana Law. . . .

The next jurisdictional issue requires us to delve into the facts. In 1989 Herzog, the plaintiff, bought the assets of Tru-Flex Metal Hose Corporation from McGowen, the defendant, and formed a wholly owned subsidiary of Herzog (also called Tru-Flex) to hold them, to which Herzog assigned the asset purchase agreement. The agreement called for annual payments from

22. The only claim a non-holder in due course takes free of is a perfected security interest in non-negotiable instruments, and then only if they are purchased for value in the ordinary course of business without notice of the security interest (§9-330). This is an Article 9 matter, and at this point don't worry what it means.

Tru-Flex to McGowen of $500,000 for five years. The two promissory notes, both demand notes, were issued by McGowen to Tru-Flex later in 1989. The parties have radically different positions on the purpose of the notes. Herzog claims that it loaned McGowen $400,000 and the notes are McGowen's promises to repay the loan. McGowen acknowledges having received the $400,000 but denies that it was a loan, contending instead that it was partial prepayment of the next year's installment due under the asset purchase agreement and that the only purpose of the notes that it gave Tru-Flex was to enable it (that is, McGowen) to postpone the realization of taxable income to the following year by making the $400,000 payment look like a loan.

The parties soon fell to squabbling and Herzog refused to make further payments under the asset purchase agreement, precipitating a suit by McGowen against Herzog in an Indiana state court for breach of contract that remains pending. At about the same time that the state court suit was brought, Tru-Flex assigned McGowen's promissory notes to Herzog, which shortly afterward brought this suit to enforce them. . . .

We come to the merits. The case was decided on summary judgment and there has been no determination of the truth of McGowen's claim that the promissory notes were never intended to be presented for payment. So we must assume that the claim is true. The question is whether, as the district judge held, solely on the basis that the notes are "clear and unambiguous," they are enforceable regardless of what the parties actually intended.

They would be if enforcement were being sought by a holder in due course, UCC §3-305, Ind. Code §26-1-3-305, but Herzog concedes that it is not that. It places its case on the parol evidence rule. The promissory notes are unambiguous—they promise Herzog a specified sum of money on demand—and their terms cannot be varied by extrinsic evidence. At first glance Herzog's argument seems a complete nonstarter. A holder of a promissory note who is not a holder in due course takes the note subject to "all defenses of any party which would be available in an action on a simple contract," UCC §3-306(b) [§3-305(b) in the Revision—Eds.], and one of those defenses, notwithstanding the parol evidence rule, is that the parties did not intend to create an enforceable contract. 2 E. Allan Farnsworth, Farnsworth on Contracts §7.4, at p. 212 (1990); James J. White & Robert S. Summers, Handbook of the Law under the Uniform Commercial Code §2-10, at p. 78 (1980). "It is well settled that whatever the formal documentary evidence, the parties to a legal transaction may always show that they understood a purported contract not to bind them; it may, for example, be a joke, or a disguise to deceive others." In re H. Hicks & Son, Inc., 82 F.2d 277, 279 (2d Cir. 1936) (L. Hand, J.); see also Nice Ball Bearing Co. v. Bearing Jobbers, Inc., 205 F.2d 841, 845 (7th Cir. 1953). The deceived others may, of course, be able to object to the attempt to prove the contract a sham, as in Central States, Southeast & Southwest Areas Pension Fund v. Gerber Truck

Service, Inc., 870 F.2d 1148 (7th Cir. 1989) (en banc), and FDIC v. O'Neil, 809 F.2d 350 (7th Cir. 1987), but that is not a factor here. More to the point, a minority of jurisdictions "have refused to admit such evidence [i.e., that the purported contract was a joke, a disguise, in short, a sham of some sort] where the purpose of the sham agreement was offensive to public policy." 2 Farnsworth, supra, §7.4, at p. 212 n.4; see Annot., "Admissibility of Oral Evidence to Show That a Writing Was a Sham Agreement Not Intended to Create Legal Relations," 71 A.L.R.2d 382, 393-397 (1960); 67 A.L.R.2d Later Case Service 555 (1984), and for an illustrative case Kergil v. Central Oregon Fir Supply Co., 213 Or. 186, 323 P.2d 947 (1958).

We prefer the majority rule, illustrated by our decision in Nice Ball Bearing Co. v. Bearing Jobbers, Inc., supra, so will apply it here in default of any Indiana cases on the question. Apart from the fact that the minority rule rewards a party to the sham agreement and imposes a punishment that may be disproportionate to the promisor's misconduct, it invites a collateral inquiry into the character of the alleged "sham." Here the party accused of shamming by his fellow shammer was angling for a tax advantage. Did that make the transaction a "sham"? Despite the doctrine of tax law that substance prevails over form, Gregory v. Helvering, 293 U.S. 465 (1935); Yosha v. Commissioner, 861 F.2d 494 (7th Cir. 1988), many transactions that would strike a nonspecialist as contrived purely to avoid taxes are entirely lawful. Must we therefore, to resolve this case, decide whether McGowen's effort to postpone its tax liability for the sale of Tru-Flex was one of them? We trust not.

But we are not done. In the face of the principle that any defenses to a contract are available in a suit on a promissory note unless the plaintiff is a holder in due course, some courts enforce the parol evidence rule more broadly in such suits than in suits to enforce ordinary contracts. Annot., "Admissibility of Parol Evidence to Show That a Bill or Note Was Conditional, or Given for a Special Purpose," 54 A.L.R. 702, 717-718 (1928). In Perez-Lizano v. Ayers, 695 P.2d 467, 469 (Mont. 1985), for example, the court refused to allow the admission of parol evidence to show that the note was a sham. One of the cases in this line is an Indiana case, Highfield v. Lang, 394 N.E.2d 204, 206 (Ind. App. 1979). But it is readily distinguishable from our case; and we have found two recent cases from other jurisdictions in which courts admitted parol evidence to show that a promissory note was not intended to be enforceable. American Underwriting Corp. v. Rhode Island Hospital Trust Co., 303 A.2d 121, 125 (R.I. 1973); Simpson v. Milne, 677 P.2d 365, 368 (Colo. App. 1983). The second was a case of a sham; the parol evidence was that the notes in suit "were executed as a fiction to satisfy plaintiff's wife, who was near death, and who strongly felt that [the defendant and his wife] still owed [the plaintiff and his wife] money from prior business transactions." Id.

Despite these last two cases and despite UCC §3-306(b), the parties have tacitly agreed that the applicability of the parol evidence rule to this case is governed not by general contract law but by a special doctrine that allows parol evidence to show, against a plaintiff who is not a holder in due course, that the delivery of the negotiable instrument that he is suing to collect was "for a special purpose." Brames v. Crates, 399 N.E.2d 437, 441 (Ind. App. 1980); UCC §3-306(c); Ind. Code §26-1-3-306(c). This approach is understandable though not inevitable. While §3-306(b) subjects the non-holder in due course to "all defenses" that the original promisor would have had, implicitly including the defense that the promise was not intended to create enforceable rights, §3-306(c) deals with some of these defenses in greater detail. This could be taken to imply that the defense that no enforceable rights were intended to be created is to be analyzed in accordance with the "special purpose" doctrine that predates the Code, though a likelier inference is that the draftsmen wanted simply to make sure that no defense was overlooked.

However this may be, Herzog argues that the special-purpose doctrine is limited to allowing the promisor (McGowen here) to defend by showing that his obligation to make good on the note was subject to a condition precedent, which is not the case here. For it is McGowen's contention not that something had to happen before Herzog could demand payment, but that Herzog could never demand payment. Parol evidence is always admissible to prove a fraud, Franklin v. White, 493 N.E.2d 161, 165 (Ind. 1986); In re Estate of Fanning, 333 N.E.2d 80, 85 (Ind. 1975); Kruse Classic Auction Co. v. Aetna Casualty & Surety Co., 511 N.E.2d 326, 330 (Ind. App. 1987), but McGowen does not contend that when Herzog agreed to the scheme for making the prepayment of the purchase installment look like a loan it intended to double-cross McGowen by demanding payment of the notes. If there was a fraud, it was against the Internal Revenue Service, though no one is arguing this. With fraud out of the picture and the scope of the parol evidence rule applicable to promissory notes conceded by McGowen to be governed by §3-306(c) rather than §3-306(b), McGowen is left with the special-purpose doctrine and Herzog concludes that a sham case is outside that doctrine, which, as we have noted, he believes to be limited to conditions precedent.

There are cases, none from Indiana, on both sides of the question whether "delivery for a special purpose" is limited to conditions precedent, although the majority view is that it is not. Compare Perez-Lizano v. Ayers, supra, 695 P.2d at 469-470, with American Underwriting Corp. v. Rhode Island Hospital Trust Co., supra, 303 A.2d at 125. Text and history can help us choose between these positions, though history more than text. Section 3-306(c) expressly recognizes a defense of "nonperformance of any condition precedent," making the "special purpose" defense redundant on Herzog's construal of it. But redundancy is built into §3-306(c), as we have seen, and maybe this is another example of it. So let us turn to history.

Until sometime after the middle of the nineteenth century, courts were highly reluctant to admit parol evidence, in suits on promissory notes, for any purpose other than to prove fraud or mistake. John Barnard Byles, A Treatise on the Law of Bills of Exchange 169 note I (4th Am. ed. 1856). A little later, they were allowing such evidence in three additional types of cases: delivery of the note together with a mortgage deed, with the note as additional security for payment of the mortgage; delivery of the note to escrow; and delivery contingent on the satisfaction of a condition precedent. Id. at 112-113 (14th ed. 1885). Some courts also allowed the admission of parol evidence "to show that a contract signed and delivered was never intended to be the real contract between the parties." Id. at 113 note o. One case—oddly enough it is factually similar to ours—used the term "special purpose" to describe the defense in a "no obligation" or "sham" case. Juilliard v. Chaffee, 92 N.Y. 529, 534 (1883). And when the English codified their law of negotiable instruments in 1882, they expressly allowed evidence (other than against a holder in due course) that delivery had been "conditional or for a special purpose only, *and not for the purpose of transferring the property in the bill.*" James W. Eaton & Frank B. Gilbert, A Treatise on Commercial Paper and the Negotiable Instruments Law 697 (1903). The meaning brought out by the words that we have italicized seems unmistakable: the "special purpose" defense encompassed all cases in which the negotiable instrument had not been intended to create an enforceable obligation. Byles, supra, at 122 (17th ed. 1911).

The American Negotiable Instruments Law—the first statute drafted by the National Conference of Commissioners on Uniform State Laws—copied the English provision word for word. Joseph Doddrige Brannan, The Negotiable Instruments Law Annotated 129 (4th ed. 1926); see also id. at 135-141. Later, however, darkness descended, and we find some authorities distinguishing among condition cases, no-obligation cases, and special-purpose cases. Annot., "Admissibility of Parol Evidence to Show That a Bill or Note Was Conditional, or Given for a Special Purpose," 20 A.L.R. 421, 490, 498-502 (1922); 4 William D. Hawkland & Lary Lawrence, Uniform Commercial Code Series 3-306:07, at p. 481 (1990). This proliferation of unhelpful distinctions was abetted by the fact that the Uniform Commercial Code, in recodifying negotiable instruments law, dropped the explanatory phrase "and not for the purpose of transferring the property in the bill" from the formulation of the special purpose defense. But this was done without any intention of changing the meaning of the defense as it had appeared in the Negotiable Instruments Law. "Notes and Comments to

Tent. Draft No. 2—Art. III," 3 Uniform Commercial Code: Drafts 186-187 (Elizabeth Slusser Kelly ed. 1984). Certainly nothing in the history of the Uniform Commercial Code suggests a purpose of abolishing the "no obligation" defense and returning to the law as it existed before the Civil War. The tendency of our law for almost a century has been to relax strict rules, perhaps because of growing (though possibly misguided and even sentimental) confidence in the ability of judges and juries to resolve factual questions (such as, What was the purpose of McGowen's notes?), with reasonable accuracy and at reasonable cost, by sifting testimony. The legal realists who, led by Karl Llewellyn, drafted the Uniform Commercial Code were leaders in the movement to soften the contours of strict common law rules. See, e.g., UCC §§2-103(1)(b), 2-204, 2-205.

It hardly matters whether the no-obligation cases are subsumed under the special-purpose defense or set off by themselves or, as seems simplest and therefore—no other values being at stake so far as we can see—preferable, assimilated to the general contract doctrine that allows parol evidence to show that a contractual-looking document was not intended to be binding. The office of the parol evidence rule is to prevent parties to a written contract from seeking to vary its terms by reference to side agreements, or tentative agreements reached in preliminary negotiations. 2 Farnsworth, supra, §7.2, at p. 197. In the case of a condition precedent the promisor is not trying to vary the terms, but to deny the enforceability of the promise by pointing to some condition that has not been fulfilled. The distinction may seem fine-spun and even arbitrary, but it has been deemed consistent with the policy behind the parol evidence rule, or at least a tolerable qualification of it. 2 id., §7.4, at pp. 211-215. Two points can be made on behalf of the distinction. The weaker, as it seems to us, is that without such an exception the rule would work dramatic forfeitures, by preventing a party from showing not merely that the terms were somewhat different from what they appeared to be but that he had never agreed to do or pay anything. The stronger point is that the parol evidence rule, properly understood, is not a rule imposed on contracting parties from without but merely an inference, drawn from the language of the document, that the parties intended it to be the complete statement of their agreement, extinguishing any agreements that might have emerged from the preliminary negotiations. Patton v. Mid-Continent Systems, Inc., 841 F.2d 742, 745 (7th Cir. 1988); 2 Farnsworth, supra, §§7.2, 7.3, at pp. 197-198. The document is unlikely to reveal whether the parties intended it to be taken seriously, and if it does not, there is no basis for applying the rule. In re H. Hicks & Son, Inc., supra, 82 F.2d at 279.

At all events, to allow parol evidence to expose a sham case such as this is alleged to be would make no greater inroads into the parol evidence rule than the cases on conditions precedent do. McGowen is not trying to change the terms in the promissory notes, but to show that the notes were not in fact intended to create a legally enforceable obligation. They were, not to put too fine a point on it, intended to fool the Internal Revenue Service. Herzog, perhaps fearing that it will be found to have been a party to this little deception, does not argue that McGowen's unclean hands should forfeit its right to make a sham-transaction defense, if there is such a defense, and we think there should be because we can think of no principled distinction between it and the condition-precedent defense that Herzog concedes is valid.

The policy of the law is to facilitate negotiability by allowing assignees of negotiable instruments to take free of defenses not obvious on the fact of the note. Northwestern National Ins. Co. v. Maggie, No. 92-1037 (7th Cir. Sept. 23, 1992). But that policy is expressed in the doctrine of holders in due course. Id. Herzog made no effort to discount the notes to one who would have been such a holder and therefore could have enforced the notes against McGowen regardless of the oral agreement not to enforce them on which McGowen relies in this suit.

The judgment is reversed and the case remanded for further proceedings consistent with this opinion.

QUESTION

How would this case be decided under the current version of Article 3? See §§3-117 and 3-105(b), plus the latter's Official Comment 2.

E. *Jus Tertii*

It is a basic rule of law that litigants must succeed or fail on the basis of their *own* rights and not the rights of others. The rights of another, called *jus tertii,* are available to other litigants only in special circumstances. Sureties, called "accommodation parties" in the Code, are permitted, with some exceptions, to raise the defenses of their principals (called "accommodated parties"); see §3-305(d). And, as we shall see when we get to the issue of restrictive indorsements, §3-206(f) permits an obligor to refuse payment if doing so would violate the terms of a restrictive indorsement.

The Code's general prohibition against using *jus tertii* is found in §3-305(c), which you should now read. Note two important things about it. The first is that the claims of another may always be asserted if that person joins the lawsuit. The second is that §3-305(c)'s last sentence permits one *jus tertii* to be asserted against a non-holder in due course: the instrument has been lost or stolen so that the current possessor is not the true owner. If this latter *jus tertii* could not be raised, then the obligor would be exposed to the possibility of double payment when the true owner showed up.

PROBLEM 137

Craig Covey was the maker of the following promissory note, which he signed in order to buy a computer:

> I, Craig Covey, promise to pay to bearer the sum of $5,000, on demand. I also promise to buy the bearer lunch on the date of presentment.

The note was given to his uncle, who had loaned him the money for the purchase. The uncle sold the note to the Stonewall Finance Company in return for a check for $4,500. Stonewall Finance Company's check bounced, and the uncle was very angry. He went down to the finance company's office and found that there was a sign on the door saying "GONE OUT OF BUSINESS." The next day the note was stolen from the office of the Stonewall Finance Company and later surfaced in the hands of Jane Eleanor, an innocent purchaser for value, who presented it to Craig for payment. In the meantime both his uncle and the Stonewall Finance Company had contacted Craig and asked him to refrain from paying the instrument, the uncle pointing to the bounced check and Stonewall to the fact that the note had been stolen from it. Is Jane a holder in due course? If not, can Craig raise the suggested *jus tertii* against her? If Craig wants to pay Jane, can his uncle stop him? See §3-602.

F. Conclusion

Reference has already been made to special statutes and rules (such as the FTC regulation) that restrict the holder in due course doctrine in consumer transactions. But these statutes do not cover the whole consumer field; for example, a couple signing a promissory note to a bank for a home improvement loan can still lose a lawsuit to a holder in due course, as we have seen. Should the doctrine be wiped out completely in consumer transactions? We've already seen the havoc it can raise in cases in which a home owner buys a home due to fraudulent inducements but cannot assert this defense against a subsequent holder in due course of the promissory note signed at the closing. What about abolishing HIDC status in commercial ventures?

Professor Grant Gilmore, one of the original drafters of the Uniform Commercial Code, has commented:

> The "holder in due course" concept was worked out by Lord Mansfield and his successors in the late eighteenth and early nineteenth centuries against a business background in which bills of exchange and promissory

> notes did in fact circulate and could be expected to pass through a number of hands before being retired. As the modern banking system developed, instruments gradually ceased to circulate. In this century nothing is rarer than a true negotiation to a third party purchaser for value—the use of negotiable notes which pass from dealer to finance company in the attempt to carry out consumer frauds is hardly a "true negotiation." The whole "holder in due course" concept could usefully have been abolished when negotiable instruments law was codified at the end of the nineteenth century. In fact it was preserved like a fly in amber both in the N.I.L. and in its successor, Article 3 of the Uniform Commercial Code. Indeed our codifications typically preserve once vital but now obsolete concepts in much the same way that our museums preserve the ancient artifacts of bygone civilizations.

G. Gilmore, The Death of Contract 108 n.18 (1974). Professor Gilmore developed this idea more fully in a fascinating article: Gilmore, Formalism and the Law of Negotiable Instruments, 13 Creighton L. Rev. 441 (1979). A leading article containing the same theme is Rosenthal, Negotiability—Who Needs It?, 71 Colum. L. Rev. 375 (1971).

In his recent book, The End of Negotiable Instruments (2012), Professor James Rogers has gone even further. He advocates the complete repeal of Article 3 of the Code! What would be the result if that extraordinary event occurred? The common law and contractual arrangements, supplemented by federal enactments (such as various banking and check regulations) would then control. Physical checks (which are decreasing in number as the twenty-first century progresses) would be controlled by the rules of Article 4 of Bank Deposits and Collections (which itself is being supplanted by federal law or organizational agreements). Promissory notes would be replaced by contractual agreements to pay debts. Thus a home mortgage's payment arrangement would be dictated by the mortgage contract, and the assignment of that contract would be all that is necessary to transfer rights to enforce the mortgage debt. The holder in due course doctrine would disappear since at common law contracts travel *with* their defenses when assigned to new owners; see Restatement (Second) of Contracts §336. Should homeowners have a defense of fraud, as did the woman in the second case in this chapter, the foreclosing entity couldn't foreclose, but would have to pass the contract back to its assignor, and so on until it was returned to the entity committing the fraud. Surely that is a happier result than allowing the fraudster to escape liability while the defrauded homeowner ends up sitting on the curb. Whether Professor Rodger's arguments will prevail is uncertain, but repealing Article 3 is an interesting idea (though it would put your authors out of work).

CHAPTER 10 ASSESSMENT: MULTIPLE CHOICE QUESTIONS

1. Rahel signed a negotiable promissory note payable to Ammu Gallery, to buy a painting for her law firm. Ammu Gallery indorsed the note to Holly Bank, who bought the note honestly, in a transaction typical for the industry. Rahel proudly displayed the painting in the firm's conference room until a discerning client alerted her that it was a forgery. Will Rahel be obliged to pay, if Holly Bank seeks payment on the note?
   a. No. Rahel could be liable only to Ammu Gallery, the person she promised to pay.
   b. No. Rahel was defrauded, a defense that can be raised even against a holder in due course.
   c. No. The painting was forged, so the seller breached warranties to Rahel, the buyer.
   d. Yes. Rahel has no defense she can raise against a holder in due course.

2. What would be the result in the previous question if Rahel had bought the painting to hang in the living room of her home?
   a. The same, because application of the holder in due course doctrine depends on Holly Bank's status, not Rahel's.
   b. Rahel could raise any defense she had against anyone seeking payment on the note.
   c. The same—fraud can always be raised as a defense, in consumer or business cases.
   d. The holder in due course doctrine applies only to loans, not sales.

3. Chacko wrote a check payable to Baba, to buy furniture for Chacko's home. Baba did not deliver the furniture as promised the next day. Baba deposited the check, without indorsing it, in his account at Valor Bank and withdrew the money. Meanwhile, Chacko stopped payment on the check, so the check was not paid when Valor Bank presented it to Chacko's Bank. Valor Bank sued Chacko. Can Chacko raise the defense of breach of contract?
   a. Yes. The holder in due course doctrine does not apply to consumer transactions.
   b. Yes. Valor Bank is not a holder in due course. Baba did not indorse the check, so Valor is not a holder.
   c. Valor Bank is not a holder in due course, because it did not give value.
   d. No. As a holder in due course, Valor Bank is not subject to the defense of breach of contract.

4. Triffin is in the business of purchasing checks that have been dishonored, paying cents on the dollar. Triffin purchases the checks from banks and check-cashers that were holders in due course. Triffin itself is not a

holder in due course, because Triffin buys the checks with notice they were dishonored. One might also argue that Triffin does not act in good faith, because Triffin's purchases are atypical for checks, Triffin pays little for the checks, and Triffin knows that at least some of the drawers may have good reason not to pay. If Triffin sues the issuer of a check, can the drawer raise defenses, such as breach of contract or unconscionability, to payment?

a. No, because that defense was against the payee, not Triffin.
b. No, because Triffin has the rights of a holder in due course.
c. Yes, because Triffin is not a holder in due course.
d. Yes. One who has promised to pay can always raise any reason that the promise should not be enforceable, such as breach of contract or unconscionability.

5. Roy is the holder in due course of a promissory note signed by Velutha. If Roy sues Velutha on the note, which defenses could Velutha raise?
   a. Velutha was defrauded, because the payee promised to loan Velutha money but never delivered the funds.
   b. Breach of contract, because the promissory note was given for some business equipment that was completely defective.
   c. Unconscionability.
   d. Velutha signed the note at a time that he was too young to make a binding legal obligation.

ANSWERS

1. *D* is the best answer. Holly Bank is a holder in due course. It is a holder because Ammu Gallery indorsed the note and delivered it to Holly Bank. It took for value, in good faith, and with no notice of Rahel's defenses. So Holly Bank would be subject to only the "real defenses," none of which applies here. *A* is wrong. The whole point of negotiability is that the signer promises to pay whomever becomes the holder of the instrument. B is incorrect because the only sort of fraud that can be raised against a HIDC is "real fraud" (signing an instrument, but reasonably not knowing what it is), not fraud in the inducement, as here. Mere breach of contract likewise is not a real defense, so *C* is incorrect.
2. *B* is the best answer. This question reminds us that the holder in due course doctrine does not apply to promissory notes signed in consumer credit sale transactions, so Rahel can raise any defense she has. *C* and *D* cite fictitious rules.
3. *D* is the best answer. This question illustrates several key points. Contrary to A, not all consumer transactions are immune to the holder in due course doctrine. The FTC rule makes the holder in due course doctrine

inapplicable to promissory notes signed for a sale or lease of goods or services to consumers (consumer credit sales). But that leaves other consumer transactions subject to the holder in due course doctrine: transactions involving checks (as opposed to promissory notes); notes signed for loans of money (as opposed to sales of goods or services); and mortgage notes (signed for sales of real estate, not goods). So consumers often have the pleasure of learning about the holder in due course doctrine.

The question also illustrates rules we have seen that ensure depositary banks may get holder in due course status. Valor Bank is a holder, even with no indorsement, because a depositary bank automatically becomes holder of a check deposited by a holder, contrary to *B*. Valor Bank also gave value, by allowing withdrawal of funds.

4. *B* is the best answer. Triffin is indeed not a holder in due course. But Triffin has the rights of a holder in due course, under the shelter rule. When an instrument is transferred, the transferee gets the rights of the transferor, including any HIDC rights (unless the transferee was actually involved in an underlying fraud). If Triffin buys a check from a HIDC, Triffin gets the rights of a HIDC. *A* and *D* respectively understate and overstate the right of a signer to raise defenses.
5. *D* is the best answer. This question illustrates how someone that signs an instrument generally gives up her right to raise defenses against a HIDC. By signing a negotiable promissory note, Velutha effectively says, "I will pay this, even if I do not get what was promised, or I am being deceived, or I am being taken advantage of. . . ." Only the real defenses may be raised against a HIDC, including infancy, making *D* correct.

Chapter 11
The Nature of Liability

It may seem odd to a lawyer to talk about defenses to a lawsuit, as the last chapter did, before talking about the various causes of action that can be brought giving rise to those defenses. We did this strange thing because holder in due course law is the primary factor that distinguishes negotiable instruments proceedings from all others, and those proceedings cannot be understood without first appreciating a concept that overarches the whole field. Now that that key issue is out of the way, we can turn to the various negotiable instrument–related legal theories that lawyers must know when clients come to them with questions triggering Article 3 of the Uniform Commercial Code.

Once a negotiable instrument is created and enters commerce, the parties thereto are automatically locked into relationships that may lead to legal liability. When a problem arises in connection with one of these instruments, the knowledgeable lawyer (and the wise student facing an exam question) asks four preliminary questions:

(1) What negotiable instrument labels (*drawer, payee, drawee, maker, indorser, guarantor*, etc.) do the parties bear?
(2) What causes of action (contractual obligation, warranty, conversion, suits "off the instrument") are available to each party?

(3) What defenses are possible?
(4) Can liability be passed to someone else?

The basic labels applied to the original parties to notes and drafts have been discussed. You will recall that a promissory note is initially a two-party instrument involving a *maker* and a *payee.* If the payee signs the instrument, whether a blank or special indorsement, he/she becomes an *indorser.* Anyone who thereafter signs his/her name to the instrument is also presumed to be an indorser (§3-204(a)). A draft always begins as a three-party instrument. A *drawer* orders the *drawee* to make payment to the order of the *payee.* If the draft is a check drawn by Carl Consumer on the Big Bank to the order of the Gas Company, the parties are, respectively, the drawer, the drawee, and the payee. If the Gas Company places its name on the back of the check, it will become an indorser, as will anyone else who signs the back of the check prior to its payment by the drawee. The labels that can be applied to other parties to the instrument (*acceptor, accommodation party, guarantor*) will be explained as they come up below.

The remainder of this segment of the book will discuss the different causes of action (legal theories) that one party can bring against another. Negotiable instruments law draws on the basic fields of contract (§§3-412 to 3-415, 4-401), property (that is, warranty rights, §§3-416, 3-417, 4-207, 4-208), and tort (primarily, conversion, §3-420) to provide the three possible legal theories on which parties can sue under the Code. In addition, of course, the parties frequently have rights against each other that arise outside of the scope of Articles 3 and 4. There is no way to catalogue all the possible non-commercial paper suits here, but the discussion immediately below introduces the most obvious one.

I. THE UNDERLYING OBLIGATION

The most common lawsuit connected with negotiable instruments, but not created by Articles 3 and 4, is a suit on the *underlying obligation* that generated the instrument. If a corporation mails a dividend check to one of its stockholders and the check is lost in the mail, the stockholder can sue on the underlying obligation (in this case, the agreement to pay the dividend) and ignore whatever rights negotiable instruments law would give.

Does this mean that in addition to the negotiable instruments suits described below, a party may always bring suit on the underlying obligation? The answer has to be no, and the following Problem illustrates why.

PROBLEM 138

Aunt Fran was unable to pay the annual rent on her hat shop, so she asked the landlord, Simon Mustache, to accept instead a promissory note from her to him for the amount of the rent, the note to be due three months in the future. Simon took the note and immediately discounted it with a local bank. A week later (and before the note matured), Simon brought suit against Aunt Fran for nonpayment of the rent (the underlying obligation being the lease agreement). Can she defend by saying that the note somehow suspended his right to sue on the underlying obligation?

The answer is yes. The common law doctrine of *merger* stated that once an instrument was offered and accepted in satisfaction of an underlying obligation, the obligation merged with the instrument, and until the instrument was dishonored, the underlying obligation was suspended (unavailable as a cause of action). This doctrine is codified in §3-310(b), which you should read carefully. Note that under §3-310(b)(1) and (2) actual payment of a check or a note discharges the underlying obligation, but until then that obligation is suspended. Once the instrument is dishonored, subsection (b)(3) divorces the underlying contract from the instrument and separate causes of action then exist for each.

PROBLEM 139

Suppose in the last Problem Aunt Fran had paid her rent by giving a cashier's check to Simon. The check was drawn by Octopus National Bank (ONB) on itself (the very definition of a cashier's check—see §3-104(g)). Simon took the check down to ONB and was dismayed to discover that the bank had failed and was now closed. He returned to Aunt Fran and demanded the rent money. What should she tell him? See §3-310(a).

Gray1 CPB, LLC v. SCC Acquisitions, Inc.

California Court of Appeal, 2014
169 Cal. Rptr. 3d 906

MOORE, J.

You cross continents and spend years trying to collect a judgment for your client. Late one Friday afternoon, the debtor's lawyer walks into your office and hands you a cashier's check for almost $13 million, covering the entire judgment and all accumulated interest. Do you accept the check or say, "no thank you, I need to make a motion for attorney fees first?" Put another way, is a bird in the hand worth two in the bush?

Gray1 CPB, LLC (Gray1), obtained a judgment against SCC Acquisitions and Bruce Elieff (collectively defendants). Almost two years later, defendants paid the amount of the outstanding judgment and accrued interest with a cashier's check. In the interim, Gray1 allegedly incurred more than $3 million in attorney fees in an effort to enforce its judgment. The fees were largely incurred in litigating a separate action against Elieff in an effort to untangle what Gray1 asserts were a number of fraudulent transactions resulting in the placement of fraudulent liens on Elieff's real property as part of a scheme to insulate Elieff's properties from the judgment.

According to Gray1, it was only when it appeared the separate action was imminently headed toward resolution in Gray1's favor that defendants gave Gray1 the cashier's check to pay the judgment. Gray1 did not immediately cash the check. It held onto the check long enough for its attorneys to file a motion for postjudgment costs, including attorney fees. Once deposited, the issuing bank honored the check.

Judgment creditors who have prevailed on a contract authorizing the award of attorney fees are entitled to postjudgment attorney fees. (Code of Civ. Proc., §§685.040, 685.070, subd. (a)(6); all statutory references are to the Code of Civil Procedure unless otherwise stated.) However, a motion for postjudgment costs must "be made before the judgment is satisfied in full." (§685.080, subd. (a).) The trial court denied Gray1's motion for postjudgment costs, finding the motion was made after the judgment had been fully satisfied. Gray1 appealed. In this appeal we are called upon to determine when a judgment paid with a cashier's check is deemed satisfied.

In addition to opposing Gray1's motion, defendants filed a motion of their own. They sought a determination that Gray1 unjustly failed to file a timely acknowledgment of full satisfaction of judgment. (§724.050, subd. (e).) The trial court denied defendants' motion, finding defendants failed to prove damages, and concluding Gray1's failure to file a timely full satisfaction of judgment was not without just cause. Defendants appealed from that order.

I. Facts

In August 2010, Gray1 obtained a judgment in excess of $9.1 million, plus interest, against defendants as a result of the defendants' failure to make good on their guaranties of a loan made to a limited liability company owned by Elieff. . . . The written guaranties contained provisions providing for the award of attorney fees. . . . The judgment provided Gray1 was entitled to attorney fees and costs to be established by a cost bill or motion. By interlineation, the court amended the judgment to reflect the award of over $1.5 million in attorney fees and more than $44,000 in costs.

Defendants made no payments on the judgment until June 8, 2012. On that date, defendants' attorney hand delivered to Gray1's attorneys a cashier's check in the amount of $12,918,654.46 and a letter. According to the letter, the cashier's check covered the amount of the judgment, including accumulated interest, and the judgment was now fully satisfied. The letter also demanded Grayl immediately file a full satisfaction of judgment. Additionally, the letter contained a notice in the language of section 724.050, subdivision (b): "'Important warning. If this judgment has been satisfied, the law requires that you comply with this demand not later than 15 days after you receive it. If a court proceeding is necessary to compel you to comply with this demand, you will be required to pay my reasonable attorney's fees in the proceeding if the court determines that the judgment has been satisfied and that you failed to comply with the demand. In addition, if the court determines that you failed without just cause to comply with this demand within the 15 days allowed, you will be liable for all damages I sustain by reason of such failure and will also forfeit one hundred dollars to me.'"

Twelve days after receiving the cashier's check, on June 20, 2012, Grayl filed a motion for postjudgment costs, including attorney fees incurred in attempting to enforce the judgment. Grayl alleged that in the two years following the judgment, it had incurred more than $3.1 million in attorney fees in efforts to collect on its judgment. On June 22, 2012, Grayl filed an acknowledgment of partial satisfaction of judgment. Grayl contended it was entitled costs (including attorney fees) incurred in attempting to enforce its judgment, and therefore, the amount paid by defendants was not in full satisfaction of the judgment.

Grayl deposited the cashier's check on June 21, 2012, the day after it filed the motion for postjudgment costs. The bank "fund[ed]" the check on June 25, 2012.

Fifteen days after hand delivering the cashier's check and letter, defendants filed a motion to compel Grayl to file an acknowledgement of full satisfaction of judgment on June 27, 2012. (§724.050, subd. (d).) The motion alleged defendants not only paid the judgment in full, but overpaid by more than $281,000, based on a miscalculation as to the date postjudgment interest started accumulating and "numerous collections and levies that Grayl has evidently already made."

The court heard the parties' respective motions on September 12, 2012. Defendants argued Grayl's motion for postjudgment attorney fees was untimely because section 685.080 requires a motion for costs, including attorney fees permitted by section 685.040, to be filed before the judgment has been fully satisfied (§§685.070, subd. (b), 685.080, subd. (a)). Defendants further asserted the judgment was fully satisfied when the cashier's check was delivered to Grayl and accepted on June 8, 2012, almost two weeks before Grayl filed its motion for postjudgment costs. Grayl conceded that had defense counsel walked into Grayl's attorney's office and paid off the outstanding judgment with a briefcase full of cash, instead of with a cashier's check, the judgment would have been fully satisfied that same day and Grayl would have been prohibited from thereafter filing a motion for postjudgment costs. Grayl argued, however, its motion was not untimely because a judgment paid by check is not satisfied until the check is ultimately honored by the issuing bank, citing section 724.010.

In a five-page ruling, the court denied as untimely Grayl's motion for postjudgment costs. The court also denied defendants' motion for damages and sanctions (§724.050, subd. (e)), finding defendants failed to present any evidence of costs, attorney fees, or other damages and that Grayl's failure to file a timely acknowledgment of full satisfaction of judgment was not without just cause.

II. Discussion

A. Grayl's Appeal

Grayl appeals, contending the trial court erred in finding its motion for postjudgment costs untimely. As we are not faced with disputed facts and this matter involves statutory interpretation, our review is de novo. (Jaffe v. Pacelli (2008) 165 Cal. App. 4th 927, 934, 82 Cal. Rptr. 3d 423.)

Under the "American rule," followed in California, "each party to a lawsuit ordinarily must pay his or her own attorney fees. [Citations.]" (Musaelian v. Adams (2009) 45 Cal. 4th 512, 516, 87 Cal. Rptr. 3d 475, 198 P.3d 560.) An exception to this rule exists where the parties have agreed to "the measure and mode of compensation of attorneys." (§1021.) For example, a contract may contain a provision providing for attorney fees in enforcing the contract. Where a contract contains such a provision, the court must fix reasonable attorney fees as an element of the costs of the lawsuit. (Civ. Code, §1717, subd. (a); §1033.5, subd. (a)(10)(A).) In this instance, the written guarantees signed by the defendants provided for "reasonable attorneys' fees," including "attorneys' fees and related costs of enforcement of" a judgment. . . .

There does not appear to be any dispute concerning Grayl's right to timely seek reasonable attorney fees as costs in efforts to enforce its judgment. That having been said, any motion for such costs must be timely made. To be timely, the motion must be made *before* the underlying judgment has been fully satisfied and within two years of the fees being incurred. (§685.080, subd. (a); Lucky United Properties Investment, Inc. v. Lee (2010) 185 Cal. App. 4th 125, 141, 110 Cal. Rptr. 3d 159; Carnes v. Zamani (9th Cir. 2007) 488 F.3d 1057, 1060; cf. §685.070, subd. (b) [memorandum of costs].) "[T]he statutory purpose of requiring that the motion for enforcement costs be brought 'before the judgment is satisfied in full' (§685.080, subd. (a)) is to avoid a situation where a judgment debtor has paid off the entirety of what he believes to be his obligation in the entire case, only to be confronted later with a motion for yet more fees. [Citation.]" (Lucky United Properties Investment, Inc. v. Lee, *supra,* 185 Cal. App. 4th at p. 144, 110 Cal. Rptr. 3d 159.) That is the present situation. . . .

"'Performance of an obligation for the delivery of money only, is called payment.' [Citation.] Payment to a judgment creditor is governed by the cases and statutes which govern commercial transactions. [Citation.]" (Long v. Cuttle Construction Co., *supra,* 60 Cal. App. 4th at p. 837, 70 Cal. Rptr. 2d 698.) In the present case, that means California Uniform Commercial Code section 3310. "Unless otherwise agreed, if a certified check, cashier's check, or teller's check is taken for an obligation, the obligation is discharged to the same extent discharge would result if an amount of money equal to the amount of the instrument were taken in payment of the obligation." (Cal. U. Com. Code, §3310, subd. (a).) . . .

The rule we announce today does no disservice to judgment creditors who have incurred postjudgment costs they wish to add to the judgment. Like Grayl, if they have not yet filed a motion for postjudgment costs at the time the judgment debtor tenders a cashier's check in full payment of the outstanding judgment, they are free to reject the payment and to file a motion for postjudgment costs. In fact, for purposes of filing a timely motion for postjudgment costs, postjudgment creditors who are provided a cashier's check may be in a better situation than those who are paid in cash. A judgment creditor must accept cash, but may reject a cashier's check and instead file a motion for postjudgment costs, including attorney fees.

This is not to say Grayl's argument is not without sympathetic appeal. If Grayl is to be believed, Elieff's slippery efforts to evade paying the judgment against him required Grayl to follow a tortuous paper (or rather, electronic) trail—with discovery battles in foreign jurisdictions—to prove the liens on Elieff's properties were fraudulent and put in place by a company run by a close associate of Elieff's based on phony loans. That being said, Grayl could have made a motion or motions for postjudgment costs, including attorney fees, prior to defendants fully satisfying the judgment nearly two years after entry of the judgment. And as stated earlier, Grayl could have refused the cashier's check and prepared its motion for postjudgment costs. Having accepted the cashier's check, the judgment against defendants was fully satisfied to the same extent it would have been had Grayl been paid in cash.

Contrary to Grayl's contention, the trial court did not "allow[] Elieff to escape his obligation to pay for" postjudgment costs, including attorney fees. The court applied the plain language of the applicable statutes. If Elieff escaped, it is not because the trial court "allowed" it, but rather because Grayl did not file its motion *before* the outstanding judgment was fully satisfied, as required by law. (§§685.070, subd. (b), 685.080, subd. (a).) Accordingly, we find defendants fully satisfied the judgment on June 8,

2012, when defendants delivered and Grayl accepted a cashier's check in an amount sufficient to cover the judgment plus accumulated interest. Grayl's motion for postjudgment costs was untimely when made 12 days later. . . .

III. Disposition

The orders of the trial court are affirmed. In the interests of justice, the parties shall each bear their own costs on appeal.

PROBLEM 140

When Aunt Fran (from the last Problem) told Simon that she was not liable for the rent as long as the note was outstanding, he got it back from the bank and tore it up. May he now sue her for the rent even though the note has not yet matured? See §§3-604, 3-310(b)(4), 3-309; Peterson v. Crown Fin. Corp., 661 F.2d 287 (3d Cir. 1981) (creditor's subjective intent irrelevant). See also Annot., 59 A.L.R.4th 617. If the cancellation had been a clerical error, what result? See Gloor v. BancorpSouth Bank, 925 So. 2d 984 (Ala. App. 2005).

Ward v. Federal Kemper Insurance Co.

Maryland Court of Appeals, 1985
62 Md. App. 351, 489 A.2d 91

Adkins, J.

The issue posed to us by appellant, Aaron Ward, is whether appellee, Federal Kemper Insurance Company, properly cancelled an insurance policy for nonpayment of a premium. The question is whether Ward owed the premium at the time of cancellation. The answer to this seemingly simple question is complicated by a problem in the law of negotiable instruments: in whose hands are the funds represented by a check that the drawer (Federal Kemper) has mailed to the payee (Ward) but that is never paid by the drawee bank because never negotiated by the payee? The facts are undisputed.

On May 19, 1981, Federal Kemper issued an automobile liability policy to Ward and his then wife (hereinafter "Ward"). Ward paid the premium in full. By its terms, the policy was to expire on November 17, 1981. On August 4, because of a change of vehicles owned by Ward, Federal Kemper sent him a check (payable to him) in the amount of $12.00, and drawn on The Citizens National Bank of Decatur, Illinois. This represented a refund of overpaid premium. Ward received the check but never negotiated it.

Soon after sending the check, Federal Kemper discovered that the proper refund should have been $4.50, rather than $12.00. On August 18, it billed Ward the difference of $7.50. Ward did not recall receiving the bill. In any event Ward never paid the $7.50, and pursuant to provisions of the policy, Federal Kemper mailed Ward a notice of cancellation effective October 11. On November 15 Ward was involved in an accident while driving the insured vehicle. The accident resulted in personal injury and property damage to him, his vehicle, and to the persons and properties of others involved in the accident. Federal Kemper declined to provide coverage.

Ward sued the insurance company in the Circuit Court for Baltimore City, seeking a declaratory judgment as to coverage. There were cross-motions for summary judgment. Because he believed that summary judgment is inappropriate in a declaratory judgment action, the hearing judge treated the proceedings as a hearing on the merits. No one objected. The judge concluded that "at the time the bill was sent . . . in the amount of $7.50, that amount was not due Kemper." He thought that "until the negotiable instrument is negotiated and paid by the drawee back [bank] Kemper has suffered no debit." Nevertheless, he went on to opine:

> I . . . conclude that Kemper proceeded properly on an assumption that its bill was being ignored in moving for cancellation. As a matter of fact, the negotiable instrument which it had issued to Mr. Ward was still outstanding and perfectly valid on its face for a period of six months by its very terms. It is not required under the statutory provisions dealing with cancellation to wait for the expiration of the six month period of the draft before seeking its set off amount due. I conclude from the stipulated facts that cancellation was proper on October 11, 1981. That being so, there was no insurance coverage . . . by Kemper . . . at the time of the accident on November 15. . . .

He granted judgment in favor of Federal Kemper.

In this court Ward contends that unless a premium is actually due and unpaid, an insurer may not cancel a policy for its nonpayment, citing Art. 48, §234A(a) to the effect that "[n]o insurer . . . shall cancel . . . a particular insurance risk . . . for any arbitrary, capricious, or unfairly discriminatory reason." Whatever the precise reach of §234A(a), Lumbermen's Mutual Casualty Co. v. Insurance Commissioner, ___ Md. ___, ___ A.2d ___, ___, No. 161, September Term, 1982 (filed February 11, 1985), we agree that an insurer may not cancel a policy for nonpayment of premium unless the premium is in fact due. See Government Employees Co. v. Insurance Commissioner, 273 Md. 467, 483, 330 A.2d 653 (1975). To put this self-evident point more directly:

> Where the propriety of the cancellation of a policy depends upon the nonpayment of a premium it necessarily follows that there is no effective cancellation when in fact the premium has been paid. For if a premium has been paid, the insurer cannot cancel for nonpayment of such premium [citations omitted].

M. Rhodes, Couch Cyclopedia of Insurance Law §67.74 (rev. 2d ed. 1983).

Federal Kemper does not dispute these propositions. The parties agree that the real issue is who had the $7.50 premium due balance that was included in the unnegotiated $12.00 check. If this money was Ward's by virtue of his possession of the check and his ability to negotiate it, then Ward owed Federal Kemper the $7.50 and the cancellation was proper. If, on the other hand, the $7.50 was still under Federal Kemper's control, because the check has not been negotiated when the policy was cancelled, the cancellation was improper. To resolve this question we must turn to the Uniform Commercial Code rather than to Art. 48A.

Ward points to §3-409(1) of the Commercial Law Article (§3-409(1) of the UCC [§3-408 in the Revision—Eds.]) which provides that:

> A check or draft does not of itself operate as an assignment of any funds in the hands of the drawee available for its payment, and the drawee is not liable on the instrument until he accepts it.

Because of this rule, he argues, his mere possession of the $12.00 check did not have the effect of transferring the $12.00 to him. Federal Kemper could have stopped payment or, for that matter, closed its account at the drawee bank prior to presentment of the check. In either of these events, he would have had nothing more than a claim against Federal Kemper for the $4.50 in fact due him; the $7.50 overpayment would at all times have remained under the insurer's control, as it in fact did. He cites Malloy v. Smith, 265 Md. 460, 290 A.2d 486 (1972), in which the Court of Appeals, by way of dictum, observed that a personal check cannot be the subject of a gift causa mortis. Referring to §3-409(1), the court explained:

> The point is, of course, that when the donor uses his own check to make the gift, there is no assignment of funds because he does not relinquish control of the sum which the check represents. A consequence of this is that a valid delivery alone will not complete the gift. To perfect the gift the check must be presented by the donee and accepted by the drawee, because the donor could stop payment, withdraw from his account the very funds which the check represents, or die before payment is made, any one of which would revoke the gift. 265 Md. at 463.

Federal Kemper counters that by virtue of §3-413 [§3-414 in the Revision—Eds.] the drawer of a check "engages that he will pay the instrument according to its tenor . . ." and further "engages that upon dishonor [as through a stop payment order] and any necessary notice of dishonor or protest he will pay the amount of the draft to the holder. . . ." According to Federal Kemper, a stop payment order may be effective to prevent payment of a check by the drawee, but that does not affect the drawer's liability to a holder in due course. Section 3-305. Had Ward negotiated the $12.00 to a holder in due course, thereby receiving value for it, Federal Kemper would have been liable to the holder in due course despite any stop payment order. First National Bank of Trinity, Texas v. McKay, 521 S.W.2d 661 (Tex. Civ. App. 1975). When Federal Kemper billed Ward for the $7.50 and when it issued the cancellation notice, it had no way of knowing whether a holder in due course had entered the picture. Thus, the argument continues, by issuing the check to Ward, Federal Kemper obligated itself to pay $12.00. And since the obligation was $7.50 more than its actual premium refund debt to Ward, Ward was obligated to pay Federal Kemper the difference. Therefore, Ward owed Federal Kemper a premium of $7.50, a sum that has never been paid.

We think Federal Kemper misapprehends the nature of a check and the relationships of the parties to it. A check is a draft or bill of exchange—an order by a drawer (Federal Kemper) to a drawee (Citizens National Bank of Decatur) to pay money to a payee (Ward). Section 3-104. B. Clark, The Law of Bank Deposits, Collections and Credit Cards Par 1.1[1] (rev. ed. 1981) (hereinafter "Clark"). As between drawer and drawee, the relationship is one of creditor and debtor. The drawer does not "own" the funds it has on deposit with the drawee. Its balance on the drawee's books represents a debt owed the drawer by the drawee. The funds are "owned" by the drawee. Id. par 2.1.

When the drawer draws a check on the drawee and delivers the check to the payee, the check ordinarily is regarded as only a conditional payment of the underlying obligation. Merriman v. Sandeen, 267 N.W.2d 714, 717 (Minn. 1978). H. Bailey, Brady on Bank Checks §1.8, 4.5 (5th ed. 1979 & 1984 Cum. Supp.) (hereinafter "Bailey"). See also Moore v. Travelers Indemnity Ins. Co., 408 A.2d 298 (Del. Super. 1979). The conditions are that the check be presented and honored. Until those conditions are met, no one is directly liable on the check itself; Clark, par 1.3. The underlying obligation represented by the check is similarly suspended until those conditions are met; §3-802(1)(b).[1] If they are not met (if, for example, the check is dishonored), an "action may be maintained either on the [check] or the obligation. . . ." Id.

The point is that the drawer is only secondarily liable on the check when he issues it. Stewart v. Citizens and Southern Natl. Bank, 225 S.E.2d 761 (Ga. App. 1976); Clark, par 1.3; §§3-122(3) and 3-413(2). As Ward correctly asserts, the delivery of Federal Kemper's check did not operate as an assignment to him of any funds in the hands of the drawee; §3-409(1). Clark, par 3.1[1]. Ward, when he received the check acquired no proprietary interest in the fund on deposit. Bailey §4.1.

1. [Now §3-310(b)(1)—Eds.]

The $12.00 check involved in this case was, of course, never dishonored. Thus, Federal Kemper never became liable directly on the check, nor was its underlying obligation (to refund $4.50 to Ward) ever actually discharged. The check was never presented to the drawee and, therefore, never paid, so the funds it represented were never transferred to Ward. In point of fact, those funds remained (and so far as we know, still remain) in the Citizens National Bank of Decatur, subject to Federal Kemper's control. Under these circumstances, we do not think that Ward owed any premium to Federal Kemper. See Owl Electric Co. v. United States Fidelity and Guaranty Co., 268 N.E. 493 (Ill. App. 1971). See also Klein v. Tabatchnik, 459 F. Supp. 707, 715-716 (S.D.N.Y. 1978), *aff'd* (as to relevant issue), 610 F.2d 1043, 1049 (2d Cir. 1979) and In re Sportsco, 12 B.R. 34 (Bkr. Ct., D. Ariz. 1981).

It is perfectly true that when Federal Kemper billed Ward, and when it sent the cancellation notice, there might have been a holder in due course lurking in the wings. That is a business risk Federal Kemper took when it proceeded as it did. The policies underlying the protections given a holder in due course, Lawrence & Minan, The Effect of Abrogating the Holder in Due Course Doctrine on the Commercialization of Innovative Consumer Products, 64 B.U. L. Rev. 325, 327-330 (1984), do not affect the underlying relationships between Ward and Federal Kemper, especially when, as here, there was no holder in due course. When Federal Kemper attempted to cancel the policy the entire premium was in its bank account; Ward owed it nothing at that time.

Accordingly, we hold that the Circuit Court for Baltimore City correctly concluded that "at the date the [premium due] bill was sent in the amount of $7.50 on August 18, 1981, it was not due." That being so, Federal Kemper could not lawfully have cancelled Ward's policy for nonpayment of that premium. Ward is entitled to a declaratory judgment to the effect that his Federal Kemper policy was in full force and effect when the accident occurred. See Jennings v. Government Employees Ins. Co., __ Md.__, __ A.2d __, No. 27, Sept. Term, 1983 (filed February 22, 1985).

Judgment reversed.

Case remanded for entry of declaratory judgment consistent with this opinion. Appellee to pay the costs.

Payment in Full Checks. One issue that's often litigated concerns a "payment in full check" sent by one party to a dispute to the other with the offer of settlement. If the other party to the dispute, the payee, cashes the check, is the dispute over? Your course in Contracts probably covered this issue in the chapter on offer and acceptance, but here is a brief précis of the rules. The underlying policy at work reflects the legal adage that "the law favors a compromise."

The common law provided that an offer of settlement was called "accord" and the other side's agreement to settle the dispute by taking the accord was a "satisfaction." If the accord is a check, the law is now governed by §3-311, which you should read. Use it to resolve the issues in the next Problem.

PROBLEM 141

Cassandra Troy was annoyed when she saw the sloppy work that Apollo Construction Company had done when it finished building her new front porch, so she subtracted $1,000 from the amount still due on the contract and sent a check clearly marked "Payment In Full" both on the front of the check and on the back where Apollo would have to indorse it, along with a cover letter expressing her disappointment at the work and explaining this was her offer to settle the dispute. Godfrey Apollo, president of the company, was outraged when he saw the check, believing that construction of the porch was first rate.

(a) If he cashes the check, is the dispute over? What if he crosses off the language about "payment in full" and writes "cashed under protest, all rights reserved"? See §1-308 and its Official Comment 3; Glassman Corp. v. Champion Bldrs., L.L.C., 83 2014 WL 2226920 (Kan. App. 2014).

(b) If Apollo can prove that Cassandra Troy is lying and had told neighbors she was delighted with the work, will cashing the check work an accord and satisfaction? See §3-311(a) and its Official Comment 4; Piney Ridge Properties, LLC v. Ellington-Snipes, 2017 IL App. 3d 160764-U, 2017 WL 5191885 (2017).

(c) If Apollo's bookkeeper cashes the check and then Apollo learns that it contained "payment in full" language, can he do anything to avoid the accord and satisfaction? See §3-311(c)(2).

(d) If you are the attorney for Apollo Construction Company and Godfrey calls you for advice as to what he should do with the check, what should you tell him?

One of your authors has a blog post entitled "The Payment-In-Full Check: A Powerful Legal Maneuver," covering these issues in more detail; if you are interested, see http://douglaswhaley.blogspot.com/2011/04/payment-in-full-check-powerful-legal.html.

II. LIABILITY ON THE INSTRUMENT

As soon as someone places a signature on a negotiable instrument, an *implied contractual obligation* is automatically made promising to pay the instrument when it matures (unless in the meantime a defense, real or personal, develops). The original version of Article 3 actually called these obligations "contracts," but the name was misleading because the legal responsibility imposed thereby did not depend on the intention of the relevant party. The so-called *contract* was imposed as a matter of law whether or not the contracting party understood the fact or extent of liability.

In the current language of Article 3 these promises are called *obligations* and not *contracts*, but the basic idea is the same. Putting one's signature on a negotiable instrument in anything other than an innocuous capacity ("witness," for example) leads to a promise *implied in law* (actual intent being irrelevant) to pay the instrument under certain circumstances. This obligation is sometimes described as liability *on the instrument*—that is, as a result of signing the instrument, and the person who could enforce that liability was the current holder of the instrument.

Before the nature of this liability in contract is explored further, let us emphasize the basic rule found in §3-401(a): "A person is not liable on an instrument unless (i) the person signed the instrument. . . ." This means that no contractual liability arises on a negotiable instrument until and unless a signature is placed thereon. What is a signature? Read the definition of *signed* in §1-201(b)(37) and the description of signatures in §3-401(b). If you now review Problems 96 and 97, you should have this concept well under control.[2]

A. *The Maker's Obligation*

The maker of a promissory note is absolutely liable on the instrument; a maker's liability has no technical implied conditions to it. The same thing is true of a bank that issues a cashier's check. This "primary" liability is codified in §3-412 (where both the maker of a promissory note and the bank issuing a cashier's check are lumped together as *issuers*).[3] If there is more than one maker, those who sign are presumed to be jointly and severally liable to the rest of the world (meaning that they can be sued individually or as a group), but they have a right to contribution from their co-makers if they are forced to pay more than their share.

2. If a forger places your name on a check, does the forgery operate as your signature? The answer is found in §3-403(a), which states that an unauthorized signature is "ineffective" as that of the person whose name is signed, but it does operate as if the forger had signed his or her real name. We will come back to this issue in the section on forgery.

3. Section 3-105(c): "Issuer" means a maker or drawer of an instrument.

PROBLEM 142

Winkin, Blinkin, and Nod signed the following promissory note:

> Oct. 1, 2022 $3,000
>
> On or after six months from date, we promise to pay to the order of *Grimms National Bank, the sum of three thousand dollars ($3,000).* We, along with all sureties and subsequent indorsers, waive all rights to presentment, notice of dishonor, and protest, and all parties hereto agree to any extension of time granted by the holder to the makers.
>
> *Wilber Winkin*
> *Barney Blinkin*
> *Harry Nod*

Grimms National Bank indorsed the note in blank and discounted it to Andersen Finance Co. When the note matured, Andersen sued only Winkin, demanding the entire amount. May he defend on the basis that Andersen should have sued all three of them, since the note contains the words "we promise to pay"? If Andersen wins, can Winkin sue Blinkin for $2,000? $1,000? See §3-116; Ghitter v. Edge, 118 Ga. App. 750, 165 S.E.2d 598 (1968).

PROBLEM 143

In an actual case, the Tips Family Trust signed a promissory note in favor of Patriot Bank secured by a mortgage on real property the family owned. The note, the security agreement, and the guaranty agreement all described the principal amount of the loan as follows:

> ONE MILLION SEVEN THOUSAND AND NO/100 ($1,700,000.00) DOLLARS

This language appears five times in the three documents, in exactly the same form each time, and no other language in the documents describes the amount of the loan. Before the note matured, the trust made payments totaling $595,586, and then defaulted and the bank sold the property for $874,125. The bank then sued the trust for the deficiency, and the trust countered with the argument that the bank had been overpaid and must remit the excess to the trust. How should this come out? Read §3-114; see Charles R. Tips Family Trust v. PB Commercial LLC, 459 S.W.3d 147 (Tex. Ct. App. 2015).

B. *The Indorser's Obligation*

Once the payee signs the back of the instrument, the payee automatically incurs the obligation the law imposes on an *indorser.* In fact, per §3-204(a), *anyone who* signs an instrument in an ambiguous capacity is conclusively presumed to assume this liability. This obligation is described in §3-415, which you should read carefully. Note that unlike the obligation of a maker, the indorser's obligation is *secondary,* in that there are certain technical conditions that must be met before the indorser can be sued on the §3-415 obligation: the instrument must have first been *presented* to the maker (if it is a note) or to the drawee (if it is a draft), there must have been a *dishonor* (by the maker or drawee), and in certain circumstances §3-503 requires that the indorser be given *notice of dishonor.*

These three rights (presentment, dishonor, and notice of dishonor) are discussed ad nauseam in the 3-500 sections of the Code. It is unfortunate, but unavoidable, that we must explore these sections at some time, but let's postpone that until after we've established the drawer's liability on a draft. For now it is sufficient if you remember that an indorser is not liable until the person primarily liable has dishonored the instrument and the indorser has been so notified. Section 3-415 settles other problems, too, as illustrated by the following Problems.

PROBLEM 144

Billy Bigelow wrote out a check payable to the order of Enoch Snow to pay for some carnival equipment. Snow cashed the check at Bascombe Check Cashing Store, indorsing his name on the back. Bascombe Store then indorsed the check and deposited it in its account at Jordan State Bank. This bank also indorsed the check and then presented it to the drawee bank, Rodgers National Bank, which dishonored it because Bigelow had no money in his account, marking it "NSF" ("Not Sufficient Funds"). The check was returned to Jordan State Bank. You are the bank's attorney, and it calls you with three questions:

(1) Bascombe Check Cashing Store, has suddenly gone out of business and there is no money in its account. Can Jordan State Bank sue Enoch Snow and, if so, on what theory? Read §3-415(a) carefully.

(2) If Jordan State Bank sues Snow, may he raise his defenses (say, that Bascombe Check Cashing Store, had failed to pay him any money when he indorsed it over to them), or is the indorser liability found in §3-415 strict liability?

(3) If the bank does recover from Snow, will he have to pay the whole amount or do the indorsers divide up the indorsement liability and share it proportionately? Cf. §§3-116, 3-205(d).

PROBLEM 145

Charlie Brown wanted to borrow $10,000 from the Peanuts National Bank, but the bank told him that it would not loan him the money unless his note was indorsed by four responsible people. Charlie explained his problem to his friend Lucy, and she signed her name to the back of the instrument. Charlie then took the note to another friend, Schroeder, who not only signed, but also persuaded his friend Pig Pen to add his name below Schroeder's. Finally, Charlie Brown had Peppermint Patty sign her name, at which point he took the note back to the bank, and it loaned him the money. When the note came due, the bank made a presentment of it to Charlie Brown and demanded payment. He had used the money in a business venture that, predictably enough, was a moral but not a financial success, and so he was unable to pay the note (a dishonor). The Peanuts National Bank gave notice of dishonor to all four indorsers, but demanded payment of Peppermint Patty alone. She resisted, claiming she was liable at most for only one-fourth of the amount ($2,500). Look at §3-415 and decide:

(a) Is she right?

(b) If she pays $10,000, can she sue Pig Pen for the entire amount or only for part? Once again look at §§3-116, 3-205(d).

(c) If she is sued, can she bring the other indorsers into the lawsuit? See §3-119 (explaining the so-called vouching in notice).

(d) If Charlie Brown comes back into the chips, can she sue him? On what theory?

Co-Suretyship vs. Sub-Suretyship. The common law presumed, unless the sureties agreed otherwise, that those signing later in time could get complete reimbursement from those signing prior in time, and this was called the presumption of *sub-suretyship.* If the sureties have agreed, expressly or impliedly, to share the liability, then they are *co-sureties* and have a right of partial contribution from each other. Where the parties have made what §3-205(d) calls an *anomalous* indorsement (one made by a non-holder—i.e., a surety), §3-116 changes the common law and now presumes that the parties are co-sureties, and hence must share the liability among themselves proportionately. See Official Comment 5 to §3-415.

Indorsers and Sureties. Whether the indorser intends it or not, the imposition of a §3-415 obligation makes the indorser an unintentional surety for the parties who have signed the instrument prior to the indorser, and the Code generally gives indorsers all the rights it gives to voluntary sureties, whom it calls *accommodation parties.*

Qualified Indorsements. How can the indorser avoid incurring the §3-415 obligation? The answer is by writing the words "without recourse" next to his or her name, preferably above it. In this manner the indorsement (technically called a *qualified* indorsement) operates to negotiate the instrument, but does not create any contractual liability. See §3-415(b).

PROBLEM 146

Marian Melody, a professional pianist, bought a piano from the Ivory Keys Music Company, signing a promissory note payable to the company for $3,000. The day after the piano was delivered, the music company discounted the note to the Friendly Loan Company for $2,700, indorsing it on the back, "Pay to the Friendly Loan Company, *Ivory Keys Music Company (Without Recourse)*." The piano fell apart, and Melody refused to pay the note when it came due. Friendly Finance sued both Melody and the Ivory Keys Music Company. What is its cause of action against each? What defenses can each defendant raise?

Practical Note. When a lawsuit is settled, the losing side will frequently send the victorious attorney a check on which the attorney and the attorney's client are joint payees. This is done to protect the attorney's lien and to help the attorney get payment from the client. When the attorney indorses such a check, the indorsement should be "without recourse." This makes it clear that the indorsement is made only to negotiate the check and that the attorney assumes no §3-415 obligation. There is no reason why the attorney (or the client for that matter) should make an unqualified indorsement and become, in effect, a surety for the drawer of the check, already known to be a loser.

C. *The Surety's Obligation*

This section must of necessity be a long one, not because the concepts herein are particularly complex, but because there is a great deal of suretyship law that one must gulp down and digest before the Code's suretyship provisions look friendlier.[4] In a negotiable instruments setting, suretyship problems come up whenever, as in the Charlie Brown Problem above, the maker must get others to "lend their names" to the maker's basic obligation. Suretyship matters can arise even in connection with checks. If you are the payee on a check drawn on Bank *A*, just see how easy it is to cash the check

4. The following brief outline of some of the basic rules of the suretyship can and should be supplemented by the two leading treatises: Stearns, Suretyship (4th ed. 1951), and Simpson, Suretyship (1950). See also the Restatement (Third) of Suretyship and Guaranty.

at Bank *B* if you do not have an account there. Bank *B* will probably not take the check unless one of its customer-depositors is willing to sign (become a surety) along with you.

It is an awesome thing to become surety for someone else, but people nonetheless do it, often with very little thought about the consequences, thus becoming the so-called fool with a pen (the Bible has a similar thought: "A man void of understanding . . . becometh surety in the presence of his friend"—Proverbs 17:18). In the desire to help out a friend or relative who is temporarily financially embarrassed (and who often assures the prospective surety "I guarantee you that you really won't have to pay"), the surety co-signs and, like it or not, understand it or not, takes on liability for the debt. To alert potential sureties to the nature of their undertaking, both the Federal Trade Commission and the Federal Reserve Board have issued regulations requiring consumer debts to carry a notice to co-signers (defined for these purposes as natural persons who are uncompensated) in the following manner:

> *Notice to Co-Signer*
>
> You are being asked to guarantee this debt. Think carefully before you do. If the borrower doesn't pay the debt, you will have to. Be sure you can afford to pay if you have to, and that you want to accept this responsibility.
>
> You may have to pay up to the full amount of the debt if the borrower does not pay. You may also have to pay late fees or collection costs, which increase this amount. The creditor can collect this debt from you without first trying to collect from the borrower.
>
> The creditor can use the same collection methods against you that can be used against the borrower, such as suing you, garnishing your wages, etc. If this debt is ever in default, that fact may become a part of your credit record.
>
> This notice is not the contract that makes you liable for the debt.

See F.T.C. Trade Regulation Rule Concerning Credit Practices, 16 C.F.R. part 444.3, effective March 1, 1985, and F.R.B. Reg. AA, 12 C.F.R. part 227, effective January 1, 1986.

In any true surety setting, there are three basic contracts involved. The first contract is the underlying obligation between the principal and the creditor. The second contract is the promise of the surety to back up the underlying obligation and see that the creditor loses nothing as a result of accepting the principal's promise on the first contract. The third contract is the promise of the principal to *reimburse* the surety if the surety is forced to pay off on the surety's promise to the creditor.[5] The contract of reimbursement is frequently implied, as where a sister co-signs for her brother and

5. This contract of reimbursement is one of the theories for Peppermint Patty's suit against Charlie Brown in Problem 145.

expects to lose no money from the transaction; when a professional surety's liability is obtained, the contract of reimbursement will be spelled out in a multi-page, fine-print document.

PROBLEM 147

Frank Family wanted to move out of his apartment and into his dream house. He hired Quickie Contractor to build the house on land Family had purchased, requiring Quickie to get a performance and payment bond guaranteeing that Quickie would do the work and pay its laborers and suppliers. Quickie got Probacker, Inc. to issue the bond guaranteeing these matters. Quickie went bankrupt halfway through the job, and Family called on ProBacker to finish the work. Which of these parties is the surety? Which the principal? Which the creditor? Identify the three contracts.

Sureties have several remedial rights in addition to the right of reimbursement. These include the rights of exoneration, subrogation, and contribution and the principle of *strictissimi juris*.

1. Exoneration

This is an equitable right by which the surety, at maturity, can compel the principal to perform instead of the surety. That is, by a bill in equity, the surety can prevent the need for a later suit for reimbursement. The basis for this right is said to be the implied duty that every principal owes to the surety to perform at the earliest moment and exonerate the surety from liability.

2. Subrogation

If the surety is forced to pay off the creditor, the surety is subrogated to whatever rights the creditor had. Put another way, the surety steps into the shoes of the creditor and is said to take an "equitable assignment" of the creditor's rights. This may be important if the creditor possesses rights the surety can take advantage of—for instance, a lien, a security interest in collateral, a priority in bankruptcy, a power to confess judgment, etc. In effect, by paying off on the second contract, the surety's right of subrogation permits the surety to become a party to the first contract and enforce it *as if the surety were the creditor.*

3. Contribution

This is a right of partial reimbursement that co-sureties have against each other for proportionate shares of the debt. If *X*, *Y*, and *Z* each sign *M*'s note for $9,000 agreeing to be co-sureties, the payee may enforce the entire obligation against any one of the three, and the right of contribution will then permit that one to sue the other two for their shares.

4. *Strictissimi Juris*

The following is a discussion of the common law rules only; as we shall see, the revision of Article 3 has drastically changed the rules.

A surety, particularly an uncompensated surety, is a *favorite of the law*, so that at common law the surety's obligation is to be construed *strictissimi juris* (of the *strictest law*), and thus the surety prevails if possible. Since the surety has agreed to back up only the first contract, the courts have held that an agreement between the creditor and the principal that changes that contract *in any detail* operates to discharge and release the non-consenting surety from further liability. Restatement of Security 128 (1941). Why? Because the modification of the first contract converts it into a new contract to which the surety did not consent. The courts even go so far as to say that a surety is discharged by a modification of the first contract that *benefits* the surety by lessening the principal's obligation. See Merchants Natl. Bank v. Blass, 282 Ark. 497, 669 S.W.2d 195 (1984) (new note given by maker containing a higher interest rate discharged surety on original note); First Natl. City Bank v. Carbonaro 1971 WL 17894 (N.Y. Civ. Ct. 1971) (surety who agreed to back loan of $4,176 discharged when promissory note filled in with only $1,656 as the amount).

Moreover, if the creditor agreed by a binding commitment to excuse the principal from liability or to give the principal extra time to pay the first contract, the Restatement (Third) of Suretyship and Guaranty would hold that a non-consenting surety is discharged unless the creditor warns the principal that this agreement works a "preservation of recourse" by the surety against the principal, meaning that the agreement in no way affects the rights of the surety against the principal.

There are theoretical reasons for these rules. By extending the time without the surety's consent, the creditor is thought to prejudice the surety's right of subrogation, but if the creditor expressly states that the surety's right of recourse is unimpaired, supposedly no prejudice occurs to the subrogation rights because the principal debtor is then alerted to the fact that the creditor's promise is conditional on the surety's rights (including subrogation) being preserved intact. The surety who dislikes this modified agreement can ignore it and exercise the usual rights, including exoneration, reimbursement, and even subrogation to the creditor's premodification position. For our purposes it is easier to memorize this black letter rule:

> If the creditor releases the principal debtor from liability on the first contract or gives the debtor a binding extension of time in which to pay, the

> surety is discharged *unless* (1) the surety consents, or (2) the creditor informs the principal of the preservation of the surety's rights against the principal.

Notice that the non-consenting surety is discharged only by a *binding* extension of time. There is all the (legal) difference in the world between the following two hypotheticals:

> (1) The note comes due, and the principal does not pay it; the creditor waits a month before suing.
> (2) The note comes due, and the creditor and principal *agree* to wait a month to enforce it, with the principal agreeing to pay an extra month's worth of interest.

In the first hypothetical the surety is not discharged even if thereby an extra month's worth of interest is added to the obligation.[6] The creditor and the principal have not *agreed* to change the original contract, and surely the surety cannot object if the creditor does not declare an immediate forfeiture. But in the second hypothetical, the surety is discharged by the new agreement unless the surety consents or the creditor adds to the agreement the *preservation of secondary obligator's recourse clause.* The Restatement (Third) of Suretyship and Guaranty, which calls the creditor the "obligee," the principal the "principal obligor," and the surety the "secondary obligor," puts it this way:

> *§129. Preservation of Secondary Obligor's Recourse.*
>
> (1) When an obligee releases the principal obligor from, or agrees to extend the time for performance of, a duty to pay money pursuant to the underlying obligation, the release or extension effect a "preservation of the secondary obligor's recourse" with respect to that duty if the express terms of the release or extension provide that:
>
> (a) the obligee retains the right to seek performance of the secondary obligation by the secondary obligor; and
>
> (b) the rights of the secondary obligor to recourse against the principal obligor (§§21-31) continue as though the release or extension had not been granted.
>
> (2) When the obligee effects a preservation of the secondary obligor's recourse in conjunction with a release or extension, the principal obligor's duties of performance and reimbursement and the secondary obligor's rights of restitution and subrogation continue as though the release or extension did not occur.

6. However, if the surety is also an indorser, a delay in presentment (discussed later in the book) may result in a discharge under §3-415(e).

There are other important rules of suretyship (for instance, a surety's promise—the second contract—must be in writing to be enforceable under the Statute of Frauds), but these rules play little part in negotiable instruments law. Section 3-419(b), for instance, completely does away with the Statute of Frauds defense as far as negotiable instruments are concerned. Instead, our study will focus on how the above rules have been varied in the law of negotiable instruments.

5. The Accommodation Party

The Uniform Commercial Code in §3-419 reserves special suretyship rights for those who deliberately lend their names to an instrument to accommodate another. These sections spell out the obligation incurred by the Code's sureties. Section 3-419 applies to an *accommodation party*, defined in subsection (a) as a party who "signs the instrument for the purpose of incurring liability on the instrument without being a direct beneficiary of the value given for the instrument." Read Official Comment 1 to §3-419. Subsection (b) informs us that the accommodation party may sign in any capacity (as maker, drawer, acceptor, or indorser), but is "obligated to pay the instrument in the capacity in which the accommodation party signs." This means that the surety (accommodation party) has the same liability as a maker if the surety signs as a maker, but the surety signing as an indorser is liable only in that capacity (and has the rights of an indorser: presentment, notice of dishonor, etc.); in addition, of course, the surety gets both statutory and common law suretyship rights.

PROBLEM 148

Consider the following promissory note:

FRONT: December 23, 2022

I, *Mary Maker*, promise to pay *$4,000* to the order of *Paul Payee* on December 25, 2022, with interest at 8 percent per annum from date.

/s/ George Generous
/s/ Mary Maker

BACK:

Pay to *Ace Finance /s/ Paul Payee*

Ace Finance comes to you early in 2023 and tells you that the note is in default, but that it failed to give notice of dishonor—a right that indorsers have but makers do not—to George Generous.

(a) May George Generous establish his status as surety against a holder in due course? See §3-419(c) with its Official Comment 3, §§3-205(d), 3-605(h).

(b) May George defend on the basis that he received no consideration for his undertaking? See §3-419(b) and its Official Comment 2.

(c) Is George an accommodation maker or an accommodation indorser? See §§3-116(a), 3-204(a); cf. Philadelphia Bond & Mortgage Co. v. Highland Crest Homes, Inc., 221 Pa. Super. 89, 288 A.2d 916 (1972) ("Thus by long established practice judicially noted or otherwise established, a signature in the lower right hand corner of an instrument indicates an intent to sign as the maker of a note or the drawer of a draft.").

It should be emphasized that Article 3's rules apply only to accommodation parties who *sign the instrument*. If the accommodation party signs a *separate* suretyship agreement but not the note itself, common law rules, not the Code, govern the result. See Official Comment 3, last paragraph, to §3-419; Uniwest Mortgage Co. v. Dadecor Condominiums, Inc., 877 F.2d 431 (5th Cir. 1989).

a. Guarantors. A *guarantor* is a surety who adds words of guaranty to his or her signature ("I hereby guarantee this instrument," for example), but words of guaranty add nothing to the suretyship obligation unless the surety has specifically guaranteed *collection* only, in which case the guarantor is given the extra protections described in §3-419(d), which you should now read.

PROBLEM 149

Suppose in the prior Problem George Generous had written the word *Guarantor* after his name. Would Ace Finance have had to sue Mary Maker first or not? See §3-419(d).

Floor v. Melvin

Illinois Appellate Court, 1972
5 Ill. App. 3d 463, 283 N.E.2d 303

ALLOY, J.

The action in the present case was instituted by Majorie Irene Floor in the Circuit Court of LaSalle County to recover money alleged to be due on a promissory note. On motion of defendant Mildred B. Melvin, executrix of the estate of Charles W. Melvin, deceased, an order was entered dismissing the claim for failure to state a cause of action. Claimant, Majorie Irene Floor, seeks reversal of the order on the theory that the deceased Charles W. Melvin was a guarantor of payment.

On April 14, 1959, Melco, Inc., an Illinois corporation, acting through its president, Charles W. Melvin, made and issued its negotiable promissory note in the principal amount of $12,000.00, payable to the order of Majorie Irene Floor. On the back of the note the following language appears: "For and in consideration of funds advanced herein to Melco, Inc., we irrevocably guarantee Majorie Irene Floor against loss by reason of nonpayment of this note." The signature of Charles W. Melvin, as well as others, appeared below such statement.

The complaint of plaintiff in this case does not allege prosecution of her claim to judgment as against the principal obligor on the note and it, also, does not allege the insolvency of the obligor, Melco, Inc. The only issue, therefore, before the court is whether, with respect to the undertaking on the back of the note, plaintiff is required to prosecute her claim against the maker of the note as a pre-condition to making a valid claim as against the estate of Charles W. Melvin.

[The court quoted §3-416, the precursor to §3-419(d).—EDS.] The quoted subsection in the portion marked as "(1)" codifies the rule of several Illinois cases including Beebe v. Kirkpatrick, 321 Ill. 612, 152 N.E. 539, and Weger v. Robinson Nash Motor Co., 340 Ill. 81, 172 N.E. 7. In the *Weger* case referred to, the guaranty contract that had been executed read (at page 85, 172 N.E. at page 9):

> We, the undersigned directors and stockholders of the Robinson Nash Motor Company, do hereby guarantee the *payment of notes* of said company given the Robinson State Bank of Robinson, Illinois, and hereby agree to be personally liable therefore and to all the conditions and requirements written in said notes . . . [emphasis ours].

The court in construing said language said, at page 90, 172 N.E. at page 11:

> A contract guaranteeing the payment of a note is an absolute contract, and by it the guarantor undertakes for a valuable consideration, to pay the debt at maturity if the principal debtor fails to do so, and upon it, if the debt is not paid at maturity, the guarantor may be sued at once. Guarantors must be regarded as original promisors, who bound themselves to pay the notes when they matured, and their duty was, on their maturity, to go to the holder and take them up, and their liability was not to depend upon the prosecution of suit against the maker.

In Beebe v. Kirkpatrick, 321 Ill. 612, 152 N.E. 539, the question was with respect to construction of the words "I hereby guarantee this loan." In support of its holding that the cited language was absolute in nature, the Supreme Court stated (at page 616, 152 N.E. at pages 540-541):

> In this state contracts of guaranty of negotiable instruments are of two kinds: Contracts guaranteeing the collection of the notes, and contracts guaranteeing the payment of the notes. A contract guaranteeing the collection

> of a note or debt is conditional in its character, and the guarantor thereby undertakes to pay the debt upon condition that the owner thereof shall make use of the ordinary legal means to collect it from the debtor with diligence but without avail. A contract guaranteeing the payment of a note or a debt is an absolute contract, and by it the guarantor undertakes, for a valuable consideration, to pay the debt at maturity if the principal debtor fails to do so, and upon it, if the debt is not paid at maturity, the guarantor may be sued at once.

Other cases, such as Dillman v. Nadelhoffer, 160 Ill. 121, 43 N.E. 378, treat the language of subsection (2) referring to "collection guaranteed." In the *Dillman* case the language before the court was "for a valuable consideration, we do hereby guarantee the collection of the within note at its maturity . . ." (at page 124, 43 N.E. at page 378). In construing this language, the Supreme Court stated that "the guaranty is not a guaranty of the payment of the note, but a guaranty of the collection of the note." The court stated (at page 125, 43 N.E. at page 379) that a contract guaranteeing the collection of a note or debt is conditional in its character and the guarantor thereby undertakes to pay the debt, "upon condition that the owner thereof shall make use of the ordinary legal means to collect it from the principal debtor with diligence, and without avail."

In the cause before us, the primary contention made by plaintiff is that the language of defendant's guarantee presents an absolute undertaking and is, therefore, a guarantee of payment within purview of subsection (1) of the statute in question. In support of that contention, Beebe v. Kirkpatrick, 321 Ill. 612, 152 N.E. 539, Hance v. Miller, 21 Ill. 636, and Empire Sec. Co. v. Berry, 211 Ill. App. 278, are cited as authority. We have indicated that in the *Beebe* case, the court found that the language "I hereby guarantee this loan" presented a guarantee of payment and not collection. The *Hance* case involved construction of language which read "For value received I guarantee payment of the within note at maturity." Consistently, the court had no difficulty in construing that language to be a guarantee of payment. In the *Berry* case, the guarantor had agreed to pay the note if the maker did not "retire" it at maturity. The court found that the word "retire" as used in the context meant "pay" and, therefore, that the guarantee was of payment and not of collection.

The language involved in each of the cases referred to by plaintiff is clearly in conformity with the law in Illinois regarding guaranty contracts. We believe, however, that plaintiff draws an erroneous analogy between guarantees appearing in those cases and that which we have under consideration in the cause before us. In our opinion, the terms of the guarantee in the instant case are made conditional upon collection of the note. While it is true that the word "collection" has not been used, in our view the guarantee as against "loss" is in effect a guarantee of collection rather than payment. At least one case of another jurisdiction, Michelin Tire Co. v. Cutter, 116 Or. 217, 240 P. 895 (1925), involved language similar to that in the instant case. There the defendant agreed to indemnify plaintiff against "any loss on account of any monies" which a certain party may owe from time to time. The court had no difficulty in concluding that the guarantee involved was of collection and not of payment in that case. . . .

A final contention made by plaintiff is that subsection "(3)" of the Illinois statute quoted earlier in our opinion to the effect that where words of guaranty do not otherwise specify, the guarantee [is] of payment could be controlling in such case. We cannot agree with such analysis since it is apparent that the use of subsection "(3)" is limited to instances where no conditional language of the type we find in the present case has been used.

We, therefore, conclude that it is apparent that the instant guarantee is one of collection and not of payment. Since plaintiff does not allege that her claim was prosecuted to judgment and execution thereon returned unsatisfied or that the maker was insolvent, she has not complied with Section 3-416(2) of the Uniform Commercial Code (Illinois Revised Statutes, Ch. 26). The trial court's dismissal of the action was, therefore, proper, and should be affirmed.

Affirmed.

STROUDER, J., and DIXON, J., concur.

To recap: the Uniform Commercial Code's *accommodation maker, accommodation indorser,* and *guarantor*—known to non-lawyers as *co-signers*—are nothing more than common law sureties dressed up with new labels, their rights partially codified. The common law rights of subrogation and reimbursement are codified in §3-419(f), which states that an "accommodation party who pays the instrument is entitled to enforce the instrument against the accommodated party. An accommodated party who pays the instrument has no right of recourse against, and is not entitled to contribution from, an accommodation party."

b. Who Is the Surety? In most cases, the form of the transaction or the language of the promissory note makes it clear which party signed for accommodation. Section 3-419(a) has a basic definition, which you should read, noting particularly the "direct benefit" test therein. Situations can arise, as the Problem below illustrates, in which the usual presumptions are turned on their head, and the issue becomes more complicated.

PROBLEM 150

When Portia Moot graduated from law school, she moved to a new city and needed to borrow money but discovered that her credit rating was so bad no one would lend her the money. She appealed to her mother, Margaret Moot, a successful doctor, and Margaret agreed to help her out. Margaret borrowed $5,000 from Octopus National Bank (ONB), signing a promissory note as maker with the bank as payee. Margaret had Portia indorse the note on the back before it was handed over to ONB in return for the money.

(a) If Margaret Moot is forced to pay this note when it matures, can she sue Portia, the indorser? Normally, the maker of the note has no cause of action against indorsers, whose §3-415(a) obligation runs to "a person entitled to enforce the instrument," defined in §3-301 as the holder (itself defined in §1-201(b)(21) as the person identified in the instrument as the person to whom it is payable, which would not include the maker).

(b) If ONB recovers its money from Portia at maturity, can Portia sue her mother, whose maker's obligation, §3-412, does run to indorsers such as Portia?

In the above Problem, Portia has made what is called an *anomalous indorsement,* §3-205(d), one that is put on the instrument by a non-holder, and that can only mean that she signed for accommodation. Anyone looking at this note should know that Portia is a surety; she is not named as the payee, but is the first person to indorse the note and must therefore have signed for some reason other than negotiation. This means that (if it had been relevant) in the above Problem the bank is conclusively presumed to know that Portia is entitled to be treated as a surety. The mere fact that the bank is presumed to know of Portia's accommodation status does not, however, keep the bank from becoming a holder in due course. A surety may prove accommodation status against a knowledgeable holder in due course or against a non-holder in due course, but if a holder in due course has no reason to know that a party is a surety, the holder in due course will take free of the suretyship defenses. See §3-605(h).

6. Tender of Payment

Read the "tender of payment" rule (§3-603), which has meaning beyond suretyship problems; indeed, you may skip the last sentence of §3-603(c), which deals with an issue to be considered later. For an excellent article on point, see Comment, Tender of Payment Under UCC §3-604: A Forgotten Defense?, 39 Ohio St. L.J. 833 (1978). Use §3-603 to solve the following Problem.

PROBLEM 151

When Saul Panzer needed to borrow money, his friend Rex Stout agreed to loan him $10,000 if Saul could get a co-signer. Saul talked Orrie Cather into signing Saul's promissory note as co-maker. The note was payable to the order of Rex Stout, who loaned Saul the $10,000 and took the note in return for the money. Stout indorsed the note and sold it at a discount to Archie Goodwin.

(a) On the date the note matured, knowing that Saul Panzer, the maker, was in financial trouble and, wanting to stop the running of interest,[7] Orrie Cather, the co-signer, went to Archie Goodwin, the current holder, and offered to pay the note, planning to seek reimbursement from Saul. Goodwin replied, "Let's give poor Saul a chance to pay it off himself." A month later, Saul went bankrupt, and Goodwin demanded that Cather pay the initial amount due plus interest for the extra month. Cather refused, and Goodwin sued, adding a claim for attorney's fees. To what is he entitled, if anything? See §3-603(c)'s first sentence; Kennedy v. Boles Investments, Inc., 53 So. 3d 60 (Ala. 2010).

(b) On the due date Saul went to Goodwin and offered to pay, but Goodwin said, "Look, I know you need the money for your other bills—pay me next month." A month later Saul went bankrupt. Can Goodwin now recover from Cather? From Stout, the payee/indorser? See §3-603(b).

(c) Instead of the above, assume that on the maturity date Orrie Cather went to Goodwin and offered to pay the debt, to which Goodwin made the same reply. A month later, Saul went bankrupt, and Orrie Cather filed for bankruptcy at the same time. Is Stout, the payee/indorser, liable to Goodwin? Cf. §3-415(a).

7. Section 3-605—*Strictissimi Juris* Again

Sureties are the beneficiaries of a number of common law maxims, among them that a "surety is a favorite of the law" and that "security follows the debt." The former you must remember to quote to the court should your client be a surety. The latter refers to the collateral (*security*) given to the creditor by the principal and means that on paying off the creditor and thereby acquiring the negotiable instrument (*debt*), the surety is also entitled to that collateral.

It follows that the surety has an interest in the creditor's handling of the collateral. Both at common law and under §3-605(e), (f), and (g) [§3R-605(d) in the 2002 revision of this section] the non-consenting surety is discharged, up to the value of the collateral, if the creditor (holder) fails to protect the collateral and if it is thereby unavailable to pay the debt.

PROBLEM 152

When Butch Byrd borrowed $10,000 from Octopus National Bank, the bank not only made him get a surety, but also demanded that the inventory

7. Section 3-112 requires the instrument to specify an interest rate or it has none.

of Butch's feed store stand as collateral. Butch talked his brother Arnold into signing the promissory note as a guarantor and signed the necessary papers for the bank to get an Article 9 security interest in the inventory. Unfortunately, the bank failed to file the Article 9 financing statement in the correct place, so when Butch had financial difficulties, other creditors prevailed over the bank's attempt to claim the inventory. The inventory was worth $6,000. What is the effect of the bank's Article 9 difficulties on Arnold's liability? See §3-605(e) and (g) [§3R-605(d) in the 2002 revision of this section]; Cliff Findlay Automotive, LLC v. Olson, 228 Ariz. 115, 263 P.3d 664 (Ariz. App. 2011).

Chemical Bank v. Pic Motors Corp.

New York Supreme Court, Appellate Division, 1982 87 A.D.2d 447, 452 N.Y.S.2d 41, *aff'd on the opinion below*, 58 N.Y.2d 1023, 448 N.E.2d 1349, 462 N.Y.S.2d 438

FEIN, J.

Pic, an established car dealership, entered into an inventory financing agreement with plaintiff Bank, pursuant to which the Bank agreed to lend funds to Pic periodically under an established line of credit on the security of Pic's inventory of automobiles as collateral. Under this form of agreement, known as floor plan financing, the borrower draws upon the line of credit for the purpose of financing the purchase of automobiles for sale. The Bank extends loans within the credit limit based on the value of the vehicles purchased by the borrower. Upon the sale of any vehicle, the borrower pays back the portion of the loan that was granted based on the value of that vehicle. Thus, the bank loan always remains secured. Sales to purchasers in the ordinary course of business are made free of the Bank's lien. As a matter of practice, the Bank conducted periodic inspections of Pic's inventory to determine whether the financed vehicles were owned by Pic and whether the loan was reduced by an appropriate payment upon sale of a financed vehicle. The Bank also followed a curtailment policy under which any loan was proportionately reduced and finally paid in full for inventory remaining unsold over specified periods of time.

Siegel had been director, president and principal stockholder of Pic for many years and had personally guaranteed the loans in writing. In 1978 Siegel sold his interest in the company to defendant Manfred Robl and resigned as an officer and director of Pic. However, it is undisputed that his guaranty continued, as agreed, during all the relevant periods of time. The guaranty reads, in pertinent part, as follows:

> NOW, THEREFORE, in consideration of the premises and of other good and valuable consideration and in order to induce the Bank from time to time,

> in its discretion, to extend or continue credit to the Borrower, *the undersigned hereby guarantees, absolutely and unconditionally,* to the Bank *the payment of all liabilities of the Borrower to the Bank of whatever nature, whether now existing or hereafter incurred,* whether created directly or acquired by the Bank by assignment or otherwise, whether matured or unmatured and whether absolute or contingent (all of which are hereinafter collectively referred to as the "Liabilities of the Borrower"). . . .
>
> The undersigned hereby consents that from time to time, before or after any default by the Borrower or any notice of termination hereof, *with or without further notice to or assent from the undersigned, any security* at any time held by or available to the Bank for any obligation of the Borrower, or any security at any time held by or available to the Bank for any obligation of any other person secondarily or otherwise liable for any of the Liabilities of the Borrower, *may be exchanged, surrendered or released* and any obligation of the Borrower, or of any such other person, *may be changed, altered, renewed, extended, continued, surrendered, compromised, waived or released in whole or in part,* . . . and *the Bank . . . may extend further credit in any manner whatsoever to the Borrower,* and generally deal with the Borrower or any such security or other person as the Bank may see fit; *and the undersigned shall remain bound under this guaranty notwithstanding any such exchange, surrender, release, change, alteration, renewal, extension, continuance, compromise, waiver, inaction, extension of further credit or other dealing.*
>
> The undersigned thereby waives (a) notice of acceptance of this guaranty and of extensions of credit by the Bank to the Borrower; (b) presentment and demand for payment of any of the Liabilities of the Borrower; (c) protest and notice of dishonor or default to the undersigned or to any other party with respect to any of the Liabilities of the Borrower; (d) all other notices to which the undersigned might otherwise be entitled; and (e) any demand for payment under this guaranty.
>
> This is a guaranty of payment and not of collection. . . .
>
> . . . [N]or in the event shall any modification or waiver of the provisions of this guaranty be effective unless in writing nor shall any such waiver be applicable except in the specific instance for which given. [Emphases added.]

In July 1979 the Bank informed Siegel that Pic was "out of trust." More than 50 percent of the inventory was unaccounted for. Pursuant to an understanding with the Bank, Siegel arranged for the sale of the remaining inventory and partial repayment was made. Following demand, the Bank instituted suit for the balance against Pic and the individual guarantors, including Siegel. Siegel appeals from the summary judgment granted against him as guarantor.

By way of defense, Siegel asserts that the deficiency was caused by the failure of the Bank to conduct regular inspections and to enforce its curtailment policy. He further alleges that two of the Bank's employees, either negligently or in complicity with Robl, submitted incorrect or false inventory reports and approved loans on nonexistent automobiles. Siegel asserts that he was assured, as a condition of his continuing guaranty upon his sale to Robl, that regular inspections and enforcement of the curtailment policy would continue. He asserts that the activities of the Bank and its employees impaired the value of the collateral, thus relieving him from liability.

Siegel argues there is a triable issue as to whether the Bank was obligated to conduct regular inspections and enforce the curtailment program, and whether the dishonesty or negligence of the Bank's employees operated to impair the collateral and thus discharge his obligation as guarantor.

It is undisputed that there is no provision in the inventory financing agreement or in the guaranty obligating the Bank to conduct inspections or to maintain the curtailment policy. The guaranty is a fully integrated unambiguous contract which by its terms could not be modified or varied by parol or by an alleged course of conduct. The guaranty expressly provides, in pertinent part:

> This is a guaranty of payment and not of collection and the undersigned further waives any right to require that any action be brought against the Borrower or any other person or to require that resort be had to any security. . . .
>
> No delay on the part of the Bank in exercising any rights hereunder or failure to exercise the same shall operate as a waiver of such rights; no notice to or demand on the undersigned shall be deemed to be a waiver of the obligation of the undersigned or of the right of the Bank to take further action without notice or demand as provided herein; nor in any event shall any modification or waiver of the provisions of this guaranty be effective unless in writing, nor shall any such waiver be applicable except in the specific instance for which given.

Thus neither the alleged prior course of conduct nor the alleged promise that it would be continued could modify the obligation of Siegel as guarantor of payment (General Phoenix Corp. v. Cabot, 300 N.Y. 87, 92; General Obligations Law §15-301, subd. 1).

Siegel expressly consented that the

> security at any time held by or available to the Bank . . . may be exchanged, surrendered or released . . . and the undersigned [defendant Siegel] shall remain bound under this guaranty notwithstanding any such . . . release, . . . compromise, . . . inaction, extension of further credit or other dealing.

It is plain that the Bank had the right to release the collateral without discharging the guarantor. If so, the negligence or dishonesty of the Bank's employees in so doing is irrelevant.

As Special Term ruled, the negligence or dishonesty of plaintiff's employees patently would not be deemed within the scope of their authority. Siegel was an unconditional guarantor of payment, not of collection, and the guaranty was not dependent upon any condition precedent other than the non-payment of the indebtedness.

The dissent relies upon Uniform Commercial Code §3-606, which provides in part:

> (1) The holder discharges any party to the instrument to the extent that without such party's consent the holder . . .
>
> (b) unjustifiably impairs any collateral for the instrument given by or on behalf of the party or any person against whom he has a right of recourse.

That section applies to commercial paper, negotiable instruments, not to a guaranty such as that here involved (UCC §3-102[1], [e]); Indianapolis Morris Plan Corp. v. Karlen, 28 N.Y.2d 30, 32. Moreover, as that case holds respecting consent to release of collateral:

> Consent may be given in advance, and is commonly incorporated in the instrument, or it may be given afterward. It requires no consideration, and operates as a waiver of the consenting party's right to claim his own discharge. (28 N.Y.2d at p. 34, quoting the Official Comment to UCC §3-606.)

In *Indianapolis Morris Plan Corp.*, supra, the lender consented to the substitution of gas consuming equipment for the mortgaged electrical cooking equipment. The debtor failed and the gas company repossessed the substituted equipment on which it had a seller's lien. The collateral security was dissipated by the substitution and the repossession of the substitute. The consent to release of security provided for in the promissory note operated to prevent the discharge of the sureties although they had no notice of these events and had not consented thereto.

Our case stands on the same footing. The consent to release of security was broad and all encompassing so as to preclude discharge of the guarantor. Under the terms of this guaranty there was no obligation to preserve and protect the collateral. The dissent's reliance upon Executive Bank [of Fort Lauderdale] v. Tighe (66 A.D.2d 70) is misplaced. That case holds only that pursuant to UCC §3-606, a guarantor's waiver of the obligation not to impair collateral will not excuse the creditor's failure properly to file the security instrument as required by law, unless the waiver expressly so provides. That issue is not here involved. (See Lafayette Bank & Trust Co. of Suffern v. Silver, 58 Misc. 2d 891.)

Similarly, Federal Deposit Insurance Corp. v. Frank L. Marino Corp., 74 A.D.2d 620, relied upon by the dissent, is not applicable. In that case the collateral was in the possession of the creditor who negligently failed to liquidate it upon the guarantor's demand. The guarantor could not be chargeable with the decline in value of the collateral. In our case the collateral was in the possession of the debtor, not the creditor, and Siegel, as guarantor, was afforded the opportunity to liquidate it, which he did.

For the same reason, Sterling Factors Corp. v. Freeman (50 Misc. 2d 715), relied upon by the dissent, is inapposite. In that case the creditor had replevied the collateral and purchased it at a price far less than its worth, without notice to the guarantors. It then proceeded to sell the collateral at a higher price without giving credit to the guarantors. This was a blatant fraud, held to preclude any recovery against the guarantors. This has nothing to do with our case, where the Bank never had possession of the collateral.

Under the express terms of the guaranty here involved, the Bank could release or surrender the collateral without notifying or discharging Siegel. It could also extend further credit to Pic on an unsecured basis without notifying or releasing Siegel. Hence the complained of actions of the Bank's employees are of no aid to Siegel. We must "take the guaranty as we find it as the surest way of determining the rights of these parties." (Corn Exchange Bank Trust Co. v. Gifford, 268 N.Y. 153, 158.)

Nothing in the agreements or in the Uniform Commercial Code provides for the release of Siegel as unconditional guarantor of payment under the circumstances. In the face of the guaranty as written there was no duty upon the creditor to preserve or protect the collateral. Where the collateral is in the possession of the debtor, inaction by the creditor, negligent or otherwise, does not release a guarantor who has executed such a waiver. A surety may waive any obligation upon the part of a creditor, including the obligation of the creditor not to impair the security (Indianapolis Morris Plan Corp. v. Karlen, supra). The parties, by agreement, may determine the standards by which the fulfillment of the rights and duties of the secured party may be measured (UCC §9-501[3]).

Accordingly, the order of the Supreme Court, New York County (Helman, J.), entered on August 12, 1980 granting plaintiff summary judgment against defendant Aaron Siegel in the sum of $189,717.17 should be affirmed with costs.

[All concur except Bloom and Milonas, JJ., who dissent in an opinion by Milonas, J.]

MILONAS, J. (dissenting). I would reverse and remand for further proceedings. . . .

Under the express terms of the agreement between Siegel and the bank, the undersigned purportedly undertook to remain bound regardless of any compromise to the security. However, where the bank's negligence has, in contravention of UCC §9-207, resulted in a breach of its duty to preserve and protect the collateral, a waiver "will not be enforced so as to bar a viable setoff or counterclaim sounding in fraud . . ." or where "based upon the creditor's negligence in failing to liquidate collateral upon the guarantor's demand . . ." (Federal Deposit Insurance Corp. v. Frank L. Marino Corp., 74 A.D.2d 620, at p. 621). As the court therein explained, to enforce such a waiver provision when there is a triable issue of fact as to the creditor's negligence would enable a creditor to shield itself from its own tortious conduct.

"The holder of security [here the inventory] is not at liberty to do any affirmative act which would impair the security and so deprive the guarantors of the benefit they might derive on a proper liquidation or upon their payment under their guaranty . . ." (Sterling Factors Corporation v. Freeman, 50 Misc. 2d 715, at p. 720). In the instant case, whether the bank can be held liable for the tortious acts of its employees presents a clear issue of fact such as to render summary judgment inappropriate. To maintain that a guarantor will always be bound on the underlying obligation, notwithstanding any negligent, fraudulent or tortious conduct on the part of the creditor, simply by the expedient of the creditor's inserting a clause to that effect in the agreement is to undermine completely the spirit of the UCC and is, in my opinion, contrary to public policy.

Order filed.

PROBLEM 153

George and Martha Washington borrowed $10,000 from the Mt. Vernon Finance Company, both signing a promissory note for the amount borrowed. To secure the note, the bank took a mortgage on Martha's vineyard, but failed to file its mortgage in the proper place. Before the note matured, Martha filed for bankruptcy, and the bankruptcy creditors were able to get the vineyard free and clear of the bank's mortgage. Is George discharged in whole or in part by §3-605(e)? By §3-605(f)? If Martha had not filed for bankruptcy, but the vineyard was still lost when the state seized it because she hadn't paid her taxes, is *she* discharged by the bank's failure to perfect its interest in the vineyard? As to all this, see Official Comment 7 to §3-605.

You will recall that at common law any change in the basic contract discharged the surety unless the surety consented. In addition, a binding agreement by the creditor not to sue the principal or to give the principal extra time to pay released the non-consenting surety unless the creditor "preserved rights" against the surety. These issues are treated very differently in Article 3, which permits certain agreements between the creditor (the current holder of the instrument) and the principal (the accommodated party) without a discharge of the surety/indorser. There is a complication, however, and it is that the 2002 revision of Article 3 substantially rewrote §3-605 to make its rules conform to those of the Restatement (Third) of Suretyship and Guaranty, which is a partial return to the rules of the common law. That 2002 revision has only been adopted in 12 or so states as of this writing, and the other states used the wording of the 1990 version of Article 3. Your instructor will tell you whether to answer the questions in the following Problem by looking at the language of the 1990 version of Article 3 or the newer 2002 version (cited in the Problem by using the letter "R"). The pre-2002 version of this section (which is the law in most states) can be found in the Appendix at the back of the book.

PROBLEM 154

When Jack Point borrowed $75,000 from Yeomen National Bank to start up his carnival business, the bank made him sign a promissory note in its favor and get a surety. Point talked his good friend Wilfred Shadbolt into signing as an accommodation maker. Is Shadbolt discharged by any of the following agreements between Yeoman National and Point?

(a) When the note matured, Point told Yeomen National that his business had gone bust and that he was thinking about filing a bankruptcy petition. Worried that it would get nothing in the bankruptcy distribution, Yeomen National persuaded him to pay all he could, a mere $5,000, and then signed an agreement with Point excusing him from having to pay the rest of the debt. The bank then demanded that Shadbolt pay the amount still due. Does Shadbolt owe it? See §3-605(b); §3R-605(a) and (g). Does the accord and satisfaction agreement between the bank and Point also bind Shadbolt, or may the latter still seek complete reimbursement from Point? See Official Comment 3 to §3-605; §3R-605(a) and its Official Comment 4.

(b) Assume instead that when the note matured, Point went to the bank and asked for more time in which to pay. The bank did this, giving Point an extra six months. No one notified Shadbolt of this extension. At the end of the six-month period, Point filed for bankruptcy instead of paying the note. Was Shadbolt discharged by the bank's actions? Would your answer change depending on whether or not Point ever had the money to pay the note at any relevant period? See §3-605(c) and its Official Comment 4; §3R-605(b) and its Official Comment 5. Who has the burden of proof on the issues? See §§3-605(b), 3R-605(h). Could Shadbolt, had he known of the extension agreement, have ignored it, paid the note, and then sued Point for reimbursement? The original statute is silent on this but the next to the last paragraph of Official Comment 4 talks about the issue and defers to the common law for the result; in the 2002 revision see §3R-605(b)(3).

(c) Assume instead that when the note was signed, the bank also made Point put up 100 shares of stock as collateral for the debt. Before the note matured Point went to the bank and asked to have the stock back, saying he needed to take advantage of a stock split the issuing corporation was offering. The bank returned the stock to him, but made him agree to pay a higher rate of interest. Has Shadbolt been discharged? Who has the burden of proof here? See §3-605(d) and (i) and its Official Comment 5; §3R-605(c) and (h) and its Official Comment 6.

(d) Is there a simple way that the bank could have avoided all these issues *ab initio*? See §3-605(i) and its Official Comment 2; §3R-605(f).

London Leasing Corp. v. Interfina, Inc.

New York Supreme Court, 1967
53 Misc. 2d 657, 279 N.Y.S.2d 209

CRAWFORD, J.

The fundamental question presented on this motion is whether a corporate officer (president) who makes a note on behalf of his corporation and, also, personally endorses that note is discharged from *personal* liability on the note by an agreement between the payee and the corporate maker, by its said president, which extends the corporate maker's time to pay the note.

This is a motion pursuant to C.P.L.R. 3213 for summary judgment against defendants Interfina, Inc., and its president, Fredrick J. Evans. On May 3, 1966, Interfina made and delivered to plaintiff a promissory note in the sum of $52,000, signed by Fredrick J. Evans, as president of Interfina, and also personally endorsed by Fredrick J. Evans. The note was not paid on its due date, August 2, 1966, and thereafter, on August 3, 15 and 19, Interfina, by its president, entered into letter agreements with the plaintiff extending the time for payment of the note. Fredrick J. Evans signed the agreements, but only in his corporate capacity.

The sum of $19,500 is due on the note and as against defendant Interfina there is no question that summary judgment should be granted.

In opposition to the motion as against him, defendant Evans contends that the extension agreements, which were not signed by him in his personal capacity, as a matter of law discharged him from personal liability on the note because he did not personally consent to the extension.

[The court quoted §3-606, the original version of what is now §3-605.—EDS.] The Code does not explicitly define the meaning of the term "consent." However, the Official Comment to §3-606 states:

> 2. Consent may be given in advance, and is commonly incorporated in the instrument, or it may be given afterward. It requires no consideration, and operates as a waiver of the consenting party's right to claim his own discharge. . . .

In the pre-Code case of National Park Bank v. Koehler (204 N.Y. 174), the court explained the rationale which underlies the rule that an endorser is discharged by the maker's agreement with the payee entered into without the endorser's consent to extend the maker's time to pay a note. The court said at pages 179-180:

> . . . It is a rule, long recognized, that an accommodation indorser, or surety, is entitled to have the engagement of the principal debtor preserved, without variation in its terms, and that his *assent* to any change therein is essential to the continuance of his obligation. The reason of the rule is that his right must not be affected, upon the maturity of the indebtedness, to make payment and, by subrogation to the creditor's place, to, at once, proceed against the principal debtor to enforce repayment. Therefore it is that any agreement of the creditor, which operates to extend the time of payment of the original debt and suspends the right to immediate action, is held to discharge the non-assenting indorser, or surety; as the law will presume injury to him thereby. The creditor may arrange with his debtor, in any way, which does not result in effecting either of these results. He may take, as collateral to the old note, new security, or other notes, and, if time is not given to the debtor, the indorser, or surety, will not be discharged. To prevent such a result, the agreement must expressly reserve all the remedies of the creditor against the indorser, or surety; in which case the latter will be in a position to pay immediately and, then, to proceed against the principal debtor. . . .

In the absence of a clear Code definition of "consent," this court is guided by the statement in Stearns Law of Suretyship (5th ed., §6.13):

> Parties to a contract may always alter it by mutual agreement and this is true of suretyship contract as others. Accordingly, if the creditor and principal modify their contract, and the surety consents thereto, he will not be discharged. Such consent need not be expressly given, *but may be implied from the surrounding circumstances or from his conduct.* [Emphasis supplied.]

The Court in In re Grottola's Estate (124 N.Y.S.2d 85) was also guided by this principle. The court stated, at page 88:

> . . . Thus the voluntary release or surrender of security by the creditor without the consent of the surety will discharge the latter to the extent of the value of the property so released. Stearns Law of Suretyship, Elder's Revision, 5th Edition, §6.46; Cohen v. Rossmoore. If, however, the surety consents to a modification of the contract between the principal debtor and the creditor he will not be discharged. Stearns Law of Suretyship, supra, sec. 6.13. The author states at page 129: "Such consent need not be expressly given, but may be implied from the surrounding circumstances or from his conduct." *Here the deceased endorser was the president and the principal stockholder of Ventura Acres, Inc., the maker of the note. Subsequent to the death of the accommodation endorser the*

> *executrix of his will, or her attorney, solicited and secured from the creditor the release of mortgage and satisfaction thereof in question. The court holds that such action on the part of the endorser's legal representative constituted a consent to the satisfaction of the mortgage held by the creditor as security for the loan in question.* Vose v. Florida Railroad Co., Stearns Law of Suretyship, supra. . . . [Emphases supplied.]

The application of this principle to the present question mandates a holding that defendant Evans consented to the extension. As a matter of fact he applied for, negotiated, signed in his corporate capacity, and received the agreements extending the time for payment. While mere knowledge or acquiescence is not, in and of itself, sufficient to prevent discharge, the defendant's conduct here far exceeded these limits and, under the special circumstances here presented, constituted consent.

Accordingly, the motion for summary judgment in the sum of $19,500 is granted as against both defendants. Submit order.

The 2002 revision to §3-605 speaks directly to this point, adding to §3R-605(f) this sentence: "Unless the circumstances indicate otherwise, consent by the principal obligor to an act that would lead to discharge under this section constitutes consent to that act by the secondary obligor if the secondary obligor controls the principal obligor or deals with the person entitled to enforce the instrument on behalf of the principal obligor."

8. New Notes for Old

PROBLEM 155

In 2022 Rex Lear borrowed $5,000 from the Kent Lending Corporation and gave them his promissory note due June 8, 2024. Rex had his daughter Cordelia sign as accommodation maker. Early in 2021 Rex defaulted on the installment payments and in return for mercy by the lending company, he signed a new promissory note dated January 11, 2024, payable to the company September 25, 2024, for the same amount but with additional collateral. The Kent Lending Corporation kept the first note as security for the payment of the second. Cordelia never signed the second note. Answer these questions:

(a) Can the payee sue on the *first* note prior to September 25, 2024? See §3-310(b)(2).

(b) If Lear does not pay the second note when it matures, can Kent sue on the *first* note, or has it been paid and discharged by the second note? See §3-310(b)(2).

(c) Assume that Cordelia can prove that the failure of the lender to enforce its rights on the first note caused her major damages in that Lear's financial situation deteriorated drastically between January 11 and September 25, 2024. Is Cordelia still liable on the first note? See §3-605(c); §3R-605(b) and (h).

PROBLEM 156

Sam Selachii was the surety on a promissory note that Marty Make had given to the Dogfish Loan Company along with a pledge of 100 shares of Titanic Telephone stock to secure the loan for $800. Shortly after receiving the loan, Marty asked for the stock back, saying that he wanted to sell it and buy other stock that he would repledge as collateral. Dogfish gave him back the stock, which Marty sold. He used the proceeds to finance a bad day at the races. A week later, Dogfish transferred the note for value to the Hammerhead Loan Company, a bona fide purchaser. Assume that Sam has been discharged under §3-605(e) [§3R-605(d)] (impairment of the collateral). Is he still liable to Hammerhead? See §§3-305(b), 3-601(b), and 3-302(b).

D. *The Drawer's Obligation*

To make this discussion more relevant, consider that checks are drafts, and the liability described next is the one you incur every time you sign a check and send it out into the world.

The drawer of a draft incurs the obligation specified in §3-414, which you should read now. It is sometimes said that the drawer's liability is *secondary* because the draft must first be presented to the drawee for payment and dishonored by the drawee before the drawer has a legal obligation to pay the instrument (unlike the liability of a maker of a note, which is *primary* since it is not subject to these conditions precedent). Why should the drawer's liability be different from that of a maker? The answer is that, with a draft, it is the understanding of all the parties that the payee will first attempt to secure payment from the drawee (a *presentment*) and only look to the drawer if the drawee refuses to pay (makes a *dishonor*). Consider, for example, that if I, your neighbor, owe you money and give you a check for the amount due, common sense tells you that you must first try to collect the check from my bank. Only if my bank refuses to pay the check can you expect me to make the check good. What are these technical rights of presentment, dishonor, and protest? They are discussed exhaustively in the 3-500 sections of the Code.

1. Presentment and Dishonor

Presentment is the demand for payment made to the maker of the note or, for drafts, to the drawee. Read §3-501 (defining and describing *presentment*). Under the NIL, the holder was required to exhibit the instrument at the moment of presentment (NIL 74), but the Code is more flexible—exhibition is required only if the presentee demands it. Read §3-501(b)(2), which sets out other rights of the presentee.

Dishonor is the refusal of the presentee to pay. Read §3-502.

PROBLEM 157

Archibald Grosvenor finally paid off an old debt to Reginald Bunthorne by giving him a check drawn on the Patience National Bank. Bunthorne took the check to the bank and demanded payment. The bank asked him to sign his name on the back, but Bunthorne refused, saying, "I will never put my name on any check Grosvenor has touched." If the bank declines to pay the check, has a technical dishonor occurred? See §§3-501(b)(3)(i), 3-501(b)(2)(iii). This may be important because Grosvenor's §3-414 obligation is conditioned on a dishonor, and he can no longer be sued on the underlying obligation that is suspended until dishonor by §3-310.

PROBLEM 158

When Grosvenor gave Bunthorne a check to pay off an old debt, Bunthorne negligently lost it behind the sofa and didn't find it for eight months. The bank it was drawn on refused to pay it because it was suspiciously old (see §4-404). Is Grosvenor still liable on this check? See §3-414(f). Would he be if the drawee bank had folded five months after the check was written but before it was presented? If Bunthorne had indorsed the check the day after it was issued to him and then cashed it at CheckCasherSupreme and that entity mislaid it for five months before the drawee bank dishonored it, is Bunthorne still liable to CheckCasherSupreme? See §3-415(e).

Messing v. Bank of America, N.A.

Maryland Court of Special Appeals, 2002
143 Md. App. 1, 792 A.2d 312, aff'd, 821 A.2d 22

KRAUSER, Judge.

This appeal focuses on one of the most expressive parts of the human body—the thumb: "thumbs up" (approval), "thumbs down" (disapproval), "thumbing one's nose" (defiance), and "thumbing a ride" (requesting transport).[8] Notwithstanding all of the things we ask of this unassuming

8. Not to mention, we should add: "thumbing through" (perusing a document), "all thumbs" (clumsiness), and "under one's thumb" (dominance and control).

two-jointed digit, appellee, Bank of America, adds one more task—personal identification. The thumbprint, if Bank of America has its way, will now be one more means by which the identity of a non-account check holder is expressed and confirmed. This idea has of course not met with universal approval, and that is why this matter of first impression is now before us.

Specifically, we are presented with the question of whether Bank of America's practice of requiring non-account check holders to provide a thumbprint signature before it will honor a check is lawful. Appellant, Jeff E. Messing, claims that it is not and filed a complaint for declaratory judgment in the Circuit for Baltimore City, requesting a declaration that the practice is illegal and an order requiring its cessation. In reply, appellee filed a motion for summary judgment. That motion was granted; appellant's complaint was dismissed; and this appeal followed.

In addition to the question of the legality of appellee's thumbprint signature program, appellant also raises questions as to whether appellee "accepted," "dishonored," or "converted" appellant's check upon presentment. . . .

BACKGROUND

On August 3, 2000, appellant attempted to cash a check for $976 at the Light Street branch office of appellee in Baltimore City. That check was made out to appellant and drawn on a Bank of America customer checking account.

Upon entering the bank, appellant handed the check to a teller. The teller then confirmed the availability of the funds on deposit, and placed the check in a computer validation slot. After "validating" the availability of those funds, the computer stamped the time, date, account number, and teller number on the back of the check. It also placed a hold on $976 in the drawer's account.

The teller then gave the check back to appellant to endorse. After he had endorsed the check, the teller asked appellant for identification. In response, appellant presented his driver's license and a major credit card. The identification information on the license and credit card was then transferred by the teller to the back of the check.

During this transaction, the teller asked appellant if he was a Bank of America customer. When he said "no," the teller returned the check to appellant and requested that he place his "thumbprint signature" on the check in accordance with appellee's thumbprint signature policy for "non-account holders." That policy, which is posted at each teller's station, requires a non-account holder, seeking to cash a check drawn on a Bank of America customer account, to provide a thumbprint signature.

The provision of such a signature is neither messy nor time consuming. A thumbprint signature is created by applying one's right thumb to an inkless fingerprinting device that leaves no ink stain or residue. The thumbprint is then placed on the face of the check between the memo and signature line.

After requesting appellant's thumbprint signature, the teller counted out $976 in cash from her drawer anticipating that appellant would comply with that request. When he refused to do so, the teller indicated that the bank would not be able to complete the transaction without his thumbprint. Appellant then asked to see the branch manager, and the teller referred him to a "Mr. Obrigkeit," the branch manager.

Upon entering the branch manager's office, appellant demanded that the check be cashed despite his refusal to place his thumbprint on the check. The branch manager examined the check and returned it to appellant explaining that because appellant was not an account holder, Bank of America would not cash the check without his thumbprint on the instrument. The requirement of a thumbprint signature from non-account holders was in accordance with the deposit agreement that Bank of America has with each of its account holders. That agreement states that Bank of America is permitted "to establish physical and/or documentary requirements" of payees or other holders who seek to cash an item drawn on a Bank of America customer's account.

Appellant then requested that the branch manager provide him with a copy of the Bank's thumbprint policy. The branch manager contacted appellee's regional headquarters and was informed that no such information was available for public distribution. After the branch manager conveyed that information to appellant, appellant left the bank. Moments later, the teller released the hold on the customer's funds, voided the transaction in the computer, and placed the $976 in cash back in her drawer.

Indignant over the bank's policy, appellant filed a complaint. . . . Appellant also requested that the circuit court order appellee to cease and desist from requiring thumbprint signatures in Maryland. . . . [W]e conclude, for the reasons set forth below, that the circuit court was legally correct in granting appellee's motion for summary judgment and dismissing with prejudice appellant's complaint.

Discussion

I.

Appellant contends that the circuit court erred in construing the "reasonable identification" requirement of C.L. §3-501(b)(2) to include a thumbprint signature if demanded by appellee, notwithstanding appellant's proffer of his driver's license and a credit card. C.L. §3-501(b)(2) provides:

> Upon demand of the person to whom presentment is made, the person making presentment must (i) exhibit the instrument, (ii) give *reasonable identification* and, if presentment is made on behalf of another person, reasonable evidence of authority to do so, and (iii) sign a receipt on the instrument for any payment made or surrender the instrument if full payment is made. (Emphasis added). . . .

While the phrase "reasonable identification" under former U.C.C. §3-505(1)(b), now codified in Maryland as C.L. §3-501(b)(2), has been addressed by the other state courts in other contexts, what constitutes "reasonable identification" under C.L. 3-501(b)(2)—particularly whether a "thumbprint signature" does—is a question that has not been addressed by any federal or state court, at least not in any reported opinion.

Appellee's thumbprint requirement is a form of "reasonable identification" for a number of reasons. First, a thumbprint signature has been accepted by the drafters of the Maryland U.C.C. as an effective, reliable, and accurate way to authenticate a writing on a negotiable instrument. "In accord with the systematic presentation of the U.C.C. and its use of consistent terminology," U.C.C. §1-201 sets forth "46 basic terms" to be used throughout the Code to "offer a starting point for the interpretation of many Code sections." 1 William D. Hawkland, Uniform Commercial Code Series, §1-201:1 (1998). The term "signed" is defined in C.L. §1-201(39) (1975, 1997 Repl. Vol.) as "any symbol executed or adopted by a party with present intention to authenticate a writing," and that definition applies throughout the Maryland U.C.C. As to what "signed" means, the Official Comment to C.L. §1-201(39) states:

> The inclusion of authentication in the definition of "signed" is to make clear that as the term is used in this Act a complete signature is not necessary. Authentication may be printed, stamped or written; it may be by initials or by *thumbprint.*

C.L. §1-201, Official Comment 39 (1975, 1997 Repl. Vol.) (emphasis added). . . .

Second, the process that a non-account holder goes through to provide a thumbprint signature is not unreasonably inconvenient. As noted, non-account holders seeking to cash a check are asked to apply their right thumb to an inkless fingerprinting device to create a "thumbprint signature." Unlike fingerprinting—which has repeatedly been upheld as an "unobtrusive" form of identification—thumbprint signatures do not require application of ink nor do they require the participation of more than one digit. In fact, appellant's thumbprint signature program uses an inkless fingerprinting device that leaves no ink stains or residue.

And third, this procedure is a reasonable and necessary answer to the growing incidence of check fraud. The American Bankers Association has reported that check fraud losses have grown, between 1995 and 1997, at an average rate of 17.5 percent. Carreker-Antinori, Provide Your Bank with a Shield of Protection against Check Fraud, Thompson Financial Publishing, at http://www.tfp.com/text/Fraudlink.pdf. "Industry estimates based on survey data show that actual losses from check fraud amounted to $512.3 million in 1997, a 5.2 percent increase over the $487.1 million estimated for 1995." Id.

As a result of the rising level of check fraud, thumbprint programs, as appellee notes, "have been endorsed by the American Bankers Association and more than thirty (30) state bankers associations including Arizona, Maryland, Missouri, Oregon, Texas, Utah and Virginia." Testifying before the United States House of Representatives as to the effectiveness of these programs, Charles L. Owens, former Chief of the Financial Crimes Section of the FBI, stated:

> We have supported implementation of inkless fingerprint policies which have been adopted by over 20 State bankers associations for non-bank customers negotiating checks. Where implemented, these procedures have successfully reduced negotiation of stolen and counterfeit checks by as much as 50 percent.

Computer Generated Check Fraud, Subcommittee on Domestic and International Monetary Policy, Committee on Banking and Financial Services, U.S. House of Representatives, May 1, 1997; see also Perkey v. Department of Motor Vehicles, 42 Cal. 3d 185, 228 Cal. Rptr. 169, 721 P.2d 50, 53 (1986) (stating that the fingerprint requirement is one of the few non-invasive reliable means of combating rampant fraud).

Finally, appellant's contention that a thumbprint does not serve the purposes of the Act is unpersuasive. We agree with appellant that a thumbprint cannot be used, in most instances, to confirm the identity of a non-account checkholder at the time that the check is presented for cashing, as his or her thumbprint is usually not on file with the drawee at that time. We disagree, however, with appellant's conclusion that a thumbprint signature is therefore not "reasonable identification" for purposes of C.L. §3-501(b)(2). . . .

III.

Appellant further asserts that the circuit court erred in holding that the appellee did not dishonor the check under C.L. §3-502(d)(1). That section provides that "if the draft is payable on demand, the draft is dishonored if presentment for payment is duly made to the acceptor and the draft is not paid on the day of presentment." Because the check "presented to [appellee] was payable on demand" and because appellee "accepted the check on August 3, 2000, but did not make payment on that date," appellant concludes that appellee "dishonored the check."

C.L. §3-502(d)(1), however, is not relevant to the instant case because the check in question, as we concluded earlier, was never accepted by appellee. In other words, appellant cites the wrong section of the U.C.C. The section that appellant should have cited is C.L. §3-502(b)(2), as it applies to dishonored "unaccepted" checks.

That section provides that if an unaccepted "draft is payable on demand . . . the draft is dishonored if presentment for payment is duly made to the drawee and the draft is not paid on the day of presentment." C.L. §3-502(b)(2). There is no dishonor, however, if presentment fails "to comply with the terms of the instrument, an agreement of the parties, or other applicable law or rule." C.L. §3-501(b)(3). In the words of one authority:

> If the presentment is not proper, payment or acceptance may be refused by the presentee and this refusal does not constitute a dishonoring of the instrument. This provision comes into play if the presentment does not comply "with the terms of the instrument, an agreement of the parties, or other applicable law or rule."

6B Anderson on the Uniform Commercial Code [Rev] §3-501:15 (3d Ed. 1998).

It is undisputed that appellee had the authority to refuse payment in accordance with the deposit agreement it had with each account holder, including with the drawer of the check in question. Pursuant to that agreement, appellee was permitted to set "physical and/or documentary requirements" for all those who seek to cash a check with appellee. And because appellee had the authority to refuse payment by agreement with its customer under C.L. §3-501(b)(2)(ii) unless "reasonable identification" was presented, appellant's failure to provide his thumbprint rendered the presentment ineffective and did not result in a dishonor of the check when appellee returned it to him. . . .

CASE REMANDED TO THE CIRCUIT COURT FOR FURTHER PROCEEDINGS CONSISTENT WITH THIS OPINION.

The Maryland Court of Appeals, the highest court in that state, affirmed, 373 Md. 672, 821 A.2d 22 (2003), noting only that an agreement between the bank and its customer has no effect on the rights of the check's presenter (though it does insulate the bank from a charge of wrongful dishonor). The court quite agreed that a drawee bank may require the presenter to give a thumbprint. Joined by Chief Judge Bell, Judge Eldridge dissented in this short opinion:

> I agree that the Circuit Court erred in failing to render a declaratory judgment. I cannot agree with the majority's holding that, after the petitioner

presented his driver's license and a major credit card, it was "reasonable" to require the petitioner's thumbprint as identification.

Today, honest citizens attempting to cope in this world are constantly being required to show or give drivers' licenses, photo identification cards, social security numbers, the last four digits of social security numbers, mothers' "maiden names," 16 digit account numbers, etc. Now, the majority takes the position that it is "reasonable" for banks and other establishments to require, in addition, thumbprints and fingerprints. Enough is enough. The most reasonable thing in this case was petitioner's "irritation with the Bank of America's Thumbprint Signature Program." (Majority opinion at p. 25.)

2. Notice of Dishonor

Indorsers are also entitled to notice of the dishonor after it occurs (but drawers are entitled to notice of dishonor only if a non-bank acceptor refuses payment of the draft; §3-414(d)). *Notice of dishonor* is defined in §3-503, which you should read.[9] Note that subsection (c) of §3-503 requires notice of dishonor to be given very quickly to be effective.

3. Protest

Protest is a technical ritual in which an official, normally a notary public, makes a formal presentment of a draft to the drawee and, upon dishonor, draws up, signs, and seals an official statement (called a *protest*) of what happened. The protest may also mention to whom notice of dishonor is given. Read §3-505(b). This ritual is no longer required, but is nonetheless sometimes done because it simplifies proof of these matters. See §3-505(a).

4. Excuse

Under some circumstances—spelled out in detail in §3-504, which you should examine carefully—these technical requirements (presentment, dishonor, notice of dishonor) can become either temporarily or completely unnecessary. For the lawyer whose client has failed to take these technical steps, §3-504 can be a bonanza—the treasure chest from which is pulled the excuse that saves the case.

These technical rights must in some situations give way to the exigencies of life. In an early case, Polk v. Spinds, 5 Cold. (45 Tenn.) 431 (1868), the advent of the Civil War made it "difficult" for the Northern holder of a promissory note signed by a Tennessee maker to make a presentment to the maker

9. *Practice Pointer*: A good attorney advises clients to give notice of dishonor to all prior parties immediately on finding out the check is being returned. See §3-503(b).

until the war ended. The Supreme Court of Tennessee held the presentment and delayed notice of dishonor excused, stating a test that is still often quoted:

> Obstacles of the kind which will excuse, need not be of the degree or extent which make travel, intercourse, presentment, impossible. It is enough if they be of the degree and character which deter men of ordinary prudence, energy and courage, from encountering them in prosecution of business, in respect of which they owe an active and earnest duty, and feel an active and earnest interest.

Id. at 433.

In reading §3-504, note that subsection (c) talks about when *delay* in taking one of these steps is excused (but the step must still be taken), and subsections (a) and (b) address themselves to situations in which the step becomes completely unnecessary.

PROBLEM 159

A promissory note contains a clause stating, "All parties to this note hereby waive all rights to presentment, notice of dishonor, and protest. . . ." Is a clause like this buried in the fine print on the front side of a note sufficient to deprive indorsers of their right to notice of dishonor? See §3-504(a)(iv) and (b)(ii).

PROBLEM 160

Frank Fortune was walking along the street, his pockets stuffed with money and checks he had won with a dazzling display of his prowess in the game of poker, when he was stopped by a creditor, one Mr. Holdit. Holdit demanded payment of a long-due $50 obligation, and Fortune was glad to indorse over to him a check for that amount that Fortune had won from Dan Deuces; Fortune was named as payee on the check. After giving the check to Holdit, Fortune thought better of the whole transaction so he contacted Dan Deuces, the drawer, the next day and persuaded him to stop payment on the check. Holdit held onto the check for six weeks and then took it to his bank, the Creditors National, and cashed it. Creditors National presented the check to the drawee bank, which dishonored it, whereupon Creditors National reclaimed its money from Mr. Holdit. Holdit, now very mad, sued Fortune on his indorser's obligation. Was Frank Fortune discharged by the delay in presentment? See §3-415(e). Was the presentment delay excused within the meaning of §3-504(a)(iv)? See Harik v. Harik, 861 F.2d 139 (6th Cir. 1988).

Makel Textiles, Inc. v. Dolly Originals, Inc.

New York Supreme Court, 1967
1967 WL 8938

SPIEGEL, J.

This is an action by the plaintiff to recover $8,000 on promissory notes executed by defendant Dolly Originals, Inc., on certain of which the names of defendants Nathan Goldberg, Richard L. Lewis, and Fred Kushner appear as endorsers.

Dolly Originals, Inc., originally borrowed $40,000; $30,000 was repaid to the plaintiff. Thereafter a promissory note in the sum of $10,000 (Pl. Ex. 1) was made to the order of the plaintiff by Dolly Originals, Inc., by Nathan Goldberg, president, and also bore the purported signature of Richard L. Lewis. The signature of Nathan Goldberg and the purported signature of Richard L. Lewis, as endorsers also appear on the back of said note. This note was not paid. Thereafter two notes each in the sum of $5,000 (Pl. Exs. 2A and 2B) were executed to the order of the plaintiff by Dolly Originals, Inc., through its president, Nathan Goldberg, and purportedly by Richard L. Lewis. The endorsement on the back of these two notes, which were given in lieu of the $10,000 note, bears the signatures of Nathan Goldberg and Fred Kushner. Five checks, each in the sum of $2,000 (Pl. Exs. 3A-3E), to the order of the plaintiff, were executed simultaneously with the two $5,000 notes and bore the signature of Nathan Goldberg, president of Dolly Originals, Inc., and the name of Richard L. Lewis. One of these checks was deposited and returned unpaid (plaintiff's exhibit 4A). None of the other four checks was deposited. No names of any endorsers appear on the back of these checks. Thereafter two other corporate checks for $2,000 were given by Dolly Originals, Inc., to the plaintiff. One of these was paid. The balance of $8,000 is now the subject of this suit.

After the trial of this action the complaint was dismissed as against the defendant Richard L. Lewis after proof that his signature was not genuine, and judgment was rendered against Dolly Originals, Inc., which offered no defense to the action. There remains only the determination of liability of the individual defendants, Nathan Goldberg and Fred Kushner, the endorsers on the notes.

The said defendants moved to dismiss the complaint at the end of the trial on the ground that the promissory notes of the corporation had never been presented for payment and thus the obligation of the endorsers was discharged; further, that subsequent checks given after the endorsement on the previous notes were taken by the plaintiff in payment of this obligation relieved the defendants of any further liability on this debt. The latter contention has no merit. A check given in payment of an obligation is merely a conditional payment and does not relieve the endorser of his liability on the obligation if the check is unpaid (Uniform Commercial Code §3-802 [§3-310(b) in the Revision—Eds.] . . .).

From all the evidence adduced upon the trial of this action, it appears that the defendant Nathan Goldberg was the president and principal officer of the defendant Dolly Originals, Inc. As such president, he executed the promissory notes and signed the corporate checks hereinabove mentioned. The promissory notes were also endorsed by him as an individual. By virtue of his active participation in the affairs of Dolly Originals, Inc., it is obvious that the defendant Nathan Goldberg well knew that the notes could not be and were not paid from corporate funds. Under these circumstances the obligation to serve Goldberg with notice of dishonor and non-payment must be deemed unnecessary, at least impliedly, within the meaning of the Uniform Commercial Code. Plaintiff's failure to present the notes for payment and give the said defendant notice of non-payment could not and did not injure nor prejudice his rights in any way. Formal notice of presentment and dishonor to Mr. Goldberg would be merely a useless gesture of advising him of a fact with which he was most familiar (UCC §§3-507, 3-511 [§3-504 in the Revision—Eds.]; J.W. O'Bannon Co. v. Curran, 129 App. Div. 90; William S. Chemical Co. v. Root, 152 N.Y.S. 368; Nemser v. Goldman, 145 N.Y.S.2d 841).

The defendant Fred Kushner was an endorser only, on each of two notes for $5,000 (Pl. Exs. 2A and 2B) above mentioned. As to said defendant Kushner, the record is void of any testimony, or proof of notice of presentment and dishonor as required under the Uniform Commercial Code. Nor is there any evidence of any activity or participation in the affairs of the corporation so as to excuse presentment or notice of dishonor.

Accordingly, the defendant Fred Kushner may have judgment against the plaintiff dismissing the complaint, and the plaintiff may have judgment against the defendant Nathan Goldberg in the sum of $8,000 with interest thereon from May 12, 1965. . . .

E. The Drawee's Obligation

PROBLEM 161

After he brought a successful Truth in Lending action against Octopus National Bank (ONB), attorney Sam Ambulance made the mistake of continuing to bank at ONB. At a time when his bank balance greatly exceeded that amount, Sam wrote an alimony check for $3,000 and gave it to his ex-wife, Sue. Because similar checks had bounced in the past, Sue hurriedly walked the check directly into the bank and presented it across the counter. The teller who took the check alerted the bank's manager, who laughed evilly as he threw it back across the counter at Sue, informing her that Sam's business was no longer welcome at ONB and that it refused to pay any more of his checks, even though there was money in the account sufficient to meet the check. You are the attorney who handled Sue's divorce, so she calls you and asks what she should do. See §§3-408, 3-401(a), 3-414, 4-402.

If you worked through all of those citations diligently, you should arrive at this conclusion: the drawee, not having signed the draft, is not liable on it. The drawee, having signed nothing, incurs no contractual obligation (though it may still be liable to the drawer under §4-402 (wrongful dishonor), which we will discuss in a later chapter).

So far, when we have mentioned *drafts*, we have really been talking only about drafts drawn on banks (checks); the drawee we have been discussing is a bank administering a checking account. But the business community makes much use of the non-bank draft in the purchase and sale of goods, particularly when the parties are in different cities.

> The seller agrees to ship buyer 10,000 widgets at $20 each, "payment against sight draft." This means that the seller will draw a draft on the buyer payable on "sight" (when the buyer first sees it). Such a procedure permits the seller to discount the draft with the seller's bank, which will indorse the draft over to a collecting bank in the buyer's city. The collecting bank will make a formal presentment to the buyer-drawee. The parties frequently arrange it so that the collecting bank has control over the goods and will turn them over to the buyer at the moment when the latter pays the draft. Thus, at the moment of payment, buyer receives the goods. No one need trust anyone else.

In the hypothetical, the seller is the drawer, and the buyer is the drawee. The payee on the draft could be any of a number of people—the seller itself, the seller's bank, or simply "bearer." The two banks that transfer the draft will presumably sign it, and as soon as they do so, they will become indorsers. If the buyer dishonors the draft on presentment, the collecting bank will send out the required notices of dishonor and then request payment on the basis of the obligations (indorser and drawer) of the prior parties.

1. The Non-Bank Acceptor

Sometimes in the sales transaction described above, the buyer will ask for time in which to pay the draft after receiving the goods. In such a case, the seller will probably want the buyer to assume liability on the instrument, so the seller will require the buyer to sign the instrument when it is presented and thus become primarily responsible for its payment. The drawee who places a signature on a draft (typically by signing it diagonally across the front) is said to have *accepted* it, and he or she incurs the obligation of an *acceptor.* See §3-413. *Acceptance* is defined in §3-409(a) as the "drawee's signed agreement to pay a draft as presented." Read §3-409.

Norton v. Knapp

Supreme Court of Iowa, 1884
64 Iowa 112, 19 N.W. 867

SEEVERS, J.

Because of the statements contained in an amended abstract, we are required to set out the petition as follows:

> That the plaintiffs sold and delivered to the defendant, about February 17, 1882, a certain flaxseed-cleaner mill, at the agreed price of eighty dollars, no part of which had been paid, and that the same was then due.
>
> That on or about April, 1882, plaintiffs drew a sight draft on defendant for the agreed price of said mill, which was in words and figures as follows:
>
> $80 La Crosse, Wis., April 18, 1882.
>
> At sight pay to the order of *Exchange Bank of Nora Springs, Iowa, eighty dollars,* value received, and charge the same to the account of
>
> *NORTON & KELLER.*
>
> To Miles Knapp, Nora Springs, Ia.

—Which was accepted by said Miles Knapp in written words and figures, on the back thereof, as follows: "Kiss my foot. MILES KNAPP." Also alleging "that said draft was still the property of plaintiff, due and unpaid, and claiming judgment for eighty dollars, interest, and costs." . . .

The amount in controversy being less than $100, the court has certified certain questions upon which the opinion of this court is desired. In substance, two of them are whether the words "kiss my foot," on the back of the draft, signed by the drawee, is a legal and valid acceptance, and whether such acceptance can be introduced in evidence without showing it was the intention to accept the draft. The rule upon this subject is thus stated in 1 Pars. Bills & Notes, 282:

> If a bill is presented to a drawee for the purpose of obtaining his acceptance, and he does anything to or with it which does not distinctly indicate that he will not accept it, he is held to be an acceptor, for he has the power, and it is his duty, to put this question beyond all possibility of doubt. . . .

The rule we understand to be, if the drawee does anything with or to the bill, or writes thereon anything, which does not clearly negate an intention to accept, then he can or will be charged as an acceptor. The question, then, is, what construction should be placed on the words "kiss my foot," written on the bill and signed by him? They cannot be rejected as surplusage. Such language is not ordinarily used in business circles or polite society. But by their use the defendant meant either to accept or refuse to accept the bill. It cannot be he meant the former; therefore, it must be the latter. It seems quite clear to us that the defendant intended by the use of the contemptuous and vulgar words above stated, to give emphasis to his intention not to accept or have anything to do with the bill or with the plaintiff. We understand the words, in common parlance, to mean and express contempt for the person to whom the words are addressed, and when used as a reply to a request, they imply, and are understood to mean, decided, unqualified, and contemptuous refusal to comply with such request. In such sense they were undoubtedly used when the defendant was requested to accept the bill. The question asked upon this point must be answered in the negative. Whether parol evidence is admissible to show the intent of the defendant, we have no occasion to determine, because no such evidence was offered, and our rule is not to determine mere abstract propositions. . . .

If the seller has agreed to give the buyer a credit period prior to payment—say, 60 days—a sight draft similar to this one is drawn:

> To Betty Buyer
>
> Sixty (60) days after sight, pay to the order of *Scott Seller $10,000.*
>
> *Scott Seller*

The seller will then discount the draft with his local bank, indorsing it over to the bank. The bank will forward it to a collecting bank in the buyer's city that will make a "presentment for acceptance" to the buyer and, if she accepts, will see that she gets the goods. When the buyer accepts, she will sign her name, usually diagonally across the face of the instrument, and the instrument will be dated, to start the 60-day period running, and returned to the collecting bank. During the 60-day period the draft (now called a "trade acceptance") may be further negotiated; it is now legally the same as an unmatured promissory note, the acceptor incurring an obligation almost identical to that of a maker. At the end of the 60 days, the holder of the draft will make a second presentment to the drawee (acceptor), this time a "presentment for payment." If the acceptor now dishonors, she can be sued on her §3-413 obligation, or the holder can proceed, after giving notice of dishonor, against the drawer and prior indorsers on their contracts. Note that if the drawee had dishonored the first presentment, the one for acceptance, she would not have been liable on the instrument because at that point she had incurred no §3-413 liability.

When a sight draft gives the drawee time for payment after sight, the holder *must* make a presentment for acceptance in order to start the running of the credit period. Read §3-502(b)(4) and the last paragraph of its Official Comment 4.

2. Checks

When the draft is a *check*, so that the drawee is a bank, the same rules apply. The drawer's writing of the check does not, absent unusual circumstances, create any immediate rights in the checking account funds, and the drawee bank has no liability to the holder of the check until it accepts it. Of course, the drawee bank is bound by the terms of its checking account agreement with its customer, the drawer. This checking account agreement is analogous to the contract of sale in the non-bank drawee situation discussed above. But the checking account agreement is a private contract between the bank and its customers and confers no rights on other parties. Read §3-408.

Galyen Petroleum Co. v. Hixson

Nebraska Supreme Court, 1983
213 Neb. 683, 331 N.W.2d 1

COLWELL, J., Retired.

Plaintiff, Galyen Petroleum Company (Galyen), appeals a summary judgment in favor of the Commercial Bank (Bank) of Bassett, Nebraska, in a suit to recover on three checks personally presented to drawee Bank by payee Galyen, upon which payment was refused, although the drawer had funds on deposit to pay some of the checks.

Galyen was a wholesale supplier of fuels to the defendant, Norman J. Hixson, who had an account in and owed Bank more than $7,000 on promissory notes. On October 1, 1975, Hixson issued check No. 2287, $3,763.25, to Galyen, which was presented through channels to drawee Bank for collection and returned unpaid for insufficient funds. On October 15, 1975, Hixson issued check No. 2304, $2,740.88, to Galyen, which was likewise presented and returned. On November 1, 1975, Hixson issued check No. 2324, $378.94, to Galyen, which was likewise presented and returned. On November 12 and 13, 1975, Galyen personally presented the three checks to Bank during regular banking hours at Bassett, Nebraska; upon each presentment, Bank unconditionally refused payment of all three checks and forthwith returned them to Galyen. Bank's records and the evidence show that at the close of business on November 10, 1975, Hixson's account had a credit balance of $3,048.46. There was no account activity on November 11, 1975. On November 12, three deposits were made to the account, $209.27, $92.90, and $443.17. After Galyen presented the checks for collection on November 12, Bank set off Hixson's account for two items of $1,006.75 and $2,700 that were credited to Hixson's note account, leaving a balance of $87.05. The credited notes were not then due. The printed part of the notes recites in part:

> Payee shall have at all times a security interest in and right of setoff against any deposit balances of the maker(s) . . . and may at the time, without notice, apply the same against payment of this note . . . whether due or not. . . .

Bank had a financing statement and security agreement from Hixson dated March 7, 1975. Hixson did not object to the setoffs. Galyen filed its petition on August 23, 1976. Hixson was discharged as a bankrupt on December 7, 1976, and dismissed as a party defendant.

Galyen claims that summary judgment was not a proper remedy here for the reason there were genuine issues of material fact concerning Bank's transactions on November 12 and 13.

Galyen assigns as error that Bank unlawfully refused payment of the checks on presentment and that it had no authority to make a setoff to credit Hixson's promissory notes where (1) the notes were not due and (2) the setoffs were exercised after presentment.

Neb. UCC §3-409(1) [§3-408 in the Revision—Eds.] (Reissue 1980) provides:

> A check or other draft does not of itself operate as an assignment of any funds in the hands of the drawee available for its payment, and the drawee is not liable on the instrument until he accepts it.

The authorities are agreed . . . that a check, of itself, and in the absence of special circumstances, is neither a legal nor an equitable assignment or appropriation of a corresponding amount of the drawer's funds in the hands of the drawee, and that therefore, in and of itself, it gives the holder of the check no right of action against the drawee and no valid claim to the fund of the drawer in its hands, even though the drawer has on deposit sufficient funds to pay it. It creates no lien on the money which the holder can enforce against the bank. [10 Am. Jur. 2d Banks §563 at 532-533 (1963).]

There are no special circumstances or agreements claimed here. The only evidence was the hearsay statement of Richard W. Galyen that Hixson told him that he had telephoned Bank and that the checks were good.

Summary judgment was a proper procedure here, and Galyen had no standing or cause of action against Bank on account of the dishonor of any of the three checks. It did have a remedy against the drawer. Neb. UCC §3-507(2) (Reissue 1980). We do not get to the question of setoffs. The summary judgment was properly granted.

Affirmed.

Section 3-408 does not mean that under no circumstances can the drawee bank become liable to the holder prior to acceptance. It was the common law rule that by special agreement the drawer could work an immediate assignment of bank-held funds so as to give the holder of the check a claim against the drawee bank prior to acceptance. See Fourth Natl. v. Yardley, 165 U.S. 634 (1897) (special agreement between drawer and payee); Ballard v. Home Natl. Bank, 91 Kan. 91, 136 P. 935 (1913) (special agreement between drawer and drawee). In Union Bank v. Safanie, 5 Ariz. App. 342, 427 P.2d 146 (1967), an oral statement by a bank officer to the payee that the drawer's check would clear when presented was held to create liability in fraud, and in Trump Taj Mahal Associates v. Bank of New York, 2003 WL 23750688 (N.J. Super. 2003), a bank that told a casino that an altered teller's check was good was held liable in an action for negligence. In a similar situation, the Nebraska Supreme Court used promissory estoppel to defeat the drawee bank; Bigger v. Fremont Natl. Bank, 215 Neb. 580, 340 N.W.2d 142 (1983). In one major UCC case finding such a special contractual liability in the drawee bank, the check was payable out of a special loan fund and was issued by the drawer after consultation with the bank, which immediately marked the account to show that the check was outstanding; this was held to create an immediate right in the payee to reach the funds, so that a stop payment order by the drawer came too late. See MidContinent Cas. Co. v. Jenkins, 2 U.C.C. Rep. Serv. 1164 (Okla. 1965). In Graybar Elec. Co. v. Brookline Trust Co., 39 U.C.C. Rep. Serv. 1721 (Boston Mun. Ct., App. Div. 1984), a bank that issued a personal money order in return for cash was required to pay it even though no signature of the bank appeared thereon; the court reasoned that the fact of issuance was an implied promise to pay the personal money order when it was presented. These causes of action would all be preserved as possibilities by §1-103.

3. Certification

The drawee bank's *acceptance* of a check is called *certification*. All of the Code sections on acceptance apply equally to certification. Read §§3-409(d) and 3-413.

PROBLEM 162

George Generous gave a check for $5,000 to the Grapes of Wrath Church as part of the church's drive to get money for a planned new building. The church did not want to cash any checks it received until it had at least $20,000 worth of pledges. On the other hand, the church didn't want contributors to be able to back out and stop payment either, so the church's lawyer advised the church directors to have all large checks certified. This, the lawyer knew, would have the effect of making the certifying bank primarily liable on the check (§3-413(a)). The church treasurer took George's check down to the drawee bank and asked to have it certified, a presentment for acceptance. The drawee bank refused, saying that its practice was never to certify gift checks.

(a) Is that a dishonor so that the church should give George notice of dishonor? See §3-409(d) and its Official Comment 4.

(b) What should the church's lawyer advise it to do now?

(c) If the bank had certified the check but later refused to pay it, could the church sue George on his drawer's obligation? See §3-414(c). Same result if George had donated a certified check that the bank later dishonored? See Official Comment 3 to §3-414; cf. §3-411.

F. Signature by an Agent

Section 3-402(a) generally defers to the common law governing an agent's signing of a contract on behalf of the principal. Thus, the agent's authority to sign the principal's name may be real (express or implied) or even apparent. See Senate Motors, Inc. v. Industrial Bank of Wash., 1971 WL 17944 (D.C. Super. 1971). The cited section also answers another question the original version of Article 3 had muddied.

PROBLEM 163

When tycoon J.B. Biggley wanted to borrow money for a business venture, he had his agent, J. Pierpont Finch, negotiate the loan from Wickets National Bank. When Finch signed the promissory note payable to the bank, he simply wrote his name as "J. Pierpont Finch, Agent," and failed to mention the name of his principal, J.B. Biggley. Is Biggley bound on this note? See §3-402 and Official Comment 1.

We shall leave the question of the scope of the agent's authority to other courses and instead concentrate on this question: when has the agent signed in so careless a fashion as to become personally liable? For instance, does the signature

Money Corporation, John Smith

make John Smith personally liable on a promissory note? Can he even introduce parol evidence to show that he is the president of the corporation and as such meant to sign only in his official capacity?

The smart way for an authorized agent to sign the instrument so as to avoid personal liability is for the agent to be careful to do two things: name the principal and unambiguously indicate that the agent is signing only in a representative capacity. See §3-402(b)(1). If the agent does one of these two things but not the other, the agent is liable to a holder in due course taking the instrument without notice that the agent was not intended to be liable, but otherwise the agent may prove that the original parties did not intend for the agent to incur liability. Official Comment 2 says that a holder in due course should be able to resolve any ambiguity against the agent.

Look at §3-402, digest the above paragraph, and then test your ability to read and comprehend a statute by resolving the Problems below.

PROBLEM 164

In the last Problem, would Finch himself be liable to a holder in due course? To Wickets National Bank?

Mundaca Investment Corp. v. Febba

New Hampshire Supreme Court, 1999
727 A.2d 990

Brock, C.J.

The defendants, Doris M. Febba, Thomas G. Scurfield, and Linda L. Kendall, appeal the Superior Court's (Smith, J.) grant of summary judgment in favor of the plaintiff, Mundaca Investment Corporation (Mundaca), holding the defendants personally liable for amounts due on two promissory notes. We reverse and remand. The defendants served as trustees of the L.T.D. Realty Trust (trust). On July 28, 1987, they purchased two condominium units for the trust. To finance this transaction, the defendants executed two promissory notes, secured by two mortgages, payable to the order of Dartmouth Savings Bank (bank). At the end of both notes below the signature line, the name of each defendant was typewritten beside the preprinted term "Borrower." Following their signatures, each of the defendants handwrote the word "Trustee." While both promissory notes state that they are secured by a mortgage, the trust is not identified on the face of the notes. The trust, however, is identified as the "Borrower" in both mortgages.

On August 19, 1993, Mundaca acquired the two notes from the Federal Deposit Insurance Corporation as receiver for the bank. By letters dated October 28, 1994, Mundaca notified defendants Scurfield and Febba that the two promissory notes were in default. Mundaca foreclosed on the condominium units and filed suit against the defendants individually for the remaining amount due on the notes. Both Mundaca and the defendants moved for summary judgment. The defendants' motion for summary judgment was denied. In granting Mundaca's motion for summary judgment, the trial court ruled that the form of the defendants' signatures—"[defendant's signature], Trustee"—did not show unambiguously that the defendants were signing in a representative capacity. See RSA 382-A:3-402(b) comment 2 (1994). The trial court then ruled that the defendants failed to meet their burden of proving that Dart-mouth Savings Bank did not intend to hold them personally liable. See RSA 382-A:3-402(b)(2) (1994). This appeal followed.

On appeal, the defendants argue that reading the notes and mortgages together shows unambiguously that they signed in a representative capacity for the trust as the identified principal, and therefore they are not personally liable under RSA 382-A:3-402(b)(1) (1994). Alternatively, the defendants contend that the trial court erred in granting Mundaca's motion for summary judgment because there was a genuine issue of material fact regarding whether the original parties intended the defendants to be personally liable. See RSA 382-A:3-402(b)(2).

The trial court applied RSA 382-A:3-402 [UCC Revised §3-402—Eds.] (1994), and the parties do not dispute that this version of the statute governs the defendants' liability. Accordingly, we will assume for purposes of this appeal that this version of the statute applies. But see, e.g., Barnsley v. Empire Mortgage Ltd. Partnership V, 142 N.H. 721, 723, 720 A.2d 63, 64 (1998). RSA 382-A:3-402 (1994) provides in pertinent part:

> (b) If a representative signs the name of the representative to an instrument and the signature is an authorized signature of the represented person, the following rules apply:
>
> (1) If the form of the signature shows unambiguously that the signature is made on behalf of the represented person who is identified in the instrument, the representative is not liable on the instrument.
>
> (2) Subject to subsection (c), if (i) the form of the signature does not show unambiguously that the signature is made in a representative capacity or (ii) the represented person is not identified in the instrument, the representative is liable on the instrument to a holder in due course that took the instrument without notice that the representative was not intended to be liable on the instrument. With respect to any other person, the representative

> is liable on the instrument unless the representative proves that the original parties did not intend the representative to be liable on the instrument.

The defendants argue that under RSA 382-A:3-402(b)(1), the handwritten term "Trustee" appearing next to their signatures on the notes shows unambiguously that the signatures were made in a representative capacity. Further, the defendants argue that while the promissory notes did not explicitly identify the trust, the notes and mortgages read together reveal that the term "Borrower" is identified as the trust. Accordingly, the defendants argue that they are not personally liable.

RSA 382-A:3-402(b)(1) requires that the form of the representative's signature show unambiguously that the signature is made on behalf of the represented person who is identified *in the instrument.* The defendants concede that the instruments in this case are the two promissory notes. The defendants, however, argue that fundamental contract law requires that the notes and mortgages be read together to interpret the contracting parties' intentions. General principles of contract law only apply to negotiable instruments if not displaced by the Uniform Commercial Code. See RSA 382-A:1-103 (1994). Accordingly, we hold that because the represented person, in this case the trust, is not identified in the *instrument* as required by RSA 382-A:3-402(b)(1), this case falls squarely under RSA 382-A:3-402(b)(2).

Pursuant to RSA 382-A:3-402(b)(2), the defendants could be personally liable in two situations: (1) to a holder in due course who takes the instrument without notice that the defendants did not intend to be personally liable; and (2) to any other party unless the defendants prove that the original parties did not intend them to be personally liable. While the trial court did not address the first situation, it ruled that the defendants failed to meet their burden of proving that the original parties did not intend them to be personally liable. The defendants contend, however, that summary judgment was inappropriate because there was a genuine issue of material fact as to the intent of the original parties. We agree. . . .

Our review of the record reveals a disputed issue of material fact as to the intent of the original parties, i.e., Dartmouth Savings Bank and the defendants. While the notes do not explicitly identify the trust as the represented party, the mortgages show that the defendants signed in a representative capacity and identify the trust as the "Borrower." See RSA 382-A:3-402(b)(1). Furthermore, the record contains conflicting affidavits by the defendants and Heidi Postupack, the bank's loan officer who handled this transaction. The defendants' affidavits claim that they intended to sign the notes as representatives of the trust. Conversely, Postupack's affidavit states that she understood that the bank intended the defendants to be personally liable, jointly and severally, on the notes. Considering this evidence in the light most favorable to the defendants, see *Barnsley*, 142 N.H. at 723, 720 A.2d at 64, we conclude that a genuine issue of material fact exists as to the bank's intent regarding the defendants' personal liability on the notes.

As noted earlier, the trial court did not address whether Mundaca was a holder in due course who took without notice that the defendants did not intend to be personally liable on the notes. See RSA 382-A:3-402(b)(2). Because the record before us is silent on this matter, we leave this issue for the trial court on remand.

The defendants also argue that the mortgages act as a defense to their alleged personal liability on the notes. This argument is without merit. The mortgages only provide a defense to the defendants' alleged personal liability on the notes to the extent that the mortgages modify, supplement, or nullify their obligation on the notes. See RSA 382-A:3-117 [UCC Revised §3-117—Eds.] (1994). The defendants argue that it is clear that the mortgages modify and supplement the notes. We disagree. What is clear is that the mortgages were issued as collateral for the notes. What is unclear by reading the notes and the mortgages is the identity of the "Borrower." We have already held that the identity of the "Borrower" is a material issue of fact in dispute.

Accordingly, we reverse the grant of summary judgment and remand this case to the trial court for further proceedings consistent with this opinion.

Reversed and remanded.

All concurred.

PROBLEM 165

The president of Money Corporation was John Smith. He signed three corporate promissory notes as follows:

(1) "John Smith." Money Corporation was not mentioned in the note.
(2) "Money Corporation, John Smith." See Genesis Capital Ventures, LLC v. Restore With Apex, Inc., 282 F. Supp. 3d 1225, 1232 (D. Colo. 2017).
(3) "Money Corporation, John Smith, President."

In each case, is he personally liable to a holder in due course of the instrument?

PROBLEM 166

Kit Fielding was the corporate president of Francis Racing Stables. The corporate checks had the words "Francis Racing Stables" printed prominently in the upper left-hand corner of the checks, but when Fielding went to sign the checks on the drawer's line, he simply signed his name and did not sign the name of the company or in any way indicate that he was signing as an agent. If the check is negotiated to a holder in due course and then dishonored by the drawee bank, may the holder in due course successfully impose personal liability on Fielding? See §3-402(c) and its Official Comment 3; Triffin v. Ameripay, LLC, 368 N.J. Super. 587, 847 A.2d 628 (2004).

Nichols v. Seale

Texas Court of Civil Appeals, 1973
493 S.W.2d 589

GUITTARD, J.

In this appeal from a summary judgment on a promissory note, the principal questions are (1) whether as between the original parties extrinsic evidence is admissible to show that the signer acted for a corporation rather than for himself, although the note does not show his representative capacity and contains only an assumed name under which the corporation was doing business, and (2) whether a statement in his affidavit that he was acting on behalf of the corporation rather than for himself is competent summary judgment proof or an inadmissible conclusion. We hold that the evidence is admissible and raises a fact issue.

The note is on a printed form beginning "I, we or either of us," and is signed as follows:

THE FASHION BEAUTY SALON
Carl V. Nichols [typewriting]
Carl V. Nichols [handwriting]

The payee sued Carl V. Nichols "individually and doing business as The Fashion Beauty Salon." Nichols filed a sworn answer denying that he signed the note in question in his individual capacity and alleging that he signed on behalf of a corporation, Mr. Carls Fashion, Inc. In response to plaintiff's motion for summary judgment, defendant Nichols filed the following affidavit:

> My name is Carl V. Nichols, and I served as President of Mr. Carls Fashion, Inc., a Texas Corporation, doing business as The Fashion Beauty Salon at 2115 Sherry Lane, Dallas, Texas, from the date of its incorporation, January 14, 1960, and I signed the promissory note attached to Plaintiff's Original Petition and marked Exhibit "A" in the capacity of officer of such corporation and in behalf of such corporation and not in my personal capacity.

The trial court rendered summary judgment against Nichols on the note. We first consider whether we must affirm that judgment on the ground that the form of the signature makes Nichols individually liable as a matter of law under §3-403(2), which provides: [the court quoted the section].

Plaintiff contends that Nichols is personally obligated under subsection (1) because the note neither "names" the corporation nor shows that Nichols "signed in a representative capacity." Admittedly, the note does not show that he "signed in a representative capacity," because it does not describe him as a corporate officer or agent or use any other language, such as "by," indicating that he was acting for someone other than himself. Neither does it "name the person represented" unless "The Fashion Beauty Salon" can be taken as naming the corporation "Mr. Carls Fashion, Inc."

We hold that use of an assumed name does "name the person represented" within the meaning of the code. This section must be read along with §3-401(2), which expressly authorizes use of an assumed name in a negotiable instrument: "A signature is made by use of any name, including any trade or assumed name, upon an instrument. . . ." The official interpretation of this section includes the following comment concerning a signature on commercial paper: "It may be made in any name, including any trade name or assumed name, however false and fictitious, which is adopted for the purpose. Parol evidence is admissible to identify the signer, and when he is identified the signature is effective." This rule applies as well when the person using the assumed name is a corporation, since corporations are expressly permitted to use assumed names by Tex. Bus. Corp. Act Ann. art. 2.05 (1956) VATS, and may sue on contracts made in assumed names. Davis v. Tex-O-Kan Flour Mills Co., 186 F.2d 50 (5th Cir. 1950), W. B. Clarkson & Co. v. Gans S.S. Line, 187 S.W. 1106 (Tex. Civ. App., Galveston 1916, *writ ref'd*). Consequently, extrinsic evidence was admissible to show that "The Fashion Beauty Salon" was an assumed name for "Mr. Carls Fashion, Inc." This conclusion is supported by Weeks v. San Angelo Natl. Bank, 65 S.W.2d 348 (Tex. Civ. App., Austin 1933, *writ ref'd*), in which a note was signed "Weeks Drug Store No. 4 by Jno. A. Weeks." The court held that this signature was ambiguous and that parol evidence was admissible to show the party's intention that the note should be the obligation of "Weeks Drug Store No. 4, Inc.," a corporation not yet organized.

Since, as we have held, a corporation is "named" within §3-403(2) by use of its assumed name, that section does not forbid extrinsic evidence to show further, as between the original parties, that the signer was not personally obligated. Such proof may be admissible, not to vary terms of the instrument or to show a mistake, but rather to explain an ambiguity with respect to the capacity of the signer. An instrument which "names the person represented but does not show that the representative signed in a representative capacity," may be ambiguous with respect to the capacity in which he signed, since, in the absence of explanatory evidence, the signature may be interpreted either as his individual signature, or as a signature on behalf of the person represented. We find the present signature to be ambiguous for that reason. Directly in point here is Canton Provision Co. v. Chaney, 70 N.E.2d 687 (Ohio App. 1945), in which checks signed "Finer Foods, Jack Chaney" were held to be ambiguous so that parol evidence was admissible to show that Chaney signed as agent for another individual doing business as "Finer Foods." See also First State Bank v. Smoot-Curtis Co., 121 S.W.2d 667 (Tex. Civ. App., Fort Worth 1938, *writ dism'd by agr.*) and Norman v. Beling, 33 N.J. 237, 163 A.2d 129 (1960), both holding that a note signed with the name of a corporation and an officer, without showing his representative capacity, is ambiguous so that the representative capacity of the individual may be shown by parol evidence. In our opinion, the ambiguity in the present note is not removed by Nichols' name in typewriting, which, whether above or below his signature, may have been used only to identify the signer in case his handwriting was not legible. Moreover, it seems to us that the conventional printed language, "I, we or either of us" only serves to increase the ambiguity. . . .

Appellant's motion for rehearing is granted, our former opinion is withdrawn, and the cause is reversed and remanded.

NOTE

On appeal, the Texas Supreme Court reversed for a procedural reason:

> Texas law provides that in order for an agent to avoid liability for his signature on a contract, he must *disclose* his intent to sign as a representative to the other contracting party. Uncommunicated intent will not suffice. Heinrichs v. Evins Personnel Consultants, Inc., No. One, 486 S.W.2d 935 (Tex. 1972); Mahoney v. Pitman, 43 S.W.2d 143 (Tex. Civ. App., Amarillo 1931, *writ ref'd*).
>
> Again viewing Nichols' affidavit broadly, it states that he signed the note as president of the corporation, thus clearly indicating his subjective intent to sign as an agent. However, nowhere does Nichols say that he disclosed his intent to Seale. Nor does his statement that ". . . I signed the promissory note . . . in the capacity of officer of such corporation and in behalf of such corporation and not in my personal capacity," intimate that this intended capacity was communicated to Seale. This is his burden in the context of the summary judgment proceedings. Consequently, Nichols has not effectively raised a fact issue upon his alleged affirmative defense of representation and Seale's motion for summary judgment must be granted.

Seale v. Nichols, 505 S.W.2d 251, 255 (Tex. 1974). See also Rotuba Extruders, Inc. v. Ceppos, 46 N.Y.2d 223, 385 N.E.2d 1068, 413 N.Y.S.2d 141 (1978).

III. OTHER THEORIES OF LIABILITY

In commercial paper law, contractual obligations arise from the voluntary act of putting one's signature on a negotiable instrument. But the Code also establishes a host of other theories imposing liability.

Subsequent chapters explore the legal relationship between a bank and its customer, and, as we shall see, these parties may sue each other for violations of the rules arising from that relationship, primarily the "properly payable" rule of §4-401 and the wrongful dishonor rule of §4-402.

In Chapter 14 we will look closely at the legal snarls following forgeries and alterations of negotiable instruments and shall there encounter causes of action based on warranty and conversion.

CHAPTER 11 ASSESSMENT: MULTIPLE CHOICE QUESTIONS

1. Marker borrowed $25,000 from Friendly Finance, signing a negotiable promissory note for that amount plus interest. Marker soon had financial woes and stopped making payments. Marker's sister offered Friendly Finance $5,000 for the note. Friendly Finance accepted the offer gladly. Marker's sister stuck the note in a safe, with no intent to recover from Marker. Several months later, Marker received a big inheritance. Friendly Finance sued Marker for the remaining $20,000 on the debt. Will Friendly Finance succeed?
   a. Yes. Marker is still liable on the portion of the debt that was not paid.
   b. No. Marker's obligation to pay the debt is suspended.
   c. Yes. Friendly Finance may enforce a note that is lost, stolen, or destroyed.
   d. Yes. If Marker's sister does not intend to enforce the note, then Marker would get a windfall if Marker did not have to pay Friendly Finance.

2. Clever Richard was discouraged, because he owed $222,321.42 on his mortgage. Then he wrote "PAYMENT IN FULL FOR ALL MORTGAGE DEBT" conspicuously on the check he sent for his monthly mortgage payment of $1,500. The check was duly paid. Ninety days has passed. Is Clever Richard's entire mortgage debt of $222,321.42 discharged?
   a. Yes, because he tendered a check to pay the debt with PAID IN FULL conspicuously written on the check.
   b. No. "PAID IN FULL" can never be used to unilaterally settle a debt.
   c. No. The amount of the debt was not disputed.
   d. Yes. Clever Richard has simply declared bankruptcy and discharged the debt.

3. Draper sent a check to Praline Produce to pay for a shipment of nuts. Praline indorsed the check over to Careless Shipping to pay off some invoices. Careless Shipping's bookkeeper stuck the check in a file and forgot about it. Eventually, Careless Shipping rediscovered the check and presented it for payment. By this time, Draper had no money in its account and the drawee bank refused to pay the check. Which of the following could make Praline Produce not liable as an indorser?
   a. If the check was not presented or deposited within 30 days of the indorsement.
   b. If Praline Producer was not given timely notice of dishonor.
   c. If Praline Producer had indorsed "Without Recourse."
   d. All of the above.

4. Which of the following could have made Draper not liable as the drawer of the check?
   a. If the check was not presented within 30 days of Draper issuing it.
   b. If Draper was not given timely notice of dishonor.
   c. If Draper had written "Without Recourse" on the memo line of the check.
   d. None of the above.

5. Shaky Shoes issued a check to Flat Feet, a supplier. Flat Feet's manager went quickly to present the check to Shaky Shoes' bank, Wingtip Bank. Wingtip Bank refused to pay. Is Wingtip Bank liable to Flat Feet?
   a. No. Wingtip Bank did not sign the check.
   b. Yes, if there were sufficient funds in Shaky Shoes' account to pay the check.
   c. Yes. A check is an unconditional order to pay.
   d. Yes, otherwise checks would be worthless.

ANSWERS

1. *B* is the best answer. Under §3-310, when Friendly Finance took the note, that suspended the underlying obligation, the debt of $25,000. That obligation remains suspended until the note is paid (which would discharge the debt) or dishonored. Even if the note were dishonored, Friendly Finance could only enforce the debt if Friendly Finance were in possession of the note. In practical terms, when Friendly Finance sold the note, Friendly Finance gave up its rights to collect the underlying debt—that's exactly how negotiability is supposed to work. So *A* is incorrect. Marker may still be technically liable on the debt, but Friendly Finance cannot enforce that suspended liability. *C* is misleading. If Friendly Finance had lost the note, it could still enforce it. But Friendly Finance transferred the note, giving up its right to enforce the note. For the same reason, *D*

is incorrect. It is up to the holder, Marker's sister, whether Marker has to pay the note.

2. *C* is the best answer. The accord and satisfaction provision of §3-311 is a mechanism to make a good faith offer to settle a dispute. It is not effective where the amount owed is not in dispute. Contrary to *A*, it cannot simply be used on just any check, where there is no dispute to settle. *B* misstates the facts. *D* is simply a fantasy. Discharge of debt in bankruptcy requires filing a case in federal bankruptcy court.

3. *D* is the best answer. The question illustrates several protections given to indorsers. Indorser liability will be negated if the check is not presented or deposited in timely fashion, §3-415(f) (as in *A*), or there is not timely notice of dishonor (per *B*), §3-415(c). Likewise, an indorser is not liable as an indorser if she indorses "without recourse." §3-415(b), (as in *C*). The reason for the without-recourse rule is that indorsement may serve different purposes: to negotiate an instrument, to guaranty payment, or to restrict payment. "Without recourse" allows someone to indorse a check in order to negotiate it, while avoiding guarantor liability.

   Note the qualification "as an indorser." Someone who indorses without recourse can still be liable on other theories, as we will see. If she deposits a check that is not paid, she would still be liable to her bank for chargeback. If she transferred a check with a forgery or alteration, or subject to a defense, she would still be liable for breach of transfer warranty.

4. *D* is the best answer, switching from "All of the above" in the last question to "None of the above" here. The drawer of a check is not afforded the same protections as an indorser, because the drawer plays different role. The indorser is indorsing a check issued by someone else. The drawer is the very person who issued the check. So the drawer does not have the same need for the check to be presented in timely fashion, because the drawer should not escape paying the underlying debt (except in the unlikely event that the drawer's bank becomes insolvent in the meantime). The drawer does not need notice of dishonor, because dishonor is usually the one responsible for the check not being paid. The drawer may not have enough money in the account, or the drawer may have stopped payment on the check. Nor should a drawer be able to write a check without recourse, because no one would be liable on the instrument. §3-414(e).

5. *A* is the best answer. Wingtip Bank simply did not sign the check, so it has not promised to pay the check. If Wingtip Bank signed the check (making it a certified check), then it would be liable. Likewise, when Wingtip Bank issues a cashier's check, it is liable on the cashier's checks.

But ordinary checks represent only an obligation of the issuer, something anyone taking a check in payment should be aware of. We will see more about the payment of checks in following chapters. We will see that, although Wingtip Bank has no liability on the check to the holder, Flat Feet, Wingtip Bank may be liable to its customer, Shaky Shoes, for wrongful dishonor of the check.

CHAPTER 12

MORTGAGES AND PROMISSORY NOTES[1]

I. INTRODUCTION

Let's begin with what a mortgage actually is. Properly defined, it is a consensual lien placed by the homeowner (called the "mortgagor") on the real estate being financed in order secure the debt incurred by the loan in favor of the lender/mortgagee. The debt is created by the signing of a promissory note; the homeowner will be the maker/issuer of the promissory note and the lending institution will be payee on the note. When someone buying a home attends the closing, three different legal documents will come into being. They are: (1) the contract by which the lender loans the money in return for getting (2) a mortgage deed on the property, and (3) a promissory note signed by the homeowner (the maker) promising to pay the mortgage amount to the lender (the payee on the note).

1. The text in this chapter is largely adapted from Douglas J. Whaley, Mortgage Foreclosures, Promissory Notes, and the Uniform Commercial Code, 39 W. St. U. L. Rev. 313 (2012), updated periodically in Whaley's blog at http://douglaswhaley.blogspot.com/2013/02/mortgage-foreclosures-missing.html.

It is important to appreciate that our law has always considered the promissory note as the primary obligation, with the mortgage contract and deed merely being security (collateral) backing up that obligation. There is a common law maxim that "security follows the debt." This means that it is presumed that whoever is the current holder of the promissory note (the "debt") is entitled to enforce the mortgage lien (the "security"). The United States Supreme Court established the basic rule early in the 1873 case of Carpenter v. Longan:

> The note and mortgage are inseparable; the former as essential, the latter as an incident. An assignment of the note carries the mortgage with it, while an assignment of the latter alone is a nullity. . . . The mortgage can have no separate existence. When the note is paid the mortgage expires. It cannot survive for a moment the debt which the note represents. This dependent and incidental relation is the controlling consideration. . . . A purported assignment of a mortgage to a bank is not proof of a transfer of a promissory note secured by the mortgage, since the mortgage follows the note but not vice versa.

83 U.S. 271, 274 (1872).

Almost every state in the country has a similar rule, so that whoever has the note is the proper owner of the property, and the mortgage simply tags along the way a tail follows the dog.

The mortgage is reified as a mortgage deed that the lender should file in the local real property records so that the mortgage properly binds the property not only against the mortgagor but also the rest of the world (this process is called "perfection" of the lien). The "mort" portion of the word mortgage comes from Latin for "death" (as in "mortician," "morgue," "mortal," etc.) because on the payment of the promissory note debt, the mortgage deed dies.

The collapse of the housing market in the middle of the first decade of the twenty-first century was a direct consequence of greedy and unwise business practices. Gullible consumers were encouraged to take out mortgages they could not afford on property that turned out to be worth far less than the mortgage indebtedness. Minority communities were particularly hard hit, often targeted by shady lenders because people of color are more likely to store their wealth in home equity in many U.S. communities. Subprime lenders frequently sold the resulting mortgages (and the promissory notes that, in theory, went with them) to other financial institutions, and these mortgages were then bundled into a mass, placed in a securitization trust, and used as the assets backing the issuance of bonds by the trust. Things went fine until real property stopped appreciating in value and its worth dropped to alarmingly low levels, with a recession that engulfed the country and, indeed, the world. Not just subprime borrowers were affected; the recession reduced the value of almost all property, and perfectly responsible mortgagors (many of whom were also laid off from their jobs) began to struggle to make payments and avoid foreclosure. According to one monitoring agency, a record number of homes received foreclosure filings in 2010 (over 2.9 million).[2] In recent years, the economy has somewhat recovered, but foreclosures are still a major problem.

The combination of subprime lending, securitization of mortgage loans, a housing market that first boomed then busted, rapacious predators who worked hard to take for themselves the equity people had built up in their homes, and foreclosure mills that operated with neither proper paperwork, nor attention to the rules of law—much less common decency—led to an explosion of laws and legal actions designed to deal with these matters. Criminal prosecutions (of which there have so far been none, which is astounding given how venal it all was) from all this will be left to other courses.

What happens to the promissory note in the meantime? In the good old days, the twentieth century, it was kept down at the bank so that when the time for payment arrived, the bank could present it to the maker, and, if the maker didn't pay, could then use legal process (or in some states self-help) to foreclose on the mortgage lien. But during the feeding frenzy that the real estate mortgage community indulged in during the last decade, more bizarre things happened. The mortgages themselves were no longer kept at the originating bank, nor were the notes. Instead, as just explained, they were bundled together with many others and sold as a package to an investment banking firm, which put them in a trust and sold bonds backed by the trust to investors (a process called "securitization"). The bankers all knew the importance of the mortgage, and supposedly kept records as to the identity of the entities to whom the mortgages were assigned. But they were damn careless about the promissory notes, some of which were properly transferred whenever the mortgage was, some of which were kept at the originating bank, some of which were deliberately destroyed (a really stupid thing to do), and some of which disappeared into the black hole of the financial collapse, never to be seen again.

There was a bright spot in all this for homeowners, however. When they stopped paying the mortgage amounts, and the current owners of the mortgages/notes tried to foreclose on the property, the rules of Article 3 of the

2. RealtyTrac Staff, Record 2.9 Million U.S. Properties Receive Foreclosure Filings in 2010 Despite 30-Month Low in December, RealtyTrac (Jan. 12, 2011), http://www.realtytrac.com/content/press-releases/record-29-million-us-properties-receive-foreclosure-filings-in-2010-despite-30-month-low-in-december-6309. This immediately followed late 2009, where the third quarter saw 937,840 homes receive some sort of foreclosure letter, which at that point was " 'the worst three months of all time.' " Les Christie, Foreclosures: "Worst Three Months of All Time," CNN (Oct. 15, 2009, 7:34 A.M.), http://money.cnn.com/2009/10/15/real_estate/foreclosure_crisis_deepens.

Uniform Commercial Code unexpectedly came to the aid of the debtors. UCC §3-301 states that the only entity that is allowed to sue on a promissory note is a "*person entitled to enforce* the instrument" (sometimes called a "PETE"). Read §3-301 and its Official Comment carefully; we will parse out its meaning as we go.

II. THE PERSON ENTITLED TO ENFORCE THE INSTRUMENT

PROBLEM 167

When Harry Potter decided to settle down and buy a house he arranged for a financing loan with Rowling National Bank, which loaned him $200,000 to buy his home and had him sign three documents at the closing: a mortgage contract by which he agreed to repay the mortgage debt to the bank or its assigns, a mortgage deed that the bank would file in the real property records to create a lien on the property in its favor, and a promissory note by which Harry agreed to pay the mortgage amount to the order of Rowling National Bank. Harry, the mortgagor, signed all of these, and the bank kept the promissory note and recorded the mortgage deed.

Three months later the bank sold the mortgage to Muggles Investment Bank (MIB) by a contract assigning the mortgage to MIB. Muggles also took possession of the promissory note. MIB then sold the note and mortgage along with a hundred other mortgages it owned to a securitization trust, which bundled the notes together in the trust corpus and then sold bonds, using the trust assets as collateral for the bonds. As the mortgages matured, they were transferred out of the trust and into the hands of the entity that would seek final payment from the mortgagor and foreclose if he did not make this payment.

All Harry knew about this was that when Rowling National Bank sold his note he was informed that he should make his monthly payment to a mortgage servicing company called the Hogwarts Agency, which he dutifully did until a bad spell of events caused Harry to lose his job. He missed six payments in a row. Harry was then contacted by the Voldemort Financial Company (VFC), which claimed to be the current owner of the mortgage. Assume that VFC can prove a regular chain of mortgage assignment contracts, and that it has a photocopy of the original promissory note. The back of the note is blank, never having been indorsed by the payee Rowling National Bank.

Does Harry's liability as the maker of a promissory note run to VFC? See §§3-412, 3-301? Rephrased, is VFC a "holder" of the note?

The Return of the Allonge. From Chapter 9 on negotiation you may remember that a piece of paper on which indorsements were written, called an allonge, was much used throughout history, with this usage falling off as instruments only infrequently passed through many hands. But the rise of the market in home mortgage promissory notes resulted in many transfers, so allonges came back into fashion and have caused much litigation. In Anderson v. Burson, 424 Md. 232, 35 A.3d 452 (2012), there were indorsements on a separate piece of paper that travelled with the note in question, but the court ignored them because, as we saw in Chapter 3, an allonge must be attached to the note in order to be valid. In Shaya v. Karam, 2014 WL 1856392 (Mich. App. 2012), the so-called allonge for a $400,000 note itself stated that "[i]t is intended that this Allonge be attached to and made a permanent part of the Note," but the allonge was only folded into an envelope along with the note. The court held it was obviously not attached, and therefore the possessor of the note could not recover the $400,000 due on the note. Given the clear attachment requirement in §3-204(a), why do you suppose that whoever created the supposed allonges in these cases failed to staple them to the notes?

PROBLEM 168

U.S. Bank seeks to enforce a promissory note as a holder in due course, relying on an indorsement on a separate piece of paper. The note and the separate piece of paper have matching holes showing they were once stapled together, but are now simply sitting next to each other in the loan file. Is U.S. Bank a holder? See Mitchell v. U.S. Bank, N.A., 2017 WL 3707274 (Mass. Land Ct. 2017). What if the allonge had been executed one day before the note? Does that pre-dating affect its validity when it's subsequently attached to the note? See Bank of New York Mellon v. Florida Kalanit, 770 LLC, 2019 WL 1781954 (Fla. App. 2019).

The Shelter Rule. The definition of a person entitled to enforce the note under §3-301 includes "a nonholder in possession of the instrument who has the rights of a holder." This is our old friend the "shelter rule," discussed in prior chapters. That concept reflects the basic idea that if I sell you something you get whatever rights I have in the object sold (you take "shelter" in my rights). This is true of negotiable instruments per §3-203(b), and holder in due course rights could pass in this fashion to someone who clearly was not a holder in due course (see Problem 127 in Chapter 10).

PROBLEM 169

The original promissory note was payable to Octopus National Bank. When ONB sold the note to First State Bank it failed to indorse the note in any way. Is FSB a "holder" of the note without this necessary indorsement? Is it a person entitled to enforce the note under §3-301? See Leyva v. National Default Servicing Corp., 255 P.3d 1275 (Nev. 2011) (to use the shelter rule the transferee must also prove the validity of the transfer from the original owner). What is the reason for giving a non-holder the rights of a holder? See page 563.

In the Harry Potter Problem, the entity trying to foreclose only had a *copy* of the original note. In Whaley's article cited in the first footnote to this chapter, he states what he calls the "Golden Rule of Mortgage Foreclosures," which is that such foreclosures cannot proceed without production of the *original promissory note* signed at the closing. The reason for this is that there might be one hundred copies of the original note, but that wouldn't allow one hundred holders to foreclose; see Dickerson v. Regions Bank, 2014 WL 1118076 (Tenn. App. 2014) (copies irrelevant where no explanation of the current location of the original promissory note); In re Veal, 450 B.R. 897 (B.A.P. 9th Cir. 2011) (dueling creditors attempting to foreclose each held only a copy of the note, but not the original, neither successful). The Uniform Commercial Code is clear that if the maker of the note pays the wrong party the maker's liability is not discharged, and the maker must still pay the true holder of the note when it is finally presented; see §3-602.

States following these rules are called "show me the note" jurisdictions (in the language of the cases), but there are other courts that disregard the rules of the UCC and allow foreclosure without production of the original note. The following two cases reflect both possibilities.

Bank of America v. Kabba

Supreme Court of Oklahoma, 2012
276 P.3d 1006

COMBS, J.

FACTUAL AND PROCEDURAL HISTORY

¶1 In a petition filed on March 11, 2010, Bank of America, NA, claiming to be the present holder of the note (hereinafter Bank of America) initiated a foreclosure action against Kabba and his wife. Bank of America claimed, at that time, to hold the note and mortgage as Successor by Merger to LaSalle Bank National Association, as Trustee under the Trust agreement for the Structured Asset Investment Loan Trust Series 2004-BNC2. A review of the note shows a blank indorsement. This blank indorsement was filed with the lower court for the first time in the motion for summary judgment. The blank indorsement was not mentioned or referenced in the original petition.

BNC Mortgage, Inc., was the original lender. Bank of America filed with the Court Clerk of Cleveland County, a document entitled "Assignment of Real Estate Mortgage" on January 17, 2011, therein claiming the assignment to be effective as of February 9, 2010. This was nine months after the filing of the petition to foreclose. Additionally, this "Assignment of Mortgage," signed by Mortgage Electronic Registrations Systems, Inc. (hereinafter MERS), as nominee for BNC Mortgage, Inc., and its successors and assigns, merely named Bank of America as Successor by Merger to LaSalle Bank National Association, as Trustee under the Trust agreement for the Structured Asset Investment Loan Trust Series 2004-BNC2. There was no mention of the note in this "Assignment of Mortgage." On June 13, 2011, Summary judgment was granted and memorialized by a Final Journal Entry of Judgment order in Bank of America's favor, against Kabba and his wife. Kabba appeals this summary judgment asserting Bank of America failed to demonstrate standing. . . .

Analysis

¶3 Appellant argues Appellee does not have standing to bring this foreclosure action. Although Appellee has argued it holds the note, there is nothing in the record that shows when Appellee became the holder. The face of the note indicates it was indorsed in blank. However, this indorsement was not filed with the petition but with the motion for summary judgment. The purported "Assignment of Mortgage" was filed after the filing of the foreclosure proceedings and was signed by MERS, and not BNC Mortgage, Inc. The "Assignment of Mortgage" at no time mentioned the note.

¶4 The issue presented to this Court is standing. This Court has previously held:

> Standing, as a jurisdictional question, may be correctly raised at any level of the judicial process or by the Court on its own motion. This Court has consistently held that standing to raise issues in a proceeding must be predicated on interest that is "direct, immediate and substantial." Standing determines whether the person is the proper party to request adjudication of a certain issue and does not decide the issue itself. The key element is whether the party whose standing is challenged has sufficient interest or stake in the outcome.

Matter of the Estate of Doan, 1986 OK 15, ¶7, 727 P.2d 574, 576. In Hendrick v. Walters, 1993 OK 162, ¶4, 865 P.2d 1232, 1234, this Court also held:

> Respondent challenges Petitioner's *standing* to bring the tendered issue. Standing refers to a person's legal right to seek relief in a judicial forum. *It may be raised as an issue at any stage of the judicial process by any party or by the court sua sponte.* (Emphasis original.)

Furthermore, in Fent v. Contingency Review Board, 2007 OK 27, footnote 19, 163 P.3d 512, 519, this Court stated "[s]tanding may be raised at any stage of the judicial process or by the court on its own motion." Additionally in *Fent,* this Court stated:

> Standing refers to a person's legal right to seek relief in a judicial forum. The three threshold criteria of standing are (1) a legally protected interest which must have been injured in fact—*i.e.,* suffered an injury which is actual, concrete and not conjectural in nature, (2) a causal nexus between the injury and the complained-of conduct, and (3) a likelihood, as opposed to mere speculation, that the injury is capable of being redressed by a favorable court decision. The doctrine of standing ensures a party has a personal stake in the outcome of a case and the parties are truly adverse.

Fent v. Contingency Review Board, 2007 OK 27, ¶7, 163 P.3d 512, 519-520. In essence, a plaintiff who has not suffered an injury attributable to the defendant lacks standing to bring a suit. And, thus, "standing [must] be determined as of the commencement of suit; . . ." Lujan v. Defenders of Wildlife, 504 U.S. 555, 570, n.5, 112 S. Ct. 2130, 2142 n.5, 119 L. Ed. 2d 351 (1992).

¶5 To commence a foreclosure action in Oklahoma, a plaintiff must demonstrate it has a right to enforce the note and, absent a showing of ownership, the plaintiff lacks standing. Gill v. First Nat. Bank & Trust Co. of Oklahoma City, 1945 OK 181, 159 P.2d 717. An assignment of the mortgage, however, is of no consequence because under Oklahoma law, "[p]roof of ownership of the note carried with it ownership of the mortgage security." Engle v. Federal Nat. Mortg. Ass'n, 1956 OK 176, ¶7, 300 P.2d 997, 999. Therefore, in Oklahoma it is not possible to bifurcate the security interest from the note. BAC Home Loans Servicing, L.P. v. White, 2011 OK CIV APP 35, ¶10, 256 P.3d 1014, 1017. Because the note is a negotiable instrument, it is subject to the requirements of the UCC. A foreclosing entity has the burden of proving it is a "person entitled to enforce an instrument" by showing it was "(i) the holder of the instrument, (ii) a nonholder in possession of the instrument who has the rights of a holder, or (iii) a person not in possession of the instrument who is entitled to enforce the instrument pursuant to

Section 12A-3-309 or subsection (d) of Section 12A-3-418 of this title." 12A O.S. 2001 §3-301.

¶6 To demonstrate you are the "holder" of the note you must establish you are in possession of the note and the note is either "payable to bearer" (blank indorsement) or to an identified person that is the person in possession (special indorsement). Therefore, both possession of the note and an indorsement on the note or attached allonge are required in order for one to be a "holder" of the note.

¶7 To be a "nonholder in possession who has the rights of a holder" you must be in possession of a note that has not been indorsed either by special indorsement or blank indorsement. Negotiation is the voluntary or involuntary transfer of an instrument by a person other than the issuer to a person who thereby becomes its holder. 12A O.S. 2001, §3-201. Transfer occurs when the instrument is delivered by a person other than its issuer for the purpose of giving to the person receiving delivery the right to enforce the instrument. 12A O.S. 2001, §3-203. Delivery of the note would still have to occur even though there is no negotiation. Delivery is defined as the voluntary transfer of possession. 12A O.S. 2001, §1-201(b)(15). The transferee would then be vested with any right of the transferor to enforce the note. 12A O.S. 2001, §3-203(b). Some jurisdictions have held, without holder status and therefore the presumption of a right to enforce, the possessor of the note must demonstrate both the fact of the delivery and the purpose of the delivery of the note to the transferee in order to qualify as the person entitled to enforce. In re Veal, 450 B.R. 897, 912 (B.A.P. 9th Cir. 2011). See also, 12A O.S. 2001, §3-203.

¶8 In the present case, Appellee has only presented evidence of an indorsed-in-blank note and an "Assignment of Mortgage." Appellee must prove that it is the holder of the note or the nonholder in possession who has the rights of a holder *prior* to the filing of the foreclosure proceeding. In the present matter the timeliness of the transfer is in question. Since Bank of America did not file the blank indorsement until it filed its motion for summary judgment it is impossible to determine from the record when Bank of America acquired its interest in the underlying note.

¶9 The assignment of a mortgage is not the same as an assignment of the note. If a person is trying to establish they are a nonholder in possession who has the rights of a holder they must bear the burden of establishing their status as a nonholder in possession with the rights of a holder. Appellee must establish delivery of the note as well as the purpose of that delivery. In the present case, it appears Appellee is trying to use the "Assignment of Mortgage" in order to establish the purpose of delivery. The "Assignment of Mortgage" purports to transfer "[f]or value received, the undersigned, Mortgage Electronic Registration Systems, Inc., as nominee for BNC Mortgage, Inc., and its successors and assigns does hereby assign, transfer and set over unto Bank of America, National Association as Successor by Merger to LaSalle Bank National Association, as Trustee under the Trust Agreement for the Structured Asset Investment Loan Trust Series 2004-BNC2, that certain real estate mortgage dated August 30, 2004, granted by Momodu Ahmed Kabba and Humu Hawah Kabba, husband and wife. . . ." This language has been determined by other jurisdictions to not effect an assignment of a note but to be useful only in identifying the mortgage. Therefore, this language is neither proof of transfer of the note nor proof of the purpose of any alleged transfer. See, In re Veal, 450 B.R. 897, 905 (B.A.P. 9th Cir. 2011).

¶10 Appellee must show it became a "person entitled to enforce" *prior* to the filing of the foreclosure proceeding. In the present case, there is a question of fact as to when and if this occurred and summary judgment is not appropriate. Therefore, we reverse the granting of summary judgment by the trial court and remand back for further determinations. If it is determined Bank of America became a person entitled to enforce the note, as either a holder or nonholder in possession who has the rights of a holder after the foreclosure action was filed, then the case may be dismissed *without prejudice* and the action may be re-filed in the name of the proper party.

Conclusion

¶11 It is a fundamental precept of the law to expect a foreclosing party to actually be in possession of its claimed interest in the note, and to have the proper supporting documentation in hand when filing suit, showing the history of the note, so that the defendant is duly apprised of the rights of the plaintiff. This is accomplished by showing the party is a holder of the instrument or a nonholder in possession of the instrument who has the rights of a holder, or a person not in possession of the instrument who is entitled to enforce the instrument pursuant to 12A O.S. 2001, §3-309 or 12A O.S. 2001, §3-418. Likewise, for the homeowners, absent adjudication on the underlying indebtedness, the dismissal cannot cancel their obligation arising from an authenticated note, or insulate them from foreclosure proceedings based on proven delinquency and therefore, this Court's decision in no way releases or exonerates the debt owed by the defendants on this home. See, U.S. Bank National Association v. Kimball, 27 A.3d 1087, 2011 VT 81 (VT 2011); and Indymac Bank, F.S.B. v. Yano-Horoski, 78 A.D.3d 895, 912 N.Y.S.2d 239 (2010).

REVERSED AND REMANDED WITH INSTRUCTIONS

Gurich, J., with whom Winchester, J. joins dissenting [omitted since it dealt with technical issues of standing in Oklahoma].

Hogan v. Washington Mutual Bank, N.A.

Supreme Court of Arizona, 2012
230 Ariz. 584, 277 P.3d 781

Berch, Chief Justice.

¶1 We granted review to decide whether a trustee may foreclose on a deed of trust without the beneficiary first having to show ownership of the note that the deed secures. We hold that Arizona's non-judicial foreclosure statutes do not require the beneficiary to prove its authority or "show the note" before the trustee may commence a non-judicial foreclosure.

I. Factual and Procedural Background

¶2 These consolidated cases involve two properties in Yavapai County purchased by John F. Hogan in the late 1990s. Each parcel became subject to a deed of trust in 2004 when Hogan took out loans from Long Beach Mortgage Company ("Long Beach"). By 2008, Hogan was delinquent on both loans, which triggered foreclosure proceedings. The trustee recorded a notice of sale for the first parcel, naming Washington Mutual Bank ("WaMu") as the beneficiary. A notice of trustee's sale recorded for the second parcel identified Deutsche Bank as the beneficiary.

¶3 Hogan filed lawsuits seeking to enjoin the trustees' sales unless the beneficiaries, WaMu and Deutsche Bank, proved that they were entitled to collect on the respective notes. The superior court granted the defendants' motions to dismiss and the court of appeals affirmed. Hogan v. Wash. Mut. Bank, N.A., 227 Ariz. 561, 261 P.3d 445 (App. 2011) ("OP"); Hogan v. Wash. Mut. Bank, N.A., 1 CA-CV 10-0385, 2011 WL 1158944 (Ariz. App. Mar. 29, 2011) (mem. Decision) ("MD"). In each case, the court of appeals held that "Arizona's non-judicial foreclosure statute does not require presentation of the original note before commencing foreclosure proceedings." OP at ¶13 (quoting Diessner v. Mortg. Elec. Registration Sys., 618 F. Supp. 2d 1184, 1187 (D. Ariz. 2009), *aff'd mem.*, 384 Fed. Appx. 609 (9th Cir. 2010)); MD at ¶19.

¶4 Hogan petitioned for review. We consolidated the cases and granted review because the cases present a recurring issue of first impression and statewide importance. We have jurisdiction under Article 6, Section 5(3) of the Arizona Constitution and A.R.S. §12-120.24 (2003).

II. Discussion

¶5 In Arizona, non-judicial foreclosure sales, or trustees' sales, are governed by statute. A.R.S. §§33-801 to -821 (2007 & Supp. 2011); *see* In re Vasquez, 228 Ariz. 357, 359 ¶4, 266 P.3d 1053, 1055 (2011). When parties execute a deed of trust and the debtor thereafter defaults, A.R.S. §33-807 empowers the trustee to sell the real property securing the underlying note through a non-judicial sale. Hogan contends that before a trustee may exercise that power of sale, the beneficiary must show possession of, or otherwise document its right to enforce, the underlying note. Nothing in our statutes, however, requires this showing. Section 33-809(C) requires only that, after recording notice of the trustee's sale under §33-808, the trustee must send the trustor notice of the default, signed by the beneficiary or his agent, setting forth the unpaid principal balance. *See also* Transamerica Fin. Servs., Inc. v. Lafferty, 175 Ariz. 310, 313-14, 856 P.2d 1188, 1191-92 (App. 1993) (recognizing that a trustee's obligation is only to mail notice to address provided). Hogan has not alleged that such notice was not given.

¶6 Hogan argues that a deed of trust, like a mortgage, "may be enforced only by, or in behalf of, a person who is entitled to enforce the obligation the mortgage secures." Restatement (Third) of Prop.: Mortgages §5.4(c) (1997); *see* Hill v. Favour, 52 Ariz. 561, 568-69, 84 P.2d 575, 578 (1938). We agree. But Hogan has not alleged that WaMu and Deutsche Bank are not entitled to enforce the underlying note; rather, he alleges that they have the burden of demonstrating their rights before a non-judicial foreclosure may proceed. Nothing in the non-judicial foreclosure statutes, however, imposes such an obligation. *See* Mansour v. Cal-Western Reconveyance Corp., 618 F. Supp. 2d 1178, 1181 (D. Ariz. 2009) (citing A.R.S. §33-807 and observing that "Arizona's [non-]judicial foreclosure statutes . . . do not require presentation of the original note before commencing foreclosure proceedings"); In re Weisband, 427 B.R. 13, 22 (Bankr. D. Ariz. 2010) (stating that non-judicial foreclosures may be conducted under Arizona's deed of trust statutes without presentation of the original note).

¶7 Hogan's complaints do not affirmatively allege that WaMu and Deutsche Bank are not the holders of the notes in question or that they otherwise lack authority to enforce the notes. Although a plaintiff need only set forth a "short and plain statement of the claim showing that [he] is entitled to relief," Ariz. R. Civ. P. 8(a)(2), the truth of which we assume when analyzing a complaint for failure to state a claim under Rule 12(b)(6), Cullen v. Auto-Owners Ins. Co., 218 Ariz. 417, 419 ¶7, 189 P.3d 344, 346 (2008), we will affirm a dismissal when "the plaintiff should be denied relief as a matter of law given the facts alleged," Logan v. Forever Living Products Int'l, Inc., 203 Ariz. 191, 193 ¶7, 52 P.3d 760, 762 (2002).

¶8 Here, assuming the truth of Hogan's factual allegations, Hogan is not entitled to relief because the deed of trust statutes impose no obligation on the beneficiary to "show the note" before the trustee conducts a non-judicial foreclosure. The only proof of authority the trustee's sales statutes require is a statement indicating the basis for the trustee's authority. *See* A.R.S. §33-808(C)(5) (requiring the notice to set forth "the basis for the trustee's qualification pursuant to §33-803, subsection A"); *see also* A.R.S.

§33-807(A) (granting the trustee the "power of sale"). Hogan's complaints do not contest that each sale was noticed by a trustee who had recorded an instrument demonstrating that it was a successor in interest to the original trustee.

¶9 Hogan further contends that the trustee, as a party seeking to collect on a note, must demonstrate its authority to do so under §47-3301 of Arizona's Uniform Commercial Code ("UCC"). But the trustees here did not seek to collect on the underlying notes; instead, they noticed these sales pursuant to the trust deeds. The UCC does not govern liens on real property. *See* Rodney v. Ariz. Bank, 172 Ariz. 221, 224-25, 836 P.2d 434, 437-38 (App. 1992). The trust deed statutes do not require compliance with the UCC before a trustee commences a non-judicial foreclosure. *See* In re Krohn, 203 Ariz. 205, 208 ¶8, 52 P.3d 774, 777 (2002) ("[D]eed of trust sales are conducted on a contract theory under the power of sale authority of the trustee.").

¶10 Hogan also claims that "the note and the trust deed go together" and "must be construed together." *See* A.R.S. §33-817 (providing that a transfer of the underlying contract operates to transfer the security for the contract). Although this is generally true, the note and the deed of trust are nonetheless distinct instruments that serve different purposes. The note is a contract that evidences the loan and the obligor's duty to repay. *See* A.R.S. §33-801(4). The trust deed transfers an interest in real property, securing the repayment of the money owed under the note. *See* A.R.S. §§33-801(4), -801(8), -801(9), -805, -807(A). The dispositive question here is whether the trustee, acting pursuant to its own power of sale or on behalf of the beneficiary, had the statutory right to foreclose on the deeds of trust. *See* Cervantes v. Countrywide Home Loans, Inc., 656 F.3d 1034, 1043-44 (9th Cir. 2011). Hogan does not dispute that he is in default under the deeds of trust and has alleged no reason to dispute the trustee's right.

¶11 Hogan suggests that if we do not require the beneficiary to "show the note," the original noteholder may attempt to later pursue collection despite a foreclosure. But Arizona's anti-deficiency statutes protect against such occurrences by precluding deficiency judgments against debtors whose foreclosed residential property consists of 2.5 acres or less, as is the case here. *See* A.R.S. §33-814(G); Mid Kansas Fed. Sav. & Loan Ass'n of Wichita v. Dynamic Dev. Corp., 167 Ariz. 122, 126, 804 P.2d 1310, 1314 (1991); Emily Gildar, Arizona's Anti-Deficiency Statutes: Ensuring Consumer Protection in a Foreclosure Crisis, 42 Ariz. St. L.J. 1019, 1020 (2010). Moreover, the trustee owes the trustor a duty to comply with the obligations created by the statutes governing trustee sales and the trust deed. *See* Patton v. First Fed. Sav. & Loan Ass'n of Phx., 118 Ariz. 473, 476, 578 P.2d 152, 155 (1978), A.R.S. §33-801(10) (providing that "[t]he trustee's obligations . . . are as specified in this chapter [and] in the trust deed").

¶12 Non-judicial foreclosure sales are meant to operate quickly and efficiently, "outside of the judicial process." *Vasquez*, 228 Ariz. at 359 ¶4 n.1, 266 P.3d at 1055 n.1 (citing Gary E. Lawyer, Note, *The Deed of Trust: Arizona's Alternative to the Real Property Mortgage*, 15 Ariz. L. Rev. 194, 194 (1973)). The legislature balanced the concerns of trustors, trustees, and beneficiaries in arriving at the current statutory process. Requiring the beneficiary to prove ownership of a note to defaulting trustors before instituting non-judicial foreclosure proceedings might again make the "mortgage foreclosure process . . . time-consuming and expensive," *id.* (internal quotation marks omitted), and re-inject litigation, with its attendant cost and delay, into the process, *see* Transamerica Fin. Servs., 175 Ariz. at 313-14, 856 P.2d at 1191-92 (citing I.E. Assocs. v. Safeco Title Ins. Co., 39 Cal. 3d 281, 216 Cal. Rptr. 438, 702 P.2d 596 (1985)).

III. CONCLUSION

¶13 For the reasons set forth above, the superior court's orders dismissing Hogan's complaints are affirmed and, although we agree with the result reached by the court of appeals, its opinion is vacated.

QUESTIONS

1. The Arizona Supreme Court more or less ignores the requirements of the Uniform Commercial Code in this decision, holding that it doesn't apply to real property foreclosures. While it's true that Article 9 [Secured Transactions] does not cover real property mortgages, Article 9 itself states that it does apply to promissory notes given in real property mortgage transactions, and that the foreclosure of the mortgage notes must comply with Article 3; Comment 6 to §9-308 specifically says: "Under this Article, attachment and perfection of a security interest in a secured right to payment do not of themselves affect the obligation to pay. For example, if the obligation is evidenced by a negotiable note, then Article 3 dictates the person to whom the maker must pay to discharge the note and any lien securing it. See Section 3-602."

2. The court holds that in Arizona the foreclosure statute governs who can foreclose and the rules of Article 3 are irrelevant. Hmm. Consider the actual language of Arizona's statute. Arizona Revised Statutes §33-807 permits a foreclosure sale "after a breach or default in performance of the contract or contracts, for which the trust property is conveyed as security, or a breach or default of the trust deed." This statute requires the court to answer the question of whether there has been a breach in the "contract" for which the property is conveyed or the trust deed. That appears to cut out the promissory note as having anything to do with that issue, but is that right? Surely if the maker of the note were current on payments to the holder of

the mortgage no one could foreclose on the deed of trust, which would only be available as a cause of action if there were a default on the mortgage obligation. To reach an answer on these matters we need to return to the issue of the merger rule.

III. THE MERGER RULE

If the plaintiff in the foreclosure suit doesn't possess the original promissory note, it's very tempting to just ignore the note and sue using the breach of the mortgage contract (or, as in Arizona, the deed of trust) as the cause of action. In the frenetic market for real property mortgages that has been with us for years, the banks that bought and sold the mortgages were much better at keeping records of who was the owner of the mortgage than they were at making sure they had possession of the promissory notes. They created a Mortgage Electronic Registration System (MERS), transferred the mortgages to MERS, and then had MERS keep track of which entity was the current assignee of the mortgage. In some cases, the assignee authorized MERS to do the foreclosure on behalf of the assignees of the mortgage (which met with mixed results in the courts as to whether MERS was the real party in interest). When the makers of the notes protested that the assignees of the mortgage and/or MERS had to produce the original promissory note because the UCC said so, there was incredulity. The UCC? Really? That course in law school we all avoided and whose rules we don't understand? Even judges (witness the Arizona Supreme Court) often threw up their hands and said something to the effect of "I'm not going to let the fusty rules of the Code slow down foreclosures in my court and let people get away without paying their mortgages just because the banks missed some technical steps like keeping track of promissory notes."

But the law is the law, and the UCC is statutory law in all U.S. jurisdictions in which foreclosures are going on. The fact that the banks stupidly misplaced the promissory notes and now can't be bothered to use their resources to find them (much less creating forged ones, which, trust us, has happened), ought not be an excuse for ignoring statutes the legislature has enacted.

PROBLEM 170

When the current assignee of the mortgage, Last National Bank, filed a foreclosure suit, the defendant demanded to see the original promissory note the defendant had signed. No one at LNB or its assignor has any idea what happened to the note. You are the attorney for LNB and you tell your client to dig deeper and find that note. The people at LNB reply that investigating this both at LNB and through all the other prior transfers registered at MERS is very expensive, but they'll give it a shot.

(a) One report from LNB's preliminary investigation suggests that the note may possibly have been scanned by a prior holder and the original then burned as part of a "paper reduction effort." Was that a good idea? See §3-604.

(b) If the note can't be found and the court insists on its production, the foreclosure will have to stop. What should LNB now do? See Restatement (Second) of Contracts §333(b), which creates a warranty at the time of assignment that the assignment is valid and there are no defenses to the assignment. What does this rule mean to your client?

(c) The attorney for LSN decides to ignore the note and just sue on the assignment of the mortgage. Can this be done? See §3-310(b)(2), the so-called merger rule, discussed below.

We dealt with the merger rule and its effect on the underlying obligation in the beginning of the last chapter. The rule states that whenever a negotiable instrument is created to pay a debt, the debt obligation is merged into the note until the note is dishonored. Discharge on the note leads to discharge on the underlying obligation. In mortgage situations, as we have seen, the maxim is that "security follows the debt," meaning here that the mortgage (the "security") goes with the "debt" (the promissory note). It is the law in all jurisdictions that the mortgage assignment is a nullity without the valid transfer of the note because the mortgage follows the note (and not the other way around). If the maker pays the note, the mortgage debt is discharged; see §3-310(b)(2). But until the note is dishonored the right to sue on the mortgage contract (the "underlying obligation") is *suspended*; §3-310(b). It cannot be the basis of a lawsuit until the note is dishonored.

In the Arizona foreclosure statute discussed after the last case, foreclosure could only be had "after a breach or default in performance of the contract or contracts, for which the trust property is conveyed as security, or a breach or default of the trust deed." In this statute surely "breach" or "default" means failure to pay the promissory note, because the other obligations are suspended until that happens. The only person who can demand payment of a promissory note is a person entitled to enforce the note, the PETE as defined in §3-301. This means in states that have renounced the "show me the note" defense and counted on the language of the foreclosure statute to authorize this result, a true reading of those statutes will demonstrate they all depend on a "default" of the mortgage obligation. As just explained, that means failure to pay the note when a PETE demands its payment.

The Uniform Commercial Code should make all states "show me the note" states.

IV. LOST NOTES

PROBLEM 171

Return to the facts of the last Problem where you are the attorney for Last National Bank and no one can find the original promissory note. It comes to your attention that the Code has another possible escape route: §3-309. Read it and decide if it will protect your client. You should know that the 2002 revision of Article 3 (adopted to date in only 12 or so states) is the version of §3-309 in your statute book. The language of the prior version (which is the law in most states) is similar but in that version (b)(1) stated, "the person was in possession of the instrument and entitled to enforce it when loss of possession occurred." That requirement of being in possession when it was lost was dropped in the revision because it was a tough burden to meet, as the following case attests.

State Street Bank and Trust Co. v. Lord

District Court of Appeals of Florida, 2003
851 So. 2d 790

STONE, J.

The issue on appeal is whether a mortgagee by assignment, State Street Bank, may pursue a mortgage foreclosure in the absence of proof that either the mortgagee, or its assignor, ever had possession of the missing promissory note. A summary judgment was entered in favor of the mortgagor, Hartley Lord. We affirm.

State Street sought to establish the promissory note and mortgage under section 71.011, Florida Statutes. State Street alleged that Hartley executed the note and mortgage and that, after multiple assignments, the documents were assigned to State Street by EMC Mortgage Corporation. Although State Street alleged in its pleading that the original documents were received by it, the record established that State Street never had possession of the original note and, further, that its assignor, EMC, never had possession of the note and, thus, was not able to transfer the original note to State Street.

The trial court correctly concluded that as State Street never had actual or constructive possession of the promissory note, State Street could not, as a matter of law, maintain a cause of action to enforce the note or foreclose the mortgage. The right to enforce the lost instrument was not properly assigned where neither State Street nor its predecessor in interest possessed the note and did not otherwise satisfy the requirements of section 673.3091, Florida Statutes, at the time of the assignment. *See* Slizyk v. Smilack, 825 So. 2d 428, 430 (Fla. 4th DCA 2002).

To maintain a mortgage foreclosure, the plaintiff must either present the original promissory note or give a satisfactory explanation for its failure to do so. §90.953(1), Fla. Stat. (2002); W.H. Downing v. First Nat'l Bank of Lake City, 81 So. 2d 486 (Fla. 1955); Nat'l Loan Investors, L.P. v. Joymar Assocs., 767 So. 2d 549, 551 (Fla. 3d DCA 2000). A limited exception applies for lost, destroyed, or stolen instruments, where it is shown that "the person was in possession of the instrument and entitled to enforce it when loss of possession occurred." §673.3091, Fla. Stat. (2002).

Section 673.3091 provides, in part:

> (1) A person not in possession of an instrument is entitled to enforce the instrument if:
>
> (a) The person was in possession of the instrument and entitled to enforce it when loss of possession occurred;
>
> (b) The loss of possession was not the result of a transfer by the person or a lawful seizure; and
>
> (c) The person cannot reasonably obtain possession of the instrument because the instrument was destroyed, its whereabouts cannot be determined, or it is the wrongful possession of an unknown person or a person that cannot be found or is not amenable to service of process.

Here, it is unrefuted that State Street was unable to meet the requirement of section 673.3091. The undisputed facts show that the note was lost before the assignment to State Street was made. This court has previously refused to allow a mortgage foreclosure under similar circumstances. In Mason v. Rubin, 727 So. 2d 283 (Fla. 4th DCA 1999), the appellant brought a foreclosure action on a second mortgage, the trial court denied the foreclosure, and this court affirmed on the basis that the appellant had failed to establish the lost note under section 673.3091. Likewise, here, where State Street failed to comply with section 673.3091, the trial court correctly entered summary judgment denying its foreclosure claim.

State Street cannot succeed under an assignment theory. We recognize that this court, and the Third District, have held that the right of enforcement of a lost note can be assigned. *See Slizyk,* 825 So. 2d at 430; Deakter

v. Menendez, 830 So. 2d 124 (Fla. 3d DCA 2002); *Nat'l Loan,* 767 So. 2d at 551. Here, however, in contrast to *National Loan, Slizyk,* and *Deakter,* there is no evidence as to who possessed the note when it was lost.

In *Slizyk,* we held that the assignee of a note and mortgage was entitled to foreclose despite his inability to produce the original documents. This court concluded that because the assignor was in possession of the notes, he had the right to enforce them. When the notes were assigned to the appellee, the right to enforce the instruments was assigned to him as well. *Id.* at 430. In contrast, here, the undisputed evidence was that EMC, the assignor, never had possession of the notes and, thus, could not enforce the note under section 673.3091 governing lost notes. Because EMC could not enforce the lost note under section 673.3091, it had no power of enforcement which it could assign to State Street. Were we to allow State Street to enforce the note because some unidentified person further back in the chain may possess the note, it would render the 673.3091 rule meaningless. We do not, and need not, reach any question as to whether *Slizyk* and *National Loan* may be applied where there is proof of an earlier assignor's possession further removed than the most immediate assignor.

We recognize that applying the statute as we do will result in a windfall to the mortgagor and a likely injustice to the mortgagee, unless it is able to obtain new evidence. In Dennis Joslin Company v. Robinson Broadcasting Corp., 977 F. Supp. 491 (D.D.C. 1997), the district court rejected the right to assign the enforcement of a lost note. Apparently, in response to that opinion, the Uniform Commercial Code was amended to delete the requirement that the transferee be in possession at the time the instrument was lost and now provides that the person seeking to enforce the instrument either was entitled to enforce the instrument when loss of possession occurred, or acquired ownership of the instrument from a person who was entitled to enforce the instrument when loss of possession occurred. *See* U.C.C. §3-309(a)(1) (2002). Florida, however, has not similarly amended its code and still requires possession either by the assignor at the time of loss or by the person seeking to enforce the note. Any remedy must, therefore, be left to the legislature.

V. CONCLUSION

The truth is that the lending mess was the result of years of sloppy practices, with greed as the fuel; no one paid any attention to details, and increasingly complex transactions led to the loss of a paper trail. But now the orgy has ended with major hangovers for the participants who paid no attention to the basic rules. The borrowers (who also have had to battle this problem at their end, when they can't figure out who is the proper party to negotiate with over repayment issues or settlement discussions) have done nothing wrong. They do owe the debt and the house is still the collateral, so they are not off the hook at all. But the courts won't let someone foreclose just because that someone thinks they are the right entity to do it, or *really, really, really* wants to foreclose. They have to prove they are a PETE by clear evidence. Wishing that they had that evidence is not enough. Indeed, as discussed above, if the buyer pays the wrong person, he/she still owes the debt.

When the consumer agrees to buys a new home and goes to the closing, the lending bank overwhelms the new homeowner with legal paper, after legal paper, after legal paper that the borrower must sign or the loan will not go through. At this end of the transaction, the bank is very careful to make sure everything is in apple pie order and that every "i" is dotted and every "t" is crossed. Perhaps it's not unfair that at the other end of the transaction when banks are attempting to take someone's home, they ought to be required to follow the law then too. As the Third Circuit has commented in a case where the foreclosing bank could not produce the necessary proof, "[f]inancial institutions, noted for insisting on their customers' compliance with numerous ritualistic formalities, are not sympathetic petitioners in urging relaxation of an elementary business practice"; Adams v. Madison Realty & Development, Inc., 853 F.2d 163 (3d Cir. 1988).

CHAPTER 12 ASSESSMENT: MULTIPLE CHOICE QUESTIONS

1. Marley borrowed $100,000 from Securitization Bank, signing a negotiable promissory note and a mortgage deed. Securitization Bank locked the note up in a vault, and a few months later sold the rights to payment to Careless Bank, with a written contract of assignment. Marley meanwhile became unemployed and stopped making monthly payments. Does Careless Bank have the right to enforce the promissory note against Marley?
   a. Yes, because the right to collect was assigned to Careless Bank.
   b. No, because Marley's obligation to pay can run only to the lender, Securitization Bank.
   c. No, because Securitization Bank did not transfer the note to Careless Bank.
   d. No, because Marley did not consent to the assignment of the obligation to pay.

2. Suppose that Marley paid Careless Bank the money owing on the mortgage loan. Then the note showed up in the hands of Titan Bank. Securitization Bank had gotten its records mixed up, and had actually sold the note to Titan Bank before erroneously (and duplicatively) selling the right to collect to Careless Bank, who qualified as a holder in due course. If Titan Bank seeks to collect the note from Marley, would Marley be liable?
   a. No. The double assignment of the note was fraud, a defense that can be raised even against a holder in due course.
   b. Yes. Marley has no defense or discharge that can be raised against a holder in due course.
   c. No. Marley has paid the note, and so is no longer liable on the note.
   d. Yes. A note is collectible until it is stamped PAID.

3. Scrooge Bank sold Fezziwig Bank a negotiable promissory note, from a mortgage loan to Dilbner. Scrooge Bank delivered the note to Fezziwig Bank, but neglected to indorse the note. Does Fezziwig Bank have the right to enforce the note against Dilbner?
   a. No, because the note is still payable to Scrooge Bank, not Fezziwig Bank.
   b. Yes, because Scrooge Bank transferred the note to Fezziwig Bank.
   c. No. Dilbner can be liable only to its lender, Scrooge Bank.
   d. Yes, because the right to collect was assigned to Fezziwig Bank.

4. Careless Bank demanded payment from Homeowner on a mortgage loan assigned to Careless Bank by Shady Lender. Homeowner's attorney notified Careless Bank that Homeowner, if sued, would raise the defense of fraudulent inducement, alleging that Shady Lender had misrepresented the terms of the loan. Preparing for a lawsuit, Careless Bank discovered that Shady Lender not indorsed the promissory note. After some prompting, Shady Lender indorsed the note to Careless Bank. If Careless Bank sues, could Homeowner raise the defense of fraud?
   a. Yes. Fraud can be raised even against a holder in due course.
   b. Yes. Careless Bank is not a holder in due course.
   c. No. Careless Bank is a holder in due course.
   d. No. Careless Bank has the rights of a holder in due course, under the shelter rule.

5. Efficiency Bank sold 300 promissory notes to Trusting Bank, all of which came from mortgage loans made by Efficiency Bank to consumers. Rather than making indorsements on the notes themselves, Efficiency Bank wrote "Pay to the order of Trusting Bank, Efficiency Bank" on 300 pieces of paper, then placed one such paper next to each promissory note in the stack of notes. Trusting Bank paid a good price for the notes, and took them all in good faith, with no notice of any problems or irregularities.

Could Trusting Bank be a holder in due course of any of the notes, in a case where the borrower had a defense arising out of Efficiency Bank's handling of the loan?

a. No, because Trusting Bank is not a holder.
b. Yes, because Trusting Bank is in possession and took for value, in good faith, and without notice of any problems or irregularities.
c. Yes, because Trusting Bank is not responsible for Efficiency Bank's behavior.
d. No, because the holder in due course doctrine does not apply to consumer transactions.

ANSWERS

1. *C* is the best answer. To be the person entitled to enforce the instrument, Careless Bank must be the holder, a transferee with the rights of a holder, or someone with the right to enforce a lost, stolen, or destroyed instrument. §3-301. An assignment of the right to collect does not make Careless any of those, so *A* is incorrect. *B* misstates the law grievously. The whole point of negotiable instruments is that the right to collect may be transferred by transferring the note. *D* likewise misstates the law. No consent of the obligor is necessary to transfer an instrument. Rather, in effect, one signing a negotiable instrument authorizes assignment of the right to collect. So a negotiable note may be assigned. But transfer of the note itself is necessary, unless the note has been lost, stolen, or destroyed). So *C* is the best answer.

2. *B* is the best answer. Marley did not pay a person who was entitled to enforce the instrument, so he does not get a discharge. See §3-602. This question illustrates why the person entitled to enforce the note must be the holder, a transferee with the rights of a holder, or a person enforcing a lost, stolen, or destroyed note. UCC §3-301. By generally requiring possession of the note to enforce the note, Article 3 protects an obligor against the risk that Marley took on here. To enforce the note, someone has to have possession of the note (be a holder or a transferee with the rights of a holder) or use the §3-309 process for enforcing a lost, stolen, or destroyed note. Under §3-309, such a person can get payment only by providing security against the possibility that a holder in due course will show up with the note and demand payment. In broader terms, this is why courts should enforce the rules of Article 3 and require banks to show the note to enforce mortgage debt: to protect borrowers who pay, against the possibility that the note will show up in the hands of a holder in due course.

3. *B* is the best answer. This question reminds us that indorsement is not necessary to transfer the note effectively. The note was payable to Scrooge

Bank. When Scrooge Bank transferred the note to Fezziwig Bank, even if not indorsing it, that transferred Scrooge Bank's rights to Fezziwig Bank. The note itself is accounted for, and so there is no risk it can show up in the hands of a holder in due course. So the requirement to actually keep track of the note is not too onerous. A transfer without indorsement is sufficient to transfer the right to payment, contrary to *A*. *C* is incorrect, because someone signing a *negotiable* promissory note is liable to whoever has the right to enforce the note.

4. *B* is the best answer. The last question reminded us that indorsement is not necessary to be able to enforce an instrument. But this one reminds us that indorsement may be necessary if one wants to be able to enforce an instrument *as a holder in due course.* To be a holder in due course, Careless Bank must be a holder, which requires being in possession of an instrument payable to Careless Bank. Careless Bank was in possession, but the note was not indorsed to Careless Bank. Shady Bank finally indorsed the note, but not before Careless Bank had notice of the defense of fraud. Careless Bank never met all four requirements to be a holder in due course (holder, value, good faith, no notice) at the same time. So, contrary to *C*, Careless Bank is not a holder in due course. Homeowner can raise any defense Homeowner has, such as fraud. *A* is incorrect, because fraud in the inducement cannot be raised against a holder in due course. Rights of a holder in due course can also be transferred, which does not require an indorsement. But that does not apply here. Shady Lender was not a holder in due course, because Shady Lender would have had notice of any fraud by Shady Lender. So the transfer from Shady Lender did not give Careless Bank the rights of a holder in due course, making *D* incorrect.

5. *A* is the best answer. This question also reviews important rules from earlier chapters and applies them in the mortgage context where these issues often arise. An indorsement may be made on an allonge, a separate piece of paper affixed to the instrument. But here the separate pieces of paper were not affixed to the notes, they were simply put next to them. Trusting Bank would therefore not be a holder of the notes, rather, a transferee with the rights of a holder. That would be sufficient for any note where the obligor had no defense to payment. But where an obligor had a defense to raise, Trusting Bank would be unable to establish holder in due course status. Nor could it use the shelter rule. If the defense arose out of Efficiency Bank's handling of the loan, Efficiency Bank would have notice of the defense and so would have no holder in due course rights to transfer to Trusting Bank. So, even though Trusting Bank took the note for value, in good faith, with no notice, it was not a holder and so not a holder in due course, contrary to *B*. *C* is incorrect,

because a party with a defense may raise it against any non-holder in due course, not just against the party whose conduct gave rise to the defense. *D* states a common misconception. The holder in due course rule does not apply to promissory notes given by consumers to purchase goods or services. But it does apply to other consumer transactions, such as mortgage loans (or promissory notes given for loans of money, or transactions where payment is by check, as opposed to a promissory note).

Chapter 13

Banks and Their Customers

A customer opens a checking account, or acquires a credit card, or uses a debit card to access this new bank account. Both federal and state laws will govern these transactions. Checks must move from one bank to another, a complex system made even more interesting in the twenty-first century by electronic conversion of these physical pieces of paper into images that zip in an instant from one bank to another. Centuries of presumptions based on paper have been rethought as e-transactions engulf the planet requiring new rules and regulations that become obsolete as they are enacted into law. To the lawyer who must master all of this, the challenge is both exciting and exasperating. How to understand it? Get a grasp on it? Master the new systems as they spring into being?

Twenty-first century casebook authors ask themselves where to begin, and come up with a comforting old answer: with the Uniform Commercial Code of course. So let's start there and, that tamed, move to on more exotic beasts.

Article 4 of the Uniform Commercial Code covers Bank Deposits and Collections, matters inextricably entwined with the rules of Article 3 on Negotiable Instruments. Section 4-102(a) provides that whenever the provisions of Article 3 conflict with those of Article 4, the latter control. This can be important in warranty actions discussed in the next chapter; §§4-207 and 4-208 will prevail over the similar provisions in §§3-416 and 3-417 if both are arguably applicable. Another matter of concern is terminology. In addition to a general definitions section in §4-104, the complicated nomenclature of Article 4 banks is laid out in §4-105. Under these definitions, a bank can bear more than one label. In §4-105, which you should examine, the Article 3 drawee bank gets a new name and becomes known as the *payor bank* (or, in the federal regulations on check collection, the *paying bank*; 12 C.F.R. §229.2(z)). The depositary bank is the *first* bank to which an item is transferred for collection; it could also be the payor bank in situations where the drawer and the payee happen to do their banking at the same institution. Any bank in the collection process, except the payor bank, can be called a collecting bank; this includes the depositary bank.

I. THE CHECKING ACCOUNT

Whenever anyone opens a checking account with a bank, two legal relationships spring into being: debtor/creditor and principal/agent. The good news is that the depositor is the creditor and the bank the debtor (!); further, the bank is an agent for payment of the principal's drafts and other instructions. We will explore these legal connections shortly.

The opening of the account creates a contract; the force of centuries imbues it with these and other characteristics. Its details may be implied—see §1-303—or may be the subject of detailed fine print. See, e.g., David v. Manufacturers Hanover Trust Co., 59 Misc. 2d 248, 298 N.Y.S.2d 847 (App. Div. 1969) (waiver of jury trial hidden in fine print of signature card upheld against charge of unconscionability). Read §4-103.

A. "Properly Payable" Rule

The basic contract between drawer and drawee, whether detailed or implied, always has at its nucleus this basic understanding: the bank may pay out the customer's money *only* if it follows the customer's orders exactly. If it does not do so, it must recredit the account. Article 4 backs up this understanding in §4-401, wherein it is stated that the bank may charge the account if the item is *properly payable*. What does *properly payable* mean here? Section 4-401(a) tells us that an "item is *properly payable* if it is authorized by the customer and is in accordance with any agreement between the customer and bank." It is easiest to understand this if you think of a check as if it were a letter addressed to the bank telling it what to do with the customer's money. The check is "properly payable" only if the bank follows the instructions of the customer *exactly*. If the bank makes a mistake and pays a check in a manner not instructed by the customer, the item is not properly payable and the bank must put the money back into the account.[1] Read §4-401.

Majestic Building Maintenance, Inc. v. Huntington Bancshares Incorporated

United States Court of Appeals, Sixth Circuit, 2017
864 F.3d 455

Clay, Circuit Judge.

Plaintiff Majestic Building Maintenance, Inc., appeals from the order entered by the district court granting the motion to dismiss of Defendant Huntington Bancshares, Inc., d/b/a The Huntington National Bank, thereby dismissing all of Plaintiff's claims against Defendant for violating the Uniform Commercial Code, U.C.C. §§4-103(a), 4-401, codified as Ohio Revised Code, O.R.C. §§1304.03, 1304.30, whereby Defendant refused to assume liability for monies paid out of Plaintiff's bank account on four fraudulent checks.

For the reasons that follow, we REVERSE the district court's order of dismissal and REMAND with instructions to allow Plaintiff an opportunity to amend the complaint and conduct discovery.

Background

A. Factual History

Plaintiff specializes in commercial cleaning services. In November 2010, Plaintiff, through its president, Luther McNeil ("McNeil"), opened a business checking account with Defendant and received a "Master Services Agreement" ("Agreement") that contained the rules and regulations for business accounts. The section of the Agreement at issue in this case states:

> [W]e have available certain products designed to discover or prevent unauthorized transactions, including unauthorized checks and ACH debits, forgeries, and alterations (all such activities referred to as "fraud"). While no such

1. Of course, there are exceptions, situations where the bank may violate the properly payable rule and live to tell about it. The bank may be able to escape liability by using any one of a number of defenses (customer negligence, subrogation, etc.), to be discussed later. What should a bank do if the check is ambiguous because, say, the written amount is not the same as the numbers on the dollar sign line? UCC §3-114 states:

> If an instrument contains contradictory terms, typewritten terms prevail over printed terms, handwritten terms prevail over both, and words prevail over numbers.

> product is foolproof, we believe that the products we offer will reduce the risk of loss to you from fraud. You agree that if your account is eligible for those products and you choose not to avail yourself of them, then we will have no liability for any transaction that occurs on your account that those products were designed to discover or prevent, nor will we have any duty to re-credit your account for any such losses.

McNeil opened the account at a computer repair shop with assistance from a representative of Defendant. At the time McNeil opened the account, he was not given a signed copy of the Agreement, nor was he advised of the details contained in the Agreement, including the nature of the fraud prevention services offered by Defendant. After opening the account, McNeil ordered hologram checks from a third party as a protective measure to avoid fraudulent activity on Plaintiff's account.

On November 24, 2014, McNeil noticed four unauthorized checks that had been debited from Plaintiff's account totaling $3,973.96. The unauthorized checks did not contain the hologram that McNeil ordered for Plaintiff's business account checks, and the check numbers on the fraudulent checks were duplicative of checks that Plaintiff had already written and that Defendant had properly paid. Within 24 hours of discovering the fraud, McNeil contacted Defendant to request reimbursement for the fraudulent checks debited from Plaintiff's account. Defendant responded in a letter stating that "reasonable care was not used in declining to use our Check Positive Pay/Reverse Positive Pay services, which substantially contributed to the making of the forged item(s)," and that "[a]s a result, we will not reimburse you for these unauthorized/forged item(s)." (R. 1-4, First Huntington Letter, Page ID # 46.) . . .

B. PROCEDURAL HISTORY

On November 20, 2015, Plaintiff filed a putative class action complaint in district court pursuant to the Class Action Fairness Act of 2005 ("CAFA"), 28 U.S.C. §1332(d), alleging that Defendant: (1) breached its obligations under U.C.C. §4-401, codified at O.R.C. §1304.30(A), when it made unauthorized payments from four fraudulent checks that were not properly payable; and (2) unreasonably shifted all liability to Plaintiff and improperly disclaimed its responsibility to act in good faith and exercise ordinary care by incorporating such terms and standards into the Agreement, in violation of U.C.C. §4-103(a), codified at O.R.C. §1304.03(A). On January 19, 2016, Defendant moved to dismiss the complaint for failure to state a claim pursuant to Federal Rule of Civil Procedure 12(b)(6). On February 19, 2016, Plaintiff responded, and on March 7, 2016, Defendant replied to Plaintiff's response.

On November 3, 2016, the district court granted Defendant's motion to dismiss. The district court held that Defendant is not liable for the loss associated with the cashing of the unauthorized checks on Plaintiff's account because the Agreement does not violate §1304.03(A) or §1304.30(A). The district court concluded that the Agreement is not manifestly unreasonable and does not absolve Defendant of its duties to act in good faith and exercise ordinary care because several provisions in the Agreement "plainly reaffirm [Defendant's] duties to act in good faith and exercise ordinary care." (R. 19, District Court's Order, Page ID # 162.) The district court thus found that the terms and conditions of the Agreement which shifted liability to Plaintiff for any fraudulent activity occurring on its account did not violate §1304.03(A) or §1304.30(A), and pursuant to the Agreement, Defendant was not liable for Plaintiff's loss. On November 23, 2016, Plaintiff timely appealed.

Discussion

. . .

A. Analysis

Plaintiff argues that Defendant violated §1304.03(A) by disclaiming all responsibility through its Agreement. Section 1304.03(A) provides that parties may vary the default provisions of the Ohio Revised Code by agreement only if that agreement does not disclaim a bank's responsibility to act in good faith and exercise ordinary care. Plaintiff further argues that Defendant violated §1304.30(A) by charging Plaintiff for four unauthorized checks. Section 1304.30(A) provides that a bank may charge a customer's account for an item that is properly payable from that account. Conversely, Defendant argues that it is not liable for the fraud on Plaintiff's account because the Agreement does not disclaim Defendant's duties to act in good faith and exercise ordinary care.

The record indicates that the provision at issue in the Agreement might improperly disclaim Defendant's basic responsibility to act in good faith and exercise ordinary care. We find that the complaint sufficiently states a claim to survive Defendant's motion to dismiss.

1. Relevant Legal Principles

Chapter 1304 of the Ohio Revised Code, Ohio's version of the Uniform Commercial Code, governs the relationship between banks and depositors. The default rule states that "[a] bank may charge against the account of a customer an item that is properly payable from that account." O.R.C. §1304.30(A). "An item is properly payable if it is authorized by the customer and is in accordance with any agreement between the customer and bank." O.R.C. §1304.30(A). "An item containing a forged drawer's signature or forged indorsement is not properly payable." U.C.C. §4-401, cmt. 1. The default rule, however, may be varied by the parties pursuant to an agreement.

Section 1304.03(A) explains that "[t]he effect of the provisions of this chapter may be varied by agreement, but the parties to the agreement cannot disclaim a bank's responsibility for its lack of good faith or failure to exercise ordinary care or limit the measure of damages for the lack or failure." Notwithstanding, "the parties may determine by agreement the standards by which the bank's responsibility is to be measured if those standards are not manifestly unreasonable." O.R.C. §1304.03(A). In other words, "regardless of the terms and conditions of the parties' contractual relationship . . . Huntington cannot remove by contract its statutory duty to act in good faith and to exercise ordinary care toward its depositors." Alotech, Ltd. v. Huntington Nat'l Bank, No. 1:13-cv-01971, 2014 WL 281973, at *4 (N.D. Ohio Jan. 14, 2014). Thus, if a bank attempts to contract out of their duty of ordinary care, then such an attempt would be considered manifestly unreasonable.

2. Sufficiency of Plaintiff's Allegations

The provision at issue, which is buried towards the end of the Agreement, refers to nondescript products Defendant has available in order to reduce the risk of fraud on a customer's account. The provision goes on to completely absolve Defendant of all liability for any fraudulent transaction that occurs on the customer's account that the anti-fraud products "were designed to discover or prevent" so long as the customer's account is eligible for such products and the customer voluntarily chose not to enroll in the products. (R. 1-1, Agreement, Page ID # 35.) The contested provision does not specify the types of products offered, what type of fraud would be prevented and/or discovered, how an account becomes eligible, whether the customer's account is eligible, or how much the products would cost the customer. Plaintiff argues that Defendant violated §1304.03(A) by attempting to absolve itself of its duties to exercise ordinary care and act in good faith by inserting the contested provision into the Agreement.

The district court dismissed Plaintiff's contention on the basis that other provisions in the Agreement "plainly reaffirm [Defendant's] duties to act in good faith and exercise ordinary care." Majestic Building Maintenance, Inc. v. Huntington Bancshares, Inc., No. 2:15-cv-3023, 2016 WL 6525387, at *3 (S.D. Ohio Nov. 3, 2016). For instance, the district court noted that the Agreement's "Limitation of Liability" section provides that Defendant "will use ordinary care in performing such Services and with processing Transactions," and that Defendant's "liability relating to any Service or Transaction shall be limited to actual proven damages sustained by Company arising directly from Bank's own gross negligence or willful misconduct." (R. 1-1 at 19.) The district court thus concluded that because other provisions in the Agreement purportedly acknowledge Defendant's duties of ordinary care and good faith, the provision at issue does not run afoul of §1304.03(A).

We find that the district court erroneously and prematurely dismissed Plaintiff's putative class action complaint. First and foremost, Plaintiff properly alleged that the provision at issue violates §1304.03(A) because it unreasonably disclaims Defendant's basic duties of ordinary care and good faith. In order to survive Defendant's motion to dismiss, Plaintiff must allege that the standards regulating Defendant's responsibility to monitor Plaintiff's account for fraudulent activity were manifestly unreasonable. *See* O.R.C. §1304.03(A). The standards regulating such conduct are discussed in the contested provision of the Agreement. (*See* R. 1-1, Agreement, Page ID # 35.) Plaintiff states a plausible claim that such standards are unreasonable; Plaintiff contends that the contested provision essentially allows Defendant to proclaim that it is not responsible for any unauthorized transaction that occurs on Plaintiff's account.

Defendant does not appear to dispute that it charges the customer additional fees for these extra anti-fraud protection services. Despite charging these extra fees, Defendant does not indicate in the Agreement that these anti-fraud products cost extra, what the costs of these products would be to the customer, and how the costs are calculated (i.e., whether the costs are different for each customer depending on the type of account, etc.). Left unanswered by the record below is whether, by charging the customer additional fees for these anti-fraud protection services, Defendant is effectively charging the customer for something it should arguably do at no additional cost—which is to exercise its ordinary duty of care.

Defendant argues that it "limited its liability only for those unauthorized transactions that the anti-fraud products were designed to detect and prevent, and only if the customer failed to avail itself of those products." (Def.'s Appellate Br. 18.) This contention is unpersuasive at this stage of the litigation given the practical effect of the provision. The provision, as mentioned above, exculpates Defendant from liability for all fraudulent transactions that occur on a customer's account as long as: (1) the customer's account was eligible for the anti-fraud products and the customer did not sign up for them; and (2) the transaction is one which the anti-fraud products "were designed to discover or prevent." (R. 1-1 at 35.)

Nowhere in the Agreement are the details of the anti-fraud products mentioned, nor is there any information on how or who determines what transactions would arguably have been detected. Given the bank customer's lack of information about the anti-fraud products, such a one-sided determination could be incredibly arbitrary. Defendant could argue that every fraudulent transaction would have been discovered or prevented by the anti-fraud products even though there is no procedure for a customer, like Plaintiff, to be involved in or contest that determination. Based on the record before us, we find that Plaintiff states a plausible claim that it was unreasonable for Defendant to absolve itself from liability for any fraudulent transaction that occurs on a customer's account when the anti-fraud products cost extra, the nature of the anti-fraud products is not revealed, and when the determination of what unauthorized transactions would have been discovered or prevented is left unexplained.

It is important to note that we are not making a determination on the merits of whether the contested provision is "manifestly unreasonable." *See* O.R.C. §1304.03(A). The district court dismissed the complaint on a motion to dismiss without giving Plaintiff the opportunity to amend its complaint or an opportunity for the parties to conduct any significant discovery. . . .

Secondly, the district court's brief analysis of the other provisions in the Agreement was unnecessary. Plaintiff's dispute was not with the other provisions in the Agreement that the district court discussed in its opinion. The complaint specifically challenged the provision related to Defendant's fraud prevention services and that provision's absolute disclaimer of liability. The district court dismissed the complaint primarily because other unrelated provisions of the Agreement "plainly reaffirm[ed]" Defendant's duties to exercise ordinary care and act in good faith. It is irrelevant whether other parts of the agreement "plainly reaffirm" Defendant's basic duties; and by so holding, the district court failed to review and properly analyze the provision being challenged. Again, Plaintiff states a plausible claim that it is unreasonable for the provision at issue to disclaim Defendant's basic duties if the customer does not enroll in and pay extra for the unspecified fraud prevention services. . . .

Conclusion

In conclusion, we find that Plaintiff has alleged facts that, if accepted as true, would be sufficient to state a claim to relief that is plausible on its face. Plaintiff's contention is quite simple: the provision at issue improperly disclaims Defendant's duties to act in good faith and exercise ordinary care. We find that Plaintiff states a plausible claim that the provision unreasonably disclaims all liability under the circumstances of this case. Because the U.C.C., and by implication the O.R.C., expressly forbids a bank from disclaiming all of its liability to exercise ordinary care and good faith, Plaintiff's complaint survives Defendant's motion to dismiss. Therefore, we hold that the district court erred in dismissing Plaintiff's complaint.

For the foregoing reasons, we REVERSE the district court's order of dismissal and REMAND with instructions to allow Plaintiff an opportunity to amend the complaint and conduct discovery.

Other courts have been more receptive to the idea that where a bank offers special protection services such as "positive pay" (a software program enabling the customer to send information to the bank about each check issued, allowing the bank to make sure all information matches before a check presented to the bank is paid) customers who do not avail themselves of this protection cannot complain about problems the program would have prevented. See Cincinnati Ins. Co. v. Wachovia Bank, 2010 WL 2777478 (D. Minn. 2010). These programs require the customer to pay a greater fee for the protection that the "properly payable" rule gives automatically. Query whether making the customer pay extra for this is okay, and whether or not the bank should just make it part of the usual contract fee for opening a checking account?

Back to the "properly payable rule" of See §4-401.

PROBLEM 172

When Portia Moot paid off a debt she owed to her law school roommate, she gave her a postdated check, dating it one week later (planning to cover it with the paycheck she would receive before that date). The roommate deposited the check in her own bank immediately, and that bank presented it to the payor bank before the date of the check. Portia's bank paid the check even though this created an overdraft (for which Portia was charged). Was the check properly payable before its date? See §4-401(c). If Portia had phoned the bank and warned it that she had written this postdated check, would it have still been properly payable? See Vincene Verdun, Postdated Checks: An Old Problem with a New Solution in the Revised U.C.C., 14 U. Ark. Little Rock L.J. 37 (1991). Banks hate postdated checks because the electronic information passed through the system does not include the date of the check. Could banks solve this problem by putting a clause in the checking account by which the customer promises not to write postdated checks and agrees that the bank will have no liability for paying a check before the date of the check? See §4-103; Aliaga Medical Center, S.C. v. Harris Bank N.A., 2014 IL App. (1st) 133645-U, 2014 WL 4415328 (Ill. App. 2014).

PROBLEM 173

Jack Point lost his checkbook. A month later his bank, Yeomen National, returned his canceled checks, including one payable to W. Shadbolt for $1,000, to which Jack's name was forged as drawer. He notified Yeoman National Bank promptly. Was this check *properly payable?* See §§3-401, 3-403. If Jack had called Yeomen National immediately on finding out that his checkbook was missing, could the bank have made him stop payment on all those blank checks and also pay a good hefty stop-payment fee on each one?

See Official Comment 1 to §4-401. The courts are clear that if a bank wrongly pays checks from a customer's bank account because that customer's name is forged to the checks, the properly payable rule is violated and the bank must recredit the account; see Moore v. Bank of America, NA, 2019 WL 2281599 (D.N.J. 2019).

PROBLEM 174

The Widow Douglas gave a check for $10.00 to Ben Rogers in return for the latter's mowing her lawn. Rogers's friend Joe Harper stole the check from Rogers, raised the amount to $1,000 by erasing the decimal point and cleverly altering the writing, and forged Rogers's signature to the back of the check. Harper presented the check for payment to the drawee bank, Clemens State Bank, which paid Harper $1,000. This reduced the balance in the Widow Douglas's account to zero and caused four other checks she had sent to her creditors to bounce. The Widow Douglas sued her bank, arguing as follows:

> Section 4-401 says that the bank may charge my account only when the item is *properly payable*. On this check I ordered the bank to pay out $10 of my funds to Ben Rogers or his order. But since Ben Rogers never signed it, he never ordered it paid to anyone, and therefore the bank did not pay in accordance with my instructions and must recredit my account. Whatever payment it made was out of the bank's own funds.

Clemens State Bank replied:

> All we are required to do is make sure that the item is apparently *properly payable*, that is, that it *appears* to contain the proper chain of endorsements. We must also, of course, act in good faith, which we have done. Mrs. Douglas paid Rogers, and if Rogers carelessly lost the check, why should that act as a windfall to Mrs. Douglas? If Mrs. Douglas is permitted to win here, she will have gotten a free lawnmowing job, and we will be out $1,000. In the alternative, even if we improperly charged this account with the entire amount, surely §4-401(d)(2) permits us to take $10 out of the account.

Which argument would prevail if you were the judge? As to the bank's "at least $10" argument, notice the word *holder* in §4-401(d). What effect does it have on the resolution of this dispute? If the bank decides to recredit the account, it will be able to recoup its loss by using the warranty theories explored in the next chapter.

Whenever a bank wrongfully takes money out of the account of its customer, it is very tempting for the customer's attorney to sue in conversion because the bank's misappropriation certainly sounds like an act of conversion. Technically, however, conversion will not lie. The reason is that when a customer puts money in the bank, that money is on *loan* to the bank; the bank becomes a *debtor* and the customer is a *creditor*. The bank cannot convert its own property any more than any debtor converts property by failing to repay the debt. Instead, the proper cause of action is for violation of §4-401 (the "properly payable" rule) or is simply an action in contract or quasi-contract (money had and received).

PROBLEM 175

You are the attorney for Octopus National Bank, and the bank has presented you with the following problem: it recently paid a check drawn on a customer's account, and there was no drawer's signature on the check. The payee on the check was a telemarketing firm that had apparently called the bank's customer, sold him some product over the phone, had the customer read off the magnetically encoded numbers at the bottom of the check,[2] and then created the check, including the magnetically encoded line. In lieu of the drawer's signature, the check is stamped "drawer's signature on file." The customer has now called and complained, apparently suffering from "buyer's remorse," and wants the account recredited with the amount of the check. There are a lot of these "pre-authorized drafts" (or "telechecks") now being created. Is the payor bank doing wrong when it honors them?

PROBLEM 176

Lemuel Gulliver opened an account with the Swift State Bank. After using the account for several years, he was away on a sea voyage for a long period of time. When he returned, a check that he had written (and dated)

2. The information magnetically encoded across the bottom of checks is printed in what are called magnetic ink character recognition (MICR—usually pronounced "mick-er") symbols so that the line can be read by automated check-processing machines. The MICR line reflects a routing number representing the drawee bank, the account number of the drawer, the check number, and certain other routing information. If you look at one of your canceled checks, you will also notice that at some point (normally done at the operations center of the depositary bank) someone put MICR numbers in the lower right-hand corner of the check, reflecting the amount of the check. This is done, of course, so that the check-processing machines can read the amount. Section 4-209 creates a warranty that this information has been correctly encoded. We will have more about the MICR line when we get to check truncation.

eight years ago was presented and paid against his account, creating an overdraft.[3] Gulliver protested the payment. Will this argument succeed? As to the old check, see §§4-401, 4-404; White & Summers §19-3; compare Granite Equip. Leasing Corp. v. Hempstead Bank, 68 Misc. 2d 350, 326 N.Y.S.2d 881 (Sup. Ct. 1971), with New York Flame-Proofing Co. v. Chemical Bank, 1974 WL 21730 (N.Y. Civ. Ct. 1974), and Charles Ragusa & Son v. Community State Bank, 360 So. 2d 231 (La. App. 1978). Did the creation of an overdraft situation keep the check from being properly payable? See §4-401(a). Does the language of that section mean that a bank must pay overdrafts? See §4-402(a). How quickly must Gulliver file suit? See §4-111; the statute of limitations for actions arising in Article 3 of the Code is found in §3-118.

B. Wrongful Dishonor

Whenever a bank makes an improper payment from an account, this debit may cause other checks written by the customer to be wrongfully dishonored. The customer may recover all actual damages whenever the bank makes a *wrongful* (which includes *mistaken*) dishonor of a check that is properly payable from the account. Read §4-402 and its Official Comment.

Twin City Bank v. Isaacs

Arkansas Supreme Court, 1984
263 Ark. 127, 672 S.W.2d 651

STEELE HAYS, J.

Twin City Bank has appealed from a judgment entered on a jury verdict against it in favor of Kenneth and Vicki Isaacs for damages sustained from the bank's wrongful dishonor of the Isaacs' checks resulting in a hold order against their account for a period of approximately four years.

On Sunday, May 13, 1979, the Isaacs discovered that their checkbook was missing. They reported the loss to Twin City promptly on Monday, May 14,

3. For consumer accounts, a bank that pays overdrafts and, by contract, charges a greater amount than is charged for returning these checks may accidentally have imposed a finance charge on the transaction. If this is done pursuant to written agreement with the customer, the bank will need to give a Truth in Lending statement to its consumer customers, or it will violate the federal Truth in Lending Act. See Regulation Z, 12 C.F.R. §1026.4(b)(2) and (c)(3). Banks earn an eye-popping amount of money from paying overdrafts and assessing fees—more than $34 billion in 2017!—doing this with 30 percent of their customers and therefore making such fees a major source of income. For a detailed discussion of this issue, see Bounce Protection: Payday Lending in Sheep's Clothing?, 8 N.C. Banking Inst. 349 (2004). We will return to this matter in Chapter 15 when we come to debit cards.

and later learned that two forged checks totalling $2,050 had been written on their account and honored by the bank on May 11 and 12. The sequence of events that followed is disputed, but the end result was a decision by the bank to freeze the Isaacs' checking account which had contained approximately $2,500 before the forgeries occurred. A few checks cleared Monday morning before a hold order was issued leaving the balance at approximately $2,000. Mr. Isaacs had been convicted of burglary and the initial hold on the account was attributable to the bank's concern that the Isaacs were somehow involved with the two forged checks. The individual responsible for the forgeries was charged and convicted soon after the forgeries occurred and on May 30, 1979 the police told the bank there was nothing to connect the Isaacs with the person arrested. Two weeks later the police notified the bank a second time they could not connect the Isaacs to the forgeries. The bank maintains it continued to keep the account frozen on the advice of its attorneys. However that may be, the Isaacs were denied their funds for some four years. The Isaacs filed suit in mid-June of 1979 for wrongful dishonor of their checks and wrongful withholding of their funds.

The jury awarded the Isaacs $18,500 in compensatory damages and $45,000 in punitive damages. The bank made a motion for a new trial pursuant to A.R.C.P. Rule 59, which was denied. From that denial the bank brings this appeal contending error on three grounds: 1) Misconduct of a juror at trial, 2) the trial court's refusal to give two requested instructions, and 3) jury error in assessing excessive damages contrary to the evidence and the law. . . .

On the issue of damages, the bank maintains there was insufficient evidence to support the $18,500 award for mental anguish, for loss of credit and loss of the bargain on a house, that the award of punitive damages should not have been given at all as there was not only insufficient proof of actual damages but insufficient evidence of malice or intent to oppress on the part of the bank. The bank does not challenge the sufficiency of the evidence of its wrongful dishonor, but contends only that there was no evidence to support an award of damages. These arguments cannot be sustained.

The statute upon which this suit was based is Ark. Stat. Ann. §85-4-402. [The court quoted §4-402.—Eds.]

The jury was instructed that if they found the bank liable they were to fix the amount of money which would compensate the Isaacs "for any of the following elements of damage sustained which were proximately caused by the conduct of Twin City Bank: 1) Any amounts of money wrongfully held by the defendant and remaining unpaid, 2) any mental anguish and embarrassment suffered by the plaintiffs, 3) any financial losses sustained by the [Isaacs]." Initially, there can be no serious question as to certain losses, the $2,000 wrongfully withheld by the bank for four years, and the value of two vehicles repossessed because the Isaacs did not have access to their funds, resulting in a loss of approximately $2,200. Additionally, after the account was frozen the bank continued to charge the account a service charge and overdraft fees on checks written before the forgeries but presented after the account was frozen. The bank does not refute these damages but argues there is no showing of any financial deprivation from loss of credit or loss of the bargain on a house the Isaacs wanted to buy, and insufficient proof of mental anguish. We find, however, that in addition to the losses previously mentioned, there was sufficient evidence to sustain damages for mental suffering, loss of credit, and sufficient demonstration of some loss attributable to the inability to pursue the purchase of a home.

Mental suffering under §4-402 of the Uniform Commercial Code is relatively new and has not been frequently addressed by other courts, but of those a majority has allowed recovery. Morse v. Mutual Federal Savings and Loan, 536 F. Supp. 1271 (Mass. 1982); Farmers & Merchants State Bank of Krum v. Ferguson, 617 S.W.2d 918 (Tex. 1981); Northshore Bank v. Palmer, 525 S.W.2d 718 (Tex. 1975); Kendall Yacht Club v. United California Bank, 50 Cal. App. 3d 949, 123 Cal. Rptr. 848 (1975); and see White & Summers, Uniform Commercial Code (1980 2d ed.) §17-4, p. 675. In general, the type of mental anguish suffered under §4-402 does not need to rise to the higher standard of injury for intentional infliction of emotional distress. Wrongful dishonors tend to produce intangible injuries similar to those involved in defamation actions. See State Bank of Siloam Springs v. Marshall, 163 Ark. 566, 260 S.W. 431 (1924). Damages of this kind are more difficult to assess with exactness. In Wasp Oil v. Arkansas Oil and Gas, 280 Ark. 420, 658 S.W.2d 397 (1983) we noted the general rule that damages may not be allowed where they are speculative, resting only upon conjectural evidence, or the opinions of the parties or witnesses, but there are instances where damages cannot be proven with exactness. In *Wasp* we recognized a different rule applies when the cause and existence of damages have been established by the evidence, that recovery will not be denied merely because the damages cannot be determined with exactness. We went on to say the plaintiff in the case at bar was not trying to prove the latter sort of damage such as *mental anguish* as a result of defamation, but loss of income.

Decisions upholding recovery for mental suffering under the code have found injury resulting from circumstances comparable to this case. In *Northshore Bank v. Palmer*, supra, for example, a $275 forged check was paid from Palmer's account. After the bank knew or should have known the check was forged, it charged Palmer with the $275 check and later wrongfully dishonored other checks. Part of the actual damages awarded was attributed to mental suffering for the "embarrassment and humiliation Palmer suffered from having been turned down for credit for the first time in his life."

In *Morse v. Mutual Federal Savings and Loan*, supra, $2,200 was awarded for "false defamatory implications arising from temporary financial embarrassment." And in *Farmers & Merchants State Bank of Krum v. Ferguson*, supra, the plaintiff's account in the amount of $7,000 was frozen for apparently one month for reasons not stated. The plaintiff was awarded $25,000 for mental anguish, $3,000 for loss of credit based on a denial of a loan, $5,000 for loss of time spent making explanations to creditors, and $1,500 for loss of use of his money. The court justified the mental suffering award because the dishonor was found to be with malice—the bank had failed to notify Ferguson that the account was frozen, some checks were honored while others were not, and the bank continued to withdraw loan payments due it during the entire time.

In this case, prior to the forgery incident the Isaacs' credit reputation with Twin City Bank was described by the bank as "impeccable" and the freezing of their funds had a traumatic effect on their lives. They obviously lost their credit standing with Twin City, and were unable to secure credit commercially at other institutions because of their status at Twin City. The Isaacs had to borrow from friends and family, and were left in a precarious position financially. They did not have use of their $2,000 for four years. The allegation relative to the loss of a house resulted from the dishonor of an earnest money check for a home they were planning to buy, ending prospects for the purchase at that time. Though there may have been insufficient proof of loss of the bargain on the house, as the bank argues, nevertheless this evidence was admissible as an element of mental suffering. The denial of credit contributed to some monetary loss as occurred in *Ferguson*, supra, in addition to its being a reasonable element of mental suffering as was found in *Palmer*, supra. There was also testimony that the financial strain contributed to marital difficulties leading at one point to the filing of a divorce suit. The suit was dropped but there was testimony that the difficulties caused by the bank's action caused substantial problems in the marriage. Finally, the Isaacs lost equities in two vehicles repossessed as a result of the withholding of their funds. One of these, a new van, was repossessed by Twin City in June, 1979, before a five-day grace period for a current installment had expired.

We believe there was substantial evidence to support the verdict. The jury heard the evidence of the amount wrongfully withheld, the loss of two vehicles, credit loss through loan denials, loss of the use of their money for four years, the suffering occasioned by marital difficulties, the inability to acquire a home they wanted, and the general anxieties which accompanied the financial strain. We recognize that our holding today presents some conflict with pre-code law by allowing recovery without exactness of proof as to damages. In *State Bank of Siloam Springs v. Marshall*, supra, a suit based on the predecessor to §4-402, we stated that the plaintiff must show the facts and circumstances which occasioned the damage and the amount thereof. However, *Marshall* itself recognized the nature of the damages in this action, and §4-402, although similar to its predecessor, has additional language which impliedly recognizes mental suffering and other intangible injuries of the type noted in *Wasp*, supra, as recoverable under this statute. See White & Summers, supra, §17-4, p. 675. To the extent that exactness in proof is not required, the law as stated in *Marshall* is displaced by §4-402.

The bank's objection to the award of punitive damages is threefold: a) The instruction on punitive damages was in accordance with A.M.I. 2217, which is intended for use in negligence cases and not applicable here; b) there was no evidence that the bank acted intentionally or with malice; and c) the verdict of $45,000 was excessive. However, we address only the question of the excessiveness of the verdict, as the other points were not raised in the trial court by objection to the instruction. Crowder v. Flippo, 263 Ark. 433, 565 S.W.2d 138 (1978); Dodson Creek Inc. v. Walton, 2 Ark. App. 128, 620 S.W.2d 947 (1981); A.R.C.P. Rule 51. . . .

The judgment is affirmed.

PROBLEM 177

Stella and Harry Squabble, after many years of constant fighting, decided to separate and seek a divorce. Stella's attorney filed the proper papers and then, to preserve Harry's financial assets in the status quo, sent a *lis pendens* (notice of litigation) to the bank in which Harry maintained an account for the barber shop he owned. The bank was uncertain what to do about the lis pendens notice, but the bank's attorney was a conservative type and advised the bank to freeze Harry's account until the divorce matter was settled. Fourteen of the barber shop's checks bounced as a result of this decision, and Harry's ulcer acted up and put him in the hospital. Harry filed suit against his bank, asking for $100,000 in damages. At trial he proved only the above facts but offered no evidence as to damages. Should the trial judge grant the defendant's motion for a directed verdict? See White & Summers §19-4.

PROBLEM 178

When Archie Goodwin received his paycheck from Nero Wolfe, his employer, he walked it into New York Metropolitan National Bank, the drawee, and presented it across the counter. The teller asked him if he had an account of his own with the bank. When he replied that he did not, the bank told him that it was the bank's policy not to pay across-the-counter checks drawn on it unless the payee had an account at the bank. Is this a wrongful dishonor? See Your Style Publications, Inc. v. Mid Town Bank & Trust Co. of Chicago, 150 Ill. App. 3d 421, 501 N.E.2d 805 (1986); Buckley v. Trenton

Savings Fund Society, 216 N.J. Super. 705, 524 A.2d 886 (1987). Could the bank solve this problem by putting a clause in the checking account agreement stating that the customer would permit the bank to refuse to pay checks presented across the counter unless the presenter had an account with the bank? See §4-103.

PROBLEM 179

Many of the maintenance workers at Football University had no checking accounts at all (the so-called "unbanked"). When they received their monthly paychecks, they physically walked them into the bank on which they were drawn and presented them across the counter for payment. The drawee bank informed them that for each check presented, the bank would extract a fee of $10 for honoring an across-the-counter-presentment. The maintenance workers are angry about this. In effect, it is a major cut in pay for many of them. They are in your law office now. Can you suggest any form of relief?

C. Death or Incompetence of Customer

The common law rule that death or incompetence of a principal revokes the authority of an agent to act used to play havoc with checking accounts. It was a sure thing that the drafters of Article 4, among them representatives of the banking industry, would enact a solution to the problem. Read §4-405 and its Official Comment.

PROBLEM 180

Howard Mortus dropped dead while walking back to his house from the corner mailbox in which he had just deposited the month's bill payments. His widow phoned the payor bank the next day and informed the bank of Howard's death. She mentioned the mailed checks and specifically asked the bank manager to keep the account, which was in Howard's name only, open to pay them. The bank manager said that the bank would pay the checks for nine more days. Later that same day, Crazy Nelly, the Mortuses' next-door neighbor, somehow got the idea that Howard had left her all his money (he didn't leave her a cent—he barely knew her) and called up the bank. She explained she was the Mortuses' neighbor and was "sure to be an heir to the estate," so she ordered the bank to stop paying checks on Howard's account. The bank consulted its attorney. Must it stop paying checks, or may it still continue to do so? If it returns checks, will it have made a dishonor? Cf. §3-502. Is it a *wrongful* dishonor so as to subject the bank to §4-402 damages?

D. *Bank's Right of Setoff*

In the late 1700s, there developed a common law lien by which a bank could unilaterally debit the account of a depositor in order to pay a debt owed to itself. This common law right, which is in existence in virtually all states today, is called the bank's right of *setoff* because one obligation (the customer's to the bank) is offset against another (the bank's to the customer). Prior to the advent of the Fair Credit Billing Act (chapter four of the Truth in Lending Act, 15 U.S.C. §§1601 et seq., effective October 28, 1975), a consumer who had a checking account with the same bank that issued him or her a credit card might be the victim of a non-notification setoff on failing to make a payment. Section 169 of the Fair Credit Billing Act now prohibits this practice in most instances involving customer credit card debts. This section is supplemented by §1026.12(d) of the Consumer Financial Protection Bureau's Regulation Z,[4] 12 C.F.R. part 1026, which explains the rules in more detail. Regulation Z §1026.12(d):

> (1) A card issuer may not take any action, either before or after termination of credit card privileges, to offset a cardholder's indebtedness arising from a consumer credit transaction under the relevant credit card plan against funds of the cardholder held on deposit with the card issuer. . . .

PROBLEM 181

When Portia Moot's financial condition became so moribund that she stopped paying all her debts, Octopus National Bank (ONB), which was annoyed that she currently owed $578 on the credit card it had issued her, simply took this amount from Portia's checking account at ONB. This caused other checks of hers to bounce, and she is furious. The Truth in Lending Act's §130, 15 U.S.C. §1640, allows her to recover actual damages, a small amount of punitive damages, and her attorney's fees for violation of the TILA rules. If she calls you, her attorney cousin, for advice, what do you say to her?[5]

4. Authority for Regulation Z was transferred from the Federal Reserve Board to the newly created Consumer Financial Protection Bureau in 2011.

5. The rest of the Regulation Z provision continues like this:

> (2) This paragraph does not alter or affect the right of a card issuer acting under state or federal law to do any of the following with regard to funds of a cardholder held on deposit with the card issuer if the same procedure is constitutionally available

Setoff[6] is recognized in the UCC in several sections that mention it in passing (§§4-201(a), 4-215(e), and 4-303), although the Code neither establishes the right nor regulates its terms. Setoff may be had only against general accounts (such as checking and savings accounts) of the depositor. When the depositor has created a *special* account for a limited purpose, the bank may not set off against it non-related debts of the depositor. See Filosa v. Pecora, 44 Ill. App. 3d 912, 358 N.E.2d 1213 (1976) (setoff not permitted against escrow account). The given reason is that for special accounts the bank is a bailee and not a debtor. See Mid-City Natl. Bank v. Mars Bldg. Corp., 33 Ill. App. 3d 1083, 339 N.E.2d 497 (1975). A bank owes a duty of fair and honorable dealing to its customers. When a bank exercises the right of setoff in an improper fashion, the courts are quick to protect the customer. See Wells v. Washington Heights Fed. Sav. & Loan Assn., 63 Misc. 2d 424, 312 N.Y.S.2d 236 (Cir. Ct. 1970).

Walter v. National City Bank of Cleveland

Ohio Supreme Court, 1975
42 Ohio St. 2d 524, 330 N.E.2d 425

This is an action in civil conversion, involving claims of priority of right to a commercial bank account of Ritzer of Austria, Inc. In the fall of 1969, Ritzer opened a commercial account with The National City Bank of Cleveland, appellant herein. On April 14, 1971, Ritzer executed a 90-day promissory note to appellant in the amount of $3,600, although Ritzer's balance sheet, as of March 31, 1971, showed the company to be insolvent.

---

to creditors generally: obtain or enforce a consensual security interest in the funds; attach or otherwise levy upon the funds; or obtain or enforce a court order relating to the funds.

(3) This paragraph does not prohibit a plan, if authorized in writing by the cardholder, under which the card issuer may periodically deduct all or part of the cardholder's credit card debt from a deposit account held with the card issuer (subject to the limitations in §1026.13(d)(1)).

It looks like all the bank need do to get around this problem and use its right of setoff is to put a clause in the bank account contract granting itself a security interest in the account to protect credit card extensions, but that won't work either. The official commentary to this Regulation Z section requires that the "consensual security interest" mentioned in subsection (2) be a separately signed writing stating that the account will be used as collateral for the credit card debt, and not merely be a clause in the credit card contract. Further, this commentary requires that the security interest in the consumer's account be open (as a matter of state law) to other creditors or the card issuer cannot claim an interest therein either. Since Article 9 of the UCC will not allow other creditors to take a security interest in consumer bank accounts—see §9-109(d)(13)—the security interest possibility is cut off.

6. Bankers, perversely, insist on calling setoff *offset*. The bankers may have won this logomachy; the Fair Credit Billing Act calls this subtraction process an *offset*.

On May 11, 1971, Robert A. Walter, appellee herein, recovered a judgment against Ritzer in the Euclid Municipal Court for $6,831.95. The following day, the appellant bank was served by mail as garnishee with an order in aid of execution. At the time of service, Ritzer had on deposit with appellant the sum of $3,651.75. The unmatured debt on appellant's promissory note totalled $3,626.25, including interest accrued. On May 24, 1971, appellant sent a letter to the Euclid Municipal Court stating that it was setting off the amount of its loan, leaving a balance of $25.50. Appellant mailed its check for the balance to the Euclid Municipal Court on July 22, 1971.

Appellee brought this action in the Court of Common Pleas of Cuyahoga County. Both parties moved for summary judgment, and judgment was granted for appellee. The Court of Appeals affirmed.

STERN, J. The appellant bank claims a right of equitable setoff of an unmatured indebtedness of its depositor, as against a judgment creditor seeking to reach the depositor's account by an order in aid of execution. Appellant concedes that it has no statutory right of setoff under R.C. 2309.19.

Setoff, both at law and in equity, is that right which exists between two parties, each of whom under an independent contract owes a definite amount to the other, to set off their respective debts by way of mutual deduction. Witham v. South Side Bldg. & Loan Assn. of Lima (1938), 133 Ohio St. 560, 562, 15 N.E.2d 149.

As a general rule, the courts have held that a bank may set off a bank account against the matured indebtedness of its depositor, although the bank has been garnished at the instance of a creditor of the depositor. Schuler v. Israel (1887), 120 U.S. 506, 7 S. Ct. 648, 30 L. Ed. 707; Bennett v. Campbell (1889), 189 Pa. 647, 42 A. 373; Annotation, 106 A.L.R. 62. In Bank v. Brewing Co. (1893), 50 Ohio St. 151, 33 N.E. 1054, it was held that a bank could set off the amount of an insolvent depositor's checking account against an unpaid and overdue note, without the knowledge or consent of the depositor, and that the bank could refuse payment of a check drawn on the account. The theory of these cases is that a bank stands in the relationship of debtor to its depositor, and has the right to apply the deposit to payment of the depositor's matured debts or obligations held by the bank, in the same way that another debtor might assert setoff as a defense to an action on the debt. Holloway v. First Natl. Bank of Pocatello (1928), 45 Idaho 746, 265 P. 699.

In fact, the exercise of setoff by a bank is often quite different from the case of a usual debtor-creditor relationship. A bank account is a debt, but one which is ordinarily subject to demand withdrawal at any time, and one which imposes clear responsibilities upon the bank depending upon the nature of the account. Historically, the bank's right to setoff derives from the bank lien of the law merchant, and that right still possesses some of the characteristics of a lien, since it permits the bank by self-help to take priority over others claiming a right to the funds on deposit.[7] Whereas, in the case of an ordinary debtor, setoff is available as an equitable and statutory defense, in the case of a bank, setoff becomes a means by which the bank, because of its position as a commercial middleman, acquires a priority of right whenever it acts as creditor for a depositor.

The courts have generally held that the bank does not have a priority of right in equity where the bank seeks to set off an unmatured indebtedness. United Bank & Trust Co. v. Washburn & Condon (1930), 37 Ariz. 223, 292 P. 1025; Gerseta Corporation v. Equitable Trust Co. of New York (1926), 241 N.Y. 418, 150 N.E. 501; Stockyards Natl. Bank of Presnall (1917), 109 Tex. 32, 194 S.W. 384. Cf. Valley National Bank of Arizona v. Hasper (1967), 6 Ariz. App. 376, 432 P.2d 924. An unmatured debt is not presently due or collectible and is not available for set-off, since set off would alter the contract made by the parties.

An exception to this rule has been made in cases where the depositor is insolvent. In Schuler v. Israel, supra (120 U.S. 506, 7 S. Ct. 648, 30 L. Ed. 708), the court noted that a defense in equity was available to a bank-debtor to prevent an insolvent depositor-creditor from obtaining payment of his debt, where an unmatured obligation was available as setoff and would be lost due to the insolvency.

The same equities do not apply in the case at bar. Here, the negotiation of a 90-day promissory note to Ritzer occurred after the date upon which, the bank itself asserts, Ritzer's balance sheet showed the company to be insolvent. In sum, the bank made a loan for a definite term to an insolvent depositor, and now claims that as a matter of equity it is entitled to priority of right to its depositor's account because of the insolvency. We disagree. The extension of credit to an insolvent was a voluntary act, whether negligent or merely lacking in sound banking practice. In the present case, no equity

7. "It is said to be a well-settled rule of the law merchant, that a bank has a general lien on all the funds of a depositor in its possession for any balance due on general account, or other indebtedness contracted in the course of their dealings, and may appropriate the funds to the payment of such indebtedness. The right to make such appropriation, it is held, grows out of the relation of the parties, as debtor and creditor, and rests upon the principle that, 'as the depositor is indebted to the bank upon a demand which is due, the funds in its possession may properly and justly be applied in payment of such debt, and it has therefore a right to retain such funds until payment is actually made.' Falkland v. Bank, 84 N.Y. 145. Though this right is called a 'lien,' strictly it is not, when applied to a general deposit, for, a person cannot have a lien upon his own property, but only on that of another; and, as we have seen, the funds of general deposit in a bank are the property of the bank. Properly speaking, the right, in such case, is that of set-off, arising from the existence of mutual demands. The practical effect, however, is the same. The cross demands are satisfied, so far as they are equal, leaving whatever balance that may be due on either as the true amount of the indebtedness from one party to the other." Bank v. Brewing Co. (1893), 50 Ohio St. 151, 158 n.59, 33 N.E. 1054, 1055 n.59.

appears which would require granting priority to the bank's unmatured obligation over the judgment of the appellee.[8]

Lack of maturity is not always permitted to defeat the right of set-off where that right is the only way to prevent clear injustice, and the courts have frequently applied equitable principles in cases of insolvency. "Where insolvency has intervened, a court will not be limited to a strict application of statutory set-off but will apply the doctrines of equity." Union Properties v. Baldwin Brothers Co. (1943), 141 Ohio St. 303, 47 N.E.2d 983 (paragraph nine of the syllabus). But no equity accrues where insolvency did not "intervene" but occurred prior to the voluntary granting of the loan sought to be set off.

The bank also claims a contractual right of set-off based upon its rules and regulations. These rules read, in part, ". . . Bank also reserves the right to apply any balance in the account to the payment of any indebtedness, direct or indirect, absolute or contingent, due or to become due and howsoever evidenced, of depositor to bank."

The signature card, signed by the corporate officers of Ritzer in 1969, states that the "depositor acknowledges receipt of a copy of the rules and regulations . . . relative to commercial accounts and agrees to be bound thereby and by any amendments and additions thereto hereafter made." The bank's claim is, in effect, that it could at any time apply any part of the funds deposited in the commercial account to the payment of the 90-day promissory note, even before the note was due, and that the garnisheeing creditor stands in the shoes of the depositor.

The 90-day promissory note executed by Ritzer in favor of the bank contains no statement that it was made upon the security of the commercial account, and contains no provision for acceleration, other than for lack of performance by the debtor. The note was secured by a security agreement in machinery and equipment,[9] but no security agreement was made with respect to the commercial account.

8. A banker's right of setoff also raises new equitable questions in situations where the bank may have several types of accounts with a depositor, including savings passbook and checking accounts and long-term certificates of deposit, and may also be a creditor for mortgage loans, installment loans, credit card, and other forms of indebtedness. It has been suggested that the setoff of a customer's indebtedness without notice or regard to his protests is not equitable and in conflict with due process and legislation protecting consumers' rights. Comment, Banking Setoff: A Study in Commercial Obsolescence, 23 Hastings L.J. 1585. See also Olsen, The Appropriation of Deposits for Debt: Levies, Liens, and Setoffs, 90 Banking L.J. 827 (1973).

9. That agreement defines "liabilities" in almost the exact terms of the rules and regulations, to include "indebtedness . . . due or to become due. . . ." It is clear that under a security agreement the rights of a secured party to enforce his security interest do not accrue until after default by the debtor. UCC §9-501.

If the language of the bank's rules and regulations is taken to mean that the bank could at any time apply the balance of the commercial account to the promissory note, those rules are in direct conflict with the contract embodied in that note. They would have the effect of converting a note payable at a definite time to one payable on demand. In this case, the later, specific terms of the promissory note control over the general language of the rules. The primary intent of the parties in executing the 90-day note was that it become due in 90 days, not upon demand, and to the extent that the earlier, general language of the rules conflicts with that intent, it must be taken to have been superseded. See 3 Corbin on Contracts, 172 n.178, Section 547; 4 Williston on Contracts (3d ed.), 816, 822, Section 624.

". . . [I]n the construction of any written instrument the primary duty of the court is to determine and give effect to the intention of the parties." United States Fire Ins. Co. v. PhilMar Corporation (1965), 166 Ohio St. 85, 87, 139 N.E.2d 330, 332.

The contract embodied in the promissory note was that the debt would become due and payable in 90 days, and the bank had no contractual right to treat the note as a demand note and set off the commercial account against the debt before maturity.

For the foregoing reasons, the judgment of the Court of Appeals is affirmed.

Judgment affirmed.

Bankruptcy and Setoff. According to §362(a)(7) of the Bankruptcy Code, the filing of a petition in bankruptcy creates an automatic stay against creditor collection activity, specifically including the exercise of the right of setoff. Individuals injured by a violation of the automatic stay may sue under §362(h) of the Bankruptcy Code and recover "actual damages, including costs and attorney fees, and, in appropriate circumstances, may recover punitive damages." Of course, the bank may apply to the bankruptcy court for relief from the stay, §362(d); and, on getting it, may exercise the right of setoff; see §553. In 1995, the U.S. Supreme Court granted some relief to banks by ruling that an *administrative freeze* on a checking account is *not* the same as a setoff and does not violate the automatic stay; Citizens Bank of Maryland v. Strumpf, 516 U.S. 16 (1995). This means that a bank could freeze the account on learning of a bankruptcy, not allowing the customer to reach the funds involved, but not taking the money for itself either, thus preserving the status quo while the bankruptcy court is asked to straighten out what is to become of the monies in the account.

E. *Customer's Right to Stop Payment*

1. Ordinary Checks

The key section on the right to stop payment is §4-403, which you should read. Official Comment 1 states:

> The position taken by this section is that stopping payment or closing an account is a service which depositors expect and are entitled to receive from banks notwithstanding its difficulty, inconvenience and expense. The inevitable occasional losses through failure to stop or close should be borne by the banks as a cost of the business of banking.

Parr v. Security National Bank

Oklahoma Court of Appeals, 1984
680 P.2d 648

REYNOLDS, J.

We are called upon to decide whether Security National Bank had a reasonable opportunity to stop payment on a check when the description received is exact in all respects except for a single digit error in the check amount. This issue has not been decided by an Oklahoma court.

Parr wrote check number 949 to Champlin Oil. She dated and mailed it September 14, 1981. The amount of the check was $972.96. On September 15, 1981, Parr ordered payment stopped by telephone. Parr gave the bank her account number, the check number, the date, the payee and the amount of the check. A 50-cent error was made in identifying the amount of the check. Parr went to the bank on September 16th or 17th and executed a written stop order dated September 15, 1981. The written stop order was also in error. Security National paid check number 949 on September 17, 1981.

Parr brought suit against Security National seeking recovery for the amount of the check, 12-percent interest on that amount, reasonable attorney's fees and costs. Security National defended by showing their computers were programmed to stop payment only if the reported amount of the check were correct. They argued Parr's 50-cent error relieved them of liability. Timeliness of notice was not an issue.

[The court then quoted §4-403(1) and the Official Comment 1 paragraph reprinted prior to the case.—EDS.]

Security National contends that whether a stop payment order has been received "in such manner as to afford the bank a reasonable opportunity to act" should be determined *after* examining how the defendant bank handles stop orders. This interpretation has found favor among highly respected legal authorities, but not among the majority of courts that have addressed this issue.

Both groups acknowledge §4-403(1) has not changed the common law rule that a stop payment order must identify the check with "reasonable accuracy." It is from this premise that courts have determined whether the description is reasonably accurate without consideration of the defendant/bank's computer program. In Elsie Rodriguez Fashions, Inc. v. Chase Manhattan Bank, 23 U.C.C. Rep. 133 (N.Y. Sup. Ct. 1978), the customer gave the bank the correct payee, check number and date but made a 10-cent error in the amount of the check. The court determined the check had been described with sufficient accuracy to allow the bank to stop payment. The opinion makes no mention of the bank's computer program. In accord with this approach on similar facts are the New York cases of Pokras v. National Bank of North America, 30 U.C.C. Rep. 1089 (N.Y. App. Term 1981), and Thomas v. Marine Midland Tinkers National Bank, 86 Misc. 2d 284, 381 N.Y.S.2d 797 (N.Y. Civ. Ct. 1976). A different result was reached by a New York court where the customer was told by the bank the stop order would not be effective unless she provided the exact amount of the check. Poullier v. Nacua Motors, Inc., 108 Misc. 2d 913, 439 N.Y.S.2d 85 (N.Y. Sup. Ct. 1981). Security National does not contend they gave notice to Parr that any discrepancy in the check amount would prevent compliance with her stop payment order.

In Delano v. Putnam Trust Co., 33 U.C.C. Rep. 635 (Conn. Super. Ct. 1981), a single-digit error in the amount of $100.00 did not prevent recovery where customer supplied bank with the correct check number, date, payee, and account number of the check. The bank's computer program required an exact match of check amount before it would stop payment. Court held bank had received sufficient information to allow it a "reasonable opportunity to act" on the stop payment order. Court stated the bank had a duty to inform its customer of the need for precision in reporting the amount before it could rely on customer's error to relieve it of liability.

The Supreme Court of Alabama denied customer's recovery in Sherrill v. Frank Morris Pontiac-Buick-GMC, Inc., 366 So. 2d 251 (Ala. 1979). Customer gave bank three descriptive elements of the check, check amount, payee and date. The check was not numbered. Two of the three pieces of information were incorrect. Court determined the check was not described with reasonable accuracy, therefore the bank was not afforded a "reasonable opportunity to act" on the stop payment order.

In FJS Electronics, Inc. v. Fidelity Bank, 431 A.2d 326 (Pa. Super. Ct. 1981), court allowed customer to prevail even though its 50-cent error in check amount prevented bank's computer from acting on stop payment order. The bank asserted §4-403 "should be read to require compliance with the procedures of a particular bank, regardless of what they are and regardless of whether the customer has been made aware of them." Id. at 328. Court determined that the drafter's policy stated in Comment 2 to §4-403 precluded such an interpretation. They reasoned:

> Fidelity made a choice when it elected to employ a technique which searched for stopped checks by amount alone. It evidently found benefits to this technique which outweighed the risk that an item might be inaccurately described in a stop order. This is precisely the type of inevitable loss which was contemplated by the code drafters and addressed by the comment quoted above. The focus of §4-403 is the service which may be expected by the customer, and a customer may expect a check to be stopped after the bank is given reasonable notice. A bank's decision to reduce operating costs by using a system which increases the risk that checks as to which there is an outstanding stop payment order will be paid invites liability when such items are paid.

We find this analysis, as well as that in *Delano,* supra, persuasive. We hold Parr described her check with reasonable accuracy, and Security National had a reasonable opportunity to act on the stop payment order.

We are aware of the burden this may place on Oklahoma banks. However, the industry has two alternatives to avoid liability if banking procedures necessitate an exact description of an item: (1) notify the customer at the time a stop order is given, or (2) seek a legislative amendment to §4-403.

We recognize Parr received the benefit of having her debt paid to Champlin Oil and will recover from Security National for failure to stop payment. To avoid this possibility of unjust enrichment, §4-407(b) subrogates the payor bank [Security National] to the rights of the payee [Champlin] against the maker [Parr]. In such a suit, an award of attorney's fees and costs to Security National would be proper under 12 O.S. 1981 §936, as Champlin would have been suing Parr on an open account if Security National had stopped payment on the check.

Trial court is reversed and this cause remanded for award of $972.96 plus reasonable attorney's fees and costs consistent with this opinion.

Reversed and remanded.

PROBLEM 182

When George and Martha's marriage turned into a wolfish nightmare they agreed to separate and seek a divorce. The couple had a joint checking account with Albee National Bank in both their names. George sent the bank a letter telling it to "freeze my checking account from further advances by anybody." The bank sent George a letter stating that it would do so. Nonetheless the bank paid a check for $20,000 that Martha drew against the account one week later. Was this a stop payment order under §4-403? See Rusnack v. Cardinal Bank, N.A., 695 F. App'x 704 (4th Cir. 2017).

PROBLEM 183

Julio Perez, newly arrived in New York from Puerto Rico, was tricked into buying a $50 refrigerator for $280. He paid the seller, Honest Juan, by check and took the appliance home in his truck. His brother saw the refrigerator, told Julio that he had been had, and advised him to call the bank to stop payment on the check. Julio phoned his bank and said, "This is Julio Perez. You must stop—do not give Honest Juan money for my check." The bank clerk who took the call asked, "Which check?" Julio replied, "Today—refrigerator check" and hung up. The bank failed to stop payment on the check, and the next day it was presented by Honest Juan and paid. Julio demanded that the money be replaced in his account, and when the bank refused, Julio retained Juanita Martinez, a lawyer, who filed suit on his behalf, contending that the check was not "properly payable" per §4-401. The complaint set out only the facts of the stop-payment order and the payment in spite of it. As a judge, how would you rule on each of the following issues raised by the bank?

(a) The stop-payment order did not give enough information to be effective. See §4-403(a); Sherrill v. Frank Morris Pontiac-Buick-GMC, Inc., 366 So. 2d 251 (Ala. 1978); White & Summers 19-5; Annot., 35 A.L.R.4th 985; Annot., 29 A.L.R.4th 228. Official Comment 5 to §4-403 says that in "describing the item, the customer, in the absence of a contrary agreement, must meet the standard of what information allows the bank under the technology then existing to identify the item with reasonable certainty."

(b) The contract of deposit that Julio initially signed stated: "Customer agrees that no oral stop-payment order shall be effective; stop-payment orders must be in writing to be effective." The bank argues that fully one-half of its customers are Spanish-speaking Americans and that oral stop-payment orders are a nightmare to try to decode. See §4-103(a); White & Summers 19-2.

(c) The contract of deposit also contained this clause: "Customer agrees that the bank shall not be liable if it mistakenly pays an item on which payment has been stopped." See Official Comment 7 to §4-403.

(d) The bank's rules require that a stop-payment order be accompanied by a $15 stop-payment fee, and Julio failed to tender such a fee. See Official Comment 1 to §4-403. Compare Opinion of Attorney General, 30 U.C.C. Rep. Serv. 1626 (Mich. 1981), with Opinion of Attorney General, 33 U.C.C. Rep. Serv. 1445 (Mich. 1981).

(e) Plaintiff's complaint is defective in that it fails to allege any loss to plaintiff as a result of the bank's alleged wrongful payment, and plaintiff carries this burden under §4-403(c). For all the bank knows, plaintiff has revoked his acceptance of the refrigerator and avoided the sale on grounds of unconscionability. See Cicci v. Lincoln Natl. Bank & Trust Co., 46 Misc. 2d 465, 260 N.Y.S.2d 100 (City Ct. 1965) (which found this argument persuasive); contra Thomas v. Marine Midland Tinkers Natl. Bank, 86 Misc. 2d 284, 381 N.Y.S.2d 797 (Sup. Ct. 1976); see White & Summers 19-6.

If the bank accidentally pays over the stop-payment order and recredits the account, it can use another important section of the Code, §4-407 (the Subrogation Rule), to step into the shoes of its customer and sue any party he or she could have sued (Honest Juan, in the above Problem). Read §4-407(3) carefully. This principle of subrogation also can help out the bank in the following situations where it is resisting the request of a customer to recredit an improper payment.

PROBLEM 184

After he had purchased a new car from Flash Motors, Thomas Crandall got the car home and discovered that it clashed with the color of his garage. He couldn't stand this, of course, so he phoned his bank, Octopus National, and placed an oral stop-payment order on the check he had written for the car. Negligently, the bank paid the check anyway. Must the bank recredit the account? See §4-407(2).

Canty v. Vermont National Bank

Vermont Superior Court, 1994
1994 WL 797862

KATZ, J.

Plaintiff Joseph Canty had a checking account with Vermont National Bank and a problem with the Internal Revenue Service. When the Internal Revenue asked him for canceled checks to document his payment of certain obligations, he forwarded the checks. The Internal Revenue redeposited those canceled checks, and Vermont National Bank paid them a second time, withdrawing the funds from plaintiff's account. Not surprisingly, plaintiff took the position that he should pay each check once, but not twice. He therefore sues, and now seeks summary judgment, asserting the Bank must recredit his account for the funds improperly withdrawn to make the second payments.

In the words of the Uniform Commercial Code, the payor bank has "paid an item under circumstances giving a basis for objection by the drawer or maker." 9A V.S.A. Sec. 4-407. It is fairly implicit in U.C.C. Sec. 4-401(1) that if an item is not properly payable, the bank may not charge the customer's account, and if it has done so, it must recredit the account. Siegel v. New England Merchants Nat. Bank, 386 Mass. 672, 437 N.E.2d 218, 221 (1982); J. White and R. Summers, Uniform Commercial Code Sec. 17-3 at 657 (2d ed. 1980). Although recrediting may constitute the usually required response, the law does permit a bank to refuse to recredit its customer's account after wrongful payment of an item by subrogating itself to the rights of the presenter of the improperly paid instrument. Id., at 660. . . .

Although a drawer bank can improperly pay on an item in several ways, its right to subrogation is inextricably entwined with its liability to its customer for improper payment. White and Summers, at 683. The customer's realization of his claim may produce unjust enrichment. Even when an item is not properly payable, for any of several reasons, the bank's payment may discharge a legal obligation of the customer, or create a right in the customer's favor against the payee. Siegel v. New England Merchants, 437 N.E.2d at 221. If the customer were permitted to retain such benefits, and recover the amount of the check as well, he would profit at the bank's expense. Id. Although plaintiff here argues that there can be no subrogation until his account is first re-credited, that appears contrary to the provisions of §4-407, which permit a bank to be subrogated to the rights of a payee, against the drawer or maker—its own customer. Manufacturer's Hanover Trust Co. v. Ava Industries, Inc., 414 N.Y.S.2d 425 (Sup. Ct. 1978) (Bank may pursue its own customer upon both subrogation and possible unjust enrichment; 4-407, comments 2 and 3). Siegel v. New England Merchants points out that the subrogation rights of 4-407 refer to those existing prior to the bank's wrongful payment of the item. 437 N.E.2d 221, n.5. Indeed, a bank may invoke subrogation under 4-407 in spite of a settlement agreement between its customer (the drawer) and payee. Swiss Credit Bank v. Balink, 614 F.2d 1269 (10th Cir. 1980). The bank may assert its subrogation rights defensively, when its depositor brings an action for wrongful debit. Siegel, 437 N.E.2d at 222; Chute v. Bank One of Akron, N.A., 460 N.E.2d 720 (Ohio App. 1983).

On the theory that one form of improper payment is functionally no different than another, the *Siegel* court analogizes the customer's right to be recredited to that existing for payment in the face of a proper stop order, which is governed by §4-403. The issue of injust enrichment is common to both. The rule of 4-403(3) is that a depositor bears the burden of proving the fact and amount of any loss. Kupersmith v. Manufacturer's Hanover Trust Co., 15 U.C.C. Rep. 696 (N.Y. Civ. Ct. 1974). Section 4-403(3) simply protects the bank against the need to prove events familiar to the depositor, *Siegel*, 437 N.E.2d 222, in this case his account status with the Internal Revenue.

Clearly there is a difference between a check which has never been paid and one which has already been paid. In the first instance, the drawer has indicated an intent to pay the payee a stated sum, presumably a voluntary and justified decision. In the second, the drawer has already made payment, and thereby satisfied his debt to the amount paid. But among payees, the Internal Revenue must be considered sui generis. One's account with the Internal Revenue is never closed. Even death does not bring immediate finality. Plaintiff argues that he "did not owe any liability to the I.R.S. *for the tax quarters to which his [ill-fated] checks related.*" (Emphasis altered.) But the scope of inquiry, in application of the equitable doctrine of subrogation, is not limited to some particular payment and its due date. Rather, given the purpose of avoiding unjust enrichment, the inquiry must be whether plaintiff depositor actually suffered any loss by the admittedly improper payment. If he did not, he may not recover, for to do so would be to enrich him twice, once on his Internal Revenue account and once on his satisfied judgment.

The purpose of most presumptions is to aid trial by shifting the burden of going forward to the party who has the best access to the facts, or who has the notably less probable side of a common question. Reporter's Notes, Rule 301, V.R. Ev. Lang v. Chase Manhattan Bank, 6 U.C.C. Rep. 1259 (N.Y. App. Div. 1969), reversed a grant of summary judgment against the bank, which was deemed not absolutely liable to its customer for paying in the face of a stop payment order, when the issue of actual loss to the customer "turns upon evidence peculiarly within the knowledge of the customer and her auto dealer. In this unfortunate situation, plaintiff customer has both the best access to the facts of his accounts with the I.R.S. and has the less probable side of the question, namely that a neutral government agency took his money without giving him any credit for it.

Given the difficulty of the bank securing information from the Internal Revenue about the account of another, the presumed regularity of its proceedings, 1 J. Weinstein and M. Berger Weinstein's Evidence, Par. 301 [03] at 301-53 (1994), citing, inter alia, Welch v. Helvering, 290 U.S. 111, 115 (1933), and the fact that we all continue to accrue liability with the Internal Revenue, we conclude that the proper disposition of this most unusual case must require plaintiff actually to prove his loss.

Saratoga Polo Assn., Ltd. v. Adirondack Trust Co., 460 N.Y.S.2d 712 (Sup. Ct. 1983), and Mitchell v. Republic Bank & Trust Co., 239 S.E.2d 867 (N.C. App. 1978), hold that a customer initially establishes a prima facie case by showing that an item was improperly paid. Thereupon the bank, exercising its subrogation rights under §4-407, has the burden of coming forward and presenting evidence of an absence of actual loss to the customer. When the bank meets the burden of coming forward with such evidence, the customer must then sustain the ultimate burden of proof. We hold that when the improperly paid item was paid to the Internal Revenue Service, we will presume an absence of actual loss to the customer; the bank has therefore met its burden of coming forward with such evidence.

We reject plaintiff's contention that the Bank must first re-credit his account, before earning any right to subrogation. Such a rule would tend to see the funds disappear while the case was ongoing. While presumably not so in this case, many of this class of cases—improperly paid checks—arise out of fraud. Requiring subrogated banks to first recredit the funds would tend to put those funds back into the hands of the miscreant, at a time when the court is still in a difficult position to know whether fraud has been practiced in the particular case at hand. Requiring recrediting as a threshold to subrogation would always arise as an interlocutory order, as there is no final judgment until all claims have been resolved. Rule 54, V.R.C.P. The effect would therefore be that the bank would have no appeal, and that the mere filing of a complaint would require the defendant to grant plaintiff the money he seeks, as a price for even litigating an affirmative defense to such recrediting. Requiring threshold recrediting of funds is not supported by *Siegel v. New England Merchants.* Moreover, a bank's §4-407 right of subrogation has been elevated above any duty to adjust its customer's account, Sunshine v. Bankers Trust Co., 34 N.Y.2d 404, 314 N.E.2d 860, 866 (N.Y. 1974), which threshold duty the New York Court of Appeals labeled a "technical mechanical requirement of common-law subrogation." As the right of subrogation has "particular approval" under our law, Lopez v. Concord Genl. Mut. Ins. Group, 155 Vt. 320, 324, 583 A.2d 602 (1990), we conclude that its value should not be diluted by requiring banks to first recredit accounts in order to gain the benefits of this venerable doctrine of equity. This is in accord with the U.C.C's intent that §4-407 was intended to provide a broad, liberal remedy that incorporated and is based upon the common law equitable principles of unjust enrichment and restitution. Swiss Credit Bank v. Balink, 28 U.C.C. Rep. at 482.

We therefore deny plaintiff's motion for summary judgment. Partial summary judgment is accorded to defendant Vermont National Bank; unless plaintiff can show actual loss by the improper second payment of his canceled checks, his claims shall be dismissed. We shall allow plaintiff 60 days to marshall his evidence regarding actual loss, and then expect either a joint status report to the clerk, a request for a pretrial conference, or a further motion for summary judgment, depending on the proof available to plaintiff.

We also grant defendant's motion to dismiss the punitive damage claims. First, we find considerable merit in the defenses raised by the bank. Second, to accept plaintiff's argument would be to telescope into one case both the merits of that case and the "malicious defense" claim inherent in the punitive damage theory. In malicious prosecution, Vermont law has always required a successful outcome in the underlying litigation before supporting punitive damages for the tort of wrongful litigation. Anello v. Vinci, 142 Vt. 583, 587, 458 A.2d 1117 (1983).

PROBLEM 185

Rupert Signer gave his fiancée, Maggie Lee, a check for $1,000 as a birthday gift. She took the check, thanked him politely, and then told him that she was getting ready to marry his best friend Charlie and "this is goodbye." Rupert left in a huff and went straight to his bank, the Careless State Bank, where he filled out a written stop-payment order on the check he had given to Maggie Lee. In the meantime, Maggie Lee indorsed the check over to Computer City in payment for a $1,000 software package she purchased there. When Computer City presented the check to Careless State Bank for payment, the bank paid it without a murmur. Rupert sued when the bank refused to recredit his account, alleging a $1,000 loss because he had tried to revoke a gift promise on which the bank now made him liable. Are either of these defenses by the bank good?

(a) Computer City was a holder in due course of Rupert's check, and he could not have refused to pay Computer City if it had presented the check to him. See Official Comment 7 to §4-403. Under §4-407, the bank is subrogated to the rights of any holder in due course of the check. Does this help the bank? See Official Comment 1 to §4-407.

(b) Same argument that Computer City was a holder in due course and that Rupert would eventually have had to pay Computer City if the bank had been able to remember to stop payment. This being true, Rupert has really suffered no loss by the wrongful payment, so he cannot recover. Cf. §4-403(c); see Seigel v. Merrill Lynch, Pierce, Fenner & Smith, Inc., 745 A.2d 301 (D.C. App. 2000).

PROBLEM 186

Same fact situation, except that Maggie Lee takes the check and deposits it in her checking account with Octopus National Bank. The balance in the checking account prior to the deposit was $.07. Later that same day, Maggie wrote a check for $1,000.07 and cashed it at her bank, thereby withdrawing all the money from her account. Octopus National Bank sent the check to the payor bank, Careless State Bank, which negligently paid the check over the stop-payment order. Can Careless State still use the above two defenses when

Rupert sues? See §§4-211, 4-210(a); Universal C.I.T. Credit Corp. v. Guaranty Bank & Trust Co., 161 F. Supp. 790 (D. Mass. 1958).

2. Cashier's, Teller's, and Certified Checks

At common law and under prior statutes there was much confusion surrounding the question of whether a customer could stop payment on a check that had been certified. The Code now makes it clear that the answer is no. A customer has no right to stop payment on a certified check. See Official Comment 4 to §4-403. The reason is that once the check is certified, the payor bank itself is the primary obligor on the instrument, §3-413(a), and the drawer has no right to require the bank to breach its acceptor's contract.[10] The same thing is true of a cashier's check (a check on which the bank is both drawer and drawee) and of a bank check (a check drawn by one bank on another, also called a *teller's check*); see §3-104(g) and (h).[11]

PROBLEM 187

Harry Flashman agreed to sell his sports car to Tom Brown if the latter paid with a cashier's check (see §3-104(g)) for $15,000, issued by Fraser National Bank. Tom purchased such a cashier's check from the bank; it was payable to the order of Harry Flashman (in such a situation, a person in Tom's position is called a *remitter*; §3-103(a)(15)). After Tom handed the check over to Harry, the latter told him that the car was parked at an address Harry gave him. Tom went to the address and found it was an automobile dump. The sports car had been wrecked and was worthless. He phoned Fraser National Bank and demanded that the bank not pay the check. Should the bank do this? See §3-411 and its Official Comment; see also §3-305(c). What can Tom do if the bank refuses to help him? See §3-202 and Official Comment 2 to §3-201.

10. The so-called Four Legals section, §4-303(a)(1), discussed later in this chapter, states that a customer loses his or her right to stop payment once the bank accepts or certifies an item. In actuality, when a check is certified by the drawee, an amount of money sufficient to pay the check when it is presented is taken from the account and held pending the second presentment; in this way the drawee bank protects itself as it undertakes the primary liability of an acceptor (§3-413).

11. Remember that the giving of an instrument on which a bank is primarily liable is an absolute payment of the underlying obligation and discharges the underlying obligor unless he or she is liable on the instrument. See §3-310(a).

Patriot Bank v. Navy Federal Credit Union

Circuit Court of Virginia, 2002
2002 WL 481129

Roush, J.

This case arises under Articles 3A and 4 of the Uniform Commercial Code, Va. Code Ann. §8.1-101, et seq. At issue is whether the defendant Navy Federal Credit Union wrongfully refused to honor a cashier's check it issued.

This matter came on for a bench trial on February 14, 2002 as a de novo appeal from the General District Court. At that time, the Court took the matter under advisement. The Court has now carefully considered the pleadings, the applicable provisions of the Uniform Commercial Code and the arguments of counsel. For the reasons stated below, judgment will be entered in favor of the plaintiff Patriot Bank, N.A. in the amount of $7,000.00, plus interest, costs, and attorney's fees.

Facts

On April 4, 2001, Thomas Peeso, a member of the Navy Federal Credit Union ("Navy FCU"), obtained a cashier's check from Navy FCU in the amount of $7,000. The check was made payable to Mr. Peeso. Mr. Peeso's account was debited for payment of the check. Mr. Peeso delivered the check to Nation's Auto Loan Center ("Nation's Auto"), a used car dealership. Mr. Peeso intended to use the check to purchase a used car for his daughter. He indorsed the check as follows:

[Peeso's Signature]
Payable to Nation's Auto Loan Center

Beneath that indorsement, was written by hand "# 180180021301"—Nation's Auto's account number at Patriot Bank.

Later on April 4, 2001, Nation's Auto deposited the check in its account at the plaintiff Patriot Bank, N.A. ("Patriot Bank"). Patriot Bank credited Nation's Auto's account in the amount of $7,000. Patriot Bank then submitted the check to Navy FCU for payment through the Federal Reserve System.

Navy FCU received the check on April 9, 2001. Navy FCU's policy requires all checks for $5,000 or more personally to be examined for regularity of indorsements before payment. A bank official examined the check and questioned the indorsements. Navy FCU returned the check to Patriot Bank on April 11, 2001 for the stated reason that "absence of endorsement guarantee required." Mr. William Oeters, the vice president of Patriot

Bank, testified that Patriot Bank wanted Navy FCU to guarantee the missing indorsement of its customer, Nation's Auto.

Several days later, on about April 18, 2001, Mr. Peeso received a telephone call from Nation's Auto. After that conversation, it was his understanding that the cashier's check was somehow "no good" and "not negotiable." Without retrieving the original cashier's check, Mr. Peeso returned to Navy FCU and asked the credit union to stop payment on the original cashier's check and issue a new cashier's check in the amount of $7,000 made payable to Nation's Auto. Although Navy FCU knew by that time that the first cashier's check had been deposited for collection at Patriot Bank and was in the collection system, Navy FCU agreed to stop payment. Navy FCU required Mr. Peeso to agree to indemnify Navy FCU for "all claims and demands that may be made upon the said credit union on account of refusing payment" of the original cashier's check. A second cashier's check was issued for $7,000, made payable to Nation's Auto.

Nation's Auto deposited the second cashier's check in a financial institution not involved in this litigation and was credited for the amount of the second cashier's check.

Shortly after April 11, 2001, Patriot Bank received the first cashier's check back from Navy FCU. Although Navy FCU returned the check for the stated reason that "absence of endorsement guarantee required" (emphasis added), Patriot Bank was uncertain what Navy FCU wanted guaranteed. Because Patriot Bank had no relationship with Mr. Peeso, who was not its customer, it was reluctant to guarantee his signature. Patriot Bank returned the check to Nation's Auto. When Patriot Bank attempted to reverse the credit it had given to its customer for the first check, however, it discovered that the account was overdrawn. All attempts to contact the customer failed. Nation's Auto had apparently ceased doing business.

Patriot Bank filed suit against Navy FCU in the General District Court on July 5, 2001. In the course of the litigation, Patriot Bank learned that Navy FCU wanted the absence of the indorsement of Nation's Auto guaranteed when it returned the first check to Patriot in April. Patriot Bank then stamped the cashier's check:

> CREDIT TO THE ACCOUNT OF THE WITHIN NAMED PAYEE IN ACCORDANCE WITH PAYEE'S INSTRUCTIONS ABSENCE OF ENDORSEMENT GUARANTEED

and resubmitted the first check to Navy FCU in August 2001. Navy FCU refused to honor the first cashier's check when Navy FCU received it with the "absence of endorsement guaranteed." By that time, payment had been stopped on the first check, the second check had been issued and paid, and Navy FCU knew that Nation's Auto was out of business.

Navy FCU stamped the first check as "refer to maker" and returned it to Patriot Bank.

Patriot Bank's Position

Patriot Bank argues that Navy FCU wrongfully refused to honor the first cashier's check on presentment. First, Patriot Bank maintains that Nation's Auto properly indorsed the check when it wrote its account number beneath "Payable to Nation's Auto Loan Center." Second, if the account number was not an "indorsement," Patriot Bank can supply the missing indorsement of its customer. No "absence of indorsement guaranteed" is required. Third, even if Navy FCU could require Patriot to guarantee the absence of indorsement, Navy FCU had no right to refuse to honor the first cashier's check when it was resubmitted in August 2001 with the requested "absence of indorsement guaranteed" language. In short, Patriot Bank argues that Navy FCU could not refuse to honor the cashier's check under the facts of this case.

Navy FCU's Position

Navy FCU contends that it acted properly when it returned the cashier's check to Patriot Bank in order for Patriot Bank to guarantee the missing indorsement of its customer, Nation's Auto. According to Navy FCU, it was observing prudent banking practices when it asked that Patriot Bank guarantee the absence of the indorsement of Nation's Auto. Navy FCU acknowledges that an issuer may not stop payment on a cashier's check. Navy FCU explains that it stopped payment on the first check as an accommodation to its customer, Mr. Peeso. Navy FCU maintains that, as between Mr. Peeso and Patriot Bank, Patriot Bank should suffer the loss.

Discussion of Authority

I. Was the cashier's check properly indorsed by Nation's Auto Loan Center?

Code §8.3A-204 defines "indorsement" in part as a "signature, other than that of a signer as a maker, drawer, or acceptor, that alone or accompanied by other words is made on an instrument." A "signature" is defined as "a name, . . . word, mark or symbol executed or adopted by a person with the present intent to authenticate a writing." Code 8.3A-401(b). Similarly, "signed" is defined as including "any symbol executed or adopted by a party with the present intention to authenticate a writing." Code §8.1-201(39). The official comment to Code §8.1-201(39) explains that "signed" is to be construed broadly:

> The inclusion of authentication in the definition of "signed" is to make clear that . . . a complete signature is not necessary. Authentication may be printed,

> stamped or written; it may be by initials or by thumbprint. . . . No catalog of possible authentications can be complete and the court must use common sense and commercial experience in passing upon these matters. The question always is whether the symbol was executed or adopted by the party with a present intention to authenticate the writing.

Code §8.1-201, Official Comment 39.

It is a reasonable inference from the evidence in this case that Nation's Auto wrote its account number at Patriot Bank on the cashier's check in order to authenticate the check for the purposes of deposit. As such, the Court concludes that the account number constitutes an indorsement as that term is defined in the Uniform Commercial Code.

The Court concludes that the cashier's check was properly indorsed when first presented to Navy FCU. Navy FCU should not have returned the check to Patriot Bank because of a missing indorsement.

II. WAS PATRIOT BANK REQUIRED TO GUARANTEE THE ABSENCE OF THE INDORSEMENT OF ITS CUSTOMER?

Even if Nation's Auto's account number did not amount to an indorsement, Navy FCU should not have returned the cashier's check to Patriot Bank for Patriot Bank to guarantee the missing indorsement of its customer.

Under Code §8.4-205.1, when a customer delivers an item to a depository bank for collection, the bank becomes a holder of the item if the customer was a holder, whether or not its customer indorses the item. The depository bank warrants to collecting banks, the payor bank or other payor, and to the drawer that the amount of the item was paid to the customer or deposited to the customer's account. The official comment to that section makes clear that "[w]hether it [the depository bank] supplies the customer's endorsement is immaterial." Code §8.4-205.1, Official Comment.

In light of Code §8.4-205.1, there was no need for Navy FCU to return the cashier's check to Patriot Bank in order for Patriot Bank to guarantee the missing endorsement of its customer, Nation's Auto. Simply by submitting the check to Navy FCU for payment, Patriot Bank warranted to Navy FCU that the item was paid to Nation's Auto or deposited into Nation's Auto's account. That warranty is the functional equivalent of supplying the missing endorsement of its customer. Therefore, Navy FCU should have honored the cashier's check when it was first presented to it for payment on April 9, 2001, before Mr. Peeso made any stop payment request.

III. COULD NAVY FCU STOP PAYMENT ON THE CASHIER'S CHECK?

The check at issue in this case is a "cashier's check" as that term is defined in the UCC. It is a "draft with respect to which the drawer and the drawee are the same bank or branches of the same bank." Code §8.3A-104(g). A customer may stop payment only on an item drawn on the customer's account. Code §8.4-403(a). The official comments to Code §8.4-403 make clear that a customer has no right to stop payment on a cashier's check: A cashier's check or teller's check purchased by a customer whose account is debited in payment for the check is not a check drawn on the customer's account within the meaning of subsection (a); hence, a customer purchasing a cashier's check or teller's check has no right to stop payment of such a check under subsection (a). Code §8.4-403, Official Comment 4.

If a bank chooses not to honor a cashier's check as an accommodation for its customer, the bank's liability is governed by Code §8.3A-411. That section provides, in pertinent part:

> If the obligated bank wrongfully (i) refuses to pay a cashier's check or certified check, (ii) stops payment of a teller's check, or (iii) refuses to pay a dishonored teller's check, the person asserting the right to enforce the check is entitled to compensation for expenses and loss of interest resulting from the nonpayment and may recover consequential damages if the obligated bank refuses to pay after receiving notice of particular circumstances giving rise to the damages.

Code §8.3A-411(b). The statute is intended to discourage the practice of banks refusing to honor a cashier's check as an accommodation to their customers. Code §8.3A-411, Official Comment 1. Attorney's fees may be awarded as part of the "expenses . . . resulting from nonpayment." Code §8.3A-411, Official Comment 2.

The issue thus becomes whether Navy FCU "wrongfully" refused to honor the cashier's check. "If the bank is not obligated to pay there is no recovery." Code §8.3A-411. Official Comment 3.

When a bank issues a cashier's check it is in essence assuming the liabilities of a maker of a promissory note. Under Code §8.3A-412, "[t]he issuer of a note or cashier's check or other draft drawn on the drawer is obliged to pay the instrument . . . according to its terms at the time it was issued." The bank is obligated to pay the check in the same way a maker is obligated to pay a promissory note. Code §8.3A-412, Official Comment 1. A bank may refuse to pay a cashier's check based on any defenses that the bank itself may have, such as if the bank was not paid by its customer for the check, unless the check is in the hands of a holder in due course. The bank may not, however, refuse to pay a cashier's check based on any defenses that the remitter[12] may have. Code §8.3A-411. Official Comment 2.

12. The "remitter" is the person who purchases the cashier's check. Code §8.3A-103(a)(11). In this case, the remitter is Mr. Peeso.

In this case, Navy FCU had no defenses to the payment of the cashier's check. Navy FCU received full payment for the check when it debited Mr. Peeso's account for $7,000 upon the issuance of the check. James Marshall, the treasurer of Navy FCU, testified that Navy FCU refused to honor the check when presented in August 2001 with the absence of Nation's Auto's indorsement guaranteed because, by that time, payment had been stopped on the first check, Nation's Auto was out of business, and the second cashier's check had been issued and paid. As discussed above, Navy FCU could not properly "stop payment" on the cashier's check. Navy FCU's other reasons for not honoring the check were defenses that properly belonged to Mr. Peeso, the remitter. A bank that issues a cashier's check may not refuse to honor the check based on defenses of the remitter.

The parties devote much argument to whether Patriot Bank was a holder in due course of the cashier's check when it submitted it for payment in August. Patriot Bank's status as a holder in due course would be relevant only if Navy FCU were asserting its own defenses to payment of the check. Because Navy FCU is asserting only the remitter's defenses, the holder in due course analysis is irrelevant.

Navy FCU conceded at trial that a bank cannot stop payment on a check under the circumstances of this case and that Navy FCU refused to honor the check as an accommodation to Mr. Peeso. Therefore, this case falls squarely within the provisions of Code §8.3A-411.

Conclusion

The Court concludes that Navy FCU wrongfully refused to honor the cashier's check. Navy FCU is therefore liable to Patriot Bank for the amount of the wrongfully dishonored check, as well as Patriot Bank's "expenses . . . resulting from the nonpayment." Patriot Bank introduced evidence of its attorney's fees expended in pursuing payment of the check. The Court will enter judgment in favor of Patriot Bank, N.A. against Navy Federal Credit Union, in the principal amount of $7,000, plus interest on the principal amount at the legal rate beginning April 10, 2001 until paid, plus attorney's fees of $5,700 and costs of $182.26. . . .

In 1991, the drafters of the Uniform Commercial Code proposed an addition to Article 3, §3-312, which provides an elegant solution to the problem of stopping payment on lost, destroyed, or stolen cashier's checks, teller's checks, or certified checks. In this procedure, the person who lost possession files with the issuing bank a *declaration of loss*, and for 90 days after the date of the check the issuing bank must pay it if it is presented by a person entitled to enforce it, but after the 90-day period has passed, the issuing bank should pay the amount of the check to the person filing the declaration of loss.

PROBLEM 188

Portia Moot agreed to buy a car from her uncle who lived in another state, but the uncle demanded a cashier's check in payment. On February 24, Portia obtained such a check for the correct amount from Octopus National Bank (ONB), which took a corresponding amount from her bank account, making the check payable to the order of Portia Moot. Portia signed her name to the back of the check and mailed it to her uncle. The uncle denied receiving the check (a lie), and Portia went down to ONB and filled out a declaration of loss on March 1. Having heard nothing during the next 90 days, on June 1, the bank refunded the money to Portia. In the meantime, the uncle cashed the check at his local bank on May 25th. Assume that the local bank qualifies as a holder in due course. What should ONB do when the local bank presents the check on June 2 and demands payment? See §3-312(b)(2) and Official Comment 3 (second paragraph). If ONB won't pay, what should the local bank do? See §§3-312(c); 3-415; Willis v. Wells Fargo Bank, N.A., 2012 WL 112942 (E.D. Va. 2012).

Losing a negotiable instrument of whatever kind is always unfortunate. Section 3-309 provides a mechanism whereby the true owner of the check can go to court and, in effect, judicially re-create it, having to post bond or give other adequate protection for the entity that will then pay the instrument. In states adopting §3-312, explored above, the two procedures are alternative possibilities; see §3-312(d) and Official Comment 1 to §3-312.

F. Bank Statements

The original version of §4-406, the Bank Statement Rule, presumed that banks were always returning canceled checks with the monthly bank statement, and this presumption proved awkward once banks moved to automation. As the next part of this chapter discusses, banks have instituted a range of measures to speed up check collection, including *check truncation* systems, in which the check itself is photographed shortly after deposit and then destroyed. In place of the check, an electronic image of the check is forwarded through the system to the payor bank, which then can make that image available to the customer for examination.

II. BANK COLLECTION

The transfer of an item (*check*) from the depositary bank to the payor bank and the remittance of the proceeds inevitably lead to legal difficulties. To facilitate the handling of the huge number of checks passed around each year, there exists a sophisticated network of banks, federal agencies, and local clearinghouses that generally make up the bank collection system. In addition to Article 4's statutory regulation, the system is governed by a federal statute on point, plus Federal Reserve regulations and clearinghouse contractual agreements, all of which are permitted to vary the rules of Article 4. See §4-103(b).

For decades, the law on this subject was contained in two enactments: Article 4 of the Uniform Commercial Code and the Federal Reserve Board Regulation J on Collection of Checks and Other Items and Wire Transfer of Funds by Federal Reserve Banks, 12 C.F.R. part 210 (which applies only if the check clears through the Federal Reserve System). But, effective September 1, 1988, a federal statute—the Expedited Funds Availability Act, 12 U.S.C. §§4001-4010, 248a [hereinafter EFAA]—superseded many of the UCC rules and resulted in an amendment to Regulation J as well. The federal statute is also supplemented by a Federal Reserve Board regulation having the force of law, Regulation CC, 12 C.F.R. 229, which will also be explained in the materials that follow (indeed, any reference to a section beginning with the numerals "229" is a reference to Regulation CC). Regulation CC is elaborated on in an official Federal Reserve Board Commentary, which is contained in Appendix E to the Regulation itself; the Commentary also has the force of law. Regulation CC should be in your statute book, likely identified as "Availability of Funds and Collection of Checks."

Thus, a lawyer wanting to understand the rules of check collection must compare the rules of the EFAA (which is almost impenetrable—it reads as if it were badly translated from German), Regulation CC (which, being drafted by the Federal Reserve, is much more readable, if soporific), and the Official Commentary in Appendix E to the regulation (which is very user-friendly, with helpful examples included).

The EFAA and Regulation CC do not completely do away with the Uniform Commercial Code rules on check collection, which still apply in any situation not covered by federal rules, and, of course, those rules were written with the UCC as a back-drop. So we begin our coverage of check collection with the Uniform Commercial Code and then look at the variations worked thereon by the EFAA and Regulation CC.

A. *Funds Availability*

It is important to appreciate that the rules that follow, both state and federal, set outside time limits on the period that banks can hold deposited funds, but they do not prohibit the depositary bank from allowing the customer *earlier* access to those funds, should the bank so decide. Earlier access is a business decision. The discussion below looks at the question of when as a *matter of legal right* the customer is entitled to the funds.

We begin with the issue of how quickly the depositor can get money back from the bank in which items are deposited. It is easiest to understand the whole process if approached from a personal point of view. So, presuming that you have had some experience with a checking account, let's use the Code to answer the basic questions.

1. Cash

If you deposit cash in your account, how quickly can you take it out again? Answer: on the next banking day. See §4-215(f).[13] The "subject to any right of the bank" language in §4-215(f) refers to the bank's right of setoff.

Banking day is defined in §4-104(a)(3) as that part of the day when the bank is "open to the public for carrying on substantially all of its banking functions."[14] As to this, see §4-108, which further refines *banking day* so as to permit a bank to establish a cutoff hour in the early afternoon and to pretend that items received after that hour were received on the next banking day. Thus, if that bank's banking day ends at 2:30 P.M., a check received at 2:31 P.M. on Friday is treated as if it were received early Monday morning (assuming neither is a holiday and the bank is not open on Saturday and Sunday). The purpose of such a rule is stated in §4-108(a).[15]

13. Section 603(a)(1), 12 U.S.C. §4002(a)(1), of the EFAA has the same requirement. The Federal Reserve Board has stated that UCC §4-215(f) is *not* preempted by the adoption of Regulation CC. 53 Fed. Reg. 32,354 (Aug. 24, 1988).

14. If a bank has a teller window open on Saturday, is this a banking day? Probably not, since the bank is not open for carrying on "substantially all of its banking functions," the statutory test. See Merrill Lynch, Pierce, Fenner & Smith, Inc. v. Devon Bank, 832 F.2d 1005 (7th Cir. 1987) (where main lobby closed, Saturday not a banking day).

15. The same rule for a cutoff hour is found in Regulation CC, except that for automated teller machines (ATMs) a bank may establish 12:00 noon as the cutoff hour for the

2. Checks

a. **Across the Counter Presentments.** If someone gives you a check and you (the payee) walk into the drawee bank and present it across the counter, how quickly must the bank pay or dishonor it? Answer: before the close of business. When an over-the-counter presentment for payment is made, §3-502(b)(2) requires the bank to make a decision that same day.

b. **"On Us" Items.** If someone gives you a check and you deposit it in your own account, how quickly may you take it out? Answer: as soon as your bank will let you, though, as discussed below, for certain kinds of checks federal law regulates this issue. If the amount is not great and you are a good customer, your bank may permit you to write checks on the deposited amount immediately, particularly if the drawer is well known and solvent (e.g., a large corporation). The real question is this: When do you have a legal *right* to draw checks on the deposited amount?

If, by coincidence, you (the payee) and the drawer each maintain an account at the same bank (that is, the depositary and payor banks are one and the same—the bankers call this an "On Us" item), §4-215(e)(2) permits you to remove the money at the opening of the *second banking day* following receipt of the item, unless, of course, in the meantime the check is dishonored, in which case you will be so notified (§§4-202(a)(2) and 3-503(c)). In this period of time, the bank, acting as the drawee-payor, will sort the check into a stack of "On Us" items and then examine the drawer's account and decide whether to pay the check.

The EFAA here makes its first major change. It speeds things up one day by requiring the depositary bank to make same-bank checks available for withdrawal on *the business day after the business day of deposit* (this is commonly referred to as "next day availability"). EFAA §603(a)(2)(E), 12 U.S.C. §4002(a)(2)(E); Regulation CC §229.10(c)(1)(vi). For "On Us" items, the bank must now make its decision to pay or dishonor overnight.

c. **"Transit" Items.** If the depositary bank and the payor (drawee) bank are *not* the same, then the check is a "transit" item and must go through some sort of multi-bank collection machinery. This can be as simple as exchanging checks with the bank across the street or as complicated

---

receipt of deposits (§229.19(a)). However, Regulation CC draws a distinction not in the UCC between "business day," meaning days other than Saturdays, Sundays, and federal holidays, and "banking day," meaning business days on which a bank is open for carrying on substantially all of its banking functions. Saturday could never be a "banking day" for Regulation CC purposes under these definitions, though it might be a "banking day" under the UCC if the bank were open for business on Saturdays. 12 C.F.R. §229.2(f) and (g).

as sending the check to the payor bank in Japan, so of course the rules are more complicated. As soon as your bank (the depositary bank) begins this process, it is called a *collecting bank*. During the process it acts as your agent (§4-201(a)).

If the depositary bank and the payor bank are in the same small town, they will typically arrange to exchange checks drawn on each other once each day. Must the banks decide which checks to pay and which to dishonor before the close of the business day, as in §3-502 above? No, because Article 4 has a special rule for interbank collection presentments, and Article 4 overrides Article 3 where they conflict; §4-102(a).

The two banks will probably maintain accounts with each other and, by contract, will agree to permit the depositary bank to debit the account of the payor bank for the amount of the deposited check, subject to the right of the payor bank to dishonor the check later and have the account recredited. Such a contract results in a *provisional settlement* (*provisional* because the so-called settlement is subject to revocation). Thus, at the time the banks exchange the checks each day, they will have already debited each other's accounts with the amounts of the presented checks. If, after receiving the checks drawn on it, the payor bank decides to dishonor one or more, it simply returns the check, and the provisional settlement for that check is wiped out (technically, *charged back*).

Suppose that Mary Depositor deposits a check on which she is the payee in her bank, which we shall call Depositary Bank. Depositary Bank will mark her account with a *provisional settlement* for the amount of the item—in effect a bookkeeping entry reflecting the hope that the check will be paid by the payor/drawee bank. During the time that the check is traveling (called the "float period" by bankers), Depositary Bank may or may not allow Mary access to the money (more about that below), but even if it lets her withdraw it, if the check is later properly returned, she will have to repay any amounts provisionally withdrawn; §4-214 (Charge Back, also discussed in detail in this chapter).

The check collection system works through computers, so the check must be magnetically *encoded* so that all the computers it will pass through can read it. The little fractional number in the upper right-hand corner of the check is the routing symbol of the drawee bank. This routing symbol, along with the drawer's account number, is already encoded across the bottom of the check on the left-hand side. The amount of the check will be encoded on the bottom right-hand side.[16]

16. The Code provides for a warranty of proper encoding; §4-209. The courts have had no problem finding liability for mis-encoding checks; see Troy Bank and Trust Co. v. Citizens Bank, 2014 WL 4851511 (Ala. 2014). Regulation CC has a similar encoding warranty in §229.34(c)(3).

If Depositary Bank and the payor bank are located in the same large city, they will probably make the provisional settlements and check exchanges through a central *clearinghouse*, which can be loosely defined as an association of local banks that has drawn up regulations and procedures to effectuate the exchange of checks. Clearinghouse rules are allowed to change the rules of the Uniform Commercial Code, including all the deadlines discussed in this chapter. That means a lawyer for a bank which is a member of a clearinghouse would be well advised to read the clearinghouse rules, with thoughts of malpractice providing the incentive to wade through them carefully.

If Depositary Bank and the payor bank are not located close to one another, Depositary Bank will send the check to the first intermediary bank, typically a Federal Reserve Bank, established by the federal government. The United States is divided into 12 Federal Reserve districts, and in the center of each district sits a Federal Reserve Bank. These Superbanks have only banks as customers (a bank for banks) and permit member banks to open accounts therein and use the efficient cross-country check collection machinery operated by the Federal Reserve Banks. In return, member banks must observe Federal Reserve Board regulations. The Federal Reserve Banks each maintain accounts with one another, which they will debit or credit as they receive checks or payment (*remittances*) from member banks.

As the check passes from one bank to another, the presenting bank will give itself a provisional settlement for the amount of the check in the account it carries with the bank to which it forwards the check (the Federal Reserve Banks do this too). Each bank has two banking days in which to pass the item on to the next bank; §4-202(b). If the payor bank pays the check, all the provisional settlements (those bookkeeping entries) along the check collection route are said to "firm up," and *now final settlement* occurs. When this happens, Mary has a legal right to the money at her end.

The Uniform Commercial Code reaches this result in a section that is difficult to read—§4-215(e). In that subsection, the beginning two small-case roman numerals refer, respectively, to (i) the superior command of federal law (i.e., the EFAA and Regulation CC), and (ii) the bank's own right of setoff. Subsection (2) discusses the rule for "On Us" items (see above), leaving subsection (1) as the relevant part covering the transit item rules described in the last few paragraphs. Read §4-215(e) carefully, remembering that provisional settlements become final settlements when the payor bank pays the check at issue.

d. **The Federal Availability Rules.** Customers objected to holds for long float periods, pointing out that of the billions of checks written every year, 99 percent are honored on first presentment, and that most of the rest are honored on second presentment (or are made good by the depositor). Customers also highlighted the facts that the banks have the use of the funds during the float period (because the bank has been given a provisional credit during collection), and that the banks were estimated to earn approximately $290 million each year from this practice.

A number of states responded to this problem by passing statutes regulating the hold on deposited funds or, at least, requiring clear disclosure of the bank's policies on the issue. New York, Illinois, California, and Massachusetts, for example, required immediate credit for small checks and for those issued by the government or banks, and specified the float periods for checks that travel various distances from the depositary bank. In 1987, the federal government got into the act, passing the EFAA and Regulation CC and preempting the state laws (except to the extent they are better for depositors than the federal rules, see Appendix F to Regulation CC).

The federal rules in most cases completely displace §4-215(e)(1), which you have just read, and have concrete answers to how long the hold for the float period can be. You should know that it can take depositary banks days to learn that a check is bad, and that banks annually lose about $1 billion on unpaid checks. Thus the depositary bank has a strong incentive not to release the deposited amount unless it is sure the check will not come bounding back.

(i) ***Next Day Availability of Special Items.*** The EFAA availability rules are designed to strike a balance between the customer's need for the funds and the risks of non-collection faced by the banks in which these funds are deposited. Congress decided that there should be *next banking day* availability[17] for items that are not likely to be dishonored, and the EFAA (§602, 12 U.S.C. §4001) and Regulation CC (see §229.10) have a list of such items:

(1) Government checks: checks issued by any branch of government, federal, state, or local;
(2) Bank checks: checks on which a bank is primarily liable (cashier, teller, and certified checks); and
(3) Wire transfers: electronically sent payment orders of the sort covered by Article 4A of the Uniform Commercial Code, and covered by Chapter 15 of this book.

There is one more addition to this list: the *$200 Availability Rule*, EFAA §603(a)(2)(D), 12 U.S.C. §4002(a)(2)(d).[18] The rule is based on the idea

17. If these items are deposited in an automated teller machine (ATM), the bank is given an extra day, and the items must be available for withdrawal on the second day after deposit; see Regulation CC §229.10(a)(2) and(c)(2).

18. The amount was raised from $100 to $200 by §1086(e) of the Dodd-Frank Wall Street Reform and Consumer Protection Act (Dodd-Frank Act) of 2010. Regulation CC is subject to the statute.

that even for riskier checks we ought to allow the customer access to a small amount immediately. Thus federal law requires the bank to make the following computation: take the aggregate of the day's deposits, from that amount subtract items already requiring next day availability, and give the customer $200 of the amount remaining.

(ii) ***Availability of Ordinary Checks.*** The following rules, from Regulation CC §229.12, may have more interest for you if you remember that they govern how fast you are allowed to make withdrawals based on checks that you deposit in your own account that are drawn on other banks. You should understand, however, that even if these rules require your bank to give you access to the deposited funds, if a check is properly returned after you have taken out the money, you will still be required to repay your own bank for the amount withdrawn (under the *charge-back* rules yet to be discussed). The rules vary depending on whether the depositor wants to take out *cash* or simply write *checks* against the deposited amounts, since checks by their very nature have a built-in float period for collection, but cash is cash and gone immediately.

First of all, the $200 availability rule allows you next day access to the first $200 deposited in any one day, whether you want it in cash or by check.

Second, the entire amount above $200 (up to $5,000 in deposits per day) must be available for check-writing purposes on the second banking day following the date of deposit. However, if the customer wants to take out cash, he/she can only get up to $400 of the amount of the check by 5 P.M. on the second banking day (with the rest of the amount available for cash withdrawal on start of business the day following).

Funds Availability Rules: Ordinary Checks Deposited on Day 0

Noncash use	Day 1	$200
	Day 2	Remainder (up to $5,000 deposits per day)
Cash	Day 1	$200
	Day 2	$400
	Day 3	Remainder (up to $5,000)

Congress, ever alert, recognized that the early availability schedules described above could be misused by some bank customers, so it gave the banks a few escape valves in EFAA §604, 12 U.S.C. §4003:

(1) New Accounts. During the first 30 days of the existence of a new account, there must be next day availability for cash or wire deposits, for government checks, and for bank-generated checks (cashier's checks, etc.). If the government check or the bank-generated check exceeds $5,000, the depositary bank may put a hold on the amount that exceeds the $5,000 for up to nine business days. There are no rules that describe the time period for the availability of ordinary checks, so the usual UCC rules would apply—see UCC §4-215(e)(1). See EFAA §604(a), 12 U.S.C. §4003(a), and Regulation CC §229.13(a). There is no requirement of $200 next day availability for new accounts; Regulation CC §229.13(a)(iii).

(2) Large Deposits. According to Regulation CC §229.13(b) and (h), only the first $5,000 of a day's deposit is subject to the normal availability rules. The excess may be held for an *additional reasonable period of time* (and five business days is presumed to be reasonable for ordinary checks; for longer periods the bank must carry the burden of establishing the period is reasonable). Deposits by cash or electronic payment are not subject to this exception for large deposits.

(3) Redeposited Checks. The normal availability rules are extended by an extra reasonable period of time (with the same five/six business days presumption) in the case of redeposited checks, unless the announced reason for the return was a missing indorsement or because the check was postdated, and these problems have been cleared up at the time of redeposit; Regulation CC §229.13(c) and (h).

(4) Repeated Overdrafts. The normal availability rules are extended by an extra reasonable period of time (with the same five/six business days presumption) for six months after the account or any combination of a customer's accounts has been repeatedly overdrawn. As to whether an account is considered to be repeatedly overdrawn, there is a two-prong test and if either prong is met, the bank may hold deposited checks for the extra period of time. Under these tests, the account is considered repeatedly overdrawn if the account balance is negative (or would have been negative if all checks or other charges to the account had been paid) on six or more banking days within the preceding six months, *or* if on two or more banking days within the preceding six months the account balance is negative (or would have been negative if all checks or other charges to the account had been paid) in the amount of $5,000 or more. See Regulation CC §229.13(d) and (h).

(5) The "Reasonable Cause" Exception. Under EFAA §604(c), 12 U.S.C. §4003(c), if the bank has "reasonable cause" to believe that a check is

uncollectible, then it may ignore the usual rules if it gives the notice to the customer, described below, telling him/her when the funds will be made available. A bank has "reasonable cause," according to the statutory language, whenever there exist "facts which would cause a well-grounded belief in the mind of a reasonable person." Such reasons must be included in the notice. The Board has elected not to expand upon the statutory language, though the Commentary does give examples of proper use of the exception. These include the fact that the bank has received a notice that the check is being returned, the fact that the check is stale (more than six months old when deposited), or that check kiting is suspected. If the bank is going to invoke this "reasonable cause" exception for cashier's, teller's, or certified checks or those drawn on a Federal Reserve Bank or those deposited at an ATM, it must use the usual times periods plus a later reasonable time (presumed to be five/six days, as above). See Regulation CC §229.13(e) and (h).

(6) Emergency Conditions. Regulation CC §229.13(f) has a rule modeled on UCC §4-109 (described at the end of this chapter in the section called "Delays") that excuses compliance with the normal availability rules due to emergencies beyond the bank's control.

(7) The Notice. Except in the "new accounts" situation, where a bank plans to take advantage of either the "large check," "redeposited check," "repeated overdrafts," or "reasonable cause" exceptions, the depositor must be notified as soon as possible of the date the funds will be made available. Appendix C to the Regulation contains model forms, including a model form of Notice of Exception to the usual availability rules. Since reliance on this form insulates the bank from any civil liability, its use is the better part of wisdom. The Federal Reserve is very insistent that banks follow whatever availability policy they disclose and not deviate from it unless the right to do so has also been disclosed.

(8) Civil Liability. Under §611 of the Act, 12 U.S.C. §4010, the bank that does not follow the statute or the regulations promulgated thereunder by the Federal Reserve Board can be sued by the injured customer for his/her actual damages, punitive damages (not greater than $1,000, nor less than $100, though in a class action the upper figure is the lesser of $500,000 or 1 percent of the net worth of the bank), plus costs of suit and attorney's fee. The suit may be brought in federal or state court within one year after the occurrence of the violation.

Variation by agreement from the rules of Regulation CC is permitted only for the check return rules of Subpart C, and such agreements only bind the specific parties to the agreement. No variation is permitted from the funds availability and disclosure requirements.

B. *Check Truncation*

1. Introduction

Consider that for the last century and the beginning of this one, banks had to daily exchange mountains of paper checks, a very inefficient system. In the last few decades, banks had experimented with a process called "check truncation" (or sometimes "check retention") in which the depositary bank simply keeps the deposited check and forwards only a description of it through the bank collection process. Specific provision is made for electronic presentment and warranties connected with same; see §§4-110 and 4-209(b).[19] In such a system, the customer never gets the check back, although it is reflected on the bank statement. In the 1990s, the bank statement rule, §4-406, was amended to require banks to send certain information back to the customer and to give the customer the right to demand a legible copy of the check for seven years after the statement was sent out.

The idea of creating an "image" of the check and sending it through bank channels instead of the original paper check had been urged for over a decade, but it was expensive to get such a system up and running, and there was a lot of resistance to the suggestion. Some banks did agree to do electronic presentment with each other. But many banks were reluctant to invest in the necessary technology—especially where it might be outdated if other banks adopted different standards. However, the September 11, 2001, attacks gave new life to this idea. Planes were grounded for five or more days that September, and many checks could not move at all from bank to bank, resulting in chaos. Check imaging was an attractive solution.

Congress passed the "Check Clearing for the 21st Century Act" or the "Check 21 Act," effective October 28, 2004. The Federal Reserve created amendments to Regulations CC and J to implement the Act, and the bulk of these regulations are found in Subpart D to Regulation CC. Check 21 permits banks to do electronic processing, without requiring banks to accept electronic presentment. Rather, a bank may make an electronic image of a check, transmit the image across the country, and either present the image or print out a substitute check, and present it for payment. Check 21 has been very successful in encouraging the use of substitute checks (and also electronic presentment, by agreement between banks). So few checks now travel around the country physically that the Federal Reserve has closed most of its check-processing centers and now sends the remaining checks through a single center in Cleveland.

19. Federal Reserve Regulation CC has a similar encoding warranty provision in §229.34(c)(3).

2. Creating the Image and the Substitute Check

a. Remote Deposit Capture. Banks engage in a practice called "remote deposit capture" (RDC), which allows their customers to use an app to photograph a check's front and back, and deposit the check image instantly through the app. The customer is often also instructed to write "void" across the original. Customers love the convenience and speed of this, and any bank that wishes to compete must now offer this service to their customers. The legal ramifications are enormous.

PROBLEM 189

MegaBank decided to speed up check processing by having its customer sign a remote deposit capture agreement by which the customer would use a cell phone and an app thereon to photograph both sides of any check the customer wished to deposit. The customer was instructed to then send the images to the bank, write "VOID" on the front of the check, and/or destroy the check. A customer named Walter White was one of the bank's customers, and when he received a $50,000 check on which he was the payee he created the required images and sent them via the app to MegaBank. Instead of following the rest of the instructions, White then indorsed the paper check and deposited it in an account he had at Heisenberg State Bank, which allowed him to withdraw $50,000 immediately. In the meantime White also withdrew the same amount from his account at MegaBank. Both the image and the paper versions of the check were presented to the payor bank on which they were drawn, and the image version of the check arrived there first, so the payor bank paid it. When the paper check arrived shortly thereafter the payor bank dishonored it, giving as its reason that this check had already been presented and paid. You are the attorney for Heisenberg State Bank, which has received the return of the paper check. Walter White has left town and can't be found. Your client wants to know who else it can sue and under what theory. Can you successfully sue the drawer of the check on the drawer's obligation in §3-414 because the paper check bounced?

The electronic presentment of checks that have been photographed as part of a remote deposit capture program created the nightmare described in the above Problem. The law originally had no obvious answer and the courts reached all sorts of bizarre results. See, e.g., 1409 West Diversey Corp. v. JPMorgan Chase Bank, N.A., 2016 WL 4124293 (N.D. Ill. 2016) (holding it was not negligent for a depositary bank to create the image without voiding the original paper check). Happily the Federal Reserve amended Regulation CC in 2018 to resolve many of the issues involved. The Regulation now expressly covers electronically created checks and requires the depositary bank that permits its customers to create such an electronic images to make sure that the images "accurately represent" the information on the front and back of the check; 12 C.F.R. §229.34 (a)(i), and that the original check won't cause problems to others. That same section creates a new warranty to be made by the depositary bank accepting an electronically created check as follows:

> (a) Warranties with respect to electronic checks and electronic returned checks.
>
> (1) Each bank that transfers or presents an electronic check or electronic returned check and receives a settlement or other consideration for it warrants that—
>
> (i) The electronic image accurately represents all of the information on the front and back of the original check as of the time that the original check was truncated and the electronic information includes an accurate record of all MICR line information required for a substitute check under §229.2(aaa) and the amount of the check, and
>
> (ii) No person will receive a transfer, presentment, or return of, or otherwise be charged for an electronic check or electronic returned check, the original check, a substitute check, or a paper or electronic representation of a substitute check such that the person will be asked to make payment based on a check it has already paid.
>
> (2) Each bank that makes the warranties under paragraph (a)(1) of this section makes the warranties to—
>
> (i) In the case of transfers for collection or presentment, the transferee bank, any subsequent collecting bank, the paying bank, and the drawer; and
>
> (ii) In the case of transfers for return, the transferee returning bank, any subsequent returning bank, the depositary bank, and the owner.
>
> (b) Transfer and presentment warranties with respect to a remotely created check.
>
> (1) A bank that transfers or presents a remotely created check and receives a settlement or other consideration warrants to the transferee bank, any subsequent collecting bank, and the paying bank that the person on whose account the remotely created check is drawn authorized the issuance of the check in the amount stated on the check and to the payee stated on the check. For purposes of this paragraph (b)(1), "account" includes an account as defined in §229.2(a) as well as a credit or other arrangement that allows a person to draw checks that are payable by, through, or at a bank.
>
> (2) If a paying bank asserts a claim for breach of warranty under paragraph (b)(1) of this section, the warranting bank may defend by proving

that the customer of the paying bank is precluded under UCC 4-406,[20] as applicable, from asserting against the paying bank the unauthorized issuance of the check.

What this all means is that the depositary bank is going to have to take steps to make sure that the paper check is not still at large once the electronically created check has taken its place. Suppose the bank is your client, future lawyer. It calls you for advice. How can it protect itself when its customers photograph the paper check and then sends the bank the electronic image?

b. Check Truncation by Banks. Under the statute, depositary banks or other banks in the collection chain have the option (not duty) to create an image of the original check and pass it on if the receiving bank agrees to accept it in that form; Regulation CC §229.2(ddd). A bank creating such an image is called a "*truncating* bank" in Regulation CC §229.2(ddd).

After truncation, the imaged check is passed along as a computer file until someone (a later bank, the bank's customer, or whoever) refuses to take the imaged version and insists on getting paper. In that case, the bank (now named a "*reconverting* bank")[21] will print out a paper version of the check. The paper version is called a "substitute check." To understand the definition of a "substitute check" in the Regulation, you should know what a "MICR line" (usually, but not always, pronounced "mick-er") is. The initials stand for "magnetic character ink recognition" and refer to the line at the bottom of all checks with the strange printing, identifying the routing information so the check can be sent to the payor bank and charged against the correct account. The depositary bank will also encode the amount of the check to the MICR line, below the drawer's signature (and our laws have long had warranties that this encoding is correct).[22] Now read the definition of "substitute check" in Regulation CC §229.2(zz).[23] If the paper reproduction of the image does not meet these standards, it will not technically qualify as a "substitute check," with important consequences as we shall see.

The reconverting bank must also add to the substituted checks all the indorsements that would have been placed on the original check had it

20. Section 4-406 of the Uniform Commercial Code requires bank customers to examine their bank statements and promptly report problems with same or be barred from complaining about forgeries or alterations on the checks. We will consider §4-406 in various other parts of this book.

21. See Regulation CC §229.2(yy).

22. UCC §4-209(a); Regulation CC §229.34(c)(3).

23. In the statute, see §5002(16).

traveled the same route as the image. Regulation CC §229.51(b) creates a duty in the reconverting check to ensure that the substitute check:

> (1) Bears all indorsements applied by parties that previously handled the check in any form (including the original check, a substitute check, or another paper or electronic representation of such original check or substitute check) for forward collection or return;
> (2) Identifies the reconverting bank in a manner that preserves any previous reconverting bank identifications, in accordance with generally applicable industry standards for substitute checks and appendix D of this part; and
> (3) Identifies the bank that truncated the original check in accordance with generally applicable industry standards for substitute checks and appendix D of this part.

3. Legal Equivalence

No one can refuse to take the substitute check, which is legally the same (for all purposes, including criminal prosecution), as the original. Customers cannot insist on getting the original back. If the parties agree to imaging without a paper copy being created, the image also has the same legal effect as the original. These rules will greatly speed up check collection, though there are some downsides to loss of the original (no fingerprints, for example, which can be important in criminal prosecutions). Section 5003(b) of the statute provides:

> A substitute check shall be the legal equivalent of the original check for all purposes, including any provision of any Federal or State law, and for all persons if the substitute check—
> (1) accurately represents all of the information on the front and back of the original check as of the time the original check was truncated; and
> (2) bears the legend: "This is a legal copy of your check. You can use it the same way you would use the original check."[24]

PROBLEM 190

Sharon Bardus paid her monthly rent in full with a check, and was considerably annoyed when the landlord sent her a letter informing her that the rent was still due and she would be assessed a late fee. When she protested, the landlord demanded to see the check she had allegedly sent in. Sharon had received that check only as an image returned as part of her monthly bank statement, but she contacted her bank, and the bank printed out a copy

24. See the similar language in Reg. CC §229.51.

of the check and sent it to her. She mailed this copy to the landlord, but received back a letter informing her that it was the landlord's policy to only accept the original cancelled check as proof of payment, so a mere copy would not be enough. Now what should Sharon do?

4. Warranty Liability

Parties passing on the substitute check make both transfer and presentment warranties that everything is on the up and up. Section 5004 of the statute states the warranties made by reconverting banks that create the substitute check and transfer it to others:

> A bank that transfers, presents, or returns a substitute check and receives consideration for the check warrants, as a matter of law, to the transferee, any subsequent collecting or returning bank, the depositary bank, the drawee, the drawer, the payee, the depositor, and any endorser (regardless of whether the warrantee receives the substitute check or another paper or electronic form of the substitute check or original check) that—
>
> (1) the substitute check meets all the requirements for legal equivalence under section 4(b); and
>
> (2) no depositary bank, drawee, drawer, or endorser will receive presentment or return of the substitute check, the original check, or a copy or other paper or electronic version of the substitute check or original check such that the bank, drawee, drawer, or endorser will be asked to make a payment based on a check that the bank, drawee, drawer, or endorser has already paid.

PROBLEM 191

When the check was truncated by the depositary bank and turned into an electronic image, the image was blurry. When the reconverting bank printed out the substitute check the account number was incorrectly listed as starting with an "8" when the original started with a "3." As a consequence the wrong account was debited for the amount of this check, causing other checks to bounce. The customer complained and the payor bank recredited the account, and calls you, the bank's attorney. Now what? See Regulation CC §229.52.

The answer is that the account holder could sue for breach of the above warranty of legal equivalence. Liability would flow back to the reconverting bank. That bank could not use the above warranty to pass the loss back to the truncating bank because that bank did not transfer a "substitute check" (a piece of paper). However, the Federal Reserve has created similar warranties for the transfer of electronic images in Regulation J §210.5(a)(3) and (4), and these warranties would operate in the same fashion. Moreover the wise attorney will make sure there is a contractual agreement in place between banks transferring and accepting images that they correctly reflect the terms of the original check, and this contractual agreement would also create liability in the truncating bank.

5. Indemnity Liability

In addition to this warranty liability, §5005 of the statute creates *indemnity* liability against banks transferring either the image or the substitute check if doing so causes *damages that could have been prevented by use of the original check*; in the Regulation see §229.53. In the above Problem, the truncating bank would have to respond to an indemnity claim because of its blurry image of the original check; if the original had been transferred, the right amount would have been debited from the correct account. It is unclear what this indemnity liability will mean in many situations, though the Official Commentary to Regulation CC gives this example:

> A drawer received a substitute check that met all the legal equivalence requirements and that was only charged once to the drawer's account, but the drawer believed that the underlying original check was a forgery. If the drawer suffered a loss because it could not prove the forgery based on the substitute check, for example because proving the forgery required analysis of pen pressure that could be determined only from the original check, the drawer would have an indemnity claim. However, the drawer would not have a substitute check warranty claim because the substitute check was the legal equivalent of the original and no person was asked to pay the substitute check more than once. In that case, the amount of the drawer's indemnity would be limited to the amount of the substitute check, plus interest and expenses, although the drawer could attempt to recover additional losses, if any, under other law.[25]

As a practical matter this means that the original check must be preserved so that it can be found in the event of trouble and produced to help resolve the difficulty. All claims must be made within 120 days after the transaction that gives rise to the claim—see Regulation CC §299.55(b)(1)—so that is the relevant period for preserving the original check. Lawsuits under Check 21 must be brought within one year after the transaction,[26] and the prudent bank may wish to hold the original checks until that statute of limitations has passed. Bankers will tell you that these periods are unrealistic

25. This is the Official Commentary to Regulation CC §229.53(b).
26. Regulation CC §229.56(c).

and that they routinely destroy most checks after 45 days or fewer. Hmm. The lawyer advises one thing to comply with the law and the bankers do another for economic reasons and also because all the other banks are doing the same ("usage of trade"). Shocking.

First Financial Bank, N.A v. Citibank, N.A.

United States District Court, Southern District of Indiana, 2012
2012 WL 3065546

William T. Lawrence, District Judge.

This cause is before the Court on the motion filed by Plaintiff First Financial Bank, N.A. ("First Financial") seeking summary judgment with regard to its claims against Defendant Citibank, N.A. ("Citibank") (dkt. no. 82). The motion is fully briefed and the Court, being duly advised, GRANTS IN PART AND DENIES IN PART the motion as set forth below. . . .

II. Background Facts

The facts relevant to the instant motion, viewed in the light most favorable to Defendant Citibank, the non-moving party, are as follow.

Defendant Misty McDonald, an attorney in Terre Haute, Indiana, deposited a check at her local First Financial bank on July 7, 2010. The check purported to be Citibank Official Check[27] No. 260356932, dated July 2, 2010, in the amount of $298,750.00; the remitter was listed as Accurate Manufactured Products Group, Inc. ("AMPG"), and the check was made payable to "Misty Y. McDonald, Attorney at Law" (the "Check"). McDonald believed the Check to be partial payment of money owed by AMPG to a company that had recently engaged her services to try to collect from AMPG.

First Financial has banking relationships with other institutions that are established by contracts. These relationships are referred to in the banking industry as correspondent banking relationships. First Financial has a correspondent banking relationship with J.P. Morgan Chase, N.A. ("Chase"), for the forward processing of checks. As relevant to this case, "forward processing" means the movement of a check that is deposited at a First Financial bank to the "paying bank" of that check. First Financial does not have a correspondent banking arrangement with Chase for the downstream processing of checks—that is, the movement of checks from paying banks back to First Financial for, among other things, providing notice of nonpayment.

27. [Bankers call cashier's checks "official checks."—Eds.]

Instead, the Federal Reserve Bank is First Financial's correspondent bank for downstream processing.

As is customary in the banking industry, First Financial created an electronic image of the Check for use in the forward and downstream processing of the Check. Pursuant to its agreement with Chase, First Financial sent the Check to Chase for forward processing. This was accomplished by including the imaged Check in a cash letter[28] to Chase dated July 7, 2010.

The following day, July 8, 2010, Chase sent an electronic image of the Check to Citibank. Citibank determined that the account number on the Check did not exist and marked it "invalid account number, account unknown." Citibank also determined that the endorsement of the depository bank (First Financial) was illegible. However, the Check contained a "Sending R/T" number on it that indicated that it had come to Citibank from Chase. Citibank therefore returned the Check for nonpayment to Chase. In order to accomplish this, Citibank sent a notice to Chase through the Electronic Advanced Return Notification System ("EARNS") at 8:34 P.M. on July 8, 2010, that indicated that the Check was being returned for an invalid account number. Citibank then sent the Check and its accompanying cash letter to the Federal Reserve Bank.

At 7:10 A.M. on July 9, 2010, Chase opened the EARNS notice that advised it that Citibank was returning the Check because it bore an invalid account number. Chase notified First Financial that the Check had been returned by sending two letters by regular U.S. mail, one dated July 9th and the other dated July 13th. First Financial did not receive either letter until at least July 14th. Chase also sent First Financial a fax bearing the image of the Check with the notice of nonpayment from Citibank on July 14th. First Financial received an EARNS notice of nonpayment on July 15th.

In the meantime, on July 9, 2010, at 12:56 P.M., First Financial completed a wire transfer for McDonald of 90% of the amount of the Check—$268,825.00—to the Bank of China in Beijing, China. When it learned that the check had been returned by Citibank, First Financial attempted to recall McDonald's wire transfer, but was notified by the Bank of China on July 19th that it had paid the beneficiary of McDonald's wire transfer on July 12th and the request to return the wire transfer would not be honored. First Financial set off funds on deposit in McDonald's accounts at First Financial in the total amount of $26,172.21, but has been unable to recover the remaining $272,577.79.

28. A cash letter is a compilation of numerous checks that is created by a bank for the purpose of packaging items for distribution to their correspondent banks in the forward or downstream processing of checks.

III. Discussion

First Financial argues that "[t]he undisputed material facts of this case demonstrate that Citibank failed to provide timely and proper notice of non-payment and return of a check, thereby breaching warranty obligations to First Financial and causing damages in the amount of the check's face value, plus interest and expenses, less those amounts mitigated by First Financial's actions." First Financial Brief at 1. First Financial therefore seeks summary judgment on all of its claims against Citibank. . . .

B. Citibank's Duties Regarding Returning the Check

Citibank's obligations with regard to the Check once it decided to dishonor it were governed by what is referred to as "Regulation CC"—a set of implementing regulations promulgated pursuant to the Expedited Funds Availability Act, 12 U.S.C. §4010 et seq. Subpart C of Regulation CC, which is found at 12 C.F.R. §229.30 et seq., sets forth a paying bank's responsibility for the return of a check; First Financial argues that Citibank violated several of Regulation CC's requirements. The Court will address each of First Financial's arguments in turn.

1. Failure to Return the Check Expeditiously

A paying bank that has decided not to pay a check must return the check "expeditiously." 12 C.F.R. §229.30(a). In order to do so, it "may send [the] returned check to the depositary bank, or to any other bank agreeing to handle the returned check expeditiously under §229.31(a)." 12 C.F.R. §229.30(a). Citibank failed to comply with this requirement when it returned the Check to Chase because Chase had no agreement with First Financial to handle returned checks expeditiously on First Financial's behalf. Citibank argues that it nonetheless complied with Regulation CC because it was unable to identify the depositary bank with respect to the Check and therefore was permitted to return the Check to Chase pursuant to 12 C.F.R. §229.30(b), which provides:

> A paying bank that is unable to identify the depositary bank with respect to a check may send the returned check to any bank that handled the check for forward collection even if that bank does not agree to handle the check expeditiously under §229.31(a).

The problem with Citibank's argument is that the evidence of record does not support its assertion that it was unable to identify the depositary bank from the information on the back of the Check. Citibank points to testimony by witnesses who say that the endorsement by First Financial was "not clear." However, Citibank also states that "[t]he image of the Check received by Citibank on July 8, 2010 is depicted in CB 00020," and the Court finds, as a matter of law, that no reasonable jury could examine CB 00020 and conclude that Citibank was unable to decipher First Financial's endorsement. Therefore 12 C.F.R. §229.30(b) did not apply to Citibank's return of the Check.

So Citibank was required to expeditiously return the Check to First Financial, and it failed to do so. The next question is what, if any, liability flows from that failure. Regulation CC provides:

> A bank shall exercise ordinary care and act in good faith in complying with the requirements of this subpart. A bank that fails to exercise ordinary care or act in good faith under this subpart may be liable to the depositary bank, the depositary bank's customer, the owner of a check, or another party to the check. *The measure of damages for failure to exercise ordinary care is the amount of the loss incurred, up to the amount of the check, reduced by the amount of the loss that party would have incurred even if the bank had exercised ordinary care.* A bank that fails to act in good faith under this subpart may be liable for other damages, if any, suffered by the party as a proximate consequence. Subject to a bank's duty to exercise ordinary care or act in good faith in choosing the means of return or notice of nonpayment, the bank is not liable for the insolvency, neglect, misconduct, mistake, or default of another bank or person, or for loss or destruction of a check or notice of nonpayment in transit or in the possession of others. This section does not affect a paying bank's liability to its customer under the U.C.C. or other law.

12 C.F.R. §229.38(b) (emphasis added). The Court has no trouble finding, as a matter of law based upon the evidence of record, that Citibank failed to exercise ordinary care when it failed to identify First Financial as the depositary bank. The inquiry, then, is the amount of First Financial's loss, if any, that would have occurred even if Citibank had exercised ordinary care and returned the Check to First Financial expeditiously.

Regulation CC provides two ways in which a paying bank can satisfy the expediency requirement. The first is the "two-day test," which provides, in relevant part:

> A paying bank returns a check in an expeditious manner if it sends the returned check in a manner such that the check would normally be received by the depositary bank not later than 4:00 P.M. (local time of the depositary bank) of . . . [t]he second business day following the banking day on which the check was presented to the paying bank.

12 C.F.R. §229.30(a)(1). Pursuant to this test, Citibank unquestionably would have satisfied its obligation to return the Check expeditiously if First Financial had received the Check by 4:00 P.M. on Monday, July 12, 2010, which

was the second business day following Thursday, July 8, the day the Check was presented to Citibank. By that time most, if not all, of the damage was already done, as McDonald wired $268,825.00 to the Bank of China on July 9. While it is certainly possible that First Financial could demonstrate that it was damaged by Citibank's failure to expeditiously return the check—if, for example, it can show that it would have been able to reverse the wire transfer had the check been returned by 4:00 P.M. on July 12—it does not point to any evidence to support such a finding. Accordingly, First Financial has not demonstrated that it is entitled to summary judgment on this claim. However, First Financial is entitled to summary judgment as to the following parts of its claim: (1) Citibank failed to comply with the requirement of 12 C.F.R. §229.30(a) that it return the Check expeditiously; and (2) Citibank failed to exercise reasonable care in complying with its obligation under 12 C.F.R. §229.30(a). Therefore, the only issue remaining for trial with regard to this claim is whether any damages were caused by Citibank's failure to return the Check expeditiously.

2. *Failure to Provide Timely Notice of Dishonor*

In addition to the obligation to return a dishonored check expeditiously, when the check at issue is for $2500.00 or more, a payor bank is required to "provide notice of nonpayment such that the notice is received by the depositary bank by 4:00 P.M. (local time) on the second business day following the banking day on which the check was presented to the paying bank." 12 C.F.R. §229.33(a). Citibank failed to satisfy this requirement, as it did not provide notice to First Financial that it was not going to pay the Check.

Again, however, Citibank's failure does not translate into liability to First Financial unless that failure proximately caused a loss by First Financial. And again, First Financial has not presented any evidence that this is the case, inasmuch as the wire transfer occurred prior to 4:00 P.M. on July 12, the second business day following the banking day on which the Check was presented to Citibank. So while First Financial is entitled to summary judgment on the issue of whether Citibank failed to comply with 12 C.F.R. §229.33—it did—the question of whether Citibank has any liability for that failure remains for trial.

3. *Incorrect Routing of the Check*

First Financial also asserts that Citibank incorrectly encoded the Check to indicate that Chase was the bank of first deposit. This, First Financial argues, constituted a breach of the warranty set forth in 12 C.F.R. §229.34(c)(3):

> Each bank that presents or transfers a check or returned check warrants to any bank that subsequently handles it that, at the time of presentment or

> transfer, the information encoded after issue in magnetic ink on the check or returned check is correct. For purposes of this paragraph, the information encoded after issue on the check or returned check includes any information placed in the MICR line of a substitute check that represents that check or returned check.

The Court is unable to discern from the evidence cited by First Financial that Citibank's actions breached this warranty. The warranty applies to "the information encoded after issue in magnetic ink" on the Check. The testimony cited by First Financial indicates that the Check was prepared for return by Citibank manually—that is, that a Citibank employee, Mr. Gandhi, manually placed information on the Check. Perhaps it is obvious to one in the banking industry, but, unfortunately, the Court is unaware whether the information Mr. Gandhi manually put on the Check was "encoded . . . in magnetic ink." Accordingly, the Court cannot determine whether Citibank breached this warranty, and First Financial is not entitled to summary judgment on this claim.

Even assuming that a breach of the encoding warranty occurred, First Financial has not presented evidence from which the Court could determine whether it suffered injury as a result of that breach. First Financial seems to assert that the EARNS notice that was sent to Chase was subject to the encoding warranty; in other words, First Financial argues that if *the Check* had been encoded properly then *the EARNS notice* would have been sent to First Financial instead of Chase and First Financial would have received the notice as quickly as Chase received it.

There are two problems with this argument. First, there is no evidence regarding when First Financial would have received an EARNS notice sent by Citibank; perhaps Citibank has a faster means of sending notices to Chase than it does to First Financial. More fundamentally, however, the plain language of 12 C.F.R. §§229.34(c)(3) appears to apply only to information encoded on a check, not to an EARNS notice. While perhaps this is incorrect (and, again, that fact might be obvious to someone in the banking industry), all the Court has to go on is the evidence to which the parties have cited, and they have cited to nothing that would contradict the plain language of the regulation. In this case, while the EARNS notice was sent to Chase, the Check itself was sent by Citibank to the Federal Reserve Bank. First Financial has submitted no evidence regarding when it would have received the Check from the Federal Reserve Bank if it had been encoded properly. All the Court knows is that the Federal Reserve Bank had agreed to return checks to First Financial expeditiously, which means that pursuant to 12 C.F.R. §229.31 it had a duty to send the Check to First Financial in a manner such that it would normally have been received by First Financial no later than 4:00 P.M. on July 12. As discussed above, that would have been too late to prevent the wire transfer. . . .

D. CITIBANK'S DUTY TO EXERCISE ORDINARY CARE

First Financial makes several arguments under the subheading "Citibank failed to exercise ordinary care and good faith in handling the Check." First, First Financial argues that had it received notice of nonpayment on July 8 when Chase received notice from Citibank, then it would have been able to stop the wire transfer. That may be true, but it is irrelevant. Citibank had no duty under Regulation CC to provide notice until July 12, and Citibank cannot be held liable under Regulation CC for failing to act as quickly as possible, but rather only for failing to comply with its obligations under Regulation CC. Therefore the relevant inquiry is not whether Citibank could have prevented First Financial's loss, but rather whether Citibank was required by Regulation CC to act in such a way that First Financial's loss would have been prevented. As set forth above, the record as it stands does not compel the conclusion that First Financial's loss would have been avoided, in whole or in part, if Citibank had complied with Regulation CC. . . .

IV. CONCLUSION

For the reasons set forth above, First Financial's motion for summary judgment is GRANTED IN PART in that the Court finds the following as a matter of law: (1) Citibank failed to comply with the requirement of 12 C.F.R. §229.30(a) that it return the Check expeditiously; (2) Citibank failed to exercise reasonable care in complying with its obligation under 12 C.F.R. §229.30(a); and (3) Citibank failed to comply with the notice requirement set forth in 12 C.F.R. §229.33. First Financial's motion is DENIED in all other respects, including whether Citibank's failures to comply with Regulation CC as just enumerated caused any injury to First Financial.

6. Expedited Recredit for Consumer

Section 5006 of the Act allows *consumers* (but not *non*-consumer customers) to get an expedited recredit to their account in certain circumstances when the consumer disputes the validity of the charge to the account. Section 7(a) of the statute provides:

> (a) Recredit Claims—
>
> (1) In General—A consumer may make a claim for expedited recredit from the bank that holds the account of the consumer with respect to a substitute check, if the consumer asserts in good faith that—

(A) the bank charged the consumer's account for a substitute check that was provided to the consumer;

(B) either—

(i) the check was not properly charged to the consumer's account; or

(ii) the consumer has a warranty claim with respect to such substitute check;

(C) the consumer suffered a resulting loss; and

(D) the production of the original check or a better copy of the original check is necessary to determine the validity of any claim described in subparagraph (B). . . .[29]

Suppose, for example, that the consumer cannot read the substitute check because the image is not clear. In that case, the consumer must report the problem within 40 days, and may demand an immediate recredit. The bank may investigate for ten business days, or if it recredits the account while it investigates, for 45 calendar days. Section 5006(a)(2) contains these time limits, which are copied from the Electronic Fund Transfer Act (the federal debit card statute we will discuss in Chapter 15):

(2) Timing of Recredit.—

(A) In General—The bank shall recredit the consumer's account for the amount described in paragraph (1) no later than the end of the business day following the business day on which the bank determines the consumer's claim is valid.

(B) Recredit Pending Investigation.—If the bank has not yet determined that the consumer's claim is valid before the end of the 10th business day after the business day on which the consumer submitted the claim, the bank shall recredit the consumer's account for—

(i) the lesser of the amount of the substitute check that was charged against the consumer account, or $2,500, together with interest if the account is an interest-bearing account, no later than the end of such 10th business day; and

(ii) the remaining amount of the substitute check that was charged against the consumer account, if any, together with interest if the account is an interest bearing account, not later than the 45th calendar day following the business day on which the consumer submits the claim.

Section 5006(d) of the statute has "Safeguard Exceptions" (copied almost word for word from the same safeguard exceptions to funds availability in Regulation CC, discussed earlier in this chapter at pages 735-737), describing situations where the bank need not recredit the account in accordance with the usual time limits.

29. Regulation CC §229.54 expands upon the statutory language.

7. Expedited Recredit for Banks

A bank that is forced to recredit a consumer's account may seek indemnity from the bank that presented the check to it. The indemnity rules are discussed above, and the procedure for an expedited recredit is given in detail in Regulation CC §229.55. It contains a requirement that all claims be made within 120 days of the original transaction giving rise to the claim, and must describe the reasons for the recredit clearly. If the claiming bank includes a copy of any substitute check as part of its claim it must take reasonable steps to make sure that copy will not get into circulation and be mistaken for the legal equivalent of the original check. Within ten business days of the recredit claim, the indemnifying bank must recredit the amount of the check, return the original check, or provide information as to why it will not do so.

8. Lawsuits and Miscellaneous Provisions

Section 5009 allows a civil action for violations of the statute with an award of actual damages (up to the amount of the check), plus costs and attorney's fees. Notice of claims must be given within 30 days after a claimant discovers the grounds for the claim or the amount of any recovery is reduced by the amount that such prompt notice would have provided; Regulation CC §229.56(d). Suit may be brought in either federal or state courts, and there is a one-year statute of limitations. The rules of Check 21 may not be varied by agreement, except for the expedited recredit provisions between banks in §229.55.

PROBLEM 192

When Jeanie Griffin went to pay for her groceries at the counter of the store, she gave the clerk a check for the relevant amount. The clerk scanned the check, turning it into an electronic file, and then returned the check to her, telling her that the amount would be debited from her checking account. Is this an Article 4 matter? A Check 21 situation?

The answer is no to both questions. Where the check is converted by a non-bank, as here, the transaction (called an "electronic check conversion" and mysteriously given the initials "ECK"[30]) is governed by the same rules we will see in Chapter 15 for debit card use. The relevant regulations for this

30. This process is also called "back office conversion" or "BRC."

situation require the merchant who has scanned the check at the point of sale ("POS") to return the original paper check to the consumer (or, if the merchant has received the check through the mail—an "accounts receivable conversion" or "ARC"—to destroy it); see Electronic Fund Transfer Regulation E, 12 C.F.R. §1005.3(b)(2), and the rules of the National Automated Clearinghouse Association.

C. *Final Payment*

A signal legal moment in the check collection rules of both Article 4 of the Uniform Commercial Code and the EFAA is the moment that a payor bank engages in *final payment* of a check. This moment is important because it fixes many of the legal rights arising under Articles 3 and 4. Following final payment, the payor bank is "accountable" for the amount of the check according to the language of §4-302(a), which means that it has lost the right to dishonor the check and must pay it to the person entitled to enforce it. If the check is properly payable (§4-401) from the drawer's account, well and good. If not, the payor bank is in a spot. The only legal theories in its favor that survive final payment are breach of presentment warranties (these have to do with forgeries and alterations, rarely at issue, discussed in the next chapter) and common law restitution, codified in §3-418, against villainous parties (who are hard to find or are often judgment-proof). Hence, this rule: Following final payment, the payor bank bears the risk of any mistaken payment not covered by one of these theories, which almost never help. Read §4-302(b).

When does final payment occur? The key section is §4-215. This section, which you should read carefully, states the events that make a payor bank "accountable" (§4-302(a)) for the item, whether it means to be or not. See Annot., 23 A.L.R.4th 203. The final payment of a check destroys the check as a cause of action. All of the Article 3 implied obligations (§§3-414, 3-415, 3-419, etc.) are at an end because the check has been paid and these obligations, being secondary, are conditioned on *dishonor* by the drawee. Once the drawee makes final payment, dishonor is no longer possible, and the drawer and indorsers are off the hook.

PROBLEM 193

Harold Sure walked into Octopus National Bank and made a presentment of a $12,000 check drawn on the bank to the head cashier, Christopher Coin, who was staffing one of the teller's windows. Coin asked

Sure (who was the check's payee) to indorse the check on the back and then tapped the computer's memory bank to check on the state of the drawer's account. The computer replied that the account contained "one thousand dollars," but Coin misread the display and thought it said "one hundred thousand dollars." He went back to the teller's window and counted out the money thoughtfully. When he was done, a nagging doubt about his vision overcame him, and—passing the money to Sure—he said, "Excuse me a minute," and rechecked the computer. This time he read the amount correctly and rushed back to his window to discover Sure still standing there, slowly recounting the money in front of him. Coin snatched the money out of Sure's hands, saying, "I'm sorry, we must dishonor the check." Sure protested, but in vain. If Sure sues, will he win? Had the bank made *final payment?* See §4-215(a)(1).

The above is an elaboration of the fact situation in a famous case, Chambers v. Miller, 13 C.B. (N.S.) 125, 143 Eng. Rep. 50 (1862). (Judge Byles, writing in this case, said, "I think it would be extremely dangerous, and would create a great sensation in the city of London, if it were held in Westminster Hall, that after a check had been regularly handed over the banker's counter and the money received for it, and in the act of being counted, the banker might treat the check as unpaid because he had subsequently ascertained that the state of the customer's account was unfavorable.")

PROBLEM 194

Sally Phillips was the payee on a $1,000 check given to her by Joseph Armstrong. She and Joe both banked at the same bank, Octopus National Bank. Sally took Joe's check to the bank and filled out a deposit slip for her checking account, putting $800 of the check in her account and taking the other $200 in cash across the counter (this is called a *split deposit*). Two hours later, while posting the check, the bank clerk discovered that Joe's account was overdrawn. Can the bank now dishonor the whole check? $800 worth? Does §4-215(a)(1) apply here? See Kirby v. First & Merchants Natl. Bank, 210 Va. 88, 168 S.E.2d 273 (1969).

PROBLEM 195

Sally Phillips was the payee on a $1,000 check given to her by Joseph Armstrong. She walked it into Octopus National Bank, on which the check was drawn, and presented it across the counter, asking for a $1,000 cashier's check payable to her order as the method of payment. The bank gave her such a check; see §§3-104(g) and 3-412. She indorsed the check over to one of her creditors, but when Octopus National Bank failed and closed its doors before the check could be presented and paid, the creditor returned the cashier's check to her and demanded payment. Must she repay the creditor? See §3-310(a). If she does repay the creditor, may she sue Joseph Armstrong either as drawer of the check, §3-414, or on the original obligation, §3-310(b)(1)? See §§4-215(a)(2) and 4-213(c).

The second method of making final payment is settling for a check and not having the legal right to revoke the settlement; §4-215(a)(2). "Settle" is defined in §4-104(a)(11) as meaning "to pay in cash, by clearing-house settlement, in a charge or credit or by remittance, or otherwise as agreed. A settlement may be either provisional or final." If there exists a right to revoke the settlement, §4-215(a)(2) does not apply. Section 4-215(a)(2) is deliberately worded vaguely since the drafters wanted to encompass all possible methods of making payment that a bank might employ: wire transfer, netting of outstanding accounts, tapping of an account, etc. As long as the bank uses one of these methods and does not reserve the right to change its mind, final payment has occurred and the payor bank is accountable for the amount of the check.

The final (and most common) method of making final payment is contained in §4-215(a)(3). Almost all checks are not presented over the counter, but come into the payor bank when presented by another bank, which will have already made a provisional settlement in its own favor for the item. In that case, final payment is made by simply holding onto the check past the deadline for returning it. Read §4-215(a)(3). What is this deadline? The answer depends on what arrangements the payor bank has made with the presenting bank. If their agreement is that presented items must be returned by 4:00 P.M. on the day following the day of presentment, then that agreement prevails. If the check is presented through a local clearinghouse, the clearinghouse rules will govern the required time of return. Absent such agreements, the "statute" mentioned in §4-215(a)(3) is the Uniform Commercial Code itself, which requires return before expiration of the midnight deadline. The "midnight deadline" referred to is not midnight of the date of presentment, as it sounds, but instead is defined thusly in UCC §4-104(a)(10):

> (10) Midnight deadline: with respect to a bank is midnight on its next banking day following the banking day on which it receives the relevant item or notice or from which the time for taking action commences to run, whichever is later.

PROBLEM 196

What is the latest the payor bank can return a check before expiration of its midnight deadline, assuming: the bank has established a cut-off hour[31] of 2:00 P.M., it is not open on Saturdays (nor, of course, on Sundays), Monday is a holiday, and the Federal Reserve Bank presents a check for $1 million on Friday at 4:00 P.M.?

Bankers must be ever alert to the possible expiration of the midnight deadline because once it has passed for a check, the check may not be dishonored and returned. When the customer of the bank is pleading for more time to cover a check overdrawing the account, the midnight deadline should be uppermost in the thoughts of a banker who is making decisions. The following is the leading case on the legal meaning of missing this deadline.

Rock Island Auction Sales, Inc. v. Empire Packing Co.

Illinois Supreme Court, 1965
32 Ill. 2d 269, 204 N.E.2d 721

SCHAFFER, J., delivered the opinion of the court: This case presents issues concerning the construction and validity of section 4-302 of the Uniform Commercial Code.

The facts were admitted or stipulated. On Monday, September 24, 1962, the plaintiff, Rock Island Auction Sales, Inc., sold 61 head of cattle to Empire Packing Co., Inc. and received therefor Empire's check in the sum of $14,706.90. The check was dated September 24, 1962, and on that day the plaintiff deposited it in the First Bank and Trust Company of Davenport, Iowa. It was received by the payor bank, Illinois National Bank and Trust Company of Rockford, Illinois, on Thursday, September 27, 1962. Empire's balance was inadequate to pay the check, but the payor bank, relying upon Empire's assurances that additional funds would be deposited, held the check until Tuesday morning, October 2, 1962. It then marked the check "not sufficient funds," placed it in the mail for return to the Federal Reserve Bank of Chicago and sent notice of dishonor by telegram to the Federal Reserve Bank. The depositary bank, the First Trust and Savings Bank of Davenport, received the check on October 4, 1962. The check was never paid. On November 7, 1962, bankruptcy proceedings were instituted against Empire and on December 13, 1962, it was adjudicated a bankrupt.

31. See §4-108.

On February 15, 1963, the plaintiff instituted this action against Illinois National Bank and Trust Company of Rockford, Empire Packing Co., Inc., and Peter Cacciatori, the officer of Empire who had signed the check. Cacciatori was not served with process, and no further action was taken against Empire after a stay order was issued by the United States District Court in the Bankruptcy proceeding. The plaintiff's case against Illinois National Bank and Trust Company of Rockford (hereafter defendant) rests squarely on the ground that as the payor bank it became liable for the amount of the check because it held the check without payment, return or notice of dishonor, beyond the time limit fixed in section 4-302 of the Uniform Commercial Code. . . .

[The court quoted §§4-302 and 4-104(a)(10).—Eds.]

The important issues in the case involve the construction and validity of section 4-302. The defendant argues that the amount for which it is liable because of its undented retention of the check beyond the time permitted by section 4-302 is not to be determined by that section, but rather under section 4-103(5) which provides that "[t]he measure of damages for failure to exercise ordinary care in handling an item is the amount of the item reduced by an amount which could not have been realized by the use of ordinary care. . . ." To support this argument it points out that other provisions of Article 4 use the words "liable," "must pay," and "may recover." Its position is that the word "accountable" in section 4-302 means that "the defendant must account for what it actually had (which is zero because there were no funds on deposit sufficient to pay the check) plus the damages (as measured by section 4-103(5)) sustained by the plaintiff as the result of the failure to meet the deadline, but for no more."

But the statute provides that the bank is accountable for the amount of the item, and not for something else. "Accountable" is synonymous with "liable" (Webster's New Twentieth Century Dictionary Unabridged, Second Edition, Webster's Dictionary of Synonyms), and section 4-302 uses the word in that sense. The word "accountable" appears to have been used instead of its synonym "liable" in order to accommodate other sections of Article 4 of the Code which relate to provisional and final settlements between banks in the collection process, and to bar the possibility that a payor bank might be thought to be liable both to the owner of the item and to another bank. The circuit court correctly held that the statute imposes liability for the amount of the item.

This construction does not create an irrational classification and so cause the statute to violate constitutional limitations. Defendant's contention to the contrary is based upon the proposition that section 4-302 is invalid because it imposes a liability upon a payor bank for failing to act prior to its midnight deadline that is more severe than the liability which section 4-103(5) imposes upon a depositary bank or a collecting bank for the same default. Of course there are no such separate institutions as depositary, collecting and payor banks. All banks perform all three functions. The argument thus comes down to the proposition that the failure of a bank to meet its deadline must always carry the same consequence, regardless of the function that it is performing.

But the legislature may legitimately have concluded that there are differences in function and in circumstance that justify different consequences. Depositary and collecting banks act primarily as conduits. The steps that they take can only indirectly affect the determination of whether or not a check is to be paid, which is the focal point in the collection process. The legislature could have concluded that the failure of such a bank to meet its deadline would most frequently be the result of negligence, and fixed liability accordingly. The role of a payor bank in the collection process, on the other hand, is crucial. It knows whether or not the drawer has funds available to pay the item. The legislature could have considered that the failure of such a bank to meet its deadline is likely to be due to factors other than negligence, and that the relationship between a payor bank and its customer may so influence its conduct as to cause a conscious disregard of its statutory duty. The present case is illustrative. The defendant, in its position as a payor bank, deliberately aligned itself with its customer in order to protect that customer's credit and consciously disregard the duty imposed upon it. The statutory scheme emphasizes the importance of speed in the collection process. A legislative sanction designed to prevent conscious disregard of deadlines cannot be characterized as arbitrary or unreasonable, nor can it be said to constitute a legislative encroachment on the functions of the judiciary. . . .

Judgment affirmed.

A payor bank that misses its midnight deadline is *strictly liable* for the amount of the check involved. It is no defense that other parties, such as the depositary bank, were negligent or did not suffer a provable loss. See First Natl. Bank in Harvey v. Colonial Bank, 898 F. Supp. 1220 (N.D. Ill. 1995); Los Angeles National Bank v. Bank of Canton, 280 Cal. Rptr. 831 (Cal. App. 1991); Hanna v. First Natl. Bank of Rochester, 87 N.Y.2d 107, 637 N.Y.S.2d 953 (N.Y. 1995). A payor bank that tries to return a check on which it has already made final payment is said to be making a "late return," which, of course, is not allowed. Regulation CC creates a *warranty of timely return* for checks, so that if a bank is guilty of making a late return it has to respond in damages; Regulation CC §229.34.

When the Federal Reserve was drafting Regulation CC, it decided to make a major alteration to the midnight deadline rule to stop the following practice. Under the Uniform Commercial Code a payor bank was required to "send" the check back before the expiration of the midnight deadline. Suppose that late in the second banking day, shortly before midnight, a payor bank made a last-minute decision to dishonor a check. The fastest way to get the check back to the presenting bank would be to wait until the armored courier could take it back the next day, but the statute did not allow that delay. "Send," as it happens, is defined in the Uniform Commercial Code to include "deposit in the mail" (see §1-201(b)(36)), and the Federal Reserve discovered that that is what the banks were doing with the checks: putting them in an envelope and then into a mailbox before midnight. Who knew when the check would actually get back to the presenting bank, but the payor bank had nonetheless complied with the law. To change this awkward procedure, Regulation CC now provides that a payor bank is permitted to miss its midnight deadline as long as it is able nonetheless to return a check to the collecting bank "on or before the receiving bank's next banking day following the otherwise applicable deadline by the earlier of the close of that banking day or a cutoff hour of 2 P.M. or later set by the receiving bank under U.C.C. 4-108"; Regulation CC §229.30(c)(1). This, in effect, gives the payor bank an extra day to return the check after the expiration of the usual midnight deadline.

First National Bank of Chicago v. Standard Bank & Trust

United States Court of Appeals, Seventh Circuit, 1999
172 F.3d 472

FLAUM, Circuit Judge.

First National Bank of Chicago, known at the time relevant to this suit as NBD Bank ("NBD"), brought an action for declaratory judgment alleging that Standard Bank & Trust ("Standard Bank" or "Standard") failed to return certain checks to NBD in a timely fashion under the Expedited Funds Availability Act, 12 U.S.C. §4010(d) & (f) ("EFAA"). Finding that the checks were returned in a timely fashion, the district court granted summary judgment to the defendant Standard Bank, and awarded it prejudgment interest on the returned checks. Standard claimed it was entitled to the average prime rate for the relevant time period. However, the district court used the three-month Treasury Bill rate—4.9241%—compounded quarterly. Both sides appeal. For the reasons set out below, we affirm the district court's decision that the checks were properly returned, but vacate the award of interest, and remand for entry of the proper measure of prejudgment interest.

Background

This litigation revolves around which party—Standard or NBD—should absorb the losses resulting from a check-kiting scheme perpetrated against both of these banks in November, 1993. On November 18, 1993, an individual presented to NBD checks with an aggregate value of $3,997,406.75, drawn on customer accounts maintained at Standard Bank, which NBD initially accepted. That day, the same person deposited $4,025,000.00 in checks at Standard, drawn on NBD customer accounts.

The following day, Friday, November 19, 1993, NBD presented the checks it received to Standard, and vice versa. LaSalle Bank, in its capacity as the collecting bank, charged both banks' accounts for the checks drawn on them, and provisionally credited each bank for the amount presented to them. On the next business day (Monday, November 22, 1993), NBD opted not to honor the checks, and returned all of the checks, totaling $4,025,000.00, to Standard Bank. Standard received notice of NBD's decision on Tuesday morning, November 23. That afternoon, Standard attempted to dishonor the checks it had received. Three of its bank officers dashed off to NBD's Operations Processing Center carrying checks totaling $3,785,441.35. The checks were received by NBD at 3:58 P.M. that day, but NBD did not credit Standard's account for that sum. On November 30, 1993, NBD filed suit, seeking a declaration that Standard Bank's return of the checks was not timely, because it neither met the "midnight deadline," nor any of the deadline's exceptions laid out in Federal Reserve Board ("the Board") Regulations appurtenant to EFAA. Standard Bank defended by arguing that its return was proper, and it counterclaimed for prejudgment interest.

On a motion for judgment on the pleadings, the district court originally found for NBD, but reversed its decision in light of a clarifying amendment[32] to the relevant Federal Reserve Regulations. The district court also decided that prejudgment interest was appropriate, but did not award the prime rate. Instead it chose a lower rate (the average T-bill rate) because of the absence of bad faith on NBD's part, and because this was a "close case." Each side appealed portions of the decision below.

I.

NBD's appeal from the district court's order granting Standard Bank's motion for judgment on the pleadings is reviewed by this court de novo. Rooding v. Peters, 92 F.3d 578, 579-80 (7th Cir. 1996).

32. When we refer to Regulation CC, we refer to the pre-clarification version of that rule. The amended version is referred to as "postclarifying amendment Regulation CC."

A.

The legal question at issue is whether Standard Bank's return of the checks comports with Federal Reserve Board Regulation CC sec. 229.30(c)(1), 12 C.F.R. Part 229 ("Regulation CC"). Regulation CC's language states:

> (c) Extension of deadline. The deadline for return or notice of nonpayment under the U.C.C. or Regulation sec. 229.36(f)(2) of this part is extended:
>
> (1) If a paying bank, in an effort to expedite delivery of a returned check to a bank, uses a means of delivery that would ordinarily result in the returned check being received by the bank to which it is sent on or before the receiving bank's next business day following the otherwise applicable deadline; this deadline is extended further if a paying bank uses a highly expeditious means of transportation, even if this means of transportation would ordinarily result in delivery after the receiving bank's next banking day.

As the text notes, Regulation CC extends the UCC's deadline, known in the vernacular as the "midnight deadline." Under the UCC, a paying bank may dishonor or revoke its provisional settlement of a check before midnight on the next business day after it received the check. UCC sec. 4-301(a)(1); Hanna v. First Nat'l Bank of Rochester, 87 N.Y.S.2d 107, 637 N.Y.S.2d 953, 661 N.E.2d 683, 686 n.2 (N.Y. 1995). While the Board favored the UCC's emphasis on expeditiously dealing with dishonored checks, it was concerned that the midnight deadline might unintentionally retard the return of checks. It noted "[b]ecause the return process must begin by midnight, many paying banks return checks by mail when a courier leaving after midnight would be faster." 52 Fed. Reg. 47119, 47123 (Dec. 11, 1987). Thus, the Board enacted the extension to the midnight deadline.

NBD argues that the Board's extension of the midnight deadline does not apply here. It primarily points to a number of statements in Regulation CC's legislative history indicating that use of the extension is limited to banks which regularly use couriers services to return checks. However, NBD is putting the cart before the horse—before we delve into the Board's commentary on Regulation CC, we must first examine its language's plain meaning.

Administrative rules are subject to the same well-known maxims of construction as legislative statutes. Alabama Tissue Ctr. v. Sullivan, 975 F.2d 373, 379 (7th Cir. 1992). As we recently noted, in statutory construction cases, "the beginning point must be the language of the statute, and when a statute speaks with clarity to an issue, judicial inquiry into the statute's meaning, in all but the most extraordinary circumstances, is finished." United States v. Kirschenbaum, 156 F.3d 784, 789 (7th Cir. 1998) (quoting Estate of Cowart v. Nicklos Drilling Co., 505 U.S. 469, 475, 112 S. Ct. 2589, 120 L. Ed. 2d 379 (1992)). If we can decipher Regulation CC's meaning on its face, there is no need to examine legislative history absent extraordinary circumstances. United States v. Hudspeth, 42 F.3d 1015, 1022 (7th Cir. 1994).

There is little in the text of the statute that supports NBD's argument that the extension is only available to banks which regularly or ordinarily use expedited delivery. Regulation CC extends the deadline when a paying bank "expedite[s] delivery of a returned check . . ." and we note the singular "a returned check" rather than the plural "returned checks." See Metropolitan Stevedore Co. v. Rambo, 515 U.S. 291, 295, 115 S. Ct. 2144, 132 L. Ed. 2d 226 (1995). Although it is not dispositive, this use of the singular suggests that Regulation CC may apply to one-time single check transactions. Far more conclusive is the structure of the second clause, which allows a bank to extend the deadline when it "uses a means of delivery that would ordinarily result in the returned check being received by the bank to which it is sent on or before the receiving bank's next business day following the otherwise applicable deadline." NBD argues, implausibly, that this mandates that a bank ordinarily or routinely use a means of expedited delivery in order to avail itself of the extension. For "ordinarily" to have such meaning, however, it would have to modify the verb "uses," causing the sentence to read: "a bank may extend the deadline if it ordinarily uses a means of delivery that would result in the returned check being received. . . ." Of course, in the actual regulation, "ordinarily" modifies the verb "would result," denoting that the bank's means of delivery must ordinarily result in return by the applicable deadline. Any other reading, including the one NBD proposes, is contrary to the clear import of the second clause.

NBD also points to Regulation CC's first clause, which allows banks to use the extension "in an effort to expedite delivery of a returned check to a bank." It argues that Standard Bank's efforts were not in "an effort to expedite delivery" of the dishonored checks. We disagree. There is no doubt that Standard Bank's executives drove the checks to NBD's processing center in order to speed up delivery.

This interpretation squares with a leading commentary on the UCC by Professors White and Summers. Analyzing the plain language of Regulation CC (before the clarifying amendment) White and Summers posed—and answered—the following hypothetical:

> Assume that the payor bank received a $100,000 check on Monday morning and that it discovers on Wednesday morning that it failed to send the check back by Tuesday midnight (the midnight deadline), but it now wishes to dishonor the check. Under the UCC the midnight deadline would have passed, and unless it had an unusual defense, payor would be liable for the $100,000. *Regulation CC* changes that. If the bank can somehow get the check back to the depositary bank before that bank's close of business on Wednesday, it escapes liability under the UCC. That appears to be the meaning of the first sentence of [Regulation CC sec. 229.30(c)].

James J. White & Robert F. Summers, Uniform Commercial Code, at 325 (4th ed. 1995) (emphasis added). Although NBD brings other scholarly points of view to our attention, those positions appear less faithful to Regulation CC's actual text than White & Summers.

We only look past the express language of a regulation when it is ambiguous or where a literal interpretation would lead to an "absurd result or thwart the purpose of the overall statutory scheme." United States v. Hayward, 6 F.3d 1241, 1245 (7th Cir. 1993). We see no ambiguity in Regulation CC which admits of the meaning NBD presses upon us. Also, a literal interpretation does not lead to an "absurd result"—there is nothing absurd about extending the midnight deadline irrespective of whether a bank avails itself of the extension once or repeatedly. Moreover, the reading we adopt does not thwart the purpose of the rule, which promoted the speedy return of dishonored checks over the postmark conscious "midnight deadline." See 52 Fed. Reg. 47112, 47140 (Dec. 11, 1987) (noting that Regulation CC "removes the constraint of the midnight deadline if the check reaches either the depositary bank or the returning bank to which it is sent on the banking day following the expiration of the midnight deadline or other applicable time for return.").

We briefly examine the rule's regulatory history for any signs that our decision would thwart the Board's intent. United States v. Mueller, 112 F.3d 277, 281 (7th Cir. 1997) (where statute is clear, examining legislative history useful to "determine if it reflects a clearly expressed legislative intention" contrary to plain meaning) (citation omitted). Regulation CC's regulatory history is not quite as clear as the text. Both sides present evidence from the available sources to support their statutory interpretations. Among other references, NBD points to Regulation CC's Official Commentary, which lists two circumstances in which the midnight deadline may be extended, one not relevant here. The putatively relevant circumstance is where "a West Coast paying bank . . . ship[s] a returned check by air courier directly to an East Coast depositary bank even if the check arrives after the close of the depositary bank's banking day." Official Commentary sec. 229.30, 12 C.F.R. Part 22, App. E (1997). This does suggest that the intent of the regulation may not have been as broad as its wording indicates. On the other hand, the commentary notes that the West Coast/East Coast bank scenario is an "example" of a highly expeditious means of delivery. 12 C.F.R. part 229, App. E. The history also states that Regulation CC "pertains primarily to air courier arrangements from West Coast banks to East Coast banks." 53 Fed. Reg. 19372, 19418 (May 27, 1988). "Pertains primarily" suggests that other exceptions exist too, and that an overly constricted reading of when the extension applies would be inappropriate. After examining the relative regulatory history, we believe it is a wash. This works to NBD's detriment, because its inability to coax strong support from the regulatory history means that it cannot overcome the clear import of Regulation CC's words. Oneida Tribe v. Wisconsin, 951 F.2d 757, 761 (7th Cir. 1991).

B.

Although our reading of Regulation CC finds little ambiguity, the Board issued a self titled "Clarifying Amendment" in 1997 to remove any doubt as to whether the midnight deadline applies to checks returned to avoid a kite. Assuming that our interpretation of the pre-clarification rule was incorrect—an assumption without which this analysis is superfluous—Standard argues that the Clarifying Amendment has retroactive effect. It was on this ground that the district court found for Standard Bank. NBD argues that the "Clarifying Amendment" was actually a legislative rule, and as such has no retroactive effect under Bowen v. Georgetown University Hospital, 488 U.S. 204, 208, 109 S. Ct. 468, 102 L. Ed. 2d 493 (1988).

The Clarifying Amendment expunged the words "in an effort to expedite delivery of a returned check to a bank" from Regulation CC sec. 229.30(c)(1). 62 Fed. Reg. 13801, 13805 (March 24, 1997). This was done to remove any doubt as to whether an inquiry into the returning bank's motives was appropriate. Id. . . .

Based on our analysis, even if the original Regulation CC did not allow Standard Bank to return the checks, we find that the 1997 Clarifying Amendment retroactively permitted the extension of the midnight deadline. Thus, the district court's finding that NBD should have honored the checks Standard delivered in the amount of $3,785,441.35 was correct. . . .

Conclusion

While we Affirm the judgment on the pleadings in favor of Standard Bank, the district court's grant of prejudgment interest is Vacated and we Remand with instructions to enter an award of prejudgment interest consistent with the average prime rate for the appropriate time period.

PROBLEM 197

Octopus National Bank, which has branches throughout the state, has one central processing center where it makes all decisions about whether to pay checks drawn on the branches. The canceled checks are returned to the branches two days after the processing center decides to pay them. Is the moment of presentment to the payer bank the moment of presentment to the processing center or the moment when the check is returned to the individual branch? See Regulation CC §229.36(b)(4).

D. *Check Return*

The major thrust of the EFAA is to require depositary banks to give customers quick access to funds represented by deposited checks. This has the effect, however, of putting the depositary banks at risk. The customer might withdraw the funds under the EFAA rules, and then the check, for whatever reason, might still be returned. The customer is required to repay the money after the check is charged back to the account (§4-214, explored later in this chapter), but all too often the money is gone and cannot be retrieved. Regulation CC therefore has a number of provisions designed to make the check collection machinery operate very quickly to forward checks for collection and return them if they are dishonored.

The Federal Notice for Large Check Return. On checks of $2,500 or more, depositary banks take the biggest risks unless they are alerted to the fact that the check is being dishonored by the payor bank. Section 229.31(c)(1) of Regulation CC therefore requires the payor bank to send a direct notice to the depositary bank any time it decides not to pay a check in the amount of $5,000 or more. The notice must include the name and routing number of the paying bank, the name of the payee, the amount, the reason for return, the date of the indorsement of the depositary bank, the account number of the depositor, the branch where the item was first deposited, and the trace number on the item of the depositary bank, unless these matters cannot be reasonably determined from an examination of the item itself. Failure of the payor bank to send the required notice makes it liable for actual damages caused (up to the amount of the item) and, if the payor bank failed to act in good faith, for other consequential damages.

How quickly must the notice be given? Regulation CC §229.33(a), in relevant part, states: "If a paying bank determines not to pay a check in the amount of $5,500 or more, it shall provide notice of nonpayment such that the notice is received by the depositary bank by 2:00 P.M. (local time) on the second business day following the banking day on which the check was presented to the paying bank. . . ." Notice may be provided by any reasonable means, including physical return of the check, a writing (which includes a copy of the check), telephone, Fedwire, telex, or other form of telegraph.

Historically, returned checks had not been handled with any great speed, and had taken far longer to get back to the depositary bank than checks being forwarded for collection traveling the same route. Regulation CC, Subpart C, has a number of provisions designed to speed up check returns, requiring what the Regulation calls "expeditious return." Section 229.31, states that the payor bank is deemed to act expeditiously if it returns the check in such a manner that it would normally be received by the depositary bank not later than 2:00 P.M. on the second business day following the original presentment to the payor bank.

Regulation CC allows returns directly to the depositary bank (thus skipping over any intermediate collecting banks), use of a route different from the one the check traveled originally, and the sending of the check through the Federal Reserve System. The reason for the return of the check must be stamped on the check itself.

E. Charge Back

These rules about final payment apply only to the actions of the payor (drawee) bank. If that bank dishonors the check and returns it to the depositary bank, the latter will expect reimbursement from its depositor no matter how many days elapsed since the check was first deposited. The bank has three ways to justify its demand for repayment: the initial contract agreement signed when the account was opened, the indorser's obligation (§3-415), and the statutory right of charge back.

Read §4-214.

PROBLEM 198

Damon owed $500 to his friend Pythias and in payment gave him a check for that amount drawn on the Bulfinch National Bank, which Pythias deposited in his account with the Dionysius State Bank on Monday, July 8. On July 11, not having heard anything, Pythias assumed that final payment had occurred and wrote checks against the augmented balance. On July 10, the check reached the Bulfinch National Bank and was marked "NSF" and returned to Dionysius State Bank the next day. Dionysius State Bank took $500 out of Pythias' account without notice, causing several other checks of his to bounce on July 15.

(a) Can Pythias sue Dionysius State Bank under §4-402 for wrongful dishonor of these later checks? See §§4-215(d), 4-215(e)(1), 4-214; Salem Natl. Bank v. Chapman, 64 Ill. App. 3d 625, 381 N.E.2d 741 (1978).

(b) Since Dionysius State Bank has failed to give a proper charge-back notice, is it liable for the amount of the item? See §4-214(a)'s second sentence.

(c) If it had given Pythias notice of dishonor, could Dionysius State Bank have recovered the $500 even if it had let Pythias withdraw all the money from his account prior to the return of the check from the payer bank? See §4-214(d)(1).

(d) Would your answer to the first question be the same if Dionysius State were both the depositary and the payor bank? See §§4-215(e)(2), 4-302; and Regulation CC §229.10(c)(vi).

(e) If the check had been returned by Bulfinch National Bank to Dionysius State Bank on September 25, could Dionysius have still charged back? See §4-214(a)'s final sentence.[33]

(f) Assume that when the check is first returned to Dionysius, the bank does not charge it back against Pythias' account, but instead again sends the check through for re-presentment, hoping this time there will be money in the drawer's account and the check will be paid. If this hope proves fruitless and the check is returned by Bulfinch a second time, does §4-214 allow Dionysius to charge back, assuming that it does so immediately on learning of the second return? See also Leibson, Handling Re-Presented Checks—Risky Business for Collecting and Payer Banks, 72 Ky. L.J. 549 (1983-1984). Charging back when the bank has no right to do so is indeed risky business. The courts in some states have shown a willingness to impose punitive damages for wrongful charge back. See Gordon v. Planters & Merchants Bancshares, Inc., 326 Ark. 1046, 935 S.W.2d 544 (1996).

All across the United States phony cashier's checks are causing major nightmares. Often the victims of these schemes are law firms (as in the Problem that follows). Cashier's checks (which bankers sometimes call "official checks"), with a bank as primarily liable, seem like a solid form of payment, and indeed they are—as long as they are not complete forgeries created by some villain and sent to the victim of a scam. Lawyers have often been unable to shift the loss to their depositary banks. See, e.g., Law Offices of Oliver Zhou v. Citibank N.A., 2017 U.S. Dist. LEXIS 35307 (S.D.N.Y. 2017); Sarrouf Law, LLP v. First Republic Bank, 35 Mass. L. Rep. 258 (2018). So many law firms have fallen for such ruses that alerts have been issued by bar associations; see Internet Scams Targeting Attorneys, State Bar of California Ethics Hotline (Jan. 2011). In addition to the loss of money (sometimes enough to sink the law firm completely), such an incident could be a violation of an attorney's duty with respect to the client trust account. See Clark

33. The rule here is actually simpler than it looks. Charge back is allowed only for provisional settlements. If the payor bank made final payment on a check, all the provisional settlements "firmed up" and became final. Charge back is not allowed to undo final settlements, and §4-214(a)'s final sentence states such a rule. When the payor bank tries to undo final payment by making a late return, the depositary bank should not accept the check back, since it has lost its right of charge back. How does the depositary bank (or any collecting bank) know whether the payor bank has made timely return? It doesn't, and in all but the rarest situation will assume that the payor bank has acted properly so that the depositary bank's right of charge back still exists. If that assumption is wrong—the payor bank did make a late return—Regulation CC §229.34 creates a warranty of timely return by the payor bank, which, having been breached, provides the needed remedy to the depositary bank.

H.C. Lacy, The Witch's Brew: Nigerian Schemes, Counterfeit Cashier's Checks, and Your Trust Account, 61 S.C. L. Rev. 753, 755 (2010).

PROBLEM 199

Samwell Tarly had a vibrant law practice in Columbus, Ohio, specializing in sports law. One morning in May of 2019 the phone rang and on the other end was Jaime Lannister, a famous wealthy California businessman who Tarly had never met but whom he knew about from the Internet and various TV appearances. Lannister told Tarly that he was negotiating to buy a newly formed professional baseball team in South Korea called "The Hodors" and wanted Tarly to handle the final purchase arrangements. The contract had already been signed and Lannister said he would forward it as well as other information about the deal (which had been reported on the Internet). He wanted Tarly to contact Khal Drogo, current Korean owner of "The Hodors," and make final arrangements to pay $12 million to Drogo immediately.

Tarly was thrilled to learn all this and he talked on the phone about the deal with Lannister for an hour. They also arranged for a legal fee to be sent by Lannister to Tarly in the amount of $20,000. Lannister explained he would send Tarly a cashier's check for $12,020,000 the next day, with the understanding that Tarly would contact Drogo in South Korea and set up a wire transfer of the money to a bank of Drogo's choosing. Tarly provided Lannister with the email address of his law firm, and Lannister immediately sent him an email with massive amounts of attachments describing the deal and explaining the professional history of "The Hodors" (there was a video about the team) and the life of Khal Drogo (another video), as well as the latter's contact information.

Tarly immediately phoned Drogo, reaching his office in Seoul, and after a couple of interoffice transfers getting the man himself on the phone. Drogo confirmed all that Lannister had said about the pending sale, and provided Tarly with the name of his bank in Korea, Rickon Chartered Bank [RCB] located in Seoul, along with an account number in the bank to which the wire transfer should be made [account #666000123]. The name on the RCB account was "Khal Drogo."

The next day Lannister's $12,020,000 cashier's check, made payable to the order of "Samwell Tarly," drawn on and by Boltan National Bank, located in Los Angeles, arrived via Federal Express at Tarly's office. Tarly walked the check down to his own bank, Octopus National Bank [ONB] in Columbus. He asked to speak to the bank manager, Bran Stark, and told Mr. Stark all about the deal. Stark helped him deposit the cashier's check in his account, and when Tarly asked how long it would take to clear, Stark replied that "cashier's checks are self-clearing and the money is available now." "I shouldn't worry at all?" Tarly asked, adding, "I will have to part with a lot of that money and

I won't do that if there is any chance that this check has problems." *"Don't worry about a thing,"* Stark replied, putting his hand on Tarly's shoulder.

Thus reassured, Tarly immediately arranged with Stark to have the $12 million wired from his account to Khal Drogo, Rickon Chartered Bank in Seoul, account #666000123.

The wire transfer for $12 million went out that afternoon, May 2, and arrived in South Korea at Rickon Chartered Bank within minutes; $12 million was deposited in Khal Drogo's account, #666000123, within an hour of the receipt thereof.

On the morning of May 3, Boltan National Bank of Los Angeles sent a message to ONB in Columbus stating it was returning the $12,020,000 cashier's check, which was "phony." Boltan National Bank had written no such check and therefore refused to honor it. The bank had made no provisional settlement for the item and had returned it within all time limits. ONB immediately took the money out of Tarly's account. When he protested, citing the conversation with the bank manager, the bank's lawyer stated that that conversation had presumed it was a real cashier's check being deposited and not a phony one.

ONB did try to recover the wire transfer, but immediately learned that the money had already been withdrawn from the Korean bank, RCB, and no one there seemed to be able to find any actual person named "Khal Drogo." The manager of RCB commented that "Khal Drogo" is not even a Korean name. No one at RCB could remember any details about the opening of this account other than it had occurred one month ago.

The real Jaime Lannister denied having ever been interested in purchasing a Korean baseball team ("I didn't know they played professional baseball in Korea," he said). He told Tarly, "Sorry, guy, but you fell for a scam." All the information in the email attachments that had been sent to Tarly were very cleverly created bogus documents and videos. There was no Hodors baseball team in Korea.

Tarly sued his own bank, ONB for reversing the credit in his account. How does this come out? See Greenberg, Trager & Herbst, LLP v. HSBC Bank USA, 17 N.Y.3d 565, 958 N.E.2d 77 (2011). How can someone receiving a cashier's check be sure it will not come bouncing back in this same horrific way? What should Tarly have done?

Valley Bank of Ronan v. Hughes

Supreme Court of Montana, 2006

334 Mont. 335, 147 P.3d 185

Justice JIM RICE delivered the Opinion of the Court.

¶1 Charles R. Hughes (Hughes) appeals the orders entered in the Twentieth Judicial District Court, Lake County, granting summary judgment to Valley Bank of Ronan (Valley Bank) and granting Valley Bank's motion in limine to exclude the testimony of Hughes' expert witness. We affirm in part, reverse in part, and remand for further proceedings.

¶2 The following issues are dispositive on appeal:

¶3 Did the District Court err by granting summary judgment against Hughes on his counterclaims?

¶4 Did the District Court err by granting summary judgment to Valley Bank on Hughes' promissory note?

¶5 Did the District Court abuse its discretion by excluding the testimony of Hughes' banking expert, Cynthia Shea? . . .

BACKGROUND

¶7 Lured by the promise of quick wealth, Hughes was conned by a "Nigerian scam." The swindlers promised Hughes a $3 million to $4.5 million commission for his aid in procuring agricultural equipment for import into Africa and then proceeded to bilk him for hundreds of thousands of dollars in advanced fees. At least some of the funds Hughes advanced were wired via the services of Valley Bank, resulting in a dispute over which party should bear the loss from the flimflam.

¶8 On Friday, March 22, 2002, Hughes received four checks from one of the con-artists and deposited them into accounts Hughes held at Valley Bank. Two of them were "official" checks, and the other two were personal checks. One official check, for $1 million, was drawn on Colonial Bank. The other official check, for $500,000, was drawn on Firstar. The personal checks were for $62,000—drawn on the account of Maximilian H. Miltzlaff—and for $70,000—drawn on a Capital One credit card account held by Sarah Briscoe and Mary Bullard.

¶9 Prior to depositing the checks, Hughes requested that Nancy Smith, a cashier and officer of Valley Bank, verify the validity of the official checks. In his deposition, Hughes described his conversation with Smith:

> Well, my question was, how long do you have to hold money to have—how long do you have to hold these checks before they're sufficient funds; I think the bank calls them collected funds. And she said, these are official checks, Chuck. These two big ones are official checks. You will be transferring these? And I said I will be transferring a large sum. We'll have to determine next week what it will be. And she says, official checks, same as cash. You can do whatever you want to do.

Smith also assured Hughes that official checks were "just like" cashier's checks. Milanna Shear, another bank employee, told Hughes to believe whatever Smith said regarding the validity of the checks. According to the deposition testimony of Hughes' wife, Barbara, Hughes had told her that "everybody at the bank assured him that the checks would be good."

¶10 On Tuesday, March 26, 2002, Hughes delivered a written request to Valley Bank to wire $800,000 to Alidh Abbas, an accountholder at the Housing Bank for Trade and Finance in Amman, Jordan. Valley Bank executed the transfer no later than 1:51 P.M. on the same day. The transfer proceeded through two intermediary banks, Wells Fargo, near Denver, Colorado, and Citibank in New York, before being sent to Amman. Upon receipt in Amman, the funds were promptly withdrawn, never to be seen again.

¶11 At about 2:00 P.M.—approximately ten minutes after initiation of the transfer—Valley Bank and Hughes learned that one of the personal checks was being returned marked "nonsufficient funds." Hughes immediately requested the wire to be stopped. No later than 3:26 P.M. Valley Bank requested that Wells Fargo reverse the wire transfer. The record is unclear about what happened during the interim between Hughes' request for cancellation and Valley Bank's attempts to comply with the request. The efforts of the several banks involved in the transfer to reverse the transaction were unsuccessful, and the later discovery that the two official checks were counterfeit resulted in Hughes' account being overdrawn by $800,000.

¶12 Valley Bank subsequently exercised its right to charge back the account and collect the $800,000 from Hughes. Allen Buhr (Buhr), Valley Bank's president, met with Hughes on March 29, 2002, to discuss Hughes' liability and suggested at that time that Hughes could be involved in a criminal prosecution for fraud. On April 11, 2002, Hughes deposited $607,838, which he had withdrawn from his retirement account, into the Valley Bank account. Also, on April 30, 2002, Hughes executed a promissory note to Valley Bank on behalf of his trust in the amount of $400,000, secured by mortgaged property. Of the $400,000 in proceeds generated by the secured note, $202,751.21 was used to pay off a previous loan against the mortgaged property, and the balance, $197,248.79, was applied to satisfy the charge-back liability in Hughes' account. Hughes was under the impression, given by Buhr, that the bank needed the note and loan agreement because it expected to be the subject of a government audit in the near future, and though Hughes thought that a new agreement might be reached after resolution of the "fraud situation," he understood that the loan may not be forgiven. The trust subsequently made the first interest payment on the note on August 1, 2002, though it was one month late. The trust made no other payments on the note, and Valley Bank sent a notice of default and acceleration on October 15, 2002. Hughes requested that the bank forebear foreclosure until the end of the year, and the bank complied. However, when Hughes failed to make any more payments on the note, Valley Bank initiated an action for judicial foreclosure. Hughes asserted counterclaims of negligence, negligent misrepresentation, constructive fraud, unjust enrichment, breach of contract, breach of the implied covenant of good faith and fair dealing, promissory estoppel, and intentional infliction of emotional distress (which was later abandoned).

¶13 On April 15, 2005, the District Court granted Valley Bank's motion in limine to exclude Cynthia Shea as an expert witness for Hughes. In an order dated April 20, 2005, the District Court granted Valley Bank summary judgment on Hughes' counterclaims. On the same day, the District Court granted Valley Bank summary judgment on its claims regarding the promissory note. From these orders Hughes appeals. . . .

Discussion

¶17 A short introduction to the check settlement process will give context to our following legal analysis. When a customer deposits a check at a bank, the bank will sometimes (but not always) credit the customer's account immediately with the face amount of the check and permit the customer to draw on the deposited funds. This practice is known in Uniform Commercial Code parlance as "provisional settlement" because the bank has not yet presented the check to the drawee bank and received payment from the check maker's account (which would constitute "final settlement"). The depositary bank, however, may "charge back" the depositor's account in the event the check is subsequently dishonored by the drawee bank. Thus, the UCC encourages the provisional settlement process by protecting a depositary bank from fraudulent or otherwise unenforceable check deposits. With this overview of the check settlement process in mind, we turn now to the specifics of the case before us.

¶18 Did the District Court err by granting summary judgment against Hughes on his counterclaims?

UCC Preemption and Ordinary Care

¶19 Hughes argues that the District Court erroneously concluded that the UCC preempts Hughes' equitable and common law claims. Hughes asserts that preemption does not occur because "[t]here are no regulations or UCC provisions which expressly regulate . . . promises and representations that bank personnel make to their customers." Further, Hughes contends that the "practical effect of the District Court's interpretation affords banks absolute immunity for negligence, fraud, misrepresentation and other acts which are not expressly addressed in the UCC. . . ."

¶20 The District Court rested its conclusion on its interpretation of §30-1-103, MCA, which reads as follows:

> Unless displaced by the particular provisions of this code, the principles of law and equity, including the law merchant and the law relative to capacity to contract, principal and agent, estoppel, fraud, misrepresentation, duress,

> coercion, mistake, bankruptcy, or other validating or invalidating cause shall supplement its provisions.

The District Court stated that the "official comments to UCC §1-103 show that preemption of common law and equitable claims is one purpose of the . . . statute. . . ." The official comment to which the District Court referred clarifies that

> while principles of common law and equity may supplement provisions of the Uniform Commercial Code, they may not be used to supplant its provisions, or the purposes and policies those provisions reflect, unless a specific provision of the Uniform Commercial Code provides otherwise. In the absence of such a provision, the Uniform Commercial Code preempts principles of common law and equity that are inconsistent with either its provisions or its purposes and policies.
>
> The language of subsection (b) is intended to reflect both the concept of supplementation and the concept of preemption.

UCC §1-103, cmt. 2. The District Court also concluded that three cases from other jurisdictions, Chase v. Morgan Guarantee Trust Co., 590 F. Supp. 1137 (S.D.N.Y. 1984), Allen v. Carver Federal Sav. and Loan Ass'n, 123 Misc. 2d 704, 477 N.Y.S.2d 537 (N.Y. App. Div. 1984), and Call v. Ellenville Nat. Bank, 5 A.D.3d 521, 774 N.Y.S.2d 76 (N.Y. App. Div. 2004), "support preemption of equitable and common law claims under the applicable UCC provisions and facts of this case."

¶21 We disagree with the District Court's interpretation of §30-1-103, MCA, and of *Chase*, *Allen*, and *Call*. A bank receiving checks from depositors must use "ordinary care"—as that term is defined and used in the UCC—in settling those checks. See §§30-4-103(3), 30-4-103(5), and 30-4-212, MCA. FN3 Section 30-3-102(1)(g), MCA, defines "ordinary care" as follows:

> "Ordinary care" in the case of a person engaged in business means observance of reasonable commercial standards, prevailing in the area in which that person is located, with respect to the business in which that person is engaged. In the case of a bank that takes an instrument for processing for collection or payment by automated means, reasonable commercial standards do not require the bank to examine the instrument if the failure to examine does not violate the bank's prescribed procedures and the bank's procedures do not vary unreasonably from general banking usage not disapproved by this chapter or chapter 4.

In its order, the District Court examined the meaning of "ordinary care" but did not distinguish the term's application to the two different actions at issue here: the settlement of the deposited checks and the alleged representations about the check settlement process. The second sentence of the definition of ordinary care specifically states that, subject to certain exceptions, a bank does not have a duty to examine instruments, in this case, checks. Pursuant to §30-1-103, MCA, and UCC §1-103, cmt. 2, such specificity preempts any common law concepts that might otherwise supplement the UCC. Thus, to the extent that Hughes' common law claims relate to Valley Bank's processing of the checks, they are preempted by the UCC.

¶22 Indeed, Hughes presents a claim directed toward the UCC-defined standard of ordinary care with respect to check processing. Hughes asserts that, by failing to comply with its own policies and the applicable federal regulations, Valley Bank inappropriately charged back his account after the dishonor of the deposited checks. However, §4-214(d), MCA, states, "[t]he right to charge back is not affected by . . . failure by any bank to exercise ordinary care with respect to the item but any bank so failing remains liable." Official Comment 5 to §30-4-214(d), MCA, expounds on this point, stating that "charge-back is permitted *even where nonpayment results from the depositary bank's own negligence.*" (Emphasis added.) Accordingly, in evaluating the propriety of Valley Bank's actions with regard to check processing, it is irrelevant whether Valley Bank exercised ordinary care in exercising its charge back rights, and the claims are preempted.

¶23 However, Hughes' claims encompass not only Valley Bank's processing of the checks but also the bank's communications to Hughes about that process. Because such communications are not addressed with specificity by the UCC, common law and equitable principles supplement the UCC and govern the legal rights and responsibilities that apply to Valley Bank's representations to Hughes, upon which Hughes allegedly relied. See §30-1-103, MCA; First Georgia Bank v. Webster, 168 Ga. App. 307, 308 S.E.2d 579, 581 (1983) (UCC does not provide relief from common law negligence; thus, common law actions are permissible.); see also Henry J. Bailey & Richard B. Hagedorn, Brady on Bank Checks ¶24.05 n.84 (8th ed. 1999). Thus, the District Court erred by concluding that the UCC preempted common law and equitable principles with respect to the alleged misrepresentations. Therefore, while Hughes bore the obligation to repay Valley Bank to satisfy the bank's right of charge-back under §30-4-214, MCA, it nevertheless is possible for Hughes to obtain a judgment to compensate him for the charge-back debt, though we express no opinion on the ultimate merits of these common law claims in this case. . . .

¶24 Although holding in favor the bank in each case, *Chase, Allen,* and *Call* do not support preemption with regard to Valley Bank's alleged misrepresentations. Rather, there is support within these decisions for this Court's determination that common law principles apply to bank communications to a depositor inquiring about the processing of checks. In each of these cases, the bank exercised its right of charge-back under UCC §4-214 and the plaintiff depositor alleged either that the bank had informed him that the deposited check had "cleared" or that the bank had led him to believe that it would clear in a certain amount of time.

¶25 The *Chase* court expressly acknowledged the possibility that common law principles could apply to the type of communications at issue here:

> [B]anks have nothing to gain by misleading customers into believing that uncleared items have cleared. Indeed, banks are usually overly cautious in giving provisional credit precisely because of the uncertainty of uncollected items. A bank could be liable for a misstatement in these general circumstances if the misstatement were part of a scheme to defraud a customer in Chase's position by, for example, a conspiracy between the bank and the party to whom Chase transferred the funds. This of course is merely one example. As discussed supra, however, [UCC] §4-214(d) simply does not hold liable for charge-back a bank whose employee inadvertently in some remark misleads a customer as to the precise likelihood that an item will clear.
>
> *The outcome might be different if a bank expressly informed a customer that it had made a final settlement on the account, but that is not the case here.*

Chase, 590 F. Supp. at 1139 n.3 (emphasis added).

¶26 The court in *Allen* also acknowledged the potential for common law liability in this context:

> We are dubious that the mere statement of a depositor that an unidentified teller told her (mistakenly) that a check had "cleared," when in fact it had not, constitutes that quantum of proof of negligence which will enable a customer to prevail against the bank under the circumstances disclosed here.

Allen, 477 N.Y.S.2d at 538. Though the *Allen* court did not distinguish the bank's duties in processing the check at issue from its duties in its communications to its depositor about that process, the language employed in the opinion suggests that some "quantum of proof" would be sufficient "to prevail against the bank" on common law claims in different circumstances.

¶27 Similarly, in *Call,* the court indicated that the "term 'cleared' . . . is not the equivalent of 'final settlement' "[34] and that, "although Mr. Call apparently assumed such, *he did not allege that this was a result of any inquiry*

34. Though it does not affect our analysis here, we pause to express bewilderment at this statement of the *Call* court. If the term "cleared" means anything in common banking usage, it is that final settlement has occurred. See Black's Law Dictionary (7th ed., 1999) (defining "clear" as "to pay (a check or draft) out of funds held on behalf of the maker 'the bank cleared the employee's check' "); see also §30-4-104(1)(j), MCA (defining "settle"), and Southside Nat. Bank v. Hepp, 739 S.W.2d 720, 723 (Mo. 1987) (final settlement occurs when "the payor bank has paid the item").

with or representation to that effect by the defendant bank." *Call*, 774 N.Y.S.2d at 79 (emphasis added). Thus, the court, though not squarely addressing the issue, left open the possibility that a bank's misrepresentation of the status of the check settlement process could lead to liability for the bank.

¶28 In each of the above cases, the defendant bank was granted summary judgment because the plaintiff depositor failed to allege facts sufficient to impute liability to the bank. However, though the bank prevailed in each case, the analyses do not support the proposition that common law and equitable principles have been preempted by the UCC. Instead, they intimate that, in certain circumstances, common law and equitable principles may supplement the UCC where the bank—though not violating its UCC-defined duty of ordinary care with respect to processing checks—breaches a duty to its depositor by misrepresenting the status of the check settlement process.

¶29 In summary, the District Court correctly determined that Valley Bank did not violate the UCC-defined duty of ordinary care in processing the checks. However, the District Court erred by failing to consider whether common law and equitable principles supplement the UCC-defined duty of ordinary care with respect to the representations about the check settlement process. Therefore, we reverse the District Court's order and remand for further proceedings on the matter. . . .

¶49 Affirmed in part, reversed in part, and remanded for further proceedings.

PROBLEM 200

Attorney Alice Practice had heard about scams in which attorneys are sent forged cashier's checks by supposedly real new clients with impressive credentials and websites, etc. When she agreed to take in payment for her services a large cashier's check that also included the settlement of the legal matter at hand, with the understanding she would deposit it to her bank account and then wire the excess of the amount over her fee to a bank nominated by her client, she was worried about doing this. When she deposited the large cashier's check she had a conversation with the bank manager in which he assured her that the wire transfer would not be made until her account was credited with funds collected from the drawee bank that had issued the cashier's check. "Don't send *my* money—send *theirs*," was her instruction, and the manager agreed. Nonetheless her bank wired the money before actually getting the funds from the drawee bank. When that bank informed her bank that the check was a forgery and returned the phony check, her bank demanded she reimburse them for the full amount of the wire transfer. How should this come out? See Cadence Bank v. Elizondo, 2020 WL 1150126 (Tex. App. 2019).

Such bogus check scams have been sent not just to businesses like law firms, but also individuals, such as students. A cashier's check may be sent as payment for an online sale, asking the student seller to deposit the check, which is larger than the expected amount, retain the sale price, and then send the "extra" money back to the seller as a wire transfer. The transfer goes through but the original check bounces, leaving the student with a huge debit to his/her bank account. Forged checks have also been sent as part of offers of employment. See Ann Carrns, Got an Unexpected Check in the Mail? It May Be Fake, N.Y. Times (Feb. 21, 2020). As the Federal Trade Commission warns, "If someone you don't know sends you a check and asks for money back, that's a scam." Id.

PROBLEM 201

When landlord Simon Mustache received a $5,400 check from his shady tenant John Weeks, who was always behind on the rent but finally produced this large check to make up his arrears, Simon deposited it immediately in his account at Last National Bank (LNB), which gave him a provisional credit for the amount. Two days later, fearful that the check would bounce, Simon phoned LNB and was told that the check had cleared, at which point Simon withdrew the money. Later that same day, the check was returned by the payor bank marked "NSF" ("Not Sufficient Funds"). The payor bank had returned the check within all required deadlines, so LNB demanded that Simon refund the amount of the check, claiming a right to charge back the amount of the check per §4-214. Simon refused, saying that the bank had assured him the check had cleared, a statement that he had relied upon, and that the bank's failure to exercise ordinary care in this regard made it liable for his damages per §4-103(e). LNB replied that since the check was worthless at all moments, Simon has *no* damages at all. How does this come out? See Wells Fargo Bank, N.A. v. FSI, Financial Solutions, Inc., 196 Cal. App. 4th 1559, 127 Cal. Rptr. 3d 589 (2011).

F. Undoing Final Payment

While UCC rights *off* the instrument (such as the right to sue for breach of the presentment warranties) survive final payment, the instrument itself is canceled by final payment, thus ending all Article 3 suits on the implied obligations created there, and the payor bank, now itself *accountable* for the check, must pay over the check's amount to the presenter. One issue that refuses to go away is whether the payor bank may resist payment, using common law theories such as mistake.

PROBLEM 202

Sandra Shirker and Frank Foxholer, two evil commercial law students, learned about the Midnight Deadline Statutes and decided to see if they could use them to create money out of thin air. Shirker, who had a checking account at the Busy National Bank, withdrew all the money in the account and, by agreement with the bank, closed it. She then wrote a $5,000 check on the account payable to Foxholer, who deposited the check in his own bank account with a different bank. At the same time, Shirker called up her old bank and talked to the vice president in charge of check payment. Shirker told him that a $5,000 check would be presented against the closed-out account but that there was "something funny" about it and Shirker would appreciate it if the vice president would call her when it came in. The vice president did so when the check came in late in the banking day, and Shirker told him that it was important that they meet. Shirker promised to come down to the bank the next day.

The following morning Shirker called the bank and said that she was delayed but was still coming and the vice president should wait. Shirker never showed up and eventually the vice president went home. On the second banking day following receipt, the Busy National Bank marked the check "Account closed" and returned it to the depositary-presenting bank, which passed it on to Foxholer, the payee. Foxholer sued the payor bank, claiming final payment had been made under §4-215(a)(3) in that the provisional settlement had not been revoked within the time allowed by §4-301, so the bank was accountable for the check under §4-302(a). Assume that Foxholer has not breached one of the §4-208 presentment warranties. All right-thinking people would agree that Foxholer should lose this suit; the only question is as to what defense the Code permits. Read §§4-302(b) and 3-418; cf. §1-304.

PROBLEM 203

When the police department of Rome, Wisconsin, opened the box of new police radios it had ordered, it was dismayed to learn that the radios were not the correct size specified in the contract. Since the police department had already sent a check, in payment to Voice of Japan, Inc., the seller, it immediately stopped payment on the check by so notifying its bank, Kelly

National Bank. Negligently, Kelly National paid the check, and, when the police department complained that the check was not properly payable, recredited the account. You are the counsel for the bank, and the head of Checking Services calls you wanting to know whether the bank can recover the amount of the check from Voice of Japan. Look at §3-418 and its Official Comment, and give your answer. Might subrogation to the police department's warranty rights also be useful to the bank? See §4-407(3).

If the bank is successful in its restitution action against Voice of Japan, the latter is entitled to get the check back for use in its dispute with the police department. Even if the check is unavailable (it has been destroyed en route by a check truncation system or was returned to the drawer, who refuses to surrender it), §§3-418(d) and 3-301(iii) give Voice of Japan the status of a "person entitled to enforce the instrument" so as to enable Voice of Japan to sue the police department on the §3-414(b) obligation of the drawer of a draft (which runs to a "person entitled to enforce the draft"). Of course, when the §3-414(b) suit is brought, the police department may raise its breach of warranty defense (Voice of Japan is not a holder in due course), which, if valid, would enable it to prevail.

G. *Delays*

Back to bank collection—and the following true story.

PROBLEM 204

In the early 1970s, a Boise, Idaho, bank's janitor mistakenly placed a box full of 8,000 unprocessed checks on a table reserved for trash. The operator of the bank's paper shredder dutifully fed the checks into his machine, turning them into quarter-inch strips. About $840,000 worth of checks underwent this ordeal. The next morning the error was discovered, and the bank hired 50 temporary employees to work six hours a day for two months to paste the checks back together (puzzle lovers were particularly welcome). At the moment of the shredding, many of the checks involved were bound to be in the process of collection. For some of the checks, the bank would be a depositary or collecting bank, and for others it would be the payer-drawee. Collecting banks are required to take action before their midnight deadline following receipt, §4-202(b), and, of course, the payor bank becomes absolutely accountable for a check not returned before the expiration of the midnight deadline. §§4-215(a)(3), 4-301, 4-302. Should the Boise bank just close down, or is there hope in §4-109(b) (delays)? See Port City State Bank v. American Natl. Bank, 486 F.2d 196 (10th Cir. 1973) (computer crash); Sun River Cattle Co. v. Miners Bank, 164 Mont. 237, 521 P.2d 679 (1974) (armored car broke down). Regulation CC §229.13(f) has a similar exemption for emergency conditions.

H. Restrictive Indorsements and Banks

Section 4-203 establishes the rule that only the collecting bank's transferor can give it binding instructions and the collecting bank need not examine the item to see whether other instructions or restrictions are contained in it. This is the *chain of command* theory of bank collection. See the Official Comment to §4-203.

PROBLEM 205

Nina Needy received her state welfare check and immediately made the following indorsement:

For deposit only
/s/Nina Needy

On her way to the bank, her purse was snatched by Max Runner, who escaped and then examined the purse's contents.

He found the check and wrote his own name below that of Nina. Max then took the check to his bank, Pursesnatchers National, and had the bank cash it. Pursesnatchers National stamped its indorsement on the check and forwarded it to the Innocent State Bank, which also indorsed the check and presented it to the drawee, the Welfare Payor Bank, which held the check past its midnight deadline. In the meantime, Nina Needy reported her loss to the state (the check's drawer), but by the time the state investigated the matter, the check had been paid. Nina consulted a lawyer. Can she sue the depositary, collecting, and drawee banks in conversion, arguing that by paying in violation of her express instruction (the restrictive indorsement "for deposit only"), the banks converted her check? Or can the banks use the chain of command sections cited above to escape liability? See §3-206(c).

People sometimes place restrictive language above their signatures, and the effect of this is to create a *restrictive indorsement*. Read §3-206. A famous case, similar in its facts to the above Problem, Soma v. Handrulis, 277 N.Y. 233, 14 N.E.2d 46 (1938), held that all three banks (depositary, intermediary, and payor) had *converted* the check by paying it in obvious violation of a restrictive indorsement. The country's bankers were horrified by the decision; they knew that, as a practical matter, it is impossible for the banks involved in the check collection process to take the time to read and investigate all the restrictive indorsements on the backs of instruments. The Code's solution is stated first in §3-206(c): Of the banks involved, *only the depositary bank* faces liability for non-compliance with the terms of a restrictive indorsement. Only at the depositary bank is the check likely to be examined by a human being (the teller). The computers that process the check thereafter cannot even read the restrictive indorsements. Read §3-206; see C & L Const. Co., Inc. v. BB & T Corp., 2005 WL 2792401 (S.D. W. Va. 2005).

I. Priorities in the Bank Account: The Four Legals

The final bank collection problem we have left is the question of priority: What gets paid first? Bankers must constantly deal with four events—notice (for instance, of a depositor's death), stop-payment orders, service of legal process (garnishment, etc.), and the bank's right of setoff—and decide whether the happening of one of these events, which bankers call *the four legals*, has priority over the payment of a check. The issue is now resolved by §4-303(a), which states in essence that the four legal events come too late, as to any given check, if that check has either been certified or the bank has taken the steps that lead to final payment of the check. Further, the four legal events are too late if they arrive after the time periods described in (a)(5). Read §4-303(a) and consider these matters.

PROBLEM 206

Joseph Armstrong had $4,000 in his checking account with the Antitrust National Bank on the afternoon of October 5 at the moment when he filed a voluntary petition in bankruptcy with the local federal district court. Early in the morning of October 6, the bank received three checks drawn on the account. One for $1,000 was presented in person by the payee and paid over the counter. Another for $500, which had been presented by another bank, was posted against the account, marked "Paid," and placed in the drawer's statement file. A third, which had also been presented by another bank on October 6, was for $3,000, and the bank was unsure what to do with it, so it placed it in a "hold pending consultation with drawer" file. At noon, Armstrong ran into Vivian Visor, the bank's head teller, while eating in the same restaurant, and since they were friends, Armstrong told Visor that the day before he had filed the bankruptcy petition. Visor expressed sympathy. At 1 P.M., just as Visor walked back into the bank, another teller made an over-the-counter payment of $500 on a fourth check. At 2 P.M., the bankruptcy trustee phoned the bank and made a formal demand that the bank freeze the account. On receiving this notice, Robert Startup, a bank vice president, checked the bank's records, found that Armstrong owed the bank $75 on a home improvement loan, and told the bank clerk to deduct this amount from Armstrong's account. Subsequently, the bank reported to the trustee that the account contained $1,925, as follows:

Oct. 5	$4,000
Oct. 6	
First Check	–1,000
	3,000
Second Check	–500
	2,500
Fourth Check	–500
	2,000
Home Improvement Loan	–75
	$1,925

The third check was marked "Not Sufficient Funds" and was returned to the presenting bank on the morning of October 10.

Consider these issues:

(a) Can the trustee in bankruptcy claim that the filing of a voluntary petition in bankruptcy on October 5 automatically froze the account of $4,000 so that the bank owes the bankruptcy estate that amount? Per §542(c) of the Bankruptcy Code the answer is no. The bank is protected as to all transfers made from the account until it had notice of the bankruptcy proceeding, although the trustee can usually recover the money from the payee per Bankruptcy Code §549(a).

(b) At what moment did the bank have notice of the bankruptcy: When Armstrong told Visor, when Visor returned to the bank, or when the phone call was received? The answer to this question will determine the validity of the payment of the fourth check. See UCC §1-202.

(c) Was the home improvement loan payment effective against the trustee? See Bankruptcy Code §553 (setoff permitted on getting relief from the automatic stay of §362(a)(7)).

(d) If you are the attorney representing the bank that presented the third check, what legal theory, if any, might attract your attention?

PROBLEM 207

The newly established Embryo State Bank hires you as counsel to the bank. After a month's operations, the bank calls you up with the following dilemma. One of its customers is Thomas Crandall, whose account currently contains $5,000. This morning, at 9:00 A.M., the bank received a bundle of checks from the bank across the street, and the bundle contained five checks drawn against Crandall's account payable to different payees and totaling $1,258. At 9:05 A.M., the bank received a bundle of checks from the nearest Federal Reserve Bank, and this bundle contained one check drawn on Crandall's account for $4,986. The dilemma: Should the bank dishonor the one big check or the five little ones? Three of the little checks are dated prior to the big check and two after. The bank is afraid that if it dishonors the big one, Crandall will quickly be sued by a major creditor. On the other hand, if it dishonors the little ones, five creditors, not just one, will think Crandall is a bum. The bank is afraid it will face §4-402 damages for wrongful dishonor. Without looking at the Code, what would you advise the bank to do? Now look at §4-303(b) and its Official Comment 7. Almost all courts considering the issue have looked at this same Comment and concluded that banks have clear authority to do as they like here, even if it results in high overdraft fees for customers; see Northampton Restaurant Group, Inc. v. FirstMerit Bank, N.A., 2012 WL 2608807 (6th Cir. 2012). There have been a number of cases attacking "high-to-low" payments in *debit card* transactions (ATMs), arguing unconscionability, to which the courts seem receptive; see, e.g., In re Checking Account Overdraft Litigation, 694 F. Supp. 2d 1302 (S.D. Fla. 2010). The Consumer Financial Protection Bureau, created by Congress in 2010, has contemplated issuing a regulation forbidding the practice, perhaps disallowing "high-to-low" payments for both check processing as well as ATM transactions, but at this writing no such regulation has been promulgated.

CHAPTER 13 ASSESSMENT: MULTIPLE CHOICE QUESTIONS

1. Okonkwo Technology issued a check to a supplier, Nwoye Semiconductor, for six-month's supply of computer chips. There was plenty of money in Okonkwo Technology's account at Careful Bank to cover the check. Careful Bank was a little nervous, however, because Okonkwo Technology owed a lot on its line of credit with the bank and was facing difficult market conditions. When Nwoye Semiconductor presented the check for payment, Careful Bank refused to pay, to conserve the money in the account. For the lack of these funds, Nwoye Semiconductor missed its monthly equipment loan payment, resulting in repossession of some key

fabrication machines and loss of revenue. Is Careful Bank liable to Nwoye Semiconductor?

a. No. Careful Bank had no obligation to Nwoye Semiconductor to pay the check, because Careful Bank did not sign the check.
b. No. Careful Bank had no obligation to anyone to pay the check.
c. Yes. Careful Bank is liable to Nwoye Semiconductor for all losses proximately caused by its wrongful dishonor.
d. Yes. Careful Bank is liable to Nwoye Semiconductor for the amount of the check.

2. On the facts of the last question, is Careful Bank liable to Okonkwo Technology?
   a. Yes. Careful Bank is liable to Okonkwo Technology for the amount of the check.
   b. No. Careful Bank held on to Okonkwo Technology's money, so it could not have caused any loss.
   c. Yes. Careful Bank is liable to Okonkwo Technology for Okonkwo's damages, if any, proximately caused by the wrongful dishonor.
   d. No. Careful Bank had no obligation to pay the check, because it did not sign the check.

3. Coyote wrote a check to Loman, happily receiving the motorcycle the two agreed upon. Coyote still tried to wriggle out of payment by issuing a stop order payment to his bank, Careless Bank, specifically identifying the check. Careless Bank absent-mindedly paid the check when presented. Is Coyote liable to Careless Bank?
   a. No. The check was not properly payable, because a stop payment order was in effect.
   b. No. Careless Bank is not entitled to payment, Loman is.
   c. Yes. A bank that pays a check is always entitled to reimbursement from its customer.
   d. Yes. The check was not properly payable, but Careless Bank may use subrogation to collect from Coyote.

4. Careless Bank's accounting books stated that Leachman has not paid her last year's mortgage payments. When Careless Bank sued Leachman, she defended by bringing her last year's bank statements from her account at Accurate Bank, which had copies of all the checks. The copies meet the requirements of Check 21. Careless Bank argued that the judge should not accept the copies, because only the original checks would be reliable evidence of payment. Should the judge accept copies of checks as evidence of payment?
   a. No. Anyone could Photoshop a plausible image of a check.
   b. No. As with promissory notes, a copy is no substitute for the original.

c. Yes. A substitute check under Check 21 is the legal equivalent of the original check.
d. Yes. Banks should afford each other professional courtesy.

5. Nyong'o decided to sell her acting trophy on Craigslist. She received an offer of $1,000 from one Maximilian. The next day, she received a letter from Maximilian with a cashier's check apparently issued by Reputable Bank, payable to Maximilian, for $3,000. She soon got a message from Maximilian: "Please cash the check, keep $1,000, wire me the other $2,000 and send the trophy. I trust you." She took the check to her bank, Careless Bank, who gave her $3,000 cash over the counter. She wired $2,000 to Maximilian, sent the trophy, and spent some of the $1,000 to treat her family to dinner. Ten days later, she saw that her bank had subtracted $3,000 from her account, leaving an overdraft. Checking her account online, she saw a notation that the cashier's check was not paid and her bank had taken back the $3,000 it gave her. Did Careless Bank have the right to do that?
   a. No. Careless Bank paid the check over the counter and is bound.
   b. No. Careless Bank should not have given her the funds until there was assurance that the cashier's check would be paid.
   c. Yes. Careless Bank, as a depositary bank, has a right of charge back, if an item deposited is subsequently not paid.
   d. Yes. Careless Bank made a mistaken payment, but may use subrogation to recover from Nyong'o.

ANSWERS

1. *A* is the best answer, stating quite correctly that Careful Bank had no obligation to Nwoye Semiconductor to pay the check, because Careful Bank did not sign the check. Careful Bank did have an obligation to pay a properly payable check. But that obligation does not run to the holder of the check, who has rights only against those who have signed the check or those who have made warranties by transferring the check. Rather, Careful Bank was obliged to its customer, Okonkwo Technology, to pay checks written on the account that were properly payable, making *B* incorrect. *C* and *D* are incorrect, because Careful Bank, for reasons stated, has no liability to Nwoye Semiconductor.
2. *C* is the best answer. As discussed above, Careful Bank is obliged to its customer, Okonkwo Technology, to pay checks that are properly payable. Where Careful Bank breached that obligation, it is liable for wrongful dishonor. The measure of liability is, unlike most negotiable instrument actions, not the amount of the check, contrary to *A*. The check was not paid, so we are not arguing about who is responsible for the amount of the check. Rather, liability is measured by the extent to which the wrongful

dishonor proximately caused damages to Okonkwo Technology, as *B* correctly states. The facts given do not show any damages to Okonkwo. There could be such damages: perhaps the bounced check will cause Nwoye Semiconductor to stop dealing with Okonkwo Technology, or cause harm to Okonkwo Technology's credit rating, or even trigger a default with one of its creditors. But unless there is a showing of harm to Okonkwo Technology, there is no liability. In most cases, there is no harm; the customer simply writes another check or pays by other means.

3. *D* is the best answer. An effective stop payment makes the check not properly payable, so Careless Bank would normally not be entitled to reimbursement. Contrary to *C*, a bank is generally entitled to reimbursement only if it pays checks that are properly payable. But a bank that pays a check by mistake may use subrogation, if it can identify another party that is receiving unjust enrichment due to the bank's mistake. Here, Coyote, who tried to stop payment on his debt he owed, would receive a motorcycle for free if Careless Bank took the loss for mistakenly paying the seller. So Careless Bank may use subrogation, in effect, stepping into the shoes of the seller to collect the agreed-upon price from Coyote.
4. *C* is the best answer. When collecting a promissory note, a copy is indeed no substitute for the original (although it may at least be evidence that at one time the person had possession of the original note). But Check 21, in order to facilitate electronic processing, permits a bank to create a substitute check, which is the legal equivalent of the original check. So the judge should accept the substitute check just as readily as the original check.
5. *C* is the best answer. This question gives an example of a common scam, one that has fooled many sophisticated people, including a fair number of lawyers. When Nyong'o handed the check to Careless Bank's teller and received cash, Careless Bank was not paying the check, contrary to A. Rather, they were taking the check as an item for deposit, to collect on Nyong'o's behalf from the drawee bank. The cash was not payment of the check; rather, it was an advance against the proceeds of the check. When an item taken for collection is not paid, the depositary bank has a right of charge back, the right to collect any amounts that have been advanced against the item. Unscrupulous people who know this, like Maximilian, are sometimes able to take advantage of those who do not, like Nyong'o.

   B has things backward. Depositary banks are under no duty to hold on to funds until an item has been paid. To the contrary, they may (and often must, under funds availability rules) make the funds available to their customers before receiving payment themselves.

   D is a red herring, put here to remind us that subrogation may sometimes be used by a drawee bank when it has paid by mistake. Such subrogation may not be used by a depositary bank.

Chapter 14

Wrongdoing and Error

Negotiable instruments represent money, and money attracts thieves. Many an employer checks the books one day to discover that mysterious checks have been written on the corporate account that no one seems to remember authorizing, or that a promissory note, supposedly in the vault, is missing. Criminals look at bank accounts and plot ways to tap them, and in this ingenious century those schemes are magnificent in their clever evilness.

When all goes wrong and the venality is uncovered those caught in the criminal's plot line must figure out who owes what to whom. There are many legal theories that are provided by the Uniform Commercial Code. The lawyer who understands these and how they fit together possesses valuable knowledge.

This course does not get involved with the substance of the crimes one might possibly commit using a negotiable instrument. Suffice it to say that it is a crime in all jurisdictions to write a check against an account known to be insufficient (or non-existent), to forge a signature to a check, or to pass (*utter*) an instrument known to be forged. It is also illegal to try to use the delay period of bank collection, the float, to create money on empty accounts. This process, known as *check kiting,* in its simplest form involves opening two bank accounts in distant locations and writing and depositing checks on the other account in each bank, increasing the amount and using the slowness of the bank collection process to create the false appearance of assets.[1] Ignoring the commercial paper crimes, this section of the book explores the legal tangles that follow in the wake of such nefarious activity.

I. FORGERY OF THE PAYEE'S NAME

A. Some Basic Ideas

It is important that you go back and review two concepts that we have already covered and make sure that they are still part of your repertoire.

The first of these was the principle explored at the end of Chapter 9 (Negotiation): the forgery of the payee's name (or of a special indorsee's name) means that no valid negotiation takes place, and therefore no one taking the instrument thereafter can qualify as a *holder.*

PROBLEM 208

When she graduated from law school, Portia Moot received a $500 check signed by her grandmother. She put it in her personal papers when she packed up to move to a new city where she planned on using it to open a checking account there. When her car containing all her belongings was stolen en route, the check went with it. The thief, Harry Villain, forged Portia's name to the back of the check and then signed his own name below hers. He deposited the check in the account he carried with Careless State Bank. Before the check was presented, Portia had her grandmother stop payment on the check, so it was dishonored and returned to Careless State Bank. By this time Harry had withdrawn the money and fled the jurisdiction. Careless State phoned its attorney. Since it gave value for the check, isn't it a holder in due course and, as such, can't it enforce the check against the grandmother per §3-414(b)? See §3-201.

1. We hesitate, for some reason, to elaborate on the how-to's of check kiting; let us note that bankers have devised methods of detecting many check-kiting schemes in their early stages. The adoption of the federal Check 21 rules eliminates much of the float period for checks and makes life harder for check kiters. For more on check kiting, see A. Brooke Overby, Allocation of Check Kiting Losses Under the UCC, Regulation CC, and the Bankruptcy Code: Reconciling the Standards, 44 Wake Forest L. Rev. 59, 63 (2009), and Thomas E. McCurnin & Peter A. Frandsen, Grounding Check Kiting with Check 21: The Civil and Criminal Ramifications of Check Kiting in the 21st Century, 125 Banking L.J. 295, 297 (2008).

As we saw at the end of Chapter 9, if a check is payable to the order of a named individual, only that person can be a holder, a status postponed until the payee acquires possession; see §1-201(b)(21). Without a valid indorsement by the payee, no later person can qualify as a holder (much less a holder in due course), and this is true no matter how many times the instrument is thereafter transferred, no matter how good the forgery appears to be, no matter how innocent the later takers, or how much value they paid. Indeed, the check is still the property of the payee whose name was forged and that person could replevy it from the current transferee.

We would get a completely different result if this check were either made out to bearer or if the payee had indorsed it in blank before the check was stolen. In that case, anyone in possession of the check would be a holder and, if otherwise qualifying, a holder in due course.

The second concept to review is the meaning of the phrase "a person entitled to enforce the instrument." Section 3-301 defines the phrase, and you should reread it now. The primary definition is that of *holder* (i.e., someone who takes pursuant to a valid negotiation), but the phrase also includes some others the law thinks worthy of protection. Subsection (ii) speaks of "a non-holder in possession of the instrument who has the rights of a holder." What does this mean? It is our old friend "the shelter rule." Consider the following.

PROBLEM 209

Assume from the last Problem that when Portia was leaving the city she owed $500 to her former roommate, Helen Midlaw, so she gave her the graduation check but forgot to indorse it. Is Helen a "holder"? When she discovers that Portia forgot to indorse the check, could she force Portia to do so? See §3-203.

Helen qualifies as a non-holder with the rights of a holder pursuant to the shelter rule of §3-203(b) and is therefore a person entitled to enforce the instrument. Another example of such a person is a depositary bank. Suppose that Portia took the check from her grandmother and deposited it, unindorsed, in the bank account she opened in the new city to which she moved. Section 4-205 gives the depositary bank Portia's holder rights and makes it a person entitled to enforce the instrument in spite of the lack of payee indorsement.

Return to the definition of "person entitled to enforce the instrument" in §3-301. There are two other possible entities that qualify per subsection (iii). The first of these is someone who has lost the instrument but who has the right to go to court to recreate it pursuant to §3-309. Consider this possibility: Portia's cat chews up the check while stuck in the car when Portia is driving across country. Portia no longer is a holder—there is nothing to hold. But she has the right to use the mechanism of §3-309 and is therefore still a person entitled to enforce the instrument. The final person so qualifying is the person described in §3-418(d); see the text following Problem 203.

B. *Warranty Liability*

After the forgers ply their trade, other parties dealing with the check must adjust their responsibilities vis-à-vis each other. There are three primary theories: the properly payable rule of §4-401, the warranties rules discussed next, and the ability of certain parties to sue in conversion (covered later in the chapter).

PROBLEM 210

Portia Moot owed $400 to her landlord, John Clark, so she handed him a check on the first of the month when they met in the lobby. John thought he had put it in his pocket, but in reality it had fluttered to the floor, where it was discovered by Harry Villain, another tenant of the building. Harry took the check down to No Questions Check Store and asked the manager to cash it for him, pretending to be John Clark, whose name he had forged to the back of the check. The manager then gave Harry $400, stamped "No Questions Check Store" under the forgery, and deposited the check in the account the store carried at Merchants Bank. Merchants Bank presented the check to Octopus National Bank, the drawee bank, and was paid. A week later, John Clark searched everywhere for the check. Finally he went back to Portia and told her he had lost it. By this time an image of the check had been returned to Portia by Octopus National Bank as part of her monthly bank statement. Portia showed it to John, and he positively declared that his signature on the back of the check was a forgery. Portia, a law student with a good grasp of the forgery rules of the Uniform Commercial Code, knew just what to do. She wrote him another check and then went down to Octopus National Bank.

(a) Can she make Octopus National Bank recredit her account? What is her theory? See §4-401.

(b) Octopus National Bank has made final payment on this check, and, as we saw in the last chapter, that ends its ability to dishonor the check. However, §4-302(b) provides that final payment does not prevent warranty liability from giving relief to the bank, specifically referring to §4-208. Read that section and answer these two questions: (1) which warranty described therein was breached, and (2) who breached it?

(c) Is it a defense to a transfer warranty lawsuit that the transferor was free of negligence and had no knowledge of a forgery, or is it strict liability? See Huntington Natl. Bank v. Guishard, Wilburn & Shorts, LLC, 2014 WL 6982566 (S.D. Ohio 2014).

Both Articles 3 and 4 contain warranty sections and they are virtually identical as a matter of substance. Sections 3-417 and 4-208 each describe *presentment* warranties and §§3-416 and 4-207 cover *transfer* warranties. The Article 3 warranties control until the check is taken for deposit, at which point the Article 4 warranties take over. This usually has no practical significance, given that the warranty liability is the same in both articles, but if an attorney needs to file a complaint, it is important that the correct article be cited.

What is the difference between *presentment* and *transfer*? The answer is easiest to understand if you think of a negotiable instrument as having three stages in its life: issuance, transfer, and presentment. Issuance (§3-105) is the creation of the instrument and its handing over to the first taker. There are no warranties made on issuance. Skipping for a moment the middle stage (transfer), the final stage in the life of the instrument is presentment: its surrender to the drawee for either acceptance or payment.[2] At that moment, presentment warranties are made by not only the entity physically making presentment but also all prior transferors (this giving the drawee a choice of defendants). Every other movement of the instrument for consideration between issuance and presentment is a *transfer* of the instrument and gives rise to the transfer warranties. Warranty suits are said to be suits "off the instrument" because they do not require possession of the instrument as a prerequisite to suit.

PROBLEM 211

Return to the facts of the last Problem. Assume that Octopus National Bank successfully recaptured its money from Merchants Bank under a theory of breach of a presentment warranty. Now Merchants Bank calls in its attorney and asks for legal advice. Can it sue the check cashing store using §4-208(a) (note the word *drawee* in subsection (a))? How does it get legal relief? See §4-207(a). What warranties have been breached? Must it give notice to the check cashing store within any given period of time? See §4-207(d). If the latter refuses to pay, how quickly must suit be commenced? See §4-111; cf. §3-118.

2. If the instrument is a promissory note, presentment is made to the maker of the note, in which case the only presentment warranty is that described in §3-417(d).

PROBLEM 212

Still using the facts of the above Problems, now assume that you are the attorney for the check cashing store. To what relief is it entitled, assuming it can find Harry Villain in a solvent condition?

When a forgery of a payee's name occurs, it is the policy of our law to use warranty theories, first presentment and then transfer, to pass the loss back to the wrongdoer (or the first person to trust the wrongdoer). Note that the check cashing store was always in the best position to discover the forgery by making Harry produce identification when he tried to cash the check.

As for damages for breach of warranty, the relevant sections in both Articles 3 and 4 are identical with, for example, §3-416(b) providing for a recovery of "the loss suffered as a result of the breach, but not more than the amount of the instrument plus expenses and loss of interest incurred as a result of the breach."

Wesseling & Brackmann, PC v. Huntington Bancshares Financial Corporation

Court of Appeals of Michigan, 2018
2018 WL 1176334

PER CURIAM.

Plaintiff appeals as of right the trial court's order granting defendant's motion for summary disposition pursuant to MCR 2.116(C)(10). For the reasons stated herein, we affirm.

I. FACTS AND PROCEDURE

This case arises from a fraudulent check scheme perpetrated against plaintiff by a fictitious client, resulting in a $58,155.20 loss to the firm. On September 24, 2014, an individual named Jason Walter contacted plaintiff through the Internet regarding legal services. Douglas J. Brackmann, an attorney and partner in the firm, responded and began communicating with Walter through e-mail and telephone. Walter ultimately retained plaintiff's services, telling Brackmann that he wished to sell a drilling rig with the assistance of a Michigan attorney.

On Friday, October 17, 2014, plaintiff received a letter of intent purportedly outlining the terms of sale for the rig. The letter included what appeared to be a cashier's check in the amount of $380,000 made out to plaintiff, and specified that $200,000 was to be wired to a company called JMS International, LLC. That same day, plaintiff deposited the check in its Interest on Lawyer Trust Account (IOLTA) with defendant.

The following Monday, October 20, 2014, Walter provided Brackmann with instructions for completing the wire transfer, and Brackmann initiated a phone call with defendant to determine the status of the check. He spoke with bank teller Heidi J. McClintic, and asked if the check had cleared the account. Although McClintic used the terms "cleared," "posted," and "available" inconsistently throughout her deposition when describing the conversation, Brackmann testified that McClintic explicitly answered: "The check is cleared. You're good to go." Based on McClintic's response, Brackmann completed the paperwork for the wire transfer.

Subsequently, Brackmann learned that the check had been dishonored. Although defendant attempted to stop the wire transfer and recovered some of the funds, $58,155.20 remained lost. As a result, plaintiff initiated this action against defendant, alleging that it should be liable for the unrecovered funds because it falsely represented to plaintiff that the fraudulent check had cleared.

In defendant's motion for summary disposition filed pursuant to MCR 2.116(C)(8) and (10), it argued that MCL 440.4207, Michigan's version of the Uniform Commercial Code (UCC) §4-207, barred recovery because plaintiff breached its warranty that the cashier's check it deposited was authentic, and defendant accepted the check in good faith. Thus, defendant contended, plaintiff should be liable for the lost funds. Ultimately, the trial court granted the motion pursuant to MCR 2.116(C)(10), finding that no genuine issue of material fact existed that defendant acted in good faith because "[defendant's] employees engaged in commercially appropriate conduct, its employee gave [plaintiff] information that was technically accurate, and the bank made every effort to recover funds lost as a result of the fraudulent cashier's check accepted and deposited by [plaintiff]."

II. Analysis

Plaintiff argues that the trial court erred by granting defendant's motion for summary disposition because a genuine issue of material fact existed regarding whether defendant acted in good faith when its employee falsely informed plaintiff that the check had cleared. . . .

Transactions involving bank deposits and collections are controlled by Articles 3 and 4 of the UCC. Mut. S & L v. Nat'l Bank of Detroit, 185 Mich. App. 591, 594; 462 N.W.2d 797 (1990). MCL 440.4207, Michigan's version of UCC §4-207, provides, in relevant part:

> (1) A customer or collecting bank that transfers an item and receives a settlement or other consideration warrants to the transferee and to any subsequent collecting bank all of the following:
>
> * * *
>
> (b) That all signatures on the item are authentic and authorized.
>
> * * *

> (2) If an item is dishonored, a customer or collecting bank transferring the item and receiving settlement or other consideration is obliged to pay the amount due on the item (*i*) according to the terms of the item at the time it was transferred, or (*ii*) if the transfer was of an incomplete item, according to its terms when completed as stated in sections 3115 and 3407. The obligation of a transferor is owed to the transferee and to any subsequent collecting bank that takes the item in good faith. A transferor cannot disclaim its obligation under this subsection by an endorsement stating that it is made "without recourse" or otherwise disclaiming liability.
>
> (3) A person to whom the warranties under subsection (1) are made and who took the item in good faith may recover from the warrantor as damages for breach of warranty an amount equal to the loss suffered as a result of the breach. . . .

Accordingly, a collecting bank may avail itself of a defense under UCC §4-207 as long as it takes a check from a customer in good faith.

There is no dispute that plaintiff transferred a cashier's check to defendant for "other consideration" and, thus, made the warranties implied under MCL 440.4207. Furthermore, there is no dispute that plaintiff breached its warranty that "all signatures [were] authentic and authorized," as the check was later dishonored as counterfeit. Therefore, the controlling issue is whether the actions of defendant during the transaction are sufficient to shift liability for the loss from plaintiff to defendant because of defendant's lack of good faith.

The UCC defines "good faith" as "honesty in fact and the observance of reasonable commercial standards of fair dealing." MCL 440.1201(2)(t). Additionally, official comments to the UCC provide further definition to the "fair dealing" aspect of good faith:

Although fair dealing is a broad term that must be defined in context, it is clear that it is concerned with the fairness of conduct rather than the care with which an act is performed. Failure to exercise ordinary care in conducting a transaction is an entirely different concept than failure to deal fairly in conducting the transaction. [UCC §3-103, official comment 4 (2002).]

We first note that good faith is "a modifier that requires a subject to modify." Gorman v. American Honda Motor Co., Inc., 302 Mich. App. 113, 133; 839 N.W.2d 223 (2013). Under UCC §4-207, good faith modifies the manner in which a bank takes a check. McClintic used the term "cleared" with regard to the check in her conversation with Brackmann three days *after* defendant accepted the check from plaintiff, and plaintiff fails to provide authority for its contention that a bank's duty of good faith with respect to a transfer warranty defense extends to specific statements made by its agents during the "processing" of a check.

Further, the caselaw plaintiff cites from other jurisdictions addressing good faith in the context of a bank's communications with a customer following acceptance of a check, is distinguishable. In those cases, the respective courts concluded that a bank's failure to follow internal procedures when taking checks, or failure to recognize common indicia of fraud, may demonstrate the bank's lack of good faith. Here, there are no facts to indicate that the check bore indicia of counterfeiting. When McClintic spoke with Brackmann, she was not looking at the check nor did she reference anything other than a computer display of the plaintiff's account summary. In fact, McClintic had never seen the check before speaking with Brackmann. Additionally, neither McClintic's nor Brackmann's testimony established that McClintic had information about the internet origin of the check. Brackmann testified that he explained to McClintic only that plaintiff had "received a check[,]" which it then deposited.

For its part, defendant argues that a bank's statement regarding the status of a check does not shift liability from the customer to the bank if the check is later dishonored. In TCF Nat'l Bank v. Adobe Liquidations, LLC, unpublished per curiam opinion of the Court of Appeals, issued November 24, 2009 (Docket No. 286335), pp. 5-7, this Court concluded that communication between a bank employee and a customer about whether a check had cleared was not enough to shift liability to the accepting bank. The Court reasoned that a bank manager's statements that the check had cleared, and subsequent actions to lift a hold on funds, "did not absolve [the defendant customer] of [its] threshold duty not to deposit a fraudulent check." *Id.* at 7. Furthermore, the defendant's counterclaim of negligence against the bank for providing such erroneous information was "irrelevant and [did] not absolve [the defendant] of his breach of statutory warranty." *Id.* at 8.

Similarly, in PNC Bank N.A. v. Martin, memorandum opinion of the United States District Court for the Western District of Kentucky, issued August 19, 2010 (No. 08-649-JBC), p. 2, cited by defendant in support of its arguments, the court concluded that statements by bank employees that a counterfeit check had cleared, even though a mistake, were "immaterial facts." In granting summary judgment for the plaintiff bank on the issue of the defendant's breach of statutory warranty, the court reasoned that "transfer warranties placed the risk of loss on [the customer], regardless of whether [the bank], [the customer], or both of them were at fault." *Id.*

This Court's unpublished decision in *TCF*, along with *PNC Bank*, support defendant's argument that its actions did not fail to adhere to reasonable commercial standards of fair dealing. First, as in *TCF*, plaintiff incurred the "threshold duty not to deposit counterfeit checks" when it transferred the check to defendant. Plaintiff was the only party in this transaction that had all the information regarding the origin and nature of the check and, thus, was the party with the closest contact to the fraudster that "ought to bear the responsibility for the loss occasioned by the [fraud]." Dominion Bank, N.A. v. Household Bank, FSB, 827 F. Supp. 463, 467 (S.D. Ohio, 1993). Defendant accepted plaintiff's deposit of the check and made funds provisionally available in accordance with the bank's procedures. Defendant notified plaintiff that the check was dishonored within two days of deposit and successfully retrieved most of the wire transfer. There is no evidence in the record that defendant was aware that the check was part of a fraudulent scheme. Therefore, as in *PNC Bank*, McClintic's statement that the check had cleared was immaterial to a determination of whether defendant acted in good faith. *PNC Bank*, unpub. op. at 2.

Furthermore, the evidence does not involve "advantage-taking" on the part of the bank. See State Bank of The Lakes v. Kansas Bakers Surety Co., 328 F.3d 906, 909 (CA7, 2003). Plaintiff was a long-time customer of defendant. There was no conceivable reason for defendant to take advantage of plaintiff by deliberately informing it that the check had cleared. Such an action would likely jeopardize a long-term business relationship with a firm that had an account with "more than $2.4 million" on deposit with the bank. Under the meaning of UCC §4-207, then, the evidence cited by plaintiff does not establish that defendant failed to act with honesty in fact and in accordance with reasonable commercial standards of fair dealing. Thus, the trial court did not err when it granted defendant's motion for summary disposition on the basis that no genuine issue of material fact existed as to whether defendant acted in good faith when its employee falsely informed plaintiff that the check had cleared.

Plaintiff's assertion that even if the relevant caselaw does not support its claim, the question of whether defendant took the check in good faith is an issue for the trier of fact, lacks merit. This Court has held that good faith is an "issue[] for the trier of fact under conflicting evidence." Cessna Fin. Corp. v. Warmus, 159 Mich. App. 706, 711, 407 N.W.2d 66 (1987). Here, in contrast to the unpublished decisions cited by plaintiff in support of its arguments, there was no evidence that defendant failed to follow its own procedures in taking the check or that its agent was aware of the nature of the Internet transaction. Therefore, there is no conflicting evidence that requires the issue to be decided by a trier of fact.

Affirmed.

C. Conversion Liability

Conversion is the civil action for misappropriation of another's property. There are many ways a negotiable instrument can be converted.

PROBLEM 213

Your employer gives you your paycheck, drawn on the employer's bank, Octopus National. You take the check down to the bank and present it across the counter. The teller takes it, walks away from the window and comes back a few minutes later empty-handed. "Yes?" she asks, looking at you blankly. "The check?" you ask. "Sorry," she says, "we are not going to pay it." "Then I want it back," you reply, planning to use it to pursue your employer on the drawer's obligation (§3-414(b)). "Sorry," she says, "we are also keeping the check." Do they have the right to do that?

PROBLEM 214

Mr. Aristotle Wellborn was walking along the street when he was surreptitiously relieved of his wallet by Art Dodger. In the wallet was a check made out to Wellborn, who had already indorsed it. Is Dodger guilty of conversion?

The original language of the conversion section in the first version of Article 3 was so poorly written that it did not appear to cover all the situations where a conversion action should lie, and the courts were forced to fill in the gaps. The 1990 Revision handled this difficulty by simply incorporating the common law of conversion as applicable to negotiable instruments (see the first sentence of §3-420(a)), and that should permit the courts to find conversion liability in both of the last Problems.

Only the person whose property rights are adversely affected may sue for conversion. For negotiable instruments the *holder* is the owner of the instrument and is the person with the property rights therein. Since at the outset only the payee can be the holder of an order instrument, only the payee has a sufficient property interest to become the plaintiff (or if the payee has negotiated the instrument to another, only that person can be the *holder* having a property interest in the instrument). Since the instrument, once delivered, gives the payee these property rights, the payee can take a number of different possible courses of action whenever the check is stolen, his or her name is forged thereon, and the instrument is paid by the drawee bank:

(1) *Conversion.* The payee can sue the drawee bank, or anyone taking the check after the forgery, in conversion. If the drawee is forced to pay the payee, the drawee will sue the check's presenter for breach of the presentment warranty that he or she was a "person entitled to enforce the instrument"; §4-208(a)(1). That person can then sue the transferee for breach of transfer warranties; §3-416(a)(1), (2), and (4). Thus the loss will pass back up the chain until it reaches the forger or, if the forger has departed for parts unknown, the first person to trust the forger. The cases are collected in Annot., 23 A.L.R.4th 855.

(2) *Drawer's Obligation.* Since the check is still the property of the payee, he or she can replevy it from its current possessor (probably the drawer, who will have it among the canceled checks), cross off the forged indorsement, sign it, and present it to the drawee bank for payment. If the drawee pays it, well and good. If not, a dishonor will have occurred, and the payee may then sue the drawer on the drawer's obligation, §3-414(b), or, certainly now, the underlying obligation.

(3) *Quasi-Contract.* Some courts considering the issue will permit the quasi-contractual action by the payee for money had and received, a cause of action that typically has a longer statute of limitations than does conversion. See Peerless Ins. Co. v. Texas Commerce Bank, 791 F.2d 1177 (5th Cir. 1986); but see AMX Enterprises, Inc. v. Bank One, N.A., 196 S.W.3d 202 (Tex. App. 2006).

(4) *Negligence.* Most courts considering the issue have not allowed a common law negligence claim against banks handling forged checks, finding that the statutory scheme of Article 3 of the Uniform Commercial Code preempts all common law theories; see Olympic Title Ins. Co. v. Fifth Third Bank of Western Ohio, 2004 WL 2009285 (Ohio App. 2004). There are a minority of decisions allowing the common law to supplement the Code; Chicago Title Ins. Co. v. Allfirst Bank, 394 Md. 270, 905 A.2d 366 (2006).

The common law had always provided that payment on a forged indorsement was conversion, see Restatement (Second) of Torts §241A, but that statement leaves a lot of substantive law to be explored. The original conversion section did not answer a host of questions that §3-420 now settles. These matters are explored by the following Problems.

PROBLEM 215

When Portia Moot learned that the check she had given to her landlord had been stolen from him, his name forged as payee, and that the check had been paid by her bank, she sued her bank in conversion. Is she the proper plaintiff in this lawsuit? If not, (1) who is, and (2) what relief does the law give her? See §§3-420(a) and 4-401(a). If the landlord (the payee) decides to bring a §3-420 action, who is liable in such a suit?

PROBLEM 216

After he won the lottery, Tim Isle decided to pay off the mortgage on his home. He mailed a check for $80,000 to Octopus National Bank (ONB), the mortgagee, but it was stolen from the mail by an unknown person, who forged "Octopus National Bank" on the back and cashed the check at Sleepy Hollow State Bank, which then collected it from the drawee bank. Since ONB, the payee, never received possession of the check, does it have sufficient property rights therein to succeed in a conversion action against Sleepy Hollow State Bank or the drawee? See §3-420(a); see also Mt. Hope Universal Baptist Church, Inc. v. Bowen, 2016 WL 6115359 (N.Y. Sup. Ct. 2016). What can the bank do? See §3-310(b).

Leeds v. Chase Manhattan Bank, N.A.

New Jersey Superior Court, Appellate Division, 2000
752 A.2d 332

WECKER, J.A.D.

Plaintiffs William Leeds and Carol Leeds, a mother and son (collectively "plaintiff" or "Leeds"), hired Louis Egnasko, Esq.[3] to represent them in connection with a mortgage foreclosure action, as well as the purchase and resale of the property in East Orange, New Jersey on which they held the mortgage. After plaintiff bought the property at the foreclosure sale, they entered into a contract to sell the property. Egnasko closed the sale and accepted a settlement check for $87,293.56 on plaintiff's behalf. The settlement check payable to William Leeds, Carol Leeds, and Isabel Gibbs,[4] was a United Jersey Bank teller's check drawn at that bank's Hackensack, New Jersey branch. Summit Bank is the successor-in-interest to United Jersey Bank (hereinafter "Summit").

Following the closing, and unknown to Leeds, Egnasko altered the settlement check by typing "* * *Louis Egnasko, as attorney for* * *" above the payee line, so that the check then read:

> * * *LOUIS EGNASKO AS ATTORNEY FOR* * *
> * * *WILLIAM LEEDS, CAROL LEEDS, ISABEL GIBBS* * *

Egnasko alone endorsed the check "for deposit only, 067003443" and deposited the check into his attorney trust account at Chemical Bank. Chemical

3. Egnasko has since been disbarred by both New York and New Jersey. Matter of Egnasko, 151 N.J. 506, 701 A.2d 701 (1997); Matter of Egnasko, 223 A.D.2d 317, 646 N.Y.S.2d 698 (App. Div. 1996).

4. Gibbs had been a record owner with the right of survivorship of an undivided one-third share of the East Orange property along with Grace Livingston and Louise Bevans, to whom Leeds made a mortgage loan. Gibbs apparently died intestate. Although Leeds alone received a deed from the Sheriff, the buyer required that Gibbs be named as a contract seller, and issued the check payable to Leeds and Gibbs, as described. The record reveals no claim by Gibbs' estate to the proceeds of the sale, and the estate is not involved in this appeal.

Bank stamped the back of the check "Endorsement guaranteed." Defendant Chase Manhattan Bank is the successor-in-interest to Chemical Bank (hereinafter "Chase"). Chase presented the check for collection in the ordinary course, and Summit honored its own teller's check. The check was negotiated between May 8 and May 16, 1996.

On June 6, 1996, Egnasko drew a check for $92,050 payable to William and Carol Leeds from an attorney trust account he held at the Trust Company of New Jersey (Trustco). This check apparently covered the proceeds of the sale of the home. Trustco honored the check drawn to Leeds, and Leeds received payment on that check. However, Egnasko's Trustco account also contained funds that Egnasko had obtained by similarly altering and depositing a check payable to Shrewsbury State Bank ("Shrewsbury"), which was intended to pay off a mortgage loan in an unrelated real estate transaction. Instead of delivering that check to Shrewsbury, Egnasko again inserted his own name, "Louis Egnasko as attorney," above the payee's name and deposited the check into his Trustco attorney trust account. Egnasko thus used funds that belonged to Shrewsbury to pay Leeds.

Facing a claim for conversion by Shrewsbury, Trustco filed suit against Egnasko and Leeds in New York, seeking repayment of monies traceable to Egnasko's fraud. Leeds filed an answer and crossclaim in the New York action on December 5, 1997, admitting receipt of the Trustco check from Egnasko, but denying that "William and Carol Leeds owe [Trustco] the traceable converted proceeds of the check delivered to William Leeds with interest. . . ."

On December 24, 1997, Leeds filed this action alleging strict liability for payment on the altered settlement check against both Chase, the depository bank, and Summit, the drawer/drawee/payor bank. In support of their motion for summary judgment, defendants argued that (1) Leeds had been paid and therefore suffered no damages; (2) Leeds would only be ordered to return that payment in the Trustco action if Leeds were found to have accepted payment with knowledge that the funds were stolen; and (3) if Leeds knowingly accepted stolen monies, the equitable doctrine of unclean hands would bar recovery against the banks. . . .

Leeds argued in opposition to summary judgment and in support of his cross-motion that Chase, as the depository bank, is strictly liable for conversion under N.J.S.A. 12A:3-420, including damages related to the cost of defending the New York suit. The motion judge granted summary judgment in favor of both Chase and Summit dismissing plaintiff's complaint. . . .

We first address Leeds' cause of action in conversion against Chase. The applicable provision of the Uniform Commercial Code (UCC), N.J.S.A. 12A:3-420a, states:

> The law applicable to conversion of personal property applies to instruments. *An instrument is also converted if it* is taken by transfer, other than a negotiation, from a person not entitled to enforce the instrument *or a bank makes or obtains*

> *payment with respect to the instrument for a person not entitled to enforce the instrument or receive payment.* An action for conversion of an instrument may not be brought by the issuer or acceptor of the instrument or a payee or indorsee who did not receive delivery of the instrument either directly or through delivery to an agent or a co-payee. [Emphasis added.]

Although the check was not actually delivered to Leeds, it was delivered to Egnasko as Leeds' attorney, with intent that title be transferred to Leeds, the payee. Thus Leeds is entitled to bring this action for conversion as one who "receive[d] delivery of the instrument . . . through delivery to an agent. . . ." N.J.S.A. 12A:3-420a. . . . It is undisputed that Egnasko was not authorized by Leeds to indorse the check and had no right to receive or enforce payment on that check.

Section 3-420a does not explicitly refer to "forgery" or "alteration," but instead addresses a class of persons who are "not entitled to enforce the instrument or receive payment." However, there can be no question that because the Summit teller's check payable to Leeds was altered by Egnasko, he was not "entitled" to payment on the instrument. Such an alteration constitutes a forgery under the Code and the common law. See N.J.S.A. 12A:3-407a. . . . By crediting Egnasko's trust account with the face amount of the check, Chase paid the check to "a person not entitled to . . . receive payment." N.J.S.A. 12A:3-420a.

As a depository bank under the Uniform Commercial Code, see N.J.S.A. 12A:4-105b, Chase is strictly liable for conversion on a forged or stolen instrument. See N.J.S.A. 12A:3-420, comment 1. Therefore, Chase is strictly liable on Leeds' claim for conversion under N.J.S.A. 12A:3-420a, because Chase "[made or obtained] payment with respect to the instrument for a person not entitled to enforce the instrument or receive payment." See New Jersey Lawyers' Fund, 303 N.J. Super. at 224, 696 A.2d 728.

The justification for strict liability upon the depository bank is that "the loss should normally come to rest upon the first solvent party in the stream after the one who forged the indorsement. . . ." 2 James J. White & Robert S. Summers, Uniform Commercial Code §18-4 at 209-10 (4th ed. 1995). See also Uniform Commercial Code, comment 3 to N.J.S.A. 12A:3-420:

> The depositary bank is ultimately liable in the case of a forged indorsement check because of its warranty to the payor bank under Section 4-208(a)(1) and it is usually the most convenient defendant in cases involving multiple checks drawn on different banks. There is no basis for requiring the owner of the check to bring multiple actions against the various payor banks and to require those banks to assert warranty rights against the depositary bank.

We are therefore convinced that the motion court improperly entered summary judgment against Leeds and in favor of Chase. We are also convinced that Chase is not entitled to summary judgment based upon the defense of payment, in light of Leeds' continuing exposure to the New York action, until that action has been resolved. If Leeds is not required in that action to disgorge the payment received from Egnasko, Chase will be entitled to set off that payment against its liability for conversion. Cf. County Concrete Corp. v. Smith, 317 N.J. Super. 50, 61-62, 721 A.2d 34 (App. Div. 1998). Leeds cannot be allowed a double recovery. If Leeds is required to disgorge, we will then address Chase's "unclean hands" defense on a complete record. That Leeds' damage claim may be limited (or even dismissed) in the future does not affect our determination of Chase's liability here and now.

We next address Leeds' cause of action in conversion against Summit. Summit is the drawer, the drawee, and the payor bank on the altered check under the Code definitions. A drawee bank is also strictly liable for conversion when it pays on a forged endorsement. . . . In Gast v. American Cas. Co. of Reading, Pa., 99 N.J. Super. 538, 541, 240 A.2d 682 (1968), we said:

> As both drawer and drawee defendant had the responsibility to make payment to the named payees on the instrument. . . . The statute [the former UCC §3-419] created an absolute right to recover in favor of plaintiffs . . . upon proof that the draft was paid on the forged indorsements. Plaintiffs' indorsements were concededly forged. It follows that defendant, having paid the draft, was rendered liable for the conversion in the face amount.

However, N.J.S.A. 12A:3-420c limits damages for conversion against

> [a] representative, other than a depository bank, who has in good faith dealt with an instrument or its proceeds on behalf of one who was not the person entitled to enforce the instrument . . . [for any more than] the amount of any proceeds that it has not paid out.

Summit is not a depositary bank in this case. Summit has paid out the entire face amount of the forged check and is not alleged to have acted other than in good faith; it therefore cannot be liable to Leeds for conversion under §3-420. Whether Summit could have been found liable for negligence, as a result of its failure to detect the alteration on its own teller's check, is not before us. Plaintiff has not pled or argued a negligence cause of action against Summit. Summary judgment is therefore affirmed in favor of Summit. . . .

We affirm summary judgment dismissing the complaint against Summit, reverse summary judgment in favor of Chase, and remand for entry of partial summary judgment on liability against Chase. A determination of damages must abide the outcome of the New York action.

The court's conclusion that §3-420(c) excuses the drawee bank from liability as a "representative" is wrong. The Official Comments to §3-420 clearly refer to the conversion liability of the drawee bank, and there is general agreement that only intermediary banks qualify as the sorts of "representatives" who are protected by subsection (c). See Levine v. Banc Alt LLC, 2019 WL 4894563 (D.N.J. 2019); White & Summers §16-4.

PROBLEM 217

The drawer made the check out to "John and Mary Doe" in order to pay a debt owed to them both. John got the check first, signed his name alone as indorser, and deposited the check in his individual checking account. His bank presented the check to the drawee bank and was paid. The issue: Is a missing signature treated the same as a forged one? Has the presenting bank breached the warranty that it is a person entitled to enforce the check? Could Mary Doe sue the banks in conversion? See §§3-110(d) and 3-420(a); Tri-County Natl. Bank v. GreenPoint Credit, LLC, 190 S.W.3d 360 (Ky. App. 2006).

Finally, you should remember that payment in violation of the terms of a restrictive indorsement ("For Deposit Only," for example) also gives rise to a cause of action in conversion; see §3-206(c) (a matter discussed in Subsection II.H of Chapter 13).

II. FORGERY OF THE DRAWER'S SIGNATURE

When a forger forges the *drawer's* signature (as opposed to that of the payee), the law reaches a completely different result than that we saw in the last section. The basic rule, the rule of Price v. Neal (below), coming to us from 1762, is that the drawee who pays or accepts a draft takes the risk of a forged drawer's signature. Later cases, however, then established the rule that the drawee does not take the risk of a forged *indorser's* signature. Canal Bank v. Bank of Albany, 1 Hill 287 (N.Y. 1841). This dichotomy still exists in our law.

Vital to an understanding of the Code's position on forgery is a grasp of the famous English case of Price v. Neal, reprinted below. Students have been telling us for years that the fact situation is too complicated to follow and, as a consequence, Lord Mansfield's opinion is meaningless. The reason for this confusion is that several key facts are unreported in the decision and have to be guessed at before the decision makes sense. To aid you in this endeavor, we have prepared our own interpretation of the facts, which you may compare with those reported in the decision.

The Facts of Price v. Neal. John Price had agreed with one Benjamin Sutton to accept and pay any drafts that Sutton drew on Price; the drafts were called *bills of exchange.* Sutton became involved in business dealings with two other men, Rogers Ruding and Thomas Ploughfor, the upshot of which was that Sutton apparently drew up two drafts on Price payable to Ruding. Both drafts were indorsed by several people before coming into the hands of Edward Neale.[5] The first draft (bill of exchange), for 40 pounds, Neale presented to Price (the drawee) for payment, and Price, via his servant, paid the draft. The second draft, also for 40 pounds, was presented for acceptance, and Price wrote on it: "Accepted, John Price," adding an order on the back to his bankers, Messieurs Freame and Barclay, telling them to pay the draft for him when it was presented for payment. We are not told who made the presentment of the second draft for acceptance, but after Price had accepted it, the draft was returned to the presenter, who indorsed it over to Neale. The latter obtained payment from Price's bankers. Subsequently, Price learned that Sutton had not really signed the drafts; his name as drawer had been forged to the instruments by a man named Lee. Price brought suit against Neale for "money had and received," demanding a return of the mistaken payments.

Price v. Neal

King's Bench, 1762
3 Burr. 1354, 97 Eng. Rep. 871

This was a special case reserved at the sittings of Guildhall after Trinity term 1762, before Lord Mansfield.

It was an action upon the case brought by Price against Neal; wherein Price declares that the defendant Edward Neale was indebted to him in 80£ for money had and received to his the plaintiff's use: and damages were laid to 100£. The general issue was pleaded; and issue joined thereon.

It was proved at the trial, that a bill was drawn as follows "Leicester, 22d November 1760. Sir, six weeks after date pay Mr. Rogers Ruding or order forty pounds, value received for Mr. Thomas Ploughfor, as advised by, sir, your humble servant Benjamin Sutton. To Mr. John Price in Bush-Lane Cannon-Street, London"; indorsed "R. Ruding, Antony Topham,

5. We worry about the "e" at the end of Neale's name—it doesn't appear in the case style, and the defendant's name is written both with and without the "e" in the opinion itself.

Hammond and Laroche. Received the contents, James Watson and Son, witness Edward Neale."

That this bill was indorsed to the defendant for a valuable consideration; and notice of the bill left at the plaintiff's house, on the day it became due. Whereupon the plaintiff sent his servant to call on the defendant, to pay him the said sum of 40£, and to take up the said bill: which was done accordingly.

That another bill was drawn as follows—"Leicester, 1st February 1761. Sir, six weeks after date pay Mr. Rogers Ruding or order forty pounds, value received for Mr. Thomas Ploughfor; as advised by, sir, your humble servant Benjamin Sutton. To Mr. John Price in Bush-Lane, Cannon-Street, London." That this bill was indorsed, "R. Ruding, Thomas Watson and Son. Witness for Smith, Right and Co." That the plaintiff accepted this bill, by writing on it, "Accepted John Price:" and that the plaintiff wrote on the back of it—"Messieurs Freame and Barclay, pray pay forty pounds for John Price."

That this bill being so accepted was indorsed to the defendant for a valuable consideration, and left at his bankers for payment; and was paid by order of the plaintiff, and taken up.

Both these bills were forged by one Lee, who has been since hanged for forgery.

The defendant Neale acted innocently and bona fide, without the least privity or suspicion of the said forgeries or of either of them; and paid the whole value of those bills.

The jury found a verdict for the plaintiff; and assessed damages 80£ and costs 40s. subject to the opinion of the Court upon this question—

> Whether the plaintiff under the circumstances of the case, can recover back, from the defendant, the money he paid on the said bills, or either of them.

Mr. Stowe, for the plaintiff, argued that he ought to recover back the money, in this action; as it was paid by him by mistake only, on supposition "that these were true genuine bills"; and as he could never recover it against the drawer, because in fact no drawer exists; nor against the forger, because he is hanged.

He owned that in a case at Guild-Hall, of Jenys v. Fawler et al. (an action by an indorsee of a bill of exchange brought against the acceptor), Lord Raymond would not admit the defendants to prove it a forged bill, by calling persons acquainted with the hand of the drawer, to swear "that they believed it not to be so"; and he even strongly inclined, "that actual proof of forgery would not excuse the defendants against their own acceptance, which had given the bill a credit to the indorsee."

But he urged, that in the case now before the Court, the forgery of the bill does not rest in belief and opinion only; but has been actually proved, and the forger executed for it.

Thus it stands even upon the accepted bill. But the plaintiff's case is much stronger upon the other bill which was not accepted. It is not stated "that this bill was accepted before it was negotiated"; on the contrary, the consideration for it was paid by the defendant, before the plaintiff had seen it. So that the defendant took it upon the credit of the indorsers, not upon the credit of the plaintiff; and therefore the reason, upon which Lord Raymond grounds his inclination to be of opinion "that actual proof of forgery would be no excuse," will not hold here.

Mr. Yates, for the defendant, argued that the plaintiff was not entitled to recover back this money from the defendant.

He denied it to be a payment by mistake: and insisted that it was rather owing to the negligence of the plaintiff; who should have inquired and satisfied himself "whether the bill was really drawn upon him by Sutton, or not." Here is no fraud in the defendant; who is stated "to have acted innocently and bona fide, without the least privity or suspicion of the forgerys and to have paid the whole value for the bills."

Lord Mansfield stopt him from going on; saying that this was one of those cases that could never be made plainer by argument.

It is an action upon the case, for money had and received to the plaintiff's use. In which action, the plaintiff can not recover the money, unless it be against conscience in the defendant, to retain it; and great liberality is always allowed, in this sort of action.

But it can never be thought unconscientious in the defendant to retain this money, when he has once received it upon a bill of exchange indorsed to him for a fair and valuable consideration, which he had bona fide paid, without the least privity or suspicion of any forgery.

Here was no fraud: no wrong. It was incumbent upon the plaintiff, to be satisfied "that the bill drawn upon him was the drawer's hand," before he accepted or paid it: but it was not incumbent upon the defendant, to inquire into it. Here was notice given by the defendant to the plaintiff of a bill drawn upon him: and he sends his servant to pay it and take it up. The other bill, he actually accepts; after which acceptance the defendant innocently and bona fide discounts it. The plaintiff lies by, for a considerable time after he has paid these bills; and then found out "that they were forged" and the forger comes to be hanged. He made no objection to them, at the time of paying them. Whatever neglect there was, was on his side. The defendant had actual encouragement from the plaintiff himself, for negotiating the second bill, from the plaintiff's having without any scruple or hesitation paid the first: and he paid the whole value, bona fide. It is a misfortune which has happened without the defendant's fault or neglect. If there was no neglect in the plaintiff, yet there is no reason to throw off the loss from one innocent man upon another innocent man: but, in this case, if there was any fault or negligence in any one, it certainly was in the plaintiff, and not in the defendant.

Per Cur'. Rule—That the postea be delivered to the defendant.

This, then, is the rule of Price v. Neal: if the drawee pays or accepts the draft, it cannot pass the risk of the drawer's signature being forged off onto prior good faith parties. Moreover, the rule has been expanded by judicial application to place on the drawee the risk of *any* mistaken payment not covered by a presentment warranty, so that, for example, the bank's payment of a check drawn against insufficient funds is a legal fait accompli (but see §4-401(a)). It is interesting to note that the finality rule of Price v. Neal has been unpopular in the courts. See, e.g., Citizens Bank v. Blach & Sons, 228 Ala. 246, 153 So. 404 (1934). It has also been criticized by lawyers such as John R.H. Kimball, an attorney for the Federal Reserve Bank of Boston, *viz:* "The rule of Price v. Neal has, I believe, outlived its rationalizations, particularly with respect to large dollar checks," Check Collection for the 21st Century, 32 U.C.C. L.J. 3, 10 (1998), and by legal commentators, both recent, White & Summers §16-7, at 770 ("We suppose it would have been too much to ask the drafters of revised Article 3 to repeal the ancient doctrine of Price v. Neal and to leave us with but one rule concerning forged signatures"), and in earlier times, Morse, Banks & Banking §464 (6th ed. 1928) ("This doctrine is fading fast into the misty past, where it belongs. It is almost dead, the funeral notices are ready, and no tears will be shed, for it was founded in misconception of the fundamental principles of law and common sense."). Morse's prediction proved too hasty; Price v. Neal is firmly imbedded in the UCC and is apparently alive and well for decades yet to come. The rule is reflected in Article 4's *final payment* statute, §4-302, which makes the payor bank *accountable* for an item that has been finally paid. In Article 3 the key section is §3-418, *a finality* rule, which is said to be a codification of Price v. Neal. Read carefully §3-418 and its Official Comments. Note that §3-418(b) also applies the finality rule to the analogous situation of makers who have paid notes on which their own signatures have been forged.

Ordinarily, the rules of the Uniform Commercial Code do not control the federal government, since the UCC is a state statute. However, as a matter of federal common law, the federal courts, including the United States Supreme Court, have applied the rule of Price v. Neal to checks drawn on the Federal Treasury and paid through the Federal Reserve System. If the government subsequently discovers that the checks are forgeries and not truly signed by the appropriate federal official, the government cannot recover its money from the banks that presented the checks. See extended discussion in ABN Amro Bank v. United States, 34 Fed. Cl. 126, 1995 WL 539779 (1995). For more on the relationship of federal law and check forgery, see page 818.

The policy reasons for the finality rule are unclear. Lord Mansfield at one point in his decision said that the drawee was guilty of "neglect" if he failed by "fault or negligence" to recognize the drawer's signature. But surely if the forgery is very skillful, the "fault," if any, is minimal. Another reason often given is that at some point it is highly desirable to *end* the transaction and have the liabilities of the parties defined and not subject to change. Professor James Rogers has argued that the proper explanation is that the drawee bank is what economists call the "cheapest cost avoider," and that, having created the system the customer must use, the drawee bank must bear its limitations. See James Steven Rogers, The Basic Principle of Loss Allocation for Unauthorized Checks, 39 Wake Forest L. Rev. 453 (2004). The bank will have insurance against losses such as this.

Decibel Credit Union v. Pueblo Bank & Trust Co.

Colorado Court of Appeals, 2000
996 P.2d 784

Opinion by Judge RULAND.

This case requires us to address which party must bear the loss for amounts paid on forged checks. Defendant, Pueblo Bank & Trust Company, appeals from the summary judgment awarded to plaintiff, Decibel Credit Union. We reverse and remand the case for further proceedings.

A thief stole blank checks furnished by Decibel to one of its checking account customers. During a period of approximately 40 days, the thief forged the signature of the customer on a series of 14 checks totaling $2,350. Each of the checks was cashed at Pueblo Bank where the thief had a bank account.

On some of the days during the 40-day period, the thief cashed more than one check per day. At no time during this period did either the thief's checking account or his ready reserve account have sufficient funds to cover the checks that were being cashed.

Pueblo Bank processed all 14 checks through the Federal Reserve System to Decibel, and Decibel timely paid the checks. Decibel's customer discovered the forgeries when he received his bank statement. The customer immediately notified Decibel. Decibel then made demand upon Pueblo Bank for reimbursement. Pueblo Bank declined, and this litigation followed.

After the complaint was filed, both parties filed motions for summary judgment. Based upon those submissions, the trial court entered judgment for Decibel.

First, the trial court concluded that Decibel had given timely notice to Pueblo Bank as soon as the forgery was discovered by its account holder. Next, the trial court determined that in submitting the checks to Decibel for payment, Pueblo Bank had triggered its responsibility under the Colorado version of the Uniform Commercial Code for both presentment and transfer warranties. The court finally determined that a breach of these warranties had occurred and that Decibel was entitled to reimbursement. This appeal followed.

I.

For purposes of the Colorado Uniform Commercial Code, Decibel was the "drawee" bank in these transactions. See §4-3-103(2), C.R.S. 1999. Pueblo Bank was the "presenting bank." See §4-4-105(6). . . .

The parties also agree on most of the legal principles from the Uniform Commercial Code that apply. Generally, a drawee bank is liable to its checking account customer for payment of a check on which the customer's signature has been forged. See §4-3-418, C.R.S. 1999; Travelers Indemnity Company v. Stedman, 895 F. Supp. 742 (E.D. Pa. 1995). Further, when the drawee bank honors the forged instrument, the payment is deemed final for a person who or an entity which takes the instrument in good faith and for value. See Bank of Glen Burnie v. Loyola Federal Savings Bank, 336 Md. 331, 648 A.2d 453 (1994); North Carolina National Bank v. Hammond, 298 N.C. 703, 709, 260 S.E.2d 617, 622 n.1 (1979). . . .

II.

Pueblo Bank asserts that under the circumstances of this case, there were no presentment or transfer warranties made to Decibel and that the trial court erred in ruling to the contrary. We agree.

A.

Presentment warranties in the Colorado version of the Uniform Commercial Code appear in §4-4-208(a), C.R.S. 1999, as follows: [The court quoted §4-208(a).].

As noted in the Official Comment to a similar section, §4-3-417, C.R.S. 1999, the warranty in subsection (a)(1) is only a warranty that there are no unauthorized or missing endorsements on the checks. Further, subsection (a)(2) does not apply because there was no alteration to the checks. Finally, there is no claim that Pueblo Bank had actual knowledge of the forged signatures, and thus subsection (a)(3) does not apply.

Indeed, as the court noted in Payroll Check Cashing v. New Palestine Bank, 401 N.E.2d 752 (Ind. App. 1980), if the warranty that all signatures were genuine applied to a bank in the position of Pueblo Bank, the final payment doctrine contained in §4-3-418 would be meaningless. This doctrine is of great importance in banking commerce because it creates certainty relative to which institution must bear the loss and thus avoids time consuming and expensive litigation. See Travelers Indemnity Company v. Stedman, supra, at 747 n.9.

Accordingly, we hold that Pueblo Bank did not extend any presentment warranty to Decibel by returning the checks to it through the Federal Reserve System. Hence, the trial court erred in concluding that presentment warranties applied for the benefit of Decibel under the circumstances of this case.

B.

The term "transfer" is defined in §4-3-203(a), C.R.S. 1999, as delivery by a party other than the maker of an instrument for the purpose of giving that party the right to enforce the check. And, §4-4-207, C.R.S. 1999, contains Colorado's version of the transfer warranties of the Uniform Commercial Code. That section provides:

> (a) A customer or collecting bank that transfers an item and receives a settlement or other consideration warrants to the transferee . . . that:
>
> (1) The warrantor is a person entitled to enforce the item;
>
> (2) All signatures on the item are authentic and authorized;
>
> (3) The item has not been altered;
>
> (4) The item is not subject to a defense or claim in recoupment . . . ;
>
> (5) The warrantor has no knowledge of any insolvency proceeding commenced with respect to the . . . drawer.

Even if we assume that a transfer is involved here, it is well established that a transfer warranty as to the genuineness of the drawer's signature does not apply for the benefit of the drawee bank. See Bank of Glen Burnie v. Loyola Federal Savings Bank, supra, 336 Md. at 344, 648 A.2d at 459 n.6; see also 5 W. Hawkland, J.F. Leary & R. Alderman, Uniform Commercial Code Series §4-207:1 n.6 (1999). Hence, the trial court erred in relying on this section to enter judgment for Decibel.

To the extent that Decibel relies upon Vectra Bank v. Bank Western, 890 P.2d 259 (Colo. App. 1995) as support for the judgment, we conclude that this case does not apply. Consistent with prior interpretations of the Uniform Commercial Code in other jurisdictions, the division in *Vectra* correctly applied the transfer warranties in a case involving forged endorsements. Here, however, the signatures of the maker have been forged. . . .

The judgment is reversed, and the cause is remanded for further proceedings consistent with the views expressed in this opinion.

Judge CASEBOLT and Judge ROY concur.

PROBLEM 218

Harry Villain climbed into the window of Portia Moot's house when she was not home and stole her checkbook. When he was alone in the quiet of his own apartment, Harry wrote out one of her checks to himself and signed her name to the drawer's line. He then cashed the check at the local check cashing store, which passed it on to Merchants Bank. Merchants then presented the check to and was paid by Octopus National Bank, the drawee. When Portia got this check back in her next monthly statement, she was very upset. She immediately demanded that the bank replace the money in her account, saying the check was not properly payable without her valid signature; §4-401(a). The bank recredited her account and then called you, its attorney. Who can it sue and under what theory? See §§4-208(a) and 3-418; Bank of America, N.A. v. Amarillo Natl. Bank, 156 S.W.3d 108 (Tex. App. 2004).

Wachovia Bank, N.A. v. Foster Bancshares, Inc.

United States Court of Appeals, Seventh Circuit, 2006
457 F.3d 619

POSNER, Circuit Judge.

This diversity suit pits two banks (for unexplained reasons, the defendant bank's parent was also joined as a defendant) against each other in a quarrel over liability for a forged or altered check.

A customer of Foster Bank named Choi deposited in her account a check for $133,026 that listed her as the payee. The check had been drawn on Wachovia Bank by a company called MediaEdge that had an account with that bank. Foster presented the check to Wachovia for payment. Wachovia paid Foster and debited MediaEdge's account. Now as it happened the actual payee of the check as originally issued had not been Choi; it had been a company called CMP Media. When CMP Media told MediaEdge that it had not received the check, an investigation ensued and revealed that Choi had somehow gotten her name substituted for CMP Media on the check she'd deposited with Foster. By the time this was discovered, Choi had withdrawn the money from her account and vanished, while Wachovia had destroyed the paper check that Foster had presented to it for payment. It had done this pursuant to its normal practice, the lawfulness of which is not questioned. It had retained a computer image of the check, but whether the image is of the original check drawn on Wachovia, with an alteration, or a forged check, cannot be determined.

MediaEdge sued Wachovia in New York for the amount of the check. That suit has been stayed pending the outcome of the present suit, in which

Wachovia seeks a declaratory judgment that Foster must indemnify it in the event that MediaEdge obtains a favorable judgment in the New York suit. Wachovia's suit is based on the Uniform Commercial Code's "presentment warranty": when a depositary bank, Foster in this case, presents a check for payment by the bank that issued the check, it warrants that the check "has not been altered." UCC §§3-417(a) 1-2, 4-208(a) 1-2; Clean World Engineering, Ltd. v. MidAmerica Bank, FSB, 341 Ill. App. 3d 992, 275 Ill. Dec. 630, 793 N.E.2d 110, 117-18 (2003); Wachovia Bank, N.A. v. FRB, 338 F.3d 318, 321-22 (4th Cir. 2003). The district court granted summary judgment for Wachovia. Foster had impleaded Choi as a third-party defendant but could not serve her because of her disappearance, so the district court dismissed the third-party claim. Foster does not challenge that ruling. . . .

The bank argues that Wachovia, because it cannot produce the paper check, cannot prove that the check was altered. For all we know, rather than the check being "altered" in the usual sense, Choi used sophisticated copying technology to produce a copy that was identical in every respect to the original check (including the authorized signature by MediaEdge's chief financial officer) except for an undetectable change of the payee's name. Had the original paper check not been destroyed, it could be examined and the examination might reveal whether the check had been forged as just described or the payee's name had been changed by chemical washing of the check or by some other method that utilized rather than replaced the original check.

The bank on which a check is drawn (Wachovia in this case) warrants to the presenting bank that the check is genuine, UCC §3-418(c); id., Official Comment 1; Henry J. Bailey & Richard B. Hagedorn, Brady on Bank Checks §28.11[1] (2006), hence not forged,[6] while as we know the presenting bank warrants that the check hasn't been altered since its issuance. When checks were inspected by hand, when copying technology was primitive, and when cancelled checks were stored rather than digitized copies alone retained, this allocation of liability was consistent with the sensible economic principle that the duty to avoid a loss should be placed on the party that can prevent the loss at lower cost. Holtz v. J.J.B. Hilliard W.L. Lyons, Inc., 185 F.3d 732, 743 (7th Cir. 1999); Edwards v. Honeywell, Inc., 50 F.3d 484, 490 (7th Cir. 1995); National Union Fire Ins. Co. v. Riggs Nat'l Bank, 5 F.3d 554, 557 (D.C. Cir. 1993) (concurring opinion). Having no dealings with MediaEdge, Foster could not determine at reasonable cost whether, for example, the drawer's

6. [This is badly phrased by the court. There is no warranty involved. What the court means is that once a drawee bank has paid a check on which the drawer's name is forged, it cannot return it. That is the rule of Price v. Neal, of course, and as to that the court is correct. — Eds.]

signature had been forged. Wachovia might be able to determine this by comparing the signature on the check presented to it for payment with the authorized signature in its files. But Wachovia would have no idea who the intended payee was, while Foster might have reason to suspect that the person who deposited the check with it was not the intended payee. And it would be in as good a position as Wachovia to spot an alteration on the check.

But this last point assumes that a payee's name would be altered in the old-fashioned way, by whiting out or otherwise physically effacing the name on the paper check. If Choi created a new check, there would be no physical alteration to alert Foster when she deposited the check with the bank. That is why Foster complains that Wachovia's failure to retain the paper check prevents determining how the "alteration" was effected—more precisely, whether it is a case of alteration or of forgery. The fact that MediaEdge acknowledges having issued a check to CMP Media is not conclusive on the question because Choi might have destroyed that check, rather than altering it, and substituted a copy that seemed perfectly genuine, with her name in place of CMP Media.

So the case comes down to whether, in cases of doubt, forgery should be assumed or alteration should be assumed. If the former, Foster wins, and if the latter, Wachovia. It seems to us that the tie should go to the drawee bank, Wachovia. Changing the payee's name is the classic alteration. It can with modern technology be effected by forging a check rather than by altering an original check, but since this is a novel method, the presenting bank must do more than merely assert the possibility of it. Granted, it is the duty of the drawee bank to take reasonable measures to prevent the forging of its checks, as by marking them in a way that a forger could not discover and therefore duplicate. But Foster has made no effort to show that retention of mountains of paper checks—which would be necessary to determine whether the original check had such a marking—would be a reasonable method of determining whether the drawee bank or the presenting bank should be liable for the loss.

Nor did Foster make any effort to show—as it might have been able to do, see Henry Bailey & Richard Hagedorn, supra, §28.3—that duplication of the entire check (that is, forgery of the check deposited with the presenting bank), rather than just physical alteration of the payee's name on the original check, has become a common method of bank fraud. Nor did it try to show that banks have, as they are allowed to do, been contracting around the provisions of the UCC relating to the warranties of drawee and presenting banks in cases such as this. Nor did it try to show what Choi's modus operandi was, assuming that she had stolen money in this way on other occasions, though such evidence may of course have been unobtainable.

Even if Foster had shown that forgery of the entire check has become a routine method of altering the payee's name, we would not adopt the rule for which it contends, which is that the drawee bank cannot enforce the presentment warranty unless it retains the paper check. The question of which bank was, in the language of economic analysis of law, the "cheaper cost avoider" would still be open. (Maybe neither bank is—which would hardly be a persuasive ground for changing a long-settled rule of law.) A depositary bank can sometimes discover an alteration of the payee's name even when there is no physical alteration in the check presented to the bank for deposit. The size of the check may be a warning flag that induces the bank to delay making funds deposited by the check available for withdrawal. E.g., Bank of America, "Frequently Asked Questions," http://www.bankofamerica.com/deposits/checksave/index.cfm?template= lc_faq_acct_info (visited July 5, 2006); Kennebunk Savings Bank, "Deposit Account Agreement," http://www.kennebunksavings.com/depositagreement.html (visited July 5, 2006). The check that Choi deposited with Foster was for a hefty $133,000, and there is no evidence that Choi had previously deposited large checks. We do not suggest that Foster was careless in deciding to make the money available for withdrawal when it did. But the uncertainties that the bank has made no effort to dispel counsel against adopting the legal change that it urges. Reform if needed in the light of modern copying technology should be left to the Uniform State Commissioners rather than engineered by a federal court in a diversity case. The judgment for Wachovia is therefore

Affirmed.

QUESTION

The court seems to think that the only problem with this check was the possible "alteration" of the payee's name, so that if there had been no "alteration," the drawee bank would have lost the case. What happened to the presentment warranty in §4-208(a)(1), and why wasn't it discussed by Judge Posner?

For years one of your authors (Whaley) wandered around the country lecturing bankers on the law of checking accounts. It amazed him that banking usage of trade ignores the rule of Price v. Neal. Over and over he was told by bankers that when the payor bank, having made final payment and then discovering the drawer's name was forged, demands repayment from the depositary bank, the latter simply coughs up the money. "We always do it that way," the banks explained. "Stop that!" Whaley would reply. "You have no right to give away your customer's money without authority, and the next time a payor bank demands its money back, ask it to specify the legal theory for its recovery." That will end that.

PROBLEM 219

In the last Problem, ONB, unhappy with being told that the depositary bank did not violate §4-208(a)(3), now asks you if the depositary bank violated §4-208(a)(1). Did it?

The answer is no, but it is a rather complicated no. Start by reading §3-403. Subsection (a) contains the basic idea that the forgery acts as if the forger had signed his or her *own* name instead of the name forged. Were that true in the above Problems, Harry Villain would be the true drawer of this check. In that case, we would have a check drawn by Harry Villain, payable to the order of Harry Villain, properly indorsed by the payee, and then properly negotiated by the check cashing store and the depositary bank. The depositary bank *was* a "person entitled to enforce the draft" of Harry Villain. In effect, the payor bank here paid the draft of a non-customer drawer. That isn't the draft they thought they were paying, but the rule of Price v. Neal puts that risk squarely on the drawee; there was nothing wrong with the negotiation. The age-old saying is that "the drawee must know the drawer's signature as a mother must know her child," and making a mistake on this cannot pass the loss back to innocent parties.

PROBLEM 220

In Problem 175 of the last chapter a drawee bank paid a check with no drawer's signature at all because the check had been created over the telephone by the telemarketing payee. When we did this Problem the last time, the relevant question was whether the check was properly payable from the drawer's bank account under §4-401 (the "properly payable" rule), and the answer (as yet unaddressed by the courts) is highly likely to be no. Thus the drawee bank must replace the money in the drawer's account (unless the subrogation rule of §4-407 can be brought into play to protect the bank). Having done so, the bank now calls you, its attorney. It wants to pass the liability back to the depositary bank. Can this be done, and, if so, under what theory?

The answer to this question is complicated by that fact that the original rules of law would place the liability here on the drawee bank as an extension of the rule of Price v. Neal: the bank has made a mistaken payment from its customer's account and must eat the loss unless the telemarketing payee can be found and made to cough up the money; see §3-418 for the cause of action against the payee here. The trouble with this result is that it is contrary to banking practices. Unaware of the rules of law, the drawee banks in this situation routinely return the preauthorized draft to the depositary bank, which debits the account of the telemarketing payee. The drafters of the UCC in 2002 proposed amendments to the presentment warranty sections that would allow the drawee bank to return what the Code now calls a "remotely-created consumer item" to the depositary bank—see §4-208(a)(4)—but these amendments have only been adopted in about 12 states as of this writing.

The Federal Reserve has now solved the problem in all U.S. jurisdictions. Effective July 1, 2006, the Fed adopted amendments to Regulation CC, 12 C.F.R. part 229. The Regulation calls these items "remotely created checks" [Reg. CC §229.2(fff)], and creates both presentment and transfer warranties that these checks were authorized by the person on whose account they are drawn in the amount specified. This allows the return of the check to the depositary bank, which is thought to be in a better position to monitor the activities of the payee than is the payor bank. See Reg. CC §229.34(d).[7]

Federal Government. The Uniform Commercial Code is a state statute and does not, of course, bind the federal government. However, as a matter of federal common law (inherited from Great Britain) the federal courts, including the United States Supreme Court, have applied the rule of Price v. Neal to checks drawn on the Federal Treasury and thereafter paid. If the government subsequently discovers that the checks are forgeries and not truly signed by the appropriate federal official, the government cannot recover its money from the banks that presented the checks. See extended discussion in ABN Amro Bank v. United States, 34 Fed. Cl. 126, 1995 WL 539779 (1995).

What steps do banks take to protect themselves from the vicious bite of Price v. Neal? In an era of check truncation and electronic presentment, many payor banks don't recapture their drawers' checks and have no opportunity to compare drawers' signatures with the signature cards (though as Check 21 imaging becomes more prevalent, the banks would be able to check the customer's signature, though most will not for economic reasons). Most banks engage in a practice called "bulk filing," in which the banks don't physically examine the checks at all if they are below a certain amount but simply file them away in bulk. If a check proves forged and the forger cannot be found, these banks recredit the drawers' accounts and look to their forgery insurance.

7. It should also be noted that the Federal Trade Commission's Telemarketing Sales Rule, 16 C.F.R. §310.3(a)(3), already requires telemarketers to obtain the customer's "express verifiable authorization" before issuing the check. One can speculate how often this is actually done.

QUESTION

If the drawer's signature is forged, but the bank pays the check anyway, the rule of Price v. Neal puts the loss on the payor bank. However, if the payee's name is forged, the loss tends to fall on the depositary bank. Are these results merely whimsical, or is there a rational reason for the two different placements of liability? In his book The End of Negotiable Instruments (2011), Professor James Rogers concludes that forgery rules placing responsibility on the banks themselves offer the optimum solution. Banks are best able to guard against or absorb the loss (if not able to pass it off to the wrongdoer), as opposed to innocent parties outside the banking system, such as the person whose name was forged. Depositary banks have the best connection to the payee and the payor bank has the same connection to the drawer.

III. VALIDATION OF THE FORGERY

Both Price v. Neal and the rule that the forged indorsement is ineffective to negotiate the instrument put a heavy burden on the drawee bank, which must frequently bear the forgery loss (or insure against it). To militate against the harshness of these rules, the basic forgery rule, §3-403(a), has an escape clause in the words "Unless otherwise provided in this Article or Article 4" and "an unauthorized signature may be ratified." This means that under some circumstances the forged signature will be treated as genuine. What are these circumstances that validate a forgery?

Ratification, a doctrine coming to us from agency law, for negotiable instrument purposes occurs when the party in question, with full knowledge of the forgery or alteration, accepts the benefits thereof or actively assents to the wrongful activity. See Rakestraw v. Rodrigues, 8 Cal. 3d 67, 500 P.2d 1401, 104 Cal. Rptr. 57 (1972); cf. Salsman v. National Community Bank, 102 N.J. Super. 482, 246 A.2d 162 (1968), *aff'd*, 105 N.J. Super. 164, 251 A.2d 460 (1969); Bank of Hoven v. Rausch, 382 N.W.2d 39 (S.D. 1986).

PROBLEM 221

George learned that his wife, Martha, had been forging his name to business checks received in his business on which he was the named payee. Except for this peccadillo, she was a model wife, and it was a good marriage, so he said nothing rather than embarrass her. Two years later his extramarital affair caused a divorce, so he decided to recover the money by bringing a conversion action against the banks that had paid money on the forged indorsements. Will his suit succeed? See Johnson v. Johnson, 2005 WL 3276177 (N.J. Super. 2005).

Ratification of supposed agency status can also occur, as where the non-agent has apparent authority due to the alleged principal's actions or inactions. See §3-402(a) and its Official Comment 1; Fulka v. Florida Commercial Banks, Inc., 371 So. 2d 521 (Fla. Dist. App. 1979) (payee estopped to bring conversion action where she knew a business associate was forging her name to checks, but kept silent); Annot., 82 A.L.R.3d 625. The major UCC case is Senate Motors, Inc. v. Industrial Bank of Washington, 1971 WL 17944 (D.C. Super. 1971). For pre-Code cases finding apparent authority in an agent to cash the alleged principal's checks, see Corbett v. Kleinsmith, 112 F.2d 511 (6th Cir. 1940); Commercial Cas. Ins. Co. v. Isabell Natl. Bank, 223 Ala. 48, 134 So. 810 (1931); Arcade Realty Co. v. Bank of Commerce, 180 Cal. 318, 181 P. 66 (1919); Rosser-Moon Furn. Co. v. Oklahoma State Bank, 192 Okla. 169, 135 P.2d 336 (1943). It is important to appreciate that the courts are slow to presume such authority. See, e.g., Taylor v. Equitable Trust Co., 269 Md. 149, 304 A.2d 838 (1973).

A. *Common Law Validation*

Hutzler v. Hertz Corp.

Court of Appeals of New York, 1976
39 N.Y.2d 209, 347 N.E.2d 627, 383 N.Y.S.2d 266

JASEN, J.

In this action against defendant tortfeasor arising out of the compromise of a personal injury and wrongful death claim made with the tortfeasor by plaintiff's attorney with the consent of the plaintiff, we are asked to decide whether defendant tortfeasor was discharged from liability where its settlement draft, naming plaintiff and her attorney as payees, was negotiated by the attorney on plaintiff's forged indorsement and the proceeds of the draft appropriated. For the reasons which follow, we hold that the tortfeasor's liability was discharged upon payment of the settlement draft by the drawee bank, the forgery notwithstanding, and that the claimant may not thereafter recover against the tortfeasor.

The parties are in agreement as to the basic facts. On June 1, 1966, Christina Hutzler was granted limited letters of administration by the Surrogate of Queens County on the estate of her husband who had perished on October 4, 1965, in an automobile accident. Through her attorney,

Daniel D. Yudow, she commenced an action against Hertz Corporation to recover damages for the personal injuries and wrongful death of her husband. After some time Yudow succeeded in settling the action with Hertz and on November 23, 1970, in consideration of that settlement, Mrs. Hutzler, after obtaining permission of the Surrogate's Court to compromise the action, executed a general release in Hertz' favor. On December 11, 1970, Hertz issued and mailed to Yudow two checks totalling $11,500, the amount of the settlement, both of which were drawn on the Manufacturers Hanover Trust Company. One of these with which we are not concerned, was in the sum of $571, made payable to "The State Insurance Fund c/o Daniel D. Yudow." The second check was for $10,929, the balance of the settlement, and was payable to "Christina Hutzler Individually And As Administratrix of the Estate of Michael E. Hutzler and Daniel D. Yudow as attorney." On December 14, 1970, Yudow, having indorsed this check with his own signature and with the forged signature of Mrs. Hutzler, deposited it in an account in his name at Manufacturers Hanover. Four months later, in April 1971, he closed the account. In the meantime, Mrs. Hutzler attempted to obtain her share of the proceeds of the settlement, but was unsuccessful in locating Yudow until June, 1973. In the interim she learned that he had closed his office and was no longer in practice.[8] Thereafter she retained her present counsel who made oral and written demand for payment on Hertz in June, 1973. Hertz produced a copy of its settlement draft and refused payment. Upon examination of the indorsements, the forgery was at once apparent to Mrs. Hutzler, and both Hertz and Manufacturers Hanover were immediately apprised of this fact. Since no satisfactory resolution could be made, Mrs. Hutzler, a short time later, commenced this action against Hertz and Manufacturers Hanover to recover the amount of the settlement check. She alleged one cause of action against Hertz for negligence in not comparing the forged signature with her signature on the settlement agreement, and two causes of action against Manufacturers Hanover, one for conversion of the check and its proceeds and the other for breach of warranty.

On cross-motions for summary judgment, Special Term granted Mrs. Hutzler judgment against Hertz for the amount of the check, and denied Hertz' motion for summary judgment. Summary judgment was also granted to the defendant bank on which the check was drawn, but no appeal was taken by the plaintiff from this part of the judgment and order. On Hertz' appeal, a divided Appellate Division modified the judgment and order "by adding to each of them a provision that the amount of plaintiff's recovery against defendant The Hertz Corporation be reduced by the amount

8. We are informed that the records of the First Department indicate that Yudow's name was stricken from the Roll of Attorneys and Counselors-at-Law, on consent, on March 22, 1972.

of the lien that attorney Yudow, had he not engaged in misconduct with respect to the settlement check, and not converted the proceeds thereof, would have been entitled to for professional services," and remitted the case for a determination of the amount of that lien. (47 A.D.2d 839.) Special Term thereupon determined the amount of the lien, and amended its earlier judgment accordingly. Hertz now appeals directly, as of right, from this amended judgment, bringing up for review with it the prior non-final order of the Appellate Division. (C.P.L.R. 5601, subd. [d].) Mrs. Hutzler cross appeals, also as of right (C.P.L.R. 5601, subd. [a], par. [iii]), claiming that the Appellate Division erred in reducing the amount of her judgment by the amount of her former attorney's lien for services rendered.

At the outset, we note that the courts of other jurisdictions have divided on the question now before us and it seems as though no majority rule can be stated. (See generally Annot., Forgery by Debtor's Agent Discharge, 49 A.L.R.3d 843, 846.) Indeed, the cases of this state have been characterized as representing in microcosm this division of authority, with no definitive statement of our rule possible. (Id., at pp.847, 859.)

As we view this case, we are concerned with two separate sets of legal relationships. The first involves a plaintiff and a tortfeasor, and the tortfeasor's payment to the plaintiff's attorney in settlement of the tort action. Reference must be made to principles of agency law in analyzing the rights and duties which arise from this set of relationships. The second concerns the relationships created when payment is made by a negotiable instrument. The rights and duties growing out of this set of relationships evolve from the law of negotiable instruments embodied principally in the Uniform Commercial Code. Only by keeping in mind that we are dealing with two separate bodies of law can we properly resolve this controversy.

We start with agency considerations. An attorney retained to collect a debt, or as here, to recover damages for personal injuries and wrongful death, normally also has at least apparent authority to receive payment from the debtor or tortfeasor once a settlement has been reached or a judgment entered. (McCoy v. Barclay, 250 App. Div. 682, 684; Moss v. Standard Brands, 68 Misc. 2d 625, 627; 2 Mechem, Agency 2180, p.1762.) This is clearly the rule, at least where payment is in cash. (See 7 Am. Jur. 2d, Attorneys at Law 102; 7 C.J.S., Attorney and Client 106, subd. c.) Having made such a payment to the creditor's or claimant's attorney, the debtor or tortfeasor can be assured that he has been discharged from liability. If the attorney absconds with the cash without paying it over to his client, the client may not thereafter compel the debtor or tortfeasor to pay a second time. (See Morrison v. Chapman, 155 App. Div. 509, 514; Burstein v. Sullivan, 134 App. Div. 623, 625.) He must instead look to the defalcating attorney.

An analogous situation develops where payment is made to the attorney for a claimant by means of a check made payable solely to the attorney.

Payment by check, sometimes referred to as "conditional payment," is not, by itself, payment of the underlying obligation. (Chatham Securities Corp. v. Williston & Beane, 41 Misc. 2d 817, 821, *aff'd,* 22 A.D.2d 260, *aff'd without op.,* 16 N.Y.2d 1016; Mansion Carpets v. Marinoff, 24 A.D.2d 947; Uniform Commercial Code §3-802, Official Comment 3 [now §3-310(b)—Eds.].) Only when the drawee bank pays on the check is payment actually effected. Thus, once the drawee bank has paid on the check the debtor or tortfeasor is discharged from the underlying obligation as fully as though he had paid the attorney cash. As where payment is in cash, if the agent appropriates the proceeds of a check for himself, the claimant may not seek repayment from the debtor or tortfeasor.

The situation becomes somewhat more complicated where the check is made payable only to the creditor or claimant, or, as here, to the claimant and attorney jointly. It is at this juncture that the agency principles just described and certain principles of the law of negotiable instruments would seem to come into conflict. Indeed, Mrs. Hutzler argues that the forged indorsement by Yudow was "wholly inoperative as that of the person [Mrs. Hutzler] whose name is signed" (Uniform Commercial Code §3-404 subd. (1)) and that Hertz' liability was therefore not discharged by its settlement draft. This argument, if accepted, would require Hertz to pay a second time.

Long ago the rule developed in this state that debtor's liability is discharged when a check payable to the creditor is wrongfully indorsed by the creditor's agent and is paid by the drawee bank, and the proceeds converted by the agent. (Sage v. Burton, 84 Hun. 267; Allen v. Tarrant & Co., 7 App. Div. 172; Morris v. Hofferberth, 81 App. Div. 512, *aff'd,* 180 N.Y. 545.) The basis for this rule is that the drawer's only obligation to the payee, upon issuance of the check, is to "see that funds are in the bank." (Sage v. Burton, supra, at p. 270.) The drawer thereafter has no obligation to examine the check for forged indorsements. (See National Surety Co. v. Manhattan Co., 252 N.Y. 247, 254.) Since checks and drafts are the usual and ordinary means of transferring money in the transaction of business, a contrary rule would add an unnecessary element of risk and uncertainty where payment is made by check to an authorized agent. Because of the time factors involved in processing a check through the depositary bank, intermediate collecting banks and the drawee bank, the discovery of the forgery by the drawer, even if possible, would often be of little practical value to the payee. Moreover, as indicated above, if a check is payable solely to the agent, there is no question that the obligation would be discharged upon payment by the drawee bank. By making the check payable to the creditor, the drawer has given the creditor a measure of protection by requiring the agent to expose himself to criminal prosecution by forging an indorsement before converting the proceeds. (See Burstein v. Sullivan, 134 App. Div. 623, 625, supra.) Therefore, as between the creditor and the drawer of the check, the party who should be required to bear the loss under such circumstances is the creditor. It is the creditor, after all, who selected a dishonest person to represent him, and he, not the drawer, should bear the risk of his unauthorized acts, having placed him in a position to perpetrate the wrong. (Sage v. Burton, 84 Hun. 267, 270, supra, Morrison v. Chapman, 155 App. Div. 509, 512, 514, supra.) The fact that the agent acted in excess of his authority in forging the indorsement is, of course, no more helpful to the creditor than is the fact that the agent who absconds with a cash payment also acts in excess of his authority. (Morrison v. Chapman, supra, at p. 514.) . . .

We note that this resolution squares with the position taken by the American Law Institute in the Restatement Second of Agency.[9] We expressly approve of that provision and hold that it correctly states the law of this state.

Returning to considerations of the law of negotiable instruments, we conclude that our holding today, in the context of the kind of relationship involved, is consistent with §3-404 of the Uniform Commercial Code [now §3-403(a)—EDS.], despite the apparent conflict noted earlier. Subdivision (1) of that section provides in part that "[a]ny unauthorized signature is wholly inoperative as that of the person whose name is signed unless he ratifies it or is precluded from denying it. . . ." Since our resolution of the issue before us is based primarily upon the principles of agency, we would hold that a person whose name is forged on an instrument by his agent is, by his unwise selection of this agent, estopped or "precluded from denying" the unauthorized signature.

Finally, we note that this rule is not unduly harsh on a person who has been defrauded in this manner by a dishonest agent. To be sure, the unfaithful agent is an unpromising defendant, and often there is little likelihood of recovering from him. However, generally the creditor could pursue

9. The relevant section is as follows

> §178. Agent Authorized to Collect a Debt . . .
>
> (2) If an agent who is authorized to receive a check payable to the principal as conditional payment forges the principal's endorsement to such a check, the maker is relieved of liability to the principal if the drawee bank pays the check and charges the amount to the maker.

This subsection is discussed in Comment c:

> If a debtor, having an account at a solvent bank sufficient to pay a check, gives to an authorized agent a check payable to the principal in accordance with business customs as conditional payment, he has performed his obligation, and any loss caused by delay because of the conduct of the agent is at the creditor's risk. Thus, if the drawee bank cashes the check after a forgery and embezzlement by the agent and charges the amount to the debtor, the latter is relieved of his debt. The creditor then would be subrogated to the right of the debtor against the bank. If, in the meantime, the bank becomes insolvent, it is the creditor and not the debtor who loses.

an action for conversion against the drawee bank. (Henderson v. Lincoln Rochester Trust Co., 303 N.Y. 27, 31; Spaulding v. First Natl. Bank, 210 App. Div. 216, 217, *aff'd without op.*, 239 N.Y. 586; Uniform Commercial Code §3-419, subd. [1], par. [c] [now §3-420(a)—Eds.].) Unfortunately, that rule does little for the plaintiff in this case as no appeal was taken from the order dismissing her conversion action against Manufacturers Hanover. Our compassion for the plaintiff cannot, however, serve as a basis for granting her relief against Hertz.

Accordingly, the amended judgment should be reversed and Hertz' motion for summary judgment granted and the complaint dismissed.

Judgment reversed, without costs, the motion by defendant The Hertz Corporation for summary judgment granted and the complaint dismissed. All concur.

QUESTION

Could the plaintiff sue the drawee bank? What would be her cause of action? See §3-420(a); Florida Bar v. Allstate Ins. Co., 391 So. 2d 238 (Fla. Dist. App. 1980).

PROBLEM 222

Donna Drawer gave her check to Paul Payee, who lost it before he indorsed it. The finder was an evil person, identity unknown, who forged "Paul Payee" to the back of the check and received payment from the drawee, Octopus National Bank (ONB). Is ONB liable to Paul Payee? See §3-420(a). If ONB pays Paul, is it also liable to Donna? See §§4-401, 4-407.

The common law handled this double liability problem by saying that it is always a defense to a negotiable instruments action to show that the money got where it was supposed to go, and, thus, the plaintiff has no damages. See Ambassador Fin. Serv., Inc. v. Indiana National Bank, 605 N.E.2d 746 (Ind. 1992); Tonelli v. Chase Manhattan Bank, N.A., 41 N.Y.2d 667, 363 N.E.2d 564, 394 N.Y.S.2d 858 (1977); Middle States Leasing Corp. v. Manufacturers Hanover Trust Co., 62 A.D.2d 273, 404 N.Y.S.2d 846 (1978). Whether approached under this idea or under §4-407's subrogation rule, the result is the same: a successful conversion action by the payee destroys the drawer's §4-401 not *properly payable* suit against the drawee.

The four Uniform Commercial Code sections that validate the wrongdoing in certain circumstances are §3-404 (the Impostor Rule), §3-405 (the Employee Forgery Rule), §3-406 (the Negligence Rule), and §4-406 (the Bank Statement Rule). They come up next, one by one.

B. *The Impostor Rule*

An "impostor"[10] is someone pretending to be someone else. The Impostor Rule in the Uniform Commercial Code validates the forgery of the *payee's* name (and only the payee's name) in the situations described in §3-404. In each of these situations, the drawer or maker has been duped by either an outsider or a trusted employee into creating an instrument on which the name of the payee is highly likely to be forged, and it is proper to put the resulting liability on the drawer/maker rather than on non-negligent parties, such as the indorsers or banks involved in collecting or paying the checks.

PROBLEM 223

Old and rich Amy Altruism was well known for her charitable contributions. One day, she answered her door to find Sandra Sting, a woman whose photograph was at that moment decorating the "wanted" posters of the country and multiple police websites, standing on the front stoop. Sandra told Amy that she was Hilda Humane, the founder of Humane's Home for Homeless Dogs, Inc., and that she wished to solicit a contribution for this worthy cause, which she described in much detail. Amy was taken in by this story, and while weeping copiously over the plight of the canine element of the world, she wrote a check for $5,000 payable to "Hilda Humane." Sandra pocketed the check, thanked her warmly, and left her quickly. She went straight to the drawee bank where, after signing "Hilda Humane" to the back of the check, she received payment. If Amy discovers that there is no such thing as Humane's Home for Homeless Dogs, Inc., can she successfully demand that her account be recredited on the theory that the check was cashed on an improper signature (not "properly payable")? See §3-404(a).

Let us next consider the issue of a double check forgery: both the drawer's and the payee's names are forged. Now what?

PROBLEM 224

Mrs. Walter Heartstrong wrote the Methuselah Life Insurance Company telling them, "I want to discontinue my life insurance policy. Please cancel

10. The word *impostor* is undergoing a spelling change. Originally, it was almost always spelled with an "or" at the end, but in recent years "er" seems to have won the day. Either spelling is now considered correct.

it and mail me the cash surrender value. I hereby certify that I have lost the policy (#112-011Z) itself or misplaced it somewhere, (signed) Walter Heartstrong." The company mailed a check to the order of "Walter Heartstrong." Mrs. Heartstrong got to the mailbox before her husband did, obtained the check, forged her husband's name on the back, and deposited the check at the Smalltown State Bank. The latter presented it to the drawee, Octopus National, which cashed it without a murmur. When Walter sues the insurance company and they call you, what would you advise? See Hicks v. Northwestern Mut. Life Ins. Co., 166 Iowa 532, 147 N.W. 883 (1914); cf. Franklin Natl. Bank v. Shapiro, 1970 WL 12588 (N.Y. Sup. Ct. 1970).

To understand §3-404(b) you need to conquer the concept of the "person whose intent determines to whom an instrument is payable" in §3-110(a) and (b). Generally, it means the person who signed the instrument, though for check-writing machines it means the person who supplied the name of the payee, whether or not authorized to do so. Apply §3-404(b) to the following Problem.

PROBLEM 225

One day it occurred to the corporate treasurer of the Business Corporation that his personal situation would be easier if he started adding fictitious employees to the payroll and took their checks each month for deposit into accounts opened under the phony names. Are such checks properly payable from the account Business Corporation has with its bank? See §3-404(b). Would the result be different if the treasurer padded the payroll with the names of real former employees and then did the same thing with these checks? If the depositary banks that took these checks were negligent in allowing the treasurer to open the accounts, would that change the result? See §3-404(d).[11]

State Sec. Check Cashing, Inc. v. American General Financial

Court of Appeals of Maryland, 2009
409 Md. 81, 972 A.2d 882

Harrell, Judge.

In this case we are asked to determine which party, as between the issuer of a check and the check cashing business that cashed it, is liable under Md.

11. There are similar comparative fault sections in each of the validation sections; see §§3-405(b), 3-406(b), and 4-406(e).

Code, Commercial Law Art. §3-404 (2002 Repl. Vol. & Supp. 2008) for the face amount of the check, when an imposter, posing successfully as another individual in securing a loan (the proceeds of which were represented by the check) from the issuer, subsequently negotiated the check at the check cashing business. We shall hold that, under the circumstances presented in this case, the issuer of the check is liable for the amount of the check.

I. Factual and Procedural Background

On 20 June 2007, American General Financial Services, Inc. ("American General") was contacted by telephone by a man, later revealed to be an imposter posing as Ronald E. Wilder (we shall refer to this person as the "imposter," though he was not known to be so at most relevant times in this case). The imposter sought a $20,000.00 loan. Based on the information supplied by him over the telephone, American General ran a credit check on Ronald E. Wilder, finding his credit to be excellent. American General informed the imposter that it would need personal tax returns for the prior two years, and asked him what he intended to do with the proceeds of the desired loan. The imposter sent by electronic facsimile to American General the requested tax returns of Mr. Wilder and explained that he wanted the loan to renovate a property he owned. On Friday, 22 June 2007, American General's District Manager received the completed loan application and tax returns, performed a cash flow analysis, and obtained approval from senior management for an $18,000.00 loan.

On that same morning, American General informed the imposter that the loan was approved. The imposter appeared at noon at American General's Security Boulevard office in Baltimore County. He proffered an apparent Maryland driver's license bearing Mr. Wilder's personal information and the imposter's photograph. He remained in the loan office for approximately thirty minutes, meeting with the branch manager and a customer account specialist during the loan closing. After all the loan documents were signed, American General issued to the imposter a loan check for $18,000.00, drawn on Wachovia Bank, N.A., and payable to Ronald E. Wilder.

Later that afternoon, the imposter presented the check to State Security Check Cashing, Inc. ("State Security"), a check cashing business. At the time the imposter appeared in State Security's office, also on Security Boulevard in Baltimore County, only one employee was on duty, Wanda Decker. Decker considered the same driver's license that the imposter presented to American General, and reviewed the American General loan documents related to the check. She also compared the check to other checks issued by American General which had been cashed previously by State Security. Deeming the amount of the check relatively "large," Decker called Joel Deutsch, State

Security's compliance officer, to confirm that she had taken the proper steps in verifying the check. Deutsch directed Decker to verify the date of the check, the name of the payee on the check, the address of the licensee, the supporting loan paperwork, and whether the check matched other checks in State Security's system from the issuer. Decker confirmed the results of all of these steps, and, upon Deutsch's approval, cashed the check, on behalf of State Security, for the imposter for a fee of 3-5% of the face value of the check.

On Monday, 25 June, the next business day after the imposter negotiated the check at State Security, the real Ronald E. Wilder appeared at the offices of American General indicating that he had been notified by the U.S. Secret Service that a person applied for a loan in his name. At that time, the true Ronald E. Wilder completed an Affidavit of Forgery. As a result of the Affidavit, Thurman Toland, the Branch Manager of American General's Security Boulevard branch, called Wachovia Bank to determine whether the $18,000.00 check had been presented for payment. Learning that the check had not been presented yet, Toland placed a "stop payment" on the check.

State Security filed a civil claim in the District Court of Maryland, sitting in Baltimore County, against American General for the face value of the check, plus interest, asserting that it was a holder in due course of American General's check, that it received the check in good faith, without knowledge of fraud, and that it gave value for the check. On 3 December 2007, the District Court conducted a bench trial. During the trial, the testimonies of Deutsch and Toland revealed three additional, potentially important points: (a) had State Security personnel called American General on 22 June 2007 to verify that American General issued a check to Ronald E. Wilder for $18,000.00, Toland would have confirmed that to be the case; (b) State Security employed a thumb print identification system for its check-cashing business, but, at the time the imposter cashed the check, it was unclear whether it was functional; and (c) although, as part of the loan application process, American General obtained names and telephone numbers of personal references from the imposter, it did not call any of the references before delivering the check.

On 19 December 2007, the District Court held in favor of American General, explaining:

> What was the one action that either party could have taken "to prevent the loss"? In the Court's view Security could have withheld payment, to the imposter, until the check cleared on the Defendant's "out of town" bank. But Security is in the business of cashing checks and charges a fee of between 3% and 5% for the check cashing service; and with a check of this amount, it probably earned a fee of approximately nine hundred ($900.00) dollars. If one is charging that type of a fee, a customer cashing a check on Friday is not

> going to wait until the following Monday to receive the proceeds. That is a risk of doing the type of business[] the Plaintiff chooses to do.

The District Court concluded that, under Md. Code, Commercial Law Art. §3-404(d), State Security had not exercised ordinary care in paying the imposter's check, and that its failure to exercise ordinary care contributed substantially to the loss.

State Security appealed to the Circuit Court for Baltimore County. A hearing was held on 24 July 2008, based on the record made in the District Court. On 8 August 2008, the Circuit Court issued its Memorandum Opinion and Order affirming the judgment of the District Court. . . .

State Security pressed on. It filed a petition for writ of certiorari with this Court, pursuant to Md. Code, Courts and Judicial Proceedings Art. §§12-305 and 12-307 (2006 Repl. Vol. & Supp. 2008), seeking review of the Circuit Court's judgment. We issued the writ. State Sec. v. Am. Gen., 406 Md. 443, 959 A.2d 793 (2008).

II. Discussion

[In a controversial portion of the opinion, the court first concluded that State Security qualified as a holder in due course and so American General could not raise its defense of fraud by the payee. The court then turned to the Impostor Rule.]

B. Commercial Law Art. §3-404

Commercial Law Art. §3-404 addresses the circumstances, among other situations, of imposters. Md. Code, Com. Law Art. §3-404. Regarding our imposter in the present case, the District Court ruled, under §3-404(d), that State Security did not exercise ordinary care in paying the check presented by him, and that the failure to exercise such care contributed substantially to the loss. The Circuit Court, in affirming that judgment, concluded that there was substantial evidence to support the District Court's finding, and therefore the District Court's finding was not clearly erroneous. . . .

The District Court determined initially and correctly that the imposter rule applies in this case because all of the pertinent requirements of Commercial Law Art. §3-404(a) were present. As noted, *supra*, §3-404(a) provides:

> (a) If an impostor, by use of the mails or otherwise, induces the issuer of an instrument to issue the instrument to the impostor, or to a person acting in concert with the impostor, by impersonating the payee of the instrument or a person authorized to act for the payee, an indorsement of the instrument by any person in the name of the payee is effective as the indorsement of the

> payee in favor of a person who, in good faith, pays the instrument or takes it for value or for collection.

Md. Code, Com. Law Art. §3-404(a). Although "imposter" is not defined in the Commercial Law Article, in Bank of Glen Burnie v. Elkridge Bank, 120 Md. App. 402, 707 A.2d 438 (1998), the Court of Special Appeals concluded that "'[i]mposter' is defined as 'one who poses as another to obtain benefits under a negotiable instrument.'" *Bank of Glen Burnie,* 120 Md. App. at 408-09, 707 A.2d at 441 (citing Black's Law Dictionary 756 (6th ed. 1991)). There is no doubt that, by appearing in person at both American General and State Security to conduct transactions, which included the presentation of a forged driver's license with the imposter's picture, but the name and personal identification information of Ronald E. Wilder, the individual in this case was a person who posed as another to obtain the benefits of the check issued by American General. There also is no doubt that, by posing as Mr. Wilder, the imposter induced American General to issue the check to him. When the imposter negotiated the check at State Security, he indorsed the check in the name of the check's payee, Ronald E. Wilder. As we have concluded already, *supra,* State Security took the instrument in good faith. Thus, our reversal of the judgments below turns on the interpretation of the remaining pertinent subsection, subsection (d), of §3-404.

As quoted, *supra,* §3-404(d) provides:

> (d) With respect to an instrument to which subsection (a) or (b) applies, if a person paying the instrument or taking it for value or for collection fails to exercise ordinary care in paying or taking the instrument and that failure substantially contributes to loss resulting from payment of the instrument, the person bearing the loss may recover from the person failing to exercise ordinary care to the extent the failure to exercise ordinary care contributed to the loss.

Md. Code, Com. Law Art. §3-404(d). "Ordinary care" is defined in §3-103(a)(7):

> (7) "Ordinary care" in the case of a person engaged in business means observance of reasonable commercial standards, prevailing in the area in which the person is located, with respect to the business in which the person is engaged. In the case of a bank that takes an instrument for processing for collection or payment by automated means, reasonable commercial standards do not require the bank to examine the instrument if the failure to examine does not violate the bank's prescribed procedures and the bank's procedures do not vary unreasonably from general banking usage not disapproved by this title or Title 4.

Md. Code, Com. Law Art. §3-103(a)(7).

Official Comment 3 to §3-404 addresses expressly the default allocation of loss in circumstances such as the present one. Comment 3 provides:

> 3. In cases governed by subsection (a) the dispute will normally be between the drawer of the check that was obtained by the impostor and the drawee bank that paid it. The drawer is precluded from obtaining recredit of the drawer's account by arguing that the check was paid on a forged indorsement so long as the drawee bank acted in good faith in paying the check. Cases governed by subsection (d) are illustrated by Cases #1 through #5 in Comment 2. *In Cases #1, #2, and #3 there is no forgery of the check, thus the drawer of the check takes the loss if there is no lack of good faith by the banks involved.* Cases #4 and #5 are forged check cases. Depositary Bank is entitled to retain the proceeds of the check if it didn't know about the forgery. Under Section 3-418 the drawee bank is not entitled to recover from Depositary Bank on the basis of payment by mistake because Depositary Bank took the check in good faith and gave value for the check when the credit given for the check was withdrawn. And there is no breach of warranty under Section 3-417(a)(1) or (3) or 4-208(a)(1) or (3). Unless Section 3-406 applies the loss is taken by the drawee bank if a forged check is paid, and that is the result in Case #5. In Case #4 the loss is taken by Corporation, the drawer, because an agreement between Corporation and the drawee bank allowed the bank to debit Corporation's account despite the unauthorized use of the check-writing machine.
>
> *If a check payable to an impostor, fictitious payee, or payee not intended to have an interest in the check is paid, the effect of subsections (a) and (b) is to place the loss on the drawer of the check rather than on the drawee or the Depositary Bank that took the check for collection. Cases governed by subsection (a) always involve fraud, and fraud is almost always involved in cases governed by subsection (b). The drawer is in the best position to avoid the fraud and thus should take the loss. This is true in Case #1, Case #2, and Case #3. But in some cases the person taking the check might have detected the fraud and thus have prevented the loss by the exercise of ordinary care. In those cases, if that person failed to exercise ordinary care, it is reasonable that that person bear loss to the extent the failure contributed to the loss. Subsection (d) is intended to reach that result. It allows the person who suffers loss as a result of payment of the check to recover from the person who failed to exercise ordinary care. In Case #1, Case #2, and Case #3, the person suffering the loss is Corporation, the drawer of the check. In each case the most likely defendant is the depositary bank that took the check and failed to exercise ordinary care. In those cases, the drawer has a cause of action against the offending bank to recover a portion of the loss. The amount of loss to be allocated to each party is left to the trier of fact. Ordinary care is defined in Section 3-103(a)(7).* An example of the type of conduct by a depositary bank that could give rise to recovery under subsection (d) is discussed in Comment 4 to Section 3-405. That comment addresses the last sentence of Section 3-405(b) which is similar to Section 3-404(d).
>
> In Case #1, Case #2, and Case #3, there was no forgery of the drawer's signature. But cases involving checks payable to a fictitious payee or a payee

> not intended to have an interest in the check are often forged check cases as well. Examples are Case #4 and Case #5. Normally, the loss in forged check cases is on the drawee bank that paid the check. Case #5 is an example. In Case #4 the risk with respect to the forgery is shifted to the drawer because of the agreement between the drawer and the drawee bank. The doctrine that prevents a drawee bank from recovering payment with respect to a forged check if the payment was made to a person who took the check for value and in good faith is incorporated into Section 3-418 and Sections 3-417(a)(3) and 4-208(a)(3). This doctrine is based on the assumption that the depositary bank normally has no way of detecting the forgery because the drawer is not that bank's customer. On the other hand, the drawee bank, at least in some cases, may be able to detect the forgery by comparing the signature on the check with the specimen signature that the drawee has on file. But in some forged check cases the depositary bank is in a position to detect the fraud. Those cases typically involve a check payable to a fictitious payee or a payee not intended to have an interest in the check. Subsection (d) applies to those cases. If the depositary bank failed to exercise ordinary care and the failure substantially contributed to the loss, the drawer in Case #4 or the drawee bank in Case #5 has a cause of action against the depositary bank under subsection (d). Comment 4 to Section 3-405 can be used as a guide to the type of conduct that could give rise to recovery under Section 3-404(d).

Md. Code, Com. Law Art. §3-404 cmt. 3 (emphasis added). As Official Comment 3 indicates, the default loss in cases involving imposters lies with the drawer because the drawer is the party that dealt directly with the imposter and thus was in the best position to detect the fraud. *Cf.* Dominion Bank, N.A. v. Household Bank, F.S.B., 827 F. Supp. 463, 466-67 (S.D. Ohio 1993) ("The loss is shifted to the drawer, because the drawer is presumed to have been in the best position to have prevented the fraud. The rationale supporting the impostor rule is essentially the same as that supporting the general rule: the party with the closest contact with the forger ought to bear the responsibility for the loss occasioned by the forgery."); N. Side State Bank v. Bd. of County Comm'rs, 894 P.2d 1046, 1053 (Okla. 1994) ("Known as the 'impostor rule,' §3-405(1)(a) creates an exception to the general notions that govern forged documents. This is so because this section places the loss on the drawer when one who impersonates a third person fraudulently induces the drawer to issue a check and places him in possession. The drawer in that scenario is in the best position to prevent forgery by exercising reasonable care in identifying the party for whom the check is to be issued.") (footnotes omitted); Fair Park Nat'l Bank v. Sw. Inv. Co., 541 S.W.2d 266, 269-70 (Tex. Civ. App. 1976) ("This interpretation is consistent with the policy of the impostor rule, which is to throw the loss resulting from dealing with an impostor on the person who dealt with the impostor, and, presumably, had the best opportunity to take precautions that would have detected the fraud, rather than on a subsequent holder, who had no similar opportunity.") (citations omitted). In certain situations, a drawer may reduce its loss by recovering damages from a person who failed to exercise ordinary care in paying the instrument or taking it for value or collection, if that failure contributed substantially to loss resulting from payment of the instrument, to the extent the failure to exercise care contributed to the loss. Md. Code, Com. Law Art. §3-404(d).

The District Court's ruling in favor of American General erred in two respects: a) the ruling is not in accord with the statutory definition of "ordinary care," in light of the uncontradicted testimony of Deutsch, State Security's compliance officer, and b) the ruling erred by shifting the default burden of loss in an imposter case to the subsequent holder, State Security, rather than the party who was in the best position to detect the fraud, the drawer, American General.

With regard to the interpretation of "ordinary care," the statutory definition of "ordinary care" contains three elements: 1) observance of reasonable commercial standards, 2) which prevail in the area in which the person is located, 3) with respect to the business in which the person is engaged. Md. Code, Com. Law Art. §3-103(a)(7). In the proceedings before the District Court, the testimony of Deutsch, the manager who "run[s] State Security Check Cashing," bore directly upon State Security's conduct on the day in question and, more generally, upon State Security's general business procedures in the check cashing business. Deutsch testified that he has been involved in the check cashing business for twenty-two years and that he had occasion to cash "large" checks in the past. American General did not challenge Deutsch's testimony on cross-examination, nor did American General offer any countervailing testimony reflecting upon State Security's conduct in light of its business practices or the location of its branch office. The only testimony American General elicited on point was through cross-examination of Wanda Decker, State Security's clerk, who testified that State Security, before disbursing, does not hold a check (regardless of the amount) to ascertain whether the funds are available. That testimony alone, however, does not diminish State Security's conduct in the matter in question. Thus, American General did not present sufficient evidence at trial to establish that State Security's conduct lacked "ordinary care" under the statutory definition.

With regard to the burden of loss, the District Court imagined that the one action either party could have taken to prevent the loss was for State Security to have withheld payment until American General's check cleared. The trial court concluded that State Security chose not to delay the payment because it earned a fee from cashing the check, and that in so doing, it ran the risk that the check may be dishonored.

Simply put, the conclusion the trial court reached does not comport with sustainable "ordinary care" analysis. That a business charges a fee for the utilization of its services, albeit here a check cashing business, for cashing the check, is not determinative of whether the conduct of that business on the occasion in question lacked "ordinary care." Under the circumstances of this case, the trial court's reasoning seems directed more towards the "good faith," rather than the "ordinary care," requirement. As Judge Easterbrook stated succinctly in State Bank of the Lakes v. Kansas Bankers Surety Co., 328 F.3d 906 (7th Cir. 2003):

> "[G]ood faith" is in a different phylum from "due care." . . . Article 3 of the UCC, which contains a definition of "good faith[,]" . . . links commercial reasonableness to "fair dealing." Avoidance of advantage-taking, which this section is getting at, differs from due care.

Id. at 909. The trial court seemed persuaded that by cashing the check for a percentage fee, State Security took unfair advantage of the situation. We have already rejected, *supra*, however, American General's claim that State Security's taking the check from the imposter in the circumstances noted above lacked "good faith."

More significantly, the trial court's ruling in favor of American General is contrary to the position emphasized in Official Comment 3 of §3-404 that "[i]f a check payable to an impostor . . . is paid, the effect of subsections (a) and (b) is to place the loss on the drawer of the check rather than on the drawee or the Depositary Bank that took the check for collection." Md. Code, Com. Law Art. §3-404 cmt. 3. This is due to the recognition that the "drawer is in the best position to avoid the fraud and thus should take the loss." Md. Code, Com. Law Art. §3-404 cmt. 3. We found no evidence in the record of this case to suggest the application of this default rule would be inappropriate. Of either party involved here, American General had the best means available by which to protect itself against the fraud, the least of which included contacting the personal references the imposter listed on the credit application, which may have helped protect American General against the fraud. We reject American General's attempt to shift the burden of the loss here to State Security on so tenuous a basis as State Security's failure to ask the imposter for his thumbprint before cashing the check, where State Security examined the same driver's license and the loan documents American General created and found satisfactory in issuing the check. *See supra* notes 14 and 18.

JUDGMENT OF THE CIRCUIT COURT FOR BALTIMORE COUNTY REVERSED; CASE REMANDED TO THAT COURT WITH DIRECTIONS TO REVERSE THE JUDGMENT OF THE DISTRICT COURT AND REMAND THE CASE TO THE DISTRICT COURT WITH DIRECTIONS TO ENTER JUDGMENT IN FAVOR OF APPELLANT; COSTS TO BE PAID BY APPELLEE.

Would the "fictitious payee" portion of §3-404(b) be applicable to Problem 225?

PROBLEM 226

Lawyer Sam Ambulance was sitting in his office when his secretary brought him his checkbook. The secretary informed him that he owed $1,500.00 to John Creditor on a debt, so he wrote out a check for that amount to John. As it turned out, Sam really didn't owe any money to John Creditor, and the secretary forged John's name to the check and pocketed the proceeds. Is this check properly payable from Sam Ambulance's account? See §3-110(a). Does it make any difference whether or not John Creditor is a real or fictitious person?

C. *The Employee Forgery Rule*

In the last Problem, §3-404(b) offers no relief because it is Sam Ambulance's intent that controls under §3-110(a), since he is the drawer of the check. Now do the Problem again, this time looking at §3-405.

Official Comment 1 to this section explains the policy here:

> Section 3-405 is based on the belief that the employer is in a far better position to avoid the loss by care in choosing employees, in supervising them, and in adopting other measures to prevent forged indorsements on instruments payable to the employer or fraud in issuance of instruments in the name of the employer. If the bank failed to exercise ordinary care, subsection (b) allows the employer to shift loss to the bank to the extent the bank's failure to exercise ordinary care contributed to the loss. "Ordinary care" is defined in Section 3-103(a)(7). The provision applies regardless of whether the employer is negligent.

PROBLEM 227

When a check for $800,000 came into Business Corporation to pay a bill owed to it by one of its buyers, the amount dazzled Lucille Larceny, the head of the bookkeeping department. She promptly forged the indorsement "Business Corporation" as payee on the back of the check, and then negotiated it through an account she opened in that name at a bank. Lucille had no authority to indorse the company name, though she was generally in charge of the handling of checks. Does §3-405 make the employer responsible for employees' forgeries where the employer is itself the *payee* (as opposed to the issuer) of the instrument? See Official Comment 1 to §3-405. See Hantz Financial Services, Inc. v. Chemical Bank, 2014 WL 5500383 (Mich. App. 2014). Would that section reach a different result if the forgeries were done by Brad Byte, who had found a check payable to his employer behind the computer he was repairing as part of his job as an in-house computer maintenance specialist?

The Official Comments to both §§3-404 and 3-405 have a number of "case" studies giving examples of fact patterns in which these rules either apply or don't, and you should read these case studies to make sure you appreciate what the drafters intended.

Auto Sision, Inc. v. Wells Fargo

United States District Court, Eastern District of Pennsylvania, 2019
375 F. Supp. 3d 627

CHAD F. KENNEY, J.

I. INTRODUCTION

Plaintiffs Auto Sision, Inc. d/b/a Collision Star ("ASI") and George Hudson (together "Plaintiffs") filed this action against Wells Fargo d/b/a Wells Fargo Bank, N.A. ("Wells Fargo") and Wells Fargo d/b/a Wells Fargo & Company (together "Defendants") for violations of 13 Pa. C.S.A. §3420 (Conversion of an Instrument) and 13 Pa. C.S.A. §3406 (Failure to Use Ordinary Care), or, alternatively, negligence. ECF No. 1. Defendant Wells Fargo moves to dismiss all claims against Wells Fargo & Company because it claims there is no basis for liability of the parent company under these facts; Counts I and II for failure to state a claim; Count III because common law negligence claims are preempted by the Pennsylvania Uniform Commercial Code; and all allegations prior to October 23, 2015 because Defendant argues they are barred by the statute of limitations set forth in 13 Pa. C.S.A. 3118(g). ECF No. 2. Plaintiffs admit in their response that all claims against Wells Fargo & Company and Count III common law negligence against both Defendants must be dismissed. ECF No. 3. Therefore, there remains only Count I, §3420 Conversion of an Instrument, and Count II, §3406 Failure to Use Ordinary Care against Wells Fargo. Plaintiffs further admit that the statute of limitations pursuant to 13 Pa. C.S.A. 3118(g) bars any instruments fraudulently indorsed and cleared by Wells Fargo prior to October 23, 2015. ECF No. 3. Thus, the Court considers Counts I and II only with respect to the allegations of fraudulent indorsement after October 23, 2015. This Court has diversity jurisdiction pursuant to 28 U.S.C. §1332.

II. Background

This matter concerns non-party Barbara Szeliga's alleged misappropriation of Plaintiffs' funds. Plaintiff ASI is a corporation that engages in the business of automotive body repair. ECF No. 1 at ¶1. Plaintiff George Hudson is the owner-operator of ASI. *Id.* at ¶2. Plaintiffs allege that non-party Albert Buccini founded an automotive body repair business, which he owned and operated until 1997, at which time he pled guilty to two counts of federal income tax evasion. *Id.* at ¶¶5-7. During and after Buccini's time as owner of this business, non-party Barbara Szeliga was allegedly employed as the business's bookkeeper. *Id.* at ¶9. When this business filed for bankruptcy, Plaintiff George Hudson purchased certain assets of the business out of the bankruptcy proceedings and entered into a five (5) year commercial lease of Buccini's premises for ASI's operation. *Id.* at ¶23. Plaintiffs allege that ASI employed Barbara Szeliga as ASI's bookkeeper allegedly based on Buccini's urging. *Id.* at ¶25. Plaintiffs allege that Buccini convinced Plaintiffs to hire Szeliga as bookkeeper as part of a scheme to misappropriate Plaintiffs' funds. *Id.* at ¶26. "At all times material hereto, . . . Szeliga was solely responsible for the handling of and accounting for . . . ASI's payments from automobile insurers." *Id.* at ¶30. Plaintiffs allege that shortly after her hiring, Szeliga "began stealing and/or misappropriating . . . ASI's assets" with Buccini's knowledge and aid, including stealing ASI's accounts receivable checks from insurers payable to ASI. *Id.* at ¶31. Szeliga then indorsed the stolen checks in ASI's name and deposited these checks into a Wells Fargo bank account for a company named United Check Cashing ("United"), a check cashing franchise, which was co-owned by Buccini, Buccini's son, and Szeliga. *Id.* at ¶19, 32-34.

In "mid to late" 2014, United went out of business, but Szeliga and Buccini did not dissolve AAB nor close United's bank accounts with Wells Fargo. *Id.* ¶¶38-39. After United went out of business, the "only moneys deposited into AAB and/or United's unlawful bank accounts were . . . ASI's misappropriated assets." *Id.* at ¶41. The Complaint alleges that "[u]pon information and belief, Defendant[] Wells Fargo knew that United has [sic] closed its operations." *Id.* at ¶43. Plaintiffs allege that in mid-2016, Plaintiff George Hudson began to suspect that Szeliga was stealing ASI's assets. *Id.* at ¶44. Plaintiffs allege that they placed a surveillance camera in ASI's offices and saw Szeliga placing a check in her blouse. *Id.* at ¶45. Plaintiffs terminated Szeliga in July 2015 and reported her and Buccini's actions to the Philadelphia Police Department. *Id.* at ¶46.

Plaintiffs allege that Wells Fargo violated 13 Pa C.S.A. §3420 "by obtaining payment with respect to the aforementioned instruments to a person not entitled to enforce the instrument or receive payment, i.e. Non-Parties, Buccini, Szeliga, and/or United." *Id.* at ¶50. Plaintiffs further allege that Wells Fargo violated 13 Pa. C.S.A. §3406 by failing to use ordinary care when it stopped requiring the United account to obtain third-party audits. *Id.* at ¶57. Plaintiffs allege that, "[u]pon information and belief," Wells Fargo "requires all cash checking entities that maintain accounts with it to obtain annual third-party audits to ensure that" Wells Fargo "is not accepting forged and/or fraudulent instruments." *Id.* at ¶53. Plaintiffs claim that "[u]pon information and belief," Wells Fargo required United to obtain these annual third-party audits until "in or around 2015." *Id.* at ¶54. Plaintiffs allege that United stopped operating its business and relinquished its license to operate to the Commonwealth of Pennsylvania in late 2014 but United continued to maintain its accounts with Wells Fargo and regularly cashed instruments with significant value. *Id.* at ¶55. Plaintiffs allege that Wells Fargo failed to use ordinary care in allowing United to continue maintaining its accounts despite having stopped operating its business and in deciding to stop requiring United to obtain annual third-party audits in 2015. *Id.* at ¶57. Plaintiffs allege that if Wells Fargo had continued to require third-party audits after 2015, it would have revealed the "illegal scheme." *Id.* at ¶58. Plaintiffs allege that Wells Fargo's failure to use ordinary care negatively impacted Plaintiffs because this "illegal scheme continued until Plaintiffs discovered the scheme in mid-2016." *Id.* at ¶59. . . .

IV. Discussion

Defendant argues that Counts I and II must be dismissed for failure to state a claim because 13 Pa. C.S.A. §3405 "places the risk of embezzlement on the employer because it is in the best position to prevent such losses" and thus Wells Fargo cannot be liable for Plaintiffs' employee's conduct under either §3420 or §3406. ECF No. 2-1 at 12. Title 13 Pa. C.S.A. §3405 states:

> (b) Rights and liabilities. For the purpose of determining the rights and liabilities of a person who, in good faith, pays an instrument or takes it for value or for collection, if an employer entrusted an employee with responsibility with respect to the instrument and the employee or a person acting in concert with the employee makes a fraudulent indorsement of the instrument, the indorsement is effective as the indorsement of the person to whom the instrument is payable if it is made in the name of that person. **If the *person* paying the instrument or taking it for value or for collection fails to exercise ordinary care in *paying or taking* the instrument and that failure substantially contributes to loss resulting from the fraud, the person bearing the loss may recover from the person failing to exercise ordinary care to the extent the failure to exercise ordinary care contributed to the loss.**

13 Pa. C.S.A. §3405(b) (emphasis added).

Defendant claims that because the Complaint alleges that Plaintiffs entrusted Szeliga with the responsibility for the handling of and accounting for instruments received by Plaintiffs for bookkeeping purposes and then fraudulently indorsed the instruments, as required by §3405, then such an indorsement was effective as if made in the name of Plaintiffs. ECF No. 2-1 at 12. Defendant cites the Third Circuit Court of Appeals in Menichini v. Grant to emphasize that the Pennsylvania Uniform Commercial Code "recognizes principals' ability to minimize agency costs and resolves the agency problem by assigning check fraud losses to the payee-employer." 995 F.2d 1224, 1230 (3d Cir. 1993); ECF No. 2-1 at 13. The Third Circuit further held that §3405 "generally denies an employer the ability to externalize the costs of employee embezzlement, 'virtually creat[ing] a bright line making fraudulent indorsements effective against the employer when employees who have "responsibility with respect to instruments" forged indorsements.'" *Menichini*, 995 F.2d at 1232; ECF No. 2-1 at 14. Thus, Defendants argue that the Complaint is clear that Szeliga's indorsements of Plaintiffs' checks were effective as if made by Plaintiffs, and thus Wells Fargo cannot be liable under §3420 and §3406. ECF No. 2-1 at 14.

In their response, Plaintiffs argued that Szeliga was not provided with the responsibility required by §3405 to exempt the bank from liability. ECF No. 3. At oral argument, however, Plaintiffs admitted that Szeliga, as bookkeeper, was a responsible party as defined in §3405(b) but claimed that §3405(b) did not act as a total bar to liability for Defendant. Transcript of March 7, 2019 Oral Argument, 6:21-24, 6:24-7:1. Plaintiffs argued that, even if Szeliga's indorsement was effective as Plaintiffs' indorsement, the last sentence of §3405(b) required Wells Fargo to exercise ordinary care in taking that instrument:

> If the **person** paying the instrument or taking it for value or for collection **fails to exercise ordinary care in paying or taking the instrument** and that failure substantially contributes to loss resulting from the fraud, the person bearing the loss may recover from the person failing to exercise ordinary care to the extent the failure to exercise ordinary care contributed to the loss.

13 Pa. C.S.A. §3405(b) (emphasis added).

Therefore, Plaintiffs argue that even if Szeliga was a responsible party with respect to the instrument and she made a fraudulent indorsement of that instrument, Wells Fargo did not "exercise ordinary care in . . . taking the instrument and that failure substantially contribute[d] to loss resulting from the fraud." *Id.* Plaintiffs primarily argue that, in failing to require United to conduct third party audits and allowing United's accounts to continue operating after United went out of business, Wells Fargo failed to "exercise ordinary care" as required by §3405.

Ordinary care is defined in 13 Pa. C.S.A. 3103 as follows:

> In the case of a person engaged in business, [ordinary care] means observance of reasonable commercial standards, prevailing in the area in which

> the person is located, with respect to the business in which the person is engaged. In the case of a bank that takes an instrument for processing for collection or payment by automated means, **reasonable commercial standards *do not require the bank to examine the instrument* if the failure to examine does not violate the bank's prescribed procedures and the bank's procedures do not vary unreasonably from general banking usage** not disapproved by this division or Division 4 (relating to bank deposits and collections).

13 Pa. C.S.A. 3103(a) (emphasis added).

Although §3405 does require Wells Fargo to exercise ordinary care in taking instruments, the facts as alleged in the Complaint do not support a finding against Wells Fargo here. Plaintiffs' argument that Wells Fargo failed to exercise ordinary care centers around Wells Fargo's purported third-party audit requirement for check cashing businesses and the fact that it allowed United to continue to maintain operating accounts after United went out of business. ECF No. 3 at 10-11.

However, Plaintiffs' argument challenges the ordinary care of Wells Fargo's auditing policies rather than its policies related to **taking the instrument** and *that* is the focus of §3405 and the bright line rule established in Menichini v. Grant, 995 F.2d 1224 (3d Cir. 1993). Plaintiffs plead no facts showing any reasonable commercial standards that Wells Fargo violated, nor any policy that Wells Fargo contravened in taking the checks and examining them. The procedures regarding auditing check cashing businesses or accounts of non-operating businesses established by Wells Fargo are not the procedures controlling "examin[ing] the instrument" and are irrelevant to the procedures for the ordinary care of "paying," "taking," and "examin[ing]" the instrument at the time of presentation. The instrument presented was, in fact, presented by a responsible party and deposited by a responsible party. Plaintiffs' responsibility for Szeliga's actions are therefore established under 13 Pa. C.S.A. §3405 and the Third Circuit's bright line rule stated in *Menichini*. Plaintiffs would have us cross this bright line and expand the concept of "ordinary care" in §3405, defined at §3103(a), to include an analysis of Wells Fargo's general banking procedures, beyond those procedures relating to the "person" taking or examining the instrument, and the law does not allow for the crossing of this line. Indeed, the statute was established to address this very circumstance, so as to "den[y] an employer the ability to externalize the costs of employee embezzlement," since the "payee-employer is normally in a better position to prevent fraudulent indorsements by its own employees—through reasonable care in the selection or supervision of employees—than a collecting bank." *Menichini*, 995 F.2d at 1233. Without a showing that Wells Fargo failed to exercise ordinary care in *taking* or *paying* the instrument, Plaintiffs cannot impose its losses based on Szeliga's fraud to Wells Fargo.

The Complaint, therefore, does not allege sufficient factual matter to state a claim for relief that is plausible on its face. Therefore, Defendant's Motion to Dismiss is granted.

V. Conclusion

For the reasons stated above, Defendant Wells Fargo's Motion to Dismiss is hereby granted. The Complaint is dismissed without prejudice.

In YF Trust v. JP Morgan Chase Bank, N.A., 2008 WL 4277902 (D. Ariz. Sept. 18, 2008), the court held that negligence in opening an account can be used to apportion loss where one of the validation rules applies. This case involved not just negligence in opening the account, but negligence in the "formation, maintenance and use" of the account; see also Miller v. Bennett, 2014 WL 2567925 (Ohio App. 2014).

NOTE ON FEDERAL COMMERCIAL PAPER LAW

As mentioned before, the Uniform Commercial Code is a *state* statute, and the federal government does not feel bound thereby. In an actual case, you may discover that, for example, the Midnight Deadline statutes and other rules of bank collection are much altered when a check is drawn on the Treasury of the United States. So it is with the padded payroll part of the Impostor Rule. While the U.S. Supreme Court decisions to date preclude the use of §§3-404(b) and 3-405, the part of these sections that deals with a true *impostor,* §3-404(a), *has* been adopted as a federal rule by lower federal courts, the Supreme Court having expressed no opinion on the issue; see Bank of Am. Natl. Trust & Sav. Assn. v. United States, 552 F.2d 302 (9th Cir. 1977); see also Comment, Federal Commercial Paper and the Common Law, 14 Tulsa L.J. 208 (1978). In United States v. Kimbell Foods, 440 U.S. 715 (1979), the Supreme Court adopted Article 9 of the Uniform Commercial Code as a matter of federal common law. This has given hope of the Court's possible federal incorporation of Articles 3 and 4 the next time the issue arises. See Official Comment 4 to §3-102 and Official Comment 1 to §4-102.

PROBLEM 228

Peter Shopper left his checkbook laying on a department store counter, and it was picked up by "Fingers" McGee. McGee wrote out a check for $100 payable to the order of "John Doe," a name he rather imaginatively made up; then he forged Shopper's name to the drawer's line. He indorsed the check "John Doe" and "Fingers McGee" and deposited the check in his own account with the Fence State Bank. The latter was paid $100 by the drawee, the Antitrust National Bank. Shopper complained to the drawee about the forgery, and the bank reluctantly recredited his account. It now wants to pass the loss on to the presenting bank, claiming that it breached the warranty that it was a person entitled to enforce the draft because of the forged indorsement of "John Doe." Has that warranty been breached, or did Fence State somehow become a *holder*? See §3-404(b), and remember the rule of Price v. Neal.

D. *The Negligence Rule*

Another situation in which a party may be estopped to complain about a forgery occurs when the person's own negligence substantially contributed to the creation of the forgery. (The same rule applies to the creation of alterations of the instrument.) The leading case establishing this negligence-as-estoppel principle is the 1827 English case, Young v. Grote, 4 Bing. 253 (Common Pleas). The Problem below is based on the facts in that case.

PROBLEM 229

Young decided to go abroad for a while, so he signed five checks and left them with his wife. After he had been gone a week, one of Young's employees, Worcester, a clerk, showed Mrs. Young how to fill out the check so as to pay employees' wages for 50 pounds. She filled out the check as directed and gave it to Worcester to cash. He inserted the numeral 3 on the check in the blank he had had Mrs. Young leave in writing the amount and cashed the check for 350 pounds with the drawee, Grote & Co. When Young returned, he sued Grote & Co. for wrongly paying that amount. In the actual case, the court gave a sexist explanation for its result, deciding that Young's negligence was in trusting a woman with a business matter (remember this was 1827): "If Young, instead of leaving the check with a female, had left it with a man of business, he would have guarded against fraud in the mode of filling it up. . . ." In our century, is it enough negligence that a space was left on the amount line to which a numeral could be added? See Official Comment 1 to §3-406.

Note that the language of §3-406 uses the doctrine of negligence only as a defense, not as a separate affirmative cause of action. The Code does not authorize an affirmative cause of action based on negligence. Read Official Comment 1, last paragraph, to §3-406, which explains why not. Affirmative negligence actions must be brought outside the Code (see §1-103) and judged by common law standards. See, e.g., Faulkner v. Hillside Bank & Trust Co., 526 S.W.2d 274 (Tex. Civ. App. 1975) (bank telling an inquirer that a stolen cashier's check was good held liable in negligence).

PROBLEM 230

Arena Auto Auction (AAA) by coincidence dealt with two customers named Plunkett Auto Sales, one in Illinois and the other in Alabama. AAA sold a car for the Alabama customer, but AAA's secretary mistakenly mailed a check to Plunkett Auto Sales in Illinois. The surprised owner of the Illinois Plunkett operation promptly cashed the check with his own bank, Park State, which forwarded the check to the drawee bank. The latter dishonored the check at AAA's request—AAA had stopped payment when it learned about its secretary's error. The Illinois Plunkett skipped the state, and the Park State Bank was left holding the check. Park State sued AAA on its drawer's obligation, §3-414(b), and the latter tried to raise the defense of mistake. Does §3-406 apply? See Official Comment 3, Case No. 2. The actual case is Park State Bank v. Arena Auto Auction, Inc., 59 Ill. App. 2d 235, 207 N.E.2d 158 (1965).

The Bank/First Citizens Bank v. Citizens and Associates

Supreme Court of Tennessee, 2002
82 S.W.3d 259

WILLIAM M. BARKER, J.

This case involves the application of Tennessee Code Annotated section 47-3-406 to determine who bears the loss of a bank's acceptance of forged instruments. The drawer issued three checks payable to a mortgage company and delivered these checks to a branch manager of that company for transfer to the main office. The manager, however, forged the endorsement of the company and deposited these checks into her personal bank account. In a suit to recover the funds, the trial court applied section 47-3-406 and found that both the drawer and the depository bank failed to exercise ordinary care. It then allocated the loss between the parties as eighty percent to the drawer and twenty percent to the bank. A majority of the Court of Appeals affirmed. On appeal to this Court, we hold that the bank may not assert that the drawer is precluded from asserting the forgery against it under section 47-3-406, because it did not show that any failure by the drawer to exercise ordinary care substantially contributed to the making of the forged endorsements. The judgment of the Court of Appeals is reversed.

Factual Background

In January 1997, Allied Mortgage Capital Company ("Allied Mortgage") opened a branch office in Cleveland, Tennessee, and shortly thereafter, it hired Ms. Frieda Gray as its branch manager for this office. In this capacity, Ms. Gray possessed the authority to conduct the day-to-day operations of the branch and to make loans. Ms. Gray was also authorized to receive, hold, and forward monies and documents to Allied Mortgage at its principal place of business in Texas.

The next month, Ms. Gray, representing herself as a branch manager of Allied Mortgage, contacted a land-development partnership, Citizens and Associates, about opening a branch office of Allied Mortgage in upper-east Tennessee. Ms. Gray hosted a seminar in Knoxville for about fifteen or twenty people to show how profitable investing in Allied Mortgage could be. Following this seminar, Citizens and Associates agreed to invest in the mortgage company in order to compl[e]ment its other land development interests. Ms. Gray stated that she would handle the transaction, and she obtained information from Citizens and Associates which she said was necessary for the main office to approve the investment.

Over the next thirty days, Citizens and Associates issued three checks to Allied Mortgage, in the total amount of $50,000.02, and it gave these checks to Ms. Gray for delivery to Allied Mortgage's main office in Texas. However, Ms. Gray did not forward the checks to the main office. Instead, she endorsed each in the name of the corporation and deposited the instruments in her personal account at The Bank/First Citizens Bank ("First Citizens Bank") in Cleveland. First Citizens Bank, as the depository bank, presented these checks to the drawee bank in Knoxville, which paid the checks and deducted the amounts paid from Citizens and Associates' account.

Citizens and Associates soon discovered that a fraud had taken place. It contacted Allied Mortgage's main office and confirmed that Allied Mortgage does not license franchises and that Ms. Gray was not authorized to negotiate franchise agreements. Citizens and Associates then contacted First Citizens Bank and demanded repayment of the face amounts of the checks, but First Citizens Bank denied any liability on the instruments. The bank then filed suit in the Bradley County Circuit Court, seeking a declaration that it possessed no liability on the three checks. Citizens and Associates filed a counterclaim against First Citizens Bank alleging that the bank failed to exercise ordinary care in taking the instruments.

Following a bench trial, the court applied Tennessee Code Annotated section 47-3-406 and found that First Citizens Bank failed to exercise ordinary care in taking the checks. More specifically, the court concluded that the bank was negligent in permitting the deposit of checks made payable to a corporation into a personal account, especially when the corporation itself did not have an account with the bank. The court also found that Citizens and Associates was negligent in delivering the instruments to Ms. Gray without first confirming the transaction with Allied Mortgage. It then allocated the loss of the instruments, as required by section 47-3-406(c), as eighty percent to Citizens and Associates and twenty percent to First Citizens Bank. A final order confirming this ruling was entered on July 11, 2000.

Citizens and Associates appealed to the Court of Appeals, and a majority of that court affirmed the judgment of the trial court. The intermediate court found that the evidence supported the trial court's findings regarding the failure of both parties to exercise ordinary care. The majority also affirmed the trial court's allocation of the loss as supported by the evidence. However, in dissent, Judge Susano concluded that First Citizens Bank should be responsible for the entire loss. He found that because Ms. Gray was "without question an employee of Allied [Mortgage] and was authorized to receive documents and checks for her employer," Citizens and Associates did not fail to exercise the ordinary care contemplated by section 47-3-406(a).

We granted permission to appeal to Citizens and Associates to resolve the proper application of Tennessee Code Annotated section 47-3-406 in this case. We now hold that First Citizens Bank may not assert the defense provided by section 47-3-406. Although we conclude that the record supports a finding that First Citizens Bank took the instruments in good faith, the bank did not show that the failure of Citizens and Associates to exercise ordinary care substantially contributed to the actual making of the forged endorsements. . . .

[The court quoted §3-406.]

Thus, viewing the statute in terms of this case, First Citizens Bank may assert that Citizens and Associates is precluded from asserting the forgery against the bank by showing (1) that it took the instruments in good faith; (2) that Citizens and Associates failed to exercise ordinary care; and (3) that this failure by Citizens and Associates "substantially contributed" to making of Ms. Gray's forged signatures. Tenn. Code Ann. §47-3-406(a). However, even if Citizens and Associates is found to be precluded from asserting the entire loss against First Citizens Bank, it may nevertheless seek to shift the burden of the loss to the bank by showing (1) that First Citizens Bank failed to exercise ordinary care in taking the instrument; and (2) that this failure substantially contributed to the loss. *See* Tenn. Code Ann. §47-3-406(b). The court may then apportion the loss to the extent "that the failure of each to exercise ordinary care contributed to the loss." Tenn. Code Ann. §47-3-406(c).

"Each of these steps in section [47-3-406] presents a question of fact, ordinarily to be resolved by the fact finder." San Tan Irrigation Dist. v. Wells Fargo Bank, 197 Ariz. 193, 3 P.3d 1113, 1118 (2000). Importantly, however, if First Citizens Bank cannot meet its initial burden of showing that Citizens and Associates is precluded from asserting the forgery against it, then the entire loss must be borne by the bank itself. *Cf.* John Hancock Fin. Servs. v. Old Kent Bank, 185 F. Supp. 2d 771, 779 (E.D. Mich. 2002) (denying preclusion under UCC section 3-406 because the bank did not show good faith in paying the instrument). We examine each of these elements in turn.

First Citizen's Bank's Good Faith Payment of the Instruments

The first issue is whether First Citizens Bank took the instruments in good faith. Citing the general code definition of "good faith" in Tennessee Code Annotated section 47-1-201(19), First Citizens Bank asserts that it has met this standard because it acted with "honesty in fact" in taking the checks. A majority of the Court of Appeals agreed, noting that the record contains no evidence that "there was any dishonesty or collusion involved in the transaction." However, although the Court of Appeals ultimately appears to have applied the correct definition of "good faith" in this context, it did not specifically examine the proper definition of this term as it applies to TUCC Article 3. Consequently, to clarify the law in this area, we undertake a more detailed analysis of this issue.

In 1990, the American Law Institute and the National Conference of Commissioners on Uniform State Laws revised Articles 3 and 4 of the Uniform Commercial Code dealing with negotiable instruments, bank deposits, and collections. Prior to these revisions, the term "good faith" was defined in these articles by the general subjective standard of "honesty in fact." However, one of the more significant revisions to Article 3 was to redefine the term "good faith" to require a party to show that it acted with "honesty in fact" in the transaction *and* that it adhered to "reasonable commercial standards of fair dealing." *See* UCC §3-103(a)(4).

In 1995, the Tennessee General Assembly substantially adopted Revised Articles 3 and 4, although, interestingly, it did not include the definition of "good faith" contained in UCC section 3-103(a)(4). Admittedly, there is some evidence that the legislature omitted the definition of this term inadvertently. For example, the legislature retained Official Comment [3] to section 47-3-103, which specifically refers to the definition of "good faith" as requiring "not only honesty in fact, but also 'observance of reasonable commercial standards of fair dealing.'" This comment is quite detailed, and it elaborates on the difference between the exercise of "ordinary care" and the observance of "reasonable commercial standards of fair dealing." One could also suppose that the inclusion of this Official Comment here is more than a mere anomaly, as comments in *three* other sections of Title 47 specifically refer to the definition of "good faith" as purportedly set forth in section 47-3-103(a)(4).

Nevertheless, "[t]his court does not lightly assume drafting error by the Legislature." *See* People v. Robles, 23 Cal. 4th 1106, 99 Cal. Rptr. 2d

120, 5 P.3d 176, 182 (2000). To the contrary, we presume that where the legislature departs from the language of a model act, it usually does so to express an intention different from the model act. *See* Heirs of Ellis v. Estate of Ellis, 71 S.W.3d 705, 713-14 (Tenn. 2002); Kradel v. Piper Indus., Inc., 60 S.W.3d 744 (Tenn. 2001). We note that the presence of the unedited comments may not be as curious as first appears, especially considering that the General Assembly has, on at least one other occasion, adopted the official UCC comments verbatim even while otherwise departing from the uniform language of the statute itself. *See* Tenn. Code Ann. §47-2-318 cmt. 3 (referring to all three alternative versions proposed by UCC section 2-318, even though the General Assembly ultimately adopted only Alternative *A*). Further, the Compilers Notes to section 47-3-103 specifically observe that the UCC's Article 3 definition of "good faith" has been omitted from the Tennessee statutes, and these Notes permit the General Assembly to correct any unintended oversight should it so desire. Consequently, we must conclude that the General Assembly intentionally omitted the UCC definition of "good faith" as it applies in Chapters 3 and 4 of Title 47, and we construe this term in accord with the general code definition to mean "honesty in fact in the conduct or transaction involved." *See* Tenn. Code Ann. §47-1-201(19).

Applying the general code definitions in this context, we agree with the lower court that the record supports a finding that First Citizens Bank took the instruments in good faith. This Court has defined the "honesty in fact" standard to mean an absence of a "knowing or reckless disregard of a customer's rights." Glazer v. First Am. Nat'l Bank, 930 S.W.2d 546, 549 (Tenn. 1996) (defining "good faith" in section 47-1-102(19)). Our review of the record reveals that while First Citizens Bank was certainly negligent in permitting the deposit of a check made payable to a corporation into an individual account, no evidence shows that it knowingly disregarded the rights of anyone. Nor does a preponderance of the evidence support a finding that the bank acted recklessly in this regard. Therefore, we conclude that the record supports the conclusions of the lower courts that First Citizens Bank took the instruments in good faith.

Citizen's and Associate's Failure to Exercise Ordinary Care and Its Substantial Contribution to the Forgery

Although the record supports a finding that First Citizens Bank took the instruments in good faith, section 47-3-406 also requires the bank to show that the drawer's failure to exercise ordinary care substantially contributed to the forgery of the instrument. Although the Court of Appeals reached a contrary conclusion, we cannot conclude that the bank has met its burden in this regard.

No reported case in this state has discussed the requirements of "ordinary care" or "substantial contribution" as they relate to the conduct of the drawer. However, the official comments shed some light on what was intended by these standards. For instance, Comment 2 to section 47-3-406 states that conduct is a substantial contribution to a forged signature if the conduct is a "contributing cause" of the signature and is "a substantial factor in bringing it about." The comment also notes that the "substantial contribution" standard "is meant to be less stringent than a 'direct and proximate cause' test" that prevailed prior to the UCC's adoption, thereby making the preclusion generally easier to establish.

Relying upon this comment, the Court of Appeals held that a drawer can be precluded under this section if the drawer negligently issues an instrument to a third party for delivery to the payee. Though the intermediate court's analysis is not without some support, several other courts have held that "only negligence which proximately relates or contributes to the forgery, *and not merely to the issuance of the checks,* would relieve a collecting bank of liability for improper payment of a fraudulently endorsed check." *See, e.g.,* Vectra Bank v. Bank W., 890 P.2d 259, 263 (Colo. Ct. App. 1995) (emphasis added).[12] Indeed, at least one court has held, as a matter of law, that the drawer's negligence in issuing the instrument, without more, cannot substantially contribute to the forgery within the contemplation of UCC section 3-406. *See* Guaranty Bank & Trust Co. v. Federal Reserve Bank, 454 F. Supp. 488, 490-91 (W.D. Okla. 1977) (addressing factual scenario in which a loan was negotiated and an instrument was delivered to a party not named as the payee).

This latter position certainly comports more closely with the plain language of section 47-3-406, which speaks only of the drawer's negligence being a substantial contribution "to the *making* of a forged signature." (emphasis added). Consequently, we agree with those cases holding that a drawer's negligence leading to the unwarranted issuance of checks will not generally

12. *See also* Bagby v. Merrill Lynch, Pierce, Fenner & Smith, Inc., 491 F.2d 192, 197 (8th Cir. 1974) ("In the final analysis, we are convinced that the meaning of §3-406 is best reflected by precluding a drawer from recovery under these or similar circumstances only where his negligent conduct contributes to the forgery, not merely to the unwarranted issuance of the checks, such as in the situation before us."); First Nat'l Bank v. MidAmerica Fed. Sav. Bank, 303 Ill. App. 3d 176, 236 Ill. Dec. 546, 707 N.E.2d 673, 678 (1999) ("The meaning of section 3-406 is best reflected by precluding a drawer from recovery under these or similar circumstances only where his negligent conduct contributes to the forgery, not merely to the unwarranted issuance of the checks." (citation and quotation marks omitted)); Twellman v. Lindell Trust Co., 534 S.W.2d 83, 90-91 (Mo. Ct. App. 1976) ("The U.C.C. seems to foresee a more direct type of contribution to a forgery. . . . We do not think that plaintiff's actions in trusting Londe and giving Londe a check which plaintiff had made payable to International Harvester could be said to have substantially contributed to Londe's forgery."); Maddox v. First Westroads Bank, 199 Neb. 81, 256 N.W.2d 647, 655 (1977) (quoting and approving *Bagby*); *Society Nat'l Bank,* 281 N.E.2d at 566 ("Even if [the drawer] had been lax in the conduct of his business affairs, mere laxity is not sufficient to prevent him from recovering against the drawee bank for the amount charged against his account and paid by the drawee over a forged indorsement, unless the lax conduct was the proximate cause of the loss.").

suffice to establish a defense under section 47-3-406. Rather, the party asserting the preclusion must show some causal relationship between the lack of ordinary care and the actual making of the forged signature, such that the drawer's negligence can be said to have substantially contributed to the ability of the unauthorized person to forge the payee's name and to pose as the intended payee. *See* Fidelity Bank v. United Nat'l Bank, 630 F. Supp. 16, 20 (D.D.C. 1985) (citing Dominion Constr., Inc. v. First Nat'l Bank, 271 Md. 154, 315 A.2d 69, 73 (1974)).

Whatever negligence Citizens and Associates may have been guilty of in issuing the three checks payable to Allied Mortgage, we cannot say that it increased the possibility that Ms. Gray would forge the endorsement of Allied Mortgage and pose as the payee of the instruments to her bank. Citizens and Associates, for example, did not leave blank the name of the payees in the various checks or make the checks payable to Ms. Gray as an agent of Allied Mortgage. *See Fidelity Bank,* 630 F. Supp. at 20. Rather, Citizens and Associates only delivered these checks to an acknowledged agent of the payee that, according to testimony by an employee of Allied Mortgage, possessed the actual authority to receive checks on behalf of the payee. Without something more, this conduct alone simply cannot be said to have substantially contributed to the making of the forged endorsements.

Consequently, while the record supports the trial court's conclusion that Citizens and Associates was negligent in issuing the checks payable to Allied Mortgage, the record does not show that this negligence substantially contributed to the ability of Ms. Gray to forge the endorsements and pose as the actual payee. Accordingly, we hold that even if First Citizens Bank took the instruments in good faith, the bank cannot assert the negligent drawer defense of section 47-3-406 because it has not shown that any failure by Citizens and Associates to exercise ordinary care substantially contributed to the making of the forged endorsements. . . . Accordingly, the judgment of the Court of Appeals is reversed.

The 1974 case of Bagby v. Merrill Lynch, Pierce, Fenner & Smith, Inc., 491 F.2d 192, 197 (8th Cir. 1974), cited in the above case's footnote, resurrected the tort doctrine of "proximate cause" (even though Official Comment 2 to §3-406 disclaims it), and one of your authors wrote a law review article attacking the court for dragging the messy "proximate cause" imbroglio into §3-406; see Douglas J. Whaley, Negligence and Negotiable Instruments, 53 N.C. L. Rev. 1 (1974). White and Summers cited the article with approval in earlier editions of their treatise, but when the issue died out, they dropped any discussion of "proximate cause," and now simply state that "where there are multiple causes of loss (not the least of which may be a deficiency in the thief's morality), one person's act could be a substantial cause even though other events might be more direct and powerful causes"; White & Summers §17-3. The subsequent rewrite of Article 3 has commanded the courts to use comparative negligence in all these forgery situations, thus recognizing there can be more than one cause of a forgery. You'd think therefore that "proximate cause" would be dead in Article 3 case law, but as the above case indicates that horror is apparently still with us.

PROBLEM 231

Lucille Larceny, corporate treasurer of Business Corporation, had the authority to indorse the corporate name to checks coming into the corporation. Over a period of months she took a number of such checks, stamped the corporate name as payee, then indorsed her own name below the corporate stamp and deposited the checks in her personal account at Busy National Bank. Is it negligent for the depositary bank to allow her to do this? See §3-307(b)(2); Al Sarena Mines, Inc. v. Southtrust Bank, 548 So. 2d 1356 (Ala. 1989); In re Lou Levy & Sons Fashions, Inc., 785 F. Supp. 1163 (S.D.N.Y. 1992), *aff'd*, 988 F.2d 311 (2d Cir. 1993).

PROBLEM 232

It was the practice of Octopus National Bank to treat checks payable to the bank as if they were payable to bearer. It did this because many check drawers made the same assumption. Whenever Business Corporation wanted to put money into a special account reserved for the payment of taxes, it wrote a check for the requisite amount, payable to the order of "Octopus National Bank," and, by use of a deposit slip with the tax account number on it, made the deposit. Lucille Larceny, the corporate treasurer of Business Corporation, wrote out a check for $250,000, payable to the order of "Octopus National Bank," cooking the books so that it appeared this amount was going into the tax account but in reality putting it into her own personal account, using a deposit slip with her account number on it. When the check cleared, Lucille disappeared with the money. Business Corporation protested to the bank and, when the bank refused to recredit its account, sued, arguing that these checks were not "properly payable" under §4-401 of the UCC. Was the bank negligent? See Olean Area Camp Fire Council, Inc. v. Olean Dresser Clark Fed. Credit Union, 142 Misc. 2d 1049, 538 N.Y.S.2d 905 (Sup. Ct. 1989) ("In charity we will withhold characterizing such conduct as 'abject stupidity' and call it merely negligence of the grossest kind"); Govoni & Sons Const.

Co. v. Mechanics Bank, 51 Mass. App. 35, 742 N.E.2d 1094 (2001); Master Chemical Corp. v. Inkrott, 55 Ohio St. 3d 23, 563 N.E.2d 26 (1990); but see Trail Leasing, Inc. v. Drovers First American Bank, 447 N.W.2d 190 (Minn. 1989) (bank is a holder in due course and takes free of the defenses of the drawer).[13] For an Annotation on the subject, see 69 A.L.R.4th 778. If the corporation were also found to be negligent in not better supervising Lucille, how does that affect the result?

PROBLEM 233

When Edwin Dennis died, he left all of his property in trust to his minor son, Patrick, whose guardianship was given over to Edwin's sister, Mame, who was named as trustee. One of the assets thus transferred was a $10,000 certificate of deposit, changed after Edwin's death so that it was payable to "Mame Dennis, as guardian and trustee for Patrick Dennis, a minor." When Mame decided to open her own catering business, she took the CD down to Babcock National Bank and pledged it as collateral for an $8,000 loan to her personally, and the bank took possession of the CD and put it in its vault. When Patrick came of age he consulted you, a former schoolmate and newly licensed attorney, and asked if he can get the CD back from the bank without having to repay the loan. See §3-307.

If Mame had used the Patrick Dennis Trust Account carried at Babcock National Bank, on which she was the named trustee, to write herself a check to pay her salary as trustee, would that be a suspicious circumstance giving rise to a claim in Patrick's favor to recover the money? See §3-307(b)(3) and its Official Comment 4.

E. *The Bank Statement Rule*

In the earlier discussion of the bank and its customer, we covered §4-406, which establishes the rule that the customer must examine the bank statement or be estopped from asserting unauthorized signatures or material alterations that could have been discovered. That section, which you should read again, is nothing more than an extension of §3-406, the

13. This decision seems terribly wrong to us. What possible value does the bank give? It is merely releasing the customer's money and parting with none of its own. Furthermore, the bank is hardly in good faith and without notice (requirements to become a holder in due course) when it is behaving this carelessly. For a case saying that the bank cannot be a holder in due course in this situation, see Mutual Service Cas. Ins. Co. v. Elizabeth State Bank, 265 F.3d 601 (7th Cir. 2001).

Negligence Rule; it establishes a specific act of negligence, failure to examine bank statements, which leads to an estoppel.

PROBLEM 234

While repairing a furnace in Rhonda Rivers' home, John Burly took advantage of her absence to sneak to her desk and tear out a blank check from the back of her checkbook. On March 25, this check cleared through Rhonda's checking account with her name forged thereto; the amount was $500. This check was returned to Rhonda on April 1. She failed to balance her checkbook until August 1 of that year, when she discovered and reported the forgery. Must the bank recredit her account? See §4-406(d)(1). Would it help or hurt the bank's position if John Burly had also had an account at the bank and had had $500 or more in this account at all times up until the end of July?

PROBLEM 235

Lucille Larceny was the administrative assistant to Howard Head, CEO of Business Corporation. Over a period of three years she stole 87 blank corporate checks from Head's checkbook, made the checks out to her brother, forged Head's name as drawer, and (with the help of her equally wicked brother) managed to take $378,000 out of the corporate account before she was caught and she and her brother, both penniless, went to jail. You are the corporate counsel for Business Corporation. How much, if anything, can it make its bank recredit? See §4-406(c), (d), (e), and (f); Spacemakers of America, Inc. v. SunTrust Bank, 271 Ga. App. 335, 609 S.E.2d 683 (2005).

Peters v. Riggs Natl. Bank, N.A.

District of Columbia Court of Appeals, 2008
942 A.2d 1163

WASHINGTON, Chief Judge:

Appellant Winston D. Peters, the personal representative of the Estate of Rhona Graves, appeals from the trial court's grant of summary judgment against his claims of breach of contract, negligence, and violations of the Electronic Funds Transfer Act ("EFTA"). Appellant claimed that appellee Riggs Bank permitted unauthorized withdrawals in the amount of $131,278.61 from his mother's account despite the fact that she had been incapacitated and later died while most of the transactions occurred. Riggs Bank denied liability, but further asserted that appellant's claims were untimely. We agree that appellant's claims are time-barred. Thus, we affirm.

I.

On October 31, 1980, Rhona Graves opened a checking account at Riggs Bank. Graves entered into a customer agreement with Riggs, which included adoption of Riggs's Rules and Regulations that covered the checking account, and executed a signature card. Graves later opened a savings account with Riggs on October 3, 1986. This account was also governed by Riggs's Rules and Regulations.[14]

At some point prior to June of 2002, Ms. Graves won a substantial amount of money in the lottery. She deposited her lump sum payment into her accounts at Riggs Bank. However, on June 8, 2002, Ms. Graves suffered a serious stroke and was hospitalized. She lost the ability to communicate. She was later transferred to a nursing home where she remained in a seriously ill condition until she died on November 9, 2002.

Between May and December of 2002, someone withdrew money from Ms. Graves's accounts through the writing of checks, phone transfers, and ATM withdrawals. Although uncertain, appellant suspects that Ms. Graves's sister, who lived with and assisted Ms. Graves for about three years between Ms. Graves's first stroke (in 2000) and her death, took the money. Appellant concedes that he does not know that his mother did not want her sister to have access to the funds, nor can he be sure that Ms. Graves did not sign the checks. However, while Ms. Graves was in the hospital, appellant told his aunt that he would bring her money to pay the household bills. Appellant claims he told his aunt not to use money from his mother's accounts.

During the 153-day period from Ms. Graves's stroke until her death, there were 73 ATM withdrawals from her account, including 72 of them at the $500.00 daily limit for withdrawals. Then, 21 additional withdrawals were made during the 41 days after Ms. Graves died, including 19 at the $500 maximum. All together, $46,547.00 was withdrawn from the account, including $10,159.50 after her death. Also, during this time, 128 checks were written, resulting in her account being debited $84,731.61. According to appellant, the signature on checks provided back to him does not match

14. Relevant to this appeal is the following provision:

> Your statement is considered correct, and we [Riggs Bank] will not be liable for payments made and charged to your account . . . unless you notify us of an error, including . . . unauthorized payment or other irregularity within (a) sixty (60) calendar days . . . of the mailing date of the earliest statement describing the charge or deposit to your account.

his mother's authorized signature on file with the bank. Six of the checks (totaling $62,000) were made out to his mother's sister, and another check was written to her daughter. Appellant asserts that during the time period of Ms. Graves's critical illness, she did not have the capacity to review bank statements, and that in any event, there is no evidence that she received any bank statements at the hospital.

After Ms. Graves died in November of 2002, appellant petitioned for letters of administration in January 2003 and received authority to open Ms. Graves's safety deposit box. In January 2003, appellant inspected the safety deposit box and discovered that his mother had won the lottery. At that time, her accounts showed balances of $2,174.18 and $159.81. On March 10, 2003, Riggs issued a check to appellant, payable to the Estate of Rhona Graves, in the amount of $2,301.12-the remaining account balance.

Appellant tried to track down the amount and location of the proceeds of Mrs. Graves's lottery winnings. He was finally appointed personal representative of the estate on April 2, 2003. Also in April, appellant discovered a Riggs bank statement from August 13, 2002 through September 12, 2002, showing that Ms. Graves's account had held $92,187.45, but closed at the end of the period with only $58,935.98. On April 16, 2003, appellant (through counsel) wrote Riggs Bank requesting more information about Ms. Graves's account. Appellant claims he had no basis for asserting that Riggs Bank had done anything improper at that time. On May 28, 2003, Riggs responded by providing appellant's counsel with copies of some account statements and other records and informed him that Riggs was still in the process of gathering further information. Riggs provided more documents on June 4, 2003.

Appellant apparently believed Riggs was investigating the withdrawals up until a November 12, 2003 meeting. By that point, Riggs had not provided results of an investigation. On November 7, 2003, appellant (through counsel) indicated to Riggs Bank that Riggs may have improperly permitted the payment on unauthorized checks and allowed unauthorized ATM cash withdrawals, but stated that appellant was awaiting the results of Riggs Bank's investigation before asserting a formal claim. According to appellant, Riggs failed to provide any further information. On August 4, 2004, appellant filed a complaint with the Superior Court, alleging breach of contract, negligence, and violations of EFTA. Appellee moved for summary judgment against appellant, claiming that appellant's claims were time-barred, as well as asserting that appellant had conceded that he could not say for certain that the checks and withdrawals had been unauthorized.

On Friday, October 14, 2005, the Honorable Michael L. Rankin held a hearing on the summary judgment motion. At the hearing, Judge Rankin, in the absence of evidence to the contrary, accepted the representations of Riggs Bank that it had sent monthly account statements to Ms. Graves, and that neither she nor appellant had notified the Bank of any unauthorized transactions in a timely manner. Judge Rankin ruled:

> In my view the defendant has the better of this argument and that it would be against the Uniform Commercial Code as applied in this case to hold the bank responsible for the loss of this money when they were sending notices of the monthly transactions, as they were required to do under their contract, to the only address that they had.
>
> In light of my view that that is the correct application of the law in this case, I'm going to enter summary judgment in favor of the defendant.

The court subsequently issued a one-page order, granting defendant's motion for summary judgment on all claims. This appeal followed.

A. UNAUTHORIZED CHECKS

Articles 3 and 4 of D.C. Code, Commercial Law and Transactions ("U.C.C.") apply to negotiable instruments, including checks. *See* D.C. Code §28:3-102(a) (2001); D.C. Code §28:3-104 (2001). Thus, the U.C.C. governs the disposition of the unauthorized checks in this case. Under the U.C.C., a person is not liable for a negotiable instrument unless he or she signed it. *See* D.C. Code §28:3-401 (2001). However, D.C. Code §28:4-406 imposes upon bank customers a duty to discover and report unauthorized signatures or alterations to the bank.[15] D.C. Code § 28:4-406(f) establishes an absolute notice requirement for customers as a pre-requisite to bringing any claim against the bank: [The court quoted §4-406(f).].

Other jurisdictions have consistently characterized this U.C.C. provision as a statute of repose, as opposed to a statute of limitations. *See* Jensen v. Essexbank, 396 Mass. 65, 483 N.E.2d 821, 822 (1985) ("The one-year period in §4-406(4) [precursor to §4-406(f)] is not a statute of limitations. . . . It is a statutory prerequisite of notice"); Indiana Nat'l Corp. v. FACO, Inc., 400 N.E.2d 202, 205 (Ind. Ct. App. 1980) (calling the provision "substantive law"). Other courts have noted that the provision constitutes a condition precedent to the customer's right to file claims against a bank. *See* National Title Insur. Corp. Agency v. First Union Nat'l Bank, 263 Va. 355, 559 S.E.2d 668, 671 (2002). According to this court, "[a] statute of repose . . . establishes an absolute time period within which legal proceedings must be initiated, regardless of when a cause of action accrues." Sandoe v. Lefta Assoc.,

15. The rationale for this U.C.C. provision is to allocate the burden of discovering forgeries to the party best able to detect the forgery: customers are more familiar with their own signatures and transactions than a financial institution that may process thousands of transactions. *See* American Airlines Employees Fed. Credit Union v. Martin, 29 S.W.3d 86, 92 (Tex. 2000).

559 A.2d 732, 736 n.5 (D.C. 1989). Based on the clear statutory language of D.C. Code §28:4-406(f)—"[A] customer who does not . . . discover and report . . . is precluded from asserting against the bank the unauthorized signature or alteration"—we hold that D.C. Code §28:4-406(f) is a statute of repose.

We must next determine whether Riggs Bank permissibly shortened the length of the statute of repose from D.C. Code §28:4-406(f)'s provision of one-year to a period of sixty days. The U.C.C. establishes that contracting parties may vary U.C.C. terms by contract:

> The effect of the provisions of this article may be varied by agreement, but the parties to the agreement cannot disclaim a bank's responsibility for its lack of good faith or failure to exercise ordinary care or limit the measure of damages for the lack or failure. However, the parties may determine by agreement the standards by which the bank's responsibility is to be measured if those standards are not manifestly unreasonable.

D.C. Code §28:4-103(a) (2001). Further, this court has noted that "'[t]he relationship between a bank and a depositor is a contractual relationship that is governed by the written agreement between the parties.'" Geiger v. Crestar Bank, 778 A.2d 1085, 1090 (D.C. 2001) (quoting Isaac v. First Nat'l Bank of Maryland, D.C., 647 A.2d 1159, 1161 (D.C. 1994)). Here, Riggs Bank and Ms. Graves entered into a contractual agreement providing, *inter alia*:

> Your statement is considered correct, and we [Riggs Bank] will not be liable for payments made and charged to your account . . . unless you notify us of an error, including . . . unauthorized payment or other irregularity within (a) sixty (60) calendar days . . . of the mailing date of the earliest statement describing the charge or deposit to your account.

Thus, following the terms of the contract, Ms. Graves had sixty days from the mailing of her account statements to discover and report unauthorized transactions.

Appellant contends that Riggs's shortening of the period to sixty days is invalid as it provides too short a period of time for a person to discover and report problems in their account, or alternatively, it effectively excuses the bank from exercising due care. However, a review of other jurisdictions reveals that courts have consistently upheld the contractual shortening of the notice provision to periods of sixty days or shorter. *See, e.g., National Title Ins. Corp. Agency, supra,* 559 S.E.2d at 672 (upholding a sixty-day notice provision); *American Airlines Employees Fed. Credit Union, supra,* 29 S.W.3d at 96 (same); Jamison v. First Georgia Bank, 193 Ga. App. 219, 387 S.E.2d 375, 376-77 (1989) (same). The contractual shortening does not alter the bank's duty to exercise ordinary care or good faith; it "merely varies" the U.C.C.'s contractual notice provision. *See National Title Ins. Corp. Agency, supra,* 559 S.E.2d at 671. Neither has appellant shown the sixty day time period to be unconscionable, as he has not demonstrated both that Ms. Graves lacked a meaningful choice in entering the contract and that the contract terms unreasonably favor Riggs Bank. *See* Riggs Nat'l Bank of Washington, D.C. v. District of Columbia, 581 A.2d 1229, 1251 (D.C. 1990) (citing Williams v. Walker-Thomas Furniture Co., 121 U.S. App. D.C. 315, 319, 350 F.2d 445, 449 (1965)). Because the U.C.C. provision allocates the duty of discovering forgeries or unauthorized transactions to the customer, a reasonable contraction of the discovery and notice period encourages due diligence by the customer in inspecting account statements; it also promotes the U.C.C.'s goal of finality. *See* Silvia v. Indus. Nat'l Bank of Rhode Island, 121 R.I. 810, 403 A.2d 1075, 1077 (1979) (discussing the policy underlying the U.C.C. statutory notice provision as one that promotes finality of transactions). Accordingly, we agree that contracting parties may permissibly shorten the notice period to sixty days.

Appellant, however, contends that the statutory notice provision should be tolled in this case because of Ms. Graves's incapacitation and subsequent death and because appellant did not discover the unauthorized transactions until months after his mother's death. In essence, appellant asks this court to read a discovery rule into D.C. Code §28:4-406(f) that would permit equitable tolling of the provision. Appellant's position is untenable: equitable tolling cannot apply to statutes of repose. "Under the discovery rule, a particular cause of action accrues when the plaintiff knows or through the exercise of due diligence should have known of the injury." Ehrenhaft v. Malcolm Price, Inc., 483 A.2d 1192, 1201 (D.C. 1984) (internal quotation omitted). However, "[a] statute of repose . . . establishes an absolute time period within which legal proceedings must be initiated, *regardless of when a cause of action accrues.*" *Sandoe, supra,* 559 A.2d at 736 n.5 (emphasis added). Therefore, if a statute of repose applies regardless of when the cause of action accrues, and the discovery rule merely alters when the cause of action accrues, then the discovery rule cannot apply to a statute of repose.[16] This logic is consistent with holdings from other jurisdictions. *See, e.g.,* Estate of Decker v. Farm Credit Servs. of Mid-America, ACA, 684 N.E.2d 1137, 1139

16. This reasoning is also reflected in Black's Law Dictionary: " 'statutes of limitations' extinguish, after [a] period of time, [the] right to prosecute accrued cause[s] of action; [a] 'statute of repose,' by contrast, limits potential liability by limiting [the] time during which cause of action can arise. It is distinguishable from [a] statute of limitations, in that [a] statute of repose cuts off right of action after [a] specified time measured from delivery of product or completion of work, regardless of time of accrual of cause of action or of notice of legal rights." Black's Law Dictionary 1411 (6th ed. 1990).

(Ind. 1997) ("While equitable principles may extend the time for commencing an action under statutes of limitation, nonclaim statutes impose a condition precedent to the enforcement of a right of action and are not subject to equitable exceptions."); Brighton, Inc. v. Colonial First Nat'l Bank, 176 N.J. Super. 101, 422 A.2d 433, 437 (App. Div. 1980) ("The one-year period limitation in §4-406(4) is not merely a statute of limitations, but a rule of substantive law barring absolutely a customer's untimely asserted right to make such a claim against the bank.").

Courts have applied this statutory bar even in cases where the result is harsh. In Siecinski v. First State Bank of East Detroit, 209 Mich. App. 459, 531 N.W.2d 768, 769 (1995), an account holder suffered a head injury, fell into a coma, and died around a month later. Prior to her death, someone presented the incapacitated woman's bank with a forged power of attorney and ultimately withdrew everything in the account (around $175,000, most of it *after* the woman had died). *Id.* The appellant in the case had been appointed personal representative and had eventually discovered the wrongful withdrawals. *Id.* The Michigan Court of Appeals concluded that its version of §4-406(4) [the predecessor to §4-406(f)] barred the action despite the fact that no one was in a position to discover the forgery. *See id.* at 770. The court concluded that the statutory language created an absolute bar and that actual receipt of customer bank statements was not required:

> Courts of other jurisdictions have held that the subsection is not a limitation statute subject to tolling under compelling circumstances but is a statutory prerequisite of notice that absolutely bars a customer's right to make a claim against the bank after one year without regard to the care or lack of care of either the customer or the bank.

Id. The court further concluded that the statutory provision barred all causes of action-thus, appellant's negligence claim failed as well. *Id.* at 770-71.

Courts have applied this reasoning against mentally incompetent plaintiffs as well. In Brown v. Cash Mgmt. Trust of Am., 963 F. Supp. 504, 504-05 (D. Md. 1997) (applying N.Y. law), the U.S. District Court in Maryland barred the plaintiff's claim in a case where a woman had opened a checking account as a co-signor with plaintiff, a mentally incompetent woman, before forging the incompetent plaintiff's signature and looting the account. Further, the bank sent statements to either the co-signor or the plaintiff's agent, but never to the plaintiff. *Id.* at 505. Nevertheless, the court held that the provision was "an unalterable condition precedent to suit" and declined to make an exception due to the plaintiff's mental state: "The certainty which the Uniform Commercial Code seeks to achieve in respect to commercial transactions would quickly dissipate if *ad hoc* exceptions to its commands were too eagerly crafted to accommodate the occasional 'hard case.'" *Id.* at 506. The North Carolina Court of Appeals reached the same conclusion. *See* Union v. Branch Banking & Trust Co., 176 N.C. App. 711, 627 S.E.2d 276, 279 (2006) ("[F]ailure of a customer or his representative to report his unauthorized signature within one year after the bank makes account statements available precludes a claim against the bank, even if the customer is incompetent (whether adjudicated or unadjudicated) during the one-year period for providing notice.").

These principles have also been applied in a number of fraud cases where the party forging checks intercepted bank statements—thus preventing the account holder from actually receiving the statements and reporting any errors. In Stowell v. Cloquet Co-op Credit Union, 557 N.W.2d 567, 569-70 (Minn. 1997), a man forged his neighbor's signature on fifty checks, misappropriated a total amount of $22,000, and stole his neighbor's credit union statements every month. In concluding that §4-406(f) applied to bar the plaintiff's claims, the court explained that the U.C.C. provision assigns the risk of non-receipt to the bank customer:

> The modern U.C.C. case law of other jurisdictions is virtually unanimous in holding that, once account statements are mailed to the account holder's proper address, the risk of nonreceipt falls on the account holder and interception of the statements by a wrongdoer does not relieve the account holder of the duty to examine the statements and report unauthorized items to the bank.

Id. at 571-72; *see also id.* at 568-69 (pointing out that the credit union processed roughly one million transactions a day, and thus provided monthly account statements, rather than manually checking individual signature cards). The court further noted that requiring actual receipt of the statements (which would be the result of placing the risk of non-receipt on the bank) "would place unreasonable financial burdens on banks and other financial institutions by forcing them to prove receipt either through the use of certified mail or by individually contacting each account holder to confirm that they had, in fact, received their account statement." *Id.* at 572. Other courts have reached the same conclusion. *See, e.g.*, Borowski v. Firstar Bank Milwaukee, N.A., 217 Wis. 2d 565, 579 N.W.2d 247, 252-53 (Ct. App. 1998) (concluding that notice provision still barred claims even where plaintiff's girlfriend forged checks (totaling around $150,000) and intercepted bank statements); PTA, Pub. Sch. 72 v. Mfrs. Hanover Trust Co., 138 Misc. 2d 289, 295, 524 N.Y.S.2d 336, 340 (N.Y. City Civ. Ct. 1988) (upholding bar of claim despite fact that forger intercepted statements, meaning that account holder had no actual receipt).

These courts based their decisions on the underlying policies of the Uniform Commercial Code: encouraging the efficiency and finality of transactions through a uniform and predictable application of the law. *See, e.g., Brown, supra,* 963 F. Supp. at 506 n.4 ("[T]he U.C.C. has the objective of promoting certainty and predictability in commercial transactions.") (internal quotation omitted); Fundacion Museo de Arte Contemporaneo de Caracas-Sofia Imber v. CBI-TDB Union Bancaire Privee, 996 F. Supp. 277, 291 (S.D.N.Y. 1998) (declining to impose actual receipt requirement because it would require banks to send account statements by certified mail); *Silvia, supra,* 403 A.2d at 1077 (discussing the policy underlying §4-406(4) as one that promotes finality of transactions). According to the U.C.C. itself, U.C.C. provisions "shall be liberally construed and applied to promote its underlying purposes and policies," including a policy "to make uniform the law among the various jurisdictions." D.C. Code §28:1-102 (2001).

Appellant urges the court to accept an exception carved out by a California appellate court. In Mac v. Bank of Am., 76 Cal. App. 4th 562, 567-68, 90 Cal. Rptr. 2d 476 (Cal. Ct. App. 1999), the court found that §4-406(f) did not apply and did not bar the claim of a personal representative to recover for unauthorized transactions that cleared after the account holder's death because §4-406(a) requires that statements be "made available to the customer," and in that case, there was no customer because the customer had died. We decline to adopt *Mac*; it functionally imposes a discovery rule inconsistent with the principles underlying statutes of repose, as well as the policies of uniformity and predictability espoused by the U.C.C. Its application to other cases would create the type of *ad hoc* exception that other jurisdictions have avoided. Further, it would impose upon banks the duty of ensuring actual receipt—a logistical problem whose extra costs would undoubtedly be passed on to the consumer. Therefore, consistent with other jurisdictions and in promotion of the underlying policies of the U.C.C., we hold that D.C. Code §28:4-406(f) is not subject to equitable tolling. Because it is undisputed that neither Ms. Graves nor appellant timely notified Riggs Bank of the unauthorized transactions, appellant's claims are barred. . . .

Accordingly, the decision of the trial court is

Affirmed.

PROBLEM 236

Francisco Calleja-Ahedo had an account at Compass Bank. An unknown fraudster contacted Compass Bank, persuading the bank to change the mailing address on the account, and issue a new debit card and set of blank checks. The malefactor depleted the account gradually over the next couple of years, which Calleja-Ahedo never noticed since he'd forgotten about the account. Does the bank statement rule prevent

Calleja-Ahedo from demanding that Compass Bank replenish the account? See Calleja-Ahedo v. Compass Bank, 508 S.W.3d 791 (Tex. App. 2016) (no, since the statements were not being sent to the customer). What if the bad actor worked in an office and altered the statements the bank properly sent there so as to hide embezzlements before the boss reviewed the statements? See Grodner & Associates v. Regions Bank, 2019 WL 1299927 (5th Cir. 2019).

PROBLEM 237

Original National Bank engaged in the practice of "bulk filing," meaning that the bank did not examine checks for forgeries if they were written for amounts less than $5,000. The bank justified this practice as necessary for economic reasons. It therefore paid a series of $3,500 checks on which a customer's signature as drawer was forged and sent them over a period of months to its customer as part of his monthly statement. The customer negligently failed to report the forgeries of his name until seven months after the first one was returned to him. When he did complain, the bank pointed to §4-406(c) and (d). The customer replied that §4-406(e) requires the bank to share the loss since it did not observe ordinary care. As to the meaning of *ordinary care*, see §4-103(c) and a definition of the term in §3-103(a)(9) that should prove very interesting to the bank's attorney. Who prevails here?

The UCC clearly states that banks are not required to examine checks and compare them to the drawer's signature on file; Official Comment 4 to §4-406 states: "The term 'ordinary care' used in subsection (e) is defined in Section 3-103(a)(7), made applicable to Article 4 by Section 4-104(c), to provide that sight examination by a payor bank is not required if its procedure is reasonable and is commonly followed by other comparable banks in the area." The courts have agreed:

> There are realities to modern banking that make signature verification impractical. Checks are processed through automation, meaning that "signature verification is a dinosaur." 2 Law of Bank Deposits, Collections, & Credit Cards §10.06 (2018). Signature cards are "a quaint historical relic with little practical force in modern banking law." A. Brooke Overby, *Check Fraud in the Courts After the Revisions to U.C.C. Articles 3 and 4*, 57 Ala. L. Rev. 351, 359-61 (2005) (describing in detail the modern-day life cycle of a check).

Grodner & Associates v. Regions Bank, 766 F. App'x 12 (5th Cir. 2019).

Clemente Bros. Contracting Corp. v. Hafner-Milazzo

Court of Appeals of New York, 2014
23 N.Y.3d 277, 14 N.E.3d 367, 991 N.Y.S.2d 14

Chief Judge LIPPMAN.

The primary issue presented is whether a bank and its customer may agree to shorten from one year to 14 days the statutory time period under UCC 4-406(4) within which a customer must notify its bank of an improperly paid item in order to recover the payment thereon. In two opinions issued over 20 years ago, this Court declined to decide this issue because it was not presented directly, but questioned whether a 14-day period could be reasonable and observed that the question "raise[d] policy considerations" (Putnam Rolling Ladder Co. v. Manufacturers Hanover Trust Co., 74 N.Y.2d 340, 349 n.2, 547 N.Y.S.2d 611, 546 N.E.2d 904 [1989]; SOS Oil Corp. v. Norstar Bank of Long Is., 76 N.Y.2d 561, 568, 561 N.Y.S.2d 887, 563 N.E.2d 258 [1990]). We now hold that, at least in this case, the parties' agreement to shorten the period was permissible.

I

In April 2007, plaintiff Clemente Brothers Contracting Corp. opened three corporate operating accounts at North Fork Bank (which subsequently merged with defendant Capital One, N.A. [collectively Capital One]) and took out a loan and a line of credit, each backed by a promissory note. Clemente Brothers could draw money on the line of credit by sending a signed drawdown request to Capital One. As a condition precedent to opening the accounts at Capital One, plaintiff Jeffrey Clemente, the company's principal, executed a personal guaranty with respect to the loan and line of credit, and Clemente Brothers passed a corporate resolution, which provided that Jeffrey Clemente was the only authorized signatory on the accounts and the only one authorized to sign drawdown requests on the line of credit.

The corporate resolution also provided,

> That unless [Clemente Brothers] shall notify the Bank in writing *within fourteen calendar days* of the delivery or mailing of any statement of account and cancelled check, draft or other instrument for the payment of money (hereinafter referred to as "Instrument") of any claimed errors in such statement, or that [Clemente Brothers'] signature upon any such returned Instrument was forged, or that any such Instrument was made or drawn without the authority of [Clemente Brothers] . . . or that it was raised or otherwise altered . . . said statement of account shall be considered correct for all purposes and said Bank shall not be liable for any payments made and charged to the account

> of [Clemente Brothers] or for any other errors in the statement of account as rendered to it.

Capital One mailed statements of account for all three of the operating accounts to the business address provided by Clemente Brothers. The monthly statements included copies of cancelled checks drawn on that account.

As for the line of credit, Capital One mailed a statement to Clemente Brothers each month showing the principal balance and the monthly interest payment, which was automatically debited from the primary operating account. Capital One has not offered any evidence that it included copies of the drawdown requests on the line of credit with the monthly statements. But the drawdowns appeared as credits on the operating account statements.

Defendant Aprile Hafner-Milazzo worked as a secretary and bookkeeper for Clemente Brothers until it was discovered that she had been forging Clemente's signature on certain Capital One bank documents, including drawdown requests on the line of credit and checks paid from one of Clemente Brothers' accounts. According to plaintiffs, Hafner-Milazzo embezzled approximately $386,000 over the course of approximately two years, from January 2008 through December 2009.

In February 2010, Clemente Brothers notified Capital One of Hafner-Milazzo's thefts. Thereafter, Capital One determined that an event had occurred that adversely affected Clemente Brothers' ability to repay its debts and, pursuant to a clause in the two promissory notes, declared all amounts due and payable.

Plaintiffs subsequently commenced this action against Hafner-Milazzo and Capital One to recover damages resulting from Hafner-Milazzo's forgeries and to prevent Capital One from forcing repayment on the loans. In its answer, Capital One interposed several counterclaims to recover amounts due under the loans and Clemente's personal guaranty.

Capital One moved for summary judgment dismissing the complaint insofar as asserted against it and on its counterclaims. Supreme Court granted Capital One's motion in its entirety and awarded it the principal sum of $1,146,262.90 on its counterclaims (Clemente Bros. Contr. Corp. v. Hafner-Milazzo, 2011 N.Y. Slip Op. 30384[U] [Sup. Ct., N.Y. County 2011]). According to the court, Capital One was "entitled to the protection afforded by UCC 4-406(4)," which precludes liability for a bank to its customer when it pays a check on a forged signature but makes statements of the account and the allegedly forged items available to the customer, and the customer fails to report the alleged forgery to the bank within one year (*id.* at *4). Here, the court observed, Clemente Brothers and Capital One, by agreement, properly abbreviated the one-year period to 14 days, within which plaintiffs failed to report each of the alleged forgeries.

The Appellate Division affirmed (Clemente Bros. Contr. Corp. v. Hafner-Milazzo, 100 A.D.3d 677, 954 N.Y.S.2d 156 [2d Dept. 2012]). This Court granted plaintiffs leave to appeal (21 N.Y.3d 856, 2013 WL 2395327 [2013]).

II

New York's version of the Uniform Commercial Code (hereinafter UCC) imposes strict liability upon a bank that charges against its customer's account any "item" that is not "properly payable" (UCC 4-401[1]; Monreal v. Fleet Bank, 95 N.Y.2d 204, 207, 713 N.Y.S.2d 301, 735 N.E.2d 880 [2000]). An "item" is "any instrument for the payment of money even though it is not negotiable but does not include money" (UCC 4-104[1][g]). Black's Law Dictionary defines "instrument" as a "written legal document that defines rights, duties, entitlements, or liabilities" (Black's Law Dictionary 869 [9th ed. 2009]). Put another way, a bank may not charge a check, or other written document defining a right to or liability for payment, bearing a forged signature against its customer's account (*Monreal*, 95 N.Y.2d at 207, 713 N.Y.S.2d 301, 735 N.E.2d 880).

The UCC nevertheless limits banks' exposure by imposing obligations on customers that, if unfulfilled, may preclude a customer's suit against the bank. When a bank sends to its customer statements of account and copies of the items paid, the customer must review those documents promptly and notify the bank of any irregularities:

> "When a bank sends to its customer a statement of account accompanied by items paid in good faith in support of the debit entries or holds the statement and items pursuant to a request or instructions of its customer or otherwise in a reasonable manner makes the statement and items available to the customer, the customer must exercise reasonable care and promptness to examine the statement and items to discover his unauthorized signature or any alteration on an item and must notify the bank promptly after discovery thereof" (UCC 4-406 [1]; *see also Monreal*, 95 N.Y.2d at 207, 713 N.Y.S.2d 301, 735 N.E.2d 880).

If the customer fails to fulfill its obligation, then the customer is precluded from asserting against the bank (1) "his unauthorized signature or any alteration on the item if the bank also establishes that it suffered a loss by reason of such failure" and (2) "an unauthorized signature or alteration by the same wrongdoer on any other item paid in good faith by the bank after the first item and statement was available to the customer for a reasonable period not exceeding fourteen calendar days" (UCC 4-406[2][a], [b]). These bars to recovery do not apply "if the customer establishes lack of ordinary care on the part of the bank in paying the item(s)" (UCC 4-406[3]).

An additional limitation, pertinent here, is found in UCC 4-406(4), which creates something akin to a statute of repose that bars a customer's claim for recovery on a wrongfully paid item when the customer fails to report the irregularity within one year after the bank provides the statement and item, regardless of either party's failure to exercise reasonable care:

> "Without regard to care or lack of care of either the customer or the bank a customer who does not within one year from the time the statement and items are made available to the customer (subsection (1)) discover and report his unauthorized signature . . . is precluded from asserting against the bank such unauthorized signature or indorsement or such alteration" (UCC 4-406 [4]).

Here, the parties shortened the one-year period to 14 days by agreement.

A

Capital One argues that UCC 4-406(4) defeats plaintiffs' claims with respect to both the operating accounts and the line of credit. But the application of UCC 4-406(4) is contingent upon the bank providing the customer with account statements and copies of the items paid under UCC 4-406(1). The parties do not seriously dispute that Capital One complied with UCC 4-406(1) with respect to the operating accounts by providing monthly statements and copies of cancelled checks. But they do dispute whether the line of credit is subject to UCC article 4 at all, and, if it is, whether Capital One complied with UCC 4-406(1).

Plaintiffs argue that the drawdown requests on the line of credit do not qualify as "items" within the meaning of UCC article 4. We disagree. The requests are written instruments formally exercising a contractual right to the payment of money from the line of credit. We do agree with plaintiffs, however, that, at least on this motion for summary judgment, Capital One cannot avail itself of UCC 4-406(4). Capital One argues that the drawdown requests should be treated as items and that it is entitled to the protections of UCC 4-406(4), but it conspicuously has not offered evidence showing that it complied with the threshold requirements of UCC 4-406(1) quoted above.

The language of the New York statute tracks the language of the original model Uniform Commercial Code (Model UCC), and has not been amended by the legislature since adoption in 1962. Section 4-406 of the Model UCC was amended in 1991 to require that the bank must provide a statement of account and "shall either return or make available to the customer the items paid *or* provide information in the statement of account sufficient to allow the customer reasonably to identify the items paid" (Model UCC [2002] §4-406[a] [maintaining 1991 language] [emphasis added]).

The Model UCC's official commentary explains that under the new language:

> "[i]f the bank supplies its customer with an image of the paid item, it complies with this standard. But a safe harbor rule is provided. The bank complies with the standard of providing 'sufficient information' if 'the item is described by item number, amount, and date of payment.' This means that the customer's duties under [what was Model UCC 4-406(4)] are triggered if the bank sends a statement of account complying with the safe harbor rule without returning the paid items" (Model UCC 4-406, Comment 1).

Many states have adopted some form of the revised Model UCC 4-406. Ohio and Illinois, for example, require only that a bank provide an account statement with information sufficient to identify an item paid (*see* Ohio Rev. Code Ann. §1304.35[A]; 810 Ill. Comp. Stat. §5/4-406[a]). But New York has not adopted the revised Model UCC.

Banks in New York, as elsewhere, must comply in good faith with UCC 4-406(1) to seek the protections of UCC 4-406(4) (*see* Elden v. Merrill Lynch, Pierce, Fenner & Smith Inc., 2011 WL 1236141, *7, 2011 U.S. Dist. LEXIS 35886, *21-22 [S.D.N.Y., Mar. 30, 2011, No. 08-Civ-8738 (RJS)] [holding that bank did not send copies of the items and did not otherwise reasonably make them available, thus precluding relief under UCC 4-406(4)]). Again, they may do this in one of three ways: supply the items to the customer with the statement of account, hold the items for the customer, or "otherwise in a reasonable manner make[] the statement and items available" (UCC 4-406 [1]). The official commentary explains that this third option is to be used only in "unusual situations" (UCC 4-406, Comment 2). But one treatise author has noted that "literal compliance with this triggering event seem[s] impossible," and argues that the bank practice of sending or posting simple account statements should be sufficient to satisfy the requirements of section 4-406(1) (*see* 5 Hawkland et al., Uniform Commercial Code Series §4-406:2 at Art. 4-988, 4-992; *accord* Barkley Clark & Barbara Clark, 1 Bank Deposits, Collections and Credit Cards ¶10.05[1][a] at 10-39-10-40 [2013]).

Here, the record does not show that the drawdown requests were provided to Clemente Brothers. Absent any record evidence or discussion in the briefs about relevant banking practice or applicable regulations on this point, we do not hold that Capital One failed to comply with section 4-406(1) as a matter of law. But neither has the bank demonstrated its compliance with the statute. Consequently, Capital One is not entitled to summary judgment on the line-of-credit claims under UCC 4-406(4), and, on remittal, the judgment in its favor must be amended accordingly pending further proceedings on these claims.

Capital One argues in the alternative, and the lower courts also reasoned, that the wrongfully paid drawdown requests did not harm plaintiff. Capital One contends that paying the drawdown requests merely effectuated a transfer of funds from one of plaintiffs' accounts to another. But this is not an accurate description of the transactions; the funds did not come from plaintiffs' account, but from the bank itself.

The line of credit was, in effect, a pre-approved loan upon which plaintiffs could draw at will. Plaintiffs did not possess any borrowed funds or owe anything in repayment in the absence of a drawdown request. Upon such a request, Capital One would transfer funds to one of plaintiffs' accounts, interest immediately would begin to accrue and plaintiffs would be liable to repay the principal. Therefore, when Capital One wrongfully paid the drawdown requests at issue in this case, plaintiffs suffered financial harm.

B

Turning to the application of UCC 4-406(4), the UCC permits parties to alter the provisions of article 4 by agreement (*see* UCC 4-103[1]). The Official Comments go so far as to say that there exists a "blanket power to vary all provisions of the Article" (*id.*, Comment 2). But that power is not boundless:

> "[N]o agreement can disclaim a bank's responsibility for its own lack of good faith or failure to exercise ordinary care or can limit the measure of damages for such lack or failure; but the parties may by agreement determine the standards by which such responsibility is to be measured if such standards are not manifestly unreasonable" (UCC 4-103[1]).

The application of these limitations raises two issues: first, whether parties can vary the one-year period by agreement; we hold that they can; and second, whether shortening the one-year period to 14 days is manifestly unreasonable; we hold that it is not, at least under these facts.

The argument that modification is not allowed is that by shortening the period, the bank is "disclaiming" its obligation to act with care or that it is limiting the measure of damages for a failure to act with care in violation of UCC 4-403(1). This argument finds some slender support in our decision in Regatos v. North Fork Bank, 5 N.Y.3d 395, 804 N.Y.S.2d 713, 838 N.E.2d 629 (2005).

Regatos involved the funds transfers provisions of UCC article 4-A. Banks are liable under article 4-A for improper funds transfers, similar to how they are liable under article 4 for improperly paid items. As for funds transfers, UCC 4-A-204 (2) provides that "the obligation of a receiving bank to refund payment . . . may not otherwise be varied by agreement."

UCC 4-A-505 contains a one-year notice period similar to that found in UCC 4-406(4). This Court held that parties could not shorten the one-year period in UCC 4-A-505 by agreement (*Regatos*, 5 N.Y.3d at 398-399, 804 N.Y.S.2d 713, 838 N.E.2d 629). The Court reasoned that shortening the one-year period effectively would "var[y]" the bank's "obligation . . . to refund payment" in violation of the plain language of UCC 4-A-204 (2) (*id.* at 402-403, 804 N.Y.S.2d 713, 838 N.E.2d 629).

Plaintiffs would have us apply *Regatos* to this case. They rely on two Appellate Division decisions that could be read as extending the logic of *Regatos* to UCC 4-406 (*see* Aikens Constr. of Rome v. Simons, 284 A.D.2d 946, 947, 727 N.Y.S.2d 213 [4th Dept. 2001]; Herzog, Engstrom & Koplovitz v. Union Natl. Bank, 226 A.D.2d 1004, 1004-1005, 640 N.Y.S.2d 703 [3d Dept. 1996]). But this result neither follows from the provisions of article 4 nor is it desirable as a policy matter.

Unlike UCC 4-A-204, UCC 4-103(1) does not prohibit a bank from altering its obligation to refund payments made in good faith. And shortening the one-year period does not violate any of the prohibitions in UCC 4-103(1). Capital One did not disclaim its responsibility to act with care by requiring its customer to notify it of an improperly paid item within 14 days of receiving the account statement. While shortening the period certainly affected Capital One's liability for improperly paid items, whether paid in good faith or not, it did not exclude all liability for negligence. Nor did the modification affect the measure of damages; it merely limited the time within which plaintiffs must provide notice of the improper charge.

Courts around the country have permitted parties to shorten the one year to various periods, from as short as 14 days to more than 60 days (*see e.g.* Gluck v. JPMorgan Chase Bank, 12 A.D.3d 305, 306, 785 N.Y.S.2d 77 [1st Dept. 2004] [60 days]; Peters v. Riggs Natl. Bank, N.A., 942 A.2d 1163, 1168 [D.C. 2008] [60 days]; Borowski v. Firstar Bank Milwaukee, N.A., 217 Wis. 2d 565, 576-580, 579 N.W.2d 247, 252-253 [1998] [14 days]). And the record and case law suggest that most banks do shorten the period.

To apply *Regatos*'s logic to this case would be to hold not only the 14-day period impermissible, but every other longer period used in the industry, be it 30 days or nine months. We perceive no good reason for creating such an inconsistency in the banking laws of the various states. We therefore hold that parties may modify by agreement the one-year period in UCC 4-406(4), as long as the modification is not manifestly unreasonable.

The modification in this case is not manifestly unreasonable. Clemente Brothers had numerous employees, regularly moved hundreds of thousands of dollars in and out of its operating accounts, and had the resources to make an informed decision about opening accounts at Capital One. Critically, Clemente was fully aware of the terms of the agreements with Capital One because Clemente Brothers passed a corporate resolution acknowledging its obligation to notify Capital One of any irregularities within 14 days of each statement of account.

It is not manifestly unreasonable to expect a company with numerous employees and hundreds of thousands of dollars under its control to monitor its accounts once a month, within 14 days of each statement, particularly where it has acknowledged its responsibility to do so in a corporate resolution. That expectation is all the more reasonable in this age, when customers can monitor their account transactions minute by minute online from around the world.

We stress, however, that our holding is limited to the case of a corporate entity that either is financially sophisticated or has the resources to acquire professional guidance. It could well be unreasonable for banks to use contracts of adhesion to impose an exacting 14-day limit on unsophisticated customers, small family businesses, or individual consumers, including, for example, the elderly, people suffering from certain disabilities, or others for whom the 14-day rule could be too unforgiving. These customers may lack the time, technology, or other resources to check their account statements within such a limited period every month. They are more susceptible to unforeseen events disrupting their routines or normal business operations. And it may be that banks need less protection on these accounts because the total assets held may be less than those of larger companies. But whether it would be *manifestly* unreasonable for these customers to be subject to a 14-day notice period, as opposed to a 30- or 60-day period, is a question for a later day.

The order of the Appellate Division should be modified, without costs, by remitting to Supreme Court for further proceedings in accordance with this opinion, and, as so modified, affirmed.

PIGOTT, J. (dissenting in part).

Uniform Commercial Code §4-406, titled "Customer's Duty to Discover and Report Unauthorized Signature or Alteration," sets forth a customer's and bank's respective duties concerning a customer's statement of account. When the bank sends the customer such a statement accompanied by items paid in good faith, the customer must "exercise reasonable care and promptness to examine the statement and items to discover his unauthorized signature . . . and . . . notify the bank promptly after discovery thereof" (UCC 4-406[1]). If the customer does not comply with that provision he or she is precluded from asserting against the bank: A customer is not precluded from asserting against a bank an unauthorized signature under subsection (2), however, "if the customer establishes lack of ordinary care on the part of the bank in paying the item(s)" (UCC 4-406[3]). UCC 4-406(4) prescribes a one-year time limit on a customer to make a claim against a bank for its payment of an altered or forged paper irrespective of whether the bank exercised ordinary care.

> "(a) his unauthorized signature or any alteration on the item if the bank also establishes that it suffered a loss by reason of such failure; and
>
> "(b) an unauthorized signature or alteration by the same wrongdoer on any other item paid in good faith by the bank after the first item and statement was available to the customer for a reasonable period not exceeding fourteen calendar days and before the bank receives notification from the customer of any such unauthorized signature or alteration" (UCC 4-406[2][a], [b]).

Plaintiff claims that Capital One had notice of defendant Hafner-Milazzo's predisposition to commit illegal acts and failed to exercise ordinary care. By boilerplate resolution, however, the bank claims to have reduced the time under which the plaintiff could assert such a lack of ordinary care from one year to the same 14-day time period as set forth in section 4-406(2), effectively repealing section 4-406(4) as it applies to its customers. The majority finds this reasonable, relying on UCC 4-103(1), which provides, as relevant here, that UCC article 4's provisions "may be varied by agreement" with the caveat "that no agreement can disclaim a bank's responsibility *for its own lack of good faith or failure to exercise ordinary care* or can limit the measure of damages for such lack or failure; but the parties may by agreement determine the *standards* by which such responsibility is to be measured if such standards are not manifestly unreasonable" (emphasis supplied).

In my view, because section 4-406(4) clearly imposes a one-year limitation on claims involving a bank's "failure to exercise ordinary care," the time period cannot be changed by agreement. To be sure, there may be a variation in standards by which a bank's responsibility is to be measured (so long as such standards are not manifestly unreasonable), but the one-year limitation remains.

The majority claims that the shortening of the period resulted in a limitation of liability, and reduced only plaintiff's time to provide notice of the improper charge (majority op. at 288, 991 N.Y.S.2d at 19, 14 N.E.3d at 372). That is mere semantics, however, because the overall effect of the time reduction is to eliminate plaintiff's opportunity to assert, after the 14-day period had passed (but before the one-year time period had elapsed) that Capital One had failed to exercise ordinary care and, consequently, recover damages as a result of that negligence. The shortening of the time period works a de facto disclaimer of liability, which is prohibited under section 4-103(1).

It is my view that just as the customer and bank in Regatos v. North Fork Bank, 5 N.Y.3d 395, 804 N.Y.S.2d 713, 838 N.E.2d 629 (2005), were prohibited from modifying by contract the one-year statute of repose set forth in UCC 4-A-505—which grants a customer one year to notify the bank of an unauthorized wire transfer—plaintiff and Capital One were prohibited from contractually shortening section 4-406(4)'s one-year time limitation. In *Regatos,* the bank received two unauthorized funds transfers totaling $600,000 and, in violation of the agreed security procedures, transferred the funds from the customer's account. When the customer notified the bank of the unauthorized transfers five months later, the bank refused to refund the money, relying on the account agreement's provision that the customer was to notify the bank of "any unauthorized signature or alteration" within 15 days (*see Regatos,* 5 N.Y.3d at 399-400, 804 N.Y.S.2d 713, 838 N.E.2d 629). Relying on UCC 4-A-204(*l*)'s language that a "bank is not entitled to any recovery from the customer on account of a failure by the customer to give notification as stated in this section," we concluded that the bank had an obligation to refund the principal so long as notice was given within one year as required by section 4-A-505 (*id.* at 402-403, 804 N.Y.S.2d 713, 838 N.E.2d 629). We explained that the policy behind UCC article 4-A was to encourage financial institutions "to adopt appropriate security procedures," and that allowing them "to vary the notice period by agreement would reduce the effectiveness of the statute's one-year period of repose as an incentive for banks to create and follow security procedures" (*id.* at 402, 804 N.Y.S.2d 713, 838 N.E.2d 629).

Likewise, UCC article 4 imposes upon a bank the obligation to act with ordinary care, which required Capital One to follow commercially reasonable security procedures to ensure it was not making payments on unauthorized checks. A reduction in the one-year period to 14 days provides little, if any, incentive for a bank to act with ordinary care. And, of course, a bank's obligation to exercise ordinary care may not be varied by agreement (*see* Aikens Constr. of Rome v. Simons, 284 A.D.2d 946, 947, 727 N.Y.S.2d 213 [4th Dept. 2001]; Herzog, Engstrom & Koplovitz v. Union Natl. Bank, 226 A.D.2d 1004, 1005, 640 N.Y.S.2d 703 [3d Dept. 1996]). But that is precisely what the corporate resolution does in this case. Prior to today, our courts have never sanctioned such a practice.

The majority approach has at least two significant drawbacks. First, it impairs the incentive the authors of UCC article 4 created for banks to exercise ordinary care in the payment of items. Second, it seems to make the outcome of cases depend upon whether the customer is a Fortune 500 company, a medium-sized one (this plaintiff is no corporate giant), a small one, or an individual. It would be better to interpret the statute in a way that obviates the need for a court to analyze whether the customer was "financially sophisticated," possessed "the resources to acquire professional guidance," was a "small family business" or an "elderly" individual (majority op. at 289, 991 N.Y.S.2d at 20, 14 N.E.3d at 373) because the rule would apply to every type of consumer. The rule proposed by the majority provides less certainty and will create more litigation because it doesn't apply to everyone in like fashion. The fact that the majority is concerned that financial institutions will "use contracts of adhesion to impose" what it acknowledges is "an *exacting 14-day limit* on unsophisticated consumers" (majority op. at 289, 991 N.Y.S.2d at 20, 14 N.E.3d at 373 [emphasis supplied]) only underscores why customers and banks should not be permitted to contractually reduce section 4-406(4)'s one-year limitation period.

Accordingly, I respectfully dissent from that part of the majority holding that a customer and bank may contractually reduce section 4-406(4)'s one-year limitations period.

Judges GRAFFEO, READ, RIVERA and ABDUS-SALAAM concur with Chief Judge LIPPMAN; Judge PIGOTT dissents in part in an opinion in which Judge SMITH concurs.

Order modified, without costs, by remitting to Supreme Court, Suffolk County, for further proceedings in accordance with the opinion herein and, as so modified, affirmed.

PROBLEM 238

When the law firm of Factory, Factory & Money (F.F. & M.) opened a checking account with Octopus National Bank (ONB), the firm members signed a deposit contract, stating that they would report all irregularities in their bank statements within 10 days of their receipt. Failure to do so resulted in a waiver of any problems with the statement. Two years later LeNore Ledger, F.F. & M.'s bookkeeper, wrote three checks to herself, each for $5,000, and forged the necessary F.F. & M. signatures to the drawer's line. The first check cleared through the bank in time to be returned with the bank statement that arrived at the law office on December 10. Ledger burned the statement and then took off for parts unknown. On January 23, Amos Factory, a senior partner, notified ONB that he could not find the December statement. When a duplicate was furnished to F.F. & M., they pointed out the first $5,000 check. By this time the other two checks had cleared through F.F. & M.'s account and were ready to be sent out in the February statement. The bank declined to recredit F.F. & M.'s account with any of the $15,000, pointing to the 10-day notice requirement in the deposit contract and to §4-406(d). F.F. & M. sued under §4-401's *properly payable* rule and argued that §4-103 invalidated the 10-day notice provision. How should this come out? See the preceding case and White & Summers 19-2, at 891-894. Would it make a difference if Ledger's forgeries were very badly done? See §4-406(e). How does the now common practice of posting check images daily on the Internet bank statement affect all of this?

Another issue that has split courts is whether the one-year bar in §4-406(f) applies when the bank has acted in bad faith. Compare Falk v. Northern Trust Co., 763 N.E.2d 380 (Ill. App. 2001) (holding one-year bar effective even where bank acts in bad faith); and Pinigis v. Regions Bank, 977 So. 2d 446 (Ala. 2007) (*contra*). We have received phone calls and emails from a number of attorneys litigating similar issues in other states. They want to know which position is right. What do you think?

PROBLEM 239

When Octopus National Bank found out about the rule of Price v. Neal (making the drawee liable for forgeries of the drawer's name unless the wrongdoer could be found), it asked its attorney what could be done to avoid this liability. The bank's attorney had the bank add a clause to the checking account agreement as follows: "Customer understands and agrees that the bank is no longer examining checks written for amounts less than $5,000, and also agrees that if the drawer's signature on such checks shall be unauthorized, the checks shall nonetheless be properly payable from the bank account, with the customer having the sole duty to pursue legal remedies against others." Is this clause valid? See §§4-103, 4-401(a), and 3-103(a)(9); James Steven Rogers, The Basic Principle of Loss Allocation for Unauthorized Checks, 39 Wake Forest L. Rev. 453 (2004); cf. Lor-Mar/Toto, Inc. v. 1st Constitution Bank, 376 N.J. Super. 520, 871 A.2d 110 (2005).

PROBLEM 240

Maximilian Money was not only very rich but also very lazy. He let the Investors National Bank handle all his affairs, the least of which was to act as drawee of his checking account. So as to save time, he signed all of his checks with a little rubber signature stamp when he first received his checkbook. Though the bank regularly sent him monthly statements, he never even opened them. At income tax time his tax lawyer discovered that his bank account was $4,000 short due to a check that had been stolen from Max and filled in to "Cash" for $4,000 over two years ago. The lawyer, as Max's agent, demanded that the account be replenished with this amount. The bank, to which $4,000 was a small matter in comparison to its income as trustee of Max's affairs, instantly complied. The $4,000 was not, however, so small a matter that it could be forgotten, so the Investors National Bank demanded repayment from the presenting bank, the Fallguy State Bank, charging breach of the §4-208(a)(2) warranty of no alteration. What result if Fallguy State refuses and suit is brought? See §4-406(f)'s last sentence and §4-208(c).

PROBLEM 241

Bertrand Balance was the payroll clerk for Tentacles Corporation, and one day in a moment of weakness he drew up 107 extra paychecks payable to phony names. He signed the payees' names to the back of every check and cashed each of the checks at various local depositary banks over the period of one month. As soon as the last one had been cashed, Balance hurriedly left the state, leaving behind only an apologetic letter explaining what he had done. The corporation immediately demanded that the money be recredited to its payroll account. The bank comes to you for advice. Tentacles Corporation is one of the bank's largest depositors, and the bank doesn't want to lose it. If it recredits the account, can it sue the depositary banks for breach of presentment warranties?

Note that (c) of §4-208 (and the corresponding (c) in Article 3's presentment warranty section, §3-417) permits the entity making presentment warranties to raise the various validation rules to avoid warranty liability. This is as it should be. If the payor bank did make proper payment in spite of the forgery/alteration because these irregularities are validated by one of the sections we have studied, then the payor bank should not be permitted to ignore the validation and pass the loss on to innocent parties such as the presenting bank. Of course, the payor bank may be reluctant to offend its wealthy depositors, as in the above Problems, and, as a business matter, may elect to eat the loss itself rather than lose their trade, but if it is going to be this nice to its customers, any damages caused thereby are self-inflicted. Any time anyone has a valid defense and fails to raise it, that person has shot himself in the foot. The proximate cause of this loss is the unwillingness to raise the defense, not the technical breach of a presentment warranty.

IV. ALTERATIONS

PROBLEM 242

Earnest Innocent went into the Mafia Loan Company and asked to borrow $100 to finance the repair of a broken tooth. The loan company advanced him the money after he signed a promissory note for this amount plus 8 percent interest per annum, payable to the order of the Mafia Loan Company on demand. After Innocent left the office, the loan officer took out his special chemicals and used them to erase the original typewritten amount ($100).

In its place he typed in $9,500. The Mafia Loan Company discounted the paper for $100 to Michael Schmidt, a self-employed commercial factor, who always bought the company's altered paper. Schmidt presented the note to Innocent for payment, and when Innocent protested, Schmidt's "collectors" broke both his arms. They said they would return the following month and would expect him to have the money ready then. Assuming Innocent can get police protection against Schmidt's "self-help" collection procedures, what legal defenses does he have? Read §3-407 carefully.

Note that §3-407(b) states that a fraudulent alteration completely *discharges* any non-negligent person whose negotiable instruments contract is changed by the alteration. The alteration in the above Problem is technically said to be a *raising* of the amount.

PROBLEM 243

George Johnson owed around $50 to Marmaduke Brown and, while making out checks to his creditors, decided to write out a check to Brown. Unfortunately, he couldn't remember how to spell Brown's name or the exact amount owed, so he simply signed his name to the drawer's line while making a mental note to fill in the rest later. He put the check in his wallet, and it was stolen along with the wallet when he was mugged the following night. The check, made out to "Cash" for $150, cleared through his checking account the next week. Johnson brought suit against his bank, demanding that the bank recredit his account since the amount was not *properly payable.* He argues that this was an alteration under §3-407 and that he was discharged by the alteration. What reply should the bank's attorney make? See §§3-115, 3-407, 3-406, and 4-401(d).

PROBLEM 244

Joseph Goodheart was the owner and manager of the Goodheart Home for the Aged. He was also the payee of a promissory note for $1,000 given him by Nick Nephew to pay for three months' care Goodheart had given to Nephew's elderly aunt, Strange Molly. One day Strange Molly, who was not responsible for her actions, sneaked into Goodheart's empty office and ransacked his files. She found her nephew's promissory note and took a pen and deftly changed the amount to $1,000,000. Does this operate, under §3-407, to discharge Nephew from his maker's obligation? What would be the result if Strange Molly had torn up and eaten the note? See §3-309 and its Official Comment.

PROBLEM 245

Lloyd Smith mailed a check for $5.00 to his friend, David Rouge, as a birthday gift. Rouge cleverly raised the amount to $500.00 and cashed it at his own bank, Octopus National Bank, which then obtained payment from Last National Bank, the drawee. When Smith received his bank statement, he immediately complained to ONB about the alteration of the check. Assuming he was not negligent in writing the check, can Smith make the bank recredit the account for $500.00, or only $495.00? See §§3-407, 4-401(d). Is the bank without a remedy? See §4-208(a).

CHAPTER 14 ASSESSMENT: MULTIPLE CHOICE QUESTIONS

1. Seward issued a check to Konstantin to purchase some land. Gorchakov stole the check, forged Konstantin's indorsement, and sold the check to Check Casher. Check Casher deposited it in its account at Crown Bank. Crown Bank presented the check to Sitka Bank, which paid the check and took the money from Seward's account. When Seward saw the statement, he notified Sitka Bank of the improperly paid check. Gorchakov is long gone. Of the innocents, who is liable to whom?
   a. Crown Bank is liable to Sitka Bank for breach of presentment warranty.
   b. Check Casher is liable to Crown Bank for breach of transfer warranty.
   c. Check Casher, Crown Bank, and Sitka Bank are liable to Konstantin for conversion.
   d. Seward is liable to Konstantin on the check.
   e. All of the above.

2. Who would be liable if Konstantin had indorsed the check himself before Gorchakov stole it?
   a. Crown Bank is liable to Sitka Bank for breach of presentment warranty.
   b. Check Casher is liable to Crown Bank for breach of transfer warranty.
   c. Check Casher, Crown Bank, and Sitka Bank are liable to Konstantin for conversion.
   d. Seward is liable to Konstantin on the check.
   e. None of the above.

3. Bering paid Steller for some livestock with a check. Steller then used software to create and print another check on Bering's account, forged Bering's signature, and deposited the check at Malaspina Bank. Steller withdrew the money and disappeared. Malaspina Bank presented the check for payment to Kotzebue Bank, who paid the check. Bering soon objected and Kotzebue recredited Bering's account. Is Malaspina Bank liable to Kotzebue Bank?

a. Yes. Malaspina Bank is liable for breach of transfer warranty.
b. Yes. Malaspina Bank is liable for breach of presentment warranty.
c. No. The forged drawer's signature does not breach the presentment warranty.
d. No. Malaspina Bank was only an intermediary, collecting the check for its customer, so makes no warranty.

4. Stevens, the bookkeeper at Mala Films, stole five checks to suppliers that Mala Films had signed and prepared for mailing. Stevens forged Mala Film's indorsement and deposited the checks in his account at Soapy Bank. Mala Film's bank, Palin Bank, paid the checks when presented. Is Palin Bank entitled to the money from Mala Films for the checks?
   a. No. The checks were not properly payable, because Palin Bank paid the wrong person.
   b. No, but Palin Bank can recover from Soapy Bank for breach of presentment warranty.
   c. Yes. The forged indorsements are validated because they were made by an employee with responsibility for checks.
   d. Yes, because Palin Bank is not expected to be able to determine whether the indorsements are authentic.

5. One fine week in May, despite good security measures, the bookkeeper at Peratovich Consulting forged a dozen checks to himself on the company account, deposited them, and absconded with the proceeds. Upon receiving its monthly statement, Peratovich Consulting immediately cried foul. Can the drawee bank, which paid the checks, recover from its customer, Peratovich Consulting?
   a. Yes. Under the bank statement rule, Peratovich Consulting takes the loss for multiple acts of wrongdoing by the same person.
   b. Yes. Under the employee forgery rule, Peratovich Consulting takes the loss for its employee's malefaction.
   c. No. The checks were not properly payable.
   d. No. Banks take the loss for all forged checks, in order to spread the loss among all customers.
   e. No. Customers take the loss for all forged checks, to encourage them to combat forgery.

ANSWERS

1. *E* is the best answer. *A* simple diagram helps to keep the characters straight in these multi-party cases:

Seward →	Konstantin →	Gorchakov →	Casher →	Crown →	Sitka
issues	steals	transfers	transfers	presents	pays

This question shows the typical allocation of loss for stolen checks bearing forged indorsements. The check was not properly payable, so Sitka Bank must recredit Seward's account, as in *A*. Sitka Bank, however, can turn around and recover from Crown Bank, as stated in *B*, because the forged indorsement meant Crown Bank was not the person entitled to enforce the instrument. Crown Bank in turn can turn around and recover from Check Casher for breach of the transfer warranty, due to the forged indorsement. Check Casher has no one to collect from, and so would take the loss, as the person who took a stolen check from the thief over a forged indorsement by the thief.

C states another way to reach the same result: Konstantin could simply recover from Check Casher for conversion, because Check Casher took a check from someone who was not the person entitled to enforce it (or Konstantin could recover in conversion from Crown Bank or Sitka Bank, who would again use warranty liability to put the loss on Check Casher).

Indeed, if we wanted, we could add, as in *D*, that Konstantin could recover from Seward, because Konstantin is still the PETE, under §3-301 and §3-309. So the answer is *E*. All of the above. No doubt you could come up with more possibilities.

2. *E* is the best answer. This question illustrates the risk of bearer paper. Remember the Laura Lawyer Problems from Chapter 9. Konstantin made the check into bearer paper by indorsing it in blank. When the check was presented, it was properly payable, contrary to *A*, because it was bearer paper payable to whomever was in possession. Likewise, there was no breach of presentment warranty, because Crown Bank was the holder, so *B* is incorrect. Check Casher would qualify as a holder in due course, so there would be no breach of the transfer warranty (no forged signature and no claim or defense that would be good against Check Casher). *C* is incorrect. Everyone took the check from a holder, so no one is liable for conversion, making *D* incorrect. Konstantin could not recover from Seward on the check under §3-309, because Seward has already paid once on the check.

   No one is liable—meaning the loss will effectively fall on Konstantin, who created the risk by making the check into bearer paper.
3. *C* is the best answer. The drawee bank typically bears the risk of loss for checks paid over a forged drawer's signature. Malaspina Bank made a presentment warranty, by presenting a check that was paid. But, contrary to *B*, a forged drawer's signature (unlike a forged indorsement) does not breach the presentment warranty (unless the warrantor knows of the forgery). The drawee bank does not get the broader transfer warranty, so *A* is incorrect. *D* is inaccurate. Depositary banks do indeed make warranties on the checks they present.

4. *C* is the best answer. This question illustrates how a validation rule can shift the loss. Normally, where a check is paid over a forged indorsement, the loss will fall on the party who took the check from the thief/forger, as in Question 1. But one of the validation rules may apply to change that result. The most frequently applied validation rule is the employee forgery rule. Where an indorsement is made by an employee with responsibility for instruments, as in this question, the employee forgery rule makes the indorsement effective. So the result is similar to Question 2—it is as if the check is bearer paper, because the forged indorsement is effective. The check is properly payable, contrary to *A*. There is no breach of presentment warranty, contrary to *B*. Note that *D* misstates the law. Drawee banks are generally not entitled to reimbursement if they pay over forged indorsements. But, as here, a rule may change that result in particular cases. Note also how helpful the employee forgery rule is to banks, because it puts the loss on employers rather than banks for embezzlement, which is a substantial portion of check fraud.
5. *C* is the best answer. The checks were not authorized by the customer, so were not properly payable. The bank statement rule may put the loss on the customer for multiple wrongdoing, but only where loss is caused by the customer's failure to make a timely report of the wrongdoing. Here, Peratovich Consulting gave timely notice. This is not a case where a forged check appeared on the statement, the customer did not give notice, and that enabled the forger to do it again. Here, the multiple checks were written close together in time. *A* is incorrect. The employee forgery rule does not apply, because that rule (like the impostor rule), only applies to forged indorsement, contrary to *B*. *D* and *E* misstate the law; sometimes banks take the loss, sometimes customers do.

Chapter 15
Electronic Banking

Some law schools have eliminated the course called "Commercial Paper" in recent years, and in the survey course of "Commercial Law" many instructors skip over Articles 3 and 4 as irrelevant to modern life, as if there were no more checks or promissory notes out there causing no end of legal difficulties. But the number of cases involving these instruments has not lessened, and, indeed, in the case of promissory notes connected with mortgage foreclosures has dramatically increased. Clients with Articles 3 and 4 problems will still appear in law offices. Try to imagine how difficult it would be to teach yourself the rules we have studied so far in this course if you had a client with a case that forced you to figure them out for the first time in your career.

It is true that many payments are made electronically these days, and this chapter explores the legal issues that arise from credit cards, debit cards, wire transfers, and other electronic forms of banking. Be warned that these matter change as bankers think up new and quicker means of moving money around, so the alert attorney who practices in this field must be careful to remain up-to-date.

Elimination of the tons of checks that daily must be carted around the world is of obvious benefit to the banks involved. (Similar concerns in connection with investment securities led to the redrafting of Article 8 of the Code so as to permit corporations to issue securities that are recorded in a computer and are not evidenced by pieces of paper, a matter we will explore in the next chapter.) The benefits to some of the banks' customers are more questionable. As electronic fund transfers (EFTs) replace checks, the consumer drawer at least faces loss of control over the account and the evidentiary nightmare of proving that computers are in error.

Our study in this chapter is divided into two parts. The first concerns the rights and duties of the parties when a consumer is permitted (or required) to use electronic fund transfers to move monies in and out of the consumer's bank account. The second looks at the wire transfers of funds between banking institutions. Both areas of EFT law are changing fast (faster than pleases casebook writers).

I. CONSUMERS AND ELECTRONIC FUND TRANSFERS

In 1968, after a decade of attempts, Congress passed the comprehensive Consumer Credit Protection Act, 15 U.S.C. §§1600 et seq. (1976). This much-amended statute is divided into titles: Title I is the Truth in Lending (TILA) Act, Title VII is the Equal Credit Opportunity Act, etc. Most of these titles authorize a federal agency, typically the Federal Reserve Board (FRB), to issue regulations having the force of law. These regulations then implement and supplement the statute and are "explained" in frequent pronouncements, official and unofficial, by the agency involved. Thus the Truth in Lending Act's statutory provisions are the bare bones on which the FRB hung its Regulation Z, now 12 C.F.R. §1026, which is the primary reference for resolving TILA disputes. In 2010, authority for Regulation Z was transferred to the newly created Consumer Financial Protection Bureau. The Truth in Lending Act and Regulation Z are relevant to our discussion because they cover three related matters: credit card liability, available defenses to credit card bills, and procedures for resolving billing disputes. Detailed exploration of these provisions awaits you in a consumer law course, but a brief look at each follows.

A. Credit Cards

1. Basic Liability

PROBLEM 246

When his sister Alice went off to California to "find herself," Clark Consumer loaned her his bank charge card. She promised to charge no more than $200 worth of purchases. Now Clark, who lives in Ohio, hasn't heard from her in months, but she has so far run up $1,800 in charges, and the charge slips mount each day. Octopus National, the bank that issued the card, says Clark is liable for all her charges until he can find her and reclaim his card. Is he? See Martin v. American Express, Inc., 361 So. 2d 597 (Ala. Civ. App. 1978); Walker Bank & Trust Co. v. Jones, 672 P.2d 73 (Utah 1983). If this were a debit card, the Electronic Fund Transfer Act would apply. What result under the implementing Regulation E, 12 C.F.R. §1005.2(m)?

In the above Problem, the use of the card was *authorized*, at least at its inception, and the consumer usually must pay the resulting bills. Where, however, the use is *unauthorized* (because, for instance, the credit card was stolen), §1026.12 of Regulation Z limits the cardholder's liability to $50 (or whatever lesser amount has been charged before the cardholder notifies the issuer of the loss), and the cardholder is not even liable for this amount unless the card issuer has notified the cardholder of the rights, the card identifies the user, and the card issuer has provided the cardholder with a means of notifying the card issuer of the loss (a telephone number, for example). Currently, by contract, many major credit card companies are waiving the right to collect the $50 maximum, and thus give their cardholders a free ride for completely unauthorized use.

Azur v. Chase Bank, USA

United States Court of Appeals, Third Circuit, 2010
601 F.3d 212

FISHER, Circuit Judge.

Francis H. Azur filed suit against Chase Bank, USA, alleging violations of 15 U.S.C. §§1643 and 1666 of the Truth in Lending Act (TILA) and a common law negligence claim after Azur's personal assistant, Michele Vanek, misappropriated over $1 million from Azur through the fraudulent use of a Chase credit card over the course of seven years. The District Court granted Chase's motion for summary judgment, and Azur appealed. We are presented here with three discrete issues for our review. First, we must determine whether §1643 of the TILA provides the cardholder with a right to reimbursement. Second, we must evaluate whether Azur's §§1643 and 1666 claims are precluded because Azur vested Vanek with apparent authority to use the Chase credit card. Third and finally, we must decide whether Azur's negligence claim is barred by Pennsylvania's "economic loss doctrine." For the reasons stated herein, we will affirm, on partly different grounds, the District Court's order granting Chase's motion for summary judgment.

I.

ATM Corporation of America, Inc. (ATM) manages settlement services for large national lenders. Azur, the founder of ATM, served as its president and chief executive officer from 1993 until September 2007, when ATM was sold. In July 1997, ATM hired Vanek to be Azur's personal assistant. Vanek's responsibilities consisted of picking up Azur's personal bills, including his credit card bills, from a Post Office Box in Coraopolis, Pennsylvania; opening the bills; preparing and presenting checks for Azur to sign; mailing the payments; and balancing Azur's checking and savings accounts at Dollar Bank. According to Azur, it was Vanek's job alone to review Azur's credit card and bank statements and contact the credit card company to discuss any odd charges. Azur also provided Vanek with access to his credit card number to enable her to make purchases at his request.

From around November 1999 to March 2006, Vanek withdrew without authorization cash advances of between $200 and $700, typically twice a day, from a Chase credit card account in Azur's name. Azur was the sole cardholder and only authorized user on the account. Although Azur recalls opening a credit card account in or around 1987 with First USA, Chase's predecessor, Azur was unaware that he had a Chase credit card.

Each fraudulent transaction included a fee of approximately $2.00 and a finance charge that corresponded to the amount withdrawn, ranging from $4.00 for a $100 advance, to $21.06 for a $700 advance. The fraudulent charges were reflected on at least 65 monthly billing statements sent by Chase to Azur, and Vanek paid the bills by either writing checks or making on-line payments from Azur's Dollar Bank checking account. When writing checks, Vanek forged Azur's signature. Over the course of seven years, Vanek misappropriated over $1 million from Azur.

The transactions occasionally triggered Chase's fraud strategies. On April 16, 2004, Chase detected its first potentially fraudulent transaction, made outbound calls to the account's home telephone number, and left an automated message on the number's answering machine. Chase received no response. On April 23, 2004, one week later, Chase detected a second potential problem and left another automated message at the same telephone number. Three days later, Chase received a call from someone that was able to verify the account's security questions and validate the card activity. Although Chase's records indicate that the caller was female, Chase did not use voice recognition or gender identification as a means of security verification. Finally, on May 14, 2005, approximately one year later, Chase detected a third potentially fraudulent transaction and called the home telephone number. As before, five days later, a return caller once again verified the account activity. The account was paid in full without protest after each incident.

On or about March 7, 2006, Azur discovered a suspicious letter requesting a transfer of funds from his checking account. After investigating, Azur and ATM discovered Vanek's fraudulent scheme and terminated her employment. On March 8, 2006, Azur notified Chase by telephone of the fraudulent use of the Chase account and closed the account. Thereafter, Azur sent Chase three pieces of correspondence relevant to this appeal: (1) a letter dated April 7, 2006; (2) an executed Affirmation of Unauthorized Use dated April 21, 2006; and (3) a letter dated May 17, 2006.

In the letter dated April 7, 2006, Azur notified Chase of the fraudulent use of the card, stated that he "is formally disputing that he is responsible for the payment of any unpaid charges and accompanying finance charges on [the] account" (App. at 48A), and requested statements, correspondence, and other documents regarding the account.

The Affirmation of Unauthorized Use, which Chase drafted and sent to Azur for execution, stated, "Any transaction(s) occurring on or after 10/09/2001 is/are also unauthorized." (*Id.* at 50A.) The Affirmation listed three credits, titled "unauthorized transactions," to Azur's account: (1) a "returned payment" in the amount of $10,000; (2) a "returned payment" in the amount of $20,000; and (3) a "fraudulent transaction" in the amount of $28,717.38. (*Id.*) Azur executed the document and returned it to Chase on April 21, 2006.

Finally, in the letter dated May 17, 2006, Azur once again notified Chase that he "continues to dispute any and all unpaid charges stemming from the [Chase account], as well as all prior fraudulent transactions on that account, which have been the subject of prior communications between you and Mr. Azur and/or his representatives." (*Id.* at 52A.)

Because Azur closed the account on March 8, 2006, the account's final billing period ended on March 6, 2006. Chase has a "policy and practice" of mailing billing statements within two days of the close of each billing cycle. . . .

A. RIGHT TO REIMBURSEMENT

Chase argues that Azur cannot recover the money already paid to Chase under §1643 of the TILA. We agree. Section 1643 does not provide the cardholder with a right to reimbursement. This is clear from the statute's language: "A cardholder shall be liable for the unauthorized use of a credit card only if. . . ." 15 U.S.C. §1643(a). "Liable" means "[r]esponsible or answerable in law" or "legally obligated." *Black's Law Dictionary* 998 (9th ed. 2009). *See also Webster's Third New Int'l Dictionary* 1302 (1993) (defining "liable" as "bound or obliged according to law or equity"). Accordingly, the statute's plain meaning places a ceiling on a cardholder's obligations under the law and thus limits a card issuer's ability to sue a cardholder to recover fraudulent purchases. The language of §1643 does not, however, enlarge a card issuer's liability or give the cardholder a right to reimbursement.

We already reached this conclusion in *Sovereign Bank,* 533 F.3d 162. *Sovereign Bank* concerned, among other things, an indemnification action by Sovereign Bank, a card "Issuer," against Fifth Third Bank, an "Acquirer," and BJ's Wholesale Club, Inc., a "Merchant," based on Sovereign Bank's assertion that it had a duty under §1643 to reimburse a cardholder's account for all fraudulent charges in excess of $50. *Id.* at 164, 174. We disagreed:

> "TILA §1643 does not impose any obligation on issuers of credit cards to pay the costs associated with unauthorized or fraudulent use of credit cards. It simply limits the liability of cardholders, under certain circumstances, to a maximum of $50 for unauthorized charges. Indeed, §1643 does not address, nor is it even concerned with, the liability of an Issuer or any party other than the cardholder for unauthorized charges on a credit card. Section 1643 imposes liability only upon the cardholder."

Id. at 175. Faced here with the same issue in a new context, we arrive at the same outcome: §1643 of the TILA does not provide the cardholder with a right to reimbursement.[1] Accordingly, to the extent that Azur requests reimbursement under §1643 for money already paid to Chase, his claim fails.

B. APPARENT AUTHORITY

Vanek's alleged apparent authority is a more difficult issue. Relying on three cases, Minskoff v. American Express Travel Related Services. Co., Inc., 98 F.3d 703 (2d Cir. 1996), DBI Architects, P.C. v. American Express Travel-Related Services. Co., Inc., 388 F.3d 886, 363 U.S. App. D.C. 365 (D.C. Cir.

1. Although other federal courts of appeals have assumed that a right to reimbursement exists, they have done so without analysis. See Minskoff v. Am. Exp. Travel Related Servs. Co., Inc., 98 F.3d 703, 707, 710 (2d Cir. 1996) (holding that the "appropriate resolution" on remand of a cardholder's §1643 reimbursement claim is that "[the card issuer] is liable for [the user's] fraudulent purchases . . . from the time the credit card was issued until [the cardholder] received the first statement from [the card issuer] containing [the user's] fraudulent charges plus a reasonable time to examine that statement."); DBI Architects, P.C. v. Am. Express Travel-Related Servs. Co., Inc., 388 F.3d 886, 888, 894 (D.C. Cir. 2004) (remanding a cardholder's §1643 reimbursement claim to determine at what point the cardholder created apparent authority in the fraudulent user). See also Asher v. Chase Bank USA, N.A., 310 Fed. Appx. 912, 919 (7th Cir. 2009) (stating, for statute of limitations purposes, that "a violation [of §1643] occurs when the card issuer notifies the cardholder that despite the cardholder's claim of fraud, the card issuer will not reimburse the cardholder for the disputed amount" in a nonprecedential opinion, which we cite solely due to Azur's reliance on the case at oral argument and in a subsequent Rule 28(j) letter) and Carrier v. Citibank (S.D.), N.A., 383 F. Supp. 2d 334, 338, 341 (D. Conn. 2005) (assuming a right to reimbursement under a card issuer's policy of "$ 0 liability for unauthorized use" but holding that the fraudulent user had apparent authority).

2004), and Carrier v. Citibank (S.D.), N.A., 383 F. Supp. 2d 334 (D. Conn. 2005), the Magistrate Judge recommended that Azur's §1643 claim be dismissed because Azur vested Vanek with apparent authority to make charges to the Chase account as a matter of law:

> "[T]he plaintiff vested Michele Vanek with apparent authority to use the account, as the repeated payment of billed charges led Chase to reasonably believe the charges were authorized. Furthermore, the plaintiff's failure to review his account statements and his lax supervision of Vanek, in whom he delegated authority to review his statements, prepare checks on the account, and discuss routine questions with the card issuer, constituted a negligent omission that created apparent authority in Vanek to incur the charges."

(App. at 17A.) The District Court agreed and dismissed Azur's §1643 claim. On appeal, Azur argues that whether he clothed Vanek with apparent authority is an issue of fact to be decided by a jury.

The application of both §§1643 and 1666 of the TILA depend, in part, on whether the fraudulent user had apparent authority to use the credit card. As stated above, §1643 provides that "[a] cardholder shall be liable for the unauthorized use of a credit card" in certain circumstances. 15 U.S.C. §1643(a). The term "unauthorized use" is defined as the "use of a credit card by a person other than the cardholder who does not have actual, implied, or apparent authority for such use and from which the cardholder receives no benefit." 15 U.S.C. §1602(o). Relatedly, §1666(a) sets forth the procedures a creditor must follow to resolve alleged billing errors. 15 U.S.C. §1666(a). Like the phrase "unauthorized use," the phrase "billing error" includes "[a] reflection on or with a periodic statement of an extension of credit that is not made to the consumer or to a person who has actual, implied, or apparent authority to use the consumer's credit card or open-end credit plan." 12 C.F.R. § 226.13(a)(1) [now 12 C.F.R. §1026.13(a)(1)—Eds.].

To determine whether apparent authority exists, we turn to applicable state agency law. *See* 12 C.F.R. Pt. 226, Supp. I ("Whether such [apparent] authority exists must be determined under state or other applicable law."); *Minskoff*, 98 F.3d at 708 (" 'Congress apparently contemplated, and courts have accepted, primary reliance on background principles of agency law in determining the liability of cardholders for charges incurred by third-party card bearers.' " (quoting Towers World Airways v. PHH Aviation Sys., 933 F.2d 174, 176-77 (2d Cir. 1991))). In this case, the parties do not refute the application of Pennsylvania law. Citing the Restatement (Second) of Agency, the Pennsylvania Supreme Court has explained as follows:

> "Apparent authority is power to bind a principal which the principal has not actually granted but which he leads persons with whom his agent deals to believe that he has granted. Persons with whom the agent deals can reasonably

> believe that the agent has power to bind his principal if, for instance, the principal knowingly permits the agent to exercise such power or if the principal holds the agent out as possessing such power."

Revere Press, Inc. v. Blumberg, 431 Pa. 370, 246 A.2d 407, 410 (Pa. 1968). Similarly, we have stated that under Pennsylvania law "[t]he test for determining whether an agent possesses apparent authority is whether a man of ordinary prudence, diligence and discretion would have a right to believe and would actually believe that the agent possessed the authority he purported to exercise." In re Mushroom Transp. Co., Inc., 382 F.3d 325, 345 (3d Cir. 2004) (quotations and citations omitted).

Although the articulation of the proper agency law standard is fairly easy, the application of that standard is difficult. Two decisions of the Second and D.C. Circuits, respectively, are instructive. In both cases, the Second and D.C. Circuits held that a cardholder's negligent omissions clothed the fraudulent card user with apparent authority under facts similar to those present in the instant case.

The Second Circuit in *Minskoff* was the first court of appeals to address this issue. Minskoff served as the president and chief executive officer of a real estate firm. 98 F.3d at 706. In 1988, the firm opened an American Express corporate credit card account and issued one card in Minskoff's name. *Id.* In 1992, Minskoff's assistant, whom the firm had recently hired, applied for and obtained an additional card to the account in her own name without Minskoff's or the firm's knowledge. *Id.* From April 1992 to March 1993, the assistant charged a total of $28,213.88 on the corporate card. *Id.* During this period, American Express sent twelve monthly billing statements to the firm's address; each statement listed both Minskoff and the assistant as cardholders and separately itemized their charges. *Id.* At the same time, American Express was paid in full by a total of twelve forged checks drawn on bank accounts maintained by either Minskoff or the firm at Manufacturers Hanover Trust (MHT), which also periodically mailed statements to the firm showing that the payments had been made. *Id.* at 706-07, 710. The assistant used the same system to misappropriate another $300,000 after applying for a platinum account. *Id.* at 707, 710. After discovering the fraud, Minskoff filed suit against American Express under the TILA. *Id.* at 707.

In determining whether or not the assistant had apparent authority to use the credit card, the Second Circuit began by differentiating between the acquisition and use of a credit card obtained through fraud or theft: "[W]hile we accept the proposition that the *acquisition* of a credit card through fraud or theft cannot be said to occur under the apparent authority of the cardholder, [that] should not . . . preclude a finding of apparent authority for the subsequent *use* of a credit card so obtained." *Id.* at 709. Then, noting that "[n]othing in the TILA suggests that Congress intended to sanction intentional or negligent conduct by the cardholder that furthers the fraud or theft of an unauthorized card user," the court held that "the negligent acts or omissions of a cardholder may create apparent authority to use the card in a person who obtained the card through theft or fraud." *Id.* Applying that reasoning to the facts before it, the Second Circuit found that Minskoff's and the firm's failure to examine any of the credit card or bank statements created, as a matter of law, "apparent authority for [the assistant's] continuing use of the cards, especially because it enabled [the assistant] to pay all of the American Express statements with forged checks, thereby fortifying American Express' continuing impression that nothing was amiss with the Corporate and Platinum Accounts." *Id.* at 710.

In *DBI Architects,* the D.C. Circuit took a narrower approach. DBI was a corporation with an AMEX credit card account. 388 F.3d at 888. In 2001, DBI appointed a new account manager of its D.C. and Virginia offices. Soon thereafter, the new manager requested that AMEX add her as a cardholder on DBI's corporate account without DBI's knowledge, although AMEX sent DBI an account statement reflecting the change. *Id.* From August 2001 to May 2002, the manager charged a total of $134,810.40 to the credit card. *Id.* As in *Minskoff,* AMEX sent DBI ten monthly billing statements—each listing the manager as a cardholder and itemizing her charges—and the manager paid AMEX with thirteen DBI checks. *Id.* Most of the checks were signed or stamped in the name of DBI's president; none were signed in the manager's own name. *Id.* Like Minskoff, DBI eventually filed suit against AMEX under the TILA. *Id.* at 888.

Acquainted with the Second Circuit's decision in *Minskoff,* the D.C. Circuit decided its case on narrower grounds. Rather than fault the cardholder for merely failing to inspect monthly credit card statements, the court focused on the cardholder's continuous payment of the fraudulent charges without complaint:

> "DBI is correct that its failure to inspect its monthly billing statements did not clothe [the manager] with apparent authority to use its corporate AMEX account. [However,] AMEX is correct that DBI clothed [the manager] with apparent authority to use its corporate AMEX account by repeatedly paying without protest all of [the manager's] charges on the account after receiving notice of them from AMEX."

Id. at 891. The court later explained its reasoning as follows:

> "By identifying apparent authority as a limit on the cardholder's protection under §1643, Congress recognized that a cardholder has certain obligations to prevent fraudulent use of its card. DBI's troubles stemmed from its failure to separate the approval and payment functions within its cash disbursement process. [The manager] had actual authority both to receive the billing statements

> and to issue DBI checks for payment to AMEX. While DBI did not voluntarily relinquish its corporate card to [the manager], it did mislead AMEX into reasonably believing that [the manager] had authority to use the corporate card by paying her charges on the corporate account after receiving AMEX's monthly statements identifying her as a cardholder and itemizing her charges."

Id. at 893. Although the court acknowledged that payment might not always create apparent authority, it held that such authority existed as a matter of law in that case:

> "[T]his is not a case involving an occasional transgression buried in a welter of financial detail. [] Nor is this a case involving payment without notice, as might occur when a cardholder authorizes its bank to pay its credit card bills automatically each month. Where, as here, the cardholder repeatedly paid thousands of dollars in fraudulent charges for almost a year after monthly billing statements identifying the fraudulent user and itemizing the fraudulent charges were sent to its corporate address, no reasonable juror could disagree that at some point the cardholder led the card issuer reasonably to believe that the fraudulent user had authority to use its card."

Id. at 893-94 (quotations and citation omitted). Ultimately, the court remanded the case to determine at what point the manager's apparent authority began. *Id.* at 894.

We agree with the D.C. Circuit's more nuanced analysis. "Apparent authority is power to bind a principal which the principal has not actually granted but which he leads persons with whom his agent deals to believe that he has granted." *Revere Press*, 246 A.2d at 410. A cardholder may, in certain circumstances, vest a fraudulent user with the apparent authority to use a credit card by enabling the continuous payment of the credit card charges over a period of time. As the D.C. Circuit reasoned, by identifying apparent authority as a limitation on the cardholder's protections under §1643, Congress recognized that the cardholder is oftentimes in the best position to identify fraud committed by its employees.

Here, Azur's negligent omissions led Chase to reasonably believe that the fraudulent charges were authorized. Although Azur may not have been aware that Vanek was using the Chase credit card, or even that the Chase credit card account existed, Azur knew that he had a Dollar Bank checking account, and he did not review his Dollar Bank statements or exercise any other oversight over Vanek, his employee. Instead, Azur did exactly what the D.C. Circuit in *DBI Architects* cautioned against: he "fail[ed] to separate the approval and payment functions within [his] cash disbursement process." 388 F.3d at 893. Had Azur occasionally reviewed his statements, Azur would have likely noticed that checks had been written to Chase. Because Chase reasonably believed that a prudent business person would oversee his employees in such a manner, Chase reasonably relied on the continuous payment of the fraudulent charges.

Many of Azur's counter-arguments are beside the point. Azur asserts that *Minskoff* and *DBI Architects* are distinguishable because the fraudulent users in those cases were cardholders on the accounts. This distinction is irrelevant: Chase's belief that the fraudulent charges were authorized did not depend on whether the fraudulent charges were made by a second cardholder; Chase's belief was contingent upon the continuous payment of the fraudulent charges—regardless of which card they were on—without objection. Azur also focuses on Chase's failure to identify the fraud. The issue, however, is whether Azur led Chase to believe that Vanek had authority to make the charges, not whether Chase's fraud-detecting tools were effective. Moreover, Vanek's ability to answer the account security questions over the telephone and the fact that Chase's fraud-detecting tools identified relatively few problems reinforce the conclusion that Chase was reasonable in believing, and did in fact believe, that the charges were authorized. In short, none of the arguments Azur has advanced persuade us to disturb the District Court's apparent authority determination.

Accordingly, we hold that Azur vested Vanek with apparent authority to use the Chase credit card, thus barring his §§1643 and 1666 claims.

[The court also held that Azur's negligence claim was barred by the "economic loss doctrine."]

NOTE

The *Azur* court first holds that a cardholder is not entitled to reimbursement from the issuer if the cardholder has paid for charges that were unauthorized. As the *Azur* court notes, other courts have assumed the contrary. Was it necessary for the court to address the issue where it next held the charges in this case were not unauthorized? Do you agree with the *Azur* court's holding on reimbursement? Where Congress wanted to state that cardholder rights did not include reimbursement, it said so. As we will see below, a cardholder's right to raise defenses against the issuer in authorized transactions is explicitly limited to amounts not yet paid. See TILA §170(b), 15 U.S.C. §1666i(b). By contrast, it seems unlikely that Congress intended a cardholder to be liable for unauthorized charges, simply because the cardholder had unknowingly paid the relevant bill. Otherwise, the $50 cap on liability for fraudulent charges offers only thin protection.

2. Asserting Defenses Against the Credit Card Issuer

PROBLEM 247

Linda Liable lived in Newark, New Jersey. One year she took a trip to San Francisco. While there, she charged her hotel bill using her bank credit card issued by Octopus National Bank in Newark, but she protested to the hotel manager that the bill was twice the amount it should have been. The hotel manager refused to listen. On her return to Newark, Linda refused to pay ONB's credit card bill for this charge; she also refused to pay for other charges: an $80 suitcase she had purchased in New York City that fell apart on the trip (the New York seller is now bankrupt) and a $25 art print ordered from Florida that had never arrived (ONB had included promotional literature on these Florida artworks in its last credit card billing). Is she liable to ONB?

To resolve this issue, see Regulation Z §1026.12(c) (implementing TILA §170, 15 U.S.C. §1666i):

> (c) *Right of cardholder to assert claims or defenses against card issuer.*
>
> (1) *General rule.* When a person who honors a credit card fails to resolve satisfactorily a dispute as to property or services purchased with the credit card in a consumer credit transaction, the cardholder may assert against the card issuer all claims (other than tort claims) and defenses arising out of the transaction and relating to the failure to resolve the dispute. The cardholder may withhold payment up to the amount of credit outstanding for the property or services that gave rise to the dispute and any finance or other charges imposed on that amount.
>
> (2) *Adverse credit reports prohibited.* If, in accordance with paragraph (c)(1) of this section, the cardholder withholds payment of the amount of credit outstanding for the disputed transaction, the card issuer shall not report that amount as delinquent until the dispute is settled or judgment is rendered.
>
> (3) *Limitations.*
>
> (i) *General.* The rights stated in paragraphs (c)(1) and (c)(2) of this section apply only if:
>
> (A) The cardholder has made a good faith attempt to resolve the dispute with the person honoring the credit card; and
>
> (B) The amount of credit extended to obtain the property or services that result in the assertion of the claim or defense by the cardholder exceeds $50, and the disputed transaction occurred in the same state as the cardholder's current designated address or, if not within the same state, within 100 miles from that address.
>
> (ii) *Exclusion.* The limitations stated in paragraph (c)(3)(i)(B) of this section shall not apply when the person honoring the credit card:
>
> (A) Is the same person as the card issuer;
>
> (B) Is controlled by the card issuer directly or indirectly;
>
> (C) Is under the direct or indirect control of a third person that also directly or indirectly controls the card issuer;
>
> (D) Controls the card issuer directly or indirectly;
>
> (E) Is a franchised dealer in the card issuer's products or services; or
>
> (F) Has obtained the order for the disputed transaction through a mail solicitation made or participated in by the card issuer.

3. Billing Errors

Under §1026.13 of Regulation Z, if the cardholder complains to the issuer of a billing error, the card issuer must acknowledge the complaint within 30 days, conduct a good faith investigation of the problem, and resolve the difficulty one way or the other within 90 days of the complaint (or within two billing cycles, whichever is less). During the interim the issuer must not treat the disputed amount as overdue or report it adversely to credit reporting agencies. Failure to honor the consumer's rights under this provision leads to the card issuer's forfeiture of up to $50 of the disputed amount and to additional liability, including attorney's fees, under §130 of the Truth in Lending Act. These penalties can be collected even if the consumer was in error and the bank was right all along.

B. Debit Cards and Other Consumer Electronic Funds Transfers

The applicability of Regulation Z to debit cards and other electronic fund transfers involving consumers was unclear until 1978 when Congress solved the problem by passing the Electronic Fund Transfer Act, 15 U.S.C. §§1693 et seq., making it the new Title IX of the Consumer Credit Protection Act of 1968. Section 904 of the Act, 15 U.S.C. §1693b, authorized the FRB to prescribe regulations to carry out the purposes of the Act, and the Federal Reserve Board responded with Regulation E, now 12 C.F.R. 1005 (authority for which has been transferred to the Consumer Financial Protection Bureau). Both can be found in your statute book. You should also know that the Federal Reserve Board published an Official Interpretation for the rules of Regulation E, 12 C.F.R. part 1005, which explains the rules in detail and gives examples. These Interpretations (which are not likely to be in your statute book but are easily found online) are appended to the Regulation's sections and have the force of law, and should therefore be consulted when difficult questions arise in practice.

PROBLEM 248

Electra Smith was employed as a clerk for the Business Corporation. One day it informed her that henceforth all her paychecks would automatically be deposited in the local bank of her choice. She chose Octopus National Bank (ONB), her usual bank. Could she have demanded a check and refused the EFT?[2]

2. This issue is resolved by §913 of the EFTA, 15 U.S.C. §1693k, reprinted below: Section 913. Compulsory Use of Electronic Fund Transfers No person may—(1) condition the

ONB informed Electra that she could pay all her bills online and that many creditors would be willing to set up an automatic monthly payment plan whereby ONB would pay routine bills unless she instructed otherwise. Electra signed such a contract with her landlord, to whom ONB agreed to transfer $900 on the first day of each month as rent. What details does ONB have to explain to her? See Regulation E §1005.7. (The government promulgated model forms for this purpose, and the bank is well advised to use them since such use shields the bank from arguments about disclosure errors. See §916(d)(2) of the Act, 15 U.S.C. §1693(l-1)(d)(2).) Consider these issues:

(a) One day ONB's computer malfunctioned and for no apparent reason deducted $1,000 from Electra's checking account and credited it to an account designated "Computer Maintenance." Several of her checks bounced as a result. Is the computer's deduction an "electronic fund transfer" under Regulation E §1005.3(b)? If so, is it also an "unauthorized electronic fund transfer" under §1005.2(m)? Is the bank liable under §910? Under UCC §4-401(a)? (Note UCC §4-104(a)(9).) Are there common law theories that she might use? As to the bounced checks, see UCC §4-402 (Wrongful Dishonor).

(b) ONB failed to pay Electra's rent on the first of January because the computer got backlogged with the huge Christmas volume. Can her landlord evict her? See §912, 15 U.S.C. §1693j. When she is evicted and sues ONB over §910, 15 U.S.C. §1693h, can the bank defend using §910(b)(1), 15 U.S.C. §1693h(b)(1)? Cf. Blake v. Woodford Bank & Trust Co., 555 S.W.2d 589 (Ky. Ct. App. 1977) (a case deciding a similar issue under UCC §4-109).

(c) One month Electra had a dispute with her landlord, so she phoned ONB and told them not to pay the next month's rent due to be transferred four days later. Is oral notice sufficient? Is her notice timely? See §907(a), 15 U.S.C. §1693e(a); Regulation E §1005.10(c). If the bank fails to stop payment, what remedy does she have? See §910, 15 U.S.C. §1693h. What damages does she have? Can she recover her attorney's fees? Compare §910(c) and §916(a) (15 U.S.C. §§1693h(c) and 1693l-1(a)).

(d) If Linda Liable in the last Problem had made purchases with point of sale (POS) EFTs, would she be able to assert her defenses against her bank under the EFTA?

---

extension of credit to a consumer on such consumer's repayment by means of preauthorized electronic fund transfers; or (2) require a consumer to establish an account for receipt of electronic fund transfers with a particular financial institution as a condition of employment or receipt of a government benefit.

PROBLEM 249

Jane Austen owned a bookstore and handled the store's financial affairs through a checking account with Octopus National Bank (ONB). If ONB grants the store an ability to pay its debts by EFTs, does the EFTA apply? See §903(2), 15 U.S.C. §1693a(2); Regulation E §1005.2(b).

PROBLEM 250

The first time Arthur Greenbaum used his access card at an all-night automated teller machine, he told the machine to give him $50 from his checking account, and it promptly did so. At the same time the ATM deducted $500 from Arthur's account and reported that Arthur had withdrawn this amount. It gave Arthur no written statement.

(a) At the end of the month Arthur's bank sent him a statement showing the status of his checking account. Should it reflect this transaction? How? See §906, 15 U.S.C. §1693d; Regulation E §1005.9(b). May it be combined with the statement required by UCC §4-406? See §906(c), 15 U.S.C. §1693d(c).

(b) If Arthur does not examine this statement for one year, does the EFTA cause him problems? Note §§909(a), 903(12), and 916(g). Does UCC §4-406(f) cause problems?

(c) If Arthur examines the statement promptly and discovers the error, what should he do? See Regulation E §1005.11(b). The bank received Arthur's notice on May 1. By what date need it act? Need it put the money back in his account during its investigation? See §908(a), (c), 15 U.S.C. §1693f; Regulation E §1005.11(c).[3]

(d) Who bears the burden of proof as to whether the ATM gave Arthur $50 or $500? See §909(b); cf. Gramore Stores, Inc. v. Bankers Trust Co., 93 Misc. 2d 112, 402 N.Y.S.2d 326 (Sup. Ct. 1978) (dispute over deposit made in a bank's night depository).

(e) What liability does the bank have simply because it never programmed the ATM to hand out written statements? See §§906(a), 916, §§1693d(a), 1693l-1; Regulation E §1005.9(a). If the ATM had been so programmed but failed to give the statement to Arthur due to mechanical failure, is this a

3. The time periods for recrediting the account that are explored here are incorporated with only small changes into the similar issue that arises under the federal Check 21 Act, discussed in Chapter 15. The fact pattern there is that a bank wrongly debits a consumer's account in connection with a substitute check or computer image of a check, and the consumer demands the amount be promptly recredited to the account.

defense? See §916(c), §1693l-1(c). Is it a defense that the ATM growled at Arthur when he walked up to it, so that he should have known it wasn't working, and thus he assumed the risk of the resulting error? Cf. §910(b)(2), 15 U.S.C. §1693h(b)(2).

(f) After receiving Arthur's complaint (and also the complaint of every single person using that particular ATM), the bank's investigation consisted solely of having a computer printout made of the transaction and mailing it to Arthur. Similar documentation was sent to each complainant. Does this satisfy §908, 15 U.S.C. §1693f? Note particularly §908(e), 15 U.S.C. §1693f(e).

Consumers use debit cards to make more than 70 percent of their small purchases nowadays, typically by the use of a *personal identification number* or PIN, though PIN-less cards are becoming more frequent. As with credit cards, debit cards and the PIN must be guarded by the customer, or life can become difficult even should the customer prevail in the resulting legal dispute. Read §909 and Regulation E §1005.6, which follows.

§1005.6 Liability of Consumer for Unauthorized Transfers

(a) *Conditions for liability.* A consumer may be held liable, within the limitations described in paragraph (b) of this section, for an unauthorized electronic fund transfer involving the consumer's account only if the financial institution has provided the disclosures required by §1005.7(b)(1), (2), and (3). If the unauthorized transfer involved an access device, it must be an accepted access device and the financial institution must have provided a means to identify the consumer to whom it was issued.

(b) *Limitations on amount of liability.* A consumer's liability for an unauthorized electronic fund transfer or a series of related unauthorized transfers shall be determined as follows:

(1) Timely notice given. If the consumer notifies the financial institution within two business days after learning of the loss or theft of the access device, the consumer's liability shall not exceed the lesser of $50 or the amount of unauthorized transfers that occur before notice to the financial institution.

(2) Timely notice not given. If the consumer fails to notify the financial institution within two business days after learning of the loss or theft of the access device, the consumer's liability shall not exceed the lesser of $500 or the sum of:

(i) $50 or the amount of unauthorized transfers that occur within the two business days, whichever is less; and

(ii) The amount of unauthorized transfers that occur after the close of two business days and before notice to the institution, provided the institution establishes that these transfers would not have occurred had the consumer notified the institution within the two-day period.

(3) Periodic statement; timely notice not given. A consumer must report an unauthorized electronic fund transfer that appears on a periodic statement within 60 days of the financial institution's transmittal of the statement to avoid liability for subsequent transfers. If the consumer fails to do so, the consumer's liability shall not exceed the amount of the unauthorized transfers that occur after the close of the 60 days and before notice to the institution, and that the institution establishes would not have occurred had the consumer notified the institution within the 60-day period. When an access device is involved in the unauthorized transfer, the consumer may be liable for other amounts set forth in paragraphs (b)(1) or (b)(2) of this section, as applicable.

(4) Extensions of time limits. If the consumer's delay in notifying the financial institution was due to extenuating circumstances, the institution shall extend the times specified above to a reasonable period.

(5) Notice to financial institution.

(i) Notice to a financial institution is given when a consumer takes steps reasonably necessary to provide the institution with the pertinent information, whether or not a particular employee or agent of the institution actually receives the information.

(ii) The consumer may notify the institution in person, by telephone, or in writing.

(iii) Written notice is considered given at the time the consumer mails the notice or delivers it for transmission to the institution by any other usual means. Notice may be considered constructively given when the institution becomes aware of circumstances leading to the reasonable belief that an unauthorized transfer to or from the consumer's account has been or may be made.

(6) Liability under state law or agreement. If state law or an agreement between the consumer and the financial institution imposes less liability than is provided by this section, the consumer's liability shall not exceed the amount imposed under the state law or agreement.

PROBLEM 251

Ebenezer Scrooge owned a bank credit card issued by Dickens National Bank, the same bank with whom he maintained a checking account. One day the mail contained a letter assigning Scrooge a PIN and explaining to him that by inserting his credit card in an ATM and punching in the PIN, he could receive immediate cash withdrawals from his checking account.

(a) Has Dickens National violated the EFTA? See §911, §1693i; Regulation E §1005.5.

(b) Scrooge threw the PIN letter in the wastebasket, from which it was removed by his employee Bob Cratchit, who stole Scrooge's card and extracted $100 from the ATM in order to buy crutches for his crippled son.

Is Scrooge liable for this withdrawal? See §§909(a), 903(1), §§1693g(a), 1693a(1); Regulation E §1005.6.

PROBLEM 252

While Carl Consumer was asleep one day, his sister Nancy sneaked into his bedroom and stole his bank card. She knew his PIN because he had once loaned her the card and authorized her to make a small series of withdrawals, but this time it was an out and out theft.[4] She took the card on April 30 and used it to take $500 from his account with Original National Bank on that same day. He missed the card when he woke up, and he rightly guessed that Nancy had taken it. Rather than notify the bank, he tried to track her down and retrieve the card. On May 5, she used the card to remove $800 from his bank account, and then she left the state. Heartsick at her perfidy, Carl slumped into a depression so severe that he could not leave his bed. On May 31, the bank sent Carl the usual bank statement; it reflected all of these transactions. On June 10, Nancy returned to the state and used the card to take $3,000 from Carl's account. A lawsuit followed. Resolve it, using §1005.6 of Regulation E, reproduced above.

PROBLEM 253

When Joseph Armstrong first received his debit card he was afraid he would forget the PIN, so he wrote it right on the card itself. If Armstrong subsequently lost his wallet, would his liability for unauthorized use increase due to his stupidity? See the Official Interpretation to §1005.6(b).

Many major debit card issuers now waive the right to collect for unauthorized charges. But the potentially unlimited liability for unauthorized charges still applies to other consumer electronic funds transfers, such as online funds transfers (as some careless individuals have learned the hard way). See The Bank Account That Sprang a Leak, N.Y. Times (Aug. 29, 2008) (where persons unknown "siphoned nearly $300,000 from his personal account at the private bank through many small electronic transfers over a 15-month period," a wealthy individual took loss for transfers made after the 60-day reporting deadline).

4. For a case saying that disclosure of the PIN for one authorized use does not make subsequent uses authorized as well, see Vaughan v. United States National Bank, 79 Or. App. 172, 718 P.2d 769 (1986).

The Dodd-Frank Act gave some relief to debit card users as of 2010 when it prohibited overdraft fees from being taken from the consumer's bank account unless the consumer had opted in to such overdraft protection; see Regulation E §1005.17. Most consumers would rather the debit card be declined in the situations where the debit is small but the overdraft fee is large, but don't understand that overdraft protection is far too expensive. One study found that 77 percent of consumers are opting in to overdraft protection. In 2013, banks earned $40 billion in overdraft fees!

One real burden facing the bank's customer in an EFT world is uncertainty as to the daily bank balance. This problem is sure to arise unless the customer keeps accurate account of all checks, charges, ATM and POS transactions, preauthorized EFTs, bank service fees, and telephonic EFTs. Furthermore, when the monthly statement arrives, the customer must be very organized to do an accurate reconciliation within the EFTA's 60-day period. The lack of documentation that is one of the benefits of EFTs for banks is making the customer's life more difficult. Some banks are experimenting with the so-called *smart card*, a debit card that has an internal memory of each transaction for which it has been used so that the card itself can do all of the consumer's recordkeeping, and some cell phones (also used for EFTs) have similar recording functions. O brave new world, that has such machines in it!

C. *Foreign Remittances*

Since 2010, the EFTA contains provisions dealing with remittances sent to foreign countries, and the Regulation E provisions are in Subpart B, §§1005.30 to 1005.36. Use those sections to resolve the next Problem.

PROBLEM 254

Fatima Ramon, who had moved to the United States from Guatemala when she married an American citizen, decided to send her mother in Guatemala $30.00 every month out of the paycheck she received from her employer. She went to Speedy International Money Service, a business that made such transfers to foreign countries, and signed an agreement to send the first $30.00 to her mother. Ramon's English is not good and she was confused about much of what happened, none of which was conducted in Spanish. When her mother later informed Ramon that the money had not arrived, Ramon went back to Speedy, where she was told that $17.00 was sent to the mother on the day after Ramon had given it to Speedy. When Ramon asked why only $17.00 had been sent, she was told that the transfer fee was $13.00.

Ramon, unhappy, then disputed that even this lower amount had made it to Guatemala. Speedy denied any responsibility for whatever had happened. Fatima Ramon, confused and disgusted, contacts you, the only lawyer she knows. What can be done?

D. Other Payment Systems

The Internet now offers payment methods of various kinds, and so far these so-called alternative payment services are unregulated or their status is unclear. PayPal, for example, claims to offer more protection than is required by the Electronic Fund Transfer Act, and, while there is an argument that the EFTA already covers PayPal and similar entities, the resolution of this is murky and must await court decisions. For a student article urging the Consumer Financial Protection Bureau to issue regulations clearing this up, see Eric Pacifici, Making PayPal Pay: Regulation E and Its Application to Alternative Payment Services, 13 Duke L. & Tech. Rev. 89 (2015).

II. WIRE TRANSFERS

The safe and efficient movement of money is now accomplished electronically through a host of systems devised by bankers and implemented by government action (the Federal Reserve System) or private agreement. Consider the advantage to the federal government of electronic payment of Social Security debts: mountains of paper (paper that can be lost or stolen) need not move clumsily through the mails. Instead, electronic signals do all the work quickly and with fewer errors. Similarly, imagine the benefits to a national retailer if the movement of money to and from its thousands of outlets can be accomplished efficiently at the end of every business day by the mere electronic adjustment of funds.

Until 1990 there was no organized body of law to deal with such transfers, though the Federal Reserve had promulgated its Regulation J, 12 C.F.R. §210, to resolve disputes internal to transfers through the Federal Reserve System.[5] But there was no guidance to resolve a host of disputes likely to occur: bank failure, computer hackers mugging the system to steal electronic dollars, glitches whereby the computer sent out duplicate order after duplicate order, etc. Nor is this a small matter; each day's wire transfers in

5. In 1991, the Federal Reserve Board amended Regulation J so that its rules are in accordance with those of Article 4A.

the United States averaged $3,000,000,000,000 (that's $3 trillion; yes, *trillion*). This number is, of course, growing.

The Federal Reserve System's wire transfer mechanism is called *Fedwire.* It electronically moves funds from one Federal Reserve bank to another at the instruction of the sending institution to the receiving institution, both of which will maintain accounts at Federal Reserve banks. These wholesale wire transactions are enormous in scale. The average Fedwire transfer is $5.4 million (compared with a $600 average for checks). In 2014, Fedwire handled 1,380,000 electronic transfers with a total value of $663,837,575 million; see http://www.federalreserve.gov/paymentsystems/fedfunds_ann.htm.

The international transfer of money is accomplished through a New York–based system called CHIPS (for "Clearinghouse Interbank Payments System," run by the New York Clearinghouse Association). Its transfers are made in U.S. dollar amounts converted from foreign currencies. The sender instructs its bank to make the wire transfer to a designated payee's account at a different receiving bank. The sending bank informs the CHIPS computer to make the transfer and then sends a verification of the proposed transfer. At the end of the banking day, settlement must occur when CHIPS informs all banks involved of their net position for the day. At this point wire transfers through the New York Federal Reserve Bank are made to adjust the accounts of all participants. CHIPS transfers are also of fantastic amounts, averaging $1,606,968,294 a day, for a total of $403,349,041,732 in 2011.

The advantages of wire transfers are their speed and safety. Typically, a receiving bank allows its non-bank customer immediate access to the funds even though settlement (and thus the actual transfer of the money) will not occur until the end of the day. If, for one reason or another (bank failure, for example), settlement never happens, the receiving bank faces the very real risk of being unable to recapture the funds.

Since many wire transfers occur in the computers before the funds are actually exchanged, all participating banks at some point during the banking day face exposures often greater than the bank's assets. If settlement is made at the end of the day, fine, but in the meantime there is a situation called *daylight overdraft,* and the rules of the various wire transfer systems may limit the amount of exposure by imposing a *debit cap*—a limit on the daylight overdraft that a participating bank may incur.[6]

An *automated clearinghouse,* or ACH, is, as its name suggests, a mechanism for the electronic transfer of recurring debits and credits between participants, typically for low-dollar/high-volume batched messages such as payrolls. There are a number of such privately created ACHs in the United

6. Sometimes called the *bilateral net credit limit.*

States, typically linking the transfers through a Federal Reserve bank.[7] ACH networks cleared 22 billion payments in 2014, totaling $39 trillion, with the bulk being transfers by the federal government to pay its routine debts (social security, veteran's benefits, employee paychecks, etc.). Transfers through the ACH are accomplished by telephone, electronic communication, or manual delivery to the ACH of a computer program containing all the relevant payment or debit instructions. The actual transfer of funds typically occurs on the day *after* the ACH receives the sender's instructions (or, by agreement, even later).

With new systems and private associations being created constantly (and old ones dropping by the wayside, their usefulness spent), the law is sorely pressed to keep up with the technology. Many of the legal disputes are resolved by contract between the participants, though a body of electronic fund transfer law is developing. We have already considered the Electronic Fund Transfer Act, which protects consumers. Non-consumer wire transfers are regulated in part by Regulation J, promulgated by the Federal Reserve Board to govern transfers using the federal system, and in part by the Uniform Commercial Code's Article 4A, "Funds Transfers." This article has now been adopted by all the states, and Regulation J has been amended so that its rules are virtually identical, thus producing one area in which we have a happy coincidence of both state and federal law.

A. *Scope of Article 4A*

While Article 4A is largely concerned with wholesale wire transfers, it is not limited to transfers by wire alone. It includes any *payment order*, whether the instruction is to be transmitted orally, electronically, or in writing; §4A-103(a)(1). A payment order *pushes* funds of the person giving the order (the *sender*) out of his or her bank account and into the bank account of the payee (the *beneficiary*). Article 4A does not cover payment instructions, such as checks, that involve the efforts of the payee to *pull* funds from the payor's bank account into the bank account of the payee. A payment order requires an electronic *credit*, not an electronic *debit*.

7. The National Automated Clearing House Association (NACHA) is an organization of such clearinghouses that regulates ACH activities through a comprehensive set of rules, now amended to incorporate Article 4A for electronic credit transfers. For example, NACHA Rule §2.2.1.1 allows fraudulent checks that are electronically processed at point of sale transactions (the grocery store that creates an image of the check, hands the original back to the drawer, and then sends the check through as an image only) to be returned to the depositary bank, and from there to the merchant, by the creation of a transfer warranty of proper authorization.

PROBLEM 255

Big Department Store was a national operation, the largest retailer of goods in the United States. Every month it paid its employees by electronic transfer of funds (through an ACH) to their bank accounts throughout the country. Every Friday it received the weekly receipts from its thousands of retail stores by instructing Big Department Store's bank to transfer to itself all the monies the retail outlets had deposited in their *Friday Receipts* accounts. Are the payroll ACH transfers *payment orders*? Are the Friday remittances? See §4A-103(a)(1); Official Comment 4 to §4A-104; Brannon v. BankTrust, Inc., 50 So. 3d 397 (Ala. 2010).

The courts have consistently held that Article 4 of the Uniform Commercial Code does not govern purely electronic capture of payment.[8] If electronic debits are not within the scope of Article 4A, what body of law covers them? Until a comprehensive law is enacted, the matter will likely be covered by Operating Letters of the Federal Reserve Banks or private agreements such as those reflected in the rules of the National Automated Clearing House Association.

PROBLEM 256

When Sheridan Whiteside, a resident of New York, agreed to buy the Mesalia Journal, a newspaper in Mesalia, Ohio from Bert Jefferson, its current owner, he instructed his bank, New York Metropolitan National Bank (NYMNB), to wire $1 million to Jefferson's bank, the Mesalia County Bank (MCB). The bank did so through Fedwire, having the Federal Reserve Bank of New York (N.Y. Fed) debit this amount from NYMNB's account with it and crediting the same amount to itself. The N.Y. Fed used Fedwire to transfer the $1 million to the account it carried with the Federal Reserve Bank of Cincinnati (Cincy Fed). Since the Mesalia County Bank did not have an account with Cincy Fed, Cincy Fed transferred the money to the account of the Lake Erie State Bank (LESB), which did, and LESB credited the $1 million into the account that MCB carried with it. MCB, in turn, placed the money into Bert Jefferson's account. All this happened in one day.

8. NACHA rules have been used by the courts to fill in the blanks; Sinclair Oil Corp. v. Sylvan State Bank, 254 Kan. 836, 869 P.2d 675 (1994). However, Article 4 does govern an electronic presentment if the item began as a check and then a truncation system stopped its physical movement and simply presented its relevant information by electronic means (called a *presentment notice*); see §4-110.

(a) Look at §§4A-103, 4A-104, and 4A-105, and put the appropriate labels on the parties: *originator, originator's bank, sender, intermediary bank, receiving bank, beneficiary,* and *beneficiary's bank.* Which of these parties gave a *payment order* as that phrase is defined in §4A-103?

(b) At what exact moment does Bert Jefferson have a legal right to the money? See §4A-404(a). Must MCB notify Jefferson that the money is in his account? See §4A-404(b). Can MCB impose a charge against Jefferson for its actions in accepting the funds transfer? See §4A-406(c) and Official Comment 5.

(c) MCB believed that Jefferson owed it $40,000 on a loan it made to him last year, so it told him that it was allowing him access to only $960,000. He protested, telling the bank that he had repaid the entire loan two weeks ago (this was true) and that he needed the $40,000 to pay off the newspaper's creditors so that the sale to Whiteside could go through. Does the bank have a right of setoff for legitimate debts that its customer owes it? See §4A-502(c)(1). If the newspaper sale collapses because Jefferson failed to pay off the creditors, what damages can he recover from MCB? See §4A-404(a).

Most funds transfers are completed on the day that the sender gives the originating payment order to his or her bank. However, in ACH transfers, as mentioned above, the usual arrangement is that the funds become available to the beneficiary on the day *after* the transfer is completed. You should also remember that the Expedited Funds Availability Act (see page 729) requires next business day availability for wire transfers. EFAA §603(a), 12 U.S.C. §4002(a); Regulation CC §229.10(b).

B. *Acceptance of Payment Orders*

A key concept in Article 4A is *acceptance* of a payment order. If a receiving bank makes a technical acceptance of such an order, it cannot change its mind and reverse the acceptance; there is no right of *charge back* simply because a bank fails to receive payment.[9] If the receiving bank does not want to make an acceptance, it must *reject* the payment order.

It is important to appreciate this: Article 4A itself *never* requires any bank to make an acceptance of a payment order. A bank, therefore, is always free to reject the payment order unless it has made a separate agreement

9. However, for ACH transfers, §4A-405(d) does permit provisional payment, revocable if the beneficiary's bank does not receive full payment from the sender. In such a case the beneficiary must be warned of this possibility and agree to it. If so, any acceptance of the payment order by the beneficiary's bank can be nullified.

otherwise. If the bank does make an agreement to accept a payment order and then wrongfully refuses to do so, the law of contracts, not Article 4A, governs its liability. See §4A-212.

If the payment order specifies a payment date,[10] no *acceptance* can occur until that date, even if the banks have made provisional settlements with each other prior to that time; §4A-209(d). A receiving bank (other than the beneficiary's bank) makes acceptance by *executing* the payment order (passing it on). The beneficiary's bank makes acceptance in one of four ways, whichever occurs first: (1) payment of the amount of the order to the beneficiary, (2) notification to the beneficiary that the amount is available for withdrawal, (3) receipt itself of full payment of the order, or (4) failure of the beneficiary's bank to reject the payment order within the time limits set forth in §4A-209(b)(3).[11] Following acceptance of the payment order, the beneficiary's bank must notify the beneficiary of the receipt of the order before midnight of the next funds-transfer business day following the payment date.[12]

Before acceptance, any credit in the beneficiary's account is provisional only (see Official Comment 2 to §4A-502). The way that a beneficiary's bank avoids liability to the beneficiary is by delaying *acceptance* of the payment order in one of the ways specified above (typically saying nothing to the beneficiary until payment is received). Once acceptance occurs, the beneficiary has a right to the funds and the debt between the originator and the beneficiary is paid. If the beneficiary's bank accepts the payment order and then, for whatever reason, fails to make payment to the beneficiary, it is liable to the beneficiary for the amount of the payment (plus interest thereon) and for any consequential damages (say, for example, the failure of the beneficiary's business) of which it was made aware, unless the beneficiary's bank proves it did not pay because of a reasonable doubt concerning the right of the beneficiary to payment; §4A-404(a).

10. Some do, some don't. If none is specified, the payment date is the date of receipt by the beneficiary's bank; §4A-401.

11. These time limits are as follows: the opening of the next funds-transfer business day following the order's payment date if the beneficiary's bank has received payment or the sender's account is fully covered by a withdrawable credit balance, unless the beneficiary's bank rejects the order before that time, or within one hour of that time, or within one hour after the opening of the sender's next business day if the sender was not immediately available to receive rejection. *Funds-transfer business day* is defined in §4A-105(a)(4) as "the part of a day during which the receiving bank is open for the receipt, processing, and transmittal of payment orders and cancellations and amendments of payment orders." Section 4A-106(a) permits the bank to establish a cut-off time for the funds-transfer business day, and treat payment orders and other Article 4A communications received after the cut-off time as if received on the next funds-transfer business day.

12. "Funds-transfer business day" is defined in the previous footnote.

Shapiro, P.A. v. Wells Fargo Bank, N.A.

United States District Court, Southern District of Florida, 2018
352 F. Supp. 3d 1226

Ursula Ungaro, United States District Judge.

This Cause comes before the Court upon Defendant's Motion for Summary Judgment (D.E. 54).

The Court has considered the Motion, the pertinent portions of the record and is otherwise fully advised in the premises. For the reasons set forth below, the motion is granted.

Background

Unless otherwise noted, these facts are undisputed.

I. The Wire Transfer

Plaintiff, Peter E. Shapiro, P.A., is a law firm whose sole principal is Mr. Peter Shapiro. D.E. 53, ¶¶1-2. The case arises out of a $504,611.13 wire transfer that Plaintiff initiated to an account at Defendant, Wells Fargo Bank. *Id.* ¶4.

Shapiro had a client, a car dealership, that needed to repay a loan, and Shapiro facilitated that transaction. *Id.* ¶¶3-9. On November 16, 2017, the client forwarded Shapiro an email from the lender's lawyer, James Messenger, containing wire transfer instructions for repaying the loan. *Id.* ¶6. That email identified Mr. Messenger's bank as M & T Bank in Syracuse, New York. *Id.* ¶7.

The next day, the client forwarded Shapiro another email purportedly from Mr. Messenger that directed repayment to a different account: a Wells Fargo account based in Texas. *Id.* ¶¶9-10. The second email stated:

> Please here are [sic] my escrow account for today [sic] payoff wire transfer instructtions. Our M & T bank [sic] is currently on audit [and] as a result can't receive funds for now. Please let the wire transfer be made to this our Wells Fargo bank [sic]. Find attached our bank details. *Id.* ¶9.

Despite receiving these two sets of wire transfer instructions, Plaintiff did not email or speak to Mr. Messenger. D.E. 53-1, 53:16-19 (Deposition of Peter Shapiro). And despite the five typographical and capitalization errors in the second email, Shapiro chose to rely on it because it was more recent. *Id.* 54:19-55:4.

The same day that Shapiro received the second email, he initiated the wire transfer to the Wells Fargo account. D.E. 53 ¶¶12-13; Ex. G. But Mr. Messenger never received the funds, because the Wells Fargo account did not belong to him. D.E. 71 ¶5. It belonged instead to someone named Chris Achebe, who promptly removed the funds from the account. D.E. 53 ¶¶17, 37. On December 14, Plaintiff's bank sent Wells Fargo a recall request, but Wells Fargo denied it because the funds were already gone. *Id.* ¶¶36.

II. WELLS FARGO'S WIRE TRANSFER PROCEDURES

Wells Fargo processes wire transfers through an electronic system called the Money Transfer System ("MTS"). D.E. 53 ¶19. When a wire transfer identifies a valid Wells Fargo account number, the MTS processes the transfer through an automated process. *Id.* ¶¶19, 24. MTS creates an automated audit trail that documents the various automated steps in the process. *Id.* ¶20. In this case, the automated audit trail included an entry that reads, "possible name mismatch in CDT party." *Id.* ¶23. This possible name mismatch entry was not seen by anybody at Wells Fargo. *Id.* ¶26. Possible name mismatch entries are common in wire transfers. *Id.* ¶28.

The wire transfer included the partial word "ATTORN." *Id.* ¶30. This triggered Wells Fargo's Office of Foreign Asset Control ("OFAC") to review the transfer for possible United States sanctions violations because of the similarity of "ATTORN" to "ATTOUN," a name which appears on the sanctions list. *Id.* This review was conducted by a person, who determined that there was no match between "ATTORN" and "ATTOUN." *Id.* ¶35. The OFAC screening process does not consider whether there is a name mismatch between the intended beneficiary and the name attached to the receiving account. *Id.* ¶33.

PROCEDURAL HISTORY

Plaintiff filed the complaint on February 5, 2018, which included one claim for violating the Uniform Commercial Code's ("UCC") wire transfer statute as adopted in Florida Statutes section 670.207, and one claim for negligence. D.E. 1. The Court dismissed the negligence claim with prejudice because it was preempted by the wire transfer statute. D.E. 14. The Court allowed the statutory claim to proceed. *Id.* . . .

DISCUSSION

As the Court noted in its order on the motion to dismiss (D.E. 14), the viability of Plaintiff's statutory claim turns on whether Wells Fargo had actual knowledge that the recipient's name and the name on the receiving account did not match. The Court explained, "[i]f Wells Fargo did not know [of the mismatch], then it was entitled to rely on the account number, and thus did not violate the statute when it transferred the funds to Chris Achebe." D.E. 14, p. 4. Wells Fargo now moves for summary judgment on the basis that there is no evidence tending to show that Wells Fargo had actual knowledge of the mismatch.

In opposition, Plaintiff first argues that Wells Fargo knew about the mismatch because it opened the receiving account in Chris Achebe's name and the automated audit trail identified a possible name mismatch. And second, it argues that the statute imposes a due diligence requirement on Wells Fargo, which the bank failed to meet.

I. THE FLORIDA BANKING STATUTES

Florida has adopted the Uniform Commercial Code's ("UCC") relevant banking statutes. This case is governed by section 670.207 of the Florida Statutes. Section 670.207 (which is materially identical to UCC §4A-207) entitled "Misdescription of beneficiary," provides, in relevant part:

> (2) If a payment order received by the beneficiary's bank identifies the beneficiary both by name and by an identifying or bank account number and the name and number identify different persons, the following rules apply:
>
> (a) [I]f the beneficiary's bank does not **know** that the name and number refer to different persons, it may rely on the number as the proper identification of the beneficiary of the order. The beneficiary's bank need not determine whether the name and number refer to the same person.
>
> (b) If the beneficiary's bank pays the person identified by name or **knows** that the name and number identify different persons, no person has rights as beneficiary except the person paid by the beneficiary's bank if that person was entitled to receive payment from the originator of the funds transfer. If no person has rights as beneficiary, acceptance of the order cannot occur.

§670.207(2) (emphasis added).

> Knowledge means "actual knowledge" and is effective for a particular transaction: from the time when it is brought to the attention of the individual conducting that transaction, and, in any event, from the time when it would have been brought to the individual's attention if the organization had exercised due diligence. An organization exercises due diligence if it maintains reasonable routines for communicating significant information to the person conducting the transaction and there is reasonable compliance with the routines. Due diligence does not require an individual acting for the organization to communicate information unless such communication is part of the individual's regular duties or the individual has reason to know of the transaction and that the transaction would be materially affected by the information.

Fla. Stat. §671.201(27); *see also* §671.201(25).

Some background is necessary to understand the purpose and effect of this statute. In 1987, Congress passed the Expedited Funds Availability Act ("EFAA"), and in 2003, it passed the Check Clearing for the 21st Century Act. *See generally* 12 U.S.C. §4001, *et seq.*; 12 U.S.C. §5001, *et seq.* Both acts were passed to expedite the transfer of funds through banks and to diminish the length of time that banks held funds between transfers. *See generally id.* Congress gave the Board of Governors of the Federal Reserve System (the "Board"), the authority to implement both acts via regulation. *See* 12 C.F.R. §229.1. To that end, the Board issued Regulation CC, which among other things, requires banks to make electronically transferred funds available to the recipient within one business day. 12 C.F.R. §229.10(b).

The Board's regulations created legal uncertainty about banks' obligations and liabilities. Judicial authority was "sparse, undeveloped, and not uniform." UCC §4A-102. Article 4A of the UCC, therefore, was drafted to provide a "clean slate." *Id.* The Article's stated purpose is to create "precise and detailed rules to assign responsibility, define behavioral norms, allocate risks and establish limits on liability. . . ." *Id.* It specifically endorses clear bright-line rules, and rejects "broadly stated, flexible principles." *Id.* Moreover, it intends for Courts to rely exclusively on the carefully balanced duties and liabilities set forth in Article 4A, and to eschew any principles of law or equity outside of Article 4A when deciding cases that fall within the statute's ambit. *Id.* The Florida Legislature adopted all of these principles when it adopted UCC Article 4A almost verbatim. *See* Fla. Stat. §670.102.

With respect to the particular provision at issue here (section 670.207), the Florida Legislature has, in great detail, explained the purpose and scope of the protection it affords banks. Comment 2 to the statute reads, in relevant part:

> A very large percentage of payment orders issued to the beneficiary's bank by another bank are processed by automated means using machines capable of reading orders on standard formats that identify the beneficiary by an identifying number or the number of a bank account. The processing of the order by the beneficiary's bank and the crediting of the beneficiary's account are done by use of the identifying or bank account number without human reading of the payment order itself. The process is comparable to that used in automated payment of checks. The standard format, however, may also allow the inclusion of the name of the beneficiary and other information which can be useful to the beneficiary's bank and the beneficiary **but which plays no part in the process of payment**. If the beneficiary's bank has both the account number and name of the beneficiary supplied by the originator of the funds transfer, it is possible for the beneficiary's bank to determine whether the name and number refer to the same person, **but if a duty to make that determination is imposed on the beneficiary's bank the benefits of automated payment are lost**. Manual handling of payment orders is both

> expensive and subject to human error. If payment orders can be handled on an automated basis there are substantial economies of operation and the possibility of clerical error is reduced. Subsection (b) allows banks to utilize automated processing by allowing banks to act on the basis of the number without regard to the name if the bank does not know that the name and number refer to different persons. "Know" is defined in Section 1-201(25) to mean actual knowledge, and Section 1-201(27) states rules for determining when an organization has knowledge of information received by the organization. The time of payment is the pertinent time at which knowledge or lack of knowledge must be determined.
>
> Although the clear trend is for beneficiary's banks to process payment orders by automated means, **Section 4A-207 is not limited to cases in which processing is done by automated means. A bank that processes by semi-automated means or even manually may rely on number as stated in Section 4A-207**.

Fla Stat. §670.207, cmt. 2. (emphasis added).

In summation, this statutory framework permits, and indeed encourages, banks to process electronic funds transfers via automated systems. Moreover, it expressly excuses banks from any duty to verify whether the recipient's name and the name on the receiving account match. *See id.* ("[I]f a duty to make that determination is imposed on the beneficiary's bank the benefits of automated payment are lost. . . . Beneficiary's Bank has no duty to determine whether there is a conflict and it may rely on the number as the proper identification of the beneficiary of the order."). And finally, this protection is not limited only to fully automated systems, but includes semi-automated systems as well. *See id.*

As discussed in more detail below, this clear protection for the beneficiary's bank undermines Plaintiff's arguments, which distilled to their essence, are an attempt to impose upon banks a duty that the statute expressly rejects.

II. CASE LAW INTERPRETING ARTICLE 4A

No court applying Florida law has squarely addressed the issue presented by this case, but numerous other states have adopted Article 4A, and courts in those jurisdictions have considered this issue. In Sliders Trading Co. L.L.C. v. Wells Fargo Bank NA, for example, the District Court for the Northern District of California confronted the same issue under an identical statute. No. 17-CV-04930-LB, 2017 WL 6539843, at *6 (N.D. Cal. Dec. 21, 2017). It held that the bank was entitled to rely on the receiving account number even when the number and name did not match. "The beneficiary's bank has no duty to determine whether the name and account number specified in the wire transfer relate to the same person." *Id.* (internal quotations omitted); *see also* Fla. Stat. §670.207 cmt. 2 ("Beneficiary's Bank has no duty to determine whether there is a conflict and it may rely on the number as the proper identification of the beneficiary of the order."). Furthermore, the court explained, "Knowledge means 'actual knowledge.' " *Id.* (citing TME Enterprs., Inc. v. Norwest Corp., 124 Cal. App. 4th 1021, 1030-31, 22 Cal. Rptr. 3d 146 (2004)).

The Tenth Circuit Court of Appeals is in agreement. While interpreting the same UCC provision adopted into New Mexico's statutes, that court explained:

> As noted, §55-4A-207(b) was designed with automated wire transfer services in mind. In a fully automated system, computer software identifies the account number on an incoming wire, searches the bank's system for a matching account number, and credits the account if a match is found. *Id.*, Official Comment 2. The efficiency benefits of an automated system are undermined if a bank is not able to rely on its automated system but must independently verify there is no conflict between a beneficiary name and an account number. Thus, the drafters of §55-4A-207 clarified that although it is possible for the beneficiary's bank to determine whether the name and number refer to the same person, it "has no duty to determine whether there is a conflict and it may rely on the number as the proper identification of the beneficiary of the order." *Id.* Significantly, the statute "is not limited to cases in which processing is done by automated means. A bank that processes by semi-automated means or even manually may rely on number as stated in Section 4A-207." *Id.*
>
> Although a bank has no duty to affirmatively search for conflicts between beneficiary names and account numbers of incoming wires, it may not escape liability if, before it pays the wire, it gains knowledge of the conflict by any means but nonetheless pays an individual who is not entitled to receive the funds. **"Knowledge" means actual knowledge, not constructive knowledge, and is determined at the time of payment.** *Id.*

First Sec. Bank of New Mexico, N.A. v. Pan Am. Bank, 215 F.3d 1147, 1152 (10th Cir. 2000) (emphasis added).

Additionally, the mere presence of information stored in an automated computer program does not create knowledge. In a different case, the Tenth Circuit held that "actual knowledge" should be given its "literal definition." Wetherill v. Bank IV Kansas, N.A., 145 F.3d 1187, 1192 (10th Cir. 1998). Thus, information stored within a bank's computer system does not create actual knowledge or a duty to investigate. *Id.* The court recognized that "[w]hile this result may at first appear harsh, to hold otherwise where the bank was unaware it was benefiting from Leitner's wrongdoing, would necessarily chill commercial transactions." *Id.*

III. APPLICATION TO THE PRESENT CASE

Here, Wells Fargo processed the wire transfer according to an automated process. True, a person reviewed the transaction for sanctions compliance, but it is undisputed that the person did not look at whether the name and account number matched. D.E. 53 ¶33. At no point in the process did anyone become consciously aware that the name and account did not match. The audit report noted a possible name mismatch, but this digitally stored information did not come to anyone's attention at the time of the transfer. *See Wetherill*, 145 F.3d at 1192 (holding that date stored in a computer system, which if inspected would have revealed wrongdoing, was not actual knowledge). There is, therefore, no evidence that Wells Fargo had actual knowledge of the mismatch.

Plaintiff argues that Wells Fargo had knowledge because it had opened the receiving account in Chris Achebe's name and it had processed a fraudulent wire to his account previously. But these facts do not create actual knowledge of a mismatch in the wire transfer at issue. They do not even create constructive knowledge of a mismatch.

Plaintiff next argues that Wells Fargo would have had knowledge if it exercised due diligence, and due diligence required Wells Fargo to put in place systems to catch name mismatches like this one. This argument fails for several reasons. First, the due diligence requirement from section 671.201(27) applies only to "the "individual conducting the transaction." *See* Fla. Stat. §671.201(27). Here, no individual conducted the transaction; it was automated. And this automation is not only permitted, but encouraged and protected by Article 4A so as to remove the possibility of human error. Fla Stat. §670.207, cmt 2.

Second, even if this due diligence standard applied here, it would not impose on Wells Fargo a duty to determine whether the name and account matched; the statute expressly relieves banks of that duty. *See* Fla. Stat. §670.207 cmt. 2 ("Beneficiary's Bank has no duty to determine whether there is a conflict and it may rely on the number as the proper identification of the beneficiary of the order."); *Sliders*, 2017 WL 6539843, at *6 ("The beneficiary's bank has no duty to determine whether the name and account number specified in the wire transfer relate to the same person."); *Wetherill*, 145 F.3d at 1192 (holding that even with constructive knowledge, there is no duty to investigate). Another case, TME Enterprises, Inc. v. Norwest Corp., is instructive. 124 Cal. App. 4th 1021, 1037, 22 Cal. Rptr. 3d 146, 150 (2004). The court there interpreted an identical UCC provision in a similar mismatch case and held that even where the transaction was reviewed by a person, the "due diligence" requirement did not override section 207. The bank, therefore, was not required to exercise due diligence in determining whether the name and account matched. *Id.* The court explained:

> [M]achines will be instructed to read the numbers and to credit the amount represented by the numbers in the numbered account **in complete obliviousness to the name on the account**. By producing a relatively certain law and

> stating clearly who bears any loss, the drafters have done all that could be asked of them.

Id. (emphasis added).

And finally, Plaintiff's proposed due diligence standard would undermine the express purpose of Article 4A by reinserting human review into a process which is intended to be quick and automated. *See* Fla. Stat. §670.207, cmt. 2 ("Manual handling of payment orders is both expensive and subject to human error. If payment orders can be handled on an automated basis there are substantial economies of operation and the possibility of clerical error is reduced.").

In sum, Wells Fargo is correct that there is no evidence that it had actual knowledge of a mismatch, and Plaintiff cannot impose a duty of care upon Wells Fargo that the statute expressly rejects. For these reasons, it is hereby ORDERED AND ADJUDGED that the Motion (D.E. 54) is GRANTED.

PROBLEM 257

During the great bank collapse of 2030, wire transfer completion became a major concern. You are the chief counsel for Octopus National Bank. If it receives a payment order from a bank whose financial status is either shaky or unknown, how can it protect itself from liability to its customers in the event that the sender fails to forward the funds (or settle at the end of the business day)? See §§4A-403, 4A-405(e) (the "doomsday" rule), 4A-209 (and its Official Comment 8).

PROBLEM 258

Octopus National Bank (ONB) made its customers sign an agreement providing that even though the bank had informed them that they were the beneficiaries of a wire transfer, no acceptance was final unless the bank itself actually received the funds. Any withdrawal of the funds prior to the bank's receipt was merely a loan by ONB to its customers, to be repaid either by receipt of the funds or, failing that, by customer repayment. Is this agreement enforceable? See §§4A-209(b)(1) (and its Official Comment 5), 4A-405(c).

C. Transmission Errors

Mistakes will happen, of course, and there are many kinds: wrong dollar amount, duplicate orders, misidentified beneficiary, etc. Fraud might also be at work: some crook might send an unauthorized payment order to sender's bank telling it to make payment to the account of the crook at another bank. Who bears the loss in these situations?

Grain Traders, Inc. v. Citibank, N.A.

United States District Court, Southern District of New York, 1997
960 F. Supp. 784

CHIN, District Judge.

Plaintiff Grain Traders, Inc. ("Grain Traders") brings this diversity action under Article 4-A of New York's Uniform Commercial Code (the "U.C.C.") and principles of common law seeking the refund of money it alleges it lost in the process of an electronic funds transfer. The funds transfer—which was to "pass" through several banks—was not completed, allegedly because defendant Citibank, N.A. ("Citibank") froze an account of one of the banks in question. Grain Traders claims that Citibank acted improperly by accepting $310,000 for a funds transfer and then failing to forward the funds in accordance with instructions, and contends that Citibank instead took the funds as a set-off against a debt owed to Citibank by one of the intermediary banks.

On the record before the court, however, no reasonable fact-finder could conclude that Citibank engaged in any conduct that would form the basis for liability under the U.C.C. or the common law. Rather, Citibank did all that it was required to do: it debited one account $310,000, credited another account $310,000, and forwarded payment instructions to the bank whose account it credited. That bank was supposed to carry out the next step in the funds transfer, but it was unable to do so because of apparent financial problems that eventually caused it to cease doing business. Likewise, the final bank in the chain also was suffering from financial problems that forced it to go out of business. Both banks were chosen by Grain Traders, not Citibank, and it was those choices—rather than any wrongdoing by Citibank—that led to the apparent loss of the $310,000.

Grain Traders's principal argument is that Citibank should not have accepted the payment order. Rather, Grain Traders argues that because Citibank knew or should have known that the next bank in the chain was experiencing financial problems, Citibank should have exercised its judgment to reject the payment order. Grain Traders's arguments, however, do not make sense and they are inconsistent with the concept of funds transfers as well as the letter and spirit of Article 4-A.

Funds transfers are high-speed means of moving large sums of money at a low cost. As the Prefatory Note to Article 4-A observes:

> There are a number of characteristics of funds transfers covered by Article [4-A] that have influenced the drafting of the statute. The typical funds transfer

> involves a large sum of money. Multimillion dollar transactions are commonplace. The originator of the transfer and the beneficiary are typically sophisticated business or financial organizations. High speed is another predominant characteristic. Most funds transfers are completed on the same day, even in complex transactions in which there are several intermediary banks in the transmission chain. A funds transfer is a highly efficient substitute for payments made by the delivery of paper instruments. Another characteristic is extremely low cost. A transfer that involves many millions of dollars can be made for a price of a few dollars. Price does not normally vary very much or at all with the amount of the transfer. This system of pricing may not be feasible if the bank is exposed to very large liabilities in connection with the transaction. . . .

U.C.C. Art. 4-A, Prefatory Note, p. 38 (McKinney Supp. 1997). Because of these characteristics—high speed and low cost—one could not expect an intermediary bank in the funds transfer to engage in due diligence to verify the creditworthiness of subsequent banks in the chain, particularly when those banks were designated by the originator itself. Indeed, in such circumstances, the risk of loss must be borne by the originator, for it was the originator's choice of an intermediary bank that led to the loss.

Grain Traders's motion for summary judgment on its claims under Article 4-A of the U.C.C. is denied and Citibank's cross-motion for summary judgment dismissing Grain Traders's claims is granted. The complaint is dismissed.

Background

A. The Facts

On December 22, 1994, Grain Traders initiated a funds transfer (the "Funds Transfer") to effectuate the payment of $310,000 to Claudio Goidanich Kraemer ("Kraemer"). (Pl. Rule 3(g) Statement ¶3). The Funds Transfer was designed to move money from Grain Traders to Kraemer in one day. The payment order issued by Grain Traders to its bank, Banco de Credito Nacional ("BCN"), stated as follows:

> WE HEREBY AUTHORIZE YOU DEBIT OUR ACCOUNT NR 509364 FOR THE AMOUNT OF US $310,000.00 AND TRANSFER TO:
>
> BANQUE DU CREDIT ET INVESTISSEMENT LTD ACCOUNT 36013997 AT CITIBANK NEW YORK IN FAVOUR OF BANCO EXTRADER S.A. ACCOUNT NR 30114 BENEFICIARY CLAUDIO GOIDANICH KRAEMER UNDER FAX ADVISE TO BANCO EXTRADER NR 00541-312 0057/318-0124 AT. DISTEFANO/M. FLIGUEIRA.

(Pargana Aff. ¶3 & Ex. C). Thus, the funds transfer was to proceed as follows: (1) Grain Traders's account at BCN was to be debited $310,000; (2) the $310,000 was then to be "transferred" to Banque Du Credit Et Investissement

Ltd.'s ("BCI") at Citibank by way of a debit to BCN's Citibank account and a corresponding credit in that amount to BCI's Citibank account; (3) the $310,000 was in turn to be "transferred" from BCI to Banco Extrader, S.A. ("Extrader") by way of an unspecified transaction between BCI and Extrader; and (4) the $310,000 was finally to be transferred to Kraemer by way of a credit to his account at Extrader.

After the payment order was issued by Grain Traders to BCN, the Funds Transfer initially proceeded as expected. BCN's account at Citibank was debited $310,000 and BCI's account at Citibank was credited $310,000. At the same time, BCN sent instructions to Citibank, directing Citibank to instruct BCI to instruct Extrader to credit $310,000 to Kraemer. (Patrickakos Aff. ¶6 & Ex. 1). Citibank in turn sent instructions to BCI on the same day, notifying BCI that Citibank had credited its account with $310,000 and instructing BCI to instruct Extrader to credit this amount to Kraemer. (Patrickakos Aff. ¶7 & Ex. 2).

Either just before or just after BCI's account at Citibank was credited with the $310,000, however, the BCI account was placed by Citibank on "hold for funds" status. (Pl. Rule 3(g) Statement ¶19). The "hold for funds" status, which was put into place because BCI's account with Citibank was overdrawn by more than $12 million, prevented BCI from making any further withdrawals from the account. (Id. ¶¶19, 22).

Kraemer apparently never received a credit to his Extrader account for the $310,000. Kraemer's affidavit, submitted by Grain Traders, states that on December 28, 1994, just six days after the attempted Funds Transfer, the government of Argentina ordered Extrader to suspend payments and that Extrader became insolvent "[s]ometime later." (Kraemer Aff. ¶5). Likewise, BCI, a Bahamian bank, ceased making payments in January 1995; it was closed by supervisory authorities in the Bahamas on July 31, 1995. (Def. Rule 3(g) Statement ¶10-12).

B. PRIOR PROCEEDINGS

Grain Traders commenced this action against Citibank in November 1995. The complaint asserts four causes of action: (1) for a refund under U.C.C. §4-A-402; (2) for a refund as well as reasonable expenses and attorneys' fees under U.C.C. §§4-A-209, 4-A-301, and 4-A-305; (3) for breach of the obligation to deal in good faith under U.C.C. §1-203; and (4) for conversion and money had and received under common law.

These motions followed. . . .

DISCUSSION

B. FUNDS TRANSFERS AND ARTICLE 4-A

Funds transfers, also commonly referred to as wire transfers, are a specialized "method of payment in which the person making the payment (the 'originator') directly transmits an instruction to a bank," generally through electronic means, "to make payment to the person receiving payment (the 'beneficiary') or to instruct some other bank to make payment to the beneficiary." §4-A-104, Official Comment 1. A funds transfer consists of one or more payment orders each instructing the next party in line as to the steps it must follow to carry out the funds transfer. Id. Hence, funds are "transferred" through a series of debits and credits to a series of bank accounts. Most often, funds transfers are used as an inexpensive and efficient method of discharging an "underlying payment obligation which arose through earlier commercial dealings between the originator . . . and the beneficiary." Sheerbonnet, Ltd. v. American Express Bank, Ltd., 905 F. Supp. 127, 130 (S.D.N.Y. 1995).

In the present case, Grain Traders was the originator of a funds transfer intended to pay $310,000 to Kraemer, the beneficiary. Grain Traders requested a series of payment orders that would "transfer" the funds from its bank, BCN, through two "intermediary" banks, Citibank and BCI and, finally into Kraemer's account at his bank, Extrader. Grain Traders asserts that Citibank did not carry out the Funds Transfer as directed and instead improperly used the funds it received as a set-off against debt owed to Citibank by BCI.

1. §4-A-402

In its first cause of action, Grain Traders claims that it is entitled to a refund of the $310,000 from Citibank under the "money back guarantee" of §4-A-402. Section 4-A-402 states:

> (3) . . . With respect to a payment order issued to a receiving bank other than the beneficiary's bank, acceptance of the order by the receiving bank obliges the sender to pay the bank the amount of the sender's order. . . . The obligation of that sender to pay its payment order is excused if the funds transfer is not completed. . . .
>
> (4) If the sender of a payment order pays the order and was not obliged to pay all or part of the amount paid [because the funds transfer was not completed], the bank receiving payment is obliged to refund payment to the extent the sender was not obliged to pay.

§4-A-402(3), (4).

Grain Traders argues that its obligation to pay BCN, and BCN's obligation to pay Citibank, was excused because the Funds Transfer was not completed. Grain Traders therefore asserts that it is entitled to a refund of its payment—pursuant to §4-A-402—from Citibank. Citibank, however, argues that Grain Traders has sued the wrong party. Citibank claims that §4-A-402 only allows a party to a funds transfer to obtain a refund from the next party or bank in line. Hence, Grain Traders may only seek a refund—if at all—from BCN. For at least four reasons, I agree with Citibank's interpretation of §4-A-402.

(i) Plain Language of §4-A-402. First, the plain language of §4-A-402 and other provisions of Article 4-A make it clear that a party to a funds transfer is only entitled to a refund from the specific party to which it made payment. Article 4-A treats a funds transfer as a series of individual transactions, each of which involve two parties dealing directly with each other. This notion is embodied in the very definition of a "funds transfer" as set forth in §4-A-104(1):

> "Funds transfer" means the series of transactions, beginning with the originator's payment order, made for the purpose of making payment to the beneficiary of the order. The term includes *any* payment order issued by the originator's bank or an intermediary bank intended to carry out the originator's payment order.

§4-A-104(1) (emphasis added). Thus, Article 4-A approaches each funds transfer not as a single payment order, but rather as a series of transactions each of which involves only the parties to the individual payment order.

After establishing this structure, Article 4-A proceeds to define the rights and duties of each bank involved in a funds transfer. First, §4-A-402(3) states that the bank that sent the payment order must pay the bank that received the payment order when the payment order is accepted. §4-A-402(3). Thus, the obligation of payment runs only from the sender bank—the bank that sent the payment order—to the bank that received the payment order. Id. This subsection further provides that the sending bank's obligation to pay the receiving bank is excused if the funds transfer is not completed. Id.

Then, §4-A-402(4) provides that when a sending bank that is not required to pay—because the funds transfer has not been completed—has already paid, the sending bank is entitled to a "refund" from the receiving bank. §4-A-402(4). Thus, these sections do not create an obligation to pay or refund a payment with respect to all the parties to a fund transfer, but instead only create an obligation between the sending bank and the receiving bank pursuant to each individual payment order making up the funds transfer. This conclusion is supported by the fact that the singular form of "bank," as opposed to the plural "banks," is used when §4-A-402 provides that "the *bank* receiving payment is obliged to refund" the payment. §4-A-402 (emphasis added). Thus, the plain language of §4-A-402 makes it clear that a right of refund lies only with respect to parties to a specific payment order and not as to all the parties to a funds transfer.

(ii) Official Comment to §4-A-402. Second, the Official Comment to §4-A-402 further underscores the intent of Article 4-A's drafters to limit the right of refund under §4-A-402 to the parties to a specific payment order. The Comment states as follows:

> The money-back guarantee [of §4-A-402(4)] is particularly important to Originator if noncompletion of the funds transfer is due to the fault of an

> intermediary bank rather than Bank A [the Originator's bank]. In that case Bank A must refund payment to Originator, and Bank A has the burden of obtaining refund from the intermediary bank that it paid.

§4-A-402, Official Comment 2. Thus, as the Comment explains, the originator is entitled to a refund from the bank to which it issued its payment order, and the originator's bank must then look to the intermediary bank—the bank to which it issued a payment order—to get a refund.

Accordingly, the Comment shows that Article 4-A's drafters intended the "money back guarantee" to apply only as between the parties to a payment order and not the parties to the funds transfer as a whole. Applied to the facts of this case, the originator—Grain Traders—would be entitled to a refund under §4-A-402(4) from its bank, BCN, but not from Citibank.

(iii) Right of Subrogation. Third, the subrogation language of §4-A-402(5) demonstrates that the originator does not, as a general matter, have a right to sue all the parties to a funds transfer. Subsection (5) deals with a situation where an intermediary-receiving bank cannot give a refund to its sending bank because the intermediary bank "suspends payment." In that case, §4-A-402(5) relieves the sending bank of its obligation to refund the payment it received. Instead, §4-A-402(5) provides that:

> [t]he first sender in the funds transfer that issued an instruction requiring routing through that intermediary bank [i.e., the one that "suspends payment"] is subrogated to the right of the bank that paid the intermediary bank to [a] refund.

Hence, the first sender to designate the defaulting bank (the bank that suspended payments) is the one that, by virtue of the subrogation, has the burden of seeking recovery.

What subsection (5) makes clear is that under §4-A-402(4) no right to a refund otherwise exists between the originator and an intermediary bank. This is evident because there would be no need for the subrogation language of subsection (5) if the originator (as the first sender) already had a right to assert a refund claim directly against all intermediary banks.

The Official Comments to §4-A-402 confirm that when it is the originator who chooses an intermediary bank that is unable, for financial reasons, to complete its part of the funds transfer, it is the originator, and not any other bank in the funds transfer, who bears the risk of loss. Comment 2 gives the following example:

> Suppose Originator instructs Bank A to pay to Beneficiary's account in Bank B and to use Bank C as an intermediary bank. Bank A executes Originator's order by issuing a payment order to Bank C. Bank A pays Bank C. Bank C fails to execute the order of Bank A and suspends payments. Under subsections [(3) and (4)], Originator is not obliged to pay Bank A and is

> entitled to a refund from Bank A of any payments that it may have made. Bank A is entitled to a refund from Bank C, but Bank C is insolvent. Subsection [(5)] deals with this case. *Bank A was required to issue its payment order to Bank C because Bank C was designated as an intermediary bank by Originator.* Section [4-A-302(1)(a)]. *In this case Originator takes the risk of insolvency of Bank C.* Under subsection [(5)], Bank A is entitled to payment from Originator and Originator is subrogated to the right of Bank A under [subsection (4)] to refund of payment from Bank C.

§4-A-402, Official Comment 2 (emphasis added).

Subsection (5) may not be precisely applicable here because it applies to a situation where an intermediary bank suspends payments and it is unclear from the record when BCI suspended payments. Nonetheless, the reasoning of subsection (5) supports the conclusion that in the present case Grain Traders must bear the risk of loss, for it was Grain Traders that chose BCI and Extrader to carry out the funds transfer. Grain Traders thus may not turn to Citibank to recover the loss suffered as a result of Grain Traders's choice of BCI and Extrader to complete the transfer.

(iv) Creation of Explicit Cause of Action by Originator Against Intermediary Bank. Finally, Citibank's argument that it owes no refund to Grain Traders finds support from the working of §4-A-305. Section 4-A-305 (2) provides that a "receiving bank" is liable to the "originator" for interest and expenses under certain circumstances. §4-A-305(2). Grain Traders points to this section as proof that all intermediary-receiving banks are liable directly to the originator for a refund. However, this section shows just the opposite. Section 4-A-305(2), which has no relationship to the refund provisions of §4-A-402, demonstrates that when the drafters of Article 4-A wanted to give the originator the right to bring a cause of action against any bank in the funds transfer chain, they knew how to make that clear. Thus, had the drafters of Article 4-A intended to allow the originator to seek a refund from any bank in the funds transfer chain, they could have made that clear also.

Accordingly, I hold that Grain Traders may not, as a matter of law, assert a claim against Citibank under §4-A-402 and hence summary judgment is granted in favor of Citibank on Grain Traders's first claim for relief.

2. §§4-A-209 AND 4-A-301

Grain Traders's second claim for relief is premised on §§4-A-209 and 4-A-301, which govern "acceptance" and "execution" of a payment order, respectively. Grain Traders alleges that because Citibank intended to use the $310,000 as a set-off to the debt owed to Citibank by BCI, Citibank did not intend to carry out the payment order received from BCN. Grain Traders argues that because of Citibank's misplaced intent, the payment order issued by Citibank of BCI did not constitute the "execution" or "acceptance" of BCN's payment order under §4-A-209 or §4-A-301. See §4-A-301 ("A payment order is 'executed' by the receiving bank when it issues a payment order intended to carry out the payment order received by the bank.") (emphasis [sic] added). Grain Traders thus concludes that Citibank is liable for its failure to properly execute BCN's payment order. I disagree.

As a threshold matter, the record shows unequivocally that Citibank properly executed the payment order that it received. It debited BCN's account $310,000; it credited BCFs account $310,000; and it forwarded instructions to BCI to instruct Extrader to credit Kraemer with $310,000. That was all that it was required to do. As §4-A-302 makes clear, an intermediary bank that accepts a payment order "is obliged to issue . . . a payment order complying with the sender's order and follow the sender's instructions concerning . . . any intermediary bank. . . ." Here, Citibank accepted a payment order from BCN that instructed it to instruct BCI to instruct Extrader to credit $310,000 to Kraemer. Citibank followed these instructions, thereby meeting its obligations, as it relayed the appropriate instructions to the next intermediary bank, BCI.

Moreover, even if Grain Traders were able to prove that Citibank failed to execute or accept BCN's payment order, it would nevertheless not be entitled to prevail on its second claim for relief. This is because neither §4-A-209 nor §4-A-301 provides a remedy for the failure to carry out a payment order. Rather, these two sections simply define the terms "acceptance" and "execution" as those terms are used in the rest of Article 4-A. If a funds transfer is not completed because one of the parties involved in the funds transfer fails to either "accept" or "execute" a payment order, the only remedy to which the originator is entitled is a refund—pursuant to §4-A-402—of any payment it made. Thus, Grain Traders's second claim for relief simply leads us back to the same place as its first claim—i.e., a claim for a refund under the "money back guarantee" of §4-A-402. Accordingly, Grain Traders's second claim for relief is dismissed for the same reasons as its first claim for relief.

C. U.C.C. §1-203[13]

In its third claim for relief, Grain Traders asserts that Citibank's actions violated §1-203. Section 1-203 imposes an obligation of good faith and fair dealing on a party's performance or enforcement of any contract or duty within the ambit of the Uniform Commercial Code. N.Y.U.C.C. §1-203. Grain Traders alleges that it is entitled to damages because Citibank violated this section. For two reasons, I disagree.

First, §1-203 only imposes an obligation of good faith and fair dealing on the performance of a "contract or duty." Id. In this case, Grain Traders

13. [Now §1-304—Eds.]

has not alleged that any contract existed between Citibank and itself. Thus, Grain Traders must be relying on a statutory duty as the predicate for its third claim for relief. The only statutory duty that applied in this case, however, is Article 4-A and, for the reasons I have already discussed, Grain Traders has failed to state a claim under that Article. Thus, there is no contract or statutory duty to which Grain Traders can argue that its good faith claim under §1-203 applies.

Second, to the extent that Grain Traders is asserting that a violation of §1-203 gives rise to an independent cause of action, its assertion is without merit, for §1-203 does not give rise to an independent cause of action. See, e.g., Super Glue Corp. v. Avis Rent A Car System, Inc., 132 A.D.2d 604, 517 N.Y.S.2d 764, 766 (2d Dep't 1987) ("the Code does not permit recovery of money damages for not acting in good faith where no other basis of recovery is present"). The Official Comment to §1-203 supports this conclusion:

> This section does not support an independent cause of action for failure to perform or enforce in good faith. . . . [T]he doctrine of good faith merely directs a court towards interpreting contracts within *the* commercial context in which they are created, performed, and enforced, and does not create a separate duty of fairness and reasonableness which can be independently breached.

§1-203, Official Comment, at Supp. p. 13. Accordingly, Grain Traders's third claim for relief is dismissed.

D. COMMON LAW CLAIMS

Grain Traders's fourth claim for relief relies on the common law torts of "conversion" and "money had and received." Grain Traders's tort claims, however, must be dismissed because Grain Traders has failed to present evidence to support either of those claims.

To prevail on either of its common law claims, Grain Traders must prove that at the time it alleges Citibank improperly kept the $310,000, Grain Traders still had a possessory interest in the funds. Lind v. Vanguard Offset Printers, Inc., 857 F. Supp. 1060, 1066 (S.D.N.Y. 1994) (under New York law, conversion "requires a showing . . . that the plaintiff had an ownership interest or an 'immediate superior right to possession of property' "); Aaron Ferer & Sons Ltd. v. Chase Manhattan Bank, 731 F.2d 112, 125 (2d Cir. 1984) (to state a claim for money *had and received* under New York Law, the plaintiff must show that "defendant received money belonging to plaintiff") (*emphasis added*). Grain Traders, however, did not have possession of the funds at the time Citibank credited them to BCFs account. This is because a depositor loses title to money deposited in a general account at the moment those funds are deposited. . . .

Rather, it debited one account $310,000 and credited another account $310,000, and it forwarded the appropriate payment instructions. That was all it was required to do. BCI should have carried out those instructions, but it was unwilling or unable to do so.

CONCLUSION

For the foregoing reasons, Grain Traders's motion for summary judgment is denied and Citibank's cross-motion for summary judgment is granted. Accordingly, the Clerk of the Court shall enter judgment in favor of Citibank dismissing the complaint with prejudice and without costs.

So ordered.

All courts considering the issue have ruled that common law theories are preempted in wire transfer cases by the statutory scheme of Article 4A (except as to matters the Article does not cover). ADS Associates Group, Inc. v. Oritani Sav. Bank, 219 N.J. 496, 99 A.3d 345 (2014), has a good discussion of this. Negligence claims in a wire transfer situation that involve issues outside the wire transfer itself are not preempted by the rule of Article 4A and will be evaluated on their own merits; Venture General Agency, LLC v. Wells Fargo Bank, N.A., 2019 WL 3503109 (N.D. Cal. 2019).

PROBLEM 259

Saul Sender agreed to buy Betty Beneficiary's business from her for the amount of $1 million, the deal to be off unless he made payment of this amount to her account (12345) at Merchants Bank on September 25. On September 24, Saul ordered his bank, Original National Bank (ONB), to wire $1 million from his account with ONB to Betty Beneficiary, Account #12345, at Merchants Bank, with a payment date of the next day. ONB executed this payment order by issuing an identical payment order to Merchants Bank, but unfortunately, it mistakenly gave the account number as 12346, though it correctly identified Betty by name. Merchants Bank notified Harry Innocent, the holder of Account #12346, that $1 million had been deposited in his account and was available for withdrawal as of September 25. Harry, delighted, withdrew the money and lit out for parts unknown. When Betty didn't receive the money, she phoned Saul on September 26 and told him that the deal was off and that she was selling the business to her brother. Saul, furious, sued his bank. Who bears what liability here?

The drafters of Article 4A discovered that the usage of trade in wire transfers was for all banks involved to look only at the account number and ignore the actual name of the beneficiary and rather than trying to change the practice, they decided to give it statutory blessing. Thus §4A-207 deals with misdescription of the beneficiary and provides that the beneficiary's bank may ignore the name specified in the payment order and deal only on the basis of the given account number (unless it was actually aware of the discrepancy, in which case it is responsible for seeing that the correct beneficiary gets the funds—see TME Enterprises, Inc. v. Norwest Corp., 124 Cal. App. 4th 1021, 22 Cal. Rptr. 3d 146 (2004)). As you might suppose, machines are much better at understanding numbers than names. Thus, in the above Problem, Merchants Bank is off the hook in this situation even though it put the money in the wrong account. Under what is called the "money-back guarantee" (see Official Comment 2 to §4A-402), Original National Bank must refund the money to its customer because it made the mistake, and then go after Harry Innocent in order to recover the money.[14] ONB is liable to its customer, Saul, though he has a duty to discover and report the problem within 90 days after his bank sends him notification of the payment or be responsible for whatever loss the bank can prove it suffered because of his delay in reporting; §4A-304. Any time a bank does not properly execute the payment order, the originator must be made whole, including interest per §4A-204(a). ONB is liable for Saul's expenses, the $1 million and interest thereon, but the bank is not liable for any consequential damages (for example, the loss of the chance to buy Betty's business) unless a written agreement between Saul and ONB provides that the bank will bear this greater loss; §4A-305 (which also provides that in certain circumstances the bank may have to pay Saul's attorney's fees—see (e)).

Corfan Banco Asuncion Paraguay v. Ocean Bank

Florida District Court of Appeal, 1998

715 So. 2d 967

SORONDO, J.

Corfan Banco Asuncion Paraguay, a foreign banking corporation (Corfan Bank), appeals the lower court's entry of a Final Summary Judgment in favor of Ocean Bank, a Florida bank.

On March 22, 1995, Corfan Bank originated a wire transfer of $72,972 via its intermediary Swiss Bank to the account of its customer, Jorge Alberto

14. Its cause of action is common law restitution ("money had and received"); §4A-207(d); HSBC Bank USA, N.A. v. A.T.A. Const. Corp., 2009 WL 1456529 (E.D.N.Y. 2009).

Dos Santos Silva (Silva), in Ocean Bank. The transfer order bore Silva's name as the recipient and indicated that his account number was 01007*0*21*0*40*0* (in fact, this was a nonexistent account). Upon receipt of the wire transfer, Ocean Bank noticed a discrepancy in this number and before depositing the money, confirmed with Silva that his correct account number was 01007*6*21*6*40*6*.[15] Ocean Bank did not, however, inform Corfan Bank or Swiss Bank of the error. Once the correct number was confirmed by Silva, Ocean Bank accepted the wire transfer and credited Silva's account.

The next day, Corfan Bank became aware of the account number discrepancy and, without first checking with either Silva or Ocean Bank, sent a second wire transfer of $72,972 to Silva's correct account number at Ocean Bank. The second transfer order did not indicate that it was a correction, replacement or amendment of the March 22nd transfer. Because the information of the transfer was correct, it was automatically processed at Ocean Bank and was credited to Silva's account. Several days later, Corfan Bank inquired of Ocean Bank regarding the two transfers, maintaining that only one transfer was intended. By that time, Silva had withdrawn the proceeds of both wire transfers. When Ocean Bank refused to repay $72,972 to Corfan Bank, this litigation ensued. Corfan Bank proceeded on two claims, one based on the §670.207, Florida Statutes (1995), which codifies as Florida law §4A-207 of the Uniform Commercial Code (UCC), and one based on common law negligence. Ocean Bank answered denying liability under the statute and also contending that the negligence claim was precluded by the preemptive statutory scheme.

The trial court, emphasizing that Florida's adoption of the UCC sections concerning wire transfers did not abrogate the basic tenets of commercial law, found that Ocean Bank had not contravened §670.207 by crediting the erroneous March 22nd wire transfer to Silva's account. Finding that Corfan Bank was the party best situated to have avoided this loss, the court held that Corfan Bank must bear that loss and, therefore, the court granted Ocean Bank's motion for summary judgment as to count one (the UCC count). Additionally, the court dismissed count two (the negligence count).

We begin with a review of the exact language of §670.207(1), Florida Statutes:

> (1) Subject to subsection (2), if, in a payment order received by the beneficiary's bank, the name, bank account number, or other identification of the beneficiary refers to a nonexistent or unidentifiable person or account, no person has rights as a beneficiary of the order and acceptance of the order cannot occur.

15. As indicated by the italicized numbers, the three sixes in the account number had been replaced with zeros on the transfer order.

Corfan Bank argues that this language is clear and unambiguous, where a name *or* bank account number, *or* other identification refers either to a nonexistent or unidentified person or a nonexistent account, the order *cannot* be accepted. Ocean Bank responds that such a "highly technical" reading of the statute is "contrary to commercial and practical considerations and common sense." It suggests that we look to the legislative intent and conclude that the "or" in the statute should be given conjunctive rather than disjunctive effect. We respectfully decline Ocean Bank's invitation to look behind the plain language of the statute and conclude that given its clarity it must be read as written.

In Capers v. State, 678 So. 2d 330 (Fla. 1996), the Florida Supreme Court stated:

> [T]he plain meaning of statutory language is the first consideration of statutory construction. St. Petersburg Bank & Trust Co. v. Hamm, 414 So. 2d 1071, 1073 (Fla. 1982). Only when a statute is of doubtful meaning should matters extrinsic to the statute be considered in construing the language employed by the legislature. Florida State Racing Comm'n v. McLaughlin, 102 So. 2d 574, 576 (Fla. 1958). . . .

In the present case, although the payment order correctly identified the beneficiary, it referred to a nonexistent account number. Under the clear and unambiguous terms of the statute, acceptance of the order could not have occurred. As the Florida Supreme Court stated in [State v. Jett, 626 So. 2d 691 (Fla. 1993)]:

> We trust that if the legislature did not intend the result mandated by the statute's plain language, the legislature itself will amend the statute at the next opportunity.

Jett, 626 So. 2d at 693.

As indicated above, the trial court dismissed count two of the complaint which sounded in negligence. The court concluded that the statutory scheme preempts the common law remedy of negligence. It is not clear whether the adoption of Article 4A of the UCC abrogated the common law cause of action for negligence relating to a wire transfer, as raised in count two of the complaint. The Uniform Commercial Code Comment following §670.102, Florida Statutes (1995), which delineates the subject matter for chapter 670, provides in part:

> In the drafting of Article 4A, a deliberate decision was made to write on a clean slate and to treat a funds transfer as a unique method of payment to be governed by unique rules that address the particular issues raised in this method of payment. A deliberate decision was also made to use precise and

> detailed rules to assign responsibility, define behavioral norms, allocate risks and establish limits on liability, rather than to rely on broadly stated, flexible principles. In the drafting of these rules, a critical consideration was that the various parties to funds transfers need to be able to predict risk with certainty, to insure against risk, to adjust operational and security procedures, and to price funds transfer services appropriately. This consideration is particularly important given the very large amounts of money that are involved in funds transfers.
>
> Funds transfers involve competing interests—those of the banks that provide funds transfer services and the commercial and financial organizations that use the services, as well as the public interest. These competing interests were represented in the drafting process and they were thoroughly considered. *The rules that emerged represent a careful and delicate balancing of those interests and are intended to be the exclusive means of determining the rights, duties and liabilities of the affected parties in any situation covered by particular provisions of the Article.* Consequently, resort to principles of law or equity outside of Article 4A is not appropriate to create rights, duties and liabilities inconsistent with those stated in this Article.

(Emphasis added). See U.C.C. §4A-102 cmt. (1977); see also, 19A Fla. Stat. Ann. 15 (U.C.C. cmt. 1995) (emphasis added). This comment suggests the exclusivity of Article 4A as a remedy. Although the commentary to the UCC is not controlling authority, see Solitron Devices, Inc. v. Veeco Instruments, Inc., 492 So. 2d 1357, 1359 (Fla. 4th DCA 1986); 1 Ronald A. Anderson, Anderson on the Uniform Commercial Code, §l-102:34-:37 (1995 Revision), we are persuaded by the expressed intent of the drafters.

In addressing this issue we restrict our analysis to the pleadings and facts of this case. In pertinent part, count two reads as follows:

> Ocean Bank owed Corfan Bank a duty of care to follow the accepted banking practice of the community, and to return the funds from the first transfer to Corfan Bank upon receipt due to the reference in the first transfer to a non-existent account number.

The duty claimed to have been breached by Ocean Bank in its negligence count is exactly the same duty established and now governed by the statute. Under such circumstances we agree with the trial judge that the statutory scheme preempts the negligence claim in this case and affirm the dismissal of count two.[16] We do not reach the issue of whether the adoption of Article 4A of the UCC preempts negligence claims in all cases.

16. We note that allowing a negligence claim in this case would "create rights, duties and liabilities inconsistent" with those set forth in §670.207. In a negligence cause of action, Ocean Bank would be entitled to defend on a theory of comparative negligence because Corfan Bank provided the erroneous account number which created the problem at issue

We reverse the Final Summary Judgment entered by the trial court in favor of Ocean Bank as to count one of the complaint and affirm the dismissal of count two. We remand this case for further proceedings consistent with this opinion.

LEVY, J., concurs.

NESBITT, J., dissenting. I respectfully dissent. I would affirm final summary judgment for Ocean Bank. In my view, the trial court's well-reasoned and pragmatic approach to the interpretation of §670.207, Florida Statutes (1995), was the best solution to the disagreement between these parties. Corfan Bank itself was negligent in handling the wire transfer in question. Corfan Bank incorrectly listed Silva's account number on the first wire transfer order and, compounding that error, Corfan sent the second wire transfer order with no indication that it was a correction of the first. These errors caused Corfan's loss.

More important, the language of §670.207 does not proscribe the actions taken by Ocean Bank. Section 670.207 precludes acceptance of a wire transfer order only if "the name, account number, or other identification of the beneficiary refers to a nonexistent or unidentifiable person or account." Considering this section in its entirety as statutory construction requires, see Fleischman v. Department of Professional Regulation, 441 So. 2d 1121, 1123 (Fla. 3d DCA 1983), it seems apparent that the part of the statute that permits the receiving bank to look to "other identification" surely allows more flexibility than the majority here would permit.

In my view, the statute question should neither be construed in the disjunctive or the conjunctive. As stated above, the construction of a statute that will reject part of it should be avoided. See Snively Groves, Inc. v. Mayo, 135 Fla. 300, 184 So. 839 (1938); or, as sometimes stated, "A court should avoid reading the statute so that it will render part of the statute meaningless." Unruh v. State, 669 So. 2d 242, 245 (Fla. 1996). There are segments of this statute that plainly permit a receiving bank to look at other identification, thus affording the receiving bank more flexibility in making the correct identification than the court recognizes today.

Ocean Bank's actions seem to better comport with the overall statutory scheme relating to funds transfers than the avenue supported by the

and then initiated the second transfer without communicating with Ocean Bank. Section 670.207 does not contemplate such a defense. (Oddly enough, allowing Corfan Bank's negligence claim in this case might actually inure to Ocean Bank's benefit). As explained in the comment, one of the primary purposes of the section is to enable the parties to wire funds transfers to predict risk with certainty and to insure against risk. The uniformity and certainty sought by the statute for these transactions could not possibly exist if parties could opt to sue by way of pre-Code remedies where the statute has specifically defined the duties, rights and liabilities of the parties.

court. The primary purpose of using a wire transfer of funds is to enable the beneficiary to get the funds quickly. Indeed, commercial or contract deadlines may be adversely impacted if the wire transfer does not go through quickly, as anticipated. We should recognize that the importance of speed in a wire transfer becomes even more critical in transactions involving different countries with, perhaps, different time zones. For example, if transmitting back Corfan was closed by the time the funds were received by Ocean Bank, Ocean Bank would not have been in a position to rectify the error until the next business day—which might well render the entire reason for the transfer moot.

Ocean Bank chose to use the beneficiary's name (which was properly included on the first wire transfer order) and "other identification of the beneficiary"—the fact that the account number given was similar to that of the beneficiary, as well as verification that the beneficiary was expecting the transfer in order to accept the wire transfer and properly credit the beneficiary's account. Ocean Bank decided that there was enough information in the first wire transfer order for it, after verification, to credit the transfer to the beneficiary's account. The order contained the beneficiary's name and account number, with a few zeros replacing the correct "6"s. This information referred not to a "nonexistent or unidentifiable person or account" but rather to an existing customer—the intended beneficiary—and to an identifiable (through "other identification") account.

I can find no common sense reason to prohibit Ocean Bank or other banks from accepting the responsibility that goes with choosing to use "other identification" in order to deposit funds into a customer's account. Basically, by verifying with Silva that he was the intended beneficiary, Ocean Bank was correcting Corfan Bank's error. Ocean Bank was seeking to aid its customer, the intended beneficiary of the funds, in getting the funds in an expeditious manner. Had Ocean Bank erroneously deposited the funds into the wrong account, it would have to face the liability associated with that decision. However, it should not face liability because it deposited the funds into the correct account—the intended beneficiary's account. Indeed, it was only because of Ocean Bank's actions that the intended beneficiary, Mr. Silva, received the funds from the first transfer.

Moreover, as the trial court emphasized, Florida's enactment of the U.C.C. did not abrogate other common law principles applicable to commercial transactions. A longstanding equitable tenet of Florida law is that, as between two innocent parties, the party best suited to prevent the loss caused by a third party wrongdoer must bear that loss. See Exchange Bank of St. Augustine v. Florida Nat'l Bank of Jacksonville, 292 So. 2d 361, 363 (Fla. 1974) ("[I]f one of two innocent parties is to suffer a loss, it should be borne by the one whose negligence put in motion the flow of circumstances causing the loss."). . . .

Here, Corfan put in issue the question of the correlative negligence of its and Ocean's actions. It is undisputed that Corfan was initially negligent in transmittal of the first wire transfer. It realized its mistake the following business day, and sent a second wire transfer with no indication it was a correction of the former. It was entirely unnecessary to transmit additional funds merely to correct the previous day's error. If it had not sent the additional funds, it is unlikely there would ever have been a dispute bringing the matter before us. Simply, Corfan Bank was in a better position to prevent the loss and, indeed, Corfan's negligence played a "substantial role" in that loss. These facts should prevent its recovery from Ocean Bank. . . .

For the above-mentioned reasons, I would affirm.

PROBLEM 260

Same facts as the last Problem, except that Saul is the one that gave his bank the incorrect account number, though he correctly listed the beneficiary's name. What result? See §4A-207(c) (and its Official Comment 3). What practical step does this section suggest to the bank?

Bank of America N.T.S.A. v. Sanati

California Court of Appeal, 1992
14 Cal. Rptr. 2d 615

Johnson, J.

In an action for unjust enrichment, money had and received, conversion, and declaratory relief, the trial court granted plaintiff's motion for summary judgment, finding that defendants had no defense to plaintiff's request for restitution for an erroneous fund transfer. Defendants appeal from the adverse judgment, claiming the trial court erroneously applied the common law pertaining to checks and negotiable instruments instead of the law specifically pertaining to funds transfers. We affirm.

Facts and Proceedings Below

In 1963 Hassan and Fatane Sanati were married in Tehran, Iran. They lived in Iran until Mrs. Fatane Sanati moved with their two children to Los Angeles in 1983. Between 1983 and 1987 Mr. Sanati spent nearly half his time living in Los Angeles. In 1987 Mr. Sanati permanently left the United States.

When Mr. Sanati left, he arranged for payments to be made to Mrs. Sanati in Los Angeles. He instructed Bank of America in London to send interest, as it accrued monthly from an account held in his name only, to an account he held jointly at Bank of America with Mrs. Sanati in Tarzana, California.

The amount of each interest payment was between $2,000 and $3,000.

On April 30, 1990, Bank of America in London erroneously sent the principal of Mr. Sanati's bank account as well as the accrued interest to the joint Sanati account in Tarzana, California. The amount of the erroneous fund transfer was $203,750. The next day Mrs. Sanati authorized her children to withdraw $200,000 from this account. These funds were then deposited into various bank accounts under Mrs. Sanati's and her children's names.

Bank of America (bank) immediately realized its error and requested reimbursement for the erroneous payment. Mrs. Sanati and her children, Babek and Haleh Sanati (collectively Sanatis or defendants) refused the bank's requests.

In July 1990, the bank filed a complaint against the Sanatis seeking restitution for the amount of the erroneous payment. Eventually Mr. Sanati's bank account in London was re-credited the amount of the principal transferred without his authority and he was dismissed as a defendant in the action. The remaining parties stipulated the funds from the erroneous transfer would be placed in a blocked account at Bank of America pending resolution of the litigation. . . .

The trial court granted the bank's motion [for summary judgment] and this appeal followed.

Discussion

I. Review of the Common Law Governing Erroneous Fund Transfers

At the time of the fund transfer in this case the law controlling the risks and liabilities of banks, beneficiaries and originators was general common law and equitable principles. Courts often borrowed concepts from Articles 3 and 4 of the Uniform Commercial Code governing commercial paper and negotiable instruments as well. This sometimes resulted in inconsistent decisions and was generally determined to be an unsatisfactory method of allocating risks and responsibilities in these widely used transactions generally involving large sums of money. Ultimately the American Law Institute developed section 4A of the Uniform Commercial Code to specifically deal with fund transfers. In 1990 the California Legislature adopted Article 4A of the Uniform Commercial Code as Division 11 of the California Uniform Commercial Code.

However, as stated, under the law in effect at the time of the fund transfer in this case, the general common law and equitable principles controlled. Under the law as it then existed, the bank was entitled to restitution from the beneficiaries for the amount of the unauthorized transfer despite its negligence under general legal principles of mistake and unjust enrichment. (Rest., Restitution, Sec. 59, com. a, p. 232; American Oil Service, Inc. v. Hope Oil Co. (1965) 233 Cal. App. 2d 822, 830; Frontier Refining Co. v. Home Bank (1969) 272 Cal. App. 2d 630, 634; Aebli v. Board of Education (1944) 62 Cal. App. 2d 706, 724-725; see also Annot., Recovery by Bank of Money Paid Out to Customer by Mistake (1981) 10 A.L.R.4th 524 Secs. 6-7 and cases collected.)

This rule, however, was subject to certain defenses. The most widely acknowledged defense to a claim for restitution for an erroneous transfer of funds was detrimental reliance by an innocent beneficiary. (Rest., Restitution Sec. 142, com. c; 1 Witkin Summary of Cal. Law (9th ed. 1987) Contracts, Sec. 94, pp.124-125; Doyle v. Matheron (1957) 148 Cal. App. 2d 521, 522.)

A less widely acknowledged defense to a claim for restitution was the "discharge for value" rule. (Rest., Restitution, Sec. 14.) This defense arises where there is a preexisting liquidated debt or lien owed to the beneficiary by the originator of the payment. If the originator or some third party erroneously gives the beneficiary funds at the originator's request, and the beneficiary in good faith believes the funds have been submitted in full or partial payment of that preexisting debt or lien and is unaware of the originator's or third party's mistake, the originator or third party will not be entitled to seek repayment from the beneficiary of the erroneously submitted funds. (1 Witkin (9th ed. 1987) Contracts, Secs., 94, 100, 102, pp.124, 129-130.) . . .

. . . Thus, under existing law the bank was entitled to seek restitution for the overpayment to defendants despite its negligence, unless defendants had detrimentally relied on the additional payment without notice of the mistake or unless the defendants had applied in good faith the additional erroneous payment to a preexisting debt or lien owed to them from Mr. Sanati.

II. THE BANK WAS ENTITLED TO JUDGMENT EVEN IF THE STATUTORY PROVISIONS GOVERNING ERRONEOUS FUND TRANSFERS CONTROLLED

On appeal defendants vigorously argue the trial court erred in applying to a fund transfer case the general common law pertaining to commercial paper and negotiable instruments.

They argue the court should have applied Division 11 of the California Uniform Commercial Code [UCC Article 4A] which governs the consequences of an erroneous execution of a payment order. Defendants also suggest that had the court applied the new law, summary judgment would have been inappropriate because there would have been a triable issue of material fact whether defendants believed in good faith the additional erroneous payment was sent in satisfaction or discharge of a preexisting debt or lien from Mr. Sanati.

Defendants' argument fails for two reasons. First, the trial court did not err in failing to apply the new fund transfer provisions of Division 11 of the California Uniform Commercial Code [UCC Article 4A]. The Legislature expressly stated that division only applied to fund transfers in which the originator's payment order was transmitted on or after January 1, 1991. (Stats. 1990, c. 125, Sec. 3.) The payment order in the present case was transmitted in April of 1990. Thus, by its terms the new fund transfer provisions of the California Uniform Commercial Code did not apply to the transfer in this case.

Secondly, even if the new fund transfer provisions were applied to this case, we conclude defendants have failed to create a triable issue of material fact whether Mr. Sanati owed them a preexisting debt or lien even assuming their good faith.

Section 11303 of the California Uniform Commercial Code [UCC §4A-303] discusses the effect of an erroneous transfer. That section merely restates existing law governing such errors and provides in pertinent part:

> (a) A receiving bank that (i) executes the payment order of the sender by issuing a payment order in an amount greater than the amount of the sender's order, . . . is entitled to payment of the amount of the sender's order. . . . The bank is entitled to recover from the beneficiary of the erroneous order the excess payment received to the extent allowed by the law governing mistake and restitution.

The comment to the Uniform Commercial Code which was incorporated into the comments in the California Uniform Commercial Code provides examples illustrating how this section should operate. The effect of the comment explicating this section is to expressly adopt the "discharge for value" rule found in §14 of the Restatement of Restitution.

The relevant comment [2] provides:

> Subsections (a) and (b) deal with cases in which the receiving bank executes by issuing a payment order in the wrong amount. If Originator ordered Originator's Bank to pay $1,000,000 to the account of Beneficiary in Beneficiary's Bank, but Originator's Bank erroneously instructed Beneficiary's Bank to pay $2,000,000 to Beneficiary's account, subsection (a) applies. If Beneficiary's Bank accepts the order of Originator's Bank, Beneficiary's Bank is entitled to receive $2,000,000 from Originator's Bank, but Originator's Bank is entitled to receive only $1,000,000 from Originator. Originator's Bank is entitled to recover the overpayment from Beneficiary to the extent allowed by the law governing mistake and restitution. Originator's Bank would normally have a right to recover the overpayment from Beneficiary, but in unusual cases the law of restitution might allow Beneficiary to keep all or part of the overpayment. For example, if Originator owed $2,000,000

> to Beneficiary and Beneficiary received the extra $1,000,000 in good faith in discharge of the debt, Beneficiary may be allowed to keep it. In this case Originator's Bank has paid an obligation of Originator and under the law of restitution, which applies through section 1-103, Originator's Bank would be subrogated to Beneficiary's rights against Originator on the obligation paid by Originator's Bank.

Thus, under this section defendants would be entitled to retain the erroneously sent funds if in good faith they believed the funds were sent to them in satisfaction of or in discharge of a valid preexisting debt or lien.

Toward this end, Fatane Sanati asserted she had a quasi community property interest in Mr. Sanati's London bank account as well as in all other property accumulated during their marriage. In an affidavit offered in opposition to the bank's motion for summary judgment Mrs. Sanati declared:

> . . . 3. I was married to Hassan Sanati, ("husband") on September 7, 1963 in Tehran, Iran where we resided until I came to Los Angeles with our two children.
>
> 4. My husband and I lived with our children, also defendants in this action, in Los Angeles since 1983. My husband was travelling in and out of the United States and until November of 1987, he had collectively spent 22 months in California during that period.
>
> 5. During our marriage we accumulated a substantial amount of money and real property, most of which was located in Iran and England.
>
> 6. My husband has always kept all of the bank accounts and most of the real property, wherever situated, in his own name.
>
> 7. Since he left in November, 1987, my children and I have been receiving interest monthly from our bank account in London, England to our account . . . at Bank of America, Tarzana branch. The account in London was opened by my husband with funds derived from our bank accounts and real property in Iran.
>
> 8. I had asked my husband on numerous occasions to transfer the London account to me in Los Angeles. Although he had agreed to do so on several occasions he had never done it.
>
> 9. My children and I have been virtual prisoners here and completely at my husband's mercy with regard to financial matters. For the last twenty-five years, my husband has always exercised complete control over all of our marital community assets worldwide.
>
> . . . 11. In May, 1990, the Bank of America in London transferred the monthly interest and the entire principal of the account to my and my husband's account in Bank of America in Tarzana.
>
> 12. I used some of these funds for the family and I removed the remainder to accounts under my control.
>
> . . . 17. Since the London account was transferred to our joint account in California, I have spoken to my husband via telephone. On several occasions,

he agreed to keep the transferred money in our joint account under both our names. However, to this date, he has not done so.

. . . 19. I have filed a petition for Dissolution of Marriage at the Los Angeles Superior Court on July 2, 1990. . . . The Summons and Complaint were personally served upon my husband, in Tehran, Iran, by Rosy Shahbodaghi, on September 24, 1990. I have instructed my counsel to enter his default therein. . . .

Thus, Mrs. Sanati's declaration raises a reasonable inference of a potential quasi community property interest in the funds in the London bank account held in Mr. Sanati's name alone. However, this evidence does not raise a reasonable inference of a preexisting debt or lien at the time of the transfer of the type recognized in those decisions applying the "discharge for value" rule.

For example, in Banque Worms v. Bank America International (S.D.N.Y. 1989) 726 F. Supp. 940, *aff'd,* (2d Cir. 1991) 928 F.2d 538, the case upon which defendants primarily rely, the debt was a bank loan. In that case the originator had an outstanding loan for $2,000,000 from Banque Worms. On the day before the erroneous transfer, Banque Worms notified the originator it was calling the loan. The next day Banque Worms received a wire transfer for $2,000,000 from Security Pacific International Bank (SPIB), the originator's bank, and applied it to the originator's outstanding loan balance.

Shortly thereafter Banque Worms received a second wire transfer from the originator's bank for $1,974,267.97 which was the amount the originator actually requested to be sent. Because it only had instructions for the latter payment, SPIB could not debit the originator's bank account for the first erroneous payment. Because Banque Worms received the payment in the good faith belief it was in response to their demand for repayment of the loan, the court held SPIB had to suffer the loss for the mistaken payment under the "discharge for value" rule.

Examples in the Restatement of Restitution describing the "discharge for value" rule describe debts that are liquidated, concrete and preexisting, not merely probable and undetermined. (E.g., Rest., Restitution, Sec. 14, com. b, illus. facts 1 [no restitution for proceeds erroneously used to pay existing mortgage on real estate]; illus. 2 [no restitution from city for property taxes paid on property not actually owned]; illus. 3 [no restitution where bank erroneously cashes customer's check given to payee in payment for services rendered]; illus. 4 [no restitution from judgment creditor for execution of judgment of wrong person's property].) No decision we are aware of has applied the discharge for value rule where the debt or lien in question was anything less than an objectively verifiable, preexisting, liquidated obligation. (See Rest., Restitution (append.), Sec. 14 and cases collected.) Indeed, allowing the rule to apply to debts or obligations any less substantial would risk destroying the certainty of the rule and allow the exception to control its application.

Consequently, it does not appear the "discharge for value" rule can be properly invoked in a case such as this where the alleged preexisting debt or lien is at best a probable yet undetermined interest in a portion of the funds in Mr. Sanati's bank account in London.[17]

The defendants do not contend they changed their position to their detriment in reliance on the erroneously transmitted funds. Nor do the defendants' opposition papers raise any other potential defense to the bank's action for restitution. Thus, in the absence of any viable defense, the bank was entitled to restitution from the beneficiaries for the erroneously transmitted funds. We therefore conclude the trial court did not err in finding the bank was entitled to judgment as a matter of law.

DISPOSITION

The judgment is affirmed. Each side to bear its costs of appeal.

D. *Unauthorized Funds Transfers*

Every payment system has a rule allocating loss in the event of unauthorized payments. A customer is not liable for unauthorized checks written on an account, unless the customer was negligent or failed to check bank statements, thus permitting multiple fraudulent checks to be written. A credit card holder is liable only for $50 of unauthorized use. A consumer is not liable for most debit transfers beyond $50, as long as the customer gives timely notice to the bank. For commercial funds transfers, UCC 4A places somewhat more risk on customers. As the following materials discuss, if the bank and the customer have agreed to use a commercially reasonable security procedure, the customer takes the loss for unauthorized transfers as long as the bank has followed the procedure in good faith. That is a significant risk for customers in a time where criminals use increasingly sophisticated means to hack into bank accounts with both technical tricks and social engineering. Many customers may not realize the risk to their bank accounts, thinking that they are only liable for actually authorized transfers.

17. This case would raise entirely different issues if, for example, there was a preexisting judgment dividing the parties' marital assets decreeing a sum certain of $200,000 or more in cash to be transferred to Mrs. Sanati as part of the settlement and that this amount was due and owing to her at the time of the erroneous wire transfer. But those are not the facts of this case. In fact, Mrs. Sanati did not file for dissolution of marriage until several months after the erroneous fund transfer.

Choice Escrow and Land Title, LLC v. BancorpSouth Bank

United States Court of Appeals, Eighth Circuit, 2014
754 F.3d 611

Wollman, Circuit Judge.

Internet fraudsters stole $440,000 from a bank account that Choice Escrow and Land Title, LLC (Choice), maintained at BancorpSouth Bank (BancorpSouth). Choice sued BancorpSouth for the lost funds, and BancorpSouth counterclaimed for attorney's fees. The questions presented in this case are thus (1) who should bear the loss of the funds from Choice's account, and (2) who should pay BancorpSouth's attorney's fees. The district court, interpreting Article 4A of the Uniform Commercial Code (U.C.C.), held that Choice should bear the loss of the funds from its account and that BancorpSouth should pay its own attorney's fees. We affirm the district court's loss-of-funds ruling, reverse its dismissal of BancorpSouth's counterclaim, and remand for further proceedings.

I.

This litigation began after an unknown third party accessed Choice's online bank account at BancorpSouth and instructed BancorpSouth to "wire" a large sum of money from Choice's account to a bank account in the Republic of Cypress. To wire money is to transfer it electronically, so named because it was once done via telegram. In a typical wire transfer, a bank's customer transmits instructions to the bank to transfer money from the customer's account to the account of a beneficiary; these instructions are called a payment order. Because the customer is not physically present at the bank, the bank uses security procedures, such as passwords and electronic tokens, to verify that the person sending the payment order is actually the customer. In this case, we confront what happens when those security procedures fail.

Choice is a Missouri company that provides real estate escrow services. When parties to a real estate transaction need a third party to hold money in escrow until closing, they give it to Choice for safekeeping. In 2009, Choice opened a trust account at BancorpSouth for this purpose: when a buyer entrusted funds to Choice, Choice deposited the funds in its account at BancorpSouth and then wired the money to the seller at closing. Choice's employees performed these tasks over the Internet using an online banking platform called InView. BancorpSouth provided Choice with four security measures designed to ensure that Choice's employees, and only Choice's employees, would be able to access Choice's account.

First, BancorpSouth required each InView user to register a unique user id and password. Whenever an employee of one of BancorpSouth's institutional customers wished to access the customer's online bank account, the employee would be prompted to enter this information. Without it, access to the account was impossible.

Second, BancorpSouth installed device authentication software called PassMark. When a customer's employee first registered for InView, PassMark recorded the IP address[18] of the employee's computer as well as information about the computer itself—information relating to, for instance, the computer's operating system, central processing unit, browser, screen, time zone settings, and language settings. Whenever any subsequent user attempted to access InView using that employee's user id and password, PassMark verified that the characteristics of that user's computer were consistent with the information PassMark had recorded about the employee's computer. In this way, PassMark verified that each InView user was accessing InView from a recognized computer. If a user attempted to access InView from an unrecognized computer, the user would be prompted to answer "challenge questions" to verify the user's identity. If the user answered these questions correctly, the new computer would be added to the list of recognized computers, and the user would be able to access InView.

Third, BancorpSouth allowed its customers to place dollar limits on the daily volume of wire transfer activity from their accounts. For instance, a customer could limit the daily volume of wire transfers to $10,000 per day, in which case any attempt to transfer more than $10,000 in a single day would be automatically denied. Choice declined to place daily transfer limits on its account.

Fourth, BancorpSouth offered its customers a security measure called "dual control." Under this system, when an InView user submitted a payment order, InView would not send the order to the bank immediately; rather, the request would create a "pending" payment order that would appear in a separate queue in InView. To send a pending payment order to the bank, a second authorized user, using a unique user id and password, would have to log in to InView and separately approve the pending payment order. If a customer declined the use of dual control, BancorpSouth required that customer to sign a waiver acknowledging that it was waiving dual control and that it understood the risks associated with using a single-control (i.e., single-user) security system.

Choice declined the use of dual control and signed the requisite waiver. Thus, Choice's account at BancorpSouth was protected only by (1) the user ID's and passwords of its employees, and (2) PassMark. Choice authorized two of its employees, Cara Thulin and Brooke Black, to use InView, and it issued each employee a unique user id and password for this purpose.

18. IP stands for Internet Protocol. An IP address is a series of numbers that identifies a computer or other device on a network.

With these security measures in place, Choice could issue a payment order by taking the following steps: First, either Thulin or Black would access BancorpSouth's website and log in to InView using her user ID and password. Second, PassMark would verify that Thulin or Black was accessing InView from a recognized computer by checking the IP address and other specifications of the computer. If the user was accessing InView from an unrecognized computer, she would be prompted to answer challenge questions. Once the user cleared PassMark, either by using a recognized computer or by correctly answering the challenge questions, she would gain access to Choice's bank account via InView. From there, the user could issue payment orders to BancorpSouth and, as long as Choice had enough funds in its account, those orders would be sent to one of six BancorpSouth employees responsible for routing Choice's payment orders. That employee would then execute the payment order based on the information contained therein, and BancorpSouth would debit the funds from Choice's account and send Choice a fax confirmation of the wire transfer.

In November 2009, Choice received an e-mail from one of its underwriters describing a "phishing" scam in which an unscrupulous person tricks an unsuspecting Internet user into downloading a computer virus, uses the virus to collect the victim's user id's and passwords, and then uses that information to issue fraudulent payment orders to the victim's bank, transferring money from the victim's account to overseas banks beyond the reach of U.S. authorities.[19] Jim Payne, the Director of Business Development at Choice, forwarded the e-mail to BancorpSouth on November 11, 2009, with the following note:

> Please read the email forwarded from one of our underwriters. They suggest a plan of action that included limiting wires to foreign banks. Can we implement this and to what extent would our liability be if fraudulent wire transfers were to occur?

Ashley Kester of BancorpSouth responded two days later:

> Hi Jim, sorry to just now be responding. I had to do some research to find out if this was possible. We are unable to stop just foreign wires, the solution is

19. As another court has explained:

> Phishing involves an attempt to acquire information such as usernames, passwords, or financial data by a perpetrator masquerading as a legitimate enterprise. Typically, the perpetrator will provide an e-mail or link that directs the victim to enter or update personal information at a phony website that mimics an established, legitimate website which the victim either has used before or perceives to be a safe place to enter information.

Patco Constr. Co. v. People's United Bank, 684 F.3d 197, 204 (1st Cir. 2012).

> dual control. We always recommend dual control on wires. We discussed this when we setup InView and you decided to waive the dual control. Would you like to consider adding it now? This is the best solution, that way if someone in the company is compromised then the hacker would not be able to initiate a wire with just the one user's information.

After Kester described the mechanics of dual control to Payne, Payne e-mailed Kester once again declining the use of dual control:

> Actually I don't think that would be a good procedure for us—lots of times Paige [Payne] is here by herself and that would be really tough unless we all shared pass words.

Sometime after this exchange, a Choice employee fell prey to a phishing attack and contracted a computer virus. This virus gave an unknown third party access to the employee's username and password and allowed the third party to mimic the computer's IP address and other characteristics, rendering InView's password prompts and PassMark's device authentication procedures ineffectual. On March 17, 2010, this third party accessed Choice's online bank account and issued a payment order instructing BancorpSouth to transfer $440,000 from Choice's account to a banking institution in the Republic of Cypress. BancorpSouth accepted and executed the payment order. After attempts to recover the funds failed, Choice sued BancorpSouth for the lost funds, and BancorpSouth counterclaimed for attorney's fees based on an indemnification agreement that it had executed with Choice.

The district court granted summary judgment to BancorpSouth after concluding that Article 4A of the U.C.C. allocated the risk of loss from the fraudulent payment order to Choice. The court then dismissed BancorpSouth's counterclaim for attorney's fees on the pleadings after concluding that the indemnification agreement at issue conflicted with the provisions of Article 4A and was thus unenforceable.

II.

We review the district court's grant of summary judgment to BancorpSouth *de novo*, viewing the evidence in the light most favorable to Choice. Hill v. Walker, 737 F.3d 1209, 1216 (8th Cir. 2013). Summary judgment is appropriate when there is "no genuine dispute as to any material fact and the movant is entitled to judgment as a matter of law." Fed. R. Civ. P. 56(a). The parties agree that Article 4A, which Mississippi enacted in its entirety in 1991, *see* Miss. Code Ann. §75-4A-101 *et seq.*, governs this dispute.

Article 4A was drafted in 1989 to account for a dramatic increase in wire transfers between financial institutions and other commercial entities, commonly called wholesale wire transfers to differentiate them from wire transfers by consumers, which are governed by a separate federal statute, *see* 15 U.S.C. §1693. At the time Article 4A was drafted, the total volume of these wholesale transfers exceeded one trillion dollars per day, *see* U.C.C. Art. 4A Refs. & Annos. prefatory note, yet "there was no comprehensive body of law—statutory or judicial—that defined the juridical nature of a funds transfer or the rights and obligations flowing from payment orders[,]" Miss. Code Ann. §75-4A-102 cmt. The drafters of Article 4A sought to create a legal framework that balanced these rights and obligations between the bank and its institutional customer. As the Official Comments note:

> Funds transfers involve competing interests—those of the banks that provide funds transfer services and the commercial and financial organizations that use the services, as well as the public interest. These competing interests were represented in the drafting process and they were thoroughly considered. The rules that emerged represent a careful and delicate balancing of those interests and are intended to be the exclusive means of determining the rights, duties and liabilities of the affected parties in any situation covered by particular provisions of the Article.

Id.

One of the liabilities balanced by Article 4A is the risk that a third party will steal a customer's identity and issue a fraudulent payment order to the bank. Generally, the bank bears this risk. Miss. Code Ann. §75-4A-204. In two circumstances, however, the bank may shift the risk of a fraudulent payment order to the customer. The first is the rare circumstance in which the bank can prove that the customer "authorized the order or is otherwise bound by it under the law of agency." Miss. Code Ann. §75-4A-202(a). This circumstance is rare because ordinarily the bank has "no way of determining the identity or the authority of the person who caused the message to be sent," and thus "[c]ommon law concepts of authority of agent to bind principal are not helpful" in determining whether a customer is bound by a payment order issued in its name. Miss. Code Ann. §75-4A-203 cmt. 1.

Because of this inadequacy, Article 4A contemplates a second circumstance in which a customer will bear the risk of a fraudulent payment order. If a bank and its customer agree to implement a security procedure designed to protect themselves against fraud, then the customer will bear the risk of a fraudulent payment order if:

> (i) the security procedure is a commercially reasonable method of providing security against unauthorized payment orders, and
>
> (ii) the bank proves that it accepted the payment order in good faith and in compliance with the security procedure and any written agreement or instruction of the customer restricting acceptance of payment orders issued in the name of the customer.

Miss. Code Ann. §75-4A-202(b). Article 4A thus permits the bank to take steps to protect itself from liability by implementing commercially reasonable security procedures. If the bank complies with these procedures in good faith and in accordance with the customer's instructions, the customer will bear the risk of loss from a fraudulent payment order. Choice concedes that BancorpSouth complied with its security procedures in accepting the March 17 payment order. Thus, BancorpSouth is entitled to summary judgment if the undisputed facts show (1) that BancorpSouth's security procedures were commercially reasonable, (2) that BancorpSouth accepted the payment order in good faith, and (3) that BancorpSouth accepted the payment order in compliance with Choice's written instructions.

A.

We first consider whether BancorpSouth's security procedures were commercially reasonable. We conclude that they were.

1.

A "security procedure" is a "procedure established by agreement of a customer and a receiving bank for the purpose of . . . verifying that a payment order . . . is that of the customer." Miss. Code Ann. §75-4A-201. As this definition makes clear, only security measures "established by agreement" are considered "security procedures" for purposes of Article 4A; security measures implemented unilaterally by the bank are irrelevant. *See* Miss. Code Ann. §75-4A-201 cmt.

There is one exception to the "established by agreement" rule. If a bank offers its customer a security procedure, and the customer declines to use that procedure and agrees in writing to be bound by payment orders issued in its name and accepted by the bank in accordance with another security procedure, then the customer will bear the risk of loss from a fraudulent payment order if the *declined* procedure was commercially reasonable. Miss. Code Ann. §75-4A-202(c). To synthesize the rule and its exception: in assessing commercial reasonableness, courts consider (1) security measures that the bank and customer agree to implement, and (2) security measures that the bank offers to the customer but the customer declines, as long as the customer agrees in writing to be bound by payment orders issued in its name in and accepted by the bank in accordance with another procedure.

Our first task is determining which of BancorpSouth's security measures fit this definition. Choice does not dispute that BancorpSouth's password prompts, daily transfer limits, and dual control system are security procedures that we may consider under Article 4A, but it asserts that PassMark does not qualify as a security procedure because BancorpSouth did not mention PassMark in any of its written contracts with Choice or formally offer Choice the option to use the software.

Notwithstanding the absence of any explicit reference to PassMark in the parties' written contracts, however, there is ample evidence that the parties agreed to implement PassMark. An agreement under the U.C.C. need not be a written contract; rather, an " '[a]greement,' as distinguished from 'contract,' means the bargain of the parties in fact, as found in their language or inferred from other circumstances[.]" Miss. Code Ann. §75-1-201. All BancorpSouth customers were required to register for PassMark when they signed up for InView. It was thus impossible for any InView user not to know that they were also using PassMark, and any customer that declined to register for PassMark would be unable to use InView. Additionally, the addendum to the Business Services Agreement between Choice and BancorpSouth states that Choice "assumes full responsibility and risk of loss for all transactions made by BancorpSouth . . . in accordance with . . . the procedures set forth in the InView User Manual(s) and Help screens." BancorpSouth posted a digital manual entitled "PassMark Login Security" on the InView portal, so PassMark was incorporated at least implicitly into the parties' written contracts. In light of these facts, we are satisfied that PassMark was "established by agreement" between Choice and BancorpSouth. We thus consider all four of BancorpSouth's security measures—password protection, daily transfer limits, PassMark, and dual control—in determining whether BancorpSouth's security procedures were commercially reasonable.

2.

In making this determination, we consider:

> the wishes of the customer expressed to the bank, the circumstances of the customer known to the bank, including the size, type, and frequency of payment orders normally issued by the customer to the bank, alternative security procedures offered to the customer, and security procedures in general use by customers and receiving banks similarly situated.

Miss. Code Ann. §75-4A-202. The commercial reasonableness standard is designed "to encourage banks to institute reasonable safeguards against fraud but not to make them insurers against fraud." Miss. Code Ann. §75-4A-203 cmt. 4. Thus, "[t]he standard is not whether the security procedure is the best available. Rather it is whether the procedure is reasonable for the particular customer and the particular bank, which is a lower standard." *Id.*

At the threshold, we reject Choice's argument that a commercially reasonable security procedure must include a process whereby a human being manually reviews every payment order submitted to the bank to ensure that no irregularities exist—what Choice calls "transactional analysis." Article

4A never mentions transactional analysis, but Choice argues that because commercial reasonableness depends on the "size, type, and frequency" of a customer's payment orders, a commercially reasonable security procedure must differentiate between payment orders based on these factors. Choice further asserts that transactional analysis is the only way to achieve this differentiation.

This argument misunderstands Article 4A's intended audience. Article 4A does not instruct the bank to consider the "size, type, and frequency" of each payment order it receives in determining if those payment orders are potentially fraudulent; it instructs the court to consider these factors in determining if a bank's security procedure is commercially reasonable—in other words, that the commercial reasonableness of a bank's security procedure depends on whether that procedure is adequate to screen payment orders of the size, type, and frequency normally issued to the bank. Such a procedure might involve "algorithms or other codes, identifying words or numbers, encryption, callback procedures, or similar security devices," Miss. Code Ann. §75-4A-201, none of which differentiate between payment orders based on their "size, type, [or] frequency." Yet notwithstanding that "[t]he concept of what is commercially reasonable in each case is flexible," Miss. Code Ann. §75-4A-203 cmt. 4, Choice argues that even all of these procedures combined would be commercially unreasonable, as none of them involve transactional analysis. This attempt to graft a rigid, foreign standard onto the commercial reasonableness inquiry is at odds with essentially all of Article 4A, and we reject it.

Nor does the record evidence establish that BancorpSouth was required to perform transactional analysis under these specific circumstances. The only person who mentioned transactional analysis was Choice's expert, who stated in his report that transactional analysis "could be a very effective aid in deterring fraudulent payment order transactions" and "would . . . be in line with Article 4A202(c)." Neither statement indicates that BancorpSouth's failure to use transactional analysis was commercially unreasonable, and at any rate Choice's expert admitted in his deposition that, under the circumstances of this case, dual control could be a commercially reasonable security procedure. BancorpSouth's Senior Vice President further testified that BancorpSouth conducts tens of thousands of wire transfers on behalf of its roughly 400,000 checking account customers and that reviewing each one of these transactions would be impracticable. Choice has presented no evidence to contradict this testimony and, indeed, has failed to present any evidence tending to show that a genuine question of fact exists as to whether BancorpSouth was required to perform transactional analysis.

Having determined that BancorpSouth was not required to perform transactional analysis, we turn to what it was required to do. We begin at the broadest level of generality, by considering "security procedures in general use by customers and receiving banks similarly situated[,]" Miss. Code Ann. §75-4A-202. Our primary authority in this endeavor is a 2005 report published by the Federal Financial Institutions Examination Council (FFIEC) called "Authentication in an Internet Banking Environment," (the Guidance), *see* Fed. Fin. Insts. Examination Council, Authentication in an Internet Banking Environment (Oct. 12, 2005), *available at* https://www ffiec.gov/pdf/ authentication_guidance.pdf. The parties agree that the Guidance provides applicable standards of commercial reasonableness in this case.

The Guidance draws a basic distinction between single-factor and multifactor authentication. As the Guidance explains, most modern security procedures involve one or more of the following three factors:

(1) Something the user knows, like a password or PIN;
(2) Something the user has, like an ATM card or smart card; and
(3) Something the user is, like a person with a unique fingerprint or biometric characteristic.

Id. at 3. Security procedures that involve only one of the above three factors, according to the Guidance, are inadequate to safeguard against modern Internet fraud. Accordingly, the Guidance recommends that financial institutions implement security procedures that use two or more of the above factors in combination. An ATM, for instance, uses a multifactor security procedure that requires the user to provide something the user has (an ATM card) as well as something the user knows (a PIN) to use the machine. BancorpSouth's security procedures also used multifactor authentication: to access InView, a BancorpSouth customer had to enter the correct password (something the user knows) and use a recognized computer (something the user has).

Of course, cyber-crime evolves rapidly, and guidance issued in 2005 may become obsolete in subsequent years. The Guidance thus states that banks should "[a]djust, as appropriate, their information security program[s] in light of any relevant changes in technology, the sensitivity of its customer information, and internal or external threats to information." *Id.* As BancorpSouth's expert acknowledged, during 2009 and 2010, cybercriminals began using more sophisticated software that could "take on the identity and internet configuration of the victim organization's personnel that were involved in the wire transfer process," emulating the computer's IP address and using the employee's passwords to bypass even multifactor security procedures. This testimony suggests that multifactor authentication alone may have been an inadequate safeguard against Internet fraud perpetrated in 2010.

BancorpSouth responded to this new threat by offering its customers dual control, which dramatically reduces the possibility of such a breach.

With dual control in place, a customer's account remains secure even if a third party manages to obtain an employee's password and IP address; to issue a payment order, that third party would have to obtain a second, wholly independent set of identifying information. Phishing scams work because one out of every few thousand recipients of a malicious e-mail will click on a link containing a virus, and the probability that two employees at the same company would fall for the same scam is quite low. Moreover, without a second user's information, any attempt by a third party to issue a payment order would alert the customer to the security breach by creating a pending payment order that no one at the company had authorized.

Accordingly, because BancorpSouth comported with the 2005 Guidance and expanded its security procedures to address security threats that arose after 2005, we conclude that BancorpSouth's security procedures comported with the standards set by "security procedures in general use by customers and receiving banks similarly situated."

This does not end the inquiry, however: we must also consider whether BancorpSouth's security procedures were suitable for Choice given "the wishes of the customer expressed to the bank" and "the circumstances of the customer known to the bank, including the size, type, and frequency of payment orders normally issued by the customer to the bank." Miss. Code Ann. §75-4A-202.

Contrary to Choice's assertion, this does not mean that a bank must always use a different security procedure for each customer. The Official Comment to §75-4A-203 states that "[a] receiving bank *might* have several security procedures that are designed to meet the varying needs of different customers" (emphasis added), but it does not make this a requirement. If a bank develops a single effective and versatile security procedure, it is not commercially unreasonable for the bank to use that security procedure for the majority of its customers and depart from the procedure only when necessary.

Choice asserts that such a departure was necessary in this case because Choice did not have enough employees on hand to use dual control effectively—in other words, that dual control was commercially unreasonable given the "circumstances of the customer known to the bank" and the "wishes of the customer expressed to the bank." As set forth above, when BancorpSouth offered Choice dual control for the second time, on November 13, 2009, Jim Payne of Choice responded, "Actually, I don't think that would be a good procedure for us—lots of times Paige [Payne] is here by herself and that would be really tough unless we all shared pass words."

Assuming that this statement is true, it does not mean that dual control was any less suitable for Choice than the single-control option Choice ultimately chose to implement. Paige Payne was not an authorized InView user, and if she was in the office by herself, she would have been unable to issue payment orders regardless of whether Choice had implemented single or dual control.

Perhaps Jim Payne intended in his e-mail to refer to either Thulin or Black, the two Choice employees authorized to use InView, instead of Paige Payne. But both Thulin and Black were full-time employees who were typically in the office during normal business hours. To the extent that Choice needed to issue payment orders outside of these hours, dual control would have been no less suitable for Choice than single control, since neither Black nor Thulin would have been in the office at that time.

Even if only one authorized InView user was in the office at certain times, dual control would not have been a major hindrance on Choice's ability to issue payment orders. Simultaneous approval of a payment order is not required under dual control; one employee may create a pending payment order in the morning, and a second employee may come into the office in the afternoon and confirm the pending payment order. Choice has not argued that it needed to be able to wire money at a moment's notice; indeed, the nature of its business suggests that Choice generally knew beforehand when it needed to wire money to beneficiaries (namely, the date of a real estate closing) and that it could plan accordingly. And even if a quick response time was necessary in some circumstances, Choice could have solved this problem by authorizing employees besides Black and Thulin to use InView.

In short, no genuine dispute of fact exists as to whether BancorpSouth's security procedures were commercially reasonable. Rather, this appears to be a case where "an informed customer refuses a security procedure that is commercially reasonable and suitable for that customer and insists on using a higher-risk procedure because it is more convenient or cheaper[,]" in which case "the customer has voluntarily assumed the risk of failure of the procedure and cannot shift the loss to the bank." *See* Miss. Code Ann. §75-4A-203 cmt. 4. Choice knew that dual control provided a reliable safeguard against Internet fraud, and it explicitly assumed the risks of a lesser procedure notwithstanding the relative ease with which it could have implemented dual control. Accordingly, we conclude that BancorpSouth's security procedures, which included password protection, daily transfer limits, device authentication, and dual control, were commercially reasonable.

B.

The risk of a fraudulent payment order remains with BancorpSouth, however, unless BancorpSouth also "proves that it accepted the [March 17] payment order in good faith and in compliance with the security procedure and any written agreement or instruction of the customer restricting acceptance of payment orders issued in the name of the customer." Miss. Code

Ann. §75-4A-202(b). Choice asserts that BancorpSouth did not accept the payment order in good faith and that it violated Choice's written instructions in doing so. We disagree.

1.

Good faith "means honesty in fact and the observance of reasonable commercial standards of fair dealing." Miss. Code Ann. §75-1-201(b)(20). This two-pronged definition has both a subjective component—honesty in fact—and an objective component—the observance of reasonable commercial standards of fair dealing. In re Nieves, 648 F.3d 232, 239 (3d Cir. 2011). We are concerned with the latter prong in this case: Choice concedes that BancorpSouth accepted the payment order honestly, but it asserts that BancorpSouth did not observe reasonable commercial standards of fair dealing in doing so.

The U.C.C.'s requirement that parties to a contract abide by reasonable commercial standards of fair dealing—and the good faith doctrine generally—is designed to ensure that each party to the contract performs its contractual duties in a way that reflects the reasonable expectations of the other party. As the Permanent Editorial Board Commentary explains:

> The principal author of the Code, Karl Llewellyn, recognized that parties develop expectations over time against the background of commercial practices and that if commercial law fails to account for those practices, it will cut against the parties' actual expectations. . . . [T]he doctrine of good faith . . . [thus] serves as a directive to protect the reasonable expectations of the contracting parties.

U.C.C. App. II Commentary 10; *see also* Restatement (Second) of Contracts §205 cmt. a ("Good faith performance or enforcement of a contract emphasizes faithfulness to an agreed common purpose and consistency with the justified expectations of the other party."). One of the challenges in applying the good faith doctrine in the Article 4A context is the apparent overlap between a bank's compliance with "commercial standards of fair dealing" and its compliance with "commercially reasonable" security procedures. It may appear at first glance that these inquiries are redundant, and some courts have suggested (although not in the Article 4A context) that this is indeed the case. *See* Watson Coatings, Inc. v. Am. Exp. Travel Related Servs., Inc., 436 F.3d 1036, 1042 (8th Cir. 2006); DBI Architects, P.C. v. Am. Express Travel-Related Servs. Co., 388 F.3d 886, 895 (D.C. Cir. 2004).

But while there may be some evidentiary overlap between the commercial reasonableness of a bank's security procedures and its compliance with reasonable commercial standards of fair dealing, we do not believe that the two inquiries are coextensive. While the commercial reasonableness inquiry concerns the adequacy of a bank's security procedures, the objective good faith inquiry concerns a bank's acceptance of payment orders in accordance with those security procedures. In other words, technical compliance with a security procedure is not enough under Article 4A; instead, as the above-quoted materials indicate, the bank must abide by its procedures in a way that reflects the parties' reasonable expectations as to how those procedures will operate.

Thus, the focus of our good faith inquiry is on the aspects of wire transfer that are left to the bank's discretion. *See* Milford-Bennington R. Co., Inc. v. Pan Am Railways, Inc., 695 F.3d 175, 179 (1st Cir. 2012) ("The good-faith obligation limits the parties' discretion in contractual performance."). Where, as here, a bank's security procedures do not depend on the judgment or discretion of its employees, the scope of the good-faith inquiry under Article 4A is correspondingly narrow. The automation of agreed-upon procedures generally ensures that those procedures will operate in a way that is consistent with the customer's expectations, as long as the procedures do not "unreasonably vary from general banking usage"—in other words, as long as they are commercially reasonable. *Watson Coatings*, 436 F.3d at 1042. We have already determined that BancorpSouth's security procedures were commercially reasonable, and we need not revisit that determination here. Rather, to establish that it acted in good faith, BancorpSouth must establish that its employees accepted and executed the March 17 payment order in a way that comported with Choice's reasonable expectations, as established by reasonable commercial standards of fair dealing.

We are satisfied that BancorpSouth has met this burden. Choice was well aware that the only time BancorpSouth employees saw its payment orders was after those orders had already cleared BancorpSouth's security procedures. Choice was also aware that the role of those employees was not to check for any irregularities but to route these payment orders to the correct beneficiaries. Jeff Jaggers, a senior vice president at BancorpSouth, testified that in his thirty years of banking experience it was "normal banking practice" for a bank's employees to route payment orders submitted in compliance with a security procedure without conducting any further review to determine if those payment orders were somehow suspicious. And even if BancorpSouth's employees should have been expected to conduct some commonsense manual review of payment orders—for instance, by flagging a payment order for $10,000,000 from a customer with only $10,000 in its account—the March 17 payment order was not so unusual that it should have raised eyebrows. BancorpSouth provided evidence that the March 17 payment order was not the largest order that Choice had ever submitted and that Choice's wire transfers followed no general pattern and varied in size from a few thousand dollars to a few hundred thousand dollars. In response, Choice asserts that the memo line of the March 17 payment order, which read "invoice: equipment," was inconsistent with Choice's business and with its past practice in issuing payment orders. Choice, of course, is a real estate escrow company with little use for equipment, and the memo line had been filled out in only 13% of Choice's previous payment orders. But the memo line's two-word description does not make the March 17 payment order so suspicious that BancorpSouth acted in bad faith by failing to notice it; if BancorpSouth's employees had to remember the business of each of BancorpSouth's 400,000 clients to ensure that the memo line of each payment order made sense, BancorpSouth would not be in business long. This is not a case where a bank "allow[ed] overdrafts totaling *$5 million* from a single account that usually ha[d] a zero balance." Experi-Metal, Inc. v. Comerica Bank, 2011 WL 2433383, at *14 (E.D. Mich. June 13, 2011). This is a case where a bank promptly executed a payment order that had cleared the bank's commercially reasonable security procedures and that the bank had no independent reason to suspect was fraudulent. Accordingly, we conclude that BancorpSouth has met its burden of establishing beyond genuine factual dispute that it accepted the March 17 payment order in good faith.

2.

The last element BancorpSouth must prove to shift the loss from the March 17 payment order to Choice is that BancorpSouth accepted the payment order in compliance with Choice's instructions. Choice attempts to shortcut the issue by arguing that BancorpSouth admitted in its answer that it had violated Choice's instructions by "Admit[ting]" the following allegation in Choice's complaint:

> 61. Choice by email on or about November 11, 2009, from Jim Payne to Ashley Kester, expressed to BancorpSouth its wish, requirement and/or instruction that BancorpSouth limit transfers to foreign banks.

According to Choice, BancorpSouth's response of "Admit" to this paragraph amounts to an admission that BancorpSouth violated Choice's "wish, requirement, and/or instruction" to limit foreign wire transfers. The merit of this argument depends on how one interprets "and/or." Choice asserts that "and/or" means "and," which is incorrect: "and/or" is an ambiguous phrase that usually means "one or the other or both." *See* Bryan A. Garner, Garner's Modern American Usage 45 (3d ed. 2009). The natural reading of BancorpSouth's admission is thus that Choice had expressed to BancorpSouth its "wish, requirement, or instruction, or some combination of the three" that BancorpSouth stop foreign wires. A judicial admission must be deliberate, clear, and unambiguous, *see* MacDonald v. Gen. Motors Corp., 110 F.3d 337, 340 (6th Cir. 1997); Rowe Int'l, Inc. v. J-B Enterprises, Inc., 647 F.2d 830, 836 (8th Cir. 1981), and Choice's use of the phrase "and/or" in its complaint renders BancorpSouth's subsequent concession anything but.

Turning to the substance of this dispute, we conclude that BancorpSouth did not violate any of Choice's instructions by accepting the March 17 payment order. The only evidence of an instruction is the November 11 e-mail from Jim Payne to Ashley Kester asking if it would be possible to stop foreign wire transfers. Payne himself agreed in his deposition that the e-mail was properly characterized as an "inquir[y]," and when BancorpSouth replied that it was "unable to stop just foreign wires," Choice did not press the issue further. This exchange does not constitute an instruction.

In sum, because BancorpSouth's security procedures were commercially reasonable, because BancorpSouth complied with its security procedures and with Choice's instructions, and because BancorpSouth accepted the March 17 payment order in good faith, the loss of funds from Choice's account falls on Choice.

III.

Finally, we turn to whether BancorpSouth is entitled to attorney's fees based on an indemnification agreement it executed with Choice. The district court dismissed BancorpSouth's counterclaim for attorney's fees on the pleadings after concluding that the indemnification provision in question conflicted with the provisions of Article 4A and was thus unenforceable. We review the dismissal of this counterclaim *de novo*. Levy v. Ohl, 477 F.3d 988, 991 (8th Cir. 2007).

The indemnification provision states as follows:

> As long as BancorpSouth has performed as provided in Section 8 above, the Customer shall indemnify and hold BancorpSouth harmless from any and all claims, damages, losses, liabilities, and costs and expenses, including reasonable attorney's fees, which relate in any manner to the Services performed under this Agreement.

"Unless displaced by the particular provisions of the Uniform Commercial Code, the principles of law and equity . . . supplement" the provisions of Article 4A. Miss. Code Ann. §75-1-103. But Article 4A preempts common law causes of action "in two specific areas: (1) where the common law claims would create rights, duties, or liability inconsistent with [Article 4A]; and (2) where the circumstances giving rise to the common law claims are specifically covered by [Article 4A]." Zengen, Inc. v. Comerica Bank, 41 Cal. 4th 239, 59 Cal. Rptr. 3d 240, 158 P.3d 800, 808 (2007). The district court, acknowledging that the issue was a "close call," held that the above-quoted indemnification provision would create rights and liabilities that were inconsistent with Article 4A because the provision "could effectively require

Choice to pay back to [BancorpSouth] those amounts that [BancorpSouth] might owe to Choice under [Article 4A]." D. Ct. Order of Aug. 30, 2012, at 3. In other words, by requiring Choice to indemnify BancorpSouth for all "damages, losses, [and] liabilities" stemming from a fraudulent payment order, the indemnification provision would frustrate Article 4A's attempts to balance this risk between the bank and its customer.

But the section of the indemnification provision dealing with "damages, losses, [and] liabilities" is not at issue in BancorpSouth's counterclaim. BancorpSouth's counterclaim seeks attorney's fees, not damages stemming from the fraudulent payment order, and Article 4A contains no provision allocating attorney's fees between the bank and its customer in the event of litigation. Although awarding attorney's fees to a bank under an indemnification agreement might reduce a customer's overall recovery against that bank, it would do so for reasons extrinsic to Article 4A's attempts to balance the risk of loss due to a fraudulent payment order. We thus conclude that the portion of the indemnification provision relating to attorney's fees is not inconsistent with Article 4A and that BancorpSouth may seek attorney's fees from Choice under this provision.

IV.

We affirm the district court's grant of summary judgment to BancorpSouth, reverse the district court's dismissal of BancorpSouth's counterclaim on the pleadings, and remand for further proceedings consistent with this opinion.

PROBLEM 261

Business Corporation paid all of its bills by funds transfers through its bank, Original National Bank (ONB). These two entities signed an agreement providing that funds transfers could be made only if the originator included in the payment order a secret code number, which would change daily according to the number assigned by a computer program accessed by both the corporation and the bank. The Business Corporation employee in charge of approving its payment orders was John Smith and he was so proud of his new job that he described it in detail (including how to access the secret code) to his wife, Mary. Mary, who was the owner of her own computer repair business, became curious whether, from the safety of her own home, her skills as a computer hacker would permit her to access Business Corporation's files, issue phony payment orders, and have ONB execute them. She was amazed how easy it all was, and by the end of the day, she had ordered ONB to transfer $830,756 to the account of her business at another bank. The next morning she withdrew the money from that account, left her husband a "Dear John" letter, and has not been heard from since. Can Business Corporation demand that ONB recredit its account for the amount she stole? See §§4A-201, 4A-202(b), and 4A-203. How long does Business Corporation have in which to demand a recredit of its account? See §4A-505; Regatos v. North Fork Bank, 5 N.Y.3d 395, 838 N.E.2d 629 (2005).

Official Comment 5 to §4A-203:

> Breach of a commercially reasonable security procedure requires that the person committing the fraud have knowledge of how the procedure works and knowledge of codes, identifying devices, and the like. That person may also need access to transmitting facilities through an access device or other software in order to breach the security procedure. This confidential information must be obtained either from a source controlled by the customer or from a source controlled by the receiving bank. If the customer can prove that the person committing the fraud did not obtain the confidential information from an agent or former agent of the customer or from a source controlled by the customer, the loss is shifted to the bank.

PROBLEM 262

Suppose, in the last Problem, the security procedure between the parties had one other wrinkle: if the amount transferred was above $500,000, the secret code had to begin with the letter "A," but the secret code itself did not tell senders this. Mary didn't know about it either (John had forgotten to mention this extra step), so when she transferred the $830,756 to her bank account, she failed to put the "A" in front of the secret code. ONB accepted the payment order anyway when it made the funds transfer to Mary's bank. Now what? See §4A-205(a)(1).

PROBLEM 263

Backwater Builders used funds transfers from its account at Schadenfreude Bank to pay suppliers, sending about seven transfers a month to local contractors, none more than $7,000. One afternoon, Schadenfreude Bank received 19 payment orders on Backwater Builders' account, ordering the transfer of a total of $450,000 to various accounts in foreign countries, most of which happen to lack extradition treaties with the United States. The staff at Schadenfreude Bank's wire transfer department recognized that the orders were likely the result of a phishing expedition, and checked that the orders all complied with the security procedure that Backwater Builders agreed to, including usernames, passwords and answers to automated challenge questions. The wire department chief smiled wryly and said, "Not my problem. Orders are in order." The staff then wired the funds abroad, never to be seen again. It turns out that Backwater Builders' trusting bookkeeper had been tricked by a phony email into submitting his username, password, and challenge question answer to some nefarious hacker. Is Backwater Builders obliged to reimburse Schadenfreude Bank? Cf. Experi-Metal, Inc. v. Comerica Bank, 2011 WL 2433383 (E.D. Mich. 2011).

E. Conclusion

Section 4A-501(a) contains an important rule for banks: "Except as otherwise provided in this Article, the rights and obligations of a party to a funds transfer may be varied by agreement of the affected party." If you, as counsel for the bank, don't like the results explained above, negotiate a contract with those involved that reaches a happier conclusion. Be warned, however, that in various places throughout Article 4A, the sections do restrict the right of the parties to change the Code's rules by agreement. For example, §4A-404(c) provides: "The right of a beneficiary to receive payment and damages as stated in subsection (a) may not be varied by agreement or a funds-transfer system rule." Thus the contract negotiated by the bank must be checked against Article 4A carefully to ensure that it does not attempt impermissible variations.[20] Banks do not charge much for the execution and acceptance of payment orders, and the system would collapse if the banks faced enormous exposure for wire transfer mishaps. Article 4A recognizes this and is animated by a spirit of bank protection. See, e.g., Official Comment 2 to §4A-305, which explains why Article 4A does not allow senders to recover consequential damages from banks for wire transfer errors. In the event of bank insolvency, banks that have accepted payment orders but not received payment must bear the loss unless a funds-transfer system (such as CHIPS) has adopted a plan for loss-sharing and the plan fails, in which case §4A-405(e) (the "doomsday" rule) provides that the payment is undone even though acceptance had occurred. Many funds-transfer systems have loss-sharing plans (typically providing for the creation of a "settlement kitty"), and they should help ease the problem of bank exposure.

---

20. There is a strong presumption in favor of the effectiveness of a rule adopted by a funds-transfer system; §4A-501(b). Such systems are particularly encouraged to adopt rules making payments provisional, and plans for the sharing of losses in the event of bank insolvency; see §4A-405(d) and (e).

CHAPTER 15 ASSESSMENT: MULTIPLE CHOICE QUESTIONS

1. Miranda forgot her credit card on a table at the Hamilton Tavern. Nadal found it there two days later. Over the next two months, Nadal used the card to run up thousands of dollars of charges at restaurants and retail stores. Miranda, meanwhile, ignored the matter. Is Miranda liable for any of the charges?
   a. Yes, for $50.
   b. Yes, for all the charges, for failure to give notice of the loss of the card.
   c. Yes, for any charges made after she received the statement on which any fraudulent charges appeared.
   d. Yes, for all charges made more than 48 hours after she lost her card.

2. Spalding ran a music talent agency. Her bookkeeper, Jones, had no permission from Spalding to write checks or use the agency credit card. Nevertheless, Jones used the card extravagantly for over a year on vacations, jewelry, and fine dining. Jones prepared a check each month to pay the credit card bill. Spalding signed the check without a glance at the bill. Spalding eventually caught on to the embezzlement. Is the credit card issuer liable to Spalding for the payments for unauthorized charges?
   a. Only for $50.
   b. Yes, for all charges made after Spalding received statements listing unauthorized charges and had a reasonable time to give notice.
   c. Yes, for all charges for which more than 60 days has passed since the statement was made available to Spalding.
   d. No. Unauthorized charges cannot be contested after the charges have been paid by the cardholder.

3. Korins purchased some antique furniture with Korins's personal credit card at Jefferson Furniture, located in Cairo, Illinois, some 400 miles from Korins's home in Lake Forest, Illinois. Korins soon realized the furniture was quite new, treated to look old. Korins had no success when requesting a refund from Jefferson Furniture. Can Korins raise the breach as a defense against paying the charge on the credit card?
   a. Yes, because the purchase was in Korins's state of residence.
   b. No, because Korins made the purchase more than 100 miles from his residence.
   c. No. Purchases with a credit card may be contested with the merchant, but not with the card issuer. Banks do not warranty furniture.
   d. Yes. Consumers always may raise defenses to payment.

4. Hughes Aircraft had a typical wire transfer agreement with Imperial Bank. Hughes Aircraft sent a payment order to its bank, Imperial Bank,

instructing the bank to transfer $1,977,000 to Maximilian H. Miltzlaff Manufacturing, Inc., Account No. 9031 9801 at Aeronautical Bank, as payment for some fuselages. Hughes Aircraft was careful to correctly state the name of the bank and, especially, the unusual name of the beneficiary. However, Hughes Aircraft made one minor error: the correct bank account was 9081 9801. Aeronautical Bank processed the order quickly, looking only at the account number, and put the money in account no. 9031 9801. The account owner, Harry Spludd, quickly took the money and disappeared. Is Hughes Aircraft liable for $1,977,000?

a. No. Aeronautical Bank cannot recover, because it could not distinguish Maximilian H. Miltzlaff Manufacturing, Inc. from Harry Spludd.
b. No. A bank that gets the account number wrong takes the loss, but customers are not charged to follow such banking practices.
c. Yes. Aeronautical Bank is entitled to rely on the account number, and is entitled to reimbursement from Imperial Bank, who in turn is entitled to reimbursement from Hughes Aircraft.
d. No. Aeronautical Bank did not process the order with due care, because it processed a transfer of $1,977,000 without checking carefully.

5. Dismayed by reports of breaches of bank account security, Belt & Suspenders Bank radically ratcheted up the security on wire transfer orders. Rather than issuing "challenge questions" (questions such as "What was your first pet's name?", for which users supply answers when setting up an account) only for payment orders that did not fit usual patterns of use or that were for large amounts, its software generated challenge questions for every payment order. The bank also lowered the threshold for reporting suspicious payment orders to its fraud team. This extra security, unfortunately, greatly increased the risk of fraud. Because challenge questions were so frequent, they were more likely to be revealed to fraudsters. Because suspicious payment warnings became so numerous, the fraud team was unable to investigate them all. As one result, phishers were able to infiltrate Patsy Architecture's account and send over $500,000 to accounts unknown. Patsy Architecture had signed an account agreement, including agreement to use of the enhanced security measures. Is Patsy Architecture required to reimburse Belt & Suspenders Bank?

a. Yes, because it had agreed to the security procedure.
b. No. Customers are only liable for funds transfers they actually authorize.
c. No, because the security procedure was not commercially reasonable.
d. No, provided that Patsy Architecture notifies Belt & Suspenders Bank within 60 days of receiving its account statement.

ANSWERS

1. *A* is the best answer. The Truth in Lending Act caps liability for unauthorized use at $50. The limit is not dependent on whether the cardholder was negligent with the card or failed to give timely notice of loss of the card or notice of the unauthorized charges upon receiving the statement, making *B*, *C*, and *D* incorrect.
2. *B* is the best answer. As set out in the *Azur* case, courts have imported notions of negligence, in a limited manner, to credit card law's $50 cap on liability. Where an employer fails to supervise an employee and fails to monitor account statements in a timely manner, courts have held the employer has given the employee apparent authority to use the card. *C* is misleading; the 60-day rule is the rule for debit cards, not credit cards. *D* likewise refers to a different rule. Where the cardholder makes authorized use of the card, but has grounds not pay the merchant, the cardholder may raise defenses against the merchant, but only until the cardholder has paid for that particular charge.
3. *A* is the best answer. Consumer credit cards, under the TILA, provide buyer protection. If a cardholder has a defense to payment against the merchant, the cardholder may raise that defense against the issuer, contrary to *C*. Banks do indeed warrant furniture and everything else purchased with consumer credit cards, in effect. There are several conditions: the cardholder must make a good faith effort to resolve the matter with the merchant, the amount of the charge must exceed $50, and the purchase must occur within the state or within 100 miles of the cardholder's residence. That last geographical limitation is met in this case, because the purchase was in Illinois, albeit 400 miles from home. It need not be both in-state and within 100 miles, contrary to *B*.
4. *C* is the best answer. UCC 4A has an unusual rule with respect to errors. A bank is entitled to rely on the account number, and may effectively ignore whether that number matches the name on the account. That sounds like a license for banks to be careless, but makes sense in practice. The rule was adopted to match banking practice. It provides a clear rule, and avoids banks' refusing payment orders for failure to correctly state the beneficiary's name. The name on the account often may not exactly match the name that the originator uses, for many reasons. Banks are charged to know the rule and follow it. Contrary to *B*, customers are likewise bound by the rule if they agree to it—and every wire transfer contract will contain a clause where the customer agrees to the rule. So, although customers may not always know it, the key part of the payment order to get correct is the account number, not the name of the beneficiary. Banks are not required to check that they match, contrary to *A* and *D*.

5. *C* is the best answer. For commercial wire transfers, a customer is indeed bound by an unauthorized payment order, provided the bank paid the order in good faith, pursuant to a commercially reasonable security procedure accepted by the customer. Customers can be liable for unauthorized payment orders, contrary to *B*. But the security procedure here was not commercially reasonable. Rather, it was so burdensome that it actually was insecure. The problem is based on an actual case, Patco Constr. Co. v. People's United Bank, 684 F.3d 197 (1st Cir. 2012). Because the security procedure was not commercially reasonable, the customer's agreement did not submit it to liability for unauthorized orders, so *A* is incorrect. *D* refers to a rule that does not apply here. For *consumer* funds transfers, under the EFTA, there is no liability for unauthorized transfers as long as notice is given within 60 days of the statement date. But this is a commercial wire transfer, governed by UCC 4A.

Chapter 16
Investment Securities

Article 8 of the Uniform Commercial Code is entitled "Investment Securities," but that fancy description is meant to describe stocks and bonds and the Article regulates their sale, transfer, and use as collateral for loans. Originally, these stocks and bonds were reflected as pieces of paper and their transfer was controlled by rules similar to those in Article 3 for negotiable instruments. But in the twenty-first century, stocks and bonds, like much else, moved into the electronic world, and most of them are now held by brokers and transferred electronically as "security entitlements."

Article 8 is something of a stepchild to the rest of the Uniform Commercial Code. White and Summers do not even cover it in their hornbook, and it is embarrassing how often the issues it addresses are litigated without Article 8 even once being cited. To avoid malpractice in this field, you should know something about its scope and general area of regulation.

The original version of Article 8 was created at a time when all investment securities were evidenced by the issuance of pieces of paper labeled as stocks or bonds (now called *certificated securities*). As corporate and government issuers moved from paper to registration of the investors' interest at the issuer's headquarters or some other central location, Article 8 was rewritten in 1978 to deal with these so-called uncertificated securities. But developments in the world of stocks and bonds made the 1978 version obsolete rather quickly because investors began holding their investments merely as bookkeeping entries on the records of their brokers, and often the brokers themselves did not hold the paper certificates either but instead had similar accounts at clearing corporations.

The 1978 Article 8 did not deal with these investment rights, leaving the law in limbo. In 1994, a new version of Article 8 made its appearance and was rapidly adopted by the various jurisdictions.[1] The 8-100s to the 8-400s deal with certificated and uncertificated securities, doing little to change the prior law, but a new part, the 8-500s, now regulates the rights that investors have in security accounts (calling these rights *security entitlements*). A wonderfully detailed "Prefatory Note" (included in most statute books reprinting Article 8) explains the evolution of the law in this area and examines the business background for investment securities and securities holding systems.

I. TERMINOLOGY

Article 8 of the Code (Investment Securities) deals with the rights and liabilities created by the issuance and transfer of stocks and bonds. These items, called *securities* in the Code, are defined in §8-102(a)(15). Under §8-103(d) all securities are governed by Article 8, not by Article 3, even if the security is technically negotiable under §3-104(a).

Essential to your comprehension of Article 8 is an understanding of the meaning of some of the technical terms, such as *registered owner*. What follows is a brief sketch of the basic business transaction that results in the creation of Article 8 paper.

Corporate securities can be divided into two main classes: *debt* securities (generally bonds or debentures and the interest coupons attached thereto), which represent the obligation of the corporation to pay the holder a specified sum, and *equity* securities (such as preferred or common shares of stock), which represent an ownership interest in the corporate enterprise. A corporation, hereinafter called the *issuer*, will make use of both types of securities to provide financing for its activities.

If the issuer is offering the securities to the public (making a *public offering*), it frequently must register them with the Securities and Exchange Commission pursuant to the Securities Act of 1933, 15 U.S.C. §§77a et seq. When printed, the securities are either signed manually, which is quite a

1. Even better, the Department of the Treasury has adopted the Revised Article 8 as a matter of federal law; see 31 C.F.R. §357.

task in the issue of, say, 100,000 shares of stock, or by facsimile (printed) signature. Debt securities are almost always placed under the control of an independent trustee, frequently a bank, called the *authenticating trustee,* who signs the securities manually, thereby expressly certifying that the item signed is one of the securities intended as part of the offering.

Debt securities may be made payable to the *bearer* or to a named person, the *registered owner* (so called because the owner's name is registered on the corporation's books as the record owner). Equity securities in this country are always issued in registered form; the registered owner then has voting rights, rights to dividends, etc. If the security is in registered form, the issuer need recognize these rights only in the registered owner. Section 8-207(a) provides:

> Before due presentment for registration of transfer of a certificated security in registered form or of an instruction requesting registration of transfer of an uncertificated security, the issuer or indenture trustee may treat the registered owner as the person exclusively entitled to vote, receive notifications, and otherwise exercise all the rights and powers of an owner.

If the registered owner sells the security, the purchaser will want to have the corporate records changed to show the purchaser as the new registered owner. To do this, the registered owner (transferor) *indorses* the instrument, by writing either on it or on a separate sheet of paper, over to the new owner, and the instrument is presented to the *transfer agent,* who may be either an employee of the corporation or a separate entity. The registered owner may simply indorse the instrument in blank, naming no transferee. This is frequently done when the registered owner is selling the security through a broker and the name of the eventual purchaser is unknown.

Prior to seeking a new registration, a blank instrument is filled in with the name of the purchaser and then submitted to the transfer agent. Of course, instruments indorsed in blank give rise to a situation that can easily become exciting when the security falls into the hands of an individual whose respect for other people's property is minimal. For this reason it has become common for registered owners who wish to sell their securities on the market to indorse them over to their brokers, who then register the security in the brokers' names.

Securities registered to a broker are said to be *street name* securities (so-called because of the broker's connection with New York's Wall Street). When the selling broker finds a purchaser, the broker submits the security to the transfer agent so that the records can be changed to switch the registered ownership from the broker (the street name) to the purchaser. As mentioned above, in today's world the actual certificate may be held only by a clearing corporation, and rights therein are passed down to lower tiers of owners by bookkeeping entries. In these indirect holding situations, the beneficial owner of the security is said to have a *security entitlement* in a *securities account* held with a *security intermediary*, who one instructs by giving an entitlement order (read §8-102(a)), in which all these terms are defined in more detail (*securities account* is defined in §8-501(a)).

To facilitate a change in the registered ownership of a certificated security, a typical security has printed on the back a transfer form more or less similar to the following language that I copied off a debenture:

> For value received, ___________ hereby sell, assign and transfer unto ___________ the within registered debenture and do hereby irrevocably constitute and appoint ___________ my attorney to transfer the said registered debenture on the books of the within named company with full power of substitution in the premises.
>
> Dated: ___________
> Signed: ___________
> In the presence of: ___________

The filling in of the third blank in the above form gives a power of attorney to the person named (frequently a broker). If no transferee is named, the transfer agent will register the security to whomever the attorney nominates; this procedure is sometimes used in lieu of the additional steps involved in registering the security in the street name. If no attorney is named and only the transferee blank (the second one above) is filled in, then the transfer agent will register the security in the name of the transferee. "Where both the name of a transferee and that of an attorney are filled in, the same person should be designated in both blanks. Otherwise, even registration in the name of the specified transferee will require instructions from, if not further indorsement by, the specified attorney." E. Guttman, Modern Securities Transfers §8-8, pp. 8-13 (4th ed. 2010). You will note that the power of attorney gives the attorney full power to substitute a new transferee. Cf. §8-308.

Another entity sometimes involved in Article 8 problems is the *registrar.* A registrar—normally, though not always, a separate entity from the issuer—has the duty to inspect proposed transfers to determine whether they will result in the issuer's having outstanding more stock than it is authorized to have, a situation called *overissue.* In effect, the registrar is an auditor of the corporate capacity of the transfer. The registrar may also be the transfer agent, the entity keeping the records and performing the physical process involved in the transfer. See Hollywood Natl. Bank v. International Bus. Machs. Corp., 38 Cal. App. 3d 607, 113 Cal. Rptr. 494 (1974); E. Guttman, Modern Securities Transfers, *supra,* ch. 10.

The practice of issuing shares of stock that are registered with the issuing company but that are not represented by a physical piece of paper results in what are called *uncertificated securities.* With uncertificated securities, the owner's interest is registered in the issuer's computer and only an initial *transaction statement* is sent to the purchaser to evidence that purchaser's right to the security. Thereafter, transfers of the uncertificated security are accomplished by the current owner's issuing *instruction* to the issuer, telling it to whom the security now belongs. Read §§8-102(a)(12) and 8-305.

II. OVERISSUE

Read §8-210 carefully.

PROBLEM 264

Colossus Corporation was authorized to issue 100,000 shares of stock at a par value of $1; it had 150,000 printed up, and the extra 50,000 were saved for the purpose of replacing the old pieces of paper as they became worn. The company sold 100,000 shares. The extra 50,000 shares were stolen by a clever thief, who negotiated them to a bona fide purchaser (BFP). Can the BFP require the corporation to recognize the 50,000 shares as valid? What remedy does §8-210 give to the BFP? See Hughes Developers, Inc. v. Montgomery, 903 So. 2d 94 (Ala. 2004).

III. THE ISSUER AND THE HOLDER

Read §§8-201 through 8-206, 8-208, and 8-407, which explain duties of the issuer and its agents.

As for §8-204, the most common restriction on transfer is the following, which is frequently printed on securities:

> The shares represented by this certificate have been exchanged exclusively with the Corporation's shareholders and have not been registered under the Securities Act of 1933. These shares may not be pledged or hypothecated and may not be sold or transferred in the absence of an effective Registration

Statement under the Securities Act of 1933 or an opinion of counsel to the Corporation that registration is not required under the said Act.

Another common restriction is that the corporation itself is to be given the right of first refusal when sale of the stock is contemplated.

Sections 8-205, 8-208, and 8-406 deal with the responsibilities of the issuer and its agents. Look at these sections in light of the following quote. Guttman's Modern Securities Transfers, *supra,* states, at §11-5, p. 11-14:

> Where the issuer relies on the manual signatures of its officers, "John Beta," who is an employee of the issuer might sign the name of "Richard Gamma, President," who is in fact the only officer authorized to sign. . . . This security is clearly not genuine under the Code definition and the issuer need not recognize it.

Do you agree? Consider the following case.

First American National Bank v. Christian Foundation Life Insurance Co.

Arkansas Supreme Court, 1967
242 Ark. 678, 420 S.W.2d 912

SMITH, J.

This is a suit brought by one of the appellees, Christian Foundation Life Insurance Company, for a declaratory judgment with respect to the validity of certain duplicate bearer bonds ostensibly issued by the First Methodist Church of Mena. That duplicate bonds were outstanding was due to the fraud of the late Lawrence Hayes, former president of Institutional Finance Company, which handled the bond issue as fiscal agent for the church. Parties to the suit include the rival owners of the duplicate bonds, the church and its trustees, the Union Bank of Mena, which acted as paying agent for the bonds, the estate of Hayes, the receiver for Institutional Finance, and the corporate surety upon Institutional Finance's qualifying bond as a securities dealer. . . .

We need state the facts only in broad outline. On January 19, 1964, the church adopted a resolution authorizing a $90,000 bond issue for the construction of a new church and employing Institutional Finance as its fiscal agent to market the bonds. On the same day the church treasurer, Bettie Jean Montgomery, in the presence of the pastor and a trustee of the church, affixed her signature to a blank sheet of paper and delivered it to Joe B. Springfield, executive vice-president of Institutional Finance, for use as a facsimile signature upon the bonds.

Two days later Springfield requested a printing company to print the bonds, which were numbered from 1 to 188 and totaled $94,000. (The record does not explain why an extra $4,000 of bonds was printed.) On

January 30 the printer delivered the bonds to Springfield. They bore the facsimile signatures of Springfield and Mrs. Montgomery, with no provision for an authenticating manual signature.

Institutional Finance sold $45,000 of the bonds to members of the church but had trouble in finding buyers for all the rest of the issue. On July 3, 1964, Hayes personally borrowed $25,000 from First American National Bank and pledged as collateral, along with other securities, $27,000 (later increased to $28,800) of the Mena church bonds. There is no sound basis for questioning the bank's standing as a good faith purchaser for value, as those terms are defined in the Uniform Commercial Code. Ark. Stat. Ann. §85-1-201 (Add. 1961). Hayes had borrowed money from the bank on a number of occasions. The bank's president, who handled this loan, understood Hayes to be an employee of a Texas dealer in church bonds and was unaware of his connection with Institutional Finance. Nothing in the transaction warned the bank that Hayes did not own the bonds.

On February 1, 1965, Hayes fraudulently ordered the printer to print $25,000 of numbered bonds that included duplicates of some of those pledged to the bank. Later in the month, Hayes, in order to complete a sale to Christian Foundation Life, had printed additional bonds in certain larger denominations requested by that insurance company. The duplicate bonds now held by Richards and Christian Foundation Life are among those obtained by Hayes in the two supplemental printings.

We find no merit in the appellant's insistence that its adversaries were not purchasers in good faith because they bought the bonds at discounts of 10 and 15 percent. We have held that the price paid for a negotiable instrument may be so grossly inadequate as to support a finding of bad faith, Hogg v. Thurman, 90 Ark. 93, 117 S.W. 1070, 17 Ann. Gas. 383 (1909), but there is no proof in this record to indicate that the discounts offered to the appellees were so great as to arouse suspicion. Nor is there evidence to sustain the appellant's argument that the purchasers of the duplicates should have been put upon inquiry by the church's apparent inability to market the entire bond issue within a period of about a year.

Hayes' dishonesty finally became known when duplicate interest coupons were presented to the Mena bank for payment. The paying agent refused to honor the coupons until their validity had been established. Hence this suit.

We think the chancellor should have found all bonds held by bona fide purchasers to be binding obligations of the church. It is plain enough that the church was careless in entrusting its treasurer's facsimile signature to Institutional Finance and in failing to take the precaution of requiring authentication of the bonds by a manual signature. By contrast, the holders of the bonds acquired them in the ordinary course of business and in circumstances entitling them to the protection afforded to bona fide purchasers.

The case is controlled by the pertinent provisions of the Uniform Commercial Code. Before the adoption of the Code the church might have been held liable by contract to one purchaser and in damages to the other, but the draftsmen of the Code point out in their Comment to our §8-205 that the Code simply validates most defective securities in the hands of innocent purchasers, refusing to prefer one such purchaser over another.

Specifically, this controversy falls within §8-205, which provides that an unauthorized signature is effective in favor of an innocent purchaser when the signing is done either by a person entrusted by the issuer with the signing of the security or by an employee of such a person or of the issuer itself. By resolution the church employed Institutional Finance as its fiscal agent to handle the sale of the bonds. The first line of the printed prospectus for the bond issue identified that concern as the issuer's fiscal agent. There can hardly be any serious contention that Hayes's wrongful use of the treasurer's facsimile signature did not fall within the purview of the Code. . . .

Reversed and remanded.

JONES, J. (dissenting). I do not agree with the conclusion reached by the majority in this case, nor do I agree with the decision of the chancellor.

Our Uniform Commercial Code §8-202(3) [now §8-202(c)—EDS.] is as follows:

> Except as otherwise provided in the case of certain unauthorized signatures on issue (Section 8-205), lack of genuineness of a security is a complete defense even against a purchaser for value and without notice.

Just what constitutes the genuineness of a security is not set out in chapter 8 of the Code on investment securities, but §1-201 contains 46 numbered general definitions, one of which is as follows: "(18) 'Genuine' means free of forgery or counterfeiting." . . .

It is my view that the duplicate bonds printed without authority and certainly with the apparent intent to defraud, were forged counterfeits of the original bonds and lacked the genuineness of the original authorized bonds, and that their lack of genuineness was a complete defense even against Christian Foundation and Reverend C.R. Richards. . . .

Under the majority holding in this case, once authority is given to an unscrupulous agent to print and sell a limited number of bonds over a facsimile signature, the principal or issuer has no further protection from being bound by such individual. A revocation of authority, or even confinement in the penitentiary, would offer no protection. Such agent or ex-agent, would be able to bind his former principal, or the issuer of bonds, for as long as such agent could find innocent purchasers and access to a printing press.

I would reverse the chancellor in this case and hold that the original bonds held by First American are genuine and legal bonds, but that the duplicates sold to Christian Foundation and Reverend Richards are forged counterfeits of the originals and are not genuine but are void as binding obligations of First Methodist.

PROBLEM 265

Titanic Telephone Company (TTC), Inc. called up the Pronto Printing Corporation (PPC) and asked Felix Pronto (founder and president) if PPC would run off 100 more of the $100 TTC bearer bonds PPC had printed in the past. PPC had previously printed 1,000 of these bonds and still had the plates. The bonds had the facsimile signatures of the TTC president, secretary, and authenticating trustee already printed on them. Felix agreed and called up Happy Clatter, the chief printer, and told him to run off 100 more of the bonds and send them by messenger to TTC. Happy ran off 200 of the bonds. He sent 100 by messenger to the offices of TTC, and he sent the other 100 as a Christmas present to his mother in Twin Falls, Idaho. Eventually, the latter bonds turned up as the property of Bing, Bong & Bell Brokerage, a purchaser for value without notice of anything unusual, which presented the bonds to TTC for payment of the interest due that year. Titanic Telephone comes to you for advice. It doesn't know whether it should treat the bonds as valid or not and is afraid that if it pays the interest, TTC's stockholders will bring suit against TTC's officers for misusing corporate funds. Give TTC your opinion as to whether the law requires TTC to honor the bonds, noting carefully §§8-202(c) and 8-205.

IV. TRANSFERS BETWEEN PURCHASERS

The proper transfer of a registered security is a three-step process: indorsement by the owner, delivery to the purchaser, and registration with the corporation in the name of the new owner. The effective transfer of a bearer security requires *only* delivery. Read §§8-304, 8-108(f), and 8-307.

Knop v. Knop

Supreme Court of Virginia, 2019

297 Va. 553, 830 S.E.2d 723

Opinion by Justice Stephen R. McCullough.

Ticonderoga Farms is a family company that owns nearly 1,000 acres of land in fast-growing Loudoun County. The shares in the company are owned by Peter J. Knop ("Father") and his three children. A dispute arose concerning what percentage of shares the children owned. The trial court concluded that—although Mr. Knop intended to make gifts of stock to his children for estate planning purposes—those gifts were never effectually made because they were never delivered to the children in the manner required by law. The trial court also rejected the children's estoppel argument. The children appeal from this ruling. For the reasons noted below, we agree with the trial court that the shares were never delivered to the children. Thus, under the law, the gifts were not completed. We further conclude that the trial court did not abuse its discretion in denying the children relief under equitable estoppel principles. Accordingly, we will affirm the judgment below.

BACKGROUND

When Ticonderoga Farms was incorporated, in 1982, Father owned almost 80% of the company. His wife, Diana Knop, and the three children, Alexandra, Peter R.Q., and William ("the children"), who were minors at the time, owned the remaining shares. Following a divorce, Diana transferred her interests to her former husband. By 1987, due to contributions by then adult children at the formation of the company and later transfers by Father, the children each owned 9.08% for a total of 27.24% of the company. Father owned the remaining shares. The company's stock book contains stock certificate stubs showing that the children each have a 9.08% ownership interest in the company and that such shares have been delivered to the children.

James Cummings, the accountant for Ticonderoga Farms, prepared the Virginia and federal income tax returns for the company for tax years 1989-2007. He also prepared the tax returns for Father and the children. He testified that Father instructed him to make gifts of stock equivalent to the maximum gift tax exclusion to the children to avoid estate taxes. Cummings testified that he followed Father's directions and prepared Schedule K-1s for the shareholders. These K-1s reflected the children's increased ownership shares and Father's decreased ownership share. The K-1s were filed with the Virginia Department of Taxation and the IRS as part of the company's income tax returns. Cummings relied on these K-1s to prepare personal tax returns for Father and the children. Father and the children filed their personal returns based on these K-1s. Father offered similar testimony, acknowledging that he intended to convey shares to them.

The forms filed with Ticonderoga's federal taxes show this rising percentage of ownership. Likewise, the forms filed in connection with Virginia taxes showed a rising percentage of ownership for the children and a decreasing ownership proportion for Father. By 2004, if the gifts were effective, the children's ownership interests in Ticonderoga had risen to a total of 44.061%, or 14.687% for each child. These ownership interests were recorded on the tax returns for that year. The federal tax returns, which were also filed with the Virginia returns, were signed under penalty of perjury.

The children also introduced into evidence a variety of emails and corporate documents authored or signed by Father in which he acknowledged the transfers and the increases in the children's ownership interests. The ownership interests reflected in these emails and documents were consistent with the interests shown in the tax returns for the corresponding years. *Compare* Pl.'s Ex. 37 and Pl.'s Ex. 188A and B (1991 returns), *with* Pl.'s Ex. 47 and Pl.'s Ex. 198A (2001 return), *with* Pl.'s Ex. 77 and Pl.'s Ex. 201A and B (2004 returns). The intended gifts of shares, however, were never reflected in stock certificates. Father testified that he never prepared the stock certificates. No ledgers were produced showing transfers of the shares.

Years later, Father decided to sell or give away some of the property to create a scenic easement. The children opposed this course of action. Under the then-existing corporate bylaws, the sale of company's real property required the approval of 90% of the ownership interests. To circumvent this requirement, Father asserted that the gifts he made to the children in the 1990s and early 2000s were not completed because he did not prepare and deliver stock certificates to the children. In other words, the children each owned the same interests they held in 1987, i.e., 9.08% of Ticonderoga each, for a total ownership share of 27.24%. Father claimed an ownership share of 72.76% of the company. Under the Virginia Stock Corporation Act, a shareholder owning more than two-thirds of a corporation can convert the corporation to another form. *See* Code §13.1-722.11(A)(5). If Father's assertion was correct, this would allow Father to convert Ticonderoga from a corporation to an LLC under the Act. In early 2015, Father noticed a series of shareholder and board of directors meetings where, relying on his claim to own 72.76% of Ticonderoga, he voted—over the children's objections—to convert Ticonderoga to an LLC. The operating agreement Father drafted for the LLC gave him total control of the company, including the ability to transfer its land without the 90% shareholder approval required by the corporate bylaws.

The children then filed a complaint in which they asked for a declaration that they each own 14.687% of Ticonderoga and that Father lacks the authority to sell Ticonderoga land without their consent. Following a bench trial, the trial court found that the children "did not testify or present any evidence that they recalled ever actually receiving a certificate, saw a certificate, or lost a certificate." App. 2456. The court also observed that the corporate stock book contains stubs indicating that there were 227 shares for each child out of a total of 2500 shares. The court noted that

> At various times, all of the [children] and certainly the [father] were in a position to update the corporate records to reflect their appropriate ownership.

> They were, at a minimum, at times, all officers, at times directors, and [Peter R.Q. Knop] was actually the president for a number of years.

The defendant was always active in the company, but the disarray of the company records cannot fall completely to the defendant.

The court credited the testimony of Mr. Cummings indicating that Father intended to give the children an ownership share greater than 9.08%. The court concluded that the children had failed to meet their burden of proving a valid *inter vivos* gift of shares.

The court found as follows:

> While plaintiffs' evidence, including tax returns, clearly reflect the defendant intended to transfer some additional percentage of his ownership share of the farm[] to the plaintiffs for estate planning and tax purposes, none of that evidence persuasively shows that there was ever an actual or constructive delivery of that additional ownership share to plaintiffs such that the defendant was divested of all dominion and control over that property and that plaintiffs were invested with such dominion and control over the property.

The trial court concluded that, under Virginia law, including the Uniform Commercial Code (UCC) and this Court's decision in Young v. Young, 240 Va. 57, 393 S.E.2d 398 (1990), no valid gifts of shares above 9.08% had been made. After the children moved the court to reconsider, the court also rejected the children's argument that the father should be estopped, under the doctrines of equitable estoppel and quasi-estoppel, from denying the gifts because he acquiesced in them for years while leading the children to believe the gifts were completed. This appeal followed.

Analysis

I. Requirements for Gifts of Certificated Shares of Stock

Under Virginia law, an *inter vivos* gift is complete where (1) there is donative intent at the time of the gift and (2) there is "such actual or constructive delivery as divests the donor of all dominion and control over the property and invests it in [the] donee." Taylor v. Smith, 199 Va. 871, 874, 102 S.E.2d 160 (1958). Proof of each element is necessary. *Id.* Donative intent without delivery is insufficient to complete a gift. Yancey v. Field, 85 Va. 756, 759, 8 S.E. 721 (1889). "[T]he burden of proof rests upon [the donee] to show every fact and circumstance necessary to constitute a valid gift by clear and convincing evidence." Rust v. Phillips, 208 Va. 573, 578, 159 S.E.2d 628 (1968).

The trial court found donative intent on the part of Father to give shares in Ticonderoga Farms to his children. The dispositive questions are whether he delivered the shares or can be estopped from denying that he gave the shares.

Code §8.8A-102 distinguishes between a "certificated security" and an "uncertificated security" by providing that the former is "represented by an instrument," Code §8.8A-102(a)(4), and the latter is "not represented by an instrument," Code §8.8A-102(a)(18). By statute, "[d]elivery of a certificated security to a purchaser occurs when. . . the purchaser acquires possession of the security certificate[.]" Code §8.8A-301(a)(1). In *Young*, we examined statutory requirements for gifts of certificated shares and concluded that, despite a father's stated intent to donate shares to his daughters, the gifts were ineffective because "[t]he prerequisite elements of delivery to, and acceptance by, the daughters, [we]re entirely lacking. . . ." 240 Va. at 64, 393 S.E.2d 398. As a consequence, "the disputed securities were never delivered to the daughters nor to anyone designated by the daughters to receive them, [and] no *inter vivos* gift was ever made." *Id.* Code §8.8A-301(a)(1) and *Young* supply the rule of decision with respect to delivery of a gift of shares of certificated stock.

A. *Recodification of the Statute Did Not Change Its Plain Meaning or Expand Its Scope*

The children point out that the General Assembly has amended the statute that was under scrutiny in *Young*. The statute we examined in *Young* provided that the "[t]ransfer of a security . . . to a purchaser occurs *only* . . . at the time he or a person designated by him acquires possession of a certificated security." 240 Va. at 63, 393 S.E.2d 398 (emphasis added). The Code now provides that "[d]elivery of a certificated security to a purchaser occurs when . . . the purchaser acquires possession of the security certificate[.]" Code §8.8A-301(a)(1). According to the children, "[t]he omission of the word 'only' in §8.8A-301 is significant." We disagree.

"It is well-settled that we determine the General Assembly's intent from the words contained in the statute." Virginia Broad. Corp. v. Commonwealth, 286 Va. 239, 249, 749 S.E.2d 313 (2013) (quoting Alger v. Commonwealth, 267 Va. 255, 259, 590 S.E.2d 563 (2004)). "When a statute is unambiguous, we must apply the plain meaning of that language." Appalachian Power Co. v. State Corp. Comm'n, 284 Va. 695, 706, 733 S.E.2d 250 (2012). "[W]hen the language of an enactment is free from ambiguity, resort to legislative history and extrinsic facts is not permitted because we take the words as written to determine their meaning." Brown v. Lukhard, 229 Va. 316, 321, 330 S.E.2d 84 (1985). The plain language of the statute provides that "[d]elivery of a certificated security to a purchaser occurs when . . . the purchaser acquires possession of the security certificate[.]" Code §8.8A-301(a)(1). The language of the statute does not leave the door ajar for any other mechanism of delivery applicable to the facts of this case.

B. The Children Failed to Prove a Constructive Delivery

The children further argue that even if there was no actual delivery, "the income tax returns filed by Ticonderoga, [Father], and the children should be considered conclusive evidence of the constructive delivery and acceptance of [Father's] ownership interests." Appellant Br. at 28. A "constructive" delivery can occur even though the recipient of the gift has not come into physical possession of the item or title to the item. For example, we have noted, by way of illustration, that "the contents of a trunk, even when they consist of bonds or other choses in action, may be given by delivery of the key of the trunk, or goods *in transitu* by delivery of the bill of lading, if the donor's intention to make the gift clearly appears." *Yancey*, 85 Va. at 760, 8 S.E. 721. In those illustrations, the giver has relinquished control over the property and placed it in the hands of the recipient of the gift.

"The essence of delivery . . . is surrender of dominion and control of the gift by the donor." Brown v. Metz, 240 Va. 127, 131, 393 S.E.2d 402 (1990). With a constructive delivery, the donor may not have turned over the actual item, but the step taken, such as turning over the key to a trunk containing the item, is sufficient for surrender of dominion and control of the gift. *Yancey*, 85 Va. at 758, 8 S.E. 721 ("The authorities uniformly hold that to render a gift effectual, the thing given, *or the means of obtaining it,* must be delivered to the donee, or to his agent, and accepted by him.") (emphasis added).

Although Code §8.8A-301(a)(1) requires the purchaser (or gift recipient) to "acquire[] possession of the security certificate," we recognized in *Young* that the possession by the purchaser or recipient of the gift "or a person designated by him" can constitute a delivery. *Young*, 240 Va. at 63, 393 S.E.2d 398. Code §§8.8A-301(a)(2)-(3), providing for other methods of delivery, are consistent with this principle. Subsection (2) provides that delivery of certificated securities may occur when "another person, other than a securities intermediary, either acquires possession of the security certificate on behalf of the purchaser or . . . acknowledges that it holds for the purchaser." Similarly, subsection (3) permits delivery when "a securities intermediary acting on behalf of the purchaser acquires possession of the security certificate. . . ." Importantly, in each of these circumstances, the donor relinquishes control.

The children contend that Father's statements on various tax documents reflecting a larger share of ownership by the children constitute a constructive delivery of certificated shares of stock. However, a statement on a tax return reflecting a gift of shares does not constitute a relinquishment of control of certificated shares by the donor. Statements on tax returns are made for purposes of assessing taxes. False or misleading statements may subject the person who makes them to civil or criminal penalties. Such statements, however, do not relinquish control of property. Statements made on a tax return do not, therefore, satisfy the element of delivery.

A simple analogy illustrates the point. A father may tell his child that he is donating his car and transferring the car title to the child. In reliance on this assertion, the child submits documentation to the taxing authority reflecting the gift. The father may likewise submit tax records reflecting the gift. At all times, however, the father retains control of both the car and the title. The father never relinquishes control of the car and, in fact, continues to drive it. In that situation, the father may have made a false or misleading statement to both the child and the taxing authority, but it is readily apparent that those statements neither surrendered dominion and control of the vehicle nor vested dominion and control of the car in the child. Without that relinquishment, there is no delivery in the eyes of the law.

The children's theory of delivery via statements made in a tax return has no basis in the controlling statute. Additionally, as Father points out, "[t]he uncertainty that would ensue if ownership claims of certificated shares could be predicated on ancillary documents other than the certificate is patent." Appellee Br. at 28. Consequently, we affirm the trial court's ruling that, despite Father's stated intention to make gifts of certificated stock to the children, the gifts were never effectually made under Virginia law.

II. ESTOPPEL AND QUASI-ESTOPPEL

The children also invoke the doctrine of estoppel to argue that Father is precluded from disavowing the ownership shares shown in the tax returns. In particular, they invoke equitable estoppel and "quasi-estoppel."

The elements necessary to establish equitable estoppel are (1) a representation, (2) reliance, (3) change of position, and (4) detriment, and the party who relies upon estoppel must prove each element by clear, precise, and unequivocal evidence.

Princess Anne Hills Civic League, Inc. v. Susan Constant Real Estate Tr., 243 Va. 53, 59, 413 S.E.2d 599 (1992). Father offers a number of responses to this assertion, but the one we find dispositive is that the children offered no evidence that they suffered any detriment from the statements in the tax returns that reflect a higher percentage of ownership by the children. As Father argues, the children offered no evidence that they "suffered any penalties, tax consequences or anything else for that matter as a result of the statements in the [c]ompany's tax returns." Appellee Br. at 40. The trial court pointed out from the bench, "[t]here's no evidence as to the tax benefit or the tax penalty with respect to [the children]." App. 2042-43. The children did not offer their tax returns into evidence. The children's arguments established the theoretical possibility of detriment, but they offered no evidence of actual detriment. The children, who bore the burden of proving equitable estoppel by clear and convincing evidence, did not carry their burden of proving prejudice.

One of the children, Peter R.Q. Knop, notes that he placed certain assets in an irrevocable trust in 2004, and that as a consequence he gave up control over his interest in the company. First, there is no evidence that this was done in reliance on the tax returns filed by the corporation that showed a greater share of ownership by the children. Peter R.Q. Knop testified that he established the trust around the time he married to protect the farm in the event of a divorce or his spouse wishing to dispose of the asset. Second, at the time he placed these assets in trust, Peter R.Q. Knop had served as President of the company for five years and was in a position to know what interests the stock ledger showed—and those ledgers showed his interest to be 9.08%. Finally, a principal's placement of assets in trust is unlikely to be a source of injury to the principal. The trust makes Peter R.Q. Knop the primary beneficiary during his lifetime. Here, again, the children had to shoulder the burden of proving both detrimental reliance and prejudice by clear and convincing evidence. The trial court rejected their equitable estoppel claim. The record fully supports the trial court's conclusion. . . .

Conclusion

For these reasons, the judgment of the trial court will be affirmed.
Affirmed.

The Article 8 equivalent of Article 3's holder in due course is called a *protected purchaser* (see §8-303), and he or she takes free of adverse claims in both direct and indirect holding systems. Section 8-303(a)(3) requires that the protected purchaser obtain *control* over the security, and while *control* is defined extensively in 8-106, the requirements are nicely summarized in Official Comment 3 to §8-303, which you should now read. It should be noted that *purchase* is defined so broadly in §1-201(b)(32) that, incredibly enough, it includes taking by *gift.* See Rogers v. Rogers, 271 Md. 603, 319 A.2d 119 (1974). *Notice* is defined in §8-105. Read it.

Note that Article 8 has a shelter rule very similar in effect to §3-203(b) in Article 3. See §8-302. Thus, even a person with notice of an adverse claim can get the rights of a protected purchaser by taking from one.

PROBLEM 266

Lynn Brown was the registered owner of 20 shares of Regional Telephone Company when the stock was stolen from her by a clever thief who forged her indorsement on the shares and sold them to Bing, Bong & Bell (B.B. & B.), stockbrokers, who purchased the shares for the brokerage firm. B.B. & B. then had the stock reregistered by Regional Telephone to its own (street) name and thereafter sold the shares to Barbara Shipek, a wealthy client who was trying to buy up all the shares of Regional Telephone that she could. When Lynn found that the shares were missing, she contacted Barbara and demanded the return of her stock. Must Barbara surrender the shares? Would B.B. & B. have had to surrender the shares if Lynn had made a demand to do so before B.B. & B. had the shares reregistered? After? See §§8-106(b), 8-108 (f) (and its Official Comment 3), 8-303 (and particularly its own Official Comment 3). Who is obviously liable to Lynn here? See §8-404.

V. REGISTRATION

When a transfer of a registered security occurs between purchasers, the transfer is *complete* upon delivery to the purchaser (§8-304(c)). But the new owner will want to have the security registered on the company's books in his or her name.[2] The impetus to registration is that until the corporate records are changed, the issuer can send dividend checks, etc., to the record owner (§8-207(a)). The seller must supply the documentation needed to register, §8-307, but does not in any way warrant that the issuer will honor the security, §§8-304(f) and 8-305(b).

On presenting the security for registration, the presenter makes the warranties stated in §8-108(f). The issuer is under a legal *duty* to register the transfer if the requirements of §8-401, which you should now read, are met; White Winston Select Asset Funds, LLC v. Professional Diversity Network, Inc., 35 Mass. L. Rptr. 584, 2019 WL 2605707 (Sup. Ct. Mass. 2019). If any of these requirements has not been satisfied, the issuer can refuse the registration.

2. The company, once it decides to change the registration, cancels the old certificate and issues a new one to the new registered owner.

PROBLEM 267

Professor Chalk was the registered owner of 50 shares of the Beaten Path Mousetrap Corporation, and he wanted to sell. The shares bore a restrictive legend like the one on pages 963-964, stating that no SEC registration had occurred and that no transfer could take place unless a registration was filed with the Securities Exchange Commission (SEC) or the owner could supply the written opinion of counsel that such a registration was unnecessary. Professor Chalk wrote the SEC and received a *No Action* letter, which is a non-binding recommendation by an SEC staff counsel that states that the counsel will not recommend that any action be taken by the Commission in connection with the transfer. He then submitted this letter to Beaten Path Mousetrap's transfer agent along with the stock and requested registration to his buyer. The transfer agent refused, claiming non-compliance with the restriction. While the dispute was going on, Beaten Path Mousetrap Corporation went bankrupt. Professor Chalk sued. Who should win? See §§8-401, 8-407; Kenler v. Canal Natl. Bank, 489 F.2d 482 (1st Cir. 1973).

The Guarantee of Signature. The transfer blanks on securities frequently contain a place for the signature of a *guarantor.* Consider the following quotations from Guttman, Modern Securities Transfers, *supra,* at §2-5, p. 2-20-2-21, §2-7 p. 2-22-2-23:

> For over a century, the legal responsibility of the transfer office was construed in extremely stringent terms. That office was and remains today fully responsible for the genuineness of the signature of the "member" purporting to transfer his interest. This responsibility is absolute. Good faith, even the highest degree of diligence and care, does not relieve the issuer from liability where the signature is not in fact genuine or, or is authorized. . . .
>
> . . . To mitigate the issuer's absolute liability in respect of genuineness of a necessary signature, commercial practice developed a working solution, the guarantee of signature. That guarantee remains today the cornerstone of the structure and the essential lubricant of the transfer process.

Read §8-306, ignoring subsections (c) and (d).

Jennie Clarkson Home for Children v. Missouri, Kansas & Texas Railway

Court of Appeals of New York, 1905
182 N.Y. 47, 74 N.E. 571

HAIGHT, J.

This action was brought to recover four registered bonds, of the par value of $1,000 each, payable in gold, in the year 1990, with 4 percent interest coupons attached, numbered respectively 8,872, 8,873, 8,874, and 8,875, issued by the defendant Missouri, Kansas and Texas Railway Company, and secured by first mortgage on the property of the company, or bonds of like amount and value, or, in default thereof, to recover the value of such bonds. The trial resulted in a judgment for the plaintiff substantially for the relief demanded in the complaint, which has been affirmed in the Appellate Division. The facts are without substantial dispute. The plaintiff, the Jennie Clarkson Home for Children, is a domestic corporation organized under the laws of this state for charitable purposes. It was the owner of the bonds in question, which by their terms were not transferable after registration, unless made on the books of the railway company by the registered holder, or by his attorney duly authorized, and noted on the bonds. They were kept in a safe deposit vault in one of the banks in the city, the president and the treasurer of the plaintiff each having a key thereto. On or about the 11th day of March, 1902, George W. Lessels, treasurer of the plaintiff, without the knowledge or consent of any of the officers or directors of the plaintiff corporation, took the bonds in question from the safe deposit vault where they were stored, for the purpose of converting them to his own use, and thereupon he took them to the office of Robert Gibson, who was a member of the stock exchange, doing business as stockbroker under the name of the limited partnership of H. Knickerbacker & Co., and asked that they be sold. The cashier of the defendant Gibson, seeing that the bonds were registered in the name of the plaintiff corporation, informed Lessels that, before the bonds could be sold, the registration must be so altered that they would be payable to bearer. Lessels asked how that could be done and he was then instructed to take them to the transfer office of the defendant railway company, and that there he could find out what was to be done in order to effect the change. Upon application to the railway company he was advised, in substance, that it would be necessary to have a resolution of the board of directors of the plaintiff corporation passed, authorizing a transfer of the bonds, and the furnishing of the company with a copy authenticated by the certificate of the secretary, under the seal of the corporation, to the effect that the copy presented was a true and correct copy of the resolution of the board and that a power of attorney would have to be executed by the corporation, authorizing the transfer of the bonds to bearer, the signature of which must be witnessed by some stock exchange house. Thereupon Lessels returned to the office of H. Knickerbacker & Co., and had the power of attorney drawn, and signed it in the name of the plaintiff, the Jennie Clarkson Home for Children, George W. Lessels, treasurer, and underneath is the statement that it was signed and acknowledged in the presence of John F. Busch, who was the cashier for H. Knickerbacker & Co., and by H. Knickerbacker & Co., which was signed by Gibson. At the same time Lessels presented to H. Knickerbacker & Co. a paper purporting to be a copy of the resolution of the board of directors, authorizing a sale of the bonds, with the certificate of the secretary, under seal, attached. But the resolution was never passed by the board of directors, the certificate of the secretary was never signed by him, and the seal affixed thereto was not the seal of the corporation. All of these papers had been forged. Upon their presentation to defendant Gibson, he caused them to be transmitted to the office of the railway company and there the bonds were changed and made payable to bearer; and then they were returned to the defendant Gibson, who sold them and paid the proceeds over to Lessels, who converted the money to his own use and subsequently absconded.

[The court then quoted Story on Agency to the effect that a principal is not bound by the actions of an agent done beyond the scope of his employment, and concluded that the treasurer was not acting within the scope of his employment while carrying out his defalcation.]

The plaintiff was the owner of the bonds in question. They had been registered by the defendant railway company. That company undertook to keep a registry of such bonds, and not to transfer them, except upon the books of the company by the direction of the owner or by his duly authorized attorney. It is deemed to have undertaken to pay the interest accruing upon these bonds, and the principal, when due, to such registered owner. The purpose of such registration was to save the owner from loss resulting from larceny or destruction of the bonds. Being registered, they could not be sold. If presented to the railway company for payment of the interest or principal by other than the registered owner, payment would be refused. They were only property in the hands of the registered owner. The bonds having been stolen from the plaintiff, it had the right to follow them and recover them wherever found. If they could not be found, it had the right to recover their value from those who had been instrumental in changing them from registered to negotiable bonds. Pollock v. National Bank, 7 N.Y. 274, 57 Am. Dec. 520. The defendant railway company knew that the bonds belonged to the plaintiff, and that it had no right to cancel the registration thereof without the authority of the plaintiff. In cancelling such registry and making them payable to bearer, thus enabling them to be sold in the market, it violated its agreement with the plaintiff, and it cannot be relieved from the effect of such violation by reason of the fact that its transfer agent was deceived by the forgeries of Lessels. So, also, did the defendant Gibson know that the bonds belonged to the plaintiff, and that they were registered, and could not be sold until the registration was changed. To some extent he assisted Lessels in procuring the registration to be changed. He advised Lessels how to obtain the information to make the change. After the requisite information had been obtained, he assisted him in drawing the power of attorney, and took part in its execution, becoming a witness thereto. He had been furnished with copies of what purported to be a resolution of the board of directors, with the false signatures of the president and secretary attached, which he transmitted, with the bonds, to the transfer agent of the railway company, to procure the change in the registry. Even after that change had been made, he still knew that the bonds belonged to the plaintiff, and that he had no right to sell them without its authority. And the fact that he was deceived by the fraudulent misrepresentations of Lessels did not relieve him from the responsibility of his acts with reference to depriving the plaintiff of them. The bonds had been traced into his hands, and the plaintiff had the right to seek them there and recover them if they were still in his possession, or if he had sold them and misappropriated the proceeds, knowing that they were the plaintiff's, to recover the value thereof from him. . . .

After the complaint in this action had been served upon the defendant railway company, it served an answer upon the defendant Gibson, in which it demanded relief as against him to the effect that, in case it was compelled to restore the bonds or pay plaintiff's claim, it should have a judgment for the amount so compelled to be paid over as against Gibson. We thus have an issue raised as between the defendants, in which the plaintiff is not interested. Under the provisions of the bonds, they may be registered in the books of the company, and, if so registered, they will thereafter be transferable only upon the books of the company by the owner in person or by attorney duly authorized. It therefore became necessary, in order to change the registry of the bonds, to have a power of attorney executed by the plaintiff. This power of attorney, as we have seen, was drawn in the office of the defendant Gibson, and executed in his presence and that of his cashier, by Lessels signing the name of the corporation thereto, and underneath his own name with the word "treasurer." It was then witnessed by Gibson and by his cashier. Both Gibson and the transfer agent of the railway company were members of the stock exchange. The trial court found as a fact "that in and by the custom among the members of the New York Stock Exchange and of railway transfer agencies in the city of New York the signature of a stock exchange house or a member thereof upon a power of attorney to transfer securities was, during all the times mentioned in the complaint, a guaranty of the correctness of the signature of the parties purporting to execute it." This finding is based upon the rule of the exchange and the testimony of the witness. The rule is as follows: "An indorsement by a member of the exchange, or a firm represented by the exchange, on a certificate is considered a guaranty of the correctness of the signature of the party in whose name the stock stands. In all cases where powers of substitution are used, the original assignment and power of attorney, and each power of substitution, must be guaranteed by a member, or a firm represented in the exchange, resident or doing business in New York." James L. Carter was sworn as a witness on behalf of the defendant railway company, and testified that he was employed by the banking house of J.P. Morgan & Co., that they were transfer agents for about 150 companies, and that there was an established custom as to the requirements upon the transfer of bonds in the city of New York, and that was to require the guaranty of a stock exchange house, or a member of the stock exchange, on the power of attorney on which the transfer is made.

As we have seen, Gibson not only witnessed the power of attorney authorizing the transfer of the bonds on the books of the railway company, but he also transmitted the bonds accompanied by such power of attorney, and with what purported to be the resolution of the board of directors, to the transfer agent of the defendant railway company to have the change of the registration made. The transfer agent, in making the change in the bonds, acted upon the papers so forwarded from defendant Gibson's house. Gibson was a member of the stock exchange in good standing, acquainted with Lessels, his customer, and he must be deemed to have become a witness to the power of attorney under the custom in force. As we have seen, the bonds stood in the name of the Jennie Clarkson Home for Children. Lessels had no power or authority to sell or transfer the bonds or to sign the plaintiff's name as attorney or agent authorizing the transfer of the bonds. The power of attorney was not, therefore, signed by the genuine or the correct signature of the corporation. Under these circumstances the courts below have held that the defendant Gibson was liable over to the defendant railway company. . . .

This much is conceded. But it is contended on behalf of Gibson that he did not, by becoming a witness, undertake to guaranty that Lessels had authority to sign the name of the corporation. This presents the real question in the case, and it really becomes one of construction as to the meaning of the rule of the stock exchange which is the basis of the custom found by the trial court. Under the rule, an indorsement by a member of the exchange on a certificate is considered "a guaranty of the correctness of the signature of the party in whose name the stock stands." If stock is held by an individual who is executing a power of attorney for its transfer, the member of the exchange who signs as a witness thereto guarantees not only the genuineness of the signature affixed to the power of attorney, but that the person signing is the individual in whose name the stock stands. With reference to stock standing in the name of a corporation, which can only sign a power of attorney through its authorized officers or agents, a different situation is presented. If the witnessing of the signature of the corporation is only that of the signature of a person who signs for the corporation, then the guaranty is of no value, and there is nothing to protect purchasers of the companies who are called upon to issue new stock in the place of that transferred from the frauds of persons who have signed the names of corporations without authority. If such is the only effect of the guaranty, purchasers and transfer agents must first go to the corporation in whose name the stock stands and ascertain whether the individual who signed the power of attorney had authority to so do. This will require time, and in many cases will necessitate the postponement of the completion of the purchase by the payment of the money until the facts can be ascertained. The broker who is acting for the owner has an opportunity to become acquainted with his customer, and may readily before sale ascertain, in case of a corporation, the name of the officer who is authorized to execute the power of attorney. It was therefore, we think, the purpose of the rule to cast upon the broker who witnesses the signature the duty of ascertaining whether the person signing the name of the corporation has authority to so do, and making the witness a guarantor that it is the signature of the corporation in whose name the stock stands. . . .

The judgment should be affirmed, with costs.

Official Comment 2 to §8-306 quotes extensively from this very case, so it still accurately states the law. The New York markets require that the guarantor be either a member of an exchange in New York (individual or corporate) or a commercial bank or trust company either located in New York or having a correspondent in New York. See N.Y.S.E. Rule 209, A.S.E. Rule Sr-47, N.Y.S.T.A. Rule 20. In theory, any person may guarantee a signature. Read Official Comment 2 to §8-402.

PROBLEM 268

Maude Raisin was 80 years old and the registered owner of 100 shares of IBM stock. Her faithful companion of 15 years was Charleyne Rikki, who, one day after being turned down for a raise, took the stock and forged Ms. Raisin's signature to it. She took the stock to Bing, Bong & Bell (B.B. & B.), stockbrokers, and asked them to sell it. B.B. & B. did so, guaranteeing the Raisin signature as part of the registration process. Maude discovered the loss, Charleyne went to jail, and Maude sued B.B. & B. on their signature guarantee. Should she prevail? See §8-306(h). Would a common law suit for conversion prevail? See §8-115 and its Official Comment 3; Decker v. Yorkton Securities, Inc., 106 Cal. App. 4th 1315 (2003). Who should she sue? See §8-404 and its Official Comment; Scott v. Ametek, Inc., 277 A.2d 714 (Del. Ch. 1971).

PROBLEM 269

Assume in the last Problem that Maude Raisin realizes that the stock had been taken and immediately contacts the issuer of the stock and alerts the issuer to the theft. When the stock is presented to the issuer later in the week, what duties does it have? See §§8-403 and 8-404. Does Maude have a duty to notify the issuer promptly? Read §8-406. If the issuer gives her a replacement for her missing stock and then the original shares turn up in the hands of a protected purchaser, what are the issuer's rights? See §8-405(b).[3]

VI. SECURITY ENTITLEMENTS

Part 5 of Article 8 deals with security entitlements in indirect holding systems. In such systems investment securities are held by one entity in an account and computer instructions are used to sell interests in the account—typically first to a bank or a stock brokerage and from there to other purchasers.

In re Estate of Rider

Supreme Court of South Carolina, 2014
407 S.C. 386, 756 S.E.2d 136

Justice BEATTY.

This Court granted a petition for a writ of certiorari to review the decision of the Court of Appeals in Rider v. Estate of Rider, 394 S.C. 84, 713 S.E.2d 643 (Ct. App. 2011), which applied the common law of agency to hold that certain financial assets were part of the decedent's probate estate. The decedent had directed his bank to transfer specified assets in his investment account to a new account for his spouse, but died before all of the assets were credited to her account. At issue in this case of first impression is whether South Carolina's Uniform Commercial Code ("UCC") or the common law of agency controls the transfer. We reverse.

I. FACTS

Charles Galen Rider ("Husband") executed an Investment Agency Agreement/Discretionary Account ("Account Agreement") with First Union

3. Under §17(f) of the Securities Act of 1934, 15 U.S.C. §78q(f) (1967), and S.E.C. Rule, 17 C.F.R. §240.17f-1, brokers and others regularly dealing with securities must comply with rigorous notification procedures for lost securities. See Pillero, Ilkson, & Yadley, Does SEC Rule 17f-1 Destroy Bona Fide Purchaser Status Under the UCC?, N.Y. L.J., Dec. 13, 1976, at 46. For a case denying protected purchaser status to a bank that failed to check with the Securities Information Center computer before buying stolen bonds, see First Natl. Bank of Cicero v. Lewco Sec. Corp., 860 F.2d 1407 (7th Cir. 1988).

National Bank of North Carolina ("First Union"), a predecessor of Wachovia Bank, N.A. ("Wachovia"), on September 27, 1993. The Account Agreement authorized First Union "to open and maintain an Agency Account" for Husband and "to hold therein, as [his] Agent, all cash, stocks, bonds, securities and other property . . . subject to" Husband's current and future written instructions. The Account Agreement stated First Union was "to provide investment review and management of the Account, taking such action as [the bank], in [its] discretion, deem[s] best . . . as though [the bank] were the owner of such property." This discretionary authority permitted First Union to buy, sell, and exercise certain rights regarding the securities in accordance with the overall investment objective selected by Husband. The terms of the Account Agreement called for its termination upon the bank acquiring actual knowledge of Husband's death, but that Husband's death "shall not affect the validity of any prior actions."

On June 8, 2005, Husband called Ruth DiLella in the Capital Management Group of what was then Wachovia and informed her that he had met with his estate attorney, who had advised him to transfer some assets to his spouse, Carolyn S. Rider ("Wife"). Husband was suffering from terminal cancer and reportedly wanted Wife to have sufficient funds to maintain her standard of living during the inevitable time that probate would be going on. Husband instructed DiLella to move $2 million in securities from his account at Wachovia and place them in a new account in Wife's name. DiLella told Husband that Wachovia would send him a list of specific securities to transfer, along with a signature page for him to sign to approve the transfer. The same day, DiLella e-mailed a list of assets totaling $2 million to Wachovia's trust department, along with Husband's instruction, so it could prepare a letter and asset listing for the client's approval.

On June 17, 2005, Husband signed the letter and returned it to the attention of Wachovia's trust administrator. The letter provided: "Please accept this letter as my authority and direction to transfer the assets listed on the following page to a new agency account to be opened for my wife, Carolyn Sue Rider." A total of $2 million in assets were listed, which included specific securities and a small sum of cash.

In response, Wachovia made a series of four transfers from June to October 2005. On June 21, 2005, four days after Husband's signing of the June 17th directive, Wachovia made the first transfer of $733,228.00 in securities (stocks) to Wife's account. On July 8, 2005, Wachovia transferred $39,672.00 in securities (stocks). That afternoon, Husband passed away in Charlotte, North Carolina, and Husband's daughter, respondent Deborah Rider McClure, notified Wachovia the same day. The next business day, Monday, July 11, 2005, Wachovia transferred $935,032.64 in securities (mutual funds) to Wife's account, and on October 20, 2005, Wachovia made a fourth and final transfer of $304,182.46 in securities (mutual funds). The total amount transferred to Wife's account was $2,012,115.00, the excess being due to the appreciation in the value of the securities.

In 2006, Thomas M. Grady, as personal representative of Husband's estate ("PR"), instituted this declaratory judgment action in the probate court for Beaufort County asking the court to determine either (1) that the securities transferred pursuant to Husband's June 17, 2005 letter to Wachovia were completed transfers on June 17, 2005 and, thus, were not includible in Husband's probate estate; or (2) that the securities transferred after Husband's death on July 8, 2005 were incomplete transfers and were includible in Husband's probate estate. The PR did not take a position, but sought guidance as to whether the UCC or the law of agency under the South Carolina common law controlled the outcome.

In its order, the probate court stated much of the argument in this case centered on whether the UCC's provision on Investment Securities applies to the securities transfer directed by Husband on June 17, 2005. The probate court stated Wife argued the UCC applies, Husband's June 17, 2005 directive was an "entitlement order" under the applicable definition in the UCC found in S.C. Code Ann. §36-8-102, the transfer was effectuated on June 17, 2005, and it was unaffected by Husband's death before completion of the transfers. In contrast, Husband's two daughters from his prior marriage, Deborah Rider McClure and Ginger C. McClure, and his two grandsons, Christian McClure and Austin McClure (collectively, "the McClure Respondents") argued, *inter alia,* that the UCC did not apply and, even if it did, it did not supplant the law of agency that governed the parties' Account Agreement. Either way, Wachovia's authority to make the transfers ended when it acquired actual knowledge of Husband's death and the disputed assets belonged to Husband's probate estate.

The probate court found the UCC controlled this securities transaction, that Husband's June 17, 2005 directive was an "entitlement order," and Wachovia was a "securities intermediary." However, it determined an entitlement order's "effective date" is a distinguishable concept from when an entitlement order is "effectuated." The probate court agreed with Wife that Husband's entitlement order was "effective" upon its issuance to Wachovia on June 17, 2005, but reasoned it still had to be carried out by Wachovia, the securities intermediary, to be "effectuated," and the UCC did not supplant the laws of property or agency, nor did it vitiate the terms of the Account Agreement.

The probate court noted Wachovia received actual notice of Husband's death on Friday, July 8th, that the second transfer of $39,672.00 was posted to Wife's account that day, and that the third transfer of $935,032.64 was posted to Wife's account the next business day, Monday, July 11th. The court stated the credible testimony at trial persuaded it that Wachovia took the necessary actions to effectuate the second and third transfers before it knew of Husband's death. The court observed, "In the commercial context of the transactions, it would be unreasonable to conclude otherwise."

The probate court concluded the first three transfers, totaling $1,707,932.64, which were posted to Wife's account on June 21, July 8, and July 11, 2005, respectively, were carried out and effectuated before Husband's death and are not part of his probate estate. However, the securities posted to Wife's account on October 20, 2005 in the amount of $304,082.46 belonged to Husband's probate estate because it was not effectuated until after Husband's death, when Wachovia's authority to act had already terminated.

Wife appealed to the circuit court, which affirmed in an order adopting the probate court's factual findings and legal conclusions. Wife appealed to the Court of Appeals, which found both the third and fourth transfers properly belonged to Husband's probate estate because they occurred after the bank had actual knowledge of Husband's death, but that no error was preserved regarding the third transfer because the McClure Respondents did not cross-appeal, so it too affirmed. Rider v. Estate of Rider, 394 S.C. 84, 713 S.E.2d 643 (Ct. App. 2011). The Court of Appeals also distinguished the "effective date" of Husband's entitlement order from the date it was "effectuated" and found the latter determinative of the question of ownership. This Court granted Wife's petition for a writ of certiorari to review the decision of the Court of Appeals. . . .

III. Law/Analysis

Wife contends the UCC addresses the subject matter at issue in this appeal, arguing only where the UCC is incomplete does the common law provide the applicable rule. *See* S.C. Code Ann. §36-1-103 (2003) ("Unless displaced by the particular provisions of this act [Title 36, the UCC], the principles of law and equity, including . . . the law relative to capacity to contract, principal and agent, estoppel, fraud, . . . or other validating or invalidating cause shall supplement its provisions."); Hitachi Elec. Devices (USA), Inc. v. Platinum Techns., Inc., 366 S.C. 163, 170, 621 S.E.2d 38, 41 (2005) ("Only where the U.C.C. is incomplete does the common law provide applicable rules.").

Chapter 8 of our state's UCC governs "Investment Securities." S.C. Code Ann. §36-8-101 (2003). It is based on the state's adoption of the revised Article 8 contained in the model Uniform Commercial Code prepared by the American Law Institute in collaboration with the National Conference of Commissioners on Uniform State Laws. Its primary purposes are to provide uniformity in the securities industry and to provide an accurate description of the realities of the securities markets, and secondarily to enhance the value-adding factors of liquidity and certainty in securities transactions. S.C.

Code Ann. §§36-8-101 to -511 cmt. at 82 (2003 & Supp. 2013) (S.C. Reporter's Introductory Comment to the 2000 Revision). Part 5 of Chapter 8, entitled "Security Entitlements," specifically governs the "indirect holding system," whereby purchasers of securities deal with intermediaries who hold securities for others, as compared to the traditional system whereby purchasers deal directly with the issuers of those securities. *See* cmt. at 83. It is noted in the Introductory Comment that these provisions "supplant a pastiche of common law rules and agreed practices." *Id.*

In the current matter, Wachovia held certain financial assets (securities) for Husband and managed those assets, subject to his oversight, pursuant to the Account Agreement, by which the bank acted as Husband's agent. This relationship thus implicates the indirect holding system set forth in Part 5 as well as general UCC provisions. Under the terms of the UCC, Husband was an "entitlement holder" with a "security entitlement" to the "financial assets" in a "securities account" maintained and managed by Wachovia for Husband's benefit in its capacity as a "securities intermediary." These and related terms are statutorily defined.

A "financial asset" includes "a security" or a share or other interest in property "which is, or is of a type, dealt in or traded on financial markets[.]" S.C. Code Ann. §36-8-102(a)(9) (2003). A "securities account" is "an account to which a financial asset is or may be credited in accordance with an agreement under which the person maintaining the account undertakes to treat the person for whom the account is maintained as entitled to exercise the rights that comprise the financial asset." *Id.* §36-8-501(a).

Wachovia is a "securities intermediary," which is defined to include "a bank . . . that in the ordinary course of its business maintains securities accounts for others and is acting in that capacity." *Id.* §36-8-102(a)(14)(ii).

Husband was the "entitlement holder," which the UCC defines as follows: "A person identified in the records of a security intermediary as the person having a security entitlement against the securities intermediary. If a person acquires a security entitlement by virtue of Section 36-8-501(b)(2) or (3), that person is the entitlement holder." *Id.* §36-8-102(a)(7).

A "security entitlement" consists of "the rights and property interest of an entitlement holder with respect to a financial asset specified in Part 5 [of Title 36]." *Id.* §36-8-102(a)(17). Section 36-8-501(b) of the UCC provides a person generally acquires a security entitlement if a securities intermediary does any of the following three things: "(1) indicates by book entry that a financial asset has been credited to the person's securities account; (2) receives a financial asset from the person or acquires a financial asset for the person and, in either case, accepts it for credit to the person's securities account; or (3) becomes obligated under other law, regulation, or rule to credit a financial asset to the person's securities account." *Id.* §36-8-501(b).

Husband, as the entitlement holder, retained the right to direct Wachovia to make changes in his account by issuing an "entitlement order," i.e., "a notification communicated to a securities intermediary directing transfer or redemption of a financial asset to which the entitlement holder has a security entitlement." *Id.* §36-8-102(a)(8).

Wachovia was statutorily required to respond to an appropriate entitlement order. *See id.* §36-8-506 ("A securities intermediary shall exercise rights with respect to a financial asset if directed to do so by an entitlement holder."); *id.* §36-8-507(a) ("A securities intermediary *shall comply* with an entitlement order if [1] the entitlement order is *originated by the appropriate person,* [2] the securities intermediary has had reasonable opportunity to assure itself that the entitlement order is genuine and authorized, and [3] the securities intermediary has had *reasonable opportunity to comply* with the entitlement order." (emphasis added)).

An "appropriate person" with respect to an entitlement order is the entitlement holder. *Id.* §36-8-107(a)(3). However, if the person "is deceased, the designated person's successor taking under other law or the designated person's personal representative acting for the estate of the decedent" is an appropriate person to initiate an entitlement order. *Id.* §36-8-107(a)(4).

The UCC further provides that "[e]ffectiveness of an . . . entitlement order is determined as of the date the . . . entitlement order *is made,* and an . . . entitlement order *does not become ineffective by reason of any later change in circumstances.*" *Id.* §36-8-107(e) (emphasis added). Subsection (e) clarifies the protection from liability of securities intermediaries who rely on appropriate persons, and "[t]his protection reflects the policy of revised Article 8 to enhance liquidity and finality in securities transactions." *Id.* §36-8-107 cmt. at 143 (S.C. Reporter's Comment to 2000 Revision).

In the Court of Appeals, the court first reviewed the terms of the Account Agreement and found the "prior actions" clause therein refers to both Husband's and Wachovia's conduct and that the plain language of the agreement showed Wachovia's authority ended upon actual knowledge of Husband's death. Rider v. Estate of Rider, 394 S.C. 84, 91, 713 S.E.2d 643, 646-47 (Ct. App. 2011). The court stated the determination whether the securities in the fourth transfer were part of Husband's estate was, therefore, determined by whether Husband's and Wachovia's conduct was sufficient to complete the transfers before Wachovia learned of Husband's death. *Id.* at 91, 713 S.E.2d at 647.

Wife argued the general agency rule that an agent lacks authority to act for a principal after a principal's death, relied upon by the McClure Respondents, does not apply to this situation because Husband's June 17, 2005 directive was an effective entitlement order under Article 8 of the UCC. *Id.* Wife contended (1) an effective entitlement order transfers the right to financial assets the date it is made and, (2) even if it does not, an entitlement order *remains effective* pursuant to the UCC provision above, which displaces the agency rule under the common law, so that actions taken to comply with the entitlement order may be completed regardless of later changes in circumstances. *Id.* at 91-92, 713 S.E.2d at 647.

The Court of Appeals rejected both of Wife's contentions and determined "the probate court properly found the [securities in] the fourth transfer are part of [Husband's] estate." *Id.* at 93, 713 S.E.2d at 648. In reaching this conclusion, the Court of Appeals stated the UCC applied, but nevertheless found the UCC's rule as to the effective date of an entitlement order contained in section 36-8-107(e) of the UCC did not fully address the subject, so it did not displace the relevant agency rule. *Id.* at 93-95, 713 S.E.2d at 648-49.

Applying the common law of agency, the Court of Appeals reasoned that an entitlement order does not complete a transfer of financial assets at the time it is made, so like other orders to agents, it is an instruction to act in the manner the principal desires, and the request is terminated by the principal's death, citing Carver v. Morrow, 213 S.C. 199, 204, 48 S.E.2d 814, 817 (1948) (stating as a general rule, an "agency terminates upon the death of the principal") and C.J.S. *Agency* §122 (2003) ("The fact that the agent has performed, as authorized, one or several acts of that which was contemplated as a single transaction does not operate to preserve or keep alive the power until the completion of the transaction."). *Id.* at 93-94, 713 S.E.2d at 648.

The court distinguished the effective date of the entitlement order from the date it was completed by Wachovia, which it defined as when the assets were credited to Wife's account, and it found the fourth transfer at issue was completed by Wachovia in October 2005, citing S.C. Code Ann. §36-8-501(b)(1) (providing a book entry by the securities intermediary to a person's account establishes a security entitlement). *Id.* at 94, 713 S.E.2d at 648. As a result, the court held the securities in the fourth transfer, having been credited after the bank's knowledge of Husband's death, are properly part of Husband's probate estate because the bank's authority under the Account Agreement had ended. *Id.* at 96, 713 S.E.2d at 649.

Several jurisdictions have observed there is a dearth of authority addressing the unique problems arising under Article 8 of the UCC. *See, e.g.*, Meadow Homes Dev. Corp. v. Bowens, 211 P.3d 743, 745 (Colo. App. 2009) (stating the "appeal raises issues of first impression under Revised UCC Article 8 (Investment Securities)" that had not previously been considered in the jurisdiction and that "have received surprisingly little attention elsewhere"); Watson v. Sears, 766 N.E.2d 784, 788 (Ind. Ct. App. 2002) ("Unfortunately, there is no discernible case law anywhere under revised Article 8 of the U.C.C. (Title 8 in Maryland)—and very little commentary—dealing with the question of the effect of an entitlement order that is authorized by only one of the entitlement holders on a joint account.").

As one legal commentator has opined, a significant body of case law has not developed for the indirect holding system, and the reported cases generally have applied whatever principles were necessary to protect an innocent investor, so they did not create well-reasoned legal doctrines to resolve the competing policies unique to the indirect holding system. Russell A. Hakes, *UCC Article 8: Will the Indirect Holding of Securities Survive the Light of Day?*, 35 Loy. L.A. L. Rev. 661, 678 (2002). "The drafters [of UCC Article 8] had the benefit of effectively starting with a clean slate." *Id.* "Troubling precedents could be overruled by the adoption of contrary concepts that matched the perceptions of those most familiar with the operation of the system-securities professionals." *Id.* "The interest and experience of securities professionals were essential to an Article 8 that could successfully govern the indirect holding system." *Id.*

"The securities industry did not want to use principles of bailment, agency, or trust law to describe the basic operations of the indirect holding system, even though agency law governs much in the relationship between the securities industry and its customers." *Id.* at 678-79. "One important goal in revising Article 8 was to simplify transfer rules for the indirect holding system." *Id.* at 679. Moreover, "[t]he drafters also caution courts not to use 'mechanical jurisprudence' but to interpret the definitions based upon the suitability of applying Article 8's substantive rules." *Id.* at 681 (citation omitted).

We agree with the Court of Appeals that the UCC does not invalidate all general principles of agency, but, as noted by the commentator above, those principles must be viewed in light of the unique nature of the indirect holding system. The UCC provisions were created to provide a uniform method of resolving issues in order to promote liquidity and finality, to be supplemented by (not thwarted by) the rules of agency and other applicable laws. *See* S.C. Code Ann. §§36-8-101 to -511 cmt. at 82 (2003 & Supp. 2013) (S.C. Reporter's Introductory Comment to the 2000 Revision) (observing the provisions in Part 5 of the UCC governing Investment Securities "supplant a pastiche of common law rules and agreed practices"); *see also* Psak, Graziano, Piasecki & Whitelaw v. Fleet Nat'l Bank, 390 N.J. Super. 199, 915 A.2d 42, 45 (Ct. App. Div. 2007) ("Indeed, the UCC displaces the common-law where reliance on the common law would thwart the purposes of the UCC." (citing Sebastian v. D & S Express, Inc., 61 F. Supp. 2d 386, 391 (D.N.J. 1999))).

In relying upon agency law to mandate that both Husband's execution of the entitlement order and full compliance by the securities intermediary exist prior to Husband's death, the Court of Appeals has created an additional requirement that does not exist under the UCC and that thwarts the purpose of the language in section 36-8-107(e) establishing a uniform effective date for entitlement orders, regardless of subsequent events. Moreover, it also overlooks the fact that under UCC section 36-8-501(b), the making of a "book entry" is but one of several means by which Wife can acquire an interest in the securities.

Once Husband issued the entitlement order and was the appropriate person, Wachovia was obligated by the UCC and the parties' Account Agreement to obey his directive. Wachovia had set up a new investment account in Wife's name and commenced the transfer of securities within a few days of Husband's request, so at that point, Wife already had a recognizable interest, even though Wachovia had not posted all of the securities to her account. The Court of Appeals, in focusing solely on the date of the "book entry," which it took to mean the date the securities were credited or posted to Wife's account, seemed to view this as the exclusive means for obtaining an interest in the securities. However, a security entitlement is created if a securities intermediary does *any* of the following three things:

> (1) indicates by book entry that a financial asset has been credited to the person's securities account;
> (2) receives a financial asset from the person or acquires a financial asset for the person and, in either case, accepts it for credit to the person's securities account; or
> (3) becomes obligated under other law, regulation, or rule to credit a financial asset to the person's securities account.

S.C. Code Ann. §36-8-501(b).

In this case, while the Court of Appeals relied on book entry under subsection (b)(1), we agree with Wife that under subsection (b)(3), Wachovia had a legal obligation to credit the securities to Wife's account. As noted in the Official Comment to §8-501 of the Uniform Act:

> Paragraph (3) of subsection (b) sets out a residual test, *to avoid any implication that the failure of an intermediary to make the appropriate entries* to credit a position to a customer's securities account *would prevent the customer from acquiring the rights* of an entitlement holder under Part 5. As is the case with the paragraph (2) test, the paragraph (3) test *would not be needed for the ordinary cases,* since they are covered by paragraph (1).

Unif. Commercial Code, Official Comment to §8-501, 2C U.L.A. 579, 581 (2005) (emphasis added).

Wachovia's failure to more quickly make the last posting to Wife's account clearly is not the ordinary case, and it falls squarely within the parameters of the residual provision in section 36-8-501(b)(3). Although the Court of Appeals treats the transfers as separate, unrelated events subject to termination under general agency law, we conclude Husband's execution of an entitlement order directing Wachovia to transfer certain specified securities to Wife is a singular act that falls squarely within the "prior act" language of the parties' agreement. Further, Wachovia's obligation to comply with Husband's entitlement order is supported by the UCC provisions examined above and comports with Article 8's goals of liquidity and finality in securities transactions. Consequently, we hold the disputed assets in this case properly belong to Wife and are not includible in Husband's probate estate.

IV. CONCLUSION

For the foregoing reasons, the decision of the Court of Appeals is reversed.

PROBLEM 270

Mr. Goldbury, an investor, told his broker, Bing, Bong & Bell (B.B. & B.), to buy him 100 shares of Utopia, Ltd. stock. The broker placed the order by having this number of shares transferred to the account it carried with Clearing Corporation. B.B. & B. then marked its books to reflect that Mr. Goldbury owned 100 shares of Utopia, Ltd.

(a) Using the definitions in §8-102, who are the *entitlement holder* and the *securities intermediary*, and what is the *security entitlement*? Who has a *securities account* as that phrase is defined in §8-501(a)?

(b) If the former owner of the 100 shares Mr. Goldbury purchased claims that they were stolen from her and somehow traces them to the account B.B. & B. has with Clearing Corporation, will she succeed in reclaiming the stock? See §8-502 and its Official Comment. If Mr. Goldbury decides to sell his stock, can the former owner announce her ownership rights to the world and thereby give such notice that no one could be free from her adverse claim? See §8-510(a) and (b).

(c) B.B. & B. became insolvent. Mr. Goldbury discovered that he was not the only owner of Utopia, Ltd. stock held by B.B. & B. but that Mr. Blushington also supposedly owned 100 shares of the same stock, according to B.B. & B.'s records. However, in violation of §8-504(a), B.B. & B. only had 50 shares of this stock in its account with Clearing Corporation. Mr. Goldbury's transaction with B.B. & B. occurred two days before Mr. Blushington's. Does that mean that he gets the entire 50 shares? See §8-503(b).

Powers v. American Express Financial Advisors, Inc.

United States Court of Appeals, Fourth Circuit, 2000
238 F.3d 414

PER CURIAM.

Amy Powers and Michael D'Ambrosia, who lived together, had a joint investment account with American Express Financial Advisors (American

Express). On the instructions of D'Ambrosia alone, American Express transferred all of the funds ($86,836.79) in the investment account to a bank account in the couple's joint name. After D'Ambrosia took all of the money, Powers sued American Express, claiming that its transfer to the bank account was ineffective because the signature of both owners of the investment account was required for a transfer of more than $50,000. The district court granted summary judgment to Powers and awarded her damages of $86,836.79, together with prejudgment interest. We affirm.

I.

Powers and D'Ambrosia began living together in 1983. On July 28, 1994, the couple opened an investment account, as joint tenants with right of survivorship, with American Express. The account was initially funded with a $15,000 transfer from the couple's joint bank account. Additions to the account were to come from D'Ambrosia's earnings. D'Ambrosia agreed to the joint account because Powers provided him with "domestic needs" and because she had contributed to improvements made to the couple's residence. To open the American Express account, Powers and D'Ambrosia filled out an investment application. In Section C of the application, Powers and D'Ambrosia checked the box next to the "Joint Tenant" provision, which reads:

> First and second clients have right of Survivorship. This is not the same as tenants-in-common. The first client's home or mailing address will be used for account-related purposes. You understand that only one signature is required for redemption requests up to $50,000.

The couple's application also directed American Express to place their money in four separate mutual funds.

On August 4, 1997, Powers and D'Ambrosia parted ways. By that time their American Express account was valued at over $80,000. Both of them contacted American Express and asked it to freeze the account. Later, in a letter dated September 26, 1997, D'Ambrosia and Powers authorized a release of the freeze and directed American Express to transfer the funds to a Prudential Securities account.

On October 15 and 16, 1997, D'Ambrosia sent American Express two separate faxes. The first, on October 15, contained a memo signed by D'Ambrosia, a copy of D'Ambrosia and Powers's statement of account at American Express, and a copy of the September 26 letter. D'Ambrosia's memo, included in the fax, changed the instructions in the September 26 letter. The memo directed American Express to close the couple's account and to mail the proceeds to D'Ambrosia and Powers's former residence in Columbia, MD. The second fax, dated October 16, also contained a memo from D'Ambrosia, a statement of the couple's account at American Express, and a copy of the September 26 letter. The memo attached to this fax again changed the instructions in the September 26 letter. The memo, signed only by D'Ambrosia, directed American Express to transfer the funds to a joint bank account held by Powers and D'Ambrosia at FCNB Bank. After receiving both faxes, American Express ignored the September 26 letter and followed the instruction in D'Ambrosia's October 16 fax memo. The company wired $86,836.79 to Powers and D'Ambrosia's FCNB joint account, and within a few days, D'Ambrosia absconded with the money.

When Powers discovered what had happened, she filed this action against American Express to recover the money. Both parties moved for summary judgment. Powers claimed that American Express transferred the funds in contravention of section 8-507(b) of Maryland's Commercial Code. See Md. Com. Law (U.C.C.) §8-507(b). Under U.C.C. §8-507(b), a "securities intermediary," like American Express, which transfers funds pursuant to an "ineffective entitlement order," is liable to an "entitlement holder" for any damages caused by the improper transfer. Powers contended that the faxes were ineffective entitlement orders because Section C of the investment application required both signatures for redemption requests over $50,000. Thus, as an entitlement holder, Powers claimed that American Express was liable to her for acting on D'Ambrosia's fax requests of October 15 and 16, 1997, which she did not sign. American Express claimed that Powers's authorization was not necessary. It claimed that D'Ambrosia's faxes constituted an effective entitlement order because, under U.C.C. §8-107(b)(l), D'Ambrosia was an "appropriate person" to order the transfer of the couple's funds.

The district court agreed with Powers that the faxes received by American Express constituted an "ineffective entitlement order." Powers v. American Express Fin. Advisors, Inc., 82 F. Supp. 2d 448, 452 (D. Md. 2000). The court recognized that Powers and D'Ambrosia were "entitlement holders" because as co-owners of the American Express account, "they were identified in the records of the securities intermediary (American Express) as having a security entitlement against the intermediary." Id. at 451. Because D'Ambrosia was an entitlement holder, the court acknowledged American Express's contention that D'Ambrosia was an "appropriate person" to give an entitlement order to American Express under U.C.C. §8-107. Id. at 451-52. The court also noted that when an "appropriate person" issues an entitlement order to a securities intermediary, the intermediary has a duty to execute the order under U.C.C. §8-507(a)(2). Id. at 452. The court decided, however, that section 8-507(a)(2) cannot be read in a vacuum because Section C of the couple's investment application with American Express requires the signatures of both investors for any redemption request above $50,000. The district court held that Section C's joint signature requirement was valid under U.C.C. §1-103. See id. at 453. Section 1-103 states that "the principles of law and equity . . . shall supplement [the U.C.C.]." Thus, "when an intermediary has agreed that the 'appropriate person' to make an order is both owners of a joint account, both owners must make the order." Id. Because Powers did not authorize or otherwise ratify the transfer of the $86,836.79 to an account at FCNB, the district court concluded that the transfer was ineffective. See id. at 452.

The district court also rejected American Express's assertion that the $50,000 threshold only applied to transfers from a single mutual fund account. See id. at 454. Because Powers and D'Ambrosia did not have more than $50,000 in any one of their four mutual funds, American Express asserted that two signatures were not required for the $86,836.79 redemption. The district court held, however, that American Express's interpretation was contrary to the plain language of Section C which states that "only one signature is required for redemption requests up to $50,000." Because the language of Section C refers to redemption requests generally and not to redemption requests out of individual funds, the district court concluded that two signatures were required for any transfer greater than $50,000. See id.

The district court summarily rejected American Express's remaining contentions. American Express claimed that Powers was barred from seeking damages under U.C.C. §8-115. According to U.C.C. §8-115, a securities intermediary is not liable to an individual who has an adverse claim to an asset that a securities intermediary transfers at the direction of a customer. The district court held that Powers was not an adverse claimant for the simple reason that she was one of two entitlement holders with respect to the account. See id. at 453. . . .

II.

After considering the joint appendix, the briefs, and the oral arguments of counsel, we are persuaded that the district court reached the correct result. We therefore affirm substantially on the reasoning of the district court. See Powers v. American Express Fin. Advisors, Inc., 82 F. Supp. 2d 448 (D. Md. 2000).

Affirmed.

CHAPTER 16 ASSESSMENT: MULTIPLE CHOICE QUESTIONS

1. Careless Corporation had already issued all the stock it had power to issue but carelessly issued and sold an extra 100 shares to Rockefeller. What are Rockefeller's rights against Careless Corporation?
   a. Zero.
   b. Careless Corporation must amend its charter to authorize the additional shares.

c. Careless Corporation must attempt to purchase substitute shares and if they are not reasonably available, refund to Rockefeller the money paid.
d. Rockefeller's shares are valid, like any other shares.

2. Oversight Corporation's comptroller was in charge of handling stock certificates, but had not authority to issue or sign them. The comptroller, however, printed up 100 share certificates, forged the signature of the necessary corporate officers on the certificates, and sold them to a good faith purchaser without notice of the wrongdoing. What are the purchaser's rights?
   a. The certificates are effective.
   b. The purchaser takes the loss, for dealing with a forger.
   c. The certificates are ineffective, but the purchaser is entitled to the money from Oversight Corporation.
   d. The purchaser should try to sell them to someone else.

3. Share certificates of Rigid Corporation bear a conspicuous notice that shares may not be sold until the corporation has made an initial public offering, which has not taken place. Happy sold 100 shares to Grumpy, but Rigid Corporation's transfer agent refused to register the transfer. Is the corporation obliged to register the transfer?
   a. Yes. The shares have been sold and now belong to Grumpy.
   b. Yes. Shares are freely transferable and such restrictions are ineffective.
   c. No. The issuer has no obligation to register a transfer that does not comply with a restriction on transfer.
   d. No. The issuer has complete discretion about what to record in its own books.

4. Durant stole Whitney's certificates for shares in Morgan Corporation. Upon request by Durant, along with Whitney's forged signature, Morgan Corporation registered the shares, enabling Durant to sell them to Dow, a bona fide purchaser without notice. What are Whitney's rights?
   a. She can collect from Morgan Corporation for wrongful registration.
   b. She can claim the shares back from Dow.
   c. Both A and B.
   d. She has no rights against Morgan Corporation or Dow, only against Durant. She should have been more careful with the certificates, which are freely negotiable.

5. Paish, a trustee, breached her fiduciary duty by selling the trust's shares in XYZ Corp. and spending the money on a trip to Antarctica. Babson, the trust's beneficiary, somehow traced the shares, which are now held in Keynes' account at Friedman Securities. Can Babson recover the shares from Keynes?

a. Yes. The shares still belong to the trust.
b. Yes. The shares would be subject to a constructive trust, due to the wrongful sale.
c. No. Keynes is protected from all claims, provided Keynes acquired the shares for value and without notice.
d. Yes, because Keynes would merely have a securities entitlement against Friedman Securities, not a right to those particular shares.

ANSWERS

1. *C* is the best answer. Under §8-210, in the event of overissue, the issuer must attempt to buy substitute shares. If they are not reasonably available, the issuer is liable for the amount last paid for the shares. The shares are not valid, because the corporation did not have power to issue them, contrary to *D*. Nor must the corporation amend its charter, so *B* is incorrect. These last two points are really matters of corporation law.
2. *A* is the best answer. Unauthorized signatures are normally ineffective, but are effective if made by an "employee entrusted with responsible handling of the security certificate." §8-205(2).
3. *C* is the best answer. An issuer is obliged to honor a transfer request that complies with §8-401, so *D* is incorrect. But §8-401 provides that an issuer need not register a transfer that is contrary to a valid restriction under §8-201, contrary to *B*. This restriction complies with §8-204, because it is noted conspicuously on the certificate. So even if the shares were purportedly sold, Rigid Corporation has no duty to recognize that sale, making *A* incorrect.
4. *A* is the best answer. Morgan Corporation is liable for wrongful registration under §8-404, due to the ineffective indorsement. This is quite similar to the rule for negotiable instruments. Whitney does not have rights against Dow, who is protected as a bona fide purchaser of registered shares, making *B* incorrect.
5. *C* is the best answer. This question is drawn from the Official Comment to §8-502, which explains that §8-502 precludes any action by Babson against Keynes under any theory, as long as Keynes acquired the security entitlement for value and without notice. Section 8-502 provides "investors in the indirect holding system with protection against adverse claims," as Official Comment 1 puts it. So claims based on ownership or constructive trust will fail, making *A* and *B* incorrect. That means Keynes has protection even though Keynes has a securities entitlement, as opposed to owning the security directly. That makes *D* incorrect.

PART 3

Payment in Documented Sales

Chapter 17
Documents of Title

If you open up your pantry, or closet, or look around the things on your desk you'll discover item after item that came there from far away—not just from other states but even from the other side of the globe: apples from New Zealand, shirts from Malaysia, numerous gadgets from China. How did they all get from there to here? Some might have been mailed or specially delivered by hand, but almost all were boxed up, put in shipping containers, and carried vast distances by plane or cargo ship or truck. The paperwork for these transactions consists of invoices and identification tags, but the primary item is a "document of title," usually a "bill of lading," which describes the goods and the details of carriage, particularly to whom they will be delivered and what conditions exist before that delivery will occur. There are international agreements about bills of lading, and a federal statute on point, and, most importantly for our purposes, Article 7 of the Uniform Commercial Code entitled "Documents of Title." Millions of these transactions take place each year and they usually go off without complications. But when the paperwork gets lost, or the goods are destroyed, or the buyer has committed fraud and the seller wants the transaction halted prior to delivery, the lawyer's phone will ring with legal questions. This chapter should give you some help with that call.

Article 7 of the Code deals with these documents of title (defined in §1-201(b)(16))—items (whether tangible paper or electronic records) issued for the purpose of actually representing title to goods. The two primary types of documents of title are bills of lading (§1-201(b)(6)) and warehouse receipts (§1-201(b)(42)).[1] Article 7 was revised in 2003,[2] primarily to allow the creation of electronic forms of documents of title, and §§7-106 and 7-105 (in that reverse order) deal with such creatures.[3]

The creation of paper representing the right of ownership of the goods became inevitable as soon as merchants wanted to borrow money and pledge goods that they owned as collateral. If the goods were large enough to store in a warehouse, the money lender was normally unwilling to take physical possession of the goods. The money lender was also normally unwilling to give the borrower possession of the collateral for fear the goods would be sold to someone else or taken by the buyer's other creditors. The solution to the problem was to store the goods with a bailee and have the bailee issue a paper stating that the goods belonged to the owner of the paper. In this fashion, the paper, representing the obligation of the bailee to deliver the goods to the holder, could be freely transferred, discounted, and rediscounted without the necessity of moving the goods into the physical control of each new owner. Any holder of the paper could surrender it and require the bailee (*issuer*) to turn over the goods. Read §7-403 carefully. Note that under subsection (c) the person claiming the goods *must* (except in the §7-503 situation discussed later) surrender the negotiable document of title for cancellation in order to receive the goods. If the document has been lost, the holder can get the goods only by procuring a court order directing the bailee to turn over the goods. Read §7-601. Documents of title are negotiable or nonnegotiable depending on whether they contain order or bearer language (§7-104). Since under §7-403(c) the bailee can demand only the surrender of negotiable paper, only negotiable documents of title truly represent absolute ownership of the goods. Nonnegotiable paper simply evidences the contract between the bailor and the bailee, which is to do whatever the contract says. Nonnegotiable documents normally state exactly to whom the bailee will deliver the goods and under what conditions. Therefore, for reasons of safety, lenders prefer to loan money against negotiable documents. With nonnegotiable documents, lenders run the risk that there has already been a delivery of the goods to someone else.

1. For treatises on point, see W. Towle, Warehousing Law (2d ed. 2001), and R. Henson, Documents of Title Under the Uniform Commercial Code (2d ed. 1990).

2. Citations in this chapter referencing Article 7 refer to the 2003 version, which has been adopted by all fifty states and the District of Columbia.

3. For an article on point, see Susan Beecher, Can the Electronic Bill of Lading Go Paperless?, 40 Intl. Law. 627 (2006). In spite of doubts about such electronic bills they are coming into use, as cases in this chapter will show.

I. *WAREHOUSE RECEIPTS*

A. *Form*

The front of a *negotiable* warehouse receipt states the name of the warehouse that is issuing the receipt and states in large type that:

> This is to certify that we have received in storage for the account of_____ in apparent order, except as noted hereon (contents, condition, and quality being unknown), the following described property, subject to all of the terms and conditions on the front or back of this contract, such property to be delivered to _____ or order, upon payment of all storage, handling, and other charges and the surrender of this Warehouse receipt properly indorsed.

Following this statement usually there are the following:

(1) a space for listing the goods stored,
(2) a statement of the warehouse company's intention to claim a lien against the goods until the storage charges are paid,
(3) a statement as to the amount of the storage charge, and
(4) the official signature of the warehouse company.

The back of the warehouse receipt contains a space in which the agent of the warehouse can note *partial* deliveries to the holder of the document (later holders can claim only the amount of goods the document shows were not delivered to prior holders). The back also has the *standard contract terms* in small print (these standard terms were adopted by a 1926 conference of experts and approved by the Department of Commerce); the terms cover the fact that the storage is on a month-to-month basis and spell out in detail the warehouse company's position as to insurance, limitation of liability, right to move the goods, etc.

A nonnegotiable warehouse receipt looks substantially the same except:

(1) It is not made deliverable to anyone. The warehouse engages to deliver the goods as per instructions received from the person storing the goods (the bailor). *Order* language is not used.
(2) There is no space on the back for notation of partial deliveries. This is because surrender of the document is not required to take out all or part of the goods. Section 7-403(c) applies only to *negotiable* documents.

Negotiable warehouse receipts normally have the word *NEGOTIABLE* stamped across their face in large letters (and the documents tend to have fancy and ornate borders, designed to make counterfeiting more difficult). Nonnegotiable documents have *NONNEGOTIABLE* stamped on the front.

Glance through §7-202.

As can be seen from the above, the warehouse receipt plays three roles: it is (1) a *receipt* for the goods, (2) a *contract* for storage, and (3) if negotiable, a *physical embodiment* of the concept of *title* to the goods.

B. *Basic Bailment Law*

All document-of-title situations start with the bailment of the goods and the issuance of a receipt by the bailee. Bailment law is relevant to fill in the gaps in Article 7 and the federal statutes. The most important bailment concept needed to supplement the Code is that the bailee is required to make proper delivery of the goods to the bailor when the bailment ends or is to be responsible for nondelivery. Section 7-403(a) gives very few excuses for nondelivery. An *unauthorized* delivery of the goods by a bailee is conversion. Restatement (Second) of Torts §234; cf. §7-601(b). Read §7-404. A "bailee is absolutely liable for misdelivering cargo, unless his mistake as to the person entitled to receive the goods was induced by the bailor." David Crystal, Inc. v. Cunard Steam-Ship Co., Ltd., 339 F.2d 295, 298 (2d Cir. 1964); Met-Al, Inc. v. Hansen Storage Co., 828 F. Supp. 1369 (E.D. Wis. 1993) ("Equitable defenses to allegations of misdelivery are disfavored."); Singer Co. v. Stott & Davis Motor Express, Inc., 79 A.D.2d 227, 463 N.Y.S.2d 508 (App. Div. 1981) ("Once a plaintiff establishes delivery of goods and the failure of the bailee to return them on demand, a prima facie case of negligence is made and the burden of coming forward with evidence tending to show due cause shifts to the bailee. . . ."); People v. Wallace, 2011 WL 1662860 (N.Y. App. Div. 2011) ("A person need not knowingly or intentionally act wrongfully for a conversion to occur"). These principles are best illustrated by one of the cases rising out of the famous Salad Oil scandal.

Procter & Gamble Distributing Co. v. Lawrence American Field Warehouse Corp.

Court of Appeals of New York, 1965
16 N.Y.2d 344, 213 N.E.2d 897, 266 N.Y.S.2d 765 21 A.L.R.3d 1320

VAN VOORHIS, J.

This is an action against a warehouse corporation based upon the nondelivery of the merchandise for which it issued its warehouse receipts. The theory of action is conversion. Plaintiff (hereafter called P & G) asserts that in the absence of any explanation of the disappearance of these goods, the defendant (hereafter called Field) is liable for the market value of this merchandise at the times when it was delivered to the warehouse. Plaintiff is correct in these contentions, we have concluded, and is entitled to summary judgment in this amount. We agree with the Appellate Division that no triable issue is presented concerning the liability of defendant, but consider that the Appellate Division erred in directing an assessment of damages and in not awarding to plaintiff the undisputed market value of the merchandise delivered to defendant at the time of its delivery, which was as high as at any subsequent time or times prior to notification to plaintiff of its disappearance. The basic issue is simple, but it has been encrusted with a complex of fact and legal argument which makes it necessary to discuss the case in more detail.

Allied Crude Vegetable Oil Refining Corp. (hereinafter called Allied) is not a party to this action, but this cause of action against defendant arose through a course of dealings between plaintiff and Allied, which traded in vegetable oils manufactured by various producers including plaintiff. Originally plaintiff sold such merchandise outright on sight draft with bill of lading attached. In the early Fall of 1962, however, in order more fully to utilize its working capital, Allied persuaded plaintiff to engage in a practice known as field warehousing. Allied had leased oil storage tanks at Bayonne, New Jersey, formerly owned by the Tidewater Associated Oil Company. These were sublet to Field, a wholly owned subsidiary of American Express Company (hereafter called Amexco), which thereupon operated as an independent warehouse company. When Allied purchased vegetable oils from plaintiff, and other producers, as it did f.o.b. seller's plant or warehouse, Bayonne, New Jersey, the oil would be shipped to Bayonne to the seller's order, and stored for the seller's account in Field's warehouses. Down payments were made, described in the contract as "Margin Requirements on Consigned Shipments," amounting to about 20% of the purchase price, at the time of receipt of the oil at Field's warehouse, and the balance by sight draft with bill of lading attached, or cash in advance of shipment to buyer, as Allied disposed of the oil.

In accordance with this procedure, plaintiff shipped 9,206,740 pounds of fully refined soybean oil under bills of lading to plaintiff itself as consignee at Bayonne, New Jersey, which was delivered for storage and safe keeping to Field at said warehouse for plaintiff's account. Field, the defendant, issued five warehouse receipts for this oil dated March 22, April 1 and April 9, 1963. Each warehouse receipt recited the number of the bill of lading for the tank car in which it had been contained, amounting in total to 151 tank carloads. Not only was the presence of this oil in defendant's tanks attested by these nonnegotiable receipts issued in plaintiff's name, but also by a series of month-end statements, issued by defendant indicating that the oil was in the warehouse. Both the warehouse receipts and these month-end statements, based on defendant's books, are evidence that the oil was received by defendant at its tank warehouse in Bayonne, New Jersey. In the absence of any evidentiary facts showing that defendant did not receive the oil in the suit, its warehouse receipts, month-end statements and books of account are conclusive against defendant on this point. Mere suspicion that the oil was stolen before reaching defendant's tanks is not sufficient to overcome this documentary evidence. . . . The usual measure of damage, in event of non-delivery of goods by a bailee, is the market value on the date of the conversion . . . not the date when the bailor learns of the loss or presents his warehouse receipt and demands his merchandise. Where, as here, the date of the conversion has not been identified, the Appellate Division has held that the value should be fixed as of the date when the bailor received notice of the loss. This, we think, was error. The circumstances regarding the loss of bailed property are more likely to be known by the bailee than by the bailor, and, where the time and manner of the loss is unknown, it ought not lie in the power of the bailee to choose the date for determining market value by electing when to notify the bailor that the goods have disappeared and cannot be accounted for. The rule that the loss is to be measured as of the time of the conversion, when the conversion date is known, should not be reshaped to designate the date when the bailor is notified of the conversion if the conversion date is unknown. That would place the bailee in a better legal position by pleading ignorance of the circumstances of the loss than if he knew or revealed the circumstances. . . .

[I]t follows that the bailor should be awarded damages measured by the highest value of the property between the date when the bailment commenced and the date when the bailor has received notice that the property has been lost. . . .

On its appeal defendant (Field) contends that there is a triable issue respecting whether it exercised reasonable care as bailee of this oil. Defendant points to section 7-204 of the Uniform Commercial Code, in effect in New Jersey at the time, providing that a warehouseman is liable for damages for loss or injury to the goods "caused by his failure to exercise such care in regard to them as a reasonably careful man would exercise under like circumstances but unless otherwise agreed he is not liable for damages which could not have been avoided by the exercise of such care." Section 7-403 of the same statute provides that the bailee must deliver the goods to a person under the document unless and to the extent that the bailee established "damage to or delay, loss or destruction of the goods for which the bailee is not liable."

These sections of the Uniform Commercial Code appear not to have altered for present purposes the prior law . . . that a warehouseman shall not be liable for loss or injury to the goods which could not have been avoided by the exercise of reasonable care, and section 8 (General Business Law, former §95), like section 7-403 of the Uniform Commercial Code, stated that a warehouseman is liable for nondelivery of bailed goods "in the absence of some lawful excuse provided by this article." Citing these sections, the Appellate Division correctly stated . . . that a warehouseman "has the burden of explanation for any loss or disappearance of the property bailed. . . . It is not enough to assert that care was taken, describing the practices used, when the disappearance of the oil remains wholly unexplained." . . . In the opinion by the present Chief Judge the rule applicable here was stated in the form of a quotation from Claflin v. Meyer (75 N.Y. 260, 264):

> If he [the bailor] proves the demand upon the warehouseman and his refusal to deliver, these facts unexplained are treated by the courts as prima facie evidence of negligence; but if, either in the course of his proof or that of the defendant, it appears that the goods have been lost by theft, the evidence must show that the loss arose from the negligence of the warehouseman. . . .

The Appellate Division well said that it is self-contradictory for a warehouseman simultaneously to assert due care and total lack of knowledge of what happened, and that it would establish an unwise rule to place a bailee in better position to be excused if he knew less about the disappearance of the goods than if he knew more. That is the underlying reason for the time-honored law of New York and New Jersey requiring a warehouseman to make an explanation of injury or loss in the case of bailed merchandise, which has been continued and not abolished by the Uniform Commercial Code.

The other points raised on the appeal by defendant Field merit but passing mention. One is that plaintiff should be obliged to accept a proportionate share of the conglomerate found on hand in the tanks of these subsidiaries of Amexco. This consisted mostly of acid soap stock, fish oil and water. These mixed fluids were not the edible fully refined vegetable oil delivered to Field by plaintiff. An argument is made that the warehouse receipts showed plaintiff's refined vegetable oil to be fungible, and granted permission to mix it with similar oil owned by other depositors. From that it is said that a warehouseman need do no more than take the word of other customers concerning the nature of the fluids which are being placed in the tanks of the warehouseman, and that if it be soap acid or fish oil then that is plaintiff's misfortune. It is a sufficient answer to that contention that plaintiff is not required to acquit the warehouse in whole or in part by taking in return a commodity or blend of commodities of a different nature from that which was deposited. . . .

No one has ever discovered exactly what happened to the missing salad oil (which was the collateral for millions of dollars worth of loans). N. Miller, The Great Salad Oil Swindle (1965).

As this case indicates, a warehouse company that issues a warehouse receipt is liable to good faith holders even if the warehouse never received the goods. Read §7-203. It is also liable if the goods are incorrectly described. A warehouse is required to keep goods separate unless they are fungible. See §7-207. If the goods are fungible, a "buyer in the ordinary course of business" can purchase the goods and get good title even though there is an outstanding negotiable warehouse receipt (§7-205).

A bailee's duty of care is that which "a reasonably careful person would exercise under similar circumstances." See, e.g., Global Strategies, Inc. v. Harbor Freight Transport Corp., 2015 WL 6737024 (D.N.J. 2015) (holding that freight storage company would be liable for its negligent failure to release, relocate, or otherwise safeguard the goods as storm approached). Read §7-204 and the following case.

Admiralty Island Fisheries, Inc. v. Millard Refrigerated Services, Inc.

United States District Court, District of Nebraska, 2007
2007 WL 4051649

Laurie Smith Camp, District Judge.

This matter is before the Court on cross-motions for partial summary judgment. The Plaintiff National Fire Insurance of Hartford as subrogee of Suram Trading Corporation filed a motion for partial summary judgment (Filing No. 67 reviving Filing No. 35), in which Admiralty Island Fisheries has joined. (Filing No. 68). The Defendant, Millard Refrigerated Services, Inc. ("Millard") has filed a motion for partial summary judgment against those Plaintiffs (Filing No. 70 and 72), and Plaintiffs Certain Underwriters at Lloyd's of London as subrogee of Icicle Seafoods, Inc., and Hartford Casualty Insurance Company, as subrogee of Global Fishing, Inc. (Filing Nos. 69 and 71) (hereafter the subrogees and subrogors will be referred to collectively as the "Plaintffs"). The cross-motions ask the Court to determine the legal effect of relevant limitation of liability clauses.

Factual Background

Millard operates cold storage warehouses throughout the country. Suram, Icicle, Global, and Admiralty have all stored seafood products in a Millard warehouse. It is undisputed that, as each truckload of seafood was delivered by the Plaintiffs to Millard warehouse, Millard issued a warehouse receipt. The warehouse receipts contain the parties' agreement regarding the storage of the seafood product.

Sometime in March 2006, Millard discovered that several pounds of seafood that were owned by the various Plaintiffs were missing. Millard conducted an internal investigation into the loss and determined that at least some of the seafood had been stolen by some of its employees. Millard ultimately terminated five of its employees for theft of seafood that was supposed be stored in the warehouse. The five employees admitted to stealing only small quantities of the seafood, which was a sufficient basis for terminating their employment. National Fire contends that Millard's former employees stole more than 94,000 pounds of seafood with a fair market value of $455,000. Millard contends that its liability for the loss is limited to 50 cents per pound, or $47,000. The issue presented on these cross-motions for partial summary judgment is whether the limitation of liability clause is enforceable, assuming that the former employees were responsible for the theft.

ANALYSIS

Consistent with the UCC, warehouse receipts may contain a limitation of liability provision that limits the warehouse operator's liability for the stored products in the case of loss or damage. Millard's warehouse receipts include a limitation of liability clause. The Plaintiffs seek a declaration from the Court that the limitation of liability clause contained on the back of the warehouse receipt is of no effect if the Plaintiffs succeed in demonstrating that Millard employees stole the seafood. The Defendant, on the other hand, asks the Court to conclude as a matter of law that the parties' contract permits Millard to limit its liability for the loss of the seafood to 50 cents per pound, regardless of whether the disappearance of the seafood is attributable to theft by the Millard employees.

THE WAREHOUSE RECEIPT

The front of the warehouse receipts in question contain the following provision, in all capital lettering:

> Limitation of liability: Unless the depositor declares a valuation higher than $.50 per pound or $12.00 per cubic foot for stored goods and such declared higher value is agreed to in writing by the warehouseman, the warehouseman's liability for loss or damage thereto shall be expressly limited as specifically set forth in Section 10(e) of the standard contract terms on the reverse side hereof.

The front of the warehouse receipt also provides:

> The goods listed hereon in apparent good order [sic], except as noted hereon (contents, condition and quality unknown) subject to all terms and

conditions herein and on the reverse hereof. Such property to be delivered to the Depositor upon the payment of all storage, handling and other charges.

On the back of the receipt is Section 10(e), copied below in the same manner that it appears in the receipt, states:

> IN THE EVENT OF LOSS, DAMAGE OR DESTRUCTION TO STORED GOODS FOR WHICH COMPANY IS LEGALLY LIABLE, STORER DECLARES THAT COMPANY'S LIABILITY FOR DAMAGES SHALL BE LIMITED TO THE LESSER OF THE FOLLOWING AMOUNTS: (1) THE ACTUAL COST TO DEPOSITOR OF REPLACING OR REPRODUCING THE DAMAGED GOOD TOGETHER WITH TRANSPORTATION COSTS TO THE WAREHOUSE, (2) THE FAIR MARKET VALUE OF THE GOODS ON THE DATE DEPOSITOR IS NOTIFIED OF LOSS, DAMAGE OR DESTRUCTION, (3) 50 TIMES THE MONTHLY STORAGE CHARGE APPLICABLE TO SUCH LOST, DAMAGED, OR DESTROYED GOODS OR (4) THE GREATER OF (I) $.50 PER POUND NET WEIGHT OF THE GOODS, EXCLUSIVE OF TARE, OR (II) $12.00 PER CUBIC FOOT, PROVIDED, HOWEVER, THAT WITHIN A REASONABLE TIME AFTER RECEIPT OF THIS WAREHOUSE RECEIPT, DEPOSITOR MAY, UPON WRITTEN REQUEST, INCREASE WAREHOUSEMAN'S LIABILITY ON PART OR ALL OF THE GOODS STORED UNDER THE WAREHOUSE RECEIPT, IN WHICH CASE AN INCREASED CHARGE WILL BE MADE BASED UPON SUCH INCREASED VALUATION; FURTHER PROVIDED THAT NO SUCH REQUEST SHALL BE VALID UNLESS MADE BEFORE LOSS, DAMAGE OR DESTRUCTION TO ANY PORTION OF THE GOODS STORED UNDER THIS WAREHOUSE RECEIPT HAS OCCURRED.

Section 10(f) states:

> The limitation of liability referred to in paragraph (e) above shall be Depositor's exclusive remedy against Warehouseman for any claim or cause of action whatsoever relating to loss, damage and/or destruction of the stored goods and shall apply to all claims including inventory shortage and mysterious disappearance claims unless Depositor proves by affirmative evidence that Warehouseman converted the good to its own use. Depositor waives any right to rely upon any presumption of conversion imposed by law. In no event shall Depositor be entitled to incidental, special, punitive or consequential damages.

(*See e.g.*, Filing No. 69, Ex. 5).

APPLICABLE PROVISIONS OF THE UNIFORM COMMERCIAL CODE

The Court finds that Uniform Commercial Code §7-204 applies to the facts presented. Section 7-204, captioned ***Duty of Care; Contractual Limitation of Warehouse's Liability,*** states:

(a) A warehouse is liable for damages for loss of or injury to the goods caused by its failure to exercise care with regard to the goods that a reasonably careful person would exercise under similar circumstances. Unless otherwise agreed, the warehouse is not liable for damages that could not have been avoided by the exercise of that care.

(b) Damages may be limited by a term in the warehouse receipt or storage agreement limiting the amount of liability in case of loss or damage beyond which the warehouse is not liable. ***Such a limitation is not effective with respect to the warehouse's liability for conversion to its own use.*** On request of the bailor in a record at the time of signing the storage agreement or within a reasonable time after receipt of the warehouse receipt, the warehouse's liability may be increased on part or all of the goods covered by the storage agreement or the warehouse receipt. In this event, increased rates may be charged based on an increased valuation of the goods.

PLAINTIFFS' MOTION FOR PARTIAL SUMMARY JUDGMENT

Because a warehouse operator would not be liable at all absent a failure of due care, a failure of due care by Millard must be established before the enforcement of the limitation of liability clause even becomes an issue. The Plaintiffs ask the Court to assume that they can prove their seafood disappeared due to employee theft. The Court might assume, for purposes of this motion, that Millard was negligent in hiring the former employees without checking their backgrounds for criminal history or in failing to maintain security over the seafood after it was deposited at the warehouse. These assumptions relate to the threshold issue of Millard's lack of due care. For purposes of this motion only, the Court will assume that Millard was negligent in failing to prevent the former employees' theft of the Plaintiffs' property.

Under Nebraska law, conversion is "any unauthorized or wrongful act of dominion exerted over another's personal property which deprives the owner of his property permanently or for an indefinite period of time." *Roth v. Farmers Mutual Insurance Company of Nebraska*, 371 N.W.2d 289, 291 (Neb. 1985). Under this definition, there is no dispute that the former Millard employees committed an intentional conversion of the Plaintiffs' property. Assuming Millard's liability arising out ordinary negligence under Section 7-204(a), the limitation of liability provision applies according to Section 7-204(b), unless the warehouse operator's liability arises out of a conversion "for its own use." The Court agrees with the observation of the commentators that "conversion for it[s] own use" as used in Section 7-204(a) must mean something more and different than simple conversion. See Comment Note No. 4, UCC §7-204 (2005) (explaining that "[c]onversion to its own use" is narrower than the idea of conversion generally" and disapproving "[c]ases such as *Lipman v. Peterson*, 575 P.2d 19 (Kan. 1978) holding to the contrary. . . .")

The limitation of liability provision applies in the presence of ordinary negligence unless there is proof that the former employees' theft, the conversion, was for the purpose of advancing Millard's interests. Enforcement of a limitation of liability clause is not a complete defense to liability, but it must be raised as would an affirmative defense because it benefits the defendant. For that reason, the Court concludes that the burden of proof should be on the warehouse operator to demonstrate that the conversion of the bailor's property was not for its own use. In reaching this legal conclusion, the Court acknowledges its rejection of Millard's attempt to place the burden on the Plaintiffs as stated in the warehouse receipts' paragraph 10(f). To place the burden of proof on the Plaintiffs, as bailors, would ignore the policy arguments that support the enforcement of limitation of liability provisions in commercial contracts.[4]

Millard has come forward with evidence that the conversion was not for its own use. Millard's general manager, Michael McTier, conducted an investigation into the Plaintiffs' losses. As a result of the investigation, five employees were fired for theft. McTier believes, based on the investigation, that all losses were caused by the former employees' theft. (Filing No. 79, McTier Dep. 159). At least one of the former employees has stated that the seafood was sold to a third party. McTier has testified that Millard did not benefit in any way from the theft.

The Plaintiffs have not come forward with any evidence to create a genuine issue of material fact regarding whether the conversion—the theft—was for Millard's own use. Plaintiffs argue that the conversion was for Millard's own purposes because it 1) was committed within the authorized space and time of the employees' employment, 2) was committed while they were performing duties for which they were hired, and 3) "was actuated, at least in part, by a purpose to serve the master [Millard]." (Filing No. 82, p. 12). The crux of Plaintiffs' argument is that Millard's interests were furthered by the

4. According to at least one commentator, there are good reasons to place the burden of proof on the warehouse operator. First, the warehouse operator is in the best position to explain the loss because the operator has taken control of the goods and has determined the manner in which they are stored. Second, placing the burden on the warehouse operator to show that it acted with due care will encourage warehouse operators to act with care and caution in the handling and storage of bailed goods and to maintain adequate tracking systems that will withstand judicial scrutiny. Third, placing the burden on operators will also have a beneficial effect on the industry because those warehouses that are unable to establish that their storage practices are reasonable will incur increased operating costs, eventually forcing poorly run facilities out of business. Last, placing the burden on the warehouses will give the operators incentive to procure insurance on all bailed goods entrusted to them which the operators can procure, presumably at a lower cost than would be incurred if each bailor had to procure its own insurance. "A Warehouse's Burden of Proof," Ralph Anzivino, *UCC Law Journal* (Spring 2004).

conversion because Millard was paying the former employees to work while they were also stealing; the former employees used Millard's equipment, including pallets, forklifts, and trucks, to accomplish the theft; and the former employees conducted the theft during hours when they were "also" working. I do not agree that these facts are evidence that the conversion was to Millard's own use. The former employees' abuse of their employment position does not automatically transform their conversion to a conversion for Millard's own use. Absent undisputed facts that the conversion was for Millard's own use, the Court concludes that the Plaintiff's motion for partial summary judgment is denied.

MILLARD'S MOTION FOR PARTIAL SUMMARY JUDGMENT

Millard also moves for partial summary judgment asking the Court to confirm the enforceability of the limitation of liability clauses in its warehouse receipts. Because there are genuine issues related to the degree of Millard's negligence, Millard's motion will be denied. The Court, assuming ordinary negligence on the part of Millard, has found that the Plaintiffs have failed to come forward with evidence to create a genuine issue regarding whether the former employees stole the seafood to further Millard's own interests. There is no evidence that the conversion was to Millard's own use. It would seem to follow that the limitation of liability clause is enforceable to limit the damages that Millard may owe to the Plaintiffs.

This case does not present a relationship involving a monopoly or parties of unequal bargaining power that might make the contract unenforceable. Where ordinary commercial relationships exist, the Eighth Circuit Court has upheld "the strong public policies of recognizing parties' liberty to contract and enforcing contracts as written." *Sander v. Alexander Richardson Investments,* 334 F.3d 712, 719 (8th Cir. 2003). The Plaintiffs had an opportunity to negotiate for a higher price per pound to be paid under the limitation of liability clause in the event of loss, but Plaintiffs did not. As a result, they were not obligated to pay the higher storage costs that likely would have come with a limitation of liability clause that was more advantageous to them. Rather, the parties agreed that the risk of loss greater than 50 cents per pound would be borne by the Plaintiffs.

However, in opposition to Millard's motion, the Plaintiffs argue that the limitation of liability clause should not be enforced as against public policy. The Plaintiffs contend that it will show at trial that Millard acted with gross negligence in failing to prevent the theft. If the Plaintiffs are able to demonstrate at trial that the failure of due care on the part of Millard constitutes gross negligence, not just ordinary negligence, then enforcement of the limitation of liability clause may be contrary to public policy. *See New Light Company, Inc. v. Wells Fargo Alarm Services,* 525 N.W.2d 25, (Neb.

1994) (holding that exculpatory clause in parties' agreement was void as against public policy to the extent that it purported to relieve fire alarm company from liability for its own gross negligence or willful and wanton misconduct). "Whether a particular exculpatory clause in a contractual agreement violates public policy depends upon the facts and circumstances of the agreement and the parties involved." Id. (noting that the greater the risk to human life and property, the stronger the argument in favor of voiding attempts by a party to insulate itself from damages caused by that party's gross negligence or willful and wanton misconduct.) "Gross negligence" has been defined as:

> [G]reat and excessive negligence; that is, negligence in a very high degree. It indicates the absence of slight care in the performance of a duty. . . . Willful and wanton misconduct exists where a defendant had actual knowledge that because of its actions, a danger existed to the plaintiff and the defendant intentionally failed to act to prevent a harm that was reasonably likely to result.

Id. at 30. Both the Plaintiffs and Millard have offered evidence relative to the degree of care exercised by Millard in connection with the seafood. There is some evidence that Millard knew of the thefts or should have known of them several months before Millard did anything about it. Because there are genuine issues of fact regarding the reasonableness of the security steps Millard took and did not take, whether Millard's conduct rises to the level of gross negligence is an issue for the jury. Accordingly, Millard's motion for partial summary judgment will also be denied.

IT IS ORDERED:

1. The Plaintiffs' Motions for Partial Summary Judgment . . . are denied; and

2. The Defendant's Motions for Partial Summary Judgment as to the Plaintiffs . . . are denied.

QUESTIONS

1. Would the court have reached the same result if the limitation was buried in the fine print on the receipt? See Keefe v. Bekins Van & Storage Co., 540 P.2d 1132 (Colo. App. 1975) (limitation effective even though not called to customer's attention); Sanfisket Inc. v. Atlantic Cold Storage Corp., 347 So. 2d 647 (Fla. Dist. Ct. App. 1977) (inconspicuous limitation held effective); Jasphy v. Osinsky, 834 A.2d 426 (N.J. Super. 2003) (limitation of liability to one dollar held unconscionable).

2. Could the bailee depend on a clause in the receipt that completely disclaimed liability for its own negligence? See §1-302; and the *XL Specialty*

Insurance case below; Blue Valley Co-op. v. National Farmers Organization, 600 N.W.2d 786 (Neb. 1999) (disclaimer in crop storage); Gonzalez v. A-1 Self Storage, Inc., 795 A.2d 885 (N.J. Super. 2000) (disclaimer in consumer goods storage).

XL Specialty Insurance Co., as Subrogee of Chowaiki & Co., Fine Art Ltd. v. Christie's Fine Art Storage Services, Inc.

Supreme Court of New York, Appellate Division, First Department, 2016
137 A.D.3d 563

Tom, J.P., Sweeny, Andrias, Gische, JJ.

Opinion

Order, Supreme Court, New York County (Saliann Scarpulla, J.), entered September 24, 2014, which, to the extent appealed from, granted defendant's motion to dismiss the complaint, unanimously reversed, on the law, without costs, and the motion denied.

Plaintiff is the insurer for Chowaiki & Co. Fine Art Ltd., a private fine art gallery. In February 2011, Chowaiki entered into a one-year managed storage agreement with defendant, Christie's Fine Art Storage Services, Inc., wherein defendant was to provide secure storage for certain of Chowaiki's fine art works at its facility in the Red Hook section of Brooklyn.

Pursuant to the terms of the agreement, Chowaiki had the option to either (a) have defendant "accept liability for physical loss of, or damage to, the Goods," or to (b) "sign a loss/damage waiver," under which Chowaiki accepted that defendant "shall not be liable for any physical loss of, or damage to, the Goods." In the event Chowaiki opted to sign the waiver, it was required to "effect and maintain adequate insurance in respect of the Goods deposited." The agreement further provided for an additional limitation of liability, stating that "even if," despite the aforementioned language, defendant was found "liable for any loss of, or damage to, the Goods," liability was not to exceed the lower of $100,000 or the market value of the goods.

Chowaiki elected to sign the waiver, which provided that Chowaiki was responsible for obtaining an "against All Risks of loss or physical damage" insurance policy covering the goods deposited with defendant. This insurance was provided by plaintiff. The waiver also absolved defendant of all responsibility for loss or damage to Chowaiki's goods, and required Chowaiki to notify its insurer of the waiver and "arrange for them to waive any rights of subrogation" against defendant with respect to any loss or damage to Chowaiki's goods while in defendant's custody.

The agreement and waiver were renewed for a second year in February 2012. In October 2012, "Superstorm Sandy" struck the New York City metropolitan area, causing major damage throughout the region.

Prior to Sandy striking, defendant notified Chowaiki via email that "extra precautions" were being taken with respect to Chowaiki's goods, specifically, that "all property on the first floor" of the building where Chowaiki's artwork was stored would be "checked to ensure all items are raised off the floor," or, if necessary, the goods would be removed to empty rooms on the upper floors of defendant's storage facility. During a prior storm (Hurricane Irene), defendant's facility flooded; however, defendant had taken measures at that time to protect Chowaiki's goods from damage. This time, however, when the facility flooded, Chowaiki's goods were damaged, apparently because the goods were left on the first floor. Plaintiff insurer reimbursed Chowaiki for its losses and commenced this action as Chowaiki's subrogee, as the policy between plaintiff and Chowaiki did not waive plaintiff's right to subrogation against defendant. Plaintiff's complaint asserted causes of action for gross negligence, breach of bailment, negligence, breach of contract, negligent misrepresentation and fraudulent misrepresentation. In lieu of an answer, defendant moved to dismiss pursuant to CPLR 3016(b), 3211(a)(1), (3), and (7), asserting four grounds for dismissal: (a) that the waiver signed by Chowaiki contained both a waiver of subrogation clause and a limitation of liability, both of which barred plaintiff's claims; (b) that even if its waiver of liability was deemed to be invalid, the agreement nonetheless limited plaintiff's damages to $100,000; (c) that plaintiff's breach of bailment claim must fail because the agreement created a lessor/lessee relationship, not bailor/bailee; and (d) that Sandy was an Act of God, which, as a matter of law, excused defendant's liability.

The motion court correctly found that the agreement between Chowaiki and defendant created a bailor/bailee relationship under article 7 of the Uniform Commercial Code and that the agreement's limitation of liability was unenforceable because it purported to exempt defendant from all liability, in contravention of then UCC 7-204(2) (UCC 7-204[b], as amended by L. 2014, ch. 505, §23, eff. Dec. 17, 2014]).

UCC 7-204(a) provides that a "warehouse is liable for damages for loss of or injury to the goods caused by its failure to exercise care with regard to the goods that a reasonably careful person would exercise under similar circumstances" and "is not liable for damages that could not have been avoided by the exercise of that care." UCC 7-204(b) provides that "[d]amages may be limited by a term in the warehouse receipt or storage agreement limiting the amount of liability in case of loss or damage beyond which the warehouse is not liable." However, such limitations on liability are limited by UCC 7-202(c), which provides that such terms must not "impair its . . . duty of care under Section 7-204. Any contrary provision is ineffective."

Here there is a question of fact concerning whether defendant, in failing to move Chowaiki's goods to either another floor, or to a location above ground level on the floor they were on, was reasonable under the circumstances. If the trier of fact finds that defendant did not act reasonably, then defendant may be liable for damages to Chowaiki's goods (*see e.g.* Modelia v. Rose Warehouse, Inc., 1968 WL 9201 [Sup. Ct., New York County 1968], *affd.* 36 A.D.2d 582, 317 N.Y.S.2d 735 [1st Dept. 1971]).

However, the court erred in finding that the waiver of subrogation contained in the agreement's loss/damage waiver is enforceable and bars this action.

Provisions purporting to exempt the bailee from liability for damage to stored goods from perils against which the bailor had secured insurance, even when caused by the bailee's negligence have been held to run afoul of the statutory scheme of UCC Article 7.

In Kimberly-Clark Corp. v. Lake Erie Warehouse, Div. of Lake Erie Rolling Mill, 49 A.D.2d 492, 375 N.Y.S.2d 918 (4th Dept. 1975), *appeal dismissed* 39 N.Y.2d 888, 386 N.Y.S.2d 393, 352 N.E.2d 580 (1976), the Court found such an exculpatory clause to be invalid. In that case, the agreement between the bailee and bailor provided that the bailor "waives any and all right of recovery from the warehouseman for losses caused by the perils covered by fire and extended coverage insurance and caused by any other perils against which customer has insured" (id. at 493, 375 N.Y.S.2d 918). In invalidating this clause, the Court noted that while UCC 7-204 permits a warehouseman to limit the *amount* of liability, it cannot completely exempt itself from liability as imposed by UCC Article 7 (id. at 494-495, 375 N.Y.S.2d 918). Quoting *Modelia,* supra, the Court stated that a warehouseman "may not contract away or lessen his responsibility except in such manner as the statute provides. . . . Any other attempted exoneration or limitation would defeat the statute and must be held void" (id. at 495, 375 N.Y.S.2d 918). It should be noted that the exoneration clause at issue in *Kimberley-Clark* was not as broad as the provisions in this case in that it did not contain an express waiver of subrogation clause or a requirement that the bailor obtain a waiver of subrogation from its insurer. The *Kimberley-Clark* Court did note that the implied waiver of subrogation in that case was nothing more than another attempt by defendant to exempt itself from all liability, which "would defeat the statute and must be held void" (see Kimberly-Clark, 49 A.D.2d at 495, 375 N.Y.S.2d 918). . . .

We have considered defendant's remaining arguments and find them unavailing.

QUESTION

Would the result be different if the clause had read: "The warehouseman shall not be liable for loss, damage, delay or demurrage caused by acts of God, . . . or by . . . flood, wind, storm, . . . or by any other cause beyond the control [of] the warehouseman, or by any cause not originating in the warehouse"? See HDI Gerling Industrie Versicherung AG v. Continental Terminals, Inc., 2017 WL 4776757 (D.N.J. 2017).

C. *Bailee's Lien*

All bailees (including warehouses and carriers) are given a statutory lien in the bailed goods to the extent of the charges for storage and expenses incident to the bailment contract (expenses necessary to preserve the goods, for instance). For warehouses, this lien is described in §§7-209 and 7-210; for carriers, §§7-307 and 7-308. These bailee's liens are possessory liens only; the bailee loses its lien if it voluntarily surrenders the goods (or wrongfully refuses to surrender them). See Darby v. Baltimore & Ohio Ry. Co., 259 Md. 493, 270 A.2d 652 (1970). If the lien is contested, the bailee must have evidence of the failure to pay. See Thompson v. T & G Relocation Systems, Inc., 2018 WL 1440683 (N.Y. Sup. Ct. 2018). If the bailor does not pay the bailee's charges, the latter may foreclose its lien by public or private sale (the rules of which are described in the above-named sections). The Code primarily requires the foreclosure sale to be held in a "commercially reasonable manner." The bailee must give the bailor proper notice of the sale. See OEC Freight (NY) v. KT Superwin Corp., 2014 WL 3887744 (S.D.N.Y. 2014). For a case exploring the details of a bailee lien foreclosure on stored household goods, see Bradford v. Muinzer, 498 F. Supp. 1384 (N.D. Ill. 1980).

D. *Delivery Orders*

You will remember that if the goods are stored under a nonnegotiable warehouse receipt, the bailee can deliver the goods without requiring surrender of the warehouse receipt. Many nonnegotiable warehouse forms state that delivery will be made "on *detached written* authority *without* the return of this receipt." When the owner (bailor) wants the order delivered, the owner simply sends a letter (called a *delivery order*) to the bailee, explaining to whom the goods are to be delivered.

Storing goods in bulk under a nonnegotiable warehouse receipt and then breaking them up into smaller units by separate delivery orders is a convenient way to merchandise commodities. The delivery orders, which need take no particular form, can be negotiable or nonnegotiable. A delivery order is negotiable if it directs the bailee to deliver the goods to someone, "or their order," or "to bearer"; otherwise, it is nonnegotiable. In many ways a delivery order is directly analogous to an Article 3 draft, only it is an order to deliver goods instead of to pay money. Like a draft, it imposes no liability on the bailee until the bailee *accepts* the order (no liability to the holder of the delivery order, that is; the bailee who refuses to accept a delivery order may be in breach of the bailment contract and, if so, is liable to the bailor). See §7-502(a)(4), especially the last sentence.

All of this ties in with how a seller of bailed goods makes *tender* to the buyer under Article 2 of the Code. Read §§2-509(2) and 2-503(4) carefully. Where a *negotiable* document of title is involved, both §§2-509(2) and 2-503(4)(a) make it clear that the risk of loss shifts to the buyer on delivery of the document if the goods conform to the contract (if not, §2-510 applies). However, these sections do *not* apply to negotiable delivery orders, which are lumped in with the rules governing nonnegotiable documents in §§2-509(2)(c) and 2-503(4)(b) ("record directing the bailee to deliver" means a delivery order). Where no documents are involved (say, a pet dog is boarded at a kennel and sold while still there), §2-509(2)(b) passes the risk of loss to the buyer on the bailee's acknowledgment of the buyer's right to possession. See Whately v. Tetrault, 29 Mass. App. Dec. 112 (1964).

PROBLEM 271

Fred Bandanna, a farmer, took two truckloads of his cotton to Rural Warehouse for storage. The first truckload of 80 bales he stored under a negotiable warehouse receipt issued by Rural. For the second truckload of 80 bales, he obtained a nonnegotiable warehouse receipt. Fred took the documents to the offices of Harold Fastbuck, a commodity merchant. Harold bought both the negotiable receipt covering the first truckload and the nonnegotiable receipt covering the second truckload of cotton from Fred. Harold asked, however, that Fred divide the 80 bales represented by the nonnegotiable receipt into two equal lots so that Harold could resell them more easily. Fred sat down and wrote out two delivery orders addressed to Rural, each requiring the warehouse to turn over 40 bales to "Harold Fastbuck or order." As soon as Fred left his office, Harold sold one of the delivery orders to another commodity merchant, Sue Fourthparty. He indorsed on the back of the delivery order "Deliver to Sue Fourthparty or order, (signed) Harold Fastbuck." Sue phoned Rural Warehouse and said that she was the owner of 40 bales of the Fred Bandanna cotton under a delivery order. The warehouse agent agreed that Sue could pick up the bales the next day. That night lightning struck the warehouse, and all the cotton burned. Who took the risk of loss as to each segment of the cotton? See §§2-509(2), 2-503(4)(b), 7-502(a)(4).

E. *Terminology: The Issuer*

Under the Code, the person primarily liable on a document of title is the *issuer* of the document. Since the *bailee* (warehouse or carrier) is almost always the person who *issues* (creates) the document, there is a temptation to think of *issuer* as synonymous with *bailee.* This would be correct except for the fact that the issuer of a delivery order (which *is* a document of title according to §1-201(b)(16)) is the *bailor.* Read §§7-102(a)(5) and 7-102(a)(8). This fact will become important later on when we get to talking about *due negotiation* and the duties of the issuer. Question: who was (were) the issuer(s) in Problem 271?

II. BILLS OF LADING

Just as warehouses issue negotiable or nonnegotiable receipts for bailed goods, carriers (such as railroads, airlines, ocean liners, and trucking firms) issue similar documents on the receipt of goods for transportation across the country or the world. These documents, called *bills of lading,* may be negotiable or nonnegotiable (depending on whether order or bearer language is used or not). As with warehouse receipts, the bill of lading is, simultaneously, a receipt for the goods, a contract of transportation, and tangible evidence of ownership of the bailed goods.

A. Federal Law

Article 7 of the Code covers only intrastate shipments. If the goods are to cross state lines, the documents issued by the carrier are governed by the Federal Bills of Lading Act (the Pomerene Act of 1916), 49 U.S.C. §81 et seq. If the goods are to cross water, they will be governed by a host of federal statutes including the Shipping Act, 46 U.S.C. §801 et seq.; the Intercoastal Shipping Act, 46 U.S.C. §843 et seq.; and (most important) the Carriage of Goods by Sea Act, 46 U.S.C. §1300 et seq. (For those of you who will have commercial bailees as clients, note at this point that all interstate carriers and warehouses are subject to federal regulation of their trade. The Federal Aviation Administration, for example, formulates rules and regulations for the airlines involved in interstate and foreign air carriage. The Department of Agriculture regulates warehouses storing agricultural products. See the United States Warehouse Act, 7 U.S.C. §241 et seq. There will also be special state statutes and regulations that deal with warehouses and carriers.)

Fortunately, the basic law set out in the Federal Bills of Lading Act is more or less the same as that in Article 7, and unless the wording is particularly crucial, language of the federal act will not be mentioned. What is important is that you remember that Article 7 does *not* apply (except by analogy) to any bill of lading issued for goods that are to leave the state. For such a bill you need to refer to the exact language of the relevant federal statutes.

B. *The Basic Idea*

Do not confuse *shipper* with *carrier* or *issuer*. The *shipper* is the original owner (bailor) of the goods who turns them over to the carrier for transportation. The *carrier* then issues a bill of lading (thus becoming an *issuer*) to the shipper. If the bill is negotiable, the carrier (issuer) will not turn over the goods at the destination until the negotiable bill of lading is surrendered (§7-403(c) applies to carriers as well as warehouses). This means that the shipper must send the bill of lading to the person who is to receive the goods (normally the buyer) before the latter can get possession of the goods. Often the shipper will not surrender the bill of lading to the buyer until the latter has paid for the goods (or has *accepted* a draft drawn on it; see the discussion below); this is called requiring *payment against documents*. As soon as the buyer pays the seller (or seller's agent), the buyer gets possession of the negotiable bill of lading and can claim the goods from the carrier. A carrier that delivers the goods to the buyer without demanding surrender of an outstanding negotiable bill of lading has converted the goods and is liable to the holder of the negotiable bill. See BII Finance Co. v. U-States Forwarding Serv. Corp., 115 Cal. Rptr. 2d 312 (Cal. App. 2002). Review §7-403(c) and read §§7-404 and 7-601(b).

C. *Form*

1. Negotiable

The word *consign* means to send or hand over goods to another. A negotiable bill of lading is called an *order bill of lading* because the goods are consigned to the "order of ________."

In bill of lading terminology, the goods are entrusted to the carrier by the *consignor* (the shipper) for delivery to the *consignee* (the person to whom the goods will belong at the end of their journey, normally the buyer). The consignee is *not* the carrier-bailee. If Sam Seller in Toledo sells goods to Betty Buyer in Atlanta via the Monopoly Railroad, using a negotiable bill of lading issued by the railroad, then Sam is the consignor, Betty is the consignee, and the Monopoly Railroad is the carrier-issuer (the agent of the consignor who carries out the consignment contract). Order (negotiable) bills of lading are yellow in color, as required by Interstate Commerce Commission (ICC) regulations.

An order bill states that the goods have been received in apparent good order, except as otherwise indicated, and states the contract of transportation (including rates), incorporating all the fine print on the back of the contract. On the front is space for describing the goods covered by the document and blanks to be filled in showing, among other things,

(1) shipper's (consignor's) name and address,
(2) to whose order the goods are consigned,
(3) the destination of the goods, and
(4) whom the carrier is to notify when the goods arrive (normally the buyer).

A negotiable bill also contains sentences like this one in large print on the front: "Surrender of this original order bill of lading properly indorsed is required prior to the delivery of the property. Inspection of such property will not be permitted by anyone prior to delivery unless permission is indorsed hereon or given in writing by the consignor." (As to inspection rights, see note §2-513(3), which agrees with this language.)

2. Nonnegotiable

A nonnegotiable bill of lading is called a *straight* bill of lading because the goods are delivered straight to the consignee whether or not the nonnegotiable bill is surrendered. Straight bills are to be printed on white paper by ICC regulation. The carrier will take the goods to their destination, notify the consignee of their arrival, and await instructions as to whom the goods are to be delivered.

Frequently the consignor consigns the goods to *itself,* thereby making the consignor and the consignee the same entity. This happens on negotiable as well as nonnegotiable bills. The reason that this is often done is to make it clear that the consignor is at all times the owner of the goods, and for that reason it is called a "shipment under reservation" (meaning a reservation of *title*). When the buyer pays for them, the seller will indorse a negotiable bill over to the buyer or, if a nonnegotiable bill is used, will issue a *delivery order* (the same as with warehouse receipts) to the carrier telling it to deliver the goods to the buyer. In effect, consigning the goods to itself gives the seller a security interest in the goods until the purchase price is paid. The Code recognizes that the *equitable* interest is in the buyer even though the legal title is in the seller. Read §2-505 carefully.

PROBLEM 272

Homer Widget, of South Bend, Indiana, the inventor of the three-dimensional widget, contracted to sell 5,000 widgets to Ned's Novelty Store in Evansville, Indiana. Homer delivered the goods to the Overnight Trucking Company, consigning the goods to himself but writing "Notify Ned's Novelty Store on arrival" on the straight bill of lading. (The carrier keeps a duplicate copy of the bill of lading with the goods; the original is, of course, turned over to the consignor.) Homer mailed the original bill to his cousin Wilbur Widget, who lived in Evansville. Along with the bill he sent a delivery order signed by himself and addressed to the trucking company telling the company to deliver the goods to Ned's Novelty Store. Homer's cover letter to his cousin stated that Wilbur should take the delivery order down to Ned at the store and turn it over to Ned only if Ned paid Wilbur cash for the goods. Wilbur did present the delivery order as Homer directed, but Ned was short on funds and could not pay. Wilbur, confused, mailed all the documents back to Homer with a letter saying Ned would not pay. Meanwhile, the goods arrived at Evansville, and John ("Slow") Burly, the company's truck driver, had to decide what to do with the widgets. Reading the bill of lading, he discovered that the consignee lived in South Bend. Checking the internet he learned that Homer Widget had no address in Evansville. Then the truck driver noticed that he was to notify Ned's Novelty Store, which did have an Evansville address, so he delivered the widgets to Ned.

(a) Was the carrier's delivery to Ned improper? Read §7-303 carefully; see Mistletoe Express Serv. v. Sanchez, 721 S.W.2d 418 (Tex. App. 1986).

(b) If the widgets were destroyed in an auto accident prior to Ned's refusal to pay, who would have had the risk of loss if the contract was "F.O.B. truck South Bend"? See §2-509(1). See also Sternheim v. Silver Bell of Roslyn, Inc., 66 Misc. 726, 321 N.Y.S.2d 965 (Cty. Ct. 1971). As to the carrier's duty of care, read §7-309(1).

(c) Would the result with regard to the risk of loss or proper delivery change if the bill of lading had been an order bill? See §§7-403(c), 2-509.

PROBLEM 273

Blue Skies Air Lines was about to deliver a shipment of frozen fish to the buyer to whom it was consigned under a straight bill issued by the airline when the phone rang. The seller-consignor was on the phone, and she forbade the delivery, telling Blue Skies to return the fish to her, since she had learned that the "buyer is a bum." If Blue Skies returns the goods to the seller, is it risking liability to the buyer? See §§7-303, 2-505, 2-705 (plus Official Comment 1 to §2-705); Clock v. Missouri-Texas R.R., 407 F. Supp. 448 (E.D. Mo. 1976).

PROBLEM 274

Jane Pitchfork, a southern Iowa farmer, had an excellent pumpkin crop (1,700 pumpkins) this year. She stored 1,000 pumpkins with the Pumpkin Warehouse, Inc., located in Des Moines, taking a negotiable warehouse receipt for 500 and a nonnegotiable receipt for the other 500. She also contracted to sell 700 other pumpkins to Peter P. Pumpkineater, who lived in Sioux City, Iowa. The terms of the contract required her to ship Pumpkineater 700 stemless pumpkins "F.O.B. railroad car Fort Madison, Iowa." Jane was too lazy to cut off the stems, but she thought Pumpkineater really would not care, so she loaded 700 pumpkins on board an Iowa Pacific Railroad car at Fort Madison, Iowa. She received a negotiable bill of lading consigned to her own order and made a proper contract for carriage of the pumpkins to Sioux City. She sold the 1,000 warehouse pumpkins to Mom's Pies, Inc., of Cedar Rapids. She indorsed the negotiable warehouse receipt over to Mom's Pies for the first 500 stored pumpkins and gave them a nonnegotiable delivery order for the other 500 stored pumpkins. Before Mom's Pies could contact the warehouse, the Iowa Pacific Railroad train carrying the pumpkins passed through Des Moines and derailed (due to the negligence of the train's engineer). The train ran off the track and went through the center of the Pumpkin Warehouse, destroying all 1,700 pumpkins. Jane Pitchfork, a dejected woman, comes to you. The railroad is, of course, going to be liable to whoever took the risk of loss as to the pumpkins. Advise Jane as to where the risk of loss is placed for each of the pumpkin transactions. See §§2-503, 2-509, 2-510, 2-601, 2-319.

D. Misdescription

Consider this problem. The bill of lading states that the boxcar contains 42 cartons of widgets. When the goods are delivered to buyer, there are only 32 cartons, or the cartons contain peanuts, or the boxcar (which was loaded and sealed by the shipper) is empty. Is the carrier liable for wrong information (misdescription) on the bill of lading if the shipper furnished the carrier with the information? The problem frequently comes up because carriers (particularly railroads) often permit the shipper to load the goods itself and then to fill out the descriptive section of the bill of lading, which the carrier then signs. Carriers defend this practice by saying that as a practical matter it is impossible for the carrier's agents to police the shipper's loading or to inventory the goods loaded. To guard against possible liability for resulting misdescription, the carrier normally states SHIPPER'S WEIGHT, LOAD, AND COUNT on the bill of lading in order to indicate that the carrier makes no warranties as to these matters. Is this language effective to eliminate the carrier's liability for misdescription? Study §7-301.

The corresponding federal law is the Federal Bills of Lading Act §22, which follows. This section has been much litigated:

> If a bill of lading has been issued by a carrier or on his behalf by an agent or employee the scope of whose actual or apparent authority includes the receiving of goods and issuing bills of lading therefor for transportation in commerce among several States and with foreign nations, the carrier shall be liable to (a) the owner of goods covered by a straight bill subject to existing right of stoppage in transit or (b) the holder of an order bill, who has given value in good faith relying upon the description therein of the goods, or upon the shipment being made upon the date therein shown, for damages caused by the nonreceipt by the carrier of all or part of the goods upon or prior to the date therein shown, or their failure to correspond with the description thereof in the bill at the time of its issue.

GAC Commercial Corp. v. Wilson

United States District Court, Southern District of New York, 1967
271 F. Supp. 242

BRYAN, J.

[The St. Lawrence Pulp & Paper Corp. borrowed money from plaintiff G.A.C., which took as collateral straight bills of lading, both interstate and intrastate, issued by defendant Norwood & St. Law. Railroad. The bills of lading indicated that St. Lawrence, as consignor, had shipped various amounts of paper products to different consignees and the plaintiff took the bills with the understanding that the goods had not yet been delivered. Plaintiff loaned St. Lawrence $254,173.42 against the bills of lading, but St. Lawrence went bankrupt anyway. To the great surprise of everyone but some of St. Lawrence's employees, the railroad cars proved to be empty. Plaintiff brought this action against St. Lawrence's officers and the Norwood Railroad.]

The method by which the alleged fraudulent scheme was carried out appears for purposes of this motion to be as follows: the bankrupt St. Lawrence, as part of its facilities in Norfolk, New York, maintained a railroad siding connected with the lines of defendant carrier which had a freight office approximately $^{1/8}$th of a mile from the siding. St. Lawrence was permitted to load freight at its spur track in preparation for shipments on defendant's line. The railroad cars were sealed by St. Lawrence with seals provided by the railroad. St. Lawrence also prepared the bills of lading on blanks furnished in quadruplicate by defendant Norwood. The bills thus prepared were then presented to Norwood's agent who signed the original and one copy without inspecting the contents of the cars. No notation such as "contents of packages unknown" or "shipper's weight, load and count" was written on the bills. The signed copies were returned to St. Lawrence and forwarded with the invoices to G.A.C. which made advances on the goods described, which, as it turned out, had not been shipped.

Since sixty of the bills of lading were issued by a common carrier for the transportation of goods in interstate commerce, the issues as to these bills are controlled by the provisions of the Federal Bills of Lading Act, 49 U.S.C. §81. This statute stands as "a clear expression of the determination of Congress to take the whole subject matter of such bills of lading within its control." . . .

Prior to the passage of the Federal Bills of Lading Act "the United States courts held that a carrier was not liable for the act of its agent in issuing a bill of lading for goods where no goods had in fact been received." Josephy v. Panhandle & S.F. Ry., 235 N.Y. 306, 310, 139 N.E. 277, 278 (1923); see, e.g., Clark v. Clyde S.S. Co., 148 F. 243 (S.D.N.Y. 1906). The liability of carriers for acts of their agents was expanded, but not drastically, by the passage of the federal legislation which draws a sharp distinction between order bills of lading and straight bills where in fact the goods are never received for shipment by the carrier. Under §22 of the Act, 49 U.S.C. §102, "[i]f a bill of lading has been issued by a carrier or on his behalf by an agent or employee . . ., the carrier shall be liable to . . . the holder of an order bill, who has given value in good faith, relying upon the description therein of the goods, . . . for damages caused by the nonreceipt by the carrier of all or part of the goods upon or prior to the date therein shown." However, the liability of the carrier for nonreceipt extends only to "the owner of goods covered by a straight bill," provided, of course, he also gives value in good faith in reliance upon the description of goods contained in the bill. See Strohmeyer & Arpe Co. v. American Line S.S. Corp., 97 F.2d 360, 362 (2d Cir. 1938).

It is clear that a party in the position of Norwood is not included within the narrow category of those liable on a straight bill under the federal legislation. In the first place there is no question that the straight bills of lading here involved are non-negotiable. [Citations omitted.] As a consequence plaintiff G.A.C., as apparent transferee of bills and invoices representing accounts receivable under the agreement with St. Lawrence, upon notification to the carrier of the transfer, could only "become the direct obligee of whatever obligations the carrier owed to the transferor of the bill immediately before the notification." 49 U.S.C. §112; see id. §109. Norwood obviously owed St. Lawrence nothing because no goods in fact were received. There was therefore no outstanding obligation to G.A.C. . . .

By no stretch of the imagination does G.A.C. qualify as an "owner of goods covered by a straight bill" who can sue the carrier under §22 of the Federal Bills of Lading Act, 39 U.S.C. §102, for representing that goods in fact had been received. The reason for this is that it is completely illusory to attempt to assign an "owner" to non-existent goods. R. Braucher, Documents of Title 23 (1958); 2 S. Williston, Sales §419a, at 576-77 (rev. ed. 1948). While the consignee is generally deemed to have title to goods shipped under a straight bill of lading, see George F. Hinrichs, Inc. v. Standard Trust & Sav. Bank, 279 F. 382, 386 (2d Cir. 1922), even he cannot sue the carrier for representing in a straight bill that non-existent goods had in fact been received. Martin Jessee Motors v. Reading Co., 87 F. Supp. 318 (E.D. Pa.), *aff'd,* 181 F.2d 766 (3d Cir. 1950). The rationale applied in *Martin Jessee Motors*—that the consignee can prevail against the carrier "only by proving its title to specific property," 181 F.2d at 767—applies a fortiori to bar the claim of G.A.C. Plaintiff's interest in the "aggregate face value of the accounts receivable pledged as security" under no conceivable reading of the statute can be deemed an "[ownership] of goods covered by a straight bill." G.A.C. is not one of the favored few who can recover under the Federal Bills of Lading Act. . . .

Plaintiff G.A.C. fares no better with respect to the two bills of lading representing intrastate shipments in New York. . . . Although the awkward term "owner" in 49 U.S.C. §102 has been replaced by the word "consignee" in the Uniform Commercial Code §7-301 . . . the change is immaterial for purposes of this case. Plaintiff, perhaps an assignee, transferee or pledgee of the non-negotiable bills, though it claims not to be, is certainly not a "consignee," which is the only party protected. 2 Anderson, Uniform Commercial Code 261 n.9 (1961); see R. Braucher, Documents of Title 23-24 (1958). Contrast U.C.C. §7-203. Thus, as with the sixty interstate bills, G.A.C. cannot successfully sue on the two intrastate bills. . . .

It is true that the result dictated by the federal legislation may lead to some inequities. A straight bill under the Federal Bills of Lading Act is obviously not a good security risk. Casenote, 63 Harv. L. Rev. 1439, 1440 (1950). The fraud of the shipper by failing to deliver goods to the carrier can result, as it did here, in misleading statements on the bills of lading, which operate to the detriment of banks and other commercial financers making advances on the basis of the bills. See Oliver Straw Goods Corp. v. Osaka Shosen Kaisha, 27 F.2d 129, 134 (2d Cir. 1928) (A. Hand, J.). Moreover, the carrier can readily prevent such a situation from arising by inserting "in the bill of lading the words, 'Shipper's weight, load, and count,' or other words of like purport" to "indicate that the goods were loaded by the shipper and the description of them made by him." 49 U.S.C. §101.

But the overriding policy considerations in the Act look the other way on the issue of liability. First, "[t]here is nothing in the statute to indicate that the mere omission of the words 'Shipper's weight, load, and count' in and of itself makes the carrier liable for damages to goods improperly loaded. The omission of the statutory words merely serves to shift upon the carrier the burden of proving that the goods were improperly loaded by the shipper, and that the damage ensued from that cause." (D.N.J. 1951); see UCC §7-301(4).[5] According to the allegations the true culprits in this case were the shipper and its agents; there is no reason to saddle defendant Norwood with liability simply because it did not insert the "Shipper's weight, load, and count" language in the bills. In addition, practicality demands loading arrangements such as those here, where the shipper places his goods aboard and seals the railroad car which the carrier has provided. Section 21 of the Act, 4 U.S.C. §101, anticipates that shippers are expected to do much of the counting and loading on their own sidings or spur tracks. The rapid flow of commerce might well be hindered if the carrier in every instance were charged with ascertaining whether in fact there were goods behind every one of its straight bills.

Moreover, denying security value to a straight bill of lading does not work a hardship upon banks and other commercial institutions. G.A.C., as a knowledgeable lender, is fully aware of the risks inherent in straight bills, and could well have required order bills to protect itself. See Chicago & Northwestern Ry. v. Stevens Natl. Bank, 75 F.2d 398 (8th Cir. 1935). It nevertheless chose to rely upon straight bills to lend money to the now bankrupt St. Lawrence at a profitable rate of interest. Wiser now, G.A.C. seeks to shift its loss to Norwood, an undoubtedly solvent defendant. The Federal Bills of Lading Act protects against this type of hindsight by requiring the lender to accept this kind of security subject to the defenses between the carrier and the shipper.

The motion of defendant Norwood for Judgment on the pleadings treated as a motion for summary judgment is granted.

It is so ordered.

Read §7-301.

In the *GAC* case, which involves a straight bill of lading, §22 of the Federal Bills of Lading Act (FBLA) does not protect GAC because there are no goods, and hence there can be no owner. Professor Robert Riegert argues that the protection given owners of straight bills by the FBLA is thus illusory and that Congress did not intend the *GAC* result. See Riegert, Rights of a

5. Now §7-301(d).—Eds.

Transferee of Document of Title Who Is Not Holder by Due Negotiation, 9 Cumb. L. Rev. 27 (1978). The UCC in §7-301 gives protection on a straight bill to the consignee. Is the *GAC* court right in saying that plaintiff is not protected by §7-301? See §7-102(a) (3).

Both the FBLA and §7-301 protect holders by due negotiation of order bills. Both acts also allow the carrier to disclaim liability under certain circumstances. For a case involving an order bill where the disclaimer did not work, see Chicago & Nw. Ry. Co. v. Stephens Natl. Bank of Fremont, 75 F.2d 398 (8th Cir. 1935). Liability for nonreceipt or misdescription under bills of lading, either negotiable or nonnegotiable, is a tricky subject. See J. White & R. Summers, 3 Uniform Commercial Code §§28.10-28.14 (6th ed. Practitioner Treatise Series 2014).

PROBLEM 275

Harry Thief went to the offices of Monopoly Railroad to see his old prison cellmate, Phillip ("Forger") Copy. Copy, under an assumed name, was currently employed by Monopoly as chief shipping clerk. Harry asked Phillip to make out some phony negotiable bills of lading representing nonexistent shipments by Harry to a buyer in California. Harry wanted to sell the bills to a bank and split the money with Phillip. Phillip made out the bills, which Harry discounted at the Octopus National Bank, and the two of them left town. When the bank sued the railroad, the latter defended on the grounds that the phony bills contain the words "Shipper's weight, load, and count." Is this defense good? See §7-301 and its Official Comment 3; Gleason v. Seaboard Air Line Ry. Co., 278 U.S. 349 (1929); cf. Societe Generale v. Federal Ins. Co., 856 F.2d 461 (2d Cir. 1988).

III. DUE NEGOTIATION

A. The Basic Concept

The word *negotiable* in our law always means that if a piece of paper is in the proper form (a typical requirement is that it be made out either to *bearer* or to the *order* of a named individual), is transferred in the proper manner, and reaches the hands of a bona fide purchaser (BFP) who has no knowledge of problems with the paper, then the BFP may enforce the paper as written and does not take subject to the usual claims or defenses. In Article 3 of the Uniform Commercial Code, the BFP who gets these extraordinary rights is called a *holder in due course.* In Article 7, the BFP is given the jaw-breaking designation of a "holder to whom a negotiable document of title has been duly negotiated" (§7-502). Note well that the whole concept applies only to *negotiable* documents and hence excludes nonnegotiable warehouse receipts and straight bills of lading. Holders of such documents get no special rights and are subject to all the usual defenses (§7-504).

Negotiation of a negotiable document of title (whether warehouse receipt, bill of lading, or delivery order) is accomplished by indorsement and delivery under rules that are virtually interchangeable with the rules for the negotiation of Article 3 drafts and notes: §§7-501(a), 7-501(b) (providing for negotiation of electronic documents of title), 7-501(c) ("Indorsement of a nonnegotiable document of title neither makes it negotiable nor adds to the transferee's rights" (emphasis added)), §7-501(d).

A person cannot become a §7-502 holder until the document has been *duly negotiated.* Due negotiation is a term of art. It is defined in §7-501(a)(5) and (b)(3), which should be read carefully at this point.

Cleveland v. McNabb

United States District Court, Western District of Tennessee, 1970
312 F. Supp. 155

Brown, C.J.

The plaintiffs here, Dr. W.B. Cleveland and his wife, Katherine Cleveland, are owners of lands situated in Fayette County, Tennessee. On January 17, 1967, these plaintiffs entered into a written lease with the defendant Jack McNabb which lease provided that, for a period of five years, the tenant McNabb would pay the landlord an annual rental amounting to fifty dollars per acre for all acreage allotted to cotton by the government and ten dollars per acre for all acreage actually planted in soybeans. (This lease is attached to the Amended and Supplemental Complaint as Exhibit A). In this action the plaintiffs sue the defendant McNabb for rent allegedly due and owing from the 1968 crop year. Further, the plaintiffs sue the defendants TFC Marketing Service, Inc., John S. Wilder and W.W. Wilder, individually and as partners doing business as Longtown Supply Company, the Commodity Credit Corporation and the United States of America to enforce landlord's liens for the value of purchased crops to the extent that such liens are necessary to satisfy any unpaid rent. It is undisputed that each of this group of defendants received crops raised by the defendant McNabb on the plaintiffs' lands. (The United States is named as a defendant because the Commodity Credit Corporation is a branch of the United States Department of Agriculture. The named defendant Ralston Purina Company has by consent been dismissed.) . . .

As stated previously, the plaintiffs also seek in this action to enforce landlord's liens for the value of crops raised on their lands in 1968 to the extent that such liens are necessary to satisfy any unpaid rent. In this connection it is stipulated that the defendant Commodity Credit Corporation made a loan on and later acquired ownership of cotton grown on the plaintiffs' lands in 1968 and that this cotton had a value of $27,155.40. . . .

To support their contention that they are entitled to liens on all crops grown on their lands in 1968, the plaintiffs rely on the Tennessee Crop Liens Statute, T.C.A. §§64-1201 to 64-1214. In particular the plaintiffs rely on the following sections: [The court quotes the statute that gives landlords a lien on all crops grown on their land to the amount of rent due, and further provides that the landlord can enforce this lien against a purchaser of the crop "with or without notice."—Eds.].

It is next contended by the defendant United States that the plaintiffs are not entitled to a lien upon crops purchased by the Commodity Credit Corporation because the Commodity Credit Corporation was a good faith purchaser for value of negotiable warehouse receipts. As a result of such negotiation, the United States contends, the Commodity Credit Corporation acquired title to the crops in question free of the plaintiffs' crop lien.

Article Seven of the Uniform Commercial Code, as adopted in Tennessee, provides that, with limited exceptions, a holder to whom a negotiable document of title has been "duly negotiated" thereby acquires title to the goods described in such documents. §7-502. The term "duly negotiated" is defined in the preceding section, §7-501, as follows: [the court quoted the version of §7-501 in effect at the time].

In addition, §1-201[6] provides in part:

> (25) A person has "notice" of a fact when . . . (c) from all the facts and circumstances known to him at the time in question he has reason to know that it exists.

The United States contends that the Commodity Credit Corporation received the warehouse receipts in question "duly negotiated." The plaintiffs, on the other hand, contend that the negotiation in question was not in the regular course of business and that the Commodity Credit Corporation, from all the facts and circumstances known to it, had reason to know of the plaintiffs' lien. Consequently it is the plaintiffs' position that the Commodity Credit Corporation did not acquire title, through due negotiation, to the crops it purchased.

The proof shows that the defendant McNabb delivered the cotton he had raised on the plaintiffs' lands and later sold to Commodity Credit

6. Now §1-202.—Eds.

Corporation to a cotton gin. After the cotton was ginned it was taken directly to a warehouse which issued a negotiable warehouse receipt for each bale of cotton it held. McNabb later received these receipts which were issued in his name as producer at the cotton gin and took them to the Agricultural Stabilization and Conservation Service office, which is the government office administrator of the cotton loan program in Somerville, Tennessee. McNabb left the warehouse receipts at this office and in return ultimately received a "loan." [Under the system, if the loan is not paid, the cotton becomes the property of the government.—EDS.]

A clerk from the ASCS office, Mrs. Sally Pat McNeil, testified that she had made no inquiry as to where the defendant McNabb had grown his cotton. The loan papers executed by this clerk show in the space designated for information concerning liens that there was no lien on the cotton grown by McNabb. Mrs. McNeil testified that she obtained this information from McNabb himself. McNabb testified that a copy of his lease with the plaintiffs was on file in the ASCS office. Further, the proof shows that the warehouse receipts referred to cotton gin tickets which in turn indicate that the cotton delivered by McNabb was grown on the plaintiffs' lands.

On this record we find that the warehouse receipts were not "duly negotiated" to the Commodity Credit Corporation so as to cut off the plaintiffs' lien. First, as the plaintiffs point out, the Department of Agriculture's own regulations, specifically 7 C.F.R. 1427.1364, require that cotton going into the loan program be lien-free. This regulation, we think, indicates that some inquiry is to be made by the local ASCS office to determine if there is a lien on cotton which is to be put into the government loan program. McNabb, as a tenant farmer (albeit a large one) could not reasonably be expected to be fully familiar with the Tennessee Lien statutes and therefore limited inquiry from him alone, even if it might reasonably be assumed that he would give an honest answer, was not sufficient, especially since Mrs. McNeil only asked McNabb whether there was a lien on the cotton he had grown, and not whether his farm land was leased. Also, as indicated, the information that McNabb was a tenant farmer was readily available to the ASCS office. Either the government office disregarded the Tennessee Lien statute or was unfamiliar with it. At any rate, we think from all the facts and circumstances known to it, the Commodity Credit Corporation had reason to know of the plaintiffs' lien. Further, we do not believe that the existence of the above-mentioned custom and usage should lead us to the conclusion that the government through its representatives had no reason to know that the lien existed.

In *McNabb,* Commodity Credit Corp. was denied §7-502 holder status because it "had reason to know." Not all courts agree on the amount of knowledge of a claim or defense that is sufficient to deprive one of the §7-502 status. Compare R.E. Huntly Cotton Co. v. Fields, 551 S.W.2d 472 (Tex. Civ. App. 1977) ("access to information sufficient to put [transferees] on notice of claims . . . is immaterial unless defendants had actual knowledge of facts and circumstances that would amount to bad faith").

Under §7-501, the negotiation must also be in the regular course of business or financing to be a due negotiation. Official Comment 1 to §7-501 provides in part:

> There are two aspects to the usual and normal course of mercantile dealings, namely, the person making the transfer and the nature of the transaction itself. The first question which arises is: Is the transferor a person with whom it is reasonable to deal as having full powers? In regard to documents of title the only holder whose possession appears, commercially, to be in order is almost invariably a person in the trade. No commercial purpose is served by allowing a tramp or a professor to "duly negotiate" an order bill of lading for hides or cotton not his own, and since such a transfer is obviously not in the regular course of business, it is excluded from the scope of the protection of subsection (a)(5) or (b)(3).
>
> The second question posed by the "regular course" qualification is: Is the transaction one which is normally proper to pass full rights without inquiry, even though the transferor itself may not have such rights to pass, and even though the transferor may be acting in breach of duty? In raising this question the "regular course" criterion has the further advantage of limiting the effective wrongful disposition to transactions whose protection will really further trade. Obviously, the snapping up of goods for quick resale at a price suspiciously below the market deserves no protection as a matter of policy: it is also clearly outside the range of regular course.
>
> Any notice on the document sufficient to put a merchant on inquiry as to the "regular course" quality of the transaction will frustrate a "due negotiation." Thus irregularity of the document or unexplained staleness of a bill of lading may appropriately be recognized as negating a negotiation in "regular" course.

A §7-502 holder gets the rights listed in that section. The FBLA is similar. Read §7-502 carefully and do the next Problem.

PROBLEM 276

Wonder Warehouse issued a negotiable warehouse receipt to "bearer" that covered 40 drums of oil. The bailor was Bonanza Petroleum Company. The receipt was pledged by Bonanza to the Octopus National Bank as collateral for a $5,000 loan. While in the bank's possession, the receipt was stolen by the bank's credit manager, Claude McStuffy, who gave it to his cousin Al McStuffy, a disreputable oil products salesman. Al presented the receipt at the warehouse, and the new agent on duty delivered the drums to him. The agent, however, also stupidly returned the receipt to Al. Al sold the drums through his business. He then took the old warehouse receipt to the Antitrust National Bank, where he pledged it as collateral for a $5,000 loan. Al and Claude then skipped town. When both banks make demand on the warehouse for the goods, does the warehouse have any defenses? Remember §7-403? Consider it; then read §7-404.

B. *The §7-503(a) Owner*

Go back to Article 2 (Sales), and read the *entrusting rule* found in §§2-403(2) and 2-403(3), which we considered when we talked about the warranty of title; see Simson v. Moon, 137 Ga. App. 82, 222 S.E.2d 873 (1975); Annot., 59 A.L.R.4th 567. An understanding of what constitutes an entrusting is essential to understand the Problem and discussion that follow.

PROBLEM 277

Albert Collector took his favorite antique grandfather clock down to the Antique Clock Store to be cleaned. The proprietor assured him it would be ready on Friday. On Thursday, Betty Shopper wandered into the store, saw the clock, and became entranced by it. She made the proprietor an offer he couldn't refuse, so he sold her the clock and she took it home. Albert Collector was furious. He consults you. Can he replevy the clock from Betty? See Lindholm v. Brant, 283 Conn. 65, 925 A.2d 1048 (2007) (reprinted in Chapter 4). Can he sue the proprietor? Using what theory (or theories)? If the proprietor had stored the clock in a warehouse, received a negotiable warehouse receipt therefor, and pledged the receipt to Last National Bank in return for a loan, could Albert Collector retrieve the clock from the warehouse? Compare §§7-403, 7-502, and 7-503.

What *real* defenses are available against a §7-502 holder? The only ones that the Code sets out are listed in §7-403(a): proper delivery to a superior claimant, nonnegligent destruction of the goods, sale to enforce bailee's lien, and "any other lawful excuse" (not further defined in the Code). Who is the *superior claimant* that §7-403(a) permits to get the goods from the bailee even though there is an outstanding negotiable document of title? The answer: a §7-503(a) owner.

A §7-503(a) owner is a person who had a legal interest or perfected security interest in the goods *prior to* the bailee's issuance of a document of title and who was in no way responsible for the creation of a situation permitting a negotiable document of title to come into existence. Read §7-503(a) carefully along with Official Comment 1. Essentially, §7-503(a) means that if the owner of goods *entrusts* them (or documents covering them) or delivers them to anyone so that that person has the *apparent* authority to deal with the goods, the owner is estopped to assert ownership against a subsequent §7-502 holder. See In re Jamestown Farmers Elevator, Inc., 49 Bankr. 661 (Bankr. D.N.D. 1985).

Where the owner has entrusted and is thus estopped, *ownership* becomes a *personal* defense, meaning it is only available against persons who do not qualify as a §7-502 holder, but is not assertable against such a holder. *But* when the owner of goods has had them, in effect, *stolen* by someone other than the owner's agent, then the owner is the very person §7-503(a) was meant to protect. A §7-503(a) owner has a superior right to the goods even against a §7-502 holder. In this case, ownership is a *real* defense (one that can be asserted against all parties, including a §7-502 holder), and the true owner can force the bailee to turn over the goods to the §7-503(a) owner without surrendering the negotiable document (though, as a practical matter, the owner will probably either have to get a court order or sign an indemnity agreement with the bailee before the latter will turn over the goods).

The policy here is that—since one of two innocent parties must bear a loss—if the owner has been even slightly at fault by permitting someone else to have the goods (and therefore apparent authority to ship or store them) or the documents, the owner should bear the loss. The owner must learn not to be so trusting in the future—or to insure against employee defalcation. But if the owner has had the goods stolen by someone not permitted to hold onto the goods, then the owner should be able to trace the goods and recover them even if they are found in the possession of a bailee.

The following case involves electronic documents of title. These are allowed by §§7-105, 7-106, and 7-501(b).

Agricredit Acceptance, LLC v. Hendrix

United States District Court, Southern District of Georgia, 2000
82 F. Supp. 2d 1379

NANGLE, District Judge.

Before the Court is defendant Hohenberg Bros. Co., Loeb & Company, Inc., Weil Brothers-Cotton, Inc., and the Montgomery Company, Inc.'s (the merchants') motion for summary judgment (Doc. 80). For the reasons that follow, defendants' motion is denied.

I. Background . . .

The defendant merchants buy cotton stored in warehouses and resell it to textile mills. Br. Supp. Defs.' Consolidated Mot. Summ. J. at 1 (Doc. 81). These transactions are generally electronic in nature, involving electronic warehouse receipts (EWRs) maintained in the central operating systems of various EWR providers. Id. at 1-2. The sale typically begins with the merchants' receipt of a recap sheet from a prospective seller, which describes a number of bales being offered for sale by grade, quantity and warehouse in which the bales are stored. Id. at 2. The merchant then telephones the seller and submits an offer involving either a fixed price or an "on call" price which is based on the price of cotton futures on the New York market. Id. Once an agreement is reached between the merchant and the seller, the seller transfers the EWRs for the bales sold into the name of the merchant, and the merchant receives a confirmation of this transaction from the EWR provider. Id. When the EWRs are in the name of the merchant, the merchant is able to obtain a list of the bales by receipt number from the central filing system by downloading the list into the merchant's computers. Id. The sale is completed when the merchant pays the seller for the cotton represented by the EWRs. Id.

These sales can also be accomplished via contract for future delivery. Id. at 5. These contracts involve the seller promising to provide some specific number of bales in the future at a provisional price. After the seller acquires the bales, it transfers the EWRs for the bales into the name of the merchant and the process proceeds as above. Id.

Thomas Hendrix's 1997 cotton crop was financed by a loan from plaintiff Agricredit Acceptance Corporation (AAC). Order dated Dec. 21, 1998, at 2. The loan was secured by the cotton crop. Id. AAC's security interest was properly perfected by filing the Security Agreement in the real estate records of the counties wherein the cotton was grown and with the County clerks' offices. Id. at 3. Sea Island Cotton Trading was designated as a selling agent through which Hendrix would sell the cotton crop, and AAC notified Sea Island of its security interest in accordance with the provisions of the Food Security Act (FSA), 7 U.S.C. §1631. Id. Hendrix's cotton crop was ginned, baled, and stored in various warehouses, including Collins Gin & Warehouse, Candler Gin & Warehouse, Goldkist, Inc., Growers Gin & Warehouse, Inc., and Bulloch Gin. Id.; Br. Supp. Defs.' Mot. Summ. J. at 3. The warehouses issued EWRs for the cotton in the central filing system of the EWR provider to which they were subscribed. Br. Supp. Defs.' Mot. Summ. J. at 3. These receipts were eventually placed in the name of Sea Island. Id. at 4; Order dated Dec. 21, 1998, at 3.

All of the defendant merchants purchased large quantities of cotton from Sea Island in 1997 and 1998, including many bales from Hendrix's

1997 crop. The merchants paid Sea Island for these bales, and the EWRs representing the bales were transferred by Sea Island into the names of the purchasing merchants. Br. Supp. Defs.' Mot. Summ. J. at 4-15. Sea Island never paid AAC or Hendrix for the cotton in violation of its obligations under the FSA notice. Order dated Dec. 21, 1998, at 4. Consequently, plaintiff AAC filed suit against the defendant merchants and others seeking foreclosure of its security interest in the Hendrix cotton, a writ of possession against anyone in possession of the cotton, and a finding of conversion and an award of damages against the cotton merchants, among other things. Id.

The defendant merchants assert that because the EWRs representing the Hendrix cotton were duly negotiated to them by Sea Island and because AAC entrusted the cotton to Hendrix with apparent authority to sell it, the cotton is no longer subject to AAC's security interest. That is, the merchants assert that duly negotiated EWRs have priority over a prior perfected security interest, especially when the secured party entrusts the collateral to the borrower. As this Court found in its Order dated December 21, 1998, the resolution of these issues depends on this Court's interpretation of the Georgia Uniform Commercial Code and its application to the facts of this case. Id. at 13-14.

II. Analysis . . .

In Georgia, a security interest in crops can only be perfected by the filing of a financing statement. O.C.G.A. §11-9-302(1)(h).[7] Generally, a perfected security interest takes priority over other liens, claims or rights to property and to security interests perfected at a later date. O.C.G.A. §§11-9-310, -312.[8] This general rule is of course subject to exception. For example, a buyer in the ordinary course of business takes free of a security interest created by his seller, O.C.G.A. §11-9-307(1). Furthermore, nothing in Article 9 of the UCC limits the rights of "a holder to whom a negotiable document of title has been duly negotiated . . . and such holders . . . take priority over an earlier security interest even though perfected," O.C.G.A. §11-9-309.[9]

A warehouse receipt is a negotiable document of title if it provides by its terms that the goods are to be delivered to bearer or to the order of a named person. O.C.G.A. §11-7-104(1)(a).[10] These receipts may be in an electronic format. O.C.G.A. §10-4-19(e). A negotiable document running to order is negotiated by indorsement and delivery. O.C.G.A. §§11-7-501(1).[11]

7. Section 9-310(a) in the 1999 revision of Article 9.—Eds.
8. Section 9-334 in the 1999 revision of Article 9.—Eds.
9. Section 9-331 in the 1999 revision of Article 9.—Eds.
10. Now §7-104(a).—Eds.
11. Now §7-501(a)(1).—Eds.

A negotiable document running to bearer is negotiated by delivery alone. O.C.G.A. §11-7-501(2).[12]

To be duly negotiated, a document of title must be negotiated "to a holder who purchases it in good faith without any notice of any defense against it or claim to it on the part of any person and for value, unless it is established that the negotiation is not in the regular course of business." O.C.G.A. §11-7-501(4).[13] Good faith is defined by reference to O.C.G.A. §11-1-201(19) as "honesty in fact in the conduct or transaction concerned." "A person has 'notice' of a fact when: (a) He has actual knowledge of it; or (b) He has received a notice or notification of it; or (c) From all the facts and circumstances known to him at the time in question he has reason to know that it exists." O.C.G.A. §11-1-201(25). Finally, in general, a person gives value for rights if he acquires them "in return for any consideration sufficient to support a simple contract." O.C.G.A. §11-1-201(44). Section 11-7-502 provides that a holder to whom a negotiable warehouse receipt has been duly negotiated acquires title to the document, title to the goods, and the direct obligation of the warehouse to deliver the goods, except as provided in O.C.G.A. §11-7-503.

Section 11-7-503[14] provides that:

> (1) A document of title confers no right in goods against a person who before issuance of the document had a legal interest or a perfected security interest in [the goods] and who neither:
>
> (a) Delivered or entrusted [the goods] . . . to the bailor or his nominee with actual or apparent authority to ship, store, or sell . . .; nor
>
> (b) Acquiesced in the procurement by the bailor or his nominee of any document of title.

Neither Article 1 nor Article 7 defines the term "entrusted." This term is used elsewhere in the UCC, however. Section 11-2-403(3) defines it as "any delivery and any acquiescence in retention of possession regardless of any condition expressed between the parties." However, Georgia courts have found that this provision only applies to owners of goods, because one cannot entrust goods one does not own. Sunnyland Employees' Fed. Credit Union v. Fort Wayne Mortgage Co., 182 Ga. App. 5, 354 S.E.2d 645, 647 (1987) (holding that party with security interest in mobile home could not be the entruster of it because party was not the owner of the home); United Carolina Bank v. Sistrunk, 158 Ga. App. 107, 279 S.E.2d 272, 274 (1981) (holding party with security interest in car could not be the entruster of it

12. Now §7-501(a)(2).—Eds.
13. Now §7-501(b)(3).—Eds.
14. The same rule is continued with slight wording changes in §7-503.

because party was not the owner of the car); McConnell v. Barrett, 154 Ga. App. 767, 270 S.E.2d 13, 15-16 (1980) (holding that non-owners cannot be entrusters and citing Adams v. City Nat'l Bank & Trust Co., 565 P.2d 26, 29 (Okla. 1977)). Acquiescence is not defined anywhere in the UCC.

C. INTERPRETATION AND APPLICATION OF THE UCC

Defendants' motion for summary judgment is based on two theories: (1) that the EWRs were duly negotiated to the merchants and pursuant to O.C.G.A. §§11-9-309, the merchants' interest in the cotton has priority over AAC's interest, Br. Supp. Defs.' Mot. Summ. J. at 16-19; Defs.' Objections to Dep. Testimony Offered by Pl. at 2-4, 6, 7-8 (Doc. 123); and (2) that AAC waived the priority of its security interest by entrusting the cotton to Hendrix pursuant to O.C.G.A. §§11-7-503, Br. Supp. Defs.' Mot. Summ. J. at 20; Defs.' Objections to Dep. Testimony Offered by Pl. at 7-8; Defs.' Resp. Opp'n AAC's Objection to Affs. at 9-12 (Doc. 120).

1. *Due Negotiation and* §11-9-309[15]

For the EWRs to be duly negotiated to the merchants, the merchants must be purchasers in good faith without notice of claims or defenses to the receipts and for value. O.C.G.A. §11-7-501(4).[16] It is undisputed that the merchants purchased the EWRs for value. Consequently, the Court must determine whether the merchants also purchased the EWRs in good faith and without notice.

Good faith as defined in Article 1[17] means "honesty in fact." Plaintiff does not dispute that the merchants acted with honesty in fact in this transaction. Rather, relying on an improper definition of good faith, AAC asserts that good faith requires the merchants to perform a lien check on the cotton before purchase. The Court finds that the "honesty in fact" definition does not require the merchants to perform a lien check on the cotton prior to purchase. Consequently, the Court holds that the merchants are purchasers in good faith as a matter of law.

However, this finding does not end the inquiry. The merchants must also be purchasers without notice of any defenses or claims to the EWRs. Plaintiff relies on the third prong of Article 1's definition of notice in arguing that the merchants' experience with the cotton industry and its willful ignorance as to the existence of liens on the cotton constitute reason to

15. Now §9-331.—Eds.

16. Now §7-501(b)(3).—Eds.

17. In the revised version of Article 1 (now the law in most jurisdictions), §1-20(b)(20) defines "good faith" as "honesty in fact and the observance of reasonable commercial standards of fair dealing," thus adding an objective component to the mix.—Eds.

know that plaintiff's defense to the EWRs existed. Pl's Resp. Opp'n Defs.' Mot. Summ. J. at 22-24 (Doc. 93). While some jurisdictions have required the existence of suspicious circumstances for a finding of "reason to know"; Colin v. Central Penn Nat'l Bank, 404 F. Supp. 638, 640-41 (E.D. Pa. 1975); others hold that willful or deliberate indifference to or ignorance of information is a basis for a finding of "reason to know;" Demoulas v. Demoulas, 428 Mass. 555, 703 N.E.2d 1149, 1167 (1998) ("If a person confronted with a state of facts closes his eyes in order that he may not see that which would be visible and therefore known to him if he looked, he is chargeable with 'knowledge' of what he would have seen had he looked.") (citations omitted); New Bedford Inst. for Savings v. Gildroy, 36 Mass. App. Ct. 647, 634 N.E.2d 920 (1994) ("Further, a holder has no duty to inquire unless 'the circumstances reveal a deliberate desire by the holder to evade knowledge of claims made by the maker.' ") (citations omitted).

The Court finds that the evidence in the record indicates that a genuine issue of fact exists concerning the merchants' notice of AAC's claims to the cotton. The merchants testified in deposition that they do not perform lien searches on cotton bought from merchants or gins. Dep. Hohenberg Bros. Co. through John D. Mitchell at 25-27 (Doc. 91); Dep. Weil Brothers-Cotton, Inc. through James A. Wade at 18-19 (Doc. 90); Dep. Loeb & Co., Inc. through James L. Loeb at 24 (Doc. 87); Dep. Montgomery Co. through Jack D. Atkins at 27-28, 42-43 (Doc. 89). However, when buying directly from the producer or when buying in a state with a central lien filing system, most of the merchants do perform lien searches. Dep. Mitchell at 25-26; Dep. Loeb at 24; Dep. Atkins at 28, 42-43. Further, when dealing with sales via contract for future delivery, the merchants include a clause in the contract requiring the seller to warrant that there are no liens on the cotton. Dep. Mitchell at 68-72. These facts imply that the merchants certainly knew of the possibility of the existence of liens. Whether their failure to search for liens amounts to deliberate indifference or ignorance to their existence, however, is less than clear from the facts presently in the record. The Court finds that this issue is one for a jury to decide.

Even if the Court finds that the merchants had no notice of AAC's claims to the cotton, this finding would not automatically provide superiority to the merchants' claims to the cotton. O.C.G.A. §11-9-309[18] provides that "Nothing in this article limits the rights . . . of a holder to whom a negotiable document of title has been duly negotiated . . . and such holders take priority over an earlier security interest even though perfected." Defendants urge the Court to hold that this Section provides that any duly negotiated EWR automatically trumps a prior perfected security interest in the goods covered by that EWR.

18. Now §9-331.—Eds.

Defendants' interpretation of §11-9-309 is in error. Such an interpretation would eviscerate the provisions of O.C.G.A. §11-7-503, which expressly provide that EWRs confer no rights in the goods covered by the EWRs against security interests existing and perfected prior to the issuance of the EWR where there has been no entrustment or acquiescence on the part of the secured party. The proper interpretation of §11-9-309 is that the Section only applies when the negotiable document holder and the secured party are both claiming an interest in the document. Farmers State Bank of Somonauk v. National Bank of Earlville, 230 Ill. App. 3d 881, 172 Ill. Dec. 894, 596 N.E.2d 173, 174-76 (1992). That is, §11-9-309 addresses disputes between competing interests in a negotiable document whereas §11-7-503 covers disputes between competing interests in the underlying goods. Accordingly, even if the EWRs were duly negotiated to the merchants, disposition of the cotton covered by those EWRs depends upon the application of O.C.G.A. §11-7-503.

2. *Entrustment*

Defendants argue that despite the Georgia courts' interpretation of §11-2-403, this Court is free to find that AAC entrusted the cotton to Hendrix by leaving it in his possession and allowing him to sell it through Sea Island. However, because Article 1 and Article 7 provide no definition for the term "entrusted," this Court must look to the Georgia courts' interpretation of that term as it is used in other sections of the UCC. Banks v. Georgia Power Co., 267 Ga. 602, 481 S.E.2d 200, 202 (1997) (stating that court is required to construe statute with reference to other statutes and decisions of the courts); Poteat v. Butler, 231 Ga. 187, 200 S.E.2d 741, 742 (1973) ("All statutes are presumed to be enacted by the General Assembly with full knowledge of the existing condition of the law . . . and their meaning and effect is to be determined in connection . . . with reference to other statutes and decisions of the courts."). Because the Georgia courts have held in the context of §11-2-403 that a secured party who does not own the goods cannot entrust them; *Sunnyland*, 354 S.E.2d at 647; *United Carolina Bank*, 279 S.E.2d at 274; *McConnell*, 270 S.E.2d at 15-16; this Court must hold similarly in the context of §11-7-503.[19] Consequently, the Court finds that plaintiff did not entrust the cotton to Hendrix as a matter of law.

Plaintiff may, however, have acquiesced in the procurement of a document of title in the cotton (namely the EWRs) pursuant to §11-7-503(1)(b).[20] When a bank knows that a farmer is attempting to sell his collateral and

19. This interpretation does not make the use of the term "entrusted" superfluous in the context of §11-7-503. Rather, that Section also applies to any persons with any legal interest in the goods which was created prior to the issuance of the document of title. When such persons are the owners of the goods, the entrustment provision would apply.

20. Now §7-503(a)(2).—Eds.

it acquiesces in his procurement of documents of title to that collateral, the bank has waived its right to assert its security interest in the collateral. Mercantile Bank of Springfield v. Joplin Regional Stockyards, Inc., 870 F. Supp. 278, 283 (W.D. Mo. 1994). The evidence presently before the Court is not sufficient to support a ruling on this issue as a matter of law. Consequently, the question of plaintiff s acquiescence is better left to a jury.

III. CONCLUSION

Because genuine issues of material fact exist,

IT IS HEREBY ORDERED that defendants' motion for summary judgment is denied.

C. *Other Transfers*

Section 7-504, which you should read as soon as you finish this paragraph, sets out the rights acquired by a transferee of a document when there has been no *due negotiation.* Section 7-505 goes on to provide that the indorser of a document of title does not make any *contract* that the bailee will honor the document, but §7-507 (which you should also glance at) provides that any transferor makes the warranties listed there. In addition, since a sale of goods is involved in the transfer of any document of title, a transferor also makes the Article 2 warranties, discussed in the earlier part of this book.

It is a basic rule of all commercial law that a transferee gets whatever legal rights the transferor had. This rule is called the shelter rule because the transferee is said to take shelter in the status of the transferor. In Article 2 (Sale of Goods) the shelter rule is found in §2-403; read it. In Article 3 (Commercial Paper) the rule turns up in §3-203(b), and in Article 8 (Investment Securities) it is reflected in §8-301. For Article 7 the rule is codified in §7-504(a). Read it, and use it to work the following Problem.

PROBLEM 278

The shipping agent for the King Cotton Manufacturing Company wrongfully took for himself 90 bales of cotton that had come under his control and stored them in the Rural Warehouse, which issued to him a negotiable warehouse receipt. This receipt he took to Octopus National Bank (ONB) and gave as security for a loan. He indorsed the receipt over to ONB. King Cotton discovered the bales were missing and investigated; the shipping agent was arrested. Shortly thereafter, ONB sold the warehouse receipt to Antitrust National Bank (ANB), which bought the document with full knowledge of the above facts. Both ANB and King Cotton made a demand on Rural Warehouse for the cotton. Rural calls you, its attorney, for advice. What do you say? Note §§7-403(c), 7-501 through 7-504, 7-603.

IV. COLLECTION THROUGH BANKS

A. "Payment Against Documents"

If the seller and buyer deal with each other on a face-to-face basis, delivery of the goods and payment of the price normally occur at the same moment, and neither party need trust the other. Where seller and buyer are separated by great distances, a seller must either trust the buyer to live up to the contract (a sale on *open account* with trust on both sides) or figure out a way to make certain that the buyer cannot get the goods until they are paid for. The easiest way to do this would be to have an agent in the buyer's city who could present the bill of lading covering the goods to the buyer but not turn it over to the buyer until cash was paid for the goods. In effect, this is the solution that sellers have adopted. See §2-503(5)(b). The *agent* that sellers typically use is a bank in the buyer's city. And, instead of a letter of instruction telling the bank-agent what to do, the seller simply draws an Article 3 draft (§3-104(e)) on the buyer (so that the buyer is the drawee) and attaches it to the bill of lading.

A draft is similar to a check; it is an instruction of payment. The seller is the drawer, and the buyer is the drawee. A simple draft will look like this:

____
(Date)

To: ______________________ ______________
(Buyer's Name) (Amount)

At sight pay to the order of ______________________________
(Payee's Name)

______________________ dollars and ___________ cents.

____
(Seller's Signature)

The payee will be whomever the seller nominates: the seller's bank, one of the seller's creditors, or even the seller itself. The only difference between this draft and your typical check is that the drawee is the buyer and not a bank.

Now that the seller has created the draft, it is combined with other papers for delivery to the buyer. The papers (which will normally include the bill of lading, a sales invoice, and, occasionally, an inspection certificate) along with the seller's draft on buyer are indorsed over to the seller's local bank for collection. Then the normal bank collection machinery in Article 4 is put into motion. Eventually, a bank in buyer's vicinity makes a formal Article 3 *presentment* of the draft (§3-501), and the buyer must either pay or dishonor. In any event, the buyer cannot get the documents (especially the bill of lading) until payment, so the seller is protected from having to trust a buyer in an arm's length transaction. If the buyer dishonors, the seller is notified by the collecting bank. The seller will then give instructions to the bank as to what to do with the goods when they arrive (the bank will be able to claim them from the carrier because it has the bill of lading; §7-403(c)).

Any draft accompanied by sales documents like those mentioned above is called a *documentary draft*. See §4-104(a)(6). The normal rules for negotiable instruments in Articles 3 and 4 apply to such drafts, but occasionally the sections make special rules for documentary drafts, e.g., §4-202(a)(2) (providing that after dishonor a collecting bank need not return a documentary draft to its transferor).

Sometimes the seller does not demand that the buyer actually pay prior to receiving the documents. Under some contracts, it is enough that buyer *accept* the draft and incur the obligation of an *acceptor* (§3-413), thus becoming primarily liable on the draft (the draft is now commonly called a *trade acceptance*). Typically, these are *time drafts* (as opposed to *sight drafts,* whereby payment is required as soon as buyer sees the draft) because they require payment in 30, 60, or 90 days after "sight" (presentment to buyer). The business reason why this is frequently done is so that the buyer can take the goods during the grace period, by manufacturing transform them into other goods, and resell them. In these transactions the seller sends the draft and documents through the banks and asks the collecting bank to call the buyer and make a presentment for acceptance. Read §4-212. The buyer shows up and accepts by writing the buyer's signature on the draft (if the buyer does not show up, the draft is dishonored). After acceptance, the draft is returned to the presenter and may be further negotiated. On acceptance by the buyer, the bank turns over the documents, and in 30, 60, or 90 days (or whatever time period the draft provides) the buyer is required to pay the draft or is in breach of the acceptor's contract. If the buyer fails to pay or accept the draft (which happens about 10 percent of the time) notice of that must immediately be sent back up the line. For an article spelling out *payment against documents* in detail, see Farnsworth, Documentary Drafts Under the Uniform Commercial Code, 22 Bus. Law. 479 (1967).

PROBLEM 279

Sam Seller in Dallas signed a sales contract to sell one ton of tennis balls to Beth Buyer in Indianapolis, "FOB truck in Dallas," $800 to be paid by a 60-day time draft on the buyer. Sam boxed the tennis balls and filled out a packaging invoice describing the goods. He drew a draft as follows:

> To: Beth Buyer
>
> Sixty days after sight pay to the order of *Sam Seller* $800.
>
> (Signed) *Sam Seller*

He took the tennis balls down to the Texas Trucking Company and asked for a negotiable bill of lading consigned to his own order, with the instructions "notify Beth Buyer on arrival." The trucking company issued the negotiable ("order") bill to Sam.

Sam then took the bill of lading, the invoice describing the goods, and the draft on Buyer down to his local bank, the Lone Star National Bank. He asked Lone Star to collect the draft. On agreeing to the bank's collection charge, Sam indorsed both the draft and the bill of lading over to the bank. Lone Star Bank then forwarded the draft and the documents to the Indianapolis State Hoosier Bank for collection. The Hoosier Bank called Beth Buyer and told her to come by the bank and get the papers. Beth came down that afternoon, wrote her name diagonally on the draft (which the bank dated and kept), and received the other documents. Read §2-514. Two days later the Texas Trucking Company showed up with the goods and promptly notified Buyer of their arrival. Buyer went down to the truck depot and surrendered the bill of lading (as required by §7-403(c)), whereupon she received the tennis balls. Now, to see how Article 2 and Article 7 fit together like one glorious puzzle, answer the following questions:

(a) Can Beth Buyer *inspect* the goods? If so, when? See §2-513.

(b) If the tennis balls are defective (Seller has breached one of his Article 2 warranties), can Buyer reject (§2-602) or revoke her acceptance (§2-608) and refuse to pay?

(c) If the cartons are empty (Sam is a crook), can Buyer sue the Texas Trucking Company, since the bill of lading states that the goods shipped are "ONE TON TENNIS BALLS"?

(d) Can Buyer sue the collecting bank because the documents did not conform to the goods shipped? Read §7-508 to answer this one.

B. *Liability of the Collecting Bank*

Sometimes a seller in the position of Sam (above) will sell (*discount*) the draft and documents to a local bank. This generally makes no difference in the resulting rights (see, for example, the last sentence of §7-508), but it does give the collecting bank a security interest in the draft and documents (§4-210(a)(3)) and therefore permits it to become a holder in due course (§4-211). Read §2-506.

The last Part of Article 4 contains four sections that deal specifically with the collection of documentary drafts. Read §§4-501 to 4-504 to see how these sections link the sale under Article 2 with the use of Article 7 documents of title.

Rheinberg Kellerei GmbH v. Brooksfield National Bank of Commerce

United States Court of Appeals, Fifth Circuit, 1990
901 F.2d 481

GARZA, J.

American bank did not notify German bank of difficulty in payment on international collection order which came due on arrival of goods in Houston; the collection order was eventually dishonored. The district court held that the American bank did not know, and had no duty to inquire, whether goods had arrived, and entered take nothing judgment. Because we find that the American bank was on notice of the possibility of dishonor and should have told the German bank of the problem in collection, we reverse.

FACTS

In January of 1986, J & J Wine, an American company, ordered a shipment of wine from a German firm, Rheinberg Kellerei GmbH, through an importer, Frank Sutton & Co.[21] Payment was to be made through an international letter of collection handled by Edekabank in Germany and Brooksfield National Bank of Commerce Bank in San Antonio ("NBC Bank").[22] On March 27, NBC Bank received the letter of collection, bill of lading and

21. The "GmbH" designation means "Gesellschaft mit beschrankter Haftung," or "company with limited liability." GmbH is a common form of corporate organization in Germany and is similar to the "Inc." designation in the American corporate system.

22. In a case like this one, international letters of collection are issued by the seller's bank (Edeka) and sent to the buyer's bank (NBC Bank), which in turn presents the letter and its documents to the buyer. To receive the documents and collect the goods, the buyer pays the amount due to its bank, which then forwards the funds to the seller's bank. Enforcement of these letters is governed by the International Chamber of Commerce's International Rules for Collection.

invoices from Edeka.[23] The letter of collection noted that payment was due "on arrival of goods in Houston harbor," and called for NBC Bank to notify Sutton "in case of any difficulty of lack payment." The invoices noted an estimated time of arrival: April 2, 1986. NBC Bank then presented the documents to J & J Wine on March 27.

There is some dispute as to what, exactly, J & J Wine told NBC Bank about its financial situation at the time, but it is sure that J & J Wine did not pay the amount due, and instead asked NBC Bank to hold the letter for a time while J & J Wine worked to raise the money for payment. NBC Bank did not notify Edeka or Sutton of J & J Wine's failure to pay on presentment. In fact, NBC Bank did nothing further until early May, when Sutton informed them that the wine was still at the Houston port and NBC Bank cabled Edeka for further instructions.

The wine had arrived in Houston on March 31, but NBC Bank did not receive notice of that. Because J & J Wine had not taken delivery of it, the wine sat, exposed, at Houston harbor in metal containers until it had deteriorated completely. U.S. Customs agents eventually sold it at auction. J & J Wine subsequently went out of business, and Rheinberg Kellerei was never paid for the wine.

Rheinberg Kellerei then brought this suit, alleging that NBC Bank had negligently failed to inform it of J & J Wine's failure to pay, and that because of that negligence, the wine had spoiled at Houston harbor. After a bench trial, the district court entered a take-nothing judgment for NBC Bank. The court reasoned that, because payment was not due until the wine's arrival, and NBC Bank had no notice of that arrival and no duty to inquire further, NBC Bank had no knowledge that J & J Wine was in breach of the payment terms. For that reason, the district court held that NBC Bank could not be held liable for failure to inform Edeka of J & J Wine's default.

Complaining that the district court improperly applied the requirements of the International Rules for Collection (the "Rules") and erred in construing the letter of collection itself, Rheinberg Kellerei brought this appeal.

DISCUSSION

I. DUTY TO INFORM

NBC Bank presented the letter of collection and the other documents to J & J Wine for payment on March 27, 1986, before the wine had arrived and before the payment was due. Rheinberg Kellerei argues that, regardless

23. The bill of lading called for notification of Sutton and M.G. Maher & Co., the customs broker, on arrival of the goods in Houston. NBC Bank was not listed on the Bill of Lading or the invoices.

of whether NBC Bank knew when the wine had arrived, once NBC Bank presented the documents, it had a duty to inform Edeka of any problem in collecting J & J Wine's payment. We agree. That duty arises both from the Rules and the collection letter itself.

A. Letter of Collection

The letter, which is the primary source of responsibility in this case, instructs NBC Bank to notify Sutton "in case of any difficulty of lack payment."[24] The district court found that section demanded notice only if there were a "lack of payment or failure to pay." Likewise, NBC Bank emphasizes that the trigger for notice is a *lack* of payment. What the court below and NBC Bank ignore is the word "difficulty." The letter did not instruct NBC Bank to notify Sutton only if there were a default, or a failure to pay, or a lack of payment. Rather, NBC Bank was called on to act also if there were any *difficulty* in collecting payment. And the request that NBC Bank hold the letter while J & J Wine sought financing certainly posed a difficulty in collection. Once NBC Bank knew that J & J Wine had asked for time to come up with the money, it should have notified Sutton in accordance with the letter's instructions.

The Rules specify that any special instructions posted on a letter of collection should be "complete and precise." General Provisions, §C. While the instructions given on this letter could have been in clearer language, they are sufficiently precise to make NBC Bank aware of its duty to notify Sutton once difficulty arose in the collection.

B. International Rules for Collection

Article 20(iii)(c) of the Rules provides that the "collecting bank [NBC Bank] must send without delay advice on non-payment or advice of non-acceptance to the bank from whom the collecting order was received [Edeka]." The court below and NBC Bank submit that section called on NBC Bank to notify Edeka if J & J Wine had not paid on the letter at the time it came due: on arrival of the goods in Houston harbor. And, they argue, since NBC Bank had no actual notice of the arrival of the goods, it did not breach that duty to notify.

The issue, it seems, is the definition of "non-payment" as it is used in Art. 20(iii)(c). Does it refer to a failure to pay on presentment? Does it require an affirmative statement of intent not to pay? Must the due date have arrived? No court has yet defined the term and its attendant duties, so we must look for guidance elsewhere.

The Rules were adopted to aid in "defining, simplifying and harmonizing the practices and terminology used in international banking." I.C.C.

24. Sutton was Rheinberg Kellerei's agent in this sale.

Banking Commission, Statement of Services to Business. They serve, for the international banking community, the same function as the Uniform Commercial Code does for domestic players. There is no reason, then, to ignore the UCC as an advisory source.

Section 4-502 of the UCC governs payment of "on arrival" drafts, such as were presented in our case. Tex. Bus. & Com. Code Ann., §4-502 (Tex. UCC) (Vernon's 1968). Under that section, a bank such as NBC Bank may, but need not, present the documents to the buyer before the goods arrive. But if the buyer does not pay at that time, the bank must notify the seller's bank: "Refusal to pay or accept because the goods have not arrived is not dishonor; *the bank must notify its transferor of such refusal* but need not present the draft again. . . ." UCC §4-502 (emphasis added). The UCC imposes on the presenting bank a duty to notify the seller's bank of any delay or failure to pay on presentment of an "on arrival" draft, *whether or not the draft is yet due.*

If §4-502 were applied to our case, NBC Bank would have a duty to notify Edeka of J & J Wine's failure to pay the letter of collection when it was presented on March 27, even though the goods were not yet in Houston harbor and the payment was not yet due. This is not to say that J & J Wine was in default at that time or had dishonored the letter. Rather, the notice is an act of prudence, an exercise in due care. And, as the aims of the Rules and the UCC are more than consistent, and both demand the exercise of due care, we find that the Rules impose the same duty. NBC Bank should have notified Edeka of J & J Wine's failure to pay at presentment, as that failure constituted a "non-payment" under Art. 20(iii)(c).

NBC Bank and the court below rely heavily on the fact that NBC Bank had no actual knowledge of the wine's arrival in Houston, and had no duty to inquire further. We agree with those premises, but do not feel they affect NBC Bank's duty to notify. That duty arose—under both the Rules and the letter itself—when J & J Wine failed to pay on presentment and asked for time. Arrival of the wine did not trigger it. And NBC Bank cannot avoid liability by hiding from knowledge of arrival and claiming that ignorance as a defense.

II. DAMAGES

State law governs the measure of damages in a case such as this one. Gathercrest, Ltd. v. First American Bank & Trust, 805 F.2d 995, 997 (11th Cir. 1986). Tex. Bus. & Com. Code Ann. §2-709(1) (Tex. UCC) (Vernon's 1968) gives the relevant standard: "the seller may recover, together with any incidental damages under the next section, the price (1) of goods accepted or of conforming goods lost or damaged . . . after risk of their loss has passed to the buyer." Risk of loss had passed to J & J Wine when the goods arrived at Houston harbor and were available for J & J Wine to take delivery. Tex.

Bus. & Com. Code Ann., §2-509(1)(b) (Tex. UCC) (Vernon's 1968). The district court found that because the wine was exposed for such a long period in Houston harbor, it was " 'over cooked' and had deteriorated, lost its original flavor, freshness, was flat and should not be sold into the market that it was intended." Since the goods were so damaged, Rheinberg Kellerei is entitled to the contract price plus the unpaid freight costs, as provided in UCC [§2-709(1)(a)].

NBC Bank is entitled to a credit for the net proceeds of any resale of the damaged wine. UCC §2-709(2). Customs agents sold the wine at auction, but we have no evidence before us of the price paid or the net amount remaining after customs fees, wharfage, and the costs of the auction were paid. For that reason, we remand this case to the district court for the limited purpose of calculating that net amount. After finding that net amount, the district court should enter judgment for Rheinberg Kellerei for the contract price plus freight charges, less the net proceeds of the customs auction.

Conclusion

NBC Bank had a duty to notify Edeka or Sutton, which was triggered when J & J Wine failed to pay the letter of collection on presentment and asked for more time. That duty arose from two sources: the Rules and the letter itself. Though payment was not due until the wine arrived in Houston harbor, that arrival was not a triggering event for the duty to arise, and lack of knowledge of it is no defense. The judgment of the district court is, therefore, reversed, and this cause is remanded for calculation of damages.

It is so ordered.

Up to this point, the text has mostly dealt with sales transactions within the United States. To understand sales of goods between sellers and buyers in different countries, Article 5 (Letters of Credit) must now be mastered. In international sales, most sales are carried out through the use of documents of title, with the added complication that letters of credit are also used. International collection of documentary drafts is regulated by Brochure 600 of the International Chamber of Commerce (2007 revision), which the banks regard as "the law." The relevant UCC Articles—4, 5, and 7—are similar to its provisions.

CHAPTER 17 REVIEW QUESTIONS

How do we distinguish negotiable and nonnegotiable documents of title?

Should a bailee surrender goods to their owner if the owner does not present the negotiable document of title?

Why do lenders prefer negotiable documents of title as collateral?
What are the consequences of unauthorized delivery of goods by bailor?
If the goods are lost without negligence of the bailor, is bailor liable for nondelivery?
When can the owner of goods recover goods that were entrusted to a merchant who then sold them?
Is a carrier liable to the consignee if the goods delivered do not match the description of the goods in the bill of lading?

ASSESSMENT: MULTIPLE CHOICE QUESTIONS

1. Frankie Knuckles operated several warehouses in Chicago. Derrick May delivered several dozen boxes of robotics equipment for storage. Knuckles issued a negotiable warehouse receipt to May. A few weeks later, despite Knuckles's state-of-the-art security and safety technology, the equipment was destroyed in an earthquake, rare for Chicago. May subsequently showed up with the warehouse receipt and demanded the equipment. Is Knuckles liable for nondelivery?
   a. Yes. A warehouse that issues a negotiable warehouse receipt is strictly liable to deliver the goods upon presentation of the receipt.
   b. Yes. A warehouse is obliged to protect against loss by carrying insurance.
   c. No. A warehouse is not liable for damage to goods, where the damage was not caused by failure to take reasonable care of the goods.
   d. No. A warehouse is not liable for loss unless the parties agree so in writing, under the doctrine of "buyer beware."

2. Jamie Principle arrived at another of Knuckles's warehouses with a truckload of printer ink for storage. The warehouse manager issued Principle a negotiable receipt for the ink. However, Principle drove away without unloading the ink. Principle later duly negotiated the receipt to Alison Limerick, who presented the receipt to Knuckles. Is Knuckles liable to Limerick for nondelivery of goods that Knuckles never received?
   a. No. Knuckles is not obliged to deliver goods that he never received.
   b. Yes. Nondelivery of the goods to the warehouse is not a defense that can be raised against a holder to which a negotiable document of title has been duly negotiated.
   c. No. The negotiable document is fraudulent and so not enforceable.
   d. Yes. Knuckles is liable as the agent for Principle.

3. Mundy burglarized Levan's home and stole a painting, *Introspective.* Mundy stored the painting in a warehouse of Knuckles, receiving a negotiable warehouse receipt. Mundy sold the painting to Collector, who gave

value in good faith. Levan learned of the painting's whereabouts and claimed it. Between Levan and Collector, who is entitled to the painting?
a. Levan, who owns the painting.
b. Collector, who owns the receipt covering the painting and has priority to the painting.
c. Collector, because the painting was entrusted to a bailee.
d. Levan, because Collector dealt directly with the thief.

4. Larchwoods Devices shipped 600 set top boxes on Reading Railroad, with a straight bill of lading consigning the goods to Bolcast Cable. Before delivery, Larchwood Devices sent an electronic message to Reading Railroad, cancelling the shipment, because of a separate dispute with Bolcast Cable about industry standards. Reading Railroad returned the goods to Larchwood Devices. Is Reading Railroad liable to Bolcast Cable for nondelivery?
a. Yes, because with a straight bill of lading, the seller may only stop delivery if the buyer is insolvent, repudiates the contract, or otherwise gives the seller the right to withhold delivery.
b. Yes, because seller no longer had title to the goods.
c. No. The shipper may cancel a shipment and the carrier is obliged to comply.
d. No. Bolcast Cable has rights under the sales contract only against the seller.

5. Sneaky Sneakers delivered a shipment of running shoes to Reading Railroad. The bill of lading listed the goods as "1,000 pairs of running shoes, Shipper's Load Weight and Count." The buyer paid for the goods after inspecting the bill of lading, but on delivery determined that only 400 pairs of shoes were shipped. Is Reading Railroad liable to the buyer?
a. No. The carrier is never liable for the sales contract between buyer and seller.
b. No. The carrier may be liable for misdescription, but not where the bill of lading indicates that the carrier makes no warranty about the description.
c. Yes. The carrier is bound by the bill of lading and cannot disclaim liability for its own misrepresentations.
d. Yes. The carrier is always strictly liable to deliver the goods promised.

ANSWERS

1. *C* is the best answer. Under §7-403(a)(2), a bailee is not liable for non-delivery on account of "damage to or delay, loss, or destruction of the goods for which the bailee is not liable." Under §7-204, "A warehouse is liable for damages for loss of or injury to the goods caused by its failure

to exercise care with regard to the goods that a reasonably careful person would exercise under similar circumstances. However, unless otherwise agreed, the warehouse is not liable for damages that could not have been avoided by the exercise of that care." So a bailee is not liable for damages to the goods unless caused by the bailee's failure to be reasonably careful. Frankie Knuckles did take reasonable care, with state-of-the-art security and safety technology, so is not liable for the goods. There is no strict liability, contrary to *A*, or a requirement to have insurance, contrary to *C*.

2. *B* is the best answer. None of the defenses good against "a holder to which a negotiable document of title has been duly negotiated" apply here. See §7-403. There was no damage to the goods, or delivery to a party with superior rights, or sale to enforce a lien, or any of the other reasons listed in §7-403. Rather, Knuckles made the error of issuing a negotiable document, which represents the right to goods, without having the goods delivered.
3. *A* is the best answer. Levan owns the painting and nothing has happened that would give Collector priority. It would be different if Levan had entrusted the painting to a dealer, who sold it contrary to Levan's agreement. In that case, entrustment would apply to give the buyer priority over the entrusting owner, Levan. But Levan did not entrust the painting. Rather, it was stolen by Mundy, who sold it to Collector.
4. *A* is the best answer. When a straight bill of lading is issued to the buyer as consignee, the buyer has the right to the goods. The seller may stop delivery in transit, but only for specified reasons, such as buyer's insolvency, failure to pay, or repudiation of the contract. §2-704(1). In turn, such a justified stoppage would excuse the carrier from its obligation to deliver. §7-403(a)(4). None of those applies, here, so Reading Railroad would be liable for nondelivery.
5. *B* is the best answer. Section 7-301(a) imposes liability on the bailee for misdescription, but allows the bailee to avoid that liability with a disclaimer such as "Shipper's Load Weight and Count," which indicates that the issuer does not know whether the description of the goods is accurate.

Chapter 18

Letters of Credit

Perhaps, upstanding citizen, you have such splendid credit that anyone would instantly grant you credit if asked, but, if so, you are a rare individual (or organization). However the only entities whose credit *is* that trustworthy are banks themselves. If someone with unknown credit wants to deal with an unknown person, the whole transaction would be easier if the credit-seeker could, in effect, have a bank back up any credit extension involved. Better yet, why not have the bank itself be the primary party making the payment promise? This concept was the impetus behind the creation of a "letter of credit," which is just what it sounds like: a letter from a bank promising credit to a stranger in a business transaction. This chapter explores the situations in which a bank might issue such a letter and explains the law governing the transaction.

There are two primary sources for this law: Article 5 of the Uniform Commercial Code and the Uniform Customs and Practice for Documentary Credits, 2007 Revision (Brochure 600 of the International Chamber of Commerce, hereinafter, the UCP). The letter of credit may effectively state that it is governed by the UCP. See, e.g., ACR Systems, Inc. v. Woori Bank, 2017 WL 532300 (S.D. N.Y., 2017). Since the two are not significantly different, we shall look primarily to the Code for study purposes. If you should get involved in a letter of credit case, however, remember to study the UCP carefully—it is recognized as a complete statement of prevailing international banking practices in the field; for the relationship of Article 5 to the UCP, see Official Comment 2 to §5-103. The leading treatise on Article 5 is J. Dolan, The Law of Letters of Credit (4th ed. 2007).

I. THE BASIC PROBLEM

Assume you are the proprietor of a business in Detroit, Michigan that makes and sells men's shirts. One day you get a letter from Germany saying: "I want to buy 50,000 shirts at $7 each United States currency, FOB Frankfurt. (Signed) *Hans Goldschnitt.*" Since you have never heard of Hans Goldschnitt, you are reluctant to ship him 50,000 shirts and risk nonpayment after the shipping costs are incurred. There are no satisfactory credit bureaus similar to Dun and Bradstreet on an international basis. How can you avoid a credit risk? The answer devised by the law merchant is for you to write Herr Goldschnitt and tell him that you will ship the goods only to a *bank* of international repute that is willing to write a letter to you making itself *primarily* and *irrevocably* liable for the payment of the contract price. If Hans Goldschnitt agrees and you agree on the other contract terms, he will go to a major German bank—say, the National Volksbank of Frankfurt (NVF)—and establish credit with the bank. Shortly thereafter you will receive a letter from the bank more or less in the following form:

NATIONAL VOLKSBANK OF FRANKFURT
Credit no. 829-411
November 20, 2024

Dear Detroit Seller:

We hereby establish our **IRREVOCABLE CREDIT** in your favor for the account of Hans Goldschnitt, our customer, up to the aggregate amount of $350,000, U.S. dollars, available by your sight draft on us, to be accompanied by the following documents:

(1) full set of clean bills of lading issued by German Ocean Lines to the order of National Volksbank of Frankfurt, notify Hans Goldschnitt;

(2) signed commercial sales invoices describing the goods;

(3) customs certificates;

(4) packing lists;

(5) inspection certificate by Grey Goods Inspection Service of New York.

Bills of lading must be dated not later than August 1, 2025; drafts must be negotiated within ten days of shipment; all drafts must be marked "Drawn Under Credit No. 829-411." Subject to UCP rules (Brochure 600). This credit will expire on October 1, 2025. We hereby agree with drawers, indorsers, and bona fide holders of drafts drawn under and in compliance with the terms and conditions of this credit to honor the same on due presentation of draft to the drawee.

Yours very truly,

National Volksbank of Frankfurt

The German bank will probably forward this letter of credit to you through a local Detroit bank (which has translation facilities and better international commercial paper routing procedures than you do). The Detroit bank will give you the letter and tell you that it is willing to transmit the documents and drafts to the German bank at the proper time. In this situation the Detroit bank is called an *adviser.* You, the Detroit seller, are the *beneficiary* of the letter of credit.

On July 6, 2025, per your contract with Hans Goldschnitt, you draw up the packing lists, invoices, and certificates required by the letter of credit and put the goods on board a German Ocean Lines ship. In return you get a *clean* (free of carrier's notation indicating a defect in the goods or packaging) bill of lading to the order of the German bank and draw a draft payable to yourself on the NVF (that is, the German bank will be the drawee). You clip all these documents together and take them down to the Detroit bank, which forwards them to the German bank and makes an Article 3 presentment for you. If the German bank decides that you have complied with the terms of the letter of credit, it will honor the draft (pay it—the money is then remitted to you by the Detroit bank) and receive all the documents. The German bank then calls Hans Goldschnitt and tells him to come pay if he wants the documents he will need to get the goods off the ship. He does so. When the goods arrive, German Ocean Lines notifies Hans pursuant to instructions on their copy of the bill of lading. He presents the bill of lading and receives the goods.

Several variations on the above are possible. If you are unwilling to wait to get your money, you may be able to sell (*discount*) the drafts to the Detroit bank. Or, as part of your initial contract with the buyer, you may have required him to get a *Detroit bank* to issue the letter of credit to you. He can do this as follows: he establishes credit with the NVF; the NVF issues a letter of credit to you through the Detroit bank and asks the Detroit bank to *confirm* it. If the Detroit bank decides to do so (and it will first investigate the credit reputation of the German bank), it will notify you that the NVF has issued a letter of credit to you and that the Detroit bank "hereby confirms it." This makes the Detroit bank a *confirmer* and liable in exactly the same fashion as the issuer. The confirming letter of credit will state that the Detroit bank will honor drafts under the letter of credit if accompanied by the listed documents. The transaction then proceeds as above, except the drafts you draw are drawn on and presented to the Detroit bank for payment. (*Note:* it is possible to draw a *time* draft on the issuing bank whereby it is given 30, 60, or 90 days—as determined by contract—following formal *acceptance* in which to pay. Such a time draft is commonly called a *banker's acceptance.*) The issuing bank may require that the draft be presented for payment not to itself but to another entity with whom it has a contractual arrangement (called a *nominated person*—see §5-102(a)(11), defining the term, and §5-107(b) and its Official Comment 4, explaining the legal status of a nominated person). This is often done, for example, when the issuer does not carry sufficient amounts of the currency called for by the credit or when the issuing bank wants a more experienced institution to examine the documents presented by the beneficiary.

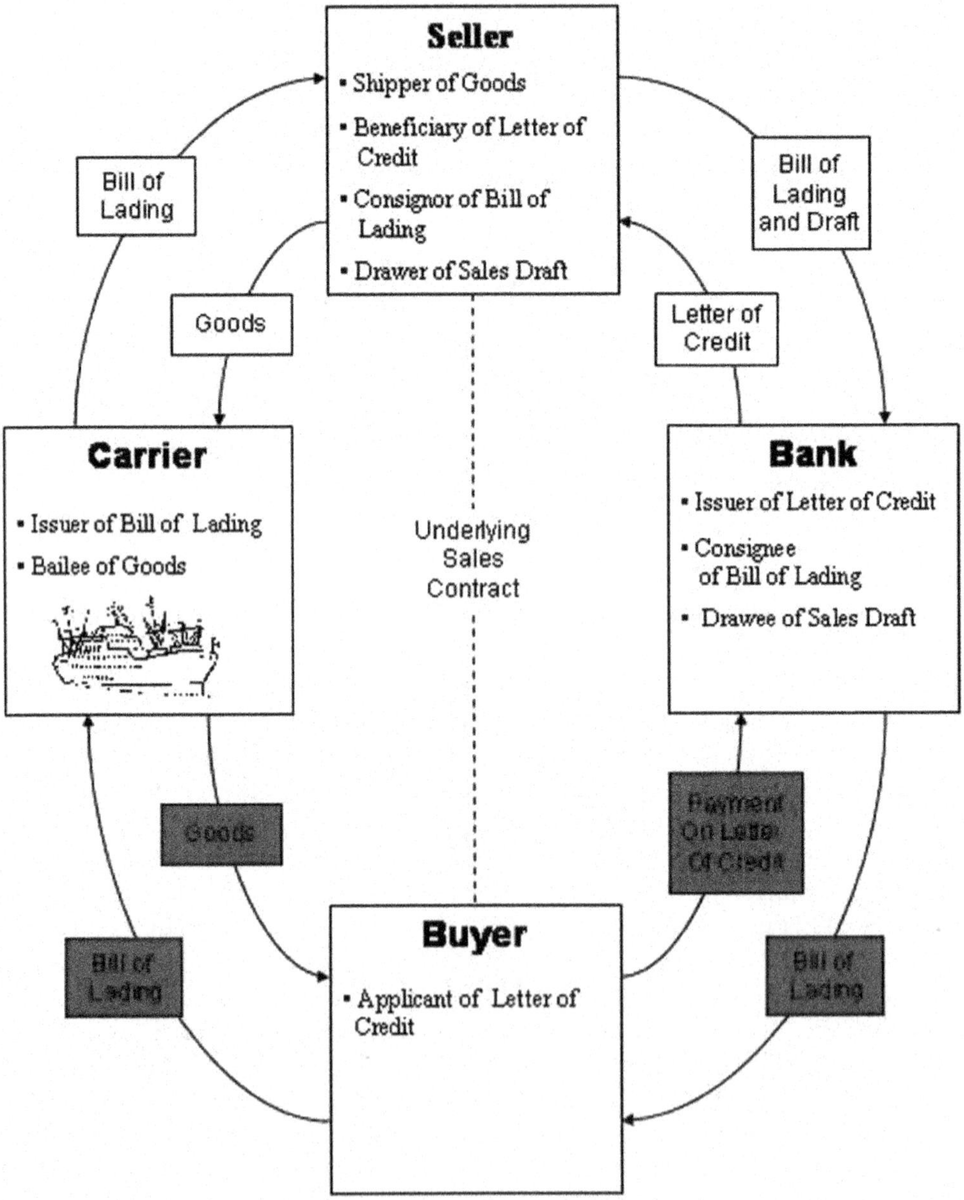

To be distinguished from the above *documentary credit* is the so-called *standby letter of credit.* A standby credit is issued by a bank to be honored only if there is default in an unrelated contract. For example, assume that a contractor agrees to build 50 apartment buildings for the owner of the lots on which the construction will occur. The owner might require the contractor to have its bank issue a standby credit in favor of the owner, to be drawn on only in the event that the contractor does not fulfill its contractual obligation. A standby credit differs from a documentary credit in that the beneficiary of the credit is not required to produce documents along with its draft against the letter of credit; instead, it typically just gives a written notice of breach. See Kirchhoff-Consigli Construction Management, LLC v. DeLuxe Building Systems, Inc., 2017 WL 3601981 (M.D. Penn. 2017). Thus, a standby credit is similar to a surety obligation (though not the same).[1] Standby letters of credit are much in use nowadays; in 2015, according to the Federal Reserve, standby letters of credit in the United States totaled over $550 billion.

PROBLEM 280

The U.S. Army wanted to order uniforms for its soldiers from Khaki Clothing, Inc., agreeing to pay a set amount on delivery. The Army, however, had had major problems in past dealings with Khaki, which was always very late at meeting delivery schedules. The purchasing officer for the Army asked the Army's attorney if the contract could contain a penalty clause, imposing a huge penalty on Khaki if it did not deliver the uniforms by the required date. The attorney, mindful of basic contracts law, opined that penalty clauses (even if disguised as liquidated damages clauses) are invalid as a matter of common law, but then he had an idea. He put a clause in the purchasing contract requiring Khaki to get a standby letter of credit in favor of the Army and requiring the issuing bank to pay a huge penalty sum to the Army in the event that Khaki did not deliver the uniforms on time. Octopus National Bank issued such a credit, but when Khaki missed the delivery deadline and the Army tried to collect the penalty specified in the credit, the bank balked and in its defense pointed to

1. It is *ultra vires* for a bank to act as a surety, so the courts have been careful to draw distinctions between suretyship and the issuance of a standby letter of credit, typically pointing to the fact that a surety is secondarily liable on the contract between the principal and the creditor, but that a bank's liability on a standby letter of credit is an independent obligation. See, e.g., State ex rel. Missouri Highway & Transp. Commn. v. Morganstein, 703 S.W.2d 894 (Mo. 1986).

the common law rule forbidding penalty clauses in contracts. Will this succeed? See Balboa Ins. Co. v. Coastal Bank (S.D. Ga. 1986); Telenois, Inc. v. Village of Schaumburg, 628 N.E.2d 581 (Ill. App. 1993); McLaughlin, Standby Letters of Credit and Penalty Clauses: An Unexpected Synergy, 43 Ohio St. L.J. 1 (1982).

Documentary letters of credit had their biggest boom in international sales right after World War II when they were used in more than half of such transactions. In the twenty-first century, only 5 percent of international sales require such credits to be issued by a bank. The reason is that a letter of credit is most useful when the seller doesn't trust the buyer to make payment (as in the Hans Goldscnitt purchase with which we began this chapter), but in this information age checking on the buyer's credit is much easier, and where the sale is to be made to a major internationally known buyer a letter of credit would just add expenses to the deal.

Standby letters of credit, however, where no documents are required and the bank pays on mere notification of default, are very popular these days, and growing in usage as those in business see the advantage of having a guaranteed payment source in the event of contractual difficulties. You, future lawyer, should consider the many situations in which having a bank as the payment source would be much better for your client than relying on some other party to pay up in the event of a dispute. Consider the next Problem.

PROBLEM 281

1. You have a family law practice and handle many divorces. It is your experience that when a divorce court orders one party, let's say the husband, to make alimony payments to the wife, your client, these payments are not always made. This is true even if the ex-husband is wealthy; there can still be bad blood between the parties, and the ex-husband may make his former wife hire a lawyer and take him to court over and over, just to annoy her. Might a standby letter of credit issued by the ex-husband's bank in favor of the wife for the payment of alimony be incorporated into the divorce decree?

2. You have a criminal law practice that often represents business clients who get caught cooking the books or misusing corporate money. When they come into your office they currently have substantial assets, but experience tells you that as their life collapses those assets have a way of disappearing and you have trouble getting paid. Could you build a standby letter of credit from the client's bank in your favor for your future fees into your retainer agreement?

II. DEFINITIONS AND SCOPE OF ARTICLE 5

Section 5-102(a)(9) addresses itself to the question of who can issue a letter of credit. Section 5-104 describes the formal requirements of such a letter (note that electronically generated letters of credit are clearly allowed; see Official Comment 3 to §5-104).

Letters of credit *not* requiring the presentation of documents are called *clean credits* because normally only drafts are tendered. See Housing Sec. Inc. v. Maine Natl. Bank, 391 A.2d 311 (Me. 1978). Perhaps the most startling use of such a letter of credit occurred in 1963, when the Royal Bank of Canada, the Morgan Guaranty Trust Co., and the Bank of America issued letters of credit totaling $106 million as security for the ransom of prisoners from the Cuban Bay of Pigs invasion. See Gerald T. McLaughlin, Remembering the Bay of Pigs: Using Letters of Credit to Facilitate the Resolution of International Disputes, 32 Ga. J. Int'l & Comp. L., 743 (2004).

Now read the definitions in §5-102. In the above hypothetical you were the *beneficiary* of the letter of credit; Hans Goldschnitt was the *applicant* (the former version of Article 5 called Hans the *customer*); the German bank was the *issuer;* and the Detroit bank was the *advisor* or *confirmer,* depending on which part of the hypothetical you are looking at. Read §5-107. Do not get these terms confused.

Now go back and reread §5-102(a)(10), which defines *letter of credit.* Note that a letter of credit can be "revocable" or "irrevocable," which means just what it sounds like. With a revocable letter of credit, the issuing bank can escape from its obligation easily. Article 7 of the UCP states that an "issuing bank is irrevocably bound to honour as of the time it issues the credit." By contrast, §5-106(a) *presumes* (if not otherwise stated) that a letter of credit is irrevocable. Remember this: *no one wants a revocable letter of credit.* To understand why, see §5-106(b); Official Comment 1 to that section comments that "revocable letters of credit offer unhappy possibilities for misleading the parties who deal with them." See Beathard v. Chicago Football Club, Inc., 419 F. Supp. 1133 (N.D. Ill. 1976). Article 2 of the UCC decrees that in sale of goods contracts, a clause requiring a letter of credit means an *irrevocable* letter of credit. Read §2-325. Circle the word *irrevocable* in subsection (3).

III. THE ISSUER—DUTIES AND RIGHTS

When the applicant comes to the issuing bank and asks to establish credit so that the bank will issue a letter of credit to the seller, the bank normally makes the applicant sign an airtight contract absolutely binding the applicant to reimburse the bank *or else.* Cf. §5-108(i)(1). When a bank issues an irrevocable letter of credit, it is under a duty to honor a draft properly drawn there under§5-108(a), so it wants to protect itself and make sure of reimbursement from the applicant. A bank owes corresponding duties to its applicant when performing its duties under the credit. Read §5-108 carefully. It is important to understand that if the issuer honors a draft that it should have dishonored, *the issuer may not seek reimbursement from its applicant.*[2] See Brenntag Intern. Chemicals, Inc. v. Norddeutsche Landesbank GZ, 70 F. Supp. 2d 399 (S.D.N.Y. 1999). An issuer in this predicament has a potential remedy in the warranty section, §5-110.

The moment of truth for the issuer occurs when the beneficiary presents a draft drawn on the issuer for the amount of the credit, accompanied by all the other items listed in the credit to be presented with the draft. In making the decision whether to pay the credit or to dishonor it (which could lead to a lawsuit alleging wrongful dishonor, with damages measured under §5-111) the issuer is only allowed to consider the documents presented by the beneficiary. What is called the "independence principle" flatly forbids the issuer to bring up matters having to do with the underlying transaction between the beneficiary and the applicant; read §5-103(d); see, e.g. Societe Anonyme Marocain De L'industrie Du Raffinage v. Bank of America N.A., 2016 WL 488665 (Sup. Ct. N.Y. 2016) (bank not required to determine facts of the underlying transaction, where beneficiary's presentation did not conform to the requirements in the letter of credit).

PROBLEM 282

At the request of its applicant, Greenbaum Construction Company, the Last National Bank issued a letter of credit to Latek Steel Company, obligating itself to pay drafts drawn against it, reflecting steel shipped to Greenbaum Construction under "Invoice #0046." Two weeks after the letter of credit was issued, the buyer and seller changed the shipment dates on the underlying contract and issued a new invoice, this one being "Invoice #0060." Latek Steel Company shipped the steel to Greenbaum Construction Company as

2. Failure of the applicant to reimburse the issuer is irrelevant as far as the beneficiary is concerned. In this situation, the beneficiary is not liable to the issuer in quasi-contract under a theory of unjust enrichment. See City Natl. Bank v. Westland Towers Apartments, 152 Mich. App. 136 (1986). The usual explanation is that the beneficiary has not in any way been unjustly enriched; it was paid for goods delivered. Section 5-108 (i)(4) clearly bars a restitution action in any situation where the defect was apparent on the face of the documents presented.

agreed and was disturbed to learn that the buyer had filed for bankruptcy two days later. However, it was reassured by the terms of the letter of credit. On Friday, March 27, it submitted a draft to Last National, accompanied by Invoice #0060, and was turned down for payment on April 1. Answer these questions:

(a) Label the parties: who is the *issuer,* the *beneficiary,* the *applicant?*

(b) What is the effect of the bank holding onto the presented draft until April 1? See §5-108(b).

(c) Remembering the doctrine of *de minimis non curat lex* ("the law does not notice small defects"), the attorney for Latek Steel argued that it had substantially complied with the letter of credit, so the bank was guilty of wrongful dishonor and ought to respond in damages under §5-111. Is this right? See Dubose Steel, Inc. v. Branch Banking & Trust Co., 72 N.C. App. 598, 324 S.E.2d 859 (1985); Dolan, Strict Compliance with Letters of Credit: Striking a Fair Balance, 102 Banking L.J. 18 (1985).

(d) Does the seller have any other remedy? See §2-702; Bankruptcy Code §546(c).

(e) What should Latek Steel have done to avoid all this? See §5-106(b). See also BasicNet S.p.A. v. CFP Services Ltd., 127 A.D.3d 157 (N.Y. App. Div. 2015).

Voest-Alpine Trading Co. v. Bank of China

United States District Court, Southern District of Texas, 2000
167 F. Supp. 2d 940

GILMORE, District Judge.

On February 16-17 and 21-23, 2000, a bench trial was held in the above-styled case. Having considered the evidence in this case and the applicable law, the Court enters the following findings of fact and conclusions of law.

On June 23, 1995, Plaintiff Voest-Alpine Trading USA Corporation ("Voest-Alpine") entered into a contract with Jiangyin Foreign Trade Corporation ("JFTC") to sell JFTC 1,000 metric tons of styrene monomer at a total price of $1.2 million. To finance the transaction, JFTC applied for a letter of credit through Defendant Bank of China. The letter of credit provided for payment to Voest-Alpine once the goods had been shipped to Zhangjiagang, China and Voest-Alpine had presented the requisite paperwork to the Bank of China as described in the letter of credit. The letter of credit was issued by the Bank of China on July 6, 1995 and assigned the number LC9521033/95. In addition to numerous other typographical errors, Voest-Alpine's name was listed as "Voest-Alpine USA Trading Corp." instead of "Voest-Alpine Trading USA Corp." with the "Trading USA" portion inverted. The destination port was also misspelled in one place as

"Zhang-jiagng," missing the third "a." The letter of credit did indicate, however, that the transaction would be subject to the 1993 Uniform Customs and Practice, International Chamber of Commerce Publication Number 500 ("UCP 500").

By the time the product was ready to ship, the market price of styrene monomer had dropped significantly from the original contract price between Voest-Alpine and JFTC. Although JFTC asked for a price concession in light of the decrease in market price, Voest-Alpine declined and, through its agents, shipped the styrene monomer on July 18, 1995. All required inspection and documentation was completed. On August 1, 1995, Voest-Alpine presented the documents specified in the letter of credit to Texas Commerce Bank, the presenting bank. Texas Commerce Bank found discrepancies between the presentation documents and the letter of credit which it related to Voest-Alpine. Because Voest-Alpine did not believe that any of the noted discrepancies would warrant refusal to pay, it instructed Texas Commerce Bank to forward the presentation documents to the Bank of China.

Texas Commerce Bank sent the documents via DHL courier to the Bank of China on August 3, 1995. According to the letter of credit, Voest-Alpine, the beneficiary, was required to present the documents within fifteen days of the shipping date, by August 2, 1995. As the documents were presented on August 1, 1995, they were presented timely under the letter of credit. Bank of China received the documents on August 9, 1995.

On August 11, 1995, the Bank of China sent a telex to Texas Commerce Bank, informing them of seven alleged discrepancies between the letter of credit and the documents Voest-Alpine presented, six of which are the subject of this action. The Bank of China claimed that 1) the beneficiary's name differed from the name listed in the letter of credit, as noted by the presenting bank; 2) Voest-Alpine had submitted bills of lading marked "duplicate" and "triplicate" instead of "original"; 3) the invoice, packing list and the certificate of origin were not marked "original"; 4) the date of the survey report was later than that of the bill of lading; 5) the letter of credit number in the beneficiary's certified copy of the fax was incorrect, as noted by the presenting bank; and 6) the destination was not listed correctly in the certificate of origin and the beneficiary's certificate, as noted by the presenting bank. The telex further stated. "We are contacting the applicant of the relative discrepancy [*sic*]. Holding documents at your risks and disposal."

On August 15, Texas Commerce Bank faxed the Bank of China, stating that the discrepancies were not an adequate basis to refuse to pay the letter of credit and requested that the bank honor the letter of credit and pay Voest-Alpine accordingly. The telex identified Voest-Alpine as the beneficiary in the transaction. Voest-Alpine also contacted JFTC directly in an effort to secure a waiver of the discrepancies but was unsuccessful.

On August 19, 1995, the Bank of China sent another telex to Texas Commerce Bank further explaining what it believed to be discrepancies between the letter of credit and the documentation presented by Voest-Alpine according to the UCP 500. In relevant part, the telex provided: "You cannot say [the discrepancies] are of no consequence. The fact is that our bank must examine all documents stipulated in the credit with reasonable care, to ascertain whether or not they appear, on their face, to be incompliance [*sic*] with the terms and conditions of the credit. According to Article 13 of UCP 500. An irrevocable credit constitutes a definite undertaking of the issuing bank, providing that the stipulated documents are complied with the terms and conditions of the credit according to Article UCP 500. Now the discrepant documents may have us refuse to take up the documents according to article 14(B) of UCP 500."

The Bank of China returned the documents to Voest-Alpine and did not honor the letter of credit.

I.

The commercial letter of credit is a payment device often used in international trade which permits a buyer in a transaction to substitute its financial integrity with that of a stable credit source, usually a bank. Alaska Textile Co., Inc. v. Chase Manhattan Bank, N.A., 982 F.2d 813, 815 (2d Cir. 1992).

"[A letter of credit] transaction usually comprises three separate contracts: '[f]irst, the issuing bank enters into a contract with its customer to issue the letter of credit. Second, there is a contract between the issuing bank and the party receiving the letter of credit. Third, the customer who procured the letter of credit signs a contract with the person receiving it, usually involving the sale of goods or the provision of some service.'" Resolution Trust Corporation v. Kimball, 963 F.2d 820, 820 (5th Cir. 1992) (quoting East Girard Sav. Ass'n v. Citizens National Bank, Etc., 593 F.2d 598, 601 (5th Cir. 1979)). The underlying principle of the letter of credit transaction is the independence of the three contracts. Philadelphia Gear Corp. v. Central Bank, 717 F.2d 230, 235 (5th Cir. 1983). The issuing bank does not verify that all the terms of the underlying contract have been fulfilled and must pay on a draft properly presented by a beneficiary, without reference to the rights or obligations of the parties to the contract. Tex. Bus. & Comm. Code Ann §5.108(a), (f)(1) (Vernon's 2000). The issuing bank need only make a facial examination of the presenting documents to determine whether the beneficiary has complied with the terms of the letter of credit, however, the bank bears the risk of any misinterpretation of the beneficiary's demand for payment. Tex. Bus. & Comm. Code Ann. §5.108(i)(4) (Vernon's 2000).

Prior to the amendments to the Texas Business and Commercial Code in 1999, a beneficiary was not required to make its presentation documents strictly comply with the letter of credit, but to present documents that on their face "appear[ed] to comply" with the letter of credit in order to receive payment. Tex. Bus. & Comm. Code Ann. §5.109(b)[3] (Vernon's 1998); see also Vest v. Pilot Point Nat'l Bank, 996 S.W.2d 9, 12 (Tex. Civ. App. 1999) (finding that the language in section 5.109 did not mandate strict compliance). The current statutory law requires an issuer to honor a presentation that, as determined by standard practice of financial institutions that regularly issue letters of credit, "appears on its face strictly to comply with the terms and conditions of the letter of credit." Tex. Bus. & Comm. Code Ann. §5.108(a), (e) (Vernon's 2000). Determination of what constitutes standard practice of financial institutions is a "matter of interpretation for the court." Tex. Bus. & Comm. Code Ann. §5.108(e) (Vernon's 2000).

The Uniform Customs and Practices for Documentary Credits, first issued in 1930 by the International Chamber of Commerce and revised approximately once every ten years since, is a compilation of internationally accepted commercial practices which may be incorporated into the private law of a contract between parties. Banco General Runinahui, S.A. v. Citibank Int'l, 97 F.3d 480, 482 (11th Cir. 1996) (citing *Alaska Textile,* 982 F.2d at 816). In this case, the parties expressly adopted the UCP 500 as the governing authority in the letter of credit. Where parties explicitly refer to the UCP 500 in their contracts, the UCP has been interpreted to apply to the transaction. *Vest,* 996 S.W.2d at 15. Accordingly, the Court will look to the UCP for guidance in analyzing whether the actions of the Bank of China were in conformity with "standard practice" of financial institutions.

The Bank of China claims that its August 11, 1995 telex to Texas Commerce Bank constituted notice of refusal under the UCP 500 because it contained the required elements listed in Article 14(d). Voest-Alpine argues that the telex did not constitute notice of refusal because there is no clear statement of refusal and because the portion of the telex that indicated that the Bank of China was contacting JFTC to seek a waiver rendered the communication ambiguous.

Article 14(d) of the UCP 500 provides:

> i. If the Issuing Bank . . . decides to refuse the [presentation] documents, it must give notice to that effect by telecommunication or, if that is not possible, by other expeditious means, without delay but no later than the close of the seventh banking day following the day of receipt of the documents. Such notice shall be given to the bank from which it received the documents, or to the Beneficiary, if it received the documents directly from him.

3. The prior version of Article 5.—Eds.

> ii. Such notice must state all discrepancies in respect of which the bank refuses the documents and must also state whether it is holding the documents at the disposal of, or is returning them to, the presenter.

International Chamber of Commerce, ICC Uniform Customs and Practice for Documentary Credits, ICC Publication No. 500 20 (1993).

According to Article 14(d), if the issuing bank elects not to honor the presentation documents, it must provide a notice of refusal within seven banking days of receipt of the documents and the notice must contain any and all discrepancies and state the disposition of the rejected documents. The section requires that if a bank wishes to reject a presentation of documents, it "*must give notice to that effect.*" (emphasis supplied)

Here, the Bank of China's notice is deficient because nowhere does it state that it is actually rejecting the documents or refusing to honor the letter of credit or any words to that effect. While it is true that under the UCP 500 the notice must contain a list of discrepancies and the disposition of the documents and the Bank of China's telex of August 11, 1995 does indeed contain these elements, this only addresses the requirements of Article 14(d)(ii). A notice of refusal, by its own terms must actually convey refusal, as specified in Article 14(d)(i). This omission is only compounded by the statement that the Bank of China would contact the applicant to determine if it would waive the discrepancies. As Plaintiff's expert, Professor James Byrne, testified, within the framework of Article 14, this additional piece of information holds open the possibility of acceptance upon waiver of the discrepancies by JFTC and indicates that the Bank of China has not refused the documents.

In the August 19, 1995 telex, the Bank of China stated, "Now the discrepant documents *may have us refuse* to take up the documents according to article 14(B) of UCP 500" (emphasis supplied). This is the bank's first mention of refusal and it is tentative at best. The use of "now" further indicates that the documents were not previously refused in the August 11, 1995 telex. Even if this second telex was sent as a notice of refusal, it came too late. The Court finds that the evidence establishes that the telex was sent on August 19, 1995. Seven banking days, the refusal period allotted by the UCP 500 Article 14(d), would have expired on August 18, 1995. International Chamber of Commerce, ICC Uniform Customs and Practice for Documentary Credits, ICC Publication No. 500 21 (1993). Accordingly, the Court finds that the Bank of China did not provide a notice of refusal within seven banking days of receipt of the presentation documents as required by Article 14(d) of the UCP 500. The Bank of China's failure to formally refuse the documents before the deadline precludes the bank from claiming that the documents are not in compliance with the terms and conditions of the credit, according to Article 14(e) of the UCP 500. Id. Although the Court could properly conclude its analysis here, the Court will analyze the discrepancies listed by the Bank of China in the August 11, 1995 telex.

II.

Voest-Alpine claims that the six remaining discrepancies cited by the Bank of China are mere technicalities and typographical errors that do not warrant the rejection of the documents. Voest-Alpine argues for a "functional standard" of compliance, contending that if the whole of the documents obviously relate to the transaction covered by the credit, the issuing bank must honor the letter of credit. The Bank of China argues that the discrepancies were significant and that if the documents contain discrepancies on their face, it is justified in rejecting them and is not required to look beyond the papers themselves.

Section 13(a) of the UCP 500 provides:

> Banks must examine all documents stipulated in the Credit with reasonable care, to ascertain whether or not they appear, on their face, to be in compliance with the terms and conditions of the Credit. Compliance of the stipulated documents on their face with the terms and conditions of the Credit shall be determined by international standard banking practice as reflected in these Articles. Documents which appear on their face to be inconsistent with one another will be considered as not appearing on their face to be in compliance with the terms and conditions of the Credit.

International Chamber of Commerce, ICC Uniform Customs and Practice for Documentary Credits, ICC Publication No. 500 19 (1993).

The UCP 500 does not provide guidance on what inconsistencies would justify a conclusion on the part of a bank that the documents are not in compliance with the terms and conditions of the letter of credit or what discrepancies are not a reasonable basis for such a conclusion. The UCP 500 does not mandate that the documents be a mirror image of the requirements or use the term "strict compliance."

The Court notes the wide range of interpretations on what standard banks should employ in examining letter of credit document presentations for compliance. Even where courts claim to uphold strict compliance, the standard is hardly uniform. The first and most restrictive approach is to require that the presentation documents be a mirror image of the requirements. See Banco General Runinahui, S.A. v. Citibank Int'l, 97 F.3d 480, 483 (11th Cir. 1996) ("This Court has recognized and applied the 'strict compliance' standard to requests for payment under commercial letters of credit. . . .'[T]he fact that a defect is a mere technicality' does not matter.") (quoting Kerr-McGee Chem. Corp. v. FDIC, 872 F.2d 971, 973 (11th Cir. 1989)); Alaska Textile Co. v. Chase Manhattan Bank, 982 F.2d 813, 816

(2d Cir. 1992) (Noting that documents that are nearly the same as those required by the letter of credit are unacceptable for presentation in a letter of credit transaction).

Second, there are also cases claiming to follow the strict compliance standard but support rejection only where the discrepancies are such that would create risks for the issuer if the bank were to accept the presentation documents. See Flagship Cruises Ltd., v. New England Merchants Nat'l Bank of Boston, 569 F.2d 699, 705 (1st Cir. 1978) ("We do not see these rulings as retreats from rigorous insistence on compliance with letter of credit requirements. They merely recognize that variance between documents specified and documents submitted is not fatal if there is no possibility that the documents could mislead the paying bank to its detriment"); Crist v. J. Henry Schroder Bank & Trust Co., 693 F. Supp. 1429, 1433 (S.D.N.Y. 1988) (where a party who has succeeded by operation of law to the rights of the beneficiary of a letter of credit, refusal was improper, even though the terms of the credit provided for payment only to the beneficiary); Bank of Cochin, Ltd. v. Manufacturers Hanover Trust Co., 612 F. Supp. 1533, 1541 (S.D.N.Y. 1985) (even under the strict compliance standard, a variance is permitted between the documents specified in a letter of credit and the documents presented thereunder where "there is no possibility that the documents could mislead the paying bank to its detriment"); *Vest,* 996 S.W.2d at 14 (noting that strict compliance does not demand "oppressive perfectionism").

A third standard, without much support in case law, is to analyze the documents for risk to the applicant. See Int'l Chamber of Commerce, Comm'n on Banking Technique and Practice, Publication No. 511, UCP 500 & 400 Compared 39 (Charles del Busto ed. 1994) (discussion of a standard that would permit "deviations that do not cause ostensible harm" to the applicant); see also Breathless Assoc. v. First Savings & Loan Assoc., 654 F. Supp. 832, 836 (N.D. Tex. 1986) (noting, under the strict compliance standard, "[a] discrepancy . . . should not warrant dishonor unless it reflects an increased likelihood of defective performance or fraud on the part of the beneficiary").

The mirror image approach is problematic because it absolves the bank reviewing the documents of any responsibility to use common sense to determine if the documents, on their face, are related to the transaction or even to review an entire document in the context of the others presented to the bank. On the other hand, the second and third approaches employ a determination-of-harm standard that is too unwieldy. Such an analysis would improperly require the bank to evaluate risks that it might suffer or that might be suffered by the applicant and could undermine the independence of the three contracts that underlie the letter of credit payment scheme by forcing the bank to look beyond the face of the presentation documents.

The Court finds that a moderate, more appropriate standard lies within the UCP 500 itself and the opinions issued by the International Chamber of Commerce ("ICC") Banking Commission. One of the Banking Commission opinions defined the term "consistency" between the letter of credit and the documents presented to the issuing bank as used in Article 13(a) of the UCP to mean that "the whole of the documents must obviously relate to the same transaction, that is to say, that each should bear a relation (link) with the others on its face. . . ." Int'l Chamber of Commerce, Banking Comm'n, Publication No. 371, Decisions (1975-1979) of the ICC Banking Commission R. 12 (1980). The Banking Commission rejected the notion that "all of the documents should be *exactly* consistent in their wording." Id. (emphasis in original).

A common sense, case-by-case approach would permit minor deviations of a typographical nature because such a letter-for-letter correspondence between the letter of credit and the presentation documents is virtually impossible. See Int'l Chamber of Commerce, Comm'n on Banking Technique and Practice, Publication No. 511, UCP 500 & 400 Compared 39 (Charles del Busto ed. 1994) (noting the difficulty in attaining mirror-image compliance). While the end result of such an analysis may bear a strong resemblance to the relaxed strict compliance standard, the actual calculus used by the issuing bank is not the risk it or the applicant faces but rather, whether the documents bear a rational link to one another. In this way, the issuing bank is required to examine a particular document in light of all documents presented and use common sense but is not required to evaluate risks or go beyond the face of the documents. The Court finds that in this case the Bank of China's listed discrepancies should be analyzed under this standard by determining whether the whole of the documents obviously relate to the transaction on their face.

First, the Bank of China claimed that the beneficiary's name in the presentation documents, Voest-Alpine Trading USA, differed from the letter of credit, which listed the beneficiary as Voest-Alpine USA Trading. While it is true that the letter of credit inverted Voest-Alpine's geographic locator, all the documents Voest-Alpine presented that obviously related to this transaction placed the geographic locator behind "Trading," not in front of it. Furthermore, the addresses corresponded to that listed in the letter of credit and Texas Commerce Bank's cover letter to the Bank of China identified Voest-Alpine Trading USA as the beneficiary in the transaction with JFTC. The letter of credit with the inverted name bore obvious links to the documents presented by Voest-Alpine Trading USA. This is in contrast to a misspelling or outright omission. See Beyene v. Irving Trust Co., 762 F.2d 4 (2d Cir. 1985) (listing beneficiary as "Soran" rather than "Sofan" was sufficient basis for refusal); Bank of Cochin, Ltd. v. Manufacturers Hanover Trust Co., 612 F. Supp. 1533 (S.D.N.Y. 1985) (omitting "Ltd."

from corporate name justified rejection). In contrast with these cases, the inversion of the geographic locator here does not signify a different corporate entity. The expert testimony of Professor Byrne supports the finding that this is not a discrepancy that warrants rejection of the presentation documents because the UCP 500 does not impose a standard of exact replication.

Second, the Bank of China pointed out that the set of originals of the bill of lading should have all been stamped "original" rather than "original," "duplicate" and "triplicate." It should be noted that neither the letter of credit nor any provision in the UCP 500 requires such stamping. In fact, the ICC Banking Commission expressly ruled that "duplicate" and "triplicate" bills of lading did not need to be marked "original" and that failure to label them as originals did not justify refusal of the documents. Int'l Chamber of Commerce, Banking Comm'n, Publication No. 565, Opinions of the ICC Banking Comm'n 1995-1996 38 (Gary Collyer ed. 1997). While it is true that this clarification by the ICC came after the transaction at issue in this case, it is clear from the face of the documents that these documents are three originals rather than one original and two copies. The documents have signatures in blue ink [*sic*—that?] vary slightly, bear original stamps oriented differently on each page and clearly state on their face that the preparer made three original bills. Further, one possible definition of duplicate is "[t]o make or execute again" and one definition of triplicate is "[o]ne of a set of three identical things." Webster's II New Riverside University Dictionary 410, 1237 (1994). While the "duplicate" and "triplicate" stamps may have been confusing, stamps do not make obviously original documents into copies.

Third, the Bank of China claimed that the failure to stamp the packing list documents as "original" was a discrepancy. Again, these documents are clearly originals on their face as they have three slightly differing signatures in blue ink. There was no requirement in the letter of credit or the UCP 500 that original documents be marked as such. The ICC's policy statement on the issue provides that, "banks treat as original any document that appears to be hand signed by the issuer of the document." (Int'l Chamber of Commerce, Comm'n on Banking Technique and Practice, The determination of an "Original" document in the context of UCP 500 sub-Article 20 (b) July 12, 1999). http://www.iccwbo.org/home/statementsrules/statements/1999/the-determination-of-an-original-document.asp. The failure to mark obvious originals is not a discrepancy.

Fourth, the Bank of China argues that the date of the survey report is after the bill of lading and is therefore discrepant. A careful examination of the survey report reveals that the survey took place "immediately before/after loading" and that the sample of cargo "to be loaded" was taken. The plain language of the report reveals that the report may have been issued after the bill of lading but the survey itself was conducted before the ship departed. The date does not pose a discrepancy.

Fifth, the Bank of China claims that the letter of credit number listed in the beneficiary's certified copy of [*sic*] fax is wrong. The letter of credit number was listed as "LC95231033/95" on the copy of [*sic*] fax instead of "LC9521033/95" as in the letter of credit itself, adding an extra "3" after "LC952." However, adding the letter of credit number to this document was gratuitous and in the numerous other places in the documents that the letter of credit was referenced by number, it was incorrect only in one place. Moreover, the seven other pieces of information contained in the document were correct. The document checker could have easily looked to any other document to verify the letter of credit number, or looked to the balance of the information within the document and found that the document as a whole bears an obvious relationship to the transaction. Madame Gao, the document checker who reviewed Voest-Alpine's presentation documents for the Bank of China, testified that she did not look beyond the face of this particular document in assessing the discrepancy. The cover letter from Texas Commerce Bank, for example, had the correct number.

Finally, the Bank of China claims that the wrong destination is listed in the certificate of origin and the beneficiary's certificate. The certificate of origin spelled Zhangjiagang as "Zhangjiagng" missing an "a" as it is misspelled once in the letter of credit, making it consistent. The beneficiary's certificate, however, spelled it "Zhanjiagng," missing a "g" in addition to the "a," a third spelling that did not appear in the letter of credit. Madame Gao first considered the discrepancy a "misspelling" rather than an indication of the wrong port, according to her notes. There is no port in China called "Zhangjiagng" or "Zhanjiagng." "Gng" is a combination of letters not found in Romanized Chinese, whereas "gang" means "port" in Chinese. The other information contained in the document was correct, such as the letter of credit number and the contract number, and even contained the distinctive phrase "by courie lukdt within 3 days after shipment," presumably meaning by courier within three days after shipment, as in the letter of credit. The document as a whole bears an obvious relationship with the transaction. The misspelling of the destination is not a basis for dishonor of the letter of credit where the rest of the document has demonstrated linkage to the transaction on its face.

Based on the foregoing, the Court finds in favor of the plaintiff, Voest-Alpine.

NOTES

1. This case was decided under the UCP 500, where the so-called *strict compliance* requirement was less markedly pronounced than it currently is

in the Uniform Commercial Code. Indeed, in the more recent UCP 600 things get even murkier. Article 14(d) states that "Data in a document, when read in context with the credit, the document itself and international standard banking practice, need not be identical to, but must not conflict with, data in that document, any other stipulated document or the credit." For the tests under the UCC, read §§5-103(d) and 5-108(a) and the following Official Comments: Official Comment 3 to §5-102 and Official Comment 1 to §5-108. Using the tests therein (which have changed since the above case), would the court have reached the same result? In determining whether there is strict compliance with the credit, §5-108(a) refers to "standard practice," as does (e). The International Chamber of Commerce has promulgated a guide as to that called "International Standard Banking Practice for the Examination of Documents Under Documentary Credits" (ICC Publication 645).

One court held that the beneficiary complied with a letter of credit requiring presentation of original letter of credit by presenting a true copy of the letter of credit, which had been issued by the issuer itself. Ladenburg Thalmann & Co, Inc. v. Signature Bank, 2015 WL 1239293 (N.Y. App. Div. 2015). The court looked to the purpose of the strict compliance rule:

> In the matter before us, there is no possibility that the presentation of a true copy of amendment 2, instead of the original, could mislead defendant to its detriment. Indeed, this copy had been prepared by defendant itself, and was provided to plaintiff by defendant's own attorney. Its accuracy was not in dispute, and there is no dispute regarding the content of the document, which merely extended the expiration date of amendment 2 and which had since been superseded by subsequent amendments. Since the submission of a true copy of amendment 2 would not compel any inquiry by the bank into the underlying transaction, the rationale for the strict compliance rule, "to protect the issuer from having to know the commercial impact of a discrepancy in the documents" (*E & H Partners*, 39 F. Supp. 2d at 284), has no applicability here.

2. As to the waiver issue in the above case, see §5-108(c); Arch Specialty Insurance Company v. First Community Bank of Eastern Arkansas, 2016 WL 4473438 (E.D. Ark. 2016) (where bank failed to give beneficiary timely notice of alleged discrepancies in presentation under letter of credit, bank was precluded relying on those discrepancies to justify failure to pay).

3. In letter of credit transactions, it should be emphasized that banks issuing the credits do not charge a great deal and therefore should be exposed to a minimum risk. If a bank is going to dishonor the credit, it should make sure that it is playing fair with all the parties involved so that in any ensuing litigation the commercial reasonableness of its actions will attract the sympathy of the court.

PROBLEM 283

Assume in the last Problem that the letter of credit issued by Last National had required that the bill of lading representing the goods be given not to Greenbaum Construction Company, the applicant, but presented to the bank itself. Assume also that Latek Steel has completely complied with all of the terms of the credit, but Last National, knowing of the applicant's bankruptcy, wrongfully refuses to pay the credit as agreed. You are the attorney for Latek Steel, and the vice president in charge of marketing calls you with some questions. The market for steel is falling rapidly. Must Latek Steel resell the steel involved in this transaction immediately, or may it wait, hoping the bank will change its mind and pay what it owes? If it does resell, does that reduce the amount it can claim as damages from Last National? As to both these matters, see §5-111 (a).

PROBLEM 284

At the request of its applicant, Octopus National Bank (ONB) issued an irrevocable letter of credit to Warren Crook, the beneficiary. The credit's terms required a bill of lading showing that the goods were loaded on board the *S.S. Titanic* by April 1, 2014. Crook cleverly drew up a phony bill of lading supposedly issued by the *Titanic* and presented it along with a draft on the bank to the issuer. ONB paid the draft. Can it collect from its applicant? See §5-108; also note §§5-110 (warranties on transfer and presentment), 5-111 (presenter's right to damages on wrongful dishonor of a draft), and 5-117 (subrogation rights of the parties). Could the applicant use the §5-110 warranties to sue the beneficiary?

PROBLEM 285

Luddite Technologies, Inc. wanted to build a new company headquarters. It hired Weekend Construction Company to do the job, requiring a standby letter of credit of $80,000 to be paid if Weekend failed to keep to the required schedule for completion of the building. At Weekend's request, Last National Bank issued such a credit in favor of Luddite, payable, according to the terms of the credit, "on default by Weekend Construction Company in meeting the attached completion schedule and the beneficiary's presentation of an affidavit to that effect along with a draft drawn on us for $80,000." Weekend Construction dutifully performed its contractual duties, but the president of Luddite, needing money, sent the required draft and affidavit to Last National, wrongfully asserting that Weekend had missed timely completion of a part of the project. Last National paid the draft without investigating the truth of the assertions in the affidavit and now seeks reimbursement from the applicant, Weekend Construction. Can Weekend resist paying under the theory that Last National did not verify the default as the letter of credit required? See §5-108(g) and its Official Comment 9. White & Summers explain: "Where the documents commit the issuer to assess facts and events outside the documents presented, they disable the independence principle and topple the wall that separates presented documents from beneficiary-applicant disputes"; §21-6-g at 1112. If Weekend Construction has gone bankrupt since the bank honored the draft, can Last National pursue Luddite Technologies to get its money back? See §§5-108(i)(4), 5-110. How quickly must it act? See §5-115.

IV. FRAUD

Sztejn v. J. Henry Schroder Bank Corp.

New York Supreme Court, 1941
177 Misc. 719, 31 N.Y.S.2d 631

SHIENTAG, J.

This is a motion by the defendant, the Chartered Bank of India, Australia and China, (hereafter referred to as the Chartered Bank), made pursuant to Rule 106(5) of the Rules of Civil Practice to dismiss the supplemental complaint on the ground that it fails to state facts sufficient to constitute a cause of action against the moving defendant. The plaintiff brings this action to restrain the payment or presentment of payment of drafts under a letter of credit issued to secure the purchase price of certain merchandise, bought by the plaintiff and his coadventurer, one Schwarz, who is a party defendant in this action. The plaintiff also seeks a judgment declaring the letter of credit and drafts thereunder null and void. The complaint alleges that the documents accompanying the drafts are fraudulent in that they do not represent actual merchandise but instead cover boxes fraudulently filled with worthless material by the seller of the goods. The moving defendant urges that the complaint fails to state a cause of action against it because the Chartered Bank is only concerned with the documents and on their face these conform to the requirement of the letter of credit.

On January 7, 1941, the plaintiff and his coadventurer contracted to purchase a quantity of bristles from the defendant Transea Traders, Ltd. (hereafter referred to as Transea) a corporation having its place of business in Lucknow, India. In order to pay for the bristles, the plaintiff and Schwarz contracted with the defendant J. Henry Schroder Banking Corporation (hereafter referred to as Schroder), a domestic corporation, for the issuance of an irrevocable letter of credit to Transea which provided that drafts by the latter for a specified portion of the purchase price of the bristles would be paid by Schroder upon shipment of the described merchandise and presentation of an invoice and a bill of lading covering the shipment, made out to the order of Schroder.

The letter of credit was delivered to Transea by Schroder's correspondent bank in India, Transea placed fifty cases of material on board a steamship, procured a bill of lading from the steamship company and obtained the customary invoices. These documents describe the bristles called for by the letter of credit. However, the complaint alleges that in fact Transea filled the fifty crates with cowhair, other worthless material and rubbish with intent to simulate genuine merchandise and defraud the plaintiff and Schwarz. The complaint then alleges that Transea drew a draft under the letter of credit to the order of the Chartered Bank and delivered the draft and the fraudulent documents to the "Chartered Bank at Cawnpore, India, for collection for the account of said defendant Transea." The Chartered Bank has presented the draft along with the documents to Schroder for payment. The plaintiff prays for a judgment declaring the letter of credit and draft there under void and for injunctive relief to prevent the payment of the draft.

For the purpose of this motion, the allegations of the complaint must be deemed established and "every intendment and fair inference is in favor of the pleading." . . . Therefore, it must be assumed that Transea was engaged in a scheme to defraud the plaintiff and Schwarz, that the merchandise shipped by Transea is worthless rubbish and that the Chartered Bank is not an innocent holder of the draft for value but is merely attempting to procure payment of the draft for Transea's account.

It is well established that a letter of credit is independent of the primary contract of sale between the buyer and the seller. The issuing bank agrees to pay upon presentation of documents, not goods. This rule is necessary to preserve the efficiency of the letter of credit as an instrument for the financing of trade. One of the chief purposes of the letter of credit is to furnish the seller with a ready means of obtaining prompt payment for his merchandise. It would be a most unfortunate interference with business transactions if a bank before honoring drafts drawn upon it was obliged or even allowed to go behind the documents, at the request of the buyer and enter into controversies between the buyer and the seller regarding the quality of the merchandise shipped. If the buyer and the seller intended the bank to do this they could have so provided in the letter of credit itself, and in the absence of such a provision, the court will not demand or even permit the bank to delay paying drafts which are proper in form. . . . Of course, the application of this doctrine presupposes that the documents accompanying the draft are genuine and conform in terms to the requirements of the letter of credit. . . .

However, I believe that a different situation is presented in the instant action. This is not a controversy between the buyer and seller concerning a mere breach of warranty regarding the quality of the merchandise; on the present motion, it must be assumed that the seller has intentionally failed to ship any goods ordered by the buyer. In such a situation, where the seller's fraud has been called to the bank's attention before the drafts and documents have been presented for payment, the principle of the independence of the bank's obligation under the letter of credit should not be extended to protect the unscrupulous seller. It is true that even though the documents are forged or fraudulent, if the issuing bank has already paid the draft before receiving notice of the seller's fraud, it will be protected if it exercised reasonable diligence before making such payment. . . . However, in the instant action Schroder has received notice of Transea's active fraud before it accepted or paid the draft. The Chartered Bank, which under the allegations of the complaint stands in no better position than Transea, should not be heard to complain because Schroder is not forced to pay the draft accompanied by documents covering a transaction which it has reason to believe is fraudulent.

Although our courts have used broad language to the effect that a letter of credit is independent of the primary contract between the buyer and seller, that language was used in cases concerning alleged breaches of warranty; no case has been brought to my attention on this point involving an intentional fraud on the part of the seller which was brought to the bank's notice with the request that it withhold payment of the draft on this account. This distinction between a breach of warranty and active fraud on the part of the seller is supported by authority and reason. As one court has stated: "Obviously, when the issuer of a letter of credit knows that a document, although correct in form, is, in point of fact, false or illegal, he cannot be called upon to recognize such a document as complying with the terms of a letter of credit." Old Colony Trust Co. v. Lawyers' Title & Trust Co., 2d Cir., 297 F. 152 at page 158, *certiorari denied,* 265 U.S. 585, 44 S. Ct. 459, 68 L. Ed. 1192. . . .

No hardship will be caused by permitting the bank to refuse payment where fraud is claimed, where the merchandise is not merely inferior in quality but consists of worthless rubbish, where the draft and the accompanying documents are in the hands of one who stands in the same position as the fraudulent seller, where the bank has been given notice of the fraud before being presented with the drafts and documents for payment, and where the bank itself does not wish to pay pending an adjudication of the rights and obligations of the other parties. While the primary factor in the issuance of the letter of credit is the credit standing of the buyer, the security afforded by the merchandise is also taken into account. In fact, the letter of credit requires a bill of lading made out to the order of the bank and not the buyer. Although the bank is not interested in the exact detailed performance of the sales contract, it is vitally interested in assuring itself that there are some goods represented by the documents. Finkelstein, Legal Aspects of Commercial Letters of Credit, p. 238; O'Meara v. National Park Bank of New York, 239 N.Y. 386, 401, 146 N.E. 636, 39 A.L.R. 747, opinion of Cardozo, J., dissenting; Thayer, Irrevocable Credits in International Commerce, 37 C.L.R. 1326, 1335.

On this motion only the complaint is before me and I am bound by its allegation that the Chartered Bank is not a holder in due course but is a mere agent for collection for the account of the seller charged with fraud. Therefore, the Chartered Bank's motion to dismiss the complaint must be denied. If it had appeared from the face of the complaint that the bank presenting the draft for payment was a holder in due course, its claim against the bank issuing the letter of credit would not be defeated even though the primary transaction was tainted with fraud. . . .

Accordingly, the defendant's motion to dismiss the supplemental complaint is denied.

Is *Sztejn* still good law? Read §5-109 and its Official Comments carefully; see Mid-America Tire, Inc. v. PTZ Trading Ltd. Import and Export Agents, 2000 WL 1725415 (Ohio App. 2000).

Note well that it has always been the law that if the draft is held by a holder in due course, the bank that issued the letter of credit is not allowed to allege the defense of fraud; see §5-109(a)(1) (expanding this idea to protect all innocent parties); Daiwa Products, Inc. v. NationsBank, N.A., 885 So. 2d 884 (Fla. App. 2004).

PROBLEM 286

Just as Octopus National Bank was about to honor a draft drawn on it by the beneficiary of its letter of credit, the bank's applicant called and demanded that the bank dishonor the draft because the beneficiary was guilty of "out-and-out fraud" on the underlying transaction between them. The bank calls you, its attorney, for advice. The documents presented along with the draft exactly match the terms of the credit, and the bank officials are sure that there is no fraud in the documents. Look at §§5-108 and 5-109, and tell the bank what you think it should do. Cf. Emery-Waterhouse Co.

v. Rhode Island Hosp. Trust Natl. Bank, 757 F.2d 399 (1st Cir. 1985) (punitive damages of $1,397,000 awarded against beneficiary who fraudulently drew against a letter of credit). If ONB dishonors the draft and this causes the beneficiary to lose millions of dollars on the underlying transaction, is ONB ever liable for *more* than the amount of the letter of credit? See §5-111.

In §5-109(a) the bank is given the option to honor or not as it wishes. As you can well imagine, banks tend to pay more attention to the applicant's request to dishonor if his name is Donald Trump than if her name is Jane Doe. The bank will not be entitled to reimbursement if it does not act in good faith. See Zeeco, Inc. v. JPMorgan Chase Bank, National Association, 2018 WL 1414119 (N.D. Okla. 2018). If the bank decides to honor the draft, the applicant has two causes of action against the seller-beneficiary: the underlying obligation (normally the contract of sale, see Article 2) and the §5-110(a)(2) warranty.

Hook Point, LLC v. Branch Banking and Trust Company

Supreme Court of South Carolina, 2012
397 S.C. 507, 725 S.E.2d 681

Justice Pleicones.

Respondent Hook Point, LLC (Hook Point) was granted a preliminary injunction preventing Appellant Branch Banking and Trust Company (BB & T) from drawing on, and defendant First Reliance Bank (First Reliance) from honoring, a $1.5 million letter of credit. BB & T appeals. We reverse.

Facts

In late 2007, Hook Point sought a loan from BB & T for the purpose of developing a subdivision on property Hook Point owned on Lake Murray called Panama Pointe. BB & T issued a commitment letter to Hook Point in September 2007 indicating that it would loan the company $5.1 million and establish a $2 million line of credit to enable Hook Point to develop the subdivision. Security for the loan included a first mortgage on the Panama Pointe property, personal guarantees of Hook Point's four principals, and a $1.5 million standby letter of credit issued by First Reliance in favor of BB & T.

Hook Point applied to and obtained a letter of credit (LC) from First Reliance that named BB & T as beneficiary. The LC was secured by a cash deposit at First Reliance of approximately $310,000, several real properties owned by a Hook Point affiliate, and personal guarantees of the Hook Point principals. Under the terms of the LC, BB & T was permitted to make draws upon presentation of a draft accompanied by

> 1) The original letter of credit.
>
> 2) A notarized, sworn statement by the Beneficiary, or an officer thereof, that:
>
> a) The Borrower has failed to perform its obligations to the Beneficiary under the Loan Agreement and Promissory Note dated November 16, 2007, executed by and between [Hook Point and BB & T];
>
> b) The amount of the draft does not exceed the amount due to the Beneficiary under the obligations; and,
>
> c) The signer has the authority to act for the Beneficiary with regard to the Letter of Credit.

The loan from BB & T to Hook Point was finalized in a loan agreement on the same day the LC was issued. Hook Point proceeded to complete infrastructure work in the development and began construction on the first home before determining that market conditions had become unfavorable to the project as originally contemplated. Hook Point defaulted on the Loan Agreement and related notes and loan documents by, among other things, failing to pay property taxes, to make interest payments due under the notes, or to pay the principal due under one note. BB & T gave Hook Point notice of default in September 2010 and accelerated the loans under the terms of the Loan Agreement on December 21, 2010. On the same day, BB & T tendered a demand letter to First Reliance, seeking to draw the full amount of the LC.

On December 23, Hook Point filed suit alleging several causes of action against BB & T, including for fraudulent misrepresentation by which BB & T induced Hook Point to enter the loan agreement. Hook Point admitted to being $70,000 in arrears on interest but argued that the terms of the agreement did not permit BB & T to draw the full amount of the LC if that exceeded the amount of interest due. It also sought an *ex parte* temporary restraining order preventing First Reliance from honoring a draft on the LC by BB & T, which the court granted. After a hearing, the court also granted a preliminary injunction against drafts on or honor of the LC beyond amounts of accrued interest, requiring extension of the LC for one year, and requiring Hook Point to post a $50,000 bond with the court. This appeal followed, and the case was transferred to this Court pursuant to Rule 204(b), SCACR.

ISSUE

Did the circuit court err when it granted a preliminary injunction? . . .

DISCUSSION

BB & T contends that the circuit court erred when it granted the preliminary injunction. We agree.

"A preliminary injunction should issue only if necessary to preserve the status quo ante, and only upon a showing by the moving party that without such relief it will suffer irreparable harm, that it has a likelihood of success on the merits, and that there is no adequate remedy at law." Poynter Investments, Inc. v. Century Builders of Piedmont, Inc., 387 S.C. 583, 586-87, 694 S.E.2d 15, 17 (2010).

On the second element, likelihood of success on the merits, BB & T argues that the grounds for refusing to honor a letter of credit are exceedingly narrow and that Hook Point has failed to show it is likely to succeed on the merits under that standard. Thus, BB & T argues that the circuit court erred when it found that Hook Point had sufficiently established this element. We agree.

A letter of credit is a financial instrument designed to reduce the need for counterparties in a transaction to trust one another by adding an intermediary bank to the transaction. This intermediary bank extends credit to one party (typically the buyer in a sales transaction[2]) so that the other need not do so. In a sales transaction, the letter of credit typically requires a seller to represent that he has shipped goods under a sales contract and to document this representation with a bill of lading in order to draw on the LC provided by the buyer. This arrangement entails risk to the buyer, who is vulnerable to loss should the seller present fraudulent documents or deliberately ship nonconforming goods. Nevertheless, the usefulness of a letter of credit depends on its being the virtual equivalent of cash. The judicial doctrine that has developed around letters of credit reflects courts' understanding of this background and the importance to commerce of respecting the terms of this financial instrument so that it remains available as a reliable means of shifting financial risk.

Specifically, this understanding is embodied in the independence principle, under which courts recognize that the obligations created in the letter of credit are independent of the obligations of the underlying contract. *See, e.g.,* Intraworld Industries, Inc. v. Girard Trust Bank, 461 Pa. 343, 357, 336 A.2d 316, 323 (Pa. 1975) ("The primary purpose of a letter of credit is to provide assurance to the seller of goods . . . of prompt payment upon presentation of documents. A seller who would otherwise have only the solvency and good faith of his buyer as assurance of payment may, with a letter of credit, rely on the full responsibility of a bank. Promptness is assured by the engagement of the bank to honor drafts upon the presentation of documents. The great utility of letters of credit flows from the independence of the issuer-bank's engagement from the underlying contract between beneficiary and customer. Long-standing case law has established that, unless otherwise agreed, the issuer deals only in documents. If the documents presented conform to the requirements of the credit, the issuer may and must honor demands for payment, regardless of whether the goods conform to the underlying contract between beneficiary and customer."); Itek Corp. v. First Nat'l Bank of Boston, 730 F.2d 19 (1st Cir. 1984) (Breyer, J.) ("Parties to a contract may use a letter of credit in order to make certain that contractual disputes wend their way towards resolution with money in the beneficiary's pocket rather than in the pocket of the contracting party. Thus, courts typically have asserted that such letters of credit are 'independent' of the underlying contract. . . . And they have recognized that examining the rights and wrongs of a contract dispute to determine whether a letter of credit should be paid risks depriving its beneficiary of the very advantage for which he bargained, namely that the dispute would be resolved while he is in possession of the money." (citations omitted)); *Roger J. Johns and Mark S. Blodgett,* Fairness at the Expense of Commercial Certainty: The International Emergence of Unconscionability and Illegality As Exceptions to the Independence Principle of Letters of Credit and Bank Guarantees, 31 N. Ill. U. L. Rev. 297, 309 (2011) ("[T]he common concern among all stakeholders is that as the ease with which letters of credit . . . can be enjoined increases their commercial utility decreases.").

Nevertheless, courts have carved out a very narrow exception to the independence principle. Aside from permitting the intermediary bank to refuse to honor forged documents presented in order to draw on the letter of credit, courts enjoin the payment of LCs for "fraud in the transaction" when "the beneficiary's conduct has so vitiated the entire transaction that the legitimate purposes of the independence of the issuer's obligation would no longer be served." *Itek,* 730 F.2d at 25 (internal quotation marks and citations omitted).

Put simply, the cases in which the "fraud in the transaction" exception has been applied are those in which the underlying transaction or the demand for payment is clearly a sham, and it is apparent that rigid adherence to the independence principle would facilitate what amounts to a scheme to defraud. In the case that established the fraud in the transaction exception, the beneficiary made an actual shipment so that the shipping documents were real, but substituted "rubbish" in place of salable bristles. Sztejn v. J. Henry Schroder Banking Corp., 177 Misc. 719, 31 N.Y.S.2d 631 (Sup. Ct. 1941). In another leading case, the beneficiary was not permitted to collect on the LC because the fall of the Iranian government so altered conditions that the contract for military equipment could not be completed, and thus there was no possibility that the original purpose of the transaction of which the LC was a part could be accomplished. In addition, no other legal recourse was available to the applicant, and the applicant had cancelled the underlying contract in compliance with its force majeure provisions, which called for cancellation of the LC upon cancellation of the underlying contract. *Itek,* supra.

Several other cases also illustrate the narrowness of the fraud in the transaction exception. *See* Intraworld Industries, Inc. v. Girard Trust Bank, 461 Pa. 343, 357, 336 A.2d 316, 325 (Pa. 1975) ("We conclude that, if the documents presented by [the beneficiary of the LC] are genuine in the sense of having some basis in fact, an injunction must be refused. . . . [N]either the trial court nor this Court may attempt to determine [the beneficiary's] actual entitlement to payment under the lease."); *see also* Roman Ceramics Corp. v. Peoples Nat. Bank, 714 F.2d 1207, 1209 (3d Cir. 1983) (permitting issuing bank to dishonor LC when it knew underlying invoice had been paid and that contrary certification was false); Dynamics Corp. of Am. v. Citizens & S. Nat. Bank, 356 F. Supp. 991, 999 (D.C. Ga. 1973) (describing court's role as limited to ensuring that the defendant could not "run off with plaintiff's money on a *pro forma* declaration which has absolutely no basis in fact"); Mid-America Tire, Inc. v. PTZ Trading Ltd., 95 Ohio St. 3d 367, 392, 768 N.E.2d 619, 641 (Ohio 2002) (affirming injunction against honor of LC where defendants repeatedly lied to and misled plaintiffs about the tires available for sale in order to pressure them into making the LC available before they "could discover the truth").

The Uniform Commercial Code (UCC) incorporated this judicially developed doctrine into Article 5, the UCC formulation of the law governing letters of credit. Thus, South Carolina's adoption of the UCC incorporated into South Carolina law the same independence principle and narrow exception limiting the enjoinment of payment of LCs to instances of egregious fraud that operates to vitiate the entire transaction. In particular, UCC Article 5, S.C. Code §§36-5-101 through-119, governs letters of credit. S.C. Code Ann. §36-5-109(b) (2003) sets forth the conditions under which a court may enjoin honor of a letter of credit as follows, in relevant part:

> If an applicant claims that a required document is forged or materially fraudulent or that honor of the presentation would facilitate a material fraud by the beneficiary on the issuer or applicant, a court of competent jurisdiction may temporarily or permanently enjoin the issuer from honoring a presentation or grant similar relief against the issuer or other persons only if the court finds that:
>
> . . .
>
> (3) all of the conditions to entitle a person to the relief under the law of this State have been met; and
>
> (4) on the basis of the information submitted to the court, the applicant is more likely than not to succeed under its claim of forgery or material fraud. . . .

For purposes of a preliminary injunction, subsection (3) effectively incorporates the requirements of the common law related to injunctions generally: that the movant show that irreparable harm will result and that no adequate remedy at law exists if the court refuses the injunction. *Poynter Investments,* supra.

Subsection (4) codifies not only the general common law requirement that the movant show a likelihood of success on the merits but also the special rule for letters of credit allowing only a narrow exception for fraud in the transaction, as discussed above. The Official Comment makes this codification explicit.

In the present case, Hook Point argues that BB & T is not entitled to draw on the LC because the commitment letter described the LC as "to be used as last resort for interest carry." Hook Point also seeks to construe as fraudulent BB & T's demand on the LC. The LC, however, by its terms requires only that BB & T represent that "[t]he Borrower has failed to perform its obligations . . . under the Loan Agreement and Promissory Note" and that "[t]he amount of the draft does not exceed the amount due to the Beneficiary under the obligation." Thus, contrary to Hook Point's arguments, the plain language of the LC permitted BB & T to use it if Hook Point defaulted under any obligation of the loan agreement and note, including an acceleration clause. Furthermore, no term in the loan agreement or note to which the LC refers limits BB & T's use of the LC to interest due. Thus, it is incontrovertible that BB & T had some basis in fact for the representations it made when it drew on the LC.

If there is any validity to Hook Point's argument that the commitment letter limited the utilization of the LC exclusively to interest, that is an ordinary contract dispute that raises no implication of fraud by BB & T sufficient to trigger the narrow fraud exception. *Dynamics Corp.,* supra. In fact, $500,000 had been reserved by BB & T from the original $5.1 million loan for the purpose of drawing down interest carry. A more plausible explanation for the "last resort" language in the commitment letter is that it was intended merely as an accommodation to the principals that BB & T would not seek to draw on the LC for interest until the reserve had been exhausted. That language, whatever it meant, is a red herring in this case as the draw on the LC was sought not only to recoup interest but as a result of multiple defaults that caused BB & T to invoke the acceleration of the entire debt.

Indeed, Hook Point's admission that BB & T was entitled to any draw on the LC for past due interest was conclusive as to the issue whether honor of the LC should be enjoined, since BB & T's entitlement to past due interest is alone some basis in fact on which BB & T could demand payment under the LC. Moreover, the strict standard required under §36-5-109(b)(4) is that the alleged fraud vitiate the entire transaction, that is, it deprives Hook Point of any benefit from the transaction. In this case, there is no dispute that Hook Point received $5.1 million from BB & T. These facts hardly parallel the receipt of "rubbish" instead of bargained-for salable bristles. *See Sztejn v. J. Henry Schroder Banking Corp., supra.*

Thus, there is no evidence Hook Point is more likely than not to succeed on a claim of material fraud so egregious as to vitiate the entire transaction as required under §36-5-109(b)(4), and the circuit court failed to evaluate the evidence under the strict standard required for injunctions against the honor of LCs. Under the proper standard, it is clear that BB & T had a sufficient basis in fact upon which to demand payment under the LC. Thus, the circuit court's finding was based upon an error of law.

Because this issue is dispositive of the case, we need not address BB & T's remaining issues. Rule 220(b), SCACR; *e.g.,* Futch v. McAllister Towing of Georgetown, Inc., 335 S.C. 598, 613, 518 S.E.2d 591, 598 (1999).

CONCLUSION

The standard under which a fraud in the transaction claim must be measured when deciding whether to enjoin honor of a letter of credit requires that the beneficiary have no colorable claim or basis in fact for asserting its rights under the letter of credit. In this case BB & T has, in our view, not only a colorable claim but an undeniable basis in fact for asserting its rights under the letter of credit. Therefore, the circuit court erred when it granted the preliminary injunction. REVERSED.

NOTE

In deciding the liability of an issuer who refuses to honor a credit, the courts have placed great emphasis on the "real" reason the issuer wants out. If that reason is that the applicant is bankrupt, so that the issuer fears no reimbursement will be forthcoming, the courts will stretch to hold the issuer liable; see ACE American Ins. Co. v. Bank of the Ozarks, 2014 WL 4953566 (S.D.N.Y. 2014). After all, fear of applicant insolvency was the very reason the seller wanted a letter of credit in the beginning. On the other hand, where the issuer hesitates because it is afraid that honoring will violate §5-108, and the issuer will lose the right to seek reimbursement from its applicant, the issuer's conduct is more likely to receive favorable treatment from the court. Cf. In re Factory Sales & Engineering, Inc., 2017 WL 4570813 (E.D. La. 2017) (beneficiary made fraudulent presentation by submitting false statement that it had terminated underlying contract). For a fascinating example of these considerations at work, compare the district and appellate court opinions in Court-aulds N. Am., Inc. v. North Carolina Natl. Bank, 387 F. Supp. 92 (M.D. N.C. 1975), *rev'd,* 528 F.2d 802 (4th Cir. 1975).

V. ASSIGNMENT

PROBLEM 287

Octopus National Bank issued a $50,000 letter of credit to Grey Goods of New York, payable to Grey Goods on presentation of a draft and certain documents demonstrating shipment of clothing to Ohio Wholesalers, the bank's applicant. Grey Goods needed money to finance its operations, so it borrowed $30,000 from Midwest State Bank, giving MSB a security interest in the proceeds of the letter of credit, and assigning the right to those proceeds to MSB, which promptly notified ONB of the assignment. Grey Goods had trouble filling the Ohio Wholesalers order, so those two parties agreed to lower the amount shipped and the price to $10,000 worth of clothing, and the letter of credit was amended to reflect this lower amount. When the clothing was shipped and the draft presented under the letter of credit, ONB was only willing to pay $10,000 to MSB. MSB calls you, its attorney. What are its rights here? See §§5-114, 5-106, and Official Comment 2 to the latter. Article 9 on Secured Transactions reaches this same result; see §9-329 and its Official Comment 2.

VI. SUBROGATION

PROBLEM 288

Ebenezer Scrooge was the sole shareholder of Scrooge and Marley, Inc., a corporation that sold coal. In early 2019, the corporation signed a $2,000,000 contract to buy mineral rights in a new coal tract in Pennsylvania from Frederick Bean, the owner of the land, agreeing that he would allow Scrooge and Marley to mine the coal in the summer of 2019, sell it to others, and then pay the $2,000,000 to Bean. In the meantime Scrooge and Marley signed a promissory note for this amount payable to Bean, guaranteed personally by Ebenezer Scrooge, due June 1, 2022. Bean also required Scrooge and Marley to get a standby letter of credit in his favor for the amount of $2,000,000, payable if the corporation defaulted on its promissory note. The corporation had Dickens National Bank issue such a letter of credit, with Bean as the beneficiary. The transaction went as planned until the market for coal collapsed after Scrooge and Marley had mined the Bean tract and found itself unable to sell that coal at a profit. When the promissory note was not paid when it came due in 2022, Bean drew a draft on the bank under the letter of credit. Dickens National Bank has this draft in hand, and calls you, the bank's attorney. Scrooge and Marley has just filed for bankruptcy, and has no assets. Must it pay the letter of credit? If it does so, can it subrogate itself to Bean's rights against Ebenezer Scrooge? See §5-117;[4] JP Morgan Chase Bank v. Cook, 318 F. Supp. 2d 159 (S.D.N.Y. 2004). Can it go after Scrooge *before* it pays Bean's draft? See §5-117(d).

Now, letter of credit students, go back to the chart on page 1056 and look at it again carefully. If you go step-by-step through the transaction—the sale of goods, the creation of the letter of credit, the draft the beneficiary drew on the bank, the bill of lading—you should see how all of it fits together it in the business world over and over again. If your practice involves documentary letters of credit this will become routine to you and be the background for any difficulties that arise.

CHAPTER 18 REVIEW QUESTIONS

Would the seller of goods more likely be the applicant or the beneficiary of a letter of credit?

Why is a revocable letter of credit of little value?

When is an issuer entitled to reimbursement from its applicant for paying a letter of credit?

Is a beneficiary entitled to payment, if it substantially, but not strictly, complies with the terms of the letter of credit?

How is the requirement of strict compliance related to the independence principle?

How does the independence principle insulate the issuer bank from the underlying transaction?

If the seller has substantially, but not strictly, complied with its obligations in the underlying sales transaction, would it be fraud for the seller to draw on the letter of credit

ASSESSMENT: MULTIPLE CHOICE QUESTIONS

1. Desktop Solutions ordered 1,000 video controllers from Larchwood Devices. Desktop Solutions arranged to have Octopus National Bank (ONB) issue a letter of credit to Larchwood Devices for the amount of the contract price. Larchwood Devices shipped the video controllers and

4. In reading that section you should know that the Restatement (Third) of Suretyship and Guaranty calls sureties and similar parties "secondary obligors," and has complicated rules explaining under what circumstances they are entitled to subrogation. See the Official Comments to §5-117.

presented to ONB the documents specified in the letter of credit (a bill of lading, an invoice, and a certificate of inspection from Ida Tech). By this time, however, Desktop Solutions had run into financial problems and would not be able to reimburse ONB if the letter of credit was paid. May ONB dishonor the presentation, for lack of sufficient funds?

a. Yes. The letter of credit is not properly payable, just like an overdrawn check.
b. Yes. ONB has no obligation to Larchwood Devices, rather only an obligation to its customer Desktop Solutions, who would be unable to perform its own obligations.
c. No. ONB's obligation to pay is independent from its right to reimbursement.
d. No. By issuing the letter of credit, ONB guaranteed the quality of the set top boxes.

2. Would ONB have the right to dishonor, if it could show that the video controllers did not meet the warranties that Larchwood Devices made about them in the sales contract?
   a. Yes. Larchwood Devices would not be entitled to payment if it shipped nonconforming goods.
   b. Yes, but ONB could only set off the amount of damages from the breach of warranty.
   c. No. ONB's obligation to pay is independent from the underlying contract.
   d. No. By issuing the letter of credit, ONB guaranteed the quality of the set top boxes.

3. Would ONB have the right to dishonor if it could show that the bill of lading showed shipment of only 500 video controllers, as opposed to the 1,000 video controllers specified in the letter of credit?
   a. Yes. Larchwood Devices would not be entitled to payment if it failed to present a bill of lading that conformed to the letter of credit.
   b. Yes, but ONB could only set off the amount of damages from the breach of contract (presumably half the contract price).
   c. No. ONB's obligation to pay is independent from the underlying contract.
   d. No. By issuing the letter of credit, ONB guaranteed the delivery of the set top boxes.

4. ONB had issued another letter of credit to Sneaky Sneakers, who presented the letter of credit along with the specified documents (a bill of lading, an invoice, customs documents, and a certificate of inspection from Footles Inspections). ONB's customer, however, notified ONB that the boxes delivered contained not the promised sneakers, but only empty

plastic bottles, some inscribed with "Size 11" and a smiley face. An ONB vice president visited the buyer's warehouse and verified the facts. May ONB dishonor the letter of credit?

a. Yes. ONB may dishonor the letter of credit if the buyer has breached the underlying contract.
b. Yes. ONB may dishonor the letter of credit in the case of fraud.
c. No. ONB's obligation to pay is independent from the underlying contract.
d. No. By issuing the letter of credit, ONB guaranteed the delivery of the set top boxes.

5. ONB also issued a $500,000 letter of credit to Gdansk Boats, in connection with the sale by Gdansk Boats of two custom-made yachts. Gdansk Boats assigned the letter of credit to Factor Finance, for a payment of $400,000. Factor Finance and Gdansk Boats notified ONB of the assignment. Gdansk Boats later modified the sales contract, making it a single custom-made yacht for $250,000. ONB, with the agreement of Gdansk Boats and the buyer, amended the letter of credit to be payable for $250,000. When the boat was delivered, Gdansk Boats presented the letter of credit to ONB, along with the required documentation (its signed certification that it had performed under the contract). How much should ONB pay, and to whom?
   a. Gdansk Boats, $250,000, because letters of credit are not assignable.
   b. Gdansk Boats, $500,000, because letters of credit are not assignable or amendable.
   c. Factor Finance, $500,000, because it did not agree to the amendment and the letter of credit had been assigned to it before the amendment.
   d. Factor Finance, $250,000, because an assignee is subject to amendment of the letter of credit.

ANSWERS

1. *C* is the best answer. The bank's obligation to pay a letter of credit is independent of its right to reimbursement. Indeed, the whole purpose of a letter of credit is for the beneficiary to be able to rely on the bank, not on the applicant, for payment. Contrary to *A*, a letter of credit is quite different from a check, which a bank may dishonor if there are insufficient funds. Contrary to *B*, and again unlike a check, a bank does have a direct obligation to the beneficiary to pay the letter of credit.
2. *C* is the best answer. A bank's obligation to pay a letter of credit is also independent of the underlying contract between the applicant and the beneficiary. Whether the beneficiary is entitled to payment on the underlying contract does not determine whether the beneficiary is entitled to payment on the letter of credit, contrary to *A* and *B*. Note that it works in

the other direction as well: if the beneficiary has performed the contract, but does not present the required documents for payment on the letter of credit, it is not entitled to payment on the letter of credit.

3. *A* is the best answer. ONB could dishonor because the specified documents have not been presented. Contrary to *C*, this result is consistent with the independence principle. ONB can dishonor not because Larchwood Devices has not performed under the contract, but because Larchwood Devices has not presented the documents specified by the letter of credit. The question illustrates how the buyer should protect itself, by specifying documents for presentment that require performing under the contract.
4. *B* is the best answer. This question illustrates the exception to the independence principle. In the case of fraud, the bank is not obliged to honor a letter of credit. It must be true fraud, not just breach of contract. But here there was fraud, delivering empty plastic bottles instead of shoes, along with taunting messages indicating knowing deception.
5. *D* is the best answer. The right to proceeds of a letter of credit may be assigned, but the assignee is subject to any amendment of the letter of credit.

PART 4

SECURED TRANSACTIONS

CHAPTER 19

INTRODUCTION TO SECURED TRANSACTIONS

"Secured Transactions" is an imposing term, but it merely refers to a business transaction in which a credit extension is protected (secured) by collateral given by the debtor to better back up the loan. Much can go wrong here: the parties may not specify the collateral exactly, or the creditor may fail to make the loan, other parties (buyers, other creditors, the debtor's trustee in bankruptcy) may make claims to the property, etc. Article 9 of the Uniform Commercial Code resolves these and other issues. It is not the most interesting subject to study, but it is logical and fits together well. And what knowledge you gain here is very important. You, future attorney, will often extend credit to your clients and it might be to your advantage to demand collateral to protect that debt. And no matter how dull secured transactions might seem in law school it will (a) likely be tested on the bar exam, (b) help you find a job, and (c) become the most fascinating subject you've ever looked at when the senior partner of your firm tells you that because you know Article 9 (from this course) you're in charge of making sure nothing goes wrong on the $5 million deal the firm is handling for its largest client.

It is understandable that someone extending credit in a sale or loan transaction wants to be sure of repayment. Some debtors are so solvent and/or trustworthy that the creditor demands nothing more than the debtor's promise to pay (sometimes called a *signature loan*); creditors doing this are said to be *unsecured.* In many transactions the creditor is less sanguine about the debtor's ability or desire to repay and may demand that the debtor either obtain a surety (called by various names: a *co-signor,* a *guarantor,* or, in Article 3 of the Uniform Commercial Code, an *accommodation party*) or *secure* the debt by nominating some of the debtor's current or future property as collateral. If the debtor defaults, the collateral may be seized and sold and the proceeds of the sale used to pay the debt.

A basic problem with mastering the law of secured transactions has always been in understanding the terminology: *lien, pledge, perfection, purchase money security interest,* etc. The terminology is complex because historically what we now call *secured transactions* have their source in many separate business devices, each with an individual set of descriptive terms. In addition, Article 9 of the Uniform Commercial Code adds a new and different nomenclature. To understand the pre-Code cases and the Code commentators' references to these pre-Code devices, it is necessary to have some minimal appreciation of how creditors protected their interests prior to the adoption of the UCC.

The core problem is that when a debtor cannot pay the bills, creditors must look to the debtor's property for whatever satisfaction they will get. These creditors must compete with other claimants for the property: donees, buyers, and (if financial death has occurred) the debtor's bankruptcy trustee. Worse yet, the creditors must compete with each other, and the law must somehow provide rules to determine who among all these individuals is to receive the property. As fast as the lawmakers create one set of statutes, those in business and their advisors think up new contractual arrangements that the statutes do not cover, and the law is chaotic until a new group of statutes can be added to those already regulating similar practices.

The original version of Article 9 of the Uniform Commercial Code, dealing with these "secured" transactions, was promulgated in 1962 and has twice been substantially rewritten: in 1972 and most recently in 1999, the version considered in this book. In most states the 1999 revision went into effect on July 1, 2001. The transition rules from the old version to the next can be found in the 9-700s. Official Comment 4 to §9-101 has a concise summary of the changes that the 1999 revision makes to the earlier version of the statute. This book also covers the minor revisions promulgated in 2010, which all 50 states, the District of Columbia, and Puerto Rico had adopted by the fall of 2020, if not yet the U.S. Virgin Islands.

We start with some basic definitions.

A *lien* is an interest in the debtor's property given by the law to protect a creditor. If the debtor voluntarily grants such an interest, a *consensual* lien is created. If a consensual lien is taken in the debtor's real property, the lien is called a *mortgage.* A consensual lien in personal property or fixtures is called a *security interest* and is governed by Article 9 of the Uniform Commercial Code. Involuntary liens can also be imposed against the debtor's property. If the lien arises from judicial proceedings (the creditor sues, recovers judgment, and sends the sheriff out to seize the defendant's property), a *judicial lien* is created. A *statutory lien* is one imposed by either a statute or the common law in favor of certain creditors the law deems worthy of protection. Examples are the liens given to landlords, to artisans repairing personal property (the garage mechanic, for example), and to a host of others, such as ostlers, innkeepers, and even attorneys. A mechanic's lien is a statutory lien in favor of those who perform construction work. And if you do not pay your taxes, the federal government will file the awesome federal tax lien, a statutory lien that reaches *all* of the taxpayer's property, a matter we treat at length in a later chapter.

Although it is impossible to make a categorical statement, generally the prior statutes regulating these matters established a hierarchy of heady contenders in the derby to divide up the debtor's assets. Assuming a claimant qualifies, a "bona fide purchaser [BFP] in the ordinary course of business" was (and still is under Article 9) a favorite in the race. Another current favorite is the bankruptcy trustee, who represents all of the bankrupt's unsecured creditors and to whom the federal bankruptcy statute gives an awesome arsenal of weapons with which to attack the supposed interests that secured creditors assert in the estate's property. Under what is called the *strong arm clause* (§544(a) of the Bankruptcy Code), as of the date of the filing of the bankruptcy petition, the trustee (and all the claims the trustee represents) is conclusively presumed to occupy the legal position of a judicial lien creditor who has levied on all of the bankrupt's property. As we shall see, secured creditors whose security interests are *unperfected* at this moment lose the right to claim the collateral. But if a creditor's claim to the property will survive the attack of the bankruptcy trustee, the creditor's security interest (lien) is said to be *perfected.* Perfection of the security interest then becomes the ultimate goal of any creditor taking an interest in the debtor's collateral. And—again this is a generality—creditors with perfected security interests not only beat out the bankruptcy trustee but also win over non-BFPs—creditors without perfected security interests, creditors whose security interests were perfected later in time, and creditors with no security interests at all (called, in bankruptcy parlance, *general creditors:* typically, for example, the corner grocer, the family doctor).

How is a creditor's security interest perfected? The answer depends on the nature of the collateral, the technical steps required by the statutes (or the courts if the legislature has not yet acted), and the particular moment in history in which the question is asked. Before embarking on a description of the major pre-Code security devices, there follows a brief outline of the bankruptcy rules against which the validity of these devices (and Article 9) must be viewed.

I. BANKRUPTCY

The United States Constitution states that Congress shall pass laws pertaining to bankruptcy; the result is the Bankruptcy Reform Act of 1978, 11 U.S.C. §§101 et seq. (hereinafter the Bankruptcy Code). There are four primary types of bankruptcy: Chapter 7, straight bankruptcy (a pure liquidation proceeding); Chapter 11, a reorganization proceeding for businesses; Chapter 12, a reorganization proceeding for farmers; and Chapter 13, a debt repayment plan for individuals. The vast majority of bankruptcies are straight bankruptcies, and over 90 percent of those are filed by individuals, as opposed to businesses. Consequently, the rest of this discussion is a sketch of the proceedings in straight bankruptcy.

To commence bankruptcy, the debtor (a *voluntary* bankruptcy) or the debtor's creditors (an *involuntary* bankruptcy) file a petition with the bankruptcy court. This is a federal court under the direction of the local federal district court. The date on which the petition is filed is important because it is the measuring moment for many of the Bankruptcy Code's sections. Along with the petition the debtor will file lists (called *schedules*), showing assets and creditors. The creditors are then summoned to a meeting (called, not inaptly, the *first meeting of creditors* or, because of its Bankruptcy Code number, a *§341 meeting*) at which they elect someone (the *trustee*) to gather up the debtor's property, sell it, and represent the creditors' interests in the distribution of the proceeds. If the debtor's property must be tended to *before* the first meeting of creditors (say, for instance, a circus goes bankrupt—someone must see to it that the menagerie doesn't run loose), a temporary custodian (an *interim trustee*), who acts until the trustee can take over, is appointed.[1]

The trustee collects the debtor's property. This can be a more complicated task than it may seem. If other people claim the property (creditors, a relative who was the recipient of a very generous birthday gift, or even the bankrupt, should there be an argument over *exempt* assets), the trustee may have to litigate the issue either before the bankruptcy judge or in the state or federal court. Property exempt from bankruptcy under federal or—in

1. The interim trustee automatically becomes the trustee unless someone else is elected trustee at the first meeting of creditors. Bankruptcy Code §702(d).

some jurisdictions—state law and worthless property (the bankrupt's cat, for example) are returned to the bankrupt. The bankrupt then petitions the bankruptcy judge for a *discharge* (read *forgiveness*) of all the scheduled debts so that the bankrupt's life can be resumed financially unburdened. With certain exceptions, bankrupts usually receive a discharge from most (but not all) debts.[2]

When the trustee gathers the estate's property, either the trustee surrenders the encumbered collateral to the secured creditors or, if the trustee elects to sell the collateral, creditors with perfected security interests get their debts paid *first* from the proceeds of the sale. The unencumbered assets of the estate are also sold, and those proceeds are used to pay the expenses of the bankruptcy proceeding, wages of the bankrupt's employees, some tax claims, certain other priority claimants, and, finally, the general creditors (who get nothing until all the above are paid in full).

The trustee need not accept the creditor's statement that the creditor has a perfected security interest; the validity (*perfection*) of the security interest is a matter of state law and will be measured by state standards. If the security interest is finally determined to be *unperfected,* the interest is destroyed, and the creditor becomes just another general (*unsecured*) creditor. Not only is the trustee armed (as has been mentioned) with the position of a perfected *lien creditor* coming into existence on the date of the petition filing (Bankruptcy Code §544(a)), but also the trustee occupies the same legal position as any actual existing creditor (Bankruptcy Code §544(b)). Further, the Bankruptcy Code codifies the old common law maxim that a debtor must "be just before he is generous." Section 547 of the Bankruptcy Code condemns as a *preference* the following type of conduct:

> On January 1, Alice owed to Tom, Dick, and Harry $1,000 each for past due loans. On May 1, she paid Tom $1,000, and the next day she filed a voluntary petition in bankruptcy.

Section 547 provides that many payments made by an insolvent debtor to an existing creditor within 90 days of the date of the filing of the petition are void as *preferences.* The trustee can recover the payment from the preferred creditor. (The fairness of §547 to Dick and Harry should be obvious.)

A final practical note worth remembering: in most bankruptcies the unsecured creditors receive *nothing.* For this reason most creditors want security (collateral) for their debts, and they want their lawyers to advise them how they can perfect that security against other creditors and the bankruptcy trustee.

2. See Bankruptcy Code §§523, 727.

II. PRE-CODE SECURITY DEVICES

Students who know nothing other than Article 9 (and, as to real property creditor conflicts, know only what they learned in their basic property course) may not appreciate the wide variety of devices the UCC replaced. Such a student may ask why all these devices, particularly those that were very similar, were needed. The answer is historical. Our legal ancestors (lawyers, judges, and legislators) had some rigid ideas about what was transferable property (a diamond ring) and what was not (a right to sue your customer if the bill wasn't paid) and about the propriety of certain business practices that now seem commonplace. We begin our study with a famous case.

Benedict v. Ratner

United States Supreme Court, 1925
268 U.S. 353

BRANDEIS, J.

The Hub Carpet Company was adjudicated bankrupt by the federal court for southern New York in involuntary proceedings commenced September 26, 1921. Benedict, who was appointed receiver and later trustee, collected the book accounts of the company. Ratner filed in that court a petition in equity praying that the amounts so collected be paid over to him. He claimed them under a writing given May 23, 1921—four months and three days before the commencement of the bankruptcy proceedings. By it the company purported to assign to him, as collateral for certain loans, all accounts present and future. Those collected by the receiver were, so far as appears, all accounts which had arisen after the date of the assignment, and were enumerated in the monthly list of accounts outstanding which was delivered to Ratner September 23. Benedict resisted the petition on the ground that the original assignment was void under the law of New York as a fraudulent conveyance; that, for this reason, the delivery of the September list of accounts was inoperative to perfect a lien in Ratner; and that it was a preference under the Bankruptcy Act. He also filed a cross-petition in which he asked that Ratner be ordered to pay to the estate the proceeds of certain collections which had been made by the company after September 17 and turned over to Ratner pursuant to his request made on that day. The company was then insolvent and Ratner had reason to believe it to be so. These accounts also had apparently been acquired by the company after the date of the original assignment.

The District Judge decided both petitions in Ratner's favor. He ruled that the assignment executed in May was not fraudulent in law; that it created an equity in the future acquired accounts; that because of this equity, Ratner was entitled to retain, as against the bankrupt's estate, the proceeds of the accounts which had been collected by the company in September and turned over to him; that by delivery of the list of the accounts outstanding on September 23, this equity in them had ripened into a perfect title to the remaining accounts; and that the title so perfected was good as against the supervening bankruptcy. Accordingly, the District Court ordered that, to the extent of the balance remaining unpaid on his loans, there be paid to Ratner all collections made from accounts enumerated in any of the lists delivered to Ratner; and that the cross-petition of Benedict be denied. There was no finding of fraud in fact. On appeal, the Circuit Court of Appeals affirmed the order. 282 Fed. 12. A writ of certiorari was granted by this Court. 259 U.S. 579.

The rights of the parties depend primarily upon the law of New York. Hiscock v. Varick Bank of N.Y., 206 U.S. 28. It may be assumed that, unless the arrangement of May 23 was void because fraudulent in law, the original assignment of the future acquired accounts became operative under the state law, both as to those paid over to Ratner before the bankruptcy proceedings and as to those collected by the receiver; and that the assignment will be deemed to have taken effect as of May 23. Sexton v. Kessler, 225 U.S. 90, 99. That being so, it is clear that, if the original assignment was a valid one under the law of New York, the Bankruptcy Act did not invalidate the subsequent dealings of the parties. Thompson v. Fairbanks, 196 U.S. 516; Humphrey v. Tatman, 198 U.S. 91. The sole question for decision is, therefore, whether on the following undisputed facts the assignment of May 23 was in law fraudulent.

The Hub Carpet Company was, on May 23, a mercantile concern doing business in New York City and proposing to continue to do so. The assignment was made there to secure an existing loan of $15,000, and further advances not exceeding $15,000 which were in fact made July 1, 1921. It included all accounts receivable then outstanding and all which should thereafter accrue in the ordinary course of business. A list of the existing accounts was delivered at the time. Similar lists were to be delivered to Ratner on or about the 23rd day of each succeeding month containing the accounts outstanding at such future dates. Those enumerated in each of the lists delivered prior to September, aggregated between $100,000 and $120,000. The receivables were to be collected by the company. Ratner was given the right, at any time, to demand a full disclosure of the business and financial conditions; to require that all amounts collected be applied in payment of his loans; and to enforce the assignment although no loan had matured. But until he did so, the company was not required to apply any of the collections to the repayment of Ratner's loan. It was not required to replace accounts collected by other collateral of equal value. It was not required to account in any way to Ratner. It was at liberty to use the proceeds of all accounts collected as it might see fit. The existence of the assignment was to be kept secret. The business was to be conducted as theretofore. Indebtedness was to be incurred, as usual, for the purchase of merchandise and otherwise in the ordinary course of business. The amount of such indebtedness unpaid at the time of the commencement of the bankruptcy proceedings was large. Prior to September 17, the company collected from accounts so assigned about $150,000, all of which it applied to purposes other than the payment of Ratner's loan. The outstanding accounts enumerated in the list delivered September 23 aggregated $90,000.

Under the law of New York a transfer of property as security which reserves to the transferor the right to dispose of the same, or to apply the proceeds thereof, for his own uses is, as to creditors, fraudulent in law and void. This is true whether the right of disposition for the transferor's use be reserved in the instrument or by agreement in pais, oral or written; whether the right of disposition reserved be unlimited in time or be expressly terminable by the happening of an event; whether the transfer cover all the property of the debtor or only a part; whether the right of disposition extends to all the property transferred or only to a part thereof; and whether the instrument of transfer be recorded or not.

If this rule applies to the assignment of book accounts, the arrangement of May 23 was clearly void; and the equity in the future acquired accounts, which it would otherwise have created, did not arise. Whether the rule applies to accounts does not appear to have been passed upon by the Court of Appeals of New York. But it would seem clear that whether the collateral consists of chattels or of accounts, reservation of dominion inconsistent with the effective disposition of title must render the transaction void. Ratner asserts that the rule stated above rests upon ostensible ownership, and argues that the doctrine of ostensible ownership is not applicable to book accounts. That doctrine raises a presumption of fraud where chattels are mortgaged (or sold) and possession of the property is not delivered to the mortgagee (or vendee). The presumption may be avoided by recording the mortgage (or sale). It may be assumed, as Ratner contends, that the doctrine does not apply to the assignment of accounts. In their transfer there is nothing which corresponds to the delivery of possession of chattels. The statutes which embody the doctrine and provide for recording as a substitute for delivery do not include accounts. A title to an account good against creditors may be transferred without notice to the debtor or record of any kind. But it is not true that the rule stated above and invoked by the receiver is either based upon or delimited by the doctrine of ostensible ownership. It rests not upon seeming ownership because of possession retained, but upon a lack of ownership because of dominion reserved. It does not raise a presumption of fraud. It imputes fraud conclusively because of the reservation of dominion inconsistent with the effective disposition of title and creation of a lien.

The nature of the rule is made clear by its limitations. Where the mortgagor of chattels agrees to apply the proceeds of their sale to the payment of the mortgage debt or to the purchase of other chattels which shall become subject to the lien, the mortgage is good as against creditors, if recorded. The mortgage is sustained in such cases "upon the ground that such sale and application of proceeds is the normal and proper purpose of a chattel mortgage, and within the precise boundaries of its lawful operation and effect. It does no more than to substitute the mortgagor as the agent of the mortgagee to do exactly what the latter had the right to do, and what it was his privilege and his duty to accomplish. It devotes, as it should, the mortgaged property to the payment of the mortgage debt." The permission to use the proceeds to furnish substitute collateral "provides only for a shifting of the lien from one piece of property to another taken in exchange." Brackett v. Harvey, 91 N.Y. 214, 221, 223. On the other hand, if the agreement is that the mortgagor may sell and use the proceeds for his own benefit, the mortgage is of no effect although recorded. Seeming ownership exists in both classes of cases because the mortgagor is permitted to remain in possession of the stock in trade and to sell it freely. But it is only where the unrestricted dominion over the proceeds is reserved to the mortgagor that the mortgage is void. This dominion is the differentiating and deciding element. The distinction was recognized in Sexton v. Kessler, 225 U.S. 90, 98, 32 S. Ct. 657, where a transfer of securities was sustained. It was pointed out that a reservation of full control by the mortgagor might well prevent the effective creation of a lien in the mortgagee and that the New York cases holding such a mortgage void rest upon that doctrine.

The results which flow from reserving dominion inconsistent with the effective disposition of title must be the same whatever the nature of the property transferred. The doctrine which imputes fraud where full dominion is reserved must apply to assignments of accounts although the doctrine of ostensible ownership does not. There must also be the same distinction as to degrees of dominion. Thus, although an agreement that the assignor of accounts shall collect them and pay the proceeds to the assignee will not invalidate the assignment which it accompanies, the assignment must be deemed fraudulent in law if it is agreed that the assignor may use the proceeds as he sees fit.

In the case at bar, the arrangement for the unfettered use by the company of the proceeds of the accounts precluded the effective creation of a lien and rendered the original assignment fraudulent in law. Consequently the payments to Ratner and the delivery of the September list of accounts were inoperative to perfect a lien in him, and were unlawful preferences.

On this ground, and also because the payment was fraudulent under the law of the State, the trustee was entitled to recover the amount. . . .

Reversed.

The evil under attack in Benedict v. Ratner is the *secret lien* that other creditors do not know about. If it is enforced by the courts, the other creditors who were deceived by the debtor's apparently unencumbered prosperity are hurt. But, although the Court in this case ruled against the creditor's security interest, most creditors took comfort from the decision because the Court had indicated methods by which the lien *would* have survived the trustee's attack. By requiring the creditor to *police* the debtor's conduct (record the mortgage, pay over collections to the creditor, etc.), the Court paved the way for increased commercial financing. Once the creditors knew what the rules were, they were more willing to extend credit.

Did the rule of Benedict v. Ratner survive the enactment of Article 9? Read §9-205 and its Official Comment 2. Article 9 solves the secret lien problem by making sure that the creditor's interest in the debtor's property is obvious so that no later creditors are deceived (typically by the filing of a notice, called a *financing statement,* in the public records, though there are other methods, such as taking possession of the collateral, that serve the same function). Note that in a sale of goods transaction it still is a bad idea for the seller to retain possession of the sold objects for a long period of time after the sale is over; read §2-402(2).

One way around the problems encountered in this famous case was to permit the creditor to have physical possession of the property (a *pledge;* see below), though this is a solution only where the collateral has tangible form, which accounts receivable, of course, do not. Other ways were suggested by the opinion itself. A very brief summary of the major devices follows.

A. *Pledge*

In a *pledge,*[3] the debtor (called a *pledgor*) gives physical possession of the collateral to the creditor (called the *pledgee*) until the debt is paid. Possession then *perfects* the creditor's interest in the collateral (even against the bankruptcy trustee). Obviously when the creditor has possession of, say, a diamond ring, the whole world is on notice that the creditor has some legal interest therein. Pledging is a superior way to perfect the creditor's security interest, but it has two drawbacks: (1) only tangible objects can be pledged,

3. A pledge is sometimes called a *hypothecation.*

and a business debtor may want to borrow money against intangible collateral (such as accounts receivable due from existing customers); and (2) for some types of collateral the debtor needs to keep possession (the machines used in manufacturing, for example). It was therefore necessary to create *non*possessory security interests.

B. Chattel Mortgage

The debtor could always mortgage land, so why not have something similar for personal property (*chattels*)? And, as with real property, the mortgage given by the debtor (the *mortgagor*) to the creditor (the *mortgagee*) was recorded in a designated place and indexed under the name of the debtor so that other potential creditors could check and see whether the collateral was encumbered. Thus, the debtor could have possession, but the secret lien problem so dreaded in Benedict v. Ratner was avoided because the mortgage was (through the recording system) witness to the creditor's very public interest in the property.

C. Conditional Sale

Here's a surprise. Without first reading the text that follows, form an opinion as to the answer to this Problem.

PROBLEM 289

Honest John sold Nancy Debts a used car for $900, to be paid off in three payments of $300 each. The contract was oral. Nancy missed the second payment, and one of Honest John's employees repossessed the car and returned it to the seller. Nancy sued Honest John for conversion. Who should win? After forming your initial opinion, read §2-702 and see if that has any bearing on your answer.

Most people assume that the unpaid seller always has a right to repossess. *This is untrue.* The unpaid seller may repossess in only three circumstances: (1) when §2-702 (which you have just read and about which more later) applies; (2) when the buyer has specifically granted the seller a *security interest* in the object sold; and (3) when the seller sues, recovers judgment, and has the sheriff seize the property as part of the execution of the seller's judgment. (When an unsecured creditor sues and acquires a judgment and then sends the sheriff out to levy on the defendant's property, the creditor is called, variously, a *judgment creditor*, a *judicial creditor*, or simply a *lien creditor*.) Of course, prior to the UCC, the seller could take a chattel mortgage in the property sold and file to record this interest, but that was a lot of trouble. Another way was to have a *conditional sale* whereby the buyer got possession of the property but the seller reserved full and complete title to it until the buyer paid in full (the *condition* in *conditional sale* was this payment before the buyer got any title). A conditional sale has the Benedict v. Ratner problem of the debtor-in-possession and a secret lien in the seller's favor, and the fictitious title retention theory had as short a life here as it did in the real property mortgage situation. The upshot was that in many states the seller's "title" was treated as nothing more than an unperfected security interest, so that the seller lost to later judicial creditors, to creditors who perfected their security interests, and to the buyer's trustee in bankruptcy. That is certainly the result in Article 9; see §9-202. In most states the seller's interest in a conditional sale had to be filed to be perfected.

Some sellers still use *conditional sale* terminology in their contracts. What effect does the seller's retention of title have under the UCC? Read §§2-401(1), second sentence, and 1-201(b)(35), second-to-last sentence in the first paragraph.

D. *Trust Receipt*

A strained use of trust law principles helped the retail automobile dealer finance (*floor plan*) purchases of vehicles from the manufacturer. In trust receipt financing, the car dealer would ask a bank to buy the cars from the manufacturer. The bank would then turn them over to the dealer after two things happened: (1) the bank filed a notice in the appropriate place announcing its intention to engage in trust receipt financing with this particular dealer; and (2) the dealer signed a *trust receipt* (thereby becoming a *trustee*; the bank was called an *entruster*), acknowledging receipt of the vehicles and granting the bank a security interest therein. As the cars[4] were sold, the bank's interest was paid off, and, when paid in full, the trust receipt was canceled. Various complications could arise, the most common of these being a sale "out of trust," meaning that the dealer did not remit the proceeds of the car sales as required by the agreement, which often happened if the bank failed to police the debtor's activities. Trust receipt financing rules were codified in the Uniform Trust Receipts Act, a very difficult statute that was adopted in two-thirds of the states.

4. Trust receipt financing was, of course, used in financing the acquisition of inventory other than automobiles but was available only where the inventory consisted of easily identifiable separate items—for instance, those having serial numbers.

E. *Factor's Lien*

The word *factor* originally meant any selling agent (wholesaler or retailer) who helped finance the principal's business. As time went on, the factor's selling function died out, and the factor became a financing entity who loaned money against inventory the manufacturer put up as collateral. In return, the factor was granted a lien (a security interest) in the inventory, but this security interest had to be filed to be perfected under most states' factor lien statutes. Most of these statutes contained this drawback: The lien did not extend to new additions to the inventory (*after-acquired property*); that is, it was not a *floating lien* that attached to the changing objects in the inventory. If the after-acquired property in the inventory was to become collateral for the factor, a new security agreement and, typically, a filing of the same were prerequisites to perfection.

F. *Field Warehousing*

In Benedict v. Ratner, the primary evil was that the debtor was in possession of property that secretly belonged to the creditor. With a pledge, possession of the collateral is in the creditor, and no deception problem arises. If the collateral is too big to be conveniently left in the creditor's possession (say, for instance, the collateral is an inventory of Christmas tree ornaments waiting for the Christmas season), one way of pulling off a pledge was for the debtor to store the goods in a warehouse and have the warehouse company issue a negotiable warehouse receipt made out to *bearer.* Such a warehouse receipt (a *document of title,* now regulated by Article 7 of the UCC) has to be surrendered before the warehouse company will turn over the goods to anyone (§7-403); in effect, this rule makes the warehouse receipt take the place of the goods, and thus the receipt was pledged to the creditor in return for the loan of money. Possession of a negotiable document of title (a warehouse receipt or a bill of lading) perfected the creditor's security interest. A *field warehouse* is the same thing as a normal warehouse with one difference: the warehouse comes to the goods instead of vice versa. If the goods are too bulky to move easily, the field warehouseman goes to the goods, stakes them out in some way, issues a warehouse receipt therefor, and guards them (even the debtor, on whose premises they remain, is not supposed to be able to get to the goods). The receipt is then pledged to a financing agency; when the debt is repaid, the warehouse receipt is returned to the debtor, who presents it to the field warehouse agent, who surrenders the goods and then packs up and leaves the debtor's property. (The field warehouse agent is frequently only temporarily hired by the field warehouse company and is actually a regular employee of the debtor. The resulting loyalty conflicts often gave rise to warehouseman misbehavior and, inevitably, lawsuits.)

G. *Conclusion*

Article 9 of the Code replaced all these devices (though some of the practices, such as a pledge or field warehousing, live on) with new rules as to creation of the security interest, the collateral to which it can attach, and the steps necessary for perfection. It is meant to be all-inclusive to cover all possible security interests in personal property and fixtures (see §9-109(c) and (d) for a list of transactions excluded from Article 9's dominion).

When Article 9 was being created, the drafters were worried that it would prove politically difficult to adopt because it did away with so many other statutes (Chattel Mortgage, Factors Act, Uniform Trust Receipts Act, and others), and replaced them with a completely new system that lawyers would have to learn. To their surprise Article 9 turned out to be a chief selling point during the state by state adoption of the Uniform Commercial Code because it was one logical system and did not require understanding a hodgepodge of other laws, and lawyers were relieved to have to master only one set of well-structured rules.

Chapter 20
The Scope of Article 9

It is particularly important for an attorney to appreciate which transactions Article 9 will apply to and those it will not. The scope provisions of the Article are considered next, starting with definitions, transactions at the borders of the Article, and exclusions from its coverage.

Article 9 focuses on secured transactions in personal property. Its rules state what a debtor and creditor must do to make the transaction effective (*attachment* or *creation*); what the creditor must do to give notice making the transaction effective against other parties, such as other creditors, buyers, or a bankruptcy trustee (*perfection*); who wins if creditors, buyers, or other parties contest rights in the collateral (*priority*); and what the creditor may and may not do to repossess the collateral and sell it to get paid (*default*).

I. SECURITY INTEREST DEFINED

Read §1-201(b)(35) (defining *security interest*) and §9-109(a) (General Scope of Article).

PROBLEM 290

Assume that a state statute gives someone doing repairs a possessory artisan's lien on the property repaired. Mr. Baker took his car into Mack's Garage for repair but, being strapped for funds, couldn't pay the full bill, and Mack wouldn't let him have the car back. Is Mack's artisan's lien an Article 9 *security interest*? See §9-109(d)(2). If, prior to the repair work, Mr. Baker signed a statement giving Mack's Garage a right to repossess the car if the bill wasn't paid, does this agreement create a *security interest* under the Code? See §9-109(a)(1).

PROBLEM 291

In need of cash, Livingstone signed an agreement with Stanley, selling his Land Rover to Stanley for $20,000, with the right to repurchase the vehicle in six months for $23,000. The Land Rover had a market value of $35,000. The agreement allowed Livingstone to continue using the vehicle during those six months. Does Article 9 apply so that steps are needed to protect these rights from later creditors wanting to seize the Land Rover? See Holland v. Sullivan, 2017 WL 3917142 (Tenn. Ct. App. 2017).

PROBLEM 292

Floyd Mutrux, one author of the musical "Million Dollar Quartet," owed money to his attorney, Gilbert Kelly. Mutrux made an agreement assigning to Kelly a percentage of Mutrux's future royalty distributions from the musical, effective until the debt was paid. Does Article 9 apply so that the attorney should take appropriate steps to protect these rights from other creditors? See MDQ, LLC v. Gilbert, Kelly, Crowley & Jennett LLP, 32 Cal. App. 5th 702, 710, 244 Cal. Rptr. 3d 211, 217 (Ct. App. 2019).

PROBLEM 293

To raise money, Farmer Brown's Fresh Vegetables Roadside Stand sold all of its accounts receivable to Nightflyer Finance Company, which notified the customers that henceforth all payments should be made directly to Nightflyer. (Note that this is not a loan from the finance company to the farmer with the accounts put up as collateral; it is an outright *sale*. If it were a loan, and if the collectible accounts exceeded the amount of the loan, the excess would be returned to Farmer Brown; in an actual sale, Nightflyer can keep the surplus. See §9-608(b).) Is this sale nonetheless an Article 9 "security interest"? See §9-109(a)(3). If so, even though Farmer Brown has no further obligations to Nightflyer, he would of necessity be termed an Article 9 "debtor." See §9-102(a)(28)(B). Then Nightflyer would have to file an Article 9 financing statement to perfect its interest against later parties. Why would the Code drafters have brought an outright sale of accounts (and *chattel paper, payment intangibles,* and *promissory notes,* all defined below) under the coverage of Article 9? Remember Benedict v. Ratner? See Official Comment 4 to §9-109; Major's Furniture Mart, Inc. v. Castle Credit Corp., 602 F.2d 538 (3d Cir. 1979).

For the practicing attorney, the possibility that a business transaction with no apparent *loan* or *collateral* may still fall within Article 9 is a matter of great concern. If the transaction creates an Article 9 *security interest,* the attorney's client had better have taken whatever steps Article 9 requires for perfection, or the client may lose the property to later creditors. If the attorney has not advised the client of this possibility, the client's thoughts may turn to malpractice actions.

A few of the obviously troublesome areas where Article 9 may or may not apply are discussed next.

II. CONSIGNMENTS

A true consignment is neither a *sale* nor a *security device*; it is a marketing procedure by which the owner of goods (the *consignor*) sends (*consigns*) them to a retailer (the *consignee*) for sale to the public. The retailer does not *buy* the goods (so no sale takes place when the consignor delivers the goods to the consignee). If the retailer cannot sell them, they are returned to the consignor. In effect, the consignee is the selling agent for the consignor, or, looked at another way, the consignee is a bailee with the ability to sell the bailor's goods. The advantages to the consignor of a true consignment over an outright sale (with reservation of a security interest so the goods can be reclaimed if the retailer does not pay for them) is that the consignor retains control over the terms of the retail sale (and thus can dictate the retail price), and, at least at common law, there is no requirement that the consignor file a notice anywhere announcing that a consignment is going on. (Why, the consignors argue, should they have to notify anyone that they have claimed an interest in their own property?) At common law, this argument tended to prevail, with the consignors able to reclaim the consigned goods from the inventory of the consignee over the objections of the consignee's other creditors; see Ludwigh v. American Woolen Co., 231 U.S. 522 (1913); In re Haley & Steele, Inc., 20 Mass. L. Rptr. 204, 2005 WL 3489869 (Mass. Super. 2005).

Nonetheless, consignments have the Benedict v. Ratner problem: the retailer appears to be the unfettered owner of goods in inventory that actually belong to someone else (the consignor). The retailer's other creditors may wish to extend credit with the inventory as collateral, but there is no place they can go to check whether some or all of the inventory is actually held on consignment.

Further, some consignments are not *true consignments* at all but are sales on credit (i.e., secured transactions) disguised as consignments in order to escape the filing requirements. If the retailer must pay for the goods whether or not able to resell them, this is not a true consignment, even if called that; it is the creation of a security interest in goods. If a *security interest* is intended, then it is not a true consignment at all; see §9-102(a)(20)(D).[1] Article 9 *must be* complied with (perfection by filing, etc.).

In the end, the drafters of the revised version of Article 9 decided to take some kinds of true consignments and treat them as Article 9 matters, thus requiring the usual steps for perfecting a security interest in someone else's inventory (see "Purchase Money Security Interests" in Chapter 24) but leaving some true consignments outside the Code (and thus protected by the common law rule that favored the consignor). Read §9-102(a)(20).

PROBLEM 294

Antiques R Us was the largest antiques store in the city, well known as a place where antique dealers could hire out space and exhibit their wares, with the store handling the sales and taking a commission on each one and returning to the dealers items that remained unsold. When the store takes out a loan from Octopus National Bank and uses as collateral "all its property," will the bank's security interest reach the items in the store that belong to the dealers if the dealers have never taken the steps required of consignors under Article 9? See §9-102(a)(20)(A)(iii); cf. Overton v. Art Finance Partners LLC, 166 F. Supp. 3d 388 (S.D.N.Y. 2016) (not consignment where art works delivered for sale to agent generally known in the field to sell works belonging to others).

1. This so-called "consignment" would typically create a purchase money security interest, requiring the steps yet to be discussed for its perfection. Because Article 9 consignments are also given this treatment, this distinction, carefully preserved in the statute, is much ado about nothing.

The "not generally known by its creditors to be substantially engaged in selling the goods of others" test from §9-102(a)(20)(A)(iii) is taken from an identical provision in the former language of §2-326, which also exempted such retail transactions from the necessity of compliance with the perfection rules of Article 9. If the consignor failed to take these steps, the consignor would frequently appeal to this factual test as a last resort but, as the case below indicates, it was a slim reed on which to lean.

In re Fabers, Inc.

United States District Court, District of Connecticut,
Bankruptcy Division, 1972
1972 WL 20789

SEIDMAN, Ref. Bankr.

The bankrupt is a retail carpet and rug merchant. On May 31, 1971, the petitioner, Mehdi Dilmaghani & Company, Inc. (dealer), shipped oriental rugs to the bankrupt on consignment. Subsequent deliveries of rugs on a similar basis were made on May 5, 1971, October 4, 1971, October 5, 1971, October 7, 1971, December 6, 1971, and December 23, 1971. All of the rugs so shipped had an identifying label attached. On each label was printed "MD. & CO., INC., Reg. No. R.N. 22956, 100% wool pile, No. ________, Quality ________, Size ________, Sq. Feet ________, Made in Iran." The consignment agreement provided that title to the rugs remained in the dealer until fully paid for; that the consignee had the right to sell the rugs in the ordinary course of business and only at a price in excess of the invoice price; that the proceeds of any sale were the property of the dealer and held in trust for the dealer; that the proceeds of any sale were to be remitted to the dealer immediately with a report of the sale; [and] that all rugs were held at the risk of the consignee.

No effort was made to comply with the provisions of the Uniform Commercial Code relating to security interests. The dealer does not assert a security interest in the rugs, claiming only that the rugs are and always were the property of the dealer under a "true consignment" and, therefore, not subject to the provisions of the Code relating to security interests. . . .

The dealer's claim is that the consignment was not intended for security and is, therefore, not subject to the requirements of Article 9. The logic of this argument escapes the court. If the dealer did not want the agreement to provide it with security for either the payment of the rugs or their return, what other purpose could there have been? The agreement describes the rugs as belonging to the dealer, but the risk of loss or damage is on the consignee. This is inconsistent with the liability of a bailee. The proceeds of the sales were to be the property of the dealer, but the consignee is described as holding the proceeds in trust. A trustee has *title* to the trust estate. The agreement impliedly permitted the consignee to mingle the proceeds with his own funds before remitting. At any rate, there was no requirement of a separate account. This is inconsistent with a true trust. . . .

The principal claim of the dealer is that the transaction was a true consignment, that at all times the consignee was acting as the agent of the dealer and, therefore, the transaction came under the exception allowed in §2-326. . . . To protect itself from the claims of creditors, the dealer could have complied with the filing provisions of Article 9, §2-326(3)(c), but it admittedly did not. The only other exceptions are compliance with an applicable Connecticut law providing for a consignor's interest by a sign (there apparently is no such law) or establishing that the consignee-bankrupt was generally known by his creditors to be substantially engaged in selling the goods of others.

In support of the latter theory, evidence was submitted that the dealer never dealt in oriental rugs prior to May 1971 and that an advertisement in the local newspapers on October 12, 1971, included a picture of Mr. Mehdi Dilmaghani together with the narrative: "By Special Arrangement, we proudly introduce: A distinctive collection of Mehdi Dilmaghani . . . renown importer of genuine handmade Oriental, India, and Petit-Point Rugs. . . ." This hardly complies with the requirement that the bankrupt "is generally known *by his creditors* to be substantially engaged in selling the goods of others." (Emphasis added.) There was no evidence of any notification to any of the bankrupt's creditors to that effect. In fact, it is found that the contrary was true. The bankrupt was not substantially engaged in selling the goods of others.

The dealer argues that the oriental rugs were not the kind of goods in which the bankrupt dealt. They may not have been of the same quality or price range as the other rugs and carpets sold by the bankrupt, but they were all of the same kind of goods—to wit: floor coverings. The trade name of the bankrupt was "Faber's World of Carpets." Other than the reference to the collection by Dilmaghani in the newspaper advertisement there was nothing to suggest any possible connection with the dealer. In fact, this advertisement is no different from that of a department store advertising a full line of "Frigidaire" appliances, or a collection of Pierre Cardin's new spring line. This is a far cry from the situation in In re Griffin, 1 U.C.C. Rep. Serv. 492, where the bankrupt had a sign in his window advertising used furniture and the court found that under the particular circumstances, this was notice that goods of others were being sold. In the instant case, there was no such notice.

There was evidence that the members of the Oriental Rug Dealers Association usually sold their rugs on consignment. This was well known to the members of the association. There was no evidence that this was the universal invariable practice in the trade, or that the creditors of the bankrupt who apparently did not deal in oriental rugs knew anything about the custom of the members of the Oriental Rug Dealers Association. As between the parties, the transaction was a consignment agreement. As to the creditors, it was a sale or return and bound by the provisions of Section 2-326. Since the petitioner does not come under the exceptions in this section, it was required to comply with the filing provisions of Article 9 to preserve its secured position. Admittedly, this was not done.

It is found that the agreement was intended for security and subject to the requirements of §2-326. There was no perfection of the security interest and the agreement did not come under the exceptions set forth in §2-326(3). Accordingly, it is held that the goods are subject to the claims of creditors, §2-326(2). The reclamation petition is denied, and it is so ordered.

PROBLEM 295

When Luke Skywalker, an artisan who handcrafted his wares, finished creating a large jeweled sword, he took it down to Weapons of the World (WOW), a large gun and weapon dealer which mostly sold items that it either manufactured itself or bought from other dealers around the globe. The sword was appraised as being worth over $25,000. Luke asked WOW to sell the sword for him. Is this an Article 9 consignment so that Luke needs to take Article 9 steps to protect himself from WOW's other creditors who have an interest in the store's inventory? Would it make a difference if one particular creditor knew the sword was on consignment? The courts have split as to this; compare TSA Stores, Inc. v. Performance Apparel Corp. (In re TSAWD Holdings, Inc.), 595 B.R. 676 (Bankr. D. Del. 2018), with Russell v. Mountain National Bank (In re Russell), 254 B.R 138 (Bankr. W.D. Va. 2000). What if Luke had agreed that WOW could show the sword but did not have authority to sell it? See Mellen, Inc. v. Biltmore Loan & Jewelry-Scottsdale, LLC, 247 F. Supp. 3d 1084 (D. Ariz. 2017).

III. LEASES

A problem similar to the applicability of Article 9 to consignments occurs when the parties disguise a secured sale as a lease.

Parties may wish to cast a transaction as a lease rather than a sale for many reasons. At various times in the tortured history of tax law (a history that is changing so fast that your authors express no opinion as to the current status of the issue under the Internal Revenue Code), rental payments on a *true lease* could be deducted from gross income, but in a *sale,* the "lessee" could take only depreciation on the object purchased. Tax lawyers developed much experience wrestling with the distinctions between a true lease and a disguised sale, witness:

> At the time of this writing, the use of many millions (and probably billions) of dollars' worth of equipment is being obtained through a medium of tax-oriented leases where the ability of the lessor to take accelerated depreciation and obtain the Investment Tax Credit [is] so crucial that the lease will not be entered into without a ruling by the Commissioner on this point, or at the very least, an unqualified opinion by tax counsel, who necessarily must err only on the side of caution. Tax counsel and administrators have developed a lore of their own for distinguishing a true lease from a disguised sale. One point of interest is their emphasis upon the necessity for the lessor's retention of a residual of significant and measurable value. Although this element is seldom stressed as such in chattel security literature, it is suggested that if UCC draftsmen ever deem it feasible to devise something better than either old U.S.C.A. section 1(2) or abandoned section 7-403, study should be directed toward the possibility of devising a formula based on the value of the residual to be returned at the end of the lease term. A rule of thumb in tax rulings and in super-cautious opinions of lessors' tax counsel is (1) that the lease must come to an end at a time when at least two years or twenty percent of the useful life of the leased item remains, and (2) that this residual must be valued at not less than 15 percent of the purchase price. The lessor's tax counsel is likely to insist that there be no options, or only an option to purchase at the market value as determined when the option is exercised. This position is based on the premise that risk of an increase or decrease in value of the residual is an incident of the lessor's ownership and that he should, therefore, bear this risk.

P. Coogan, Leases of Equipment and Some Other Unconventional Security Devices: An Analysis of UCC Section 1-207(37) and Article 9, 1973 Duke L.J. 909, 966-967. For other IRS tests, see Rev. Rul. 55-540, 1955-2 Cum. Bull. 39; Rev. Proc. 75-21, 26 C.F.R. §601.201 (1975). The same issue comes up when books must be maintained:

> From an accounting point of view, the true lease has had the advantage to the lessee of providing him with "off balance sheet financing." That is to say, the lease obligates him to pay rent and not to buy goods. Accordingly, the leased property is not shown as an asset on the lessee's balance sheet, and, consistently, the obligation to pay rent is not listed as a liability. This treatment tends to improve the balance sheet ratios commonly used in determining the lessee's financial strength. Additionally, the obligations of a lessee under a true lease usually are not subject to restrictions on the amount

of money he may borrow contained in existing loan agreements, corporate charters and so forth.

W. Hawkland, The Proposed Amendments to Article 9 of the UCC—Part 5: Consignments and Equipment Leases, 77 Com. L.J. 108, 113 (1972). The tax/accounting tests tend to focus on the "intention of the parties" and on two other factors: (1) the "equity" the lessee builds in the leased property; and (2) the value of the property surrendered to the lessor at the end of the term.

Finally, for various statutory reasons, lessors fare better in bankruptcy than do sellers. See discussion in In re Grubbs Constr. Co., 319 B.R. 698 (Bankr. M.D. Fla. 2005).

The drafters of the Uniform Commercial Code deal with the issue in the complicated definition of "security interest" in §1-203. The drafters' task was to give some concrete guidance to the difference between a sale on credit disguised as a lease (security interest) and a true lease. Take a deep breath and wade through that definition now, with the hope that the following materials will make it seem less formidable than appears at first glance.

What are we to make of this definition? The happiest thing about it (despite its size) is that it does draw some bright lines to help attorneys distinguish leases from secured transactions:

1. If at the end of the lease period the lessee becomes the owner of the property for little or no consideration, a secured transaction and not a lease has been created.
2. If the contract contains a clause that permits the lessee to terminate the lease at any time and return the leased goods, a true lease has resulted. Such a right of termination is not an attribute of a sale of goods.
3. If the lease is for the entire economic life of the leased goods, with or without renewal, a disguised sale has occurred. This is sometimes called the *junk pile* test because goods that are worthless at the end of the lease are simply tossed out.

Other than that, each lease must be evaluated on its own. It does not necessarily answer the central question if the lessee pays consideration equal to or even greater than the fair market value of the leased goods as long as the lease does not cover the total economic life of the goods. Nor does the lessee's assumption of major duties (taxes, risk of loss, etc.) necessarily indicate either a lease or a sale of goods.

Use the definition and the above tests to answer the following Problem.

PROBLEM 296

BIG Machines, Inc., leased a duplicating machine to Connie's Print Shop. The lease was for five years, and the rental payments over this period exactly equaled the current market price of the machine. The lease contract further provided that at the end of the five years Connie's Print Shop could purchase the machine outright by paying BIG Machines $5. BIG Machines did not file an Article 9 financing statement. Thereafter Connie's Print Shop borrowed money from the Octopus National Bank and signed a security agreement with the bank granting it an interest in all of the print shop's "equipment." Octopus National duly perfected its security interest by filing a financing statement in the appropriate place. When Connie's Print Shop failed to repay the loan, Octopus National seized all the shop's equipment, including the duplicating machine. In the lawsuit Octopus National Bank v. BIG Machines, Inc., who gets the machine? Read §1-201(b)(35); see In re Price, 2017 WL 4119031 (Bankr. E.D.N.C. 2017) (agreement to pay one dollar at end of lease to regain possession was nominal and indicated a secured sale had taken place); In re Lasting Impressions Landscape Contractors, Inc., 2017 WL 4127833 (Bankr. D. Md. 2017) (likely a secured sale, not a true lease, where "only a fool would fail to exercise the purchase option").

Gibraltar Financial Corp. v. Prestige Equipment Corp.

Supreme Court of Indiana, 2011
949 N.E.2d 314

SULLIVAN, Justice.

The parties to this lawsuit claim rights to a punch press used in the manufacturing business of now-defunct Vitco Industries, Inc. Gibraltar Financial Corp. holds a perfected security interest in Vitco's tangible and intangible property, including its equipment. The other parties claim that the security interest does not cover the press because the press was not Vitco's equipment; rather, it had been leased to Vitco by Key Equipment Finance, Inc. We find that genuine issues of material fact exist regarding whether the press was leased.

BACKGROUND

Vitco Industries, Inc., was a manufacturer of porcelain enameled goods in Napanee, Indiana. In April, 2004, Vitco paid $243,000 for a punch press to use in its business. Roughly eight months later, in December, 2004, Vitco entered into a transaction with Key Equipment Finance, Inc. ("Finance"), in which Finance paid Vitco the same amount, $243,000, and Finance and

Vitco executed a contract under which Vitco was entitled to use the punch press in exchange for monthly payments. Finance and Vitco called this contract a "Master Lease Agreement," which we will refer to in this opinion as the "Lease." Consistent with the lease nomenclature, Finance did not file a financing statement in connection with the transaction.

The Lease had the following terms:

- Term: Six years.
- Rent: $3,591.91 per month ($43,102.92 per annum).
- Net Lease Terms: Vitco was required to maintain insurance, pay all personal property taxes, bear all risk of loss, and perform all repairs and maintenance with regard to the press.
- Early Buyout Option ("EBO"): Vitco was entitled to buy the press after five years for $78,464.70 (32.29% of the total cost of the equipment), a price that the Lease recited represented "the parties['] present best estimate of the fair market value of the Equipment on the EBO Date determined by using commercially reasonable methods which are standard in the industry." Appellant's App. 121.
- End-of-Term Options: In the event Vitco did not exercise the EBO, Vitco was required to continue paying monthly rent during the sixth year (total of $43,102.92). At the end of the Lease's six-year term, Vitco could do one of four things:
  (1) buy the press for fair market value; or
  (2) renew the Lease for the fair market renewal rental value; or
  (3) continue the Lease month-to-month at the current monthly rental rate; or
  (4) return the press to Finance (in which case Vitco would pay for the press's removal and return to Finance, or Finance could attempt to sell the press directly from Vitco's facility).

For purposes of the End-of-Term Options, the Lease defined "fair market value" as "the Equipment's value as determined between Lessor and Lessee, based upon a price which would be obtained in an arm's-length transaction between an informed and willing lessor or seller . . . and an informed and willing lessee or buyer." Id. at 114.

Vitco never made it to the point where it could exercise the EBO or otherwise complete the terms of the Lease. By 2007, Vitco was no longer in business and had defaulted under the Lease.

Independent of its dealings with Finance, Vitco had entered into several loan agreements with Gibraltar Financial Corp. pursuant to which it had granted Gibraltar a security interest in virtually all of its tangible and intangible property, including its equipment. It is undisputed that Gibraltar perfected its security interest. In a separate lawsuit filed against Vitco in July,

2007, Gibraltar was awarded possession of the collateral in which it had a perfected security interest, including Vitco's equipment. Gibraltar sold that equipment and credited Vitco with the sale proceeds, but Vitco still owed Gibraltar almost $580,000.

In the meantime, Finance repossessed the press and sold it in July, 2007, for $160,000 to National Machinery Exchange, Inc. ("NME"), in a joint venture with Prestige Equipment Corp.

In May, 2008, Gibraltar filed this action against Prestige to recover the value of the press, alleging that Prestige had acquired the press subject to Gibraltar's security interest. A series of third-party complaints and amendments followed, as detailed in the margin. The parties agreed after a pretrial conference that the dispute turned on whether the Lease was a true lease (as argued by the Defendants) or a sale subject to a security interest (as argued by Gibraltar). The trial court granted summary judgment in favor of the Defendants after concluding that the Lease was a true lease.

The Court of Appeals affirmed the trial court's grant of summary judgment. Gibraltar Fin. Corp. v. Prestige Equip. Corp., 925 N.E.2d 751 (Ind. Ct. App. 2010). Gibraltar sought transfer to this Court, arguing, in part, that the decision of the Court of Appeals in this case conflicted with the prior decision of the Court of Appeals in Gangloff Industries, Inc. v. Generic Financing & Leasing Corp., 907 N.E.2d 1059 (Ind. Ct. App. 2009). We have granted transfer to reconcile any conflict between these two cases and to clarify Indiana law in distinguishing true leases from sales subject to security interests. . . .

DISCUSSION

I

Court decisions, treatises, and articles on commercial law are replete with declarations of the difficulty in distinguishing between "true" leases and sales subject to security agreements. For example, the court in the epic WorldCom bankruptcy case was forced to observe that though the concepts of lease and security agreement "are rather easily defined, the means to distinguish between them in a rigorous manner has often eluded the courts." WorldCom, Inc. v. Gen. Elec. Global Asset Mgmt. Servs. (In re WorldCom, Inc.), 339 B.R. 56, 64 (Bankr. S.D.N.Y. 2006). For their part, White and Summers say that whether a transaction in the form of a lease is characterized as a lease or a sale subject to a security interest is "one of the most frequently litigated issues under the Uniform Commercial Code." 4 James J. White & Robert S. Summers, Uniform Commercial Code 17 (6th ed. 2010).

Our review of the history of these disputes suggests that much of the difficulty arose under the pre-1987 version of the Uniform Commercial Code ("U.C.C."), a uniform law adopted in some version by all 50 states.

See In re Edison Bros. Stores, Inc., 207 B.R. 801, 809 n.7 (Bankr. D. Del. 1997) (noting that the U.C.C. has been adopted by all 50 states). The pre-1987 U.C.C. emphasized the subjective intent of the parties entering into a lease agreement at the time the agreement was made. The Official Comment to post-1987 U.C.C. §1-203 discusses this problem:

> Reference to the intent of the parties to create a lease or security interest led to unfortunate results. In discovering intent, courts relied upon factors that were thought to be more consistent with sales or loans than leases. Most of these criteria, however, were as applicable to true leases as to security interests. . . . Accordingly, [the 1987 revision of the U.C.C.] contains no reference to the parties' intent.

U.C.C. §1-203 cmt. 2 (2001) (formerly U.C.C. §1-201(37)), 1 U.L.A. 28 (2004).

The parties agree that this dispute is governed by Colorado law. Two sections of the U.C.C. as adopted by Colorado are applicable here. First, the Colorado U.C.C. defines the term "lease" as follows:

> "Lease" means a transfer of the right to possession and use of goods for a term in return for consideration, but a sale, including a sale on approval or a sale or return, or retention or creation of a security interest is not a lease. . . .

Colo. Rev. Stat. §4-2.5-103(j) (2010). The key thing to note about this definition is that it specifies that a transaction creating a lease and a transaction retaining or creating a security interest are mutually exclusive. E. Carolyn Hochstadter Dicker & John P. Campo, FF & E and the True Lease Question: Article 2A and Accompanying Amendments to UCC Section 1-201(37), 7 Am. Bankr. Inst. L. Rev. 517, 521 (1999).

Colorado has adopted the following provision of the U.C.C. that sets forth rules for distinguishing a transaction creating a lease and a transaction retaining or creating a security interest: [The court quoted §1-203.] . . .

II

Although Colorado §1-203(a) provides that "[w]hether a transaction in the form of a lease creates a lease or security interest is determined by the facts of each case," §1-203(b) dictates that if its specifications are met, the transaction will be deemed to have created a security interest. Thus, Colorado §1-203(b) provides that if its bright-line test is met, the issue is decided—the transaction has created a security interest and no further inquiry is required.

The bright-line test of §1-203(b) has two prongs which, if both satisfied, dictate that a transaction creates a security interest. The first prong is satisfied "if the consideration that the lessee is to pay the lessor for the right to possession and use of the goods is an obligation for the term of the lease and is not subject to termination by the lessee." Colo. Rev. Stat. §1-203(b). As one commentator has observed, this prong is satisfied if the lease "requires the lessee to make rental payments to the lessor 'come hell or high water.'" Dicker & Campo, supra, at 534 (footnote omitted).

The Defendants maintain that the Lease was subject to early termination by Vitco by virtue of Vitco being able to terminate the lease by exercising the EBO. But the Court of Appeals rejected this argument, pointing out that a termination clause differs from a buyout clause. *Gibraltar*, 925 N.E.2d at 755-56. We agree with the Court of Appeals and its analysis on this point—the consideration Vitco was obligated to pay was an obligation for the term of the lease and was not subject to termination by Vitco. Thus, the first prong of the bright-line test is satisfied.

The second prong of the bright-line test of §1-203(b) is satisfied if any one of the four "Residual Value Factors" listed in §1-203(b)(1) through (4) are found to exist. In re QDS Components, Inc., 292 B.R. 313, 332 & n.9 (Bankr. S.D. Ohio 2002). Gibraltar acknowledges that the first three factors do not apply to the Lease. Appellant's Br. 18. But it contends that the fourth factor does, arguing that the Lease provided Vitco with "an option to become the owner of the goods for no additional consideration or for nominal additional consideration upon compliance with the [Lease]." Colo. Rev. Stat. §4-1-203(b)(4). If so, both prongs of the bright-line test would be satisfied and the transaction would have created a security interest.

As discussed under Background, supra, the Lease gave Vitco two opportunities to become the owner of the punch press—at the end of the Lease and upon exercise of the EBO.

At the end of the Lease, Vitco had the right to purchase the press for its "fair market value"; no specific amount was provided. Did this provision give Vitco the right to buy the press "for no additional consideration or for nominal additional consideration"?

The statute provides that "[a]dditional consideration is not nominal if: . . . the price is stated to be the fair market value of the goods determined at the time the option is to be performed." 322 Colo. Rev. Stat. §4-1-203(d)(2).

The price "stated" for Vitco to purchase the press at the end of the lease was its "fair market value," in so many words, and so the consideration in this circumstance was not nominal. As such, the provisions of the end-of-term option did not cause the transaction to create a security interest.

The provisions of the EBO, however, were quite different. Under the EBO, Vitco had the right to buy the press after five years for the specific amount of $78,464.70. And as described in Background, supra, the Lease did declare that the parties agreed that this amount represented their best estimate of what the fair market value of the equipment would be on the EBO date. The Defendants argue that this language had the effect of "stat[ing]" that Vitco could purchase for fair market value within the meaning §1-203(d)(2). For the same reason the provisions of the end-of-term option did not cause the transaction to create a security interest, the Defendants contend, so too for the EBO.

The Court of Appeals rejected this contention, holding that "the EBO applie[d] a fixed price [(the $78,000 amount)] to the value of the Punch Press rather than permitting the price to be determined at the time the option [was] to be performed." *Gibraltar,* 925 N.E.2d at 757. The Court of Appeals was correct in concluding that for §1-203(d)(2) to operate, the fair market value of the goods must be determined at the time the option is to be performed. But, at the same time, §1-203(e) directs that " 'reasonably predictable' . . . fair market value . . . shall be determined with reference to the facts and circumstances at the time the transaction is entered into." Even if we were to conclude, reading these two provisions together, that fair market value could be specified in advance under the Fair Market Value Test, we think that for the Defendants to be entitled to summary judgment on this point, they were required to set forth material facts demonstrating that the $78,000 price constituted the expectations of Vitco and Finance at the time the transaction was entered into as to what the fair market value of the punch press would be on the EBO date.

Except for the recitation in the contract itself, there was no evidence presented to the trial court of the expectations of Vitco and Finance at the time the transaction was entered into as to what the fair market value of the punch press would be on the EBO date. There was evidence presented by Gibraltar's expert that the value of the press near the time of the EBO date was at least $100,000. Appellant's App. 229. And there was evidence that after Vitco's default, Finance sold the press for $160,000 approximately two-and-a-half years after the Lease was executed. Id. at 110. While these facts are not relevant to establishing the expectations of Vitco and Finance at the time the transaction was entered into, they are enough to keep us from crediting the contract recitation alone as reflecting the parties' actual expectations. We agree with the Court of Appeals that Finance failed to establish that the $78,000 EBO price is not nominal under the Fair Market Value Test.

While the Court of Appeals did not find §1-203(d)(2) applicable here, it came to the ultimate conclusion that Vitco did not have an option to become the owner of the punch press for only nominal additional consideration upon compliance with the EBO. It reached this result by applying the test embodied in the first sentence of §1-203(d)—referred to in the cases as the "Option Price/Performance Cost Test"—and concluding that the $78,000 price was greater than Vitco's reasonably predictable cost of performing if the EBO was not exercised. *Gibraltar,* 925 N.E.2d at 756-57 (citing *In re QDS Components,* 292 B.R. at 335). We agree. Had Vitco declined to exercise the EBO, it would have been required to pay an additional approximately $43,000 in rent. The only evidence in the record indicates that the cost to return the punch press would have equaled approximately $19,500, although that figure was not estimated at the time the parties entered into the agreement. Appellant's App. 228. In any event, the $78,000 price is not less than even the sum of these two amounts and, therefore, not nominal within the meaning of §1-203(d). *Gibraltar,* 925 N.E.2d at 757; see also *In re QDS Components,* 292 B.R. at 335-340 (detailing the proper method of applying the "Option Price/Performance Cost Test" of §1-203(d)).

To review, we have applied the objective, bright-line test of §1-203(b) and concluded that the Lease did not create a security interest per se. Even though it was not subject to termination by Vitco, compliance with the Lease required Vitco to pay more than nominal consideration to become the owner of the press. This is because the $78,000 EBO price was not less than Vitco's reasonably predictable cost of performance under the Lease had the EBO not been exercised within the meaning of the Option Price/Performance Cost Test of §1-203(d).

III

A

Under the objective, bright-line test of §1-203(b), the Lease did not create a security interest per se. But because §1-203(a) provides "[w]hether a transaction . . . creates a lease or security interest is determined by the facts of each case," the facts of this case may nevertheless dictate that the Lease did create a security interest. *In re WorldCom,* 339 B.R. at 70; Sankey v. ABCO Leasing, Inc. (In re Sankey), 307 B.R. 674, 680 (Bankr. D. Alaska 2004) (citing *In re QDS Components,* 292 B.R. at 333).

If a court finds that a transaction did not create a security interest per se, it must then "consider the economic reality of the transaction in order to determine . . . whether the transaction is more fairly characterized as a lease or a secured financing arrangement." Duke Energy Royal, LLC v. Pillowtex Corp. (In re Pillowtex), 349 F.3d 711, 719 (3d Cir. 2003). Unfortunately, the U.C.C. does not provide any explicit test or methodology for assessing the economic reality of the transaction. As a result, the cases contain a plethora of formulations and approaches which we will briefly survey.

The majority of courts and commentators recite that the principal inquiry in this regard is "'whether the lessor has retained a *meaningful reversionary interest* in the goods.'" *In re WorldCom,* 339 B.R. at 71 (emphasis in original) (citation omitted). However, again, the U.C.C. does not provide for assessing whether a lessor has retained a "meaningful reversionary interest." *In re QDS Components*, 292 B.R. at 341. Nevertheless, the *WorldCom* court explained the rationale for the "meaningful reversionary interest" test as follows:

> If the lessor does not possess a meaningful reversionary interest, the lessor has no interest in the economic value or remaining useful life of the goods, and therefore the lessor transferred title to the goods, in substance if not in form. In other words, the parties did not create a lease where the putative lessor does not have the interest, the entrepreneurial stake, in the goods that a true lessor would have.

339 B.R. at 72. But as the *WorldCom* court itself acknowledged, this reasoning by itself is "circular." Id. In point of fact, the absence of any accepted method of determining whether a meaningful reversionary interest exists renders such a determination more a statement of conclusion—that the transaction is a lease—than a method of analysis.

For its part, the Court of Appeals recognized that the cases provide no " 'consistent set of factors for identifying a lessor's residual interest.' " *Gibraltar*, 925 N.E.2d at 758 (quoting In re Gateway Ethanol, L.L.C., 415 B.R. 486, 504 (Bankr. D. Kan. 2009)). Following the *Gateway* court, it "decline[d] to apply a laundry list of factors identified by other courts [and instead focused] on the economic factors of the Lease."[2]

In sorting through these various formulations, we first conclude that the U.C.C. has rejected the laundry list approach in an apparent effort to "overrule a series of bad decisions under the pre-1987 version of section 1-201(37)." 4 White & Summers, supra, at 30. This was done because many of the factors considered under the old approach were just as applicable to true leases as they were to security interests. *Kimco Leasing*, 656 N.E.2d at 1218 n.15; *In re QDS Components*, 292 B.R. at 326.

Nonetheless, the U.C.C. does not explicitly prohibit consideration of these factors. Rather, it provides that "[a] transaction in the form of a lease does not create a security interest *merely because*" of the presence of any

2. Similar to the Court of Appeals in this case, the Indiana Tax Court has rejected the "laundry list" approach and instead identified two considerations in determining whether the lessor retained a meaningful residual interest: "1) whether the lease contains an option to purchase for no or nominal consideration, and 2) whether the lessee develops equity in the leased property such that the only sensible decision economically for the lessee is to exercise the purchase option." Kimco Leasing, Inc. v. State Bd. of Tax Comm'rs, 656 N.E.2d 1208, 1218 & n.15 (Ind. Tax Ct. 1995); see also *In re QDS Components*, 292 B.R. at 342-43 (noting that California law considers similar factors). We note that the first consideration duplicates the second prong of the bright-line test contained in §1-203(b)(4). See *In re QDS Components*, 292 B.R. at 343 n.20 (noting the redundancy in considering the nominality of the option price a second time in the meaningful-residual-interest analysis).

one or more of the six factors. Colo.Rev.Stat. § 1–203(c)(1)–(6) (emphasis added). Indeed, the Court of Appeals in Gangloff Industries, Inc. v. Generic Financing & Leasing, Corp. relied on this language in concluding that certain factors were not prohibited from consideration. 907 N.E.2d at 1066 n.8; see also In re WorldCom, 339 B.R. at 71 (noting that the factors are "characterized as not sufficient alone to establish that a security interest has been created." . . . Leading scholars, on the other hand, have opined that with the exception of the first,[3] the conditions are not only "not enough," but are simply not relevant in distinguishing between true leases and security interests. 4 White & Summers, supra, at 33.

B

To be entitled to summary judgment, the Defendants bear the burden of demonstrating the absence of any genuine issue of material fact as to whether the economic realities of the transaction dictate that it is a lease as a matter of law. Ind. Trial Rule 56(C). The Court of Appeals concluded that the Defendants were entitled to summary judgment because Finance had retained a meaningful reversionary interest in the punch press. This was so, according to the Court of Appeals, primarily because the equipment would still have had significant value had Vitco decided to return it at the end of the six-year Lease. It reached this conclusion because the useful life of the punch press was apparently fifteen to twenty years. *Gibraltar*, 925 N.E.2d at 758.

The putative lessor in the *Pillowtex* case made a similar argument. In that case, the Third Circuit found

> that under certain circumstances, the fact that transferred goods have a useful life extending beyond the term of the transferring agreement could reveal the transferor's expectation of retaining residual value in those goods. Such an inference would only be proper, however, where the evidence showed a plausible intent by the transferor to repossess the goods.

In re Pillowtex, 349 F.3d at 720. In *Pillowtex,* the court found no likelihood that the transferor would repossess the fixtures in question because their removal would have been prohibitively expensive. Id. at 720-21. That is certainly not the situation with the punch press. But *Pillowtex*'s analysis does lead us to conclude that the punch press's useful life extending beyond

3. The first condition considers the amount of rent the lessee is required to pay as compared to the fair market value of the goods at the time the lease is entered into. Colo. Rev. Stat. §1-203(c)(1). We agree with these scholars that the exclusion of the first condition is "puzzling" because "[n]ormally one would assume that when [the first condition] is met the parties have a secured sale, not a lease." 4 White & Summers, supra, at 30-31.

the term of the Lease does not by itself establish that the transaction was a true lease.

C

In the end, we "focus on economics." U.C.C. §1-203 cmt. 2 (2001), 1 U.L.A. 29 (2004). This includes "all the economic factors which drove the transaction and which were the prime impetus to the ultimate decision to enter into the transaction and the reasons for structuring the transaction as it was done." Am. President Lines, Ltd. v. Lykes Bros. Steamship Co., Inc. (In re Lykes Bros. Steamship Co., Inc.), 196 B.R. 574, 580 (Bankr. M.D. Fla. 1996); see, e.g., United Airlines, Inc. v. HSBC Bank USA, N.A., 416 F.3d 609, 617 (7th Cir. 2005) (finding as determinative the measure for rent, the presence of a balloon payment, the effect of prepayment, and the lessee already having the asset and using it for an extension of credit); Kentuckiana Med. Ctr. LLC v. The Leasing Group Pool II, LLC (In re Kentuckiana Med. Ctr. LLC), No. 10-93039-BHL-11, 2011 Bankr. LEXIS 1702, 2011 WL 1750769, at *7 (Bankr. S.D. Ind. May 6, 2011) (noting that the leases were structured in such a way as to make lessee's cost of returning the collateral exceed the cost of purchasing it); In re Grubbs Constr. Co., 319 B.R. 698, 720 (Bankr. M.D. Fla. 2005) (noting the key factor for entering into the transaction was the effective interest rate charged for financing); *Gangloff Indus.*, 907 N.E.2d at 1065 (citing evidence that consideration was based on the price plus interest divided by months). Other factors may include, but are not limited to, the total amount of rent required of the lessee, whether the lessee acquired equity or any pecuniary interest in the goods, the useful life of the goods, the practical limitations on the lessee's ability to remove and return the leased goods, and the ability of the lessor to market the equipment. In re Uni Imaging Holdings, LLC, 423 B.R. 406, 418-20 (Bankr. N.D.N.Y. 2010) (citing *In re Gateway Ethanol*, 415 B.R. at 505); *In re WorldCom*, 339 B.R. at 74; *In re Grubbs* Constr. Co., 319 B.R. at 718-721.

At least some of these factors are present in this case. Pointing toward the transaction creating a security interest is the fact that Vitco already owned the punch press when it entered into the Lease with Finance (and it may have used it as security for an extension of credit). Pointing toward the transaction creating a lease are the useful life of the punch press, the absence of limitations on its removal, and the ability of Finance to market it.

What we are not able to determine, however, is whether the payment provisions of the Lease are more indicative of a lease or of a secured financing arrangement. We know that the purchase price of the press at the time of the transaction was $243,000. We know that Vitco had the option of purchasing it after five years for a total outlay of roughly $294,000 (60 monthly payments of $3,591.91 plus the EBO price of $78,464.70). And we know that if Vitco had not exercised the EBO, it would have been required to make twelve additional monthly payments totaling $43,102.92 (a total outlay of roughly $259,000), and thereafter it could have purchased the punch press for its then-appraised value.

The economics of the transaction can certainly be cast to demonstrate a lease: The parties agreed that Vitco would lease the punch press for 72 months at $3,592 per month with an option to buy at fair market value at the end. Under this approach, the EBO is an aside—an agreement as to the option price if Vitco wanted to exercise the option after 60 months.

On the other hand, the economics could also be cast to demonstrate a sale subject to a security interest: Vitco agreed to buy the punch press for $294,000 with 60 monthly payments of $3,592 plus a balloon payment of $78,000. Under this approach, the language regarding the sixth year was mere surplusage—paying the $78,000 was the only economically sensible course for Vitco to take.

A bankruptcy case discussed by both sides in their briefs illustrates this point. In that case, a construction company had entered into several equipment leases. In re Grubbs Constr. Co., 319 B.R. at 698. Under the leases' early buyout options, the "price was determined in advance and in no way depended on a future valuation." Id. at 720-721. In holding that the equipment leases had created security interests, the court found that "the only economically sensible course for [the company], absent default, was to exercise the Early Buyout Option" and acquire the equipment. Id. at 721.

As the movants for summary judgment, the Defendants had the burden of establishing the absence of any genuine issue of material fact as to the economic realities of the transaction dictating that it was a lease as a matter of law. To do so required evidence of the expectations of Vitco and Finance at the time the transaction was entered into as to such factors as the value of the punch press on the EBO and lease expiration dates, the discount rate, and whether the "only economically sensible course" for Vitco would have been to exercise the EBO. We regret having to remand this case for further proceedings, but the authorities are clear that "[f]oresight not hindsight controls." 4 White & Summers, supra, at 33; see also *In re Uni Imaging Holdings*, 423 B.R. at 417 ("In determining whether 'additional consideration' is nominal, the Court is to examine the economic realities of the transaction and the expectations of the parties concerning the projected value of the equipment at the time they entered into the agreement. . . ." (citing *In re Gateway Ethanol*, 415 B.R. at 500)). We see no way of resolving this case without this evidence. Because such evidence was not presented, summary judgment was not appropriate.

CONCLUSION

For the foregoing reasons, the judgment of the trial court is reversed and the case is remanded for proceedings consistent with this opinion.

In close cases the advising attorney may wish to tell the lessor (or the alleged consignor in quasi-consignment problems) to play it safe and file a financing statement even if it is believed that a true lease/non-consignment has been created. This may create a danger, however, that the Article 9 filing is an admission (for tax/accounting purposes) that only a secured transaction is involved. To avoid this admission problem, the drafters gave us §9-505, which is a "fail-safe" provision, allowing the protective filing without it being in any way an admission that a secured transaction is intended.

IV. OTHER TRANSACTIONS

PROBLEM 297

When Mercy Hospital's administrators decided to build a new addition, they hired a general contractor named Crash Construction Co. and required it to get a surety to guaranty the performance of the construction job and the payment of all the workers and material suppliers (to avoid a mechanic's lien on the hospital). Standard Surety issued such a performance and payment bond covering Crash's obligation to Mercy Hospital. To finance the construction, Crash borrowed money from Octopus National Bank (ONB) and gave as collateral the right to collect the progress payments from Mercy Hospital as they came due. ONB duly filed an Article 9 financing statement. Halfway through the job, Crash went bankrupt, and Standard Surety had to finish and pay off the employees and suppliers. At this point, by virtue of the common law right to *subrogation* (the equitable right given to sureties to step into the legal shoes of persons they have paid), Standard Surety claimed a superior right to unpaid monies retained by Mercy Hospital, which were to be paid to Crash. ONB also claimed this fund, pointed to its filed security interest, and stated that Standard Surety's subrogation right was only an unfiled Article 9 security interest. Who should win? See New Mexico State Highway and Transp. Dept. v. Gulf Ins. Co., 996 P.2d 424 (N.M. App. 1999); Comment, Equitable Subrogation—Too Hardy a Plant to Be Uprooted by Article 9 of the UCC?, 1971 U. Pitt. L. Rev. 580.

V. EXCLUSIONS FROM ARTICLE 9

Read §9-109(c) and (d).

A. Federal Statutes

It is no surprise that the Uniform Commercial Code, a state statute, cannot displace federal law. From the way §9-109(c)(1) is worded, however, note that the UCC *does* apply to the extent that the federal statute does not answer the problem presented. See G. Gilmore, Security Interests in Personal Property, ch. 13 (1965) (hereinafter G. Gilmore); for a list of such statutes, see J. White & R. Summers, Uniform Commercial Code (6th ed. 2010) [hereinafter White & Summers, a leading treatise on the meaning of the UCC] §22-11. With the exception of the federal tax lien statute, Internal Revenue Code §§6321-6325, most federal statutes (for example, the Ship Mortgage Act of 1920 and the Civil Aeronautics Act's provisions on security interests in aircraft) do not cover the field and are constantly supplemented by Article 9 provisions in litigation.

In United States v. Kimbell Foods, 440 U.S. 715 (1979), the Supreme Court decided that, as a matter of *federal* law, the relative priority of private consensual liens arising in favor of the U.S. government under various lending programs is to be decided under non-discriminatory state law (i.e., the UCC), unless a federal statute clearly provides otherwise.

For the practitioner, the important thing to remember is that certain matters must be researched on a federal as well as a state level. Ship mortgages, aircraft titles, railroad equipment, and some interstate commercial vehicles (such as trucks and buses registered with the Interstate Commerce Commission) are, in part, governed by federal statutes. Creditors (and their attorneys) who simply think an Article 9 filing will perfect their interest in, say, an airplane, end up as unsecured creditors whose only cause of action may be against their state-law–minded attorneys. See Feldman v. Chase Manhattan Bank, N.A., 368 F. Supp. 1327 (S.D.N.Y. 1974) (assignment of airplane lease with Article 9 filing not effective against bankruptcy trustee where creditor failed to file with FAA as required by Federal Aviation Act). Exciting efforts are under way to create an international registration system for rail, planes, and satellites, and some parts of the plan are already in place; see http://www.unidroit.org/work-in-progress-studies/studies/security-interests.

Further, certain federal statutes may void some security interests. Section 125 of the Truth in Lending Act, 15 U.S.C. §1635 (1980), for instance, destroys any security interest taken in a consumer's home as part of many credit transactions if the credit seller does not notify the consumer of a three-day right to rescind the contract (and supply the consumer with other truth-in-lending disclosures). This does not apply to first mortgage liens taken on the property.

Some federal statutes may be more friendly to creditors than Article 9. In one case Magnacom Wireless bought FCC radio spectrum licenses on credit, but was unable to pay the price when due. The FCC revoked the licenses and resold them, for $249 million more than Magnacom owed. Had Article 9 applied, Magnacom would have been entitled to the surplus, but under governing federal law, the FCC was entitled to keep the surplus. See In re Magnacom Wireless, LLC, 503 F.3d 984 (9th Cir. 2007).

NOTE ON INTELLECTUAL PROPERTY AS COLLATERAL

Strangely enough, there is great confusion as to whether security interests in various types of intellectual property are to be perfected under federal or state law. The federal trademark, patent, and copyright statutes all provide that security interests may be recorded in the relevant federal office (the U.S. Patent and Trademark Office or the Copyright Office). But none of the three statutes is clear on whether federal filing is required to perfect the security interest. Courts have reached a variety of conclusions on the issues. See In re Together Dev. Corp., 227 B.R. 439 (Bankr. D. Mass. 1998) (trademarks should be filed under Article 9); In re Cybernetic Services, Inc., 252 F.3d 1039 (9th Cir. 2001) (patents should be filed under Article 9); Rhone-Poulenc Argo, S.A. v. DeKalb Genetics Corp., 284 F.3d 1323 (Fed. Cir. 2002) (stating that federal filing would govern priority in patent rights); In re World Auxiliary Power Co., 303 F.3d 1120 (9th Cir. 2002) (security interest in *unregistered* copyrights should be filed under Article 9); In re Peregrine Entertainment, Ltd., 116 B.R. 194 (C.D. Cal. 1990) (security interest in *registered* copyrights should be filed in Copyright Office). The matter is of some real practical importance. If a UCC filing is all that is required, one filing in the name of the debtor will do it for all the intangible rights he/she owns; if a federal filing is necessary, it will have to be done for *each* patent, copyright, or trademark, a much more expensive undertaking. Cf. White & Summers §22-11.

PROBLEM 298

Pollution Solutions, Inc., took out a loan from Octopus National Bank (ONB), putting up as collateral its copyrights, patents, and trademarks. Where *should* ONB file to be sure it has a perfected security interest? No one knows where ONB *must* file to perfect its security interest, but the question here is slightly different. As a lawyer, what would you have your client do?

Philko Aviation, Inc. v. Shacket

United States Supreme Court, 1983
462 U.S. 406

Justice White delivered the opinion of the Court.

This case presents the question whether the Federal Aviation Act of 1958 (Act), 49 U.S.C. §§1301 et seq., prohibits all transfers of title to aircraft from having validity against innocent third parties unless the transfer has been evidenced by a written instrument, and the instrument has been recorded with the Federal Aviation Administration (FAA). We conclude that the Act does have such effect.

On April 19, 1978, at an airport in Illinois, a corporation operated by Roger Smith sold a new airplane to respondents. Respondents, the Shackets, paid the sale price in full and took possession of the aircraft, and they have been in possession ever since. Smith, however, did not give respondents the original bills of sale reflecting the chain of title to the plane. He instead gave them only photocopies and his assurance that he would "take care of the paperwork," which the Shackets understood to include the recordation of the original bills of sale with the FAA. Insofar as the present record reveals, the Shackets never attempted to record their title with the FAA.

Unfortunately for all, Smith did not keep his word but instead commenced a fraudulent scheme. Shortly after the sale to the Shackets, Smith purported to sell the same airplane to petitioner, Philko Aviation. According to Philko, Smith said that the plane was in Michigan having electronic equipment installed. Nevertheless, Philko and its financing bank were satisfied that all was in order, for they had examined the original bills of sale and had checked the aircraft's title against FAA records. At closing, Smith gave Philko the title documents, but, of course, he did not and could not have given Philko possession of the aircraft. Philko's bank subsequently recorded the title documents with the FAA.

After the fraud became apparent, the Shackets filed the present declaratory judgment action to determine title to the plane. Philko argued that it had title because the Shackets had never recorded their interest in the airplane with the FAA. Philko relied on §503(c) of the Act, 49 U.S.C. §1403(c), which provides that no conveyance or instrument affecting the title to any civil aircraft shall be valid against third parties not having actual notice of the sale, until such conveyance or other instrument is filed for recordation with the FAA. However, the District Court awarded summary judgment in favor of the Shackets, 497 F. Supp. 1262 (N.D. Ill. 1980), and the Court of Appeals affirmed, reasoning that §503(c) did not preempt substantive state law regarding title transfers, and that, under the Illinois Uniform Commercial Code, Ill. Rev. Stat., ch. 26, §§1-101 et seq., the Shackets had title but Philko did not. 681 F.2d 506 (CA7 1982). We granted certiorari, ____ U.S. ____ (1982), and we now reverse and remand for further proceedings.

Section 503(a)(1) of the Act, 49 U.S.C. §1403(a)(1), directs the Secretary of Transportation to establish and maintain a system for the recording of any "conveyance which affects the title to, or any interest in, any civil aircraft of the United States." Section 503(c), 49 U.S.C. §1403(c), states:

> No conveyance or instrument the recording of which is provided for by [§503(a)(1)] shall be valid in respect of such aircraft . . . against any person other than the person by whom the conveyance or other instrument is made or given, his heir or devisee, or any person having actual notice thereof, until such conveyance or other instrument is filed for recordation in the office of the Secretary of Transportation.

The statutory definition of "conveyance" defines the term as "a bill of sale, contract of conditional sale, mortgage, assignment of mortgage, or other instrument affecting title to, or interest in, property." 49 U.S.C. §1301(20) (Supp. V, 1981). If §503(c) were to be interpreted literally in accordance with the statutory definition, that section would not require every transfer to be documented and recorded, it would only invalidate unrecorded title *instruments,* rather than unrecorded title *transfers.* Under this interpretation, a claimant might be able to prevail against an innocent third party by establishing his title without relying on an instrument. In the present case, for example, the Shackets could not prove their title on the basis of an unrecorded bill of sale or other writing purporting to evidence a transfer of title to them, even if state law did not require recordation of such instruments, but they might still prevail, since Illinois law does not require written evidence of a sale "with respect to goods for which payment has been made and accepted or which have been received and accepted." Ill. Rev. Stat., ch. 26, §2-201(3)(c).

We are convinced, however, that Congress did not intend §503(c) to be interpreted in this manner. Rather, §503(c) means that every aircraft transfer must be evidenced by an instrument, and every such instrument must be recorded, before the rights of innocent third parties can be affected. Furthermore, because of these federal requirements, state laws permitting undocumented or unrecorded transfers are preempted, for there is a direct conflict between §503(c) and such state laws, and the federal law must prevail.

These conclusions are dictated by the legislative history. The Senate, House, and Conference committee reports, and the section-by-section analysis of one of the bill's drafters, all expressly declare that the federal statute "requires" the recordation of "every transfer of any interest in a civil aircraft." The Senate report explains: "This section requires the recordation with the Authority of every transfer made after the effective date of the section, of any interest in a civil aircraft of the United States. The conveyance evidencing *each such transfer* is to be recorded with an index in a recording system to be established by the Authority." Thus, since Congress intended to require the recordation of a conveyance evidencing *each transfer* of an interest in aircraft, Congress must have intended to preempt any state law under which a transfer without a recordable conveyance would be valid against innocent transferees or lienholders who have recorded.

Any other construction would defeat the primary congressional purpose for the enactment of §503(c), which was to create "a central clearing house for recordation of titles so that a person, wherever he may be, will know where he can find ready access to the claims against, or liens, or other legal interests in an aircraft." Hearings Before the House Comm. on Interstate and Foreign Commerce, 75 Cong., 3d Sess., 407 (April 1, 1938) (testimony of F. Fagg, Director of Air Commerce, Dept. of Commerce). Here, state law does not require any documentation whatsoever for a valid transfer of an aircraft to be effected. An oral sale is fully valid against third parties once the buyer takes possession of the plane. If the state law allowing this result were not preempted by §503(c), then any buyer in possession would have absolutely no need or incentive to record his title with the FAA, and he could refuse to do so with impunity, and thereby prevent the "central clearing house" from providing "ready access" to information about his claim. This is not what Congress intended.

In the absence of the statutory definition of conveyance, our reading of §503(c) would be by far the most natural one, because the term "conveyance" is first defined in the dictionary as "the action of conveying," i.e., "the act by which title to property . . . is transferred." Webster's Third New International Dictionary 499 (P. Gove ed. 1976). Had Congress defined "conveyance" in accordance with this definition, then §503(c) plainly would have required the recordation of every transfer. Congress' failure to adopt this definition is not dispositive, however, since the statutory definition is expressly not applicable if "the context otherwise requires." 49 U.S.C. §1301. Even in the absence of such a caveat, we need not read the statutory definition mechanically into §503(c), since to do so would render the recording system ineffective and thus would defeat the purpose of the legislation. A statutory definition should not be applied in such a manner. Lawson v. Suwannee S.S. Co., 336 U.S. 198, 201 (1949). Accordingly, we hold that state laws allowing undocumented or unrecorded transfers of interests in aircraft to affect innocent third parties are preempted by the federal Act.

In support of the judgment below, respondents rely on Matter of Gary Aircraft Corp., 681 F.2d 365 (CA5 1982), which rejected the contention that §503 preempted all state laws dealing with priority of interests in aircraft. The Court of Appeals held that the first person to record his interest with the FAA is not assured of priority, which is determined by reference to state law. We are inclined to agree with this rationale, but it does not help the Shackets. Although state law determines priorities, all interests must be federally recorded before they can obtain whatever priority to which they are entitled under state law. As one commentator has explained, "The only situation in which priority appears to be determined by operation of the [federal] statute is where the security holder has failed to record his interest. Such failure invalidates the conveyance as to innocent third persons. But recordation itself merely validates, it does not grant priority." Scott, Liens in Aircraft: Priorities, 25 J. Air L. & Com. 193, 203 (1958). Accord, Sigman, The Wild Blue Yonder: Interests in Aircraft Under Our Federal System, 46 So. Cal. L. Rev. 316, 324-325 (1973) (although recordation does not establish priority, "failure to record . . . serves to subordinate"); Note, 26 Wash. & Lee L. Rev. 205, 212-213 (1979).

In view of the foregoing, we find that the courts below erred by granting the Shackets summary judgment on the basis that if an unrecorded transfer of an aircraft is valid under state law, it has validity as against innocent third parties. Of course, it is undisputed that the sale to the Shackets was valid and binding as between the parties. Hence, if Philko had actual notice of the transfer to the Shackets or if, under state law, Philko failed to acquire or perfect the interest that it purports to assert for reasons wholly unrelated to the sale to the Shackets, Philko would not have an enforceable interest, and the Shackets would retain possession of the aircraft. Furthermore, we do not think that the federal law imposes a standard with which it is impossible to comply. There may be situations in which the transferee has used reasonable diligence to file and cannot be faulted for the failure of the crucial documents to be of record. But because of the manner in which this case was disposed of on summary judgment, matters such as these were not considered, and these issues remain open on remand. The judgment of the Court of Appeals is reversed, and the case is remanded for further proceedings consistent with this opinion.

So ordered.

NOTE

For the resolution of this case on retrial, see Shacket v. Philko Aviation, Inc., 841 F.2d 166 (7th Cir. 1988) (second purchaser, alas, still lost because of failure to investigate suspicious circumstances).

B. Landlord's Lien and Other Statutory Liens

Subsections (d)(1) and (2) of §9-109 exclude statutory liens (like the one in Problem 290) from Article 9; but what about the following situation?

PROBLEM 299

When Christopher Morley opened his bookshop, the landlord wanted security for the rent. They signed a lease agreement providing that all of the inventory (the books) would be subject to a lien in the landlord's favor and could be seized and sold if Christopher defaulted on the rent payments. Is the landlord's lien required to be perfected under Article 9? See Persky, Shapiro, Salim, Esper, Arnoff & Nolfi Co., L.P.A. v. Guyuron, 2000 WL 1867407 (Ohio App. 2000).

C. *Wage Assignments*

Claims to wages were once a fertile source of collateral, but special statutory regulation has all but killed off wage assignments. Thus, some states absolutely prohibit the assignment of future wages (see, e.g., Ala. Code tit. 39, §201; such assignments are *void*); some permit them in limited circumstances if the employer consents (see, e.g., Del. Code Ann. tit. 5, §2115; N.C. Gen. Stat. §95-31); and some states require the consent of both the employer and the spouse (see, e.g., Ind. Code §22-2-7). Employers always disliked having to bother with direct payments to an employee's creditors (and further disliked the idea that employees had little or no equity left in their own paychecks). The special statutes on the matter survive the enactment of Article 9; §9-109(d)(3).

PROBLEM 300

Carl Jugular was an independent insurance agent who sold policies for many companies, though his primary sales were the life and automobile policies of the Montana Insurance Association (MIA). In order to float a loan to buy a car, Carl gave the lending bank a security interest in "all present and future commissions earned or to be earned" from the MIA. Does Article 9 cover this assignment? See Massachusetts Mut. Life Ins. Co. v. Central Pa. Natl. Bank, 372 F. Supp. 1027 (E.D. Pa. 1974).

D. *Non-Financing Assignments*

The §9-109(d)(4) through (7) exclusions of some transfers of accounts, chattel paper, payment intangibles, and promissory notes are each meant to be an exclusion of all such assignments of a non-financing nature. See

G. Gilmore §10-5. Generally, as we have seen, such sales would be Article 9 matters, but in the listed situations no one would think to comply with Article 9, and the possibility of the deception of later parties is small.

PROBLEM 301

When David Vargo sold his lucrative art business to Manny Flowers, he sold not only all the tangible assets but his outstanding accounts receivables as well. Must the buyer take the steps required by Article 9 of a secured party? See §§9-102(a)(72)(D) and 9-109(d)(4). If Vargo received a commission to paint the portrait of the city's mayor but decided he was too busy to perform the task and (with the mayor's permission) transferred the job (and the right to the payment for it) to another artist, must the new artist take Article 9 steps? See §9-109(d)(6). When one of Vargo's clients refused to pay for a delivered painting, Vargo sold the account to Trash Collection Agency. Must Trash comply with Article 9? See §9-109(d)(5). Finally, pressed by his art supplies store for payment of his outstanding tab, Vargo transferred to the store the money due him from a client whose portrait he had painted the month before. Must the art supplies store take Article 9 steps? See §9-109(d)(7).

E. *Real Estate*

Except for fixtures, real estate security interests are not covered by Article 9, but what happens when the paperwork creating them (the mortgage and the promissory note the debtor signs) is used as security when the mortgagee seeks a loan?

PROBLEM 302

Local Loan Company (LLC) needed to borrow money, and Octopus National Bank agreed to loan it the requisite amount, taking into ONB's possession as collateral the real property mortgages and accompanying promissory notes given to LLC by its borrowers. Need ONB do anything either in the real property recording office or under the UCC's Article 9 to protect its interest in this collateral? Compare §9-109(d)(11) and (b); read Official Comment 7 to §9-109; see the helpful discussion in R. Bowmar, Real Estate Interests as Security Under the UCC: The Scope of Article Nine, 12 UCC L.J. 99 (1979); and see §§9-203(g) and 9-308(e). See Prime Fin. Servs. LLC v. Vinton, 279 Mich. App. 245, 260 (Mich. Ct. App. 2008). If the collateral consisted of contracts to sell real estate and receive payments, would Article 9 apply? See In re Blanchard, 819 F.3d 981 (7th Cir. 2016).

F. Other Exclusions

PROBLEM 303

Octopus National Bank issued Connie Consumer a credit card. As collateral for the credit card debts, ONB took a security interest in all items she purchased using the card, as well as in her personal checking account with the bank. Does Article 9 apply to the bank's rights in this account? See §9-109(d)(13).

Would Article 9 apply if she used her consumer bank account as collateral for a business loan? See §9-102(a)(26).

PROBLEM 304

Debtors assigned to Octopus National Bank "all sums recovered by Debtors, directly or indirectly," from their lawsuit against Meep Corporation for breach of a sales contract. Meep Corporation settled the lawsuit, and agreed to pay Debtors the claimed amount. Is the assignment subject to Article 9? See §9-109(d)(9). See Goldberg & Connolly v. New York Cmty. Bancorp, Inc., 565 F.3d 66 (2d Cir. 2009).

Section 9-109(d) lists some other items that are excluded from Article 9 coverage in whole or in part (insurance, certain tort claims, etc.). We will consider these matters as they arise in other contexts.

CHAPTER 20 ASSESSMENT: MULTIPLE CHOICE QUESTIONS

1. UCC Article 9 provides a comprehensive scheme for regulating security interests in personal property. To which of the following transactions would Article 9 apply?
   a. Pemulis Auto borrowed money from Wolters Bank, with the parties agreeing that Pemulis Auto's inventory, equipment, and accounts receivable would be collateral for the loan.
   b. Von Richthofen provided aerial photography services for Konstantin Farms, to guide irrigation and planting decisions. A state statute gave

Von Richthofen a lien on Konstantin "Farms'" crops, to secure payment for those services.
c. Williams Bank purchases the accounts receivable of Fitzherbert Spa, which are the debts owed by customers for spa services.
d. Turing, unable to sell his Enigma supercomputer on eBay, delivers it to a local electronics retailer. The parties agree that if the retailer sells the Enigma, they will split the proceeds, and if not Turing will take the Enigma back.
e. All of the above.

2. To which of the following transactions does Article 9 apply?
   a. Baldwin put up his house on Strivers Row as collateral for a loan from Empire Bank.
   b. Stewart used her life insurance policy as a security for a debt to Fateful Finance.
   c. Darrow, a lawyer, assigned a long-unpaid account receivable, for collection to Persistent Servicing.
   d. Cannon leased a car for a day.
   e. None of the above.

3. Sasha had a samovar, which had been in the family several generations. He took it to Karl's Konsignments, who agreed to attempt to sell it on Sasha's behalf, for a percentage. Not long after, Karl's Konsignments went into bankruptcy. If Article 9 applied, as we will see in later chapters, that means Sasha would lose the samovar to the bankruptcy trustee. Did Article 9 apply?
   a. Yes. Article 9 applies to consignments.
   b. No. This transaction did not fit in the Article 9 definition of consignments, because it was a consignment of consumer goods.
   c. No. Sasha did not borrow money from Karl's Konsignments.
   d. No. Karl's Konsignments did not borrow money from Sasha.

4. Pemulis Auto offers to sell Lloyd, an Uber driver, a Somme Sedan for a down payment of $1,000, along with 36 monthly payments of $400. Lev likes those terms, but would prefer a lease, on the theory that he could deduct the lease payments as a business expense. So Pemulis Auto offers a Lease Agreement, under which Lloyd ("Lessee") pays down $1,000 and is obliged to make 36 monthly lease payments of $400 to Pemulis Auto ("Lessor"), and then will have an option to purchase the car for $1. The Lease Agreement further provides that if Lev fails to make the payments, Pemulis Auto may repossess the car. Lev signs and hands over $1,000. Pemulis Auto signs the papers to have the car registered in Lloyd's name and reminds him to get insurance on the car. Is the transaction subject to Article 9?

a. No. It is a lease, not a secured loan, consignment, sale of accounts, or agricultural lien.
b. Yes. In substance, the transaction is a sale of the car on credit, with the car serving as collateral.
c. No. Article 9 does not apply to cars, which are regulated by Lemon laws and the like.
d. No. Article 9 does not apply to true leases, and the parties have drafted an agreement using only lease terminology.

5. Chang Equipment was negotiating a one-year loan of $50,000 at 10 percent interest from Nightflyer Finance, putting up equipment worth $120,000 as collateral. Nightflyer wished to avoid the complexities of debtor-creditor law. Creatively, the parties crafted the following transaction. Chang Equipment agreed to sell the equipment to Nightflyer for $50,000, although Chang Equipment retained use of the equipment. In one year, Chang has the option to buy the equipment back for $55,000. If it does not buy the equipment back, Nightflyer gets the equipment. Does Article 9 apply to the transaction?
   a. Yes. The transaction, in substance if not form, is a secured loan.
   b. No. The transaction is a sale of equipment with an option to buy back, with no debt or collateral.
   c. No. The transaction is a true lease.
   d. No. Article 9 applies only to consumer transactions.

ANSWERS

1. *E* is the best answer. Section 9-109 states the transactions to which Article 9 applies. Answer *A* is a classic secured transaction, a party agrees to use personal property as collateral for a debt, covered by §9-109(a). But §9-109 makes Article 9 apply more broadly, to transactions that also raise issues common to secured transactions. *B* is an agricultural lien, therefore covered by §9-109(b). *C* is a sales of accounts, within §9-109(c). Even though that is not a secured transaction, it is brought within Article 9 in order to require Williams Bank to comply with the protections that Article 9 provides, such as notice to other creditors (thereby avoiding the secret lien of Benedict v. Ratner). *D* is a consignment. This transaction is also not a secured transaction. The retailer is not borrowing money and the Enigma is not collateral. But the hazard of the secret lien still exists: the retailer's creditors might not realize that the Enigma does not belong to the retailer. Bringing such consignments within Article 9 means that Turing will (as later chapters will discuss) need to file a UCC financing statement to maintain priority in the Enigma, should other creditors go after the Enigma or should the retailer file bankruptcy.

2. *E* is the best answer. This question gives some of the transactions excluded from Article 9 by §9-109. There was already well-established law dealing with mortgages, so Article 9 excludes transactions where the collateral is real estate. Insurance as collateral is specifically excluded. Although assignments of accounts generally are made subject to Article 9, some assignments are excluded because the protections of Article 9 are not necessary. The assignment of an account for collection is excluded. That is not an assignment of which Darrow's creditors need notice. True leases are not secured transactions, although a lease that has the effect of a secured transaction is within Article 9. A one-day car rental is a true lease, not a disguised secured transaction.
3. *B* is the best answer. Article 9 generally applies to consignments, but its definition of consignment excludes various consignments to which the policy of giving notice to creditors is weaker. See §9-102(20). The definition excludes consignments where the consignor and consignee have the same name (so creditors would likely not be affected), where the consignee is an auctioneer (whose creditors would not expect to go after the goods the auctioneer sells for others), or where the creditors know the consignee generally takes goods on consignments (and so the creditor do not need notice of that fact). It also excludes consignments of less than $1,000 in value and excludes consignments (as in this question) of consumer goods, because we do not expect consumers to know about Article 9 and comply with it.
4. *B* is the best answer. Article 9 applies to "a transaction, regardless of its form, that creates a security interest in personal property or fixtures by contract." §9-109(a). Regardless of the legal form used (lease, sale, trust, assignment, etc.), Article 9 will apply if the substance of the transaction is that personal property is used as collateral for an obligation. Here, the form of the transaction was a lease, but the substance was a secured sale. The business deal was that Lev was obliged to pay for the car and was entitled to keep it, subject to Pemulis Auto's right of repossession in the event of default. In substance, that is a sale of a car on credit, with the car serving as collateral. It was not a true lease, contrary to *D*. *C* is misleading. Other laws apply to cars, but they do not displace Article 9.
5. *A* is the best answer. The transaction is just the secured loan under another name. The terms are the same: Nightflyer hands over $50,000 and in one year Chang Equipment pays $55,000 or loses its equipment. *C* and *D* are red herrings. Although the parties used only sales terms, the substance governs over form, contrary to *B*.

   What difference does it make that Article 9 applies? The following chapters will tell, but here is a preview. Article 9 requires that Nightflyer Finance would have to file a UCC financing statement to give constructive notice to the world of its security interest in the equipment. If Nightflyer

Finance does not do so, it will lose its right to the collateral if Chang Equipment goes into bankruptcy, or sells the equipment, or is faced with a judgment creditor after the equipment. In addition, Article 9 limits the rights of a creditor on default. Nightflyer Finance would not be entitled to simply keep the equipment (worth $120,000) if Chang Equipment did not make its payments (of $55,000). Article 9 imposes other rules that Nightflyer Finance might violate if it does not realize that Article 9 applies. This chapter, then, introduces an important skill for any lawyer that deals with transactions, whether negotiating, closing, or litigating them. A lawyer must recognize whether Article 9 applies, irrespective of the business terms the parties use, and protect her client accordingly.

CHAPTER 21

THE CREATION OF A SECURITY INTEREST

The client tells the attorney, "Protect my interest in the collateral," and that instruction triggers the rules of this chapter. The attorney immediately begins thinking about how the law classifies this collateral and what steps are required to make sure the client's interest will prevail over other claimants to the property. It is easy to make mistakes at this stage and create very unhappy clients.

I. CLASSIFYING THE COLLATERAL

Article 9 divides *collateral* (defined in §9-102(a)(12)) into many different categories:

Goods (read §9-102(a)(44); cf. §2-105):
Consumer Goods (read §9-102(a)(23));
Equipment (read §9-102(a)(33));
Farm Products (read §9-102(a)(34)); and
Inventory (read §9-102(a)(48)).

Quasi-Tangible Property (pieces of paper used as collateral):
Instruments (read §§9-102(a)(47) and 3-104).[1]
Investment Property (stocks and bonds and rights to accounts containing same) (read §9-102(a)(49));
Documents (warehouse receipts and bills of lading) (read §§9-102(a)(30) and 1-201(b)(16));
Chattel Paper (read §9-102(a)(11)); and
Letter of Credit Rights (read §9-102(a)(51)).

Intangible Property (property having no significant physical form):
Accounts (read §9-102(a)(2));
Commercial Tort Claims (read §9-102(a)(13));
Deposit Accounts (read §9-102(a)(29));
General Intangibles (read §9-102(a)(42));
Health-Care–Insurance Receivables (read §9-102(a)(46)—these are a subcategory of "accounts"); and
Payment Intangibles (read §9-102(a)(61)—these are a subcategory of "general intangibles").

Note that *equipment* is defined not according to its usual meaning but rather as a catchall category for any goods that do not fit into the other three goods categories. Similarly, *general intangibles* include all intangible collateral not falling into another category.

Classification of the collateral is central because many provisions of Article 9 make legal distinctions based on the type of collateral. For example, the technical steps required to *perfect* a security interest in a negotiable instrument, a family car, or a hardware store's inventory are completely different, as we shall explore when we address the issue of perfection.

It is important to note that it is the *debtor's* announced use of the collateral that determines its classification.

PROBLEM 305

Fill in the blanks with the proper classifications of these items of collateral:

(a) A professional pianist's piano: ______________ (see In re Symons, 1967 WL 8983 (Ref. Bankr., E.D. Mich. 1967)).

1. Promissory notes, defined in §9-102(a)(65), are a subcategory of instruments.

(b) Cattle fattened by a farmer for sale: ____________ (see In re Cadwell, Martin Meat Co., 1970 WL 12561 (Ref. Bankr., E.D. Cal. 1970)); the farmer's tractor: ____________ (see Central Natl. Bank v. Wonderland Realty Corp., 38 Mich. App. 76, 195 N.W.2d 768 (1972)); the farmer's chickens: ____________ (see United States v. Pete Brown Enter., Inc., 328 F. Supp. 600 (N.D. Miss. 1971)); manure from the dairy herd: ____________ (see Miller, Farm Collateral Under the UCC: "Those Are Some Mighty Tall Silos, Ain't They Fella?" 20 S.D. L. Rev. 514, 526 (1975)).

(c) A mobile home: ____________ (compare §9-102(a)(53)).

(d) A right to sue someone for breach of contract: ____________ (see Friedman, Lobe & Block v. C.L.W. Corp., 9 Wash. App. 319, 512 P.2d 769 (1973)); a right to sue someone for negligence arising out of an automobile accident: ____________ (see §9-109(d)(12)); a right to sue a corporation for wooing away a trusted employee: ____________ (see §9-102(a)(13)); a security interest in a lawsuit plaintiff has already won and that has been reduced to a settlement agreement: ____________ (see §9-109, Official Comment 15).

(e) Pencils and other stationery supplies used by Sears or a similar large retailer in its credit offices: ____________ (see §9-102, Official Comment 4(a), fourth paragraph).

(f) A liquor license: ____________ (see In re Chris-Don, Inc., 308 B.R. 214 (Bankr. D.N.J. 2004)); a right to the return of a security deposit held by a landlord: ____________ (see United States v. Samel Ref. Corp., 461 F.2d 941 (3d Cir. 1972)); a newspaper carrier's right to payments for papers already delivered: ____________ ; a newspaper carrier's right to payments for papers to be delivered in the future: ____________.

(g) Curtains bought by a lawyer for the law office: ____________ (see In re Bonnema, 1967 WL 9011 (N.D. Ohio 1967)). What if after purchasing the curtains the lawyer decides to use them at home? Do they become consumer goods? See §9-507(b) and the next case; cf. In re McClain, 447 F.2d 241 (10th Cir. 1971).

(h) Aunt Augusta loaned her nephew $5,000 with an oral agreement he would repay the money the following year. If she wants to use this agreement as collateral, how would it be classified?

(i) Patents, trademarks, and copyrights: ____________ (see, e.g., Matter of Roman Cleanser, 43 B.R. 940 (Bankr. D. Mich. 1984)).

(j) Lottery winnings: ____________ (see Tex. Lottery Commn. v. First State Bank of DeQueen, 254 S.W.3d 677 (Tex. App. 2008)).

(k) Bitcoin: ____________ (see §1-201(a)(24), §9-102(2), (42), (49), (76)).

(l) Hay grown, raised, harvested, and packed in bales by farmer: ____________ (see In re Ollis, 2019 WL 1313397 (Bankr. D.S.C. 2019)).

In re Troupe

United States District Court, Western District of Oklahoma,
Bankruptcy Division, 2006
340 B.R. 86, 2006 WL 689515

T.M. Weaver, Chief Judge.

Presented by the parties' cross-motions for summary judgment is the issue of whether the debtors' tractor, in which the defendant has a purchase money security interest, is consumer goods under Article 9 of the UCC. If it is, the defendant's security interest is perfected even though the defendant did not file a financing statement. If not, the defendant's security interest is unperfected and subject to avoidance. Because of representations in the security agreement regarding the debtors' intended personal use of the tractor, and for the other reasons herein stated, the court concludes that the tractor is consumer goods and that the defendant has a perfected security interest.

The Chapter 7 Trustee (the "trustee" or "plaintiff") brought this action against the defendant (the "creditor" or "Deere") seeking to avoid Deere's security interest in the tractor pursuant to Sections 544, 549 and 550 of the Bankruptcy Code. The trustee contends that Deere's admitted failure to file a financing statement renders Deere's purchase money security interest unperfected. The trustee asserts that the tractor was used and intended to be used for business, rather than personal, purposes and thus was not consumer goods under Article 9. The defendant maintains that the debtors' primary intended and actual use of the tractor was for personal, family and household purposes and hence was consumer goods. The parties acknowledge that a purchase money security interest in consumer goods is perfected upon attachment, without filing a financing statement. Conversely, they agree that with respect to non consumer goods, the filing of a financing statement is required for perfection of a non-possessory purchase money security interest. . . .

Undisputed Facts

The following material facts are undisputed:

1. On September 24, 2004 (the "petition date"), the debtors filed their voluntary Chapter 7 bankruptcy petition.

2. On the petition date, Robert O. Troupe and Dawn Lynn Troupe (the "debtors") owned a 2001 John Deere 4300 MFWD tractor, with loader and blade (collectively, the "tractor").

3. The debtors purchased the tractor from Deere's dealer on or about July 13, 2001.

4. At the time of the purchase, the debtors lived on a 10-acre tract of land in Colorado.

5. Prior to the purchase of the tractor, the debtors applied for credit with Deere and submitted a credit application dated July 2, 2001.

6. The credit application signed by the debtors stated that the debtor Robert O. Troupe ("Robert") was not self-employed but was employed in a management position with an automotive company earning a gross salary of $4,500 per month. The credit application also stated that the debtor Dawn Lynn Troupe ("Dawn") was employed as a professional auto body estimator earning a gross income of $36,000 per year.

7. The debtors each worked at least 60 hours per week at their respective places of employment. Dawn testified on deposition that she worked approximately 75 hours per week at her job as an estimator and two other part-time jobs that she held at the same time.

8. Before purchasing the tractor, the debtors told the Deere's dealer's salesman that the debtors wanted to purchase a tractor to be used to fill irrigation ditches on their land. They also stated they wanted the tractor to be small enough to go through the gate of a horse stall. Dawn testified on deposition that she also represented to the salesman that they wanted to use the tractor for moving dirt, hay and snow.

9. Deere financed the debtors' purchase of the tractor. In connection with the financing, the debtors and Deere executed a security agreement by which the debtors granted to Deere a purchase money security interest in the tractor.

10. At the top of the first page of the executed security agreement, there were boxes labeled "Personal" and "Commercial," respectively. An "x" was placed in the box labeled "Personal," while the "Commercial" box was left blank.

11. The security agreement contained the following provision on the first page:

> Unless I otherwise certify below, this is a consumer credit transaction and the Goods will be used primarily for personal, family or household purposes. (bold type on security agreement)

12. The security agreement also contained on the first page a conspicuous rectangular box running the entire width of the printed page within which appeared the following:

> COMMERCIAL PURPOSE AFFIDAVIT. I/We being first duly sworn, affirm and represent to Seller and its assignees that this is a commercial credit transaction, as the Goods listed above will be used by the undersigned in his/her/its business primarily for commercial purposes and will not be used primarily for personal, family or household use.
>
> Buyer's (Debtor's) Signature Buyer's (Debtor's) Signature

The above signature lines were left blank.

13. The purchase price of the tractor was $16,539.00.

14. At the time of their purchase of the tractor, and for the several years thereafter, the debtors boarded horses and raised cattle and pigs on their acreage. This activity was done while they were working at their full-time jobs.

15. The debtors testified that they intended their farming and ranching activity on their acreage to be profitable financially.

16. On the debtors' tax returns for the years 2001, 2002 and 2003, the debtors took a deduction for depreciation on the tractor. The tax returns reflected that the tractor was used 100 percent for business.

17. The debtors' tax returns for each of the above years showed a substantial loss from ranching.

18. Marketing information on the website of the defendant shows the subject tractor to be in the category of residential equipment.

19. In their affidavits submitted in support of the trustee's motion for summary judgment, the debtors represented that their actual use and intended use of the tractor was for the business purpose of farming and ranching.

20. The debtors' deposition testimony is that the tractor was used 90 percent of the time for personal purposes and 10 percent for business. They considered personal use as being work performed on the homestead as opposed to work done to make a living.

Conclusions of Law and Discussion

This court has jurisdiction over this adversary proceeding pursuant to 28 U.S.C. §157, 1334 and 11 U.S.C. §544 and 550. This is a core proceeding under 28 U.S.C. §157(b)(2)(F).

The trustee brings this action asserting his rights under the "strong arm clause" of §544(a)(1). Under this provision, the trustee has the rights and powers of a hypothetical lien creditor who held a judicial lien on the property in question at the time of the commencement of the bankruptcy case, whether or not there actually is such a creditor. By exercising these rights, a trustee may avoid liens on property that a lien creditor without notice could avoid. Id.

In bankruptcy proceedings, state law governs issues of validity and priority of security interests [citing cases]. The parties do not dispute that Colorado law applies here. Under C.R.S. §4-9-317(a)(2), the holder of an unperfected security interest is subordinate to the rights of one who became a lien creditor before the security interest was perfected. A lien creditor includes a trustee in bankruptcy. C.R.S. §4-9-102(52). Thus, Deere must have held a perfected security interest to prevail over the trustee in bankruptcy. It is not disputed that if the tractor is classified as consumer goods under the UCC, Deere held a perfected purchase money security interest despite the fact that a financing statement was not filed. C.R.S. §4-9-309(1). If the tractor is not consumer goods, however, Deere is not perfected. C.R.S. §4-9-310.

Consumer goods are "goods that are used or bought for use primarily for personal, family or household purposes." C.R.S. §4-9-102(23). The other possible classification for the tractor, and the one supported by the trustee is that of equipment. Equipment is defined as "goods other than inventory, farm products or consumer goods." C.R.S. §4-9-102(33).

The classification of collateral is to be determined as of the time of the creation of the security interest. The classification does not change because of a later change in the manner in which the collateral is used [citing cases]. If the law were otherwise, a secured party would be required to continually monitor the use that was being made of the collateral.

From reviewing the affidavits of the debtors submitted in support of the trustee's motion for summary judgment, and their deposition testimony, it is not completely clear what oral representations the debtors may have made to Deere's dealer regarding their intended use of the collateral. Robert says he told the salesman that he needed a tractor that was large enough to move dirt to fill irrigation ditches on his land, but small enough to get through a horse stall door. Dawn says she told the salesman they wanted the tractor to do a number of other things on their land in addition to filling the irrigation ditches. Yet nowhere in the debtors' sworn testimony is there any evidence that they told Deere's representative that the tractor was to be used in any type of commercial activity.

The debtors state that they were in the farming and ranching business on their 10-acre tract. They testified that they boarded horses and raised some livestock. Their intention was to make a profit, they said. Their income tax returns reflected that they were involved in ranching, although it was not a profitable endeavor. While the tax returns indicated that the tractor was used 100 percent for business purposes, the debtors' deposition testimony is that 90 percent of the use was personal. Assuming that all of this testimony is true, it nevertheless relates to events subsequent to the attachment of the security agreement. The focus, however, must be on the intended use of the collateral when the security interest was granted.

At the outset, the debtors gave no indication to Deere that they were engaged in a business activity. Their credit application represented that they were both employed, together earning $90,000 per year. Robert represented in the credit application that he was not self-employed. They worked long hours at their jobs—Robert 60 hours per week and Dawn about 75 hours per week.

The security agreement that the debtors signed reflected that it was a "Personal" rather than a "Commercial" transaction. The body of the document stated unequivocally that it was a consumer credit transaction and that the tractor was intended to be used for personal, family or household purposes.

The case law is clear that where a debtor makes an affirmative representation in loan documents that he or she intends to use goods primarily for personal, family or household purposes, the creditor is protected even if the representation turns out to be erroneous. 1 Barkley Clark, The Law of Secured Transactions Under the Uniform Commercial Code ¶12-02[3] (rev. ed. 2005). (". . . just about every case that has dealt with this issue holds that the dealer . . . can rely on the debtor's written 'consumer representation'"). In Sears, Roebuck & Co. v. Pettit (In re Pettit), 18 B.R. 8 (Bankr. E.D. Ark. 1981), the debtor bought goods for use in his rental business. Yet the debtor did not inform the seller of his intended use. The security agreement "affirmatively and unambiguously represented that the debtor was purchasing the collateral for personal, family or household purposes." Id. at 9. The bankruptcy court rejected the admission of extrinsic evidence to contradict the unambiguous representation in the security agreement of the debtor's intended use of the collateral. The *Pettit* court held that the seller's purchase money security interest was properly perfected without filing a financing statement, observing that the secured party was not required by the UCC to monitor the debtor's use of the collateral in order to determine its proper classification. In accord is McGehee v. Exchange Bank & Trust Co., 561 S.W.2d 926, 930 (Tex. App. 1978) ("[T]he intent of the debtor-purchaser at the time of the sale when . . . [the] security instrument attached to the collateral is controlling, and no creditor is required to monitor the use of the collateral in order to ascertain its proper classification.")

The rationale of *Pettit* is compelling. A debtor who makes representations in a security agreement regarding the intended use of the collateral should be bound by those representations. That is especially true where the debtors fail to inform the creditor that they intend to use the collateral for other than personal, family or household purposes. The classification of the collateral, for purposes of perfection of the security interest, is determined when the security interest attaches. The later use of the collateral for another purpose than as stated in the security agreement is irrelevant in determining whether the security interest is perfected.

According to the security agreement here, the debtors intended to use the tractor as consumer goods. Deere was entitled to rely on the debtors' representation. The debtors did not inform Deere of a different intended use. Therefore, Deere's purchase money security interest was perfected when it attached, and the filing of a financing statement was not required. The security interest remains perfected despite any subsequent use for purposes other than consumer, if indeed there was such other use.

The trustee argues that he should not be bound by the debtors' representations in the security agreement because the debtors did not know of the representations. However, one who signs an agreement is bound by its terms, although ignorant of them, absent fraud or false representation.

Elsken v. Network Multi-Family Security Corporation, 49 F.3d 1470 (10th Cir. 1995). As there is no allegation of fraud or false representation regarding the security agreement, this argument is without merit.

For these reasons, the court holds that Deere has a perfected purchase money security interest in the tractor. Accordingly, the defendant's motion for summary judgment is granted, and the plaintiff's motion for summary judgment is denied.

QUESTIONS

What will be the result where a car buyer tells the seller he wants the car for personal family use, but is lying and really plans to resell it on his own lot? See Balon v. Cadillac Auto. Co., 113 N.H. 108, 303 A.2d 194397 (1973). Some creditors contemplating a loan to the debtor require that the debtor fill out an application that explains the intended use of the collateral. Is this legally wise from the creditor's point of view?

PROBLEM 306

Wheeler made a loan to Montreal, Maine & Atlantic Railway ("MMA"). The security agreement and financing statement described the collateral as, among other things, "payment and accounts." An MMA freight train laden with oil derailed, causing havoc. MMA filed a claim under its business interruption insurance policy for lost business income. Is the insurance claim collateral of Wheeler? See §§9-102(a)(2), 9-109(d)(8); In re Montreal, Maine & Atl. Ry., Ltd., 799 F.3d 1, 4 (1st Cir. 2015).

PROBLEM 307

Mercy Hospital needs financing and calls you, its attorney, with this question. Many of its patients are members of various health plans, and when they come in for treatment, they sign paperwork authorizing the hospital to seek payment from their health insurance coverage provider. The hospital always has a large number of such receivables in the process of collection. When the hospital borrows money, can it use the monies due it from the various health plans as collateral? See §§9-109(d)(8) and 9-102(a)(46).

PROBLEM 308

Passport Credit Card Company issued millions of credit cards internationally, sending them to cardholders, who then used them in millions of transactions with merchants. The merchants would then send the resulting paperwork to Passport for reimbursement (minus Passport's fee). You are the attorney for Passport. When Passport needs to borrow money, can it use these credit card transactions as collateral? See §9-102(a)(2). Remember that the outright sale of such property by Passport is also an Article 9 transaction; §9-109(a)(3).

A hotel puts up its "accounts" as collateral for a loan. Many hotel guests pay with credit cards. Does the creditor have a security interest in the hotel's right to collect from the credit card company? See U.C.C. §9-102, Official Comment 5.d; In re Lexington Hosp. Grp., LLC, 2017 WL 5035081, at 10 (Bankr. E.D. Ky. 2017).

PROBLEM 309

Fill in the blanks with the proper collateral classifications:

(a) Milk in the hands of the farmer: ____________; in the hands of the grocery store: ____________; in the hands of the grocery store's customer who is buying for consumption: ____________. Would your answer to the second question change if "restaurant" were used in place of "grocery store"? See §9-102, Official Comment 4(a), second paragraph.

(b) A certificate of deposit issued by a bank: ____________ (compare §3-104(j), §9-102(a)(47), and Southview Corp. v. Kleberg First Natl. Bank, 512 S.W.2d 817 (Tex. Civ. App. 1974)). Would it make a difference if the certificate of deposit was transferable? See In re Perez, 440 B.R. 634 (Bankr. D.N.J. 2010), and Official Comment 12 to §9-102. An *airbill* issued by an airline as a receipt for frozen shrimp shipped by air: ____________ (see §1-201(b)(6)); the receipt given to a farmer by a silo operator when the farmer stored grain there: ____________.

(c) Rare coins bought by a hobbyist for addition to his collection: ____________ (see In re Midas Coin Co., 264 F. Supp. 193 (E.D. Mo. 1967), *aff'd,* 387 F.2d 118 (8th Cir. 1968)).

(d) A tax refund: ____________ (see In re American Home Furnishings Corp., 48 B.R. 905 (Bankr. W.D. Wash. 1985)).

(e) A debenture bond issued by a corporation: ____________ (see §§8-102(a)(15) and 9-102(a)(49)); a right to 100 shares of stock recorded on the books of the debtor's stockbroker: ____________ (see §8-102(a)(17)).

(f) The checking account you have at your bank: ____________ (see §9-102(a)(29)).

(g) A computer program: ____________ (see §9-102(a)(44)).

(h) The monthly rental obligations owed to a landlord, who wants to use these obligations as collateral for a loan: ____________ (compare §§9-102(a)(2),

9-109(d)(11)); the promissory notes signed for the tenants to pay their rent: ____________ (§§9-102(a)(47), 9-109(b)).

Morgan County Feeders, Inc. v. McCormick

Colorado Court of Appeals, 1992
836 P.2d 1051

[Neil Allen made an agreement with James McCormick to sell him 56 head of cattle Allen owned. The cattle were subject to a perfected security interest in favor of Morgan County Feeders, Inc., which seized the cattle prior to their delivery to McCormick. Items sold in the "ordinary course of business" (i.e., *inventory*), as we shall see, pass to the buyer free of even perfected security interests; pieces of *equipment* generally do not. After stating the facts and noting that the trial court had ruled in favor of Morgan County Feeds, Judge Rothenberg continued as follows.]

McCormick first contends that the trial court erred in determining that the cattle purchased by Allen were equipment, rather than inventory. We disagree.

Under the Uniform Commercial Code, "goods" are defined as "all things which are movable at the time the security interest attaches. . . ." Section 4-9-105(1)(f), C.R.S. (1991 Cum. Supp.) [now §9-102(a)(44)—Eds.]. Goods are classified under four major types which are mutually exclusive. These include: consumer goods; equipment; farm products; and inventory. . . .

Here, the parties agree that the cattle constitute "goods" under the Uniform Commercial Code. They further agree that the cattle are not "farm products." Thus, the remaining issue surrounding the cattle is whether they should be designated as inventory or equipment. The distinction is important because buyers of inventory in the ordinary course of business take free of perfected security interests. [See §9-320—Eds.]

Section 4-9-109(2), C.R.S. [now §9-102(a)(33)—Eds.], provides that goods are equipment:

> if they are used or bought for use primarily in business (including farming or a profession) . . . or if the goods are not included in the definitions of inventory, farm products, or consumer goods.

In contrast, §4-9-109(4), C.R.S. [now §9-102(a)(48)—Eds.], provides that goods are inventory:

> if they are held by a person who holds them for sale or lease or to be furnished under contracts of service or if he has so furnished them, or if they are . . . materials used or consumed in a business. Inventory of a person is not to be classified as his equipment.

In ascertaining whether goods are inventory or equipment, the principal use of the property is determinative. Section 4-9-109, C.R.S. (Official Comment 2). The factors to be considered in determining principal use include whether the goods are for immediate or ultimate sale and whether they have a relatively long or short period of use in the business. Section 4-9-109, C.R.S. (Official Comment 3); First Colorado Bank & Trust v. Plantation Inn, Ltd., 767 P.2d 812 (Colo. App. 1988).

Goods used in a business are equipment when they are fixed assets or have, as identifiable units, a relatively long period of use. They are inventory, even though not held for sale, if they are used up or consumed in a short period of time in the production of some end product. First Colorado Bank & Trust v. Plantation Inn, Ltd., supra. . . .

At trial, the court determined that the longhorn cattle were "equipment" and not "inventory" because: "Allen did not acquire or hold them for the principal purpose of immediate or ultimate sale or lease. . . . Instead, the cattle were to be used principally for recreational cattle drives. . . . While Allen might have occasionally leased the cattle to other entrepreneurs, it was his intention to utilize the cattle principally in his own recreational business." Thus, the court concluded that McCormick bought the cattle subject to Morgan County Feeders' security interest.

Although we recognize that the classification of cattle as "equipment," rather than "inventory," is highly unusual, we also recognize that the evidence presented to the trial court disclosed unusual circumstances, and we conclude that the record supports the court's classification.

Allen testified that his purpose for purchasing the longhorn cows was to use them on cattle drives and that these cows have a relatively long period of use in comparison to rodeo calves and feeder cattle. Several other witnesses also testified that Allen had stated his intent to use the longhorn cows for recreational cattle drives. Thus, the trial court was justified in rejecting McCormick's contention that the cattle were purchased only for rodeos. And, it did not err in finding that, under these unique circumstances, the cattle should be classified as "equipment."

In light of this conclusion, we need not address McCormick's additional contention that the trial court erred in finding that McCormick was not a buyer in the ordinary course of business. . . .

The judgment is affirmed.

PROBLEM 310

Sam Ambulance was a lawyer who loved speculative investments. When Elvis Presley died, Ambulance managed to acquire one of the musician's guitars. He decided to keep it for years and let it appreciate in value (he did not himself play the guitar). If Ambulance uses the guitar as collateral for a loan needed to run his law practice, how is the guitar classified?

A Few Words About Chattel Paper. Chattel paper is an artificial construct of Article 9. Suppose, for example, that you run an automobile dealership and your business successfully sells a lot of cars each month on credit. The purchasers sign promissory notes in your favor and also sign a security agreement giving your dealership a security interest in the sold vehicle so that you (or your assignee) can repossess it in the event of default. This set of papers, taken collectively, is called *chattel paper* (note that it includes an instrument therein). Read §9-102(a)(11).[2] There is a huge market for such paper, so when your dealership needs money it can either sell the chattel paper outright or use it as collateral for a loan from a lending institution. Either way it is an Article 9 transaction and will require the purchaser/lending institution to take the steps required by Article 9 to protect its security interest in the paper; §9-109(a).

PROBLEM 311

How would you categorize the car lease contracts that Dime-A-Minute Rental Cars uses as collateral when it borrows money from a bank? If Dime-A-Minute moves into the computer age and stops using paper entirely, can the electronic version of this paperwork be used as collateral? See §9-102(a)(31) and its Official Comment 5(b). Article 9 provides that a secured party will be protected as to such electronic chattel paper if it has "control" over the paper, but, given that there is no actual writing, how could this possibly be done? Read §9-105.

PROBLEM 312

The State of Montana has enacted a statute giving unpaid crop dusters a lien on the crops of the farmer; Montana Statutes §71-3-901. This, of course, is a statutory lien (since it arises by statute and is not created by the consent of the debtor—the farmer). Is this nonetheless an Article 9 transaction requiring compliance with the usual Article 9 rules? See §§9-102(a)(5), 9-109(a)(2) and (d)(2).

2. This is just one example of chattel paper, which is defined broadly enough to encompass the sale of most security interests from one secured party to another. Because the buying secured party takes possession of the paper, that is usually sufficient to satisfy the Article 9 rules on attachment and perfection.

II. TECHNICAL VALIDITY OF THE FORMS

The creation of an Article 9 security interest typically involves two documents: the *security agreement* and the *financing statement.* The security agreement is the *contract* between the debtor and the creditor by which the debtor grants to the creditor (the *secured party*) a security interest in the collateral. See §9-102(a)(74).[3] The financing statement is the *notice* that is filed in the place specified in §9-501 (and indexed under the debtor's name) in order to give later creditors an awareness that the collateral is encumbered. Thus, the purpose of the security agreement is to create property rights between the debtor and the creditor, and the purpose of a financing statement is to create property rights in the creditor against most of the rest of the world.

This section of the book explores the technical requirements for valid security agreements and financing statements. While not inherently interesting in and of themselves, these sections deserve your close attention. Much of the litigation involving Article 9 of the Code could have been avoided if the attorneys had done their jobs carefully when the documents were created. Imagine that you are a new associate at a major law firm that has just landed a multimillion-dollar account requiring Article 9 compliance. The senior partner confirms that you studied secured transactions in law school (this course) and puts you in charge of making sure that the client's interests are perfected in this big-ticket transaction. The partner tells you, unnecessarily, that the whole firm is trusting you not to make any mistakes. Now read §§9-203(a) and (b), 9-502(a), 9-509(a) and (b), and 9-521. *Record* (a new term in the 1999 revision) is defined broadly in §9-102(a)(70) with the hope that it will encompass all the possible future ways of memorializing legal arrangements.

A. *The Security Agreement*

Where the collateral is in the possession of the secured party (a *pledge*), no written security agreement is required by law (though one is probably still desirable for evidentiary reasons). Where, however, the property is to leave the creditor's control, §9-203 becomes relevant and creates technical problems.

3. The 2010 revisions to Article 9 inserted a new definition of "public organic record" at §9-102(a)(68), so the numbers of the following subsections are all increased by 1.

If the collateral is not in the secured party's possession or control, the §9-203 security agreement must (1) be authenticated by the debtor (*authenticate* is defined in §9-102(a)(7)) and (2) describe the collateral (plus the land if timber is involved). The security agreement need not be in any particular form or contain any particular words. Cf. §1-201(b)(3), defining *agreement.* It needn't call itself a security agreement. See Official Comment 3 to §9-203 on the admissibility of parol evidence to establish the security nature of apparently absolute transactions.

PROBLEM 313

When Frederick Bean bought a new computer on credit from Centerboro Office Supply, before he could take it home the store made him sign a "Conditional Sale Contract," by which he agreed that title to the computer would remain with the store until he had fully paid for his purchase. The contract described the computer, but nowhere did it mention a security interest. Does the contract qualify as a security agreement under §9-203? See §1-201(b)(35), and §2-401(1), second sentence; Sommers v. International Bus. Machs., 640 F.2d 686 (5th Cir. 1981).

A good security agreement will, of course, spell out much more than §9-203 requires. It should identify the parties, describe the collateral, contain a grant by the debtor to the creditor of a security interest in the collateral, and specify the contractual understandings of the parties—in particular, naming what events will constitute *default* to permit the creditor to realize on the security interest by repossessing the collateral. Many more desirable clauses will be suggested by the materials that follow.

B. The Financing Statement

The financing statement—commonly called by its form number, "UCC-1"—is the document filed in the appropriate public office by the creditor (secured party) to *perfect* the creditor's rights in the collateral against later parties. Under the 1999 revision, the requirements for a financing statement have been significantly simplified. Per §9-502(a) it need be signed by no one (though the debtor must have *authorized* it, which follows automatically from the signing of the security agreement; §9-509), but it must identify the parties and indicate what collateral is covered. If realty interests are involved (timber, fixtures, minerals to be extracted from the ground), §9-502(b) adds other requirements—particularly that it describe the realty and the record owner of the realty (if he or she is not the obligor) and indicate that it be filed in the real property records (so that the filing officer sees that it gets to the right place).

In addition, §9-516 lists other things that need to be in the financing statement before the filing office will accept it. Read that section. Note, however, that if the filing office does take the financing statement not containing these things, the financing statement is effective nonetheless.

The financing statement has as its function the giving of notice to later creditors as to what property of the debtor is encumbered by prior liens. Consequently, the financing statement does not typically contain many details of the underlying transaction. Such things as the amount of the loan, the time periods of repayment, etc., are not required to be described in the financing statement. If later curious parties are to discover these details, they must find them out from the original parties, not the public record. This is facilitated by the fact that the financing statement will have on it the addresses of the debtor and secured party, so that those searching the files know how to contact the original participants and discover the current state of the described encumbrance.

Security agreements and financing statements serve different purposes, but they have several problems in common: who the *debtor* is, what a sufficient *description of the collateral* is, etc. Some of these issues are resolved identically for both documents, and some are not. The most common specific problems are explored next.

C. The Debtor's Identity

When the financing statement is filed (typically in the Secretary of State's office), it will be indexed under the debtor's name. Because later possible creditors will search the records under that name, it is particularly important that it be correct.

PROBLEM 314

Harry Fellini ran a movie theater called "Fellini's Art Theater," but, because he was the sole proprietor, that was a trade name. He gave a security interest in the business's equipment to Sharkteeth Finance Company. The financing statement calls for a listing of the "debtor's name."

(a) Should the parties use the business name or individual name? Read §9-503.

(b) If the theater were run as a partnership, would the partnership's name be used as the debtor's name? See §9-503(a)(6) and (b)[4] and its Official Comment 2.

Determining the name of an individual has proven to be a nightmare for lenders, their attorneys, and the courts. The 2010 amendments to Article 9 gave the states two options to resolving the issue: in §9-503(a)(4)'s Alternative A [sometimes called the "Only If Rule"] or Alternative B [the "Safe Harbor Rule"]. To these alternative possibilities §9-506(a) adds that a financing statement that is in error but not "seriously misleading" is nonetheless effective, but that issue is complicated by the "search engine" test of §9-506(c), defining "seriously misleading" in a cyber fashion. Use these citations to resolve the following Problem.

PROBLEM 315

Bob Wolton had always used "Bob" as his first name even though his birth certificate lists him as "Robert Edward Wolton." All of Bob's public records used "Bob Wolton," and that is the name on his driver's license. When Bob applied for a loan from a credit union, using his valuable comic book collection as collateral, will the credit union be perfected in an Alternative A state if its financing statement identifies him as "Bob Wolton"? In an Alternative B state? What if his driver's license lapses and he fails to get another one? Is the credit union now perfected in either state?

If a debtor signed a security agreement with the debtor's nickname rather than the name on the debtor's driver's license, would the security agreement be effective? Cf. In re Smith, 2017 WL 5198149 (Bankr. D.N.M. 2017).

In re John's Bean Farm of Homestead, Inc.

United States Bankruptcy Court, Southern District of Florida, Miami Division, 2007

378 B.R. 385

LAUREL M. ISICOFF, Bankruptcy Judge.

[Creditor filed its financing statement under the name of "John Bean Farms, Inc.," instead of the Debtor's actual name of incorporation, "John's Bean Farm of Homestead, Inc."]

4. Before the 2010 revisions to Article 9 this issue was governed by §9-503(a)(4)(A) and (B).

The matter under consideration is one of first impression in this district and concerns the degree of error necessary to render a financing statement "seriously misleading" under revised Uniform Commercial Code section 9-506, as adopted in Florida. . . .

PERFECT FINANCING STATEMENTS UNDER REVISED ARTICLE 9

A primary purpose of revised section 9-506 of the UCC, adopted in Florida as Fla. Stat. §679.5061, was to replace the former reasonableness standard with a clearer standard based on the computerized search logic of the filing office. This represents a significant shift from the prior law. Enacted to clarify the sufficiency of debtors' names in financing statements, the revision was "designed to discourage the fanatical and impossibly refined reading of statutory requirements in which courts occasionally have indulged themselves." Fla. Stat. §679.5061 cmt. 2. See In re Kinderknecht, 308 B.R. 71, 75 (B.A.P. 10th Cir. 2004) ("The intent to clarify when a debtor's name is sufficient shows a desire to foreclose fact-intensive tests, such as those that existed under former Article 9 of the UCC".).

Courts in other states that have adopted revised Article 9 have recognized and emphasized the purpose and importance of this change in the search standard. The Supreme Court of Kansas analyzed its own state's adoption of revised UCC sections 9-503 and 9-506 (which adoption is virtually identical to the Florida language) and noted the importance of the accuracy of the name and the reasons behind the shift in focus of the revised Article 9:

> [T]he express provisions of the revised amendments read *in pari materia,* and the Official UCC Comments are all in accord that the primary purpose of the revision of the name requirement is to lessen the amount of fact-intensive, case-by-case determinations that plagued earlier versions of the UCC, and to simplify the filing system as a whole. The object of the revisions was to shift the responsibility to the filer by requiring the not too heavy burden of using the legal name of the debtor, thereby relieving the searcher from conducting numerous searches using every conceivable name variation of the debtor.

Pankratz Implement Co. v. Citizens Nat'l Bank, 281 Kan. 209, 227, 130 P.3d 57, 68 (Kan. 2006). Accord In re F.V. Steel and Wire Co., 310 B.R. 390, 393-94 (Bankr. E.D. Wis. 2004) ("A rule that would burden a searcher with guessing at misspellings and various configurations of a legal name would not provide creditors with the certainty that is essential in commercial transactions".).

Under revised Article 9 what debtor misnomer is "seriously misleading" is statutorily defined as that which would not be discovered using the state's standard search logic. Thus, under the Safe Harbor provision, the discoverability of a financing statement expressly delimits permissible error. A financing statement is effective if a computer search run under the debtor's correct name produces the financing statement with the incorrect name. If it does not, then the financing statement is ineffective as a matter of law. This new standard is intended to

> reflect[] a balance between the need for some flexibility to allow for human error on the part of filers . . . and the avoidance of a rule that would cast an altogether inappropriate burden on searchers to have to try to divine potential errors and make searches under not only the correct name but also "foreseeable" or "likely" errors that a filer might have made[.]

Harry C. Sigman, Twenty Questions About Filing Under Revised Article 9: The Rules of the Game Under New Part 5, 74 Chi. Kent L. Rev. 861, 862-63 (1999). See also Steven O. Weise, An Overview of Revised Article 9, in the New Article 9 Uniform Commercial Code 7 (Corinne Cooper ed., 2d ed. 2000).

> Revised Article 9 contains a statutory rule to determine when a mistake [sic] the debtor's name is so incorrect as to make the financing statement ineffective. The financing statement is effective if a computer search run under the debtor's correct name turns up the financing statement with the incorrect name. If it does not, then the financing statement is ineffective as a matter of law. The court has no discretion to determine that the incorrect name is "close enough."

Id. (as quoted in In re F.V. Steel and Wire Co., 310 B.R. at 393-94).

Post-revision case law is fairly well settled that the burden is squarely on the creditor to correctly identify the name of the debtor.

> Revised Article 9 requires more accuracy in filings, and places less burden on the searcher to seek out erroneous filings. The revisions to Article 9 remove some of the burden placed on searchers under the former law, and do not require multiple searches using variations on the debtor's name. Revised Article 9 rejects the duty of a searcher to search using any names other than the name of the debtor indicated on the public record of the debtor's jurisdiction of organization.

In re Summit Staffing Polk County, Inc., 305 B.R. 347, 354-55 (Bankr. M.D. Fla. 2003). See Receivables Purchasing Co. v. R&R Directional Drilling, LLC, 263 Ga. App. 649, 652, 588 S.E.2d 831, 833 (Ga. 2003) ("[A] party filing a financing statement now acts at his peril if he files the statement under an incorrect name".).

The majority of cases decided under revised Article 9 are unforgiving of even minimal errors. In In re Tyringham Holdings, Inc., 354 B.R. 363 (Bankr.

E.D. Va. 2006), the creditor filed a financing statement covering 65 pieces of jewelry totaling $310,925 worth of consigned inventory. However, the creditor listed the name of the debtor as "Tyringham Holdings" rather than the debtor's legal corporate name, "Tyringham Holdings, Inc." Although the name error merely omitted the corporate suffix "Inc.," an official search under the debtor's actual name did not reveal the creditor's financing statement and the court held that, therefore, the financing statement was ineffective to perfect the security interest. The *Tyringham* court reasoned:

> [w]hile application of the filing office's standard search logic may lead to situations where it appears a relatively minor error in a financing statement leads to a security interest becoming unperfected, it is not that difficult to ensure that a financing statement is filed with the correct name of the debtor. Little more is asked of a creditor than to accurately record the debtor's name, and according to the statute, failure to perform this action clearly dooms the perfected status of a security interest.

354 B.R. at 368. Similarly, in Pankratz Implement Co. v. Citizens Nat'l Bank, 281 Kan. 209, 130 P.3d 57, the debtor purchased a tractor from the creditor, signed a security agreement, and the creditor misspelled the debtor's name on the financing statement by omitting a "d"—listing the debtor as "Roger House" instead of his legal name "Rodger House." The Supreme Court of Kansas upheld summary judgment invalidating the prior interest represented by the faulty financing statement. In Host Am. Corp. v. Coastline Fin., Inc., 2006 U.S. Dist. LEXIS 35727, 2006 WL 159614 (D. Utah 2006), the court held that a financing statement was seriously misleading where the debtor, whose name was "K.W.M. Electronics Corporation" was identified in the financing statement as "K W M Electronics Corporation."

This canvas of history, commentary and application sets the background against which the adequacy of Klein's financing statement must be judged.

THE KLEIN FINANCING STATEMENT IS SERIOUSLY MISLEADING

Both the Trustee and Klein rely on In re Summit Staffing Polk County, Inc., 305 B.R. 347. In that case Chief Judge Glenn determined that a financing statement that identified the debtor as "Summit Staffing, Inc." rather than by the debtor's correct name of "Summit Staffing of Polk County, Inc." was not seriously misleading because, although using the standard search logic for Florida did not produce a page on which the financing statement appeared, the searcher only had to push the "previous" button one time and the financing statement was listed. Chief Judge Glenn held that the "reasonably diligent searcher" standard survives in some part. "Although Revised Article 9 does not require that a searcher exercise reasonable diligence in the selection of the names to be searched or the number of searches to conduct, the revisions to Article 9 do not entirely remove the duty imposed on a searcher to be reasonably diligent." Id. at 355. In Chief Judge Glenn's view, some burden is placed on the searcher to employ "reasonable diligence in examining the results of the search." Id.

In the *Summit Staffing* case, a creditor, Associated Receivables, filed a financing statement listing the debtor as Randy A. Vincent and "Summit Staffing," a sole proprietorship, as an additional debtor. Summit Staffing was subsequently incorporated as "Summit Staffing of Polk County, Inc." The corporation later filed for relief under Chapter 7 of the Bankruptcy Code. The Chapter 7 Trustee conducted a UCC search through the Florida Secured Transaction Registry website using the actual corporate name of the debtor, Summit Staffing of Polk County, Inc., and found no financing statement relating to the debtor's assets. The name "Summit Staffing" appeared at the top of the page displayed when a search under the debtor's correct name was made. By selecting the "previous" command to display the results page with alphabetical listings immediately prior to the page displayed, the Associated Receivables financing statement appeared. In determining the financing statement was not seriously misleading, and that Florida's standard search logic revealed the faulty financing statement, Chief Judge Glenn wrote:

> When a search is conducted in the Florida Secured Transaction Registry, a listing of debtors' names is produced. The listing is an alphabetical listing, and 20 names are displayed. If the debtor's actual name is produced, it is at the top of the list. If the debtor's name is not found, the next succeeding name on the alphabetical list is at the top of the list. To see the next preceding name on the alphabetical list, the searcher must use the "Previous" command on the screen. In fact, at the top of the list is the statement: "Use the Previous and Next buttons *to display additional search results.*" (Emphasis supplied.) This statement directs the searcher to use the "Previous" command to see the immediately preceding names on the alphabetical list.
>
> Certainly the searcher should do this. Since the name immediately following Summit Staffing of Polk County, Inc. is produced at the top of the alphabetical list, and since the filing office's directions state that the searcher should use the "Previous" command to display additional search results, clearly a searcher should check the preceding names on the alphabetical list.

305 B.R. at 353-354. However, Chief Judge Glenn noted that the obligation to push the "previous" button is not limitless.

> Although it is clear that a searcher should check the immediately preceding names as well as the immediately succeeding names on an alphabetical list if there is not an exact match of the debtor's correct name, the issue of "reasonableness" develops at some point because the listing is an alphabetical listing. Although only three names begin with "Summit Staffing," there are

> several screens of debtors' names, with 20 names per screen, that begin with "Summit." Moreover, since the listing is an alphabetical listing, it is conceivable that one could use the "Previous" command to go to back to the beginning of the alphabetical list.

Id. at 354.

Here, the Trustee conducted a search of the Registry's online database. Using the Debtor's correct name, the Trustee's search yielded no matches. (Tr.'s Mot. Summ. J. Ex. CP 3.) It is undisputed that when the Debtor's correct name was inputted as the search term, the listing of 20 names on the initial search result screen did not disclose the Klein financing statement. (Tr.'s Mot. Summ. J. P 21; Klein Resp. n. 25.) Klein's financing statement was only found by striking the "previous" command 60 times. (Tr. Mot. Summ. J. P 22; Dubon Aff. PP 4-5; Klein Resp. n. 25.)

The Trustee relies on *Summit Staffing* arguing the case demonstrates that only the initial search result screen generated when the Debtor's correct name is input counts as the search result and, since Klein's financing statement did not appear on the initial page displayed, the financing statement is seriously misleading. Moreover, the Trustee argues, even if the search result goes beyond the initial result screen, then, as Chief Judge Glenn stated in *Summit Staffing,* the obligation to expand the search beyond the initial page displayed must be reasonable.

Klein also relies on *Summit Staffing.* Klein correctly points out that in *Summit Staffing,* the disputed financing statement did not appear on the initial page displayed, but rather the page displayed when the searcher pushed the "previous" command once. Thus, Klein argues, the results of "standard search logic" in Florida means something other than the initial result screen. However, Klein goes on to argue that Chief Judge Glenn improperly imposed a "reasonableness" requirement on the searcher's duty, that the statute is unambiguous, and has no "reasonableness" limitation. Since, by pushing the "previous" command (60 times) the Klein financing statement did eventually appear, Klein argues the financing statement is not seriously misleading.

The Trustee argues "[t]o require a secured creditor to search through numerous pages of names would defeat the salutary purpose of revised Article 9 and set dangerous precedent." (Tr. Mot. Summ. J. P 23.) Klein counters that since the plain language of the statute has no reasonableness requirement the court cannot impose a requirement that the statute doesn't provide. "Adding a reasonableness requirement would inevitably result in a situation where courts would have to delve into a host of case by case factual issues that were never contemplated by the legislative, and indeed, would require the courts to effectively rewrite the Safe Harbor Provision [Fla. Stat. §679.5061] in a manner that conflicts with the plain language." (Klein Resp. 11.) Thus, according to Klein's interpretation of the statute, any financing statement filed, no matter how far it may appear from the proper listing, would be sufficient so long as the statement could be found at some point in the pages preceding or following the initial displayed page. Under this interpretation, absent any reasonableness as to the distance between a proper and improper listing, a searcher would have to look through every page of the online database to determine whether or not a financing statement exists.

The crux of the dispute between the Trustee and Klein is what constitutes the search result using Florida's standard search logic. If my answer to this question is something other than the initial displayed page, then I must determine whether there is a limit on how much a searcher must search past the original display page. The debate between the Trustee and Klein centers on the meaning of "a search of the records of the filing office under the Debtor's correct name, using the filing office's standard search logic. . . ." As noted, the Trustee argues this refers to the initial page result; Klein argues there is a difference between a "search result" and a "display."

The only "search logic" in Florida is statutorily defined as a search by the debtor's name or document number. In order to determine what is the result of inputting that search logic, it is necessary and appropriate to understand what the Registry explains is a "result." The Registry, at its website, www.floridaucc.com, has a list of frequently asked questions. One of the questions listed is "How do I do my own search on the Internet." The answer to that question is:

> You can access the UCC filed records for the Florida Secured Transaction Registry on the Internet at: www.floridaucc.com. Click on the "Search" option. Choose one item in the "Select Search Type" box, then enter the appropriate data in the "Name/Document Number" box, and click on "search." *The exact name or number or the nearest alphabetical or numeric entry will be displayed.* Click on the number of the entry(ies) you are interested in.

Florida Secured Transaction Registry, UCC Frequently Asked Questions, http://www.floridaucc.com/faq.html (emphasis added). The same website has a Help menu that explains "UCC Filing Inquiry by Debtor Name." That section states in pertinent part:

> These transactions provide a list of UCC filings on the Florida Secured Transaction Registry beginning with the name that is closest to the key entered. This list also includes the document number and the type of each record. There are several inquiry functions available using the Debtor's Name, all of these inquiry functions will provide the user with an alphabetic listing beginning with the name closest to the key entered.

Id. at http://www.floridaucc.com/help.html#name.

I agree with Klein that the statute is unambiguous. Moreover, I agree with Klein that the statute does not include a reasonableness requirement. Indeed, as explained in great detail above, the very purpose of this statute was to eliminate the need for, indeed, the ability of, a judge to inject himself or herself in the determination of what is seriously misleading. However, I disagree with Klein's assertion that the initial page displayed is not the result of applying Florida's standard search logic. Florida's standard search logic is set by statute. The search logic clearly leads to one result—a single page on which names appear. For those, including Klein, that argue the search result is something more, the Registry website makes clear they are wrong. The Registry's own website unambiguously describes the page displayed when the search data is input as the result of the search. Nothing in the Registry's information page mentions the use of the "previous" or "next" page key in connection with conducting a search using the search criteria. Since it is undisputed that Klein's financing statement did not appear in the search result when the Debtor's correct name was input, the financing statement is seriously misleading and summary judgment in the Trustee's favor is appropriate.

Although I have found that Fla. Stat. §679.5061 is unambiguous, and that there is no implicit or explicit obligation of a searcher to go beyond the search result, I feel compelled to address what I view as Klein's incredible argument that the Florida statute unambiguously requires a searcher to scroll through the pages of the UCC search until the nonconforming financing statement is located. If Klein is correct, that the "search result" means something other than the page displayed when the required data is input, it does not follow that the statute requires a limitless search through the UCC database.

Klein argues that the case law is clear—when a statute is unambiguous on its face, it must be applied as written. However, Klein cavalierly casts aside as inapplicable the equally long and well established case law on statutory construction that reminds us—

> When applying the plain and ordinary meaning of statutory language "produces a result that is not just unwise but is clearly absurd, another principle comes into the picture. That principle is the venerable one that statutory language should not be applied literally if doing so would produce an absurd result."

Miedema v. Maytag Corp., 450 F.3d 1322, 1326 (11th Cir. 2006) (quoting Merritt v. Dillard Paper Co., 120 F.3d 1181, 1188 (11th Cir. 1997)).

Klein's argument that Florida's Safe Harbor provision clearly recognizes his financing statement was not seriously misleading, notwithstanding that it was listed 60 pages prior to the displayed search result (that is 1,200 entries), asks this Court to apply a meaning to the Safe Harbor provision that is "clearly absurd." Such an interpretation would eviscerate the purpose of the statute—that is, to create a framework for the perfection of security interests that is less arbitrary, that includes statutory guidance for simplifying the search, while allowing for "minor" errors.

Accordingly, if I am incorrect, and in fact, the Florida search result includes more than the initial page displayed, then, in order to interpret section 679.5061 so as to avoid an absurd result, I would be compelled alternatively to hold, as did Chief Judge Glenn, that there is a reasonable limit to the search, which I find is no more than one page "previous" or "next" from the initial result screen. Since Klein's financing statement appears 60 pages from the initial display, not one page, it is seriously misleading.

PROBLEM 316

EDM Corporation routinely did business as "EDM Equipment," and was commonly known by that name, so when the lender filed its financing statement it listed the debtor as "EDM CORPORATION D/B/A EDM EQUIPMENT." Does this correctly identify the debtor's name, and, to answer this question, is there something else you need to know? See Official Comment 2; In re EDM Corp., 431 B.R. 459 (B.A.P. 8th Cir. 2010). In resolving this Problem it may be useful for you to see a common administrative rule used by most states as to search logic. Here is the one from Ohio:

Ohio Administrative Code §111-11-62 Search Methodology

Search results are produced by the application of search logic to the name presented to the filing officer. Human judgment does not play a role in determining the results of the search.

The following rules apply to searches:

(A) There is no limit to the number of matches that may be returned in response to the search criteria.

(B) No distinction is made between upper and lower case letters.

(C) Punctuation marks and accents are disregarded.

(D) Words and abbreviations at the end of a name that indicate the existence or nature of an organization as set forth in the "Ending Noise Words" list as promulgated and adopted by the international association of corporation administrators are disregarded.

(E) The word "the" at the beginning of the search criteria is disregarded.

(F) All spaces are disregarded.

(G) For first and middle names of individuals, initials are treated as the logical equivalent of all names that begin with such initials, and first name and no middle name or initial is equated with all middle names and initials.

For example, a search request for "John A. Smith" would cause the search to retrieve all filings against all individual debtors with "John" or the initial "J" as the first name, "Smith" as the last name, and with the initial "A" or any name beginning with "A" in the middle name field. If the search request were for "John Smith" (first and last names with no designation in the middle name field), the search would retrieve all filings against individual debtors with "John" or the initial "J" as the first name, "Smith" as the last name and with any name or initial or no name or initial in the middle name field.

(H) After using the preceding rules to modify the name to be searched the search will reveal only names of debtors that are contained in unlapsed financing statements and exactly match the name requested, as modified.

[Here is the list of "Ending Noise Words":

IACA List of Ending Noise Words pursuant to Rule 503.4

The following words and abbreviations indicate the existence or nature of an entity. These business endings will be ignored in a UCC search.

• Agency • Association • Assn • Associates • Assc • Assoc • Attorneys at Law • Bank • National Bank • Business Trust • Charter • Chartered • Company • Co • Corporation • Corp • Credit Union • CU • Federal Savings Bank • FSB • General Partnership • Gen part • GP • Incorporated • Inc • Limited • Ltd • Ltee • Limited Liability Company • LC • LLC • Limited Liability Partnership • LLP • Medical Doctors Professional Association • MDPA • Medical Doctors Professional Corporation • MDPC • National Association • NA • Partners • Partnership • Professional Association • Prof Assn • PA • Professional Corporation • Prof Corp • PC • Professional Limited Liability Company • Professional Limited Liability Co • PLLC • Railroad • RR • Real Estate Investment Trust • REIT • Registered Limited Liability Partnership • RLLP • Savings Association • SA • Service Corporation • SC • Sole Proprietorship • SP • SPA • Trust • Trustee • As Trustee

Punctuation and accents are disregarded. "And" and "&" are disregarded.]

PROBLEM 317

When World Wide Widgets was formed it filed a corporate name document with the State Corporate Registration Office, as required by law. That document identified the company as "World Wide Wigets, Inc." (a typographical error), but the State's database correctly listed the company as "World Wide Widgets, Inc." and that was the name in the State's Index of Registered

Corporations. What is the corporation's name for Article 9 filing purposes? See §§9-503(a)(1), 9-102(a)(68).

In re PTM Technologies, Inc.

United States Bankruptcy Court, Middle District of North Carolina, 2011
452 B.R. 165

WILLIAM L. STOCKS, Bankruptcy Judge.

* * *

On July 15, 2010, the Plaintiff [PTM Technologies, Inc.] filed an adversary proceeding against Maxus Capital, seeking to avoid its lien pursuant to 11 U.S.C. §544(a) on the basis that it was unperfected. That same day, the Plaintiff also filed an adversary proceeding against GE Capital, seeking to avoid its lien on the same basis. The Motion seeks summary judgment on these section 544(a) claims.

PTM Technologies, Inc. is a duly organized corporation and that its jurisdiction of organization is North Carolina, the state in which it was organized. PTM Technologies, Inc. is the actual registered name of PTM Technologies, Inc. in the office of the Secretary of State of North Carolina.

In 2008, PTM Technologies, Inc. sought certain financing from Maxus Capital, and the parties closed on four separate loans subject to a master security agreement. These documents granted Maxus Capital a security interest in the collateral described in the loan documents. Certain of these loans then were sold and assigned to GE Capital.

On August 23, 2010, GE Capital filed a proof of claim in the amount of $5,185,283.35. The documents attached to the proof of claim include a UCC financing statement that was filed in the North Carolina Secretary of State's office on May 7, 2008. The financing statement incorrectly listed the Debtor's name as "PTM Tecnologies, Inc."—omitting the "h" in "Technologies." The financing statement that was filed in the Secretary of State's office by Maxus Capital on the same date also incorrectly listed the Debtor's name by omitting the "h" in "Technologies."

The North Carolina Secretary of State maintains a website that may be accessed over the internet. One of the services available on that website is "UCC Research" that enables users to search the UCC financing statements that are on record with the Secretary of State. Navigating to the page of the website at which UCC searches may be conducted involves clicking on an entry on the opening page of the website entitled "UCC Records." That takes a user to a page on the website that lists the UCC "Business Services" available on the website. One of the business services listed is "UCC Research."

By clicking on "UCC Research" a user accesses the website page on which research regarding UCC financing statements may be conducted. Two types of searches are available on the research page, namely, the "Standard RA9" search and the "Non-Standard RA9" search. When the research page is accessed, the Standard RA9 search is selected automatically. A standard search is then available by inserting the name of the organization in question and clicking on the word "Search." In order to conduct a non-standard search, it is necessary to click on "Non-Standard RA9."

The parties agree that a search of the Secretary of State's records under the Debtor's correct name, using the "Standard RA9" search, does not reveal the GE Capital or the Maxus Capital financing statement. The parties also agree that a search of the Secretary of State's records under the Debtor's correct name, using the "sounds like" feature of the "Non-Standard RA9" search does reveal the financing statements filed by GE Capital and Maxus Capital.[5]

ANALYSIS

In 2001, North Carolina adopted Revised Article 9 [RA9] of the Uniform Commercial Code, which included UCC sections 9-503 and 9-506(b) and (c). Under N.C. Gen. Stat. §25-9-503, if the debtor is a registered organization, a financing statement sufficiently provides the debtor's name only if it lists the debtor's correct name as indicated on the public record. It is undisputed that the GE Capital and Maxus Capital financing statements do not sufficiently provide the debtor's name under this section because they misspell the Debtor's name and thus do not list the Debtor's name as it is shown in the public record in the Secretary of State's office.

N.C. Gen. Stat. §25-9-506(a) provides that "[a] financing statement substantially satisfying the requirements of this Part is effective, even if it has minor errors or omissions, unless the errors or omissions make the financing statement seriously misleading." Generally, "a financing statement that fails sufficiently to provide the name of the debtor in accordance with G.S. 25-9-503(a) is seriously misleading." N.C. Gen. Stat. §25-9-506(b). However, N.C. Gen. Stat. §25-9-506(c) provides a safe harbor for certain financing statements that fail to use the debtor's correct name.

> "If a search of the records of the filing office under the debtor's correct name, using the filing office's standard search logic, if any, would disclose a financing statement that fails sufficiently to provide the name of the debtor in accordance with G.S. 25-9-503(a), the name provided does not make the financing statement seriously misleading.

5. When a user clicks on the Non-Standard search, the next step is to chose one of five types of searches, namely, "Starting with," "Sounds Like," "All words," "Exact Match" and "Any Words."

The issue in this proceeding is whether the GE Capital and Maxus Capital financing statements fall within the safe harbor provided under N.C. Gen. Stat. §25-9-506(c). Based upon the undisputed facts presented, the court concludes that the financing statements do not fall within the safe harbor provided by section 25-9-506(c) and that the Plaintiff's Motion should be granted and the Defendants' Cross-Motions denied.

The 2001 amendments were designed to eliminate the inconsistency that had developed in the court decisions regarding whether an error in the debtor's name made a financing statement seriously misleading. The amendments in Revised Article 9 eliminate such inconsistency by creating a clear delineation for determining when an incorrect name makes a financing statement seriously misleading. If the debtor's name is incorrect, then the financing statement is seriously misleading, unless a search using the filing office's standard search logic, if any, would nevertheless reveal the defective financing statement.

N.C. Gen. Stat. §25-9-526 gave the Secretary of State authority to "adopt and publish rules to implement the Secretary of State's responsibilities" under sections 25-9-503 and 25-9-506. Pursuant to this authority, the Secretary of State has adopted rules dealing with UCC searches that are found in Title 18 of the North Carolina Administrative Code and which may be accessed on the UCC search page of the Secretary of State's website by clicking on "Administrative Rules." These rules include 18 N.C.A.C. 5B.0503 which is entitled "Rules Applied to Search Requests," and which provides:

> Search results shall be produced by the application of standardized search logic to the name presented to the filing officer. Human judgment shall not play a role in determining the results of the search. The following rules shall apply to searches:
>
> (1) There shall be no limit to the number of matches that may be returned in response to the search criteria.
>
> (2) No distinction shall be made between upper and lower case letters.
>
> (3) Punctuation marks and accents shall be disregarded.
>
> (4) Words and abbreviations at the end of a name that indicate the existence or nature of an organization as set forth in the "Ending Noise Words" list as promulgated and adopted by IACA shall be disregarded. This list may be viewed or obtained by contacting the UCC Section.
>
> (5) The word "the" at the beginning of the search criteria shall be disregarded.
>
> (6) For first and middle names of individuals, initials shall be treated as the logical equivalent of all names that begin with such initials, and first name and no middle name or initial shall be equated with all middle names and initials. For example, a search request for "John A. Smith" shall cause the search to retrieve all filings against all individual debtors with "John" or the initial "J" as the first name, "Smith" as the last name, and with the initial "A" or any name beginning with "A" in the middle name field. If the search request

were for "John Smith" (first and last names with no designation in the middle name field), the search shall retrieve all filings against individual debtors with "John" or the initial "J" as the first name, "Smith" as the last name and with any name or initial or no name or initial in the middle name field.

(7) After using the preceding paragraphs of this Rule to modify the name to be searched, the search shall reveal only names of debtors that are contained in unlapsed financing statements and, exactly match the name requested, as modified.

Under this regulation, the seven rules stated therein constitute the "standardized search logic" that "shall" be applied to searches performed by the Secretary of State. As such, these rules describe the standard search logic employed in the North Carolina Secretary of State's office and hence constitute "the filing office's standard search logic" for purposes of N.C. Gen. Stat. §25-9-506(c). This means that if a search using these seven rules would reveal the defective GE Capital and Maxus Capital financing statements, then they would be saved by the safe harbor provision of section 25-9-506(c); conversely, if such a search would not reveal the financing statements, then the financing statements are seriously misleading as a matter of law under N.C. Gen. Stat. §25-9-506(b).

Rule 5B.0503 essentially creates a two-step process for applying the seven enumerated rules to the filing records. 18 N.C.A.C. 5B.0503. First, rules (1) through (6) are applied to ensure there is no limit on the number of matches returned and to expand the possible search results by treating the debtor's precise name more leniently. These rules expand the possible results by removing any distinction based on capitalization, disregarding punctuation marks, disregarding noise words such as "Company" at the end of the debtor's name, removing the word "the" from the beginning of a debtor's name, and modifying the debtor's name to account for initials if the debtor is an individual. Second, after applying the above rules to modify the debtor's name "the search shall reveal only names of debtors that are contained in unlapsed financing statements and, *exactly match the name requested,* as *modified.*" (Emphasis supplied). Under this search logic, the GE Capital and Maxus Capital financing statements clearly would not be disclosed in a search under the Debtor's correct name. A search using this search logic would modify the name to reveal a financing statement with incorrect capitalization, such as "ptm technologies, inc." It would disregard punctuation, and thus reveal a financing statement with no punctuation or different punctuation. It would remove ending noise words, and thus reveal a financing statement under the name "PTM Technologies." However, none of the rules defining the standard search logic would modify the debtor's name to correct for the missing "h" in the debtor's name. Thus, a search of the filing office's records under the debtor's correct name, using the foregoing standard search logic, would not reveal the defective financing statements filed by GE Capital and Maxus Capital, since after modifying the name accordingly, the name in the defective financing statements would not "exactly match the name requested." It follows, therefore, that the safe harbor of N.C. Gen. Stat. §25-9-506(c) is not available to GE Capital and Maxus Capital.

The same result flows from the results that occur when a "Standard RA9" search is conducted under the correct name of PTM Technologies, Inc. The designation of the "Standard RA9" search alternative as "Standard" sufficiently identifies that search alternative as the one employing the standard search logic described in Rule 5B.0503 and adopted as such by the Secretary of State. A "Standard RA9" search thus also dictates a decision in favor of the Plaintiff since the parties agree that a "Standard RA9" search at the Secretary of State's website does not reveal the defective financing statements. The parties also agree that a "Non-Standard RA9" search using the "sounds like" feature will reveal the financing statements. Given these results, in order for the Defendants to prevail on the merits, they would have to establish that the "Non-Standard RA9" search utilizes the "standard" search logic, while the "Standard RA9" search does not, a proposition that is illogical and contrary to the undisputed facts before the court.

Conclusion

Since the safe harbor of N.C. Gen. Stat. §25-9-506(c) does not apply, the GE Capital and Maxus Capital financing statements are seriously misleading as a matter of law, pursuant to N.C. Gen. Stat. §25-9-506(b), and therefore are insufficient to perfect the security interests claimed by GE Capital and Maxus Capital. The Plaintiff's Motion therefore should be granted and the Defendants' Cross-Motions denied. A separate order so providing is being entered pursuant to Rule 9021 of the Federal Rules of Bankruptcy Procedure.

The strict requirements for the debtor's name have caused losses from what might seem like reasonable errors by creditors. See In re Nay, 563 B.R. 535 (Bankr. S.D. Ind. 2017) (financing statement ineffective where debtor's name listed as "Ronald Mark Nay," but debtor's driver's license identified him as "Ronald Markt Nay"); Fishback Nursery, Inc. v. PNC Bank, N.A., 2017 WL 6497802 (N.D. Tex. 2017) (financing statement ineffective where creditor inserted a comma before the "LLC" abbreviation); United States Securities and Exchange Commission v. ISC, Inc., 2017 WL 3736796 (W.D. Wis. 2017) (financing statement ineffective where creditor inserted extra space in creditor's corporate name, i.e., "ISC, Inc." rather than "ISC, Inc.").

PROBLEM 318

Barbara Song borrowed $50,000 from Octopus National Bank (ONB) in order to start a business called "Barb's Interiors," interior design being her specialty. ONB and Ms. Song signed a security agreement showing her as the debtor and giving ONB an interest in the inventory and equipment. ONB duly filed a financing statement. Subsequently, Ms. Song married Fred Dancer, and she changed her name to Barbara Dancer. She borrowed another $50,000 from the Nightflyer Finance Company, which loaned her the money after searching the records under "Dancer" and finding no prior encumbrances on the business's inventory and equipment. Did ONB lose its security interest because it failed to refile when her name changed? See §9-507(c) and its Official Comment 4.

PROBLEM 319

The Last National Bank filed a financing statement in the proper place to perfect its security interest in the accounts receivable of the American Electronics Store. When the latter ran into financial difficulty, its assets were sold to a new electronics concern, Voice of Japan, which moved into the same retail location. Must Last National refile to keep its security interest perfected in (1) the accounts actually transferred by American Electronics to Voice of Japan or (2) accounts thereafter acquired by Voice of Japan? See §9-507(a) and its Official Comment 3. Do we get the same result if American Electronics Store merges with Voice of Japan and the new entity is called "Voice of Electronics, Inc."? See §§9-102(a)(56), 9-203(d) and (e) and its Official Comment 7, and 9-508. What if the opposite happens, and the debtor remains the same, but Last National assigns its interest in the debtor's accounts to Octopus National Bank? Need the records be changed? Read §§9-310(c) and 9-511. Is Octopus National's interest superior to that of Last National's creditors? Consider that the transfer of the security interest from Last National to Octopus National is itself the transfer of an account or chattel paper; see Official Comment 4, Example 2 to §9-310.

PROBLEM 320

When Robin Oakapple found he could not get a loan unless he had collateral, he got permission from his foster brother, Richard Dauntless, to use Richard's yacht as collateral. Should the lender make both sign the security agreement (only Robin signed the promissory note)? Which of these parties is the "debtor" and which the "obligor"? Compare §§9-102(a)(28)(A) and 9-102(a)(59). Under whose name should the financing statement be filed?

D. Description of the Collateral

One of the great fears of those opposed to Article 9's original adoption was that it would lead to creditor overreaching in demanding too much collateral.

PROBLEM 321

Peter Poor signed a security agreement and financing statement in favor of the Total Finance Company, giving the company a security interest in "all personal property debtor now owns or ever owns or even hopes to own between now and the end of the world or his death, whichever occurs first." Does this perfect an interest in his guitar? Compare §§9-108 and 9-504. Why would the drafters have drawn this distinction between the description in the security agreement and that in the financing statement?

PROBLEM 322

A financing statement states: "This Financing Statement also relates to an obligation secured by a security interest in collateral and is evidenced by the Mortgage referred to above and the All-Assets Security Agreement executed on September 28, 2015." Does the financing statement perfect a security interest in collateral listed in the All-Assets Security Agreement? See In re Lexington Hosp. Grp., LLC, 2017 WL 5035081, at 11 (Bankr. E.D. Ky. 2017).

In re Grabowski

United States District Court, Southern District of Illinois, Bankruptcy Division, 2002
277 B.R. 388

Kenneth J. Meyers, Bankruptcy Judge.

This case involves a priority dispute between defendants Bank of America and South Pointe Bank ("South Pointe") regarding their security interests in three items of farm equipment owned by the debtors.

Both lenders filed financing statements perfecting their interests. Bank of America, the first to file, described its collateral in general terms and listed the debtors' business address, rather than their home address where the collateral was located. South Pointe, by contrast, described the collateral more specifically and included the debtors' home address. South Pointe contends that Bank of America's description was ineffective to perfect the Bank's security interest in the equipment and that South Pointe has a superior interest by reason of its subsequently filed financing statement.

The facts are undisputed. In April 2001, debtors Ronald and Trenna Grabowski of Dubois, Illinois, filed this Chapter 11 proceeding to reorganize their farming operation in Washington and Perry counties, Illinois. The debtors have been engaged in farming at this location for the past 30 years. Beginning in 1993, the debtors also owned and operated a John Deere farm equipment business, Grabowski Tractor-Benton, Inc., at 12047 Highway 37, Benton, Illinois. During this time, debtor Trenna Grabowski, a certified public accountant, moved her accounting practice to the Benton dealership. Although the dealership was sold in 1999, Trenna Grabowski continues to conduct her accounting practice from the Benton location.

The debtors' schedules include a list of items of equipment used in their farming operation. The debtors filed the present proceeding to determine the validity, priority, and extent of liens held by various lenders in this equipment. Subsequently, the lenders reached an agreement concerning their respective interests in the farm equipment with the exception of three items. (See Stip., Doc. No. 20, filed February 1, 2002.) These items, as to which a dispute remains between Bank of America and South Pointe, consist of a John Deere 925 flex platform, a John Deere 4630 tractor, and a John Deere 630 disk. (See Stip. at 3-4.)

Bank of America claims a prior security interest in this equipment by virtue of a security agreement signed by the debtors in December 1998. The Bank's financing statement, filed on December 31, 1998, identifies the debtors as "Ronald and Trenna Grabowski" and lists their address as "12047 State Highway #37, Benton, Illinois 62812." The financing statement describes the Bank's collateral as:

> All Inventory, Chattel Paper, Accounts, *Equipment* and General Intangibles[.]

(See Supplmntl. Stip., Doc. No. 15, Ex. B, filed Jan. 22, 2002) (emphasis added).

South Pointe subsequently obtained a lien on the debtors' equipment in January 2000. South Pointe's financing statement, filed January 18, 2000, identifies the debtors as "Ronald and Trenna Grabowski" at "P.O. Box 38, Dubois, Illinois 62831" and describes South Pointe's collateral as:

> JD 1995 9600 combine . . . , *JD 925 FLEX PLATFORM* . . . , *JD 4630 TRACTOR* . . . , *JD 630 DISK 28' 1998* . . . referenced in South Pointe's financing statement.

(See Supplmntl. Stip., Doc. No. 15, Ex. C, filed Jan. 22, 2002) (emphasis added).

South Pointe asserts that Bank of America's financing statement, although prior in time, was insufficient to perfect the Bank's interest because it failed to place other lenders on notice of Bank of America's interest in the subject equipment. Specifically, South Pointe notes that the Bank's financing statement contained the address of the debtors' farm equipment business rather than that of the debtors' home where their farming operation is located and, further, that it failed to mention any specific items of equipment or even make reference to "farm equipment" or "farm machinery." South Pointe argues that, based on this description, a subsequent lender would reasonably conclude that Bank of America's intended security was the personal property of the debtors' business rather than equipment used in the debtors' farming operation. South Pointe maintains, therefore, that the Bank's financing statement did not reasonably identify the Bank's collateral as required to fulfill the notice function of a financing statement under Illinois' Uniform Commercial Code. . . .

The UCC sets forth the requirements for a creditor to obtain and perfect a security interest in personal property of the debtor.

Section 9-203 governs the attachment and enforcement of security interests through the parties' execution of a security agreement, while §9-502 relates to the requisites of a financing statement filed to perfect the creditor's interest against the interests of third parties. Both sections call for a description of the debtor's property. However, the degree of specificity required of such description depends on the nature of the document involved—whether it is a security agreement or financing statement—and the purpose to be fulfilled by such document. See 9A Hawkland, Uniform Commercial Code Series, [Rev.] §9-108:2, at 291-92; [Rev.] §9-108:2, at 294-96 (2001). While a security agreement defines and limits the collateral subject to the creditor's security interest, a financing statement puts third parties on notice that the creditor may have a lien on the property described and that further inquiry into the extent of the security interest is prudent. See Signal Capital Corp. v. Lake Shore Natl. Bank, 273 Ill. App. 3d 761, 210 Ill. Dec. 388, 652 N.E.2d 1364, 1371 (1995).

Section 9-108 sets forth the test for sufficiency of a description under the UCC, stating:

> (a) . . . a description of personal . . . property is sufficient, whether or not it is specific, *if it reasonably identifies what is described.*

810 Ill. Comp. Stat. 5/9-108(a) (emphasis added) (2001) (see former §9-110, 810 Ill. Comp. Stat. 5/9-110 (2000)). Examples of descriptions that meet this "reasonable identification" test include identification by "category" or by "type of collateral defined in the UCC." See §9-108(b)(2), (3). In addition, identification "by any other method" is sufficient, "if the identity of

the collateral is objectively determinable." See §9-108(b)(6). Only a super-generic such as "all the debtor's assets" or "all the debtor's personal property" is insufficient under the "reasonable identification" standard of §9-108. See 810 Ill. Comp. Stat. 5/9-108(c).

While §9-108 provides a flexible standard for determining the sufficiency of a description in a security agreement, §9-504 provides an even broader standard with regard to a financing statement. This section states:

> A financing statement sufficiently indicates the collateral that it covers if the financing statement provides:
> (1) a description of the collateral pursuant to Section 9-108; or
> (2) *an indication that the financing statement covers all assets or all personal property.*

810 Ill. Comp. Stat. 5/9-504 (2001) (emphasis added). Thus, in the case of a financing statement, a creditor may either describe its collateral by "type" or "category" as set forth in §9-108 or may simply indicate its lien on "all assets" of the debtor.

This exceedingly general standard for describing collateral in a financing statement, which is new to the UCC under revised Article 9, is consistent with the "inquiry notice" function of a financing statement under previous law. A financing statement need not specify the property encumbered by a secured party's lien, but need merely notify subsequent creditors that a lien may exist and that further inquiry is necessary "to disclose the complete state of affairs." Uniform Commercial Code Comment 2, 810 Ill. Comp. Stat. 5/9-502, Smith-Hurd Ann. at 385 (West Supp. 2002); see Matter of Little Brick Shirthouse, Inc., 347 F. Supp. 827, 829 (N.D. Ill. 1972); In re Swati, 54 B.R. 498, 501 (Bankr. N.D. Ill. 1985). In the present case, Bank of America filed a financing statement indicating it had a lien on the debtors' property consisting of "all inventory, chattel paper, accounts, equipment, and general intangibles." Despite the generality of the Bank's description, it was sufficient to notify subsequent creditors, including South Pointe, that a lien existed on the debtors' property and that further inquiry was necessary to determine the extent of the Bank's lien. For this reason, the Court finds no merit in South Pointe's argument that the description of the Bank's collateral was too general to fulfill the notice function of a financing statement under the UCC.

South Pointe asserts, however, that it was misled by the incorrect address contained in Bank of America's financing statement and "reasonably concluded" that the only equipment subject to the Bank's lien was that located at the debtors' farm equipment dealership. The Court disagrees that such conclusion was "reasonable." The debtors' business address was not part of the Bank's description of its collateral and, thus, did not serve to limit the collateral subject to the Bank's lien as South Pointe argues. In fact, Bank of America's financing statement indicated the Bank had a lien on the debtors' "equipment," with no indication that its interest was confined to equipment located in a particular place. Rather than serving to describe the Bank's collateral, therefore, the debtors' address merely provided a means by which subsequent lenders could contact the debtors to inquire concerning the Bank's lien. See 9 Hawkland, supra, §9-402:11, at 724-25.

While a subsequent creditor should not be imposed upon to be a "super-detective" in investigating prior secured transactions, the debtors' address in this case was an accurate and ready means of contacting the debtors. The Court notes, moreover, that even though the mailing address on the Bank's financing statement was that of the debtors' business, the debtors' names were listed as "Ronald and Trenna Grabowski," not "Grabowski Tractor-Benton, Inc.," the name of the debtors' business. Accordingly, the Court finds that a reasonably prudent lender would not be misled into believing that the collateral listed was property of the debtors' business, rather than that of the debtors individually.

For the reasons stated, the Court concludes that Bank of America's financing statement was sufficient to perfect its security interest in the subject farm equipment and that the Bank's interest, being prior in time, is superior to that of South Pointe. Accordingly, the Court finds in favor of Bank of America and against South Pointe on the debtors' complaint to determine validity, priority, and extent of liens in the debtors' farm equipment.

PROBLEM 323

Jeanne Angell sold 20 cows to Richard Baker, a dairy farmer, on credit. With each cow, Angell delivered a Certificate of Registration issued by Holstein Association USA, Inc. Each certificate stated the name of the cow, and included a sketch of the cow with its distinctive markings. Some of the certificates included handwritten ear tag identification numbers. Baker granted Angell a security interest in the cows for the unpaid price. Angell filed a financing statement, stating a name and ear tag identification number for each cow.

Some time later, it turned out that only four of the cows had ear tags with numbers that matched the financing statement. Ten cows had no tag and six cows had tags with numbers not matching those listed in the financing statement. Missing and inaccurate ear tags are common in the dairy industry. The cows, however, could be identified by name, using the certificates. Did the financing statement sufficiently describe the 20 cows? See In re Baker, 465 B.R. 359 (Bankr. N.D.N.Y. 2012). See also In re Wharton, 563 B.R. 289, 298

(B.A.P. 9th Cir. 2017) ("This note is partially secured by 1965 Corvette automobile" held sufficient to identify particular car).

In re I80 Equipment, LLC

United States Court of Appeals, Seventh Circuit, 2019
938 F.3d 866

BRENNAN, Circuit Judge.

This interlocutory bankruptcy appeal presents a matter of first impression for our court: whether Illinois's version of Article 9 of the Uniform Commercial Code requires a financing statement to contain within its four corners a specific description of secured collateral, or if incorporating a description by reference to an unattached security agreement sufficiently "indicates" the collateral. The bankruptcy court ruled that a financing statement fails to perfect a security interest unless it "contains" a separate and additional description of the collateral. Given the plain and ordinary meaning of the Illinois statute, and how courts typically treat financing statements, we disagree and reverse.

I

The facts necessary to resolve this appeal are straightforward. The debtor, I80 Equipment, LLC, is a business in Illinois that purchased and refurbished trucks for resale. I80 Equipment obtained a commercial loan from First Midwest Bank. To ensure repayment, the parties executed an agreement on March 9, 2015, which granted First Midwest a security interest in substantially all of I80 Equipment's assets. These were described in twenty-six listed categories of collateral, such as accounts, cash, equipment, instruments, goods, inventory, and all proceeds of any assets. To perfect its interest in I80 Equipment's assets, First Midwest timely filed a financing statement with the Illinois Secretary of State. The financing statement purported to cover "[a]ll Collateral described in First Amended and Restated Security Agreement dated March 9, 2015 between Debtor and Secured Party."

Two years later, I80 Equipment defaulted on the loan and filed a voluntary bankruptcy petition under Chapter 7. The court appointed a trustee to manage the bankruptcy assets. First Midwest sued the trustee, seeking to recover $7.6 million on the loan. It also filed a declaration that its security interest in I80 Equipment's assets was properly perfected and senior to the interests of all other claimants, including the trustee. The trustee countered that First Midwest's security interest was not properly perfected because its financing statement did not independently describe the underlying collateral, but instead incorporated the list of assets by reference to the parties' security agreement. The trustee also asserted a counterclaim to avoid First Midwest's lien pursuant to §544(a) of the Bankruptcy Code. Both parties moved for judgment on the pleadings.

The bankruptcy court agreed with the trustee and ruled that "[a] financing statement that fails to contain any description of collateral fails to give the particularized kind of notice" required by Article 9 of the UCC. With First Midwest's consent, the trustee sold the estate's assets for approximately $1.9 million and holds the net proceeds pending resolution of this dispute. The parties jointly certified under 28 U.S.C. §158(d)(2)(A) that an immediate appeal of the bankruptcy court's decision to this court would materially advance the progress of the case, and this court granted the parties' petition.

On appeal, neither the validity of the loan nor the legitimacy of First Midwest's security interest is in question. The trustee maintains only that First Midwest's lien is avoidable because the financing statement failed to properly indicate the secured collateral, and First Midwest disagrees.

II

We review de novo questions of statutory interpretation. *In re Robinson*, 811 F.3d 267, 269 (7th Cir. 2016); *United States v. Webber*, 536 F.3d 584, 593 (7th Cir. 2008). When answering a novel question of state law, we look to "relevant state precedents, analogous decisions, considered dicta, scholarly works, and any other reliable data tending convincingly to show how the highest court in the state would decide the issue at hand." *Pisciotta v. Old Nat'l Bancorp*, 499 F.3d 629, 635 (7th Cir. 2007). Here, we apply the UCC as interpreted by Illinois courts and governed by Illinois law. *See In re Blanchard*, 819 F.3d 981, 984 (7th Cir. 2016); *see also Helms v. Certified Packaging Corp.*, 551 F.3d 675, 678 (7th Cir. 2008).

In Illinois courts, statutory construction starts with the statutory language itself. *People v. Grant*, 402 Ill. Dec. 387, 52 N.E.3d 308, 313 (2016). If that language—given its plain and ordinary meaning—is clear and unambiguous, "the court must give it effect and should not look to extrinsic aids for construction." *In re Robinson*, 811 F.3d at 269; *see also Home Star Bank & Fin. Servs. v. Emergency Care & Health Org.*, 379 Ill. Dec. 51, 6 N.E.3d 128, 135 (2014) (when construing a statute, "[i]t is improper for a court to depart from the plain statutory language by reading into the statute exceptions, limitations, or conditions that conflict" with the expressed text); *LaSalle Bank Nat'l v. Cypress Creek 1, LP*, 242 Ill.2d 231, 351 Ill. Dec. 281, 950 N.E.2d 1109, 1113 (2011) (when plain language is "clear and unambiguous, we will apply it as written"); *Webber*, 536 F.3d at 593 ("When the plain wording of the statute is clear, that is the end of the matter.").

We can give statutes their plain and ordinary meaning by applying contemporaneous dictionary definitions, *Landis v. Marc Realty, LLC*, 235 Ill.2d 1, 335 Ill. Dec. 581, 919 N.E.2d 300, 304 (2009), and by reading the statutes in their entirety. *Home Star Bank*, 379 Ill. Dec. 51, 6 N.E.3d at 135 (statutory "[w]ords and phrases should not be viewed in isolation, but should be considered in light of other relevant provisions of the statute"). As the Illinois Supreme Court has explained: "A court must view the statute as a whole, construing words and phrases in light of other relevant statutory provisions and not in isolation. Each word, clause, and sentence of a statute must be given a reasonable meaning, if possible, and should not be rendered superfluous." *People v. Perez*, 385 Ill. Dec. 41, 18 N.E.3d 41, 44 (2014) (citation omitted); *see also In re Melching*, 589 B.R. 846, 848–52 (Bankr. S.D. Ill. 2018) (court considered "the entire statutory scheme" when interpreting Illinois exemption statute). We apply these principles of interpretation to the statutes in this case.

A

At issue here is the text of Article 9 of the UCC, 810 Ill. Comp. Stat. 5/9-101, *et seq.* (2001). In relevant part, §9-502 requires that a financing statement: (1) provide the name of the debtor; (2) provide the name of the secured party or its representative; and (3) *indicate the collateral covered by the financing statement* (emphasis added).

According to §9-504, "[a] financing statement sufficiently indicates the collateral that it covers if the financing statement provides: (1) a description of the collateral pursuant to Section 9-108; or (2) an indication that the financing statement covers all assets or all personal property." Section 9-108 further explains that a description of the secured property does not need to be specific but must "reasonably identif[y]" what is described. Section 9-108 gives six distinct methods by which a description of collateral reasonably identifies the secured property: (1) specific listing; (2) category; (3) type; (4) quantity; (5) mathematical computation or allocation; or (6) "*any other method, if the identity of the collateral is objectively determinable*" (emphasis added).

A financing statement that substantially satisfies these requirements is effective, even if it has minor errors or omissions that are not "seriously misleading." 810 Ill. Comp. Stat. 5/9-506(a). But if a financing statement fails these basic requirements, the lender's interests are subject to avoidance under §544(a) of the Bankruptcy Code.

We must decide whether the statutory language of Article 9 requires that the four corners of the financing statement include a specific description of the secured collateral (either by type, category, quantity, etc.), or if incorporating such a description by reference to a security agreement sufficiently "indicates" the collateral.

The text of §9-108 provides six ways to indicate collateral in a financing statement—including by "any other method"—so long as the identity of the collateral is "objectively determinable." This expands the pre-2001 Article 9 requirements under which a financing statement must: (1) give the name of the debtor or the secured party; (2) be signed by the debtor; (3) include the secured party's address; and (4) *contain a statement indicating the types, or describing the items, of collateral. See* 810 Ill. Comp. Stat. 5/9-402(1) (2001) (emphasis added).

In 2001, the Illinois version of the UCC was revised to no longer require that the financing statement "contain" a description of the collateral; after revision the statement must only "indicate" collateral. Under the revisions, "[a]n indication may satisfy the requirements of Section 9-502(a), even if it would not have satisfied the requirements of former Section 9-402(1)." 810 Ill. Comp. Stat. Ann. 5/9-504 cmt. 2. This pared-down approach reflects the notice function of Article 9:

> This section adopts the system of "notice filing." What is required to be filed is not, as under pre-UCC chattel mortgage and conditional sales acts, the security agreement itself, but only a simple record providing a limited amount of information (financing statement). . . . The notice itself *indicates* merely that a person may have a security interest in the collateral indicated. Further inquiry from the parties concerned will be necessary to disclose the complete state of affairs.

810 Ill. Comp. Stat. Ann. 5/9-502 cmt. 2 (emphasis added). With this context, the ordinary meaning of "indicate" is to serve as a "signal" that "point[s] out" or "direct[s] attention to" an underlying security interest. That plain reading of the text allows a party to "indicate" collateral in a financing statement by pointing or directing attention to a description of that collateral in the parties' security agreement.

This interpretation reflects how we and other courts have understood the UCC's notice function. For example, we have recognized that Article 9 ensures "adequate public notice" of liens and security interests, *In re Blanchard*, 819 F.3d 981, 988 (7th Cir. 2016), and that "the goal of the filing system is to make known to the public whatever outstanding security interests exist in the property of debtors." *Id.* at 986 (citing *In re Hoeppner*, 49 B.R. 124 (Bankr. E.D. Wis. 1985)); *see also Helms v. Certified Packaging Corp.*, 551 F.3d 675, 679 (7th Cir. 2008) ("The purpose of the financing statement is to put third parties on notice that the secured party who filed it may have a perfected security interest in the collateral described, and that further inquiry into the extent of the security interest is prudent.") (citations and quotations omitted); *In re Grabowski*, 277 B.R. 388, 391 (Bankr. S.D. Ill. 2002) (holding the same). This is so Article 9 does not "create a windfall for a bankruptcy estate or a minefield for lenders." *In re Blanchard,* 819 F.3d at 988–89 (citation omitted).

The financing statement itself is an "abbreviation of the security agreement." *Helms,* 551 F.3d at 679. "It is a streamlined paper to be filed for the purpose of giving notice to third parties of the essential contents of the security agreement." *Id.* (citation omitted); *see also Grabowski,* 277 B.R. at 391 (financing statement not required to share same level of detail as security agreement).

The security agreement defines and limits the collateral, while the financing statement puts third parties on notice that a creditor may have an existing security interest in the property and further inquiry may be necessary. *In re Grabowski,* 277 B.R. at 391. In recognizing this distinction between financing statements and security agreements, this court has said:

> The purpose of the financing statement is to place would-be subsequent creditors on notice that a creditor has a security interest in the debtor's property; it is the security agreement . . . that defines that interest and by defining limits it. . . . The security agreement embodies the intention of the parties and is the document which creates the security interest. . . . The financing statement on the other hand need not particularize in detail the collateral secured under the security agreement because in accordance with the "notice filing" concept adopted under the [UCC] a financing statement serves to give notice that the secured party who filed may have a security interest in the collateral and that further inquiry with respect to the security agreement will be necessary to disclose the complete state of affairs.

Helms, 551 F.3d at 680 (citations and quotations omitted). "Hence less detail is required in the financing statement." *Id.*

While financing statements and security agreements both must describe the collateral, "the degree of specificity required of such description depends on the nature of the document involved—whether it is a security agreement or a financing statement. . . ." *In re Grabowski,* 277 B.R. at 390–91. The "prudent potential creditor would [] request[] a copy of the security agreement," *Helms,* 551 F.3d at 680, and "need look no further than the security agreement" to resolve questions about the adequacy of the collateral description. *Id.* at 681. The different treatment of these two documents highlights the distinct function each serves under Article 9: the financing statement provides notice of an underlying security interest, while the security agreement creates and specifically defines that interest.

B

Bankruptcy courts for all three districts in Illinois have recognized this distinction and have noted that incorporation by reference is an available method for describing collateral. The Southern District of Illinois bankruptcy court has held that a financing statement was sufficient to perfect a bank lender's interest "[d]espite the generality of the Bank's description" of collateral. *In re Grabowski*, 277 B.R. at 392. In *Grabowski*, Bank of America filed a financing statement indicating it had a lien on the debtor's property consisting of "all inventory, chattel paper, accounts, equipment, and general intangibles." *Id.* at 391-92. The court rejected the subsequent creditor's argument that the description was "too general," finding it still "fulfill[ed] the notice function of a financing statement under the UCC," even though the financing statement misstated the debtor's property address and did not otherwise specifically identify the security interest. *Id.* at 392. The court noted that "only a super-generic" description—such as "all the debtor's assets" or "all the debtor's personal property" without any limiting factor—is insufficient under the reasonable identification standard of §9-108. *Id.* at 391. The court found "[t]his exceedingly general standard for describing collateral in a financing statement" reflects the traditional notice function a financing statement was designed to serve. *Id.*

The Central District of Illinois bankruptcy court in *In re Duesterhaus Fertilizer* ruled that a financing statement with a collateral description incorporated by reference to the previous financing statement was insufficient under Article 9 because the previous statement had lapsed. 347 B.R. 646 (Bankr. C.D. Ill. 2006). The new financing statement included "no indication of collateral whatsoever," and even the reference to the previous, lapsed statement did not specify that a description of the collateral subject to the security interest could be found there. *Id.* at 650. Even so, the court embraced incorporation by reference as an available method for indicating collateral, at least in new or "continuing" financing statements: "Absent an express state law requirement that the continuation statement contain a description of collateral, reference to another document in the same public record would appear to meet the notice requirements." *Id.* at 651.

Two years before *In re Duesterhaus*, the bankruptcy court for the Northern District of Illinois suggested incorporation by reference may satisfy the UCC's collateral description requirements for financing statements. *In re Macronet Group, Ltd.*, 2004 WL 2958447 (Bankr. N.D. Ill. 2004). Ultimately the court held that the lender's security interest failed to attach to the debtor's collateral. *Id.* at *5. But that decision was based on the absence of an authenticated underlying security agreement from which the identity of the collateral could be objectively determined, not the lender's choice to indicate the collateral by reference to the agreement. *Id.* ("[I]t may be true that incorporating a collateral description in a separate document, such as a form financing statement, by reference into a security agreement could qualify as 'any other method' of identification pursuant to UCC section 9-108. . . .").

The approach of these courts to financing statements supports the conclusion that incorporation by reference is permissible in Illinois as "any other method" under §9-108, so long as the identity of the collateral is objectively determinable. That requirement is met here by the security agreement's detailed list of the collateral. The financing statement covers: "All Collateral described in First Amended and Restated Security Agreement dated March 9, 2015 between Debtor and Secured Party." There is no dispute that the financing statement names (as terms defined earlier in the document) both the debtor (I80 Equipment) and the secured party (First Midwest). The statement has not lapsed and includes the date and precise title of the underlying document. It describes the security interest by referencing "[a]ll [c]ollateral" as described in the underlying security agreement between the parties. For its part, the security agreement references twenty-six independent categories of collateral covered by the agreement, including accounts, cash, equipment, goods, financial assets, deposits, investments, instruments, inventory, and all proceeds of any assets. Although a subsequent creditor is not expected to be a "super-detective" while investigating prior secured transactions, *In re Grabowski*, 277 B.R. at 392, the financing statement in this case "notif[ied] subsequent creditors that a lien may exist and that further inquiry [was] necessary to disclose the complete state of affairs." *Id.* at 391 (quotations omitted).

III

The plain and ordinary meaning of Illinois's revised version of the UCC allows a financing statement to indicate collateral by reference to the description in the underlying security agreement. This interpretation is reinforced by how Illinois bankruptcy courts construe these statutes. For these reasons, we hold that the trustee is not entitled to avoid First Midwest's lien under the Bankruptcy Code.

We Reverse and Remand for further proceedings in the bankruptcy court.

PROBLEM 324

When you sign up for a credit card the agreement will often have this clause: "Cardholder hereby grants the Issuer a security interest in all goods purchased on your Account." Does this sufficiently describe the law books you subsequently buy with the card? Compare In re Murphy, 2013 WL 1856337 (Bankr. D. Kan. 2013), and In re Cunningham, 489 B.R. 602 (Bankr. D. Kan. 2013).

PROBLEM 325

The financing statement described the collateral as:

> All assets of the Debtor including, but not limited to, any and all equipment, fixtures, inventory, accounts, chattel paper, documents, instruments, investment property, general intangibles, letter-of-credit rights and deposit accounts now owned and hereafter acquired by Debtor and located at or relating to the operation of the premises at 100 River Rock Drive, Suite 304, Buffalo, New York, together with any products and proceeds thereof including, but not limited to, a certain Komori 628 P+L Ten Color Press and Heidelberg B20 Folder and Prism Print Management System.

After the financing statement was filed and payment commenced the debtor moved everything in the business to a new location in Buffalo. No one thought to amend the financing statement. Will this description be sufficient to give the creditor a valid interest in the same assets at the new Buffalo location? See In the Matter of Sterling United, Inc., 674 Fed. Appx. 19, 21 (2d Cir. 2016).

PROBLEM 326

Polly Travis owned a clothing store that was doing quite well, so she decided to open branches all over the state. She borrowed money to do so from Longhorn State Bank, which took a security interest (according to the filed financing statement) in "all inventory, accounts receivable, equipment, instruments, general intangibles, and personal property." The bank also made her pledge her extensive collection of jewelry to the bank, making her bring it from her home and putting it in the vault. A year later, she asked to have the jewelry back so that she could wear it to a social occasion, and the bank gave it to her. Before she could return it to the bank, another creditor seized it by judicial process. You are the lawyer for Longhorn State Bank. Is their interest in the jewelry perfected by the filed financing statement? What will be your argument? See In re Boogie Enters., Inc., 866 F.2d 1172 (9th Cir. 1989); Merchants Natl. Bank v. Halberstadt, 425 N.W.2d 429 (Iowa App. 1988).

A much-discussed issue facing the drafters of the Uniform Commercial Code was the wisdom of permitting debtors to encumber not only their current property, but also property that they would acquire in the future. In the end, freedom of contract prevailed, and debtors are allowed (with one exception involving consumer goods, discussed later) to use future as well as current property as collateral for a credit extension. Where this is done, the so-called "floating lien" arises, because the creditor's lien will attach to new property without the signing of any further paperwork. Read §9-204(a).

PROBLEM 327

The security agreement and the financing statement both described the collateral as "inventory." Does this limit the security interest to existing inventory only, or does the security interest extend to replacement for the original collateral? See In re Filtercorp, Inc., 163 F.3d 570 (9th Cir. 1998). If the security agreement had said "inventory now owned or after acquired" but the financing statement had simply mentioned "inventory," does this perfect a security interest in after-acquired inventory? See Official Comment 3 to §9-108 and Official Comment 2 to §9-502; Kubota Tractor Corp. v. Citizens & S. Natl. Bank, 198 Ga. App. 830, 403 S.E.2d 218 (1991) (similar issue where collateral was "all farm equipment"). The same problem arises if the collateral consists of accounts receivable. See In re Shenandoah Warehouse Co., 202 B.R. 871 (Bankr. W.D. Va. 1996).

PROBLEM 328

Mark Escoto, a dentist, gets a loan from a patient to fund litigation arising out of defective construction of Escoto's home. Escoto signs a promissory note providing that the loan will be due in three years or upon settlement of the litigation. The note further states:

> Escoto et al. further pledge any and all personal possessions holdings and items of value as security and collateral for payment of this note and by this note grant Lender-Hillsman the right to remove any and all possessions of Escoto et al. to be sold as necessary to recover debt in full and to effect garnishment of any paycheck, settlement monies, or other assets without the need of a court order regarding the same.

Escoto comes into funds as a result of settling the lawsuit. Do the settlement funds become collateral of the patient creditor? See In re Escoto, No. 2:13-AP-01058-MKN, 2017 WL 1075046, at *4 (B.A.P. 9th Cir. 2017).

Section 9-108 (read it along with its Official Comment 2) speaks to the faulty description problem in both the security agreement and the financing statement. The test adopted by the courts is the one from the Official Comment: "whether the description does the job assigned to it, i.e., make possible the identification of the thing described." Marine Midland

Bank-Eastern Natl. Assn. v. Conerty Pontiac-Buick, Inc., 77 Misc. 2d 311, 352 N.Y.S.2d 953 (Sup. Ct. 1974). Or, because later potential creditors will be doing the records searching, would a "reasonable person" be put on inquiry as to the identity of the collateral? Ray v. City Bank & Trust Co., 358 F. Supp. 630 (S.D. Ohio 1973). The UCC adopts a system of *notice filing,* so that the description in the financing statement must be sufficient to alert the searcher to the necessity for further inquiry. "The description need only inform, it need not educate," *Marine Midland Bank,* supra, at 960; see also Official Comment 2 to §9-502.

PROBLEM 329

The financing statement's description said "Various Equipment, see attached list." No list was attached. Is the statement sufficient to perfect a security interest in the debtor's equipment? See Chase Manhattan Bank v. J. & L. Gen. Contractors, Inc., 832 S.W.2d 204 (Tex. App. 1992).

PROBLEM 330

The security agreement stated that the collateral was "machinery, equipment, furniture and fixtures." To this list the financing statement added "inventory and accounts receivable." The parties are all willing to testify that the loan was intended to be secured by inventory and accounts receivable as well as by the items listed in the security agreement. Other creditors object. Does the secured party's interest reach inventory and accounts receivable? See §9-203(b) and In re Martin Grinding & Mach. Works, Inc., 793 F.2d 592 (7th Cir. 1986) ($233,000 lost as a result of this error!).

PROBLEM 331

The loan officer at Octopus National Bank has sent you, the bank's attorney, an e-mail with the following question. The bank is planning to make a loan to Luddite Technology, Inc., and wants to take a security interest in all of the equipment of the debtor. However, Luddite's most important piece of equipment is the very expensive Abacus-12, which designs computer hardware. Should the security agreement be drafted to say that the debtor grants a security interest in "the Abacus-12 plus all other equipment," "all equipment, particularly the Abacus-12," or simply "all equipment"? Or do you have a better phraseology?

PROBLEM 332

The security agreement stated that the tractor buyer granted a security interest to "______________," but the seller forgot to fill in his name. The seller later filed a financing statement showing he had a secured interest in the buyer's tractor. Is the purported document with the blank a §9-203 security agreement? What about the financing statement? What about both? See In re Bollinger Corp., 614 F.2d 924 (3d Cir. 1980).

NOTE

To meet all the above objectives, the wise creditor will:

1. Make sure all the forms are correctly filled out in all particulars;
2. check the debtor's technical legal name now and in the immediate past and make sure it is correctly listed on all documents, and given the 2010 amendments to Article 9, take a close look at the debtor's driver's license;
3. refile if the debtor's name changes in any way;
4. describe the collateral as accurately and completely as possible in all documents; and
5. inquire into the source of the debtor's title to ensure that the former owner's creditors have no valid claims.

III. ATTACHMENT OF THE SECURITY INTEREST

Attachment is the process by which the security interest in favor of the creditor becomes effective against the debtor. *Perfection* is the process by which the creditor's security interest becomes effective against most of the rest of the world. The steps involved in attachment are described in §9-203. They are:

1. a security agreement must be "authenticated" (defined in §9-102(a)(7) to mean "signed" or the electronic equivalent), or the creditor must have possession or control of the collateral, pursuant to an oral agreement with the debtor;
2. the creditor must give *value* (defined in §1-204—after all, you shouldn't get a security interest unless you've done something to deserve it); and

3. the debtor must have some rights in the collateral (one cannot give a security interest in property one does not own or have some legal interest in).

Read both §§9-203 and 9-204.

PROBLEM 333

If the creditor agrees to provide value to a third party on the debtor's request, will the security interest still attach to the debtor's property? See Royce v. Michael R. Needle, P.C., 2019 WL 2189261 (N.D. Ill. 2019).

Border State Bank of Greenbush v. Bagley Livestock Exchange, Inc.

Court of Appeals of Minnesota, 2004
690 N.W.2d 326

LANSING, Judge.

This action arises from a dispute over the enforceability of a security interest and the interpretation of the cattle-sharing agreement that underlies the security interest. The district court, apparently relying on an incorrect argument that an ownership interest was necessary for the security interest to attach, made no findings on the disputed provisions of the agreement. We therefore reverse the district court's order directing a verdict against the bank, which attempted to enforce the security interest in a conversion claim, and remand for the court to address the disputed provisions. We affirm, however, the jury verdict adjudicating the claims between the cattlemen on the breach of the underlying cattle-sharing agreement. The record contains competent evidence to sustain the verdict, the special-verdict form conveyed a correct understanding of the law, and the damages assessed by the jury do not require remittitur.

FACTS

Bert Johnson, doing business as Johnson Farms, and Hal Anderson entered into an oral cattle-sharing contract in December 1997. Approximately one month later, they memorialized the oral contract in written form. Under the written instrument, Anderson agreed to care for and breed cattle owned by Johnson and Johnson would receive a "guaranteed" percentage of the annual calf crop. The contract further provided that the cattle Johnson placed with Anderson were "considered to be owned by Johnson Farms and any offspring is to be sold under Johnson Farms' name." The contract required Johnson Farms and Anderson mutually to agree when the calves would be sold and within thirty days of receiving money for the sale, Johnson Farms to pay the "remainder" to Anderson "for his keeping of [the] cattle."

In the fall of 1998 and 1999, calves bred under the contract were sold under the provisions of the written contract. Anderson testified that in October 1999, Johnson asked him to care for additional cattle on the same terms. Anderson initially declined, explaining to Johnson that he was ending his cattle business because of adverse personal circumstances. Anderson said that his father had died, his mother was in a nursing home, his partner, Linda Peterson, was caring for an ill family member, he had no additional help at his farm, he had insufficient feed for the cattle, and he had not planted hay for the coming winter. Nevertheless, according to Anderson, they continued to discuss their cattle-sharing contract, and he eventually agreed to continue based on certain modifications: (1) the share percentage would be a straight 40/60 split, without Johnson's "guaranteed" percentage; (2) Johnson would provide feed, including beet tailings; (3) Johnson would provide additional pasture; and (4) the agreement would include approximately 500 cattle, instead of the original 151 cattle.

Johnson testified that he discussed the cattle-sharing agreement with Anderson in October 1999 and that he agreed to send Anderson beet tailings, which were free to him, so long as Anderson paid the cost of shipping. Johnson also testified that he and Anderson agreed that approximately 500 cattle would be cared for under the cattle-sharing agreement, rather than the original 151 cattle. But Johnson denied that he had agreed to provide feed, other than the beet tailings, and denied that he had agreed to change the provision that "guaranteed" that his percentage of the calf crop would be calculated on the initial number of cows regardless of whether each produced a calf that survived.

In March 2000, Anderson negotiated with Border State Bank for loans totaling $155,528. To secure these loans, Anderson granted Border State Bank a security interest in, among other things, all of Anderson's "rights, title and interest" in all "livestock" then owned or thereafter acquired.

After the modification of the cattle-sharing contract, Johnson made a number of shipments of beet tailings to Anderson. When Johnson stopped the shipments, he sent checks totaling $55,000 to Anderson for the purchase of feed. In November 2000, Anderson encountered difficulty caring for the cattle due to heavy rainfall and lack of feed. The cattle were reclaimed by Johnson, but the calves remained with Anderson for sale. At trial, Anderson testified that some of the cattle that Johnson reclaimed were actually Anderson's cattle or were cattle that belonged to Evonne Stephens, another person with whom Anderson had a cattle-sharing contract.

In December 2000, 289 calves that had remained with Anderson were sold at Bagley Livestock Exchange. The livestock exchange knew of Border State's security interest in Anderson's livestock but, after discussing the agreement with Johnson, determined the security interest did not attach to the calves. The livestock exchange issued a check to Johnson Farms in the amount of $119,403. Thereafter, Johnson gave Anderson a check for $19,404, representing Anderson's share of the sale proceeds, less $55,000 that Johnson claimed as repayment for money advanced to Anderson to purchase feed.

Border State Bank sued Bagley Livestock Exchange and Johnson, contending that they had converted Border State Bank's perfected security interest in the calves sold in December 2000. In a third-party complaint, Johnson sought indemnity from Anderson, in the event that Border State Bank was successful on its conversion claim. Anderson served a counterclaim against Johnson, asserting breach of contract.

These claims were tried to a jury in September 2003. Following Border State Bank's case-in-chief, Johnson and Bagley Livestock Exchange moved for a directed verdict. The district court granted the motion, finding that, under the cattle-sharing agreement, Johnson did not "grant" Anderson an "ownership interest" in the calves. Border State Bank appeals from the directed verdict on its conversion claim.

Following the directed verdict, Anderson presented evidence on his breach-of-contract counterclaim against Johnson, and the counterclaim was submitted to the jury. In response to special-verdict questions, the jury determined that the written contract between Anderson and Johnson had been modified, Johnson breached the contract, and Johnson's breach directly caused damages to Anderson in the amount of $92,360. Johnson moved for judgment notwithstanding the verdict (JNOV), or, in the alternative, a new trial or remittitur. The district court denied Johnson's posttrial motions. Johnson appeals from that denial.

Issues

I. Did the district court err by issuing a directed verdict against Border State Bank?

II. Does the record contain competent evidence to sustain the verdict?

III. Did the district court abuse its discretion by denying Johnson's motion for new trial?

IV. Did the district court abuse its discretion by submitting to the jury a special-verdict form that conveyed an incorrect understanding of the law?

V. Were the damages assessed by the jury so unjustified that the district court abused its discretion in denying the posttrial motion for remittitur?

ANALYSIS

I. . . .

Article 9 of the Uniform Commercial Code, incorporated into Minnesota law, provides that a security interest attaches to collateral, and is enforceable against the debtor or third parties, when (1) value has been given; (2) the debtor "has rights in the collateral or the power to transfer rights"; and (3) the debtor has signed a security agreement that contains a description of the collateral. Minn. Stat. §336.9-203(b) (2002). To perfect the security interest, both the security agreement and financing statement must contain an adequate description of the collateral. Prod. Credit Assn. of W. Cent. Minn. v. Bartos, 430 N.W.2d 238, 240 (Minn. App. 1988). We liberally construe descriptions in the security agreement and financing statement because their essential purpose is to provide notice, not to definitively describe each item of collateral. World Wide Tracers, Inc. v. Metro. Prot. Inc., 384 N.W.2d 442, 447 (Minn. 1986).

The parties do not dispute that Anderson signed a security agreement and that value was given. The security agreement stated that the collateral included, in part, "all livestock owned or hereafter acquired" and Anderson's "rights, title and interest" in such livestock. The financing statements covered "all livestock," whether "now owned or hereafter acquired, together with the proceeds from the sale thereof." The parties also do not dispute the validity of these descriptions or the assertion that "livestock" includes cattle and calves. What is disputed is whether the bank's security interest attached to the 289 calves sold in December 2000 under Anderson and Johnson's cattle-sharing agreement. See Wangen v. Swanson Meats, Inc., 541 N.W.2d 1, 3 (Minn. App. 1995) (stating that if security interest attaches to collateral transferred to third party, secured party may repossess collateral or maintain action for conversion), review denied (Minn. Jan. 25, 1996).

In directing a verdict against Border State Bank's conversion claim, the district court did not issue a written order. The district court, instead, briefly stated the decision on the record at the conclusion of Border State Bank's case-in-chief, following arguments by counsel. Johnson's attorney couched his argument in terms of "who actually owned these cattle." The attorney for the cattle exchange cast his argument in terms of a "mutual mistake of fact as to the ownership" and also referred to an "ownership interest." Anderson's attorney, in response, argued that "[m]erely titling something in somebody's name" does not determine "ownership interest." And the bank's attorney asserted that the provisions in the contract did not "indicate who owns [the] calves." The district court stated on the record that the cattle-sharing contract had not "granted" Anderson an "ownership interest" in the calves, specifically finding that "the modifications testified to by Mr. Anderson in the light most favorable to Border State Bank do not modify the terms of the agreement such that an ownership interest is granted." Based on the arguments presented, the district court apparently determined that, for Border State Bank's security interest to attach, Johnson would have had to grant Anderson an interest equivalent to ownership.

The provisions of the Uniform Commercial Code's Article 9, incorporated into Minnesota law, refer to "rights in the collateral," not solely the "ownership" of the collateral. Minn. Stat. §336.9-203(b)(2) (stating security interest may attach to collateral if "the debtor has rights in the collateral or the power to transfer rights in the collateral"). Rights in the collateral, as the term is used in Article 9, include full ownership and limited rights that fall short of full ownership. Minn. Stat. Ann. §336.9-203 U.C.C. cmt., para. 6 (West 2002) ("A debtor's limited rights in collateral, short of full ownership, are sufficient for a security interest to attach."); see also Greenbush State Bank v. Stephens, 463 N.W.2d 303, 306 (Minn. App. 1990) (explaining that "ownership" under the UCC can be shared, with each party possessing its own bundle of interests"), review denied (Minn. Feb. 4, 1991). Simply stated, the UCC "does not require that collateral be owned by the debtor." State Bank of Young Am. v. Vidmar Iron Works, Inc., 292 N.W.2d 244, 249 (Minn. 1980).

Other jurisdictions have cautioned against an interpretation that ownership rights are necessary for the attachment of a security interest. For purposes of the UCC, "sufficient rights" arise with far less than full ownership. Kinetics Tech. Intl. Corp. v. Fourth Natl. Bank of Tulsa, 705 F.2d 396, 398-99 (10th Cir. 1983). Ownership or title is not the relevant concern under Article 9; "the issue is whether the debtor has acquired sufficient rights in the collateral so that the security interest would attach." Fricke v. Valley Prod. Credit, Assn., 721 S.W.2d 747, 753 (Mo. Ct. App. 1986). The "rights in the collateral" language is a "gateway through which one looks to other law to determine the extent of the debtor's rights." Am. Bank & Trust v. Shaull, 678 N.W.2d 779, 788 (S.D. 2004). Thus, "[a]ll or some of owner's rights can be transferred by way of sale, lease, or license [and a] person with transferable rights can grant an enforceable security interest in those rights." Id. at 788, n.4. A "security interest will attach to the collateral only to the extent of the debtor's rights in the collateral"; mere possession of the collateral is insufficient to support an attachment, but the debtor need not have full ownership. Pleasant View Farms, Inc. v. Ness, 455 N.W.2d 602, 604 (S.D. 1990). "The common conceptualization of property rights as consisting of a bundle of sticks is helpful in understanding when a debtor has sufficient rights in an asset to grant an enforceable Article 9 security interest." First Natl. Bank of Philip, S.D. v. Temple, 642 N.W.2d 197, 204 (S.D. 2002) (quotation omitted).

The district court did not analyze the modified cattle-sharing contract to determine the nature of Anderson's rights in the calves or whether

Anderson's interests or rights were sufficient to permit attachment of a security interest. We conclude that the standard relied on by the district court is inconsistent with Minnesota law. The application of the incorrect standard prematurely terminated the analysis of the cattle-sharing agreement, which is necessary to determine whether Anderson's rights in the collateral were sufficient for the bank's security interest to attach. Findings of fact that are controlled or influenced by errors of law are not final and must be set aside. Webb Bus. Promotions, Inc. v. Am. Elecs. & Entm't Corp., 617 N.W.2d 67, 73 (Minn. 2000). Because the district court applied a standard of ownership that is inconsistent with Minnesota law, its finding that the security interest did not attach was influenced by an error of law.

In applying the correct legal standard, the district court must initially determine whether the cattle-sharing agreement is ambiguous. Turner v. Alpha Phi Sorority House, 276 N.W.2d 63, 66 (Minn. 1979). The agreement suggests ambiguity by stating that the cattle provided by Johnson continue to be "owned" by Johnson, but, with respect to the calves, requiring only that they are to be sold in Johnson's "name." When contract language is susceptible to more than one meaning, the interpretation of the contract becomes a question of fact. Trondson v. Janikula, 458 N.W.2d 679, 681 (Minn. 1990). The parties whose interests are affected by this determination should have a full opportunity to argue whether the cattle-sharing contract is ambiguous. For these reasons, we reverse the district court's order that directed the verdict on Border State Bank's conversion claim. On remand, the district court shall consider the cattle-sharing agreement to determine whether Anderson had "rights" in the calves, to which the bank's security interest attached. . . .

DECISION

Minn. Stat. §336.9-203(b) (2002) refers to "rights in the collateral." The district court applied the wrong legal standard by limiting its inquiry to whether Anderson owned the cattle and erred in failing to address whether the debtor held "rights" in the collateral under the cattle-sharing agreement. We reverse the directed verdict on the bank's conversion claim and remand for further proceedings. Because the record contains competent evidence to sustain the verdict, the special-verdict form conveyed a correct understanding of the law, and the damages assessed by the jury did not so greatly exceed adequate compensation as to require remittitur, we affirm the district court's denial of Johnson's posttrial motions.

Affirmed in part, reversed in part, and remanded.

PROBLEM 334

Roy Gabriel decided to go into the music business and borrowed $35,000 from Octopus National Bank (ONB) in order to open his shop, named Gabriel's Trumpets. On January 6 he signed a security agreement with the bank, giving ONB an interest in all "existing and after-acquired inventory in the store." That same day he received the money. On January 6 his inventory consisted of four guitars and a pitch pipe. Gabriel did have a contract with Triumphant Trumpet Manufacturing Company (TTMC) to sell him 40 trumpets, which he paid for in advance of the delivery date (March 30). On March 15 TTMC packaged the 40 trumpets and marked them "For Shipment to Gabriel's Trumpet Store." On March 30 TTMC shipped them to Gabriel, who received them that day and displayed them in the store.

(a) On what day or days did the bank's security interest *attach* (that is, become effective) to the guitars, pitch pipe, and trumpets? See §9-203(a) and read §2-501. (Why is it relevant?) Cf. Cyber Solutions International, LLC v. Priva Security Corp., 2017 WL 3599578 (W.D. Mich. 2017).

(b) Does your answer change if we add the fact that the bank filed a proper financing statement covering Gabriel's inventory on January 7? Can a financing statement be filed before the security agreement is signed? Attached? See §9-502(d). Why would a creditor wish to file a financing statement before the security interest had attached? See §9-322(a)(1).

(c) If the bank did not advance any money until March 31 (the date the bank actually saw the trumpets in the store), and if the bank did not make any commitment (see §9-102(a)(69)) to advance any money until that date, when did the security interest attach?

PROBLEM 335

Daniel Huron loaned Jennifer Ontario money to buy a car. They agreed over the phone that the car would be collateral for the debt. After Huron sent a form to the Registry of Motor Vehicles, he was listed as a creditor on the car's certificate of title. Does he have a security interest in the car? Compare In re Crandall, 346 B.R. 220 (Bankr. M.D. Fla. 2006), with In re Westermeyer, 2012 WL 2952176 (Bankr. C.D. Ill. 2012).

PROBLEM 336

ACRO, Inc., owed considerable funds to its bank. The bank subsequently obtained possession of valuable promissory notes belonging to ACRO, and, because the transactions were closed in the bank's offices, the notes were put in the bank's vault. Did the notes become collateral for ACRO's debt to the bank? See In re ACRO Bus. Fin. Corp., 357 B.R. 785 (Bankr. D. Minn. 2006); In re Debaeke, 2011 WL 5563543 (Bankr. E.D. Mich. 2011).

In re Howell Enterprises, Inc.

United States Court of Appeals, Eighth Circuit, 1991
934 F.2d 969

ROSENBAUM, J.

It all started simply enough. Howell Enterprises, Inc. (Howell) and Tradax America, Inc. (Tradax) both sell rice. A customer, Bar Schwartz Limited (Bar Schwartz), wanted to buy some rice and pay for it with a commercial letter of credit. But Bar Schwartz could not buy rice from Howell because Howell would not accept the commercial letter of credit as payment. This means of payment was acceptable to Tradax, but Bar Schwartz refused to buy rice from Tradax for reasons of its own. So, Howell and Tradax came up with a plan—Tradax would sell its rice to Bar Schwartz under Howell's name. This seemingly simple solution created the complex legal problem now before the court, a problem the parties clearly did not contemplate when the transaction took place.

I. BACKGROUND

Howell is an Arkansas corporation engaged in the business of buying, selling, storing, and milling rice. On June 20, 1986, Howell borrowed $2,100,000 from the First National Bank of Stuttgart, Arkansas (First National), and granted the bank a security interest in all accounts receivable.

Tradax is a New York corporation engaged in the business of buying and selling rice in the United States and abroad. Tradax transacted business with Howell on a regular basis in 1987. One of those transactions engendered this lawsuit.

On February 25, 1987, a contract was signed in the name of Howell, under which rice would be sold by Tradax to Bar Schwartz. Payment was to be accomplished by a one-year commercial letter of credit. Names were used interchangeably throughout the transaction: Tradax was listed as the owner on some shipping documents and on one bill of lading; Howell was listed on another bill of lading and on the certificate of origin; Tradax prepared the shipper's export declaration, but identified the shipper as Howell; Tradax paid the shipping and loading expenses and the brokerage fees, but sometimes did so under Howell's name.

Critical to this controversy, Howell listed the Bar Schwartz transaction as an account receivable on its books, with a corresponding and equivalent account payable to Tradax. Tradax documented the transaction on its books as a sale to Howell, but did not invoice Howell for a sale.

The rice was successfully, but not uneventfully, delivered to Bar Schwartz.[6] In due course, Howell sent an invoice to Bar Schwartz for the purchase price of the rice. On April 29, 1987, Bar Schwartz arranged for the letter of credit to be issued, naming Howell as beneficiary.

On June 18, 1987, Howell presented the letter of credit and the necessary supporting documents to First National. It was understood that Howell would transfer the proceeds to Tradax when the letter of credit matured, in May, 1988. But on April 4, 1988, before the maturity date, Howell filed for Chapter 11 bankruptcy. Upon the filing of the bankruptcy, First National came forward to claim its perfected security interest in Howell's accounts receivable. The Bar Schwartz letter of credit was swept into the bankruptcy.

Tradax brought this complaint before the bankruptcy court on May 9, 1988, asserting that Bar Schwartz's letter of credit was not one of Howell's accounts receivable and therefore was not subject to First National's security interest. Tradax alternatively argued that the letter of credit was subject to a constructive trust in favor of Tradax.

In an order, entered September 8, 1989, the bankruptcy court ruled that Tradax did have an equitable interest in the letter of credit and its proceeds as beneficiary of a constructive trust. The bankruptcy court then looked to the UCC as adopted in Arkansas to define First National's security interest in "all accounts receivable." Section §4-9-106 of the Arkansas Statutes defines "account" as "any right to payment for goods sold." The bankruptcy court ruled that because the letter of credit could be characterized as a "right to payment," First National had a perfected security interest in the letter of credit. The bankruptcy court, faced with two competing claims to the letter of credit, found that First National qualified as a bona fide purchaser for value and held an interest superior to Tradax's equitable interest.

Tradax appealed to the district court, which affirmed on April 16, 1990. On appeal, Tradax argued that the district court erred in ruling that the Bar Schwartz letter of credit was an "account" or evidence of a right to payment to Howell, that First National had a security interest in the letter of credit and that First National was entitled to prevail on general equitable principles.

6. A short time after the rice was loaded on a barge, Tradax determined that the ship which would carry the rice overseas was delayed. Tradax arranged a swap with Sunrice, another rice trading company, whereby the original barge-load was sold in exchange for a barge-load of rice available at a later date. The second load of rice was loaded aboard the ocean-going vessel on May 26, 1987.

II. Discussion

As the second reviewing court, we review the bankruptcy court's legal conclusions de novo and its factual findings under the clearly erroneous standard. Wegner v. Grunewaldt, 821 F.2d 1317, 1320 (8th Cir. 1987). The parties, in this case, do not dispute the factual findings of the bankruptcy court. This case turns, instead, on the legal characterization of the Bar Schwartz letter of credit. As such, our review is de novo.

Both parties acknowledge that First National had a perfected security interest in Howell's accounts receivable. As the parties would frame the issue, if the letter of credit is an account receivable, First National is entitled to its proceeds; if not an account receivable, the asset goes to Tradax.

The court eschews the parties' categorical inquiry. A letter of credit is an instrument of commerce, which is sui generis.[7] Its unique character is reflected in the fact that Article 5 of the UCC is devoted to letters of credit. The court is disinclined to go beyond the UCC and decide this case on unnecessarily broad grounds. Analysis reveals that the court need not answer whether a letter of credit can ever constitute an account. It is clear that this particular letter of credit was never intended to be an account and was listed as such purely by happenstance.

In this court's view, the primary and relevant inquiry is whether or not First National's undisputed security interest can reach that particular line item in Howell's accounts receivable identified as the Bar Schwartz account. With this inquiry in mind, the court turns to the specific facts of this case.

Arkansas has adopted the UCC secured transactions and letters of credit provisions. Ark. Stat. Ann. §§4-9-101 to 4-9-507; 4-5-101 to 4-5-117. Under Arkansas Statutes, §4-9-203, a security interest cannot attach unless "the debtor has rights in the collateral." The courts below found that Howell had a legal interest in the Bar Schwartz account receivable, subject to Tradax's equitable interest. This court has a less expansive view of Howell's rights.

Howell's only claim to the Bar Schwartz account receivable is by reason of its arbitrarily having elected to record the Bar Schwartz letter of credit on its receivable ledger. Tradax had no opportunity to know of or protest

7. Letters of credit are means of guaranteeing payment for sales of goods. Here, the seller did not wish to deliver goods without assurance of payment; likewise the buyer did not want to pay prior to receiving the goods. The letter of credit resolved this difficulty by substituting a stable third party's, here a bank's, credit for that of the buyer. Upon receiving the letter of credit, the seller delivers the requested goods to a common carrier and obtains a payment-authorizing document in return. The seller presents the letter of credit and the required documentation to the issuing bank to collect payment. After honoring the letter of credit, the bank is entitled to reimbursement and a fee from the buyer. Upon reimbursement, the bank gives the bill of lading to the buyer who then can present it to the common carrier and receive the goods. See generally 2 J. White & R. Summers, Uniform Commercial Code §19-1 (3d ed. 1988) [now vol. 3, §26-1(a) (5th ed. 2008)—Eds.].

this infelicitous listing. More critically, Tradax had no notice that Howell's accounts receivable were encumbered by First National's security interest. The lower courts determined, as matters of fact, that the only agreement between Tradax and Howell was that Howell would allow Tradax to use its name on pertinent documents. Howell did not, and could not, claim any right in the Bar Schwartz account or the proceeds of the letter of credit, because the rice was always owned by Tradax.

Certainly Howell acquired physical possession of the letter of credit, but mere possession of such a document is insufficient to establish a right to collateral upon which to base a security interest. Rohweder v. Aberdeen Production Credit Assn., 765 F.2d 109 (8th Cir. 1985); Pontchartrain State Bank v. Poulson, 684 F.2d 704, 707 (10th Cir. 1982); Montco, Inc. v. Glatzer, 665 F.2d 36, 40 (2d Cir. 1981). Howell was involved in this transaction for the sole and limited purpose of serving as a conduit for Tradax's sale to Bar Schwartz.

This lawsuit, however, became inevitable when Howell mistakenly attempted to "book" the deal. The court finds this factual occurrence to be of no legal effect; the fact of booking this transaction as an account receivable did not make it an account receivable in law. Howell did not own and could not legitimately encumber any interest in the Bar Schwartz account, regardless of the bookkeeping procedure it chose.

Finally, the court declines to embrace the "equitable" theory referenced by the courts below. Each suggested that Tradax was a "culpable" party and was, perforce, responsible for the legal consequences here. Certainly, Tradax and Howell sought to hide the identity of the true seller from Bar Schwartz. But no legal consequences flow from this fact. Legal arrangements through undisclosed partners, agents, and proxies are not unknown in the marketplace. The court finds no reason, based solely on an undisclosed but legal arrangement, to require Tradax to pay twice, with no hope of recompense, for the same barge of rice by permitting First National to execute its security interest on the Bar Schwartz account. Moreover, while First National was an innocent third party in this transaction, First National has shown no detrimental reliance on Howell's accounting error.

III. Conclusion

For the foregoing reasons we reverse the judgment of the district court and remand the case for entry of judgment in favor of Tradax.

PROBLEM 337

To get a loan from Mutsy, Mason signed a security agreement putting up his partnership interest in MMC partners. The partnership agreement has a clause providing that partnership interests may not be assigned. Does the partnership interest become Mutsy's collateral? In re Mason, 2019 WL 1472947 (E.D.N.C. 2019).

Clark v. Missouri Lottery Commission

Missouri Court of Appeals, Western District, 2015
463 S.W.3d 843

JOSEPH M. ELLIS, Judge.

Appellant Gary Clark appeals from the Circuit Court of Cole County's grant of summary judgment in favor of Respondent Community Bank of El Dorado Springs ("Community Bank"). Appellant contends that the circuit court erroneously granted summary judgment because §313.285.12 of the State Lottery Law prohibits the assignment of lottery prizes, thereby making the assignment of his lottery payments, which he used to secure two loans from Community Bank, invalid. For the following reasons, the judgment is affirmed.

The following facts are undisputed. In 2006, Appellant won the Missouri Lottery "Lifetime Riches" prize. The prize entails Appellant receiving $50,000.00 per year for the rest of his life with a minimum payout of thirty years. On October 3, 2007, Appellant entered into a loan agreement with Community Bank in which Appellant granted Community Bank a security interest in the "Assignment of all Missouri Lottery Payments" in exchange for a $100,000.00 loan.

On October 16, 2007, Appellant executed a document titled "Missouri Lottery Payments" in which he agreed "to have all funds from the Missouri Lottery payable to [him] to be deposited in an account" at Community Bank. The document further states that the payments would be deposited into that account "for the purpose of securing payment of each and every debt, liability or obligation of every type or description which [he] may now, or at any time hereafter owe to" Community Bank. The document then states that Appellant understands Community Bank "has full authority and withdrawal rights on this account" and that Appellant "may not revoke this agreement." Attached to the bottom of the document is an acknowledgement of the agreement by the Missouri Lottery.

On July 13, 2010, Appellant executed a consolidated loan agreement with Community Bank in which he granted a security interest in the "Missouri Lottery Payment Assignment" in exchange for a $713,670.96 loan. Under the 2010 loan agreement, Appellant agreed to make twelve installment payments of $500.00 and one final balloon payment of $708,170.96 on July 15, 2011.

On September 3, 2013, Appellant filed a petition for declaratory judgment against Community Bank and the Missouri Lottery Commission. In his petition, Appellant alleged that the "Missouri Lottery Payments" agreement constituted an unlawful assignment of lottery proceeds and, therefore, was void. Appellant requested that the circuit court declare the "Missouri Lottery Payments" agreement void and unenforceable and that the Missouri Lottery Commission be directed to make all future payments to Appellant.

In answering Appellant's petition, Community Bank denied that the assignment was unlawful and filed a counterclaim for declaratory judgment. In its counterclaim, Community Bank alleged that the agreement was a lawful assignment under §400.9-406 of Missouri's Uniform Commercial Code ("UCC"). Community Bank requested that the circuit court declare the "Missouri Lottery Payments" agreement binding on the parties and that the Missouri Lottery Commission continue to pay all lottery proceeds to the designated bank account as long as Appellant owes money to Community Bank.

On January 21, 2014, Community Bank filed a motion for summary judgment in which it contended that it was entitled to judgment as a matter of law because the lottery payments were validly assigned pursuant to §400.9-406. Community Bank alternatively argued that, even if the assignment was void, Appellant should be estopped from claiming the agreement was invalid. In his response to Community Bank's statement of uncontroverted facts, Appellant did not "refute or contest," inter alia that he was "in default in payments under the 2010 loan agreement." However, Appellant filed a counter-motion for summary judgment asserting that he was entitled to judgment as a matter of law because §313.285 prohibits the assignment of lottery proceeds thereby making the assignment void.

On September 15, 2014, the circuit court entered summary judgment in favor of Community Bank. In doing so, the circuit court concluded that the loan agreements between Appellant and Community Bank are valid and enforceable and that the Missouri Lottery Commission should continue to pay all prize monies to the designated account.

Appellant now appeals from the circuit court's grant of summary judgment. "[W]e review the grant of summary judgment de novo." Kershaw v. City of Kansas City, 440 S.W.3d 448, 452 (Mo. App. W.D. 2014) (citing ITT Comm. Fin. Corp. v. Mid-Am. Marine Supply Corp., 854 S.W.2d 371, 376 (Mo. banc 1993)). "Summary judgment is appropriate when there is no genuine issue of material fact and the moving party is entitled to summary judgment as a matter of law." Rapp v. Eagle Plumbing, Inc., 440 S.W.3d 519, 522 (Mo. App. E.D. 2014) (citing Rule 74.04(c)). This Court will review the record and all reasonable inferences therefrom in the light most favorable to the non-movant. *Kershaw*, 440 S.W.3d at 452.

In his sole point, Appellant contends that the circuit court erred in granting summary judgment because the assignment of his lottery proceeds, and the loan agreements resulting therefrom, were invalid in that §313.285.1 prohibits the assignment of lottery proceeds. In doing so, Appellant asserts that §400.9-406 did not impliedly repeal §313.285.1's prohibition against assigning lottery prizes. Rather, Appellant avers that the two statutory provisions must be read together and, to the extent they conflict, §313.285.1 prevails, as it is the specific statute with respect to Missouri lottery prizes. Appellant's argument, however, is contradicted by the plain language of §400.9-406.

Appellant is correct that the State Lottery Law limits the assignment of Missouri lottery prizes. Section 313.285.1 provides, in pertinent part, that "[n]o prize, nor any portion of a prize, nor any right of any person to a prize awarded shall be assignable[.]" Section 313.285.3 further provides: "Notwithstanding any other provision of this section, any person pursuant to an appropriate judicial order may be paid the prize to which the winner is entitled." Therefore, under the State Lottery Law, lottery prizes are unassignable without "an appropriate judicial order." Section 313.285 was last amended in 1993.

In 2001, however, Article 9 of the UCC was amended and defined the term "account" as "a right to payment of a monetary obligation," including "winnings in a lottery or other games of chance operated or sponsored by a state, governmental unit of a state, or person licensed or authorized to operate the game by a state or governmental unit of a state." §400.9-102(a)(2). More importantly, §400.9-406(f) provides:

> [A] rule of law, statute, or regulation, that prohibits [or] restricts . . . the assignment or transfer of, or creation of a security interest in, an account . . . is ineffective to the extent that the rule of law, statute or regulation . . . [p]rohibits [or] restricts . . . the assignment or transfer of, or the creation, attachment, perfection or enforcement of a security interest in, the account[.]

Accordingly, pursuant to §400.9-406(f), any statute that prohibits or restricts the assignment of an account, which includes lottery winnings, is ineffective. Section 400.9-406(f), therefore, renders §313.285.1 ineffective to the extent that it prohibits or restricts the assignment of lottery prizes.[8]

8. Although not binding upon this Court, we recognize that the Texas Supreme Court similarly concluded that the plain language of the UCC indicated the legislature's intent that the UCC provisions permitting the assignment of accounts, including lottery prizes, prevail over Texas's State Lottery Act. Tex. Lottery Comm'n v. First State Bank of DeQueen, 325 S.W.3d 628, 639 (Tex. 2010) (construing Tex. Bus. & Com. Code §9.406(f) (2010), which contained the same language found in §400.9-406(f)). The Texas legislature subsequently

Appellant recognizes that lottery prizes are included in the UCC's definition of an "account" and that §400.9-406 makes "accounts" assignable. Nevertheless, Appellant contends that §313.285.1 prevails over §400.9-406(f) because, to the extent that two statutes relating to the same subject matter conflict and "one statute deals with the subject in general terms and the other deals in a specific way, . . . the specific statute prevails over the general statute." State ex rel. Taylor v. Russell, 449 S.W.3d 380, 382 (Mo. banc 2014) (internal quotation omitted). Appellant asserts that §313.285 constitutes the more specific statute with respect to Missouri lottery prizes and, thus, prevails over §400.9-406.[9]

Appellant's argument relies on a rule of statutory construction. But the plain language of §400-9.406 is quite clear, and therefore we need not resort to principles of statutory construction. "If the intent of the legislature is clear and unambiguous, by giving the language used in the statute its plain and ordinary meaning, then we are bound by that intent and cannot resort to any statutory construction in interpreting the statute." Goerlitz v. City of Maryville, 333 S.W.3d 450, 455 (Mo. banc 2011) (internal quotation omitted). Section 400.9-406(j) provides: "This section prevails over any inconsistent provisions of any statutes, rules, and regulations." The legislature, therefore, expressly provided that §400.9-406 prevails over any other inconsistent statute. Moreover, the current version of §313.285.1 was adopted prior to the enactment of the 2001 amendments to Article 9 of the UCC. Accordingly, to the extent that §313.285.1's prohibition on the assignment lottery prizes is inconsistent with §400.9-406(f), §400.9-406(f) prevails.

Thus, it follows that, despite §313.285.1, Appellant's assignment of his lottery proceeds to Community Bank in order to secure the two loans constitutes a valid assignment. The circuit court, therefore, did not err in granting summary judgment in Community Bank's favor. Point denied. . . .

Judgment affirmed.

---

amended Tex. Bus. & Com. Code §9.406 in 2013 to provide an exception for its state lottery act.

9. In further support of this argument, Appellant cites to a California case in which an appellate court upheld the state's limitations on the assignment of lottery winnings on the basis that the specific provisions of California's lottery act controlled over the more general provisions of the UCC. See Stone Street Capital, LLC v. Cal. State Lottery Comm'n, 165 Cal. App. 4th 109, 80 Cal. Rptr. 3d 326, 333 (2008). Although Appellant encourages us to apply the same rationale here, the California lottery statute at issue in *Stone Street Capital* contained specific provisions allowing assignment of lottery winnings in particular circumstances; the court relied on those provisions in concluding that the lottery statute was the more specific enactment. Id. No similar provisions appear in §313.285.

PROBLEM 338

Antos got a loan from Magnolia Financial Group, signing a security agreement putting up as collateral Antos's interest in a settlement agreement of certain litigation. The settlement agreement, however, has a clause stating that the rights under the agreement may not be assigned. Does Magnolia have a security interest in the funds received under the settlement? Magnolia Fin. Grp. v. Antos, 2017 WL 4286126 (E.D. La. 2017).

CHAPTER 21 ASSESSMENT: MULTIPLE CHOICE QUESTIONS

1. Bruce Banner gets a loan for his biotech business, putting up as collateral his precision scientific instruments. What category of collateral are the instruments?
   a. Instruments.
   b. Inventory.
   c. Equipment.
   d. General intangibles.
   e. All of the above.

2. Banner gets his loan from Hector. The parties make an oral agreement, sealed with a handshake. Hector delivers the money. Banner promises that the instruments are collateral for the debt, although Banner will retain them and use them in the lab's work. If called on to testify, Banner would freely testify to the agreement. Is the security agreement effective to create a security interest? Meaning, for example, will it stand up if Banner goes into bankruptcy or another creditor gets a judgment against Banner?
   a. Yes, because Banner does not deny the effectiveness of the agreement.
   b. Yes, because Hector has performed and so may enforce the agreement.
   c. Yes, if Banner can provide evidence that the money was delivered, such as an account statement.
   d. No, because there was no agreement signed by Banner and Hector was not in possession of the collateral.

3. Pemulis Auto delivered a car to Lloyd under a Lease Agreement, which provided that Lloyd would own the car after making the required payments. Because such a transaction is in substance a secured sale on credit, Article 9 applies to the transaction. Does that mean that Pemulis Auto would have no effective security interest, because the parties signed a Lease Agreement, not a security agreement?

a. Pemulis Auto will not have an effective security interest, for lack of a signed security agreement.
b. Pemulis Auto has an effective security agreement, because the Lease Agreement will qualify as a security agreement.
c. Pemulis Auto will not have a security interest, because it did not provide value.
d. Pemulis Auto will not have a security interest, because Lloyd has no interest in the collateral.

4. Maximilian M. Miltzlaf signed a security agreement to put up his art collection as collateral and got a loan from Slippup Bank. Slippup Bank filed a UCC financing statement, but misspelled the debtor's name as "Maximilian M. Milztlaf." A search of the state's UCC records using its standard search logic under the debtor's correct name does not disclose the financing statement. Is the financing statement effective?
   a. Yes. Even though the debtor's name was slightly misspelled, it was not seriously misleading.
   b. No. The error is deemed seriously misleading, because a search using the correct name does not disclose the statement filed with the incorrect name.
   c. It depends on whether other creditors had been misled by the inaccurate filing.
   d. It depends on whether a search with the incorrect name would disclose the financing statement filed under the correct name.
   e. Yes, as long as the collateral is described correctly. The debtor's name is not important.

5. Assume the financing statement is not effective. Does Slippup Bank have an enforceable security interest?
   a. No. The financing statement is what makes the security interest enforceable.
   b. No. Slippup Bank is an unsecured creditor.
   c. Yes. Slippup Bank has a security interest that is enforceable against Maximilian M. Miltzlaf, but would probably lose its security interest if Miltzlaf went into bankruptcy or another of Miltzlaf's creditors got a judgment lien on the art collection.
   d. Yes. The security agreement is all that is necessary to give Slippup Bank rights in the art collection that will stand up against anyone else.

ANSWERS

1. *C* is the best answer. Instruments are not necessarily instruments. Rather, in classifying collateral, we look to the definitions in the UCC. "Instruments," under §9-102(47), are promissory notes, checks and

the like. Here, the precision scientific instruments are goods (movable things, §9-102(44)). Goods has four subcategories. The precision instruments are not inventory, because they are not held for sale, §9-102(48). They are not farm products, as §9-102(34) quickly confirms. They are not consumer goods, because Banner does not have them for personal, family or household use. §9-102(23). They must then fall into the residual category of goods, equipment. See §9-102(33). They are not remotely general intangibles, which is the residual category for things that do not fall into any of the other defined categories of collateral.

2. *D* is the best answer. Article 9 has a stricter writing requirement than contract law. Sales contracts, for example, may be enforced without a signed writing if the party admits the existence of the contract or if the goods have been accepted. §2-201. But an enforceable security agreement requires either a signed writing or that the creditor is in possession of the collateral. §9-203.
3. *B* is the best answer. To have an enforceable security agreement, the creditor must meet three requirements, under §9-203:
   —a signed security agreement or creditor in possession of the collateral by agreement;
   —value has been given;
   —debtor has rights in the collateral.

   The Lease Agreement will qualify as a security agreement. Article 9 reaches out to cover all transactions that, in effect, create a security interest in personal property. Consistent with that, the definition of "security agreement" is forgiving, covering any agreement that has the effect of creating a security interest in personal property. §9-102(74). Pemulis Auto has given value—not money, but the car. Lloyd has rights in the car, which has been delivered by Pemulis Auto. All three requirements are met and so Pemulis Auto has an enforceable security interest. As later chapters will discuss, Pemulis Auto may find that it faces difficulties if it fails to perfect the security interest or if it does not follow Article 9's rules about enforcing the security interest.
4. *B* is the best answer. The key piece of information in a UCC financing statement is the debtor's name, contrary to *D*, because the records are principally searched using the debtor's name to see if the debtor's property is encumbered. A seriously misleading finance statement is not effective, even if no one was affected, contrary to *C*. For the debtor's name, the UCC provides a test of whether the error was seriously misleading: if a search using the right name discloses the financing statement filed under the incorrect name, then it was not seriously misleading. Even though the error was only switching two letters, it resulted in a search

that did not disclose the statement with the incorrect name. The filing was seriously misleading and so ineffective, contrary to *A*. *D* puts the test backwards.

5. *C* is the best answer. As stated above, to have an enforceable security interest, the creditor needs to meet three requirements: (1) signed security agreement or collateral in possession; (2) value has been given; (3) debtor has rights in the collateral. Slippup Bank has met all three requirements. None of them requires that an effective financing statement has been filed. So Slippup Bank has an enforceable security interest (which also means that its security interest has "attached"). See §9-203.

   What about that ineffective financing statement? A financing statement is not necessary for the security agreement to be enforceable *against the debtor*. But, as later chapters discuss, it may be necessary to make the security interest effective *against other claimants*. Filing a financing statement perfects the security interest. By filing, the creditor gives notice to others of its claim. If the creditor does not perfect, as we will see, it will likely lose to other claimants: Miltzlaf's bankruptcy trustee, another creditor that attaches a judgment lien to the art collection, or a buyer of the art collection. Creditors file financing statements in order to retain priority in the collateral, even if the debtor goes into bankruptcy, if the collateral is attached by a judgment creditor, or if the collateral is sold.

Chapter 22
Perfection of the Security Interest

We are all striving for perfection, of course, but in secured lending the term has a specialized meaning. A creditor's security interest in the debtor's collateral is "perfected" when the creditor has taken all the steps required by the law to give that creditor top-dog priority in that collateral. Later entities may make subsequent claims to the collateral (other creditors, the debtor's trustee in bankruptcy, buyers of the collateral, etc.), and the creditor wants its attorney to make sure that no steps have been missed and that creditor's interest will trump these other claimants. It's easy to make missteps here, missteps that conjure up the ugly word "malpractice." Learning the basics and making sure they are complied with time after time is very important. Lawyers fresh out of law school and familiar with this course will do fine, but as time passes errors may occur as the lawyer gets busy, delegates the duties to assistants, or life inevitably becomes more complicated. Keeping up vigilance here, year after year, will be difficult, but whoever said the practice of law is easy?

If a security interest is *perfected,* it is senior to most later creditor interests (especially that of the trustee in bankruptcy, should the debtor go bankrupt). Read §9-308 carefully. Note particularly that a security interest must first *attach* before perfection is possible. (If you think about it, this is an obvious requirement: a security interest must be effective between the debtor and the creditor before it has legal meaning as to other parties.)

The UCC's most common means of perfection is by having the secured party (the creditor) file a financing statement in the appropriate place. In fact, §9-310 presumes that the filing of a financing statement is the usual way of perfecting a security interest in the debtor's property. However, the Code does permit perfection in other ways too. Perfection of security interests in tangible collateral (goods, instruments, documents, and chattel paper) may be accomplished by the creditor's taking physical possession of the collateral (a common law *pledge*; see below). Further, for some types of collateral the security interest is *automatically* perfected without filing *or* possession; attachment is all that is required. For some goods, such as vehicles, a security interest usually must be perfected by having a notation made on the certificate of title. Finally, perfection for some types of collateral can be accomplished by achieving "control" over the collateral. The legal steps involved in all these sorts of perfection choices are considered next.

I. PERFECTION BY POSSESSION (PLEDGE)

If the collateral is in the physical possession of the creditor, the world at large is alerted to that creditor's possible interest in the property, and no other notice is therefore required. Obviously, only collateral having physical form can be possessed. Read §9-313 and its Official Comments 2, 3, and 4. The Code drafters did not attempt to define "possession," leaving that to the common law. Professors White and Summers comment that possession "is a notoriously plastic idea"; White & Summers §23-8(b) at 1207.

PROBLEM 339

Your client, Archibald Gracie, owns The White Star of England, a famous large diamond currently on display at the Astor Museum in New York. Molly Brown, a wealthy Colorado investor, has agreed to buy the diamond from Gracie, and she has made a substantial down payment, with an agreement to make three more payments before she gets possession. Gracie and Brown have signed the purchase agreement, which contains a clause granting him a security interest in his own diamond until she has made all the required payments. His question to you is this: Can he perfect a security interest in the diamond by simply notifying the Astor Museum of the sale and telling the museum to hold it for his benefit until she makes payment in full, thus creating an escrow arrangement in which possession is held by the escrow agent? See §9-313(c), (f), and (g).

Sometimes the collateral is so large that possession by the secured party is too awkward. In that case it may be possible to store the goods in a warehouse and get a negotiable warehouse receipt representing the goods. Such a receipt is regulated by Article 7 of the Uniform Commercial Code, where an important provision, §7-403(c), provides that the warehouse cannot surrender the goods unless the recipient turns over any outstanding warehouse receipt (a *document of title*—the same rule applies to negotiable bills of lading, another kind of document of title). Read §9-312(c). Sometimes, as in the next Problem, it is more convenient for the warehouse to come to the goods instead of vice versa, a practice called *field warehousing*.

PROBLEM 340

Kiddie Delight, Inc., a manufacturer of toys, wanted to borrow money and use its inventory of toys as collateral. It called up Fred's Field Warehouse Company, and Fred's came to the plant, put the inventory in a locked room, and posted a sign on the door saying "Contents of Room Under Control of Fred's Field Warehouse." Fred's then issued a negotiable warehouse receipt deliverable to the order of Kiddie Delight. Fred's hired Mort Menial, the Kiddie Delight janitor, as its local warehouse custodian (Mort was paid $1 a week by Fred's to mind the goods; he continued to receive his normal paycheck from Kiddie Delight). Kiddie Delight pledged the warehouse receipt (a *document*) to Mammon State Bank in return for a loan. Kiddie Delight went bankrupt shortly thereafter.

(a) By having possession of this document, did the bank have a perfected security interest in the inventory? See §9-312(c) and Official Comment 3 to §9-313.

(b) Assume the warehouse receipt is validly issued and effective. If the bank and Kiddie Delight signed a written security agreement covering the warehouse receipt and the inventory it represented and if the bank gave Kiddie Delight the money, does the bank have a perfected security interest in the warehouse receipt even *before* the bank gets possession of it? See §9-312(e) (this is called *temporary perfection*—see Official Comment 9).

(c) If Kiddie Delight (prior to bankruptcy) wanted to get the warehouse receipt back from the bank in order to present it to the warehouseman (Mort), get the goods, clean them, return them to the field warehouse, and get back the receipt for rehypothecation to the bank, will the bank lose its perfection if it turns the document over to the debtor? Read §9-312(f).

(d) If the bank loses its perfection, who would you advise it to sue? See §7-204(a).

PROBLEM 341

Octopus National Bank (ONB) made a loan to Pi Solutions, Inc., secured by Pi's patent on a solar-powered night light. ONB learned that it is unsettled whether a security interest is perfected by filing in the state UCC office or the federal patent and trademark office. ONB had a brainwave. Rather than filing, can ONB perfect with a pledge—taking possession of Pi's patent certificate? See In re Coldwave Systems, LLC, 368 B.R. 91 (Bankr. D. Mass. 2007).

PROBLEM 342

Karate, Inc., was a self-defense training school. It pledged 36 of the promissory notes given it by its customers to Nightflyer Finance Company in return for a loan. The parties signed a security agreement, and the finance company took possession of the notes. A month later, Karate, Inc.'s president, Arnold Sun, asked Nightflyer to let him have back one of the notes so that he could present it to the customer for payment (an Article 3 *presentment*). The finance company gave him the note on April 6. Sun put it in his desk at the school and forgot about it. On October 12, the karate school went bankrupt. Does the bank have a perfected security interest in any or all of the promissory notes? See §9-312(g) and (h). Could the finance company have protected itself by filing a financing statement as to the promissory notes? See §9-312(a).

NOTE

The primary use of §9-312(e) and (f) occurs in letter of credit transactions (UCC Article 5), wherein the issuing bank receives a bill of lading (a *document*) covering the goods and turns it over to the buyer (*debtor*) so the buyer can get the goods from the carrier, sell them, and reimburse the bank. During the 20-day period the bank's security interest in the document remains perfected even though the document is out of its possession. Under §5-118, a section added to Article 5 by the 1999 revision of Article 9, the issuer of a letter of credit will always have a security interest in bills of lading presented under the letter of credit until the issuer is reimbursed by its customer (the *applicant*).

II. AUTOMATIC PERFECTION

Automatic perfection means that the secured party need only make sure that its security interest has *attached,* and perfection is thereby accomplished without the need for any further steps. The materials below explore the situations in which this occurs.

A. Purchase Money Security Interest in Consumer Goods

The various transactions qualifying for automatic perfection are listed in §9-309. The first of these we will study is the automatic perfection given to purchase money security interests in consumer goods; read §9-309(1). The reason for having an automatic perfection of purchase money security interests in consumer goods without requiring either filing or possession was partly historical (it had always been done that way) and partly practical. Consumer goods are unlikely to be used as collateral *twice,* so there are rarely any later creditors to protect. Filing costs money, and it is simply not worth it for merchants to file to perfect a security interest in every nickel and dime sale (note that there is no automatic perfection for motor vehicles—see §9-311(a)(2); security interests in them require definite steps for perfection, typically notation of the lien interest on the certificate of title once the vehicle leaves the dealer's inventory).

To qualify for automatic perfection under §9-309(1), the security interest in consumer goods must qualify as a *purchase money* interest, a term defined in §9-103. A purchase money security interest (PMSI) is granted to sellers or lenders whose willingness to extend credit permitted the debtor to acquire the collateral. Such creditors obviously have a superior equity in the collateral vis-à-vis other creditors, and the Code therefore frequently affords them special considerations.

PROBLEM 343

Bilko Siding, Inc., put aluminum siding on Mr. and Mrs. Brown's home. They signed a contract on August 4, giving the company a security interest in all their currently owned appliances, machines, art works, sports equipment, and furniture, plus those acquired in the future. On September 25, the Browns went to First Finance Company and borrowed $80 for the stated purpose of buying a sewing machine. They signed a security agreement with the finance company, granting it a security interest in the machine. First

Finance did not file a financing statement. The Browns bought the machine on October 11. They filed for bankruptcy on October 12. Bilko, First Finance, and their trustee all claim the machine.

(a) Did Bilko's security interest attach to the sewing machine? See §9-204(b); In re Johnson, 1973 WL 21366 (Bankr. D. Neb. 1973) (creditor's security interest in "all consumer goods" held totally invalid because the bankruptcy judge found the after-acquired property clause overbroad, unconscionable, and unfair as it had an *in terrorem* effect on consumers). What did the bankruptcy judge in this last-cited opinion mean? And why, in the first place, would Bilko want a security interest in a used sewing machine (which, after all, has little resale value)?

(b) Was the loan agreement a *purchase money security interest* even though First Finance was a lender and not the seller of the machine? See §9-103(a)(2).

(c) Would it have been a purchase money security interest if the Browns had used the $80 to pay a liquor bill and had used $80 from their savings account to buy the sewing machine? How can finance companies protect themselves from the debtor's misuse of the funds advanced? See §3-110(d).

(d) Assuming the $80 was used for the announced purpose, who gets the sewing machine?

Congress thought it was outrageous to allow creditors to take a nonpurchase money security interest in consumer goods that the consumer would otherwise want to claim as exempt from creditor process, so §522(f) of the Bankruptcy Code permits the debtor in bankruptcy to avoid such security interests. This has led to a much-litigated issue: If a purchase money transaction has later been renegotiated and either consolidated with other debts or new money loaned, does it retain its purchase money character so as to escape avoidance under Bankruptcy Code §522(f)? The next case illustrates the problem.

In re Short

United States Bankruptcy Court, Southern District of Illinois, 1994
170 B.R. 128

KENNETH J. MEYERS, Bankruptcy Judge.

Debtors Robert and Dawn Short seek to avoid the lien of American General Finance, Inc. ("American") as a nonpossessory, non-purchase money security interest impairing an exemption claimed by them in household goods. See 11 U.S.C. §522(f)(2). American objects that its lien is a purchase money security interest not subject to avoidance under §522(f)(2) and that its lien retained this status even though the original note granting such interest was consolidated with another obligation of the debtors, with the goods in question serving as collateral for the entire amount. The debtors respond that this refinancing destroyed the purchase money character of American's lien and that the lien, therefore, may be avoided under §522(f)(2).

The facts are undisputed. On June 20, 1992, the debtors entered into a retail installment contract with Anderson Warehouse Furniture for the purchase of bedroom furniture. Under the contract, no interest was charged for one year and no payments were due until June 20, 1993, at which time the entire balance of $2,880 became due. The contract, which granted a security interest in the bedroom furniture purchased by the debtors, was assigned to American on the date it was signed. The debtors made no payments under this contract.

On July 16, 1993, the debtors executed a note with American in which they consolidated the June 20 contract obligation with another note to American for $3,642.33 dated June 22, 1992. The July 16 note in the amount of $7,337.30 provided funds to pay off the June 20 and June 22 notes, with the remaining balance applied to pay credit life and disability insurance premiums. The July 16 note, providing for an interest rate of 21.90 percent, was to be paid in monthly installments, with the final payment due in July 1997.

A disclosure statement accompanying the note described the collateral for the July 16 note as a "continued purchase money interest" in the debtors' bedroom furniture and, on a separate line, listed numerous other recreational and household items owned by the debtors. There was no indication that these latter items served as collateral for the June 22 note or that American had a purchase money security interest in them.

The debtors made one payment under the July 16 note of $248.38 and a partial payment of $146. On January 4, 1994, the debtors filed their Chapter 7 bankruptcy petition. The debtors then moved to avoid American's lien on household goods, including the bedroom furniture, under §522(f)(2).

Discussion

Section §522(f)(2) allows a debtor to avoid the fixing of a lien on property that would otherwise be exempt if such lien is a non-possessory, non-purchase money security interest.[1] The Bankruptcy Code does not define

1. Section 522(f)(2) provides in pertinent part:

> (f) [T]he debtor may avoid the fixing of a lien on an interest of the debtor in property to the extent that such lien impairs an exemption to which the debtor would have been entitled . . . if such lien is —
>
> (2) a nonpossessory, nonpurchase-money security interest in any —
>
> (A) household furnishings . . . that are held primarily for the personal, family, or household use of the debtor. . . .

11 U.S.C. §522(f)(2).

"purchase money security interest" or specify how a lien's purchase money status is affected by refinancing or consolidation with other debt. Reference must be had, therefore, to the state law definition of "purchase money security interest" in §9-107 of the Uniform Commercial Code. See Pristas v. Landaus of Plymouth, Inc. (In re Pristas), 742 F.2d 797, 800 (3d Cir. 1984).

That section provides:

> A security interest is a "purchase money security interest" *to the extent* that it is
>
> (a) taken or retained by the seller of the collateral to secure all or part of its price; or
>
> (b) taken by a person who by making advances or incurring an obligation gives value to enable the debtor to acquire rights in . . . collateral.

810 ILCS 5/9-107 (emphasis added).

Under this definition, a seller obtains a purchase money security interest by retaining a security interest in goods sold. A financing agency, such as American in the present case, obtains a purchase money security interest when it advances money to the seller and takes back an assignment of chattel paper. See Uniform Commercial Code, §9-107, cmt. 1 (1993); Raymond B. Check, The Transformation Rule Under §522 of the Bankruptcy Code of 1978, 84 Mich. L. Rev. 109, 126 n.104 (1985) (hereinafter Check, Transformation Rule).

In this case, American clearly had a purchase money security interest in the debtors' bedroom furniture when it accepted an assignment of the debtors' contract on these goods. Debtors contend that this interest was canceled when their original note of June 20 was consolidated with other indebtedness and the note was paid by renewal. American argues, however, that its purchase money lien survived despite this refinancing and that it retained a nonavoidable purchase money security interest in the debtors' bedroom furniture to the extent of the balance remaining on the original note for purchase of the collateral.

There is a split of authority among the circuits concerning whether a purchase money security interest is extinguished when the original purchase money loan is refinanced through renewal or consolidation with another obligation. One line of cases holds that a purchase money security interest is automatically "transformed" into a nonpurchase money interest when the proceeds of a renewal note are used to satisfy the original note. See Matthews v. Transamerica Financial Services (In re Matthews), 724 F.2d 798, 800 (9th Cir. 1984); Dominion Bank of Cumberlands v. Nuckolls, 780 F.2d 408, 413 (4th Cir. 1985); In re Keeton, 161 B.R. 410, 411 (Bankr. S.D. Ohio 1993); Hipps v. Landmark Financial Services of Georgia, Inc. (In re Hipps), 89 B.R. 264, 265 (Bankr. N.D. Ga. 1988); In re Faughn, 69 B.R. 18, 20-21

(Bankr. E.D. Mo. 1986). Because the collateral now secures an antecedent debt rather than a debt for purchase of the collateral or, in the case of a renewal note consolidating debt or advancing new funds, secures more than its purchase price, these courts hold that the resulting lien on the purchased goods no longer qualifies as a "purchase money security interest" under §9-107. Following such refinancing, then, the lien may be avoided in its entirety under §522(f)(2).

The second line of cases, rejecting the "all or nothing" approach of the transformation rule, holds that a lien may be partially purchase money and partially non-purchase money and that the purchase money aspect of a lien is not automatically destroyed by refinancing or consolidation with other debt. See Billings v. Avco Colorado Industrial Bank (In re Billings), 838 F.2d 405, 409 (10th Cir. 1988); *Pristas,* 742 F.2d at 801 (3d Cir. 1984); Geist v. Converse County Bank (In re Geist), 79 B.R. 939, 941 (D. Wyo. 1987); In re Hemingson, 84 B.R. 604 (Bankr. D. Minn. 1988); In re Parsley, 104 B.R. 72, 75 (Bankr. S.D. Ind. 1988). This view, referred to as the "dual status" rule, is premised on the language of §9-107, which provides that a lien is a purchase money security interest "to the extent" that it is taken to secure the purchase price of collateral. Accordingly, the purchase money security interest taken under the original note is preserved to the extent of the balance remaining unpaid on the original purchase money loan. See Russell v. Associates Financial Services Co. (In re Russell), 29 B.R. 270, 273-274 (Bankr. W.D. Okla. 1983).

Courts adopting the "dual status" rule note that it gives effect to the substance of the refinancing transaction.

> Though in form the original note is canceled, its balance is absorbed into the refinancing loan. To the extent of that balance, the purchase money security interest taken under the original note likewise survives, because what is owed on the original note is not eliminated[;] it is merely transferred to, and increased in amount by, another obligation. The refinancing changes the character of neither the balance due under the first loan nor the security interest taken under it.

Associates Finance v. Conn (In re Conn), 16 B.R. 454, 459 (Bankr. W.D. Ky. 1982); see *Russell,* 29 B.R. at 273.

The difficulty with the dual status rule lies in determining the extent of the purchase money interest remaining after refinancing. See *Pristas,* 742 F.2d at 801; Coomer v. Barclays American Financial, Inc. (In re Coomer), 8 B.R. 351, 353-354 (Bankr. E.D. Tenn. 1980). When a purchase money loan has been consolidated with non-purchase money debt and payments have ensued, some method of applying payments between the purchase money and non-purchase money portions of the refinanced loan is necessary so that the purchase money collateral secures only its own price and does not remain as collateral for the entire obligation. See Mulcahy v. Indianapolis Morris Plan (In re Mulcahy), 3 B.R. 454, 457 (Bankr. S.D. Ind. 1980). This problem has led some courts to find that purchase money status is forfeited if no method of allocation has been supplied, either by the parties' contract or by statute. See *Coomer,* 8 B.R. at 355; *Mulcahy,* 3 B.R. at 457; cf. *Pristas,* 742 at 802 (apportionment formula supplied by statute); Matter of Weigert, 145 B.R. 621, 623 (Bankr. D. Neb. 1991) (parties' agreement provided allocation formula). Other courts have adopted a judicial "first in, first out" method of allocation, under which payments are applied sequentially to purchase money debts in the order in which they were incurred. See In re Clark, 156 B.R. 693, 695 (Bankr. S.D. Fla. 1993); *Parsley,* 104 B.R. at 75; Matter of Weinbrenner, 53 B.R. 571, 579-580 (Bankr. W.D. Wis. 1985); *Conn,* 16 B.R. at 458; In re Gibson, 16 B.R. 257, 267-268 (Bankr. D. Kan. 1981); see generally Bernard A. Burk, Preserving the Purchase Money Status of Refinanced or Commingled Purchase Money Debt, 35 Stan. L. Rev. 1133, 1144-1146 (1983) (hereinafter Burk, Preserving Purchase Money Status).

Having considered the rationales for both the "automatic transformation" and "dual status" rules, this court finds that the dual status rule more closely adheres to the statutory language of §9-107 while effectuating the policy behind §522(f)(2). The "to the extent" language of §9-107 clearly contemplates that a lien may be partially purchase money and partially non-purchase money, depending on the circumstances of its creation. Thus, if a lender makes two separate loans—one for the purchase of goods, the other a cash advance—and retains a security interest in the purchased goods for both loans, the resulting lien is both purchase money (for the outstanding balance of the purchase money loan) and non-purchase money (for the amount remaining on the cash advance loan). No reason appears why the purchase money character of the first loan should disappear if the two loans are later consolidated, so long as the amounts attributable to the two loans may be separated. See Check, Transformation Rule, at 128.

Section 522(f)(2), moreover, with its distinction between purchase money and non-purchase money liens, was designed to permit debtors to avoid liens attached to household goods already owned by them rather than liens on collateral purchased with the money advanced. See *Russell,* at 274. Congress limited this avoidance option to non-purchase money interests in order to protect those lenders whose credit enabled the debtor to acquire the collateral in the first place. Check, Transformation Rule, at 127. When a purchase money loan is refinanced, the creditor is not committing the type of overreaching that §522(f)(2) aims to prevent, as the purchased goods remain as collateral for the loan. Thus, application of the dual status rule, with its recognition of the continued existence of the creditor's purchase money interest after refinancing, preserves the legislative balance between debtors' and creditors' rights in exempt property that is the purpose of §522(f)(2). See id.; In re Billings, 838 F.2d at 409-410.

Courts in the Seventh Circuit have not embraced either the transformation or the dual status rule but have, for the most part, taken a case by case approach which examines whether the debtor's obligation has been so changed by the refinanced loan that the resulting lien can no longer be characterized as a purchase money security interest. See In re Hatfield, 117 B.R. 387, 389-390 (Bankr. C.D. Ill. 1990) (quoting from In re Hills, No. 86-72037, slip op. at 4-5 (Bankr. C.D. Ill. July 29, 1987)); In re Gayhart, 33 B.R. 699, 700-701 (Bankr. N.D. Ill. 1983); Matter of Weinbrenner, 53 B.R. at 579-581; Johnson v. Richardson (Matter of Richardson), 47 B.R. 113, 117 (Bankr. W.D. Wis. 1985); but see In re Parsley, 104 B.R. at 75 (applying "dual status" rule). Under this approach, a refinanced loan is determined to be either a renewal of the original purchase money obligation, in which case the purchase money lien survives, or a novation, which extinguishes the purchase money character of the loan, depending upon the degree of change in terms and obligation between the two loans. See *Hatfield,* 117 B.R. at 390 ("the greater the degree of change in obligation . . . the more likely a novation will be found").

While the "middle of the road" approach of these courts lacks the certainty of a well-defined rule such as the transformation or dual status rule, this approach is not surprising given the diversity of fact situations presented in cases examining the purchase money character of refinanced loans. In the case of a simple refinancing that merely extends the repayment period of a loan—with a reduction in the amount of monthly payments and the same interest rate and security, strict application of the automatic transformation rule works an obvious injustice to the lender who has acted to benefit the borrower. See *Gayhart,* 33 B.R. at 700-701; *Hatfield,* 117 B.R. at 390. At the other end of the spectrum, when a purchase money loan is refinanced for new consideration and the second note involves different security and terms, this change may be seen to evidence the parties' intent to enter into a new obligation that cannot be characterized as a purchase money loan. See *Hills,* slip op. at 5 (refinanced note involving fresh advance of funds constituted a novation). Thus, courts that employ a case by case approach attempt to give effect to the parties' intent as derived from the facts of a particular transaction.

The facts of this case support a finding that American retained a purchase money lien on the debtors' bedroom furniture under either the dual status rule of the Tenth and Third Circuits or the case by case approach of bankruptcy courts in this circuit. As noted above, the problem under the dual status rule is allocating payments between the purchase money and non-purchase money aspects of a loan following consolidation in order to determine the extent to which the purchase money lien survives refinancing.

The problem under the case by case approach is to determine whether the facts evidence the parties' intent to continue the purchase money character of the original loan.

In this case, the debtors had made no payments on the original purchase money loan of June 20 at the time they agreed to consolidate this obligation with another, non-purchase money note of June 22. Since the entire purchase price of the collateral remained unpaid, it is unlikely the parties intended to extinguish the debtors' obligation under the first note or to change its character. Rather, the purchase money note of June 20, a no-interest note with one annual payment, was essentially "extended" by the consolidation note of July 16 to allow for monthly payments at a commensurately high interest rate. Thus, the July 16 note merely enabled the debtors to pay the original purchase price of the bedroom furniture over a longer period of time. Despite the change in interest rate and repayment terms, the purchase money character of the loan had not become blurred by repeated refinancings, see Slay v. Pioneer Credit Co. (In re Slay), 8 B.R. 355, 358 (Bankr. E.D. Tenn. 1980) ("at some point the number of transactions between the lender and the debtor destroys any claim that the debt is part purchase money"), and the essential character of American's interest in the purchase money collateral remained intact.

The parties' intent to continue the purchase money character of American's lien following consolidation was specifically stated in the documentation for the July 16 note, in which the security was described as a "continued purchase money interest" in the debtors' bedroom furniture. Cf. In re Billings, 838 F.2d at 109 (loan document expressly stating intent to continue the purchase money security interest showed parties did not intend to extinguish the original debt and security interest). While such a statement would not be sufficient, of itself, to preserve purchase money status upon refinancing, it adds weight to the Court's conclusion that the parties considered the new note to be a continuation of the debtors' original purchase money obligation. This statement of intent distinguishes the present case from In re Hills, in which the court found a novation based on the fact that the parties' note consolidating a purchase money obligation with non-purchase money debt did not identify the purchased goods as collateral and stated that the creditor was "not being given a 'security interest in the goods or property being purchased.'" *Hills,* slip op. at 1. Based on the parties' express statement of intent in this case and the fact that no payments had been made on the original purchase money loan at the time of refinancing, the Court finds that the parties intended to continue the purchase money status of American's lien in the July 16 note consolidating debt.

The problem of determining the extent of American's purchase money lien following consolidation is complicated only slightly by the fact that the debtors made one monthly payment and a partial payment on the consolidated note before their bankruptcy filing. If the debtors had made no payments at all, the purchase money portion of the consolidated debt would be the amount owing on the purchase money debt at the time of the consolidation. See In re Slay, 8 B.R. at 358. The *Slay* court, noting the difficulty of apportioning payments between the purchase money and non-purchase money parts of a consolidated loan, ruled that normally a creditor's purchase money status is forfeited upon consolidation with non-purchase money debt. However, the court found an exception to this general rule based on the fact that the debtors in *Slay* had made no payments following consolidation. Id.

It would be ironic if the debtors' payments here of $248.38 and $146 on a note that included $2,880 in purchase money debt would cause American's lien to lose its purchase money status completely. Neither the parties' contract nor an applicable statute provides a method for allocating payments between the purchase money and non-purchase money portions of the consolidated debt. However, courts of equity are peculiarly suited to the task of allocating payments, see In re Weinbrenner, 53 B.R. at 580 (citing Luksus v. United Pacific Insurance Co., 452 F.2d 207, 209 (7th Cir. 1971)), and have, in other contexts, supplied an allocation method when the parties failed to do so. See Burk, Preserving Purchase Money Status, at 1160, 1163 n.107 (creditor's burden to prove security interest extends only to production of facts and documents necessary to application of tracing rule). Therefore, in the absence of contractual or legislative direction, the Court will allocate the debtors' payments to determine the amount still owing on the purchase money debt—and, hence, the extent of American's purchase money lien—following consolidation. See In re Conn, 16 B.R. at 458.

Under the "first in, first out" allocation method employed by most courts, payments are deemed applied to the oldest debts first, with the result that purchase money liens are paid off in the order in which the goods are purchased. See *Parsley,* 104 B.R. at 74; *Conn,* 16 B.R. at 458. Once the purchase price of an item has been paid, any security interest remaining in it becomes a nonpurchase money security interest and is avoidable under §522(f)(2). The purchase price includes the cost of the item and any financing charges and sales taxes attributable to that item. *Parsley*; see Burk, Preserving Purchase Money Status, at 1178 (charges that would be considered part of the purchase money obligation of the original sale are accorded similar status after refinancing). In this case, there were no financing charges on the June 20 purchase money loan, as it was interest-free for the one-year term of the loan. The $2,880 amount of the loan presumably included sales taxes on the purchase of the bedroom furniture. Accordingly, the debtors' payments of $248.38 and $146 will be applied to reduce the unpaid purchase price of $2,880, resulting in a continued purchase money lien on the bedroom furniture of $2,485.62. The debtors' motion to avoid lien is granted to the extent of American's remaining nonpurchase money lien on this furniture.

NOTES

1. Why would Congress have enacted §522(f), which permits the debtor to avoid non-possessory, non-purchase money security interests in certain items? What policy is at work to restrict the use of such collateral in lending? Note that Bilko Siding, Inc., in the last Problem, attempted to do this. Because most used consumer goods have little resale value, why would creditors ever want the debtor to use them as collateral?

2. Both the Federal Trade Commission and the Federal Reserve Board have issued regulations forbidding creditors from taking non-possessory security interests in household goods unless they are purchase money security interests. See F.T.C. Trade Regulation Rule Concerning Credit Practices, 16 C.F.R. part 444.2(4), effective March 1, 1985; F.R.B. Reg. AA, 12 C.F.R. part 227, effective January 1, 1986. These rules should be in your statute book under the heading "FTC Credit Practices Rule."

3. The 1999 revision of Article 9 now provides that in non-consumer goods cases, the "dual status" rule prevails, and creates methods of allocating the payments so as to ascertain what portion of the purchase money debt survives. Read §9-103(e) through (g). But these rules do not obtain where the collateral is consumer goods, leaving cases like the one you have just read as arguably good law. Read §9-103(h) and its Official Comment 8. Why did the drafters not extend the statutory change to consumer goods? Surely the lenders here have typically done no evil and therefore ought not to lose their purchase money status in bankruptcy because of a technical misstep. Nonetheless, one of the major compromises made by the drafters of the 1999 Article 9 revision was to exempt consumer goods transactions from most of the Article 9 rules, leaving the resolution of these issues to other statutes or common law decisions.

PROBLEM 344

Facade Motors decided to buy an expensive Oriental rug for its main office. It selected one from the stock of Treasures of Persia, Inc., which let Facade Motors take the rug back to the office to try it out to see if it wanted to buy the rug. All of the equipment of Facade Motors was covered by a perfected floating lien in favor of Octopus National Bank. As soon as Facade gets possession of the rug (and before it makes up its corporate mind whether it wants to buy it), does the bank's lien attach? See §2-326(1) and (2). Facade Motors did decide to purchase the rug, so it signed a contract to do so with

Treasures of Persia, Inc., making a down payment at the time it did so. To finance the rest of the installment payments, Facade Motors borrowed the necessary amount from Nightflyer Savings and Loan, giving it a security interest in the rug. Does Nightflyer's security interest qualify as the purchase money kind? See §9-103(a), its Official Comment 3, and the next case.

General Electric Capital Commercial Automotive Finance, Inc. v. Spartan Motors, Ltd.

New York Supreme Court, 1998
246 App. Div. 2d 41, 675 N.Y.S.2d 626

FRIEDMANN, J.

This appeal arises from a dispute between two automobile finance companies as to which had a superior security interest in two Mercedes-Benz cars—part of the inventory of the defendant Spartan Motors, Ltd. (hereinafter Spartan), a now-defunct car dealership. The issue presented is whether by advancing Spartan the funds to purchase the vehicles after Spartan itself had already paid for and received them, the defendant General Motors Acceptance Corporation (hereinafter GMAC) thereby acquired a purchase money security interest in the merchandise that could defeat a previously-perfected security interest in all of Spartan's inventory held by the plaintiff, General Electric Capital Commercial Automotive Finance, Inc. (hereinafter GECC). We conclude that under the circumstances presented here, GMAC has established that its post-purchase advance entitled it to a purchase money security interest in the disputed collateral such that its lien enjoyed priority over GECC's prior "dragnet" lien.

FACTS

On Sept. 28, 1983, a predecessor of GECC entered into an "Inventory Security Agreement" with Spartan in connection with its "floor plan" financing of the dealership's inventory. By assignment of that agreement, GECC acquired a blanket lien (otherwise known as a "dragnet" lien) on Spartan's inventory to secure a debt in excess of $1,000,000. "Inventory" was defined in the agreement as "[a]ll inventory, of whatever kind or nature, wherever located, now owned or hereafter acquired, and all returns, repossessions, exchanges, substitutions, replacements, attachments, parts, accessories and accessions thereto and thereof, and all other goods used or intended to be used in conjunction therewith, and all proceeds thereof (whether in the form of cash, instruments, chattel paper, general intangibles, accounts or otherwise)." This security agreement was duly filed in the Office of the Dutchess County Clerk and with the New York State Secretary of State.

On July 19, 1991, Spartan signed a new Wholesale Security Agreement with GMAC, in which the latter agreed to finance or "floor-plan" Spartan's inventory. According to its terms, Spartan covenanted, inter alia, as follows:

> In the course of our business, we acquire new and used cars, trucks and chassis ("Vehicles") from manufacturers or distributors. We desire you to finance the acquisition of such vehicles and *to pay the manufacturers or distributors therefor.*
>
> We agree upon demand to pay to GMAC *the amount it advances or is obligated to advance to the manufacturer or distributor* for each vehicle with interest at the rate per annum designated by GMAC from time to time and then in force under the GMAC Wholesale Plan.
>
> We also agree that to secure collectively the payment by us of *the amounts of all advances and obligations to advance made by GMAC to the manufacturer, distributor or other sellers,* and the interest due thereon, GMAC is hereby granted a security interest in the vehicles and the proceeds of sale thereof ("Collateral") as more fully described herein.
>
> The collateral subject to this Wholesale Security Agreement is new vehicles held for sale or lease and used vehicles acquired from manufacturers or distributors and held for sale or lease. . . .
>
> We understand that we may sell and lease the vehicles at retail in the ordinary course of business. We further agree that *as each vehicle is sold, or leased, we will faithfully and promptly remit to you the amount you advanced or have become obligated to advance on our behalf to the manufacturer, distributor or seller* (emphasis supplied).

It is not disputed that GMAC's security agreement was duly filed. In addition, by certified letter dated July 17, 1991, GMAC officially notified GECC of its competing security interest in Spartan's inventory, as follows:

> This is to notify you that General Motors Acceptance Corporation holds or expects to acquire purchase money security interests in inventory collateral which will from time to time hereafter be delivered to Spartan Motors Ltd. of Poughkeepsie, New York, and in the proceeds thereof.
>
> Such inventory collateral consists, or will consist, of the types of collateral described in a financing statement, a true copy of which is annexed hereto and made a part hereof.

On May 7, 1992, Spartan paid $121,500 of its own money to European Auto Wholesalers, Ltd. to acquire a 1992 600 SEL Mercedes Benz. Six days later, on May 13, 1992, GMAC reimbursed Spartan and the vehicle was placed on GMAC's floor plan.

On July 7, 1992, Spartan paid $120,000 of its own money to the same seller to acquire a second 1992 600 SEL Mercedes. Two days later, on July 9, 1992, GMAC reimbursed Spartan for that amount and placed the second vehicle on its floor plan. The two vehicles remained unsold in Spartan's showroom.

A few months later, on or about Oct. 2, 1992, GECC commenced this action against Spartan, seeking $1,180,999.98, representing money then due to GECC under its agreement with Spartan. Claims were also made against the principals of Spartan, upon their guarantees, as well as against GMAC and Mercedes-Benz of North America, Inc. (hereinafter MBNA), to determine lien priority in the collateral.

After commencement of the litigation, Spartan filed a bankruptcy petition and ceased doing business. GECC, GMAC, and MBNA took possession of and liquidated their respective collateral pursuant to a prior agreement between the parties. Among the assets appropriated and sold by GMAC were the two Mercedes-Benz automobiles, which were auctioned for $194,500.

Since commencing this action, GECC has apparently settled its claims against all of the defendants except GMAC, which it has accused of converting the two Mercedes-Benz vehicles in violation of GECC's antecedent security interest.

The court granted GECC's motion for summary judgment (and, upon reargument, adhered to its original determination), finding persuasive GECC's argument that a literal reading of GMAC's security agreement with Spartan, in conjunction with the wording of Uniform Commercial Code §9-107(b) [now §9-103(a)(2)—Eds.], required a holding that GMAC had a purchase money secured interest *only* to the extent that it paid funds *directly* to "manufacturers, distributors and sellers" of Spartan's inventory *in advance* of the transfer of the merchandise to the car dealership. The court reasoned that because "[n]owhere in the contracts of adhesion signed by Spartan with GMAC is there an obligation by GMAC to *reimburse* Spartan for funds used to purchase automobiles" (emphasis supplied), GECC's previously-perfected security interest in all of Spartan's inventory should prevail.

We now reverse and, upon searching the record, grant summary judgment to GMAC.

Analysis

A perfected purchase money security interest provides an exception to the general first-in-time, first-in-right rule of conflicting security interests. Thus, a perfected purchase money security interest in inventory has priority over a conflicting prior security interest in the same inventory. . . . However, as the Supreme Court, Dutchess County observed, the purported purchase money security interest must fit within the Uniform Commercial Code definition to qualify for the exception.

Uniform Commercial Code §9-107 [now §9-103—Eds.] defines a "purchase money security interest" as a security interest:

(a) taken or retained by the seller of the collateral to secure all or part of its price; or

(b) taken by a person who by making advances or incurring an obligation gives value to enable the debtor to acquire rights in or the use of collateral if such value is in fact so used.

The issue here is therefore whether GMAC's payment as reimbursement to Spartan after it had acquired the two Mercedes-Benz vehicles on two different occasions qualifies as an "advance" or "obligation" that enabled Spartan to purchase the cars, such that GMAC acquired a purchase money security interest in the vehicles. The arguments against finding a purchase money security interest under these circumstances are basically twofold: Firstly, of the few courts to construe Uniform Commercial Code §9-107(b), many have been reluctant to decide that a purchase money security interest has been created where, as here, title to and possession of the merchandise have passed to the debtor before the loan is advanced. Secondly, the literal wording of the agreement between GMAC and Spartan appears to accord GMAC purchase money secured status only when the finance company paid Spartan's "manufacturer, distributor or other seller" directly. As the supreme court noted, nothing in GMAC's contract with Spartan appears to contemplate any obligation on the part of the financier to "reimburse" the auto dealership for funds that the latter had already expended to purchase merchandise. These two interrelated arguments will be discussed seriatim.

(1) WHETHERAFTER-ADVANCED FUNDS MAY QUALIFY FOR PURCHASE MONEY SECURITY STATUS UNDER UNIFORM COMMERCIAL CODE §9-107(B)

Research indicates that there is no judicial authority in New York construing the application of UCC §9-107(b) vel non, to circumstances such as those presented here. Indeed, there has been little judicial discussion in any jurisdiction of the applicability of UCC §9-107(b) to a creditor's subsequent reimbursement of a debtor for an antecedent purchase of collateral.

Accordingly, it is appropriate to examine the legislative history of UCC §9-107(b), to arrive, if possible, at the intent of the framers.

Professor Grant Gilmore, one of the original drafters of UCC Article 9 (see, MBank Alamo Natl. Assn. v. Raytheon Co., 886 F.2d 1449, 1459), has explained that UCC §9-107(b) was enacted at least in part to liberalize the rather rigid traditional rules, e.g., regarding the circumstances under which purchase money secured status could be obtained by a creditor who enables a debtor to acquire new inventory (see, Gilmore, The Purchase Money Priority, 76 Harv. L. Rev. 1333, at 1373 [1963]).

For example, whereas under pre-Code law a person who advanced the purchase price on a buyer's behalf directly to the seller would be found to have a purchase money interest in the items so acquired, no such security interest was guaranteed to the person advancing money to a buyer who then used the funds to pay for merchandise (see, e.g., Manlove v. Maggart, 111 Ind. App. 398, 41 N.E.2d 633; Hughbanks, Inc. v. Gourley, 12 Wash. 2d 44, 120 P.2d 523). Under UCC §9-107(b), however, if a financier can show both that his advance was made for the purpose of enabling the debtor to acquire the collateral and that it was in fact so used, he will be accorded purchase money secured status (Gilmore, The Purchase Money Priority, supra, at 1373).

Similarly, under pre-Code law the *sequence* of the transfers was dispositive. Indeed, as Professor Gilmore noted, even 9-107(b), on its face, seems to assume "the sequence of loan first and acquisition second or . . . that the loan and acquisition take place simultaneously." Where, for example, "the buyer pays the price (or writes a check) on Monday and borrows that amount from the secured party on Tuesday," the secured party is faced with the obvious difficulty of satisfying both the " 'to enable' " and the " 'in fact so used' " prongs of the statute (Gilmore, at 1374). However, under the Code, "in . . . the hypothetical [case] just put a court could reasonably find that the secured party had acquired a purchase money interest. If the loan transaction appears to be *closely allied* to the purchase transaction, that should suffice. The evident intent of paragraph (b) is to free the purchase money concept from artificial limitations; rigid adherence to particular formalities and sequences should not be required" (Gilmore, at 1374, emphasis supplied; see also, 2 Gilmore, Security Interests in Personal Property, §29.2, at 782; Anderson, Uniform Commercial Code, §9-107:26, at 529; White and Summers, Uniform Commercial Code, §33-5, at 325-326 [Practitioner's 4th ed.][2]).

If under UCC §9-107(b) neither the chronology of the financing nor the configuration of the cash flow is, without more, dispositive (see, e.g., Clark, The Law of Secured Transactions Under the Uniform Commercial Code, §3.09[2][a]), how can we tell if a loan transaction is sufficiently "closely allied" to a purchase transaction to qualify for purchase money status?

One factor that courts have considered is simple temporal proximity—that is, whether the value is given by the creditor "more or less contemporaneously with the debtor's acquisition of the property" (see, e.g., Matter of Brooks, 1980 WL 98467 [U.S. Bankr. Ct., D. Me.]). However, it should be noted that early drafts of UCC §9-107 contained an additional paragraph (c), which envisioned a purchase money interest to the extent of value advanced for the purpose of financing new acquisitions within 10 days of the debtor's receiving possession of the new goods, *even though the value was*

2. [Now §33-4, at 331-334 (6th ed. 2010)—Eds.]

not in fact used to pay the price. The paragraph was deleted according to the sponsors, because it extended the purchase money interest too far (see, Gilmore, The Purchase Money Priority, supra, at 1374, n.97, citing 1956 Recommendations of the Editorial Board for the Uniform Commercial Code §9-107). It appears, then, that mere closeness in time is but another mechanical circumstance to be considered—a significant clue, but not one dispositive of the relationship between the transactions.

The authorities are agreed that the critical inquiry, as in all contract matters, is into the intention of the parties (see, e.g., Township of Stambaugh v. Ah-Ne-Pee Dimensional Hardwood, 841 F. Supp. 803; New West Fruit Corp. v. Coastal Berry Corp., 1 Cal. App. 4th 92, 1 Cal. Rptr. 2d 664, 668; see also, Anderson, Uniform Commercial Code, supra, at 529). "In determining whether a security interest exists, the intent of the parties controls, and that intent may best be determined by examining the language used and considering the conditions and circumstances confronting the parties when the contract was made" (Baldwin v. Hays Asphalt Constr., 20 Kan. App. 2d 853, 856, 893 P.2d 275). In assessing the relationship of the transactions, the test should be whether the availability of the loan was a factor in negotiating the sale, and/or whether the lender was committed at the time of the sale to advance the amount required to pay for the items purchased (see, Matter of Hooks, 40 B.R. 715 [U.S. Bankr. Ct., M.D. Ga.]; Anderson, Uniform Commercial Code, supra, at 529; Clark, The Law of Secured Transactions Under the Uniform Commercial Code, §3.09[2][a] [rev. ed. 1993]).

Applying these principles to the matter before us: (1) The record establishes that GMAC's reimbursements to Spartan following its two Mercedes-Benz purchases were only six and two days apart, respectively. (2) GECC does not dispute GMAC's contention that a post-purchase reimbursement arrangement was common in the trade, as well as routine in Spartan's course of dealing with GMAC and its other financers, depending upon the circumstances of the purchase. For example, GMAC employee Philip Canterino, who handled GMAC's account with Spartan, has averred without contradiction by GECC that although it was customary for GMAC to pre-pay a car manufacturer before it delivered new vehicles to Spartan's showroom, in a case of the sort at issue here—where the vehicles were difficult to obtain from the manufacturer but were readily available from a distributor—it was not uncommon for GMAC to reimburse Spartan after the cars had been delivered to Spartan's showroom, upon Spartan's presentation of proof of clear title. In the language of Uniform Commercial Code §9-107(b): GMAC was committed to give value to enable the car dealership to acquire rights in the collateral. The value so extended was intended to and in fact did enable Spartan to acquire the two Mercedes-Benzes, as GECC does not seriously suggest that without GMAC's backing Spartan could have afforded to purchase the expensive vehicles. Accordingly, the literal requirements of Uniform Commercial Code §9-107(b) are satisfied, notwithstanding the inverted purchase-loan chronology (see, e.g., Matter of McHenry, 71 B.R. 60 [U.S. Bankr. Ct., N.D. Ohio]; Thet Mah & Assocs. v. First Bank of N. Dakota, 336 N.W.2d 134 [Sup. Ct., N.D.]). Because GMAC's loans were "closely allied" with Spartan's inventory acquisitions, GMAC enjoys a purchase money security interest in the contested merchandise (see, e.g., Matter of Hooks, supra).

Concededly, in making assessments of this sort, courts have considered an important factor to be whether or not title had passed to the borrower before the loan was issued (see, e.g., DeKalb Bank v. Purdy, 205 Ill. App. 3d 62, 562 N.E.2d 1223 [purchase money status clear where title to cattle did not pass until creditor advanced payment]; Matter of Hooks, supra [creditor had purchase money security interest where legal ownership in cows was not transferred to the debtor until loan closed]). This is because, where the borrower already possesses all possible rights in the collateral, the value extended by the creditor looks more like a loan procured to satisfy a preexisting debt than an advance "enabl[ing] the debtor to acquire rights in . . . the . . . collateral" (UCC 9-107[(b)]). However, it seems ill-advised to create an artificial rule premised upon this circumstance, as there will be cases where a purchase money arrangement will not be established even though title has not passed, and other cases, like the one before us, where the passing of title is irrelevant to the creditor's demonstration that the value he extended was closely allied to the purchase of the collateral. In this regard, it is worthy of note that the *Hooks* court, and to some degree the *DeKalb* court as well, treated the passage of title as merely one element to consider—albeit a significant one—in applying the "closely allied" test to arrive at the parties' intentions (see, e.g., Matter of Hooks, supra, at 340-341; DeKalb Bank v. Purdy, supra, at 1226-1227).

A classic case holding the opposite, North Platte State Bank v. Production Credit Assn. (189 Neb. 44, 200 N.W.2d 1), relied upon by GECC, is distinguishable for many reasons. There, the borrower took a loan from the plaintiff bank approximately one and one-half months after purchasing certain cattle, without informing the bank that the loan was intended for any particular purpose. The *North Platte* court noted that the debtor had merely borrowed money several weeks after acquiring title to and possession of a herd of cattle in order to discharge an antecedent debt. Although the "closely allied" test was not discussed by the *North Platte* court, which focussed instead on the pre-loan passage to the debtor of all rights in the collateral, the case is in fact an illustration of a failure to meet that test's requirement (see also, e.g., First Interstate Bank of Utah, N.A. v. I.R.S., 930 F.2d 1521; Valley Bank v. Estate of Rainsdon, 117 Idaho 1085, 793 P.2d 1257; ITT Commercial Finance Corp. v. Union Bank & Trust Co. of N. Vernon, 528 N.E.2d 1149 [Ind. App.]; Wade Credit Corp. v. Borg-Warner Acceptance Corp., 83 Or. App. 479, 732 P.2d

76; Matter of Manuel, 18 B.R. 403 [U.S. Bankr. Ct., D.S.C.]). In contrast to the matter before us, there was no pretransaction meeting of the minds between debtor and creditor; the bank was not "obligated" to give value to enable the debtor to acquire rights in the collateral; and the purchase and loan transactions were not close in time, but were nearly two months apart. Put somewhat differently, in North Platte the availability of the loan was not a factor in the debtor's negotiation of the sale; and the plaintiff bank was not committed at the time of the sale to advance the amount required to pay for the items purchased.

In addition, the *North Platte* court's conclusion that the plaintiff had not acquired a purchase money interest in the debtor's collateral was reinforced by the "even more fundamental" consideration that the plaintiff had neglected to file its security interest within 10 days of the debtor's receiving possession of the merchandise, as required by Uniform Commercial Code §9-312(4) (North Platte State Bank v. Production Credit Assn., 189 Neb. 44, 200 N.W.2d 1, 6; see also, White and Summers, Uniform Commercial Code, supra, at 326[3]). Here, in contrast, it is not disputed that GMAC timely filed its purchase money security interest in Spartan's inventory, and that in July 1991 it notified GECC of that interest.

(2) WHETHER GMAC'S LIEN IS CIRCUMSCRIBED BY THE PRECISE LANGUAGE OF ITS AGREEMENT WITH SPARTAN

It is well established that the terms of a written security agreement may be amplified by "other circumstances including course of dealing or usage of trade or course of performance" (UCC 1-201[(3)]; see also, UCC 1-205, 2-208; New West Fruit Corp. v. Coastal Berry Corp., supra). Here, GECC does not deny that, although the written terms of GMAC's contract with Spartan *appeared* to contemplate a single method of inventory-financing (i.e., GMAC's payment to Spartan's sellers in advance of the purchase transaction), *in fact* it was not at all unusual for the parties to pursue the same end by somewhat different means (i.e., GMAC's post-transaction reimbursement to Spartan for its inventory purchases), as GMAC employee Canterino repeatedly explained.

Generally, the express terms of an agreement and a differing course of performance, course of dealing, and/or usage of trade "shall be construed whenever reasonable as consistent with each other" (UCC 1-205[(4)], 2-208[(2)]). Only when a consistent construction would be "unreasonable" must express terms control over course of performance, and course of performance prevail over course of dealing and usage of trade. GMAC's election on some occasions to fund Spartan's floor-planning by reimbursing the

3. [Now at 334-335 (6th ed. 2010) — Eds.]

car dealership for its purchases can hardly be considered inconsistent with its decision on other occasions to accomplish the same goal by following the strict wording of the contract and pre-paying the supplier directly. Rather, it is only reasonable to consider these two methods of financing to be entirely compatible with one another.

In any event, it is well established that a written contract may be *modified* by the parties' post-agreement "course of performance" (UCC 2-208[(1)], [(3)]; see, e.g., Farmers State Bank v. Farmland Foods, 225 Neb. 1, 402 N.W.2d 277; see also, Rose v. Spa Realty Assoc., 42 N.Y.2d 338, 343-344; Maynard Ct. Owners Corp. v. Rentoulis, 235 A.D.2d 867; Indemnity Ins. Co. of N. Am. v. Levine, 168 A.D.2d 323, 326; Recon Car Corp. of N.Y. v. Chrysler Corp., 130 A.D.2d 725, 729). In this regard, GECC offered no rebuttal to the testimony and affidavit of GMAC's employee who had handled the financier's account with Spartan, to the effect that it was the custom in the trade, as well as in GMAC's course of dealing with Spartan and others, for the financier to reimburse the debtor following delivery of the merchandise to the debtor's showroom, and upon presentation by the debtor of proof of clear title.

There is no merit to GECC's suggestion that, because Spartan and GMAC had diverged in practice from the literal language of their contract, GECC lacked notice of the inventory covered by GMAC's security interest. . . .

CONCLUSION

Accordingly, the supreme court erred when it found that, having financed the two vehicles at issue here by way of reimbursements—"the very opposite of an advance"—GMAC did not acquire a purchase money security interest pursuant to Uniform Commercial Code 9-107(b). Rather, since GMAC has established—and GECC does not deny—that GMAC was "obligated" to give value to enable Spartan to acquire rights in the two Mercedes-Benzes, and the purchase and loan transactions were only days apart, it is clear that Spartan's purchase and GMAC's subsequent reimbursement were sufficiently "closely allied" to give GMAC a purchase money security interest in the subject vehicles. Under these circumstances, we conclude, upon searching the record, that GMAC is entitled to retain the proceeds of the sale of the two contested vehicles and to summary judgment against GECC (see, CPLR 3212[(b)]). . . .

B. Certain Accounts and Other Intangibles

Read §9-309(2) and Official Comment 4's first paragraph. The courts have split over whether the major test is "significant part" (a percentage test) or "casual or isolated transaction" (the Official Comment test). See White & Summers §23-7. A creditor is ill advised to rely on §9-309(2) and not file; it is simply too dangerous to take the chance that a court will find that the section applies. Grant Gilmore, one of the drafters of the original Article 9, concluded that the exemption was meant to protect assignees who don't normally take such assignments and are therefore unlikely to file. Under his test the assignee must be "both insignificant and ignorant." G. Gilmore, Security Interests in Personal Property §19.6 (1965). One court adopted his test and permitted the assignee to establish his "insignificance and ignorance" so as to have a perfected interest without filing, E. Turgeon Constr. Co. v. Elhatton Plumbing & Heating Co., 110 R.I. 303, 292 A.2d 230 (1972).

In re Wood

United States District Court, Western District of New York, 1986

67 B.R. 321

TELESCA, J.

This appeal is from the order of the Bankruptcy Court holding that the security interest and the accounts assigned to the plaintiff, Edwin M. Larkin, by the debtors is unsecured due to the lack of perfection by filing under the Uniform Commercial Code. Specifically, the decision of the court below determined that the transaction in question did not fall within the exemptions from filing contained in UCC §9-302(1)(e).

The facts are relatively simple. Both the plaintiff and the defendant are practicing attorneys. They have had a continuing professional and personal relationship spanning a number of years. On or about March 15, 1977, Mr. Larkin loaned to his friend and attorney, Robert F. Wood, the sum of $10,000. The debtors executed a demand promissory note at that time including provision for the payment of interest. No payment was made on the note by either of the debtors for a period of five years. By letter agreement dated on or about June 3, 1982, the debtors agreed to pay to Mr. Larkin the sum of $1,000 within ten days of May 28, 1982, to be applied towards the payment of accrued interest. Subsequent payments would also be applied first to interest and then to reduction of the principal balance. In the agreement, the debtors also agreed to a limited assignment of the proceeds that might be due the debtors from two litigations in which the debtors were engaged. The litigations provided for contingency fee agreements between Mr. Wood and his clients. The assignment of the contingency proceeds contained restrictions on the assignee's right to disclose the existence of the assignment to any third parties, including the clients, or to participate in the prosecution of the underlying litigations or any settlement negotiations.

On September 9, 1983, the debtors filed voluntary petitions pursuant to Chapter 11 of the Bankruptcy Code. In this proceeding, the debtors seek to avoid the security interest of Larkin and the proceeds subsequently received by the debtors from the settlement of the litigations.

In reaching its decision, the Bankruptcy Court reviewed numerous court decisions relating to the interpretation of U.C.C. §9-302(1)(e) [now §9-309(2)—Eds.]. Relevant language is:

> (1) A financing statement must be filed to perfect all security interests except the following. . . .
>
> (e) an assignment of accounts which does not alone or in conjunction with other assignments to the same assignee transfer a significant part of the outstanding accounts of the assignor; . . .

The official Comment 5 to the above section explains the policy as follows:

> The purpose of the subsection (1)(e) exemptions is to save from ex post facto invalidation casual or isolated assignments: some accounts receivable statutes have been so broadly drafted that all assignments, whatever their character or purpose, fall within their filing provisions. Under such statutes, many assignments which no one would think of filing might have been subject to invalidation. The subsection (1)(e) exemptions go to that type of assignment. Any person who regularly takes assignments of any debtor's accounts should file. . . .

After reviewing the cases and learned articles on the subject, the Bankruptcy Court concluded that the appropriate standard to be applied in interpreting UCC §9-302(1)(e) is a combination of both the "percentage test" and "casual and isolated transaction test." Both tests need to be reviewed in conjunction with all of the facts and circumstances involved in the relationship between the parties and the transactions in which they are engaged. See, generally, 85 A.L.R.3d at 1050, 1053-1054, 1062. See also, White and Summers, Uniform Commercial Code §23-8.[4]

No hard and fast rule interpreting UCC §9-302(1)(e) can be established in view of the unlimited variety of facts and circumstances present in private lending transactions. A standard utilizing either or both the percentage test and the casual and isolated transaction test ought to be employed. . . .

This court elects to follow the policy stated in In re B. Hollis Knight Company, 605 F.2d 397, 401 (8th Cir. 1979):

> Both of the policies underlying the two tests appear to be valid limitations on the scope of UCC §9-302(1)(e). The language of the section would not permit an assignee to escape the filing requirements if he received a large portion of an assignor's accounts whether or not the transaction was an isolated one.

4. [Now §23-78 (6th ed. 2010)—Eds.]

Nor is it unfair to require a secured party who regularly takes such assignments to file, since the comments to UCC §9-302(1)(e) indicate that the section was designed as a narrow exception to the filing requirement—not applicable if the transaction was in the general course of commercial financing.

The Bankruptcy Court correctly determined that the burden of meeting each test is on the assignee. Miller v. Wells Fargo Bank Intl. Corp., 406 F. Supp. 452 (S.D.N.Y. 1975). The court then held that Larkin failed to meet his burden in either test.

This court will not disturb the Bankruptcy Court's finding that the assignee Larkin failed to meet his burden to demonstrate the size of the assignment made by the debtor in this case in relation to the debtor's other outstanding accounts at the time of the assignment was not significant. However, in reviewing the application of the casual and isolated transaction test, the court below incorrectly held that by reason of the fact that Mr. Larkin was an attorney at law, he should be familiar with the importance of perfecting security interests by filing and that this imputed professional knowledge excluded him as one of the members of the class protected under UCC §9-302(1)(e). This was an erroneous interpretation of the casual and isolated transaction test and is not supported by any reported authority.

The casual and isolated transaction test requires the court to examine the circumstances surrounding the transaction, including the status of the assignee, to determine whether the assignment was, in fact, casual and isolated. Architectural Woods, Inc. v. State of Washington, 88 Wash. 2d 406, 562 P.2d 248 (1977). The underlying rationale behind the test is that it would not be unreasonable to require a secured creditor to file if he regularly takes assignments of a debtor's accounts, but it would be unreasonable if this was not a usual practice. However, the authorities are clear that where the assignee is regularly engaged in commercial financing and routinely accepts assignments of accounts, perfection by way of filing under the UCC is required regardless of the actual amount of the accounts assigned. In re B. Hollis Knight Co., supra.

In reviewing the reported authority, the distinguishing fact in determining whether or not the *status* of the assignee required filing for protection turned on whether or not the assignee was involved in commercial lending or regularly took assignment of accounts. The court, however, cited no authority for the stated proposition that attorneys who accept the security interest in an account are excluded from this exception to the filing requirement, nor has research revealed any. This court is unable to find any authority which characterizes attorneys as a group which are ineligible to engage in casual and isolated assignments of accounts under UCC §9-302(1)(e).

The record in this case clearly establishes that Larkin was not a commercial lender engaged in regularly accepting assignments from debtors.

He made one loan to the debtors and subsequently obtained one assignment of the proceeds of two cases as collateral for the repayment of the loan. The record amply supports the conclusion that this was a casual and isolated transaction between two individuals who maintained a personal and professional relationship. That requires a finding that Larkin was not regularly engaged in the business of taking accounts, and therefore, he clearly falls within the exemption from filing under UCC §9-302(1)(e). It was an error for the Bankruptcy Court to hold otherwise. . . .

The Bankruptcy Court's holding that plaintiff's claim was unperfected and unsecured is reversed. Plaintiff had a perfected security interest in the two accounts as of June 4, 1982. This case is remanded to the Bankruptcy Court for proceedings not inconsistent with this opinion, including reconsideration of plaintiff's motion for contempt.

So Ordered.

Now read all of §9-309, extending the same automatic perfection to the transfer of a number of types of intangible or quasi-intangible collateral.

PROBLEM 345

Octopus National Bank sold all the promissory notes it was holding in its vault to Last National Bank. Remember that the *sale* of promissory notes is an Article 9 transaction (with the seller being the "debtor" and the buyer the "secured party"—see §9-109(a)(3)). Must Last National file a financing statement or make sure it has possession in order to perfect its security interest in the notes? See §9-309(4).

The sale of debt is big business; there is a huge market for the transfer of payment obligations of all kinds. Often investors will create a trust to buy up debts from others (mortgages, promissory notes, accounts receivable, etc.), and then sell stock in this trust (the whole process is called *securitization*). Similarly, credit card companies can sell the credit card account receivables to others; banks making big loans can sell off parts thereof to other bankers (called a *loan-participation* agreement); and banks can extend loans to mortgage lenders, taking a security interest in the underlying mortgages (*mortgage warehousing*). The financial world is busy creating all sorts of new financing mechanisms and markets for the transfer of debt.

When debts are sold, they are sometimes transferred "with recourse," and sometimes "without recourse." The difference has to do with which party assumes the risk of non-collection. If the sale is "with recourse," then if the underlying obligors do not make full payment of the debts sold, the original seller must make up the deficiency. If the sale is "without recourse," then the buyer of the debt assumes both the risk that the debts won't be paid and gets any surplus if more is collected than the selling price.

It is important to appreciate this: The automatic perfection rules for the sale of some types of debt—§9-309(3) and (4)—apply only if a true *sale* is taking place. If the seller of the debt keeps any of the indicia of ownership, there is an argument that a "sale" has not taken place. In that case, automatic perfection will not work, and the so-called "buyer" must take the usual steps for perfection (possession, filing a financing statement) in order to prevail over other claimants to the obligations sold. If the transfer was "with recourse," it looks more like merely a loan than an outright sale, so the buyer is arguably not automatically perfected when its interest attaches. In doubtful cases, as always, the smart thing to do is to file a financing statement or take possession of the promissory notes and thus be assured of perfection. See White & Summers §23-7; In re Commercial Money Center, Inc., 350 B.R. 465 (B.A.P. 9th Cir. 2006) ($47 million worth of payment intangibles lost when the court deemed the transaction a loan rather than a sale and the buyer failed to perfect by filing).

PROBLEM 346

When Nightflyer Finance Company (NFC) loaned $20,000 to Portia Moot to enable her to expand her law practice, she gave the finance company a security interest in her accounts receivable (the monies her client owed her), which NFC promptly perfected by filing a financing statement in the appropriate place. One of these accounts has a surety, the mother of the client, who promised Portia that she would pay the debt if the client did not. What must NFC do to perfect its interest in the surety obligation of the mother? See §§9-102(a)(78), 9-102(a)(72), 9-203(f), and 9-308(d). Note that under the cited definitions, the same rule for automatic perfection extends to letters of credit that support the original transaction.

III. PERFECTION BY FILING

The basic supposition of §9-310 is that except for the transactions listed therein, the *filing* of a "financing statement" is the exclusive method of perfection of the creditor's security interest.

A. *The Mechanics of Filing*

Under the original version of Article 9, the filing rules were quite complicated and often required dual or sometimes even triple filing of financing statements in both local and statewide offices. This made some sense in the pre-computer age, when the state offices were hard to get to and the searches were often done manually by rifling through paper records. The UCC now mandates central filing (typically in the office of the Secretary of State) for almost all financing statements, with local county filing only for matters having to do with realty: minerals to be extracted from the earth, timber, or fixtures; see §9-501.

PROBLEM 347

Hamlet Corporation borrowed $100,000 from the Elsinore Finance Company and gave it a security interest in the corporation's equipment. The parties properly filled out a financing statement; W. Shakespeare was mentioned on the financing statement as the president of Hamlet Corporation. Elsinore gave the financing statement and the filing fee to a clerk at the Secretary of State's office. The clerk, Ophelia Nunnery, had just announced her intention to quit to her fellow office workers and was not paying attention to her job as she indexed the financing statement under "Shakespeare" instead of "Hamlet." One year later, another finance company loaned Hamlet Corporation more money, taking a security interest in the same equipment (the second finance company had checked the records and discovered nothing under "Hamlet Corp."). Since priority of creditors in this situation depends on order of filing (§9-322(a)(1)), did Elsinore "file" first, or did it bear the risk of clerical error? See §§9-516(a), 9-517 (and its Official Comment 2); In re Masters, 273 B.R. 773 (Bankr. E.D. Ark. 2002); In re Butler's Tire & Battery Co., 1975 WL 22897 (Bankr. D. Or. 1975), *aff'd on opinion below,* 1976 WL 23725 (D. Or. 1976) (creditor not protected where creditor's error caused filing official's mistake); The Feed Store, LLC, 2018 WL 1320168 (Bankr. N.D. W. Va. 2018) (financing statement effective, although filing office erroneously assigned number already in use and so did not index correctly). Whichever creditor loses should sue the state for negligence. Some states have set aside a fund from the filing fees with which to pay judgments against the filing officer.

Where perfection depends not on filing a financing statement, but rather on having the security interest noted on the certificate of title, the rule may demand more of the creditor. See In re Hicks, 491 F.3d 1136 (10th

Cir. 2007) (creditor not perfected, where it properly filed Notice of Security Interest with certificate of title agency, but agency issued certificate of title that did not have notation of security interest).

NOTE

An attorney who files a financing statement should retain proof of what was filed, where it was filed, and when it was filed, in case people or computers in the UCC office misdirect or lose the financing statement. For online filings, the UCC office will typically return an electronic confirmation and a downloadable copy of the filing. The careful attorney will print out copies for the file, because those digital files may go astray over the years. As of 2020, filings may be made online in every state, as well as Puerto Rico and the U.S. Virgin Islands. Some states (as of summer 2020, Colorado, Delaware, New Jersey, and North Dakota) no longer accept paper filings, although many accept attached files. See Paul Hodnefield, UCC Electronic Filing Methods and Capabilities by State (updated July 27, 2016), https://www.iaca.org/wp-content/uploads/UCC-E-File-Info-by-State.pdf. Paper filings are sometimes more convenient, such as when the creditor attaches documents. For paper filings, always pay whatever extra amount is necessary to have duplicate copies of the financing statement made, stamped, and returned to you (or get an acknowledgment of the filed written record). See §9-523 for the procedure.

B. Other Filings

A financing statement is effective for five years and then it lapses unless a continuation statement is filed (*public finance transactions*—defined in §9-102(a)(67), and *manufactured home transactions*—defined in §9-102(a)(53), are effective for 30 years). Read §9-515. The filing office is commanded by statute to keep records of lapsed financing statements for an additional one-year period; see §9-522. If the secured party *assigns* the security interest to another creditor, the two creditors may (it is not compulsory) file an assignment statement; read §9-514. If the debtor and secured party want to free some of the collateral from coverage under a filed financing statement, see the procedure provided for in §9-512.

PROBLEM 348

Octopus National Bank (ONB) had a security interest in the equipment of the Weekend Construction Company for which it filed a financing statement in the proper place on May 1, 2020. Antitrust National Bank (ANB) took a security interest in the same collateral and filed its financing statement on May 2, 2020, in the same place.

(a) How long is a financing statement effective? See §9-515(a).

(b) If ONB files a continuation statement on May 1, 2024, is its perfected position continued? See §§9-515(d), 9-510(c). Pre-revision decisions called this the problem of "premature renewal."

(c) If ONB never files a continuation statement at all, after May 1, 2025, does it nonetheless retain its priority over ANB (who, after all, always thought of itself as junior to ONB's prior filing and would get a windfall if it suddenly prevails)? See §9-515(c).

(d) If ONB fails to file a continuation statement in time, so that its perfection lapses, but a week later files another financing statement, is it still senior to ANB? See Signature Credit Partners, LLC v. Casaic Offset & Silkscreen, Inc., 2012 WL 1999494 (W.D. La. 2012) (no).

(e) Is an attorney who fails to file a continuation statement guilty of malpractice? See Barnes v. Turner, 278 Ga. 788, 606 S.E.2d 849 (Ga. 2004).

PROBLEM 349

When Portia Moot paid off her debt to Last National Bank, which had loaned her $3,000 to buy a computer for her law office (and had taken a purchase money security interest therein, for which it had duly filed a financing statement), she wanted the bank to clear up the records down at the filing office. Does she have this right? See §9-513. What can she do if they stiff-arm her? See §§9-509(d)(2), 9-625(b) and (e)(4).

One happy idea codified in the 1999 revision of Article 9 is called the *open drawer* concept of file searches. What this means is that later searchers are given absolutely everything related to the original financing statement (amendments, assignments, deletions, continuation statements, termination statements, etc.) when they do a search, so that they have complete information as to the current status of the filed transaction. Note that the definition of *financing statement* includes an original filing and *all related amendments;* §9-102(a)(39). Section 9-519(c) requires the filing office to index the filing under the debtor's name and the file number and associate all related filings to the original filing. Thus, when a later searcher requests the financing statement per §9-523(c), the entire file will be forthcoming. Section 9-522(a) requires the filing office to maintain all filings until at least one year after the filing has lapsed with respect to all secured parties of record; §9-519(g) prohibits the removal of a debtor's name from the index until one year after complete lapse. When you put all this together, you have the "open drawer" system where a "drawer" is created for each new financing statement into which all related filings are deposited. Most states make electronic filings immediately available to searchers, although they may not yet be certified as filed. Everything stays in the searchable drawer until a year after lapse. That is not to say that everything in the drawer is legally effective. A valid termination might have been filed by all secured parties of record. But note that the effectiveness of the termination (or any other filing, for that matter) cannot be ascertained from the public record, as it needs to have been properly authorized to be effective. For a complete discussion of this and other issues related to the filing system, see Darrell W. Pierce, Revised Article 9 of the Uniform Commercial Code: Filing System Improvements and Their Rationale, 31 UCC L.J. 16 (1998).

The case that follows should cause you to tremble. The misstep involved caused the law firm's client to lose a financing statement for the collateral securing a $1.5 billion loan!

In re Motors Liquidation Company

United States Court of Appeals, Second Circuit, 2015
777 F.3d 100

PER CURIAM:

We assume familiarity with our prior certification opinion, Official Committee of Unsecured Creditors of Motors Liquidation Co. v. JP Morgan Chase Bank, N.A. (In re Motors Liquidation Co.), 755 F.3d 78 (2d Cir. 2014), and the resulting decision of the Delaware Supreme Court, Official Committee of Unsecured Creditors of Motors Liquidation Co. v. JPMorgan Chase Bank, N.A., 103 A.3d 1010 (Del. Supr. 2014). We restate the most salient facts.

BACKGROUND

In October 2001, General Motors entered into a synthetic lease financing transaction (the "Synthetic Lease"), by which it obtained approximately $300 million in financing from a syndicate of lenders including JPMorgan Chase Bank, N.A. ("JPMorgan"). General Motors' obligation to repay the Synthetic Lease was secured by liens on twelve pieces of real estate. JPMorgan served as administrative agent for the Synthetic Lease and was identified on the UCC-1 financing statements as the secured party of record.

Five years later, General Motors entered into a separate term loan facility (the "Term Loan"). The Term Loan was entirely unrelated to the Synthetic Lease and provided General Motors with approximately $1.5 billion in financing from a different syndicate of lenders. To secure the loan, the lenders took security interests in a large number of General Motors' assets, including all of General Motors' equipment and fixtures at forty-two facilities throughout the United States. JPMorgan again served as administrative agent and secured party of record for the Term Loan and caused the filing of twenty-eight UCC-1 financing statements around the country to perfect the lenders' security interests in the collateral. One such financing statement, the "Main Term Loan UCC-1," was filed with the Delaware Secretary of State and bore file number "6416808 4." It "covered, among other things, all of the equipment and fixtures at 42 GM facilities, [and] was by far the most important" of the financing statements filed in connection with the Term Loan. Official Comm. of Unsecured Creditors of Motors Liquidation Co. v. JPMorgan Chase Bank, N.A. (In re Motors Liquidation Co.), 486 B.R. 596, 603 n.6 (Bankr. S.D.N.Y. 2013).

In September 2008, as the Synthetic Lease was nearing maturity, General Motors contacted Mayer Brown LLP, its counsel responsible for the Synthetic Lease, and explained that it planned to repay the amount due. General Motors requested that Mayer Brown prepare the documents necessary for JPMorgan and the lenders to be repaid and to release the interests the lenders held in General Motors' property.

A Mayer Brown partner assigned the work to an associate and instructed him to prepare a closing checklist and drafts of the documents required to pay off the Synthetic Lease and to terminate the lenders' security interests in General Motors' property relating to the Synthetic Lease. One of the steps required to unwind the Synthetic Lease was to create a list of security interests held by General Motors' lenders that would need to be terminated. To prepare the list, the Mayer Brown associate asked a paralegal who was unfamiliar with the transaction or the purpose of the request to perform a search for UCC-1 financing statements that had been recorded against General Motors in Delaware. The paralegal's search identified three UCC-1s, numbered 2092532 5, 2092526 7, and 6416808 4. Neither the paralegal nor the associate realized that only the first two of the UCC-1s were related to the Synthetic Lease. The third, UCC-1 number 6416808 4, related instead to the Term Loan.

When Mayer Brown prepared a Closing Checklist of the actions required to unwind the Synthetic Lease, it identified the Main Term Loan UCC-1 for termination alongside the security interests that actually did need to be terminated. And when Mayer Brown prepared draft UCC-3 statements to terminate the three security interests identified in the Closing Checklist, it prepared a UCC-3 statement to terminate the Main Term Loan UCC-1 as well as those related to the Synthetic Lease.

No one at General Motors, Mayer Brown, JPMorgan, or its counsel, Simpson Thacher & Bartlett LLP, noticed the error, even though copies of the Closing Checklist and draft UCC-3 termination statements were sent to individuals at each organization for review. On October 30, 2008, General Motors repaid the amount due on the Synthetic Lease. All three UCC-3s were filed with the Delaware Secretary of State, including the UCC-3 that erroneously identified for termination the Main Term Loan UCC-1, which was entirely unrelated to the Synthetic Lease.

A. *General Motors' Chapter 11 Bankruptcy Filing*

The mistake went unnoticed until General Motors' bankruptcy in 2009. After General Motors filed for chapter 11 reorganization, JPMorgan informed the Committee of Unsecured Creditors (the "Committee") that a UCC-3 termination statement relating to the Term Loan had been inadvertently filed in October 2008. JPMorgan explained that it had intended to terminate only liens related to the Synthetic Lease and stated that the filing was therefore unauthorized and ineffective.

On July 31, 2009, the Committee commenced the underlying action against JPMorgan in the United States Bankruptcy Court for the Southern District of New York. The Committee sought a determination that, despite the error, the UCC-3 termination statement was effective to terminate the Term Loan security interest and render JPMorgan an unsecured creditor on par with the other General Motors unsecured creditors. JPMorgan disagreed, reasoning that the UCC-3 termination statement was unauthorized and therefore ineffective because no one at JPMorgan, General Motors, or their law firms had intended that the Term Loan security interest be terminated. On cross-motions for summary judgment, the Bankruptcy Court concluded that the UCC-3 filing was unauthorized and therefore not effective to terminate the Term Loan security interest. *In re Motors Liquidation Co.*, 486 B.R. at 647-48.

B. *Prior Certification Opinion*

On appeal to this Court, the parties offered competing interpretations of UCC §9-509(d)(1), which provides that a UCC-3 termination statement is effective only if "the secured party of record authorizes the filing." JPMorgan reasoned that it cannot have "authorize[d] the filing" of the UCC-3 that identified the Main Term Loan UCC-1 for termination because JPMorgan neither intended to terminate the security interest nor instructed anyone else to do so on its behalf. In response, the Committee contended that focusing on the parties' goal misses the point. It interpreted UCC §9-509(d)(1) to require only that the secured lender authorize the act of filing a particular UCC-3 termination statement, not that the lender subjectively intend to terminate the particular security interest identified for termination on that UCC-3. The Committee further argued that even if JPMorgan never intentionally instructed anyone to terminate the Main Term Loan UCC-1,

JPMorgan did literally "authorize[] the filing"—even if mistakenly—of a UCC-3 termination statement that had that effect.

In our prior certification opinion we recognized that this appeal presents two closely related questions. First, what precisely must a secured lender of record authorize for a UCC-3 termination statement to be effective: "Must the secured lender authorize the termination of the particular security interest that the UCC-3 identifies for termination, or is it enough that the secured lender authorize the act of filing a UCC-3 statement that has that effect?" *In re Motors Liquidation Co.*, 755 F.3d at 84. Second, "[d]id JPMorgan grant to Mayer Brown the relevant authority—that is, alternatively, authority either to terminate the Main Term Loan UCC-1 or to file the UCC-3 statement that identified that interest for termination?" *Id.*

Recognizing that the first question—what is it that the UCC requires a secured lender to authorize—seemed likely to recur and presented a significant issue of Delaware state law, we certified to the Delaware Supreme Court the following question:

> Under UCC Article 9, as adopted into Delaware law by Del. Code Ann. tit. 6, art. 9, for a UCC-3 termination statement to effectively extinguish the perfected nature of a UCC-1 financing statement, is it enough that the secured lender review and knowingly approve for filing a UCC-3 purporting to extinguish the perfected security interest, or must the secured lender intend to terminate the particular security interest that is listed on the UCC-3?

Id. at 86. The second question—whether JPMorgan granted the relevant authority—we reserved for ourselves, explaining that "[t]he Delaware Supreme Court's clarification as to the sense in which a secured party of record must authorize a UCC-3 filing will enable us to address . . . whether JPMorgan in fact provided that authorization." *Id.* at 86-87.

C. *The Delaware Supreme Court's Answer*

In a speedy and thorough reply, the Delaware Supreme Court answered the certified question, explaining that if the secured party of record authorizes the filing of a UCC-3 termination statement, then that filing is effective regardless of whether the secured party subjectively intends or understands the effect of that filing:

> [F]or a termination statement to become effective under §9-509 and thus to have the effect specified in §9-513 of the Delaware UCC, it is enough that the secured party authorizes the filing to be made, which is all that §9-510 requires. The Delaware UCC contains no requirement that a secured party that authorizes a filing subjectively intends or otherwise understands the effect of the plain terms of its own filing.

Official Comm. of Unsecured Creditors of Motors Liquidation Co., 103 A.3d at 1017-18. That conclusion, explained the court, follows both from the unambiguous terms of the UCC and from sound policy considerations:

> JPMorgan's argument that a filing is only effective if the authorizing party understands the filing's substantive terms and intends their effect is contrary to §9-509, which only requires that "the secured party of record authorize [] the filing." . . .
>
> Even if the statute were ambiguous, we would be reluctant to embrace JPMorgan's proposition. Before a secured party authorizes the filing of a termination statement, it ought to review the statement carefully and understand which security interests it is releasing and why. . . . If parties could be relieved from the legal consequences of their mistaken filings, they would have little incentive to ensure the accuracy of the information contained in their UCC filings.

Id. at 1014-16 (first alteration in original) (footnote omitted).

Discussion

The Delaware Supreme Court has explained the sense in which a secured party must "authorize[] the filing" of a UCC-3 termination statement. What remains is to answer the question we reserved for ourselves in our prior certification opinion: Did JPMorgan authorize the filing of the UCC-3 termination statement that mistakenly identified for termination the Main Term Loan UCC-1?

In JPMorgan's view, it never instructed anyone to file the UCC-3 in question, and the termination statement was therefore unauthorized and ineffective. JPMorgan reasons that it authorized General Motors only to terminate security interests related to the Synthetic Lease; that it instructed Simpson Thacher and Mayer Brown only to take actions to accomplish that objective; and that therefore Mayer Brown must have exceeded the scope of its authority when it filed the UCC-3 purporting to terminate the Main Term Loan UCC-1.

JPMorgan's and General Motors' aims throughout the Synthetic Lease transaction were clear: General Motors would repay the Synthetic Lease, and JPMorgan would terminate its related UCC-1 security interests in General Motors' properties. The Synthetic Lease Termination Agreement provided that, upon General Motors' repayment of the amount due under the Synthetic Lease, General Motors would be authorized "to file a termination of any existing Financing Statement relating to the Properties [of the Synthetic Lease]." J.A. 2151. And, to represent its interests in the transaction, JPMorgan relied on Simpson Thacher, its counsel for matters related to the Synthetic Lease. No one at JPMorgan, Simpson Thacher, General Motors, or Mayer Brown took action intending to affect the Term Loan.

What JPMorgan intended to accomplish, however, is a distinct question from what actions it authorized to be taken on its behalf. Mayer Brown prepared a Closing Checklist, draft UCC-3 termination statements, and an Escrow Agreement, all aimed at unwinding the Synthetic Lease but tainted by one crucial error: The documents included a UCC-3 termination statement that erroneously identified for termination a security interest related not to the Synthetic Lease but to the Term Loan. The critical question in this case is whether JPMorgan "authorize[d] [Mayer Brown] to file" that termination statement.

After Mayer Brown prepared the Closing Checklist and draft UCC-3 termination statements, copies were sent for review to a Managing Director at JPMorgan who supervised the Synthetic Lease payoff and who had signed the Term Loan documents on JPMorgan's behalf. Mayer Brown also sent copies of the Closing Checklist and draft UCC-3 termination statements to JPMorgan's counsel, Simpson Thacher, to ensure that the parties to the transaction agreed as to the documents required to complete the Synthetic Lease payoff transaction. Neither directly nor through its counsel did JPMorgan express any concerns about the draft UCC-3 termination statements or about the Closing Checklist. A Simpson Thacher attorney responded simply as follows: "Nice job on the documents. My only comment, unless I am missing something, is that all references to JPMorgan Chase Bank, as Administrative Agent for the Investors should not include the reference 'for the Investors.'" J.A. 921.

After preparing the closing documents and circulating them for review, Mayer Brown drafted an Escrow Agreement that instructed the parties' escrow agent how to proceed with the closing. Among other things, the Escrow Agreement specified that the parties would deliver to the escrow agent the set of three UCC-3 termination statements (individually identified by UCC-1 financing statement file number) that would be filed to terminate the security interests that General Motors' Synthetic Lease lenders held in its properties. The Escrow Agreement provided that once General Motors repaid the amount due on the Synthetic Lease, the escrow agent would forward copies of the UCC-3 termination statements to General Motors' counsel for filing. When Mayer Brown e-mailed a draft of the Escrow Agreement to JPMorgan's counsel for review, the same Simpson Thacher attorney responded that "it was fine" and signed the agreement.

From these facts it is clear that although JPMorgan never intended to terminate the Main Term Loan UCC-1, it authorized the filing of a UCC-3 termination statement that had that effect. "Actual authority . . . is created by a principal's manifestation to an agent that, as reasonably understood by the agent, expresses the principal's assent that the agent take action on the principal's behalf." Restatement (Third) of Agency §3.01 (2006); *accord Demarco v. Edens*, 390 F.2d 836, 844 (2d Cir. 1968). JPMorgan and Simpson

Thacher's repeated manifestations to Mayer Brown show that JPMorgan and its counsel knew that, upon the closing of the Synthetic Lease transaction, Mayer Brown was going to file the termination statement that identified the Main Term Loan UCC-1 for termination and that JPMorgan reviewed and assented to the filing of that statement. Nothing more is needed.

CONCLUSION

For the foregoing reasons, we REVERSE the Bankruptcy Court's grant of summary judgment for the Defendant and REMAND with instructions to the Bankruptcy Court to enter partial summary judgment for the Plaintiff as to the termination of the Main Term Loan UCC-1.

This decision caused a sensation not so much for its legal result, which seems clearly right, but for the astounding amount of money that was lost over a clerical error. Would the law firm have to reimburse its client, in your judgment, for the money lost? What if it doesn't have that much money? How can your law firm—future attorney—avoid this sort of misstep? How much malpractice insurance should you buy when you start your practice? One court soon followed *Motors Liquidation.* See In re Wheeler, 2017 WL 6568758 (Bankr. W.D. Ky. 2017) (financing statement became ineffective when bank mistakenly filed termination statement, although bank attempted to amend the termination within minutes).

Motors Liquidation held that JPMorgan had terminated its UCC-1 financing statement covering "equipment and fixtures" at some 42 GM facilities. All was not lost, however. JPMorgan also had fixture filings covering fixtures at those facilities. Nor was all saved. The rest of the story is in the section on Fixtures in Chapter 24.

PROBLEM 350

When attorney Sam Ambulance handled a divorce for a client, he incurred the wrath of her ex-husband, Andrew Anarchist, president of the Freeman Common Law Movement, a group that did not recognize the authority of the state or federal government. The irate ex-spouse filed 42 phony financing statements in the public records to show that all of Sam's assets were security for various nonexistent loans in favor of Anarchist, the secured party of record. What can Sam do to clear up these clouds on his title to his property (which the common law would have regarded as defamation)? See §§9-513, its Official Comment 3, 9-518, its Official Comment 2, and 9-625(b) and (e)(3) and (4); United States v. Orrego, 2004 WL 1447954 (E.D.N.Y. 2004).

Prison inmates frequently file fraudulent UCC-1 financing statements against prosecutors and prison officials. Some penitentiaries have declared UCC materials contraband, and confiscated them after lockdowns and searches. See Monroe v. Beard, 536 F.3d 198 (3d Cir. 2008) (addressing First Amendment issues of inmates' access to legal materials).

Recent years have seen an increase in bogus UCC-1 filings for such purposes as harassment and fraud. See National Association of Secretaries of State, State Strategies to Subvert Fraudulent Uniform Commercial Code (UCC) Filings (updated June 2019). When a fraudulent financing statement is filed against someone, that person may file an information statement or a termination statement. See §9-513(c)(4), §9-5-518. But such filings are not a complete solution, because the fraudulent financing statement remains in the file, which may leave the situation unclear to other parties. In response, some states have enacted procedures to allow filing offices to refuse or remove unauthorized filings. Some states permit expedited court procedures to expunge such filings. The office may have authority to reject fraudulent financing statements rather than accepting them for filing. The office may also have authority to remove bogus financing statements from the records after filing. The fees for the procedures are generally low and the procedure is expedited, in order to permit removal quickly. The filing party is afforded notice and an opportunity to be heard, to preserve fairness and due process.

Statutes in some states allow a party to recover damages, costs, and attorney's fees from the person making the fraudulent filing. Making a bogus filing is now a crime in many states. See People v. Cratty, 2013 WL 967803 (Mich. Ct. App. 2013) (upholding conviction for making fraudulent filings against judges, lawyers, and court officers involved in home foreclosure case).

The website of the State of Maryland's office for UCC filings makes clear that the costs to make a fraudulent filing may go well beyond the filing fee of $25:

> NOTE: UNDER MD CRIMINAL LAW, A PERSON WHO FILES IN THE PUBLIC RECORDS OF THE DEPARTMENT OF ASSESSMENTS AND TAXATION A LIEN OR ENCUMBRANCE AGAINST THE PERSONAL PROPERTY OF ANOTHER THAT IS BASED ON A FALSE, FICTITIOUS OR FRAUDULENT STATEMENT IS GUILTY OF A MISDEMEANOR AND SUBJECT TO IMPRISONMENT NOT EXCEEDING ONE YEAR OR A FINE NOT EXCEEDING $10,000 OR BOTH FOR THE FIRST OFFENSE.

At the federal level, Congress passed the Court Security Improvement Act, 18 U.S.C. §1521:

> Whoever files, attempts to file, or conspires to file, in any public record or in any private record which is generally available to the public, any false lien or encumbrance against the real or personal property of an individual described in [18 U.S.C.] section 1114, on account of the performance of official duties by that individual, knowing or having reason to know that such lien or encumbrance is false or contains any materially false, fictitious, or fraudulent statement or representation, shall be fined under this title or imprisoned for not more than 10 years, or both.

Filing a bogus UCC-1 financing statement with a lengthy, incoherent description of collateral might not have met the requirements of the U.C.C. but supported a criminal conviction under the federal statute. See United States v. Reed, 668 F.3d 978, 984 (8th Cir. 2012).

IV. PERFECTION BY NOTATION ON CERTIFICATE OF TITLE

PROBLEM 351

Coco buys a Corvette, signing a security agreement making the car collateral for payment of the price. The dealer retains possession of the certificate of title and set of keys. Would that perfect the dealer's security interest? In re Wharton, 563 B.R. 289 (B.A.P. 9th Cir. 2017). If the dealer filed a financing statement indicating the car as collateral, would that perfect its security interest? See §9-311(b). If the dealer retained possession of the car, would that perfect its security interest? See §9-311(b). Or maybe the security interest perfects automatically, if the transaction is a purchase money security interest in consumer goods? See §9-309(1).

Suppose Bank makes a loan to a car dealer, secured by the car dealer's inventory of cars. Must the Bank get its security interest noted on every car that comes through the dealership, in order to be perfected in case the dealer goes under? See §9-311(d).

Every state requires notation on the certificate of title to perfect a security interest in cars. Some states require certificates of title for goods such as boats, farm tractors, or mobile homes (also known as manufactured homes or trailer homes). States also vary as to form, some using paper titles, some electronic, some both. Most states have the creditor hold the certificate of title until the debt is paid, while others permit the debtor to hold title.

V. PERFECTION BY CONTROL

In addition to the possibility of filing a financing statement, for certain types of collateral the secured party may achieve perfection of the security interest by gaining control over the collateral. Section 9-314(a) provides that a "security interest in investment property, deposit accounts, letter-of-credit rights, or electronic chattel paper may be perfected by control of the collateral under Section 9-104, 9-105, 9-106, or 9-107." *Control* generally means that the secured party has taken the steps described in these sections, so it is obvious to anyone investigating the state of the collateral that the secured party has rights therein. We will investigate perfection by control when we take up the issue of priority in Chapter 24.

CHAPTER 22 ASSESSMENT: MULTIPLE CHOICE QUESTIONS

1. Ataturk Gallery offered to put up an Old Master painting, *Portrait of a Merchant,* as collateral to get a loan from Beaux Finance. Ataturk Gallery, however, was reluctant to allow Beaux Finance to file a UCC financing statement to perfect the security interest, regarding such a filing as déclassé. The parties agreed that Beaux Finance would perfect its security interest by possession of the painting, but Ataturk Gallery also wished to continue displaying the painting in its gallery. So the parties decided that the security agreement would provide that Ataturk Gallery was in possession of the painting as the agent for Beaux Finance. Would that be effective to perfect the security interest?
   a. No. A creditor cannot perfect by possession if the creditor simply leaves the debtor in possession of the collateral.
   b. Yes. Beaux Finance would be in possession, through its agent, Ataturk Gallery.
   c. No filing is necessary to perfect, because a painting is consumer goods.
   d. No filing is necessary to perfect, because the transaction is a purchase money security interest.

2. Miyazaki borrowed money from Beaux Finance to purchase a painting, *The Howl,* for his home, signing an agreement making the painting itself

collateral for the debt. Beaux Finance did not bother filing a financing statement. Does Beaux Finance have a perfected security interest?

a. No, because it did not file a financing statement.
b. Yes, because it has constructive possession through the debtor, Miyazaki.
c. Yes, because the security interest in this transaction will perfect without filing or possession by the creditor.
d. No, because an expensive painting is not consumer goods.
e. No. Beaux Finance was not the seller, so the transaction is not a purchase money transaction.

3. Beaux Finance had a painting as collateral in yet another transaction. Khan Biologics purchased *Triple Helix* from Ataturk Gallery, borrowing the funds from Beaux Finance and signing a security agreement. Once again, Beaux Finance did not file a UCC-1 financing statement. Is the security interest perfected?
   a. Yes, because it is a purchase money security interest.
   b. No, because the painting is not consumer goods.
   c. No, because Ataturk Gallery did not sign the security agreement.
   d. No, because paintings are certificate of title goods.

4. After a year or so, Beaux Finance realizes its error with respect to the Khan Biologics loan. Fortunately, during that time, nothing has happened that would give someone else priority over Beaux Finances' security interest. As later chapters discuss, Beaux Finance could have lost its unperfected security interest if Khan Biologics filed bankruptcy, or sold the painting, or was subject to a judgment lien. Breathing a sigh of relief, Beaux Finance filed a financing statement on September 1, 2022. To retain its perfected status, when should it file a continuation statement?
   a. A continuation statement is not necessary here. A continuation statement is only necessary where the debtor continues to acquire new collateral, such as with a security interest in all the debtor's inventory or accounts.
   b. Immediately, to ensure no lapse occurs.
   c. After five years from the date of the loan.
   d. Within the last six months of five years from the date of filing the financing statement.

5. Suppose that Beaux Finance fails to file a continuation statement. What practical effect would it have, when the financing statement expires?
   a. The debt would be cancelled and Beaux Finance would be left with nothing.
   b. The debt would become an unsecured debt, meaning Khan Biologics would still owe the money but Beaux Finance would no longer have the painting as collateral.

c. Beaux Finance would still have a security interest in the painting, but it would be unperfected.
d. No effect whatsoever.

ANSWERS

1. *A* is the best answer. A creditor can perfect a security interest without filing a financing statement, if the creditor is in possession of the collateral. Possession is a flexible concept. The first case many students encounter in law school is Pierson v. Post, on whether possession of a fox was secured by giving chase to it or by actually killing it. Article 9 does not define "possession," and some courts have recognized constructive possession through an agent. But courts would not consider the creditor to be in possession here, because such a rule would make filing unnecessary. Creditors could simply always agree that the debtor is in possession on their behalf. Creditors would not need to file, and other creditors would not receive the notice that filing provides, one of the key aspects of the Article 9 system.

   The other answers review an important rule. A creditor perfects without filing, with a purchase money security interest in consumer goods. But that rule does not apply here, because the transaction is not a purchase money security interest (Ataturk Gallery already owns the painting and is not borrowing to acquire it) and is not consumer goods (Ataturk Gallery has the painting for business purposes, not as consumer goods). *C* and *D* are therefore incorrect.
2. *C* is the best answer. A creditor generally needs to file or possess to perfect the security interest, but there are a good number of exceptions. This question illustrates one of the most common: a security interest will perfect without filing for a purchase money security interest in consumer goods. A purchase money creditor may be either a vendor (who sells the collateral) or a lender (who funds the purchase), contrary to *E*. Consumer goods are any goods acquired for personal, family or household purposes, even luxury goods, contrary to *D*.
3. *B* is the best answer. This variation emphasizes a key distinction. A security interest perfects automatically in a purchase money security interest *in consumer goods*. The collateral here is not consumer goods, rather a painting acquired by a business, which would be inventory (probably not in this case) or equipment. Students (and sometimes lawyers) often learn the rule for purchase money security interests in consumer goods and apply it too broadly, to every purchase money security interest that they spot. *C* and *D* are quite off base. Only the debtor need sign the security interest, and Ataturk Gallery is not even a party to the loan transaction. No filing is necessary, or even effective, for goods like cars that require a

notation on the certificate of title for perfection. But no state has paintings as certificate of title goods, contrary to *D*.

4. *D* is the best answer. A financing statement will expire after five years after filing, unless a timely continuation statement is filed. That rule applies whether there is after-acquired collateral or not, contrary to *A*. But the drafters wanted to prevent creditors from filing continuation statements right after financing statements were filed, which would lead to zombie financing statements that were effective long after the loan had been paid. A continuation statement is effective only if filed within "six months before the expiration of the five-year period," §9-515(c), contrary to *B*. Beaux Finance must remind itself to file anywhere between 4½ to 5 years after the date of filing (not the date of the loan, the second inaccuracy in *C*).
5. *C* is the best answer, reminding us of the difference between a perfected and unperfected security interest. The financing statement serves to perfect the security interest. If it becomes unperfected, that does not negate the security interest, rather makes it unperfected. Beaux Finance could still enforce the security interest (take possession of the painting and sell it) if Khan Biologics defaulted on the debt. But if a third party claimed an interest in the painting (a bankruptcy trustee, buyer of the painting, or rival creditor), Beaux Finance would likely lose that priority contest, as later chapters will discuss. Beaux Finance, if it allowed the financing statement to expire, should file a new one and become perfected again.

Chapter 23
Multistate Transactions

A secured transactions lawyer's life would be easier if all Article 9 matters took place in one state, but that world doesn't exist. Instead the debtor and the creditor may live in different jurisdictions while the collateral is in a third. Which state's law controls and what happens if things change: after the deal is done the debtor moves to another state or the collateral is transferred there? In this chapter these issues and more are our area of study.

I. GENERAL CHOICE OF LAW RULES

Section 1-301 includes the Code's general choice of law provision. It permits *party autonomy,* so that those involved in the transaction may agree to be bound by the law of any state or nation bearing a "reasonable relation" to the transaction. Article 9 has its own overriding conflicts provisions, chiefly §9-301, and when Article 9 dominates the problem, this section is controlling. The original Article 9 rules had very complicated choice of law provisions. The law of the state where the collateral was located generally governed. But a debtor may have collateral in many states. Some collateral moves from state to state. Intangible collateral does not have a location. So there had to be special rules for all those cases.

Things are much simplified in the 1999 revision, which primarily adopts a *domicile* approach and looks to the law of the *debtor's location* as the state in which the steps for perfection need to be taken. See §9-301(1). However, if the collateral has physical form, the law of the jurisdiction in which the collateral is located will govern issues involving priority and other Article 9 matters; §9-301(1) and (3). So, the secured party looks to the jurisdiction in which the debtor is located as the *place* of perfection but the jurisdiction of the collateral's physical location to resolve *questions* of perfection or priority as to that collateral.

All 50 states (as well as the District of Columbia, the Commonwealth of Puerto Rico, Guam, and the U.S. Virgin Islands, along with an increasing number of Native American tribes) have adopted the Uniform Commercial Code. The rules are often the same in all relevant jurisdictions, so courts need not decide which jurisdiction's law governs. But choice of law becomes an issue where jurisdictions have non-uniform variations. In addition, every jurisdiction has a different rule for where the financing statement should be filed.

PROBLEM 352

Mary Bush lived in a home she owned in Cheyenne, Wyoming but she also wanted to buy a large sailboat in Cleveland, Ohio and planned to keep the boat there after the purchase for use in her charter fishing business. Ohio law provides that whenever a buyer has paid more than 75 percent of a debt secured by a boat, the creditor's security interest automatically is stripped from the boat. Wyoming has no such rule. If a creditor loans Mary money to buy the sailboat and takes a security interest in it, where should the creditor file the financing statement? When Mary has paid 75 percent of the debt, will the creditor's security interest still be attached to the boat?

Sections 9-301 through 9-306 have some special choice of law rules for certain kinds of collateral: minerals to be extracted from the ground (§9-301(4)), agricultural liens (§9-302), goods covered by a certificate of title (§9-303, considered in detail below), deposit accounts (§9-304), investment property (§9-305), and letter of credit rights (§9-306). The provisions of these sections generally choose the law where these types of collateral are located to resolve the relevant issues.

PROBLEM 353

Peripatetic Corporation was organized under the laws of the State of Delaware but has its large retail store outlet in New Jersey. Further, the corporation was really a husband-and-wife type of business, and they did all the corporate paperwork at their home in Baltimore, Maryland (where they also kept the corporate records). Their corporate stationery used their home address. When the corporation borrows money against its accounts receivable, in which state should the financing statement be filed? See §9-307(b) and (e). If the corporation was registered and had its only place of business in the Republic of Jahala, a Pacific island nation, where should the financing statement be filed? See §9-307(c).

Section 9-307(a) gives some guidance as to where a debtor's place of business is located, and the courts have developed a number of tests for this issue (still applicable where the debtor is not a registered organization). In re Mimshell Fabrics, Ltd., 491 F.2d 21 (2d Cir. 1974) (principal place is "frequent and notorious" to "probable potential creditors"); In re Carmichael Enters., 334 F. Supp. 94 (N.D. Ga. 1971) (the "factual" principal place of business). See also this oft-quoted passage from In re McQuaide, 5 U.C.C. Rep. Serv. 802, 806-807 (Ref. Bankr., D. Vt. 1968):

> "Place of business" is defined in 48 C.J. 1213 §3 as an agency, an office; a place actually occupied, either continually or at regular periods, by a person or his clerks, or those in his employment; a place devoted by the proprietor to the carrying on of some form of trade or commerce; a place where people generally congregate for the purpose of carrying on some sort of traffic, or where people are invited or expected to come to engage in some sort of mercantile transaction; a place where a calling for the purpose of gain or profit is conducted; a place where business is carried on by persons under their control and on their own account; some particular locality, appropriated exclusively to a local business, such as a farm, store, shop, or dwelling place; that specific place within a city or town at which a person transacts business. *An occasional use or occupation of a place for business purposes is not sufficient to constitute it as a place of business.* (Emphasis in original.)

Under §9-307(c), if the debtor is located abroad, the creditor files in that jurisdiction only if it has the equivalent of Article 9, a system for filing non-possessory security interests in public records. Otherwise the creditor files in the District of Columbia. Most jurisdictions do not have a filing system equivalent to Article 9. See Dayka & Hackett, LLC v. Del Monte Fresh Produce N.A., Inc., 2012 WL 234142 (Ariz. App. 2012); Arnold S. Rosenberg, Where to File Against Non-U.S. Debtors: Applying U.C.C. §9-307(c) [Rev.] to Foreign Filing, Recording and Registration Systems, 39 UCC L.J. 109 (2006). Some countries have systems similar to Article 9, or even copied from Article 9. Albania, for example, modeled its secured transactions law on that of Saskatchewan, which in turn was modeled on Article 9. Other formerly communist countries have adopted a version of Article 9 as part of reforming their legal system for a market economy. Other countries follow a wide range of approaches. The 1804 Napoleonic Code, the basis for many civil law legal systems, "eliminated all nonpossessory security interests in movables, ironically out of the drafters' despair at ever being able to design an effective registration system." Id. That approach persists in some civil law jurisdictions, although others have been driven by commercial practices to adopt registration systems for personal property used as collateral.

NOTE

For perfectly obvious reasons, when in doubt, file everywhere.

PROBLEM 354

Factory, Factory & Money is a legal partnership that has its only place of business in Chicago, Illinois where Octopus National Bank, which has a security interest in the accounts receivable of the firm, had filed its financing statement. If the law firm makes a permanent move to Washington, D.C., on January 1, 2021, does the bank lose its perfection or does it have a grace period in which to refile in the new jurisdiction? Read §9-316(a). If the law firm *merges* with a law firm in D.C. with the new D.C. firm assuming all the debts of the former one, is the time period the same? See §9-316(a)(3). Is the creditor protected as to collateral debtor acquires between the move or merger and during the applicable time period? See §9-316(h) and (i).[1]

PROBLEM 355

Suppose that Factory, Factory & Money, the Chicago law firm in the last Problem, had two creditors before its permanent move to D.C., each of which had a perfected security interest in the firm's accounts receivable—Octopus National Bank, which had filed its financing statement first, and Last National Bank, which had filed second, both creditors filing in Chicago early in the year 2021. When the move occurred on January 1, 2022, Last National promptly refiled in D.C. before the end of March of that year, but Octopus National was careless and didn't realize that the firm had moved until that September. If Octopus National Bank files in D.C. in September, will it retain its priority over Last National? See §9-316(b) and its Official Comment 3. Note the definitions of *purchase* and *purchaser* in §1-201(b)(29) and (30).

1. These two provisions were added in the 2010 revisions to Article 9.

II. CERTIFICATES OF TITLE

Grant Gilmore, one of the principal drafters of the original version of Article 9, wrote a famous treatise on its meaning, Security Interests in Personal Property (1965). In his treatise he had this to say about automobile financing:

> The automobile, in addition to its potentialities as an instrument of destruction and an agent of social change, has been one of the great sources of law in the twentieth century. As the most expensive chattel ever to come into general use, it generated novel methods of secured financing. Its unique mobility, combined with the high resale value of used cars, made theft both easy and profitable.
>
> From a legal point of view there is nothing interesting in the situation where *A,* a thief, steals *B*'s car and sells it to *C: A,* if apprehended, will go to jail and *C,* if found, can be forced to return the car to *B.* However, the fact that most automobile purchases are financed under some kind of security device has led to a refined version of automobile theft which is legally much more interesting than the crude business of smash and grab. Under the refined version, *A* buys a car, making the smallest possible down payment and executing a chattel mortgage, a conditional sale contract or an Article 9 security agreement for the balance in favor of *B. A,* representing the car to be free from liens, now sells it to *C,* who buys it, we may assume, in good faith and without actual knowledge of *B*'s interest. *C* is typically a used car dealer, so that a further complication is introduced when *C* resells to *D,* who also buys in good faith and without notice. *A*'s behavior is criminal and legally uninteresting; if caught, he will and should go to jail. The sales to *C* and *D,* however, begin to be worth thinking about since *A,* who is a criminal, albeit a refined one, is also in some sense an owner of the car, with some kind of title to it, and our legal system has always sharply distinguished between the lot of the good faith purchaser from a thief without title (who gets nothing) and that of the good faith purchaser from a person with a defective title (who may get perfect title, despite the intervening fraud or crime).

Section 20.1, at 550-551. For the protected status of a good faith purchaser buying from someone with voidable title, read §2-403(1) (and remember that *purchaser* is broadly defined in Article 1 to include any voluntary transferee—creditors as well as buyers).

PROBLEM 356

Lyle Saylor was a trucker who lived and worked in the State of Michigan. When his old rig wore out and he decided to buy a completely new truck, he went to Pennsylvania and purchased a truck on credit from Ringer Truck City. Because the State of Indiana charged a great deal less for licenses and other registration fees, Saylor told the dealership that he lived in Indiana and that the truck would be domiciled there. He gave Ringer Truck City the address of his sister, who did live in Indiana. Indiana law requires that lien interests be noted on the certificate of title, a step that Ringer Truck City duly took when it procured the Indiana certificate. When Saylor went bankrupt a year later, the trustee in bankruptcy argued that Ringer Truck City was unperfected because it had not gotten a Michigan certificate of title and had its lien interest noted thereon, as Michigan law required. Ringer Truck City argued that it was entitled to believe the debtor when he told the company that he lived in Indiana. How should this come out? See §9-303(a); In re Stanley, 249 B.R. 509 (D. Kan. 2000).

Metzger v. Americredit Financial Services, Inc.

Court of Appeals of Georgia, 2005
273 Ga. App. 453, 615 S.E.2d 120

Bernes, Judge.

Theresa Metzger appeals from an order entered by the Superior Court of Clayton County granting partial summary judgment to Americredit Financial Services, Inc. on her claim for conversion based on the alleged wrongful repossession of her vehicle. Metzger contends that the Superior Court erred by failing to conclude that she took her vehicle free of Americredit's security interest under the special good faith purchaser rule for goods covered by a certificate of title set forth in OCGA §11-9-337(1). We agree and reverse.

The underlying facts are not in dispute. On or about October 1, 2002, Americredit repossessed a 1997 Ford Taurus from Metzger, who had purchased the vehicle from a used car dealership in March of 2002. Metzger did not realize that Americredit had a prior lien on the vehicle or that it had been repossessed. As a result, she reported the vehicle as stolen to the police.

Metzger later learned that Americredit had obtained a security interest in the vehicle in 1998, when the company financed James Strong's purchase of the vehicle in the State of New York. The New York certificate of title issued to Strong reflected Americredit's security interest in the vehicle.

Strong later moved from New York to Georgia and submitted a "MV1Z" application form, along with the existing title and the required fee, to the Cobb County tag agent for the Georgia Department of Motor Vehicles ("DMV") in order to convert the existing New York certificate of title to a Georgia one. The DMV processed the application, but as a result of a clerical data entry error, the DMV issued a Georgia certificate of title that did not reflect Americredit's security interest in the vehicle.

Strong later transferred the vehicle to an automobile dealer owner, and the vehicle thereafter passed through a non-dealer owner and additional dealer owners before Metzger purchased it in March of 2002. None of the subsequent Georgia certificates of title issued for the vehicle in connection with these transfers reflected Americredit's security interest.

After Metzger purchased the vehicle and registered it with the DMV, Americredit, having finally located the vehicle, repossessed it from Metzger's residence and sold it at auction. Once she learned from the police department that her vehicle had been repossessed rather than stolen, Metzger filed suit against Americredit in the Superior Court of Clayton County. She contended that Americredit wrongfully repossessed her vehicle and kept her personal belongings contained therein, and, as a consequence, should be held liable for conversion, negligence, deceptive trade practices, breach of the peace, breach of good faith, racketeering, unjust enrichment, and breach of sale.

Metzger subsequently filed a motion seeking partial summary judgment on her claim of conversion. Americredit filed its response and a cross motion for summary judgment on all of Metzger's claims. The Superior Court denied Metzger's motion for partial summary judgment and granted summary judgment in favor of Americredit on Metzger's conversion claim only. The Superior Court concluded that Americredit had a perfected security interest in the vehicle that it could enforce against Metzger. Metzger now appeals from that order.

"When reviewing the grant or denial of a motion for summary judgment, this Court conducts a de novo review of the law and the evidence. . . ." (Citation and punctuation omitted.) Osman v. Olde Plantation Apartments on Montreal, LLC, 270 Ga. App. 627, 607 S.E.2d 236 (2004). In order to establish a claim for conversion, "the complaining party must show (1) title to the property or the right of possession, (2) actual possession in the other party, (3) demand for return of the property, and (4) refusal by the other party to return the property." (Citation omitted.) Johnson v. First Union Nat. Bank, 255 Ga. App. 819, 823(4), 567 S.E.2d 44 (2002). The sole issue regarding Metzger's conversion claim is whether Metzger had the exclusive right of possession to the vehicle, making Americredit's seizure unlawful, or whether Americredit's security interest instead empowered it to practice self-help and repossess the vehicle from Metzger. See, e.g., Fulton v. Anchor Savings Bank, FSB, 215 Ga. App. 456, 468(5), 452 S.E.2d 208 (1994). Because the material facts are undisputed, resolution of this issue turns on our interpretation of the applicable statutory framework.

"[I]n construing [Georgia statutes], we apply the fundamental rules of statutory construction that require us to construe a statute according to its terms, to give words their plain and ordinary meaning, and to avoid a construction that makes some language mere surplusage." (Citation omitted.) Slakman v. Continental Cas. Co., 277 Ga. 189, 191, 587 S.E.2d 24 (2003). See also City of Atlanta v. Yusen Air & Sea Svc. Holdings, Inc., 263 Ga. App. 82, 84(1), 587 S.E.2d 230 (2003). With these rules in mind, we turn to the Motor Vehicle Certificate of Title Act, OCGA §40-3-1 et seq. (the "Act"), which provides the exclusive procedure for perfecting a security interest in a motor vehicle in Georgia. Staley v. Phelan Finance Corp. of Columbus, 116 Ga. App. 1, 1-2, 156 S.E.2d 201 (1967).

Under the Act, a security interest in a motor vehicle is perfected, at the latest, on the date when the application documents for obtaining a certificate of title are delivered to the DMV or local tag agent, so long as the application documents properly reflect the existence of the security interest:

> (b)(1) A security interest is perfected by delivery to the commissioner or to the county tag agent of the county in which the seller is located, of the county in which the sale takes place, of the county in which the vehicle is delivered, or of the county wherein the vehicle owner resides, of the required fee and:
>
> (A) The existing certificate of title, if any, and an application for a certificate of title containing the name and address of the holder of a security interest; or
>
> (B) A notice of security interest on forms prescribed by the commissioner.

Perfection occurs on that date, irrespective of whether the certificate of title subsequently issued by the DMV fails to reflect the security interest:

> (b)(2) The security interest is perfected as of the time of its creation if the initial delivery of the application or notice to the commissioner or local tag agent is completed within 20 days thereafter, regardless of any subsequent rejection of the application or notice for errors; otherwise, as of the date of the delivery to the commissioner or local tag agent. The local tag agent shall issue a receipt or other evidence of the date of filing of such application or notice. When the security interest is perfected as provided for in this subsection, it shall constitute notice to everybody of the security interest of the holder.

OCGA §40-3-50(b). "Compliance with the filing requirements of the Act has the effect of imputing constructive notice to all who may subsequently acquire an interest in or lien against the property." (Citation and punctuation omitted.) Cobb Center Pawn & Jewelry Brokers, Inc. v. Gordon, 242 Ga. App. 73, 75(2), 529 S.E.2d 138 (2000).

Based on this statutory language and case law, it might appear that because Strong delivered proper application forms reflecting Americredit's security interest to the Cobb County tag agent, Americredit could enforce its security interest against Metzger, who under OCGA §40-3-50(b)(2) would have constructive notice of the security interest despite the clerical error contained in the Georgia certificate of title that was later issued. However, OCGA §40-3-50 contains three statutory exceptions:

> (a) *Except as provided in Code Sections 11-9-303, 11-9-316, and 11-9-337,* the security interest in a vehicle of the type for which a certificate of title is required shall be perfected and shall be valid against subsequent creditors of the owner, subsequent transferees, and the holders of security interests and liens on the vehicle by compliance with this chapter.

(Emphasis supplied.) OCGA §40-3-50(a).

Significantly, one of those exceptions, OCGA §11-9-337, states:

> If, *while a security interest in goods is perfected by any method under the law of another jurisdiction,* this state issues a certificate of title that does not show that the goods are subject to the security interest or contain a statement that they may be subject to security interests not shown on the certificate:
>
> *(1) A buyer of the goods, other than a person in the business of selling goods of that kind, takes free of the security interest if the buyer gives value and receives delivery of the goods after issuance of the certificate and without knowledge of the security interest. . . .*

(Emphasis supplied.) OCGA §11-9-337(1). An explanation of this provision is set forth in Comment 2 to Uniform Commercial Code §9-337:

> This section affords protection to certain good-faith purchasers for value who are likely to have relied on a "clean" certificate of title, i.e., one that neither shows that the goods are subject to a particular security interest nor contains a statement that they may be subject to security interests not shown on the certificate. Under this section, a buyer can take free of, and the holder of a conflicting security interest can acquire priority over, a security interest that is perfected by any method under the law of another jurisdiction. . . .

UCC §9-337 cmt. 2.

In the present case, the undisputed evidence of record shows that the six requirements of the statutory exception contained in OCGA §11-9-337(1) have been met. First, the parties agree that, at the time that Strong filed his application for a Georgia certificate of title with the Cobb County tag agent, Americredit had previously perfected its security interest in the vehicle under New York law, and the security interest remained perfected. Second, the certificate of title issued by the DMV to Strong failed to show that the vehicle was subject to a security interest. Third, Metzger is not a person in the business of selling automobiles. Fourth, Metzger gave value for the vehicle. Fifth,

Metzger received delivery of the vehicle after issuance of the Georgia certificate of title by the DMV erroneously omitting reference to Americredit's security interest. Sixth and finally, Metzger was without knowledge of the security interest that Americredit held in the vehicle. Thus, Metzger was entitled to invoke OCGA §11-9-337(1). It necessarily follows that Metzger took the vehicle free of Americredit's security interest.

However, Americredit contends that two additional statutes found in Georgia's Uniform Commercial Code, OCGA §§11-9-303 and 11-9-316, indicate that Metzger took the vehicle subject to the security interest. Based on these two statutes, Americredit argues that the special good faith purchaser rule set forth in OCGA §11-9-337(1) has no application in this case, because its perfected security interest in Metzger's vehicle was no longer governed by New York law once the proper application documents and required fee for a Georgia certificate of title were submitted to the Georgia DMV by James Strong. Thus, in Americredit's view, OCGA §11-9-337(1) does not apply under the circumstances here because the erroneous Georgia certificate of title was not issued "while" its security interest in the vehicle was perfected "under the law of another jurisdiction."

Americredit's statutory argument is based on a strained reading of the interplay between OCGA §§11-9-303, 11-9-316(d) and (e), and 11-9-337. OCGA §11-9-303, entitled "Law governing perfection and priority of security interests in goods covered by a certificate of title," is a choice of law provision, as its title suggests. OCGA §11-9-303(b) provides that:

> Goods become covered by a certificate of title when a valid application for the certificate of title and the applicable fee are delivered to the appropriate authority. Goods cease to be covered by a certificate of title at the earlier of the time the certificate of title ceases to be effective under the law of the issuing jurisdiction or the time the goods become covered subsequently by a certificate of title issued by another jurisdiction.

Section 11-9-303(c) then provides that "[t]he local law of the jurisdiction under whose certificate of title the goods are covered governs perfection." These provisions indicate that even when a security interest in goods has been perfected in another state, Georgia law determines perfection and priority issues once the goods become "covered" by a Georgia certificate of title, which occurs when a valid application and fee are submitted to the Georgia DMV.

Once it becomes clear that Georgia law governs because the goods are covered by a Georgia certificate of title, the next question is whether the security interest previously perfected in another state remains perfected. That issue is addressed by OCGA §11-9-316, entitled "Continued perfection of security interest following change in governing law," specifically subsections (d) and (e), which deal with certificates of title. These subsections set forth the general rules for when a security interest perfected in another state remains perfected in Georgia, once the goods are "covered" by a Georgia certificate of title.

"A statute must be construed in relation to other statutes of which it is a part, and all statutes relating to the same subject-matter, briefly called statutes in pari materia, are construed together, and harmonized wherever possible, so as to ascertain the legislative intendment and give effect thereto." (Punctuation omitted.) City of Buchanan v. Pope, 222 Ga. App. 716, 717(1), 476 S.E.2d 53 (1996). When read in pari materia with OCGA §11-9-303 and 11-9-316(d) and (e), OCGA §11-9-337(1) gives protection to a good faith purchaser for value who is not "in the business of selling goods of that kind," when there is continued perfection of the security interest under OCGA §11-9-316(d) and (e), but the Georgia certificate of title fails to reflect the security interest. Consequently, in the present case, although Americredit's security interest in the vehicle remained perfected at the time that Metzger purchased the vehicle, that security interest could not be enforced as against Metzger, a good faith purchaser as that term is defined in OCGA §11-9-337(1), since the security interest was not properly reflected on the Georgia certificate of title.

Furthermore, "a specific statute will prevail over a general statute, absent any indication of a contrary legislative intent, to resolve any inconsistency between them." (Punctuation and emphasis omitted.) Hooks v. Cobb Center Pawn & Jewelry Brokers, 241 Ga. App. 305, 309(6), 527 S.E.2d 566 (1999). OCGA §11-9-316(d) and (e) are general statutory provisions addressing continued perfection of an out-of-state security interest once goods become covered by a Georgia certificate of title. In contrast, OCGA §11-9-337(1) sets forth a more specific rule addressing what occurs in the unique circumstance where the Georgia certificate of title that covers the goods erroneously fails to reflect the security interest originally perfected in another state. Because OCGA §11-9-337(1) is the more specific statute, it controls, even if there were a perceived inconsistency between the various statutory provisions. Accordingly, Americredit's statutory interpretation argument is unavailing. . . .

For these reasons, we reverse the partial grant of summary judgment in favor of Americredit. We remand to the superior court to enter summary judgment in favor of Metzger on her conversion claim.

PROBLEM 357

When Nick Dunne bought his wife Amy a new car, he financed it through Flynn Bank, which made sure its security interest in the car was noted on the certificate of title that Missouri issued with her name as the record owner. Before the loan was paid off Amy forged a letter to the Missouri Department of Motor Vehicles supposedly from Flynn Bank stating that the loan had been repaid, after which the State issued her a new certificate of title showing no lien on the vehicle. Amy then left her husband, moved to New York, and sold the car to Desi Collings, an old boyfriend who knew nothing about the car's history. He obtained a clean certificate of title from the State of New York. When Flynn Bank discovered what was going on it tracked the car down and repossessed it in New York. When Collings pointed to the UCC provisions you have just studied the bank replied that it's a basic rule of law that a thief cannot pass good title. How does this come out? See Mercedes-Benz Financial v. Powell, 2014 WL 3844013 (Mich. App. 2014).

PROBLEM 358

May 10, Holly Tourist, a resident of Dallas, Texas, bought a new car on credit while on vacation in Norman, Oklahoma, from Norman Car Sales, Inc. (NCS). Oklahoma law required lien interests to be noted on the certificate of title as a condition of perfection, which NCS did on May 12. On May 14, Holly drove the car to Dallas, and that same day she re-registered the car there and received a Texas certificate. Somehow she was able to do this without surrendering the Oklahoma certificate (though Texas law apparently required her to turn in the old certificate before a new one should have been issued). Texas required lien interests to be noted on the certificate of title as a condition of perfection, but the Texas certificate showed no liens of any kind thereon. On May 26, Holly sold the car to her neighbor, William Innocent, who paid full value therefor without knowledge of NCS's interest. On May 28, learning of the sale to William, NCS arranged for the car to be repossessed from in front of his house. Assuming that her resale of the car was a "default" so as to entitle NCS to repossess, decide which of them is entitled to the car. See §§9-303 and its Official Comment 6, 9-316(d) and (e) and its Official Comment 5, and 9-337 and its Official Comment. Note that §9-337 favors non-business buyers; a used car lot buying an out-of-state vehicle is not entitled to the same protection. Why would the drafters have made this distinction?

BMW Financial Services, N.A., LLC v. Felice

Appellate Court of Illinois, Second District, 2017
2017 Ill. App. 2d 160397, 75 N.E.3d 368, 412 Ill. Dec. 388

Presiding Justice HUDSON delivered the judgment of the court, with opinion.

¶1 Plaintiff, BMW Financial Services, N.A., LLC (BMW Financial), filed a replevin complaint in the circuit court of Du Page County, seeking possession of a 2011 Porsche Panamera. The complaint named Richard D. Felice as defendant, but an amended complaint named both Felice and Auto Showcase, Inc. (Auto Showcase), as defendants. Felice was later dismissed from the action. BMW Financial and Auto Showcase filed cross-motions for summary judgment. The trial court granted BMW Financial's summary judgment motion, denied Auto Showcase's motion, and awarded possession of the Porsche to BMW Financial. Auto Showcase filed a timely notice of appeal. We affirm.

¶2 I. Background

¶3 For purposes of their cross-motions for summary judgment, BMW Financial and Auto Showcase stipulated in writing to the following material facts. On or about March 13, 2012, Bruce Grant executed a retail installment contract for the purchase of the Porsche. The retail installment contract granted a security interest in the Porsche to BMW Financial. On or about April 4, 2012, the Secretary of State issued an original certificate of title for the Porsche, naming BMW Financial as the first lienholder. Grant later submitted a "lien release letter" to the Secretary of State. BMW Financial did not execute the lien release letter, nor did it ever authorize the release of its security interest. On November 16, 2012, the Secretary of State issued a duplicate certificate of title to Grant. The duplicate certificate did not name BMW Financial as a lienholder. However, the duplicate certificate stated, "This is a duplicate certificate and may be subject to the rights of a person under the original certificate." On or about November 20, 2012, Grant sold the Porsche to Auto Showcase for $47,000. He executed the assignment of title on the duplicate certificate. Auto Showcase conducted computerized searches of the Secretary of State's records. Those searches did not reveal the existence of any liens on the Porsche.

¶4 On November 29, 2012, Auto Showcase sold the Porsche to Felice for $59,000. By letter dated January 30, 2013, BMW Financial advised the Secretary of State that the lien release letter submitted by Grant was fraudulent. BMW Financial asked the Secretary of State to "accept this letter as notice that any further attempt to title the [Porsche] without showing [BMW Financial's] lien should be denied." Auto Showcase later brought a *mandamus* action in the circuit court of Du Page County to compel the Secretary of State to issue a certificate of title naming Felice as the owner of the Porsche. The court entered judgment in favor of Auto Showcase, and the Secretary of State issued a certificate of title to Felice. BMW Financial was not a party to the *mandamus* action. BMW Financial subsequently commenced the replevin action giving rise to this appeal. Felice was dismissed after Auto Showcase repurchased the Porsche from him.

¶5 II. Analysis

* * *

¶7 A. PERFECTION OF SECURITY INTEREST

¶8 The primary purpose of a replevin proceeding is "to test the right of possession of personal property and to place the successful party in possession of that property." Koerner v. Nielsen, 2014 Ill. App (1st) 122980, ¶12, 380 Ill. Dec. 230, 8 N.E.3d 161. It is undisputed that BMW Financial's right of possession depended on whether Auto Showcase acquired title to the Porsche subject to BMW's security interest. "As a general rule, the holder of a perfected security interest has an interest in the secured property, and the proceeds from the sale thereof, which is superior to the interests of unsecured creditors of the debtor and subsequent purchasers of the secured property." Herman v. First Farmers State Bank of Minier, 73 Ill. App. 3d 475, 477, 29 Ill. Dec. 787, 392 N.E.2d 344 (1979). The perfection of security interests in motor vehicles is governed, in part, by section 3-202(b) of the Illinois Vehicle Code (Vehicle Code) (625 ILCS 5/3-202(b) (West 2014)), which provides, "[a] security interest is perfected by the delivery to the Secretary of State of the existing certificate of title, if any, an application for a certificate of title containing the name and address of the lienholder and the required fee. The security interest is perfected as of the time of its creation if the delivery to the Secretary of State is completed within 30 days after the creation of the security interest or receipt by the new lienholder of the existing certificate of title from a prior lienholder or licensed dealer, otherwise as of the time of the delivery." Section 3-107(a)(3) of the Vehicle Code (625 ILCS 5/3-107(a)(3) (West 2014)) provides, in pertinent part, that a certificate of title shall contain "the names and addresses of any lienholders, in the order of priority as shown on the application." Section 3-108 of the Vehicle Code (625 ILCS 5/3-108 (West 2014)) provides that "[t]he certificate of title shall be mailed or delivered to the first lienholder named in it or, if none, to the owner."

¶9 BMW Financial acquired a security interest in the Porsche pursuant to the retail installment contract with Grant. BMW Financial perfected its security interest by applying for a certificate of title that noted its lien on the Porsche. The certificate of title was issued on April 4, 2012. Auto Showcase subsequently purchased the Porsche from Grant on or about November 20, 2012. Had Grant actually paid off his car loan, BMW Financial would have been obligated to execute a release of its security interest and deliver the release and the certificate of title to Grant. 625 ILCS 5/3-205(a) (West 2014). Grant could have then transferred the Porsche to Auto Showcase by executing an assignment of title in the space provided for that purpose on the original certificate. 625 ILCS 5/3-112(a) (West 2014). Instead, he submitted a false release to the Secretary of State, obtained a duplicate certificate of title (see 625 ILCS 5/3-111(a) (West 2014)) that did not identify any liens on the vehicle, and executed the assignment of title on the duplicate certificate.

¶10 Auto Showcase maintains that the assignment via the duplicate certificate of title was not subject to BMW Financial's security interest. We disagree. Auto Showcase relies, in part, on section 9-303(b) of the Uniform Commercial Code (UCC) (810 ILCS 5/9-303(b) (West 2014)), which provides, "Goods cease to be covered by a certificate of title at the earlier of the time the certificate of title ceases to be effective under the law of the issuing jurisdiction or the time the goods become covered subsequently by a certificate of title issued by another jurisdiction." Auto Showcase argues that "the issuance of the duplicate Certificate of Title * * * *which removed BMW* [*Financial*] *'s lien*, must control the determination of possession." (Emphasis added.) Auto Showcase cites no authority for the proposition that the issuance of a duplicate certificate somehow renders the original certificate ineffective under Illinois law. Indeed, Auto Showcase's argument contorts the meaning of the adjective "duplicate." Section 3-111(a) of the Vehicle Code (625 ILCS 5/3-111(a) (West 2014)) provides for the issuance of a duplicate certificate "[i]f a certificate of title is lost, stolen, mutilated or destroyed or becomes illegible." Furthermore, section 3-111(a) provides that the duplicate certificate "shall contain the legend 'This is a duplicate certificate and may be subject to the rights of a person under the original certificate.'" *Id.* That language would be meaningless if, as Auto Showcase argues, the original certificate were no longer effective. Consequently, we reject Auto Showcase's assertion that, by issuing the duplicate certificate, the Secretary of State "removed" BMW Financial's lien.

¶11 B. UNIFORM COMMERCIAL CODE

¶12 Auto Showcase also relies on section 9-337 of the UCC (810 ILCS 5/9-337 (West 2014)) in support of its contention that it holds title free and clear of BMW Financial's security interest. Section 9-337 provides, in pertinent part:

> "If, while a security interest in goods is perfected by any method under the law of another jurisdiction, this State issues a certificate of title that does not show that the goods are subject to the security interest or contain a statement that they may be subject to security interests not shown on the certificate:
>
> (1) a buyer of the goods, other than a person in the business of selling goods of that kind, takes free of the security interest if the buyer gives value and receives delivery of the goods after issuance of the certificate and without knowledge of the security interest; and

> (2) the security interest is subordinate to a conflicting security interest in the goods that attaches, and is perfected under Section 9-311(b), after issuance of the certificate and without the conflicting secured party's knowledge of the security interest." *Id.*

¶13 Section 9-337 clearly does not apply here. By its terms, section 9-337 applies only to a security interest perfected under the law of another jurisdiction; BMW Financial's security interest was perfected under Illinois law. Although Auto Showcase insists that it should not matter whether the security interest was perfected under Illinois law or the law of another jurisdiction, we cannot simply ignore the plain language of the statute. Miller v. Sarah Bush Lincoln Health Center, 2016 Ill. App (4th) 150728, ¶17, 404 Ill. Dec. 615, 56 N.E.3d 599. That said, we recognize that courts "are not bound by the literal language of a statute if that language produces absurd or unjust results." People v. Johnson, 2013 Ill. App (1st) 120413, ¶17, 374 Ill. Dec. 149, 994 N.E.2d 1086. "In such an instance, we may modify, alter or supply words to 'obviate any repugnancy or inconsistency with the legislative intention.' " *Id.* (quoting Community Consolidated School District No. 210 v. Mini, 55 Ill. 2d 382, 386, 304 N.E.2d 75 (1973)). Auto Showcase argues that limiting section 9-337 to security interests perfected in other jurisdictions "would achieve absurd results within interstate commerce." We disagree. The following comment accompanying section 9-303 of the UCC is illuminating:

> Ideally, at any given time, only one certificate of title is outstanding with respect to particular goods. In fact, however, sometimes more than one jurisdiction issues more than one certificate of title with respect to the same goods. This situation results from defects in certificate-of-title laws and the interstate coordination of those laws, not from deficiencies in this Article. As long as the possibility of multiple certificates of title remains, the potential for innocent parties to suffer losses will continue. At best, this Article can identify clearly which innocent parties will bear the losses in familiar fact patterns.

810 ILCS Ann. 5/9-303, Uniform Commercial Code Comment 6, at 474 (Smith-Hurd 2004).

In enacting section 9-337, the General Assembly evidently discerned a need to afford special protection against hidden lien interests arising under the laws of other states. We see nothing absurd in distinguishing between interstate and intrastate priority conflicts. In any event, section 9-337 is inapplicable because the duplicate certificate clearly indicated, as required by section 3-111(a) of the Vehicle Code (625 ILCS 5/3-111(a) (West 2014)), that others might have rights under the original certificate.

¶14 Auto Showcase contends that it "researched the Certificate of Title presented by Grant using all available commercial means for determining whether any encumbrance remained on the vehicle, finding none." According to Auto Showcase, to hold in favor of BMW Financial "would effectively negate the legal significance of Illinois duplicate certificates of title and the ability for consumers and dealers to rely upon records of the Secretary of State." But it is equally true that to hold in favor of Auto Showcase would effectively negate the ability of creditors to rely on the statutory mechanism for protecting their lien rights. And although we sympathize with the plight of a purchaser in Auto Showcase's position who has examined the Secretary of State's vehicle records to confirm that title is unencumbered, Auto Showcase cites no statutory authority or case law for the proposition that errors in those records affect either the validity or the priority of a security interest that was perfected in accordance with section 3-202(b) of the Vehicle Code. . . .

¶19 III. Conclusion

¶20 For the foregoing reasons, the judgment of the circuit court of Du Page County is affirmed.

¶21 Affirmed.

PROBLEM 359

Joseph Armstrong bought a yacht in his home state that did not use certificates of title for boats and that required filing for perfection in such collateral, a step that the financing bank, Octopus National Bank (ONB), duly took. Armstrong then moved to a state that required all security interests on boats to be noted on certificates of title issued by that state, but he never took the time to get such a certificate. Does ONB's perfection in the second state last as long as its filed financing statement is still effective or for only four months? See §9-316(b)(2). Suppose that the opposite situation occurs: Armstrong starts in a title state and ONB's interest is duly noted on that state's certificate. Armstrong moves to a state that has no certificates of title at all for boats, ONB never files there, and Armstrong never re-registers the yacht. Now what result? See §9-303 and its Official Comment.

CHAPTER 23 ASSESSMENT: MULTIPLE CHOICE QUESTIONS

1. Clark lives in Gardiner, Montana. She runs tours into Yellowstone National Park, Wyoming using equipment that she leaves in Yellowstone. Her business office is in Driggs, Idaho. Old Faithful Finance signed her

up to a line of credit, secured by her equipment. To perfect the security interest, where must Old Faithful Finance file its financing statement?
a. Montana, the location of the debtor's residence.
b. Wyoming, the location of the debtor's business activities.
c. Idaho, the location of the debtor's principal office.
d. Wyoming, the location of the collateral.
e. None of the above.

2. Old Faithful Finance will also make a loan to Lewis to purchase some pricey kayaks, for Lewis's use as a hobby in Yellowstone. Lewis lives and works as a park ranger in Yellowstone and has a post-office box in Idaho, used for eBay sales of collectibles. To perfect the security interest in the kayaks, where should Old Faithful Finance file its financing statement?
   a. Montana, the location of the debtor's residence.
   b. Wyoming, the location of the debtor's business activities.
   c. Idaho, the location of the debtor's principal office.
   d. Wyoming, the location of the collateral.
   e. None of the above.

3. Another Gardiner resident, Floyd, is the sole shareholder of a small corporation, Discovery Corps, which does construction in Montana and Wyoming. Discovery Corps is incorporated in Delaware. The business office is in Montana. If Old Faithful Finance makes Discovery Corps a loan secured by its equipment, where is it necessary for Old Faithful Finance to file its financing statement, to perfect its security interest?
   a. Montana, the location of the debtor's residence.
   b. Delaware, the location of the debtor.
   c. Montana and Wyoming, the location of the debtor's business activities.
   d. Montana, the location of the debtor's principal office.
   e. Montana and Wyoming, the location of the collateral.
   f. None of the above.

4. Hadfield Explorers, a Canadian corporation, has an office in Montana and does business at drilling sites in Wyoming, Montana, and Idaho. Hadfield Explorers has its chief executive office and most of its operations in the province of Alberta, Canada. When Old Faithful Finance lends to Hadfield Explorers taking a security interest in its equipment and accounts, where should it file the financing statement?
   a. In Alberta, if Alberta has the equivalent of an Article 9 filing system; otherwise in Washington, D.C.
   b. Montana, the location of its U.S. office.
   c. Wyoming, Montana, and Idado, the locations of its U.S. property.
   d. Wyoming, Montana, and Idado, the locations of its U.S. places of business.

5. Garcia, a trucker living in Gardiner, put up her 16-wheeler as collateral for a loan from Old Faithful. Garcia should have registered her truck in Montana, but has a valid certificate of title issued by Illinois. If Old Faithful, not realizing that Garcia lives in Montana, had itself listed on the Illinois certificate of title, would that perfect its security interest?
   a. No, because the certificate of title would not count, as coming from the wrong state.
   b. No, because the notation would not put Garcia's Montana creditors on notice.
   c. Yes, because if a certificate of title is issued, then it governs perfection in the vehicle.
   d. No notation is necessary, because the security interest perfects automatically.

ANSWERS

1. *A* is the best answer. The present version of Article 9 takes the simplest approach to determining governing law for filing the financing statement. Traditional property law would call for filing in the state where the property is located. But a debtor may have collateral in multiple states, collateral may move from state to state, and some collateral has no location, if it is intangible rights like accounts. The present version of Article 9 shifted from using the location of the collateral to the location of the debtor, to simplify things. It then defines the location of the debtor in ways likely to give a single place to file. An individual is located at the individual's principal residence, which tends to remain relatively stable over time.
2. *E* is the best answer. This question reminds us that sometimes it is not necessary to file, and so, not necessary to figure out where to file. This transaction is a purchase money security interest in consumer goods, so the security interest perfects without filing. No filing is necessary to perfect the security interest, making *E* the best answer. Note that, although it is not necessary to file in order to be perfected, the creditor may file for other reasons, such as to have priority over a buyer of the consumer goods (as the next chapter discusses), in which case the creditor should file in the state of the debtor's residence, Montana.
3. *B* is the best answer. Contrary to *A*, the debtor here is Discovery Corps, the corporation, not the individual that owns the corporation's shares, Floyd. Article 9 takes the clearest approach possible for corporations: a corporation is located in the state where it is organized. Discovery Corps is a Delaware corporation, so Old Faithful Finance should file its financing statement in Delaware. This approach makes life simpler for creditors. Under the previous version of Article 9, the creditor would have to

identify all states where the debtor had collateral and file in each state, and also figure out where to file for intangible collateral, and continue to keep track in case collateral changed jurisdictions. Now the creditor need simply check the Secretary of State's office for the relevant state to confirm that the debtor is incorporated there (and this also helps get the debtor's name correct on the financing statement, because the debtor's name is the name on its incorporation documents).

4. *A* is the best answer. If the debtor is located in a foreign jurisdiction, then the filing statement must be filed there—if the jurisdiction has the functional equivalent of the Article 9 filing system. As it happens, Canada does have such a system, so Alberta would be the place to file. Civil law jurisdictions (which include most jurisdictions in the world) do not, and for those transactions the filing would be in the District of Columbia.
5. *C* is the best answer. For certificate of title goods such as vehicles, perfection must be achieved by making a notation on the certificate of title, not filing a financing statement. Since vehicles already have a system for making public record of claims to ownership, Article 9 simply has a creditor use that system to give notice of the security interest in the vehicle. Article 9 again takes the simplest approach. If a certificate of title has issued, that state's law governs, even "if there is no other relationship between the jurisdiction under whose certificate of title the goods are covered and the goods or the debtor." §9-303(a),(c). The Illinois certificate of title governs.

Chapter 24
Priority

When the secured party files its financing statement it is with the hope that its legal rights in the collateral will prevail over other parties. It is the job of the lawyer to make sure that that hope is fulfilled, or at least that the client is aware of what other interests might trump a perfected security interest. The attorney must know those risks well, and this chapter explores possible problems (the collateral is sold, other creditors file a financing statement, the debtor files for bankruptcy, the debtor merges with another entity, etc.) and highlights what can be done to lessen their effects.

I. SIMPLE DISPUTES

When the debtor's financial situation collapses, the creditors all scramble to seize the debtor's assets. The legal issue of *priority* decides which creditor gets what. A basic priority provision is §9-317, which lists the parties prevailing over an *unperfected* security interest (one that has attached but that the creditor has failed to take the steps required for perfection). Read it and work through these Problems.

PROBLEM 360

Epstein's Bookstore borrowed $10,000 from Octopus National Bank (ONB), signing a security agreement giving the bank a floating lien over the store's inventory. ONB, due to negligence, never got around to filing the financing statement. Martin's Travel Service was an unpaid creditor of the bookstore that sued on the debt and recovered a judgment against the store. It then had the sheriff levy on the inventory. ONB learned of this and calls you, ONB's attorney. Does ONB or Martin's Travel Service get paid first when the inventory is sold? See §9-317(a)(2), and the definition of *lien creditor* in §9-102(a)(52). Compare United States v. Cox, 2008 WL 2397615 (W.D.N.C. 2008). If, instead of a judgment creditor seizing the goods, Epstein's Bookstore had filed a bankruptcy petition while ONB's lien was still unperfected, what result? What result if, instead, Epstein's Bookstore had sold the inventory to a good faith buyer? See §9-317(b).

PROBLEM 361

Coke Travel Agency used its accounts receivable as collateral for a loan from the Mansfield State Bank, but the bank failed to file the financing statement that Coke Travel Agency had authorized because the bank's attorney lost the statement in the maze of papers on her desk. Six months later, Coke Travel Agency needed another loan and applied for one from the Bentham National Bank, which searched the files, discovered that there were no financing statements recorded for Coke Travel Agency as debtor, and took a security interest in the agency's accounts receivable. Bentham National Bank did file a financing statement in the proper place. Which bank has the superior interest in the collateral? See §9-322(a)(2) and Official Comment 3 to §9-317.

The major Article 9 priority section is §9-322(a)(1), which you should read after you finish this paragraph. Use it to resolve the Problems that follow.

PROBLEM 362

Jay Eastriver ran a clothing store and needed money. He went to two banks, the First National Bank and the Second State Bank, and asked each to loan him money using his inventory as collateral. They each made him sign a security agreement. First National Bank filed its financing statement first, on September 25, but did not loan Eastriver any money (nor did it make any commitment to do so) until November 10. On October 2, Second State both loaned Eastriver the money and filed its financing statement. Eastriver paid neither bank. Answer these questions:

(a) Did both banks have a perfected security interest, assuming they filed in the proper place? That is, is it possible for two creditors to have perfected security interests in the same collateral?

(b) Remembering that attachment is a prerequisite to perfection, §9-308, and that attachment cannot occur until the creditor gives value, decide which bank has the superior right to the inventory. See Example 1 in Official Comment 4 to §9-322.

(c) If either bank had *knowledge* of the transaction between Eastriver and the other bank at the time it perfected, does that affect its priority? See St. Paul Mercury Ins. Co. v. Merchants & Marine Bank, 882 So. 2d 766 (Miss. 2004).

(d) Suppose First National Bank had filed its financing statement *before* the debtor signed its security agreement. Subsequently, Second National Bank filed an authorized financing statement to perfect its security interest in the same collateral. Next, the debtor signed a security agreement with First National Bank, which counted on the existing financing statement to perfect its interest in the identical collateral. Which bank would have priority? See Official Comment 4 to §9-322 (the third paragraph); In re Adoni Group, Inc., 530 B.R. 592 (Bankr. S.D.N.Y. 2015).

PROBLEM 363

When First National Bank took a perfected security interest in the inventory of Jay Eastriver's clothing store, the security agreement provided that the inventory would secure not only the current loan "but all future advances of whatever kind." Six months later, First National loaned Eastriver an additional $10,000 and had him sign a new promissory note for that amount. Do the existing filed financing statement and security agreement need to be altered in any way, or are they sufficient as is to protect the bank? See §9-204(c) and its Official Comment 5.

Assume that after First National made Eastriver the first loan and filed its financing statement, he then borrowed more money from Second State Bank, using the same inventory as collateral, and this lender also filed a financing statement in the correct place. Eastriver then paid off the loan to First National completely, but the bank never filed a termination statement. A month later, First National loaned Eastriver more money. The parties signed a new security agreement, but no new financing statement was filed. First National's attorney reasoned that the earlier financing statement would protect the later loan's priority, even though this loan was not contemplated when the first financing statement was filed. Is this right? Second State would prefer that the court rule that the first financing statement was "spent" when the underlying debt was paid off, and could not be used to give a top priority to a later uncontemplated loan. See §9-323(a) and its Official Comment 3, Example 1, and Official Comment 2 to §9-502. Often a security agreement will have in it a clause stating that the collateral protects not only this loan, but all future advances as well; see §9-204(c). If such a future advances clause had *not* been in the original security agreement that Eastriver signed with First National, does that affect the answer at all? See In re K&P Logging, Inc., 272 B.R. 867 (Bankr. D.S.C. 2001); Korea Trade Ins. Corp. v. Neema Clothing, Ltd., 2015 WL 363569 (S.D.N.Y. 2015) (financing statement mentioning the amount of the original loan protected loans made later in excess of that amount).

PROBLEM 364

Phillip Philately pledged his valuable stamp collection to the Collectors National Bank (CNB) in return for a loan (he gave CNB an oral security interest in the collateral; no financing statement was filed). The bank put the stamp collection in its vault. Philately later borrowed money from his father, Filbert Philately, and gave him a signed security agreement in the same stamp collection. The father filed a financing statement in the proper place. Answer these questions:

(a) Who has priority between CNB and the father?

(b) If Phillip goes to the bank and takes the collection home so that he can add new stamps but does then return it, does the answer change? At common law the pledgee could return the collateral to the pledgor for a "temporary and limited purpose" without losing its perfection. See G. Gilmore §14.5. Has this doctrine survived the enactment of the Code? See §9-313(d). Is §9-312(f) relevant?

(c) If CNB makes Phillip sign a security agreement and then turns the collection over to him but never files a financing statement, who wins? See §9-308(c). What should CNB have done?

Section 9-204(c) broadly authorizes future advance clauses in the security agreement. Does it also give the drafters' imprimatur to the so-called "dragnet clause," a clause purporting to expand the security interest to cover unrelated obligations owed by the debtor to the creditor? Professor Gilmore thought not and, in §35.6 of his treatise, proposed that the courts develop a test based on the intention of the parties and a requirement that the later obligation be "related," "similar," or "of the same class" as the original transaction. Under prior versions of Article 9, the courts often followed this recommendation—see the case below. Is it still good law? See Official Comment 5 to §9-204.

PROBLEM 365

Howard "Red" Poll decided to go into the cattle business and borrowed $65,000 from the Brangus National Bank to finance part of the purchase of the initial herd. Poll signed a security agreement using the cattle as collateral for this "and all other obligations now or hereafter owed to the bank." A financing statement covering this transaction was filed in the appropriate place. Two years later, Poll received a charge card from the same bank and used it to finance a trip to Australia to look over cattle ranching there. When he failed to pay the credit card bill, the bank repossessed the cattle (even though his payments on the cattle purchase loan were current). Did the bank's security interest in the cattle encompass the credit card obligation? Would it make a difference if he had gone to Australia in search of the perfect wave for surfing? See In re Johnson, 9 B.R. 713 (Ref. Bankr., M.D. Tenn. 1981) (consumer goods held not to secure future advances of a business nature in spite of dragnet clause); Kimbell Foods, Inc. v. Republic Natl. Bank, 401 F. Supp. 316 (N.D. Tex. 1975) ("The true intention of the parties is really the sole and controlling factor in determining whether future advances were covered by the original agreement . . . [or] would have to be reperfected."); John Miller Supply Co. v. Western State Bank, 55 Wis. 2d 385, 199 N.W.2d 161 (1972) (adopts the Gilmore tests); Note, Future Advances Financing Under the UCC: Curbing the Abuses of the Dragnet Clause, 34 U. Pitt. L. Rev. 691 (1973).

In re Zaochney

United States District Court, District of Alaska, Bankruptcy Division, 2011
2011 WL 6148727

MEMORANDUM ON MOTION TO VALUE SECURITY INTEREST

Donald MacDonald IV, Bankruptcy Judge.

The debtor filed a motion to value the security interest of Alaska USA Federal Credit Union in a 2008 Chevrolet Impala. Alaska USA contends that the Impala is encumbered by a purchase money lien as well as by sums due on a credit card, through dragnet clauses found in its loan documentation. The debtor alleges that the dragnet clauses are unenforceable. I agree with Alaska USA and find the dragnet clauses valid. The debtor's motion will be granted, in part. Alaska USA's secured claim is valued at $12,950.00. However, the vehicle is collateral for both the debtor's car loan and her credit line loan.

The debtor signed a two-page credit line loan agreement with Alaska USA on September 12, 2009. On the first page, above the debtor's signature, the agreement had bold headings for a series of 11 paragraphs. One paragraph, headed "Cross-Collateralization," states:

> Collateral pledged as security for other loans I have now or in the future with Credit Union will also be security for this agreement. This cross-collateral provision does not apply to my principal dwelling or household goods pledged as security for other loans.

The debtor says she signed this agreement because employees at Alaska USA told her it was a one-time offer to obtain credit at a favorable rate. She alleges that there was no discussion of the cross-collateral provision when she signed the agreement. She says personnel at the credit union also told her during this visit that she could obtain a car loan.

Ten days after receiving the credit line, the debtor purchased a car from Alaska Sales and Service. She financed the purchase through Alaska USA. The retail installment sales contract provided that the "Seller intends to assign this contract to Alaska USA Federal Credit Union." The sales contract had a large box in the lower right hand corner with Alaska USA's logo. It stated: "Questions?" and listed Alaska USA's P.O. Box and two separate phone numbers. In her supporting memorandum, the debtor confirms that she knew, at the time she made the purchase, that the financing would be through Alaska USA.

On the front page of the sale contract, above the box containing the debtor's signature, is a provision regarding a security interest. It states:

> Security Interest. You are giving a security interest in the goods or Property Being Purchased as described above. As permitted by law the goods or Property Being Purchased secures other obligations now or hereafter owed by you to the Creditor and other Collateral held by the Creditor, including funds on deposit with the Creditor, secures this Contract (see reverse side under Security).

The reverse side of the sales contract contains a paragraph in fine print labeled "*Security.*" It provides, in part:

> As provided by law, the Collateral for this contract secures other obligations you owe now or later to the Creditor, and other Collateral the Creditor presently holds or later obtains, also secures this contract. This cross-collateralization provision does not cover or extend to your principal dwelling or household goods pledged as security for other loans.

The debtor filed for chapter 7 relief on August 4, 2011. The only creditor listed on Schedules D and F is Alaska USA. The debtor lists two secured debts owed to the credit union: a mortgage on a residence for $220,000.00 and her obligation on the 2008 Chevrolet Impala of $12,000.00. She also lists two unsecured debts owed to the credit union: a deficiency balance of $4,836.22 on a repossessed 2005 Chevrolet Trailblazer and $5,000.00 for her credit line.

The debtor sought to reaffirm her car loan. Alaska USA places a value of $12,950.00 on the vehicle and the debtor does not dispute this. Alaska USA contends the vehicle secures not only the balance due on the Impala, $11,097.87, but also roughly $1,852.13 of the outstanding balance on the credit line. The debtor disagrees. She contends the Impala is collateral only for the vehicle loan.

In *Alaska Fur Gallery,*[1] I found a cross-collateralization clause in a commercial contract to be valid and enforceable. I went on to state:

> My conclusion here is limited to commercial transactions. Consumer debtors are held to a less stringent standard than commercial debtors. In a consumer transaction, courts may still look to the "true intent" of the parties. Other considerations, such as good faith, overreaching or unconscionability, might also alter the outcome. These are issues left for another day.

According to the debtor, that day has arrived and this court must now strike down the cross-collateral provisions found in the Alaska USA loan documents. I respectfully decline to do so for a number of reasons.

The debtor argues that the Alaska Supreme Court's decision, Lundgren v. National Bank of Alaska,[2] applies here. *Lundgren* involved a dragnet clause in a second deed of trust against commercial real property. The court found that such clauses deserved strict scrutiny, and adopted guidelines for determining whether these clauses could be enforced. However, the court also indicated that UCC policy considerations were not relevant to its determination of the impact of the dragnet clause in the deed of trust.

Lundgren is distinguishable from this case. No deed of trust is involved. While courts in other jurisdictions have applied a *Lundgren*-type analysis to UCC transactions, the Alaska Supreme Court has not. Additionally, *Lundgren* was decided prior to the nationwide adoption of amendments to the UCC in 2001. AS 45.29.204 was amended effective July 1, 2001, fourteen years after the *Lundgren* decision was issued. AS 45.29.204(c) permits a security agreement to "provide that collateral secures . . . future advances or other value, whether or not the advances or value are given pursuant to the commitment." The Official Comment to U.C.C. §9-204, the corresponding subsection of the Uniform Commercial Code, indicates that *Lundgren*'s dragnet rationale is inapplicable to UCC cases. The Comment states:

> **Future Advances; Obligations Secured.** Under subsection (c) collateral may secure future as well as past or present advances if the security agreement

1. Alaska Fur Gallery v. First National Bank Alaska (In re Alaska Fur Gallery, Inc.), 457 B.R. 764 (Bankr. D. Alaska 2011).
2. 756 P.2d 270 (Alaska 1987).

> so provides. This is in line with the policy of this Article toward security interests in after-acquired property under subsection (a). Indeed, the parties are free to agree that a security interest secures any obligations whatsoever. Determining the obligations secured by collateral is solely a matter of construing the parties' agreement under applicable law. *This Article rejects the holdings of cases decided under former Article 9 that applied other tests, such as whether a future advance or other subsequently incurred obligation was of the same or a similar type or class as earlier advances and obligations secured by the collateral.*

To support her position here, the debtor has cited cases that preceded the 2001 amendments to the UCC. Those cases applied an analysis similar to the one adopted in *Lundgren*. In a recent memorandum disposition, the Ninth Circuit BAP indicated that such cases have been superseded by the adoption of U.C.C. §9-204.[3] However, the BAP remanded that case for determination of certain factual issues pertaining to enforceability of the cross-collateralization clause. These issues included whether applying the clause would be unconscionable or violate the duty of good faith under the UCC.

In a few published decisions issued after the UCC amendments, courts have declined to enforce a cross-collateralization clause on facts distinguishable from the ones found here. In In re Keeton,[4] the bankruptcy court found that a dragnet clause in a loan taken out by joint debtors and secured by a vehicle did not operate to secure the credit card liability of just one of the debtors. The court's rationale was that, where the loan defined "debtor" to mean both of the debtors, there was no indication that the parties intended the vehicle to secure the separate and individual obligations of just one of the debtor[s]. Similarly, in First National Bank of Izard County v. Garner,[5] an Arkansas appellate court declined to apply a dragnet clause in a loan taken out by three debtors, secured by real property and a tractor, so that it would encompass a subsequent loan taken out by just one of the debtors individually. The court found that the subsequent loan was entirely unrelated to the first loan and could not have been within the contemplation of the parties at the time the first loan was taken out. Finally, in Wooding v. Cinfed Employees Federal Credit Union,[6] the court found that the debtor's credit card debt was not secured by a vehicle that was collateral for an earlier loan. The court found there was no meeting of the minds with respect to the cross-collateralization provisions found in the loan documents because the credit card application signed by the debtor provided only for a security interest

3. Frontier Fin. Credit Union v. Dumlao (In re Dumlao), 2011 WL 4501402 at 5 (9th Cir. B.A.P. Aug. 5, 2011) (mem. disposition).

4. 2008 WL 686938 (Bankr. M.D. Ala. Mar. 10, 2008).

5. 167 S.W.3d 664 (Ark. App. 2004).

6. 171 Ohio App. 3d 665, 872 N.E.2d 959 (Ohio App. 1 Dist. 2007).

in her accounts and there was no evidence that the debtor had received the underlying credit card agreement. Further, the loan documents were ambiguous and there was nothing in them to indicate that the vehicle would secure the credit card account as well.

In other cases decided subsequent to the amendment of the UCC, courts have enforced cross-collateralization provisions in a consumer context, with the result that credit lines or deficiency balances were secured by the debtor's vehicle.[7] One court did so in spite of finding that the loans were adhesion contracts.[8] Another court stated that a debtor's failure to read the loan documentation was an inadequate defense to the enforcement of these provisions.[9]

Here, the loan documents signed by the debtor plainly state that collateral pledged for one loan will secure other existing or future loans extended by the credit union. The dragnet provisions are not embedded in fine print and are in simple English. Although I did indicate, in *Alaska Fur Gallery,* that different standards for interpreting a dragnet clause might be applied in consumer transactions, a debtor must provide the court with something more than a citation to *Lundgren* and the assertion of an adhesion contract. The debtor here has not submitted any evidence that the "true intent" of the parties was anything other than as set forth in the documents. Nor has she submitted any evidence of bad faith, overreaching or unconscionability.

I conclude that the dragnet clauses found in the debtor's loan documents with Alaska USA are valid and enforceable. The debtor's vehicle is valued at $12,950.00. Because Alaska USA is owed less than this, $11,097.87, on the vehicle loan, it wants to use the balance of the equity in the vehicle to secure roughly $1,852.13 of the outstanding balance on the debtor's credit line. It may do so under the terms of the loan documents. The debtor's motion to value security interest is granted, in part. Alaska USA's secured claim is valued at $12,950.00.

An order and judgment will be entered consistent with this memorandum.

PROBLEM 366

Aware of difficulties with cross-collateralization clauses, rancher Howard Poll was always careful to keep his consumer obligations (from his Visa card,

7. See In re Hobart, 452 B.R. 789 (Bankr. D. Idaho 2011); In re Shemwell, 378 B.R. 166 (Bankr. W.D. Ky. 2007); In re Nagata, 2006 WL 2131318 (Bankr. D. Hawaii Jul. 20, 2006); In re Watson, 286 B.R. 594 (Bankr. D.N.J. 2002)

8. *Watson,* 286 B.R. at 602-603.

9. *Hobart,* 452 B.R. at 801 n.29.

using the objects purchased as collateral) with a different bank than the one that financed his ranching operations (with a traditional loan, using his cattle as collateral). Each bank had him sign security agreements that provided that the collateral nominated for each debt would also protect "any and all debts, now existing or after-acquired" owed to the same creditor. Howard was therefore distressed to learn that when the two banks merged, the new bank's loan officer now insisted that his cattle also protect the debts he owed on his Visa card. Is that right?

PROBLEM 367

HTG put up most of its assets as collateral for a loan from CTF and "all other obligations of ours to you, however and whenever created, arising or evidenced, whether direct or indirect, through assignment from third parties in the ordinary course of your business, absolute, contingent or otherwise, now or hereafter existing or due to become due." HTG later sold phony invoices to CTF. Is CTF's right to recover for fraud secured by the collateral? See Ehrlich for Hoffmans Trade Grp. LLC v. Commercial Factors of Atlanta, 567 B.R. 684, 690 (N.D.N.Y. 2017).

II. PURCHASE MONEY SECURITY INTERESTS

A. The Basic Rule

The seller who extends credit to the buyer or the lender who advances the money to enable the buyer to purchase the collateral has a special equity in it in the eyes of the law. If the parties sign a security agreement, the seller/lender gets a *purchase money security interest* (PMSI). Read §9-103. Even though the goods become subject to an existing security interest when they come into the buyer's possession, the PMSI is given priority. This is true in spite of the fact that the PMSI is later in time to earlier perfected interests. Where the collateral is consumer goods, no further steps are required for a PMSI therein to prevail over prior or later interests. See §9-309(1). All other PMSIs must be perfected during a 20-day "grace period" following the buyer's possession of the goods in order to take advantage of a relation-back of priority to that date. Read §§9-317(e) and 9-324(a) carefully. Section 9-324(b) has a special rule for PMSIs taken in goods that are to become part of the buyer's *inventory*, and §9-324(d) has a similar one for a PMSI in *livestock*, but we'll defer consideration of those rules for a few pages.

PROBLEM 368

When Paramount Homes finished building "Utopia, Ltd.," its newest fancy apartment complex, it had to furnish the clubhouse, so it sent its construction manager, Bill Gilbert, to Sophy's Interiors, a furniture store, where he made $2,000 worth of credit purchases and signed a security agreement on behalf of Paramount Homes in favor of the seller. The agreement was signed on June 8; the goods were delivered that same day. Bill failed to mention that all his employer's equipment was designated as collateral on an existing security agreement and financing statement in favor of Sullivan National Bank. This agreement contained an "after-acquired property" clause, which stated that later similar collateral coming into the buyer's estate would automatically fall under the bank's security interest. (See §9-204(a).) The policy of Sophy's Interiors was not to file financing statements for its credit furniture sales.

(a) Why might it have such a policy? Is it wise here?

(b) On June 10, which creditor will have priority in the furniture? On June 30?

In re Wild West World, L.L.C., Debtor

United States Bankruptcy Court, District of Kansas, 2008
2008 WL 4642266

Robert E. Nugent, United States Chief Bankruptcy Judge.

Memorandum Opinion

On November 17, 2005 debtor [Wild West World] entered into a purchase agreement with Larson to purchase the Ride for $190,000. Pursuant to the express terms of the purchase agreement, Texas law governs the construction and enforcement of the purchase agreement. Paragraph 5 of the Terms and Conditions of the purchase agreement provides:

> 5.1 Title to the goods shall remain with the Seller until Seller actually receives payment in full for the goods, unless otherwise expressly provided in the terms appearing on the face of this Contract.
>
> 5.2 Seller shall retain a security interest on the goods sold on credit to Buyer, including all rides sold to Buyer, all parts, attachments and additions thereto now or hereafter acquired and all replacements and substitutions therefore and all proceeds from the sale of such rides, including accounts receivable, until paid in full by Buyer (the "Ride"). Seller may file any financing statements or their equivalent in any jurisdiction at any time it deems necessary to maintain its interest, with or without the signature of Buyer; Buyer agrees to execute any financing statements and any amendments thereto

required by Seller and hereby specifically authorizes Seller to file such statements with its signature.

The undisputed practice in the amusement ride industry is that title to a ride does not pass until the ride has been paid in full. Pursuant to the purchase agreement, delivery of the Ride to debtor was scheduled for November 15, 2006 and the Ride was actually delivered no later than March 5, 2007. Larson filed its financing statement on the Ride with the Kansas Secretary of State's office on June 8, 2007. Larson filed a proof of claim in this bankruptcy for the unpaid balance on the Ride in the amount of $164,824.

First National loaned over $6 million to debtor for the construction of the Wild West World amusement park. In conjunction with the construction loan, debtor and First National entered into a commercial security agreement in which debtor granted a blanket security interest in debtor's property. First National filed its financing statement with the Kansas Secretary of State on March 24, 2006 perfecting a security interest in all business assets of the debtor. First National's lien secures a claim of $6,507,871.

During the pendency of this bankruptcy, the Ride was liquidated and debtor holds net proceeds of $85,800, plus accrued interest. The prevailing party in this adversary will be entitled to these sale proceeds.

Analysis and Conclusions of Law

A. Seller's Reservation of Title and UCC §2-401

Larson asserts that notwithstanding its delivery of the Ride to debtor in March 2007, it reserved title to the Ride pursuant to the explicit terms of the purchase agreement and industry practice and that title to the Ride did not pass to debtor until the Ride was paid in full. Larson therefore reasons that debtor had no interest in the Ride to which a security interest (including First National's) could attach and therefore, its ownership interest in the Ride is superior to First National.

First National counters that §2-401 of the Uniform Commercial Code limits a seller's ability to reserve title once the seller has delivered the goods to the buyer. It relies upon In re Samuels & Co. First National contends that once the goods are delivered, the effect of reserving title is to give the seller a security interest in the goods delivered. It further argues that since Larson did not timely perfect its purchase money security interest, Larson's interest in the Ride is inferior to First National's interest.

The parties disagree on the interpretation of §2-401. The pertinent parts of the UCC text of §2-401 titled "Passing of Title; Reservation for Security; Limited Application of This Section," states:

> Each provision of this Article with regard to the rights, obligations, and remedies of the seller, the buyer, purchasers, or other third parties applies irrespective of title to the goods except where the provision refers to such title. Insofar as situations are not covered by the other provisions of this Article and matters concerning title become material, the following rules apply:
>
> (1) Title to goods cannot pass under a contract for sale prior to their identification to the contract (Section 2-501), and unless otherwise explicitly agreed, the buyer acquires by their identification a special property as limited by this Act. *Any retention or reservation by the seller of the title (property) in goods shipped or delivered to the buyer is limited in effect to a reservation of a security interest. Subject to these provisions and to Article 9,* title to goods passes from the seller to the buyer in any manner and on any conditions explicitly agreed on by the parties.

Texas' version of §2-401, while containing lettered paragraphs rather than numbered paragraphs, is identical to the UCC official text. For ease of reference, the Court will simply reference §2-401 in this opinion.

The Court has carefully reviewed the parties' case authorities and concludes that *Samuels,* cited by First National, is a correct interpretation of the law. Although *Samuels* involved an unpaid seller's reclamation claim vis-à-vis the buyer's creditor claiming a security interest in after-acquired property, that factual distinction has no bearing on the outcome of the case at bar. The pertinent legal conclusion in *Samuels* applicable here is that the interest of an unpaid seller in goods already delivered to a buyer is subordinate to the interest of the holder of a perfected security interest in those same goods. That legal conclusion is based upon the Fifth Circuit Court of Appeals' interpretation of UCC §2-401. As the Fifth Circuit observed:

> However, the U.C.C. specifically limits the seller's ability to reserve title once he has voluntarily surrendered possession to the buyer: "Any retention or reservation by the seller of the title (property) in goods shipped or delivered to the buyer is limited in effect to a reservation of a security interest." §2.401(a).

Samuels holds that this limitation applies whether the sale is a cash sale or a credit sale. The *Samuels* court went on to address the perceived unfairness to the unpaid seller.

> Any seeming unfairness to [sellers] resulting from the Code's operation is illusory, for the sellers could have protected their interests, even as against [a third party's] prior perfected interest, if they had merely complied with the U.C.C.'s purchase-money provisions. [Citations omitted.] The Code favors purchase-money financing, and encourages it by granting to a seller of goods the power to defeat prior liens. The seller at most need only (1) file a financing statement and (2) notify the prior secured party of its interest before delivery of the new inventory. The procedure is not unduly complex

> or cumbersome. But whether cumbersome or not, a [seller] who chooses to ignore its provisions takes a calculated risk that a loss will result.
>
> In the instant case [sellers] did not utilize §9.312's purchase-money provision. The sellers never perfected. Thus, in a competition with a perfected secured party they are subordinated, and in this case, lose the whole of their interests. [citations omitted].

Numerous other courts across the country are in accord with *Samuels* and interpret §2-401 in a like fashion. Section 2-401(1) negates the ability to delay passage of title beyond delivery. Any express agreement of the parties or reservation of title in the seller is limited by §2-401(1). Moreover, §2-401(1) cannot be varied by custom and usage in the trade, course of dealing, or agreement.

The Court rejects Larson's argument that because it has expressly reserved title until full payment under the purchase agreement, it avoids the operation of §2-401(1). Larson seizes upon the "unless otherwise explicitly agreed" language in the first sentence and the "title . . . passes . . . in any manner and on any conditions explicitly agreed on by the parties" language in the third sentence of §2-401(1). However, it ignores the prefatory language in the statute: "*Subject to these provisions* and to Article 9, title to goods passes from the seller to the buyer in any manner and on any conditions explicitly agreed on by the parties." It could not be any clearer to this Court that the ability to expressly agree on when title passes to the buyer is *subject to* the second sentence of §2-401(1). The limiting operation of reservation of title found in the second sentence of §2-401(1) is triggered by delivery. Delivery of the goods is the key. It is only when the seller has delivered the goods to the buyer that a seller's express reservation of title is limited to retention of a security interest. If there has been no delivery, the express reservation of title may be enforced.

The Court therefore concludes that Larson is an unpaid credit seller of the Ride to debtor. Larson's reservation of title until the Ride was paid in full, by both the express terms of the purchase order and by industry custom and practice, is negated and limited by operation of §2-401(1). Because Larson voluntarily delivered the Ride to debtor prior to payment in full, Larson retained only a security interest in the Ride.

B. PRIORITY BETWEEN LARSON AND FIRST NATIONAL—UCC §9-322 AND §9-324

Having concluded that Larson retained only a security interest in the Ride, the Court next determines priority between the two competing security interests in the Ride—Larson versus First National.

The general rule of priority between parties claiming a perfected security interest in the same property is "the first-to-file." This general rule is set forth in Kan. Stat. Ann. §84-9-322(a)(1) (2007 Supp.). Likewise, a perfected security interest takes priority over an unperfected security interest in the same collateral.

Kan. Stat. Ann. §84-9-324(a) (2007 Supp.) provides an exception to the general priority rules and creates a special priority for purchase money security interests. It elevates the holder of a purchase money security interest over a perfected non-purchase money security interest in the same collateral, provided the purchase money creditor perfects its security interest within twenty days of delivery of the collateral to the debtor. This special priority rule for purchase money security interests applies even if the non-purchase money security interest was perfected by filing prior to the purchase money security interest.

Here, there is no dispute that Larson held a purchase money security interest in the Ride. The uncontroverted facts establish that the debtor received possession of the Ride no later than March 5, 2007, when Larson delivered the Ride to debtor. Thus, Larson had until March 25, 2007 in which to file its financing statement to perfect its purchase money security interest in the Ride and obtain special priority status under §84-9-324(a). The uncontroverted facts further establish that Larson did not perfect its purchase money security interest in the Ride until June 8, 2007, outside the 20-day period from delivery. Accordingly, Larson is not entitled to special priority over First National as the holder of a purchase money security interest.

This means that the Court must fall back to the general priority rules in §84-9-322(a)(1) to determine the priority between Larson and First National. The undisputed facts establish that First National perfected its blanket security interest by filing a financing statement on all of debtor's "business assets" (including the Ride) on March 24, 2006. Since Larson did not perfect its security interest in the Ride until filing its financing statement on June 8, 2007, First National was the "first-to-file" and its security interest is prior to Larson's.

By failing to timely perfect its purchase money security interest after delivery of the Ride, Larson finds itself in the same unfortunate position as the unpaid seller in *Samuels*. Larson failed to avail itself of the special priority and protection afforded holders of purchase money security interests and must suffer the loss. . . .

Conclusion

Pursuant to UCC §2-401(1)'s limiting operation, Larson's reservation of title to the Ride that it sold and voluntarily delivered to debtor effected only a reservation of a security interest in the Ride. As the first to file its financing statement on the Ride, First National's perfected security interest in the Ride is prior to and superior to Larson's competing perfected security interest under Kan. Stat. Ann. §84-9-322(a)(1). Because Larson failed to perfect its security interest within 20 days of delivery of the Ride to debtor, it is not entitled to special priority as the holder of a perfected purchase money security interest in the Ride under Kan. Stat. Ann. §84-9-324(a). Accordingly, First National has priority to the Ride proceeds and is entitled to summary judgment on its claim against Larson for the amount of the Ride proceeds, together with accrued interest thereon. A Judgment on Decision shall issue this day.

SO ORDERED.

PROBLEM 369

Video Wonder, an electronics store, had granted a floating lien over its inventory and equipment to Last National Bank, which perfected its security interest by filing a financing statement in the appropriate place. Needing a guard dog for the store, Video Wonder's manager responded to an ad in the newspaper placed by Agatha Shaw, who was selling her beloved German Shepherd, Fang. She had bought him for protection when he was but a pup, but he had proven too much for her, having seriously injured a meter-reader and two mail carriers. She checked out the store carefully before agreeing to sell Video Wonder the dog, saying she wanted a good home for Fang. He cost the store $1,200. The manager agreed to send her $100 a month until the dog was paid for, at which time she agreed in writing to sign over Fang's papers. Ms. Shaw and the manager agreed that the store would not get any title to Fang until all the payments had been made. Fang proved to be a fine watchdog for the store, but when Video Wonder stopped making payments to all creditors two months later, Last National Bank seized all of the store's assets, including Fang. Agatha Shaw is upset. She calls you, her attorney. Is there any hope for her? Can she argue that the bank's security interest only attached to Video Wonder's equity in the dog, or that until Video Wonder had paid the entire debt, it had no property interest to which the bank's floating lien could attach? See ITT Indus. Credit Co. v. Regan, 487 So. 2d 1047 (Fla. 1986); First Natl. Bank v. Quintana, 733 P.2d 858 (N.M. 1987).

PROBLEM 370

Hart Farm Equipment leased a construction backhoe to Farmer Bean for a six-month period with the understanding that Farmer Bean would be given the option to purchase the backhoe at any time during that period, and, in fact, the lease at one point called this a "sale on approval." Farmer Bean's equipment was already subject to a perfected floating lien in favor of Octopus

National Bank. Three months after the delivery of the backhoe, Farmer Bean agreed to buy the backhoe, and Hart Farm Equipment filed its financing statement the next day, claiming its purchase money security interest. Who wins in the priority battle between Hart Farm Equipment and Octopus National Bank? See §2-326(2); Official Comment 3 to §9-324.

PROBLEM 371

Danica Entropy traded in her SUV for a hybrid Maxwell Demon at Cash For Clunkers, Inc., at a time when she still owed Cash For Clunkers $15,000 on the SUV, which is now worth $10,000. To finance this transaction, Danica borrowed $25,000, secured by the Maxwell Demon, from Octopus National Bank, which made her a hybrid loan of $20,000 to pay the price of the new Maxwell Demon and $5,000 to pay off her "negative equity" in the old SUV. Does Octopus National Bank have a purchase money security interest for the full amount? See the following case.

In the Matter of Faith Ann Peaslee and Others

Court of Appeals of New York, 2009
13 N.Y.3d 75, 913 N.E.2d 387

PIGOTT, J.

The United States Court of Appeals for the Second Circuit, by certified question, asks us to decide whether "the portion of an automobile retail installment sale attributable to a trade-in vehicle's 'negative equity' [is] a part of the 'purchase-money obligation' arising from the purchase of a new car, as defined under New York's U.C.C.?" (547 F.3d 177, 186 [2d Cir. 2008].) We find that it is.

I.

On August 28, 2004, Faith Ann Peaslee entered into a retail installment contract for the purchase of a 2004 Pontiac Grand Am. As part of the transaction, Peaslee traded in her vehicle, which had a negative trade-in value, or negative equity, of $5,980.[10] That amount was rolled into the financing of her new car along with other charges, resulting in financing totaling $23,180. The lien against the trade-in was paid off by the dealer, and the dealer's security interest in the new vehicle was assigned to GMAC, LLC.

10. In automobile industry parlance, "negative equity" occurs when the trade-in vehicle is subject to a lien that exceeds the vehicle's value.

Nearly two years after purchasing her new vehicle, Peaslee filed for chapter 13 bankruptcy and a trustee was appointed to handle the estate. As part of her bankruptcy plan, Peaslee proposed that she retain possession of the vehicle and that, pursuant to United States Bankruptcy Code (11 U.S.C.) §506(a)(1),[11] GMAC's secured claim would be reduced to $10,950, representing the alleged retail value of the vehicle. Under Peaslee's proposal, the remaining amount owed to GMAC, $6,954.95, would be treated as an unsecured claim.

GMAC objected to this characterization of its claim and argued that, pursuant to the "hanging paragraph" set forth in Bankruptcy Code §1325(a), it was entitled to have the entire $17,904.95 treated as a secured claim. The "hanging paragraph," which was enacted as part of the Bankruptcy Abuse Prevention and Consumer Protection Act of 2005, states, in pertinent part, that

> "[f]or purposes of paragraph (5), [Bankruptcy Code] section 506 shall not apply to a claim described in that paragraph *if the creditor has a purchase money security interest securing the debt that is the subject of the claim,* the debt was incurred within the 910–day [sic] preceding the date of the filing of the petition, and the collateral for that debt consists of a motor vehicle (as defined in section 30102 of title 49) acquired for the personal use of the debtor" (emphasis supplied).

The trustee moved to have the Bankruptcy Court determine that GMAC had a secured claim of $10,950 and only an unsecured claim for the balance. The Bankruptcy Court did just that, and held that the term "purchase money security interest" (PMSI), as set forth in New York's Uniform Commercial Code, did not include negative equity (358 B.R. 545, 558 [Bkrtcy. W.D.N.Y. 2006]). The United States District Court for the Western District of New York reached the opposite conclusion (373 B.R. 252, 258-261 [Bkrtcy. W.D.N.Y. 2007]). The Second Circuit, noting that Congress failed to provide a definition of purchase-money security interest either in the hanging paragraph or elsewhere, concluded "that state law governs the definition of PMSI in the hanging paragraph" and certified to us the question of whether the New York Uniform Commercial Code considers that portion of a retail installment sale attributable to the negative equity of a trade-in vehicle to be part of the purchase-money obligation arising from the sale of a new car (547 F.3d 177, 184, 186 [2008]).

For the reasons that follow, we answer the question in the affirmative.

11. This provision states, in pertinent part, that

> "[a]n allowed claim of a creditor secured by a lien on property in which the estate has an interest . . . is a secured claim to the extent of the value of such creditor's interest in the estate's interest in such property . . . and is an unsecured claim to the extent that the value of such creditor's interest . . . is less than the amount of such allowed claim."

II.

"A security interest in goods is a purchase-money security interest . . . to the extent that the goods are purchase-money collateral with respect to that security interest" UCC 9-103[b][1]). Purchase-money collateral is defined as "goods or software that secures a purchase-money obligation incurred with respect to that collateral" UCC 9-103[a][1]). A purchase-money obligation is "an obligation of an obligor incurred as all or part of the *price of the collateral or for value given* to enable the debtor to acquire rights in or the use of the collateral if the value is in fact so used" UCC 9–103[a][2] [emphasis supplied]).

III.

Addressing "price" first, although that term is not defined by New York's UCC, the expansive examples given in an official comment concerning what items constitute the "price of the collateral" indicate that the term "price" should be afforded a broad interpretation. Specifically, with respect to a purchase-money obligation,

> "'*price*' of collateral or the 'value given to enable' includes obligations for expenses incurred in connection with acquiring rights in the collateral, sales taxes, duties, finance charges, interest, freight charges, costs of storage in transit, demurrage, administrative charges, expenses of collection and enforcement, attorney's fees, and *other similar obligations*" (UCC 9-103, Comment 3 [emphasis supplied]).

The list of examples in Comment 3 that clarify "price" is representative, not exhaustive, and cannot be read to limit those "other similar obligations" to the 10 items preceding that term, all of which are clearly either transaction costs and/or components of price. Indeed, the phrase "and other similar obligations" intimates that "price" under New York's UCC is broad enough to encompass negative equity financing. For instance, just as "finance charges" and "interest" constitute obligations that are paid over and above the vehicle's actual cost (such charges being incurred as part of the overall financing of the vehicle), negative equity is likewise part of the overall price of a new vehicle. Moreover, negative equity constitutes an obligation that fits comfortably within the "other similar obligations" language in Comment 3, particularly in regard to automobile sales because the negative equity from the trade-in is often "rolled in" as part of the overall price of the newer vehicle to facilitate the transaction. It follows, then, that under New York's UCC negative equity constitutes "an obligation . . . incurred as all or part of the price of the collateral."

This broad interpretation of the term "price" to include negative equity furthers New York's policy that the UCC "be liberally construed and applied to promote its underlying purposes and policies," including "the continued expansion of commercial practices through custom, usage and agreement of the parties" ([UCC §1-305]). After all, the parties to the instant transaction agreed that the negative equity from the older vehicle would be "rolled-in" as part of the purchase price of the newer vehicle, not an uncommon practice in the realm of automobile sales (see In re Graupner, 537 F.3d 1295, 1303 [11th Cir. 2008]), thereby furthering the policy of facilitating commercial transactions. Indeed, to exclude negative equity as part of the "price" would serve to hinder commercial practices rather than facilitate them.

Additionally, and not inconsequentially, New York has defined "price" in its Motor Vehicle Retail Installment Sales Act (MVRISA) to include negative equity (see Personal Property Law §301[(6)]). Under the MVRISA, "cash sale price" can "include the unpaid balance of any amount financed under an outstanding motor vehicle loan agreement or motor vehicle retail installment contract or the unpaid portion of the early termination obligation under an outstanding motor vehicle retail lease agreement" (id.).

IV.

Turning to "value given," we likewise disagree with the trustee's contention that negative equity is not related to the acquisition of collateral because it is merely a payoff of an antecedent debt such that it cannot be deemed "value given to enable the debtor to acquire rights in or the use of the collateral if the value is in fact so used" (UCC 9-103[(a)][(2)]).

By paying off the outstanding debt on the trade-in, a lender is giving "value" to the debtor in order to allow, or "enable," the debtor to purchase, or "acquire rights in," the vehicle (see In re Price, 562 F.3d 618, 625 [4th Cir. 2009]). When a lender finances the purchase of a new vehicle and a portion of that financing pays off the negative equity owed on the trade-in (i.e., "the value is in fact so used" [UCC 9-103(a)(2)]), that loan constitutes a purchase-money obligation of the buyer, the purchased vehicle constitutes purchase-money collateral, and the security interest obtained by the lender is a PMSI.

V.

Finally, Comment 3 instructs that the existence of a PMSI also "requires a close nexus between the acquisition of collateral and the secured obligation" (UCC 9-103, Comment 3); and that requirement has plainly been met here. Without a payoff of the trade-in debt, the buyer will generally not be able to consummate the purchase of the newer car, and the financing of the negative equity is thus integral to the completion of the sale (see generally *Graupner*, 537 F.3d at 1302).

Here, Peaslee's debt to GMAC was incurred at the time of the trade-in, under the same retail installment contract and for the same purpose of purchasing the Grand Am. Simply put, the financing of the negative equity was "inextricably linked to the financing of the new car" (In re Petrocci, 370 B.R. 489, 499 [Bkrtcy. N.D.N.Y. 2007]), thereby satisfying the "close nexus" requirement under the New York UCC.

Accordingly, the certified question should be answered in the affirmative.

NOTE

This question about whether financing "negative equity" in a car loan eliminates the status of the financing creditor as the holder of a "purchase money security interest" has primarily arisen in bankruptcy cases, as the above case indicates. All of the federal Circuits eventually agreed that such a creditor does get acquire a PMSI, until the Ninth Circuit broke ranks, and, over a strong dissent, denied such status if negative equity is part of the loan; see In re Penrod, 636 F.3d 1175 (9th Cir. 2011). Eventually the United States Supreme Court will have to settle the issue since it has the final say as to the meaning of the Bankruptcy Code.

B. Inventory and Livestock

The inventory financier will have a perfected interest in existing and after-acquired inventory, in effect a floating lien over the mass of changing goods available for sale by the debtor to others. If the debtor buys new inventory and gives the seller a purchase money security interest therein, the original financier is seriously hurt if (a) it does not know of the purchase money interest but instead thinks *all* the inventory is collateral in which it has priority, and (b) the purchase money interest is held to prevail over the already perfected interest in after-acquired inventory. To protect the first creditor, §9-324(b) provides a notification procedure that the purchase money secured creditor must follow in order to take the normal priority. See White & Summers §25-4(c); G. Gilmore §29.3.

PROBLEM 372

The Merchants Credit Association held a perfected security interest in the inventory of Harold's Clothing Store. Harold went to a fashion showing in New York and contracted to buy $4,000 worth of new clothes for resale; the seller was to be Madame Belinda's Fashions, Inc., which took a purchase money security interest in the clothes on December 10, the date of sale. Madame Belinda herself wrote the Merchants Credit Association on December 11 and informed the credit manager of the sale. He protested but did nothing. Madame Belinda filed on December 11; the goods were delivered to the store on December 12.

(a) Who has priority?

(b) Would your answer change if Madame Belinda's notice wasn't received until December 13?

(c) If the notice was received on December 11, as above, is it sufficient to permit Madame Belinda to keep selling goods to Harold for an indefinite period thereafter or only for this one transaction? See §9-324(b)(3); T. Gluck & Co., Inc. v. Craig Drake Mfg., Inc., 2013 N.Y. Misc. LEXIS 2384 (N.Y. Sup. Ct. 2013).

How does it help the creditor with the prior perfected interest in the inventory to get notice if that creditor still ends up junior to the purchase money creditor? The Code drafters decided that if the prior creditor has notice, it can take whatever steps are called for to protect its interest. The creditor may not care that the debtor is encumbering the inventory with PMSIs believing that the inventory will sell for enough to make all the creditors happy. Or, if the creditor does care, it can call the loan (or forcefully explain to the debtor the folly of continuing to subordinate the creditor's security interest by such purchases). In any event, alerted by the §9-324(b) notice as to what is going on, the prior creditor must watch out for itself and cannot complain if the purchase money creditor prevails as to the inventory covered by the notice.

Kunkel v. Sprague National Bank

United States Court of Appeals, Eighth Circuit, 1997
128 F.3d 636

John R. Gibson, Circuit Judge.

In this appeal two creditors, Hoxie Feeders, Inc., and Sprague National Bank, both claim first priority security interests in the same cattle. The district court affirmed the bankruptcy court's summary judgment for Hoxie holding that Hoxie's purchase money security interest had priority over Sprague's earlier security interest in the cattle. Kunkel v. Sprague Nat'l Bank, 198 B.R. 734, 735 (D. Minn. 1996). As an alternative holding for Hoxie, the district court held that Sprague did not have a security interest in the cattle because the debtor lacked "rights in the collateral," as required by the Uniform Commercial Code. Id. at 739. On appeal, Sprague alleges that the district court erred in interpreting and applying various provisions of the UCC governing sales and secured transactions. We reverse the district court's holding that Sprague did not have a security interest in the cattle but affirm its judgment for Hoxie because Hoxie's security interest is senior to Sprague's security interest.

Beginning in 1990, Sprague made a number of loans to John and Dorothy Morken pursuant to certain loan agreements and promissory notes. The Morkens executed a security agreement in favor of Sprague covering their inventory, farm products, equipment, and accounts receivable presently owned or thereafter acquired. Sprague filed with the Kansas Secretary of State a UCC-1 financing statement regarding the collateral located in Kansas. Sprague contends that the Morkens' debt to Sprague currently exceeds $1.9 million.

Hoxie is in the business of financing and selling cattle and operating a feedlot near Hoxie, Kansas. In five transactions between February and April 1994, John Morken purchased interests in approximately 1900 head of cattle from Hoxie. Hoxie financed Morken's cattle purchases. For each transaction, Morken executed a loan agreement and promissory note in favor of Hoxie and a security agreement granting Hoxie a purchase money security interest (PMSI) in the cattle, which were identified by lot number when the documents were executed. In addition, Hoxie was paid $100 per head by either Morken or a company in which he owned an interest. The invoices for the cattle transactions recited that the cattle were shipped to Morken, Hoxie, or both.

Hoxie did not file a UCC-1 financing statement with the Kansas Secretary of State but instead perfected its security interest by taking possession of the cattle pursuant to feedlot agreements between Morken and Hoxie. The feedlot agreements stated that the cattle belonged to "the Party of the First Part," meaning Morken, and acknowledged that Morken had delivered the cattle to Hoxie, although Morken never had physical possession of the cattle. Under the feedlot agreements, the cattle were to remain on Hoxie's feedlot for purposes of care and feeding. The feedlot and loan agreements authorized Hoxie to sell the cattle in its own name for slaughter, to receive direct payment from the packing house, and to deduct the feeding and purchase expenses from the sale proceeds and then remit the balance to Morken. Hoxie's general manager acknowledged, however, that he needed Morken's authority to sell the cattle, and that Morken determined at what price the cattle would be sold. The loan agreements recited that Morken bore all risk as to the profit or loss generated by feeding and selling the cattle.

On June 10, 1994, Morken and his wife filed a Chapter 11 bankruptcy case under Title 11 of the United States Bankruptcy Code. After the bankruptcy case was commenced, Hoxie sold the cattle to Iowa Beef Processors for slaughter. After deducting amounts owed to Hoxie for the care and feeding of the cattle, approximately $550,000 in sale proceeds remained. It is these funds which are subject of competing claims by Sprague and Hoxie.

After the cattle sales, the Morkens' bankruptcy trustee commenced an adversary proceeding in the bankruptcy court to determine which party—Sprague or Hoxie—was entitled to the net sale proceeds. Hoxie and the trustee subsequently reached a settlement. Hoxie and Sprague filed cross-motions for summary judgment regarding entitlement to the funds.

The bankruptcy court granted Hoxie's motion for summary judgment and denied Sprague's motion. It held that both Sprague and Hoxie had perfected security interests in the cattle but Hoxie's interest had first priority under the Kansas UCC, Kan. Stat. Ann. §84-9-312(3) [now §9-324(b)—Eds.]. This UCC provision gives "superpriority" to a creditor with a PMSI in inventory if certain conditions are met, including the requirement that the creditor must send a specified notification to any competing secured party. The competing secured party must receive the notification within five years before the debtor receives possession of the inventory. Although Sprague [*sic*—Hoxie] did not send its statutory notification to Hoxie [*sic*—Sprague] until March 1995, long after the cattle had been sold and slaughtered and the adversary proceeding commenced, the bankruptcy court held that the timing of the notification was nevertheless sufficient because "the Debtor never obtained possession and never will."

Sprague appealed to the district court, which affirmed the bankruptcy court's summary judgment in favor of Hoxie. The district court held that a creditor that has perfected its security interest in inventory through possession, rather than by filing, is not required to provide notification of its PMSI to competing secured creditors to attain "superpriority." According to the district court, the "superpriority" provision presumes that the creditor perfected by filing and that the debtor has possession of the inventory. The court concluded that this presumption was strong evidence that the notification requirement did not apply to a PMSI creditor that perfects by possession. 198 B.R. at 737-738.

As an alternative holding, the district court ruled that Sprague did not even have a security interest in the cattle because delivery of the cattle to Morken had not been completed and, therefore, no "present sale" had occurred. The court explained:

> Under Kansas law, a delivery may be completed although the goods remain in the possession of the seller if the seller's possession "is as an agent or at the request of the buyer under an agreement to store or care for the property, *and nothing further remains to be done by either party to complete the sale.*" Lakeview Gardens, Inc. v. Kansas, 221 Kan. 211, 557 P.2d 1286, 1290-91 (1976) (emphasis added). Here, something further was required, payment to Hoxie under the loan agreement.

Id. at 739. Because the transactions were not a "present sale," the court reasoned that Morken did not have "rights in the collateral," as required by the Kansas UCC, Kan. Stat. Ann. §84-9-203(1)(c), to convey a security interest in the cattle to Sprague. Morken's interest in the cattle was only a "remedial" interest against Hoxie; such an interest was inadequate to support Morken's alleged grant of a security interest to Sprague. Id. at 739-740.

I.

. . . The issues on appeal are: (a) did Sprague have a perfected security interest in the cattle?; (b) did Hoxie have a "super-priority" purchase money security interest which had priority over Sprague's interest in the cattle?; and (c) was Hoxie entitled to the proceeds from the sale of the cattle to IBP?

II.

The district court held that Sprague did not have a security interest in the cattle because Morken did not have "rights in the collateral" sufficient for a security interest to attach. We reverse on this issue.

Under the UCC, a security interest is not enforceable against the debtor or third parties, and does not attach, unless and until the following three requirements are met: (a) either the secured party has possession of the collateral by agreement with the debtor (as is the case here) or the debtor has signed a security agreement; (b) value has been given; and (c) "the debtor has rights in the collateral." Kan. Stat. Ann. §84-9-203(1). Only the last requirement is at issue in this case.

The phrase "rights in the collateral" is not defined in the UCC. "If the debtor owns the collateral outright, it is obvious that the security interest may attach. . . ." B. Clark, The Law of Secured Transactions Under the Uniform Commercial Code ¶2.04[1], at 2-43 (Rev. ed. 1993). It is also well settled, however, that "rights in the collateral" may be an interest less than outright ownership, but must be more than the mere right of possession. See id.; see also 4 J. White & R. Summers, Uniform Commercial Code 126 (4th ed. 1995) ("It follows that almost any 'rights in the collateral' will suffice under 9-203."). The concept of "title" is not determinative. See Kan. Stat. Ann. §84-9-202. "An agreement to purchase can give rise to sufficient rights in the debtor to allow a security interest to attach, regardless of whether the debtor has technically obtained title to the property." United States v. Ables, 739 F. Supp. 1439, 1444 (D. Kan. 1990). Courts consider factors such as the extent of the debtor's control over the property and whether the debtor bears the risk of ownership. See, e.g., Kinetics Tech. Intl. Corp. v. Fourth Natl. Bank, 705 F.2d 396, 399 (10th Cir. 1983) (debtor's control); Chambersburg Trust Co. v. Eichelberger, 588 A.2d 549, 552-553 (Pa. Super. Ct. 1991) (debtor had risk of ownership). The debtor need not have possession in order to pledge the property; the UCC expressly contemplates that the secured party may retain possession of the collateral. See Kan. Stat. Ann. §84-9-305 [now §9-313—Eds.].

The district court looked to Article 2 of the UCC, which governs sales, to determine whether Morken had "rights in the collateral." It was appropriate to consider Article 2 principles. "In many cases the secured creditor may turn to Article 2 of the UCC to measure the debtor's 'rights' with respect to collateral." Kan. Stat. Ann. §84-9-203 Kan. cmt. (1996). The district court erred, however, in its interpretation of Article 2 and its conclusion that the cattle transactions did not bestow Morken with "rights in the collateral." As will be seen, the cattle were sold and delivered by Hoxie to Morken and Morken thus acquired "rights in the collateral."

A "sale" is the passing of title from buyer to seller for a price. Kan. Stat. Ann. §84-2-106(1). Where delivery of the goods is made without moving the goods, title passes from buyer to seller at the time parties contracted if the goods are identified at that time. Id. §84-2-401(3)(b). When identification occurs, the buyer acquires a "special property" and, importantly, any title interest retained by the seller is limited to the reservation of a security interest. Id. §84-2-401(1). Physical receipt of the goods by the debtor is not necessary; rather, a sale may take place if the goods are constructively delivered to the buyer through delivery to the buyer's agent or bailee. "Delivery is not required for a 'sale' to take place, and the buyer does not even need any right to possession of the goods in question." B. Clark, The Law of Secured Transactions ¶3.04[2], at 3-48.

In this case, the cattle were identified in the invoices and other transaction documents, and the parties agreed that delivery would be made to Morken by delivering the cattle to Hoxie at its feedlot. The feedlot agreements recited that the cattle belonged to Morken. Morken solely bore the risk that the venture would not generate a profit. Hoxie became a bailee of the cattle because it took "delivery of property for some particular purpose on an express or implied contract that after the purpose has been fulfilled the property will be returned to the bailor, or dealt with as he directs." M. Bruenger & Co., Inc. v. Dodge City Truck Stop, Inc., 675 P.2d 864, 868 (Kan. 1984) (quoting 8 C.J.S. Bailments §1). Even though Hoxie had the right to deduct the costs of purchasing and caring for the cattle from the sale proceeds, the parties viewed Morken as owner of the cattle, and Morken determined when cattle would be sold and at what price. In sum, Morken became the owner of an interest in the cattle, and Hoxie's interest in the cattle was therefore limited to that of a bailee and secured party.

In similar circumstances, other courts have held that the debtor acquired "rights in the collateral" even though the debtor received only constructive delivery of the cattle to a feedlot. See, e.g., The Cooperative Fin. Assn., Inc. v. B & J Cattle Co., 937 P.2d 915, 917, 920-921 (Colo. Ct. App. 1997) (debtor acquired rights when cattle were delivered to a third party feedlot; secured creditor prevailed over unpaid cattle seller); O'Brien v. Chandler, 765 P.2d 1165, 1168-1169 (N.M. 1988) (same); see also The Hong Kong & Shanghai

Banking Corp. v. HFH USA Corp., 805 F. Supp. 133, 142-143 (W.D.N.Y. 1992) (physical possession of the collateral is not necessary for the debtor to have rights).

Hoxie contends that the sale transactions were not completed because it had the right to stop delivery of the cattle upon discovering Morken's insolvency. See Kan. Stat. Ann. §84-2-702. Hoxie lost its Article 2 right to stop delivery, however, when the cattle were constructively delivered to Morken and Hoxie acknowledged to Morken in the feedlot agreements and other transaction documents that Morken had purchased the cattle and Hoxie was holding them for Morken for feeding and sale purposes. See id. §84-2-705(2)(b); see also Abilene Natl. Bank v. Fina Supply, Inc. (In re Brio Petroleum, Inc.), 800 F.2d 469, 472 (5th Cir. 1986) ("the Code makes clear that a seller's right to stop goods in transit may continue after delivery and until the buyer is in actual, physical or constructive possession of them"); Ramco Steel, Inc. v. Kesler (In re Murdock Mach. & Engr. Co.), 620 F.2d 767, 773 (10th Cir. 1980) (same).

Moreover, in some circumstances, the debtor can transfer greater rights in the collateral to a third party than the debtor himself holds. Thus, "[a] person with voidable title has power to transfer a good title to a good faith purchaser for value." Kan. Stat. Ann. §84-2-403(1). "Purchase" includes taking an interest in property by mortgage, pledge, or lien. Id. §84-1-201(32). Therefore, a secured party such as Sprague can be a "good faith purchaser" which can acquire an interest in the collateral greater than the interest of the debtor, Morken, and superior to the interest of an unpaid seller such as Hoxie. The leading case on this point is Stowers v. Mahon (In re Samuels & Co., Inc.), 526 F.2d 1238 (5th Cir.) (en banc) (per curiam), *cert. denied,* 429 U.S. 834 (1976), pitting a creditor with a security interest in the debtor's cattle against the unpaid seller of the cattle. The court held that the secured creditor's interest was superior to the unpaid seller's interest under UCC §2-403 which "gives good faith purchasers of even fraudulent buyers-transferors greater rights than the defrauded seller can assert." Id. at 1242. As to whether the debtor had "rights in the collateral," the court reasoned that the UCC's priority scheme of elevating a "good faith purchaser" over an unpaid seller necessarily requires that the debtor had "rights in the collateral" even though it had not paid for the cattle:

> The existence of an Article Nine interest presupposes the debtor's having rights in the collateral sufficient to permit attachment, §9-204(a). Therefore, since a defaulting cash buyer has the power to transfer a security interest to a lien creditor, including an Article Nine secured party, the buyer's rights in the property, however marginal, must be sufficient to allow attachment of a lien.

Id. at 1243. Thus, the debtor had "rights in the collateral," even though it had not paid the seller for those cattle.

In summary, when the dust had settled after each of the five cattle transactions: (a) a sale had occurred; (b) Hoxie had constructively delivered the cattle to Morken and had possession of the cattle on Morken's behalf; (c) Morken had title to and owned the cattle; (d) the only interest retained by Hoxie in the cattle was a security interest and interest as bailee; (e) Hoxie's UCC Article 2 remedy of refusing to deliver the cattle had been cut off; and (f) Morken had "rights in the collateral" sufficient for Sprague's security interest to attach. Accordingly, we hold that Sprague had a perfected security interest in the cattle and reverse the district court on this issue.

III.

Having determined that Sprague held a perfected security interest in the cattle, we now turn to the priority dispute between the two secured creditors, Sprague and Hoxie. We hold that Hoxie attained purchase money security interest "superpriority" under the Kansas UCC, Kan. Stat. Ann. §84-9-312(3), and has priority over Sprague's interest.

Section 9-312 of the UCC sets forth rules for determining priorities among conflicting security interests in the same collateral. See Kan. Stat. Ann. §84-9-312. The general priority scheme is that the first creditor to perfect its security interest beats later perfected security interests. See Kan. Stat. Ann. §84-9-312(5)(a). There is an important exception to this "first-to-perfect" rule for a purchase money security interest. A PMSI in inventory has "superpriority" over an earlier perfected interest if: (a) the PMSI is perfected at the time the debtor receives possession of the inventory; (b) the PMSI creditor gives written notification to all holders of competing security interests which had UCC-1 financing statements on file when the PMSI creditor filed its UCC-1; (c) the competing secured creditor receives the notification within five years before the debtor receives possession of the inventory; and (d) the notification states "that the person giving the notice has or expects to acquire a purchase money security interest in inventory of the debtor, describing such inventory by item or type." Id. §84-9-312(3).

Sprague contends that the §84-9-312(3)'s "superpriority" status cannot be attained by a creditor that has perfected its security interest in inventory by possession, rather than by filing a UCC-1 financing statement. It emphasizes language in this UCC section and its commentary that refers to perfection by filing and the debtor receiving possession of the inventory. See Kan. Stat. Ann. §84-9-312(3) & Official UCC cmt. 3. We observe, however, that there is no language expressly excluding a creditor that has perfected by possession from taking advantage of this UCC section. More importantly, there is no sound policy reason to distinguish between perfection by filing and possession, and to provide the former, but not the latter, the opportunity to attain "superpriority." The common law of pledge—perfection by possession—predates, and was incorporated by, the UCC. In addition, pre-UCC law afforded special priority to purchase money security interests, and this has been carried over into the UCC. See B. Clark, The Law of Secured Transactions ¶3.09[1], at 3-100 ("the purchase money priority . . . breaks up what would otherwise be a complete monopoly on the debtor's collateral"). Thus, the UCC, as it stands today, does not reflect any intent to penalize a PMSI creditor by depriving it of the opportunity to attain "superpriority" simply because of its means of perfection.

We believe that there is a more logical explanation for UCC §9-312(3)'s contemplation that a creditor with a security interest in inventory would likely perfect by filing rather than possession. Inventory are goods "held for immediate or ultimate sale." Kan. Stat. Ann. §84-9-109 [now §9-102(a)(48) —Eds.] & Official UCC cmt. 3. The debtor typically needs its inventory to run its business and is not in a position to allow a third party, such as its lender, to possess the inventory. Therefore, the situation here—in which the creditor has possession of the inventory—will arise only rarely. The fact that the "superpriority" provision of §84-9-312(3) does not expressly refer to perfection by possession does not establish that its scope is limited to perfection by filing. The UCC was not drafted to address every possible factual situation, but, rather, was "intentionally designed to allow room to grow," Kan. Stat. Ann. §84-1-102 Kan. cmt. 1 (1996), and to accommodate the "expansion of commercial practices." Id. Official UCC cmt. 1.

Having concluded that it was possible for Hoxie to use §84-9-312(3) to attain "superpriority," we must now decide whether it did so by fulfilling the statutory requirements. The only requirement at issue here is the timing of Hoxie's PMSI notice, which was received after the cattle were sold and slaughtered and this litigation was commenced. We believe that this issue turns on the meaning of "possession" in the context of §84-9-312(3). As explained above, the UCC treats constructive possession as analogous to actual possession in certain circumstances. If Morken's constructive possession triggered the notification requirement, then Hoxie's notification was untimely because Sprague received the notification after Morken received constructive possession of the cattle. On the other hand, if "possession" is limited to actual possession, Hoxie's notice was timely because Sprague received it before Morken could ever receive actual possession.

Professor Grant Gilmore, the primary drafter of UCC Article 9, provides guidance on the meaning of "receives possession" in §84-9-312(3). Professor Gilmore's treatise Security Interests in Personal Property has been described as "an invaluable source of legislative intent because he is the fountainhead in this area." B. Clark, The Law of Secured Transactions ¶1.01[2][c], at 1-8. In that treatise, Professor Gilmore states that "'[r]eceives possession' is evidently meant to refer to the moment when the goods are physically delivered at the debtor's place of business—not to the possibility of the debtor's acquiring rights in the goods at an earlier point by identification or appropriation to the contract or by shipment under a term under which the debtor bears the risk." II G. Gilmore, Security Interests in Personal Property §29.3, at 787 (1965). In light of Professor Gilmore's comments, we interpret UCC §9-312(3)'s notification requirement to be triggered by actual possession of the inventory by the debtor. Because Sprague received Hoxie's notification within five years before Morken could have received actual possession, that notification was timely.

Sprague complains that the purpose of §84-9-312(3) is frustrated by granting "superpriority" to a PMSI without requiring pre-perfection notification to prior filed secured creditors. It contends that debtors on the brink of insolvency will now have the motive to create "secret liens" to the detriment of prior perfected secured creditors. The notification requirement, however, was not intended to allow other secured creditors veto power over the extension of new credit because the notification does not have to be given before the PMSI is acquired. The notification is required to state "that the person giving the notice *has* or expects to acquire a purchase money security interest in inventory of the debtor, describing such inventory by item or type." Kan. Stat. Ann. §84-9-312(3)(d) (emphasis added). Thus, the PMSI creditor can wait to notify competing secured creditors after it has acquired and perfected its security interest. The Official UCC Comment explains that the notification protects the inventory financier from making additional advances to the debtor in the mistaken belief that it is secured by inventory which, in fact, has been financed by a third party with a PMSI in that inventory. If the inventory financier "has received notification, he will presumably not make an advance; if he has not received notification (or if the other interest does not qualify as a purchase money interest), any advance he may make will have priority." Kan. Stat. Ann. §84-9-312 & Official UCC cmt. 3.

Our holding is consistent with this purpose in the context of this case. Sprague did not extend further credit in reliance on the cattle serving as its collateral; in fact, Sprague had not made any loans to Morken since at least a year before Morken acquired an interest in these particular cattle. We stop short, however, of holding, as did the district court, that a PMSI creditor that perfects by possession of inventory does not ever have to send a statutory notification. It is not necessary to reach that issue because Hoxie timely sent its statutory notification. A different fact pattern in another case might justify a different conclusion. See Scallop Petroleum Co. v. Banque Trad-Credit Lyonnais, 690 F. Supp. 184, 192 (S.D.N.Y. 1988) (PMSI creditor was required to send notification even though debtor never had possession of the inventory). . . .

[The court also concluded that Hoxie prevailed as to the proceeds of the sale.]

In conclusion, we reverse the district court's holding that Sprague did not have a security interest in the cattle, but affirm its judgment that Hoxie's security interest has priority over Sprague's security interest.

This case should continue to be good law even after the 1999 revision was adopted. Official Comment 5 to §9-324 states that if "the debtor never receives possession, the five-year period never begins, and the purchase-money security interest has priority even if notification is not given."

The revised version of Article 9 extends the superpriority procedure for gaining a PMSI security interest in inventory to a PMSI in the debtor's livestock (see §9-324(d)), and, in Appendix II to the 1999 revision, gives the states the option to use the same procedure for creditors taking a PMSI in the debtor's future crops (there called a *production money security interest*).

PROBLEM 373

Hans Racing Equipment bought much of its inventory from Standard Auto Wholesales, Inc., which always took a purchase money security interest in the goods sold to Hans and which filed a financing statement on the same day. Hans also borrowed money from the Matching Dishes National Bank (MDNB) to finance the purchase of inventory from wholesalers, part of which was used to pay off Standard Auto. MDNB filed a financing statement, claiming a security interest in Hans's inventory. On March 28, Hans contracted to buy $3,000 in goods from Standard, making a down payment of $1,500 and giving Standard a purchase money security interest in the goods for the rest. On that same day, he borrowed the $1,500 down payment from MDNB and also gave the bank a purchase money security interest in the same goods. Both creditors knew of the other, so they both sent written notice to each other. The goods were delivered to Hans on April 2. Which creditor has priority? See §9-324(g) and its Official Comment 13 (termed by some, "vendor beats lender").

Similar problems arise, of course, with consignments. Even true consignors hoping to prevail over perfected interests in the inventory of the consignee must follow a notification procedure of this type. See §9-103(d) and Example 3 in Official Comment 3 of §9-319.

PROBLEM 374

Barbara Shipek was pleased and flattered when Tim Isle, owner of Isle's Fine Art Works, asked her if he could exhibit and sell some of her pottery. She gave him five of her favorite pieces. The next day she took a party of friends down to the store to see the display and was astounded to learn that Octopus National Bank (ONB), which had a perfected floating lien on the store's inventory, had foreclosed and seized everything in the store, including Barb's pottery. Can ONB do this to her? Murphy v. Southtrust Bank of Ala., 611 So. 2d 269 (Ala. 1992).

III. CONTROL AND PRIORITY

The 1999 revision of Article 9 created the idea of *control* as a means of perfection. White & Summers explain the basic concept best by telling us that "'control' is to intangibles as 'possession' is to goods"; White & Summers §23-4. Taking the steps for control, described below, gives the world some notice at least that the creditor has legal rights in the intangible property that must be respected.

A. Control over Investment Property

The 1994 version of Article 8, concerning investment securities, dealt not only with traditional stocks and bonds represented by actual pieces of paper (*certificated securities;* see §8-102(a)(4)), and similar rights against the issuing corporation that are merely registered in a computer at that corporation (*uncertificated securities;* see §8-102(a)(18)), but also with the widespread practice of holding securities in an account with a stockbroker, with the investor's rights reflected merely by a bookkeeping entry in the stockbroker's records (called a *securities entitlement*; see §8-102(a)(17)).[12] Article 9 lumps all these methods of holding securities, along with similar rights in commodity contracts and accounts, and names them *investment property.* Read §9-102(a)(49).

How is a security interest taken in investment property? There are two ways: the filing of a financing statement and/or the taking of *control* over the investment property, with the latter trumping the former (that is, a secured party who has control has priority over one who has merely filed; see §9-328(1)). *Control* is defined in §8-106, with similar rules for commodity contracts in §9-106(b). Generally, one has control over a certificated security by taking delivery of it along with any necessary indorsements; §§8-106(a), (b),

12. The stockbroker may not itself have possession of the actual certificates either, but may only have rights to an account it carries with a clearing corporation or bank, where the actual certificates are physically located. In this case the broker has a security entitlement in the latter account, and its rights pass through to its investor free of the claims of most creditors of either upper-tiered party; see §8-503(a).

and 8-301(a). The same is true of uncertificated securities (see §8-106(c)), only here *delivery* is artificially defined in §8-301(b) as making sure that the secured party is registered as the stock owner in the records of the issuing corporation. In the context of indirect holding, *control* requires that the secured party take steps to make sure that it can reach the rights of the debtor in the event that it needs to foreclose, as is illustrated in the following Problem.

PROBLEM 375

Mr. Goldbury instructed his stockbroker, Bing, Bong & Bell (BB&B) to buy 100 shares of Utopia, Ltd., stock and place it in his account at BB&B. Bing, Bong & Bell bought the shares and kept them in the account it held at Clearing Corporation but marked its records to indicate that Mr. Goldbury was really the owner of this number of shares of the stock. In this case, Article 8 would deem Mr. Goldbury an *entitlement holder* who has a *securities entitlement* in a *security account* with a *securities intermediary;* see §8-102, which defines all these terms (*securities account* is in §8-501(a)). Mr. Goldbury went to Octopus National Bank (ONB) and asked to borrow money using the above 100 shares as collateral. You are the counsel for ONB and are in charge of making sure that the bank's security interest is perfected, which means getting "control" over the securities entitlement. Look at §8-106(d) and its Official Comment 4, and advise the bank. Which of the possible methods is the safest for your client?

Then answer these two questions:

(a) If another creditor also gets control over the rights to the 100 shares, which has priority? See §9-328(2).

(b) If Mr. Goldbury borrows money from BB&B after ONB has control and grants BB&B a security interest in all stocks held in his account with them, is BB&B's security interest superior to ONB's? See §9-328(3) and Official Comment 4, Example 5.

For all these issues of control and perfection of security interests in investment property, the Official Comments to both §§8-106 and 9-328 contain a wealth of information, including Examples aplenty, to which you are referred in the event of an actual legal dispute.

B. *Control over Deposit Accounts*

Similar rules govern the use of bank accounts as collateral. Prior to the 1999 revision of Article 9, it was unclear whether a bank account could stand as collateral for debts owed to anyone other than the bank in which the account was maintained (and, subject to non-uniform amendments, the prior version of Article 9 excluded deposit accounts from its scope). The revision allows a perfected security interest in such accounts by a creditor obtaining control over the account. Consumer accounts may not be used as collateral for consumer debts (though they could be so used for non-consumer debts); see White & Summers §22-9.

PROBLEM 376

Computer World, Inc., desires to borrow money from Investment Bank of America, which will grant it a revolving line of credit, secured in part by the bank account that Computer World maintains at Last National Bank. You are the attorney for Investment Bank of America. Advise the bank how it can perfect its security interest in this bank account and which of the methods of control specified in §9-104 would be the safest form of security. If Computer World later borrows money from Last National Bank and grants the bank a security interest in the account carried there, would Last National have priority over your client? See §9-327(3) and (4). To gain control of an account, is it sufficient that the creditor is an authorized signatory on the account? See In re Anderson, 2019 WL 1227925 (D. Md. 2019).

C. *Control over Letters of Credit Rights*

Letters of credit (the subject of Article 5 of the Uniform Commercial Code) are an increasingly popular means of financing various transactions. If one party does not trust the other to make payment at an agreed upon time, that party may require that the payment be made directly by a bank of good repute. If this is done, the bank that is persuaded to do so will issue a letter of credit to the person to whom payment is to be made (called the *beneficiary*) specifying the circumstances under which the bank will honor drafts drawn on it by that person. The other party to the transaction who persuades the bank to issue the letter of credit (the bank's customer) is called the *applicant.* The beneficiary may use its rights under the letter of credit as collateral for a different loan with a different creditor, who will then want to perfect its security interest in the rights represented by the letter of credit.

PROBLEM 377

Computer World agreed to sell 10,000 computers to Football University for the sum of $25,000, with Football University agreeing to obtain a letter of credit for this amount in favor of the seller. Shortly thereafter Computer World received a letter of credit from Octopus National Bank (ONB) naming Computer World as the beneficiary and stating that it would honor drafts drawn on the bank in favor of Computer World for the amount of $25,000 on presentation of an invoice showing shipment of the computers to the university by September 25 of that year. Computer World comes to you, its attorney, in February of the same year with the following problem. It needs to borrow $10,000 from some lender in order to finance the construction of the computers by the required deadline. It wants to use the letter of credit as collateral for this loan. How can the new lender obtain a perfected interest in the rights represented by the letter of credit? See §9-107. When Computer World asked ONB if it would agree to an assignment of the proceeds of the letter of credit to Computer World's lender, the bank not only refused but pointed to clauses in the letter of credit that provided a number of things: (1) the right of Computer World to draw drafts on the bank was not transferable; and (2) the letter of credit specifically forbade the beneficiary (Computer World) the right to make an assignment of the proceeds of the letter of credit and *voided* the letter of credit if the beneficiary made such an assignment without the bank's consent. What can Computer World tell potential lenders who might be willing to loan it money if the letter of credit rights could be used as collateral? Remember, as you read the cited sections that follow, that the obligation from Football University to Computer World is an *account*. See §§5-114, 9-308(d), 9-102(a)(78), 9-409, and the latter's Official Comments.

IV. BUYERS

Section 9-201(a) states what White & Summers called Article 9's "Golden Rule" (White & Summers §24-12 (3d ed. 1998)):

> Except as otherwise provided by the Uniform Commercial Code, a security agreement is effective according to its terms between the parties, against purchasers of the collateral and against creditors.

Section 9-320(a) is one of the sections that fit in the "except" language of §9-201; so is §9-317(b), which lists other buyers who win out over the *unperfected* secured party in some circumstances. A corollary to §9-201's "Golden Rule" is §9-315(a)(1):

> (a) Except as otherwise provided in this article and in Section 2-403(2):
>
> (1) a security interest or agricultural lien continues in collateral notwithstanding sale, lease, license, exchange, or other disposition thereof unless the

secured party authorized the disposition free of the security interest or agricultural lien. . . .

PROBLEM 378

Betty Consumer bought a television set from Distortion TV, Inc., a retail store. A month later, Distortion went bankrupt, and a minor functionary from the Octopus National Bank (ONB) showed up on her stoop and asked her to turn over the set. He explained that ONB held a perfected security interest in all of Distortion's inventory and that since Distortion had not paid off its debts to ONB, the bank was repossessing.

(a) What should Ms. Consumer tell the bank's flunky? See §9-320(a).

(b) Would it matter if she had known that ONB had a perfected security interest in Distortion's inventory? See White & Summers §25-8(b); Official Comment 3 to §9-320.

(c) Would it matter if she bought at a "Liquidation Sale" and was informed by the store's owner that the store planned to file a bankruptcy petition the following week? See In re Fritz-Mair Mfg. Co., 16 B.R. 417 (Bankr. N.D. Tex. 1982).

(d) What if Ms. Consumer had put the TV on "layaway" and had paid 50 percent of the price but permitted Distortion to keep the TV (she signed a contract obligating herself to pay the balance), and then the store filed for bankruptcy? Read §2-502 and its Official Comments. The Bankruptcy Code also offers such consumers some relief in §507(a)(7), which gives layaway buyers a priority payment up to the amount of $3,025 per individual.

International Harvester Co. v. Glendenning

Texas Supreme Court, 1974
505 S.W.2d 320

WILLIAMS, C.J.

This appeal is from a take nothing judgment in a suit to recover damages for wrongful conversion of three tractors.

International Harvester Company and International Harvester Credit Corporation (both hereinafter referred to as International) brought this action against Don Glendenning in which it was alleged that International was the holder of a duly perfected security interest in three new International Harvester tractors; that such security agreements had been executed in favor of International by Jack L. Barnes, doing business as Barnes Equipment Company, an International Harvester dealer; that Barnes and Glendenning had entered into a fraudulent conspiracy wherein Glendenning had wrongfully purchased the three tractors from Barnes; that Glendenning was not a buyer in the ordinary course of business; that he did not act in a commercially reasonable manner and did not act honestly, therefore taking the tractors subject to International's security interest. It was further alleged that Barnes and Glendenning had wrongfully conspired to convert the ownership of the tractors and to deprive International, by fraud and deceit, of its ownership of the tractors by virtue of their security interest therein in that (1) Glendenning acquiesced in falsifying a retail order form so that it was made to indicate receipt of $16,000 in cash and the trade-in of two used tractors allegedly worth a total of $8,700, while in fact both Glendenning and Barnes knew that Glendenning had only paid the sum of $16,000 in cash, a sum far below the market value of the tractors; (2) Glendenning, in the furtherance of the conspiracy and unlawful conversion, represented to a representative of International that he, Glendenning, had, in fact, traded certain used tractors to Barnes, which was untrue; and (3) Glendenning removed the new tractors in which International had a security interest to the State of Louisiana where he sold the same and converted the proceeds to his own use and benefit. International sought damages in the sum of $24,049.99 which was alleged to be the reasonable value of the tractors on the date of conversion.

Glendenning answered by a general denial and with the special defense to the effect that he purchased the tractors in the ordinary course of business and that such purchase was made in good faith and without any knowledge of any security interest held by International. The court submitted the case to the jury on one special issue:

> Do you find from a preponderance of the evidence that on the time and occasion in question, the defendant, Don Glendenning, was a buyer in the ordinary course of business?

In connection with this issue the court instructed the jury that the term "buyer in ordinary course of business" means "a person who in good faith and without knowledge that the sale to him is in violation of the ownership rights or security interest of the third party in the goods buys in the ordinary course from a person in the business of selling goods of that kind."

The court instructed the jury that the term "good faith" means "honesty in fact in the conduct or transaction concerned."

The jury answered the special issue "Yes." . . .

[The court quoted §§9-307(1) (the predecessor to §9-320(a)), 1-201(b)(9), and 1-201(b)(19) and noted that "whether a sale is in the ordinary course of business is a mixed question of law and fact."]

The material testimony presented to the court and jury may be summarized, as follows:

At the time of the trial of this case appellee Glendenning was a farmer in Collin County. He described himself as being not only a farmer but a trader. He said that he frequently traded tractors and other farm equipment as well as anything else from which he could make a profit. He has had almost twenty years' experience in the business of buying and selling farm tractors. In the early 1950s he owned an International Harvester dealership in Frisco, Collin County, Texas. From 1956 to 1960 he was a salesman for International Harvester. After leaving International he began trading farm equipment of his own, using some of the implements on his own farm and holding others strictly for resale. For many years he had been familiar with International Harvester's custom of "floor-planning" tractors and other farm equipment. By this plan International would supply tractors and other equipment to the dealers who, in turn, would give International a note and security agreement to protect International in its investment. When a dealer sold a piece of equipment from the floor he would pay International the amount due. He also testified that he knew that when used tractors were taken as trade-ins by International Harvester dealers such used tractors were also mortgaged or covered by the security agreement to International. He admitted that International Harvester always kept close tabs to see what was wrong with the used tractors and that International always wanted to know what its dealers traded for in connection with new equipment sales. Glendenning acknowledged that any false information contained on a retail order form would provide incorrect information concerning the transactions to International Harvester, or any other lender.

Glendenning said that he had known Jack L. Barnes, an International Harvester dealer, for two or three years and during that time he had bought several tractors from him. In the early part of July 1971 Barnes, and Joe Willard, another friend, came to his home in Collin County and talked to him about buying some tractors. He said that Barnes had eight tractors to sell but that he was only interested in buying three of the machines. Barnes described the tractors and told Glendenning that he wanted $18,500 for the three. Glendenning declined that offer but told Barnes that he would give $16,000 cash for the three. Barnes accepted the offer.

At the time of this transaction Glendenning knew that the three tractors were reasonably worth $22,500. Willard went to Vernon, Texas, and got the tractors and delivered them to Mr. Glendenning's home. Glendenning asked Willard to bring him a bill of sale when he returned with the tractors. Willard received from Barnes an instrument entitled "Retail Order Form" dated July 5, 1971, which recited that Glendenning had purchased from Barnes three tractors for the total price of $24,700 with a cash payment of $16,000 leaving a balance of $8,700. The instrument recited that Glendenning had traded in four tractors with values totaling $8,700 so that the total consideration of $24,700 was shown to have been paid.

Glendenning said that the next day Barnes came to his home to get payment for the tractors. At that time Glendenning requested a "bill of sale" and he watched Barnes fill in another retail order form similar to the one that he had obtained from Willard the day before. This order form stated that Glendenning had traded in four tractors worth $8,700 in addition to payment of $16,000 in cash making a total purchase of $24,700. After Barnes had completed filling out this form and signed the same Glendenning said that he put his signature on the instrument also. He then gave Barnes $16,000.

Concerning the contents of the retail order form Glendenning said that at the time Barnes filled in the blanks indicating that Glendenning was trading in four tractors he knew that he was not trading anything and that he did not question Barnes about the trade-in information contained in the form. He admitted that he did not ask Barnes whether the tractors which he purchased were free and clear nor did he call International to determine whether or not such company had a mortgage on the tractors. Glendenning admitted that he knew that the information contained in the printed form concerning trade-ins and total consideration for the sale of the three new tractors was false; that he knew of this falsification when he signed the order form; and that he also knew that such falsification would mislead any creditors relying on the document such as a dealer, a manufacturer or a bank lending money with the equipment as collateral. He admitted that at the time of the transaction in question Barnes was probably "trying to come out even" or that he did it to make his books balance. Glendenning admitted that he was suspicious of the manner in which Barnes prepared the order form and confessed that his actions amounted to dishonesty. He said that to his knowledge he had never before signed an order form with false trade-ins. He admitted that such action was "unusual."

A few days after the transaction a Mr. McKinney, collection manager for International Harvester Company, and a representative of International Harvester Credit Corporation, telephoned Glendenning concerning the transaction in question. In that conversation Glendenning told McKinney that he had traded four tractors to Barnes in addition to paying $16,000 cash for the three new International tractors. Glendenning testified that he knew that he had lied to Mr. McKinney concerning the trade-ins and that such oral misrepresentation or lie was dishonest.

After receiving the tractors Glendenning removed them to a barn near Alexandria, Louisiana, although it was his usual practice to place equipment on his own premises or at another dealer's place of business. He subsequently sold the three tractors in Louisiana.

As a part of his direct examination Glendenning testified that he considered the deal to be a purchase of three tractors for $16,000; that he had no side agreement with Barnes; that he thought he was making a good deal; and that he was acting in good faith.

At the very beginning of this trial appellee Glendenning confessed the validity of appellant's cause of action against him based upon fraud, conspiracy and conversion, but sought to evade legal liability by assuming, pursuant to Tex. R. Civ. P. 266, the burden of going forward and establishing his sole defense that he was a buyer in ordinary course of business within the meaning of §9.307(a) (1968). This assumption carried with it the additional burden of establishing by competent evidence that Glendenning acted in good faith and without knowledge that the sale to him was in violation of the ownership rights or security interest of a third party. Good faith, as the court correctly charged the jury, means honesty in fact in the conduct or transaction concerned. In an effort to establish this affirmative defense and thereby evade liability, appellee Glendenning testified on direct examination with the broad conclusory statement that he had acted in good faith. However, this subjective and conclusory statement was immediately annihilated by factual evidence falling from the lips of Glendenning himself.

Appellee Glendenning's own testimony immediately removes him from the category of an innocent Collin County farmer who seeks to purchase one or more tractors in the ordinary course of business. By his own testimony he has had many years of experience as a tractor dealer, a salesman and one of the most active traders of farm equipment in Collin County. Based upon this experience he is knowledgeable in the very nature of business done by International by "floor-planning" its equipment. With all of this knowledge and information in his possession he purchased the equipment for considerably less than its value, made no investigation of International's security interest, acquiesced in the falsification of the retail order form showing nonexistent trade-ins, and misrepresented the particulars of the transaction to International's representative by stating that there were, in fact, trade-ins. He confesses that his actions were dishonest.

Thus it is evident to us that Glendenning's own testimony, which is the only material testimony offered, is entirely devoid of honesty in fact and completely negates his contention that he was a buyer in the ordinary course of business within the meaning of the Texas Business & Commerce Code.

While we have been unable to find any Texas authorities decided under this specific provision of the Business & Commerce Code a recent Uniform Commercial Code release notes that the good faith requirement was added "to make it clear that one who buys dishonestly is not within the definition. The 'without knowledge' addition spells out one important type of dishonesty." UCC Release No. 27-1973, 6 Bender's Uniform Commercial Code Service §1-201 at 1-29 (1965).

The complete picture revealed by all of the material testimony in this case reveals a definite pattern of lies, deceit, dishonesty and bad faith. We find no competent evidence in this record to support the jury's answer to the special issue submitted and therefore the same should have been set aside and disregarded by the trial court. . . .

Even where the Code is silent about a "good faith" requirement, §1-304 imposes one. There is a growing body of UCC law that says that good faith is a condition precedent to any protection under the statute. "Bad faith," a phrase not defined in the Code, can alter the usual Article 9 priorities. See Limor Diamonds, Inc. v. D'Oro by Christopher Michael, Inc., 558 F. Supp. 709 (S.D.N.Y. 1983).

PROBLEM 379

Deering Milliken was a textile manufacturer. It routinely sold textiles on credit to Mill Fabrics, a firm that finished the textiles into dyed and patterned fabrics. It was Mill Fabrics' practice to resell the fabrics to Tanbro Fabrics, a wholesaler. While the textiles were still in Deering's warehouse, Mill Fabrics contracted to buy them from Deering, signing a security agreement to that effect and giving Deering a financing statement, which it duly filed. In turn, Mill Fabrics sold the textiles to Tanbro, which paid Mill Fabrics for them, but delayed taking delivery for a few weeks, so that the fabrics remained in Deering's possession. Deals of this kind were common in the textile industry, and all parties knew of the others' interest. Unfortunately, Mill Fabrics became insolvent and never paid Deering for the textiles, and Deering therefore refused to deliver them to Tanbro. The latter sued. Who should prevail? See §9-320(e) and its Official Comment 8.

In re Western Iowa Limestone, Inc.

United States Court of Appeals, Eighth Circuit, 2008
538 F.3d 858

HANSEN, Circuit Judge.

I.

Western Iowa Limestone, Inc. (WIL) owned several quarries throughout Iowa, and it began marketing agricultural lime as a by-product of its operations in 2004. It marketed the ag lime through six fertilizer and chemical dealers, who resold the ag lime at retail. In January 2005, one of WIL's dealers, Independent Inputs, LLC, purchased 5,000 tons of ag lime from WIL, and in February 2005, two other dealers, Paul Leinen and Leinen, Inc.

(collectively "Leinen" and hereinafter, together with Independent Inputs, referred to as "Dealers"), purchased a total of 13,400 tons of ag lime. The Dealers paid for the ag lime at the time of the purchases, and each of the bills of sale noted that the ag lime would remain at the quarry until the Dealers sold the ag lime to their ultimate customers. This arrangement was beneficial to WIL, which also provided trucking services. WIL maintained its ag lime in a single fungible pile on its premises. The ag lime that the Dealers purchased likewise remained in the fungible pile until resold to their customers and removed from the premises.

WIL filed a petition under Chapter 11 of the Bankruptcy Code on December 12, 2005. At that time, Independent Inputs had resold and removed 416 tons of ag lime from WIL's premises, and Leinen had removed 1,406 tons. United Bank of Iowa is WIL's largest secured creditor, and it had a security interest in all of WIL's assets, including its inventory, accounts receivable, and proceeds, to secure a $6 million loan. The ag lime remaining on WIL's premises was sold in the bankruptcy proceedings as part of its inventory, and the Dealers filed a joint objection to the proposed distributions from the sale of the inventory, claiming priority over United Bank as buyers in the ordinary course of business (BIOC) to the extent of the value of the ag lime they had purchased but had not yet removed from WIL's premises. Independent Inputs' claim was for $35,522, and Leinen's claims were for $89,508.

The bankruptcy court initially determined that the Dealers failed to establish BIOC status under Iowa law because they did not take physical possession of the ag lime or have a right to recover the goods under Article 2 of the Iowa Uniform Commercial Code (Iowa UCC) as required by Iowa Code §554.1201(9). On a motion to alter or amend, the bankruptcy court reversed itself, concluding that the Dealers had taken constructive possession of the ag lime and had satisfied the requirements for BIOC status under §554.1201(9). United Bank appealed, and the BAP reversed, concluding that the Dealers did not constructively possess the ag lime under Iowa law for purposes of a priority contest between a secured creditor and a purchaser. Because the BAP concluded that the Dealers did not have constructive possession of the ag lime, it avoided the separate issue of whether constructive possession satisfies the requirement of "tak[ing] possession" contained in §554.1201(9). The Dealers appeal from the BAP's decision.

II. . . .

Under Iowa's UCC law, "a buyer in ordinary course of business . . . takes free of a security interest created by the buyer's seller, even if the security interest is perfected and the buyer knows of its existence." Iowa Code §554.9320(1). Thus, the Dealers take free of United Bank's prior security interest if they meet the definition of a BIOC. "Buyer in ordinary course of business" is defined by the Iowa UCC as

> a person that buys goods in good faith, without knowledge that the sale violates the rights of another person in the goods, and in the ordinary course from a person . . . in the business of selling goods of that kind. A person buys goods in the ordinary course if the sale to the person comports with the usual or customary practices in the kind of business in which the seller is engaged or with the seller's own usual or customary practices. . . . Only a buyer that takes possession of the goods or has a right to recover the goods from the seller under Article 2 may be a buyer in ordinary course of business. "Buyer in ordinary course of business" does not include a person that acquires goods in a transfer in bulk or as security for or in total or partial satisfaction of a money debt.

Iowa Code §554.1201(9).

Relevant to this appeal, BIOC status requires that the sale comport with the usual or customary practices for the kind of business involved and that the buyer take possession of the goods. (The Dealers do not claim that they had a right to recover under Article 2.) We begin with the central issue of this case—that is, whether a buyer who purchases fungible goods from a seller but leaves the goods at the seller's premises satisfies the requirement that the buyer "take[] possession of the goods." Id. We must determine whether constructive possession is within the meaning of the statute, and if so, whether the circumstances of this case amount to constructive possession sufficient to confer BIOC status.

The penultimate sentence of the definition of a BIOC requires that the buyer either "take[] possession" or "ha[ve] a right to recover the goods from the seller under Article 2." Id. The requirement was added to the Uniform Commercial Code (UCC) in 1999, and the Iowa legislature adopted the revised UCC provision verbatim in 2000. The term "possession" is not defined in the Iowa UCC, and §554.1201(9) does not elaborate on what is meant by "tak[ing] possession." Iowa courts "determine legislative intent from the words chosen by the legislature. . . . Absent a statutory definition or an established meaning in the law, words in the statute are given their ordinary and common meaning by considering the context within which they are used." City of Waterloo v. Bainbridge, 749 N.W.2d 245, 248 (Iowa 2008) (internal marks omitted). Iowa courts look beyond the statute's express terms only when the language is ambiguous. "A statute . . . is ambiguous if reasonable minds could differ or be uncertain as to the meaning of the statute." Id. Language that is "plain, clear, and susceptible to only one meaning" is unambiguous. Id.

Section 554.1201(9) refers only to "possession," not to "physical possession" or "constructive possession." In the context of §554.1201(9), both physical possession and constructive possession are plausible meanings of the bare term "possession," and we conclude that the term is ambiguous as used in §554.1201(9). See First Nat'l Bank in Lenox v. Lamoni Livestock Sales Co., 417 N.W.2d 443, 447 (Iowa 1987) ("'Ambiguity in the word *possession* dates from the introduction into the law of the concept of *constructive possession.*'" (quoting Jacobson v. Aetna Cas. & Sur. Co., 233 Minn. 383, 46 N.W.2d 868, 871 (Minn. 1951)). We therefore apply the rules of statutory interpretation to ascertain the Iowa legislature's intent in requiring a buyer to take possession before being considered a BIOC.

In interpreting a statute, the Supreme Court of Iowa looks to the common law to construe undefined terms. See *Lamoni Livestock Sales,* 417 N.W. 2d at 447-48; S & S, Inc. v. Meyer, 478 N.W.2d 857, 860 (Iowa Ct. App. 1991) ("Unless displaced by the UCC, . . . the common law supplement[s] its provisions."). In *Lamoni Livestock Sales,* the court interpreted the term "possession" in the context of comment 4 to Iowa UCC §554.9109, which distinguished between the characterization of goods as farm products or inventory depending on whether the goods were "in the possession of a debtor engaged in farming operations" or had "come[] into the possession of a marketing agency." Iowa Code §554.9109, cmt. 4 (1987). The court relied on the concept of constructive possession to hold that livestock in the physical possession of a sale barn (or marketing agency) was nonetheless constructively possessed by the farmer who placed the livestock with the sale barn because the farmer retained ownership of the livestock. *Lamoni Livestock Sales,* 417 N.W.2d at 448. The Supreme Court of Iowa noted that possession is not defined in the UCC and looked to property law concepts for an analogy. Id. at 447-48; see also Iowa Code §554.9313, cmt. 3 (recognizing that "possession" is not defined and "adopt[ing] the general concept as it developed under former Article 9," which applied the principles of agency).

There is no reason to believe without some explicit indication that Iowa courts would construe the undefined term "possession" to include constructive possession in some sections of the Iowa UCC and not in others. See Iowa Code §554.1103(2) ("Unless displaced by the particular provisions of this chapter [referring to the Iowa UCC], the principles of law and equity, including the law of . . . principal and agent . . . supplement its provisions."). Where the Iowa legislature intended to supplant the common law in the UCC, it specifically provided so. For example, in defining "control" for purposes of a certificated security in §554.8106, the comments specify that control has a particularized meaning and is not to be interpreted by reference to other bodies of law. See Iowa Code §554.8106 cmt. 7. The comment provides that "[i]n particular, the requirements for 'possession' derived from the common law of pledge are not to be used as a basis for interpreting subsection (c)(2) or (d)(2)" of §554.8106. Id. Rather, "[t]hose provisions are designed to supplant the [common law] concepts of 'constructive possession' and the like." Id. This comment recognizes that the Iowa legislature intended courts to look to the common law to interpret undefined terms contained in the Iowa UCC, and that under the common law of Iowa, possession includes constructive possession.

The transfer of possessory rights as between the buyer and the seller is a logical point at which to sever the security interest held by the seller's lender when the seller sells its goods in the ordinary course of its business. See U.C.C. §1-201, cmt. 9 ("The penultimate sentence prevents a buyer that does not have the right to possession as against the seller from being a buyer in ordinary course of business."); 9 William D. Hawkland, Richard A. Lord, Charles C. Lewis, & Frederick H. Miller, Hawkland UCC Series Art. 9 Appendix (Part II) (2008) (suggesting that under the "amendment, a buyer will become a [BIOC] when the buyer becomes entitled to a possession remedy"). Construing possession to include constructive possession is consistent with this demarcation and with the purpose of the BIOC status. If §554.1201(9) required physical possession to the exclusion of constructive possession, then a buyer who completed a sales transaction and placed goods with a bailee would not be considered a BIOC, but would continue to be subject to the lender's security interest. In this scenario, as between the buyer and the seller, the seller has no authority for regaining possession of the goods from the bailee, and the buyer clearly has the superior possessory interest as compared to the seller. Further, at this point, the lender is secured by the proceeds of the sale and no longer needs the security provided by the goods themselves. See GMAC Bus. Credit, L.L.C. v. Ford Motor Co. (In re H.S.A. II, Inc.), 271 B.R. 534, 541 (Bankr. E.D. Mich. 2002) ("[T]he reason that a security interest does not continue in collateral that is sold to a buyer in ordinary course is that the security interest continues in the proceeds, thus protecting the secured creditor."); see also 4 White & Summers—Uniform Commercial Code §33-8(b) ("Normally a lender with a security interest in inventory intends the debtor to be able to sell the inventory free and clear.").

In this situation, we see no reason for the buyer not to receive the inventory free of the lender's security interest even though the buyer took constructive rather than physical possession of the goods. The outcome should not differ based on whether the bailee is a third party or is the seller, where, as here, the buyer completes the sales transaction, the buyer takes delivery of the goods at the seller's premises, and the buyer and the seller explicitly agree that the seller will hold the goods for the buyer, such that the buyer constructively possesses the goods. See Kunkel v. Sprague Nat'l Bank, 128 F.3d 636, 643 (8th Cir. 1997) (applying Kansas law and holding that under the UCC, a seller loses its Article 2 right to stop delivery when the goods are constructively delivered to the buyer via a bailee, even when the bailee is the seller); see also Havens Steel Co. v. Commerce Bank, N.A. (In re Havens Steel Co.), 317 B.R. 75, 87 (Bankr. W.D. Mo. 2004) (holding that constructive possession satisfies the "take possession" requirement under Missouri's UCC §1-201(9)). We hold that "possession" as used in Iowa UCC §554.1201(9) includes constructive possession.

Having determined that the requirement in Iowa UCC §554.1201(9) may be met through constructive possession, we turn to the separate issue of whether the Dealers satisfied the requirements of constructive possession under Iowa law. The bankruptcy court concluded that the Dealers had constructive possession of the ag lime, but the BAP disagreed. According to the BAP, under Iowa law a buyer has constructive possession of goods held by the seller only if the buyer takes "some visible and apparent step to inform the world of the change in possession from the [seller] to the [buyer]." In re W. Ia. Limestone, Inc., 375 B.R. at 525-26 (discussing Boothby & Co. v. Brown, 40 Iowa 104, 1874 WL 609 (1874); McAfee v. Busby, 69 Iowa 328, 28 N.W. 623 (Iowa 1886)). The Dealers assert that adoption of the UCC in the 1960s by the Iowa legislature rendered these cases inapplicable, and that more recent cases support their position that they could take constructive possession of the ag lime without notice to the secured creditor.

We agree with the Dealers that *McAfee* and *Boothby* do not control on the issue of whether constructive possession under Iowa law requires notice to the world of the change in ownership. Both cases involved application of an Iowa statute that specifically required notice when a seller retained actual possession: "'no sale or mortgage of personal property, where the vendor or mortgagor retains *actual possession* thereof, is valid against existing creditors or subsequent purchasers *without notice,* unless a written instrument conveying the same is executed and acknowledged like conveyances of real estate, and filed for record.'" *McAfee,* 28 N.W. at 623 (quoting Iowa Code §1923 (1873)) (emphasis added). Iowa Code §1923 explicitly required notice when the vendor retained actual possession. In *McAfee,* a husband claimed to have gifted a carriage to his wife to avoid a prior security interest. Id. at 623-24. The court determined that the husband retained actual possession based on the facts that the carriage was used for and by the entire family and that, at that time in Iowa's history, personal property used in the house occupied by the husband and wife was deemed to be in the possession and control of the husband. Id. at 624 (distinguishing Pierson v. Heisey, 19 Iowa 114 (Iowa 1865), where a father who gifted a piano to his daughter did not retain actual possession though the piano remained in his home because "[t]here was no pretense 'the father used the property as his own'"). *Boothby* relied on the same statute. See *Boothby,* 40 Iowa 104, 1874 WL 609, *1. Section 1923 was subsequently transferred to Iowa Code §556.3 and repealed by the Iowa legislature in 1965. See Iowa Code §556.3, historical notes (noting the repeal by Acts 1965 (61 G.A.) ch. 413, §10102). Notably, this was the same time that the Iowa legislature initially adopted Iowa's UCC. See Iowa Code

§554.1201, historical notes (noting that the section was added by Acts 1965 (61 G.A.) ch. 413, §1201).

Section 1923's notice requirement that applied to vendors who retained actual possession is no longer on Iowa's books. Without that statutorily mandated notice, we are left to determine what constitutes constructive possession under Iowa law, and particularly whether the BAP correctly concluded that notice to the world is required before a buyer can constructively possess goods left with the seller. The Supreme Court of Iowa has described constructive possession as follows: "[C]onstructive possession of personal property by its owner exists where the owner has intentionally given the actual possession—namely, the direct physical control—of the property to another for the purpose of having him do some act for the owner to or with the property." *Lamoni Livestock Sales Co.,* 417 N.W.2d at 447-48. Ultimately, the court's discussion of constructive possession focused on the knowledge and agreement of the parties rather than notice to the world; where the parties agreed that one would hold direct physical control for another for the purpose of doing some act for the owner, the owner retained constructive possession. Id.; see also Gass v. Hettinga (In re Estate of Hettinga), 514 N.W.2d 727, 730 (Iowa Ct. App. 1994) (citing *Lamoni Livestock Sales* for the proposition that "[w]here the owner retains constructive possession, the party to whom bare physical control of the property had been entrusted for the owner's purpose does not have possession but only custody"); cf. U.C.C. §1-201, cmt. 9 (explaining that the possession "requirement relates to whether *as against the seller* the buyer or one taking through the buyer has possessory rights").

Although construing a different section of the Iowa UCC, we find the court's discussion of constructive possession in *Lamoni Livestock Sales* instructive. The court relied on non-UCC law to construe the undefined term "possession," indicating that nothing peculiar to §554.9109 warranted giving constructive possession a specialized meaning under that provision of Iowa's UCC law. Further, possession was determinative of whether a security interest continued or had been extinguished in *Lamoni Livestock Sales,* much the same as it is in the context in which we face it. We see no reason to treat constructive possession differently for purposes of §554.1201(9) than the Supreme Court of Iowa treated it for purposes of §554.9109. Finally, we are bound by a state supreme court's construction of its own law, and even where there is no case directly on point by a state's highest court, we look to "relevant state precedent, analogous decisions, considered dicta, and any other reliable data" to determine how the Supreme Court of Iowa would construe Iowa law. See HOK Sport, Inc. v. FC Des Moines, L.C., 495 F.3d 927, 935 (8th Cir. 2007). We therefore use the concept of constructive possession under Iowa law as developed by the Supreme Court of Iowa's most recent discussion of it.

In this case, the bankruptcy court found that the ag lime was in existence at the time of the January and February bills of sale and that the identification by weight in each of the bills of sale sufficiently identified the ag lime to the contracts. (See Add. at 40 ("The product, in a particular pile, was identified to the contract. . . .").) See also Iowa Code §554.2105(4) (2005) (providing that an undivided share in an identified bulk of fungible goods is sufficiently identified to a contract when the portion to be sold is identified by weight). The parties specifically contemplated that title would pass at the time of the bill of sale and that delivery would take place at WIL's quarry, where the ag lime would remain. (See Appellants' App. at 535, 536, & 542, each bill of sale containing the language: "And 'Seller,' in further consideration of the transfer and assignment, agrees to allow 'Buyer' to leave said Processed Ag Lime at the Logan Quarry until shipped to their clients.") The Dealers each filed affidavits stating that they inspected the ag lime and accepted it at WIL's place of business. It is undisputed that the Dealers paid for the ag lime at the time of acceptance. The bankruptcy court below found that title to the ag lime passed to the Dealers at the time of the sale, and United Bank does not contend otherwise. See Iowa Code §554.2401(3)(b) (2005) (providing that "[u]nless otherwise explicitly agreed where delivery is to be made without moving the goods, if the goods are at the time of contracting already identified and no documents are to be delivered, title passes at the time and place of contracting"); Sam & Mac, Inc. v. Treat, 783 N.E.2d 760, 764 (Ind. Ct. App. 2003) (explaining that title (and with it a possessory interest) passes from seller to buyer at the time and place the seller delivers the goods as agreed by the parties). Notably, this occurred in January and February of 2005, and each of the Dealers, without restriction, removed portions of the ag lime from WIL's premises as it was resold to the Dealers' customers.

United Bank argues only that it had no notice of the sale of the inventory. Because notice is not a requirement for constructive possession under Iowa law, the BAP erred in concluding that constructive possession required notice to the world. We hold that the Dealers constructively possessed the ag lime left at WIL's quarry based on the completed sale, the identification of the ag lime to the contract, and the agreement in the bill of sale between the Dealers and WIL that the ag lime would remain on WIL's premises until resold. See In re Havens Steel Co., 317 B.R. 75 at 87 (holding that the buyer's "possessory rights, arising from [its] payment for and title to the steel, were sufficiently strong to imbue [the buyer] with constructive possession of the steel, in the context of [Missouri UCC] §1-201," where the steel was identified to the contract but held at the seller's warehouse).

Finally, United Bank argues that even if the Dealers took possession of the ag lime, they still are not entitled to BIOC status because the sales of ag lime were not conducted in a manner that was customary in WIL's business or in the industry. See §554.1201(9) (to qualify as a BIOC "the sale [must] . . . comport[] with the usual or customary practices in the kind of business in which the seller is engaged or with the seller's own usual or customary practices"). In the bankruptcy court proceedings, United Bank asserted that it was unusual for customers to prepay the ag lime contracts and to leave the ag lime on the quarry's premises. The bankruptcy court found that although WIL was new to the business of processing and selling ag lime through dealers, the sales to the Dealers were conducted in a manner that was "a usual and customary practice in the industry." (Add. at 36.)

We conclude that the bankruptcy court's finding is not clearly erroneous. The evidence in the record consists primarily of contradictory affidavits filed by Gary Hopp, President and owner with his wife, Dianna, of WIL, and by Pete Horne, acting CFO and a director of WIL. Mr. Hopp attested that most customers bought ag lime on credit and took immediate delivery, although a few customers prepaid their ag lime contracts and left the ag lime on the quarry's premises in early 2005. Mr. Horne attested that Dianna and Gary Hopp directed him to develop a product development and marketing plan for the ag lime that was being produced as the by-product of a large asphalt project in late 2004; that he developed a plan to market the ag lime through exclusive dealerships; and that prepaid contracts became the normal custom for WIL as a result of the newly developed marketing plan. He also attested that it was standard practice in the agricultural fertilizer business to conduct business in a similar manner. Faced with the contradictory affidavits, the bankruptcy court credited Mr. Horne's affidavit and found the transactions at issue to be usual and customary in the industry. This finding was further supported by the affidavits of Doug Welsh and Robert Bryant, who were also dealers of ag lime for WIL and who, like the Dealers here, paid for the ag lime in full and left the lime on WIL's premises until sold to their customers. There being no other evidence in the record about the customary practices in the ag lime business, we cannot say that the bankruptcy court clearly erred in crediting one affidavit over the other. See Dixon v. Crete Med. Clinic, P.C., 498 F.3d 837, 847 (8th Cir. 2007) ("Where there are two permissible views of the evidence, the factfinder's choice between them cannot be clearly erroneous.") (internal marks omitted).

III.

Because the Dealers satisfied the requirements of being buyers in the ordinary course of business under Iowa Code §554.1201(9), we reverse the decision of the BAP and affirm the September 26, 2006, order of the bankruptcy court.

There is quite a list of qualifications (culled from §9-320(a) and §1-201's definition of "buyer in the ordinary course of business") that a buyer must meet to purchase free of a prior security interest in the purchased property:

> (1) He/she must be a buyer in the ordinary course of the seller's business (i.e., buying the seller's inventory in the routine way),
> (2) who does not buy in bulk (that is, does not buy an entire inventoried business) and does not take the interest as security for or in total or partial satisfaction of a preexisting debt (that is, the buyer must give some form of "new" value),
> (3) who buys from one in the business of selling goods of that kind (that is, cars from a car dealer, i.e., inventory),
> (4) who buys in good faith and without knowledge that this purchase is in violation of others' ownership rights or security interests, and
> (5) who does not buy farm products from a person engaged in farming operations,
> (6) the seller's creditor must part with possession (the issue in the above Problem), and
> (7) the competing security interest must be one "created by the buyer's seller."

PROBLEM 380

Octopus National Bank (ONB) had a perfected security interest in all cars on Smiles Motors' lot. Smiles owed $5,000 in past due insurance premiums to its insurance agent, Howard Teeth, who showed up one morning to buy a new car from Smiles. The president of Smiles first gave Howard a check for $5,000, but Howard endorsed it back over to Smiles when he saw a new car he wanted to buy. Is Howard a §1-201(b)(9) "buyer in the ordinary course of business" so as to take free of ONB's security interest? See Chrysler Credit Corp. v. Malone, 502 S.W.2d 910 (Tex. Civ. App. 1973). If Howard then sold the car, would Howard be liable to ONB for conversion? See In re TXNB Internal Case, 483 F.3d 292 (5th Cir. 2007).

PROBLEM 381

Arthur Greenbaum bought a new car on credit from Lorri's Car City, which took a purchase money security interest in the vehicle, perfecting same by notation of its lien interest on the certificate of title, as required by state law. Arthur was a used car dealer by profession, but he had purchased the car for his own private use. Nonetheless, he frequently parked the car on his lot, and one day sold it for cash to Ann Matheson, a customer in search of a good used car. Arthur did not mention to her that it was his personal car. When everyone learned what had happened, Ann sued Lorri's Car City, demanding that it release the title. What result? See Blue Ridge Bank and Trust Co. v. Hart, 152 S.W.3d 420 (Mo. App. 2005). Would a "benevolent sale of tractors from father to son for less than a quarter of their value" fall within the ordinary course of business? See Sec. Natl. Bank of Sioux City v. Welte, 924 N.W.2d 877 (Iowa Ct. App. 2018).

PROBLEM 382

Wonder Spa, Inc. pledged 50 of its promissory notes to the Conservative State Bank and Trust Company (CSBTC) in return for a loan. The bank took possession of the notes. The spa asked to have ten of the notes back for presentment to the makers for payment, and the bank duly turned over the notes, which Wonder Spa sold (*discounted*) to Octopus National Bank (ONB), a bona fide purchaser without knowledge of CSBTC's interest. This resale was in direct violation of the spa's agreement with CSBTC. Which bank is entitled to the instruments? Read §§9-312(g) and 9-331. Is ONB one of the parties protected by §9-331? See §§3-302 and 3-305.

Subsection (b) to §9-320 appears at first glance to apply to more situations than it really fits. It is meant to cover only a rare transaction: a sale of *consumer goods* by a *consumer* to a *consumer*. This is because the language of the statute clearly requires that the seller have acquired the goods for personal, family, or household purposes (i.e., "consumer goods"), and that the buyer is buying them for the same purposes. White & Summers §25-8(d); Balon v. Cadillac Auto. Co., 113 N.H. 108, 303 A.2d 194 (1973); Everett Natl. Bank v. Deschuiteneer, 109 N.H. 112, 244 A.2d 196 (1968). In such a sale the buyer takes free of the seller's creditor's security interest only if the buyer is both ignorant of it *and* if there is no financing statement on file.

PROBLEM 383

Andy Audio bought a stereo receiver on credit from Voice of Japan, Inc., an electronics store, giving it a purchase money security interest in the receiver. Voice of Japan did not file a financing statement. Six months later, when Andy still owed Voice of Japan $300, he held a garage sale and sold the receiver to Nancy Neighbor for $200 cash. If Andy stops making payments to Voice of Japan, can it repossess the receiver from Nancy? See §9-320(b) and its Official Comment 5.

NOTE

Even though a purchase money security interest in consumer goods is automatically perfected on attachment, per §9-309(1), the above Problem is meant to suggest the wisdom of filing a financing statement in big-ticket consumer transactions (such as the sale of a yacht or a famous painting) lest the creditor suffer the same fate as Voice of Japan when the consumer sells the collateral to another consumer.

PROBLEM 384

The Repossession Finance Company had a perfected (filed) security interest in the equipment of White Truck Ice Cream (WTIC), Inc. (the company sold ice cream from trucks that traveled through the city's neighborhoods). Though technically a corporation, WTIC was in actuality a family business, and Bill White-Truck himself frequently drove one of the trucks. One day while making his rounds, Bill met Frank Family, a consumer who asked about buying an ice cream–making machine for his family. Bill promptly sold him one of the machines the company owned, for which Frank paid cash. When WTIC failed to make its payments, the finance company lived up to its name and repossessed all equipment. When Frank refused to turn over the ice cream machine, Repossession sued him for conversion (a tort that does not require *scienter* or guilty knowledge for its commission). Answer these questions:

(a) Does he lose? Compare §§9-201, 9-401(b), and 9-315(a)(1) and Production Credit Assn. v. Nowatzski, 90 Wis. 2d 344, 280 N.W.2d 118 (1979); Bell Fin. Cmty. Credit Union v. Nagy, 862 N.E.2d 726 (Ind. Ct. App. 2007).

(b) Would we get a different result if the bank's interest were unperfected at the time of the sale? See §9-317(b).

(c) Would we get a different result if the bank knew and approved of the sale? Compare §9-315(a)(1); RFC Capital Corp. v. EarthLink, Inc., 2004 WL 2980402 (Ohio App. 2004).

PROBLEM 385

Paul Pop was a rock singer to whom Octopus National Bank (ONB) loaned $8,000 so he could buy stereo equipment for his road show. On April 2, Paul purchased the equipment, and on April 10, ONB filed its financing statement in the proper place. However, in the interim, on April 8, Paul sold the equipment to Used Stereo Heaven, which bought with no knowledge of the bank's purchase money security interest. Does ONB or Used Stereo Heaven have the superior claim to the equipment? Compare §§2-403, 9-201, and 9-317(e).

PROBLEM 386

When Farmer Bean borrowed a large amount of money from Farmers' Friend Financing Company (FFFC), he was required to sign a security agreement by which he promised not to sell the crop that was the collateral for the loan without the written consent of FFFC. Nonetheless, every year he sold the crop to the same buyer and remitted the proceeds to FFFC without getting its written consent. Does the buyer take free of the security interest of the secured party under §9-320(a)? If FFFC never protested what was going on year after year as the security agreement was violated, can it be said to have *waived* its security interest? Can a security interest be waived? See §9-315(a)(1) and the following famous case.

Clovis National Bank v. Thomas

New Mexico Supreme Court, 1967
77 N.M. 554, 425 P.2d 726

OMAN, J.

This is a suit by plaintiff-appellant for alleged conversion of cattle by defendant-appellee. The parties operate their respective businesses in Clovis, Curry County, New Mexico, and will be referred to as plaintiff and defendant.

In its capacity as a bank, plaintiff, on March 27, 1963, loaned the sum of $8,800 to a Mr. W.D. Bunch. To evidence and secure the indebtedness he gave plaintiff a promissory note and a security agreement by which he granted a security interest in about 46 head of cattle belonging to him and branded "W D Bar." On April 11, 1963, a further security agreement, granting a security interest in 102 head of cattle, was given by him to plaintiff as additional security for the loan of March 27, and as security for additional loans to be made to him by plaintiff from time to time.

On July 29, 1963, he deposited $3,507 with plaintiff. This money represented proceeds from the sale by him of 35 head of cattle covered by the security agreements. $3,300 of this amount was applied by plaintiff on the indebtedness then owing by him.

On October 29, 1963, he deposited with plaintiff the sum of $5,613.17, the total amount of which was applied to his indebtedness, and which amount represented proceeds from the sale by him of 56 head of cattle covered by the security agreements. This deposit consisted of two checks given by defendant, who is a licensed commission house and market agency and as such handled the sale of the cattle for him.

Plaintiff admitted to being aware that Mr. Bunch was making sales of cattle covered by the security agreements.

In about September 1963, he made application to plaintiff for an additional loan with which to purchase additional cattle and with which to carry his cattle through the winter. An investigation was made by plaintiff during September, to determine the feasibility of granting this additional loan. Plaintiff approved the loan, and cattle were acquired by him and paid for by drafts drawn on plaintiff. By November 12, 1963, the additional cattle had been acquired.

On November 12, a new note in the principal amount of $21,500 and a new security agreement covering 283 head of cattle branded W D Bar were given by him to plaintiff to evidence and secure his then indebtedness. This indebtedness in the amount of $21,500 represented $2,007.67 still owing on the original note of March 27, $2,743.10 credited to his checking account on November 12, and amounts loaned or advanced to him during the intervening period. The security agreement was duly recorded in both Curry and Quay counties and in part provided:

> DEBTOR FURTHER REPRESENTS, WARRANTS, AND AGREES THAT: . . .
>
> Without the prior written consent of Secured Party, Debtor will not sell, . . . or otherwise dispose of the collateral. . . .

Thereafter, cattle covered by the November 12 security agreement were consigned to defendant by Mr. Bunch for sale on his behalf at public auction. The plaintiff had no actual knowledge of these sales and had not given any express consent to Mr. Bunch to make the sales. He remitted no part of the proceeds from these sales to the plaintiff for application on his indebtedness. The sales were of 45 head of cattle on February 20, 1964, 95 head on May 14, 1964, and one head on May 21, 1964. The total value of these cattle was $16,450.34, and plaintiff sought recovery from defendant of this amount under the first cause of action of its complaint.

Mr. Bunch has a son by the name of William D. Bunch, Jr., also known as Bill Bunch, Jr., who will be referred to either by name or as the son. The son was the owner of a brand referred to as "Swastika K." Some time prior to July 15, 1964, at least 90 head of cattle were acquired by either Mr. Bunch or his son and were branded Swastika K. There was some evidence tending to show that these cattle, at least to some extent, were actually property of the father. No security agreement was ever given by either the father or the son by which a security interest in cattle branded Swastika K was granted to the plaintiff, unless in some way it can be held that they were covered by the security agreement of November 12.

On July 15, 1964, plaintiff requested that Mr. Bunch sell the remainder of his cattle, including the Swastika K cattle. On the following day, 90 head of Swastika K cattle were trucked to defendant's place of business for sale and were carried on the defendant's records as belonging to Bill Bunch, Jr. Plaintiff knew the cattle were at defendant's place of business to be sold and told defendant that plaintiff claimed some interest in the cattle. Defendant was not told the nature or extent of the claimed interest of plaintiff in these cattle.

The cattle were sold on July 16. Plaintiff was aware of the sale and advised defendant that it would be "nice" if the check in payment for these cattle could be made payable to one or both of the Bunches and to the plaintiff. At no time did the plaintiff demand payment or request that defendant not make payment to Bill Bunch, Jr.

Bill Bunch, Jr., consulted the local brand inspector and solicited his aid in securing payment from the defendant. The brand inspector advised defendant that the Swastika K brand was recorded in the name of Bill Bunch, Jr., and that insofar as the Cattle Sanitary Board was concerned, payment could be made to him.

An attorney also called defendant on behalf of Bill Bunch, Jr., concerning payment for the cattle, and demand was made by Bill Bunch, Jr., upon defendant to pay him the proceeds from the sale of the cattle. This the defendant did on July 22. This payment was in the amount of $7,777.84, which is the amount of plaintiff's claim against defendant under the second cause of action.

On this same date, plaintiff filed suit against W.D. Bunch and William D. Bunch, Jr., wherein plaintiff sought to recover from the father on the note of November 12, and sought to recover from the son the said sum of $7,777.84. In this proceeding plaintiff filed an affidavit in support of an application for a writ of garnishment, wherein it was asserted that the defendant was indebted to William D. Bunch, Jr. No claim was made that the proceeds from the sale belonged to plaintiff, but rather plaintiff asserted that the proceeds belonged to William D. Bunch, Jr., and, as already stated, tried to reach these proceeds by garnishment, which came too late. The present suit was then filed against defendant on August 31, 1964.

The plaintiff asserts thirteen separate points relied upon for reversal. However, the ultimate conclusions upon which the judgment for defendant rests are (1) the plaintiff consented to the sales of W D Bar cattle covered by the security agreement of November 12, and thus waived any possessory rights it may have had in these cattle, and (2) the plaintiff had no perfected security interest in the Swastika K cattle, and failed to prove an unperfected security interest in these cattle of which defendant had knowledge.

Insofar as the sales of the W D Bar cattle are concerned, the trial court found plaintiff, as a matter of common practice, usage and procedure, permitted Mr. Bunch to sell cattle covered by the security agreements of March 27 and April 11, and consented to receipt of the sale proceeds by Mr. Bunch. It also found that plaintiff, by common practice, custom, usage and procedure, permitted and consented to the sales of W D Bar cattle covered by the security agreement of November 12, and permitted and consented to the receipt by Mr. Bunch of the proceeds from these sales.

The trial court concluded that plaintiff had permitted, acquiesced in, and consented to these sales; that by its conduct, plaintiff had waived any possessory rights it may have had in and to these cattle; that defendant did not wrongfully convert cattle in which plaintiff had an enforceable security interest; and that defendant was not responsible for the debtor's failure to remit the proceeds of the sales to plaintiff.

We agree with the findings and conclusions of trial court. Insofar as consent and waiver on behalf of plaintiff are concerned, in addition to the facts recited above, the plaintiff's officers testified that it was the custom and practice of plaintiff to permit a debtor, who has given cattle as collateral, to retain possession and to sell the collateral without ever obtaining prior written consent of plaintiff, and that at no time in its dealings with Mr. Bunch between the time of the making of the note on November 12, 1963, and the sale of cattle on May 21, 1964, did plaintiff demand of him that he obtain prior written consent before making a sale.

It is true there was some testimony that the collateral was not released from the lien until the debtor actually delivered the proceeds of the sale to plaintiff, but, as testified to by one of the plaintiff's officers, the debtor never contacts the plaintiff and secures permission to make a sale, but the sale is made and plaintiff relies upon the debtor to bring the proceeds to plaintiff to be applied on the indebtedness. This practice is followed because 99% of the people with whom plaintiff deals are honest and take care of their obligations.

The general rule of liability of an auctioneer, who sells, in behalf of his principal, property subject to a mortgage lien, is stated as follows in the annotation at 96 A.L.R.2d 208, 212 (1964):

> According to the overwhelming weight of authority, an auctioneer who sells property on behalf of a principal who has not title thereto, or who holds the property subject to a mortgage or other lien, or who for other reasons has no right to sell such property, is personally liable to the true owner or mortgagee for conversion regardless of whether he had knowledge, actual or constructive, of the principal's lack of title or want of authority to sell, in the absence of facts creating an estoppel or showing acquiescence or consent on the part of the true owner or mortgagee. . . .

The trial court, in addition to holding plaintiff had consented to and acquiesced in the sales and had waived his possessory rights in the cattle, concluded plaintiff was estopped from recovery by reason of its conduct. The plaintiff and the amicus curiae have both made strong attacks on this conclusion. We are inclined to agree that the essential elements of an estoppel are lacking. We do not, however, predicate our decision upon estoppel, but rather upon consent and waiver.

The plaintiff, if not expressly consenting to the questioned sales, certainly impliedly acquiesced in and consented thereto. It not only permitted Mr. Bunch, but permitted all its other debtors who granted security interests in cattle, to retain possession of the cattle and to sell the same from time to time as the debtor chose, and it relied upon the honesty of each debtor to bring in the proceeds from his sales to be applied on his indebtedness.

Plaintiff was fully aware of its right to require its written authority to sell or otherwise dispose of the collateral, but it elected to waive this right. Waiver is the intentional abandonment or relinquishment of a known right. Smith v. New York Life Ins. Co., 26 N.M. 408, 193 Pac. 67; Miller v. Phoenix Assur. Co. Ltd., 52 N.M. 68, 191 P.2d 993.

In Farmers' Natl. Bank v. Missouri Livestock Comm. Co., 53 F.2d 991 (8th Cir. 1931), suit was brought by the holder of chattel mortgages for alleged conversion of cattle by a livestock commission house. Although the facts are dissimilar from those of the present case, that case does stand for the principle that consent may be established by implication arising from a course of conduct as well as by express words, and that consent to a sale operates as a waiver of the lien or security interest. See also Moffet Bros. & Andrews Comm. Co. v. Kent, 5 S.W.2d 395 (Mo. 1928).

In First Natl. Bank & Trust Co. v. Stock Yards Loan Co., 65 F.2d 226 (8th Cir. 1933), the effect of a course of conduct on the part of a mortgagee, such as was followed by the mortgagee in that case and such as was followed by plaintiff in the present case, was stated to be:

> . . . When a mortgagee under a chattel mortgage allows the mortgagor to retain possession of the property and to sell the same at will, the mortgagee waives his lien, and this is true whether the purchaser knew of the existence of the chattel mortgage or not.

The fact that plaintiff may have intended that the proceeds from the sales of cattle covered by the security agreements should be remitted to plaintiff by Mr. Bunch for application on his indebtedness did not change the waiver. When plaintiff consented to the sales and the collection of the proceeds of the sales by him, it lost its security interest in the collateral and was then looking to him personally for payment. . . .

The collateral here in question—livestock, falls within the classification of "farm products," and these products are expressly excluded from the classifications of "equipment" and "inventory." Section 9-109(3), N.M.S.A. 1953. By excluding "farm products" from the classifications of "equipment" and "inventory," and by expressly providing in §9-307(1) [now §9-320(a)—EDS.], N.M.S.A. 1953, that a buyer in the ordinary course of business of farm products from a person engaged in farming operations does not take free of a security interest created by the seller, the draftsmen of the code apparently intended "to freeze the agricultural mortgagee into the special status he has achieved under the pre-code case law." 2 Gilmore, Security Interests in Personal Property 714 (1965).

It would only seem logical and consistent that if the buyer from one engaged in farming operations takes subject to the security interest, then the selling agent is subject to the rights of the secured party in the collateral. This is consistent with the foregoing cited authorities. See also United States v. Union Livestock Sales Co., 298 F.2d 755 (4th Cir. 1962); United States v. Matthews, 244 F.2d 626 (9th Cir. 1957).

Section 9-306(2) [now §9-315(a)(1)—EDS.], N.M.S.A. 1953 provides:

> Except where this article otherwise provides, a security interest continues in collateral notwithstanding sale, exchange or other disposition thereof by the debtor unless his action was authorized by the secured party in the security agreement or otherwise, and also continues in any identifiable proceeds including collections received by the debtor.

No section of the code provides otherwise as to farm products. Thus, the holder of the security interest in farm products has the same protection under the code which he had under the pre-code law, and the cattle broker is still liable to the secured party for conversion of the collateral. United States v. Sommerville, 211 F. Supp. 543 (W.D. Pa. 1962), *aff'd on other grounds,* 324 F.2d 712 (3d Cir. 1963), *cert. denied,* 376 U.S. 909 (1964). See also 2 Gilmore, Security Interests in Personal Property 715 (1965).

Also, under the code the secured party may consent to the sale of the collateral, and thereby waive his rights in the same. See Official Comment No. 3, §9-306, and Official Comment No. 2, §9-307 [in the 1999 revision, see Official Comment 2 to §9-315, second paragraph—EDS.]. There being no particular provision of the Code which displaces the law of waiver, and particularly waiver by implied acquiescence or consent, the code provisions are supplemented thereby. Section 1-103, N.M.S.A. 1953. The defendant cannot be held liable for a conversion of the W D Bar cattle, because plaintiff consented to and acquiesced on the sales thereof, and thereby waived its rights in this collateral. . . .

It follows from what has been stated that the judgment should be affirmed. It is so ordered.

CHAVEZ, C.J., and NOBLE and COMPTON, JJ., concur. CARMODY, J. (dissenting). [Omitted.][13]

NOTE

This case and the waiver issue it presents have an uneasy history. The difficulty is created by the rule in §9-320(a) that a buyer in the ordinary course from one selling farm products does not take free of the secured party's interest in the products sold. Why would the Code drafters have done this? The answer lies in the special deference always shown to farmers as debtors.

The importance of farming to our society has created any number of rules favoring agricultural borrowers. It is crucial that financial institutions be encouraged to loan money to farmers, and §9-320(a) is an example of a statute that reflects this policy. If the lenders can follow the collateral into the hands of an innocent buyer, they are more secure and therefore more likely to make the original loan to the farmer. In truth, a farmer's sale of the annual crop is more like an Article 6 *bulk sale* (the sale of a large part of the inventory) than the typical retail sale that §9-320(a) usually covers, so the buyer from a farmer ought to be more careful to make sure that everything is squared with the farmer's lender. On the other hand, §9-320(a) catches all buyers, even auctioneers and commission merchants, and involves them in policing the relationship between the farmer and the bank, and these buyers bitterly resented fulfilling this function.

Where the bank was aware that the farmer was routinely ignoring the security agreement's requirement of written consent, the courts were, like in the *Clovis* case, especially likely to find a waiver of the security interest. Later courts generally (though not always) followed *Clovis*. See the case law summary in Anon, Inc. v. Farmers Prod. Credit Assn., 446 N.E.2d 656 (Ind. App. 1983). Some courts developed a "conditional consent" test whereby the waiver was ineffective unless the condition under which it was made (typically payment of the proceeds to the secured party) was complied with. See, e.g., Baker Prod. Credit Assn. v. Long Creek Meat Co., 97 Or. 1372, 513 P.2d 1129 (1973). Other courts, noting that the bank's "waiver" was

13. The New Mexico legislature responded by amending the UCC to provide that course of dealing or trade usage could not have the effect of waiving a security interest in farm products. The court did not consider the proper definitions in §1-303; had it, would the result have changed? Compare Official Comment 2 to §1-303 with §1-303(f).

really nothing more than the acceptance of a *fait accompli* ("I sold the collateral even though I said I wouldn't; here's the money."), did not permit such a "course of dealing" to override the express selling prohibition of the security agreement. See §1-205(4); Wabasso St. Bank v. Caldwell Packing Co., 251 N.W.2d 321 (Minn. 1976).[14] For the position of revised Article 9 on this issue, see Official Comment 2, second paragraph, to §9-315. Courts are more likely to find a waiver of the security interest in the *collateral* than they are to find a waiver of the right to *proceeds* of the sale, and those are two different issues; see discussion in Peoples Trust & Sav. Bank v. Security Sav. Bank, 815 N.W.2d 744 (Iowa 2012).

The answer of many states to the sale of farm products was to enact a statute creating a system whereby a buyer would take free of the security interest of the farmer's creditor if the buyer first jumped through certain hoops. These statutes proved to be the model for a federal statute that has now replaced them and has completely preempted the farm products exclusion in UCC §9-320(a), §1324 of the Food Security Act of 1985 (hereinafter FSA), 7 U.S.C. §1631. (This statute is in your statute book.) The FSA contemplates the following schema: the security agreement between the farmer and the bank requires the farmer to furnish the bank with a list of prospective buyers of the farm products (see §1631(h)(1)), and the farmer agrees not to sell to anyone else unless the farmer notifies the bank in writing at least seven days before the sale (§1631(h)(2)). The bank then sends a direct notice to the listed buyers informing them of any payment instructions the bank wants to impose; the notice must contain the details mentioned in §1631(e)(1)(A). If the buyers follow the payment instructions, they take free of the bank's security interest (§1631(d) and (e)). In addition to the above, the state may establish a central filing system for the registration of financing statements covering farm products.[15] Buyers then register with the central filing office, which

14. One other matter: Fair or not, it is the rule that no agent of the United States government has actual or apparent authority to waive the government's security interests. United States v. Hughes, 340 F. Supp. 539 (N.D. Miss. 1972). Where the federal government is the farmer's creditor, the courts are quick to find conversion despite the buyer's lack of knowledge; FDIC v. Bowles Livestock Commn. Co., 739 F. Supp. 1364 (D. Neb. 1990). For an informative discussion of the meaning of conversion in Article 9, see Mammoth Cave Prod. Credit Assn. v. Oldham, 569 S.W.2d 833 (Tenn. App. 1977).

15. Nineteen states have central filing systems; see the list at http://www.gipsa.usda.gov/Lawsandregs/cleartitle.html. The financing statement to be filed in the central filing system must be more detailed than the usual one filed under the UCC. See §1631(c)(4) for the definition of effective financing statement, which must include, among other things, the Social Security number of the debtor, the amount of farm products covered, and their location. See Sanford, The Reborn Farm Products Exception Under the Food Security Act of 1985, 20 UCC L.J. 3 (1987). The central filing system indexes these financing statements by four different categories, including *crop year.* See §1631(c)(2). "Attorneys for agricultural lenders have recently found themselves pondering such questions as: What is the 'crop year' of a pig?" Reiley, State Law Responses to the Federal Food Security Act, 20 UCC L.J.

regularly sends them a list of the relevant financing statements concerning the types of farm products they wish to buy. Or the central filing office will respond to buyers' inquiries within 24 hours as to the existence of any financing statements covering farm products they wish to purchase; §1631 (c) (2). If the buyers then obtain either a release or a waiver from the secured parties (or follow their instructions as to payments), the buyers take free of the security interests in the farm products. See White & Summers §25-9.

PROBLEM 387

Farmer Bean borrowed money from Octopus National Bank (ONB), which had him sign a security agreement covering his crops. The security agreement forbade him the right to sell his crops without the written consent of the bank. It also required him to give the bank a list of potential buyers of the crop. Farmer Bean did so. The list was of the five buyers to whom he had sold his crop (or parts thereof) in the past. The bank sent a written notice complying with §1631(e)(1) to each of the listed buyers, telling them that all payments for Farmer Bean's crops should be by check made payable to ONB. One buyer not on the list was Rural Silo, Inc., a grain merchant that contracted to buy all of Farmer Bean's 2016 wheat crop. Rural Silo knew that Farmer Bean had borrowed money from ONB and that ONB had filed a financing statement to perfect its security interest (the state had not created an FSA central filing system). It bought the crop from Farmer Bean and paid him cash for it at his request. Is Rural Silo, which after all knew all about ONB's security interest, a *buyer in the ordinary course* as defined in §1631(c)(1)? See Lisco State Bank v. McCombs Ranches, Inc., 752 F. Supp. 329 (D. Neb. 1990); Ashburn Bank v. Farr, 206 Ga. App. 517, 426 S.E.2d 63 (1992). Does Rural Silo take free of the bank's security interest? See §1631(d). Does the bank have any other remedy here? See §1631(h)(3).

Farm Credit Bank of St. Paul v. F&A Dairy

Wisconsin Court of Appeals, 1991
165 Wis. 2d 360, 477 N.W.2d 357

CANE, J.

F&A Dairy (the dairy) appeals a judgment in favor of Farm Credit Bank of St. Paul for conversion of secured farm property. The dairy raises

260 (1988). The regulations adopted pursuant to the Act have shed some light on this and other mysteries; see 9 C.F.R. §205.107 (*crop year* of an animal is the year in which it is born or acquired).

four issues on appeal: (1) The trial court erred by basing its decision on §9-307, in contravention of 7 U.S.C. §1631 (1988), which the dairy claims preempts state law; (2) the dairy took free and clear of the bank's security interest because the bank did not meet the notice requirements of §1631; (3) the bank was not in possession or entitled to immediate possession of the secured property and, thus, could not maintain an action for conversion; and (4) the trial court's decision was unfair, inequitable and contrary to the policy behind §1631. . . .

John and Barbara Bonneprise own and operate a dairy farm. The Bonneprises borrowed $300,000 from Farm Credit Bank of St. Paul. As collateral for the loan, the bank obtained and perfected a security interest covering the Bonneprises' milk and all accounts arising from the sale or other disposition of their milk and milk products. The Bonneprises were selling milk to Land O' Lakes Dairy. In return for waiver of its lien, the bank executed an assignment with Land O' Lakes and the Bonneprises whereby Land O' Lakes would pay the bank $4,333 per month from the Bonneprises' milk proceeds.

In August 1988, the Bonneprises switched dairies and began selling their milk to F&A Dairy. After the bank received no payment in August, it found out that the Bonneprises had switched dairies. The Bonneprises refused to make an assignment directing the dairy to make payments to the bank. By letter dated August 22, 1988, the bank notified the dairy of its previous assignment with Land O' Lakes and demanded payments of $4,333 in accordance with the assignment. Also, the bank enclosed a copy of the assignment, a product lien notification statement and a copy of its financing statement filed in accordance with the UCC. Four days later the bank notified the dairy of its perfected security interest in the Bonneprises' milk and all accounts arising from the sale or other disposition of their milk and milk products and enclosed a copy of the security agreement.

The dairy refused to pay the bank $4,333 per month for milk sales during August, September, October and November.[16] The reasons it gave for not paying the bank were that there was no assignment between the bank, the Bonneprises and the dairy, and that John Bonneprise directed it to pay him and not the bank. Each of these months' sales to the dairy exceeded $4,333.

The trial court found that the bank had an effective perfected security interest covering the sale of the Bonneprises' milk to the dairy. It also found that the Bonneprises defaulted on their payments to the bank in August 1988, and, therefore, the bank was entitled to immediate possession

16. The milk sales from December 1988 and following are not in issue because they were placed in escrow.

of the secured property. The trial court concluded that the dairy bought the Bonneprises' milk subject to the bank's security interest under §1631 because the bank met the §1631 notice requirements. It further concluded that the dairy was guilty of converting the sum of $4,333 per month during September, October, November, and December (constituting proceeds from the August, September, October, and November milk sales), totaling $17,332. The trial court entered judgment in the amount plus 5% interest from the date of conversion to the date of judgment, and costs.

PREEMPTION

[The court concluded that 7 U.S.C. §1631 (Food Security Act) preempted what is now §9-320(a).]

APPLICATION OF 7 U.S.C. §1631

Next, we address whether the dairy purchased the Bonneprises' milk subject to or free of the bank's security interest, under §1631. The application of a statute to a particular set of facts is a question of law that we review de novo. Cleaver v. DOR, 158 Wis. 2d 734, 738, 463 N.W.2d 349, 351 (1990).

Section 1631(d) provides that a buyer of farm products takes free of a security interest except as provided in §1631(*e*). Subsection 1631(*e*) provides in part:

> *(e) Purchases subject to security interest*
> A buyer of farm products takes subject to a security interest created by the seller if—
> (1)(A) within 1 year before the sale of the farm products, the buyer has received from the secured party . . . written notice of the security interest organized according to farm products that—
> (i) is an original or reproduced copy thereof;
> (ii) contains,
> (I) the name and address of the secured party;
> (II) the name and address of the person indebted to the secured party;
> (III) the social security number of the debtor . . .;
> (IV) a description of the farm products subject to the security interest created by the debtor . . .; and . . .
> (V) [contains] any payment obligations imposed on the buyer by the secured party as conditions for waiver or release of the security interest; and
> (B) the buyer has failed to perform the payment obligations. . . .
> (Footnote omitted.)

If the bank has met the §1631(e) notice requirements, including notice of any payment obligation, and the dairy failed to perform the payment obligations, it purchased the milk from the Bonneprises subject to the bank's security interest.

Here, the bank sent letters and documents to the dairy containing a copy of the security agreement creating the security interest in the milk and accounts from its sale, the bank's name and address, the Bonneprises' names and address, John Bonneprise's social security number and a reasonable description of the secured property and where it was located. It also demanded the monthly sum of $4,333.

The dairy argues that the bank did not meet the "payment obligation" notice requirement because its payment obligation was ambiguous. We disagree. Under its perfected security interest and by giving proper notice under §1631(e), the bank was entitled to receive all proceeds from the sale of the Bonneprises' milk, not merely the payment amount of $4,333. See Miracle Feeds, Inc. v. Attica Dairy Farm, 129 Wis. 2d 377, 385 N.W.2d 208 (Ct. App. 1986). The requirement of giving notice of "any payment obligations" is merely to allow the bank, if it wishes, to accept a lesser amount of milk sale proceeds and to waive its lien for the balance of the proceeds. The bank's documents and letters sent to the dairy provide sufficient notice that it had a lien on the Bonneprises' milk and proceeds from its sale, and that it demanded payment of $4,333 per month as a waiver of its lien.

The dairy also argues that the bank's payment obligation notice required an assignment from the Bonneprises directing it to pay a specific amount to the bank because the lien notification statement sent to the dairy referred to such an assignment. It further argues that because there was no such assignment, the notice requirements of §1631(e) are not met and it therefore takes free of the bank's security interest.

Subsection (e) does not require an assignment to be filed with the buyer. Although the bank's lien notification statement arguably requires such an assignment, the lack of an assignment does not allow the dairy to take free of the bank's security interest. If we were to view only the lien notification statement without an assignment, arguably the bank would be entitled to all proceeds from the milk sales because there would be no payment obligation for waiver of its lien. However, reviewing the correspondence and documents sent to the dairy, the only reasonable construction is that the bank was demanding payment of $4,333 per month in lieu of receiving the Bonneprises' milk and all proceeds arising from its sale. Thus, we hold that the bank adequately informed the dairy of "any payment obligations . . . as conditions for waiver" under §1631(e).

Section 1631(e) requires that the notice be given within one year before the sale of the farm products. The bank's notice was given in late August. The Bonneprises began selling their milk to the dairy earlier in August.

Thus, the notice was given before the September, October, and November sales, but not before the August sales. Consequently, we hold that the bank's notice was timely only as to the September, October, and November milk sales, covering the October, November, and December proceeds. We therefore reverse that portion of the judgment pertaining to the August milk sales and September proceeds.

In addition to proper notice, §1631(e) requires that the buyer failed to perform the payment obligations of the secured party. At no time did the dairy make a payment of $4,333, or any other amount, to the bank. Thus, we conclude that the dairy, having proper notice of the bank's security interest and payment obligations as conditions for waiver for the September, October, and November milk sales, failed to comply with those payment obligations. Consequently, the bank met all the requirements of §1631(e), and the dairy takes subject to the bank's security interest.

CONVERSION

Next, the dairy contends that the bank cannot succeed on its action for conversion because it was not in possession or entitled to immediate possession of the secured property, and because it did not allege in the complaint that the Bonneprises defaulted on their loan. The issue of whether a particular set of facts fulfill a particular legal standard is a question of law that we review de novo. State v. Trudeau, 139 Wis. 2d 91, 103, 408 N.W.2d 337, 342 (1987). An action for conversion is the proper means for a secured party to enforce its security interest against a transferee. United States v. Fullpail Cattle Sales, 640 F. Supp. 976, 980 (E.D. Wis. 1986) (applying state law). Conversion is the wrongful or unauthorized exercise of dominion or control over a chattel. PCA v. Equity Coop Livestock Sales Assn., 82 Wis. 2d 5, 10, 261 N.W.2d 127, 129 (1978). A plaintiff in a conversion action must prove that he was in possession of or entitled to immediate possession of the chattel that was converted. Id.

The bank did not receive the August payment from the Bonneprises' milk sales. Thus, as of August, the Bonneprises were in default on their payments and, under §9-503 [now §9-609—EDS.], the bank had the right to immediate possession of the secured property. The bank established that the Bonneprises had defaulted on their required payments from August through December. Thus, we conclude that the bank was entitled to immediate possession of the Bonneprises' milk proceeds, and the dairy wrongly exercised control over them by not giving the required proceeds to the bank. . . .

Because we conclude that 7 U.S.C. §1631 preempts §9-307, and §1631 applies to the facts in this case, we need not consider the dairy's argument that the trial court's decision was contrary to equity, fairness and the policy behind §1631. Therefore, we hold that the bank is entitled to recover the proceeds from milk sales in September, October, and November, plus interest. The matter is therefore remanded to the trial court to modify the judgment consistent with this opinion.

By the Court—Judgment affirmed in part; reversed in part and cause remanded with directions. No costs to either party.

PROBLEM 388

Mr. and Mrs. Halyard purchased a large sailboat with money borrowed from the Boilerplate National Bank (BNB), which took a security interest therein and promptly filed a financing statement in the proper place. The Halyards sold the boat to Oil Slick Boat Sales, Inc., a used boat concern, telling Oil Slick of the bank's interest and of the necessity of making monthly payments to the bank. Oil Slick turned around and resold the boat to Mr. and Mrs. Blink, innocent people who paid full value for the boat believing Oil Slick had clear title. When BNB did not receive its usual monthly payment, it investigated, found the boat, and repossessed it. Has the Blinks' property been converted, or don't they fit into §9-320(a)? Element Fin. Corp. v. Marcinkoski Gradall, Inc., 2017 WL 1175879 (Fla. Dist. Ct. App. Mar. 29, 2017). What does "created by the buyer's seller" mean in §9-320(a)? See White & Summers §25-8(b). Does Article 2's "entrusting" rule, §2-403, help the Blinks? What is §2-403's relationship with Article 9? See White & Summers §25-8(c); Conseco Finance Servicing Corp. v. Lee, 2004 WL 1243417 (Tex. App. 2004). The "created by the buyer's seller" language will often cause trouble for buyers buying goods from a used merchandise dealer. Why would the drafters have favored the original creditor in this situation over a buyer in the ordinary course? If the Blinks lose this lawsuit, whom should they sue, and what is their theory? See §2-312. Can Oil Slick use the same theory against the Halyards?

V. LEASES

In resolving the Problems that follow, it should be noted that according to §2A-103(1)(j) (defining *lease*): "Unless the context clearly indicates otherwise, the term includes a sublease."

PROBLEM 389

The Highbid Construction Company gave a security interest to Octopus National Bank (ONB) in all of its construction equipment "now owned or after-acquired." ONB filed a financing statement in the proper place. Two years later, Highbid was in the middle of an enormous construction project at Football University when a number of its key employees quit, leaving it very short-staffed. To avoid breach of contract, it became necessary to farm out the project to someone else, though Highbid had never done this before. The president of Highbid reached an agreement with Newcomer Construction Company, one of its subcontractors on the Football University job, by which Highbid would lease all of its construction equipment to Newcomer for the length of the Football University project so that Newcomer could finish the job for Highbid. Use the rules of Article 2A to answer the following question: Is the lessee subject to ONB's existing security interest in the equipment? See §§2A-307, 2A-103(1)(o), 9-321(c).

PROBLEM 390

When the Football University project was completed, the lease described in the last Problem ended, and the machinery was returned by the lessee to Highbid Construction Company. Things were going so well for Highbid that it was able to pay off all of its loans in full and free all of its assets from the security interests that had encumbered them. Highbid's lawyer advised the company that for both tax and accounting reasons it would be better if Highbid leased the new grading machine that it had recently purchased rather than owning it outright. To accomplish this, Highbid's attorney worked out a deal by which Octopus National Bank (ONB) would purchase the grading machine from Highbid and then lease it back to Highbid. The term of the lease was exactly equal to the useful life of the grading machine.

Two months after this arrangement had come into being, Highbid's president absconded with the company's liquid assets, leaving the company in bad financial shape and needing to borrow some money. ONB refused to advance further funds, so Highbid looked elsewhere. The new president of Highbid went to Antitrust National Bank (ANB) and sought a loan, offering the grading machine as collateral. He was able to produce a bill of sale showing that Highbid had purchased the grading machine a mere three months ago when it was involved in the Football University contract. He did not tell ANB about the subsequent sale and leaseback arrangement that Highbid had with ONB. After ANB checked the public records and found no evidence of a security interest in the grading machine, it had Highbid sign the necessary Article 9 documents and a promissory note, loaned the money, and filed its financing statement in the appropriate place.

When Highbid defaulted on its lease payments, ONB repossessed the grading machine, at which point ANB claimed the superior interest therein.

ANB's attorney argued that ONB was a party to fraud in that the sale and leaseback helped Highbid create the false appearance of assets.

How does this come out? See §§2A-307, 2A-308(3), and 1-203, and compare §2-402(2) in Article 2. Would you reach the same result if the lease agreement between Highbid and ONB provided the lessee with a right of termination at any time?

VI. ARTICLE 2 CLAIMANTS

PROBLEM 391

Jack Gladhand was a traveling salesman dealing in many kinds of office supplies. He needed new luggage to carry his samples and bought a set from Alligator Fashions, which reserved a security interest therein and filed a financing statement. A month later, in the middle of a hot sales deal, Jack sold all of his samples and the luggage to Mark Impulse, a compulsive buyer. Jack told Mark (who paid cash for the goods) that the luggage was genuine alligator (a lie—he knew it was lizard). When Mark discovered the truth, he revoked his acceptance of the goods pursuant to §2-608 and claimed a security interest in the goods. Read §2-711(3). On learning of Jack's resale to Mark and of the latter's revocation of acceptance, Alligator Fashions decided to call the loan and repossess the luggage. Who is entitled to the luggage? See §9-110.

The rights of an unpaid seller are governed by both Article 2 and Article 9. If the seller gets a security agreement covering the item sold, a purchase money security interest (§9-103) arises, and Article 9 handles the priority in §9-324(a) and (b). If the seller extends credit to the buyer but fails to reserve a security interest, §2-702 applies. Finally, if the buyer gets the goods and pays with a check that is then dishonored (NSF—not sufficient funds), the seller's rights are governed by §§2-403, 2-507, and 2-511 (which you should now read), not by §2-702.

PROBLEM 392

Guy Baldwin was a successful author who decided to self-publish his latest book and market it directly to retailers. He received an order for 200 copies from Cowskin Book Chain, and he shipped off the books immediately, along with an invoice for their price. Two days later, he learned that Cowskin was hopelessly insolvent and unable to pay any creditors. What can he do? See §2-702. Suppose that two weeks before he shipped the books, Cowskin had sent him a letter lying about its financial condition; now how long does he have to make his reclamation demand? If he gets the books back, can he sue Cowskin for the wasted shipping costs? See §2-702(3). If Cowskin's inventory was subject to a perfected security interest in favor of a bank, which thereby had a floating lien on the inventory, could he still reclaim the books? See §§2-702(3) and 2-403(1); In re Nitram, Inc., 323 B.R. 792 (Bankr. M.D. Fla. 2005). Note that the definition of a *purchaser* in §1-201(b)(29) and (30) includes any voluntary transferee, which would encompass secured parties. What should Baldwin have done? See §9-324(b).

If, in the last Problem, the buyer had filed a bankruptcy petition shortly before receiving the books, Bankruptcy Code §546(c) might allow him to recover the books from the bankruptcy trustee:

> (1) Except as provided in subsection (d) of this section and in section 507(c), and subject to the prior rights of a holder of a security interest in such goods or the proceeds thereof, the rights and powers of the trustee under sections 544(a), 545, 547, and 549 are subject to the right of a seller of goods that has sold goods to the debtor, in the ordinary course of such seller's business, to reclaim such goods if the debtor has received such goods while insolvent, within 45 days before the date of the commencement of a case under this title, but such seller may not reclaim such goods unless such seller demands in writing reclamation of such goods—
>
> (A) not later than 45 days after the date of receipt of such goods by the debtor; or
>
> (B) not later than 20 days after the date of commencement of the case, if the 45-day period expires after the commencement of the case.
>
> (2) If a seller of goods fails to provide notice in the manner described in paragraph (1), the seller still may assert the rights contained in section 503(b)(9).

In re Arlco, Inc.

United States Bankruptcy Court, Southern District of New York, 1999
239 B.R. 261

ARTHUR J. GONZALEZ, Bankruptcy Judge.

On June 6, 1997, Arley Corporation ("Arley") and Home Fashions Outlet, Inc. ("Home Fashions" and together with Arley, the "Debtors") each filed a petition under chapter 11 of title 11 of the United States Code (the "Bankruptcy Code"). Arley was engaged in the business of manufacturing, importing, and wholesaling home furnishings, window coverings, bedcoverings, and linens which were sold to retailers, one of which was Home Fashions, Arley's wholly-owned subsidiary. Home Fashions operated retail outlet stores in Massachusetts and California. In addition, the Debtors maintained business and corporate offices, a showroom, and a design facility in New York. They also maintained business offices in Massachusetts and manufacturing facilities in Massachusetts, North Carolina, South Carolina, and California.

On September 15, 1997, pursuant to 11 U.S.C. §363, the Court approved an asset purchase agreement for the sale of substantially all of the Debtors' assets as a going concern. The asset purchase agreement included a requirement that the Debtors change their corporate names contemporaneously with the closing of the sale transaction. Thus, Arley changed its name to Arlco, Inc. and Home Fashions changed its name to HFO, Inc. On August 6, 1998, the Debtors' chapter 11 cases were converted to chapter 7. Thereafter, Robert Fisher, Esq. was appointed as chapter 7 trustee (the "Trustee").

Galey & Lord, Inc. ("Galey") is a fabric manufacturer. Prior to the filing of the Debtors' petitions, Galey, in its ordinary course of business, sold textile goods on credit to Arley. On May 16, 1997, Galey sent a letter to Arley by fax, overnight courier, and certified mail (the "May 16th Letter") demanding that Arley return the merchandise it "received during the applicable periods referred to in [§2-702 of the Uniform Commercial Code]" and notifying Arley that "all goods subject to [Galey's] right of reclamation should be protected and segregated by [Arley] and are not to be used for any purpose whatsoever." Subsequently, on May 21, 1997, Galey sent the Debtor an additional notice detailing each invoice issued to Arley within the 10-day period prior to May 16, 1997 for the goods allegedly subject to reclamation. Since early 1995, CIT Group/Business Credit Inc. ("CIT") has held a perfected security interest in substantially all Arley's assets, including accounts receivable and inventory.

On June 9, 1997, prior to the sale of the Debtors' assets, Galey commenced an adversary proceeding against Arley seeking reclamation of the textile goods referred to in the May 16th Letter. On June 11, 1997, Galey filed an Amended Complaint. Currently before the Court are motions for summary judgment filed by Galey and by the Trustee, respectively.

In its summary judgment motion, Galey maintains that it has complied with all the statutory requirements for establishing a valid claim for reclamation. The Trustee refutes Galey's contention and opposes entry of summary judgment in favor of Galey. Rather, the Trustee maintains that his arguments support entry of summary judgment in Arley's favor. The three principal reasons advanced by the Trustee in opposition to Galey's motion and in support of his own motion are that 1) the reclamation notice was legally deficient, 2) Galey failed to prove what goods Arley still had on hand when

Galey made its demand, and 3) Galey's right to reclamation is subject to CIT's perfected security interest. In addition, Arley contends that there are factual disputes that preclude entry of summary judgment in favor of Galey.

DISCUSSION

The purpose of 11 U.S.C. §546(c) is to recognize any right to reclamation that a seller may have under applicable nonbankruptcy law. In re Victory Markets Inc., 212 B.R. 738, 741 (Bankr. N.D.N.Y. 1997). Section 546(c) does not create a new, independent right to reclamation but merely affords the seller an opportunity, with certain limitations, to avail itself of any reclamation right it may have under nonbankruptcy law. Id.; Toshiba America, Inc. v. Video King of Illinois, Inc. (In re Video King of Illinois, Inc.), 100 B.R. 1008, 1013 (Bankr. N.D. Ill. 1989). Pursuant to §546(c), a seller may reclaim goods it has sold to an insolvent debtor if it establishes:

(1) that it has a statutory or common law right to reclaim the goods;
(2) that the goods were sold in the ordinary course of the seller's business;
(3) that the debtor was insolvent at the time the goods were received; and
(4) that it made a written demand for reclamation within the statutory time limit after the debtor received the goods.

Victory Markets, 212 B.R. at 741. The reclaiming seller has the burden of establishing each element of §546(c) by a preponderance of the evidence. *Victory Markets,* 212 B.R. at 741. Thus, in addition to establishing the requirements necessary to obtain reclamation under common law or any statutory right for such relief, the seller seeking reclamation under §546(c) must prove that it sold the goods in the ordinary course of business and it made a written demand within ten days of the receipt of the goods. Pester Refining Co. v. Ethyl Corp. (In re Pester Refining Co.), 964 F.2d 842, 845 (8th Cir. 1992). Moreover, Bankruptcy Code §546(c) limits the definition of insolvency to that found in 11 U.S.C. §101(31). *Video King,* 100 B.R. at 1013.

In addition, to be subject to reclamation, goods must be identifiable and cannot have been processed into other products. Party Packing Corporation v. Rosenberg (In re Landy Beef Co., Inc.), 30 B.R. 19, 21 (Bankr. D. Mass. 1983). It has also been noted that "an implicit requirement of a §546(c) reclamation claim is that the debtor must possess the goods when the reclamation demand is made." Flav-O-Rich, Inc. v. Rawson Food Service, Inc. (In re Rawson Food Service, Inc.), 846 F.2d 1343, 1344 (11th Cir. 1988). . . . However, it is not clear "whether possession is an element under §546(c) of the Bankruptcy Code or in establishing an independent right of reclamation under nonbankruptcy law to be recognized under §546(c)." *Video King,* 100 B.R. at 1014. Logic dictates that, if not possession, the debtor should at least have control over the goods if it is to be required to return them. For the same reason, if the goods are not identifiable, the debtor could not identify or extract the goods to return them to the reclaiming seller. The issue concerning control of the goods or the identifiable nature of the goods would be relevant whether or not the reclaiming seller is seeking the goods in a bankruptcy context. Thus, it appears that these elements are requirements under the "independent right of reclamation under non-bankruptcy law." *Video King,* 100 B.R. at 1014.

Section 546(c) also affords the bankruptcy court broad discretion to substitute an administrative claim or lien in place of the right to reclaim. *Pester,* 964 F.2d at 845. This discretion gives the court needed flexibility and permits it to recognize the reclaiming creditor's rights while allowing the debtor the opportunity to retain the goods in order to facilitate the reorganization effort. Id.

Uniform Commercial Code ("U.C.C.") §2-702, as enacted in various jurisdictions, ordinarily forms the statutory right upon which sellers base their reclamation demand. Thus, as previously noted, the reclaiming seller must establish the requirements of the relevant U.C.C. section and remains subject to its limitations. Pursuant to U.C.C. §2-702(3), the seller's right to reclamation is "subject to" the rights of a good faith purchaser from the buyer. *Pester,* 964 F.2d at 844. . . . That the right of a reclaiming creditor is subordinate to that of a good faith purchaser does not automatically extinguish the reclamation right. *Pester,* 964 F.2d at 846. Rather, the reclaiming creditor is "relegated to some less commanding station." *Leeds,* 141 B.R. at 268.

Most courts have treated "a holder of a prior perfected, floating lien on inventory . . . as a good faith purchaser with rights superior to those of a reclaiming seller." See *Victory Markets,* 212 B.R. at 742 [many citations omitted]. Galey argues that the courts that have found parties with secured interests in inventory to be good faith purchasers have merely referred to the definitions of good faith purchaser under the U.C.C. §1-201(19), (32), and (33). Galey contends that because U.C.C. §2-702(3) refers to the reclaiming seller's interest as being subject to the interest of a good faith purchaser "under this Article," only parties acquiring their interests under Article 2 of the U.C.C. are the type of good faith purchasers encompassed within the protection of U.C.C. §2-702(3). Therefore, Galey contends that parties acquiring security interests under Article 9 of the U.C.C. are not included. Galey also points to the Seventh Circuit decision in In re Reliable Drug Stores, Inc., where the court, in dicta, noted that there was room for debate as to whether a party with a security interest qualified as a good faith purchaser. 70 F.3d 948, 949 (7th Cir. 1995).

U.C.C. §2-702(3) provides that the right to reclamation is "subject to the rights of a buyer in ordinary course or other good faith purchaser under this Article (Section 2-403)." However, neither U.C.C. §2-403 nor any other section in Article 2 defines "good faith purchaser." U.C.C. §2-403 is entitled

"Power to Transfer; Good Faith Purchase of Goods; Entrusting" and concerns the power certain parties have to transfer goods and the rights of certain parties who acquire those goods. While the section makes reference to these various parties, it does not define who they are. In fact, the only definition provided in U.C.C. §2-403 is of the term "entrusting." To derive the definition of "good faith purchaser," reference must be made to several subsections of U.C.C. §1-201, which provides general definitions applicable to the entire U.C.C. First, "good faith" is defined as "honesty in fact in the conduct or transaction concerned." U.C.C. §1-201(19). This is further refined when dealing with a merchant because U.C.C. §2-103(1)(b) requires the "observance of reasonable commercial standards of fair dealing in the trade." A "purchaser" is defined as one "who takes by purchase," U.C.C. §1-201(33), and "purchase" is defined to include "taking by sale, discount, negotiation, mortgage, pledge, lien, issue or re-issue, gift or any other voluntary transaction creating an interest in property." U.C.C. §1-201(32). Thus, the definition of purchaser is broad enough to include an Article 9 secured party, which then qualifies as a purchaser under U.C.C. §2-403. See *Samuels & Co.,* 526 F.2d at 1242. The reference in U.C.C. §2-702(3) to "the rights of a buyer in ordinary course or other good faith purchaser under this Article (Section 2-403)" does not mean to imply that reclaiming sellers are only subject to interests acquired under Article 2. Rather, the focus is on the rights of the listed parties under Article 2. Under this reading, the purpose for the reference to U.C.C. §2-403 is clear. U.C.C. §2-403 provides, in part, that "[a] person with voidable title has power to transfer a good title to a good faith purchaser for value." As included in the U.C.C. §1-201(44) definition, "value" is considered to be given for rights if they are acquired "as security for or in total or partial satisfaction of a pre-existing claim." Thus, under Article 2—specifically U.C.C. §2-403—the party who qualifies as a "good faith purchaser" as defined under U.C.C. §1-201 and gives "value," as defined in U.C.C. §1-201(44), acquires greater rights than the party transferring the goods to it had. Therefore, U.C.C. §2-403 gives a transferor, even one who has acquired goods wrongfully, the power to transfer the goods "to a Code-defined 'good faith purchaser.'" *Samuels & Co.,* 526 F.2d at 1242. Thus, in the instant case, if CIT qualifies as a good faith purchaser pursuant to U.C.C. §1-201 and gave value pursuant to U.C.C. §1-201(44), then pursuant to U.C.C. §2-403, even if Arley had voidable title to the goods, it could transfer good title under Article 2 to CIT. Further, if CIT obtained the goods in this manner, the demand of a reclaiming seller is subject to CIT's interest. U.C.C. §2-702(3). . . .

Galey also directs the Court's attention to dicta in *Reliable Drug,* 70 F.3d at 949-50, where the court noted that, although there was substantial case law holding that properly perfected lienholders were good faith purchasers, legal scholars debated the issue. The *Reliable Drug* court observed that one view was that "[U.C.C. §2-702(2)] gives a vendor the rights of a purchase-money security holder for 10 days, and the purchase-money lender undoubtedly beats a creditor with a security interest in after-acquired inventory." Id. at 950 (citing Thomas A. Jackson & Ellen Ash Peters, Quest for Uncertainty: A Proposal for Flexible Resolution of Inherent Conflicts Between Article 2 and Article 9 of the Uniform Commercial Code, 87 Yale L.J. 907, 965-70 (1977-78)). The law review article is premised on the view that a party with a security interest should only be considered a good faith purchaser for value if it has suffered detrimental reliance by extending new value. The authors of the article acknowledge that a prior secured lender with an after-acquired property interest "meets the apparently literal requirements of a good faith purchaser for value." 87 Yale L.J. at 965. Nevertheless, they argue that the "open-ended" language of U.C.C. §2-403, a comment to the section, and "the pervasive weighing of equities in Article 2" should "justify relying on [a] more flexible approach." 87 Yale L.J. at 966, 968.

However, if the language of a statute is plain, the court's role "is to enforce it according to its terms." U.S. v. Ron Pair Enterprises, Inc., 489 U.S. 235, 241, 109 S. Ct. 1026, 1030, 103 L. Ed. 2d 290 (1989). The Uniform Commercial Code includes "value" as being given for goods if they are acquired "as security for or in total or partial satisfaction of a pre-existing claim." U.C.C. §1-201(44). The state legislature is the appropriate forum to address the issue of whether or not the statute should be amended to allow a reclaiming seller priority against a prior secured lender with an after-acquired property interest who has not advanced new funding. However, this Court is required to interpret the statute as written and, based on our earlier analysis of the relevant sections of the Uniform Commercial Code as currently drafted, a creditor with a security interest in after-acquired property who acted in good faith and for value, which includes acquiring rights "as security for or in total or partial satisfaction of a pre-existing claim," U.C.C. §1-201(44), is a good faith purchaser to whose claim that of a reclaiming seller is subject.

The Court now turns to whether CIT acted in good faith. The U.C.C. definition of good faith is "honesty in fact," U.C.C. §1-201(19), which "for Article Two purposes, is 'expressly defined as . . . reasonable commercial standards of fair dealing.'" *Samuels & Co.*, 526 F.2d 1238 (5th Cir. 1976) (citing U.C.C. §§1-201, Comment 19; 2-103(a)(2)).

Galey argues that a determination as to CIT's good faith cannot be made on summary judgment because there is a factual issue as to CIT's good faith. However, Galey has not challenged the validity of the lien nor has it asserted that there was any misconduct by CIT. Neither has it alleged that CIT acted in bad faith in its dealings with Arley. Rather, Galey argues that CIT was aware that Arley was having financial problems and stopped advancing funds to Arley without informing Galey of its decision. Therefore it appears that Galey's argument is that Arley was aware that other creditors would be impacted by its decision to stop funding Arley.

However, the secured creditor with a floating lien remains a good faith purchaser even if it terminates funding with knowledge that sums are owed to third parties, as long as the decision concerning the funding was commercially reasonable. *Samuels,* 526 F.2d at 1244. There is no allegation that the contract obligated CIT to advance any additional funds. The "honesty in fact" element does not require a secured creditor to continue to fund a business with enormous debt and continuous losses. Id.; Mitsubishi Consumer Electronics America, Inc. v. Steinberg's, Inc. (In re Steinberg's, Inc.), 226 B.R. 8, 11 (Bankr. S.D. Ohio 1998). Rather, a decision to stop funding such an enterprise is "clearly reasonable." *Samuels,* 526 F.2d at 1244. An entity that advances funds secured by a valid lien on all the borrower's assets is a good faith purchaser absent a showing of misconduct by the secured creditor. Pillsbury Co. v. FCX, Inc. (In re FCX, Inc.), 62 B.R. 315, 320 (Bankr. E.D.N.C. 1986). The burden is on the reclaiming seller to show misconduct by the secured creditor. *FCX, Inc.,* 62 B.R. at 322. Some courts have framed the issue as an absence of bad faith. *Victory Markets,* 212 B.R. at 742 (citing cases). Others as the secured creditor's lack of good faith. *Steinberg's Inc.,* 226 B.R. at 11 (citing cases). Under any formulation, the reclaiming seller bears the burden of proof under §546(c). Id.; *Victory Markets,* 212 B.R. at 741. . . .

Galey's conclusory assertions concerning the absence of good faith by CIT are not sufficient to create the fair doubt required to show that the issue is genuine. Galey makes no allegation of misconduct by CIT in its negotiations with Arley or in its compliance with the terms of the financing agreement with Arley. CIT has not set forth any basis upon which to question CIT's good faith. Thus, there is no genuine issue of material fact concerning whether CIT acted in good faith. Moreover, there is no factual dispute on the issue of whether CIT gave value and qualifies as a good faith purchaser for value, pursuant to the Code's definitions of the various terms. Therefore, the Court grants summary judgment on the issue and finds that CIT qualifies as a good faith purchaser for value.

As previously noted, while a seller's right to reclamation is subject to the rights of a good faith purchaser, the reclamation right is not automatically extinguished. Relying on this principle, Galey argues that, pursuant to §546, it is entitled to either an administrative claim or lien in lieu of its right to reclamation. Galey maintains that if it is denied this relief, its claim effectively is extinguished by the presence of a good faith purchaser. Further, Galey contends that because there will be surplus collateral once CIT has been paid in full, that collateral should be used to pay Galey's reclamation claim and it should get its administrative claim or lien on that surplus.

The Trustee counters that it is not arguing that a reclaiming seller's claim is extinguished. Rather, the Trustee argues that when the goods subject to a reclamation demand are liquidated and the proceeds are used to pay the secured creditor's claim, the reclaiming seller's subordinated right is rendered valueless. The Trustee maintains that once the secured creditor is paid in full, the reclaiming seller is only entitled to reclamation when the surplus collateral remaining consists of the very goods sold by the reclaiming seller or the traceable proceeds from those goods.

Courts differ on the treatment to be afforded reclaiming sellers subject to the superior rights of good faith purchasers. Some courts have awarded a reclaiming seller, who otherwise meets the criteria to qualify as a reclaiming seller but is subject to a superior claim, an administrative claim or replacement lien for the full amount of the goods sought to be reclaimed. *Sunstate Dairy,* 145 B.R. at 345-46; In re Diversified Food Service Distributors, Inc., 130 B.R. 427, 430 (Bankr. S.D.N.Y. 1991). However, the majority view appears to be some method of assuring that the reclaiming seller only receive what it would have received outside of the bankruptcy context after the superior claim was satisfied. *Pester,* 964 F.2d at 847; *Leeds,* 141 B.R. at 269; *Blinn,* 164 B.R. at 448; *Victory Markets,* 212 B.R. at 744. Thus, it is only when the reclaiming seller's goods or traceable proceeds from those goods are in excess of the value of the superior claimant's claim that the reclaiming seller will be allowed either to reclaim the goods or receive an administrative claim or lien in an amount equal to the goods that remain after the superior claim has been paid. . . .

Thus, while the reclaiming seller's claim is not automatically extinguished, the reclaiming seller is also not automatically granted an administrative claim or lien in the full amount sought when it is subject to the rights of the good faith purchaser. *Victory Markets,* 212 B.R. at 743. Rather, the reclaiming seller's right to reclaim depends on the value of the excess goods remaining once the secured creditor's claim is paid or released. Id.

As the bankruptcy filing does not enhance the reclaiming seller's rights, the Court should determine what would have happened to the reclaiming seller's claim in a nonbankruptcy context. The parties concede that under state law the secured creditor would have the option of proceeding against any of its collateral. Therefore, the secured creditor may choose to foreclose on the goods sold by the reclaiming seller if these goods can be readily liquidated. When the secured claim, or a portion of it, is paid out of the goods sought to be reclaimed, the right to reclaim is rendered valueless. *Pester,* 964 F.2d at 847. Thus, "in the non-bankruptcy context, the secured creditor's decision with respect to its security interest in the goods will determine the value of the seller's right to reclaim." *Pester,* 964 F.2d at 847. Id. Here, following the Debtors' filing, CIT decided not to seek relief from the Court to pursue those remedies available to it to secure the immediate liquidation of all the Debtors' assets. Rather, it supported the Debtors' efforts to sell its inventory including any Galey goods in the ordinary course of its business. As a result, all of the goods which Galey sought to reclaim were sold and the proceeds used to pay CIT. Moreover, even after CIT received payment from the sale of the goods, there was still a balance due it. Thus, Galey's reclamation claim was rendered valueless. . . .

Finally, because this Court finds that Galey is not entitled to an administrative claim or replacement lien in as much as any right to reclamation it might have was subject to CIT's security interest and was rendered valueless by CIT's interest, it is unnecessary for the Court to reach the issue of whether Galey otherwise complied with all the requirements for a right to reclamation.

Conclusion

CIT, as the holder of a perfected security interest in substantially all Arley's assets including accounts receivable and inventory, is a good faith purchaser for value. Galey's interest as a reclaiming seller in the goods it sold Arley is subject to CIT's rights as a good faith purchaser. Galey's reclamation claim was rendered valueless because the proceeds from the disposition of the Galey goods were used to pay CIT's secured claim. Therefore, the value of any right Galey has to an administrative claim or replacement lien, pursuant to §546, is zero. . . .

The Trustee is to settle an Order consistent with this Memorandum Decision.

QUESTION

What could the seller have done in this situation in order to prevail over the floating lien that CIT had on the buyer's inventory? See §9-324(b).

PROBLEM 393

Octopus National Bank (ONB) held a perfected security interest in all the cattle owned by Family Farms of Iowa, Inc. (a mom-and-pop operation). When it became obvious that the farm was failing financially, ONB decided to pull the plug. Before it did so, it wanted to make sure that the cattle were well fed, so the ONB officer in charge of loan management called Cow Chow, Inc., and encouraged it to make another delivery of cattle feed to Family Farms, even though it had not been paid for its last two deliveries. ONB did not mention that it was about to foreclose on the fattened cattle, which it did as soon as they had consumed most of the new delivery (for which Cow

Chow billed Family Farms in the amount of $10,000). Cow Chow was an unsecured creditor, which ONB well knew. Is ONB required to give Cow Chow any of the money it realizes from the foreclosure sale? See §§1-103 and 1-304; Ninth Dist. Prod. Credit Assn. v. Ed Duggan, Inc., 821 P.2d 788 (Colo. 1991); see also Feresi v. The Livery, LLC, 2014 WL 7530260 (Cal. App. 2014) (breach of fiduciary duty destroys perfected security interest).

VII. STATUTORY LIEN HOLDERS

Just as the buyer in the ordinary course of business is a favorite of the law, those doing repairs in the ordinary course of business are frequently given priority over previously perfected consensual security interests. Read §9-333 and its Official Comments.

PROBLEM 394

The Repossession Finance Company (RFC) had a perfected security interest in Hattie Mobile's car (RFC's lien was noted on the certificate of title as required by state law). The car broke down on the interstate one day, and Hattie had it towed to Mike's Greasepit Garage, where it was repaired. State law gave a possessory artisan's lien to repairpersons. The garage told Hattie it was claiming such a lien, but when she pleaded with the manager, he let her drive the car to work after she assured him that she would return the car to the garage for storage every night (fortunately, she lived across the street). Repossession found out about this practice and, deeming itself insecure (§1-309), accelerated the amount due and repossessed the car from the parking lot in front of Hattie's place of business.

(a) Which creditor has the superior interest in the car under §9-333? Forrest Cate Ford v. Fryar, 62 Tenn. App. 572, 465 S.W.2d 882 (1970).

(b) If the car had been in Mike's possession when the conflict arose, would it matter under §9-333 that the finance company never gave its consent to the repairs? See Williamsport Natl. Bank v. Shrey, 612 A.2d 1081 (Pa. Super. 1992); Annot., 69 A.L.R.3d 1162.

(c) Once Mike's released the car to Hattie, did its lien reattach whenever she returned it to the garage? See M&I W. State Bank v. Wilson, 172 Wis. 2d 357, 493 N.W.2d 387 (Ct. App. 1992).

If the garage's charges are unconscionably high, does the lien still prevail? See §1-304; G. Gilmore §33.5, at 888: "To be entitled to priority under [§9-333] the lienor must have furnished services or materials 'in the ordinary course of his business.' This limitation should be read as tantamount to a requirement of good faith. . . . Section [9-333] is designed to protect the honest lienor and not the crook."

VIII. FIXTURES

Article 9 of necessity had to make special rules for the creation and perfection of a *fixture*—the legal bugaboo that hangs in limbo somewhere between chattel mobility and realty attachment. See, e.g., §9-109(a) ("[T]his Article applies . . . to: (1) any transaction . . . that creates a security interest in personal property *or fixtures*. . . .") and §9-501(a)(1)(B) (directing that fixture filings be made in the real property records).

The Code has only the most limited definition of *fixtures:* "'Fixtures' means goods that have become so related to particular real property that an interest in them arises under real property law," §9-102(a)(41), and "A security interest does not exist under this article in ordinary building materials incorporated into an improvement on land," §9-334(a). Obviously pre-Code state law defining *fixtures* is very important. State law tests range from a pure *annexation* test (measured by the difficulty of removal) to an "intention of the parties" test (for which the leading case is Teaff v. Hewitt, 1 Ohio St. 511 (1853)). Moreover, some courts have developed different categories of fixtures. *Trade fixtures* are items of personal property necessary to the conduct of the tenant's business but not permanently affixed to the realty. They remain the tenant's and may be removed when the tenancy ends. Generally, the UCC courts treat a trade fixture as equipment and not as a true fixture, In re Factory Homes Corp., 333 F. Supp. 126 (W.D. Ark. 1971), though the wide-awake lawyer will advise dual filings. A similar idea is the *assembled industrial plant* doctrine, which has it that all items connected with the operation of a going business are fixtures (primarily a Pennsylvania way of thinking; for the doctrine's clash with the UCC, see In re Griffin, 182 B.R. 8 (Bankr. M.D. Pa. 1995)). For general treatise discussions of the meaning of *fixture,* see 8 Powell on Real Property §57 (Michael Allan Wolf ed., 2014); 5 Thompson on Real Property §46 (David A. Thomas ed., 2d ed. 2007); Friedman on Contracts & Conveyances of Real Property §3A:5 (James C. Smith ed., 7th ed. 2011).

In re Motors Liquidation Company

United States Bankruptcy Court, Southern District of New York, 2017
576 B.R. 325

MEMORANDUM OPINION REGARDING FIXTURE CLASSIFICATION AND VALUATION

Martin Glenn, United States Bankruptcy Judge.

I. Introduction

The Defendants are a group of Old GM's creditors referred to as the Term Lenders, who initially held a security interest in approximately $1.5 billion of Old GM's assets, with a perfected security interest resulting from a UCC-1 Statement filed in Delaware. In earlier stages of this litigation (described below), the perfected security interest of the Term Lenders resulting from the Delaware UCC-1 filing was terminated when a UCC-3 Termination Statement was mistakenly filed in Delaware. Despite the filing of the UCC-3 Termination Statement in Delaware, the Defendants allege that, at the time of the 363 Sale they held a perfected security interest in over 200,000 fixtures at GM plants because of twenty-six Fixture Filings in counties where disputed assets were located. The Defendants argue that these fixtures should be valued according to their replacement cost new less depreciation, as part of a going-concern business. The Avoidance Action Trust, on behalf of Old GM's unsecured creditors, disputes whether most of these assets are indeed fixtures, and if they were, it argues that they should be valued at their liquidation value.

It is impractical, to say the least, to litigate issues with respect to each of the over 200,000 disputed assets. Therefore, in pretrial proceedings, the Court directed the parties to designate forty representative assets to be the subject of this trial. The Court indicated that it would issue an opinion regarding which assets are fixtures and how to value them. The parties agreed that after the issuance of this Opinion, they would attempt to settle as to the remaining disputed assets. In an effort to provide guidance to the parties in resolving the remaining disputes, the Court includes extensive factual detail in this Opinion. Where possible, the Court has articulated broad principles of both fixture and valuation law to serve as guiding principles for the more than 200,000 assets that remain in dispute.

A. FIXTURES

The representative forty assets were located at General Motors facilities in Michigan and Ohio. Disputed assets were located in other states as well, but the disagreement between the Plaintiff and Defendants touches on the fundamental nature of manufacturing assets located at GM's plants: which ones were "fixtures" that remained subject to the Term Lenders' perfected security interests when the chapter 11 cases were filed; and, for those fixtures, what are the appropriate valuation principles?

The Defendants maintain that hundreds of thousands of General Motors assets were fixtures that remained part of the Lenders' perfected security interest after the UCC-3 Termination Statement was filed in Delaware. The Plaintiff disagrees, and argues that just about every asset located inside General Motors facilities was not a fixture. The forty "representative" assets are characteristic of thousands of other GM assets. Hopefully, with the benefit of this Opinion, the parties will be able to resolve the balance of their dispute through settlement.

The Representative Assets selected by the parties range from enormous stamping presses and machining equipment, to high-tech robotic arms, to long and winding conveyor systems, and even include a software program. The assets, many of which the Court observed in operation during a site-visit with the parties, perform a wide assortment of tasks. Presses stamp sheet metal into auto body parts; robots conduct precision welding generating a cascade of sparks along an intricate assembly line; and sophisticated paint sprayers coat auto parts in a state-of-the-art paint shop described at trial as truly "beautiful."

Throughout this case, several principles have emerged from both the case law and the nature of the assets involved that have assisted the Court in making its ultimate determinations. First, the presence of a concrete pit, specialized foundation, or trench attendant to an asset weighed heavily in favor of finding that an asset was a fixture. As borne out by the case law, the permanence of concrete evidences both a strong level of attachment, and also a forceful intent that an asset remain in place permanently. Second, given the highly interconnected nature of the assets in the manufacturing and assembly process at these facilities, the Court found it useful to look at the level of integration and interconnectedness that an asset had with the production and assembly process and surrounding assets. An asset highly integrated into the assembly line or manufacturing process, including with respect to other assets adjacent or attached to it, cannot be easily removed or relocated without bringing the manufacturing and assembly to a halt, and are stronger indications that the asset was intended to remain in place permanently as an accession to the realty. This is particularly true where a group of assets fit together in a specific amalgamation, and one or more of the assets is installed in concrete. On the other hand, an asset standing on its own, separate from the manufacturing and assembly process and other assets, necessarily has a lower level of integration with the assembly line and manufacturing process, and there is a lesser indication of an intent for permanence. These principles, explained more fully below, will hopefully assist the parties as they endeavor to resolve the disputes surrounding the remaining assets in question.

. . .

B. OHIO'S THREE-PART FIXTURE TEST

Ohio, like Michigan, has a three-part test: (1) "annex[ation] to some extent to the realty"; (2) "application to the use or purpose to which the realty to which it is attached, is devoted"; and (3) "actual or apparent intention upon the part of the owner of the chattel in affixing it to the realty to make such chattel a permanent part of such realty." Holland Furnace Co. v. Trumbull Sav. & Loan Co., 135 Ohio St. 48, 52, 19 N.E.2d 273 (1939) (citing Teaff v. Hewitt, 1 Ohio St. 511 (1853)).

. . .

VII. CONCLUSIONS OF LAW REGARDING THE 40 REPRESENTATIVE ASSETS

A. THE PRESSES

1. The Leased Presses are not Fixtures

The AA Transfer Press and the B3-5 Transfer Press (together, the "Leased Presses") are leased, not owned, by GM and the Defendants concede that they therefore hold no security interest in them. (JPTO ¶66.) In both leases, Old GM agreed that the Leased Presses would "retain the character of personal property" and "shall not become part of any real property." (PX-220 at 38; PX-283 at 41.) Nevertheless, the Defendants argue that the Leased Presses are fixtures, no doubt because there are numerous similar presses among the 200,000 remaining assets still to be resolved. The Defendants argue that because the Leased Presses were installed before the leases were entered into, the leases—in which GM agreed that the Leased Presses would remain personal property—have no bearing on GM's intent at the time of installation. The Court disagrees.

The B3-5 Transfer Press was put into service in December 2003—the same month that the sale/leaseback provision was entered into. (PX-220 at 38 (dated December 10, 2003).) The AA Transfer Press was put into service in September 2003 and the sale/leaseback provision was entered into under three months later, also in December 2003. (PX-283 at 41 (dated December 23, 2003).) Miller testified that "the planning for installation of a press . . . begins several years before the in-service dates." (Miller Direct ¶68.) It is hard for the Court to believe that a sophisticated financial agreement such as the sale/leaseback agreements would not also be negotiated and drafted during that same timeframe. In the context of a years-long installation process, the Court finds that the execution of the sale/leaseback agreement within days or even a few months of the press's installation is a strong indicator of GM's intent at the time of installation. The Court can think of few more "objective, visible" indicators of intent than a nearly contemporaneous agreement to maintain the asset as personal property. See *Mich. Nat'l Bank*, 293 N.W.2d at 627. While other factors may weigh in favor of a finding of intent to make the asset a permanent accession to the realty (as discussed below regarding the other three presses), those factors are trumped by the plain, objective language of the leases.

Accordingly, the intent prong of the Michigan three-part fixture test has not been met for either the AA Transfer Press or the B3-5 Transfer Press, and the Court finds that Representative Assets Nos. 32 and 33 are not fixtures. The Court notes that, but for the leases, the Leased Presses share substantially the same characteristics as the remaining three presses the Court rules below are fixtures.

2. The Remaining Three Presses Are Fixtures

Representative Assets Nos. 29, 30, and 31 are not subject to leases, and the Plaintiff agrees that all three presses are attached to the realty. (See Goesling Direct ¶60.)

The adaptation prong of the three-part test has clearly been met for all three presses. All of the presses were installed in 16- to 20-foot pits excavated in the concrete foundations of the plants in which they were located—part of an installation process that took years to plan and execute. (Miller Direct ¶68.) Special concrete pillars supporting the presses were anchored to the bedrock beneath the plants. All of the presses were served by hard utility and piping connections integrated with the rest of the facilities, along with supporting assets such as overhead cranes and underground conveyors. (Id. ¶¶109, 125, 138.)

The Court also finds that it was GM's intent at the time of installation of the non-leased presses that they would become a permanent accession to the realty. Importantly, all three presses were vital to the operations of the plants in which they were located, and were integrated with the rest of the assembly lines of which they were a part. All of the presses were extremely large and extremely heavy: the TP-14 Transfer Press and Danly Press both weighed over 700 tons and stood three stories tall, while the GG-1 Transfer Press weighed over 1,100 tons and stood three stories tall. (Id. ¶¶85, 103, 133.) It took years to plan their installation and create the custom foundations necessary to run the presses, and would take months to remove them. (See JPTO ¶¶103-04 (TP-14 Transfer Press and Danly Press both took at least three months to remove).) Removal of a press would leave behind its 16- to 20-foot foundation pit. (See, e.g., Miller Direct ¶110 (describing "the large pit that would be left behind" if the Danly Press were removed).) It is unreasonable to suggest, as Goesling does, that such pits are not "damage" to the realty: the facility cannot be repurposed until the pit is filled in and a new foundation is poured. (See id. (noting that the floor would need to be "healed" before the area could be used).)

The Court has considered the Plaintiff's arguments regarding the Danly Press, and comes to the same conclusion as the other non-leased presses. The Danly Press was originally put into service in October 1980 at the GM Indianapolis stamping plant, was idled in place 23 years later when the press line was taken out of production because of a design change, and was moved to LDT in 2003. (JPTO ¶104; Miller Direct ¶¶112-13; Trial Tr. (Miller) at 1127:13-28:22.) The combination of the idling of the press line at the GM Indianapolis plant, and the opening of the LDT plant, created an "extraordinary situation" in which the rare movement of a press made economic sense. (Miller Direct ¶114.) It took three to six months to remove the Danly Press from the GM Indianapolis plant and prepare it for shipment, and after it was removed GM needed to repair the damage to the facility's floor. (Trial Tr. (Miller) at 1128:23-30:7.) GM then excavated a pit for the Danly Press into the floor at LDT. (Id. at 1130:24-31:12.) The cost, time, and effort to move the Danly Press and reinstall it at LDT weigh in favor of GM's intent for permanence, not against. The Court is also convinced that the Danly Press is an integral part of the production line at LDT. The Danly Press is a "tryout press," used to validate large dies for the production presses. If the Danly Press were removed, GM would have to take a production press offline to test dies, causing significant disruption. (Miller Direct ¶116; Trial Tr. (Miller) at 1126:4-24.)

B. THE CONVEYOR SYSTEMS

Nine of the forty Representative Assets are conveyors or conveyor systems. Warren Transmission houses the Power Zone Roller Conveyor (Representative Asset No. 3) and the Button Up and Test Conveyor (Representative Asset No. 35). Lansing Delta Township houses the Paint Dip Conveyor (Representative Asset No. 6), the Skid Conveyor (Representative Asset No. 16), the P & F Conveyor (Representative Asset No. 17), the Wheel & Tire Delivery Conveyor (Representative Asset No. 20), the Skillet Conveyor System (Representative Asset No. 21), and the Vertical Adjusting Carriers (Representative Asset No. 18). The Defiance Foundry houses the Core Delivery Conveyor (Representative Asset No. 26).

1. The Modularity of the Conveyor Systems Does Not Suggest That the Conveyors Are Not Fixtures

With respect to the conveyor assets, the Plaintiff relies heavily on the argument that the conveyor systems are comprised of individual segments that are delivered separately to a facility, then assembled on site to fit the specifications needed to run the conveyor system in conjunction with other assets. Specifically, the Plaintiff argues that this "modularity" makes removal of the conveyors easier, rendering them less "permanent." (See Plaintiff's Post-Trial Brief ¶661 ("The sectional/modular nature of the conveying equipment . . . and the methods of attachment all allow for removal of the asset without damage to the building or the equipment."))

The Court finds this argument unpersuasive. The conveyor systems are hundreds of feet long, and wind throughout the facilities, often ascending and descending to different floors. Due to the size, weight, and vast dimensions of so many of these conveyors, it would be impossible to assemble them entirely prior to delivery in GM's plant; they are simply too large to be transported by road or rail to GM's facilities. (Stevens Direct ¶132.) It would be wholly impossible to deliver such a conveyor system already intact, and the modular nature of the conveyors is necessary for installation, and says very little, if anything, about the intent of GM regarding the permanence of the conveyor assets.

2. *The Conveyors Are Attached to the Realty*

The parties agree that the Skid Conveyor (Representative Asset No. 16), the P & F Conveyor (Representative Asset No. 17), the Paint Dip Conveyor (Representative Asset No. 6) the Wheel & Tire Delivery Conveyor (Representative Asset No. 20), the Skillet Conveyor System (Representative Asset No. 21), the Core Delivery Conveyor (Representative Asset No. 26), the Power Zone Roller Conveyor (Representative Asset No. 3), the Button Up and Test Conveyor (Representative Asset No. 35) are all attached to the realty. (Goesling Direct, Ex. A at 344.)

The Plaintiff maintains that the Vertical Adjusting Carriers (Representative Asset No. 18) at the Lansing Facilities is not attached to the realty as the carriers themselves are not permanently affixed to the building, but instead ride along the top of a rail and are connected to it by gravity. (Trial Tr. (Stevens) at 165:18-167:23; Goesling Direct ¶115.) The rail for the Vertical Adjusting Carriers is attached to white steel beams within the facility that is in turn bolted to the building. (Trial Tr. (Stevens) at 165:18-167:23; Goesling Direct ¶118.)

But even "slight" physical attachment can suffice. *Wayne Cty.*, 563 N.W.2d at 678; see also, e.g., In re Joseph, 450 B.R. at 692 (mailbox hanging on two screws was attached to house). Assets can be constructively attached even if not directly attached to the realty if they are "part of, or accessory to, articles which are so annexed." *Wayne Cty.*, 563 N.W.2d at 680 (citation omitted). Put another way, assets are deemed "constructively annexed" if "their removal from the realty would impair both their value and the value of the realty." Id. at 679.

The Vertical Adjusting Carriers are constructively attached because they are plainly "part of" the vertical adjusting carrier system, which includes the rails on which the carriers rest, and the removal of the carriers would completely halt the flow of production in the assembly plant.

Accordingly, each of the conveyor systems is attached to the realty.

3. The Conveyors Are Highly Integrated into the Assembly Process

Naturally, given that these conveyor systems move parts and components along the production line and throughout a facility, driving the production process forward, these systems are highly integrated into the production process with many other assets. And to be sure, production would cease altogether if any of the conveyor assets were removed from the facility. For example, Mr. Stevens repeatedly oversaw the work of teams who had to specially design equipment layout and conveyors to fit within a particular space or column configuration (or had to specially design a particular space to fit the equipment and conveyors). (Stevens Direct ¶39.) Many conveyors must run for thousands of feet to allow multiple repeated operations to be performed in a complex, highly choreographed assembly process. (Id.) And the layout of the conveyors for the 6-speed transmission line at Warren Transmission was customized specifically for the tight layout of the renovated Warren building. (Trial Tr. (Deeds) at 732:23-733:7; Deeds Direct ¶¶45, 60, 178.) The conveyor assets therefore demonstrate an exceptionally high level of integration and interconnection with other manufacturing assets.

Courts have held that assets somewhat similar to the conveyor systems at issue here are fixtures. The Bankruptcy Court in the Western District of Michigan held that a chairlift on a ski hill was a fixture when the chairlift was attached to the realty by concrete and bolts and specially engineered to the use of the realty. See *Cliff's Ridge*, 123 B.R. at 759-60. Like a conveyor belt, a chair lift is a mechanical system operating on a straight or tilted plane, with the essential purpose of moving physical objects.

The *Cliff's Ridge* court determined that the chairlift fulfilled the first element of the test, because "[t]he chairlift was attached to the realty. Concrete pads were poured in the realty prior to the erection of the chairlift. Towers were then bolted to the concrete pads, cables were strung, and about 100 chairs were attached to the cables." Id. at 759. The court also held that the second element of the fixture test was fulfilled, noting that "the chairlift was engineered to be erected on the realty and the chairlift was specially modified to be attached to the realty." Id. ("The court finds the chairlift was adapted to the ski hill real property for its use and purposes.") (internal citation omitted). The *Cliff's Ridge* court determined that the third element was fulfilled because "[i]n two financing statements dated December 14 and December 15, 1982, filed by First National, it is stated, 'The goods are to become fixtures on 11-24-82.'" *Cliff's Ridge*, 123 B.R. at 759. The court further noted that, "[u]nder Michigan law, attachments to realty to facilitate its use become part of the realty and, if done by the owner, are presumed to be permanent." Id. (citation omitted).

Regarding the adaptation element, like the chairlift in *Cliff's Ridge*, GM's conveyors in Michigan were designed and engineered for the realty on which they were installed. See *Cliff's Ridge*, 123 B.R. at 756 (noting that "[t]he chairlift was specially engineered and modified for a slope on the ski hill real property"). As noted above, these conveyors wind and curve throughout the assets of the facilities in which they reside, and are absolutely critical to the integrated manufacturing processes. For example, defense expert Deeds testified that Asset No. 3 "is a critical component of the transmission housing line at Warren Transmission," and "[Asset No. 3's] layout was driven by the specific dimensions of the machining area at the Warren Transmission facility, with a custom layout." (Deeds Direct ¶¶55, 60.) Deeds also testified that Asset No. 35 "is a necessary, customized component of the final assembly line for completed transmissions . . . and was also specifically designed for the layout of Warren Transmission's assembly area," with a glass wall built around the Asset "to separate the assembly building process from the shipping dock." (Id. ¶178.) Defense expert Steven Topping testified that Asset No. 6 "is a necessary part of the ELPO Process, which is a critical step in the paint-shop process," and that "the facility was clearly customized to support this Conveyor." (Topping Direct ¶47.) This in particular emphasizes the nature in which the realty and asset are integrated and adapted.

This goes to demonstrate that each of the conveyors are essential to driving the production process forward, and are "a necessary or at least a useful adjunct to the realty, considering the purposes to which the latter is devoted." *Wayne Cty.*, 563 N.W.2d at 680. The adaptation element for each of the conveyors is therefore satisfied.

And because of the extremely high level of integration that the conveyor systems have with other assets and the realty itself, as well as the high level of attachment that most of these conveyors have with the realty (in some cases, by thousands of bolts), there is strong evidence that GM intended these conveyors to remain in place for their useful lives such that the production process would continue. The presumption that GM intended for the conveyors to remain in place permanently has not been overcome.

Accordingly, the Court finds that each of the conveyor assets are fixtures.

C. THE ROBOTS

The robots present unique challenges for the Court. The robots are much smaller than the presses and machining assets. They are also relatively easy to remove (Trial Tr. (Thomas) at 837:7-838:17), and there is a robust secondary market for these types of robots. (See Sofikitis Dep. Tr. at 97:1-4; Levy Dep. Tr. at 60:18-61:1.) And additionally, robots are reprogrammable, rendering them more versatile than some of the other assets. (Trial Tr. (Thomas) at 842:25-843:4.)

But as discussed below, some of the robots are highly interconnected and integrated with other assets along the manufacturing process. And each of these robots serves an essential function, without which the production process could not continue.

1. Representative Asset Nos. 39 and 12

The CB 91 Robot at the Defiance Foundry unloads engine cores from the CB 91 core making machine. The asset delivers each core to several work stations before delivering a complete core sub-assembly to a conveyor for further processing. The sub-assemblies are used later in the iron casting process at Powertrain Defiance. The asset was put into service in March 2005. (JPTO ¶112.) The Body Shop Robot LAZN-150R1 at the Lansing Facilities applies spot welds to join together body panels into a complete vehicle body outer frame.

The parties agree that both of these robots are attached to the realty (Goesling Direct, Ex. A at 344)—the CB 91 Robot, on account of the lag bolts affixing the assets steel plate mount to the floor (Goesling Direct ¶346; see also Trial Tr. (Thomas) at 834:19-835:14; 838:18-24), and the body shop robot on account of the bolts affixing it to the overhead structure to which it is attached. (Goesling Direct ¶¶146-47.)

Moreover, both of these robots are highly interconnected with other assets, and serve critical functions along the manufacturing process. The body shop robot, for example, works in conjunction with a number of other robotic arms to perform welding operations as components are shuffled past on a conveyor system. With all of these welding robots working together with conveyor systems and other manufacturing processes, the high level of integration among these assets and the realty demonstrate an intent on the part of GM that this complex formulation of assets remain in place permanently.

Under Michigan's adaptation prong, the body shop robot is used "in the regular course of its business," and integral to the LDT plant, and the purpose for which it was built. *Cincinnati Ins.*, 166 F. Supp. 2d at 1180. And given the presumption that this asset was installed with an intent to remain permanently, coupled with the fact that the LDT operations could not go forward without it, the intent prong is likewise satisfied.

The body shop robot is therefore a fixture, as all three prongs are satisfied.

The CB 91 Robot likewise is highly interconnected with other assets. The CB 91 first removes the core from the core machine, then transports it to a "definning stand" in the cell that removes residual sand from the core, then moves the core to a specialized "turntable" where operators assemble two cores, and once assembly is complete, the Robot picks up the assembled cores and transports them to an unload dip conveyor that takes the cores to a dip tank for coating in advance of casting. (Thomas Direct ¶92 & Ex. A at 27; JX-1588; JX-1592; see also Trial Tr. (Thomas) at 801:3-23.)

Removing the CB 91 from this production flow would halt the entire process, rendering the other assets in the cell useless. And given that the realty in which this asset is located is a foundry, designed specifically for producing parts for use in automobiles, the adaption prong under Ohio law is met as this robot is "essential to the use or purpose of the realty" because the entire line had been "integrated into the factory." *Mid-Ohio Mechanical, Inc.*, 862 N.E.2d at 547. And for the same reasons that GM intended for the body shop to remain in place, so too does the evidence demonstrate that GM intended for the CB 91 Robot to remain in place for its useful life.

Accordingly, because all three prongs of the fixture test are met for the CB 91 Robot and the body shop robot, the Court concludes that they are fixtures.

XI. Conclusion

The Court's Opinion sets forth in considerable detail the findings of fact and conclusions of law with respect to each of the Representative Assets.

The court held that most but not all of the collateral was fixtures. The parties settled shortly thereafter. See Infamous GM Bankruptcy Case, Triggered by Colossal UCC Filing Error, Is Settled for $231 Million, Clarks Secured Transactions Monthly (May 1, 2019) ("Assuming the settlement is approved, the final chapter in this 'most colossal UCC filing error' litigation will have been written. One UCC-3 prepared and filed in error cost the Term Loan lenders $231 million plus untold millions in attorney's fees.").

NOTE

See White & Summers §25-5(a). Then there is this oft-quoted passage from Strain v. Green, 25 Wash. 2d 692, 695, 172 P.2d 216, 218 (1946):

> [W]e will not undertake to write a Treatise on the law of fixtures. Every lawyer knows that cases can be found in this field that will support any position that the facts of his particular case require him to take. . . . [T]here is a wilderness of authority. . . . Fixture cases are so conflicting that it would be profitless . . . to review . . . them.

PROBLEM 395

As stated above, in differentiating among goods (subject to UCC filing), fixtures (subject to UCC and realty filing), and ordinary building materials (subject only to realty filing), courts look to three tests: (1) actual physical annexation to the realty, (2) application or adaption to the use or purpose to which the realty is devoted, and (3) intention of the person making annexation to make a permanent accession to the freehold. Decide how each of the following would be characterized:

1. The furnace that heats the building and water;
2. The pipes that carry the hot water through the walls;
3. A couch that has been sitting in the living room for 20 years,
4. A lavish designer bathtub, handcrafted and carefully set in the corner, see In re Ryan, 360 B.R. 50 (Bankr. W.D.N.Y. 2007);
5. Security cameras, tracks, wiring, and equipment for wireless Internet access; see In re Marble Cliff Crossing Apartments, LLC, 484 B.R. 175 (Bankr. S.D. Ohio 2012).

In theory, your basic property course taught you to tell fixtures from non-fixtures with more refinement. Our main concern is resolution of priority disputes between those who have a security interest in the fixture and those who have or acquire an interest in the realty to which the collateral is affixed. Read §9-334 carefully, and then consider these Problems.

PROBLEM 396

Monopoly Railway went to Octopus National Bank (ONB) and asked to borrow money, using as part of the collateral its extensive network of railroad track (rails and ties), which winds through 12 western states. ONB consults you. The track is installed in a total of 117 counties. Must it file a financing statement in each one? See §§9-501(b) and 9-102(a)(81).

PROBLEM 397

Simon Mustache decided to erect an apartment building on a vacant lot he owned, so he borrowed $4 million from Construction State Bank (CSB), to which he mortgaged the real estate "and all appurtenances or things affixed thereto, now present or after-acquired." Simon and CSB signed the mortgage, which contained a legal description of the realty and stated that the debt financed the construction, and the mortgage was filed in the real property recorder's office. Is the mortgage effective as a financing statement? See §9-502(c). During construction of the apartment building, Simon Mustache bought a furnace on credit from Blast Home Supplies, giving Blast a security interest in the furnace that described the real estate. Where should Blast file its financing statement? See §9-501. Is there a technical sentence that needs to be in this financing statement? See §9-502(b)(2). Why would the drafters have added such a requirement? Even if Blast files a proper financing statement in the right place before the furnace is installed, will Blast prevail over CSB? See §9-334(d) and (h), and Official Comment 11. If CSB's interest is not perfected, will Blast prevail? See §9-334(e)(1). What can Blast do to ensure itself of priority? See §§9-334(f)(1), 9-339.

Suppose a security agreement and fixture filing also listed as collateral a liquor license owned by Simon for a bar in the building. Would the fixture filing perfect a security interest in the liquor license? See §9-501(a); In re Tam of Allegheny LLC, 575 B.R. 131 (Bankr. W.D. Pa. 2017).

PROBLEM 398

Would your answer to the last Problem's priority disputes change if the object in question were a refrigerator? What if it were a computer that Simon purchased for use in his office (which is located in the apartment building)? (Note: some states would consider the computer a *fixture* under the *industrial plant* doctrine; see the discussion above.) See §9-334(e)(2) and (f)(2), and Official Comment 8.

Lewiston Bottled Gas Co. v. Key Bank of Maine

Maine Supreme Judicial Court, 1992
601 A.2d 91

CLIFFORD, J.

Plaintiff Lewiston Bottled Gas Company (LBG) appeals from an order of summary judgment entered by the Superior Court (Androscoggin County, Perkins, J.) in favor of defendant Key Bank of Maine in this declaratory judgment action brought to determine the rights of the parties with respect to ninety heating and air-conditioning units installed in the Grand Beach Inn at Old Orchard Beach. We agree with the Superior Court that Key Bank's mortgage gives it priority over LBG's purchase money security interest in the units and we affirm the judgment.

In July 1986, Key Bank loaned $2,580,000 to William J. DiBiase, Jr. The loan was secured by a mortgage on the real estate owned by DiBiase located on East Grand Avenue in Old Orchard Beach. The mortgage, which covered after-acquired fixtures, was properly recorded in the York County Registry of Deeds. On June 10, 1987, DiBiase incorporated Grand Beach Inn., Inc. (Grand Beach) for the purpose of constructing and operating the Grand Beach Inn on DiBiase's East Grand Avenue property. DiBiase was the president and sole shareholder of Grand Beach and at all relevant times was the owner of the property.

On June 15, 1987, Grand Beach contracted to purchase ninety heating and air-conditioning units from LBG. The contract provided that the units would remain the personal property of Grand Beach notwithstanding their attachment to the real property. On June 16, Grand Beach granted to LBG a purchase money security interest in the ninety units. Financing statements disclosing the security interest and identifying the debtor as "Grand Beach Inn, Inc., William J. DiBiase, Jr., President" and describing the real estate upon which the units were located as "Grand Beach Inn, East Grand Avenue, Old Orchard Beach, ME 04064" were filed with the Secretary of State and also recorded in the York County Registry of Deeds. In each place, they were indexed under the name "Grand Beach Inn, Inc." Nothing, however, was indexed under DiBiase's name. In September and October 1987, the units were installed in the exterior walls of each room in the Inn.

On June 29, 1987, Key Bank made a second loan to DiBiase secured by a second mortgage on the same property, also covering after-acquired fixtures and also properly recorded. The title search undertaken by Key Bank in the York County Registry of Deeds prior to the execution of the mortgage failed to disclose the financing statement and the existence of LBG's security interest in the units because LBG's financing statement was indexed under the name "Grand Beach" even though DiBiase was the record owner of the property at the time.

In May 1989, Key Bank foreclosed on both its mortgages. LBG was not joined as a party-in-interest because Key Bank was unaware of LBG's interest in the units until after the foreclosure was commenced. The parties agreed to allow the foreclosure to proceed and to litigate the issue of title to the heating and air-conditioning units later. Key Bank was the successful bidder at the foreclosure sale. LBG then filed the present complaint against Key Bank seeking a declaratory judgment that its purchase money security interest in the units had priority over the interest of Key Bank. The Superior Court granted summary judgment to Key Bank concluding that the heating and air-conditioning units were fixtures and that Key Bank's properly recorded mortgages had priority over LBG's unperfected security interest. This appeal followed. . . .

II. Units as Fixtures

11 M.R.S.A. §9-313(1)(a) [the predecessor to §9-334—Eds.] (1964 & Supp. 1991) provides that "[g]oods are 'fixtures' when they become so related to particular real estate that an interest in them arises under real estate law." That interest arises when the property is (1) physically annexed to the real estate, (2) adapted to the use to which the real estate is put, that

is, the personal and real property are united in the carrying out of a common purpose, and (3) annexed with the intent to make it part of the realty. Boothbay Harbor Condominiums, Inc. v. Department of Transp., 382 A.2d 848, 854 (Me. 1978) (citing Bangor-Hydro Elec. Co. v. Johnson, 226 A.2d 371, 378 (Me. 1967)).

The evidence compels a conclusion that, under the first prong of the three-part fixture test, the units were physically annexed to the real estate. The heating and air-conditioning units were installed when the Inn was under construction and are part of the walls of the building. The units are attached by bolts and although they could be removed, their removal would create a large hole in the walls of each room. See Roderick v. Sanborn, 106 Me. 159, 162, 76 A. 263 (1909) (property need not be permanently fastened to realty to be physically annexed).

As to the second prong of the test, it is undisputed that the units, although they are catalogue items and not specially made for the Grand Beach Inn, were adapted to the use of the real estate as the Grand Beach Inn. The real estate was designed and built as an inn to accommodate overnight guests. The heating and air-conditioning units help create a livable atmosphere for those guests by providing heat and cooling to the rooms. The personal and real property, therefore, are united in the carrying out of a common enterprise. See *Bangor-Hydro,* 226 A.2d at 376. The fact that the units are catalogue items, and not custom-made, does not preclude them from being fixtures.

The intent of the person annexing the personal property to the real estate is the third and most important of the three prongs of the fixture test. *Bangor-Hydro,* 226 A.2d at 377. LBG contends that summary judgment was improperly granted to Key Bank because the agreements between DiBiase and LBG granted to LBG a purchase money security interest in the units and expressly stated that the units would remain personal property and therefore demonstrated DiBiase's intent that the units remain personal property. We disagree.

In determining the intent of the parties as to whether a chattel annexed to real estate becomes a fixture, it is not the hidden subjective intent of the person making the annexation that must be considered but rather "the intention which the law deduces from such external facts as the structure and mode of attachment, the purpose and use for which the annexation has been made and the relation and use of the party making it." *Bangor-Hydro,* 226 A.2d at 378. The agreement DiBiase made with LBG to have the heating and air-conditioning units remain personal property cannot be considered against Key Bank on the fixtures issue because Key Bank was not a party to those agreements and was unaware of them. Vorsec Co. v. Gilkey, 132 Me. 311, 314, 170 A. 722 (1934); Gaunt v. Allen Lane Co., 128 Me. 41, 46, 145 A. 255 (1929).

The objective manifestation of intent in this case, as evidenced by the physical annexation of the units to the walls of the building and their adaptation to the use of the real estate as an inn, leaves no genuine dispute that the units are fixtures and part of the Grand Beach Inn real estate.

III. LBG's Failure to Perfect Its Security Interest

Because the heating and air-conditioning units were fixtures and part of the real estate, they became subject to Key Bank's mortgages pursuant to §9-313. Key Bank's first mortgage takes priority over LBG's security interest in the units unless LBG's security interest falls within one of the exceptions found in §9-313. 11 M.R.S.A. §9-313(7) (Supp. 1991). The only relevant exception in this case is §9-313(4)(a) [now §9-334(d)—Eds.], which states:

> (4) A perfected security interest in fixtures has priority over the conflicting interest of an encumbrancer or owner of the real estate where:
>
> (a) The security interest is a purchase money security interest, the interest of the encumbrancer or owner arises before the goods become fixtures, the security interest is perfected by a fixture filing before the goods become fixtures or within 10 days thereafter, and the debtor has an interest of record in the real estate or is in possession of the real estate.

The security interest of LBG was a purchase money security interest. 11 M.R.S.A §9-107 (1964). The record clearly demonstrates, however, that it was not properly perfected and does not otherwise come within any recognized exception that would give it priority over Key Bank's first mortgage.

A security interest is perfected when it has attached and all of the applicable steps required for perfection have been taken. 11 M.R.S.A. §9-303(1) (1964). To perfect a security interest in a fixture, the secured party must file a "fixture filing." "A 'fixture filing' is the filing in the office where a mortgage on the real estate would be filed or recorded of a financing statement covering goods which are or are to become fixtures and conforming to the requirements of section 9-402, subsection (5)." 11 M.R.S.A. §9-313(1)(b) (Supp. 1991). Section 9-402(5) (Supp. 1991) requires that, in addition to the general requirements for financing statements set forth in §9-402(1) (the name and signature of the debtor, the name and address of the secured party and a description of the collateral), the fixture filing must contain a description of the real estate and, if the debtor does not have an interest of record in the real estate, "the financing statement must show *the name of a record owner*." 11 M.R.S.A. §9-402(5) (emphasis added).

In this case, LBG's financing statement was correctly filed in the York County Registry of Deeds, identified the debtor as "Grand Beach Inn, Inc., William J. DiBiase, Jr., President," and contained a description of the real estate that we assume is adequate. Because it failed to identify DiBiase as the record owner of the property, however, the financing statement does not comply with §9-402(5).

As a general rule, a financing statement is sufficient if, in all the circumstances, the filing would give a title searcher sufficient notice to justify placing a duty upon the searcher to make further inquiry concerning the possible lien. In the Matters of Reeco Elec. Co., 415 F. Supp. 238, 240 (D. Me. 1976). In this case, the financing statement was indexed under "Grand Beach Inn, Inc." A title searcher would not be expected to check the index for "Grand Beach Inn, Inc." at a time when the property is owned by DiBiase. Because LBG failed to perfect its security interest in the heating and air-conditioning units pursuant to §9-402(5), the rights of Key Bank as mortgage holder of the real estate to which the units are affixed take priority over LBG's unperfected security interest.

The entry is: Judgment affirmed.

All concurring.

PROBLEM 399

Simon Mustache (of the last Problem) failed to pay his attorney, Susan Mean, so she sued him, recovered judgment, and levied on the apartment building and its contents. Will Simon's creditors holding security interests in the fixtures prevail if they have perfected by fixture filings? See §9-334(e)(3). What if those creditors filed financing statements in all the correct places *except* the real estate records? See Official Comment 9 to §9-334; In re Allen, 221 B.R. 232 (Bankr. S.D. Ill. 1998).

PROBLEM 400

After the building was complete, Tuesday Tenant moved in. Not liking the refrigerator Simon had installed, she had him remove it, and she bought another refrigerator on time from Easy Credit Department Store, which reserved a security interest therein but never filed a financing statement. Assume state real property laws permit Construction State Bank's after-acquired property mortgage to reach fixtures installed by lessees. (If they do not, Easy Credit will always prevail. See §9-334(f)(2).) Will Easy Credit be entitled to priority if it is forced to repossess? See §9-334(e)(2)(C) and Official Comment 8, third paragraph.

PROBLEM 401

Assume Tuesday (last Problem) bought a trash compactor on credit from Easy Credit Department Store and had her kitchen area remodeled to accommodate it. It was installed on May 5. Easy Credit comes to you on May 7.

Is it entitled to automatic perfection of its security interest in consumer goods here? See Official Comment 3 (last sentence) to §9-309. Suppose it has a financing statement indicating the debtor is Tuesday. Should the statement contain Simon Mustache's name too? Why? See §9-502(b)(4). Will Easy Credit prevail over CSB if it files on May 10? See §9-334(d). Will it prevail over Simon's landlord's lien?

PROBLEM 402

Assume that Blast Home Supplies held a perfected security interest in Simon's furnace and that this interest was entitled to priority over CSB, the real estate mortgagee. If Simon defaults on his payments, what liability does Blast have to CSB if removal (repossession) of the furnace will do $1,000 damage to the building's structure and if to replace it Simon (or CSB) will have to spend $8,000? See §9-604 and its Official Comment 2. What are CSB's rights? See the last sentence of §9-604(d). Is Blast liable to Simon for the damage to the building caused by the furnace's removal?

Maplewood Bank & Trust v. Sears, Roebuck & Co.

New Jersey Superior Court, Appellate Division, 1993
625 A.2d 537

COLEMAN, P.J.A.D.

This appeal requires us to decide whether a first mortgage lender or a fixture financier is entitled to priority in the funds realized from a foreclosure sale of the mortgaged premises. We hold that a first mortgage is entitled to priority in such funds.

Plaintiff Maplewood Bank and Trust is the holder of a first purchase money mortgage dated September 20, 1988, and recorded on October 5, 1988, on premises owned by defendants Edward and Terre Capers. The original mortgage debt was for $121,000. On May 31, 1989, Sears, Roebuck and Company (Sears) filed a financing statement covering a completely new kitchen, consisting of "new countertops, cabinets, sinks, disposal unit, dishwasher, oven, cooktop and hood," installed in the mortgaged premises at the request of the Capers after they executed a security agreement. The financing statement, known as the UCC-1 form, filed by Sears gave notice that Sears had a security interest in the new kitchen installed in the mortgaged premises in the sum of $33,320.40.

On August 18, 1989, the Capers executed a second mortgage on the previously mortgaged premises to defendant New Jersey Savings Bank for the sum of $34,000. That mortgage was recorded on August 23, 1989.

When the Capers eventually defaulted in the payments due plaintiff and Sears, plaintiff declared the entire unpaid balance on the mortgage was due. Nonpayment of the entire balance plus interest prompted plaintiff to file its complaint for foreclosure on November 5, 1990, and an amended complaint on or about December 6, 1990. Sears filed an answer and a counterclaim. Sears sought a declaration that its debt was "prior to the mortgage of the plaintiff" and, among other things, to compel plaintiff to "pay [Sears] the amount due on its Agreement." The essence of the counterclaim was that under N.J.S.A. 12A:9-313 [now §9-334—Eds.], Sears was entitled to priority over the plaintiff in the funds realized from the anticipated foreclosure sale. Sears' answer and counterclaim were stricken on July 26, 1991, and the matter proceeded as an uncontested foreclosure action. A final judgment in foreclosure was entered on February 28, 1992.

Sears has appealed the dismissal of its counterclaim. It argues that the priority given Sears as a purchase money security interest holder under the Uniform Commercial Code "applies to the proceeds of a judicial sale instituted" by a purchase money mortgagee. This is the same issue Sears raised in Orange Savings Bank v. Todd, 48 N.J. 428, 430 (1967), wherein Sears asserted that it was entitled to priority over the purchase money mortgagee "in the funds realized on foreclosure." Ibid. The Supreme Court concluded that although the briefs raised "interesting and important questions under the secured transactions provisions of the Uniform Commercial Code (N.J.S.A. 12A:9-101 et seq.), we find no present occasion to deal with any of them in view of the position now taken by the parties." Ibid. In the present case, we have considered the contention raised by Sears and conclude that it is unsound and must be rejected.

It is undisputed that the new kitchen Sears installed and financed satisfies the definition of a fixture under N.J.S.A. 12A:9-313(1)(a). It is also undisputed that Sears obtained a purchase money security interest in the fixture to secure full payment. See N.J.S.A. 12A:9-107(a) [now §9-103—Eds.]. Sears perfected its security interest by filing a financing statement (UCC-1) covering the fixtures in the Hunterdon County Clerk's Office where the first mortgage held by plaintiff was recorded. N.J.S.A. 12A:9-313(b) and N.J.S.A. 12A:9-402(5) [now §9-502—Eds.].

The purchase money security interest of Sears attached to the goods or chattels before they became affixed to the realty as fixtures. N.J.S.A. 12A:9-313(4)(a). By perfecting the security interest, Sears was able to make its security interest in the fixtures permanent, or until paid or discharged. The point to be made is that Sears' security interest is limited to the fixtures and does not extend to the realty otherwise.

By statute, Sears' purchase money security interest, when perfected, "has priority over the conflicting interest of an encumbrancer or owner of the real estate." N.J.S.A. 12A:9-334(4). This concept was expressed more clearly in the version of the statute which predated the 1981 amendments. The prior version of N.J.S.A. 12A:9-313(2) provided "A security interest which attaches to goods before they become fixtures takes priority as to the goods over the claims of all persons who have an interest in the real estate except as stated in subsection (4)." This means the purchase money security interest of Sears in the goods or chattels which became fixtures gives it a "super priority" as to those goods or chattels which became fixtures.

Next we must focus upon the remedies available to a purchase money security interest lienholder upon default by the debtor. Sears contends it should be entitled to receive from the proceeds obtained at the foreclosure sale, the difference between the value of the realty with the new kitchen and the value of the realty after the new kitchen has been removed. We reject this entire approach as an inappropriate remedy absent authorization by statute. The Uniform Commercial Code, as adopted in New Jersey, provides at N.J.S.A. 12A:9-313(8) [now §9-604—Eds.] that:

> When the secured party has priority over all owners and encumbrancers of the real estate, *he may* on default, subject to the provisions of subchapter 5, *remove his collateral from the real estate* but he must reimburse any encumbrancer or owner of the real estate who is not the debtor and who has not otherwise agreed for the cost of repair of any physical injury, but not for any diminution in value of the real estate caused by the absence of the goods removed or by any necessity of replacing them. . . . (Emphasis added.)

Thus based on the plain language of §9-313(8), Sears has two options: removal of the fixtures or foregoing removal of the fixtures.

New York, the only other jurisdiction which has addressed the issue, rejected Sears' argument. In Dry Dock Savings Bank v. DeGeorgio, 305 N.Y.S.2d 73 (1969), the defense asserted a lien superior to the mortgage by reason of a properly filed fixture financial statement covering aluminum siding on a house which was the subject of a foreclosure action. The mortgage was recorded prior to the time the fixture financial statement was filed.

The court held that under §9-313 the purchase money security interest holder may remove his fixtures from the real estate, but must reimburse any owner or encumbrancer for the cost of repair. Id. at 75. The court observed: "He merely has the right to remove the goods after posting security to repair any damage. This may turn out to be a somewhat Pyrrhic victory, giving the lienor a pile of dubious scrap not worth the labor of getting it off the house, repairing nail holes, etc. . . . [Removal] may hurt the mortgagee without doing the lienor any corresponding good. However, that is something for the parties to consider and beyond the control of the court." Ibid.

In Nu-Way Distributing Corp. v. Schoikert, 355 N.Y.S.2d 475 (N.Y. App. Div. 1974), plaintiff instituted an action to recover the price of fixtures (kitchen cabinets, etc.) sold by plaintiff, after the goods or chattels had been installed in the realty as fixtures. The Appellate Division construed §9-313 "as merely providing the creditor with the statutory right of repossession, provided that he first comply with the security provision of the statute." Id. at 476.

The Appellate Division opined that even if the purchase money security interest holder failed or did not desire to repossess the fixtures upon default, that lienholder was not entitled to maintain an action for the purchase price against a subsequent purchaser of the real property. Ibid. The court further held that the same rule would apply even in cases where the fixtures are custom-made and would be of no use or value should they be repossessed. The underlying rationale for the rule was that such a lienholder as the one involved in *Nu-Way* must be assumed to have known and understood the risk he was taking.

Sears' approach has been adopted only in Louisiana and there it was based on the legislature's definitive modification of §9-313(8) by adding the following language:

> A secured party may also demand separate appraisal of the fixtures to fix his interest in the receipts of the sale thereof in any proceedings in which the real estate is sold pursuant to execution upon it by a mortgagee or other encumbrancer. [Uniform Commercial Code §9-313, 3 U.L.A. 332 to 23 (1992) (Action in Adopting Jurisdictions).]

The most compelling authority supportive of Sears' position is an article "An Integrated Financing System for Purchase Money Collateral: A Proposed Solution to the Fixture Problem Under Section 9-313 of the Uniform Commercial Code" by Morris G. Shanker. 73 Yale L.J. 795 (1964). In this article, Professor Shanker states "[w]here the fixture secured debt is not paid, removal of the fixture seems to be the favorite means of foreclosing on the fixture security interest." Id. at 804.

The article goes on to cite certain instances where the fixture secured party may prefer not to exercise his removal rights. For example, if an elevator was designed for a specific building, it would have little or no value apart from that building. Ibid. Other cited examples include situations where a fixture secured party should be required to use judicial foreclosure proceedings even though he has the right of removal. For example, a secured party should not be free to remove a heating system in a large apartment building in the dead of winter, even where the debtor defaulted.

Shanker opines that "the Code, as it now stands, probably authorizes the fixture secured party to employ judicial foreclosure proceedings to enforce his security interest" in lieu of removal of the fixtures. Ibid. He states that limiting the remedy to the right to remove or choosing not to remove, in no way detracts from the fixture secured party's paramount security interest in his collateral; it merely requires him to enforce his security interest in a sensible and equitable fashion. Id. at 805.

We decline to adopt the creative approach articulated by Professor Shanker. Such action, in our view, would be legislating. We prefer the approach followed in Louisiana where the legislature, upon its preference and initiative, provided the innovative remedy sought by Sears. To adopt Sears' argument in the absence of legislation, would mean that a mortgagee's security interest could be impaired substantially without the legislature pronouncing an intention to do so. Any modification of long established fundamental property rights of purchase money mortgagees must be done in some straightforward manner and may not be implied from the existing statute. The fact that fixtures may be custom-made does not require any different result. See *Nu-Way,* supra, 355 N.Y.S.2d at 476.

We are also persuaded that Sears is not entitled to any remedy, other than removal of the fixtures, based on equitable principles. Sears knew its remedy was limited to removal upon default. Indeed, the Retail Installment Contract and Security Agreement prepared by Sears and signed by the Capers provided that the Capers were giving Sears a "security interest under the Uniform Commercial Code in all merchandise purchased under this contract . . . [and] *the security interest allows Sears to repossess the merchandise*" in the event the Capers did not make payments as agreed. (Emphasis added.)

Summary judgment in favor of plaintiff is affirmed.

NOTE

Professor Shanker appears to have prevailed on this issue because revised Article 9 has very different rules for repossessing fixture creditors in §9-604, and Official Comment 3 to that section specifically states that it was meant to overrule the case you have just read. But what does that mean in the context of the facts of the case? What could Sears do if §9-604 had been the law when the case was decided? See Timothy R. Zinnecker, The Default Provisions of Revised Article 9 of the Uniform Commercial Code: Part I, 54 Bus. Law. 1113, 1124-1128 (1999).

It should also be noted that a creditor who is repossessing a fixture is bound by all the usual repossession rules that we will study in Chapter 27 (and therefore cannot breach the peace; see §9-609, for example).

PROBLEM 403

Farmer Bean had filed a mortgage on his home in favor of Rural State Bank. The mortgage stated that it extended to the realty and all things "growing on, or attached thereto, now in existence or in the future." When Farmer Bean borrowed money to plant this year's crop, he gave a security interest in the crop to Seeds, Inc., the purchase money lender. If the latter files its financing statement in the appropriate place, will it prevail over Rural State's mortgage lien? See §9-334(i), and its Official Comment 12.

PROBLEM 404

When Farmer Bean bought a doublewide trailer from Traveling Homes, Inc., for $100,000, he had it towed to a vacant lot on his farm with police protection en route and large WIDE LOAD signs attached. That was the only trip the doublewide made in its life. It was then placed on a foundation that had been built on the vacant lot, attached to various utilities for electricity and water, and Farmer Bean built a fancy deck that he extended out the front door of the trailer. If you are the attorney representing the bank that loaned Farmer Bean the money to buy the doublewide, what steps should be taken to perfect its purchase money security interest in the collateral: a real estate mortgage? a fixture filing under Article 9 of the Uniform Commercial Code? or notation of the bank's interest on a certificate of title issued for the doublewide? See §9-334(e)(4); compare In re Kroskie, 315 F.3d 644 (6th Cir. 2003) (certificate of title controls), with In re Gregory, 316 B.R. 82 (Bankr. W.D. Mich. 2004) (real property laws trump Article 9 rules); White & Summers §25-5(b)(5); Mark R. Koontz, Manufactured Homes Under U.C.C. Revised Article 9: A New Conflict Between Certificates of Title and Financing Statements, 80 N.C. L. Rev. 1829 (2002).

IX. ACCESSIONS AND COMMINGLING

When goods are affixed to other goods (as opposed to realty), an *accession* occurs, and the rights of the creditors are regulated by §9-335. A similar problem arises when goods are so combined with other goods (eggs in a cake mix, for example) that they cannot be recovered. See §9-336 on *commingling.* Article 9's contribution to the solution to these problems can only be completely understood in light of centuries of property law development. A lawyer embroiled in litigation should review the basic common law rules. See 2 Thompson on Real Property §13.04(g)(6) (David A. Thomas ed., 3d ed. 2014).

PROBLEM 405

When Jane Witherspoon filed her bankruptcy petition she was living in a manufactured home that was in no way attached to the realty on which it sat. In the bankruptcy proceeding Life-Master Financing Company claimed a security interest in the home and all accessions pursuant to a security agreement. The accessions were not separately listed in the security agreement, but LifeMaster argued they included a porch Jane had had installed, as well as storm windows, a heater, carpeting, a built-in dishwasher, a replacement bathtub, a refrigerator, a stove, one air conditioner unit for the bedroom window, smoke detectors, and drapes. Which of these items, in your opinion, are accessions and which are not? See §9-335(d) and its Official Comment 7; In re Eaddy, 2016 WL 745277 (Bankr. D.S.C. 2016).

X. *FEDERAL PRIORITIES FOR DEBTS AND TAXES*

A. *The Federal Priority Statute*

Most of the federal statutes concerning secured transactions are registration acts only and say little or nothing about priorities in the collateral. There are two major exceptions: the general federal priority statute, 31 U.S.C. §3713, and the Federal Tax Lien Act, which is part of the Internal Revenue Code (§§6321 to 6323).

The federal priority statute (enacted originally in 1797!) is a broadly worded grant of pre-bankruptcy priority for *all* federal claims (no matter how they arise: as tax matters, contract debts, federal insurance loans, guaranties, etc.), so these claims are paid first when a debtor becomes insolvent. It is a truism that governments, when making laws, always protect themselves before others.

Priority of Government Claims 31 U.S.C. §3713

(A)(1) A Claim oftThe United States Government shall be paid first when—

(A) a person indebted to the Government is insolvent and—

(i) the debtor without enough property to pay all debts makes a voluntary assignment of property;

(ii) property of the debtor, if absent, is attached; or

(iii) the act of bankruptcy is committed; or

(B) the estate of a deceased debtor, in the custody of the executor or administrator, is not enough to pay all debts of the debtor.

(2) This section does not apply to a case under title 11 [bankruptcy].

(b) A representative of a person or an estate (except a trustee acting under title 11) paying any part of a debt of the person or estate before paying a claim of the Government is liable to the extent of the payment for unpaid claims of the Government.

The statute makes no exceptions to absolute federal priority, but the courts have subordinated the federal claim to an earlier lien (judicial, statutory, and consensual) if the lien is *choate,* a word dating back to 1534 and meaning "complete or perfected." The United States Supreme Court, in a maddening series of cases, has refused to clarify the current meaning of *choate,* so it is difficult to predict when an earlier perfected lien will be sufficiently choate to prevail over the federal debt. Lower federal courts have held that most security interests perfected under Article 9 are sufficiently choate to come ahead of the United States' claim. Pine Builders, Inc. v. United States, 413 F. Supp. 77 (E.D. Va. 1976). There is general agreement, however, that a security arrangement claiming a floating lien on after-acquired property or claiming a priority for future advances is inchoate and inferior to the federal claim. G. Gilmore §40.5. It is clear that if the Federal Tax Lien Act, discussed next, applies to a dispute then it and not the Federal Priority Statute resolves the issues involved. It should also be noted that the Bankruptcy Code provides that federal tax debts get all sorts of special treatment in a bankruptcy proceeding, including surviving an individual debtor's discharge (as to income tax debts owed for the last three years); 11 U.S.C. §523(a)(1).

B. *Tax Liens—Basic Priority*

A federal tax lien arises on *assessment* and covers all of the taxpayer's property, real or personal, presently owned or after-acquired. It is a secret lien, because it may happen that no one knows of the assessment except the IRS, but the tax lien nevertheless binds the property, and the government wins out over all parties claiming an interest in the property except those listed in §6323(a): "any purchaser, holder of a security interest, mechanic's lienor, or judgment creditor." To prevail over such persons, the federal tax lien must be *filed* in the place designated under state law See I.R.C. §6323(f). This is usually the state's Secretary of State Article 9 filing system, but not always: "In the following sixteen states, a notice of federal tax lien is filed in an office other than the office in which UCC financing statements are filed: Alaska Ohio Indiana Pennsylvania Kentucky Rhode Island Maryland South Carolina Massachusetts Tennessee Missouri Utah New Jersey Vermont New Mexico West Virginia. In the following three additional states, notices of federal tax lien and UCC financing statements are filed in the same office but are, apparently, not indexed together, so that a separate search of each database is necessary: Florida Georgia Illinois." Department of the Treasury, Internal Revenue Service, Guidelines for Processing Notice of Federal Tax Lien Documents, https://www.irs.gov/pub/irs-pdf/p1468.pdf.

C. *Tax Liens and After-Acquired Property*

PROBLEM 406

Octopus National Bank (ONB) had a perfected security interest in the inventory, accounts receivable, instruments, and chattel paper of an automobile dealership named Smiles Motors, to which the bank made periodic loans. Smiles Motors failed to pay its federal taxes, and the IRS filed a tax lien in the proper place on October 1. On the first days of November and December new shipments of cars arrived at Smiles's lot, and all during the year Smiles continued to sell cars on credit, generating chattel paper and accounts receivable. Does the filing of the tax lien cut off ONB's floating lien in whole or in part? Is this issue in any way affected by the bank's knowledge of the tax lien filing?

The answer to this Problem is that §6323(c) of the Internal Revenue Code expressly permits *commercial financing security* (defined at the end of the section) to fall under an existing perfected security arrangement and take priority over a filed federal tax lien if the new collateral is acquired by the taxpayer-debtor in the 45 days following the tax lien filing. The statute, like most of the tax code, is written in almost impenetrable language, but that is what it means. While §6323(c)(2)(A) requires that the loan has to be made without knowledge of the tax lien filing, the lender's later discovery of the tax lien filing in no way affects the priority of its floating lien during the 45-day period; see Treas. Reg. §301.6323(c)-1(d) (1976). Section 6323(c) reads:

> (c) Protection for certain commercial transactions financing agreements, etc.
>
> (1) *In general.* To the extent provided in this subsection, even though notice of a lien imposed by section 6321 has been filed, such lien shall not be valid with respect to a security interest which came into existence after tax lien filing but which—
>
> (A) is in qualified property covered by the terms of a written agreement entered into before tax lien filing and constituting—
>
> (i) a commercial transactions financing agreement,
>
> (ii) a real property construction or improvement financing agreement, or

(iii) an obligatory disbursement agreement, and—

(B) is protected under local law against a judgment lien arising, as of the time of tax lien filing, out of an unsecured obligation.

(2) *Commercial transactions financing agreement.* For purposes of this subsection—

(A) Definition: The term "commercial transactions financing agreement" means an agreement (entered into by a person in the course of his trade or business)—

(i) to make loans to the taxpayer to be secured by commercial financing security acquired by the taxpayer in the ordinary course of his trade or business, or

(ii) to purchase commercial financing security, (other than inventory) acquired by the taxpayer in the ordinary course of his trade or business; but such an agreement shall be treated as coming within the term only to the extent that such loan or purchase is made before the 46th day of tax lien filing or (if earlier) before the lender or purchaser had actual notice or knowledge of such tax lien filing.

(B) Limitation on qualified property. The term "qualified property," when used with respect to a commercial transactions financing agreement, includes only commercial financing security acquired by the taxpayer before the 46th day after the date of tax lien filing.

(C) Commercial financing security defined. The term "commercial financing security" means (i) paper of a kind ordinarily arising in commercial transactions, (ii) accounts receivable, (iii) mortgages on real property, and (iv) inventory.

To take advantage of this 45-day period, Uniform Commercial Code §9-323(b) also creates a similar 45-day rule in which advances made by a perfected Article 9 creditor prevail over the intervening interest of a judicial lien creditor.[17]

Plymouth Savings Bank v. U.S. I.R.S.

United States Court of Appeals, First Circuit, 1999
187 F.3d 203

Cudahy, Senior Circuit Judge.

Jordan Hospital ("Hospital") owed Shirley Dionne ("Dionne") $75,000. Dionne, in turn, was indebted to the Plymouth Savings Bank ("Bank") and the Internal Revenue Service ("IRS"), both of which held valid liens on the

17. Similarly, §9-323(d) creates a 45-day period that protects non-ordinary course buyers from future advances made with knowledge of the purchase or more than 45 days after the purchase. There is an identical rule for leases in §9-323(f). All of this will be explored in Problem 408.

money the Hospital owed Dionne. The Hospital deposited the money with the district court, and we must now decide who is entitled to it. The problem is simply to determine which of the two liens has priority. We hold that the Bank's lien may trump the IRS's and therefore reverse the district court's grant of summary judgment in favor of the IRS.

Most of the facts are not in dispute. Dionne owned and operated the Greenlawn Nursing Home, a 47-bed state-licensed facility. On September 22, 1993 and apparently before extending credit, the Bank filed a financing statement with the state of Massachusetts describing and giving notice of its security interest in Greenlawn and other assets of Dionne. On April 13, 1994, Dionne executed an $85,000 promissory note in favor of the Bank. As security for the loan, Dionne granted the Bank a security interest in all of her tangible and intangible personal property individually, as well as in her capacity as a sole proprietor doing business as Greenlawn. Paragraph 2 of the agreement specifically granted the Bank: all cash and non-cash proceeds resulting or arising from the rendering of services by Dionne; all general intangibles including proceeds of other collateral; and all inventory, receivables, contract rights or other personal property of Dionne. On or about December 1, 1994, Dionne defaulted on her $85,000 obligation to the Bank, leaving some $65,465 unpaid.

Dionne's financial troubles did not end there. She failed to make Federal Insurance Contribution Act, 26 U.S.C. §3101, et seq. (FICA), payments of $19,639 for the second quarter of 1994. The IRS assessed liability on September 19, 1994 and filed a federal tax lien in the district court on December 19. Dionne again failed to make FICA payments of $62,767 for the fourth quarter of 1994. Liability was assessed on February 2, 1995 and a lien was filed on February 14.

On March 31, 1995, Dionne signed a contract in which she agreed to help the Hospital obtain a license to operate a skilled nursing facility in exchange for $300,000, payable in three installments. Dionne would receive $25,000 when she signed a letter of intent, $200,000 when Massachusetts approved a license and the final $75,000 two years after the license-approval date. With Dionne's assistance, by mid-May 1995 the Hospital had received approval for its license and had paid Dionne the first two installments, totaling $225,000. (In practical effect, it appears that Dionne transferred her Greenlawn license to the Hospital.) The Hospital never paid Dionne the $75,000 balance.

The Bank sued the Hospital in Massachusetts state court to recover the unpaid balance of its loan to Dionne. Considering cross-motions for summary judgment, the state court ruled for the Bank. It found that, pursuant to the contract between Dionne and the Hospital, the $75,000 constituted cash proceeds arising from the rendering of personal services by Dionne. Because the security agreement between the Bank and Dionne expressly covered "proceeds" of services, the court held that the Bank had a secured interest in the money. The court rejected the Bank's argument that the security interest attached to the nursing home license or to proceeds of the transfer of that license. Instead of awarding the $75,000 to the Bank, however, the court directed the Bank to bring a declaratory judgment action to determine whether its interest in the money had priority over that of other lien-holders.

Ever diligent, the Bank brought such an action—this one—which the IRS subsequently removed to the district court. The Hospital, content to let the Bank and the IRS do battle, deposited the $75,000 with the district court and exited from the action. The Bank and the IRS filed cross-motions for summary judgment, each asserting that its lien trumped the other's. The court sided with the IRS. The Bank's right to recover as against the government depended on when Dionne had performed the services required by the contract, the district court stated. And, although the record on the timing of Dionne's performance was sparse, the court determined that it was undisputed that she had not helped the Hospital secure approval of a nursing home license within the 45 days following the tax lien filing as required by the Federal Tax Lien Act, 26 U.S.C. §§6321, 6323(c) (FTLA). See Dis. Ct. Mem. Op. & Order at 18-19. Accordingly, the district court held that the IRS's two liens were superior to the Bank's lien. The Bank appeals this decision, and we review de novo the district court's grant of summary judgment in favor of the government. . . .

When an individual fails to pay her taxes after a demand has been made, the FTLA grants the United States a lien "upon all property and rights to property, whether real or personal, belonging to such person." 26 U.S.C. §6321. The lien also attaches to property acquired by the delinquent taxpayer after the initial imposition of the lien. See, e.g., Glass City Bank v. United States, 326 U.S. 265, 267, 66 S. Ct. 108, 90 L. Ed. 56 (1945). Section 6323 of the FTLA, however, gives certain commercial liens priority over federal tax liens. Pursuant to §6323(a) and as defined in §6323(h), for example, tax liens are subordinate to security interests in a taxpayer's property that is "in existence" before the government files notice of the tax lien. (Subsection 6323(f) details the filing requirements.) And §6323(c) extends the priority of these prior security interests to certain "qualified property" that the taxpayer acquires even after the government has filed a notice of the tax lien. The scope of this safe harbor for after-acquired property under §6323(c) is at issue here. Mindful that we are entering "the tortured meanderings of federal tax lien law, intersected now by the somewhat smoother byway of the Uniform Commercial Code [UCC]," Texas Oil & Gas Corp. v. United States, 466 F.2d 1040, 1043 (5th Cir. 1972), we lay out the pertinent provisions with as much specificity as we can apply.

To fall within §6323(c)'s safe harbor for after-acquired property, a security interest must be in "qualified property covered by the terms of a written agreement entered into before tax lien filing," including "commercial transactions financing agreement[s]." 26 U.S.C. §6323(c)(1)(A)(i). The security interest must also be superior, under local law, to a judgment lien arising out of an unsecured obligation. See id. at §6323(c)(1)(B). A "commercial transactions financing agreement" is defined as "an agreement (entered into by a person in the course of his trade or business) . . . to make loans to the taxpayer to be secured by commercial financing security acquired by the taxpayer in the ordinary course of his trade or business," id. at §6323(c)(2)(A)(i), and must be entered into within 45 days of the date of the tax lien filing. See id. at §6323(c)(2)(A). "Commercial financing security" can include, among other things, "paper of a kind ordinarily arising in commercial transactions" and "accounts receivable," id. at §6323(c)(2)(C), and it must be "acquired by the taxpayer before the 46th day after the date of tax lien filing." Id. at §6323(c)(2)(B).

The relevant Treasury regulations include still more definitions. "Paper of a kind ordinarily arising in commercial transactions" means "any written document customarily used in commercial transactions," and includes "paper giving contract rights." 26 C.F.R. §301.6323(c)-1(c)(1). For purposes of the FTLA, a "contract right" is "any right to payment under a contract not yet earned by performance and not evidenced by an instrument or chattel paper." Id. at §301.6323(c)-1(c)(2)(i). "An account receivable is any right to payment for goods sold or leased or for services rendered which is not evidenced by an instrument or chattel paper." Id. at §301.6323(c)-1(c)(2)(ii).

Because Dionne signed the personal service contract with the Hospital exactly 45 days after the IRS filed notice of the second tax lien (February 14-March 31),[18] the fighting issue is whether by so doing she "acquired" rights to the $75,000, the money the Hospital owed Dionne and deposited with the district court. See 26 U.S.C. §6323(c)(2)(B). If, by signing the contract, Dionne acquired rights to the money, then the Bank's lien trumps the IRS's. For, if that is the case, it is undisputed that the Dionne-Hospital contract is commercial financing security within §6323(c)(2)(C) and that the Dionne-Bank agreement is a commercial transactions financing agreement within §6323(c)(1)(A)(i) & (c)(2). In this scenario, the Bank's security interest is in qualified property, and the $75,000 would fall within the safe harbor for after-acquired property. On the other hand, if Dionne did

18. The Bank does not claim that its lien should take priority over the first tax lien, filed on December 19, 1994. The duel here is between only the second tax lien (filed on February 14, 1995, and covering FICA payments of $62,767 for the fourth quarter of 1994) and the Bank's lien.

not acquire the rights to the money when she signed the contract, the IRS's lien takes priority.

The Treasury Department (of which the IRS is a part) has provided an answer. Recall that the potential qualified property here is the contract between Dionne and the Hospital, which granted Dionne certain rights to payments when she performed certain services. Before the 46th day after the tax lien was filed (that is, before April 1, 1995), if Dionne had acquired anything, she could only have acquired a contract right, not an account receivable, because she had yet to perform any services. See 26 C.F.R. §301.6323(c)-1(c)(2)(i) & (ii). The regulations provide that a "contract right . . . is acquired by a taxpayer when the contract is made." Id. at §301.6323(c)-1(d). So, Dionne acquired the right to be paid for services to be rendered in the future at the time she entered into that contract. In statutory terms, the commercial transactions financing agreement (the Dionne-Bank agreement), which was entered into well before the tax lien filing, covers the Bank's loan (the $85,000) to the taxpayer (Dionne). The loan in turn was secured by commercial financing security (the Dionne-Hospital contract). The Dionne-Hospital contract conferred contract rights (the right to be paid $75,000 two years after Massachusetts approved a nursing home license for the Hospital) and was acquired by the taxpayer within 45 days of the tax lien filing. See 26 U.S.C. §6323(c)(2)(A) & (B). The contract, and the rights (even if conditional) under it, are therefore qualified property covered by the Bank's security interest and protected by §6323(c)'s safe harbor.

Of course, the Bank is interested in the money, not the contract right. The regulations again point the way. "Proceeds" are "whatever is received when collateral is sold, exchanged, or collected." 26 C.F.R. §301.6323(c)-1(d). The regulations further provide: "Identifiable proceeds, which arise from the collection or disposition of qualified property by the taxpayer, are considered to be acquired at the time such qualified property is acquired if the secured party has a continuously perfected security interest in the proceeds under local law." Id. Recall that the commercial financing security (the Dionne-Hospital contract and the rights under it) is simply collateral for the loan (the Bank's $85,000 loan to Dionne). So, where the collateral is a contract giving contract rights, the proceeds of those rights, like the rights themselves, are considered to have been acquired at the time the contract was made. This is so even though the right to proceeds under the contract does not become unconditional until the contract is performed. Pursuant to the Treasury regulations, the conditional right to the proceeds relates back to the time the contract was formed and executed. Therefore, Dionne acquired the rights to the proceeds of the contract right on March 31, 1995, exactly 45 days from the date of the tax lien filing.

In this case, however, the proceeds of the contract right are simply an account receivable, the right to payment of $75,000 for services rendered by Dionne. See 26 C.F.R. §301.6323(c)-1(c)(2)(ii). And herein lies the rub. The IRS argues that, pursuant to the regulations, a taxpayer acquires an account receivable "at the time, and to the extent, a right to payment is earned by performance." Echoing the district court, the IRS correctly points out that Dionne did not earn a right to payment before the 45 days. See Appellee's Br. at 18. But the contract and the rights under it, rather than the account receivable, are the qualified property at issue here, and the regulations provide that the proceeds of qualified property are deemed to be acquired at the time the qualified property is acquired. The regulations do not distinguish between forms of proceeds. Well then, the IRS parries, the account receivable cannot be "proceeds" because the contract was not "sold, exchanged, or collected." See 26 C.F.R. §301.6323(c)-1(d). Had Dionne sold the contract, the IRS says, the Bank's lien would reach the proceeds of that sale; but performance (rendering the services) does not amount to a sale. See Appellee's Br. at 18. This ingenious quibble is unconvincing. Dionne's rendering of the contracted-for services effectively "exchanged" her contract right, converting it into an account receivable. See 26 C.F.R. §301.6323(c)-1(d). The IRS has given us no good reason, nor can we find any basis in commercial reality, to distinguish between a "sale" or an "exchange" and a conversion by performance for this purpose. In fact, performance would seem to be necessary for the production of proceeds even if there were a sale or exchange of the contract. We therefore conclude that the account receivable, the right to the $75,000, is the proceeds of the contract right.

To this, the IRS responds by complaining that we have expanded too far §6323(c)'s safe harbor for after-acquired property. It cites legislative history which it claims suggests that Congress intended §6323(c)'s protections to extend only to property that was collected within 45 days of the tax lien filing. See Appellee's Br. at 17 (citing S. Rep. No. 1708, 89th Cong., 2d Sess. (1966), at 2, 8). We find this argument unpersuasive. As an initial matter, this Senate Report does not directly address commercial financing secured by contract rights, the precise issue here. The Report does indicate, however, that the FTLA was "an attempt to conform the lien provisions of the internal revenue laws to the concepts developed in [the UCC]." S. Rep. No. 1708, 89th Cong., 2d Sess., at 2. The Treasury regulations reflect this intent by providing definitions for FTLA terms that closely track UCC definitions of like terms. For example, the FTLA definitions of "contract right" and "account receivable" match the pre-1972 revision definitions of "contract" and "account," compare, e.g., 26 C.F.R. §301.6323(c)-1(c)(i) & (ii) with Mass. Gen. Laws Ann. ch. 106, §9-106 (West 1998) (Official Reasons for 1972 Changes), and the two definitions of the term "proceeds" are almost identical, compare 26 C.F.R. §301.6323(c)-1(d) with Mass. Gen. Laws Ann. ch. 106, §9-306(a) (West 1988) [now §9-102(a)(64)—Eds.] (defining "proceeds" as "whatever is received upon the sale, exchange, collection or other disposition of collateral or proceeds"). Our conclusion that the Bank's security interest in the contract rights covers the proceeds of those rights—even if the proceeds are accounts receivable—is compatible with still other provisions of the UCC. See, e.g., Mass. Gen. Laws Ann. ch. 106, §9-306(2) (West 1980) [now §9-315—EDS.] (providing that security interests extend to the proceeds of all secured property). In all events, whatever Congress intended, the regulations make it clear that, so long as the contract was entered into within 45 days of the tax lien filing, the rights under that contract and all of the proceeds of those rights fall within §6323(c)'s protective bounds.

This conclusion can hardly come as a surprise to the IRS. The IRS has advanced the same arguments which it uses here in cases analogous to this one, and has lost each time (except, of course, below). See Bremen Bank & Trust Co. v. United States, 131 F.3d 1259 (8th Cir. 1997); State Bank of Fraser v. United States, 861 F.2d 954 (6th Cir. 1988); In re National Fin. Alternatives, Inc., 96 B.R. 844 (Bkrtcy. N.D. Ill. 1989). Each of these cases, like this one, turned neither on a clever interpretation of the FTLA nor on a thorough scouring of the Congressional records in an attempt to divine intent, but instead on a plain reading of the regulations. It is that simple: the regulations governing §6323(c) say that contract rights and the proceeds thereof are acquired at the time the parties enter into the contract. It matters not that the proceeds of that contract right might be accounts receivable because the regulations do not distinguish among different kinds of proceeds. The IRS, which promulgates these regulations, has had ample opportunity to rewrite them to better suit its desired interpretation of the statute. (Congress, of course, might yet disagree.) To our knowledge, it has made no such effort. . . .

Because we find that the Bank's lien may trump the IRS's, we REVERSE the district court's grant of summary judgment in favor of the IRS. The case is REMANDED to the district court for proceedings consistent with this opinion.

PROBLEM 407

Six months after the IRS filed a tax lien against her, Charlene McGee bought a fire extinguisher system for her horse stables. She purchased the system on credit from King Protection Enterprises, which reserved a purchase money security interest in itself and perfected it. Is the IRS's lien superior to King's purchase money security interest? See Rev. Rul. 68-57, 26 C.F.R. §301.6321-1; In re Specialty Contracting & Supply, Inc., 140 B.R. 922 (Bankr. N.D. Ga. 1992).

D. *Tax Liens and Future Advances*

After the filing of the tax lien, the taxpayer's financing creditor may make a new loan, expecting it to be secured by an existing perfected interest in the collateral listed in the security agreement. If the secured party is aware of the filed tax lien, it almost certainly will refuse to make the advance, but if the lien is undiscovered and the advance is given, which has priority—the IRS or the lender?

Section 6323(d) of the Internal Revenue Code gives protection to future advances made without knowledge of the tax lien in the 45 days after its filing if the advance is collateralized by a perfected security interest in existing property of the taxpayer, such as equipment. It provides:

> (d) 45-day period for making disbursements.
>
> —Even though notice of a lien imposed by section 6321 has been filed, such lien shall not be valid with respect to a security interest which came into existence after tax lien filing by reason of disbursements made before the 46th day after the date of tax lien filing, or (if earlier) before the person making such disbursements had actual notice or knowledge of tax lien filing, but only if such security interest
>
> (1) is in property (A) subject, at the time of tax lien filing, to the lien imposed by section 6321, and (B) covered by the terms of a written agreement entered into before tax lien filing, and
>
> (2) is protected under local law against a judgment lien arising, as of the time of tax lien filing, out of an unsecured obligation.

PROBLEM 408

Marie Medici owned a hat factory. She financed her business through a series of loans from the Richelieu State Bank pursuant to an agreement by which she gave the bank a security interest in all of the factory's equipment, and the bank agreed to loan her money from time to time "as it thinks prudent." A financing statement covering the equipment was filed in the proper place. On August 1, she owed the bank $1,500 (having paid back most of the prior loans). The equipment consisted of two machines: the Habsburg Hat Blocker (worth $7,000) and the Huguenot Felt Press (worth $5,000). On that date, the United States filed a federal tax lien against all of Medici's property. On August 31, the bank loaned her another $10,000. Answer these questions:

(a) Assuming the bank did not know of the tax lien on August 31, does the bank or the United States have priority in the equipment, and to what amount? See I.R.C. §6323(d). What if the bank did know?

(b) Assume there is no tax lien, but on August 15 Louis Dupes paid Medici $5,000 cash for the Huguenot Felt Press, and on August 31 the bank loaned her the $10,000. Does the purchase cut off the bank's security interest? Does it matter whether or not the bank knew of the sale prior to the August 31 loan? See §§9-323(d) and (e), 9-102(a)(69).

(c) Instead of buying the machine, as in the last paragraph, assume that Dupes is another creditor of Medici. On August 15, he levied execution on the felt press pursuant to a judgment. If he did this with full knowledge of the bank's security interest and if with notice of his levy the bank still loans Medici the $10,000 on August 31, does Dupes or the Richelieu State Bank have the superior interest in the felt press as to the future advance? See §9-323(b). If the bank did not know of the levy by Dupes on August 15 but loaned Medici an additional $5,000 on October 15, who would have priority as to this advance?

CHAPTER 24 ASSESSMENT: MULTIPLE CHOICE QUESTIONS

1. Jin-Qua loaned $200,000 to Noble House, a Tennessee business which was in a financial jam. The parties signed an effective security agreement, granting Jin-Qua a security interest in Noble House's inventory, equipment, and accounts. Jin-Qua was not in the business of asset-based lending and did not know to file a UCC-1 financing statement. Eighteen months later, with its debts greater than its assets, Noble House filed bankruptcy. The debt to Jin-Qua was $222,000, including interest. The collateral was worth about $400,000. Will Jin-Qua's collateral ensure that Jin-Qua is paid?
   a. Yes, because Jin-Qua has an effective security interest.
   b. No, Jin-Qua will, in effect, lose its right to the collateral and be just another unsecured creditor in the bankruptcy.
   c. Yes, because there is no showing that the failure to file a financing statement induced other creditors to lend to Noble House, so they cannot show any reliance injury.
   d. Yes, because Jin-Qua can file a financing statement and become perfected, with priority over other claimants to the collateral.

2. On January 1, Baker Long Distance negotiated a line of credit from Kimetto Finance, signing a security agreement putting up its inventory and accounts as collateral. Kimetto Finance quickly filed its financing statement on that day, but dallied in actually handing over funds. It had no obligations under the agreement to lend. Frustrated, Baker Long Distance signed an agreement with Mutai Bank on February 1, likewise giving a security interest in its inventory and accounts. Mutai Bank the same day filed its financing statement and loaned $200,000. A few weeks

later, on March 1, Baker Long Distance borrowed $250,000 under its line of credit with Kimetto Finance. About a year later, Baker Long Distance refused demands by both lenders to repay. Its business setbacks meant the collateral was worth only about $200,000. Which lender has priority in the collateral?

a. Kimetto Finance, because it filed before Mutai Bank filed or otherwise perfected.
b. Mutai Bank, because it loaned first.
c. Mutai Bank, because it perfected first.
d. The lenders would share pro rata, having the same status as perfected secured creditors.

3. Khufu Construction got a construction project loan from Luxor Bank, secured by Khufu's state-of-the-art equipment. Luxor duly perfected its security interest by filing a financing statement covering Khufu Construction's "equipment, now-owned or after-acquired." A few months later, Khufu Construction purchased a Seismic Earthmover excavator on credit from Normous Machines, who duly filed its own financing statement the day after delivery. If Khufu Construction runs into problems, which creditor will have priority in the Seismic Earthmover?
   a. Luxor Bank, because it was first to file or perfect.
   b. Luxor Bank, because it perfected first.
   c. Normous Machines, because it has a perfected purchase money security interest.
   d. Luxor Bank, because Normous Machines has a purchase money security interest, but the collateral is not consumer goods.
   e. Luxor Bank, because Normous Machines did not file before delivering the collateral.

4. Khufu Construction, short of cash, sold the Seismic Earthmover to Great Wall Construction, who paid the market price for such a machine, in good faith, with no knowledge of the security interests of Normous Machines and Luxor Bank. Does Great Wall Construction take the machine free of the creditors' security interests?
   a. Yes, because it paid market price in good faith without notice.
   b. Yes, because it was not a party to the security agreements creating the security interests.
   c. No. The security interest generally remains with the collateral when sold, and none of the exceptions to that rule applies here.
   d. Yes. If the collateral is sold, the creditor lose its security interest but is entitled to claim the money received as its collateral.

5. Selassie Gallery gets a much-needed loan to fund operating expenses from Nile Bank. Selassie Gallery signs an agreement making its inventory

of art collateral for the debt, and promising not to sell any artwork without permission from Nile Bank. Shortly thereafter, Selassie Bank sells a painting to Moulson in a typical art gallery transaction. Does Moulson take the painting subject to Nile Bank's security interest?

a. Yes, because the sale violated the security agreement.
b. Yes, because a security interest continues in collateral despite sale.
c. No, because Moulson is protected as a buyer in the ordinary course of business.
d. No, because a good faith buyer takes free of a security interest.

ANSWERS

1. *B* is the best answer. This question illustrates how UCC Article 9 sets the basic structure for finance in the United States. Someone who makes a loan or sells goods or services on credit, may do so unsecured or secured. An unsecured creditor merely has a legally enforceable promise of payment. If the debtor has no assets to enforce that promise against, the unsecured creditor may be out of luck. A secured creditor has a claim on specific property of the debtor to get paid. To maintain its rights against not just the debtor, but other claimants to the collateral, the secured creditor must put the world on notice by perfecting the security interest, such as by filing a UCC-1 financing statement.

   A secured creditor that fails to perfect, as did Jin-Qua, will likely lose a priority contest to a bankruptcy trustee, or a perfected creditor, or a purchaser of the collateral. See §9-317. Someone who becomes a lien creditor takes priority over an unperfected security interest. §9-317. Lien creditors include judgment creditors who have attached the collateral and, most importantly, a bankruptcy trustee as of the moment the bankruptcy petition is filed. §9-102(52). Once the lien creditor has established priority, it retains it over a subsequently perfected security interest. §9-317. By these rules, Article 9, for most personal property collateral, draws the line between secured and unsecured creditors.

   To put things in context, remember Benedict v. Ratner from Chapter 19. The court held that an assignment of accounts as collateral was not effective, because it was fraudulent as to the other creditors, because they did not know the property would not be subject to their claims. Article 9 was subsequently enacted to, among other things, permit secured creditors to have security interests enforceable against other creditors (and bankruptcy trustees and buyers of the collateral), provided secured creditors gave notice, by perfecting the security interest. Filing a financing statement is a deceptively important task for a creditor and its lawyers.
2. *A* is the best answer. Mutai Bank did loan first. It also perfected first. A creditor's security interest perfects when it has attached and the

creditor has done whatever is necessary to perfect. When Mutai Bank made its loan and filed on February 1, it had then attached (meeting the three requirements of security agreement, value, debtor having rights in the collateral), and perfected (by filing). As of that date, Kimetto Finance's security agreement had not attached, because Kimetto Finance had not yet given value. Rather, Kimetto Finance's security agreement attached and perfected on March 1, when it finally loaned money, giving value. But priority does not go to first to perfect or first to loan, contrary to *B* and *C.* As between perfected creditors, priority generally goes to the first to file or perfect. §9-322(a)(2). Mutai Bank's priority date is February 1. Kimetto Bank's priority date is January 1, giving it priority over Mutai Bank.

That result may seem unfair, where Mutai Bank loses priority even though it loaned money to Baker Long Distance and perfected, before Kimetto Finance made its loan. But Article 9's rule provides a clear method of establishing priority. Mutai Bank, before lending, could simply have searched the UCC records, which would have disclosed that Kimetto Finance already established priority in Baker Long Distance's inventory and accounts. The date of filing is a public record, clearer and easier to establish than the dates of signing security agreements and making loans. Creditors must know the priority rules and act accordingly.

3. *C* is the best answer. In a priority dispute between two perfected creditors, the general rule is that priority goes to the first to file or perfect. But §9-234 gives special priority to a purchase money security interest (PMSI). If the collateral is not inventory or livestock, the PMSI takes priority as long as it is perfected no later than 20 days after the debtor receives the collateral. §9-234. Contrary to *D,* the rule applies to PMSI's generally, not just to a PMSI in consumer goods. Contrary to *D,* the creditor gets a grace period, if the collateral is not inventory or livestock, receiving priority as long as the creditor perfects within 20 days of delivery of the collateral. That grace period applies here, where the collateral is equipment.

   If the collateral is inventory or livestock, the PMSI creditor may still get priority, but to do so, before the debtor receives the collateral, must perfect and give the other creditor notice.
4. *C* is the best answer. A security interest generally "continues in collateral notwithstanding sale, lease, license, exchange, or other disposition thereof." §9-315(a)(1). There are several exceptions to that rule, but none of them apply here. The creditor could consent and release its security interest. Id. The security interest could be unperfected. §9-317(b). The transaction could be a consumer-to-consumer sale, §9-320(b) or a sale to a buyer in the ordinary course of business. §9-320(a). This question at first might sound like a buyer in the ordinary course of business transaction. But that exception is narrower than it sounds, as set out

in the list of qualifications after the *Western Limestone* case, culled from §9-320(a) and §1-201(b)(9). Applicable here is the requirement that the buyer purchase goods "from a person . . . in the business of selling goods of that kind." Khufu is in the construction business, not in the business of selling equipment. The buyer in the ordinary course rules does not protect all good faith buyers, contrary to *A*. Rather, it protects a buyer purchasing goods from someone in the business of selling such goods, such as someone buying construction equipment from a construction equipment retailer.

5. *C* is the best answer. A sale to a mere good faith buyer will be subject to the security interest, as the last question illustrated, contrary to *D*. But a sale to a buyer in the ordinary course of business will be free of the security interest, provided all the requirements of §9-320(a) and §1-201(b)(9) are met. Those requirements are met here, so Moulson would take free of the security interest. The sale breached the security agreement, but the buyer is protected as long as the buyer did not know that the sale breached the agreement. §1-201(b)(9). The question illustrates how the buyer in the ordinary course rule encourages customers to buy from merchants, by freeing them from wondering if the merchant's inventory is someone's collateral.

CHAPTER 25

BANKRUPTCY AND ARTICLE 9

When a debtor enters the bankruptcy court seeking financial relief, a creditor is likely to get nothing unless the court recognizes the validity of the security interest held by that creditor in an asset of the debtor. Federal law in the form of the Bankruptcy Code allows the debtor's trustee in bankruptcy (or, in Chapter 11 reorganizations, a similar entity called the "debtor in possession") to use various theories, explored below, to attack the security interest. If those attacks fail, the creditor's rights in the collateral continue, and such a creditor is likely to retrieve the collateral (or its value) from the bankruptcy proceeding before it is over. It is the job of the creditor's attorney to be aware, from the creation of the security interest, of issues that might arise in bankruptcy and take appropriate steps to lessen their effect.

I. THE TRUSTEE'S STATUS

The filing of a bankruptcy petition creates an automatic stay of any further creditor collection activity. Bankruptcy Code §362. Thereafter, creditors must pursue whatever rights they have in the bankruptcy proceeding only. The rule is clear: filing a bankruptcy petition stops all creditor actions done without the permission of the bankruptcy court, and violations lead to contempt of court citations. Courts are split on whether a creditor violates the automatic stay by simply retaining a vehicle that was repossessed before bankruptcy. Compare, e.g., In re Fulton, 926 F.3d 916 (7th Cir. 2019), and WD Equipment LLC v. Cowen (In re Cowen), 849 F.3d 943 (10th Cir. 2017). If a financing statement is effective when debtor goes into bankruptcy, it is not necessary to file a continuation statement to preserve perfection, according to In re Essex Construction, LLC, 2018 WL 4656206 (Bankr. D. Md. 2018) (applying the "freeze rule," meaning that bankruptcy freezes the parties in the position they held at the filing).

The trustee in bankruptcy is given a number of useful rights in resisting or attacking creditors' claims. As we have seen, the so-called "strong arm clause" imbues the trustee with the state law status of a hypothetical judicial lien creditor who acquires a lien on all of the debtor's property as of the moment of the filing of the bankruptcy petition. Bankruptcy Code §544(a) (reprinted below). Because state law, here §9-317(a)(2) of the Uniform Commercial Code, allows such a lien creditor to avoid unperfected security interests, the trustee may do so too. In addition, §558 gives the trustee the benefit of whatever defenses the debtor would have had against the creditor's claim, so that, for example, if the debt is barred by the Statute of Frauds or a statute of limitations, the trustee may assert these matters. Under §544(b) of the Bankruptcy Code, the trustee is imbued with the rights and position of any unsecured creditor who has a claim against the estate. In the cryptic and often criticized opinion of Moore v. Bay, 284 U.S. 4 (1931), the Supreme Court, per Oliver Wendell Holmes, held, however, that the trustee gets better rights than the creditor represented because the trustee's claim is not limited to the amount of the actual creditor's claim but rather is the size of the entire estate.

§544. Trustee as Lien Creditor and as Successor to Certain Creditors and Purchasers

(a) The trustee shall have, as of the commencement of the case, and without regard to any knowledge of the trustee or of any creditor, the rights and powers of, or may avoid any transfer of property of the debtor or any obligation incurred by the debtor that is voidable by—

(1) a creditor that extends credit to the debtor at the time of the commencement of the case, and that obtains, at such time and with respect to such credit, a judicial lien on all property on which a creditor on a simple contract could have obtained such a judicial lien, whether or not such a creditor exists; . . .

or

(3) a bona fide purchaser of real property, other than fixtures, from the debtor, against whom applicable law permits such transfer to be perfected, that obtains the status of a bona fide purchaser and has perfected such transfer at the time of the commencement of the case, whether or not such a purchaser exists.

(b) The trustee may avoid any transfer of an interest of the debtor in property or any obligation incurred by the debtor that is voidable under applicable law by a creditor holding an unsecured claim that is allowable under section 502 of this title or that is not allowable only under section 502(e) of this title.

PROBLEM 409

Lew Sun, a Korean, moved to Chicago and opened a Korean restaurant called "Seoul Food." He had many unsecured creditors (food sellers, linen services, employees, etc.). On April 17, he went to the International State Bank and got a loan of $10,000, and signed a security agreement in favor of the bank, secured by an interest in Sun's equipment. On April 18, one hour before the bank filed the financing statement, Sun filed a bankruptcy petition in the federal court.

(a) Can the trustee avoid the bank's security interest under §544(a) of the Code?

(b) What result if the bank had filed its financing statement two seconds before the bankruptcy petition was filed?

(c) If the bank's interest had been a *purchase money security interest,* would the filing of the bankruptcy petition have cut off the usual 20-day grace period? See §546(b) of the Code, which follows.

§546. Limitations on Avoiding Powers

. . . (b)(1) The rights and powers of the trustee under section 544, 545, or 549 of this title are subject to any generally applicable law that—

(A) permits perfection of an interest in property to be effective against an entity that acquires rights in such property before the date of such perfection; or

(B) provides for the maintenance or continuation of perfection of an interest in property to be effective against an entity that acquires rights in such property before the date on which action is taken to effect such maintenance or continuation. . . .

In re Duckworth

United States Court of Appeals, Seventh Circuit, 2014
776 F.3d 453

HAMILTON, Circuit Judge.

In these appeals we consider whether a secured lender can use parol evidence against a bankruptcy to save a security agreement from a mistaken description of the debt to be secured. The security agreement here said that the collateral secured a promissory note made on a given date. The date was a mistake. The borrower had executed a promissory note but two days after the stated date. This is the sort of mistake that can be corrected as between the original parties to the loan by reforming the instrument based on parol evidence.

We have previously held, however, that under Illinois' enactment of the Uniform Commercial Code a secured lender cannot use parol evidence *against a bankruptcy* to correct a mistaken description of the collateral in a security agreement. In re Martin Grinding & Machine Works, Inc., 793 F.2d 592, 595 (7th Cir. 1986). Similarly, the First Circuit has held that a lender cannot use parol evidence against a bankruptcy to change or add to the debts secured by the security agreement, relying on the same provisions in Massachusetts' enactment of the UCC. Safe Deposit Bank & Trust Co. v. Berman, 393 F.2d 401, 402-03 (1st Cir. 1968). The reasoning of these cases persuades us that the lender in these appeals was not entitled to use parol evidence against the bankruptcy to correct the mistaken description of the debt to be secured. We therefore hold that the security agreement did not give the lender a security interest in the specified collateral that could be enforced against the trustee. We reverse the judgments of the district courts and remand for further proceedings in the bankruptcy court.

I. Factual and Procedural Background

The parties filed cross-motions for summary judgment based on the following undisputed facts. On December 15, 2008, David L. Duckworth borrowed $1,100,000 from the State Bank of Toulon. The transaction was executed through a promissory note that was dated and signed on December 15 and an Agricultural Security Agreement dated two days earlier, December 13, 2008. The security agreement said that Duckworth granted the State Bank of Toulon a security interest in crops and farm equipment. The promissory note referred to the security agreement. The security agreement identified the debt to be secured, but the identification had a critical mistake. The security agreement said that it secured a note "in the principal amount of $_______ dated *December 13, 2008.*" But there was no promissory note dated December 13. Both the December 15 promissory note and the security agreement were prepared by the bank's loan officer.

In 2010, Duckworth filed a petition for bankruptcy protection under Chapter 7 of the bankruptcy code. Appellant Charles E. Covey was appointed trustee. The bank filed two complaints in bankruptcy court to initiate adversary proceedings. On cross-motions for summary judgment, the bankruptcy court held that the mistaken date in the security interest did not defeat the bank's security interest and that the security agreement of December 13, 2008 secured the note of December 15, 2008. The bankruptcy court issued two decisions in favor of the bank, one for proceeds from the sale of Duckworth's crops and another for proceeds from the sale of some of his farm equipment. The trustee appealed both bankruptcy court orders to the district court, where the appeals were assigned to different judges. Both district judges affirmed, and the trustee has appealed, in No. 14-1561 regarding the crop sale and in No. 14-1650 regarding the equipment sale. The issue before us is whether the mistaken date in the security agreement defeats the banks' asserted security interest in the crops and farm equipment.

II. Analysis

We review *de novo* a grant of summary judgment, meaning we decide the questions of law without giving deference to the decisions of the district court or the bankruptcy court. See In re ABC-Naco, Inc., 483 F.3d 470, 472 (7th Cir. 2007). The trustee argues that the security agreement unambiguously identified the debt to be secured, but did so only for a nonexistent debt and therefore failed to grant a security interest to secure the note of December 15, 2008. Even if the mistake in the security agreement might be corrected as between the original parties to the loan, the trustee argues, parol evidence of such a mistake cannot be used against a bankruptcy trustee to save the faulty security agreement.

The bank argues that the security agreement is enforceable against the original borrower and should also be enforceable against the trustee. The bank relies on the terms of the security agreement itself, parol evidence of the original parties' intent, and Illinois' "composite document" rule to save its security interest. The bank also contends that its transaction with the debtor satisfied the minimum requirements for an enforceable security interest under Illinois' enactment of the Uniform Commercial Code and therefore the security interest is effective against the trustee.

We first parse the terms of the security agreement and conclude that it cannot be construed to secure the December 15, 2008 note. We then consider the parol evidence argument. We conclude that although the evidence could have supported reformation of the security agreement as between the original parties, the evidence cannot be used against the bankruptcy trustee to reform the security agreement or otherwise to correct the mistaken identification of the debt to be secured. Nor does the composite document rule save the bank's security interest here. Finally, we examine the governing statute, Article 9 of the Uniform Commercial Code, and determine that it directs us to enforce the agreement according to its terms, which fail to secure the debt to the bank.

A. THE TERMS OF THE SECURITY AGREEMENT

The security agreement is governed by Illinois law, except where federal law might preempt it. Illinois adopts the familiar principle that an unambiguous contract is interpreted by the court as a matter of law without use of parol evidence. Air Safety, Inc. v. Teachers Realty Corp., 185 Ill. 2d 457, 236 Ill. Dec. 8, 706 N.E.2d 882, 884 (1999).

The relevant provisions of the security agreement are unambiguous as applied to these facts. The security agreement grants the bank a security interest "to secure the Indebtedness," which is defined as "the indebtedness evidenced by the Note or Related Documents." The security agreement then defines the "Note" as "the Note executed by David L. Duckworth in the principal amount of $_______ dated December 13, 2008, together with all renewals of, extensions of, modifications of, refinancings of, consolidations of, and substitutions for the note or credit agreement." In the security agreement, the dollar amount of the loan was left blank.

The bank faces two textual obstacles in arguing that the terms of the security agreement secure the debt embodied in the December 15 promissory note. First, the security agreement refers clearly to a December 13 promissory note that the parties agree never existed. The promissory note that the Bank seeks to secure was signed and dated on December 15.

Second, the Bank cannot rely on the security agreement's "Related Documents" provision to incorporate the December 15 promissory note. The relevant definitions in the security agreement are essentially circular. The definition of "Indebtedness" points the reader to "Related Documents," which are defined as documents "executed in connection with the Indebtedness." The "Indebtedness" is defined in turn as the debt evidenced by the "Note or Related Documents," and the Note again is defined as "the Note executed . . . dated December 13, 2008." These circular definitions thus offer no escape from the mistaken date. On its face, the security agreement secures only a December 13 promissory note that never existed. The text of the security agreement does not incorporate the promissory note dated December 15 or the description of the debt contained therein.

B. PAROL EVIDENCE AGAINST THE TRUSTEE?

To cure the mistaken date in the security agreement and connect it to the December 15 promissory note, the bank relies primarily on parol evidence, from outside the four corners of the document. The bank relies on the December 15 promissory note itself and testimony regarding the bank's and the borrower's intentions.

The bank offers two related theories for reading the security agreement as securing the December 15 note. First, the bank contends that parol evidence is generally admissible to assist in interpreting the security agreement, which it asserts is ambiguous. Second, the bank argues that we should use the composite document rule to read the security agreement and the December 15 note together because the two documents were executed as part of the same transaction. See, e.g., Tepfer v. Deerfield Savings & Loan

Ass'n, 118 Ill. App. 3d 77, 73 Ill. Dec. 579, 454 N.E.2d 676, 679 (1983) (documents executed by same parties in course of same transaction are "construed with reference to one another because they are, in the eyes of the law, one contract"). Both arguments attempt to justify the use of evidence external to the security agreement itself.

The testimony of both the bank officer who prepared the documents and borrower Duckworth makes clear that the bank made a mistake in preparing the security agreement. We are confident that the bank would have been able to obtain reformation—even of an unambiguous agreement—against the original borrower if he had tried to avoid the security agreement based on the mistaken date. See Fisher v. State Bank of Annawan, 163 Ill. 2d 177, 205 Ill. Dec. 520, 643 N.E.2d 811, 814 (1994) (reformation action available where clear and convincing evidence shows parties made a mutual mistake); Suburban Bank of Hoffman-Schaumburg v. Bousis, 144 Ill. 2d 51, 161 Ill. Dec. 289, 578 N.E.2d 935, 939 (1991) (same); Harley v. Magnolia Petroleum Co., 378 Ill. 19, 37 N.E.2d 760, 765 (1941) (same).

A bankruptcy trustee is in a different position, however. A bankruptcy trustee is tasked with maximizing the recovery of unsecured creditors. See In re Vic Supply Co., 227 F.3d 928, 931 (7th Cir. 2000). To assist in this task, trustees may exercise the so-called strong-arm power: the trustee is deemed to be in the privileged position of a hypothetical subsequent creditor and can avoid any interests that a hypothetical subsequent creditor could avoid "without regard to any knowledge of the trustee or of any creditor." See 11 U.S.C. §544(a). The strong-arm power is a "blunt information-generating tool" that encourages lenders to give public notice of their security interests by harshly penalizing those who fail to do so. Jonathan C. Lipson, *Secrets and Liens: The End of Notice in Commercial Finance Law,* 21 Emory Bankr. Dev. J. 421, 450-51 (2005) (criticizing the strong-arm power, "a necessary evil," as perhaps "more troublesome for its over- and under-inclusiveness than for its basic goals"); see also Barkley Clark & Barbara Clark, *The Law of Secured Transactions Under the Uniform Commercial Code* §6.02(1)(a) (3d ed. 2011) ("The strong-arm clause is the ultimate Article 9 enforcer."); *id.,* §6.02(1)(b) ("As a matter of public policy, the [strong-arm] rules penalize secret liens and encourage lenders to give public notice of their security interests.").

The bank argues that constructive notice may still be imputed to a trustee using the strong-arm power. The concept of constructive notice comes from state real property law and defines the property rights of good faith purchasers. See In re Crane, 742 F.3d 702, 706-07 (7th Cir. 2013). A good faith purchaser cannot avoid the claims of creditors who have complied with state recording laws that provide public notice of the ownership of and liens on property. For that reason, constructive notice constrains a trustee who seeks to use the specific strong-arm power of a good faith purchaser of property.

See 11 U.S.C. §544(a)(3); In re Sandy Ridge Oil Co., 807 F.2d 1332, 1336 (7th Cir. 1986).

But the trustee here does not need to assume the role of a good faith purchaser to avoid the lender's interest. The trustee can use other strong-arm provisions and stand in the shoes of other subsequent creditors, to which the limitations of constructive notice do not apply. The trustee may avoid the bank's security interest by acting as a hypothetical judicial lien creditor. 11 U.S.C. §544(a)(1). Such a trustee, unconstrained by constructive notice, may "void a security interest because of defects that need not have misled, or even have been capable of misleading, anyone." In re Vic Supply Co., 227 F.3d at 931.

We therefore must treat the trustee as if he were a hypothetical later lien creditor and ask if the bank has a valid security interest that could be asserted against such a creditor. We conclude that the bank's asserted security interest is not valid against such a later creditor. Such a creditor would be entitled to rely on the text of a security agreement, despite extrinsic evidence that could be used between the original parties to correct the mistaken identification of the debt to be secured.

We find guidance principally from our prior decision in *Martin Grinding* and the First Circuit's decision in Safe Deposit Bank and Trust Co. v. Berman. Those decisions emphasize the importance of third parties' ability to rely on unambiguous documents—even if the original parties can show they contain mistakes—to determine the validity and priority of security interests.

In *Martin Grinding*, we held that parol evidence about the original parties' intentions could not be used to correct a mistake in a security agreement by adding, over a bankruptcy trustee's objection, to the agreement's written list of the collateral securing a loan. The lender had failed to list inventory and accounts receivable as collateral in the security agreement. We enforced the unambiguous security agreement according to its terms:

> That the security agreement omits any mention of inventory and accounts receivable is unfortunate for the Bank, but does not make the agreement ambiguous. Since the security agreement is unambiguous on its face, neither the financing statement, nor the other loan documents can expand the Bank's security interest beyond that stated in the security agreement.

793 F.2d at 595. We recognized that the result was contrary to the intentions of the original parties. We explained, though, that the result should promote economy and certainty in secured transactions more generally, a central goal of Article 9 of the Uniform Commercial Code. *Id.* at 596 (Article 9 was intended to enable "'the immense variety of present-day secured financing transactions . . . [to] go forward with less cost and with greater certainty.'"),

quoting Ill. Rev. Stat. ch. 26, ¶ 9-101 Uniform Commercial Code Comment (comment to version of UCC in effect in 1986).

The rigid rule allows later lenders to rely on the face of an unambiguous security agreement, without having to worry that a prior lender might offer parol evidence (which would ordinarily be unknown to the later lender) to undermine the later lender's security interest. *Martin Grinding,* 793 F.2d at 596-97. On the other hand,

> if parol evidence could enlarge an unambiguous security agreement, then a subsequent creditor could not rely upon the face of an unambiguous security agreement to determine whether the property described in the financing statement, but not the security agreement, is subject to a prior security interest. Instead, it would have to consult the underlying loan documents to attempt to ascertain the property in which the prior secured party had taken a security interest. The examination of additional documents, which the admission of parol evidence would require, would increase the cost of, and inject uncertainty as to the scope of prior security interests, into secured transactions. *See California Pump & Manufacturing Co.,* 588 F.2d [717, 720 (9th Cir. 1978)]; *H & I Pipe & Supply Co.,* 44 B.R. [949, 951 (Bankr. M.D. Tenn. 1984)]. Therefore, although the rule excluding parol evidence works results contrary to the parties' intentions in particular cases, it reduces the cost and uncertainty of secured transactions generally.

Id. at 597 (footnote omitted).

In these appeals, the bank would have us limit *Martin Grinding* to prohibit use of parol evidence to correct mistakes only in identifying *collateral* but to allow its use to correct mistakes in identifying the *debt* to be secured. The bank notes that such identification of collateral is expressly required by the Illinois enactment of the Uniform Commercial Code, see 810 Ill. Comp. Stat. 5/9-203(b)(3)(A), while the statute does not similarly require identification of the debt to be secured.

We reject the bank's suggested limitation, finding persuasive guidance from our colleagues in the First Circuit in Safe Deposit Bank and Trust Co. v. Berman, 393 F.2d 401, which addressed a mistake in identifying the debts to be secured. In that case the borrower took out a series of loans over several years. All the promissory notes referred to the same original security agreement for collateral. The problem was that the original security agreement itself identified only a single promissory note as the debt to be secured. By the time the borrower declared bankruptcy, that single promissory note had been paid off. By the terms of the security agreement itself, therefore, there was no debt to be secured and thus no security interest.

Like the bank here, the lender argued that the notes showed that the parties intended to create a security interest securing all the later loans. The bankruptcy and district courts had agreed with the trustee, however, that the lender could not use parol evidence against the trustee to show that it had a security interest in the collateral to assure payment of the later loans.

The First Circuit affirmed, albeit "reluctantly because the result is commanded not by fireside equities but by the necessary technicalities inherent in any law governing commercial transactions." 393 F.2d at 402. The First Circuit noted that collateral could be used to secure future debts if the security agreement provided as much. (A so-called "dragnet" clause in a security agreement can include such later loans to the borrower, see UCC §9-204(c) (security agreement may provide that collateral secures "future advances or other value"), but the intent to secure later loans must be explicit in the security agreement.) The First Circuit held that the absence of such language could not be cured by parol evidence, at least as against the bankruptcy trustee. This was so even if the evidence showed that the original parties had intended to include such language. In other words, parol evidence could not be used to add a dragnet clause where the original security agreement did not include one.

Recognizing that its decision was contrary to the evident intent of the original parties to the loans, the First Circuit concluded that the more general effects of the lender's proposed cure would be worse than sticking to the text of the security agreement:

> In a commercial world dependent upon the necessity to rely upon documents meaning what they say, the explicit recitals on forms, without requiring for their correct interpretation other documents not referred to, would seem to be a dominant consideration. If security agreements which on their face served as collateral for specific loans could be converted into open-ended security arrangements for future liabilities by recitals in subsequent notes, much needless uncertainty would be introduced into modern commercial law.

393 F.2d at 404; accord, Texas Kenworth Co. v. First Nat'l Bank of Bethany, 564 P.2d 222, 226 (Okla. 1977) (refusing to interpret security agreement as securing future advances of credit; "potential creditors who do inquire should be able to rely upon the security agreement itself in determining what obligations are secured").

In both *Safe Deposit Bank and Trust* and the case before us, the lender made a mistake and failed to ensure that the security agreement properly identified the debt to be secured. We do not see a sound basis for distinguishing between the mistaken identification of the debt in our case and the mistaken failure to add a "dragnet" clause in *Safe Deposit Bank and Trust.*

The bank points out that even a hypothetical later lender who finds the recorded financing statement has a duty to inquire further to see the security agreement itself. That is certainly correct, as far as it goes. But the bank argues that the later lender would be obliged to inquire still further. We see no basis for imposing on the later lender a legal duty to inquire beyond the face of an unambiguous security agreement, at the risk of losing the priority of its lien based on parol evidence concerning the dealings between the original parties.

The bank argues, though, that if it had been asked for the security agreement, it surely would have shown the later lender both the security agreement and the promissory note of December 15, despite the erroneous date in the security agreement. That reasoning is not consistent with *Martin Grinding* or *Safe Deposit Bank and Trust.* We also rejected the same argument in Helms v. Certified Packaging Corp., 551 F.3d 675, 680 (7th Cir. 2008), where we reaffirmed that a subsequent creditor is justified in relying on the security agreement alone. In that case, the publicly filed financing statement listed collateral that was not specified in the security agreement itself. We held that the security agreement controlled. A creditor need look no further than the security agreement: "A prudent potential creditor would have requested a copy of the security agreement because that, and not what an employee of an existing creditor might tell the potential creditor over the phone, is the security interest that the parties to the security agreement had agreed to create." *Id.*

That argument applies with even more force where the parol evidence that a party seeks to use to enlarge the security interest consists of a separate and private document (the note of December 15) that is not identified in the security agreement, rather than a publicly available financing statement as in *Helms.* See also Caterpillar Financial Services Corp. v. Peoples Nat'l Bank, N.A., 710 F.3d 691, 696 (7th Cir. 2013) (explaining that between two conflicting descriptions of the collateral, the "security agreement is controlling").

The bank also argues that we should overlook the erroneous date in the security agreement because it was just a small error that would have been easy to discover. We disagree. We find no limiting principle that would allow the courts or parties to distinguish reliably between small errors and big ones. Under the reasoning of *Martin Grinding, Helms,* and *Safe Deposit Bank and Trust,* parol evidence cannot be used to correct even the seemingly minor clerical error in the security agreement. We must hew to the "necessary technicalities inherent in any law governing commercial transactions," even when the result is harsh. *Safe Deposit Bank & Trust Co.,* 393 F.2d at 402. We therefore do not think that parol evidence, contemporaneously executed or not, can be used to undermine the ability of later lenders (or bankruptcy trustees) to rely on unambiguous security agreements.

C. THE BANK'S STATUTORY ARGUMENT

Seeking to steer clear of the parol evidence problem, the bank also contends that it has a security interest enforceable against the trustee because the transaction satisfies the statutory requirements for enforcing a security interest. The bank relies on Illinois' enactment of UCC §9-203(b), which provides in relevant part, and subject to exceptions that do not apply here: [A] security interest is enforceable against a debtor and third parties . . . only if:

> (1) value has been given;
> (2) the debtor has rights in the collateral . . . ; and
> (3) . . . the debtor has authenticated a security agreement that provides a description of the collateral. . . .

810 Ill. Comp. Stat. 5/9-203(b). (Paragraph (b)(3) offers three alternative ways to satisfy its requirements by giving the secured party possession or control of the collateral, but they do not apply here.) The bank asserts that its security interest is enforceable against the trustee because the bank gave value, borrower Duckworth had rights in the crops and farm equipment, and the parties authenticated a security agreement that described the collateral.

The trustee responds that another provision in the UCC, section 9-201, provides that the terms of a security agreement must be enforced as written: "Except as otherwise provided in the Uniform Commercial Code, a security agreement is effective according to its terms between the parties, against purchasers of the collateral, and against creditors." 810 Ill. Comp. Stat. 5/9-201(a). The trustee argues that the UCC thus points us to the terms of the agreement, and the bank must lose because those terms fail to secure the debt the bank relies upon.

The trustee has the better reading of the UCC. Section 9-203 cannot cure the security agreement's failure to identify correctly Duckworth's debt to the bank, at least against a later lender or the trustee. We have previously read these two sections of the UCC together, concluding that section 9-203's requirements for enforcing a security interest are an exception to section 9-201's general rule that a security agreement is effective according to its terms: "An agreement that violates section 9-203 may not be effective according to its terms." In re Vic Supply Co., 227 F.3d at 932; see also UCC §9-201, official comment 2 ("It follows that subsection (a) does not provide that every term or provision contained in a record that contains a security agreement or that is so labeled is effective.").

Section 9-203 sets out minimum requirements that must be satisfied to enforce a security interest. It does not provide a mechanism for rescuing a lender from its mistakes in drafting a security agreement. A security interest that satisfies section 9-203's requirements may be enforced, but only according to the terms of the security agreement. The bank's argument to the contrary is puzzling. It urges that its interest must be "enforceable" under section 9-203. But enforceable how, if not according to the agreement's terms? Section 9-203 provides no gap-filling terms for when a security agreement fails. We see no reason to invent them merely because the bank made a mistake in preparing its security agreement. . . .

Accordingly, we hold that the mistaken identification of the debt to be secured cannot be corrected, against the bankruptcy trustee, by using parol evidence to show the intent of the parties to the original loan. Nor do the other loan documents themselves provide a basis for correcting the error against the trustee. Later creditors and bankruptcy trustees are entitled to treat an unambiguous security agreement as meaning what it says, even if the original parties have made a mistake in expressing their intentions. The judgments of the district courts are REVERSED and the cases are REMANDED for proceedings consistent with this opinion.

This case should remind you of the case earlier in the book, In re Motors Liquidation Company, in which a law firm accidentally filed a termination statement it did not mean to file and potentially lost the client $1.5 billion. Here the amount of the loan was a mere $1.1 million, but still. . . .

II. PREFERENCES

As a debtor's financial situation deteriorates, many unfortunate things often occur before everything skids into bankruptcy. The rules against preferential transfers are designed to combat two evils: (1) a feeding frenzy by the creditors, as they seize everything in sight while there is still something to seize, and (2) the debtor's decision to pay off a favorite creditor and stiff the others.

A *preference* is a "transfer" (defined in the Bankruptcy Code to include the creation of a security interest in the debtor's property) made or suffered by the bankrupt to pay or secure a pre-existing debt within the 90-day period preceding the filing of the bankruptcy petition,[1] which has the effect of giving the transferee (the creditor) a greater payment than the creditor would get under the usual bankruptcy distribution. The trustee can avoid such preferential transfers under §547 of the Bankruptcy Code, reprinted below, if the debtor was insolvent at the time of transfer, which is presumed in the

1. The preference period is *one year* before the filing of the petition if the transfer is to an *insider*, defined broadly in §101(31) of the Bankruptcy Code to include relatives, partners, co-habitors, attorneys, officers of corporations, and others.

90-day period. An Article 9 creditor who delays perfection until the 90 days before bankruptcy is frequently met with a trustee who is wielding §547 as a weapon.

If the creation of a security interest is deemed preferential, the trustee can cancel it, thus turning the preferred creditor into an unsecured (read *unpaid*) one. Other transfers of the debtor's property (for instance, a cash payment) are returned to the bankrupt's estate at the trustee's insistence.

§547. *Preferences*

(a) In this section—

(1) "inventory" means personal property leased or furnished, held for sale or lease, or to be furnished under a contract for service, raw materials, work in process, or materials used or consumed in a business, including farm products such as crops or livestock, held for sale or lease;

(2) "new value" means money or money's worth in goods, services, or new credit, or release by a transferee of property previously transferred to such transferee in a transaction that is neither void nor voidable by the debtor or the trustee under any applicable law, including proceeds of such property, but does not include an obligation substituted for an existing obligation;

(3) "receivable" means right to payment, whether or not such right has been earned by performance; and

(4) a debt for a tax is incurred on the day when such tax is last payable without penalty, including any extension.

(b) Except as provided in subsections (c) and (i) of this section, the trustee may avoid any transfer of an interest of the debtor in property—

(1) to or for the benefit of a creditor;

(2) for or on account of an antecedent debt owed by the debtor before such transfer was made;

(3) made while the debtor was insolvent;

(4) made—

(A) on or within 90 days before the date of the filing of the petition; or

(B) between ninety days and one year before the date of the filing of the petition, if such creditor at the time of such transfer was an insider; and

(5) that enables such creditor to receive more than such creditor would receive if—

(A) the case were a case under chapter 7 of this title;

(B) the transfer had not been made; and

(C) such creditor received payment of such debt to the extent provided by the provisions of this title.

(c) The trustee may not avoid under this section a transfer—

(1) to the extent that such transfer was—

(A) intended by the debtor and the creditor to or for whose benefit such transfer was made to be a contemporaneous exchange for new value given to the debtor; and

(B) in fact a substantially contemporaneous exchange;

(2) to the extent that such transfer was in payment of a debt incurred by the debtor in the ordinary course of business or financial affairs of the debtor and the transferee, and such transfer was—

(A) made in the ordinary course of business or financial affairs of the debtor and the transferee; or

(B) made according to ordinary business terms;

(3) that creates a security interest in property acquired by the debtor—

(A) to the extent such security interest secures new value that was—

(i) given at or after the signing of a security agreement that contains a description of such property as collateral;

(ii) given by or on behalf of the secured party under such agreement;

(iii) given to enable the debtor to acquire such property; and

(iv) in fact used by the debtor to acquire such property; and

(B) that is perfected on or before 30 days after the debtor receives possession of such property;

(4) to or for the benefit of a creditor, to the extent that, after such transfer, such creditor gave new value to or for the benefit of the debtor—

(A) not secured by an otherwise unavoidable security interest; and

(B) on account of which new value the debtor did not make an otherwise unavoidable transfer to or for the benefit of such creditor;

(5) that creates a perfected security interest in inventory or a receivable or the proceeds of either, except to the extent that the aggregate of all such transfers to the transferee caused a reduction, as of the date of the filing of the petition and to the prejudice of other creditors holding unsecured claims, of any amount by which the debt secured by such security interest exceeded the value of all security interests for such debt on the later of—

(A)(i) with respect to a transfer to which subsection (b)(4)(A) of this section applies, 90 days before the date of the filing of the petition; or

(ii) with respect to a transfer to which subsection (b)(4)(B) of this section applies, one year before the date of the filing of the petition; or

(B) the date on which new value was first given under the security agreement creating such security interest;

(6) that is the fixing of a statutory lien that is not avoidable under section 545 of this title;

(7) to the extent such transfer was a bona fide payment of a debt for a domestic support obligation;

(8) if, in a case filed by an individual debtor whose debts are primarily consumer debts, the aggregate value of all property that constitutes or is affected by such transfer is less than $600; or

(9) if, in a case filed by a debtor whose debts are not primarily consumer debts, the aggregate value of all property that constitutes or is affected by such transfer is less than $5,000.

(d) The trustee may avoid a transfer of an interest in property of the debtor transferred to or for the benefit of a surety to secure reimbursement of such a surety that furnished a bond or other obligation to dissolve a judicial lien that would have been avoidable by the trustee under subsection (b) of this section. The liability of such surety under such bond or obligation shall be discharged to the extent of the value of such property recovered by the trustee or the amount paid to the trustee.

(e)(1) for the purposes of this section—

(A) a transfer of real property other than fixtures, but including the interest of a seller or purchaser under a contract for the sale of real property, is perfected when a bona fide purchaser of such property from the debtor against whom applicable law permits such transfer to be perfected cannot acquire an interest that is superior to the interest of the transferee; and

(B) a transfer of a fixture or property other than real property is perfected when a creditor on a simple contract cannot acquire a judicial lien that is superior to the interest of the transferee.

(2) For the purposes of this section, except as provided in paragraph (3) of this subsection, a transfer is made—

(A) at the time such transfer takes effect between the transferor and the transferee, if such transfer is perfected at, or within 30 days after, such time, except as provided in subsection (c)(3)(B);

(B) at the time such transfer is perfected, if such transfer is perfected after such 30 days; or

(C) immediately before the date of the filing of the petition, if such transfer is not perfected at the later of—

(i) the commencement of the case; or

(ii) 30 days after such transfer takes effect between the transferor and the transferee.

(3) For the purposes of this section, a transfer is not made until the debtor has acquired rights in the property transferred.

(f) For the purposes of this section, the debtor is presumed to have been insolvent on and during the 90 days immediately preceding the date of the filing of the petition.

(g) For the purposes of this section, the trustee has the burden of proving the avoidability of a transfer under subsection (b) of this section, and the creditor or party in interest against whom recovery or avoidance is sought has the burden of proving the nonavoidability of a transfer under subsection (c) of this section.

(h) The trustee may not avoid a transfer if such transfer was made as a part of an alternative repayment schedule between the debtor and any creditor of the debtor created by an approved nonprofit budget and credit counseling agency.

(i) If the trustee avoids under subsection (b) a transfer made between 90 days and 1 year before the date of the filing of the petition, by the debtor to an entity that is not an insider for the benefit of a creditor that is an insider, such transfer shall be considered to be avoided under this section only with respect to the creditor that is an insider.

PROBLEM 410

On June 8, Business Corporation borrowed $80,000 from Octopus National Bank (ONB) and gave the bank a security interest in its equipment (worth $100,000). On July 18, ONB filed a valid financing statement in the proper place. The next day, Business Corporation filed its bankruptcy petition. Can the trustee destroy ONB's secured position and turn it into a general creditor under the theory that the delayed perfection is a preference? What if the bank had waited a longer period before filing? See In re Power, 2018 WL 1887318 (Bankr. D. Idaho 2018) (40-day delay by car lender in perfecting not substantially contemporaneous, hence a preference). If ONB *had* perfected on June 8 but the debtor made some extraordinary payments to ONB in the 90-day period before the filing of the petition, could the trustee use §547 to make ONB pay that money back into the estate? See White & Summers §24-4(a). Finally, again assume that ONB had perfected on June 8 but that the collateral was only worth $60,000 (the debt was still $80,000, so the bank is undersecured). Would routine payments made to service this debt be preferential? See §547(c)(2); Union Bank v. Wolas, 502 U.S. 151 (1991).

PROBLEM 411

On November 1, the Piggy National Bank loaned Kermit $1,000 to buy a banjo he wanted for his nightclub act, making him sign a security agreement and a financing statement. He bought the banjo on November 15, and the bank filed the financing statement in the proper place on December 5. Kermit filed his bankruptcy petition the next day. Is the *transfer* of the security interest in his banjo a preference? See §547(c)(3). If the bank's security interest was not of the *purchase money* variety but was simply a loan made on November 1 secured by "equipment now owned or after-acquired, with the banjo bought by Kermit (using his own money) on November 15 and the bank filing its financing statement on December 5, what result? See §547(e)(2); White & Summers §24-4(a).

PROBLEM 412

In early 2020, John Carter borrowed $1,000 from the Barsoom World Bank; it was a *signature loan* (i.e., no collateral). On September 25, 2020, John made a $500 payment to the bank (assume that this payment is not in the ordinary course), but on October 4 he borrowed $300 more from the bank, giving it a security interest in his sword collection. The bank never filed a financing statement, and John filed a bankruptcy petition on November 8, 2020. How much, if anything, can his bankruptcy trustee recover from the bank? See §§544(a)(2), 547(c)(4); White & Summers §24-5.

The Moment of "Transfer." Sometimes it is obvious when a transfer of the debtor's property occurs (the debtor gives a diamond ring to a creditor on Monday at 3:00 P.M., for example), but where the transfer is accomplished by creating a security interest in the property, when does it occur? Section 547(e) has rules concerning this. For real property (other than fixtures), the transfer is said to happen when a bona fide purchaser could no longer prevail over the creditor, which in almost all cases is the moment of the filing in the real property records. See §547(e)(1)(A). For personal property and fixtures, §547(e)(1)(B) chooses the moment when a judicial lien creditor could not achieve priority over the creditor, which under §9-317 is the moment of perfection (usually the filing of a financing statement). However, even here the Bankruptcy Code gives the creditor a break that state law may not because it creates a 30-day grace period from the moment of attachment (the "time such transfer takes effect between the transferor and the transferee"). If perfection is accomplished during this federal grace period, a relation back occurs to protect the transfer from the trustee's attack. See §547(e)(2)(A).

III. THE FLOATING LIEN IN BANKRUPTCY

Section 60 of the former Bankruptcy Act condemned as a preference the creation of a security interest within four months of the filing of the bankruptcy petition unless the creditor advanced new money for the collateral as it was acquired. A question of immense concern to creditors who lent against inventory or accounts receivable was whether their security interest in the collateral acquired in that four-month period would be preferential. Even though the UCC clearly permits after-acquired property to be covered automatically by the security interest, the Code is drafted so that the security interest cannot *attach* or be *perfected* until the debtor acquires an interest in the property and, arguably, *that* occurs within the four-month period; §§9-203, 9-308(a). Under both the prior and the current versions of the Bankruptcy Act, *perfection* of the security interest is the moment of "transfer" in preference disputes, and thus the argument is that the collateral first falling under the floating lien during the preference period is recoverable by the trustee as a preferential "transfer" securing an old debt.

Everyone crossed their fingers and waited for a federal appellate court to hear a bankruptcy challenge to an Article 9 floating lien. The Seventh Circuit spoke first. In Grain Merchants of Ind., Inc. v. Union Bank & Sav. Co., 408 F.2d 209 (7th Cir. 1969), the court upheld the floating lien's validity as to the property falling under it during the preference period, though the court noted that in the case at bar there was both inflow and outgo of collateral during the relevant time period, and the creditor had thus not improved its position by getting an increased amount of collateral prior to bankruptcy.

The Bankruptcy Code's solution to this after-acquired property/preference issue is found in §547(c)(5). The test found therein, while alarming at first view, is remarkably simple in operation. It commands the courts to compare the debt/collateral difference at two points: 90 days before the filing of the petition (or the first date within that period where a debt was owed if the loan was made within the 90-day period), and the date of the filing of the petition. There is a preference to the extent that the creditor's position has improved within this period.

PROBLEM 413

The Last National Bank had a perfected security interest in the inventory of the Epstein bookstore, which owed the bank $20,000. On March 1, the inventory was worth $8,000. On May 28, when Epstein filed for bankruptcy, the inventory was worth $20,000 because the store had purchased several new shipments for cash in the interim. What can the trustee do about the bank's claim? What if the bank first loaned Epstein $20,000 on May 1, when the inventory was worth $12,000, though worth $20,000 when the petition was filed on May 28?

In re Smith's Home Furnishings, Inc.

United States Court of Appeals, Ninth Circuit, 2001
265 F.3d 959

Cynthia Holcomb Hall, Circuit Judge.

Plaintiff-appellant Michael Batlan ("trustee") appeals the district court's judgment affirming the decision of the bankruptcy court. Batlan filed an action to recover payments made by a chapter 11 debtor to defendant-appellee Transamerica Commercial Finance Corporation ("TCFC"). The bankruptcy court found that the payments were not avoidable transfers under 11 U.S.C. §547(b). We agree with the bankruptcy court and the district court that the trustee did not satisfy his burden of showing that TCFC received a greater amount by virtue of the payments than it would have received in a hypothetical chapter 7 liquidation.

Factual and Procedural Background

Smith's Home Furnishings, Inc. ("Smith's"), sold furniture, electronic goods, and appliances at 19 stores in Oregon, Washington, and Idaho. TCFC was one of Smith's primary lenders for almost a decade. TCFC financed Smith's purchase of some merchandise (the "prime inventory"), consisting mainly of electronic goods and appliances. TCFC's loans were secured by a first-priority floating lien on the prime inventory and the proceeds from it. Thus, the prime inventory served as collateral for TCFC's loans to Smith's.

Under the loan agreements, TCFC extended credit to Smith's by granting approval to various manufacturers. After receiving approval, the manufacturers shipped merchandise to Smith's. When Smith's sold a product financed by TCFC, it paid TCFC the wholesale price of that product.

Smith's did not segregate its sales receipts. Instead, Smith's deposited all its sales proceeds into commingled bank accounts at the end of each day. First Interstate Bank ("the Bank"), Smith's revolving-line-of-credit financier, swept the accounts daily, leaving the accounts with overnight balances of zero. The next day, the Bank advanced new funds to Smith's if sufficient collateral was available. Smith's then paid its operating expenses and creditors, including TCFC.[2]

During 1994, Smith's suffered substantial losses. Consequently, in March 1995 TCFC reduced Smith's line of credit from $25 million to $20 million. Over the next few months, TCFC reduced Smith's line of credit twice more, down to $13 million by August. During the same period, TCFC required substantial pay-downs of Smith's debt; Smith's paid TCFC most of its available cash in a series of 36 payments, totaling more than $12 million, between May 24, 1995, and August 22, 1995.

On August 18, 1995, TCFC declared a final default, accelerated the entire debt due from Smith's, and sought a receiver for the company. For the first time, TCFC also sought to require Smith's to segregate the proceeds from its collateral.

2. Because of these procedures, the allegedly preferential payments, which we will describe below, were not made directly from the proceeds of the sales of TCFC's collateral.

Smith's voluntarily initiated bankruptcy proceedings under chapter 11 of the Bankruptcy Code on August 22, 1995 (the "petition date"). As of that date, Smith's owed $10,728,809.96 to TCFC. TCFC took possession of its collateral and liquidated it, receiving $10,823,010.58.

On October 11, 1995, the case was converted to a chapter 7 liquidation and Batlan was appointed as trustee. The trustee discovered the $12,842,438.96 in payments that Smith's had made to TCFC during the 90 days before the petition date (the "preference period"). Believing that the payments were preferential, he asked TCFC to return the money to the bankruptcy estate. When TCFC refused, the trustee initiated this adversary proceeding, seeking to avoid the payments as preferential transfers, under 11 U.S.C. §547(b), and to recover the money for the benefit of other creditors of Smith's, under 11 U.S.C. §550(a).

The parties stipulated that the payments met the first four elements of a preferential transfer under 11 U.S.C. §547(b)(1)-(4).... The parties proceeded to trial to determine whether the payments met the fifth element of the preferential transfer statute, 11 U.S.C. §547(b)(5), and whether TCFC could establish an affirmative defense under 11 U.S.C. §547(c)(5).

On September 10, 1998, the bankruptcy court ruled, in a letter opinion, that the trustee had failed to meet his burden of proof in showing that the payments were preferential transfers. The court reasoned that, because the value of the collateral on the petition date ($10,823,010.58) exceeded the amount of TCFC's claim on the petition date ($10,728,809.96), TCFC was oversecured by $94,200.62. As a result, the court concluded that, because TCFC was a floating-lien creditor, the trustee was required to prove that TCFC was undersecured at some time during the preference period in order to avoid the transfers. The court also ruled that TCFC's collateral should be valued at liquidation value ($10,823,010.58) and that liquidation costs should be deducted from the liquidation value in computing the value of the collateral, but that the trustee had failed to present credible evidence of TCFC's liquidation costs. Because the bankruptcy court concluded that the trustee had not proved that the transfers were preferential, the court did not address TCFC's affirmative defense under §547(c)(5).

The trustee filed a motion for reconsideration. In response, the bankruptcy court amended its opinion to correct typographical and computational errors, but otherwise confirmed its judgment. The trustee timely filed an appeal to the district court, raising the same issues that it raises in this appeal. In a published opinion, Batlan v. Transamerica Commercial Finance Corp., 237 B.R. 765, 776 (D. Or. 1999), the district court affirmed the bankruptcy court's decision "in all respects." This timely appeal followed....

DISCUSSION

I. "GREATER AMOUNT" TEST

This case requires us to interpret two sections of the Bankruptcy Code, 11 U.S.C. §§547(b)(5) and 547(g). 11 U.S.C. §§547(b) permits a trustee to "avoid any transfer of an interest of the debtor in property" when certain conditions are met. One of the conditions is that the transfer enable the creditor to receive more than such creditor would receive if:

> (A) the case were a case under chapter 7 of this title;
> (B) the transfer had not been made; and
> (C) such creditor received payment of such debt to the extent provided by the provisions of this title.

11 U.S.C. §547(b)(5). TCFC and the trustee dispute whether the 36 payments made during the preference period enabled TCFC, as a result of the 36 payments, to receive more than if the payments had not been made and TCFC had received payments only pursuant to a chapter 7 liquidation. Section 547(g) places the burden of proof on the trustee to show all of the conditions of §547(b). Thus, the trustee must show that the creditor received a greater amount than it would have if the transfer had not been made and there had been a hypothetical chapter 7 liquidation as of the petition date. If the trustee shows that TCFC received a greater amount by virtue of the 36 payments, then the payments are avoidable as preferential transfers. See In re Lewis W. Shurtleff, Inc., 778 F.2d 1416, 1421 (9th Cir. 1985). The trustee contends that he satisfied his burden because: 1) the 36 payments plus the amount that TCFC received from the post-petition sale of its collateral is greater than the amount received from the post-petition sale of the collateral standing alone; and 2) TCFC has not traced the source of the allegedly preferential payments to sales of its collateral. We disagree with both of the trustee's arguments.

A. THE ADD-BACK METHOD DOES NOT SATISFY THE TRUSTEE'S BURDEN WHEN THE PAYMENTS COME FROM COLLATERAL SECURED BY A FLOATING LIEN

The trustee tried to satisfy his burden under §547(b)(5) by adding the amount of the 36 payments to the amount TCFC received as a result of the post-petition sale of its remaining collateral. The trustee then compared this amount to the obviously smaller amount of the post-petition sale by itself and concluded that TCFC must have received a greater amount because of the payments. Some bankruptcy courts have used the same "add-back" method employed by the trustee to determine the status of a creditor on the petition date. See In re Al-Ben, Inc., 156 B.R. 72, 75 (Bankr. N.D. Ala. 1991) (adding alleged preferences to the amount of unpaid balance at the petition date to find the creditor's secured status); In re Estate of Ascot Mortgage, Inc., 153 B.R. 1002, 1018 (Bankr. N.D. Ga. 1993) (adding pre-petition amounts received to what would have been received under a chapter 7 liquidation).

We agree with the bankruptcy court and the district court, however, and conclude that the "add-back" calculation does not satisfy the trustee's burden in this case. Pre-petition transfers to a creditor that is fully secured on the petition date are generally not preferential because the secured creditor is entitled to 100 percent of its claims. See In re LCO Enterprises, 12 F.3d 938, 941 (9th Cir. 1993). This is not a hard and fast rule. As the bankruptcy court in this case noted, payments that change the status of a creditor from partially unsecured to fully secured at the time of petition may be preferential. See Porter v. Yukon Nat'l Bank, 866 F.2d 355, 359 (10th Cir. 1989). Moreover, a transfer may be avoided when the creditor is fully secured at the time of payment, but is undersecured on the petition date. See In re Estate of Sufolla, Inc., 2 F.3d 977, 985-86 (9th Cir. 1993). The trustee failed to show, however, that TCFC was undersecured *at any time* during the preference period. Instead, the evidence submitted showed that as of the petition date, the value of the collateral held by Smith's exceeded its indebtedness to TCFC. If TCFC was never undercollateralized, then TCFC could not have received more by virtue of the 36 payments than it would have received in a hypothetical liquidation without the payments.

It is important to understand that TCFC did not loan one fixed amount to the debtor; instead, TCFC held a "floating lien." A floating lien is a financing device where the creditor claims an interest in property acquired after the original extension of the loan and extends its security interest to cover further advances. The floating lien is a lien against a constantly changing mass of collateral for a loan value that will change as payments are received and further advances are made. See 3 Norton Bankr. L. & Prac. 2d §57.23. The cases the trustee cites applying the "add-back" method do not deal with floating liens. It is not correct to assume that the 36 payments gave TCFC more than it would have received if the payments had not been made. Instead, under a floating lien arrangement, those payments are used to liquidate part of the debtor's debt. Then, new credit under the floating lien is extended and is secured by new collateral. It is not enough for the trustee to show that the 36 payments plus the amount received upon dissolution exceeded the amount of TCFC's secured claim as of the petition date. Since collateral and indebtedness changed throughout the preference period, these values do not prove that TCFC received more by virtue of the payments than it would have received without them. Under §547(b)(5), the trustee must show that the amount of indebtedness under the floating lien was greater than the amount of collateral at some point during the 90-day period. See In re Schwinn Bicycle Co., 200 B.R. 980, 992-93 (Bankr. N.D. Ill. 1996) ("At no point in time did the collateral value fall below the outstanding debt, and therefore TIFCO was not preferenced in having received payments on its secured debt.").

The trustee contends that the existence of the floating lien means that the burden is shifted to TCFC under §547(c)(5). Section 547(c)(5) provides an affirmative defense for creditors when the trustee has successfully demonstrated that the creditor received more from the payments than under a hypothetical liquidation. Section 547(c)(5) insulates the transfer of a security interest in after-acquired property, i.e., a floating lien, provided that the creditor does not improve its position during the preference period. In effect, the trustee contends that the existence of a floating lien means that he does not have to prove that the creditor was undersecured at some point during the 90-day period and therefore received more by virtue of the payments than the creditor would have if the creditor had waited for a chapter 7 liquidation.

We reject the trustee's argument. A floating lien does not shift the burden of showing avoidability to the creditor. The trustee still has to satisfy his burden under §547(b)(5). The Tenth Circuit has addressed the question of what needs to be shown by a trustee to avoid a transfer financed by the sale of inventory subject to a floating lien. See In re Castletons, 990 F.2d 551 (10th Cir. 1993). In *Castletons,* the creditor held a floating lien on the debtor's inventory, accounts receivable, and proceeds. The trustee sought to avoid the payments given by the debtor to the creditor during the preference period. The Tenth Circuit affirmed the district court's holding that the trustee failed to show that the creditor received more from the challenged payments than it would have received in a chapter 7 liquidation. It explained:

> [A]ll payments to [the creditor] came from assets already subject to its security interest. It is further uncontested that the nature of [the creditor's] security interest in debtor's assets was never altered during the preference period. Under these circumstances, it cannot be said, as §547(b)(5) requires, the transfers enabled [the creditor] to receive more on its debt than would be available to it in a Chapter 7 distribution.

Id. at 555. Essential to the court's holding was its recognition that the creditor held a floating lien:

> While the identity of individual items of collateral changed because of sales and subsequent acquisitions of new collateral, the overall nature of [the creditor's] security interest remained the same.

Id. at 556.

It is true that other courts have evaluated floating lien cases by proceeding directly to the §547(c)(5) affirmative defense without a discussion of the requirements of §547(b)(5). See In re Wesley Indus., 30 F.3d 1438, 1443 (11th Cir. 1994); In re Lackow Bros., Inc., 752 F.2d 1529, 1530-31 (11th Cir. 1985). But in those cases, the parties had stipulated or the bankruptcy court had found that the creditor was undersecured as of the petition date. In other words, the §547(b)(5) burden had already been satisfied so it did not need to be discussed. The trustee in this case never showed that TCFC was undersecured at any point during the 90-day period and the bankruptcy court determined that TCFC was fully secured as of the petition date. The trustee did not satisfy his burden. See Richard F. Duncan, Preferential Transfers, the Floating Lien, and Section 547(c)(5) of the Bankruptcy Reform Act of 1978, 36 Ark. L. Rev. 1, 20 (1987) ("[I]t is not necessary to reach the question of application of section 547(c)(5) until after the trustee has met his burden of proving all of the necessary elements of a preference under section 547(b)."); James J. White & Daniel Israel, Preference Conundrums, 98 Com. L.J. 1, 4 (1993) ("It is important to remember, however, that 547(c)(5) applies only to a creditor who is undersecured ninety days before bankruptcy. The creditor who is fully secured cannot be attacked under 547(b). There is no initial deficiency and later transactions cannot improve the creditor's position.").

B. THE BURDEN OF TRACING THE FUNDS USED TO MAKE THE PREFERENTIAL PAYMENTS IS ON THE TRUSTEE

The trustee contends that its use of the "add-back" method is correct because TCFC has not shown that the source of the allegedly preferential payments was sales of TCFC's collateral. In *Castletons,* it was undisputed that all of the preference period payments came from sales of assets subject to the creditor's floating lien. See In re Castletons, 990 F.2d at 555. In this case, however, the payments came from a commingled account that contained monies from the sales of other goods not subject to TCFC's lien. When Smith's made a sale, the proceeds were deposited into commingled bank accounts. Smith's bank swept the accounts daily, leaving them with zero balances overnight. Thus, the challenged payments were not made directly from the proceeds of the sales of TCFC's collateral. On the other hand, there is no evidence indicating that Smith's did not sell off enough of TCFC's collateral to account for all of the challenged payments. . . .

[W]e believe that it is part of the trustee's §547(b)(5) burden to trace the funds used to make the payments to sales of merchandise not subject to TCFC's liens. See In re Robinson Bros. Drilling, Inc., 6 F.3d 701, 703 (10th Cir. 1993) ("Under 11 U.S.C. §547(g), a trustee seeking to avoid an allegedly preferential transfer under §547(b) 'has the burden of proving by a preponderance of the evidence every essential, controverted element resulting in the preference.'") (quoting 4 Collier on Bankruptcy ¶547.21[(5)]

at 547-93 (15th ed. 1993)); cf. In re Prescott, 805 F.2d 719, 726-27 (7th Cir. 1986) (placing burden on trustee to establish value of collateral and to show that value of collateral was less than the amount of indebtedness at time of transfer). One might argue that the creditor will be in a better position than the trustee to prove whether or not the alleged preferential payments came from the proceeds of the sale of its own collateral. On the other hand, in bankruptcy, it is the trustee who accedes to the debtor's books and records and has easier access and a better ability to divine the financial activities of the debtor in its last months of operation. Regardless of which side is better equipped to decipher the debtor's final financial actions, we hold that the language of the statute places the burden of demonstrating the source of such preferential payments squarely on the trustee.[3] See In re Lease-A-Fleet, 151 B.R. at 348 ("It is therefore an unfortunate fact of life that a preference plaintiff must effectively prove a negative (that the defendant is not a totally secured creditor), even though the secured creditor is the party with most access to proof of the validity of its own security interests.").

Commingled funds or not, §547(b)(5) places the burden on the trustee to show that the payments at issue came from a source other than sales of TCFC's collateral. Here there is no suggestion that any sales of products funded by TCFC were not subject to TCFC's priority lien. Instead, both parties stipulated that TCFC held a valid security interest in Smith's property. It is true that the route the payment took to TCFC was indirect, but we are not prepared to release the trustee from his burden under §547(b)(5) simply because the payments did not, demonstrably, come directly from sale of TCFC's collateral. See In re Compton Corp., 831 F.2d 586, 591 (5th Cir. 1987) ("The federal courts have long recognized that '[t]o constitute a preference, it is not necessary that the transfer be made directly to the creditor.'") (quoting National Bank of Newport v. National Herkimer County Bank, 225 U.S. 178, 184, 32 S. Ct. 633, 56 L. Ed. 1042 (1912)). It is up to

3. Our decision furthers the paramount policy behind §547: equality of distribution among creditors of the debtor. See In re Schwinn Bicycle Co., 200 B.R. 980, 993 (Bankr. N.D. Ill. 1996). If a floating lien creditor genuinely did not profit from a preference period transfer, then the creditor should not be forced to disgorge those payments. We agree with the dissent that §547 also tries to dissuade creditors from rushing to extract payments from the debtor shortly before bankruptcy. We do not think that our decision controverts this policy or that this is a case involving a race to the debtor's assets. The trustee offered no evidence that TCFC was less than 100 percent secured at the time of any of the 36 payments. For the payments it made to TCFC, the debtor received additional financing to keep its business afloat. Rather than encouraging a race to dismember the debtor, our decision to place the burden on the trustee to show that TCFC did not receive more by virtue of the payments than it would under a hypothetical liquidation encourages TCFC and other creditors to continue extending credit under floating liens.

the trustee to show that the payments did not come from TCFC's collateral before he can use the add-back method to satisfy his §547(b)(5) burden. . . .

CONCLUSION

We affirm the decision of the bankruptcy court in all respects.
[The forceful dissent of Judge GRABER is omitted.]

IV. FRAUDULENT TRANSFERS

Under §548 or §544(b) of the Bankruptcy Code, the trustee can avoid any "transfer" (including the creation of an Article 9 security interest) that is a *fraudulent transfer.* The law as to what is or is not a fraudulent transfer has been developing for centuries, but is generally summarized in the Uniform Voidable Transactions Act (UVTA), which most states have adopted. There, an existing or later creditor (and the bankruptcy trustee, per §544(b)) may avoid two types of fraudulent transfers: those where the transferee from an insolvent debtor does not give "reasonably equivalent value in exchange," and those where the transferor and the transferee have the *actual intent* to defraud the debtor's creditors.

Fraudulent conveyances may be easy to identify.

James H. Rice Co. v. McJohn

Supreme Court of Illinois, 1910
244 Ill. 264

On October 6, 1902, the James H. Rice Company, a corporation, filed its bill of complaint in the superior court of Cook county against Joseph McJohn and Edward McJohn, charging that on September 17, 1902, complainant recovered a judgment against said Joseph McJohn in the circuit court of Cook county for $1801.60; that prior to the rendition of the said judgment Joseph McJohn was the owner of certain real estate in Cook county, which was improved by a three-story brick building; that on September 20, 1902, an execution was issued upon said judgment and delivered to the sheriff of said county; that on August 7, 1902, prior to the rendition of the judgment but after the indebtedness upon which it was rendered had accrued, Joseph McJohn conveyed the said real estate to Edward McJohn for a pretended consideration of one dollar; that said conveyance was a mere sham and was made with intent to defraud complainant and other creditors of Joseph McJohn out of their just demands; that no consideration was paid by Edward McJohn therefor, and that the premises are now held by Edward McJohn in trust for Joseph McJohn and for the purpose of preventing a levy and sale of the premises under said execution; that Joseph McJohn has no personal or real estate liable to levy and sale, except the premises aforesaid, on which the sheriff could levy and realize said judgment; that the sheriff has frequently requested Joseph McJohn to pay said judgment or to turn out property upon which he could levy, but Joseph McJohn has refused to do so. The bill made Joseph McJohn and Edward McJohn defendants, and prayed that they might be required to answer and state the facts and circumstances attending the said conveyance, the amount paid thereon by Edward McJohn and the purpose of the conveyance; that upon a hearing the said conveyance and deed be set aside and declared null and void; that a receiver be appointed, with the usual powers and duties of a receiver; that the sheriff be directed to proceed to levy upon and sell the premises for the satisfaction of complainant's judgment, and for such other and further relief as equity may require.

[The court set aside the conveyance as "fraudulent and null and void."]

PROBLEM 414

When Arnold Austin retired as an international diplomat, he was famous but much in debt. He decided to make money by writing his memoirs, which were certainly best-seller material. He gave a security interest in the right to receive royalty payments from his publisher to his wife as collateral for "the many debts I owe her," and she filed a financing statement in the proper place five months before Arnold filed his bankruptcy petition. Can the trustee avoid this security interest? (At common law, one of the *badges of fraud*—situations in which fraud is presumed—was a voluntary transfer made by the debtor to a family member. United States v. West, 299 F. Supp. 661 (D. Del. 1969).) See G. Gilmore §45.3.1; King v. Ionization Intl., Inc., 825 F.2d 1180 (7th Cir. 1987).

Sometimes, whether a fraudulent conveyance has occurred is less clear.

Aptix Corp. v. Quickturn Design Systems, Inc.

United States Court of Appeals, Federal Circuit, 2005
148 Fed. Appx. 924

GAJARSA, Circuit Judge.

[Mohsen founded Aptix and was the majority shareholder, chief executive officer, and chairman of the company. Quickturn obtained a judgment of some $4.2 million against Aptix, arising out of a patent dispute. With Aptix unable to borrow funds from other sources, Aptix and Mohsen entered into a security agreement whereby Aptix granted Mohsen a security interest in all of its assets in exchange for certain loan funds. Prior to that time, Mohsen had loaned at least $2 million to Aptix on an unsecured basis. Pursuant to the security agreement, Mohsen loaned Aptix at least $9.7 million on a secured basis.]

The district court applied California's fraudulent transfer statute in determining that the security interest granted to Mohsen should be voided. That statute reads:

> (a) A transfer made or obligation incurred by a debtor is fraudulent as to a creditor, whether the creditor's claim arose before or after the transfer was made or the obligation was incurred, if the debtor made the transfer or incurred the obligation as follows:
>
> (1) With actual intent to hinder, delay, or defraud any creditor of the debtor.
>
> (2) Without receiving a reasonably equivalent value in exchange for the transfer or obligation, and the debtor either:
>
> (A) Was engaged or was about to engage in a business or a transaction for which the remaining assets of the debtor were unreasonably small in relation to the business or transaction.
>
> (B) Intended to incur, or believed or reasonably should have believed that he or she would incur, debts beyond his or her ability to pay as they became due.

Cal. Civ. Code §3439.04(a). Section 3439.04 has been construed to mean that a transfer is fraudulent if the provisions of either subdivision (a)(1) regarding actual intent or subdivision (a)(2) regarding the circumstances of the transfer have been satisfied. Annod Corp. v. Hamilton & Samuels, 100 Cal. App. 4th 1286, 1294, 123 Cal. Rptr. 2d 924 (2002); see also Mejia v. Reed, 31 Cal. 4th 657, 664, 3 Cal. Rptr. 3d 390, 74 P.3d 166 (2003) (treating current subdivisions (a)(1) and (a)(2) as separate criteria for finding a fraudulent transfer).

The court relied on subdivision (a)(1) of §3439.04 in finding that Aptix made the transfer to Mohsen with the actual intent to hinder or defraud Quickturn. *Aptix,* slip op. at 5. In so finding, the district court identified three "badges of fraud" that supported an inference of fraudulent intent. At the time the court issued its order, the badges of fraud were not statutory, but appeared in the Legislative Committee commentary to §3439.04. In 2004, the California legislature added subsection (b) to §3439.04 which codified the following nonexclusive list of the badges of fraud:

> (b) In determining actual intent under paragraph (1) of subdivision (a), consideration may be given, among other factors, to any or all of the following:
>
> (1) Whether the transfer or obligation was to an insider.
>
> (2) Whether the debtor retained possession or control of the property transferred after the transfer.

> (3) Whether the transfer or obligation was disclosed or concealed.
>
> (4) Whether before the transfer was made or obligation was incurred, the debtor had been sued or threatened with suit.
>
> (5) Whether the transfer was of substantially all the debtor's assets.
>
> (6) Whether the debtor absconded.
>
> (7) Whether the debtor removed or concealed assets.
>
> (8) Whether the value of the consideration received by the debtor was reasonably equivalent to the value of the asset transferred or the amount of the obligation incurred.
>
> (9) Whether the debtor was insolvent or became insolvent shortly after the transfer was made or the obligation was incurred.
>
> (10) Whether the transfer occurred shortly before or shortly after a substantial debt was incurred.
>
> (11) Whether the debtor transferred the essential assets of the business to a lienholder who transferred the assets to an insider of the debtor.

Cal. Civ. Code §3439.04(b). The three badges of fraud relied on by the district court now appear as items (1), (4) and (9) on the codified list. The district court determined that while Aptix was insolvent it granted a security interest to an insider and that that transfer occurred just before a substantial judgment was to be entered against Aptix. *Aptix,* slip op. at 5.

Before the district court, Mohsen argued that he should not be punished for simply lending money to Aptix so that it could continue as a going concern. The district court rejected this argument finding that Aptix and Mohsen had

> an arrangement by which Dr. Mohsen lends Aptix money, which Aptix uses to pay employee salaries and essential creditors in an effort to keep functioning. . . . Dr. Mohsen receives money back from Aptix on demand. . . . This setup allows . . . Aptix to pay unsecured creditors as it sees fit, while effectively avoiding its obligations toward a judgment creditor that holds a judgment lien.

Id. Thus, the district court concluded that the arrangement was "not as innocent as Dr. Mohsen suggests." Id.

On appeal, Mohsen takes issue with both the district court's factual findings and the legal principles it applied. Mohsen's factual challenge is fundamentally a reassertion of the argument rejected by the trial judge, namely that the granting of the security interest to Mohsen was intended to benefit not defraud creditors by keeping Aptix operational. Borrowing a concept from bankruptcy cases, Mohsen argues that the on-going operation of Aptix was a "legitimate supervening purpose" such that the confluence of three badges of fraud was insufficient to establish actual intent to defraud.

Mohsen's reliance on the concept of a "legitimate supervening purpose" is misplaced. The concept is typically applied in bankruptcy cases where courts have held that in assessing whether a transfer constitutes a fraudulent conveyance under 11 U.S.C. §548(a)(1), the confluence of several badges of fraud can establish "conclusive evidence of actual intent to defraud, absent 'significantly clear' evidence of a legitimate supervening purpose." Acequia, Inc. v. Clinton (In re Acequia, Inc.), 34 F.3d 800, 806 (9th Cir. 1994) (quoting Max Sugarman Funeral Home Inc. v. A.D.B. Investors, 926 F.2d 1248, 1255 (1st Cir. 1991)). Once multiple indicia of fraud are established, the burden shifts to the transferee to prove that there was a "legitimate supervening purpose" for the transfer at issue. Id. There is no bright line test for what constitutes a legitimate supervening purpose; the issue is simply whether the presumption of fraud has been adequately rebutted. See In re Bateman, 646 F.2d 1220, 1223 n.4 (8th Cir. 1981) ("The burden which shifts now upon a showing of reasonable grounds is not a burden of going forward with the evidence requiring the bankrupt to explain away natural inferences, but a burden of proving that he has not committed the objectionable acts with which he has been charged." (quoting Shainman v. Shear's of Affton, Inc., 387 F.2d 33, 37 (8th Cir. 1967))).

Here, Mohsen attempts to rebut the presumption of fraudulent intent by focusing on the reason that Aptix needed to borrow money from Mohsen, i.e. it could not obtain funding elsewhere, and its ultimate use of the money, i.e. to pay employees and other creditors. Although Mohsen's argument may explain why Aptix entered into the loan arrangement with Mohsen, it does not explain why it was necessary for Aptix to grant Mohsen a security interest in substantially all of its assets when Mohsen had never required such an interest for his past loans. It also does not address the district court's express finding that the arrangement was not as innocuous or well-intentioned as Mohsen suggests. Mohsen failed to rebut the circumstantial inference arising from the badges of fraud and, therefore, it was not clear error for the district court to conclude that Aptix granted the security interest with the actual intent to defraud Quickturn.

Mohsen's legal arguments are also without merit. First, he argues that California law protects the right of debtors to "pay one creditor in preference to another, or . . . give to one creditor security for the payment of his demand in preference to another." Cal. Civ. Code §3432. Mohsen fails to recognize, however, that the section of the California Civil Code on which he relies does not insulate debtors who make transfers with the intent to defraud creditors not party to the transaction. Kemp v. Lynch, 8 Cal. 2d 457, 460-61, 65 P.2d 1316 (1937) (a transfer that appears to be a lawful preference, but which is made with a fraudulent intent will be vitiated); Roberts v. Burr, 135 Cal. 156, 159, 67 P. 46 (1901) (stating that a debtor may pay one creditor in preference to another in the absence of fraud).

Similarly, Mohsen argues that Aptix did not have the requisite fraudulent intent because it entered into the security agreement in order to benefit some of its creditors. This argument reads §3439.04(a)(1) as if it requires that the debtor intend to defraud *all* of its creditors, whereas the language actually used in the statute mandates only that the debtor act with the actual intent to "defraud *any* creditor" (emphasis added).

Finally, Mohsen asserts a defense under Cal. Civ. Code §3439.08(a), which states that a "transfer or an obligation is not voidable under subdivision (a) of Section 3439.04, against a person who took in good faith and for a reasonably equivalent value or against any subsequent transferee or obligee." Mohsen argues that the security interest should not be voided because Aptix engaged in the security agreement in a good faith effort to stay in business and the amount of money loaned to Aptix exceeded the value of the security granted in return. This argument fails for two reasons. First, it appears that Mohsen did not invoke §3439.08(a) in the proceedings before the district court and he is therefore prevented from raising the statutory defense for the first time on appeal. Singleton v. Wulff, 428 U.S. 106, 120, 49 L. Ed. 2d 826, 96 S. Ct. 2868 (1976); United States v. Carlson, 900 F.2d 1346, 1349 (9th Cir. 1990). Even if this argument were properly before us, Mohsen only identifies evidence tending to show Aptix's good faith in entering into the transaction and points to no evidence showing that Mohsen himself acted in good faith as required by the statute. Cal. Civ. Code §3439.08(a). Mohsen's heavy reliance on the California case Annod Corp. v. Hamilton & Samuels, 100 Cal. App. 4th 1286, 123 Cal. Rptr. 2d 924 (2002) does not address the flaws in his argument.

In *Annod,* the court applied §3439.08 to find that a law firm had not engaged in a fraudulent transaction when it executed partnership draws pursuant to a pre-existing partnership agreement rather than pay an outstanding judgment for unpaid rent. 100 Cal. App. 4th at 1293-94. Mohsen makes much of the court's conclusion that the partners had received the draws in good faith in part because "if the draws were not paid, none of the former partners would have continued working and generating revenue for the struggling law practice." Id. at 1293. Mohsen asserts that under *Annod* transactions engaged in with the purpose of keeping a struggling business afloat cannot constitute fraudulent transactions. In making this assertion, Mohsen ignores the extensive additional evidence relied on by the court as the complete basis for finding that the partners acted in good faith. Id. at 1296 (focusing on evidence that the payments made were substantially less than previous draws, represented undermarket values for the services performed, and were consistent with the partner's significant efforts to increase funds available to creditors). *Annod* does not stand for the proposition that a transfer made to enable an enterprise to stay in business cannot constitute a fraudulent transaction. Contrary to Mohsen's assertions, the district court did not err as a matter of law in determining that Aptix's grant of a security interest to Mohsen was a voidable transaction under California law.

NEWMAN, Circuit Judge, dissenting.

I respectfully dissent. Dr. Mohsen loaned over nine million dollars to the company he had founded and operated, secured by the assets of the company. My colleagues hold that the purpose of making the secured loan was to defraud future creditors, based on two undisputed facts: that Dr. Mohsen expected an adverse attorney fee award in favor of Quickturn, and that his previous smaller loans to his company were unsecured. I cannot agree that the requirement of security for the larger loans establishes fraudulent intent. . . .

Precedent illustrates instances of fraudulent intent. In Kemp v. Lynch, 8 Cal. 2d 457, 460-61, 65 P.2d 1316 (1937) an ostensibly lawful preference made with "the understanding that it shall be a mere simulated transfer" was fraudulent. See also Bank of Cal. v. Virtue & Scheck, Inc., 140 Cal. App. 3d 1026, 1039, 190 Cal. Rptr. 54 (1983) (collecting cases) ("California courts have consistently treated a secret reservation in the grantor as potent evidence of fraud"). Unlike *Kemp,* here there was no simulated transfer, but regular monthly loans to meet payroll and other operating obligations. The facts of this case are more analogous to those of *Wyzard,* in which a secured loan was taken in order to pay an existing debt when it became known that an adverse judgment was imminent; the court held that there was no fraud in a transfer made "with recognition that the transfer will effectively prevent another creditor from collecting on his debt." *Wyzard,* 23 Cal. App. 4th at 1189-90 (concluding that the facts did not raise a triable issue of fact as to fraud, notwithstanding the existence of three factors of fraud); see also *Annod Corp.,* 100 Cal. App. 4th at 1299 (no triable issue of fact, despite three factors of fraud).

Aptix granted Dr. Mohsen a security interest; the money was needed and used for legitimate business purposes. The panel majority states that this "does not explain why it was necessary for Aptix to grant Mohsen a security interest" when "Mohsen had never required such an interest for his past loans." Maj. op. at 9. It is surely not fraudulent to obtain security for a loan of over nine million dollars, whatever the relationship between the lender and the recipient. Knowledge of a potential adverse judgment does not establish fraudulent intent when making a loan to meanwhile keep the company alive and operating. See *Wyzard,* 23 Cal. App. 4th at 1189 (a transfer in anticipation of liability, "with recognition that the transfer will effectively prevent another creditor from collecting on his debt," is not fraudulent).

V. NON-CONSENSUAL LIENS AND THE TRUSTEE

Section 547(b) of the Bankruptcy Code condemns as preferential all judicial liens acquired by a creditor within the 90 days preceding the bankruptcy filing if taken while the bankrupt was insolvent.

As for statutory liens (the garage mechanic, etc.), they are effective under §545 against the trustee if (a) they would be good against a BFP and (b) they do not arise only on insolvency. The reason for this last rule—statutory liens that arise only on insolvency are void against the trustee—is this: originally the Bankruptcy Code permitted the separate states to specify which general creditors would get priority payments when the bankrupt's estate was distributed. When that power was taken away from the states, the states battled back by rewriting their priority statutes as statutory lien statutes—providing, for example, that unpaid employees would have an automatic lien on the employer's assets if the employer became insolvent but not otherwise. Because Congress didn't want the states to be able to dictate priorities in a federal insolvency proceeding, §545 and its predecessor were redrafted to avoid this type of statutory lien.

CHAPTER 25 ASSESSMENT: MULTIPLE CHOICE QUESTIONS

1. Antonio Credit loaned $100,000 to Prospero, a chemist, secured by Prospero's patent rights. Antonio Credit was uncertain whether to perfect by filing in the relevant state UCC office or in the United States Patent and Trademark Office. A wise creditor would have filed in both offices. Antonio Credit simply dithered. A few days later, after disastrous losses in his investment portfolio, Prospero filed bankruptcy, with his debts far greater than his assets. What is the effect on Antonio Credit's security interest?
   a. The unperfected security interest will be effectively nullified and Antonio Credit will be an unsecured creditor.
   b. There will be no effect, because no one has relied on the filing or lack thereof.
   c. The security interest and debt are both nullified.
   d. No effect, because the bankruptcy trustee will be bound by the security agreement.

2. Sycorax Gallery had sold Prospero a painting, *The Cyclone*, for his business office. The sale was on credit, but the parties did not bother with the formalities of Article 9. Rather, Sycorax Gallery delivered the painting under a Conditional Sales Contract, which provided that the painting belonged to Sycorax Gallery until fully paid for, required Prospero to pay the price over time, and gave Sycorax Gallery the right to take the painting back if the price was not paid. Prospero filed bankruptcy a few days before the first payment was due, some months later. The due date has now passed. Is Sycorax Gallery entitled to get the painting back?

a. Yes. The painting is the property of Sycorax Gallery, so is not property of Prospero's bankruptcy estate.
b. Yes. Prospero's creditors have claims against Prospero's property, not against Sycorax Gallery's property.
c. No. Sycorax Gallery simply had an unperfected security interest in the painting, and will suffer the same fate as Antonio Credit.
d. No. The transaction will be nullified as a fraudulent conveyance.

3. Caliban had loaned $40,000 to Prospero, with a perfected security interest in accounts of Prospero worth about $25,000. Dubious about Prospero's investments, Caliban had been very concerned about whether Prospero would be able to repay the debt, given that Caliban was undersecured, the collateral being worth about $15,000 less than the debt. So Caliban was delighted to receive a payment of $15,000 from Prospero, reducing the debt to $25,000. A few weeks later, Prospero filed bankruptcy. Caliban thought, "I was lucky. I've been paid $15,000 and will be entitled to the other $25,000 as a perfected creditor in bankruptcy." Will Caliban emerge fully paid?
a. No. Caliban will be obliged to return the $15,000 payment, as a preferential transfer.
b. Yes. Caliban did not collude, so the $15,000 payment is not a preferential transfer.
c. No. Even perfected creditors must share their collateral with other creditors in bankruptcy.
d. Yes. The payment occurred prebankruptcy, so the bankruptcy trustee has no powers to reverse it.

4. Another creditor of Prospero was Miranda, owed $33,000 with a perfected security interest in about $55,000 worth of equipment and general intangibles. A week before bankruptcy, Prospero had paid the debt in full. Will Miranda be required to return the $33,000 to the bankruptcy trustee?
a. Yes, it was clearly a preferential payment, made just before bankruptcy.
b. Yes, but Miranda will fare well as an oversecured creditor in bankruptcy.
c. No, because the payment is not avoidable under §547.
d. No, and Miranda will also be entitled to her $55,000 in collateral.

5. Shortly before bankruptcy, Prospero realized that he would end up with virtually nothing and his creditors would divide his assets. Not so fond of his creditors, he wired his remaining $40,000 in funds to a favorite niece as a graduation present. Prospero had no intention of getting the money back from her. Will the niece be able to retain the money?
a. Yes. She is not a creditor, so it is not a preferential transfer.
b. Yes. It is a bona fide gift, not an attempt to hide funds, so is not a fraudulent conveyance.

c. No. The trustee may recover the payment as a fraudulent transfer.
d. No, because she did not file a UCC financing statement.

ANSWERS

1. *A* is the best answer. The federal Bankruptcy Code gives effect to state law in §9-317, which gives priority to a lien creditor, such as a bankruptcy trustee, over an unperfected security interest. In short, an unperfected security interest gets wiped out in bankruptcy. The debt becomes unsecured, and Antonio Credit will have a claim in the bankruptcy proceeding as an unsecured creditor. In a typical bankruptcy proceeding, after the secured creditors and the administrative expenses are accounted for, there is nothing left for the unsecured creditors. But sometimes there are assets left over to divide among the unsecured creditors. Antonio Credit can now hope that Prospero's investments and other assets, including those patent rights, miraculously gain value during bankruptcy.
2. *C* is the best answer. This question ties Chapter 20, on the scope of Article 9, to bankruptcy. If a party to a transaction does not recognize that Article 9 applies, the party may fail to comply with Article 9 and suffer the consequences later. Article 9 applies to any transaction that, in substance, creates a security interest in personal property by agreement. The transaction here was a conditional sale in form, but a secured sale in substance, so Article 9 applies. To perfect, Sycorax Gallery could simply have filed a financing statement. It did not, and so was unperfected, meaning in bankruptcy it will become unsecured. Article 9 prevails over the party's agreement, so the painting was no longer Sycorax Gallery's property, contrary to *A* and *B*. Rather, it became Prospero's painting, subject to Sycorax Gallery's security interest. This question emphasizes a basic skill of any lawyer that deals with transactions.
3. *A* is the best answer. A creditor that receives payment may have to return it, if the debtor files bankruptcy within the next 90 days (or even one year, for insiders). Contrary to *D*, the bankruptcy trustee may recover some transfers of the debtor's property in the prebankruptcy period. This payment meets all the requirements of §547 of the Bankruptcy Code: a transfer of the debtor's property during the prebankruptcy period that put the creditor in a better position than would have otherwise occurred in bankruptcy. Without the payment, Caliban would have had a $40,000 claim secured by $25,000 in collateral, so would have been undersecured in bankruptcy by $15,000. With the payment, Caliban has a $25,000 claim, fully covered by $25,000 in collateral. None of the exceptions apply (not an ordinary course payment, not a contemporaneous exchange of value such as a cash sale, not followed by new value from the creditor, or any of the other exceptions in §547). Contrary to *B*, even innocent creditors

are subject to the rule; no collusion or bad faith need be shown. An unsecured or undersecured creditor that gets payment may need to cross its fingers for the next 90 days.

4. *C* is the best answer. Section 547 does not authorize the bankruptcy trustee to recover all transfers of the debtor's property in the prebankruptcy period. A key requirement is that the transfer have preferential effect, enabling the creditor to receive more than the creditor would have in a liquidation bankruptcy. §547(c). An oversecured creditor, like Miranda, will be fully paid in bankruptcy. The payment did not make her better off than bankruptcy would have, unlike a payment to an undersecured or unsecured creditor. There are also several exceptions that protect some creditors who receive transfers with preferential effect. It is unnecessary to consider them here, where the transfer does not even meet the initial requirement of preferential effect.
5. *C* is the best answer. The niece was not a creditor, so the issue of preferential transfers or perfected security interests do not arise. But the trustee also has the power under Bankruptcy Code §548, to recover fraudulent transfers, broadly defined as any transfer made by the debtor, within two years before bankruptcy, while insolvent, without receiving reasonably equivalent value. The transfer here meets all those requirements. Fraud need not be shown, contrary to *B*.

   Note that in addition to §548, the bankruptcy trustee may also use state law to recover fraudulent transfers, such as transfers made with intent to hinder creditors. State law often permits the trustee to attack transfers made more than two years before bankruptcy.

Chapter 26

Proceeds

Should the debtor, with or without the blessing of the secured creditor, sell the collateral or trade it for some other item, the creditor wants its security interest transferred to whatever is left in its place when the collateral moves on. Article 9 phrases this as giving the creditor an interest in "proceeds" of the collateral. Consider, for example, a security interest in a retailer's inventory. As that inventory is sold in the usual course of business the creditor now is most concerned in reaching the payments given to the retailer. This right to proceeds is an important cog in the machinery of financing, and this chapter explores what the creditor must do to make sure the proceeds belong to that creditor.

I. THE MEANING OF PROCEEDS

Proceeds is defined in §9-102(a)(64) (*cash proceeds,* a subcategory of proceeds is defined in §9-102(a)(9)), and the priority rules for proceeds are contained in §9-315. Read those sections.

PROBLEM 415

When Rosetta Stone bought a new car from Champollion Motors, Inc., she traded in her five-year-old car, made a $200 down payment by giving the dealer her check, and signed a promissory note for the balance payable to the dealership. Rameses National Bank had a perfected security interest in Champollion Motors' inventory.

(a) Does that security interest continue in the car once it is delivered to Ms. Stone? See §9-320(a).

(b) Under §9-315(a) the bank's security interest will continue in *proceeds,* as defined in §9-102(a)(64). What are the proceeds of the car sale?

(c) Is the attachment of the creditor's security interest in the proceeds automatic, or must they be claimed in the original security agreement? See §9-203(f).

Farmers Cooperative Elevator Co. v. Union State Bank

Iowa Supreme Court, 1987
409 N.W.2d 178

LARSON, J.

Rodger Cockrum operated a farm and hog confinement operation in Madison County, Iowa. For several years financing for a substantial portion of the operation came from [Union] State Bank of Winterset (Union State). In February 1981, Union State loaned Cockrum a large sum of money and took a security agreement covering

> all equipment and fixtures, including but not limited to sheds and storage facilities, used or acquired for use in farming operations, whether now or hereafter existing or acquired; all farm products including but not limited to, *livestock, and supplies used or produced in farming operations whether now or hereafter existing or acquired. . . .*

(Emphasis added.)

In December 1983 and January 1984, Cockrum entered into several purchase money security agreements with Farmers Cooperative Elevator Company (CO-OP) for livestock feed. See Iowa Code §554.9312 (1983). For each transaction, CO-OP filed a financing statement with the Secretary of State, which stated:

> This is a purchase money security interest which covers Collateral described as all feed sold to Debtors by Secured Party and all of Debtors' feeder hogs now owned or hereafter acquired including . . . additions, replacements,

> and substitutions of such livestock, including all issues presently or hereafter conceived and born, the products thereof, and the proceeds of any of the described Collateral.

Cockrum defaulted on his obligations to both Union State and the CO-OP. CO-OP commenced an action against Cockrum seeking possession of collateral. (International Barter Corporation was also joined as a defendant, but its petition under chapter 11 of the Bankruptcy Act stayed further proceedings against it, and it is not involved in the present action.)

Union State filed a statement of indebtedness and requested that its security interests be established as a first security lien on Cockrum's hog inventory and any sale proceeds therefrom. CO-OP responded by filing an amendment to its petition, joining Union State as a defendant and alleging that its right to the hogs is superior to Union State's.

On CO-OP's motion to adjudicate law points, the district court ruled that Union State's security interest in the hogs was prior and superior to the CO-OP's. CO-OP has appealed from that decision.

We first address CO-OP's argument that its interest in the livestock and proceeds therefrom is superior to Union State's under section 554.9312(4) [now §9-324(a)—Eds.]. That section provides:

> A purchase money security interest in collateral other than inventory has priority over a conflicting security interest in the same collateral or its proceeds if the purchase money security interest is perfected at the time the debtor receives possession of the collateral or within twenty days thereafter.

"Purchase money security interests" are defined in section 554.9107 [now §9-103—Eds.]:

> A security interest is a "purchase money security interest" to the extent that it is
>
> a. taken or retained by the seller of the collateral to secure all or part of its price; or
>
> b. taken by a person who by making advances or incurring an obligation gives value to enable the debtor to acquire rights in or the use of collateral if such value is in fact so used.

Union State concedes that CO-OP held a purchase money security interest in the feed. The question, however, is whether such a priority interest continues in livestock which consume the feed.

In essence, one who takes a purchase money security interest under section 554.9107(a) is the equivalent of the old conventional vendor—a seller who has, in effect, made a loan by selling goods on credit. See J. White & R. Summers, Uniform Commercial Code §25-5, at 1043 (2d ed. 1980).

Put more simply, a purchase money security interest "is a secured loan for the price of new collateral." Henderson, Coordination of the Uniform Commercial Code with Other State and Federal Law in the Farm Financing Context, 14 Idaho L. Rev. 363, 375 (1978). In this case, CO-OP took the purchase money security interests to secure the price of the feed, not the hogs. Consequently, by definition, CO-OP does not have a purchase money security interest in the hogs.

CO-OP, nevertheless, argues that their priority interest in the feed continues to be superior in the hogs pursuant to section 554.9203(3) because the hogs are "proceeds" of the feed. That section provides, "[u]nless otherwise agreed a security agreement gives the secured party the rights to proceeds provided by section 554.9306." Subsection 1 of section 554.9306 defines proceeds to include "whatever is received upon the sale, exchange, collection or other disposition of collateral or proceeds."

CO-OP contends that the "other disposition of collateral" language in section 554.9306 [now §9-315(a)—Eds.] includes ingestion and the biological processes involved when livestock consume feed, and as a result, fattened livestock are proceeds of the feed they consume. Such an argument was rejected in a case on all four hooves, so to speak. In First National Bank of Brush v. Bostron, 564 P.2d 964, 966 (Colo. App. 1977), the court emphasized that "[the livestock producer] received nothing when he disposed of the collateral by feeding it to the . . . cattle . . . the collateral was consumed, and there are no traceable proceeds to which the security interest may be said to have attached."

We agree with the result reached by the Colorado court. Ingestion and biological transformation of feed is not a type of "other disposition" within the contemplation of section 554.9306. For UCC purposes, the hogs are not proceeds of the feed.

CO-OP also argues that it should prevail over Union State pursuant to section 554.9315(1) [now §9-336—Eds.], which provides in part:

> If a security interest in goods was perfected and subsequently the goods or a part thereof have become part of a product or mass, the security interest continues in the product or mass if
>
> a. the goods are so manufactured, processed, assembled or commingled that their identity is lost in the product or mass. . . .

CO-OP contends that its superior interest in the feed continued in the hogs because the feed became commingled with the hogs.

Section 9-315 of the Uniform Commercial Code is probably the least litigated and discussed section of article 9. See Hawkland Uniform Commercial Code Series §9-315:01, at 256 (1986) (hereinafter Hawkland).

The only reported case examining this question is *Bostron*. There, the court concluded

> that cattle are neither a "product" nor a "mass" as these terms are used in the statute. The reference in subsection (a) to "manufactured, processed, assembled, or commingled" precludes any other interpretation. The feed which the cattle ate did not undergo any of these transformations, that is, it was not manufactured, processed, assembled or commingled with the cattle. . . . Once eaten the feed not only loses its identity, but in essence it ceases to exist and thus does not become part of the mass in the sense that the Code uses the phrase.

Bostron, 564 P.2d at 966.

Examining the *Bostron* decision and the question presented by the present case, one Uniform Commercial Code commentator has said:

> Other than section 9-315, no Code provision clearly suggests a contrary result, and section 9-315 does not seem to apply since the goods have not been manufactured, processed or commingled. Rather, their identity has been lost through ingestion, a process apparently not contemplated by section 9-315.

Hawkland at 262.

When construing a statute, we search for an interpretation that is sensible, workable, practical and logical. Emmetsburg Ready Mix Co. v. Norris, 362 N.W.2d 498, 499 (Iowa 1985). CO-OP's argument, although creative, stretches the language of section 554.9315 beyond our interpretation guideposts.

Because of our disposition on the merits, we need not address Union State's procedural issues. We have considered all arguments raised and find no error.

Affirmed.

PROBLEM 416

Octopus National Bank (ONB) made a loan to Dairy, Inc., secured by Dairy's equipment. The equipment was then sold to Cheeseworks, Inc., which later sold the equipment to Buttercups, Inc. Was the money that Cheeseworks received as proceeds of the sale subject to ONB's security interest? See Border State Bank, N.A. v. AgCountry Farm Credit Servs., FLCA, 535 F.3d 779 (8th Cir. 2008). Can ONB successfully claim that its collateral now includes both the equipment, now owned by Buttercups, and the money received as proceeds of the equipment? See §9-315(a); Commercial Credit Group, Inc. v. Process, Inc., 2017 WL 4214085 (E.D. Ark. 2017).

While Article 9 does not usually apply to security interests taken in an insurance policy as collateral (the common law or other statutes regulate these transactions), insurance payments that qualify as *proceeds* are regulated by the Code; §9-109(d)(8). For example, if the collateral is a car that is destroyed in a traffic mishap and the car owner receives compensation from an insurance company, the insurance money is *proceeds,* and any security interest in the car attaches to these monies.

Helms v. Certified Packaging Corp.

United States Court of Appeals, Seventh Circuit, 2008
551 F.3d 675

Posner, Circuit Judge.

Sarah Michaels, Inc., a manufacturer of bath products and a customer of a packaging manufacturer named Certified Packaging Corporation, declared bankruptcy together with affiliated corporations unnecessary to discuss separately. The trustee in bankruptcy brought an adversary proceeding against Certified seeking to avoid transfers that Michaels had made to that company to pay for packaging. The trustee obtained a default judgment for some $2 million but in an effort to collect the judgment collided with LaSalle Bank, which, as the assignee of a loan to Certified, claimed a security interest in Certified's assets. LaSalle in turn assigned its claim to CPC Acquisition, which is the successor to Certified and which has intervened in the bankruptcy proceeding to assert the priority of its lien over the trustee's judgment lien. For the sake of simplicity we'll pretend that LaSalle was and remains the lender to Certified and thus the adversary of the trustee in bankruptcy.

In December 2000, after LaSalle had made the loan, a fire broke out at one of Certified's plants and damaged equipment in it. The plant was shut down for several weeks, and the business losses resulting from the shutdown greatly exceeded the damage to Certified's property. Certified brought two lawsuits (both in Illinois state courts) in the wake of the fire. One was against its insurance broker, Rothschild, for negligence in having failed to list the plant on a business-losses insurance policy that Rothschild had procured for Certified. That suit was settled for $88,000 after deduction of attorneys' fees. The trustee contends that the settlement money should belong to the bankrupt estate, LaSalle that the money should belong to it as proceeds of the collateral damaged in the fire. The bankruptcy judge agreed with the trustee but was reversed by the district judge, and the trustee appeals.

Certified's other suit was against Commonwealth Edison and claimed that the fire had been due to Com Ed's negligence in maintaining one of its power lines. In that suit, which is pending, Certified seeks damages of $2,000,000 for property damage and business losses, the latter accounting for about 90 percent of the claimed damages. The bankruptcy judge, seconded by the district judge, ruled that the business-losses part of Certified's claim against Com Ed belongs to the trustee in bankruptcy, not to LaSalle. The cross-appeal challenges that ruling.

So we must decide whether the negligence claim against Rothschild for business losses, and the parallel claim against Certified, or either, or neither, are part of LaSalle's security interest. The issues are governed by the Uniform Commercial Code, as interpreted by the Illinois courts.

The loan agreement between LaSalle and Certified gave LaSalle a security interest in the equipment damaged in the fire. If a suit against someone who steals or damages collateral eventuates in an award measured by the diminution in the value of the collateral caused by the defendant's wrongdoing, so that the award restores the original value of the collateral, the award, like an insurance payment for damaged collateral, constitutes "proceeds" of the collateral and is therefore covered by the lender's security interest. UCC §§9-102(a)(64)(D) (proceeds include, "to the extent of the value of collateral, claims arising out of the loss, nonconformity, or interference with the use of, defects or infringement of rights in, or damage to, the collateral"), (E); McGonigle v. Combs, 968 F.2d 810, 828-29 (9th Cir. 1992); In re Wiersma, 324 B.R. 92, 106 (B.A.P. 9th Cir. 2005), reversed on other grounds, 483 F.3d 933 (9th Cir. 2007); In re Territo, 32 B.R. 377, 379-80 (Bkrtcy. E.D.N.Y. 1983); Richard F. Duncan et al., The Law and Practice of Secured Transactions: Working with Article 9 §2.05[3], pp. 2-57 to 2-58 (2008); R. Davis Rice, "McCullough v. Goodrich & Pennington Mortgage Fund, Inc.: Are Secured Creditors Really 'Secure' from Third Party Impairment of Collateral?," 59 S. Car. L. Rev. 455, 467-70 (2008); Lynn M. LoPucki & Elizabeth Warren, Secured Credit: A Systems Approach 205-06 (2d ed. 1998).

If Certified's suit against Com Ed succeeds, it will be as if Com Ed had converted some $200,000 of the collateral for LaSalle's loan and was therefore obliged to repay it; and "an action for conversion is a proper remedy for a secured party to bring against a third party when its collateral has been disposed of by the debtor." Taylor Rental Corp. v. J.I. Case Co., 749 F.2d 1526, 1529 (11th Cir. 1985); see also UCC §9-315, comment 2; Bartlett Milling Co., L.P. v. Walnut Grove Auction & Realty Co., 665 S.E.2d 478, 488-89 (N. Car. App. 2008); Farmers State Bank v. Easton Farmers Elevator, 457 N.W.2d 763, 766 (Minn. App. 1990). And so the judgment obtained in that suit would constitute proceeds of the collateral up to its value. That is why LaSalle's entitlement to the property-damage component of Certified's claim against Com Ed is unchallenged, and it is why if Rothschild, the insurance broker, had failed to obtain insurance coverage for damage to the physical assets that secured LaSalle's loan, the claim against the broker rather than for loss of business would be a claim to proceeds of the collateral.

But the claim against Rothschild *was* for failure to obtain business-loss insurance, and we do not see how compensation for that failure can be considered proceeds of collateral. The usual proceeds of collateral are the money obtained from selling it. By a modest extension, as we have just seen, they are money obtained in compensation for a diminution in the value of the collateral. But replacing a business loss is not restoring the value of damaged collateral. There is no necessary relation between the value of collateral and a business loss that results from its being destroyed or damaged—as this case illustrates: the business losses exceeded the impairment of the value of the collateral ninefold. The claim of a secured creditor to the proceeds of collateral cannot exceed the value of the collateral. UCC §9-102(a)(64)(D), (E); In re Tower Air, Inc., 397 F.3d 191, 199 and n.10 (3d Cir. 2005); In re Stevens, 130 F.3d 1027, 1030 (11th Cir. 1997). Recall the qualification in the definition of proceeds in UCC §9-102(a)(64)(D): "to the extent of the value of collateral."

The district judge was therefore wrong to treat the $88,000 settlement of Certified's claim against Rothschild for failing to procure business-loss coverage as proceeds of damaged collateral. . . .

NOTE

When the collateral is gone but the debtor still has money, creditors may press various theories to claim it as proceeds of their collateral. Compare, e.g., BMW Financial Services, NA, LLC v. Rio Grande Valley Motors, Inc., 2012 WL 4623198 (S.D. Tex. 2012) (funds from settling lawsuit held to be proceeds of underlying franchise rights); In re Wright Group, Inc., 443 B.R. 795 (Bankr. N.D. Ind. 2011) (customers' payments to play golf were not proceeds of golf course equipment).

PROBLEM 417

Farmers' Friend Credit Association loaned Farmer Bean money secured by his crops. In 2020 the federal government paid Farmer Bean not to grow any crop that year. Is the government payment the "proceeds" of the crop? See PHI Fin. Serv. v. Johnston Law Office, 2016 WL 308944 (N.D. 2016); Annot., 79 A.L.R.4th 903.

II. PRIORITIES IN PROCEEDS

PROBLEM 418

IPC (USA) delivered oil on consignment to Pettit Oil, but did not file a financing statement to protect its interests. Sure enough, Pettit Oil went into bankruptcy. IPC (USA) will be treated as an unsecured creditor as to the consigned oil (i.e., lose it to the bankruptcy trustee). How about proceeds of consigned oil? Will IPC (USA) recover any cash or accounts receivable that Pettit Oil has from sales of consigned oil? See §9-319(a); In re Pettit Oil Co., 917 F.3d 1130 (9th Cir. 2019).

PROBLEM 419

The Aquarius Auto Audio Shop (AAAS) sold and installed stereo systems in cars. Its inventory was financed by the Canis Major Bank and Trust Co., which had a perfected security interest in present and after-acquired inventory. When Aquarius sold the systems, it sometimes was paid cash, sometimes extended credit without signed contracts, and sometimes made credit customers sign contracts promising payment and granting AAAS a security interest in the systems. When Aquarius needed further financing, it took a later loan from the Cassiopeia Finance Company, granting the lender a security interest in its accounts receivable and its chattel paper. Cassiopeia knew all about the prior loan and inventory security interest of the Canis Major Bank at the time it filed its financing statement in the proper place. Aquarius defaulted on both loans, and both secured parties claimed the accounts and chattel paper (only Canis Major claimed the inventory). Canis Major's theory was that the accounts and chattel paper were *proceeds* of the inventory. The chattel paper was in Cassiopeia's possession; it had not yet collected any of the accounts receivable. Who should prevail? See §§9-315, 9-330(a), 9-322(a) and (b); White & Summers §25-10(a). What result where the accounts receivable financer filed first?

PROBLEM 420

Shadrach Heating and Air Conditioning, Inc., borrowed $15,000 from the Meshach Merchants Financing Association (MMFA) in order to purchase a new furnace for its own home office. When one of its important clients needed an identical furnace in a hurry, Shadrach Heating sold it its own new furnace, which it installed in the client's place of business. The $17,000 check it received in payment was put into Shadrach's checking account (balance prior to this deposit: $81) with the Abednego State Bank. Thereafter, Shadrach made one further deposit of $5,000, followed a week later by a withdrawal of $5,040.

(a) Are proceeds from the furnace sale still in the bank accounts? See Universal C.I.T. Credit Corp. v. Farmers Bank, 358 F. Supp. 317 (E.D. Mo. 1973) (the general rule is that "in tracing commingled funds it is presumed that any payments made were from other than funds in which another had a legally recognized interest," called the *lowest intermediate balance* rule). Section 9-315(b) permits tracing of *identifiable* proceeds; see also Official Comment 3 to this section. Note §4-210(b).

(b) If Shadrach Heating defaults on its loan repayment to MMFA and also on an unsecured promissory note currently held by the Abednego State Bank, can the bank exercise its common law right of setoff and pay itself out of the checking account, or is its setoff right junior to MMFA's security interest in the proceeds? See §9-340.

(c) What can a creditor claiming an interest in proceeds do to protect itself from setoff by the debtor's bank?

(d) If the depositary bank has a security interest in proceeds deposited in the debtor's account, but honors a check that depletes the account, may it still recover the money as traceable and identifiable proceeds? See §9-315's Official Comment 7, §9-332(b), and In re Cumberland Molded Products, LLC, 2009 WL 2208582 (Bankr. M.D. Tenn. 2009).

Yaddehige v. Xpert Technologies, Inc.

Court of Appeals of Michigan, 2019
2019 WL 1746077

Before: Jansen, P.J., and Meter and Gleicher, JJ.

Per Curiam.

Plaintiff appeals as of right the trial court's order granting summary disposition to defendant and dismissing plaintiff's Uniform Commercial Code (UCC) and unjust-enrichment claims. We affirm.

This case concerns certain assets of Legacy Group Lighting, LLC, doing business as Creative Lighting Solutions (CLS) that were dispersed to defendant out of CLS's deposit account. Plaintiff alleges that he loaned CLS $3 million in 2013 and that, as collateral for the loan, CLS granted plaintiff a security interest in "all assets of CLS." In 2016, defendant obtained a judgment against CLS for $199,680 in a separate action. CLS satisfied this judgment with money from the deposit account.

Plaintiff then sued defendant, arguing that he held a perfected, first-priority security interest in the money used to satisfy the judgment. Plaintiff alleged that defendant's retention of the money would amount to unjust enrichment and sought an injunction preventing defendant from collecting on the judgment with collateral securing plaintiff's loan. The trial court granted summary disposition in defendant's favor, concluding, in pertinent part, that MCL 440.9332 protects persons who receive transfers of money from a debtor when those funds are subject to a preexisting security interest. This appeal followed.

On appeal, plaintiff argues that the trial court erred in its conclusion that MCL 440.9332 precluded plaintiff's UCC and unjust-enrichment claims. "We review de novo a trial court's grant or denial of summary disposition." Tomra of North America, Inc. v. Dep't of Treasury, 325 Mich. App. 289, 293-294; ___ N.W.2d ___ (2018). "A motion for summary disposition under MCR 2.116(C)(10) tests the factual sufficiency of the claim, and is appropriately granted when, except as to the amount of damages, there is no genuine issue as to any material fact, and the moving party is entitled to judgment as a matter of law." Id. at 294. MCL 440.9332 provides:

> (1) A transferee of money takes the money free of a security interest unless the transferee acts in collusion with the debtor in violating the rights of the secured party.
>
> (2) A transferee of funds from a deposit account takes the funds free of a security interest in the deposit account unless the transferee acts in collusion with the debtor in violating the rights of the secured party.

Plaintiff does not argue that defendant colluded with CLS to violate plaintiff's security interests. Additionally, plaintiff does not argue that defendant does not qualify as a "transferee" for the purposes of MCL 440.9332.[1] Rather, plaintiff argues that the protections set forth in MCL 440.9332(2) apply only to a security interest in the deposit account itself. As a necessary corollary to this argument, plaintiff appears to concede, as he must, that under MCL 440.9332(2) defendant accepted the transfer free of plaintiff's alleged security interest in the deposit account itself.

Plaintiff, however, alleges that his secured interest in "all assets of CLS" extends to CLS's "accounts receivable" and "cash." Plaintiff points out that, under MCL 440.9315(b), a "security interest attaches to any identifiable proceeds of collateral." According to plaintiff, the money in the deposit account was the "proceeds" of CLS's accounts receivable and cash, meaning that plaintiff's security interest extends to these funds under MCL 440.9315(b). Plaintiff argues that, because MCL 440.9332(2) applies only to a security interest in the deposit account itself, defendant's judgment interest in the money in the deposit account must yield to plaintiff's higher-priority interest in that money as proceeds of secured collateral. Plaintiff's argument is without merit.

First, plaintiff has failed to set forth any evidence establishing that the money in the deposit account is actually identifiable cash proceeds of collateral securing his loan. Plaintiff argues that the affidavit of CLS's vice president establishes that the money in the deposit account was the proceeds of secured

1. See Orix v. Kovacs, 167 Cal. App. 4th 242 (2008) (concluding that a judgment creditor qualifies as a transferee).

collateral but this affidavit only states that CLS and plaintiff entered into a loan agreement. The deposit account is mentioned nowhere in the affidavit.

Second, assuming arguendo that the money in the deposit account was the proceeds of secured collateral, plaintiff fails to acknowledge MCL 440.9332(1), which provides that a "transferee of money takes the money free of a security interest unless the transferee acts in collusion with the debtor in violating the rights of the secured party." (Emphasis added). Subsection (1) provides the same protection as subsection (2), but is not limited to a security interest in the deposit account. See MCLA 440.9332, comment 2. Rather, subsection (1) protects a transferee from a security interest in the money itself. To the extent that defendant argues that MCL 440.9315(b) compels a different result when the money is cash proceeds, comment 7 to MCLA 440.9315 belies that argument, clarifying that in many cases "a purchaser or other transferee of the cash proceeds will take free of the perfected security interest"—citing MCL 440.9332(1) and (2) as examples. Accordingly, assuming arguendo that plaintiff held a first-priority security interest in the cash proceeds contained in the deposit account, defendant was protected from that security interest under MCL 440.9332(1). Therefore, because there is no material question that plaintiff accepted transfer of the money in the deposit account free of any security interest alleged by plaintiff, the trial court properly dismissed plaintiff's UCC-related claims.

Regarding plaintiff's remaining claim, unjust enrichment "is defined as the unjust retention of money or benefits which in justice and equity belong to another." Tkachik v. Mandeville, 487 Mich. 38, 47-48; 790 N.W.2d 260 (2010) (internal citation and quotation marks omitted). As already explained, plaintiff has not established that the transfer at issue violated his alleged security interests. Moreover, plaintiff has not shown that the transfer has caused him any harm. Plaintiff acknowledges that CLS has made "regular monthly payments" to him against the loan "over the past several years" and does not argue that the transfer will prevent CLS from continuing to do so. Similarly, plaintiff has not argued that the transfer left CLS with insufficient collateral to fully secure the loan. Accordingly, plaintiff has failed to set forth a genuine issue of material fact that defendant's retention of the transfer resulted in an inequity to plaintiff. See Karaus v. Bank of New York Mellon, 300 Mich. App. 9, 22-23; 831 N.W.2d 897 (2012). Thus, the trial court properly dismissed plaintiff's unjust-enrichment claim under MCR 2.116(C)(10).

Affirmed.

PROBLEM 421

Armstrong Bank held a perfected security interest in the deposit account of Tuscany Energy. Anticipating a legal struggle with its creditors, Tuscany hired a law firm and paid the firm a hefty retainer from the deposit account. Is Armstrong Bank entitled to recover the funds from the law firm? See §9-332; In re Tuscany Energy, LLC, 581 B.R. 681 (Bankr. S.D. Fla. 2018). What if funds from the deposit account had been transferred into another account of the debtor, a "lock-box" account established for the benefit of another one of debtor's creditors? See In re Tusa-Expo Holdings, Inc., 811 F.3d 786 (5th Cir. 2016).

Does §9-332 apply to transfer of bitcoin?

PROBLEM 422

Octopus National Bank loaned $200,000 to Big Department Store and took a security interest in its inventory "now owned or after-acquired," which it perfected by filing a financing statement on July 5. Antitrust National Bank loaned $100,000 to Total Store, Inc., and took a security interest in its inventory "now owned or after-acquired," which it perfected by filing a financing statement on September 25. Without the consent of either creditor, the two retailers merged the following year, when the inventories of both were worth $300,000. The new entity was named Total Department Store. Which bank has priority in this situation? See §§9-102(a)(56), 9-203(d) and (e), 9-508 (and its helpful Official Comments), 9-325, 9-326, and the latter's Official Comments; White & Summers §25-11(a); Jean Wegman Burns, New Article Nine of the UCC: The Good, the Bad, and the Ugly, 2002 Ill. L. Rev. 29, 70-75.

Read §9-315(d) carefully, and work your way through the following Problem.

PROBLEM 423

On August 2, when the filed financing statement in favor of the Last National Bank covered "all business machines," the debtor engaged in the transactions listed below. Decide for each transaction if the bank should take action before August 23 or if the financing statement is sufficient as filed:

(a) The debtor traded a computer for another computer.

(b) The debtor traded another computer for a painting to be hung in the office.

(c) The debtor traded a duplicating machine for a used car (and state law requires a lien interest in a vehicle to be noted on the certificate of title as the sole means of perfection).

(d) The debtor sold a calculator to a friend for cash and that same day used the cash to buy a painting to hang in the office.

(e) The debtor sold an adding machine for $500 and put the cash in a bank account at a different bank; on August 2, that bank exercised its right of setoff against the account. See §9-340.

(f) The debtor sold a coffee maker for $200 and gave the money to a Salvation Army volunteer that same day; see §9-332(a).

PROBLEM 424

Balboa Bank & Trust Company floor-planned the inventory of Erickson Motors and perfected its security interest in the inventory (and proceeds) by filing in the proper place. See §9-311(d). Erickson Motors sold a car on credit to John Smith, who paid $1,000 down and signed a contract obligating him to pay $25,000 more. The car dealership assigned this contract and the promissory note Smith signed to the Cartier Finance Company, which took possession of these items and notified Smith he was to make future payments to Cartier. Smith made no payments at all because the car had serious mechanical difficulties, and eventually the parties cancelled the transaction and the car was returned to Erickson Motors on September 11. On September 12, a representative of Cartier Finance Company came to the dealership and took possession of the car, claiming it was *proceeds* from the contract of purchase, which Cartier still had. Balboa Bank objected and claimed a superior interest in the car, asserting its priority in the inventory of the dealership. Who prevails here? See §9-330(c) and its Official Comments 9 and 10.

For a complete review of priority problems, some involving proceeds and some not, read Official Comments 4 through 9 of §9-322. If you can understand them all, you are on top of the subject matter of this course.

CHAPTER 26 ASSESSMENT: MULTIPLE CHOICE QUESTIONS

1. Bond Manufacturing, in need of cash, sold some of its milling equipment for $10,000. At the same time, Bond Manufacturing missed a loan payment to Seizure Finance, who held a perfected security interest in Bond Manufacturing's equipment. Seizure Finance declared default and demanded that Bond Manufacturing hand over the $10,000. Bond Manufacturing refused, contending that Seizure Finance was still entitled to go after its collateral in the hands of the buyer and had a security interest only in equipment, not cash. Is the $10,000 collateral of Seizure Finance?

a. No, unless the security agreement grants a security interest in equipment and also cash.
b. No, because the sale did not eliminate the security interest in the equipment.
c. Yes, because the $10,000 is identifiable proceeds of collateral.
d. Yes, under equitable considerations.

2. Bond Manufacturing had another piece of equipment, the Miller CNC, which it used to produce circuit boards. The machine was destroyed by fire, but was insured. The insurance company wrote Bond Manufacturing a check for the replacement value of the machine. Was the check proceeds of Seizure Finance's collateral?
   a. Yes, because it is payment for the time the machine was indisposed.
   b. Yes, because it is a product of the collateral.
   c. No, because it was not received upon sale or other disposition of the collateral.
   d. No, unless the security agreement covers checks.
   e. Yes, because it is insurance payable by reason of damage to the collateral.

3. Bond Manufacturing sold a piece of equipment, receiving $19,000. Seizure Finance did not pay attention for about a year, by which time the money had been spent, and was no longer traceable using accounting methods. Did Seizure Finance lose its security interest in those proceeds?
   a. No, the debtor cannot unilaterally destroy a security interest.
   b. Yes, the security interest continues only in identifiable proceeds.
   c. No, Seizure Finance would be entitled to claim as proceeds any cash Bond Manufacturing had.
   d. Yes, a security interest in proceeds in collateral lasts only 20 days.

4. Bond Manufacturing, increasingly entrepreneurial, traded another piece of manufacturing equipment for a sports car. Bond Manufacturing appeased the angry Seizure Finance by acknowledging that the car was proceeds of Seizure Finance's collateral, although the parties took no action to note the security interest on the certificate of title. Two months later, Bond Manufacturing finally staggered into bankruptcy. Seizure Finance had a security interest in the car, as collateral. But was it a *perfected* security interest (we know what happens to an unperfected security interest in bankruptcy)?
   a. Yes. Seizure Finance had a perfected security interest in the collateral and so will have a perfected security interest in the proceeds, the car.
   b. Yes, provided that Seizure Finance perfected its security interest by filing a financing statement.
   c. No, this security interest in proceeds became unperfected after 20 days.
   d. No, a security interest cannot be perfected in proceeds.

5. Boxcar Bank had a purchase money security interest in Furniture Retail's inventory. Paper Finance had a security interest in Furniture Retail's chattel paper. Furniture Retail often sold furniture on credit, receiving in return sales contracts under which the buyer promised to pay and put up the furniture as collateral. Furniture Retail delivered the contracts to Paper Finance, who kept them locked in a vault. If Boxcar Bank claimed such contracts as proceeds of inventory and Paper Finance claimed the contracts as chattel paper, who takes priority?
   a. First to file or perfect.
   b. Boxcar Bank, who had a purchase money security interest.
   c. Paper Finance, as a chattel paper creditor.
   d. The creditors would share equally.

ANSWERS

1. *C* is the best answer. When the collateral is sold (or otherwise disposed of), the creditor automatically has a security interest in identifiable proceeds. §9-315(a)(2). That right arises under the statute, and need not be included in the security agreement, contrary to *A*, although security agreements often include "proceeds" in the granting clause. Proceeds include anything acquired upon the sale, so the $10,000 sum is identifiable proceeds. The creditor is entitled to proceeds and, in general, retains the security interest in the collateral. §9-315(a)(1), (2). Contrary to *B*, the creditor has a right to proceeds even if it retained its security interest in the transferred collateral. That sounds as if the creditor's collateral will double in value, but in practice many factors prevent that. Some buyers take free of the security interest, some buyers would be difficult to track down, and often the proceeds are not tracked.
2. *E* is the best answer. Proceeds is broadly defined in §9-102(64) to include insurance payments for lost or damaged collateral.
3. *B* is the best answer. A practical limitation on the security interest in proceeds is that it applies only to "identifiable proceeds of collateral." Often, as here, a debtor receives proceeds of collateral but later they become untraceable. Creditors can protect against this in the security agreement, by getting a security interest in bank accounts or other collateral, or requiring debtors to track proceeds (such as by having a lock-box account at a bank).
4. *C* is the best answer. If the security interest is perfected in collateral, the creditor has a security interest perfected in the proceeds—but only for 20 days, unless one of the following apply:
   i. The creditor filed for the collateral and could have filed for proceeds category (and the proceeds were not acquired for cash proceeds);

ii. the proceeds are identifiable cash proceeds; or
iii. the security interest is perfected within 20 days.

A security interest in a car cannot be perfected by filing, so (i) does not apply. The car is not cash proceeds, so (ii) does not apply. Seizure Finance could have complied with (iii) and remained perfected by getting its security interest noted on the certificate of title. But it did not, so its security interest is unperfected—and so ill-fated in bankruptcy.

5. *C* is the best answer. This question serves simply to illustrate a very specific priority rule. Section 9-330(a) provides:

> A purchaser of chattel paper has priority over a security interest in the chattel paper which is claimed merely as proceeds of inventory subject to a security interest if:
>
> (1) in good faith and in the ordinary course of the purchaser's business, the purchaser gives new value and takes possession of the chattel paper or obtains control of the chattel paper under Section 9-105; and
>
> (2) the chattel paper does not indicate that it has been assigned to an identified assignee other than the purchaser.

Because inventory finance and chattel paper finance are important and potentially conflicting commercial practices, Article 9 provides a specific rule to resolve priority.

CHAPTER 27
DEFAULT

In what is perhaps the only portion of secured transactions law where things can get exciting, Part 6 of Article 9 presents us with the rules on default and foreclosure. In this segment if a debtor ceases to make payments the creditor must take action to enforce its rights in the collateral. Even in our civilized times this can involve pitched battles during ugly encounters. For example, in Griffith v. Valley of the Sun Recovery & Adjustment Bureau, 613 P.2d 1283 (Ariz. App. 1980), the repossessor was held liable in negligence for the actions of the debtor's neighbor who used a shotgun to shoot a bystander during a repossession melee. It is the job of the lawyers involved to make sure that everyone obeys the rules Article 9 lays down to ensure the process is fair to everyone, and, when things go awry, to know who bears what responsibility.

I. *PRE-DEFAULT DUTIES OF THE SECURED PARTY*

PROBLEM 425

Andy Doria was the owner of 100 shares of Titanic Telephone, which he pledged to the Morro Castle National Bank as collateral for a $10,000 loan. At the time of the pledge, the stock was selling for $100 a share.

(a) If the stock began to fall in value and if on November 4, when it was selling at $80 a share, Andy called the bank and told the bank to sell, is the bank responsible if it does not and the stock bottoms out at $1.50 a share? Read §9-207; see, e.g., Layne v. Bank One, Ky., N.A., 395 F.3d 271 (6th Cir. 2005).

(b) Would it help the bank's position if the pledge agreement contained a clause saying that the bank was not responsible for its own negligence in dealing with the stock? Read §1-302(b); see Brodheim v. Chase Manhattan Bank, N.A., 75 Misc. 2d 285, 347 N.Y.S.2d 394 (Sup. Ct. 1973); G. Gilmore, ch. 42.

(c) Andy's dealings with the bank became more complicated, and eventually the bank held, as pledgee, Andy's stocks in five different companies. One of these, Lusitania Foundry, offered a stock split option that had to be exercised by December 31, so Andy wrote the Morro Castle National Bank and, explaining that his records had become confused, asked the bank how many shares of Lusitania Foundry it held. The bank replied that it possessed 50 shares (this was a typographical error; it actually held 150). Andy tendered 50 shares of equivalent stock to the bank in exchange for a return of 50 shares of Lusitania Foundry, on which he then exercised the stock option, which proved very profitable. On January 3, Andy learned he owned 100 more shares that the bank held; it was too late to take the stock option on these shares. Does Andy have a cause of action against the bank under §9-207? Under §9-210? What damages can he recover? See §9-625(b) and (f).

(d) May a creditor in possession sell the collateral, in the absence of default or authorization in the security agreement? See Segovia v. Equities First Holdings, LLC, 2008 WL 2251218 (Del. Super. Ct. 2008).

PROBLEM 426

Mazie Minkus borrowed $2,000 from the Mount Brown State Bank and, as collateral, pledged to the bank her stamp collection (valued at $2,000). She used the money for a South American vacation. While she was away, the bank, which was located in an unstable geological area, was destroyed in an earthquake. The stamp collection went with it. Fortunately, the bank was fully insured by a policy with the Gibbons Insurance Company, which, inter alia, paid the bank $2,000 for the loss of the stamp collection. Gibbons then notified Mazie that she should pay the $2,000 debt to the insurance company, which was using the doctrine of subrogation to step into the shoes of the bank. Need she pay? See §9-207(b)(2); G. Gilmore §42.7.

II. DEFAULT

PROBLEM 427

Northern Aviation Co. has made timely payments on its debt to Crowley, but failed to get insurance on the collateral airplanes, as required by the security agreement. Failure to get insurance is defined as one of the events triggering default. Can Crowley take possession of the airplanes and sell them to pay the debt? See §§9-601, 609; Crowley v. Northern Aviation, LLC, 441 P.3d 407 (Alaska 2019).

State Bank of Piper City v. A-Way, Inc.

Illinois Supreme Court, 1987
115 Ill. 2d 401, 504 N.E.2d 737

WARD, J.

The plaintiff, State Bank of Piper City, filed a complaint in the circuit court of Iroquois County against the defendant, A-Way, Inc., to enforce its security interest in grain and the proceeds from sales of grain held by the defendant on account for a debtor of the plaintiff. The circuit court granted the defendant's motion to dismiss the complaint and denied the plaintiff's motion to vacate the order of dismissal. On the plaintiff's appeal, the appellate court reversed and remanded (135 Ill. App. 3d 1010), and we granted the defendant's petition for leave to appeal (103 Ill. 2d R. 315). . . .

In February 1982, the plaintiff was awarded a judgment in the amount of $131,083.91 against William C. Brenner upon his default on promissory notes that had been secured, under article 9 of the Uniform Commercial Code (UCC) (Ill. Rev. Stat. 1979, ch. 26, par. 9-101 et seq.), by a security interest in grain owned by Brenner which was stored in the defendant's warehouse. In a supplementary proceeding to enforce its judgment (Ill. Rev. Stat. 1981, ch. 110, par. 73), the plaintiff served the defendant with a citation to discover assets that it held on Brenner's behalf. The defendant responded by an affidavit acknowledging the accuracy of an attached ledger sheet with information regarding Brenner's account. The ledger sheet listed, inter alia, the number of bushels of grain the defendant held for him, 5,141.20, and the costs of drying and storing the grain. The plaintiff then moved for a citation order requiring the defendant to pay the plaintiff $5,141.20, confusing the number of bushels with their value, "as partial satisfaction for the judgment entered" in its suit against Brenner. The court held a hearing at which the defendant failed to appear, and allowed the plaintiff's motion. Acting upon the order, the defendant sold the grain, obtaining $11,310.64; of that amount, the defendant remitted $5,141.20 to the plaintiff and applied the balance to outstanding charges on Brenner's accounts.

Approximately eight months later, realizing its mistake, the plaintiff brought this action under article 9 of the UCC (Ill. Rev. Stat. 1979, ch. 26, par. 9-101 et seq.), to enforce its security interest in the proceeds of the grain sale over and above $5,141.20. The court dismissed the plaintiff's complaint on the grounds that the doctrines of merger and res judicata barred the suit. As stated, the appellate court reversed the dismissal.

The defendant first contends that the trial court properly dismissed the plaintiff's complaint under the doctrine of merger and that any rights the plaintiff had under the promissory notes of Brenner merged into the judgment, extinguishing any interest it had in the grain. "The general rule is, that by a judgment at law or a decree in chancery, the contract or instrument upon which the proceeding is based becomes entirely merged in the judgment. By the judgment of the court it loses all of its vitality and ceases to bind the parties to its execution. Its force and effect are then expended, and all remaining legal liability is transferred to the judgment or decree. Once becoming merged in the judgment, no further action at law or suit in equity can be maintained. . . ." (Doerr v. Schmitt (1941), 375 Ill. 470, 472, quoting Wayman v. Cochrane (1864), 35 Ill. 152, 154; Rock Island Bank & Trust Co. v. Stauduhar (1978), 59 Ill. App. 3d 892, 900.) Second, under principles of res judicata, it says, citing Hughey v. Industrial Com. (1979), 76 Ill. 2d 577, 582-583, that the plaintiff is barred from bringing the present action because the issue now raised could have been litigated in the citation proceeding.

The defendant's contentions have not been directly addressed by this court. We judge that, under the language of article 9 of the UCC (Ill. Rev. Stat. 1979, ch. 26, section 9-501(1)(5)) and from constructions in other jurisdictions, these contentions are without merit.

Section 9-501(1) [now §9-601—Eds.] of the UCC serves to broaden the options available to a secured creditor upon a debtor's default. . . . Section 9-501(1) of the UCC states:

> When a debtor is in default under a security agreement, a secured party has the rights and remedies provided in this Part [concerning default]. . . . He may reduce his claim to judgment, foreclose or otherwise enforce the security interest by any available judicial procedure. . . . The rights and remedies referred to in this subsection are cumulative.

(Ill. Rev. Stat. 1979, ch. 26, par. 9-501(1).)

When a secured creditor has chosen to reduce his claim to judgment "the lien of any levy which may be made upon his collateral by virtue of any execution based upon the judgment shall relate back to the date of the perfection of the security interest in such collateral" (Ill. Rev. Stat. 1979, ch. 26, par. 9-501(5)) and serve as a continuation of the secured creditor's original perfected security interest (Ill. Ann. Stat., ch. 26, par. 9-501(5), Uniform Commercial Code Comment, at 322 (Smith-Hurd 1974)). Thus, a secured creditor's effort to collect its debt through the judicial process will not "operate to destroy his security interest vis-à-vis the debtor or to impair its priority [interest] over third parties" (2 G. Gilmore, Security Interests in Personal Property sec. 43.7, at 1209-1210 (1965); [citations omitted]).

The doctrine of merger does not, contrary to the defendant's argument, preclude a secured creditor from enforcing its security interest in the property given as collateral.

In Ruidoso State Bank v. Garcia (1978), 92 N.M. 288, 587 P.2d 435, cited above, a secured creditor earlier had brought suit to enforce its security interest in two vehicles which it had previously levied upon in satisfaction of a judgment against its debtors upon their default on promissory notes. The vehicles, however, had been released upon a trial court's finding that they were exempt property. Subsequently the secured creditor brought the suit involved. The debtors argued, inter alia, that by foreclosing on the notes the secured creditor caused the security agreements executed by the debtors to merge in the judgment, precluding their subsequent enforcement. The court rejected this contention, holding:

> Merger does not apply here for the reason that the Bank[, the secured creditor,] had two separate causes of action. It could sue and reduce the debt to judgment. In that case the debt would be merged into the judgment. However, the debt would be carried forward so that the Bank's rights under the security agreement would not be destroyed. The security agreements, under the statutory prohibition [i.e., under article 9 of the UCC], would not be merged into the judgment.

Ruidoso State Bank v. Garcia (1978), 92 N.M. 288, 290, 587 P.2d 435, 437. . . .

Here even though the notes merged in the judgment precluding further action on the notes (Doerr v. Schmitt (1941), 375 Ill. 470, 472; Rock Island Bank & Trust Co. v. Stauduhar (1978), 59 Ill. App. 3d 892, 900), that merger did not preclude the plaintiff from bringing this action to enforce its security interest in the grain. That security interest was provided for in security agreements separate from and independent of the notes. The security agreements provided that upon the debtor's default the secured creditor "shall have all of the rights and remedies of a secured party under the Illinois Uniform Commercial Code," remedies which are, as previously stated, "cumulative." Furthermore, the "lien of any levy," which was made upon the grain pursuant to the plaintiff's judgment against Brenner, related back to the time of perfection of the security interest. (Ill. Ann. Stat. ch. 26, par. 9-501(5), Uniform Commercial Code Comment, at 322 (Smith-Hurd 1974).) Thus, the merger of the note in the plaintiff's judgment against Brenner and the plaintiff's citation to discover assets proceeding did not affect the plaintiff's security interest in the remaining grain-sale proceeds.

The defendant next contends that the plaintiff is barred under res judicata from bringing the present action against A-Way, Inc.:

> The doctrine of res judicata provides that "a final judgment rendered by a court of competent jurisdiction on the merits is conclusive as to the rights of the parties and their privies, and, as to them, constitutes an absolute bar to a subsequent action involving the *same* claim, demand or cause of action." (Emphasis added.) [Citation.] When res judicata is established "as a bar against the prosecution of a second action between the same parties upon the same claim or demand . . . it is conclusive not only as to every matter which was offered to sustain or defeat the claim or demand, but as to any other matter which might have been offered for that purpose. . . ." Housing Authority for La Salle County v. YMCA (1984), 101 Ill. 2d 246, 251-252.

Because of the provision under article 9 of the UCC for multiple and cumulative remedies upon the debtor's default, res judicata will not bar a secured creditor from exhausting his remedies under the UCC. . . .

Although the decisions cited involved successive actions against a debtor in default, there is no reason not to apply the same principles to situations, as here, involving third parties. Not to do so would defeat the purpose of article 9 in providing a secured creditor with multiple remedies upon a debtor's default.

That the order entered in the citation proceeding against the defendant was a final order (Illinois Brewing & Malting Co. v. Ilmberger (1910), 155 Ill. App. 417, 418) does not, under res judicata, preclude the plaintiff from bringing the present action. The order was entered in execution of the plaintiff's judgment against Brenner. Here, the plaintiff is acting in its capacity as a secured creditor attempting to enforce its article 9 security interest in the surplus proceeds from the sale of the grain, proceeds which it mistakenly omitted in the citation proceeding. The action of the plaintiff in the citation proceeding does not bar the plaintiff from proceeding here.

The defendant argues too that if the plaintiff is permitted to proceed with this action it will suffer undue hardship because it has applied the proceeds remaining from the sale to its other accounts of Brenner. The argument appears to border on effrontery. The defendant in the argument admitted that it knew the amount of the plaintiff's judgment against Brenner; that it was aware that the plaintiff had made a mistake in requesting that it pay the plaintiff 5,141.20 dollars instead of bushels; and that it did not disclose to the plaintiff the amount it received from sale of the grain. These may have been considerations in the defendant's not appearing at the citation proceeding. If we were to conclude that fraud had been present, which under our analysis we need not do, res judicata, of course, would not be applicable.

Hughey v. Industrial Com. (1979), 76 Ill. 2d 577, 583; McNely v. Board of Education (1956), 9 Ill. 2d 143, 151-152.

For the reasons given, we hold that the trial court erred in dismissing the complaint. The judgment of the appellate court reversing and remanding the cause is affirmed.

Judgment affirmed.

The secured party's Part 6 Article 9 rights come into being whenever there has been a *default* by the debtor. The Code, however, does not define *default,* and the only judicially recognized form of default is failure to pay the debt on time; see Cofield v. Randolph County Commn., 90 F.3d 468 (11th Cir. 1996). Since the Code is silent on the meaning of the term, the security agreement must fill in the blanks. It is the lawyer's job to draft the security agreement so as to cover the possible exigencies with appropriate clauses triggering default and the ability to foreclose. One way to do this is by a specific definition of the term *default,* so that it includes not only failure to pay on time but also failure to perform any of the terms of the agreement. *Default* may also be defined to cover certain specific problems: death of the debtor, an assignment for the benefit of creditors, institution of any insolvency proceeding, impairment of the collateral, etc.

A practical point that debtors (and law students) sometimes overlook: Even if the debtor is making all the loan payments on time, there will be default if another default event specified in the security agreement occurs, such as failure to provide proof of insurance for the collateral or failure to pay other creditors on time (called a "cross-default clause"). See, e.g., Regions Bank v. Thomas, 422 S.W.3d 550 (Tenn. Ct. App. 2013) (failure to provide proof of insurance on collateral was default under loan contract, permitting repossession and sale of aircraft).

If through inadvertence, mistake, or deliberate bad faith the creditor repossesses when there is no right to do so, the creditor is guilty of conversion (and breach of contract) and will have to pay all damages caused thereby. In re Martin Specialty Vehicles, Inc., 87 Bankr. 752, (Bankr. D. Mass. 1988).

Some security agreements provide simply that default is the failure to observe the conditions and promises of the security agreement and then include an acceleration clause similar to this one:

> The parties agree that if at any time the secured party deems itself insecure because in good faith it believes the prospect of payment or performance is impaired, it shall have the right to declare a default and accelerate payment of all unpaid sums or performance or, at its option, may require the debtor to furnish additional collateral.

Read §1-309 carefully.

PROBLEM 428

When Mr. and Mrs. Bankruptcy bought a mobile home from Nervous Motors, Inc., they signed a purchase money security agreement in favor of the seller that contained an acceleration clause identical to the one above. Which of the following events, in your opinion, is sufficient to trigger the proper use of the clause?

(a) A very bad financial quarter for Nervous Motors, Inc.?

(b) A serious drop in the state of the economy?

(c) Knowledge that the Bankruptcys have been talking to a lawyer (could the seller here make use of §2-609)?

(d) A report (which simple investigation would show to be false) that the Bankruptcys have failed to pay their grocery bills for the last two months?

(e) An anonymous phone call that states the Bankruptcys are getting ready to move the mobile home to Mexico?

(f) The confiscation of the mobile home and the arrest of the Bankruptcys for possessing marijuana? See Blaine v. General Motors Acceptance Corp., 82 Misc. 2d 653, 370 N.Y.S.2d 323 (Sup. Ct. 1975). See §1-309 and its Official Comment; G. Gilmore §43.4. In First Natl. Bank in Libby v. Twombly, 689 P.2d 1226 (Mont. 1984), the court awarded punitive damages for a bad faith acceleration.

(g) Would §1-309 be relevant at all if Mr. and Mrs. Bankruptcy had signed a demand promissory note (one that permits the creditor to call the loan anytime the creditor wishes)? See the Official Comment to §1-208 and Solar Motors, Inc. v. First Natl. Bank of Chadron, 4 Neb. App. 1, 537 N.W.2d 527 (1995).

The courts stretch to protect the debtor whenever the secured party's "insecurity" is unwarranted. See Lane v. John Deere, 767 S.W.2d 138 (Tenn. 1989). For particularly outrageous conduct on the part of the creditor, punitive damages are favored. See Annot., Punitive Damages for Wrongful Seizure of Chattel by One Claiming Security Interest, 35 A.L.R.3d 1016.

Klingbiel v. Commercial Credit Corp.

United States Court of Appeals, Tenth Circuit, 1971
439 F.2d 1303

BROWN, J.

When Vern Klingbiel (Purchaser) went outside his home in St. Louis, Missouri, on the morning of June 22, 1966, he found his brand new (1966) Ford Galaxie 500 gone. Later he was to learn that in the dark of night and with skillful stealth the car—despite its being fully locked—had been taken away, not by some modern auto rustler, but by an anonymous representative of the Automobile Recovery Bureau acting for Commercial, the installment finance company, which was described with remarkable accuracy as a "professional firm." Little did he know that with this sudden, unexplained disappearance of an automobile, which—with all its chrome and large mortgage—was still his, so much had been unleashed. First, of course, was his anguish at his loss. More significant for us, time, tide, litigation, trial, victory and appeal was to instruct him in the intricacies of the fine print of the purchase mortgage contract he signed and, perhaps to his awe, the Uniform Commercial Code.

A Kansas jury, under the Judge's careful instructions, which we find to be unexceptionable, did not think much of this treatment and by its verdict awarded some small actual damages plus punitive damages in a sum almost twice the purchase price of the car.

Fleeing from this judgment as a matter of principle, if not principal, Commercial quite naturally and properly seeks a haven in the terms of the contract[1] and, as an anchor to windward, the acceleration and good faith provisions of the Kansas Uniform Commercial Code. We find the attack unavailing and affirm.

WHAT HAPPENED

The case was tried largely on stipulated facts. On May 26, 1966, Vern Klingbiel, a resident of St. Louis, Missouri, entered into an installment contract with Dealer for the purchase of a new Ford Galaxie automobile. This installment contract showed a time sales price of $4,907.56. Purchaser made a down payment of $400, tendering to Dealer a personal check in the amount of $300 and a second check in the amount of $100, the latter being signed in his wife's name. This left a time balance of $4,507.56, to be paid

1. For convenience of reference the bracketed numbers are inserted (e.g., [i] [a] [b] [c] etc.):

> This Mortgage may be assigned by Seller [Dealer], and when assigned, all rights of Seller shall vest in its assignee [Commercial] and this Mortgage shall be free from any claims or defenses whatsoever which Purchaser may have against Seller . . . [i] If Purchaser [a] defaults on any obligation or breaches any agreement or warranty under this Mortgage, or [b] if Seller should feel itself or Vehicle insecure, [c] the unpaid portion of the Time Balance and any expense (including taxes) shall without notice, at the option of Seller, become due forthwith. [ii] Purchaser agrees in any such case [a] to pay said amount to Seller, upon demand, or [b] at the election of Seller, to deliver Vehicle to Seller. [iii] This Mortgage may be foreclosed [a] in any manner provided by law, or [b] Seller may, without notice or demand for performance or legal process, except such as may be required by Law, lawfully enter any premises where Vehicle may be found, and take possession of it. [iv] Seller may retain all payments made by Purchaser as compensation for the use of the Vehicle while in Purchaser's possession. [v] Any personal property in Vehicle at the time of repossession which has not become a part thereof may be held temporarily by Seller for Purchaser, without liability thereof. . . . All rights and remedies hereunder are cumulative and not alternative.

in 36 equal, successive monthly installments of $125.21, the payments to commence on June 26, 1966, under the mortgage contract containing the acceleration and enforcement provisions (see Note [1] supra). Commercial shortly became the assignee, on a dealer recourse basis, for the consideration of $3,400.

Subsequently, but before Purchaser's first monthly installment became due, Commercial felt itself insecure, and it directed the Automobile Recovery Bureau of St. Louis, Missouri to repossess the automobile. On June 22, 1966—four days before Purchaser's first monthly installment was due and at a time when he was not in default—the repossessing professionals, without notice, demand, communication, or correspondence with Purchaser, removed his locked automobile from the front of his house in the dead of night, [and] delivered it to Commercial[2] along with Purchaser's personal property. . . .

Out of the Verbal Wilderness

The skillful Trial Judge having been aware that this contract . . . was not written for those who run to read discerned its true meaning by recognizing its true sequential structure. Unlike Commercial which assumes that the right to accelerate without notice or demand is synonymous with the right to repossess without notice or demand, the Judge carefully distinguished between the two. Acceleration, he charged, was permissible without notice or demand. But upon acceleration Commercial then had to make demand or give notice to Purchaser so that the admitted failure of notice/demand . . . made Commercial's repossession an unlawful conversion.

The Court's instruction tracked the terms of the contract correctly. Though under clause [i][b] (note [2], supra) "Time Balance" might from acceleration become due at any time without notice, if Commercial felt itself insecure, the very next provision in the contract provides "[ii] Purchaser

2. Purchaser did not have the slightest idea that his car had been repossessed. He notified the police that it was missing, in the belief that it had been stolen, and it was the police who finally uncovered what had actually transpired.

Even the austere stipulation vividly portrays Commercial's conduct and presages its predicament:

> On June 22, 1966, Automobile Recovery Bureau, St. Louis, Missouri, at the telephone direction and request of Commercial Credit Corporation, without notice, demand, communication or correspondence with plaintiff, some time during the night, took the locked 1966 Ford Galaxie automobile off the street in front of plaintiff's home, and delivered the car to Commercial Credit Corporation at St. Louis, Missouri. Commercial Credit Corporation had no communication, either written or oral, with plaintiff prior to taking the automobile. Commercial Credit Corporation requested, ordered, authorized and directed the repossession of the 1966 Ford Galaxie 500 automobile from Vern Klingbiel because it felt itself, or vehicle, insecure.

agrees in any such case [a] to pay said amount to Seller, *upon demand,* or, [b] at the election of Seller, to deliver vehicle to Seller." (Emphasis added.) Clause [ii][a][b] with its alternative stated in the disjunctive does not speak in terms of rights which Commercial has. Rather it speaks in terms of *actions* which Purchaser must take depending on the choice opted by Commercial. It could require Purchaser to pay off in full or it could require redelivery. But before Purchaser was bound to do either Commercial had first to indicate which course was required. The two words, "upon demand," are not only conspicuous, they are unavoidable.

Not yet overborne, Commercial would further have us construe the contract so as to declare that no notice was necessary prior to repossession by falling back on clause [iii][b] which provides: "[iii] This mortgage may be foreclosed [a] . . . or [b] Seller may, without notice or demand for performance or legal process, . . . lawfully enter any premises where Vehicle may be found, and take possession of it."

This is equally unavailing. At the outset, this clause follows—does not precede—but follows clause [ii] which, [a][b] as we have held, calls for notice/demand before Purchaser is required to act upon a declared acceleration. Equally important, in the sequential structure of the contract this refers only to a *foreclosure.* This means that there must be a default on the part of the Purchaser. This can take the form of Purchaser's failure to perform as in [i][a] or an acceleration under [i][b]. Certainly in the case of predefault acceleration, as a result of the manner in which this contract is constructed, clause [ii][b] in effect calls for notice/demand to precipitate a default. The failure or refusal of Purchaser after such notice/demand would, of course, be a [i][a] default, thus setting in train the foreclosure provisions of [iii][a] or [b], including *at that stage* even the most stealthy repossession by night riders. But this privilege is not available by skipping from [i][b] to [iii][b] over the head of [ii][a][b]. . . .

We think there was evidence, if believed by the jury, to warrant the inference of more than simple inadvertence or a technical conversion. There was first the circumstance of the stealthy retaking without notice of any kind, although notice clearly was called for as we have held. At that time Purchaser was not in default. Further, Purchaser's own personal property was taken along with the automobile. This was never returned to him, nor did he receive recompense for it. In fact, Commercial never even contacted Purchaser to inform him of the repossession. He had to find out through his own effort and investigation. There are many other factors unnecessary to catalogue which sustain the punitive damage finding.

This leaves only the objection to the Court's instruction on actual damages. Clearly there was sufficient evidence to cover the three elements submitted by the Court for the loss of value of the automobile, Purchaser's personal property, and the loss of the vehicle for an intervening period.

The objection is pointed at the term "actual value" rather than market value of the car. Assuming, but not deciding that it was error, such error was harmless. The "actual" damages awarded totalled $770. Of this sum $120 was for the loss of Purchaser's personal property, which Commercial fully concedes is correct. Purchaser's testimonial estimate of the loss from the loss of use of the car, which clearly is a permissible element of damages, was approximately $500. Thus, this leaves only $150 for the loss of value of the automobile itself. This modest recovery does not demonstrate any harm.

Affirmed.

NOTE

On default, the debtor's attorney should read the security agreement carefully to see if expressly or impliedly it gives the debtor a right to notice before repossession. Conversely, the secured party's attorney should make sure the security agreement avoids statements like "upon demand," which may give rise to such an implication.

Where a bank pursued its foreclosure remedy under the guise of a state attachment procedure that was clearly unconstitutional, the plaintiffs in Guzman v. Western State Bank of Devil's Lake, 540 F.2d 948 (8th Cir. 1976), took the unusual step of suing under the Civil Rights Act, 42 U.S.C. §1983, and recovered nearly $10,000 in actual damages and $30,000 in punitive damages. The court expressly found the bank guilty of bad faith.

PROBLEM 429

Natty Birdwhistle bought a car with money borrowed from Carpe Diem Finance Company (which perfected its interest in the car). The security agreement provided that "time was of the essence" and that the acceptance by the finance company of late payments was not a waiver of its right to repossess. Natty always paid 10 to 15 days late. One month, Carpe Diem Finance had had enough, and it sent a man out who took the car (using a duplicate set of keys) from the parking lot of the factory where Natty worked. Has a default occurred? See §1-303(d) and (f); Moe v. John Deere Co., 516 N.W.2d 332 (S.D. 1994); G. Gilmore §44.1, at 1214: "[C]ourts pay little attention to clauses which appear to say that meaningful acts are meaningless and that the secured party can blow hot or cold as he chooses." If Carpe Diem's conduct has waived the right to repossess if Natty is late, what can it do to reinstate the "time is of the essence" clause? See §2-209(5); Hendrickson v. Fifth Third Bank, 2019 WL 652417 (D. Minn. 2019).

NOTE ON CREDIT INSURANCE AND DEFAULT

If the debtor has died or become ill or disabled, so that the credit insurance taken out at the time the original contract was signed should pay the debt, there is authority for the proposition that the secured creditor must look first to the credit insurance before repossessing. Owens v. Walt Johnson Lincoln Mercury, Inc., 281 Or. 287, 574 P.2d 642 (1978); Corbin v. Regions Bank, 574 S.E.2d 616 (Ga. App. 2002).

III. REPOSSESSION AND RESALE

Section 9-609 authorizes the secured party to skip going through judicial processes and to repossess the collateral on the debtor's default if this can be done without a "breach of the peace." For the meaning of that elusive term, see White & Summers §26-7; Census Fed. Credit Union v. Wann, 403 N.E.2d 348 (Ind. App. 1980); Comment, Breach of Peace and Section 9-503 of the Uniform Commercial Code—A Modern Definition for an Ancient Restriction, 82 Dick. L. Rev. 351 (1978); Annot., What Conduct by Repossessing Chattel Mortgagee or Conditional Vendor Entails Tort Liability, 99 A.L.R.2d 358. Grant Gilmore:

> In the financing of business debtors repossession causes little trouble or dispute. In the underworld of consumer finance, however, repossession is a knock-down, drag-out battle waged on both sides with cunning guile and a complete disregard for the rules of fair play. A certain amount of trickery seems to be accepted: it is all right for the finance company to invite the defaulting buyer to drive over to its office for a friendly conference on refinancing the loan and to repossess the car as soon as he arrives. It is fairly safe for the finance company to pick up the car on the street wherever it may be parked, although there is always a danger that the buyer will later claim that he had been keeping a valuable stock of diamonds in the glove compartment. But the finance company will do well to think twice before allowing its man to break into an empty house, even though a well-drafted clause in the security agreement gives it the right to do exactly that. And if the housewife, who is invariably pregnant and subject to miscarriages, sits on the sofa, stove, washing machine or television set and refuses to move, the finance company man will make a serious mistake if he dumps the lady or carries her screaming into the front yard. Juries love to award punitive damages for that sort of thing and the verdict will often be allowed to stand.

G. Gilmore §44.1, at 1212-1213.

For many types of collateral, the creditor is unlikely to use self-help repossession. Repossessing the inventory of a store or the equipment on a construction company would be difficult without breaching the peace, unless the debtor cooperates. But one type of collateral is often left unattended on public streets overnight: vehicles. Some two million cars are repossessed each year. Many of the reported judicial decisions on repossession involve cars.

Smith v. AFS Acceptance, LLC

United States District Court, Northern District of Illinois, 2012
2012 WL 1969415

Elaine E. Bucklo, District Judge.

Plaintiffs Rosalind Smith and Rashai Jackson sued defendants AFS Acceptance, LLC ("AFS") and Equitable Services, Inc. ("Equitable") for various statutory and common law claims arising out an incident that occurred on August 16, 2010. . . . AFS has moved to dismiss the claims against it: (1) violation of Article 9, §609(b)(2) of Illinois' Uniform Commercial Code ("Repossession Statute") (Count II); (2) negligence (Count III); and (3) willful and wanton behavior (Count IV). In addition, Equitable has moved to dismiss all five claims against it: (1) violation of the Fair Debt Collection Practices Act, 15 U.S.C. §1692 (Count I); (2) violation of 810 ILCS 5/9-609(b)(2) (Count II); (3) negligence (Count V); (4) willful and wanton behavior (Count VI); and intentional infliction of emotional distress (Count VII). For all the following reasons, both motions are denied in part and granted in part.

Afs's Motion To Dismiss

AFS argues that I should dismiss Count II, which alleges a violation of the Repossession Statute, because plaintiffs failed to allege facts establishing an agency relationship between AFS and Equitable. Plaintiffs respond that, regardless of the relationship between AFS and Equitable, AFS is liable for the actions taken on its behalf.

Under the Repossession Statute, a secured party, after default, has the right to take possession of the collateral without judicial process so long as the secured party "proceeds without breach of the peace." 810 ILCS 5/9-609(b)(2). Comment 3 to the Repossession Statute states, "In considering whether a secured party has engaged in a breach of the peace, however, courts should hold the secured party responsible for the actions of others taken on the secured party's behalf, *including independent contractors* engaged by the secured party to take possession of collateral." 810 ILCS 5/9-609,

Comment 3 (emphasis added). According to Comment 3, a secured party may be liable for the actions of another, even if no agency relationship exists. Here, plaintiffs allege that AFS loaned money to Smith for the purchase of the vehicle. Plaintiffs also allege that Equitable acted on AFS's behalf. Thus, plaintiffs' allegations are sufficient to claim that AFS, as a secured party, may be liable under the Repossession Statute for the actions of Equitable. *See* Thompson v. Gateway Financial Services, Inc., No. 10 CV 7658, 2011 WL 1429207, at *2 (N.D. Ill. Apr. 14, 2011) (relying on Comment 3 to find that the secured party may be liable for actions taken by independent contractor with no agency relationship); Williams v. Republic Recovery Service, Inc., No. 09 C 6554, 2010 WL 3732107 at *3-4 (N.D. Ill. Sept. 16, 2010) (same). Thus, Count II stands. . . .

Equitable's Motion to Dismiss

Equitable moves to dismiss the FDCPA claim against it. First, it argues that plaintiffs have failed to provide sufficient facts to show that Equitable is a "debt collector" under the Act. Plaintiffs respond by pointing to Section 1692a(6) which states that "[f]or the purpose of section 1692f(6) of this title, ["debt collector"] also includes any person who uses any instrumentality of interstate commerce or the mails in any business the principal purpose of which is the enforcement of security interests." 15 U.S.C. §1692a(6). At this stage, plaintiffs' allegations that Equitable is a "debt collector" for purposes of §1692a(6) is sufficient.

Section 1692f(6) prohibits "[t]aking or threatening to take any nonjudicial action to effect dispossession or disablement of property if— (A) there is no present right to possession of the property claimed as collateral through an enforceable security interest; (B) there is no present intention to take possession of the property; or (C) the property is exempt by law from such dispossession or disablement." Plaintiffs allege that defendants "did not have a present right to possession of the vehicle" because Equitable's "attempt to repossess the vehicle "constituted a 'breach of the peace' in violation of 810 ILCS 5/9-609(b)(2)." Am. Compl. ¶27. "In other words, if the debt collector violated the self-help repossession statute, by breach of the peace or otherwise, then the collector had no present right to possession of the property under §1692f(6)." Fleming-Dudley v. Legal Investigations, Inc., No. 05 C 4648, 2007 WL 952026, at *5 (N.D. Ill. Mar. 22, 2007).

The Illinois Commercial Code allows a secured party to use self-help repossession "without judicial process, if it proceeds without breach of the peace." 810 ILCS 5/9-609(b)(2). Under Illinois law, "breach of the peace" as used in the statute "connotes conduct which incites or is likely to incite immediate public turbulence, or which leads to or is likely to lead to an immediate loss of public order and tranquility." Chrysler Credit Corp. v. Koontz, 277 Ill.

App. 3d 1078, 214 Ill. Dec. 726, 661 N.E.2d 1171, 1173 (Ill. App. Ct. 1996). "Whether a given act provokes a breach of the peace depends upon the accompanying circumstances of each particular case." *Id.* at 1174.

Plaintiffs allege that the vehicle was parked in a driveway at Rosalind Smith's mother's house. "Unknown Repossession Agents" backed a tow truck up the driveway and "began to hook the vehicle up." Am. Compl. ¶11. One of Rosalind's children noticed the agents hooking the vehicle up to the tow truck. Rosalind's mother and children, including Rashai Jackson, ran outside to see what was going on. When Rosalind's mother asked the agents what was going on, they told her they were taking the vehicle for nonpayment of the loan. Then, Rashai Jackson opened the door to the vehicle and got into it. The agents continued to hook the vehicle up to the tow truck and then raised the rear of the vehicle with Rashai still in the vehicle and with the door of the vehicle open. The agents started to tow the vehicle out of the driveway with Rashai still in the vehicle. Rosalind then yelled for the agents to stop towing the vehicle and to put it down because her daughter was in the vehicle. Rosalind then jumped into the vehicle with her daughter. The agents continued to tow the vehicle out of the driveway and into the street. Police officers were called to the scene and told the agents to stop towing the vehicle and the agents complied. Rosalind and Rashai exited the vehicle. The police officers told the agents to return the vehicle to its original place in the driveway. Throughout this incident, Rosalind's mother, children, and individuals from neighboring residences yelled at the agents to stop towing the vehicle away with individuals in the vehicle and the vehicle's doors open.

I conclude that plaintiffs have put forward sufficient allegations concerning a "breach of the peace" to survive a motion to dismiss. While plaintiffs certainly played a role in any breach of the peace, Equitable's employees, despite the fact that plaintiffs jumped into the vehicle, raised the rear of the vehicle and actually towed the vehicle away from the driveway with two individuals in the vehicle and the doors open. All this was done while plaintiffs' family members and neighbors yelled at the agents to stop towing the vehicle. Equitable makes much of the fact that the plaintiffs themselves played a role in any breach by first jumping into the vehicle, but totally fails to address the fact that its own employees continued to tow the vehicle down the street *with the two women in the back*. In addition, they did so with a group of people yelling at them to stop. Finally, the police were called to the scene to restore order. Equitable has put forward no cases like this one where both parties contributed, in part, to the breach of the peace. The language of the statute states that the secured party can repossess secured property so long as the secured party "proceeds without breach of the peace." Nothing in this language suggests that the fault for any breach must lie solely with the party doing the repossessing, and Equitable has failed to present any authority to the contrary.

Thus, plaintiffs' claim under the FDCPA and Smith's standalone claim for a violation of 810 ILCS 5/9-609(b)(2) survive Equitable's motion to dismiss. And, as above, the claim under 810 ILCS 5/9-609(b)(2) is limited to Smith, as Jackson was not a debtor or an obligor. . . .

Finally, plaintiffs allege a state law claim of intentional infliction of emotional distress against Equitable. To state a claim for intentional infliction of emotional distress, plaintiff must show that: "(1) defendant's conduct was extreme and outrageous; (2) the defendant intended to inflict severe emotional distress or knew that there was at least a high probability that his conduct would inflict severe emotional distress; and (3) the defendant's conduct did cause severe emotional distress." Naeem v. McKesson Drug Co., 444 F.3d 593, 604-05 (7th Cir. 2006).

"Conduct is extreme and outrageous only if the conduct has been so outrageous in character and so extreme in degree as to go beyond all possible bounds of decency." Van Stan v. Fancy Colours & Co., 125 F.3d 563, 567 (7th Cir. 1997) (internal quotations and citations omitted). The standard for determining whether one's conduct is outrageous is whether an average person in the community would find the conduct outrageous. Restatement (Second) of Torts, §46, cmt. d, at 73 (1965). The Seventh Circuit has also suggested that the following factors may be considered: whether the defendant had control or power over the plaintiff, whether the defendant reasonably believed its goal was legitimate and whether the defendant was aware that the plaintiff was peculiarly susceptible to emotional distress. Franciski v. Univ. of Chi. Hospitals, 338 F.3d 765, 769 (7th Cir. 2003).

While this is a close call, plaintiffs' IIED claim survives Equitable's motion to dismiss. The conduct alleged—towing two women down the street with the doors opened—is sufficiently outrageous in nature as to constitute a basis for recovery under intentional infliction of emotional distress. There is no suggestion that the tow truck operators were unaware of the women's presence in the vehicle, and thus the most likely explanation of the agents' behavior is that they intended to severely frighten the women. An average member in the community could certainly think it outrageous for tow truck operators to proceed with a repossession with two individuals in the vehicle. I acknowledge that the two women jumped into the car, likely in an attempt to stop the towing. A reasonable person could conclude, however, that what followed on the part of the towing agents was "extreme in degree." As Equitable points out, the tow truck operators arrived at the scene with the "legitimate" goal of repossessing the vehicle. However, a defendant's "reasonable belief that his objective is legitimate does not provide a defendant carte blanche to pursue that objective by outrageous means." McGrath v. Fahey, 126 Ill. 2d 78, 127 Ill. Dec. 724, 533 N.E.2d 806, 809 (Ill. 1998). The tow truck operators obviously exerted control over the plaintiffs in that they controlled the time and location in which plaintiffs could safely exit the vehicle. Given the facts (as alleged by plaintiffs), plaintiffs' claim survives at this stage.

For all of the foregoing reasons, AFS's motion to dismiss is granted in part and denied in part. Likewise, Equitable's motion to dismiss is granted in part and denied in part.

Particularly in consumer debtor cases where the repossession violates Article 9 of the Code will the complaint allege, as the one in the case above did, violation of other statutes or common law tort theories. Most states have a Consumer Sales Act (called by various names) that give injured consumers actual damages, punitive damages and attorney fees, and the federal government has the Fair Debt Collection Practices Act, 15 U.S.C. §1692, which does the same thing for outrageous behavior in debt collection.

QUESTION

This court clearly holds that if the secured party hires an independent contractor to repossess then the secured party is liable for whatever misconduct the independent contractor commits. But what if the debtor sues the independent contractor itself for committing a breach of the peace or other forbidden activity during the repossession? Does §9-609 create liability in that case? See Nelson v. BMW Fin. Serv. NA, 2015 WL 8328073 (D. Minn. 2015).

PROBLEM 430

Don Jose was in charge of repossession for Carmen Motors. One Monday morning, the dealership told him that cars owned by four debtors (Escamillo, Micaela, Zuniga, and Morales) were to be picked up because the buyers had missed payments. Look at §9-609, and answer this question: is Carmen Motors required to give the debtors *notice* that they are in default before repossessing? Don Jose visited each of the debtors with the following results:

(a) Don Jose found Escamillo's car parked in his driveway at 2:00 A.M.; he broke a car window, hot-wired the car, and drove it away. Has a breach of the peace occurred? See Giles v. First Virginia Credit Services, Inc., 560 S.E.2d 557 (N.C. App. 2002). What if Escamillo heard the window break, rushed out, and began yelling? May Don Jose continue the repossession, or must he quit? If he goes away, may he try again later that night? Compare Darren Trucking Company v. Paccar Financial Corp., 2019 WL 3945103 (D. Md. 2019)(slightest debtor objection breaches the peace); Chrysler Credit Corp. v. Koontz, 277 Ill. App. 3d 1078, 1081 (1996) (mere "Don't take it" statement by the debtor not enough to make repossession breach the peace).

(b) Don Jose showed up at Micaela's house accompanied by his brother (an off-duty sheriff who was wearing his sheriff's uniform). Don Jose told Micaela that he was repossessing the car, and she said nothing. Has a breach of the peace occurred? See Official Comment 3 to §9-609; Hyman v. Capital One Auto Fin., 306 F. Supp. 3d 756 (W.D. Pa. 2018) (use of police officers in repossession breaches the peace); accord First & Farmers Bank v. Henderson, 763 S.W.2d 137 (Ky. App. 1988) ($75,000 punitive damages). See also In re Bolin & Co., LLC, 437 B.R. 731 (D. Conn. 2010) (the presence of a police officer did not breach the peace where the officer was not there to help with the repossession).

(c) When no one was at home, Don Jose broke into Zuniga's garage through the use of the services of a locksmith. The garage lock and door were undamaged. A clause in the contract provided that the secured party had the right to enter the debtor's premises to remove the property. Does the repossession comply with §9-609? See §9-602(6); Pantoja-Cahue v. Ford Motor Credit Co., 375 Ill. App. 3d 49, 872 N.E.2d 1039 (2007); White & Summers §26-7.

(d) Don Jose phoned Morales and said that the car was being recalled because of an unsafe engine mount. Morales brought the car in that morning. When the time came to pick up the car, Don Jose simply smiled, said "April Fool; it's been repossessed!" and refused to return it. Is the repossession valid? Compare Cox v. Galigher Motor Sales Co., 213 S.E.2d 475 (W. Va. 1975), with Ford Motor Credit Co. v. Byrd, 351 So. 2d 557 (Ala. 1974), commented on in 40 Ohio St. L.J. 501 (1979).

Repossession Technology. Automobile repossession in the twenty-first century has developed a new tactic employing a "starter interrupt device." This invention allows the creditor to push a button on a computer and suddenly the car won't start. The debtor is usually called immediately and told that the car can be reactivated by making a payment, which (with kids who need to get to school, or a boss at work looking at empty desk) the debtor usually does immediately. Often the repossession has beeps that warn the debtor that the repo is coming soon, and, in theory, the debtor has also been given a code that can be punched into the car's computer to restore the vehicle to mechanical health for a 24-hour period even without a payment (very useful in emergencies). To avoid accidents the starter interrupt device is not supposed to work when the car is running (though stories circulate of cars swerving uncontrolled through traffic or stalled at traffic lights turning green). Enthusiastically embraced by creditors, this quasi-evil innovation has most often been used in subprime automobile financing, but is now expanding into more general application, and may soon be exposing supposedly well-to-do drivers who can't get out of their reserved parking spaces at work.

Hilliman v. Cobado

New York Supreme Court, 1986
499 N.Y.S.2d 610

HOREY, J.

By an order to show cause the plaintiff has brought on a motion for injunctive relief. In particular the plaintiffs seek an order of this court that the defendant return 26 cattle which the defendant seized and removed from the plaintiffs' farm premises. While not specifically denominated as a motion brought under the provisions of CPLR 6301 it is clear that the motion in issue falls within the parameters of that section.

The factual background giving rise to the motion is this: the defendant sold the plaintiff a herd of cattle. Sale was initially to be effected under an instrument denominated a "collateral security mortgage" dated February 1, 1984. Under the terms of this instrument the sale was secured by a mortgage on the farm realty of the plaintiff purchaser. However, before delivery of the cattle, the defendant demanded additional security interest in the cattle to be sold.

As a consequence of this demand a second instrument entitled "chattel mortgage" dated February 8, 1984 was executed by plaintiffs. Under the terms of this instrument the defendant was given a chattel mortgage interest in "68 cows and 1 bull."

Both instruments had the same provisions for payment of the indebtedness (sale price) which was $48,200. Payment was to be made by plaintiff by even monthly payments of $1,000. Interest was provided at 11% per annum.

After the delivery of the cattle to the plaintiff, the plaintiff under a claim of right culled a number of the cattle delivered. The defendant took exception to this practice. As a result of negotiations a third instrument was executed. This was also denominated a "chattel mortgage." It is dated June 20, 1985. Under the terms of this instrument the collateral is recited to be "37 replacement cows." The balance due was fixed at $39,552.77. Provision for payment of this reduced amount continued as previously provided, viz., $1,000 per month with the balance drawing interest at 11% per annum. The court regards it as significant that the plaintiff has never been in default on the required contract payments. . . .

After the second chattel mortgage no specific default was alleged by the defendant. Inferentially it appears that he continued to be disturbed by the plaintiff's practice of culling poorer cattle from the herd. Suddenly without any prior warning, the defendant Cobado and two deputy sheriffs arrived at the premises of the plaintiff, Szata. Mr. Szata, a cripple, proceeding with the aid of a cane and his wife went out of their home to meet Cobado and the deputies. It was then that the deputies advised Mr. and Mrs. Szata that

Cobado "was here to repossess the collateral under the terms of the security agreement."

Mr. Szata immediately replied that he was not in default and that Cobado was to leave the premises immediately and could not have the cattle.

Mr. Szata attempted to engage Cobado in conversation to no avail. Cobado simply turned and ran to the barn saying "to hell with this we're taking the cows."

Cobado entered the barn and started releasing the cattle from their stanchions.

A brief conversation ensued between Deputy Buchardt and Mr. and Mrs. Szata. Deputy Buchardt told them that Cobado had a violent temper and a reputation for violence. The Deputy also told Mr. Szata that if he (Szata) got out of line he would be arrested.

After an unfruitful attempt to call their attorney, Mr. and Mrs. Szata went to the barn and again told Cobado to stop. Cobado simply laughed at them and continued to release the cattle and drive them around in the barn.

At this time while Cobado was beating the released cattle and trying to herd them through a small opening in the barn door a Fay Hilliman, the mother-in-law of Mr. Szata and the mother of Mrs. Szata arrived at the barn. She joined the Szatas in ordering Cobado to desist. Cobado ignored them and continued to push the cattle through the barn opening.

Before the cattle were loaded onto the trucks assembled, Lt. Ernie Travis of the Cattaraugus County Sheriff's Department appeared on the scene. He advised Cobado that if he, Cobado, left with the cattle he would be arrested. Cobado ignored the warning and when he left with the cattle he was arrested for possession of stolen property. Later Mr. Szata was charged with fraudulent sale of mortgaged property. As of the argument of the motion at bar no disposition had been made of either criminal charge. . . .

The second instrument executed, viz., the first chattel mortgage dated February 8, 1984, securing "68 cows and 1 bull" contained the following provisions for seizure, to wit:

> In conjunction with, addition to or substitution for those rights, secured party, at his discretion, may (1) *enter debtor's premises peaceably* by secured party's own means or with legal process and take possession of the collateral, or render it unusable or dispose of the collateral on the debtor's premises and the debtor agrees not to resist or interfere. . . .

(p. 2 chattel mortgage dated February 8, 1984.) Italics added.

The third instrument, executed, viz., the second chattel mortgage dated June 20, 1985 contains an identical provision for seizure as that in the chattel mortgage of February 8, 1984, set forth above.

The quoted provisions from the two chattel mortgages follow an immediate prior contract provision also referable to default and repossession which provided that upon default "the *secured party will have all the rights,* remedies and privileges *with respect to repossession,* retention and sale of the collateral and disposition of the proceeds *as are accorded to a* secured party by *the applicable section of the UCC* respecting 'default' in effect as of the date of the security agreement."

This court finds nothing in conflict between the clause in each chattel mortgage providing the secured party with the right to enter "debtor's premises peaceably" and the immediate prior provision in those chattel mortgages stating that the secured party has those rights as to repossession which are accorded under the UCC. This is for the reason as we have seen that the repossession rights granted under the UCC may only be exercised "without breach of the peace" §9-504 UCC [now §9-609—Eds.].

Since the motion turns to consideration of "breach of the peace" we look to decisional law for definition of that term.

In People v. Most, 171 N.Y. 423 (Ct. of Appeals 1902, Opn. by Vann, J.), our highest court stated that a breach of the peace was well known at common law. The court then defined it as follows:

> It is a disturbance of public order by an act of violence, or by any act likely to produce violence, or which by causing consternation and alarm, disturbs the peace and quiet of the community.

171 N.Y. 423 at 429.

The right to self help by way of repossession is an assignment of the exclusive power of the sovereignty of a state. This is true because it represents a delegation of the exclusively governmental function of resolving disputes. See generally Sharrock v. Dell Buick, 45 N.Y.2d 152 at 162 and Fuentes v. Shevin, 407 U.S. 67 at 93. The delegation of the right of repossession to a secured party is not a carte blanche one. Rather it is specifically limited and exercisable only without a breach of the peace. Its exercise should be strictly confined to those situations, rare as they may be, when the repossession can be accomplished peaceably. Physical confrontation or the threat thereof is not necessary to effect a breach of the peace.

Certain it is that in ignoring the order of the purchasers to desist and remove himself from the premises; in ignoring the admonition of Lt. Travis of the Sheriff's Department to desist; in demonstrating his contempt for all restraint by his statement "to hell with this we're taking the cows"; by proceeding to release the cows, beating and herding them to the trucks, without heed of the warning that his continuance would result in his arrest, the defendant Cobado not only engaged in conduct which was likely to produce violence and consternation but did in fact produce violence, consternation and disorder.

This court finds as a matter of fact and law that the retaking of the plaintiff's cattle was a "breach of the peace."

Accordingly the decision of the court is that the defendant Cobado forthwith at his cost and expense redeliver the cattle repossessed by him to the plaintiff inclusive of any calves born to those cattle during his possession thereof.

PROBLEM 431

Octopus National Bank (ONB) financed Mary Melody's purchase of a new car, in which it perfected its security interest. The loan agreement provided that on default, the bank had all the rights listed in Part 6 of Article 9 of the UCC and that the parties agreed that the bank would not be liable for conversion or otherwise if there were other items in the car at the time it was repossessed. Mary missed a payment, and ONB's agent took the car in the dead of night from its parking place in front of her home. She protested the next day, claiming that her golf clubs were in the trunk. ONB looked there but couldn't find the clubs. When she sued, ONB defended on the basis of the security agreement's exculpatory clause. Is it valid? See Ford Motor Credit Co. v. Cole, 503 S.W.2d 853 (Tex. Civ. App. 1973). If ONB finds the clubs and returns them promptly on her demand, is the bank still guilty of conversion? See Thompson v. Ford Motor Credit Co., 324 F. Supp. 108 (D.S.C. 1971).

PROBLEM 432

Repossession agent Paul Chambers, seeking to repossess a particular Ford Expedition, parked in a tow truck near the debtor's house. He saw the debtor back the Expedition out of the driveway and then leave it on the street with its motor running, while the debtor went back into the house. Chambers quickly towed the car off. Less than a minute later, he stopped to check the Expedition and saw two children in the backseat. He immediately drove the Expedition back to the debtor's house and returned the children and the vehicle to the now-distraught debtor. Did Chambers violate Article 9? See Chapa v. Traciers & Assocs., 267 S.W.3d 386 (Tex. App. 2008).

PROBLEM 433

Octopus National Bank declared a default on Jessica Napoleon's car loan, and Napoleon showed up at ONB to surrender the vehicle. May ONB decline to take it and instead just sue Napoleon for the debt? See §9-601 and Chemtex, LLC v. St. Anthony Enters., 490 F. Supp. 2d 536 (S.D.N.Y. 2007).

It is important to remember that if the debtor files a petition in bankruptcy, §362 of the Bankruptcy Code creates an automatic stay of any creditor collection activity. This automatic stay forbids not only repossession but also even more prosaic attempts to collect the debt, such as dunning letters. The automatic stay does not depend on formal court notice that the bankruptcy petition has been filed; it is in effect from the moment of the filing. Creditor action taken without knowledge of the filing must be undone on learning that the debtor's bankruptcy has already occurred. But any true information that reaches the creditor from whatever source that the bankruptcy has been filed invokes the protection of the automatic stay. Deliberate creditor conduct thereafter violating the stay would not only be in contempt of court, but could also lead to the invocation of §362(k): "An individual injured by any willful violation of a stay provided by this section shall recover actual damages, including costs and attorneys' fees, and, in appropriate circumstances, may recover punitive damages." Let the lender beware.

PROBLEM 434

Wonder Spa gave Antitrust National Bank (ANB) a security interest in its accounts receivable and chattel paper in return for a loan. When Wonder Spa missed two payments in a row, ANB notified the spa's customers that future payments should be made directly to the bank. Does the bank have this right? Read §9-607 and its Official Comment 2; see §9-406(c). If the spa stops opening its doors, need its former customers keep paying ANB? (The spa contracts did not mention the possibility that the contracts would be assigned.) See §9-404(a); G. Gilmore, ch. 41. The ability of customers to raise defenses against the finance company is bound up in the law of negotiable instruments—see Unico v. Owen, 50 N.J. 101, 232 A.2d 405 (1967), the leading case—and special consumer protection statutes, e.g., Uniform Consumer Credit Code §3.404, and regulations such as the FTC's Holder in Due Course rule, 16 C.F.R. §433 (1975); Annot., 39 A.L.R.3d 518. Section 9-403(e) carefully preserves any other rule of law that protects consumers from waiving their rights to assert their defenses against assignees of their obligations.

After repossession, the secured party may in some circumstances (§§9-620 to 9-622, explored below) simply keep the collateral and give up further remedy (this is called *strict foreclosure*). More typically the repossessing creditor will resell the collateral and, if the resale does not pay the debt in full, then sue the debtor for any *deficiency* (or, if the resale more than pays the debt, return the *surplus* to the debtor[3]).

Section 9-610 and the sections that follow it regulate the resale. Note that in most cases §9-611(c) dictates that the secured party must give the debtor *notice* of the time and place of the sale. The reason for this notice is twofold: on getting it, the debtor may elect to use the §9-623 right of redemption (about which more later), or the debtor can attend the sale or send potential buyers who will enter real bids and, by actively competing in the bidding, bring a fair price for the collateral. The notice requirement is much litigated: What must it say, whom must it go to, and what happens if it is not given? These issues are raised by the Problems below, which also consider another §9-610 matter, the §9-610(b) mandate that "every aspect of a disposition of collateral, including the method, manner, time, place, and other terms must be commercially reasonable." As to the meaning of *commercially reasonable,* see G. Gilmore §44.5.

PROBLEM 435

Is notice required if the creditor sells securities in its customer's account, before default, as authorized by the security agreement? See Kinzel v. Bank of America, 850 F.3d 275 (6th Cir. 2017).

PROBLEM 436

After Nightflyer Loan Company had repossessed Lynn Brown's car, it decided to advertise it for bids in a local newspaper. Is this a private or a public sale? See Official Comment 7 to §9-610. How much in advance of the resale must she be given notice? See §§9-611, 612. What should the notice say? See §9-614 (for the notice to be given to non-consumer debtors, see §9-613). Must it state whether it is a public or private sale? See Boulevard Bank v. Malott, 2013 WL 324041 (Mo. App. 2013). If the car were to be sold in an Internet auction, would it be sufficient to give notice of the web address of the auction and the physical address of the auction company? See Moore v. Wells Fargo Constr., 903 N.E.2d 525 (Ind. App. 2009). If a sale is private, would the notice need to specify such information as whether the seller will use websites, what advertising will be used, and whether a retail, wholesale, or salvage market will be used? See Volvo Financial Services v. Williamson, 2017 WL 4708136 (S.D. Miss. 2017).

3. You can imagine how often this happens. "Like neutrinos, surpluses are believed to exist but are never observed," White & Summers §26-13 at 1357.

After the resale, Nightflyer simply sent her a statement saying that the amount she now owed was $3,200. She is unsure how Nightflyer came up with this figure, and comes to you, her attorney/cousin, for advice. What are her rights here? See §§9-616, 9-625(c) and (e). The price obtained at the resale seems suspiciously low to her. How relevant is that? See §9-627(a). She suspects that the reason the sale brought so little is that the only bidder was Nightflyer Loan Company itself. Can they do that? See §§9-610(c), 9-615(f), and 9-626(a)(5); White & Summers §26-10(d). If she succeeds in reducing the amount she owes, can she also get actual damages for the harm they have caused her? See §9-625(d); White & Summers §26-13(e).

PROBLEM 437

Mr. and Mrs. Miller decided to open a restaurant, for which purpose they needed $80,000. They went to Apocalypse National Bank, which agreed to loan them the money if they (1) got a surety, (2) signed an agreement giving the bank a security interest in the restaurant's equipment and inventory, and (3) pledged to the bank additional collateral having a value of $20,000 or more. The Millers got Mrs. Miller's father (Mr. Stuhldreher) to sign as surety; they signed the security agreement; and they borrowed $20,000 worth of stock from Mr. Miller's cousin, Mr. Layden. The stock was registered in Layden's name at the time it was pledged to the bank, but the bank had it reregistered in the bank's name so that it could be sold easily in the event of default. The bank did, however, file its financing statement in the appropriate office. Subsequently, the Millers borrowed another $5,000 from Northbend Credit Union, which also took a security interest in the restaurant's equipment, and filed a financing statement. The restaurant then became involved in an unfortunate food poisoning incident, and business fell off dramatically. The Millers (who were in the midst of a divorce) missed two payments on the loan. The bank sent its collection agent, Mr. Crowley, out to the restaurant, and he repossessed the assets he found there. Mr. Crowley sent a written notice to Mr. Miller (who he knew was now living in a hotel), telling him that the stock would be sold on the open market (no specific date given) and that the restaurant equipment would be sold at public auction on December 1 at the offices of the Crowley Collection Agency. Crowley phoned Mr. Stuhldreher (the surety) and told him the same thing. He sent a written notice to Mr. Layden (the stock owner), but the letter came back marked "Moved—No Forwarding Address." If asked, either Mr. or Mrs. Miller would have supplied Crowley with Layden's new address. Crowley sold the stock for $10,000 on the open market (that was its current selling price) and auctioned off the restaurant equipment on December 1 for $500 (only one bid was received—Crowley himself was the bidder; he later resold the equipment to other restaurants for $10,000). Crowley turned over the proceeds from the two sales ($10,500 total) to Apocalypse National Bank, which then brought suit against the Millers and Mr. Stuhldreher for the deficiency. Answer these questions:

(a) Is a surety entitled to a notice under §9-611? That is, is he a *debtor*? Read §§9-102(a)(28)(A), 9-102(a)(72), 9-611(c). Was Mr. Layden a *debtor* too? See Official Comment 2a to §9-102. Does the *oral* notice to Mr. Stuhldreher satisfy §9-611(b)? See §§1-201(b)(36), 9-102(a)(7), and 9-611's Official Comment 5.

(b) Were any parties entitled to notice of the *stock* sale? See §9-611(d). How about the sale of the equipment? See §9-611(c). If no notice was sent to Northbend Credit Union before the equipment was sold, did Mr. Crowley himself take free of its security interest when he bought the equipment at the foreclosure sale? See §9-617. Did the buyer take free of its security interest when he bought the equipment from Crowley? See §2-403(1).

(c) Is the notice sent to Mr. Miller sufficient as to Mrs. Miller? See Tauber v. Johnson, 8 Ill. App. 3d 180, 291 N.E.2d 180 (1972).

(d) Does §9-611 require the creditor, to whom a notice is returned by the post office, to take further steps to notify the debtor? See Official Comment 6; Auto Credit of Nashville v. Wimmer, 231 S.W.3d 896 (Tenn. 2007).

(e) Since the restaurant equipment is also named as collateral on the junior filed financing statement, must the bank notify that secured party of the resale? See §9-611(c) and (e).

(f) Who has the burden of proof as to the commercial reasonableness of the sales? See §9-626(a)(2). What is commercially reasonable and what is not? Compare Bank Leumi USA v. GM Diamonds, Inc., 149 A.D. 3d 662 (N.Y. App. Div. 2017) (held commercially reasonable where creditor had two experts appraise the value of the diamonds, solicited bids from four potential bidders, and took the highest of three bids submitted, which was near the appraised value from two experts hired by creditor), and In re Comprehensive Power, Inc., 578 B.R. 14, 42 (Bankr. D. Mass. 2017) ("The Trustee has pleaded sufficient facts to support a claim under Article 9 of the UCC, including that: (i) Moog did not employ a process intended to generate a reasonable sale price and the sale price obtained was substantially less than that which the parties had previously valued the Debtor's assets and less than the assets would have been appraised for if an appraisal conducted; (ii) Moog conducted the auction sale as a formality to consolidate its control the Debtor's assets; (iii) Moog failed to adequately market the property; (iv) Moog was the sole bidder at a sale conducted on only fourteen days' notice and other potential purchasers were deprived from acquiring the Debtor's assets; and (v) Moog deprived the Debtor of six-month "runway" to obtain alternative financing and the Debtor was damaged as a result.").

(g) If Crowley had given the equipment sale no publicity, has a *public* sale occurred, and, if so, was it *commercially reasonable*? See §9-610, Official Comment 7.

(h) When a secured party repossesses goods and sells them at a foreclosure sale, will this give rise to the Article 2 sales warranties being made to the purchaser at the sale? See §§2-312, 9-610(d) and (e), and the latter's Official Comment 11.

(i) Suppose that, rather than repossession occurring, the Millers had sold the collateral, with the consent and encouragement of the secured creditor, Apocalypse National Bank. Would the creditor have to give notice to other creditors who have filed financing statements covering the collateral? See Bremer Bank v. Matejcek, 916 N.W.2d 688 (Minn. Ct. App. 2018).

R & J of Tennessee, Inc. v. Blankenship-Melton Real Estate, Inc.

Court of Appeals of Tennessee, 2005
166 S.W.3d 195

ALAN E. HIGHERS, J.

This case involves a lawsuit filed by a secured party against a guarantor seeking a deficiency judgment following a foreclosure sale. The guarantor argued that the secured party was not entitled to a deficiency because he was given inadequate notice and the sale was conducted in a commercially unreasonable manner. Following a hearing, the trial court awarded the secured party a deficiency judgment. We reverse and remand to the trial court for further action consistent with this opinion.

I. FACTUAL BACKGROUND AND PROCEDURAL HISTORY

On February 23, 2000, Walden Blankenship ("Mr. Blankenship"), as acting president of Blankenship-Melton Real Estate, Inc. ("Blankenship-Melton"), entered into a loan transaction with the Bank of Henderson County (the "Bank"). In exchange for the Bank loaning Blankenship-Melton $40,133, Blankenship-Melton executed a security agreement granting the Bank a security interest in a 1999 Bryant boat, a New Holland tractor, a 1999 Ford F150 truck, and a 1994 mobile home. The agreement called for Blankenship-Melton to pay off the loan by June 18, 2000.

The collateral used to secure the loan was purchased by Blankenship-Melton prior to entering into the loan in question. According to Mr. Blankenship, Larry Melton, a director of Blankenship-Melton, purchased the truck new for an amount between $23,000 and $24,000, and the vehicle's title listed Blankenship-Melton as the owner. Mr. Blankenship purchased the tractor used as collateral, as well as a tiller, a bush hog, and a boom pole, for an amount between $17,000 and $18,000. Mr. Blankenship also stated that Blankenship-Melton paid approximately $15,000 for the double-wide mobile home when they purchased it. At the time the loan agreement was entered into in February of 2000, the Bank estimated the value of all of the collateral to be at least $40,000.

Contemporaneously with the execution of the promissory note, Mr. Blankenship executed a guaranty agreement promising to remain personally liable on the promissory note owed to the Bank. The guaranty agreement identified Mr. Blankenship's home address as "2820 Shady Hill Road, Lexington, TN, 38351." In addition, Larry Melton and his son, Steve Melton, the secretary of Blankenship-Melton, also executed personal guarantees to secure the loan. The Bank renewed the loan on two separate occasions, extending the due date for six months each time. At some point, the loan went into default. During this period of time, Mr. Blankenship asserted that he communicated with the Bank and asked the Bank to foreclose on the collateral. Stan Reynolds, a representative of the Bank, did not recall Mr. Blankenship making such a request. Regardless of this dispute, Mr. Blankenship never personally paid any amounts toward the outstanding loan amount.

Johnny Melton is the majority shareholder and president of R & J of Tennessee, Inc. ("R & J" or "Appellee"). Larry Melton and Steve Melton approached Johnny Melton explaining that this particular note had come due and asked for help with some outstanding loans Blankenship-Melton owed to the Bank. On November 6, 2001, Johnny Melton, acting as agent for R & J, purchased the promissory note from the Bank for $26,455.39. At the time R & J purchased the promissory note from the Bank, Blankenship-Melton was already in default on the loan, and the Bank had already begun to institute foreclosure proceedings on the collateral. In addition, only the truck, tractor, and mobile home were left as collateral to secure the note.[4] When R & J purchased the note, Steve Melton had been living in the trailer which was used as collateral, and he never paid rent to Blankenship-Melton during his periods of occupancy. Larry Melton had possession of the Ford truck and drove it on a daily basis. The tractor remained in Larry Melton's possession and was stored at his personal residence. According to Johnny Melton, at the time R & J purchased the note, the tractor was inoperable due to mechanical problems.

In June of 2002, Johnny Melton, acting as agent for R & J, began the foreclosure process. On June 11, 2002, Johnny Melton sent a notice to Mr.

4. Prior to assigning the promissory note to R & J, the Bryant boat was sold and the proceeds applied toward the outstanding debt. As a result, the Bank released the boat as collateral securing the loan.

Blankenship indicating that the collateral would be sold at a public sale on June 21, 2002. According to Johnny Melton, Steve Melton and Larry Melton continued to use the collateral during this period of time. R & J sent the notice of sale by certified mail to Mr. Blankenship at the address listed in the promissory note. Mr. Blankenship, however, had subsequently moved and conceded that he never notified the Bank of his new home address. According to Johnny Melton, similar notices were also sent to Larry Melton and Steve Melton. Johnny Melton also posted a copy of the notice of sale at R & J's office, the courthouse, and on the collateral. The envelope containing the notice to Mr. Blankenship, which was introduced as an exhibit at trial, indicated that the postal service attempted to deliver the notice to Mr. Blankenship at his old address on June 13 and 18, 2002. Despite having not received a return receipt indicating successful delivery of the notice, R & J went ahead with the sale of the collateral on June 21, 2002. On June 28, 2002, the postal service returned the notice to R & J marked "not deliverable as addressed."

On the date of the public sale, only Johnny Melton, on behalf of R & J, and Larry Melton were present, and only Johnny Melton placed a bid on the collateral. R & J purchased the mobile home for $8,000, the Ford truck for $11,000, and the tractor for $1,000. Johnny Melton stated that he used his previous experience in the banking industry and mobile home business to assess the value of each item of the collateral at the time of the sale. On August 26, 2002, Johnny Melton, on behalf of R & J, filed a lawsuit against Mr. Blankenship in the General Sessions Court of Henderson County, seeking a deficiency judgment in the amount of $13,388.40 pursuant to the personal guaranty. The general sessions court found in favor of Mr. Blankenship, and R & J appealed the decision to the Circuit Court of Henderson County. Following a de novo bench trial, the circuit court entered a deficiency judgment against Mr. Blankenship in the amount of $10,847.29.

Mr. Blankenship filed a timely notice of appeal to this Court and presents the following issues for our review:

I. Whether Appellant, Walden Blankenship, was given statutorily sufficient notice regarding the public sale of the collateral pursuant to section 47-9-611(b) of the Tennessee Code;
II. Whether Appellee, R & J of Tennessee, failed to dispose of the collateral in a commercially reasonable manner under section 47-9-610(b) of the Tennessee Code and to exercise good faith pursuant to section 47-1-203 of the Tennessee Code;
III. Whether Appellee, R & J of Tennessee, exercised reasonable care pursuant to section 47-9-207(a) of the Tennessee Code in preserving and exercising custody of the collateral used to secure the loan at issue; and

IV. Whether the trial court erred in finding that no evidence was introduced at trial regarding the condition and value of the tractor on the date of the foreclosure sale as it relates to Appellee's bid.

In addition to the issues raised by Appellant, we are also asked to review the following issue raised by Appellee:

V. Whether Appellant, Walden Blankenship, waived the objections to the foreclosure sale which he now raises on appeal according to the terms of the personal guaranty.

For the reasons contained herein, we reverse the decision of the trial court. . . .

III. Waiver of Objections

R & J asserts on appeal that Mr. Blankenship has waived his right to contest the sufficiency of the foreclosure sale and notice based upon the terms of the personal guaranty. The applicable provision of Tennessee's version of the Uniform Commercial Code provides:

> *Waiver.*—
> (a) WAIVER OF DISPOSITION NOTIFICATION. A debtor or secondary obligor may waive the right to notification of disposition of collateral under §47-9-611 only by an agreement to that effect entered into and authenticated *after default.*

Tenn. Code Ann. §47-9-624(a) (2003) (emphasis added). Accordingly, we find this issue to be without merit. See Tropical Jewelers, Inc. v. Nationsbank, N.A., 781 So. 2d 392, 396 (Fla. Dist. Ct. App. 2000).

IV. Notice of Sale

The loan transaction at issue in this case is governed by Tennessee's version of Article 9 of the Uniform Commercial Code, codified at section 47-9-101 et seq. of the Tennessee Code. See Nationsbank v. Clegg, No. 01-A-01-9510-CH-00469, 1996 WL 165513, at *1, 1996 Tenn. App. LEXIS 214, at *3 (Tenn. Ct. App. Apr. 10, 1996). The question of whether the notice given by R & J in this instance was sufficient is a question for the trier of fact, and R & J bears the burden of proof on this issue. Id. at *13; see also Tenn. Code Ann. §47-9-626(2) (2003). The trial court found, and the parties do not dispute, that Mr. Blankenship never received actual notice of the sale. After reviewing the Appellant's Brief, we have come to the conclusion that Mr. Blankenship is arguing, in essence, that section 47-9-611(b) of the

Tennessee Code requires that a person in Mr. Blankenship's position must receive actual notice of the disposition of the collateral prior to a public sale in order for the notice to be adequate under Tennessee's version of Revised Article 9 of the Uniform Commercial Code.

In support of this argument, Mr. Blankenship points to the mandatory language "shall" in the applicable statute which provides:

> Notification of Disposition Required. Except as otherwise provided in subsection (d), a secured party that disposes of collateral under §47-9-610 shall send to the persons specified in subsection (c) a reasonable authenticated notification of disposition.

Tenn. Code Ann. §47-9-611(b) (2003). Section 47-9-611(c), setting forth the persons to be notified before a secured party disposes of the collateral, provides that, in order "[t]o comply with subsection (b), the secured party shall send an authenticated notification of disposition to . . . any secondary obligor."[5] Tenn. Code Ann. §47-9-611(c)(2) (2003). Alternatively, R & J asserts that it sent the notice to Mr. Blankenship at the address he listed on the personal guaranty, and, therefore, he should bear the responsibility for not receiving the notice since he failed to notify the Bank of his change in address.

5. A "secondary obligor" is defined as "an obligor to the extent that: (A) the obligor's obligation is secondary; or (B) the obligor has a right of recourse with respect to an obligation secured by collateral against the debtor, another obligor, or property of either." Tenn. Code Ann. §47-9-102(71) (2003). The official comment to the definition section to Article 9 of the Code provides, in relevant part, as follows:

> Determining whether a person was a "debtor" under former section 9-105(1)(d) required a close examination of the context in which the term was used. To reduce the need for this examination, this article redefines "debtor" and adds new defined terms, "secondary obligor" and "obligor." In the context of part 6 (default and enforcement), these definitions distinguish among three classes of persons: (i) Those persons who may have a stake in the proper enforcement of a security interest by virtue of their nonlien property interest (typically, an ownership interest) in the collateral; (ii) those persons who may have a stake in the proper enforcement of the security interest because of their obligation to pay the secured debt; and (iii) those persons who have an obligation to pay the secured debt but have no stake in the proper enforcement of the security interest. Persons in the first class are debtors. Persons in the second class are secondary obligors if any portion of the obligation is secondary or if the obligor has a right of recourse against the debtor or another obligor with respect to an obligation secured by collateral. One must consult the law of suretyship to determine whether an obligation is secondary.

Tenn. Code Ann. §47-9-102 cmt. 2 (2003). In the instant case, Mr. Blankenship qualifies as a secondary obligor. See Hardy v. Miller, No. M1998-00940-COA-R3-CV, 2001 WL 1565549, at *2, 2001 Tenn. App. LEXIS 898, at *5-6 (Tenn. Ct. App. Dec. 10, 2001); Robert M. Lloyd, The New Article 9: Its Impact on Tennessee Law (Part II), 67 Tenn. L. Rev. 329, 353 (2000) (discussing the manner in which Revised Article 9 eliminates the controversy over whether notice of sale must be sent to a guarantor).

The trial court held that the notice provided to Mr. Blankenship in this case was sufficient. In support of his position that the notice in this instance was inadequate, Mr. Blankenship directs our attention to two facts. First, he points to the fact that R & J proceeded with the sale despite having not received any indication that the notice had been delivered to Mr. Blankenship. Second, Mr. Blankenship asserts that Johnny Melton had actual knowledge of Mr. Blankenship's correct home address and failed to send the notice to that address. Mr. Blankenship points to a copy of a complaint filed in federal court on June 21, 2002, the day of the public sale. The complaint, attached to Mr. Blankenship's Amended Motion to Alter or Amend Judgment or for a New Trial submitted to the circuit court below, named Mr. Blankenship as a defendant and correctly listed his current address as 341 Box Road, Darden, Tennessee, 38328. After conducting a hearing, the trial court issued an order denying Mr. Blankenship's motion.

The decision as to whether to grant a motion for new trial or to alter or amend a final judgment based on newly discovered evidence is entirely within the discretion of the trial judge. Collins v. Greene County Bank, 916 S.W.2d 941, 945 (Tenn. Ct. App. 1996) (citing Seay v. City of Knoxville, 654 S.W.2d 397, 400-01 (Tenn. Ct. App. 1983)). We review a trial court's decision in this regard under an abuse of discretion standard. Chambliss v. Stohler, 124 S.W.3d 116, 120 (Tenn. Ct. App. 2003) (citing Bradley v. McLeod, 984 S.W.2d 929, 933 (Tenn. Ct. App. 1998)). In applying this standard this Court has stated: It is clear that a finding of an abuse of discretion cannot be based simply upon an appellate court's determination that it would have decided the question differently. Whiton v. Whiton, No. E2000-00467-COA-R3-CV, 2002 WL 1585630, at *7, 2002 Tenn. App. LEXIS 512[,] at *21 (Tenn. Ct. App. July 18, 2002). Rather, this standard requires that we determine "whether the lower court's exercise of its discretion went beyond the bounds of a fair exercise of discretion." Id. Davis v. Estate of Johnnie Rex Flynn, No. E2001-02480-COA-R3-CV, 2002 WL 31174229, at *9, 2002 Tenn. App. LEXIS 702, at *23 (Tenn. Ct. App. Sept. 30, 2002). The federal complaint was filed on June 21, 2002, and the trial in this matter occurred on July 28, 2003. We presume that Mr. Blankenship received service of the federal complaint prior to the trial of this matter in the court below. "The moving party must demonstrate that the new evidence was not known prior to or during the trial and that it could not have been ascertained by the exercise of reasonable diligence." *Collins,* 916 S.W.2d at 945; see also *Seay,* 654 S.W.2d at 399. Accordingly, we find that the trial court did not abuse its discretion in denying Mr. Blankenship's motion partially based on the information contained in the federal complaint. In turn, we are constrained to reviewing only the evidence presented at trial when determining whether the notice sent to Mr. Blankenship was sufficient under section 47-9-611(b) of the Tennessee Code.

The official comment to section 47-9-611(b) provides that "[t]he notification must be reasonable as to the manner in which it is sent, its timeliness (i.e., a reasonable time before the disposition is to take place), and its content." Tenn. Code Ann. §47-9-611 cmt. 2 (2003). Mr. Blankenship does not contest that R & J failed to send the notice in a timely fashion. See Tenn. Code Ann. §47-9-612. Rather, he contests whether the notice was sent in a reasonable manner when it was addressed to an address where he no longer lived. In addition to the timing of the notice, the reasonableness of the notice also encompasses a consideration of where the notice was sent. Commercial Credit Corp. v. Cutshall, 1979 WL 30031 (Tenn. Ct. App. 1979).

Section 47-9-611 of the Tennessee Code "leaves to judicial resolution, based upon the facts of each case, the question whether the requirement of 'reasonable notification' requires a 'second try,' i.e., whether a secured party who sends notification and learns that the debtor did not receive it must attempt to locate the debtor and send another notification." Tenn. Code Ann. §47-9-612 cmt. 6 (2003). We begin by examining the definitions of the key terms contained in section 47-9-611(b) of the Tennessee Code. The term "send" is defined as follows:

> "Send," in connection with a record or notification, means:
>
> (A) to deposit in the mail, deliver for transmission, or transmit by any other usual means of communication, with postage or cost of transmission provided for, addressed to any address reasonable under the circumstances; or
>
> (B) to cause the record or notification to be received within the time that it would have been received if properly sent under subparagraph (A).

Tenn. Code Ann. §47-9-102(75) (2003). The definition section applicable to Tennessee's version of Article 9 does not define "notice," but we find guidance in the general definition section of the Code, which provides:

> A person "notifies" or "gives" a notice or notification to another by taking such steps as may be reasonably required to inform the other in ordinary course whether or not such other actually comes to know of it. A person "receives" a notice or notification when:
>
> (A) It comes to his attention; or
>
> (B) It is duly delivered at the place of business *through which the contract was made or at any other place held out by him* as the place for receipt of such communications[.]

Tenn. Code Ann. §47-1-201(26) (2003) (emphasis added).

The policy justifications for providing notice to a debtor are equally applicable to a secondary obligor, and can be stated as follows:

> We think the provision for notice in connection with a sale is intended to afford the debtor a reasonable opportunity (1) to avoid a sale altogether

> by discharging the debt and redeeming the collateral or (2) in case of sale, to see that the collateral brings a fair price. A notice that does not afford him this reasonable opportunity is not reasonable notification and a sale under it is not commercially reasonable.

Intl. Harvester Credit Corp. v. Ingram, 619 S.W.2d 134, 137 (Tenn. Ct. App. 1981) (citing Mallicoat v. Volunteer Fin. & Loan Corp., 57 Tenn. App. 106, 415 S.W.2d 347, 350 (1966)).

In support of his argument that the notice given was not reasonable, Mr. Blankenship relies on our decision in Mallicoat v. Volunteer Finance & Loan Corp., 57 Tenn. App. 106, 415 S.W.2d 347 (1966). In *Mallicoat,* the secured party sent a notice of sale to the debtor by certified mail, but the notice was returned to the secured party undelivered. *Mallicoat,* 415 S.W.2d at 349. After receiving the returned notice, the secured party continued to conduct a sale of the collateral and sued the debtor for a deficiency judgment. Id. In finding the notice in that case insufficient under the predecessor statute to section 47-9-611, we stated:

> In view of the undisputed proof in this case that the debtor did not receive the notice and that the secured creditor was aware that he had not received it, it is our opinion the creditor not only failed to show a compliance with the Act but that the record affirmatively shows a lack of compliance and a conscious disregard of the debtor's right to notice. The property was not perishable. The debtor lived in Knoxville where the creditor had its place of business and sold the property. In addition, the creditor had information as to where the debtor was employed and where his parents lived. Yet, the sale was allowed to proceed without any further effort to comply with the notice requirement.

Id. at 350; see also First Tenn. Bank Natl. Assn. v. Helton, No. 03A01-9501-CV-00026, 1995 WL 515658, at *2, 1995 Tenn. App. LEXIS 339, at *5-6 (Tenn. Ct. App. May 23, 1995).

Courts throughout the country vary as to whether the secured party has the burden of proving that the debtor or a secondary obligor received actual notice of a pending sale. See Richard C. Tinney, Annotation, Sufficiency of Secured Party's Notification of Sale or Other Intended Disposition of Collateral Under UCC §9-504(3), 11 A.L.R.4th 241, §§14-16 (2003). Many of our sister states interpret the notice provision to require only that the creditor send notice. See Underwood v. First Ala. Bank of Huntsville, 453 So. 2d 742, 745 (Ala. Civ. App. 1983); Hall v. Owen County State Bank, 175 Ind. App. 150, 370 N.E.2d 918, 925 (1977); McKee v. Miss. Bank & Trust Co., 366 So. 2d 234, 238 (Miss. 1979); Commerce Bank of St. Louis v. Dooling, 875 S.W.2d 943, 946 (Mo. Ct. App. 1994); First Natl. Bank & Trust Co. of Lincoln v. Hermann, 205 Neb. 169, 286 N.W.2d 750, 752 (1980). Our decision in *Mallicoat,* however, demonstrates that Tennessee requires more than a mere "sending" in order for a secured party to be in compliance with the statute. James J. White & Robert S. Summers, Uniform Commercial Code §26-10, at 987 (1972).

At the other end of the notice spectrum, we have held that the notice requirement is satisfied when the following occurs:

> The sending of notice, certified, return receipt requested, is commercially reasonable. When a plaintiff forwards notice to the debtor's proper address, certified, return receipt requested, and the notice is received at that address and returned signed by someone at the address, it is reasonable for plaintiff to assume that the defendant received the notice.

Caterpillar Fin. Services Corp. v. Woods, No. 89-326-II, 1990 WL 15230, at *3, 1990 Tenn. App. LEXIS 117, at *7-8 (Tenn. Ct. App. Feb. 22, 1990). Our case law makes clear that "the creditor will not be forced to take responsibility for lost mail or the debtor's refusal to accept properly delivered mail." Nationsbank v. Clegg, No. 01-A-01-9510-CH-00469, 1996 WL 165513, at *5, 1996 Tenn. App. LEXIS 214, at *14 (Tenn. Ct. App. Apr. 10, 1996). Yet, we have also made clear that:

> While absolute proof of receipt of notice may not be required in every instance, a creditor, who only makes one attempt to contact the debtor, and is left uncertain of receipt of the notice, has not fulfilled its obligation to the debtor when it proceeds with a disposition less than two weeks from mailing its first notice.

Id. 1996 WL 165513, at *5, 1996 Tenn. App. LEXIS 214, at *15-16.

We disagree with Mr. Blankenship's assertion that section 47-9-611(b) requires the secured party to prove that the secondary obligor actually received the notice. See Commercial Credit Corp. v. Cutshall, 1979 WL 30031 (Tenn. Ct. App. 1979). Based on the facts presented to the trial court below, however, we find the trial court's holding that notice in this case was sufficient under the statute to be erroneous as a matter of law. We are mindful that Mr. Blankenship bears some responsibility for not receiving notice in this case. See The Cent. Trust Co. of Northeastern Ohio v. Snair, No. CA-5818, 1982 WL 5437, at *1, 1982 Ohio App. LEXIS 15214, at *2-3 (Ohio Ct. App. June 23, 1982); Gen. Motors Acceptance Corp. v. Horn, No. 5861, 1978 WL 216247, at *3, 1978 Ohio App. LEXIS 11155, at *5 (Ohio Ct. App. July 20, 1978). However, R & J sent the notice to Mr. Blankenship on June 11, 2002, and conducted a sale ten days later on June 21, 2002, without receiving any indication as to whether the notice actually reached Mr. Blankenship. We find, therefore, that this amounts to unreasonable notice under the statute and reverse the trial court's holding on this issue. See Nationsbank v. Clegg, No. 01-A-01-9510-CH-00469, 1996 WL 165513, at *5, 1996 Tenn. App. LEXIS 214, at *15-16 (Tenn. Ct. App. Apr. 10, 1996).

V. Commercial Reasonableness of the Sale of the Collateral

Lack of reasonable notice to a secondary obligor is one factor bearing upon whether the sale of the collateral was commercially reasonable. See Mallicoat v. Volunteer Fin. & Loan Corp., 57 Tenn. App. 106, 415 S.W.2d 347, 351 (1966); Gen. Motors Acceptance Corp. v. Middleton, No. 02A01-9103-CH-00033, 1991 WL 206517, at *4, 1991 Tenn. App. LEXIS 820, at *7 (Tenn. Ct. App. Oct. 16, 1991). "However, notice by itself is not conclusive on the question of whether a sale was commercially reasonable." Decatur County Bank v. Smith, No. CAW1999-02022COAR3CV, 1999 WL 1336042, at *3, 1999 Tenn. App. LEXIS 864, at *9 (Tenn. Ct. App. Dec. 27, 1999). We note that the remaining issues presented by Appellant for our review focus upon whether Appellee conducted the sale of the collateral in a commercially reasonable manner. Accordingly, we will discuss these issues collectively in this section of the opinion.

"After default, a secured party may sell, lease, license, or otherwise dispose of any or all of the collateral in its present condition or following any commercially reasonable preparation or processing." Tenn. Code Ann. §47-9-610(a) (2003). As a secured party conducting a public sale, R & J also had the right to purchase the collateral at the sale. Tenn. Code Ann. §47-9-610(c)(1) (2003). In carrying out the sale of the collateral R & J was bound by two standards. "First, in exercising his rights upon default the secured party is bound by the good faith requirement applicable throughout the Uniform Commercial Code." *Decatur County Bank*, 1999 WL 1336042, at *3, 1999 Tenn. App. LEXIS 864, at *6 (citing Tenn. Code Ann. §47-1-203). The second requirement that R & J was bound to follow addresses the procedures used in selling the collateral and provides:

> Commercially reasonable disposition. Every aspect of a disposition of collateral, including the method, manner, time, place, and other terms, must be commercially reasonable. If commercially reasonable, a secured party may dispose of the collateral by public or private proceedings, by one (1) or more contracts, as a unit or in parcels, and at any time and place and on any terms.

Tenn. Code Ann. §47-9-610(b) (2003); see also Am. City Bank of Tullahoma v. W. Auto Supply Co., 631 S.W.2d 410, 419 (Tenn. Ct. App. 1981). This Court has defined "commercially reasonable" as follows:

> The requirement that the property be disposed of in a "commercially reasonable" manner seems to us to signify that the disposition shall be made in keeping with prevailing trade practices among reputable and responsible business and commercial enterprises engaged in the same or a similar business.

Mallicoat v. Volunteer Fin. & Loan Corp., 57 Tenn. App. 106, 415 S.W.2d 347, 350 (1966); see also Tenn. Code Ann. §47-9-627(b) (2003). The trial court found that R & J conducted the sale in good faith and in a commercially reasonable manner. We disagree.

Like notice, review of a sale of collateral to determine whether it was conducted in good faith and in a commercially reasonable manner is an inquiry dependent upon the facts of each case. In reviewing the facts of this case, we are cognizant of the following:

> Rather than viewing in isolation specific details of the sale of the debtor's collateral, it is the aggregate of circumstances in each case which should be emphasized in reviewing the sale. The elements of manner, method, time, place and terms cited by the Uniform Commercial Code are to be viewed as necessary and interrelated parts of the whole transaction.

In re Four Star Music Co., Inc., 2 B.R. 454, 463 (Bankr. M.D. Tenn. 1979) (citations omitted).

This court has often looked to the following factors when attempting to ascertain whether a foreclosure sale was conducted in a commercially reasonable manner:

> Although the statute has not attempted to define the parameters of the term "commercially reasonable," case law has specified six factors by which the statute requirements may be measured:
> (1) the type of collateral involved; and
> (2) the condition of the collateral; and
> (3) the number of bids solicited; and
> (4) the time and place of sale; and
> (5) the purchase price received or the terms of the sale; and
> (6) any special circumstances involved.

Decatur County Bank v. Smith, No. CAW1999-02022COAR3CV, 1999 WL 1336042, at *2, 1999 Tenn. App. LEXIS 864, at *7-8 (Tenn. Ct. App. Dec. 27, 1999) (quoting In re Four Star Music Co., Inc., 2 B.R. 454, 461 (Bankr. M.D. Tenn. 1979)). "The burden of proving that a sale of collateral is commercially reasonable under these statutes is on the secured party seeking the deficiency judgment." *Decatur County Bank*, 1999 WL 1336042, at *3, 1999 Tenn. App. LEXIS 864, at *7.

Mr. Blankenship argues that the timing of the sale demonstrates it was conducted in a commercially unreasonable manner. In support of his position, he points to the fact that R & J delayed in conducting a sale of the collateral for seven and one-half months after purchasing the note. Mr. Blankenship notes that at the time R & J purchased the note it had already been in default for some time.

The official comment to section 47-9-610 of the Tennessee Code provides:

> *Time of Disposition.* This article does not specify a period within which a secured party must dispose of collateral. This is consistent with this article's

> policy to encourage private dispositions through regular commercial channels. It may, for example, be prudent not to dispose of goods when the market has collapsed. Or, it might be more appropriate to sell a large inventory in parcels over a period of time instead of in bulk. Of course, under subsection (b) every aspect of a disposition of collateral must be commercially reasonable. This requirement explicitly includes the "method, manner, time, place, and other terms." *For example, if a secured party does not proceed under section 9-620 [§47-9-620] and holds collateral for a long period of time without disposing of it, and if there is no good reason for not making a prompt disposition, the secured party may be determined not to have acted in a "commercially reasonable" manner.* See also section 1-203 [§47-1-203] (general obligation of good faith).

Tenn. Code Ann. §47-9-610 cmt. 3 (2003) (emphasis added). Mr. Blankenship directs our attention to this Court's holding in Nationsbank v. Clegg, No. 01-A-01-9510-CH-00469, 1996 WL 165513, 1996 Tenn. App. LEXIS 214 (Tenn. Ct. App. Apr. 10, 1996), where we stated:

> Of concern to this Court is the fact that the secured parties in this instance permitted an automobile to sit idly for over 13 months after default. The UCC does not state particular time limits for a secured party to take possession of the collateral, or to proceed with a sale following the taking of possession. The determination of whether delay is commercially unreasonable requires consideration of all surrounding circumstances, including market conditions, the possible physical deterioration of the collateral, its economic deterioration through obsolescence, and the time required to assemble the collateral and prepare it for sale. . . .
>
> We have found no evidence in the record, or other authority which indicates that the 13 month delay in selling the automobile, a depreciating asset, is "in keeping with the prevailing trade practices among reputable firms engaged in similar business activities," in Tennessee. Thus, the delay appears unreasonable to this Court. . . .
>
> In exercising its rights upon default, Nationsbank is bound by the good faith requirement applicable throughout the Uniform Commercial Code. Tenn. Code Ann. §47-1-203. American City Bank of Tullahoma v. Western Auto Supply, 631 S.W.2d 410, 420 (Tenn. App. 1981). The obligation of good faith required the secured parties in this instance to have sold the car with greater haste.

Nationsbank, 1996 WL 165513, at *3-4, 1996 Tenn. App. LEXIS 214, at *8-10 (citations omitted).

In response, R & J contends that, unlike the facts in *Nationsbank,* the collateral in this case did not sit unused during the period leading up to the sale. To the contrary, Larry Melton continued to drive the truck, and Steve Melton continued to live in the mobile home. Only the tractor remained unused since it was inoperable at the time of the foreclosure sale.

"The policy of the Uniform Commercial Code, as to the disposition of collateral, is to balance and protect the rights of both debtor and creditor, while maximizing the recovery from the disposition of the collateral for the benefit of all parties." *Nationsbank*, 1996 WL 165513, at *3, 1996 Tenn. App. LEXIS 214, at *8 (citations omitted). Upon reviewing the entire record, we find that the evidence clearly preponderates against the trial court's finding that the sale of the collateral conducted by R & J in this case was commercially reasonable. Once a debtor or secondary obligor raises the issue of the commercial reasonableness of a sale, the secured party, in this case R & J, bears the burden of proving that the sale was carried out in a commercially reasonable manner. Decatur County Bank v. Smith, No. CAW1999-02022COAR3CV, 1999 WL 1336042, at *3, 1999 Tenn. App. LEXIS 864, at *7 (Tenn. Ct. App. Dec. 27, 1999). R & J failed to carry this burden at trial.

In addition to the failure to provide adequate notice, R & J failed to offer a reasonable explanation as to why it waited in excess of seven months to conduct a sale of the collateral, during which time Larry Melton and Steve Melton were allowed to continue using the collateral. See *Nationsbank*, 1996 WL 165513, at *3-4, 1996 Tenn. App. LEXIS 214, at *8-10. Contrary to

R & J's position, we note that use of the items of collateral in this case would cause them to depreciate more rapidly, not less. Mr. Blankenship also raises a related issue regarding R & J's handling of the collateral after it purchased the note in question. Mr. Blankenship asserts that, by allowing Steve Melton and Larry Melton to continue to use the collateral over the seven and one-half months before the sale, R & J increased the amount of the deficiency. According to Mr. Blankenship, in addition to constituting bad faith on the part of R & J, this amounts to a violation of section 49-9-207(a) which provides, in relevant part, as follows:

> *Rights and duties of secured party having possession or control of collateral.*—
> (a) DUTY OF CARE WHEN SECURED PARTY IN POSSESSION. Except as otherwise provided in subsection (d), a secured party shall use reasonable care in the custody and preservation of collateral in the secured party's possession.

Tenn. Code Ann. §47-9-207(a) (2003). We agree with Mr. Blankenship that the actions by R & J relating to the use and custody of the collateral constitute an additional factor demonstrating that the disposition of the collateral in this case was commercially unreasonable. See Farmers & Merchants Bank v. Barnes, 17 Ark. App. 139, 705 S.W.2d 450, 453 (1986) (holding a sale of collateral commercially unreasonable where the collateral remained in the custody of the original owner who was permitted to continue using it for six months prior to the sale); The Bank Josephine v. Conn, 599 S.W.2d 773, 775 (Ky. Ct. App. 1980) (finding a sale of collateral commercially unreasonable where the secured party did not dispose of the collateral for four to five weeks after repossessing it, thereby allowing it to deteriorate further prior to the sale).

We also agree with Mr. Blankenship that R & J's actions in allowing Larry Melton and Steve Melton to continue to use the collateral prior to the sale constituted bad faith. Johnny Melton's own testimony, indicating that Larry Melton and Steve Melton also continued to retain possession of the collateral after the sale, supports this conclusion:

> *Q:* Who keeps the vehicle for you, Mr. Melton?
> *A:* Larry Melton still takes care of it.
> *Q:* Yes. The tractor, where is the tractor at?
> *A:* It's still at their place.
> *Q:* At the Melton place?
> *A:* At the Melton place.
> . . .
> *Q:* Where is the mobile home at currently?
> *A:* It's still on the property where it was.
> . . .
> *Q:* Is Mr. Larry Melton living in that mobile home?
> *A:* Not that I'm aware of.
> *Q:* Who is living in it?
> *A:* Steve is living in it.
> *Q:* Okay. Steve Melton?
> *A:* Uh-huh.

Providing notice of a public sale to the general public corresponds with additional factors related to the procedures employed by the secured party in conducting the sale. When a secured party undertakes to dispose of the collateral by public sale, advertising of some sort should be conducted in order to increase competitive bidding and maximize proceeds. Gezon Motors v. Gould, 1976 WL 23727 (Mich. Dist. 1976). Although R & J posted a notice of sale at the courthouse and on the collateral, the record also indicates that R & J never advertised the sale in a public newspaper or utilized an experienced auctioneer. See First Tenn. Bank Natl. Assoc. v. Helton, No. 03A01-9501-CV-00026, 1995 WL 515658, at *3, 1995 Tenn. App. LEXIS 339, at *7-8 (Tenn. Ct. App. May 23, 1995); see also U.S. v. Warwick, 695 F.2d 1063, 1073 (7th Cir. 1982); Benton v. Gen. Mobile Homes, Inc., 13 Ark. App. 8, 678 S.W.2d 774, 776 (1984). Given the nature of the collateral, this is another factor indicating the sale was not conducted by R & J in a commercially reasonable manner. Leasing Serv. Corp. v. Broetje, 640 F. Supp. 51, 53 (E.D. Wash. 1986) (finding a public sale commercially reasonable, despite the fact that the secured party was the only bidder present, where the secured party properly notified the debtor and advertised the sale in newspapers in the area of the sale); Kobuk Engg. & Contracting Services Inc. v. Superior Tank & Constr. Co-Alaska, Inc., 568 P.2d 1007, 1011 (Alaska 1977) (holding that a sale was not commercially reasonable where the secured party merely gave a copy of the notice to the court clerk for posting on a bulletin board and did not advertise in the newspaper in the area where the collateral was to be sold); The Bank Josephine v. Conn, 599 S.W.2d 773, 775 (Ky. Ct. App. 1980) (stating that a sale was commercially unreasonable where the secured party failed to prove where he posted notices, did not advertise in any newspapers, and was the only bidder at the sale).

In addition to being the only bidder at the sale, R & J also valued the collateral instead of seeking an independent appraisal. Johnny Melton did testify that he had prior experience in the banking and mobile home industries which he used to value the collateral. We note that an independent appraisal may not be required in every case. When coupled with the other facts present in this case, however, R & J's failure to do so in this instance is an additional factor indicating that this sale was not conducted in a commercially reasonable manner. See In re Cummings, 147 B.R. 738, 746 (D.S.D. 1992) (holding that a secured party failed to conduct a sale in a commercially reasonable manner where he did not obtain an appraisal, exerted minimal effort to notify potential buyers, and failed to give notice to the debtor); In re Thomas, 1973 WL 21424 (W.D. Va. 1973) (stating that the fact that the secured party failed to obtain an independent valuation of the collateral by a third party was a factor supporting the commercial unreasonableness of the sale); Kobuk Engg. & Contracting Services, Inc. v. Superior Tank & Constr. Co., Alaska, Inc., 568 P.2d 1007, 1011 (Alaska 1977) (expressing the opinion that, had the secured party conducted an independent appraisal of the collateral, a finding of commercial reasonableness would be more likely); Jefferson Bank & Trust Co. v. Horst, 599 S.W.2d 201, 203 (Mo. Ct. App. 1980) (finding a public sale of a mobile home commercially reasonable where the secured party obtained an independent appraisal).

The aggregate of circumstances in this case demonstrates that the sale of the collateral conducted by R & J was not conducted in good faith or in a commercially reasonable manner as required by Article 9 of Tennessee's Uniform Commercial Code.

VI. Effect of Failure to Conduct a Commercially Reasonable Sale and Provide Sufficient Notice

Because R & J failed to provide Mr. Blankenship with adequate notice under section 49-9-611, Mr. Blankenship may be entitled to certain statutory damages. Tenn. Code Ann. §47-9-625 (2003). We remand this case to the trial court and instruct the court to determine what damages, if any, Mr.

Blankenship is entitled to pursuant to section 47-9-625 of the Tennessee Code due to R & J's failure to provide adequate notice. . . .

On remand, the trial court must also conduct an additional inquiry. Tennessee follows the "rebuttable presumption rule" which governs a creditor's failure to comply with Tennessee's version of the Uniform Commercial Code.

Under Tennessee law, in the event the creditors foreclose upon security interest in collateral and conduct a commercially unreasonable sale, there is a presumption that the debtor is damaged to the extent of the deficiency claimed. The fact of an unreasonable sale does not result in the extinguishment of any deficiency whatsoever. Federal Deposit Insurance Corp. v. Morgan, 727 S.W.2d 500 (Tenn. Ct. App. 1986). This presumption shifts the burden of proving to the creditor the amount that should reasonably have been obtained through sale conducted according to the law. ITT Industrial Co. v. Rector, 1982 WL 170990 (Tenn. Ct. App. 1982)]. The presumption is a presumption of law, and is a burden shifting device, requiring the party who is in a better position, to go forward with the evidence. Where evidence is presented sufficient to rebut the presumption, creditors are entitled to recover the deficiency. Id. Decatur County Bank v. Smith, No. CAW1999-02022COAR3CV, 1999 WL 1336042, at *3, 1999 Tenn. App. LEXIS 864, at *9-10 (Tenn. Ct. App. Dec. 27, 1999). "It is the burden of the secured party to rebut this presumption and failure to rebut the presumption with evidence of fair market value in the record results in denial of the secured party's claims for deficiency judgment." In re Frazier, 93 B.R. 366, 372 (Bankr. M.D. Tenn. 1988) (citations omitted); see also Fed. Deposit Ins. Corp. v. Morgan, 727 S.W.2d 500, 502 (Tenn. Ct. App. 1987) (citing United States v. Willis, 593 F.2d 247, 260 (6th Cir. 1979)); Empire S., Inc. v. Repp, 51 Wash. App. 868, 756 P.2d 745, 750-51 (1988).

At trial, the parties presented conflicting testimony regarding the value of the collateral on the date of the foreclosure sale. In rendering a judgment below, the trial court listed the proceeds from the foreclosure sale in its tabulation of the deficiency owed R & J, but the court failed to state whether this amount constituted the fair market value of the collateral on the date of the sale. Therefore, we are unable to determine what the fair market value of the collateral was on the date of the foreclosure sale and whether R & J overcame the presumption that the amount received at the sale equaled the debt owed. See In re Frazier, 93 B.R. at 372. On remand, the trial court is instructed to determine whether R & J presented sufficient proof in this regard and is entitled to a deficiency judgment. See Provident Employees Credit Union v. Austin, 1981 WL 138032 (Tenn. Ct. App. 1981). If the trial court determines that R & J has overcome the presumption and is entitled to a deficiency, then the trial court is instructed to determine whether the deficiency should be offset by any damages due Mr. Blankenship pursuant to section 47-9-625 of the Tennessee Code. See *Gen. Motors Acceptance Corp.*, 1991 WL 206517, at *4, 1991 Tenn. App. LEXIS 820, at *11-12.

VII. Conclusion

For the foregoing reasons, we reverse the trial court's decision. We remand this case to the trial court with instructions to determine whether the Appellant is entitled to damages against Appellee consistent with this opinion. We also instruct the trial court to determine whether Appellee is entitled to a deficiency and, if so, the amount that the deficiency should be offset by Appellant's damages, if any, consistent with this opinion. Costs of this appeal are taxed against Appellee, R & J of Tennessee, Inc., for which execution may issue if necessary.

To the extent that this case holds that the creditor must do any sort of checking to see that the notice was actually received, it was overruled by Auto Credit of Nashville v. Wimmer, 231 S.W.3d 896 (Tenn. 2007) ("To require every creditor to verify receipt of notification in every situation would place an unreasonable burden on them, making secured transactions in this state unduly cumbersome").

For recent examples of a commercially reasonable sale and an unreasonable one, compare Bank Leumi USA v. GM Diamonds, Inc., 149 A.D.3d 662 (N.Y. App. Div. 2017) (held commercially reasonable where creditor had two experts appraise the value of the diamonds, solicited bids from four potential bidders, and took the highest of three bids submitted, which was near the appraised value from two experts hired by creditor), and In re Comprehensive Power, Inc., 578 B.R. 14, 42 (Bankr. D. Mass. 2017) ("The Trustee has pleaded sufficient facts to support a claim under Article 9 of the UCC, including that: (i) Moog did not employ a process intended to generate a reasonable sale price and the sale price obtained was substantially less than that which the parties had previously valued the Debtor's assets and less than the assets would have been appraised for if an appraisal conducted; (ii) Moog conducted the auction sale as a formality to consolidate its control the Debtor's assets; (iii) Moog failed to adequately market the property; (iv) Moog was the sole bidder at a sale conducted on only fourteen days' notice and other potential purchasers were deprived from acquiring the Debtor's assets; and (v) Moog deprived the Debtor of six-month "runway" to obtain alternative financing and the Debtor was damaged as a result.").

PROBLEM 438

Car dealers sometimes engage in a shady practice called "yo-yo financing." The buyer is persuaded to take a "spot delivery" of the car being purchased, but is warned that the deal is off if the seller is unable to secure financing for the buyer. If the financing goes through, well and good, but if not the buyer must surrender the car or work out some other means of payment, and, if necessary the seller will hunt the car down and bring it back to the dealership using a spare set of keys and then sell it to some other customer. Is this an Article 9 transaction? See §2-401(1). If so, is the car dealer at risk of damages under §9-625(c)(2) if no notice is given of the subsequent resale of the car? See Cappo Management V, Inc. v. Britt, 282 Va. 33, 711 S.E.2d 209 (2011). If the customer, on learning of the failure of the financing, voluntarily returns the keys to the dealership, is any subsequent sale of the car governed by the repossession rules of Article 9? If the car dealer resells the car, must the car dealer return the first buyer's down payment (if any)? See §9-615(d). Another issue that has arisen with yo-yo financing is whether the purchaser of the car has any ownership interest in it so that the dealership's security interest could even attach during the period when it is unclear if financing will be forthcoming; see In re Byrd, 546 B.R. 434 (Bankr. D. Idaho 2016).

Yo-yo financing is sometimes called "bait and switch" financing because the buyer thinks he/she has bought a new car only to be told to return it because the financing mysteriously fell through. When the buyer returns to the dealership, a new deal is often offered with worse terms for the buyer. If the buyer won't return the car, threats are often made that police will be called, the buyer's employer will be informed (or the base commander if the buyer is in the service), etc. Out and out fraud and lies are common. Courts may take a dim view of these practices—witness the Supreme Court of Virginia's opinion cited above. For an expanded discussion of yo-yo financing, see http://www.edmunds.com/car-loan/dont-fall-prey-to-spot-delivery-scams-and-yo-yo-financing.html. In In re Lewis, 2019 WL 2158832 (Bankr. W.D. La. 2019), a predatory dealer, after repossessing a car, held a "phantom" sale to make it seem as if the car had been sold, to avoid handing the car over to the debtor's bankruptcy trustee. The court held that the dealer had violated Article 9 and was obliged to give the debtor the fictional surplus from the sale.

PROBLEM 439

The Bunyan State Bank held a perfected security interest in the logging equipment of the Blue Ox Timber Company. When Blue Ox defaulted on its loan repayment, Bunyan repossessed the equipment. The sale was held the next day in the middle of a snowstorm. The equipment sold for very little (there was only one bidder, and he complained that it was hard to know the condition of the equipment because it was so dirty, being covered with mud from the backwoods). Bunyan sued Blue Ox for the amount still due. Answer these questions:

(a) Was the notice period too short? See §9-612. See, e.g., In re MarMc Transp., Inc., 469 B.R. 84 (Bankr. D. Wyo. 2012). Would if affect the notice requirement if the collateral were perishable, such as a load of tomatoes? See §9-611(d)?

(b) Is the secured party required to wash the collateral prior to sale? See §9-610(a); Weiss v. Northwest Acceptance Corp., 274 Or. 343, 546 P.2d 1065 (1976); Timothy R. Zinnecker, The Default Provisions of Revised Article 9 of the Uniform Commercial Code: Part I, 54 Bus. Law. 1113, 1149-1151 (1999).

(c) Did it violate §9-610(b) to conduct the sale in the snowstorm? Liberty Natl. Bank & Trust Co. v. Acme Tool Div. of the Rucker Co., 540 F.2d 1375 (10th Cir. 1976).

PROBLEM 440

When you explained to your client, Repossession Finance Company, all the rights that debtors have when the creditor seizes the collateral and resells it, the president of the company asked you to draft a clause in the security agreement waiving these rights. How should you do this? See §9-602 and its Official Comment. Can guarantors (as opposed to the primary debtor) waive these rights? See §9-602, Official Comment 4; Kraenzler v. Brace, 321 Wis. 2d 265, 773 N.W.2d 481 (2009).

PROBLEM 441

Facade Motors granted a security interest in its inventory to Octopus National Bank (ONB), which duly perfected by filing a financing statement in the proper place. Subsequently Facade Motors granted an identical security interest to Nightflyer Finance Company to get short-term credit. When Facade failed to repay the second debt, Nightflyer repossessed the inventory and sold it. Must it somehow account to ONB for the proceeds of the resale? Does the buyer at the resale take free of the security interest of the senior creditor? See §§9-608 (and its Official Comment 5), 9-615(g), and Official Comment 5 to §9-610; note §§9-617, 2-312, 9-610(d) and (e). How can the resale creditor avoid making the warranty in §2-312?

Penalties for Non-compliance. Amazingly, under the prior version of Article 9, it was unclear what the penalty was for a secured party who did not follow the required rules when disposing of the collateral, and the states reached differing results, with many resolving the matter by non-uniform statutes. Some courts held that failure to comply resulted in a forfeiture of the creditor's right to collect a *deficiency* (the difference between the amount owed and the amount realized at the foreclosure sale)—this was called the *absolute bar* rule. Others (like the Tennessee decision reprinted above) allowed a deficiency but made the creditor overcome a *rebuttable presumption* that had the rules been followed, there would have been no deficiency and allowed the creditor to pursue the debtor for the amount still due only if the creditor could overcome this presumption by adequate proof.

PROBLEM 442

Facade Motors repossessed the car that Portia Moot used in her law practice but failed to send her any notice of the foreclosure sale, which brought only half the amount she still owed on the car. May it still sue her for the deficiency? See §9-626(a) and its Official Comments. What are Portia's rights? See §9-625. If Portia had purchased the car for her *personal* use, what is the rule? See §9-626(b). Why would the drafters have done this?

Coxall v. Clover Commercial Corp.

Civil Court, City of New York, 2004
4 Misc. 3d 654, 781 N.Y.S.2d 567

JACK M. BATTAGLIA, J.

On October 21, 2002, Jason Coxall and Utho Coxall purchased a 1991 model Lexus automobile, executing a Security Agreement/Retail Installment Contract. The "cash price" on the Contract was $8,100, against which the Coxalls made a "cash down payment" of $3,798.25 and financed the balance of $4,970. Apparently simultaneously with the sale, the Contract was assigned to Clover Commercial Corp., whose name was printed on the top and at other places. Although Majestic Capital Inc. is designated as the "Seller" and "Dealer" in the assignment, at trial the parties referred to the seller of the automobile as Jafas Auto Sales. Title to the vehicle was put in Jason Coxall's name.

The Coxalls were required by the Contract to make monthly payments of $333.68 each, beginning November 21, 2002. No payments were made, however, because Jason Coxall experienced mechanical difficulties with the vehicle soon after purchase. On February 19, 2003, Clover Commercial took possession of the vehicle, and on the next day mailed two letters to Jason Coxall; in one, Clover told Mr. Coxall that he could redeem the vehicle with a payment of $5,969.28, exclusive of storage charges and a redemption fee;

in the other, Clover gave Mr. Coxall notice that the vehicle would be offered for private sale after 12:00 noon on March 3, 2003.

On March 3, 2003, the Lexus was sold back to Jafas Auto Sales for $1,500. On April 22, 2003, Clover Commercial wrote to Jason Coxall demanding that he pay a "remaining balance" of $4,998.09.

Jason Coxall commenced Action No. 1 with a Summons with Endorsed Complaint dated April 29, 2003 that states the nature and substance of the cause of action as "automobile illegally repossed [sic]," and seeks damages of $8,000 with interest from February 19, 2003. Clover Commercial was served on May 2, and filed its Answer on May 20. Despite the filing, the action was placed on the Part 12 calendar for inquest to be held on June 27.

Meanwhile, with a Summons and Verified Complaint dated June 16, 2003 and filed on June 25, Clover Commercial commenced Action No. 2 against Jason Coxall and Utho Coxall, seeking $4,630.62 with interest from October 21, 2002 plus reasonable attorney fees. The Verified Complaint alleges that "Plaintiff is the holder for value of a promissory instrument dated 10/21/02 duly executed and delivered and/or guaranteed by the defendant(s)." These documents show Clover Commercial's attorney to be E. Hope Greenberg, the same attorney who signed Clover's Answer in Action No. 1 approximately one month earlier. . . .

[The trial court ruled in favor of the creditor, but on appeal this court found that the notice was only given to one of the two debtors and that the resale of the car had not been proven by the creditor to be commercially reasonable, particularly in light of the low sale price and other suspicious circumstances. The court then turned to a consideration of the effect of these failures on the creditor's ability to continue its pursuit of the debtors.]

Deficiency

When the secured party has disposed of the collateral in a commercially reasonable manner after sending reasonable notification to the debtor, the debtor will be liable for any deficiency if the proceeds of the disposition are not sufficient to satisfy the debt and allowed expenses. (See Revised UCC §9-615[(d)]; see also Former UCC §9-504[(2)].) Former Article 9 was silent, however, on whether the secured party that had failed to send reasonable notification or had not disposed of the collateral in a commercially reasonable manner or both, as here could obtain a deficiency judgment against the debtor. . . .

"Three general approaches emerged. Some courts have held that a noncomplying secured party may not recover a deficiency (the 'absolute bar' rule). A few courts held that the debtor can offset against a claim to a deficiency all damages recoverable under former Section 9-507 resulting from the secured party's noncompliance (the 'offset' rule). A plurality of courts considering the issue held that the noncomplying secured party is barred from recovering a deficiency unless it overcomes a rebuttable presumption that compliance with former Part 5 would have yielded an amount sufficient to satisfy the secured debt." (Official Comment 4 to Revised UCC §9-626.)

In New York, the departments of the Appellate Division were not in agreement as to which of the approaches to follow, with the Second Department alone adopting the "absolute bar" rule. [Citations omitted.]

Revised Article 9 resolves the conflict and uncertainty for transactions other than consumer transactions by adopting the "rebuttable presumption" rule. (See Revised UCC §9-626[a][3].) The limitation of the "rebuttable presumption" rule to non-consumer transactions "is intended to leave to the court the determination of the proper rules in consumer transactions," and the court "may continue to apply established approaches." (Revised UCC §9-626[(b)].)

It is clear, therefore, that the "rebuttable presumption" rule is now the law in the Second Department for non-consumer transactions. The question remains, however, whether the "absolute bar" rule is to be applied in these actions, involving, as they do, a consumer transaction. A review of the legislative history provides no guidance. The Report of the New York State Law Revision Committee that accompanied Revised Article 9 through enactment states only that, "[w]ith respect to consumer defaults, Revised Article 9 makes no recommendation whatsoever, leaving the courts free to shape a remedy as is appropriate in each case." (The New York State Law Revision Commission, 2001 Report on the Proposed Revised Article 9, at 158.)

Up to now, New York courts have not distinguished between consumer and non-consumer transactions in fashioning rules where the enforcement provisions of Article 9 were silent, suggesting that the "rebuttable presumption" rule will be adopted for all transactions. But at this time, for a court sitting in the Second Department, there is an "absolute bar" rule that has not been legislatively displaced by Revised Article 9.

Having found, therefore, that Clover Commercial failed to comply with both the reasonable notification and commercially reasonable disposition requirements of Article 9, the "absolute bar" rule precludes it from recovering a deficiency from the Coxalls. Even if, however, the "rebuttable presumption" rule were to be applied, the result would be the same. Clover introduced no evidence of "the amount of proceeds that would have been realized had [it] proceeded in accordance with the provisions of" the Code relating to disposition of the collateral. (See Revised UCC §9-626[(a)][(3)][(B)].)

Specifically, Clover Commercial provided no evidence as to the fair market value of the Lexus on the date of the sale, either by reference to "blue book" value, appraisal, sales of similar vehicles or other measure. (See Long Island Trust Co. v. Williams, 133 Misc. 2d at 754, 507 N.Y.S.2d 993;

see also Central National Bank v. Butler, 294 A.D.2d at 882, 741 N.Y.S.2d 643 ["certified appraised value"]; Kohler v. Ford Motor Credit Co., Inc., 93 A.D.2d at 208, 462 N.Y.S.2d 297 ["book value of the vehicle"].) Moreover, Clover's witness, Adam Greenberg, acknowledged that Clover considered the Lexus to be of sufficient value to serve as collateral for the secured debt, which, at the least, was the amount financed, $4,970.

Although Clover Commercial cannot recover for any deficiency, it may recover "the sums owed to it prior to the repossession as well as the repossession charges." (See Avis Rent-A-Car System, Inc. v. Franklin, 82 Misc. 2d at 67, 366 N.Y.S.2d 83.) Clover's failure to comply with the enforcement provisions of Article 9 "would not discharge the [Coxalls] from all liability under the contract." (See Stanchi v. Kemp, 48 A.D.2d at 974, 370 N.Y.S.2d 26; see also Bank of China v. Chan, 937 F.2d 780, 788 [(2d Cir. 1991)].) At the time of repossession, three monthly payments of $333.68 were unpaid for a total due of $1,001.04; and the Contract provided for a 10% late charge for each payment not made when due, for an additional charge of $100.11. Clover is entitled, therefore, to $1,101.15 for payments in default and related late charges.

The Contract also provides that the debtor must pay the "cost of repossession, storage and preparation for sale" and "an attorney's fee of up to 15% of the amount due . . . unless the court sets a smaller fee." Clover Commercial includes $325 in its computation of the deficiency, which apparently is intended as a charge for repossession, storage, and preparation charges, but, unlike the late charge, the amount is not specified in the Contract, and no evidence was submitted to explain or support it. Similarly, there was no evidence to support an award of attorney fees. (See Orix Credit Alliance, Inc. v. Grace Industries, Inc., 261 A.D.2d 521, 521-522, 690 N.Y.S.2d 651 [2d Dept. 1999].)

Coxall's Claim Against Clover

Jason Coxall no longer has his Lexus. His down payment was $3,798.25, and he owes $1,101.15 for overdue payments. In effect, approximately four months' use of the vehicle has cost him approximately $5,000, not including alleged repair and towing expenses. Of course, "the debtor who precipitated the sale by defaulting on a debt is certainly not to be freed lightly from default." (Siemens Credit Corp. v. Marvik Colour, Inc., 859 F. Supp. at 692.) Nonetheless, does Mr. Coxall have a remedy for Clover Commercial's failure to comply with Article 9, beyond being relieved of any liability for a deficiency?

"Under common law, prior to the enactment of the Uniform Conditional Sales Act, the seller was under no obligation upon the retaking of the goods on buyer's default to make return of partial payment or any part thereof." (Laufer v. Burghard, 146 Misc. 39, 42, 261 N.Y.S. 364 [Sup. Ct., Erie County 1932].) "A retaking of the property by a conditional vendor is not a rescission of the contract so as to require the vendor to place the buyer in a former position and return the consideration received under the contract." (Id. at 45, 261 N.Y.S. 364.) If, however, the repossessing seller failed to comply with obligations imposed by statute after taking possession, a return of all or part of the payments made by the buyer was mandated. (See Rivara v. James Stewart & Co., 241 N.Y. 259, 262, 267, 149 N.E. 851 [1925], aff'd, 274 U.S. 614, 47 S. Ct. 718, 71 L. Ed. 1234 [1927]; La Rocca Builders, Inc. v. Sanders, 230 A.D. 594, 597, 245 N.Y.S. 262 [1st Dept. 1930].)

Under Article 9, "a person is liable for damages in the amount of any loss caused by a failure to comply" with the statute. (Revised UCC §9-625[(b)]; see also Former UCC §9-507[(1)].) "Damages for violation of the requirements of [the statute] . . . are those reasonably calculated to put an eligible claimant in the position that it would have occupied had no violation occurred." (Official Comment 3 to Revised UCC §9-625.) There are, however, both supplements to and limitations on this general liability principle.

"[A] debtor . . . whose deficiency is eliminated or reduced under Section 9-626 may not otherwise recover . . . for noncompliance with the provisions . . . relating to enforcement." (Revised UCC §9-625[(d)].) This provision "eliminates the possibility of double recovery or other overcompensation," but "[b]ecause Section 9-626 does not apply to consumer transactions, the statute is silent as to whether a double recovery or other overcompensation is possible in a consumer transaction." (Official Comment 3 to Revised UCC §9-625.) Respected commentators "argue that double recoveries should be denied in consumer cases too." (See White and Summers, Uniform Commercial Code, §25-13, at 919 [5th ed. 2000].[6])

The law in New York under Former Article 9 allowed a debtor to recover any loss resulting from the secured party's noncompliance, even though the secured party was deprived of recovery for a deficiency because of noncompliance. (See Liberty Bank v. Thomas, 222 A.D.2d 1019, 635 N.Y.S.2d 912 [4th Dept. 1995].) Here again, since Revised Article 9 does not displace existing law for consumer transactions, this Court must apply the pre-revision law. At the least, denial of a deficiency to the noncomplying secured party should not preclude the debtor's recovery of the statutorily-prescribed minimum damages. (See Matter of Calvin Angel, 142 B.R. 194, 198-99 [S.D. Ohio 1992]; Wilmington Trust Co. v. Conner, 415 A.2d 773, 781 [Del. 1980].)

Revised Article 9, like its predecessor, "provides a minimum, statutory, damage recovery for a debtor . . . in a consumer goods transaction" that "is

6. [Now §26-13 at 1358 (6th ed. 2010) — Eds.]

designed to ensure that every noncompliance . . . in a consumer-goods transaction results in liability." (See Revised UCC §9-625[(c)]; Official Comment 4 to Revised UCC §9-625; Former UCC §9-507[(1)].) The debtor may recover "an amount not less than the credit service charge plus 10 percent of the principal amount of the obligation or the time-price differential plus 10 percent of the cash price." (Revised UCC §9-625[c].) The statute "does not include a definition or explanation of the terms" used in the damage formula, but "leaves their construction and application to the court, taking into account the . . . purpose of providing a minimum recovery." (Official Comment 4 to Revised UCC §9-625.)

Here, according to the Contract, the time-price differential is $1,036.24 and 10% of the cash price is $810, for a total statutory damage recovery of $1,846.24. Mr. Coxall is entitled to this recovery even if he sustained no actual loss from Clover Commercial's failure to comply with Article 9. (See Davenport v. Chrysler Credit Corp., 818 S.W.2d 23, 31-32 [Tenn. App. 1991]; Erdmann v. Rants, 442 N.W.2d 441, 443 [N.D. 1989]; First City Bank-Farmers Branch, Texas v. Guex, 677 S.W.2d 25, 29 [Tex. 1984].) But, although Clover Commercial failed to comply with both the requirement for reasonable notification and the requirement for a commercially reasonable disposition, it is obligated for only one statutory damage remedy. (See Dunn v. Security Pacific Housing Services, 1996 Del. Super. Lexis 428, *10-11 [Super. Ct., New Castle]; Crosby v. Basin Motor Co., 83 N.M. 77, 79, 488 P.2d 127, 129 [1971].)

Mr. Coxall would also be entitled to the value of the personal property that, he says, was contained in the vehicle when it was repossessed, but which has not been returned to him. (See Fitzpatrick v. Bank of New York, 125 Misc. 2d 1069, 1076, 480 N.Y.S.2d 864 [Civ. Ct., Queens County 1984].) But Mr. Coxall introduced no admissible evidence of that value.

Disposition

In Action No. 1, judgment is rendered in favor of Jason Coxall against Clover Commercial for $745.09, representing the difference between Mr. Coxall's statutory damages of $1,846.24 and Clover's Commercial's damages for breach of the Contract of $1,101.15, with interest from March 3, 2003, plus costs. . . .

Military Loans. Ever since the Civil War federal law has appreciated that those called to military active duty have a reduced income and may have significant difficulty meeting current payment obligations. Consequently, the Servicemembers Civil Relief Act, 50 App. U.S.C. §§501 et seq., has broad rules covering all loans to servicemembers, protecting them, for example, from default judgments, evictions, and termination of various benefits such as life insurance without adequate notice. It converts all existing loan interest rates to a maximum of 6 percent during the period of active duty, and excuses any requirement for ever paying the excused interest (so that payments reduce principal). Many states have statutes protecting members of the military in their financial dealings, and these statutes frequently give terrific protection to service personnel during their military career.

IV. REDEMPTION AND STRICT FORECLOSURE

Centuries of property law have established the right of the defaulting debtor to recover the collateral by curing the default. The courts of equity first enforced this right of *redemption,* and it has become a common maxim that the courts will not permit anything to "clog the equity of redemption." See G. Gilmore §43.2; Indianapolis Morris Plan Corp. v. Karlen, 28 N.Y.2d 30, 268 N.E.2d 632, 319 N.Y.S.2d 831 (1971).

Hutzenbiler v. RJC Investment, Inc.

Supreme Court of Montana, 2019
395 Mont. 250, 439 P.3d 378

Justice Beth Baker delivered the Opinion of the Court.

¶1 Charlene Hutzenbiler appeals an order of the Thirteenth Judicial District Court, Yellowstone County, granting RJC Investment, Inc. ("RJC") summary judgment on Hutzenbiler's claim to an accounting and recovery of surplus proceeds on the resale of her mobile home after she returned it to RJC. We restate the dispositive issues as follows:

1. Did the Release between Hutzenbiler and RJC terminate application of the Uniform Commercial Code's requirement for an accounting and surplus after RJC sold the collateral?
2. Did the District Court err in determining that the Release constituted an acceptance of the collateral in full satisfaction of Hutzenbiler's secured obligation?
3. Is RJC entitled to summary judgment on other statutory or equitable grounds?

We reverse the District Court's summary judgment order and remand for further proceedings.

PROCEDURAL AND FACTUAL BACKGROUND

¶2 Hutzenbiler entered into an Installment Sale Contract and Security Agreement (the "Contract") with Cherry Creek Development, Inc. ("Cherry Creek") to purchase a mobile home in March 2010. The purchase price of the mobile home was $47,500. Cherry Creek retained a security interest in the mobile home to secure Hutzenbiler's payment obligations. Hutzenbiler paid $3,800 down and agreed to pay $483 per month for fifteen years to pay off the remaining $43,700 balance, with payments due on the 19th of each month. The Contract provided that a late fee would be charged for any payment that was five days past the due date. Cherry Creek assigned the Contract to its parent company, RJC.

¶3 Hutzenbiler acknowledges that she made some of her payments late but disputes that she "missed" payments or was in default. On December 10, 2015, Hutzenbiler vacated the mobile home and allowed RJC to take possession of it. Hutzenbiler signed a Full Release of Contract (the "Release"), under which she relinquished all rights to the mobile home. The Release reads in its entirety as follows:

> I/We *Charlene L. Hutzenbiler* herby [sic] release all rights to the manufactured home located at 8 Lapin St. N, Billings, MT 59105 described by serial number HY12485 am [sic] releasing myself and removing my name off of the contract currently in place with RJC Investment, Inc. and Cherry Creek Development, Inc. I am fully aware that by signing this I am completely removing my rights to all aspects of the home and I will not be entitled to any rights of this home or refund of all money applied to the home including but not limited to the down payment, and all payments made on the home and the lot up to this day.

(Emphasis in original). The Release was executed by Hutzenbiler and by Roy Clause, as President of Cherry Creek and RJC. When the Release was executed, Hutzenbiler owed $34,499.01 under the Contract.

¶4 RJC resold the mobile home in February 2016, without notice to Hutzenbiler, for $45,500. Hutzenbiler's counsel requested an accounting of the sale from RJC, but RJC failed to provide one. RJC did not refund any surplus to Hutzenbiler and claims none was owed. Hutzenbiler sued RJC for failing to provide for an accounting of the results of the resale of the mobile home pursuant to §30-9A-616(2)(a)(ii), MCA; for failing to pay her the surplus proceeds of the mobile home's resale pursuant to §30-9A-615(4)(a), MCA; and alleging that the trial court should apply all her payments to the principal, providing for a larger surplus, because RJC failed to comply with the Retail Installment Sales Act (RISA), Title 31, chapter 1, part 2, MCA.

¶5 RJC moved for summary judgment, asserting that the Release terminated the underlying Contract and any further application of Uniform

Commercial Code ("U.C.C.") Article 9.[1] RJC argued that even if Article 9 still applied, the parties' execution of the Release constituted an acceptance of the mobile home in full satisfaction of Hutzenbiler's obligations. RJC argued in the alternative that, because RJC was unaware that Hutzenbiler remained a debtor, it could not remain liable under the U.C.C. RJC alternatively argued that Hutzenbiler was equitably estopped from pursuing her claims because she made false representations that she would not pursue her rights under the U.C.C. when she signed the Release.

¶6 The District Court granted RJC's motion for summary judgment, holding that Hutzenbiler did not state a claim upon which relief could be granted under any reading of Montana law. The court reasoned that "[t]his identical issue was previously heard . . . in Kapor v. RJC Investment, Inc.," Thirteenth Judicial District Cause No. DV 17-0311, and concurred with the district court's opinion and order in that case. The District Court did not address RJC's other alternative arguments.

Standard of Review

¶7 We review de novo a district court's grant or denial of summary judgment, applying the criteria of M. R. Civ. P. 56. Yorlum Props., Ltd. v. Lincoln County, 2013 MT 298, ¶12, 372 Mont. 159, 311 P.3d 748. Summary judgment "should be rendered if the pleadings, the discovery and disclosure materials on file, and any affidavits show that there is no genuine issue as to any material fact and that the movant is entitled to judgment as a matter of law." M. R. Civ. P. 56(c)(3). We view the evidence in the light most favorable to the party opposing summary judgment, and we draw reasonable inferences in favor of the party opposing summary judgment. Maier v. Wilson, 2017 MT 316, ¶15, 390 Mont. 43, 409 P.3d 878. Where the material facts are undisputed, we "identify the applicable law, apply it to the uncontroverted facts, and determine who prevails." *Yorlum Props., Ltd.*, ¶12. The determination whether a party is entitled to judgment on the facts is a conclusion of law, which we review for correctness. *Yorlum Props., Ltd.*, ¶12.

Discussion

¶8 1. Did the Release between Hutzenbiler and RJC terminate application of the Uniform Commercial Code's requirement for an accounting and surplus after RJC sold the collateral?

¶9 The District Court held that Article 9 did not apply after the Release was executed because it severed all security interests created under the original contract. Because the U.C.C. no longer applied, the District Court determined that Hutzenbiler had no right to any surplus from the repossession sale. Hutzenbiler argues that Article 9 imposed duties on RJC that survive the discharge of the security interest, including the duty to account for the proceeds and expenses of the sale and the duty to pay her the alleged surplus. The parties disputed facts concerning Hutzenbiler's payments on the contract. Because it addressed the issues the parties presented and concluded that Article 9 no longer applied after the Release was executed, the District Court did not determine whether Hutzenbiler was in default or analyze her claims further.

¶10 *Kapor* involved similar facts and a virtually identical release to the one Hutzenbiler signed. In *Kapor,* the trial court granted RJC's motion for summary judgment after it determined that Article 9 no longer applied once Kapor executed the release, and even if Article 9 applied, the release constituted an acceptance of the collateral in full satisfaction of the secured obligation. We held, "Except as allowed under other U.C.C. provisions, [a party's] discharge or release [of obligations under a secured transaction for the sale of a mobile home] cannot [] waive or vary [the creditor's] duty to account for or [the debtor's] right to receive any surplus proceeds from the resale of the mobile home." *Kapor,* ¶13. Sections 30-9A-608(1)(d) and -615(4)(a), MCA, provide that a "secured party shall account to and pay a debtor for any surplus" from proceeds of the sale of collateral. Section 30-9A-602(5), MCA, expressly forbids a debtor from waiving protections the U.C.C. provides for payment of surplus proceeds of collateral.

¶11 Pursuant to §30-9A-616(2), MCA, when the debtor is entitled to a surplus or a consumer is liable for a deficiency, a creditor must provide a debtor with an explanation of how the proceeds obtained from the sale of collateral were applied to the debtor's account. In every consumer-goods transaction, the debtor is entitled to know the amount of a surplus or deficiency and the basis upon which it was calculated. Section 60-9A-616, MCA, cmt. 2. Section 30-9A-210(2)(a), MCA, also provides that a secured party is required to provide an accounting explanation within 14 days of receipt of request. Section 30-9A-602(2) and -602(9), MCA, expressly forbid either party from waiving the protections the U.C.C. provides for the accounting explanation.

¶12 We held in *Kapor* that "[t]he Release did not, by its express terms, lift the parties' relationship from that of debtor and creditor under U.C.C. Article 9 or render obsolete the protections afforded a debtor under §§30-9A-608(1)(d) and -615(4)(a), MCA." *Kapor,* ¶14. "Article 9 may still require the creditor to account for a surplus realized from the collection of an account or from the disposition of the collateral." *Kapor,* ¶14 (internal citation and quotations omitted).

¶13 The Release that Hutzenbiler executed is substantively identical to the release that Kapor executed. The Release cannot waive or vary Hutzenbiler's right to an accounting or to receive surplus proceeds, if any, from resale of the mobile home. The Release also did not terminate the application of the U.C.C. altogether. The parties were free to discharge their obligations to one another, but that discharge could not waive the protections provided in the U.C.C. *Kapor*, ¶13. *Kapor* is controlling.

¶14 The statutory requirements are triggered when the debtor defaults. See §30-9A-601, MCA (explaining that "this part" governs the secured party's rights after default). That question remains to be decided here. Despite the Dissent's invitation, we decline to conduct an independent review of the summary judgment record to decide sua sponte whether Hutzenbiler was in default. That issue was not litigated by the parties, developed in the record, decided by the District Court, or briefed on appeal. See Pilgeram v. GreenPoint Mortg. Funding, Inc., 2013 MT 354, ¶¶20-21, 373 Mont. 1, 313 P.3d 839 (explaining that we do not consider new arguments for the first time on appeal because it would be fundamentally unfair to the parties).

¶15 The record indicates that the parties disputed whether Hutzenbiler had defaulted on her obligations, but neither party made an argument regarding the effect of any default or lack thereof. Clause stated in his affidavit that, "From 2013 through 2015, Hutzenbiler repeatedly failed to meet her obligations under the Contract, and failed to make her monthly payments on numerous occasions." (Emphasis added.) Hutzenbiler asserted in her summary judgment response that "[t]here are disputed facts concerning the Plaintiff's payments on the contract," and that she had not "missed" payments as averred by Clause but had made all of her payments within the "statutory" grace period. It seems odd, indeed, that Hutzenbiler would maintain she never defaulted when that well could defeat her U.C.C. arguments. Also odd, if in fact supported in the existing record, is that RJC has not argued Hutzenbiler's lack of default to refute her claims. We simply take the case in the procedural posture presented and will not speculate on the arguments, if any, the parties may have regarding Hutzenbiler's default or its effect on the statutory requirements. The District Court erred when it granted RJC summary judgment on the ground that the U.C.C. no longer applied after Hutzenbiler signed the Release.

¶16 2. Did the District Court err in determining that the Release constituted an acceptance of the collateral in full satisfaction of Hutzenbiler's secured obligation?

¶17 The District Court alternatively held that even if Article 9 does apply, the Release constituted full satisfaction of the parties' respective obligations under the contract in accordance with §30-9A-620(1), MCA. Hutzenbiler argues that the Release did not satisfy the requirements of strict foreclosure because the Release did not contain any language releasing the claims of RJC. Hutzenbiler adds that the Release was signed before she was in default, and strict foreclosure therefore is not permitted. RJC responds that the undisputed facts establish strict foreclosure in compliance with the statute.

¶18 Addressing the same arguments on identical release language, we held in *Kapor*: "[T]here must be mutual agreement between the parties; the statute does not allow a creditor to obtain a debtor's relinquishment of rights without accepting the collateral in satisfaction of the debt and waiving its right to pursue a deficiency." *Kapor,* ¶24. "Although explicit language may not be required, the document must indicate at least that [the creditor] was giving up its right to seek a deficiency from [the debtor] or was accepting the collateral in full satisfaction of the obligation." *Kapor,* ¶27.

¶19 *Kapor* requires a like conclusion in this case. Whether Hutzenbiler was or was not in default, the plain language of the Release is insufficient for strict foreclosure. As in *Kapor,* RJC did not include any language in the Release that it accepted the collateral in satisfaction of the obligation, that it released Hutzenbiler from all her obligations, or that it relinquished its right to pursue a deficiency judgment against her if the mobile home sold for less than the owed principal. The District Court erred in granting RJC summary judgment on the ground that RJC satisfied the elements of the acceptance of collateral in full satisfaction pursuant to §30-9A-620, MCA.

¶20 3. Is RJC entitled to summary judgment on other statutory or equitable grounds?

¶21 RJC argues that the District Court could have granted summary judgment on the alternative ground that the exculpatory provision of the U.C.C. absolved RJC of any liability because RJC had no reason to believe Hutzenbiler remained a debtor after signing the Release. Section 30-9A-628(2), MCA, provides that a secured party is not liable because of its status as a secured party unless the secured party knows that the person is a debtor. See also §30-9A-605(1), MCA. The Official Comments explain that without this provision "a secured party could incur liability to unknown persons and unknown circumstances that would not allow the secured party to protect itself." Section 30-9A-628, MCA, cmt. 2. An example of an unknown debtor is when "a secured party may be unaware that the original debtor has sold the collateral subject to the security interest and that the new owner has become the debtor." Section 30-9A-605, MCA, cmt. 2. Hutzenbiler was not an "unknown" debtor. Cherry Creek assigned RJC the Contract that Cherry Creek and Hutzenbiler entered to create the debtor/creditor relationship, and RJC collected payments from Hutzenbiler under that Contract. RJC is not entitled to summary judgment under §§30-9A-605(1) or -628(2), MCA.

¶22 Finally, RJC argues that the District Court also could have granted RJC summary judgment on the ground that Hutzenbiler was equitably estopped from asserting her claims because of her alleged false representations through the Release that she would not seek remedies under the U.C.C. We resolved this issue in *Kapor,* ¶¶31-37. The same holding applies. RJC is not entitled to summary judgment on other statutory or equitable grounds.

CONCLUSION

¶23 The District Court erred in granting RJC summary judgment on the grounds that Article 9 no longer applied after the Release was signed and that the Release satisfied the elements of strict foreclosure. Because the District Court held the U.C.C. inapplicable, it did not reach the merits of Hutzenbiler's claims; nor do we. The case is remanded to the District Court for further proceedings consistent with this Opinion.

We Concur:
MIKE MCGRATH, C.J.
INGRID GUSTAFSON, J.
JAMES JEREMIAH SHEA, J.

Justice LAURIE MCKINNON, dissenting.

¶24 I agree with the Court that the District Court erred when it failed to first determine whether Hutzenbiler was in default before holding Title 30, MCA, did not apply to Hutzenbiler and RJC's relationship after they signed the Full Release of Contract ("2015 Agreement"). Notwithstanding, based on the existing record, I would hold Hutzenbiler was not in default when she signed the 2015 Agreement. Therefore, she is not entitled to any surplus from the mobile home's sale provided for under Title 30, chapter 9A, part 6, MCA ("Part 6"), which governs default in secured transactions. Furthermore, even if Hutzenbiler was in default, then the District Court's alternative conclusion—that Hutzenbiler and RJC executed a strict foreclosure—was correct. Accordingly, I would affirm the District Court's order granting summary judgment in favor of RJC.

¶25 The Court states that the District Court must decide the question of default on remand, but it provides no guidance to the District Court for how to evaluate whether Hutzenbiler was in default, and it fails to paint a clear picture of why the issue of default is so important to begin with. Thus, I will explain its importance here: if Hutzenbiler was not in default when she executed the 2015 Agreement, she is not entitled to any surplus from the mobile home's sale. Further, the parties do not dispute any material facts, and Hutzenbiler's payment record and security agreement are part of the record on appeal. The record establishes that Hutzenbiler was not in default when she executed the 2015 Agreement. Where the material facts are undisputed, we "identify the applicable law, apply it to the uncontroverted facts, and determine who prevails." *Yorlum Props., Ltd.*, ¶12.

¶26 Part 6 governs default in secured transactions. Default triggers certain rights provided under Part 6 for both secured parties and debtors, but those rights do not exist before default. Section 30-9A-601(4), MCA ("Except as otherwise provided . . . *after default*, a debtor and an obligor have the rights provided in this part and by agreement of the parties." (emphasis added)); §30-9A-601(1), MCA ("*After default,* a secured party has the rights provided in this part and, except as otherwise provided in [§]30-9A-602, [MCA,] those provided by agreement of the parties." (emphasis added)). For example, a secured party may take possession of collateral after default, but it may not do so before. Section 30-9A-609(1)(a), MCA; *see Padin v. Oyster Point Dodge,* 397 F. Supp. 2d 712, 725 (E.D. Va. 2005) (interpreting Virginia's version of §30-9A-609, MCA: "A secured party may take possession of the collateral, but only after default." (emphasis in original)). Similarly, a debtor is only entitled to a surplus under §§30-9A-615 and 616, MCA, after default, because the statutory mechanisms that lead to a surplus—for example, the secured party's possession and disposition of the collateral under §§30-9A-609 and 610, MCA—can only occur after the debtor defaults.

¶27 Part 6 provides fundamental protections for debtors and specific statutory procedures that secured parties must follow to possess and dispose of collateral after a debtor is in default. These protections are especially important because a debtor in default is in a substantially inferior bargaining position. See Walker v. Grant Cty. Sav. & Loan Ass'n, 304 Ark. 571, 803 S.W.2d 913, 916 (1991) ("One clear policy reason underlying Article 9 default provisions is the protection of post default debtors from the potential of overbearing tactics and intimidation by secured parties. After default the secured party is unquestionably in a position of control and even dominance."). However, when the debtor is not in default, the debtor and creditor can mutually agree to exchange the collateral and terminate their security agreement without triggering Part 6. And this makes sense: when the debtor is not in default—when the parties hold more balanced positions of bargaining power—the parties must be able to exchange the collateral, terminate their security agreement, and go their separate ways without concern that the default procedures of Part 6 will impede their ability to do so. Debtors have a significant interest in avoiding the negative consequences of a default proceeding.

¶28 How courts should define default varies from case to case. Neither Title 30, MCA, nor the UCC define the term "default." Black's Law Dictionary defines "default" as "[t]he omission or failure to perform a legal or contractual duty; esp., the failure to pay a debt when due." Default, Black's Law Dictionary (10th ed. 2014). In most cases, however, default is simply "whatever the security agreement says it is." 4 James J. White, Robert S. Summers, & Robert A. Hillman, Uniform Commercial Code: Practitioner Treatise Series §34:5, at 530 (6th ed. 2015) (internal quotations and footnotes omitted). Thus, in order to determine whether a party is in default, courts should look first to the security agreement itself. Here, the parties' original security agreement ("2010 Security Agreement") states what the parties agreed would constitute a default: "Default. If [Hutzenbiler] fails to perform any of the covenants or promises called for hereunder, such failure shall, at the election of [RJC], constitute a default in performance of this agreement."

¶29 Notwithstanding, a security agreement may provide debtors with an opportunity to cure a default, acting to reverse the events that led to it. When a debtor cures a default, the debtor returns both parties to their pre-default positions. See In re Taddeo, 685 F.2d 24, 26-27 (2d Cir. 1982) ("Curing a default commonly means taking care of the triggering event and returning to pre-default conditions. The consequences are thus nullified."). Accordingly, an effective cure eliminates a default and its attendant consequences. After a debtor cures, the debtor is simply no longer in default. In re Entz-White Lumber & Supply, Inc., 850 F.2d 1338, 1342 (9th Cir. 1988) (holding that after a debtor cures the default, the debtor "is entitled to avoid all consequences of the default . . ."). Courts sometimes refer to the period of time the security agreement allows the debtor to cure a default as a "cure period." See Rathblott v. PeopleStrategy, Inc., 2016 WL 861348, *3, 2016 U.S. Dist. LEXIS 28864, at *8-9 (E.D. Pa. 2016).

¶30 The 2010 Security Agreement provides the following cure period: "If [Hutzenbiler] fails to cure any such default within THIRTY (30) days after written notice thereof to [Hutzenbiler], [RJC] may, without further notice or period of grace, declare the entire unpaid balance of the purchase price, principal and accrued interest, immediately due and payable." In other words, if Hutzenbiler defaulted—for example, by failing to make a payment—the 2010 Security Agreement gave Hutzenbiler thirty days to cure the default before RJC could accelerate her outstanding debt. And once Hutzenbiler cured it, she was no longer in default.

¶31 In the District Court, while the parties disputed whether Hutzenbiler was in default when she signed the 2015 Agreement—a legal conclusion—they did not dispute any material facts. Specifically, they did not dispute Hutzenbiler's payment history. Hutzenbiler failed to make timely payments several times over the course of her relationship with RJC. She ultimately made every payment within 30 days of the due date, though, curing each default. She wrote a check for what would become her final payment to RJC on November 23, 2015. After RJC deposited Hutzenbiler's check, Hutzenbiler's account was current, and the next payment was not due under the terms of the 2010 Security Agreement until December 19, 2015. That fact is crucial—because Hutzenbiler's account was current, she was not in default when she executed the 2015 Agreement. Through the 2015 Agreement, Hutzenbiler agreed to transfer ownership of the mobile home to RJC in exchange for terminating the 2010 Security Agreement and forgiving the remaining balance Hutzenbiler owed RJC. And Hutzenbiler executed the 2015 Agreement when she was not in default—when she and RJC shared more balanced positions of bargaining power. Accordingly,

I would hold Hutzenbiler is not entitled to whatever surplus RJC derived from the mobile home's sale.

¶32 Finally, even if Hutzenbiler was in default, I would hold Hutzenbiler and RJC executed a strict foreclosure under §30-9A-620, MCA, following similar reasoning from my dissent in *Kapor.* See *Kapor,* ¶¶46-61 (McKinnon, J., dissenting). In the 2015 Agreement, the phrase "releasing myself and removing my name off the contract currently in place with RJC" is clear and unambiguous language indicating the parties were agreeing to release Hutzenbiler from her obligations and terminate their contract. By holding that RJC did not consent to accepting the mobile home in satisfaction of Hutzenbiler's obligation, the Court once again elevates form over substance, as it did in *Kapor.* See *Kapor,* ¶¶49, 54, 61 (McKinnon, J., dissenting). Even if the 2015 Agreement's language is ambiguous, the surrounding circumstances—just like the circumstances in *Kapor*—indicate Hutzenbiler was attempting to give up any rights she had in the mobile home, transfer her rights to RJC, and terminate the security agreement with RJC, just like a debtor would in strict foreclosure. The 2015 Agreement could have no other purpose but to relieve the parties from the terms of the security agreement. Like *Kapor,* this case simply involves a debtor and a creditor, through a signed agreement, attempting to consent to a transfer of collateral to the creditor in full satisfaction of the debtor's obligation. See §30-9A-620, MCA. The Court, however, renders the 2015 Agreement meaningless.

¶33 From the record before the Court, including the 2010 Security Agreement and Hutzenbiler's payment history, Hutzenbiler was not in default when she executed the 2015 Agreement. I disagree with the Court that remand is necessary to resolve the issue. Hutzenbiler is not entitled to any surplus RJC derived from the mobile home's sale under Part 6, and specifically §§30-9A-615 and -616, MCA. Furthermore, even if Part 6 applies, Hutzenbiler and RJC executed a strict foreclosure. I would affirm the District Court's conclusion that Hutzenbiler was not entitled to a surplus. I dissent.

Justice Jim Rice and Justice Dirk Sandefur join in the dissenting Opinion of Justice McKinnon.

PROBLEM 443

When Paul Morphy borrowed $2,000 from the Lasker State Bank in order to finance a trip to Iceland, the bank made him sign an agreement giving the bank a security interest in Paul's private yacht. He agreed to repay the loan at the rate of $200 a month. He took the trip and on his return made the first payment on time. He failed to make the second payment on the due date, and the next day the bank repossessed the yacht. Paul raced to the bank with the late payment. He had $200 in cash, which he tendered. The bank refused to take the money. The bank's loan officer, a Mr. Anderssen, pointed to an acceleration clause in the security agreement that made the entire amount due if a payment was missed. Anderssen demanded the total unpaid balance. Need Paul pay off everything? See §9-623 along with its Official Comment 2. There is pre-revision authority for the proposition that misdescription of the redemption rights bars any action for the deficiency. First Natl. Bank v. DiDomenico, 302 Md. 290, 487 A.2d 646 (1985).

Strict foreclosure occurs when the creditor repossesses the collateral and simply keeps it in satisfaction of the debt. No deficiency is sought. The debtor (or other creditors having junior security interests) may not be pleased with strict foreclosure in all situations. Read §§9-620 to 9-622.

PROBLEM 444

Art Auctions, Inc. (AAI), sold Dudley Collector a $5,000 painting by Smock Pallet, a famous artist. Dudley paid $1,000 down and agreed to pay over $1,000 a month thereafter. The finance charge was $151.20; the annual percentage rate was 18 percent. The contract contained a clause saying that in the event of default, AAI could repossess the painting and keep it without reselling it or, at its option, could resell it and sue for the deficiency. Dudley made three more payments and then missed the last one, being temporarily short of funds. AAI, without notice, sent one of its agents to Dudley's home. Dudley's teenage son let the agent in, and he simply removed the painting from the wall and walked out, saying, "Thank you." Dudley immediately tendered $1,000 to AAI and demanded the painting. AAI refused (the painting is now worth $20,000). Four months later, Dudley filed suit. What is the basis of his cause of action, and to what relief is he entitled? See §§9-620(e) and (f), 9-625(b) and (c).

Here the creditor will make a huge profit by the use of strict foreclosure. Is that relevant? See McDonald v. Yarchenko, 2013 WL 3809512 (D. Or. 2013). Must the notice of strict foreclosure inform the debtor of the need to object within 20 days? See Born v. Born, 304 Kan. 542 (2016).

If Dudley had made only one payment and then defaulted, causing AAI to repossess, could AAI have sent him a proposal that it would keep the painting and forgive *half* the remaining debt only? See §9-620(g).

PROBLEM 445

When Repossession Finance Company declared a default and repossessed all the office equipment of attorney Portia Moot, as allowed by the security agreement, the company then did nothing with the collateral except let it sit in a storage room for 17 months. Finally, it conducted a resale with appropriate notices and then sued Portia for the deficiency. She defended by arguing that actions speak louder than words and that, in effect, by doing nothing for such a long period, the finance company had constructively elected strict foreclosure and had forfeited any right to a deficiency. Is this correct? See Official Comment 5 to §9-620; Jefferson Loan Co., Inc. v. Session, 397 N.J. Super. 520, 938 A.2d 169 (2008) (failure to resell the repossessed vehicle for four years deemed "commercially unreasonable"); but see Key Equipment Fin. v. Southwest Contracting, Inc., 2015 WL 5159073 (D. Colo. 2015) (resale almost two years after repossession held commercially reasonable where explainable). Can a creditor be liable where for months it declined to repossess the collateral on request of debtor, then eventually repossessed and sold? See WM Capital Partners, LLC v. Thornton, 525 S.W.3d 265 (Tenn. Ct. App. 2016).

Reeves v. Foutz & Tanner, Inc.

New Mexico Supreme Court, 1980
94 N.M. 760, 617 P.2d 149

Sosa, C.J.

These suits were brought as separate actions but were consolidated by the Court of Appeals because the issues were essentially the same. The trial court held for plaintiffs, the Court of Appeals reversed, and we reverse the Court of Appeals.

Plaintiffs Reeves and Begay are uneducated Navajo Indians whose ability to understand English and commercial matters [is] limited. Each of them pawned jewelry with the defendant whereby they received a money loan in return for a promise to repay the loan in thirty days with interest. The Indian jewelry left with defendant as collateral was worth several times the amount borrowed. The plaintiffs defaulted and defendant sent each of them a notice of intent to retain the collateral, though Reeves claimed she never received notice. The retention was not objected to by either plaintiff. Defendant then sold the jewelry in the regular course of its business.

The question we are presented with is whether a secured party who sends a notice of intent to retain collateral, in conformance with §9-505 of the Uniform Commercial Code [now §9-620—Eds.], may sell the collateral in its regular course of business without complying with §9-504 [now §9-610—Eds.]? We decide that the secured party in this case could not sell the collateral without complying with §9-504.

The Uniform Commercial Code provides a secured party in possession with two courses of action upon the default of the debtor. Section 9-504 provides generally that the secured party may sell the collateral, but if the security interest secures an indebtedness, he must account to the debtor for any surplus (and the debtor must account for any deficiency). Section 9-505(2) provides the secured party with the alternative of retaining the collateral in satisfaction of the obligation. Under this section, the secured party must give written notice to the debtor that he intends to keep the collateral in satisfaction of the debt. The debtor is then given thirty days to object to the proposed retention and require the sale of the property according to §9-504.

In the present case we will assume that defendant gave proper notice to both Reeves and Begay of its intention to retain the collateral and that neither objected within thirty days. The trial court found that the defendant, in accordance with its normal business practice, then moved the jewelry into its sale inventory where it was sold to Joe Tanner, president of defendant corporation, or to Joe Tanner, Inc., a corporation owned by Joe Tanner and engaged in the sale of Indian jewelry. There was no accounting to plaintiffs of any surplus. The trial court also found that the defendant did not act in good faith in disposing of the jewelry, taking into consideration the relative bargaining power of the parties.

The defendant argues that the trial court should be reversed because it applied §9-504. It essentially argues that once it complied with §9-505(2) and sent the notice of intent to retain, it could do as it pleased with the property once the thirty days had elapsed without objection. The debtor-creditor relationship terminates, they claim, and the creditor becomes owner of the collateral.

The plaintiffs argue that the trial court was correct in applying §9-504 to require that any surplus from the sale of collateral be returned to the debtor. They urge that the intention of the secured party should control and where he intended to sell the collateral and did sell the collateral in the normal course of business, he must comply with §9-504 which governs sales of such collateral.

Neither party to this action has cited a case which has dealt directly with the issue here, but amicus has referred us to a Federal Trade Commission case on the subject where it was stated:

> In the Draftsmen's Statement of Reasons for 1972 Changes in Official Text, the Draftsmen summarized the purpose of §9-505 as follows:
>
> > Under subsection (2) [9-505(2)] of this section the secured party may in lieu of sale give notice to the debtor and certain other persons that he proposes to retain the collateral in lieu of sale.
>
> The foregoing language strongly suggests that waiver of surplus and deficiency rights under §9-505 is appropriate only when prompt resale of repossessed collateral in the ordinary course of business is not contemplated by the creditor. . . . That being so, use of §9-505 by an automobile dealer,

> particularly one not disposed to pursue deficiency judgments, would appear calculated solely to extinguish surplus rights of consumers, which we do not believe was the intended purpose of §9-505.

In the Matter of Ford Motor Company, Ford Motor Credit Company, and Francis Ford Inc., 93 F.T.C. Rep., 3 C.C.H. Trade Reg. Rep. 21756, 21767 (FTC Docket No. 9073, Sept. 21, 1979). The Commission went on to say that a creditor of this type is not foreclosed from using §9-505(2) so long as he intends to retain the collateral for his own use for the immediately foreseeable future, rather than to resell the collateral in the ordinary course of business. We agree with the approach used by the Federal Trade Commission.

The Court of Appeals reasoned that once the creditor elected to retain the collateral, and followed the mechanics of §9-505, the property became his to keep or to sell. We do not find fault with this reasoning, but it misses the point. Defendant can do as he pleases with the property, but where he intends to sell the property in the regular course of his business, which is in substance selling the property as contemplated by §9-504, he must account for a surplus in conformity with §9-504.

The defendant also argues that plaintiffs could have objected to the retention, thus forcing a sale in compliance with §9-504. But because there was never any actual intent to retain under §9-505(2), the failure of plaintiffs to timely object does not foreclose their claim. Moreover, the fact that plaintiffs could have objected means nothing in this context; their objection would only have served to cause a sale of the goods, which sale was already intended by defendant.

The defendant also argues that the trial court erred in finding that it acted in bad faith. We need not reach this question because bad faith was not material to the trial court's conclusions of law and judgment, which we find to be proper.

The defendant next claims error in the fact that the trial court allowed interest on the judgment from November 1, 1974. The date is the approximate day on which the loss took place and is apparently not controverted. The amount due the plaintiffs was a sum certain once the jewelry was sold, as calculated according to the provisions of §9-504. It was not error for the court to allow prejudgment interest or to allow interest as a portion of the damages. Sundt v. Tobin Quarries, 50 N.M. 254, 265, 175 P.2d 684, 690-691 (1946).

The judgment of the trial court is affirmed.

QUESTION

Is this case right? Does the court mean that any time the creditor elects to use §9-620, that creditor is forbidden the right to resell the collateral in the ordinary course of its business? After this decision, and assuming the court would reach the same result under the revision of Article 9, can it be said that §9-620 is a dead letter in New Mexico?

CHAPTER 27 ASSESSMENT: MULTIPLE CHOICE QUESTIONS

1. Ickx purchased a Le Mans hybrid car on credit from Formulaic Motors, signing a security agreement, which provided that default would occur upon failure to make scheduled payments, upon failure to maintain insurance, or upon other events. Ickx made all payments in timely fashion but carelessly let the insurance expire. One morning, the car had disappeared from in front of Ickx's home. Ickx reported the car stolen to the police, who responded that Formulaic Motors had repossessed the car. Repo agents routinely keep police informed of their activity, to avoid misunderstandings when they spirit vehicles away. Can Formulaic Motors legally repossess Ickx's car, when Ickx has not missed a single payment?
   a. No, Formulaic Motors violated Article 9 by making a commercially unreasonable repossession.
   b. No, a creditor cannot repossess the car where the debtor is not in default in payment.
   c. Yes. Upon default as defined by the parties, the creditor may take possession of the collateral.
   d. Yes. Until paid for, the car belongs to the seller, Formulaic Motors.

2. Ickx contends that, even if Formulaic Motors was entitled to repossess the car, it was required to give him prior notice. There was no emergency that prevented giving him notice and a car is not perishable goods, like fruit. Did Formulaic Motors violate Article 9 by failing to give prior notice?
   a. Yes, to take possession of the collateral, a creditor must give notice and proceed in a commercially reasonable manner.
   b. Yes, Article 9 requires good faith in all aspects, which would include giving prior notice of taking possession.
   c. No. Prior notice of repossession is not required by Article 9.
   d. No. Formulaic Motors can deal with its collateral as it pleases at all times.

3. Formulaic Motors repossessed the car of another defaulting debtor, Lauda. The security agreement provided that Formulaic Motors was permitted to use any means necessary to get the car, in the event of default. Formulaic Motors' agent broke through the garage door with an axe at 3 A.M., smashed the driver's side window of the car, pushed away Lauda, who had jumped out of bed, and warned neighbors with a megaphone not to intervene. Is Formulaic Motors in violation of Article 9?

a. No. Its actions were authorized by Article 9 and the contract between the parties.
b. Yes. It breached the peace and the contract provision that authorized such actions would not be effective.
c. No, creditors are entitled to repossess the collateral, including taking any necessary measures.
d. Yes. A creditor must get a court order in order to take possession of the collateral.

4. Formulaic Motors sent Prost notice that it would conduct a private sale of Prost's car, which Formulaic Motors had repossessed. The car had a market value of about $30,000 and the debt was $20,000. Formulaic Motors sold the car to a favorite customer for $21,000, applied $20,000 to the debt and gave Prost the surplus of $1,000. Prost is not satisfied. Is Formulaic Motors liable to Prost?
   a. No. Prost had notice the car was to be sold, so could have prevented the sale by paying off the debt.
   b. No. As with real estate foreclosure, sales of collateral are usually low-ball sales.
   c. Yes. Formulaic Motors failed to sell the collateral in a commercially reasonable manner.
   d. Yes. Formulaic Motors cannot sell someone else's car.

5. Jacob Finance held a security interest in the inventory of Marvelous Products, but with a subordinate position to another creditor, Esau Finance, who had filed an earlier financing statement. When Marvelous Products failed to make several payments, Jacob Finance took possession of the inventory. Before selling, Jacob Finance gave all required notices, including notice to Esau Finance. Jacob Finance sold the inventory and applied the proceeds of the sale to pay off most of the debt. Esau Finance demanded that Jacob Finance hand over enough of the sale proceeds to pay off Esau Finance, because Esau Finance had priority. Is the junior creditor required to give the senior creditor first cut of the proceeds of the collateral sale?
   a. Yes, that is exactly what priority means.
   b. No. The junior creditor may apply the proceeds to its own debt, and if there is money left over, return it to the debtor.
   c. Yes, the senior creditor is entitled to all of the sale proceeds.
   d. No. Article 9 is strictly first come, first served.

ANSWERS

1. *C* is the best answer. The creditor may take possession of the collateral upon default. Default is not defined in Article 9, rather should be defined

by the parties in the security agreement, which is normally drafted by the creditor. Contrary to *B*, the parties may define default to go well beyond a failure to make timely payments. There was a default here under the security agreement, so Formulaic Motors was entitled to take possession. Contrary to *A*, unlike an insecurity clause that requires the creditor to be insecure about its chances of being repaid, which would require a good faith or reasonable belief that the collateral was at risk, this default clause required only a lapse in the insurance.

2. *C* is the best answer. When a creditor *sells* the collateral, the creditor must give prior notice and proceed in a commercially reasonable manner. §9-610, §9-611. But those requirements do not apply to the preliminary act of taking possession, contrary to *A*. Rather, §9-609 permits a creditor to take possession, provided it does so without a breach of the peace. Repossession without notice is a common commercial practice permitted by Article 9, so would not be a violation of the obligation of good faith, contrary to *B*.
3. *B* is the best answer. This question illustrates two key rules. First, on default, a creditor may take possession of the collateral, without judicial process, provided there is no breach of the peace. §9-609. Second, most of the creditor's obligations with respect to default, such as the requirement that there be no breach of the peace in a repossession, may not be effectively varied in the parties' security agreement. §9-602(6).

   The requirement that there be no breach of the peace eliminates self-help repossessions for many creditors. If the collateral is inventory locked in a store or jewelry in the debtor's bedside drawer, then taking possession without the debtor's consent would require a breach of the peace. Such creditors are not out of luck. The debtor should abide by its contract and hand over the collateral. If not, creditors are well versed in obtaining rapid judicial relief.

   One important category of collateral, however, has wheels and is often left sitting invitingly on the street: vehicles. The creditor must still avoid breaching the peace. What constitutes a breach of the peace is often hard to determine. Is taking the car at 2 in the morning a breach of the peace, because neighbors might think it's a theft, or no breach, because it's a quiet time when likely no one will notice? This question used an extreme set of facts to make sure that there was a breach of the peace.
4. *C* is the best answer. A creditor may sell the collateral after default, contrary to *D*, but must do everything in a commercially reasonable manner. §9-610. Giving notice that a sale will occur is not sufficient, contrary to *A*. "Every aspect of a disposition of collateral, including the method, manner, time, place, and other terms, must be commercially reasonable." §9-610(b). Selling the car at a sub-market price to a favored party, without

any bidding or attempt to get better offers, would not even be close to a commercially reasonable sale.

Formulaic Auto will be liable for damages. See §9-625. Another issue is whether Prost will get the car back. A good faith buyer at an Article 9 sale takes free of the debtor's interest, even if the creditor violated Article 9. If the buyer was reasonably unaware of Formulaic Motor's violation, then the buyer may have acted in good faith. If the buyer knew Formulaic Motor was selling it someone else's car at a submarket price, then the buyer may have acted in bad faith.

5. *B* is the best answer, which may be a surprise until we review the relevant rules. When a creditor sells the collateral, the creditor must apply the proceeds to, in order, the expenses of sale, the creditor's debt, the debt of creditors *subordinate* to the selling creditor (none, in this case) and give any surplus to the debtor. §9-615(a). The selling creditor is not obliged to give anything to creditors who have priority to the selling creditor. In this case Jacob is not required to give any sale proceeds to Esau. It sounds illogical that the junior creditor may sell the collateral without giving any proceeds to the senior creditor, until we consider the effect of the sale. When a creditor sells the collateral, the buyer takes the property free of the interests of the selling creditor, any creditor subordinate to the selling creditor, and the debtor. §9-617(a). The interests of creditors senior to the selling creditor are unaffected and remain with the collateral in the hands of the buyer. In other words, the junior creditor cannot sell the collateral free of the senior interest, but does not have to give any of the sale proceeds to the senior creditor, who keeps its interest in the collateral. So in this case, Jacob sold the inventory subject to Esau's security interest but does not have to give any money to Esau, who can still seize the inventory and sell it if there is a default (and a default sale of the inventory no doubt triggered a default under Esau's security agreement).

   Another rule comes into play. A selling creditor (Jacob) would violate the warranty of title unless it informed the buyer of Esau's security interest before the sale, or the parties agreed to exclude that warranty. §9-610(d). Potential buyers would naturally discount the price they were willing to pay, because they would still have to see that Esau was paid off, to own the collateral free of claims. The best practice, if a junior creditor is selling, is to enter into an agreement with the senior creditor beforehand, in order to sell the goods free of all security interests for the best price.

APPENDIX

1990 VERSION OF §3-605

[This is the 1990 version of this section, which is the law in all jurisdictions (as of the summer of 2015) except Arkansas, District of Columbia, Indiana, Kentucky, Michigan, Minnesota, Mississippi, Nevada, New Mexico, Oklahoma, South Carolina, and Texas.]

§3-605. Discharge of Indorsers and Accommodation Parties

(a) In this section, the term "indorser" includes a drawer having the obligation described in Section 3-414(d).

(b) Discharge, under Section 3-604, of the obligation of a party to pay an instrument does not discharge the obligation of an indorser or accommodation party having a right of recourse against the discharged party.

(c) If a person entitled to enforce an instrument agrees, with or without consideration, to an extension of the due date of the obligation of a party to pay the instrument, the extension discharges an indorser or accommodation party having a right of recourse against the party whose obligation is extended to the extent the indorser or accommodation party proves that the extension caused loss to the indorser or accommodation party with respect to the right of recourse.

(d) If a person entitled to enforce an instrument agrees, with or without consideration, to a material modification of the obligation of a party other than an extension of the due date, the modification discharges the obligation of an indorser or accommodation party having a right of recourse against the person whose obligation is modified to the extent the modification causes loss to the indorser or accommodation party with respect to the right of recourse. The loss suffered by the indorser or accommodation party as a result of the modification is equal to the amount of the right of recourse unless the person enforcing the instrument proves that no loss was caused by the modification or that the loss caused by the modification was an amount less than the amount of the right of recourse.

(e) If the obligation of a party to pay an instrument is secured by an interest in collateral and a person entitled to enforce the instrument impairs the value of the interest in collateral, the obligation of an indorser or accommodation party having a right of recourse against the obligor is discharged to the extent of the impairment. The value of an interest in collateral is impaired to the extent (i) the value of the interest is reduced to an amount less than the amount of the right of recourse of the party asserting discharge, or (ii) the reduction in value of the interest causes an increase in the amount by which the amount of the right of recourse exceeds the value of the interest. The burden of proving impairment is on the party asserting discharge.

(f) If the obligation of a party is secured by an interest in collateral not provided by an accommodation party and a person entitled to enforce the instrument impairs the value of the interest in collateral, the obligation of any party who is jointly and severally liable with respect to the secured obligation is discharged to the extent the impairment causes the party asserting discharge to pay more than that party would have been obliged to pay, taking into account rights of contribution, if impairment had not occurred. If the party asserting discharge is an accommodation party not entitled to discharge under subsection (e), the party is deemed to have a right to contribution based on joint and several liability rather than a right to reimbursement. The burden of proving impairment is on the party asserting discharge.

(g) Under subsection (e) or (f), impairing value of an interest in collateral includes (i) failure to obtain or maintain perfection or recordation of the interest in collateral, (ii) release of collateral without substitution of collateral of equal value, (iii) failure to perform a duty to preserve the value of collateral owed, under Article 9 or other law, to a debtor or surety or other person secondarily liable, or (iv) failure to comply with applicable law in disposing of collateral.

(h) An accommodation party is not discharged under subsection (c), (d), or (e) unless the person entitled to enforce the instrument knows of the accommodation or has notice under Section 3-419(c) that the instrument was signed for accommodation.

(i) A party is not discharged under this section if (i) the party asserting discharge consents to the event or conduct that is the basis of the discharge, or (ii) the instrument or a separate agreement of the party provides for waiver of discharge under this section either specifically or by general language indicating that parties waive defenses based on suretyship or impairment of collateral.

OFFICIAL COMMENT

1. Section 3-605, which replaces former Section 3-606, can be illustrated by an example. Bank lends $10,000 to Borrower who signs a note under which Borrower is obliged to pay $10,000 to Bank on a due date stated in the note. Bank insists, however, that Accommodation Party also become liable to pay the note. Accommodation Party can incur this liability by signing the note as a co-maker or by indorsing the note. In either case the note is signed for accommodation and Borrower is the accommodated party. Rights and obligations of Accommodation Party in this case are stated in Section 3-419. Suppose that after the note is signed, Bank agrees to a modification of the rights and obligations between Bank and Borrower. For example, Bank agrees that Borrower may pay the note at some date after the due date, or that Borrower may discharge Borrower's $10,000 obligation to pay the note by paying Bank $3,000, or that Bank releases collateral given by Borrower to secure the note. Under the law of suretyship Borrower is usually referred to as the principal debtor and Accommodation Party is referred to as the surety. Under that law, the surety can be discharged under certain circumstances if changes of this kind are made by Bank, the creditor, without the consent of Accommodation Party, the surety. Rights of the surety to discharge in such cases are commonly referred to as suretyship defenses. Section 3-605 is concerned with this kind of problem in the context of a negotiable instrument to which the principal debtor and the surety are parties. But Section 3-605 has a wider scope. It also applies to indorsers who are not accommodation parties. Unless an indorser signs without recourse, the indorser's liability under Section 3-415(a) is that of a guarantor of payment. If Bank in our hypothetical case indorsed the note and transferred it to Second Bank, Bank has rights given to an indorser under Section 3-605 if it is Second Bank that

modifies rights and obligations of Borrower. Both accommodation parties and indorsers will be referred to in these Comments as sureties. The scope of Section 3-605 is also widened by subsection (e) which deals with rights of a non-accommodation party co-maker when collateral is impaired.

2. The importance of suretyship defenses is greatly diminished by the fact that they can be waived. The waiver is usually made by a provision in the note or other writing that represents the obligation of the principal debtor. It is standard practice to include a waiver of suretyship defenses in notes given to financial institutions or other commercial creditors. Section 3-605(i) allows waiver. Thus, Section 3-605 applies to the occasional case in which the creditor did not include a waiver clause in the instrument or in which the creditor did not obtain the permission of the surety to take the action that triggers the suretyship defense.

3. Subsection (b) addresses the effect of discharge under Section 3-604 of the principal debtor. In the hypothetical case stated in Comment 1, release of Borrower by Bank does not release Accommodation Party. As a practical matter, Bank will not gratuitously release Borrower. Discharge of Borrower normally would be part of a settlement with Borrower if Borrower is insolvent or in financial difficulty. If Borrower is unable to pay all creditors, it may be prudent for Bank to take partial payment, but Borrower will normally insist on a release of the obligation. If Bank takes $3,000 and releases Borrower from the $10,000 debt, Accommodation Party is not injured. To the extent of the payment Accommodation Party's obligation to Bank is reduced. The release of Borrower by Bank does not affect the right of Accommodation Party to obtain reimbursement from Borrower or to enforce the note against Borrower if Accommodation Party pays Bank. Section 3-419(e). Subsection (b) is designed to allow a creditor to settle with the principal debtor without risk of losing rights against sureties. Settlement is in the interest of sureties as well as the creditor. Subsection (b), however, is not intended to apply to a settlement of a disputed claim which discharges the obligation.

Subsection (b) changes the law stated in former Section 3-606 but the change relates largely to formalities rather than substance. Under former Section 3-606, Bank in the hypothetical case stated in Comment 1 could settle with and release Borrower without releasing Accommodation Party, but to accomplish that result Bank had to either obtain the consent of Accommodation Party or make an express reservation of rights against Accommodation Party at the time it released Borrower. The reservation of rights was made in the agreement between Bank and Borrower by which the release of Borrower was made. There was no requirement in former Section 3-606 that any notice be given to Accommodation Party. Section 3-605 eliminates the necessity that Bank formally reserve rights against Accommodation Party in order to retain rights of recourse against Accommodation Party. See

PEB Commentary No. 11, dated February 10, 1994 [Appendix II, Vol. 3A Uniform Laws Annotated, Master Edition or ULA Database on Westlaw].

4. Subsection (c) relates to extensions of the due date of the instrument. In most cases an extension of time to pay a note is a benefit to both the principal debtor and sureties having recourse against the principal debtor. In relatively few cases the extension may cause loss if deterioration of the financial condition of the principal debtor reduces the amount that the surety will be able to recover on its right of recourse when default occurs. Former Section 3-606(1)(a) did not take into account the presence or absence of loss to the surety. For example, suppose the instrument is an installment note and the principal debtor is temporarily short of funds to pay a monthly installment. The payee agrees to extend the due date of the installment for a month or two to allow the debtor to pay when funds are available. Under former Section 3-606 surety was discharged if consent was not given unless the payee expressly reserved rights against the surety. It did not matter that the extension of time was a trivial change in the guaranteed obligation and that there was no evidence that the surety suffered any loss because of the extension. Wilmington Trust Co. v. Gesullo, 29 U.C.C. Rep. 144 (Del. Super. Ct. 1980). Under subsection (c) an extension of time results in discharge only to the extent the surety proves that the extension caused loss. For example, if the extension is for a long period the surety might be able to prove that during the period of extension the principal debtor became insolvent, thus reducing the value of the right of recourse of the surety. By putting the burden on the surety to prove loss, subsection (c) more accurately reflects what the parties would have done by agreement, and it facilitates workouts.

Under other provisions of Article 3, what is the effect of an extension agreement between the holder of a note and the maker who is an accommodated party? The question is illustrated by the following case:

Case #1. A borrows money from Lender and issues a note payable on April 1, 1992. B signs the note for accommodation at the request of Lender. B signed the note either as co-maker or as an anomalous indorser. In either case Lender subsequently makes an agreement with A extending the due date of A's obligation to pay the note to July 1, 1992. In either case B did not agree to the extension.

What is the effect of the extension agreement on B? Could Lender enforce the note against B if the note is not paid on April 1, 1992? A's obligation to Lender to pay the note on April 1, 1992 may be modified by the agreement of Lender. If B is an anomalous indorser Lender cannot enforce the note against B unless the note has been dishonored. Section 3-415(a). Under Section 3-502(a)(3) dishonor occurs if it is not paid on the day it becomes payable. Since the agreement between A and Lender extended the due date of A's obligation to July 1, 1992 there is no dishonor because A was not obligated to pay Lender on April 1, 1992. If B is a co-maker the analysis is somewhat different. Lender has no power to amend the terms of the note without the consent of both A and B. By an agreement with A, Lender can extend the due date of A's obligation to Lender to pay the note but B's obligation is to pay the note according to the terms of the note at the time of issue. Section 3-412. However, B's obligation to pay the note is subject to a defense because B is an accommodation party. B is not obliged to pay Lender if A is not obliged to pay Lender. Under Section 3-305(d), B as an accommodation party can assert against Lender any defense of A. A has a defense based on the extension agreement. Thus, the result is that Lender could not enforce the note against B until July 1, 1992. This result is consistent with the right of B if B is an anomalous indorser.

As a practical matter an extension of the due date will normally occur when the accommodated party is unable to pay on the due date. The interest of the accommodation party normally is to defer payment to the holder rather than to pay right away and rely on an action against the accommodated party that may have little or no value. But in unusual cases the accommodation party may prefer to pay the holder on the original due date. In such cases, the accommodation party may do so. This is because the extension agreement between the accommodated party and the holder cannot bind the accommodation party to a change in its obligation without the accommodation party's consent. The effect on the recourse of the accommodation party against the accommodation party of performance by the accommodation party on the original due date is not addressed in §3-419 and is left to the general law of suretyship.

Even though an accommodation party has the option of paying the instrument on the original due date, the accommodation party is not precluded from asserting its rights to discharge under Section 3-605(c) if it does not exercise that option. The critical issue is whether the extension caused the accommodation party a loss by increasing the difference between its cost of performing its obligation on the instrument and the amount recoverable from the accommodated party pursuant to Section 3-419(e). The decision by the accommodation party not to exercise its option to pay on the original due date may, under the circumstances, be a factor to be considered in the determination of that issue. See PEB Commentary No. 11, dated February 10, 1994 [Appendix II Vol. 3A Uniform Laws Annotated, Master Edition or ULA Database on Westlaw].

5. Former Section 3-606 applied to extensions of the due date of a note but not to other modifications of the obligation of the principal debtor. There was no apparent reason why former Section 3-606 did not follow general suretyship law in covering both. Under Section 3-605(d) a material modification of the obligation of the principal debtor, other than an extension of the due date, will result in discharge of the surety to the

extent the modification caused loss to the surety with respect to the right of recourse. The loss caused by the modification is deemed to be the entire amount of the right of recourse unless the person seeking enforcement of the instrument proves that no loss occurred or that the loss was less than the full amount of the right of recourse. In the absence of that proof, the surety is completely discharged. The rationale for having different rules with respect to loss for extensions of the due date and other modifications is that extensions are likely to be beneficial to the surety and they are often made. Other modifications are less common and they may very well be detrimental to the surety. Modification of the obligation of the principal debtor without permission of the surety is unreasonable unless the modification is benign. Subsection (d) puts the burden on the person seeking enforcement of the instrument to prove the extent to which loss was not caused by the modification.

The following is an illustration of the kind of case to which Section 3-605(d) would apply:

Case #2. Corporation borrows money from Lender and issues a note payable to Lender. X signs the note as an accommodation party for Corporation. The loan agreement under which the note was issued states various events of default which allow Lender to accelerate the due date of the note. Among the events of default are breach of covenants not to incur debt beyond specified limits and not to engage in any line of business substantially different from that currently carried on by Corporation. Without consent of X, Lender agrees to modify the covenants to allow Corporation to enter into a new line of business that X considers to be risky, and to incur debt beyond the limits specified in the loan agreement to finance the new venture. This modification releases X unless Lender proves that the modification did not cause loss to X or that the loss caused by the modification was less than X's right of recourse.

Sometimes there is both an extension of the due date and some other modification. In that case both subsections (c) and (d) apply. The following is an example:

Case #3. Corporation was indebted to Lender on a note payable on April 1, 1992 and X signed the note as an accommodation party for Corporation. The interest rate on the note was 12 percent. Lender and Corporation agreed to a six-month extension of the due date of the note to October 1, 1992 and an increase in the interest rate to 14 percent after April 1, 1992. Corporation defaulted on October 1, 1992. Corporation paid no interest during the six-month extension period. Corporation is insolvent and has no assets from which unsecured creditors can be paid. Lender demanded payment from X.

Assume X is an anomalous indorser. First consider Section 3-605(c) alone. If there had been no change in the interest rate, the fact that Lender gave an extension of six months to Corporation would not result in discharge unless X could prove loss with respect to the right of recourse because of the extension. If the financial condition of Corporation on April 1, 1992 would not have allowed any recovery on the right of recourse, X can't show any loss as a result of the extension with respect to the amount due on the note on April 1, 1992. Since the note accrued interest during the six-month extension, is there a loss equal to the accrued interest? Since the interest rate was not raised, only Section 3-605(c) would apply and X probably could not prove any loss. The obligation of X includes interest on the note until the note is paid. To the extent payment was delayed X had the use of the money that X otherwise would have had to pay to Lender. X could have prevented the running of interest by paying the debt. Since X did not do so, X suffered no loss as the result of the extension.

If the interest rate was raised, Section 3-605(d) also must be considered. If X is an anomalous indorser, X's liability is to pay the note according to its terms at the time of indorsement. Section 3-415(a). Thus, X's obligation to pay interest is measured by the terms of the note (12%) rather than by the increased amount of 14 percent. The same analysis applies if X had been a co-maker. Under Section 3-412 the liability of the issuer of a note is to pay the note according to its terms at the time it was issued. Either obligation could be changed by contract and that occurred with respect to Corporation when it agreed to the increase in the interest rate, but X did not join in that agreement and is not bound by it. Thus, the most that X can be required to pay is the amount due on the note plus interest at the rate of 12 percent.

Does the modification discharge X under Section 3-605(d)? Any modification that increases the monetary obligation of X is material. An increase of the interest rate from 12 percent to 14 percent is certainly a material modification. There is a presumption that X is discharged because Section 3-605(d) creates a presumption that the modification caused a loss to X equal to the amount of the right of recourse. Thus, Lender has the burden of proving absence of loss or a loss less than the amount of the right of recourse. Since Corporation paid no interest during the six-month period, the issue is like the issue presented under Section 3-605(c) which we have just discussed. The increase in the interest rate could not have affected the right of recourse because no interest was paid by Corporation. X is in the same position as X would have been in if there had been an extension without an increase in the interest rate.

The analysis with respect to Section 3-605(c) and (d) would have been different if we change the assumptions. Suppose Corporation was not insolvent on April 1, 1992, that Corporation paid interest at the higher rate during the six-month period, and that Corporation was insolvent at the end of the six-month period. In this case it is possible that the extension and the additional burden placed on Corporation by the increased interest rate may have been detrimental to X.

There are difficulties in properly allocating burden of proof when the agreement between Lender and Corporation involves both an extension under Section 3-605(c) and a modification under Section 3-605(d). The agreement may have caused loss to X but it may be difficult to identify the extent to which the loss was caused by the extension or the other modification. If neither Lender nor X introduces evidence on the issue, the result is full discharge because Section 3-605(d) applies. Thus, Lender has the burden of overcoming the presumption in Section 3-605(d). In doing so, Lender should be entitled to a presumption that the extension of time by itself caused no loss. Section 3-605(c) is based on such a presumption and X should be required to introduce evidence on the effect of the extension on the right of recourse. Lender would have to introduce evidence on the effect of the increased interest rate. Thus, both sides will have to introduce evidence. On the basis of this evidence the court will have to make a determination of the overall effect of the agreement on X's right of recourse. See PEB Commentary No. 11, dated February 10, 1994 [Appendix II Vol. 3A Uniform Laws Annotated, Master Edition or ULA Database on Westlaw].

6. Subsection (e) deals with discharge of sureties by impairment of collateral. It generally conforms to former Section 3-606(1)(b). Subsection (g) states common examples of what is meant by impairment. By using the term "includes," it allows a court to find impairment in other cases as well. There is extensive case law on impairment of collateral. The surety is discharged to the extent the surety proves that impairment was caused by a person entitled to enforce the instrument. For example, suppose the payee of a secured note fails to perfect the security interest. The collateral is owned by the principal debtor who subsequently files in bankruptcy. As a result of the failure to perfect, the security interest is not enforceable in bankruptcy. If the payee obtains payment from the surety, the surety is subrogated to the payee's security interest in the collateral. In this case the value of the security interest is impaired completely because the security interest is unenforceable. If the value of the collateral is as much or more than the amount of the note there is a complete discharge.

In some states a real property grantee who assumes the obligation of the grantor as maker of a note secured by the real property becomes by operation of law a principal debtor and the grantor becomes a surety. The meager case authority was split on whether former Section 3-606 applied to release the grantor if the holder released or extended the obligation of the grantee. Revised Article 3 takes no position on the effect of the release of the grantee in this case. Section 3-605(b) does not apply because the holder has not discharged the obligation of a "party," a term defined in Section 3-103(a)(8) as "party to an instrument." The assuming grantee is not a party to the instrument. The resolution of this question is governed by general principles of law, including the law of suretyship. See PEB Commentary No. 11, dated February 10, 1994 [Appendix II Vol. 3A Uniform Laws Annotated, Master Edition or ULA Database on Westlaw].

7. Subsection (f) is illustrated by the following case. X and Y sign a note for $1,000 as co-makers. Neither is an accommodation party. X grants a security interest in X's property to secure the note. The collateral is worth more than $1,000. Payee fails to perfect the security interest in X's property before X files in bankruptcy. As a result, the security interest is not enforceable in bankruptcy. Had Payee perfected the security interest, Y could have paid the note and gained rights to X's collateral by subrogation. If the security interest had been perfected, Y could have realized on the collateral to the extent of $500 to satisfy its right of contribution against X. Payee's failure to perfect deprived Y of the benefit of the collateral. Subsection (f) discharges Y to the extent of its loss. If there are no assets in the bankruptcy for unsecured claims, the loss is $500, the amount of Y's contribution claim against X which now has a zero value. If some amount is payable on unsecured claims, the loss is reduced by the amount receivable by Y. The same result follows if Y is an accommodation party but Payee has no knowledge of the accommodation or notice under Section 3-419(c). In that event Y is not discharged under subsection (e), but subsection (f) applies because X and Y are jointly and severally liable on the note. Under subsection (f), Y is treated as a co-maker with a right of contribution rather than an accommodation party with a right of reimbursement. Y is discharged to the extent of $500. If Y is the principal debtor and X is the accommodation party subsection (f) doesn't apply. Y, as principal debtor, is not injured by the impairment of collateral because Y would have been obliged to reimburse X for the entire $1,000 even if Payee had obtained payment from sale of the collateral.

8. Subsection (i) is a continuation of former law which allowed suretyship defenses to be waived. As the subsection provides, a party is not discharged under this section if the instrument or a separate agreement of the party waives discharge either specifically or by general language indicating that defenses based on suretyship and impairment of collateral are waived. No particular language or form of agreement is required, and the standards for enforcing such a term are the same as the standards for enforcing any other term in an instrument or agreement.

Subsection (i), however, applies only to a "discharge under this section." The right of an accommodation party to be discharged under Section 3-605(e) because of an impairment of collateral can be waived. But with respect to a note secured by personal property collateral, Article 9 also applies. If an accommodation party is a "debtor" under Section 9-105(1)(d), the accommodation party has rights under Article 9. Under Section 9-501(3)(b) rights of an Article 9 debtor under Section 9-504(3) and Section 9-505(1), which deal with disposition of collateral, cannot be waived except as provided in Article 9. These Article 9 rights are independent of rights under Section 3-605. Since Section 3-605(i) is specifically limited to discharge under Section 3-605, a waiver of rights with respect to Section 3-605 has no effect on rights under Article 9. With respect to Article 9 rights, Section 9-501(3)(b) controls. See PEB Commentary No. 11, dated February 10, 1994 [Appendix II Vol. 3A Uniform Laws Annotated, Master Edition or ULA Database on Westlaw].

Table of Cases

Italic type indicates principal cases

Table of Statutes

Montana Statutes

Nevada Revenue Statute

New York General Business Law

North Carolina, General Statutes

Ohio Administrative Code

Restatement (Second) of Contracts

Restatement (Second) of Torts

Securities Act of 1933

Securities and Exchange Commission

Servicemembers Civil Relief Act

Ship Mortgage Act of 1920

Shipping Act

Treasury Department Regulations

Truth in Lending Act

Uniform Commercial Code

Index